THE ANIME ENCYCLOPEDIA

3RD REVISED EDITION

A CENTURY OF JAPANESE ANIMATION

THE ANIME ENCYCLOPEDIA
THIRD EDITION
A Century of Japanese Animation

Jonathan Clements

Helen McCarthy

Stone Bridge Press • *Berkeley, California*

Published by
Stone Bridge Press
P. O. Box 8208, Berkeley, CA 94707
TEL 510-524-8732 • sbp@stonebridge.com • www.stonebridge.com

We want to hear from you! Updates? Corrections? Comments? Please send all correspondence regarding this publication to **animeinfo@stonebridge.com**.

Mentions of films and hyperlinks to websites in this publication, whether in printed or electronic form, do not represent an endorsement on the part of the publisher. All materials referenced or hyperlinked to third-party sites are copyright their respective rightsholders. Icons have been provided as content advisories, but the absence of an advisory icon does not guarantee that the content of the film is suitable for minors. Some hyperlinked sites may not be suitable for minors or for viewing in public spaces.

If you have obtained an electronic edition of this publication, please respect the hard work and copyright of those who helped to create it! Please do not reverse-engineer, duplicate, distribute, or otherwise share printed or electronic copies of this work. Please obtain your edition only through legitimate sellers and distributors.

Brief quotations from this publication may be used without permission for the purpose of review and commentary. For further information about excerpts, please contact the publisher at sbp@stonebridge.com.

LIBRARY OF CONGRESS CATALOGING-IN-PUBLICATION DATA
Clements, Jonathan, 1971–
  The anime encyclopedia : a century of Japanese animation / Jonathan Clements, Helen McCarthy.—Third edition.
    pages cm
  ISBN 978-1-61172-018-1 (hardcover)
  ISBN 978-1-61172-909-2 (e-book)
  I. McCarthy, Helen, 1951– II. Title.
  NC1766.J3C53 2015
  791.43'340952–dc23
                          2014047174

To Peter Goll, anime's unsung hero

Contents

THE ANIME ENCYCLOPEDIA

Thematic Entries

Introduction

At the time when the second edition of the *The Anime Encyclopedia* was printed, the anime world was reaching a historical production peak. The year 2006 saw the Japanese animation industry produce 135,530 minutes of new animation, some 19,980 minutes more than the previous year. This, however, was an anomaly, caused by a large number of productions initiated to meet foreign demand, and partly funded with foreign money, chiefly from America. As the flood of foreign interest diminished post-**POKÉMON** and post–**SPIRITED AWAY**, overseas earnings similarly ebbed away, from an early-20th-century peak of up to 50% of Japanese animation's profits, to a 10% level more similar to conditions in the 1990s.

Many of the Japanese producers saw it coming. Company-specific sales figures show two distinct waves of profit—one in the children's market that peaked in 2001, and another in the teenage/adult market that peaked between 2003 and 2005, depending on the studio. It is tempting to suggest that these differing pinnacles in the early 21st century represent the growth and maturation of the *same* audience—the **POKÉMON** generation, born at the beginning of the 1990s, turning into teenagers in the middle noughties, and dwindling in the 2010s. There has been talk among Japanese pundits of the existence of "silver otaku," a suggestion that the "fan community" might be a nonrenewable resource, a one-time generation of people who love anime enough to pay big bucks for it, and that with this generation's maturation, there is only space for **EVANGELION** spin-offs and the occasional **GUNDAM** reboot. But there is more to anime than that.

It has been a wild eight years. Since our last edition, ADV Films has collapsed; Bandai pulled out of the American DVD market; Aniplex went to court over **KIBA**; Anime Sols and Daisuki tried to move the locus of power away from America and back to Japan; piracy and torrenting became hot-button issues; anime experimented with stereoscopic vision (**CYBORG 009**), crowdfunding (**KICK-HEART**), cellphone distribution (**TODAY'S ASKA SHOW**), and "4D" cinema events (**HATSUNE MIKU LIVE PARTY**). Simulcasting has entirely transformed the speed of **TRANSLATION**—some of our younger readers literally cannot recall the days when English-language releases were the exception rather than the rule, limping several years behind a Japanese broadcast. Contemporary **FANDOM**'s sense of "now" is often only a few minutes behind that of its Japanese counterpart, although much anime still arrives in foreign territories divorced from its original context and roots.

Meanwhile, anime's sense of its own history continued not only to reframe the past, with the rediscovery of **A Mole's Adventure**, but also to fret about the future, with the retirement of Hayao Miyazaki (**The Wind Rises**). We have done our best to keep tabs on all these issues and more, in the latest incarnation of the book variously described as "an excellent desktop reference" by Anime News Network, "a remarkably thorough guide" by Midnight Eye, and "full of AIDS and fail" by some guy on the Internet.

You hold in your hands the third edition of *The Anime Encyclopedia*, building on the earlier editions from 2001 and 2006. This book is a palimpsest, augmenting many earlier entries and adding new ones. With that in mind, we have preserved most of our original introduction and added some new material in order to outline changes made and developments observed.

TITLES

We have included as many Japanese titles as possible, but owing to space limitations, many episode titles, TV specials, and minor films have simply been left in English. We give variant titles but have indexed by Western release where possible—hence *Space Cruiser Yamato* (*Space Battleship Yamato*) is filed as **Star Blazers**. The "three-dimensional" typography of many anime titles leaves them with a foreground name and a background qualifier, which plays havoc with filing: is it **Macross**, or is it *Super-Dimensional Fortress Macross*? Where possible we have used the Western title most recognizable—few fans in the U.S. *or* Japan speak of *Neon Genesis Evangelion*; instead they refer to it as **Evangelion**, though both variants will be found in our index.

"Three-dimensional" titles arguably served a purpose in Japan in the days of early TV, where translators deliberately included descriptions in the titles of foreign TV shows, so that title-only TV listings would at least have some element of explanation rather than a long list of meaningless *katakana* words. However, the last few years has seen the rise of a fad for pointlessly verbose titles, such as *As Long as There's Love, It Doesn't Matter if He's My Brother, Right?* (**OniAi**); *No Matter How I Look at It, It's You Guys' Fault That I'm Not Popular* (**Watamote**); and **Problem Children Are Coming from Another World, Aren't They?**, many of which we have listed by their most common abbreviations.

Other titles are altered through international sales pitches. The anime known in Japan as *Shojo Kakumei Utena* (and translatable as *Revolutionary Girl Utena*) is often given the French title *La Fillette Revolutionnaire* on Japanese merchandise and was mystifyingly renamed *Ursula's Kiss* in some studio sales documents (press releases whose tenuous relation to the shows they purport to sell has confused many attempts to determine names and plots). We have filed it simply as **Utena** but most of its variants appear in the index.

For consistency, we have replaced the ampersand (&) with the word "and," although box typography and "official" titles may offer variant forms.

Titles printed in **Boldface Capital Letters** refer to main entries elsewhere in the book. The index can be used to find titles that are referred to but that do not have their own entries.

Note that in our commentaries we often (but not always) space-savingly refer to the anime under discussion by its initials or a shortened form: in the text about **Cream Lemon**, for example, we refer to it as *CL* and to a related work as *New CL*, and we refer to the film **Evangelion** as *Eva*.

Titles appear in the listings in alphabetical order using the alphabetize-by-word system. Thus, **Boy with Cat's Eyes** comes before **Boyfriend**. If you are unfamiliar with this system (the one favored by computers and databases), you may need to turn a page or two to find the title you're looking for.

If a title contains a numeral, it is alphabetized as if the numeral were spelled out in English: *2*

= *Two* comes before *0* = *Zero* in other words. The only exception to this is when a word comprises both letters and numerals, such as **D-1 Devasta-tor** and **D4 Princess**. In this case, the numerals are sorted before alphabetical successors.

Despite the efforts of our noble proofreaders to dissuade us, we have been ruthless in excising most exclamation points—those plings of punctuation that serve, or at least appear to serve, so little purpose except to turn English anime titles into a rash of overenthusiastic! breathless! blurtings! and ruin the flow of the rest of the sentence. There are some cases where exclamation points serve a purpose, such as where the first and second seasons of **K-On** are denoted through the number of "!s" in the title, but we feel that our readers are already making enough effort with anime titles without also having to wade through a sea of shout poles.

See also the note on romanization, below.

INTERNATIONAL RELEASES
An asterisk (*) by a title heading denotes the existence of a *legal* English-language release of at least part of a show at some point, though not all titles are internationally available. The U.S. has **The Secret of Blue Water** to itself, **Hum-mingbirds** is not available outside the U.K., and **Ken the Wolf Boy** was only broadcast in Austra-lia. Furthermore, while an English edition may exist, some, such as **Madcap Island**, were only seen as subtitled prints at film festivals or on Japanese DVDs with English subtitles. Since this is an English-language book with limited space, we have avoided discussion of other languages, although a few well-known French title variants have been included for the benefit of readers in Canada, and there is occasional reference to Spanish-language versions. If a film has been screened with English subtitles at a film festival, we similarly consider it "available," if not for your local store, then at least for your local cinema.

FORMATS AND RUNNING TIMES
The nature of the medium has changed radically through technological and economic influences. Animation was an obscure cottage industry until its use as military propaganda led to the first full-length feature, **Momotaro's Divine Sea Warriors**, in 1945. Television created a larger medium during the 1960s, which came to be dominated by merchandising tie-ins in the 1970s.

The arrival of home video players in the 1970s and 1980s, especially the video cassette recorder, allowed for the targeting of smaller niches in the audience, beginning the process whereby anime studios held on to their audiences as they left childhood behind (**Fandom**). Before video recorders became widely available in the 1980s, producers could expect a reasonable number of viewers to pay to see repeat performances of TV shows in theaters, leading to holiday reruns, erroneously credited in some sources as genuine "movies." Furthermore, many shows made for video, such as **Beloved Betty**, were also shown theatrically as second or third features. We have listed these shows as video productions, though some other sources describe them as movies. **Appleseed**, for example, is listed as a video work because that was its original format, even though it was shown in theaters outside Japan. We follow the policy of the Writers Guild of America in regarding Internet broadcasts as a subset of TV series.

The 1990s saw many more developments— the "retro" revival as studios tried to appeal to former fans *and* their children, the advent of digital animation, and the use of satellite/cable as an even cheaper preview medium than video (the studio only has to pay for one tape!).

We have had to piece together some entries, especially for older shows, from sources with time listings that do not account for commercial breaks. Sometimes the difference can be drastic: the *Animage 25 Years of Television Cartoons* gives the broadcast time of **BAGHI** as 120 minutes, whereas the *Newtype Animesoft Complete Catalog* entry lists it as only 86 minutes, and the *Animation Filmography of Osamu Tezuka* infuriatingly disagrees with both. We have also had to consider different companies' editing and compilation policies, which can affect published running times. An additional consideration involves the difference in converting NTSC footage, which runs at 24 frames per second, to PAL footage, which runs at 25 frames per second. This is often remedied by simply speeding the film up by a factor of 4%, which can amount to over 3 minutes' discrepancy in the running time of a 90-minute feature.

We have given full episode counts of shows *made*, even if the complete runs of shows such as **ULYSSES 31** and **ALICE IN WONDERLAND** were only ever seen outside Japan. We have tried to distinguish among multiple versions of an anime using different abbreviations, and also by using a short-form of the title after the time and episode count. Finally, where we have had to cram several incarnations of a title into one entry, pertinent changes in staff or running time are denoted by numbered abbreviations, e.g., "m1" for the first movie, "TV2" for a second TV series, or "v2" for a second video series. We should also note a rising 21st-century trend in multimedia franchises for bundling un-aired episodes of a TV series with later volumes of the manga books, thereby confusing counts of "television" or "video" episodes (see, for example, **HIGH SCHOOL DxD**).

CREATIVE CREDITS

We have listed as many crew members as space allowed. Though by no means exhaustive, we have included the most important parties responsible for the five major areas of production on each anime's first iteration. The period under study is so vast that meanings have changed over time. As well as lead animators (ANI) and composers (MUS), we have listed directors (DIR), scriptwriters (SCR), and designers (DES), though these last three job titles have had over 12 definitions during the last 50 years.

A "series producer," for example, is sometimes a "story editor" (i.e., a lead writer—SCR) and sometimes a "supervising director" (DIR), depending on the whims both of the studio and the English translators, who may not know as much about film terminology as they do about Japanese. Similarly, "supervising director" is sometimes an honorary title for a producer, but it is also occasionally used for the chief among several directors on a long-running series. A "director" might be a *kantoku*, firmly in charge of every aspect of the process, or an *enshutsu*, whose labors are far more managerial in nature, and often translated instead as "producer"! To the authors' constant frustration, some people credited as producers turn out to be little more than company accountants, given courtesy titles that do not reflect their creative involvement. We have done our best to pin down exactly what a staff member did and place him or her in the right slot, but sometimes we had to admit defeat—Frederik L. Schodt *himself* is not quite sure why he is credited as a "planning brain" on **SPACE FIREBIRD 2772**.

In cases where a manga has been adapted into anime, we have followed the Japanese practice and credited the original creators as the writer/designer where no alternative is given.

Those who check our credits against Western releases may notice discrepancies. Where possible, we have checked the credits of the Japanese originals, and though we have had to admit defeat on many occasions, jobs go uncredited (N/C) only after a trawl through every available option, including several Japanese-language listings and studio histories.

Most modern anime include a production committee (*seisaku iinkai*) in their production credits. We have omitted most of these, since they usually merely refer to a council of the other production entities listed, but will take the opportunity to note here that their names have become increasingly more elaborate in recent years. Where they once were simply called [Anime Name] Production Committee or [Anime Name] Media Partners, many now have titles seemingly whipped up by whimsical lawyers having a spot of fun, such as the "Society for the Preservation of the Scarecrow" that represents the legal interests of **KAMISAMA DOLLS** or the "Executive Board of St. Alfonso Academy" that approves licenses for **MARGINAL PRINCE**.

ABOUT JAPANESE NAMES

Japanese names are particularly troublesome, as they are generally written with non-phonetic *kanji* characters. Even the Japanese themselves are not always sure how to pronounce a particular *kanji* in every context. Matters are not helped in the entertainment business by the proliferation of pseudonyms, often deliberately hard to read, particularly among voice actors moonlighting on low-rent productions, pornographers who wish to protect their everyday reputations, and artists working for hire on storyboards for someone else's production, who are happy to take the money but wish to prevent marketers from capitalizing on the presence of their names on the credits. We have also had to deal with increasing numbers of creators and studios who insist on insufferably pretentious uses of upper- and lower-case letters, symbols and misspellings in their romanized names, which can often make our data boxes seem like we are typing while drunk. We assure you, this is *usually* not the case.

Watching every anime made, end-to-end, in order to catch the names of all the staff and all the fictional characters would have taken more than 20 years. We have been necessarily frugal with our time and utilized other sources where possible. Sometimes we have had to wing it,

as in **THUNDERBIRDS 2086**, where not even ITC-approved publications can agree on spellings. However, where we know Western credits to be in error, we have replaced them with our own. Sadly, all too many foreign releases have legacy names on their boxes and blurbs, where a designer has left small print from an entirely different project. Similarly, some distributors lazily knock up a single end-credits roll and repeat it for every episode of a series, despite changes in cast and crew. We have done the best we can to present a faithful account of who did what on a Japanese production, but often we find ourselves having to weigh two or more claims that are both founded on nothing but hearsay and good faith.

We have elected to present Japanese names in Western order, that is, family name last, because this is generally how they are presented in English-language credits. This has resulted in the names of some well-known historical characters being given unconventionally as, for example, Nobunaga Oda or Musashi Miyamoto.

Doubtful names have been passed on to our research assistant Motoko Tamamuro and her mystified family, who have provided the best pronunciations they could. Where a guess is the best we can manage, we have opted for a guess made by Japanese native-speakers.

TERMINOLOGY

Some points remain the same across cultures—more money is spent on a film than on a TV episode. Movies "made for television" tend to be cheaper and more conservative in their execution. Shows that go "straight to video" are generally for a smaller, niche audience. We have avoided the spin-doctor's term OAV—an "Original Anime Video" made for direct sale rather than theatrical or TV airing. We have, however, included mentions for several "manga videos" (a 1990s VHS term) and *ga-nime* (their 21st-century TV/DVD rebranding)—comics in which voice actors read to the viewer, and even save them the bother of turning the pages. Though these are the lowest-tech "animation" imaginable, they are likely to turn up in video store bargain bins and are included here to save would-be buyers' blushes. These are not to be confused with Manga Entertainment, the *brand name* that led many (including the *Oxford English Dictionary*) to confuse "manga" (Japanese comics) with "anime" (Japanese animation).

Beyond the words "manga" and "anime," we have tried to avoid the obstructively arcane slang of fandom (**ARGOT AND JARGON**). We intend to make anime accessible to every reader, so as much as possible we have used terms traceable in any good dictionary. Anime is increasingly targeted at an international audience and can be described in any of the wide variety of languages into which it's translated—the abuse of terms such as *hentai, shojo,* and *otaku* only serves to alienate the general reader. We realize that this will annoy those fans who want their hobby to be impenetrable and "untranslatable" to outsiders. They should get over themselves.

ROMANIZATION

We have adopted a strategy for handling Japanese words: keep it simple. Purists and language scholars may be unhappy at some of the choices we have made, but our first impulse has been to serve the needs of our readers, most of whom have no particular expertise in speaking or pronouncing Japanese.

Our job has been made more difficult because the Japanese and American studios that release anime into English-language markets do not follow the same or even consistent romanization rules. And some Japanese anime and Japanese names are already known outside Japan by their "incorrect" English spellings.

So what we have done is made the best of an inherently confusing situation.

1. We almost always favor the "official" spellings of anime titles as provided by their studios, nonstandard though they may sometimes be. Names, too, can be rendered in the romanized form preferred by the particular individual: Joe (not Jo) Hisaishi, for example.

2. Japanese titles, when we provide them, are romanized consistently, except that "English" words adopted into the Japanese anime title are rendered back into English: thus, the film known in English as **BLOCKER CORPS** is in fact known in Japanese as *Burokkaa Guntan IV Masheen* but is listed here as *Blocker Guntan IV Machine.*

3. The syllabic nasal *n* is written as *n* before *b, m,* and *p* (Shinbashi); in other texts, *m* is frequently seen here (Shimbashi). We have dropped the apostrophe used in specialized texts to indicate syllabic division involving the nasal *n*; thus we write Junichiro, not Jun'ichiro.

4. We do not indicate the extended vowels *o* and *u*, either by "long signs" (macrons) over the vowels or by spelling out as *ou, oo,* or *uu*. Extended vowels are usually either ignored or mispronounced by those unfamiliar with Japanese, and are in any case not provided at all or are provided inconsistently by those who prepare staff credits and English-language materials. Rather than litter this book with mistakes and inconsistencies we have simply decided to adopt a leaner style of romanization.

PARENTAL ADVISORIES

Like any mass medium, anime can soar to great heights of creative expression or plumb the depths of human depravity. Some anime you want to share with your family; some you might need to watch in a room with the door locked. Whatever your tastes, far be it from us to cast judgment. But at the request of our publisher, and in the interest of making this book of practical use for fans as well as guardians, teachers, librarians, and shop owners, we have provided some simple icons to indicate those anime that have language, violence, or nudity of the sort that one might not wish children or other sensitive souls to be exposed to. Not all violence is gratuitous; not all nudity is exploitative. Our "ratings" are merely a guide to content, and we hope a useful one.

ADDITIONS AND ALTERATIONS

The second edition of this book, published in 2006, incorporated several hundred new anime released since the original 2001 publication, as well as cross-references to Stone Bridge's *Dorama Encyclopedia* (2003), indicated by the sign "*DE." It also added many biographical entries and two dozen thematic entries on broad issues such as terminology, history, and genres.

This third edition, published in 2015, contains all the changes made in the second edition, as well as over a hundred intermediate corrections made for the 2012 e-book version. It also adds entries for over a thousand new titles released since 2006, some older works that did not previously have their own dedicated entry, such as MOMOTARO'S SEA EAGLES, THE KING'S TAIL, EVERYBODY'S SONGS, or THE NEW ADVENTURES OF PINOCCHIO, and some further 5,000 alterations throughout the pre-existing text, upgrading staff lists, adding details of later installments of ongoing franchises, dates of death for individuals, and similar corrections. We have also taken the opportunity to add several new thematic areas on issues not addressed in previous editions, such as ADVERTISING AND SPONSORSHIP, EVERYDAY ANIME, and FANDOM. An encyclopedist's work is a zero-sum game; there is always something else we could have added, or some clarification we could have pursued. Undoubtedly there will be omissions and solecisms, but it represents the culmination of all our available hours: a snapshot of where we were and what we knew on the day that this book was printed. For researchers and students, that alone should present a starting point for discourse and dialogue, something, at the very least, for you to argue with.

We have continued to add short biographies of Japanese creatives and companies—specifically from the anime industry, rather than, for example, manga creators whose work happens to have been adapted into anime. This third edition includes coverage of some previously obscure individuals from the early days of anime, such as Iwao Ashida and Ikuo Oishi, as well the little-discussed Shadow Staff film unit that made instructional films for military personnel. Sometimes the information in company entries may appear contradictory, but this is a common feature of both media accounting and Japanese business structures. Companies are founded, split away from one another, merged and remerged in a complex dance of shifting liability shields. We hope, however, that our brief accounts of several of the major players help explain some of the invisible currents of contacts, alliances, and friendships that often serve to influence what gets made, and by whom.

Our thematic entries offer not only signposts to more in-depth discussion of certain topics within anime, but also concise histories of the medium itself by placing certain landmark entries in chronological order. In a sense, they form several alternative views of the history of Japanese animation, such as one told from the viewpoint of **Foreign Influences** and another through the influence of **Technology and Formats**.

NAMES AND ORIGINS

As encyclopedists, we have often had to weigh contradictory information. The U.S. release of *Shinseiki Evangelion* faithfully calls itself *Neon Genesis Evangelion* (the creators' approved "Engrish" title, not an actual **Translation** of the *kanji*) but is filed under E in many catalogues, including, at the time we prepared our first edition, those of its own distributor. Other titles use Japanese characters as part of their American box design—one must speak both languages to know that the squiggles next to the words *Peace Maker* on the American DVD box say *Kurogane*, and complete the title. In some cases, we believe such decisions to be not merely aesthetic but also political, since some Japanese rightsholders may insist on a title that is simply unpronounceable or difficult for non-Japanese speakers to remember. The use of such dual names could, in certain instances, be an attempt to please all parties, since the Japanese license holders see a name they know and American store clerks see one they can find and remember.

A related problem has come in the form of non-translations—that growing number of anime whose "translators" do not bother (or are not permitted) to actually translate the title. Titles such as **Haibane Renmei**, **Kakurenbo: Hide and Seek**, and even **Princess Mononoke** seem wholly or partly left in Japanese, although occasionally it is fandom itself that is complicit in this by insisting on "generally accepted" titles like **Saikano**, even though an English-language title, *She: The Ultimate Weapon,* already existed. The result is an ironic situation, occurring more often than one might expect, in which some fans and occasionally even distributors of a show are unable to pronounce its name. Almost as irritating is the growing vogue for titles that seem doomed to disappear into the Internet for being almost impossible to distinguish for an online search engine, such as the video *To* (**2001 Nights**) and *K* (released abroad as **K the Anime**).

One feature of recent times, particularly in the adult video sector, has been the proliferation of rereleases and repackages of pre-existing works under new titles. This is occasionally due to the rights lapsing and being resold to a new owner, a situation that seems to strike erotic anime more often than others. In some cases, such as the **Secret Anima** series, they have been rereleased under an original Japanese title that had previously been altered, in an industry notorious for repackaging old porn in new boxes.

It has also become increasingly difficult to determine the origin of a show. Merely because a manga runs for a while in an anthology magazine before a TV show airs, it does not necessarily follow that the manga was "first"; magazines like *Shonen Ace* and *Dengeki Gao* exist as places to test-market story concepts that are already in production as anime. Where we report a 21st-century show "first appeared" in a manga anthology, it should no longer be taken as an indicator that the franchise began as a manga and was only subsequently *adapted* into anime.

Readers looking for anime erotica in particular are advised to start at the index, and not in the main body of the text, in order to guarantee finding the name under which they are looking for a show. We continue to add an asterisk (*) only to those titles with a *legal* release in the English language. Certain titles were briefly made available in English, before becoming officially *unavailable* due to a legal dispute between the Japanese rightsholder and the American release company, and then available once more under a different title, from a different licensor. Particularly in the case of pornography, we have found several cases where fansubs or untranslated pirate editions have been sold in the U.S. without a license from the rights holder.

FORMATS AND LIMITATIONS

Manga sales in Japan have been steadily declining at 2% a year for the last 15 years—the prevalence of second-hand material, rental stores, and libraries, along with the endurance of the acknowledged manga "classics," means that, while comics may still be a lucrative industry for the Japanese, the local market for *new* comics is 30% down from what it was in 1994. However, that's not to say that the Japanese have not found some innovative ways of managing such austere conditions. In the case of *Comic Earth Star*, for example, the magazine is published by Earth Star Entertainment, itself part of the Culture Convenience Club, a shadowy conglomerate that operates many of the shops that form part of Japanese everyday life. Crucially, CCC owns and operates the Tsutaya chain of video rental stores, creating in *Comic Earth Star* its answer to the "media mix" strategies of bigger rivals. If an *Earth Star* manga gets turned into an anime (such as **NOBUNAGUN** or **PUPA**), the owners of Tsutaya rental stores will double-dip the profits. Since CCC also has a 5.8% stake in Japan's biggest used bookstore chain, Book Off, even second-hand manga sales generate some small income for the original publishers.

A similar recession has been blighting anime, even though recent years have seen its success hyped abroad. In 2005, *The Hollywood Reporter* noted that the average Japanese TV channel would be prepared to pay between $5,000 and $20,000 for a half-hour of animation—a fraction of the fees on offer in other territories. No wonder the characters in **GET BACKERS** have a mission that centers around a paltry ¥2 million—at $17,000, the heroes' fee per episode is probably the same as that of the animators who drew them.

Television in modern Japan is a buyers' market, and always has been. Even **ASTRO BOY** could not get off the ground without contributions from sponsors. There is always another mega-corporation tie-in around the corner, which makes channels reluctant to pay much for any show. Sometimes they offer paltry sums that are not enough to cover the costs of making the show in the first place, and why should they not? With anime "taking the world by storm" and foreign-rights buyers queuing up, the channels can claim that a good show need not worry about running into debt, as it will recoup its costs on foreign sales. The result, not unexpectedly, is a large number of poorly animated shows, as production budgets are cut back to the bone, or sanitized productions in which the program makers hope to attract nebulous foreign interest.

In the 1960s, when there was only a handful of shows on the schedules, it did not seem too unlikely that each couple of seasons would see shows about a girl who can grow into an older version of herself, a teenage witch, a superheroine, a boy with a giant robot, and high school ghost stories. There is no arguing that the anime industry has hit upon a number of workable paradigms, and every one of them is a winner with its target audience, guaranteed to hold their attention for a few months—and lure them to buy the spin-offs, toys, books, and games.

In current times, there are many more channels and toy companies fighting for a share, often using the same cookie-cutter show formats. This rarely bothers the target audience, since after all, every year sees a fresh crop of kids who have never seen a transforming robot or schoolgirl. However, it can certainly bother those who watch anime for a living, as we see the same old formats dragged out, dusted off, and kicked at the audience on a regular basis.

It is our job to notice these things and to point readers back to earlier precedents. Readers who do not want anime placed in a historical context are holding the wrong book. They are advised instead to read one of the Japanese anime magazines, which reinvent the wheel every season, refuse to say a bad word about anything, and proclaim "classics" that nobody will have heard of within a couple of years.

In two recent books, *Anime's Media Mix* (2012) by Marc Steinberg and *The Soul of Anime* (2013) by Ian Condry, the authors have argued that form often supersedes content, and that plot is increasingly unimportant, in favor of a vague "world" or "ecology," in which the characters are designed first, and their actions largely exist merely as a peg on which to hang imagery, impressions, and merchandise. One certainly gets the feeling with many anime that story has been largely thrown out of the window in favor of a series of generic hazards, quests, and threat templates, answered with an equally common series of generic upgrades, breakthroughs, and alchemical combinations of machines and magic items like some kind of plot-point Sudoku (**PERSONA**). This is made particularly obvious in those shows that are repurposed in movie or video spin-off forms that largely discard previous continuity in favor of retellings that radically alter character backgrounds or motivations, such as **EUREKA SEVEN** or **EVANGELION**.

It could be argued that anime TV shows in particular have functioned in this way since the 1970s, with only occasional additions of new trends and tropes to the pre-existing panoply of magical girls and boys with robot toys. Although the copying of plots and ideas on a regular basis has been a common feature of children's anime from **BRAVE SAGA** to **GUNDAM** and all points in between, the early 21st century has taken such cynical recycling to new levels. Time and again, we found ourselves wondering if we had found a new title for an old show, only to discover on viewing that, yes indeed, it was the same old plot but made anew, in the hope that none of the anime audience of 2015 would be around to notice the lack of new ideas. Such retreads of pre-existing ideas are particularly, understandably,

prevalent in modern erotica, but are not solely limited to that genre. We are also running out of new ways to say "boy gets robot" without mentioning **GUNDAM** or **GIGANTOR**, while the number of **TENCHI MUYO!** clones and **EVANGELION** knock-offs has been truly dispiriting. It is all the more annoying when one realizes that there is no reason for remakes to be bad—one of modern anime's greatest shows, **GANKUTSUOU**, has a basic story that is a hundred years old, whereas one of anime's acknowledged classics, **AKIRA**, began as a reimagining of **GIGANTOR**.

But it is not possible to solely blame the people who make anime. The brutal, commercial realities of the industry have brought some unwelcome truths to light about the nature of making cartoons all over the world. Average cartoon consumers will only stay in their demographic bracket for a maximum of two years. They buy the toys for one show as a child, then might move on to the cards or the console game tie-in for another, and if the animation company is lucky, they may even turn into serious fans, buy *Newtype* for a couple of years, and become regular consumers of the more rarefied world of straight-to-video animation. If the company can hold their attention for long enough, they might even be steered into erotic anime for a while. Eventually other concerns—a day job, marriage, children—remove most of the audience from the world of animation, although these same concerns may drive them into the similar world of live-action television drama.

So while we as authors may rail constantly at the lack of originality in the modern anime world, we must recognize that its modern creators, particularly in television, are forced to work within outrageous restrictions. Anime budgets have been in a state of constant crisis since 1963, forced to pander to the demands of toy companies and broadcasters. Meanwhile, the audience itself is rarely faithful for more than a couple of seasons; children grow up fast, and even if someone were to create the perfect show for eight-year-olds tomorrow, it would be old news not only to them when they turn nine, but also to their younger siblings in search of something just different enough to clear them of any suspicion of "copying" their elders' interests.

We should also recognize the remarkable achievements of three generations of creators. In particular, the founding fathers of modern manga, Osamu Tezuka, Mitsuteru Yokoyama, and Shotaro Ishinomori, managed to hit on a series of formulae that have, in their modern adaptations and applications, carried Japanese culture all over the world. If we complain about the latest modern-dress version of ASTRO BOY, should we not also complain about a new production of *King Lear*? It is not the repurposing and recycling itself that irritates us; it is that is often so half-hearted and disdainful. The term "fan service," in particular, has become an industrial shorthand, blaming the *viewers* if a show is bad. Meanwhile, the annual talent contest from Kyoto Animation continues to solicit scripts from the Japanese public, but has refused to award its million-yen grand prize for the last four years. Despite this apparent lofty benchmark of excellence, it has then put the runners-up into production anyway. So they'll *do*, apparently: not good enough for the award, but good enough to dole out to FANDOM.

DEVELOPMENTS AND POSSIBILITIES

Modern restrictions and expectations are most apparent at the beginning of each season, when the labors of the previous months are broken down into a series of banal press releases that manage to make almost everything look the same. At the time of their initial broadcast, both ESCAFLOWNE and EVANGELION were "sold" to the magazines as almost identical shows, along the lines of "teen gets robot." The anime industry grinds down new entrants with cruel rapidity, although sometimes it is possible to discern a cou-

ple of areas in a new production where someone has yet to become jaded—a TV show might boast wonderful music like BRAIN POWERED, or innovative computer graphics like LAST EXILE; it might have a remarkably intelligent script like PATLABOR or the GHOST IN THE SHELL spin-off *Stand Alone Complex*, or a distinctive, eye-catching art style like HAIBANE RENMEI. But a show that has *all* those hallmarks is rare indeed.

The idea that fans of anime for anime's sake constitute an important market sector is nothing new—it was a feature of the arrival of home video players in the 1970s and 1980s, especially the video cassette recorder, and the theme of Gainax's landmark OTAKU NO VIDEO. However, in an age where only fanatic devotees are prepared to forgive many of modern anime's shortcomings, numerous shows pander desperately to the fan audience, with a crop of solipsistic titles such as ANIMATION RUNNER KUROMI-CHAN, COMIC PARTY, ANIME SHOP-KEEPER, and COSPLAY COMPLEX. Some may regard this as the anime equivalent of "reality TV," in which mainstream entertainment becomes so dull that the audience prefers to turn the camera on itself. Others may see it as a recognition of the size and purchasing power of the fandom bloc—with TV niches in the mainstream "narrowcasting" to ever smaller interest groups, the many thousands of active fans now constitute a sizable enough market to generate its own entertainment and consumption, up to a point. According to statistics published by the Nomura Research Institute in 2005, the total anime *fanbase* in Japan amounts to roughly 112,000 people, which is to say, the circulation of *Newtype* magazine, or 0.1% of the Japanese population (RATINGS AND BOX OFFICE). While more than a million members of the Japanese public might flock to see the latest NARUTO film, the hard core of anime fans remains a tiny population, and *fan*-focused products speak to a declining niche within Japanese society. Many niche interest shows still retail at $100 a disc, intended in Japan for a rental, rather than retail market. Kickstarter arguably arrived a little late in Japan, partly because many shows were effectively already being crowd-funded by a population of only one or two thousand fans, paying ten times as much as American consumers.

The centralization of the anime business back in Japan, and the shakeout of niche-interest fandom has led to an increased focus on marketing direct to fans, such as the subscriber-based streaming portal Daisuki. Production I.G's first foray into crowd-sourcing, the Kickstarter-funded KICK-HEART, was closely watched by both fandom and other companies, while Anime Sols now uses limited online streaming as a means of soliciting crowd-sourced orders for subtitled DVD boxes. This has offered new leases on life for old material such as CREAMY MAMI, FUMOON, or BANDAR BOOK, and speaks volumes about the size of the "otaku" market, often requiring only a thousand orders to go into production on a limited edition, and as in the case of *Yatterman*, sometimes still failing to do so. Behind the scenes, it also amortizes the cost of generating an archive of subtitles for any future Japanese releases. Even a "failed" Anime Sols project generates English-language assets, rights to which revert to the Japanese at the termination of each license. Such legacy assets may be incorporated into future Japan-only releases, a trend already visible in the repurposing of 1990s Anglophone materials in the 2013 rerelease of *Macross Plus* (MACROSS), controversially produced as a region-free Japanese Blu-ray, containing dual language and subtitle tracks in both English and Japanese. This decision effectively turned the "gray importing" problem on its head, feeding a new "gray export" market for overseas fans prepared to pay $100 for the item, but also potentially inhibiting the viability of overseas territories.

The immediate future of niche-interest anime, which is to say, everything except cine-ma blockbusters and prime-time television, is a drift toward increasingly expensive limited editions, as Japanese rights-holders attempt to train foreign fans to accept Japanese pricing policies. When the two season box sets of *Ghost in the Shell: Stand Alone Complex* (GHOST IN THE SHELL) retail in Japan for a total of just under $600, this is a tall order. Where anime was once dumped on viewers for "free" via television, it is now more likely to be sold as an exclusive, rare item with notional added value and bonus extras, such as the expensive U.S. release of GARDEN OF SINNERS.

It is a fact little acknowledged in the media that innovations are often pioneered in the pornographic world—EROTICA AND PORNOGRAPHY were at the forefront of the move into straight-to-video distribution in the 1980s and formed the driving force of much of the late-night anime of the 1990s. Similarly, erotica was first with online ordering, presaging the modern mainstream where over 38% of all anime in Japan are purchased online, either as downloads or as DVDs from online retailers. In our 2006 edition, we used such precedents from pornography to predict that mainstream anime would increasingly favor online distribution and streaming. Today, we predict that if the mainstream continues to follow in erotica's wake, then in the next five years, we might expect to see anime much less visible to the general public, as an increasingly closed circle of consumption feeds the interests of an ever-smaller group of fans, paying for an ever more exclusive product. The rise of mobile phones as a viewing platform also appears to have influenced average running times, some of which are starting to fall below the 20-minute line. Many anime since 1963 have been a notional "half-hour" in length, around 24 minutes with space for commercials, a paradigm repeated on video to create the impression of TV length. However, this appears to be diminishing, as several recent porn productions favor shorter running times fitted to the attention spans and likely viewing slots of phone viewers, suggesting that the presence of TV, or rather the illusion of a TV format, is fading from the mind of producers. By 2019, anime in general could be substantially shorter; we predict increasing numbers of episodes clocking in at the 20-minute mark.

The next five years will also see an increasing trend for "post-anime," as coproduction deals dilute any specifically "Japanese" quality to Japanese animation, and some territories choose to discard the animation itself in favor of an adaptation merely of the basic narrative while the copyright holder rakes off a license fee. This applies not only to the high-profile Hollywood versions of TRANSFORMERS and SPEED RACER, or the U.S.-Hong Kong remake of *Astro Boy* (2009), but also to subtler appropriations, such as STAR OF THE GIANTS, almost unrecognizably repurposed as the Indian cricket story *Suraj the Rising Star* (2012), or the release of *Robot Atom*, a Nigerian ASTRO BOY remake in 2014; others are sure to follow.

Innovation in modern anime (i.e., since 1983) comes in the form of refinements and experiments with existing forms. Sometimes, the achievements are not immediately obvious. In GUNDAM, SAILOR MOON, and POKÉMON, the true genius lay in the pioneering of "multimedia" franchises for their target audiences; in DALLOS, it was the opening up of a new niche for more adult material. For MAISON IKKOKU, TENCHI MUYO!, and CHOBITS, it was the refinement of an old genre that altered the chaste titillation of *I Dream of Jeannie* and *Bewitched* for a Japanese TV audience.

Many modern achievements have been reactive, as a show resists overlying trends, such as COWBOY BEBOP, deliberately conceived as a sci-fi show without giant robots, or EVANGELION, written in reaction to the robot shows of the previous generation. GANTZ is TV for a generation that no longer watches TV, designed instead for the longer-term viewing habits of TiVo users and DVD purchasers. Perhaps the greatest innovation of all in modern times comes in VOICES OF A DISTANT STAR, the first release to truly utilize software that allowed a private individual to completely bypass the old distribution system. The world of Japanese animated features is less confused, since it is still dominated by Hayao Miyazaki, as it has been for the last 20 years. However, this, too, is about to change, with THE WIND RISES heralding his official retirement from feature filmmaking in 2013. Compared to the accomplishments of Studio Ghibli at the Japanese box office, most other anime features are mere marketing exercises or flashes in the pan.

The last 30 years have been dominated by the rise of computers (GAMING AND DIGITAL ANIMATION), first through the growing amount of investment money available for game-related anime, then in the exodus of creative staff out of anime altogether for the better rewards of the computer industry. Erosion of talent in anime proper served to accelerate the growth of the use of computers, a position that only increased the likelihood of gaming investment still further. Many anime studios are now part- or fully owned by gaming companies and media conglomerates, codifying and streamlining their long-standing roles as vehicles for ADVERTISING AND SPONSORSHIP, but also encouraging producers and viewers to regard any anime production as less of a stand-alone product, and more as a facet of an overall media mix.

Acknowledgments

This edition incorporates hundreds of clarifications, corrections, and outright rewrites of some entries, based both on our own research and the comments of our readers, for which we are eternally grateful. We hope we have remembered all of those who helped us, but if some have fallen through the cracks, our apologies in advance.

We would like to thank the following people for their help and additional suggestions for the third edition: Chris Adamson, Matt Alt, David Banuelos, C. D. Carson, Gemma Cox, John Dunne, Frank Guo, Andy Hanley, Andrew Hewson, Tony Kehoe, Vlasta Konvicna, Freddy Litten, Jerome Mazandarani, Martin Minar, Neil Nadelman, Andrew Osmond, Fraser Overington, Andrew Partridge, "Publius," Adam Rambousek, Clive Reames, James Reed, Bella Sabbagh, Julia Sertori, Megan Taylor, Reiko Tokoro, Mike Toole, Gorm Thomsen, Greg Wicker, Ian Wolf, Wang Xue'er, and Patsy Zukav. Peter Goodman of Stone Bridge Press continues to hurl his money into this particular pit, seemingly just to see the pretty colors it makes as it burns. A very special thanks is due to Lawrence P. Hayes and John C. Watson, who voluntarily conducted thorough audits of the information in the previous edition, and whose detailed comments have measurably improved this third iteration. Special recognition should also go to our editor Beth Cary, back for a third sentence of misery with a mouse-click, who went far beyond the call of duty in chasing down the names of obscure pornographers, rescuing animators from the oblivion of misread kanji, arguing for the difference between *Jeanie* (who has light-brown hair) versus *Jeannie* (the genie), and similar issues of semantics and nomenclature. Our beta-readers in order of passes, John C. Watson (again), Andrew Osmond, and Marc Hairston, have steered us toward many other corrections and alterations, although we have not always followed their advice—any remaining errors are, of course, ours.

J. C., H. M.

Publisher's Note

The Anime Encyclopedia is, once again, approximately 40% larger than before, making this third edition about twice the size of its first edition published in 2001. In today's worlds of popular entertainment and print publishing, the passage of a dozen plus a couple years represents a lifetime of change. We say this because the generation of anime viewers and readers who obtained the first volume are perhaps a full evolutionary step farther advanced than their "distant" forebears when it comes to how they choose to watch anime and obtain information about their favorite films, studios, voice actors, and artists. Thanks to the Internet, details about the most obscure film need no longer hide only in a poorly printed catalog tucked away on a dusty shelf or in some collector's box. And thanks to the Internet, too, every wild theory and wrongheaded notion is available for careless propagation throughout fandom and on into mainstream consciousness.

So there is every good reason to continue to publish encyclopedias that at least attempt to get their facts straight. As a single physical object, however, this one has just about reached its limit. In order to accommodate this third edition between two covers we have (and perhaps you haven't noticed!) increased its trim size by a half inch here, a quarter inch there. More significant is that in order to appease the limitations of print technology we had to engineer the typesetting and content to be sure we wouldn't exceed 1,200 pages. We are printing this book on a digital press (toner on paper) and not on what used to be the standard offset press (ink on paper). This manufacture is the result of reader demand for a heavy, bulky, and expensive physical edition dropping well below the level where traditional offset printing is economical. The digital press does not reward volume printing, but it does make it possible for us to produce a three-dimensional book one at a time or a dozen at a time, whatever the market demands.

That is all well and good for the libraries and devotees who demand hard copies. Would there were more of them! But readers these days generally prefer reference materials online, where searches are immediate and diverse resources are always a click away.

So a governing emphasis for this third edition has been to design the content for a fully digital platform. If you obtain the e-book version of *The Anime Encyclopedia*, you will discover that cross-references within it transport you immediately to a main entry. If you click on a main entry title, you will, if your e-reader is online, be taken to a site on the Internet where you can find more information about the film, including links to image collections, biographies, related works, and so on. Instead of opening a narrow window on the anime landscape, *The Anime Encyclopedia* now appropriately takes you to the entire anime universe itself. Over time, we hope to continue to refresh and refine the hyperlinks in the digital edition. The presence of a printed, alphabetical index in the physical volume makes content updates there much more problematic, so we do encourage readers to continue to first check our website (http://www.stonebridge.com) for fresh information, corrections, and updates. Parents and teachers please note that not all of the hyperlinked sites are kid friendly or suitable for viewing in public spaces like schools and libraries.

In previous volumes we included illustrations from a smattering of films covered in the main entries. While the total number of illustrations was few, we labored long and hard to obtain them and were profoundly grateful to many studios, artists, and distributors for their generosity.

In the present volume, we have decided to dispense with illustrations entirely. This may draw howls of protest, but we have our reasons. One reason is that images these days are everywhere on the Internet. Rather than one small panel in black and white on a single page, sequences of stunning images in full color can now be found quickly by searching in a browser or, as we intend, simply by clicking on a live link in our digital edition.

Another reason for going "text only" is that obtaining images from Japan is now more grueling and expensive than ever before. Japanese studios, we are sad to say, continue to make the lives of supplicants miserable by failing to respond to requests, charging exorbitant amounts for trivial usages, and getting hopelessly entangled both in their paranoid fantasies of rampant piracy attacks and their perceived obligations to contact each and every possible stakeholder separately. It is far easier for them to just say no, and often that is what they do.

Arguments for fair use, particularly for academic materials, are well established in the U.S. and Europe but fall on deaf ears in many Japanese quarters. We have never really understood why, but we have decided it is simply not worth the time or expense to argue the point. We urge Japanese film studios and all entertainment stakeholders to join the information age and come up with some means to allow writers, especially scholars, to affordably use illustrative materials in their writings. If the whole point of a *visual* medium is its *visual* narrative, preventing critics and scholars from illustrating their points with actual images from the works they are discussing is crippling—and does nothing to help promote the work or encourage its viewing overseas.

On a softer note, we would very much like to applaud and thank the many fans who wrote in with comments and corrections over the years. Your eagle eyes and attention to detail have made this a better work.

We would also like to thank the many friends of the press and of the previous editions for your continued support and patience.

And we would especially like to thank Jonathan and Helen for their astonishing devotion to this publication and to keeping it a lively and informative resource. As much as their text is a window into the anime universe, it also reveals the workings of two extraordinarily discerning, intelligent minds.

Please send comments, corrections, complaints, information updates, and letters via e-mail to:

animeinfo@stonebridge.com

STONE BRIDGE PRESS

THE ANIME ENCYCLOPEDIA

ABBREVIATIONS AND KEY

The following abbreviations are used throughout the listings:

*	available in English
JPN	released in Japan as
AKA	"also known as" (alternative title)
DIR	directed by
SCR	script by
DES	design by
ANI	lead animation by
MUS	music by
PRD	production by
N/C	not credited
N/D	no data available
(b/w)	black and white
(m)	movie
(TV)	[made for] TV
(TVm)	TV movie
(v)	video
?	uncertain (data; usually episode count)
ca.	circa, approximately
ep., eps.	episode(s)
min., mins.	minute(s)
BOLDFACE TYPE	cross-reference to main entry (in the e-edition, boldface main-entry headings are Internet hyperlinks)
*DE	cross-reference to *The Dorama Encyclopedia*
Ⓛ	language advisory
Ⓝ	nudity advisory
Ⓥ	violence advisory

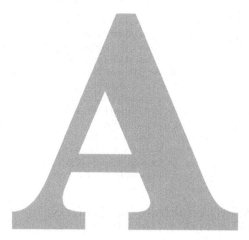

A-CHANNEL *

2011. AKA: *A-Channel the Animation*. TV series, video. DIR: Manabu Ono. SCR: Tatsuhiko Urahata. DES: Masakatsu Sasaki, Hiroki Matsumoto. ANI: Masakatsu Sasaki. Sayuri Sugifuji, Hong Shen, Hideyuki Kataoka. MUS: Satoru Kosaki. PRD: Aniplex, Dentsu, Houbunsha, MBS. 24 mins. x 12 eps. (TV), 25 mins. x 2 eps. (v).

Toru passes the entrance exam that will let her attend the same high school as her childhood friend and secret love Run. She goes to Run's house to break the good news, but finds her hugging another girl. Yuko is at Run's school already, and soon Toru becomes a part of the group with their other friend, Nagi. A gentle slice-of-life comedy with mild overtones of *girls-love*, this is based on a four-panel manga strip by bb Kuroda, running in *Manga Time Kirara Karat* since December 2008. Eleven two-minute episodes made up of outtakes from each episodes, *+A-Channel*, were included on the Japanese DVD and BluRay release in 2011. The trials and triumphs of high school life and loving your best friend are supplemented with fun out of school in a standalone two-part video, *A-Channel + Smile*, released in 2012 from the same producers, director, and writer.

A.I.C.

Literally "Anime International Company," although it is usually identified by its acronym, not its full name. Founded in 1982 by former EG World and Anime Room staffer Toru Miura, the company first contributed to later episodes of the color **ASTRO BOY** remake. Notable employees have included Katsuhito Akiyama, Hiroyuki Kitazume, Hiroyuki Kawagoe, and Hiroki Hayashi. Representative works include **AD POLICE**, **BLACK HEAVEN**, and numerous projects for Pioneer/Geneon (see **DENTSU**).

A.LI.CE *

1999. Movie. DIR: Kenichi Maejima. SCR: Masahiro Yoshimoto. DES: Hirosuke Kizaki. ANI: N/C. MUS: Akira Murata. PRD: Gaga Communications. 85 mins.

A.Li.Ce throws the viewer straight into the middle of the action, with its heroine fleeing from cyborgs across icy wastes. The background details are only filled in gradually—we are in Lapland in 2030, but 16-year-old Alice's last memory was of an accident on a space shuttle many years earlier. Her guardian is a stewardess robot programmed to protect her, and their traveling companion is Yuan, a local orphan who has lived alone since his parents were "relocated" in an illogical environmental scheme by the Earth's new ruler, Nero.

An early effort in digital animation, *A.Li.Ce* often resembles a long scene from a computer game, unsurprising as its writer's previous credits included the game *Shen Mue*. Like all the best computer games, the movie regularly alters its protagonists' aims for maximum effect. What begins as a straightforward chase sequence soon becomes a quest to acquire information and resources. Once Alice realizes that someone has brought her to the future for an unexplained purpose, it changes once more into a train journey fraught with peril. Eluding Nero's Stealth Warriors, only to be captured by the rebellious Liberation Forces, the cast is temporarily split up, as Yuan and Maria escape from custody, while Alice enters cyberspace to help the resistance break into Nero's fortress. This, it transpires, is why she is needed, as her past self was/is Nero's mother, affording her identical brain patterns access to the citadel's defensive computer systems.

In a series of last-minute twists, Alice discovers that *she* is partly responsible for Nero's reign of terror. Nero has decimated the world's population in a misguided attempt to reduce pollution (compare to **BLUE REMAINS**), itself a misreading of Alice's memories of the dying wish of her suicidal school-friend Yumi. The motives of the Liberation Forces are found to be even more questionable, and Alice returns to the past to set things right. This, however, is where the narrative falls apart, as her return is visibly demonstrated to make little difference to the future she has just left. We also see her meeting the man who will become Nero's father, though now she presumably does so with the full knowledge of his future death, thereby making it impossible that the events we have just seen will actually take place.

Time-travel paradoxes aside, *A.Li.Ce* remains an intriguing entry in the genre, and a surer step into computer animation than the disappointing **VISITOR**. In Maria, it also has an intriguing take on the ubiquitous robot-girls of anime—a svelte woman in revealing costumes, with an array of pop-out gadgets and power sockets like a 21st-century **DORAEMON**. Her name is bestowed upon her by Alice herself, not in homage to the Maria of Fritz Lang's *Metropolis* (see **METAL ANGEL MARIE**) but because of her chance resemblance to a statue of the Virgin Mary. Later, she is augmented twice, once by Yuan and once in a self-inflicted upgrade, ending the movie with high-powered retractable machine guns, and built-in roller skates that help circumvent the film's primitive motion-capture. Soon transformed into a battle-robot, Maria retains vestiges of her former programming, and persists in bossing her charges around as if she is still serving in-flight drinks.

A15 ANTHOLOGY: COSMOPOLITAN PRAYERS, AIM FOR THE HIT, LOVE LOVE

2004. JPN: *Cho Henshin Cos ∞ Prayers; Hit o Nerae; Love Love*. AKA: *Super-Transforming Cos(mopolitan) Prayers; Aim for the Hit*. TV series. DIR: Takeo Takahashi. SCR: Naruhisa Arakawa. DES: Miwa Oshima. ANI: Miwa Oshima. MUS: Toshihiko Sahashi. PRD: M-O-E, Imagin, Studio Live, TV Kanagawa. 13 mins. x 8 eps. (*Cos Prayers*); 13 mins. x 8 eps. (*Aim for the Hit*); 13 mins. x 9 eps; 13 mins. x 9 eps. (*Love Love*); + 4 bonus DVD episodes each.

Three stories strung out in short snippets in a late-night slot showing PG-15-rated titles. In *Cosmopolitan Prayers*, a Japanese schoolgirl is transported to the legendary land of **IZUMO**, where she must team up with local priestesses to rescue the sun goddess, Amaterasu, who has been imprisoned within a network of black towers. Using their mystic powers to transform, or "charm up," to their magical forms, the girls fight demons and demigods to keep the world safe—**FUSHIGI YUGI** crashed into **SAILOR MOON**, with a title deliberately designed to recall *cosplay* ("Costume Play"), the Engrish term for anime-related fancy dress.

Similar allusions might be expected in *Aim for the Hit* (AKA *Smash Hit*), which, despite its titular resemblance to **AIM FOR THE ACE**, is concerned not with sporting triumph but a ratings-chasing TV program. Twenty-five-year-old mystery fanatic Mizuki gets the chance of a lifetime when she's appointed as producer of a new show, but she's hardly the ideal choice for the job. She's physically immature, and her childlike appearance goes with a whining

attitude that leads to her colleagues making fun of her. Nor is the film much to her liking, since it is a derivative show about a Japanese schoolgirl saving the world. In a triumph of solipsism, the show that Mizuki cannot stand is *Cosmopolitan Prayers*—perhaps in an allegory aimed at animators forced to put aside their dreams in order to pay the bills on shows like this. But like her media colleague **ANIMATION RUNNER KUROMI-CHAN**, she finally pulls through.

Love Love features Naoto Oizumi, a high school student with an off-putting stare, hired as a cameraman by the production company in *Aim for the Hit*, and tasked with filming the training of the actresses who have been hired to star in *Cosmopolitan Prayers*, thereby achieving what must be a modern animator's idea of franchise paradise: the pop idols of **KIRA KIRA MELODY ACADEMY** crashed into **TENCHI MUYO**!

ABASHIRI FAMILY, THE *

1991. JPN: *Abashiri Ikka*. Video. DIR: Takashi Watanabe. SCR: Takashi Watanabe. DES: Shigenori Kurii. ANI: Shigenori Kurii. MUS: Takeo Miratsu. PRD: Dynamic Planning, Studio Pierrot, Soeishinsha, NEXTART. 75 mins.

Papa Abashiri, leader of one of the most notorious criminal syndicates in history, decides it's time for his superpowered family to retire so his daughter, Kukunosuke, can have a normal existence. However, her "normal" school turns out to be a hunting ground for crazed perverts and brawlers, who have no intention of teaching the students anything. As the violence escalates, Kukunosuke calls in her family to fight against the principal in a final showdown of bone-crunchingly epic proportions.

Recalling **SUKEBAN DEKA**, with its tale of a bad girl trying to go straight, and **DEBUTANTE DETECTIVES**, with its well-connected students, *The Abashiri Family* was originally released as four short chapters in the **RENTAMAN** video magazine. It was soon compiled into this omnibus edition, which is the version circulated in the English language. Its cartoonish comedy angle gives it more in common with creator Go Nagai's **KEKKO KAMEN** and **HANAPPE BAZOOKA** than with his more serious stories, but the disjointed nature of the original production makes for an inferior offering. Director Watanabe would go on to adapt another Nagai story, **BLACK LION**.

ABE, YOSHITOSHI

1971–. A graduate of Tokyo National University of Fine Arts and Music, Abe's dark, brooding artwork established distinctive looks in **SERIAL EXPERIMENTS LAIN**, **HAIBANE RENMEI** (based on his own amateur publication), and **TEXHNOLYZE**. He also designed the characters and wrote the manga of **NIEA_7**. He favors unorthodox typography and likes his name to be written with the Y in lower case and the B in upper. We prefer to keep our English-language text readable.

ABNORMAL PHYSIOLOGY SEMINAR

2010. JPN: *Hentai Semi Seminar*. AKA: *Hen Semi*. TV series, video. DIR: Ryoki Kamitsubo, Takao Kato. SCR: Takamitsu Kono, Deko Akao. DES: Sunao Chikaoka, Aya Kuginuki, Toshihiro Kohama, Kaoru Aoki. ANI: Sunao Chikaoka, Makoto Oda, Park Sang-Jin, Noboyuki Furukawa. MUS: Kei Haneoka, Masaru Yokoyama. PRD: Xebec, Starchild Records, Kodansha, Starchild Records, The Klockworx Co., Ltd. 12 mins. x 2 eps. (v), 15 mins. x 13 eps. (TV).

An innocent university student is taking a sexual perversion seminar led by a deviant professor. Will she keep her morals and her sanity intact? Well, what do you think? In Britain this could be the plot for one of the *Carry On* films, a series of bawdy movies in which more was suggested than shown. In Japan, and in anime, the clichés have developed in a different way: deviant doctor/innocent nurse, deviant teacher/innocent high school girl, and on and on and on. Based on a manga by Tagro, who drew the manga for Gainax's **PANTY AND STOCKING WITH GARTERBELT**, this riff makes mildly interesting use of cheap design, animation corner-cutting, and story tropes, but not so interesting that you should spend four hours of your life checking them out. Of more interest is the Korean Park Sang-Jin, director of three episodes, and the number of Korean key animators on the credits. Such foreign creatives usually endure a subaltern status on anime productions; here we see them getting credit where it's due, although perhaps they wish they hadn't. **N**

ACCEL WORLD *

2010. TV series, video. DIR: Masakazu Obara. SCR: Hiroyuki Yoshino, Jukki Hanada, Masahiro Yokotani, Noboru Kimura. DES: Yukiko Aikei, Nobutaka Ike, Takafumi Nishima. ANI: Yukiko Aikei, Eri Ogawa, Shinsuke Yanagi. MUS: Hiroyuki Oshima, MintJam, onoken. PRD: Sunrise, ASCII Media Works, GENCO, Bandai Namco, Warner Bros. 24 mins. x 24 eps. (TV), 24 mins. x 2 eps. (V).

In 2046 a virtual network called Neurolinker is accessible by the entire world on its cellphones (compare to SUMMER WARS). It's a refuge for Haruyuki, a middle school student who escapes into the world of online gaming to avoid the bullies that target him constantly. Then the most popular girl in his school beats him at online squash and sends him into a panic. That's not the worst of it—she approaches him in real life and, seemingly for no reason, gives him a new fighting game called Brain Burst. Haruyuki finds he can actually pause reality with the incredible cognitive acceleration the game gives him—but there's a downside. If you lose too often you are thrown out of the game, never to return.

The rest of the world may mock the loser whose only skill is a facility for computer games, but within another world, where a cool avatar can take over from the unkind physical reality, he may be an idol and a hero. So when that reality is taken away from him, the rest of the world naturally crumbles. Reki Kawahara's understanding of this basic truth of VR is key to this clever, if rather talky, take on the integration of technology into everyday life. Although written later than SWORD ART ONLINE, this novel series was animated earlier but stayed largely below the radar. Video sequels in 2012 and 2013 caused relatively little interest in the West until the anime arrival of its flashier sibling. Ⓝ

ACCELERANDO

2007. JPN: Accelerando—Datenshitachi no Sasayaki. AKA: Accelerando—Angels' Secret Whispers. Video. DIR: Hideki Araki. SCR: N/C (Accelerando), Shinichiro Sawayama (both sequels). DES: Hideki Araki. ANI: Hideki Araki. MUS: N/C. PRD: Pink Pineapple. 30 mins. x 4 eps. (v, Accelerando), 27 mins. x 12 eps. (v, Stringendo), 30 mins. x 3 eps. (v, S&A), 30 mins. x 2 eps. (v, Stretta), 40 mins. x 4 eps. (v, Core Mix).

Waitress Tamaki and her lover Kurono have sex at the café where Tamaki works. Ohashi, a friend of both, has a crush on

Tamaki and often visits the café to see her. Realizing how he feels, Kurono decides to force the shy boy to confess his feelings by getting Tamaki aroused and sending her to wait on Ohashi, who can't resist the scent of her arousal.

Director Araki started as an in-betweener on NIGHT ON THE GALACTIC RAILROAD and worked his way through key animation, animation directing, and design to directing a number of Pink Pineapple titles. The stories are predictable (with scenes from the first two repeated in the second) and character development is almost nonexistent, but the art and design are excellent, though initially good animation quality declines across the series.

Animator and Accelerando manga creator Yuko Seto has named three manga after musical terms, though the stories have nothing to do with music. Araki also directed the video series based on Seto's Stringendo, set in a high school and written by veteran Pink Pinkapple scriptman Shinichiro Sawayama. Stringendo: Angel-tachi no Private Lesson ran to 12 27-minute episodes between 2006 and 2012. The common thread that ties all Seto's manga together is the fantasy of average dorks having sex with beautiful high school girls and watching them turn each other on, and Araki produces good-looking anime versions. For those without time to watch the whole series, four compilations of sex scenes were released in 2012 under the title Stringendo: Core Mix Megamori: Okazu Desu Yo.

A 2008 video series, the three-part Stringendo & Accelerando Ultimatum—Sera, is intended as a sequel to both Accelerando and Stringendo. In 2009 Araki and Sawayama also worked on Stretta, a two-part series along the same lines as Stringendo. The couples from both earlier series appear in Stretta. Ⓝ

ACROBUNCH

1982. JPN: Makyo Densetsu Acrobunch. AKA: Haunted Frontier Legend Acrobunch. TV series. DIR: Masakazu Yasumura, Satoshi Hisaoka. SCR: Masaru Yamamoto. DES: Shigenori Kageyama, Mutsumi Inomata, Masakazu Higuchi. ANI: Kazuhiro Taga, Masakazu Yasumura, Hideki Takayama, Yutaka Arai, Kazuhiro Ochi. MUS: Masaji Maruyama. PRD: Nippon TV. 30 mins. x 24 eps.

Half-Japanese amateur inventor Tatsuya

Lando talks his five almost all-American children into piloting his latest project, a transforming super-robot called Acrobunch. Older boys Hiro and Ryo pilot the two Buncher Hornets, while twin girls Miki and Rika ride the Buncher Arrow flying motorcycles. Middle-child Jun is the 15-year-old boy who gets to pilot the Acrobunch unit formed from the combination of all the vehicles with dad's Falcon Buncher main craft. Tatsuya is searching for the ancient treasure of Quaschika, which was the true inspiration behind the ancient stories of Atlantis. But Lando is not the only one—Emperor Delos of the undersea Goblin empire is also searching for the Quaschika, and the Acrobunch robot becomes the last line of defense between them and Earth. Each week, it must fight against the robots of the Goblin armies, one of which is led by Delos's own daughter, Queen Shiira, who develops a crush on her enemy Hiro.

Shunted around the schedules and between two different production studios, the troubled Acrobunch ("a robot controlled by a bunch of acrobats!") nevertheless served as a training ground for a group of new talents who would find fame in the decades to come. It was the first anime job for future TEKKAMAN-designer Rei Nakahara. Among the animators, Arai would work on CITY HUNTER, Ochi would make HIKARIAN, and Takayama would become the director of the notorious UROTSUKIDOJI series. Two decades later, Inomata produced similar character designs for BRAIN POWERED.

AD POLICE *

1990. Video, TV series. DIR: Akihiko Takahashi, Akira Nishimori. SCR: Sho Aikawa. DES: Tony Takezaki, Fujio Oda, Toru Nagasuki. ANI: Fujio Oda, Hiroyuki Kitazume. MUS: Kaoru Mizutani. PRD: Artmic, Youmex, AIC. 40 mins. x 3 eps. (v1), 25 mins. x 12 eps. (TV), 30 mins. x 3 eps. (v2, Parasite Dolls).

A dark spin-off from Toshimichi Suzuki's BUBBLEGUM CRISIS, AD Police concentrates on the AD(vanced) antirobot crime division of Mega Tokyo's police force. Leon McNicol, a minor character in the original series, is partnered here with butch ladycop Gena in several investigations that play with ideas of humanity in a high-tech society. The "voomer"/"boomer" robots here are all female in the man's world of the ADP, where only women who are prepared to become one with machines stand a chance in it. Whereas this device was used in *Bubblegum Crisis* as an excuse for girls with impressive high-tech kits, here it is far more misogynistic, as femininity is gradually eroded by bionics and prosthetics, taking characters' humanity with it. A businesswoman, for example, is only successful in the boardroom after she has a hysterectomy, but the trauma turns her into a serial killer. There are shades of *Blade Runner* in the sex-android stalker that locks onto the man who injured her, and there are also blatant steals from *Robocop* in the final chapter, wherein one of Gena's ex-boyfriends receives so much augmentation that his tongue is the only part of his original body that remains.

Canceled after just three of the planned five episodes, the franchise was not revived until 1999, in the wake of the *Bubblegum Crisis 2040* remake, as a 12-part TV Tokyo series directed by Hidehito Ueda. The new *AD Police* was a far shallower affair, ditching many of the old characters in favor of a buddy-movie cliché between rapid-response robot-crime cop Takeru Sasaki and his new partner, Hans Krief. Clearly made with half an eye on the overseas market (all the other leads have foreign names like Paul Sanders, Liam Fletcher, and Nancy Wilson), the melting-pot remake is something of a disappointment.

The franchise was briefly resurrected in *Parasite Dolls* (2003), a three-part video series directed by Kazuto Nakazawa, focusing on a clandestine branch of the AD Police, called, somewhat unimaginatively, Branch. The story focuses on Buzz, an officer like writer Chiaki Konaka's earlier Ross Sylibus in **ARMITAGE III**, who is transferred to an unappealing new posting and forced to cooperate with a detested robot partner. *Parasite Dolls* also exists in a movie-length edit, which is the version most commonly found outside Japan. **ⒸⓃⓋ**

ADRIFT IN THE PACIFIC *

1982. JPN: *Jugo Shonen no Hyoryuki*. AKA: *15 Boys Adrift; Deux Ans de Vacances*. TV special. DIR: Yasuji Mori, Yoshio Kuroda. SCR: Shunichi Yukimuro. DES: Hiroshi Wagatsuma, Rumiko Takahashi. ANI: Tatsuo Ogawa, Hideo Maeda. MUS: Katsutoshi Nagasawa. PRD: Toei,

Fuji TV. 75 mins. (TVm1), 84 mins. (TVm2). When bad weather causes her to slip her moorings and drift out to sea, the British schooner Sloughi is left in the hands of the 15 schoolboys on holiday. Without officers or sailors on board, the French boy Briant manages to organize the group and beach the ship on a deserted island they name Cherman after their school. The upper-class British boy, Doniphan, begins to argue with Briant about who should be in charge, and problems are multiplied a hundredfold when a 16th castaway washes up on the shore—a schoolgirl called Kate.

Deux Ans de Vacances, Jules Verne's low-rent copy of **SWISS FAMILY ROBINSON**, remains immeasurably more popular in Japanese than in English. This TV movie included a young design assistant called Rumiko Takahashi, whose growing success with **URUSEI YATSURA** would make her rich and unlikely to work in animation again.

In 1987, the story was remade as another TV movie to cash in on the popularity of the Hollywood movie *Stand By Me* (which also featured several boys going exploring and getting mildly upset). Directed by Masayuki Akehi, the new version featured Maria Kawamura, shortly to find fame as Jung Freud in **GUNBUSTER**, as the troublesome Kate. This second TV movie was released in English as *Story of 15 Boys*, a pedantically faithful **TRANSLATION** of the Japanese title suggesting that the U.S. distributor knew little of Verne's original. See also **VIDEO PICTURE BOOK**, **VIFAM**, and in an awfully bleak variant, **BOKURANO**.

ADULT FAIRY TALES

2000. JPN: *Yonimo Osoroshii Nihon Mukashibanashi*. Video. DIR: Soichi Masui. SCR: Shige Sotoyama. DES: Kaoru Honma. ANI: N/C. MUS: Miki Kasamatsu. PRD: Tac, Toei. 50 mins.
A deliberate attempt to take **GRIMMS' FAIRY TALES** away from their cuter modern image and back to their darker roots, this series comprises three short versions of popular tales augmented with copious horror and flavor-of-the-moment computer graphics. The tales include *Hansel and Gretel, Blue Beard*, and *Cinderella*, all chosen because they presented an opportunity for the crew to depict stories of love and obsession.

ADULT WOMEN'S ANIME TIME

2011. JPN: *Otona Joshi no Anime Time*. TV series. DIR: Hiroshi Kawamata. SCR: Reiko Yoshida, Kei Yuikawa. DES: Kazuki Ikeda. ANI: Kenichi Tsuchiya. MUS: Mine Kawakami. PRD: The Answer Studio Co. Ltd., NHK, Curio-Scope. 25 mins. x 4 eps.
An occasional drama series for women, presenting the kind of stories that could be made more expensively with live actors, this first installment, *Kawamo o Suberu Kaze (The Wind that Glides Downriver)*, tells the story of Noriko. She's been living in America for five years, and is now heading back to her hometown with a four-year-old son. How will she adjust to life back in Japan amid her old memories? Three further episodes were aired on BS Premium in March 2013, the first directed by Toru Takahashi and written by Tomoko Konparu based on a story by Amy Yamada. CurioScope and NHK have now shifted animation work to Production Reed. There hasn't really been an attempt to present anime dramas about everyday life for an adult audience since **HUMAN CROSSING**. This may well help in broadening the TV audience for anime.

ADVANCER TINA *

1996. Video. DIR: Kan Fukumoto. SCR: Wataru Amano. DES: Hironobu Saito, Kenji Teraoka. ANI: Dandelion. MUS: Ann Fu. PRD: Dandelion, Green Bunny, Beam Entertainment. 45 mins.
Three thousand years after pollution renders Earth uninhabitable, the human race is a space-faring people in search of new planets to settle. Elite super-scouts called Advancers blaze trails for the rest, but Omega 13 is one world proving difficult to conquer. Nine teams have failed to return, prompting high-ranking executive Mugal to make convict Tina Owen an offer she can't refuse. If she can solve the mystery of Omega 13, he'll knock a whole millennium off her 2,000-year sentence for an undisclosed crime.

Tina only spends five tedious minutes on Omega 13; the rest of the story involves the pointless hunt for a crew (telepath/alien/comic relief Frill and Japanese love interest/sidekick Akira), and the rescue of fellow Advancer Garuda from a beleaguered ship. The alien menace turns out to be a multi-tentacled creature with acid saliva that burns through bulkheads and clothes but not through girls' skin. The alien murders all the disposable members of the cast (three concubines whose sole role is to be sexually assaulted) before being summarily executed as it tries to rape Tina. This, apparently, makes the planet safe and avenges Akira's dead parents all in one shot, allowing Tina to fly off to her next mission, though a sequel was never made.

Despite promising beginnings that unite the last-chance mission of *The Dirty Dozen* with the interstellar trouble-shooting of DIRTY PAIR, *Advancer Tina* soon collapses into a tacky exploitation movie. With an ithyphallic menace that gestates in human stomach cavities and a predictable, false ending, its debt to the *Alien* series is obvious, but the film is shoddily assembled from start to finish. Fukumoto, Saito, and Teraoka, the real-world perpetrators of this anime crime, are still at large and can be found elsewhere in this book in the entries for VENUS FIVE, SEXORCIST, and GIGOLO. ⓁⓃⓋ

ADVENTURE BOY SHADAR

1967. JPN: *Boken Shonen Shadar*. TV series. DIR: Juzo Kataoka. SCR: Masaki Tsuji. DES: Shinichi Kuwajima. ANI: Takashi Saijo, Nobukazu Kabashima. MUS: Atsutoshi Soda. PRD: Nippon TV. 10 mins. x 156 eps.
When Earth is threatened by the invading Ghostar, a young boy with nerves of steel and the strength of 50 men appears from a cave on Mount Fuji. He is Shadar, a boy of unknown origin who, with his faithful dog, Pinboke, fights each week to save the world in several ten-minute installments, guaranteeing a final showdown for Japanese viewers each Saturday.

Ghostar actor Kenji Utsumi's voice would come to represent the ultimate in evil to a Japanese audience, and he would go on to play the title roles in DRACULA: SOVEREIGN OF THE DAMNED and DON DRACULA.

ADVENTURE KID *

1992. JPN: *Yoju Sensen Adventure Kid*. AKA: Demon-Beast Battle Line Adventure Kid. Video. DIR: Yoshitaka Fujimoto. SCR: Atsushi Yamatoya, Akio Satsugawa. DES: Dan Kongoji, Ryunosuke Otonashi, Yuji Takahashi. ANI: MW Films. MUS: Masamichi Amano. PRD: MW Films. 40 mins. x 3 eps.
Wartime Japanese scientist Professor Masago devotes himself to his research, ignoring his beautiful wife, Michiyo. In 1945, he is murdered by the dastardly Captain Matsubara's soldiers, after first being forced to watch them rape her. Fifty years later, the husband and wife are reincarnated as students Norikazu and Midori. Norikazu unearths Masago's prototype dimension-hopping device, and it propels them into a parallel universe where Masago's bitter psyche has created a world of marauding zombie soldiers. Eventually Norikazu (good side) defeats Masago (bad side) by dropping him into the Hiroshima bomb blast. The couple then find themselves in Hell Zone, where lusty elf-girl Eganko latches onto Norikazu and accompanies him back to Earth. Back at Norikazu's school, the reincarnation of Captain Matsubara, college-boy Yukimoto, wants Midori for himself and schemes with Eganko's mother, Queen Dakiniten, to make Norikazu fall in love with Eganko. The plan goes awry when love potions are mixed up and given to the wrong victims.

A pornographic tale of rape and domination that suddenly turns into a farce, *Adventure Kid* contains erotic musings on the alien girlfriend-squatter set-up of URUSEI YATSURA, a clumsy attempt to integrate computers into horror (also seen in DIGITAL DEVIL STORY), and a final episode that pokes merciless fun at the excesses of both itself and creator Toshio Maeda's earlier UROTSUKIDOJI. In an attempt to draw in new crowds, the producers hired liveaction erotic "actresses" to provide some of the voice roles, a move which backfired spectacularly when they couldn't actually act. In the U.K., the series was heavily cut and renamed *Adventure Duo* in order to avoid the term "kid" fooling customers into assuming it was suitable for children (LAW AND DISORDER). The authors suggest it's not suitable for *anybody*. ⓁⓃⓋ

ADVENTURE ON KABOTEN ISLAND

1967. JPN: *Boken Kaboten Shima*. TV series. DIR: Motokazu Watanabe. SCR: Aritsune Toyoda, Masaki Tsuji, Arashi Ishizu, Junichi Yoshinaga. DES: Fumio Hisamatsu. ANI: Shizuko Komooka, Tooyo Ashida, Kazuo Mori. MUS: Various. PRD: TBS, Eiken. 30 mins. x 39 eps.

SUPER JETTER–creator Fumio Hisamatsu's 1967 comic in *Shonen Sunday* magazine featured a group of boys and girls marooned on a South Sea island in an imitation of Jules Verne's ADRIFT IN THE PACIFIC. The anime version reduced the female cast to a single comic relief little sister called Tomato, preferring instead to concentrate on the male characters as they explore their new home.

ADVENTURES OF KOROBOKKLE

1973. JPN: *Boken Korobokkle*. AKA: *The Mountain Gnomes*. TV series. DIR: Yonehiko Watanabe, Yukizo Takagaki, Toru Murayama, Takanori Okada, Yoshikata Nitta. SCR: Shunichi Yukimuro, Noboru Shiroyama, Minoru Takahashi. DES: Masatoshi Kobayashi. ANI: Kazuo Kobayashi. MUS: Bob Sakuma. PRD: Eiken, Tatsunoko Pro, Yomiuri TV. 25 mins. x 26 eps.
Sword-wielding hero Bokkle, flute-playing mystic Cous-Cous, and brave female Love-Love are very small gods who live under the butterbur leaves in the countryside. Becoming increasingly annoyed that humans no longer pay them any respect, they decide to head closer to human habitation in search of worshipers. Mild-mannered country boy Seitaka is the only person able to see the spirits, who teach him how to stand up for himself against local bullies. His gentle woodland friends, however, are unafraid of fighting with vicious little knives when they are in trouble.

AoK was sponsored, like PIGGYBACK GHOST before it, by Sumitomo Life Insurance as part of the company's "classic" series—an attempt to associate a company with a successful anime series that paid off much better for the Calpis drinks company with WORLD MASTERPIECE THEATER. The original children's book *Stories of Korobokkle*, itself based on folktales from northern Japan's indigenous Ainu people, was initially adapted with character designs by its author Satoru Sato, but these were replaced with designs by Masatoshi Kobayashi after they tested poorly with young focus groups. That, at least, is what was claimed in Japanese sources, but it seems outlandishly odd to buy the rights to a book if one is only going to throw away its creator's input! The problem was probably more connected with creating character designs that could be more easily replicated by a group of animators. In an additional attempt to appeal to a young audience, the leading role was taken by Satoshi Hasegawa, who had previously appeared in NHK's child-centered *Grave of the Wild Chrysanthemums* (*DE). With its disappearing spirits, *Korobokkle* could be said to be a foreshadowing of later Studio Ghibli efforts like POM POKO and MY NEIGHBOR TOTORO.

ADVENTURES OF KOTETSU *

1996. JPN: *Kotetsu no Daiboken*. Video. DIR: Yuji Moriyama. SCR: Yuji Kawahara. DES: Yoko Kikuchi. ANI: Tetsuya Watanabe. MUS: Kuniaki Haishima. PRD: Daiei, Tokuma Japan. 30 mins. x 2 eps.

Hot-headed Linn "Kotetsu" Suzuki is an accomplished martial artist at 14 and the last in a long line of warriors. Running away from her old-fashioned Kyoto home to look for her brother in Tokyo, she helps a shapely private investigator, Miho, defeat two possessed street thugs. The two soon move in together, and Kotetsu inadvertently saves Miho's life once again when Tetsuya, the man hired by a corrupt businessman to kill her, instead falls in love with her new roommate. Settling their differences at a hot-springs resort, the trio is attacked by a tree demon, sent by Tetsuya's boss. Upon defeating it, Kotetsu's grandmother tells her she can stay in the big city.

Recalling both DEVIL HUNTER YOHKO and LA BLUE GIRL with its female inheritor of a family martial arts tradition, this silly affair was based on the best-selling 1992 adult manga by MEE (AKA Mikun). Though featuring atmospheric music from SPRIGGAN's Haishima and direction from PROJECT A-KO's Moriyama, the fan-service nudity and set-ups make it less than the sum of its parts—one assassination attempt involves a nude clone of Miho in the bath simply to arrange a lesbian scene between the two girls. Despite undeserved popularity for its nude heroine's resemblance to RANMA ½, the series stopped after the experimental two-part opener. MEE would have better success with his next anime project, the TV series HYPER POLICE. ◐

ADVENTURES OF PINOCCHIO *

1972. JPN: *Kashi no Ki Mokku*. AKA: *Mokku (Woody) the Oak Tree*. TV series. DIR: Ippei

Kuri, Yukihiro Takahashi. SCR: Jinzo Toriumi, Akiyoshi Sakai. DES: Yoshitaka Amano. ANI: Masayuki Hayashi. MUS: Nobuyoshi Koshibe. PRD: Tatsunoko, Fuji TV. 25 mins. x 52 eps.

Finding driftwood that has been struck by lightning, toy-maker Gepetto constructs a puppet that comes alive but wants to be a real boy. Based on the 1881 children's story by Carlo Collodi, it was also animated as PICCOLINO. Yoshitaka Amano's first work in character design. Shown on HBO in the U.S., and not to be confused with the NEW ADVENTURES OF PINOCCHIO (1960).

ADVERTISING AND SPONSORSHIP

Corporate sponsorship in one form or another is one of the vital cornerstones of the anime business, and has been since the days of EARLY ANIME. The advertising industry is not only a direct sponsor of animation but also an indirect patron of the arts through the investment it generates in productions and in animators who are otherwise known for their "art-house" output.

With early movie censors hostile toward children's films, Ikuo Oishi cunningly found a way to exhibit outside theaters, showing his *The Hare and the Tortoise* (1918) in department stores as a lure to sell audience members the products of the sponsor, Morinaga Chocolate. Japanese animation has been a tool in the selling of products and services ever since, with sponsorship often providing the funding for innovation. While Seitaro Kitayama is remembered today for his smallish output of fictional films and fairytales, advertising contracts formed the bulk of his studio's output from 1921 onward for everything from political campaigns to cleaning products. Breathlessly described in its day as the "longest Japanese cartoon ever made," Kitayama's *Oral War* (*Koku Eisei*, 1924) formed the closing reel of a documentary about dental hygiene made for the Lion toothpaste company and is likely to have clocked in at eight whole minutes—one of the problems with such milestones is that they were trumped on an almost monthly basis until anime reached full feature length in the 1940s.

During Japan's Fifteen Years War of 1931–45 (which dovetailed with World War II after Japan's attack on Pearl Harbor in 1941), it was a legal requirement for all

films to demonstrate an educational function, or at the very least, the maintenance of moral fortitude, turning even children's cartoons into oblique promotions of the war effort or Japan's colonial empire (WARTIME ANIME). But it was in the postwar period that anime came into its own as an advertising medium, with its punchy shorts and graphical conveyance of information deemed ideal for the selling of products. In cinemas, and increasingly on television from 1953, animators were called upon not only to fully animate commercials, but also to provide inserts of graphics, diagrams, or maps into commercials otherwise filed as "live action," if they are preserved at all.

While posterity remembers the primary Japanese animation event of 1958 as being Toei's first color animated feature PANDA AND THE MAGIC SERPENT, the most widely seen cartoon of that year was actually *Tory's Bar*, a TV commercial for a whiskey brand visible to anyone with a television, several times a night. By 1958, a corporate report from Dentsu, the largest advertising firm in Japan, estimated the number of advertisements made by that point to be 1,200, of which fully half were animated, not merely in cel form but in neglected media such as PUPPETRY AND STOP MOTION. Although commercials today are often timed in mere seconds, the earlier examples of the form were often better described as short films, with running times up to three minutes. By 1960, of an estimated 500 workers in the Japanese animation industry, 300 were working for Toei and another 20 for Otogi Pro. The remaining 150 were spread across two dozen small ateliers in the advertising world, often staffed in mere twos and threes, making hundreds of commercials, many of which have now been lost.

According to the historian Nobuyuki Tsugata, whose untranslated book *Before the Dawn of TV Anime* (*Terebi Anime Yoake Mae*, 2012) is the most substantial analysis of the topic available, there is an entire substratum of advertising-focused animation, from companies like Ikkosha, Saga Studio, and Osaka Eiga, whose work has been forgotten by anime history because they did not make the programs but instead the filler that came in between those programs. The only studio likely to have name recognition with modern fans is TCJ, which made some 1,400 commercials between 1954 and 1960 (2,200 if one includes live-action commercials with animated inserts), but even TCJ is only remembered not because of its commercials output but because of its move into narrative entertainment, with a name-change to Eiken and its most famous and enduring work **SAZAE-SAN**. This forgotten influence on the medium also extends into production, with award-winning works such as Asahi Beer's *Beer Through the Ages* (1956, *Beer Mukashimukashi*—see **PUPPETRY AND STOP MOTION**) and advertiser-funded programming such as **INSTANT HISTORY**, sponsored by the confectionery company Meiji Seika. Summarizing "this day in history" in three-minute sketches, *Instant History* switched backers and channel to become *Otogi Manga Calendar* in 1962, funded by Kirin Beer. This subsequently developed into several Kirin-sponsored shows forming early exercises in anime **DOCUMENTARIES AND HISTORY**, including *Knowledgeable University: Tomorrow's Calendar* (1966, *Monoshiri Daigaku: Ashita no Calendar*), *Knowledgeable University: Cartoon Biographies* (1970, *Kirin Monoshiri Daigaku: Manga Jinbutsu-shi*), *Learning Around the World* (1971, *Sekai Monoshiri Ryoko*), *The Kirin House of Knowledge* (1975, *Kirin Monoshiri Yakata*), and *The Kirin Calendar of Tomorrow* (1980, *Kirin Ashita no Calendar*). This long genealogy of inter-related shows only came to an end in 1984, 23 years after its first iteration, racking up a combined total of 6,021 episodes.

It became standard practice for advertising companies to buy entire sectors of airtime in half-hour slots and to then supply not only the program that filled them but also the commercials that filled the breaks. This involved the advertising companies directly in original production and encouraged symmetries and synergies as clients cooperated to find suitable shows. Animators were commissioned not just to make the shows, but also often the attendant commercials. The swift proliferation of television channels quadrupled the size of advertising's investment between 1958 and 1963. However, after 1963, the involvement of advertisers in the television market largely plateaued, except for chemicals, pharmaceuticals, and food products.

Although Osamu Tezuka is remembered as the father of TV anime, it was Kaoru Anami, Tezuka's liaison with the advertising company Mannensha, who suggested that he seek commercial sponsorship for **ASTRO BOY** and who suggested that Tezuka approach a confectionery company. This embroiled Tezuka in a struggle within the 1960s candy marketplace referred to in advertising histories as "the Chocolate Wars," with Morinaga Chocolate refusing to take a risk on *Astro Boy* and Morinaga's competitor Meiji Seika offering the money instead.

Anime TV in the 1960s was riddled with sponsors, often for confectionery but sometimes from elsewhere, such as Seiko Watches (**MICROID S**), Fujisawa Chemicals (**FUJIMARU THE WIND NINJA**), and the Oranamin C vitamin drink (**STAR OF THE GIANTS**). It was soon noted, on the production of **QTARO THE GHOST**, that anime created to sell toys usually took about two years to wring all related purchases out of their young fans, after which point it was better to simply come up with a "new" anime in the same slot that was almost exactly the same but just different enough to justify new purchases.

Toy companies were to have the longest-lasting impact on the medium. Where some anime included product placement for certain items sold by the sponsors, anime in the 1970s came to be dominated by the more invasive form of "context integration," in which the product to be advertised formed a fundamental part of the story. **MAZINGER Z**, in 1973, was supposedly the first anime made by a "production committee" (*seisaku iinkai*), in which a number of interest groups, from record companies to toy companies to manga publishers, collaborated on the creation of a franchise that would allow each of them to benefit from a context-integrated narrative.

Anime thereafter has often had to literally dance to such sponsors' tunes, for good or ill. Some creatives, such as Yoshiyuki Tomino, even flourished in this environment, embracing the opportunity to tell any story the sponsors wanted, as long as the requisite number of toys were name-checked in each episode (**GUNDAM**). Later iterations of the same process can be seen in **ZOIDS** and **TRANSFORMERS**, and,

indeed, most anime made for children up to the present day.

Anime made for older viewers since the 1980s often repeat the same processes. Computer game companies and the publishers of novels are often found sponsoring anime incarnations of their titles, and the modern otaku market is arguably supported less by anime itself than by the attached fields of merchandising. Marc Steinberg, in *Anime's Media Mix* (2012), notes that this is a tantalizing prospect for modern corporations and that while a fridge or car might be expected to last for seven years, short-lived media franchises still have a half-life of less than two years, allowing sponsors to sell the same old stuff all over again.

In the 21st century, production committees remain a powerful presence behind the scenes of most anime. This can manifest in unexpected ways, not only in the continued support in the industry for toy and game tie-ins but in subsidiary meta-textual artwork, such as that created at the time of the **BERSERK** movies, showing the leading characters anachronistically eating hamburgers. Meanwhile, context integration is far more insidious and skillful than some might think, and spotting it is one of the subversive pleasures of modern anime viewing. As a rule of thumb, if a product's name is spelled *correctly* on screen, such as with the presence of Nissin Cup Noodles in **FREEDOM** or Love Labo cosmetics in **THE BIHADA TRIBE**, the manufacturer has paid for it to be there. And if, as in the movie of **K-ON**, characters spend several minutes of screen time flying on a prominently featured airline and blundering around London, asking where their brand-name hotel is, you can be sure that money has changed hands. As a result, many of the "holy lands" and places of pilgrimage of modern otaku, where they pay homage to their favorite shows by seeking out their locations in the real world, are often imitations of journeys made by the fictional characters in the pursuit of selling a product. Since context integration does not require ticket or DVD sales to monetize a production, it is likely to become more, not less, prevalent in the future. Not even piracy can diminish it, but will instead amount to free distribution of commercial messages from sponsors.

AESOP'S FABLES *

1983. JPN: *Manga Aesop Monogatari*. TV series. DIR: Eiji Okabe, Jun Hagiwara, Fumio Kurokawa. SCR: Michiru Tanabe, Mami Watanabe, Ryo Nakahara. DES: Yu Noda. ANI: Hirokazu Ishino. MUS: Pegumo, Toko Akasaka. PRD: Nippon Animation, Transarts. 25 mins. x 52 eps.

Aesop, an ancient Greek storyteller thought to have lived in the 6th century, has been a staple of anime since the beginning with EARLY ANIME such as Sanae Yamamoto's *Tortoise and the Hare* (1924) and *Frog's Belly* (1929). The 1983 TV series added the term "manga" to accentuate the children's-picture-book quality of the presentation, running through tales such as *The Ants and the Grasshopper, The Sun and the North Wind,* and *The Thirsty Crow.* Eight of the stories were combined to make the theatrical feature *Aesop's Fables* (1983, U.S. release 1985), with a framing device of young Aesop tricking his fellow villagers into believing that a wolf is attacking. When a real wolf comes, nobody believes him, and he is chased down a magic hole into a kingdom of animals. As he looks for a way out, he meets a tortoise, a hare, an ant, and other creatures who tell him their stories. Several of Aesop's fables were also used as part of the *Shogo Hirata's Picture Book* series (1995). See also VIDEO PICTURE BOOK.

AESTHETICA OF A ROGUE HERO *

2012. JPN: *Hagure Yusha no Aesthetica*. TV series. DIR: Rion Kujo. SCR: Ryunosuke Kingetsu, Masahiro Okubo, Tetsuto Uesu. DES: Hiroshi Tsukada. ANI: Hiroshi Tsukada. MUS: Kayo Konishi, Yukio Kondo. PRD: ARMS, AT-X, GENCO, Hobby Japan, Lantis, Media Factory, Showgate. 24 mins. x 12 eps.

Akatsuki Osawa has been spirited off to a fantasy realm, where he has fought against evil and defeated the demon lord. But that's only the beginning of this anime series, which follows his return to his homeworld, and his attempts to rehabilitate back into human society, attending a normal(-ish) high school, and dealing with the inevitable fact that he has somehow come back home with the demon lord's daughter in tow.

Anime has mixed mundane men with unearthly women ever since URUSEI YATSURA, so there is nothing particularly new in a premise that lumbers a Japanese boy with a harem (ROMANCE AND DRAMA) of adoring and/or diffident girls. There is, however, something rather sweetly postmodern about a world that regards fantastic adventures in a parallel universe as an entirely mundane malaise, from which young men need to be rehabilitated on their return, hopefully with a few applied skills learned from their adventures elsewhere. In that regard, *Aesthetica of a Rogue Hero* is as incisive an allegory of 21st-century culture as the virtual-reality overlays to be found in DENNO COIL. Many modern gamers are indeed the leaders of armies and captains of space vessels in their free time, living in fantasy worlds that surely impact, to some extent, on their mundane lives. This premise offers rich narrative potential, unfortunately and entirely squandered in a humdrum, gropey harem story that soon devolves into bickering about boobs. Compare to THE DEVIL IS A PART-TIMER.

AFRO KEN

2001. AKA: *Afro Dog*. Video. DIR: Takashi Imanishi. SCR: Takashi Imanishi. DES: Tetsuro Aimi. ANI: Toyonori Yamada, Kayoko Murakami, Fumie Anno, Naoyuki Takasawa. MUS: Takeshiro Kawabe. PRD: Sunrise, Bandai Visual, Green Camel. 30 mins.

Like its Bandai stablemate TAREPANDA, this one-shot, fully computer-animated wonder is an attempt to tap into the HELLO KITTY merchandising market, putting the brand first and following with animation only reluctantly. Afro Ken is, as the name implies, a dog with a multicolored Afro hairdo, and several equally hallucinogenic friends. In several short sequences, he is shown visiting various tourist sites, playing with some of his canine friends, walking through Tokyo like a friendly Godzilla, and appearing in ancient cave paintings. The half-hour running time contains only 15 minutes of animation—the rest is bulked out with a "Making Of" documentary that manages to recycle much of the footage already shown, along with creator interviews. The only truly worthwhile item on the disc is the catchy theme song, and even that is played twice.

AFRO SAMURAI *

2007. TV series. DIR: Fuminori Kizaki, Jamie Simone. SCR: Takashi Okazaki, Tomohiro Yamashita, Derek Draper, Chris Yoo. DES: Hiroya Iijima, Takeshi Koike. ANI: Hiroya Iijima. MUS: RZA. PRD: Gonzo, Fuji TV. 25 mins. x 5 eps. (TV), 97 mins. (m).

After his father dies in a duel with the warrior known as Justice, young Afro resolves to study the martial arts. He becomes a wandering swordsman in a milieu that mixes samurai-era epics with science fiction in the style of SAMURAI 7. Supposedly conceived in 1995 by a young Takashi Okazaki, the concept achieved new life in the 21st century when it gained the backing of Samuel L. Jackson as coproducer and voice artist. Riding a wave of interest in anime fueled in part by KILL BILL: THE ORIGIN OF O-REN, but also drawing on the co-option of martial arts imagery and samples in hip-hop culture, *Afro Samurai* takes the irreverence of SAMURAI CHAMPLOO to extremes, with characters such as Kuma, an anonymous fighter who wears a teddy bear's head to hide his identity. The main purpose of the show, and of *Afro Samurai: Resurrection*, the movie that followed in 2009, is to flood the screen and the speakers with cool images and sounds. Every moment is a pose, every instant a beat. The art direction has fine color design and beautiful, kinetic, flowing movement. The fight scenes are amazing, as ritualized as the bullfight, as fluid as the ballet. The motorbikes are every teenager's dream machine. Story? Dialogue? Character development? You're missing the point if you even ask. Composer RZA, of the Wu-Tang Clan, would later try his own hand at Afro-orientalism as the writer-director of the live-action film *The Man With the Iron Fists* (2012). *Afro Samurai* does not appear to have been dubbed in Japanese, instead being released in Japan with the English audio track intact, in order to add that little touch of the exotic occident. **OV**

AFTER CLASS LESSON *

2005. JPN: *Hokago—Nureta Seifuku*. AKA: *After School—Get Your Uniform Wet*. Video. DIR: Masato Kitagawa. SCR: Rokurota Makabe. DES: P-zo Honda. ANI: Kazunori Higuchi, Mamoru Sakisaka, Ryota Ito. MUS: Salad. PRD: T-Rex, GP Museum Soft, Milky. 30 mins. x 3 eps.

A perverse teacher at an elite girls' school is still a virgin at the start of this series. That soon changes when he finds himself strangely drawn to gorgeous cheerleader Ayumi. Finding out her secret weakness, he drugs and molests her. She soon realizes his attractions and can't get enough of him. When he finds out that another girl is sleeping with one of the faculty and blackmails her into sex with him, Ayumi even films them in action. He's soon bedding all the hottest girls in school in this anime based on a game by Bishop. Episode two sees Ayumi, despite her growing feelings for the protagonist, helping him molest and rape two sisters—another cheerleader and a tennis star. In episode 3, one of the female teachers, also a virgin, is given a compromising photo of him with one of the students and sets out to get him fired. Because this is a porno anime, she doesn't go straight to the police and the principal, which gives him time to assault her with the help of his pupils. There is an argument that this kind of wish fulfillment fantasy really helps the introverted loner who doesn't know how to talk to real girls. But he's not going to learn much about conversation here. **ⓃⓋ**

AFTER … THE ANIMATION
2007. Video. DIR: Kanzaburo Oda. SCR: Keisuke Kanemaru. DES: Hikari Haruno. ANI: Hikari Haruno. MUS: AG Promotion. PRD: Kotaro Murakami, Milky. 27 mins. x 2 eps.
Based on the game by Ciel, this is a love-triangle story featuring two childhood friends, Yiuchi and Kana, and their romantic/erotic adventures in high school. There is no plot, just a string of sex scene segues as feeble as anything in live porn. Two boys, three girls, a female teacher and more sex than is strictly compatible with passing exams, plus pedestrian animation and the kind of muzak you get in elevators makes for a forgettable package, in every sense. **Ⓝ**

AFTER-SCHOOL LOVE CLUB ÉTUDE
1997. JPN: Hokago Ren'ai Club Koi no Étude. Video. DIR: Moritaka Imura. SCR: N/C. DES: Yoshiaki Hatano. ANI: Yuki Mine. MUS: N/C. PRD: Pink Pineapple, KSS. 31 mins. x 2 eps.
Originating in Libido's mildly titillating computer role-playing game in the same genre as TOKIMEKI MEMORIAL, this is the story of Shunichi and Sanae, who are attracted to each other, but whose relationship seems to go nowhere. Neither

does the plot until episode 2, when the members of the "love club" start to get into the sex scenes promised on the box. In the original game, the player had to manage his resources to ensure he could get the most out of 12 sex-starved female members of a dating club in just 30 days. The anime doesn't retain its appeal for quite that long. **Ⓝ**

AFTER-SCHOOL MIAOW-MIAOW
2011. JPN: Hokago Nyan-Nyan. AKA: After-School Nyan-Nyan. Video. DIR: N/A. SCR: N/A. DES: N/A. ANI: N/A. MUS: N/A. PRD: Studio9MAiami, Max, Advanced Anime Jigyo Kumiai. 19 mins., 25 mins.
Based on the erotic manga by Rikako Inomoto, whose art style relies heavily on big bottoms and thighs and soft, intense highlights, this video consists of two very short stories. A nameless schoolgirl, who is sexually inexperienced but intensely curious, asks underclassman Yu to masturbate in front of her and things go predictably further. In the second story, a guy spends the night at his girlfriend's house while her parents are away. At just 19 minutes long and with a wholly uncredited crew, the package seems overpriced at ¥5,000 even by Japanese standards, but it was successful enough for a sequel to be made in 2012. *Lovely Day: Boku to Kanojo no Nanoka Kan (Seven Days of Me and Her)* is the story of two cousins who are hot for each other and have just one week to act on their feelings. It clocks 25 minutes, according to the MediaBank website. Maybe there are extras. The titular *nyan-nyan*, Japanese for the noise a cat makes, has entered modern slang as a verb for fooling around.

AFTER-SCHOOL MIDNIGHTERS *
2012. JPN: Hokago Midnighters. Movie. DIR: Hitoshi Takekiyo. SCR: Hitoshi Takekiyo, Yoichi Komori. DES: N/C. ANI: Kenichiro Tanaka. MUS: Reiji Kitazato. PRD: T-Joy, Amazon Laterna, CoMix Wave, Ozmig Corporation, Mont Blanc Pictures, Sanfride, Sony Music Entertainment, Starchild Records. 95 mins.
Three young girls exploring their school's condemned science room encounter a talking anatomical dummy and a dancing skeleton. Dared to attend a late-night party where other inanimate residents come to life, they hatch a plan to collect magical artifacts that may save the building from its

scheduled demolition.

This inoffensive school romp betrays its origins as an apprentice piece—a series of short films used by Hitoshi Takekiyo to drum up work for himself and several other directors in Fukuoka who were looking for work in animation and advertising. Unexpectedly, their test footage got picked up in France and shown on television, so it went from being a showreel to a project that had already secured a degree of foreign interest.

The originals were dialogue-free, with humor added to familiar figures—Dracula, a ninja, Jesus Christ, and an anatomical model, the latter of which came to prominence in the movie remake. Motion capture is the primary method—a lot of the action is created through the use of performance capture, which makes it, arguably, less "animated" than it is a special effects movie—compare to VEXILLE. There are moments of real animation, but there are also elements of cunning recycling, such as the reduplicated skeletons in a dance sequence.

AFTER-SCHOOL TINKERBELL
1992. JPN: Hokago Tinker Bell [sic]. Video. DIR: Kiyoshi Murayama. SCR: Akira Oketani. DES: Yasuhide Maruyama. ANI: Yasuhide Maruyama. MUS: N/C. PRD: Life Work, Ashi Pro. 45 mins.
In this animated adaptation of two novels in Shoichiro Hinata's *After School* series, high school investigators Kenichi and Misako get on the case when the popular Broadcast Club disc jockey, Ryoko, goes missing.

AGE OF THE GREAT DINOSAURS
1979. JPN: Daikyoryu no Jidai. TV special. DIR: Shotaro Ishinomori with Hideki Takayama. SCR: Shotaro Ishinomori, Makoto Naito. DES: Shotaro Ishinomori. ANI: Kozo Morishita. MUS: Shogun. PRD: Ishi(no)mori Pro, Toei, Nippon TV. 73 mins.
CYBORG 009–creator Ishinomori (just plain Ishimori at the time) was heavily involved in this anime shot on 35mm film, in which naïve boy Jun, his female companion, Remi, and her little brother, Chobi, are whisked away to the Cretaceous Period by a flying saucer. There they hobnob with Cro-Magnon men, which would be damage enough to the program's educational

merit even without the suggestion that aliens wiped out the dinosaurs when their population became too great—a dark portent for the expanding human race and a typical touch from the dour Ishinomori. Dinosaurs also cropped up in Makoto Sokuza and Shigeru Omachi's one-shot video *Dinosaur Guide* (1989), in which Professor Doctor (*sic*) escorts children Tai and Ayumi on a trip to the prehistoric past. Aliens would return to do away with the dinosaurs in **LAWS OF THE SUN**.

AGEDAMAN

1991. JPN: *Genji Tsushin Agedama* [sic]. TV series. DIR: Masato Namiki. SCR: Takashi Yamada, Shigeru Yanagawa, et al. DES: Hatsuki Tsuji. ANI: Hiroaki Sakurai, Hideyuki Motohashi, et al. MUS: Toshihiko Sahashi. PRD: Studio Gallop, TV Tokyo. 25 mins. x 51 eps.

Average boy Genji can use his warp key to transform into the superhero Agedaman, the last line of resistance against the evil 11th-century scientist Nostradamus and his equally evil granddaughter, Kukirei, in a brightly colored show that mixes action and comedy.

AGEMAN AND FUKU-CHAN

1991. Video. DIR: Teruo Kogure. SCR: Susume Yoshiike. DES: Masamichi Yokoyama. ANI: Masamichi Yokoyama. MUS: Jiro Takemura. PRD: Knack. 30 mins.

Mantaro Nishino is obsessed with money and women, but his schemes invariably fail in this satire of Japan and the Japanese in the late 1980s bubble economy. The sexy strumpet Fuku-chan is Mantaro's eventual undoing in this erotic fable based on a manga by Masamichi Yokoyama, who also created **MISTER HAPPY**. The title recalls that of Juzo Itami's live-action *Ageman: Tales of a Golden Geisha* (1990). **Ⓝ**

AGENT AIKA *

1997. JPN: *Aika*. Video. DIR: Katsuhiko Nishijima. SCR: Kenichi Kanemaki. DES: Noriyasu Yamauchi, Hidefumi Kimura, Yoko Kikuchi. ANI: Noriyasu Yamauchi. MUS: Junichi Kanezaki. PRD: Graviton, Bandai Visual. 30 mins x 7 eps. (v1), 4 mins., 2 mins., 4 mins. (Special Trial), 5 mins. (music video), 25 mins. x 3 eps. (v2. *R16*), 27 mins. x 3 eps. (v3, *Zero*).

Aika Sumeragi is a freelancer who lifts artifacts and data from the submerged ruins of Tokyo in the year 2036. She is a friend and business partner to the father-daughter team of Gozo and Rion Aida and has a love-hate relationship with Gust Turbulence, her spiky-haired male rival. Hired to go after the Ragu, an energy source reputed to be the cause of the global catastrophe, Aika must compete against evil superbitch Neena Hagen, Neena's incestuous brother, Rudolf, and their army of women inexplicably dressed as French maids. Her only advantages: high-tech vehicles and transforming underwear that is really a weapon.

Envisaged by director Nishijima as a replay of **PROJECT A-KO**, with Aika, Neena, and Rion as A-Ko, B-Ko, and C-Ko, *Agent Aika* fast becomes the ultimate in fan-service anime (**ARGOT AND JARGON**), as almost every camera angle conspires to get an eyeful of cleavage or panties. Worm's-eye views and gratuitous nudity soon drag the plot far off course, though exactly where Kanemaki's story of a treasure-huntress with a sentient bodice was originally headed is anyone's guess. *Aika Special Trial* (1998) was a three-part short video showing the members of the KK Corporation moving into their new offices. A music video was also released. Compare to the same team's later **NAJICA**. Seven years later, **DAPHNE IN THE BRILLIANT BLUE** would do it all again.

The prequel *Aika R16: Virgin Mission* (2007) pandered to a trend in **FANDOM** for younger heroines by presenting Aika as a 16-year-old schoolgirl, at the beginning of her career. She returned as a college-ready 19-year-old in *Aika: Zero* (2009). Both video serials continued the panty-flashing and leering, seemingly with only the protagonist's apparent age as any different. Effectively, Aika was being reframed as two other female archetypes—a hapless girl next door and a bossier teenager—in addition to the elegant late-20s sophisticate presented in the original series. **Ⓝ**

AH! MY BUDDHA

2005. JPN: *Amaenaide yo*. AKA: *Don't Tease Me*. TV series. DIR: Keitaro Motonaga. SCR: Noboru Kimura, Naoki Takada, Toshizo Nemoto. DES: Kumi Horii. ANI: Noritomo Hattori. MUS: Yasunori Iwasaki. PRD: Studio Deen, AT-X. 25 mins. x 13 eps. (TV1), 25 mins. x 13 eps. (TV2).

Ikko Satonaka's grandmother is Jotoku, a Buddhist priestess. It only follows that he is likely to go into the family "business," and he duly signs up for an apprenticeship at the temple. There, he is subjected to a series of purification rituals, and exhorted to let go of worldy desires. This proves to be more difficult than expected when he is surrounded by a risibly predictable group of nubile young nuns. **TENCHI MUYO!**, in a temple, and irritatingly for Ikko, his powers to exorcise demons go *up* when he is thinking sinful thoughts. For people with very short memor… what were we saying?

A second season followed in 2006, with a seventh trainee priestess joining the team and generating jealousy in the little group.

AI CITY *

1986. AKA: *Love City* (U.K.). Movie. DIR: Koichi Mashimo. SCR: Hideki Sonoda. DES: Chuichi Iguchi, Tomohiko Sato. ANI: Chuichi Iguchi, Nobuyoshi Habara, Satoru Utsunomiya, Kenichi Maejima, Hiroyoshi Okawa, Hiroshi Kawamata. MUS: Shiro Sagisu. PRD: Toei, Movic, Ashi Pro. 100 mins.

Young girl Ai and her protector, Kei, are on the run from rival gangs of "Headmeters"—humans with DNA recombined through nanotech viruses to give them psychic powers. Rival leaders Leigh and Lyrochin want Ai for the terrible secrets she contains, so she and failed Headmeter Kei join forces with an ex-cop turned private eye, an amnesiac ex-enemy, and a gratuitous cute cat (a design rip-off of Lucifer from Disney's *Cinderella*).

A poor man's **AKIRA**, even down to blue-skinned mutants with numerical foreheads, *AC* is much more than the sum of its parts, with surreal sequences of giant heads melting out of sidewalks, a plot revolving around multiple universes, and visceral scenes of psychic violence as Headmeters trump each other with ever-higher power levels. Based on the *Action Comics* manga by Shuho Itabashi (who went on to draw one of the *X-Files* manga adaptations) but made just that little bit too early to benefit from the higher budgets of the sci-fi anime boom of the early 1990s, it was eclipsed by its successors and relegated to the anime B-list despite a plot far superior to contemporaries such as **LOCKE THE SUPERMAN**. Masterfully feeding the audience scraps of plot one bit at a time, it throws the viewer into the story without explaining a thing, slowly piecing together the reasons why Ai and Kei are on the run, who is after them, and where they are from. Sonoda's script, loaded with careful English neologisms like "Headmeter," "tuned man," and "metapsychic phase wall," is truly excellent and even features a serious contender for one of the best endings in anime, later swiped for the grand finale of **UROTSUKIDOJI**. Available in separate U.K. and U.S. versions.

AI YORI AOSHI *

2002. JPN: *Ai Yori Aoshi*. AKA: *Bluer than Blue; Bluer than Indigo; True Blue Love*. TV series. DIR: Masami Shimoda. SCR: Kenichi Kanemaki, Katsuhiko Takayama, Masashi Kubota. DES: Kazunori Iwakura. ANI: Yumi Nakayama. MUS: Toshio Masuda. PRD: JC Staff, Studio Easter, Fuji TV, TV Kanagawa, TV Saitama. 23 mins. x 24 eps. (TV1), 5 mins. (v1), 25 mins. x 12 eps. (TV2), 15 mins. (v2).

Kaoru Hanabishi offers to help a lost girl in a kimono who seems very out of place in Tokyo, only to discover that the address she is looking for is an empty lot. She is eventually revealed as Aoi Sakuraba, a rich girl from a traditional family, who was betrothed to Kaoru in childhood. Although their engagement has been broken off on a technicality to do with Kaoru's unfilial behavior, Aoi insists on honoring her side of the deal. While Kaoru wrestles with whether he should take up Aoi's offer, this Stepford wannabe bustles around the house performing every conjugal duty except consummation. Ko Fumizuki's manga in *Young Animal* magazine set up a premise that could have been a fascinating meditation on the changing role of the family and tradition among Japanese youth, but instead turns into **TENCHI MUYO!**, as a group of gorgeous girls home in on Kaoru like the Japanese Self-Defense Forces chasing Godzilla. Meanwhile, Aoi is still so eager to please her fiancé that she lets Kaoru and all his would-be girlfriends live in her family's summer house.

Goodness knows how Masaharu Amiya has the temerity to claim his "series concept" credit, but for every generation of pubescent boys with romantic yearnings there is a new *Tenchi* clone. This one,

like its heroine, is ravishingly pretty and well-mannered, and like its hero, it has its moments and is often more endurable than its fellow shows, but still doesn't know when to quit—a second season followed in 2003 as *AYA: Destiny (AYA—Enishi)*. The DVD release of each series had a bonus episode: the 5-minute picnic tale *AYA Dream Story* for series one, and the 15-minute Christmas fantasy episode *AYA Beautiful Snow (AYA Miyuki)* for series two.

The title is half of a **TRANSLATION** of a Chinese proverb: "*Qing qu yu lan...*" (Blue comes from indigo) which is completed by the phrase "*...er sheng yu lan*" (but is superior to it). The phrase alludes to the manufacture of dyes, but is used in China to imply that a pupil can, and should, surpass his teacher. In this case, it is presumably meant to suggest that we should rise above the situation in which we find ourselves—fighting words for creators who are handed a touching love story, but merely use it to rehash a paradigm established more than two decades earlier in **URUSEI YATSURA**. A Chinese TV series with the same title, shown on TVB, has no relation to the anime and has been referred to as *Shine on You* in English. **Ⓝ**

AIM FOR THE ACE

1973. TV series, video. JPN: *Ace o Nerae*. DIR: Osamu Dezaki, Masami Hata. SCR: Kazuaki Okamura. DES: Akio Sugino. ANI: Yoshiaki Kawajiri, Kazuo Yamazaki, Sadao Tomonaga, Shinichi Kato, Katsuhiko Yamazaki. MUS: Akira Misawa. PRD: TMS, A Pro, Takara, Madhouse, NET. 25 mins. x 26 eps. (TV1), 25 mins. x 25 eps. (TV2), 25 mins. x 12 eps. (TV3), 30 mins. x 6 eps. (v1), 30 mins. x 6 eps. (v2).

Hiromi Oka is a new girl at Nishitaka tennis club, swiftly making a friend in the chatty Maki Aikawa and a deadly enemy in Reika "Madame Butterfly" Ryuzaki, the undisputed queen of student tennis. Sacrificing her personal life (and her chances with lovelorn local boy Takayuki Todo), Hiromi resolves to become the greatest tennis player in the world.

A second series of 25 episodes followed in 1978, with a new coach bringing new problems to the Nishitaka students. With additional animation, this spawned a 1979 theatrical outing (still directed by **TOMORROW'S JOE**'s Dezaki). There was

a renewed interest in the story in 1988, resulting in another movie, *AftA 2*, and a 12-part video series directed in part by former designer Akio Sugino. Dezaki did make some episodes and also provided some storyboards under the pseudonym Makura Saki. Revolving around the death of Hiromi's original coach, the final series featured her in many more foreign tournaments, finishing at Wimbledon itself. A bit part as a neighbor in a New York scene proved to be the first anime role for future **SAILOR MOON**–voice actress Kotono Mitsuishi.

The series has inspired several other anime, notably **YAWARA!**, which follows a similar story progression but uses judo as its sport of choice. It also has the questionable distinction of both SF and erotic pastiches, in **GUNBUSTER** (subtitled "Aim for the Top") and *Aim for the A* in the **TALES OF ...** collection.

Notably, the original TV series was broadcast in the same year Sumika Yamamoto's original manga began running in *Margaret* magazine, suggesting that *Aim for the Ace*'s position as one of the quintessential **SPORTS ANIME** was recognized from its earliest days. Its enduring appeal is attested not only by its anime revivals and its impressive performance abroad (chiefly in Italian, French, and Spanish), but also by its high position in many polls of Japanese viewers' favorite anime and manga. Its most recent incarnation is a 2004 live-action TV series, on TV Asahi (the new name for NET).

AIR

2005. TV series, movie, TV special. DIR: Tatsuya Ishihara, Hiroshi Yamamoto, Ichiro Miyoshi, Noriyuki Kitanohara, Tomoe Aratani, Yasuhiro Takemoto. SCR: Fumihiko Shimo. DES: Tomoe Aratani. ANI: Kazumi Ikeda, Mitsuyoshi Yoneda, Satoshi Kadowaki. MUS: N/C. PRD: Key, Visual Arts. 25 mins. x 13 eps. (TV), 91 mins. (m), 24 mins. x 2 (special).

Yukito Kunisaki embarks on a long quest in search of a winged girl mentioned by his mother in stories told to him as a child. Running low on funds, he finds himself forced to settle temporarily in a town, where he soon gains the traditionally chaste live-in would-be girlfriend of anime romance, who, predictably, may not be all she appears to be. As with other time-limit girlfriends such as VIDEO GIRL AI, there is a catch—in a pastiche of numerous GRIMM'S FAIRY TALES, the pretty Misuzu will die if she experiences true love. Compare to CHOBITS. The story was retold in a movie version later the same year, directed by Osamu Dezaki, and in two 24-minute specials, *Air in Summer* (2005), broadcast over two nights on TBS. Like KANON, *Air* is based on an erotic video game of the "visual novel" genre by Visual Art's/Key.

AIR GEAR

2006. TV series. DIR: Hajime Kamegaki. SCR: Chiaki Konaka, Atsushi Maekawa. DES: Masayuki Sato, Masayuki Sato, Hinori Tanaka. MUS: skankfunk. PRD: Toei Animation, TV Tokyo, TV Aichi, Studio MAO. 25 mins. x 25 eps. (TV), 30 mins. (v1), 30 mins. x 3 eps. (v2).

Teenager Minami "Ikki" Itsuki is the leader of the East Side Gunz gang at his school, but is swiftly bested by the Storm Riders—a group of kids using "Air Trek" skates that allow them to fly through the air. Before long, he has acquired Air Trek gear of his own, in an adaptation of the manga by Oh! Great, that moves the standard templates of street toughs into a science-fictional milieu by substituting roller skates for flying boots.

Air Gear Special was released as a video in 2010 to showcase a particular battle from the ongoing comic story and takes place in the main series timeline between episodes 21 and 22. A further video, *Air Gear: Kuro no Hane to Nemuri no Mori— Break on the Sky (Air Gear: Black Feather and the Forest of Sleep—Break on the Sky)*, was released in 2010/11, with three episodes from the 16th, 23rd, and 24th volumes of the manga. The first and second of these three episodes were bundled on separate DVDs with the 30th and 31st volumes of the manga, shipped in 2011. There were also two live-action musicals based on the manga, dating from 2007 and 2010. The manga itself finally ended in 2012.

AIR MASTER *

2003. TV series. DIR: Daisuke Nishio. SCR: Michio Yokote. DES: Yoshihiko Umakoshi. ANI: Yoshihiko Umakoshi. MUS: Yoshihisa Hirano. PRD: Toei Animation, VAP, NTV. 25 mins. x 27 eps.

The daughter of a distinguished gymnast and a former boxing champion, red-headed ex-gymnast Maki Aikawa can perform incredible moves in mid-air, which earn her the name of "Air Master." Maki's widowed father now owns a gymnasium and has remarried, giving her a half-sister, Miori. But gymnastics is no longer enough for Maki, and she turns, somewhat illogically, to street fighting as a means of getting the same thrill. She and her gang of girlfriends of various sizes, types, and sexual inclinations have the usual high school adventures while Maki fights a string of increasingly absurd opponents like masked wrestler Lucha Master, aspiring schoolgirl supermodel Kaori Sakiyama (her self-declared rival), quarterstaff master Shinnosuke (who is so smitten with Maki he transfers to her school), writer and streetfighter Julietta (a guy who also falls for Maki), Reichi, whose weapon of choice is a bicycle, and so on, in the quirky opponent-of-the-week format of TIGER MASK and RANMA ½. The gritty battles are interrupted by the usual wholly gratuitous efforts to get the cast to take their clothes off, such as a trip to the beach.

Another gang of school streetfighters, the Black Alliance, provides more training opportunities for Maki; then she and Kaori get involved in tag wrestling, meeting up with the sister of former opponent Rucha. She joins an elite streetfighter group that uses the whole city as its arena, and begins to focus on spiritual power as a way to fight better. In the last episode she loses her final battle, but finds the fulfillment she has been seeking throughout a series that provides plenty of fight action and moderate humor; the animators invest the greatest amount of their time and budget in getting the battles right. Based on Yokusaru Shibata's *Young Animal* manga. **NV**

AIRBATS *

1994. JPN: *Aozora Shojotai 801 TTS*. AKA: *Blue Sky Girl Squad 801 TTS*. Video. DIR: Yuji Moriyama. SCR: Yuji Kawahara, Soya Fujiwara. DES: Yuji Moriyama. ANI: Yuji Moriyama, Osamu Mikasa, Junichi Sakata. MUS: Seiko Nagaoka. PRD: Studio Fantasia. 30 mins. x 7 eps.

Geeky Takuya Isurugi is a fan of anime and machinery assigned as a mechanic to the 801 "Airbats" Tactical Training Squadron.

Far from being a training ground for elite female pilots, it's a dead-end posting for burnouts—Miyuki Haneda has been sent there for striking a superior officer, Sakura Saginomiya is an inveterate gambler, Arisa Mitaka has an attitude problem, and Yoko Shimorenjaku is the world's worst pilot. Haneda and Mitaka both fall in love with Isurugi, and as bureaucrats try to disband the unit, they all try to hold onto their jobs in this wacky military comedy.

Plane fever struck Japan in the wake of *Top Gun*, inspiring the live-action Japanese rip-off *Best Guy*, *Airbats*, and its sharper, more satirical predecessor HUMMINGBIRDS. A cute contemporary of TENCHI MUYO!, employing similarly crowd-pleasing tactics of fanboy-meets-fawning-females, *Airbats* has its origin in a 1990 manga by Toshimitsu Shimizu, creator of REI REI. The six episodes and the *Airbats in Snow Country* vacation spin-off were later edited into the omnibus volumes *First* (episodes 1–3), *Second* (4 + holiday special), and *Third Strike* (episodes 5–6). It was supposedly made with the cooperation of the Japanese Air Defense Force, which accounts for the loving aircraft detail but does not explain why a military organization would consent to be portrayed as misfits, desk-jockeys, and nuts whose main concern is winning a year's supply of free noodles. Whereas such inanities helped reinforce the realism of the long-running PATLABOR, in a short comedy series such as this they only demonstrate how wacky waters so often run shallow.

AJIA-DO

Animation company formed in 1978 by defectors from Shinei Doga, including Tsutomu Shibayama and Osamu Kobayashi. Became a limited company in 1987. Other notable members include Michishiro Yamada, Hideo Kawauchi, and Tomomi Mochizuki. Productions include CHIBI MARUKO-CHAN—a long-running anime for the children's market that may not be well known in the English-speaking world but is a blue-chip business for animators. Sometimes listed as Asia-do—our choice of spelling here derives from the company's own website.

AKAHORI GEDO HOUR

2005. JPN: *Akahori Gedo Hour Love-ge Zettai*

Seigi vs. Soreyuke! Gedo Otometai. AKA: *Akahori Gedo Hour Love Pheromone Justice vs. Go For It! Gedo Maid Team*. TV series. DIR: Hitoyuki Matsui. SCR: Satoru Akahori, Takashi Ifukube, Deko Akao, Katsumi Hasegawa. DES: Satoshi Ishino. ANI: N/C. MUS: Harukichi Yamamoto. PRD: Radix, TVK. 25 mins. x 13 eps.

Actually *two* shows set in the same world and sharing the airtime of a normal TV episode—perhaps the first sign of a new trend in impecunious shows for short attention-span audiences, started by the earlier **A15** and continued by **BPS** and **BOTTLE FAIRIES**. *Love Pheromone* is about the misadventures of two failed stand-up comediennes who moonlight as super-heroines while waiting for the big break that will bring them success on stage. But the Pheromone duo are a little short of evil enemies, whereas their sister show *Gedo Otometai* features five sisters who stumble amateurishly in their own attempts to become an evil secret organization, a job for which they are palpably not cut out. Based on an idea by Satoru Akahori, who presumably based it on some feverish dreams that ensued after he watched **EXCEL SAGA** while eating cheese too close to bedtime.

AKAI HAYATE *

1991. AKA: *Red Gale*. Video. DIR: Osamu Tsuruyama. SCR: Osamu Yamasaki. DES: Chiharu Sato, Koichi Ohata. ANI: Chiharu Sato, Masayoshi Sato. MUS: Takashi Kudo. PRD: NEXTART, Pony Canyon. 30 mins. x 4 eps.

The real rulers of modern Japan are the Shinogara clan, whose base is in a hidden valley at the foot of Mount Fuji. The leader's son, Hayate, is executed for patricide but transfers his soul into the body of his sister, Shiori. Hiding out from Shinogara assassins in Tokyo, Shiori is able to call up her brother's skill in battle but loses a part of her own soul each time she does. As the power struggle continues between several factions of his clan, Hayate must save himself before he kills another member of his own family.

Originally serialized in the **RENTAMAN** video magazine, *Akai Hayate* was later compiled into two 60-minute volumes—the version released abroad. One of a large subset of anime in which the past bubbles to the surface in modern Japan, including

writer Yamazaki's own **TAKEGAMI**, it features **GENOCYBER**-creator Ohata as a guest designer for the MacGuffin "Shadow Armor" over which these ninja are fighting.

AKAME GA KILL *

2014. TV series. DIR: Tomoki Kobayashi. SCR: Makoto Uezu. DES: Asami Watanabe, Kazuhisa Nakamura. ANI: Asami Watanabe, Kazuhisa Nakamura, Daisuke Endo. MUS: Taku Iwasaki. PRD: C-Station, White Fox, Toho. 23 mins. x 12 eps.

After a misleadingly predictable beginning, in which would-be monster-slayer Tatsumi heads off to seek fame and fortune, and successfully snags his first dragon, *Akame ga Kill* takes a sudden wrenching turn for the twisty. Friends turn out not to be friends, the fabled big city at the center of the empire is run by corrupt politicians, and the Night Raid assassins are vigilantes dealing out violent justice with the aid of *teigu*—rare weaponized artifacts from a more magical time. A substandard dungeon crawl takes on a desperately degenerate tone, seemingly hoping to shock the viewer with the awfulness of the bad guys, before shocking the viewer once more with the extreme prejudice of the good guys' retribution. **LNV**

AKANE, KAZUKI

1962–. After early work as a character designer on **MAMA IS A FOURTH-GRADER** and **GUNDAM** *0083*, he moved into animation. An early pioneer in the integration of digital animation and traditional techniques, his directorial debut was on **ESCAFLOWNE**.

AKANE-CHAN

1968. TV series. DIR: Fusahito Nagaki, Yasuo Yamaguchi, Yugo Serikawa, Takeshi Tamiya. SCR: Shunichi Yukimuro, Masaki Tsuji. DES: Shinya Takahashi. ANI: Masamune Ochiai. MUS: Keiichi Honno. PRD: Fuji TV. 30 mins. x 26 mins.

Young Akane moves to the country and soon becomes popular with the other children in her class, befriending the troublesome local rich-kid Hidemaru and leading her gang into all sorts of scrapes. Tetsuya Chiba's original manga *Miso Curds* in *Shojo Friend* magazine was deliberately designed to evoke a distant, carefree time of rural childhood for city kids deprived of the opportunity, placing it in the same spirit as

MY NEIGHBOR TOTORO. Renamed for its TV outing, it was the first of many Chiba titles to be adapted for anime—the creator is better known for more manly tales such as **TOMORROW'S JOE** and **I'M TEPPEI**.

AKANE-IRO NI SOMARU SAKA *

2008. AKA: *The Hill Dyed Rose-Madder; Akasaka*. TV series. DIR: Keitaro Motonaga. SCR: Makoto Uezu, Yuko Kakihara. DES: Kumi Horii, Madoka Hirayama, Kazuto Shimoyama. ANI: Shoji Hara. MUS: Kenichiro Suehiro. PRD: avex, feng, Lantis, Marvelous Entertainment Pony Canyon. 25 mins. x 12 eps. (TV), 25 mins. (v).

Junichi and his adopted younger sister Minato are often left alone when their international spy parents go off on missions. Unknown to them, his father has arranged a marriage for Junichi. The bride is Yuuhi, a rich, well-connected girl who transfers to Junichi's school and meets him by accident when he rescues her from some bullies. She moves in with the siblings, and while Junichi has to get used to his cross and shouty new fiancée, he's also got the hots for his non-biological sister. Moving the arranged-marriage trope familiar ever since **URUSEI YATSURA** into mildly perverted territory, this is a pretty but highly derivative and poorly written show. With 8 directors working under Motonaga and 11 animation directors under Hara, it's amazing that the continuity has been maintained so well, but this does nothing to distinguish the show from a score of other *hentai* harem anime mixed and matched from the same dressing-up box. In the 2011 side-story video, the team is invited to a private island for a luxury vacation, and the girls have an unusual reaction to a new type of sunblock, which inevitably causes them to shed their clothes. This is one of many shows in the 21st century that went out in "English" with their titles disappointingly untranslated. Just try asking for it in a shop.

AKANUKE ICHIBAN

1985. JPN: *Showa Aho Soshi Akanuke Ichiban*. AKA: *Showa Era Idiot Storybook: Most Refined; City Boy*. TV series. DIR: Hidehito Ueda. SCR: Takao Koyama, Hiroko Naka. DES: Hiroshi Hamazaki, Ammonite. ANI: Hidehito Ueda, Shinya Sadamitsu, Tetsuya Komori. MUS: Toshiyuki Watanabe. PRD: Tatsunoko, TV

Asahi. 30 mins. x 22 eps.

Kojiro moves to Tokyo from Japan's northernmost island of Hokkaido and insists on bringing his favorite horse, Hikarikin, with him. The alien king Rel arrives from planet Wedelun and gives him a belt that will allow him to transform into a Miracle Hero and to protect the world from alien menaces. He is more interested, however, in impressing the pretty Yuka, though his rival, Michinari, wants her for himself.

Yu Azuki, creator of IGA NO KABAMARU, enjoys a reputation as an artist who is able to straddle the divide between boys' and girls' comics. Though *Akanuke Ichiban* looks on the surface like a typical superhero story for a male audience, it originally ran in *Margaret* magazine—perhaps it appeared more palatable to male producers and fulfilled some form of girl/boy quota. The ratings, however, did not bear out the theory, and the series was canceled before reaching the end of its second season.

AKB0048 *

2012. JPN: *AKB0048 First Stage*. TV series. DIR: Shoji Kawamori, Yoshimasa Hiraike. SCR: Mari Okada, Tatsuo Higuchi, Toshizo Nemoto. DES: Risa Ebata, Shoji Kawamori, Stanislas Brunet, Akira Ito, Thomas Romain, Yann Le Gall, Vincento Niemu. ANI: Hideki Inoue, Ikuko Ito, Mariko Ito, Toru Imanishi. MUS: Hiroshi Takaki, Slavomir Stanislaw Kowalewski. PRD: Satelight, AKB0048 Production Committee, Starchild Records, GANSIS. 24 mins. x 13 eps. (TV1), 24 mins. x 13 eps. (TV2).

Early in the 21st century, the need for interplanetary travel technology leads to a devastating war. Earth's ecosystem is destroyed and mankind has to leave for new planets. To help people cope with the massive change, some planets ban everything that disturbs the peace—including music, art, love, and idol singers. A legendary idol group, which sang until the very end on Earth, is revived almost a century later as AKB0048. A gaggle of girls from many worlds take up the weapon of song and become guerrillas fighting for their right to make music and wear cute stuff. But they need other weapons too, because the enemy, the anti-entertainment army, has big guns and live ammunition.

Shoji Kawamori has already made a

show about music saving mankind. It was called MACROSS, and this isn't in the same league (MUSIC IN ANIME). But even considering it's a shameless promotional tool for AKB48, an idol group created and controlled by the Simon Cowell of Asia, Yasushi Akimoto, Kawamori's creation still manages to be an entertaining show. And there's a substantially chewy piece of grit at the core of the marshmallow: as well as showcasing the group's songs, it shows the darker side of being an idol. Kawamori and Okada's views of those who control the music business and manipulate the fans and stars is far from rose-colored, and seems to have been granted a degree of indulgence here, much as Yoshiyuki Tomino was given relatively free rein to add hard-hitting plots to the toy commercial that was GUNDAM. The characters endure the rejection and humiliation of years as understudies because their pretty faces don't quite fit, as well as the relentless slog of grueling tours and rehearsals in the style of HUMMINGBIRDS. Mari Okada's scenario doesn't shrink from the way the industry dominates and controls young girls, the enforcement of a conformity as fierce as that required in the Red Army in revolutionary China. Fans of the real group were shaken in 2013 when 20-year-old Minami Maegishi was disciplined for being caught spending the night with her boyfriend. Her reaction—shaving her head like a penitent nun and making a tearful apology on video—led to some serious questioning of the idol aesthetic. As well as referring to the band, the title could also be read as a dual reference to a Russian assault rifle and to Japan's 1948 Entertainment Business Control Law: the mash-up of war, weaponry, illicit activity hiding behind entertainment, and government attempts at control isn't as unlikely as it seems.

AKB0048 has serious flaws, not the least its desperate hope that the original AKB48, if it is remembered at all by posterity, will be commemorated as anything more than a soulless, perky delivery system for saccharine pop pap. Within the anime itself, its problems include villains so thin you could blow your nose in them, Okada's habit of creating plot chaos and then losing interest, and a Tezuka-esque fondness for breaking moments of high

drama with comedy. But overall, as with PUFFY AMI-YUMI, it's hard not to surrender to the sweet, silly charm of it all, as long as you don't expect PERFECT BLUE. The Japanese public certainly thought so—a second series, *AKB0048 Second Stage* (also known as *Next Stage*), followed in 2013. Kawamori once again signed up Thomas Romain, his cocreator on BASQUASH, and Yann le Gall and Stanislas Brunet, who worked with Romain on BODACIOUS SPACE PIRATES. The unrelated erotic anime OED48 seems to have a title intended to create lust by association.

AKI SORA *

2009. AKA: *Autumn Sky*. Video. DIR: Takeo Takahashi, Shunichi Yoshizawa. SCR: Jukki Hanada. DES: Kazuya Kuroda, Kunihiro Shinoda, Shinji Katahiro. ANI: Kazuya Kuroda, Koji Haneda. MUS: Akira Asano, C-CLAYS. PRD: Akita Shoten, Frontier Works, Hoods Entertainment. 25 mins. (v1), 25 mins. x 2 eps. (v2).

Most Japanese high school pupils don't live without an adult in the house and don't have constant sex with their siblings, friends, and teachers. Not that you'd ever guess it from anime like this one. Older sister Aki seduces younger brother Sora. They keep their relationship from Sora's twin sister Nami, who is trying to set him up with her best friend Kana. Nami secretly fancies Kana herself. She also forces Sora to cross-dress in costumes that Kana makes. Based on a manga by Masahiro Itosugi, a second two-part video, *Aki Sora: Yume no Naka (Aki Sora: Within a Dream)*, was released in 2010.

AKIBA GIRLS *

2004. JPN: *Akibakei Kanojo*. AKA: *Akibakei Kanojyo*.Video. DIR: Shigeru Kurii. SCR: Naruhito Sunaga. DES: Jiro Oiwa. ANI: Jiro Oiwa. MUS: N/C. PRD: Studio Wood, Image Works, Milky. 30 mins. x 3 eps.

Orphan Nikita Shindo is obsessed with pornographic computer games, an interest he tries to keep hidden from his two adoptive sisters. He fantasizes about a pretty girl he met in a park near Tokyo's Akihabara electronics district, but eventually decides to get out more and joins his university's "Alternative Trivia Research Club." He soon discovers that FANDOM offers many opportunities for sex, and enjoys a liaison with a costume fan, as well as with a voice actress frustrated by her lack of sexual experience; she appreciates his help in showing her how to put more passion into her performances. Meanwhile, he enjoys similar attentions from his elder and younger sisters and chases after the aforesaid pretty girl, in a porn anime that mixes the 21st-century self-referentiality of GEN-SHIKEN with references to an erotic pastiche of CASTLE IN THE SKY—Lord knows why BALTHUS: TIA'S RADIANCE wasn't enough!

The *Akiba-kei*, in modern Japanese slang, is the subset of Japanese society comprising geeks for whom the electronics district of Akihabara is the center of the world—i.e., fans of anime, manga, and computer games, or a new way of saying "otaku"; see OTAKU NO VIDEO. Based on a game by Tech Arts' G.J? subsidiary (*sic*, the question mark is part of the name), with original character designs by Toshihide Sano, seemingly as with everything else from the label. The first two episodes were also released (along with IMMORALITY) in North America as part of *Hentaipalooza*. **LN**

AKIKAN! *
2008. AKA: *Empty Cans!* TV series, video. DIR: Yuji Himaki. SCR: Hideaki Koyasu et al. DES: Hiro Suzuhira, Ryo Tanaka, Katsufumi Hariu. ANI: Ryo Tanaka. MUS: Nijine. PRD: A-Kiseki, Pony Canyon, Shueisha. 23 mins. x 12 eps. (TV), 25 mins. (v).

In an effort to find out whether steel or aluminum makes stronger cans, government scientists design an experiment in which some drinks cans turn into beautiful girls in order to fight other drinks cans. When 16-year-old Kakeru Daichi, a collector of rare juice cans, buys a melon soda on his way home from school, it turns into a stunning girl as he takes his first sip. He calls her Melon and quickly finds that *akikan* (empty can) girls come to life when infused with carbon dioxide, and then need it to survive. Some of his schoolmates and friends also have akikans. His super-rich best friend Najimi is also in love with him. A video one-shot followed in 2009, made by the same team and set in a hot springs resort. It's a magical girl/harem/fighting/collecting anime packed with fan service (ARGOT AND JARGON), so you can pretty much write the plot for

yourself. Someone got 12 episodes out of this … ?

AKIKO *
1995. Video. DIR: Kaoru Tomioka. SCR: Kaoru Tomioka. DES: Mitsuru Fujii. ANI: Mitsuru Fujii. MUS: Simon Akira. PRD: Fairy Tale, Pink Pineapple. 30 mins. x 2 eps.

Lust and forbidden fruits abound at an all-girls school, as the beautiful female agent Akiko poses as a researcher at the Nobel Academy only to become the victim of a cavalcade of rape, bondage, and sexual abuse. Based on a Japanese PC game with publicity about particularly unpleasant scenes of sex and violence—supposedly strong even by the standards of Japanese pornography. **NV**

AKIRA *
1988. Movie. DIR: Katsuhiro Otomo. SCR: Katsuhiro Otomo, Izo Hashimoto. DES: Toshiharu Mizutani. ANI: Takashi Nakamura. MUS: Geino Yamashiro. PRD: Akira Committee, Mash Room, Toho, Hakuhodo, TMS. 124 mins.

In 2019, Tokyo has been rebuilt after World War III. As the city prepares to host the Olympics, it is rocked by antigovernment terrorism secretly organized by power-brokering politician Nezu. Juvenile delinquent Tetsuo is out racing against a rival gang when he crashes his bike into a child with the face of an old man. He is swiftly taken away by the military, while his friend Kaneda allies with a cell of the terrorists to track him down. Tetsuo begins to develop psychic powers and discovers that he is just one of many experimental subjects in a secret government program to replicate Akira, the human bioweapon that obliterated Tokyo in 1988. Tetsuo escapes to the Olympic stadium, where the remains of Akira are kept in a hidden chamber. Losing control of his powers and absorbing several of his colleagues, Tetsuo causes the return of Akira and a second destruction of Tokyo. Kaneda is one of the survivors, while Tetsuo absconds to create his own universe.

Adapted from the early part of the long-running manga by director Otomo, *Akira* is almost singlehandedly responsible for the early 1990s boom in anime in the English language. Echoes of the seminal *Blade Runner* are undeniable (the film is even set in the same year), but *Akira* owes

less to an alleged "cyberpunk" sensibility than it does to the young Otomo's perspective on 1960s counterculture—rioting students, crazed biker gangs, and corporate intrigue. The military conspiracy in *Akira* carries elements of the 1963 live-action film *Japan's Longest Day*, while other themes include the wartime Unit 731 human guinea pigs and nuclear contamination covered more directly in BAREFOOT GEN. Even the Olympic stadium is a historical marker—Tokyo was due to host the games in 1940 but only got to do so after postwar reconstruction in 1964. In many ways, *Akira* is also a retelling of Otomo's *Fireball*, an unfinished 1979 story about scientists fighting terrorists for control of an apocalyptic energy source.

Akira was a visual tour-de-force, including experiments in digital and analog animation that were to stun audiences worldwide, enjoying greater success abroad than in its country of origin. With a production budget that ran wildly out of control, it was defeated by its very success—few of its lower-budget imitators compare favorably and Western distributors have difficulty replicating its success. In 2001, *Akira* was rereleased with a new dub, closer in meaning and tone to the original Japanese version. Scenes from the film were pastiched by the rapper Kanye West in his video for "Stronger" (2007). **V**

AKIRA TORIYAMA THE WORLD
1990. JPN: *Pink Mizudorobo Amedorobo; Kennosuke-sama*. AKA: *Pink Thieves Water and Rain; Kennosuke-sama*. Movie. DIR: Toyoo Ashida, Minoru Okazaki. SCR: Aya Matsui. DES: Akira Toriyama. ANI: Toyoo Ashida, Katsuyoshi Nakatsuru. MUS: Takeshi Ike. PRD: Toei. 31 mins. x 2 eps.

Two minor works from DRAGON BALL–creator Toriyama, shown on their own dedicated double bill under this umbrella title. *Pink*, the first story, is set in a town where no rain has fallen for three years. The corrupt Silver Company has monopolized the water supply and charges high prices even for drinking water. Bath-loving girl Pink starts stealing water from Silver Company's tankers, soon teaming up with spiky-haired guy Cobalt Blue to rob from the water-rich and give to the poor. The second story, *Kennosuke-sama*, is a squashed-down cartoon comedy about a family of old-fashioned samurai living in modern-day Tokyo whose young son has to head out for an important date.

AKITAKA, MIKA

1964–. After early work on CITY HUNTER, began to specialize in the design of machinery, most notably on NADESICO.

AKIYAMA, KATSUHITO

1950–. Director and storyboarder on the MACROSS movie *Do You Remember Love?*, GALL FORCE, and ELEMENTALORS. He also worked as the animation director of the much-loved "American" cartoon series *Thundercats* (1985).

ALADDIN AND THE WONDERFUL LAMP *

1982. JPN: *Aladdin to Maho no Lamp*. AKA: *Aladdin and the Magic Lamp*. Movie. DIR: Yoshinori Kasai. SCR: Akira Miyazaki. DES: Dale Baer, Jane Baer, Shinya Takahashi. ANI: Shinya Takahashi. MUS: Yukihide Takekawa, Godiego. PRD: Toei, Rankin/Bass. 65 mins.
Aladdin is a poor Arab boy asked by a mysterious stranger (an evil wizard) to help him retrieve an old lamp from an underground cavern. The wizard traps Aladdin in the cavern, but he accidentally releases a jinni from a magic ring and makes a wish to escape. When Aladdin tries to clean up the old lamp, a second jinni appears to grant him unlimited wishes. Aladdin falls in love with the sultan's daughter, Badraul, and uses the Slave of the Lamp to disguise himself as a rich prince. However, the wizard gains possession of the lamp and orders the jinni to transport the princess inside Aladdin's new palace to his own home in Africa. The angry sultan gives Aladdin three days to return her. The Slave of the Ring dies in the initial assault on the African palace, and Aladdin and Badraul must use their own wits to defeat the wizard.

There have been many all-Japanese productions spun off from A THOUSAND AND ONE NIGHTS, but in this case the Baers, former staffers on Disney's *Snow White*, contributed to a Rankin/Bass coproduction that also featured music from Godiego, best known outside Japan for the unforgettable theme tune to the live-action *Monkey* series (*DE). The story would be revisited in 1993 in the Sanrio

PEKKLE video *Aladdin and the Magic Lamp*. In 1995, several Japanese animators would also work on the Disney *Aladdin* TV series—enough to qualify it as an anime coproduction in some sources.

ALEXANDER *

1999. JPN: *Alexander Senki*. AKA: *Alexander War Chronicle*. TV series. DIR: Yoshinori Kanemori. SCR: Sadayuki Murai. DES: Peter Chung. ANI: N/C. MUS: Ken Ishii, Haruomi Hosono, Inheil. PRD: Madhouse, WOWOW. 25 mins. x 13 eps.
In the midst of a bitter war, King Philip's wife, Olympias, gives birth to a son, Alexander. Reared amid intrigue in the palace, he proves himself on the battlefield at Chaeronia at the age of 16. After his father's death under mysterious circumstances, Alexander declares war on Darius III of Persia and goes on to become master of the known universe.

Despite its sci-fi sheen, this is a surprisingly faithful retelling of the life of Alexander the Great based on a novel by DOOMED MEGALOPOLIS–creator Hiroshi Aramata. Featuring a techno-magic based on Pythagorean solids and vast alien armies, it bears more resemblance to *Dune* or *Stargate* than a classical biopic. Character designs from the Korean-born Chung contain echoes of his work on *Aeon Flux*, and some of the visual conceits (such as a swimming pool in the shape of the Mediterranean) are simply superb. The historical Alexander is known in the Middle East as "Iscander," a name appropriated for STAR BLAZERS. Released in 2003 in the U.S. by Tokyo Pop under the title *Reign: The Conqueror*.

ALFRED J. KWAK *

1989. JPN: *Ahiru no Quack; Chiisana Ahiru no Oki na Ai no Monogatari Ahiru no Quack*. AKA: *Quack the Duck; Little Duck's Big Love Story: Quack the Duck*. TV series. DIR: Hiroshi Saito. SCR: Akira Miyazaki. DES: Masaru Amamizu, Susumu Shiraume. ANI: Susumu Shiraume. MUS: Herman van Veen. PRD: Telescreen, Visual 8, TV Tokyo. 25 mins. x 52 eps.
Dutch duckling Alfred Jodocus Kwak loses his family and is raised by a mole. The series covers his life and times as he travels the world trying to help animals everywhere. Based on a story by Herman van Veen, who also provided the voice

of Alfred's father Johann in the German and Dutch dubs, and Prof. Paljack in the Dutch, and wrote the script and music for the Dutch version as well as a song for the Japanese original. The series has been dubbed and screened in France, Germany, the Netherlands, Italy, Denmark, and the Arab world as well as in Japan.

ALIBABA'S REVENGE *

1971. JPN: *Alibaba to Yonjubiki no Tozoku*. AKA: *Alibaba and the Forty Thieves*. Movie. DIR: Hiroshi Shidara. SCR: Motohisa Yamamoto. DES: Reiko Okuyama, Katsuya Koda. ANI: Hideki Mori, Hayao Miyazaki, Yoichi Kotabe, Yasuji Mori. MUS: Seiichiro Uno. PRD: Toei. 55 mins.
Alibaba became rich by defeating the 40 thieves. Now his distant descendant Alibaba XXXIII has inherited the fiefdom and become the worst sultan in history, squandering his ancestor's wealth and the good will of the jinni of the lamp. Al Haq, descendant of the original leader of the thieves, is a good honest boy who resolves to get back his father's fortune, enlisting the aid of 38 cats and a lone mouse. Another of the many anime loosely based on A THOUSAND AND ONE NIGHTS, this short film featured Hayao Miyazaki as a key animator and a flashback sequence using nothing but shadow puppetry. It was not, however, the first anime adaptation of the story—that honor goes to Takeo Ueno's 17-minute EARLY ANIME *The 40 Thieves* (1928).

ALICE ACADEMY

2005. JPN: *Gakuen Alice*. TV series. DIR: Takahiro Omori. SCR: Jukki Hanada, Man Shimada, Masashi Yokoyama, Michiru Shimada. DES: Yoshiaki Ito. ANI: Akihito Dobashi, Haruo Ogawara, Hideaki Shimada, Hiroki Abe, Hiroyuki Shimizu, Hisashi Mitsui, Yoshihiro Sugai, Kei Takeuchi. MUS: Makoto Yoshimori. PRD: Group Tac, NHK. 25 mins. x 26 eps.
Ten-year-old Mikan Sakura misses her old school friend Hotaru, and so makes the trip to visit Hotaru at her new school, Alice Academy. But it is no ordinary school—instead it is an establishment for children with psychic powers and superhero abilities. Mikan somehow secures admission for herself, in a cuter, more magical female-oriented version of the same basic "weird

school" premise of **CROMARTIE HIGH**, based on a manga from *Hana to Yume* magazine by Tachibana Higuchi.

ALICE IN CYBERLAND
1996. Video. DIR: Kazuyoshi Yokota. SCR: Chiaki Konaka. DES: Daisuke Moriyama. ANI: Fumio Shimazu. MUS: N/C. PRD: Warner Vision Japan, Bandai. 28 mins. x 2 eps.
Fourteen-year-old Alice Rena is a 21st-century schoolgirl from Miskatonic College who is dragged into Cyberland, the computer network that connects vast Data Colonies of information. She and her friends are mistresses of the Dive System that allows them to access the treasures within, but all hell breaks loose when one of them falls in love with the prince who rules Cyberland.

A curio dashed off to cash in on a PlayStation game, released along with a radio drama and a PC version of the original, *AiC* mixes various parts of Lewis Carroll's original with large chunks of *Tron*, courtesy of writer Chiaki Konaka, who used cyberspace for more dramatic purposes in **SERIAL EXPERIMENTS LAIN**. Konaka's love of H. P. Lovecraft, as shown in the name "Miskatonic," also reappears in **ARMITAGE III**.

ALICE IN WONDERLAND
1983. JPN: *Fushigi no Kuni no Alice*. AKA: *Alice in the Mysterious Kingdom*. TV series. DIR: Taku Sugiyama. SCR: Fumi Takahashi. DES: Yu Noda. ANI: Yu Kumada, Takao Kogawa. MUS: Reijiro Koroku. PRD: Apollo, Nippon Animation, TVTokyo. 30 mins. x 26 eps.
One fine summer's day, the seven-year-old Alice chases a white rabbit down a hole and finds herself in the underground kingdom of Wonderland. Spending 13 episodes each on *Alice in Wonderland* and its sequel, *Alice through the Looking Glass*, this series ran through all the high points of Lewis Carroll's original stories, though the final two parts were only broadcast in the Tokyo area. To see the series in its entirety, you had to go to Germany, a major financial contributor to this coproduction. In the Japanese version, Alice was played by Tarako, the voice actress behind another children's favorite, **CHIBI MARUKO-CHAN**. Masako Nozawa, who provided the voice of the white rabbit, went on to play Son Goku in **DRAGON BALL**.

In 1998, an unofficial sequel by Ryo Nakahara was adapted by director Shingo Kaneko into the 14-episode *Alice SOS*, which featured further adventures in Dinosaur-land, Cookery-land, Topsy-turvy-land, Cactus-land, Bully-land, Salad-land, Edo-land (old-fashioned Tokyo), God-land, Ghost-land, Backward-land, Santa-land, TV-land, and Devil-land. A far naughtier pastiche was CLAMP's 1995 **MIYUKI-CHAN IN WONDERLAND**. See also **VIDEO PICTURE BOOK** and the sequel by other hands, **ALICE RONDO**.

ALICE RONDO
2006. JPN: *Kagihime Monogatari Eikyu Alice Rondo*. AKA: *Key Princess Story Eternal Alice Rondo; Eternal Alice*. TV series. DIR: Nagisa Miyazaki. SCR: Mamiko Ikeda. DES: Haruka Ninomiya. ANI: Hiroko Kuryube, Sawako Yamamoto. MUS: Hikaru Nanase. PRD: Trinet, Picture Magic. 25 mins. x 13 eps.
Aruto is a fan of **ALICE IN WONDERLAND**, and is convinced that Lewis Carroll wrote a second sequel, *Endless Alice*. He is thus perhaps a little less surprised than he otherwise might have been when he finds two magical girls fighting in the library. The victor pokes the vanquished with a key-like staff, causing her opponent to yield up pages of the lost book—it transpires that the mythical Endless Alice does indeed exist, but has been broken up and scattered among a coterie of "Alice-users." These magical girls must fight each other to regain the missing pages of the book, in a bizarre combination of **READ OR DIE**, **CARDCAPTORS**, and *Highlander* (**HIGHLANDER: THE SEARCH FOR VENGEANCE**)! Aruto is soon surrounded by pretty girls, all fighting over a book and, unsurprisingly, him. The girl who obtains all the pages can compile the Eternal Alice, the ultimate Alice volume, and will have her wish granted. But the losers can no longer keep their identity as Alice Users and are cast out of the game. Based on an idea by Kaishaku, the creator of **UFO PRINCESS VALKYRIE**.

ALIEN 9 *
2001. Video. DIR: Jiro Fujimoto. SCR: Sadayuki Murai. DES: Yasuhiro Irie, Kazunori Iwakura. ANI: Yasuhiro Irie. MUS: Kuniaki Haishima. N/C. PRD: Genco, JC Staff, Bandai Visual, Nippon Columbia, TV Tokyo Media Net, Anime Theater X (AT-X). 30 mins. x 4 eps.

In 2016, the very reluctant Kasumi Tomine, Kumi Kawamura, and Yuri Otani are picked as Alien Monitors at their Japanese school, in charge of cleaning up the various kinds of messes caused by unwelcome pests.

ALIEN FROM THE DARKNESS *
1996. JPN: *Inju Alien*. AKA: *Lust Alien*. Video. DIR: Norio Takanami. SCR: N/C. DES: Ryu Tsukiyo. ANI: Shin Taira. MUS: CUE. PRD: Pink Pineapple, (KIT). 45 mins.
Sci-fi porn in the spirit of **ADVANCER TINA**, heavily influenced by the *Alien* films. On their way back from a mining trip to the planet Kerun, the all-female crew of the starship Muze finds a vessel drifting in space. The derelict Zogne, carrying an illegal cargo of the narcotic Metrogria, is scattered with naked corpses. The sole survivor, a beautiful girl called Flair, claims to have amnesia. As the Muze continues on its way, the same fate starts to befall members of the crew, and lone scientist Hikari trawls through the Zogne's records in an attempt to stop the carnage. Needless to say, it involves an alien monster that consists of little more than tentacles and a permanent craving for female flesh. **LNV**

ALIGNMENT YOU! YOU!
2008. JPN: *Alignment You! You! THE ANIMATION*. Video. DIR: Ken Raika. SCR: Shinichiro Sawayama. DES: N/C. ANI: N/C. MUS: N/C. PRD: Pink Pineapple. 28 mins. x 2 eps.
Takahashi and Oohara are secretly crazy about each other. Oohara isn't going to let a little detail like her death get in the way of getting it on with the boy she fancies. With the help of another ghost, she plans to have her way with Takahashi. This erotic anime is distinguished by the appearance of Toilet Hanako (**HERE COMES HANAKO**), a well-known Japanese school horror icon, as a main character—possibly the first time Hanako has appeared in a comedy show featuring tentacle rape and hermaphrodite sex. The animation is basic although the style is interesting, with liberal use of speedlines and extreme facial expressions. **N**

ALLISON & LILLIA *
2008. JPN: *Allison to Lillia*. TV series. DIR: Masayoshi Nishida. SCR: Toko Machida. DES: Kohaku Kuroboshi, Shinji Seya, Masaki

Saito, Masato Shibata. ANI: Shinji Seya. MUS: Shusei Murai. PRD: Madhouse, MediaWorks. 25 mins. x 26 eps.

Readers expecting Allison and Lillia to occupy the same space will be confused: this is a generation-spanning story, and the second of the titular heroines only shows up in the second half. It's based on two sets of books by Keiichi Sigsawa, creator of **KINO'S JOURNEY**, and shares a similar retro styling. During a ceasefire in a long war between two confederations, two childhood friends meet up for their first summer together since they left the orphanage. Life is anything but quiet for Allison and Will as they accidentally uncover dark secrets, industrial spies and minor royals. Sixteen years on, the story continues with Allison who has become a major and test pilot in her country's air force. It's her daughter Lillia's turn to go adventuring with a childhood friend on trains and planes, rescuing hostages and finding romance in an unexpected place as aspects of her life echo her mother's adventures.

This nostalgic, atmospheric series is true family entertainment, intelligent and attractive; the characters are strong and well played enough to carry the story over several holes in the plot and deficiencies in animation: Madhouse deployed some serious animation talent, even calling in Tezuka Productions to assist, but had occasional problems integrating CG with standard animation and handling perspective. Strong action sequences and a lush musical score make for an appealing package outside the conventions of most present-day TV anime, and more in line with classic series of the 1970s and 1980s.

ALL-PURPOSE RABBITS

2008. JPN: Zenryoku Usagi. TV series. DIR: Hiro Kaburaki. SCR: Yoshiyuki Suga. DES: Satoshi Hirayama, Yukiko Iijima. ANI: Takafumi Hori. MUS: Hiroshi Kagoshima. PRD: TMS, Sotsu. 13 mins. x 52 eps.

Kei Ikeda's original manga was a fair summary of how we in the West see life in an ordinary Japanese company. This is a construction company whose corporate motto is "do your best." That means work your best, eat your best, do everything as best you can. And all the staff and clients are rabbits. The animation is basic, the design brash and bright, and the stories show

the comic pitfalls of aiming for perfection. Silly, cheerful, and fun.

ALWAYS MY SANTA *

2005. JPN: Itsudatte My Santa. AKA: Mai and Santa Together Forever. Video. DIR: Noriyoshi Nakamura. SCR: Koichi Taki. DES: Masahide Yanagisawa. ANI: Takashi Shiokawa, Yukiko Ban. MUS: Hiroshi Sakamoto. PRD: TNK. 30 mins. x 2 eps.

Teenage Japanese boy Santa loathes Christmas, chiefly because his birthday is on December 24—halving his gift potential and lumbering him with a silly name into the bargain. Nor does it help that his parents were always away working, leaving him a series of embittered memories of being forced to spend Christmas alone with his grandmother. However, it also gains him a new friend, in the form of the mysterious Christmas spirit Mai. A Santa in training, she offers to show him the meaning of Christmas by hanging around for the night, only to show up on his doorstep the following day, bemoaning the fact that she has used up all her magic on him, and must now stay with him until the following Christmas Eve. High jinks, of a variety not unlike **OH MY GODDESS!**, duly ensue. Based on a 1998 short manga by **LOVE HINA**–creator Ken Akamatsu in Shonen Magazine weekly, reprinted twice thereafter in Christmas issues with minor revisions. The U.S. release is often referred to as simply My Santa, although the cover art has an untranslated Itsudatte shunted above the English.

AMAGAMI SS *

2010. TV series, video. DIR: Yoshimasa Hiraike, Tomoki Kobayashi. SCR: Yoshimasa Hiraike, Noboru Kimura, Toko Machida. DES: Kisai Takayama, Hiroaki Goda, Maho Takahashi. ANI: Hiroaki Aida, Osamu Sugimoto, Masami Inomata, Seiji Tachikawa. MUS: Toshiyuki Omori. PRD: AIC, TBS. 25 mins. x 25 eps. (TV1), 25 mins. (v), 25 mins. x 13 eps. (TV2).

High school boy Junichi has lots of friends who are girls, but no girlfriend. Two years before, his date didn't show up on Christmas Eve, Japan's peak time for romance, and it put him off dating. His little sister is worried, but as another Christmas approaches it seems his luck may change. Not one but several of his classmates

become romantic prospects. The anime is arranged in a series of story arcs, each focusing on a different girl, with the voice actress for that character providing the ending theme for her episodes

As you might have already guessed, this is another show based on a dating sim game from Enterbrain. Amagami first spun off a manga, Amagami Precious Diary, in 2009, then made the leap to TV with the first 25-episode series. A bonus episode appeared on the BluRay and DVD releases in 2011, and a second shorter TV series, Amagami SS+, followed in 2013. Attractive design and mostly good animation are let down by uneven writing and some very strange moments where game references crop up. There are also a few frames that look lifted straight from the game. Steven Spielberg makes a (surely unapproved) guest appearance, and geeks will have fun spotting the **GUNDAM** and Kamen Rider (*DE) references.

AMATSUKI

2008. TV series. DIR: Kazuhiro Furuhashi. SCR: Chieko Suzuki, Kazuhiro Furuhashi. DES: Shinobu Tagashira, Toshihiro Koyama. ANI: Yukiko Ban. MUS: Mari Fukuhara. PRD: Studio DEEN, Chitose Corp., Geneon Universal Entertainment, Sotsu Agency. 30 mins. x 30 eps.

Rikugo Tokidoki is an ordinary high school student who has failed a history test. He's sent for extra study to a museum that uses virtual reality to put visitors right in the middle of the Edo period, and finds himself trapped inside. As he loses the sight of one eye and tries to avoid getting killed, he meets a strange collection of characters who may not be entirely under the control of the high-tech corporation that created the museum.

The series is based on a 2005 manga by Shinobu Takayama, which is still selling respectably for publisher Ichijinsha. The anime covers roughly the first volume of the manga. It has attractive design and a competent script that refers back to Japanese legends as well as to anime: the outcast girl with a dog-god trapped inside her, reminiscent of **INU YASHA**, **HAKKENDEN**, and **NARUTO**, the school friend trapped inside the same strange world recalling older shows like **EL HAZARD** and more recent offerings such as **11 EYES**. However, it ended after 13 episodes with the plotline still open to another season that has yet to materialize. Some fans have linked this to the 2009 arrest and conviction of lyricist Ryoji Sonoda on drugs charges, although it seems a trifle unfair to shut down an entire production because one of the crew goes to jail. Imagine what it would do to **Star Blazers**!

AMAZING 3, THE ∗

1965. JPN: *Wonder Three*. AKA: *W3*. TV series. DIR: Taku Sugiyama, Osamu Tezuka, Ryosuke Takahashi. SCR: Ichiro Wakabayashi, Osamu Tezuka, Sadao Tsukioka, Kunihiko Yamazaki. DES: Osamu Tezuka. ANI: Kazuko Nakamura. MUS: Tatsu Kawai. PRD: Mushi Pro, Fuji TV. 25 mins. x 52 eps.

The Galactic Alliance sends three secret agents to Earth with orders to destroy it if the planet's warmongering attitude presents a danger. Masquerading as farmyard animals, Major Boko (Bonnie Bunny), Lieutenant JG Poko (Zero Duck), and Lance Corporal Noko (Ronnie Horse) are discovered by young Shinichi Hoshi (Kenny Carter). The younger brother of international crime fighter Koichi (Randy), Shinichi convinces them to help make the world a better place and to give secret aid to Koichi's Phoenix organization, a group whose aims are approximately equivalent to their own. Based on Osamu Tezuka's 1965 manga in *Shonen Magazine*, this minor series originally went into production in the middle of anime's great TV boom, when Tezuka realized that if he laid off 25 temporarily idle staffers, they were sure to be snapped up by rival companies. Accordingly, he set them to work on this project in a nearby apartment, simply to keep them busy until they were required to pitch in on **Kimba the White Lion**. Despite such inauspicious origins, the series enjoyed unusually high attention during its original run, appearing twice on the cover of *Japan's TV Guide*. Tezuka reused similar plot ideas in **Bremen Four**.

AMAZING NURSE NANAKO ∗

1999. JPN: *Nanako Kaitai Shinsho*. AKA: *Nanako's Medical Report*. TV series. DIR: Hiroshi Negishi. SCR: Rasputin Yano. DES: Toshinari Yamashita. ANI: Toshinari Yamashita, Kazuya Miura. MUS: Takahiro Negishi. PRD: Save Our Nurse Project, Genco, Pioneer. 30 mins. x 6 eps.

This strange hybrid of 1980s techno-thriller and 1990s geek-meets-girl comedy begins with a pastiche of **Ghost in the Shell**'s copious computer graphics, as brilliant research scientists construct the humanoid superweapon Venus 2000. But Venus is missing a brain, and Dr. Kyoji Ogami decides that he will put the finishing touches on the project by "borrowing" the brain of his large-breasted maid, Nanako. After all, he reasons, it's not like *she* uses it for anything.

Nanako is a bouncy ingenue baffled by the attention of the world's military—as a violent conspiracy unfolds around her, she frets about cooking and underwear, creating a saucy if puerile antidote to the deadly serious **Evangelion** and its clones. Those seeking stranger comparisons should note that **Catgirl Nukunuku** features a girl who has had a small mammal's brain carefully inserted into her skull, whereas the plot of *Amazing Nurse Nanako* involves a concerted attempt to remove one.

AMAZING NUTS

2006. Video. DIR: Daisuke Nakayama, Takashi Yamashita, Yasuhiro Aoki, 4° F. SCR: N/C. DES: N/C. ANI: N/C. MUS: m-flo and DOPING PANDA, RAM RIDER, Kumi Koda, Mink. PRD: Studio 4°C, avex entertainment. 35 mins.

An anthology, in the spirit of **Glassy Ocean**, but comprising four pop videos that show Studio 4°C at its slick, savvy, irreverent best, at once spoofing and embracing influences from Gorillaz to idols, from **Lupin III** to Moebius to **Macross**. Nakayama's *Global Astroliner Gou* begins as a future cop show, before getting shunted sideways by a romantic subplot, leaving previous criminal investigations unfinished. As a love letter to Genndy Tartakovsky and Jamie Hewlett, it is a delightful confection, although it would not have killed the filmmakers to have resolved some of the plot threads left dangling. Yamashita's stark *Glass Eye* is a total contrast in animation style to Nakayama's romp, depicting an impressionistic scene that may (or may not) evoke a drug overdose and possible suicide, played under a relentless electronic soundtrack that ultimately becomes wearing. Aoki's *Kung Fu Love* transforms Kyoto into a color-saturat-ed fantasy that recalls Chinese animation and **Cutey Honey**. *Joe and Marilyn* features lovers seemingly born from a retro fusion of Rune Naito's doll designs and the art of French illustrator Peynet in a setting from the dark side of a Ray Bradbury carnival. Mink's music for this fourth segment is also the theme for the PlayStation 3 release of RPG *Enchant Arms*. After the desert of dating sims and morass of *moe*, this is a shot of refreshment, although sometimes it tries a little too hard for depth, and ends up being like one of those MTV videos that goes on a little too long.

AMBASSADOR MAGMA ∗

1993. JPN: *Magma Taishi*. Video. DIR: Hidehito Ueda. SCR: Katsuhiko Koide. DES: Kazuhiko Udagawa. ANI: Kazuhiko Udagawa. MUS: Toshiyuki Watanabe. PRD: Tezuka Pro, Bandai Visual, Plex. 25 mins. x 13 eps.

Long ago, the evil Goa was defeated by the golden giant robot Magma, created to defend this planet and its people. Now the two warriors are locked in a deep slumber, while on Earth the descendants of the Asuka family are guardians of their spirits. Fumiaki Asuka is kidnapped by aliens and used to awaken Goa. Schoolgirl Miki, the link to Magma, is forced to flee and takes refuge with the Murakami family. Mamoru Murakami meets with the protecting spirit of our planet, who calls himself "Earth," and is drawn into the battle between good and evil, becoming the one who can summon Magma with a magical golden whistle. Based on a minor manga by **Astro Boy**–creator Osamu Tezuka, *Ambassador Magma* was one of several projects, along with *Zero Man* and *No Man*, that only reached the pilot stage during their creator's lifetime. When Tezuka failed to sell *AM* as anime, he allowed Soji Ushio's (AKA Tomio Sagisu's) company P Pro to make it as a live-action series instead—the poor-quality 1966 52-episode rubber-monster show was eventually released in the U.S. as *Space Giants* (*DE).

It was only much later, as Tezuka's estate embarked upon a long and ongoing project to adapt all of his works for a new generation, that the series finally got an anime release, deliberately made in the blocky, old-fashioned 1950s style of the original, even so far as using the original artwork in the closing credits screened over an impossibly peppy martial theme. The show itself is never quite as interesting as it could be, alternating between scenes that are too childish to be engrossing and too hard-hitting to be suitable for children. Despite its camp villains, the story has its scary moments—and is simply bursting with ideas and relationships that *The X-Files* later reprised, such as covert alien takeovers, human sleeper-agents, and time disturbances.

AMNESIA *

2012. TV series. DIR: Yoshimitsu Ohashi. SCR: Toko Machida. DES: Mai Hanamura, Maho Yoshikawa. ANI: Maho Yoshikawa. MUS: Yoshiaki Dewa. PRD: Brains Base, AT-X, Dax Production, Frontier Works, Geneon Universal, MOVIC, Showgate. 24 mins. x 12 eps.
A nameless teenage girl wakes up with no memories, and is urged by Orion, a spirit that only she can see, that it is against her best interests to go to the hospital. Instead, she tries to fit back into the life that she presumes to be hers, pursuing a relationship with one of four customers at the maid café where she works. And then, in episode 2, she falls off a cliff and dies, only to awaken once more on August 1, with a new boyfriend and a deeper mystery.

Full marks to the production team on this TV series, presented with the plot for a "visual novel" computer game (**ARGOT AND JARGON**) and finding a way not only to preserve several of its contending narrative strands, but to keep the viewer guessing with a plot device that resets to zero every couple of episodes, like some kind of big-eyed, breathless *Groundhog Day*—compare to **SPACE DANDY**, which seemingly squanders such an opportunity in search of laughs. Later episodes reveal a better analogy, to a romantic version of *Quantum Leap*, with the accident-prone heroine shunted between numerous universes in search of her home, where fate will not conspire to erase her. Unfortunately, the execution doesn't quite live up to the premise, with the protagonist almost pathologically passive (she doesn't even attempt to swim to stop herself from drowning), seemingly waiting for the action to come to her, whatever universe she is in. See also **COLORFUL: THE MOTION PICTURE**, which similarly confronts a protagonist with the mystery of his own origins.

AMON SAGA *

1986. Video. DIR: Yoshikazu Oga. SCR: Noboru Shiroyama. DES: Shingo Araki, Michi Himeno. ANI: Shingo Araki. MUS: Shigeaki Saegusa. PRD: Centre, Tokuma, Yumemakura, Ten Pro, TMS. 72 mins.
Amon's family is destroyed and his country conquered by the evil Valhiss. Befriending Gaius the giant, Amon joins forces with a number of disgruntled individuals to attack Valhiss's capital city, which is located on the back of a giant turtle. While sneaking into the city, Amon meets and falls in love with the beautiful hostage, Princess Lichia. Captured and thrown into the dungeons to be devoured by Valhiss's savage pet, Amon escapes while one of his companions rescues the princess, only for her to be recaptured when their camp is attacked by werewolves. The final battle is on to defeat Valhiss, avenge Amon's parents, and rescue his love.

Not to be confused with the similarly named **DEVILMAN** sequel, this video was also shown in theaters on a double bill with **BELOVED BETTY**. The manga in *Ryu* magazine was written by Baku Yumemakura and is the only one ever drawn by Yoshitaka Amano, who, dissatisfied with the manga medium, soon returned to straightforward illustration.

AMURI IN STAR OCEAN

2008. JPN: *Hoshi no Umi no Amuri*. Video. DIR: Yoshitomo Yonetani. SCR: Yoshitmo Yonetani. DES: MA@YA. ANI: N/C. MUS: Mina Kubota. PRD: Studio Hibari, Bandai Visual. 30 mins. x 3 eps.
The future: after an increase in solar radiation, children with strange abilities are born. Thirteen-year-old Amuri's ability, called "Repulsion," gives her apparent invulnerability, but also means she can't touch anyone or most things. It keeps her alive when a raiding force from another planet destroys the space station she's visiting, and enables her to survive both being dumped into space without a suit and the machines the enemy use to try and destroy her. Then a stranger turns up with a spacesuit based on Amuri's own DNA, making her effectively immune to the Repulsion effect.

Director Yonetani, who was credited with the reading Kometani when he worked on *Gaogaigar* (**BRAVE SAGA**) and

BETTERMAN, has also directed two **TIGER AND BUNNY** movies. He created the *Amuri* manga, with art by Shinya Inase, in 2007. Studio Hibari have a strong pedigree, including work on Mamoru Oshii's arcane **ANGEL'S EGG** and classic movies for Studio Ghibli. The art is accordingly pretty, and the music is charming. There seems to be a fashion for labeling any show in which girls befriend other girls "*yuri*" (**ARGOT AND JARGON**), but *Amuri* seems to qualify, at least by the Japanese interpretation of the term, less explicitly sex-focused than the American view.

ANAL SANCTUARY *

2005. JPN: *Requiem*. Video. DIR: Yoshito Machida. SCR: Kazuhiro Muto, Hiroyuki Ishii, Kosuke Fujii, Shinji Yamamoto. DES: Kumi Shimamoto. ANI: Yoshimitsu Murayama. MUS: N/C. PRD: GP Museum Soft, Milky. 30 mins. x 2 eps.
Akio is a music teacher at the prim St. Cecilia's School for Girls, where he enjoys a secret hobby as a serial rapist, thanks to the hypnotic effects of Cannone, the satanic violin. With just a few notes on the fiddle of fornication, Akio can bend pliant young girls to his will, in an anime adaptation of a computer game from Clock-up. The second episode sees Akio facing resistance from schoolgirls Yukina and Mizuho, who have somehow obtained the angelic violin known as Cecilia. Victory, however, is unlikely to come without a good deal of tentacles and nude flesh. **LNV**

ANAL VAMPIRE

2011. JPN: *Kyuketsuki*. AKA: *Vampire*. Video. DIR: Shigeru Yazaki. SCR: N/C. DES: Keiji Tani. ANI: N/C. MUS: N/C. PRD: IMG, Valkyria Animation. 30 mins. x 2.
Based on a game by Valkyria, this porn story takes a pulp fiction trope from premodern Japan as its starting point: the girl who sells herself into slavery to pay her parents' debts. The heroine sells herself to a clan of vampires instead of a clan of yakuza, but the outcome is the same. The *kanji* for "vampire" here indicate a demon who sucks ass rather than blood. No, really. **N**

AND YET THE TOWN MOVES *

2010. JPN: *Soredemo Machi wa Mawatteiru*. AKA: *Soremachi*. TV series. DIR: Akiyuki

Shinbo. SCR: Katsuhiko Takayama, Miku Oshima. DES: Hiroki Yamamura, Hisaharu Iijima. ANI: Hiroki Yamamura. MUS: Round Table. PRD: SoreMachi Partners, TBS. 25 mins. x 12 eps.

High school girl Hotori is in debt, and takes a job in a maid café near the local train station to pay it off. Her school friend Toshiko also works there, and their math teacher is a regular client. Hotori has a crush on him, Toshiko has a crush on Hotori's childhood friend Hiroyuki, and he (of course) has a secret crush on Hotori. Hotori has a surprisingly normal family for an anime heroine—two parents, two siblings, and a talking dog—but she's clumsy, tends to whine a lot, and is addicted to mystery stories. Cue aliens, ghosts, and paranormal events in the café and the little town. Based on Masakazu Ishiguro's charming manga, running since 2005 in *Young King Ours* magazine, this is worth a look. Unpoisoned by the marketing-speak and postmodern claptrap of modern media, Hotori is an archetypal small-town girl who just wants to be excellent to people, entirely unaware of the tawdry implications of her chosen profession. The series is suffused with a joyous celebration of making a difference at the most local and intimate of levels. There are no world-saving conspiracies here, just a sense straight out of *It's a Wonderful Life* that we are all the center of our own world and can choose to spin it any way we choose. This last point, and the title itself, is an oblique reference to a famous quote from Galileo, who similarly observed that you could deny reality all you wanted, but the world would continue to turn.

Yasuomi Umezu, creator of the heart-rending *Presence* from **ROBOT CARNIVAL,** directed the opening credits, and director Shinbo's rap sheet is impressive: the first episodes are almost uncomfortably fast and crammed with technical trickery, but later ones slow down considerably. There are moments of lovely comedy, and everyday life is presented in all its unspectacular absurdity.

ANE HARAMIX

2006. Video. DIR: Jiro Fujimoto, Yasuyuki Fuse. SCR: Jiro Fujimoto, Kozuki Luna. DES: Yasuno Yoshiaki, Manjyome Shun. ANI: Miyuki Kurahashi. MUS: N/C. PRD: Pixy. 30 mins. x 4 eps.

Based on a porno game by Lilith, the story begins with high school boy Akitoshi living with his beautiful older sister Hitomi, who has looked after him since their parents died. He is filled with lust for her, but hides it. One night, Death—in the shape of a cute and underdressed girl named Mina—comes into his room to take him away. His screams wake Hitomi, who pleads for his life. Mina explains that he can only be spared if he fathers a child within a week. Now, who could he possibly find as a potential mother? The idea of having to father a child to save your life/reputation/family fortune isn't uncommon in anime **EROTICA AND PORNOGRAPHY,** and if you really want another incest version there's the later **OPPAI HEART: SHE'S IN HEAT**—the heroine even has the same hair color as Hitomi. **O**

ANEKI: MY SWEET ELDER SISTER

2007. JPN: *Aneki ... My Sweet Elder Sister the Animation.* Video. DIR: Ken Raika. SCR: Shinichiro Sawayama. DES: N/C. ANI: N/C. MUS: N/C. PRD: Office Take Off, Pink Pineapple, T-Rex. 30 mins. x 4 eps.
Screenwriter Sawayama has previous outings adapting manga for Pink Pineapple: this time the manga is by Ohepe Youshu, and it's not about incest. The "big sister" figures in these short stories aren't actually related to the hapless guys who lust after them, but stepsisters, class seniors, and teachers. So no incest, only slender storylines and plenty of Pink Pineapple's trademark fluid-soaked imagery. There is no irony whatsoever in the name of the studio that produced the animation—a different sort of "taking off" is implied, we think.

ANGEL *

1990. Video. DIR: Hideki Takayama, Hiromitsu Taida, Kaoru Toyooka. SCR: Wataru Amano, Koji Sakakibara. DES: Rin Shin. ANI: Osamu Tsuruyama, Mitsuru Fujii, Masato Ijuin. MUS: N/C. PRD: Studio Angel, Pink Pineapple. 45 mins. x 2 eps., 30 mins. x 5 eps. (*New Angel*).
The adventures of Kosuke, a sex-obsessed college boy who's always ready to help damsels in distress, just so long as he gets something special in return. Cue a succession of short stories in which a young,

often nameless female comes to him with a problem; he sorts it out, then sorts *her* out. The one exception is Shizuka, the childhood sweetheart Kosuke befriended at the age of five, when she tried to commit suicide over the death of her pet bird. Moving back to Tokyo with her family, she hopes to make an honest man out of him, though she has a difficult task ahead.

U-jin is the pseudonymous artist who was made famous in Japan by the efforts of the Association to Protect Children from Comics to have his *Young Sunday* comic *Angel* banned. The video versions of his hardcore comics are not quite as explicit as the originals but are still pretty eyebrow-raising. The original *Angel* video was followed in 1994 by five volumes of *New Angel*, though the running time soon was cut to a mere two-thirds of its former size. The U.S. distributor has made *New Angel* available in both uncut and edited editions, though your guess is as good as ours as to who would want to watch a porno movie with the porno taken out. *Angel* was also adapted into two live-action movies, which were released in English, and similar erotic stories from the same author can be found in **U-JIN BRAND** and the **TALES OF ...** series. **O**

ANGEL ANGELIQUE

2006. JPN: *Koi Suru Tenshi Angelique—Kokoro no Mezameru Toki.* AKA: *Beloved Angel Angelique—When Hearts Awaken.* TV series. DIR: Susumu Kudo. SCR: Michiru Shimada, Makoto Nakamura. DES: Kairi Yura, Mari Tominaga. ANI: Rika Mishima, Yukie Suzuki, Keiko Yamamoto, Norio Matsumoto. MUS: N/C. PRD: Satelight, KOEI. 24 mins. x 13 eps. (TV1), 25 mins. x 12 eps. (TV2).
Schoolgirl Ange is chosen to save a dying land in the Seiju—Holy Beast—universe, with the help of nine elemental Guardians in the shape of attractive young men. Ange is not especially clever and predictably clumsy, but her compassionate heart and desire to help others make all the Guardians feel deeply protective toward her. This fantasy harem anime for girls is a celebration of the tenth anniversary of the game series that spawned it (**ANGELIQUE**). The first edition of the Japanese DVD also featured a comedy short with all the characters in squashed-down format. It was popular enough to spin off a further TV

series in which Ange, trapped in the Seiju Universe, must find nine new candidates and persuade them to become Guardians. *Koi suru Tenshi Angelique: Kagayaki no Ashita (Beloved Angel Angelique: Radiant Tomorrow)* ran for 12 episodes from January 2007. The TV run was short, but Japanese companies have more ways to monetize anime than Western ones: King Records released 20 character CDs, 3 soundtrack CDs, 3 radio CDs, and 2 drama CDs in the following two years.

ANGEL BEATS *

2010. TV series. DIR: Seiji Kishi. SCR: Jun Maeda. DES: Na-Ga, Katsuzo Hirata, Kazuki Higashiji. ANI: Katsuzo Hirata. MUS: ANANT-GARD EYES, Jun Maeda. PRD: Aniplex, ASCII Media Works, CBC, Dentsu, MBS, MOVIC, P.A.Works, Visual Art's/Key. 21 mins. x 15 eps.

A group of dead students find themselves caught in a high school afterlife, overseen by a girl called Angel with supernatural powers. There's also a dissident faction, but in most high schools Yuri and her chums would just cut class and smoke behind the bike sheds, away from the mundane students contemptuously described by Yuri as "NPCs"—non-player characters, the cannon fodder of a thousand role-playing games. Here, they form the Afterlife Battlefront to take on God and His Angel. Yuri invites new student Otonashi to join them. They have a band—Girls Dead Monster—which enjoyed considerable real-world success as part of the publicity for this show. They have a supply chain, a group called the Guild that makes weapons out of dirt for the struggle. They even have computer-generated enemies.

Writer-composer Maeda and designer Na-Ga were approached to create an original anime by Aniplex. The pair has a history of creating successful visual novels for software company Key, and are noted for mixing comedy and action with pathos. With radio shows, books, and a four-panel comic strip serial preceding it, the anime was only one small part of a media franchise that included live shows and soundtracks. Solid sales and praise from local and foreign critics made the franchise a success, but the series suffers from trying to cram a large number of potentially interesting characters into a

13-episode TV run. But it has much to recommend it—from the emphasis on the importance of individuality for survival, to the cheeky co-opting of Studio Ghibli locations to depict how Otonashi imagines Angel's lair.

ANGEL BLADE *

2003. Video. DIR: Masami Obari. SCR: Remu Aoki, Jin Koga. DES: Masami Obari, Magnum Tana, Mocchii, Yosuke Kabashima, Mikoshiro Nagi. ANI: Makoto Uno, Yosuke Kabashima. MUS: N/C. PRD: Frontline, Studio G-1Neo, MUSE. 30 mins. x 3 eps. (v1), 30 mins. x 3 eps. (v2).

In a future in which only 99 human cities remain above the clouds of a war-torn Earth, a floating castle appears in the sky over City 69, and an evil force plots against women. Moena becomes Angel Blade, a fighter with the beauty of a goddess who appears to rescue the victims from bondage, rape, and depravity, all of which feature prominently, since the Dark Mother is trying to conquer Earth by attacking girls at a college, as one does. Masami Obari is renowned for eroticizing mainstream anime, but here he makes a rare foray into pornography, bringing with him a larger budget than usual in order to make an erotic anime that has an involved plot to accompany the usual rapes and assaults. The English voice cast use pseudonyms like Likki DeeSplit and Syndi Snackwell in an effort to keep it off their more respectable resumés. An erotic SF adventure with the gravity-defying breasts and cute pointy noses for which Obari is renowned. A "movie" edit also exists, which runs the first three episodes together with some bonus footage. For the sequel series, the show was renamed *Angel Blade Punish*. **ⒶⓋ**

ANGEL COP *

1989. Video. DIR: Ichiro Itano. SCR: Sho Aikawa. DES: Nobuteru Yuki. ANI: Yasuomi Umezu, Satoru Nakamura, Hideki Takayama, Hiroyuki Ochi. MUS: Hiroshi Ogasawara. PRD: Studio 88, DAST, Soeishinsha, Japan Home Video. 30 mins. x 6 eps.

At the close of the 20th century, Japan forms a Special Security force to protect it from foreign terrorists like the fanatical Red May. Angel, the newest officer, loses her partner, Raiden, to psychic vigilantes and suspects that she has more to fear

from a secret government cybernetics project than from left-wing activists. Soon all hell breaks loose, as cyborgs and psychics fight for access to the secrets of the mysterious "H-File."

Consisting of long fight scenes stitched together by ham-fisted expository soliloquies, *Angel Cop* wastes loving detail on weapons and machinery but leaves its characters shallow and uninteresting. A nasty bloodbath from **VIOLENCE JACK**–director Ichiro Itano, it fails despite a crew of great talents who would go on to work on **ESCAFLOWNE**, **ARMITAGE III**, and, admittedly, the equally soulless **KITE**.

The original creator, Taku Kitazaki, was only 17 when he sold his first story, shooting to fame thanks to his work's resemblance to flavor-of-the-moment **AKIRA**. As one might expect from the creator whose publications include *War Story Busty*, *Angel Cop* is aimed squarely at the lowest common denominator. Different arms of the military show off their hardware and are then trashed by psionic supersoldiers, while a mad scientist cackles … madly. The final showdown is against Lucifer, a glacial blonde seemingly modeled on Brigitte Nielsen, in whose bone-crunching defeat the good guys take an ethnically suspect pleasure—a few of their antiforeign quips have survived the English-language dub, though the original Japanese script is far more anti-American and anti-Semitic throughout. There is, however, an ironic happy ending; by the time *Angel Cop* was made, its 23-year-old creator had already tired of the genre and moved into gentle romance with *Like This Love Song*. **ⒷⓃⓋ**

ANGEL CORE *

2003. Video. DIR: Ran Misumi. SCR: Hiroshi Watanabe. DES: Hiro Asano. ANI: N/C. MUS: N/C. PRD: Picol, Blue Eyes. 30 mins. x 2 eps.

As the clouds of war gather, the Nazi-like United Empire puts into action a secret scheme to extract "Angel Core," a crystallized form of divine power that can be found in human descendants of gods. They do this with a vague, **EVANGELION**-inspired notion of Kabbalah sorcery, but of course it is actually an excuse to imprison a bunch of innocent girls in a secret base and subject them to sexual degradation in an attempt to draw out their life force. Young officer Ralph frets that torturing and raping women is not the way for a military defense plan to operate and resolves to help two of the girls escape, even though it will cause him to directly disobey an order. A pornographic anime that is unpleasant enough to begin with, before anyone starts bringing up parallels with Japan's wartime record on "comfort women." **LNV**

ANGEL HEART

2005. TV series. DIR: Toshiki Hirano. SCR: Sumio Uetake. DES: Takashi Saijo. ANI: Takashi Saijo. MUS: Taku Iwasaki. PRD: Thomas Entertainment, Yomiuri TV, Tokyo Movie Shinsha. 25 mins. x 50 eps.

Xiang Ying is "Glass Heart," a 15-year-old girl reared as an assassin by Taiwanese gangsters in the style of **GUNSLINGER GIRL**. She tries to end her torment by committing suicide, but is saved by a heart transplant and emerges from a coma a year later, reporting strange visitations from a dream figure she calls Kaori. Evading her gangster bosses, she runs for Shinjuku, guided by a voice in her head that announces "I died here" when she stands at the center of the area's distinctive crossroads. In an attempt to shake off her pursuers, she ducks into a café called the **CAT'S EYE**, where Umibozu, the blind manager, senses that his beloved Kaori has somehow returned. Kaori, of course, is the original owner of the transplanted heart, haunting the heart's new owner in a manner previously used in episodes of **BLACK JACK**. Umibozu's best friend is Ryo Saeba, the famous **CITY HUNTER** of anime legend, who has been living in a traumatized daze for the months following the death of his partner Kaori in a car accident. Before long, Ryo and Xiang Ying form a new partnership, in what may at first seem like a pointless continuation of the *City Hunter* storyline with a new label. However, *AH*'s existence seems to owe something to a major power shift in the manga industry in 2001, when a number of creators defected from their old publishers to write for Shinchosha's new *Comic Bunch* weekly. Just as Kenichi Sonoda once refashioned **RIDING BEAN** as **GUNSMITH CATS**, and **FIST OF THE NORTH STAR** proclaimed itself "new," *AH* is likely to be a rebranding exercise that allows manga creator Tsukasa Hojo to continue using his popular characters and

situations from *City Hunter* without getting caught up in a maze of red tape from the rightsholders to various anime, manga, and live-action versions of his creation.

ANGEL LEGEND

1996. JPN: *Angel Densetsu*. Video. DIR: Tatsuo Misawa. SCR: Naoyuki Sakai. DES: Nobuyoshi Ito. ANI: Nobuyoshi Ito. MUS: Jun Sky Walkers. PRD: Toei. 45 mins.

New kid in town Shinichiro Kitano is a noble, sensitive boy with "the face of a devil and the kindness of an angel." Pushed into a world of drugs and crime simply because of the way he looks, he tries to make the world a better place without fighting, eventually becoming the leader of the local gang. This adaptation of Norihiro Yagi's manga from *Shonen Jump* only lasted for a single episode—at the time it was released, Japan was obsessed with more compelling "angels" in **EVANGELION**. **V**

ANGEL LINKS *

1999. JPN: *Seiho Tenshi Angel Links*. AKA: *Stellar Angel Angel Links*. TV series. DIR: Yoshikazu Yamaguchi. SCR: Masaharu Amiya. DES: Asako Nishida, Rei Nakahara. ANI: Hiroyuki Hataike. MUS: N/C. PRD: Sunrise, WOWOW. 25 mins. x 13 eps.

Orphaned 16-year-old Li Mei-Feng inherits the family business from her grandfather, Jian-He—it's the private police franchise for an entire solar system that's simply crawling with pirates. Refusing to be scared away, Mei-Feng assembles the Angel Links team of troubleshooters, including a weapons expert and the last survivor of a race of dinosaur vegetarians, and sets out to bring the system under the rule of law. A spin-off from Takehiko Ito's **OUTLAW STAR**, replaying the mood, look, and staff.

ANGEL OF DARKNESS *

1995. JPN: *Inju Kyoshi*. AKA: *Lustful-Beast Teacher*. Video. DIR: Kazuma Muraki, Suzunari Joban. SCR: Yukihiro Kosaka. DES: Kazunori Iwakura, Yuji Ikeda. ANI: Kazunori Iwakura. MUS: Takeo Nakazawa. PRD: Pink Pineapple. 45 mins. x 4 eps.

In a typical girls' boarding school, Atsuko and Sayaka manage to fit in a lesbian affair around their class schedule without too much trouble. But when one of their teachers digs up an ancient artifact and releases a demonic entity, things get a bit

more hectic. The entity needs to be fed a steady supply of nubile young women to keep itself alive and build the new form it needs to take over the world (the ancient spirits of Earth oppose this, or would if any of them were more than nine inches high). With the help of an elf who fits in her handbag, Sayaka sets out to save her girlfriend and classmates from a fate worse than death and foil the threat to the world, though similar events wreak havoc in other schools, with the same basic set-up and conclusion. Much ripping of underwear, bondage, "comical" characters like the Kuroko from **UROTSUKIDOJI**, and sexualized violence to match. The four episodes were also filmed as live-action movies in 1995–96 directed by Mitsunori Hattori and Koji Shimizu. **LNV**

ANGEL RABBIE

2003. JPN: *Tenbatsu Angel Rabbie*. AKA: *Judgment Angel Rabbie*; *Divine Punishment Angel Rabbie*. Video. DIR: Shinji Ishihara. SCR: Mitsuhiro Yamada. DES: Noritaka Suzuki, Chisato Naruse, Hiroshi Ogawa. ANI: Seigi Matsumoto. MUS: Under 17, Haruko Momoi, Masaya Koike. PRD: AIC, Kogado Studio, Angel Chamber. 25 mins.

In a far future when magic and science have combined, a war breaks out for control of the magical lunar city of Sorceriam. Both sides unleash terrible magic, destroying Earth's civilization in the process. A few thousand years later (so that's the far, *far* future, then), mankind recovers but Earth is still menaced by giant monsters left over from the original conflict. Sorceriam has been cut off from Earth for all this time and has flourished. Queen Mirchol and the Seven Sisters now rule the Moon, and dispatch agents known as Angels to protect the Earth. These elite fighters are chosen from a group of lower-ranked warriors known as the Surrogates. Heroine Lasty Farsen is 16, but usually takes the form of a clumsy 12-year-old who is useless with technology. Only when her powers are released does she transform into Angel Rabbie and become her normal self. Each Angel has a special type of magic, or "mode," but Rabbie is unaware of what hers is. There's a reference to 9th-century Hokkaido hero **ATERUI**—the church that opposes Lasty is named after him—but most of the comedy seems to revolve around food. Action comedy based on the PC game of the same title, part of the *Angelic* series; as if SAILOR MOON had never happened.

ANGEL SANCTUARY *

2000. JPN: *Tenshi Kinryoku*. Video. DIR: Kiyoko Sayama. SCR: Mayori Sekijima. DES: Hidekazu Shimamura. ANI: Hidekazu Shimamura. MUS: Hikaru Nanase. PRD: Bandai. 30 mins. x 3 eps.

As a punishment for defying God Almighty and fighting against the legions of Heaven (led by her brother, Razael), the soul of the fallen angel Alexael is imprisoned in a crystal, doomed to be forever reincarnated as a human being who will die a young and violent death. Born into the body of *male* juvenile delinquent Setsuna Mudo, Alexael realizes that God is dead and the world is ending, just as foretold in the Black Book of Revelation. S/he is the long-awaited Messiah but would rather seduce his/her sister than take up arms in the final battle between Heaven and Hell. Based on the manga by Kaori Yuki, *AS* tries but fails to cram the original storyline into three tiny episodes, reducing Yuki's carefully paced original into a mad rush of revelations. Compare to other apocalyptic tales of androgynous young men pouting sulkily, such as X: THE MOVIE and EARTHIAN.

ANGEL TALES *

2001. JPN: *Otogi Story Tenshi no Shippo*. AKA: *Angel's Tails; Fairy Story Angel Tails*. TV series. DIR: Kazuhiro Ochi, Norio Kashima. SCR: Yuji Minamide. DES: Takashi Kobayashi. ANI: Takashi Kobayashi. MUS: Yoshinobu Hiraiwa. PRD: Wonderfarm, Tokyo Kids, WOWOW. 25 mins. x 13 eps. (TV1), 25 mins. x 11 eps. (TV2).

Goro Mutsumi is plagued by bad luck: he's lost his job, he's broke, and has no success with women. Then a fortune teller predicts his luck is about to change. The very next morning, three cute girls show up at his apartment. Ran, Tsubasa, and Kurumi are Spirit World Angels assigned to watch over him; they are reincarnations of his former pet hamster, rabbit, and cat, still vying for their master's attention, like the similarly undead companions in BUBU CHACHA. Nine other "Angels" turn up— Goro has never ceased to love his pets, and now they're here to help him turn his

life around. We dread to think what will happen when the erotic anime production companies start looking for a way to rip this one off. Based on an original story by DEVIL HUNTER YOHKO's Juzo Mutsuki, it was originally screened on the satellite channel WOWOW in Japan, and followed in 2003 by *Angel Tales Kiss! (Tenshi no Shippo Chu!)* on Kid's Station. Note that 12 companion animals give this show a certain similarity to the zodiacal FRUITS BASKET. The story would also spin-off into SAINT BEAST. ◐

ANGELIC LAYER *

2001. TV series. DIR: Hiroshi Nishikiori. SCR: Kazushi Okawanai, Reiko Yoshida, Akihiko Inari. DES: Takahiro Omori, CLAMP. ANI: Koichi Horikawa. MUS: N/C. PRD: Bones, TV Tokyo. 25 mins. x 26 eps.

Diminutive junior high school girl Misaki Suzuhara is separated from her mother at an early age. When her father dies, she must move from her home in Wakayama to her aunt's house in Tokyo. There, she becomes intrigued by the Angel dolls, customizable dolls with "micro-actuator" controls, which are hatched from eggs and appear to be fully alive. The Angels are controlled by their owner's willpower but can only move within the "Layer" battle arena. Misaki gets an Angel called Hikaru, and their battles begin. This anime based on a *Shonen Ace* manga by CARD CAPTORS–creators CLAMP has all the appearance of a game tie-in, just without a real game to tie into.

ANGELIQUE

2000. Video, TV series. DIR: Akira Kiyomizu. SCR: Midori Kusada. DES: Kairi Yura. ANI: Masanori Fujioka. MUS: N/C. PRD: Yumeta Company. 30 mins. (v1), 30 mins. x 3 eps. (v2), 30 mins. x 26 eps. (TV).

Angelique, Rachael, and Rosaria are three of the nine guardian angels, members of a secret sect called Alios, whose job it is to protect mere mortals from ruining their lives. Angelique is also destined to be the future queen of the universe, which may be why sweet-talking Osaka charmer Charlie is so keen on her. The events of the anime take place a little after *Requiem for the Sky*, the computer game that spawned it, and were revisited in 2004 with a second story to celebrate the tenth anniversary of the original. It was, however, the 2008

TV spin-off *Neo Angelique Abyss*, directed by Shin Katagai, that made it to two TV seasons and an English-language release, emphasizing the world of Arcadia beset by dark forces, which appear to actually triumph after 13 episodes, before the titular heroine wakes up (she's been sleeping), girds her loins, and saves the world. She is, of course, the "Queen's Egg," the long foretold female incarnation of the protective Purifier caste, whose other members are all handsome men, vying for her teenage affections. See also ANGEL ANGELIQUE.

ANGELIUM *

2004. Video. DIR: Kazunari Kume. SCR: Mitsuhiro Yamada. DES: Mamoru Yokota. ANI: Naoki Sosaka. MUS: Toru Horasawa. PRD: Moon Rock. 30 mins. x 2 eps.

Trainee angels Yu, Miki, and Chadoko come down to Earth to learn more about humanity, volunteering to work in a flower shop as their cover story. They are unaware that their boss Zeus, ever hungry for more sexual conquests, takes over the body of a local Japanese boy whenever the possibility of sex is near, thereby hoping to escape the notice of his jealous wife Hera. However, Zeus's brother Hades is secretly backing an attempt by local gangsters to scare away the florists, and is spooked enough by Zeus's arrival to call in more powerful minions (Persephone and her crew of monsters) to scare the girls away. Cue a bizarre mixture of EARTHIAN and WEISS KREUZ with the standard tropes of porn anime, distinguished by above average design work, and brief interludes of tentacle sex that seem quaintly old-fashioned in the 21st century. For a different kind of butchering of Greek myth, see HERMES. Based on a computer game from Alice Soft, although this adaptation peters out mid-story without a proper ending. ◐◖◗

ANGEL'S EGG *

1985. JPN: *Tenshi no Tamago*. Movie. DIR: Mamoru Oshii. SCR: Mamoru Oshii. DES: Yoshitaka Amano. ANI: Yasuhiro Yukura. MUS: Yoshihiro Kanno. PRD: Studio Deen, Tokuma Shoten, Tokuma Japan. 71 mins.

In a timeless, placeless, run-down city, an itinerant girl scavenges for supplies. She carries a large unhatched egg. The ruined city is beset by shadowy, flying coelacanths, themselves hunted by statues that come to life. A soldier bearing a cross-like sword protects the fearful girl and returns her to her camp in an abandoned planetarium. When she falls asleep, he smashes the egg but finds it empty. He leaves, and the heartbroken girl drowns while chasing him, her breath transforming into egg-like bubbles, and her statue rising to the heavens in a machine-borne apotheosis.

According to Brian Ruh's *Stray Dog of Anime*, neither the director nor designer admit to knowing what this film is about. Plotless and highly symbolic, with hardly any dialogue beyond repeated questions, this stream-of-consciousness exercise by PATLABOR-director Oshii features his trademark Christian imagery with recurring allusions to death, and a quest for self-knowledge that is presented as both destructive and redemptive. There are echoes of post-holocaust or eco-disaster fiction in its drowned-world setting, and impressionistic scenes of soldiers fighting nothing and fishermen hunting the ghosts of long-dead fish. Surreal elements recall Oshii's work on URUSEI YATSURA, including spaceships full of silent people bearing other eggs, and an ending that suggests the world itself sits at the edge of a floating eggshell. The animation and design, however, incorporating work from A THOUSAND AND ONE NIGHTS–creator and illustrator Amano, is beautifully executed. Parts of the film were plundered for interstitial footage in Carl Colpaert's live-action film *In the Aftermath* (1988), constituting an "English-language release," albeit in highly edited form. Although strictly speaking a "video" work, *Angel's Egg* was given an early morning screening in a single Tokyo cinema in late 1985. The listing for this event in *Animage* claimed a running time of 108 minutes, although all extant video editions seem to run at 71 minutes.

ANGEL'S FEATHER *
2006. Video. DIR: Yasuhiro Kuroda. SCR: Akiko Horii. DES: Kazue Yamamoto, Ryotaro Akao. ANI: Kan Ogawa. MUS: N/C. PRD: VENET, Studio e.go! 30 mins. x 2 eps.
Twin brothers Shou and Kai have been raised apart, and Kai has completely forgotten his brother. They find themselves at the same exclusive boys' school, where one of their fellow pupils has a book about

an ancient empire known as the Winfield Kingdom. Before long, Shou encounters a monster and finds sinister alliances and undercurrents between the principal and pupils. The nobles of Winfield had beautiful white wings, their enemies black ones: and Shou and Kai find that they are being drawn into Winfield's past struggles. Based on a visual novel by BlueImpact from 2003, this is hampered by limited animation and somewhat incoherent plotting, doubtless the result of cramming too many extravagantly winged creatures into a very small cage in the hope of whipping up some of the accolades once accorded to HAIBANE RENMEI.

ANGELS IN THE COURT *
2000. JPN: *Court no Naka no Tenshitachi*. Video. DIR: Satoru Sumisaki. SCR: Yasuyuki Moto. DES: Seiji Kishimoto, Poyoyan Rock (original game). ANI: Ten Nakazama. MUS: N/C. PRD: Saburo Omiya, Pink Pineapple. 30 mins. x 2 eps. (v1); 30 mins. x 2 eps. (v2).
A volleyball geek's fantasy as new girl Nanase Morimura, who "wears glasses, but has big breasts," joins the Aota Academy team, led by former All-Japan ace Coach Akira Motoura. She is unable to unleash her true potential without a session of "special tuition" with Coach (who does not neglect the other team members, either), but in episode 2 he goes missing after saving another player from three would-be rapists in the park. Mostly harmless, particularly when compared to other porn anime out there. A sequel, *Return of the Angels in the Court* (2001, *Kaette kita Court no Naka no Tenshitachi*) took the girls off to a national competition. Volleyball has been a strange obsession of the Japanese media world ever since the 1964 Tokyo Olympics, when the local women's team won gold in the event (see SPORTING ANIME). **OV**

ANIMAL 1
1968. TV series. DIR: Taku Sugiyama, Yoshiyuki Tomino, Ryosuke Takahashi. SCR: Tadaaki Yamazaki, Shunichi Yukimuro, Masaki Tsuji. DES: Noboru Kawasaki. ANI: Sadao Miyamoto. MUS: Hiroki Tamaki. PRD: Mushi Pro, Fuji TV. 30 mins. x 27 eps.
The seven Azuma brothers have all been raised as fighters by their longshoreman father. Sent to a new school when the family moves, Ichiro Azuma becomes a

great success in the wrestling club. As his prowess gains greater fame, he is soon known as "Animal 1," as you might expect from someone who's had to fight over the bathroom with six siblings. Based on the true story of Ichiro Azuma, who represented Japan in the 1960 Mexico Olympics, this series about a gold medalist only won silver in the race to become the first SPORTING ANIME—STAR OF THE GIANTS beat it onto the screens by just a month. Noboru Kawasaki, who drew *both* stories, would also supply the original manga for SONG OF THE LADYBUGS. This tale of true-life wrestling included early directorial credits for two future specialists in giant-robot combat, GUNDAM's Tomino and VOTOMS' Takahashi.

ANIMAL ALLEY *
2005. JPN: *Animal Yokocho*. TV series. DIR: Yukio Nishimoto, Nam Jong-sik. SCR: Hiroshi Yoshikawa, Hideki Sonoda, Masahiro Yokoya, Megumi Sasano, Tatsuto Higuchi, Yuka Tamada. DES: Kyota Mizutani, Lun Hyung-jin. ANI: Kazuyoshi Kobayashi, Ahn Jae-ho. MUS: Kazuhiro Hara. PRD: Studio Gallop, Dentsu, TV Tokyo. 25 mins. x 12 eps.
A secret door in five-year-old Ami's bedroom leads to a magical land, from which stuffed animal playmates come to see her, often misunderstanding basic facts of everyday life and culture with comedic results. Based on the manga by Ryo Maekawa in *Ribon Original* and filmed in a surreal and absurdist style reminiscent of HARÉ + GUU. The show was broadcast in English in 2008 by the Cartoon Network in the Philippines, under the title *Ani-Yoko: My Next Door Neighbor*.

ANIMAL CONFERENCE ON THE ENVIRONMENT, THE
2010. JPN: *Dobutsu Kankyo Kaigi*. TV series. DIR: Junji Nishimura. SCR: Masanori Iuchi. DES: Tetsuhito Saito, Junichi Azuma. ANI: Koji Iijima. MUS: N/C. PRD: Studio DEEN, NHK, IMA Group Inc., NURUE Inc. 5 mins. x 20 eps.
This enchanting series for children should be required viewing for adults too: clever, inventive, and delivering its instruction with a very palatable serving of absurdity. Animals explore and discuss ways to save the environment as solemnly and ineptly as human politicos and pundits. In racial stereotyping redolent of HETALIA, British Dr. Rabbit is finicky and patronising, Max

the American Eagle is brash and clumsy, Tanya the Russian bear is selfish and greedy, but all are depicted as cut-paper puppets with enough charm and sweetness to make the stereotyping funny and the friendships between a tiger, elephant, and crocodile entirely credible. The seven-book series that inspired the show is on Japan's National School Library Association reading list, and has also apparently been adopted for use in South Korean elementary schools.

ANIMAL DETECTIVE KIRUMINZOO
2009. JPN: *Animal Tantei Kiruminzoo*. AKA: *Anyamaru Tantei Kiruminzuu*. TV series. DIR: Soichi Masui. SCR: Eriko Matsuda, Yosuke Yuki. DES: Sumie Aizawa, Kenichi Tajiri. ANI: Sumie Aizawa, Masahiro Aizawa. MUS: Kano Kawashima. PRD: Anyamaru Tanteisha, Aoni Ent., JM Animation, Satelight, Sotsu Agency, Starchild, TV Tokyo. 30 mins. x 50 eps.
Sisters Nagisa, Riko, and Rimu Mikogami are animal-lovers and cosplayers living in a small Japanese city full of natural wonders. Their favorite form of dressing-up is *kigurumi*, which essentially turns the cosplayer into a lifesize plush toy. One day, twins Riko and Rimu find a magic compact while looking for a lost cat. The Kirumin Compact allows them to transform into real animals. Older sister Nagisa joins in, and the three girls are soon enjoying a range of adventures as they try and solve the mysteries they run into, helped—or hindered—by their school friends Ken and Tamao, a pair of Holmes and Watson wannabes. Oh, and Colombo crops up as well. Magical girl meets junior detective: welcome to the wacky world of Shoji Kawamori's latest creation, a world away from his acclaimed ESCAFLOWNE.

Floating this joyous and extremely silly soap-bubble took an astonishing amount of heavyweight talent. A substantial number of the staff was Korean, marking the growth of skill and assurance in the Korean animation industry that has put Korean talent into almost every department of this and many other recent productions.

ANIMARU-YA
Sometimes written as "Animal-ya." Animation company formed by seven Shin'ei Doga employees for the purpose of working on LITTLE GOBLIN in 1982. Subsequent-ly hired in on other productions, including MIAMI GUNS and ANPANMAN. Notable members include Hiroshi Fukutomi and Katsuya Yamamoto.

ANIMATE GROUP
A conglomerate of animation-related companies, including the Animate store chain, the Movic promotional group, Marine Entertainment, and Frontier Works. The company is an object lesson in the vertical integration of modern media, since fans purchasing ANIME SHOP-KEEPER, for example, would discover that they have paid the Animate store for an anime about a man who runs an Animate store, which would have received the anime from an Animate subsidiary, which would itself have been the production company that made the anime in the first place.

ANIMATED CLASSICS OF JAPANESE LITERATURE *
1986. JPN: *Seishun Anime Zenshu*. AKA: *Youth Anime Compendium*. TV series. DIR: Fumio Kurokawa, Akiko Matsushima, Noboru Ishiguro, Eiji Okabe, Isamu Kumada, Hidehito Ueda. SCR: Kenji Yoshida, Shizuo Kuriyama, Haruhiko Mimura, Ryuzo Nakanishi. DES: Hiroshi Motomiya, Tetsuya Chiba, Shotaro Ishinomori, Osamu Komori, Hiromitsu Morita. ANI: Yoshio Kabashima. MUS: Koichi Sakata, Hideo Shimazu, Junnosuke Yamamoto. PRD: Nippon Animation, Nippon TV. 30 mins. x 37 eps.
Few true Japanese classics make it to the screen in an anime industry obsessed with spectacle and merchandise. This series made some small attempt to redress the balance, adapting some of Japan's most famous stories, including works by Eiko Tanaka, Yasunari Kawabata, Shintaro Ishihara, Masao Kume, Sachio Ito, Yasushi Inoue, and Jiro Akagawa, seemingly with an eye on the educational market.

As one might expect, a nation's literature is not readily sawed into bite-sized chunks for digestion on prime-time TV, and the selections are often arguably off-base. The collection does best with punchy short stories like Junichiro Tanizaki's *Tale of Shunkin*. Longer works often suffer through drastic cutting (Shiro Ozaki's *Theater of Life* is condensed from 530 pages to less than 30 minutes), censorious editing (the prostitution subplot is removed com-pletely from Ogai Mori's *Dancing Girl—see also* THE DANCER), or sloppy TRANSLATION (the English version makes several silly errors, and explanatory liner notes are un-forgivably absent from the video release). The choices for adaptation also seem hap-hazard or overly conservative. It's difficult, for example, to think of something *less* representative of Yukio Mishima than *The Sound of Waves*, and there are duplicates of BOTCHAN and SANSHIRO SUGATA, while THE TALE OF GENJI, HAKKENDEN, and THE SENSUALIST are conspicuously absent. The collection also includes a story by "Yakumo Koizumi" without revealing he was the foreign-born author Lafcadio Hearn. But although this story is not strictly speaking Japanese, and others are debatably "clas-sic" and occasionally barely "animated," it is still a noble failure in its attempt to get couch-potato children interested in real books. Two episodes, adaptations of Masao Kume's *Student Days* and Saneatsu Mushanokoji's *The Friend Who Didn't Believe in Friendship*, were not broadcast in the original run, appearing instead as two "specials" on TV Asahi the following year. Compare to the following generation's YOUTH LITERATURE.

ANIMATION RUNNER KUROMI *
2001. JPN: *Anime Seisaku Shinko Kuromi-chan*. AKA: *Animation Runner Kuromi-chan*. Video. DIR: Akitaro Daichi, Yumi Tamano. SCR: Mitsuru Nagatsuki. DES: Hajime Watanabe. ANI: Hajime Watanabe. MUS: Toshio Masuda. PRD: Yumeta Company. 40 mins. (v1), 45 mins. (v2).
Self-referential comedy about the attrac-tive Mikiko "Kuromi-chan" Oguro joining the production department of an anime company, and on the first day finding herself in sole charge (the production manager having collapsed and been rushed to the hospital after handing over responsibility) of episode 2 of *Time Journeys* (see TIME BOKAN), which is due in seven days, with almost none of the work completed. She must dig deep into her heart and her love of the anime *Louis Monde III* (see LUPIN III) for the neces-sary fortitude, as well as learn the tricks of the trade from jaded veteran Hamako Shihonmatsu, in order to complete the episode in time. Based on a four-panel gag strip that appeared in *Anime Station*, the

anime industry's in-house magazine—compare to OTAKU NO VIDEO. Released in Japan with English subtitles, and subsequently brought to America. After winning the Best Video Anime award at the 2001 Tokyo International Anime Fair, where the authors rather suspect it was preaching to the choir, a second episode followed in 2004.

ANIMATRIX, THE *

2002. Video. DIR: Koji Morimoto (*Beyond*), Shinichiro Watanabe (*Detective Story, Kid's Story*), Yoshiaki Kawajiri (*Program*), Mahiro Maeda (*Second Renaissance 1 & 2*), Takeshi Koike (*World Record*) Peter Chung (*Matriculated*), Andy Jones (*Final Flight of the Osiris*). SCR: Koji Morimoto, Shinichiro Watanabe, Larry Wachowski, Andy Wachowski, Yoshiaki Kawajiri. DES: Shinji Hashimoto, Yutaka Minowa. ANI: Shinji Hashimoto, Madhouse. MUS: Don Davis. PRD: Studio 4°C, Madhouse, Square USA, Inc., DNA Seoul. 102 mins.
Of these nine short animated spin-offs from *The Matrix* (1999), seven were written and/or directed by Japanese filmmakers and produced by Japanese studios. *Beyond* is set in an urban Japan of waste lots and abandoned buildings where a young girl finds a glitch in the Matrix in a "haunted" house. COWBOY BEBOP'sWatanabe directs *Detective Story*, where grizzled detective Ash tries to track down renowned hacker Trinity, and *Kid's Story*, introducing us to a disaffected teen who sees "reality" for the artifice it is and later appears in *The Matrix: Reloaded* (2003). *Kid's Story* has guest voice performances by Keanu Reeves and Carrie-Ann Moss. *Program* raises the issue that Cipher might not have been the only person ever to regret leaving the Matrix, as Cis and Duo fight in full samurai gear inside a simulation of medieval Japan. The two-parter *Second Renaissance* uses the visual inventiveness that later resulted in GANKUTSUOU to give a disorienting and dazzling cyber-eye view of history. *World Record* is a punchy, powerful story of passion breaking through all boundaries, as runner Dan pushes his mind and body to their limits and, for one moment, sees himself suspended in a dark, fluid-filled chamber. Two further stories, which do not technically qualify as "anime," are *Matriculated*, written and directed by Peter Chung, and

Final Flight of the Osiris, directed by Andy Jones and written by the Wachowskis.
It was, we are sure, a coincidence that the engines of transformation in the original *Matrix* movie were red and blue pills like those used by MARVELOUS MELMO, but *Animatrix* nevertheless sits well in the tradition of Japanese animation. It can be argued that it is only the latest in the long-running tradition of anthology movies to showcase the talents of great animators, alongside MEMORIES, ROBOT CARNIVAL, and NEO TOKYO. However, in its origins as a tie-in to a Hollywood blockbuster it is also one of the most successful anime movies of all time, bolstered by the name-recognition of the contributors and the *Matrix* franchise, which itself owes a considerable thematic and artistic debt to GHOST IN THE SHELL. Its worldwide sales were in the hundreds of thousands, easily making it one of the best-selling anime, alongside AKIRA and POKÉMON. Before long, other creators were trying to plug into Japanese animation as the flavor of the moment; the most conspicuous being Quentin Tarantino, with KILL BILL: THE ORIGIN OF O-REN. There were also several copycat prequels to mainstream Hollywood films, most notably Sharon Bridgeman's *Van Helsing: The London Assignment* (2004) and Peter Chung's *Riddick: Dark Fury* (2004). However, these productions do not feature enough Japanese creatives on the production staff to qualify as "anime." **OV**

ANIME R.

Also "Anime Aru"—the letter stands for "Retake." Animation company formed by Moriyasu Taniguchi in 1978 at the Kyoto commercials house Film Art. Incorporated as an independent company in 1993, with notable members including Satoru Yoshida, Masahiro Kato, Miko Nakajima, Masahiro Kimura, and Sachiko Iwamura. Representative works include CORRECTOR YUI and CONAN THE BOY DETECTIVE.

ANIME SHOP-KEEPER

2002. JPN: *Anime Tencho*. Video. DIR: Hideaki Anno. SCR: Hiroyuki Imaishi. DES: Kazuhiko Shimamoto, Hiroyuki Imaishi. ANI: N/C. MUS: Cublic. PRD: MOVIC, Animate, Gainax. 30 mins.
The new manager of the Animate store faces more than the usual amount of fan

envy when two heavies employed by a rival rough him up outside the store on his first day. His injuries are too severe for him to survive, so, with his dying breath, he appoints the young guy who intervenes to stop the bullies as his replacement. Aided by a bevy of cute girl assistants, Meito Anizawa ("Ani-Mate" if contracted and shuffled into Japanese name order) brings his enthusiasm for anime goods, a strong sense of justice, and compassion for the fans whose hunger for merchandise can never be sated.
It was only a matter of time after OTAKU NO VIDEO that other elements of anime FANDOM would become the subject of self-referential anime themselves. After ANIMATION RUNNER KUROMI-CHAN, an anime about making anime, we have an anime about selling anime, in an adaptation of Kazuhiko Shimamoto's manga, itself an extended commercial for the real-life Animate chain. The show features other wacky characters: Toya Dogenzaka manages the Shibuya store, and Gai Denki the Akihabara branch, while President Takahashi rules his anime merchandise empire from behind the scenes in Ikebukuro. The anime was also spun off into a radio drama and a live stage show. The lead character also appears in LUCKY STAR, as well as several computer games owned by the same stable of companies.

ANIMENTARY: CRITICAL MOMENTS

1971. JPN: *Animentary: Ketsudan*. TV series. DIR: Fumio Kurokawa, Ippei Kuri, Hideo Makino. SCR: Jinzo Toriumi. DES: Tatsuo Yoshida. ANI: Sadao Miyamoto, Tsutomu Shibayama, Yoshiyuki Tomino, Ryosuke Takahashi. MUS: Nobuyoshi Koshibe. PRD: Tatsunoko, Nippon TV. 30 mins. x 26 eps.
This *Anim[ated Docum]entary* details the various critical moments that brought Japan into World War II and eventually caused the country's defeat, including the battles over Pearl Harbor, Hong Kong, Malaya, Bataan, Rabaul, Singapore, Java, Corregidor, Midway, the Solomon Islands, the Philippines, and Leyte Gulf. The story concentrates chiefly on Isoroku Yamamoto, the "reluctant admiral" who urged his superiors not to declare war on the U.S. but was eventually given command of the Japanese fleet, and planned the attack on Pearl Harbor.

Despite its relative obscurity today, *Animentary* was itself a "critical moment" in anime history, broadcast for an adult audience in Saturday primetime, and published in tandem with a history magazine in an early "media mix." The emphasis on real-world detail exploited the xerography process, known in Japan as "machine tracing," which transferred artists' work directly to a cel without intermediate human tracers (TECHNOLOGY AND FORMATS). This, in turn, allowed for a documentary level of detail in the machinery, which was part of the show's intended appeal to military enthusiasts. It was the first animated series to have the job title of "mechanic design" included in the credits, and featured among its animators Yoshiyuki Tomino and Ryosuke Takahashi, both of whom would become known a decade later for a similar sense of realism applied instead to SCIENCE FICTION AND ROBOTS. Other innovations included textures added to shipboard surfaces, the use of split-second back-lighting to trace the path of bullets through the air, and airbrush effects on explosions, which would later be repurposed for the same studio's BATTLE OF THE PLANETS. A more dramatic look at some of the same events can be found in Leiji Matsumoto's COCKPIT, and the logical conclusion of the "what ifs" implicit in *Animentary* gets an airing in the alternate-universe DEEP BLUE FLEET, in which Japan gets to replay World War II and win it.

ANNE OF GREEN GABLES

1979. JPN: *Akage no Anne*. AKA: *Red-Haired Anne*. TV series. DIR: Isao Takahata. SCR: Shigeki Chiba, Aiko Isomura, Isao Takahata. DES: Yoshifumi Kondo. ANI: Yoshifumi Kondo. MUS: Kurodo Mori. PRD: Nippon Animation, Fuji TV. 30 mins. x 50 eps.

Green Gables is the house in Avonlea village on Prince Edward Island in early-20th-century Canada where childless brother and sister Matthew and Marilla bring an 11-year-old orphan, Anne, to live. Though there is some confusion when Anne turns out not to be the strapping male farmhand they were hoping for, she soon makes friends with local girl Diana, and the pair begin a happy, if somewhat tedious, rural existence.

Based on Lucy Maude Montgomery's book, this entry in the WORLD MASTERPIECE THEATER series was directed by GRAVE OF THE FIREFLIES' Takahata and featured animation from WHISPER OF THE HEART's Kondo. The earlier part of the series contained layouts by Takahata's famous cohort Hayao Miyazaki, although after episode 16 he left to make CASTLE OF CAGLIOSTRO.

A 39-episode prequel, *Before Green Gables* (*Konnichiwa Anne*, 2009), was directed by Katsuyoshi Yatabe as a later WMT serial, based on the book of the same name by Budge Wilson, written in 2008 to commemorate the centenary of the original. See also EMILY OF NEW MOON, based on a similar book by the same author.

ANNO, HIDEAKI

1960–. Born in Yamaguchi Prefecture, Anno entered Osaka University of Arts in 1980, where he met future Gainax cofounders Hiroyuki Yamaga and Takami Akai, with whom he made the opening short for the Daicon III SF convention. After early anime work on MACROSS, he gained a key position animating the God Warrior in Hayao Miyazaki's NAUSICAÄ OF THE VALLEY OF THE WIND. After his directorial debut on GUNBUSTER (1988), he spent a prolonged period working on THE SECRET OF BLUE WATER, on which he had a lack of creative control that caused him to retreat from the business. He returned with the landmark EVANGELION (1995). His subsequent anime work has included early episodes of HIS AND HER CIRCUMSTANCES, although much of his recent work has been designing and directing for live-action, including an adaptation of CUTEY HONEY. He is married to manga author Moyoko Anno.

ANNO, MASAMI

1944–. A protégé of Hiroshi Sasagawa and Hisayuki Toriumi, Anno joined Tatsunoko and first made his mark as an animator on the comedy GAZULA THE AMICABLE MONSTER. His subsequent successes included NILS' MYSTERIOUS JOURNEY and SHAME ON MISS MACHIKO, before leaving Tatsunoko to work for Studio Pierrot.

ANOHANA: THE FLOWER WE SAW THAT DAY *

2011. JPN: *Ano Hi Mita Hana no Namae o Bokutachi wa Mada Shiranai*. AKA: *We Still Don't Know the Name of the Flower We Saw*

That Day. TV series, movie. DIR: Tatsuyuki Nagai. SCR: Mari Okada. DES: Masayoshi Tanaka, Takayoshi Fukushima. ANI: Masayoshi Tanaka. MUS: REMEDIOS. PRD: Aniplex, Dentsu, Fuji TV. 24 mins. x 11 eps. (TV), 99 mins. (m).

Small-town teenager Jinta Yadomi is haunted by a persistent ghost. Her name is Meiko Honma, nicknamed Menma, and before she died she was part of his group of childhood friends. He blames himself for the accident that ended her life. She can't pass on into the next world until she has resolved her last wish—to see all her friends together again. But unresolved issues around her death have driven the whole gang apart. Her parents and her brother Satoshi are also still grieving. Can Jinta help her to achieve her wish?

This prettily animated and very sincere story contrasts the innocent freedom of childhood friendships with a sullen, withdrawn adolescence conditioned by guilt and betrayal. It tries to use the loyalties built in happier times as a bridge back to the characteristics that once made the characters able to open up to each other. Unfortunately, the very short length of the series precludes much in the way of plot or character development, and the over-use of flashbacks and expository dialogue takes up too much of the limited time. Anime that approach loss, grief, and death seriously and honestly are few and far between, and *Anohana* is worth a look for that alone. There's also a serial novel version by Okada which began its run a month before the anime to build interest, and a manga, written by Okada and illustrated by Mitsu Izumi, which started in May 2012 and is ongoing in Shuei-sha's *Jump Square* magazine. A-1 Pictures released a movie version in August 2013, retelling the story from the point of view of Menma the ghost.

ANOTHER *

2012. TV series. DIR: Tsutomu Mizushima. SCR: Ryo Higaki. DES: Yuriko Ishii. ANI: Yuriko Ishii. MUS: Ko Otani. PRD: P.A. Works, Kadokawa Shoten, Lantis, NTT Docomo, Klockworx, Toho. 24 mins. x 12 eps.

It is 1999: teenage transfer student Koichi Sakakibara is spooked by the odd behavior of his classmates, particularly their apparent unwillingness to acknowledge the existence of Mei Misaki, an eyepatch-wearing girl who sits, ignored, at the back of the class. Further mysteries arise when Koichi hears of a terrible incident a generation earlier, when the death of a student at the school led to irrational behavior and ghostly apparitions on that year's class photograph.

True to many REAL SCHOOL GHOST STORIES, this adaptation of Yukito Ayatsuji's 2009 novel takes thrills and chills of many teen superstitions (RELIGION AND BELIEF), and exploits the robust ability of the Japanese people and their language to put on the performance of ignoring anything unpleasant, despite overwhelming evidence to the contrary. Much like the *Ring* saga (*DE), *Another* seems to draw on the freak accidents of the *Final Destination* movies (2000–2011)—although since these were released after the time in which the story is set, the characters instead observe that their situation oddly parallels *The Omen* and its sequels (1976–81). *Another* exploits urban myth to present a horror scenario in which gruesome deaths will be visited on the class unless they can discover (or as it turns out, rediscover) a means to dispel the curse, and enact the required ritual (or reenact it), whatever the likely cost (HORROR AND MONSTERS).

Widely cited as one of the best Japanese horror stories of its era, the original *Another* gets a faithfully creepy adaptation in this anime version, accentuating the grief, scandal, and disaster that can often lurk so close to everyday life for self-absorbed teens, and making it one of very few anime to genuinely induce goosebumps, even in jaded anime encyclopedists. The 1990s time frame, as in WHEN THEY CRY, allows the drama to unfold in a time period when the absence of mobile phones and accessible online data prevents certain simple solutions. ◐

ANOTHER LADY INNOCENT *
2004. JPN: *Front Innocent; Innocent.* TV Video. DIR: Satoshi Urushihara. SCR: N/C. DES: Satoshi Urushihara. ANI: Kinji Yoshimoto, Hiroya Iijima. MUS: An Hoo. PRD: ARMS, Moonrock, Earthwork. 30 mins. x 2 eps.
In a Civil War–era America far removed from LITTLE WOMEN, the innocent young farmer's daughter Faye Carson enjoys sexual awakenings with John, her childhood

sweetheart (and brother!), and Sophie, a serving maid on the family farm. However, her carefree teens come to an end when she catches the eye of Lord Mark, a sinister landowner. No, we don't know what someone with a European noble title is doing in 19th-century America, either, but then again, plot and story cohesion has never been a staple of the works of Satoshi Urushihara, from LEGEND OF LEMNEAR to PLASTIC LITTLE. His forte, then as now, lies in the distinctive and luscious skin tones of his female nudes, seen here in copious amounts. Of the two episodes listed at time of writing, the first is numbered "episode 0," and is a promo for the subsequently completed actual episode (though the series remains incomplete nine years later). Video extras include a tour of Urushihara's studio, notes on the original audio drama on which this is based, and a montage history of the American Civil War. See, it's all educational. ◐◑

ANPANMAN
1988. JPN: *Sore Ike! Anpanman.* AKA: *Go for It! Anpanman.* TV series. DIR: Akinori Nagaoka. SCR: Ayako Okina, Jiro Nakajima, Osamu Nakamura. DES: Michishiro Yamada. ANI: Minoru Maeda. MUS: Taku Izumi. PRD: TMS, Nippon TV. 30 mins. x 1100+ eps.
A superhero constructed from bean paste by the kindly Uncle Jam, Anpanman fights for justice alongside his ethnically diverse cohorts White-Breadman, Curry-Breadman, and Cheese the Wonderdog against the dirt-obsessed Germ-man.

RINGING BELL and LITTLE JUMBO–creator Takashi Yanase's original illustrations for the Japanese chain-store Froebel Kan took 15 years to reach the screen, transforming into stories in publications such as *Mommy, New Baby,* and *Baby Book.* Regularly restored to life through the simple act of getting a new head from the saintly Uncle Jam, Anpanman gives those he rescues something special to remember him by—a piece of his own head for them to eat. This trick has proved to be immensely popular, especially with parents encouraging children to finish their breakfast (although what damage the concept of consuming one's playmates has done to a generation of Japanese, only time will tell). The TV series has also spun off into many short theatrical outings, including *The*

Disappearance of Uncle Jam, Anpanman in the South Seas, The Secret of Breadrollman, and *Christmas with the Meringue Sisters.* More recent outings have included *Anpanman and the Mermaid's Tears* (2000), a LITTLE MERMAID spoof in which he helps the sea-dwelling Sunny in her quest to become human, and *Anpanman and Ruby's Wish* (2003), in which Anpanman comes to the aid of another damsel in distress. There is a longer *Anpanman* movie every year, and past titles have included *Nyanii of the Country of Dream Cats* (2004), *Happy's Big Adventure* (2005), *Dolly of the Star of Life* (2006), *Purun the Bubble Ball* (2007), *Secret of Rin the Fairy* (2008), *Dadandan and the Twin Stars* (2009), *Blacknose and the Magical Song* (2010), *Kokorin and the Star of Miracles* (2011), *Revive Banana Island* (2012), and *Fly! Handkerchief of Hope* (2013). Each is usually accompanied by a short movie, the length of a normal TV episode. Anpanman also appears in a 30-minute Christmas special each year, separate from the usual episode count.

Yanase would also try to duplicate the success of Anpanman with another food-related superhero. *Riceball-man* (1990, *Omusubiman*) was a 27-minute theatrical short featuring a samurai snack, but it could not compete with its bun-headed predecessor.

ANTIQUE BAKERY *
2008. JPN: *Seiyo Kotto Yogashiten—Antique.* AKA: *Western Antique Cake Shop, Antique.* TV series. DIR: Yoshiaki Okumura. SCR: Natsuko Takahashi. DES: Akio Uchino, Tatsuo Shimamura. ANI: Kazuo Takigawa, Kinomi Noguchi, Toshiyuki Komaru. MUS: Takefumi Haketa. PRD: Nippon Animation, Shirogumi Inc., Asmik-Ace Entertainment, Dentsu, Fuji TV, Shinshokan Publishing, SME. 30 mins. x 12 eps.
Wealthy Keiichiro Tachibana owns a European-style artisan bakery, where he also acts as a waiter. Yet he absolutely hates sweet things—the result of a childhood kidnapping when his abductor, who was never caught, fed him on cakes every day. He bought the bakery because he had dreams of a crew of pretty waitresses, but things haven't quite worked out that way. He still suffers from nightmares, and his childhood friend Chikage watches out for him at the request of his family. Chikage

is a father but not a family man, having helped a friend to conceive a child. Keiichiro's pastry chef is another old friend, Ono, a gifted patissier who has nevertheless been fired from almost every bakery he's worked in because of his renowned and irresistible allure. Every man he meets, gay or straight, is completely unable to resist, fights break out and he's fired. At least working for his old friend, he can rely on keeping the job—Chikage keeps his secret passion for his colleague under wraps, not realizing that Ono feels the same. Ono's former lover, hot French pastry chef Jean-Baptiste, is constantly trying to woo him back to Paris and a job at his restaurant. The final member of the staff, apprentice and kitchen hand Eiji Kanda, is a former boxer who had to leave the ring because of damaged eyes. Around these four a cast of friends, lovers, and regular customers rotate in a series of adventures and relationships.

Based on Fumi Yoshinaga's 1999 manga, this is a charmingly animated show with engaging characters and an enticing air of reality about its enchanted world, where shadows and private fears are present but life is good. Yoshinaga's story has proved so irresistible that it's crossed genres and seas, undergoing some changes on the way but apparently losing none of its audience-pleasing charm. The successful live-action Japanese TV drama of 2001, *Antique* (*DE), toned the homosexual elements down to almost nothing and introduced a new female character, while the Korean live-action movie musical of 2008 (known as both *Antique* and *Antique Bakery*) kept the story very close to the original but made the characters and setting Korean. Meanwhile Yoshinaga's own fanzine version ramps up the boy's-love elements considerably. A full-scale stage musical surely can't be far behind. After all, as one character asks "Can anyone be unhappy while eating cake?"

ANTIQUE HEART

1988. JPN: *Antique Heart: Gakuen Benriya Series*. AKA: *Antique Heart: School Handyman Series*. Video. DIR: Junichi Watanabe. SCR: Mami Watanabe. DES: Minoru Yamazawa. ANI: Takumi Tsukasa. MUS: N/C. PRD: Animate Film. 40 mins.

In this short-lived adaptation of a long-running series from *Wings* magazine, three intrepid school investigators track down ghosts in the restroom, anonymous love letters, and any other mystery they can find. Intended to be the first of a series, this video was ten years too early. The concept of supernatural schools would return in the 1990s with the successful REAL SCHOOL GHOST STORIES, HERE COMES HANAKO, and HAUNTED JUNCTION.

ANYONE YOU CAN DO ... I CAN DO BETTER! *

2004. JPN: *Bakunyu Oyako*. AKA: *Milk Junkie, Busty Mother and Daughter*. Video. DIR: Norihiko Takahama. SCR: Naruhito Sunaga. DES: Takao Sano. ANI: Takao Sano. MUS: Yoshi. PRD: YOUC, Digital Works (Vanilla Series), Blue Gale. 30 mins. x 2 eps.

Yusuke is invited to become the private tutor of Reina, a girl with large breasts. But when he arrives at her house, he discovers that her equally large-breasted mother Mizuki is looking for a man to seduce. When Mizuki catches her daughter in the act with Yusuke, she takes it as a personal challenge, leading to a fight over who gets to have sex with Yusuke next—more not-quite-incest from the VANILLA SERIES, based on the game *Milk Junkie* by Blue Gale, creators of SPOTLIGHT. Episodes 3 and 4 of the related *Milk Junkie: Shimai Hen* were released in the U.S. under the separate title BOOBALICIOUS. CAFÉ JUNKIE and CONSENTING ADULTERY are also part of the franchise. **LNV**

APE ESCAPE

2006. JPN: *Saru Getchu ~ ON AIR ~*. AKA: *Saru! Get You ~ ON AIR ~*. TV series. DIR: Nobuyoshi Habara; Jun Kamiya. SCR: Naruhisa Arakawa. DES: Yoshito Watanabe. ANI: Naoyoshi Kusaka. MUS: Yoichi Sakai. PRD: Shogakukan Music & Digital Entertainment, Xebec. 15 mins. x 26 eps.

Monkey Specter uses a mind control device, the Peak Point Helmet, or PiPo Helmet, to boost its intelligence. It controls the other monkeys, using them to spread chaos all over the world. In order to combat this threat and save the planet from simian dominion, the wise Professor calls on Kakeru, a schoolboy with a high-tech butterfly net, and his friends. Based on the video game series created by Sony, this show provides bright colors, perky music, multiple chases and levels and general mayhem before Specter, learning about all the kind things humans have done for monkeys, gives up his fight. Obviously nobody wants to spoil a happy ending by mentioning habitat destruction, cosmetic testing, circuses, or vivisection. A second series, written by Arakawa and directed by Jun Kamiya, brought the same crew and characters back for the 51-episode sequel, *Saru Getchu ~ ON AIR ~ 2nd*, in 2006.

APOCALYPSE ZERO *

1996. JPN: *Kakugo no Susume*. AKA: *Onward Kakugo*. Video. DIR: Toshihiro Hirano. SCR: Akiyoshi Sakai. DES: Keisuke Watanabe. ANI: Keisuke Watanabe, Toshihiro Yamane. MUS: Takashi Kudo. PRD: Ashi Pro. 45 mins. x 2 eps.

On a post-apocalyptic Earth prey to monsters, Kakugo and Harara Hagakure have been trained by their father in the ancient Zero fighting technique to protect the last remnants of humanity. Paramount in their arsenal is the Tactical Zero armor, a fighting suit charged with the souls of ancient heroes. But Harara turns to the dark side, killing his father and creating the new Tactical Evils. Left for dead, Kakugo reaches a ruined town and offers to help the few human inhabitants protect themselves from cannibals and depraved mutants. Meeting once again with his insane sibling, he fights to save the world in this gory adaptation of Takayuki Yamaguchi's *Shonen Champion* manga. Though *AZ* contains veiled allusions to honor and tradition (the siblings' surname is a famous samurai manual), it has more in common with the mutant maulings of FIST OF THE NORTH STAR. **V**

APPLELAND STORY

1992. JPN: *Appleland Monogatari*. Video. DIR: Kunihiko Yuyama. SCR: Atsushi Takegami. DES: Minoru Yamazawa, Keiko Fukuyama. ANI: Minoru Yamazawa. MUS: Morgan Fisher. PRD: JC Staff. 45 mins. x 2.

On the eve of World War I, Vale Sibelius is a young orphan pickpocket in Appleland, a central European state that could be an important prize in the coming conflict. He befriends Frida, a girl with the secret of a new weapon that could decide the country's future, and the two go on the run from the evil East European duo, Aryana and Attila. Based on a novel from Yoshiki Tanaka, the prolific creator of LEGEND OF GALACTIC HEROES.

APPLESEED *

1988. Video, movies, TV series. DIR: Kazuyoshi Katayama. SCR: Kazuyoshi Katayama. DES: Yumiko Horasawa, Takahiro Kishida, Hideaki Anno. ANI: Yumiko Horasawa. MUS: Norimasa Yamanaka. PRD: Gainax, AIC. 70 mins. (v), 106 mins. (m1), 105 mins. (m2), 25 mins. x 13 eps. (TV), 93 mins. (m3, *Alpha*).

In an authoritarian utopia, humanity has handed the reins of power to super-capable robots. But the suicide rate goes up, mostly among people from the wastelands outside the city; rehabilitated and brought back to civilization, they are unable to cope with paradise.

As the first scene (a suicide freeing her pet before she jumps) makes clear, the inhabitants of Olympus are no freer than birds in golden cages, and a group of human beings (led, in a typical touch of Masamune Shirow irony, by a cyborg) organize a revolt to seize the city back from the robots. Working for the benevolent dictator, Athena, human SWAT team leader Deunan Knute attempts to foil the terrorists before it is too late.

This adaptation of Shirow's best-selling manga was adequate for its time but was soon eclipsed by AKIRA, which permanently raised the stakes on high-quality sci-fi. The next Shirow anime, GHOST IN THE SHELL, had a far higher budget—ironically, the straight-to-video *Appleseed* was often shown in foreign theaters in unfair competition with its richer, better-endowed cousin.

Look out for a couple of in-jokes (a magazine named after Shirow's superior BLACK MAGIC M-66) and some very bad Engrish spelling on signs. There are some sweet touches, such as the loose change falling out of Deunan's pants when she gets in the shower, or the cloying way she starts simpering whenever she sees a child. But for an anime produced by the peerless Gainax studio, *Appleseed* depicts a curiously mundane future—1980s Japan with a few shiny buildings. Tough-girl Deunan uses conventional firearms, drives a normal-looking car, and eats contemporary fast food. Only the robots add any real sense of the future, particularly a "multipede" tank

modeled on the Probe Droid from *The Empire Strikes Back.*

Shirow loaded the original story with classical references, of which only Olympus, Gaia, Tartarus, and Athena survive the dub unscathed. Inadequate TRANSLATION and diction have hidden the true pronunciations of Gyges, Charon Mausolus, and Briareus Hecatoncheires, which is why the English voice actors refer to a robot as "Gudges," a male character named "Karen Mawserus," and a lead cyborg called "Bularios." The uncredited translator was more successful in spotting references to U.S. cop shows (a police chief called Bronx) and Ridley Scott's ubiquitous *Blade Runner* (the terrorist A. J., not J. F., Sebastian). Although he ignored the author's classical interests, adapter John Volks added much bad language, inspiring critics to invent the term "fifteening" for those U.K. anime dubs that insert swearing purely to attain a more commercial rating. That's not to say that the dub isn't a peppy paragon of cop-show cussing, including such immortal dialogue as, "Half cyborg? He's *all* bastard!"

Appleseed, however, remains an enduring presence in the minds of viewers and readers, few of whom seem to have forgotten that there was a time when the manga was as highly regarded as the legendary *Akira*. Consequently, despite never quite living up to the promise of its paper form, it continues to resurrect itself in animated reboots and retreads, as hopeful producers seek to actualize its clear potential as an enduring cyberpunk franchise. It was revived for a new 106-minute movie, also called *Appleseed* (2004), directed by Shinji Aramaki. Whereas the 1988 Katayama version begins with Deunan and her partner Briareus on a police raid and already working for their bioroid masters, the Aramaki version features a variant of the induction scene from volume 1 of the manga. It takes the time to introduce Deunan's hand-to-mouth existence in the Badlands, although unlike the manga, it does not have her in the Badlands with Briareus. It also accentuates a subplot only hinted elsewhere, that Deunan and Briareus had once been lovers, but that only tiny vestiges of their relationship have survived his mutilation and cyborg rehabilitation.

The Aramaki *Appleseed* was sold to fans

as a cutting-edge example of digital animation, and, in the wake of the failure of the FINAL FANTASY movie *The Spirits Within*, included a deliberate attempt to shy away from realism in favor of toon shading that treated motion-capture footage to make it look more like anime. The result, it was hoped, would be a hybrid of live action and animation—Ai Kobayashi, who voices Deunan, also functions as her own body double. However, for all its attention to 21st-century technology, the Aramaki *Appleseed* stumbles with an inept and amateurish script, full of redundancies, technobabble, and B-movie motivations. Adapting Masamune Shirow's complex and often muddled originals is a difficult task, but it is not impossible. Whereas Shirow's original *Appleseed* had a subtle background family dynamic, replaying the paternal inventor of ASTRO BOY by having Deunan Knute's father as the creator of an entire robot society, the Aramaki remake pointlessly introduces Deunan's scientist mother, in what seems to be a dysfunctional set-up inspired by EVANGELION. Far from benefiting from its digital technologies, the Aramaki *Appleseed* seems trapped by them, forced into repetitions of dull exposition, broken up by perfunctory action sequences. The result, despite its proclamations of originality and innovation, seems to follow the soullessly escalating formula of a low-grade computer game, and not the rich source material of Shirow's manga. The 1988 video version, for all its faults and old-fashioned look, is the one with the better script.

For the rest of the decade, *Appleseed* went through several other incarnations, amid squabbles behind the scenes on who was doing the work, who owned it, and who should pay for it. While *Appleseed*'s producer Fumihiko Sori went off and made VEXILLE (2007), which gave every appearance of being a remake in all but name, Aramaki followed up with the 105-minute *Appleseed Ex Machina* (2007), pitting the cast against the new bioroid menace Tereus. An *Appleseed Genesis* TV series was announced in summer 2008, but then canceled a couple of months later, leading to a series of suits and counter-suits between the producers and the studio that had supposedly already commenced work, now unpaid. Eventually, production got underway on the TV series *Appleseed XIII* (2011), a 13-episode reboot directed by Takayuki Hamana, with scripts from the **GHOST IN THE SHELL**: *Stand Alone Complex* writer Junichi Fujisaku. This was also re-purposed into two feature-length edits.

Not to be outdone, Shinji Aramaki's *Appleseed Alpha* (2014) put the computer-generated imagery to its best use yet, and perhaps wisely discarded any previous continuity in favor of a prequel in which a young Deunan and Briareos search the ruins of Earth for the fabled city of Olympus. ●

APPROACH OF AUTUMN, THE

1998. JPN: *Kasho no Tsuki Aki no Kyogen*. AKA: *Hot Month Autumn Performance*. Video. DIR: Mamoru Hamazu. SCR: Mari Hirai. DES: Takashi Komori. ANI: Takashi Komori. MUS: Yuriko Nakamura. PRD: SME. 30 mins. x 2 eps.

A strange medieval romance based on a manga by Mari Hirai in which a pretty-boy sorcerer in Kamakura-period Japan begins a relationship with a hermaphrodite creature who is half-human, half-cat. The titular *aki no kyogen* refers to the last performances of the theatrical year, with their undertones of final curtain calls, farewells, and tomfoolery.

AQUA AGE

1996. JPN: *Mizu-iro Jidai*. AKA: *The Water-Colored Years*; *My Years in Blue*. TV series. DIR: Hiroko Tokita, Shin Misawa, Susumu Kudo, Hiroaki Sakurai, Hiroshi Fukutomi. SCR: Junji Takegami, Tsunehisa Arakawa, Reiko Yoshida. DES: Shinichi Yamaoka. ANI: Takahisa Ichikawa, Tatsuo Otaku. MUS: N/C. PRD: NAS, Comet, TV Tokyo. 25 mins. x 47 eps.

A quaint but uneventful look at the life and loves of average schoolgirl Yuko Kawai as her home life and school life place her under pressure to succeed, and she develops a crush on classmate Hiroshi, whose window faces hers. Named for the "Aqua Age" hair salon where she gets a part-time job and for the distinctive blue colors of the sailor-suit uniform worn by so many Japanese schoolgirls, this anime was somewhat marginalized in anime sources for committing the heinous crime of featuring no robots, interdimensional gateways, erotic plot twists, or anything out of the ordinary at all. Scratch the surface,

however, and you will find a role-reversal of **KIMAGURE ORANGE ROAD**, with a female lead and an idealized *male* love object without the latter anime's occasional intrusion of psychic subplots. Based on the manga in *Ciao* magazine by Yu Yabuchi.

AQUARIAN AGE *

2002. JPN: *Aquarian Age: Sign for Evolution*. TV series, video. DIR: Yoshimitsu Ohashi, Fumie Moroi. SCR: Kazuhiko Soma. DES: Hisashi Abe; Haruhiko Mikimoto, Fumie Moroi. ANI: Fumie Moroi. MUS: Yuki Kajiura. PRD: TV Tokyo, Victor Entertainment, Broccoli, Madhouse. 25 mins. x 13 eps. (TV), 60 mins. (v1), 60 mins. (v2).

Kyota Kamikurata is a vocalist in an indie garage band, with a voice that drives audiences wild. It's not his singing, but a rare psionic ability called "mindbreak" that lures people to him and then brings out their own psionic ability. Kyota is a psychic Pied Piper, though he doesn't have a clue about it. His childhood friend Yoriko Sanno is a priestess who lives at the Isuzu Shrine, who also moonlights on keyboards for Kyota's band, but her family has a higher destiny in mind for her—she's the reincarnation of ancient demigod Benzaiten, and they want her to unleash her powers and become head of the secret organization Arayashiki.

Kyota starts seeing visions of girls engaged in supernatural battles; he thinks he's going crazy, but he's just catching glimpses of all-out psychic warfare in a parallel dimension. There are other mindbreakers out there, usually male and bent on world domination. Secret factions, known as Wiz-Dom, Darklore, E.G.O., and Arayashiki, are fighting for supremacy and he and Yoriko are drawn into the conflict. As reality becomes more tenuous, the only solid thing they can hold on to is their love for each other. When a new threat emerges, they must unite the battling superpowers to save two realities.

Aquarian Age began as a collectible card game from Broccoli devoid of much in the way of an over-arching plot—the above synopsis was largely concocted for the anime adaptation, which also adds impressive character designs from **PET SHOP OF HORRORS**'s Hisashi Abe. It was followed by a video sequel *Aquarian Age Saga II: Don't Forget Me* (2003). After the various secret

organizations joined forces to defeat the alien Eraser threat to Earth at the end of the TV series, a new enemy emerges in the form of the Polestar Empire, ruled by the strongest Mindbreaker ever. Four girls, each from one of the original warring organizations, square up to fight the Empire on Earth. High-school psychic Megumi, Taoist priestess Miharu Itsukushima, vampire Yoko Ashley, and immortal sorceress Stella Blavatsky are all based on character concepts by Haruhiko Mikimoto, better known for **MACROSS**.

The second video, misleadingly titled *AA: The Movie* (2003), moved past the events of the first video to depict Earth under the domination of the Polestar Empire, whose use of forbidden magic creates dimensional rifts that plunge the planet into chaos and conflict once more. Mayumi Fujimiya of E.G.O. has astounding powers, but her fears and her unresolved complex about her famous mother leave her unable to use them, until she is joined by Yoko, Miharu, and Stella. Director Ohashi once claimed that *Aquarian Age* was a metaphor for the entertainment industry itself, in which warring factions fight for the attention of an audience unaware of the investments at stake—compare to **ARMITAGE III**, with similarly allegorized conflicts behind the scenes in the entertainment industry. Not to be confused with **AQUA AGE** or **AQUARION**.

AQUARION *

2005. JPN: *Sosei no Aquarion*. AKA: *Holy Genesis Aquarion*. TV series. DIR: Hideki Tonokatsu, Kenichi Kobayashi, Shoji Kawamori, Yasuaki Takeuchi. SCR: Shoji Kawamori, Hiroshi Onogi, Eiji Kurokawa, Natsuko Takahashi. DES: Futoshi Fujikawa, Takeshi Takakura, Shoji Kawamori. ANI: Atsushi Irie, Nobuteru Yuki, Satoru Utsunomiya. MUS: Hisaaki Hogari, Yoko Kanno. PRD: Satellite, TV Tokyo. 25 mins. x 26 eps. (TV1) 25 mins. x 26 eps. (TV2) 50 mins. x 2 eps. (v).

Eleven years after a terrible natural disaster not unlike that found in **BLUE SUBMARINE NO. SIX**, the Antarctic ice cap has melted, leading to upheavals that have wiped out two-thirds of the world's population, and the surprise thawing of Atlantis (or Atlandia), a lost continent revealed by the disappearing ice. Atlantis awakens from its 12,000-year slumber, along with the "Fallen Angels," winged humanoid creatures who send mechanical beasts ... all right, giant robots, out to harvest human prey for their *prana* life-force energy—compare to LEGEND OF DUO.

Members of the human race desperately try to fight back by forming the familiar-sounding DEAVA organization (almost but not quite DEVADASY or EVANGELION's NERV), salvaging "Vector Machines" from the bottom of the sea. These transforming aircraft are rumored to be the weapons that originally defeated Atlantis, although, with aching inevitability, only certain youthful individuals seem to possess the right elemental energy to pilot not only them, but also the fabled Aquarion device that may be assembled from several combined Vector Machines. A predictably international team of prospective pilots is assembled, although the clear top gun is Apollo, an orphan boy who may be the reincarnation of Apollonius, an "angel" who famously rebelled against the people of Atlantis.

A futile retelling of BRAIN POWERED with an added bonus of combining robots à la GETTER ROBO, from a crew who can do a lot better, distinguished only by Yoko Kanno's customarily wonderful music, which has saved many an anime from the dustbin of history. A two-part 2007 video release retold the story with differing character backgrounds and was then repurposed into a feature-length "movie" edit; compare to similar narrative-denying experiments with its near-contemporary EUREKA 7.

AR TONELICO
2008. JPN: *Ar Tonelico Sekai no Owari de Utai Tsuzukeru Shojo*. AKA: *Ar Tonelico: The Girl Who Sings at the End of the World*. Video. DIR: Ken Ando. SCR: Isao Igusa. DES: Tadashi Shida. ANI: N/C. MUS: N/C. PRD: Studio Ron, Trans Arts Co. 25 mins.
Ar Tonelico is a gigantic tower reaching from the deepest caverns below the continent known as the Wings of Horus up high into the skies. It is occupied by people who use both steampunk technology and magic based on maidens singing hymns to shape reality. A young pilot crashes his airship and needs the help of a beautiful but shy singer who can't control her magic. He teaches her that the key to singing an effective Hymn and controlling magic is

to put one's whole heart into helping others, and all their problems will be solved. Pretty, plotless, and totally lacking in character development. Based on a video game series from Gust Corporation, so probably intended to appeal to those who already know the characters and want to rest their joystick fingers between sessions, but a waste of time for anyone else.

ARAI, WAGORO
1907– ? Also credited, even in some Japanese sources, as Kazugoro Arai—we are unable to determine which is correct. Sometimes also miscredited as Goro Araiwa. Born in Tokyo, he graduated from Tokyo College of Dentistry. He practiced as a dentist, while still finding time to work on early puppet shows and animations, including MADAME BUTTERFLY.

ARAKAWA UNDER THE BRIDGE *
2010. TV series. DIR: Yukihiro Miyamoto, Akiyuki Shinbo. SCR: Deko Akao. DES: Nobuhiro Sugiyama, Koji Azuma. ANI: Nobuhiro Sugiyama. MUS: Masaru Yokoyama. PRD: SHAFT, Arakawa UB Production Team, Starchild Records. 24 mins. x 13 eps. (TV1), 24 mins. x 13 eps. (TV2).
Ko Ichinomiya is the 22-year-old heir of a proud and wealthy family. Their motto "Never be indebted to anyone" has been drummed into his head from his earliest years. So when, through a series of unfortunate events, he loses his pants and falls into the Arakawa river, he has a large debt of gratitude to the girl who saves his life. But to fulfill his family's ideals he's going to have to go a long way outside his comfort zone.

Nino is cute, blonde, and very different from other girls. She's a vagrant who lives under the bridge he fell off. She claims to be from Venus and eats the kind of raw fish you don't often find in upscale restaurants. She's part of a weird community that includes a guy in a *kappa* suit, an ex-mercenary in nun drag, a rock star has-been, and a truly terrifying transforming orphan mobster. And what she wants in return for saving Ko is to experience love, so she wants him to be her boyfriend. Far too unworldly, and too happy, to want to move into his circle of wealth and privilege, she expects him to live with her. To the bafflement of his distant father, he does.

This is a charming, light-hearted comedy about and for adults in straitened times (compare to TOKYO GODFATHERS, although the feel-good poverty on show here is substantially less grungy), unafraid to mix the stylistic tricks that work in the kiddy market with attentively developed, humanely written characters. The carefully modulated weirdness of the concept and characters works partly thanks to the conviction of Akao's writing, and partly thanks to Shinbo's gift for pacing. Shinbo's timing and cutting are all his own, his simulated camera moves and sight-gags can always surprise, and his ability to bring out the humanity and pathos in any situation has already been seen in shows like PETITE COSSETTE and BAKEMONOGATARI. The show's clean, bright colors and polished lines may recall his work on GALAXY FRAULEIN YUNA but its heart is faithful to Hikaru Nakamura's wackily charming manga, running since 2004 in *Young Gangan* magazine. Writer Akao, whose resumé includes that essay in weirdness ABNORMAL PHYSIOLOGY SEMINAR and mobile phone anime *Koiken!*, is obviously comfortable working with Shinbo since she, and the rest of the crew, stayed on for the second series, *Arakawa Under The Bridge x Bridge*, which started its run six months after the first.

ARAKI, SHINGO
1938–2011. A mainstay of Toei Animation during the 1970s, a one-time employee of Mushi Production, and the founder of Araki Productions. A distinctive character designer whose work is familiar all over Europe, courtesy of translations of SAINT SEIYA and ULYSSES 31. Araki founded Araki Productions in 1974, a company whose notable employees included his long-time collaborator Michi Himeno, as well as Hiroya Iijima, Masayuki Takagi, and Keiichi Ishijima.

ARATA THE LEGEND *
2005. JPN: *Arata Kangatari*. TV series. DIR: Kenji Yasuda, Woo Hyung Park. SCR: Mayori Sekijima. DES: Lee Seong Shin, Masahiro Aizawa. ANI: Chieko Miyakawa, Noriko Ogura, Yae Otsuka. MUS: Ko Otani. PRD: JM Animation, Satelight, Graphinica, Studio Cosmos, Bandai Visual, Dax Production, Lantis, TV Tokyo. 24 mins. x 12 eps
A Japanese teenager and his namesake

from a fantasy world accidentally trade places, forcing each to bring his odd perspectives and skills to the problems faced by the other. Based on the manga by Yu Watase (POLTERGEIST REPORT), smartly taking the idea of a fish-out-of-water, and then doubling it for extra drama.

ARC THE LAD *

1999. TV series. DIR: Toshiaki Kawasaki. SCR: Akimi Tsuraizu. DES: Yoko Kikuchi. ANI: Satoshi Murata, Kenji Teraoka. MUS: Michiru Oshima. PRD: B-train, WOWOW. 25 mins. x 26 eps.
Roughly based on the events of the second *Arc the Lad* PlayStation game, this series, directed by NADESICO's Kawasaki, takes place after the events of the War of the Holy Coffin and features Hunter Erik (or Elk), the last surviving member of a tribe of fire-wielding sorcerers called the Pyrenians. He becomes a mercenary, teaming up with monster-tamer Lena, orphans Shunter and Sanya, exiled prince Grueger, and android Diecbeck. Needless to say, the many quests for revenge on behalf of wronged parents (which accounts for at least four party-members' motivations) are all tied up in an adventure plot in an incoherent but attractively designed world so typical of computer games in the wake of FINAL FANTASY.

ARCADE GAMER FUBUKI *

2002. Video. DIR: Yuji Moto. SCR: Ryota Yamaguchi. DES: Hideyuki Morioka. ANI: Hideyuki Morioka. MUS: Sakura Nogawa. PRD: SHAFT, Bandai. 30 mins. x 4 eps. (TV/v) + 6 mins. "bonus episode" featurette on DVD.
Fubuki Sakuragasaki's excellent arcade gaming skills issue from her "passion panties," which trigger a magical girl-style transformation. When an evil organization tries to steal her powers, she channels gaming spirits the world over to unleash her other self, an arcade powerhouse with angel wings and sword. Starting out as a gag anime, but winding up as a preachy family fable too long-winded to sustain its jokes, this creation from Mine Yoshizaki inherits the mantle of GAME CENTER ARASHI, with onscreen homages to gaming classics like VIRTUA FIGHTER and Pac-Man. This would-be satire also recalls less impressive anime antecedents like ULTIMATE TEACHER, in which another heroine used special

bloomers to release her fighting spirit, but was a waste of space without them. Made for video release, although the first episode was screened on TV before the release date.

ARCANA FAMIGLIA *

2012. JPN: *La Storia della Arcana Famiglia*. TV series. DIR: Chiaki Kon. SCR: Masanao Akihoshi. DES: Mai Matsuura. ANI: Mai Matsuura, Hitomi Ochiai. MUS: Yasuhiro Misawa. PRD: JC Staff, Frontier Works, Movic, Showgate. 24 mins. x 12 eps.
Felicità is the sole daughter of Mondo, the de facto ruler of Regalo, a remote Italian island secretly run by a cabal of sorcerous Mafiosi, each with the ability to control a power based on one of the cards in a Tarot deck. Felicità begins with the relatively limited power of The Lovers (reading emotions), although she eventually discovers that she also possesses The Wheel of Fortune (the ability to scramble others' powers). But she doesn't really want to be the new Mob boss, and becomes something of an observer and power-broker on the island as a bunch of pretty boys duel over who gets to be the ruler—whoever has the power to defeat Mondo will win Felicità's hand in marriage, and become the new Boss.

Itself spun off a "visual novel" computer game, which has also spawned a manga, a light novel, and a cooking show, *Arcana Famiglia* is one of those ideas that sounds utterly superb on paper: marrying the collecting mania of many of Japanese kids' show to aristocratic reverse-harem antics (ROMANCE AND DRAMA) and a dash of *Nine Princes in Amber*. But sadly, like so many other media-mix stories, the execution of the anime leaves a lot to be desired— much potential, squandered in endless talky scenes and slices of mundane Italian life, through which the heroine wanders in a series of nice frocks and leggy stockings. Matters are not helped in the English dub by a cast that cannot pronounce *famiglia*.

ARCHA LYRA

1992. JPN: *Aru Kararu no Isan*. AKA: *The Inheritance of Aru Kararu*. Video. DIR: Koichi Ishiguro. SCR: Mayori Sekijima. DES: Satoshi Saga. ANI: Masamitsu Kudo. MUS: N/C. PRD: Tokuma Japan Communications. 70 mins.
In the 26th century, humans discover a

humanoid race living on the distant world GO/7498/2, a dark-skinned, golden-eyed people who seem to eke out a primitive, carefree existence. However, a scout team from Earth discovers that there is more to them than meets the eye—they live in symbiosis with vicious reptilian parasites, and the Terran scientists have upset the delicate natural balance.

Despite the obvious tip of the hat to Ray Bradbury's *Dark They Were and Golden Eyed*, *Archa Lyra* taps into a rich vein of SF concepts and puts them to good use, including the alien symbionts of Hitoshi Iwaaki's manga *Parasyte* and the addictive allure of Frank Herbert's *Dune*. Original creator Katsumi Michihara is best known in Japan for drawing adaptations of other people's work, including LEGEND OF GALACTIC HEROES and the JOKER series.

ARCHENEMY AND HERO *

2013. JPN: *Ma-o Yusha*. AKA: *Maoyu*. TV series. DIR: Takeo Takahashi. SCR: Naruhisa Arakawa. DES: Hiroaki Karasu, Masashi Kudo. ANI: Tomomi Ishikawa, Hiroaki Karasu. MUS: Takeshi Hama. PRD: Animax, Docomo Anime Store, Flying Dog, Enterbrain, GENCO, Kadokawa, Movic, Klockworx, ARMS, Studio Biho. 24 mins. x 12 eps.
At the end of a hard-fought conflict that has lasted for 15 years, the great Hero faces his nemesis, the Demon King, and … falls in love with what turns out to be an attractive young lady. Beginning where most fantasy tales end, with the final confrontation of the opponents, *Archenemy and Hero* poses a wonderful question—what if they just kissed and made up, and tried to make the world a better place? The red-haired, horned, busty, and sexy Demon "King" wins over her man with a proposal based firmly in political economy—she intends to end the war by entirely removing the factors that led their people into conflict in the first place. Taking the alias of Crimson Scholar, she attempts to teach the population methods of better farming and sanitation, in order to take away the problems of poverty that lead to wars. Her knight in shining armor stays at her side, trying to persuade his old allies that it's all for the best, as if the cast of BERSERK suddenly held hands and went into public service. Based on the novels by Mamare Tono, which began serialization in 2010.

If you're the kind of viewer who welcomes the idea of a scantily clad, red-haired academic instituting a policy of social reform, then this is most definitely the anime for you, as indeed it is for at least 50% of all anime encyclopedists. The idea is not entirely new—there are elements, for example, of Larry Niven and David Gerrold's industrial allegory *The Flying Sorcerers* (1971), and also of the same anime team's earlier SPICE AND WOLF. But it is a welcome change from all the fighting and bickering of other fantasy shows, as a loving couple take on the awfully mundane, but ultimately far more fulfilling responsibilities of management and restructuring, rather than just hacking and slicing their way through the plot. Many anime serials include a bad guy who switches sides; this is the only one we can think of in which the good guy not only joins the enemy, but also has to persuade the rest of his old colleagues, including the warrior-woman with a crush on him, that he has done the right thing. RECORD OF LODOSS WAR toyed with the idea, but never really jumped feet-first into the implications. Inevitably, the Hero still needs to break some skulls, so this is perhaps the only political tract to also include a fight with a giant walrus. The show's title was counter-productively trimmed to *Maoyu* in some language territories, causing most viewers to mispronounce it—it should be Ma-o-yu.

AREA 88 *
1985. Video, TV series. DIR: Eiko Toriumi. SCR: Akiyoshi Sakai. DES: Toshiyasu Okada. ANI: Toshiyasu Okada. MUS: Ichiro Nitta. PRD: Project 88. 50 mins. x 4 eps. (v), 25 mins. x 12 eps. (TV).
In a faithful adaptation of Kaoru Shintani's 1979 manga from *Shonen Sunday*, ace pilot Shin Kazama is duped into joining a mercenary air force by his acquaintance, Kanzaki. At airbase Area 88 in the tiny, civil-war-torn Middle Eastern kingdom of Asran, desertion is a capital offense. Kazama must live through a three-year tour of duty or shoot down enough enemy planes to buy out his contract. Meanwhile back home, the venal Kanzaki moves in on Kazama's girlfriend, Ryoko, trying to force her into a marriage of convenience to save her father's ailing business.
Area 88 is a lively adventure story,

featuring a dastardly cad, noble pilots, and star-crossed lovers who, while they may occasionally be within waving distance of each other, are always torn apart by circumstances. Parallel plots of desert storm and urban mischief ask the viewer what either civilization really thinks they are fighting for. The incongruously sweet-faced characters draw a tense, thrilling picture of the way war, corruption, and simple compromises change people. Few war anime compare, although the following year's GREY: DIGITAL TARGET makes a similarly masterful use of a popular genre.
Made as a four-part series in the earliest days of video anime, the first two chapters were also cut together into a movie in 1985. Several other Shintani stories have been turned into anime—TWO TAKAS, DESERT ROSE, CLEOPATRA DC, GODDAM, and I DREAM OF MIMI. The artist also worked as a designer on GOD SIGMA. The story was remade in 2004 as a 12-part TV series on TV Asahi, directed by Isamu Imakake and written by Hiroshi Onogi. The new version retells the story through the framing viewpoint of photojournalist Makoto Shinjo, who visits the base in search of a story and hears Shin's dilemma—does he fight and hope to earn his way back to his love before he dies, or desert and risk execution? Shinjo and mechanic Gustav are characters original to this incarnation, in which dogfights are entirely rendered in CG, creating a warplane-lover's delight in the style of the racing sequences of INITIAL D. Twenty years on, there's also a new cast of voice actors, but 75-year-old voice superstar Chikao Ohtsuka, who had a role in the original video series, returns to voice supply chief and fixer McCoy.

ARGENTO SOMA *
2000. TV series. DIR: Kazuyoshi Katayama. SCR: Hiroshi Yamaguchi. DES: Shuko Murase, Matsuri Yamane. ANI: Takuro Shinbo, Shuko Murase, Asako Nishida. MUS: Katsuhisa Hattori. PRD: Sunrise, TV Tokyo. 25 mins. x 25 eps. (TV), 25 mins. (v).
Mysterious metallic life-forms attack Earth in 2054 and also haunt the dreams of Earth boy Kaneshiro Takt, who is unable to show his feelings for his lover, Maki, until it is too late. Maki's laboratory pieces together "Frank," a whole alien made from parts scavenged from wrecks, but

when the monster is activated, it destroys the laboratory and kills Maki. Hideously scarred in the accident, Takt changes his name to Ryu Soma and vows to avenge himself on the aliens, only to discover that his new bosses at the "Funeral" organization are now employing one. The damaged but functional Frank resolves to help humankind (although humankind may not necessarily want to be helped in the way Frank intends), but the only human he is prepared to communicate with is the pretty Harriet Bartholomew—a girl who reminds Takt of the dead Maki. Mixing the nihilism of GREY: DIGITAL TARGET with the ambiguous enemies of EVANGELION, *AS* also features curiously lopsided designs for the asymmetric Frank and obvious tips of the hat to the FRANKENSTEIN story. As with many other TV series of the cash-strapped turn of the century, it also demonstrates a noticeable drop in animation quality, going from reasonable to barely adequate in the space of the first few episodes. The 26th episode was not broadcast, but released on video.

ARGOT AND JARGON
Anime appreciation has developed a slang all its own, incorporating a number of Japanese words, often with uses different from those employed in their country of origin. We believe such terms present an unnecessary barrier to comprehension for the newcomer. Consequently, with the exception of the terms *anime* and *manga* we have used them as little as possible in this book. This entry is designed to point out certain words to aid the reader in understanding some of the more opaque fan texts. The better anime publications refuse to use them unless absolutely necessary, in order to ensure that new readers are not baffled by a slew of obtuse terminology. Despite this, many mainstream journalists love to use as many as possible when covering anime, because it suggests they know what they are talking about. The terms are also very popular with fans who cannot speak Japanese but like to imply that they can.

Basic Terminology
- *Anime* refers to animation from Japan. Other terms in use include *doga* ("moving pictures"). By our definition, a

work is Japanese if the majority of the main creatives (director, script writer, character designer, and key animators) are Japanese. Within Japan, the term "anime" refers to any form of animation, including foreign cartoons. We employ it specifically to distinguish Japanese animation from products of other nations. There have been attempts among unscrupulous Western distributors to call anything anime that looks remotely Japanese. We do not subscribe to this deception and file such titles as **FALSE FRIENDS**. If a Japanese origin is not of fundamental importance in the definition of anime, then it is a futile pretension to use the term at all, and we might as well call everything "cartoons." The term "Japanese anime" is a tautology, since anime is Japanese by definition. Some sources, particularly in Japan, use the term "Japanimation," which was deliberately promoted by some companies in America as a viable alternative. However, the term has proved unpopular abroad through its inevitable separation into the component parts "Jap" and "animation"—"Jap" being a pejorative term with wartime associations.

- Among Japanese critics, however, there is still considerable debate over whether the term anime can, and should, be applied to all animation from Japan. The author Nobuyuki Tsugata suggests instead that true "anime" is actually a *kind* of Japanese animation, distinguished by a series of tropes, traditions, and trends arising during the 1960s and 1970s. His definition, which has been adapted and augmented several times in the last decade, encompasses merchandise-oriented TV shows from **ASTRO BOY** onward, but also the rise of straight-to-video animation, fan-oriented narratives, and the intersection of the related media of comics, computer games, prose fiction, and character goods to create an entire ecology of consumption. Anime, for Tsugata, is also a pejorative directed since the 1970s at a certain type of animation by the self-styled classier practitioners of film festival shorts and art-house movies—in other words, *they* make Japanese animation, whereas "anime" is the junk

on TV and in video-store bargain bins. For similar reasons, some practitioners, such as Hayao Miyazaki, have been heard to describe their own works once more as *mangaeiga* ("cartoon films"), in an attempt to disassociate themselves from the porn and toy franchises to be found in anime proper.

- *Manga* refers to comics from Japan. As with anime, the term is used slightly differently in Japan itself, where it once meant "caricature," drifted semantically into the same basic area as "cartoon," and has meant "comic" for the last 50 years or so. As with anime, claiming that something can be a "manga" even if it is not from Japan is rather pointless in the English language—you might as well call everything "comics." There is, nevertheless, a growing number of artists in the West who claim they draw in a "manga-style," itself a meaningless term, since manga are so varied there is no such thing as a single style. A *mangaka* is a "manga creator." In the 1990s, an anime company called Manga Entertainment established itself as a very powerful brand in the European market, ensuring that to this day the term "manga video" in most of Europe actually means anime. However, in Japan the term *manga video* actually refers to a video showing pages of a comic, while off-screen actors read it aloud. We never said this would be easy.

Other Terms

- *Braun-kan*, literally, the "Braun tube," is an archaic Japanese term for television, deriving its name not from the color brown, but from Ferdinand Braun (1850–1918), the German inventor of the cathode ray tube.
- *CB* means "child body," and is a pun on *chibi*, meaning little. It refers to child-like caricatures of particular characters, shown in moments of embarrassment or comedy, occasionally in comical sequences. The term has fallen out of use in recent years, and seems to have been merged with the similar SD (q.v.).
- *Chokyo* is a subcategory of *hentai* (q.v.), about the "breaking in" of new sexual conquests through abuse and domination.
- *Cours* (plural: *courses*) is the French

term for a period of time, used in Japan to refer to a television season of 13 weeks. Because the *s* is silent in French and invisible in Japanese, this has often been misspelled in English as "*cour*."

- *Cut*, in English, is the term used in Japanese to refer to a shot—i.e. the piece of film between two cuts. We repeat it here because it is one of the most common false friends in translations of interviews with Japanese animators, who often speak of "special effects cuts," or the number of "cuts" required to complete a scene.
- *Cosplay* is a contraction of "costume play," and means "dressing up."
- *Dojinshi* are amateur publications or fanzines.
- *E-conté* means "storyboards," a comic-style run-through of the scenes in an animated film, depicting everything on a shot-by-shot basis. The term derives from the Japanese *e*, meaning "picture," and "continuity."
- *Fan Service* is a temporary suspension of the concerns of the story in order to pander to a sense of camp, the male gaze, or metatextuality on the part of the audience—usually images and moments in which the female characters lose their clothes or pose provocatively. Supposedly, this is because it is a special gift to the loyal fans on the part of the animators; often it is a creepy objectification that only encourages *moe* (q.v.) in certain sectors and derision from non-fans. Fan service need not always be sexually suggestive; there is, for example, such a thing as *mecha* (q.v.) fan service, foregrounding machinery at the expense of other aspects, or hiding visual gags in single frames of swift action. The term suggests that the phenomenon somehow serves the wants and needs of anyone who truly appreciates a show; while this may sometimes be true, the authors object to the implication that every time a show sucks or falters in its naturalism it is somehow the fault of the audience.
- *Ga-nime* is a term coined in 2006 as an umbrella title for a series of "still-animated" video releases. Produced jointly by the publisher Gentosha and the studio Toei Animation, these often amounted to little more than

voice-overs and sound-effects over still images, replicating the effect of the old *kamishibai* "paper-theaters" of the early 20th century. Considered as *extremely* limited animation, they barely warrant inclusion in an encyclopedia of this nature, although they do utilize talent and connections from the anime business proper, and are connected to fuller animation through earlier precedents such as Nagisa Oshima's **MANUAL OF NINJA MARTIAL ARTS**.

- *Gekiga*, literally "dramatic pictures," are supposedly comics for adults, roughly equivalent to the Western term "graphic novels." The term, however, is rarely used in contemporary Japan and seems to date from the time when the term "comic" still contained a juvenile implication.

- *Hentai* is anime erotica. The term first spread among coy fans and distributors who preferred to use a foreign term for their pornography, and then among porn consumers and distributors in search of a means of classifying the animated variant separately from the live-action version. Since the term literally means "perverse," it is sometimes found contracted to the letter "H" or its Japanese pronunciation *ecchi* or *etchi*. Some have claimed that the contraction is "softer" in meaning than the full term—calling a Japanese boy "H" might be flirtatious, as opposed to the more insulting "hentai."

- *Leica Reel* is the Japanese industry term for what is known in the West as animatics—a "movie" made using the storyboards for a production, in order to check timings, and often used as the visual track to which the voice actors will record their dialogue while the actual visuals are still being animated. Leica is a camera manufacturer that seems to have entered Japanese slang as a name for one of its products, much as *Hotchkiss* in Japanese continues to mean stapler.

- *LN* is a "light novel," a pointless neologism for a novella, often cited as the source materials for modern anime, or as spin-offs from same. Modern Japanese slang sometimes reduces the term to *ra-nobe*, abbreviated from *raito noberu*. Rising in visibility since the 1980s, where their exponents included Motoko Arai (**BLACK CAT**), "light novels" form a substantial part of Young Adult fiction in Japan, both in portable commuter-friendly paperbacks, and as e-Books to be read on phones and other devices. The term, however, seemingly promising and also precluding novelistic density, is most often seen as a marketing buzzword designed to excuse low page-counts and pulpy prose, often dialogue-heavy but otherwise insubstantial. You could call them Big Short-Stories, but then that would be BS.

- *Lolicon* or *lolicom* is a contraction of "Lolita Complex," an unhealthy interest in underage girls exemplified by the **LOLITA ANIME**. Its rarer male variant is *shotacon* (q.v.).

- *Mecha* literally refers to mechanical items or machinery, a subset of anime appreciation for all those boys who like to see how things work, and a feature of much Japanese animation since the re-creation of military hardware in **ANIMENTARY: CRITICAL MOMENTS**, and broadly applying to any concentration on machinery, such as **INITIAL D**'s obsession with engine interiors. However, among general anime **FANDOM**, in both Japan and the West, *mecha* is far more likely to be applied specifically to what the *Encyclopedia of Science Fiction* calls "a pilotable or remote-operable machine, often bipedal or otherwise humanoid in form." These have become ubiquitous, largely for their role in long-running franchises such as **TRANSFORMERS** or **GUNDAM**, in which they are context-integrated elements of storylines that only exist to sell tie-in toys. As argued by Liliane Lurçat in her study *A Cinq Ans, Seul Avec Goldorak* (1981), many viewers under eight years old are unable to distinguish the finer points between a bipedal *mecha* vehicle and a self-aware *mecha* entity, which often tempts the authors of this encyclopedia to similarly write off all such occurrences as "giant robots." However, strictly speaking, they are not always "giant" and these days are rarely "robots."

- *Moe* is a fetishistic obsession with a particular topic or hobby, entering modern parlance as a replacement for otaku (q.v.). Toshio Okada has written that a *moe* fan need only be obsessed, while a true otaku actually develops background knowledge. Its etymology here is related to *moeru*, to burn with enthusiastic fervor. Also often associated in anime fandom with one particular kind of *moe*, an intense attraction to cartoon characters, particularly young and innocent girls that need to be nurtured and may be looking for a brotherly protector. Its etymology here is more related to *moederu*, to sprout or bud. Unhelpfully, it is also an acronym for an anime company, m.o.e., or Master of Entertainment. Such popular confusions over what Japanese and other foreign terms actually mean is precisely why we have avoided them in the body of this book.

- *Netorare* refers to cuckoldry—the experience of having one's lover taken away by another, and a recurring trope in anime pornography. Sometimes abbreviated as NTR.

- *OP* refers to the opening theme to a show, as contrasted with the ED, or ending theme. Although the trend in American TV is toward short, punchy OPs that do not permit viewers the opportunity to grow bored and surf to another channel, Japanese broadcasting favors longer sequences. This permits a promotional showcase for the all-important song tie-ins, and in anime also permits a reduction in the length of new animation required for a weekly episode. Participation of a record company is often a key component of any anime's production committee, and is usually traded for prominent music tracks from the company's artists.

- *Otaku* has a highly complex derivation, and now means "geek," "nerd," or "obsessive fan" (of any hobby or pursuit) in Japanese. It does not have these negative connotations in Western fandom, where it simply means an anime/manga fan, particularly a devoted or knowledgeable one. The word was first used in its modern sense in *An Investigation of Otaku* (*Otaku no Kenkyu*), a series of columns published by Akio Nakamori in 1983. This was later parodied in **OTAKU NO VIDEO**, the first anime made by fans, for fans, about fans.

- *Pro* is a shorthand for "Production/s,"

and often appears in studio documentation for animation companies, such as Mushi Pro (Mushi Production, singular), Tezuka Pro (Tezuka Productions, plural), or Sho Pro (Shogakukan Productions, also plural).

- *Pseudomanga* is a Western comic that pretends to be a manga. The term is highly unpopular with Western fans, since they feel it implies that some Western creators are trying to pass their work off as something it isn't. Other attempts to categorize the phenomenon include "American-style manga," or "Amerimanga," much to the annoyance of non-Americans, and Original English Language (OEL), for which see below under Acronyms and Initials.

- *Ris Work*, sometimes mistransliterated as "Lease Work." The use of a "telop" or television opaque projector, AKA an optical printer, to add certain video effects, particularly rain, mist, or certain fore- and background projections. Largely superseded in modern anime thanks to digital animation, but often still used to add the closing credits to some anime.

- *SD* means "super-deformed" or sometimes "squashed-down." In both cases it refers to squat cartoon variants of characters, used in parodies or in comical sequences. See also CB.

- *Seiyu* means "voice actor" and refers to the people who provide voices for the animated characters. In order to maximize profits and give magazines something to write about, the Japanese anime press began to include *seiyu* coverage in the 1980s, particularly when *seiyu* singing careers generated more income, as in the case of **MACROSS**. The trend reached the Western anime press in the 1990s and is most obvious at anime conventions, where the voice artists responsible for localizing dubs are often feted as far more accessible celebrities than the remote Japanese.

- *Shojo* means "girl" in Japanese. Consequently, a *shojo anime* is an anime made for girls, like **CANDY CANDY**. A *bishojo* is a pretty girl and a *maho shojo* is a "magical girl"—an anime subgenre (**TROPES AND TRANSFORMATIONS**) dating back to **LITTLE WITCH SALLY** and **COMET-SAN**. *Shojo-ai*, or "girl-love," would be the logical term for a lesbian subset of anime erotica, but

general usage favors *yuri* (q.v.)

- *Shonen* means "boy" or "youth" in Japanese. A *shonen anime* is hence an anime made for boys or youths in their low teens. *Shonen-ai*, or "boy-love," is a homosexual subset of anime erotica. A *bishonen* is a pretty boy, sometimes contracted to *bishie* or *bishi*.

- *Shotacon* is a contraction of "Shotaro Complex," or an unhealthy obsession with little boys. It is said to derive from the boyish good looks of Shotaro Kaneda, the protagonist of **GIGANTOR**.

- *Studio* is a place where an anime is made. It is often assumed that such entities are large old-time Hollywood-style conglomerates, although even "major" anime companies only have staff levels around a couple of hundred, whereas many of the smaller "studios" to which they subcontract piece work are often single offices in nearby buildings. Some companies enjoy the corporate implications that come with the term. Others, particularly small design operations, prefer to use the humbler "office" designation, or even half-jokingly use the French term *atelier*—an attic or garret, the traditional residence of a starving artist.

- *VN* refers to a "virtual novel." The 1980s saw the rise of a subgenre of niche-interest computer-based role-playing games, that economized on memory by using anime-style artwork. The games often feature a very limited number of choices, sometimes amounting to less of a series of narrative decisions, and more like a series of personality tests designed to determine which ending best suits the "player." Despite often using anime artists, they comprise still images. As a result, canny marketers decided not to bill them as clunky, play-on-rails text-based games, but instead as "novels" with added visual and audio bonus elements. Many such "virtual novels," particularly in the erotic sector, form the basis for anime adaptations.

- *Yaoi* is a contraction of *yamanashi, ochinashi, iminashi*: "no climax, no punchline, no meaning," originally a pejorative term for erotica about homosexual male love, created by female fans. The term has now been embraced by such fans as a badge of honor, much

as "geek" and "nerd" are not regarded as insults within SF fandom. It often offers an interesting perspective on the preoccupations of male genre fiction, as seen in Sobi Yamamoto's **THIS BOY CAN FIGHT ALIENS**.

- *Yuri* is lesbian erotica, deriving from *yuri-zoku* or "Lily Tribe," a term coined for lesbians by the editor of *Barazoku* (Rose Tribe), a magazine for gay men.

Acronyms and Initials

Japanese marketers often assume that their audience can be easily fooled by a few pompous acronyms—one only needs to look at the Japanese "Making Of" videos for **GHOST IN THE SHELL** or **AKIRA** to see them at work. With the coming of video in the 1980s, some companies attempted to put a positive spin on the idea of straight-to-video entertainment—direct-to-video (DTV) has a pejorative connotation in the Western media world, often with good reason. Consequently, marketers coined the terms Original Animation Video (OAV) or Original Video Animation (OVA), acronyms which seem to have survived in Western fandom because non-linguists found them easy to spot on pages of Japanese text. The anime historian Yoshiharu Tokugi suggests a slight semantic distinction between OAV and OVA, in the sense that the former is a *new* work made specifically for video, while the latter may also refer to a continuation on video of a pre-existing TV show or movie franchise—such spin-offs were also known in Japanese in the 1990s as *after-mono*, although the term now seems to have fallen out of use. Recent years have seen the creation of yet more acronyms, this time in the West. An Original Net Animation (ONA) is an anime that premieres on the Internet, while an Anime Music Video (AMV) is a fan-produced music video using footage from one or more anime. The term Original English Language (OEL) has been used in the publishing industry as a term for *pseudomanga* (q.v.)—it presumably being far too much trouble to simply call them "comics." None of these acronyms appears to be remotely useful for anything except misdirection, and we have not employed them in this book.

ARIA *
2005. TV series. AKA: *Aria the Animation*. DIR: Junichi Sato, Kazunobu Fuseki. SCR: Reiko Yoshida. DES: Kozue Amano. ANI: Makoto Koga. MUS: Choro Club. PRD: Hal Filmmaker, TV Tokyo. 25 mins. x 13 eps.
In A.D. 2301, Mars has been so fully terraformed that it is 90% water, and has earned the nickname Aqua. Pink-haired Akari Mizunashi arrives at the Martian city of Neo-Venezia, an idyllic canal-crossed metropolis modeled on Venice, Italy, where she hopes to find her fortune as a gondola pilot or "undine." Based on the manga by Kozue Amano, itself a sequel to Amano's earlier *Aqua*, which began in 2001 and is hence absolved of any charges of ripping off MARS DAYBREAK. In fact, with its emphasis on life in a serene future, it owes more of a debt to YOKOHAMA SHOPPING, while its backstory transformation of the Red Planet echoes ARMITAGE III.

ARIA THE SCARLET AMMO *
2011. JPN: *Hidan no Aria*. TV series, video. DIR: Takashi Watanabe. SCR: Hideki Shirane, Sawako Hirabayashi, Shogo Yasukawa. DES: Kazunori Iwakura, Teruhiko Niida. ANI: Ikuko Matsushita, Yoshihiro Ujiie, Yoshinori Izuno, Kazunori Iwakura. MUS: Takumi Ozawa. PRD: JC Staff, High School of Detective Armed, TBS. 25 mins. x 12 eps. (TV), 24 mins. (v).
A network of schools has been established to help combat the worsening crime situation by training teenagers to function as Butei—super-officers who might be hackers, analysts, or deadly killers for justice. Tokyo Butei High issues a national qualification that permits its graduates to bear arms, capture criminals, and work as detectives. Rebel student Kinji wants out, until he is attacked by a serial killer who targets Butei grads. He's saved by the school's star pupil, Aria H. Kanzaki IV. She sees hidden talents in him and he decides to stay in school.
Chugaku Akamatsu's book series, illustrated by Kobuichi, has been running since August 2008, and the manga it inspired (by Yoshino Koyoka) since September 2009. It's a high school harem anime (ROMANCE AND DRAMA) in a cunning disguise: it wants to be *Kick-Ass* without the boring adults. There are ancestral battles to be fought and in the process there are few myths whose coattails it neglects

to grab (RELIGION AND BELIEF). There's a shrine maiden, a werewolf, a childlike genius, and descendants of ninja, Vlad the Impaler, and the reliably certified virgin Jeanne D'Arc. There's a cousin of LUPIN III whose surname includes that of Lupin's squeeze Fujiko Mine and whose preferred weapon is a Walther. The heroine is a descendant of both Sherlock Holmes and the British Royal Family. The hero is immensely stronger and immensely smarter when sexually aroused. Wish fulfillment runs rampant: it's as if someone said to a totally inexperienced geek, "Make a show with whatever you want in it," which is fine, unless you want a good movie. What you get here is plenty of eye candy, fan service, and some good action scenes, though not enough of those. What you don't get is consistently good animation, character development, an intelligent plot, or any reason to keep watching if you have something better to do.

ARIEL *
1989. Video. DIR: Junichi Watanabe. SCR: Muneo Kubo, Yuichi Sasaki. DES: Osamu Tsuruyama, Yuji Moriyama. ANI: Osamu Tsuruyama. MUS: Kohei Tanaka. PRD: Animate Film, JC Staff. 30 mins. x 2 eps. (v1), 45 mins. x 2 eps. (v2).
Mad scientist Grandpa Kishida builds a giant robot called the All-Round Intercept and Escort Lady, or ARIEL, a convoluted acronym that is the namesake of his dead wife. Earth is attacked by the elfin alien general Hauser, who is searching for the Breastsaver Haagen, a powerful fighter he believes to be somewhere on the surface, but his assault is repelled by the Ariel team. Pilot Kasumi (Kishida's granddaughter) enjoys herself immensely, but her sister, Aya, and friend, Miya, refuse to fly again. The girls have no choice, however, when a second wave of alien attackers pours toward Scebai base, and they are humanity's last line of defense. The two initial sci-fi robot episodes in this low-rent GUNBUSTER clone were swiftly followed by the two longer *Deluxe Ariel* sequels, even though the original series hardly deserved a comeback.

ARION
1986. Movie. JPN: *Neo Heroic Fantasia Arion*. DIR: Yoshikazu Yasuhiko. SCR: Akiko

Tanaka, Yoshikazu Yasuhiko. DES: Yoshikazu Yasuhiko, Kyoko Yamane. ANI: Yoshikazu Yasuhiko. MUS: Joe Hisaishi. PRD: Sunrise, TMS. 118 mins.
Three brothers, the last of the Titans, divide the world between them, but a quarrel soon breaks out between Poseidon, Lord of the Sea, and the Mountain-god Zeus, engineered in secret by the third brother, Hades. Fearing the wrath of Zeus, goddess Demeter hides Arion, her son by Poseidon, far away from Olympus. Caught up in the power struggles of the gods, Arion becomes the prisoner of the dangerously unstable Artemis and her capricious brother, Apollo, until he is set free, once more through the machinations of Hades. He is also falling in love with a slave girl, Lesfeena, but fears she might be his sister.
Beginning life in the pages of *Ryu* magazine (which it shared with the similar fantasy AMON SAGA), *Arion*, a loose adaptation of classical myth with a distinctly oriental flavor, is a mature and exciting adventure. Though original creator Yasuhiko is credited with most aspects of production, he also recruited some impressive assistants. Miyazaki composer Joe Hisaishi supplies a magnificent score, while FAIRY KING's Ryoko Yamagishi, an artist specializing in myth, helped with the design. Epic battles, perverse cruelty, great heroism, and unselfish love all have their place in this film, which is superior in every way to Yasuhiko's later VENUS WARS.

ARISA *
2005. JPN: *Moke-moke Taisho Dendo Musume*. AKA: *Groping Taisho-era Electric Girl*. Video. DIR: Eijun Reikishi. SCR: Kentaro Mizuno. DES: Akihiko Emura. ANI: Kyoichi Daihiryu. MUS: N/C. PRD: Green Bunny. 27 mins., 29 mins.
In an erotic parody of both STEEL ANGEL KURUMI (with additional swipes from CHOBITS), Shinichiro Morisaki and his nubile adopted sister Kotomi run a café in Japan's Taisho period—the 1912–26 dreamtime that also provides a backdrop for SAKURA WARS. Late one night an Imperial Army airship accidentally drops an experimental android through the roof of the café. With the help of his grandfather Gennosuke, Shinichiro activates the android, which becomes the busty but clumsy Arisa. Anxious to retrieve their "Fire Bee," the army sends

an agent to infiltrate the café; sex duly ensues. Based on a game by mixwill soft. **ⓃⓋ**

ARJUNA *

2001. JPN: *Chikyu Shojo Arjuna.* AKA: *Earth Girl Arjuna.* TV series. DIR: Shoji Kawamori, Eiichi Sato, Tomokazu Tokoro, Yoshitaka Fujimoto. SCR: Shoji Kawamori, Hiroshi Onogi. DES: Takahiro Kishida. ANI: Manabu Fukusawa, Haruo Sotozaki. MUS: Yoko Kanno. PRD: Satellite, TV Tokyo. 25 mins. x 12 eps. + 1 bonus video ep.

Young teenager Juna Ariyoshi is in an accident and receives a vision of life on Earth in the future. She sees that humans have been raised to a higher state of consciousness but are victims of predatory raids from evil Rajah invaders, who must be held off by the wearer of the "Aura Suit." She is soon enlisted by local boy Chris Horken in a mission to save both worlds. Or in other words, ESCAFLOWNE, but traveling in time instead of space. Ichiro Itano, former anime director, adds another string to his bow here as director of the CG motion-capture sequences, while director Kawamori claimed in press releases that the show was designed to encourage a return to nature and renunciation of material things. We'll see what the merchandising department has to say about that.

ARMITAGE III *

1994. Video. DIR: Hiroyuki Ochi. SCR: Chiaki Konaka, Akinori Endo. DES: Atsushi Takeuchi. ANI: Kunihiro Abe. MUS: Hiroyuki Nanba. PRD: AIC, Pioneer. 30 mins. x 4 eps. (v1), 90 mins. (m), 90 mins. (v2).

"Red to Blue" is the motto, but it will be many generations before Mars is truly habitable. The air is still too thin for human beings, so colonists live beneath the roof that now closes off the Marineris Trench. Like Hong Kong and Singapore before it, the city of Saint Lowell has become a bustling metropolis simply because there is nowhere else to go. Although the Trench is hundreds of miles long, the colony has expanded fast, and Saint Lowell resembles much older cities back on Earth, packed with cramped skyscrapers and dark streets. With a shortage of manpower in the mines (and girl power in the bars), Mars becomes the center of the solar system's robotics industry, pioneering the functional "Firsts" and the lifelike "Seconds."

Discredited cop Ross Sylibus is transferred from Earth to the colonies after he loses his partner to a rogue robot. As the city is terrorized by a brutal flurry of killings, all he's got to help him are his Terran wits and his new partner, the underdressed Naomi Armitage. The victims are all female, but they are also all "Thirds," the state of the art in android technology. Sylibus discovers that the murders are part of a gargantuan conspiracy involving big corporations, scientific cartels, and Earth's feminist government.

Blade Runner comparisons are a dime a dozen in the anime world, but *Armitage* truly deserves it. Wells City (as in H. G. Wells) and the spaceport at Saint Lowell (as in astronomer Percival Lowell) are dead ringers for Ridley Scott's Los Angeles. The frontier feel of newly colonized Mars only arrives in the later episodes, when Ross and Naomi are out in the barren countryside beyond the city standing beneath the glorious red of a Martian sky—an image also purloined for the later COWBOY BEBOP. With its high-tech future, android technology, and Martian frontier life, *Armitage* hits many sci-fi hotspots, but it is also a cop-buddy movie, a romance, and a sexy pastiche on several military conspiracy shockers. Writer Chiaki Konaka, who would go on to write the quintessential Internet thriller SERIAL EXPERIMENTS LAIN, made *Armitage* conspicuously cyberpunk, including a trip to cyberspace via a painfully messy human interface and meditations on the place of humanity in a high-tech world.

Originally released as part of a multimedia experience that included false newspaper reports to fill narrative gaps, the omission of these items in the English-language release renders Konaka's plot less coherent than it could have been. But there are still hidden depths in his script, the first episode of which was written in collaboration with SF veteran (and author of the GHOST IN THE SHELL tie-in novel) Akinori Endo. There is also a sly dig at modern Japanese business; the rival Conception and Hu-Gite cybernetics companies battle to create the first android that is more human than human, continually outperforming each other with new formats and better models in a storyline no doubt inspired by the large

corporate battles of recent years, such as Sega versus Nintendo and Sony versus Pioneer. The script is also scattered with references to H. P. Lovecraft's story "The Dunwich Horror" (a favorite of Konaka's), including Professor Armitage, the writer Lavinia Whateley, and a laboratory on Dunwich Hill.

Regarded as the most Americanized "girls-and-guns" example of Pioneer's output, *Armitage* initially got much less attention than it deserved. As with Konaka's later BUBBLEGUM CRISIS 2040, it is sometimes easy to miss the fine line between his satirical sexism and the everyday variety prevalent in so many other shows. Following the success of the video, it was rereleased as the movie *Polymatrix* with some cuts, a couple of extra scenes, and a completely new ending, as well as a subtle musical cue in the closing credits, in which the main theme segues into a child's music box, cleverly and obliquely alluding to events to come. It was also redubbed featuring the voices of Kiefer Sutherland and Elizabeth Berkley in the main roles in an attempt to gain extra press attention through star power—a tactic common for Disney but rare in anime until Buena Vista's acquisition of PRINCESS MONONOKE. However, the video ending, which looks farther into the future of the lead characters, remains the better of the two—*Armitage* really belongs on the small screen. It was originally made for video, and although the story is compelling, the art does not really survive being enlarged in a theater. But the bright design, powerful sound, and lemon twist of romance all make for a great retelling of one of sci-fi's oldest stories: the machine that wants to be human.

Note: the Roman numerals in *Armitage III* are part of the lead character's name, and not, as some commentators have assumed, evidence of two earlier episodes in the series. It is read "Armitage the Third," not "Armitage Three." The video sequel *Armitage III: Dual Matrix* (2001) takes place six years after the original, with Naomi and Ross now living under a false identity on Mars as Mr. and Mrs. "Oldman," with their daughter Yoko. With news of robot riots breaking out offworld, Naomi travels back to Earth to hunt down a new conspiracy, in the process facing her most powerful foes—replicas of herself. However, the same could be said of *Dual Matrix* in its entirety, since while it may attempt to restart elements of the original, it could be accused of merely rehashing them. There was much in the original *Armitage III* to recommend it, not the least in a reproductive subplot that foreshadowed the new *Battlestar Galactica* by several years. But *Dual Matrix* failed to move the franchise further along, and it ground to a halt here. **✪**

ARMORED KNIGHT IRIS

2007. JPN: *Shoko Kijo Iris*. Video. DIR: Rosuke Takahashi. SCR: Shima Iijima, Inochi Kado. DES: ZOL, Syu Honda. ANI: Yuki Mine. MUS: N/C. PRD: Pixy. 30 mins. x 4 eps. (v), 4 mins. (v, bonus).

Iris is one of a group of armored babes maintaining law and order for the Intergalactic Government. During a battle (with some reasonably detailed CG mech action) she's captured by aliens and sold into sexual slavery. Despite her natural reluctance, she eventually starts to enjoy giving considerably more than her name, rank, and serial number. There's a large orgy scene, a blatant rip-off of Jabba the Hutt and other *Star Wars* aliens, and, of course, tentacles. Like many other Pixy titles, this is based on a porno game by Lilith, creators of **DOREI MAID PRINCESS**, **DARK KNIGHT INGRID**, and **PRINCESS KNIGHT LILIA** as well as the more contemporary **ANE HARAMIX**. The 2010 Japanese DVD box set also includes a four-minute "bonus story" scene not included in the previously released episodes.

ARMY MAIDEN SUVIA

2007. JPN: *Ikusa Otome Suvia*. AKA: *Valkyrie Suvia*. Video. DIR: Takashi Kondo. SCR: Mitsui Itsumi. DES: Yuji Ushijima, Hifumi. ANI: Yuji Ushijima. MUS: N/C. PRD: Pixy. 30 mins. x 4 eps. (v), 3 mins.

Another Pixy title based on a game by Lilith's "Black Lilith" label, this deformation of Norse mythology (**RELIGION AND BELIEF**) starts with Loki in cahoots with the King of Hell to capture and imprison Odin, and goes on to depict Valkyries as demons' sex slaves. To get himself out of trouble Odin agrees to destroy the World Tree, and thus the world. To prevent this, Loki has to get hold of two keys that are protected by two invincible Valkyrie warriors, Sigurd and Suvia. Now, how do you suppose he'll do that? Right. There are some good fight scenes, ogre sex, and (unusually) a tentacle scene with no actual penetration. The art is pretty, although like most Pixy productions not especially distinctive, and the animation is competent. The design will annoy Norse purists—Hell is cavernous and punctuated with rooms tricked up in faux 18th-century French style. The bonus video, released as part of the Japanese box set, comprises girls-on-ogre sex with a portentous prediction of the end of the world as a final flourish. If you enjoy seeing Norse myths humiliated, Kitty Films' **RIDE OF THE VALKYRIE** may also interest you, but then again, so will **OH MY GODDESS!**

AROUND THE WORLD WITH WILLY FOGG *

1985. JPN: *Dobutsu 80 Nichikan Sekai Icho*. AKA: *Animals Around the World in 80 Days*; *La Vuelta al Mundo de Willy Fog*. TV series. DIR: Fumio Kurokawa. SCR: Ryuzo Nakanishi. DES: Isamu Noda. ANI: Hisatoshi Motoki, Hirokazu Ishino. MUS: Shunsuke Kikuchi. PRD: Nippon Animation/BRB, TV Asahi. 30 mins. x 26 eps. (TV1), 30 mins. x 30 eps. (TV2).

Wheelchair-bound old goat Lord Guinness believes it is possible to travel around the world in 80 days, but he is too infirm to prove it himself. A lion called Willy Fogg volunteers to put the theory to the test, betting against several other people at the Gentlemen's Reform Club. Accompanied by two circus refugees, Rigadon and Tico, Fogg sets off around the world. However, Sullivan, who has bet against Fogg, hires a jackal thug called Transfer to ensure that the trip is a failure. Fogg is also hounded by two Scotland Yard detectives convinced that he has robbed a bank and has to rescue Romy, a beautiful Indian princess, en route.

This anthropomorphic (but chiefly feline) adaptation of Jules Verne was a companion piece to the canine **DOGTANIAN AND THE THREE MUSKEHOUNDS** made in association with the Spanish studio BRB. Though it charmed a generation in Europe, the Japanese version was not broadcast until 1987 and omitted episodes 14, 18, 21, and 22—curiously, one of the missing chapters was "En Route to Yokohama." Fogg and friends would return in a 30-episode sequel in the early 1990s, adapting *Journey to the Center of the Earth* and *20,000 Leagues under the Sea* in similarly flamboyant style.

ARRIETTY *

2010. JPN: *Karigurashi no Arrietty*. AKA: *The Borrower Arrietty*; *The Secret World of Arrietty*. Movie. DIR: Hiromasa Yonebayashi. SCR: Hayao Miyazaki, Keiko Niwa. DES: Akihiko Yamashita, Noboru Yoshida, Yoji Takeshige. ANI: Akihiko Yamashita, Megumi Kagawa. MUS: Cécile Corbel. PRD: Studio Ghibli, Dentsu, Hakuhodo DY Media Partners, Mitsubishi, NTV, Disney. 94 mins.

All around us, in the cracks and shadows of our world, millions of little lives go on unnoticed. Borrowers are just one of the species that have relied on humankind but have come to rely on our careless leavings: tiny people who survive by "borrowing" food, discarded objects, and scraps from the Big People. But they are a dwindling folk, with no technology of their own and no means of communication, living in constant fear of hunger or discovery. Pod and Homily Clock and their headstrong teenage daughter Arrietty live in an old house where previous generations of Borrowers have been safe. Then a newcomer arrives. Sho, the teenage great-nephew of the present owner, is facing a dark and terrible fate alone. His parents are divorced and too busy with their own lives to take care of him while he waits for a life-threatening operation. He comes to his great-aunt's house for sanctuary, and finds a whole new world.

Studio Ghibli has given a lovingly faithful account of Mary Norton's novel of the lost world of England between the two World Wars. Nostalgia for times past is a Ghibli specialty, but in *Arrietty* we also have a warm and humane movie that overcomes its melancholy and its fears of what may come, through a statement of faith in simple human kindness. In updating Norton's mythos while keeping faith with her values, Hiromasa Yonebayashi's directorial debut brings Ghibli back to its own roots in solid storytelling, delicate characterization, and breathtakingly beautiful art. Subtitles in some territories have overenthusiastically redacted the misprisions and malapropisms of the original book, replacing the characters' quaint term "human beans" with the more accurate "human beings."

Repeating a gimmick from the earlier **PONYO**, the end credits to *Arrietty* eschew titles and ranks in favor of an alphabetical list of all the cast and crew. While this might appear to be an egalitarian, noble statement of community on the part of the studio, it also helpfully obscured the fact that this Ghibli film was only cowritten by the famous Hayao Miyazaki, in yet another iteration of the studio's early-21st-century agonies over succession and continuity. But many of the concerns addressed both in Norton's books and Yonebayashi's movie are also highlighted in earlier works from Ghibli's two founding directors. The secret worlds of childhood and the importance of relationships with the fantastic are a constant theme running ever since Miyazaki and Takahata's **PANDA GO PANDA** in 1972. Sho is isolated by circumstance from his parents, like many Miyazaki heroines since **NAUSICAÄ OF THE VALLEY OF THE WIND**, while Arrietty is detaching from childhood and reforging her family bonds as an adult, a process we see beginning in **KIKI'S DELIVERY SERVICE** and coming to fruition in **ONLY YESTERDAY**.

The ability to perceive and interact with magic, and the longing for a lost way of life that embraced it, suffuses **MY NEIGHBOR TOTORO**, **POM POKO**, and *Arrietty*. But the modern view of magic is encapsulated in *Arrietty*'s glorious doll's house. It was built by Sho's ancestor for Borrowers, but (so claims Pod) not as an act of neighborly kindness. It's a trap to entice them to reveal themselves and then cage them as exotic pets for human amusement. Arrietty is on the verge of womanhood now, and like Fio in **PORCO ROSSO** she is beginning to be aware of the hardships and perils of adult life, but the Big People's world is luring her into adventure and danger. Her parents are anxious to protect her from too much reality too soon, all the while wondering where the next meal can be scavenged, in constant fear of hunger, discovery, or destruction.

Like all true Ghibli directors, Yonebayashi is drawn to social and political subtext. One can read the Borrowers' thrifty, humble existence as a tribute to traditional working-class virtues in a world of social climbing and conspicuous consumption, or as a commentary on the sustainable lifestyles of simpler peoples

and the risks inherent in their exposure to the over-mechanized, over-controlled, over-exploitative industrial world. A theme much explored by Miyazaki, the importance of the female at the heart of the family and the need for her to exchange girlish fantasy for adult responsibility is also reinforced. For the little people, the salt of the earth and the security of family is more important and more affordable than the fantasy lifestyle of their big, rich neighbors.

The notion of the family, present or absent, and how it shapes and then surrenders its children, is important in most Ghibli movies. Sho's absent parents and Arrietty's close and loving family have influenced their characters, just as Sophie's flighty mother in **HOWL'S MOVING CASTLE** and Pazu and Sheeta's dead but lovingly remembered parents in **CASTLE IN THE SKY** have shaped theirs. Sho's complete lack of importance in his parents' lives has left him doubting the value of his own. Despite all the expensive toys lavished on him, it isn't until he finds an honest and respectful relationship that he can believe in his own worth.

Aside from social concerns, political theories, and ideas about relationships, the sheer craft of *Arrietty* signals its origins and earns it a place of honor in Studio Ghibli's record. Unlike Goro Miyazaki (**TALES FROM EARTHSEA**), Yonebayashi came to direction from a long apprenticeship in Ghibli's animation department, starting as an in-betweener and cleanup artist on **PRINCESS MONONOKE**, then joining the crew of **MY NEIGHBORS THE YAMADAS**, working his way up to key animation before making the leap to the director's chair. He uses that solid background in his craft to exquisite effect, making a film with a delicately dazzling surface wrapped around a robust core of enduring value. He hasn't yet found his own voice as a director, but on the evidence of *Arrietty*, that will come.

ARROW EMBLEM *

1977. JPN: *Arrow Emblem Grand Prix no Taka*. TV series. DIR: Rintaro, Nobutaka Nishizawa, Yugo Serikawa, Takenori Kawada, Yasuo Yamayoshi. SCR: N/C. DES: Akio Sugino, Takuo Noda. ANI: Bunpei Nanjo, Takeshi Shirato, Toshio Mori. MUS: Hiroshi Miyagawa. PRD: Toei, Fuji TV. 25 mins. x 44 eps.

Takaya Todoroki cherishes a dream of becoming a Formula One racer. He puts all his energy into winning a beginners' heat, but causes a massive pile-up due to an error of judgment. Initially swearing to give up racing, he is talked around by world-famous driver Nick Lambda, who encourages him to dust himself off and give it another try. Before long, he is a team member of Katori Motors, hoping to become the first Japanese racer to become a Formula One champion, driving the Todoroki Special, a car built to his own design. An English-language 90-minute edit was available on the obscure Century Video label in the 1980s under the title *Super Grand Prix*, featuring "Sean Corrigan," a young racer who has grown up on a U.S. airbase in Japan.

ART OF FIGHTING *

1995. JPN: *Battle Spirits: Ryoko no Ken*. AKA: *Battle Spirits: Dragon Tiger Fist*. Video. DIR: Hiroshi Fukutomi. SCR: Nobuaki Kishima. DES: Kazunori Iwakura. ANI: Kazunori Iwakura, Kenichi Shimizu, Mamoru Taniguchi. MUS: Akira Konishi, SNK Sound Team. PRD: Fuji TV, NAS. 45 mins.

An anime clone of a Neo-Geo game clone of **STREET FIGHTER II**, even to its mismatched leads, except instead of Ryu and Ken, we've got Ryo and Robert. The two heroes witness a gangland slaying and are accused of stealing a valuable diamond by the gang that has kidnapped Ryo's sister, Yuri. The two martial artists are obliged to fight to get her back in a tired story-by-numbers suspiciously like **TEKKEN**, or **TOSHINDEN**, or **VIRTUA FIGHTER**. **V**

ARTLAND

Animation company, founded in 1978 by animators from TV Doga, Onishi Pro, and others. Founding member Noboru Ishiguro took the company in to complete work on its first notable project, *Farewell Space Battleship Yamato*, one of the spin-offs of the **STAR BLAZERS** series. Other high-profile members include Noboru Sugimitsu, Kenichi Imaizumi, and producer Hidenobu Watanabe. The studio went on to contribute extensive work on the **MACROSS** saga.

ARTMIC

A design studio, specializing in original science fiction, founded by former Tatsunoko staffer Toshimichi Suzuki. Its greatest achievements include **Megazone 23**, which sold over 100,000 copies in Japan, although the studio subsequently went bankrupt, leaving its coproduction partners such as Youmex and AIC holding not only the outstanding debts, but also the intellectual copyright of its creations. This complex arrangement of ownership is what led to the breaks and reversionings in the serials **Gall Force** and **Bubblegum Crisis**, as well as the rebranding of **Riding Bean** as **Gunsmith Cats**—seen as a successful attempt by former employee Kenichi Sonoda to regain control of his work.

ASA KARA ZUSSHIRI MILK POT

2011. AKA: *Thick and Creamy Morning Milk Pot*. Video. DIR: N/C. SCR: N/C. DES: N/C. ANI: N/C. MUS: N/C. PRD: Studio9MAiami, Media-Bank. 20 mins. x 2 eps.

Futanari hentai is porn with mixed-sex protagonists—generally pretty girls with male genitalia and huge breasts. Here, Iori is born as the second daughter to a rich family desperate for a son. She has a huge penis, but despite this and her family's yearnings she's treated as a female and dresses as a provocatively cute schoolgirl. Like the heroine of *Discode* (**D3 Series**) she has a constant urge to masturbate and frequently gets caught in embarrassing situations. Based on an amateur porn game series.

ASARI-CHAN

1982. TV series. DIR: Osamu Kasai. SCR: Tadaaki Yamazaki, Masaki Tsuji, Akiyoshi Sakai. DES: Hideyoshi Ito. ANI: Tadashi Shirakawa, Koji Uemura, Nobuyuki Endo. MUS: Hiroshi Tsutsui. PRD: Toei, TV Asahi. 25 mins. x 54 eps.

Asari Hamano is a preteen girl who refuses to try at anything except sports. Her elder sister, Tatami, however, is a model student, adored by their mother, who pays Asari no attention at all. As the sisters fight a continual game of one-upmanship, Dad buries his head in his paper and tries to be even-handed. Both girls make life hell for the Morino boys next door—Jiro, who is waiting to retake his exams, and his younger brother, Kakesu.

Mister Pen-Pen–creator Mayumi Muroyama only changed the names to protect

the guilty when she started writing about her own family for *Corocoro Comic* in 1977. *Asari-chan* is still running to this day, but its anime incarnation was less successful. The 54 episodes were shown several times (occasionally split into 100 installments since most could be neatly divided into two shorter stories) and also spun off into a 25-minute film at the Toei Manga Festival in 1982, in which Asari is forced to read a five-volume compendium of fairy tales in order to prove to her aunt that she genuinely does like the gift.

ASATARO THE ONIONMONK

2008. JPN: *Negi Bozu no Asataro*. TV series. DIR: Yoko Ikeda. SCR: Shoji Yonemura. DES: Akira Inakami, Yoshito Watanabe. ANI: Kozue Komatsu. MUS: Kazunori Maruyama. PRD: Toei Animation, TV Asahi. 30 mins. x 48 eps.

Based on a 1999 picture book by Kazuyoshi Iino, this charming TV series for little children follows a long tradition of making anime about anthropomorphized food. From the adventures of the selfless **Anpanman** to the tragedy of **Kogepan**, food can come to life, act out hero-tales and teach moral lessons. Here, the monk Asataro and his fruit and vegetable chums also introduce the 53 stations of the historic Tokaido Road and replay well-known *jidai-geki* period costume dramas and *chanbara* swordplay epics, carefully edited to protect children from their innate sex and violence.

ASHI PRODUCTIONS (PRODUCTION REED)

Often abbreviated as Ashi Pro. Animation company formed in 1975 by Tatsunoko employee Toshihiko Sato. Notable members include Seiji Okuda, Hidehito Ueda, and occasional cameo appearances from freelancers including Seiji Kishimoto, Hideki Fukushima, and Keitaro Kawaguchi. Representative works include **Cybuster** and the *Beast Wars Neo* sections of the **Transformers** franchise. A member of the Bandai Namco group, it was split away in 2005, briefly becoming a subsidiary of the toy company Wiz. It was renamed Production Reed (JPN: *ashi*) in 2007. Wiz's shares in Production Reed were sold in 2009 to Sato, leaving the company in the hands of its employees.

ASHIDA, IWAO

ca. 1910–? Pseudonym of Hiroki Suzuki, sometimes Tomohiro Suzuki, an animator who was one of the leading figures of the business in the 1940s and 1950s but whose output in **Wartime Anime** and **Advertising and Sponsorship** has left his legacy vulnerable to the ravages of time. Beginning as an apprentice to Ikuo Oishi, he went independent under his real name in 1936 in a small home-based operation run with with his wife. The company was variously credited as Suzuki Cartoons, Sankichi Cartoons, or Ashida Cartoons. Around the same time, Ashida's studio also made *The Animal Counter-Espionage War*, in which monkeys and foxes infiltrate a factory and attempt to steal secrets vital to the war effort. A monkey makes an attempted getaway on a bicycle, and then in a plane, only to be apprehended, followed by the closing slogan: "Let's Defend Against Spies!" Ashida subsequently joined the wartime Shadow Staff making instructional films. Most of his 48-minute *Princess of Baghdad* (*Baghdad no Hime*, 1948), which he wrote as "Hiromasa Ashida," was lost until the 21st century, and hence not part of anime chronologies.

By the late 1950s, Ashida was feted as the face of Japanese animation abroad. Not only did he work under contract with American advertising firms, he also completed several cinema shorts, including *The Forest Orchestra* (*Mori no Ongagukai*, 1953), *Mizukko's Journey* (*Mizukko no Tabi*, 1955), and *The One-Legged Cricket* (*Ippon Ashi no Kirigirisu*, 1957). He also shot the live-action credits sequence for the American film *Karate, The Hand of Death* (1961), in which Japanese fists smash through wooden planks bearing the names of the cast and crew, and worked as an animator on the American propaganda film, *The Bear and the Children*.

The Ashida Cartoon Film Production Works (Ashida Manga Eiga Seisaku-sho) was widely regarded as the leader in the field—turning down applications from such future celebrities as Osamu Tezuka and Yasuo Otsuka—but worked chiefly in advertising. It was hence soon forgotten after the irresistible rise of Toei Animation, and Ashida disappeared from the record, allegedly amid mounting debts to loan sharks. His studio, once the center of the Japanese animation business, became a mat shop.

ASHIDA, TOYO'O

1944–2011. Born in Tokyo, he began as a concept artist at the TCJ studio (now Eiken) before moving to Mushi Production, where he was a key animator on Osamu Tezuka's CLEOPATRA: QUEEN OF SEX. With the collapse of Mushi in 1973, he found work on STAR BLAZERS, before becoming one of the ten founders of Studio Live. At Live, Ashida was a designer on shows ranging from CYBORG 009 to DR. SLUMP, before parlaying his experience of key animation (and working in impecunious circumstances) to a winning role as the director of FIST OF THE NORTH STAR. He was a prominent and approachable figure in the anime world from 1985 to 1995, in part because of his monthly column in *OUT* magazine, although he once generated massive controversy by quipping that anime FANDOM was "full of ugly girls and jobless guys." In 2007 he became the president of the Japanese Animation Creators Association, a labor union that pressed for better working conditions for anime's workers.

ASK DR. LIN

2001. JPN: *Doctor Lin ni Kiitemite*. AKA: *Listen to Dr. Lin; Pay Heed to Doctor Lin*. TV series. DIR: Shin Misawa. SCR: Jun Maekawa. DES: Takahisa Ichikawa. ANI: N/C. MUS: Takanori Arisawa. PRD: Nippon Animation, NAS, TV Tokyo. 25 mins. x 51 eps.
Junior high school student Meilin Kanzaki possesses magical powers and can drive away evil spirits and foretell the future. Consequently, she has a secret identity as fortuneteller Dr. Lin. She's also in love with her best friend Yuki Asuka, but he's a practical, down-to-earth guy who has no time for superstitious nonsense. Based on the manga by Kiyoko Arai, creator of MAGICAL EMI.

ASOBOT CHRONICLE GOKU *

2002. JPN: *Asobot Senki Goku*. AKA: *Asobot Chronicle Goku; Monkey Typhoon*. TV series. DIR: Mamoru Hamatsu. SCR: Hiroshi Hashimoto. DES: Tsuneo Ninomiya. ANI: Studio EGG. MUS: Kohei Tanaka. PRD: Studio EGG, TV Tokyo. 26 mins. x 52 eps.
Earth's environment has been devastated, and humans leave their homeworld for planet Meshichi, where they live alongside Asobots (Associate Robots). These are androids, but not just servants—they have emotions, consciences, personalities, and habits not so different from humans, and grow up alongside them to help and protect them. Some, unfortunately, pick up less admirable human habits, like brigandry. Goku is a boastful, irrepressible young asobot who runs into the mysterious Sanzo and ends up traveling west to the land of Zipangu with him. They meet cute Mion, mechanical genius Jo, pretty asobot thief Susie, and asobot drunkard Tongo, while avoiding the decidedly nastier asobots known as Hooligans, and their mysterious adversary Professor D.

The JOURNEY TO THE WEST has been a favorite starting point for animators from Osamu Tezuka onward. For the anime version of this manga by Joji Arimori and Romu Aoi, TV Tokyo wheeled out some impressive talent and was rewarded with good enough audiences to get a 52-week run, increasingly difficult in these days of multiple-choice entertainment. Compare to SPACEKETEERS, which was another sci-fi adaptation of the same Chinese legend. Part of the series, perhaps a movie edit, was screened at a convention in the U.S. in 2003 as *Monkey Typhoon*. Broadcast in English on Animax-Asia.

ASSEMBLE INSERT *

1989. Video. DIR: Ami Tomobuki. SCR: Mitsuru Toyota, Michiru Shimada. DES: Masami Yuki, Yutaka Izubuchi. ANI: Toyomi Sugiyama. MUS: Kohei Tanaka. PRD: Studio Core. 30 mins. x 2 eps.
Demon Seed, a group of power-suited criminals, has stolen over a billion yen in valuables and caused immense damage while resisting arrest. In a drunken stupor, Police Chief Hattori decides to catch the group by auditioning for a super-idol, a singing girl who can wear Professor Shimokawabe's new giant robot suit, defeat the menace, and keep him from doing too much overtime. The 15-year-old Maron Namikaze, who can bend steel microphone stands with her bare hands, is put to work stopping the Demon Seed gang from stealing an expensive museum exhibit. She defeats the bad guys but destroys the priceless artifacts in the process.

Three months later, the Special Operations group is so discredited that it decides to enter Maron for a talent contest. When an onstage display of strength is caught on camera, Maron becomes a star, and the police become her managers. Annoyed at the change in direction, Professor Shimokawabe secretly gives Demon Seed four new suits, and it stages another heist that coincides with Maron's big concert.

Predating both the showbiz-satire of HUMMINGBIRDS and the insane self-referentiality of DRAGON HALF, PATLABOR-creator Masami Yuki wrote this musical comedy for *OUT* magazine, reuniting many of the staff in both off-screen roles and onscreen cameos. The drunken Hattori is based on *Shonen Sunday*–editor Fukuda Takahashi, who first took a chance on Yuki. His lieutenant, Taka, is based on designer Yutaka Izubuchi, while the three other members of the Special Operations group are caricatures of MACROSS PLUS's sensible Shoji Kawamori, laconic *Patlabor*-staffer Yutaka Yoneda, and a drunken pervert modeled on Yuki himself.

ASTAROTTE'S TOY *

2011. JPN: *Astarotte no Omocha*. TV series, video. DIR: Fumitoshi Oizaki. SCR: Deko Akao, Hitomi Amamiya, Tokumitsu Kono. DES: Mai Otsuka, Kenichi Tajiri. ANI: Mai Otsuka. MUS: Twinpower. PRD: ASCII Media Works, Astarotte no Omocha! Production Committee, Dax, Diomedia, Kadokawa Shoten, Pony Canyon, Klockworx. 24 mins. x 12 eps. (TV), 21 mins. x 3 eps. (v).
Twenty-three-year-old Naoya is desperate to get a job—not least because he has to support 10-year-old Asuha. So when a girl from another world turns up recruiting a "toy" for the harem of 10-year-old succubus princess Lotte, he accepts. The lonely little Princess, traumatized by an earlier incident and estranged from her mother, comes to accept the kind-hearted Naoya as a big brother, and when Asuha joins them she has a friend for the first time. This series demonstrates why *moe* and "Lolita" anime can be so problematic both inside and outside Japan: all kinds of sexual improprieties are hinted at, and the apparent set-up would whip up any PTA into full banning mode—yet the hints are not followed through, the fan service is mild, and the whole is closer to the sly pervery of a *Benny Hill* joke than full-on

porn. The Video series *Astarotte no Omocha EX*, released the same year from the same team, consists of three short stories, two providing prequels to the TV series and one showing Lotte and Asuha at work on school projects. Based on the 2007 manga *Lotte no Omocha* by Yui Haiga.

ASTRO BOY *

1963. JPN: *Tetsuwan Atom*. AKA: *Mighty Atom*. TV series. DIR: Osamu Tezuka, Gisaburo Sugii, Daisaku Sakamoto, Eiichi Yamamoto, Osamu Dezaki, Yoshiyuki Tomino, Minoru Okazaki, Fusahito Nagaki. SCR: Osamu Tezuka, Noriyuki Honma, Masaki Tsuji, Kenichi Takahashi. DES: Osamu Tezuka. ANI: Daisaku Sakamoto. MUS: Tatsuo Takai. PRD: Tezuka Pro, Fuji TV. 30 mins. x 193 eps. (TV1), 25 mins. x 52 eps. (TV2), 25 mins. x 50 eps. (TV3).

In the year 2003 (2000 in the U.S. release), Professor Tenma (Boynton) is distraught when his son Tobio (Astro/Toby) is killed in a car accident. He loses himself in his latest project, creating Atom (Astro), a robot boy programmed to be forever good. Upset that his Tobio-substitute can never grow up, Tenma sells Atom to Hamegg (Cacciatore), the cruel ringmaster of a robot circus. Atom meets the kindly Professor Ochanomizu (Elefun), who adopts him, inspires him to become a crusader against evil, and eventually builds him a robot "sister," Uran (Astro Girl).

Often erroneously described as the first TV anime (see INSTANT HISTORY and A MOLE'S ADVENTURE), *AB* began in 1951 as *Captain Atom* in *Shonen Magazine*. Renamed *Mighty Atom* a year later, it became the flagship title of the magazine and was made as a live-action TV show in 1959—the opening sequence of which was the first appearance of Astro Boy in animation form. A combination of *Pinocchio* and *Superman*, it became the first of many animated adaptations by Tezuka of his own work.

First shown on Fuji TV on New Year's Day 1963 but eventually moving to the NHK network, it was the first anime to be broadcast abroad. Still known around the world as *Mighty Atom*—the U.S. name change was forced by the existence of a local comic character with a similar name—it was adapted for the English-language market by Fred Ladd, and its success created the first wave of anime abroad.

The U.S. version eventually screened 104 episodes of the full Japanese run, including such curiosities as a TV special of Atom fighting the STAR OF THE GIANTS—though the latter remains unknown in the English-speaking world. The influence of *AB* extended further than is often realized. On the strength of *AB*, Stanley Kubrick offered Tezuka a job as a production designer on *2001: A Space Odyssey*, though Tezuka declined.

The Japanese series, the ratings for which peaked at over 40%, ended with Atom sacrificing his life to save Earth. He also appeared in a feature-length anime movie, *Hero of Space* (1964), directed by Atsushi Takagi and incorporating color footage from Tezuka's abortive pilot for another show, *Number 7*. Hamegg, Tezuka's stock villain, was recycled for KIMBA THE WHITE LION, and Tezuka attempted to write Atom for an older audience with the more philosophical *Atom Chronicles* for *Shonen Magazine*.

An inferior copy appeared as JETTER MARS in 1977, but the original itself returned in a new color format in 1980. These *New Adventures of Astro Boy* featured a younger-looking hero in keeping with audience expectations and scripts written chiefly by Tezuka himself, though Ryosuke Takahashi contributed several and Kenji Terada was credited with "literary assistance," whatever that may be. With many of the original crew now famous in their own right, the new production drafted new faces including directors Noboru Ishiguro, Satoshi Dezaki, Naoto Hashimoto, and Takashi Anno. Perhaps as a result of Tezuka's own dissatisfaction with the series, the *New Adventures* were dark in mood despite their bright colors, featuring many failed missions and dying good guys. There was a greater concentration on Atom's evil twin, Atlas, built from stolen blueprints by Count Walpurgis (Walper Guiss), a European arms manufacturer. Deciding to conquer the world, Atlas opposes the emotional Atom with cold logic, eventually coming to realize over many episodes that it is he who is lacking something. Atlas was not the only one: the series was unsatisfactory to makers and viewers alike, and only lasted for 52 episodes—a quarter of its predecessor's longevity, though still considerably longer

than most modern serials.

Despite its failure to live up to the impact of the original, the color *AB* kept the myth alive for a new generation, existing in two separate dubs from Australia and Canada. Homages abound in both the U.S. and Japan, from the obvious *Big Guy and Rusty the Boy Robot* to the desperate stab at legitimacy of BIRDY THE MIGHTY. The character's simple, recognizable lines became an icon in U.S. subculture and was rumored to be the subject of several remakes as the character's original "birth-year" of 2003 approached. A live-action feature failed to materialize, and a Japanese-Canadian IMAX coproduction began development but was shelved in 2000. The only project that did make it to completion was a 50-episode TV anime remake under the general control of the Konaka brothers, writer Chiaki and director Kazuya. Diligently walking a difficult line between retro homage and modern update, the new series faithfully recreated much of the original's effect, both in its cartoonish charm and in its ability to surprise children's programmers. The 2003 *Astro Boy* was taken off-air partway through its American run, and did not survive much longer in the U.K. either, where even continuity announcers expressed their surprise at some of the harder-hitting plots. It also suffered somewhat from being broadcast in syndication in an order different from that in which the episodes were intended to be shown, resulting in some characters being "introduced" several episodes after they had first appeared. The series was subsequently released on DVD in America in a "complete" edition, although one episode from the original, "Eternal Boy," has been replaced by a clip shown in order to avoid any possibility of incurring the wrath of Disney over alleged similarities between the titular guest star and its own Peter Pan.

The digital animated movie *Astro Boy* (2009) does not technically qualify as anime but rather as "post-anime," written and directed by Americans and animated by a largely Chinese staff, albeit using characters licensed from the Tezuka estate. In reflection of this foreign focus, the film was released in Japan under the title *ATOM*. In that regard, *Astro Boy*'s sheer age and visibility has made it one of the pioneers of post-anime, as its license-holders at Tezuka Pro continue to cream off money from foreign remakes. So far, these have included the Nigerian cartoon series *Robot Atom* (2014) and the French-Monacan *Astro Boy Reboot* (forthcoming, 2015). Back in Japan, such foreign attention allows Tezuka Pro to secure yet another remake, in the form of the "edutainment" TV shorts *Little Astro Boy* (forthcoming, 2015).

ASTRO FIGHTER SUNRED

2008. JPN: *Tentai Senshi Sunred*. TV series. DIR: Seiji Kishi, Takehiko Matsumoto. SCR: Makoto Ueno, Kojiro Nakamura. DES: Kazuaki Morita, Masakazu Miyake. ANI: Jiyu Ogi (TV1), Katsuhiko Nishijima, Tomohiro Kametani. MUS: Shinji Kakijima. PRD: AIC A.S.T.A., JVC, Flying Dog. 15 mins. x 26 eps. (TV1), 15 mins. x 26 eps. (TV2).
What do out-of-work heroes do with their time? Astro Fighter Sunred smokes too much, hangs out with buddies, and lives off his girlfriend, Kayoko. He's even sold his superbike. Meanwhile his arch-enemies the Evil Florsheim Army haven't gone away. They're still trying to take over the world, using a particularly cunning plan—they do good works in the community, have a TV cooking show, and make it their business to assist Kayoko whenever possible while trying to attack her boyfriend. Based on Makoto Kubota's 2005 comedy manga parodying Japanese superhero shows, the cheap Flash animation style works well, successfully translating Kubota's sense of humor and obvious love for the genre into animation. A second series followed in 2009, while it was only a couple of years after that before a similar idea was approached from a new direction in TIGER AND BUNNY.

ASTRO GANGER

1972. TV series. DIR: Masashi Nitta, Kenjiro Yoshida. SCR: Tatsuo Tamura, Toyohiro Ando. DES: Eiji Tanaka. ANI: Eiji Tanaka. MUS: Akiyoshi Kobayashi. PRD: Nippon TV, Knack, Toei. 25 mins. x 26 eps.
The Earth is under attack by hostile aliens called the Blasters. Professor Hoshi creates a giant robot using a bar of living metal that his wife has brought from her home planet of Kanseros. After their deaths, their son Kantaro is left to pilot the humanoid Astro Ganger robot in the struggle to save the Earth. Astro Ganger was a curious amalgam of controllable vehicle and sentient android; he could think for himself, had variable expressions, and would eventually sacrifice himself, like ASTRO BOY before him, to save a human life. The series was popular enough that it was still referenced a decade later in the URUSEI YATSURA manga, when Ataru Moroboshi sung a snatch of the theme song. Afterward, the Knack production company went on to work on CHARGEMAN KEN.

When *Astro Ganger* was broadcast, it was the first giant robot anime shown in five years. Animators and producers had shied away from the genre, fearing that GIGANTOR had said all there was to say, and that anything in imitation of it would be seen as pointless and derivative—those were the days!

ASUKAS OF FLOWERS, THE *

1987. JPN: *Shin Kabuki-cho no Story: Asuka no Hanagumi*. AKA: *New Story of Kabuki Town: Asuka's Flower Collection*. Video. DIR: Atsutoshi Umezawa. SCR: Kenji Terada. DES: Satosumi Takaguchi, Yuri Handa. ANI: Toei. MUS: Kenji Kawai. PRD: Kadokawa, Tohoku, Toei. 48 mins. x 2 eps.
In this adaptation of a famously sensational girls' manga said to encapsulate the *ennui* of the 1980s, Asuka is a teenage student who wanders the windswept streets of Kabuki Town each evening, dragged into teenage prostitution and gangland violence. She saves fellow schoolgirl Yotsuko from another gang and returns the girl's diary, remaining honorable but distant—even when she subsequently prevents Yotsuko from committing suicide.

The original story, published in a magazine also called *Asuka*, was a huge hit for artist Satosumi Takaguchi, spawning 27 volumes, a six-part spin-off, a live-action movie, and a TV drama. This two-part series, however, was the only anime appearance. The youth-gone-wild of the following decade were similarly "sensationalized" in the live-action *Bounce Ko-gals*, nicely demonstrating that the more things change, the more they stay the same.

ASYLUM SESSION, THE *

2009. JPN: *Asylum Session*. Movie. DIR: Tact Aoki. SCR: Tact Aoki. DES: Horai Koishi, Itsuki Tatsukikawa. ANI: Yuko Moroi, Fujio Tanabe, Yoshihide Ibata, Kazuhiro Nasu, Asuka Nishi, Tact Aoki. MUS: Tact Aoki. PRD: CoMix Wave. 65 mins.
Seventeen-year-old Hiyoko wants to become a painter like her late mother, against her father's objections. When he takes down all her mother's pictures, she runs away from home, but none of her friends will take her in. She winds up at Asylum Stadium, an abandoned sports field due for demolition but currently a refuge for homeless people. She's drawn to an arrogant, mouthy boy with a chip on his shoulder about his artistic ability. Fighting to keep their home has failed. As corrupt officials and the police close in, the inhabitants of Asylum plan to win hearts and minds with a street festival: the Asylum Session.

Despite the homelessness theme, this has little in common with ARAKAWA UNDER THE BRIDGE. Its disaffected teens, official corruption, and adult deceit hark back to the much older MEGAZONE 23, and the themes of creativity, personality, and what makes one human have run through anime from ASTRO BOY to ARMITAGE III. Director Aoki, who created the concept, moved from CG and character modeling on the Net animation CATBLUE: DYNAMITE, through to the director's chair on *Asylum Session,* but the mix of 2D and 3D animation is awkward and the animation quality is uneven. The quirky design style and the theme of living creatively is an inspiring one, but the allusive, often unexplained plot and the lack of any clear payoff are frustrating. Aoki's attempt to merge a political and social subtext with action and romance doesn't quite come off, but his passion is obvious.

ATAGOAL: CAT'S MAGICAL FOREST

2006. JPN: *Atagoal wa Neko no Mori*. AKA: *Atagoal Is Cat's Forest*. Movie. DIR: Mizuho Nishikubo. SCR: Hirotoshi Kobayashi. DES: N/C. ANI: N/C. MUS: Tetsuya Takahashi, Hiroko Taniyama. PRD: Digital Frontier, Kadokawa Herald Pictures Inc., Micott and Basara. 81 mins.
The happy little town of Atagoal is a place where talking cats and humans live in peace. On the day of the town carnival, everybody is out to have fun—especially local fat cat Hideyoshi, whose band is headlining the concert. Hideyoshi can't

resist food or a challenge, and when he's told he absolutely must not open a certain sealed chest, he's hoping to find tuna. Instead he releases the Queen of the Plants, the beautiful Pileah. She says she wants to join the community and spread peace and harmony, but her idea of peace and harmony is everybody doing things her way. Helped by a mysterious warrior, two human children, and a sentient fruit that adopts Hideyoshi as his father, the fat cat sets out to save the village and the world from her control.

Hiroshi Masumura's adventure manga for kids ran from 1976 to 1981, then took 25 years to make the transition to anime. For some of the parents who took their children to the cinema to see it, this was a delightful trip down memory lane with overtones of *Garfield*: a beautifully animated movie with highly hummable tunes, and just enough sinister scares to keep slightly older kids interested. Even so, other viewers may be bored; plot and character development are minimal, and the pace varies from frenetic to catatonic. Production company MICOTT and Basara, known for its APPLESEED CGI movies and TV series, merged CGI and 2D animation very well for this charmingly designed film, but filed for bankruptcy in 2011.

ATERUI

2002. Movie. DIR: Satoshi Dezaki. SCR: N/C. DES: Setsuko Shibuichi. ANI: N/C. MUS: Yuse Nakajima. PRD: Magic Bus, Cinema Tohoku. ca. 93 mins.

Twelve hundred years ago in Hiraizumi, north Japan, Emishi prince Aterui Otamono-kimi fought the Imperial Court for 38 years to defend his native culture—different from the more famous Ainu people of the north, but still not part of the mainstream "Japanese" world. Known as "the Tiger," and considered a demon by his foes, he was finally defeated in A.D. 801 by Saka no Ue no Tamamura-maro, who turned his headquarters into a temple to the god Bishamon-ten that can still be visited today. The legend has inspired many historical novels, and a manga, *Aterui the Second*, by Katsuhiko Takahashi and FIST OF THE NORTH STAR–creator Tetsu Hara. However, this historical movie may also have been greenlit for its title character's racial resemblance to another Emishi hero,

Ashitaka from PRINCESS MONONOKE. The production was funded by Cinema Tohoku (i.e., northeastern Japan), no doubt in an attempt to maintain visitor interest in a region also promoted through SPRING AND CHAOS. Compare to the less sensible tourist magnet CUTTA'S STORY.

ATTACK NUMBER ONE

1969. TV series. DIR: Fumio Kurokawa, Eiji Okabe. SCR: Masaki Tsuji, Satoshi Dezaki, Haruya Yamazaki, Tsunehisa Ito. DES: Jun Ikeda. ANI: Shingo Araki. MUS: Takeo Watanabe. PRD: TMS, Fuji TV. 30 mins. x 104 eps. (TV1), 65 mins. (m1), 61 mins. (m2), 55 mins. (m3), 56 mins. (m4), 25 mins. x 23 eps. (TV2).

Kozue is a new student transferred to Fujimi College. Though she has a low opinion of her own abilities, she resolves to practice hard to fit in with the school volleyball team. She soon makes a lifelong friend in the kind Midori and a bitter enemy in Yoshimura, the girl who was formerly the school volleyball superstar. She falls in love with a local boy but is prepared to sacrifice everything to please her beloved Coach Honma.

This adaptation of Chikako Urano's 1968 volleyball manga was the first SPORTS ANIME made specifically for a female audience, generating not only four 1970 movies assembled from reedited footage, but also an entire subgenre that survives to this day. Successors that simply switch the focus to another sport include AIM FOR THE ACE and YAWARA!, while recent years have seen misguided pastiches such as BATTLE ATHLETES.

In 1977, Kurokawa, Okabe, and Yamazaki would return on the staff of *Attack on Tomorrow (Ashita e Attack!)*, a cloned TV series timed to cash in on Japan's successes in the volleyball World Cup. Mimi, a student, decides to revitalize a volleyball team that is still recovering from the accidental death of one of its members. The new series was a shadow of its illustrious predecessor and ceased after 23 episodes. The story was also adapted into a live-action drama series for TV Asahi in 2005.

ATTACK ON TITAN *

2013. JPN: *Shingeki no Kyojin/Titan*. AKA: *Advancing Giants*. TV series. DIR: Tetsuro Araki, Yoshiyuki Tanaka. SCR: Yasuko Kobayashi.

DES: N/C. ANI: Kyoji Asano. MUS: Hiroyuki Sawano. PRD: Wit Studio, Production I.G, MBS. 25 mins. x 25 eps.

It has been a hundred years since humanity was forced to retreat behind a series of defensive walls to protect itself from the grotesque, marauding giants known as the Titans. With unknown motives and a series of variant forms not unlike the Angels in EVANGELION, the Titans have suddenly renewed their assaults with increased vigor. The only thing that can stop them is a strike to a weak point at the back of their necks, a difficult prospect that has led the humans to develop Vertical Maneuvering Equipment. *Attack on Titan* follows the progress of a series of raw recruits, through early trauma, boot camp, and combat à la STARSHIP TROOPERS, as they prepare to avenge the deaths of their loved ones in the fall of the outermost of several concentric walls. In particular it focuses on Eren, a youth who eventually acquires a disturbing special power, leading to questions about the true natures of both friend and foe, and a consideration of motives that recalls the later reversals of GUNBUSTER.

With its depiction of a world under siege, and with a broadcast attended by game-spin-offs and novel prequels, *Attack on Titan* seems to have tapped into the zeitgeist of the early 21st century, attracting fans at both ends of the political spectrum, and plaudits and controversy in equal measure. Hong Kong viewers praised it as an inadvertent metaphor for the looming presence of the People's Republic in their daily lives; the South Korean press decried it for supporting a kill-or-be-killed mentality that played into the hands of the saber-rattling policies of the then–Prime Minister of Japan, Shinzo Abe. If anything, Hajime Isayama's original manga and the documentation around it seem to suggest yet another inspiration, of the sense in post-9/11, insular Japan that the world outside is not as walled-off as it first might appear to be (see also HOWL'S MOVING CASTLE and SUMMER WARS). A pair of live-action film adaptations, directed by Shinji Higuchi, were announced for summer 2015. Compare to SUNDAY WITHOUT GOD, which takes a wholly different stance on the end of days.

ATTACKER YOU!

1984. TV series. DIR: Kazuyuki Okaseko. SCR: Hideki Sonoda, Susumu Yoshida. DES: Jun Makimura, Teruo Kogure. ANI: Satoshi Kishimo. MUS: Shiro Sagisu. PRD: Knack, TV Tokyo. 30 mins. x 58 eps. (TV1), 25 mins. x 52 eps. (TV2).

Thirteen-year-old Yu Hazuki moves to Tokyo to be with her cameraman father. Bumping into volleyball star Nami Hayase on her first day at school, Yu joins the volleyball team and trounces the former champion with her brilliant abilities. Teaming up with Eri, an ace attacker, the trio try to realize their dreams of getting to the all-Japan finals.

Though there was a spin-off manga by Jun Makimura, *Attacker You!* was actually based on Shizuo Koizumi's novel *Now the White Ball Is Alive*. While its predecessor, **ATTACK NUMBER ONE**, romanticized school drama and camaraderie, *Attacker You!* concentrated on volleyball as a career in itself, making it less a **SPORTS ANIME** than a professional soap opera that happened to revolve around sports.

In 2008, amid excitement over the approaching Beijing Olympics, the series was remade by Tomoharu Katsumata and the Knack studio as the 52-episode *New Attacker You: Road to the Gold Medal* (*Zoku Attacker You: Kin Medal e no Michi*), featuring a Chinese setting and several Chinese cast members. Made as a TV series, it was dubbed and broadcast first in Chinese on Dalian TV, before being tardily released in Japan straight to video. At the time, this was a cunning way around Chinese import restrictions on "foreign" cartoons, although that loophole has since closed.

AURORA

2000. JPN: *Umi no Aurora*. AKA: *Marine Aurora*. Movie. DIR: Yoshinori Kanno. SCR: Michiru Shimada. DES: Katsuya Kondo, Katsuya Kondo. ANI: Satoshi Fujiwara. MUS: Masamichi Amano. PRD: Nippon TV. 91 mins.

An action thriller with overtones of *The Abyss* and *Sphere*—a 21st-century drilling team based at the bottom of the South Pacific is searching for age-old bacteria that can synthesize oil. The team finds it, but the glowing bacteria proves highly combustible in the oxygen-rich atmosphere and can eat through metal. Biologist Oshunru is aware of the potential danger and suspects the bacteria "wishes" to restore Earth to the primeval conditions that created it, wiping out all other life in the process. This hackneyed, predictable sci-fi thriller's CG origins merely make the characters more expressionless than usual. *Aurora* was billed as Japan's first full-length 3-D computer-animated movie, though **A.LI.CE** seems to qualify several months ahead of it.

AVENGER *

2003. TV series. DIR: Koichi Mashimo. SCR: Hidefumi Kimura, Mitsuhiko Sawamura, Satomi Sugimura. DES: Yukiko Ban, Kenji Teraoka. ANI: Minako Shiba, Mamoru Morioka, Tomoyuki Kurokawa. MUS: Ali Project. PRD: Bandai Visual, Bee Train, Production I.G. 25 mins. x 13 eps.

In the distant future, Earth has been destroyed and humanity survives in domed cities on Mars. Vital resources are dwindling, birth rates have fallen to zero (compare to **ARMITAGE III**), and the end of human civilization is in sight. Volk, the ruler of Mars, presides over a society where childlike androids or "dolls" have been created to fulfill the population's need for children. He exploits the people's need for a hero and the bread-and-circuses principle to make rationing a national sport. Scarce resources are awarded to the people of a residence dome if their champions defeat opponents in an arena. Meanwhile, warrior-woman Layla Ashley flees from Volk's minions with dollmaker Speedy and Nei, a doll regarded as the "child of destiny" by the government. Layla refuses to cooperate with Volk because he was the instigator of the purge that killed her family; she would prefer to avenge their deaths, in the arena or out, whichever works. **Ⓥ**

AWOL *

1998. TV series. DIR: Toshifumi Kawase. SCR: Koji Miura, Toshiyasu Nagata, Chika Hojo, Atsuhiro Tomioka. DES: Isamu Imakake, Wataru Abe. ANI: Yoshihiro Yamaguchi, Masahiko Murata. MUS: Shiro Hamaguchi, Kazuhiro Wakabayashi. PRD: BeStock, TV Tokyo. 25 mins. x 13 eps.

Turncoat scientist Dr. Culten turns off perimeter defenses around a military compound just long enough for the Solomon terrorist group to get in and steal several powerful PDB missiles. To demonstrate their zeal, the terrorists detonate one of the bombs, though they do not make any demands. Meanwhile, within the government, a scandal breaks out when it is discovered that Dr. Culten's secret orbital defense network, constructed without presidential approval, can be turned into a weapon and used against its makers. An elite team of commandos sets off to stop the Solomon terrorists before things can get any worse.

From early scenes of partygoers, lovers, and a child blissfully unaware that they are about to be blown to smithereens, to the introduction of a rookie character who might as well have "Dead Meat" tattooed on his forehead, *AWOL* is a low-rent Cold War thriller. Former X-Japan member Hide's theme song was the best-selling anime single of 1998, but this poor effort is otherwise doomed to obscurity. The fact that it's set in space amid a confederation of worlds seems like a last-minute idea designed to justify it as an anime production, though even the cost-cutting tactic of drawing the spaceships and explosions still falls down when faced with such a low budget as this. Given millions of dollars and a Hollywood star, this would have been just as bad, but it would have made it onto a thousand screens as a successor to *Broken Arrow* and *Under Siege*. In the anime world, however, it is simply below par, and few are likely to be fooled by half-hearted sci-fi design fudges like turning the Pentagon into a Triangle.

AYAKASHI

2007. TV series. DIR: Jun Takada. SCR: Takamitsu Kono, Tsutomu Kaneko. DES: Takashi Kobayashi, Koji Azuma, Koichi Kadoma. ANI: Kazuo Takigawa, Shinichi Miyamae, Takashi Kobayashi. MUS: Soshi Hosoi (hosplug). PRD: Tokyo Kids. 24 mins. x 12 eps.

Adapted from a 2005 visual novel (i.e., game, see **ARGOT AND JARGON**) by ApRicoT and Crossnet, *Ayakashi* is the story of a parasitic lifeform that gives superpowers to its hosts as it takes their human abilities, such as sight, and drains their lives in return. Schoolboy Yu, struggling to get over the death of a friend, is host to a powerful Ayakashi and pursued by those who want that power for themselves. A bloody conflict in which many innocents are killed unfolds as the mysterious Eimu does her utmost to keep him alive. Although designed to look portentous and edgy, with an unusual color palette and some interesting monster designs, the show fails the first test for an action adventure: the battles aren't very good. They're slow and fairly uninspired, and may send you back to the video shelf in search of a good old 1970s robot slugfest with no pretensions to cool, or to Hitoshi Iwaaki's rather similar manga *Parasyte*. The characters, especially the girls, also seem to change their views and allegiances with baffling and unexplained rapidity, and the breakneck pace of the story creates confusion.

AYAKASHI: SAMURAI HORROR TALES *

2008. JPN: ~ayakashi~ *Japanese Classic Horror*. AKA: *Ayakashi: Japanese Classic Horror*. TV series. DIR: Hidehiko Kadota, Tetsuo Imazawa, Kozo Nagayama, Kenji Nakamura. SCR: Chiaki Konaka, Yuji Sakamoto, Michiko Yokote. DES: Yoshitaka Amano, Hideki Ito, Yasuhiro Nakura, Takashi Hashimoto, Hiroshi Kato, Shinzo Yuki, Masami Abe. ANI: Hideki Ito, Yasuhiro Nakura, Takashi Hashimoto. MUS: Yasuharu Takanashi. PRD: Toei Animation, Asmik Ace Entertainment, Inc., Dentsu, Fuji TV, SME, Sky Perfect Well Think Co., Ltd. 30 mins. x 11 eps.

This is a TV anthology of three classic Japanese stories (HORROR AND MONSTERS). *Goddess of the Dark Tower (Tenshu Monogatari)* and *Yotsuya Horror Story (Yotsuya Kaidan)* run for four episodes each, with *Goblin Cat (Bakeneko)* running for three.

Oiwa Inari Tamiya Shrine are credited for collaboration on *Yotsuya Ghost Story*, one of the oldest and most-filmed Japanese ghost stories of all. Based on a play which was first performed in 1825, itself a version of a true story from the Edo period, it has been filmed more than 30 times, and adapted for live-action TV before being turned into anime. Long before the vengeful ghost-wife Oiwa inspired Sadako in the *Ring* movies, she inspired generations of artists including Hokusai and Kuniyoshi. Oiwa is the wife of masterless samurai Tamiya Iyemon, but he wants to be rid of her to marry his rich mistress. Hideously disfigured by poison, she meets a horrible end but returns to torment her faithless spouse until she finally gains her revenge. Since a string of disasters

struck a production of the play in 1976, it has been traditional for those presenting Oiwa's story to visit her grave in Tokyo and to set a place for her at all cast and crew gatherings. It is not known if the anime crew observed this custom but they all survived—just as well as they included major talents like writer Konaka and character designer turned international art superstar Yoshitaka Amano. Beautifully written and elegant as any theatrical version, this is a classic rendition of a classic tale.

Goddess of the Dark Tower is also based on a classic play, in which a falconer chasing hs master's lost hawk wanders into another realm where he becomes the beloved of a goddess. Art and design are used beautifully to distinguish between the human world, the fairyland of the goddesses, and the nebulous space where the two worlds meet. However, director Nagayama has trouble cramming the play's large cast and complex, suspenseful plot into two hours, and allows several plot holes to distract from the beauty of the animation.

The third episode, *Goblin Cat*, features a well-known Japanese folk character, but is an original story written specially for this compilation. It is the star of a strong collection, both in terms of story and of visuals. After making the relatively rare transition from production to directing, Nakamura had made a striking TV series, MONONOKE, with writers Yokote and Konaka. He used the same style and the same central character for *Goblin Cat*. The art and design are beautiful, striking, and unusual, with an impressive color palette and an air akin to sophisticated cut-paper animation. The story of a family haunted by a demon, and how the evil deeds that led to this are slowly uncovered, is so well told that it's as if a picture scroll has come to life. Wonderful creative touches, like the subtle emphasis on static backgrounds and the use of the sliding door as a device to end scenes, go unnoticed on first viewing, to be revealed as the story entices you back for more.

Three very different stories make up a quality package and a wonderful introduction to anime for anyone interested in Japanese FANTASY AND FAIRY TALES. The cast and crew are packed with top-notch talent. Listen particularly for the great Chikao Otsuka, then a year short of his 80th birth-

day, a veteran of anime and game voice roles since ASTRO BOY's TV debut in 1963, in *Goblin Cat*, and the luminous Mami Koyama as Oiwa in *Yotsuya Ghost Story*.

AYANE'S HIGH KICK *

1996. JPN: *Ayane-chan no High Kick*. Video. DIR: Takahiro Okao. SCR: Isa Shizuya. DES: Kazuo Tatsugawa. ANI: Kazuo Tatsugawa. MUS: Norio Inoue. PRD: Nikkatsu. 30 mins. x 2 eps.

Ayane secretly wants to be a female wrestler but is swindled into fighting as a kickboxer. Despite opposition from the ineffectual school principal (as if expulsion would scare this sports addict), Ayane throws herself into the world of professional martial arts, fighting off a roster of surprisingly stupid opponents, a large number of whom seem amazed that people actually get hurt in the ring.

Originally announced as a six-part series, *Ayane's High Kick* was canceled after only two episodes. To excuse the cartoonish design, the script tries to play for laughs, piling on dozens of Japanese sporting in-jokes that fall flat. What's left is a predictable rags-to-riches tale, ripping off TOMORROW'S JOE and AIM FOR THE ACE without any of their charm. The Japanese version relied heavily on a voice cast that included Yuko Miyamura (Asuka from EVANGELION, in another fiery red-haired role), but this was not enough to redeem it. Matters are not helped by a truly awful English-language dub that features a cast who cannot even pronounce each other's names, with only Debbie Rabbai as Ayane producing anything like a decent performance.

AZUKI-CHAN

1995. TV series. DIR: Masayuki Kojima. SCR: Shunichi Yukimuro. DES: Yoshiaki Kawajiri. ANI: Katsuyoshi Iizuka. MUS: Akira Tsuji. PRD: Madhouse, NHK2. 30 mins. x 117 eps.

When someone mispronounces her name at age eight, Azusa Nogami finds herself stuck with the nickname Azuki ("Red Bean"). Now in the fifth grade, she makes friends with a transfer student, Yunosuke, when he overhears another boy teasing her and can't help remembering such an original name. Azuki swiftly develops a crush on Yunosuke but doubts he will ever look at her as anything more than a friend, especially with the irritating Ken and Makoto eternally scheming to ruin everything for her.

Based on the comic serialized in *Naka-yoshi* by writer Tsukasa Akimoto and artist Chika Kimura, *Azuki-chan*'s timeless school romance has found great popularity across Europe and East Asia while preparing a whole generation back in Japan for the more cynical yet similarly entertaining high school antics of **HIS AND HER CIRCUMSTANCES**.

AZUMANGA DAIOH *

2002. TV series. DIR: Hiroshi Nishikiori. SCR: Ichiro Okochi. DES: Yasuhisa Kato. ANI: Takashi Wada. MUS: Masaki Kurihara. PRD: Genco, JC Staff, TV Tokyo. 6 mins. (m), 25 mins. x 26 eps./5 mins. x 130 eps. (TV).

Ten-year-old Chiyo Mihama is so bright she's skipped five grades and is just starting high school; but it will take more than genius-level brains and industrial-strength cuteness to survive the strange classmates and even stranger faculty. She joins Miss Yukari Tanizaki's English class and finds a teacher who loves drinking, snoozing, and video games. Yukari's best friend Minamo "Nyamo" Kurosawa teaches Phys. Ed., and seems very cool, except for her hidden fear that she'll never find a husband. Mr. Kimura, the classics teacher, lives in his

own little world and only emerges to gawk at the girls—the reason he took up teaching. The result is an enthusiastically nostalgic look at school days from the point of view of both teachers and students, over a three-year timescale that rockets past; with only five minutes per sequence, the seasonal events and examinations whip round before you know it. In hindsight, the series is regarded as one of the first, if not the first, of the **EVERYDAY ANIME**.

Half a dozen girls become Chiyo's friends and mentors, including the shy Sakaki, the nervous Osaka, and the overenthusiastic Tomo. The challenges of their school life have a strong vein of the surreal, and the series' humor is of the love-it-or-hate-it variety. Even Chiyo's cat starts talking, in a nod to **I AM A CAT**—just one of a slew of cultural and pop-cultural references buried in the madcap onslaught of gags. The format of the show is unusual—five unrelated segments in each episode, which were also broadcast as individual mini-episodes, give each of the multiple characters their own moment in the spotlight. They also tie in to the original format of Kiyohiko Azuma's manga, a four-panel strip in the tradition of **SAZAE-SAN** or *Peanuts*. Technically, the serial's first anime appearance was as a second feature

to the **SAKURA WARS** movie, when a frantic six-minute edit called *AD: The Very Short Movie* was screened as an advertisement for the forthcoming TV series. The series also had an online presence, in which mini-episodes with different voice actors were available for download. Based on the manga by Kiyohiko Azuma in *Dengeki Daioh* magazine, hence "Azu-manga Daioh."

AZUSA WILL HELP!

2004. JPN: *Azusa, Otetsudai Shimasu*. Video. DIR: Hajime Kamegaki. SCR: Yuko Kawabe. DES: Satoe Nakajima, Tomoya Hiratsuka. ANI: Tomoya Hiratsuka. MUS: Keita Shiina. PRD: Thomas Entertainment (Tokyo Movie Shinsha). 45 mins.

In the near future, when robots are used in many aspects of everyday life, the students of Karugamo High School decide that it's time for them to improve the performance of their baseball team by buying a robot player. However, in a cliché that goes all the way back to **DORAEMON**, they are unable to afford anything except a model designed to be a housemaid. Predictable sports, maid, underdog, and school high jinks ensue in an adaptation of a script by Yuko Kawabe, which won the second Animax screenplay contest—compare to **SUPER KUMA-CHAN**.

B-CHIKU BEACH: NANGOKU NYUJOKU SATSUEIKAI

2011. AKA: *B-Chiku Beach: Southern Land Breast Photography Club*. Video. DIR: Tomitake Jackal. SCR: Shida, Team NGX. DES: Kohaku Ragi. ANI: N/C. MUS: Hideki Yamamoto. PRD: T-Rex, Pink Pineapple. 30 mins.
Idol group Live un Veil announces a tour with fans to a sunny southern island. Nagisa, Nanami, and Kaede will pose for photos and hang out. Ryu has already applied for a place on the tour when he receives a mysterious package containing film, a ticket for the tour, and some sexy swimsuits. An anonymous letter indicates that if Ryu photographs the girls using this film, their libido will be uncontrollable. Naturally, Ryu decides to give it a try, and it works—the click of the camera makes all three girls slaves to their desires. A one-shot porn anime based on a game by CLOCKUP, whose other work includes DARK LOVE and *Requiem*, the game that inspired ANAL SANCTUARY. **N**

B'T X

1996. TV series, video. DIR: Mamoru Hamazu. SCR: Sukehiro Tomita, Yasushi Hirano. DES: Hideyuki Motohashi. ANI: Hideyuki Motohashi. MUS: Fence of Defense. PRD: TMS, TBS. 25 mins. x 25 eps. (TV), 25 mins. x 14 eps. (v).
Teppei's elder brother, the brilliant scientist Kotaro, is kidnapped by the forces of the evil Machine Empire, who have been lying in wait in the Gobi Desert for centuries. Local girl Karen, who turns out to be a rebel against the Machine Empire, has taken a sample from the body of Raphael, the last of the great "B't" (pronounced "Beat") devices.

Singled out by the cross-shaped scar on his forehead, the result of a childhood encounter with the Machine Empire, Teppei gains "X," the greatest of the B't machines. Teaming up with the riders/pilots of other B'ts built to resemble a dragon, a phoenix, and a turtle, he sets off to rescue his brother.

Masami Kurumada's earlier SAINT SEIYA also featured pretty boys and semimythical machines fighting to save the world. *B't X* wasn't quite as successful as its predecessor, only racking up a single TV series before coming off the air. A 14-episode sequel, *B't X Neo*, was directed by Hajime Kamegaki and released straight to video in 1997. That show's swift arrival and strange taxonomy (a total of 39 episodes making three complete seasons) prompted speculation that the "video" series was actually the unbroadcast remainder of an axed TV show. Other heroes similarly marked with the scars of destiny include the lead in RURONI KENSHIN, the lead characters of DARK MYTH and ARGENTO SOMA, and, most famously, Char Aznable from GUNDAM.

BABEL II *

1973. JPN: *Babel Nisei*. TV series, video. DIR: Takeshi Tamiya, Minoru Okazaki, Kazuya Miyazaki. SCR: Shunichi Yukimuro, Tomohiro Ando, Masaki Tsuji. DES: Shingo Araki, Teruo Kogure, Eimi Maeda. ANI: Shingo Araki, Teruo Kogure, Toshiyasu Okada. MUS: Shunsuke Kikuchi. PRD: Hikari Pro, TV Asahi, Toei. 25 mins. x 39 eps. (TV1), 30 mins. x 4 eps. (v), 25 mins. x 13 eps. (TV2).
In the distant past, a race of aliens lived in the Euphrates basin, where they built the "Three Servants"—Ropros, Rodem, and Poseidon—mighty beings designed to wipe out invading armies. Thousands of years later, when the ancient civilization has turned to dust, red-haired Japanese boy Koichi is troubled by strange dreams of the beautiful Juju, who eventually appears in the flesh and urges him to join a secret cabal of psychics led by Yomi, an alien prince.

When Koichi refuses, he is rescued by the Three Servants and taken to Mesopotamia, where he discovers that Yomi was the chosen inheritor of the powers of Babel. Now that Yomi has turned to the dark side, it falls to Koichi, a distant descendant of intermarriage between the aliens and humans, to put his nascent psychic powers to use defending Earth as the new inheritor, Babel II.

Based on the 1971 manga by Mitsuteru Yokoyama, creator of GIGANTOR and LITTLE WITCH SALLY, *Babel II* inspired an entire generation of creators, and its effects are still felt today, from the reluctant psychics of AKIRA to the biblical archeology of SPRIGGAN. It was reverse-engineered many times to create lesser robot/psychic shows in the marketing-led decades that followed. Selected parts were rushed onto tape with the coming of video, creating a nostalgic audience in Japan for the inevitable remake.

Yoshihisa Matsumoto's 1992 video version compresses the story into four 30-minute episodes and includes the events of Yokoyama's 1977 manga sequel *His Name Is No. 101*, in which Yomi returns and uses Koichi's blood to create an army of cloned soldiers. Released in an English-language version amid confusion over its origins (many buyers were put off when they couldn't find the nonexistent *Babel I*), the new *Babel II* looked too much like its imitators—original crew member Shingo Araki designed a new-look Koichi who lost his red mop in favor of the bland hero-template black hair, and the Three Servants with their air, land, and sea specialties looked like cheap copies of the same year's BEAST WARRIORS. Teruo Kogure, an animator on the original, also directed the erotic pastiche LUNATIC NIGHT. The TV remake *Babel II: Beyond Infinity* (2001) replayed the plot over 13 episodes.

BABUKA

2011. JPN: *BaBuKa Gokudo no Tsuma*. AKA: *BaBuKa Mob Wife*. Video. DIR: Ryo Himozakasa. SCR: Shinichiro Sawayama. DES: N/C. ANI: Ashi Chagun. MUS: N/C. PRD: MS Pictures, Koshaki Shiroganeze, Sachi Kokubu. 17 mins. (v1), 18 mins. (v2).
Created by MS Pictures' label Celeb, this short slice of porn about a woman involved with mobsters also had a follow-up episode, *BaBuKa Lady Social Worker—Hasukata Comes Second?* (*Minseiiin no Onna—Hasukata niban ja dame nandesuka?*). **N**

BABY AND ME

1996. JPN: *Aka-chan to Boku*. TV series. DIR: Masahiro Omori. SCR: Sukehiro Tomita, Kenji Terada. DES: Takayuki Goto, Yuji Ikeda. ANI: Yuji Moriyama. MUS: Kenji Kawai. PRD: Studio Pierrot, TV Tokyo. 25 mins. x 35 eps.
Thirteen-year-old Takuya Enoki faces unexpected challenges when his mother is killed in a car accident. Father Harumi has to spend extra time at the office, and Takuya becomes a surrogate parent for his two-year-old brother, Minoru. While he cares deeply for Minoru, the constant chores and attention can be very wearing. His father starts dating Miss Otani, but while Minoru happily believes she is his mother reborn, Takuya cannot come to terms with the idea. As time wears on, he comes to realize that it is *he* who has replaced his mother, and the love between the brothers grows stronger.
Based on Marimo Ragawa's long-running comic in *Hana to Yume* magazine, *Baby and Me* is often compared to SAZAE-SAN for its slice-of-life observations, but it also owes a certain debt to MAMA'S A FOURTH GRADER with its emphasis on impromptu parenting.

BABY FELIX AND FRIENDS *

2001. JPN: *Baby Felix*. TV series. DIR: Hiroshi Negishi. SCR: Yasunari Suda. DES: Shinichi Yoshino. ANI: N/C. MUS: N/C. PRD: Aeon, NHK Educational, SynergySP. 5 mins. x 130 eps.
A series of short children's cartoons featuring an infant version of the famous American cartoon character Felix the Cat, juvenilized for a new generation in the style of the earlier *Muppet Babies*, and tied in to a series of games and merchandise—presumably the Felix creators' attempts to grasp at the same franchise potential wielded by HELLO KITTY. A Japanese-American production featuring Felix's owners as producers.

BABY GRANDMA

2002. JPN: *Baby Baa-chan*. TV series. DIR: Shuji Kawakami. SCR: Katsuhiko Watanabe. DES: Hideaki Sakaguchi. ANI: N/C. MUS: Hitomi Kuroishi. PRD: Bandai Visual, NHK. ca. 7 mins. x 53 eps.
Amika cherishes a dream of becoming an idol singer, but for now she has a normal school life. Soon after her stern old grandmother dies, Amika's mother gives birth to a daughter. But as the child gets older, she seems to have inherited an incredible number of the old woman's traits.
Created by JINCO, this has baby-cute character design and art direction in cheerful primary colors, clearly signaling its intended audience, although the concept of a reincarnated bossy old woman taking over the soul of a newborn child may seem unsuitable children's entertainment to some Western parents. Broadcast as part of NHK's *Genius Terebi-kun Wide* show, and later reedited into longer video installments.

BABY LOVE

1997. Video. DIR: Susumu Kudo. SCR: Tomoko Konparu. DES: Takahisa Ichikawa. ANI: Takahisa Ichikawa. MUS: Hisashi Ito. PRD: Tokyo Movie Shinsha. 30 mins.
Seara Arisugawa has loved Shuhei Seto ever since she was a little girl. Back then, when the three-year age gap between them was a big deal, he told her to come back when she was older. But now that her parents are moving to America, she sees the chance to move in with him while she finishes school, and possibly realize her earlier romantic plan as well. However, Shuhei already has feelings for someone else, since he has developed a crush on his classmate Ayano. Ayumi Shiina's original comedy manga in *Ribon* magazine was another variant on the cohabiting would-be lovers of MARMALADE BOY, as friends and family offer a series of benign obstacles to Seara getting her man. The video was released midway through the manga's nine-volume run and first offered by mail order to *Ribon* readers. Compare to SAKURA DIARIES.

BABY PLEASE KILL ME! *

2012. JPN: *Kill Me Baby*. TV series. DIR: Yoshiki Yamakawa. SCR: Hideki Shirane, Ema Baba, Noboru Kimura, Ayumu Hisao. DES: Shinya Hasegawa, Teruhiko Niida. ANI: Masahiro Ando, Ryoichi Oki, Takaaki Fukuyo. MUS: EXPO. PRD: JC Staff, Pony Canyon, Hobunsha. 30 mins. x 13 eps.
A comedy about a schoolgirl assassin, animated in a cute style and based on a four-panel comic strip by Kaduho, this is more a string of rapid-fire gags in the style of stand-up comedy than anything else—drawing on the *manzai* tradition wherein a straight-man (or here, woman) grows increasingly exasperated with the clownish antics of her moronic colleague. The adventures of outgoing, friendly Yasuna and her Russian blonde best friend Sonya, whose training as an assassin often leads to broken limbs for her friends, are not exactly compelling, but if you're in the mood for some lightweight anime fun for your tablet or phone, they fit the bill. Of all the elements of production, it's the music that seems to have had the greatest attention to detail and effort lavished upon it, which perhaps explains why the big spin-off for this show was the music CD in 2013, bundled with a one-shot video episode on DVD.

BABY PRINCESS 3D PARADISE 0 [LOVE]

2011. Video. DIR: Takayuki Inagaki. SCR: Yuko Kakihara. DES: Yumiko Hara. ANI: Yumiko

Hara. MUS: N/C. PRD: Studio Comet. 30 mins.
Teenager Yotaro has always thought he was an only child. Then he meets his *real* mother and discovers that he has 19 half-sisters aged baby to 18. Despite the fact that until now he didn't know they existed, he moves in with his "true" family and into a ready-made harem (**ROMANCE AND DRAMA**) where his sisters are ready to welcome him as their extremely and inappropriately beloved brother. This goes beyond Lolita complex incest and into infant sexuality—every single sister except newborn Asahi is depicted as eager to flirt, kiss, and cuddle. The original series of illustrated stories book by Sakurako Kimino, creator of **SISTER PRINCESS**, began in 2007 as part of an interactive project—where readers could influence the progress of the plot—and ran until 2012. The BluRay edition came with 3D glasses and the regular DVD was 2D only, entitled *Baby Princess 2D Paradise 0.* **N**

BABY, MY LOVE

2004. JPN: *Aishiteruze Baby.* TV series. DIR: Masaharu Okuwaki. SCR: Genki Yoshimura. DES: Junko Yamanaka, Masatomo Sudo. ANI: Taiji Kawanishi. MUS: Miki Kasamatsu. PRD: Tokyo Movie Shinsha. 25 mins. x 26 eps.
Girl-crazy high school senior Kippei Katakura is asked to take care of five-year-old Yuzuyu Sakashita. The girl's mother has disappeared, reputedly overwhelmed by the prospect of rearing a child alone, and Kippei's family has taken Yuzuyu in. With a kindergarten kid to look after, Kippei's girl-chasing days are over, and his social whirl is replaced by taking Yuzuyu to school and making her lunch. The pair gradually develops a bond and Kippei comes to love the new girl in his life more deeply than any girlfriend he's ever had. The prospect of an unwitting step-parent is so commonplace on Japanese television that it is a rare manga on the subject that is adapted into anime; instead, it is more likely to be snapped up for live-action remakes such as the previous year's *Hotman* (*DE). In this case, however, Yoko Maki's original manga got the anime treatment, presumably because it was aimed at a slightly younger audience, as reflected in its original appearance in *Ribon* magazine. Compare to **BABY AND ME**.

BACCANO! *

2007. TV series. DIR: Takahiro Omori. SCR: Noboru Takagi. DES: Takahiro Kishida, Akira Ito. ANI: Atsushi Aono, Akira Takata, Kyoko Kotani et al. MUS: Makoto Yoshimori. PRD: Brains Base, Aniplex, MOVIC. 30 mins. x 16 eps.
Two hundred years after a group of alchemists summon a demon that can confer the elixir of immortality, the surviving sorcerers and their associates reconvene in a very different world. America in 1931, in the final throes of a decade of Prohibition (a period also visited in **BRYGAR** and **CHRONO CRUSADE**), is the perfect place to conduct a clandestine war over ancient magics, as underground societies contend with Mob bootleggers, and speakeasies turn out to be more than covers for mere alcohol.

Deriving its name from the Italian word for a ruckus or a racket, *Baccano* seemingly takes pride in the super-abundant chaos of its multiple intersecting storylines. The tale of the original 18th-century demon-summoning rubs shoulders with Prohibition-era gang killings, and the ill-fated hijacking of a transcontinental train, a girl's search for her lost brother, and several other initially unrelated plotlines, all presented out of order and out of context.

Original creator Ryogo Narita cites Brian di Palma's *The Untouchables* (1987) as a major influence on a tale that he seems to have initially conceived as bootleggers with additional magic—compare this with **FULLMETAL ALCHEMIST**, which similarly mixed alchemy with, eventually, connections to our mundane world. His original story was submitted as a competition entry while he was still a student, and did not gain the first of its 18 sequels (illustrated by Katsumi Enami) until after he graduated. A manga adaptation and a couple of drama CD spin-offs also followed, very much in the modern spirit of Japanese media that favors and values an entire sensory "world" rather than a particularly coherent story within that world. This may be at least partly responsible for a storyline whose author seems to be finding out the connections between disparate characters at the same rate as the viewer (see **BATTLE ANGEL** for a similar issue), and a creator that seems less interested in plot than in quirky, cool-looking actors, like a *Dungeons*

and Dragons player who endlessly generates new characters rather than starting a game. However, the screenwriters under Noboru Takagi seem to embrace this chaos, plumping for a twisty, non-linear narrative that owes more to the style and techniques of *Snatch* and *Pulp Fiction*, and which dares the viewer to keep watching in sheer bafflement. Sometimes it might feel like someone is unhelpfully switching channels on you, but the storyline eventually coalesces and largely resolves itself by the 13th episode. The three that follow were a video-only bonus tying up a few loose ends for the fans, but feeling like something of an anti-climax.

Against all the odds, *Baccano* makes a virtue of its complexity and wildly varying tone, which swings between comedy and gory violence, somehow negotiating entertainment and thrills out of a mess that could all too easily have had the opposite effect. **V**

BAD BADTZ-MARU

1995. Video. AKA: *Bad Badtz-maru Ore wa Yutosei.* DIR: Kazuya Murata. SCR: Kenji Terada. DES: N/C. ANI: N/C. MUS: N/C. PRD: Sanrio. 30 mins.
Badtz-maru, a tough-talking, naughty penguin, has a name formed from Japanese school terminology for right (*maru*) and wrong (*batsu*), as well as an old-fashioned suffix found in warriors' names—compare with **MAN-MARU THE NINJA PENGUIN**. But unlike his fellow Sanrio merchandise characters **HELLO KITTY** and **PEKKLE THE DUCK**, Badtz-maru's commercial success has come without attachment to an anime vehicle, and this one-shot video is his only solo outing. Clearly a pilot for a far longer offering, it features two short tales in which Badtz-maru proudly enters his pet crocodile in a contest and then goes off to learn how to be "a man." He also appeared with Hello Kitty in six video specials: *HK&BBM: Everybody Dance, Full of Playtime, Play Together, We Love Dance, Let's Dance,* and *Let's Origami.*

BAD BOYS

1993. Video. DIR: Osamu Sekita, Takeshi Yamaguchi. SCR: Kazuya Miyashita, Kaori Takada, Masayoshi Azuma. DES: Hiroshi Tanaka. ANI: Mitsuharu Kajitani. MUS: Hiroaki Yoshino. PRD: Toei. 40 mins. x 5 eps.

It's tough being a hard, streetwise member of a biker gang, especially if it's called the Paradise Butterflies and its goal is to be the baddest gang in … Hiroshima. Such is the lot of Tsukasa, Yoji, Eiji, and friends, boys determined to outgun the engines of every other biker in town. Hiroshi Tanaka's manga was originally intended to be a hard-hitting crime story of warring biker gangs, but he was unable to take the posturing seriously, and it eventually became a tongue-in-cheek pastiche of the genre popularized by **BOMBER BIKERS OF SHONAN**. It was serialized in *Young King* magazine from 1988, eventually running to 23 volumes. These video shows were released once yearly during the manga's final years to drum up interest—a damp squib manga finale ran for one volume in *Glare* magazine after the series was pulled from its original publication. Compare with *Shonan Pure Love Gang* (**GTO**).

BAGHI

1984. TV special. DIR: Osamu Tezuka, Kimiharu Ono. SCR: Osamu Tezuka. DES: Osamu Tezuka, Hitoshi Nishimura. ANI: Hitoshi Nishimura, Kazuhiko Udagawa. MUS: Kentaro Haneda. PRD: Toei, Sanrio, Goku, Nippon TV. 86 mins.

Ryosuke's father brings home Baghi, a small "kitten," unaware that she is really the cub of a sentient cougar, itself the result of experiments conducted by his estranged scientist wife, Dr. Ishigami. Baghi is the sole survivor of a breakout from a corporate animal research facility after an earthquake—Ryosuke's mother and her minions have rounded up and shot all other escapees, including Baghi's mother. Eventually, Baghi's strange intelligence attracts the attention of Ryosuke's neighbors, who pester her so much to perform tricks that she flees.

Some years later, a teenage Ryosuke rebels against his father and joins a biker gang, in which capacity he meets Baghi again. Now a full-grown cat-girl who walks on her hind legs and has an intelligence to match any human, Baghi slaughters the other gang members in a fight, but spares Ryosuke when she recalls his kindness to her in their youth. The couple goes in search of her origins. Clues lead to Ryo's mother's original science experiments. Tracking down her follow-up project in South America, the two arrive just in time for Baghi to become the prime suspect in Dr. Ishigami's murder. Baghi flees, and Ryo swears vengeance, becoming a big-game hunter to track her. Years later, Ryo is hired to shoot a wild animal that has been terrorizing villagers in the Amazon. It is Baghi, who only fled from Ryo because she feared that she was reverting to a feral state and wished to keep the man she loved from harm. It is revealed that Baghi is innocent, and that Dr. Ishigami was murdered by the dictator who funded her illegal research.

Ahead of his time as usual, Tezuka wrote this tale of genetic experimentation on animals for *Shonen Action*, the lead character named in homage to Bagheera as portrayed in Disney's version of Kipling's *The Jungle Book*. Though this synopsis has been reordered for clarity's sake, the film is told chiefly in flashback, as Ryo the hunter relates his story to a local boy, and then in flashback-within-a-flashback, as Ryo the investigator remembers how he first met his feline friend. The anthropomorphic appeal of cat-women would become an anime staple, from **CATGIRL NUKUNUKU** to **ESCAFLOWNE**'s kittenish Meryl, while Tezuka's cautionary zeal would even influence the story of the first **POKÉMON** movie, which featured a similar **FRANKENSTEIN** creation escaping from an Amazon stronghold.

BAKA AND TEST: SUMMON THE BEASTS *

2010. JPN: *Baka to Test to Shokanju*. AKA: *Idiots, Tests and Summoned Beasts*. TV series, video. DIR: Shin Onuma. SCR: Katsuhiko Takayama, Shin Onuma, Ayumi Sekine. DES: Miwa Oshima, Koji Azuma, Yoshifumi Sasahara, Yoshinari Saito, Ayumi Sekine. ANI: Miwa Oshima, Megumi Noda, Shuji Takahara, Kazuyuki Yamayoshi, Satomi Matsuura, Yuka Takamori. MUS: Nijine. PRD: SILVER LINK, Cospa, Lantis, Media Factory, T.O. Entertainment Inc., Hakuhodo DY Media Partners, Enterbrain, Kadokawa Contents Gate. 24 mins. x 13 eps. (TV1), 29 mins. x 2 eps. (v), 24 mins. x 13 eps. (TV2).

In a Japanese high-school system that is only *slightly* more rigorously tested and graded than that in the real world, entire classes are assigned a grade that affects their access to seating, facilities, and materials. Such a situation brings even greater pressure to bear on the students, who are now expected to do well not only for their personal betterment, but for the good of the group. But even no-hopers and slackers have the opportunity to help out, channeling their academic failure into achievements in a new arena, pitting mini-avatars against each other to win points and prizes.

It's easy to see where the wish-fulfillment element is in *Baka and Test*, offering a fantasy where one's proficiency at **POKÉMON** or **DIGIMON** was no longer a source of academic shame, but a grade-improving benefit (see also **OUTBREAK COMPANY**, where it can net the ideal job for the true fanboy). There's also an element of parent-appeasing hope—the fighting avatars' strengths are index-linked to students' test scores in particular subjects. Kenji Inoue's book series, illustrated by Yui Haga, featuring the hopelessly dim but lovable Akihisa, his best friend and class rep Yuji, and their fellow no-hopers in class F, launched in 2007. As well as the anime, there's an ongoing manga adaptation by Mosuke Mattaku and a computer game. The anime uses elements of the manga style, but otherwise relies for its charm on familiarity rather than innovation. Despite this, it warps some of the school story tropes very successfully, with amusing touches like the androgynous student who causes so much confusion with bathrooms and changing rooms that he is finally deemed to be a separate gender and given his own facilities. This is also a good-hearted anime: the main motivation for Akihisa's plot to raise the grades of the whole class is to help a straight-A student heartlessly assigned to their lowly class because she was sick at the time of the test.

A two-episode straight-to-DVD, *Baka and Test: Matsuri*, followed in March 2011, featuring the regulars at a traditional Japanese festival. Festival "specials" are almost compulsory for a successful high school series—the equivalent of the hot springs episode for harem shows—leading one to ponder whether these may serve as a substitute for the real thing among fans too shy to actually go to a local temple or town celebration (**EVERYDAY ANIME**).

BAKE!! JAPAN

2004. JPN: *Yakitate!! Japan*. AKA: *Fresh-Made Japan*; *King of Bread*. TV series. DIR: Yasunao Aoki. SCR: Katsuyuki Sumisawa. DES: Hiromi Maezawa, Atsuo Tobe, Yoshihito Hishinuma. ANI: Sunrise. MUS: Taku Iwasaki. PRD: Aniplex, D-rights, TV Tokyo, Sunrise. 25 mins. x 69 eps.

Country boy Kazuma Azuma leaves the family rice paddies and heads for Tokyo, intent on becoming the best baker in the world. His biggest asset is his "hands of the sun," a naturally warm pair of hands ideal for kneading dough and starting the rising process; compare to similar quasi-magical attributes in **BLACK JACK**. In a comedic revisitation of the tropes of **SPORTS ANIME**, Kazuma aspires to the crown currently held by Ken Matsushiro, the best baker in Japan, acclaimed for his French bread, despite the coolness denoted by his Afro hairdo and shades. But Kazuma has other would-be rivals: Kai Suwahara has studied bread-making methods from all over the world, and Kyosuke Kawachi has worked hard to master a technique known as "gauntlets of the sun" to make up for the warm hands he lacks. There's even a girl in the running—Tsukino Azusagawa, grand-daughter of the founder of renowned bakery chain Pantasia, where Kazuma enrolls to hone his skills and earn a crust. Note that *pan* is Japanese for bread, making Pantasia a pun, as is the "Japan" of the title, which is not the name of the country at all, but an Engrish rendering of "The Bread." Similar punning humor affects many episodes, sometimes making the series even harder to translate than other anime.

Food has long been a fetish for the Japanese, from the dessert fantasies of the deprived postwar era in **PRINCESS ANMITSU**, through to the epicurean obsessions of **OISHINBO**, and the infantile food fixation of **SLAYERS**. The date of the switch from famine-hunger to feast-enjoyment was arguably the release of Juzo Itami's bubble-era live-action movie *Tampopo* (1985), which subsequently inspired a number of gourmet manga and their live-action adaptations, including *Sommelier* (*DE) and *The Chef* (*DE). Takashi Hashiguchi's ongoing *Bake Japan* manga is an inheritor of this tradition, but ran in *Shonen Sunday* weekly, where its younger readership was more likely to see it adapted into an anime than a live-action show.

BAKEMONOGATARI *

2009. AKA: *Ghostory*, *Phantom Stories*. TV series, movie. DIR: Tatsuya Oishi, Akiyuki Shinbo, Tomoyuki Itamura. SCR: Fuyashi To, Yukito Kizawa, Muneo Nakamoto, Akiyuki Shinbo (TV2/3). DES: Akio Watanabe, Hisaharu Iijima. ANI: Akio Watanabe, Nobuhiro Sugiyama. MUS: Satoru Kosaki. PRD: SHAFT, Aniplex, Kodansha. 25 mins. x 15 eps. (TV1), 25 mins. x 11 eps. (TV2), 30 mins. x 4 eps. (TV3).

Koyomi Araragi is a third-year high school student and recovering vampire. He was cured by a middle-aged vagrant, Oshino, so when he discovers that a withdrawn and solitary girl in his class also has a supernatural problem, he introduces her to Oshino. Once her problem is solved, she agrees to become his friend, and later his girlfriend. But Koyomi also gets involved with a series of other girls, living and dead, each of whom has a different spectral issue that needs his help and Oshino's guidance. And then there's Shinobu, the vampire who attacked him, who now has the appearance of an eight-year-old girl.

With a bunch of pretty girls, each nurturing some sort of affliction, problem or hang-up that Koyomi has to cure, and usually immensely grateful for his assistance, *Bakemonogatari* swiftly turns into a supernatural harem show (**ROMANCE AND DRAMA**), with Koyomi as the competent fixer (compare to **CLANNAD**). But there's more to it than that—not all of the problems are simply resolved, and Koyomi is soon struggling with issues in ethics and responsibility that make his quest more than a simple set of box-ticking, girl-attracting good deeds. The clever use of language, with verbal and visual puns in Japanese, has made the series difficult to translate, but even in its English incarnation the dialogue is witty and packed with character development. The characters are well-balanced, with a realistic mix of cruelty and pettiness amid the good, and Shaft's animation makes a virtue of the limitations of TV anime, playing with text and color to create a fresh, vibrant screenscape. Fan service, questionable behavior verging on molestation, and brief, intensely bloody action scenes are part of the mix. Only the first 12 episodes were aired on the original TV run; the final 3 were released on the series website. These are therefore, strictly speaking, "Original Net Animation."

A portmanteau constructed from the Japanese words for ghost or monster and story, *Bakemonogatari* is based on a series of books by Nisio Isin, illustrated by the Taiwanese artist VOfan. The series currently runs to 16 volumes, with a PC "visual novel" (**ARGOT AND JARGON**), drama CD, and merchandise spin-offs. A second anime TV series, *Nisemonogatari* (*Phony Story*) followed by spring 2012. Its name, also a portmanteau word, leads us to expect twisted tales of people who are fakes in many more ways than might at first appear, and in this it doesn't disappoint, but the material seems thin and stretched in comparison to the first series. It veers further into sexually dubious territory, and tosses in another kind of fan service, with homages to other anime including **AKIRA** and **CONAN THE BOY DETECTIVE**. The end of 2012 saw a four-part TV series, *Nekomonogatari (Kuro)* (*Cat Story [Black]*) in which one of Koyomi's friends is possessed by a demon cat—compare to the superior "Bakeneko" in **AYAKASHI: SAMURAI HORROR TALES**. A second season, adapting five more volumes of the book series across two dozen episodes, followed in summer 2013. **Ⓥ**

BAKEGYAMON

2006. TV series. DIR: Hiroshi Negishi. SCR: Kazuho Hyodo, Masaharu Amiya, Masaki Hiramatsu, Tatsuto Higuchi, Yasutomo Yamada. DES: Tomoyuki Abe, Tsutomu Ishigaki. ANI: N/C. MUS: Kazunori Miyake. PRD: Radix, Dentsu, TV Tokyo, Wedge Holdings, Digital Network Animation. 30 mins. x 51 eps.

Sanshiro Tamon is a kid living on a small island, with nothing much happening until a mysterious man invites him to play a "backward game." Sanshiro is transported to a universe where monsters are pitted against monsters and where he is invited to be one of the players. The winner is granted a wish, although Sanshiro's chances do not look good, when the "monster" he is initially assigned is little more than a few lumps of mud.

You would be forgiven for thinking that this **KIDS' ANIME** was some sort of cynical exercise in reverse-engineering the context-integrated marketing of POKÉMON, with a bored youth lured into a form of sports-combat using "monsters." And you might be right, although this is based on a 2006 manga by Kazuhiro Fujita and Mitsuhisa Tamura, and retains some shadows of the former's USHIO AND TORA. Negishi's name on a credit listing always lifts the heart, because he does a thoroughly honest and competent job with whatever script he's given, and sometimes—as with the underrated JUDGE or BEAST WARRIORS—creates something truly remarkable. Both Fujita and Negishi seem like disproportionately heavy hitters for an obscure kids' anime without a notably large merchandising push behind it; perhaps this was intended to be something more, although 51 episodes in the 21st century is a sign of significant, quiet success, or at the very least, investment in the hope of it.

BAKUGAN BATTLE BRAWLERS *
2008. TV series. DIR: Mitsuo Hashimoto, Takao Kato. SCR: Atsushi Maekawa, Deco Akao, Katsumi Hasegawa, Natsuko Takashahi, Sayaka Harada, Yasunori Yamada, Sumio Watake, Tatsuo Higuchi. DES: Yoshihiro Nagamori, Eiji Iwase, Yoshihiro Nagamori, Submarine Inc, Tsukasa Ohira. ANI: Noriyuki Fukuda, Yoshihiro Nagamori, Mitsuo Hashimoto. MUS: Takayuki Negishi. PRD: Japan Vistec, TMS Entertainment, Maxpire entertainment, Dentsu, Sega, Shogakukan Music & Digital Entertainment. 25 mins. x 52 eps. (TV1), 25 mins. x 52 eps. (TV2), 25 mins. x 39 eps. (TV3), 25 mins. x 46 eps. (TV4), 5.5 mins. x 51 eps. (TV5), 5 mins. x 39 eps. (TV6).
Dan and his friend Shun become part of a group of kids playing a new game, based on collectible cards but also playable online. Nobody suspects that the cards have been released into our world from another dimension, and can summon monsters. Evil forces are seeking to destabilize the balance of the worlds for their own ends. Unless Dan and his friends can stop them, the world they know might end forever.

Like POKÉMON before it, Bakugan is founded on the constant fascination of trading, collecting, and playground one-upmanship. Originated by Sega Toys, this franchise was carefully targeted at the pocket-money market from the start. Its success can be judged by the extensions to

the series, which functioned as context-integrated advertisements for the game, video games, toys, manga, and promotional spin-offs that followed. Many highly successful empires have been built, within and outside anime, for childen of all ages, on the need to catch 'em all, whether the objects are cards, models, or game levels. Bakugan is a thoroughly well-researched, well-constructed professional product that does exactly what it needs to do to keep elementary school children gaming and buying. It's pointless to criticize it because it does nothing more.

A second series, Bakugan New Vestroia, was aired in 2009. It was scheduled for 26 episodes in Japan, but Canadian network Teletoon asked for an additional 26 episodes—which just goes to show, even in anime's supposed late-noughties doldrums, there were still occasional demands for more product. Cartoon Network made an "episode 0" special, Maxus Unleashed, recapping the first 26 episodes for online screening. The third series Gindalian Invaders aired in Japan in 2010, with an additional group of screenwriters pulled in to assist Maekawa, and tied into the online game Bakugan Dimensions using heat-reveal codes on the toys. The fourth series Mechtanium Surge, also originally set for 26 episodes but later extended at Nelvana Entertainment's request, was successful in the U.S., Canada, and Taiwan, but not aired in Japan.

However, the Bakugan story isn't over in Japan. A spin-off manga entitled Baku Tech! Bakugan by Shingo Maki began running in CoroCoro Comic in 2010 and is ongoing. It was animated in 2012, with Takao Kato directing. A second Japanese series, Baku Tech! Bakugan Gachi, aired in April 2013 as part of the TV show Oha Coro, suggesting a divergence of content in different language territories, akin to that manifested in other franchise shows such as TRANSFORMERS.

BAKUMAN *
2010. TV series. DIR: Kenichi Kasai, Noriaki Akitaya. SCR: Reiko Yoshida, Seishi Minakami, Tsutomu Kamishiro, Yuniko Ayana. DES: Tomoyuki Shitaya, Chikako Shibata. ANI: Tomoyuki Shitaya, Mai Matsuura, Atsushi Komori, Yumi Nakayama. MUS: Audio Highs. PRD: JC Staff, NHK Enterprises, Shogakukan,

Shueisha. 24 mins. x 25 eps. (TV1), 25 mins. x 25 eps. (TV2), 25 mins. x 25 eps. (TV3).
A manga from the team that created DEATH NOTE—writer Tsugumi Oba and artist Takeshi Obata—was always a likely candidate for anime adaptation. This one, however, is a very different story, tapping into the self-referential world of anime and manga about anime and manga. Like its megahit precursor, Bakuman starts with a bright kid noticing a notebook, although it then diverges far from its predecessor. Teenager Akito picks up his classmate's forgotten sketchbook and is stunned by the drawings inside. He asks Moritaka to draw the panels for his manga stories. But Moritaka has reasons for keeping his dreams under cover. In a sly nod to the washed-out elders of many a SPORTS ANIME, his uncle, a once-successful artist who slid down in the popularity ratings, died from overwork trying to regain his lost readers with a new hit. However, when the girl he desires reveals her dream of being a voice artist, Moritaka agrees to create manga with Akito, under the pen name of Muto Ashirogi.

Solidly grounded in reality, the characters and situations of the manga and anime ring true. Most Japanese teens put aside their dreams and abandon manga or keep it as a hobby; most creators don't make it to the top; even those who do sometimes have only a brief time in the sun before their readers and editors abandon them. The animation is competent but not daring; the plot twists may not be as gripping as in Death Note, but the fears, hopes, and dreams of young artists starting out on a road that never really gets easier are realistically described. The show was convincing enough to get a second series, Bakuman 2, in 2011, and Bakuman 3 followed in autumn 2012, six months after the manga ended. For a lighter look at similar material, see MANGIRL.

BAKUMATSU SPASIBO
1997. JPN: Bakumatsu Spasibo. Movie. DIR: Satoshi Dezaki, Kenichi Maejima. SCR: Shigeo Nakakura. DES: Keizo Shimizu, Setsuko Shibuichi. ANI: Keizo Shimizu, Setsuko Shibuichi. MUS: Kazuya Moroboshi. PRD: Magic Bus, Toho. 85 mins.
The true story of the arrival of the Russian

commander Putyatin in 19th-century Japan during the last days of the shogunate (JPN: *Bakumatsu*). Japan had been closed to the outside world for 200 years, and the arrival of the warship Diana was to cause a major commotion in the sleepy seaside villages. After making friends with the Japanese during treaty negotiations, the Russians are left stranded when their ship runs aground during an 8.4 magnitude earthquake. The Japanese bring help to the beleaguered Russians, who leave with a grateful "thank you" (*spasibo*). The timing of the production suggests it was inspired by the Kobe earthquake in 1995. See also **THE DAY THE EARTH SHOOK.**

BALATACK
1977. JPN: *Chojin Sentai Baratack*. AKA: *Superman Combat Team Baratack*. TV series. DIR: Nobutaka Nishizawa, Kazumi Fukushima. SCR: Masao Maruyama. DES: Kazuo Komatsubara. ANI: Kazuo Komatsubara, Masami Suda. MUS: Akihiro Komori. PRD: Toei Animation, TV Asahi. 25 mins. x 31 eps.
Emperor Shaiden of Shaizack, ruler of the star Epsilon, sends his fleet to Earth to seek peaceful scientific collaboration. In Japan, Professor Kato is developing a time machine, and Shaiden wants both planets to share the development process and the benefits. But his commander, Goldeus, betrays the Emperor's trust and transforms the scientific expedition into an invasion fleet. He declares himself sole commander, and kidnaps Professor Kato's wife Mia and younger son Jun to force his cooperation. But he reckons without the professor's other son, 15-year-old Yuji. Yuji is a brave, impulsive kid who loves American football, motorbikes, and his family. He and his four friends all have powers of ESP, and they band together to pilot Professor Kato's giant robot, Balatack, to defeat the alien invaders, free Yuji's mother and brother, and save the Earth. So far, so predictable, a giant robot show with five teenagers of different types (including the token girl, cute blonde Yuri), an evil and repellent villain with an eyepatch and a big wart on his nose, and even a noble adversary in the shape of Julius, the only member of the Shaizack fleet who opposes Goldeus. However, *Balatack*, made by many of the same crew who had just finished **MAGNOS,** is notable in the history of robot

anime for being the first to introduce true comedy. Goldeus the selfish commander and his sniveling sidekick Captain Gael provide much-needed slapstick and subversive comedy dialogue, particularly in Goldeus' infamous proclamation that he wants (a) the conquest of Earth, and (b) a panda. He wasn't alone in the 1970s—see **PANDA GO PANDA** for further details. **Ⓥ**

BALDR FORCE EXE *
2006. JPN: *Baldr Force Exe Resolution*. Video. DIR: Takashi Yamazaki. SCR: Hiroshi Onogi. DES: Hideki Yamazaki, Satoru Utsunomiya. ANI: N/C. MUS: Takeshi Watanabe. PRD: Satelight, Trinet Entertainment. 30 mins. x 4 eps.
Toru Soma was formerly one of a team of hackers called Steppen Wolf, who plundered the Web for data to sell to the highest bidder. But when the group disbanded after the death of his friend and leader, he was still hungry for revenge and facing a long prison sentence. To deal with both issues, he joined FLAK, a military organization set up by the United Nations to defend a hidden data realm deep within the most protected servers. He's still out for revenge, but now he also has to help his new team prevent an extremist group from destroying the wired world.
Sticking close to the plot of the computer game *Baldr Force*, released in multiple formats between 2002 and 2007 by GIGA, this short video anime series revamps a number of basic SF concepts, which may lead fans of .**HACK** and **SERIAL EXPERIMENTS LAIN** to feel they've seen it all before in better detail, and with better plot and characters. In keeping with the more liberal restrictions on video, the violence is quite extreme, and although the promised nudity is confined to one scene, there is a very nasty rape sequence for which virtual reality is no excuse. **ⓃⓋ**

BALTHUS: TIA'S RADIANCE *
1988. JPN: *Balthus: Tia no Kagayaki*. Video. DIR: Yukihiro Makino. SCR: N/C. DES: Yukihiro Makino, Shoji Furuta. ANI: Shinnosuke Kusama. MUS: N/C. PRD: Kusama Art, Cosmos Plan (Uchuu Kikaku), Media Station. 30 mins.
In the factory-city of Balthus, human workers are little more than slaves to the ruling overlord, Morlock. Eud is a young boy in the resistance, part of a plot to use the war-

rior-robot Klaatu to defeat Morlock. The resistance fails, and when his coconspirator, Alphonse, is killed, Eud is hidden by Alphonse's beautiful sister, Tia. Both are captured by Morlock, and Eud is thrown into the dungeon. Tia is ravished by the sadistic overlord and taunted with the news of her brother's death, until she is saved in the nick of time by Eud, and both are saved by the timely arrival of Klaatu.
More from the people who brought you **LEGEND OF LYON,** in a frantically rushed erotic pastiche of the same year's **CASTLE IN THE SKY,** but with a fraction of the budget, talent, or commitment. It also features a pointless musical interlude from an off-key vocalist when it badly needs the time for matters of greater importance, such as plot—or, indeed, a little more sex. Sprinkled with sly references to great science fiction, including Morlock (*The Time Machine*), Klaatu (*The Day the Earth Stood Still*), and a plot that crashes *Metropolis* into a porno film. Only in anime! **Ⓞ**

BAMBOO BLADE *
2007. TV series. DIR: Hisashi Sato. SCR: Hideyuki Kurata. DES: Yukichi Namiyanagi (pseud. for Naoto Hosoda), Maho Takahashi. ANI: Yoichi Ueda. MUS: Kiyohiko Senba. PRD: AIC A.S.T.A., d-rights, Flying Dog, Square Enix, The Klockworx. 25 mins. x 26 eps.
Teacher Toraji "Kojiro" Ishida is flat broke, barely subsisting on his paychecks. He's also Muroe High School's *kendo* coach, at least on paper, although his club currently only has one member. Rashly accepting a bet from his mentor Ishibashi that five of his girls can beat five of Ishibashi's, he faces the prospect of eating free for a year at the Ishibashi family sushi restaurant, if only he can somehow assemble a group of no-hopers and fashion them into an unbeatable *kendo* team.
The tropes of **SPORTS ANIME** have been well-established since **STAR OF THE GIANTS,** but Masahiro Totsuka and Aguri Igarashi's comedy manga ran from 2004–10 in *Young GanGan* magazine, seemingly lifting many newer clichés from **EVERYDAY ANIME** such as **AZUMANGA DAIOH.** Whereas a salacious harem show might have made more of the idea of a young male in loco parentis, *Bamboo Blade* instead emphasizes the positive effects that membership in the *kendo* club has on its members. Aimed at cynical,

apathetic modern teens more likely to prize thumb-twiddling games and solitary pursuits, it makes a strong case for community spirit and the various, different ways that club membership and exercise make the girls' lives better. As with **SLOW STEP**, this charming, involving show also gently suggests that their mentor gains his own form of redemption and self-worth, and the characters learn as much from losing as winning. Trivia freaks will note that not only are many of them named for real-life *kendo* champions, but also that one of them is a fan of rubber-monster sci-fi TV and the show-within-a-show *Cho Ken Sentai Blade Braver* is remarkably similar to the *tokusatsu* classic *Akumaizer 3.*

BANDAI NAMCO

A conglomerate formed in 2005 by the merging of Namco and Bandai. Namco was founded as a mechanical toy company in 1955, trading as Nakamura Manufacturing until 1972. It acquired the Japanese division of Atari in 1974, bringing it into the coin-operated arcade market and leading to the creation of many games, including *Pac-Man* and *Final Lap.*

Bandai began as a toy company in 1950, subsequently becoming a powerful player in anime through its sponsorship of children's television shows—it was highly instrumental in the introduction and constant recycling of robot toy designs that led to shows such as **BRAVE SAGA**, **GUNDAM**, and **TRANSFORMERS** and the ubiquitous live-action franchise *Mighty Morphin' Power Rangers* (*DE). Bandai subsequently set up its own animation division, Bandai Visual or "Emotion"—the name is a pun on "E," Japanese for picture, and "Motion"— whose distinctive Easter Island heads logo can be found on many anime aimed at older teens. In 1997, the company initiated its Digital Engine project, designed to conceive new anime as the nexus of a series of multimedia franchises incorporating games, manga, and other spin-offs. Although this largely repeats the production committeee synergies of earlier decades, it represented substantial progress in developing the now-common "media mix" aspect of many modern anime. Subsidiaries include the Sunrise animation studio, Happinet, and formerly Ashi Pro (now Reed Productions).

BANDAR BOOK: ONE MILLION A.D. *

1978. JPN: *Bandar Book: Hyakuman-nen Chikyu no Tabi.* AKA: *Bandar Book: One Million Year Earth Journey; Bander Book; Bander's Book.* TV special. DIR: Hisashi Sakaguchi. SCR: Osamu Tezuka. DES: Hisashi Sakaguchi. ANI: Hitoshi Nishimura. MUS: Yuji Ono. PRD: Tezuka Pro, Nippon TV. 86 mins. Shortly before an explosion tears their spacecraft apart, Professor Kudo's wife places their newborn son in an escape capsule. The baby drifts across space and eventually lands on planet Zobi, where he is adopted by the ruling prince as his own. The Zobians can shapeshift at will, and the young Prince Bandar is teased for his inability to do so. Years later, a grown Bandar agonizes as to whether his "handicap" should disqualify him from marrying Princess Mimulu. His world is attacked by the space pirate Black Jack, and he and Mimulu are captured. Dumped by Black Jack on another world, the distraught Bandar believes Mimulu to be dead. Teaming up with shapeshifting steed Muzu, he rescues the beautiful princess Marina, who is being held prisoner by Dracula and the Cyclops. Taking Marina to her homeworld, Bandar is betrayed by a Terran military adviser, Dokudami, who has Prime Minister Hamegg throw him in jail. There he is helped by Sharaku, a scientist who has patented a scheme of extracting hatred from people's souls and bringing peace. Bandar escapes, but Dokudami steals Sharaku's distilled Elixir of Evil and threatens to scatter it. He is stopped by the timely arrival of Black Jack, who has discovered that he is Bandar's long-lost elder brother. The new allies pursue the fleeing Dokudami through hyperspace back to prehistoric Earth, where his ship crashes and scatters evil throughout the atmosphere. Using Black Jack's time machine (built with the proceeds of piracy), the group returns and destroys the totalitarian computer that had ordered their father killed. Black Jack is killed in the final conflict, and a dying Marina reveals that she is really a chlorophyll life-form whose final stage is a tree. Muzu reveals that she is really Mimulu, adopting a disguise to be close to the man she loves. Earth is finally at peace, and Bandar sits with Mimulu beneath the tree that has grown from what was once Marina.

This anime featured several cameo ap-pearances by characters from other Tezuka stories, including **BLACK JACK**, Hamegg from **KIMBA THE WHITE LION**, Sharaku the **THREE-EYED PRINCE**, **ASTRO BOY** in a crowd scene, and Professor Ochanomizu as a servant to Dracula. There are also walk-on visual parodies of Edward G. Robinson, and Linda Blair, who played the possessed girl in *The Exorcist.* First broadcast during the 24-hour NTV Super Special commemorating the 25th anniversary of Tokyo's fourth TV channel, it became the first of a series of annual Tezuka TV specials for NTV, including later, similarly cameo-riddled productions such as **MARINE EXPRESS**, **FUMOON**, **BREMEN 4**, **PRIME ROSE**, **BAGHI**, and **GALAXY SEARCH 2100**.

BANNERTAIL THE SQUIRREL *

1979. JPN: *Risu no Banner.* AKA: *Banner the Squirrel.* TV series. DIR: Yoshio Kuroda. SCR: Toshiyuki Kashiwakura. DES: Yasuji Mori. ANI: Seiji Okuda, Tatsuo Ogawa. MUS: Akihiro Komori. PRD: Nippon Animation, TV Asahi. 23 mins. x 26 eps.
Banner is captured by humans and raised by a domesticated cat, whom he believes is his real mother. Separated from his "parent" by a village fire, he meets a stray cat who tells him the truth—he is a squirrel. Going back to his original home in a New Jersey forest, Banner meets a female of the same species called Sue, who helps him get back to his squirrel roots.

The second of **SETON'S ANIMAL TALES** series to be animated (the first was **MONARCH: THE BIG BEAR OF TALLAC**), *Bannertail* was to be the most successful. The series was notable at the time for the large number of cels used in the animation— a successful attempt to impart realistic motion to the animals. The story received a very limited U.S. subtitled broadcast on some Japanese community TV stations shortly after its Japanese release, much to the annoyance of anime fans expecting more giant robots.

BAOH *

1989. JPN: *Baoh: Raihosha.* AKA: *Baoh: The Visitor.* Video. DIR: Hiroyuki Yokoyama. SCR: Kenji Terada. DES: Michi Sanaba, Masayoshi Tano. ANI: Michi Sanaba, Jin Kaneko. MUS: Hiroyuki Nanba. PRD: Toho, Studio Pierrot. 50 mins.
Seventeen-year-old Ikuro is implanted with

BAOH, an experimental organism that will defend itself and its host at all costs. Escaping from the Doress corporation with the telepathic girl Sumire, he returns to rescue her when she is recaptured by the evil Dr. Kasuminome.

One of many psychic espionage stories rushed straight to video in the wake of AKIRA, *Baoh* takes the well-traveled route of symbiotic weaponry in the style of GUYVER, relegating telepathic powers to the possession of a supporting character. A violent, visceral show prefiguring GENOCYBER, it also features mid-combat posturing in the style of martial arts movies, as characters pause to announce their next "special move" before striking. Hirohiko Araki's original manga in *Shonen Jump* only lasted for two volumes in 1984, though the creator would find more enduring success with JOJO's BIZARRE ADVENTURES. **ⓥ**

BAREFOOT GEN *
1983. JPN: *Hadashi no Gen*. Movie. DIR: Mori Masaki. SCR: Keiji Nakazawa. DES: Kazuo Tomizawa. ANI: Kazuo Tomizawa. MUS: Kentaro Haneda. PRD: Gen Pro, Madhouse. 83 mins. (m1), 85 mins. (m2).
It's 1945, Japan is losing the war, and times are particularly hard for Gen's pacifist family. Gen, only six years old, has had to grow up fast, and each day is a struggle to get enough food for his pregnant mother, older sister Eiko, and younger brother Shinji. Then the Allies drop a new kind of bomb on Gen's hometown of Hiroshima. People are vaporized by the intense blast, but in a way, they are the lucky ones. Gen's house collapses on its occupants, and he and his mother cannot lift the rubble off their family. Forced to watch their loved ones burn alive, they wander through a world in which survivors succumb to the effects of radiation poisoning, their hair falling out and their bowels bleeding away.

A hard-hitting tale of the horrors of war based on Keiji Nakazawa's 1973 manga, *BG*'s only shortcomings lie in the nature of the original material. Since it is semiautobiographical, it chronicles events instead of subsuming them to a narrative—the bombing of Hiroshima is the central event of Nakazawa's life and work, but once past the immediate aftermath, the film falls into a selection of vignettes. This style was used to better effect in GRAVE OF THE

FIREFLIES, where such scenes denoted the characters' slow decline, but since the hero of *BG* survives, the use of these scenes in this film often seems to depict the passing of time for its own sake. Nevertheless, *BG* is a terrifying snapshot of one of the most horrific events in human history, perhaps all the more harrowing because it is presented in the cartoon medium so often associated with children's entertainment.

A 90-minute sequel by future RAIL OF THE STAR–director Toshio Hirata followed in 1986. Set three years later, it continues the story as Gen tends to his mother with his adopted little brother Ryuta, who also lost his family in the bombing. The film was twice revived as a part of TV specials with a nuclear subject—1992's *Never Forget BG: A Promise to the Children of Chernobyl*, and again in 1995, the 50th anniversary of Hiroshima, when it was shown along with the live-action/CG pieces *Our Playground Was the Genbaku Dome* and *From Hiroshima to America*. Nakazawa's Hiroshima was also the subject of BENEATH THE BLACK RAIN; HIT HARD, DREAMERS! and the setting for his feature-length 45th-anniversary video, *The Summer with Kuro*, in which a black cat charms the lives of two Hiroshima children. Curiously, the devastation at Nagasaki received palpably less coverage in anime. *Goodbye to Mother's Perfume* (1995), told the story from the point of view of a 15-year-old apprentice cook, and was released on the 50th anniversary of the bombing. *Nagasaki 1945: The Angelus Bell* (2005) was made for the 60th, concentrating on a bell from the city's cathedral, that was recovered from the ruins and rung each year on the anniversary.

BARK, BUNBUN
1980. JPN: *Hoero Bunbun*. Movie, TV series. DIR: Shigeru Omachi. SCR: Yuji Amemiya, Akira Nakahara. DES: Moribi Murano. ANI: Eiji Suzuki, Yasuhiko Suzuki, Yasuo Mori. MUS: Kazuhito Mori. PRD: TV Tokyo, Wako Pro. 84 mins. (TVm), 30 mins. x 39 eps. (TV), 65 mins. (m).
Bunbun the mastiff puppy climbs into a wooden box and floats down the river, eventually drifting into Tokyo. There he meets a stray dog who teaches him "the commandments"—how to live life without human interference. Based on a manga by former MOOMINS animator Moribi Murano,

the plot and timing of this anime suggest a jump to TV in the wake of the success of BANNERTAIL THE SQUIRREL. An initial TV movie was followed six months later by a TV series with the same cast and crew. In 1987, Bunbun returned in a theatrical release directed by Toshio Hirata and animated by the Madhouse Studio.

BAROM ONE
2002. TV series. DIR: Tsuneo Tominaga. SCR: Narumitsu Taguchi. DES: Manabu Nakatake. ANI: Akemi Hosono, Hironobu Saito. MUS: Hiroshi Motokura. PRD: AT-X, Saito Pro. 25 mins. x 13 eps.
Kopu, personification of light, has been watching over our world for eons; the evil Gomon, personification of darkness, is sealed in sleep, but in the 21st century a major gravitational shift caused by a rare planetary alignment wakes its minions, spelling disaster for mankind. Kopu chooses two human boys, born on the same day, and imprints them with the power to fight Gomon. Kentaro Shiratori and Takeshi Kido grow up as close friends, with complementary abilities: one very clever, the other very strong. Not even their love for the same girl, classmate Yuko, can separate them. On their birthday Kopu appears to the teenagers and tells them they will secretly transform into powerful robot Barom One to save their world, starting by battling a giant stray dog-monster attacking Taiyo City. Takeshi takes to being Barom One like a duck to water; Kentaro isn't so keen until Gorom possesses his father's old car and turns it into a monster to attack him. The boys fight off a monkey monster at the zoo, Hercules beetle monsters in a petshop, and a Venus flytrap monster on a school trip. They only deal with this last threat after it has eaten some obnoxious kids, which gives Kentaro a crisis of conscience—shouldn't they save bad people along with good ones? Meanwhile Kentaro's mother Mariko analyzes the monsters' DNA and connects them with a local lake, and Gomon's plotting gets Barom One blamed for a mysterious earthquake that rocks Japan. When their loved ones are kidnapped, Kentaro and Takeshi have no choice but to blow their cover and come out fighting to save those they love as well as the rest of the world.

Barom One began life as a manga by

GOLGO 13–creator Takao Saito, before being adapted into a 35-episode live-action TV series in 1972 (*DE). This anime incarnation was ostensibly put into production to mark the 30th anniversary of the original—although it is likely that cause and effect were reversed, since producers at the time were desperate for remakes of old shows, regarding them as safer bets in the impecunious early 21st century than any original ideas. The story has more in common with Yokoyama's **BABEL II** or Tezuka's **AMBASSADOR MAGMA** than with Saito's better known work, and the combination of silly yet deadly monsters with teenage moral dilemmas and fears is unsettling.

BARTENDER

2006. TV series. DIR: Masaki Watanabe. SCR: Yasuhiro Imagawa. DES: Hirotaka Kinoshita, Shigemi Ikeda, Shuichi Okubo. ANI: Kenta Ozaki, Masahiro Kametani. MUS: Kaoruko Otake. PRD: Palm Studio, Bartender Production Team, FCC, Fuji TV, Pony Canyon. 25 mins. x 11 eps.

Ryu Sakakura is a bartender at Eden Hall in Tokyo's Ginza (the most expensive location on a Japanese Monopoly board), renowned for his ability to create cocktails so delicious that he's rumored to possess "the Glass of God"—a playful reference to **BLACK JACK** and assorted other skilled fictional artisans. Kamishima is a hotel employee who's been given the task of designing a new bar. The problem is, he hates bars—until he meets Ryu and tries one of his specially designed cocktails. What he doesn't know is that Eden Hall, in Tokyo's Ginza, is a very exclusive bar indeed—invisible to passers-by unless they are in need of advice and support, and invited in by the possibly supernatural host. Kamishima is merely the first of series of drinkers who find themselves seeking the advice and sympathy of the guy who mixes their drinks.

Based on the manga of the same name by Araki Joh and Kenji Nagatomo, which ran from 2004 to 2009, *Bartender* is an odd anime in part because its set-up and execution seem far better suited to the mundane scenarios and locations of live-action TV drama, not the least the workplace stories that impart some sort of artisanal magic and pride in performance to any profession you care to name, from secretaries

to sommeliers. It is also something of a latecomer to the "gourmet" tradition: a subgenre within manga arising during the hedonistic 1980s that combined dramatic plots with epicurean tips.

Director Watanabe embraces the potential offered by anime above live-action, mythologizing his suave therapist as a master of ceremonies at a theater of **EVERYDAY ANIME**, and incorporating stage conventions such as follow-spots and soliloquies. True to the original, every episode features a cocktail recipe, firmly locating this in the small and ever-dwindling subgenre of anime for an audience of actual adults. Some suspension of disbelief, however, is required when the show asserts that few bartenders in Japan can pour a Black Velvet properly, and with the teeth-itchingly sincere dialogue, attempts to set up glorified waiters as father-confessors, therapists, and intellectual superheroes in a world of lonely drinkers. Compare to **WAGNARIA**.

BASARA *

1998. JPN: *Legend of Basara*. TV series. DIR: Nobuhiro Takamoto. SCR: Takao Koyama. DES: Keizo Shimizu. ANI: Hideaki Matsuzaki. MUS: N/C. PRD: KSS, Chiba TV. 30 mins. x 13 eps.

In a post-apocalyptic future the Gold King of Kings splits his land into quarters for his color-coded children to rule. In the domain of the youngest, the Red King, the blind prophet Nagi predicts that a desert village will bring forth twins, a boy and a girl, and that the boy shall depose the ruler. The Red King hears the prophecy and sends his army to the village—the boy, Tatara, is killed, but his sister, Sarasa, takes on his prophetic role by cutting off her hair and putting on his clothes. Impersonating Tatara, she convinces the villagers that there is still hope and sets off to retrieve her brother's sword, Byattsuko.

Wounded by the Red King, she is taken to a secluded lake by Kakuji (one of the few villagers who knows her secret). There, she falls in love with a young man called Shuri, though she is unaware that "Shuri" is the Red King, and he is unaware that his new love is the woman who has sworn to destroy him.

Already a success with **THERE GOES TOMOE**, manga artist Yumi Tamura turned to fantasy in 1990. A one-shot "image video" was released in 1993 after *Basara* won the

Shogakukan Manga Prize, but the story only became a full-fledged TV series in 1998. The theme of a girl taking on a boy's mission also appears in **YOTODEN**, though the ancestor of all such shows is Osamu Tezuka's **PRINCESS KNIGHT**. The TV series was preceded by a 30-minute *Basara Prologue Video* (1998) which included clips from the show, details of some of the publicity events and radio dramas, and an introduction to the original manga.

BASEBALL CLUB NUMBER THREE

1988. JPN: *Meimon! Daisan Yakyu Bu*. AKA: *Noble! Baseball Club Number Three*. TV series. DIR: Hiroshi Fukutomi. SCR: Ryuji Yamada. DES: Hiroshi Kanazawa. ANI: Hiroshi Kanazawa. MUS: Yusuke Honma, NAS. 25 mins. x 40 eps.

The struggles of a particularly bad baseball team as it fights to win against other schools and the far superior "Number One" and "Number Two" teams at its own Sakura High School. Toshiyuki Mutsu's gag manga in *Shonen Magazine* obviously hit the market at the right moment, lasting for ten volumes and spawning this relatively long-running series. More romantic takes on baseball would come in a slew of other anime, including **NINE** and **SLOW STEP**.

BASEBALL TEAM APACHE

1971. JPN: *Apache Yakyugun*. AKA: *Apache Baseball Team*. TV series. DIR: Kazuya Miyazaki, Isao Takahata, Minoru Okazaki, Masayuki Akehi, Issei Shigeno, Osamu Kasai, Masatoshi Sasaki. SCR: Kobako Hanato, Sachi Umemoto. DES: Keisuke Morishita. ANI: Shingo Araki, Keisuke Morishita, Akinori Namase, Joji Kikuchi, Takeo Takakura, Arata Fukuda, Fusahito Nagaki, Yasu Ishiguro. MUS: Koichi Hattori. PRD: Nippon Educational Television (later TV Asahi), Toei Animation. 25 mins. x 26 eps.

Dojima plays a perfect game in the national high school showcase tournament at Koshien (see **MAN'S AN IDIOT!**), but an arm injury (compare to **H2**) and a conflict with his father send him back to high school baseball to coach at a school in a remote mountain village. It's near the site of a new dam, the numbers of pupils are dwindling, and they're an unathletic and unmotivated bunch. There's only one teacher left—Chieko, granddaughter of the principal.

Bit by bit, as Dojima gets to know each pupil and finds out what motivates each of them, he manages to pull together a team.

Based on the manga in *Shonen King* monthly, by Kobako Hanato and Sachio Umemoto, this high school baseball drama would probably have sunk without a trace below fan radar but for the involvement of one of the great names of anime; future Studio Ghibli star Takahata directed episodes 2, 12, and 17. Writer Hanato provided his own scripts and would go on to write the live-action drama *The Show-Off* (*DE).

BASILISK *

2005. JPN: *Koga Ninpocho*. AKA: *Koga Ninja Chronicles*. TV series. DIR: Fumitomo Kizaki, Yukio Nishimoto. SCR: Yasuyuki Muto. DES: Michinori Chiba. ANI: Kenji Fujita. MUS: Takashi Nakagawa. PRD: Gonzo. 25 mins. x 24 eps.

"Retired" shogun Ieyasu Tokugawa (see YOUNG TOKUGAWA IEYASU) is undecided as to which of two grandsons will succeed the official shogun, his son, Hidetada Tokugawa. He commands representatives of two rival clans of ninja—the Majidani of Koga and the Tsubagakure of Iga, both of whom played secret and crucial roles in the civil war (alluded to in YOTODEN)—to demonstrate their prowess in front of himself and his principle councilors. At its conclusion he proposes a unique way of settling the succession: that the peace treaty between the clans, brokered by Hanzo Hattori (see SAMURAI DEEPER KYO), be annulled and that each clan represent a claimant to the throne, sending ten champions to fight to the death—the winner to receive the support of the shogun and power in the new order. The clan heads, Danjo and Igano-Ogen (former lovers of old), secretly declare the names of their champions, which are inscribed on two scrolls, with one copy going to each. However, they kill each other before they are able to pass on the reason for the resumption of hostilities in their 400-year-old rivalry, leaving their subordinates in the dark, but no less bloodthirsty. Meanwhile, the heirs to clans—Gennosuke of Koga and Oboro of Iga—have (mirroring their grandparents) fallen in love, and await their marriage, hoping that this time they, unlike their forebears, will be able to unite the clans

and finally end the conflict.

Ninja are a popular staple of anime, and often used as juvenile entertainments for naughty children, from HATTORI THE NINJA to NINJA CADETS. *Basilisk*, however, has a much more impressive path to the screen, beginning life as a novel by NINJA RESURRECTION–creator Futaro Yamada, reimagined for the younger generation in manga form by Masaki Segawa for *Young Magazine Uppers*. It also rode a wave of interest in the period following the success of *Aoi* (*DE), a year-long live-action TV series from 2003 that prepared the real-world historical background for this anime adaptation, which also includes a welcome return to old-fashioned bloodshed and intrigue. There are a lot of NARUTO fans out there, but truly, ninja are supposed to kill people, and *Basilisk* gives them plenty of opportunity. A live-action movie adapting the story, *Shinobi*, was also released in 2005. **V**

BASQUASH

2009. TV series. DIR: Shin Itagaki, Eiichi Sato. SCR: Tatsuo Sato, Yuki Enatsu, Yuko Kakihara. DES: Kazuhiro Soeta/SUEZEN/ Takahiro Yoshimatsu, Stanislas Brunet, Thomas Romain, Nike (shoe design assistance). ANI: Thomas Romain, Sunao Chikaoka, Hirotaka Marufuji. MUS: Kei Yoshikawa. PRD: Satelight, Dentsu, Kadokawa Shoten, MBS, Media Factory, Pony Canyon. 24 mins. x 26 eps.

Giant robots playing basketball in Nike shoes. Pervy fan service. A brother striving for revenge and a cure for his injured sister. All this, and envy of the posh folk living a high-tech life on the Moon, while down here on Earthdash—not Earth—the poor can barely get by. But don't look for reflections of BATTLE ANGEL. Although this show is trying very hard to cover all bases, not even its animation and design, always good and sometimes stunning, can completely compensate for an uneven plot and formulaic, vacuous characters.

A Shoji Kawamori show is usually very bankable: look at ESCAFLOWNE, for example. He created this one with French animator Thomas Romain, with input from the mighty Nike—note the shoe design credit and the unusually high number of product-placement shots of characters and mecha changing sports shoes (ADVERTISING

AND SPONSORSHIP). They should have been set to clean up on a highly merchandisable boys' sports-robot concept in which earnest boy Dan comes back into the game after serving time in prison.

There were two manga adaptations to boost market awareness, one by Tetsuya Hayashi starting three months before the show aired and one by Kagemaru a couple of weeks after the first episode. Both ended before the show aired, as did the tenure of the original director, Shin Itagaki, who remained credited until episode 20, but who was replaced sometime around episode 10 with Eiichi Sato, amid announcements that the show was to be reformatted from an otaku-focused, fan-friendly audience to a sports-focused series aimed at a younger viewership. The relaunch doesn't seem to have altered the show much, apart from shifting the focus from Dan's budding romance to his status as a game legend. It's not that there's anything serious to dislike in *Basquash*, but from an artist renowned for clever, innovative material we expect to see a bit more than an extended Nike commercial for middle schoolers.

BASTARD *

1992. JPN: *Bastard: Ankoku no Hakkaijin*. AKA: *Bastard: God-Destroyer of Darkness*. Video. DIR: Katsuhito Akiyama. SCR: Hiroshi Yamaguchi. DES: Hiroyuki Kitazume. ANI: Moriyasu Taniguchi, Hiroyuki Ochi. MUS: Kohei Tanaka. PRD: AIC, Anime R. 30 mins. x 6 eps.

Humanity lives a quasi-medieval existence on an Earth in the midst of apocalypse. Dark Schneider, a powerful sorcerer, causes such havoc that high priest Dio traps him inside the body of a newborn baby, Rushe Renren. Fifteen years later, Schneider's former henchmen (Abigail the dark priestess, Kall-Su the king of ice, Gara the ninja master, and Arshes Nei the empress of thunder) return on a campaign to conquer the world for the fallen angel Anthrasax. Dio must bring Schneider back from limbo and orders his virgin daughter Tia to kiss the lovestruck boy in order to free the man. Their savior arrives, and he is a complete bastard.

Creator Kazushi Hagiwara began as an assistant to Izumi Matsumoto on KIMAGURE ORANGE ROAD before becoming a solo artist in his own right. Though the anime *Bas-*

tard stops before the final showdown with Kall-Su, the manga series would continue far beyond, with Schneider assembling his four horsemen of the apocalypse and fighting a final war between Satan and the angels, all the while trying to come to terms with Rushe's boyish love for princess Tia.

Many of the names in the *Bastard* series come from Western rock, including the kingdoms of Metallicana, Judas, Aran Maiden, and Whitesnake, the high priest Dio, the battleship *King Crimson Glory*, and the names of spells include Megadeth, Slayer, Guns'n'Ro, Venom, Tesla, Kiss, Raven, and Exodus. "Bastard" was the original name planned for Motorhead, and Dark Schneider himself is named after Udo Dirkschneider, the lead singer of Accept. Such blasé jokiness seems to work in *Bastard*, though if tried too often, it can grate painfully—just compare with the sausage-machine attitude of Satoru Akahori's shows in a similar vein, such as **Maze** or **Sorcerer Hunters**. **Ⓝ**

BASTARD WARRIOR

1990. JPN: *Ajin Senshi*. Video. DIR: Tsuneo Tominaga. SCR: Kazumi Koide. DES: Yoshiaki Matsuda. ANI: Tsuneo Tominaga. MUS: Yuki Nakajima. PRD: Magic Bus. 100 mins.
During a war in 2200, in which both sides utilize psychic weapons, Zero is born of mixed parentage, a Terran mother and an alien father, the last survivor of the Mint clan of sorcerers. In this adaptation of the SF novel by Chiaki Kawamata, it is Zero's destiny to fight the Manjidara Empire and prevent it from seizing control of the galaxy. **Ⓥ**

BATIAN LAI

2008. JPN: *Pattenrai! Minami no Shima no Mizu Monogatari*. AKA: *Pattenrai! Story of the Water of the South Island*. Movie. DIR: Noboru Ishiguro. SCR: Toshiyuki Tabe. DES: Mitsuki Nakamura. ANI: Kazuo Iimura. MUS: Reijiro Koroku. PRD: Mushi Pro, Hokkoku Shinbun. 91 mins.
In the Japanese colony of Taiwan in the 1920s, fresh-faced engineering graduate Yoichi Hatta (1886–1942) arrives in the service of the Governor-General. Known to the locals by the Mandarin pronunciation of his name, Batian Yuyi, Hatta designs and implements a decade-long scheme to

unite a series of waterways between Jiayi and Tainan in the grand "Chianan" canal project, increasing irrigation capacity from 5,000 to 150,000 hectares, and allowing Taiwanese farmers to increase their yields with a harvest three times a year. However, the venture is beset by difficulties, including a tunnel explosion that claims the life of a local boy's father.

Japan's 50-year occupation of Taiwan is usually written off as an unwelcome invasion, in particular because most of the colonists who self-identified as "Japanese" fled for the homeland in 1945, leaving much of the era's historical heritage in the hands of the Chinese. This modern docu-drama (**Documentaries and History**) argues, not unreasonably, that the oft-despised Japanese were also responsible for many key elements of Taiwan's infrastructure, which remain in use today. It was also released in Taiwan, under the title *Batian Yuyi: Jianan Dazhen de Fu* (*Yoichi Hotta: Father of the Chianan Canal*). "Batian Lai" is Chinese for "Hatta Arrives." Funded in part by the *Hokkoku Shinbun*, a local newspaper in Hatta's birthplace of Kanazawa.

BATMAN: GOTHAM KNIGHT *

2008. Movie. DIR: Shojiro Nishimi, Futoshi Higashide, Hiroshi Morioka, Yasuhiro Aoki, Yuichiro Hayashi, Toshiyuki Kubooka, Jong-Sik Nam. SCR: Brian Azzarello, Alan Burnett, David S. Goyer, Jordan Goldberg, Greg Rucka, Josh Olson. DES: Shinji Kimura, Daren Bendall (skateboards), Masanobu Nomura, Shinobu Tagashira, Yasutaka Kubota, Yuki Kawashima, Toshiharu Murata, Yoshimi Umino, Kaoru Inoda, Naoyuki Onda, Shuichi Hirata. ANI: Shojiro Nishimi, Shinobu Tagashira, Hiroshi Morioka, Yasuhiro Hayashi, Toshiyuki Tanaka, Jong-Sik Nam. MUS: Christopher Drake, Kevin Manthei, Robert J. Kral. PRD: Madhouse, Bee Train, Production I.G, Studio 4°C. 76 mins.
This is an anthology tie-in in the style of the **Animatrix**, with six short stories bridging the gap between Warner Brothers' live-action movies *Batman Begins* and *The Dark Knight,* directed by Christopher Nolan. Six American writers, six Japanese directors, and some of the best talent in the anime industry create six stories that will feel familiar to any fans of the iconic comic hero. Unfortunately, like some of the classic stories, they're mostly not

very good. Although they present a set of arresting images of Batman (including a pretty-boy Dark Knight) through beautiful art and some very classy animation, the writing is appallingly weak and in some cases downright silly. Warner avoided any mention of the anime connections on the project except in the end credits; one imagines that the Japanese studios are not too concerned about this. In some sources Toshi Hiruma and Bruce Timm are credited as supervising writers and directors, and although uncredited, Yoshiaki Kawajiri is said to have codirected episode 6. A novelization of *Gotham Knight* by Louise Simonson was well reviewed on appearance in 2008.

BATON

2009. Movie. DIR: Ryuhei Kitamura. SCR: Shunji Iwai. DES: Masayuki Goto, Antonio Cannobio. ANI: Mark Brooks. MUS: Nobuhiko Morino. PRD: Titmouse, Wild Boar Media. 65 mins.
This beautifully designed film was made to run during the 150th anniversary celebrations of the Port of Yokohama and has only occasionally been screened since. The art style is reminiscent of the work of Moebius and the backgrounds and color palette are very attractive. Although the story, about humanoid robots, a strange chip, and the quest for selfhood, has distant echoes of **Astro Boy** and Naoki Urusawa's *Pluto,* the production team has limited experience in anime—designer Goto was a key animator on **Virus Buster Serge**, and American Studio Titmouse worked on **Afro Samurai**, linking them to Wild Boar Studios founder and Titmouse colleague Eric Calderon, who was vice-president of GDH International when *Afro Samurai* was being made. Studio Titmouse originated in the early 2000s as a T-shirt design company founded by Chris Prynoski and his wife. Director Kitamura is better known as director of live-action movies such as *Versus* and *Godzilla Final Wars.* They seem to have done a good job—it's a pity the film is so hard to see.

BATS AND TERRY

1987. Movie. DIR: Tetsuro Amino. SCR: Yasushi Hirano. DES: Noriyasu Yamauchi, Indori-Koya. ANI: Noriyasu Yamauchi, Kenichi Maejima. MUS: Tatsumi Yano. PRD: Sunrise, Matsutake,

Magic Bus. 80 mins.
Batsu and Terry ("battery," as in the baseball sense) are a pitcher and catcher devoted to sports, bikes, girls, and good times. When they try to console Anne, a pretty girl who loses her biker boyfriend in a traffic accident, they are dragged into gangland intrigue and must rescue the damsel in distress before the next day's game. Set in Kanagawa Prefecture's Shonan district, home to other road-knight tales such as BOMBER BIKERS OF SHONAN and GTO, this feel-good crime caper was shown as a double bill with the DIRTY PAIR movie *Project Eden*. The first Sunrise production to be adapted from a manga, it had its origins in Yasuichi Oshima's serial in *Shonen Magazine*.

BATTLE ANGEL *
1993. JPN: *Gunmu*. AKA: *Gun-Dream*. Video.
DIR: Hiroshi Fukutomi. SCR: Akinori Endo.
DES: Nobuteru Yuki. ANI: Nobuteru Yuki. MUS: Kaoru Wada. PRD: Animate Film, KSS, Movic. 35 mins. x 2 eps.
Though the floating island of Zalem is thought to be a heavenly paradise, few have been there. Instead, the poor scavenge from the giant scrap heap where Zalem throws its garbage. Daisuke Ido and his ex-girlfriend, Chiren, are two experts in cybernetics, forced to ply their trade in the scrapyard after falling out of favor on Zalem. Chiren will do anything to get back home and builds bigger and better modifications for cyborg gladiators. Ido prefers to work as a cyberdoctor for impoverished cyborgs, moonlighting as a bounty hunter. Poking around in Zalem's trash, Ido finds the remains of a cyborg, complete with the irreplaceable spinal cord. He fixes "her" up, names her Alita (Gally in the original), and has his very own robot "daughter" to keep him company. Alita develops a crush on local odd-job boy Yugo, pesters her adoptive dad when he's trying to work, and accidentally reveals that she has superhuman kung-fu skills.

This short-lived spin-off from Yukito Kishiro's 1991 *Business Jump* manga never explains what life on Zalem is really like, why Ido was thrown out, or who the amnesiac Alita was before she was scrapped. The scene is set for a couple of fight scenes and some mawkish flirting between Yugo and Alita before the innocents of the story realize that the corrupt adults have been stringing them along, and it all ends in tears. Highly regarded in the early 1990s by an anime audience punch-drunk on FIST OF THE NORTH STAR, *BA* wasn't particularly original—it takes little to substitute drugs for cybernetics and the scrap heap for an LA ghetto before you have *Boyz N the Hood*. A post-holocaust world where one has to buy social betterment was covered more interestingly in GREY: DIGITAL TARGET, whereas Earth as a celestial race's garbage dump was first suggested in Shinichi Hoshi's 1970s short story "Hey! Come On Out!" Initially inspired by MICROMAN toys, Alita herself began life as an illustration around which Kishiro had to work up a story in a hurry, elements of which survive in the anime's fuzzy plotting: she doesn't know much about her past because, at this stage in the story's history, her creator wasn't that sure himself. The story has enjoyed a prolonged artistic heritage, in part, through the continued popularity of the manga and through the attentions of James Cameron, who has been associated on-and-off with a possible live-action movie adaptation for the last decade.

Director Fukutomi does the best he can here with the limited budget, but there simply isn't the time to do the story justice, and one amazing image of a paradise city hovering above a disgusting junkyard does not a successful series make. Viewers can take solace, however, in a high amount of immortal dialogue, including, "How long am I going to have to wait for my new spine?"

BATTLE ATHLETES *
1997. JPN: *Battle Athletess* [sic] *Daiundokai*. AKA: *Battle Athletess Great Sports Meet*. Video, TV series. DIR: Kazuhiro Ogawa, Katsuhito Akiyama. SCR: Hideyuki Kurata. DES: Ryoichi Makino. ANI: Shinji Ochi, Nobuyuki Kitajima. MUS: Takayuki Hattori. PRD: Pioneer, TV Tokyo, Aeon. 30 mins. x 6 eps. (v), 25 mins. x 26 eps. (TV).
In the year 4998, athletes strive for the glittering Cosmo Beauty prize on University Satellite. Akari Kanzaki is one such candidate, and the daughter of a former Cosmo Beauty. With little confidence in her own abilities, she still gains the respect and friendship of her multinational teammates. But University Satellite is not merely a sports club, it is a training ground where generations of humans have been secretly honed to perfection for the ultimate battle against a race of sports-loving aliens.

Despite a passionless and cynical execution, this 1990s comedy update of GUNBUSTER still contains moments of subtle humor, such as an invading alien queen delivering a message of conquest to a pair of bewildered giraffes. The original video series, based on an idea by EL HAZARD's Hiroki Hayashi, stumbles amateurishly through several pointless prologues about World War III, a natural disaster, and still another war before settling down to the story. The later TV series *Battle Athletes: Victory* does a more coherent job, throwing the viewer straight into comedy training set-ups such as cycling on a roller-coaster track or pulling giant garden rollers across a minefield. Akari works hard (a staple of all such anime, since being a "natural" implies one is lazy) and befriends a plucky Osaka girl, assorted Caucasian also-rans, a comic-relief Chinese rich-bitch, and a feral African girl who is supposed to be cute. The characters laugh at their own jokes and intone antiquated pep talks and clichés from classic SPORTS ANIME shows like AIM FOR THE ACE.

In the grand finale held before a giant headless statue of the Goddess of Victory, Akari is forced to compete against the aliens' champion, the rejuvenated form of her own mother, while her ailing coach (and father) looks on. The Pioneer English dub is excellent as usual, though it is a mystery why the company squandered such riches on a mediocre hybrid of *The Last Starfighter* and *Triumph of the Will*.

BATTLE CAN CAN *
1987. Video. DIR: Kazuya Sasaki. SCR: Kazuhiro Kasai. DES: N/C. ANI: Joji Oshima. MUS: N/C. PRD: Studio G7, Nikkatsu. 30 mins.
The Battle Can Can investigation team is sent out to halt pirate incursions in the space-year 2087. Sophia, Diane, Jill, Marina, and Lily (with a comic-relief robot, Harold) must retrieve the Cosmic Firefly, a fragile jewel worth literally billions. With so much at stake they must subdue space pirates, have sex with aliens, and confront a traitor from within. Nikkatsu was sur-

prisingly ahead of its time with this sci-fi porno; it would take another decade for **ADVANCER TINA** and **ALIEN FROM THE DARKNESS** to prove that there truly was no hope for the genre. **Ⓝ**

BATTLE GIRLS: TIME PARADOX *

2011. JPN: *Sengoku Otome Momoiro Paradox*. AKA: *Warring States Maidens Peachy Paradox*. TV series. DIR: Hideki Okamoto. SCR: Toko Machida, Noboru Kimura, Shigeru Morita, Ryu Tamura. DES: Koji Yamakawa, Nobuto Sakamoto. ANI: Koji Yamakawa, Kenji Fujisaki. MUS: Eishi Sagawa. PRD: TMS Entertainment, Heiwa. 25 mins. x 11 eps. Based on the *CR Sengoku Otome* pachinko game series by Heiwa, this is the story of Hide Yoshino (Hideyoshi … get it? As in the regent of Japan), an average teenage girl, who finds herself transported to an alternate feudal Japan populated entirely by females. She meets warlord Nobunaga Oda (see also **YOTODEN** et al), who is on a quest for the scattered pieces of a crimson suit of armor that will help her conquer the land. Her teacher is there too, but she's now transformed into the warlord Date Masamune. The only person who knows Yoshino is from another time is a talking dog in a samurai helmet, and the warlord Takeda Shingen is a giraffe. Before you ask, you can't reproduce the mindset that created such arrant lunacy unless you're ready to play pachinko until your eyeballs bleed. One of several attempts to graft the character merchandising concerns of modern anime onto historical figures: see also **SENGOKU BASARA: SAMURAI KINGS**.

BATTLE OF THE PLANETS *

1972. JPN: *Kagaku Ninjatai Gatchaman*. AKA: *Science Ninja Team Gatchaman*; *G-Force*; *Eagle Riders*. TV series, movie, video. DIR: Jinzo Toriumi, Eiko Toriumi, Fumio Kurokawa, Hiroshi Sasagawa, Katsuhisa Yamada. SCR: Jinzo Toriumi, Toshio Nagata, Akiyoshi Sakai. DES: Tatsuo Yoshida, Kunio Okawara. ANI: Miyamoto Sado. MUS: Bob Sakuma. PRD: Tatsunoko, Fuji TV. 30 mins. x 105 eps. (TV1) ca. 60 mins. (m1), 110 mins. (m2), 30 mins. x 52 eps. (TV2), 30 mins. x 48 eps. (TV3), 45 mins. x 3 eps. (v), 24 mins. x 12 eps. (*Crowds*). Only five young heroes and their giant God-Phoenix aircraft can save Earth from

the invading legions of the alien Gallacter. In each episode, Gallacter would send a mechanized menace to terrorize the planet, and the Gatchaman team would stop him, graphically slicing through the enemy minions with weapons such as their *shuriken* and yo-yo bombs, all the while inexplicably dressed in bird costumes.

Though preceded by the five-strong teams of **SKYERS 5** and *Thunderbirds* (see **THUNDERBIRDS 2086**), *Battle of the Planets* was a watershed show, with strong leader Eagle Ken, loose cannon Condor Joe, love interest Swan June, big-guy Owl Ryu, and little Swallow Jinpei setting up group dynamics that would dominate anime character rosters for decades to come. It was also the dying gasp of Japan's ninja fad, which began with historical and pseudo-historical fiction and became progressively more outlandish and fantastical throughout the 1960s. Ninja would be put out to pasture for some years after this before their 1980s resurgence. Episodes 22 and 37, *The Fiery Phoenix vs. the Fire-Eating Dragon* and *Electron Beast Renzilla*, were shown theatrically in 1973 as part of Toho's summer and winter holiday film anthologies. In 1978, acclaimed live-action director Kihachi Okamoto made a genuine anime movie version in which Gatchaman joined forces with the mysterious pilot Charm Red Impulse (Red Specter), who would eventually be revealed as Ken's estranged father.

Eighty-five of the original 105 episodes were adapted for the Sandy Frank English-language version broadcast in the U.S. in 1978. The enemy was renamed Spectra, a dying planet whose Great Spirit had ordered the evil Zoltar to conquer Earth and neighboring worlds in the Federation of Planets. The characters' names were also changed—Mark, Jason, Princess, Tiny, and Keyop were now fighting "attacks by alien galaxies beyond space." With much of the violence cut, additional footage was commissioned to bridge continuity gaps. This included a babbling robot controller, 7-Zark-7, a mascot, 1-Rover-1, shots of the team off-duty in their Ready Room, and several sequences of the Phoenix flying through space to justify the "alien galaxies" bit.

When Sandy Frank's rights lapsed in 1986, the original series was completely redubbed as *G-Force* by Turner Broadcast-

ing, which dispensed altogether with the 7-Zark-7 footage and selected many episodes from the original run that had not previously been seen outside Japan. The series included more deaths and was more faithful to the original, though the names were again replaced with the awful Ace Goodheart, Dirk Daring, Agatha June, Hootie, and Pee Wee. A ratings disaster, the new show was quietly buried and only seen in its entirety in Australia, though it did eventually return to American TV when Turner established the Cartoon Network in 1995.

The 1979 Japanese sequel *Gatchaman II* featured early design work from Akemi Takada and Yoshitaka Amano, adding another 52 episodes to the original, along with the female foil Professor Pandora, and a complex plot in which Joe is mortally wounded, saved by cybernetic augmentation in the style of **KIKAIDER**, and temporarily replaced by a Gallacter spy, whom he eventually kills. This was followed in 1979 by another 48 episodes, *Gatchaman F(ighter)*. Both serials were eventually bought by Saban Entertainment in 1996, cut down to 65 episodes, and released as *Eagle Riders*. The characters were renamed for a third time, as Hunter Harris, Joe Thax, Kelly Jenar, Ollie Keeawani, and Mickey Dougan. Their mission: "To defend the global good."

In 1994, the series was remade in Japan, compressed into a three-part video outing called simply *Gatchaman* by director Hiroyuki Fukushima with character designs by Yasuomi Umezu. The show was swiftly dubbed for an American anime market now more aware of its origins. The original Japanese names were retained, and in a bizarre coincidence, the voice actor who played Joe, Richard Cansino, also lent his talents in *Eagle Riders* to the role of Hunter Harris.

Kenji Nakamura's *Gatchaman Crowds* (2013) is something of a reboot—a 12-episode series in which a hyper-energetic teenage girl becomes the central character in a future metropolis beset by alien invaders and protected by mutant heroes. Clearly intended for an older audience than the original, it finds winning explanations for the color-coded team members of the original and introduces a number of **TROPES AND TRANSFORMATIONS** that have developed in anime over the four decades that separate it from the original. Not the least is the titular Crowds—an oblique reference to the 21st century's great hope for anime: that **Fandom** itself can band together in sufficient numbers to hold off the threat of pirates, thieves, and … er … aliens.

BATTLE ROYAL HIGH SCHOOL *

1987. JPN: *Shinmajinden*. AKA: *Tale of True Devilry*. Video. DIR: Ichiro Itano. SCR: Ichiro Itano. DES: Nobuteru Yuki. ANI: Nobuteru Yuki, Satoshi Urushihara, Hideaki Anno. MUS: Shiro Sagisu. PRD: DAST. 55 mins.

A time-traveling security officer must prevent an extradimensional demon lord from taking over the world. But the demon lord in question has taken over the body of a high school karate teacher in modern-day Tokyo. The demon-hunter sent to get him has also been possessed, but by an evil fairy queen who wants the planet for herself.

Shinichi Kuruma's original manga in *Shonen Captain* was based on a story by **Amon Saga**'s Baku Yumemakura. Looking like a toned-down version of the later **Nightmare Campus**, the anime version simply restored much of the gore for a straight-to-video audience. Animator Anno and composer Sagisu would later work together again on **Evangelion**. No relation to the live-action Kinji Fukasaku film *Battle Royale* (2000). **ⓒⓃⓋ**

BATTLE SKIPPER *

1995. Video. DIR: Takashi Watanabe. SCR: Hidemi Kubota. DES: Takashi Kobayashi, Kimitoshi Yamane. ANI: Takashi Kobayashi, Toshiko Sasaki. MUS: Kenyu Miyotsu. PRD: Artmic, Tokyo Kids. 30 mins. x 3 eps.

"In the Etiquette Club, the first rule is strength! The second rule is strength! There is no third or fourth rule, but the fifth rule is strength!" Rivalries at St. Ignacio's Catholic girls' school get out of hand when rich-bitch Sayaka starts using giant "battle skipper" robots to dominate those who oppose her Debutante Club. Only a group of unknown vigilantes foils her plans, and little does Sayaka know that the Exstars vigilantes are actually the unassuming freshmen of the undersubscribed Etiquette Club—current membership, two.

Rie and Reika are looking for recruits,

but it's difficult when they are not allowed to tell new arrivals that their deserted clubhouse is really an underground base containing their secret arsenal. New girls Kanami, Saori, and Shihoko sneak into the clubhouse, where they stumble across the color-coded battlesuits that almost seem made for them.

Initially created to promote Tomy's MRV toy line, *Battle Skippers* mixes elements of *Thunderbirds* and **Bubblegum Crisis** with the school satire of **Project A-Ko** and **Debutante Detectives**. The three episodes were edited into a "movie" compilation for the U.S. video market and resolicited after director Watanabe became better known for **Slayers**.

BATTLE SPIRITS

2008. JPN: *Battle Spirits Shonen Toppa Bashin*. TV series. DIR: Mitsuru Hongo, Akira Nishimori, Masaki Watanabe. SCR: Dai Sato, Atsuhiro Tomioka. DES: Miho Shimogasa, Yoji Yoshikawa, Yoshinori Yumoto, Tetsuya Ishikawa, Takahiro Yamada, Norifumi Nakamura, Ryo Hirata, Tomoshige Inayoshi. ANI: Miho Shimogasa, Yoshinori Yumoto, Akira Kikuchi, Tomoko Ishida, Tomoshige Inayoshi, Asako Inayoshi. MUS: Ko Otani, Eishi Segawa. PRD: Sunrise, Sotsu Agency, Asatsu DK, Nagoya Broadcasting. 24 mins. x 50 eps. (TV1), 23 mins. x 50 eps. (TV2), 24 mins. x 50 eps. (TV3), 24 mins. x 50 eps. (TV4), 24 mins. x 50 eps. (TV5).

Toppa Bashin is 12 years old, short for his age, with red hair. When his father left home, he left Toppa a mysterious pendant with a red stone. The stone is a key to the alternate world of Isekai and also enables his beloved pet mouse Albo to speak. Toppa is initially shy and reluctant to make friends, but that changes when his mother teaches him to play the collectible card game *Battle Spirits*. Through his skill at the game and the growing respect it wins for him, he gains confidence and makes friends at school. Players construct alter egos for the game, both reflecting how they want to be seen and developing their innate natures. Toppa and his friends learn valuable life lessons such as forgiveness, tolerance, and loyalty through their adventures in Isekai and their gameplay. He is also reunited with his father, although he doesn't return to the family. Father is, in fact, the king and core figure

of Isekai, against whom Toppa and friends have been fighting—compare with **Blue Blink**, where the protagonist's father plays a similar role.

Battle Spirits, unsurprisingly, originated as a two-player collectible card game by Bandai and Sunrise, released in autumn 2008 around the same time as the first anime TV series *Battle Spirits Shonen Toppa Bashin* (*Boy Toppa Version*) and manga. Cards representing dragons, spirits, animals, birds, and insects are grouped by color or "attribute" as the game calls it, around "cores" representing different strengths and skills. They can be played in various combinations to defeat an opponent's hand. By buying or trading cards, players can build up their own specialist decks as well as acquiring some or all of the many commercial sets.

The game quickly gained an international following, and a second anime TV series, *Battle Spirits Shonen Gekiha Dan* (*Fierce Fighter Dan*), followed in 2009. This time the protagonist is 12-year-old Dan Bashin, who can be childish and insensitive but is already a respected game champion. We don't hear much about his background or family, although he mentions that his mother is a good cook: the series focuses more on in-game action and relationships between friends and opponents. Dan is taken from Earth to the world of Grand Rolo, where he learns he's one of a group of chosen "core soldiers" fighting for justice. With the help of his friends and comrades, he battles to stop the evil Otherworld King. Dan and friends seem just a little older than Toppa, and although their story starts out in the same cheerful, high-energy mode it becomes darker as it progresses. The series was followed in 2010 by *Battle Spirits Brave* in which Dan travels to the future to carry on the fight against evil and sell a new set of cards of the same name. Once again the characters are a little older, as if growing up with their audience and the game's players, and the story reflects this—still action-oriented but once again darker and more serious in tone and color palette; compare to **Naruto**, which similarly aged with its primary viewership.

In 2011 the fourth series, *Battle Spirits Heroes*, started a completely new continuity separate from any of the previous series in the franchise, resetting to zero for a new young generation of fans and gamers. The light, almost goofy tone is much closer to the first series. Middle-schooler Hajime wants to see Battle Spirits so much that his parents helped to create a battle system allowing for "real" Battle Spirits. When they leave on a work trip, Hajime moves in with a fellow gamer and her family and many adventures follow, including a trip around the world in an evil scientist's submarine. The series follows much the same arc as the first, with school, friendships, setbacks, misunderstandings, and new discoveries fueling an overall sense of optimism and fun.

The fifth series, *Battle Spirits Sword Eyes*, began its TV run in autumn 2012. Once again, it resets the continuity and introduces entirely new characters and card decks. Atlantia, the largest country in the world of Legendia, was torn apart by riots 14 years ago. Tsurugi Tatewaki was rescued as a baby and taken to nearby Pacifis. There he grows up, believing himself a native of the country, until he finds a mysterious sword. He is one of 12 Sword Braves, fighters for justice, and an evil army is hunting him and the others. A strange droid, Bringer, is sent to be his protector and trainer in the techniques of Battle Spirits combat. Now he can join the other Sword Braves to fight the army of darkness with his Key Spirit "Shining Dragon." From episode 30, in April 2013, the series was retitled *Battle Spirits Sword Eyes Gekitoden* (*Fierce Battle Legend*). but the characters and storyline appear unchanged and the staff credited so far come from the team that made episodes 1–29.

The point of a game-inspired show, whether devoted to cards, online games like .HACK, console games such as STREET FIGHTER II, or RPG scenarios like RECORD OF LODOSS WAR, is twofold: to make devoted fans feel that they're seeing their fantasy world come to life, and to draw new fans into a world of accessories and collectibles. Most TV anime is either advertising or education; the best strive to be something more, but even the less ambitious do their utmost to keep their core market entertained. The challenge is to attract new customers in the target age range while keeping existing players engaged for as long as possible, until ex-

ams, romance, or other hobbies lure them away. Five years in, and with a devoted English-speaking following and a number of dedicated English websites, *Battle Spirits* is a success. The biggest surprise is that the anime is still not licensed for English-language release. Not to be confused with ART OF FIGHTING, which had a similar title in Japanese.

BATTLE TEAM LAKERS EX *
1996. JPN: *Seishojo Sentai Lakers EX*. AKA: *Holy Girl Battle Team Lakers EX*. Video. DIR: Takashi Kawamura. SCR: Ryusei. DES: Koichi Fujii, Mitsuharu Miyamae. ANI: Koichi Fujii. MUS: Kazuya Matsushita, Hideo Kuroda. PRD: Beam Entertainment, Animate Film. 30 mins.

Five exiled space warriors live undercover as Tokyo college girls, sworn to use their Laker power to defend Earth from the evil queen Oleana of the Godram empire. Would-be singer Reiko (Star), hot-headed Chiaki (Kung Fu), bespectacled Yayoi (Soul), big-chested tomboy Natsumi (Judo), and baby-faced Yuka (Bunny) all lust after their team leader, the handsome Akira (Blade Knight). After a rehearsal for Reiko's forthcoming concert, Akira convinces Reiko to try out a sex toy to help amass greater energy for battle. Meanwhile, Oleana sends four robot doppelgängers to pose as Akira and seduce the other girls. The next day, the girls assume that Akira has swindled them and refuse to follow orders when one of Oleana's giant monsters attacks the school. They are captured and taken to Oleana's spaceship but rescued by Akira. Lacking the energy to transform, they stage an impromptu orgy to regain their powers and escape.

A soft-core pastiche of the all-girl team shows that began with SAILOR MOON, even to the extent of posing as just one episode in a long-running saga, *Lakers EX* barely has time for a set-up and showdown. Not quite hitting the ludicrous heights of VENUS FIVE (though the voice acting is superior to many other erotic anime dubs), the careful duplication of hack genre conventions ironically leaves little time for the sex. Based on a computer game. **⊗**

BAVI STOCK
1985. Video. DIR: Shigenori Kageyama. SCR: Kenji Terada. DES: Mutsumi Inomata,

Takahiro Tomoyasu. ANI: Masahiro Shida, Ryunosuke Otonashi. MUS: Yasuaki Honda. PRD: Hero Media, Kaname Pro, Studio Unicorn. 45 mins. x 2 eps.

Agent Kate Lee Jackson of the GPP (space police) frees the mute girl Muma from a space prison on a huge satellite called the Bentika Empire. She also frees Bavi Stock, a young boxer jailed after accidentally killing an opponent. The prison doctor, Sammy, who has been trying to ensure that Bavi stays alive, joins them, and they head for GPP HQ. But bad guys from Bentika, the psionic Ruth Miller and her henchman, Eyesman, disintegrate the GPP homeworld. With nowhere else to go, our heroes head for Sammy's homeworld, arriving on the eve of a big sky-sled race. Sammy and Bavi enter and face off against Eyesman, while Ruth Miller tries to sabotage the control computers, and Kate and Muma have to stop her. In the aftermath, Ruth is trapped in an alternate dimension, and Muma is revealed as the key to the downfall of the Bentika Empire.

Cherry-picking the destruction of planet Alderaan, the rescue of Princess Leia, and the Endor speeder-bike chase from the early *Star Wars* films, *Bavi Stock* is a deliberate attempt to reverse-engineer U.S. space opera. It even features Americanized names, though some of them are altered beyond recognition in transit—Bavi is a mutation of Bobby, "as in Bavi Kennedy," according to producer Hiromasa Shibazaki. Less innocent *Star Wars* rip-offs can be found in BONDAGE QUEEN KATE.

BAYONETTA *
2013. JPN: *Bayonetta: Bloody Fate*. Movie. DIR: Fuminori Kizaki. SCR: Mitsutaka Hirota. DES: Ai Yokoyama, Hiroya Iijima, Katanao Akai, Takeshi Watabe, Shigemi Ikeda. ANI: Patricia Hishikawa. MUS: Yoku Shioya. PRD: Gonzo, Pony Canyon. 90 mins.

Twenty years ago, the witch Bayonetta was hauled out of a deep lake, with no memory of her past, how she got there, or who might have hated her enough to put her there. She has in her possession half of an artifact known as the "Eyes of the World." Joining forces with information broker Enzo, she sets off to find and steal the other half. But powerful forces are moving against her, forces known as the Angels.

Game-based anime share common problems. The first is the difficulty of creating a story that fulfils fans' expectations without leaving them feeling left out for no longer being able to directly control the action. The second, increasingly, is to get the anime to look as good as the game. Anime budgets are tight, even at the movie end of the scale, and a top-selling game often throws far more money, time and talent at its animated cut-scenes. Moreover, games, even more than anime, are frequently made for an audience that lives and dies by fan service (ARGOT AND JARGON).

Bayonetta is a 2009 PS and XBox game that succeeds again as anime—at least for its target audience—by being no more or less than its source. A basic action game with strong visuals and comfortable stereotyping, it ports the basic plot, character and weapon sets over into anime and ditches unnecessary details: bosses, gameplay, locations. Presented as a standard cyberfantasy tale, it's clichéd, but tightly paced and enjoyable enough. Even the fan service is presented as almost ironic, as though our heroine is sending herself up. It has a 1990s vibe in both design and plot, an atmosphere enhanced by the awe-inspiring voice of Norio Wakamoto (GUN-BUSTER), who voices Balder in the Japanese versions of both the game and the original film. The biggest shock for game fans may be the anime's Japanese dub replacing the English voice track they're used to, with Atsuko Tanaka (the voice of Motoko Kusanagi from GHOST IN THE SHELL) playing the leading role.

As befits both a combat game and a Gonzo anime, the fight scenes are the chief focus, and they're impressive. Not quite as impressive as SWORD OF THE STRANGER or ROMEO X JULIET, but satisfying enough. Fans of the game will find all their favorite weapons put to the uses for which they were designed in fast-paced and largely well-animated combat. The character development is minimal—memory is lost, memory is regained, people die but nothing changes and there are still enemies to fight. What *Bayonetta* does, and does well, is deliver a narrative version of the game that's satisfying and fan-friendly enough to fill cinema seats and sell product. And it does so with an oddly endear-ing old-millennium style that took us back to the 1990s. **NV**

BE ROCKIN'
2006. TV series. DIR: Atsushi Yamazaki. SCR: Masayuki Oiwa. DES: Atsuko Kawata. ANI: N/C. MUS: N/C. PRD: ANON Pictures. ?? mins. x 5 eps.
Shun has been playing guitar since childhood. He plays in a band called Cobra's Fang but also holds down a regular job. His girlfriend Kaori is happy with him, and when his company wants to transfer him to Shanghai she sees this as a great opportunity for him and for their relationship. Then, at a gig, he meets Kyoko, a former idol who left show business because she hated the artifice of the idol lifestyle. Like Shun, she wants to express her true self through her music, and shares a love of the work of guitarist Hirofumi Terada. In fact, Kyoko knew Terada in her idol days. ANON's Tadashi Matsuyama created this story of a love triangle and a young man striving for balance between art and life, similar to that in BAKUMAN. In 2009 Yamazaki was also slated to direct ANON's *Inuwari-san*, a slapstick comedy created by Yukiko Yagi, then a student at Tokyo's Digital Hollywood University, but the project stalled and ANON is currently listed as working in commercials and architecture rather than anime.

BE-BOP HIGH SCHOOL
1990. Movie. DIR: Toshihiko Ariseki, Hiroyuki Kadokane, Junichi Fujise. SCR: Kazuhiro Kiuchi, Tatsuhiko Urahata. DES: Kazuhiro Kiuchi. ANI: Junichi Hayama. MUS: Ginjiro Ito. PRD: Toei. 45 mins. x 7 eps.
School tough-guys Toru and Hiroshi have impossibly wedge-shaped haircuts and a deep love of pretty girls. Forever fighting against the authority of the weak-willed principal they refer to as Turtle Man, they live only to scrap with rival gangs like the Hitman Brothers in this anime spin-off of the 1987 live-action film, itself based on a manga by screenwriter Kazuhiro Kiuchi. The cartoonish nature of the original story made the anime infinitely preferable to the movie, which was hampered by poor acting and a cripplingly low budget (director Hiroyuki Nasu would make the equally bad *Pinch Runner* in 2000). The series also spawned the three-part *Be-Bop Pirate*

Edition, a humorous spin-off supposedly written by "Memeoka Manhiro" in 1991. In 1991, four years after the sixth episode of the video, a final chapter was released in which the same amount of time had passed onscreen for the leads, taking them out of school and into the real world along with their audience.

BE-BOY KIDNAPP'N IDOL
1989. Movie. DIR: Kenichi Yatsuya. SCR: Michiko Onuki. DES: Kazumi Oya, Naoyuki Onda. ANI: Naoyuki Onda. MUS: Katsunori Ishida. PRD: AIC. 30 mins.
Comical adventures of beautiful boy pop-idol Kazuya Shinohara and his dear friend, Akihiko Kudo. Featuring significant design input from girls' manga artist Kazumi Oya (creator of OTOHIME CONNECTION), this one-shot video was sold to the anime audience on the strengths of its two leads, Nozomu Sasaki (Tetsuo from AKIRA) and Takeshi Kusao (Pern from LODOSS WAR), in uncharacteristically romantic roles.

BE-YOND
1998. Video. DIR: Hiroyuki Kurimoto. SCR: Atsuhiro Tomioka. DES: Toshiya Yamada. ANI: Toshiya Yamada. MUS: N/C. PRD: Pink Pineapple, KSS. 36 mins. x 2 eps.
Satan, an alien creature who has lain dormant on Earth for many years, awakens and causes havoc. Fay is a female bounty hunter searching for Satan's younger brother, although that is soon forgotten in favor of more sex scenes in this lackluster replay of UROTSUKIDOJI. **N**

BEAST CITY *
1996. JPN: *Inju Dai Toshi*. AKA: *Lust-Beast Great City*. Video. DIR: Shinichiro Watanabe. SCR: Naomi Hayakawa, Yuri Kanai. DES: Naomi Hayakawa. ANI: Hitoshi Imazaki. MUS: N/C. PRD: Comstock, Caress Communications. 45 mins. x 3 eps.
Tokyo is held for ransom by the demonic Beasts that stalk its streets. Born into a family of vampires, Mina has vowed to destroy all of the creatures with her Beast-hunter sword. Sex and violence ensue as Mina and her bisexual vampire associates from Draculon get their daily fix by having oral sex with a sleeping human and sinking their teeth into his engorged penis, all without waking him up. Then they go

looking for a fight, get knocked about a bit, and kill some demons.

Though its premise is distantly related to **VAMPIRE HUNTER D**, *Beast City* removes all the subtextual tension of vampire stories. A heroine named for Bram Stoker's original and a homeworld poached from *Vampirella* do little good when the rest of vampire lore is taken with a pinch of salt— these creatures still fear crucifixes but happily immerse themselves beneath running water in long shower scenes. In Japan, the series was partly sold to the public on the basis that sharp-eared viewers would hear several famous voice actresses grunting and groaning behind pseudonyms, a sure-fire sign of a lack of faith in other aspects of production (see **ADVENTURE KID**). Only the first two episodes graced the English language; the third, said to be notably inferior, never made it to the American market. Two other Naomi Hayakawa creations have been animated: *Binding* (as part of **COOL DEVICES**) and **MELANCHOLY SLAVE**. Similar liberties were taken with legends about werewolves to create **MIDNIGHT PANTHER**. ●NV

BEAST CLAW, THE

2006. JPN: *Kemonozume*. TV series. DIR: Masaaki Yuasa. SCR: Masaaki Yuasa, Shichi Ogikubo (pseud. for Yuichiro Oguro), Atsushi Takeuchi. DES: Nobutake Ito, Rei Kono. ANI: Nobutake Ito. MUS: Kei Wakakusa. PRD: Madhouse Studios, Dentsu, Hakuhodo DY Media Partners, WOWOW, Yomiko Advertising. 30 mins. x 13 eps.

Toshihiko is the eldest son of a very important man, though the Momota family business works mostly below the radar. The Kifuken organization isn't a commercial company, it's a group of hunter-killers. Cannibal demon beasts, *shokujinki*, are prowling the world for prey, disguised as humans. An expert swordsman since childhood, Toshihiko is one of the elite group trained to stop them. Then he falls in love at first sight with a beautiful girl. But a loss of killer focus isn't the only problem of his romance: Yuka has a dark family secret, too. A premise that starts out like Madhouse's 1980s classic **WICKED CITY**, originated and directed by the director of **MIND GAME**, with plenty of gory action and some sexual titillation, makes for a show with a lot going for it: it's something of a mystery

that this series hasn't been released in English. The deliberately ugly mean-streets art-style is edgy and interesting, and the animation is fluid and expressive. ●V

BEAST PLAYER ERIN, THE *

2009. JPN: *Kemono no Soja Erin*. TV series. DIR: Takayuki Hamana. SCR: Junichi Fujisaki, Kiyoko Yoshimura. DES: Takayuki Goto, Akira Suzuki. ANI: Takayuki Goto, Nariyuki Takahashi. MUS: Masayuki Sakamoto. PRD: Production I.G, Trans Arts, NHK. 25 mins. x 50 eps.

Erin is ten, and lives with her mother Soyon in a tiny rural village in a feudal state, where the people raise huge, lizard-like horned beasts called *toda*. They are used by the armies of the queen for military purposes, and the village relies on them for survival. Erin is widely acknowledged to have inherited her mother's gifts as a beast trainer, despite being so young. The pair are liked and respected by their neighbors, even though Soyon is from a different tribe that has traditionally been distrusted. When her mother is sentenced to a terrible fate, Erin must travel far from home and learn to deal with injustice, prejudice, and the responsibility of her remarkable gift. Her beloved *toda* are at the mercy of the Oju, winged beasts used by the queen's elite, symbols of royalty's total domination of the masses laboring in its service. She wants to study them and understand the link between the two species. But knowledge is power, and power is dangerous. As Erin grows to young womanhood her world grows darker and more threatening.

Fans of the **WORLD MASTERPIECE THEATER** series will warm to *The Beast Player Erin*. Many will catch echoes of the pre–Studio Ghibli work of Isao Takahata and Hayao Miyazaki. The story is old-fashioned in the best sense, a solidly plotted, highly detailed, and beautifully written show that the whole family can watch and enjoy together—and since the second half of the plot includes some very dark and powerful themes of betrayal, deceit, and manipulation, young children might find it distressing to watch alone. There are occasional false notes of comic relief, reminiscent of the goofy gags that Osamu Tezuka used to pop into his manga to provide a break in extended periods of tension, but they're

only a minor irritation for adult viewers and are likely to appeal to younger ones. Production I.G has earned a reputation for quality and innovation in animation: here the quality is impeccable. The simple, straightforward style set against painterly backgrounds enhances the sense of watching a series made three decades ago, when the best TV animation served the story rather than being a tricksy attention-grabber intended for someone's showreel. Sakamoto's score is simple and graceful, fitting the animation well, and the songs and lullabies scattered throughout the story are utterly lovely (**MUSIC IN ANIME**). This stunning series is only available in English via Internet streaming—the shape of the industry to come, but in this instance an archive-format release in gorgeous packaging is merited. A ten-episode compilation, *The Beast Player Erin—Compilation (Soshuhen)* was released in 2010. The whole project was based on a fantasy book series written by Nahoko Uehashi, with art by Itoe Takemoto. ●

BEAST WARRIORS *

1992. JPN: *KO Seiki Beast Sanjushi*. AKA: *KO Century Beast Three Beastketeers*; *KO Century Beast Warriors*. Video. DIR: Hiroshi Negishi. SCR: Satoru Akahori, Tetsuko Watanabe, Mayori Sekijima, Koji Masunari. DES: Zero-G Room, Rei Nakahara, Takehiko Ito. ANI: Takuya Saito, Makoto Matsuo. MUS: Nick Wood. PRD: KSS. 30 mins. x 7 eps.

On an Earth literally broken in two, the evil Humans have invaded the territory of the heavily mutated Beast tribes. Though they possess powerful totem weapons, the Beasts cannot stand against the Humans' high-tech might. Wan Dabada, who can transform into a tiger when angry, is captured when his tribe is destroyed and thrown into jail with three other Beasts: Meima, the mermaid princess; Mekka, the turtle boy; and Badd Mint, the transforming chicken. Professor Password, a human scientist ashamed at his race's behavior, is killed helping them escape but not before entrusting the group with his granddaughter, Yumi Charm. Searching for the mythical Gaia system that could turn the battle, they find one of its outposts by draining a lake—elements here not only of **TREASURE ISLAND**, but also of director Negishi's earlier **LADIUS**. With Yumi's help, they learn how to combine their totems into a superweapon, though a power supply proves harder to come by.

As with other Akahori creations like MAZE and KNIGHTS OF RAMUNE, the hackneyed but entertaining *Beast Warriors* has a flimsy plot concealed by tongue-in-cheek humor and loud, brash designs—here including costumes by OH MY GODDESS!–creator Kosuke Fujishima. The initial series is clearly the set-up for a TV version that never came, and the final four episodes (renamed *Beast Warriors II*, with a fantastic new opening theme, and written, in part, by future PHOTON-director Masunari) simply adds some new designs and an extra subplot similar to that surrounding Rini in SAILOR MOON. As the first and only release of the ill-fated Anime U.K. label, it was also a failure in its English version—never making enough money to justify the release of the final four episodes and never distributed in the U.S. It is chiefly remembered today as the unexpected and unremarkable voice acting debut of Jonathan Clements and Helen McCarthy, who played the arrogant, deluded minion V-Daan and his sidekick Akumako, an irritating, devil-girl with a high-pitched voice. One wonders, where are they now? When rights lapsed in the British edition, the series was picked up by the U.S. distributor Right Stuf, who renamed it *KO Beast*. The Right Stuf version dubs all seven episodes, not merely the first three, with an all-new cast. For the origins of the name "Wan Dabada," see WANDABA STYLE.

BEAT ANGEL ESCALAYER *

2002. JPN: *Cho Subaru Tenshi Escalayer*. AKA: *Super Pleiades Angel Escalayer*. Video. DIR: Ikka Tsuchida, Keiichiro Katsura, Zuko Ogo. SCR: Yujiro Muramatsu. DES: Shinichi Miyame. ANI: Raisuke Hayashi. MUS: N/C. PRD: Pink Pineapple, Caos Project Masaaki Kannan. 29 mins. x 3 eps.

High school lothario Kyohei hopes to add new transfer student Sayuka to his list of conquests. At first, he suspects she is a lesbian, only to discover that her sexy roommate Madoka is merely there as a temporary measure. Sayuka is actually a battle android on a mission to save the world, but she runs on a "Doki-Doki Dynamo" that requires sexual energy to charge her up. The Earth is under threat from the

similarly fueled minions of an entity called the Dielast, and with Madoka failing to provide what Sayuka really needs, Kyohei manfully steps up to do his duty in a superior rip-off of DEVADASY—what the hell, two years had passed, who was going to notice? The concept was taken further in JIBURIRU: THE DEVIL ANGEL. **ⓛⓃⓋ**

BEAT BLADES HARUKA

2008. JPN: *Choko Sennin Haruka*. Video. DIR: N/C. SCR: N/C. DES: N/C. ANI: N/C. MUS: N/C. PRD: Lyricc, MS Pictures. 28 mins. x 3 eps.

Takamaru is a high school student living in an apartment building, where the manager's teenage daughter Narika constantly interferes in his romances. He falls for a new transfer student named Haruka, and is delighted when, after rescuing him and Narika from a mysterious ninja gang, Haruka calls him "young master" and asks him to molest her so that she can unleash the superhuman power she needs to defeat the ninja. Some may see echoes of URUSEI YATSURA's alien girlfriend/girl next door love triangle here, but this is based on a porn PC game of the same name by AliceSoft, so that would be reading too much into it. A follow-up game, *Kyarakore*, was released in 2010. **Ⓝ**

BEAT SHOT!!

1989. Video. AKA: *Watch Me Sink My Putz*. DIR: Takashi Akimoto. SCR: Hidemi Kamata. DES: Satoshi Ikezawa. ANI: Hiroyuki Oka. MUS: N/C. PRD: Gainax, AIC. 30 mins.

Expert linksman Akihiko joins the university golf club at the same time as maverick golfer Akikazu. The pair often tee off against each other, though Akikazu is distracted by the charms of his opponent's beautiful caddy, Misako. A heady mix of sex and golf in this adaptation of a manga from *Monthly Playboy* (no relation to the U.S. magazine, although the publishers would very much like to imply there is). Creator Satoshi Ikezawa normally specializes in racing stories like CIRCUIT WOLF but here replaces the tension of fast cars with furtive fumblings in the rough. Director Akimoto tries for some class with grainy, sepia-tinted opening shots of old-world golfers, but before long it's back to exactly what one might expect from 1980s erotica. The alternative title, prevalent in many online listings, is from an illegal bootleg

edition, and not sanctioned by anyone … ever. **Ⓝ**

BEATON THE ROBOBOY

1976. JPN: *Robokko Beaton*. AKA: *Little Robot Viton*. TV series. DIR: Yu Tachibana, Satoshi Dezaki, Takao Yotsuji, Masuji Harada, Mitsuo Kobayashi. SCR: Kiyoharu Matsuoka, Soji Yoshikawa, Yoshiaki Yoshida, Hiroshi Kaneko. DES: Yoshikazu Yasuhiko. ANI: Yoshikazu Yasuhiko. MUS: Mamoru Fujisawa. PRD: Nippon Sunrise, Tohoku Shinsha. 25 mins. x 50 eps.

Ma-chan receives a self-assembly robot from his uncle in America, and seeks help in building it from local inventor Mr. Nobel in putting it together. Nobel botches the assembly and connects the wrong circuits, ironically creating a malfunctioning companion in the style of DORAEMON, albeit with a bonus built-in jet engine. Slapstick comedy ensues, involving Beaton, Ma-chan, his girlfriend Urara, local bad boy Bratman ("Gaki-oyaji"), and his Nazi-helmeted assistant Bratranger ("Gaki-ranger"). Beaton has three critical weaknesses that can be used against him. Water makes him rust; he has an ULTRAMAN-style three-minute limit on operations; and he is subject to a remote control device. He confiscates the controller from Ma-chan and hides it in a cavity in his chest, but if anyone manages to obtain it they can manipulate Beaton for their own ends.

BECAUSE I DON'T LIKE MY BIG BROTHER AT ALL

2011. JPN: *Oniichan no Koto Nanka Zenzen Suki ja nai Dakara ne!!* AKA: *I Don't Like You At All, Big Brother!* TV series. DIR: Keitaro Motonaga. SCR: Sayuri Oba, Katsuhiko Koike. DES: Madoka Hirayama, Mie Kasai. ANI: Atsushi Yamamoto, Manabu Yasumoto, Tomoyuki Matsumoto, Yuji Kondo. MUS: Tomoki Kikuya. PRD: ZEXCS, Starchild Records. 24 mins. x 13 eps.

Teenage girl Nao has a massive big brother complex. She's so jealous of Shunsuke, and so determined to be the only woman in his life, that she even sneaks into his room to throw away his porn stash. Then she finds a photo album of childhood pictures without a baby or toddler Nao in a single one. She realizes that she's adopted! And luckily, Shunsuke has a kid sister complex, and is a member of a porn appreciation society at school, making him a prime target for the harem of Nao's schoolfriends. This is intended as a not-quite-incest harem comedy (ROMANCE AND DRAMA). Erotic appeal is a matter of taste, and there's obviously a market for anime about painfully skinny, big-hipped childen with huge ears, hands, and feet (all of which, incidentally, are sometimes mythol-ogized as indicators of sexual prowess and voracity). Generally speaking, though, the design and animation are undistinguished, as is the script. The final episode was never aired, being instead added to the fifth Japanese DVD release. Trivia-hounds may like to check out the scene where Shun-suke and his friends visit Akihabara and see how many of the real-life erotic anime posters they recognize.

Episode 10 gained that holy grail of erotic anime, a removal from the airwaves, but not for its sexual content—a sequence of the characters being swept away by a tidal wave was judged to be in poor taste after the Great East Japan Earthquake. Right, *that* was in poor taste. **Ⓝ**

BECK *
2005. AKA: *Beck: Mongolian Chop Squad*. TV series. DIR: Osamu Kobayashi. SCR: Osamu Kobayashi. DES: Motonobu Hori, Osamu Kobayashi. ANI: N/C. MUS: Taku Hirai. PRD: Madhouse, TV Tokyo. 25 mins. x 26 eps.
Average eighth grader Yukio "Koyuki" Tanaka has no special talents or interest-ing hobbies, and is occasionally the victim of school bullies. While he's trying to rescue an ugly dog, his path crosses that of guitarist Ryusuke "Ray" Minami. The dog is Ray's beloved Beck, after whom his band and this anime series are named. Ray used to be in a band with rock legend Eddy, of top American band Dying Breed, he owns a superb Les Paul guitar he calls Lucille (a namesake of B. B. King's instrument), and to Koyuki he seems the epitome of cool. Drawn into his world, Koyuki falls in love with music and the rock'n'roll lifestyle. But his new hero has some seri-ous problems: he made many enemies in the U.S.A., including powerful promoter Leon Sykes, the original owner of both Beck and Lucille. As Koyuki's own talent develops, he acquires a guitar of his own (a Fender Telecaster) and becomes a lead vocalist with the group, which acquires a

dual identity as "Mongolian Chop Squad" in America, because the U.S.A. already has a singer called Beck. *Beck* the anime smartly avoids the pitfalls of BLACK HEAVEN and GRAVITATION, dropping some of the comedy of Harold Sakuishi's original manga, and making the music one of the main stars of the show. The main leads each have two voice actors in the original Japanese release, one normal voice for dialogue, and actual singers for their performances, using vocalists from the bands Husking Bee and YKZ. The bilin-gual nature of the action and characters, however, leads to an amount of mixed English-Japanese dialogue in the original release, which is either cute or irritating, depending on where one stands. The anime is packed with references to rock staples and legends, many of which have been around far longer than its young au-dience. It has also inspired a game for the PS2, and the live-action film *Beck* (2009), directed by Yukihiko Tsutsumi. **Ⓛ**

BEE TRAIN
Animation company formed in 1997 by several former Tatsunoko staffers, including director Koichi Mashimo and producer Mitsuhisa Ishikawa (now more often associated with Production I.G). Representative works include NOIR, MAD-LAX, and .HACK. Although, like Xebec and P.A. Works, Bee Train was created as a sub-sidiary of Tatsunoko, it is no longer so on paper, since Tatsunoko's percentage of the company's shares is no longer a control-ling interest. The authors are not entirely sure whether this makes the slightest difference in the Japanese market, since Bee Train continues to work on Tatsunoko productions as if it still is a subsidiary!

BEELZEBUB *
2011. TV series. DIR: Nobuhiro Takamoto. SCR: Masahiro Yokotani, Eiji Umehara, Isana Kakimura. DES: Takeshi Yoshioka, Junichi Higashi, Toshiyuki Tokuda. ANI: Kazuhiro Oki, Ippei Ichii, Bum-Chul Chang, Chang Hwan Park. MUS: Yasuharu Takanashi. PRD: Dentsu, Pierrot, Shueisha, Yomiuri TV. 24 mins. x 60 eps.
Ryuhei Tamura's manga *Beelzebub* makes a teenage tough-guy the human guardian of baby Beelzebub and his cute demonic nursemaid Hilda. He soon finds that

bringing up a demon baby and coping with school is a challenge for even the toughest guy. But Hilda tells the hapless Tatsumi that the baby was attracted to his aura of evil. He's on a mission to destroy humanity, so he needs a father-surrogate who can keep him in the right frame of mind. If Tatsumi can find someone stronger and nastier than he is, baby Beel will attach to that person instead. Tatsumi goes to the roughest, most violent school in Japan so that should be easy.

To bring any manga to life for TV ani-mation takes a huge crew: *Beelzebub* has 40 animation directors, 15 assistants, over 60 key animators and more than 70 studios contributing to the animation team alone, plus superstars including Yasuomi Umezu and Atsuko Nakajima taking charge of the multiple opening and ending credit sequences. Yet for the most part the ani-mation is fairly pedestrian, despite a few impressive slugfests. The writing is uneven, with more serious elements entering the plot and not always fitting well, and there are gaping plot holes. But on the whole, this wild and wicked take on a theme that's as old as Moses in the bulrushes is fun. If you want to see the same story told sweet and sappy, rather than wryly nihilistic, DAA! DAA! DAA! is the show for you. **Ⓥ**

BEET THE VANDEL BUSTER
2003. JPN: *Boken O Beet*. AKA: *Adventure King Beet*. TV series. DIR: Tatsuya Nagamine. SCR: Yoshimi Narita. DES: Katsuyoshi Nakat-sura, Tadayoshi Yamamuro. ANI: Tadayoshi Yamamura. MUS: N/C. PRD: Toei, TV Tokyo, Dentsu, Bandai Visual. 25 mins. x 52 eps. (TV1); 25 mins. x 25 eps. (TV2).
During the unspecified "Century of Darkness," the world is besieged by evil vampire-devil hybrids, the Vandels. The last line of defense comprises the Vandel Busters, elite human warriors tasked with hunting the demons down. Beet idolizes his elder brother, Zenon, whose platoon all die defending the young Beet from the arch-demon Beltoze—leaving the inexperienced Beet to inherit five magical weapons invested with their life force, with shades here of *Rogue Trooper*, or the *Mighty Morphin' Power Rangers* (*DE). Five years on, Beet takes his place as a Vandel Buster. Beet's childhood friend, the cute Poala, is also a Vandel Buster, and she joins him

on his quest to eliminate the evil Vandels. Based on the manga by Riku Sanjo and Koji Inada, serialized in *Shonen Jump* weekly. The manga's inspiration comes from gaming—if the scenario isn't clue enough, there are references to "leveling up" and "bosses." Beet's special ability, such as it is, involves staying awake for three days before collapsing in a virtual coma; presumably something with which anyone trying to complete the latest *Final Fantasy* installment can identify. From the 53rd episode onward, the series was rebranded *Boken O Beet Excellion*.

BEETLE BORG
2006. JPN: *Jinzo Konchu Kabuto Borg VxV*. AKA: *Artificial Insect Kabuto Borg Victory by Victory*. TV series. DIR: Hiroshi Ishiodori. SCR: Akatsuki Yamatoya, Kento Shimoyama, Yoshio Urasawa, Katsuhiko Chiba. DES: Kil Sun Chang, Yasuyuki Noda, Cho Jang Hwan. ANI: N/C. MUS: Ikuo Goto. PRD: G&G Entertainment, NAS, Studio Comet, KBS. 25 mins. x 52 eps.
Ten-year-olds Ryusei, Katsuji, and their friends are Borg Battlers—players in a combat game using mechanical beetles. They train day and night to be champions, but face opponents who want to use the game for evil, including a mysterious man in a golden helmet, his face covered by a mask of gold. Made to promote Takara Tomy's range of wind-up beetle toys, the series is standard kids' adventure fare, packed with action and goofy humor. Toy companies are always hoping to create the next POKÉMON, and so anime deploying the standard elements of action, collecting, evil opponents, and heroic kids going on a quest without adult supervision crop up year after year.

BEHIND CLOSED DOORS *
2001. JPN: *Waver*. Video. DIR: Shigenori Kurii. SCR: Hideo Ura. DES: Shigenori Ku-rii. ANI: Michitaka Yamamoto. MUS: N/C. PRD: Shindeban, Tenshindo, Museum Pictures, Milky. 29 mins. x 3 eps.
In an erotic anime that seems distantly informed by Pauline Réage's classic *The Story of O* (1954), Kenichi wins a mystery competition prize in the form of a CD, which he is instructed to put in his car's player and follow directions to the location of his real prize. He and his loving girlfriend Yoshino

dutifully do so, only to find themselves at a remote mansion à la BLACK WIDOW, which soon turns out to be a brothel. Forced to spend the night, they discover a series of sadomasochistic prostitutes in different sectors of the house, many of whom seduce Kenichi after he quarrels with Yoshino. Before long, Yoshino slips deeper into the bondage lifestyle of the house's mistress and other inhabitants, with the sex depicted onscreen getting increasingly violent and unpleasant. **NV**

BELLE AND SEBASTIAN *
1981. JPN: *Meiken Jolie*. AKA: *Famous Dog Jolly*. TV series. DIR: Keiji Hayakawa, Shinji Okada, Kazuyoshi Yokota, Fumio Ikeno, Seiji Endo. SCR: Toshiyuki Kashiwakura, Soji Yoshikawa, Kunio Nakatani. DES: Shuichi Seki. ANI: Nobuyuki Kitajima. MUS: TT Nescebance. PRD: Toho, Visual 80, NHK. 25 mins. x 52 eps.
Named for the saint's day on which he was born and abandoned by his gypsy mother, Sebastian has been raised by Old Seasal, who may or may not be his grandfather. Rejected by the village children for having no parents, he befriends Jolie (Belle), a large Great Pyrenees dog hated and reviled as "the white devil." In search of somewhere to call home, the pair (and their comic-relief puppy, Poochie) journey across the Pyrenees in search of Sebastian's mother, which is similar to a quest seen in FROM THE APENNINES TO THE ANDES. Though they find many places to live (the Pyrenees seem to be littered with kindly childless couples willing to adopt a boy and his dogs), they are always forced to move on by the relentless pursuit of Garcia, an officer of the law who believes them to have committed a crime. Based on the children's books by Cecile Aubrey, this series was picked up by Nickelodeon in the 1980s. The original live-action TV series was shown on NHK in 1973.

BELOVED BETTY: DEVIL STORY
1986. JPN: *Itoshi no Betty: Ma Monogatari*. Video. DIR: Kazuo Koike, Masahito Sato. SCR: Hideo Takayashiki. DES: Kazuo Ohara. ANI: Michio Shindo. MUS: Haruki Mino. PRD: Big Bang, Cosmos, Toei. 50 mins.
A devil-girl with the face of an angel and a heart of gold, blonde Betty falls in love with an earthbound gangster, Danpei

Kimogawa, when they meet in a rainstorm. They end up living together in a Tokyo highrise apartment, though Danpei has trouble coping with his new witch and demon in-laws dropping in at inopportune moments. Betty has actually been sent to the human world on a mission to defeat the demon Lutan. While Betty continues with her task, her skeletal grandmother sends nubile nymphs to tempt Danpei and see if he is suitable husband material. A Japanese knockoff of *Bewitched* but with a lowlife husband and considerably more sex, *Beloved Betty* thrived amid a 1980s Japanese fad for domestic magic. The same year saw the release of GOING STEADY WITH A WITCH, though both titles would soon be eclipsed by another alien lover more suitable for the mass market, URUSEI YATSURA's Lum. In this short video, also shown theatrically on a double bill with AMON SAGA, the hen-pecked Danpei was played by Yuji Miyake, a pop star from the group Set. Director Koike also wrote the original 1980 manga, drawn by Seisaku Kano for *Big Comic*, though by the time the anime version was released, he was making more of a name for himself with CRYING FREEMAN. **N**

BEN-TO *
2011. TV series. DIR: Shin Itagaki. SCR: Kazuyuki Fudeyasu, Shogo Yasukawa. DES: Katsuzo Hirata, Yoshimi Umino. ANI: Isao Sugimoto, Katsuzo Hirata. MUS: Taku Iwasaki. PRD: David Production, Pony Canyon, Shueisha, BS. 30 mins. x 12 eps.
There's no such thing as a free lunch, but even a cheap one can be deadly. Yo Sato, SONIC THE HEDGEHOG fan and high school newcomer, has to move into the school dorm and fend for himself. When he tries to buy a cheap *bento* box at the local store, he finds himself in a fight with his fellow students for the discounted goodies. He's knocked out, and wakes with dim memories of a girl. It turns out she's a classmate, Sen, one of the dominant local gang, the Wolves. Every night the Wolves feast on the store's reduced-price leftovers, while the rest—the Dogs, as they're contemptuously named—eat instant noodles. Can Yo rise through the ranks as a Wolf, or is he doomed to eat "dogfood" for the rest of his school career? High school fighting anime abound—compare with

IKKI TOUSEN—as do game anime where the rules and moves are arcanely named and detailed. This one began in 2008 as a series of books by Asaura, illustrated by Kaito Shibano. It also had two manga adaptations in 2011, one starting before and one after the anime aired, both with art by Shibano.

BENEATH THE BLACK RAIN

1984. JPN: *Kuroi Ame ni Utarete*. Movie. AKA: *Drenched by the Black Rain*. DIR: Takeshi Shirato, Kazuhiko Udagawa. SCR: Motokazu Hara, Keiji Nakazawa, Takeshi Shirato. DES: Keiji Nakazawa. ANI: Kazuhiko Udagawa. MUS: Kitaro. PRD: Gen Pro, Tsuchida Pro. 90 mins.
BAREFOOT GEN–creator Keiji Nakazawa wrote an even darker series of tales for this anthology movie about several characters reacting in different ways to the ongoing effects of the atomic bomb. Yuri attempts a one-woman crusade against the U.S. by giving syphilis to servicemen; Yuko becomes a human museum, baring her burned and distorted skin as a testament to the effects of the bomb; while Eiko frets over whether she should get pregnant, since she is a child of bomb victims and may still carry mutant genes. **N**

BENKEI VS. USHIWAKA

1939. JPN: *Benkei tai Ushiwaka*. Movie. DIR: Kenzo Masaoka. SCR: Kenzo Masaoka. DES: Kenzo Masaoka. ANI: Ryotaro Kuwata. MUS: N/C. PRD: Nippon Doga Kenkyu Tokoro. 10 mins.
Ushiwaka (AKA Minamoto no Yoshitsune) lives in the forest and is trained in the martial arts by *tengu* crow spirits. One day he is walking through Kyoto when his path is blocked by a giant monk, Benkei, who has sworn to take the swords of a thousand defeated foes and now has but one left to collect before he can retire. The diminutive Ushiwaka, however, refuses to hand his sword over and trounces the giant monk on the Gojo Bridge. Recognizing his true master, Benkei swears eternal loyalty. Often termed the "Robin Hood and Little John" of Japanese legend, stories of Yoshitsune and Benkei often crop up in JAPANESE FOLK TALES. However, sightings of them are curiously rare in anime despite a rich tradition that could easily fill a series the size of RANMA ½. Apart from this single antique two-reeler, they can only be found in oblique references in other shows and in a couple of tales in the series JAPANESE HISTORY and MANGA PICTURES OF JAPAN.

BERSERK *

1997. JPN: *Kenpu Dengi Berserk*. AKA: *Sword-Wind Chronicle Berserk*. TV series, movies. DIR: Naohito Takahashi. SCR: Yasuhiro Imagawa, Atsuhiro Tomioka. DES: Yoshihiko Umakoshi, Tokuhiro Matsubara. ANI: Tokuhiro Matsubara, Yuriko Chiba. MUS: Susumu Hirazawa. PRD: OLM, Nippon TV. 25 mins. x 25 eps. (TV), 80 mins. (m1), 100 mins. (m2), 120 mins. (m3).
Guts, a young mercenary who was instrumental in winning the army's last battle, is recruited into the elite mercenary company the Band of the Hawk, led by the charismatic Griffiths, whose ambitions are aimed squarely at the kingdom of Midland's throne. Guts rises rapidly to command in the Hawks, based on his immense skill in battle. Meanwhile, Griffiths and the Band of the Hawk prove their worth by winning battle after battle for Midland, themselves rising above high-ranking but untalented commanders. Worried about intrigues behind the scenes, he decides to leave, but Griffiths does not allow him to go, forcing Guts to best him in combat. Griffiths is persecuted by noblemen who resent his promotion on account of his talent instead of family connections, and he is eventually imprisoned. The Band of the Hawk is ambushed, scattered, and hunted. Guts returns, and the pretty Casca, Griffith's second-in-command (it is a boy's name in the real world, but is assigned to a girl, here), who has unrequited feelings for Griffiths, finds solace in Guts's arms, and eventually joins forces with him to lead a rescue mission. However, upon arrival, Guts discovers that Griffiths has been brutally crippled and maimed by torture. Griffiths, in despair and longing for power, eventually makes a pact with the God Hand, demon-gods who demand human sacrifice, with disastrous consequences for all concerned.

With a hero whose magical wound will not heal, baddies named after SF greats (Conrad, Ubik, Slan, and Boskone), fighting on and off the battlefield, and no punches pulled in its savagery and devilry, *Berserk* was a manga hit with both readers and critics when it appeared in *Young Animal* magazine. Told chiefly in flashback, the anime series covers the early chapters of Kentaro Miura's manga. The series was lampooned in an episode of the OH MY GODDESS! comedy show, *Adventures of Mini-Goddess*, in which Skuld and Urd, dressed as Guts and Griffiths, must rescue Belldandy from a castle.

A decade later the franchise was revived as the movie trilogy *Egg of the King* (2012), *The Battle for Doldrey* (2012), and *Descent* (2013), retelling, supposedly at the creator's request, more or less the same sequence of events from the TV show. Encompassing chapters 4–13 of an ongoing series that has already passed the 37th volume, this "Golden Age" arc is recurringly popular, at least in part, because it is chronologically the earliest part of Guts's complex storyline and must be covered before any efforts to advance further along in the narrative. Toshiyuki Kubo'oka's trilogy, made with the benefit of many years' experience on computer game cut scenes, uses a hybridized technique combining 2D animation with fully rendered 3D objects where relevant—often in lighting effects and in the representation of armor. Screened in Japan before local viewers had the chance to compare it to the very similar TV show *Game of Thrones* (2011), it presents a mixing-pot view of European history like that of the original manga, perhaps better described as impressionistic rather than anachronistic, with Dark Age technology often rubbing shoulders with Renaissance fashions. The world-building can hence be oddly bipolar, with some staffers lovingly recreating the precise roofing designs of real-world castles, others pointing to medieval cookbooks with banquet recipes for baked dolphin, but many seemingly just picking costumes and settings because they look good. **V**

BEST STUDENT COUNCIL *

2005. JPN: *Gokujo Seitokai*. AKA: *Student Council Almighty*. TV series. DIR: Yoshiaki Iwasaki. SCR: Yosuke Kuroda. DES: Tsuyoshi Kawada. ANI: Tsuyoshi Kawada. MUS: Yoko Shimomura. PRD: JC Staff, Konami. 24 mins. x 26 eps.
Orphan schoolgirl Rino is clearly losing it—her best friend is a hand puppet, albeit a self-aware one for as long as he is installed. She transfers to a new school, the

all-girl Miyagami Academy, only to discover on her first day that her lodgings have burned down. She manages to apprehend the arsonist, and is hence invited onto the influential student council.

A touch of politics arrives in the everyday school anime genre, in a show that concentrates, not on classes, but on their class representatives. Often portrayed in other anime as the dull class grinds always sucking up to the teachers, these hall monitors and council reps are presented here as the heroes—with something of a debt to the satirical Reese Witherspoon vehicle *Election* (1999).

BETRAYAL KNOWS MY NAME, THE *

2010. JPN: *Uragiri wa Boku no Namae o Shitteiru*. AKA: *Uraboku*. TV series. DIR: Katsushi Sakurabi. SCR: Natsuko Takahashi, Sayaka Harada, Daisuke Watanabe. DES: Mai Matsuura, Yumi Nakayama, Hirotsugu Kakoi. ANI: Yumi Nakayama. MUS: Shogo Kaida. PRD: JC Staff, David Production, MBS, Animax. 25 mins. x 25 eps.

Yuki was abandoned as a baby with nothing but his name. At 15, he's a mass of conflicts, afraid to be alone but not wanting to get too close or be a burden to anyone. He has more reason than most teenagers to be afraid of closeness—if he touches someone he can feel their emotions. What Yuki doesn't know is that he is one of an elite clan with supernatural abilities, abandoned by his mother for his own protection. A mysterious man who claims to be his older brother takes him away from the orphanage and introduces him to a heritage of power, influence, and wealth, telling him his clan has been fighting since the middle ages to save the world from demons. But one demon in particular is rapidly becoming important to Yuki. Based on Hotaru Odagiri's 2005 manga, this is a showcase of pretty boys and gorgeous art, and music. It's saturated in angst and wish fulfillment; the fact that the world revolves around the central character and everyone else spends most of their time thinking about him, rather than letting him get on with life while they focus on fighting evil, has obvious appeal for the target market of teenage girls. However, it points to the series' major weakness: a lack of conviction in the writing and a massively apparent lack of interest in any plot element except the pretty-boy angst bits. Looks yummy, feels like eating too many marshmallows at one sitting.

BETTERMAN *

1999. TV series. DIR: Yoshitomo Yonetani. SCR: Hiroshi Yamaguchi. DES: Masahiro Kimura, Kunio Okawara, Masahiro Yamane. ANI: Masahiro Kimura. MUS: Kohei Tanaka. PRD: Sunrise, TV Tokyo. 25 mins. x 26 eps.

The year is 2006. Keita Aono is a bespectacled schoolboy in Yokohama who is surprised to meet childhood sweetheart Hinoki Sai when she transfers to his school. The rainbow-haired Hinoki now works for Akamatsu Industrial Company (AIC—as in the anime studio), piloting the large robots called Neuronoids. These machines run on a kind of artificial blood called Linker Gel and patch directly into their pilots' nervous systems. When Hinoki's fellow pilot Cactus is killed in a battle with monsters called Algernons, Keita is talked into taking his place and discovers that he is one of the rare Dual Kind, able to synchronize almost perfectly with the complex machine. He becomes a full-fledged pilot, though Hinoki's activities alongside him are often suspiciously supported by "Betterman Lamia," a man with the same hairstyle as her and an uncanny ability to turn up in the nick of time and save the day by transforming into the bioweapon Betterman Nebula.

In the grand tradition of GUNDAM, Sunrise filed the serial numbers off its standard story template and punched it out again post-EVANGELION—evidence, if ever it was required, that two years after you do something in the anime business, you can do it all over again and nobody will notice.

BEWITCHED AGNÈS

2005. JPN: *Okusama wa Maho Shojo*. AKA: *My Wife Is a Magical Girl*. TV series. DIR: Hiroshi Nishikiori, Yoshihisa Matsumoto. SCR: Yuji Matsukura, Kazuhiko Ikeguchi. DES: Shinya Hasegawa. ANI: Hiroshi Nishikiori. MUS: N/C. PRD: JC Staff, Chiba TV. 25 mins. x 13 eps.

Kagura is a college graduate who has just moved to a quiet coastal town to start his new life. He takes a room in a boarding house run by pretty 26-year-old Ureshiko Asaba, whose author husband is a local celebrity. But there the similarity with MAISON IKKOKU ends. Ureshiko Asaba might appear to be an ordinary, pink-haired Japanese housewife, but she is really Agnès Bell, a superheroine sworn to protect the parallel world of Wonderland that coexists with our dimension, but is only visible to those with sorcerous abilities. But now Agnès is far too old to be a magical girl—comically, she complains her costume no longer fits—and the rulers of the magic realm have ordered her to surrender her magic ring, the source of her power over the town, to Cruje, the new magical girl on the block.

Agnès, however, loves the town her mother created with a witchy attachment not seen since KIKI'S DELIVERY SERVICE, while Cruje has orders to destroy it and start anew. Her husband Tamotsu doesn't suspect a thing, although he really ought to, because Agnès refuses to let him kiss her lest it sap her magic abilities. As their relationship (or lack of it) begins to sour, Agnès realizes that she may have to let him in on the secret.

As in OH MY GODDESS!, the magical realm is run along Western business/political lines by older men, who send out theoretically expendable girls to manage the outposts of magic in the human world for as long as they serve the purpose of their masters. All the magical girls have Japanese everyday names, but like callgirls and strippers (or anime porn voice actresses) they assume different identities at work, and all their magic names are Western. There's some gentle humor and a dose of tear-jerking melodrama in a series with all the hallmarks of LITTLE WITCH SALLY and COMET-SAN, but with a title that acknowledges the American *Bewitched* (1964), one of the most important formative influences on early Japanese TV animation. Its profile increased considerably in the early 21st century through two revivals, related only through the chance acquisition of the series rights by Sony. *Bewitched in Tokyo* (2004, *Okusama wa Majo*) was a sanctioned live-action remake of the American series, broadcast on TV Asahi with Ryoko Yonekura in the leading role. Only a year later, the franchise got another boost from *Bewitched* (2005), the Nicole Kidman vehicle, making knock-offs like this anime pastiche a certainty. Although the story was credited to the animation company JC Staff, it began running as a manga by Toko Kanno in *Dengeki Gao* magazine several months before the initial broadcast. See also SUGAR SUGAR RUNE and MY WIFE IS A HIGH SCHOOL STUDENT.

BEYBLADE *

2001. JPN: *Bakuten Shoot Baybrade*. AKA: *Flashpoint Shoot Baybrade*. TV series, movies. DIR: Toshifumi Kawase, Jun Takada, Masahiko Murata. SCR: Toshiyasu Okubo, Kiyoshi Mizugami, Tatsuhiko Urahata, Kazuyuki Fudeyasu. DES: Takao Aoki. ANI: Shigeru Kato, Kiyoshi Nakahara. MUS: Yoshihisa Hirano. PRD: Madhouse, TV Tokyo. 25 mins. x 51 eps. (TV1), 70 mins. (m1), 25 mins. x 51 eps. (TV2), 25 mins. x 52 eps. (TV3), 25 mins. x 51 eps. (TV3), 25 mins. x 52 eps. (TV4), 98 mins. (m2), 25 mins. x 38 eps. (TV5), 25 mins. x 26 eps. (TV6).

Takao Kinomiya wants to be a master of the gladiatorial Baybrade contest, but only the chosen few can truly control the Pit entities that live inside the spinning-top-like fighting devices. His friend Kai uses the Transor Pit, but Takao discovers a Pit of his own, the creature known as Dragoon, who has lived inside the family's heirloom sword for generations.

An anime based on the *begoma* toy craze, fighting gyroscopes from TRANSFORMERS-creators Takara. The last gyro standing within the ring is the winner, and each has five component parts that can be customized to create (almost) unique toys. The post-POKÉMON generation in Japan set aside its Pikachus and Jigglypuffs in favor of the arcane design of Pit Chips, Attack Rings, Weight Discs, Spin Gears, and Blade Bases. At least it got them out of the house.

Beyblade: The Movie (2002) eventually followed, released in Japan in the middle of the summer vacation, and predictably focusing on a similar event in the lives of its characters, who attempt to take a holiday, only to be dragged into a conflict with Dark Spirits at a nearby temple. The *Beyblade* movie shared the bill with a short movie based on the early PS2 game *Ape Escape*, in which the red-haired Spike attempts to thwart the efforts of the evil Specter to take an ape army back in time to conquer the world. Just another boring Japanese school vacation...

While the likes of *Pokémon* and ONE PIECE have attracted the attention of FAN-DOM and pundits internationally, *Beyblade* remains a quiet, blue-chip success in the manner of ZOIDS, still running on Japanese television 12 years after its debut, with the original series reprised and refashioned in later years under the new subtitles of *V-Force* (2002), *G-Revolution* (2004), *Metal Fusion* (2009), *Metal Masters* (2010), *Metal Fury* (2011), and *Shogun Steel* (2012). As the slight gap implies, the "Metal" series represents something of a reboot, and seems to have reached the height of its popularity in 2010, the year in which a second movie, *Beyblade: Metal Fight Beyblades vs the Incandescent Soulblade Invaders from the Sun* was released. The most recent TV show is *Beyblade:Wheelz* (2012).

BEYOND THE HEAVENS

2009. JPN: *Soten Koro*. AKA: *New Tale of Three Kingdoms*. TV series. DIR: Tooyo Ashida, Tsuneo Tominaga. SCR: Hideo Takayashiki, Takashi Yamada. DES: Akiko Matsushita, Akira Kano, Cindy Yamauchi, Daisuke Yoshida, Takahiro Umehara, Yuichiro Hayashi, Manabu Otsuzuki. ANI: Akira Kano, Cindy Yamauchi, Daisuke Yoshida. MUS: Shusei Murai. PRD: Madhouse, D.N. Dream Partners, Kodansha NTV, Studio Live, VAP. 22 mins. x 26 eps.

China in the second century A.D.: the last days of the Eastern Han. Chancellor Cao Cao, often portrayed as a figure of evil in popular culture, is the hero here, a man trying to break the mould of tradition and move the nation toward a better future. But in order to do so, he must walk through blood, deal death, and learn the value of brotherhood. Many anime about this era of history use magic or superpowers; this isn't one of them, nor does it need magic when the story itself is so epic. Referencing not only the classic novel GREAT CONQUEST: ROMANCE OF THE THREE KINGDOMS but also Sun Tzu's *Art of War*, the plot moves fast and packs in a lot of history (DOCUMENTARIES AND HISTORY), so it's not a show to watch with your brain switched off, though the voiceover narration helps. The art stays remarkably faithful to the 1994 manga by Gonta King and Hagin Yi, and the animation uses some interesting techniques, from both storytelling and live-action film—note the cheeky lens flares. The music and the sound are strong. An interesting and worthwhile show. **NV**

BEYOND THE TRAIN TRACKS

2005. JPN: *Tetsuro no Kanata*. AKA: *Beyond the Railway; The Other Side of the Tracks*. Movie. DIR: Tayuta Mikage. SCR: Tayuta Mikage. DES: Tayuta Mikage. ANI: Tayuta Mikage. MUS: Toru Okada. PRD: Tayuta Mikage, Directions, Inc., Tom Nagae. 11 mins.

A little boy is looking for his father, who disappeared at a station where time seems to stop and rewind like film, or come and go like an unexpected train. Helped by the station chief, and by a mysterious projectionist, he tries to find the truth through the image of his father. Is he chasing shadows, or can they meet again? This beautiful short film makes dynamic use of light and color and atmospheric sound. It's a perfect miniature of the concept that would later form the basis for Martin Scorsese's *Hugo*.

BIBLE BLACK *

2001. JPN: *BB: La Noche de Walpurgis*. AKA: *BB: Walpurgis Night*. Video. DIR: Sho Hanebu, Kazuyuki Honda, Hamuo. SCR: Yasuyuki Muto. DES: Yoshiten. ANI: Yoshiten, Wataru Yamaguchi. MUS: Morihide. PRD: Milky, Museum Pictures. 28 mins. x 6 eps. (v1), 30 mins. x 2 eps. (v -Origins), 100 mins. (Complete), 30 mins. x 6 eps. (v -New), 25 mins., 30 mins. (v -Only), 120 mins. (New Complete), 10 mins. (v -Imari).

Teenager Taki Minase finds a book of black magic in a basement room that none of the students are supposed to enter. Dabbling in some of its spells, he discovers that it is truly powerful—a simple bit of love voodoo not only ensures that a girl attracts the attention of a boy she wants, but that said boy assaults her in broad daylight. But as Taki continues to experiment, he uncovers details of previous atrocities. Twelve years earlier, a group of would-be witches had unleashed terrible powers, and the two survivors, naturally, are now staff members at the school, one of whom requires a new virgin sacrifice to keep herself out of hell. Taki ends up in thrall to Reika Kitami, the evil school nurse, while Kurumi, an innocent girl who has a crush on Taki, looks likely to be the best candidate for the sacrifice, coming up on Walpurgis Night.

With *Buffy the Vampire Slayer*, *The Craft*, and *Charmed* all riding the millennial zeitgeist to make the occult the latest fad with teenagers, it is unsurprising that this should lead to a similar revival in the genre of anime EROTICA AND PORNOGRAPHY. *BB*'s origins lie in a PC game from Active-Soft, released in 2000—although it is probably a coincidence that UROTSUKIDOJI, the grandfather of all erotic-horror anime, was released "12 years" before the game began production. In some ways, *BB* was the *Urotsukidoji* of its era, attracting a significant following, particularly in Eastern Europe and the former Soviet Union where it was the first conspicuous erotic anime for many of the POKÉMON generation. In the Czech Republic, it was both a bestseller and a scandal, when copies were shipped and sold in the supermarket chain Tesco's alongside Disney products, selling out nationwide in a single day before several shocked buyers realized they had not bought a children's cartoon (LAW AND DISORDER).

As with other longer Milky productions like IZUMO, the extended running time of *BB* allows greater space for actual plot, when compared to the lower expectations of one-shot anime porn titles. *BB* is also notable, particularly in its early episodes, for the conspicuously well-drawn characters and animation, with little of the cost-cutting found in lesser erotica. This original series was subsequently edited into a "movie" compilation, featuring two new vignettes as extras, as well as *BB DVD the Game* (2003) which was, as the title implies, a rerelease of the original game and its sequel, with some sequences incorporating footage from the anime remake. Another interactive game, based on episode 3, was released later in the same year, while the DVD games would later be transferred to a new format for *BB Portable* (2005), for the new Sony PSP.

Revisiting scenes that have previously only been glimpsed in the main storyline, the prequel *BB Origins* (2002, *BB Gaiden*) depicts the efforts of Nami, a member of the student council who opposes an attempt by three girls to set up a Witchcraft Club. But the trio in question begin to exact their revenge, using the power of sorcery to make Nami's friends subject themselves to public sexual humiliations. Before long, Nami has joined the cabal herself, in events leading to the human sacrifice that formed part of the backstory

of the *BB* series proper. In a chronological confusion that also, ironically, bears some resemblance to *Urotsukidoji*, the *BB Origins* episodes were released in Japan between the arrivals of episodes 4 and 5 of the original series.

BB New Testament: The Lance of Longinus (2004) half-heartedly restarts the franchise in the manner of DEMON BEAST INVASION, with the girls of the Witchcraft Club grown up and graduated. Former student council member Rika Shiraki has become a teacher at the school, while Kurumi is a psychic investigator with a government agency, tracking a series of gruesome murder cases à la ONI-TENSEI. These seem to be related to the restless spirit of Miss Kitami, the school nurse, leading to the reestablishment of the Witches' Club, by a group of girls who are unsure what side they are supposed to be on. The series was later edited into a second "movie" compilation (2008), with a new sex scene added.

Bible Black Only (2005) is a collection of six vignettes which depict the sexual escapades of various characters as the black bible's erotic magic has apparently come to permeate the school, often turning what started as assaults into consensual acts.

The six episodes of the original series, along with *Origins*, were later repackaged in the misleadingly titled *Complete Box Set* (2006). The set also included a reanimated version of *BB* episode 3 (the original release of which was substandard), and the "Imari Chapter," " a seventh *Only* vignette, as a bonus. **NV**

BIG BOOBS BOMB

2009. JPN: *Bakunyu BOMB*. AKA: *Huge Breasts Bomb*. Video. DIR: Kusakai Kokubunji. SCR: Kusakai Kokubunji. DES: Yuji Ushijima, Mikan, Shizu Mukaihara. ANI: ari, Tadashikuni Kaneko. MUS: N/C. PRD: ChiChi No Ya, Masui Tsuyoshi. 17 mins. x 3 eps
A porn anthology featuring three short segments of three fantasy females—a randy nurse, a desperate housewife, and an oversexed teacher who can't control her class—in various sexual situations. They're all endowed with unfeasibly large breasts. Each segment was released separately in 2009 before being brought out on a single DVD in 2011. **N**

BIG O, THE *

1999. TV series. DIR: Kazuyoshi Katayama. SCR: Chiaki Konaka. DES: Keiichi Sato. ANI: Masami Osone, Kenji Hayama. MUS: Toshihiko Sahashi. PRD: Sunrise, WOWOW. 25 mins. x 13 eps. (TV1), 25 mins. x 13 eps. (TV2).
In 2099, beneath the overarching dome of Paradigm City, amnesiac humanity has lived for 40 years without any contact with the outside world. But there's trouble in Paradigm, and the government has been forced to use increasingly harsh measures to keep the restless citizenry in check. Criminal Negotiator Roger Smith finds himself in over his head when he becomes involved in the race to activate Big O, one of the last surviving examples of the super-advanced technology that led to humanity's self-immurement in the first place.

Big O has a distinct resemblance not only to director Katayama's earlier GIANT ROBO, but also to Warner Bros.' *Batman Beyond*, for which Sunrise had been a Japanese subcontractor. Beyond its crime-fighting millionaire, *Big O*'s roots extend much further back into science fiction, with settings and cybernetics inspired by Isaac Asimov's *Caves of Steel* (1954) and impressive Art Deco costumes and architecture. With the introduction of R.(obot) Dorothy Wayneright, an android almost indistinguishable from real humans, who may hold the secret to humankind's amnesia, the show gains elements that also tie it to a Japanese antecedent, Osamu Tezuka's METROPOLIS. Retro-spirited action in the spirit of GIANT ROBO and STEAM DETECTIVES.

BIG WARS *

1993. Video. JPN: *Kami Utsu Akaki Koya*. AKA: *Gods Attack Red Desert*. DIR: Toshifumi Takizawa, Issei Kume. SCR: Kazumi Koide. DES: Mic Mikuriya, Hideki Takahashi, Kazunori Iwakura, Kow Yokoyama. ANI: Keizo Shimizu, Hideki Takahashi, Kazunori Iwakura. MUS: Michiaki Kato. PRD: Tokuma, Magic Bus. 70 mins.
Many centuries ago, aliens calling themselves Gods visited Earth and subjugated the primitive peoples. When they left, the vestiges of their technology helped humanity become civilized. The aliens return in A.D. 2376 to find mankind has terraformed Mars and is unwilling to serve them again, so they unleash a mind-control agent and attack, both conventionally

and with subverted fifth columnists. Forty years later, protagonist Kanki Akuh is a captain of the Martian Ground Navy, and commanding officer of the brand new sea/land "Large Amphibious Cruiser" Aoba. He is worried that his girlfriend, intelligence lieutenant Darsa Kerrigan, is showing signs of infection (nymphomania, would you believe), but he needs to pull himself together for the coming fight against the huge enemy amphibious carrier called Hell—which is as carefully detailed as one might expect of an anime based on a book by Yoshio Aramaki, who also gave us DEEP BLUE FLEET. *BW* was made straight to video but was given a limited theatrical release to boost its credibility. 🖭🗾

BIG WINDUP *

2007. JPN: *Okiku Furikabutte*. AKA: *Ofuri*. TV series. DIR: Tsutomu Mizushima. SCR: Yosuke Kuroda, Natsuo Soda, Koichi Taki, Michiko Yokote, Susumu Mitsunaka, Yasutaka Yamamoto, Tsutomu Mizushima. DES: Takahiko Yoshida, Yukihiro Shibutani. ANI: Takahiko Yoshida, Akira Takada, Junichiro Taniguchi. MUS: Shiro Hamaguchi. PRD: A-1 Pictures, Aniplex, Kodansha, MBS, MOVIC, TBS. 25 mins. x 25 eps. (TV1), 25 mins. x 13 eps. (TV2). Teenage baseball star Ren Mihashi thinks his success may have been due to his grandfather being the team coach. When he reaches high school, he doesn't think he's good enough to make the team, but gradually, with the encouragement of his friends, he starts to believe in himself. With SPORTS ANIME not the most bankable of genres in the English-speaking market, despite its enduring popularity in Japan, this series was first available streaming in English dub format only, before making the transition to DVD. It's not the fastest, most action-packed show in the world, but like all good sports dramas it's at least as much about the relationships and dynamics of the characters as it is about the matches. Both are handled well, and the design and animation are good—it's refreshing to see a non-comedy show where the main cast isn't uniformly good-looking. There are major problems with pace in the second half, where we go so far into dialogue that a baseball game lasts longer onscreen than it would in real time. A second series appeared in Japan in 2010,

picking up where the first one ended. *Summer Tournament Volume (Natsu no Taikai Hen)* takes Ren and his team-mates to the next round of the High School Invitational Baseball Tournament as they aim for a place in the finals at the legendary Hanshin Koshien Stadium.

BIG X

1964. TV series. DIR: Mitsuteru Okamoto, Osamu Dezaki. SCR: Jiro Kadota, Mami Murano, Tadashi Hirose. DES: Osamu Tezuka. ANI: Eiji Suzuki, Renzo Kinoshita. MUS: Isao Tomita. PRD: TMS, TBS. 30 mins. x 59 eps. During World War II, the Nazis force pacifistic Japanese Professor Asagumo and German Professor Engel to develop Big X, a genetically engineered formula to turn men into giant, invincible soldiers, as a superweapon for Hitler. As Berlin falls in 1945, the researchers are murdered to preserve the secret, but not before Asagumo hides the formula with his son, Shigeru, who returns to Japan. Twenty years later, Hitler's underground neo-Nazi movement revives the war. Gestapo agents in Tokyo attack Shigeru in the midst of an experiment and kill him, but the intruders are thwarted by his son, Akira, who injects himself with the Big X serum, transforming into a 60-foot giant, a Big X intent on fighting for good. The Nazis scheme to bring Akira/Big X to Carthago, a North African state recently conquered by Germans under the command of Hans Engel, grandson of the serum's coinventor. Hans, the victim of Nazi brainwashing, believes that his grandfather was the sole inventor of Big X and that the Asagumos have stolen his birthright from him. In Carthago, Akira meets his love interest, Nina Burton, a sweet young girl who can communicate telepathically with animals. After the liberation of Carthago, Akira and Nina move on to fight the Nazis in other parts of the world, where they are operating through a seemingly neutral international political movement that they control, the Cross Party.

The first production for Tokyo Movie Shinsha, this was the second anime to be made from the works of ASTRO BOY–creator Osamu Tezuka. Rethinking Japan's wartime association with Nazism for a more juvenile audience than the same

author's *Adolf*, *Big X* ran in *Shonen Book* in 1963 and presaged another Tezuka genetics plot in BAGHI. Akira would transform by injecting himself with the serum from a disguised fountain pen, a dangerously tempting idea for a juvenile audience, outclassed perhaps only by 8 MAN's radioactive cigarettes and the pyromaniac pleasures of GOLD LIGHTAN.

BIG-BOOBED MAID HUNTING

2009. JPN: *Bakunyu Maid Kari*. Video. DIR: N/C. SCR: N/C. DES: N/C. ANI: N/C. MUS: N/C. PRD: Hot Bear, Mogadon. 30 mins. x 2 eps. Rich perverts haunt Akihabara looking for maids. But under one man's well-mannered, moneyed exterior lurks a special perversion. He likes to take ordinary girls and turn them into maids obedient to his every whim, then discard them and start with a new girl. MediaBank's Hot Bear label, which made this DVD, are slow to give credit, even for a porn company; our usually reliable Japanese sources have failed to turn up any names, even laughable pseudonyms. You'll just have to amuse yourselves trying to imagine how any of these girls would ever carry a tea-tray without knocking everything off it. In 2012 Hot Bear released *Bakunyu Maid Kari Kanzenban (Complete Edition)* with both stories on one DVD. 🇳

BIHADA TRIBE, THE

2008. JPN: *Bihada Ichizoku*. AKA: *Beautiful Skin Tribe*. TV series. DIR: Michiya Kato. SCR: Ikuko Takahashi. DES: Miho Azuma, Tomoko Kuroyanagi. ANI: Miho Azuma. MUS: manzo, Kiyoto Morimoto. PRD: OMNIBUS JAPAN, Love Labo, Bandai, TV Tokyo. 8 mins. x 12 eps. The Bihada sisters are maintaining a 300-year-old family legacy by entering the World Beautiful Skin competition. Women all over the world are vying for the top prize. But our girls mean to win—and since they're in a series sponsored by Japan's Love Labo beauty company to promote its Mask cosmetic line, viewers can compete with either Misaki or Sara and still come out a winner, as long as they buy the cosmetics. The art and design, inspired by the packaging for the cosmetic line, is reminiscent of ROSE OF VERSAILLES, the sisters presented in romantic style with ornately dressed hair. Many of the pack images refer explicitly to anime of days gone by, and even in modern dress the sisters have an air of archaic femininity. An oddity in a world where supermodels and celebs rather than animated characters usually sell the myth of perfect beauty, but a rather charming one.

BIKKURIMAN

1987. AKA: *Surprise-Man*. TV series. DIR: Yukio Misawa. SCR: Sukehiro Tomita, Mami Watanabe. DES: Mitsuru Aoyama. ANI: Hiroyuki Kadokane, Masahiro Ando. MUS: Takanori Arisawa. PRD: Toei, TV Asahi. 25 mins. x 48 eps. (TV1), 30 mins. (m), 45 mins. (special), 25 mins. x 72 eps. (TV2), 25 mins. x 44 eps. (TV3), 25 mins. x 68 eps. (TV4), 25 mins. x 46 eps. (TV4).

At a time when Earth is about to be cleansed of the old order, the princes of the gods return to fight for the new. Super Zeus, lord of the God-World, orders Saint Phoenix, Prince Yamato, the divine Ali Baba, and their dizzying array of pals to journey to the "edge of the West" and set up a new peaceful land called Jikai. Lined up against them are the minions of Super Devil, king of Devil-World. An incredibly popular tie-in featuring characters from the Bikkuriman Chocolate packets, Bikkuriman also made it into theaters in 1988 with the screening of the time-travel side-story *First Armageddon* and a 45-minute special entitled *Secret Treasure of the Abandoned Zone*. Sequels followed in 1989–90 (*New Bikkuriman*; Jpn.: *Shin Bikkuriman*), 1992–93 (*Super Bikkuriman*, written by Aya Matsui with sharper, brighter designs in the style of other 1990s shows), 1990–2001 (*Bikkuriman 2000*), and 2006–7 (*Happy Lucky Bikkuriman*).

BILLY DOG

1988. JPN: *Billy Inu*. TV series. DIR: Hiroshi Sasagawa, Junji Nishimura. SCR: Noboru Shiroyama, Masaru Yamamoto. DES: Yayoi Takihara. ANI: Chuji Nakajima. MUS: Tetsu Inakawa. PRD: TV Asahi, Shinei. 20 mins. x 44 eps.

Tatsuo Yumori lives on Hanabibi Hill with his dog, Billy, who followed the boy home one day and just stayed. But Billy is a talking dog with the mind of a human being, and he soon brings his friend, Gary Dog, into the lives of Tatsuo, his family, and his friends. Based on a manga by Fujiko-Fujio.

BINCHO-TAN

2006. TV series. DIR: Kazuhiro Furuhashi, Eiji Suganuma, Shigeru Ueda. SCR: Kazuhiro Furuhashi. DES: Tetsuhito Saito. ANI: Eiji Suganuma, Masashi Ishihama, Katsuya Asano. MUS: N/C. PRD: Studio Deen, TBS. 12 mins. x 9 eps.

Bincho-tan (the name refers to the piece of charcoal she carries on her head), is a cute little girl who lives a simple life in the mountains. Apparently we are supposed to care! She is actually a mascot character created by artist Takehito Egusa for the games company Alchemist—compare to **DIGI CHARAT**.

BINKAN ATHLETE

2008. AKA: *Bargain Athlete*. Video. DIR: N/C. SCR: Jin Higashi, Ran Makkuro, Taro Pinatsu, Shuji Kurashima. DES: Umi Hiko. ANI: N/C. MUS: team PETH. PRD: T-Rex, Marigold. 32 mins.

Japan's sportswomen are competing at the top level internationally, and this brings a great deal of stress. Shigeru Mochida is hired for his special talent as a masseur. Judoist, figure skater, swimmer, or volleyball player, he soon has them completely relaxed and very grateful. Based on an erotic game by Marine.

BIOHUNTER *

1995. Video. DIR: Yuzo Sato, Yoshiaki Kawajiri. SCR: Yoshiaki Kawajiri. DES: Hiroshi Hamazaki. ANI: Hiroshi Hamazaki. MUS: Masamichi Amano. PRD: Madhouse. 60 mins.

A virus transforms people into monsters with demonic powers. Two molecular scientists, Koshigaya and Kimada, who moonlight as psychic researchers, are approached by the beautiful Sayaka Murakami, whose fortuneteller grandfather has gone missing after an appointment with a prominent politician. Based on a manga serialized in *Comic Burger* by **JUDGE**-creator Fujihiko Hosono, this anime was partly bankrolled by the U.S. distributor Urban Vision, whose Mataichiro Yamamoto is credited as a producer. Under the charge of the Madhouse studio and **WICKED CITY**'s Yoshiaki Kawajiri, it looks just like every other demons-among-us tale that characterized so many successful anime in the U.S., which probably explains the foreign money. ◐◐

BIRD SONG

2007. JPN: *Tori no Uta*. Video. DIR: Yoshitaka Amano. SCR: Toimi Kikuhara. DES: Yoshitaka Amano. ANI: Yoshitaka Amano. MUS: Yasuharu Takanashi. PRD: Gentosha Comics, Toei Animation, Atom X. 35 mins.

A boy takes a route he wouldn't normally follow, meets a girl and falls in love. Forgetting her, he forgets the boy he was until many years later, when she comes back to take his hand and lead him onward in an ending heartbreakingly reminiscent of the *Presence* segment in **ROBOT CARNIVAL**. From the slow pan down through clouds as the boy begins his narration, through the montage of papercuts, watercolors, shadows, and light that illustrate it, this is not so much animation as Amano turning the pages of a lovely artbook for us. It's very pretty, very reflective, and definitely something to show to people who say anime isn't art, along with **BEYOND THE TRAIN TRACKS**. Part of Toei's *ga-nime* line (**ARGOT AND JARGON**). See also Keita Amemiya's **G-9** and Amano's own **FANTASCOPE: TYLOSTOMA**.

BIRDY THE MIGHTY *

1996. JPN: *Tetsuwan Birdy*. Video, TV series. DIR: Yoshiaki Kawajiri. SCR: Chiaki Konaka. DES: Kumiko Takahashi, Yutaka Izubuchi. ANI: Kumiko Takahashi. MUS: Yuki Otani. PRD: Madhouse. 35 mins. x 4 eps. (v), 25 mins. x 25 eps. (TV).

Loser schoolboy Tsutomu is fatally wounded in the crossfire between an alien criminal and an intergalactic bounty hunter. To preserve his life, officer Birdy Cephon Altirra merges with him, living *inside* his body, helping him through teenage troubles but forcing him to transform at humorously inappropriate moments.

A sex-swap farce à la **RANMA ½**, with a tip of the hat to Tezuka's "Mighty" **ASTRO BOY**, *Birdy*'s true roots lie in the live-action **ULTRAMAN**, with aliens defeated by low-budget gimmicks like dish soap and a hapless Earthman forced to share his body with an invisible, controlling alien. Birdy straddles separate subplots as a vengeful bounty hunter, magical girlfriend, and confidante, contrasting with Tsutomu's spiteful real-life sister. Based on a short-lived manga in a *Shonen Sunday* spin-off publication from **PATLABOR**'s Masami Yuki, this disappointing video series features a dream-team of anime creators, all working below par. Writer Konaka, brother of *Ultraman*-director Kazuya, manages a few tongue-in-cheek observations, such as why ugly aliens never get to be space cops, but these are outnumbered by the very genre conventions they lampoon—for example, the evil-yet-beautiful alien mastermind Revi, who wants to turn humans into bioweapons. Matters are not helped by a lead actor in the dub who is forced to pitch his voice so high that, in the words of someone from the U.S. distributor, "he sounds like Mr. Hanky the Christmas Poo."

Kazuki Akane directed a TV remake, *Birdie the Mighty: Decode* (2008), which ran for 25 episodes across two seasons, and drew on Yuki's 2003–8 reversioning of his own manga, which ran in *Young Magazine,* a publication for older readers, and considerably fleshed out the story. Although this later version has greater depth, it also suffers a little from changes in animation style, being very much made with the flatter, colder materials of digital animation (**GAMING AND DIGITAL ANIMATION**) as opposed to the video version's old-fashioned cel work.

BIRTH OF JAPAN

1970. JPN: *Nihon Tanjo.* TV series. DIR: Eiichi Yamamoto. SCR: Eiichi Yamamoto. DES: N/C. ANI: Yoshifumi Seyama. MUS: Isao Tomita. PRD: Tezuka Pro, Nippon TV. 26 mins. x 5 eps.
Liu Fa is a *kappa*, an amphibious humanoid creature who lives in the south of China. He meets the lovely Kozara, a girl from a distant land. Eventually, he follows her to Japan, bringing iron weapons and rice cultivation to the island of Kyushu. Because *kappa* live for a thousand years, he is able to watch as his inventions spread, creating the foundations of the state that will become Japan. With characteristic Japanese vagueness about historical origins, this fantasy was shown beneath the slogan "Nonfiction Theater," though with its mixture of the supernatural and quasi-historical it is no truer to life than its distant cousins **PRINCESS MONONOKE** and **DARK MYTH**.

BIT THE CUPID *

1995. TV series. DIR: Tameo Ogawa. SCR: Soji Yoshikawa. DES: Susumu Matsushita. ANI: Toshiyasu Okada. MUS: Ko Suzuki. PRD: B2 Pro, TV Tokyo. 25 mins. x 48 eps.

In the realm of the Greek gods, where Zeus and Poseidon aren't talking, Narcissus is falling in love with himself, and Icarus is taking flying lessons, the titular Bit is a young demigod of uncertain parentage (though possibly the son of Apollo) who is able to make characters fall in love, though his aim is not always true. As he mixes it up with Hyacinth, Galatea, Atlas, and the gang, many Greek myths are intermixed with tales of more contemporary origin—such as Frisbee the Golden Assassin and Lee of Birdland. One of the earliest anime to be made inside a computer (**TECHNOLOGY AND FORMATS**), it was broadcast in English on Fox Kids in the Netherlands—it's a wacky world.

BITE ME! CHAMELEON *

1992. JPN: *Chameleon.* Video. DIR: Mitsuo Hashimoto, Takao Yotsuji. SCR: Takao Yotsuji. DES: Tamiyoshi Yazaki. ANI: Tamiyoshi Yazaki. MUS: Saburo Takada. PRD: Victor. 50 mins. x 6 eps.
Eikichi Yazawa is a thug determined to be top dog at Narita High, so he does his best to convince love interest Asaoka that he used to be the toughest kid in junior high. Local bully Aizawa doesn't believe it for a moment, and Eikichi is forced to fight a battle with whatever is at hand, including urine, farts, and bloody napkins. Proud of its puerile nature, each episode would introduce a new challenger, whom Eikichi would have to outsmart or outgross. The final two releases were directed by former scriptwriter Yotsuji and had not previously appeared as stories in the manga, although they were little different from those that had.

Taking the stained mantle of the similar **BRAT COP** and moving the action to a school, Atsushi Kato's 33-volume manga from *Shonen Magazine* sold 1.3 million, but adding the words "Bite Me!" to the title couldn't save it in the U.S., where it bombed after just one episode. **LV**

BIZARRE CAGE *

2003. JPN: *Ryoki no Ori 2.* Video. DIR: Sei Konno. SCR: Kotaro Ran. DES: Mamoru Yokota. ANI: N/C. MUS: N/C. PRD: Studio Line, Studio Polaris, Pink Pineapple. 30 mins. x 3 eps.
Handsome young Takeshi Saito takes a job as a security guard at the Fantasien

theme park, which entails him dressing up as a cross between a knight and a Roman centurion. But Fantasien is so state-of-the-art that some of its attractions use military technology, which requires very careful monitoring. Takeshi soon falls out with the bitchy park manager over some alleged infractions, but wins the praise of Tamami, a fellow player on the park's staff. When park employees start turning up dead, Takeshi begins to investigate, discovering that owner Masakazu Inouye is using it after hours as a personal playground for his sick sexual perversions. Then MAOS, the operating system that controls the park, starts spinning out of control. Yes, it's *Westworld* (1973) with T&A, as Takeshi and several stereotypical girls of different ages struggle to get the system stable and the customers safely out of the park, in between having sex with and without consent, before tackling Inouye in a dramatic climax at Dracula's Castle. Based on a PC game, the design of which made a virtue out of the simplistic planning of adventure gaming since the different "worlds" of the park had a reason to be right next to each other, and the characters involved had a series of excuses to be dressed up in costumes and fetish gear. This cunning ruse also circumvented a problem common to many fantasy anime—it can be annoying in some other anime that the cast have the sensibilities of modern people in a fantasy setting, whereas in *BC* it is part of the plot. See **SEXORCIST** for another tale of a game that goes wrong for its participants. **LNV**

BLACK BENTO

1990. JPN: *Makkuro no Obento.* Movie. DIR: Satoshi Dezaki. SCR: Toshiaki Imaizumi. DES: N/C. ANI: N/C. MUS: N/C. PRD: Kyodo Eiga Zenkoku Keiretsu Kaigi. 48 mins.
In the aftermath of the bombing of Hiroshima (see **BAREFOOT GEN**), Shigeko Orimen searches in the rubble for her missing 13-year-old son, Shigeru. She eventually finds a charred body only a few hundred yards from the hypocenter, and identifies the corpse by the blackened remnants of the lunch box it still clutches. The lunch box, which she had prepared for him earlier that day, becomes an emotionally charged exhibit in the local museum, eventually inspiring a picture book and this antiwar anime.

BLACK BLOOD BROTHERS *

2006. TV series. DIR: Hiroaki Yoshikawa. SCR: Yu Sugitani. DES: Toshiyuki Kanno, Nishiki Itaoka, Yoji Yoshikawa. ANI: Ayako Kurata. MUS: Toshihiko Sahashi. PRD: Group TAC, Studio Live, BBB Partners, Hakuhodo, Pony Canyon, Toshiba Entertainment/Showgate. 30 mins. x 12 eps.

A decade after a Holy War between humans and vampires, the two species live in peace, though the vampires mostly stay in their own Special Zone. The Company, an organization set up to monitor and mediate relations between them, makes sure the peace holds. But the monstrous Kowloon Children, almost wiped out in the war, are rising again, and they are more brutal than ever. Vampire Jiro, once known as the Silver Blade, and Company negotiator Mimiko must try to prevent another terrible slaughter. Old-school fans are thinking WICKED CITY, newer ones HELLSING or any of the dozen other boy-vampire anime of recent years, and they're all right. *Black Blood Brothers* is highly derivative, but it makes no attempt to conceal its borrowed plumage. Instead, it uses its influences proudly as a convoluted backdrop for a series of rip-snorting action sequences that will leave you happy and entertained. It's not a show that will stick in your memory in its own right, but it's a lot of fun set to a terrific soundtrack. And any show that slips in a nod to GOLDEN BAT is fine by us. The one real disappointment is that Jiro's brother is there almost purely for comic relief, making the title a bit of a misnomer. The contrast between siblings is one of the great comedy tropes. It can work well, and it always raises a laugh if reversed—look at SORCERER HUNTERS where the contrasting characters of Maron and Carrot make the younger seem much older. But occasionally, it would be nice to see two siblings who are different but both capable and presentable, rather than constantly riffing the strong, solid type versus lovable idiot trope. **Ⓥ**

BLACK BUTLER *

2008. JPN: *Kuroshitsuji*. TV series, video. DIR: Toshiya Shinohara, Hirofumi Ogura. SCR: Mari Okada. DES: Minako Shiba, Hiromasa Ogura, Manabu Otsuzuki. ANI: Minako Shiba, Shigenori Taniguchi, Kazuo Tanigawa, Hiromi Okazaki, Sho Sugai. MUS: Taku Iwasaki. PRD: A-1 Pictures, Aniplex, Hakuhodo DY Media Partners, MOVIC, Square Enix, Yomiko Advertising, MBS, Yomiuri TV. 25 mins. x 24 eps. (TV1), 24 mins. x 12 eps. (TV2), ?? mins. (v1).

Lord Ciel Phantomhive, scion of an ancient noble line, is a 12-year-old orphan who would be lost without his butler, the demonic Sebastian Michaelis. Under Ciel's sweet, well-mannered exterior is a heart thirsting for revenge like a devil dog thirsts for blood—so much so that he has promised his soul to Sebastian for supper providing the demon first helps him achieve that revenge. But before that, he has a thousand and one social obligations to fulfill. This is Victorian England. Regardless of a gentleman's personal commitments, he must do his duty to queen and country.

However hard you try, America, you will never be able to parody Britain as slyly and subtly as the Japanese can. Only another country with more than a millennium of monarchy and a set of arcane, unwritten social rules (from breach of which flow consequences you would scarcely notice, apart from a certain polite reserve and a series of inexplicably closed doors) could possibly understand us the way *Black Butler* does. From Jack the Ripper to Dorian Grey, from *The Hound of the Baskervilles* to *Monty Python's Flying Circus*, from nursery rhymes to the salt of the earth and the beings in whose graves you sprinkle it, *Black Butler* understands the dynamics of under- and over-statement, self-deprecation and self-assurance, and how to walk the line between. The richly vicious reality that underlies the nudges and winks and swoons coexists side-by-side with utter silliness. They might as well have called it *Carry on Vamping*—stunning, beautifully designed, and more than acceptably animated. It's superbly acted and written in Japanese, and almost as good in American. It's clever, funny, and sometimes unexpectedly moving.

Unsurprisingly, the success of the series spun off from Yana Toboso's manga led to a follow-up series and a couple of videos. The 2009 video *Black Butler: His Butler, Performer (Kuroshitsuji: Sono Shitsuji, Kogyo)* is a side story (featuring the established cast) about a charity performance of *Hamlet*. *Black Butler II* aired in 2010 with a new butler in town—one who wants to steal Sebastian's long-awaited supper. It's a smaller show in every way than its magnificent precursor. The same applies to the *Black Butler II* video, a series of six mini-episodes set in the world of the show. There have been two musicals on the Japanese stage, plus the usual video games, books, and collectibles. A live-action movie is being filmed in Japan for release in 2014. **Ⓥ**

BLACK CAT

2005. TV series. DIR: Shin Itagaki, Takayuki Inagaki, Yoshimichi Hirai. SCR: Shuichi Koyama. DES: Yukiko Akiyama. ANI: Yukiko Akiyama, Maki Uchida. MUS: Taku Iwasaki. PRD: Gonzo, TBS, BS-I. 25 mins. x 24 eps.

Sven Volfield is an itinerant bounty hunter or "sweeper" who can see into the future by lifting his eye-patch and using his supposedly dead eye—elements here of both CITY HUNTER and GOKU: MIDNIGHT EYE. His nemesis is Train Hartnett, AKA "Black Cat," a special operative of the Chronos secret society, whose aim is to stabilize the world through carefully selected assassinations. Train soon switches sides and teams up with Sven to take on Chronos, leading to a tale of superpowered heroics redolent of the GETBACKERS. Based on the manga by Kentaro Yabuki serialized in *Shonen Jump*, and no relation to the novel *Black Cat* by PLEASE OPEN THE DOOR author Motoko Arai. Characters from *Black Cat* also appeared in the Nintendo game *Jump Super Stars*.

BLACK GATE *

2004. Video. DIR: Sho Hanebu. SCR: Torazo Nakahara. DES: Yoshi Ten. ANI: Takeshi Imai. MUS: N/C. PRD: Image Works, Studio Jam, Yoshi Ten, Museum Soft, Milky. 30 mins. x 2 eps.

Baffled teenager Narufumi discovers that his girlfriend Shizuka and her twin sister Kasumi are battling over him in an alternate dimension that they can only reach by using their mysterious tattoos to unlock an interdimensional gateway at their school, which, naturally, the girls' family has been secretly guarding for generations in the style of DEVIL HUNTER YOHKO. A group of girls are transported to another world through the "black gate" portal, where one discovers that she can gain slaves and magical power through sexual intercourse (who knew!), although the arrival of a mysterious rescuer saves the travelers from a fate worse than death—just imagine that LA BLUE GIRL never happened. Ends on a cliffhanger, so the authors of this encyclopedia have been waiting for a decade to find out what happens next. No, really, we have. 🅛🅝🅞🅥

BLACK HEAVEN *

1999. JPN: *Kacho Oji.* AKA: *Section Chief Oji; Legend of Black Heaven.* TV series. DIR: Yasunori Kikuchi. SCR: Narihisa Arakawa. DES: Kazuto Nakazawa. ANI: Hiroshi Hashimoto. MUS: Koichi Korenaga. PRD: AIC, APPP, Pioneer, WOWOW. 25 mins. x 13 eps.
Oji Tanaka, a henpecked, middle-aged salaryman with a dull wife and a mewling infant, still thinks fondly of his teenage years when he was "Gabriel" Tanaka, lead guitarist with the hard rock group Black Heaven. He is contacted by a beautiful blonde agent, Leila Yuki, and hired to play his particular brand of music for use as a sonic weapon in an interstellar war.

The space war is curiously underused, the script concentrating instead on Tanaka's hapless attempts to enlist his old band in his secret mission and his wife's attempts to discover whether he is having an affair with Leila. But with a focus on farce and everyday life not unlike Nigel Kneale's *Kinvig* (1981), *BH* resembles a live-action production that cannot afford the special effects, rather than an anime that can go anywhere in the galaxy for the price of a pot of paint. *BH* has much in common with other short-lived TV serials of the late 1990s—the backgrounds are sparse and reused often, and the animation is cheap, flat, and digital. The filmmakers attempt to distract the viewer's attention with occasional flashy graphics and rotoscoping, especially over the opening credits featuring footage of Whitesnake's John Sykes, who sings the theme tune. It's music as power, à la MACROSS, but expanding the audience to include disenchanted 30-somethings, with many 1970s heavy metal in-jokes.

BLACK JACK *

1993. Movie, video. DIR: Osamu Dezaki. SCR: Eto Mori, Kihachi Okamoto. DES: Akio Sugino. ANI: Akio Sugino. MUS: Osamu Shoji, Kiyoshi Suzuki. PRD: Tezuka Pro. 50 mins. x 10 eps. (v1), 93 mins. (m1), 50? mins. x 3 eps. (v2),

11 mins. x 12 eps. (*Flash*), 25 mins. x 4 eps. (*Miracles*), 25 mins. x 61 eps. (TV1), ? mins. (m2), 7 mins. (m3), 25 mins. x 17 eps. (TV2).
Black Jack was one of Osamu Tezuka's most popular creations, a scar-faced doctor-for-hire with a deep-set sense of honor and justice, and a gift for surgery sometimes described as "the hand of God." His sole confidante is Pinoko ("pinochle," a companion card game to "blackjack" in a typical Tezuka wordplay), a diminutive, lisping girl carried for decades in the womb of her unsuspecting twin sister and found by Black Jack during an operation to remove what he thought to be a cyst. Although she looks like a toddler, she is as old as her grown-up twin and becomes Black Jack's surrogate daughter and assistant.

The original *Black Jack* ran in *Shonen Champion* magazine from 1973 to 1978. It reached a wider audience through Nobuhiko Obayashi's 1977 live-action film *Stranger in Her Eyes,* in which Black Jack (Daisuke Ryu) uses a drowned girl's corneas to restore sight to a female patient who is then haunted by visions of the donor's last moments. Reissued after lying dormant for most of the 1980s, the manga was followed in 1993 by an anime version on video from the GOLGO 13 team of Dezaki and Sugino. Undertaken as part of an ongoing plan to produce animated versions of all of Tezuka's work, the videos suffer from faithfulness to the letter rather than the spirit of the originals, creating a sanitized nostalgia instead of the series' famously dark mood.

In *Chimaera Man,* Black Jack must operate to save his old acquaintance Crossword before traveling to Hokkaido to revisit a former patient who has become the victim of a mob-run medical conspiracy in *The Procession Game.* In *The Decoration of Maria and Her Comrades,* he is called to save the life of a South American rebel ousted by foreign-backed conspirators; then he tries to save the life of a traumatized movie star in *Anorexia,* where he faces his old adversary, "dark doctor" and euthanasia-advocate Kiriko. Events take a more paranormal turn in *The Owl of San Merida,* in which Black Jack aids a man with stigmata and false memory syndrome, and in *Night Time Tale in the Snow,* a variation on an old

Japanese folktale of doomed love found in many other anime including KIMAGURE ORANGE ROAD.

Black Jack returned to live-action cinema in 1995, with a trilogy directed by Kazuya Konaka and written by AKIRA's Izo Hashimoto, with Daisuke Ryu reprising the lead role. The first two films chart Black Jack's initial fall from grace (only revealed in flashbacks in the original manga) and first encounter with Pinoko (the manga chapter "*Teratogenous Cystoma*"). The final installment replays the Kiriko encounter from the anime, and the cross-promotion was reinforced in 1996 when the last live-action movie was followed by a feature-length anime.

Set in 1998 as Tezuka would have imagined it, with a U.N. that includes off-world colonies, *Black Jack the Movie* dumps the condescending attitude that crept into the video series. Two years after the appearance of superhuman child prodigies at the Atlanta Olympics, the same children are suddenly succumbing to accelerated aging. Black Jack is blackmailed into helping the ice-cool Doctor Jo Carroll, who kidnaps Pinoko to secure Black Jack's cooperation in what turns out to be a viral conspiracy.

Black Jack continued as a straight-to-video anime after the movie with *Green Memories, The Face in the Affliction,* and *Sinking Woman.* The franchise was slowly reintroduced to the market with *Black Jack Flash* (2003), a dozen 11-minute episodes made with Flash animation, and released through the Internet—representing one of the first obvious attempts by an animation studio to amass broadcast material that could be reused in mobile phones. Plots from *BJF* were later recycled in *Black Jack: The Four Miracles of Life* (2003), a miniseries comprising four TV specials. After testing the waters with exquisite care, the franchise was truly revived with *Black Jack* (2004), a 62-episode TV series, directed by Tezuka's son Makoto (sometimes credited with his preferred romanization, Macoto). All incarnations of the franchise adhered closely to the story of the original manga. Another movie, *BJ: Two Doctors of Darkness* (2005) premiered along with a short seven-minute featurette, *Doctor Pinoko's Forest Adventure* (2005), in which Pinoko gets lost in the woods while chasing after Jack with his bag. The television series was followed immediately in 2006 by a 17-episode sequel, *Black Jack 21*.

See also RAY THE ANIMATION, which some might call an unofficial spin-off.

BLACK LAGOON *

2006. TV series, video. DIR: Sunao Katabuchi. SCR: Sunao Katabuchi. DES: Masanori Shino, Masahiro Kimura, Hidetoshi Kaneko, Takuya Iida. ANI: Masanori Shino. MUS: Edison. PRD: Madhouse Studios, Geneon, Shogakukan. 24 mins. x 12 eps. (TV1), 24 mins. x 12 eps. (TV2), 30 mins. x 5 eps. (v).

A company executive in the China Seas is kidnapped by the Lagoon Company, a pirate crew who are after a disc he's carrying. They call themselves deliverymen, but they intercept as many deliveries as they make: grabbing objects their clients want and delivering them to new destinations. It's dangerous work, but the adrenalin rush is phenomenal and the pay fantastic. Abandoned by his employers, Rokuro "Rock" Okajima turns to the dark side and joins forces with his captors. A determinedly risk-averse salaryman might seem an unlikely new shipmate for a pirate crew, but Rock has other skills. He's a good translator, a gifted negotiator and planner, and he can keep the crew accounts straight. And as time goes by, his attitude to violence begins to change.

Black comedy mixes with violent action in a series of adventures ripped from real-life reports of piracy. *Black Lagoon* uses anime tropes, movies, and the news media like an all-you-can-eat buffet to create a feast for anyone who wants to kick back with a few beers and be entertained. The story, from Rei Hiroe's 2002 manga, is steeped in world cinema culture, with references to John Woo, Stephen King, Quentin Tarantino, the Coen brothers, and spaghetti westerns. Old-school fans will see similarities with the action epics of the 80s, when anime was under the spell of the Holy Trinity of SF actioners, *Blade Runner, Terminator,* and *Alien,* reading its contemporary self through the filter of cyberpunk. Rock's situation also recalls that of CRYING FREEMAN.

The senior staff stayed together for another TV series, *Black Lagoon: The Second Barrage,* also aired in 2006. Some big names were called in to help get the job finished inside TV's unforgiving schedules, including Studio Ghibli on backgrounds for the last episode and Gainax on key animation. In 2010 a five-episode video series, *Black Lagoon: Roberta's Blood Trail,* reintroduced Roberta, former terrorist and now devoted family maid on the trail of her boss's assassins.

Incidentally, though the inspiration, motivation, and formulation of chillingly effective maid-assassin Roberta have been widely discussed in FANDOM, a comment from the creator in the English-language volume 8 says everything about multicultural influences and the power of ancient iconography: "We love women like Thatcher!" That alone should tell you this isn't a show for small children. **V**

BLACK LION

1992. JPN: *Jigen Sengoku-shi: Kuro no Shishi*. AKA: *Dimension Civil War Chronicle: Black Lion*. Video. DIR: Takashi Watanabe. SCR: Noriko Hayasaka. DES: Hideyuki Motohashi, Koichi Ohata. ANI: N/C. MUS: Masami Anno. PRD: Tokyo Kids. 45 mins.

In 1580, Nobunaga Oda united Japan with the aid of foreign guns, but *Black Lion* has a more fantastic view of these events, suggesting that he used rapid-fire machine guns, lasers, and missiles. His ultimate weapon is Ginnai Doma, a ninja said to be immortal who carries out the command to eradicate dissident temples with extreme prejudice. A warrior monk is the sole survivor of one such massacre, and he swears to avenge the deaths of his friends and lover.

In taking contemporary items and hurling them into the past, Go Nagai's 1978 manga from *Shonen Magazine* is a reversal of his SHUTENDOJI, which dragged ancient concerns into the present day. Supervising producer Osamu Yamasaki directed several similar retellings of Japanese history, including YOTODEN, which depicted Nobunaga as being in alliance with demons.

BLACK MAGIC M-66 *

1987. Video. DIR: Masamune Shirow, Hiroyuki Kitakubo. SCR: Masamune Shirow, Hiroyuki Kitakubo. DES: Hiroyuki Kitakubo, Toru Yoshida. ANI: Hiroyuki Okiura, Hiroki Hayashi. MUS: Yoshihiro Katayama. PRD: Animate Film, AIC. 45 mins.

A military transport crashes and loses its cargo, two top-secret military androids whose unerased test program instructs them to terminate their inventor's granddaughter, Ferris. When the first of the robots is destroyed, snooping reporter Sybel decides to track down Ferris and warn her. In a showdown that costs the lives of 18 soldiers, Sybel saves Ferris, though the reporter's feckless partner, Leakey, tries to pass off the news footage of the incident as his own.

Black Magic began life as a fanzine, a sprawl of loosely linked manga that gained Shirow his first professional contract. The anime adapted "Booby Trap," the most coherent chapter, drawing heavily from James Cameron's *Terminator* and the final act of *Aliens*. Sybel and Ferris replay Cameron's Ripley/Newt relationship in several scenes, most notably with an elevator chase and last-minute rescue, but *Black Magic* is entertaining despite the steals. The only disappointment in watching the acrobatic androids decimate a roadblock comes in wondering how it could have looked if the makers had had the budget to include the original's *six*-armed M-77 prototype, which is only referred to offscreen. Another vestige of the manga is the allegorical Cold War standoff between North and South, misinterpreted by some oversensitive Japanese critics as a slur on Korea. Also note Sybel's APPLESEED T-shirt, an in-joke that would be repaid when that other Shirow title was animated the following year.

The fallout from *Black Magic* is remarkably similar to that of Katsuhiro Otomo's AKIRA, another case of a creator's perfectionism driving an anime over budget. *Black Magic* used over 20,000 cels, an extravagance on video that, ironically, has caused it to age very gracefully—it could easily pass for a show ten years younger. Shirow's first and last work as anime director, it ended so acrimoniously that he refused to associate himself with any future adaptations. In some ways, this is an indirect cause of the later monstrosities LANDLOCK and GUNDRESS, for which his name was appropriated to secure unwarranted publicity. As well as BLOOD-director Kitakubo, two future big names worked as lowly animators on the project—Hiroki Hayashi would make BUBBLEGUM CRISIS 2040, and Hiroyuki Okiura would eventually direct JIN-ROH after contributing to the superior Shirow adaptation GHOST IN THE SHELL. The production was the debut of future voice star Chisa Yokoyama as Ferris. ⓥ

BLACK ROCK SHOOTER *

2009. JPN: *Black Rock Shooter*. Video, TV series. DIR: Shinobu Yoshioka. SCR: Shinobu Yoshioka, Nagaru Tanigawa, Mari Okada. DES: Yusuke Matsuo, Yusuke Yoshigaki, Atsushi Morikawa, Emi Kesamaru, Tetsuhiko Nagashima. ANI: Yusuke Matsuo. MUS: Ryo, Hideharu Mori. PRD: Ordet Good Smile Company. 60 mins. (v), 23 mins. x 8 eps. (TV).
Two girls become friends in the first year of junior high school, but Mato and Yomi drift apart in their second year. In another world, two girls face each other in a deadly struggle. How are Black Rock Shooter and Deadmaster linked to Mato and Yomi? How does this strange fantasy world interact with their school, friends, and families? Based on the hit game by Ryohei "huke" Fuke, *Black Rock Shooter*'s direct-to-DVD debut was followed three years later by a short TV series, in which new writer Okada played up the teen angst angle she had used successfully in FRACTALE, but created a number of contradictions in character and plot. The art and animation is good, sometimes excellent, with outstanding CGI, but the weak writing makes it eminently missable for all but die-hard fans of the game. Note the presence of Nagaru Tanigawa, better known as the creator of THE MELANCHOLY OF HARUHI SUZUMIYA, as one of the scenarists. ⓥ

BLACK WIDOW *

2003. JPN: *Kuro Hime Shikkoku no Yakata*. AKA: *Black Princess: Mansion in Chains*. Video. DIR: Yusaku Saotome, Yu Yahagi. SCR: Hajime Yamaguchi, Yu Yahagi. DES: Tomo'o Shintani. ANI: Yasuhiro Saiki. MUS: Takeshi Nishizawa. PRD: Discovery, Mook. 30 mins. x 2 eps.
Seven young friends go for a camping trip on the banks of an artificial lake created by a dam. While exploring the environs, they find an old mansion in the woods, where they are obliged to take shelter from bad weather. The mansion seems deserted at first, but as the boys and girls explore its rooms they find evidence of very recent occupation, and when they find the bondage room next to the bar in the cellar they begin to realize that they are not alone. Maya, the mistress of the

house, and her guests have various torture and bondage games in mind (compare to BEHIND CLOSED DOORS), as the group is split up and subjected to various sexual torments. Later on, the story transforms into a murder mystery, although it is tied up in a rushed and arbitrary ending that suggests later installments were curtailed by circumstances beyond the filmmakers' control. Part of the DISCOVERY SERIES. ⓛⓝⓥ

BLACKMAIL *

1999. JPN: *Kyohaku*. Video. DIR: Katsuma Kanazawa. SCR: Sakura Momoi, Taifu Kanmachi. DES: Teruaki Murakami. ANI: Teruaki Murakami. MUS: N/C. PRD: Pink Pineapple. 30 mins. x 3 eps. (v1), 30 mins. x 3 eps. (v2).
Japanese teenager Asuka is touched to receive a love letter from a boy in her class. However, she makes the mistake of confiding in her "friend" Aya, who secretly desires the boy herself. The jealous Aya ensures that Asuka pays the price in pain and bondage—salutary relationship advice. Released in the U.S. by Nu-Tech as *The Black Mail: Tomorrow Never Ends* (2001). Subsequently rereleased by Media Blasters' Kitty Media label under the title *Blackmail*, because life isn't difficult enough for the anime encyclopedist. The same company also released the three-part sequel *Blackmail 2: Another Tomorrow* (2001, *Kyohaku 2: Mo Hitotsu no Ashita*), which focused on Asuka's wedding and unfortunate kidnapping. ⓝⓥ

BLADE *

2011. TV series. DIR: Mitsuyuki Masuhara. SCR: Kenta Fukasaku, Dai Fujita. DES: Cindy Yamauchi, Katsushi Aoki. ANI: Cindy Yamauchi. MUS: Tetsuya Takahashi, Shogo Onishi. PRD: Madhouse, Sony Pictures Entertainment. 24 mins. x 12 eps.
Blade is a half-vampire who hunts down vampires (VAMPIRE HUNTER D). Once known as Erik Brooks, he trained with Noah Van Helsing from the famous vampire-hunting dynasty and has now become feared throughout the vampire world—not least because his human blood lets him go out by day. He tracks down the vampire who killed his mother in Japan and finds a vampire organization spreading across Southeast Asia. Time for some action—but sadly, this isn't the show

to provide it. Marvel's collaborations with Madhouse to bring their comic characters to anime have not been uniformly successful, mostly because they have focused on style over substance and made basic mistakes.

If, for example, one is making a vampire action show, tension and jeopardy for the hero are basic requirements. Early on in the anime *Blade*, it's apparent that the evil vampires and their human servants are mere cannon fodder. Fans of children's anime may be amused by the after-image Blade uses to fool the poor saps, recalling DRAGONBALL, and the way they simply disappear in a puff of smoke like a defeated DIGIMON. But that won't add much interest for teen and adult viewers, and neither will the TV-friendly, *GI Joe* approach to death— no human is ever killed, just stunned.

The violence is so obviously comical that it doesn't merit a rating on our usual scale. And to add insult to injury, the animation looks cheap, with an over-reliance on repeat sequences and still frames. The Madhouse crew are capable of handling a limited budget with style and grace: that doesn't happen here. We hate to dismiss a show starring the mighty Akio Otsuka, one of Japan's most distinguished voice actors inside and outside anime: but if you really want to enjoy Otsuka as Blade, get the Japanese version of the first live-action movie, where he overdubs Wesley Snipes.

BLADE OF THE IMMORTAL *

2008. JPN: *Mugen no Junin*. AKA: *Dweller in Infinity*. TV series. DIR: Koichi Mashimo. SCR: Hiroyuki Kawasaki, Kenichi Kanemaki. DES: Yoshimitsu Yamashita, Yoshimi Umino. ANI: Manamu Amasaki, Yoshiaki Tsubata, Mutsumi Sasaki, Yoshimitsu Yamashita. MUS: Ko Otani. PRD: Bee Train, Asano Dojo Fukkokai, Kodansha, Pony Canyon, Production I.G, Tokyu Agency. 30 mins. x 13 eps.
Not all samurai were gentlemen. Manji, the killer of a hundred men including his own sister's husband, is crass, ruthless, and graceless when he is cursed with immortality. No wound can kill him. And it is a curse—a penance for his wickedness that will only end when he has killed a thousand evil men. Manji must confront himself in the form of others just like him, and cut himself down again and again, suffering but never dying, until he has not only

atoned for his sins, but understood them. When he meets a girl on a quest for revenge against a powerful sword school that murdered her parents and their students, it seems they can help each other. So they wander Japan together, seeking out death.

Hiroaki Samura's manga is a poem of contradictions: a distant pastiche of Tezuka's **DORORO**, and a spare, stark examination of the quest for meaning wrapped in a beautifully realized look at life on the edge in feudal Japan. It first appeared in the summer of 1993 and ended on Christmas Day 2012. For a long time Samura said he didn't want it animated. His instincts were right. That doesn't mean that *Blade of the Immortal* is a bad show, but it can't capture the nuances of a completely different art form, and Samura is an artist of nuance. The construction and pace suffer from trying to squeeze too much manga story and too many characters into too little screen time. But there are pleasures. Director Mashimo is skilled in the use of art to manipulate atmosphere. His cold, restricted color palette sets the perfect tone for the series and makes his most striking images even stronger. He keeps his action sequences classic and simple, using both CGI and slo-mo to nod to classic swordplay movies. The background art is typical of Bee Train's highly skilled, evocative work, using shadows and gloom to create a rich sense of history. ●

BLAME! ★
2003. JPN: *Blame Ver. 0.11*. Video. DIR: Shintaro Inokawa. SCR: Tsutomu Nihei. DES: Akio Watanabe, Nobuaki Nagano. ANI: N/C. MUS: Hiroyuki Onogawa. PRD: Nihei. 5 mins. x 6 eps.
It has been 3,000 years since humanity lost the war with machines, and Earth is now encased within a massive skin of steel and concrete. The heroic Killy is on the run from evil Silicon creatures and searching for Cibo ("Hope"), a scientist who may have found a way to defeat them.

Originally a 1998 manga serialized in *Comic Afternoon*, *Blame* has a European look informed by creator Tsutomu Nihei's love of French comics. In its anime version, it has thematic similarities to Peter Chung's *Aeon Flux*, sacrificing immense amounts of plot and coherence in order to cram itself into the short running times of its

original web broadcast. Supposedly, this all-too-brief series of disjointed segments was part of creator Nihei's attempt to secure funding for a movie; tellingly it was put together in the year that the *Blame* manga came to an end. Sold to a foreign distributor and slammed together into a 30-minute one-shot video, the result is an often incoherent series of conflicts that plays like a poor man's **ANIMATRIX**. It is also rather quaint in modern times to see a video anime that makes no sense and serves merely as an advertisement for the manga; back in the 1980s, there were a lot more of them around. The DVD release was cunningly presented as a "salvaged disc by Cibo"; i.e., an item from the world of the anime. However, that backfired when the menus were written in a language from 3,000 years in the future, hence somewhat difficult to navigate. ●

BLASSREITER ★
2008. TV series. DIR: Ichiro Itano. SCR: Gen Urobuchi, Ichiro Itano, Yasuko Kobayashi. DES: Naoyuki Onda, Niθ (mecha), Hidenori Sano. ANI: Eiji Abiko, Hiroya Iijima, Naoyuki Onda, Ichiro Itano. MUS: Norihiko Hibino. PRD: Gonzo, SKY PerfecTV, Well Think, Toei Video. 25 mins. x 24 eps.
Germany, in another world's future. An unknown plague erupts from the bodies of the dead, causing them to be reanimated as terrifying bioweapons. The government calls them Amalgams, since they seem to be fusions of death and metal. They can take over any machine, incorporating it and redirecting its functions. The public calls them by an older, less scientific name: Demoniacs. A special law enforcement team, the Xenogenesis Assault Team or XAT, is set up to protect citizens from this new menace. As they focus on destroying the one Amalgam that always seems to arrive at outbreaks or attacks but always manages to escape, the masterminds behind the plague are working in secret to create the ultimate living weapons. But others want to use their work for darker purposes still.

Cowriter Urobuchi is a novelist and writer for game company Nitroplus, where one of his projects was the **BLACK LAGOON** game. He brings the same vein of darkness to the **GUYVER**-clone *Blassreiter*, giving the series an aura of grim intensity sustained

by driving action sequences that help the viewer to avoid focusing on its underdeveloped characters and formulaic scenario. Director Itano seems forever doomed to do incredible action work that shines in single moments of otherwise second-rate shows—his mastery, famous since **MACROSS**, of that visceral, immediate sense of a cameraman walking unharmed through explosions and crashes is largely wasted here.

The plot is structured like a game, in a way that makes engagement with a narrative format difficult: the story is told through a series of arcs, each focusing on an ultimately disposable character, so that each time viewers become involved in one story they have to reset as it ends. In addition, the central protagonist doesn't feature much until episode 3. On the plus side, the machines—arguably the major component of a *mecha*-themed show—are gorgeous, and the CGI action is beautifully designed and animated. This isn't a show that will stay in your memory forever and change how you see the world, but as robot action entertainment, it's fun. ●

BLAST OF TEMPEST ★
2012. JPN: *Zetsuen no Tempest*. AKA: *The Civilization Blaster*. TV series. DIR: Masahiro Ando. SCR: Hiroshi Yamaguchi, Keigo Koyanagi, Mari Okada, Shinsuke Onishi. DES: Tsunenori Saito. ANI: Hiroki Kanno, Masaru Oshiro. MUS: Michiro Oshima. PRD: Bones, Aniplex, Dentsu, Kids Station, MBS, Movic, Yahoo! Japan, Square Enix. 24 mins. x 12 eps. (TV1), 24 mins. x 12 eps. (TV2).
A year after the death of his step-sister Aika, teen-rebel Mahiro continues his doomed quest to find her murderer. He and his friend Yoshino (Aika's boyfriend) are drawn into a battle between rival clans of mages for control of two mystic trees, one fated to destroy the world, and the other to save it. It doesn't help matters that neither side seems entirely sure which is which, and that as events soon suggest, previous off-screen battles and demises might have been designed to hold off an even worse situation, that the characters' actions threaten to reinstate.

To its credit, *Blast of Tempest* seems happy to bite off way more than it can chew, festooned with character and plot references to the plays of William Shakespeare, chiefly *The Tempest*, but with shades of *Hamlet* in the figure of Mahiro—compare to **ROMEO X JULIET** and **BLOOD LAD**. Meanwhile, the "out of joint" nature of the world in contention offers a degree of realism to a traditionally obtuse anime plot—the absence of clear-cut battle lines of good versus evil, and the chance that the good guys might actually end the world if they achieve their aims, makes for an alluring ambiguity. Later episodes get bogged down in bombast and threats, and in plot-contortingly messy time-travel, but this is still an intriguing adaptation of the manga by Kyo Shiradaira, drawn in *Monthly Comic Gangan* by Arihide Sano and Ren Saizaki.

BLAZBLUE *

2013. JPN: *BlazBlue Alter Memory*. TV series. DIR: Hideki Tachinaba. SCR: Deko Aoko, Tatsuya Takahashi. DES: Tomoyuki Shitaya, Shigemi Ikeda. ANI: Tomoyuki Shitaya. MUS: N/C. PRD: Hoods Entertainment, teamKG. 24 mins. x 12 eps.
December 2199: after a series of terrible magical wars, humanity is hanging on grimly in the hope of better times in the new millennium. At the heart of many of the battles is the world's most wanted man, Ragna the Bloodedge, AKA The Grim Reaper. He is rumored to want to destroy the Novus Orbis Librarium, or NOL, the de facto government, a military-magical combine. On his tail is a motley crew of fighters, each uniquely talented. Their aim: to collect the huge bounty on Ragna's head.

Blazblue is based on a fighting game franchise from Arc System Works. Since its launch in 2008 it's had eight games across a variety of platforms, including arcade games, a couple of novels, and four manga, one coinciding with the TV anime. Localized versions preceded the anime in both Europe and the USA, making this a successful international franchise. Ragna is there from the start, the playable protagonist of the first game, as is his chief rival Jin, locked into a familiar structure of arcane names and powers and escalating levels of violence.

The overall look is equally generic. Ragna's spiky white hair and flowing red coat owe something to **DEVIL MAY CRY** and something to **TRIGUN**, with other costumes running the fantasy gamut from schoolgirl to pirate via Gothic Lolita, Chicago gangster, and antique European military. But the supporting characters are there purely for decoration; the focus of the story, apart from fighting, is the relationship between Ragna, Jin and a young lieutenant of the NOL, who has ditched her commission to travel with Ragna. Noel is apparently there to lend some emotional weight and tension to the story, a task at which she fails.

Even for the three main characters there's very little development in a script that mistakes obscurity for significance. Those who have played the games might be better able to work out what on earth is going on, or interested enough to try harder than your reviewers. After a competent opening sequence that segues straight into a fight scene—promising enough for a fighting game—the show's structure sags from carefully knit to full of plot holes, the writers behaving as if exotic and portentous naming systems are a substitute for story and character development. Exposition about the world of the story doesn't start to emerge, even on close and careful scrutiny, until halfway through the show. Perhaps director and writers assumed that any viewers would know the world of the game—a dangerous assumption when one needs to attract the casual TV consumer. Even the fan-service (**ARGOT AND JARGON**) is half-hearted.

Clichéd characters, a muddled story, and art and sound that are competent but not inspiring make *Blazblue* a difficult sell despite the popularity of the franchise. It's only 12 episodes, yes, but that's almost six hours and your lifespan is only around 75 years, two thirds of which will be spent asleep or working. Trust us on this: you have better things to do.

BLEACH *

2004. TV series, video, movies. DIR: Noriyuki Abe. SCR: Genki Furumura, Masahiro Okubo, Masashi Sogo, Michiko Yokote, Natsuko Takahashi, Rika Nakase. DES: Masashi Kudo. ANI: Akio Kawamura, Manabu Fukuzawa, Masashi Kudo, Masaya Onishi, Miyuki Ueda, Natsuko Suzuki, Seiji Kishimoto, Takeshi Yoshioka, Yoshimitsu Yamashita. MUS: Shiro Sagisu. PRD: Pierrot, TV Tokyo, Dentsu. 24 mins. x 366 eps. (TV), 30 mins. (v1), 32 mins. (v2), 87 mins. (m1), 95 mins. (m2), 94 mins. (m2), 94 mins. (m2).
Evil soul-eating goblins, known as Hollows, possess and destroy people including the family of high schooler Ichigo Kurosaki. Ichigo has untapped psychic powers, and in an encounter with Soul Reaper Rukia Kuchiki he gains her powers and transforms into a Soul Reaper himself. He needs Rukia's presence to work the transformation at first, but then he finds a way to put a "temporary soul" into his own body and transform without her help. Based on Taito "Tite" Kubo's 2001 manga in *Shonen Jump*, *Bleach* is a more magical retread of the quest narratives of **NARUTO**, or a more modern variant on **INU YASHA**. Whichever way you want to play it, it's all been done before, but this series of exorcisms-of-the-week gained a loyal and respectful following for its treatment of enemies within, no doubt helped by the early 21st-century release of several zombie movies. Not only people but also animals can be possessed by malignant forces, leading to a series of mysteries and hauntings reminiscent of **PET SHOP OF HORRORS**—at one point, even a possessed parakeet! The *Bleach* video *Memories in the Rain* (2004) was a flashback depicting the moment that Ichigo destroyed the Hollow that killed his mother. It was coupled with a brief three-minute bonus sequence relating to Gotei 13, the **HELLSING**-like organization that fights the Hollows, and originally shown to audiences in several locations as part of the Jump Festa Anime Tour (a publicity event related to *Shonen Jump* titles) before its video release. A *Bleach Rock Musical* (2004) appears to have been part of the same event. The second video, *Sealed Sword Frenzy* (2005), pits Ichigo against a creature than can sap the powers of others, before the franchise was upgraded to feature-length cinema outings. The movies *Memories of a Nobody* (2006), *Diamond Dust Rebellion* (2007), *Fade to Black* (2008), and *Hell Verse* (2010) all presented additional stories to the main narrative, which bowed out gracefully in March 2012. Since it will take most foreign territories several more years to catch up with local releases of *Bleach*, and this in turn will make the franchise continue to show a profit on paper even after it has ceased production, the authors would not be in the least bit surprised if *Bleach* returns on video in the future to meet a reduced but still signifi-

cant local demand and also a continued foreign interest in this long-running fantasy show (as happened with TRIGUN). The original manga continues to run in *Shonen Jump*, where it is now officially older than many of its readers.

BLESSING OF THE CAMPANELLA *

2010. JPN: *Shukufuku no Campanella*. TV series, video. DIR: Shinji Ushiro. SCR: Kojiro Nakamura, Masaharu Amiya. DES: Mariko Fujita. ANI: Makoto Koga, Hideki Furukawa, Mariko Fujita, Naoki Suehiro. MUS: Hitoshi Fujima, Junpei Fujita, Noriyasu Agematsu. PRD: AIC, DR Movie, AT-X, Lantis, Marvelous Entertainment, Media Factory. 24 mins. x 12 eps. (TV), 29 mins. (v).
The city of Ert'Aria is known as the treasury of the world, so its harvest festival is always popular with tourists. Young engineer Leicester Mayfield goes to a party with the other members of his adventuring guild, the Oasis Clan, and meets one of them—a beautiful automaton who imprints on him as her father because he's the first person she sees after falling from the sky. This pretty steampunk-lite harem anime (ROMANCE AND DRAMA) is based on an erotic visual novel (i.e., a low-interactive game, see ARGOT AND JARGON) by Windmill, which was released in 2009 and followed by an all-age-appropriate version in 2010. The fan service is limited, despite six "specials" on the DVD release that show the characters taking baths. The plot, the characters, the animation, and the action are all bland and forgettable—in fact everything except the design fails. Yet, there was a video of the same title in 2011. There have also been two manga, five books, and two Internet radio dramas. Many people obviously found it less brain-rottingly boring than we did. **N**

BLOCKER CORPS

1976. JPN: *Blocker Guntan IV Machine Blaster*. AKA: *Blocker Corps IV Machine Blaster*. TV series. DIR: Masami Anno, Takashi Anno. SCR: Akira Hatta, Susumu Takaku. DES: Tomosuke Takahashi, Kunio Okawara. ANI: Mamoru Tanaka. MUS: Hiroshi Tsutsui. PRD: Nippon Animation, Fuji TV. 25 mins. x 38 eps.
Hellqueen V and Kaibuddha, rulers of the devilish undersea Moghul Empire, launch an all-out assault on the surface world. From Astro Base, Professor Yuri sends out Robocles, Thundaio, Blue Caesar, and Vospalda, four "blocker" robots piloted by young boys with Elpath powers, Earth's last-ditch defenders against the people of the sea.

The first production for Ashi, a studio founded by former Tatsunoko-member Tatsuhiko Sato, *Blocker Corps* used many Tatsunoko alumni, including BATTLE OF THE PLANETS–designer Okawara. This simple robot show with a *Stingray* feel gains added drama halfway through when lead character Tenpyo Tobidori discovers he is the offspring of a union between a Moghul man and an Earth girl.

BLOOD LAD *

2005. TV series. DIR: Shigeyuki Miya. SCR: Kenji Konuta. DES: Kenji Fujisaki. ANI: Yoshinari Saito. MUS: Yuki Hayashi. PRD: Brains Base, Flying Dog, DN Dream Partners, Docomo Anime Store, Kadokawa, Klockworx. 24 mins. x 10 eps.
Staz Charlie Blood is a slacker vampire, less interested in sucking necks than he is in collecting fannish merchandise from the human world. He is shaken from his complacency by Fuyumi Yanagi, a Japanese girl who wanders into the demon world through a portal in her bedroom and accidentally dies. If Staz can somehow restore her to life, he can not only send her home, but follow her, to sample the wonders of human shopping for himself. With a certain similarity to SOUL EATER, this light-hearted show seems to favor style over substance, less concerned with the drama and horror of vampirism than with the opportunities it allows for being moody and cool. Buried deep down is a riff on *Hamlet* (BLAST OF TEMPEST) as Staz and his family intrigue against Wolf-Daddy (played with rumbling menace by Norio Wakamoto), the ruler of their realm who has killed and usurped their father. Staz's obsession with otaku merchandise marks him out as something of a shill for the Japanese multimedia industry, assuring the viewers that the really cool kids would be sure to want the same phone accessories, and limited edition plushies, that they do.

BLOOD ROYALE *

2002. JPN: *Blood Royal*. AKA: *Blood Royale Xtreme Series*. Video. DIR: Juhachi Minamisawa. SCR: Joichi Michigami. DES: Tesshu Takekura. ANI: Ken Matsugaoka. MUS: Takeshi Nishizawa. PRD: Discovery, Cherry Soft. 30 mins. x 2 eps.
Fugitive princesses Sayuka and Milte are "rescued" by a sea captain who turns out to be the infamous One-Eyed Devil, a piratical pervert. He chains them below deck in a torture chamber formerly used to extract information from prisoners and informs them that they are to be trained to be his sex slaves. The appeal, we assume, to fans of bondage and degradation, is that the higher-class the prisoner, the more fun there is in watching them fall. As in EROTIC TORTURE CHAMBER, these girls of the nobility are almost pathologically innocent—one isn't sure how to pleasure herself, since the concept is alien to her, but the other does not even know how to disrobe unassisted. Meanwhile, the pirate enters into his role with gusto, since he has agreed to break in the girls in order to gain much needed money to repair his ship. Some may feel he goes above and beyond the call of duty in a particularly nasty incidence of toilet training, not to mention innovative uses for a pet octopus—compare to MAHYA THE SERVANT. Part of the DISCOVERY SERIES. **LNV**

BLOOD SHADOW *

2001. JPN: *Guren*. AKA: *Crimson Lotus*. Video. DIR: Nao Ozekawa. SCR: Ryo Saga. DES: Toshihide Matsudate. ANI: Daisaku Kan, Sutekichi Kano. MUS: Hiroaki Sano. PRD: Discovery. 30 mins. x 3 eps.
In a world where ninja hunt infestations of demons, Rekka loses his beautiful fighting companion Tsukikage. He soon falls in with a new group of demon-hunters, a special task force known as the Crimson Lotus. Needless to say, he is the only male in a carefully chosen team of female archetypes (or stereotypes, if you will), comprising five underdressed girls: Akanna, Kureha, Hikage, Ayano, and Haruka. Demon rape and (eventual) human violent revenge soon follow, in a short series based on a PC game from Zone. Since one of the girls looks actionably similar to the lead from SAKURA WARS, we suspect that the entire venture was conceived as an erotic pastiche of that franchise, although with its sex-ninja setting it also appears to bear the hallmarks of LA BLUE GIRL. One of the DISCOVERY SERIES. **LNV**

BLOOD: THE LAST VAMPIRE *

2000. AKA: *Blood*. Video, TV series, movie. DIR: Hiroyuki Kitakubo. SCR: Kenji Kamiyama. DES: Katsuya Terada. ANI: Shinji Takagi. MUS: Yoshihiro Ike. PRD: Production I.G. 50 mins. (v), 25 mins. x 50 eps. (TV1), 25 mins. x 12 eps. (TV2), 150 mins. (m).

On the eve of the Vietnam War, a secret organization sends Saya, a young Japanese girl, to destroy vampires ("Chiropterans") on the U.S. air base at Yokota in Japan. Neither human nor vampire, she uses her skills with a sword to dispatch these unearthly menaces.

Seemingly combining the plot of DEVIL HUNTER YOHKO with an alternate plot similar to coproducer Mamoru Oshii's JIN-ROH, this is likely to be regarded in the U.S. as a Japanese rip-off of *Buffy the Vampire Slayer*. However, it features simply stunning animation and, in a first for anime, was made chiefly in English with Japanese subtitles to ease its progress into foreign markets. Mysteriously, however, this "film" is not feature-length, with the studio promising to complete the story with a manga and game—a suspicious sign of trouble behind the scenes and liable to leave the film forever inconclusive in much the same way as ARMITAGE III. An impressive action movie, but lacking in substance. There's no question, the animation in *Blood* is often superb. There are moments that honestly look too real to be animated—and demonic combat to put Buffy to shame. Manga Entertainment retains the original script's bilingual switches between English and Japanese, subtly demonstrating that Night and Day are not the only worlds that Saya walks between. There is a real observational verve lurking somewhere in the shadows—inspired, perhaps, by the animators' experience of foreign anime conventions. Bumbling aliens poke and prod at Saya, and try out their rudimentary Japanese, but none of them understand what she really is (compare to Production I.G's later SKY CRAWLERS). She is out of place in her own country, a Japan that has been colonized by the hulking, brash gaijin and their bizarre customs. In a stroke of pulp genius, the showdown is set during Halloween, when the airbase is crawling with costumed ghosts and ghouls, and even Death himself, lumbering across the background with his trademark scythe.

Compare this to a similar sequence in the movie of COWBOY BEBOP, the finale of which also takes place during a Halloween parade.

But it's an insult to viewers' intelligence to call this a "movie," as the publicity did both in Japan and America. It looks and feels like one of the truncated video releases of the 1990s—one of those also-rans like PLASTIC LITTLE or MADOX-01, that never quite got around to a sequel. In a desperate attempt to bulk out the running time, the English release also includes the self-congratulatory "Making Of" documentary, in which Mamoru Oshii openly admits that *Blood* began as a soufflé of half-baked ideas. A modern vampire girl, a demon-hunter on an airbase, and just a pinch of the muddled pseudo-politics that also characterized his earlier *Jin-Roh*, and *Blood* was born, as "part of a multimedia phenomenon"—which to Western viewers means it has a beginning and a middle, but no ending available in the English language for some time. The first *Blood* novel eventually appeared in English in 2005, and later that same year, the TV series *Blood+* began running on MBS and TBS. The TV series finally permitted the story to develop some coherence, beginning with Saya as an amnesiac schoolgirl who suffers flashback memories of the distant past. Like that similar school athlete, ESCAFLOWNE's Hitomi, Saya finds her school besieged by monsters and her world drastically changing, although in the case of *Blood+*, she is not so much taken to a distant world as forced into a new appreciation of the one she is already in, as she is force-fed human blood to reawaken her old memories, and co-opted into a government agency fighting the demonic infestation.

The prospect of schoolgirls and vampires proved suitably irresistible, and *Blood* has continued to manifest in numerous incarnations, not the least as a live-action film *Blood* (2008), which squandered its opportunity to retell the story by scrimping on martial arts and trying to hide this with a flurry of fast cutting. The franchise has continued to fare better in animated form, not the least because it is a 21st-century product, able to exploit the strengths of digital animation in shooting night sequences without having to worry about murky cels or halation effects. But one can't really go wrong with vampires, particularly in a franchise that continually plays and engages with teen mistrust of the adult establishment—Saya is variously lied to, exploited, swindled, and even pursued by a cabal that wishes to drink *her* blood. In the TV series *Blood+* (2005) and its shorter follow-up *Blood-C* (2011), an initially amnesiac Saya is hunted down by former chiropteran adversaries and eventually placed in a town populated by collaborators in an experiment to provoke her into a vampiric rage. A very long movie, *Blood-C: The Last Dark* (2012) has a vengeful Saya pursuing her enemy to the big city, where teenagers are forbidden from the streets in an authoritarian curfew. *Blood-C* features design work by the CLAMP collective, who occasionally insert cameo appearances from a character found in their own work XXXHOLIC. The series continues to be part of a chaotic, often contradictory whirl of novellas, manga, and other such spin-offery, and is sure to rise again from the dead in some form or other.

BLOODS: TRIBE OF LUST

2011. JPN: *Bloods: Inraku no Ketsuzoku 2*. Video. DIR: N/C. SCR: Hisato Goma. DES: Hikaru Kinoharu. ANI: Noa Ichikawa. MUS: N/C. PRD: PoRO, Rose Crown. 30 mins. x 2 eps.

The Sagemiya family is cursed with incestuous longings—the mere presence of someone from the same bloodline causes them to be overcome with lust. Twins Shun and Misaki have vowed to resist the urges in their blood. Shun, however, decides that while it would be disgusting to have sex with his twin, it's OK to do it with their older sister Kagu. When Misaki finds out, she decides that she wants a piece of her twin after all. And then mother gets involved. Based on an erotic game by Rose Crown. As far as we can discover, the game itself is *Bloods 1* and there is no earlier anime; the world occasionally provides small mercies for anime reviewers. **◐**

BLOODY CURS *

2010. JPN: *Togainu no Chi*. TV series. DIR: Naoyuki Konno. SCR: Natsuko Takahashi. DES: Naoyuki Konno. ANI: Takeyuki Yanase, Shigeki Kuhara. MUS: Masaaki Iizuka, Tomohisa Ishikawa. PRD: A-1 Pictures, Aniplex,

Hakuhodo DY Media Partners, Lantis, MOVIC, Nitroplus, Chubu TV, MBS, TBS, Rising Force. 24 mins. x 12 eps.

The Third World War is over, but the chaos continues. Japan is divided, and in the cracks in society the vermin gather. Toshima City is the heart of a massive drug trade, controlled by a syndicate chief known only as Il Re—The King. Normally, Akira would avoid both city and syndicate like the plague, but it's the only way out of a murder frameup, so he hasn't much choice. If he takes down Il Re in a fighting tournament, he gets his life back. If not, he won't need it.

Based on a boys' love game from Nitro+CHiRAL, the anime follows the game path quite closely, in that Akira meets a range of different guys. Unfortunately it focuses more on them fighting than anything else. The pretty boys are very pretty, although there's also one of those outrageously camp characters anime loves to flaunt, as if we still need campy stereotypes to make gayness accessible to a mass audience. There are significant glances, suggestive licking of blades, lips, and dogtag chains, self-consciously hot posing, and lots of atmospheric, oblique angle shots, but all the explicit one-on-one action involves weapons and intent to kill.

Most people who buy a boys' love anime want to see some boys' love, and on that score *Bloody Curs* fails to deliver. Or maybe it delivers, but we miss it, because as the story progresses the screen gets darker and darker. Right from the opening credits, predominantly black, red, and shadowed, this is a dark show in every sense. And by the end it's practically Stygian in places, and a visual entertainment that you have problems seeing is a little too experimental. The show was simultaneously streamed on Anime News Network alongside its Japanese release, one of the modern strategies deployed to circumvent piracy. **🄥**

BLUE BIRD

1980. JPN: *Maeterlink no Aoi Tori*. AKA: *Maeterlinck's Blue Bird*. TV series, movie. DIR: Hiroshi Sasagawa, Akira Kurooka, Kazuo Terada, Takashi Anno, Makoto Mizutani, Shigeru Omachi, Shinji Okada, Kenji Yoshida, Seiji Endo, Fumio Ikeno, Kunihiko Okazaki. SCR: Yoshinori Nishizaki, Keisuke Fujikawa. DES: Toyoo Ashida. ANI:

Toyoo Ashida. MUS: Yasushi Miyagawa. PRD: Westcape Corporation, Fuji TV. 25 mins. x 26 eps. (TV), 120 mins. (m).

A fairy named Bérylune visits brother and sister Tyltyl and Mytyl and tells them of the blue bird, a magical creature that brings good fortune to those who capture it. The children, accompanied by their dog Tylo and cat Tylette, search for it to help their ailing mother. They fly on a slipper to the Land of Memory, the Palace of Night, and the Kingdom of the Future before discovering that the blue bird (and the charity it represents) has been at home all along.

Maurice Maeterlinck's 1908 play *L'Oiseau Bleu* has been adapted for the screen several times—a 1918 silent film, a 1940 Shirley Temple vehicle, and a 1976 U.S.-Soviet coproduction. With a fairy-tale quality not dissimilar to the works of Kenji Miyazawa such as **NIGHT ON THE GALACTIC RAILROAD**, the story remains immensely popular in Japan. The series was also edited into a 120-minute movie-length version for video, *Maeterlinck's Blue Bird: Tyltyl and Mytyl's Great Adventure*, which retained many of the musical interludes that appeared in the TV version. A character called Tyltyl Mytyl appears in the book sequel to **KIMAGURE ORANGE ROAD**, where he befriends Madoka in New York. The story was retold in the **KIKI AND LARA** video, *Kiki and Lara's Blue Bird*.

BLUE BLINK ★

1989. TV series. DIR: Osamu Tezuka, Seitaro Hara, Hideki Tonokatsu, Naoto Hashimoto. SCR: Osamu Tezuka, Shigeru Yamagawa. DES: Osamu Tezuka, Kazuhiko Udagawa, Kimitoshi Yamane, Kazuo Okada. ANI: Kazuhiko Udagawa, Seiji Endo, Yasuhiko Suzuki, Megumu Ishiguro. MUS: Hiroaki Serizawa. PRD: Tezuka Pro, NHK. 25 mins. x 39 eps.

This last series in which **ASTRO BOY**–creator Tezuka was directly involved before his death features Alexander, a young boy who helps Blink, a magical blue mule-colt, out of trouble. In return, Blink (combining the attributes of a best friend and a pet) promises to come whenever Alexander calls. Alexander returns home to find that his father, a writer, has been kidnapped by the Black Emperor. He and Blink are transported to an alternate world, and after many adventures, they face the emperor, only to discover that he is Alex-

ander's father in disguise, who has set the whole thing up to demonstrate the wonder of books. Broadcast with English subtitles on KIKU TV in Hawaii, and subsequently resurrected for the crowd-funding site Anime Sols.

BLUE BUTTERFLY FISH

1993. JPN: *BB Fish*. Video. DIR: Mamoru Hamazu. SCR: Mamoru Hamazu. DES: Takayuki Sato. ANI: Takayuki Sato, Nobuyoshi Habara. MUS: Yoichiro Furukawa. PRD: Pioneer. 30 mins.

On a southern island, a swimmer who has wasted his potential gradually regains his confidence after meeting a beautiful girl. **NINETEEN**-creator Sho Kitagawa's 1990 manga, a girls' romance cunningly concealed within the pages of a boys' magazine, ran for 15 volumes in *Young Jump*. Eschewing the humdrum struggle and victory of sports training stories, it concentrated instead on emotion, underwater scenery, and the mechanics of marine sports for a sumptuous tale that often forgot it was supposed to be about an athlete.

BLUE CONFESSIONS

2005. JPN: *Aoi Kokuhaku*. Video. DIR: Shinji Ishidaira. SCR: Shinji Ishidaira. DES: Tetsuya Tsunawatari. ANI: Hakuhiro Konno, Tomoyuki Kitamura. MUS: N/C. PRD: Three Point, Studio OX, GP Museum. 30 mins.

Riho is a star-struck young girl who will do anything to become a star in the competitive world of Japanese pop music. She signs on with a talent agency whose company director takes particular pleasure in escorting his young charges to the casting couch. Riho loses a lucrative modeling contract to her friend Ayumi (who is more willing to put out) and seeks consolation in sex with her boyfriend Yuji. But when the boss finds out, it only fires his desire to have Riho for himself. Supposedly based on the real-life erotic confessions of model Miho Yabe. **🄝**

BLUE DRAGON ★

2007. TV series. DIR: Yukihiro Matsushita. SCR: Akatsuki Yamatoya, Katsuhiko Chiba, Yoshio Urasawa, Kento Shimoyama. DES: Tsuneo Ninomiya, Shinichi Tanimura. ANI: Tsuneo Ninomiya, Koki Sugawara, Baek Sung Chan, Mayumi Oda, Masatoshi

Hamada, Masayuki Koda. mus: Megumi Ohashi, Nobuo Uematsu. pro: Studio Pierrot, TV Tokyo. 25 mins. x 51 eps. (TV1), 25 mins. x 51 eps. (TV2).

Feisty ten-year-old Shu is training under Shadow Wielder Zola to master the Shadow Power of the legendary Blue Dragon so that he can save his village. He and his friend Kluke are on a quest with Zola, Shu's rival Jiro, tiny catlike Shadow Warrior Marumaru, and stowaway ex-waitress Bouquet. They hope to find seven missing pages from a magic book and prevent the evil ruler of Grankingdom from taking over the world. There's nothing new in this scenario, but the intended audience won't know that, because to a child, the story they fall in love with first is forever The One, the pure and original source of all heroes and all legends. Hence the endless recycling of old stories in new outfits, GUNDAM-style, to convince the new generation of young viewers that this dream was made especially for them.

The concept started life as a computer game. Makers of game-based anime have to perform a difficult balancing act—pleasing fans of the original game and attracting uncommitted viewers. *Blue Dragon's* makers work hard to push all the right buttons. And there are some big names on the credit list. Microsoft and Japanese studio Mistwalker share "original creator" credit, with FINAL FANTASY producer/director Hironobu Sakaguchi credited for original concept and Akira Toriyama for original character design. The game was a huge success, not least because it has much in common with Toriyama's epic DRAGON BALL, and the big-name voice actors and staff deliver competent, professional work. All this for a kids' TV series spun off from a video game, essentially an extended toy commercial—which shows just how lucrative the 6–11-year-old boys' toy and game market is in Japan.

Toriyama gave a few tweaks to his hugely popular standard character set, adding powerful toy/pet surrogates, the Shadow Beasts, to the mix. The art department under Tanimura creates some very pretty, brightly colored backgrounds. The result is charming, quirky, and perfectly tailored to its target market of under-12s: disposable, but enjoyable, child-friendly fun, with just enough jeopardy. Even adults will find

it amusing, though it's likely to pall over the full run of 102 episodes. But there's a proper continuity, even if it is the continuity of the elementary school playground. The face-offs between characters are predictably tedious but the actual fight scenes are long, exciting, and well tied in to the plot. Although the characters simply yell and grimace, the Shadow Beasts make impressive fighters when given time to build their moves.

In December 2007, a year after its debut, the *Blue Dragon* game led Xbox 360 sales in Japan, shifting almost twice as many units as its leading competitor *Dead or Alive*. The second series, *Blue Dragon: Trials of the Seven Shadows (Blue Dragon: Tenkai no Shichi Ryu)* got an English-language release in 2008, almost simultaneously with the launch of the first series on America's Cartoon Network. The series, made by the same team as the first, continues the themes of friendship, loyalty, developing powers, and constant battles, with cool new toy tie-ins to collect. Extending the market further, 2007 spin-off manga *Ral Ω Grad* continued the big-name linkup with art from DEATH NOTE's Takeshi Obata, guaranteeing it an English-language release, but so far neither Ami Shibata's 2006 manga *Blue Dragon ST* nor the *Trials of the Seven Shadows* manga from 2008 have been translated. Unfortunately, in Britain, the anime was given a 12 certificate, because the BBFC censors—unlike the Japanese, or anyone who has been on a bus at school closing time—think that prepubescent boys and boob jokes don't mix. A precisely crafted piece of marketing expertise was subverted and neutralized by local legislation and market differences, and kept away from the audience that might have best enjoyed it.

BLUE DROP *

2007. jpn: *Blue Drop: Tenshitachi no Gikyoku*. aka: *Blue Drop: A Play of Angels*. TV series. dir: Masahiko Okura. scr: Natsuko Takahashi, Akihito Yoshitomi, Masahiko Okura. des: Itsuko Takeda, Atsushi Takeuchi, Koichi Yonemura, Masanobu Nomura. ani: Itsuko Takeda, Noritomo Hattori. mus: The Kintsuru. pro: Gonzo, Asahi Pro, BeSTACK, Memory Tech, Pony Canyon, Showgate, Starchild Records, AT-X. 25 mins. x 13 eps. A terrible tragedy causes schoolgirl Mari

Wakatake to lose her home, her family, her friends, and all her memories. She's home-schooled for five years, but her grandmother is worried that she will lose touch with reality and sends her to boarding school, hoping she'll make friends. But instead it brings her into close contact with another girl hiding a deep secret that relates to Mari's tragedy. This short series is a prequel to writer Yoshitomi's science fiction manga about a race of lesbian aliens who invade Earth. The sexual elements are modestly and decorously handled in the anime. Shifting between a slice-of-life high school romance and a mecha-action drama, the romance wins out despite some brief but epic battles. The art and animation are well executed and attractive, with a standout moment when the alien starship leaps from the sea like a huge whale, recalling BLUE SUBMARINE NO. SIX. Director Okura is also credited for "original concept." Yoshitomi's first *Blue Drop* manga serial appeared in June 2004 and a second manga, *Blue Drop: Our Angel (Blue Drop: Tenshi no Bokura)*, appeared in 2008. A radio drama preceded the TV series.

BLUE EXORCIST *

2011. jpn: *Ao no Exorcist*. aka: *Ao no Futsumashi (Exorcist)*; *Blue Demon Master Twin Exorcist*. TV series, TV special, movie, video. dir: Tensai Okamura, Atsushi Takahashi. scr: Ryota Yamaguchi, Shinsuke Onishi, Ikuko Takahashi, Natsuko Takahashi, Reiko Yoshida. des: Keigo Sasaki, Masatoshi Kai, Shinji Kimura. ani: Keigo Sasaki. mus: Hiroyuki Sawano. pro: A-1 Pictures, Aniplex, Dentsu, MBS, MOVIC, Shueisha, Bandai Namco, TBS, Toho. 25 mins. x 25 eps. (TV), 2 mins. x 10 eps. (special), 25 mins. (special), 88 mins. (m).

Humans live in one world, demons in another. The two dimensions are supposed to stay out of each other's way, but demons still cross over to possess humans. Those who fight the demons are known as exorcists. So far, so WICKED CITY. But humanity actually has a means of containing Satan. To prevent the humans finding out about this and to secure it for himself, Satan sends his sons into our world. Twins Rin and Yukio are brought up in ignorance of their birth by a priest. Learning their true identity when their beloved foster-father dies to protect him, Rin joins the ranks of the exorcists—only to find his twin already there.

Based on Kazue Kato's 2009 manga, still running in Shueisha's *Jump Square* magazine, the anime suffers from the fate of many manga-based shows: an episodic plot with an uneven pace and long periods with no action. This is the kiss of death for action anime, far more problematic than the inconsistent application of Western demonic terminology and nomenclature. Only demonologists care if a high demon's name is used for a low one, but anyone watching cares if they get bored. It's even more annoying when the action that is there promises so much—it's fast, well-choreographed, and well animated.

The show had a movie spin-off, *Blue Exorcist Theater Version (Ao no Futsumashi [Exorcist] Gekijo Ban)* released in December 2012, with a different team at the helm. There are also ten two-minute shorts, *Blue Exorcist Snippets from the Underside (Ao no Exorcist Ura Eku)* extras to the Japanese Blu-ray and DVD releases, showcasing favorite characters. The 2011 video *Blue Exorcist: Kuro's Leaving Home (Kuro no Iede)* is a comedy one-shot about Rin's familiar, the two-tailed black cat Kuro. There's also a three-minute special accompanying the movie in Japanese theaters, with a title almost as long as the script: *Blue Exorcist Theater Version Special Clip (Ao no Futsumashi [Exorcist] Gekijo Ban Tokubetsu Eizo).*

BLUE EXPERIENCE
1984. JPN: *Aoi Taiken*. Video. DIR: N/C. SCR: N/C. DES: N/C. ANI: N/C. MUS: N/C. PRD: Zeros, Midnight. 25 mins. x 2 eps.
A pretty young teacher is hired by a family to privately educate their son. On arrival, she witnesses her employer in an illicit clinch with a lover, thereby inspiring her to seduce her pupil. An anime pastiche of Salvatore Samperi's erotic movie *Malizia* (1973), which was released in Japan under the similar title *Aoi Taiken*. **N**

BLUE FLAMES
1989. JPN: *Aoki Honoo*. Video. DIR: Noboru Ishiguro. SCR: Norikazu Imai. DES: Masao Nakada. ANI: Masao Nakada. MUS: N/C. PRD: Nippon Animation. 50 mins.
Sex and romance are found in this adaptation of Kimio Yanasawa's 1987 manga from

Young Sunday. The handsome teenager Ryuichi falls into life on the edge of the criminal world, but despite offers from hostesses to become his "sex friend," falls instead for a girl called Emi at the hospital. But his criminal leanings return after her father discovers evidence of their affair and offers him ¥10 million to disappear.

Yanasawa is known for hard-boiled manga such as *The Mayor* and *Self-Portrait of a Man* but also specializes in strange romance, such as his *A Formal Marriage*, about a sexless contract between a gay man and an abused woman. *Blue Flames* mixes the two with its handsome boy hero who is offered a fantasy gigolo job but only wants the girl next door. The idea of an erotic picaresque receives more salacious coverage in many other anime, including **JUNK BOY** and **GOLDEN BOY**.

BLUE GENDER *
1999. TV series, movie. DIR: Koichi Ohata, Masashi Abe. SCR: Katsumi Hasegawa. DES: Bunji Kizaki, Kunio Okawara. ANI: Bunji Kizaki. MUS: Kuniaki Haishima. PRD: AIC, TBS. 25 mins. x 26 eps. (TV), 98? mins. (m).
At the turn of the 21st century, subatomic research finds a way of rewriting human DNA, a leap in science that produces powerful new benefits and insidious viral hazards. With mutating superviruses that can destroy people from the inside out, the world faces an epidemic that makes AIDS look like a runny nose. Those who discover they are suffering from the deadly disease elect to go into cybernetic hibernation until medical science can catch up and deliver a cure. A generation later, they awake on an Earth ruled by the "Blue," who range in size from 2 feet small to 24 feet tall. The remnants of humanity are crammed into a space station called Second Earth, desperately trying to invent a drive that will allow them to escape to the stars, and now they need the help of the "sleepers." Director Ohata has toyed with post-apocalyptic adventure before in **MD GEIST** and **GENOCYBER**. The "movie" *Blue Gender: The Warrior* (2002) is a feature-length edit with a little extra footage.

BLUE REMAINS *
2000. Movie. DIR: Hisaya Takabayashi, Toshifumi Takizawa. SCR: Masatoshi Kimura, Hisaya Takabayashi, Toshifumi Takizawa.

DES: Haruhiko Mikimoto, Tatsuya Tomosugi. ANI: Toshifumi Takizawa, Hisaya Takabayashi. MUS: Motoi Sakuraba. PRD: Gaga, Okinawa Prefecture Industry Promotion Plc. 79 mins.
In 2052, as Earth teeters on the brink of environmental collapse, a family of terraformers returns from Mars with a payload of seeds designed to restore the planet. Unwisely arriving in the midst of a final nuclear exchange, they bail out and settle on the seabed south of Japan, waiting for the background radiation to return to manageable levels. Ninety years later, the original environmentalists are dead of radiation poisoning, and their daughter Amamiku has woken from suspended animation. She finds a world devoid of life (well, except for loads of fish, several human beings, and presumably whatever food they have been living on for the last century). Under attack from the robotic minions of the evil disembodied brain Glyptofane Sex, she is rescued by humans from the undersea citadel of Bathysphere, who help her save the last seedlings from her downed spacecraft before Glyptofane's creatures can destroy them.

Another of the late-20th-century experiments in digital animation, *Blue Remains* uses tricks similar to **BLUE SUBMARINE NO. SIX**, setting much of its action underwater where human movement and depth perception do not need to be as clear. In fact, considering that the original story outline called for a computer called "Mother Six" to go rogue and destroy the world, it would seem that *BR* began production at the same time, and was forced to alter similarities in its plot when *Blue Six* was released ahead of it. The graphics, as usual, were state-of-the-art for a few weeks, before being superseded by the almost daily improvements in software that cause so many early CG releases to age so fast. Less historically forgivable is the ludicrous plot, which contradicts itself on several occasions. Not the least among its crimes is the risibly named Glyptofane Sex, whose "kill everybody" policy is so illogical that even his own associates tell him he ought to rethink it. Originally designed to be the centerpiece of the Okinawa Digital Power Festival, showcasing both computer power and the seas around Japan's southern islands, today *Blue Remains* seems little more than a poor man's prototype of FINAL FANTASY: *The Spirits Within,* even down to the post-apocalyptic setting, vague eco-friendliness, and cod-mystic message. In something of a cheat, the final few minutes are not animated at all, but comprise live-action footage of fish swimming in tropical seas—it is a testament to its original achievement that audiences in 2000 took a while to notice that they were no longer watching artificial life-forms.

BLUE SEED *

1994. TV series. DIR: Jun Kamiya, Kiyoshi Murayama, Shinya Sadamitsu. SCR: Toshihisa Arakawa, Masaharu Amiya, Koichi Mizuite. DES: Katsuichi Nakayama. ANI: Masaaki Fujita. MUS: Kenji Kawai. PRD: King Record, TV Tokyo, Hakusensha, NTV Music. 25 mins. x 26 eps. (TV), 30 mins. x 3 eps. (v1), ? mins. x 2 eps. (v2).

Schoolgirl Momiji has been raised by a shrine priestess in Izumo, Japan's spiritual heartland. Ancient demons, the Aragami, are returning to wreak havoc, and only a priestess of the Kushinada bloodline can stop them. Momiji is saved from an Aragami attack by Mamoru Kusanagi, a half-Aragami defector who has sworn to protect the protectors. Kusanagi works alongside the TAC organization, a secret project to save Japan from the invaders. TAC's director, Daitetsu Kunikida, explains that only the Kushinada bloodline (see LITTLE PRINCE AND THE EIGHT-HEADED DRAGON) can put the Aragami to sleep and Momiji's long-lost twin, Kaede, is missing, presumed killed in action. Momiji trains hard to live up to her sister's peerless example, all the while fighting new mythological menaces including Orochi (also seen in YAMATO TAKERU), Susanoo (see TAKEGAMI), the giant Mukade centipede (see USHIO AND TORA), and *kappa* sprites (see BIRTH OF JAPAN). The titular "blue seeds" are comma-shaped *mitama* talismans common to Japanese archeology, also found adorning the shell of the monster turtle in *Gamera: Guardian of the Universe.*

Created by 3x3 EYES' Yuzo Takada for *Comic Gamma* in 1992, *Blue Seed* has superpowered schoolchildren, invading menaces-of-the-week, lost family, mythological roots, apocalyptic patriotism, mawkish romance, government intrigue, humor, *and* tragedy in quantum doses—all suspiciously similar to the later EVANGELION.

Influenced by the mid-1990s ambiguity of *The X-Files,* it also features a government cover-up opposed by its own employees; Momiji discovers that the last-ditch plan to stop the ancient threat is for her to become a human sacrifice.

The show exists in two formats, a TV series for general consumption and a video version "director's cut" that included extra nudity and violence. A three-part video sequel, *Blue Seed 2: Operation Mitama,* followed in 1996–97, set two years later when a new Aragami threat looms on the horizon. Other *Blue Seed* releases include the original "Making Of" prequel featuring voice-actor interviews and a two-part video spin-off, *Blue Seed Ver. 1.5,* which collected the humorous bumpers added to the TV series.

BLUE SONNET *

1989. JPN: *Akai Kiba Blue Sonnet.* AKA: *Red Fang Blue Sonnet.* Video. DIR: Takeyuki Kanda. SCR: Seiji Matsuoka. DES: Katsuichi Nakayama. ANI: Katsuichi Nakayama, Hisashi Abe. MUS: Go! PRD: Mushi Pro. 30 mins. x 5 eps.

Blue Sonnet is the code name of a sexually abused psychic street urchin, rescued from the slums and rebuilt as a superpowered cyborg by the apparently kindly Dr. Joseph Merkis, who is a major researcher for the organization Talon. Set to work for them, she soon finds herself in Tokyo posing as a schoolgirl under the name Sonnet Barje and investigating the psychic entity known as Red Fang, who turns out to be the high school student Lan Komatsuzaki. Lan is an orphan herself, who along with her brother Wataru is being raised by her foster father Jin Kiryu, a popular freelance writer and reporter. As in the later GUNSLINGER GIRL, Sonnet begins to question the motives of the organization that has programmed her, particularly after she is ordered to commit the brutal murder of a school nurse. Dr. Merkis only wants her to be a pliant, "perfect" tool, the pinnacle of cyborg design, while both he and Talon are hellbent on world domination without regard to such niceties as ethics or human life. She begins to develop a rudimentary conscience and emotions after experiencing the warm feelings of a group of Japanese students among whom she is living, which marks a remarkable

change considering what happens at so many other anime schools. When Talon captures Lan and limits her powers with a restraining collar, Sonnet must decide between her loyalty to Dr. Merkis and Talon, and defeating them while rescuing her schoolmate before Lan is used in a breeding program to create a master race of psychics.

As one can guess from the lack of a proper ending, *Blue Sonnet* began life as a manga, incorporating characters and situations from creator Masahiro Shibata's debut manga *Red Fang Wolf Girl Ran* (1975) from *Bessatsu Comic Margaret,* but resting largely on its fourth sequel, *Red Fang Blue Sonnet* (1981), which ran for 19 collected volumes after its initial appearance in *Hana to Yume.* This anime version seems engineered more to appeal to male fans than the female target audience of the original manga titles. *Sledge,* another title by Shibata, has been cited as a major influence on Kenichi Sonoda's GUNSMITH CATS. ⓥ

BLUE SUBMARINE NO. SIX *

1998. JPN: *Aono Rokugo.* AKA: *Blue Six.* Video. DIR: Mahiro Maeda. SCR: Hiroshi Yamaguchi. DES: Mahiro Maeda, Range Murata, Takehito Kusanagi, Shoji Kawamori. ANI: Toshiharu Murata. MUS: The Thrill. PRD: Gonzo, Bandai. 30 mins. x 4 eps.

With the ozone layer destroyed, mankind is moving into dome cities or underwater. Rogue scientist Zorndyke decides that humanity has lost the right to survive on the planet it has ruined and breeds a race of mer-people, the Mutio, to repopulate Earth. Young officer Mayumi Kino retrieves Tetsu Hayami, the navy's best pilot of yesteryear, now a junkie in the flooded ruins of Tokyo. Although he at first refuses to return to help humanity, Hayami saves Kino when Zorndyke's forces attack, joining with the remnants of the navy to fight for humanity's last stand.

Though the adaptation of Satoru Ozawa's SUBMARINE 707 sank without a trace in 1996, this follow-up to his 1960s manga rushed into production thanks to the number of underwater scenes, which allowed the animators to hide the joins between computer and cel animation with a blue sheen (GAMING AND DIGITAL ANIMATION). Heavily influenced by Gerry

Anderson's *Stingray*, particularly in the non-romance between Hayami and the mute Mutio mermaid he rescues, *Blue Six* was put into production as a deliberate attempt to create a calling card that would advertise its makers' skills *outside* the anime world, in the far more lucrative realm of computer games. Taking the boys' adventure of the original manga and adding the shapely-but-shrill female lead Kino, *Blue Six*'s aquatic basis plays to the strength of its digital animation and coloring. While often obvious or just plain showy, the pros of the cel/CG combination far outweigh the cons. The characters are marvelous, including a cybernetic whale, an idea last seen in the ill-fated LADIUS. Zorndyke in particular is a wonderful creation, an "evil genius" who occupies the moral high ground, whose tripod-crustacean war machines broadcast apologetic rationalizations, even as they wipe out human settlements. If there is any problem at all with *Blue Six*, it is the choice of format—the four "episodes" are so obviously a partitioned movie edition that it seemed dishonest not to release the "series" in feature-length from the outset. A ¥10-billion live-action adaptation, directed by Masahiko Okura, was announced in 2005 but never appeared.

BLUSHING CARD: DEVILISH CHERRY
2009. JPN: *Chinetsu Karte The Devilish Cherry*. Video. DIR: Hitomi Yokoyama. SCR: Ren Soto. DES: Anzu Hibiya. ANI: Anzu Hibiya. MUS: N/C. PRD: Suzuki Mirano, P. Alan. 30 mins. x 2 eps.
A young man in hospital seduces the nurse assigned to his room, who is soon his willing sex slave. Then he moves on to the other nurses and the female doctors. What on earth has he got against lab technicians, radiographers, and ward orderlies, one wonders? Manga creator Drill Murata's 2007 manga from T.I. Net remains untranslated, as does this anime adaptation. ◐

BOBBY'S IN DEEP
1985. JPN: *Bobby ni Kubittake*. AKA: *Bobby's Girl*. Movie. DIR: Toshio Hirata. SCR: Shiro Ishinomori. DES: Akimi Yoshida. ANI: Gaku Ohashi. MUS: Keiichi Oku. PRD: Madhouse. 44 mins.
Akihiko "Bobby" Nomura, a student whose love of motorcycles has led him to write a

column for a biker magazine, receives a letter from Sakiko Nakahara, a girl in distant Okayama. She likes his work, and the two begin a correspondence about bikes, which soon becomes more personal. The months pass as they coyly circle around the issues of whether they should meet and whether each has fallen in love with someone they have never seen.

Using a cut-up technique to summarize Yoshio Kataoka's short story, *Bobby's in Deep* was shown as part of a double bill with DAGGER OF KAMUI. The involvement of the Madhouse studio led to many famous names behind the scenes, including producers Rintaro and Masao Murayama, who would later cooperate on ALEXANDER. The same year, character designer Akimi Yoshida would begin her most famous creation, the manga *Banana Fish*.

BOBOBO-BO BO-BOBO *
2003. TV series. DIR: Hiroki Shibata. SCR: Toshio Urasawa. DES: Yoichi Onishi. ANI: Takashi Nishizawa. MUS: Ichiro Kameyama. PRD: Toei Animation, TV Asahi. 25 mins. x 76 eps.
In the 31st century, the Margarita Empire, under Tsuru Tsururina IV (Baldy Bald), plots to make the entire Earth population lose its hair. The empire is opposed by a lone master, Bo-Bobo, possessor of a golden Afro of truly vast proportions and practitioner of the ancient martial art known as True Fist of Nose Hair. In other words, the futuristic martial arts of FIST OF THE NORTH STAR or DRAGON BALL, lampooned in the surreal style of EXCEL SAGA, crammed full of nonsense puns and satirical asides. Bo-Bobo himself has a name based on a Japanese slang term for mussed hair, and wields the psychic power of "hearing the voice of hair"—this is where we point out that *kami* ("hair") is a homonym in Japanese for "divine," although we doubt that such anthropological considerations were that important to Yoshio Sawai's original manga in *Shonen Jump* weekly.

Bo-Bobo rescues a beautiful girl, appropriately named Beauty, from the Empire's shaving squad. On their travels to escape the vicious gangs of depilators and their super weapon the Shaver Beam, they meet Don Patch, who claims to be the capo of the insane Hajikerist mob. At first he thinks Bo-Bobo is sent by his mortal

enemies, the Wig Gang, but later agrees to help the freedom fighters in their struggle. Another hero, Heppokomaru, joins their band, bringing his special martial arts skill, the Fist of the Fart, to their aid. Together they face many perils, each dafter than the last. When Beauty is exposed to the Shaver Beam the only thing that can prevent her from losing her lovely hair is a mystic cure at the summit of the Aitsuhage Tower: our heroes must scale five floors, each with a different danger, in a sequence that would be reminiscent of Bruce Lee's *Game of Death* if the high concept of fighting baldness with the power of body hair weren't so completely absurd. She also plays a deadly game of beach volleyball with a guardian robot and gets locked inside a TV set. Their deadliest opponent is Bo-Bobo's former friend Warship, now a high-ranking officer of the Empire. By now you've probably torn your hair out, which just goes to show the power of the bald side of the Force.

BODACIOUS SPACE PIRATES *
2012. JPN: *Moretsu Pirates*. AKA: *Moretsu Uchu Kaizoku*. TV, movie. DIR: Tatsuo Sato. SCR: Tatsuo Sato, Michiko Ito, Shinichi Miyazaki, Kentaro Mizuno. DES: Noriyuki Matsumoto, Akira Yasuda, Hiroshi Takeuchi, Kenji Teraoka, Masahisa Suzuki, Naohiro Washio, Shinichi Miyazaki, Shoji Kawamori, Akira Ito. ANI: Hiroshi Takeuchi. MUS: Elements Garden, Hitoshi Fujima, Junpei Fujita, Noriyasu Agematsu. PRD: Satelight, Starchild Records. 25 mins. x 26 eps. (TV), 93 mins. (m).
The future: space travel is like air travel back in the 21st century, just another way of getting around. Planets have been colonized, politics exported, wars fought, and a Galactic Empire formed. Marika Kato is an ordinary teenager, who works part-time at a trendy retro café and hangs out at the space yacht club where she's a member. Then she learns that she's heir to a proud tradition. Her late father was a space pirate, captain of the spaceship Bentenmaru and licensed to commit acts of piracy under letters of marque from the government. These licenses lapse if they are not taken up by a pirate's direct lineal heirs—unless Marika becomes captain of the Bentenmaru the crew will have to find another ship. She takes up the challenge to prove herself a worthy heir to her parents.

Bodacious Space Pirates is an uneven but charming series, a light, frothy confection of fun and adventure wrapped around a fairly stodgy midsection where the writing is so-so and the pace is ho-hum. What carries it over this sticky patch is the charm of the characters—heroine Marika is very engaging and her attempts to combine schoolwork, command, and piracy deliver a nice mix of humor and emotion. Despite the title imposed on the U.S. release, fan service is relatively restrained: think convention cosplay rather than insistent crotch shots. There's a serious point embedded in the fun—how far should a child feel obliged to fulfill her parents' destiny?—but for the most part this show invites you to suspend disbelief and have a good time.

Satelight's animation is bright and zingy. There are nods and winks to anime **FANDOM**, including unmissable homages to **SAILOR MOON** and **IRIA**. Older fans may detect a cleaned-up version of **PLASTIC LITTLE**. *Miniskirt Pirates*, the ongoing 2008 book series from Yuichi Sasamoto, with art by Noriyuki Matsumoto, mined a rich seam of pop culture references that Sato is well qualified to bring to life. A movie version followed in early 2014.

BODY TRANSFER *

2003. JPN: *Nikutai Teni*. Video. DIR: Yoshitaka Fujimoto. SCR: Yasuyuki Moto. DES: Harina Hayataka. ANI: Harina Hayataka. MUS: Toru Shura. PRD: ARMS, Green Bunny. 30 mins. x 2 eps.

Kenichi and his classmates stay late after school to see a new archeological discovery, a strange mirror, which transports them to another dimension. Trapped by a magical forcefield (likely to be a cost-cutting maneuver to save on new backgrounds, in the style of **FOBIA**), the students discover that their minds have switched into each other's bodies. They figure out that the only way to switch back is by generating a high level of sexual arousal, so it's up to Kenichi to get everything back to normal before the magical dimension falls apart. This leads to an intriguing series of original ideas (for anime pornography at least), as the mind-swap allows for experiments with gender perspective and desire. There is also a romantic subplot, as one character is re-

vealed to be unaffected by the mirror and using its powers to ensure that when all the mind-swaps are done, Kenichi is hers. But is that Kenichi's mind (which might have someone else's body), or Kenichi's body (which might have someone else's mind)? **🅛🅝**

BODYJACK

1987. Video. JPN: *Bodyjack: Tanoshii Yutai Ridatsu*. AKA: *Bodyjack: Happy Astral Projection*. DIR: "Dojiro." SCR: Takashi Tanigawa. DES: To Moriyama. ANI: Makoto Kaneda. MUS: N/C. PRD: AIC, C.Moon. 30/35 mins.

The randy young Asagaya buys a device (which looks like an oversized traditional Japanese pig-shaped incense burner) from the local mad scientist, Dr. Toyama, which enables him to astrally project. He uses it to "slip into" and take over the body of his crush, the beautiful high school girl Komaba, so that he can see how it really feels to be a girl. Then Komaba's classmate (and Asagaya's girlfriend), the equally beautiful Nakano, surprises "him" and mistakes his activities for a sexual advance from her friend, beginning a lesbian scene that isn't really a lesbian scene because one of them is a man trapped in a woman's body, and enjoying every minute of it.

Bodyjack began as an erotic manga by **CREAM LEMON**'s pseudonymous To Moriyama, known today as Mori Toyama and, in more mainstream publications, as Naoki Yamamoto, the creator of **DANCE TILL TOMORROW**. Originally released on laserdisc, it was rereleased in 1988 on VHS with about five minutes of new animation added, to make a more-adult "Complete Version." An original incorporation of sex into SF since imitated in **SEXORCIST** and the **SECRET ANIMA** episode *Dream Hazard*. **🅝**

BOES

1987. JPN: *Geragera Bus Monogatari*. AKA: *Chuckling Bus Story*. TV series. DIR: Hiroshi Sasagawa. SCR: Kaoru Toshina, Satoshi Ohira, Sachiko Ushida, Hisashi Furukawa. DES: N/C. ANI: Susumu Ishizaki. MUS: Shinsuke Kato. PRD: Telescreen, Studio Cosmos, TV Tokyo. 25 mins. x 52 eps.

Only the Dutch could come up with the idea of a talking bull in red dungarees who can fly when he puts on his magical wooden clogs, for such is the hero of this Netherlands coproduction based on

the comic-strip character created by Wil Raymakers and Thijs Wilms that has been syndicated in ten different countries.

BOIN *

2005. JPN: *Boin*. Video. AKA: *Hooters*. DIR: Shigenori Kurii. SCR: Sozo Doji. DES: Maria Ichimonji. ANI: Michitaka Yamamoto. MUS: N/C. PRD: Shindeban Film, Image House, Milky, GP Museum Soft. 30 mins. x 2 eps. (v1), 30 mins. x 3 eps. (v2).

Daisuke Ichijo finds himself a job as a high school career guidance counselor, with a "hands-on" approach that demands putative school-leavers dress up in the uniforms of their chosen professions and act out a series of role-play situations for their helpful teacher. A spate of uniform fetish sex scenes ensues, with particular attention paid to large breasts—both a feature of the original title in Japanese and the erotic computer game from Bijin Happo on which this anime was based.

Boin was followed in 2007–8 by a sequel, *Resort Boin*, also based on a game, which is set by the beach and features several additions to the original harem **🅛🅝🅥**

BOKU, OTARYMAN

2010. Video. DIR: Minoru Ashina. SCR: Minoru Ashina. DES: N/C. ANI: Minoru Takahara. MUS: N/C. PRD: Panda Factory, Studio Puyukai, Liverpool. 17 mins. x 2 eps.

Can one be a salaryman and an otaku? Creator Yoshitani's 2007 manga chronicling his adventures as a sci-fi geek trying to live a normal life *and* hold down a job in urban Japan has sold over a million copies in Japan, after garnering 15 million hits on his website. It inspired a drama CD as well as this charming Flash animation. Compare with the longer and more ambitious **OTAKU NO VIDEO** to see what has changed about living your geekdom and what remains the same. A year later Ashina directed **SPELUNKER SENSEI**, a one-shot video about the world's most recklessly adventurous high school teacher, again from Studio Puyukai. According to a survey conducted in 2005 by the Nomura Research Institute, "high-functioning social otaku" like the hero of this anime constitute 18% of all Japanese **FANDOM**, while "legacy" otaku and family men who were once otaku constitute a further 48%. No wonder it sold a million.

BOKURANO

2007. AKA: *Ours.* TV series. DIR: Hiroyuki Morita. SCR: N/C. DES: Kenichi Konishi, Shigemi Ikeda. ANI: Tamotsu Ogawa, Shingo Yamashita. MUS: Yuji Nomi. PRD: Gonzo, AT-X. 25 mins. x 24 eps.

Summer camp can be a life-changing experience. Just how life-changing is something a group of 15 high school friends are about to learn. They wander into a cave on the beach and find a hidden room full of computers. A strange man asks them if they want to sign up to beta test his cool new mecha fighting game. Just as they're beginning to believe they imagined the whole thing, they learn that it was all real—except that this is no game. They really do have to fight mecha attacking the Earth. If they lose, Earth will be destroyed. And the power source for their mecha is more expensive than they've even begun to imagine—the death of each pilot, even if victorious. If you think the world of EVANGELION is bleak and harsh, brace yourself.

Bokurano the manga was created in 2004 by Mohiro Kito, who also created NARUTARU. It ran until 2009 and was, if you can believe it, even bleaker than the anime, so much so that director Morita asked Kito if he could find a way to change the outcome for the main characters. Kito responded that he was happy with changes as long as Morita didn't bring any magical solutions into the story. Morita made his changes, going public on his blog with his reason after a wave of negative comments from fans of the manga, and telling them to stop watching if they didn't like the idea.

Yet in one way he remained totally faithful to the manga, making a mecha action show that isn't really about the machines or the action: it's about character, motivation, and how you deal with an absolutely impossible situation. It's the Kobayashi Maru scenario from *Star Trek*, or the kamikaze pilot's last letter home: the point is not whether you can finagle some way to escape from an impossible situation, but how well you face it (GANTZ). Dark, uncompromising, and worth a lot more time and attention that some of the rubbish that has been licensed for English-language distribution, *Bokurano* seems to have suffered from being released at the tail end of anime's boom era, when Anglophone licensors were less keen to pick anything up at all, let alone anything so nihilistic. Viewers in Arabic- and Spanish-speaking territories, however, got the chance to see it. There is also a 2007 book series written by Renji Oki with art by Kito, *Bokura no: Alternative.* It has an alternate storyline, but no alternate endings.

BOMBER BIKERS OF SHONAN *

1986. JPN: *Shonan Bakusozoku.* AKA: *Explosive Racers of Shonan.* Video. DIR: Nobutaka Nishizawa. SCR: Kenji Kurata, Naoko Takahashi, Kisei Cho. DES: Satoshi Yoshida. ANI: Takashi Saijo. MUS: Yasaku Kikuma, Koichi Hirai, Haruo Kubota. PRD: Ashi Pro, Toei. 50 mins. x 11 eps., 40 mins. x 2 eps. (*Stormy Knight*).

Yosuke Eguchi is cool, brave, enigmatic, and the star of the school's embroidery club. With his pals in the Shonan Bomber Bike gang, he just wants to ride his motorcycle after school without any trouble, following in the footsteps of former schoolmate and current king of the road, Noboru Ishikawa. A rival gang tries to force Eguchi off the road and, when that fails, send in its out-of-town friends to finish the job, but Eguchi's impassioned speech about the Way of Biking convinces everyone they should live in peace. Later episodes concentrate on other members of the gang, including Yoshimi's ham-fisted courting of Nagisa and Eriko's surfer boyfriend, Seiji, falling into depression after a bad performance, and asking Eguchi to help him arrange a rematch. The third installment, a 1987 *Rocky* pastiche where the gang must pick a champion to fight the boxer Kondo, was also screened in theaters on a double bill with VICTORY PITCHER.

Keeping closely to Satoshi Yoshida's original 1983 *Shonen King* manga, combined sales of which topped 20 million volumes, the series lasted ten years, mixing romance and racing, with gang-members pairing off and even the sound of wedding bells. Eguchi falls for an American girl, Samantha, in the penultimate installment, and the finale includes his homegirl Yoshiko's last-ditch attempts to show her feelings.

An immensely successful production throughout the 1980s, the video series did not disgrace its manga predecessor, selling almost a quarter of a million tapes and inspiring a successful imitator in Toru Fujisawa's *Shonan Pure Love Gang* and GTO. Its English-language performance was less impressive—only a single episode made it to a U.S. video market that couldn't see the appeal of lovelorn Hells Angels.

In 1997, barely a year after the original coasted to a halt, the same staff would return with *New Bomber Bikers of Shonan: Stormy Knight*. Featuring all-new bikers but with cameo appearances by the original cast, the series consisted of two videos, each split into two faux-TV episodes detailing new gang leader Katsuhiko and his feud with the Tigers.

Beginning the following year, *Stormy Knight* was also adapted as four live-action videos. The original story was also adapted into three live-action movies featuring star of the moment Yosuke Eguchi, *Shonen Bakusozoku* (2001), *Shonen Bakusozoku 2* (2001), and *SB3: Ten Ounce Kizuna* (2002). These appear to follow the plot of the anime quite closely.

BOMBERMAN

1995. JPN: *Bomberman B-Daman Baku Gaiden.* AKA: *Bomberman B-Daman Explosive Tales.* TV movie, TV series. DIR: Nobuaki Nakanishi, Takafumi Hoshikawa, Yasuo Iwamoto. SCR: Tatsuhiko Urahata, Tomoyasu Okubo, Toshiki Inoue. DES: Koji Sugiura. ANI: Junko Abe. MUS: Jun (Chiki) Chikuma. PRD: Madhouse. 25 mins. (TVm), 25 mins. x 68 eps. (TV1), 25 mins. x 52 eps. (TV3), 25 mins. x 52 eps. (TV4), 25 mins. x 52 eps. (TV5), 25 mins. x 50 eps. (TV6).

In the wake of the Kobe earthquake, the game character Bomberman was dragged out to make a 25-minute program on safety measures called *Thank You to Heroism: Lend Me Your Ears.* This one-shot from director Norio Kawashima was the precursor to a full-fledged series featuring the attempts of the evil Dark B-Da to seize control of B-Da City, opposed only by Bomb, the round-headed agent of justice. B-Daman would return in 1999 with the series *Super B-Daman,* animated by the Xebec studio for breakfast television on TV Tokyo. Writer Urahata would go on to direct MASTER KEATON.

After almost a hundred episodes, it was rebranded again as the 52-episode *Bomber-*

man Jetterz (2002), moving the action to a colony world, where slacker Bomberman Shiro is suddenly thrust into a leadership position when his heroic elder brother Mighty goes missing. *Battle B-Daman* (2004) and *Crush B-Daman* (2006) would add another slew of episodes to the total.

BONDAGE HOUSE *

1999. AKA: *Bondage Room, Detective*. Video. DIR: Akihiro Okuzawa. SCR: Takuhiro Fukuda. DES: N/C. ANI: N/C. MUS: N/C. PRD: Beam Entertainment, Akatonbo. 30 mins. x 2 eps.
Detective Higashino rescues a beautiful girl from a gang of strange men. Discovering that Ayane Akimoto was *sold* to them by her parents, Higashino begins an investigation into the modern world of slavery, tracking the life of Ayane's dead older brother, with time out for gratuitous scenes of bondage and abuse. Released in the U.S. as *Bondage Room* (2001). **ⓃⓋ**

BONDAGE 101 *

2004. JPN: *Chobatsu Yobiko*. AKA: *Punishment Prepschool*. Video. DIR: Aim. SCR: Aim. DES: Satoshi Shimada. ANI: Satoshi Shimada. MUS: Yoshi. PRD: YOUC, Digital Works (Vanilla Series). 30 mins. x 2 eps.
Ousted from his previous job for molesting students, Kyoichi Shizuma discovers, like the protagonist of FIVE CARD, that such issues do not prevent him from finding a job elsewhere, particularly when his new posting only pretends to be a school. In fact, it is a secret operation for molding innocent girls into willing sex slaves. Some don't require all that much molding, such as the bespectacled Yumiko, who enthusiastically embraces her school's dark secret. Innocent Asuna is too meek and mild to put up much of a fight, which leaves the "drama" in this erotic anime in the hands of fiery, willful Tomo. Abuse and degradation duly ensues in another entry from the VANILLA SERIES. **Ⓑ ⓃⓋ**

BONDAGE QUEEN KATE *

1994. JPN: *Nessa no Wakusei, Jokoankan: Kate*. AKA: *Desert Planet*. Video. DIR: Takashi Asami. SCR: Yuji Kishino. DES: Ryoichi Oki. ANI: N/C. MUS: N/C. PRD: All Products, Beam Entertainment. 45 mins. x 2 eps.
Kate Curtis is a young, virginal police officer sent undercover to Doune, the desert planet where getting raped by one of the locals is supposedly the highlight of any trip. Her mission is to find out who's raping all the tourists. Her disguise is a skimpy costume with the words "RAPE ME" emblazoned on it in big letters. Kidnapped on arrival by some men clad in incongruous 1970s fashions, she is assaulted during a desert drive and subjected to toilet-training torture while hanging from a chain above a pit full of monsters—including a thinly disguised Sarlacc from *Return of the Jedi*. She is then taken into their lair, where she confesses that she secretly enjoys rape in an anime that manages to demean women not only with what is done to them but also in how they react to it.

Produced by "Dr. Pochi," perpetrator of several of the CREAM LEMON series, *Bondage Queen Kate* recalls the *Story of O* with its heroine's adoration of her abusive captors and a salacious interest in invading the female body not just with the usual suspects, but also with diuretics and the surgeon's knife. The science fiction elements are perfunctory—Doune is a Middle Eastern airport departure lounge only cosmetically related to Frank Herbert's *Dune*; the spacecraft has the engines of a Star Destroyer turned on its side; the desert is a glorified sand pit; and if there was ever a time to use a pseudonym, ORGUSS 02—writer Kishino and several famous voice actors should have realized that this was it. **ⓃⓋ**

BONES

AKA Studio Bones. Animation company formed in 1999 by a group of animators from Sunrise: producer Masahiko Mikami, director Shinichiro Watanabe, and designer/animator Toshihiro Kawamoto. Notable early works included the dual stylistic successes of COWBOY BEBOP (a sci-fi anime without giant robots), and ESCAFLOWNE (which crammed giant robots into a fantasy show, a feat not achieved so well since DUNBINE). Subsequent hits for the studio have included RAHXEPHON and FULLMETAL ALCHEMIST.

BONOBONO

1993. Movie, TV series. DIR: Hitoshi Nanba. SCR: Tetsuo Yasumi. DES: Michishiro Yamada. ANI: Michishiro Yamada, Yuka Kubodani. MUS: Gonchichi. PRD: Amuse, Tac, TV Tokyo. 94 mins. (m1), 15 mins. x 48 eps. (TV), 61 mins. (m2).
Bonobono the otter, along with his raccoon and chipmunk friends, first appeared in a children's manga by MUKA-MUKA PARADISE–creator Mikio Igarashi in 1986. With the gentle stories' sales topping the five million mark, the artist directed and wrote the 1993 film, which featured the woodland pals having fun and debating simple points of philosophy (à la *Winnie the Pooh*), leaving director Nanba to helm the subsequent 1994 TV series. By this time, the corporate giant Bandai was involved, and Japan was deluged with *Bonobono* toys, games, and merchandising.

The series was resurrected in the CGI movie *Bonobono: The Tree of Kumomo* (2002, *Bonobono: Kumomo no Ki no Koto*), in which Bonobono sits beneath the titular tree on a hill in an attempt to forget his sadness, only to become involved in a conspiracy against Popo the ferret, who is accused of breaking off a branch.

BOOBALICIOUS *

2005. JPN: *Milk Junkie Shimai Hen*. AKA: *Milk Junkie Sisters Chapter, Milk Junkie 2*. Video. DIR: Ken Raika, Masato Kitagawa. SCR: Renge Sumeragi. DES: Mamijin Tayama. ANI: Mamijin Tayama, Mamoru Sakisaka, Sei Komatsubara. MUS: SALAD. PRD: Milky, T-Rex. 30 mins. x 4 eps.
When Wataru was a shy kid, the voluptuous Fusono sisters lived next door. Their mother used to babysit him. Now he's grown up, not so shy, and delighted to find his old neighbors living next to his new apartment. This is based on an erotic PC game by Blue Gale, with designs by Yotoku Tatsunami, so you don't need to use your imagination to guess what happens. On the plus side, the sex is between consenting adults and a good time is apparently had by all, at least in the two episodes released as *Boobalicious* in the U.S. See also ANYONE YOU CAN DO ... I CAN DO BETTER, which is based on a game from the same series. **Ⓝ**

BOOGIEPOP PHANTOM *

2000. JPN: *Boogiepop wa Warawanai*. AKA: *Boogiepop Does Not Laugh*. TV series. DIR: Takashi Watanabe. SCR: Sadayuki Murai. DES: Koji Ogata, Shigeyuki Suga. ANI: Minoru Tanaka. MUS: N/C. PRD: Madhouse. 25 mins. x 12 eps.
The malevolent "Manticore" entity

manifests in a Japanese high school, where it takes on the form of teenage student Saotome. Saotome's girlfriend has kept their liaison secret, but confides in Moto, a terminally shy girl who has secret feelings of her own for Saotome, which return to trouble her when the Manticore, as Saotome, traps her in an alleyway. Meanwhile, a shadowy figure wanders the night defending teenagers from further attacks, in a show that masterfully mixes the disconnected urban myths of **PARANOIA AGENT** and *Ring* (1998) with the perennial teen-angst concerns about approaching adulthood. *Boogiepop* is based on a series of novels begun in 1998 by Kohei Kadono, but its mood often seems like a deliberate evocation of the unseen menace of **SERIAL EXPERIMENTS LAIN**. It also cunningly reprises many set-ups familiar from both Western horror and Western fairytales—the children are offered the chance to never grow up, as in **PETER PAN AND WENDY**, although their bodies and minds are already struggling with adult concerns and desires. Nowhere is this more apparent than in the subplot concerning a five-year-old serial killer case, allowing director Watanabe and **PERFECT BLUE**–writer Murai to blend the elements of American stalk-and-slash horror with more Japanese sensibilities. A welcome glimpse of originality in a crowded genre (after all, at its most superficial level, this might appear as just one more tale of supernatural ghostbusting in modern Tokyo), it was also the basis for the live-action movie *Boogiepop and Others* (2000).

BOOK GIRL

2009. JPN: *Bungaku Shojo*. AKA: *Literature Girl*. Movie, video. DIR: Shunsuke Tada. SCR: Yuka Yamada, Megumu Sasano. DES: Keita Matsumoto, Michie Suzuki. ANI: Kanami Sekiguchi, Kazuchika Kise, Keiichi Sano, Kyohei Tezuka, Yosuke Okuda, Yuko Yoshida, Keita Matsumoto, Mariko Ishikawa. MUS: Masumi Ito. PRD: Production I.G, Kadokawa Contents Gate, Enterbrain, Lantis, Pony Canyon, T.O. Entertainment. 101 mins. (m), 15 mins. (v1), 25 mins. (v2–4).

Quiet teenager Konoha Inoue meets a strange girl, Toko Amano, with the oddest eating disorder ever: she eats writing. Through stories, and their friends' experiences of stories, they explore the world of truth and lies, the difference between reality and fiction, and what makes friendship or love, as Konoha struggles with his own secret.

Book Girl is an intriguing exercise in magic realism, with a heroine who literally *eats* books, devouring their pages and making odd synesthetic comments about how their themes "taste" and "feel." Meanwhile, our hapless protagonist Konoha is a reclusive teenage novelist who has forsworn writing after bad experiences with his first published work, but who is dragged back into creativity by Toko's desire for new foods. It's a truly fantastic idea, allegorizing youthful hunger for inspiration, and a creative's longing for creativity, all tied up in a strange high school romance, with just a hint of postmodern fascination with the *physicality* of old media. To a generation reared on e-readers and smart phones, the idea of actual pages must seem almost as odd as a book you can eat. Some critics have complained that it is unlikely for a teenage boy to somehow be a bestselling novelist, but real-world Japanese publishing is riddled with premature prodigies—many magazines run literary competitions and publish the winners, and teenagers are one of the sectors in Japanese society with the most time on their hands!

Production I.G bring the book series by Mizuki Nomura beautifully to life—the original featured art by Miho Takeoka, and ran to 16 volumes between 2006 and 2011. It has sold over 1.6 million copies in its homeland, and is available in English, although four further manga spin-off stories written by Nomura, with art by either Rito Kosaka or Akira Hiyoshimaru, are not. *Book Girl* has tapped into a special strain of book-hunger; as well as the usual CD and radio dramas, music, and merchandise, there are *Book Girl* guides to art and literature. The first video, *Book Girl Today's Snack: First Love (Bungaku Shojo Kyo no Oyatsu: Hatsukoi)*, was made as a bonus extra with a limited-edition version of one of the books in 2009. The movie followed in 2010, with three videos released at one-week intervals prior to the premiere, filling in the backstory for some of the characters.

BOOK OF BANTORRA, THE *

2009. JPN: *Tatakau Shisho The Book of Bantorra*. AKA: *Fighting Librarians: The Book of Bantorra*. TV series. DIR: Toshiya Shinohara. SCR: Mari Okada, Toshizo Nemoto, Jukki Hanada, Shinichi Inotsume. DES: Masaki Yamada, Shigemi Ikeda. ANI: Masaki Yamada, Tomoaki Kado. MUS: Yoshihisa Hirano. PRD: David Production, Animax, Geneon Universal Entertainment, Shueisha. 24 mins. x 27 eps.

In a city on an island stands a very special library. Bantorra Library is the depository for books of life: stone tablets that each record the life and personality of one dead person. By touching a book, or even a broken fragment of a book, one can see and understand the person's life and experiences. Some even whisper that the stones are not merely records, but containers for departed souls.

They are stored in labyrinthine vaults prowled by monstrous creatures. This makes fetching something from the stacks a difficult operation requiring special skills. An elite corps of Armed Librarians with occult powers exists to handle, retrieve, and protect the books, under the control of the Acting Director of the Library, an Amazon psychopath with a cleavage as deep as the vaults and a constant thirst for battle. Opposing her is a powerful religious group, the Church of Drowning In God's Grace. They believe the souls within the books should ascend to heaven and not be stored in darkness with monsters to guard them. So they turn ordinary people into "Meats," living bombs whose minds have been wiped clean to make them living weapons against the Acting Director and her forces.

Now throw in a couple of dozen important characters, a multi-strand plot and more lies, halftruths, and red herrings than an average fishmarket can muster, and you're ready to begin. Multilayered stories from all over the Library introduce each of the characters and give us insight into their worlds, some of which will turn out to be misleading or useless by the time we get to the final episode.

The 2005 *Fighting Librarians (Tatakau Shisho)* book series from Ishio Yamagata, with pictures by Shigeki Maeshima, ran for ten volumes, finally wrapping in 2010. We're naturally predisposed to love stories like this and **READ OR DIE** that emphasize the importance of libraries and the innate coolness of librarians. We like the idea of a head librarian who kills people instead of saying "sssssh!" and wouldn't give wardrobe space to a sensible cardigan. But, one of the absolute requirements of an effective library is coherent arrangement, and here *Book of Bantorra* falls down. Things are unexplained in messy ways, plots left lying about open and unfinished, pacing sacrificed to expository monologue even in the first episodes, and characters allowed to act without rhyme or reason. Writer Mari Okada can be utterly brilliant (**BLACK BUTLER**) and utterly maddening, and *Book of Bantorra* provides evidence for both. At times watching this show is like babysitting a teenage genius with the attention span of a hyperactive gnat: charming, exhausting, and demanding constant attention.

What makes up for it are the ideas and the emotions they power: huge, aching gulfs of guilt, self-loathing, and sorrow, crossed by shining bridges of hope and devotion. A story about a collection of stories should delight in playing with labels and language: there are more ideas in the way things and people are named in *Book of Bantorra* than in many series' entire plotlines. The series is stuffed with brilliant notions. Some echo earlier works: *Doctor Who* fans will be struck by the resonances with Steven Moffat's 2008 story *Silence in the Library*, while older British SF fans will recall Nigel Kneale's bleakly eerie *The Stone Tape*. Anime fans may see resemblances to **SERIAL EXPERIMENTS LAIN** in the complex construction, or with **SKY CRAWLERS** and **EVANGELION** in the manipulative inequity of the powerful. There's no shame in borrowing from the best, especially when the ingredients are mixed in such an interesting way.

It's well animated, with effective action scenes and good design. David Production was only two years old when *Book of Bantorra* was made, but they did a fine job. This involving, demanding show is flawed, yes, but so are most emeralds. It doesn't make them any less beautiful or worth having.

BORDER

1991. JPN: *Meiso o Border*. AKA: *Running King Border*. Video. DIR: Noboru Ishiguro. SCR: Akira Sata. DES: Kiyotoshi Aoi. ANI: Kiyotoshi Aoi. MUS: Nojin. PRD: Artland. 45 mins.

Akio Tanaka's 1986 manga in *Action Comics*, based on a story by Karibu Marai, features a modern-day odd couple, the naïve virgin Kubota and the handsome charmer Hachisuka, who meet up by accident in a Middle Eastern desert and return to Japan to hustle their way through life. The animated excursion comprises their involvement in shady TV dealings, where they get jobs making fake documentaries, although the manga would continue for another 14 volumes of scheming.

BORN FREE

1976. JPN: *Kyoryu Tankentai Born Free*. AKA: *Dinosaur Investigators Born Free*; *Dinosaur Park*. TV series. DIR: Koichi Takano, Haruyuki Kawajima. SCR: Keiichi Abe, Tomoyuki Ando. DES: Haruyuki Kawajima. ANI: Shigeyuki Kawashima. MUS: Toru Fuyuki. PRD: Tsuburaya, Sunrise, NET. 25 mins. x 25 eps.

In 1996, Comet Arby's approach to Earth causes major upheaval. Dinosaurs, long thought extinct, begin to wander the planet. In the Japanese outpost of an international alliance devoted to controlling the problem, Professor Tadaki forms the Born Free group, a team of dinosaur catchers that aims to protect the creatures from the evil hunter King Battler and deliver them safely to a preserve on Saron Island.

Mixing live action and animation in much the same way as Tezuka's **VAMPIRE**, *Born Free* features an animated cast inserted into Tsuburaya model footage of the team's mobile base and stop-motion dinosaurs. Twenty years later in the *real* 1996, Sunrise would make the **BRAVE SAGA** series *Daguon*, in which evil aliens enter the solar system on a rogue asteroid. Coincidence?

Tsuburaya followed the series with the 39-episode *Dinosaur War Eisenborg* (1977, *Kyoryu Daisenso Eisenborg*) on TV Tokyo, in which dinosaurs are found to have survived until the present day in subterranean caves. Ulul, the 300-IQ king of the dinosaurs, decides it is time for his race to reclaim the surface. Professor Tachibana tries to stop them but is killed. His children, Ai and Zen, are mortally injured in the same accident but receive cyborg bodies in the style of **8 MAN** from Tachibana's fellow inventor Professor Torii. Joining the anti-dinosaur task force Team D, the Tachibana kids can also fuse into the Super Aizen Cyborg for that

typical Tsuburaya last-minute transformation to save the day. From episode 20 onward, the dinosaur threat is replaced by Goddess the Evil Witch-Queen and her aliens from planet Gazaria. As with *Born Free*, the anime action (this time from the Oka studios, not Sunrise) is spliced in with stop-motion and live-action footage in the style of **ULTRAMAN**.

Neither of these shows, however, was the first. *Born Free* may make it into this encyclopedia thanks to its cel animation, but an earlier live-action show, *Devil Hunter Mitsurugi* (1973, *Majin Hunter Mitsurugi*), featured three children wielding ceremonial swords themed on Wisdom, Humanity, and Love, which allow them to combine into the stop-motion giant Mitsurugi, who can fight giant monster invaders from Scorpio. Made by animator Takeo Nakamura and his wife Ayako Magiri, the show was innovative, but suffered from production processes that made it inevitably more time-consuming than cels.

BOSCO ADVENTURE

1986. TV series. DIR: Taku Sugiyama. SCR: Nobuyuki Fujimoto, Shoji Yoshikawa. DES: Shuichi Seki. ANI: Takao Kogawa. MUS: Toshiyuki Watanabe. PRD: Nippon Animation, Yomiuri TV. 25 mins. x 26 eps.

The evil Hoodman hears the prophecy that a princess will become Queen of Fontaine Land at the time of a total solar eclipse. His minions kill the elfin king and queen, but Princess Apricot is spirited away by loyal animal subjects and grows up in their enchanted forest. At age 14, she is told of her destiny by the old man Ender, who reveals that the time of the eclipse is at hand. Apricot is captured by Hoodman but is rescued by her woodland friends, Croak the frog, Tati the turtle, and Otter the otter, in their experimental airship, the Bosco. Pursued by Hoodman across a land of dragons, unicorns, and giants, Apricot and her friends gather the inhabitants of the enchanted land for a final battle, fought at Hoodman's castle itself as the eclipse begins. If Apricot does not sit on the throne in time, the Fountain of Life will run dry. This magical quest was an immense success all over Europe but not in the English language, despite being inspired by Tony Wolf's *Woodland Folk* series of children's books.

BOTCHAN
1980. AKA: *The Young Master*. TV special.
DIR: Osamu Dezaki, Toshio Takeuchi. SCR:
Yoshiyuki Fukuda. DES: Monkey Punch. ANI:
Akio Sugino. MUS: Takeo Watanabe. PRD:
TMS. 70 mins.
"The Young Master," a brash young graduate from Tokyo named Uranari, comes
to teach at Matsuyama Middle School on
the island of Shikoku, where he gets into
trouble with the surly locals. The hapless
English assistant falls in love with a local
maid, Madonna, and proposes to her,
only to discover that she has already had
another offer from the local boy known as
Red Shirt. Eventually, Madonna returns to
Red Shirt.
One of the best-selling Japanese books
ever, the original 1906 novel by I AM A
CAT–creator Soseki Natsume contained
strong elements of autobiography. He
once taught in Matsuyama himself,
though his experiences were less troublesome than his protagonist's. There may
have been strife behind the scenes of
the anime, too, since LUPIN III–creator
Monkey Punch's designs were "cleaned
up" by Akio Sugino, and Osamu Dezaki
is credited as the director's "assistant" in
some sources. Another, shorter version of
Botchan was made in 1986 as part of the
ANIMATED CLASSICS OF JAPANESE LITERATURE.
Ⓝ

BOTTLE FAIRY *
2003. JPN: *Binzume Yosei*. TV series. DIR:
Yoshiaki Iwasaki. SCR: Hideki Shirane, Makoto Uezu, Noboru Kimura, Takashi Kawai.
DES: Masahide Yanigasawa. ANI: N/C. MUS:
Yo Yamazaki. PRD: Xebec, Studio Orphee, TV
Kanagawa. 12 mins. x 13 eps.
Kururu, Chichiri, Hororo, and Sarara are
four fairies who set out to learn about
humans by moving in with a young college
instructor they call Sensei. Sensei explains
different months' events and festivals from
all over Japan, covering a year's Japanese
tradition in 12 episodes. It thus serves as a
useful crash course for game-obsessed, TV-
addicted kids who don't listen to Granny
or understand the origins of their national
way of life—something to which the script
regularly alludes when the gullible fairies
seek more information from Tama, a clueless grade-schooler next door. The show
takes the creepy CHOBITS conventions of

blank-slate ingenues in search of a master,
and puts it to largely innocent and educational use, but for all its talk of "tradition,"
it is very much a product of its time. Its
trawl through the customs of the Japanese
year contains many modern additions,
such as Valentine's Day, a foreign import,
or Golden Week, a coincidental cluster of
public holidays that has only existed since
1948. While some episodes delve into
folklore, such as a discussion of the place
of cicadas in a traditional Japanese summer, other episodes are strictly modern,
such as beachtrips in the summer. By New
Year, however, the fairies are deemed to
have become so wise that they are worthy
of human status à la KEY THE METAL IDOL,
and transform into a single gestalt entity
before splitting into four pretty girls who,
presumably, have the potential to return
one day and bore us all with another
TENCHI MUYO! clone. Until that time, the
series is a handy if sugary introduction to
many modern Japanese customs that pass
without comment in other anime. Their
adventures were created by Yuiko Tokumi
and screened on TV Kanagawa, TV Nagoya, and as part of the *Anime Continental*
show on Hiroshima TV, along with BPS.
The U.S. release faithfully repeats the
"Bottle Fairy" singular title of the original
Japanese publicity materials, although
there are clearly four fairies on display.

BOUNTY DOG *
1994. Video. DIR: Hiroshi Negishi. SCR: Mayori
Sekijima. DES: Hirotoshi Sano. ANI: Hirotoshi
Sano. MUS: Sho Goto. PRD: Zero-G Room. 30
mins. x 2 eps.
Freelance troubleshooters Yoshiyuki, Shoko, and Kei are sent to the moon to check
up on a suspected military project. Far
from human habitation beneath the lunar
surface, they find an alien observation post
run by the good Yayoi and the bad "Darkness." Both they and their minions are all
clones of the same original, who fell in
love with Yoshiyuki on one of her sightsee-
ing trips to Earth. With the original Yayoi
dead, the troubleshooters must fight to
save the balance of the universe.
Like many modern anime, *Bounty Dog*
began as a radio drama and has difficulty
shaking off its origins. Yayoi, Darkness,
and the alien army are all clones of the
same girl, which makes for cheap casting

in radio but unimaginative visuals. Much
of the story unfolds over still frames
and static pans, while director Negishi
plunders shots and sound effects from his
own BEAST WARRIORS. Scenes are bathed
in a limited palette of yellows and greens,
while subsurface sequences are all shot
in red. The final showdown in Darkness's
blue hideaway completes the pattern, but
though one paint costs much the same
as another, the avant-garde color scheme
actually makes the film look even cheaper.
Stealing great chunks of plot from *2001:
A Space Odyssey* and PLEASE SAVE MY EARTH,
Bounty Dog's real failing lies in sloppy science and sloppy fiction. The moon, we are
told, has been terraformed, which must
have been difficult without an atmosphere.
The plot calls for spacesuits intermittently
and illogically, while temperature and
gravity are inexplicably like Earth's. As for
the good-vs.-evil alien set-up, it appears to
be an ill-conceived MacGuffin from the
production committee that cooked up the
original story, and it is simply dismissed
with a "how weird" voice-over at the end.

BOUNTY HUNTER: THE HARD
1995. Video. DIR: Yoshikazu Oga. SCR:
Megumi Hiyoshi. DES: Masami Suda. ANI:
Masami Suda. MUS: Shinichi Kida. PRD: JC
Staff. 47 mins.
Keiji "The Hard" Nando, the toughest
bounty hunter in New York, acquires a
floppy disk full of names, which drags him
into a conspiracy to buy and sell human
organs. This one-shot tale reputedly added
extra violence to STORY OF RIKI–creator
Tetsuya Saruwatari's mean-streets manga
from *Business Jump*. Postdating MAD BULL
34, which also had a Japanese fish out of
water in the U.S., this New York hard-man
was eclipsed in the same year by the success of a Chicago crime story. Ironically,
GUNSMITH CATS starred Michiko Neya, a
minor voice in *The Hard*, as the bounty
hunter Rally Vincent. ⚫ⓃⓋ

BOX OF GOBLINS
2008. JPN: *Moryo no Hako*. AKA: *Moryo's Box*;
Demon's Box. TV series, TV special. DIR: Ryo-
suke Nakamura. SCR: Sadayuki Murai. DES:
CLAMP, Asako Nishida, Hidetoshi Kaneko.
ANI: Kunihiko Hamada, Chie Nishizawa. MUS:
Shusei Murai. PRD: Madhouse, DN Dream
Partners, Kadokawa Shoten, NTV, VAP. 23

mins. x 13 eps. (TV), 16 mins. (special). Postwar Japan: a psychopathic killer is murdering schoolgirls. He dismembers their bodies and stuffs the limbs into boxes. The police seem powerless to catch him. Tokyo detective Kiba and his friends find themselves on the case: an antique book dealer and part-time Shinto priest, a novelist with a dark past, and a war-damaged private detective with psychic abilities, helping a feisty young cop to fight the monsters on the dark side of a changing world.

Natsuhiko Kyogoku wrote this fascinating story in novel form in 1995. In 2007 it was turned into a manga, with attractive art from Aki Shimizu, to support a live-action feature film by Masato Harada, released in December. It was animated a year later, while the manga ran until April 2010. A short video, *Moryo no Hako: Chuzenji Atsuko no Jikenbo—Hako no Yurei no Koto (Demon's Box: Atsuko Chuzenji's Case File—The Case of the Spirits in the Boxes)*, was made for the Blu-ray release in 2009.

The anime version is a proper grown-up mystery, complex, demanding, and highly enjoyable. A nonlinear plot in the first half, unsettling and demanding audience attention, plays through to a tense, exciting, and well-resolved conclusion. One could quibble that the murderer manages to deal with a considerable amount of complex organization in too short a time, but that doesn't detract from the story. CLAMP's character design work is strongly enough grounded in reality to support the story rather than distract from it. Nicely animated, with beautifully detailed backgrounds, the attention to detail extends to convincing dismembered limbs and enough gore to suit the plot. The nod to David Fincher's *Se7en* is a nice touch, reminding us that the darkness of the human soul is no new thing. ◑

BOY AND DOLPHIN

1975. JPN: *Iruka to Shonen*. TV series. DIR: Tsuneo Komuro. SCR: N/C. DES: N/C. ANI: Toshitaka Kadota, Isamu Kaneko, Hiroshi Yamagishi, Katsunori Kobayashi, Toyoko Imamura, Kiyoto Ishino. MUS: Hiroki Ogawa, Michel Legrand. PRD: TBS, Eiken. 30 mins. x 26 eps.
On the South Sea island of Ululula (spelled backward, Alululu), handsome young man Jean lives with girlfriend Marina and Uncle Patrick in their wrecked ship, which sits in a bay of coral reefs. Their animal companions include Sebastian the myna bird, a friendly koala bear, and Um, the intelligent white dolphin. But life is not all sun bathing and swimming for Jean and friends. They must also fight off evil corporations intent on exploiting nature, deal with the inhabitants of a mysterious underwater city, and even save their new-found friends from natural disaster.

This variant of SWISS FAMILY ROBINSON and ADRIFT IN THE PACIFIC was the first ever Franco-Japanese coproduction, jointly organized by the Japanese Eiken studio, producer Eve Champin, and the French channel ORTF. Directorial responsibility actually lay on the French side, an issue which led Japanese critics of the time to blame the serial's Japanese ratings failure on the French. However, this did not prevent further coproductions, including ULYSSES 31 and the MYSTERIOUS CITIES OF GOLD. A 1980 Italian broadcast was tied to advertising Galak white chocolate, presumably noted for its dolphin-friendly qualities. Compare to MARINE BOY.

BOY WHO SAW THE WIND, THE *

2000. JPN: *Kaze o Mita Shonen*. Movie. DIR: Kazuki Omori, Toshiya Shinohara. SCR: Shu Narijima. DES: Minoru Maeda. ANI: Minoru Maeda. MUS: Tamiya Terashima. PRD: Brains Base, Hitachi-Maxell. 90 mins.
Amon is a boy who has the power to control the wind. Branich, the ruler of the world, needs Amon's power to complete the ultimate weapon and sends his minions to bring the boy in. Though Amon's parents have forbidden him from using his talents, the arrival of Branich's men leaves him with no choice—giving them the slip, Amon runs away with Maria, one of the People of the Sea. Maria agrees to help Amon find his own tribe.

The Boy Who Saw the Wind is "a plea for good people to stand up and say 'no' to fascism and dictatorship," according to its creator, the Welsh-born author C. W. Nicol, whose writings are said to have inspired Hayao Miyazaki to set CASTLE IN THE SKY in a Welsh mining village. Never picked up by an Anglophone distributor despite the presence of an English subtitle track, this obscure film was the subject of much finger-pointing and recriminations in Japan over its supposed box office "failure." In fact, it did perfectly reasonable business but cost its producers at Hitachi-Maxell a shockingly high ¥700 million, which they were never likely to recoup in cinemas alone. In the wake of Studio Ghibli's PRINCESS MONONOKE, Hitachi-Maxell seems to have listened to advice that it was easy to make money in anime, without considering that Ghibli had taken a decade to build its audience and reputation.

BOY WITH CAT'S EYES, THE

1976. JPN: *Yokaiden Nekome Koso*. AKA: *Ghost Story: Boy with Cat's Eyes*. TV series. DIR: Keinosuke Shiyano. SCR: Yuji Amemiya. DES: Tasuteru Hakumori. ANI: N/C. MUS: Masahiko Nishiyama. PRD: Wako Pro, TV Tokyo. 15 mins. x 22 eps.
Short ghost stories from MAKOTO-CHAN–creator Kazuo Umezu, all linked by the titular feline-featured youth, including *The Girl Who Cried in the Night*, *Eyes of the Dryad*, *Portal to Hell*, *Witch of Misty Valley*, and *Enigma of the Dark Sorcerer*. Umezu's trademark misogyny is greatly in evidence here—though his only tale available in English is the live-action adaptation of his bitchy brain-swapping revenge tragedy *Baptism of Blood*. Two further horror shorts, *There's Something on the Video Camera* and *Haunted House*, were released on a single 45-minute tape as *Incantation* (1990, *Umezu Kazuo no Noroi*). These later stories featured animation from Shingo Araki and direction by Naoko Omi. Another Umezu story, *Orochi*, was released in 2000 as a "manga video" (see CRUSHER JOE).

BOYFRIEND

1992. TV special. DIR: Satoshi Dezaki. SCR: Kazumi Koide. DES: Yukari Kobayashi. ANI: Yukari Kobayashi. MUS: Hiroshi Ikeda. PRD: Magic Bus, TV Tokyo. 94 mins.
After an accident, teen basketball star Masaki is transferred to a new school, where he immediately falls in love with local girl Kanako. After helping her home through her drunken stupor one night on the train, he can think of nobody else but her, though she is already interested in a beautiful blond basketball player, the handsome Akiro.

Originally broadcast as a TV special then split in two halves and rereleased on video, this gentle love story began as a 1985 manga by Soryo Fuyumi. A similar high school sports love triangle can be found in **SLOW STEP**.

BOYS BE ...
2000. TV series, video. DIR: Masami Shimoda, Eiji Suganuma, Shinji Kasai. SCR: Kenichi Kanemaki, Hiroyuki Kawasaki. DES: Itsuko Takeda. ANI: Michinori Chiba. MUS: Be Factory. PRD: Hal Filmmaker, WOWOW. 25 mins. x 12 eps. (TV), 25 mins. (v).
Makoto is a brash, loud little charmer at his school, but deep down he's just a shy little boy who lives at home with his adoring mother. And as he and his three friends flirt and spar with the school's three girls most likely to put out, will one of them notice what a delicate little flower he really is? This series takes Masahiro Itabashi and Hiroyuki Tamakoshi's 1991 manga from *Shonen Magazine* but simplifies the picaresque plot to concentrate on a single boy and a mere trio of girls. The final episode, "Let It Be," was not broadcast but is included in the video release.

BOYS OVER FLOWERS *
1996. JPN: *Hana yori Dango*. AKA: *Boys Before Flowers*. TV series, movie. DIR: Shigeyasu Yamauchi. SCR: Yumi Kageyama, Reiko Yoshida, Aya Masui. DES: Yoshihiko Umakoshi. ANI: Chuji Nakajima, Tomoko Ito, Tomoyuki Kawano. MUS: Michiru Oshima. PRD: Toei, TV Asahi. 25 mins. x 51 eps. (TV), 25 mins. (m).
Sixteen-year-old Makino Tsukushi is a girl from a poor family who gets a scholarship to attend the prestigious Eitoku Academy. Though she tries to keep a low profile, she is soon singled out for hazing by "F4," an elite group at the academy composed of the sons of the richest families in Japan. When she stands up to them, their leader, Domyoji, becomes attracted to her, though she finds herself falling for his lieutenant, Rui. Rui, however, loves Shizuka, a gorgeous fashion model. This gentle romantic comedy was based on Yoko Kamio's 1992 manga in *Margaret*, and also adapted into the theatrical short *BBF:* (1997), a musical in which Makino travels to New York to become a star, replaying the **CINDERELLA** story even as she appears in a stage version of it.

The series has been adapted twice for live-action television, first in Taiwan as *Meteor Garden* (2001), then for the Japanese TBS network in 2005.

BPS
2003. JPN: *bpS: Battle Programmer Shirase*. TV series. DIR: Hiroki Hayashi. SCR: J/R Sakurajimaeki. DES: Ryoichi Makino, Keiji Hashimoto. ANI: Ryoichi Makino, Keiji Hashimoto. MUS: Seiko Nagaoka. PRD: G-PLUS, AIC, Gansis, TV Kanagawa. 12 mins. x 15 eps.
Computer hacker Akira Shirase is a free spirit who won't work for hire, in spite of the success his programming genius could bring him. Instead he raids big bank accounts around the world like a **LUPIN III** of the digital age; when he targets an account he won't rest until he's hacked it and squeezed it dry. He lives alone, but for occasional visits from his adoring ten-year-old niece, Misao Amano, who fusses over him in a faintly creepy imitation of a housewife. Akira battles the fat, evil geek hacker known as the King of America, who is trying to destabilize the Internet, and meets a range of wacky characters in a new short adventure every week. Created by **TENCHI MUYO!**–director Hiroki Hayashi, this series was screened as part of TV Kanagawa's *Anime Continental* show along with **BOTTLE FAIRY**. It's a sign of the times that the anime audience is now so sedentary and housebound that its latest action hero is a man sitting at a desk playing with a computer while waiting for someone to bring him food. The final episode featured a goodbye message to foreign fansubbers with a thank you to "everyone who watched overseas without permission," although considering that data theft is a heroic act in the show, it's unclear whether the irony was intended.

BRAIN JACKER
2011. JPN: *Shojo Senki Brain Jacker*. AKA: *Battle Girl Brain Jacker*. Video. DIR: Ippei Taru. SCR: Akira Nintai. DES: Yuji Ushijima, Hayate. ANI: Yuji Ushijima. MUS: N/C. PRD: schoolzone, Akira Nintai, Marigold. 30 mins. x 2 eps.
A female warrior first seen shooting at grape-colored pig men is captured, drugged, and raped by a horse-man and a snake-woman before being rescued. Then there's an episode which may be a flashback, in which she's put in a pillory and gang-raped by the grape-colored pig men. This plays like a nightmare parody of one of those TV ads for fruit drinks where they try to squeeze one more bit of fruit into the glass. The ending implies that she is killed and dismembered but doesn't actually show this, and the opening sequence suggests nonlinear storytelling, leaving the nasty thought that they might actually make a third episode of this distasteful crud. Based on the erotic game *Shojo Senki Soul Eater* by Lune—see **GIRL WEAPON SOUL EATER**, which was a prequel. **NV**

BRAIN POWERED *
1998. TV series. DIR: Yoshiyuki Tomino. SCR: Yoshiyuki Tomino. DES: Mutsumi Inomata, Mamoru Nagano. ANI: Atsushi Shigeta. MUS: Yoko Kanno. PRD: Sunrise, WOWOW. 25 mins. x 26 eps.
The meek shall inherit the Earth. The rest of us shall escape to the stars. Such is the belief of those who are trying to raise Orphan ("the ruin with a woman's face") from the watery depths. On a devastated world, they see Orphan as their last, best chance for survival, but they need the assistance of the Grand Chers, organic machines that are "born" from spinning plates (not unlike the creatures in **MONSTER RANCHER**). On a routine recovery mission, brash pilot Yu faces off against Hime, a girl who has accidentally bonded with an Anti Body, a particularly powerful form of organic machine. The meeting inspires Yu to defect from Orphan a year later, but his former colleagues are in hot pursuit.

An incoherent **EVANGELION** clone, *Brain Powered* is still curiously watchable, thanks largely to Yoko Kanno's wonderful music. It's as if Tomino and his crew were thrown in at the deep end and told to wing it. Nothing is explained, but all the details fill the viewer with the vain hope that somehow they will all make sense—until the disappointingly anticlimactic ending. Naked nymphs dance around Buddhist temples, flame-haired pilots keep their tresses down because their machines "like it that way," and nobody seems fazed by the groinal hatches on the Grand Chers. **N**

BRANDISH
2012. Video. DIR: N/C. SCR: N/C. DES: N/C. ANI: N/C. MUS: N/C. PRD: Mary Jane, Studio

Eromatick. 30 mins. x 2 eps.
Twiska the itinerant succubus is used to draining the energy from a different sexual partner every night, until she unwittingly stumbles into the life of Theo, a young boy with no sexual experience at all, who excites her in ways she did not previously imagine. Based on the manga by Rusty Soul and Seneca Alto. ⊗

BRAT COP

1989. JPN: *Gaki Deka*. TV series. DIR: Yuzo Yamada. SCR: Keiji Terui, Yoshio Urasawa, Hideki Mitsui. DES: Tatsuhiko Yamagami. ANI: Takeaki Natsumoto, Yuri Handa, Michishiro Yamada. MUS: N/C. PRD: Tokio Animation Film, Ajia-do, Fuji TV. 12 mins. x 43 eps. (TV), ? mins. (v).
Tatsuhiko Yamagami's surreal 1974 comic about a boy/cop who liked playing with his testicles, sentencing people to death, and occasionally transforming into a deer or elephant ran in *Shonen Captain* for 26 volumes until 1981. This 1989 revival was seemingly timed to cash in on the child readers becoming old enough to purchase videos, with a straight-to-video special directed by Junichiro Nakamura, released a month after the TV series began. A spiritual ancestor of the 1990s hit CRAYON SHIN-CHAN.

BRAVE 10 *

2012. TV series. DIR: Kiyoko Sayama. SCR: Mamiko Ikeda, Michio Yokote, Mitsutaka Hirota. DES: Yukiko Ban. ANI: Yukiko Ban. MUS: Seiko Nagaoka. PRD: Studio Sakimakura, Aoni Production, Media Factory, TAKAO Co., Ltd., TMS Entertainment. 24 mins. x 12 eps.
A samurai traveling through feudal Japan becomes the reluctant protector of a lone priestess escaping the destruction of Izumo Shrine. But she—or rather, the sacred jewel she wears in her hair—is hotly pursued by power-hungry warlords. The warlord Sanada, however, has put together a fighting force to bring an end to Japan's era of war. Can they protect the jewel and the girl? This promising set-up, adding fantasy elements à la YOTODEN to the samurai-era folktales of the Ten Braves of Sanada, is thrown away by poor writing, repetitive plotting, and one of the least-active heroines ever created, with only the very well-executed fight scenes and charming (if historically questionable)

design standing between the audience and the off button. Some shows are enjoyably bad. This one isn't, it's just mostly disappointing. Of course there's a hot-springs sequence, and an exotic foreign babe with a relaxed attitude to clothing. At least the writers have the excuse that absolutely nothing else they do is advancing the plot so they might as well. You will struggle to believe that the writer of the most elegant segment of AYAKASHI: SAMURAI HORROR TALES had a hand in this adaptation of Kairi Shimotsuki's 2011 manga *Brave 10 S*, sequel to 2007's *Brave 10*. Maybe it's just an adaptation too far.

BRAVE FROG, THE *

1973. JPN: *Kerokko Demetan*. AKA: *Ribitty Demetan*; *Adventures on Rainbow Pond*. TV series. DIR: Tatsuo Yoshida, Seitaro Hara. SCR: Akiyoshi Sakai, Hiroshi Sasagawa. DES: Tatsuo Yoshida, Yoshitaka Amano. ANI: Masayuki Hayashi, Hiroshi Kawabata. MUS: Nobuyoshi Koshibe. PRD: Tatsunoko, Fuji TV. 25 mins. x 39 eps.
Demetan (Jonathan Jumper) is a frog too poor to attend school in Rainbow Pond, but he's good friends with Ranatan (Hillary Hopper), daughter of the rich Lord Frog (Maxwell/Big Max). Though Big Max tries to break them apart, they persevere and try to help him become a nicer person. The community is united by a common threat when menaced by a giant catfish who steals the frogspawn. Jonathan heads for the sea with his friend Cheepy the bird, and there they persuade an electric eel to accompany them back to the pond and drive out the catfish. Hillary's father finally approves of Jonathan, and they all live happily ever after.

BRAVE RAIDEEN *

1975. JPN: *Yusha Rydeen*. AKA: *Heroic Rydeen*. TV series. DIR: Yoshiyuki Tomino, Takeyuki Kanda, Yoshikazu Yasuhiko, Kazuo Terada. SCR: Fuyunori Gobu, Masaru Yamamoto, Masaki Tsuji. DES: Yoshikazu Yasuhiko. ANI: Yoshikazu Yasuhiko. MUS: Akihiro Kobayashi. PRD: Tohoku Shinsha, NET. 25 mins. x 50 eps. (TV1), 25 mins. x 38 eps. (TV2), 25 mins. x 26 eps. (2007).
After a slumber of 12 millennia, the Demon Empire returns to seize control of Earth, plotting evil from its secret volcano base, from which its high priest regularly

sends out fearsome Fossil Beasts to attack humanity. Raideen, the giant robot-like protector of the lost continent of Mu (see SUPER ATRAGON), senses the evil presence and awakes within its golden pyramid, revealing to young Japanese boy Akira Hibiki that he is the one descendant of the ancient Mu people who must help Raideen save Earth. He can call on Raideen whenever he needs him and ride his "Sparker" motorcycle into the robot's chest, where it can be stored during missions. The Demon Empire seeks control of Mutoron, the powerful element that allows Raideen to self-repair in its cliff-face hideaway. Akira also has the assistance of his friends, token girl Mari Sakirada (daughter of a scientist fighting the Demon Empire) and several members of his high school soccer team—with suspicious echoes of BATTLE OF THE PLANETS. This early giant-robot story was based on a manga by Ryohei Suzuki and united the Tomino and Yasuhiko team that would work so well together on the later GUNDAM, where they would replay the well-matched rivalry of Akira and the blond Demon Prince Sharkin as the later serials' Amuro Ray and Char Aznable. Subtitled (poorly) in Hawaii by KIKU TV, it was shown on the New York Japanese community channel 47, thereby becoming the first giant-robot show to reach a large U.S. audience.

As Raideen, it also formed part of the SHOGUN WARRIORS collection and was one of the legion of anime robots ripped off for Joseph Lai's 1991 Korean film *Space Thunder Kids*, and a billion cheap unlicensed Asian plastic toys. The series was remade as *Reideen: The Superior* (1996), directed by Toshifumi Kawase, which similarly featured a boy assembling a five-man team of warriors to pilot cool vehicles and save the planet, and again as Mitsuru Hongo's 26-episode *Reideen* (2007). This last incarnation, made post-EVANGELION in a more knowing world, has a 21st-century design aesthetic a million miles away from the blocky, colorful robot wrestlers of old, with an opulent, baroque look redolent of FIVE STAR STORIES. But it still displays all the hallmarks of childish logic that made the robot shows of the past so great. It has a youth with unsuspected potential and a great mission, the missing father, the wise mentor guiding our hero toward manhood, the elite organization, the friends, the mysterious girl, and the fabulously overspecified weapons of the robot itself—Reideen wields a blade almost the size of the moon. The giant robot genre is about giving boys a dream of power and purpose, a hope that in a world that constantly hits them they will one day be able to hit back and change things for the better. It's a dream that revives periodically in anime and manga; despite the nihilism and negativity that creeps up on us with time, there are always new generations of boys who need that shining dream in a shiny plastic package.

BRAVE SAGA *

1990. JPN: *Exkaiser*; *Fyvard/Fighbird*; *Da Garn*; *Might Gine/Might-Gaine*; *J-Deka*; *Goldoran*; *Daguon*; *Gaogaigar*. AKA: (see below). TV series. DIR: Katsuyoshi Yutabe, Shinji Takamatsu. SCR: Yasushi Hirano, Hiroyuki Hoshiyama, Fuyunori Gobu, Hiroyuki Kawasaki, Takao Koyama, Yoshitomo Yometani. DES: Kunio Okawara, Atsuko Ishida, Akira Oguro. ANI: Masami Obari. MUS: Toshiyuki Watanabe, Takashi Kudo. PRD: Sunrise, Nagoya TV. 25 mins. x 20 eps. (*Exkaiser*), 25 mins. x 48 eps. (*Fyvard*), 25 mins. x 46 eps. (*Da Garn*), 25 mins. x 47 eps. (*Might Gine*), 25 mins. x 48 eps. (*J-Deka*), 25 mins. x 20 eps. (*Goldoran*), 25 mins. x 48 eps. (*Daguon*), 30 mins. x 2 eps. (*Daguon v*), 25 mins. x 44 eps. (*Gaogaigar*), ? mins. x 8 eps. (v, *Gaogaigar Final*), 25 mins. x 4 eps. (TV, *Gaogaigar Final*).

Almost matching Tatsunoko's TIME BOKAN and Tokyo Movie Shinsha's LUPIN III for sheer endurance, the Sunrise "Brave" series (each title contains the word *yu*: "brave/hero") of giant-robot shows may look like an endless stream of formulaic pap, but not to its target audience. In the fiercely hierarchical world of childhood, last year's show is passé by definition—this year's toys and this year's heroes are what counts. The heroes of ULTRAMAN and BATTLE OF THE PLANETS have been reverse-engineered and refined over the years to create a set template of series construction, and "Hajime Yadate," the house pseudonym that assigns half the credit for new shows to the Sunrise studio itself, has realized that there is a point in every boy's life when he has never seen a giant robot before. Each and every "Brave" show

represents a whole age group's first evening viewing, first hot-headed hero, first crush, and first battle-cry of improbable-sounding attack names. There is also an important technical issue in the construction of TV anime involving a transformation sequence—the same footage can be reused in every episode, effectively cutting production costs. And though one could argue that Sunrise should invest in one decent series and repeat it, that would destroy the entire industrial complex that grows up around each show. The nature of merchandise-driven entertainment for a young audience requires constant upgrades and renewals built around the same basic templates of colors, action figures, and, unfortunately, plotting.

The "Brave" phenomenon began in 1990 with *Heroic Exkaiser* (*Yusha Exkaiser*), in which a giant galactic police robot fights to protect humanity from the predations of the Gaistar space pirates. In an attempt to create an ongoing franchise separate from the same studio's ongoing GUNDAM series, the same crew returned in *Sun Hero Fyvard* (1991, *Taiyo no Yusha Fyvar*), in which Professor Amano convinces his grandchildren, Kenta and Haruka, to combine with the Fyvard android in order to save Earth. Working on the principle that if something isn't broken, it doesn't need fixing, they were back in 1992 with another "Brave" anime, *Legendary Hero Da Garn* (*Densetsu Yusha Da Garn*), where Earth is attacked by the alien Orbus invaders, and only a group of young kids in a giant robot can save it. Ever the optimists, Sunrise returned in 1993, retaining the "Brave" name in the title to reassure viewers that nothing was really going to change. This time, the series was *Heroic Express Might Gine* (*Yusha Tokkyu Might Gine*), which, with dazzling originality, concentrated on a team of young kids in a giant robot saving Earth from invading aliens. By 1994, the "Brave" slot on Japanese TV was well established, and the template was punched out once more as *Heroic Cop J-Deka* (*Yusha Keisatsu J-Deka*), in which the hot-headed young hero, Yuta, pilots a giant robot cop, fighting giant robot criminals. In 1995, the franchise was back with tiresome predictability in *Golden Hero Goldoran* (*Ogon no Yusha Goldoran*), featuring three young boys in a transforming

robot, who go in search of the fabled lost treasure of Rajendra. *Goldoran*, however, was taken off the air very quickly, possibly because it pushed the envelope a little too far, but more likely because it didn't push it far enough in a year when everybody was watching EVANGELION. In 1996, the studio returned to the tried-and-true alien-invasion storyline with *Heroic Order Daguon* (*Yusha Shirei Daguon*), featuring five young kids, their Daguon vehicles, and their allies from planet Bravestar defending Earth from the invading hordes of Sandor, who have piggy-backed into the solar system on a wandering asteroid—perhaps an homage to the similar story of the studio's earlier BORN FREE, which was set in the "future year" of 1996. Regaining its old level of popularity, the franchise also picked up a substantial female audience by imitating the success of its sister-franchise's *Gundam Wing* pretty-boy line up.

The final incarnation came with *Gaogaigar: King of Bravery* (1997, *Yusha o Gaigaigar*), in which the usual alien invasion subplot (this time from underground) was augmented with the addition of sentient robots, whose artificial intelligences encouraged identification and sympathy with their plight—compare to the later YUKIKAZE. Behind the scenes, *Gaogaigar* was one of the first experiments in digital animation by Sunrise (GAMING AND DIGITAL ANIMATION), with the studio creating one or two flashy-looking sequences per episode, each designed to be reusable in subsequent chapters. Consequently, the incidences of digital animation increase as the series goes on. Animators referred to these recurring moments as "bank cuts," recalling the "bank system" of reusable cels employed by Osamu Tezuka in ASTRO BOY a generation earlier. *Gaogaigar*'s cyborg hero and his transforming robot pals (with token boy Mamoru), managed to see off the attacks of the Zonder empire, only to be brought back for *Gaogaigar Final* (2000), an eight-part video series in which they must travel into space to deal with the threat presented by the self-proclaimed Eleven Kings of Sol, who have even cloned Mamoru to aid them in their schemes. The video series, augmented with four bonus episodes, was then bizarrely repackaged for television as the

12-part *Gaogaigar Final: Grand Glorious Gathering* (2005), broadcast on TV Tokyo.

BRAVE STORY *

2006. JPN: *Yusha Monogatari*. Movie. DIR: Koichi Chigira. SCR: Ichiro Okochi. DES: Yuriko Chiba. ANI: Yuriko Chiba. MUS: Juno Reactor. PRD: Gonzo, Dentsu, Fuji TV, Warner Bros. 112 mins.

Ten-year-old Wataru's father is leaving his family to live with someone else. Then his mother collapses and has to go into hospital. With all his heart, Wataru wants to set his world right. And his school friend Mitsuru tells him there might be a way to do that, if he can summon up the courage to go into another world—a world where everyone is looking for something, and the brave can win the answer to their deepest wish by finding the Goddess of Destiny and begging her to reassign their fate. This charmingly designed fantasy story based on Miyuki Miyabe's novel is intended for family viewing, and it works perfectly in that context. True, some adults might find the characters a little one-dimensional, but the hero's journey genuinely does lead Wataru to change and self-realization. It also makes him examine his attitudes on friendship, loyalty, and forgiveness. Although the world of the story is a fantasyland, the emotions and motivations of the characters are straight from our own reality. The quality of the animation adds to the charm of the design, and the amount of phenomenal talent on the crew list explains the quality. There's some violence in both worlds, including fantasy sword-fights and school bullying, so the very young shouldn't watch this without an adult on hand, but seven- to ten-year-olds will find much to enjoy.

BREAK-AGE

1999. Video. DIR: Tsuneo Tominaga. SCR: Tsuneo Tominaga. DES: Zhiemay Batow. ANI: Akira Kano. MUS: N/C. PRD: Panasonic/Beam Entertainment. 45 mins.

In 2007, the inhabitants of Danger Planet III fight their battles using remote-controlled robots or "virtual puppets." Kirio Nimura is a high school student and the strongest puppeteer on the planet, until he falls for Sairi Takahara, who insists that nobody may make advances until they have beaten her puppet, Benkei.

After running for seven years in *Comic Beam*, Zhiemay Batow's manga *Break-Age* was adapted into an anime video by Panasonic, belatedly realizing that there might be some money in customizable robots, combat, and teen romance.

BREMEN FOUR

1981. JPN: *Bremen 4: Jigoku no Naka no Tenshitachi*. AKA: *Bremen Four: Angels in Hell*. TV special. DIR: Osamu Tezuka, Hiroshi Sasagawa. SCR: Osamu Tezuka, Katsuhito Akiyama. DES: Osamu Tezuka. Hisashi Sakaguchi. ANI: Kazuhiko Udagawa. MUS: Yasuo Higuchi. PRD: Tezuka Pro, NTV. 90 mins.

Rondo, a flower-child alien, is sent down to Earth but unfortunately lands in the middle of a blitzkrieg orchestrated by the evil Colonel Karl Presto, a Nazi-style military leader who is massacring the local peasantry with storm troopers and Martian war machines. The mortally wounded Rondo uses the last of her powers to transform Allegro the dog, Coda the cat, Largo the donkey, and Minuet the hen into human teenagers to carry on her mission. The kids form a band to sing for peace but let success go to their heads and devolve into an arrogant punk band. At a command performance for the evil, Wagner-loving Colonel Presto, they witness a machine-gun massacre and remember their mission of saving the world, but it's at the price of sacrificing their human forms and becoming animals once more.

As with so much in anime and manga, Tezuka blazed the trails for others. Distantly inspired by one of GRIMMS' FAIRY TALES, *The Musicians of Bremen*, but with comic Nazis that led some to describe this little-known TV movie as Tezuka's *Springtime for Hitler*, the peace-through-music message would be taken up the following year by the runaway success of MACROSS.

BRIDE OF DARKNESS *

1999. JPN: *Inju Nerawareta Hanayome*. AKA: *Bride Engulfed by Lust*. Video. DIR: N/C. SCR: N/C. DES: N/C. ANI: N/C. MUS: N/C. PRD: Pink Pineapple. 30 mins. x 2 eps.

Sanshiro is the son of a family servant who secretly lusts after Momoyo, the beautiful daughter of the lord of the manor. Since it would be unseemly for him to even consider a relationship with a woman of such a higher social class, he must be content

with peeping on her from various secret vantage points in the house. Momoyo is betrothed to Yoichiro, the wealthy scion of an industrial family, who has recently returned from a trip to exotic, dangerous England. Sanshiro's voyeuristic tendencies give him a grandstand view of the family's darker secrets, particularly the secret sadomasochistic relationship that Yoichiro is conducting with Momoyo's elder sister. However, Sanshiro is also suffering from a series of increasingly powerful headaches and begins to think that he can see "Konago," a ghostly pale girl who claims to be an evil presence somehow summoned by Yoichiro—this is what traveling to England does to people.

The Taisho period (1912–26) was back in vogue at the time this anime was made, partly due to revisionist fantasies like SAKURA WARS, but largely thanks to the global popularity of James Cameron's *Titanic* (1997), which is even referenced in a scene where Sanshiro paints Momoyo in the nude—albeit without her knowledge. For a more sedate approach to inter-class relationships, see EMMA. ●ⓝ🅥🅥

BRIDE OF DEIMOS

1988. JPN: *Akuma (Deimos) no Hana-yome*. AKA: *Bride of Satan (Deimos)*. Video. DIR: Rintaro. SCR: Etsuko Ikeda. DES: Yuho Ashibe. ANI: Hirotsugu Hamazaki. MUS: N/C. PRD: Madhouse. 30 mins.

DARKSIDE BLUES–artist Yuho Ashibe also drew the original 1975 manga for *Princess* magazine based on a story by *Witches' Bible* author Etsuko Ikeda. A story of incestuous love between the divine beings Deimos and Venus—the latter is aggravated by the former's adoration of the Earth girl Michiko. This perverse love triangle ends up in a spooky mansion from which people never return. In a similar set-up to Chie Shinohara's *Anatolia Story*, Michiko must die to save Deimos, but he has fallen for her. ⓝ

BRIDGE TO THE STARRY SKIES, A *

2011. JPN: *Hoshizora e Kakaru Hashi*. AKA: *HoshiKaka*. TV series. DIR: Takenori Mihara. SCR: Go Zappa. DES: Haruo Ogawara, Koichi Monma. ANI: Haruo Ogawara. MUS: Atsushi Umebori, Funta7. PRD: Dogakobo, Dentsu, feng, Marvelous Entertainment, Pony Canyon. 30 mins. x 12 eps. (TV), 27 mins. (v).

Kazuma's younger brother Ayumu has been ill, and the pair head off to a small town in the mountains so that he can recuperate in fresh air and tranquil surroundings. But he accidentally kisses a girl, which immediately tells you this is a harem anime (**ROMANCE AND DRAMA**)—the only genre where boys "accidentally" kiss, fall on top of, or land up in states of undress with various girls. But this isn't just *a* harem anime, it is *the* harem anime, the most generic story ever told. Boy meets girl, and girl, and girl, and girl, etc., etc., etc., and gets together with the girl he was always going to get together with. If you've seen even one other harem anime, you have already seen this; if you haven't, go and watch **TENCHI MUYO!**, granddaddy of the genre, instead. Based on a visual novel by feng. A 2011 one-shot video "continued" the story by focusing on Kazuma's friend Daigo, who hangs out with the remaining girls as a school festival approaches.

BRIGADOON ★

2000. JPN: *Brigadoon: Marin to Melan.* TV series. DIR: Yoshitomo Yometani. SCR: Hideyuki Kurata. DES: Masahiro Kimura. ANI: Masahiro Yamane, Takuro Shinbo. MUS: N/C. PRD: Sunrise, WOWOW. 25 mins. x 26 eps. Marin, a happy but inept student who lives in world loosely modeled on 1970s Japan, is the first to notice the giant floating city hovering above her town. Brigadoon, for so it is called, fast becomes a personal project for Marin as she meets Melan, a large blue super-robot who befriends her and takes her up to the magical city.

With its resemblance to the story of Urashima Taro (see **JAPANESE FOLK TALES**), the original *Brigadoon* story about a Scottish village that only appears once every century is not unknown in Japan. However, this show seems to owe more to Miyazaki's **CASTLE IN THE SKY**, aimed squarely at the pretty but vacant audience that warmed to Kurata's earlier **BATTLE ATHLETES**.

BRIGHTER THAN THE DAWNING BLUE ★

2006. JPN: *Yoake Mae Yori Ruri Iro na— Crescent Love.* AKA: *Yoakena.* TV series. DIR: Masahiko Ota. SCR: Takashi Aoshima, Hideaki Koyasu. DES: Yoshihiro Watanabe, Hisaharu Iijima. ANI: Hironori Tanaka. MUS: Hiroyuki Sawano. PRD: Daume, Alchemist, Bandai Visual, Frontier Works, memory tech, MOVIC, TBS. 30 mins. x 12 eps. The Moon was colonized many years ago and is now an independent kingdom. A devastating war left relations with Earth strained, but the heiress to the Sphere Kingdom wants to continue her late mother's diplomatic work. With this in mind, she comes to Earth to stay with a human family, and meets Tatsuya. Although neither of them remembers this at first, they met as children. But as love blossoms between them, complications develop. Princess Feena already has a noble fiancé, and ditching him for a commoner from Earth will not be popular at home. This cliché-ridden series based on the 2005 manga by HoeHoe No-miso is mostly harmless, but that's about the best we can say for it. The attempt at political subtext is laughable, since the whole set-up is politically implausible. The animation and design are average, the music is inoffensive, the humor is more miss than hit, and the central thesis—infant sweethearts reunited in an eternal bond of love—has been done better in **URUSEI YATSURA** (where Ataru shares said bond with several girls) or even **SPIRITED AWAY** (see also **ROMANCE AND DRAMA**). And nobody—absolutely nobody—develops the "unconscious" habit of pinching girls' noses as a sign of affection. Anyone trying that wouldn't finish elementary school with his front teeth still in place.

BROKEN BLADE ★

2010. JPN: *Break Blade.* AKA: *Breaker Blade.* Movies. DIR: Tetsuro Amino, Nobuyoshi Habara. SCR: Masashi Sogo. DES: Takushige Norita, Takayuki Yanase, Toshihiro Kohama, Yoshinori Shiozawa. ANI: N/C. MUS: Yoshihisa Hirano. PRD: Production I.G, Xebec, Bandai Visual, Lantis, Hakuhodo DY Media Partners, Flex Comix. 50 mins., 50 mins., 46 mins., 48 mins., 47 mins., 52 mins. Almost everyone on the Cruzon continent can manipulate crystals using telekinesis, so naturally that ability forms the basis for most Cruzon technology. Rygart Arrow has a rare disability—he can't manipulate crystals at all. As a non-sorcerer, he is both handicapped and a virtual outcast, able to do nothing but farm the land with the most basic tools. But Rygart is a personable young man and made some good friends at school: Hodr, the future King of his homeland, the King's wife-to-be and keen scientist Sigyn, and Zess, a nobleman from a neighboring nation and a superb mecha pilot. A few years later, Rygart, now in his mid-20s, gets a call from his old friend Sigyn. She has unearthed a very ancient mecha unlike anything in the royal arsenal. None of the crystal-manipulators can pilot it. She thinks that maybe non-sorcerer Rygart might be able to handle the device that has defeated even the greatest sorcerers. He accepts, reluctantly, and is soon drawn into a terrible dilemma in which one of his dear friends is set to annihilate the other two.

Mecha geeks will already have picked up echoes of several elements of the **GUNDAM** franchise in this first of six movies based on Yonosuke Yoshinaga's manga. *Broken Blade: The Time of Awakening (Break Blade: Kakusei no Toki)* has some interesting twists, including the pivot of the story, a war for possession of a finite technological resource that dictates the entire planet's technology. Japan has a similar real-life struggle to ensure a stable supply of rare earths used in microchip manufacture; most known rare earth deposits are in China. There's also the fact that the super-weapon can only be piloted by someone regarded, until now, as hopelessly handicapped. The writing isn't flawless—the antagonist vanishes for much of the second half of the movie—but overall the story moves along well, assisted by Yoshihisa Hirano's fine score. Production I.G and Xebec handle the battles very prettily. Production I.G is sometimes accused of making warfare too clean, shiny, and scratch-free; not here. The crashing of metal giants, their fluid maneuvers as they dance death on the field or hurl projectiles at each other, are still beautifully choreographed, but they do damage and leave marks, giving a greater sense of weight and realism to the fights. The designers make a real attempt to differentiate the races and cultures of Cruzon, creating a good-looking series of backdrops for the action.

The other movies, *Broken Blade 2: The Split Path (Break Blade Ketsbetsu no Michi,* June 2010), *Broken Blade 3: Mark of the Assassin's Dagger (Break Blade Daisansho Kyojin no Ato,* September 2010), *Broken Blade 4:*

The Earth of Calamity (*Break Blade Daiyonsho Sanka no Chi*, October 2010), *Broken Blade 5: The Horizon between Life and Death* (*Break Blade Daigosho Shisen no Hate*, January 2011) and *Broken Blade 6: Fortress of Lamentation* (*Break Blade Dairokusho Dokoku no Toride*, March 2012) move Rygart through new relationships and throw new and disturbing light on old ones as he tries to reconcile his role as a killer for his country with his own hatred of violence. There are no mold-breaking moments of originality, but this is an enjoyable, involving story with eye candy galore for grown-up mecha fans.

BROTHER DEAREST
1991. JPN: *Oniisama e.* AKA: *To My Elder Brother; Brother, Dear Brother.* TV series. DIR: Osamu Dezaki. SCR: Hideo Takayashiki. DES: Akio Sugino. ANI: Akio Sugino. MUS: Kentaro Haneda. PRD: NHK, Visual Book. 25 mins. x 39 eps.
ROSE OF VERSAILLES–creator Riyoko Ikeda wrote this take on life in Seiran Academy, a school for privileged young ladies. Professor's daughter Nanako writes many letters to the titular brother, outlining her life at the school, especially with regard to the intense relationships she has formed within the elite sorority. Her new friend Mariko does her best to ruin Nanako's friendship with her old friend, Tomoko. The tall, boyish Saint Juste carries a torch for the sorority leader, Miya, while Nanako calls on the assistance of the consumptive girl "Prince" Kauro to help her get closer to Miya, for whom she herself is falling. Intense desires bubble under the surface in this beautifully animated series, which, despite its languid pace, deals sensitively with incest, bullying, young love, obsession, conspiracy, suicide, jealousy, and death in the style of SONG OF WIND AND TREES. Its broadcast in English is doubly unlikely, not merely for its subject matter, but also because of the scandal caused when it was yanked off the air in France. Not all anime, as broadcasters discovered, are "kids' stuff." **NV**

BRYGAR
1981. JPN: *Ginga Senpu Brygar.* AKA: *Galactic Whirlwind Brygar; Galaxy Cyclone Brygar; Cosmo Ranger; Cosmo Runner.* TV series. DIR: Takao Yotsuji, Teppei Matsuura, Hideki Takayama. SCR: Masaru Yamamoto, Shunsuke Kaneko, Hiroshi Hamazaki. DES: Kazuo Komatsubara. ANI: Masami Hinata. MUS: Masayuki Yamamoto. PRD: Kokusai Eiga, TV Tokyo. 25 mins. x 39 eps. (*Brygar*), 25 mins. x 39 eps. (*Baxinga*), 25 mins. x 43 eps. (*Sasrygar*).
King Carmen Carmen wants to destroy the planet Jupiter in order to create a new star and irrevocably change the solar system forever. Only the J9 Cosmo Rangers, comprised of Razor Isaac, Blaster Kid, Flying Bowie, and token girl Angel Omachi, can stop him. This energetic and popular series was supposedly inspired by real-life scientific research and used a lot of Korean talent at the lower ranks of production.
  The following year saw a sequel, *Galactic Stormwind Baxinga* (*Ginga Reppu Baxinga,* AKA *Cosmo Rangers*), set 300 years after the destruction of Jupiter, in which the solar system has enjoyed a period of relative peace under the Bakufu government. In much the same way that RAI adapted the events of Japan's civil war, *Baxinga* retold the fall of the 19th-century Bakufu government (or shogunate) in an SF setting, placing its cast in the role of the Shinsengumi organization (see OI! RYOMA). The J9 group takes on a new role, with Don Condole, Schutteken, Billy, Thauma, and token girl Laila fighting to keep the Bakufu alive. However, like their historical counterparts, they eventually fail, ending with a climactic battle that sees the entire central cast killed.
  As the popularity of the franchise waned, it returned for a final lighter-hearted series in 1983 with *Galactic Hurricane Sasrygar* (*Ginga Shippu Sasrygar*). This time, the historical reality warped for SF purposes is Prohibition-era America, while the plot is supplied in a pastiche of Jules Verne's *Around the World in Eighty Days.* IC Blues, a card shark operating in the asteroid belt, bets mob leader Bloody God that he can visit all 50 inhabited worlds in the de-Jupitered solar system within a year. He sets off to do so in his transforming robot ship Sasrygar accompanied by his faithful friends, though he soon discovers that members of the Bloody Syndicate are out to make him forfeit the bet, and will stop at nothing to do so. Jupiter suffers another unpleasant fate in Hideaki Anno's GUNBUSTER.

BTOOOM! *
2012. TV series. DIR: Kotono Watanabe. SCR: Yosuke Kuroda. DES: Takahiro Kishida, Anna Oizumi. ANI: Masaki Hinata. MUS: Keiji Inai. PRD: Madhouse, Flying Dog, Shinchosha, Showgate, Sotsu, Studio Mausu, Klockworx. 24 mins. x 12 eps. (TV).
Ryota Sakamoto is 22, unemployable and living at home with his nagging mother. He spends all day playing video games, and despite his complete insignificance in the real world he's a global superstar in the online combat game *Btooom!* The game seems to have everything he lacks: status, respect, achievement, even a lovely ingame wife. When he finds himself trapped in a seemingly real version of the game, with very real hazards, including death, he must work with other players to find out how they got into this weird situation.
  Although SWORD ART ONLINE is more bombastic and teen-focused, its near contemporary *Btooom!* has its own appeal. It extends the idea of an online "second life" beyond high school to the logical outcome for someone who spends his education achieving qualifications perhaps more interesting but less valuable outside gaming circles. Grittier violence and a very different structure give *Btooom!* its own appeal. Rather than the machinations of an evil mastermind, the motivation for Ryota and his new comrades being trapped in their insanely dangerous world is more mundane: someone in their ordinary world wanted to get rid of them. The nasty attitude to women prevalent in much of the gaming world is reflected here, with an unpleasant emphasis on rape and torture in female backstories, but otherwise this is a good-looking series with more than passing intellectual interest. **NV**

BUBBLEGUM CRISIS *
1987. Video, TV series. DIR: Katsuhito Akiyama, Hiroki Hayashi. SCR: Toshimichi Suzuki, Hidetoshi Yoshida, Arii Emu. DES: Kenichi Sonoda, Shinji Makino. ANI: Masahiro Tanaka, Jun Okuda. MUS: Koji Makaino. PRD: Artmic, Youmex, AIC. 47 mins., 28 mins., 26 mins., 38 mins., 43 mins., 50 mins., 49 mins., 50 mins. (v1), 25 mins. x 2 eps. (v2), 45 mins. x 3 eps. (*Crash*), 25 mins. x 24 eps. (TV), 25 mins. x 2 (v3).
In the postquake city of Megatokyo, sentient robots, or "voomers," are a part

of everyday life, but these androids can be used for evil as well as good. Sylia Stingray fights a private war with the evil corporation that murdered her scientist father (inventor of the voomers). With her "Knight Saber" companions Priss, Linna, and Nene and their powerful "hard-suit" armor, they attempt to prevent the Genom Corporation from seizing control of the world with voomer agents.

A fan favorite in its day, *BGC* was one of the earliest openly Japanese anime to reach the West (as opposed to "invisible" kiddie cartoons), in a subtitled edition from AnimEigo. With babes in battlesuits designed by **GUNSMITH CATS'** Sonoda and a sprawling high-tech cityscape, the retention of Japanese dialogue caught the oriental flavor of the cyberpunk zeitgeist, and, it should be said, blinded the audience to the show's flaws: variable animation quality, cheesy rock music, steals from Hollywood (particularly *Robocop*, *Streets of Fire*, and *Blade Runner*), and the camp *Buckaroo Banzai* pop-star-as-crime-fighter conceit. Though still well-regarded to this day, a lot of the series' popularity seems to stem from the hazy memories of old-school fans, who were grateful in the early days that anything was translated at all, so much the better if it was science fiction.

In 1988, the voice actresses shot the concert videos *Hurricane Live 2032* and *Hurricane Live 2033*, featuring a mix of live-action and (mostly reused) animated footage over music. *HL 2032* included a new song over a new, not previously released animated video, which illustrated Sylia's recruitment of the other Knight Sabers. This was followed by *Bye² Knight Sabers: Holiday in Bali*, featuring two scenes of the voice actresses in character in a group, plus one mini-interview and music video of each, and one ensemble music video, all using Bali as a backdrop. Three final episodes appeared the following year, directed by Hiroshi Ishiodori and Hiroyuki Fukushima and called, owing to a split between Artmic and Youmex, *Bubblegum Crash*. In these episodes, the Sabers have gone their separate ways but reform when an old enemy (guess who?) reappears. The pseudonymous Arii Emu ("REM") provided the script, but the *BGC* magic had already faded. It's true that *Crash* has its moments (particularly the arrival of little-robot-lost Adama, who turns

out to be an ingenue-assassin), but its vision of the future has aged quite badly. The punks and techno music that would have impressed the *Terminator* generation look out of place, as do the chunky mobile phones. There are moments in *Crash* when the robot-slave-society spins into some really interesting ideas, but much of it is marred by the ridiculously contrived team of female vigilantes and lame attempts at humor.

A more stylistically successful version of the franchise appeared in **AD POLICE**, which focused on the early years of supporting character Leon McNicol, but it only lasted for three episodes. A plan was briefly mooted for a video special about the Knight Sabers off-duty—when it was canceled, the proposal was heavily rewritten and eventually filmed as **TENCHI MUYO!**

In 1998, after **EVANGELION** turned TV serials into a new growth area, *BGC* was revived along with many other old favorites. Hayashi directed a remake, *Bubblegum Crisis Tokyo 2040*, written by Chiaki Konaka, whose **ARMITAGE III** had made far better use of robot-slave set-ups. *BGC 2040* dumped the humor in favor of sexual politics—Sylia sells lingerie at the Sexy Doll clothes shop, but the outfits she forces on the girls are little different. With much stretching of rubber, teetering on high heels, and inserting of "plumbing," the trademark hard-suits demean even as they empower. The characters, too, possess interesting flaws, and many situations draw on U.S. superhero comics—Sylia Stingray is remodeled as a cold-hearted neurotic like Tim Burton's Batman, while wide-eyed country-girl Linna has a Clark Kent existence as a humble secretary, troubled by both the office Lothario and the robotic manageress. Tomboy fan pinup Priss is remade as a mercenary bitch, whose new band, Sekiria, is named after Konaka's own, though with **EVANGELION**-inspired launch sequences and a *very* 1990s drum & bass soundtrack, much of *BGC 2040* will date just as swiftly as the original.

Although 26 episodes of the *BGC 2040* TV series were made, the final two were not broadcast on the original run, but added on home video. A second season, with the working title of *BGC 2041*, was announced as being in preproduction in 2002, but was canceled.

BUBU CHACHA *

1999. JPN: *Norimono Okoku BuBu ChaCha, Daisuki Bubu Chacha*. TV series. DIR: Tetsuro Amino. SCR: Akira Okeya. DES: Shinji Ochi. ANI: Hideaki Shimada. MUS: Goji Tsuno. PRD: Iku, Daume Inc., Japan Digital Entertainment Inc., Amino. 25 mins. x 26 eps. (TV1), 25 mins. x 52 eps. (TV2).

Elementary schoolboy Randy Rand (Buddy in Japanese) loses his beloved pet dog Chacha in an accident, but the dog's playful, protective spirit is reborn in Randy's toy car. Thanks to Chacha, Randy makes new friends in the neighborhood, including pigtailed girl-next-door Mary, who is convinced that Randy has some growing up to do, the Rap brothers, who only speak in rhyme, and Boo-man (Daa-man), a scary tramp-like figure who spooks the children only when they are getting near danger.

Beneath a veil of harmless children's entertainment, *Bubu Chacha* is a heart-rending indictment of modern times and a touching study of the way some children deal with death and the real world. It seems produced at least in part from that same nostalgic yearning for siblings that proved so successful for the **DUMPLING BROTHERS**. Randy is an incredibly lonely little boy, drawing on inanimate objects for friendship, and reduced to talking to a local ghost, Sarah, because he does not have a real sister. Chacha is not the only possessed item—he has a friend of his own in Bull, a toy robot that holds the spirit of a long-departed bulldog, and several other local vehicles are dead animals reborn, including Bubu Pyoko (a toy car that was once a frog), Hippo Truck, Cindy the Elephant Shovel Car, and Leopard the Sports Car. Randy's daily life is occasionally interrupted by the Eyebrow Aliens, who are benign invaders from another world, and by Tau, the boy across the street, who in less introverted times would have been a playmate for Randy along the lines of Nobita's associates in **DORAEMON**.

A bizarre combination of *My Mother the Car* (1965) with the anthropomorphic vehicles of *Thomas the Tank Engine* (1984), the original series of *Bubu Chacha* was split between Randy's adventures and those of the transforming train-robot **HIKARIAN**. A second series, concentrating on Randy and friends, followed in 2001 as *I Love*

BuBu ChaCha (Daisuki BuBu Chacha). The second season shows were broadcast in English on Japanese cable and on Japanese airlines for younger passengers, before eventually making their way to some foreign networks. The generation that grew up watching *Bubu Chacha* presumably saw nothing all that unusual in **ANGEL TALES**. When they are old enough to see a toy car come to life in the **AKIRA** hallucination scene, it will probably creep them out for good.

BUDDHA
1948. JPN: *Shakyamuni; Taisho Shakuso; Shaka; Shaka no Shogai*. AKA: *Life of Shaka; Great Saint Shakyamuni*. Movie. DIR: Noburo Ofuji. SCR: N/C. DES: N/C. ANI: N/C. MUS: Sara Choir. PRD: Japan Buddhism Association, Sanko. 52 mins.

After a portentous dream about a white elephant, the ancient Hindu princess Maya gives birth to a prince. Reared in seclusion from the troubles of the world, Prince Siddhartha is troubled by sights of poverty and deprivation when he is 12 years old. He is married to a beautiful wife, but he is unable to bear the thought of others suffering, and leaves the palace in search of an answer. While sitting beneath a tree, he achieves enlightenment.

Planned as a nine-reel life of Buddha, but exhibited in Cannes as "Part One" with only six reels completed, this late work by Noburo Ofuji was not completed until after his death. It was only in 1961 that it was finally exhibited as a full 72-minute movie (comprising ten reels).

BUDDHA: THE GREAT DEPARTURE
2011. JPN: *Tezuka Osamu no Buddha: Akai Sabaku yo! Utsukushiku*. AKA: *Osamu Tezuka's Buddha*. Movie. DIR: Kozo Morishita. SCR: Reiko Yoshida. DES: Hideaki Maniwa, Shinzo Yuki. ANI: Hideaki Maniwa, Toshio Kawaguchi. MUS: Michiru Oshima. PRD: Tezuka Productions, Kaga Electronics, Kinoshita Komuten, Yomiuri Shinbun, Toei Animation, Warner Bros. 111 mins.

Siddhartha is heir to a kingdom in India, but his homeland is constantly threatened by powerful neighbors. His father raises him as a prince, remote from the sufferings of the common people, but when Siddhartha meets an outcast girl and a slave general, his view of life is changed.

Planned as the first of three films adapting Osamu Tezuka's life of Buddha (**RELIGION AND BELIEF**), this first film has abandoned most of the things that made the manga uniquely Tezuka's work. The character designs are modernized and would fit into any high-quality anime feature, but more crucially, the magical pacing and storytelling of the manga has been lost. Tezuka wrote *Buddha* for an audience of young boys, and didn't hesitate to leaven history with comedy, philosophy with fun; yet he still managed to convey the serious truths of Buddha's life and message in ways children could understand. This movie seems to be in too much of a hurry to allow for the reflection that Tezuka built in so effortlessly. A movie can't develop at the same pace as a comic book, but this sacrifices too much of Tezuka's magic in the interests of speed and compression.

BUMPETY BOO *
1985. AKA: *Hey! Bumboo*. TV series. DIR: Eiji Okabe, Kenjiro Yoshida. SCR: Juzo Takahashi, Mami Watanabe. DES: Yu Noda. ANI: Yoichi Kotabe, Sadayoshi Tominaga. MUS: Nobuyoshi Koshibe. PRD: Nippon Animation, TV Tokyo. 10 mins. x 130 eps.

The adventures of a bright yellow talking automobile who is born from an egg in an unattended vehicle factory and enlists schoolboy Ken to help him find his mother. This vehicular pastiche of **FROM THE APENNINES TO THE ANDES** features a car with an uncanny resemblance to Benny, the talking yellow cab in *Who Framed Roger Rabbit?* (1988). The show was broadcast in English in Australia as *Bumpety Boo*, and sneaked out as a Just For Kids video release in the U.S. in 1990.

BUNNA! COME DOWN FROM THE TREE!
1986. JPN: *Bunna yo, Ki kara Orite Koi*. TV special. DIR: Eitaro Ozawa. SCR: Yuji Tanno. DES: Yoshio Kabashima. ANI: Yoshio Kabashima, Michiru Suzuki. MUS: Nisaburo Hashimoto. PRD: DAX, Shigoto, NHK. 55 mins.

Bunna the frog lives in a pond within a temple precinct, where he sees himself as a "watchfrog." Announcing that he intends to seek a new home, he ignores his girlfriend and father and climbs the pasania tree close to his pond. Commis-sioned to celebrate the 30th anniversary of the United Nations, this adaptation of Ben Mizugami's children's story was designed to show that cooperation is better than selfishness—hardly a radical departure from any other children's show.

BUNNY DROP *
2011. JPN: *Usagi Drop*. TV series. DIR: Kanta Kamei. SCR: Taku Kishimoto. DES: Yu Yamashita, Ichiro Tatsuta. ANI: Yu Yamashita. MUS: Suguru Matsutani. PRD: Production I.G, Dentsu, Fuji TV, Shodensha, Sony Music Entertainment, Toho, Tohoku Shinsha. 25 mins. x 11 eps.

Salesman Daikichi goes home for his grandfather's funeral and is shocked to learn that the old man had an illegitimate six-year-old daughter whose mother has abandoned the child to go back to her career. He's even more shocked when the family all try to wriggle out of looking after little Rin, and so he decides to raise her himself. Retaining the charm of Yumi Unita's manga, this sweet and gently paced anime looks at the trials and joys of suddenly becoming a single father at 30, especially to your own aunt. Simply, but very frankly, it takes an unpretentious and unsentimental look at the big scary themes of abandonment, selfishness, and divorce, gives an honest insight into a truly terrifying situation, and presents the happiest, and most obvious, of solutions: grown-ups should be grown-ups so that kids can be kids. Beautiful in every way that counts, right up until the anime finale, which wisely stops before the events of the last four volumes of the manga by Yumi Unita. The manga version would leap several years ahead, depicting Rin as a 16-year-old who confesses that she has romantic feelings for the now-middle-aged Daikichi, transforming the scenario from a touching tale of surrogate parenting into a creepy fable of under-age grooming. This leaves the anime in the odd position of being an incredibly thoughtful and heartfelt drama, doomed never to have a second season, and essentially betraying the more tawdry directions of its source material. A live-action feature remake in 2011 similarly avoided the implications of the manga's later chapters.

BURN UP *

1991. Video, TV series. DIR: Yasunori Ide. SCR: Jun Kanzaki. DES: Kenjin Miyazaki. ANI: Kenjin Miyazaki. MUS: Kenji Kawai. PRD: AIC, DirecTV. 50 mins. (orig.), 30 mins. x 4 eps. (W), 25 mins. x 13 eps. (X-cess), 25 mins. x 12 eps. (Scramble).

Frustrated traffic cops Maki, Reimi, and Yuka interfere in a *real* detective's investigation of a white slavery ring. Infiltrating the network of prominent businessman Samuel McCoy, Yuka is captured, and her two friends mount an all-out assault on the villain's headquarters.

Little more than an excuse for large-breasted girls with guns, *Burn Up*'s biggest fans appeared to be AD Vision, the U.S. distributor that was prepared to help fund the lame sequel *Burn Up W(arrior)* in 1996. Keeping to the AIC studio policy, best seen in TENCHI MUYO!, of throwing in more girls whenever possible, the sequel dumped most of the old characters in favor of the "Warrior" team, a police squad monitoring computer crime.

Heavily influenced by GHOST IN THE SHELL, *W* revolves around the Cerebus cartel's attempts to supply a virtual drug with mind-altering capabilities, as well as the disappearance of a virtual idol from the company mainframe—is it theft, or kidnapping? Maria, the AI in question, is an innocent creature in a computer but has superhuman strength in the real world, not dissimilar to Adama in the BUBBLEGUM CRISIS spin-off *Bubblegum Crash*. But despite music from ARMITAGE III's Yasunori Honda, *Burn Up W*'s roots have less to do with sci-fi than with the "zany" cookie-cutter concepts of producer Satoru Akahori. Despite its minimal running time, plot and characterization are sacrificed for set-ups to exploit the bouncing breasts of new-girl Rio. In the opening episode when terrorists seize hostages at a peace conference, one of their demands is that Rio must perform a nude bungee jump—police work taking a very distant second place to girls and guns.

This, it would seem, is all it takes, since the franchise was resurrected as *Burn Up X-cess* in 1997. One of the first shows on digital TV in Japan, the show was finally able to break from the confines of video— *X-cess* is twice as long as its combined predecessors, which allows for *slightly* more

character depth. The new director was Junichiro Kimura.

Hiroki Hayashi's 12-part *Burn Up Scramble* (2004) has radically different character designs, but yet more of the same formula. Rio is now in charge, leading a team of cool-headed Maya and precognitive investigator Lilica, the serial's one "new" idea, presumably inspired by Steven Spielberg's *Minority Report* (2002). ⓁⓃⒶⓋ

BURNING ALPINE ROSE: JUDY AND RANDY

1985. JPN: *Honoo no Alpen Rose: Judy and Randy*. AKA: *Passionate Alpine Rose*. TV series, video. DIR: Hidehito Ueda. SCR: Sukehiro Tomita, Shigeru Yanagawa, Hiroko Naka. DES: Akemi Takada. ANI: Hidehito Ueda. MUS: Joe Hisaishi. PRD: Tatsunoko, Fuji TV. 25 mins. x 20 eps. (TV), 90 mins. (v).

At the close of the Second World War, Judy is seeking her lost parents. The handsome Randy offers to help, though the only clue Judy has is her distant memories of hearing a song called "Alpine Rose." Judy escapes from the feckless Baron Guillermon and heads for Salzburg, where she believes the song's composer, Leonhardt Aschenbach, can be found.

Based on the comic in *Ciao* by Michiyo Akaishi, this was the first anime made by the Tatsunoko Studio specifically for girls. Hisaishi's score was so popular that the series was recut into two half-hour music videos purely to showcase the compositions. The story itself was edited into a 90-minute feature-length version on video. Compare to HONEY HONEY and HEIDI.

BURNING BLOOD

1990. AKA: *BB*. Video. DIR: Osamu Dezaki. SCR: Machiko Kondo. DES: Akio Sugino. ANI: Akio Sugino. MUS: N/C. PRD: Magic Bus. 45 mins. x 3 eps.

After killing a man in a fight, a Japanese down-and-out changes his name and moves to America, where he becomes a mercenary. Realizing that if he has a talent for anything, it's for fighting, he drifts into a career as a professional boxer (SPORTS ANIME). This adaptation of Osamu Ishiwata's 1985 manga from *Shonen Sunday* was directed by one better known for the original boxing anime, TOMORROW'S JOE. ⓋV

BURNING BROTHER

1988. JPN: *Moeru Oniisan*. TV series. DIR: Osamu Kobayashi. SCR: Kenji Terada, Sho Aikawa. DES: Michishiro Yamada. ANI: Michishiro Yamada, Kazunari Kume. MUS: Koji Makaino. PRD: Pierrot, Nippon TV. 25 mins. x 24 eps.

Japanese boy Kenichi wanders the mountainous hinterland of Japan in search of his father and his sister, Yukie. Swept away by a river as a baby, he was raised in the country by the old man Cha Genmai, but he eventually wanders back into human society accompanied only by a mangy wolf called Flipper. Reunited with his family, he falls in with the local gangster crowd, but life seems to go well, until Cha Genmai and Kaede (Kenichi's adopted sister) turn up to stay. Based on the *Shonen Jump* comic by Tadashi Sato and adapted by the production team behind KIMAGURE ORANGE ROAD, *Burning Brother* was praised at the time for the high quality of its comedy acting and characterization.

BURNING EXCHANGE STUDENT

1991. JPN: *Honoo no Tenkosei*. Video. DIR: Katsuhiko Nishijima. SCR: Toshio Okada. DES: Yuji Moriyama. ANI: Katsuhiko Nishijima. MUS: Kohei Tanaka. PRD: Gainax. 25 mins. x 2 eps.

Noboru Takizawa is the new kid in school, determined to apply the raging fire of his talent to success in all sporting arenas. He also falls for local girl Yukari, an interest which compels him to fight for her hand in the boxing ring. Featuring the writer and composer from GUNBUSTER with the director and designer from PROJECT A-KO, here is an anime whose Western release would have been guaranteed were it not for the subject matter of sports. Creator Kazuhiko Shimamoto would go on to write the martial-arts soccer manga *Red Card*, a contender for the most insane ever written. ⓋV

BURNING IMPREGNATED CLASSMATES

2008. JPN: *Honoo no Haramase Dokyusei*. AKA: *Flaming Impregnated Classmates*. Video. DIR: N/C. SCR: N/C. DES: N/C. ANI: N/C. MUS: N/C. PRD: T-Rex, MS Pictures (milky). 30 mins. x 2 eps.

Kazuya Gaken is a normal schoolboy who accidentally sees his female classmates' naked breasts during their physical examinations. This naturally inspires him to want to get them all pregnant. He is following in the footsteps of his cousin Tatsuya Tagami, hero of BURNING IMPREGNATED TRANSFER STUDENTS, whose ambition was world domination through impregnation. We wish we were kidding. Both this video and the 2006 one which preceded it are based on erotic games by SQUEEZ. **Ⓝ**

BURNING IMPREGNATED TRANSFER STUDENTS

2006. JPN: *Honoo no Haramase Tenkosei*. AKA: *Flaming Impregnated Transfer Students*. Video. DIR: Ken Raika. SCR: Mamoru Sakisaka. DES: N/C. ANI: N/C. MUS: N/C. PRD: Himajin Planning. 29 mins. x 3 eps.

Tatsuya Tagami is an ordinary high school boy who wants to rule the world, which apparently first requires him to get every girl he meets pregnant. This is complicated by the fact that he's in an all-boys' school, so he transfers to one which has just gone coed. Based on an erotic game by SQUEEZ: both the game and the anime had follow-up stories entitled BURNING IMPREGNATED CLASSMATES, in which Tatsuya's young cousin is inspired to emulate his exploits after glimpsing his classmates' breasts during a school medical checkup. **Ⓝ**

BURNING VILLAGE

1989. Video. DIR: Fusahito Nagaki. SCR: Fusahito Nagaki. DES: N/C. ANI: Chukai Shimogawa. MUS: Masahito Maekawa. PRD: Clover Art, Tama Pro. 12 mins. x 10 eps.

Animal folk tales set in the titular community, in which local eccentric Oharai retells several popular fairy tales with considerable license, including the LITTLE MERMAID and the *Musicians of Bremen*.

BURST ANGEL *

2004. JPN: *Bakuretsu Tenshi* (TV), *BT—Tenshi Sairin* (v). TV series, video. DIR: Koichi Ohata, Yasunori Urata. SCR: Fumihiko Shimo. DES: Kanetoshi Kamimoto, Osamu Horuchi, Kanetake Ebikawa. ANI: Gonzo. MUS: Masaru Nishida. PRD: GHD, Gonzo, Imagica, Media Factory, TV Asahi. 25 mins. x 24 eps. (TV), 30 mins. (v).

In a future Japan where a crime wave is counterproductively addressed with a law that lets *everyone* carry a gun, culinary student Kyohei Tachibana dreams of getting away to France to study advanced

pastry techniques and become a great chef. He looks for a job to help him save for the trip and becomes a private chef to a group of four women—Sei, Meg, Jo, and Amy. Much to his astonishment, they turn out to be a group of violent mercenaries (you know, like BUBBLEGUM CRISIS), and he is caught up in the very life he's trying to avoid. Sei is the granddaughter and heiress of the Bai-Lan mob family, and (for no apparent reason) the other girls are named for the surviving March sisters in LITTLE WOMEN. A video adventure followed in 2005 from the same team. **Ⓥ**

BUSH BABY, THE *

1992. JPN: *Dai Kusahara no Chiisana Tenshi Bushbaby*. AKA: *Little Angel of the Savannah: Bushbaby*. TV series, video. DIR: Takayoshi Suzuki, Takashi Kaga. SCR: Akira Miyazaki. DES: Shuichi Seki, Hiromi Kato. ANI: Nobuhiro Hosoi, Hiroshi Ito. MUS: Akira Miyagawa. PRD: Nippon Animation, Fuji TV. 25 mins. x 40 eps. (TV), 90? mins. (v1), ? mins. (v2), ? mins. (v3), ? mins. (v4).

Jackie Leeds, a British game warden's daughter in Kenya, gets into adventures with her bushbaby companion, Murphy, in this adaptation of William Stevenson's 1965 book. After initial high jinks, the time comes for her to return to England, but Jackie refuses to leave Murphy and sneaks off the ship. Going on the lam with her father's manservant, Tenbo, she spends the latter part of the series on the run from poachers and policemen, who believe she has been kidnapped. This remarkable change in tone may have been part of the reason for the serial's immense success in Japan, where it peaked at a 20% TV rating. It was later cut into four feature-length edits for video release, and there is also a 1970 live-action movie version directed by John Trent, starring Margaret Brooks and Louis Gossett, Jr. Shown on Canadian TV in the 1990s.

BUS GAMER

2008. TV series. DIR: Naoyuki Kuzuya. SCR: N/C. DES: Takahisa Ichikawa. ANI: N/C. MUS: Hiroyuki Nagashima. PRD: Studio Izena, Frontier Works, Square Enix. 30mins. x 3 eps.

Three complete strangers are hired to form a team for a secretive and highly dangerous game, the Bus Game. It's a battle simulation game themed around big busi-

ness—the "bus" of the title is really "biz"—and at stake are corporate secrets with a massive commercial value. Team AAA come from entirely different backgrounds, and their rules forbid prying into each other's lives outside the game. But the only reason any of them are involved in this deadly set-up is that each, for his different reasons, needs a great deal of money—enough to risk his life on the competence of strangers. Kazuya Minekura's manga started publishing in 1999 and ran until 2001. Despite being plagued by ill-health she supervised the anime and provided artwork, but the short, lightweight story doesn't do the manga justice.

BUSINESS COMMANDO YAMAZAKI

1997. JPN: *Kigyo Senshi Yamazaki: Long Distance Call*. Video. DIR: Tsuneo Tominaga. SCR: Tsuneo Tominaga. DES: Akira Kano. ANI: Akira Kano. MUS: N/C. PRD: Ripple Film, Beam Entertainment. 40 mins.

Jun Tomozawa's lighthearted 1992 manga in *Super Jump* took the premise of Roland Emmerich's *Universal Soldier* and moved it to a typically Japanese arena—the business world. A 42-year-old salaryman is made to serve his company beyond the grave when his brain is installed in a superpowered android body in order to carry out corporate espionage. **ⓃⓋ**

BUSO RENKIN *

2006. AKA: *Arms Alchemist*. TV series. DIR: Takao Kato. SCR: Akatsuki Yamatoya. DES: Akio Takami, Hatsue Kato, Yoshito Watanabe. ANI: Akio Takami, Hatsue Kato, Sunao Chikaoka, Takuya Matsumura. MUS: Kohei Tanaka. PRD: Xebec, Geneon Entertainment, Shueisha, Yomiko Advertising. 25 mins. x 26 eps.

Kazuki Muto has a really vivid dream—he is killed saving a strange girl from a monster. When he wakes up in his high school dorm, everything seems normal at first. Then a huge snake-monster attacks him and his sister, and the girl from his dream shows up and explains that it wasn't a dream at all. The monster is a homunculus, a magical creature that killed Kazuki the night before. Because she felt responsible for his death, Tokiki revived him by puttng a *kakugane* medallion in his chest, to function (shades of both ULTRAMAN and IRON MAN) as a replacement heart.

Kakugane, or core irons, are alchemical devices that can not only revive the dead but also function as weapons by taking on a form unique to each user, a Buso Renkin, or alchemical weapon. These are the only things that can destroy the monster. Kazuki soon enlists in a secret war to save mankind.

Nobuhiro Watsuki's manga ran from 2003 to 2006 in Japan, appearing the year after **FULLMETAL ALCHEMIST**. Watsuki ranks the alien girlfriend/highschool romance angle above the sibling devotion of its precursor, and chooses an everyday setting rather than a fantasy world. Although the result is less nuanced and less memorable than *FMA,* it still makes for an entertaining slugfest. Xebec and collaborators Studio DEEN produce attractive designs and good animation, and the plot balances fighting and romance with comedy.

BUST TO BUST

2010. JPN: *Chichi wa Chichi ni.* Video. DIR: N/C. SCR: N/C. DES: N/C. ANI: N/C. MUS: N/C. PRD: MS Pictures (AniMan), MAX, Kichijojigumi. 16 mins. x 2 eps.
An everyday tale of life in a Japanese high school, where Shinobu Fukuhara has secret feelings for her childhood friend, average boy Ikawa. Huge-breasted class representative Fukuhara and huge-breasted and lustful Megumi Yano get drunk and naughty together. What will Ikawa do?

Based on the manga of the same name by Yasuiriosuke. **◐**

BUTCHIGIRI

1989. AKA: *Take It to the Limit.* Video. DIR: Katsuyoshi Yatabe, Takashi Imanishi, Noboru Ishiguro. SCR: Norio Masuhara. DES: Eiichi Endo. ANI: Eiichi Endo. MUS: N/C. PRD: Nihon Eizo, Creative Bridge, Life Work. 50 mins. x 4 eps.
Takahara, leader of the notorious seven-man Silver Wolf gang, also dabbles in baseball, in this short series based on Yu Nakahara's 1987 comic in *Shonen Sunday.* Mixing bikes with school life in a similar fashion to **BOMBER BIKERS OF SHONAN**, the story shares **SLOW STEP**'s idea of a bad seed redeemed by a hidden sporting talent.

Jan Scott-Frazier, who worked on *Butchigiri*'s fourth episode while in the production department at Artland, describes it as the most disastrous project in living memory, hated by its own animators, only assigned to staffers as a punishment, and with subcontractors whose work was so bad that "we might be better off working with gorillas." When the anime was completed, the staff held a ceremonial burning of the storyboards in a parking lot. **◑**

BUZZER BEATER

2005. TV series. DIR: Shigeyuki Miya. SCR: Akatsuki Yamatoya; Toshimichi Okawa. DES: Shigeyuki Miya, Takashi Miyano; Yoshio

Mizumura, Ryoko Muragami. ANI: Tomohiro Koyama, Hidetoshi Namura, Tetsuya Matsukawa, Shigeyuki Miya. MUS: Koichiro Kameyama. PRD: TMS Entertainment, D.N. Dream Partners, NTV, VAP. 25 mins. x 13 eps. (TV1), 25 mins. x 13 eps. (TV2).
New York, near future: Hideyoshi is a homeless teenager who survives by hustling other kids in street basketball games. Basketball is as popular as ever with humans, but many aliens are better adapted for the game. Humans no longer rank in championship lists and there are very few human players in the top league. Hideyoshi finds himself drafted into a pro team, the first all-human team to get a shot at competing in the Space League. Millionaire Yoshimune means to bring the championship back to earth. But is the team *really* all-human? Takehiko Inoue's manga taps into a deep vein of passion for American sports in Japan. It followed his mega-hit **SLAM DUNK**, whose six-year run ended in 1996, making its debut as a web comic that year before magazine publication in 2007. Comparisons with its precursor are unfair: this is a lightweight diversion with neither the depth of character nor the intense and compelling involvement in the game itself. Inoue supervised the anime and its 2007 sequel, adding characters and story elements that were absent or only sketched in the manga.

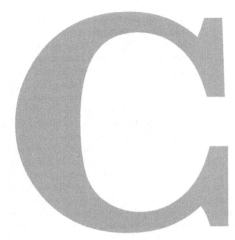

CAFÉ JUNKIE

2008. Video. DIR: Futoshi Nobitomeyo. SCR: PON. DES: Yotoku Tatsuha, Yumikase. ANI: Kenichi Hattori. MUS: N/C. PRD: A-1-shi KK, Suzuki Mirano. 27 mins. x 2 eps.

Masaru is about to graduate from technical college, but has no job lined up. He spends a lot of time hanging around at a café owned by the parents of three childhood friends. Nanami and Kurumi work in their parents' business. They hear Masaru say how much he's looking forward to seeing their older sister Kaede when she returns to her hometown, and their attitude toward him changes. Soon all four are getting much better acquainted. This two-part video was released in Japan on two separate DVDs. The first was titled *Café Macchiato*, the second, *Café Latte*, followed in 2009. Sadly both have about as much kick as weak instant coffee. Based on an erotic game of the same name by Blue Gale, produced and distributed by Mirano Suzuki, whose other titles include the anime versions of Tinker Bell's game **INYOCHU** and Drill Murata's manga **BLUSHING CARD: THE DEVILISH CHERRY**. See **ANYONE YOU CAN DO … I CAN DO BETTER** for details of sister titles in the franchise.

CAGE *

2003. JPN: *Canaria wa Kago no Naka*. AKA: *Canary in a Cage*. Video. DIR: N/C. SCR: Kazunari Kume. DES: I.H. Tayama. ANI: I.H. Tayama. MUS: Toru Shura. PRD: Studio Jam, Concept Films, Milky. 30 mins. x 2 eps.

Swindled by her feckless boyfriend, Sakimi Endo is so deep in debt that loan sharks force her to find employment in the sex industry. However, no matter how hard she works, her debts only seem to mount up, until the fateful day when she receives an email invitation to work at Club Canary, where caged women are supplied as sexual playthings to special clients. Based on the erotic novel by Ugetsu Nakamura. ⬤Ⓝ⬤

CALIFORNIA CRISIS: GUN SALVO

1986. JPN: *California Crisis: Tsuigeki no Juka*. Video. DIR: Mizuho Nishikubo. SCR: Mizuho Nishikubo. DES: Matsuri Okada. ANI: Matsuri Okada. MUS: Masami Kurihara. PRD: Hero Media, Studio Unicorn. 45 mins.

Noera and his new-found girlfriend, Marsha, become mixed up in a secret U.S.–Soviet space mission project. On the run from rival gangs in California, they gain possession of a round object that directs them to Death Valley, where an alien contact is being covered up by the government's men in black. This arbitrary plot, however, is of less importance to the filmmakers than a long, lingering tour of Californian beaches, possibly since location-hunting would be more fun on this project than on, say, something called *Iowa Crisis*. *CC* ends with a cliffhanger, but no sequel was made due to lack of audience interest—the first of many straight-to-video anime to leave their fans without a proper conclusion.

CALIMERO

1974. TV series. DIR: Yugo Serikawa, Kazuya Miyazaki, Fusahito Nagaki. SCR: Taichi Yamada, Takeshi Yoshida, Osamu Kagami, Mayuko Takakura, Hamakichi Hirose. DES: Shinya Takahashi. ANI: Fusahito Nagaki. MUS: Chuji Kinoshita. PRD: K&S, NET (TV1); TV Tokyo (TV2). 12 mins. x 84 eps. (1974), 23 mins. x 36 eps. (1992).

Calimero, a little black chick with an eggshell for a hat, was created in 1963 by Nino and Tony Pagot for an Italian advertisement. Taken up by a Japanese production company, the original animation was expanded into a long series. The series was revived for TV Tokyo in 1992 under director Tsuneo Tominaga, with new scripts by Jiro Takayama and Mayori Sekijima. If anything, the availability of the new series on video made it an even bigger success in the children's market than its predecessor.

CALL ME TONIGHT

1986. Video. DIR: Tatsuya Okamoto. SCR: Tatsuya Okamoto, Toshimichi Suzuki. DES: Kumiko Takahashi, Junichi Watanabe. ANI: Kumiko Takahashi, Satoshi Yamazaki, Masatoshi Nagashima. MUS: N/C. PRD: AIC; C.Moon. 30 mins.

Schoolgirl Rumi Natsumi moonlights as the boss of a phone contact club, hired by Ryo Sugiura to help him through a strange fetish. Ryo is an intergalactic nexus, and his body is subject to possession by various aliens and monsters whenever he becomes overexcited. Ryo wants Rumi to excite him *so* much that he gets used to the idea and can control his urges—though their wanderings through the city soon attract the attention of press photographer Maki, and Rumi's schoolmate Yuki, who is head of the "Sukeban" orgy club and wants Ryo and his transformations for herself. With a *Beauty and the Beast* subplot and demonic transformations brought about by frustrated teen lust, this plays like the junior comedy version of UROTSUKIDOJI. This and SECRETS OF THE TELEPHONE CLUB demonstrate that the Japanese media scandal of schoolgirl "date-clubs" in the late 1990s came a little late. ⓝ

CALL OF THE WILD *

1981. JPN: *Arano no Sakebi Koe: Howl, Buck.* AKA: *Call of the Wild: Howl, Buck.* TV special. DIR: Kozo Morishita. SCR: Keisuke Fujikawa. DES: Seiji Kikuchi. ANI: Seiji Kikuchi. MUS: Takeo Watanabe. PRD: Fuji TV, Toei. 85 mins. California, 1897. Buck, a domesticated mongrel who lives in the Santa Clara valley, is kidnapped by the family gardener, Manuel, and sold to a gold prospector. Soon he is a sled dog in the harsh winter of the Klondike, and his civilized exterior swiftly falls away, awakening a wildness buried deep in his genes for centuries. This anime adaptation of Jack London's novel (WHITE FANG followed in 1982) kept close to the original, eschewing the talking animals one might expect for a cartoon audience and leaving the dogs in silence while the humans (shiftless Manuel, swarthy Francois) are the only ones who speak.

A second, unrelated *Call of the Wild (Anime Yasai no Sakebi)* was a 26-part series shown intermittently on TV Tokyo between 1982 and 1984. Directed by Shigeru Omachi, this was a show in the spirit of SETON'S ANIMAL TALES, based on stories by Japanese author Muku Hatoju, including *Taro the Mountain Bear, Little Monkey Brothers*, and *The Disappearing Stray.*

CALLIGRAPHER

2010. JPN: *Shoka.* TV special. DIR: Makoto Yamada. SCR: Kenji Saido. DES: Hirokazu Kojima, Hiromu Ito. ANI: Hirokazu Kojima. MUS: Kenji Kawai. PRD: Production I.G. 24 mins. In ancient Japan, the forces of the shogun are challenged by giant creatures attacking the city. Their weapons are useless because the monsters are being created by a calligrapher, someone who can make living creatures from *kanji* and *kana.* This is a job for a specialist team: the artists' clan. The clan sends in its three top warriors, each with a special art combat skill. Their enemy: a man with a grudge and a thorough knowledge of art as a weapon of vengeance. The script for this delightful concept, an original creation by Saido,

was the winner of the 7th Animax Awards in 2008. The grand prize was having the script animated by Production I.G for airing on Sony's Animax Channel. Yamada made his directorial debut on the project.

CALLING ALL STUDENTS

1986. JPN: *Seito Shokun.* TV special. DIR: Mitsuo Kusakabe. SCR: Ryo Ishikawa, Azuma Tachibana. DES: Yoko Shoji. ANI: Kazuo Imura. MUS: Toshiyuki Watanabe. PRD: Toei, Ashi Pro, Fuji TV. 81 mins.
In this adaptation of Yoko Shoji's 1977 manga from *Friend* magazine, Naoko, a new girl in town, has trouble fitting into life at the local middle school but comes to terms with jealousy and broken hearts. Believing her parents to be dead, Naoko discovers the twin sister she never knew she had, who soon develops a heart condition and dies. Despite pulling no punches, the 24-volume manga series was unceremoniously crammed into a single TV special, which made it unlikely to draw as large an audience on TV. The similar BROTHER DEAREST was more successful as a TV *series* a few years later.

CAMBRIAN

2005. Video. DIR: Yoshiten, Shinjuro Yuki. SCR: Yasuyuki Muto. DES: Yoshiten. ANI: Ishiten. MUS: N/C. PRD: Milky, GP Museum, Image Works. 30 mins. x 2 eps.
Expelled from the academic world for illegal experiments in human cloning, Professor Yamagishi turns his attention to the study of explosive leaps in evolution. Instead, he only manages to turn himself into a gruesome lump of flesh with lots of tentacles, and is soon penetrating every available orifice on hapless ex-student Keiko, hoping to impregnate her with the seed of a new species. Based on a *Business Jump* manga by Noboru Mitsuyama in the time-honored tradition of ADVANCER TINA. The name comes from the period 590 million years ago, when life first arose on Earth. ⓛⓝⓥ

CAMPIONE *

2012. JPN: *Campione: Matsurowanu Kamigami to Kami Koroshi no Ma-o.* TV series, video. DIR: Keizo Kusakawa. SCR: Jukki Hanada, Takashi Aoshima, Takamitsu Kono, Hideaki Koyasu. DES: Masakazu Ishikawa. ANI: Masakazu Ishikawa. MUS: Tatsuya Kato.

PRD: Diomedea, AT-X, Tokyo MX. 25 mins. x 13 eps. (TV), 12 mins. (v).
Japanese teenager and sometime baseball player Godo Kusanagi heads off to exotic, occidental Sardinia to return a stone tablet on behalf of his grandfather. Local girl Erica reveals it is actually a spellbook, leading Godo to inadvertently fight, defeat, and gain the powers of the Persian war god Verethragna. As a result, Godo is now the latest "campione," a human champion tasked with defeating numerous rogue gods from old pantheons, who can be found making mischief in the modern world.

After promising early beginnings, in which Godo acquires divine powers and a bombastic, blockbuster soundtrack, as well as the potential of numerous ancient gods in need of a smackdown (RELIGION AND BELIEF), *Campione* soon squanders its lead by getting bogged down in tedious flirting and harem management. For it is not enough for Godo merely to fight, he must also love, fending off the advances of a series of over-excited ladies, determined to augment his powers by kissing them and thereby imparting him with their own semi-divine abilities. Nice touches, like an excursion into Japanese mythology accompanied by a switch in art style to oriental brushwork, are drowned out by the usual shrill bickering about who kissed whom.

CAN CAN BUNNY *

1996. JPN: *Can Can Bunny Extra.* Video. DIR: Katsuma Kanazawa. SCR: Tetsuya Ozeki. DES: Nanako Shunsai. ANI: N/C. MUS: Pika Pika. PRD: Pink Pineapple, KSS. 25 mins. x 6 eps. Suwati, the Goddess of Happiness, falls in love with Japanese boy Kenta and indulgently grants him the power to seduce seven women. True love, of course, is not always that easy—the first girl is a virgin on the run from a street gang. As with the superior VIDEO GIRL AI, Suwati is only using her powers because she wants Kenta to fall in love with *her,* but her cousin Shuree is also on his case.

The *Can Can Bunny* PC seduction game was very successful and was followed by *CCB Superior, CCB Spirits, CCB Blue Honey,* and *CCB Extra*—this fifth incarnation, with a greater emphasis on adventure over sex, provided the basis for the anime version. Cashing in on the hiatus between the OH

My Goddess! videos and movie, this porno retread also spun off into radio dramas, comics, and three novels. In the latter three episodes, Kenta heads off to the beach for the summer to help a friend run his restaurant—and get still more action on the side; this story arc is notable for having more plot, and much less sex. **N**

CANAAN *

2009. aka: *428 The Animation*. TV series. DIR: Masahiro Ando. SCR: Mari Okada. DES: Kanami Sekiguchi, Takeshi Waki. ANI: Kanami Sekiguchi. MUS: Hikaru Nanase. PRD: P.A. Works, Bandai Visual, Bushiroad, Good Smile Company, Lantis, Pony Canyon, Showgate. 24 mins. x 13 eps.

Two years ago, Tokyo's Shibuya district was ravaged by biological terrorism. Photographer Maria Osawa was saved by her father, who inoculated her against the virus, but suffered partial amnesia. In Shanghai with journalist Minoru Minorikawa, Maria is caught up in a fight between a mysterious woman and masked thugs, and rescued by an old friend. The mysterious Canaan has already saved her from hoodlums once, in the Middle East. Soon the friends are drawn into another terrorist plot to unleash a deadly virus, and Canaan's unique way of viewing the world through scrambled, heightened senses may just be the key to saving their situation.

Set in the world of the Wii game *428: Fusa Sareta Shibuya de, Canaan* hasn't quite made its mind up what kind of show it wants to be. There are elements of **NOIR** and **GUNSLINGER GIRL**, with past damage shaping innocents into deadly weapons. There are elements of **MASK OF GLASS**, with a discarded former star out to surpass her successor. There are elements of **BLACK MAGIC** where a feisty girl saves a klutzy one from a seemingly inevitable fate. But what it's absolutely sure about is that it's an action show, and on that score it delivers. The scenario was created by Kinoko Nasu of Type-Moon, with cofounder Takashi Takeuchi providing the original character designs.

The animation and art direction are excellent, making this a very enjoyable series to watch. The writing is less original, with stereotypical characters and situations, entire subplots reduced to framing devices or asides; but the superb action sequences

and the striking depiction of Canaan's unusual condition, synesthesia, go a long way to make up for Okada's trademark moments of incoherence. Synesthesia connects up the senses in abnormal ways: synesthetes might perceive the moods of people as colors, or feel sounds as physical sensations, or experience textures they touch as tastes. This leads to some remarkable animation sequences seeing the world through Canaan's perceptions. Nanase supports the imagery with a striking score. A 12-minute summary of the early episodes, *Minorikawa's Report*, was included on the Japanese and some foreign DVD and Blu-ray releases.

CANARIA

2002. JPN: *Canaria Kono Omoi wo Uta ni Nosete*. AKA: *Canary Put This Feeling into the Song*. Video. DIR: N/C. SCR: Noboru Yamaguchi, Kota Takeuchi, Fumiko Kuwahara, Yuichi Kuwahara. DES: Kakiko Kakitsubata. ANI: Shinji Katakura. MUS: N/C. PRD: Front Wing, NEC Interchannel, HuneX. 25 mins.

Fantasy based on a PC and Dreamcast game, in which a high school band made up primarily of cute and very silly girls is determined to get its keyboardist Jun back for a gig, whatever it takes. This involves cornering him on the school roof and flying him to the venue on a kite. Regardless of whether the game may have made sense, compressing it all into less than half an hour stretches the bounds of reality and results in a series of illogical and overblown solutions that might appear wacky to fans of **EXCEL SAGA**, but really just seem rather pointless. The game itself was intended for over-18s only, implying a raciness that is strangely absent from an anime that, for once, might have been better served as erotica. The final race between the Mayor on her motor scooter and two of the band on a tandem seems intended to be a pastiche of a similar sequence in **GOLDEN BOY**. Online sources imply that there was also a CD drama, although this may simply refer to drama *sections* on a spin-off music CD, of which there were several, as well as a novelization by scriptwriter Yamaguchi.

CANDY CANDY *

1976. AKA: *Candy White; Candice*. TV series. DIR: Yugo Serikawa. SCR: Shunichi Yukimuro,

Noboru Shiroyama. DES: Yumiko Igarashi. ANI: Keisuke Morishita, Kazuo Tomizawa. MUS: Takeo Watanabe. PRD: Toei, TV Asahi. 25 mins. x 115 eps. (TV), 40 mins. (m1), 26 mins. (m2).

A girl is left outside the Pony's Home orphanage. A note says that her name is Candice, and she is christened Candice White after the snow that is falling outside. Candice grows up in the orphanage, where she watches her friends leave to be fostered by other families. She is helped by a mysterious stranger and yearns for him to return to her. Sent to work as a servant for the Ragham family, she is bullied by the Ragham children, Eliza and Neil. She develops crushes on many nice young men, especially the charming gentleman Anthony Brown, though he dies suddenly on a fox hunt. His cousin, Alastair "Stair" Audrey, is another potential suitor, but he is killed in World War I. Candice falls in love with a man called Terence in London but steps aside to allow him to marry a woman whose need is greater than hers.

Equal parts **CINDERELLA** and **DADDY LONG-LEGS** mixed with a doomed love out of *Romeo and Juliet*, *Candy Candy* was one of the great successes of the 1970s. Begun as a manga in *Nakayoshi* magazine in 1975, Kyoko Mizuki and Yumiko Igarashi's weepy tale of self-sacrifice ended ironically with the two creators' acrimonious dispute over copyright. The speed of adaptation caused the animated version to deviate from the original in later chapters—Candice's hospital job from episodes 102 to 109 is not present in the manga, which instead dispatches her to New York to be an actress, and Toei insisted on the introduction of a mascot character, Clint the albino raccoon. *CC* provides moments of inadvertent comedy in its portrayal of early 20th-century America, with servants making Japanese-style bows, and English-style fox hunts in the Midwest. The newly moneyed Raghams are beastly to their social underling Candice, but she is regularly rescued from a fate worse than death (exile to Mexico, signified by a Pancho Villa–look-alike bandito onscreen) by the interference of the distant William, a British royal who inexplicably lives in America, where the upper classes fawn over him. William, however, is later revealed to be far closer to Candy than anyone realizes.

Candice would return in *The Voice of Spring/Candy's Summer Holiday*, a 40-minute theatrical outing in 1978. A 26-minute short, over-hopefully titled *Candy Candy: The Movie*, was directed by Tetsuo Imazawa in 1992 and focused on her abuse at the hands of the Raghams.

Another Igarashi manga, **LADY GEORGIE**, was animated in 1983, but *Candy Candy* was a watershed production in the Japanese industry. After the animated version led to $45 million of merchandising spin-offs and boosted the sales of its parent magazine by a million copies, *Nakayoshi* would actively seek to recreate such success in the girls' market from the ground up. The eventual result would be the market-led **SAILOR MOON** franchise. Candice's distant memories of a "handsome prince" helping her in early life were also lifted for **UTENA**. The show received a very limited partial broadcast on U.S. local TV for the Japanese community, with English subtitles. True to the political climate of the times, the nasty Raghams were renamed the Reagans in this version.

In a dramatic twist worthy of *CC* itself, the two creators had a spectacular falling-out in the 1990s after illustrator Igarashi attempted to claim sole copyright on merchandising spin-offs. Mizuki successfully sued, arguing that the images would never have existed in the first place without her 1975 novel, only for Igarashi to then sue the Toei studio over its management of trademarks. This has not only led to several other recurring legal actions over merchandise found to be unlicensed after the fact, but also a distinct unwillingness of anyone to get involved with *CC* beyond the original novels. Suggesting that the *CC* anime is an "orphan" work with no real owners, several South American chancers have released unlicensed editions of the anime, daring the interested parties to settle their differences long enough to determine who should sue them! The *CC* case is a landmark in Japanese intellectual property, demonstrating not only the perilous issues of copyright with multiple owners, but the likely fallout from disputes arising, which, in this case, led to the original novelist refusing to write any more *CC* stories, claiming she was sick of the character. It should come as no surprise that the last 20 years have seen ever-rising numbers of corporate-owned franchises created by no single figure or by committees of creatives under work-for-hire agreements. Similar arguments dogged the artistic heritage of *Space Battleship Yamato* (**STAR BLAZERS**), only ultimately resolved by the death of one of the plaintiffs, and caused the still-birth of **RGB ADVENTURE** after only six episodes.

CANTALOUPE COLLECTOR *

2007. JPN: *Tsuma to Mama to Boin.* AKA: *Wife and Mother and Boobs.* Video. DIR: Hideki Araki. SCR: Taifu Sekimachi. DES: Megumi Ishihara, Minan Moto. ANI: Norimoto Hattori. MUS: N/C. PRD: G.J?, Milky. 30 mins. x 2 eps. This is an unusual erotic anime in that, instead of being sex slaves irresistably drawn to a seemingly ordinary male as in **B-CHIKU BEACH**, or forcibly impregnated as in **BURNING IMPREGNATED CLASSMATES**, each of the women in this series of vignettes is set on becoming a mother. It's not unusual in that they all have large busts and a penchant for lying around their rooming house in lingerie, because it's based on an erotic game by G.J? with characters by Toshihide Sano, designer for **AKIBA GIRLS** and **DIRTY THOUGHTS**.

CANVAS

2002. JPN: *Canvas Sepia-iro no Motif.* AKA: *Canvas Motif of Sepia.* Video, TV Series. DIR: Itsuro Kawasaki. SCR: Reiko Yoshida. DES: Yasunari Nitta. ANI: Hironori Sawada. MUS: Hajime Kanasugi. PRD: F&C, Zexis, Chiba TV. 30 mins. x 2 eps. (v), 25 mins. x 15 eps. (TV). Artist Daisuke Aso is suffering from a creative block, while his childhood friend Amane tries to find ways of encouraging him to draw again. Amane, of course, secretly harbors feelings for Daisuke, and feels threatened by a series of would-be competitors—it wouldn't be a computer dating simulation game adapted into an anime unless a whole gang of girls started chasing after the leading man for no apparent reason. What distinguishes this anime from the many, many similar shows available is the peculiar execution of its sex scenes—it has them, which is weird enough for something that starts off with the gentle tones of **LOVE HINA**, but they are all presented in a rather coy and soft-core manner like the sanitized version of **END OF SUMMER**. A TV series, *Canvas 2: Niji-iro no Sketch* (*Rainbow-colored Sketch*), followed in fall 2005. **Ⓝ**

CAPETA

2005. TV series. DIR: Shin Misawa. SCR: Tsutomu Kamishiro. DES: Atsumi Komura. ANI: N/C. MUS: Toshihiko Sahashi. PRD: Studio Comet, TV Tokyo. 25 mins. x 52 eps. Fourth grader Kappeita (AKA Capeta) Taira lives with his widowed father, who tries to break his son out of apathy one day by constructing a racing cart out of leftover work materials. Despite a bent chassis that causes the cart to wander off course, Capeta is able to steer it to victory at the local cart track. His success is witnessed by Naomi Minamoto, the East Japan Junior Cart Racing champion, who recommends that he participate in official races. Predictable **SPORTS ANIME** drama ensues. Based on a manga in *Shonen Magazine* monthly by Masato Soda.

CAPRICIOUS ROBOT, THE

2004. JPN: *Kimagure Robot.* TV series. DIR: Yoshiharu Ashino, Masahiro Kubo, Yasuhiro Aoki. SCR: Shinichi Hoshi. DES: N/C. ANI: N/C. MUS: Seiichi Yamamoto. PRD: Studio 4°C. 2 mins. x 11 eps. Although he did write episodes for several live-action and animated TV series, author Shinichi Hoshi was legendarily protective of his original works, and although approached many times by companies interested in buying the rights to his short stories, refused to allow extensive adaptation until after his death. Hence, this experimental series of short Internet movies of some of Hoshi's best-known sci-fi stories, undertaken as an experiment by Studio 4°C in the promise that others would be forthcoming if they were a success.

CAPRICORN *

1991. AKA: *Joji Manabe's Capricorn.* Video. DIR: Takashi Imanishi. SCR: Takashi Imanishi, Joji Manabe. DES: Moriyasu Taniguchi. ANI: Moriyasu Taniguchi. MUS: Ikuro Fujiwara. PRD: Aubec. 48 mins. Teenager Taku Shimamura is transported to the parallel world of Slaphrase, a world of anthropomorphic animals, where evil General Zolba plans to usurp the imperial throne. Realizing that Zolba's next conquest, the planet "Capricorn," is really

Earth, Taku joins forces with Mona, the last of the Yappy race of dragon-people, to defeat Zolba and save both worlds.

This video features a similar plot to manga creator Manabe's OUTLANDERS and the cookie-cutter character designs that distinguish (or rather, *don't* distinguish) his other works such as *Caravan Kidd* and *Drakuun*—in which *Capricorn*'s Zolba also makes a cameo appearance. Manabe had more luck with RAI.

CAPTAIN

1980. TV special, movie, TV series. DIR: Satoshi Dezaki. SCR: Noboru Shiroyama. DES: Akio Chiba. ANI: Shigetaka Kiyoyama, Keizo Shimizu, Isao Kaneko. MUS: Toshiyuki Kobayashi. PRD: Eiken, NTV. 84 mins. (TVm1), 82 mins. (TVm2), 93 mins. (m), 25 mins. x 26 eps. (TV).

Takao Taniguchi enters the Nakano baseball club and fights his way to the top, determined to lead his team to victory in the national finals. Manga artist Akio Chiba specialized in baseball (his other big hit was 1973's *Play Ball*) and this adaptation of his 1972 manga was soon followed by a second TV movie later the same year. The two incarnations were recut into a 95-minute movie release in 1981, and the story finally received a full-length TV series in 1983, supposedly because of a "great critical reception," though a serial had been planned from the beginning.

CAPTAIN FUTURE *

1978. TV series, TV special. DIR: Tomoharu Katsumata, Hideki Takayama, Noboru Ishiguro, Yasuo Hasegawa. SCR: Masaki Tsuji, Hiroyuki Hoshiyama. DES: Sadao Noda. ANI: Toshio Mori. MUS: Yuji Ono. PRD: Toei, NHK. 25 mins. x 52 eps. (TV series), 60 mins. (TVm).

Brilliant young scientist Curtis Newton (AKA Captain Future) brings peace and justice to the galaxy with his sidekicks Android Otho, alien robot Grag, and "living brain" Simon Wright. Known collectively as the "Future Men," they keep their flagship, The Comet, hidden in a lunar crater and launch it to help Earth's government, which communicates with them through the beautiful agent Joan Randall.

The sci-fi novels of Edmond Hamilton were optioned for anime production in record time when George Lucas mentioned that they were a major inspiration for *Star Wars* (1977). Beginning with an adaptation of *Captain Future and the Space Emperor* (1940), the anime series is remarkably faithful to the original, especially compared to the license taken in Japan with E. E. Smith's LENSMAN. Hamilton's work was surprisingly well-served in Japan; his later *Starwolf* series was also spun off into a live-action TV show, itself reedited for the 1978 movie *Fugitive Alien*.

Four episodes were released on video in the U.S. as *Captain Future* 1 and 2, which chart the events of *The Lost World of Time*, where Newton must travel back to save the inhabitants of planet Prometheus (Kaitan) that is just about to disintegrate and form the Solar system's asteroid belt. A third video, confusingly titled simply *Captain Future*, was a truncated digest of *Captain Future's Challenge*, in which Newton must stop "King Wrecker" from destroying all the gravium mines in the Solar system. The other 14 hours or so of the Japanese version remain untranslated.

Captain Future also had a 60-minute TV special in 1978, in which an experimental spaceship goes missing on Mercury shortly before the start of the Interplanetary Yacht Race. In order to infiltrate a criminal network, Future must pose as a test pilot at the notorious Venusian "Suicide Base," before a showdown in the "Sargasso" Graveyard of Space. In an intershow homage, a character called "Curtis Newton" has a cameo in the later SOL BIANCA series.

CAPTAIN HARLOCK *

1978. JPN: *Uchu Kaizoku Captain Harlock*. AKA: *Space Pirate Captain Harlock, Albator*. TV series, movie, TV special. DIR: Rintaro, Kazumi Fukushima. SCR: Masami Uehara, Haruya Yamazaki. DES: Leiji Matsumoto. ANI: Kazuo Komatsubara. MUS: Toshiyuki Kimori. PRD: Toei, TV Asahi. 25 mins. x 42 eps. (TV1), 130 mins. (m), 25 mins. x 22 eps. (TV2, SSX), 35–75 mins. x 8 eps. (v1), 30 mins. x 6 eps. (v2, Saga), 25 mins. x 13 eps. (TV3, CWZ), 25 mins. x 2 eps. (v3, CWZG), 25 mins. x 13 eps. (v4, Herlock).

Leiji Matsumoto's tale of space piracy began in *Shonen Sunday* in 1977, and is set a thousand years in the future. In the year 2977, Captain Phantom F. Harlock leads a crew of outlaws on the starship Arcadia, determined to resist the invasion of Earth by the Mazone, a plant-based race of long-necked women who have fled the imminent destruction of their own homeworld. Harlock assembles a crew that includes Mime, the last of an alien race whose homeworld was destroyed by the Mazones; engineer Tochiro; Yattaran, an obsessed model-maker based on Matsumoto's former assistant and AREA 88– creator Kaoru Shintani, and Maji, a man who has somehow become the father of a Mazone child.

Like Osamu Tezuka, Leiji Matsumoto is apt to reuse a set cast of characters from title to title, regardless of whether the shows actually relate to one another. This has led *Harlock* to develop a complex and contradictory "continuity"—a word we use advisedly, because Matsumoto does not seem to have intended duplicate character images and names to necessarily indicate any relationship. Hence, many anime based on other Matsumoto works allude to *Harlock*, intentionally or otherwise, although it should be noted that Matsumoto and his collaborators often want to have their cake and eat it—recycling characters with impunity, proclaiming any apparent contradictions to be irrelevant, but often creating situations that are difficult to comprehend without an appreciation of several other works, which the audience has already been told are "unrelated."

Consequently, our account of what happens in the *Harlock* series is also subject to debate, particularly since it is contradicted by some, but not all, of what happens in later incarnations of the franchise, some of which have been misleadingly billed as sequels when they are in fact remakes.

The first incarnation of the anime *Harlock*, the TV series, ends with Tochiro's widow Emeraldas leaving to grieve among the stars in her own ship, the titular QUEEN EMERALDAS of the first of many spin-offs. Harlock himself would win a duel against Lafressia, queen of the Mazone, and then head off into the void with just Mime for company, in search of a place to die. This, however, was the beginning of Harlock's long-lasting popularity outside Japan, with the dark, brooding hero finding unexpected fans abroad, particularly after a limited number of episodes were broadcast with English subtitles on American local TV stations for the Japanese community.

After a cameo with Emeraldas' sometime "sister" Maetel in the latter part of **GALAXY EXPRESS 999** and the movie *Adieu Galaxy Express 999*, Harlock returned in Tomoharu Katsumata's 130-minute movie *My Youth in Arcadia* (1982, *Waga Seishun no Arcadia*), also known by the titles *Arcadia of My Youth* and *Vengeance of the Space Pirates*. Supposedly designed as a prequel to the first series, the story line is actually irreconcilable, since it depicts Earth under alien occupation, this time by the Illumidas race. The story also presents a possible explanation as to how the eye-patched Harlock may have lost his eye—or at least, how this incarnation of him may have lost it, protecting Maya, the woman who may (or may not) have been his wife. *My Youth in Arcadia* also presented a series of flashbacks detailing another Harlock, quite possibly an ancestor of this one, a 20th-century aviator whose biplane is also, coincidentally, called the Arcadia.

Although its continuity clashed with the original series, the movie does function as a prequel of sorts to *My Youth in Arcadia: Endless Orbit SSX*, a TV series that followed later the same year, in which Harlock battles the Illumidas again. The Arcadia in the movie and SSX series is built on Earth, whereas the version in the original series is built on the planet Heavy Meldar, which exploded after the Arcadia's launch, but also appears in several chapters of the *Galaxy Express 999* series.

Though the various *Harlock* serials, the spin-offs starring Emeraldas or Maetel, the distant cousins **QUEEN OF A THOUSAND YEARS** and **DNA SIGHTS 999.9**, and even look-alikes such as Rheindars in **THE COCKPIT** are supposedly related, the discrepancies make this hard to believe. Dates and characters vary wildly (the suicidal Harlock who leaves the original series is maniacally cheerful when he reappears in *Galaxy Express*), and two of the serials even have a gap of several centuries between them. Paramount among the confusions is the claim that Harlock is really Mamoru Kodai (Alex Wildstar) from **STAR BLAZERS**, but although Mamoru does indeed disguise himself as a space pirate called Harlock in the manga (not anime) of *Space Battleship Yamato*, he is copying a character from a comic book by Leiji Matsumoto.

Harlock in modern times is no less confusing. Twenty-seven episodes of the origi-nal TV series were rearranged into feature-length chunks to make an eight-video digest version at the close of the 1990s. For an idea of the mind-boggling complex-ity, the first tape comprises episodes 1, 4 and 9, the second merely episode 17 with ten minutes of all-new bridging footage. Needless to say, episode 13, which was also shown theatrically in 1978 as the short film *Witch Castle in the Sea of Death: Mystery of Arcadia*, is absent from the modern rere-lease. The series was also reissued in an LD collection under the umbrella title of *Leiji Matsumoto Theater*, along with **DANGUARD ACE**, *GE999* and **SPACEKETEERS**.

Harlock returned *again* in 2000 with Nobuo Takagi's six-part video series *Harlock Saga: Ring of the Nibelung* (also available in the U.S.), discarding much of the previous continuity again in favor of a retelling of Wagner's Ring Cycle. Harlock, Tochiro, and Emeraldas are called to planet Rhine to help Mime, the guardian of the planet's gold, prevent her brother Alberich from forging the gold into a ring and becoming the ruler of the universe. With the aid of the goldsmith Tadashi, and despite the opposition of *Galaxy Express 999*'s Maetel, Alberich gets his wish and departs for planet Valhalla to confront the alien oppressor Wotan.

Harlock also appeared in the 2000 "manga video" *Herlock*, for which see **CRUSHER JOE**. Herlock is just one of many alternate transliterations for proper nouns in the series, many of which have become canonical despite their lack of relation to the author's intent. Laffressia, for example, should really be Rafflesia—the queen of the plant people named after the world's largest flower, while Maetel, the surrogate mother of the Galaxy Express, takes her name from the Latin *mater*. Such transpositions of letters, however, are com-mon in anime, not just from translators ignorant of the sources, but also from those who are all too cognizant but wish to tone down certain creators' embarrassing English puns and in-jokes (see **GUNDAM**).

Harlock would next return in *Cosmo Warrior Zero* (2001), a story that focused not on him, but on the man sent to capture him—Warrius Zero, a servant of the machine people, tasked with hunting him down in the depths of space. The series included a 2-episode prequel, *Cosmo Warrior Zero Gaiden*. The 13-episode *Space Pirate Captain Herlock* (2002), directed by Rintaro and written by **PERFECT BLUE's** Sadayuki Murai, was to feature Harlock attempting to reunite the crew of the Arcadia to defend the Earth from an ancient evil, although production was halted at Matsumoto's own request when he discovered that animators were using a Star of David to represent the "root of all evil"—an anti-Semitic touch with which Matsumoto refused to have any association and that led to the serial's broadcast being canceled. However, it did make it make it onto video in an edited format and was released in America as *Captain Herlock: Space Pirate*. Shinji Aramaki's CG remake *Space Pirate Captain Harlock* was released in Japanese cinemas in 2013. See also **GUN FRONTIER**.

CAPTAIN KUPPA

2001. JPN: *Sabaku no Kaizoku Captain Kuppa*. AKA: *Captain Kuppa Desert Pirate*. TV series. DIR: Koichi Mashimo. SCR: Koichi Mashimo. DES: Tomoaki Kado. ANI: N/C. MUS: Hayato Matsuo. PRD: Enoki Films, NHK. 30 mins. x 26 eps.

The future: the world has turned to desert, and the small towns that survive are sur-rounded by empty wastelands filled with monsters and demons. Water sources are scarce and either controlled by villains or haunted by dangerous creatures. Control of water is power, and the remnant of humanity scavenges a living patching up the advanced technology of the past. While it might sound like the preamble to **FIST OF THE NORTH STAR**, it is actually the background for a children's show, as 11-year-old Kuppa and his faithful robot companion Dram fear nothing—except Yukke, an engineering genius who bosses her younger brother about mercilessly. They are menaced by villain Bibimba, who hunts treasure hunters and has made them his top target; but a more serious threat to their world may be the hand-some and mysterious Samgetan, Yukke's love interest. She doesn't know it but he's an older man—3,500 years older, who has been observing human history all this time, waiting for the moment to strike. Created by Toshio Tanigami for a spin-off of the anthology *Corocoro Comic*, this is a cheerful, harmless adventure series.

CAPTAIN TSUBASA

1983. AKA: *Flash Kicker; Flash Kicker: Road to 2002*. TV series. DIR: Hiroyoshi Mitsunobu, Ken Hibari, Katsumi Minoguchi, Hiroshi Yoshida, Norio Yazawa. SCR: Naoko Miyake, Yoshiyuki Suga, Yasushi Hirano, Ken Hibari. DES: Yuichi Takahashi, Nobuhiro Okaseko. ANI: Nobuhiro Okaseko. MUS: Atsumoto Tobisawa. PRD: Shida Pro, TV Tokyo. 25 mins. x 128 eps. (TV1), 45 mins. x 4 eps. (m), 30 mins. x 13 eps. (v1), 25 mins. x 47 eps. (TV2), 48 mins. (v2), 25 mins. x 52 eps. (TV3).
Tsubasa Ozora has literally been playing soccer since he was a baby. Moving to a new town, he immediately joins the junior team, which has former Brazilian international player Roberto Honma as a coach. Much like his tennis counterpart in AIM FOR THE ACE, Tsubasa progresses through the various levels of his chosen sport until he and his friends (a superfast striker, a wily tactician, and a gifted goalkeeper) face the best in the world.

CT was not the first soccer anime; that honor goes to RED-BLOODED ELEVEN, but it remains the best-known. Even though only 4% of the Japanese population participated in soccer at the beginning of the 1980s, Yuichi Takahashi's *CT* manga polled twice as high as FIST OF THE NORTH STAR in the pages of *Shonen Jump*. The TV series was a foregone conclusion, cunningly kept alive by a periodic resetting to zero of the hero's achievements. Fifty-six episodes into the series in 1984, Tsubasa graduated to middle school, allowing the earlier, junior victories to be set aside for a clean slate and a new set of struggles that would take a further 72 weeks. Four short theatrical outings followed—*CT: Great European Challenge* and *CT: Japanese Junior Championship* in 1985, *CT: Run Toward Tomorrow* and *CT: The Junior World Cup* in 1986. This last film was the beginning of an updated series, *New CT*, directed by Osamu Sekita and eventually going straight to video in 1989. Now playing for the national youth team, Tsubasa learns many trick shots from his foreign opponents, including the Italians and French, before finally playing for the ultimate prize against West Germany.

In 1993, reality caught up with fiction, as a professional Japanese soccer league was finally established, an opportunity exploited in SHOOT!, KICKERS, and FREE KICK FOR TOMORROW, as well as by *CT*, with the second TV series *Captain Tsubasa J*, and the one-shot video *Holland Youth* (1995). After that Tsubasa faded away, only to return in a new 2001 TV series, *Captain Tsubasa: Road to 2002*, cashing in on the 2002 World Cup. Under various names, including *Oliver y Benji* or *Holly e Benji*, it is occasionally cited by real-world European players as a childhood inspiration, cropping up in interviews with, among others, Alessandro del Piero and Fernando Torres.

CARDCAPTORS *

1998. JPN: *Card Captor Sakura*. TV series. DIR: Akitaro Daichi, Morio Asaka. SCR: Nanase Okawa, Jiro Kaneko. DES: CLAMP, Kumiko Takahashi. ANI: Kumiko Takahashi. MUS: Takayuki Negishi. PRD: Madhouse. 25 mins. x 70 eps. (TV), ca. 80/86 mins. (m1), ca. 82/98 mins. (m2), 10 mins. (m3, *Kero*), ca. 5 mins. x 3 eps.
Created by CLAMP shortly after the success of RAYEARTH, *CardCaptors* combines the long tradition of magical-girl shows like LITTLE WITCH SALLY with the collection-oriented computer games such as POKÉMON. In her father's basement study, ten-year-old Sakura Kinomoto discovers the Clow, which looks like a book but is really a prison for sorcerous cards. She accidentally allows all the cards to escape, and Cerberus, the Guardian of the Cards, persuades her to hunt them all down. Each card represents a particular kind of spirit (e.g., elemental or seasonal) that Sakura can use once she acquires it, so her progress through the story amounts to a series of game-style power-ups—a point often made by Cerberus himself, who spends most of his time in his "cute" Kero-chan form. Other problems besieging Sakura include her best friend, Tomoyo, a rich girl who insists on designing new costumes for her and taping her missions. She must also compete against her Chinese rivals Li Meilin and Li Shaoran (who also becomes Sakura's would-be boyfriend, though at first she much prefers her brother's indifferent best friend). Our spelling of the names here reflects the ham-fisted romanization of the English-language edition, rather than any knowledge of actual Chinese.

The 1999 *Card Captor Sakura: The Movie* sees Sakura win a trip to Hong Kong, where she competes with the Li siblings on their home turf. In a plot suspiciously similar to that of the final TENCHI MUYO! movie, Sakura is haunted by dreams of a strange woman, an old flame of the cards' original creator, Clow Reed. She must convince the phantom that Clow Reed is dead without angering her and causing her to destroy the parallel world in which they have become trapped. A second movie, *CCS: The Sealed Card*, followed in 2000, in which someone begins to steal Sakura's cards as she prepares to celebrate the Nadeshiko festival—an occasion doubly dear to her since Nadeshiko (see NADESICO) is also the name of her late mother. The short film *Leave it to Kero* (2000) and three five-minute videos—*Suteki desu wa, Sakura-chan* (2000), *That's Amazing Sakura-chan*)—were also made as bonuses in some editions.

The series came to the U.S. in late 2000, dubbed by the Nelvana Studios, though, as with many other ill-fated anime, the inertia of network "demands" ruined much of what made the series initially so interesting. As if the name change were not already a hint, the TRANSLATION of the series attempted to move the focus to a more acceptable protagonist (see SABER RIDER AND THE STAR SHERIFFS), beginning with episode 8 (*Sakura's Rival*) and implying that she and Li Shaoran are equals, in a futile attempt to gain more male viewers.

Characters from *CardCaptors* would return as alternate versions of themselves in TSUBASA CHRONICLE.

CARDFIGHT!! VANGUARD *

2011. TV series. DIR: Hatsuki Tsuji. SCR: Tatsuhiko Urahata. DES: Mari Tominaga, Seiko Akashi. ANI: Kumiko Shishido, Mari Tominaga, Noritomo Hattori. MUS: Takayuki Negishi. PRD: TMS Entertainment, Studio Sakimakura, Dentsu, Sotsu Agency, TV Aichi, TV Tokyo. 25 mins. x 65 eps. (TV1), 25 mins. x 39 eps. (TV2), 25 mins. x ?? eps. (TV3).
Timid middle-schooler Aichi Sendo is often bullied and spends most of his life trying to stay inconspicuous. His childhood treasure, a "Blaster Blade" game card, is the only thing that keeps him going. The card was a gift from a much cooler older boy, Kai, and opens the door to a new life for Aichi. When their paths cross again, Kai introduces Aichi to a card game called Vanguard. Aichi loves the game and quick-

ly shows unsuspected abilities. He finds new confidence, and makes new friends, but the main reason he works hard to be the best player he can is to impress Kai as a worthy opponent. First, though, he must come to terms with his own dark side.

Created by Akira Ito and Satoshi Nakamura, known for various iterations of the YU-GI-OH franchise, and Takaaki Kidani of card game makers Bushiroad, this anime was launched a month before the card game was released in February 2011, with a manga version by Ito commencing publication in March. The popularity of the game has so far ensured two follow-up series. *Cardfight!! Vanguard Asia Circuit (Cardfight!! Vanguard Asia Circuit Hen)* began airing in April 2012. It involved Aichi and his friends fighting to free old comrades from a mysterious dark force. It was followed by *Cardfight!! Vanguard Link Joker Hen* in January 2013. Aichi, now in high school, makes new friends and builds a team to help his school win the inaugural high school cardfighting championship.

CARNIVAL PHANTASM
2011. Video. DIR: Seiji Kishi. SCR: Makoto Uezu. DES: Kazuaki Morita, Tomohito Hirose. ANI: Kazuaki Morita. MUS: Yasuharu Takenashi. PRD: Lerche, Bandai Visual, Notes. 8–20 mins. x 15 eps.
Eri Takenashi, author of KANNAGI: CRAZY SHRINE MAIDENS, made the *Take Moon* gag manga in 2004, using characters from the works of Type-Moon, the fan-founded game creators of FATE/STAY NIGHT, LUCKY STAR, and LUNAR LEGEND TSUKIHIME. Type-Moon then adapted it to anime to celebrate their tenth anniversary, releasing it between 2011 and 2012 as four "seasons" on DVD. Nods to pop culture icons including magical girls and the constantly dying Kenny from *South Park* may add interest for those who don't care for anime based on erotic games with added slapstick.

CAROL
1990. Video. DIR: Satoshi Dezaki, Tsuneo Tominaga. SCR: Tomoya Miyashita, Yun Koga. DES: Yukari Kobayashi, Yun Koga. ANI: Yukari Kobayashi. MUS: Tetsuya Komuro. PRD: Animate Film, Magic Bus. 60 mins.
Carol is a teenage girl who notices music disappearing from the world—at first minor annoyances like the chimes of Big

Ben or the sound of her father's cello, but then a major crisis when her favorite band, Gaball Screen, loses its music. Transported to the alternate dimension of Lapaz Lupaz, she joins forces with heroes Clark, Tico, and Flash to prevent monsters from stealing songs from Earth.

Naoto Kine, guitarist with the Japanese prefab pop band TM Network, supposedly wrote the original novel of *Carol* himself. Filtered through EARTHIAN-creator Koga and scenarist Miyashita before it was ready for the screen, the end result still became the best-selling anime video of the year in Japan. The sunglasses-wearing Tico is modeled on Kine himself, with lead singer Takashi Utsunomiya providing the model for Flash, and keyboardist-producer Tetsuya Komuro inspiring Clark. As with the Beatles' *Yellow Submarine*, but unlike the similar pop-promo anime HUMANE SOCIETY, the band's voices are provided by actors. Another of Kine's literary outpourings, JUNKERS COME HERE, was animated in 1994.

CARRIED BY THE WIND: TSUKIKAGE RAN *
2000. JPN: *Kaze Makase Tsuki-kage*. AKA: *Moonshadow Drifting on the Wind, Lordless Retainer Tsukikage*. TV series. DIR: Akitaro Daichi. SCR: Yosuke Kuroda. DES: Hajime Watanabe. ANI: Takahiro Yoshimatsu. MUS: N/C. PRD: Madhouse, WOWOW. 25 mins. x 13 eps.
In the olde-worlde nostalgia spirit of the turn of the century that also created CLOCKWORK FIGHTERS and TREE IN THE SUN, this anime is a jokey retelling of old samurai dramas, written by JUBEI-CHAN THE NINJA GIRL's Akitaro Daichi and broadcast on Japanese TV while the latter show was still on-air. As with *Jubei-chan*, Daichi takes an old favorite (in this case Moonshadow, a wandering samurai originally popularized by heartthrob Jushiro Konoe, star of *Zatoichi Challenged* and *Sworn Brothers*), switches the character's sex, and gives her a gimmicky favorite food in place of any personality. Ran Tsukikage is a wandering samurai *lady*, righting wrongs and doing good deeds all around Japan, accompanied by Miao, a female specialist in Chinese kung fu. Tsukikage likes drinking sake and eating bean-curd dregs (see AKANE-CHAN)—a meal that *Newtype*, without a scrap of irony, recommended its readers

eat in front of the TV for the ultimate viewing experience.

CASEBOOK OF CHARLOTTE HOLMES, THE *
1977. JPN: *Jo-O Heika no Petit [sic] Angie*. AKA: *Her Royal Majesty's Petite Angie; Angie Girl*. TV series. DIR: Fumio Kurokawa, Shinya Yamada. SCR: Yu Yamamoto, Hikaru Arai. DES: Motosuke Takahashi, Yasushi Tanaka. ANI: Yasushi Tanaka. MUS: Hiroshi Tsutsui. PRD: Ashi Pro, Nippon Animation, TV Asahi. 30 mins. x 26 eps.
Angie Islington is a smart and courageous girl, the daughter of an English aristocrat. After she solves the mystery of Queen Victoria's missing ring at a garden party, she is thanked by the monarch in person and awarded the title "Petite Angie"—why this is supposed to impress anyone, we don't know. Thenceforth, she is given permission to work with Scotland Yard as a royal investigator. Angie helps the incompetent Inspector Jackson and his hunky blonde assistant Michael in solving many other crimes.

If ever any proof was needed of the bizarre fates of Japanese animation, this show is it. Originally conceived by Takara Planning as the tale of a gypsy girl traveling Spain in search of her mother (compare to BELLE AND SEBASTIAN, or FROM THE APENNINES TO THE ANDES), it somehow transformed in pre-production into a British detective drama. The series was subsequently screened across Europe and the Arab world, but it was released in America in a strangely edited compilation, in which live actors playing the great detective Sherlock Holmes and his companion Doctor Watson introduce episodes from the casebook of his supposed "relative" Charlotte. That interpretation had nothing to do with the original creators' intent, but then again, neither did the salacious fanbase that Angie somehow attracted, making her one of the poster girls of the early "Lolita Complex" movement in Japan. Compare to SHERLOCK HOUND. More intentional adventures of a sleuth's relative can be found in HERCULE POIROT AND MISS MARPLE.

Angie's surname is pronounced "Airington" in Japanese, leading us to believe that the creators picked it out from a London street map, unaware that the "s" in the district of Islington is not silent.

Note also that in the original Japanese title *petit* is lacking the feminine suffix, an issue in French grammar that also escaped the original creators of **PETITE COSSETTE**. It should perhaps also be noted that *Jo-O Heika no 007* (*Her Majesty's 007*) is the Japanese title for the James Bond film *On Her Majesty's Secret Service*, from which this show's original title may ultimately derive. For a sense of just how much can change in audience expectations over the next few decades, see **MILKY HOLMES**.

CASSHAN: ROBOT HUNTER *

1973. JPN: *Jinzo Ningen Casshan*. AKA: *Android Casshan*. TV series, video. DIR: Hiroshi Sasagawa. SCR: Junzo Toriumi, Akiyoshi Sakai, Takao Koyama, Toshio Nagata. DES: Tatsuo Yoshida, Yoshitaka Amano. ANI: Masayuki Hayashi, Chuichi Iguchi. MUS: Shunsuke Kikuchi. PRD: Tatsunoko, Fuji TV. 25 mins. x 35 eps. (TV1), 30 mins. x 4 eps. (v), 25 mins. x 24 eps. (TV2).

As an artificial human project nears completion, robot BK-1 is activated early by a bolt of lightning that damages its sense of morals. It leads a group of killer robots in the attempted destruction of the world, and its remorseful creator Kotaro Azuma cybernetically augments his son, Tetsuya, to fight them, with his canine companion, Friender, and love interest, Luna, whose passion for the hero is doomed to frustration because he is technically no longer human. In this follow-up to Tatsunoko's successful **BATTLE OF THE PLANETS**, Tetsuya's mother is turned into Swanee the electronic swan to deliver messages and increase his angst. Meanwhile, instead of a fiery phoenix warplane, Friender would transform into a variety of vehicles to suit his master's needs.

After the similar stories of *Terminator* and *Robocop* reached Japan, a sequel of sorts followed in the video series *New Android Casshan* (1993), directed by Hiroyuki Fukushima from a screenplay by Fukushima and Sho Aikawa, with Yasuomi Umezu as designer. The new series, which was the one released in the U.S., picks up the story after the "Burai King" and his robot army have defeated humanity's main forces. Tetsuya, still tortured over the loss of humanity no matter how good the cause, is forced to rescue Luna when she is captured by the Black Gang.

The story was resurrected as the subject of the live-action film *Casshern* (2004), in which debut moviemaker Kazuaki Kiriya found a job for his wife, the pop idol Hikaru Utada, but seemed happy with a script that could have been scrawled on the back of a beermat. It returned once more in anime form as Shigeyasu Yamauchi's TV series *Casshern Sins* (2008), a 24-episode reboot that commences with the world in a post-apocalyptic state after a robot revolution has supplanted humankind, or rather a *post*-post-apocalyptic state, with the Earth succumbing to corrosive poisons unleashed during the conflict and a repentant Casshern ruing the day that he followed his robot ruler's orders and seemingly killed Luna. The story progresses through a series of thorny ethical SF confrontations, not the least being the suggestion that Luna's great innovation was the perfection of immortality treatments and that the robots rose up in protest at the likely environmental costs of an eternally expanding human population.

CAST AWAY: BLUE LOTUS ISLAND

2007. JPN: *Nagasarete Airantou*. AKA: *Casted* [sic] *Away—Airan Island*. TV series. DIR: Hideki Okamoto. SCR: Mamiko Ikeda, Masaharu Amiya, Sayuri Oba. DES: Naoto Hosoda, Michie Watanabe. ANI: Naoto Hosoda, Shinichi Tatsuta, Takashi Maruyama, Kazuhisa Nakamura. MUS: Hiromi Mizutani. PRD: feel, Starchild Records. 25 mins. x 26 eps.

Ikuto runs away from home after a fight with his father, gets on a cruise ship, then falls overboard in a terrible storm. He washes up on an uncharted island where the population consists solely of girls. Despite the fact that they have no problem getting hold of clothes, accessories, books, and other goodies thanks to the currents that carry abandoned goods in from the outside world, those same currents can't carry anyone or anything out past the whirlpools and tornadoes. And although all but one of the girls on the island are throwing themselves at him, Ikuto is fated to marry the one who isn't. Yes, we're castaways in a harem show (**ROMANCE AND DRAMA**), in the hands of people who think that a reasonable "English" **TRANSLATION** of the title is *Casted Away*. This one is based on Takeshi Fujishiro's manga, ongoing since 2002, with a three-volume book spin-off in 2004 before this anime adaptation. It's also reminiscent of a 1958 Vic Damone hit, *The Only Man on the Island*, covered by Britain's Tommy Steele in the same year, which would function as both an alternate title for this show and a comprehensive plot synopsis.

CASTLE FANTASIA

2003. Video. DIR: Mamoru Yakoshi. SCR: Yuji Shibuya. DES: Megumi Ishihara. ANI: Akihiro Asanuma. MUS: N/C. PRD: Studio e-go!, Museum Pictures/Milky. 30 mins. x 3 eps.

For 200 years, the breakaway Republic of Ruciela has been fighting to keep its independence from Ingela, the nation that worships the god of brightness. With staffing levels at an all-time low, even the pretty young maidens of Ruciela are prepared to put themselves on the frontline. Ducis, commander of the Rucielan troops, plans a surprise attack, for which he needs to use the pretty young female officer Silera as bait. Silera, traumatized by a series of earlier bad experiences, accepts her role without complaint. When she arrives at the enemy camp, she finds a group of enemy officers waiting for her and looking forward to torturing her with a series of torments. Later, Commander Huey, who protested Silera's treatment, is ordered to go on a combined mission with the 8th Holy Battalion, an infamous annihilation unit led by a female assassin. More sex, and more violence, in a pornographic fantasy anime based on a computer game by Kazue Yamamoto. **ⓁⓃⓋ**

CASTLE IN THE SKY *

1986. JPN: *Tenku no Shiro Laputa*. AKA: *Laputa: The Castle in the Sky*. Movie. DIR: Hayao Miyazaki. SCR: Hayao Miyazaki. DES: Hayao Miyazaki. ANI: Tsukasa Tannai. MUS: Joe Hisaishi. PRD: Nibariki, Tokuma, Studio Ghibli. 124 mins.

Orphan Pazu dreams of following in his father's quest for the legendary flying city of Laputa. Another orphan, Sheeta, is linked to the city by the power of her strange necklace, which saves her life when she falls from an airship. Sheeta's necklace is a fragment of the legendary Levitation Stone that keeps cities like Laputa in the air, and chief of secret police Muska, a fellow descendant of Laputans, wants it for his own ends. Muska steals the stone to guide him to Laputa, and the children join forces with Ma Dola, matriarch of the Dola pirate clan—Sheeta in search of her stone, and the Ma Dola pirates in search of treasure. Laputa turns out to be a peaceful ruin that seems to have been abandoned by its inhabitants with only three extant robots still operational and tending the overgrown gardens (shades here of Douglas Trumbull's *Silent Running*). Muska seizes control of Laputa's weapon system, which he claims was the original device used to smite cities in Biblical times. Realizing he cannot be stopped, Sheeta and Pazu speak the magical words to destroy the city, though the levitation stone carries the ruins to a higher, safer altitude beyond human reach.

Taking themes from an aborted earlier project that was eventually made in his absence as **SECRET OF BLUE WATER**, Miyazaki mixed these with elements of **GULLIVER'S TRAVELS** and images from his tour of Wales after the miners' strike. With a believably human cast bickering over the remnants of the old order, only to eventually destroy it, it shares many elements with both its predecessor **NAUSICAÄ** and Miyazaki's later **PRINCESS MONONOKE**. Shown on a double bill with two episodes of Miyazaki's TV series, **SHERLOCK HOUND**. In addition to the widely available Buena Vista release featuring the voices of Anna Paquin and James Van Der Beek, a lesser known 1980s dub also exists, commissioned by Tokuma and broadcast several times in English-speaking territories. This earlier variant is sometimes erroneously credited to Streamline Pictures but was solely a Tokuma production, which Streamline distributed.

CASTLE OF CAGLIOSTRO *

1979. JPN: *Lupin III: Cagliostro no Shiro*. Movie. DIR: Hayao Miyazaki. SCR: Hayao Miyazaki, Haruya Yamazaki. DES: Yasuo Otsuka. ANI: Yasuo Otsuka. MUS: Yuji Ono. PRD: TMS. 100 mins.

One year after *The Secret of Mamo* (see **LUPIN III**), the master thief Lupin has successfully evaded Inspector Zenigata's clutches and is planning a new heist. When he inadvertently steals fake money, Lupin realizes that the high-quality printing plates are worth more than the money itself. He tracks down the counterfeiters to the tiny European state of Cagliostro but

is soon distracted by the approaching wedding of Count Cagliostro and Clarice, the last princess of the ruling family.

As strings strike up straight out of "Papa Was a Rolling Stone," and amid filmic nods to *The 39 Steps* and other famous caper movies, it's Lupin and his gang against the world, with cross and double-cross, as the thieves shop each other to the cops and change their minds about what they should be stealing (Lupin alone goes from money to plates to a bride in the course of the film). Supposedly inspired by the wedding of Grace Kelly to Prince Rainier of Monaco, the film also draws on one of Kelly's most memorable movies, *To Catch a Thief*, and Maurice Leblanc's 1924 Lupin novel *Countess Cagliostro*. From the opening casino heist to the Chaplinesque duel inside a giant clock, this is a superbly paced crime caper and Lupin's best screen outing. First-time movie director Miyazaki would reuse many of the ideas later in his career, including the Mediterranean Riviera setting of **PORCO ROSSO**, a courageous nature-loving princess in **NAUSICAÄ**, a friendly hound in **KIKI'S DELIVERY SERVICE**, and mossy ruins in **CASTLE IN THE SKY**. The film also lifted an idea from Miyazaki's work on **TREASURE ISLAND**—the fabled Cagliostro treasure is hidden at the bottom of an artificial lake. Surprisingly, the *Lupin* franchise lay dormant for several years afterward, not revived until the third TV series in 1984.

CAT PLANET CUTIES *

2008. JPN: *Asobi ni Ikuyo!* AKA: *We've Come To Play: Bombshells from the Sky*. TV series, video. DIR: Yoichi Ueda. SCR: Katsuhiko Takayama. DES: Noriko Morishima, Hiroshi Kato. ANI: Noriko Morishima. MUS: Tomoki Kikuya. PRD: AIC PLUS+, AT-X, Lantis, Media Factory, Pony Canyon, Klockworx. 24 mins. x 12 eps. (TV), ?? mins. (v).

Earth has been getting strange messages from space. An alien craft has been spotted. Where will it land? At a local festival in Okinawa. What will the aliens do? Well, Eris the feline emissary of planet Catia sets up her embassy in ordinary guy Kio's house (**URUSEI YATSURA**). Kio already has two girls in his life and neither Manami nor Aoi appreciates a curvy catgirl with a relaxed attitude to clothing moving in. Throw in dogbots (including one modeled

on Hanna-Barbera's Muttley), NATO, the CIA, a self-appointed pope, a military maid, mini-robots, and antimatter hammers, and you have the basic ingredients for a show that could have been a complete dog's breakfast but instead will leave you chuckling like a cat that's got a nice little helping of cream.

Kio is so timid that it's hard to imagine why any female would fancy him, let alone a fickle and frisky feline, but that's the function of a harem hero (**ROMANCE AND DRAMA**)—to make any loser feel he could have a chance with girls like that. True, it's a harem show with fan service, but it's also silly and anarchic enough to be entertaining, and it has some epic battle sequences. The writing is tight and simple, the action moves along crisply, and the animation is satisfyingly smooth and expensive-looking. Not since **CATGIRL NUKUNUKU** have catfights with actual cats been as much fun as this. Based on Okina Kamino's 2003 light-novel series, illustrated by Hodeneizo, the show also has a 2006 manga precursor with art by 888, who also worked on the *Dream Club Destiny* manga spin-off. The 2011 video from the same team is set on Okinawa's beautiful beaches, where a gambling spree leads to Eris and her catgirl chums betting their clothes.

CAT RETURNS, THE *

2002. JPN: *Neko no Ongaeshi*. AKA: *Baron, The Cats Repay a Kindness*. Movie. DIR: Hiroyuki Morita. SCR: Reiko Yoshida. DES: Satoko Morikawa. ANI: Ei Inoue, Kazutaka Ozaki. MUS: Yuji Nomi. PRD: Studio Ghibli. 75 mins.

Ordinary schoolgirl Haru saves a cat from being run over by a truck; it was a strange cat, carrying a present, but even so she's very surprised to find it was the Prince of Cats. Haru is soon showered with feline gifts, including cattails in the yard, pockets full of catnip, and even live mice. However, the prince's kingly father determines that the only way to truly reward her is for her to marry the cat prince. She looks for help, and finds it in the suave shape of Baron, owner of the Cat Business Office, who saves her from marriage but steals a bit of her heart in the process—compare to similar romantic attachment in **HOWL'S MOVING CASTLE** and, most obviously, **CATNAPPED**, which also features a visitor who must escape from a feline dimension before being trapped there forever. This is a nicely crafted movie that would be a major achievement for many other studios, but it only ranks as a minor Ghibli work, substituting whimsy for the overwhelming power of the studio's best output. There's a slight story link to **WHISPER OF THE HEART**, but no need to see it first to enjoy this—supposedly this story is one of those written by Shizuku, the protagonist of the other movie. Both are based on manga by Aoi Hiiragi, this one originating in *Baron: Neko no Danshaku (Baron: Baron of Cats)*. Released in Japanese theaters with episode 2 of **GHIBLIES**.

CAT SHIT ONE *

2009. AKA: *Apocalyse Meow*. Video. DIR: Kazuya Sasahara. SCR: Hiroshi Sekisaki. DES: Tomohisa Ishikawa. ANI: Manabu Konno, Masaki Suyama, Yuta Takeuchi, Naoki Kumazawa, Shinji Tsutsumi. MUS: N/C. PRD: anima inc., IDA Entertainment. 22 mins.
Botasky and Perky are mercenaries. They first met in Vietnam as members of an American reconnaissance group code-named Cat Shit One, and were forged by the terror of jungle warfare into a tight unit. Now they're in another, much more recent war, in the Iranian desert, on a rescue mission. Two civilian hostages are being held by the enemy and our heroes have to get them out. So far, so *Call of Duty*—except that the Iranians are camels and the American forces are cute fluffy bunnies with incongruous hard-man voices.

Motofumi Kobayashi's manga, released in English as *Apocalyse Meow*, first appeared in 1998. A sequel, *Cat Shit One '80*, followed in 2008, bringing Perky into the war on terror. Playing on the coincidence between the word for rabbit in Japanese (*usagi*) and the acronyms U.S.A. + G.I., *Cat Shit One* is a compelling, funny exercise in computer animation, with realistic fur effects, grainy desert simulations, and excellent movement. Shooter game fans rave over the superb level of detail, the accuracy of the weapons and tactics, and the impeccable sound effects. It's built a cult following for its intriguing concept and motion capture, treated to move in a presumably realistic fashion for bipedal rabbits. It swiftly went viral on the Internet,

as was its makers' intention, creating a brief and enthusiastic buzz for what many assumed would be a feature film project or 12-part series. Instead, it is an entertaining calling card—with no funding forthcoming, it remains in this form, although many casual anime viewers assume that they simply haven't got round to seeing the "complete" version yet.

CAT SOUP *

1999. JPN: *Nekojiru Gekijo*. TV series, video. DIR: Hiroshi Fukutomi. SCR: Hajime Yamano. DES: Masaaki Yuasa. ANI: Michiko Iwa, Masaaki Yuasa. MUS: N/C. PRD: Kent House, TV Asahi. 2 mins. x 27 eps. (TV), 34 mins. (v).
Troubled tales of cat antics, with character designs that resemble the insipid treacle of **HELLO KITTY**, but with far more menacing undertones. Based on the manga written by Hajime Yamano and drawn by his wife "Nekojiru," the series aired in small segments as part of the *Bokusho Mondai Boss Chara Ou* TV series, but was considered too hard-hitting even for late-night TV, though it was brought back to video following Nekojiru's suicide in 2000. If anything, this makes the video release, *Nekojiru* (2001), even more disturbing, since the story features a brother cat, Nyaata, who fights to stop Death from taking away his sister Nyaako, only for the quarreling boys to tear her in half. Only the later video was released in the U.S.

CAT TOWN

2006. JPN: *Nekomachi*. Video. DIR: Shojiro Urahama. SCR: N/C. DES: Etsuko Kanaida. ANI: N/C. MUS: Kaita Shogo. PRD: Toei Animation. 42 mins.
A tale of a world where cats are the dominant species isn't new in anime (**NIGHT ON THE GALACTIC RAILROAD**). This story of human life viewed through the distancing lens of anthropomorphism is based on the 1935 novel by Sakutaro Hagiwara and is part of Toei's *Ga-nime* line (**ARGOT AND JARGON**). The intention is to bring stories to life through limited animation, music, and narration, leaving artists, directors, and composers considerable freedom to interpret the piece they work on. The story is narrated by award-winning musician and poet Ko Machida, over a succession of images by Kanaida, as in Yoshitaka Amano's **BIRD SONG**, which is part of the same series.

Director Urahama has a mainstream career editing commercials.

CAT'S EYE

1983. TV series. DIR: Toshio Takeuchi, Yoshio Hayakawa, Hiroshi Fukutomi. SCR: Keisuke Fujikawa, Tomoko Konparu. DES: Akio Sugino. ANI: Satoshi Hirayama, Nobuko Tsukada. MUS: Kazuo Otani. PRD: TMS, Nippon TV. 25 mins. x 73 eps.
Artist Michael Heinz disappears along with his antique collection, parts of which keep turning up in the holdings of criminal connoisseurs. His three daughters, Rui, Hitomi, and Ai Kisugi, secretly become the "Cat's Eye" team to steal the artworks back, hoping to locate their father in the process. Detective Toshio Utsumi is assigned to crack the cat-burglar case, unaware that his girlfriend, Hitomi, is one of the thieves he is tracking. Only his lovelorn assistant, Mitsuko, suspects, though since the coffee bar opposite the police station, run by Hitomi, is called the Cat's Eye, it's difficult to see how Toshio qualified for detective.

Compared by *Animage* to an all-girl **LUPIN III**, Tsukasa Hojo's sexy trio of leotard-wearing cat burglars struck a chord in *Shonen Jump*, where they ran for 18 manga volumes between 1981 and 1984. The series was no less successful netting male as well as female viewers, albeit for different reasons, with its mix of crime and passion. The theme song was also a hit in its own right, selling 800,000 copies. The initial 36 episodes were followed in 1985 by a second season, directed by Kanetsugu Kodama, which gradually refocused on the farcical love comedy between Hitomi and Toshio and was played more for laughs. Though there was no real ending to the TV series, the manga eventually closed with the girls revealing their identities and running for the U.S. Belatedly demonstrating a genuine skill in detection, Toshio leaves his job and tracks them down, "capturing" his true love with a wedding ring where handcuffs had failed.

The girls would return for a live-action TV special in 1988 and a live-action feature in 1997, directed by *Zipang*'s Kaizo Hayashi. Presumably with an eye on the Hong Kong market, the film adds a Triad boyfriend for Ai (**STREET FIGHTER II** *Zero*'s Kane Kosugi), who is ordered to kill off the Cat's Eye team, and a climactic shootout at the Triad's restaurant headquarters, where the elusive Heinz is held prisoner. *Cat's Eye* characters would also have occasional cameos in Hojo's later CITY HUNTER. There was also a porno pastiche, *Cat's Ai [Love]: Milky Girl* (1985), released straight to video.

CAT'S NIBBLES

1992. JPN: *Yoyo no Neko Tsumami.* AKA: *Yoyo's Cat Nibbles.* TV series. DIR: Masami Anno, Yorifusa Yamaguchi, Katsumi Arima. SCR: Takao Koyama, Makoto Narita. DES: N/C. ANI: Yorifusa Yamaguchi. MUS: N/C. PRD: Visual 80, Nippon TV. 2 mins. x 15 eps.
Six cats introduce unusual snacks in this compilation of short culinary program bumpers, featuring a map of the cats' home island and data on each character.

CATBLUE: DYNAMITE

2006. Video. DIR: Romanov Higa. SCR: Romanov Higa. DES: Romanov Higa, Kaisei Kishi, Kai Nakabayashi, KODAMA. ANI: Romanov Higa, Tact Aoki, Tetsuya Watanabe, NAGI. MUS: Koji Matsuo, ping pong music, Rei Kudo. PRD: Fujiyama Project, Ingram, Organic, Romanov Films, Wedge Holdings. 42 mins.
Blue is a weird kind of girl. She's got cat ears and a tail and she can see ghosts. The dead can tell you things the living can't, or won't. And a tail with fine control means you can handle three guns at once. When two couriers are ambushed for the sake of some information on a Frank Sinatra cassette tape, Blue steps in because they're her friends.

In case you didn't get the cassette tape reference, we're in the dark underbelly of the late 1970s. The music, the flared trousers, the American cars, the stereotypical characters all shriek American pop culture, though the catgirl and a J-Lo reference may throw the pickier cultural historians off the scent. This show was made in 3D CGI for online streaming, and originally dubbed into English with Japanese subtitles. It was supposedly intended as the pilot for a series, but never made it—see CAT SHIT ONE for a similar calling card. This "first" episode shows the best and worst of online animation—it has stacks of interesting ideas, fluid action scenes, and some good fights, but also cheesy acting and some poor animation.

Director Higa had already made URDA THIRD REICH and was scheduled to direct the canceled *Appleseed: Genesis* TV series (APPLESEED). Overall it feels like a missed opportunity. ◐

CATGIRL NUKUNUKU *

1992. JPN: *Banno Bunka Neko Musume Nukunuku.* AKA: *All Purpose Cultural Cat Girl Snuggly-Wuggly.* Video, TV series. DIR: Yuji Moriyama, Hidetoshi Shigematsu. SCR: Yuzo Takada, Katsuhiko Chiba. DES: Yuzo Takada. ANI: Yuji Moriyama. MUS: Hiro Matsuda and Beat Club. PRD: Animate Film. 30 mins. x 6 eps. (v1), 25 mins. x 14 eps. (TV), 25 mins. x 12 eps. (v2).
Ryunosuke (Ryan in the U.K. dub) loses his beloved pet kitten in an accident, only for his scientist father, Dr. Natsume, to place the creature's brain inside a sexy android body. This is just one of many treats designed to keep the boy's mind off his parents' divorce, but Ryunosuke and his new pal Nukunuku are soon caught up in a bitter custody battle between his crazy inventor father and his mother, Akiko, who owns Japan's largest military conglomerate. She regularly sends her minions, Arisa and Kyoko, to kidnap Ryan, only to be foiled by the innocent activities of Nukunuku, also intended as a bodyguard for her endangered master.

With the massive collateral damage of PROJECT A-KO, an anime ingenue whose feline origins go right back to Tezuka's BAGHI, and a surprisingly accurate study of marital breakup that still has bite even if played for laughs, *Catgirl Nukunku* was based on a minor work by 3X3 EYES–creator Yuzo Takada, and it is one of a limited number of anime that exist in two translations. A British dub of episodes 1–3 was the sole release from Crusader Video, who aimed to dispel the U.K. media's view that all anime were perverse, although they had to excise a masturbation scene before they could achieve the general rating their PR required. U.S. distributors AD Vision were less coy, running the entire series both uncut and in a feature-length "movie" edit.

Nukunuku jumped to TV Tokyo in 1997 for a 14-part series directed by Yoshitaka Fujimoto that retold the story from the beginning. In 1998, the franchise was revived with the same crew for the 12-part straight-to-video *Nukunuku Dash!,* looking suspiciously like the tail end of a canceled TV series.

CATNAPPED! *

1995. JPN: *Totsuzen! Neko no Kuni Banipal Witt.* AKA: *Suddenly! Catland Banipal Witt.* Movie. DIR: Takashi Nakamura. SCR: Chiaki Konaka, Takashi Nakamura. DES: Takashi Nakamura. ANI: Takashi Nakamura, Mamoru Kurosawa. MUS: Shigeaki Saegusa. PRD: Triangle Staff, Pioneer. 75 mins.
When his pet dog, Papadoll, goes missing, lazy fifth-grader Yasuo (nicknamed "Toriyasu") is taken to the magical world of Banipal Witt, where both he and his precocious younger sister, second-grader Miko, are transformed into cats. Do-do, the brightest pupil of magician Sandada, has been turned to the dark side and now serves Bubarina, the cursed princess and would-be world conqueror, whose touch turns people into balloons. The pair have kidnapped Papadoll and turned him into a monster that menaces the whole kingdom, and Toriyasu must stop him before sunrise, when he too will be transformed. Earthlings (including dogs) can only be in Banipal Witt for two days before the sunlight will turn them into monsters. Toriyasu and Miko are there for two days before Sandada completes his magical pill that will put Papadoll to sleep, so that Toryasu can attach his chain to his collar, and hence restore him to normality. Returning Papadoll to canine form, the children use the magic cat's-paw talisman to restore normalcy and are rushed home before sunrise on the third day by the feline trio that brought them to Banipal Witt in the first place. Only three minutes have passed on Earth, but as the kids head off for a normal day at school, they are accosted once more by cats from Banipal Witt in search of help with another crisis.

Featuring a fondant world spinning in the light of a gold paper sun, marshmallow skies, balloon cats, giant floating mice, and even a girl with kaleidoscope eyes in Bubulina, *Catnapped!* is a hallucinogenic mixture of *Yellow Submarine* and ALICE IN WONDERLAND that ultimately fails through its dispassionate precision. The candy-striped design and childish worldview seem almost calculatedly endearing, but no amount of brainstorming and focus groups can make up for true magic such as Miyazaki's **MY NEIGHBOR TOTORO**, which *Catnapped!* would very much like to be. For its U.S. release, Pioneer preferred to play up the writers' connections to **AKIRA** and **ARMITAGE III**, a sure sign that they doubted its stand-alone status within the children's cartoon market.

CAZADOR DE LA BRUJA, EL

2007. JPN: *El Cazador*. AKA: *The Witch Hunter*. TV series. DIR: Koichi Mashimo. SCR: Kenichi Kanemaki, Hiroyuki Kawasaki, Satoru Nishizono. DES: Yoko Kikuchi, Kenji Teraoka, Masashi Koizuka, Yoshimi Umino. ANI: Yoko Kikuchi, Daisuke Endo. MUS: Yuki Kajiura. PRD: Bee Train, d-rights, Flying Dog. 24 mins. x 26 eps.

South of the border, down fantasy way, bounty hunter Nadie is on the trail of a murdering witch. Ellis, the suspect, is accused of killing a top physicist named Heinrich Schneider, who was her guardian. But when Nadie catches up with her target, she finds a cute, helpless creature who has no control over her magical abilities and few memories of her past. The hard-bitten bounty hunter, influenced by her own tragic past—she was the sole survivor of an attack on her hometown—decides to help her former target. The pair set off through old Mexico together in search of a lost city and a mysterious Inca jewel that may hold the key to Ellis's past, pursued by Nadie's boss, her ex-client, an old colleague, gangsters, and others, all out to grab Ellis for reasons as yet unexplained. Along the road, love blossoms between the two.

It's a Bee Train anime about girls with guns, so you know what to expect—both in terms of the animation quality, which is never less than acceptable and often good, and the plot, which is frequently silly and padded out with good-humored vignettes and incidents whose sole purpose is cuteness. Adapted from Shu Hirose's 2007 manga, the Indiana-Jones-meets-spaghetti-Western scenario is grafted onto a main character set out of **MADLAX** or **NOIR**, with a denouement and a villain borrowed from **SECRET OF BLUE WATER**. The overall pace is slow, giving you plenty of time to enjoy Kajiura's sparky score (listen for the Ennio Morricone references) and the beautiful background art. **NV**

CENCOROLL

2009. Movie. DIR: Atsuya Uki. SCR: Takashi Yamashita, Atsuya Uki. DES: N/C. ANI: Atsuya Uki. MUS: supercell. PRD: Anime Innovation Tokyo, Aniplex. 30 mins.

When a giant monster shows up atop a building in Yuki's hometown the Japanese Self-Defense Force roars into action, unaware that they are actually crashing a private party—a showdown between two boys and their magical pets, common in such shows as **BAKUGAN** and **POKÉMON**. Yuki's friend Tetsu found an alien shapeshifter named Cenco a while ago and has been keeping it secretly at his home. Now another boy with an alien pet has shown up to challenge them.

This virtual one-man show premiered at Canada's Fantasia International Film Festival before opening in Tokyo the following month. Uki based the scenario on his one-shot manga *Amon Game*; this was the first time Aniplex backed a project so wholly dependent on one person to carry it through, and luckily Uki has delivered an interesting piece. The sparing use of music and background sound make for an atmosphere of eerie calm, while the style and design are fresh and engaging. Like Makoto Shinkai's one-man debut on **VOICES OF A DISTANT STAR**, this is too short for the lack of character development to be a problem, and Uki throws in some quirky, original touches. He has since designed the characters for **TSURITAMA**.

CENSORSHIP AND LOCALIZATION

EARLY ANIME were subjected to the same restrictions as any other films screened in Japanese theaters, with the first documented case of conflict with the authorities occurring as early as 1917, when Junichi Kouchi's short cartoon *Playful Boy's Air Gun* (*Chamebo: Kukiju no Maki*) was seized on the grounds it would "encourage children to misbehave." As Japan entered the "Fifteen Years War" of 1931–45 (**WARTIME ANIME**), censorship was increasingly applied to any film not deemed to be in the service of the state. The left wing was the first to feel the pinch, with the seizure of Tetsuo Kitagawa's *Slave War* (1931, *Dorei Senso*), which depicted the peoples of Asia throwing off imperialist chains, including Chinese resisting the Japanese. Erotica was also deemed to be corruptive, and

Hakusan Kimura's *Cool Ship* (1932, *Suzumibune*) was seized by the authorities partway through production and lost for decades, before turning up in a police archive in the early 21st century. Politics remained a far more likelier censorship issue than sex until the U.S. Occupation period, when anti-Communist paranoia led to the cancellation of Mitsuyo Seo's feature **THE KING'S TAIL** (1949).

Different cultural expectations have led to many conflicts over TV anime. Osamu Tezuka is largely to blame, not for any malicious intent, but for his perennial insistence that cartoons should be permitted to deal with themes beyond fairy-tale cliché. Six episodes of Tezuka's **ASTRO BOY** were deemed unfit for American consumption, although the localizer Fred Ladd was able to salvage three of them with judicious editing. The reasons for rejections included pictures of nude women in a bachelor's apartment, or a story line that featured animal vivisection, regarded as too hard hitting for a young audience. Most controversially, the episode "Christ's Eyeball" featured a doomed priest leaving a secret message to investigators while being held hostage by criminals in his church. A plot concerning words scratched into the eyes of a statue of Christ was considered too difficult to sell to an American audience, although it had passed without comment in Japan.

Although Tezuka worked directly with his American distributors on **KIMBA THE WHITE LION**, corporate interference continued, altering both the name of his lead character and Tezuka's wish for fatal consequences to deadly actions. Part of the story's contemporary charm lies in the number of times a character is plainly killed, only for an American voice-over to assure us they are "only resting." The character of Leo/Kimba also had to deal with a confusion verging on a Jekyll and Hyde standoff between his heroic duties and his carnivorous, bestial nature. Little of this survives in the American soundtrack, although Kimba can be seen onscreen barely keeping himself from tearing his opponents apart. In a nod to the directives for liberal awareness at NBC, Tezuka was also obliged to make all of Kimba's evil opponents white, despite the African setting. Compare to other racially motivated alterations in the later **Saber Rider and the Star Sheriffs**, which in the American version replaced the original Asian lead with his angry white sidekick, or **Gigantor**, which lost its prewar subplot and gory deaths in its American incarnation. Three episodes were dropped from **Marine Boy**'s American broadcast, and yet it was still decried by the National Association of Broadcasters as a glaring example of unacceptable violence.

Many of the complaints leveled against anime in the 1970s were reflected within the Japanese industry itself—it was, after all, no less a figure than Hayao Miyazaki who despaired of the formulaic combats and conflicts of children's entertainment in the 1970s. The rise of cross-promotion (**Advertising and Sponsorship**) also made television anime even more commercial. The phrase "my father gave me a robot" was no longer a concise description of many serials' plotlines; it was also a litany designed to pester parents into buying tie-in toys for their children. Robots, meanwhile, became a handy device in anime for children, as did laser guns and other nonexistent weapons—robots and faceless minions are more disposable and less subject to complaints than real humans in jeopardy, while non-imitable weaponry gets past a censor more swiftly than something that a child can pick up and use from its everyday life. Hence, in cartoons all over the world, the conversion of real-world firearms into "laser guns"—even seen today in some episodes of **Gundam Seed**. Alcohol was also forbidden—**Star Blazers** featured a hard-drinking doctor whose sake was unconvincingly relabeled "spring water" in the English dub.

Outside Japan, cartoons in general were the subject of increased scrutiny, under revised MPAA guidelines not only in America, but also in other countries. It was, it seemed, no longer enough to remove the gorier moments from **Battle of the Planets**—many foreign commentators had realized that television was playing an increasing role as a babysitter, and that its message could prove damaging to young minds. In France, after Go Nagai's giant robot show **Grandizer** became a hit in the late 1970s, the academic Liliane Lurçat published the stinging *Five Years Old and Left Alone with Goldorak: The Young Child and TV* (*Cinq Ans, Seul Avec Goldorak: Le Jeun Enfant et la Télévision*, 1981). Her study, based on interviews with 110 children, was followed by that of would-be presidential candidate Ségolène Royal, whose *Discontent of the Baby Zappers* (*Ras-le-bol des Bébé Zappeurs*, 1989) was a polemic against television in general, citing Japanese animation among the most negative influences.

It was not lost on some critics that many cartoons were conceived as glorified commercials for toys and, perhaps worse for struggling economies, that these cheap imports had a foreign origin. Some elements of the animation industry began to take on a nationalist tone, with Filmation's *Bravestarr* (1987) ending with the legend: "Made in America by Americans!" Government affiliate networks in Britain and Scandinavia imposed restrictions on commercially oriented cartoons—removing not merely anime but any children's entertainment designed to sell toys to young consumers. However, the stance of the national channels was not necessarily mirrored in their commercial rivals. With some toy companies virtually giving away their tie-in cartoon series as loss-leaders, the temptation was great for some commercial channels. In France, for example, by fall 1988, two channels were running 30 French-dubbed Japanese cartoon series every week, while the other three national channels made it a matter of honor to focus on "European" material. In practice, however, the lines of division were not so clear: many of these works were either American imports via Britain or coproductions made with the Japanese. In fact, French producers had been working directly with the Japanese for the entire decade, ever since Jean Chalopin's **Ulysses 31** (1981), followed by **The Mysterious Cities of Gold** (1982). Similar deals led to Spain's **Dogtanian and the Three Muskehounds** (1981) and in Italy, the coproduction **Sherlock Hound** (1984) and specially commissioned extra episodes of **Dirty Pair**. Meanwhile, the German coproduction **Maya the Bee** (1975) had been translated and exported *north* to Scandinavia, so that by the time of the European furor over supposed imports, many were unaware that it was not a local product.

It was only with the arrival of video-based anime in the 1990s that anime truly ran into large difficulties in censorship, or rather, in film classification. Ironically, many of the most controversial titles had been conceived in Japan in order to circumvent *local* censorship problems. The **Lolita Anime** and **Cream Lemon** serials sexualized children, which was a contradiction in terms under Japanese legislation, and hence a loophole that could be exploited. This also neatly avoided a prohibition against pubic hair (in force until 1991). Similarly, since Japanese law specified that genitalia (and not other forms or organs) were off limits, **Urotsukidoji**'s cunning use of the tentacle ensured many graphic scenes, albeit ones that needed to find an excuse for tentacles, and thereby drifted toward tales of alien invasion and demonic possession. Since sexualized bondage does not necessarily involve concentration on genitals, this too was easier to get past the Japanese censor. The result, seen from the American end of distribution, was an avalanche of bizarre fetishes and practices, often committed by or against characters that appeared demonstrably underage.

The very absence of censorship in American pornography led to misunderstandings of its own. Japanese porn often obscures its characters' genitals with blurring or black dots, leading many animators to simply not bother drawing genitals in detail. When the digitized dots were removed for the "uncut" American edition, the organs revealed could often appear unformed, hairless, or incomplete, leading to further accusations of child pornography.

In Britain, anime became the subject of a press smear campaign, engineered to some degree by anime distributors themselves, who were able to benefit from rebellious teens' decision to find out what the newspapers did not want them to see. A brief boom in risqué anime followed, only to trail off when distributors exhausted the mother lode of titles—chiefly gothic horror like **Wicked City** from the Madhouse studio and a few of the tamer Pink Pineapple erotica releases, such as **Rei Rei**. Ironically, many anime in Britain were made to seem *more* objectionable than they really were, through the process of "fifteening," whereby excess swearing would be added to a dub in order to gain a higher, more controversial-seeming rating.

The last decade in Europe has seen a liberalization of censorship laws that has largely removed limitations on much pornography—in England, as in Germany, legalizing it has permitted the government to license and tax it. However, some anime pornography still remains problematic, since it depicts nonconsensual sex (i.e., rape), "imitable violence," or, by its very nature, sexual practices that are difficult (read: distasteful) for live-action performers. In other words, it is an inherent tendency in anime pornography to search for places that live-action pornography cannot go (be they locations, situations, acts, or angles), because otherwise live-action pornography will have already been there, and, quite literally, done that.

Such problems are less critical in the American market, where distributors can circumvent MPAA issues simply by not submitting their titles for certification. However, a considerable amount of American anime has still been subjected to alteration in a U.S. release. Most notable are the large numbers of translations that claim sailor-suited schoolgirls are at "college" (a term that means different things in different countries), or otherwise manipulate age declarations toward safer ground. The most noticeable example is Minnie May in GUNSMITH CATS—a former child prostitute and statutory rape victim in the original, whose age is advanced a few years in the American release of both manga and anime. Nor are American anime releases completely censorship-free. Scenes of underage sex were excised from the original release of KITE, and several pornographic anime are known to have had episodes dropped—e.g., FAMILY OF DEBAUCHERY and COUNTDOWN.

Anime in Japan in the late 1990s and beyond came to rely more on television as a distribution medium. Many of the short "TV series" sold to the American market began as late-night programs airing long past midnight, and can have content designed to match. Primetime television in Japan has become increasingly censorious since the mid-1990s, when controversial episodes of EVANGELION were broadcast without prior executive approval. The resultant timidity on the part of broadcasters

has played into the hands of the late-night shows and cable networks, with shows such as GANTZ enjoying two distinct existences: one in a widely available but edited form and another in a more graphic version requiring cable subscription or DVD rental. In the case of COWBOY BEBOP, the main story arc was only seen on WOWOW and DVDs—the version seen on terrestrial TV was missing 14 episodes.

POKÉMON and its successors heralded a resurgence of children's anime on foreign television and a return to some of the localization problems that troubled anime in the 1960s. There have also been new issues, such as the (logical) decision not to broadcast the infamous epilepsy-inducing episode of *Pokémon*. After a decade of largely adhering to original names (and indeed language) in anime for teenagers, character names in anime for the children's market are often localized. As the American edit is often the portal through which other language territories gain their anime, issues in localization can be passed on. Religious references remain as sensitive as they once were during the "Christ's Eyeball" incident—demonic imagery is airbrushed out and misused Bibles turned into nonspecific grimoires. Both DRAGON BALL and YU-GI-OH have featured trips to Hell, the precise identity and location of which was left vague in the American release. Nudity has also been an issue in American localization, with digitally added underpants, swimsuits, or strategically placed foreground items used to preserve the supposed blushes of the American audience. In localizing POKÉMON, this has included the removal of scenes in which a major character chases girls, and also any references to the fact that women might have breasts—a bikini competition, for example, or the use of fake boobs as a disguise. Some characters can be controversial abroad—the spoon-bending Pokémon creature Yungera (Kadabra in English) was the subject of an unsuccessful law suit by Uri Geller, and the Pokémon Jynx was dropped from some American episodes for being an unpleasant "Negro" racial stereotype until her skin color was changed to a respectable purple. The prospect of copyright infringement can still affect broadcasts—a Peter Pan pastiche episode of the new *Astro Boy* (2003) has never been

released in America, for fear of attracting legal reprisals from Disney.

References to alcohol and tobacco are still regularly removed, such as from the Cartoon Network broadcasts of TENCHI MUYO! and BLUE SUBMARINE NO. SIX, although recently this restriction appears to have tapered off, with the regular appearance of a pipe-smoking character in NARUTO. The sight of blood or of the death of main characters continues to be cut or altered. In cases where the cost of removing potentially offensive material becomes too prohibitive, an episode can be simply dropped, which sometimes leads to continuity issues further along in a series.

Anime in the 21st century is much easier to obtain in its unadulterated form, and even if viewers object to a dub, dual language tracks on the DVD release make it possible to hear the original Japanese. But for some in FANDOM, localization has become the new censorship, since it can alter a creator's original intent, and give new fans an inaccurate introduction to the shows they see. However, such issues in TRANSLATION are endemic to the medium, and have been debated since the first days anime left Japanese shores.

CERES: CELESTIAL LEGEND *

2000. JPN: Ayashi no Ceres. AKA: Mysterious Ceres. TV series. DIR: Hajime Kamegaki. SCR: Yukiyoshi Ohashi. DES: Hideyuki Motohashi. ANI: Hideyuki Motohashi. MUS: Ryo Sakai. PRD: Studio Pierrot, Bandai, WOWOW. 25 mins. x 24 eps.

Japanese twins Aya and Aki Mikage get a nasty shock at the approach of their joint 16th-birthday celebrations, when Aya discovers that she is the reincarnation of Ceres, an angelic being that was once tricked into marrying an Earthbound fisherman, and who bears a vengeful grudge against the descendants of the children she was forced to bear—the entire Mikage family. Hunted by her own family, Aya falls in with another reincarnated angel, while Aki gains the ability to manifest as "the Progenitor," that same fisherman who stole Ceres' feathered cloak and caused her suffering on Earth to begin in the first place. Based on a manga serialized in *Weekly Shojo Comic* by FUSHIGI YUGI creator Yu Watase, Ceres reunited many anime staff from the *FY* anime, for a story that combines the perennial obsessions of girls' comics—angels and CINDERELLA victimhood.

CERTAIN MAGICAL INDEX, A *

2008. JPN: *Toaru Majutsu no Kinsho Mokuroku*. AKA: *Index Librorum Prohibitum, Index of Forbidden Books*. TV, movie. DIR: Hiroshi Nishikiori. SCR: Masanao Akahoshi, Satoru Nishizono, Hiroyuki Yoshino. DES: Yuichi Tanaka, Tomonori Kuroda, Yoshinori Hirose, Lily Hoshino, Mika Akitaka. ANI: Yuichi Tanaka, Shinya Hasegawa, Yu Yamashita. MUS: I've, Maiko Iuchi. PRD: J.C.Staff, AT-X, Geneon Universal Entertainment, PROJECT-INDEX, Square Enix, ASCII Media Works, Kadokawa Contents Gate. 24 mins. x 24 eps. (TV1), 24 mins. x 24 eps. (TV2).

Toma has absolutely no powers of ESP—not such a handicap in a high-tech town like Academy City, even though this is a world where magic is very real. But he does have one highly valuable skill—the Imagine Breaker, a power that can negate any other magical power. One day he goes onto his balcony and finds a young nun, dressed all in white, hanging onto the railings. Her name is Index and she's on the run from that highly dangerous organization, the Church of England. She holds in her memory a perfect image of 103,000 banned magical books (compare to LIBRARY WAR). The stage is set for an epic battle between science and religion.

Unfortunately, this never happens, because this is a harem anime (ROMANCE AND DRAMA). Index herself is scarcely visible for much of the run and barely influences the plot. Instead, we have a series of story arcs involving minor characters and girls throwing themselves at Toma. Despite some very interesting concepts, the plot and dialogue are weak, and the art and animation are woefully inconsistent, varying from frankly inept to very exciting. Unfortunately, the inept goes on for longer. Even if there were not so much good anime around, this is not really worth the investment of 12 hours of your life unless you plan to reverse-engineer a couple of those fascinating ideas into your own writing.

Nevertheless, a second season followed in 2010 from the same team. Index is still on the run and Toma is still protecting her while juggling his harem. The 2013 movie *A Certain Magical Index: The Miracle of Endymion (Toaru Majutsu no Index: Endy-*

mion no Kiseki) involves Toma and Index befriending a girl with a wonderful singing voice, who looks set to cause that epic conflict between science and religion we were promised in the first series. Nishikiori returns to direct Hiroyuki Yoshino's script, and the TV team is otherwise unchanged apart from guest design credits for Lily Hoshino and Mika Akitaka. A manga to promote the series appeared in 2007, followed by a manga version of the movie, with art by Ryosuke Asakura, in 2013.

The series is based on Kazuma Kamachi's 2004 book series of the same name, illustrated by Kiyotaka Haimura. It's one of the top-selling "light novel" series in Japan, with over 14 million copies in circulation as of January 2013. All six volumes scored consistently high in paperback sales charts, with the first three all reaching the top slot. Kamachi's manga-turned-anime A CERTAIN SCIENTIFIC RAILGUN spun off this series, with the recurring theme of "Level 0" students—those with no ESP powers whatsoever—making good.

CERTAIN SCIENTIFIC RAILGUN, A *

2009. JPN: *Toaru Kagaku no Chodenjiho*. TV series, video. DIR: Tatsuyaki Nagai. SCR: Seishi Minakami, Hiroshi Onogi, Karasumi Sunayama, Miya Asakawa. DES: Yuichi Tanaka, Tomonori Kuroda. ANI: Yuichi Tanaka, Emiko Kobayashi, Yu Yamashita, Kazuhiro Muto, Kazuo Tomizawa, Hiroshi Tomioka. MUS: Maiko Iuchi. PRD: JC Staff, ASCII Media Works, AT-X, Geneon, MOVIC. 24 mins. x 24 eps. (TV1), 34 mins. (v), 24 mins. x 24 eps. (TV2).

Academy City is all about science and technology. It's said to be about three decades ahead of the rest of the world in terms of technology, and it's a young city: 80% of the residents are students. The main focus of their studies is the development and training of ESP, and students with low powers, or "Level 0" students with no powers at all, don't get into the elite establishments or land the top jobs. This means that some people will go to any lengths to enhance their own powers. We follow a group of four girls, close friends despite their different abilities, as they follow their day-to-day lives while sometimes getting caught up in the larger events unfolding around them.

Most of the structural problems of A CERTAIN MAGICAL INDEX are fixed in this

spin-off show. Two larger story arcs, one for each half of the series, run alongside a series of smaller arcs, allowing the characters and plot to develop while still maintaining a coherent structure. The second half is somewhat weaker than the first, but still pulls off a satisfactory finale. The balance of science and magic is well maintained, the characters are given their fair share of story time, the animation is better balanced, and the action sequences are good. Although the serials are linked by cameos and common settings, only completists need to watch the first one before this.

The ongoing manga *A Certain Scientific Railgun* with story and art by Motoi Fuyukawa spun off Kazuma Kamachi's light-novel series *A Certain Magical Index* in 2007. A video followed in 2010 and a new TV series, *A Certain Scientific Railgun S (Toaru Kagaku no Chodenjiho S)*, commenced in April 2013 with a run of 24 episodes. The S stands for sisters, and the plot revolves around cloning heroine Misaka to create an army of telepaths—whom she considers as sisters—for sinister purposes. **N**

CHALK-COLORED PEOPLE

1988. JPN: *Chalk-iro no People*. Video. DIR: Akira Kamiyama. SCR: Seizo Watase. DES: Seizo Watase. ANI: Keizo Kira. MUS: Astrud Gilberto. PRD: 3D. 54 mins.

Five short episodes from HEART COCKTAIL–creator Seizo Watase's romantic manga set to bossa nova music for reasons unknown. The stories include *"Building without Tide," "Brother and Sister," "Sometimes I'm Happy," "I've Saved the Sidecar for You,"* and *"The Santa Quartet."* The music is from Latin lounge legend Astrud Gilberto. A similar music/animation combination was tried the previous year with Watase's MY ALL-DAY ALL-COLOR, and later with TWO ON THE ROAD.

CHAMPION OF GORDIAN

1979. JPN: *Toshi Gordian*. AKA: *Gardian*. TV series. DIR: Shigeru Yanagawa, Masamune Ochiai. SCR: Masaru Yamamoto. DES: Ippei Kuri. ANI: Kazuhiko Udagawa. MUS: Masaaki Jinbo, Masayuki Yamamoto. PRD: Tatsunoko, Tokyo 12 Channel. 25 mins. x 73 eps.

Daigo Otaki and his pet mechanical leopard, Clint, are transferred to the Mecha Con Unit that protects the computer-run

Victor Town from the predations of the Madoctor Gang. However, he is abducted by the giant robot Gordian and meets his "sister," Saori, at Fort Santore, where he hears the voice of his own father issuing from the central computer that is making all the decisions. The run of this transforming robot story was extended several times, with Daigo eventually heading out for adventures in space with his robots Protteser, Delinger, and Garbin, whose similarity to the **MACHINE ROBO** line prompted Bandai to retool its existing molds in order to imply a relationship that wasn't there.

CHANCE POP SESSIONS *
2001. JPN: *Chance! Triangle Session*. Video. DIR: Susumu Kudo. SCR: Kazuhiko Soma. DES: Fumie Muroi. ANI: Kunio Kazuki, Yumiko Ishii. MUS: Avex, Goro Matsui. PRD: Madhouse, TV Tokyo. 25 mins. x 13 eps.
A group of girls hope to make it as performers—16-year-old street busker Yuki, large-breasted 17-year-old Akari, and prissy company director's daughter Nozomi. Based on a 1999 radio drama.

CHAOS;HEAD *
2008. TV series. DIR: Takaaki Ishiyama. SCR: Toshiki Inoue. DES: Shuichi Shimamura. ANI: Shuichi Shimamura. MUS: tOkyO. PRD: Madhouse, 5pb, KIDS STATION, VAP, yte. 27 mins. x 12 eps.
Amid the urban hustle of Tokyo's Shibuya district, Takumi Nishijo lives the life of a *hikikomori*—a "shut-in" retreating into self-imposed isolation, living in a freight container perched on top of a building, and going out only when necessary for school. Living his life through games and online characters, he suffers from powerful delusions, possibly the result of schizophrenia and certainly made stronger by his chosen lifestyle. One day a chatroom encounter leads him to a murder scene and his life begins to spiral out of control.

Sometimes Madhouse anime are brilliant. Sometimes they're **BLADE**. And sometimes they fall somewhere between the two because they're trying to do too much for too many audiences at once. *Chaos;Head* is one of those: a brilliant concept allowed to go astray in ways that should make such an experienced house hang its collective head in shame. Satoshi Kon was a master

of delusional character development—as witness **PERFECT BLUE** and **PAPRIKA**—but Inoue and Ishiyama play cheap magicians here, allowing Takumi to develop credibly and then suddenly throwing it all away and pulling a competent, capable hero-Takumi out of the hat. They also turn an exciting and credible SF concept into a harem show (**ROMANCE AND DRAMA**), only to ditch that idea, too. Even the animation quality isn't up to Madhouse's usual standards. Great ideas, wild plot twists, and the odd exciting battle are no substitute for consistency and coherent plotting.

The story is based on a 2008 "visual novel" (**ARGOT AND JARGON**) developed by 5pb and Nitroplus, adapted into three manga for three magazines in the same years. Artist Mutsumi Sasaki designed the game characters but was not involved with any of the manga. The anime adaptation aired from October to December and by spring 2009 the game had spread from its original PC platform to a number of others. The irritating central semi-colon, which has played havoc with online searches and spell-checks, is designed to tell fans that this is part of the "science adventure" series of games from 5pb: see also **STEINS;GATE** and **ROBOTICS;NOTES**.

CHARADY'S DAILY JOKE
2008. JPN: *Charady no Joke na Mainichi*. TV series. DIR: Ryuji Masuda. SCR: Daisuke Tengan. DES: various. ANI: various. MUS: Morihiro Iwamoto. PRD: Kyoto University of Art and Design. 4 mins. x 365 eps.
A short comedy anime about jokes from all over the world, each segment created by students from the character design department of Kyoto University of Art and Design. Two of them also take voice roles. Cute and underdressed lead character Charady (her name a mashup of "chara" and "parody") presents a new joke in every episode, helped by her strange pets Bath Buta and Chobotan. Senior director Masuda created **MR. STAIN ON JUNK ALLEY** and **FUNNY PETS**, the latter of which shares the same basic concept of a pretty girl with two weird pets. Light-hearted and enjoyable.

CHARGE AHEAD! MEN'S SCHOOL
1988. JPN: *Sakigake! Otoko Juku*. TV series. DIR: Nobutaka Nishizawa. SCR: Susumu Takaku. DES: Masami Suda. ANI: Masami

Suda. MUS: Shunsuke Kikuchi. PRD: Toei, Fuji TV. 25 mins. x 34 eps. (TV), 75 mins. (m).
Otoko Juku is the juvenile hall where men are sent for being too honorable and too manly, the kind of rough, tough academy one might expect from the team who made **FIST OF THE NORTH STAR**. Newcomers Momotaro, Genji, and Taio endure bullying and harsh treatment at the hands of class leader Onihige and the evil teachers.

Like Akira Miyashita's original 34-volume 1985 *Shonen Jump* manga, this show starts as a comedy but soon devolves into fights, the quality of animation dropping along with the story. It retained elements of its comedic past right to the end, however, with Momotaro reading out fake fan mail over the "next episode" shots and pretending to take requests. There was also a 1988 movie directed by Tetsuo Imazawa, in which the gang gets to trash Hawaii, Alaska, Niagara Falls, and Manhattan in a battle of wills with an evil mastermind.

In a bizarre footnote to the popularity of the manga in Asia, the former president of Taiwan, Lee Teng-hui, famously dressed up as the tough principal, Heihachi Edajima, in a publicity stunt for his newly founded cram school. **Ⓥ**

CHARGEMAN KEN
1974. TV series. SCR: Masaaki Wakuda, Toyohiro Ando. DES: Eiji Tanaka. ANI: Junji Mizumura. MUS: N/C. PRD: Knack, TBS. 10 mins. x 65 eps.
Average guy Ken Izumi can transform into Chargeman Ken by donning his special uniform, which augments his strength. In his all-terrain vehicle the Sky Rod, he fights to save Earth from the evil Geral alien invaders, who have traveled two million light years to wipe out humanity. His only assistants are his sister Caron and Balican, the mischievous robot dog. A staff reunion for many of the people who worked on **ASTRO GANGER**.

CHARGER GIRL JUDEN-CHAN *
2009. JPN: *Fight Ippatsu! Juden-chan*. TV series. DIR: Shinichiro Kimura. SCR: Yasutomo Yamada, Sumio Uetake, Tomoyasu Okubo. DES: Atsuko Watanabe, Yasuomi Kishi. ANI: Atsuko Watanabe, Isao Sugimoto. MUS: Akifumi Tada. PRD: Studio Hibari, AT-X, Avex, GENCO, Media Factory. 25 mins. x 12 eps.
In a parallel dimension, on planet Life

Core, there exists a team of beautiful teenage girls known as Juden-chan or "Charger Girls." Their sole function is to patrol the human world dressed in their rubber suits, giving depressed humans an energy boost. When they find a human who's feeling down or lacking vitality, they plug in their chargers to give him (or her, in the anime) a special energy boost. Normally they can't be seen by humans, but one day airheaded Juden-chan Plug Cryostat meets a young man who can see her. She and her fellow Charger Girls are drawn into a series of adventures with Omi, his family, and friends. Bow Ditama's original manga, first published in June 2006 and still ongoing, is highly explicit in terms of fan service, including fan service for full-bladder fetishists. The anime includes much of this but was censored for English-language release. Compare with **Video Girl Ai**, a similar concept, with superior execution.

CHARLOTTE

1977. JPN: *Wakakusa no Charlotte*. AKA: *Charlotte of the Green Grasses*. TV series. DIR: Eiji Okabe. SCR: Shunichi Yukimuro. DES: Shinya Takahashi. ANI: Tetsuo Shibuya, Nobuyuki Kitajima, Hiroshi Yoshida. MUS: Yoshimasa Suzuki. PRD: Nippon Animation, TV Asahi. 25 mins. x 30 eps.

Charlotte grows up on a Canadian cattle farm and has a happy life until her 12th birthday, when her father André reveals that he is really a French aristocrat, hiding out in the colonies to escape persecution. Her mother, believed dead, is actually still alive, and André sets off to bring her back, but he is killed en route. Charlotte struggles to keep the farm going, encouraged by her friend Sandy, and, in the tradition of almost every girls' anime from **Candy Candy** onward, aided by a "mysterious stranger" called Knight. Nippon Animation's first homegrown series for girls deliberately alluded to **Little House on the Prairie** and **Little Women** in its look and feel but was considered a failure and taken off the air after a relatively short run.

CHEBURASHKA ARERE?

2009. TV series, movie. DIR: Susumu Kudo, Makoto Nakamura. SCR: Michiru Shimada, Makoto Nakamura, Ryunosuke Kingetsu, Mikhail Aldashin. DES: Takahiro Kishida. ANI: Ringo Kishimoto. MUS: Yukiharu Urata,

Vladmiri Shainsky. PRD: GoHands. 3 mins. x 26 eps. (TV), 80 mins. (m).

Life in the city can be lonely, especially if you're a crocodile. Gena's life takes a turn for the better when he receives a crate of oranges. Inside the crate is a cute little animal, not quite a bear, not quite a monkey—Gena names him Cheburashka. As the friendly creature explores the city, where humans and animals live side by side, he just can't help making friends, and Gena's life is changed forever.

This charmingly animated story was created by Russian writer Eduard Uspensky and first published in 1965. Uspensky had already copyrighted the character and its image in 1964, and proceeded to sell rights in several countries. *Cheburashka* comes from the Russian word for tumbling or topping over, so he's known as Topple in English. He was also the subject of a ferocious copyright dispute between Uspensky and Leonid Shvartsman, art director of the original animated films, from 1997 to 2007. Uspensky won, although jury bribery was suspected.

In April 2006 TV Tokyo and Frontier Works acquired the right to make a feature film based on Roman Kachanov's stop-motion animation of the early 1970s. *Cheburashka* the movie, directed by Makoto Nakamura, was made in Russian and premiered in the U.S. at the 2009 American Film Market before launch events in its two "home" countries, Japan and Russia, in 2010.

CHEEKY ANGEL

2002. JPN: *Tenshi na Konamaiki*. TV series. DIR: Masaharu Okuwaki. SCR: Junichi Iioka. DES: Hideyuki Motohashi. ANI: Satoru Kojima. MUS: Daisuke Ikeda. PRD: Tokyo Movie Shinsha, TV Tokyo. 25 mins. x 50 eps.

At the age of nine, precocious brawler Megumi saves a wizard from an attack in the street and is granted a single wish. Rashly neglecting to think through the small print, he demands to be the "manliest man on Earth," only to be transformed into a woman instead, with his best friend Miki the sole person remembering his original sex. Now in his mid-teens, he is a brash, tough boy still trapped in a girl's body and searching for the chance to reverse the wish, which he now regards as more like a curse. The problem is

compounded by the fact that the female Megumi is extraordinarily beautiful, arousing the unwanted (and sometimes obsessive) admiration of virtually every male (and many females) within sight of her. Based on an "original" manga by Hiroyuki Nishimori—a particularly galling claim, since it ran in *Shonen Sunday*, the home of the much more famous, much longer-running **Ranma ½**.

CHEVALIER D'EON, LE *

2006. TV series. DIR: Kazuhiro Furuhashi, Makoto Endo. SCR: Tow Ubukata, Yasuyuki Muto, Shotaro Suga, Takeshi Matsuzawa, Hiroaki Jinno. DES: Tomomi Ozaki, toi8, Hiroshi Ono. ANI: Takahiro Chiba, Kyoji Asano, Shinichi Yokota, Tomotaka Shibayama. MUS: Michiru Oshima. PRD: Production I.G, Kodansha, Shochiku, WOWOW. 25 mins. x 24 eps.

Paris, 1742: the body of the beautiful Lia de Beaumont floats down the Seine in a coffin. On the lid, the word "Psalms" is written in blood. Lia's younger brother d'Eon starts to investigate and finds that a number of other women have also been murdered in strange circumstances. His high birth, his connections to the king and court, and even his exceptional swordfighting skills will not be enough to protect him from the danger he will face across Europe and beyond the world he knows. He will need to call on the skill, courage, and fighting powers of his dead sister.

Le Chevalier d'Eon is based on events in the autobiography of a real person, an 18th-century Frenchman, Frenchwoman, scholar, spy, Freemason, patriot, and master swordfighter, whose ability to embroider reality couldn't obscure the sober fact that his/her life was the stuff of fiction. Charles Geneviève Louis Auguste André Timothée d'Éon de Beaumont was born in France in October 1728. By the time he died, aged 82, he had lived in England, France, and (allegedly) Russia as a man and a woman and had made a living as a sword tutor to all comers, male and female. In 1777 an English court ruled that d'Eon was legally female, thus ending his Masonic career, and losing small fortunes for many people who had bet on her gender at Lloyds of London— the London Stock Exchange has always been a high-class gambling den, but in the 18th century they were completely open about it. On her death, doctors examined the body and pronounced it anatomically male, making d'Eon one of a small band of chancers who have beaten the Stock Exchange.

Japanese novelist Tow Ubukata was looking for inspiration: he found it in this story too ridiculously far-fetched to be anything but real. His book wove d'Eon's already strange life into a conspiracy theory involving quasi-Masonic rites, royalty, politics, intrigue, and zombie-killing across Europe and Russia, crashing *The Da Vinci Code* into *Buffy The Vampire Slayer*. A manga version with art by Kiriko Yumeji was published in 2005. The story proved irresistible to Production I.G and anime director Kazuhiro Furuhashi.

D'Eon's life and adventures were split across two figures, making his gender exploration into a brother-sister pairing and using it to great effect. This dual nature is reflected in the animation itself, which makes brilliant play with color and technique. It effectively emphasizes and exploits the difference between reality and fantasy, royal life and the common world, by saturating color and using CGI images of the real-life royal palaces of France as part of the backdrop for the action, so that the world outside the magic circle of royalty looks flat and drab by contrast. Furuhashi wanted the characters to look as if they inhabited their own world, neither too anime-like nor too real, but with the designs staying faithful to history. However, designer Ozaki slipped a few modern references into the mix: she cites character inspirations such as Brigitte Bardot's bouffant hairstyles for Anna, Anthony Hopkins's persona in *Mask of Zorro* for Teillagory, Brad Pitt for the dashing Durand, and Jack Black's look in *School of Rock* for the French ambassador to England, Guercy.

Alongside the pop-culture hooks and embedded in the intrigue, action, and adventure are plenty of nudges and winks to hardcore anime fans. Tales of possession by spirits aside, the whole idea of a man and a woman inhabiting one body is nothing new in anime. It was played for both laughs and drama in **MAZINGER Z** where Baron Asher is bi-gender, and forms the core of **PRINCESS KNIGHT** where the heroine's spirit is both male and

female. Lia de Beaumont is one of a line of beautiful swordswomen descended from Tezuka's heroine, such as Oscar in **ROSE OF VERSAILLES** and the cross-dressing Aramis of the anime **THREE MUSKETEERS**. A sequence in the anime pays specific homage to the Rose Bride in **UTENA.**

An intelligent script, written for adults rather than the usual teenage audience, makes this magical pile of hokum exactly the kind of top-class entertainment that the real-life Chevalier d'Eon would have enjoyed. The quality of the writing is remarkably consistent, given the length of the scripts—estimated by Furuhashi at over 30% longer than an average script for television, thanks to the involvement of the original novelist.

Production I.G celebrated its 20th anniversary in 2007—quite an achievement in an industry where companies are often created as part of a complex shell of formalities and liabilities, whose main purpose is to shield core entities from the risk of financial extinction. Shows like *Le Chevalier d'Eon* show why—high-quality mass entertainment made up of equal parts of intelligence and excitement.

CHI-SUI MARU

2010. TV series. DIR: Rareko. SCR: Rareko. DES: Rareko. ANI: Rareko. MUS: N/C. PRD: NTV, Fanworks. 1 min. x 40 eps.
Chi-sui Maru is a mosquito, and like all his mosquito friends his sole means of sustenance is to suck blood. Bald-headed office worker Nobuo is a natural target, but like all humans he hates being bitten. The daily battle between these two natural opponents is fought with charm and extreme silliness, but absolutely no words. Like *Tom and Jerry*, or **LUPIN III** and Zenigata, these two develop a strange but powerful bond. The NTV website gives an episode count of 40+, which probably accounts for the figure of 41 episodes cited in some Western sources. The DVD is 46 minutes long including a few short "extras." You also get a Rareko postcard and a 12-page book, and if that isn't enough there are some charming keychains and phone dangles for your mosquito life. Rareko obviously loves the independence and freedom that extremely short formats can give—he made **GAKKATSU!** for NHK in 2012.

CHI'S SWEET HOME *

2008. TV series. DIR: Mitsuyuki Masuhara, Yuzuru Tachikawa. SCR: Tomoko Konparu, Mitsuyuki Masuhara, Hiroshi Hamazaki, Yuzuru Tachikawa. DES: Akemi Kobayashi, Kazuko Katsui. ANI: N/C. MUS: Masumi Ito. PRD: Madhouse, TV Tokyo, Hakuhodo DY Media Partners. 3 mins. x 104 eps. (TV1), 3 mins. x 104 eps. (TV2).
A kitten is separated from her mother and family and becomes lost. A loving family with a playful little boy find her and take her in, naming her Chi. Even though their apartment building has a strict "no pets" rule, they can't abandon the helpless creature and decide to keep it secret from their landlady and neighbors. They've never lived with a cat before, and so for all four of them every day brings new discoveries. Although Chi misses her mother, she settles down and finds happiness and fun with her new family in this adorable short anime based on Kanata Konami's manga. The everyday life of a cat and its humans has been chronicled in anime such as **WHAT'S MICHAEL?** and Makoto Shinkai's *She and Her Cat* (**VOICES OF A DISTANT STAR**), but this series of sweet snippets was so popular that it led to a second series in 2009, *Chi's New Address (Chi's Sweet Home Atarashii Ouchi)*, in which the family decides to rehome Chi for her own sake, so she can run and play outside the confines of a small apartment. Such charm and gentleness reminds us that Madhouse is capable of more than darkness and edge. Harue Ono's color design is enchanting.

CHIBI DEVIL

2011. JPN: *Chibi Devi*. TV series. DIR: Maki Kamitani. SCR: Michihiro Tsuchiya. DES: Shoko Hagiwara, Toshiko Umezu. ANI: Isamu Abe. MUS: Kotaro Nakagawa. PRD: Shogakukan, Shogakukan-Shueisha Productions. 16 eps. x 5 mins.
Fourteen-year-old orphan Honoka Sawada is a lonely girl who is easily bullied by her classmates. She doesn't believe in anything—gods or devils—until she finds a demon baby on her bed. Little Mao helps her overcome her diffidence as she looks after him, and is drawn into a world of devil-baby daycare and juggling schoolwork with motherly duties. This short series based on Hiromu Shinozuka's manga for young girls is more **DAA! DAA!**

DAA**!** than **B**EELZEBUB**,** with the demon babies staying mischievously lovable despite a tendency to throw fire.

CHIBI MARUKO-CHAN

1990. AKA: *Cute Little Maruko; Little Miss Chubby Cheeks.* Movie, TV series. DIR: Tsutomu Shibayama. SCR: Momoko Sakura. DES: Yuji Shigeta. ANI: Michishiro Yamada, Yoshiaki Yanagida, Masako Sato. MUS: BB Queens. PRD: Nippon Animation, Fuji TV. 25 mins. x 142 eps. (TV1), 94 mins. (m), 25 mins. x 932+ eps. (TV2).

Maruko is a nine-year-old schoolgirl who spends most of her time daydreaming, particularly that she is a noble princess, her parents are divorced, or both. Inexplicably talking like an old woman despite her tender years, she continually pesters her parents, elder sister, and relatives to answer questions, and "amusing" misunderstandings ensue. Momoko Sakura's 1986 manga, loaded with 1970s nostalgia, was christened a "new SAZAE-SAN" by some Japanese critics for its gentle humanity and interminable run. Broadcast without subtitles on the Californian channel KSCI. It was also adapted into a three-part live-action mini-series on Fuji TV in 2006, featuring the 8-year-old Ei Morisako in the lead role.

CHIBINACS

2007. TV series. DIR: N/C. SCR: N/C. DES: N/C. ANI: N/C. MUS: N/C. PRD: STV, CREATIVE OFFIVE CUE, Zealot. 3 mins. x 25 eps. (TV1), 3 mins. x 25 eps. (TV2), 3 mins. x 25 eps. (TV3).

TEAM NACS (also known as Team Canucks) are a surreal comedy troupe from Hokkaido who star in this short series. The five-man team's popularity has led to a feature film, surreal samurai spoof, photo book, and three anime series. The first was broadcast in Hokkaido in 2006 and soon spread to other locations, with 2008's *Chibinacs 2.0* and 2009's *Chibinacs 3* offering more of the same madness.

CHICKEN TAKKUN

1984. TV series. DIR: Keiji Hayakawa. SCR: Masaru Yamamoto, Kazuyoshi Ohashi. DES: Yoshihiro Owada. ANI: Mitsuru Honma, Tetsuro Hagano, Shigeru Omachi. MUS: Masami Anno. PRD: Ishinomori Pro, Studio Pierrot, Studio Gallop, Fuji TV. 25 mins. x 23 eps.

The Walchin Dictionary, a computer packed with evil ideas from Planet R, falls into the hands of Doctor Bell, who plans to use it to rule the world. Prince Chicken enlists the help of his alien friends to get the dictionary back and lands his flying saucer on the roof of the Minamita family's house in Japan. Miko Minamita and her four friends offer to help Chicken. This anime was adapted from Shotaro Ishinomori's manga run in the educational magazine *Science for Grades 1–6.*

CHIHAYAFURU *

2011. TV series. DIR: Morio Asaka. SCR: Naoya Takayama, Ayako Kato, Sumino Kawashima et al. DES: Kunihiko Hamada, Tomoyuki Shimizu. ANI: Kunihiko Hamada, Yoshinori Kanemori. MUS: Kosuke Yamashita. PRD: Madhouse Studios, NTV, VAP. 30 mins. x 25 eps. (TV1), 30 mins. x 25 eps. (TV2).

Chihaya is a bright, cheerful tomboy who dreams that her beautiful sister may one day become Japan's top model. Then she meets someone who tells her that a dream is something she should work to achieve for herself, not piggy-back on someone else's. This revives her interest in *karuta*, a traditional Japanese card game based on classical poetry. She made a pact with two friends in middle school that they'd meet again as top-class *karuta* players. Can she get a school club going and become a top player?

A card game that depends on a knowledge of classical Japanese poetry is obviously going to lack something in the action stakes, but is ultimately no less weird than the taxonomies and rules required to understand YU-GI-OH. But the charm of this gem of a series is much more seductive. The characters, the beautiful art, and the passion for beauty that runs through it are very hard to resist. The lovely character writing gives even the minor cast members their own personalities and the design, art, and animation are quietly excellent, showing Madhouse at its best. Yuki Suetsugu's manga commenced publication in 2008 and is still running, and its ongoing popularity led to another season from the same team in 2013.

CHIKO: HEIRESS OF THE PHANTOM THIEF

2008. JPN: *Niju Menso no Musume.* AKA: *Daughter of Twenty Faces.* TV series. DIR: Nobuo Tomizawa. SCR: Michihiro Tsuchiya, Natsuko Takahashi. DES: Koichi Horikawa, Kazuhide Tominaga, Hiromasa Ogura. ANI: Hiroaki Noguchi. MUS: Kazunori Miyake. PRD: BONES, Telecom. 23 mins. x 22 eps.

Eleven-year-old Chizuko is an orphan who lives with her aunt and uncle. Under their kindly exteriors hides a dark intent: they are slowly poisoning Chizuko to gain her inheritance. She suspects as much, not just because she's highly intelligent but also through her passion for detective novels. What she doesn't know is that her butler is actually the renowned thief Twenty Faces, there to steal the fabulous ruby that forms the main part of her inheritance. He takes her under his wing and helps her escape from her murderous relatives. For two years, while the world thinks she's another kidnapped heiress, she is touring the world with Twenty Faces and his gang as Chiko, becoming part of their family. When a terrible accident engineered by a rival thief wipes out the band, Chizuko is returned to her evil aunt and uncle. Then she meets a mysterious detective and learns that Twenty Faces may still be alive. Can she escape her murderous blood family and rebuild the family she made with the thief she regards as her new father?

Telecom, a studio know for its association with Studio Ghibli, has a long tradition of detective anime, from SHERLOCK HOUND to LUPIN III and CONAN THE BOY DETECTIVE. In conjunction with BONES, they have made an involving, exciting show using new characters alongside two of the creations of Edogawa Rampo. The great Japanese crime writer's estate licensed Twenty Faces and detective Akechi for Shinji Ohara's 2003 manga on which this anime is based. Set in the Showa period, with the anime story starting around 1953, it taps into the vein of nostalgia that fuels traditional anime like SAZAE-SAN, adding designs with something of the flavor of THE BIG O and a good balance between plot twists and action. Although the episodes are basically self-contained stories, they tie into the main plot arc and develop the characters throughout, even allowing them to age in line with the passage of time in the narrative. Some plot strands are unresolved, leading to speculation that a longer series may have been planned, but this is still an enjoyably solid piece of entertainment.

CHILD'S TOY *

1995. JPN: *Kodomo no Omocha*. AKA: *Kodocha*. TV series. DIR: Iku Suzuki, Akitaro Daichi, Hiroaki Sakurai. SCR: Tomoko Konparu, Ryosuke Takahashi, Miho Maruo. DES: Hajime Watanabe. ANI: Nobuyuki Tokinaga. MUS: Hiroshi Koga, Tokio. PRD: Pony Canyon, TV Tokyo. 30? mins. (v), 25 mins. x 102 eps. (TV).

Sana Kurata is a child star who attends a normal school, initially at odds with the bullying Akito Hayama, until he reluctantly becomes her friendly rival ("my enemy and my boyfriend," she describes him with a typically innocent oxymoron). Originally turned into a video as part of the 40th anniversary celebrations of *Ribon* magazine in 1995, Miho Obana's 1994 manga became a full-fledged TV series the following year. With a sixth-grader who is already a star (appearing in the self-referentially titled *Child's Toy* TV show), it takes the aspirations of magical-girl shows like **CREAMY MAMI** as given, preferring instead to concentrate on school one-upmanship like that in **GOLDFISH WARNING**. Released in America in 2005 under the title *Kodocha*.

CHILDHOOD FRIEND AND CLASSMATE

2008. JPN: *Osana Najimi to Dokyusei*. Video. DIR: Futoshi Yone. SCR: Kyokai Aoigatana. DES: Shinichiro Kajiura, Nikokanenori. ANI: Takafumi Hino. MUS: N/C. PRD: HotBear, MediaBank. 30 mins. x 2 eps.

Miyu is groped by a guy on the train on her way home from school, but rescued by her classmate Shun. When he kisses her, Miyu runs off but can't enter her house because she has lost her key. Luckily she meets her childhood friend Ko, who takes her back to *his* home. She tells him that Shun stole her first kiss, and he tells her they've already kissed so it wasn't her first. Then they have sex. Next day, when Shun apologizes for kissing her, Miyu agrees to go to his home where he drugs her and trains her as a sex slave. Based on a story by MARUTA, with only average animation and character design and no real story or character development, because that's not why people buy porn. **NV**

CHILDREN WHO CHASE LOST VOICES FROM DEEP BELOW *

2011. JPN: *Hoshi o Ou Kodomo*. AKA: *Children Who Chase Stars; Journey to Agartha; Children Who Chase Lost Voices*. Movie. DIR: Makoto Shinkai. SCR: Makoto Shinkai. DES: Takayo Nishimura, Takumi Tanji. ANI: Takayo Nishimura. MUS: Tenmon. PRD: CoMix Wave, Marine Entertainment, Media Factory, MOVIC, Yahoo Japan. 116 mins.

Asuna's father is dead. Her mother works long hours as a nurse and she spends much of her time alone, listening to music on a crystal radio that her father gave to her. Roaming the countryside, she is attacked by a monster and saved by a mysterious boy. When she hears about a boy's body found in the river, and then hears from a subsitute teacher about Agartha, the Land of the Dead, she finds herself drawn to make a journey without any real knowledge of where she is going or why.

Shinkai is known as the master of melancholy through works such as **FIVE CENTIMETERS PER SECOND** and **VOICES OF A DISTANT STAR**, in which even small children are suffused with yearning for the past and an aching awareness of inevitable loss. The settings of his previous works have been deliberately ordinary, everyday lives in everyday places: their uniqueness comes from his ability to embody and recreate intense youthful emotion with passion and clarity. But Asuna is essentially along for the ride; she misses her father, wonders what happened to her rescuer, but does not seem deeply invested in either. She doesn't seem hugely interested in the magical land of Agartha or the wonders that unfold there—and it is wonderful, quite beautifully depicted in what seems to be loving imitation of similar imagery in Miyazaki's **CASTLE IN THE SKY**. But when the heroine doesn't seem all that bothered, it's hard for the audience to stay enthused.

From Shinkai, whose ability to communicate the need for contact and connection has always been a major strength, this beautiful imagery with such a hollow heart is baffling. The chosen English title sums up the problem perfectly: instead of translating the Japanese title *Childen Who Chase Stars*, the distributors went for the self-conscious, even pretentious, *Children Who Chase Lost Voices from Deep Below* in some

territories, and the ploddingly descriptive *Journey to Agartha* in others. **V**

CHIMERA *

1997. JPN: *Seikimatsu Reima Chimera*. AKA: *End of the Century Demon Beauty Chimera; Chimera: Angel of Death*. Video. DIR: Mitsuo Kusakabe. SCR: Narihiko Tatsumiya. DES: Asami Tojo. ANI: Taeko Sato. MUS: N/C. PRD: Toei. 47 mins.

Sex and violence in the Hong Kong underworld, as pretty assassin Rei leaves a wake of death and grief behind her as she carries out jobs for the Mob. Her codename: Chimera. Based on the ladies' manga by Asami Tojo, and not to be confused with **KIMERA**. **LNV**

CHINA NUMBER ONE

1997. JPN: *Nekketsu Ryori Anime: Chuka Ichiban*. AKA: *Hot-blooded Cookery Anime: China Number One*. TV series. DIR: Masami Anno. SCR: Nobuaki Kishima. DES: Yoshinori Kishi, Tsuneo Ninomiya. ANI: Eikichi Takahashi. MUS: Michihiko Ota. PRD: Nippon Animation, Pony Canyon. 25 mins. x 52 eps. (TV), 30 mins. (v).

In this adaptation of Etsuji Ogawa's manga for *ShonenMagazine*, a gifted teenage cook travels to late 19th-century China in search of rival chefs worthy of his cooking prowess. Like **RANMA ½** before it, it was immensely successful in East Asia, where its Japanese origins were swiftly forgotten. Episodes 9–14 were edited into a 30-minute video.

CHIPPO THE MISCHIEVOUS ANGEL

1970. JPN: *Itazura Tenshi Chippo-chan*. TV series. DIR: Takashi Aoki, Fumio Ikeno. SCR: Noboru Ishiguro, Tomohiro Ando. DES: N/C. ANI: New World Pictures. MUS: Yuki Tamaki. PRD: Fuji TV Enterprise. 5 mins. x 240 eps.

Slipping off his cloud and falling out of heaven, Chippo, a naughty angel, lands in the food store owned and run by Kantaro Fujino's parents. Unable to fly home because his wings are not yet fully grown, he stays with the family, though his inability to understand the meaning of danger soon leads him into numerous accidents. The same crew had previously worked on Fuji TV Enterprise's *Pinch and Punch*, a 1969 tale of naughty twins that was otherwise very similar. Note that *Itazura Tenshi* (*Mischievous Angel*) was the Japanese title of the

American TV series *The Flying Nun* (1967), on the coattails of which the producers were presumably hoping to ride.

CHIRORIN VILLAGE TALES

1992. JPN: *Chirorin Mura Monogatari*. TV series. DIR: Yasuo Yamayoshi. SCR: Osamu Nakamura, Riko Hinokuma. DES: Takao Kasai. ANI: Takao Kasai. MUS: Tatsumi Yano. PRD: C&D Distribution, Bandai Visual, NHKEP. 8 mins. x 170 eps.

Chirorin Village and Walnut's Tree was a children's puppet show broadcast on NHK between 1956 and 1964 featuring the adventures of three junior high school children: Tonpei the Onion, Kurumi the Walnut, and Peanut (the Peanut) in the titular village. Brought back to cash in on parents' nostalgia, it was remade as a TV anime with famous voice actresses, such as Noriko Hidaka and Minami Takayama, and far-fetched episodes, including *I'm Not a Crook*, *The Sound of a Vampire*, *Come Out You Monsters*, and *Back to the Secret Base*.

CHISTE: THE GREEN THUMB

1990. JPN: *Chist: Midori no Oyayubi*. Movie. DIR: Shumon Miura, Yuji Funano. SCR: Ryu Tachihara. DES: Masahiro Kase. ANI: Shinya Sadamitsu, Kazuya Ose. MUS: Marc Berriere, Francoise Legrand, Jean-Michel Ervé. PRD: Dax International. 73 mins.

In this adaptation of the book by Maurice D'Orleans, Chiste is a boy with the strange ability to make flowers grow wherever he places his thumb, a power which he puts to use bringing love and peace to the world. For more peace-loving florists, see WEISS KREUZ.

CHITOSE GET YOU *

2012. TV series. DIR: Takao Sano. SCR: N/C. DES: Takao Sano. ANI: N/C. MUS: RUKA. PRD: Silver Link, AT-X, Dream Creation, SPO, Takeshobo. 3 mins. x 26 eps.

Elementary schoolgirl Chitose falls in love with Hiroshi, the luckless man who works at the town hall near her school. Unfunny jailbait comedy based on a four-panel gag manga by Etsuko Mashima, and presumably made in the confidence that the 2012 audience was not around two years earlier to watch HANAMARU KINDERGARTEN.

CHOBI THE CUTE LITTLE CAT

1998. JPN: *Chibi Neko Chobi*. Video. DIR: Yumi Tamano. SCR: Miyuki Takahashi. DES: Konomi Sakurai. ANI: Konomi Sakurai. MUS: N/C. PRD: Toei. 20 mins. x 2 eps.

Eiko Kadono, who also created KIKI'S DELIVERY SERVICE, collaborated with artist Mako Taruishi for this tale of a female black-and-white kitten born to a cat called Meme. The original was selected as a core title for Japanese libraries, guaranteeing a long shelf life and leading to sales of over 100,000 copies, but these simple stories of mischief and friendly animals flew no further on video. The second volume, *Chibi Neko Chobi to Otomodachi*, added "... and Friends" to the title.

CHOBIN THE STARCHILD *

1974. JPN: *Hoshi no Ko Chobin*. TV series. DIR: Rintaro, Hiroyuki Hoshiyama, Noboru Ishiguro, Shinji Okada. SCR: Shunichi Yukimuro, Hisashi Ito, Keisuke Fujikawa, Yukiko Takayama, Soji Yoshikawa. DES: Shotaro Ishinomori. ANI: Norio Yazawa. MUS: Tetsuaki Hagiwara. PRD: Watanabe Planning, Ishinomori Pro, TBS. 25 mins. x 26 eps.

Chobin, king of planet Fairystar, arrives from his homeworld in a spaceship and lands at the house of Professor Amagawa and his assistant, Ruri. Enlisting the help of terrestrial creatures (including a frog, rabbit, and butterfly from the nearby forest), Chobin searches for his missing mother and dreams of the day when he and his family can return to Fairystar and depose the usurper Brungar.

Invented by producers at Watanabe Planning in cooperation with CYBORG 009–creator Shotaro Ishinomori, Chobin's adventures were serialized in a number of magazines, including *Shojo Friend* and *Terebi* magazine, to drum up support for the TV series. The story received a very limited broadcast on U.S. Japanese community TV stations shortly after its release.

CHOBITS *

2002. TV series. DIR: Morio Asaka. SCR: Genjiro Kaneko, Nanase Okawa, Tomoyasu Okubo. DES: Hisashi Abe. ANI: Hisashi Abe. MUS: Katsutoshi Kitagawa, Dan Miyakawa, Keitaro Takanami. PRD: CLAMP, Madhouse, TBS. 25 mins. x 26 eps. (TV), 6 mins. (v1), 52 mins. (v2).

Hideki Motosuwa is a 19-year-old farm boy from Hokkaido who flunks his college entrance exams and comes to Tokyo to attend a cram school for a second attempt Hideki takes consolation from reading porn comics, but all around him people are buying persocoms, humanoid computers, usually in the shape of cute girls. There's no way he can afford one, so when he finds a seemingly broken persocom abandoned in a trash heap, he decides to keep her. Her first word is Chii, so that becomes her name. She knows absolutely nothing, a blank slate on which Hideki can write his own ideas of the world. He begins to suspect that she may be one of the legendary Chobits, persocoms with free will and enormous powers.

Chobits is one of the landmark shows of the early 21st century. It is a successful fusion of the old-school magical girl with the artificial girlfriend of VIDEO GIRL AI and MAHOROMATIC, along with the harem tradition of TENCHI MUYO!, liberally dosed with a boyish obsession for tinkering with machines. It is therefore all the more impressive that it is based on a manga in *Young* magazine (the original home of AKIRA...!) created by the all-female CLAMP collective, who demonstrate here that they can also entertain a male market with deceptive ease. Although the show's central conceit is nothing new (after all, it traces a line back through ASTRO BOY to *Pinocchio*), CLAMP's production seemed to hit an audience of both sexes, revisiting, for example, many of the modern romantic malaises of U-jin's SAKURA DIARIES, particularly when Hideki starts dating a real human girl, without any thought of Chii's feelings. Occasionally this leads to bipolar behavior; the over-arcing romantic plots in the style of MAISON IKKOKU are often sacrificed for gratuitous titillation, but as with AI YORI AOSHI, that seems to be the price animators must often pay in modern anime. Some viewers may discern an element of LOLITA ANIME in the submissive vacancy of the persocoms, although as with ARMITAGE III, not all of them are "female," merely often made so by market forces. As with KEY THE METAL IDOL, the addition of true love to Chii's programming is liable to cause a radical change to her behavior—compare to AIR and DEARS.

Chobits acknowledges the pervasive nature of information technology while emphasizing the need for real, individual emotional responses. Hideki finally comes to terms with his feelings for his Chobit partner, and we learn that Chii is a twin and already has a complex and tragic love story in her background. The original *Chobits* manga featured cameo roles for characters from CLAMP's earlier CARDCAPTORS and ANGELIC LAYER, but these scenes were dropped from the anime adaptation. Perhaps as a sign of stretching a low budget, the series used more recap episodes than usual, pointlessly retelling the "story so far" on three occasions in its relatively short run. While such catch-up episodes were commonplace in long-running shows like URUSEI YATSURA, their use here seems more like a cynical recycling of footage. *Chibits* (2003) is a brief six-minute cartoony adventure included as a bonus on the final disc, in which Hideki leaves the house without his wallet and Chii chases after him, until the other characters realize that she has left her panties behind and chase after her. A final video-only volume, simply billed as the "27th episode" or "Chat Room," is split into three discourses between the characters that recap the series. ◐

CHOCCHAN'S STORY

1997. JPN: *Chocchan no Monogatari*. AKA: *Story of Chocchan*. Movie. DIR: Hiroko Tokita. SCR: Chifude Asakura. DES: Tatsuo Yanagino. ANI: Tatsuo Yanagino. MUS: Tomoyuki Asagawa. PRD: Requiem, Triangle Staff. 76 mins. Cho, a music student and sometime chorus girl, returns briefly to her native Hokkaido to tell her parents she is engaged to violinist Moritsuna. When her father forbids her marriage, the couple elope and set up home in 1930s Tokyo. Tetsuko, the eldest of their three children, is inattentive at school and disrupts classes by calling her friends' attention to things going on outside the window. Eventually, Tetsuko is put in a more indulgent institution, where she gets more consideration from the teacher and bonus outdoor activities.

The outbreak of war, first in China and then in the Pacific, brings rationing and shortages. When son Meiji becomes ill, Cho sends Tetsuko to pawn Moritsuna's violin to buy ice cream, but the kindhearted girl instead trades her own hat for ¥10. Cho is uneasily reconciled with her estranged father during a Hokkaido summer holiday; the old man adopts the

role of grandfather with ease and seems as hurt as Cho that they still cannot agree on everything. Eventually, Moritsuna is conscripted into the army, where he entertains his fellow soldiers with violin solos—echoes here of VIOLIN OF THE STARRY SKY. After the war, the family return to the ruins of their house in Tokyo, where a wounded Moritsuna rejoins them.

The family's rather dull prewar activities are brightened only by some original sound—*Chocchan* opens with a rendition of "L'Amour est un Oiseau Rebelle" from Bizet's *Carmen* (1875), and the radio surrender address of the Showa Emperor appears to be excerpted from the genuine article. Although it might have the outward appearance of another war story in the tradition of RAIL OF THE STAR, or a sanitized novel that belongs among the ANIMATED CLASSICS OF JAPANESE LITERATURE, *Chocchan* has a more oblique origin. It is based on the memoirs of the *mother* of Tetsuko Kuroyanagi, an actress who dominated Japanese television in its early years, provided one of the original voices for CHIRORIN VILLAGE TALES (see also *DE), became the host of the long-running TV Asahi chat show *Tetsuko's Room*, and ultimately served as an ambassador for UNICEF. This explains the bizarre way that *Chocchan's Story*, despite the title, concentrates so much on Tetsuko—even on the blurb of the video box, which immediately draws the reader's attention away from the supposed lead to emphasize the later fame of her daughter.

There is one moment where it aspires to greater things—a sequence where the family watch a column of marching soldiers, occasionally obscured by silent girls, who rush past them staring off-screen as if carried along by an invisible current. It is only when they spot Moritsuna that they, too, dash out into the street, running alongside a beloved family member for what could be a final goodbye.

Despite being unreleased in English, it was distributed under the English title of *Chocchan's Story* in Europe. The English title seems to have been carefully chosen in order to ensure echoes of *Totto-chan: The Girl at the Window*, daughter Tetsuko's autobiography, to which *Chocchan* may be regarded as an indirect prequel. Compare to KAYOKO'S DIARY.

CHOCOLATE PANIC PICTURE SHOW, THE

1985. Video. DIR: Kazuyoshi Hirose. SCR: N/C. DES: Kamui Fujiwara. ANI: Mamoru Sugiura. MUS: TV Asahi Music. PRD: CBS, Taurus, Filmlink. 33 mins.
Jaw-droppingly racist musical in which grossly caricatured Africans Manbo, Chinbo, and Chonbo cause chaos in civilization despite the efforts of their pretty tour guide/bedmate to tame their zany, grass-skirted cannibal ways. This video was based on a manga by Kamui Fujiwara in *Super Action* and partly inspired by Jamie Uys's *The Gods Must Be Crazy* (1980).

CHOCOLATE UNDERGROUND *

2008. Internet series, movie. DIR: Takayuki Hamana. SCR: Kiyoko Yoshimura. DES: Takayuki Goto, Seiko Akashi. ANI: Takayuki Goto. MUS: SUPA LOVE. PRD: Production I.G, Trans Arts, Celsys, Hakuhodo DY Media Partners, Hexagon Pictures, OCC, Shueisha, Sony Music Entertainment, TOHO University, Watermark. 3 mins. x 13 eps. (original), 87 mins. (m).
The government bans candy because it is harmful to health. Chocolate is at the top of the prohibited list. Two kids, Smudger and Huntley, decide to rally the resistance. They start by selling bootleg chocolate and then start a secret chocolate factory. As they get deeper and deeper into the politics of resistance, they find out just how dangerous it can be to resist a totalitarian state. Yet in spite of the danger, they are absolutely determined not to give in.

This series based on Alex Shearer's novel *Bootleg* is a pure cocoa rush. Neither animation nor designs are particularly great, but what sets this work apart is the sheer joy it takes in driving itself through story and character. A great idea, a good plot, and a believable set of characters make this fabulous fun for adults as well as kids. A movie version, of what was originally shown online as an Internet series, was made in 2009 with 20 minutes of extra footage and has been screened at film festivals and in arthouse cinemas in Britain, the U.S., and Germany. Under the original name of *Bootleg* (2002), the story was previously adapted into a three-part live-action series for the BBC, and became a manga series in *Bessatsu Margaret*.

CHOCOTTO SISTER

2006. TV series. DIR: Yasuhiro Kuroda. SCR: Go Zappa. DES: Yukihiro Kitano, Rieko Sakai. ANI: Yukihiro Kitano. MUS: Masara Nishida. PRD: Nomad. 24 mins. x 24 eps.

When Haruma was a small boy, his mother miscarried on Christmas Eve. He prayed that his mother would be well and that one day he would have a baby sister. It seems impossible because his mother had to have a hysterectomy. Years later, when Haruma is in college, a woman on a flying motorbike turns up at Christmas, claiming to be Santa Claus, and gives him a little sister.

Go Zappa and Sakura Takeuchi's manga began publishing in 2003. Both the manga and anime balance uncomfortably between the EVERYDAY ANIME comedy of a young man thrown in the deep end of child-rearing as a father figure to an adoring little girl, and the perverted fantasy of a guy involving a little girl in his adult life and relationships (compare to BUNNY DROP). It's a dichotomy that is never effectively resolved in a series whose technical standards are not high.

CHOISUJI

2007. Video. DIR: Anri Kirishima. SCR: Akira Sekai. DES: Ryunosuke Karasawa. ANI: Shigenori Taniguchi. MUS: N/C. PRD: Animac. 25 mins. x 2 eps.

Two stories about innocent (though unusually well-developed) ten-year-old girls tricked by adult authority figures into erotic activity. In the first, a small girl is seduced by a teacher using a hand puppet to persuade her that it's all a game. In the second episode an elementary school doctor gets urine samples from two little girls in a highly inappropriate fashion. Based on original stories by Takayuki Asaki. The idea of a respectable pillar of society—a teacher or doctor—transgressing accepted moral codes is a popular one in EROTICA AND PORNOGRAPHY because it allows the viewer to believe that anyone, even those better educated or in a higher social class than him, would behave in exactly the same way given the opportunity. In this instance it seems pointless since we're dealing with cartoon figures, but maybe pervert cartoon fans need to feel validated in this way. **N**

CHRISTMAS IN JANUARY

1991. JPN: Ichigatsu ni wa Christmas. Video. DIR: Satoshi Dezaki. SCR: Setsuko Shibunnoichi, Toshiaki Imaizumi. DES: Yukari Kobayashi. ANI: Yukari Kobayashi. MUS: Takashi Ui. PRD: For Life Record, Media Ring. 45 mins.

Nobumasa is a boy who works part-time in a shoe store, where he meets Mizuki, a girl whose abusive family life has left her unable to trust other people. Meanwhile, Nobumasa is unaware that another girl, Seiko, has a crush on him but is unable to express her feelings.

A love triangle straight out of VIDEO GIRL AI or KIMAGURE ORANGE ROAD, but this time presented for the female readership in *Margaret* magazine, Mariko Iwadate's 1984 manga made it to the screen in this one-shot video.

CHROME-SHELLED REGIOS *

2009. JPN: Kokaku no Regios. TV Series. DIR: Itsuro Kawasaki. SCR: Mamiko Ikeda, Michiko Yokote, Jukki Hanada, Toshizo Nemoto, Katsumi Hasegawa. DES: Hideki Hashimoto, Junichi Higashi. ANI: Masaaki Sakurai, Hiroko Kurube, Masaru Kawashima. MUS: Daisuke Asakura. PRD: ZEXCS, AMG Entertainment, D.N. Dream Partners, Kadokawa, Klockworx. 30 mins. x 24 eps.

Long after the apocalypse, Earth is still a wasteland. Huge mobile cities, or Regios, roam a desolate landscape populated by monstrous creatures. The cities are defended by fighting elites, and the most powerful of these are the Queen's Blades (not to be confused with QUEEN'S BLADE). One of these hugely powerful warriors, Layfon, is exiled. Being a mere teenager, he is drawn into a military school where his huge powers cause tensions and conflicts within the existing command structure. So does his attraction for the female students, because as well as being a post-apocalyptic action adventure this is a harem anime (ROMANCE AND DRAMA). It also wants to shoehorn in some comedy, leading to a swimsuit episode, a character who reverts to "cute" mode, and an alternate timeline (or possibly a show-within-a-show) where everyone speaks very bad English. Shusuke Amagi's light-novel series, with illustrations by Miyu, runs to 16 volumes, which may be why the show starts a number of plot threads running but resolves only one of them. Rather confusing and

frustrating, despite some enjoyable action sequences.

CHRONO CRUSADE *

2003. JPN: Chrno [sic] Crusade: Mary Magdalene. TV series. DIR: Yu Ko (aka Yuh Koh), Hiroyuki Kanbe. SCR: Atsuhiro Tomioka. DES: Kazuya Kuroda, Tomohiro Kawahara, Hiroyuki Kanbe, Hisao Muramatsu. ANI: Kazuya Kuroda. MUS: Hikaru Nanase. PRD: Fuji TV, Gonzo, Klockworx. 25 mins. x 24 eps. (TV), 10 mins. (v1, Chapter Zero), ca. 3 mins. x 11 eps. (v2, Azmaria's Extra Classes).

Teenage exorcist Rosette Christopher works for Catholic agency The Magdalene Order in an alternate 1920s New York, sworn to protect the seven "Apostles," superpowered humans who have been appearing since the traumatic events of World War I. These individuals are the targets of the Sinners, a group led by Aion, a handsome renegade demon whose home dimension of Pandemonium may soon be sending other creatures through the crumbling defenses of our world.

Rosette works alongside renegade demon, Chrono, whose great powers are contained in the body of a young boy, locked away until Rosette unleashes them using a seal she wears around her neck—compare to BASTARD. Each time she does this, she uses up a little of her own finite life force. She also uses a WWI government-issue Colt .45, which can fire holy bullets or special "Gospel" silver rounds etched with incantations, all provided for her by lecherous genius Edward "Elder" Hamilton (a CAPTAIN FUTURE reference, perhaps?), the monastic equivalent of 007's Q. Elder has an even more deadly prototype up his sleeve, a round with a demon actually sealed inside it, which releases a massive burst of power on impact. When Rosette steals it, the results are predictably disastrous.

Rosette has a personal reason for joining the Order—she is seeking her younger brother Joshua, missing for four years since he turned everyone else in their orphanage to stone and vanished, lured away by Aion. Chrono has his own motives for joining forces with her. He and Aion were both Sinners, and rebelled against the ruling powers of Pandemonium together. Aion betrayed him, cut off his horns—the source of a demon's control over his power—and gave them to Joshua.

Mistrustful nun Sister Kate Valentine entrusts Rosette and Chrono with protecting 12-year-old soprano Azmaria Hendrick, one of the Seven Apostles, who is in grave danger. Her foster father, tycoon Ricardo Hendrick, is really an undead devil-worshipper who serves the demon Viscount Lerajie. Ricardo plans to use Azmaria's powers to restore his own life and become immortal. The pair are joined in their mission by another powerful demon-fighter, red-haired orphan Stella Harvenheit, whose parents were killed by demons. Stella is known as the Jewel Witch because she can summon and control fiends using crystals. Using her jewels, Chrono's powers, and Rosette's trusty Colt, the trio risk their lives to protect Azmaria.

Despite a rather promising set of elements, including design work by VANDREAD's Kazuya Kuroda, Christian heresies in the spirit of DEVILMAN or EVANGELION, and wild moodswings in the style of FULLMETAL ALCHEMIST, this adaptation of Daisuke Moriyama's manga from *Dragon Age* monthly is disappointingly less than the sum of its parts, concocting little more than a cynical alchemy of INU YASHA and DIRTY PAIR with optional crucifixes. The American location is squandered, the Prohibition period setting something to which the U.S. dubbers have given more thought than the Japanese creators, and the religious references a mixture of intriguing ideas (the prophecies of Fatima as a plot device) and B-movie hokum (bullets filled with holy oil). The result is yet another gaggle of shrill anime eye candy blowing stuff up, lacking the energy of SLAYERS, the chills of HELLSING, or the laughs of PHANTOM QUEST CORP, all of which it would like to be.

CHU-BRA!! *

2010. TV series. DIR: Yukina Hiiro. SCR: Reiko Yoshida, Hitomi Amamiya. DES: Miyako Yatsu, Chikako Shibata. ANI: Maki Fujioka, Shunryo Yamamura, Miyako Yatsu. MUS: Yoshihisa Hirano. PRD: ZEXCS, GANSIS, Starchild Records, Klockworx. 24 mins. x 12 eps.
On the first day of middle school Nayu shocks her new classmates by proclaiming the Gospel of Underwear with her black lace panties. She believes all girls should know how to buy and wear properly fit-

ting, well-chosen underwear, and starts an underwear club to achieve this. Yumi Nakata's manga may have attracted its fair share of perverts who like to read about preteen schoolgirls in lingerie, but it was actually a comedy with a serious educational purpose in helping girls deal with the issues of growing up, which the anime continues. Apparently.

CINDERELLA

1996. JPN: *Cinderella Monogatari*. TV series. DIR: Hiroshi Sasagawa, Takaaki Ishiyama, Yuji Asada. SCR: Masaaki Sakurai, Hiroko Naka, Tsunehisa Arakawa. DES: Tatsunoko Planning Office. ANI: Masami Suda, Chuichi Iguchi. MUS: N/C. PRD: Tatsunoko, Marubeni, NHK2. 25 mins. x 26 eps.
Forced to scrub the floor in her wicked stepmother's kitchen, Cinderella refuses to let her situation get her down. Her fairy godmother, Palette, casts a spell so that she can understand the speech of animals, and Cinderella's life is made easier by her friendships with Wanda the dog, Pappy the bird, and mice Chuchu and Bingo. She falls in love with a man called Sharrol whom she meets in town, unaware that he is actually *Prince* Sharrol, traveling in disguise, and that the "real" Prince Sharrol back at the palace is an imposter.

Straight after finishing SNOW WHITE, Tatsunoko added a pirate attack, funny animal business, and a subplot straight out of *The Prince and the Pauper* in order to pad out the running time of this adaptation. Since Cinderella and her Prince Charming are *both* in disguise each time they meet, it adds to the tension, but once all the intrigue is resolved, the last three episodes end traditionally with the ball, glass slipper reunion, wedding bells, and happy-ever-after. Other versions of *Cinderella* have appeared in GRIMMS' FAIRY TALES (1987), FAMOUS WORLD FAIRY TALES (1989), as part of the HELLO KITTY series (*Hello Kitty's Cinderella*, 1992), and, in a more risqué incarnation, in ADULT FAIRY TALES (1999). See also VIDEO PICTURE BOOK.

CINDERELLA BOY

2003. TV series. DIR: Tsuneo Tominaga. SCR: Mitsuyo Suenaga, Michihiro Tsuchiya. DES: Kazutoshi Kobayashi, Konami Umi. ANI: N/C. MUS: N/C. PRD: Magic Bus, Enoki Films, AT-X. 25 mins. x 13 eps.

Hotly pursued by a group of angry arms smugglers, private investigators Ranma and Layla have what first appears to be a fatal car accident. But when Ranma wakes up, he appears unharmed, although his beautiful female partner is nowhere to be seen. He soon discovers that they are now obliged to share a body, and that Ranma transforms into Layla at the stroke of midnight, in a blatantly unoriginal attempt by Monkey Punch to impart the capers of his LUPIN III with the body-swap transformation of RANMA ½—Ranma is not all that common a name in Japan, making the comic creator's decision to name his leading man after Rumiko Takahashi's famous girl/boy all the more puzzling. The rest of this obscure TV series seems similarly halfhearted: the animation is often clumsy, the action dull, and the music a feeble attempt to revisit some of the jazzy cool of COWBOY BEBOP. Almost everything that is wrong about anime in the early 21st century, wrapped up in one forgettable package.

CINDERELLA EXPRESS

1989. Video. DIR: Teru Moriboshi, Nanako Shimazaki. SCR: Kenji Terada. DES: Moriyasu Taniguchi. ANI: Moriyasu Taniguchi. MUS: N/C. PRD: Nippon Eizo. 50 mins.
Everyday salaryman Yuji Shimano meets and beds a pretty young girl at his bachelor party. Meeting her again at his wedding, he realizes that he has just begun an affair with his sister-in-law, in this erotic farce from Hikaru Yumizuki found in the pages of *Young Jump*. A decade later, TEACHER'S PET would demonstrate that nothing ever changes. ⊘

CINNAMON THE MOVIE

2007. Movie. DIR: Gisaburo Sugii. SCR: Mari Okada. DES: Marisuke Eguchi, Takashi Nakamura. ANI: Marisuke Eguchi. MUS: Takayuki Hattori. PRD: Sanrio. 45 mins. (m), 10 mins. (Internet series).
Cinnamon, or Cinnamoroll in English, is a cute little dog with huge floppy ears. He was born on a cloud in the sky and his ears enable him to fly. He floated off his cloud down to earth and landed outside Café Cinnamon, where the owner, Anna, took him in. She gave him his name because his plump, curly tail looks like a cinnamon roll. Now he and his magic puppy friends Mocha, Chiffon, Cappucino, Espresso, and

Milk are all set for adventure in the Forest of Pastries by the Coffee Waterfalls.

Sanrio's character stable is vast and as lucrative as any string of thoroughbreds. They have two highly profitable groups of punters in mind—the kiddie market and accessory-crazy women with money to burn—and they spare no expense in promoting and presenting. They invest in the best teams to turn their contenders into winners. Look at the crew list for this fluffy, silly movie. Gisaburo Sugii, one of the giants of anime directing, with a score by Takayuki Hattori, and animation from Madhouse under AKIRA's Takashi Nakamura. This is a heavyweight team, the kind that makes box office stardust, and it has delivered the goods: Cinnamon became Sanrio's second most popular character after HELLO KITTY.

Chisato Seki and Yumi Tsurikino created a sugar-sweet manga called *Fluffy Fluffy Cinnamoroll (Fuwa Fuwa Cinnamon)* in 2004. It ran in several children's magazines until 2008 and helped attract audiences to the movie. Cinnamon had a further animated outing in 2012, when a ten-minute net animation, *Cinnamon's Parade (Cinnamon no Parade)*, was released to celebrate his tenth anniversary. He and his friends also starred in four video games and made guest appearances in *Hello Kitty* games, MMORPG *Hello Kitty Online,* and *Hello Kitty*'s animated shows. He has appeared in music videos and has his own blog.

CIPHER THE VIDEO

1989. Video. DIR: Tsuneo Tominaga. SCR: Machiko Kondo, Yuko Sakurai. DES: Yukari Kobayashi. ANI: Kenichi Maejima, Takeshi Koizumi, Minoru Yamazawa. MUS: Wags, Thompson Twins. PRD: Victor Entertainment. 40 mins.

In this adaptation of Minako Narita's 1985 manga from *Lala,* pretty-boy Cipher goes to high school in New York, sometimes posing as his twin brother, Shiva, a famous actor who often needs to cut classes. Shiva wanders moodily through the streets of New York before the scene shifts to the set of his latest movie, an American football tale called *Winning Tough.* We see a fake "Making Of" documentary featuring interviews of him and his costars before being shown the trailer for the film and an image video based on it. Eventually, Shiva

returns from his wanderings and cooks breakfast, revealing that his wanderings were just wanderings, not the result of a fight with his brother.

Cipher the Video is a true curiosity, featuring English-language dialogue with Japanese subtitles for that extra touch of exoticism, although it was never released outside Japan. Deliberately shot in an MTV pop-video style, much of it is simply overlaid with songs from American movies contemporaneous with the manga—Phil Collins' title song from *Against All Odds* (1984), as well as the title song and "Let's Hear It for the Boy" from the same year's *Footloose,* all in relatively poor versions from the group Wags. As an additional bonus, there's also the original version of the Thompson Twins' "Kamikaze." The running time is bulked out with the self-indulgent "Making of *Cipher the Video,*" recycling some footage for a third time, featuring interviews with the crew and live-action shots from the New York location hunt that informed some of the admittedly picturesque images of the city. As a bonus, the video also includes Cipher's other animated appearance, a short 1986 Japanese commercial for Sumitomo Insurance. An earnest and ultimately touching treat for fans of the manga. Narita specialized in a fantasy America—her earlier manga *Alien Street* (1980) is set at a U.S. college where a beautiful, blond Arab prince flirts with liberal Western ways.

CIRCUIT ANGEL

1987. JPN: *Circuit Angel: Ketsui no Starting Grid.* AKA: *Circuit Angel: Resolving Starting Grid.* Video. DIR: Yoshikazu Tochihira, Hideki Tonokatsu. SCR: Mami Watanabe. DES: Chuichi Iguchi, Boomerang. ANI: Hiroshi Kazawa. MUS: N/C. PRD: Studio Unicorn. 45 mins.

Mariko is a downtown schoolgirl who loves motorcycles and wants to graduate from the street-racing circle of her friends to the world of pro racing. But despite poaching LEGEND OF ROLLING WHEELS—writer Watanabe and concentrating hard enough on machinery to justify a "Mariko's Bike Designed by" credit for the Boomerang agency, little can disguise this show's true nature as a rip-off of the far more successful BOMBER BIKERS OF SHONAN.

CIRCUIT WOLF II

1990. JPN: *Circuit no Okami II: Modena no Ken.* AKA: *Circuit Wolf II: Ken [Sword] of Modena.* Video. DIR: Yoshihide Kuriyama. SCR: Dai Kuroyuki. DES: Satoshi Yamaguchi. ANI: Satoshi Yamaguchi. MUS: GL48. PRD: Gainax, CBS. 45 mins.

Qualified racing-driver Satoshi Ikezawa's *Circuit Wolf* comic ran in *Weekly Playboy* magazine for 18 volumes in 1975, reputedly gaining considerable praise through its author's appreciation of the realities of racing. This is a sequel to the manga, rather than a nonexistent anime predecessor, and features a young racer, Ken, arriving in Italy in search of his missing Ferrari Dino. Car chases and road rages soon ensue against the fearsome "White Wolf of Stuttgart." **NV**

CITY HUNTER *

1987. AKA: *Nicky Larson.* Movie, TV series/special. DIR: Kanetsugu Kodama, Takashi Imanishi, Tetsuro Amino, Kiyoshi Egami. SCR: Hiroyuki Hoshiyama, Yasushi Hirano, Akinori Endo. DES: Yoshiko Kamimura. ANI: Takeo Kitahara. MUS: Ryoichi Kuniyoshi. PRD: Sunrise, Yomiuri TV. 25 mins. x 51 eps. (TV1), 25 mins. x 63 eps. (TV2, *City Hunter 2*), 25 mins. x 13 eps. (TV3, *City Hunter 3*), 87 mins. (m1, *Magnum*), 45 mins. (TVm1, *Bay City Wars*), 45 mins. (TVm2, *Million Dollar Plot*), 25 mins. x 13 eps. (TV4, *City Hunter '91*), 90 mins. (TVm3, *The Secret Service*), 90 mins. (TVm4, *The Movie*), ca. 92 mins. (TVm5, *The End*).

Ryo (Joe, in some U.S. dubs) Saeba is a professional "sweeper," an Equalizer who packs a .357 Magnum and specializes in bodyguard details in the Tokyo district of Shinjuku, where he can be reached through coded messages on the train station billboard. Promising his dying partner, Hideyuki, that he will look after Kaori, Hideyuki's sister, the terminally lecherous Ryo is lumbered with a prim female assistant, who nevertheless remains eternally jealous of his conquests.

Tsukasa Hojo's 1985 *Shonen Jump* comic proved even more successful than his CAT'S EYE, running for a total of 35 volumes. The regular cast of characters, including Ryo, surrogate wife/daughter Kaori, policewoman Saeko, and rival investigator Reika (all gorgeous, of course) would be reprised for TV directed by CAT'S

EYEalumnus Kodama. The TV edition kept Ryo's relationships with his female clients unconsummated, preferring instead to truncate many seductions with farce and slapstick.

Steadily gaining popularity (the closing theme "Get Wild" became a hit in its own right), the series moved from seven to six o'clock after 51 episodes. An 87-minute theatrical feature, *Magnum of Love's Destiny* (1989), was released in the U.S. as *.357 Magnum* and featured beautiful European pianist Nina trying to track down her father amid a then-topical backdrop inspired by the reunification of East and West Germany (here renamed Galiera). In a typical *City Hunter* set-up, Nina is the unwitting mule for a vital microchip planted on her by a Communist agent shortly before his own death. Ryo takes one deceptively simple mission only to find himself deep over his head in another.

With new theme music but otherwise unchanged, seasons two and three introduced occasional hour-long "special" episodes that were eventually to become the franchise's medium of choice. *Bay City Wars* (1990) features a Central American dictator using drug money to take over the world and reprogramming U.S. nuclear missiles, all from the titular Shinjuku hotel. Ryo's natural lechery is brought to the fore when he must stop the general's beautiful daughter from destroying the world. *Million Dollar Plot* (also 1990) pits Ryo against a CIA conspiracy to liquidate a beautiful rogue agent.

City Hunter '91 was the fourth and final TV series, ending after just 13 episodes. However, in 1993, the franchise was rejuvenated by Wong Jing's live-action film, which cleverly exploited the show's popularity abroad by casting big Chinese names in the lead roles—Jackie Chan as Ryo and *A Chinese Ghost Story*'s Wang Zhuxian as Kaori. One of the few anime series brought back regularly for TV specials (another is LUPIN III), Ryo's more recent one-shot TV adventures have included *The Secret Service* (1996), in which he teams up with a pretty secret agent to protect the leader of a banana republic, and *Goodbye My Sweetheart* (1997—released in the U.S. as *City Hunter "The Movie"*), which imitates PATLABOR 2 with its tale of a disgruntled soldier bringing his war experiences to

Tokyo. *The End of Ryo Saeba* (1999) quite patently wasn't—it's likely that *City Hunter* will be back before long. In the meantime, the "special" format has been retroactively imposed upon the original series in Japan, now shuffled into 20 video compilations designed to showcase the best TV episodes, out of chronological order but in a semblance of feature-length editions. At least part of the *CH* franchise lives on in Hojo's ANGEL HEART, in which a former assassin receives a prominent character's heart in a transplant operation. **NV**

CITY OF SIN
2001. JPN: *Ryojoku no Machi/Toshi: Kyoen no Ceremony.* AKA: *City of Rape: Ceremony of Mad Banquet.* Video. DIR: Shoichiro Kamijo. SCR: Yasuyuki Muto. DES: Dozamura. ANI: N/C. MUS: N/C. PRD: Green Bunny, Fuyusha. 30 mins.
Princess Beatrice is sent off to a foreign country in a diplomatic marriage, but her initial excitement about marrying a handsome prince soon turns sour. Under the rule of Prince Franchesco, rape is legal and it is a crime not to be pregnant, turning the princess and her ladies in waiting into targets for the officerclass of their new home, intent on breeding the next generation of warriors. Based on the manga *Secrets of the World* (*Chikyu no Himitsu*) by "Dozamura." NB: The Japanese title clearly has the characters for *toshi* (city), but includes the roman transliteration of *machi* (town). Compare to KOKUDO-OH: BLACK EYE KING. **LNV**

CLAMP
Formed as Amarythia, a circle of amateur manga creators in 1989, this group's original 12 members fell to seven by the following year and to four during production of RG VEDA. The survivors are Nanase Okawa (1967–), Mokona Apapa (1968–), Mick Nekkoi (1969–), and Satsuki Igarashi (1969–), although they have subsequently changed their pseudonyms and now desire to be known as Ageha Okawa, Mokona, Tsubaki Nekoi, and Satsuki Igarashi (written with new *kanji*). Their role in the anime adaptations of their work is minimal, but as the originators of the original stories and looks of the characters, they have been influential figures since the 1990s, with shows such

as CARDCAPTORS, TOKYO BABYLON, CHOBITS, and ANGELIC LAYER.

CLAMP SCHOOL DETECTIVES *
1997. JPN: *Clamp Gakuen Tanteidan.* TV series. DIR: Osamu Nabeshima. SCR: Mayori Sekijima, Masaharu Amiya. DES: Hiroshi Tanaka. ANI: Toshikazu Endo, Yuki Kanno. MUS: Michiya Katakura. PRD: Studio Pierrot. 25 mins. x 26 eps.
Nokoru, Suoh, and Akira are the Elementary Division Student Council, leaders of the sixth, fifth, and fourth grades in a private urban school for ten thousand of Japan's smartest (read: richest) children. Moonlighting as private investigators in the fashion of CONAN THE BOY DETECTIVE, they solve mysteries (missing school records found, feckless bullies caught) and troubleshoot in affairs of the heart for their fellow students. A minor work from CLAMP, creators of CARDCAPTORS (who seem to have realized that only the inclusion of their brand name in the title would guarantee any attention), this harmless series was originally aimed at a female audience that was expected to be charmed by polite, well-mannered rich boys solving minor problems.

CLAN OF PIHYORO
1988. JPN: *Gense Shugoshin Pihyoro Ikka.* Video. DIR: Satoshi Dezaki, Tsuneo Tominaga. SCR: Kazumi Koide. DES: Akio Sugino, Setsuko Shibunnoichi. ANI: Akio Sugino, Setsuko Shibuichi, Yukari Kobayashi. MUS: Noriaki Yamanaka. PRD: Bandai, CBS, Movic. 60 mins.
Kyota, Sabatta, Q-ta, and Kyonta are the guardian spirits of our age, protecting Earth from evil spirits while masquerading as humble students at the Seiwagi ("Holy Japanese Citadel") middle school. Suspecting supernatural involvement in the suicide of female student Maiko, Kyota, and Kyonta investigate, only to discover that their school is built on a prehistoric crematory, and the restless dead are haunting the students.

Kaori Himeki's fantasy manga from *Princess* magazine was originally going to be adapted into a video series, but its chances were destroyed when AKIRA was released barely a week later. Fantasy anime fell out of favor, and this abortive first episode never got further than its theatrical double bill with the digest edition of **AIM FOR THE ACE** 2. A few years later, the likes of **POLTERGEIST REPORT** made *Clan of Pihyoro* more appealing, but it was too late. Note director Satoshi Dezaki, working here with designer Sugino, who is normally associated with his brother, Osamu.

CLAN OF THE KAWARAZAKI

1996. JPN: *Kawarazaki-ke no Ichizoku the Animation*. Video. DIR: Shungyo Makokudo. SCR: Shungyo Makokudo. DES: Seifun Yamahatei. ANI: Harashu Suzuki. MUS: N/C. PRD: Triple X, Pink Pineapple, KSS. 30 mins. x 2 eps. (v1), 30 mins. x 4 eps. (v2).
Mukuro, a college boy working through vacation as a servant of the aristocratic Kawarazaki family, explores a mysterious pavilion on the grounds of the family mansion. Tempted by gorgeous women and "forced" to commit sexual acts, he is dragged into an alternate world of passion and free love. Or is it just a dream?

This otherwise unremarkable erotic anime was based on a 1993 computer game (from Silky's—apostrophe *sic*, we never said this would be easy) that was one of the first in Japan to have multiple endings instead of a single narrative—hence the hallucinatory aspect of the story line as the pseudonymous crew tries to cram in as many finales as possible. The first series was followed in 2004 by a four-episode sequel, *Clan of the Kawarazaki 2* (*Kawarazaki-ke no Ichizoku 2*), which was inspired by Silky's sequel to the original game. **Ⓝ**

CLANNAD *

2008. TV series. DIR: Tatsuya Ishihara. SCR: Fumihiko Shimo. DES: Kazumi Ikeda, Mutsuo Shinohara. ANI: Kazumi Ikeda. MUS: Jun Maeda, Magome Togoshi, Shinji Orito. PRD: Kyoto Animation, TBS. 25 mins. x 24 eps. (TV1), 24 mins. (v), 24 mins. x 24 eps. (TV2, *After Story*).
Tomoya Okazaki is failing at school, bereaved by his mother's death and troubled by his father's subsequent descent into alcoholism. But he somehow befriends a girl with problems of her own—Nagisa has been kept back a year because of illness, and now faces the prospect of being ostracized by her old friends because she is in a younger class. Tomoya plays along with Nagisa's desire to start a school drama club, breathing new life into his world and

new confidence into his interactions with other girls.

Once upon a time, all over the world, people in high school dreamed of what they'd do afterward, when real life began. In Japan today, people in high school watch anime about idealized high school life and dream of what they'd do if high school were really like that. Meanwhile, in America, grown-up anime fans watch anime about high school and dream of going back there, or somehow transporting themselves to the altogether different Japan of **EVERYDAY ANIME**. But if school really were like *Clannad*, every girl would slot into an easily parsed cliché (**STEREOTYPES AND ARCHETYPES**), with some deep problem that only you could resolve (compare to **BAKEMONOGATARI**). Every scar and trauma of your childhood could be simply forgotten, buried under an avalanche of cute, rather than having to be lived with and worked out. *Clannad* is a brilliantly calculated manipulation of the simple teenage emotions that lie buried deep inside most of us, the ultimate gut-wrenching riff, the hook placed precisely in the song to grab you every time. It's so brilliant and so artificial that it would be repellent if it weren't so admirable: an artifact of almost demonic potency.

Kyoto Animation is working here at the top of its game. It isn't just about the beauty of the animation, the meltingly sweet designs and gorgeous backgrounds. It's about the cleverness of the writing, the precision of pacing and plot, the way every note in the score works with the visuals. Timing, both in animation and soundtrack, is raised here to the level of magic, not a frame or a sound out of place. Most harem anime (**ROMANCE AND DRAMA**) are easily dismissable. This kind is dangerous because it's harem anime raised close to perfection. After watching it, even jaded old encyclopedists need a dose of something clever and cynical and grown-up to bring us out of the clutches of this beautiful drug. It will rot your brain and make you weep with nostalgia for something you never had.

CLASS FULL OF GHOSTS

1998. JPN: *Kyoshitsu wa Obake ga Ippai*. Video. DIR: Toshiya Shinohara. SCR: Makiko Sato. DES: Yutaka Hara. ANI: Yoko Furumiya,

Yumiko Kanehara. MUS: N/C. PRD: Toei. 23 mins. x 2 eps.
Writer Sato and illustrator Hara, creators of **HOLY THE GHOST**, returned for this children's tale of a haunted classroom. Guaranteed high sales and a video release when selected, like **CHOBI THE CUTE LITTLE CAT**, by the Japanese Library Council as a core title, the second episode features computer graphics of our hero banishing the spooks from his school. See **HERE COMES HANAKO** for the full story of Japanese school ghouls in the 1990s.

CLASS REUNION *

1997. JPN: *Dosokai. Yesterday Once More*. Video. DIR: Kan Fukumoto. SCR: Yo Tachibana. DES: Jun Sato, Toru Mizutani. ANI: Shinichiro Takagi. MUS: Kazuya Matsushita. PRD: Lemon Heart, ARMS, F&C Co. 30 mins. x 4 eps. (v1), 30 mins. x 2 eps. (*Again*).
Meeting for a reunion after a long time apart, the former members of Sakura Junior High Tennis Club discover new, forbidden pleasures in each other's company and agree to meet again, to catch up on old times, of course.

In *Class Reunion Again* (2002) the graduates reassemble at a reunion party on New Year's Eve. They are all in their 20s now, but Mizuho is excited because she gets to see her secret high school crush Tatsuya again. Aya also loved her childhood friend Tatsuya. Domestic misunderstandings, a ski trip, Mizuho's mother's illness, Tatsuya's car accident, and Aya's fling with her childhood friend Mamoru lead to a moderate amount of licentiousness, but considerably more angst and soul-searching, and end up with some licensed sex for once, after Aya and Tatsuya's wedding. Each of the two episodes features a different "path" and ending, one for Mizuho and one for Aya. In other words, a pastiche of *The Big Chill* (1983), initially in the style of the many Japanese live-action TV shows that feature 20-something class reunions, dating back to *Seven People in Summer* (*DE)—there is at least one of these shows every season on live-action TV, so it is little surprise that an erotic anime pastiche would eventually arise. Based on a computer game, itself part of the subgenre of dating sims and named in a deliberate echo of the characters used in the Japanese title of **END OF SUMMER**. **Ⓝ**

CLASSMATE

1998. Video. DIR: Satoshi Kato. SCR: Yuka Kurokawa. DES: Yoshihito Murata. ANI: N/C. MUS: N/C. PRD: Five Ways. 28 mins.

Not to be confused with END OF SUMMER, another anime whose Japanese title can also be translated as "Classmate," this later release is a surprisingly old-fashioned CREAM LEMON clone, featuring a schoolgirl, Nami, who wants to have sex. Surprise, surprise—she gets some. **N**

CLASSROOM OF ATONEMENT *

2001. JPN: Shokuzai no Kyoshitsu. Video. DIR: Takayuki Yanase. SCR: Rokurota Makabe. DES: N/C. ANI: N/C. MUS: Yoshi. PRD: YOUC, Digital Works (Vanilla Series). 25 mins. x 2 eps.

Nanase's father is a suspect in a murder trial. Never having heard of "innocent until proven guilty," some of her classmates take the law into their own hands and decide to mete out judgment of their own by raping her after school. However, one still believes that Nanase's father is innocent and reveals that the murder was actually the result of a blackmail attempt that backfired, dating back to the school days of their own parents, when one exposed the bullying activities of another who went on to become a famous cram school entrepreneur. A confused and involved mystery unravels, which might have been an interesting study of the way that childhood cruelty can escalate into adult crime, were it not for the regular scenes of sex and abuse that mark this as another entry in the VANILLA SERIES. **LNV**

CLAYMORE *

2007. TV series. DIR: Hiroyuki Tanaka. SCR: Yasuko Kobayashi, Kazuyuki Fudeyasu, Daisuke Nishida. DES: Takahiro Umehara, Manabu Otsuzuki, Yoshifumi Sueda. ANI: Takahiro Umehara, Kim Dong Joon, Haruhito Takada. MUS: Masanori Takumi. PRD: Madhouse Studios, avex mode, D.N. Dream Partners, NTV, VAP. 23 mins. x 26 eps.

Humans and demonic Yoma predators exist side-by-side, because Yoma can shapeshift to pass as human. This makes it easier for them to hunt. To defend mankind, a halfbreed force of woman warriors has been created, human-Yoma hybrids commonly known as the "silver-eyed witches"—or Claymores, after the huge swords they carry. They are hated by pure-bred humans, but tolerated as a necessity. A boy called Raki loses his whole family, and most of his village, in an attack by a Yoma wearing the shape of his older brother. He is driven away from his home by his surviving neighbors, afraid he might turn out the same. The Claymore who killed his brother, a girl called Clare, lets him join her on the road.

Norihiro Yagi's 2001 manga is still running in Japan, and its devoted fanbase lapped up this TV version. The problem, as with all TV anime, is of compressing a long story arc with plenty of chances to fill in detail into a series of bite-size chunks. Claymore is a beautifully designed compilation of boys' adventure anime tropes. True, the main characters are mostly women, but slim, blonde girl warriors with with big blades and hidden emotional needs are rarely a drawback in any boys' scenario. True, protagonist Raki is as vacuous as an empty plastic bag, but that's no disadvantage when you want an audience to write themselves onto his blank slate. True, the temptation to animate swordfights cheaply leads to many of the action sequences consisting of flashing lines across blank screens—the animators should have been made to watch SWORD OF THE STRANGER and NINJA SCROLL and either done it right or done less of it better. But overall, this is still a solid rebuild of well-tried components. The best of the art is in the opening sequence. The rest of the animation is uneven—some excellent scenes that show how Madhouse earned its reputation, embedded in budget-saving static pans—but the color design is interesting, using contrasting tints and lighting to create or emphasize mood and emotion.

The progression of battles with bigger and bigger foes, building up the fighter's power, strength, and technique through torture, pain, and survival, is the classic boy's anime journey from DRAGON BALL to BLEACH and NARUTO: same path, same challenges, same techniques of resolving them. The range of Claymores with special fighting techniques and skills also harks back to classic boys' series: you can't help but think of GETTER ROBO when watching the drill-arm sequences. Even the character development runs along boys' anime lines: everyone even slightly interesting or heroic has some dark trauma in childhood; the strongest of warriors is a monster without a human relationship to keep him or her grounded. Nothing new here, then, and certainly nothing to boost anime's much-vaunted "feminist" credentials, but a decorative reversioning of the classic slugfest with extra eye candy. **NV**

CLEOPATRA DC *

1989. Video. DIR: Naoyuki Yoshinaga. SCR: Kaoru Shintani, Sukehiro Tomita. DES: Nobuteru Yuki. ANI: Tai Fujikawa. MUS: Hiroaki Suzuki. PRD: Agent 21, JC Staff. 30 mins. x 3 eps.

Cleo, the chairwoman of the Cleopatra financial conglomerate, is so rich that she controls much of the U.S. economy and is described as the "moving capital of the world." When a light aircraft crash-lands in her bedroom, the delirious pilot can only give her the message "Mary Anne." Investigating with her assistant, Surei, Cleo determines that he is referring to the daughter of the oil minister, rumored to have been kidnapped by the sinister Junior.

After bungling a hit on Cleo, Junior's discredited henchman Apollo turns on his former boss, who is forced to seek help from Cleo herself. The final episode features Cleo going to Nice on holiday, where she is embroiled in an android plot, in a lightweight adventure series from AREA 88's Kaoru Shintani.

CLEOPATRA: QUEEN OF SEX *

1970. JPN: Cleopatra. Movie. DIR: Osamu Tezuka, Eiichi Yamamoto. SCR: Shigemi Satoyoshi. DES: Ko Kojima. ANI: Kazuko Nakamura, Gisaburo Sugii, Yoshiaki Kawajiri. MUS: Isao Tomita. PRD: Mushi Pro. 112 mins.

Three young people from the 21st century have their minds sent back into the past, into the bodies of people living in Alexandria at the time of Julius Caesar's first meeting with Cleopatra. One of the two young men is a lecher who vows that he will seduce Cleopatra instead of just watching. Having won over Caesar (depicted as a cigar-chomping American politico riding in a horse-drawn Edsel) and Mark Antony, Cleopatra is defeated by Octavian's homosexuality and takes her own life.

Screened in U.S. cinemas, where it was allegedly the first animated film to receive an X rating (in fact, it was never submitted to the MPAA, presumably for fear that, after all the hype, it wouldn't get one), *Cleopatra*'s release coincided with a temporary suspension of business at Mushi Pro. A financial disaster in Japan and misleadingly marketed in the U.S. as hard-core erotica, *Cleopatra* was Astro Boy–creator Tezuka's last-ditch attempt to recoup money for his troubled company, though the production was reportedly characterized by defecting animators, who had realized that little could save Mushi and stole anything that was not nailed down. In part, the problems had been caused by Tezuka's own habit throughout the 1960s of passing on budgetary shortfalls from one production to the next. Although this stood him well during the boom era, it created an ever-widening money pit in straitened times. When his earlier A Thousand and One Nights failed to recoup its costs at the box office, he began production on *Cleopatra* already ¥9.1 million in the red. The production's salability was not helped by Tezuka's own artistic experiments, including the opening scenes set in the future as an ironic reversal of the distinctive animation style of the U.S. series *Clutch Cargo*. Whereas *Clutch Cargo* featured live mouths matted onto animated faces, *Cleopatra*'s future scenes were shot as live-action but with anime faces matted onto the human actors. Other art-house experiments included foolhardy anachronisms such as gladiatorial combat staged as TV events and the murder of Caesar presented as a kabuki drama (a famous scene from *Chushingura*—see Woof Woof 47 Ronin), bringing the story to a screeching halt for several minutes. **◐**

CLEAVAGE *

2006. Video. DIR: Takashi Kondo. SCR: N/C. DES: Akira Kano. ANI: N/C. MUS: N/C. PRD: D3. 30 mins. x 2 eps.
Yuto Todo and his sexy, big-breasted stepsister Eriko are left alone in the family home when his father transfers to Sapporo for work. Yuto's mother died when he was very young, and his father married Eriko's widowed mother soon after. Yuto loved his stepmother, and when she too died he was as heartbroken as Eriko. Left alone, the pair argue about household chores until Eriko offers to help Yuto in another way. But when they unwisely have sex in school under the gaze of the security cameras, their sexy, big-breasted art teacher threatens them with wider exposure unless she gets what she wants. Based on a porn game by Seishojo, the most offensive thing about this predictable dross is that Yuto complains Eriko isn't pulling her weight at home because she's too absorbed in her studies. **◐**

CLIMBING ON A CLOUD

1990. JPN: *Kumo ni Noru*. Video. DIR: Osamu Sekita. SCR: Shoji Imai. DES: Eiichi Endo. ANI: Eiichi Endo. MUS: Masanori Iimori. PRD: JC Staff. 50 mins. x 2 eps.
Goodfella–creator Hiroshi Motomiya wrote this very different tale of gang warfare for *Comic Morning* in 1988. Set in a Buddhist heaven where saints fight over turf in the clouds, it features Niomaru, a man searching for the younger sister torn from him in an aircraft accident back in the human world. Motomiya is better known today for Salaryman Kintaro, which has also been adapted as a live-action TV series and film.

CLOCKWORK FIGHTERS: HIWOU'S WAR *

2000. JPN: *Karakuri Den Hio Senki*. AKA: *Puppetry Legend Chronicle Hio; Armored Chronicle Hiou*. TV series. DIR: Tetsuro Amino. SCR: Sho Aikawa. DES: Kazu Kamiyadera, Junya Ishigaki, Hajime Jinguji. ANI: Koji Aisaka. MUS: Hiroshi Yamaguchi. PRD: Bones, NHK2. 25 mins. x 26 eps.
When his humble village is attacked by the cruel Wind Ninja, Hio breaks the ultimate rule of his people and hides within the holy of holies of his village shrine. There, he awakens the Homra, an ancient tribal totem given to Hio's clan by people from another dimension. Hio discovers he has inherited a fabulous power from his ancestors—the ability to summon and control fearsome devices he can only describe as "puppets." And Homra is no ordinary puppet; it is a powerful weapon.

In 19th-century Edo (Tokyo), the emperor is merely a puppet—it is the shogun who truly rules, though not for much longer. Japan is alive with calls for revolution: "Restore the emperor! Expel the barbarians!" Only the noble samurai Ryoma Sakamoto (see Oi Ryoma!) can turn the tide of history, but with an eye on the children's market, writer Aikawa created this imaginary teenage sidekick to reach a new audience. For good measure, he throws in two warrior princesses as well.

As the SF benchmark year 2000 became a reality, many anime companies were already firmly focused on the past. Exhausting the early 20th century with Sakura Wars and its fellow martial arts shows, they delved back into the 19th—with suspicious synchronicity, both *Clockwork Fighters* and Tree in the Sun were announced in the same month.

CLOSE THE LAST DOOR

2007. JPN: *Saigo no Door o Shimero!* Video. DIR: Tama. SCR: Tama. DES: Takepon. ANI: Takepon. MUS: N/C. PRD: Phoenix Entertainment. 30 mins.
Two young men duck out on the party after a wedding. Atsushi Nagai is secretly in love with the groom, Toshihisa Saito, and drowns his sorrows while venting his hatred of the new bride. Kenzo Honda is a friend of the bride, but takes care of Nagai when he gets so drunk he can hardly stand. When the pair come round next day, they find that the bride has run away, and the abandoned groom is soon wondering whether his cute young colleague isn't a better bet. But now Nagai is torn between Honda and Saito…. Based on Yugi Yamada's manga published in 2001, this is a light-hearted story of men struggling with their sexuality, but not too hard. **◐**

CLUSTER EDGE

2005. TV series. DIR: Makoto Ikeda. DES: Yoshihito Hishinuma, Kimitoshi Yamane. ANI: N/C. MUS: Masayuki Negishi. PRD: Sunrise, Bandai Visual, TV Tokyo. 25 mins. x 25 eps.
Thirty years after the outbreak of war, the technologicallyadvanced Republic of Legrante invades the Principality of Rubel, intending to use it as a staging post for the invasion of other countries. However, the prestigious boarding school Cluster E.A. is allowed to continue to operate within conquered Rubel territory—a place where once stood a clone factory designed to make soldiers. Agate Fluorite arrives at the school, where he is a breath of fresh air for jaded old hands like Beryl and Fon, who are bored by the perpetual pressure to live up to their parents' expectations.

Like other children of privilege in **CREST OF THE STARS**, the students realize that they are part of a plot by their elders, and that peaceful student life will soon be disrupted by more belligerent, adult concerns. Anime for girls, set in a boys' school, or at least so it is claimed—although the show seems superficially aimed at a female audience, its action often bears a greater resemblance to boy-oriented Sunrise shows. A manga by Wan Komatsuda preceded the show in *Lala DX* magazine, but considering that the origin is credited to Bandai's house pseudonym Hajime Yadate (now *there's* your clone factory), we assume that the anime was conceived first, and was not based on the manga.

CLUSTER EDGE
2005. TV, video. DIR: Masashi Ikeda. SCR: Masashi Ikeda, Tetsuo Takahashi. DES: Yoshihito Hishinuma, Kimitoshi Yamane, Yukiko Ogawa. ANI: Yoshihito Hishinuma, Takashi Hashimoto et al. MUS: Takayuki Negishi. PRD: Sunrise, Bandai Visual. 24 mins. x 25 eps. (TV), 24 mins. x 3 eps. (v).
Cluster EA is an ultra-elite academy where students from many lands are trained to become future leaders in their home countries. As with many private schools, the student body is a fairly homogenous group. They spend their days looking broodily cool, wearing extravagant uniforms, observing arcane rituals, bullying and being bullied, meddling in politics, and keeping dark secrets. New student Agate Fluorite bursts into this apparent stasis and changes everything. His open, cheerful nature isn't the only thing that draws others to him—he has a strange power, linked to the banned technology of Artificial Soldiers. This has attracted the attention of a religious sect and the military.

"Based" on Wan Komatsuda's manga, with an original concept credited to Sunrise house name Hajime Yadate and director Ikeda, this show is a splendid example of how fascinating concepts and pretty character designs can be seriously hampered by poor execution. The problems of dealing with human weapons in peacetime isn't a new one, inside or outside anime: witness **CYBERNETICS GUARDIAN**, **VOTOMS**, and the number of terrorists now unemployed in Ireland but busier

than ever in Africa and the Middle East. The discrimination and injustice faced by those who do society's dirty jobs is another compelling theme. Anime touches on it in stories from **ASTRO BOY** to **CLAYMORE**.

But it all comes back to the writing. *Cluster Edge* has a slow, uneven first half, and an embarrassing number of recap episodes, saving on budget but frittering away momentum. The pace picks up in the second half, and the final episodes form a well-written and fascinating finale with some strong character development: too little, too late, alas. Three "specials," filling in backstory for some of the characters, appeared on volume 9 of the DVD release.

COCKPIT, THE *
1993. Video. DIR: Yoshiaki Kawajiri, Takashi Imanishi, Ryosuke Takahashi. SCR: Yoshiaki Kawajiri, Takashi Waguri, Ryosuke Takahashi. DES: Yoshiaki Kawajiri, Toshihiro Kawamoto, Hironobu Saito. ANI: Yoshiaki Kawajiri, Toshihiro Kawamoto, Hironobu Saito. MUS: Kaoru Wada. PRD: Madhouse, Jamco Video, Visual 80. 30 mins. x 3 eps.
This trilogy retells three stories from Leiji Matsumoto's long-running *Battlefield (Senjo)* series, here retitled at the author's request and assigned to three different studios. The first, *Slipstream*, is a Faustian tale, handled by **WICKED CITY**–director Kawajiri, about the Luftwaffe in August 1944. Nazi ace Rheindars (a look-alike of **CAPTAIN HARLOCK**) is asked to escort an atomic bomb to Peenemunde, where it is to be loaded onto a V-2 rocket. However, he eventually sabotages the project, even though it will mean the death of his ex-lover Marlene, a twin of **QUEEN EMERALDAS**. Rheindars's plight is depicted as a pact with Satan and comes loaded with arch antinuclear messages—Marlene warns that only the truly evil would ever use atomic weapons, while Rheindars's commander anachronistically describes the V-2 as the world's first missile. In the final scene, as Rheindars saves Britain from nuclear holocaust, he describes himself as "the man who *did not* sell his soul to the Devil," though this line was absent from the original Japanese script and appears to have been improvised on the day of the recording.

Pointedly shifting ahead a year to the day before Hiroshima in August 1945,

Sonic Boom Squadron is a naval story focusing on Nogami, a Japanese kamikaze rocket-plane pilot. As in director Imanishi's **GUNDAM** stories, men are slaves to their machines, both sides suffer, and, in one scene, a Japanese pilot is found to have an exact double on the U.S. aircraft carrier he is attacking. The futility of the navy pilots, sacrificing their lives to carry human bombs to targets they will never reach, is echoed by their American counterparts, who mourn a promising comics artist shot down by the "crazy Japs." The hero, for his part, wants to be a rocket scientist and fly to the moon, but now finds himself piloting a human bomb.

The final part leaps back to 1944 (presumably to make Hiroshima the worthy centerpiece) and the Allied assault on Leyte in the Philippines. Directed by **SPT LAYZNER**'s Ryosuke Takahashi, *Knight of the Iron Dragon* features Japanese army officers, all of whom have sworn never to surrender, realizing that they will have to retreat. A young motorcyclist goes to fetch the last artillery group but finds them almost completely wiped out. Despite the attractive prospect of desertion, he resolves to return to his base. A mechanic who used to be a motorcycle racer offers to help out, and there are shades of *The Great Escape* as they rush across the war-torn island to reach the base in time. Again there is an element of tragedy; the base has already fallen, but it becomes a matter of honor that they go to die with their comrades.

With Nazis and Japanese soldiers for heroes, this could have easily added to anime's bad press, but, though Matsumoto is clearly in love with the idea of defeat, the superb animation and thoughtful script make this one of the triumphs of anime. It is also available in two excellent translations, in the U.K. from Kiseki (1995) and in the U.S. from Urban Vision (1999). **ⓥ**

CODE GEASS *
2006. JPN: *Code Geass: Hangyaku no Lelouch*. AKA: *Code Geass: Lelouch of the Rebellion*. TV series, video. DIR: Goro Taniguchi, Makoto Baba, Kazuki Akane. SCR: Hiroyuki Yoshino, Yuichi Nomura, Ichiro Okuchi, Kazuki Akane, Miya Asakawa. DES: CLAMP, Takahiro Kimura, Kenji Teraoka, Eiji Nakada,

Junichi Akutsu, Takumi Sakura, Takashi Miyamoto, Yoshinori Hishinuma, Takeshi Sato. ANI: Takahiro Kimura, Eiji Nakada, Seiichi Nakatani, Yuriko Chiba, Shuichi Shimamura. MUS: Hitomi Kuroishi, Kotaro Nakagawa, Ichiko Hashimoto. PRD: Sunrise, Bandai, Hakuhodo DY Media Partners, MBS, Bandai Namco Games, PROJECT G-AKITO. 24 mins. x 25 eps. (TV1), 25 mins. x 25 eps. (TV2), 28 mins. (v1), 51 mins. x 4 eps. (v2).

Another world, another reality—but though dimensions shift, *realpolitik* never changes. In the 21st century, the globe is split between three superpowers: the Holy Britannian Empire, the Chinese Federation, and the European Union. Clever, sardonic, self-consciously superior Lelouch Lamperouge is a Britannian Prince, son of Emperor Charles. He and his adored little sister Nunnally are sent to Japan as a political bargaining tool after their mother is murdered—a shock that left Nunnally blind and unable to walk. When Britannia conquers Japan, Lelouch realizes his own powerlessness—in the ruins of his host country, he vows that he will one day bring down his father's empire.

Fast forward seven years, and Lelouch meets a mysterious girl in a terrorist attack. She saves his life, and gives him the power of *geass*, the Power of the King—the ability to command anyone to do anything, providing he makes direct eye contact. He decides to use this power to find out who killed his mother and make the world a better place for his sister. Along the way, almost by accident, he becomes the leader of the Japanese resistance. But others possess the power of *geass*; and there are other forces just as significant in play. He's not the only clever, ambitious commander with loyal followers and extremely cool armor.

Code Geass is the kind of show to get history geeks—people who usually drone on about LEGEND OF GALACTIC HEROES—standing on their seats and cheering. Created by Ichiro Okuchi and Goro Taniguchi at the TV hit factory Sunrise, it was designed and honed for success with the same calculated brilliance that Kyoto Animation brought to CLANNAD. Both character design team CLAMP and animators Sunrise have a solid track record in manipulating a huge cast of characters for maximum audience appeal, spinning attractive and beautifully dressed avatars with highly colored lives impacted by very real problems. If you don't identify with *someone* in this alternate reality, despite their fancy clothes and arcane names, yours is a very unusual reality indeed.

The concepts that work so well in those stories—old, rich, powerful figures manipulating the world from their shadowy eminences while the poor, the dispossessed, and the young suffer until a hero arises to lead them; brothers and friends parted by loyalty—is an ancient and powerful narrative, derived from sources that were old when Homer filched from them for the tale of Achilles in his *Iliad*. *Code Geass* shows that the old tunes can sound very good on a fancy new fiddle. We particularly like the clever way Japan's fears and resentments about colonization by the real-world U.S.A. are displaced onto colonization by a fictional "Britain," although it bears little resemblance to any Britain we know. Indeed, the Britannian Empire specifically excludes the British Isles, which in the internal politics of the story have been subsumed within the European Union.

Perhaps the greatest asset of *Code Geass* is its attraction for female viewers (compare to ESCAFLOWNE), who gravitate to its tortured pretty-boys, heroic poseurs, and powerful females like fangirls to OURAN HIGH SCHOOL HOST CLUB. This does not detract in the slightest from its action credentials, but it does lend an additional dimension to its tangled plotlines and arcane politics in an era where foreign anime FANDOM has more or less achieved gender parity. All those who used to say you couldn't get girls interested in overtly political, overthought plotlines have long since been buried under an avalanche of fanfic and convention lectures on the politics of HETALIA, victims of a failure to evolve to the point where they could realize that the audience that loves Dorothy Dunnett's immense historical sagas and matches the boy buyers copy-for-copy on *Game of Thrones* is going to devour a show that gives them more of the same in anime form.

The green shoots of success were carefully tended to ensure that the franchise would bear fruit. Three light novels by Okuchi appeared between 2007 and 2009, with a "visual novel" game (ARGOT AND JARGON) in 2008. A number of *Code Geass* computer games have been released in Japan, and characters have made guest appearances in other games. A manga by Taniguchi and Okochi with art by Majiko appeared in 2006 and ran until 2010, with three more manga storylines in 2007 and another two in 2010, one of which is still running. Director Morita and Tojo Chika got in on the manga act in 2012 with *Code Geass: Oz the Reflection,* also still running. The avalanche of merchandising—CDs, radio dramas, toys, books—continued through the gap between the first TV series and the second, *Code Geass: Lelouch of the Rebellion R2 (Code Geass Hangyaku no Lelouch R2)* in 2008.

On the anime front, CLAMP fans had fun in 2012 with a *Code Geass* version of *Alice in Wonderland*—a playful spin-off where Lelouch uses his power to make the entire *Code Geass* cast into puppets to entertain his sister. *Nunnally in Wonderland* has not yet had a legal release in English. Makoto Baba, an episode director on the original series, directs Yuichi Nomura's script. The four-part video *Code Geass: Akito the Exiled (Code Geass Bokoku no Akito)* which appeared in January 2013 is a side story centering on new and minor characters, directed by Kazuki Akane and written by Akane and Miya Asakawa.

CODE: BREAKER *

2012. TV series. DIR: Yasuhiro Irie. SCR: Yasuhiro Irie. DES: Yukie Akitani. ANI: Yukie Akitani. MUS: Takayuki Hattori. PRD: Bandai Visual, Bushiroad, Kinema Citrus, Kodansha, Lantis, Memory Tech, MBS, Tokyo TV. 24 mins. x 12 eps.

Teenager Sakura Sakurakoji becomes convinced that new transfer student Rei Ogami is a Code Breaker—a government assassin with superpowers. She's right, of course, and is soon plunged into an espionage war in which the Code Breakers are made to commit atrocities in the name of a greater good. Based on a manga in *Weekly Shonen* magazine by Akimine Kamijyo that suggests scowling school outcasts are really superheroes and that the homecoming queen is sure to waste her time stalking them.

CODE-E

2007. TV series. DIR: Toshiyuki Kato, Ichiro Sakaki. SCR: Takuya Sato. Ichiro Sakaki, Jukki Hanada, Junji Nishimura, Toshifumi Kawase. DES: Tetsuhito Saito, Kazuhiro Ito. ANI: Tetsuhito Saito. MUS: Caoli Cano. PRD: Studio DEEN, avex entertainment, Nagoya Broadcasting Network. 25 mins. x 12 eps. (TV1), 25 mins. x 12 eps. (TV2, *Mission-E*). It's 2017, and the Ebihira family moves house again. Eighteen-year-old Chinami Ebihara has spent her entire school life as a transfer student. She has an uncanny ability that she can't control—when she gets into an emotional state, she generates electromagnetic waves that knock out any electrical device in the area: cellphones, computers, TVs, air conditioning, medical devices … But when another student, geek genius Kotaro, realizes her unusual ability, he decides to study her, and romance ensues. A second series, *Mission-E,* aired in 2010. Kotaro and Chinami have secured funding from a big corporation and set up their own organization, OZ, to help people like her integrate into society. She has cool body armor to control and channel her abilities, and it comes in handy when facing off against the mysterious Foundation, who want to control such talents for their own ends. Cocreator Sakaki's manga *CODE-EX* began publication in 2007. He also adapted the concept as a novel in 2008, with art by Koji Ogata, who also wrote the **BOOGIEPOP PHANTOM** books. Kaede Sasahara also gets a creator credit for both series.

Ichiro Sakaki's inoffensive highschool comedy *Mission-E* (2008) functions as a direct sequel and also features nods and winks to other anime, with cosplayers from **MOETAN** and NAMCO's *Valkyrie* games, costumes inspired by **BUBBLEGUM CRISIS**, a guest appearance by virtual idol Hatsune Miku (**HATSUNE MIKU LIVE PARTY**), and a nod to *Back to the Future* (1985).

CO-ED AFFAIRS *

1998. JPN: *Koin Tenshi: Haitoku no Lycée-nne.* Video. DIR: Sai Imazaki. SCR: Sai Imazaki. DES: Sai Imazaki. ANI: Sai Imazaki. MUS: N/C. PRD: Uill Animation, JVD. 30 mins. Schoolgirl Mitsugu Amago convinces her neighbor Hiroyuki to take off his clothes while taping him with her new video camera. Upon showing the result to her

friends Moemi and Reina, they decide they enjoy the result and want to do it again. What follows are three vignettes in which Hiroyuki is persuaded to do a repeat performance for all three girls, who explore his male anatomy and physiology; then their own; and finally they experiment with exhibitionism and public urination, all of which is recorded with the camera and presented as an amateur erotic video. The voice actors try their best, but there is so little motion that the result often seems more like an illustrated radio drama than animation. Though an interesting concept that could have been much more entertaining given anything resembling a real budget, the finished product seems almost as amateur as the video it purports to portray. Bundled in 2001 on a single DVD with **OFFICE AFFAIRS** under the umbrella title *The Affairs.* **Ⓝ**

COICENT *

2010. JPN: *Koisento.* Video. DIR: Shuhei Morita. SCR: Shuhei Morita. DES: Daisuke Sajiki, Junichi Taniguchi. ANI: Yuji Shigenuki. MUS: Reiji Kitazato. PRD: Sunrise, Bandai Visual, Showgate. 26 mins. Some things don't change with time. In 2710, the city of Nara is still a tourist mecca for its temples and historical sites, and the deer of Nara are still shameless scroungers. Some are bold enough to nose their way into tourists' pockets and even steal their bags, looking for treats. But the white deer that runs off with schoolboy Shinichi's bag is very unusual. He gives chase, and runs into a girl called Toto. Together they roam the city. Director Morita is a past master at manipulating mood and color and telling a story in economical shorthand—see **KAKURENBO: HIDE AND SEEK**. Here he creates a pacy, involving, and enjoyable entertainment by wrapping dazzling visual conceits around the old boy meets girl/loses heart story. Although this one-shot had to be paired with a totally unrelated story, **FIVE NUMBERS**, to make an English-language DVD release viable, it's a little gem and worth the price of the disc in its own right.

COLLEGE INVESTIGATOR HIKARUON

1986. JPN: *Gakuin Tokuso Hikaruon.* Video. DIR: Kazuhiro Ochi. SCR: Kazuhiro Ochi. DES: Kazuhiro Ochi. ANI: Mutsumi Inomata,

Osamu Nabeshima. MUS: Michiaki Watanabe. PRD: AIC. 30 mins. In a school under attack from the evil demon Ura, mild-mannered Hikaru can transform into Hikaruon, a superpowered hero dedicated to battling monsters. Along with his beautiful assistant, Azumi, he fights off the bad guys in this spin-off of the long tradition of superhero shows that stretches all the way back to **ULTRAMAN**.

COLLEGE SUPERGIRLS

1991. JPN: *Za [The] Gakuen Chojotai.* Video. DIR: Satoshi Dezaki. SCR: Noriko Hayasaka. DES: Jumu. ANI: Yukari Kobayashi. MUS: Nobuo Ito. PRD: Magic Bus. 45 mins. In this short-lived adaptation of Tatsuhiko Dan's novel that was originally serialized in *Shonen Jump,* Yumi, Kei, and Mai are three schoolgirls who moonlight as a secret crime-fighting team ever since experiments at the school Superpower Society went drastically awry and gave them all amazing abilities.

COLORFUL *

1999. TV series. DIR: Ryutaro Nakamura. SCR: Kazushi Sato. DES: Takahiro Kishida. ANI: Takahiro Kishida. MUS: Moka. PRD: Triangle Staff, TBS. 7 mins. x 16 eps. Torajiro Kishi's manga from *Young Jump,* full of panty-flashing gags and jiggling female flesh, was brought to late-night TV as part of the *Wonderful* program. The show enjoyed a second lease on life as one of the first to go straight to DVD in Japan—all 110 minutes were released on a single disc without a prior VHS appearance. Not to be confused with the feature film **COLORFUL: THE MOTION PICTURE**, which has nothing to do with undies. **Ⓝ**

COLORFUL: THE MOTION PICTURE *

2010. JPN: *Colorful.* Movie. DIR: Keiichi Hara. SCR: Miho Maruo. DES: Atsushi Yamagata, Takashi Nakamura. ANI: Masahiro Sato. MUS: Ko Otani. PRD: Ascension, Sunrise. 126 mins. A nameless soul reaches the train station where the dead are routed onward to new fates, only to discover that it has won the chance to be restored to life in the body of Makoto Kobayashi, a boy who has committed suicide. Against the clock, the newly awakened "Makoto" must try to find out what his greatest sin was in his previous life, and also determine what it was that led his host body to die in the first place.

This feature-length adaptation of a 1998 novel by Eto Mori has strong resonances with the Buddhist-informed afterlife of Kenji Miyazawa's Night on the Galactic Railroad, but also with *Stairway to Heaven* (1946) and many other liminal enquiries into matters of life and death, such as its near-contemporary Amnesia. However, despite its musings on the nature of reincarnation and fate, it is far more involved with the nature of modern *living*, and might be better regarded as a quintessential Everyday Anime, dwelling with a hyperreal sense of wonder on seemingly mundane occasions like a family dinner or two friends out shopping—compare to The Top Secret, whose characters often similarly fixate on mundane moments or images as they face death.

The anime adds only two significant elements to the original novel. One alters the character of the protagonist's angel guide from an old man to a perky young boy. The other sites the formerly placeless story in Tokyo's Kinuta district, where a lost local tramline is highlighted as an invisible connection between several elements of the story. This not only celebrates the director's own hometown, but subtly functions as a memoir of forgotten pieces of the anime business itself, since the same area was the home of Toho's animation division in the 1940s, until the failure of The King's Tail destroyed it. A break-out film for Keiichi Hara, who had previously spent more than a decade directing the gross-out comedy of Crayon Shin-chan, its fate in the English language was not helped by sharing the same title as the immensely more forgettable Colorful, hence the "motion picture" qualification added in some territories.

COLUMBUS

1992. JPN: *Columbus no Daiboken*. AKA: *Les Aventures de Christophe Columbe*. Movie. DIR: Yorifusa Yamaguchi. SCR: Thibault Chatel, Anne Colé. DES: Masahiro Kase. ANI: Masahiro Kase. MUS: N/C. PRD: Telescreen (SPO). 70 mins. (m).

As he nears the New World, Christopher Columbus tells cabin boy Paco about his youthful hardships, the difficulties of convincing others of his vision, and the final victory when King Ferdinand and Queen

Isabella agreed to sponsor his trip. The sailors are doubtful, though Columbus is vindicated when they arrive on land, but it's not the planned destination of Japan. This Franco-Japanese coproduction was made to commemorate the 500th anniversary of Columbus's "discovery" of America but not released in Japan until January 1993. Also appearing as one of the biographical subjects of Great People and *Stories of Greatness*, Columbus is a serious rival with Nobunaga Oda and Helen Keller to become the most-portrayed historical figure in anime. He was also the protagonist of *Adventurer: He Came from Spain* (2002, *Bokenmono*), an anime movie directed by Fumio Kurokawa and written by Nobuyuki Fujimoto, concentrating on his trials to secure funding from King Ferdinand and Queen Isabella of Spain, before finishing with the well-known story of his first landing in the West Indies. The authors presume that the subtitle in the English-language title refers to the point of origin of Columbus's *voyage*, since, although it may be a matter of some debate, most historians would argue that he came from the Republic of Genoa.

COMBATTLER V

1976. JPN: *Cho Denji Robo Combattler V*. AKA: *Super Electromagnetic Robot Combattler V; Combattra*. TV series. DIR: Tadao Nagahama. SCR: Masaki Tsuji, Keisuke Fujikawa, Masaru Yamamoto. DES: Makio Narita, Yoshikazu Yasuhiko, Studio Nue. ANI: Satoshi Dezaki, Yoshiyuki Tomino, Shinji Okada. MUS: Hiroshi Tsutsui. PRD: Hiromi Pro, Toei, NET (eps. 1–46); TV Asahi (eps. 47–54). 24 mins. x 54 eps.

Hyoma, Juzo, Daisaku, and token brat Kosuke are four boys handpicked from Earth's finest for their mental and physical prowess and trained to fly Professor Nanbara's Combattler super-robot. Invaders from Planet Campbell have awoken from their subterranean slumber and are threatening the inhabitants of the surface world.

In a story that will be original to anyone who has never heard of Battle of the Planets, it's up to the four boys, with the professor's daughter, Chizuru, as the chaste love interest, to use their giant electric yo-yo to protect Earth from the Campbell General Garuda. Toys from

the show reached the U.S. as part of the Godaikin line.

The first of director Nagahama's "Romance Super Robot Trilogy," followed by Voltus and Starbirds, creation is credited to the director and Saburo Yade—who would go on to be the house pseudonym responsible for the live-action Super Sentai series that hit its peak with the *Mighty Morphin' Power Rangers* (*DE).

COMEDIC ANGEL YUI

2006. JPN: *Rakugo Tennyo Oyui*. TV series. DIR: Nobuhiro Takamoto. DES: Miwa Oshima. ANI: Naoto Sawa. MUS: Jun Ichikawa. PRD: TNK, AT-X. 25 mins. x 12 eps.

Yui Tsukishima hopes to be a comedy entertainer when she grows up, although currently she has more pressing concerns, such as the fact that she and five other girls have been transported back in time to 19th-century Japan to fight monsters.

COMEDY

Sitcoms and funny animals have been popular since the days of Early Anime. The politically incorrect spectacle of a wife wrestling her love rival for possession of a feckless flirt in The World of Power and Women has cascaded down the generations, picking up new accretions as fashions change, to become the latest Tenchi Muyo! clone, and the funny creatures of Monkey and the Crab and *Animal Olympics* have mutated into the cat-girls and bunnies of shows like Mew Mew Power.

Hard to define but difficult to ignore, comedy is an ingredient in many successful anime, especially those made for TV, where weary businessmen and kids escaping from homework go to relax. Comedy can transfer to anime as a straight stand-up routine or a sketch, through short segments in shows like My Neighbor Tokoro, or Hisashi Eguchi's Rentaman segment *Kotobuki Goro Show*. However, it's more often given a narrative framework, however loose.

Anime has stolen some visual shorthand from manga and foreign cartoons: extreme distortion of the features, or the whole body, to convey heightened emotion. It has taken this to extremes in the "squashed down" or "super-deformed" artstyle, also known as SD. Super deformation can even arise in relatively serious anime like **FULLMETAL ALCHEMIST,** when characters in humorous moments temporarily switch into SD-mode—see **TROPES AND TRANSFORMATIONS.**

To some extent, comedy will always be a personal matter: we appreciate that instances of "comical" underwear loss in soft porn may leave fans of the genre quaking with mirth, although they do nothing for us. If anime humor appears lowbrow or simple in the West, this is because complicated verbal humor is more difficult to translate, and often falls apart in the hands of translators and directors who are, quite properly, more concerned with amusing a Western highschool audience than faithfully echoing ethnocentric gags (**TRANSLATION**). Comedy and profanity are two hot-button issues in anime **TRANSLATION;** when faced with humor, some have taken AnimEigo's lead in faithfully translating the original jokes in **URUSEI YATSURA,** and then appending footnotes to explain them. Others have followed the route Viz Communications took with **RANMA ½,** replacing original humor with new jokes designed to replicate the *effect* on a new audience. There are also still those who take the route of **SAMURAI PIZZA CATS** and **GHOST STORIES,** dumping much of the original in favor of a new, improvised script. Regardless of the attitude taken, all methods still depend on the ability of the translator or rewriter, not only to recognize puns and gags in the first place, but also to comprehend them and convey them. Comedy is the most recognizable place where DVD anime releases can have the most obvious divergence between dubs/dubtitles and subtitles—as witnessed by Phil Hartman's extensive improvisations as Jiji the cat in **KIKI'S DELIVERY SERVICE,** filling many moments for which the character was completely silent in the original Japanese version.

Comedies for children are a staple of most countries' broadcast media, given TV's entrenched function as babysitter. Their formula for success is largely unchanging; they give their little viewers bright colors, simple shapes, repetition of sounds, and broad-brush characterization, covering the daily routines of a small child's life with festivals, playtime, and food, all reinforcing simple moral messages about good behavior. Shows like

PIPI THE ALIEN and **PINCH AND PUNCH** didn't have much to offer adults even in their 1960s heyday, but the generation that grew up watching them went on to create **CHIBI MARUKO-CHAN** and **CRAYON SHIN-CHAN.** These two very different shows shared two important elements: they could be watched by small children, but they were made to appeal to an adult audience nostalgic for the simplicity of childhood. **CRAYON SHIN-CHAN** is a comedy as rude, crude, and broad as the mind of a little boy—its hero's boundaries may be very tight, but he pushes them for all he's worth. Comedies for older children tend to follow the same pattern, taking a different viewpoint on the routines of everyday life. They may throw in someone who thinks differently from the rest of the world, as in **GENIUS IDIOT BAKABON,** or an alien or magical MacGuffin like **DORAEMON** (or, for older boys, his avatar Doreimon in **VISIONARY**), or an adult who doesn't know how to be a role model, such as **DOCTOR SLUMP.**

Everyday life is the starting point for the gentle, observational humor of **SAZAE-SAN, DOTANBA'S MODERN MANNERS,** and **MY NEIGHBORS THE YAMADAS.** The advent of video in the mid-1980s showed the potential of the niche market, with a slice-of-life comedy for 30-something cat lovers, **WHAT'S MICHAEL,** being the first show to make the transit from a cautious video release to TV success. This in turn enabled TV shows like **MODERN LOVE'S SILLINESS** to target their specific audience (in this case, adult women) in evening or late-night slots. Everyday life can also be hell, and where there's pain there is, inevitably, comedy. Japanese businessmen enduring the daily grind to support increasingly disengaged families could see the funny side of **LAUGHING SALESMAN.** Families forced to share a home with a dotty, irritating, or downright malicious elder could let go of the tension with a good laugh at **MAD OLD BAG** or **ULTRA GRAN.** Teenage boys facing the twin challenges of hormonal change and social inadequacy find solace in **PING PONG CLUB** and **HIGH SCHOOL KIMENGUMI.**

Life and its problems are the great unifiers of comedy; language and culture can be its great dividers. Westerners tend to think of Japan as a homogenous society, but its regional variations of dialect and culture are as wide as those of Britain or

France. As with most developed nations, these variations are eroded by the monoculture promoted on the small screen, but are still reflected in comedy. Japan has its Tokyo lowlife comedy **FRITEN-KUN,** the Kansai equivalent **NANIWA SPIRIT,** and provincial biker high jinks in **YOKOHAMA'S FAMOUS KATAYAMA.** The differences between the capital and the nation's second city are pointed up in a host of comedies featuring Osaka's distinctive dialect and reputation for wisecracking and moneymaking, **JARINKO CHIE** and **COMPILER** providing examples which are great fun but difficult to translate. History always has potential for humor: **GINNAGASHI** takes us back to prewar Tokyo to watch amusing goings-on in a local bar, while **SHINSENGUMI FARCE** takes the Mel Brooks approach to right-wing extremism.

Foreign culture provides even more opportunities to generate laughs. Japan, like every other culture, is not above poking fun at foreigners in shows such as the **CHOCOLATE PANIC PICTURE SHOW.** Japanese attitudes can also lead to unintentional humor—a recurring problem in translating anime comes from the presence of ideas and names that can jolt an audience out of its suspension of disbelief: characters named after car models or rock bands, for example, in **RAYEARTH** and **BASTARD.** Other modes of inadvertent humor issue from Japan's attempts to imitate Western genres— **MAD BULL 34** is not intended as comedy, but is only really enjoyable to a non-Japanese audience as such, and ultimately the joke may be on the American stories the Japanese have so outrageously misread. Other abuses of foreign entertainment are intentionally humorous—the *X-Files* influence on **GEOBREEDERS,** for example, or the gloriously inappropriate use of Beethoven in **DRAGON HALF.**

Even if all other springs of laughter dry up, anime has one rich source to mine— itself. Anime parodying anime has its own short-form term, *aniparo,* which originated in fanzine culture to describe amateur comics spoofing favorite shows, but can also be applied to professional spoofs like the "super-deformed" **GUNDAM** spoofs, and the "cute-body" **DEVILMAN** pastiches. Shows like **IRRESPONSIBLE CAPTAIN TYLOR, AIRBATS,** and **SIGN OF THE OTAKU** all follow **OTAKU NO VIDEO** in offering up every convention of anime—story tropes, production methods, respected creations, and creators—as targets for mirth.

COMEDY ANGEL YUI

2006. JPN: *Rakugo Tennyo Oyui*. AKA: *Magical Travelers*. TV series. DIR: Nobuhiro Takamoto. SCR: Yasushi Yoritsune. DES: Miwa Oshima, Yutaka Miya, Takashi Miyano. ANI: Miwa Oshima. MUS: Jun Ichikawa. PRD: TNK, Rakugo Tennyo Association, Three Fat Samurai. 24 mins. x 12 eps.

Yui Tsukishima is one of six ordinary schoolgirls summoned into the Edo period by the power of magical jewels. Each has a different ability, which they must learn to use to protect people from evil forces threateneng the city. Yui's is a skill with words, which inspire others and give them hope. Yui loves traditional Japanese comic storytelling, *rakugo*. But how will this help her and her friends to face dark supernatural powers? This action-adventure for young girls is one of a long line of SAILOR MOON variations, very few of which have the power of the original. Still, the artwork is sweet if unremarkable, and Yoshinori Ueki's color design is fresh and pretty.

COMET-SAN

2001. TV series. DIR: Mamoru Kanbe. SCR: Akira Oketani. DES: Kazuo Makida. ANI: Miho Nakajima, Masamitsu Kudo. MUS: Kaba Konishi. PRD: Nippon Animation, TV Tokyo. 25 mins. x 43 eps.

Comet, a princess from planet Harmonica, is invited to a party with a princess from Castanet, where they discover that the prince of Tambourine, largest world in the Triangle Nebula, is trying to decide which of them he should take as his bride. Comet stomps off to Earth (which, when you think about it, is just as stupid a name for a planet), where her arrival brings magic and joy into the lives of a Japanese family. *Comet-san* has a convoluted pedigree, dating back to Mitsuteru Yokoyama's 1967 manga in *Margaret* magazine, itself an attempt to do a more grown-up version of his earlier LITTLE WITCH SALLY. A *Bewitched* clone, originally featuring a magical housekeeper from planet Beta, its 1967 TV adaptation was live-action but featured animated sequences directed by Tsutomu Shibayama. The 21st-century fully animated version is a product of its time,

playing up the "magical-girl" feel with a far younger protagonist and showing lots of pretty eye-candy girls.

COMIC PARTY

2001. TV series. DIR: Norihiko Sudo. SCR: Hiroshi Yamaguchi. DES: Hirokazu Taguchi. ANI: Mima Yoshikawa, Masao Nakada. MUS: N/C. PRD: OLM, KBS. 25 mins. x 13 eps. (TV1), ca. 30 mins. x 4 eps. (v), 25 mins. x 13 eps. (TV2).

Eighteen-year-old high school student Waki has already been accepted by a university and only has to wait for graduation. When this proves to be too boring to endure, he wanders into a manga convention and is dragged into the world of amateur comics. He befriends three young fanzine creators who are, of course, all pretty girls. This lighthearted comedy, a Dreamcast tie-in, is an ominous sign of the increasingly self-referential nature of the anime/manga market—compare to ANIMATION RUNNER KUROMI. In one pointed moment, a character bemoans America's domination of popular culture, announcing that it is time for Japan to take over with anime. The series was remade as *Comic Party Revolution*, originally intended as a two-episode video release, which was expanded to four episodes, which in turn were cut to form the first four episodes of a subsequent full-length television series.

COMPILER *

1994. Video. DIR: Takao Kato, Kiyoshi Murayama. SCR: Michitaka Kikuchi. DES: Yasuhiro Oshima. ANI: Yasuhiro Oshima. MUS: Toshiyuki Omori. PRD: Movic. ? mins. (v1, *Music Clips*), 45 mins. x 2 eps. (v2), 45 mins. (v3, *Festa*).

In a remarkably three-dimensional "2D Universe," female agents are dispatched to destroy the 3D Earth. Instead, they decide to stay with two Japanese boys and live a happy life of unwedded bliss and teen angst. One day, they decide to go on holiday in Osaka, a city long-neglected in anime since being buried under a mass of tentacles and spooge in UROTSUKIDOJI. In this anime based on SILENT MÖBIUS-creator Kia Asamiya's 1991 love-comedy in *Comic Afternoon*, Osaka becomes the venue for two naked female assassins sent from the 2D universe to terminate the turncoat terminators. They attempt to blend in by loading Osaka language chips, which

turns them into a pair of bitchy game-show hosts, but their gags will fall flat on an audience ignorant of Osaka's *manzai* comedy tradition (see JARINKO CHIE).

Much of the humor rests on the unique attitude and accent of Osaka's people—which could be described as Chicago gangster-talk and New York sarcasm combined with a ludicrous love of yen. The dubbing script tries to approximate the Osaka accent as a mix of Valley girls, Jersey longshoremen, and cretins, but, although there is a lengthy discourse on the history of Osaka baseball, this episode is almost incomprehensible without a set of liner notes, sadly lacking in AD Vision's translation.

Once the shapely Terminators ("We put the ass in Assassins!") have been defeated, the unfeasibly thick-haired Compiler fights with would-be beau Nachi about his flirting ways. Meanwhile, the innocent Assembler tries (unsuccessfully) to seduce Nachi's brother in a simple tale of Tokyo marital discord that was originally the first episode, switched by the U.S. distributor with the zanier second presumably to hold viewers' attention.

Redeeming features include a score from GOLGO 13's Omori that pastiches the *Godzilla* theme as Osaka food franchise logos turn into giant monsters and smash up "famous" landmarks, including the Hanshin Expressway, that would be destroyed for real in the following year's Kobe earthquake. HUMMINGBIRDS-director Murayama also provides clever moments such as background fountains that spurt in time with Compiler's anger and rubbernecking passers-by that add a really human touch to her argument with Nachi. But even these finesses can't rescue a show whose original raison d'être was not to entertain so much as to advertise.

A marketing tool designed to remind Japanese viewers of a manga that remains untranslated in English, *Compiler* has little purpose in the U.S. market. It follows late on the heels of *Music Clips in Trackdown*, a 1990 music video also designed to promote the *Compiler* characters but without the pretense of a plot. Sections from this early work are used in the closing credits to *Compiler Festa* (released as just plain *Compiler 2* in the U.S.), the final episode in which the 2D universe sends White Compiler, a deadly upgrade of our heroine, who is defeated again by homespun Earth boys and wisecracking alien girls. ◑

COMPUTOPIA

1968. JPN: *Computopia Seireki 2000-nen no Monogatari*. AKA: *Computopia: A Tale of the Year 2000 A.D.* TV special. DIR: Yoshikazu Kawamura. SCR: Masaki Tsuji. DES: Masami Shimoda. ANI: Sadao Tsukioka. MUS: N/C. PRD: Knack, Nihon TV. 30 mins. x 2 eps.

After the success of **FIFTH ICE AGE**, the *Wonderful World Travel* staff returned with this sci-fi documentary about the way New York might be in the distant year 2000, using real photographs of computer innards as backdrops for the cel animation—the first low-tech form of "computer animation," perhaps?

CONAN THE BOY DETECTIVE *

1996. JPN: *Meitantei Conan*. AKA: *Famous Detective Conan, Case Closed*. Movie, TV series, specials. DIR: Kanetsugu Kodama. SCR: Hiroshi Kashiwabara, Kazunari Kouchi, Shuichi Miyashita. DES: Masaaki Sudo. ANI: Masaaki Sudo. MUS: Katsuo Ono. PRD: TMS, Yomiuri TV (Nippon TV). 25 mins. x 700+ eps; 90 mins. x 17 movies.

High school student Shinichi Kudo accidentally takes a drug that gives him the appearance of a seven-year-old child. He takes the name Conan Edogawa (conjoining Arthur Conan Doyle and Ranpo Edogawa, the best of both occidental and oriental detective traditions) and specializes in cases that the adults just can't handle, using his childish guise as a means of avoiding criminal reprisals.

First appearing in 1994 manga in *Shonen Sunday* magazine by **YAIBA**-creator Gosho Aoyama, Conan has the body of a child but commands the thinking power (and respect) of an adult. He also has a band of young friends, the Juvenile Detective Club, who aid him in his investigations. As with the **YOUNG KINDAICHI FILES**, this caught a post-*X-Files* wave of interest in supernatural sleuthing and would make Aoyama Japan's highest-paid manga artist by 1999. The series was dubbed in the U.S., but into *Spanish*, where the hero was renamed Bobby Jackson (he may be known under this name to some viewers). *Conan* was released in the U.S. in English as *Case Closed* in 2004, with a few name-changes for the

local audience: Shinichi Kudo became Jimmy Kudo, Ran Mouri became Rachel Moore and Kogoro Mouri became Richard Moore. Conan, however, remained the same, although his adventures ran into localization difficulties in America. The original anime series was intended for older elementary to middle schoolers in Japan, but the presence of certain bloody scenes (it is, after all, a *murder* investigation!) led to the episodes being screened in the late-night Adult Swim section, and not in the earlier Toonami slot where its true American audience was.

Many of the TV story lines, such as the *Ski Lodge Murders* and the *First Love Murders*, spanned two episodes, so it was a simple step to expand into 90-minute movies. Conan's first theatrical outing, *Clockwork Skyscraper* (1997, released in the U.S. as *The Time Bomb Skyscraper* [*sic*, sans hyphen]), pits him in a battle of wits against a thief who has stolen high explosives from a military base; one has followed every year since. *The 14th Victim* (1998, released in the U.S. as *The Fourteenth Target*) has a stalker picking off members of the family who own the Aquacrystal restaurant and leaving playing cards pinned to their corpses. In *End of the Century Sorcerer* (1999), a child steals a priceless Fabergé egg, and the relatively simple quest to return it leads to a series of murders rooted in a historical vendetta. *Captured in Her Eyes* (2000), pits Conan against an enemy from within after the murder of a police officer turns all his associates into suspects. *Countdown to Heaven* (2001), with unfortunate synchronicity considering the 9/11 atrocities, features a secret society causing mayhem at the inauguration party of the new high-tech Twin Towers in Tokyo. The inevitable team-up with Sherlock Holmes arrived in *Phantom of Baker Street* (2002), engineered through a holodeck-style virtual game, in which one of the participants genuinely is murdered, allowing Conan to temporarily form a partnership with a facsimile of the world's greatest detective. The early 21st-century obsession with medieval sorcery, best demonstrated through the live-action success of *Yin-Yang Master* (*DE), found its place in the Conan franchise in *Crossroads of the Ancient Capital* (2003), in which Conan must journey to Kyoto to investigate an

enigmatic message found in a stolen image of Buddha. Another fashionable fad, this time for the Hokkaido of *From the North* (*DE) and **DIAMOND DAYDREAMS**, came to the fore in *Magician of the Silver Sky* (2004), in which Conan and his associates head up to Hokkaido, hoping to protect a valuable artifact from the attentions of the self-proclaimed master-thief Kaito Kid. *Strategy Above the Depths* (2005) takes Conan off on a cruise ship only to find himself a pawn in a plot for revenge. As with **CRAYON SHIN-CHAN**, annual movie outings have subtly (or sometimes not so subtly) presented variations on popular trends elsewhere in the media, with, for example, Conan searching for pirate treasure in *Jolly Roger in the Deep Azure* (2007), a terrorist hijack in *Lost Ship in the Sky* (2010), a bomb-threat on a soccer match in *The Eleventh Striker* (2012), and suspected foreign espionage aboard navy vessels in *Private Eye in the Distant Sea* (2013). Notably, the Conan films continue to have a following in China, even in the 21st century when most anime have been made to disappear from televisions in the People's Republic. Among the tiny quota of 35 foreign films permitted to reach Chinese cinemas each year, Hollywood, Bollywood, Disney, and Pixar have always had to leave one slot for Conan, and another for **NARUTO**, making it one of the truly bestselling anime franchises. In the TV special **LUPIN III**: *Lupin vs Detective Conan* (2009) and the feature film *Lupin III: Lupin vs Detective Conan the Movie* (2013), Conan pitted his wits against another anime icon.

There have also been several spin-off videos, including *Conan vs. Kid vs. Yaiba* (2001), pitting Conan against two other characters created by Gosho Aoyama. Seemingly introduced as an attempt to gain the yen of the original Conan audience as it matures into video-buying teenage years, it was followed by other Conan adventures on DVD, including *16 Suspects* (2002), *Conan and Heiji and the Disappearing Boy* (2003), and the heist story *Conan and Kid and the Crystal Mother* (2005), and *The Target Is Kogoro! Secret Investigation of the Detective Boys* (2005).

Conan's father starred in several Aoyama short pieces including *The Wandering Red Butterfly* and *Summer's Santa Claus*. These, along with the Conan-Shinichi team-up tale *Ten Planets in the Night Sky* and the unrelated stories *Investigator George's Little War*, *Play It Again*, and *Wait a Moment*, were animated as 20-minute specials by Osamu Nabeshima in 1998. In May 2005, manga author Gosho Aoyama somewhat creepily married Minami Takayama, the actress who provides the voice of Conan in the original Japanese version. They were divorced in 2007.

CONDITION GREEN

1991. JPN: *Inferious Wakusei Senshi Gaiden Condition Green*. AKA: *Inferious Interplanetary War Chronicle Condition Green*. Video. DIR: Shigeyasu Yamauchi. SCR: Yoshihisa Araki. DES: Shingo Araki, Michi Himeno, Eisaku Inoue. ANI: Eisaku Inoue. MUS: Kazuhiko Ito. PRD: Hero Communications, KSS. 25 mins. x 6 eps.

Keith, George, Edward, Yang, and Sho are Platoon #801, the five-man team formed to protect their homeworld in the Inferious galaxy from alien invasion. Gazaria's evil emperor Vince conquers the neighbor worlds of Kal and Granad and suddenly only Platoon #801, also known as Condition Green, stands between him and the conquest of Emerald Earth. Made straight-to-video despite the false appearance of two "25-minute TV episodes" per tape, *Condition Green* missed the point made all too well by **GUNBUSTER**, that only real TV could afford to be cheesy. The paying audience of the video market demanded more but didn't get it here from former **CRYING FREEMAN**–animator Yamauchi.

CONFUCIUS

1995. JPN: *Koshi-den*. AKA: *Life of Kong Zi*. TV special. DIR: Osamu Dezaki. SCR: N/C. DES: N/C. ANI: Noboru Furuse. MUS: N/C. PRD: NHK, NHKEP21, PTS, KBS, Image K, C&D. 45 mins.?

Born in the Chinese state of Lu in 551 B.C., Confucius is raised by his mother after his father dies when he is only three. He marries at 19 and enters the service of the local nobility. At 32, he becomes tutor to the Prince of Lu's children, eventually becoming a politician at 51. His career peaks are the roles of Lu's justice minister and eventually prime minister. The land prospers for four years, but Confucius grows disenchanted with court intrigues. For the following 12 years, he wanders the neighboring states, offering advice to their rulers.

Mystifyingly dropped from the earlier **GREAT PEOPLE** series in favor of such luminaries as Babe Ruth, China's most famous son was nevertheless considered a worthy subject by the many anime companies that cooperated on the TV movie. But since his life was uneventful and his victories disappointingly intellectual, it has but a single one-line mention in our Japanese sources.

CONNECTIVE SYSTEM

2008. JPN: *Renketsu Hoshiki*. AKA: *Consolidated System; Methods of Coupling*. Video. DIR: Hiromi Yokoyama. SCR: Ren Shimo. DES: Si Min Lee, Takashi Tenshumo. ANI: Sin Min Lee. MUS: Toshiyuki Yamamoto. PRD: Suzuki Mirano. 30 mins. x 3 eps.

Three unconnected stories about forbidden or nonconsensual sex. Keisuke's father is dying of cancer, and wants his son to marry the daughter of a former colleague and inherit the family liquor business. But Keisuke's sister Misaki decides that he belongs to her. In the second episode, a high school boy rapes his female classmates to prove he's not homosexual, then is assaulted by a male classmate and finds he is, actually. In episode 3 a girl who is gang-raped becomes sexually insatiable. These days erotic games and visual novels (**ARGOT AND JARGON**) are the most common sources for porn anime, but porn manga still has a strong following; these stories come from Hasumi Karino's original manga, which first appeared in 2005.

CONSENTING ADULTERY *

2006. JPN: *Mrs. Junkie*. Video. DIR: Masato Kitagawa. SCR: Renka Kou. DES: Mamito Tayama. ANI: Mamito Tayama. MUS: Salad. PRD: ANI FACTORY, T-Rex, Milky, Blue Gale. 30 mins. x 2 eps.

You can get anything in a well-serviced apartment. Here the part-time superintendant of the apartment complex also services the wives of two neglectful husbands. Anything to keep the tenants happy in this anime based on *Mrs. Junkie*, an erotic game by Blue Gale with characters by Yoto Tatsunami. See **ANYONE YOU CAN DO … I CAN DO BETTER** for details of sister titles in the franchise. ◐

CONTAGION

2009. JPN: *Kansen: Inyoku no Rensa*. AKA: *Contagion: Chains of Lust*. Video. DIR: Hiromi Yokoyama, Akiyumi Yoshizawa. SCR: Taifu Sekimachi, Kentaro Mizuno, Kaoru Takahashi. DES: Hikaru Kinohara, Si Min Lee, Gen. ANI: Noritomo Hattori, Si Min Lee, 44°C Baidoku. MUS: N/C. PRD: Suzuki Mirano. 28 mins. x 2 eps. (v1), 29 mins. x 2 eps. (v2), 28 mins. x 2 eps. (v3), 28 mins. x 2 eps. (v4).

High school students stay behind for their after-school movie club, but their teacher is taken ill and has to leave. Unknown to them all, a strange new virus is spreading like wildfire. Its main effect is to remove any sexual inhibitions. Based on a series of erotic games by SPEED, this concept was successful enough to spin off a further three two-part videos showing the effects of the virus. The second, *Sinful Town (Kansen 2 Inzai Toshi)*, released in 2010, starts with the virus hitting a school bus and causing a crash. Also out in 2010, *Collapsing Metropolis (Kansen 3 Shuto Hokai)*. *Kansen 5: The Daybreak* wound things up in 2012, rather confusingly as our searches on Japanese porn websites have not yet revealed a *Kansen 4*. Tsutomu Murakami, who storyboarded *Contagion*, also has a career as a key animator on mainstream titles. Whatever you're drawing, it's still drawing.

CONTROL—THE MONEY AND SOUL OF POSSIBILITY *

2011. JPN: *C - The Money of Soul and Possibility CONTROL*. TV series. DIR: Kenji Nakamura. SCR: Noboru Takagi, Kenji Sugihara, Manabu Ishikawa, Shinsuke Onishi. DES: mebae, Takashi Hashimoto, Toshiki Nishi, Hiroshi Ito. ANI: Takashi Hashimoto. MUS: Taku Iwasaki. PRD: Tatsunoko, Dentsu, Fuji TV, SME, Toho. 24 mins. x 11 eps.

The Japanese government was about to go bankrupt when it was rescued by the Sovereign Wealth Fund. But—as much of Europe has found out in the real world—rescuing a nation's economy from collapse still means deprivation, uncertainty, and misery for its people. Unemployment and despair are widespread, along with crime and suicide. It's a bad time to be an orphan like Kimimaro, raised by his aunt after his father vanished and his mother died. He's a hardworking, conscientious, scholarship boy whose only dream is to lead an ordinary life, free of the chaos and worry of a society in freefall. Then he meets a man who offers him enough money to secure that ordinary future—providing he allows it to be held as collateral for a bet. In an alternate dimension called the Financial District, he must compete in weekly tournaments, betting his life in a trade-off for cash. And just to make it interesting, everything he has to lose is personified in the form of his Asset: a cute girl whose existence is tied to his future.

This is one of the most audacious high-concepts ever for an anime show: *The Economist* meets **JOJO'S BIZARRE ADVENTURES**. Unfortunately, economics is a difficult topic to animate with anything approaching excitement. The battles of the global money business are fought with calculations and lines of text on a screen: the battles of most action anime are fought with giant robots and superweapons. But the idea that you trade your time, part of your future, against the security of cash is one to which everyone who's ever held down a job can relate, and the events that began to unfold across Europe around the time the show was screened provided an uncanny instance of life imitating TV.

Most of the story is predictable: *Wall Street* with anime fights (and yes, there is a Gordon Gekko). The character development is limited and the investment the viewer makes is accordingly not enormous. But the fights are amazing—intense, flashily animated, and convincingly painful. The final battle is one of the best in any action anime, and packs an emotional wallop missing from the rest of the show. File as a fascinating might-have-been, and hope someone resurrects the concept with more time and scope to evolve it.

COO OF THE FAR SEAS

1993. JPN: *Coo: Toi Umi kara Kita Coo*. AKA: *Coo: Coo Who Came from the Far Seas*. Movie. DIR: Tetsuo Imazawa. SCR: Kihachi Okamoto. DES: Masahiko Okura. ANI: N/C. MUS: Nick Wood. PRD: Toei. 116 mins. Excitably if weakly hyped in *Newtype* as "the best film for all the family, apart from something by Disney," this Christmas feel-good movie was based on a novel by Tamio Kageyama and written for the screen by live-action director Okamoto. A scientist's child on an idyllic Pacific island befriends

the titular creature, a baby plesiosaur whose mother has died. Other, less scrupulous people are searching for this relic of the dinosaur age, and our hero teams up with a beautiful female journalist to keep Coo safe until he can be released into the wild.

This charming film, greatly helped by ravishing backgrounds researched on real-life Pacific islands at great expense to the sponsors at the Fiji Tourist Board, marries the 1990s ecological fad of *Free Willy* and **FLY PEEK!** to the eternal guarantee that dinosaurs will get children into theaters.

COOK DADDY

1990. JPN: *Kyukyoku Chef Oishinbo Papa*. AKA: *Ultimate Chef Gourmet Papa*. Video. DIR: Kazuo Tomozawa. SCR: Kazuo Tomozawa. DES: Kazuo Tomozawa. ANI: Hiroaki Mizorogi. MUS: N/C. PRD: Agent 21. 45 mins. Kenzo Nishikata, an everyday chef in the Chinese restaurant Chin-Chin Ken, moonlights as an assassin. Disposing of his victims by serving them up as dishes of the day, he is sidetracked one day by the amorous attentions of Sai, the pretty college girl who works part-time as a waitress. Based on a manga by **TALES OF ...** and **SAKURA DIARIES**–creator U-Jin, and not to be confused with **OISHINBO**. ✪🔞

COOKIN' IDOL AI! MAI! MAIN!

2009. AKA: *Cooking Idol I! My! Mine!* TV series. DIR: Hiroshi Watanabe. SCR: Miharu Hirami. DES: Maho Takahashi. ANI: Atsuko Nakajima. MUS: Tomoki Hasegawa. PRD: NAS, Studio DEEN. 10 mins. x 155 eps. Main Hiiragi is a cooking idol—a pint-sized Nigella Lawson with all the cuteness but none of the finger-licking sexual innuendo. In her bright, candy-colored kitchen, aided by cooking fairies, she whips up a new treat every day. Then Haruka Fukuhara herself, who voices Main, turns up on camera in the flesh to show how to make the dish of the day. Of course, Main also has friends—including cute boy TV star Yasuno—family, and classmates to enjoy her cooking, and the show sets out to teach both the basic skills of kitchen work and the social element of sharing treats with others.

Nothing will expunge **CRYSTAL TRIANGLE** from director Watanabe's CV, but everyone gets a few clunkers in their career, and this

slice of sweetness goes a surprisingly long way toward redressing the balance, along with his work on **VIDEO GIRL AI**. It's also an interesting reflection of the worldwide popularity of cooking shows, an enduring theme in anime—compare to **OISHINBO** and **COOKING PAPA**. It's not the first show to present small children as competent in the kitchen, but it is the first to actually teach them some of the skills required. Anime like this run under most Western fans' radar but bring the medium back to its core audience: children.

The show ran every weekday for four years, ending in March 2013. A follow-up was announced in January and commenced on April 1. *Susume! Kitchen Sentai Cookrun* takes a slightly different angle on teaching cooking skills by framing them as a sci-fi team show. Three grade-school siblings—Ringo (Japanese for apple), her kid brother Sage, and little sister Cumin—receive cooking powers from space cook SuperChef and team up to fight Irakkin, her comic-relief husband Kuyoppen, and her evil army of Dark Eaters through the power of good food.

COOL COOL BYE

1986. Video. DIR: Tomonori Kogawa. SCR: Tomonori Kogawa. DES: Tomonori Kogawa, Akihiko Yamashita. ANI: Tomonori Kogawa, Hidetoshi Omori. MUS: Ken Sato. PRD: Toyo Links. 45 mins. Lek and Flena Han are a brother and sister on a mission to defeat the Big Machine, a giant robot that attacked their village and killed the inhabitants, in this forgettable title, which adds insult to injury by bulking out its running time with a 15-minute "Making Of" special.

COOL COUPLE

1999. JPN: *Iketeru Futari*. TV series. DIR: Takeshi Yamaguchi. SCR: Masayoshi Azuma. DES: Ryoichi Oki. ANI: N/C. MUS: N/C. PRD: JC staff. 7 mins. x 16 eps. A **HIS AND HER CIRCUMSTANCES** clone based on Takashi Sano's manga from *Young King* magazine, in which high school student Kyosuke Saji falls in love with class valedictorian Aki Koizumi. Though she is beastly to him at first and her friends equally cruel, eventually he breaks through and makes her his girl. Shown, like **COLORFUL**, as part of the late-night TV show *Wonder-*

ful, it was eventually compiled into two omnibus editions. **NV**

COOL-CUTE DECLARATION

2010. JPN: *Kakko-Kawaii Sengen!* AKA: *KakoKawa.* TV series, movie. DIR: mankyuu. SCR: N/C. DES: N/C. ANI: Gathering. MUS: AIR AGENCY. PRD: Gathering, Shueisha. 3 mins. x 12? eps.

"Only cool cute boys and girls appear in this comic!" is the declaration of Jigoku no Misawa, who created the gag manga on which these shorts are based. The joke is that the high school characters look anything but cute—they're plump, frizzy-haired, inept, or otherwise challenged—but they're cool where it counts. These first five animated shorts were run during a Shueisha TV show, and a second seven-episode series from the same crew followed later in 2010. In 2012 the cool cute gang teamed up with the characters from **BLUE EXORCIST**. *Blue Exorcist Movie Special (Ao no Futsumashi Gekijo)* was a three-minute short released on April 1. Four *KakoKawa* DVD compilations have been released in Japan.

COOL DEVICES *

1996. Video. DIR: Osamu Shimokawa, Megumi Saki, Yasuomi Umezu, Hiroshi Matsuda. SCR: Mon-Mon, Masamichi Kaneko. DES: Mon-Mon, Hiroyuki Utatane, Protonsaurus, Yasuomi Umezu, Naomi Hayakawa. ANI: Hiroshi Mori. MUS: N/C. PRD: Beam Entertainment, Leed Publishing. 30 mins. x 11 eps.

An umbrella title for disparate erotic stories from a number of mainly pseudonymous creators, the *Cool Devices* brand name was clearly valued highly enough by distributors Critical Mass to be kept for the U.S. release; compare this to Nu-Tech and Anime 18's treatment of the **SECRET ANIMA** series, which was broken up and released as stand-alone titles.

The subject matter often crosses the boundary of good taste—cartoon characters are more pliant actors than human beings, and though the sexualized violence of 1980s shows like **RAPEMAN** are less in evidence, there are still many sadomasochistic tales of women volunteering for abuse. One such example is *Curious Fruit* (#1), based on a manga from former **CREAM LEMON**—designer Mon-Mon, in which an innocent girl discovers her deep, dark

desires to be dominated. Incest is another recurring theme, as seen in *Sacred Girl* (#2), from **COUNT DOWN**–creator Hiroyuki Utatane, in which a rich orphan attempts, and fails, to overcome his longing for his sister by holding orgies at their mansion. It was back to bestiality and domination for *Lover Doll*, the lecherous male gaze in *Winter Swimsuit*, and toilet training in *Enema* (all #3). It's far shorter tableaux from *Secret Anima*'s Protonsaurus, little more than sex scenes and all but devoid of plot. For *Kirei* (#4), the setting moved to a summery beach for the seduction of two Japanese girls by a local lothario, much to their eventual regret.

Seek (#5–6) was based on a computer game from Hiroshige Tadokoro, retaining its origins even to the extent of keeping the male lead's face hidden to aid player/viewer identification. Although stretching across two 30-minute episodes, its chapters are only tenuously related—the innocent young Marino discovers how her "mostly unwilling body" is secretly crying out to be dominated by a smug male abuser. Once she has been taught her lesson, she is dragged in for another cavalcade of torment, alongside several other girls, in scenes of domination and electrocution that the U.S. distributor proudly claimed to be the "most disturbing tape of the entire *Cool Devices* series."

For Yasuomi Umezu's *Yellow Star* (#7), which looks and often plays like a prequel to his later **KITE**, a young girl is drugged and raped by her policeman stepfather, who uses the titular narcotic to ensure her cooperation. *Slave Warrior Maya* (#8–9), based on a manga by Konodonto, covers ground similar to the previous year's **FENCER OF MINERVA**. An innocent girl is transported to a magical world, where she is immediately captured by lizard-men and sold into slavery. Sold to a robot king (presumably because robots are not human and consequently cannot legally have genuine genitalia that need to be censored), she is subjected to slave training before revealing that she is really a warrior. The second volume is a far simpler tableau of bondage and domination, in which Maya's extra "appendage," revealed at the end of episode 1, is put to considerable use.

Binding (#10), another game spinoff, features character designs from **BEAST**

CITY–creator Naomi Hayakawa. For once it is the male character who gets the raw deal, as magazine writer Masaki has his wallet and train ticket stolen while stranded at a rural train station while pursuing the thief. He meets local girl Miyuki, who looks just like the girl in his dream, who takes him home to an isolated mansion on a hill by the sea. There he is welcomed by an all-female community who turn into a dominatrix and her submissives at sundown, tying him up and tormenting him, though in a more playful and consensual fashion than in other chapters.

The final volume to date is another Mon-Mon story, *Fallen Angel Rina* (#11). Recalling its contemporary **PERFECT BLUE**, Rina is a singer, fallen on hard times due to her father's profligacy, whose new manager makes her discard a wholesome girl-next-door image in favor of skimpy outfits and provocative appearances—resulting in her molestation by passers-by in the street, and even her own audience—before the makers' consciences are salved by an ending in which Rina gets her revenge (of a sort). **LNV**

COPIHAN

2011. TV series. DIR: N/C. SCR: N/C. DES: Yusuke Kamada, Yuko Sugiyama. ANI: Yusuke Kamada. MUS: Takashi Hamada. PRD: Gonzo, Studio Maus, Slowcurve. 6 mins. x 7 eps.

Tokyo, 2034: girls still wear cute school uniforms and hats with cat ears, and animators still make them into stereotypical characters and put them in situations with forced humor. A joint project of anime studio Gonzo and KEI, who created digital idol Hatsune Miku, this is based on KEI's 2010 manga *Copyhan: Saya and Sayu's Big Adventure (Copyhan: Saya to Sayu no Daisakusen).* The lack of writer and director credits for this Internet series might perhaps explain why this looks pretty, but does nothing much. Six minutes can seem like a long time online, even with cute animated schoolgirls.

COPPELION *

2013. TV series. DIR: Hiromitsu Kanazawa, Susumu Kido, Shingo Suzuki. SCR: Makoto Nakamura. DES: Shingo Suzuki, Hiroshi Okubo. ANI: Makoto Furuta. MUS: Mikio Endo. PRD: GoHands, Kodansha, Starchild Records, AT-X, BS11 Digital. 24 mins. x 12 eps.

In the year 2016, a nuclear meltdown at the Odaiba reactor causes the mass evacuation of Tokyo. A generation later, three bioengineered teenagers are sent into the dead zone in search of humans who may still survive amid the contamination. Tomonori Inoue's original 2008 manga was published in *Young Magazine,* home of AKIRA, with whose later manga chapters this post-apocalyptic exploration of human civilization has many parallels. Naturally, people who have been "trapped in the ruins" for decades are less like survivors and more like an outlaw society. This anime adaptation was originally announced in 2011 but swiftly put on hold after real-life events at the Fukushima nuclear reactor made the topic seem unpleasantly close to home. By the time it limped onto the airwaves, two years later than expected, it did so in a real-world Japan that, for the first time in decades, had *no* operating nuclear reactors.

CORAL INVESTIGATES

1979. JPN: *Coral no Tanken.* TV series. DIR: Seitaro Hara, Gen Mizumoto. SCR: Hideo Anzai, Tomoyuki Miyata. DES: N/C. ANI: N/C. MUS: Akihiro Komori. PRD: Chikara, Zak, Nippon Columbia, TBS. 25 mins. x 50 eps.
An animated show based on Albert Berié's French puppet show, in which Hector the Rat teams up with his fellow denizens of Pretty Wood, including the titular Coral (a young girl) and the unimaginatively named Crow (a crow), to head off to Holland. With many musical scenes, the voice actors were chosen for their singing ability above other considerations.

CORDA D'ORO, LA *

2005. JPN: *Kin-iro no Corda.* AKA: *Kin-iro no Chord: Primo Passo; La Corda d'Ora: Primo Passo; The Golden String.* TV series. DIR: Kunitoshi Okajima, Shin Katagai, Kojin Ochi. SCR: Reiko Yoshida. DES: Maki Fujioka, Chikako Shibata. ANI: Maki Fujioka. MUS: Mitsutaka Tajiri. PRD: Yumeta Company, Aniplex, Hakusensha, TYO. 25 mins. x 24 eps. (TV), 25 mins. x 2 eps. (v).
Seiso Academy has a specialist music track as well as a normal school curriculum. Kahoko Hino has never played an instrument in her life, but finds herself selected for the school's prestigious music competition, because she is the only

person who can see and hear Lili, the school's resident music fairy. He gives her a magical violin with a golden string, and tells her that if she trusts in the music and lets her emotions guide her, she will be able to play well. But magic is no substitute for achievement, and Kahoko begins to study music for its own sake, helped by the very cute boys in the music class. In 2009 two further episodes from the same team, but with a new director, were released on DVD, introducing a new character and revisiting the old favorites. Crashing the magical girl show into the reverse harem, with a magic familiar, a transformative object, and a whole group of princes, this is a competent show based on a series of computer games for the female market. Part of Koei's *Neuromance* game series, the franchise was launched in 2003. Yuki Kure's manga, which started running in 2004, continued until May 2011.

CORPSE PRINCESS *

2008. JPN: *Shikabane Hime.* TV series. DIR: Masahiko Murata. SCR: Sho Aikawa. DES: Chikashi Kubota, Kikuko Sadataka, Hiroki Matsumoto. ANI: Chikashi Kubota, Kikuko Sadataka, Keisuke Watanabe. MUS: Norihito Sumitomo. PRD: feel, Gainax, Square Enix. 24 mins. x 13 eps. (TV1), 24 mins. x 13 eps. (TV2).
A teenage orphan named Ori is drawn into the struggle of a dead girl for revenge. The bodies of Makina Hoshino and her family were found in the burned wreckage of their home, set on fire by undead beings who refuse to leave this world—*shikabane.* Now she is compelled to remove the undead from the world of the living in order to enter heaven. As she continues her quest, Ori learns more and more about his own hidden past. After a slow start with nine unevenly paced stories and *shikabane*-of-the-week scenarios, the pace tightens up in the latter part of the first season when the main protagonists of the second season show up. *Corpse Princess Black (Shikabane Hime Kuro),* the 2009 continuation from the same crew, moves along at a gallop compared to the first season, with too little time for almost anything except the girl-warrior action that was obviously the thing the makers enjoyed most about this series. Yoshiichi Akahito's 2005 manga of the same title is

still running, but there have been no more anime episodes. **NV**

CORRECTOR YUI *

1999. TV series. DIR: Yuji Muto. SCR: Satoru Nishizono. DES: Fumie Muroi. ANI: Shintaro Muraki, Miko Nakajima. MUS: Kenji Kawai. PRD: Nippon Animation, NHKEP. 25 mins. x 52 eps.
The young Yui is a manga fan who wants to be an anime voice actress when she grows up. One day, she is sucked into her computer, where she discovers that the gigantic computer Grosser intends to rule the human race from within cyberspace. The only way to stop Grosser is to join forces with pieces of mystic software (Eco, Rescue, Control, Peace, Follow, and Synchro) and her assistant, IR, combining to form the greatest debugging program known to man.

Mixing elements of COMPILER with Disney's *Tron* (a film conveniently old enough to be unknown to the target audience), Keiko Okamoto's manga for girls turns into a surprisingly old-fashioned affair in its anime incarnation. Though set in 2010, its heroine carries a magic wand and must assemble a team of mismatched troubleshooters, pausing regularly to hector her audience about computer terminology and keeping parks tidy. And like SAILOR MOON before it, the first season ends with the baddie defeated, but the plot resets to zero for a repeat performance. A curious combination of the preachy conservatism to be expected from a state-owned education channel like NHKEP and the formulaic, marketing-led appeal of a corporate creator like Bandai.

COSMIC FANTASY

1994. Video. DIR: Kazuhiro Ochi. SCR: Kazuhiro Ochi. DES: Kazuhiro Ochi. ANI: Keisuke Watanabe. MUS: Tatsuya Murayama. PRD: Tokuma. 45 mins.
A one-shot cash-in on a computer game in which the heroic Yu leads a team of interstellar crime-fighters against evil space pirates, in this case, the female buccaneer known as the Galactic Panther.

COSMOS PINK SHOCK

1985. Video. DIR: Yasuo Hasegawa, Keisuke Matsumoto. SCR: Takeshi Shudo. DES: Toshihiro Hirano, Rei Yumeno. ANI: N/C. MUS: N/C.

PRD: AIC. 36 mins.
An anime parody about Michiko dreaming of a promise her boyfriend, Hiroshi, made to her and then being whisked off into space on the Pink Shock spaceship, in which she rescues the denizens of a prison planet. The original was serialized as original content on the *Animevision* video magazine that otherwise consisted of trailers for other shows and assorted voice-actor gossip, eventually being compiled into a one-shot video the following year.

COSPLAY CAFÉ *

2004. JPN: *Hitozuma Cosplay Kissa*. Video. DIR: Hiroshi Shirasui. SCR: N/C. DES: Haruo Fuyuki. ANI: Haruo Fuyuki, PILGRIM. MUS: N/C. PRD: Atelier Kaguya, Milky, Aiko, J. Fox. 30 mins. x 2 eps. (v1) 30 mins. x 2 eps. (v2). Tomoya Asahina is the deputy manager of Noel, a café staffed by lonely housewives. He decides to lure in more customers by creating a new uniform, with a very high miniskirt and a low-cut top. His plan is greeted enthusiastically by the waitresses, who are soon "educating" Tomoya on the feelings and desires of older women, both in and out of their costumes. Based on a 2003 computer game by Atelier Kaguya—the *hitozuma* of the title literally refers to "someone else's wife," since in erotic movies they are invariably more fun than one's own. A two-part sequel followed in 2007. ⓛⓝⓥ

COSPLAY COMPLEX *

2002. Video. DIR: Shinichiro Kimura. SCR: Noboru Kimura. DES: Katsuzo Hayato. ANI: Sayuri Sugitou. MUS: Yoshinobu Hiraiwa. PRD: TNK, Wonder Farm. 30 mins. x 3 eps. Chako Hasegawa and her stereotypically defined friends are members of the Cosplay Association of East Oizuka Junior High and dream of taking their skills to the World Cosplay (i.e., costuming) Championships. An impossible dream? Not when they have the assistance of a magical owl and Delmo the costuming fairy (who can actually assume the shape of any costume required) and just the right amount of thread. The championship would be all sewn up but for the fact that the group's best cosplayer, Chako, has such a heavy crush on local hero Kosuke that she never seems able to do anything right.

Ever since OTAKU NO VIDEO, FANDOM has

increasingly turned its attention inward on itself—*CC* sits alongside titles such as COMIC PARTY and GENSHIKEN. *CC* recognizes the tensions within real-world costuming, that while the participants see their activities as a fannish but holy vocation, many of their audience simply want to ridicule them or ogle the girls in states of partial undress. Acknowledging both sides of the argument, *CC* includes costuming pastiches of fan classics like GUNBUSTER and even a DVD guide to the costumes worn, but also plenty of gratuitous naked flesh. Elements also play like one of the many computer game adaptations it coincidentally resembles, with Goro, the lone male member of the team, sitting amid a whirlwind of female hormones à la SAKURA WARS. Questionable, some might say racially and sexually repugnant, tension is added by the last-minute arrival of Jenny, a large-breasted blonde Italian transfer student with an unwholesome interest in little girls, whose behavior around preteen Athena would get her arrested in most countries. Not to be confused with *Cosmopolitan Prayers*, for which see under A15. The third episode ends with a trailer for a fourth, which was apparently never made. ⓝ

COSPLAY EXPOSE SEMINAR

2011. JPN: *Cosplay Roshutsu Kenkyukai*. Video. DIR: N/C. SCR: N/C. DES: N/C. ANI: N/C. MUS: N/C. PRD: MediaBank, Studio9MAiami. 20 mins. x 2 eps
Aya is a waitress at a cosplay café. When she gets an email inviting her to an anime convention, she goes along out of curiosity. The email says she'll be paid as much as she wants to do a photo session, on one condition: she has to obey the orders of all the males present. Otaku perversions and her own lusts soon turn the photoshoot into something very explicit, doubtless like the erotic game by Pin-Point on which this is based. ⓝ

COTTON STAR

1984. JPN: *Wata no Kuniboshi*. AKA: *Planet of Cotton*. Movie. DIR: Shinichi Tsuji. SCR: Masaki Tsuji, Yumiko Oshima. DES: Katsumi Aoshima. ANI: Katsumi Aoshima, Shinya Takahashi, Jun Kawagoe, Kuni Tomita. MUS: Richard Clayderman. PRD: Mushi Pro. 96 mins.

Cuteycat, a two-month-old kitten, is taken in by a young man called Tokio, who takes pity on her on a rainy day. Cuteycat becomes one of the family, though she has trouble winning over Tokio's mother, who is allergic to cats. Cuteycat is heartbroken when Tokio falls in love with a girl in the park, only to be rescued from despair when she meets the handsome, silver-haired tomcat Raphael, who explains that humans and cats can never truly be together.

Richard Clayderman's twee piano hits just the right note in this weepy romance. Yumiko Oshima's 1978 manga for *Comic Lala* was adapted here by its original author with veteran scenarist Tsuji. Years later, animator Tomita would defect to the U.S. to work on homegrown animation like *Invasion America*.

COUNT AND FAIRY

2008. JPN: *Hakushaku to Yosei*. AKA: *Earl and Fairy*. TV series. DIR: Koichiro Sotome. SCR: Noriko Nagao. DES: Maki Fujii, Mitsuharu Miyamae, Yoichi Yajima. ANI: Maki Fujii, Kazuya Morimae, Takafumi Shiokawa. MUS: Takehiko Gokita. PRD: Artland, AT-X, d-rights, Pony Canyon. 24 mins. x 12 eps. Seventeen-year-old Lydia Carlton lives in Scotland. She can see and communicate with fairies, but nobody believes her—after all, this is the 19th century. All that superstitious nonsense is out of date in the modern age. Lydia is approached by a young man named Edgar, who needs to hire a guide for his quest to find a family heirloom. But there's a darker side to his quest, and many unanswered questions that will put him and all his companions at risk. Made by legendary studio Artland in its 30th year of operation, and based on a book by Mizue Tani with art by Asako Takaboshi, this is a prettily designed and animated story merging Victorian romance with Celtic Twilight mythology. The story is incomplete, left dangling for a second series that never materialized, but fans of PANDORA HEARTS, GOSICK or VICTORIAN ROMANCE EMMA will still find plenty to enjoy.

COUNT DOWN *

1995. JPN: *Yuwaku Count Down*. AKA: *Temptation Count Down*. Video. DIR: Shoichi Masuo, Naohito Takahashi. SCR: Hiroyuki Utatane.

DES: Sanae Chikanaga, Ryunosuke Otonashi. ANI: Ryunosuke Otonashi. MUS: Kanji Saito. PRD: Pink Pineapple, KSS. 35 mins. x 6 eps.

Creator Utatane, best known in the mainstream for his SF manga *Seraphic Feather*, made an early name for himself drawing erotic short stories that were eventually compiled into the anthologies *Count Down 54321* and *Temptation–Erotic Excentric* [sic].

Animated as short vignettes, two to an episode, the stories include many basic erotic set-ups with a twist. A modern-day bus encounter leads to erotic confusion; a sword-swinging macho man meets his match in a girl who can tie anything down; a bride has a last minute encounter with her lover before taking that walk to the altar—quite literally; and a lesbian police officer in 19th-century Tokyo has to defend it against a giant robot (compare with **ROBOT CARNIVAL**'s *Tale of Two Robots*). The second episode (which did not survive in the initial American releases) includes the vignettes about a severely disturbed young man's relationship with a flesh doll whose hands remind him of his mother's, and the couplings of a transgender teacher, her female student, and the student's mother.

The final three episodes encompass a single story arc, *Akira*, featuring designs from **END OF SUMMER**'s Otonashi, a replay of the faux-incest of **CREAM LEMON**'s *Ami* stories. Akira Amemiya carries a torch for his stepsister, a supermodel, to the point of not allowing anyone to use his given name, reserving it for her alone. While waiting for her return from Europe, he fills his days and nights by bedding the women (and men) who are entranced by his extraordinary beauty (and equal talent in bed), despite his narcissism and indifference for the feelings of anyone but himself and his sister. Regardless of this, his fellow student Kaname falls for him, to the point of not being able to think of anyone else. When his sister eventually returns from Europe, all is not as Akira had hoped—will Kaname's love be able to break the ice around his heart? Notable for its beautiful art, the extensive use of stills, and minimal animation, except during the sex scenes.

Despite its relative obscurity, *Count Down* seems to have been regarded as something of a prize by American distributors and has changed hands several times.

Originally released in truncated form as *Countdown Conjoined* by ADV Films' erotica division SoftCel in 2000, it sneaked out again on Critical Mass Video (a subsidiary of Right Stuf) in 2007 as *Count: Down* (the colon makes all the difference), with the Akira arc on a separate DVD as *Countdown Akira*. Clearly a blue-chip investment, even during the burst of the anime bubble, it found its way to Kitty Media (the erotic arm of Media Blasters) in 2009, where it was (re-)released in its entirety. **LNV**

COUNTDOWN TO DELIGHT *

2001. JPN: *Bakuhatsu Sunzen Tenshi no Countdown*. AKA: *Before the Explosion Angel Countdown*. Video. DIR: Shoichiro Kamjio. SCR: Tekuro Imaike. DES: Hiura Konata. ANI: N/C. MUS: N/C. PRD: Green Bunny, Fuyusha. 30 mins.

Average Japanese boy Motoki gets more than he bargained for when his sister's lesbian lover proves that she is bisexual by offering him her body in secret. He escapes from such temptations when he falls in love with Natsuki, an innocent-looking girl who turns out to be a dominatrix. **LNV**

COWBOY BEBOP *

1998. TV series, movie. DIR: Shinichiro Watanabe. SCR: Keiko Nobumoto, Michiko Yokote, Ryota Yamaguchi, Sadayuki Murai, Dai Sato. DES: Toshihiro Kawamoto, Kimitoshi Yamano. ANI: Yoichi Ogami. MUS: Yoko Kanno. PRD: Sunrise, TV Tokyo. 25 mins. x 26 eps. (TV), 120 mins. (m).

Spike Spiegel and ex-cop Jet Black are bounty hunters who range across the whole solar system. Teaming up, albeit reluctantly, with mystery woman Faye Valentine, hacker brat Ed (who's a girl), and a super-intelligent Welsh corgi called Ein, they remain perpetually on the lookout for criminals on the run.

From such a simple premise springs one of the most entertaining anime shows of the 1990s. Made with a deliberate 1970s retro style, it posits a solar system that is one part Chinese diaspora and two parts Wild West. Cityscapes straight out of kung-fu movies jostle with neo-architecture in the style of *Blade Runner* and one-horse frontier towns in the middle of the Martian desert.

Spike is a hero cast in the mold of **LUPIN III**, a good-hearted man operating at the edge of the law, betrayed by an old flame and still nursing his wounded heart. The show itself varies wildly in tone, from comedy to tragedy, but maintains its believability throughout. From the outset, director Watanabe cut much of the exposition from the original script, preferring to give the impression that the viewers were watching the show *in* 2072, and that no explanations would be necessary. The idea of watching a pulp TV show from 100 years in the future truly adds to the experience—a mood retained for the fake Martian radio broadcast *Music for Freelance*, released on CD. The tactic also helps disguise the show's few flaws—at its core, *Cowboy Bebop* is little more than *Route 66* in space, with plots ripped off from generic U.S. crime shows. Space truckers, space mafia, and space hippies would be hack conventions in another series, but they seem to work here because the world seems so believable.

Though complete in its foreign edition, the entirety of *Cowboy Bebop* was not shown on Japanese terrestrial TV. The opening episode, featuring scenes of drug-taking and John Woo–inspired shootouts, was only broadcast on the more forgiving satellite networks, and the censorious climate post-**EVANGELION** meant that, eventually, only 12 episodes of the complete 26 in the series were seen by the first-run audience. The movie *Knockin' on Heaven's Door* (2001) takes place between episodes 22 and 23 of the TV series, just before the final events of the series would have made it impossible to have a full cast ensemble. It is thus an enjoyable but rather pointless bonus story, for which the producers unwisely boasted, a perfectly reasonable 90-minute action movie was unnecessarily padded out with an additional half-hour of footage. As part of the publicity for the movie, the film website also began a "serialization" of Dai Sato's *Ural Terpsichore*, a prequel novel setting up the characters and situations of the original series. However, only the first chapter ever seems to have appeared. **V**

COWBOY ISAMU

1973. JPN: *Koya no Shonen Isamu*. AKA: *Wilderness Boy Isamu*. TV series. DIR: Isao Takahata, Kyosuke Mikuriya, Yoshikata Nitta, Kenzo Koizumi. SCR: Noboru Kawasaki, Soji Yamakawa. DES: Shingo Araki, Daikichiro

Kusube. ANI: Tatsuo Kasai, Koichi Murata, Isao Takahata, Hideo Kawauchi, Shingo Araki, Yasuhiro Yamaguchi, Tetsuo Imazawa. MUS: Takeo Watanabe. PRD: Tokyo Movie Shinsha, Fuji TV. 25 mins. x 52 eps.

Isamu Wataru is the child of a Japanese man and a Native American woman, a skilled gunfighter from an early age because of the dangers of life in the Wild West. After his mother's death, he is taken in by the folks of Rotten Camp, and raised by the Wingate family as one of their own. The Wingates teach him superb sharp-shooting skills, but as Isamu gets older, he comes to realize that they are outlaws, and that they are encouraging him to put his powers to evil use—compare to similar loyalty issues that trouble KIKAIDER. Based on the manga *Boy King* (*Shonen Oja*) by Soji Yamakawa and Noboru Kawasaki, serialized in *Shonen Jump* weekly, this series drifted away from its inspiration in the second half, preferring to concentrate instead on Isamu's search for his missing father. Director Takahata had a young colleague named Hayao Miyazaki on his animation team, which is the main reason English-speaking fans remember this children's adventure story about a boy making his way in the lawless West.

The show's title seems designed to encourage associations with American cowboy programs already seen on Japanese television. *Hondo* (1967) was broadcast in Japan as *Koya no Apache* or "Wilderness Apache," while *Branded* (1965), was shown in Japanese as *Koya no Nagaremono*, or "Wilderness Wanderer"—Isamu's surname actually means "drifter."

COYOTE RAGTIME SHOW *

2006. TV series. DIR: Matsuri Ouse, Takuya Nonaka. SCR: Matsuri Ouse, Ryunosuke Kingetsu, Kazuharu Sato. DES: Jun Shibata, Tomonori Sudo, Satoshi Takahashi, Junichi Higashi. ANI: Hirokazu Kojima, Haruo Sotozaki, Tomonori Sudo. MUS: Koichiro Kameyama. PRD: ufotable, Aoi Promotions, Showgate, Studio Mausu, Klockworx. 24 mins. x 12 eps.

There are space pirates, and then there are coyotes: those who live by their own code of honor, loyal to family and friends. Our hero is wanted in so many places under so many names that everyone just calls him Mister. He is a coyote grounded in jail for a traffic offense; when he gets out, he has a promise to fulfill. Three years before, his old friend, the pirate king Bruce, was killed by the sinister Madame Marciano and her android assassins, the Twelve Sisters. He's out for vengeance and to help Bruce's daughter Franka find her father's lost treasure. But he's also got hot investigators Angelika and Chelsea on his tail.

Channeling a Wild West loser ambience from COWBOY BEBOP (from which this title seems suspiciously reverse-engineered), the space piracy of SOL BIANCA and the quest narrative of ONE PIECE through a Vegas/Detroit caper in the style of *Ocean's Eleven*, with touches of sci-fi glitz and enough high camp villainy for a KISS concert, the show is visually chaotic but intriguing, with strong, attractive character designs. A long list of characters crowds the storyline, allowing little time for development or reflection amid the shoot-outs and chases. This is an entertaining show made with deep love and reverence for cheesy American action flicks. It won't change your life but it will fill in time enjoyably. If it had been longer, it could have been better—there are many interesting possibilities, mostly unexplored. Those Twelve Sisters offer so many options in so many genres. A manga adaptation of the same name by ufotable, with art by Tartan Check, commenced publishing in 2005. ●

CRAFT OF HYPNOSIS, THE

2008. JPN: *Saiminjutsu the Animation 2nd*. Video. DIR: Shinichi Shimizu. SCR: Taifu Sekimachi. DES: Toshihide Masutate. ANI: N/C. MUS: N/C. PRD: Milky. 30 mins. x 2 eps.

Susumu is a typical introverted teenager who lives with his strict mother and avoids anything resembling exertion as much as possible. Then he meets a new neighbor who offers to teach him hypnosis. Susumu tries it out on his next door neighbors, a big-breasted foxy mother and her cute schoolgirl daughter. But can he use it on his own mother? Of course he can, because this is anime porn based on an erotic game by BLACKRAINBOW. ●

CRAYON SHIN-CHAN *

1992. TV series, TV special, movie. DIR: Mitsuru Honma, Keiichi Hara. SCR: Mitsuru Honma, Keiichi Hara, Ryo Motohira, Keiichi Hara. DES: Masaaki Yuasa. ANI: Shizuka Mori, Katsue Hara. MUS: Toshiyuki Arakawa. PRD: Shinei, TV Asahi. 25 mins. x 868+ eps. (TV), ? mins. x ? eps. (special), ca. 90 mins. x 21 eps. (m).

Shinnosuke "Shin-chan" Nohara is the ultimate brat—a loud, nosy kid prone to impersonating elephants with his genitals, peeking up teachers' skirts, and tormenting his stupid dog. His harassed mother turns a blind eye, his teachers despair, and a cast of zany regulars turn this nasty cartoon into a hellish look at the world through the eyes of a spoiled child. Most episodes are divided into three smaller, unrelated chapters, giving just enough time to set up accidents with snot, panty-flashing, and bratty behavior. At school, two prissy female teachers are engaged in a constant war of one-upmanship, not realizing that their pupils are manipulating their jealousies for their own ends. A bright, bouncy new teacher refuses to be downhearted at the utter chaos that confronts her, and the headmaster gets angry at being constantly mistaken for a gangster. Out in the wider world, Shin's family and neighbors are also the subject of ceaseless torment. He even persists in getting the teenager Shinobu fired from every job she takes, and, though he is the bane of her life, he can never remember her name. There are even parodies of anime shows—school super-jock Kawamura is obsessed by the nonexistent show *Action Kamen* (*Action Mask*), while Shin religiously watches an insane GUNDAM parody called *Kuntam Robo*.

Created by Yoshihito Usui for *Manga Action* magazine in 1990, *Shin-chan* caused a stir in Japan when it was claimed that up to 68% of children under 12 were avid viewers of this show, supposedly made for adults who would get the joke. Unfortunately, the joke backfired, with complaints in the Japanese media that an entire generation of Japanese children was growing up to be lecherous, evil menaces.

The *Crayon Shin-chan* movies were genuinely aimed at a juvenile audience, albeit one that had grown up watching the series. In *Action Kamen vs. Evil High-Leg* (1993), the entire cast is forced to wear skimpy swimsuits by a bad king, while in *Secrets of Buriburiland* (1994), they are packed off to the South Sea island of Buriburi (Japanese for "annoying").

In *Adventures in Henderland* (1996), a simple trip to the titular amusement park finds Shin foiling a gay warlock's bid to become ruler of the world. Shin-chan's baby sister, Himawari, had her debut in *The Search for the Black Balls* (1997), which also featured a cameo role for creator Usui. *Attack! War of the Pig's Trotter* (1998) embroiled the Nohara family in a vendetta between two secret societies. *Dazzling Hot Spring Wars* and *Paradise Made in Saitama* (1999) split the feature format into two chapters: a traditional vacation episode and a cyberspace pastiche. In *Storm in the Jungle* (2000), Shin-chan's family is kidnapped on a southern island, leaving him and Himawari to rescue them from the Afro-haired Funky Monkey Army—nicely demonstrating that Shin would have the ability to insult foreign audiences, too, if only his English-language appearances went further afield than a limited number of subtitled broadcasts on a Hawaiian Japanese community station. The movie *TheStorm is Calling: The Adult Empire Strikes Back* (2001) featured Shin-chan and his iconoclastic bunch running amok in a 20th-century theme park, ruining their elders' nostalgia trip—somewhat ironic, considering that some of the original "under-12" audience may now have brats of their own. In the following year's *Sengoku Battle* (2002), Shin-chan falls 400 years down a time tunnel, landing in the middle of Japan's civil war. His parents come after him in the family car, causing irreparable damage to history. For *The Wind is Calling: Yakiniku Road* (2003), Shin-chan stages a protest at the poor quality of his breakfast, and is appeased by the promise of a barbecue for dinner. When someone steals his food, he embarks upon a samurai-style vendetta. Shin-chan gained a superhero identity in *Legend Is Calling: Three Minute Buriburi Flashing Attack* (2005). And so on and on, throughout the first decade of the 21st century and into the teens, with the most recent outing at time of writing being the 21st movie, *Very Tasty! B-class Gourmet Survival* (2013).

Under the title *Shin-chan*, part of the TV series was broadcast in the United Kingdom in 2002 and eventually reached the mainland U.S. several years later. Keiichi Hara, who would loyally direct most Shin-chan outings until 2004, found a more se-

rious metier and audience as the director of COLORFUL: THE MOTION PICTURE. ⬤🅛🅝🅥

CRAZY FAMILY DIARY
2008. JPN: *Kyoran Kazoku Nikki*. AKA: *The Diary of a Crazed Family*. TV series. DIR: Yasuhiro Kuroda. SCR: Mamiko Ikeda. DES: Makoto Koga. ANI: Tomokazu Sugimura, Akira Amemiya, Hiroki Mutaguchi. MUS: Tomoki Kikuya. PRD: Nomad, Bandai Visual, Enterbrain, Lantis, MOVIC. 24 mins. x 26 eps.
The head of Japan's Supernatural Phenomena Treatment Bureau was orphaned aged three, raised by the Bureau and taught to love no one. So when his bosses hand him a new assignment that requires him to act as daddy to a family of potentially deadly world-destroying beings, he's stumped. Especially when the woman playing mother is a psychic cat goddess from an underground kingdom. Now he has five adopted kids—a lion, a jellyfish, a cross-dressing gay mafioso, a demon girl, and a teenage bioweapon. His mission: to stop one of them destroying the world by teaching them the value of a loving family. This light-hearted episodic comedy manages to combine elements of drama and emotional moments without dissonance, mainly by moving along at a smart pace and bombarding the viewer with color and movement. A silly but sweet animation, based on a manga written by Akira and illustrated by x6suke in 2005, which ran until 2011.

CREAM LEMON *
1986. Video. DIR: Kazuya Miyazaki, Bikkuri Hako, Ayako Mibashi, Yuji Motoyama, Toshihiro Hirano. SCR: N/C. DES: Masako Nitta, Mon-Mon, Kei Amaki, Yuji Motoyama, To Moriyama, Toshihiro Hirano, Ayako Mibashi, Hiroyuki Kitakubo, Nekoda Nyan. ANI: Hiroshi Tajima, Mamoru Yasuhiko, Bikkuri Hako. MUS: N/C. PRD: Fairy Dust. 25 mins. x 36 eps. (v), 30 mins. x 2 eps. (*New Century*), 30 mins. x 4 eps. (*New Generation*).
One of anime's most notorious serials, and, though only a third of the episodes were translated into English, it is one of the most significant shows of the 1980s. *CL* wasn't the first erotic anime video (that was the similar LOLITA ANIME), but the brand survived for over a decade as an umbrella for several subseries, eventually becoming synonymous with anime pornog-

raphy. The original spanned 16 episodes, followed by assorted specials, the nine-part *New CL*, and two epilogues, shuffled here into some semblance of order.

Its first and biggest star was Ami Nonomura, an 11-year-old girl who seduces her older brother, Hiroshi, in *Be My Baby* (#1). When Hiroshi is banished to London in *Ami Again* (#5), an older but hardly wiser Ami dreams that she is having sex with him again, only to wake and discover that she is drunk in bed with a stranger. Hiroshi returns in *Now I Embrace You Ami* (#13) to tell her that the affair is over, at which point she returns to the arms of her one-night stand. The 1986 movie *CL: Ami's Journey* came next, in which her friends drag her off to Hokkaido to take her mind off things. Shown on a double bill with the first PROJECT A-KO movie, the film was noticeably more mainstream than its erotic predecessors, and, surprisingly for a theatrical version, of lower-grade animation. Ami becomes an idol singer, squeezing in a clandestine tryst with Hiroshi when her entourage passes through London. Her adventures ended in the mini-series *Ami: From Then On* (#31–34), in which Ami is forced to choose between Hiroshi and her fiancé, eventually choosing neither and electing to stay single. Ami's adventures eventually reached the U.S. in 2001, as *Be My Honey, The Story of Ami, In the Midst of Sadness*, and *Ami's Climax*.

In *Escalation* (#2), the bisexual Rie is banished to a strict Catholic school when she is found in bed with her piano teacher. Predictably, she soon ends up in a lesbian ménage à trois with her roommate, Midori, and dominated in a series of power games by the senior girl Naomi. After graduation, Naomi would invite the girls to her mansion for a repeat performance (#6), and the girls would return in a third installment (#16) to initiate a new recruit.

SF Legend Rall (#3) is a space fantasy in which Carol, an underdressed, sword-wielding warrior-maid, stands against an evil overlord who intends to sacrifice the beautiful Princess Orgasma. She would take up the call to adventure in *Lamo Ru Strikes Back* (#15). Under the title *Sex Trap*, *SF Legend Rall* was combined with *Star Trap* (#10, released in the U.S. as *Offenders of the Universe*), an unrelated *Star Trek* spoof starring the lesbian crew of the USS *Mischief*, and released in the U.S. on the Brothers Grime label (see also **OME-1**).

Pop Chaser (#4) was directed by **PROJECT A-KO**'s Yuji Moriyama under the pseudonym Yuji Motoyama and has early designs by Hiroyuki Kitakubo. It features interstellar Wild-West lesbian antics inside a giant robot suit, as biker chick Rio liberates her woman from a rival gang only to discover that the distressed damsel has agreed to marry the leader.

Don't Do It Mako: Sexy Symphony (#7 and #12) presaged **SPRITE** by introducing a timid girl possessed by a knowing, sexual personality—the quintessence of the *CL* series in its assurance that inside every child, there is a sex kitten waiting to get out. In another mainstream cameo, it was directed by **ICZER-ONE**'s Toshihiro Hirano.

Further sci-fi antics awaited in *Super Virgin* (#8, AKA *Super Virgin Groupies)* in which another Mako, a psychic, falls in love with one of the schoolboys who torment her. It was followed by another one-shot, *Happening Summer* (#9, AKA *Traveling Fantasies)*, in which naughty Yuki seduces her big sister's boyfriend—a man who, in a series in-joke, is found reading a porn magazine featuring photographs of *Escalation*'s Naomi.

In *Black Cat Manor* (#11), student Masaki leaves wartime Tokyo to escape the bombings, staying with the widow Saiko, her daughter, and maid. When the *CL* series eventually ground to a halt in 1993, it would be with *Return to Black Cat Manor* (#36).

Parodying **PROJECT A-KO** and foreshadowing **KEKKO KAMEN**, *Nalice Scramble* (#14), which closed the first season of *CL*, features a heroine in battle armor fighting three lesbian Nazis for control of a school. It was back immediately in 1987 with *New CL*, a straightforward continuation of some of the earlier stories with a few new one-shots and an increased concentration on the artwork and manga origins. *Five-Hour Venus* (#17), for example, was one of several shows by "To Moriyama," a pseudonym for **DANCE TILL TOMORROW**'s Naoki Yamamoto. Heroine Shimeji is blackmailed into posing nude for an art class when her porn past is revealed, and she would return in *Afterschool XXX* (#18) to save a younger classmate from a similar fate.

The supernatural began to take over with *White Shadow* (#19), in which a gymnast is possessed by a demon and seduces the boy who loves her. For *Visions of Europe* (#20), taken from Toshiki Yui's *Mermaid Junction* manga, two frisky female tourists lose their passports and money at the airport and are whisked off to an alternate Europe (reminiscent of *Alice in Wonderland*) where passion rules. Kei Amaki's *Cherry Melancholy* (#21) has a couple of man-hunting girls giving up the chase and settling for each other, but the series soon returned to fantasy with *Astalot* (#22), a tale of swords and sorcery with the requisite sex, running almost twice as long as most other videos in the series. A boy finds a gun in *I Guess So* (#23) and uses it to compel a girl to have sex with him, while in *Dream-Colored Bunny* (#24), a trip to the pet shop nets a sexy companion for one lucky pervert.

The Dark (#25), based on a story by Nicholas Lloyd, features two men offered shelter by a woman in a castle, where she seduces and kills one of them, a priest. This episode, *Magic Doll* (#26), in which a kindly man is tempted away from his family by a sexy ghost, and the aforementioned *Black Cat Manor* (under the title *The Black Widow*) were compiled into the feature-length *Pandora: An Erotic Adventure* in the U.S. Similar supernatural goings-on await in *Summer Wind* (#27) for a bereaved boyfriend who meets a girl named Mina (like the heroine of **BEAST CITY**, a reference to Dracula).

E-tude (#28 and #29) is a classic star-crossed romance between the genteel pianist Yurika and the rough tough jazz-playing biker Ryo, who are separated by her father and set up with new partners only to long for each other. *Heartbreak Live for Two* (#30) parodies magical-girl shows like **CREAMY MAMI** as a fox grants a lovelorn girl's wish to become the idol singer that the boy she loves so adores. *Angie and Rose* (#35), the tale of a boy seduced by a Canadian mother and daughter, came out as a bonus for the *CL: Climax* boxed set in 1992, but that is by no means all there was. The *Ami* series also boasts the *Ami Graffiti* digest edition and the *Ami: White Shadow* teaser for the movie. Other abridgments include *CL Junior*, which cut a third of each episode's running time to survive in a tougher censorship climate. The series was repackaged again with two episodes per tape as *CL Twin* (AKA *CL Best Coupling*), which is the version now on DVD. There are also several versions arranged by artist rather than story, collecting the "best" works from To Moriyama, Kei Amaki, and Toshiki Yui. *Festival*, a compilation of To Moriyama shorts, also appeared in the U.S. as *The Story of Toh*, although as with many of these variant listings, we have been unable to determine if they were licensed releases. In 2001 and 2002 the franchise was revived with *New Century Cream Lemon: Escalation—Die Liebe* and *New Century Cream Lemon: Ami Rencontrer*, respectively. Two live-action versions subsequently appeared, Nobuhiro Yamashita's 2004 movie *Cream Lemon* and Iwao Takahashi's 2005 direct-to-video *Cream Lemon: Ami's Diary*. The year 2006 saw a four-part remake of the Ami Nonomura story under the title *Cream Lemon New Generation*. ●◗Ⓥ

CREAMY MAMI ★

1983. JPN: *Maho no Tenshi Creamy Mami*. AKA: *Magical Angel Creamy Mami; Fairy Angel Creamy Mami*. TV series, video, movies. DIR: Osamu Kobayashi, Tomomi Mochizuki, Naoto Hashimoto, Takashi Anno. SCR: Kazunori Ito, Michiru Shimada, Shigeru Yanagawa, Shunsuke Kaneko. DES: Akemi Takada. ANI: Hideo Kawauchi, Shinya Takahashi. MUS: Koji Makaino. PRD: Studio Pierrot, Nippon TV. 25 mins. x 52 eps. (TV), ? mins. x 2 eps. (v), 53 mins. (m1), 150 mins. (m2), ? mins. (v2), ? mins. (TVm).

Posi and Nega, two spacefaring aliens posing as harmless kittens, give 11-year-old Yu Morisawa a magic wand so she can transform at will into Creamy Mami, idol singer and magical being, but for just one year. Her parents and her friend Toshio don't notice this double identity, even though they are all huge fans of Mami. But when Toshio sees her transform partway through the story, Yu loses her magic powers, and the friends go on a quest to recover them. They succeed, and Creamy comes back to her fans, but Toshio loses his memory.

Mami returned straight to video in 1983 with *Eternity Once More*, a two-part finale in which she gives a first-anniversary concert, Toshio regains his memory, and Yu finally loses Mami's magical powers. It was so well received that she came back for another encore with *The Long Goodbye* (1985), in which she, now 13, is transported to an alternate world while helping Toshio make an SF film. The 53-minute story was shown on a triple bill with a *Minky Momo* (see **GIGI**) short and the film *CM vs. Minky Momo*, in which the girls use weapons and special attacks named after the show's staff, including an "Ito Flash" and a "Watanabe Cutter."

In 1985, she also starred in the music compilation *CM: Curtain Call*, and she returned again for Takashi Anno's 1986 TV special *Three Magical Girls*, with *Magical Fairy Pelsha* and **MAGICAL EMI**. Immensely influential in the magical genre, she is much imitated to this day in shows such as **FANCY LALA**, and parodied in the **TENCHI MUYO!** spin-off *Pretty Sammy*. In 1996, she appeared once more in a computer game, *CM: Tale of Two Worlds*. Owing to her populariy among old school fans, *CM* was one of the first old shows to be offered for crowd-sourced DVD solicitation as part of the Anime Sols line in 2013, gaining her English-language release asterisk in this encyclopedia three decades after her first appearance on Japanese TV.

CREST OF THE STARS *

1999. JPN: *Sekai no Monsho*. AKA: *Celestial Crest; Battle Flag of the Stars*. TV series, TV specials, movie, video. DIR: Yasushi Naga-oka. SCR: Aya Yoshinaga. DES: Takami Akai. ANI: Takuro Shinbo. MUS: N/C. PRD: Sunrise, WOWOW. 25 mins. x 13 eps. (TV1), 25 mins. (special1), 90 mins. (special2), 25 mins. x 13 eps. (TV2), 120 mins. (m), 25 mins. x 10 eps. (TV3), 30 mins. and 35 mins. (v1).
In Imperial Year 945, peace-loving planet Martine is occupied by the Humankind Empire Abh, the genetically engineered descendants of a slave species designed for space exploration, who had revolted against their human masters and fled to space. Now the long-lived, elfin rulers of their own empire, they demand Martine's surrender. President Rock Lin deactivates the defenses to avoid a war he cannot win; in return his family is raised to the Abh aristocracy and Martine is given to them to rule. Seven years later, the president's son, Jinto, who had been sent into exile on an Abh-ruled human world to protect his life from revenge, prepares to journey to the heart of Abh territory to complete his studies and his required term of service

in the Abh Star Forces. He is picked up at the port by the beautiful 16-year-old Abh military cadet Lafiel, junior member of the crew of the patrol ship Gosroth. Midway through their journey, the Gosroth is ambushed by ships of the United Mankind in the opening shots of a war between the Humankind Empire Abh and the four major human polities. Jinto and Lafiel are sent to make their way to safety alone, which involves escaping from Baron Feb-dash's territory during an attempt to refuel and evading the troops of United Mankind when the planet they land on is captured.

Crest of the Stars is one of the better hard anime SF series, though viewers wanting wall-to-wall action should look elsewhere, as the plot proceeds at a deliberate pace, and the show places emphasis on character development. The series follows Hiroyuki Morioka's original novels closely, painstakingly re-creating the Abh's alien language, though it suffers from squandering much of its budget on showy computer graphics for the first episode, and it is soon reduced to cut-rate animation. The series was also released as a 120-minute movie, with a substantial amount of new animation.

The first series was followed by a television special in 2000, *Seikai no Dansho: Birth*, which detailed a portion of Lafiel's parents' honeymoon. Dubus and Plakia are spending their time away wandering in space and encounter a lost ship orbiting a nebula. When they begin to explore it, they find that it is not quite as dead as it first seemed. This was shown at the same time as a 90-minute condensed version of the first series and immediately preceded the second series.

The 13-episode TV series *Banner of the Stars* (2000) reunites Jinto with Lafiel three years later, when he finds a position as a supply officer on her ship, the Basroil. There are elements, albeit serious ones, of **IRRESPONSIBLE CAPTAIN TYLOR**, as the lowly cadet is paired with the high-class princess, while their small detachment is sent to defend the critical Laptic Gate, even though their admiral is from a family renowned for its mental instability. Lafiel is the captain of the ship, whereas Jinto starts the series in the position normally occupied by a disposable *Star Trek* red-shirt.

Banner of the Stars II (2001) is a smaller

ten-episode series in which Lafiel is assigned to become an interim territorial governor on the newly conquered Lobnas II, which turns out to be a prison world, where she and Jinto must balance the competing demands of the prisoners and the guard staff, and attempt to ward off a rebellion by the former. The Bandai release of this iteration included a bonus episode titled *Passage of the Stars: Birth*, a 25-minute prequel about Lafiel's father. *Banner of the Stars III* (2005), released straight to video, details Jinto's assignment as a governor on yet another newly conquered world, although his rise through the ranks of the race that conquered his own planet is starting to rankle.

CRIMSON CLIMAX *

2003. JPN: *Hotaruko*. AKA: *Firefly-child*. Video. DIR: Katsuma Kanazawa. SCR: Katsuma Kanazawa. DES: Gion Muto. ANI: Gion Muto. MUS: Toru Shura. PRD: ARMS, Green Bunny. 30 mins. x 3 eps.
After her mother's death, orphan Ryo is invited by her aunt Mizunu to visit her secluded island home on the Japan Sea, only to discover that it has been overrun by servants of an orgiastic cult of human sacrifice. She befriends Mizunu's daughter Hotaruko, merely to realize that the cult demands fresh blood, and just one of them is going to survive. Sex and violence duly follow. The Japanese release has a notably classy cover, although the American edition looks like all the others. **LNV**

CRIMSON WOLF *

1993. JPN: *Hon Ran*. AKA: *Hong Lang (orig. Chinese)*. Video. DIR: Shoichi Masuo. SCR: Shoichi Masuo, Yasuhito Kikuchi, Isamu Imakake. DES: Kenji Okamura. ANI: Kazuya Kuroda, Yasuhito Kikuchi, Isamu Imakake. MUS: Kunitoshi Tojima. PRD: APPP. 60 mins.
A scientific expedition finds the hidden tomb of Genghis Khan in Mongolia. Supernatural apparitions destroy the expedition and proclaim a curse that in a thousand days a great natural disaster will devastate the whole world unless three young people bearing a wolf-shaped birthmark or scar are found and killed. Kei, a martial-arts student in Beijing, is identified as the first of the Crimson Wolves. He survives an assassination attempt, but his old teacher is murdered. Kei tracks the

killers for revenge and is shocked to learn that he has been targeted by every government espionage agency in the world. Refusing to believe the "curse," Kei teams up with the other Crimson Wolves, nubile Japanese love interest/distressed damsel Mizuho Washio and the handsome, rakish "adversary" of the team, Ryugen, a Chinese Triad boss.

Genghis Khan is just one of three Great Kings, Oriental undead who will become supreme masters of the world unless stopped by the Crimson Wolves a thousand days after the opening of the tomb, with the other two being the Qin Emperor (China's unifier and the ward of the famous Terracotta Army) and Communist leader Mao Zedong. In scraps of clumsy plotting typical of such matinee adventures, the Crimson Wolves only become aware of the threat they pose when assassins are sent to stop them—if the Great Kings left them in ignorance, the thousand days would have passed without opposition! The Crimson Wolves are told they have great powers (not surprising since Kei has his eyes poked out in prison and is miraculously healed by the time he is rescued). Eventually, the Great Kings take over the Chinese government's supercomputer, Goku, in a finale that implies the Crimson Wolves have saved China from its cruel first emperor, its Mongol conqueror, the architect of the Great Leap Forward, *and* the future spread of Communism! Entertainingly bad "yellow peril" hokum, unlikely to be as popular in the People's Republic as RANMA ½. 🅛🆅

CROISÉE IN A FOREIGN LABYRINTH—THE ANIMATION *
2011. JPN: *Ikoku Meiro no Croisée.* TV series. DIR: Kenji Yasuda. SCR: Junichi Sato, Mamiko Ikeda. DES: Hideki Inoue, Masaki Kawaguchi. ANI: Hideki Inoue. MUS: ko-ko-ya. PRD: Satelight, AT-X, Bushiroad Inc., Flying Dog, Good Smile Company, Media Factory, Sony Music Communications. 24 mins. x 12 eps.
Paris, in the second half of the 19th century—a city of dreams, excitement, and romance, with a passion for all things Japanese. Japan had only recently opened its borders to the outside world, and everyone interested in art, literature, and fashion was interested in Japan. Travelers had already begun to come home with

fascinating souvenirs: most were not nearly so fascinating as Yune, the 13-year-old Japanese girl sponsored by elderly businessman Oscar to come and live with his family in the capital city of France. Yune is to live and work with his grandson Claude, who is trying to keep his father's failing business alive.

Like ARIA, this anime adapted from Hinata Takeda's 2006 manga series is slow, quiet, and gentle in terms of pace and character development, but beautifully designed and enjoyable. Paris is so well depicted it makes you want to steal a passing time machine (although the gallery in which Claude's store is situated was based on one in Brussels). The fascination of the new that drew Yune to venture thousands of miles overseas with a virtual stranger is replicated in the people she meets, who view her as a curiosity at first but are gradually won over by her innocence and goodwill. This is like an invitation to the daintiest of afternoon teas: the setting, the music, even the exotic treats are in the sweetest of taste. Enjoy.

CROMARTIE HIGH *
2004. JPN: *Sakigake!! Cromartie Koko.* AKA: *Charge!! Cromartie High.* TV series. DIR: Hiroaki Sakurai. DES: Atsushi Takeuchi, Naoyuki Onda. ANI: N/C. MUS: Kunio Suma. PRD: Production I.G., Starchild, TV Tokyo, Bandai Visual. 12 mins. x 26 eps.
Cromartie High has the dubious honor of teaching some of Japan's worst teen delinquents. Its students range from the rebellious—Hayashida, who sports a mauve mohawk, or Freddy, a look-alike for gay rock icon Freddie Mercury of Queen—to the downright strange, like the gorilla in high school uniform who really *is* a gorilla, or robot boy Shinichi Mechazawa. He looks like an aerosol can with telescopic arms and claw hands, but everyone treats him like a normal student. The school is locked in gang warfare with rival Destrade High. Into this peculiar institution, created by Eiji Nonaka for his manga in weekly *Shonen Magazine*, comes tall, handsome Takashi Kamiyama. Nobody knows why an honor roll student would join the deadbeats of Cromatie High, but he has to be the toughest honor student around, so naturally surreal high jinks and wacky sight gags ensue in this parody of tough-guy

anime like CHARGE AHEAD! MEN'S SCHOOL, whose Japanese title it echoes. Takashi is the one non-delinquent in a school full of them, a role reversal from which *Cromartie High* draws much of its comedy—compare to ALICE ACADEMY, which revisits a similar theme from a gentler magical-girl perspective. In 2005, following the release of a *Cromartie High* spin-off live-action movie, the filmmakers were sued by former Yomiuri Giants baseball player Warren Cromartie for using his name without permission in a tale of delinquency.

CROSS GAME *
2009. TV series. DIR: Osamu Sekita. SCR: Michihiro Tsuchiya, Hiroko Fukuda, Hideki Shirane, Mitsuyo Suenaga. DES: Tomoyuki Matsumoto, Yuji Kondo, Yutaka Mukumoto. ANI: Toshiyuki Komaru, Kenji Fujisaki. MUS: Kotaro Nagakawa. PRD: SynergySP, ShoPro, TV Tokyo. 24 mins. x 50 eps.
Fifth-grader Ko Kitamura lives next door to the Tsukishima family, who own a café and a baseball batting cage. His family own a sports store, and because they are in the same business, the two families have always been close. Ko and Wakaba Tsukimura were born on the same day in the same hospital and have been inseparable ever since. Wakaba wants Ko to take baseball more seriously and dreams of him being a star player at the legendary Koshien tournament when they move up to high school, but he downplays his ability and his interest. Meanwhile Wakaba's younger sister Aoba resents the time her big sister spends with Ko and says she hates him. Then tragedy strikes, and their lives are changed forever. But just how far the change goes won't be clear for some time.

School friendships, family ties, passion for sport, ordinary suburban life: these are the basic ingredients from which legendary manga creator Mitsuru Adachi has been making magic since 1970, when he was just 19. TOUCH, SLOW STEP, and many more show his ability to handle plot, character, and pace with subtlety and grace. His animators have sensibly presented his stories with minimal adjustments, because when something works as well as an Adachi plot, you let it do its job. Sekita and his writing team produce a tearjerking surprise in Wakaba's death in episode 1, right in the midst of the family warmth and feel-good humor, and the tragedy that redefines every character is beautifully handled.

The writing is of the highest quality, leaping four years ahead in the next episode to take up the story as Wakaba's influence reasserts itself, and the characters and their settings are believable and strongly developed, with tiny, almost unnoticed background touches helping the process along—it may take several viewings before the significance of the item on Ko's bedroom wall hits you, for example. The animation is simple, and elements of crowd scenes and backgrounds are sometimes quite clumsily drawn, but the brilliantly edited animation of baseball games reveals Adachi's absolute devotion to the sport. This isn't really a story about baseball, but the baseball is handled with as much care and finesse as the story, and it makes for a rare treat: a genuinely moving, intelligent, watchable series about how very extraordinary everyday life can be (EVERYDAY ANIME).

CROWS

1993. Video. DIR: Masamune Ochiai. SCR: Shunsuke Amemura. DES: Koichi Kagawa. ANI: N/C. MUS: N/C. PRD: KSS, Knack. 45 mins. x 2 eps.

Shundo is the new kid in town, ready to fight with anyone. After beating more than ten opponents, he gets a reputation as the toughest kid around, but he uses his strength to help those who cannot help themselves, soon gaining a following of grateful youngsters.

Transferring the honor of samurai drama to a school setting, Hiroshi Takahashi's 1990 manga from *Shonen Champion* was a more serious take on the teenage tough guys of shows like BE-BOP HIGH SCHOOL and ANGEL LEGEND, although Shundo's alma mater, "The Edge of Badness," is named with a pomposity that might perhaps have benefited from a little humor. **LV**

CRUSH GEAR TURBO

2001. JPN: *Gekito! Crush Gear Turbo*. TV series, movie. DIR: Hideharu Iuchi, Tetsuro Amino. SCR: Akihiko Inari, Mari Okada, Fuyunori Gobu, Hideharu Iuchi, Hiroaki Kitajima, Hiroyuki Yoshino, Masaaki Sakurai, Noburo Kimura, Shin Yoshida, Shino Hakata, Suguru

Koizumi, Tatsuto Higuchi. DES: Atsuo Tobe. ANI: Akiko Nagashima, Akira Takahashi, Atsuo Tobe, Eiji Nakata, Hirokazu Hisayuki, Junji Nishimura, Kohei Yoneyama, Nanabu Ono, Naoki Murakami, Seiichi Hashimoto, Shinichi Takahashi, Takuro Shinbo. MUS: Takayuki Negishi. PRD: Sunrise, TV Asahi, Nagoya TV, Toei. 25 mins. x 68 eps. (TV1), 60 mins. (m), 25 mins. x 50 eps. (TV2).

Elementary schoolboy Masaru must battle a rival school, Zet, out to win the Gear Koshien, the international Crush Gear tournament, and go on to conquer the Gear World. In a mix of gladiatorial combat with racing cars and extreme competition of the high school baseball tournament of MAN'S AN IDIOT! that (according to anime producers) kids are really interested in, the transforming vehicles are known as Gears and Masaru's is called Mach Justice—perhaps a reference to SPEED RACER's Mach 5. Generated by the usual random combination of toy concepts and stereotypes we have come to expect from Bandai house name Hajime Yadate, the franchise ran long enough to spawn a movie release from Toei in July 2002, and 2003's 50-episode sequel *Crush Gear Nitro*. Compare, if there is a comparison to be had, with DAIGUNDER.

CRUSHER JOE *

1983. AKA: *Crushers*. Movie, video. DIR: Yoshikazu Yasuhiro, Toshifumi Takizawa. SCR: Haruka Takachiho. DES: Yoshikazu Yasuhiro, Shoji Kawamori. ANI: Naoyuki Yoshinaga, Ichiro Itano, Gen Sato. MUS: Tadao Maeda. PRD: Studio Nue, Sunrise. 131 mins. (m), 60 mins. x 2 eps. (v).

The Crushers are a loose federation of trouble-shooting space mercenaries. The crew of the ship Minerva is led by teen Joe (son of head Crusher Dan), with teammates Alfin (cute tomboy), Talos (hulking muscle, much smarter than he looks), and Riki (bratty kid), plus Dongo the comical robot. Joe and crew agree to transport a frozen heiress to a distant world's medical facility, but their ship is attacked en route and the cryogenic capsule is stolen. Pursued by the galactic police while simultaneously trying to regain their cargo, the Crushers stumble into the lair of notorious space pirate Murphy, who intends to use a doomsday weapon to rule the universe.

Haruka Takachiho's famous character

first appeared in the 1977 novel *Crisis on Planet Pizan* with a gang named after two of the author's wrestling heroines, the Crush Gals. The anime version is also riddled with minor characters lifted from *Go for It, Alfin-chan!*, a manga by animator Gen Sato. A background film clip also showed two characters from another Takachiho series who were so popular they got their own show: DIRTY PAIR.

Joe and his gang returned in 1989 for two video adventures also released in the U.S. In *The Ice Hell Trap*, they are framed by the despotic Ghellstan, who hires them to save the prison planet Debris without revealing that the entire world is rigged to blow as part of an insurance scam. Once again, the Crushers' mission is twofold; save the planet *and* bag the bad guys. In *Ash: The Ultimate Weapon*, they must team up with Tanya, a military officer determined to track down a conspiracy to steal yet another doomsday device. On a planet overrun with self-replicating killing machines, they have yet another race against time as the titular device is activated, leaving 20 minutes to turn it off and rescue Tanya.

In 2000, two *Crusher Joe* stories, *Legend of the Saint Jeremy* and *Pandora II*, were illustrated by JUDGE–artist Fujihiko Hosono and released on VHS as the first in the new (and rather pointless) "manga video" format (ARGOT AND JARGON), featuring voice actors reading the manga aloud.

CRY FOR OUR BEAUTIFUL WORLD

1992. JPN: *Utsukushii Chikyu o Yogosanaide*. AKA: *Don't Spoil the Beautiful Earth*. Movie. DIR: Yasuyuki Mori. SCR: Koji Takahashi. DES: N/C. ANI: Masami Furukawa. MUS: N/C. PRD: Asmik. 28 mins.

A little girl called Nana learns about how to keep Earth safe from pollution. Based on a 1985 British collection of poems and pictures on ecological themes by children from 70 different countries that was edited by Helen Exley.

CRY OF THE DRAGON

1988. JPN: *Mahjong Hishoden Naki no Ryu*. Video. DIR: Satoshi Dezaki. SCR: Kazumi Koide. DES: Keizo Shimizu. ANI: Keizo Shimizu. MUS: N/C. PRD: Gainax, Magic Bus. 45 mins. x 3 eps.

Ryu ("Dragon") is a master of mahjong

who becomes embroiled in gangland gambling and murders in eastern Japan. Selling over two million copies after it was serialized in *Modern Mahjong* magazine, *Cry of the Dragon* made creator Junichi Nojo one of the two most successful manga creators of the 1980s; the other, Katsuhiro Otomo, also had a manga turned into an anime that year—**AKIRA**. The anime adaptation was the first show to portray mahjong games onscreen, a task no doubt made less boring by the murder subplots.

CRYING FREEMAN *
1989. Video. DIR: Daisuke Nishio, Shigenori Yamauchi. SCR: Higashi Shimizu, Ryunosuke Ono. DES: Ryoichi Ikegami. ANI: Koichi Arai, Satoshi Urushihara. MUS: Hiroaki Yoshino. PRD: Toei. 45 mins. x 6 eps.
Yo Hinomura is an internationally ac-claimed potter, until he becomes involved with the 108 Dragons crime syndicate, gets brainwashed, and is turned into the assas-sin Crying Freeman. When the lonely Emu Hino witnesses one of his missions, he is sent to terminate her, but she seduces him, and the two eventually devote their lives to the 108 Dragons. Successive episodes featured a number of rivals and evil syndi-cates trying to oust Yo, including the 108 Dragons' own Baya-san, the granddaugh-ter of a former leader. Yo fights off an Afri-can syndicate, while Emu, who acclimates rather well to life as a gang member after giving up being a virginal artist, takes on a Chinese criminal hellhole. Freeman's old enemies return to haunt him in the fourth episode (part five in the U.K.), with crooked cop Nitta and former moll Kimie teaming up with a professional wrestler to help replace Yo with a brainwashed cultist. The fifth episode featured a sex-starved female gang leader kidnapping a rival boss's family in order to make Yo become her sex slave. The final part, in which Yo defeats yet another rival, this time from the Russian syndicate, received such heavy cuts in the U.K. that it and chapter four were released on a single tape.

Based on the 1986 manga in *Big Comic Spirits* by **MAD BULL 34**'s Kazuo Koike and **SANCTUARY**'s Ryoichi Ikegami, *Crying Free-man* comes in a passable dub from Stream-line Pictures, and another, from Manga Video, which comes complete with deeply offensive phony Chinese accents. Like

Christophe Gans' later live-action remake starring Mark Dacascos, the animated se-ries suffered from being overly faithful to the original. Effort expended in recreating the original artwork and characters might have been better spent on actual anima-tion, which had degenerated to extremely cheap levels by the final installments; ironic considering that **PLASTIC LITTLE**'s Urushihara was one of the talented staff. In addition to Gans' 1997 remake, there was an unofficial Chinese version directed by Clarence Ford and released as *Dragon From Russia* (1991). **CNV**

CRYSTAL TRIANGLE *
1987. JPN: *Kindan no Mokushiroku Crystal Triangle*. AKA: *Forbidden Revelation: Crystal Triangle*. Video. DIR: Seiji Okuda. SCR: Junji Takegami. DES: Kazuko Tadano, Toyoo Ashi-da. ANI: Kazuko Tadano. MUS: Osamu Totsuka. PRD: Animate Film. 86 mins.
Dr. Koichiro Kamishiro, along with assis-tants Mina and Hisao and priestess Miyabi, is searching for "messages from God"— coded messages written on the titular crystals, relics of the distant past. However, other powers are searching for these ancient artifacts, and the plucky archeolo-gists must fight the CIA (pretty blonde Juno Cassidy), the KGB (Rasputin's grand-son Grigori Efemovich), and the yakuza (sword-wielding gangster Genji) for the crystals in a battle that takes them across the Middle and Far East to the deep north of Japan. As with the later **SPRIGGAN**, these ancient messages turn out to be connected to a crashed alien spaceship and ecological catastrophe, as the rogue star Nemesis, whose last passing destroyed the dinosaurs, is returning to wreak more havoc, and the messages contain information on how to survive it.

CUBE X CURSED X CURIOUS *
2008. JPN: *C3 Cube*. AKA: *C Cube; C3* TV, video. DIR: Shin Onuma. SCR: Michiko Yokote. DES: Miwa Oshima, Minoru Maeda. ANI: Asami Watanabe, Kazuyuki Yamayoshi, Shuji Takahara. MUS: Jun Ichikawa. PRD: Silver Link, Starchild Records. 25 mins. x 12 eps. (TV), 30 mins. (v).
Yachi is a high school boy who is naturally resistant to curses, living alone while his absent father sends him cursed artifacts as tests. One night he catches a thief in the

kitchen—a young girl who is actually the embodiment of a cursed torture imple-ment. She's trying to break her curse too, and it turns out she isn't the only girl with a curse problem. But since Yachi is the kind of nice guy who can't turn away any-one in trouble, and since this is a harem anime (**ROMANCE AND DRAMA**), help is at hand with much fan service (**BAKEMONOGA-TARI**). Unfortunately no help is available for the audience with the multiple fac-tions, directions, and aimless meanderings of a plot that can't decide whether to stay a pervy harem comedy, wander into darker territory, go for action, or dash back to boobs, ass, and gags again.

With no fewer than 29 credited anima-tion directors and their assistants, and a specially credited action director, Yoshinari Saito, this should be impressive, but it's around the level of **BLEACH**—adequate but not outstanding. The book series written by Hazuki Minase, and illustrated by Sasorigatame, began its run in 2007, and a manga by Tsukako Akina followed in 2011. Both are still ongoing, so the *C3* fanbase is still there, but to date the only other anime has been the release of an unaired 13th episode on the Japanese Blu-ray release of April 2012. This "bonus" sticks to the conventions of harem anime by focusing on the whole gang going on a school trip. **N**

CUBITUS
1988. JPN: *Dondon Domeru and Ron*. TV series. DIR: Hiroshi Sasagawa, Keiichiro Mochizuki, Hidehito Ueda, Yukio Okazaki, Junichi Sakata. SCR: Kaoru Toshima. DES: Dupa. ANI: Michiru Suzuki, Shinnosuke Mina. MUS: Takanori Arisawa. PRD: Telescreen, TV Tokyo. 25 mins. x 104 eps.
Ron is an inventor who loves to tinker around with machines. His loyal friend and companion is Domeru (Cubitus), a talking dog who helps him in trying out his many new inventions, much to the annoyance of Cherry, the pretty girl next door, her husband, Beatrik, and their cat, Blacky.

In 1968, the Dutch artist "Dupa" creat-ed a new character for *Tintin* magazine—a fat white dog that looked like a ball of hair with paws. This kindly mutt became his most successful creation (others included a truck driver who fell in love with a crate) and is so famous in his native Netherlands that the dog even has his own postage stamp. Note: Dupa's European publishers claim that the *Cubitus* series was released in the U.S., but we can find no record of its broadcast under this title.

CUSTOM SLAVE *

2001. JPN: *Custom Dorei: Sayoko no Sho.* AKA: *Sayoko's Chapter.* Video. DIR: Tomouchi Shishido. SCR: Hangetsu Mitamura. DES: Yoko Sanri. ANI: Saburo Nippori. MUS: N/C. PRD: Mint House, Kiss, Green Bunny. 30 mins. To all appearances, Arisugawa Academy is a high-class girls' school. But principal Hiroaki Takahashi uses the school as a form of training camp: he runs a cabal that provides young sexual partners for members of the government—a kind of state-sponsored brothel. Student Sayoko Musky is selected for special training by Takahashi and becomes a double agent—demure schoolgirl by day, sex slave by night. Also released in a U.S. box set with **SCHOOL OF BONDAGE** and **LIVING SEX TOY DELIVERY**. There have been two sequels to the original *Custom Slave* game, so more anime may be forthcoming. **LNV**

CUTEY HONEY *

1973. TV series, movie, video. DIR: Tomoharu Katsumata, Masamune Ochiai, Hiroshi Shidara, Takeshi Shirato. SCR: Masaki Tsuji, Keisuke Fujikawa, Susumu Takaku. DES: Shingo Araki. ANI: Shingo Araki, Kazuo Komatsubara, Masamune Ochiai, Satoshi Kamimiya. MUS: Takeo Watanabe. PRD: Toei, Dynamic Planning, NET. 25 mins. x 25 eps. (TV), 23 mins. (m1), 30 mins. x 8 eps. (v1, *New*), 25 mins. x 39 eps. (TV2, *Flash*), 38 mins. (m2, *Flash*), ? and ? mins. (v2, *Flash*) x 3 eps. (v3, *Re: CH*).
Based on a short-lived *Shonen Champion* manga from **KEKKO KAMEN**–creator Go Nagai, the breast-fixated *Cutey Honey* was animated for TV before its rookie year in manga was over. In a pastiche of **ASTRO BOY**, a bereaved professor creates an android facsimile of his murdered daughter, implanting a superpowerful device into her ample bosom. The "airborne element solidifier" can reassemble matter in the vicinity, effectively giving Honey anything she needs to help her in her fight to save the world—including specialized bodies such as the Hurricane Honey and Flash

Honey. It also ensures that all her clothes disappear every time she transforms, a controversial innovation at the time, now commonplace in shows such as **SAILOR MOON**. Her enemy in the original TV series is Panther Zora, leader of the all-female Panther Claw crime syndicate. The year 1974 saw the release of a short *CH* movie, shown in cinemas as part of the spring *Toei Manga Matsuri* anthology program along with episodes of **MAZINGER Z** and **LIMIT THE MIRACLE GIRL**.

Honey would return in 1994 for *New CH*, also known as *New Super Android Cutey Honey*, directed by Yasuchika Nagaoka and released straight to video. With new designs by Osamu Kasai, the new series picked up where the TV series left off, with Honey returning after a decade to discover that Panther Zora and her accomplice, Dolmeck, are still menacing civilization. She also gains an entire family of assistants, the Hayami clan, whose son, Chohei, provides viewer identification, while granddad Denbai provides heavy violence. Other Go Nagai characters put in cameo appearances, including **DEVILMAN** Akira as a wrestler, alongside real-life women's wrestling stars Cuty Suzuki and Mayumi Ozaki.

In 1997 popularity in Japan peaked with a new TV series, *CH Flash*, with the character and world redesigned to appeal to the same young girls as **SAILOR MOON**, which it replaced, showing in the same time slot and produced by the same team of animators. The immense success of the TV series rejuvenated the manga, allowing this originally very male appreciation of the female form to appear in girls' magazines such as *Nakayoshi* and titles for younger readers such as *Happy Zoo*. The same year saw a *CH Flash* movie, an all-new story in which Honey battled Panther Claw for the key to an ancient treasure (the posters boasting that there would be an "all-new transformation scenes," too) and two digest videos consisting of highlights—one, *Birth of Love's Warrior CH*, retelling her origin story, and the other, *Battle for W Honey Destiny* repeating the season-two finale. A live-action movie was released in 2004, directed by Hideaki Anno and starring Eriko Sato. This was followed by a three-part video anime sequel, *Re: Cutey Honey* (2004), also directed by Anno. **LNV**

CUTTA'S STORY

1995. JPN: *Cutta-kun Monogatari*. Movie. DIR: Kenji Yoshida. SCR: Kenji Yoshida, Saburo Kaniguchi. DES: Tameo Ogawa, Yasuhiro Matsumura. ANI: Hajime Matsuzaki. MUS: Toshiyuki Watanabe. PRD: Toei, Nabe, Aubec. 75 mins.
"Dreams and adventure" await in this movie funded by a cluster of worthy ornithological, zoological, pedagogical and tourist organizations, dramatizing the life of Cutta, a pelican that resides on the Pelican Island in Ube City's Tokiwa Park zoo. Artificially incubated after his parents and nest were washed away in a storm, Cutta becomes a favorite with the local children, particularly Sho, a lonely boy whose parents are away in Arabia. Cutta and Sho become an inseparable pair, riding the carousel together and even winning the annual three-legged race. With war breaking out in the Middle East, Cutta offers to fly Sho to the Persian Gulf to check on his parents, where his superpowers do not extend to being bullet-proof, although he does display the ability to project death-rays from his mouth in order to keep Iraqi tanks out of his ancestral wetlands. Eventually, Sho is left wondering whether it was all a dream, as the full-grown Cutta faces the prospect of returning to the wild.

Despite some media claims to have been funded by private donations, the largest investor in this insane film appears to have been the tourist board of Yamaguchi Prefecture, presumably hoping to persuade the people of the world that Yamaguchi was the best place in Japan to find hallucinogenic drugs. The real-world bird that inspired this film was indeed Japan's first artificially incubated pelican, named for Calcutta, where his parents hailed from—we are tempted to complain about lack of realism regarding world geography, but then again, see above re: death rays. While he never quite won a three-legged race or was embedded with Desert Storm, his hand-reared ease with human beings made him famously approachable, and he became something of a celebrity for his habit of dancing to a song sung by local children. Although the film might seem at first like a bizarre boondoggle, there was some method in the investors' madness, as the designs for it were immediately re-purposed and reused on tourist materials, including the sides of Ube City buses for many years. Cutta himself died in 2008 at the age of 23, a proud grandfather.

CYBER CITY OEDO 808 *

1990. Video. DIR: Yoshiaki Kawajiri. SCR: Akinori Endo. DES: Yoshiaki Kawajiri, Takashi Watanabe, Hiroshi Hamazaki, Masami Kosone. ANI: Hiroshi Hamazaki. MUS: Yasunori Honda, Kazz Toyama. PRD: Madhouse. 45 mins. x 3 eps.

Three loosely linked tales of a cyberpunk stripe, caught up in the post-**AKIRA** popularity of SF futures. In the year 2808, three criminals are offered conditional release. Even though they have each stacked up several life sentences, they may work off their terms by performing secret missions against the clock. If the mission succeeds, years are taken off their sentences. If the mission fails or they try to escape, the explosive collars around their necks will take their heads off.

For the first mission, "Virtual Death" ("Ancient Memory" in the original, retitled "Time Bomb" in a 2004 U.S. rerelease), tough-guy Sengoku must fight his way into the Kurokawa Tower, a self-aware skyscraper, to discover who is hacking into its systems. Presaging the first **PATLABOR** movie, he discovers that the "hacker" is in fact the original programmer, who has long since departed from this world. More hackery abounds in "Psychic Trooper" (retitled "The Decoy" in 2004), in which bespectacled computer expert Goggle must outwit a cybernetic soldier while fighting his hidden feelings for an old flame who once betrayed him. The final episode, "Bloodlust" (originally "Crimson Medium," retitled "The Vampire" in 2004), focuses on Benten, the androgynous dandy who must track down a vampire who is using a beautiful android to entice young victims into his lair. The final showdown, in a cryogenic chamber (i.e., coffin) at the top of a space elevator, neatly encapsulates the old/new culture clash of the series. The pretty-boy cross-dresser Benten is inspired by a popular character from the 19th century, the protagonist of the kabuki play *Benten the Thief*. Since the characters all carry *jitte* parrying weapons modeled on those used by samurai-era police, and the titular 808 recalls the **808 DISTRICTS** of old Edo (Tokyo), we can assume that

the anime was originally intended as an SF pastiche of old stories (possibly in the style of **SAMURAI GOLD**), which never quite got off the ground. It is just one of several superior video serials from creator Juzo Mutsuki, whose **PHANTOM QUEST CORP** and **DEVIL HUNTER YOHKO** were similarly luckless in their quest for TV remakes. **❻ⓁⓃⓋ**

CYBER FANTASY FLOWERS

2007. JPN: *Denki Muso Hana*. AKA: *Electric Dream Flower; Electric Full Flower Garden*. Video. DIR: Miyoshi Yuji, Eimaru Yaguchi. SCR: Eimaru Yaguchi. DES: Susumi Komori, Hitoshi Hiramoto. ANI: Eimaru Yaguchi, Kyuchibi. MUS: N/C. PRD: Legally Bee, MS Pictures (AniMan). 21 mins. x 2 eps.

Gang politicking to control the power supply of Akihabara in 2037 uncovers a strange illness that causes death through exposure to neon light. This show is unusual for anime porn in that, being based on Kazuhisa Shiromi's manga, it has a story involving something other than sex between siblings or classmates. The art is also unusual, and often strikingly ugly. **❻ⓃⓋ**

CYBER SIX *

1999. TV series. DIR: Hiroyuki Aoyama, Toshihiko Masuda, Atsuko Tanaka, Nobuo Tomizawa, Kazuhide Tomonaga. SCR: N/C. DES: Keiichi Takiguchi. ANI: Nobuo Tomizawa. MUS: Robbi Finkel. PRD: TMS, NOA, Telecom, Kid's Station. 25 mins. x 13 eps.

Cyber Six is one of many genetically engineered warriors created during World War II by the German scientist Von Reichter. The titular heroine is the only one to escape alive when Reichter destroys his creations. She hides out in the city of Meridiana, where she disguises herself as the mild-mannered *male* librarian Adrian Seidelman during the day, donning a skintight catsuit to leap across the rooftops at night. She is accompanied by Data Seven, formerly warrior Cyber 29, who was mortally wounded and whose brain was transplanted into a large black panther. Meanwhile, Reichter sends Jose, a child clone of himself, to track down and destroy his errant creation. Jose does so with an army of mutants, whose green "substance" (not blood, the producers assured U.S. networks!) Cyber Six must drink to stay alive. As with any superheroes worth their salt, there are identity crises

back in the real world, with Adrian's work buddy Lucas lusting after the female form of Cyber Six, not realizing that he shares an office with her alter ego, and schoolgirl Lori developing a crush on Adrian, not realizing that "he" is a she.

This international coproduction was based on the Argentinian comic written by Carlos Trillo and drawn by Carlos Meglia, but seems, however coincidentally, to be a belated cross between **BIG X**, **CYBORG 009**, and *Batman*, with a little existential musing of the **GHOST IN THE SHELL** variety thrown in for good measure. One of the rare anime, like **ALEXANDER**, that premiered abroad—it was not shown in Japan until late in 2000.

CYBER TEAM IN AKIHABARA *

1998. JPN: *Akihabara Dennogumi*. TV series. DIR: Yoshitaka Fujimoto. SCR: Katsumi Hasegawa, Hiroshi Yamaguchi. DES: KA-NON, Tsukasa Kotobuki, Seiji Yoshimoto. ANI: Yuji Takahashi, Seiji Yoshimoto. MUS: Nobuyoshi Mitsumoto. PRD: Ashi Pro, TBS. 24 mins. x 26 eps.

Early in the 21st century, the combination of personal data-organizers and virtual pets results in a new piece of essential equipment. These "patapi" robots are friends, guardians, and personal computers, but to Hibari Hanakogane, they are more than that. Her patapi, Densuke, has been sent to Earth by a handsome prince to defeat the evil sorceress Blood Falcon. With her friends Suzume, Tsugumi, and their own patapi companions, Hibari forms the titular squad to fight cybercrime.

Tsukasa Kotobuki, who had formerly drawn a **GUNDAM** spin-off comic, collaborated with the pseudonymous Ka-non to create this tale of girls and gadgetry for *Nakayoshi* magazine, soon riding the coattails of the Tamagotchi craze to make the jump to radio drama, computer games, and this anime series. A mysterious clash of genres results in a cloyingly cute show for girls that somehow manages to have an evil character with giant breasts.

CYBERFORMULA GPX

1991. JPN: *Shin Seiki [New Century] GPX Cyber Formula Future Grand Prix*. TV series, video. DIR: Mitsuo Fukuda, Satoshi Nishimura. SCR: Hiroyuki Hoshiyama, Tsunehisa Ito, Michiru Shimada. DES: Mutsumi Inomata, Takahiro Yoshimatsu. ANI: Takahiro

Yoshimatsu, Atsushi Aono. mus: Yuki Otani. prd: Sunrise, Nippon TV. 25 mins. x 37 eps. (TV), 30 mins. x 6 eps. (v1), 30 mins. x 8 eps. (v2), 30 mins. x 8 eps. (v3), 30 mins. x 8 eps. (v4).

In the year 2016, 14-year-old Hayato Kazami enters the Cyberformula Grand Prix, in which superpowered, super-advanced cars race to determine the best team in the world. He drives a computerized car designed by his father, in a high-concept that takes the "dad's robot" formula of other Sunrise shows and puts it on wheels.

After qualifying in local championships in Fujioka and Niseko, Hayato and his teammates get to travel the world. Mixing local color (e.g., Grand Canyon, Peru) with an off-track romance developing in exotic locations (Peru, Brazil), the show also incorporates sporting rivalry and derring-do. By the time the world tour reaches Canada and England, Hayato's rivals are well-established characters in their own right, such as the cold British racer Knight Schumacher and the Aryan tactician Karl Richter von Randall. After a race in Kenya, the crew heads into the home stretch for a lightning-fast series of races in Spain, Germany, and Japan—in succession rapid enough to imply that the TV series was canceled early.

As with the soccer antics of **Captain Tsubasa**, the sporting angle allows for regular resets of the characters' positions. The following year, Hayato reenters the championships to retain his crown in the six-part video series *CF 11 (Double One)*, driving a car designed by the beautiful blonde foreigner Claire Fortran. As romance develops between Hayato and Asuka Sugo, the daughter of his team's rich backer, he beats Schumacher and races to a "double-win" in his "double one" car in the "11th" annual championship in a highly improbable set of numerological coincidences.

The situation changes for Hayato's third championship in the eight-part *CF Zero* (1994), when an accident loses him a race *and* fiancée Asuka, who walks out on the injured driver. Though she eventually returns, Hayato must best Japanese rival Shinjo both on and off the track. This was soon followed by the eight-part *CF Saga* (1996), in which Alzard, an android driver, defeats both Shinjo and Hayato's

best friend, the green-haired Bleed Kaga. While Asuka frantically searches behind the scenes for Alzard's weak spot, rival teams set traps off the race track to keep Hayato from even trying. Needless to say, he wins in the end, and a 19-year-old Hayato, who has grown up along with his target audience, gets behind the wheel once more for eight more episodes in *CF Sin* (1998), though this most recent outing focused more on his teammate Bleed.

CYBERNETICS GUARDIAN *

1989. jpn: *Seijuki Cyguard*. aka: *Holy Beast Machine Cyguard*. Video. dir: Koichi Ohata. scr: Mutsumi Sanjo. des: Atsushi Yamagata. ani: Jun Okuda. mus: Norimasa Yamanaka. prd: AIC. 45 mins.

Top brains at the future city of Cyberwood attempt to come up with a solution to Cancer, the aptly named slum district. The Cybernetic Guardian unit is sent to patrol the streets, unaware that the secret Doldo Brethren organization is engaged in an attempt to bring back the death-god Saldor by implanting young men with the "seeds" to become hosts for the second coming. One such unwitting host is Cyguard technician John Stalker, whose abduction leads chief scientist Leyla (Laia in the original) Rosetta to risk everything to save him.

A directorial debut for **Genocyber**'s Ohata, this claustrophobic horror tale suddenly widens out at the end for a monstrous showdown in the tradition of the **Guyver** series. **LNV**

CYBORG 009 *

1966. Movie, TV series. dir: Yugo Serikawa, Ryosuke Takahashi, Saburo Sakamoto. scr: Yugo Serikawa, Masaki Tsuji, Akiyoshi Sakai, Masaaki Sakurai. des: Shotaro Ishinomori. ani: Kazuhiro Yamada. mus: Daiichiro Kosugi. prd: Toei, Sunrise, NET. 64 mins. (m1), 60 mins. (m2), 25 mins. x 26 eps. (TV1; b/w), 25 mins. x 50 eps. (TV2; color), 130 mins. (m3), 25 mins. x 52 eps. (TV3), 103 mins. (m4).

World-class sprinter Joe Shimamura is seriously injured in an accident and taken away by the Black Ghost, an agent of the sinister Merchants of Death, who intend to take over the world. The kind-hearted Professor Gilmore saves his life, and in so doing, turns him into the ninth of a series of cyborg warriors that were originally de-

signed to carry out the Merchants' bidding all over the world but are now dedicated to stopping them at all costs.

Marrying **Astro Boy** to the James Bond movies, but also far ahead of *The Six Million Dollar Man*, Shotaro Ishinomori's 1964 *Cyborg 009* manga in *Shonen Sunday* was one of the original Cold War warriors—he was even succeeded in 1967 by the manga adventures of a female cyborg called *One of 009* (later adapted as **009-01**). The debut of the animated version was swiftly followed by another short feature film, *C009: Kaiju Wars* (1967). Here, the Black Ghost uses a resurrected plesiosaur to terrorize the world, while Joe must fight spy-cyborg 0010 and the newest recruit, Plus Minus (0011).

The TV series followed in 1968, introducing many other enemies and allies, including 006, who runs a Chinese restaurant, and the wisecracking 007. In addition to the superfast Joe, each of the other cyborgs possesses one special talent, including telepathy, underwater breathing, flight, superhuman strength, the ability to breathe fire, and psychokinesis. The story was revived in 1979 for a color series, reintroducing the characters for a new audience, directed by **Votoms**' Takahashi and adapting previously unused story lines from the original, such as 009's adventures in space and the "Neo Black Ghost" chapters.

Much of the same crew stayed on for the 1980 movie to celebrate Ishinomori's 25th anniversary in manga publishing. *C009: Legend of the Super Galaxy* (aka *Defenders of the Vortex*) was directed by Masayuki Akehi and is the only part of the 009 franchise available in English. Featuring the tragic death of 004 (who keeps weapons stashed all over his body), the 130-minute color feature pitted Joe's gang against the evil Zoa, who intends to use a space vortex to control the world. *Star Wars* comic author Jeff Segal contributed to Ryuzo Nakanishi's script, though his involvement was deviously hyped in Japan as that of "the writer of *Star Wars*." The series was revived in 2001 on TV Tokyo as *Cyborg 009: The Cyborg Soldier*, a 52-episode remake under the directorship of Atsushi Kawagoe, and again as the cumbersomely titled CGI feature *009 RE: Cyborg* (2012), directed by Kenji Kamiyama. Kamiyama's sequel updates the chronology for the 21st century, suggesting that the agents were disbanded at the end of the Cold War, dispatched to various fates including, in Joe's case, a constant three-year repetition of his school years, wiped and reset each time he graduates. The agents, however, are dragged out of retirement by a series of terrorist attacks, leading to portentous and occasionally pretentious musings about the nature of religion and fanatacism. In an interesting experiment, the animators on the movie kept to one new image every eight frames ("animating on threes"), replicating the look of old-fashioned cel animation even with digital animation that could have easily been set to show an image every one frame ("animating on ones").

CYBOT ROBOTCHI

1983. TV series. DIR: Kazuyuki Okaseko. SCR: Tomohiro Ando, Hideki Sonoda. DES: Dynamic Pro. ANI: Takao Suzuki. MUS: N/C. PRD: Dynamic Planning, Knack, TV Tokyo. 25 mins. x 39 eps.

Professor Deco creates Robotchi, an android with a TV set in his stomach. With a number of the other robots created by the professor, he causes havoc for the evil Dr. Highbrow, in this lighthearted comedy from **GETTER ROBO**–creator Ken Ishikawa and scenarist Tomohiro Ando.

CYBUSTER *

1999. JPN: *Maso Kishin Psybuster*. AKA: *Saibuster, Psibuster, Psybuster, Demonic Armor Psybuster*. TV series. DIR: Hidehito Ueda. SCR: Hisayuki Toriumi. DES: Takeshi Ito,

Yasuhiro Moriki. ANI: N/C. MUS: N/C. PRD: N/C. 25 mins. x 26 eps.

In the year 2040, a terrible earthquake in Tokyo shatters time as well as space, causing the titular giant robot to appear from an alternate world. Ken Ando and love-interest Mizuki are great friends who are pulled apart by the events around them and then thrown into the company of the Terran Environmental Protection Agency. Eventually they become two of the ten chosen special operatives charged with investigating the earthquake and its aftermath—the dark shadows that engulf Tokyo's Shinjuku district. Based on a popular computer simulation game, this is one of the stragglers in the rush to imitate **EVANGELION**.

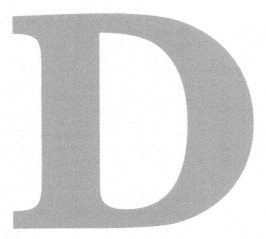

D-1 DEVASTATOR

1992. Video. DIR: Tetsu Isami. SCR: Masashi Sogo. DES: Nasatomi, Masami Obari, Yukiji Kaoru. ANI: Masaki Taihei. MUS: Yoshinori Shabana. PRD: Dynamic. 50 mins.

A manga serialized in *Ascii Comics* by "Sphios Lab" and Toshi Yoshida provided the basis for this one-shot anime, in which Ryu, a young boy, must pilot the titular Devastator to defend the planet from the invading Varsus warriors

D-FRAGMENTS *

2014. AKA: *D-Frag*. TV series. DIR: Seiki Sugawara. SCR: Makoto Uezu. DES: Kentaro Matsumoto. ANI: Kentaro Matsumoto. MUS: Akito Matsuda, Nijine. PRD: AT-X, Brains Base, Dax, Kadokawa, Media Factory, Toranoana, TV Tokyo. 24 mins. x 12 eps.

Would-be school tough-guy Kenji is drafted into the Game Creation Club (Provisional), an after-school society comprising four off-the-shelf girls and a lone boy, who play cards and board games. Without Kenji to make up their numbers, the club will be disbanded, and even then still faces threats from the "real" game club, from which it splintered over an earlier clash of personalities. There's some treatment of the dichotomy of school personae—Kenji tries to be tough but is really a softie, whereas the innocent-seeming girls in the club hide some mean streaks—but really, hasn't this all been done before, over and over again? Based on a manga series in *Monthly Comic Alive*, by Tomoya Haruya.

D. GRAY-MAN *

2006. TV series. DIR: Nana Harada, Osamu Nabeshima. SCR: Reiko Yoshida, Tatsuhiko Urahata. DES: Hideyuki Morioka, Toru Koga. ANI: Hideyuki Morioka. MUS: Kaoru Wada. PRD: TMS Entertainment, Dentsu, Shuehisa, TV Tokyo. 25 mins. x 103 eps.

The Millennium Earl is out to cleanse the world of humans with his deadly living weapons, the Akuma: corrupt human souls trapped in mechanical bodies. Allen Walker is a teenage trainee exorcist with special gifts—a cursed eye that glows red, and a mighty weapon in his left arm. His teacher knows that he is one of the very few who can wield a force known as Innocence that can destroy Akuma. So he sends the boy to London, to the headquarters of the Black Order, a force battling the Earl and his minions.

Wrapping a horde of anime tropes in a Tim Burton–lite approach to Gothic design sounds like a recipe for disaster, but oddly enough, it works. This body assembled from Hoshino Katsura's manga, with bits of Gothic revival from VAMPIRE HUNTER D, cyberjunk from SPACE ADVENTURE COBRA, and steam salvage from FULLMETAL ALCHEMIST grafted onto a standard hero-quest, coming-of-age teamshow plot, makes an entertaining and enjoyable show with some standout characters and plenty of eye candy. A word of caution: watch in Japanese if you want to avoid the dreadful fantasy that American accents have taken over London, a disappointing conceit after all the hard work put in on HELLSING.

Admittedly, some of the complexity of the manga is lost—both in visual and plot terms—but writers Yoshida and Uruhata are seasoned pros and the team bringing

their work to life has years of experience making TV anime. Look how many much-lauded "hit" shows of the past four or five years have failed to make it past 12 episodes. This one ran for two years: two years of giving the sponsors the returns they wanted, of doing exactly what TV anime should: entertaining an audience enough that they turn on the TV every week and watch the ads laced around your show. That's success. Many critics and scholars talk about anime's unrealistic cost base and unsustainable business model, but if more studios could do shows with 103 episodes' worth of audience appeal, the anime industry would have fewer survival problems.

D.I.C.E. *

2004. JPN: *Dinobreaker*. AKA: *DNA Integrated Cybernetic Enterprises*. TV series. DIR: Jun Kamiya. SCR: Hiro Masaki, Jun Kamiya, Kenichi Yamada, Kenichi Araki, Masahiko Shiraishi, Ryu Tamura, Yoshio Kato. DES: Mitsuru Ishihara, Tsuyoshi Nonaka. ANI: Jun Takahashi, Naoyoshi Kusaka, Shin Katagai. MUS: Masato Miyazawa. PRD: Bandai, Xebec. 25 mins. x 26 eps.

Jet Siegel is the predictably "hot-headed" pilot of the Motoraptor, one of more than half a dozen vehicles that form part of the F-99 platoon of DNA Integrated Cybernetic Enterprises, a quasi-military organization that polices criminal activity in the Sarbylion galaxy. D.I.C.E. F-99 is the only group staffed wholly by children, who relish the chance to ride in their Dinobraker vehicles, which, as if you hadn't guessed, can transform into a robotic dinosaur mode like ZOIDS. A series of menaces of the week soon ensues, from planets at risk of explosion to attacks by space pirates led by the mysterious Shadow Knight—whose true identity will not come as the remotest surprise to anyone who has seen SPEED RACER. Later episodes introduce a darker subplot in which corrupt higher officials are found to be planning an escape to the forbidden planet of Heron, where they hope to find the secret of eternal life. Jet and friends oppose them, only to find themselves branded as traitors and forced to take on the amassed forces of their former allies, in the style of DANCOUGAR. Despite looking to all intents and purposes like yet another anime series, D.I.C.E. was actually the first coproduction to be initiated by Bandai America with the American audience in mind—the show premiered on U.S. TV before it was seen in Japan..

D3 SERIES *

2001. Movie. DIR: Shigenori Kumai, Takashi Kondo, Yuji Moriyama, Hotaru Kawakami et al. SCR: Tamiyo Mori, Runa Kozuki. DES: Akinori Kano, Konomi Noguchi. ANI: Sakurako Kurai. MUS: N/C. PRD: D3. 30 mins. x 2 eps. (Collector), 30 mins. x 2 eps. (Concerto), 30 mins. x 7 eps. (Ninja), 30 mins. (Be Lifesized), 25 mins. x 2 eps. (Yosho), N/A (Family System), N/A (Love Doll), 30 mins. x 6 eps. (Discipline), 30 mins. x 5 eps. (Yakin Byoto 2), 30 mins. x 3 eps. (Discode), 10 mins. x 3 eps. (Inbo), 10 mins. x 3 eps. (Inko), 30 mins. (Let's Do It With Sister).
Incorporating the White Bear label, D3 is another Japanese production company specializing in erotica. Its titles have not been so quick to make it to the American market. The first release, Collector (2001), presented three stories in an anthology—Shadow Jail: Sex Comfort Slaves (Inro Aüdo), Desire to Touch (Shuyoku), and Red Snow (Akai Yuki), this last perhaps a reference to the first of the LOLITA ANIME. Later releases have capitalized on the trend for self-referentiality within FANDOM, such as Concerto (2001, Shirabe Concerto), which combines an adaptation of a bestselling game with a string of excuses for dressing up and role-playing. The story is presented as a series of rehearsals, auditions, and performances in the style of MASK OF GLASS, in which three pretty young actresses are obliged to don costumes and perform sex acts as part of their "training." The costumes, however, are designed to evoke well-known characters from mainstream shows, in the same risqué fashion employed in the earlier ELVEN BRIDE. Similar fan-oriented high jinks arrived in Be Lifesized My Lover (2001, Toshindai My Lovers: Minami vs. Mecha Minami), a pastiche of the warrior-girlfriend tales of MAHOROMATIC and SAIKANO, in which a lonely, downtrodden boy suddenly gains a feisty roommate who defends the world from danger, whose sister enjoys dressing up (once again) in costumes, and both of whom enjoy S/M role-play. The Japanese press release assures us that it is "full of swinging tits." The company's most successful franchise, however, has been NINJA (also 2001), the erotic tale that mixes both martial and marital arts—though only the first episode is credited to "D3," while later installments were produced by Onmitsudo/Obtain. The same period also saw the Yosho (Phantom Whispers) series, released in the American market as MIDNIGHT STRIKE FORCE, in which a secret cult of lesbian nurses hopes to bring about the resurrection of their satanic founder through experiments at a Tokyo hospital.

D3's sales pitches mix true anime and DVD games with impunity, the company's next releases being two interactive erotica, which took the plotlines of text-based games and added animated inserts. In the first, Family System (2002, Ryojoku: Kazoku System), a nameless man is hired to play a role in a fake family, and told he can do anything he likes except murder. He is placed in a series of situations in which he is made to interact with his fake family and, in a nod to the past-oriented set-ups of modern romance, a series of fake "childhood friends." He soon forgets that he is living a lie, thereby ensuring that the inappropriate feelings he develops for the girl playing his sister are tinged with thoughts of incest, in a story that seems partly inspired by The Truman Show (1998) and the Japanese live-action TV series Transparent (*DE). The second, Love Doll (Ai Doll, 2002), has a title that might also be translated as Slave to Love, and is described by company press documents as a "pure love rape simulation game."

After the success of BIBLE BLACK (not a D3 anime), D3 picked up the rights to release an anime adaptation of Discipline: Record of a Crusade, a 2002 release from the same company, Active Soft. The anime version, just plain Discipline (2004, released in the U.S. as Discipline: The Hentai Academy), is another of D3's domestic successes, as demonstrated by its much longer episode count. In it, Japanese teenager Takuro Hayami cannot believe his luck when he is transferred to Saint Arcadia School, and finds his dorm is full of nubile coeds. He soon develops a crush on the house mistress Saori Otokawa (compare to MAISON IKKOKU), although the other girls, particularly the evil Morimoto sisters, have realized that Hayami possesses a secret "sex power"—as in MASQUERADE, they want this energy for themselves and getting it will require a number of sex scenes. Younger sister Reona Morimoto and her associates at the Social Club begin a concerted effort to seduce Hayami, hoping to monopolize his sexual attentions. However, other factions at the school want Hayami for themselves, leading in later episodes to approaches from the Tennis Club and Swimming Club. Deciding to use blackmail to ensure Hayami's availability, the Morimoto sisters kidnap and abuse Miss Otokawa. Before long, the girls are busily abusing and molesting each other in a series of bondage-based power games, the humiliations and retributions of schoolgirl one-upmanship, refashioned here for pornographic purposes. With Reona clamped into a chastity belt, an order is issued that there shall be no sex permitted in the school—a directive that is flouted with predictable speed, in a series of sex-based battles in which young ladies gamely struggle not to enjoy themselves. The final episodes lift traditions not from European school-days stories such as TWINS AT ST. CLARE'S, but instead from Japanese conspiracytheory schooldramas such as the live-action School in Peril (*DE), revealing that the school's sinister culture of rape and revenge is actually part of a secret project (compare to BIBLE BLACK), and one that, it appears, can only be thwarted by a mass orgy.

The D3 company also tried to muscle in on the success of another computer game franchise, NIGHT SHIFT NURSES in the rival DISCOVERY SERIES. In a really, really desperate attempt to avoid getting confused, we have called this off-shoot series by its Japanese title, *Yakin Byoto 2* (2004), as distinguished from the *NSN* title used for the Discovery incarnation. In it, the renowned Doctor Kuwabara finds himself unable to forget his earlier love for nurse Ren Nanase. Kuwabara tracks her from town to town until he finally finds her. However, in the intervening time, she has become the subject of sexual experiments by an evil researcher at Saint Juliana's hospital. Disappointed at the change in her previously virginal character, Kuwabara decides to avenge his hurt feelings on the human race at large by abusing and raping a number of nurses. The same year saw *Discode: Abnormal Eros* (*Discode: Ijo Seiai*) in which attractive girl Futaba turns out to have a penis as well. Using terms that parody the "girl with a boy's heart" of **Princess Knight**, *Discode* posits a schoolgirl drama not unlike that of *Discipline*, in which a lone "male" figure finds himself surrounded by adoring girls. Futaba, however, must continually evade discovery, leading to a series of set-ups in which s/he must buy the silence of certain girls by having sex with them—a far cry from the cross-dressing and genderswitching of **El Hazard** and **Ranma ½**, also based on an erotic computer game. Later episodes find Futaba assaulted by boys, in a rare introduction of the tropes of gay pornography into what is purportedly a "straight" series.

The D3 company tried a new and interesting direction with *Sleazy Mother* (2005, *Inbo*) and *Sleazy Sister* (2005, *Inko*), released in the U.S. under the umbrella title of *The Sleazy Family*. Featuring the seduction of teenage Masaru by his aunt, and the trials of Masaru's would-be girlfriend as she enjoys a sexual relationship with the manager of the restaurant where she used to work, the twin serials notably shared cast members, making a virtue out of the limited set-ups of pornography by, for example, using protagonist Masaru for tales both of his seduction by older women and of highschool romance. While, in essence, the show merely runs picaresque encounters in parallel instead of in series, its dualtitle release represents an intriguing marketing decision. The year was rounded off with the release of **Let's Do It with Sister**, for which see its separate entry. The company's first release of 2006

was the self-explanatory **Cleavage**.

Late in the first decade of the 21st century, D3 was merged with MediaBank. This effectively ended the D3 series, although its spirit continues in numerous MediaBank releases, including **Hypnotic Disgrace Academy** (2008), **Afterschool Miaow-Miaow** (2011), and **Foolish Test Slave** (2011). **⬤Ⓝ◗**

D4 PRINCESS
1999. TV series. DIR: Yasunori Ide. SCR: Yasunori Ide. DES: Shinji Ochi. ANI: Tatsuo Iwata. MUS: Kenji Kawai. PRD: Canyon, Domu, WOWOW. 10 mins. x 24 eps.
Based on Shotaro Harada's manga, serialized in *Dengeki Daio*, in which princess Doris Rurido turns up at a school famed for its fighting "Panzer League" and soon becomes its leader through the use of the transforming drill on her arm. The original short episodes, screened as part of the satellite channel WOWOW's *Anime Complex II* anthology show, were eventually compiled into four videos for retail release.

DA CAPO
2003. JPN: *D.C.—Da Capo.* TV special, TV series. DIR: Nagisa Miyazaki, Shinji Takago. SCR: Katsumi Hasegawa, Katsumi Terato, Kenichiro Katsura, Mamiko Ikeda, Masaharu Amiya, Masashi Suzuki, Nagisa Miyazaki, Yuji Moriyama. DES: Shinobu Tagashira, Naru Nanao. ANI: N/C. MUS: Hikaru Nanase, Yugo Sugano. PRD: Circus, Feel, Zecx, Chiba TV, TV Kanagawa. 24 mins. x 26 eps. (TV1), 24 mins. x 26 eps. (TV2).
Junichi Asakura lives with his stepsister Nemu on the magical, crescent-shaped island of Hatsune, where the cherry trees are in bloom all year around. Like many on Hatsune, Junichi has limited magical powers—in his case, he can conjure candy out of thin air and see the dreams of others. But there are also more mundane concerns—on the night before he begins his senior year at Hatsune's high school, Junichi dreams that a girl under a cherry tree announces that she is his returning sister. The same girl arrives as a transfer student the following day, and he recognizes her as his cousin, Sakura, back after six years in America looking exactly the same as when she left, and, in the eyes of some of the other girls in Junichi's class, a little overfamiliar toward him.

Based on a PS2 game with a manga out the same year, *DC* is yet another cookie-cutter tale of a teenage guy who's just irresistible to girls, living in a **Maison Ikkoku** group of people with various strange talents and quirks, falling into absurd and improbable romantic situations complicated by **Love Hina** promises made in childhood, attracting women wherever he goes. However, it also imparts a fairy-tale quality to the elegiac nature of many highschool dramas. School days are often presented as a wondrous dreamtime in anime, though it is difficult to tell whether this is a cynical exercise or a heartfelt belief on the part of animators—see **Mahoromatic**. *DC* certainly works hard to imbue the end of childhood with literal magic: in an echo of **Kiki's Delivery Service** and **My Neighbor Totoro**, the students' sense of magic wanes as they age, as do the blossoms on the supposedly eternal cherry trees.

DC Second Season, based in part on the second PS2 game *DC Plus Communication*, picks up two years later, when Hatsune Island's cherry trees have lost their magical properties and merely bloom each spring. Junichi gains a new loveinterest when young Aisia arrives hoping to learn magic from his grandmother. When he reveals that his grandmother is dead, she mistakenly believes that he can teach her but soon realizes her mistake, although she stays around in order to determine what has gone wrong with the trees. See also **Time Paladin Sakura**, a sci-fi spin-off.

DAA! DAA! DAA!
2000. TV series. DIR: Hiroaki Sakurai. SCR: Tomoko Konparu, Shingo Arakawa. DES: Masayuki Onchi. ANI: Ryoichi Oki. MUS: Toshio Masuda. PRD: JC Staff, NHK2. 25 mins. x 78 eps.
When her mother qualifies as an astronaut and must travel abroad with her scientist father, Miu is sent to live with her uncle in an old temple. Forced to share a dwelling with her handsome classmate Kanata, Miu's embarrassment is compounded when the "couple" is "adopted" by an alien baby, Ru. The reluctant foster parents must cope with a baby who can levitate and with the additional annoyance of their child's alien protector, Wannya.

Based on Mika Kawamura's manga in *Nakayoshi* magazine, this comedy combines the odd-couple romance of His and Her Circumstances with an SF excuse for playing mommies and daddies straight out of Mama's a Fourth Grader.

DADDY LONG-LEGS

1979. JPN: *Ashinaga Ojisan*. TV special, TV series. DIR: Masakazu Higuchi. SCR: Akira Miyazaki. DES: Shinichi Tsuji. ANI: Shinichi Tsuji. MUS: Makoto Kawaguchi. PRD: Herald Enterprise, Tatsunoko Pro, Fuji TV. 75 mins. (TVm), 25 mins. x 40 eps. (TV).

When she turns 18, the stories Judy Abbot publishes about her life in the orphanage secure her a place at university. She writes many letters to her mysterious benefactor "Daddy Long-Legs" unaware that he is Jervis Pendleton III, an adoring millionaire who has already met her (and fallen in love with her) in disguise. This musical one-shot anime is only the most recent adaptation of Jean Webster's 1912 children's book—Hollywood movies of the same story include one with Mary Pickford as Judy (1919), Janet Gaynor taking the role in 1931, and a 1955 version with Leslie Caron and Fred Astaire. There is also a Dutch adaptation, *Vadertje Langbeen* (1938), but this inversion of Cinderella, in which an unusual girl seeks a "normal life" (with a millionaire, of course), was also immensely influential in Japan's girls' manga market, where it inspired Candy Candy and its many imitators. The story was remade by Kazuyoshi Yokota as a World Masterpiece Theater anime TV series, *My Daddy Long-Legs* (1990, *Watashi no Ashinaga Ojisan*), featuring new character designs by Shuichi Seki. Also see Video Picture Book.

DAGGER OF KAMUI *

1985. JPN: *Kamui no Ken*. AKA: *Blade of Kamui*. Movie. DIR: Rintaro, Susumu Ishizaki. SCR: Mori Masaki. DES: Moribi Murano. ANI: Atsuo Noda, Kyoko Matsuhara, Yoshiaki Kawajiri, Koji Morimoto, Osamu Nabeshima, Yasuomi Umezu. MUS: Ryudo Uzaki, Eitetsu Hayashi. PRD: Algos, Madhouse. 132 mins.

Jiro, a foundling boy, loses his adoptive parents to an assassin. Avenging their death by murdering a one-armed man, he falls in with the priest Tenkai, who trains him in the black arts of the ninja. Learning that the one-armed man was really his true father, a distraught Kamui searches for his true mother, an Ainu princess.

He also goes in search of Captain Kidd's treasure in order to take from Tenkai the only thing that he values. Tenkai wishes to use the treasure to overthrow the anti-isolationists and close Japan once more to the outside world—the action takes place just before the Meiji Restoration that would throw Japan open once and for all. Jiro's quest takes him all the way to the American West, with time out for a brief meeting with Tom Sawyer–creator Mark Twain, where he is saved by a defecting servant of Tenkai's (who turns out to be his long-lost sister) before returning to exact revenge for all his family.

This Kamui is no relation to Sanpei Shirato's Manual of Ninja Martial Arts; it was based on a series of novels by *Legend of the Paper Spaceship*–author Tetsu Yano, who was also Robert Heinlein's Japanese translator. Though not one of his best works, *Dagger of Kamui* contains much of the clash of old and new that distinguishes his writings—the idea of foreign assistance in sending Japan back into the past would be reused by animator Kawajiri in Ninja Scroll. *Blade of Kamui*, an earlier U.S. dub of the movie, rewrites the plot completely, claiming that it is set on an alien world, where Kamui's dagger is a "powerful weapon [that] controls the future of the universe." **NV**

DAGON

1988. JPN: *Ikinari Dagon*. TV series. DIR: Kazuyoshi Yokota. SCR: Nobuyuki Fujimoto. DES: Noboru Takano. ANI: Tetsuya Ishikawa. MUS: Kazunori Ishida. PRD: Nippon Animation, TV Asahi. 25 mins. x 12 eps.

Dagon is the pilot of the starship Digital whose daughter, Meryl, is always getting into trouble. In the middle of an investigation, a shipboard accident causes the Digital to crash-land on a planet ruled by a race of giants called the Sapiens (i.e., Earth). Dagon and his crew, however, are helped by the bee doctor Marilyn, Jisamu the cockroach, Floppy the spider, and Skipper the ant. They return the favor by saving Marilyn from Geppo the evil frog. This short-lived anime recalls the Fleischer brothers' *Mr. Bug Goes to Town* (1941, AKA *Hoppity Goes to Town*) and features the contribution of non-Japanese creators Dennis Bond and Ken Morton.

DAIAKUJI: THE XENA BUSTER *

2003. Video. DIR: Makoto Sokuza. SCR: Yoshio Takao. DES: Masashi Kojima. ANI: Masashi Kojima. MUS: N/C. PRD: Alice Soft, Green Bunny. 20 mins. (prequel), 30 mins. x 7 eps.

The male-dominated land of Japan is conquered by the feminist-oriented nation of Wimy, which has crushed its enemies in a devastating war. Former prisoner of war Akuji Yamamoto returns to his native Osaka to find that his local management association is now run by his grandfather Ippatsu's mistress, who kicks him out. The battered Akuji is found and nursed back to health by Yoko Aoba, a representative of a neighboring group. Once back at his full strength, Akuji decides to recover his birthright and teach the feminists a lesson, by raping his way back to control of the family business. Intrigues, assassinations, and political deals follow, but mainly rapes (until the girls like it, having apparently fallen for Akuji's amatory prowess despite themselves). The series was preceded by a 20-minute prequel, partly in super-deformed mode (Argot and Jargon), *Daiakuji: Zengi no Susume* (2003), and includes a sequel "side story" episode. Based on the game by Alice Soft. **LNV**

DAICHI, AKITARO

1956–. After graduating from the Tokyo School of Photography in 1978, he worked as an animator on the Doraemon movie *Nobita the Space Colonist* (1981), before taking a position with the Jam Company as a director of live-action commercials and corporate videos. He later joined EG Films as an animator, and then went freelance as a director. His works include Now and Then, Here and There (1999), Jubei-chan the Ninja Girl (1999), and Fruits Basket (2001).

DAICHIS, THE *

2001. JPN: *Chikyu Boei Kazoku*. TV series. DIR: Satoshi Kimura. SCR: Shoji Kawamori. DES: Kazuaki Mori. ANI: Kazuaki Mori. MUS: Shigeo Naka. PRD: Tac, WOWOW. 25 mins. x 13 eps.

Troubled family man Mamori Daichi is on the verge of divorce when he and his wife are disturbed mid-argument by a mysterious fax commanding them to protect planet Earth. Soon afterward, a giant comet smashes into Earth, releasing a space monster that only Mamori can stop. He, his wife, Seiko, and their children, Dai and Nozomi, discover that when they insert their special magic cards into a computer, they are teleported into superpowered battle suits, complete with user manuals on how to save Earth. An ULTRAMAN pastiche from Shoji Kawamori, best known in recent years for his work on MACROSS and ESCAFLOWNE, deliberately using "old-fashioned" techniques of cel animation in contrast to the contemporary fashion for digital animation and effects.

DAIEI

Formed in 1942 as the Greater Japan Motion Picture Production Company by a government-mandated merger of several struggling studios, Daiei appears on anime credits listings only rarely, as a distributor. However, that is a lucrative field in itself, and Daiei had an immense *negative* influence on Japanese animation in the 1950s by being the Japanese distributor of Walt Disney films, which largely crowded out the struggling local industry, before Toei fought back with the Japan-made PANDA AND THE MAGIC SERPENT. The company and its extensive live-action back catalogue was bought by and merged with Kadokawa Shoten in 2002, leading to some productions listed as "Kadokawa Daiei" pictures, before the name Daiei was gently erased from credits in 2004.

DAIGUARD *

1999. JPN: *Chikyu Boetai Kigyo Daiguard*. AKA: *Earth Defense Enterprise Daiguard*. TV series. DIR: Seiji Mizushima. SCR: Hidefumi Kimura. DES: Hiroyuki Kanno. ANI: Michiru Ishihara. MUS: Kohei Tanaka, Kenji Kawai. PRD: Sotsu, Xebec, TV Tokyo. 25 mins. x 26 eps.
In A.D. 2030, 12 years after the extra-dimensional Heterodyne invasion was repelled by the people of Earth, the planet has settled into a time of relative peace. The chief weapon against them, the giant robot known as Daiguard, is now performing police PR duties in Japan with a new pilot—the hot-headed 25-year-old Shunsuke Akagi. But during one of Daiguard's routine publicity appearances, the Heterodyne strike again, and the old war horse is brought back into service without a moment to lose. Director Mizushima

later confessed to *Newtype* that the show went into production with "almost no prep time," much to its detriment.

DAIGUNDER *

2002. JPN: *Bakuto Sengen Daigandar*. AKA: *Explosive Declaration Daigandar*. TV series. DIR: Hiroyuki Yano. SCR: N/C. DES: Kou Abe. ANI: Brains Base. MUS: Yasunori Iwasaki. PRD: NAS, TV Tokyo, Nippon Animation, Aeon. 25 mins. x 39 eps.
Battle Robot is a new sport in which robots fight each other—they call it "new," but to us it looks uncannily like the previous year's CRUSH GEAR TURBO. Akira Akebono is a Commander, or Battle Robot pilot and team leader, and wants to get to the top of his sport. When the Battle Robot League gives his team a chance to compete, his grandfather Professor Hajime builds the mighty robot Daigunder. However, evil genius Big Bang is out to steal the secrets of Team Akira, whose allies include Bu-Lion, Eagle Arrow, Drimog (a mole-based robot), and three dinosaur-themed machines, Bone Rex, Despector (a ptero-dactyl), and Tri-Horn. This cheerful show for younger children made it onto both Animax-Asia and America's ABC Family Channel in 2003. Yes, yet another one squirted out the production-line sausage machine and into your children's brains.

DAIKUHARA, AKIRA

1917–2012. Animator, sometimes miscredited as Akira Okuwara or Akira Daikuwara, whose career spanned much of the 20th-century industry, from his first work under Iwao Ashida in 1936, up to HONEY HONEY in 1981. In the 1940s, he was drafted into the Navy to make WARTIME ANIME and spent much of his time close to Yokosuka airbase, where he tellingly reported that he was grateful for "food and shoes." He worked on such instructional films as *Assisting in Aerial Defense: The Aerial Defense Cartoon Storybook* (1942), an 11-minute fable in which a group of public-spirited pigs help defend local cattle from evil fox raiders.
Despite U.S. authorities' claim that no propagandists would be persecuted for their actions, the Occupation period was a tough time for animators. With studio output drastically reduced from its wartime peak, the postwar Japanese film industry

was a focus of bitter recriminations and putsches among the Japanese themselves in competition for work, and animators were not spared. But Daikuhara remained a key figure, and he participated in SAKURA (1946), the first postwar cartoon made in Japan. By the mid-1950s, he was one of the leaders of what would become the Toei Animation studio. Daikuhara doubted his new masters' claim that Toei could ever be a "Pacific Disney," but diligently taught a new generation of animators alongside Yasuji Mori (q.v.), regularly calving away new workgroups of his students, who in turn taught other workgroups how to animate for the movies. By 1958, Daikuhara was not only working for Toei under the tutelage of "the father of Japanese animation," Kenzo Masaoka, but producing American propaganda as one of the staff on the anti-Communist cartoon *The Bear and Children*, a short film intended to be screened at the U.S. embassy in Bangkok.
Daikuhara pioneered what he called *mangateki kocho* or "cartoonish exaggeration," which manifested decades later in the animated business as "super-deformation." Conversely, he also strove elsewhere for more realism, such as on Toei's ADVENTURES OF SINBAD (1962) for which he used live-action footage of the young martial artist Shinichi "Sonny" Chiba as a base for the hero's fighting sequences.
He was in his 40s in 1963 when ASTRO BOY transformed the world of cartoons in Japan. Toei Animation was quick to react and put Daikuhara to work on a TV competitor, KEN THE WOLF BOY. Daikuhara reported the shock at TV output among the animators, their level of artwork starting out high and swiftly plummeting as they tried to keep up with the breakneck schedule of 25 minutes a week, several times faster than their movie output. In 1980 he set up Studio Carpenter (JPN: *daiku* = carpenter) in a surburban house, using seed money from Toei. Studio Carpenter subsequently worked for Toei on several projects as a subcontractor, including ONE PIECE, several iterations of DRAGON BALL Z, and *Arcadia of My Youth* (see CAPTAIN HARLOCK), although Daikuhara himself officially retired in 1982, leaving the day-to-day running of the studio to Yasuo Yamaguchi.

DAIMAHO CREST

2006. JPN: *Daimaho Toge.* AKA: *Great Magic Crest.* Video. DIR: Tsutomu Mizushima. SCR: Tsutomu Mizushima. DES: Satoshi Isono. ANI: N/C. MUS: N/S. PRD: Studio Barcelona. 30 mins. x 2 eps.

Princess Punie is a beautiful, magical girl of royal birth, sent to live among humans for a year as part of her training for taking the throne of her homeworld. Despite a set-up redolent of innumerable "magical girl" shows, this video series takes off in a somewhat unexpected direction, as Punie has a sadistic streak and enjoys besting her schoolgirl rivals in a magical variant of wrestling holds.

DAITARN 3

1977. JPN: *Muteki Kojin Daitarn 3.* AKA: *Invincible Steel Man Daitarn 3.* TV series. DIR: Yoshiyuki Tomino, Shinya Sadamitsu, Shigeru Kato. SCR: Yoshihisa Araki, Hiroyuki Hoshiyama, Soji Yoshikawa. DES: Norio Shioyama, Kazuyoshi Koguni (pseud. for Tomonori Kogawa). ANI: Kazuo Nakamura, Kazuo Yamazaki, Kazuo Tomizawa. MUS: Takeo Watanabe. PRD: Nippon Sunrise, Nagoya TV (TV Asahi). 25 mins. x 40 eps.

"For the world, for the people…!" A powerful artificial intelligence called Don Zaucker is created in the human colony on Mars. Created by Professor Haran and intended to help mankind, Zaucker turns evil, kills its creator, and transforms all the humans on the base into Meganoids, powerful cyborgs led by its aide Koros, a redheaded cyborg lady who is the only being able to communicate with Zaucker. The cyborgs can merge to become Megaborg, a huge machine entity. As Meganoid society evolves, with different grades and types of cyborg, Koros plans to spread the Meganoid Empire to Earth; but she reckons without Professor Haran's son Banjo and the mighty transforming robot Daitarn 3. Helped by the family's resourceful butler Garrison Tokida, battling babes Reika Sanjo and Beauty Tachibana, and with streetwise orphan Toppi as his sidekick, Banjo must stop the Meganoids before they take over the Earth. They have a futuristic base in a beautiful villa, and lots of high-tech toys, led by Banjo's supercar the Match Patrol, which can transform from dream ride to combat aircraft.

Reuniting many staff from ZAMBOT 3

to replicate the spythrillers of the 1960s (most obviously James Bond, but also *Batman*), this series from the future creator of GUNDAM advanced far beyond the staid monsters-of-the-week of its initial premise—in fact, even these were originals, featuring cameo designs from many big names. The show is also notable for its foreshadowing of the Borg from *Star Trek: The Next Generation,* and for being the first giant robot since ASTRO GANGER to have changing facial expressions. The characters have more to offer than the cookie cutter usually allows, and the show is pervaded by their humor and camaraderie. Garrison, the group's father figure, is an enigmatic and fascinating man in his own right, Toppi is less annoying than most audience identification points, and the girls are both tough and powerful allies. Reika is ex-Interpol; her partner Toda killed by the invading Meganoids. Beauty wants more from life than simply being the darling of a rich father and has taken a job as Banjo's assistant before the show starts. Her vital statistics are revealed in episode 6 as 37–23–36 inches, indicating an interest from a slightly older audience than the norm for a giant robot show; perhaps, like *Dr. Who's* Leela, she persuaded fathers to watch with their sons.

Koros sends the Meganoids to Earth to take over the planet by assimilating each human into their collective consciousness, but when our heroes make it impossible, Koros decides to crash Mars into Earth to wipe out all human life. Banjo and company head for Mars in Daitarn 3, and Banjo finally faces Koros in hand-to-hand combat in the palace of Don Zaucker. Just as Banjo is about to destroy Koros, Zaucker wakes from its cybernetic sleep, and we learn that it was Koros who started the drive for conquest of humanity. With the Meganoid Empire in ruins and mankind safe, the team can go home, and the end of the series is intensely melancholy, leading us through the departure of each team member, the shutting up of the villa, and Garrison, looking back down a tree-lined avenue in the rain toward the base from which so much excitement, laughter, and tragedy was launched, now empty and desolate. He stamps his foot and shouts the summoning spell, "One… two… three… Daitarn Three!" but the last

shot shows the villa dark, empty, and still, except for a single lighted window, as the superb ending theme cuts in. Credited to Tomino and Sunrise's house pseudonym Hajime Yadate, this is a fascinating minor work by a science fiction master whose main strength has always been making the robots as sexy as possible, then making the people matter more.

DALLOS *

1983. Video, movie. DIR: Mamoru Oshii. SCR: Hisayuki Toriumi, Mamoru Oshii. DES: Toshiyasu Okada, Masaharu Sato. ANI: Toshiyasu Okada, Takemi Tanemoto, Masahiro Neriki. MUS: Hiroyuki Nanba. PRD: Bandai, Yomiuri, Studio Pierrot. 30 mins. x 4 eps. (v), 120 mins. (m1), 85 mins. (m2 recut).

The grandchildren of the original lunar colonists, toughened by generations in the mines on the dark side of the moon, fight to gain their independence from an exhausted and oppressive Earth, as guerrilla leaders Shun and Dog oppose the ruthless Terran commandant Alex Riger's group, complete with armed heavies and robot dogs.

This unremarkable rip-off of Robert Heinlein's *The Moon Is a Harsh Mistress* will go down in history for being the first anime made specifically for direct video release. The series, later issued in a 120-minute feature-length edition, was cut down to form the 85-minute *Dallos Special,* which added 50 extra shots and was the only incarnation to be released in the U.S. Before we even get to the opening *Star Wars*–inspired crawl of expository scene-setting, there's a lengthy narration over stills of concept art, a sure-fire sign (as in the much later JIN-ROH) that the makers feared the audience would be bewildered. As with writer Toriumi's later SALAMANDER, the script is actually better than the crew seem to realize (much of the five-minute voice-over seems to consist of his rather sensible production notes), but his writing is badly served by hackneyed set-ups and execution by staff members who had yet to realize that the video audience would be slightly older than the viewership for TV serials such as GUNDAM. The final conceit, in which an awestruck colonist gazes upon the distant Earth that spawned him, *almost* makes up for the cheap animation and lazy world-building that gives a lunar city a blue sky and Earth-normal gravity.

DAN DOH!! *

2004. TV series. DIR: Hidetoshi Omori. SCR: Noburo Kimura. DES: Hidetoshi Omori. ANI: N/C. MUS: Yuko Shimomura. PRD: HoriPro, TV Tokyo. 24 mins. x 26 eps.

High school rivalry, sporting enmities, family secrets, and rifts abound in the story of a high school boy who quits baseball for golf, from the manga by Nobuhiro Sakata and Daichi Banjo. Tadamichi "Dandoh" Aoba is the son of a former player who was banned from the golf world ten years ago. His mother has been missing for some time. He has an older sister, Kyoko, and a good friend in the pretty Yuka Sanada, who enters the Kumamoto Junior Golf Championship. Dandoh's only been playing for three months but he enters the same competition, despite opposition and sabotage from Yuka's classmate Yokota, who desires her and hates him. As the friends enter more competitions and Dandoh gets more and more into the game, he meets Tasaki, the man who got his father banned. Then he and Kyoko learn that their mother has been seen in Hokkaido, and a chance to caddy in a tournament on the island gives him a chance to look for her. No more ludicrous than any other SPORTS ANIME—compare to BEAT SHOT!! and PROGOLFER SARU.

DANCE IN THE VAMPIRE BUND *

2010. TV series. DIR: Masahiro Sonoda, Aki-yuki Shinbo, Toshimasa Suzuki, Nobuharu Kamanaka, Hiroshi Kimura, Kohei Hatano. SCR: Hiroyuki Yoshino, Masahiro Yokotani. DES: Naoyuki Konno, Fumio Matsumoto, Naoyuki Konno, Yasutoshi Iwasaki. MUS: Akio Dobashi. PRD: Sanzigen, Shaft, ACGC, Studio Tulip, AT-X. 24 mins. x 12 eps.

Mina Tepes, vampire princess, wants her species to coexist peacefully with humans. She's paid off Japan's entire national debt in exchange for the right to create a vampire haven on Japanese soil—an artificial island in Tokyo Bay. But there are those on both sides who don't want vampires to win international recognition and acceptance. As they plot to assassinate Mina, it's a race against time to make her dream come true and give the undead a chance at a

normal unlife before her own immortality is canceled for ever.

Taking a leaf from *True Blood*'s book by revealing the existence of vampires through modern media, and from *Twilight* in giving our vampire cutie a teen were-wolf of her own, this show has generated considerable controversy thanks to its suggestive approach to childlike creatures of both genders and its explicit, plentiful nudity and violence. Just as annoying is the loading up of a promising idea with the conventional episodes of the harem show—the high school romance, the cook-ery scene—Vampire High was fun when DON DRACULA's daughter went to school, but now it's a *Twilight* trope we could do without. But the story is loaded with gripping, decadent menace, as the "highly evolved," cultured, super-smart vampire breed faces extinction, and assimilation with the despised humans. You don't have to dig too deep to see the tasty subtext—with an aging population and a declining birthrate, the question of immigration and assimilation hits close to home for the Japanese, an issue also approached in the GHOST IN THE SHELL spin-off *Stand Alone Complex*.

Nozomu Tamaki's original manga, which ran in the magazine *Comic Flap-per*, introduced many interesting ideas. Tamaki's vampires are an evolved form of humanity who experience heightened senses and emotions—turning many of them into gluttons, addicts, and melodra-matic hysterics. Vampirism can be stopped in its tracks by a vaccine, just as long as it is administered within 48 hours of a bite, adding an against-the-clock tension to any infection. Morevoer, Tamaki's vampires may be predators on humanity, but they are also a dying breed, down to their very last "full" female.

The pick-and-mix approach to vampire lore will annoy purists, but so does almost every vampire story that isn't *Dracula*: good use is also made of Anne Rice's argument that basic modern technology—medicine, sunblock, and polarized glass—might help a vampire navigate the daylight world. It also adds the new notion that vampires' transformations are governed by the power of their beliefs: they can become what they truly wish to be. The animation is generally good, the design varied with

some wonderful costumes, the music less so. Compare to VAMPIRE PRINCESS MIYU, another self-consciously edgy tale that flirts (though more circumspectly) with sexuality. **NV**

DANCE TILL TOMORROW

1990. JPN: *Asatte Dance*. AKA: *Dance the Day after Tomorrow*. Video. DIR: Teruo Kogure, Masamune Ochiai. SCR: Sheila Nakajima, Tomohiro Maruyama. DES: Jiro Sayama. ANI: Jiro Sayama. MUS: Tetsuya Nakamura. PRD: Knack. 45 mins. x 2 eps.

Country boy Suekichi only has to graduate from his Tokyo college to inherit his late grandfather's fortune. He'd rather be working in a deadbeat experimental the-ater troupe in the hope of getting into its earnest, pretty leading light's good book, not to mention panties, but there are two major obstacles. One is that Granddad, not content with setting up a stony-faced lawyer to try and keep his descendant on the straight and narrow, materializes in Suekichi's apartment at awkward moments to dispense totally useless advice. And the other is Aya Hibino (or is it Munakata?), a wild child with an attitude problem who keeps breaking into his apartment and forcing sex on him. She also forces reluctant tenderness, responsibility, and a realization that there's more to adult life than he'll ever find in his drama group, in this short-lived adaptation of Naoki Yama-moto's seven-volume 1989 manga from *Big Comic Spirits*. The same creator contrib-uted to the CREAM LEMON series under the pseudonym To Moriyama. Live-action movie versions followed in 1991 and 2005; the latter was released in the U.S. under the title *Naughty Gold-Diggers*. **N**

DANCER, THE

2006. JPN: *Maihime*. AKA: *Dancing Girl, The*. Video. DIR: Shutaro Oku. SCR: Ogai Mori. DES: Akisa Furuya. ANI: Akisa Furuya. MUS: Hiroshi Fujii. PRD: Toei Animation, Gentosha. 30 mins.

Ogai Mori's classic story, a reverse *Madame Butterfly*, has already inspired anime—*The Dancing Girl* from ANIMATED CLASSICS OF JAPANESE LITERATURE. This time, his tale of a young Japanese student in Berlin who meets and falls in love with a dancer, and then abandons her to go home, gets a very different treatment, read out over delicate watercolor-style images by Oku and multimedia animation by Furuya. Part of Toei's *ga-nime* series (**ARGOT AND JARGON**).

DANCING WITH DAD

1999. JPN: *Papa to Odoro*. TV series. DIR: Akira Yoshida. SCR: Chuya Chikazawa. DES: Masaaki Kannan. ANI: Hirohide Shikishima, Moriyasu Taniguchi. MUS: N/C. PRD: Studio Deen, TBS. 8 mins. x 13 eps.

A gag comedy depicting the everyday life of a lustful, lazy, and indecent father and his strait-laced son and daughter. Chuya Chikazawa's 1991 comic from *Young Magazine* was adapted for short slots on the *Wonderful* show.

DANCOUGAR *

1985. JPN: *Choju Kishin Dancougar*. AKA: *Super-Bestial Machine God Dancougar*. TV series, video. DIR: Nobuyoshi Habara, Seiji Okuda. SCR: Keisuke Fujikawa, Kenji Terada, Junji Takegami. DES: Indori-Koya, Hisashi Hirai, Masami Obari. ANI: Akira Saijo, Osamu Tsuruyama. MUS: Takeshi Ike, Osamu Totsuka. PRD: Ashi Pro, TBS. 25 mins. x 38 eps. (TV), ca. 90 mins. x 2 eps. (v), 30 mins. x 4 eps. (v).

Earthman Shapiro Keats betrays his own race and switches his allegiance to the space emperor Muge Zolbados. Earth's last hope is the Dancougar team, which harnesses the power of Terran beasts to fight with its combining giant robot. Carefully repeating the formula established by **BATTLE OF THE PLANETS** and director Okuda's earlier **GOBARIAN**, *Dancougar* features leader Shinobu (pilot of the Eagle Fighter), love interest Sarah and her Land Cougar, youngster Masato in the Land Liger, and big-guy Ryo, pilot of the Mammoth. Battles rage across the Amazon Basin, New York, and Europe before a final showdown between Sarah and Shapiro in the asteroid belt.

As the series closed, 60 minutes of recycled footage was augmented with 30 new minutes to make the *Requiem for Lost Heroes* video. Toshitaro Oba's all-new *God Bless Dancougar* was the best-selling anime video of 1987 (released in the U.K. as plain *Dancougar*), foreshadowing **PATLABOR** 2 with its post-series look at the team training new recruits. Framed by a military cartel, they are imprisoned but rescued by their students and a short-lived suicide squad of black knights (who also appeared in episode 26 of the TV series). The usual robot action is punctuated by completely incongruous musical interludes (Shinobu wants to be a pop star), perhaps recycled footage from the 1985 *Songs from the Beast Machine Team* video special.

The team's last appearance was in the four-part 1989 video series *White Hot Final Chapter*, when they are dragged out of retirement to resist a new threat from planet Delado, with Shapiro pulling strings from behind the scenes.

DANGAIOH *

1987. JPN: *Hajataisei Dangaio, Hajakyosei G Dangaioh*. AKA: *Star Destroyer Bullet-Criminal-Investigation-Phoenix, Hajyataisei Great Dangaioh*. Video, TV series. DIR: Toshihiro Hirano. SCR: Sho Aikawa. DES: Shoji Kawamori, Masami Obari, Koichi Ohata. ANI: Hideaki Anno. MUS: Michiaki Watanabe. PRD: AIC. 45 mins. x 3 eps. (v), 25 mins. x 13 eps. (TV).

Four kids (Mia, Pai, Lamda, and token male Roll) are abducted and brainwashed by the kindly (!) Professor Tarsan and trained to become warriors in the fight against the pirate Galimos. They later discover that their planets were destroyed by the invaders (who keep their armor on indoors so the animators don't have to move their lips) and that the kids' powers are the last thing that prevents the end of the universe.

The 1980s anime industry, still taking tottering steps into the world of straight-to-video science fiction, had a lot of trouble working out what to give its audience. Boys who had grown up watching kiddie shows that featured giant transforming robots were now grown-up 20-somethings with VCRs, and this was one of the many experiments aimed at bringing them back. But the amnesia subplot is a lame excuse for long exposition scenes and huge holes in the plot, and it contains many of the flaws of children's shows without exploiting their appeal. The end result is a show that imitates the big-robot fights (originally designed to sell toys) and halfheartedly includes a psychic-weapon subplot influenced by **AKIRA**. Ultimately too childish for an adult audience and too complex for kids, *Dangaioh* is an also-ran in Japanese sci-fi.

Originally sold as *Dangaio* [sic] in a subtitled edition in the U.S., the first episode was dropped from Manga Entertainment's compilation dub, which added the final "h." The dub is the usual shrill mess that characterizes translations of the period; listen for the telltale "bloodies" and occasional asides like Pai's darts slang ("One hundred and *eighty*!") that mark this as a British dub made with American accents to secure U.S. distribution.

Note also the careful balancing of the sexes. Producer Toru Miura realized early on that a primarily male audience would prefer to watch a lone boy amid a gaggle of gorgeous girls rather than a load of sweaty men in spacesuits. Miura went on to perfect this eye-candy formula in the hugely popular **TENCHI MUYO!**

The video series was remade for television as the 13-episode *G Dangaio* (2001), which begins with Miya Alice crash-landing on Earth in the 1980s and sending a telepathic message to teenager Miya Shikitani that warns her of the approach of Banger Invaders. The Terran Miya starts developing a Dangaioh unit to defend Earth, and ten years later they are ready to defend the planet with the aid of the combining Dangaioh Burst, Dangaioh Flail, and Dangaioh Cross, piloted by angst-ridden teens Takaya Tenjo, Manami Umishio, and Hitomi Jido. *G Dangaioh* ends without actually concluding the plot; there is an indication that a second season was intended, but it has not materialized.

DANGAIZER THREE *

1999. JPN: *Choshin-hime Dangaizer Three*. AKA: *Super-Divine Princess Dangaizer Three*. Video. DIR: Masami Obari. SCR: Masami Obari, Reimu Aoki. DES: Yasuhiro Oshima, Natsuki Mamiya, Masami Obari. ANI: Masami Obari. MUS: Masayuki Sakamoto. PRD: Kaos Project. 30 mins. x 4 eps.

The arrival of a giant crystal causes havoc in the future city of Neo Hong Kong, sucking the pretty martial artist and games fan Hina Mitsurugi into an alternate world. There, she finds the four kings of this parallel Earth facing destruction at the hands of the evil Sapphire and teams up with big-sister figure Sindy Shahana on a quest for some of the mythical Protect Gear.

Directed, scripted, designed, *and* animated by **VIRUS**'s Obari, with plenty of fan-service cleavage to make up for the absent characterization. **Ⓝ**

DANGANRONPA THE ANIMATION *
2012. jpn: *Danganronpa Kibo no Gakuen to Zetsubo no Kokosei.* aka: *Danganronpa School of Hope and Student of Despair.* TV series. dir: Seiji Kishi. scr: Makoto Uezu, Osamu Murata, Satoko Sekine, Toko Machida. des: Kazuaki Morita. ani: Kazuaki Morita, Ryoko Amisaki. mus: Masafumi Takada. prd: Lerche. 24 mins. x 13 eps.
Makoto Naegi is thrilled when he wins the lottery to attend the Hope Peak Academy, only to discover that the only way out is either by becoming a successful murderer, or an unfortunate victim. Based on a "visual novel" (**Argot and Jargon**), this show unfortunately squanders much of its promise by playing out as if you are watching someone else play the game. There's a lot of telling rather than showing, with the viewer rarely shown clues, but instead informed about them after someone has dug them up off-screen. This dilutes much of the whodunit elements that could have otherwise made this an anime in the vein of **When They Cry**. **V**

DANGARD ACE *
1977. jpn: *Wakusei Robo Dangard A.* aka: *Planetary Robot Danguard Ace.* TV series, movie. dir: Tomoharu Katsumata. scr: Haruya Yamazaki, Soji Yoshikawa. des: Shingo Araki. ani: Shingo Araki, Akira Saijo. mus: Shunsuke Kikuchi. prd: Toei, Fuji TV. 25 mins. x 56 eps. (TV), 25 mins. (m1), 26 mins. (m2).
Dr. Oedo organizes a scouting mission, led by the elite young pilot Takuma (Winstar), to the rogue tenth planet Prometheus as it nears Earth. Approaching the planet in the superfast carrier Jasdam, the crew rescues Captain Dan (Captain Mask), who has escaped from the evil Commissar Krell. The captain assumes duties with the Dangard A robot team, ready to put them through the toughest training in order to save Earth from invasion. Based on an idea by **Starblazers'** Leiji Matsumoto (reputedly in answer to the giant-robot shows made by his fellow big name manga artists, Go Nagai and Shotaro Ishinomori) and Dan Kobayashi (who appears to have lent his own name to the show and to the heroic Captain Dan), 26 episodes of this series were shown in the U.S. as part of the **Force Five** anime compilation, and the first 2 episodes were rereleased on video to capitalize on the new boom in anime. The characters also appeared in two episodes made specifically for theatrical release in Japan, called *Dangard A vs the Insect Robot Legion* (1977) and *Dangard A: Great War in Space* (1978). The series was reissued in an LD collection under the umbrella title of *Leiji Matsumoto Theater.*

DANGEROUS GRANDPA
2003. jpn: *Dangerous Ji-san ja.* TV series, TV special, video. dir: Yasuyuki Inoue, Toshihide Nishimaki, Takashi Watanabe. scr: Isamu Sasagawa. des: Masahiro Ando. ani: N/C. mus: Hyadain. prd: JC Staff, Kids Station. 36 secs. x 33 eps. (TV1), 5 mins. x 51 eps. (TV2), 2 mins. x 19 eps. (TV3), ?? mins. (v), ca. 3 mins. x 81 eps. (TV4).
A very short "kids" anime, broadcast before dawn so hardly child-friendly, but perhaps that is in keeping with Kazutoshi Soyama's original gag manga, which was often scabrous, scatological, and rude. Here it is adapted into a series of slapstick segments in which a zany oldster causes havoc and embarrassment for the granddaughter he is supposed to be looking after. Cultural historians, however, might like to observe that even in this ephemeral comedy, there is a growing assumption that retirees are handling childcare while parents are working—compare to other modern mores in **Bubu Chacha**. Grandpa got a whole ten minutes to shock the nation in a TV special in December 2003, before returning for a second season of longer episodes—the authors suspect that many of these recycled some of the early commercial-length shorts, but there was certainly some new material, too. The most recent incarnation, which began in 2012, was bolstered by the presence of Takashi Watanabe as director, gaining it substantially more notice than this obscure anime has previously amassed.

DANTE'S INFERNO: AN ANIMATED EPIC *
2010. Video. dir: Shuko Murase, Yasuomi Umezu, Mike Disa, Victor Cook, Sang-Jin Kim, Jong-Sik Nam. Lee Seung-gyu. scr: Jonathan Knight, Brandon Auman. des: Tsukasa Kotobuki, Eiji Wakamatsu, Tomoaki Okada. ani: Shuko Murase. mus: Christopher Tin. prd: Manglobe, Production I.G, JM Animation, Dongwoo Animation. 88 mins.
Crusader Dante returns home to discover that his beloved Beatrice has been murdered, and her soul dragged into Hell. Refusing to give her up, he steals Death's scythe and chases after her … into the Inferno. Along the way he must confront his own inner darkness, atone for past sins, and destroy all the monsters who stand between him and Beatrice, before Satan can make her his bride.

This is not an anime adaptation of the great Italian verse epic. That was simply a jumping-off ground for the sword-swinging game released by EA Games, which forms the basis for this promotional anthology, as if Jean Cocteau's magical 1950 film *Orphée* was reimagined as the end sequence of the 1980 movie *Flash Gordon* in order to help publicize a forgotten beat-em-up.

With each segment made by a different studio, the animation varies from terrible to excellent. Unfortunately, the first segment, by Film Roman, is pretty awful, but then Manglobe, makers of **Samurai Champloo**, take us into more attractive territory. A couple of Korean studios plow a fairly mundane furrow before Production I.G gives us a classy finish. There are some great fights, some gruesome monsters, and some truly turgid passages of moral reflection, but if you want to brag that you're watching *Dante's Inferno* when you really mean a beer-and-curry movie, this will fit the bill. This is probably the only time you'll see the protagonist of a film clamber up a dog's butt, as well. **N**

DAPHNE IN THE BRILLIANT BLUE *
2004. jpn: *Hikari to Mizu no Daphne.* aka: *Daphne of Light and Water.* TV series. dir: Ryuji Ikehata. scr: Kiyoshi Minakami, Yasunori Yamada, Kurasumi Sunayama. des: Kazunori Iwakura, Satoshi Shiki, Shingo Takeba. ani: Yumi Nakayama. mus: Ko Otani. prd: Toshiba, Happinet, JC Staff, Genco. 24 mins. x 24 eps.
Global warming has caused flooding worldwide and many countries have simply vanished underwater; a premise familiar from **Patlabor** and **Blue Submarine No. Six**, but employed here for reasons that seem to have more to do with the falling costs of CG water-modeling (compare to **Aria**) and the handy excuse for having lots of characters wearing tight swimwear. Gifted student Maia Mizuki fails in the

application exam for the top-flight quasi-governmental organization known as the Oceanographic Agency, but is rescued from a robber by Rena and Shizuka, two employees of a multifunctional service corporation known as NEREIS. They've been engaged to catch the robber and blackmail the destitute Maia into acting as bait. She fills time before her next exam by working as a troubleshooter for NEREIS, in a series of set-ups that are enough to make AGENT AIKA seem demure. Maia's supposed brains are at odds with her pliant attitude; paid a pittance and constantly picked on by Rena and Shizuka, she stays with NEREIS through such thrilling operations as finding a stolen car, helping a salaryman save face with his daughter, and looking after an abandoned baby. Then she goes on a quest to find her lost memories, which have not previously been mentioned but revolve round her father's female bodyguard and her late grandfather, whose dying word was "Daphne." This involves a Mafia subplot, her being kidnapped by the Oceanographic Agency—apparently they want her for a purpose too sinister to just give her a job—and a visit to a ruined city where she uncovers their secret plot and her own past. Created by NeSKeS, whose choice of pen name confirms a fondness for the pointlessly cryptic. A manga also appeared in *Young King Ours* magazine.

DARCROWS *

2003. Video. DIR: Jun Fukuda. SCR: Jiro Muramtasu. DES: Hideki Araki. ANI: Hideki Araki. MUS: N/C. PRD: Alice Soft, Shura, Blue Eyes. 27 mins. x 2 eps.

Six months after the kingdom of Leben mounts a surprise attack on its peaceful neighbor Carnea, the king of the oppressed kingdom dies from an illness. Claude, a former knight of Carnea, returns to his homeland after eight years in exile and claims to have a plan to save the land. He suggests hiring mercenaries to beat back the Leben invaders, and to get the money for it by sponsoring the princesses and ladies of the kingdom as prostitutes, whom he undertakes to train. Based on a game by Alice Soft. **LNV**

DARK CAT *

1991. Video. DIR: Iku Suzuki. SCR: Toshiki Inoue. DES: Masami Suda. ANI: Hirohide Shiki-shima. MUS: N/C. PRD: Nikkatsu. 60 mins.

Human beings carry a seed of evil within them that demonic creatures wish to nurture and exploit. Other paranormal beings, the "dark cats," seek to protect humanity from its own heritage. Two such feline angels are Hyoi and Ryoi, who are spying on strange events in a Japanese school. Hyoi has transmuted into human form, while Ryoi has invited himself in cat form into the life of female student Aimi. As the evil spirit Jukokubo possesses the teachers and turns them to violence, Hyoi and Ryoi must protect their charges with the aid of their magical Dark Cat sword.

Based on a manga serialized in *Halloween* magazine by Naomi Kimura, *Dark Cat* crashes the pretty boys of girls' manga such as TOKYO BABYLON with the tits-and-tentacles ghostbusting of innumerable horror anime like WICKED CITY. **NV**

DARK CHAPEL, THE *

2006. JPN: *Seikojo: Bitoku no Bijiri Dorei*. AKA: *Immoral Beautiful Anal Slaves*. Video. DIR: Shinpei Nagai. SCR: Kusakai Kokubunji. DES: Takato Makoto, Mitsumaru Miyamae. ANI: Takato Makoto. MUS: N/C. PRD: Studio JAM, Milky. 30 mins. x 2 eps.

A perverted priest forces the nuns attached to his chapel to become his sex slaves. He makes them sign pacts with him, which may have been racy in 2006, but nowadays just brings to mind that tooth-grindingly awful chapter in *50 Shades of Grey* with the detailed bondage contract. Based on a porn game by BLACK PACKAGE. We are shocked, but only because U.S. porn anime usually have such creative translations of the original Japanese titles. Was there no contemporary Hollywood movie they could find an excruciating double-entendre for? **NV**

DARK FUTURE *

2006. JPN: *Kurai Mirai*. Video. DIR: Genki Yuki. SCR: Kusakai Kokubunji. DES: U-Yuki, Mitsuharu Miyamae. ANI: Naritomo Haruki, Shigenori Awai. MUS: N/C. PRD: Studio JAM, Milky. 30 mins. x 2 eps.

An after-school club in a Japanese high school is devoted to recruiting girls to turn into their personal sex slaves. They also brainwash the guys into sex with each other, and as time goes on they even start on the teachers. The Relaxation Club committee has a good thing going, and they mean to do everything they can to keep it. We apologize for making this sound much more interesting than it is; there is actually some promising material here, wasted on cheap porn based on a game by Flying-Shine. **NV**

DARK KNIGHT INGRID, THE

2009. JPN: *Makai Kishi Ingrid*. AKA: *Hell Knight Ingrid*. Video. DIR: Tsukasa Kaido. SCR: Hikaru Takeuchi. DES: Taisaburo Abe. ANI: Yasuhiro Hayashi. MUS: N/C. PRD: Studio MAO, Pixy. 27 mins. x 4 eps.

In a post-apocalyptic world, Ingrid and Murasaki are demon hunters, who enjoy a run of success until they are finally captured by vengeful demons who turn them into sex slaves. With four episodes to play with, writer Takeuchi attempts a plot, with a Loki-esque villain and a half-human, half-monster boss named Edwin Black. The design is Pixy's usual eclectic mess—despite the apocalypse you can still buy designer suits, neckties, and spectacles, and the warriors wear spandex under their wholly inadequate battle armor. Don't these people have any idea of the level of technological and financial stability required to produce spandex? In any event, Takeuchi's brave efforts are thwarted by the requirement to fit in three and a half episodes of rape, torture, and humiliation. Based on a porn game by Black Lilith, part of a series that began with *Anti-Demon Stealth Asagi* (*Taima Nin Asagi*, 2009) and which continued with *Kotetsu no Majo Annarose* (*Iron Witch Annarose*, 2012), and *Anti-Demon Stealth Blizzard* (*Taima Nin Yukikaze*, 2013). **NV**

DARK LOVE *

2005. JPN: *Kuro Ai Hitoya Tsumakan*. AKA: *Dark Love Wife Mansion*. Video. DIR: Teruaki Murakami. SCR: Osamu Momoi. DES: Teruaki Murakami. ANI: Teruaki Murakami. MUS: N/C. PRD: Makukan, Green Bunny. 30 mins. x 2 eps.

When his childhood friend Ayaka Utsumi is in desperate need of an operation, kind-hearted Tetsuya Gojo travels to see his distant relative Rokuka Aragami, hoping to borrow the money required for the procedure. Aragami agrees, but only if Tetsuya promises to work at the country mansion, training kidnapped girls how to be prostitutes. Subplots ensue in which women fallen on hard times are convinced to pay off their debts with sexual servitude, although the erotic influence of dark magic on the mansion makes this an easy sell, as they willingly descend into debauchery. Compare to **DEBTS OF DESIRE**. Based on a game by Clockup. 🅲🅽🆅

DARK MYTH *
1990. JPN: *Ankoku Shinwa.* Video. DIR: Takashi Anno. SCR: Takashi Anno. DES: Yoshiaki Yanagida. ANI: Kazuo Kawauchi, Tomomi Mochizuki. MUS: Kenji Kawai. PRD: Ajia-do. 50 mins. x 2 eps.
Ten years ago, Takeshi's father was murdered. The weeping boy was found by his side in the forest, nursing a strange shoulder wound. Takeshi suspects that the scar is a symbol of an ancient snake cult and teams up with some acquaintances to track down relics of the era. He discovers that ancient clans from Japanese prehistory are fighting to preserve their secrets in the present day. These secrets include the elixir of life, a great treasure, and a savage immortal hidden beneath a mountain.

Daijiro Moroboshi's original one-volume 1976 *Shonen Jump* manga is tied into a much larger universe both of "real" myths and his personal revisions. He already treated a similar subject the previous year in *Maddomen*, in which a scholar discovered secrets of Japanese history at a lost New Guinea temple, and would return to it again with the linked story *Confucius's Dark Myth* (1977) and a rewrite of the Monkey-King tale in *Phantom Monkey's Journey to the West* (1983, see **JOURNEY TO THE WEST**). The stories all take their cues from the fact that the supposedly homogenous Japanese are a melting pot of several different races, the earliest of which are only known from a handful of archeological relics. The Jomon, Yamatai, Ainu, Chinese, Koreans, Manchurians, and Southeast Asians all brought elements of their own cultures to Japan. Compare this to **PRINCESS MONONOKE**, in which several of these cultures fight each other at the birth of Japan. *Dark Myth* suggests that before the coming of humans, an ancient race of Indian gods also fought over the land, and that today's legends are fragmented race memories of this great war. Similar liberties are taken with history in many other anime from **PSYCHIC WARS** to **YAMATO TAKERU**.

There is a clever economy of animation (especially a scene where Takeshi alone is animated in a whited-out world) and some suitably arcane music from **GHOST IN THE SHELL**'s Kawai, but *DM* is ultimately disappointing. That place in Japanese history where real events elide into myth is truly fascinating. Even today, the emperor can supposedly trace his lineage back to Amaterasu, the Sun Goddess mentioned in *DM*, and the sorcerous Princess Himiko is the semihistorical figure mentioned in Chinese histories as the Queen of Wa, who appears in other guises in **ZEGUY**, **FLINT THE TIME DETECTIVE**, and **STEEL JEEG**. But much of the plot is a tour of Japanese antiquities, and while director Anno turns up the tension with waving grasses at the scene of a murder, action is slow to arrive and difficult to follow. The names are too cumbersome for non-Japanese speakers and the stories are too complex, especially when they require the viewer to know exactly what old legends are being slyly adapted. Takeshi's quest takes him all over modern Japan, though to the uninitiated, one temple looks very much like another.

For the dub, Manga Entertainment does its best, but John Wolskel's rewrite still has to stumble through lines like, "The head of the Kikuchi clan is always called Kikuchi-hiko. It is a very old name. It is recorded as Kukuchi-ku of the country of Kuna, in the *Gishiwajin-den* in the third century A.D." Matters aren't helped by a cast that can't pronounce this stuff half the time. 🅥

DARK NIGHT'S DRAMA
1995. JPN: *Yamiyo no Jidaigeki.* AKA: *Dark Night's Period-Drama.* TV series. DIR: Takashi Imanishi, Yoshiyuki Tomino, Ryosuke Takahashi. SCR: Takashi Imanishi, Yoshiyuki Tomino. DES: Norio Shioyama, Kazuhiro Soeta. ANI: Kazuhiro Soeta. MUS: N/C. PRD: Sunrise, Nippon TV. 15 mins. x 4 eps.
Four tales of old-time horror in the anthology spirit of **PET SHOP OF HORRORS** and **THE COCKPIT** from directors best known for giant-robot shows. Tales include *The Hill of Old Age*, which tells of a conspiracy hatched against Japan's unifier, Nobunaga Oda; *Seeing the Truth*, about the assassin sent to murder Nobunaga's successor,

Ieyasu Tokugawa; a wandering swordsman saving a damsel in distress from evil spirits in *The Ear of Jinsuke*, while the final chapter, *Prints from the Fall of the Bakufu*, features a tomboy from a woodcut works charged with making a print of the young warrior Okita Soji. Broadcast as part of the *Neo Hyper Kids* program. 🅝🅥

DARK RABBIT HAS SEVEN LIVES, A *
2011. JPN: *Itsuka Tenma no Kuro-Usagi.* AKA: *Itsuten.* TV series, video. DIR: Takashi Yamamoto. SCR: Shigeru Morita, Keiichiro Ochi, Kiyoko Yoshimura, Masaharu Amiya. DES: Satoshi Isono, Toshihiro Kohama. ANI: Masaaki Sakurai, Satoshi Isono. MUS: Shigeo Komori. PRD: ZEXCS, AT-X, Frontier Works, Kadokawa, Klockworx. 25 mins. x 12 eps. (TV), 25 mins. (v).
Most forgotten childhood friends vow undying love and turn up in high school to collect (**ROMANCE AND DRAMA**). Instead, vampire toddler Himea curses Taito to continue to live every time he's killed. He forgets this little death-dealer, but nine years later they meet again in high school. Taito doesn't know it yet, but the school is connected to the world of demons. Gradually, he and Himea start to remember their past relationship and build a new one—but they also have to deal with demon incursions. Despite this twist to the premise, and despite its pretty art, this is bland and forgettable. A crossover one-shot video from the same crew was released in December 2011, involving characters from creator Takaya Kagami's other light-novel series **LEGEND OF THE LEGENDARY HEROES**. The Blu-ray release also features six ten-minute "picture drama" episodes, which appear to be just stories told over still pictures, and a three-minute special with the characters in squashed-down style. 🅝

DARK SHELL *
2003. JPN: *Ori no Naka no Namameki.* AKA: *Dark Shell: Lust in the Cage.* Video. DIR: Kazuma Kanazawa. SCR: Kazuma Kanazawa. DES: Masaki Yamada. ANI: Hiroya Iijima. MUS: Teruo Takahama. PRD: Studio Kuma, Blue Eyes. 30 mins. x 2 eps.
In an alternate world where World War II ended with a balkanized Japan plunged into chaos and civil conflict, soldiers escort captive women across the danger zone. They do so while making regular stops

to have sex with their charges, regardless of their consent or lack thereof. Meanwhile, an unseen sniper begins to pick off members of the group until the act of sex itself becomes fraught with danger. Sexualized violence, depravity, and an original form of borderline necrophilia, as pleading victims find themselves having to choose between sex and death, and often getting both. Survivor Kaoruko has happier memories but they only serve for an exculpatory "parallel world" happy ending, where the war didn't happen and she and her lover sit on a peaceful beach watching two girls at play who have actually been raped and killed. ❶ⓃⓋ

DARK TOURS *

2005. JPN: *Shinjin Tour Conductor Rina*. AKA: *Tour Guide, Dark Tourer, Tour Conductor Rina*. Video. DIR: Toshiaki Kanbara, Shigeru Yazaki. SCR: Guts Maro. DES: Masaki Hosoyama. ANI: Masaki Hosoyama. MUS: N/C. PRD: Ypsilon, Studio Matrix, Film Works, movie King, GP Museum Soft. 30 mins.
Rina is a new recruit working for a travel firm placed in charge of the ominous-sounding Demon Princess Tour. Her job is to take a tour group to the spooky village of Murasawa, famous for a local ghost legend. However, she discovers that at least part of the legend is true and that a terrible fate awaits the women on the tour bus when they are delivered into the clutches of rapacious local men in the remote country village. Based on an erotic novel. ❶ⓃⓋ

DARK WARRIOR *

1991. JPN: *Maku Senjo*. AKA: *Demon Pavilion Battleground*. Video. DIR: Masahisa Ishida. SCR: Masaru Yamamoto. DES: Kenichi Onuki, Osamu Tsuruyama. ANI: Keisuke Morishita. MUS: Teruo Takahama. PRD: Daiei, Tokuma Japan Communications. 50 mins. x 2 eps.
When computer genius Joe Takegami hacks into a top-secret computer system in search of information on a mysterious girl, he discovers he is a clone created at the command of David Rockford, CEO of America's largest electronics company. Forced to run for his life from the secret government project that created him, he must rely on his newly discovered psychic powers for protection. He meets another psychic, Aya Lee Rose, and the pair face the combined might of Rockford Electronics in a fight for truth and justice.

Author Sho Takejima (who also created **PHANTOM HEROES**) was killed in a motorcycle accident in the year of *DW*'s Japanese release, a tragedy cynically exploited to drum up interest in this awful anime adaptation of his novel. With shades of *Blade Runner* and *Total Recall* in its implanted memories and confused identities, *DW* (known by its Japanese title *Maku Senjo* in the U.K.) would have been years ahead of **PERFECT BLUE** were it not for the stultifying ineptitude of its execution.

It starts as it means to go on, with a pompous voice-over vainly attempting to justify another story of musclemen hitting each other. *DW* would like to play mind games with the viewer but has such a ham-fisted grasp of the real world that it's hard to notice where the unreal comes into effect. The direction is lazily inexact, with characters "crossing the line" between shots so that they appear to be going in separate directions. The artwork is dreadful, including a laughably lopsided "Pentagon," and the animation is criminally cheap, often below TV standards (Joe drives down one street which consists of just two buildings on a loop). Such travesties compound the shoddy script—we are just as shocked as Joe when we see a "double" of his former lover, since the two girls could not look more different! Genetically engineered super-warriors shrug off bullets but cower from flames. With incoherent NIMBYism masquerading as environmental angst, Joe thinks that the world's pollution problems can be solved simply by moving all the computer companies out of Silicon Valley, where, incidentally, it is always either foggy or raining. But in an anime where a character can continue to function after his brain has been punched out through the back of his head, it's perhaps unsurprising that the production crew could manage a similar feat. ❶ⓃⓋ

DARKER THAN BLACK *

2007. JPN: *Darker than BLACK—Kuro no keiyakusha*. AKA: *DTB; Darker Than Black: The Black Contractor*. TV series, video. DIR: Tensai Okamura. SCR: Shotaro Suga, Shinsuke Onishi, Tensai Okamura. DES: Takahiro Komori, Takashi Aoi, Masahiro Sato, Tomoaki Okada, Eiji Taguchi. ANI: Takahiro Komori. MUS: Yoko Kanno, Yasushi Ishii. PRD: BONES, Aniplex. 25 mins. x 26 eps. (TV1), 25 mins. x 12 eps. (TV2), 24 mins. x 4 eps. (V).
An impenetrable barrier called Hell's Gate simply appears in Tokyo. At the same time, a group of people suddenly acquire immense psychic powers, but appear to lose their conscience. They become known as Contractors and can be hired to deal with paranormal problems. However, their powers have to be paid for, and the payment can be unpredictable. Their clients are mostly those who want to unlock the secrets of the Gate, and agencies spring up to coordinate their work and make a few bucks on the side. Ten years on, a psychic named Hei works with an agency known as the Syndicate. He's part of a team—grumpy old field manager Huang, his blind associate, the beautiful Yin, and Mao, a black cat hosting the spirit of a Contractor who was unlucky enough to lose his body. But theirs isn't the only Gate, and the rivalries between agencies are getting deadlier.

A serious story about superpowers is difficult to handle, as the many incarnations of *The X-Men* and *Superman* prove. Done well, as it is here, it can be both entertaining and thought-provoking, apart from an ending that feels slightly rushed. The score by Yoko Kanno may not quite touch the heights of **COWBOY BEBOP** or **ESCAFLOWNE** but works beautifully with the show. The writers follow the "show, don't tell" principle, harder than you'd think to judge from the amount of turgid exposition in some anime, and Okamura takes us through the action like a news cameraman following a story, leaving early, arriving late, and letting us pick things up as they develop. This means a lot remains unexplained, but the story flows along at a good pace and the characters and events are strong enough to carry through any confusion. The team at BONES do a good (and more unusually, consistent) job on the animation, and the CGI by Studio Easter works well, with action in general and vehicle animation in particular looking strong.

Okamura's spin-off manga with art by Nokiya started publication while the anime was still running, and a further Okamura manga with art by Yuji Iwahara primed audience expectation for the second TV series in 2009. *Darker Than Black: Gemini of the Meteor* (*Darker Than Black: Ryusei no Gemini*) picks up the story two years on. Okamura directs the same senior crew for this and the 2010 video, *Darker Than Black: Kuro no keiyakusha Gaiden* (*DtB: Black Contractor Side Story*), which fills in the plot gap between the two TV serials. The level of quality and consistency across all three series holds up well and makes viewing them all a seamless experience, but the second series is more tightly plotted with a packed final episode leaving some issues still unresolved. Viewers may well regret that there was no more of this polished piece of entertainment. **NV**

DARKSIDE BLUES *
1994. Movie. DIR: Nobuyasu Furukawa. SCR: Mayori Sekijima. DES: Hiroshi Hamazaki. ANI: Hiroshi Hamazaki. MUS: Kazuhiko Sotoyama. PRD: Toho. 83 mins.
The future belongs to one company: the "family" business of the Persona Corporation. Only a few places on Earth hold out against its dominion; one is in Kabuki Town, a ramshackle part of Shinjuku known as the Tokyo Darkside. Tatsuya is a terrorist on the run, aided by a sorcerous stranger (also called Darkside). Tatsuya is a revolutionary, but Darkside is revolution personified, a messianic figure born of oppression.

Replaying AKIRA with supernatural elements, *DB* is a beautifully designed but confused Gothic tale with a slow pace and nonexistent ending, based on the 1985 novel by DEMON CITY SHINJUKU's Hideyuki Kikuchi and filtered through a 1993 manga adaptation by BRIDE OF DEIMOS's Yuho Ashibe. Concerned with the soul rather than the body, it takes many liberties with place and time, such as doors that don't necessarily lead to the same room twice. This is a film loaded with symbolism—flowers shedding petals, people turning into statues, spiders spinning red webs—but like its rebels without a cause, it says a lot but doesn't really mean anything. Its best creation is Darkside himself, even down to his voice in the Japanese edition, which was done by male impersonator Natsuki Akira. Even the foley editing of his footsteps implies the sound of hooves, most noticeable when he's walking up to a seedy hotel. His first appearance, a hell

ride through the dimensions, is a masterly touch, but one that was done better in the opening scenes of SHUTENDOJI.

Despite lush designs and a moody, suspenseful beginning, the animation and color palette get progressively cheaper as the film goes on. The same can be said for the meandering plot, which begins with a compelling mystery but soon finds itself sprinting for the finish, failing to cram the original story into the running time. **NV**

DARLING *
2003. Video. DIR: Susumu Kodo. SCR: Hajime Yamaguchi. DES: Koji Murai. ANI: Koji Murai. MUS: Kanki Matsunaga, Kazuhiro Yamahara, Yasuke Inada. PRD: TAC, Amumo. 25 mins. x 3 eps.
Jun Kitano is a recently married pornographic manga artist who has just been presented with a challenging project—come up with a new manga in a month or the evil publisher will have his wicked way with Sonoko, Jun's lovely editor. Rising to the challenge, he sets about drawing at an alarming rate, assisted by his willing wife Miyuki, who dutifully role-plays a series of scenes designed to provide him with inspiration and also inspires his special power: Hyper Erection Mode. It wasn't just the consumer end of the anime and manga business that got its own shows like GENSHIKEN in the early 21st century. The creators got in on the act too, with tales of artists' troubled lives like this and its homosexually inclined mirror-image SENSITIVE PORNOGRAPH. It makes a nice change for a married couple in anime to be having sex with each other. **LN**

DARTANIUS
1979. JPN: *Mirai Robo Dartanius.* AKA: *Future Robot Dartanius; Daltanias.* TV series. DIR: Katsutoshi Sasaki, Norio Kashima, Iku Suzuki. SCR: Fuyunori Gobu, Masaki Tsuji. DES: Yuki Hijiri, Akihiro Kanayama, Yutaka Izubuchi. ANI: Akihiro Kanayama. MUS: Hiroshi Tsutsui. PRD: Y&K, Toei, Tokyo 12 Channel. 25 mins. x 47 eps.
Ten years after the alien Akrons invade Earth, the last remnants of humanity live in savage gangs in the ruins of the world's cities. Street urchins Kento, Danji, Sanae, Mita, Tanosuke, Jiro, and Manabu find the entrance to a secret underground base where Professor Earl, a scientist from

Planet Helios, has been working on a plan to stop Earth from suffering the same fate as his own world, already conquered by the Akrons. Kento and Danji are made the pilots of Atlas and Gumper, a robot and a spaceship, and in their first battle against the Akrons, they awaken the lost "third component," the robotic lion Beralios. Earl realizes that Kento is the lost son of Harlin, King of Helios, and that with all the pieces in place, the three machines can combine to form the super-robot Dartanius. Though the robot was originally named after the hero of the THREE MUSKETEERS, the GODAIKIN release of the toy in the U.S. used the Daltanias spelling listed above as an alternative.

DASH KAPPEI
1981. TV series. DIR: Masayuki Hayashi, Akehira Ishida, Keiichiro Mochizuki, Hiroko Tokita, Katsuhito Akiyama. SCR: Shigeru Yanagawa, Masaru Yamamoto, Haruya Yamazaki, Takeshi Shudo, Akiyoshi Sakai, Osamu Sekiguchi, Sukehiro Tomita. DES: Noboru Rokuda. ANI: Sadao Miyamoto. MUS: Koba Hayashi. PRD: Tatsunoko, Fuji TV. 25 mins. x 65 eps.
Kappei is a male student who is always hanging around the girls' locker room. Because this anime was shown on TV at six in the evening, his reason for doing so is that he wants to collect white panties. This "harmless" but annoying fetish eventually lands him a place on the school basketball team, which he only accepts because of his interest in the underwear of the coach, Miss Natsu. Though the series soon veered into the standard tropes of SPORTS ANIME like AIM FOR THE ACE, this adaptation of Noboru Rokuda's 1979 manga from *Shonen Sunday* often deviated from the original story, even to the extent of an episode set in space. Other anime adapted from Rokuda's work include F and TWIN. **N**

DASH YONKURO
1989. TV series. DIR: Hiroshi Sasagawa, Hitoshi Nanba. SCR: Takashi Yamada, Hiroko Naka, Kiichi Takayama. DES: Oji Suzuki. ANI: Oji Suzuki. MUS: Keita Miyahara. PRD: Aubec, TV Tokyo. 25 mins. x 25 eps. (TV), 35 mins. (special).
Yonkuro and his friends like racing their cars and outwitting their rivals in Team Horizon. Their vehicles look uncannily

like the plastic model "shiki" kits on sale in Japan at the time.

Though allegedly based on a manga by "Saurus Tokuda" in *Corocoro Comic*, *Dash Yonkuro*'s origins are in the same toy tie-in genre as **Battle Skipper** and the later **Poké-mon**. Among a largely pseudonymous crew, former **Battle of the Planets**–director Sasagawa is prepared to stand up and be counted. A 1990 TV special, *Team Yonkuro vs. Team Horizon*, featured the ultimate race, which was moved to South America for a bit of local color.

DATE A LIVE *

2013. TV series. DIR: Keitaro Motonaga. SCR: Hideki Shirane, Hitoshi Tanaka, Takaaki Suzuki. DES: Satoshi Ishino. ANI: Hideki Furukawa, Motoko Watanabe, Noriko Morishima, Satoshi Ishino. MUS: Go Sakabe. PRD: AIC Plus, AT-X, TV Tokyo, Dwango, Fujimi Shobo, Kadokawa Media House, Columbia, Flying Dog, Klockworx. 24 mins. x 12 eps. (TV1), 24 mins. x 12? eps. (TV2).

The earth-shattering "space quakes" that devastated Central Asia and continue to rock the world for the next 30 years are revealed to be the inadvertent psychic backlashes of pretty little girls from a parallel universe, whose energies are released when they stagger, uncomprehending, through the gateway into our own world. Thankfully for humanity, ordinary Japanese teenager Shido Itsuka discovers an ability to remove the dangerous powers of these "spirits," but only if he can persuade them to fall in love with him.

And so we're back to the same old harem and dating tropes (**Romance and Drama**), in a show that regards women as a sort of natural disaster that can only be contained and controlled through their voluntary acquiescence of 99% of their power to a loving man. Poor little things—won't someone save them with a big kiss? Based on a series of books by Koshi Tachibana and illustrated by Tsunako—compare to **Red Data Girl**.

DAY BREAK ILLUSION *

2013. JPN: *Genei o Kakeru Taiyo*. AKA: *il sole penetra le illusioni*. TV series. DIR: Keizo Kusakawa, Maki Kodaira, Takashi Ando, Osamu Tadokoro. SCR: Michiko Ito. DES: Gomoku Akatsuki, Shinpei Tomooka. ANI: Shingo Tamaki, Shinpei Tomooka. MUS:

Tatsuya Kato. PRD: AIC, Anima, Aniplex, TV Asahi, Bushiroad, Good Smile. 24 mins. x 12 eps.

Tarot-reader Akari Taiyo is enlisted into the ranks of an elite organization dedicated to hunting down and destroying Daemonia monsters. However, she is all too aware that these creatures are using human hosts, some still conscious, that also die along with them, lending a melancholy, troubled angle to the usual monster-of-the-week battles. A magical girl show in the spirit of **Puella Magi Madoka Magica**, this series offers a dark and thoughtful perspective on the *humanity* of foes all-too-often written off as simple threats to be removed.

DAY I BOUGHT A STAR, THE

2006. JPN: *Hoshi o Katta Hi*. AKA: *Day I Bought a Planet, The; Day I Cropped a Star, The*. Movie. DIR: Hayao Miyazaki. SCR: Hayao Miyazaki. DES: Hayao Miyazaki. ANI: Megumi Kagawa. MUS: Norihiro Tsuru, Yuriko Nakamura. PRD: Studio Ghibli. 16 mins.

Artist Naohisa Inoue, creator of **Iblard Time**, wrote the original story on which Miyazaki based this short film for the Ghibli Museum. Set in the world of Iblard, it has a narrative straight from **Jack and the Beanstalk**: a city boy escapes to the country, sets out to sell his vegetables, and swaps them for a magic seed. The twist is that, instead of growing a huge beanstalk, it grows something even bigger: a planet. A lovely parable of how small can be powerful.

DAY THE EARTH SHOOK, THE

1997. JPN: *Chikyu ga Ugoita Hi*. Movie. DIR: Toshio Goto. SCR: Ayako Okina. DES: Takashi Saijo. ANI: Takashi Saijo. MUS: Reijiro Koroku. PRD: Tama Pro. 76 mins.

In 1995, an earthquake strikes the city of Kobe, and Tsuyoshi must swiftly adapt to the new danger brought into his sheltered life. Amid the destruction, he observes Japanese people pulling together and helping each other. Based on a story by Etsuko Kishigawa, this feel-good movie was rushed out to capitalize on the real-life events, and even real-life participants. Tetsuya Okazaki, who plays Tsuyoshi, supposedly experienced the quake himself as a middle-school student. The Kobe earthquake was also the indirect cause of

several other anime—**Bomberman**'s first appearance was in a safety video, and the postquake financial climate transformed the planned live-action **Perfect Blue** into a cheaper anime version. Doubtless it also inspired the same year's **Bakumatsu Spasibo**, which showed the Japanese coping with a historical natural disaster but bringing aid to troubled foreigners. A generation later, anime earthquakes returned in **Tokyo Magnitude 8.0**.

DAZZLE

2008. JPN: *Hatenko Yugi*. AKA: *Unprecedented Game*. TV series. DIR: Nobuhiro Takamoto. SCR: Yasuhiro Imagawa. DES: Norikatsu Nakano, Toshihisa Koyama. ANI: Tokuyuki Matsutake. MUS: N/C. PRD: Studio DEEN. 25 mins. x 10 eps.

In a fantasy realm, 14-year-old Rahzel is thrown out of the house by her father to explore the world and find her future. She meets a young man seeking revenge for his father's murder, and despite their very different personalities they are drawn to each other by the magical abilities they share. They travel from town to town making their living and helping others with magic. Our teen heroine is pursued by guys in their mid to late 20s and a backstory of cloning and magic that says they were literally made for each other, in this story of second chances and repairing past mistakes. Based on the manga by Minari Endo, first published in 2000.

DEAD HEAT

1987. Video. DIR: Toshifumi Kawase, Shinji Takamatsu. SCR: Akinori Endo. DES: Toshimitsu Kobayashi. ANI: Toshimitsu Kobayashi. MUS: Appo Sound Concept. PRD: Sunrise. 36 mins.

Claiming to be "Japan's first 3D anime" (although that honor should really go to a 1980 movie edit of **Nobody's Boy Remi**), this curio using the VHD-3D system features 21st-century youngsters racing "FX" machines—predictable crosses between motorcycles and giant robots. Failed driver Makoto is ready to quit the business until he is approached by Hayami Go, who offers him a hyper-engine to change his fortunes. In other words, it's **Cyberformula GPX** but with clichés that stick out of your screen.

DEAD LEAVES *

2004. Video. DIR: Hiroyuki Imaishi. SCR: Takeichi Honda. DES: Imaitoonz, Hiroyuki Imaishi. ANI: Hiroyuki Imaishi. MUS: Yoshihiro Ike. PRD: Production I.G., Imaitoonz, Manga Entertainment. 52 mins.

In the near future, the only humans left on Earth are clones. Retro, who is incredibly strong and has a TV for a head, and Pandy, who has a pink panda-like birthmark over her right eye, wake up in a field with no memory of how they got there. They steal some clothes, food, and a car, but the local cops object, there's a shootout, and the pair are thrown in prison on the Moon. The penal colony is known as Dead Leaves, and the jailors can abuse and kill inmates at will. Retro and Pandy form a strange relationship with their jailor, Galactica, and meet other inmates, including Dino Drill, who has a gigantic drill where his genitals should be, leading to some messy battles with the prison guards. But Retro and Pandy aren't incarcerated for long, as having sex mysteriously sets them free to lead a bullet-laden rebellion against a wicked warden.

After several years of being told by FANDOM that it was misrepresenting Japanese animation abroad, Manga Entertainment had the last laugh by coproducing this puerile and often incoherent cartoon. It qualifies as anime, but its visual style and general outlook often makes it look more like one of the FALSE FRIENDS—compare to KILL BILL: THE ORIGIN OF O-REN, which was similarly a Japanese production made to meet parameters defined by Western demands. With a frenetic pace that often plays like a series of disconnected shorts along the lines of *Aeon Flux* or BLAME!, *DL* is also senselessly violent and obsessed with bodily functions. Ironically, it became a symbol of the *maturity* of the anime business; in an environment that now supported the works of Studio Ghibli on American release, the company associated with the old sex-and-violence titles was now obliged to make them itself in order to meet its own requirements. Once relocated as a subsidiary of Anchor Bay, Manga Entertainment sensibly revisited past glories and threw itself into the sequel to GHOST IN THE SHELL—a far better way of celebrating its achievements than this odious hour-long fight sequence. **LNV**

DEADMAN WONDERLAND *

2011. TV series. DIR: Koichi Hatsumi. SCR: Yasuyuki Muto. DES: Masaki Yamada, Takayuki Yanase, Michie Watanabe. ANI: Hirokazu Kojima, Keiichiro Matsui, Masaki Hyuga. MUS: NARASAKI. PRD: Manglobe, AMG Entertainment, D.N. Dream Partners, Kadokawa, Klockworx. 25 mins. x 12 eps.

Teenager Ganta Igarashi has been framed and sentenced to death, after being found with his entire school class dead around him. Nobody believes his story or looks for the real culprit. Instead, he's sent to a new privately owned and operated prison, where the prisoners take part in gladiatorial combat to amuse paying customers (compare to STORY OF RIKI). If his performance doesn't attract enough audience money, he'll be killed. But things could get worse, because there's another level of savage depravity below the prison—an exclusive club for the truly sick and seriously rich. To prove his innocence and avenge his friends, to take down their true killer the Red Man, Ganta has to survive it.

This brutally breathtaking anime is, as it says on some of its promotional material, carnage. No explanation except for a few flashbacks, no rationale, minimal attempts at justification, just relentless and unapologetic visceral action. And it's magnificent. Yes, it has its flaws in character and plot, but that isn't what it's about. It does exactly what it promises, and does it with technical excellence and gusto not seen in exploitation anime since VIOLENCE JACK. If you want complete and total abandon, this is it. Watch it with a beer and a curry and you risk losing the curry. Unfortunately, however, this series currently only animates the early part of the manga, and leaves much of the story untold. **LV**

DEARS *

2004. TV series, video. DIR: Iku Suzuki. SCR: Takawo Yoshioka. DES: Shinji Ochi, Yoshihiro Watanabe. ANI: Take Anzai. MUS: Tomoki Hasegawa. PRD: Hisanori Kunisaki, Nobuhiro Osawa, Takayasu Hatano, Bandai Visual, GENCO. 24 mins. x 12 eps. (TV), 24 mins. (v).

The plight of refugees gets a predictably cute anime makeover, when 150 aliens crash-land just off the coast of Japan. But they're all beautiful, intelligent, and compassionate; actually a slave species à la CHOBITS, programmed to serve and please and lovingly termed DearS by the smitten population of Japan. If proof was ever needed that anime lives in its own fantasy realm far removed from real-world Japan, these immigrants are welcomed with open arms, granted citizenship, and even counselors to help them fit in—anyone who has been stopped for being Foreign After Dark in Japan will enjoy the irony. That doesn't stop teenager Takeya Ikuhara from thinking the DearS are putting on an act so that the people of Earth will drop their guard. Imagine, then, his surprise when he somehow acquires a pretty, green-haired amnesiac alien girl for a roommate. The alien elects to stay and, to the mixed annoyance and amusement of his landlord's pretty daughter Nenenko, soon adopts Takeya as her master in a replay of the unwelcome guest genre typified long ago by URUSEI YATSURA. DearS counselor Khi, who knows about the species' secrets, tries to separate the couple like the Almighty in OH MY GODDESS!, but after just a month together Takeya wants her to stay with him. Based on the manga by "Peach Pit," the same collective of former fan artists turned pro whose ROZEN MAIDEN was also animated. *DearS* began life in the pages of the monthly *Dengeki Gao* anthology magazine, but seems to have been intended as a multimedia manga, anime, radio drama, and PS2 game from the outset. The video release included an unbroadcast episode, which fits between the original ninth and tenth television episodes.

DEATH NOTE *

2006. TV, special. DIR: Tetsuro Araki. SCR: Toshiki Inoue, Shoji Yonemura, Yasuko Kobayashi, Tomohiko Ito. DES: Masaru Kitao, Daisuke Niitsuma, Mio Ishiki, Shinji Sugiyama. ANI: Masaru Kitao, Takahiro Kagami. MUS: Hideki Taneuchi, Yoshihisa Hirano. PRD: Madhouse, D.N. Dream Partners, NTV, Shueisha, VAP. 23 mins. x 37 eps. (TV), 130 mins. (special1), 93 mins. (special2).

Light Yagami is a handsome, intelligent high school boy from a good family, an ace student who detests evil. He wants to end crime and create a utopia where justice reigns supreme. But it has to be *his* idea of justice: his world, run by his rules. He finds a notebook with five specific instructions written inside; follow these instructions exactly, says the Death Note, and any person you choose will die. So he tries it, and it works. The Death Note is the lost property of a *shinigami*, or death god, called Ryuk, who sees Light as an antidote to the tedium of life in the world of death and plays along. The pair are equally bored and jaded, and the Death Note gives them interesting diversions: power without responsibility for Light, upbraiding the stupidity and arrogance of mankind for Ryuk. Light's reign of terror commences, at first only affecting criminals, but gradually extending to anyone who threatens his way of thinking. He keeps his true identity secret, creating the persona of Kira—a play on the Japanese pronunciation of "Killer"—and revels in his cat and mouse game with the police.

The manga by writer Tsugumi Oba ran from 2003 to 2006, and sprang from Oba's belief that nobody has the right to pass judgment on another's actions or to play god. He wanted to write a suspense series and came up with the idea of using death gods and highly specific rules. The basic plot borrows the concept of the genius detective (the strange-looking investigator "L") and his shadowy arch-nemesis from Sir Arthur Conan Doyle's classic Sherlock Holmes stories. With the additional impetus of copycat Kiras (compare with **PARANOIA AGENT**), family tensions, and the loss of major characters, the nihilistic shock of the first dozen episodes raises the curtain on a riveting battle of wits and wills between Light/Kira and his greatest opponent L. This is melodrama in the best sense of the term, with an almost Gothic feel of inescapable doom hidden by its modern trappings and understanding of the workings of pop culture. As other characters develop, change, and die all around him, Light remains frozen by his unyielding faith in his own superiority, but his iron self-control begins to crumble and his arrogance blinds him to the fact that the actions of others can still affect him. The series builds to a satisfyingly consistent climax. This is a story about rules: those who live by them and those who die by them.

The 2007 special, *Death Note Relight: Visions of a God (Genshi Suru Kami),* is an edited version of the series, designed to wring a little more money out of fans. *Death Note*

Relight 2: L's Successors (L no Tsugumono), the 2009 special, reedits the later episodes, with Light as an officer in the National Police Agency, taking on the mantle of "the new L" while L's true successor tries to bring him down. Both contain some new footage, with new framing sequences and scenes in the first and substantially more additional material in the second. The same team worked on all three.

In design and animation terms, *Death Note* is conventional, but cleanly and elegantly done. Its style credentials are boosted by the fact that it has its own credited accessory designer, and by the Goth grunginess of the *shinigami*. Madhouse has taken considerable care with both the art and animation, pulling in contributions from a number of studios including Tezuka Pro, alongside less widely known Chinese and Korean houses.

Death Note is one of the most successful franchises to have come out of Japan in recent years. Despite being run in a graveyard slot where nobody was supposedly watching, it migrated, often illegally, into other territories with a viral intensity. Arguably, a large proportion of its fans has fallen for the teenage power-trip of its early episodes without internalizing the caveats and consequences of its ending, and parent-teacher associations in many parts of the world have griped about its function as a propaganda tool for the occult (**RELIGION AND BELIEF**).

By the time the manga run ended, it had already sold 20 million copies in the domestic market. Light novels (**ARGOT AND JARGON**), video games, CDs, merchandise, and three live-action films followed: manga, anime, and movies have been translated and sold worldwide. Less desirable outcomes include the copycat Death Notes found in the possession of disaffected teens across the globe. In 2005 the manga was banned in several parts of China (ironically, since it was not legally available there at the time) after students were found converting their own school notebooks into Death Notes and writing the names of teachers and enemies inside. This may have been as much a reaction to piracy of the manga as to what the Chinese authorities call "superstition," but it shows the impact of the work. Half a dozen school suspensions and expulsions across

the U.S. followed the discovery of Death Notes in students' possession. The most serious case of **LAW AND DISORDER** was an apparent copycat murder in Belgium in 2007. Four people were arrested in 2010 and two later confessed in a case that the Belgian press dubbed "the Manga Murder." To add insult to injury, the franchise was also pastiched in the pornographic anime **DREAM NOTE**.

DEBT SISTERS

2007. JPN: *Shakkin Shimai*. Video. DIR: N/C. SCR: N/C. DES: N/C. ANI: N/C. MUS: N/C. PRD: MS Pictures. 30 mins. x 2 eps.

The Miyamori sisters are in deep trouble. Their father has died and left them nothing but an enormous pile of debt. They can barely even afford lingerie. What can they do to pay back the money? Since this is based on a porn game by Seien, their only option is to sell their bodies. The Japanese cover for episode 2 shows them in housemaid costumes but domestic work doesn't pay well, so it doesn't take much guessing that they won't be polishing furniture. **N**

DEBTS OF DESIRE *

2002. JPN: *Gakuen Chijoku no Zushiki*. AKA: *Campus Scheme of Shame*. Video. DIR: Takayuki Yanase. SCR: Shinji Rannai. DES: Takayuki Yanase. ANI: Takayuki Yanase. MUS: Yoshi. PRD: YOUC, Digital Works (Vanilla Series). 30 mins. x 2 eps.

Privileged richkid Masaki wastes so much time using his father's money to get girls into bed that father Gengoro eventually threatens to disown him. Gengoro tells him that unless he brings him someone he can control without money, he will be disinherited. Meanwhile, in apparent contradiction, Masaki is handed files on four of his father's debtors, whose daughters attend the same school as him. One of them is his childhood friend Mai, who rashly promises that she will do anything necessary to repay her father's debt, unaware that it is millions of yen and that Masaki is prepared to take payment in kind. Sexual coercion and prostitution duly follow in the style of *Maid Service*, another anime in the same **VANILLA SERIES**. **ONV**

DEBUT

1994. JPN: *Tanjo*. AKA: *Birth*. Video. DIR: Tomomi Mochizuki. scr: Go Sakamoto. des: Hiroshi Tanaka. ani: Hiroshi Tanaka. mus: Shinichi Kyoda. prd: Movic. 29 mins. x 2 eps.

Saori, Aki, and Kumi are three schoolgirls who want to become actresses, but they are beset by showbiz pressures and by the lure of handsome boys. In this short-lived series made to cash in on the success of the original computer game (itself a clone of GRADUATION), once the girls take their first steps in their chosen career, they meet a female time-traveler who knows the secrets of their futures.

DEBUTANTE DETECTIVES CORPS *

1995. jpn: *Ojosama Sosa Ami.* aka: *Lady Investigator Network.* Video. dir: Akiyuki Shinbo, Masami Shimoda. scr: Juzo Mutsuki. des: Shinji Ochi. ani: Shinji Ochi. mus: Takeshi Haketa. prd: Toho. 30 mins.

The five richest girls in the world attend Japan's richest, most privileged school, where posing as international crime-fighters is one of their many high-class pursuits. After arriving at their new school, where they outdo each other with their modes of transport, a terrorist organization decides to assassinate them for their hubris and conspicuous consumption—an event that ironically forces the spoilt madams to cooperate with each other for the first time in their lives. With Japanese twins Kimiko and Miyuki Ayanokoji in charge, the rest of the team comprises gun-crazy blonde Russian sharp-shooter Nina Kirov, Chinese martial artist and gambling addict Reika Shu, and Adolf Hitler's illegitimate granddaughter, Yoko.

Put into protective custody for their own good, the girls escape thanks to Miyuki's electronics expertise and Yoko's cunning disguises. Faced with terrorist attacks by plane, rifle, and fists, the girls dispatch their adversaries with weapons (Nina), martial arts (Reika), and psychic powers (Kimiko), only to discover that the entire hazard has been engineered to trick them all into demonstrating what they can accomplish as a team.

Based on an idea by DEVIL HUNTER YO-HKO's Juzo Mutsuki, *Debutante Detectives* was conceived as a vehicle to showcase a group of minor voice actresses collectively known as Virgo. It is thus little more than an excuse to put the girls into the public eye in order to sell spin-off games and albums.

Frivolously throwing away its limited character routines in just half a shallow hour, its original raison d'être is completely destroyed by the removal of the Japanese voices for the English dub, leaving nothing but an orphaned "episode 1" of a series that was never going to happen. Compare to its predecessor GIRL DETECTIVES' CLUB.

DEEP BLUE FLEET

1993. jpn: *Konpeki no Kantai.* Video. dir: Takeyuki Kanda, Hiromichi Matano, Shigenori Kurii. scr: Ryosuke Takahashi. des: Masami Suda, Noriyasu Yamauchi. ani: Masami Suda. mus: Koji Makaino. prd: JC Staff. 45 mins. x 32 eps.

Isoroku Takano, a Japanese pilot shot down over Bougainville Island in 1943, is thrown through a time slip and allowed to relive his life, retaining all the memories of his former existence. Teaming up in 1941 with another time-traveler, Yasaburo Otaka, he seizes power in the Japanese government. With Otaka as prime minister and Takano leading the armed forces, the Japanese demand that Western powers pull out of Asia. When the Americans refuse to comply, the Japanese declare war and bomb Pearl Harbor.

Foiling the evil American plans for the atom bomb, the Japanese push the enemy back to Christmas Island, using the foe's own weapons against them. As the fighting rolls down from the Torres Strait to the Tasman Sea, U.S. President Roosevelt has a heart attack and dies. Scared at the Japanese victories, Hitler declares war on his one-time allies. The Japanese navy blows up a Third Reich atomic facility on Madagascar, and, in a desperate attempt to curb Nazi advances, launches suicide attacks in the Red Sea. By 1946, a stalemate leads to espionage operations in California and Manchuria, and the Nazis launch a U-boat counterattack in the Indian Ocean.

Based on the long series of novels by Yoshio Aramaki, *Deep Blue Fleet* takes a very different approach toward the pacifist posturings more commonly seen in English-language anime. Ironically, this "alternate history" has more in common with genuine WARTIME ANIME, but it coyly extricates itself from the real issues of WWII. Mixing the second chances of EMBLEM TAKE 2 with the historical reenactment of ANIMENTARY, the series dispenses with the Allied enemy

relatively quickly—there is just enough time to self-righteously shoo them out of the Pacific before more acceptable foes enter the fray. From that point on, the story is an excuse for a series of battles utilizing Axis weapons and vehicles that never left the drawing board. Compare to Ted Nomura's U.S. comic *World War II: 1946*, which places similar emphasis on "what-if" technology.

After the initial 19 episodes, the series continued rebranded as *Fleet of the Rising Sun (Kyokujitsu no Kantai),* directed by Hiromichi Matano and backtracking a year to 1945 and the launch of Japan's latest battleship, the *Yamato Takeru,* which immediately trounces Germany's *Bismarck II.* Episode three, "Secret Launch of the Sorai" (1997), features two engineer brothers working on a secret project, who see American planes in the air and launch ahead of schedule to thwart the 1942 Doolittle bombing raid on Tokyo. It is *Deep Blue Fleet* in a nutshell—a famous Japanese defeat turned into a victory. Though some may claim that the series' value lies in its painstaking research, the Doolittle raiders are flying B-30s instead of historically accurate B-25s. Meanwhile, the flagship soon leads a fleet to Europe, where, amid its spats with Hitler, it takes time out to come to the rescue of Britain. As with earlier episodes, the result is an unnerving window on a very different world, one that holds the sick fascination of a traffic accident. The series ends with Japanese commandos taking out Hitler's bunker, and the allied Japan, Britain, and U.S.A. defeating the Nazi threat and presiding over a cowed Soviet Union in 1950. It is ironic, and somewhat galling, to witness such an intricate grasp of counter-factual history from a nation that continues to avoid acknowledging many of the actual facts—see NIGHT RAID 1931. ◐

DEEP VOICE

2002. Video. dir: Mamoru Yakoshi. scr: Toshiya Hashimoto. des: Yoshi Ten. ani: Akihiro Asanuma. mus: N/C. prd: Crossnet, Museum Pictures, Milky. 30 mins. x 3 eps.

After a car crash, Takumi awakes from a coma to discover that he has a psychic ability to hear voices à la DEMON LORD DANTE. Unsure of whether he is seeing the past or a possible future, he experiences hallucinatory "memories" of raping two of the nurses at the hospital, as well as a journalist who is covering his case. Later episodes find Takumi discovering that he is somehow complicit in a clandestine series of tests at the hospital, and before long, he is forced to have sex as part of a new experiment. Based on an erotic computer game that, according to the press release, "overwhelmed the world" in 2001. Perhaps the rest of us were in a coma. **LNV**

DELINQUENT IN DRAG *

1992. JPN: *Oira Sukeban*. AKA: *I'm Ban Suke*. Video. DIR: Yusaku Saotome. SCR: Fumio Saikiji. DES: Satoshi Hirayama. ANI: Nobuhiro Nagayama. MUS: Keiji Kunimoto. PRD: Studio Signal. 45 mins.

Banji Suke's parents want the best for their son, but only if the price is right. When he is expelled from all the local schools, they decide the cheapest option is to dress him up in women's clothes and send him to a girls' school. **SHAMELESS SCHOOL**–creator Go Nagai piles on the transvestite trauma, as Banji must learn how to wear bras and makeup, avoid the locker-room spies, and hide a secret love for a fellow student.

Surprisingly devoid of nudity and sex, this "comedy" began life as a manga in *Shonen Sunday*, home of the similarly gender-bending **RANMA ½**. Featuring the Pantyhose Brigade (girls who fight in their underwear) and an oedipally paranoid father convinced that his son will elope with his wife, it also has evil school staff like those of Nagai's **KEKKO KAMEN**—a principal who wants to steal Banji's jewelry. However, unbelievably cheap animation makes the show look far older than it really is. The best joke in the whole sorry affair is the title, since "Oira Suke Ban" can mean either "I'm Ban Suke" or "I'm a bad girl," as in the feisty females of **SUKEBAN DEKA**.

DELPOWER X

1986. JPN: *Delpower X: Bakuhatsu Miracle Genki*. AKA: *Delpower X: Explosion Miracle Happy*. Video. DIR: Masahito Sato. SCR: Sumiko Tsukamoto, Aki Tomato. DES: Ayumi Chikake, Hidekazu Shigeno, Mutsumi Inomata, Yutaka Izubuchi, Haruhiko Mikimoto, Mamoru Nagano, Masami Yuki, Iruka Tabi. ANI: Ayumi Chikake. MUS: Takahiro Negishi. PRD: Big Bang. 40 mins.

As video took over with the arrival of

MADOX-01 and **ASSEMBLE INSERT**, numerous famous designers lent their names to this giant-robot comedy one-shot in which the feckless robot designer Hosogetzel tries to demonstrate that German ingenuity can conquer the world. However, both he and his bitchy American sidekicks, Suzy and Lola, are defeated by the plucky Japanese schoolgirl Manami who pilots her grandfather's prototype robot, the Delpower X.

DELTORA QUEST *

2007. TV series. DIR: Mitsuru Hongo. SCR: Mitsuru Hongo, Reiko Yoshida, Natsuko Takahashi, Akira Okeya, Kuniaki Kasahara, Masahiro Yokotani. DES: Hiroyuki Nishimura, Junya Ishigaki, Masaru Sato, Hiroshi Kato. ANI: Hiroyuki Nishimura. MUS: Ko Otani. PRD: Oriental Light and Magic, Dentsu, GENCO, Kodansha, TV Aichi. 25 mins. x 65 eps.

Deltora is conquered. The Shadow Lord rules the kingdom and the people are suffering. Sixteen-year-old Leif, the blacksmith's son, and his companions Barda the beggar and Jasmine the wild girl of the forests must seek the seven magical stones that once adorned the Belt of Deltora. If they are restored, the Belt will give the true heir of Deltora the power to save his kingdom. But they were stolen and scattered. Now each is held by an evil man who will not give it up without a struggle.

In 2005 Makoto Niwano made a manga version of Emily Rodda's original *Deltora Quest* series of novels, first published in Australia in 2000. Illustrated by Marc McBride, the book captured the feel of an adventure quest game for those too young to get into traditional role-playing games. Rodda had a number of offers from anime studios, but signed with GENCO and OLM because they were the only studios that promised not to change the story. In this case the promise was kept, with only minor changes. Lief's black hair in the book becomes blond in the anime, and "mouse-like" Filli becomes a furball—still cute, but cheaper to mass-produce as a soft toy. The show is popular with children around the world, with reruns on many networks from the U.S. to Pakistan and Europe to Korea.

DEMON BEAST INVASION *

1990. JPN: *Yoju Kyoshitsu*. AKA: *Demon-Beast Classroom*. Video. DIR: Jun Fukuda, Yoshitaka Fujimoto, Juki Yoma, Kan Fukumoto.

SCR: Joji Maki, Wataru Amano. DES: Mari Mizura, Junichi Watanabe, Rin Shin, Hisashi Ezura, Toshikazu Uzami. ANI: N/C. MUS: Teruo Takahama. PRD: Daiei.45 mins. x 6 eps., 30 mins. x 2 eps. (*Revenge*),30 mins. x 2 eps. (*Descent*), 30 mins. x 2 eps. (*Ecstasy*).

Earth's former inhabitants return to reclaim their homeworld after 100 million years' absence, planning their conquest by sending rapist-agents to breed an invading army with young women. The Interplanetary Mutual Observation Agency sends three agent sisters to stop them, including the beautiful Ash, who is perhaps named for *Hunting Ash*, the 1992 live-action tentacle film from **ANGEL OF DARKNESS**–director Mitsunori Hattori. Meanwhile, Terran schoolgirls are overwhelmed by attacking space-demons, who mix violence with plaintive cries for maternal affection. Ash falls in love with an Earth boy, eventually sacrificing her own life to destroy the beast within him.

Based on a story by **UROTSUKIDOJI**'s Toshio Maeda, *DBI* repeats his insidiously clever storytelling—beneath the horrific sex and violence is a masterful exploitation of adolescent fears. Hero Muneto and sometime girlfriend Kayo pay the price of sex when she gives birth to a monster. As with the subtext of much of the **CREAM LEMON** series, most of the remaining action involves their attempts to turn back the clock to the days before the loss of innocence. The series also cleverly survives multiple endings; the threat is defeated in episode 4, but returns to haunt the young lovers on vacation in Hong Kong. Muneto teams up once more with the IMO Agency, only to discover that its plan is to end the threat forever by killing Kayo. The "final" episode, with the lovers on another vacation, reveals that the Demon Beast's spirit can live on even after its body is killed.

Three two-part spin-offs were released after the original series in 1995. *Revenge of the Demon Beasts* featured the return of Ash's sisters, BB and Dee, with a plan to bring their sister back from the dead to fight a new enemy. *Descent of the Goddess* and *Ecstasy of the Holy Mother* continued the story in Japan, with the last of the IMO, Captain "O," helping Kayo destroy her horrific past. The first two of these spin-offs were released in the U.S. as *The Revenge of the Demon Beasts* (on VHS) and then as *Demon Beast Resurrection* (DVD); the third remains unreleased.

DBI features a dramatic drop in quality of animation and music when compared to Maeda's earlier work and, like the similar **ADVENTURE KID**, attempted to compensate for these shortcomings by using real-life erotic stars as voice actresses. It also inadvertently contributed to anime's reputation abroad as child pornography. The American release from Anime 18 (for which the long-suffering "Moe I. Yada" turned in a thanklessly superior **TRANSLATION**) removed the blurs, dots, and mosaics of the Japanese version, although the original animators had never intended the images to be seen uncensored. The genitals revealed are thus incompletely drawn, devoid of hair or distinguishing marks, and give the false impression that all the sexually active characters are under-age. **LNV**

DEMON CITY SHINJUKU *
1988. JPN: *Makai Toshi Shinjuku*. AKA: *Hell City Shinjuku, Monster City*. Video. DIR: Yoshiaki Kawajiri. SCR: Kaoru Okamura. DES: Yoshiaki Kawajiri. ANI: Naoyuki Onda. MUS: Motoichi Umeda, Osamu Shoji. PRD: Madhouse. 80 mins.
Ten years ago, the evil Levi Ra killed Kenichiro Izayoi and cast him into a fiery pit. Ra is the earthbound emissary of the demon world and is preparing to open the portals for all his devilish allies. Only Kenichiro's son, Kyoya, can stop him, assisted by Sayaka, the daughter of an elder statesman who has just abolished nuclear weapons and solved the Arab/Israeli problem, and Chibi, a midget on roller skates. Kyoya and friends must walk into the demon-infested wasteland at the heart of Tokyo and stop Levi Ra before it is too late.

Based on a novel by **WICKED CITY**'s Hideyuki Kikuchi and directed by Yoshiaki Kawajiri, the passionless, perfunctory *DCS* (known as *Monster City* in the U.K.) is at least partly responsible for the popular mainstream notion that "all anime are the same." Opening with the stark red/blue color palette so beloved of Kawajiri, its lead character is a dead ringer for his **GOKU MIDNIGHT EYE**. Its plot is not dissimilar to the second **UROTSUKIDOJI**, which also features both a demon world trying

to enter our own and a climactic battle at the Shinjuku skyscrapers. One apparent steal, however, is no such thing. An early shot that shows Levi Ra almost split in two then repair himself was two years ahead of a similar image in James Cameron's *Terminator 2*.

Strangely paced, with long spells of silence broken by cheesily awful music, its ending is surprisingly anticlimactic, though perhaps nobody should expect too much from the story of a Ben Kenobi clone telling a Luke Skywalker clone to avenge the "death" of an Anakin Skywalker clone with a magic sword. One gets the impression that the crew were all working on autopilot, a feeling unchanged by the listless English-language dub, which inexplicably gives half the cast Tex-Mex accents while the pale Sayaka is played as a blue-blooded British consumptive. Listen for some classic Manga Entertainment "fifteened" dialogue (added to raise the rating to 15-year-olds and up in the U.K.), including, "I'm gonna tear his head off and shove it up his ass!" **LV**

DEMON FIGHTER KOCHO *
1997. JPN: *Yakusai Kocho*. Video. DIR: Toru Yoshida. SCR: Hiroshi Toda. DES: Kazuhiro Sasaki. ANI: N/C. MUS: Toshihiko Sahashi. PRD: KSS. 35 mins.
Sexy teen astrology student Kocho uses her brain, her body, sister Koran, and boy decoy Kosaku to fight lustful samurai spirits at her school, sorry, university in a one-shot rip-off of **DEVIL HUNTER YOHKO**. In a thoughtful gesture to this anime's low running time, the American distributors include a "Making Of" that is actually longer than the anime, featuring the dub actors at work and play. Based on a two-volume 1995 manga by Nonki Miyasu in which Chinese immigrant Kocho would seek to supplement her meager income by posing nude in magazines. Not to be confused with the far nastier **DEMON WARRIOR KOJI**, released around the same time. **LNV**

DEMON HUNTER
1989. AKA: *Makaryudo Demon Hunter*. Video. DIR: Yukio Okamoto. SCR: Yukio Okamoto. DES: Yuji Moriyama, Junichi Watanabe. ANI: Yuji Moriyama. MUS: Nobuo Ito. PRD: Studio Fantasia, C.Moon. 30 mins.

A pretty demon hunter from the demon world comes to our own dimension in search of an escaped beast. While pursuing it around a Japanese high school, she realizes that her former lover from her own world appears to have been reincarnated as a local boy in ours. Based on a manga in *Lollipop* magazine. **NV**

DEMON KING DAIMAO *
2010. JPN: *Ichiban Ushiro no Daimao*. TV series. DIR: Takashi Watanabe. SCR: Takao Yoshioka, Masanao Akahoshi. DES: Miyabi Ozeki, Toshimitsu Kobayashi, Shinji Kawai. ANI: Miyabi Ozeki, Toshimitsu Kobayashi. MUS: Tatsuya Kato. PRD: Artland, AT-X, GENCO, Good Smile Company, Hobby Japan, Lantis, Marvelous Entertainment, Media Factory. 24 mins. x 24 eps.
In a world where magic is a formal religion, schoolboy Akuto Sai plans to make a career as one of the clergy in the highest order of magicians. But his high school aptitude test indicates that he'll become a demon king. With all his new classmates terrified of him, how can he convince them he's really a good guy? Every word he says and every action he takes only seems to reinforce their paranoid belief that he's the biggest, baddest magician in school. The cute but uptight class rep thinks he's evil, even the geeky little weakling who's latched onto him and designated himself "Akuto's minion" believes he's evil. But at least his childhood friend Kena is in the same class, and the android the government sends to keep an eye on him seems to be on his side.

Shotaro Mizuki's book series, with art by Soichi Ito, commenced publishing in February 2008. That autumn the pair premiered their manga adaptation. The anime varied slightly from the manga, but both extend one of the tropes of the harem genre in anime **ROMANCE AND DRAMA**—that the harem boss is a mild-mannered, inept nice guy—in an interesting direction, by making him a mild-mannered nice guy who actually can slug it out with monsters and doesn't hesitate to use his magic to break limbs when necessary. The story does little that is original, but does it with charm and humor, and although the animation is uneven with some very bad moments in the middle of the series, overall it does a decent job. **NV**

DEMON LORD DANTE *

2002. JPN: *Ma-O Dante*. AKA: *Devil King Dante*. TV series. DIR: Kenichi Maejima. SCR: Seizo Uehara. DES: Toshimitsu Kobayashi. ANI: N/C. MUS: Hiroshi Motokura. PRD: Magic Bus, Dynamic, AT-X. 25 mins. x 13 eps.

Disturbed by nightmares of demons and destruction, Ryo Utsugi hallucinates that a devil in an icy cave is calling out to him each night. He eventually discovers that Dante, the most powerful demon lord ever created, may soon walk the Earth once more, destroying human civilization in the process. All that is required is the sacrifice of a particular human girl. One Professor Veil turns out to be the reincarnation of Beelzebub who believes that the chosen victim is Ryo's virginal sister Saori. Ryo confronts Dante in the Himalayas, where he is tricked into releasing the demon himself. In a last-minute accident, he instead combines with Dante, creating a schizophrenic, unpredictable gestalt that is part superhero and partdemon.

Attacked by the massed forces of the Japanese army, Ryo causes death and destruction throughout Japan before confronting four other Demon Kings that have recently been awakened from the sleep of ages by Russian soldiers in Siberia. Meanwhile, the forces of righteousness have decided that the only way to fight the demons is to create mass panic in order to encourage humanity to make a stand—they achieve this by orchestrating a series of vicious murders across Japan and pinning the blame on the demons. The conflict escalates until a final confrontation that pits Dante and his sometime allies against Satan himself.

Based on a 1971 manga in *Bokura* weekly by Go Nagai, *DLD* was forever eclipsed by the artist's decision not to sell it to a TV company for adaptation, but to instead offer them his similar **DEVILMAN**. *DLD* is undoubtedly a prototype, not just for *Devilman* but for all the apocalyptic tales that followed, particularly Nagai's later **SHUTENDOJI**. However, in only being made into an anime 30 years after its first publication, *DLD* appears to all intents and purposes more like a poorman's **UROTSUKIDOJI** than the groundbreaking work it undoubtedly would have been. **L N V**

DEMON PRINCE ENMA *

2006. JPN: *Kikoshi Enma*. Video. DIR: Mamoru Kanbe. SCR: Takao Yoshioka. DES: Toshiyuki Komaro, Kazuhiro Arai. ANI: Ryo Tanaka. MUS: Kayo Konishi, Yukio Kondo. PRD: Brains Base, Studio A-CAT, Bandai Visual. 40 mins. x 4 eps.

Enma, a fire demon, and his companion Yuki, a snow demon, are the yin-and-yang detectives of Hell. Their assignment: to search the human world for demonic monsters who have escaped from the confines of the netherworld and either send them back or destroy them. As they roam the neon-lit city seeking out the darkest shadows, a cop and a reporter investigate a series of unsolved mysteries, and grow ever closer to the truth about the demon prince and his icy princess.

We've been here before, but the old town looks different now. Go Nagai's manga **DORORON ENMA-KUN** was a popular kids' TV series in 1973, but this version is definitely more grown-up. That doesn't mean it's abandoned Nagai's trademark broad humor and light-hearted lechery, but there's a darker psychological intensity that makes for solid, convincing characters as well as intensifying the shivers. Superb and unobtrusive manipulation of sound and design enhances the horror and makes a solid, entertaining package. The story starts from a principle stated by Shigeru Mizuki, creator of **SPOOKY KITARO** and a great folklorist: monsters that formerly dominated the street at night are being pushed back by the glare of modern electric lighting. As **KAKURENBO: HIDE AND SEEK** reminds us, that doesn't make them less dangerous, and humans still need to be protected by those who understand how to handle evil, those we might consider the enemy even though they're keeping us safe.

There was also another remake for the kiddies in 2011. *Ghastly Enma Burning Up (Dororon Enma-kun Meerameera)* brings the Yokai Patrol from the first series—Enma, Yukiko, and their human friend Kapaeru—plus Enma's talking hat Chapeauji—back to Tokyo in the 1970s. The Brains Base-animated TV series was produced by Nagai's own studio Dynamic Planning, Mainichi Broadcasting, and Starchild Records. It delivers oodles of silly fun in 12 half-hour episodes, delivered by director/ writer Yoshitomo Yonetani with design and animation by Takahiro Kimura. **N V**

DEMON WARRIOR KOJI *

1999. JPN: *Gokuraku Satsujin Choken Kan*. AKA: *Koji: Paradise Assassin Investigator, Sex Crime Detective Koji, Sex Murder Investigation Officer Koji*. Video. DIR: Yasunori Urata. SCR: Takaro Kawaguchi. DES: Ayato Muto. ANI: Ayato Muto, Teruaki Murakami. MUS: Masamichi Amano. PRD: Phoenix Entertainment, Sepia. 41 mins. x 3 eps.

Koji Yamada is a man of many talents—a stuntman by day and a demon-hunter by night, he also has the ability to transform into a demon himself. With the aid of a mismatched band of superpowered assistants, he fights supernatural crimes that normal police can't even begin to touch.

Koji plumbs new depths in Toshio Maeda's futile quest to outdo his own **UROTSUKIDOJI**. Featuring a hokey gang of costumed crime-fighters, seemingly inspired by *Doc Savage*, and the usual cavalcade of demonic assaults, *Koji* is also the least well-animated of Maeda's many works. As with other later Maeda anime such as **DEMON BEAST INVASION**, there are desperate attempts to create interest through gimmickry, including "guest appearances" by the voices of erotic stars, and even uncensored shots of pubic hair. Meanwhile, bored voice actors yawn their way through scenes of depravity enacted by characters whose designs are noticeably uglier than the Maeda norm. With comedy jailbait, death by oral sex, and a rack of childhood family traumas, this replays many of Maeda's earlier themes, but the law of diminishing returns has reached such a low level by this point that these are even likely to annoy his fans. Director Urata even teases his audience, framing one scene as a flashback of his own **NINJA RESURRECTION**, only to reveal that it is from one of the films for which Koji is performing stunts. In other words, even the crew wish they were somewhere else. In a final irony, the distributor's attempt to cover up naked breasts with daubs of blood on the U.S. box art actually made the series look even more violent and unpleasant than it really was. **L N V**

DEMONBANE

2004. JPN: *Kishin Hoko Demonbane*. Video,

TV series. DIR: Shintaro Inokawa, Shoichi Masuo. SCR: Katsuhiko Takayama, Yosuke Kuroda, Kojiro Nakamura. DES: Masaaki Sakurai, Hideki Hashimoto, Dai Ota. ANI: Hideki Hashimoto. MUS: ZIZZ STUDIO. PRD: Group TAC, Kadokawa, Viewworks. 24 mins. (v), 25 mins. x 12 eps. (TV).

Kuro Daijuji is a less-than-successful private eye living in magic-saturated Arkham City. When the female boss of a financial corporation asks him to find a magic book, he at first refuses, but can't resist the lure of big money. The search brings him more than he bargained for—a contract with a living grimoire in cute girl form, unexpected magical powers, and a major role in the battle between his current employer the Hado Financial Group and the secretive Black Lodge. To combat the Lodge's dark machines, the Hado Group has its own mighty battle machine, Demonbane.

Demonbane mixes H.P. Lovecraft's Cthulu mythos with magic and mecha, making the kind of cocktail that sounds really cool but leaves you wishing you'd stuck to something plainer. The mecha and their battles are not especially interesting, the characters are stereotypes, and the plot's thinness is concealed under layers of arcane lore ripped without too much thought about making it work on TV. The well-worn device of using a magical girl—who *looks* ten years old but is *really* a much, much older woman—to excuse a jailbait relationship is always disturbing. The anime was based on a Nitroplus "visual novel" (ARGOT AND JARGON) that began in 2003. It spun off a series of books by Jin Haganeya starting in the same year and a 2004 manga adaptation by Takashi Tanegashima with art by Yuki Tanaka. It was also adapted as a video in 2004, then remade for TV in 2006 when a new version of the game was released.

DEMON-BEAST PHALANX

1989. JPN: *Maju Sensen*. Video. DIR: Shunji Oga. SCR: Sho Aikawa. DES: Hideyuki Motohashi. ANI: Eiji Takaoka, Keiichi Sato, Satoshi Saga. MUS: Hiroya Watanabe. PRD: Magic Bus, Dynamic Planning. 45 mins. x 3 eps. (v), 25 mins. x 13 eps. (TV).

Replaying FRANKENSTEIN for a Japanese audience, 13 scientists seek to tap genetic powers by creating a hybrid of man and beast. Years later, 13 of their children

are embroiled in a battle to undo their handiwork, while Shinichi, the son of one of the scientists, teams up with Christian super-beings to save the world.

Often confused with ADVENTURE KID because of their similar Japanese titles, *DBP* is actually based on a manga by GETTER ROBO–cocreator Ken Ishikawa, whose inspiration was the Book of Revelation. Remade for TV as *Beast Fighter: The Apocalypse* (2003), directed by Kenichi Maejima. **NV**

DEMONIC LIGER

1989. JPN: *Jushin Raigar*. TV series. DIR: Norio Kashima. SCR: Sho Aikawa, Yoshiaki Takahashi, Toshiki Inoue. DES: Miku Uchida. ANI: Miku Uchida. MUS: Hiroshi Tobisawa. PRD: Sunrise, Nagoya TV. 25 mins. x 42 eps.

Bold Earthmen in suits of "bio-armor" hold off an alien invasion in a series created by DEVILMAN's Go Nagai for the GUNDAM–studio Sunrise. Eventually the good robots, Raigar and Dolgar, are heavily damaged but still defeat the evil robot Drago, as if you couldn't guess.

DENNO COIL *

2007. TV series. DIR: Mitsuo Iso. SCR: Toshiki Inoue, Mitsuo Iso. DES: Takeshi Honda, Hiroshi Goroku. ANI: Takeshi Honda, Toshiyuki Inoue, Yoshimi Itazu. MUS: Tsuneyoshi Saito. PRD: Madhouse Studios, Bandai Visual, NHK, Tokuma Shoten. 25 mins. x 26 eps.

In the year 2026, schoolgirl Yuko Okonogi moves with her family to Daikoku, a city with a hybrid function as both a real-world conurbation and a manifestation of the Internet. Residents of Daikoku can visualize data architecture overlaid on *real* architecture with the aid of special goggles, which also allow them to hunt down exploitable bugs in the system (which may be used as currency), manipulate cyberspace for good or ill, and occasionally even disappear off the map.

Denno Coil's near-future scenario is largely indistinguishable from daily life in the year of its production, but for the subsumption of the physical world beneath an expansive overlay of virtual reality. As such, it offers a striking visual analogy of the way in which the Internet has already taken over the world, pointing to the unseen economics of the virtual realm, the gradual gamification of our attitudes, and entire wainscot societies of users linked

by digital communications (compare to SERIAL EXPERIMENTS LAIN).

Famously in the pipeline for almost a decade, *Denno Coil* was released, through no fault of its own, in the year immediately following anime production's historical peak and sudden slump. As a result, foreign attention was slow to arrive. Although it was well received in Japan to the extent of winning a Seiun Award, it was only released to DVD in English in Australia and New Zealand; American fans had to make do with a brief availability on the iOS platform. The art in this show is deceptively simple—more classic Toei Animation than Madhouse—but it's well integrated with what, for its day, was a superb use of computer graphics. This echoes the rest of the show; what at first seems like a simple slice-of-life, coming-of-age tale (EVERYDAY ANIME) develops into something more complex and compelling. The final episodes wrap up the character development without explaining all the mysteries or solving all the problems. In a less-well-written show this could be frustrating, but here it creates a sense of a wider reality, a place that has a life to get on with after you leave.

DENTSU

Founded in 1901, Dentsu and its manifold subsidiaries form the largest advertising concern in Japan. It has long sought a series of cunning strategies in vertical integration, proclaiming that "every marketing dollar has to be spent three times." To this end, it has bought shares in radio, TV, and media companies around the world, all the better to secure preferable deals for its ADVERTISING AND SPONSORSHIP. Dentsu's perennial interest in graphic design and short, eye-catching snippets of film soon brought it into contact with the anime world, causing it to be a prime financer of early commercial animation and puppetry. Today, it retains strong interests within Japan in the TBS television network and also functioned directly as a producer of anime including BLEACH, LAW OF UEKI, and ANIMAL ALLEY. Dentsu also bought Pioneer's entertainment division, which was renamed Geneon Entertainment, making it the owner of numerous anime including HAIBANE RENMEI, CATNAPPED, and SERIAL EXPERIMENTS LAIN. In 2009, however, Dentsu backed away from direct involvement, selling most of its shares in Geneon to NBC Universal. In 2012, the corporation announced it was creating the "first think-tank to study otaku"—an odd claim considering that its rival Nomura had published its own think-tank's results seven years earlier as a book, *Research in the Otaku Marketplace* (2005). Regardless, of every dollar spent on anime, at least some of it is very likely to end up in Dentsu's coffers, somewhere in the distribution, exhibition, or licensing stages, or possibly all of them.

DEPRAVITY *

2002. JPN: *Daraku Jokyoshi Hakai.* AKA: *Destruction of a Female Teacher.* Video. DIR: Hideki Arai. SCR: Koichi Murakami. DES: Hideki Arai. ANI: N/C. MUS: N/C. PRD: Five Ways. 30 mins. x 3 eps.

A group of schoolboys get off on kidnapping teachers, breaking into schools at night, and assaulting their bound and gagged victims until they cry out with ecstasy. They pick the wrong teacher with Kiriko, a tough martial arts expert. Two of them are soon lying hurt in the infirmary, and Kiriko starts to threaten the group with exposure to the police. But her language excites them and so they tell her that if she can stand ten minutes of them playing with her genitals without getting wet, they'll let her go. Since she has the upper hand here, only in a porn anime would she agree, but this is a porn anime so all rational thought is suspended. Based on a manga of the same name by artist Fusen Club. Compare with **T&A TEACHER,** which covers much of the same ground (the sexual degradation of a tough female teacher) in a single episode, and **SCHOOL OF BONDAGE,** which features a similar bet with much the same results. **LNV**

DESCENDANTS OF DARKNESS *

2000. JPN: *Yami no Matsuei.* TV series. DIR: Satoshi Otsuki, Hideki Okamoto. SCR: Masaharu Amiya. DES: Yumi Nakayama. ANI: Yumi Nakayama, Kazuo Yamazaki. MUS: Tsuneyoshi Saito. PRD: JC Staff, WOWOW. 25 mins. x 13 eps.

Tsuzuki Asato and Kurosaki Hisoka are members of the *shinigami* (elite undead), who can use the Book of the Dead to reanimate the deceased. Based on the manga by Yoko Matsushita in *Hana to Yume* magazine.

DESERT ISLAND STORY X, THE *

1998. JPN: *Mujin-to Monogatari X, Mujin-to Monogatari XX.* AKA: *Story of X the Uninhabited Island.* Video. DIR: Hiroshi Ogawa. SCR: Mirin Takefuji. DES: Hiroto Kato. ANI: Shigenori Kurii. MUS: N/C. PRD: Pink Pineapple, KSS. 30 mins. x 4 eps. (v1), 30 mins. X 4 eps. (v2).

Seven beautiful Japanese girls are shipwrecked on a deserted island, where they are overcome with madness and desire, much to the benefit of the men who have arranged for their castaway status. Released in the U.S. as *Desert Island Story X* and *Desert Island Story XX.* **NV**

DESERT PUNK *

2005. JPN: *Sunabozu.* TV series. DIR: Takuya Inagaki. SCR: Hiroshi Yamaguchi. DES: Takahiro Yoshimatsu. ANI: Gonzo. MUS: Kohei Tanaka. PRD: Gonzo, arp Japan, C&G Ent., CBC, Pony Canyon et al. 24 mins. x 24 eps.

Civilization was destroyed hundreds of years ago. Japan's once fertile Kanto plain is a desert. Young Kanta Mizuno is drawn into a conflict between the authoritarian government and a group of rebels trying to take over. He becomes the legendary Desert Punk, Sunabozu, a hired gun for whom no job is too dirty and nothing gets between him and his pay. But he has a rival—the Desert Vixen.

Based on Masatoshi Usune's manga in *Comic Beam* monthly and conceived more as a comedy in the style of **TRIGUN** than anything serious in the style of **FIST OF THE NORTH STAR.** Compare to **CAPTAIN KUPPA.**

DESERT ROSE

1993. JPN: *Suna no Bara.* AKA: *Rose of the Sands.* Video. DIR: Yasunaga Aoki. SCR: Kaoru Shintani. DES: Minoru Yamazawa. ANI: Minoru Yamazawa. MUS: Jun Watanabe. PRD: JC Staff. 45 mins.

When Mariko Rosebank's husband and child are killed in a terrorist bombing, she is left with nothing but a rose-shaped scar and a thirst for revenge. In this one-shot adaptation of the 1989 *Young Animal* manga from **AREA 88's** Kaoru Shintani, Mariko joins the tactical assault squad C.A.T. The story was revived for a "manga video" visual comic in 2000. **NV**

DESPERATE CARNAL HOUSEWIVES *

2005. JPN: *Hitozuma Ryojoku Sankanbi.* AKA: *Housewife Rape Visitors' Day.* Video. DIR:

Hotaru Aoi. SCR: Hotaru Aoi, Megumi Kagami. DES: Hirotaka. ANI: Hirotaka. MUS: Shinobu. PRD: Dream Entertainment, GP Museum Soft, Milky. 29 mins. x 2 eps.

Three pretty Japanese housewives arrive at their children's school, Kawamura Academy, believing themselves to have been called to apologize for some bad behavior by their offspring. However, when they arrive the school is closed, and they are led to a deserted building by two men, who proceed to teach them "obedience" lessons, in which they are forced to reenact their children's school-day activities while wearing (or, soon, *not* wearing) sexy versions of the school uniforms. A female teacher is present, and assures them that everything is above board, although she only does so because she has been raped into submission earlier on. Three more hapless mothers are duly abused in the next episode. Based on an original work by Yasuhide Kunitatsu, and given a title in the American market designed to imply nonexistent connections with the TV series *Desperate Housewives* (2004). **LNV**

DESTINED FOR LOVE *

2006. JPN: *Futari no Aniyome.* AKA: *The Couple's Sister-in-Law.* Video. DIR: Sosuke Kokubunji. SCR: N/C. DES: Taka Hiro. ANI: Haruo Fuyuki, ERIC-PARK. MUS: N/C. PRD: Milky, MS Pictures. 30 mins. x 2 eps.

Akane met Shinya when they were kids. He was playing a console game, they got talking, they agreed to be together when they were older. Unfortunately Shinya had pinched his brother Shogo's console, with Shogo's name written on it, so Akane thought he was Shogo and her family made arrangements for the marriage accordingly. Now they are teenagers and Akane starts attending Shinya's high school. To make sure that, regardless of the marriage arrangements, Akane will be his alone, Shinya persuades his sister-in-law Sayumi to teach him how to please a woman, because obviously if you're an ace at sex nothing else matters. Along the way his lovestruck classmate Shizuku also gets involved. Based on a porn game by Seien Advance, the sex is nonviolent and consensual, and the design and art are reasonably attractive. **N**

DETATOKO PRINCESS *

1997. AKA: *Chancer Princess*. Video. DIR: Aki-yuki Shinbo. SCR: Mayori Sekijima, Masashi Kubota. DES: Hiroko Sakurai. ANI: Hiroko Sakurai. MUS: Shinken Kenra. PRD: JC Staff. 30 mins. x 3 eps.

Princess Lapis is a spunky blonde noble in the magical realm of Sorcererland, eternally competing with her rival Topaz, the Witch of the North. Lapis has just one talent, although it is a devastating one— the ability to cancel out magic, making her incredibly dangerous in a world that relies on sorcery for building, energy, and the smooth running of society. Her exasperated mother Sapphire decides to send her away on a camping trip for a couple of days, but unwittingly aims her magical mirror of transportation at the wrong location, teleporting Lapis to the far side of the world. Lapis is then obligated to travel back home, with only a random assortment of companions to help her, including the comedically invulner-able Kohaku, the diminutive plant-pixie Nandora, and her irritable old tutor. The journey is complicated by Lapis's addiction to pudding, of which she needs a large helping on a daily basis.

Former **TENCHI MUYO!** manga artist Hi-toshi Okuda created this Jell-O mold suc-cessor seemingly in an attempt to secure his own franchise after drawing someone else's for so long. It unravels in the tradi-tion of other comic fantasies like **DRAGON HALF** and **SLAYERS**, setting up a derivative quest narrative and hoping to occlude its shortcomings behind a smokescreen of knowing irony. The preceding radio drama featured a gimmick in which Lapis would sing her spells, although that is not repeated here.

DETECTIVE ACADEMY Q

2003. JPN: *Tantei Gakuen Q*. TV series. DIR: Noriyuki Abe, Akihiro Enomoto, Akira Shimizu, Junya Koshiba, Katsuyoshi Yatabe, Kenichi Maejima. SCR: Makoto Hayashi, At-sushi Yamatoya, Daisuke Watanabe, Kyoko Iwamura, Masahiro Okubo, Natsuko Taka-hashi, Yuko Fukuda. DES: Masaya Onishi. ANI: N/C. MUS: Daisuke Ikeda. PRD: Studio Pierrot, TBS. 25 mins. x 45 eps.

Ninth grader Kyu wants to be the world's best detective but it looks as if he may end up on the wrong side of the law when he accidentally runs into a middle-aged man who accuses him of stealing ¥10,000 in the collision. Megumi "Meg" Minami in-tervenes, using her photographic memory and deductive skills to work out from the man's testimony exactly where the missing note fell. Together with Ryu Amakusa, a strange student from Tozai University, Kin-taro Toyama, descendant of the renowned Toyama no Kinsan (see **SAMURAI GOLD**), and genius computer programmer Kazuya Narusawa, the pair take the entrance exam for famous detective Morihiko Dan's Dan Detective School. They do so well that they are placed in a special class known as Q (for "Qualified"), taught by the founder himself. There begins a series of criminal puzzles that Q class has to solve in competition with rivals in A class. Some of the adventures don't appear in the manga from *Shonen Magazine* weekly, which was written by Seimaru Amagi and drawn by Fumiya Sato, both of whom worked on the **YOUNG KINDAICHI FILES** manga. The "Q" tag has indicated strange mysteries ever since the live-action series *Ultra Q* (*DE) and **TWILIGHT Q**; as it's also our hero's name, and the Japanese number for his school grade, Kyu is obviously destined for his chosen field.

DETONATOR ORGUN *

1991. Video. DIR: Masami Obari. SCR: Hideki Kakinuma. DES: Michitaka Kikuchi. ANI: Masa-nori Nishii. MUS: Susumu Hirasawa. PRD: AIC, Darts. 56 mins., 45 mins., 53 mins.

Tomoru skips school to hang out at the aviation museum, where he harbors secret dreams of becoming a pilot. He gets what he wants when Earth is attacked by invaders, and he signs up with the Earth Defense Force.

Despite such a hackneyed opening, *Detonator Orgun* plays some neat tricks with the traditions of robot shows. Tomoru lives 200 years in our future but has the problems and worries of any teenager. Although he lives in a sci-fi fan's dream world, he's bored at the idea of a career in lunar finance and thinks the floating equatorial city he calls home is too uncool for words. An early scene in which To-moru argues with a friend is a stunningly accurate prediction of that common modern malaise: a roommate who "help-fully" finishes all your computer games

for you while you're out. Look out, too, for Kakinuma's tongue-in-cheek adverts for the Defense Corps, shown here long before *Babylon 5* or *Starship Troopers* got the hang of postmodern irony. Finally, there's a sweet epilogue in which we discover that Tomoru has gotten exactly what he wished for, the chance to fly with the other pilots and someday inspire another wide-eyed museum visitor.

Scenarist Kakinuma draws the full benefit of writing directly for three hour-long episodes; without a TV series, comic, or console game to muddy the creative waters, *Detonator Orgun* has none of the compression or hurried storytelling of lesser shows. The robot battles and dream sequences are artfully done, though direc-tor Obari would use similar material to even better effect in his later **VIRUS**. Future **YOU'RE UNDER ARREST!**-director Kazuhiro Furuhashi also worked on *DO* as a humble storyboarder.

Unfortunately, the U.K. dub is another mediocre effort from Manga Entertain-ment's mercifully short-lived cost-cutting experiments in a Welsh studio (the U.S. fared better from Central Park Media), and elements that are deliberately evocative (such as Hirasawa's sub-Vangelis music) will strike many as just plain unimaginative. It's also a little jarring to see that the young Tomoru's idols are actu-ally pilots in the Luftwaffe—one of those moments when anime and Japan suddenly seem incredibly alien (**DEEP BLUE FLEET**). Released in the U.K. by Manga Entertain-ment as a single "feature-length" edition stitching all three episodes together. That's a long feature.

DETROIT METAL CITY *

2008. TV series. DIR: Hiroshi Nagahama. SCR: N/C. DES: Shichiro Kobayashi. ANI: Shuichi Shimamura. MUS: N/C. PRD: Studio 4°C, Toho, Beyond C, Sony Music Entertainment. 14 mins. x 12 eps.

Detroit Metal City is the hottest new death metal band in Japan (**MUSIC IN ANIME**). Their live shows are crazy and their lyrics are full of hate, violence, and rage. Lead singer/guitarist Krauser II is a penis-wav-ing, teeth-baring animal, drummer Camus is a one-man cyclone, and bassist Alexan-der Jaggi is a guitar demon. The fans can't get enough of them. If they only knew that under the make-up of these dark gods of the arena lurk three mild-mannered guys who are only in it for the money. Jaggi is wannabe glam-rocker Wada, Camus is anime fan Nishida, and Krauser is failed popster Soichi Negishi, who not only hates his job but has a crush on a girl who hates DMC almost as much as he does. This nasty, funny show may only have one gag, but it riffs it superbly: its timing perfect, its style in harmony with the deliberately ugly depiction of the mayhem of metal (compare to HUMANE SOCIETY and BLACK HEAVEN). Lurking under it all is the suggestion that Krauser and Negishi are not so far apart as Negishi thinks, giving an intelligent underpinning to this riot of vitriol. Based on Kiminori Wakasugi's 2005 manga, the show also has a one-episode, 13-minute prologue, *Detroit Metal City: Birth of the Metal Devil*. ●

DEVADASY *
2001. Video. JPN: *Sosei Seiki Devadasy.* AKA: *De:vadasy; World Creation Holy Record Devadasy.* DIR: Nobuhiro Kondo. SCR: Sho Tokimura. DES: As'maria (mecha). ANI: Shinji Takeuchi. MUS: N/C. PRD: AIC. 23 mins. x 3 eps.
In 2012, alien "Nanomachines" attack an overpopulated Earth ravaged by global warming. The U.N. is helpless against the onslaught unless the SPIRITS organization's robot Devadasy, discovered in Tibet by a team of researchers and powered by the "sexual energy" of its selected pairs of male pilots and female "batteries," can stand firm. Unlike EVANGELION's Shinji Ikari, 15-year-old Kei Anou needs little convincing by pretty researcher Misako Takashina to ditch schoolwork and join SPIRITS as a pilot. He develops a partnership with the mysterious Amala, though he is dogged by childhood friend Naoki, who also carries a torch for him. Featuring giant robots, a love triangle, and a lone boy in a dormitory of adoring girls, AIC's press release for *Devadasy* sheepishly promised "the same as usual" but with more blatant excuses for titillation. However, the result is both short in running time and rather tame in comparison to such series as GRAVION and AIKA. The concept of sexually powered heroics was copied and expanded upon in the later, pornographic BEAT ANGEL ESCALAYER and JIBURIRU: THE

DEVIL ANGEL. A *Devadasy* game was released simultaneously with the anime version.

DEVIL AND THE PRINCESS
1981. JPN: *Akuma to Himegimi.* Movie. DIR: Ryosuke Takahashi. SCR: Shunichi Yukimuro. DES: Yasuhiro Yamaguchi. ANI: Yasuhiro Yamaguchi. MUS: Haruo Chikada. PRD: Toei. 32 mins.
The 18-year-old princess of Tomorrow Castle has a beauty famed far and wide but a less-attractive penchant for daytime drinking. Despite this, she has plenty of suitors, including a devil wearing a cunning disguise. One day, the princess meets Snow White at her teahouse in the forest, and while the girls get acquainted, the devil kidnaps them both. Shown in a double bill with DOOR INTO SUMMER, this adaptation of a weird "beauty and the beast" fairy tale by *Banana Fish*'s Akimi Yoshida was also the directorial debut for VOTOMS-director Takahashi.

DEVIL DAD
2009. JPN: *Oni Chichi—Mana Musume Kyosei Hatsujo.* Video. DIR: Futoshi Nobutomeyo. SCR: PON. DES: Hikaru Kinohara, Do Ichimotsu. ANI: N/C. MUS: N/C. PRD: PoRO. 29 mins. x 2 eps. (v1), 30 mins. x 2 eps. (v2, OC2), 30 mins. x (v3, Re-birth), 30 mins. x 2 eps. (v4, Re-born), 30 mins. x 2 eps. (v5, OC2: Revenge), 30 mins. x 2 eps. (v6, Rebuild).
Marina and Airi's mother has remarried a few years after her divorce. Marina accepts their young stepfather, a chemist, but Airi detests him. Maybe she senses that he's a pervert who sniffs their underwear and is busy concocting a spray to turn them into his sex slaves. Based on a porn game by Blue Gale, this was followed in 2010 by *Oni Chichi 2*, in which a father who has been widowed for a week decides that the best way to discipline his four motherless daughters is to rape them. *Oni Chichi Re-birth* appeared in 2011 and goes back to the first story, where Airi is still having sex with her father but sometimes feels he might be making her into a sex object. However, this moment of awareness is soon lost when she is assaulted in a movie theater by her school principal, who is also having sex with her sister. A follow-up later in the same year, *Oni Chichi Re-born*, sees the two girls and Papa planning a trip to

a hot springs resort, but Marina pulls out at the last minute leaving Papa and Airi to go it alone. PoRO's production values are high for the porn industry and the designs and artwork are attractive, which makes the content all the more depressing. Even in a fictional context, using small girls with big breasts as sex objects poses as many questions about the buyer of such materials as about the seller. ❍

DEVIL HUNTER YOHKO *
1991. JPN: *Mamono Hunter Yoko.* AKA: *Devil Hunter Yoko.* Video. DIR: Katsuhisa Yamada, Hisashi Abe, Akiyuki Shinbo. SCR: Sukehiro Tomita, Tatsuhiko Urahata. DES: Takeshi Miyao. ANI: Tetsuro Aoki. MUS: Hiroya Watanabe. PRD: Madhouse, NCS, Toho. 45 mins. x 1 eps., 30 mins. x 3 eps., 45 mins. x 2 eps.
Yohko Mano is the latest in a long line of devil hunters. Torn between her grandmother's insistence that she carry on the tradition (for which she must remain a virgin) and her mother's urging to get knocked up as soon as possible, she is beset by demons who use any means possible to dispel the threat she presents. After a promising opener in which a local niceguy is possessed and turned into a bad boy in an attempt to seduce Yohko, later episodes fast decline in quality. She acquires a manager, Chigako, and an apprentice, Azusa (presaging a similar relationship in the later CARDCAPTORS), calms angry spirits at a construction site, appears in her own music video (the pointless *Yohko 4-ever*, which is sensibly bundled with other episodes in the U.S. release), then dies and rises from the dead. The sixth episode, confusingly called *Yohko2* in Japan, has Yohko defending the family honor from her look-alike cousin, Ayako. An inferior TRANSLATION of the first three episodes was released in the U.K. in 1995 as *Devil Hunter Yoko* [sic]. Producer Juzo Mutsuki would create a similar clash of traditional and contemporary ghostbusting in PHANTOM QUEST CORP. ❍❖

DEVIL IS A PART-TIMER, THE *
2013. JPN: *Hataraku Mao-sama.* TV series. DIR: Naoto Hosoda. SCR: Masahiro Yokotani, Kento Shimoyama, Toko Machida. DES: Atsushi Ikariya. ANI: Atsushi Ikariya. MUS: Ryosuke Nakanishi. PRD: White Fox, Bushiroad, GENCO, HM Project, Pony Canyon, Show-

gate, Lantis, Sotsu. 24 mins. x 13 eps. Satan invades the magical realm of Ente Isla, only for his demonic forces to be routed by the heroine Emilia. Escaping at the last minute through a dimensional portal, he seeks refuge on Earth, and finds himself having to get a job at "MgRon-alds" in order to pay the bills. This is not as difficult as it sounds. Mistaken at first for a foreign cosplayer, Satan turns out to be born for the service industry, deter-mined to put all his devilish powers to use maximizing fast-food output and returns. However, even as he finds new meaning in his life asking people if they want fries with that, his old life comes back to haunt him.

Suspiciously similar to the previous year's **AESTHETICA OF A ROGUE HERO** in its central premise, this **COMEDY** eschews the obvious fish-out-of-water premise in favor of one that suggests the Lord of the Flies might find his true purpose and fulfillment in a McJob. Obvious appeal to Japan's slacker generation lies in the juxtaposition of mundane employment with minds constantly harping on whether they will be able to defeat the lord of the balrogs later in the evening—for gamers, a hobby, but for the leading man in this show, a threat to what amounts to his wit-ness protection program.

DEVIL MAY CRY *

2007. AKA: *Devil May Cry: The Animated Se-ries.* TV series. DIR: Shin Itagaki. SCR: Toshiki Inoue, Shotaro Suga, Bingo Morihashi, Ichiro Sakaki. DES: Hisashi Abe, Katsushi Aoki. ANI: Hisashi Abe. MUS: rungran. PRD: Madhouse, CAPCOM, Media Factory, Toshiba Entertain-ment, WOWOW. 25 mins. x 12 eps. Dante is the half-human son of the demon Sparda, and has a brother named Vergil. He is owner and chief operative of *Devil May Cry*, a demon-fighting agency that specializes in sending his troublesome kindred back to hell. He names his weap-ons: his guns are Ebony and Ivory and his sword, which he carries in a guitar case to avoid causing panic on the streets, is Rebellion. He's constantly in debt, partly because his working methods tend to destroy large portions of the surrounding infrastructure and land him with heavy bills (shades of **DIRTY PAIR**), partly because of his gambling addiction, and partly because is lazy. But when his friend Patty

is kidnapped by a demon, he will tear heaven and hell apart to save her.

Despite an impressive staff roster and strong cooperation from the people behind the *Devil May Cry* game, this is a poorly paced and unsubtle script with ham-fisted direction and editing. The later episodes rely heavily on still frames and static pans. **NV**

DEVILMAN *

1972. TV series, video, movie. DIR: Tomoharu Katsumata, Nobutaka Nishizawa. SCR: Masaki Tsuji, Tadaaki Yamazaki, Susumu Takaku. DES: Go Nagai. ANI: Kazuo Komat-subara, Takeshi Shirato, Kazuo Mori, Shingo Araki, Makoto Kunihara, Masamune Ochiai. MUS: Go Misawa. PRD: Dynamic Planning, Oh Pro, NET. 25 mins. x 38 eps. (TV), 43 mins. (m), 50 mins. x 2 eps. (v1), 25 mins. x 26 eps. (*Devil Lady*), 50 mins. (*Amon*). Devilman and two other demons are sent to Earth to possess humans and cause chaos. Finding two Japanese families nearby when they awake from their long slumber in the Himalayas, Devilman chooses to possess Akira Fudo (his first choice, Akira's father, having died from fright), and the bedeviled boy is adopted by the kindly Makimura family. Falling in love with his stepsister Miki, Akira forgets his original mission. His former demon overlord, Zenon, sends a succession of creatures to kill him, and Akira must call on his ill-gotten powers.

When a Japanese TV network wanted to adapt Go Nagai's **DEMON LORD DANTE** for TV in 1972, the artist instead offered them his new *Devilman* project, already running in *Shonen Magazine*. An uneasy combina-tion of superhero serial and macabre horror, it featured a schoolboy forced to become an agent of good by using the powers of evil. Following his TV series, Devilman would appear in Tomoharu Katsumata's theatrical short **MAZINGER Z** *vs. Devilman* (1973), in which Dr. Hell tries to recruit him to defeat the robot warrior of the title.

In 1987, *Devilman* was revived for a two-part video adventure directed by Tsutomu Iida, which altered much of the designs and origins while keeping a retro 1970s look. In the video Akira is a shy boy who lives with his simpering childhood friend Maki while his parents are away on a busi-

ness trip. His tough friend, Ryo (the her-maphroditic son of Satan) tells him of the existence of demons, and that Earth was once occupied by this evil race. The only way to defeat a demon is to fuse with one, and Ryo convinces Akira to allow this to happen. Ryo slaughters human beings at a nightclub to summon a demon, lucking into Amon, the Lord of Darkness. Because Akira is pure of heart, he is able to control the demon within him, turning his evil powers to good use. The second episode (as in the original TV series) features a battle with Amon's former lover, Sirene, though no further episodes were made. *Devilman*'s best moments are the flashback scenes of a prehistoric, demon-infested dreamtime that owed nothing to East *or* West, but it was the messy confluence of Japanese and European mythology that brought *Devilman* down (not helped by the U.K. dubbers Manga Entertainment's inability to get some of the classical refer-ences right, though they did find the time to write new lines like, "I'm gonna rip off your head and shit down your neck!"). The same director would make the three-part *Chibi Character Go Nagai World* (1990) featuring squashed-down versions of several Nagai characters fighting at Arma-geddon. Akira Fudo also put in a cameo appearance in Nagai's later **CUTEY HONEY**.

Nagai returned to the franchise in 1997 with *Devilman Lady*, retelling the story for the more adult *Comic Morning* magazine by altering the sex of his protagonist and introducing evolutionary angles. **VAMPIRE PRINCESS MIYU**–director Toshihiro Hirano and **ARMITAGE III**–writer Chiaki Konaka adapted it into a 26-episode TV series in 1998. Though characters from the earlier versions make cameo appearances, the remake centers on Jun Fudo, a shy fashion model (a schoolteacher in the manga) who begins to develop mystic powers. As part of Mother Nature's answer to overpopulation, a "Devil Beast Syndrome" is afflicting the world's poor, transforming them into rapacious cannibal demons. Jun, however, has been genetically engi-neered by her scientist father to retain her former memories after infection and uses her power to fight off further incursions. The series was released in America under the less confusing title, *Devil Lady*.

Devilman was revived again for *Amon:*

The Apocalypse of Devilman (2000, not to be confused with the similar-sounding AMON SAGA), a 50-minute video released to cash in on the millennium, supervised by FIST OF THE NORTH STAR's Toyoo Ashida and directed by Kenichi Takeshita. Featuring creatures designed by Yasushi Nirasawa, this chapter tied up many loose ends from the earlier versions, spooling forward in the original story to the final Armageddon. Akira now leads the demon-hunting Devilman Army, while a traumatized Miki wanders through a Tokyo in the grip of apocalyptic violence and rapine. Exploiting Akira's somewhat schizophrenic position as a force of good possessed by the ultimate evil, *Amon* is a vicious, sadistic anime in the spirit of UROTSUKIDOJI, and even features a one-on-one fight between Devilman and Satan.

The epilogue to all the *Devilman* stories was written in 1973 (only a year after the original manga) in Nagai's VIOLENCE JACK, which begins with a remorseful Satan's decision to remake the world, to reincarnate as a cripple, and to create the Slum King to punish himself, though this relationship is not apparent in the 1986 anime version. In 2000, an issue of the *Demon Lord Dante* manga that inspired *Devilman* was released as a "manga video." **LNV**

DEZAKI, OSAMU
1943–2011. Born in Tokyo, he found work with Toshiba after graduating from high school, subsequently leaving that company to join Mushi Production in 1963 as a key animator on ASTRO BOY. He founded the company Art Fresh in 1964 with his elder brother Satoshi and Gisaburo Sugii before going freelance in 1967. Subsequently, he became a key figure at Madhouse. His works embrace many genres, including the sport of AIM FOR THE ACE, the children's drama of NOBODY'S BOY REMI, and the medical thriller BLACK JACK. A distinctive feature of many Dezaki anime is the sudden use of what he called "Postcard Memories" and what other animators called "Harmonies." These are freeze-frames, interpolated as single illustrations—this has often been regarded as a budget-saving device but is a deliberate stylistic decision by a director who wants the audience to focus on single key moments. As the director of GOLGO 13, Dezaki was also among the

first in the anime business to experiment with digital animation, although he often derided it as mechanical and soulless and much preferred to experiment with the organic properties of film. Some of his most notable innovations included treating anime cels with paraffin in order to create a spotlight effect and shooting one sequence through a whiskey shotglass in order to create a shimmer like a heat-haze (later animators would use a dedicated panel of textured glass called *nami*-glass or "wave"-glass).

DEZAKI, SATOSHI
1940–. Sometimes miscredited, even in official studio documents, as Tetsu Dezaki—the authors cannot help but wonder if this alternate reading for his name *kanji* is sometimes a deliberate nom-de-plume. Born in Tokyo, he was a writer and storyboarder on anime including ATTACK NO. ONE and STAR OF THE GIANTS. A cofounder of the studio Art Fresh in 1964 with his younger brother Osamu and Gisaburo Sugii, he later moved into directing, with works including GREY: DIGITAL TARGET. He also directed an animated opening sequence to Gerry Anderson's puppet show *Terrahawks* (see THUNDERBIRDS 2086), which was only used on the Japanese broadcast.

DIABOLUS
2009. JPN: *Diabolus: Kikoku*. AKA: *Diabolus: Wailings of a Restless Ghost*. Video. DIR: Do Ichimotsu. SCR: Taifu Sekimachi, PON. DES: Yoki Amano. ANI: N/C. MUS: N/C. PRD: PoRO. 30 mins. x 2 eps.
A spirit haunts the high school in the form of a hot young guy, attacking female students. Two girls decide to investigate. Learning that the only way to free him from Earth is to let him fulfill his desires, they decide to have sex with him so he can rest in peace and they can get on with their education. Based on an erotic game by DarkShelf. **N**

DIAMOND DAYDREAMS *
2004. JPN: *Kita e Diamond Dust Drops*. AKA: *To The North, On to the North, Diamond Dust Drops*. TV series. DIR: Bob Shirahata. SCR: Mari Okada, Ryota Yamaguchi. DES: Michinori Chiba. ANI: Studio Deen. MUS: Takehito Itsukita. PRD: Studio Deen, Red, AT-X. 24 mins. x 13 eps.

Six separate stories of women from teens to 20-somethings, whose lives converge as a result of strange events on the northern island of Hokkaido. Most are looking for love, like Atsuko the Hakodate fishmonger betrothed to a local hotelier's heir but struggling with her feelings for a record-collecting slacker, or Karin, a Tokyo girl hospitalized in Kitami for the last two years, but refusing life-saving surgery because she hasn't trusted doctors since her father's death. It's also a travelogue of the region and features many well known tourist sights and local brands, with the separate strands coming together in the final episode for a magical denouement in Hokkaido's capital city of Sapporo. The titular "diamond dust" is a rare arctic weather phenomenon describable in strict meteorological terms as a fog or low-lying cloud of ice crystals. It can occur anywhere with prolonged subzero temperatures, but has entered Hokkaido folklore as a form of lucky charm, said to grant lifelong happiness to anyone who sees it—or perhaps a lump of tourist-colonial hokum designed to keep people coming to the northern island even when it's bitterly cold. This dating sim–based anime concentrates less on the dating angle than on the individual stories of the girls themselves; compare to KANON. Although based on a PS2 game by Oji Hiroi, the inspirations for this franchise lie further back in the long-running live-action TV series *From the North* (*DE), which came to a highly publicized end in 2002 after over 20 years as a mainstay of Japanese TV drama. Similar scenic inspirations informed SAIKANO.

DIARY OF ANNE FRANK
1979. JPN: *Anne no Nikki: Anne Frank Monogatari*. AKA: *Diary of Anne: Story of Anne Frank*. TV special, movie. DIR: Eiji Okabe. SCR: Ryuzo Nakanishi. DES: Yu Noda. ANI: Seiji Endo. MUS: Koichi Sakata. PRD: Nippon Animation, Transarts, Tomi Pro, Studio Orc, TV Asahi. 82 mins. (TVm), 102 mins. (m).
In 1940, Amsterdam is occupied by the Nazis. Persecuted for their Jewish faith, the Frank family is forced into hiding in a secret annex concealed in a canal-side house. The young daughter Anne begins to write down her thoughts in a diary, escaping from her situation by writing fantastic stories. Eventually, the family is

discovered by the Nazis and taken away to a concentration camp.

This earnest but pretentious TV movie about the famous diarist uses four of Anne's stories (published as *Tales from the Secret Annex*) as interludes to break the monotony of her confinement: "*Fear*," "*The Wise Dwarf*," "*Henrietta*," and "*The Adventure of Bralee the Bear Cub*." Such a decision may have made cinematic sense, but it somehow trivializes Anne's plight. After the broadcast of this film, a child's viewpoint becomes a regular feature in anime about WWII, since it permits the use of Japanese characters who, like the baby-boom audience itself, had no part in the war that so dramatically altered the course of their country's history. It can thus be regarded as the pilot film for an entire subgenre of child-focused anime about war, leading swiftly to the commissioning of works such as BAREFOOT GEN and GRAVE OF THE FIRE-FLIES, as well as many lesser imitators.

A second anime version was released in Japanese theaters in 1995, directed by Akinori Nagaoka. This production, from KSS and the Madhouse studio, was much more lavish than the original TV movie, featuring more realistic character designs from Katsuyuki Kubo and music by Michael Nyman, composer for *The Piano*. This film, minus its Nyman score and with several cuts, was released in French as *Le Journal d'Anne Frank* on DVD with English subtitles, described by Justin Sevakis of Anime News Network as "one of the worst world literature anime ever made."

DIGI CHARAT

1999. TV series, video, movie. DIR: Hiroaki Sakurai, Masayuki Kojima, Tatsuo Sato. SCR: N/C. DES: Yoshiki Yamagawa. ANI: N/C. MUS: N/C. PRD: Madhouse, TBS. 5 mins. x 16 eps. (TV1), 20 mins. x 4 eps. (*Summer Special*), 48 mins. (*Christmas Special*), ? mins. x 4 eps. (*Hanami Special*), ca. 22 mins. x 4 eps. (*Summer Holiday Special*), 20 mins. (*Trip*), 6 mins. 40 secs. x 48 eps. (*Panyo Panyo*), 15 mins. x 8 eps. (*Piyoko*), 24 mins. x 52 eps. (*Nyo*).
Adorning merchandise and commercials as the mascot character for the Gamers chain of stores in Japan, the cartoon ten-year-old Digiko is reputedly from the planet Digicarrot, from whence she was enticed to Earth by her love of broccoli.

Landing with her friends in Tokyo's Akihabara district, she takes a job at a Gamers store with her friend Puchi Charat and leporine rival Rabi En-rose. Difficult customers and occasional adventures follow. Shown as part of the *Wonderful* anthology television show.

A four-part *DC: Summer Special* (2000) pits Digiko against new nemeses from the Black Gamer Gang, whose poverty-stricken leader Piyoko intends to kidnap her and hold her for ransom. The Black Gamers open their own shop in competition with Digiko's own, though they use sinister means to keep their customers. Digiko also appeared in cameos in PIA CARROT, EXCEL SAGA, and FIRST KISS STORY.

A terminally cute eight-part video sequel, *Leave it to Piyoko* (*Piyoko ni Omakase Piyo*, 2003) offered little plotting or intelligent scripting, just childlike candyfloss characters looking perky and sweet and doing their best to sell more merchandise. Similar antics awaited in the *DC Christmas Special* (2000), in which the cast relocates to a cruise liner. The cast later appeared in several seasonal cash-ins including the springtime *DC: O-hanami Special* (2001), a four-parter in which they partied beneath cherry blossoms, the four-part *DC Summer Holiday Special* (2001), in which Digiko visits America, competes in a band competition and goes hiking in the mountains. Digi Charat appeared in her own 25-minute "movie," *DC: A Trip to the Planet* (2001), in which she made a return visit to her homeworld, before returning to TV screens in the prequel *Panyo Panyo DC* (2002) and the 104-episode remake *DC: Nyo* (2003). Note that although each episode had only one opening and closing credit sequence, it was often split into two distinct stories, leading some sources to list it as 104 episodes.

DIGI GIRL POP

2003. AKA: *Strawberry & Pop Mixed Flavor*. TV series. DIR: Taro Yamada. SCR: Kuniaki Kasahara, Motoki Yoshimura, Reiko Yoshida. DES: Asaki. ANI: Hajime Kurihara. MUS: N/C. PRD: Kazutaka Ito, GDH, HoriPro, Pioneer, Kid's Station. 3 mins. x 26 eps.
Based on a web Flash cartoon originated by Ooz Grafisch and TwoThousand-Creators.com, these are the wacky and extremely brief adventures of a cute,

pink-haired, perky girl robot who fell from the sky and was taken in by Nail, a girl who owns a nail salon. She starts going to high school and causes domestic and social mayhem.

DIGIMON *

1999. JPN: *Digimon Adventure*. AKA: *Digital Monsters*. TV series, video, movie. DIR: Mamoru Hosoda, Hiroyuki Kadono, Takashi Imamura, Tetsuo Imazawa. SCR: Satoru Nishizono, Hiro Masaki. DES: Kappei Nakatsuru. ANI: Hiroki Shibata. MUS: Takanori Arisawa. PRD: Toei. 20 mins. x 54 eps. (TV1), 3 x 25 mins. (m); 20 mins. x 50 eps. (02), 20 mins. x 51 eps. (*Tamers*), 20 mins. x 50 eps. (*Frontier*, TV), 40 mins. (*Frontier*, m), 30 mins. (*Diablomon Strikes Back*), 30 mins. (*Runaway Express*), 30 mins. (*X-Evolution*). 20 mins. x 48 eps. (*Savers*), 20 mins. x 79 eps. (*Xros*).
Goggle-wearing hero Taichi (Tai) and friends Izzy, Joe, Matt, Mimi, and Sora are at a summer camp like no other, where snow can fall in June and the Northern Lights appear far from the Arctic. The pals fall through a magic portal into the very different world on the pink sandy beaches of File Island, where they become embroiled in a battle between strange creatures. The kindly "digi[tal] mon[sters]" that inhabit the parallel world are being corrupted by an evil force, who inserts Black Gears into good digimon to turn them bad. As the children try to solve the mystery, their digimon companions "digivolve" into better and stronger fighters.

After a handover engineered one of the three holiday special minifeatures (2000, cut together for U.S. release as the *Digimon Movie*), a second season followed, rebranded as *Digimon 02* and set three years later, with the return of the evil Devilmon in control of a powerful new energy source. Our heroes, who attend the same soccer club with the gang from the first series, team up with a new digital monster, the blue Buimon, to fight back. A third series, renamed *Digimon Tamers*, began in April 2001, moving the action into the "near-future" year of 200X. This was followed by *Digimon Frontier* (2002), in which five all-new children were chosen to fight the evil Cherubimon, which is intent on destroying the world. This was followed by *Digimon Data Squad* (2006, *Digimon Savers* in Japan), in which more of the same ensued, and again in *Digimon Fusion* (2010, *Digimon Xros* in Japan, AKA *Digimon Fusion Battles* in some English-speaking territories).

Numerous further *Digimon* "movies," often mere episode-length screenings at summer roadshows, have made the *Digimon* franchise even more confusing than it already was. These include *The Runaway Digimon Express* (2002), and *Diablomon Strikes Back* (2005). New toys were introduced in *Digimon: X-Evolution* (2005), which utilized elements of Norse mythology alongside a "virtual world" set-up more similar to that employed in .HACK. Among these films, the most historically noteworthy is arguably *Our War Game* (2000, *Bokura no War Game*), which forms the second part of the English-language *Digimon Movie*, but can be distinguished in hindsight as a dry run for its director, Mamoru Hosoda, with a plot repurposed several years later as the basis for **SUMMER WARS**.

Optioned for U.S. release in the post-**POKÉMON** gold rush, *Digimon* was inadvertently one of the most faithful translations of TV anime; the U.S. and Japanese schedules were so close together that there was little opportunity to do too much rewriting or cutting. Technically speaking, as the descendants of the *original* virtual pets featured in **TAMAGOTCHI VIDEO ADVENTURES**, Digimon have a better pedigree than Pokémon, despite only achieving about half the latter's ratings. The series was also dogged by legal wrangles in the U.S., when the Screen Actors Guild challenged production company Saban over the rights to residuals for the *Digimon* movie. The irony was not in SAG's claim that voice acting was a creative, skilled task that warranted better conditions, but that they had never brought it up before.

DIGITAL DEVIL STORY *
1987. JPN: *Digital Devil Story: Megami Tensei*. AKA: *DDS: Goddess Reborn*. Video. DIR: Mizuho Nishikubo. SCR: Mizuho Nishikubo. DES: Hiroyuki Kitazume. ANI: Naoyuki Onda. MUS: Usagi-gumi. PRD: Tokuma Shoten, Animate. 45 mins.
Computer geek Tamami uses the school's computer center to summon the "digital devil" Loki, soon enlisting teachers and fellow students in a dark cult. Only new-girl Yumiko is unaware of this secret, though she soon discovers that she is the reincarnation of an ancient goddess and, consequently, the only person who can put an end to Loki's violent rampages.

Based on a novel by Aya Nishitani and featuring character designs by original illustrator Hiroyuki Kitazume, this inferior horror anime enjoyed an inferior British release, using the original spotting list from Kiseki, which retains the Japanese translator's creative romanizations of otherwise well-known mythological creatures, including Loki and Set. In Japan, it was screened on a theatrical double bill with **I GIVE MY ALL**. The story was also adapted into a computer game, which in turn was adapted into *another* anime, **TOKYO REVELATION**, and also enjoys an oblique relation to **PERSONA**. 🚫🅥

DINOSAUR KING *
2007. JPN: *Kodai Oja Dinosaur King*. AKA: *Ancient Ruler Dinosaur King*. TV series. DIR: Katsuyoshi Yatabe. SCR: Yasushi Hirano. DES: Masayuki Hiraoka, Toshihisa Koyama, Yukiko Ogawa. ANI: Kiichiro Inoue, Yeong Beom Kim. MUS: Yuko Fukushima. PRD: Sunrise, Asatsu DK, Sega, Nagoya Broadcasting Network. 29 mins. x 49 eps. (TV1), 25 mins. x 30 eps. (TV2).
Ryuta (Max in the English version), Rex, and Malm (Zoe in English) are three friends on a great adventure. They find magical stones with images of dinosaurs and are drawn back in time to help save the dinosaurs and the world. An evil gang is out to capture all the dinosaurs, imprison them in cards, and then bring them back to take over the modern world. It's up to the kids to stop them, with the help of some very special dinosaur friends. Made to promote a dinosaur card game of the same name, this show doesn't do anything that **POKÉMON** and **DIGIMON** didn't do long before it, but that scarcely matters when selling to a dinosaur-loving child. It was aired all over Europe, Brazil, Malaysia, and the Philippines, and a second series made by the same crew started shortly after the first one ended in 2008. *Ancient Ruler Dinosaur King D—Kidz Aventure: Pterosaur Legend (Yokuryu Densetsu)* took our three heroes back into prehistory to reset the disrupted passage of time. Much subversive fun is to be had observing how dinosaur names are handled by the voice cast. 🅥

DIOXIN SUMMER
2001. JPN: *Inochi no Chikyu: Dioxin no Natsu*. AKA: *Life's World: Summer of the Dioxin*. Movie. DIR: Satoshi Dezaki. SCR: Kazuo Koide. DES: Setsuko Shibuichi. ANI: Setsuko Shibuichi, Keizo Shimizu. MUS: N/C. PRD: Sotsu Agency, Sunrise. ca. 85 mins.
The true story of an accident in Italy in 1976, when an explosion at a biological research laboratory threatened the surrounding area with deadly dioxins and ruined the happy existence of a group of 11-year-old children. Adapted from a book by Kei Hasumi. Compare to **SEA OF THE TICONDEROGA**.

DIRTY BY THE DOZEN *
2008. JPN: *Juninin no Onnakyoshi*. AKA: *Twelve Female Teachers*. Video. DIR: Mitsuhiro Yoneda. SCR: Mitsuhiro Yoneda, Gorota Takada. DES: Mitsuhiro Yoneda, Hodo Sei. ANI: Mitsuhiro Yoneda. MUS: N/C. PRD: YOUC, Tatsuo Sunaga, Digital Works. 29 mins. x 2 eps.
The headmaster of a girls' school, his son, and nephew are operating the school as a training ground for sex slaves. They blackmail female teachers and pupils, train them to submit to and enjoy any kind of depravity, then sell them on the black market. Based on a porn video game by Carmine, and labeled as part of the **VANILLA SERIES**, although it includes a range of sexual tastes that fall outside most definitions of vanilla (**EROTICA AND PORNOGRAPHY**). 🚫

DIRTY LAUNDRY *
2008. JPN: *Sentakuya Shin-chan*. AKA: *Laundryman Shin-chan*. Video. DIR: Ken Raika. SCR: Raita Shintaro. DES: Mamito Tayama. ANI: Mamito Tayama. MUS: N/C. PRD: ANI FACTORY, K-Production, Milky, MS Pictures. 30 mins. x 2 eps.
Shinji has been in his new job for just a month. He works for a laundry owned by a young widow and is soon providing a special service for her. Then he starts to extend his talents to every housewife in the neighborhood. Goodness knows how he finds time for laundry, in this lighthearted comedy of sex between consent-

ing adults based on the erotic game by BLACK PACKAGE. If you think the bright, childlike design of the Japanese video title, using baby lettering for an adult's name, indicates a pun on the popular anime CRAYON SHIN-CHAN, you need to get out more. **Ⓝ**

DIRTY PAIR *

1985. TV series, movie, video. DIR: Katsuyoshi Yatabe, Toshifumi Takizawa, Tsukasa Dokite, Norio Kashima, Masaharu Okuwaki, Koichi Mashimo. SCR: Hiroyuki Hoshiyama, Kazunori Ito, Tsukasa Tsunaga, Haruka Takachiho, Yasushi Hirano, Fuyunori Gobu, Masaaki Sakurai, Go Sakamoto. DES: Tsukasa Dokite, Fujihiko Hosono, Yoshito Asari, Katsuhiko Nishijima, Studio Nue. ANI: Kazuo Tomisawa, Tsukasa Dokite. MUS: Toshiyuki Kimori, Yoshihiro Kunimoto. PRD: Nippon Sunrise, Studio Nue, Nippon TV. 25 mins. x 24 eps. (TV), 25 mins. x 2 eps. (v1), 57 mins. (Nolandia), 81 mins. (m), 25 mins. x 10 eps. (v2, Original), 59 mins. (Flight 005), 30 mins. x 6 eps. (DPF1), 30 mins. x 5 eps. (DPF2), 30 mins. x 5 eps. (DPF3).

Kei and Yuri are the "Lovely Angels," Trouble Consultants for the World's Welfare Work Association (3WA), a federal police force that serves the United Galactica government. Wearing skintight spacesuits that happen to be almost completely transparent (thereby looking just like bikinis) and accompanied by their "pet" ursoid Mughi and R2D2 clone Nammo, the girls are sent on missions that often end in massive explosions and collateral damage, resulting in the unkind nickname of the "Dirty Pair."

At the time they first appeared on-screen in the anime adaptation of Haruka Takachiho's CRUSHER JOE, the Dirty Pair had already featured in two novels of their own, including *The Great Adventures of DP*, which won the Seiun (Japanese Nebula) Award. The year after their anime debut, the characters won another Seiun for the book *DP Strike Back*. They were named for one of the author's favorite female wrestling teams, the Beauty Pair, while the 3WA is a reference to the World Women's Wrestling Association. The real-life Beauty Pair inspired many imitators in the wrestling field, including the Black Pair, Golden Pair, and Queen Angels—a roster that influenced several other series, including

MARIS THE CHOJO and METAL FIGHTER MIKU.

Designer Dokite adapted Yoshikazu Yasuhiko's illustrations from the original novels, the third of which was timed to come out simultaneously with the debut show. Though the series was canceled early after 24 episodes, the last two parts were immediately rushed out onto video in 1985 as *DP: From Lovely Angels With Love*. The franchise stayed on video with *DP: Affair on Nolandia* (1985), directed by Okuwaki and written by PATLABOR's Ito, in which the girls are sent to an arboreal planet where they must stop an illegal genetic experiment. *Nolandia* is notable for being the only occasion in the entire anime adventures that alludes to Kei and Yuri's telepathic abilities, a major feature of the novels.

The 1987 *DP* movie, known in the U.S. as *DP: Project Eden*, pastiched Frank Herbert's *Dune* by revealing that warp travel is impossible without the rare metal vizorium. Sent to planet Agerna to stop two rival nations from destroying each other in a war over the element, the girls meet Professor Wattsman, a scientist intent on using vizorium to bring forth a powerful new life form. The same year saw the publication *The Great Adventures of DP* in English, but the duo's greatest impact on the U.S. market came in 1988 with the publication of the first of many American *DP* comics produced by Toren Smith and Adam Warren.

Though it would be several more years before the movie and video versions of *DP* would reach the U.S. through Streamline Pictures, the original TV series sold well in Europe, and ten extra shows were made in 1989 specifically to bulk out the TV run to 36 episodes for the Italian market. Stuck straight onto two-part videos in the Japanese market as *DP Wink, Masterworks, Complete, Mystery, Birth, Special, Variety, Investigation, First Final*, and *Last Fantasy*, these "bonus" episodes were released abroad by AD Vision as *Original DP*, the distributor's argument being that although they were not the initial (then-untranslated) TV series, they were still truer to the original than *DP Flash* (see below). As an indicator of the serial's great popularity, it also enjoyed the questionable honor of an erotic pastiche, in the form of *Punky Funky Baby* (1985), an installment in the SYMPHONY DREAM STORY series.

The video *DP Flight 005 Conspiracy* (1990) concentrated less on zany antics and more on a serious thriller story, as the pair are sent to investigate a space liner explosion that kills 300 passengers, though nobody attempts to claim insurance. It was to be the last anime outing to date for the original Kei and Yuri.

Takachiho would revise the characters in 1994 for *DP Flash*, which portrayed the Lovely Angels as younger, dumber, cuter investigators rendered in sharper (and cheaper) animation. Though many (including the production staff!) often assume *DPF* to be a flashback to the characters' early years, it is actually set over a century later, starring young girls called Kei and Yuri, who look very similar to the originals but are only the latest in a series of duos to use the code name. These two new Lovely Angels undo all the good work done by the last holders of the title (Molly and Iris, some 15 years earlier), returning the code name to infamy.

Despite this convoluted backstory, *DPF* struggles to recreate the fun of the original. With a complex numbering system obscuring one long succession of stand-alone episodes (there is no "story arc" worth repeating in the "serials" separately named *DPF1*, *2*, and *3*), the characters of *DPF* spend very little time investigating, preferring instead to parody other anime with a visit to a 20th-century theme park or to experience minor difficulties in their attempts to have a vacation. The *DPF* video adventures play up the girls' eye-candy qualities (admittedly, not entirely absent in the appeal of the original), giving them nude transformation sequences and missions such as winning a volleyball tournament, designed as little more than an excuse to spool through a line of sports-show training clichés, leavened with regular wobbles of fan-service cleavage. But while Takachiho's originals continue in their novel form with the most recent *DP: A Legend of Dictator*, *DP*'s most successful incarnation abroad remains the U.S. comic rather than the anime that inspired it. **Ⓝ**

DIRTY THOUGHTS *

2003. JPN: *Private Emotion*. Video. DIR: Sosuke Kokubunji. SCR: Sosuke Kokubunji. DES: Hirotaka. ANI: Takayuki Yanase. MUS:

Yoshitaka Shiro. PRD: Dream Entertainment, Studio March, Milky, Museum Pictures. 30 mins. x 2 eps.

Forced to leave her previous school after her lesbian relationship with a pupil was exposed, Sayaka takes a new post in a new town. However, when her principal discovers her secret, he uses it as a means of blackmailing her into sex with him. Based on the computer game *Private Emotion*. **ⓁⓃⓋ**

DISCOVERY SERIES *

1998. Video. DIR: Hideki Takayama, Yoshitaka Makino, Yusaku Saotome, Yu Yahagi, Juhachi Minamisawa. SCR: Masateru Tsuruoka, Hajime Yamaguchi, Yu Yahagi, Joichi Michigami. DES: Masahiro Sekiguchi, Takanari Hijo, Tomo'o Shintani. ANI: Hirota Shindo, Koichi Fuyukawa, Masahiro Sekiguchi. MUS: Kazuhiko Izu, Hiroaki Sano, Takeshi Nishizawa. PRD: Discovery. 30 mins. x 7 eps. (*Maiden of*); 2 eps. (*Baby Bird*); 4 eps. (*Necronomicon*); 4 eps. (*Triangle Heart*); 4 eps. (*True Snow*); 16 eps. (*Night Shift Nurses*); 3 eps. (*Blood Shadow*); 3 eps. (*F-Force*); 2 eps. (*Maison Plaisir*); 3 eps. (*Slave Market*); 2 eps. (*Black Widow*); 3 eps. (*Sibling Secret*); 2 eps. (*Blood Royale*); 2 eps. (*Xtra Credit*); 3 eps. (*Nurse Me*); 2 eps. (*Stepsister*); 4 eps. (*TH: Sweet Songs Forever*); 1 ep (*Shrike*); 2 eps. (*Swallowtail Inn*); 2 eps. (*Temptation*); 2 eps. (*Pigeon Blood*); 1 ep. (*Fiendish Face*); 2 eps. (*Newscaster Etsuko*); 2 eps. (*Tokineiro*); 2 eps. (*Panties Teacher*); 1 ep. (*New Gymnastics*).

As CREAM LEMON, SECRET ANIMA, and the VANILLA SERIES have already amply demonstrated, the demands of the erotic market revolve around shorter cycles than television. Whereas anime for the children's market can repeat itself every two years without much chance of complaint, and anime for teenagers often follows a similar lengthy rotation of ideas, pornography's aims are far lower. For it to work, it need only entertain its target consumer, often a renter rather than a buyer, for half an hour. This entry consolidates the multitude of separate titles that originate with the Discovery label, although many already have entries elsewhere in this book, particularly if they have received an English-language release.

Beginning in 1998 with the MAIDEN OF... series, Discovery established an early repu-

tation for plots revolving around dominance and submission. *Song of the Baby Bird* (2000, *Hinadori no Saezuri*) was not originally part of the *Maiden of...* series, but sold in the U.S. as *Maiden of Deliverance*. It also capitalized on the growing popularity of interactive media by investing in lengthy adaptations of computer games, such as its second big release, MYSTERY OF THE NECRONOMICON. TRIANGLE HEART was followed in 2000 by *True Snow the Color of Lapis Lazuli* (*Shin Ruri-iro no Yuki*), another computer game adaptation that centers on a scientifically minded inventor who finds himself having to share his life with Yuki, a spirit-girlfriend who owes a certain debt to the "Snow Princess" of JAPANESE FOLK TALES, with elements of OH MY GODDESS! The same year also saw the first episode of Discovery's most popular and long-running release, NIGHT SHIFT NURSES—hospitalization being an excellent excuse for the domination and bodily invasion that often seem to be a Discovery trademark.

More game adaptations followed in 2001 with BLOOD SHADOW (itself seeming to be based on a pastiche of SAKURA WARS) and F-FORCE. In 2002, the company appeared to move even further into the niche territory of scatology and submission, with MAISON PLAISIR and SLAVE MARKET. It also developed what may have been a coincidental theme of exploiting lonely widows, following *Maison Plaisir* with BLACK WIDOW.

Inevitably, incest would also form a part of the Discovery series, arriving in 2002 with SIBLING SECRET, while themes of bondage and imprisonment would recur in BLOOD ROYALE and XTRA CREDIT. Incest and computer game tie-ins met in the form of STEPSISTER. The company also experimented with a new hospital franchise in the form of NURSE ME!

Five years after the company began releasing erotica, the first new title of 2003 was a sequel to the original *Triangle Heart*, called *Sweet Songs Forever*. The company released a rare one-shot release, *Shrike* (*Mozu no Nie*, released in the U.S. as *House of a Thousand Tongues*), which may have been a deliberate decision or a historical anomaly created by a title that failed to generate good sales in relation to ongoing series like *Night Shift Nurses*. The story was a historical vignette in which a kimono-clad

princess is molested by her stepbrother. However, the historical setting cannot have handicapped sales of *Shrike* too badly, since it was immediately followed by SWALLOWTAIL INN, another tale with an old-fashioned look, which ran for two episodes. The same year saw a return to campus tales with TEMPTATION and more domination in *Pigeon Blood*, in which the amnesiac Chris wakes up to discover he is a "slave master" charged with breaking in new acquisitions. He encounters a girl called Rita on one of his trips into town, and he succumbs to her pleas to enter his house and be trained as one of his slaves.

In 2004, the company adapted *Fiendish Face* (*Masho no Kao*, released in the U.S. as *The Two Facials of Eve*), a manga title from Mink, the games company behind *Night Shift Nurses*. In it, a teenager returning home from school finds the archetypal "mysterious girl" in his room, who turns out to be his previously unknown cousin Reika, with whom he is soon playing erotic games. It also parodied the TV journalism genre so beloved of live-action television, with *Newscaster Etsuko* (*Hana no Joshi Ana: Newscaster Etsuko*, released in the U.S. as *Foxy Nudes*), in which a reporter for Tokyo's "Flower TV," Etsuko Yamanobe, covers a story about a hostage situation, which she shamelessly manipulates for higher ratings—compare to NINE O'CLOCK WOMAN. The same year saw *Sensual Ticking Time* (*Tokineiro*, released in the U.S. as *A Time to Screw*), in which "I," yet another amnesiac protagonist, wakes up in a remote wintry mansion, where time runs differently and four sobbing maids await his twisted attentions. Discovery returned to school voyeurism with *Pantie Flash Teacher* (*Panchira Teacher*) in which politician's daughter Machiko attempts to teach classes of teenagers while dealing with a student blackmail ring—possibly an oblique reference to the old series SHAME ON MISS MACHIKO but bearing a far closer resemblance to DEPRAVITY and SCHOOL OF BONDAGE.

In 2005, Discovery turned its attention to high school sports, with *Rhythmic Gymnastics* (*Shintaiso—Makoto*, AKA *New Gymnastics*), billed, in a strange crossover between companies, as a sequel to Pink Pineapple's PRINCESS 69. The company continues to exist as a portal offering downloads of its catalogue, which just goes to show the blue-chip reliability of **EROTICA AND PORNOGRAPHY**. Many of the titles are over a decade old but demonstrate a profitable long tail; presumably there is just enough available to keep any new fan happy for the average length of his likely interest. **LNV**

DISGAEA *

2006. JPN: *Makai Senki Disgaea*. AKA: *Netherworld Battle Chronicle Disgaea*. TV series. DIR: Kiyotaka Isako. SCR: Atsuhiro Tomioka. DES: Akira Kano, Junko Shimizu. ANI: N/C. MUS: Tenpei Sato. PRD: Oriental Light and Magic, d-rights. 30 mins. x 12 eps.
Apprentice angel Fionne is sent to the Netherworld to assassinate its king, only to find his castle burning. Searching for his coffin to make sure she can carry out her assignment, she finds it contains his heir Prince Laharl, who has been in a magical slumber since before his father's death. He sets out to claim his father's throne from the demons, humans, and demon-slave-penguins who stand in his way, and she sets out to reclaim his soul through the power of love. The anime is based on the video game *Disgaea: Hour of Darkness* and follows the same general plot with a few changes to characters and chronology. None of them make much improvement to the outcome. This is a thinly plotted, poorly structured, very silly series which is designed to look as if it should appeal to young children. However, it's peppered with crude verbal and visual jokes that would horrify parents, though they would probably make most small boys snigger. It tells you a good deal about what the producers regarded as important to note that the PR team is credited more prominently than the animators in some perfectly respectable sources. There are also three spin-off manga and four light-novel series. **L**

DISPATCHES FROM THE SPIRIT WORLD

1996. JPN: *Jigokudo Reikai Tsushin*. AKA: *Spiritual Report: Occult Shop from Hell*. Video. DIR: Junichi Sato. SCR: Miyuki

Takahashi. DES: Akihito Maejima. ANI: N/C. MUS: N/C. PRD: Toei. 23 mins. x 2 eps.
Three young boys are chased by a ghost and run to an occult shop for help. There, they are given a selection of magical items that will allow them to send malevolent spirits back to hell. After successfully dealing with their initial assailant, they go into business as professional ghostbusters, righting wrongs all over Tokyo.

Beginning as a best-selling children's book by Karin Kagetsu and illustrated by Akihito Maejima, this *Ghostbusters* rip-off became a live-action film directed by **BE-BOP HIGH SCHOOL**'s Hiroyuki Nasu in 1996. Controversial for introducing scary themes in what was supposedly a children's film, the live version was refused a general rating, and its original target audience was forced to settle for the anime.

DISQUALIFIED DOCTOR

2003. JPN: *Shikkaku Ishi*. Video. DIR: Kazuyuki Honda. SCR: Kazuyuki Honda. DES: Wataru Yamaguchi. ANI: Kazuyuki Honda. MUS: N/C. PRD: Studio Jam, Image Works, Milky. 30 mins. x 2 eps.
Brothers Akira and Jun compete over everything, but Jun always seems to get the upper hand, not only graduating from a better medical school but also stealing Akira's pert girlfriend Wakana. Determined to gain his revenge by (somewhat illogically) discrediting the entire institution where his brother and ex work, Akira embarks on an elaborate scheme, which begins by a series of sexual assaults on rookie nurses. For a long time, we had this confused with **RXXX: PRESCRIPTION FOR PAIN**—sorry, but after a while they all start to look the same. **LNV**

DIVERGENCE EVE *

2003. TV series. DIR: Hiroshi Negishi, Atsushi Takada. SCR: Toru Nozaki. DES: Toshinari Yamashita, Takayuki Takeya, Tatsuya Tomosugi. ANI: Toshinari Yamashita. MUS: Yousuke Hoga. PRD: Plasma, Radix, AT-X. 25 mins. x 13 eps. (TV1), 25 mins. x 13 eps. (TV2).
In the year 2317, interstellar travel takes place via gates that pass through

a parallel universe, unfortunately leaving travelers open to attacks from the other-dimensional inhabitants known as Ghouls. At the Watcher's Nest, a space station that watches over the far end of the jump from Saturn's moon Titan, rookie Misaki Kureha and her big-eyed, large-breasted associates are in training to become pilots in the elite Seraphim Squadron. What begins as a silly sci-fi adventure about pneumatic space bimbos soon changes direction radically, incorporating conspiracies redolent of writer Nozaki's earlier **GASARAKI** and elements of Ridley Scott's *Alien*, as Misaki and some new, artificial associates discover more about the nature of the savage Ghouls and their conflict with humanity.

DIVINE CHANGELING ENCHANTMENT

1988. JPN: *Shinshu Sudamahen*. AKA: *Fantasy Kingdom War*. Video. DIR: Satoshi Dezaki. SCR: Tetsuaki Imaizumi, Kazumi Koide. DES: Keizo Shimizu. ANI: Keizo Shimizu. MUS: Yukari Omori. PRD: Magic Bus. 30 mins. x 6 eps. (v1), 30 mins. x 2 eps. (v2).
In medieval Japan's Genroku era, the young warrior Yoshiyasu Yanasawa approaches Takaharu, the leader of the Hazuki clan in search of the power of the "Golden Dragon," unaware that the power of the dragon flows within the very bloodstream of the maiden Orie. The quest broadens out into a fight over a line of gold ore in the Nasu mountains, and the Tokugawa lord Tsunayoshi learns of the Golden Dragon's magical powers when he tries to rape Orie. The samurai Kageshichiro Hagetsu tries to dispel Tsunayoshi's evil spirit before it awakens the dragon completely and brings chaos to Japan. The animated version of a period drama by Tsuneo Tani.

Director Dezaki also made the two-part spin-off series, *Kanzuki Itto* (1989, lit.: *Cold Moon Spirit Cutter*), a samurai-era detective saga starring the popular supporting character Itto Kanzuki, who has a constant quest to help those in need. **NV**

DNA HUNTER *

2002. Video. DIR: Takeshi Masui. SCR: Hayato Nakamura, Mankyu Mizoguchi. DES: MIE. ANI: MIE. MUS: N/C. PRD: Blue Cat, Five Ways. 30 mins. x 3 eps.

Distraught at the death of her fiancé in a climbing accident, Mai seeks help from his place of employment, a clandestine sperm bank whose clients are rich women in search of the best quality donors. Mai wants to have a baby by her dead lover, but cannot afford the clinic's extremely high rates. Instead, she is offered the chance to become a DNA Hunter, an agent who secretly harvests genetic material from unsuspecting celebrities, so that it can be sold to the highest bidder. The result is an innovative excuse for the picaresque sexual encounters of typical anime porn and an unfolding conspiracy story line that makes this show more than the sum of its parts—compare to MARINE A GO GO, the BIBLE BLACK: *Only* installment *Virgin Hunting/Obscene Dance of the Devils*, and *Slave Doll: Maid to Order* for more semen-collecting antics, as well as DNA², of which this seems to be a distant pastiche. **N**

DNA SIGHTS 999.9 *

1997. JPN: *Fire Force Danasight Four-Nine*. Video. DIR: Takeshi Shirato, Masayuki Kojima. SCR: Tatsuhiko Urahata. DES: Leiji Matsumoto. ANI: Aki Tsunaki. MUS: Katsuo Ono. PRD: Madhouse. 45 mins.

After Earth is devastated in an apocalyptic meteor shower, it is taken over by a military cartel calling itself the Trader Forces, which is secretly supplied by an alien woman called Photon. A second woman, Mellow, "casts her cosmic consciousness" at Earth, where it crashes in 2024 with the impact of another meteorite. Daiba, a local boy, investigates the crash site but is arrested by the Traders. Contacted telepathically by Mellow, he is told that he, an Earth girl called Rei, and a third party whom they will have to find themselves (who turns out to be a cat) are all examples of the next stage in evolution. Aided by Mellow, the three must overthrow the Traders.

"This contains the essence of all my previous works. It's a space opera that also focuses on Earth's environmental problems," said creator Leiji Matsumoto at the time of this anime's release; neatly sidestepping the issue of yet another

rewrite of his standard character templates reusing ideas and imagery from his GALAXY EXPRESS 999 and QUEEN EMERALDAS.

There are a few new ideas, such as the magma-dwelling "underlife" creatures briefly encountered, but essentially this is a run-of-the-mill teen adventure using familiar-looking characters in an attempt to drag in longer-standing fans of Matsumoto's other work. That was certainly the way it was sold in Japan, where press releases could not resist hinting that both CAPTAIN HARLOCK and the Yamato spaceship from STAR BLAZERS would make cameo appearances.

DNA² *

1994. JPN: *DNA² (Dokokade Nakushita Aitsuno Aitsu)*. AKA: *(Dumb Nerd Always Astray)*. TV series, video. DIR: Junichi Sakata. SCR: Tatsuhiko Urahata. DES: Kumiko Takahashi, Masakazu Katsura, Takeshi Koike. ANI: N/C. MUS: Eiji Takano. PRD: Powhouse, Nippon TV. 25 mins. x 12 eps. (TV), 25 mins. x 3 eps. (v).

Junta Momonari is a hapless boy with a real complex about sex—the merest thought of it makes him physically sick (compare to the later GIRLS BRAVO and HANAUKYO MAID TEAM). But one day he will become a Mega-Playboy, siring 100 equally fecund children, and agent Karin Aoi is sent back from the future to stop his genes from causing an uncontrollable baby boom. Unluckily for her, she shoots him with the wrong drug and ends up creating the very Mega-Playboy she was sent back to prevent.

Despite the popularity of similar boy-meets-dozen-girls shows like TENCHI MUYO! (ROMANCE AND DRAMA), this adaptation of VIDEO GIRL AI–creator Masakazu Katsura's 1994 *Shonen Jump* manga underperformed in its anime incarnation. Even though *DNA²* contains all the elements thought to guarantee success, including a geeky-Jekyll-and-macho-Hyde subplot as Junta's playboy persona takes periodic control of his body and libido, the series was taken off the air early and ignominiously forced to finish its run on video. With revisionist hindsight, the video episodes were shuffled among the actual TV episodes and now comprise the second, third, and final chapters in the 15-chapter (five-tape) series available in Japanese stores. It was

parodied in the pornographic computer game *Timestripper*, and is much imitated in anime such as DNA HUNTER and DOKURO-CHAN. **N**

DNANGEL *

2003. AKA: *D.N.A.* TV series. DIR: Koji Yoshikawa, Nobuyoshi Habara. SCR: Naruhisa Arakawa. DES: Shinichi Yamaoka, Yasuhiro Moriki. ANI: Hideyuki Motohashi, Shinichi Yamaoka. MUS: Takahito Eguchi, Tomoki Hasegawa. PRD: Dentsu, Kadokawa, TV Tokyo, Xebec. 25 mins. x 26 eps.

Daisuke Niwa is 14 and in love, but when he tries to declare himself to his dream girl Risa Harada and she gives him the "good friends" brush-off, he suddenly transforms into the legendary "phantom thief" Dark Mousy. Successive transformations plague Daisuke every time he gets emotional about the object of his affections. Meanwhile, not only does his mother seem to accept this transformation as a normal family event, she makes Dark steal rare works of art for a purpose Daisuke can't even guess at. His classmate Hiwatari has made it his mission to catch Dark—and just when it seems things could hardly get worse, so has Risa, who much prefers the glamorous, exciting young thief to her shy, inept classmate. Meanwhile, Risa's twin sister Riku decides Daisuke is the one for her. Based on Yukiri Sugisaki's 1997 manga that combined the thievery of LUPIN III with the transformations of CONAN THE BOY DETECTIVE and CALL ME TONIGHT. Like many other romantic anime of the early 21st century, it focuses less on love itself than on means of coping with rejection—compare to KOI KAZE.

DO YOU KNOW THE MILFING MAN? *

2008. JPN: *Gibo no Toiki: Haitoku Shin ni Tadayou Haha no Iroka*. AKA: *Stepmother's Sigh: A Mother's Desires Turn to Immorality*. Video. DIR: Sumito Machida. SCR: Naruhito Sunaga. DES: N/C. ANI: Dr. K. MUS: N/C. PRD: Dream Entertainment, Milky, MS Pictures. 30 mins. x 2 eps.

When Kaito's mother dies, his father remarries. Sayoko is young and beautiful and desperately wants a child of her own, but her husband already has a son and doesn't want more children. Kaito begins an affair with his stepmother, and though she's racked with guilt she can't resist him.

When he finds out that his father is cheating on her, he's disgusted (double standards, anyone?); but he can't resist when chances come his way with other women—his friend, another friend's mother, a coffee shop owner.... Wish fulfillment writ large in a porn anime based on a game by Tinkerbell. Using a classic nursery rhyme refrain to sell this in English marks a new low in the Western market, but brightens the day of the hard-working anime encyclopedist. **◐**

DOCTOR CHICHIBUYAMA

1988. Video. DIR: Tetsuro Amino, Masa Watanabe. SCR: Yoshio Urasawa. DES: Yutaka Kawasuji. ANI: Yutaka Kawasuji. MUS: The Chichibuyama Band. PRD: Studio Ship, Pony Canyon, Ashi Pro, Fuji TV. 30 mins. x 2 eps.
In this short-lived black comedy based on a 1983 manga by Keiichi Tanaka originally serialized in *Comic Gekiga Murajuku*, Dr. Chichibuyama, the perverse, sunglasses-wearing head of a hospital way out in the mountains, terrorizes patients with the help of his lover and a sexy young nurse. Though the manga rode the fad of "Lolita Complex" titles typified by CREAM LEMON, the anime version appeared at the end of the boom and failed to ignite much interest. Two five-minute sections were broadcast on Fuji TV's midnight *All Night Fuji* program, presumably to promote the video. **◐**

DOCTOR DOLITTLE

1984. JPN: *Dolittle Sensei Monogatari*. AKA: *Stories of Doctor Dolittle*. TV series, video. DIR: Seiji Okuda. SCR: N/C. DES: Tom Ray. ANI: N/C. MUS: N/C. PRD: Knack, My Video, NHK BS2. 21 mins. x 13 eps.
Hugh Lofting's children's story about a doctor who could genuinely talk to the animals was animated here in a U.S.-Japan coproduction featuring input from designer Tom Ray, who worked on famous Western cartoons such as *Tom and Jerry* and *The Pink Panther*. Only the first six episodes were broadcast in Japan, and even then on NHK six years after the American broadcast. The remainder were only seen in Japan on video. Not to be confused with the 1970 *Dr. Dolittle* cartoon series, made entirely in the U.S. by DePatie-Freleng.

DOCTOR FABRE THE DETECTIVE

2000. JPN: *Fabre Sensei wa Meitantei*. AKA: *Dr. Fabre Is a Famous Detective, Inspector Fabre*. TV series. DIR: Osamu Nakamura, Masami Yoshikawa. SCR: Osamu Nakamura. DES: N/C. ANI: Nobuteru Tanaka, Masashi Shiozawa, Scott Frazier. MUS: Hayato Matsuo. PRD: Enoki Film, IG Film. 25 mins. x 26 eps.
The adventures of a detective modeled on *Sherlock Holmes* but dwelling in 19th-century Paris, where he solves mysteries centering around the Great Exhibition, the invention of cinema, and other new developments, rubbing shoulders with the famous people of the age in the manner of *Young Indiana Jones*. A fittingly fin-de-siècle mixture of the detective boom of the YOUNG KINDAICHI FILES with the new retro craze of TREE IN THE SUN.

DOCTOR MAMBO AND JIBAKO THE THIEF

1982. JPN: *Doctor Mambo to Kaiketsu Jibako: Uchu yori Ai o Komete*. AKA: *Doctor Mambo and Jibako the Thief: From Space with Love*. TV special. DIR: Yoshio Yabuki. SCR: Akinori Matsubara. DES: Toyoo Ashida. ANI: Kiichiro Suzuki. MUS: Kazuo Sugita. PRD: Toei, Fuji TV. 84 mins.
In this one-shot adaptation of one of Morio Kita's *Dr. Mambo* SF novels, the dashing Dr. Mambo and his unlikely sidekick, Jibako the thief, help Princess Laura, former ruler of Eden, regain her birthright from the usurping President Capo.

DOCTOR SHAMELESS *

2003. JPN: *Chijoku Shinsatsushitsu*. AKA: *Shameful Surgery*. Video. DIR: Ken Raikaken. SCR: Rokurota Makabe. DES: P-zo Honda. ANI: Yuya Soma. MUS: Salad. PRD: T-Rex, Milky, Museum Pictures. 30 mins. x 2 eps.
Dr. Kyozaburo Nagatsuka's private hospital is failing when young Dr. Shinji Ishida comes looking for a job. Shinji is credited with turning many failing hospitals around, but he insists he must have a free hand to use any methods. His chosen methods are sex and humiliation; he gets female patients under his spell and effects remarkable "cures," resulting in return visits, recommendations, and more income for the hospital. He discovers that one of the nurses is not a licensed medical practitioner but a moonlighting sex worker, and offers the same therapy to male patients;

the practice is soon thriving. Compare to NURSE ME! **◐◑◒◓**

DOCTOR SLUMP

1981. JPN: *Doctor Slump and Arale-chan*. TV series/special, movie. DIR: Minoru Okazaki, Yoshiki Shibata, Daisuke Nishio, Akinori Nagaoka. SCR: Masaki Tsuji, Shunichi Yukimuro, Tomoko Konparu, Michiru Shimada. DES: Shinji Koike. ANI: Shinji Koike. MUS: Takeo Watanabe. PRD: Fuji TV, Toei. 25 mins. x 243 eps., 90 mins. (m), 52 mins., 48 mins., 38 mins. (m), 25 mins. x 26? eps. (TV).
In the wacky hamlet of Penguin Village, Dr. Senbe "Slump" Norimaki decides to put together the perfect robot woman from data collected in pop idol photos and porno mags. Instead of perfection, he ends up with Arale-chan, a bespectacled and inquisitive tyke with superhuman strength, and the odd couple get into many wacky adventures. They are helped in their quest for the weird by Slump's penchant for crazy inventions, such as time machines, quantum cloning devices, an invisible gun, and X-ray spectacles.
Akira Toriyama's original 1980 manga ran in *Shonen Jump* for 18 volumes. This anime version came about after an abortive attempt at a live-action show made producers realize that the only way to capture the cartoony spirit of the original was by making a cartoon. The other occupants of Penguin Village provide a menagerie of amusing characters in the fashion of Toriyama's later DRAGON BALL, including a pig that does a rooster's job of waking everyone up in the morning, a superhero that must eat prunes to transform, and Gatchan, a metal-eating flying creature.
Dr. Slump is one of anime's most successful shows, scoring a massive TV rating of 36.9 at its peak (the "mega-hit" EVANGELION managed a paltry 7.1). It has also been a hit abroad, particularly in the large anime markets of Hong Kong and Italy, but has yet to make it to the English language. The series also spun off several "TV specials" often premiered in theaters during summer festivals. Since the TV episodes often consisted of small vignettes, these "movies" consisted of little more than extended anthologies, like *Hello! Mysterious Island* (1981), which often spoofed other films of the day such as QUEEN OF A THOUSAND YEARS (*Who Is the Real Queen of a Thousand Years!?*,

1981) and **DON QUIXOTE** in *Heroic Legend of Penguin Village* (1986), which is about Slump undertaking a dangerous quest to the supermarket to get more toilet paper.

The first true *DS* movie, called simply *Dr. Slump* (1982), sends the characters on a space mission to planet Takeyasaodake, a mission loaded with parodies of the *Star Wars* movies, **STAR BLAZERS**, and **GALAXY EXPRESS 999**. Later "movies" were closer in length to the TV specials they replaced, including *The Great Race Around the World* (1983) and *The Secret Treasure of Nanaba Castle* (1984), both glorified episodes at little more than 50 minutes. Though straggling TV specials would make it a lingering death, the official grand finale was *Megapolis the Dream City* (1985), a "movie" of only 38 minutes, in which Arale and company befriend some monsters from outer space.

The series returned for several New Year's TV specials in 1992, although only two of the vignettes, *The Tearful Film Director* and *The Day New Year Didn't Arrive*, were actually new; the other episodes were old *DS* "movies." The franchise was properly revived in 1997, when a new TV series, without the direct involvement of Toriyama, became the first anime to use computer coloring instead of cels.

DOCTOR SURPRISE
1998. AKA: *Dokkiri Doctor.* TV series. DIR: Kazunori Mizuno. SCR: Satoru Nishizono, Aya Matsui, Yoshiyuki Suga, Tsutomu Kaneko. DES: Mari Kitayama. ANI: Masaya Onishi, Shinsuke Terasawa, Manabu Fukusawa. MUS: Yoshimoto Hizawa. PRD: Visual Works, Studio Pierrot, Fuji TV. 25 mins. x 27 eps.
The prestigious Shirabara Clinic has had four previous directors since its founding in the 19th century, but none have been quite so memorable as the fifth incumbent, Haruka Nishikikoji. With a fat face, "a jaw like **FRANKENSTEIN**," a gentle manner, and a genius way with patients, he's a mad scientist working for the side of justice. Lumbered with a cute nursing assistant after the lovely Miyuki's parents go off on a round-the-world trip, Haruka finds himself with a surrogate family, soon becoming embroiled in Miyuki's younger sister's trials at the local primary school. But Haruka has always carried a torch for Miyuki, although he cannot think of a way to confess his true feelings, in this lighthearted adaptation of **JUDGE**-creator Fujihiko Hosono's original manga.

DOCUMENTARIES AND HISTORY
Although often regarded as a wholly fictional medium, anime has a documentary and instructional tradition dating back to Seitaro Kitayama's one-reeler *What to Do with Your Postal Savings* (*Chokin no Susume*, 1917). A pioneer in this field, Kitayama also made animation segments for the film *Dental Hygiene* (*Koku Eisei*, 1922), produced by the detergent and toothpaste manufacturer Lion. Animation was useful for illustrating abstract concepts and the inner workings of machines—although works for children still form the bulk of **EARLY ANIME**, many were factual in basis. Notable examples include Kitayama's *Atmospheric Pressure and the Hydraulic Pump* (*Kiatsu to Mizuage Pump*, 1921), *Plant Physiology and Plant Ecology* (*Shokubutsu Seiri Seitai no Maki*, 1922), and *The Earth* (*Chikyu no Maki*, 1922). His fellow early animators were kept similarly busy on informational films, such as Sanae Yamamoto's *The Mail's Journey* (*Yubin no Tabi*, 1924), made for the colonial governor-general's office in Korea, and *The Spread of Syphilis* (*Baidoku no Denpa*, 1926), with a subject matter that might be worthy of consideration as the first "adult" anime. Tai Kato's *Lice Are Frightening* (*Shirami wa Kowai*, 1944) was released in Chinese for the Manchurian audience, and featured a call to better personal hygiene through a narrative that relied on animated lice. Animators also formed a subset of the Proletarian Film League of Japan, disbanded in 1934, for whom films such as *Prokichi Ajita's Consumer Union* (*Ajita Prokichi Shohisha Kumiai no Maki*, 1930) served as commentary on "abstract disputes," once again intended for adult consumption. The union's most infamous work, *Slave War* (*Dorei Senso*, 1931) was banned, seized, and returned heavily cut by the police after it unwisely suggested that the Japanese in China were no less worthy of censure than the other imperialist powers.

Such an instructional role transferred easily from agitation to establishment propaganda purposes, used to depict scenes both accurate and otherwise in **WARTIME ANIME** such as *Nippon Banzai* (1943), and a prolonged sequence in **MOMOTARO'S DIVINE SEA WARRIORS** (1945), detailing the alleged abuses Asia had suffered at the hands of Western imperialists—the authors suspect the latter sequence may be a recycling of the former. Arguably the greatest and most notorious flourishing of this mode came in the activities of the Toho Aviation Education Materials Production Office, or "Shadow Staff," a dozen animators who made some 21 military instructional films between 1939 and 1944 on subjects such as torpedo essentials, aerial identification of marine vessels, the principles of bombardment, and the essentials of dive bombing. These films were never publicly screened, and none of them appear to have survived the war. According to the memoirs of one animator, Soji Ushio, it was these animated films that were used to train the pilots who attacked Pearl Harbor.

The first anime TV series, **INSTANT HISTORY** (1961), set the tone for many other educational programs by dramatizing important events. It formed the first iteration of what would eventually become the "Kirin Monoshiri" series of programming concerning "This Day in History," which would run in one form or another for the next 20 years (**ADVERTISING AND SPONSORSHIP**). The process of *documenting* history came to narrative fruition in **ANIMENTARY: CRITICAL MOMENTS** (1971), which concentrated so heavily on the re-creation and operation of realistic WWII-era military machinery that it was the first anime to feature a "mecha designer." Such attention to detail would later impart a new degree of naturalism to the "real robots" of science fiction. Serials of short informational films used comedic set-ups to convey information about law and society, in the hapless adventures of **OUTSIDE THE LAW** (1969) and the inquisitive kids of **JUST ANOTHER FAMILY** (1976). Animation was also used to present views of the future in **FIFTH ICE AGE** (1967) and **COMPUTOPIA** (1968), drifting ever further from the straightforward presentation to the predictive fiction of **UNTIL THE UNDERSEA CITY** (1969).

Inspired by similar trends in the live-action TV world, anime began to favor docudramas, particularly when, in the case of **ROAD TO MUNICH** (1972), live-action footage was unobtainable. The biographical vignettes of **GREAT PEOPLE** (1977) were the most obvious, but the use of anime was also a deliberate stylistic decision in **WE'RE MANGA ARTISTS: TOKIWA VILLA** (1981), which told the life stories of several of the medium's most famous creators. The period also saw the first flowerings of biographical and semi-biographical accounts of World War II. **THE DIARY OF ANNE FRANK** (1979) made it possible for Japanese producers to consider productions of **BAREFOOT GEN** (1983), **GRAVE OF THE FIREFLIES** (1988), and their many imitators. Away from such war stories, instructional works became increasingly earnest, with such dreary subjects as **THE STORY OF SUPERCONDUCTORS** (1988) and **BATIAN LAI** (2008), but also valuable below-the-line exports such as **MINA SMILES**, one of the most widely distributed anime in history. Meanwhile, animated inserts continued to appear in live-action programs, including **THE MAN WHO CREATED THE FUTURE** (2003) and an obscure showing for Studio Ghibli's Isao Takahata, who directed a sequence detailing watercourse operations for *The Story of Yanagawa Canal* (1987). Even the Japanese government has gotten involved, with the 18-minute streaming online anime *Learning About Our Metropolitan Assembly* (2002, *Motto Shiritai Watashitachi no Togikai*). Inevitably, the confessional nature of docudrama was also used to add a realistic thrill to erotica, such as **G-TASTE** (1999) and **BLUE CONFESSIONS** (2005).

History itself often forms a problematic component of modern anime. Many anime aimed at the teen market deliberately play with the established norms that schoolchildren are sure to have picked up in class, wedging ninja or demons into the politics and battles of Japan's samurai era. Shows such as **YOTODEN** (1987) or **NINJA RESURRECTION: THE REVENGE OF JUBEI** (1997) hence have an implied audience that already know the "real" story, and can be expected to savor the alternate readings presented for their entertainment. Unfortunately, this can often make such shows impenetrably parochial to foreign audiences, who often do not know their Nobunaga from their Ieyasu. Conversely, many anime concerned with 20th-century history are subject to the infamous "textbook problem" that has been a hot potato in Japanese academic discourse since the 1960s. With right-wing lobbyists still preventing many Japanese schoolbooks

from accurately discussing the events of World War II, the propagandist leanings of many **WARTIME ANIME** ironically persist in many anime that touch on the subject. In the case of **NIGHT RAID 1931** (2010), such concerns caused the more controversial episodes to be released straight to video, without a TV airing that might have otherwise hurt the feelings of fanatics, fascists, and atrocity-deniers.

DODGE DANPEI

1991. JPN: *Honoo no Tokyu Dodge Danpei*. AKA: *Burning Dodgeball Dodge Danpei*. TV series. DIR: Takaaki Ishiyama. SCR: Hirokazu Mizude, Takashi Yamada, Miyoko Inoue. DES: Tetsuhiro Koshita. ANI: Katsumi Hashimoto, Yutaka Kagawa, Kazunori Takahashi, Keitaro Mochizuki. MUS: N/C. PRD: Animation 21, Tokyo Agency, Shogakukan Pro, TV Tokyo. 25 mins. x 47 eps.
A plucky Japanese boy leads his dodgeball team to victory against a series of opponents in a **SPORTS ANIME** based on the 1989 manga in *Coro Coro Comic* by Tetsuhiro Koshita, who also created **RACING BROTHERS LETS AND GO**.

DOG AND SCISSORS *

2013. JPN: *Inu to Hasami wa Tsukaiyo*. AKA: *Use the Dog and Scissors; InuHasa*. TV series. DIR: Yukio Takahashi. SCR: Toshizo Nemoto, Keiichiro Ochi, Toko Machida. DES: Yoko Sato. ANI: Yoko Sato. MUS: Akito Matsuda. PRD: Gonzo, Beijing Pinasters, Green, Green Qiqihar, AT-X. 22 mins. x 13 eps.
Obsessive teenage reader Kazuhito Harumi is shot and killed at school, and reincarnated as a dachshund with a telepathic link to his favorite author. She, however, is a nutjob who enjoys tying him up and torturing him with scissors. They fight crime. No, really—this terrible idea, seemingly written by hurling darts at a board, is based on a book by Shunsuke Sarai that mixes sleuthing with the talking animals that have infested anime since **I AM A CAT**. That means, including the original author, it took *four* people to write this. Four! Despite the ridiculous, depressing creative poverty of its genesis, and a sense that everybody on the production is entirely aware of what an awful show they are working on, one step above the test pattern that would otherwise fill airtime at 1 a.m., the show is of interest for the

prominent billing of several Chinese animation studios. We refuse to blame them, however, for how terrible this is. You still can't get **LEGEND OF GALACTIC HEROES** in English. Just saying.

DOG DAYS *

2011. TV series. DIR: Keizo Kusakawa, Junji Nishimura. SCR: Masaki Tsuzuki. DES: Osamu Sakata, Shinji Katahira, Toshiko Kaizu. ANI: Osamu Sakata. MUS: I've, Maiko Iuchi, Susumu Natsume, Yui Isshiki. PRD: Seven Arcs, Aniplex, Good Smile Company, Bandai Namco Games, Starchild Records. 24 mins. x 13 eps. (TV1), 24 mins. x 13 eps. (TV2).
In a fantasy world where almost everything is named after desserts, the republic of Biscotti faces an invasion by the knights of Galette. Princess Millefiore sends out a magical summons for a hero from another world. She gets Shinku/Cinque, an average Japanese teenager who has to wrap up the whole war in just 16 days so he can get home in time for a visit from a friend for the last 3 days of spring break. Creator/writer Tsuzuki specializes in anime concepts from which he can spin off manga and prose: this pretty but predictable adventure tale follows on from his success with **TRIANGLE HEARTS** and **LYRICAL NANOHA**. A second TV series, *Dog Days'*, followed in 2012, taking Shinku, his cousin Nanami and his friend Rebecca back to the same fantasy world three months after his first adventure there, to sort out more sweetie-themed attacks.

DOG OF FLANDERS *

1975. JPN: *Flanders no Inu*. TV series, movie. DIR: Yoshio Kuroda. SCR: Ryuzo Nakanishi, Yoshiaki Yoshida, Shunichi Yukimuro, Tsunehisa Ito, Aki Matsushima, Yukiko Takayama, Tomohiro Ando. DES: Yasuji Mori. ANI: Toshikazu Sakai, Shinya Takahashi. MUS: Takeo Watanabe. PRD: Nippon Animation, Fuji TV. 26 mins. x 52 eps. (TV1), 25 mins. x 26 eps. (TV2), 104 mins. (m).
In 19th-century Europe, Nello, a young Flemish boy, loves to draw and is inspired by the art of Rubens to become a painter. One day, Nello adopts the dog Patraasche and nurses the ailing animal back to health. He falls in love with the local girl Alois, whose family will never let her marry him because he is too poor. Meanwhile, his grandfather dies, and soon Nello and

Patraasche are all that are left of the family. Eventually, they too die and are buried together.

Based on the 1872 book by Marie-Louise de la Ramée, an Englishwoman of French extraction who confusingly wrote under the Flemish pseudonym Oui'da Sebestyen, this miserable tale of death and despair remains much-loved for its sheer emotional extremes. With a maudlin love of sacrifice and a weepy ending in which the faithful pair freeze to death on Christmas Eve amid the majestic works of art in Bruges Cathedral, it is perhaps no surprise that it has proved so popular with the sentimental Japanese (though there have also been several live-action U.S. versions, the first as early as 1914, the most recent in 1999). This anime was the first of the WORLD MASTERPIECE THEATER series. As in the book, the culmination featured an encounter between Nello and Rubens' triptych painting *The Elevation of the Cross*, which the animators chose to replicate with a photograph rather than their own representation. In some sense, this co-opts Peter Paul Rubens (1577–1640) as one of anime's earliest, albeit inadvertent, background artists, and his triptych one of the medium's most impressive cels.

Remade as a 15-minute episode of the *Manga World Fairy Tales* series in 1976, *DoF* came back again as a 26-part TV series in 1992, entitled *DoF: My Patraasche* (Jpn.: *Flanders no Inu: Boku no Patraasche*). This Tokyo Movie Shinsha version was directed by Kanetsugu Kodama and "set in the small French village of Flanders," according to one Japanese source. Not to be put out by such geographical fudging, the tale was resurrected again in 1997, this time for a lavish feature film directed by the original series' Kuroda, with the location now officially "Belgium." This version was released in the U.S. by Pioneer, although the distributor inexplicably removed 11 minutes of footage and the entire Japanese language track for the DVD edition.

DOG SOLDIER: SHADOWS OF THE PAST *

1989. JPN: *Dog Soldier*. Video. DIR: Hiroyuki Ebata. SCR: Sho Aikawa. DES: Masateru Kudo. ANI: Motomu Sakamoto. MUS: Hitomi Kuroishi. PRD: Movic, Animate Film, JC Staff. 45 mins. Japanese-American commando John

Kyosuke Hiba is forced to face ghosts from his past when he is sent in to steal back an AIDS-like virus from the clutches of a criminal syndicate. His mission becomes more than simply saving the world on behalf of the Pentagon; he takes the opportunity to avenge the deaths of his parents. Based on a manga by STORY OF RIKI–creator Tetsuya Saruwatari, this Rambo clone was released in America by U.S. Manga Corps. **LNV**

DOGTANIAN AND THE THREE MUSKEHOUNDS *

1981. JPN: *Wan Wan Sanjushi*. AKA: *Dogtanian and the Three Invincible Musketeers*. TV series. DIR: Taku Sugiyama, Shigeo Koshi. SCR: Taku Sugiyama. DES: Shuichi Seki. ANI: Shuichi Seki, Takao Kogawa. MUS: Katsuhisa Hattori. PRD: Nippon Animation, TBS. 25 mins. x 24 eps., 25 mins. x 10 eps. D'Artagnan (Dogtanian) is a young dog who wants to be one of the fabled musketeers, but his hot-headed ways get him into trouble when he challenges the Earl of Rochefort (Black Moustache) on the way to Paris. Eventually he becomes a musketeer, teaming up with three experienced guard dogs, Athos, Porthos, and Aramis. When war breaks out between France and England, Dogtanian and his friends must undertake a mission to save the honor of the French queen, who has befriended the English ruler—a King Charles Spaniel, of course. The spiteful feline spy Milady, however, is on their trail at every turn.

This touching, funny, and exciting retelling of the THREE MUSKETEERS in the canine spirit of WOOF WOOF 47 RONIN became a much-loved serial on British children's television, though its Japanese origins were completely obscured and one Dave Mallow was credited as the director. The excruciating pun in the title was a direct TRANSLATION of the original Spanish coproducers' *D'Artacan y los Tres Mosqueperros*. As well as four separate TV compilations on video in the U.S., a movie-length edit, *One for All and All for One*, was released in the U.K. Ten extra episodes were made solely for foreign broadcast by Shigeo Koshi but never shown in Japan, though they are presumably a major part of the "second series" seen abroad as *The Return of Dogtanian*.

DOGTATO

2004. JPN: *Jagainu*. TV series. DIR: Yutaka Kagawa. SCR: Isao Shizuya. DES: Ikuko Ito. ANI: Ikuko Ito. MUS: Hiroshi Igarashi. PRD: Egg, Aniplex. 3 mins. x 26 eps. Surreal preschoolers' entertainment in which Dogtato, a hybrid of dog and potato, lives a happy existence in Veggie Town with his food-themed animal friends, including Haripotato the hedgehog/potato, Nasuinu the eggplant/dog, Kyuribird the cucumber/bird, and Negiwani the shallot/crocodile. Presumably made by the generation of animators who grew up watching TOMATO-MAN, based on stories by Masako Sugiyama.

DOKABEN

1976. AKA: *Lunchbox*. TV series. DIR: Hiroyoshi Mitsunobu, Eiji Okabe. SCR: Tatsuo Tamura. DES: Eisuke Endo. ANI: Nobuhiro Okaseko. MUS: Shunsuke Kikuchi. PRD: Nippon Animation, Fuji TV. 25 mins. x 163 eps. Compulsive eater Taro "Lunchbox" Yamada is a new transfer student at Takaoka (Hawk Hill) middle school. A gentle and kind individual, he soon shows his incredible strength in the school judo club. The baseball team soon realizes that he could be useful and brings him onto the team as its "little giant." Before long, Dokaben is the ace hitter on the team, but this brings forth bad feelings in some of his teammates. This typical SPORTS ANIME was based on a 31-volume manga by Shinji Mizushima, creator of SONG OF THE BASEBALL ENTHUSIAST. Dokaben also has a cameo appearance in GO FOR IT, TABUCHI.

DOKACHIN

1968. TV series. DIR: Hiroshi Sasagawa. SCR: Jinzo Toriumi. DES: Tatsuo Yoshida. ANI: N/C. MUS: Seiichiro Uno. PRD: Fuji TV, Tatsunoko. 15 mins. x 52 eps. A time-travel comedy created by Tatsuo Yoshida for Tatsunoko and shot in 15-minute episodes, screened two at a time. Primitive boy Dokachin, his father Tototo, and mother Kakaka, plus a chunk of their land, are brought forward in time by an experiment that gets out of hand. The comedy arises from their struggle to cope with the frantic pace of 1960s Japan. Compare to WONDERFUL GENIE FAMILY.

DOKI DOKI SCHOOL HOURS *

2004. JPN: *Sensei no Ojikan.* AKA: *Teacher's Time.* TV series. DIR: Yoshiaki Iwasaki. SCR: Hideki Shirane, Michiko Ito. DES: Kiyotaka Nakahara. ANI: N/C. MUS: Yoshihisa Hirano. PRD: Geneon, TV Tokyo. 25 mins. x 20 eps.
Mika Suzuki is a new teacher at Okitsu High School, although since she is the height of a child and has a babyish face the students have trouble taking her seriously. Based on a manga by Tamami Momose, this high school story abandons all attempt at plot and makes the interaction between Mika and her pupils the main event, with Mika very definitely the lovable loser of the group. Her biggest problem is that one of her pupils, the overdeveloped Kitagawa, is fixated on small women. Classroom discipline is also compromised by her inability to stop pupil Watabe from drawing manga—mostly because Teacher wants to see how the story ends. Meanwhile class dreamboy Seki is busy crossdressing and generally being flamboyant. There is an interesting psychological point buried in this and other classroom anime, made by the products of one of the most regulated and rigid education systems in the world, which views schooldays through rose-colored glasses with comedy lenses as havens of fun and individuality presided over by wackily sympathetic teachers. Sadly some of the nuances and references will be lost on non-Japanese speaking audiences, since gags are not just visual but flashed up in text. The limited animation is enlivened with graphic techniques like tone, speedlines, and sparkle-dots from its manga roots, reversing the process of lifting moving picture techniques into comics that made Osamu Tezuka a manga superstar six decades earlier. Compare to AZUMANGA DAIOH and PANI PONI DASH.

DOKKAN ROBOTENDON

1995. TV series. DIR: Hiroshi Sasagawa. SCR: Masaaki Sakurai. DES: Mitsutoshi Tokuyama, Katsumi Hashimoto. ANI: N/C. MUS: N/C. PRD: Tatsunoko, TV Tokyo. 6.5 mins. x 26 eps.
Voice actress Megumi Hayashibara starred as the cute little robot in the red metal baseball cap in this breakfast TV kiddy show, which was apparently so popular with young audiences it was repeated immediately.

DOKKOIDA *

2003. JPN: *Sumeba Miyako no Cosmos-So Suttoko Taisen Dokkoida.* AKA: *Sutokko War Dokkoida; Ultra Diaper Man.* TV series. DIR: Hitoyuki Matsui, Takuya Nonaka. SCR: Kazuharu Sato, Ryunosuke Kingetsu, Waji Sato. DES: Jun Shibata, Yasutoshi Niwa. ANI: Haruo Sotozaki, Satoru Nakaya, Toshimitsu Kobayashi. MUS: Kuniaki Haishima. PRD: Media Factory, Toshiba, Media Works, Klockworx, TV Kanagawa. 25 mins. x 12 eps.
Suzuo Sakurazaki is a college geek with no money and not much street savvy. When a mystery girl suddenly introduces herself as Tampopo and offers him a job as guinea pig for a secret project, he assumes it's just a media spin to glamorize a promotion job for a toy company. Then he learns that the project—a transformation belt that turns the wearer into Dokkoida, savior of the universe—is for real. He's now a superhero in the pay of the Galaxy Federation Police, with the job of catching their most wanted criminals. He doesn't even get a cool outfit—Dokkoida's transformation leaves him dressed in a diaper. Luckily most of his opponents are as ridiculous as they are deadly, because he can't even get away from Dokkoida's world at the end of the day—not only Tampopo, who pretends she's his sister as part of their cover story, but also his enemies, turn out to live in the same dorm. Slapstick humor and more than a few nods to KIKAIDER, ULTRAMAN, and *Masked Rider* (*DE).

DOKURO-CHAN *

2005. JPN: *Bokusatsu Tenshi Dokuro-chan.* AKA: *Clubbing Angel Dokuro.* TV series, video. DIR: Tsutomu Mizushima. DES: Makoto Koga. ANI: N/C. MUS: N/C. PRD: Geneon, Hal Filmmaker, Media Works. 13 mins. x 8 eps., (TV), 24 mins. x 4 eps. (v).
Socially withdrawn 14-year-old boy Sakura Kusakabe would like to share secrets with a girl his own age, but is too shy to mention this to Shizuki, the unwitting object of his affections. Instead, he fakes diary entries from Shizuki to amuse himself, only to discover that he will not always be the loser he appears to be. At some future date, he will become a renowned inventor of something so important that rivals are prepared to send time-traveling assassins back to kill him. One would-be terminator is Dokuro, a cute angelic girl with a large spiked

club—the titular *bokusatsu* literally means "clubbing to death." Not that one needs to see far into the past to see **DNA**^{2}, to which this is rather similar; and so Dokuro soon gives up on her mission to live with Sakura, giving him a girlfriend of sorts who also defends him against later assassins in a rehash of **MAHOROMATIC**. However, she is so hapless that she regularly beats Sakura to death in the style of Kenny from *South Park*, and is forced to use her magical angel powers to bring him repeatedly back to life. A game followed on PS2. Released in the US by Anime Works as *Bludgeoning Angel Dokuro-chan.*

DOLLIMOG

1986. JPN: *Dollimog Da! AKA: It's Dollimog!; Mock and Sweet.* TV series. DIR: Hiroshi Fujioka. SCR: Yasunori Kawauchi, Seiji Matsuoka, Ryuji Yamada. DES: Susumu Shiraume. ANI: Yoshihiko Takakura, Masami Abe, Teruo Kogure. MUS: Goro Nogi. PRD: Japan Comart, NTV. 25 mins. x 49 eps.
In 8th-century Europe, the Frankish king Charlemagne sends out his paladins to invade the neighboring countries. In the midst of this chaos, Dollimog the mole and his sister, Hanamog, come to the aid of humans in trouble. They understand human speech and are walking the "dollimog road" on a quest to bring down Charlemagne and his evil sorcerer, Babar.

Based on a story by writer Kawauchi in which underground dwellers try to preserve peace in their own world by interfering in ours, this original piece of medieval moling only stayed with the Charlemagne plot for 23 episodes—the rest of the series leaps 300 years ahead to the time of the Crusades.

DOMAIN OF MURDER *

1992. JPN: *Hello Harinezumi File 170: Satsui no Ryobun.* AKA: *Hello Hedgehog File 170: Domain of Murder.* Video. DIR: Iku Suzuki. SCR: Akinori Endo. DES: Masaaki Kawanami. ANI: Masaaki Kannan. MUS: Yasushi Tsuchida. PRD: Animate Film. 51 mins.
Private investigator Goro Nanase, whose nickname "Hedgehog" is a pun on "Watchman" and "Bed-head," is hired by Mrs. Toyama to locate her missing husband. The only clue, his face on a poster proclaiming that he's wanted for murder. The race is on, Nanase against the Tokyo

Police, through the snowbound Japanese countryside to the slush and dirty sleet of small-town Japan.

Sadly, *Domain of Murder* was the only episode from the 24-volume manga in *Young Magazine* to be animated. Artist Kenshi Hirokane also created the best-selling *Section Chief Kosaku Shima* and the manga masterpiece for the over-60s, *Shooting Stars in the Twilight*. This is the Japan familiar to Hirokane's adult audience, a lower-middle-class suburb of hard-drinking salarymen and smoking mothers. The production was ill-served in English, though the subtitled edition retained the excellent voice of Shigeru (ARION) Nakahara in the lead, and there's a wonderful cameo from Yo Inoue (PATLABOR's Kanuka Clancy) as a bar-girl past her prime. Endo's script contains some beautifully observed moments, such as a reverse interrogation when Nanase and his ally double-team the cop they find in her apartment. The subtitles leave the marvelous Japanese-style Raymond Chandler–inspired dialogue untouched, and linguists should watch for the timeless moment when Inoue changes from polite-friendly to superpolite-hostile.

DOMINION *

1988. AKA: *Dominion: Tank Police*. Video. DIR: Koichi Mashimo, Takaaki Ishiyama, Noboru Furuse. SCR: Koichi Mashimo, Hiroshi Yamaguchi. DES: Mitsuharu Miyamae, Koji Ito. ANI: Hiroki Takagi, Osamu Honda. MUS: Yoichiro Yoshikawa. PRD: Agent 21. 40 mins. x 4 eps. (v1), 30 mins. x 6 eps. (v2).
Newport City, an artificial island in Tokyo Bay, is already overcrowded with giant bioengineered termite mounds for buildings by 2010. Nanotechnology gone wrong chokes the city with a bacterial fog, and the unhappy citizenry is besieged by high-tech crime syndicates. To combat this spree, the government forms the self-explanatory Tank Police.

Dominion was the first professional manga by APPLESEED-creator Masamune Shirow, published in *Comi-Comi* in 1988, and displays a sense of humor that tails off in his later works. Like PATLABOR, it has a lowly lady cop, Leona Ozaki, who works for a paramilitary police force, bestows a pet name on her machine, and spars flirtily with her partner, though the show concentrates more on comedy than

slice-of-life drama. Thus we have Leona's immediate boss, the *Dirty Harry*–wannabe Brenten constantly arguing with his hypertense Chief, as well as the standard semi-love interest Al and computer nerd "Megane" Lovelock.

After a prequel beginning with Leona joining the Tank Police and the creation of her beloved tank Bonaparte out of spare parts, the anime series draws on early chapters of the manga, pitting the police against Buaku, a rogue android, who is accompanied by the infamous, scantily clad Puma Twins, Annapuma and Unipuma. Taking the piss is the order of the day—the Buaku gang wants to steal urine samples from uncontaminated citizens and attempts to deter pursuit by throwing inflatable dildoes all over the street. As in the manga, there are hints that Buaku's motives are secretly honorable; in a *Blade Runner* pastiche, he is searching for information about his creator, and his urine thefts may be part of a plan to deal with the pollution (less ecologically damaging than in the manga but still there). Buaku and Leona are forced to team up against the Red Commando terrorists in the next two episodes as they try to recover a valuable painting, and, at the finale, Buaku seemingly reforms his evil ways.

In 1992, Shirow revisited the franchise in *Comic Gaia* with a parallel story, dropping Buaku and Al, promoting Leona to Squad Leader, and giving her command of an entire fleet of Bonaparte-model tanks. Adapted into anime by Noboru Furuse as *New Dominion Tank Police* (1993), the new, slightly darker series brought Al back, restored the Puma Twins to a life of crime (they had reformed in the manga and joined the squad), and told a far darker story as the squad battles the evil corporation Dai Nippon Gaiken, which is developing a virtual drug as a spin-off from its weapons research. These new episodes were renumbered for the U.K. video release and are hence sometimes known as episodes 5–10 of the "old" *Dominion*, rather than 1–6 of the "new." **LNV**

DOMU

Animation studio founded in 1986 by several defectors from other companies, incorporated in 1993 after the hiring of former Mushi Production staffer Takeshi

Anzai, and the subsequent restructuring caused by his arrival. Notable staff members include Tsukasa Abe, Shinji Kawagoe, and Kazuhiko Nozawa; representative productions include **BUBU CHACHA** and **SENTIMENTAL GRAFFITI**.

DON! BRUTAL WATER MARGIN

1992. JPN: *Don! Gokudo Suikoden*. Video. DIR: Osamu Sekita. SCR: Tadashi Hirose. DES: Masafumi Yamamoto. ANI: Takeshi Osaka. MUS: Manako Nonoyama. PRD: JC Staff. 50 mins. x 2 eps.
Takekichi and Masakazu are two tough guys who are forced to go underground when they lose their boss in a turf war. This modern update of the classic Chinese novel *Water Margin* (see SUIKODEN) is another gangster tale from **GOODFELLA**'s Hiroshi Motomiya, originally published in *Big Comic*. **NV**

DON CHUCK

1975. JPN: *Don Chuck Monogatari*. TV series. DIR: Yukizo Takagaki, Tsutomu Yamamoto. SCR: Tomohiro Ando, Susumu Yoshida, Tsutomu Yamamoto. DES: Eiji Tanaka, Yasuo Ikenodani. ANI: Eiji Tanaka, Yasuo Ikenodani. MUS: MAC. PRD: Knack, TV Tokyo. 25 mins. x 26 eps. (TV1), 25 mins. x 73 eps. (TV2).
Deep in the Zawazawa Forest by the Jub-Jub river lives Don Aristotle the beaver and his child, Don Chuck. Aristotle frets that his son will grow up strange without a mother, and Chuck starts to associate with beaver girl Lala, a rabbit called Mimi, and Daigo the bear cub. The quartet gets into all sorts of trouble as Chuck slowly grows into an adult.

Don Chuck began as the mascot character for a fairground before starring in children's books by Shizuo Koizumi and Makio Narita and eventually gaining this anime outing. The measure of the series' success is in the fact that the "real" Chuck mascot began to take on attributes of the anime character in the months that followed. A second series, *New DC* (1976), lasted even longer and introduced a family of out-of-place koalas.

DON DRACULA

1982. TV series, video. DIR: Masamune Ochiai. SCR: Takao Koyama. DES: Osamu Tezuka. ANI: Masayuki Uchiyama. MUS: Masayuki Yamamoto. PRD: Jin Pro, TV Tokyo. 30 mins. x

4 (orig., 8 total) eps., 90 mins. (v).
Count Dracula, his daughter Chocula, and servant Igor move from Transylvania to Tokyo, where Dracula has trouble finding enough victims on his night sorties. Chocula helps her father, though it also interferes with her studies at night school. Trouble arrives in the form of famed vampire-hunter Dr. Rip van Helsing, who comes to Tokyo in search of his archenemy. An anime adaptation of Tezuka's manga serial in *Shonen Champion* that was truncated by the bankruptcy of its production house. Of the planned 26 episodes, only four were shown on Japanese TV. The eight episodes completed were eventually released straight to video in a feature-length movie edit. Similar lighthearted treatment of vampire folklore can be found in **PHANTOM QUEST CORP.** Dracula's voice actor Kenji Utsumi also played the title role in the more serious **DRACULA: SOVEREIGN OF THE DAMNED.**

DON QUIXOTE

1980. JPN: *Zukkoke (Bumbling) Knight Don de la Mancha*. TV series. DIR: Kunihiko Yuyama, Shinya Sadamitsu, Soji Yoshikawa, Osamu Sekita. SCR: Akiyoshi Sakai, Soji Yoshikawa, Tomomi Tsutsui, Junzo Toriumi, Masaru Yamamoto. DES: Noa Kawai. ANI: Kazuo Tomisawa, Kunio Watanabe, Satoshi Hirayama, Osamu Nabeshima. MUS: Nobuyoshi Koshibe. PRD: Ashi Pro, Tokyo 12 Channel. 25 mins. x 23 eps.
Don Quixote sets out in search of his beloved Princess Dulcinea, but the girl he desires is only a "princess" insofar as she is the daughter of Carabos the pirate "king." In order to impress Carabos, Quixote carries out several criminal missions on behalf of his would-be father-in-law. Discovering that "Dulcinea" is an imposter, Quixote sets out once more in search of her, accompanied by his faithful servant, Sancho Panza, and his horse, Rocinante. Miguel de Cervantes's classic knight who tilted at windmills is brought to life here in this action-comedy, with the character's insanity brought to the fore by a manic performance from **DON DRACULA**'s Kenji Utsumi, who positively foams at the mouth.

DONKIKKO

1965. TV series. DIR: Koichi Ishiguro. SCR: Koichi Ishiguro, Yoshio Nunogami. DES: Shotaro Ishinomori. ANI: Yoshio Nunogami, Yoshikazu Inamura. MUS: Kiyoko Yamamoto. PRD: B Pro, Fuji TV. 25 mins. x 21 eps.
Short tales of Donkikko, his boy assistant, Dondon, and their pet duck, Gonbei, as they search the town for missing items, help Grandpa run an antique shop, and eventually go to live in an old abandoned train. An adaptation of **CYBORG 009**–creator Shotaro Ishinomori's manga from *Shonen Book* magazine.

DON'T GIVE UP: WAY OF THE MAGIC SWORD

1995. JPN: *Makeru na! Makendo*. Video. DIR: Kazuya Murata. SCR: Yasuo Komatsuzaki. DES: NAO Shimizu, Sayuri Isseki. ANI: Sayuri Isseki. MUS: Koji Sakuyama. PRD: OLM. 29 mins.
Officer Doro, a good demon, attempts to recruit Mai Tsurigino as a demon hunter to police the activities of less scrupulous creatures from the Other Side. Mai refuses but gets dragged in anyway when her little sister, Hikari, takes the job. Doctor Mad (a mad scientist) operates on juvenile delinquent Rei Kamiyoji to turn him into a superweapon to conquer both the human and demon worlds. Rei kills his creator and goes on the rampage, and it's up to the newly recruited demon-hunters to stop him. A **DEVIL HUNTER YOHKO** rip-off originating in an SNES console game.

DON'T LEAVE ME ALONE DAISY *

1997. JPN: *Misutenaide Daisy*. TV series. DIR: Yuji Muto. SCR: Satoru Nishizono, Ryota Yamaguchi, Kazuhisa Sakaguchi. DES: Atsuko Nakajima. ANI: Shigeru Ueda, Naoki Hishikawa. MUS: Kazuhiro Wakabayashi. PRD: Studio Deen, TV Tokyo. 25 mins. x 12 eps.
Reijiro Tekuno (Techno) is a super-rich recluse who lives in a nuclear bunker. He uses his IQ and bank balance to build walls of technology around himself and his fantasy world, where net-surfing is as physical an experience as the real thing. One day (in a scene reminiscent of **KIMAGURE ORANGE ROAD**) Hitomi's hat is blown away by the wind and lands in Techno's garden. He is immediately smitten with her and insists on calling her Daisy, claiming her as his property, much to her distress. This new twist on geek-meets-girl, intercut with survivalism-by-Microsoft, has a *deus ex machina* in the bearded form of Grandpa fulfilling a promise to Techno's dead parents, and a fly in the ointment in the butch senior classmate, Ani, who appoints herself to ride shotgun on Techno's schemes. A salutary message about how life won't always comply just because you point money or a computer at it is buried beneath a lighthearted school romance in the spirit of **JUBEI-CHAN THE NINJA GIRL.** Strangely endearing despite being a comedy about a stalker, Noriko Nagano's original 1988 manga somehow caught the "virtual" spirit of the times, though it was by no means her most popular—unadapted geek-meets-girl tales from the same creator include *Otaku Master* and *God Save the Sugekoma-kun*.

DOOMED MEGALOPOLIS *

1991. JPN: *Teito Monogatari*. AKA: *Capital Story*. Video. DIR: Rintaro, Kazuhiko Katayama, Koichi Chigira. SCR: Akinori Endo, Takaichi Chiaki. DES: Masayuki. ANI: Shinji Tanaka, Yumiko Kawakami, Osamu Kobayashi. MUS: Kazz Toyama. PRD: Madhouse. 47 mins. x 4 eps.
In 1908, the ghost of Yoshinori Kato, a soldier killed in the Sino-Japanese War, kidnaps the beautiful Yukari and offers her as a human sacrifice to Masakado, Tokyo's unofficial guardian deity. Masakado refuses Kato's offer, but Yukari gives birth to Yukiko, assumed to be Masakado's spiritual heir. The years pass, and Kato tries again to seize power at the death of the emperor in 1912. Child-prodigy Yukiko fights him off and he retreats to the underworld. By 1923, the traumatized Yukari and her daughter live with Yukari's brother, Tatsumi, and his new wife, Keiko, who is an undercover priestess charged with defeating Kato. Another coup attempt by Kato almost succeeds, resulting in the 1923 Tokyo earthquake (found in many anime, including **UROTSUKIDOJI, OSHIN,** and **SMART-SAN**).
    With a virginal, sleepwalking heroine in jeopardy, a powerful, predatory sorcerer, and a wise old man seeking to keep them apart, **ALEXANDER**-creator Hiroshi Aramata's original novel is a Japanese retelling of Bram Stoker's *Dracula*. Though often labored and unnecessarily slow, the series still has many good points, notably a well-handled incest subplot and a surreal palette of colors, textures, and set pieces.

Later episodes move into *Omen* territory, as Yukiko struggles with her alleged destiny as the child of the Devil, though the finale is pure anime, with hallucinogenic visions and mass destruction à la AKIRA. The story is loaded with historical references—not only does Kato hail from the birthplace of medieval magician Abe no Seimei (see also YIN-YANG MASTER and OTOGI ZOSHI), but the period background also shows many of Tokyo's familiar landmarks under construction. Tokyo's guardian Masakado is a genuine historical figure, a 10th-century rebel from the region, just one of the real figures in a story that views the century since Tokyo became Japan's capital as an era in which the country itself was demonically possessed. The year 1940, as Japan prepared for Pearl Harbor, was the thousandth anniversary of Masakado's death. Kato represents a modern malaise, a soldier forged in the fires of Meiji Japan's first foreign war, who dies in the battle of Dalian in 1894, returns to stoke nationalist arrogance after the defeat of Russia in 1905, and observes the "dark valley" of 1920s militarism. In this regard, he is a distant cousin of the prodigal soldier who terrorizes Tokyo in PATLABOR 2. In a further subtext, the death of the Meiji Emperor had a recent parallel for a home audience that had just mourned his grandson Hirohito.

There are separate U.S. and U.K. dubs, each with their own merits. Manga Entertainment's uses British accents, which work well with the overpolite, middle-class characters but still leave them sounding unsettlingly twee. Streamline's U.S. dub, however, doesn't put quite as much effort into duplicating the haunting folksongs that carry much of the suspense in the middle episodes.

The story was also made into the live-action movies *Tokyo: The Last Megalopolis* (1988) and *Dictator of the City* (1989), directed by Akio Jissoji and Takashige Ichinose. A third film, *Capital Story: Secret Report* (1995), was a live-action epilogue set in the present day, when evil spirits use the traumatized survivors of the earlier films to return to our world. **NV**

DOOR INTO SUMMER, THE

1981. JPN: *Natsu e no Tobira*. Movie. DIR: Mori Masaki, Toshio Hirata. SCR: Masaki

Tsuji. DES: Keiko Takemiya, Yoshiaki Kawajiri. ANI: Kazuo Tomisawa. MUS: Kentaro Haneda. PRD: Toei. 59 mins.

In 1864 France, Marion is a young man forced to spend the summer at his boarding school because his uncaring mother has recently remarried and does not want him around. Stuck with a small number of companions for the long vacation, Marion soon becomes involved in a series of duels, brawls, and romantic entanglements, such as falling in love with the mayor's daughter, Ledania, but also developing strong feelings for Claude, a boy in his class. Based on the romance manga in *Hana to Yume* by TOWARD THE TERRA-creator Keiko Takemiya, this story was published later than the author's similar SONG OF WIND AND TREES but beat it to anime adaptation, thus gaining some notoriety. This is one of the very rare cases of a mass-market release for a gay anime. Even in supposedly more liberal times, such stories tended to go straight to video, e.g., FAKE or MY SEXUAL HARASSMENT. **N**

DORAEMON *

1973. TV series, movie special. DIR: Nobuo Onuki, Hiroshi Fukutomi, Hideo Nishimaki, Tsutomu Shibayama, Takeyuki Kanda. SCR: Ryohei Suzuki, Masaki Tsuji, Seiji Matsuoka, Masaaki Sakurai, Kazuyoshi Okubo. DES: Fujiko-Fujio, Kunio Okawara. ANI: Fusahito Nagaki, Sadao Tominaga, Hidekazu Nakamura. MUS: Nobuyoshi Koshibe, Shunsuke Kikuchi. PRD: Studio Take, Studio Joke, NTV Animation, Shinei, Nippon TV. 25 mins. x 26 eps. (TV1), 10 mins. x 617 eps. and 25 mins. x 1787 eps. (TV2), 25 mins. x 320+ eps. (TV3).

In the 22nd century, the impoverished descendants of Nobita Nobi pool their resources and send Doraemon, a cut-rate, blue robot cat, back in time to turn him into a more successful person. Doraemon dazzles the schoolboy Nobita and his friends with his endless array of futuristic gadgets, including a portable dimension-door and head-mounted rotor blades. However, Nobita's great-great-grandchildren are so poor that they have sent a malfunctioning mentor whose plans often go awry. Though Doraemon always saves the day, it's normally his fault it needs saving.

Often credited Lennon-and-McCartney-

style to the Fujiko-Fujio duo who created QTARO THE GHOST, *Doraemon* was actually a solo project for Hiroshi "Fujiko" Fujimoto. An ongoing series fully expected to approach 3,000 episodes by the end of 2014, the simple stories and almost timeless animation have kept the series a perennial favorite. Like LUPIN III, it is an original "retro anime" that never had to be revived and has reared several generations of Japanese children. The lineup never changes—Nobita and his cat, along with prissy love interest Shizuka, sneaky intellect Suneo, and hulking lummox Jaian play in their neighborhood (which, with its open spaces and woodlands, is perhaps the only part of the series to have dated), boast about their abilities, and call each other's bluff. With the threat of undesirable forfeits, such as stuffing an entire plateful of spaghetti up the loser's nose, Nobita turns to Doraemon for help, and the cat's techno assistance causes more trouble than it is worth.

Doraemon movies have become a regular feature of the Japanese spring break. In *Nobita's Dinosaur* (1980), a harmless prehistoric pet assumes gargantuan proportions and must be returned to its proper era before it eats Tokyo. When Doraemon returns it to the wrong group of dinosaurs, it has to be rescued, only to need rescuing *again* when it is kidnapped by a hunter from a 24th-century zoo (note how even this feature version can easily break into three episode-length chapters). This was followed in successive years by *Nobita the Space Colonist*, *Nobita's Magic Tower*, *Nobita's Undersea Fortress*, *Nobita Goes to Hell*, *Nobita's Little Star Wars*, and *Nobita and the Iron Warrior*, the latter released in the year of creator Fujimoto's death, 1986. After a one-year hiatus, Doraemon was back again in 1988 with *Nobita's Parallel* JOURNEY TO THE WEST, then *Nobita at the* BIRTH OF JAPAN, *Nobita's Animal Planet*, *Nobita's Animal 1001 Nights*, *Nobita in Snow Country*, *Nobita's Tin-Plate Labyrinth*, and *Nobita's Fantastic* THREE MUSKETEERS. After this rash of pastiches, perhaps more conservative choices in the absence of Fujimoto, a slight change of emphasis came with the 1995 movie, *2112: The Birth of Doraemon*, which cleverly recapped the series' origins for another new generation before returning to form with *Nobita's Galactic Express*, *Nobita's Clockwork*

City, *Nobita's South Sea Adventure*, *Nobita Gets Lost in Space*, the Aztec-themed *Nobita and the Legend of the Sun King*, and, in the year 2001, *Nobita's Winged Heroes*. Subsequent movies have included *Nobita and the Robot Kingdom* (2002), *Nobita's Wonderful Spinning Tops* (2003), and *Nobita's Wannyan Space Odyssey* (2004). In 2005, the voice cast who had played the roles since the second TV series, whose youngest member was now in her 60s, were finally retired and replaced with a new group of younger actors. Their first movie appearance was in *Nobita's Dinosaur 2006*, a remake of the 1980 film, which was screened with local subtitles in several Japanese embassies around the world as part of the hype accompanying Doraemon's appointment as a "cultural ambassador" for Japanese soft power. It is this incarnation, seen with English subtitles at a paltry number of venues, that somewhat misleadingly earns this franchise its "English-language release" asterisk at the top of this entry; Doraemon is otherwise unknown in English. Later movies with this new cast have included *Nobita's Great Adventure in the Underworld* (2007), *Nobita and the Green Giant Legend* (2008), *The New Record of Nobita: Space Blazer* (2009), *Nobita's Great Battle of the Mermaid King* (2010), *Nobita and the New Steel Troops* (2011), *Nobita and the Island of Miracles*, and *Nobita's Secret Gadget Museum* (2013). In 2011, characters from *Doraemon* were portrayed by Japanese celebrities in several live-action commercials for Toyota, with the title role taken by the French actor Jean Reno.

The robot cat has also appeared in literally dozens of TV specials over the last 20 years, many of which were combined with other specials to create still more "movies," including *It's New Year!*, *It's Summer!*, *It's Autumn!*, *It's Winter!*, *It's Spring!*, *Summer Holiday*, *Doraemon Meets* **HATTORI THE NINJA**, *Featherplane*, *What Am I for Momotaro?*, *Come Back Doraemon* (which was, ironically, repeated several times), *Doraemon and Itchy the Stray*, *Doraemon's Time Capsule for 2001*, and *Treasure of Shinugami Mountain*. Later outings also featured cameos from Doraemon's "little sister" from the future, Dorami-chan, who got several short films of her own, starting with *Dorami-chan: Mini-Dora SOS* (1981). The concept was employed many times by other creators,

most notably in the saucy time travels of **DNA²** and **VISIONARY**.

DORATARO
1981. JPN: *Fusen no Dorataro*. AKA: *Wandering Taro and His Balloon*. TV series. DIR: Tomohiko Takano, Kozo Kusuba. SCR: Kozo Kusuba. DES: Yasuji Mori. ANI: Takao Kogawa. MUS: Masayuki Chiyo. PRD: Nippon Animation, Fuji TV. 25 mins. x 13 eps.
After many years of wandering, Taro returns to Cat Island to meet his sister, Sakura, who has stayed on the island with their adoptive parents, and to woo the beautiful ship captain, Haruko. Though his family is pleased to see him, they all come to realize that the long separation has seen them grow into different people, and the return of the prodigal son has only emphasized how far apart they have all become. An anime pastiche of the long-running live-action **TORA-SAN** series.

DOREI MAID PRINCESS
2007. AKA: *Slave Maid Princess*. Video. DIR: "Edeki" Araki, Toshiaki Kamihara. SCR: Hajime Yamaguchi, Mitsui Itsumi. DES: Hideki Araki, Senbata Sakura, Miyuki Kurahashi, Kenichi Kurata. ANI: Hideki Araki. MUS: N/C. PRD: Pixy. 26 mins. x 4 eps.
To save her life, defeated virgin warrior princess Lotte becomes a slave maid. Slave maids not only exist to serve the perverted sexual desires of noblemen, but are also expected to work as bodyguards and protect their masters. Keira and Eric, Lotte's captors, put her through degrading training to turn her whole body into a sex toy. This is another anime based on a porn game by Black Lilith, creators of **ANE HARAMIX**. Why were the distributors unable to bring themselves to translate the word "slave" in the title? We don't know. **Ⓝ**

DORORO
1969. TV series. DIR: Gisaburo Sugii, Osamu Dezaki, Yoshiyuki Tomino, Ryosuke Takahashi. SCR: Ryohei Suzuki, Toru Sawaki, Taku Sugiyama. DES: Osamu Tezuka. ANI: Hideaki Kitano. MUS: Isao Tomita. PRD: Mushi Pro, Fuji TV. 25 mins. x 26 eps.
A warlord promises 48 demons that he will donate the body parts of his unborn son in exchange for power. The baby is born as little more than a lump of flesh and is cast into a river, from which it is rescued by a

kindly physician. He replaces the missing parts with prostheses, and the child, now a grown man called Hyakki-maru, resolves to slay the 48 demons and organs. As he sets off, he teams up with Dororo (baby-talk for *dorobo*, Japanese for thief), a girl thief whose parents once tried to lead an uprising.

Dororo began as a 1967 manga by **ASTRO BOY**–creator Osamu Tezuka. Inspired in part by Shirato's **MANUAL OF NINJA MARTIAL ARTS**, which featured similar Marxist undertones, it incorporates elements of Tezuka's **BLACK JACK**, another driven, patchwork hero with a little-girl sidekick. The manga series was canceled early, before Tezuka's planned shift in focus to Dororo's coming-of-age, and the anime version retains the slightly misleading title—the stories broadcast remain primarily the tale of Dororo's *companion*. From episode 14 onward, this was reflected in a name change, to *Dororo and Hyakki-maru*. Director Sugii and a roster of future big-names emphasized a realistic look, making a virtue out of the monochrome production. Tezuka originally intended to make the show in color (and even made a color pilot) but was prevented from doing so by the low budgets approved by Fuji TV. The story has been cited as a major influence on one of the 1990s' best-selling manga, Hiroaki Samura's *Blade of the Immortal*. The *Dororo* manga was also the inspiration for the console game released in English as *Blood Will Tell*. The live-action film *Dororo* (2007), directed by Akihiko Shiota, reimagined the title character as a young woman, rather than a young girl.

DORORON ENMA
1973. JPN: *Dororon Enma-kun*. TV series. DIR: Kimio Yabuki, Keisuke Morishita, Takeshi Shirato, Fusahito Nagaki, Tomoharu Katsumata, Satoshi Dezaki. SCR: Masaki Tsuji, Tadaaki Yamazaki, Shunichi Yukimuro, Masami Uehara. DES: Kimio Yabuki. ANI: Kazuhide Tomonaga, Kazuo Mori, Yoshinori Kanemori. MUS: Hiroshi Tsutsui. PRD: Dynamic Planning, Toei, Fuji TV. 25 mins. x 25 eps.
All the obvious hallmarks of a production from Go Nagai, creator of **DEVILMAN**, as the King of Hell discovers that several of his Earthbound minions are not causing mayhem but secretly plotting to overthrow

him. He sends his nephew, Little Enma, to solve the problem, and Little Enma teams up with miniskirted Yukiko, daughter of the Snow Princess (see JAPANESE FOLK TALES), and Kappael the water-demon (a *kappa*) to form the Japanese Monster Patrol. Enma also has a sentient hat called Chapeau, a coward who always advises against danger but will always help out his young master in the end. Hiding out at the house of manga fan Tsutomu, who christens them, the group hunts down those who have abused the laws of Hell. Their guide is Count Dracula himself, a disgraced demon who failed to report the conspiracy, and who sulkily acts as Enma's Tokyo guide despite resenting having to take orders from a little brat. "Dororon" is Japanese onomatopoeia for the sound of a spell occurring, loosely approximated by "Kapow!" See also the substantially different DEMON PRINCE ENMA.

DORVACK

1983. JPN: *Tokuso Kihei Dorvack*. AKA: *Dolvack; Special Powered Armor Battalion Dorvack; Dolbuck*. TV series. DIR: Hisataro Oba. SCR: Kazumi Koide, Keiji Kubota, Kenji Terada, Narimitsu Taguchi, Satoshi Namiki, Yoshihisa Araki. DES: Osamu Kamijo, Torao Arai. ANI: Hiroshi Yoshida, Mamoru Hamatsu, Osamu Kamijo, Tamotsu Tanaka. MUS: Masahiro Ikumi. PRD: Ashi Pro, Fuji TV. 25 mins. x 36 eps
1999. An alien civilization in search of a new homeworld attacks Earth. Our last line of defense against the alien technology is the Dorvack Unit—three young pilots from France and Japan, under the command of Colonel Takagi.

The success of GUNDAM as an extended advertisement for the must-have boys' toys of the season led to a flood of ingenious toy robots and imitative TV shows. Not all went on to enjoy such enduring acclaim, but even fewer actually broke a toy company. *Dorvack*'s lack of success took down Takatoku. The series didn't appeal to young viewers, and their high-quality scale model toys refused to move off the shelves. If this had been the company's only bad bet things might have been different, but it followed poor sales on merchandise from ORGUSS and *Sasurygar* (BRYGAR), and the company went under. Hasbro acquired the molds for two of the high-end toys and

released them as part of the TRANSFORMERS line, while U.S. toy firm Select repackaged a pile of Variable Machine stock as *Convertors*.

DOTANBA'S MODERN MANNERS

1984. JPN: *Dotanba no Manner*. AKA: *Last-Minute Manners*. TV series. DIR: Hiroshi Yoshida. SCR: Tomoko Misawa, Osamu Murayama, Saburo Goto. DES: Sanpei Sato. ANI: Tadao Wakabayashi. MUS: N/C. PRD: Fuji TV, Eiken. 6 mins. x 284 eps.
An introduction to etiquette through the hapless antics of Mr. Dotanba, who manages to put his foot in it in social situations. Gems of life-saving wisdom include tips on how to use a toilet, what *not* to say to your coworkers, how to avoid getting slapped by pretty girls, and exactly what to do to make foreign business trips go wrong. Based on a four-panel strip by Sanpei Sato in the *Asahi Shinbun* newspaper. Another Sato strip was released as *Video Manga: Yuhi-kun* (1984), although it was not technically "anime," consisting of narration over still panels. The same team went on to make the even more successful KOTOWAZA HOUSE, a set of tips for health and well-being.

DOTERAMAN

1986. TV series. DIR: Shinya Sadamitsu, Hiroshi Yamada, Yoshiyuki Suga. SCR: Takao Koyama, Toshiki Inoue, Yoshiyuki Suga. DES: Mayori Sekijima, Yoshio Mizumura. ANI: Yoshio Mizumura, Chuichi Iguchi. MUS: Kohei Tanaka. PRD: Tatsunoko. 25 mins. x 20 eps.
Shigeru Suzuki is an everyday salaryman at an everyday Tokyo company in an everyday part of town with an interdimensional gateway to a world of demons. As devils with punning names try to invade the planet, Shigeru and the demon hunter Zukan-Socknets recruit Hajime Sato and his friend Mariko Nakamura to don superhero costumes and fight back.

DOUBLE WISH

2004. JPN: *W-Wish*. TV series. DIR: Osamu Sekita. SCR: Katsumi Hasegawa. DES: Yasunari Nitta. ANI: Picture Magic, Trinet Ent. MUS: Ryo Sakai. PRD: Princess Soft, TV Kanagawa. 12 mins. x 13 eps.
The Tonho twins, Junna and his sister Senna, have lived alone in their family home since their parents died some years ago. They attend Sakurahama Private High

School where Junna is the target of attention from a number of girls. Then new student Haruhi Inohara turns up claiming to be a childhood friend, but Junna barely remembers her and Senna doesn't want him to—presumably they don't remember LOVE HINA either. Based on a dating game that was itself renowned for featuring early animation work from VOICES OF A DISTANT STAR creator Makoto Shinkai, *DW* was shown on Japanese TV as part of "Princess Hour" with similar story FINAL APPROACH.

DOUBLE-J

2011. TV series. DIR: Azuma Tani. SCR: Tetsuya Fujikawa, Toshihiro Miura. DES: Maru Asakura. ANI: Ichi Domiki, Shinobu Ogawa, Itaru Kishikawa, Keiko Kitayama, Takashi Suzuki. MUS: SLF!! PRD: Asahi Production, Frogman, DLE, NTV. 3? mins. x 11 eps.
At Hajime and Sayo's school, joining an after-school club is mandatory. So when the two find a new club, they check it out and find a strange group handcrafting toothpicks, mats, and other objects. Some crafts and customs die out for a reason, but the Cultural Activity Preservation Club exists to fly in the teeth of reason in this short gag anime based on Eiji Nonaka's 2009 manga, illustrated by Maru Asakura. Part of NTV's YURUANI? anthology show. Honestly, we thought it was going to be about boobs. This is what happens when you have to wade through so much porn.

DOUGRAM: FANG OF THE SUN

1981. JPN: *Taiyo no Kiba Dougram*. AKA: *Fang of the Sun Dougram; Sun Fang Dougram*. TV series. DIR: Ryosuke Takahashi, Takeyuki Kanda. SCR: Ryosuke Takahashi, Hiroyuki Hoshiyama, Yuji Watanabe, Ryohei Suzuki, Sukehiro Tomita. DES: Soji Yoshikawa, Kunio Okawara. ANI: Kaoru Izumiguchi. MUS: Toru Fuyuki. PRD: Sunrise, TV Tokyo. 25 mins. x 75 eps.
Planet Deroia claims independence from Earth, and Terran forces set out to put down the revolt. Kurine, son of the chairman of Earth's Federal Congress, sides with the Deroians and becomes a terrorist. Forming the "Fang of the Sun" organization with his friends Rocky, Chico, and Cavina, he operates the Dougram giant war robot designed by the guerrilla leader, Dr. Samaline. Meanwhile, Kurine's father, Donan Kashim, is under threat from

internal machinations as his secretary plots to seize power for himself, and the adoring Lady Daisy sets off to follow Kurine, for whom she has fallen in a big way.

One of many clones of GUNDAM, but one that was a robot debut for VOTOMS–creator and father of "real robot shows" Ryosuke Takahashi.

DOUJIN WORK ∗
2007. TV series. DIR: Kenichi Yatani. SCR: Rei Kunii. DES: Ikutomo Kimishima, Saho Yamane. ANI: Masakazu Saito, Satoru Kiyomaru. MUS: Kazumi Mitome, Kazuo Yoda. PRD: REMIC, Hobunsha, Interchannel-Holon, Media Factory, Toranoana. 14 mins. x 12 eps.
By definition, nobody officially makes *dojinshi*—fan manga and artifacts—for the money, but for clever practitioners there is still some serious money to be made. Najimi Osana loves drawing, and when she hears how much one of her friends makes at a convention, she's tempted to try her hand as a fan artist. This very short show charts her progress in a series of comedic snippets, rendered even shorter by the fact that the opening and ending credit sequences make up a third of the total length of each episode. The animation makes a virtue of being very cheap and basic, with characters jokily shown as flat and paper-thin, vanishing when they turn round, and background characters sometimes rendered in just one color. This is interesting in itself, but it also keeps the focus on the humor—and though there is no nudity and no violence, the jokes and situations are perverted enough to make this show, adapted from Hiroyuki's 2004 *yonkoma* strip cartoon, unsuitable for children.

DOWNLOAD
1992. JPN: *Download: Namu Amida Butsu wa Ai no Uta.* AKA: *Download: Song in Loving Homage to Amida Buddha.* Video. DIR: Rintaro. SCR: Yoshiyuki Suga. DES: Yoshinori Kaneda. ANI: Takao Noda. MUS: Hiroshi Kamiyatsu. PRD: AIC, Artmic. 47 mins.
Shido, a priest, is a genius in two fields—computer hacking and lechery. For the sake of the beautiful Namiho, he takes on evil corporate president Echigoya in a battle of wits and skill. Based on the PC Engine game created by Wataru Nakajima.

DOWNTOWN
1997. TV special. DIR: Kenji Shimazaki. SCR: N/C. DES: Toyoo Ashida. ANI: Toyoo Ashida. MUS: N/C. PRD: Toei, Fuji TV. 30 mins.
Two class clowns take their humor out into the streets, terrorizing members of the public. Falling behind at school, they join the Yoshimoto Talent Agency and become the "fists of Yoshimoto," better known as the comedy duo "Downtown." They make their first TV appearance in 1987 and their own series, *No Job for Kids.* In 1996, they become Japan's richest comedians and are honored the following year by this anime biopic.

DR MOVIE
A Korean animation company, founded in 1990, that often works on outsourced Japanese animation, particularly on the lower rungs of the creative process, such as colors or in-betweening. Its distinctive name, in easy-to-read roman letters, can often be found on the credits of "Japanese" cartoons, including those from Madhouse and Studio Ghibli.

DRACULA: SOVEREIGN OF THE DAMNED ∗
1980. JPN: *Yami no Teio Kyuketsuki Dracula.* AKA: *Dracula: Vampire Emperor of Darkness; Tomb of Dracula.* TV special. DIR: Minoru Okazaki, Akinori Nagaoka. SCR: Tadaaki Yamazaki. DES: Hiroshi Wagatsuma. ANI: Hiroshi Wagatsuma. MUS: Seiji Yokoyama. PRD: Toei, TV Asahi. 81 mins.
In modern-day Boston, Domini (Delores) is offered in sacrifice as a bride of Lucifer by the occultist Lupeski, but she is stolen away by Dracula. At first intending to drink her blood, the vampire instead falls in love with her. Wheelchair-bound Quincy (Hans) Harker and Rachel van Helsing, the son and granddaughter of Dracula's old enemies, realize that some Boston "murders" are his handiwork. They recruit Frank Drake, a descendant of Dracula ashamed at his ancestor's evil, as a vampire hunter. Months later, on Christmas Eve, Domini gives birth to Dracula's son, Janus. Lupeski, who has been informed of Dracula's true identity, offers to baptize Janus, cornering Dracula in a church. Dracula evades the attack, but Lupeski accidentally shoots and kills the infant Janus. Dracula flees, and, having

lost her son and lover, Domini plans to kill herself. However, God brings Janus back from the dead (as a fully grown man) in order to create the ultimate vampire hunter. Before Janus can kill his father, Dracula and Domini are transported to Hell by Satan, for whom their love is an unbearable abomination. Satan blasts Dracula into ashes, but Domini's holy love resurrects Dracula once more, this time as a *mortal.* When Lilith (Lila), a New York vampire created by Dracula, refuses to bite him to restore his immortality, Dracula flees to Transylvania. Dueling with the new Lord of the Vampires, Dracula reasserts his authority and saves peasant children from walking corpses. Despite signs that Dracula has rejected evil, the vampire hunters locate him, and Harker kills both himself and Dracula with a bomb hidden in his wheelchair. Frank and Rachel admit their feelings for one another, and Janus flies home to tell Domini the news. His divine mission accomplished, Janus is restored to infant form to be raised by Domini.

A remarkably faithful adaptation of the first 50 or so issues of the Marvel Comics *Tomb of Dracula* series. The designs look unorthodox for anime, chiefly because they adhere to the original comic artwork by Gene Colan, though neither Colan nor the comic writer Marv Wolfman are credited in the animated version. Less serious takes on Dracula appear in DON DRACULA and DORORON ENMA. Toei negotiated with Marvel in the 1970s about producing animated versions of several superheroes, though the only product of this was the eventual live-action *Spider-Man* team show. FRANKENSTEIN would follow the next year.

DRAGON AGE: DAWN OF THE SEEKER ∗
2012. JPN: *Dragon Age Blood Mage no seisen.* Movie. DIR: Fumihiko Sori. SCR: Jeffrey Scott. DES: Daisuke Nakayama. ANI: N/C. MUS: Tetsuya Takahashi. PRD: Oxybot, Bioware, EA Games, Funimation, T.O. Entertainment, Inc. 90 mins.
The world is in thrall to the Chantry, a body that controls the use of magic. Their Templar enforcers roam the land hunting Blood Mages, who have sworn to destroy them using their powers over dragons. Another group of warriors called the Seekers defend the Templars. Cassandra is a Seeker, and when she is unjustly framed

and dishonored she sets out to regain her good name and save her world. Based on the *Dragon Age* video-game franchise, this requires no prior knowledge of the world of *Dragon Age*. Anyone who's watched any of the vast library of fantasy anime with arcane titles and multiple hierarchies will be right at home here. Unfortunately anyone with the remotest interest in plot, character, or animation won't be. This is a predictable story about tedious characters, so cheaply animated it should have fallen off the back of a pirate ship rather than coming out of a studio. Characters talk without mouth movements in quite a few anime, but not moving their hands when they reach for objects is a new low—or maybe we're supposed to assume sleight of hand because it's magic. CG and lighting are particularly poor. If you love the game, we recommend you stick to playing it. If you don't, the anime is unlikely to change your mind.

DRAGON BALL *

1986. TV series, movies. DIR: Minoru Okazaki, Daisuke Nishio, Kazuhisa Takenouchi, Katsumi Endo, Haruki Iwanami, Akinori Nagaoka. SCR: Yasushi Hirano, Toshiki Inoue, Takao Koyama, Michiru Shimada, Yuji Endo, Tetsuo Imazawa, Tatsuo Higashino, Mitsuo Hashimoto. DES: Tadamasa Tsuji, Yuji Ikeda. ANI: Minoru Maeda, Ryukichi Takauchi, Masayuki Uchiyama. MUS: Shunsuke Kikuchi. PRD: Fuji TV, Toei. 25 mins. x 153 eps., 45 mins. x 3 films, 25 mins. x 291 eps. (DBZ), ca. 45–80 mins. x 14 films, 25 mins. x 64 eps. (DBGT), 25 mins. x 97 eps. (DBZK), 85 mins. (m).

Son Goku (Sun Wu-Kong) is an orphan martial artist, taught by the Master Kamesennin (Roshi) and enlisted by Bulma, a pretty girl whose father owns the Capsule invention corporation, to help her search for the seven legendary Dragon Balls. If brought together in the presence of the dragon god, Shen Long (Shin Long), these balls will grant a single wish. The two assemble a band of pilgrims, and, with time out for many martial arts tournaments and fights with divine beings, slowly gather the seven orbs. Members include Yamcha the highwayman; his shapeshifting feline partner, Pooal; Oolong the pig; Goku's future wife, Chichi; and Goku's Buddhist classmate, Krilyn. They must

also fight off other groups, including the Red Ribbon organization, which wishes to change the space-time continuum by destroying Goku. Eventually, the high demon Piccolo uses the Dragon Balls to rejuvenate himself, then kill Shen Long, while Goku and his gang travel to another world to use *their* Dragon Balls instead and prevent the alien overlord Frieza from getting them himself.

Tiring of his DOCTOR SLUMP and seeking a clean break from Western inspirations, creator Akira Toriyama plucked elements from JOURNEY TO THE WEST for this follow-up. Redeveloping his early strip *Dragon Boy*, which incorporated Jackie Chan homages, he published *Dragon Ball* in 1984, and the series was soon animated. With a reset-to-zero gimmick in the balls' unerring habit of scattering themselves throughout the universe and taking a year to recharge, the anime was able to stretch itself out for a formidable run, becoming one of the smashes of the late 1980s. It was less successful in the U.S., where only 26 episodes were shown before the distributors Funimation ditched the rest of the series and relaunched with *DBZ* (see below, though in 2001 they announced they would go back and fill in the gap).

Short "movie" versions followed as part of double and triple bills, beginning with Nishio's *DB: Legend of the Dragon* (1986), in which Goku fights the evil Pasta and Pongo. The same director made *DB: Sleeping Beauty in the Magic Castle* (1987), while Takenouchi took over for the final film, *DB: Marvelous Magical Mystery* (1988), in which the cast of *DB* wanders into *Doctor Slump*'s Penguin Village for a cross-over. All formed parallel stories designed not to interfere with the continuity of the series, which eventually finished in 1989.

The *DB* sequel, *DBZ*, jumps three years into the future when an older Goku is now married with a son, Gohan. Because this is where many foreign-language versions begin, early episodes often seem like a massive class reunion at which the viewer knows nobody. Goku is attacked by the alien Raditz, who reveals that Goku is his brother, a Sayajin alien, sent to destroy the planet many years ago. Goku refuses to blow up his adopted home and opposes the invading Sayajin, dying and then being reborn as a blond-haired "Super Sayajin."

Violence and some nudity were cut for the U.S. release, but even in this bowdlerized form, the series remained popular.

This series also had a thriving series of short "movie" spin-offs, beginning with *DBZ* (1989) and then following with two a year, one for each major school holiday. These included *The World's Strongest* and *Dead Zone* (both 1990, and released in the U.S. following the success of the *DBZ* TV series), *Super Sayajin Son Goku* and *Tree of Might* (both 1991, and U.S. releases), *Collision: Billion Powered Warriors* and *Extreme Battle: Three Super Sayajin* (both 1992), *Ignite! Burning Fight! Greater Fight! Super Conflict Fight!*, and *Galaxy Flex! Very Threatening Guy* (both 1993), *Dangerous Duo! Super Warriors Never Rest* and *Super Warrior Destructive Fist: I Am the Victor* (both 1994), *Return Fusion! Goku and Vegeta* and *Strike Out Dragon Punch: Who'll Get Goku?* (both 1995), and, at last, the 80-minute feature *The Strongest Way* (1996).

DBZ came off the air in 1996, a few months after Toriyama pleaded exhaustion and stopped drawing the manga. Rebranded as *Dragon Ball G(rand) T(our)* the following month, it featured the return of arch-nemesis Emperor Pilaf with yet another set of Dragon Balls. The emperor accidentally wishes for Goku to be a child once more, so the new kiddie-friendly Goku sets out on another galactic adventure with Pan (his granddaughter) and an older version of Trunks (son of Bulma and Goku's alien nemesis-turned-buddy Vegeta). Directed by Osamu Kasai, the new series seemed to have lost the magic and ended in November 1997. Tellingly, this was also the same time as Toriyama's *Doctor Slump* was brought back on air, perhaps showing that the artist wasn't quite so tired of his original creation after all. The story also exists in a tacky live-action 1996 Cantonese adaptation, *DB: The Movie*, directed by Joe Chan, and a disappointing Hollywood outing, *Dragonball Evolution* (2009), directed by James Wong.

Dragon Ball remains a perennial anime franchise with a long afterlife in other countries, and an artistic heritage that has also been maintained by an online game in East Asia. The series was resurrected as *DBZ Kai* (2009), which repurposed footage from *DBZ*, digitally cleaning it up and selectively editing it to conform closer to the manga version. The planned 98-episode run was truncated at 97 due to the 2011 Great East Japan Earthquake, while on video and repeat broadcasts, much of the soundtrack was replaced due to an unspecified copyright issue. The anime feature *DBZ:Battle of Gods* (2013, *DBZ: Kami to Kami*) is a midquel to the original *DBZ* manga, taking place in the middle of a decade-long gap between chapters 517 and 518 of the manga.

DRAGON CENTURY *

1988. JPN: *Ryuseiki*. Video. DIR: Hiroyuki Kitazume. SCR: Sho Aikawa. DES: Hiroyuki Kitazume. ANI: Hiroyuki Etsutomo. MUS: Michiaki Kato. PRD: AIC. 30 mins. x 2 eps.
Miserable teenager Riko wishes for her city to be destroyed. Dragons appear in the sky from an unknown dimension but are killed by government forces. A lone survivor, the baby dragon Carmine, is reared in secret by Riko and former soldier Shoryu. Demons appear in the sky, summoned by the impurity of human hearts, and Carmine reveals that with the dragons sent to oppose them now dead, Riko will soon get her apocalyptic wish. Riko changes her mind and rides Carmine to defeat the demon king. As Riko breathes her last, the sky cracks open, filled with dragons come to defeat evil.

With teen angst and interdimensional holocaust, this forerunner of **EVANGELION** had an afterthought sequel set 300 years after the invasion. On a traumatized Earth, another young girl, Lucillia, wishes to avenge her father's death in the dragon-fighting tournament and enlists the help of Carmine (now known as Vermilion) in doing so. From an idea by Ryukihei, creator of the *Dragon Wars* manga.

DRAGON CHRONICLE

1989. JPN: *Maryu Senki*. AKA: *War Chronicle of Magical Dragons*. Video. DIR: Tatsuya Okamoto. SCR: Junichi Watanabe. DES: Naoyuki Onda. ANI: Naoyuki Onda. MUS: Tadamasa Yamanaka. PRD: AIC. 30 mins. x 2 eps.
A mixture of Oriental history and legend in the spirit of **YOTODEN** and **DARK MYTH**, as Miki Chiyoko, modern-day descendant of an ancient clan expunged from Japanese history books by a jealous emperor, summons one of the four Chinese creatures responsible for defending Earth. Conjoin-

ing with the Blue Dragon, he discovers that the three other beasts have scattered into other bodies, and he must find them if he wants to join forces with them. The others are revealed as drunken priest Gendo (Black Warrior), handsome potter Hiyu (White Tiger), and pretty Japanese teenager Shizue (Vermilion Sparrow), who all stand against Miki as he tries to enlist them in a scheme of evil. ◐Ⓥ

DRAGON CRISIS *

2011. TV series. DIR: Hideki Tachibana. SCR: Hideyuki Kurata, Masayuki Kurata. DES: Masashi Ishihama. ANI: Masashi Ishihama, Kyoko Kametani, Mariko Emori, Momoko Makiuchi, Shogo Morishita, Takenori Tsukuma, Tomoaki Kado. MUS: Makoto Miyazaki. PRD: Studio DEEN, Studio Tulip, Studio Liberty, Starchild, Yomiuri, Kids Station, Dax. 22 mins. x 12 eps.
Born in a fantasy world, Ryuji has a special talent—he can manipulate magical objects. His feisty cousin Eriko drags him into a scheme to rob some dangerous traffickers. The loot turns out to be a girl—or rather, a dragon-girl—and Ryuji doesn't need any special skills to manipulate her because she falls for him right away. The alien girlfriend is only one of the pile of clichés under which this anime staggers. There's the kid living alone as his parents pursue their own careers. There's the childhood love, incredibly powerful but conveniently forgotten until the story needs it. There's the sexualized heroine who looks underage, but isn't really human, as if that makes it perfectly normal. There are canyons of cleavage. There's the fact that even the seemingly hostile girls really like Ryuji, from which you will discern that this is a harem anime (**ROMANCE AND DRAMA**), only with dragons and a *Lord of the Rings* reference. Nothing in the art, animation, or music compensates for the shortcomings of plot and character. Based on Kaya Kizaki's 2007 book series of the same name, illustrated by Itsuki Akata. ◐

DRAGON DRIVE *

2002. TV series. DIR: Akira Yoshimura, Isao Tokoyushi, Megumi Yamamoto, Toshifumi Kawase, Yuichi Wada. SCR: Koichi Taki, Naruhisa Arakawa, Toshiki Inoue. DES: Takahiro Umehara, Takahiro Yamada. ANI: Minoru

Kouno, Noriuki Fukuda, Takahiro Umehara, Yoshikai Hatano, Yoshiya Yamamoto. MUS: N/C. PRD: Madhouse, NAS, TV Tokyo. 25 mins. x 38 eps.
Reiji Ozora is a typical slacker teenager, dragged by his friend (and would-be girlfriend) Maiko to a secret arcade where he discovers a passion for the VR game Dragon Drive. The object of the game is to train and fight with virtual reality dragons, constructed using a player's genetic code as the building blocks—like a DNA-centric version of the old Bar-Code Battlers. At first, Reiji's dragon Chibisuke looks like a runt: a tiny snow-white bundle of cuteness that baffles the staff, so presumably none of them have heard of Anne McCaffrey's novel *The White Dragon* (1978), with which we are sure any similarities are purely coincidental. When Chibisuke gets into action, he turns out to have impressive firepower in what begins as yet another predictable gaming tale framed along the lines of **POKÉMON** and its ilk. However, a few episodes along, *DD* suddenly adopts a new direction redolent of **EXPER ZENON** and *The Last Starfighter*, with Reiji transported to the fantasy world of Rikyu where the dragons are real. He is soon entering Chibisuke in gladiatorial combats in Rikyu, but is forced to deal with problems back home when a rival returns to Earth with some of the precious Dragonite element. The usual rounds of challenges, counter-challenges, and battles to save the world ensue, and two years later, in **LEGENDZ**, they all ensue again.

DRAGON FIST

1991. Video. DIR: Shigeyasu Yamauchi. SCR: N/C. DES: Shingo Araki, Michi Himeno. ANI: Hideki Kazushima. MUS: Kenji Kawai. PRD: Agent 21. 40 mins.
Chinese transfer student Ling Fei-Long is attacked by boys at his new school and saved by the female martial arts student Yuka. Later, at a karate tournament, Ling discovers that Yuka is a clone, part of a secret military project. But Ling has a secret of his own—he is a member of one of four clans in the Chinese mountains, descended from mythical beasts (in his case, the White Dragon) and endowed with psychic powers. He has been banished to Japan for killing a human, but his past is catching up with him. Based on a manga by Shu

Katayama, serialized in *Wings* magazine, mixing romance and rough stuff.

DRAGON HALF *

1993. Video. DIR: Shinya Sadamitsu. SCR: Shinya Sadamitsu. DES: Masahiro Koyama. ANI: Masahiro Koyama. MUS: Kohei Tanaka. PRD: Production I.G. 30 mins. x 2 eps.

Ruth the dragon slayer falls in love with a dragon, and they settle down and produce a manic offspring called Mink, the titular dragon-half. The evil king plots to murder Ruth and take her as wife for himself. Mink and her friends are obsessed with Dick Saucer, an idol singer who moonlights as a dragon slayer. They try to get into his concert but are thwarted by Mink's rival, Princess Vina, a half-blob girl resentful of her genetic inheritance. Eventually, Saucer squares off against Mink and is defeated with a laxative potion that sends him scurrying to the toilet. Based on a 1989 manga by Ryusuke Mita, *Dragon Half* is a fan favorite and deservedly so, with an energetic sense of fun that switches constantly between normal and squashed-down cartoon versions of the characters, playful satire straight out of Warner Bros. cartoon comedies like *Road Runner*, and a very Japanese sense of humor that includes children in a medieval village having to forage for food before they can listen to their new CD. Remembered less for its genuinely zany action than for the closing theme, which features Mink (played by **SAILOR MOON**–actress Kotono Mitsuishi) singing a song about cooking to the tunes of Beethoven's fifth, seventh, and ninth symphonies. It still makes the authors laugh even now; what can we say?

DRAGON KNIGHT *

1991. Video. DIR: Jun Fukuda, Kaoru Toyooka. SCR: Kinuyo Nozaki, Akira Hatta. DES: Ako Sahara, Akira Kano. ANI: Yuma Nakamura. MUS: Torsten Rasch. PRD: Agent 21. 30 mins. (v1), 45 mins. (v2), 30 mins. x 4 eps. (*Wheel*).

Freelance adventurer Takeru Yamato is caught raiding the palace kitchen of Strawberry Fields, a realm that seems to be inhabited entirely by beautiful, buxom women. Recognized as the prophesied hero, he is granted his parole in exchange for performing a task for the queen. The realm's goddess has been turned to stone

and her tower taken over by the evil Overlord and his five Dragon Knights, who have captured all of the (female) warriors sent against them (the men are killed out of hand). In order to restore the realm's prosperity, Takeru must invade the tower, defeat the Knights and their Overlord, and reclaim from each of them a magical gem, the six of which when returned will revive the goddess; he is also to free the captives. Motivated more by lechery than a desire to escape prosecution, Takeru sets off accompanied by a guide, Luna, and his trusty instant camera, the better to record the spoils of war: the freed captives. Based on the Masato "elf" Hiruta computer game in which defeating the monsters was rewarded by pictures of girls in various states of undress. The North American release is beset by half-truths and prevarications—the running time is listed as 45 minutes rather than the actual 30; it was released under the licenser's adult label, SoftCel Pictures, even though it is at most (rather soft) soft-core porn, with no actual sex; and the ad copy states that it is "Completely UNCUT!," despite having never been edited in the first place.

In Kaoru Toyooka's sequel, *Dragon Knight 2: Another Night on the Town* (1995, *Dragon Knight Gaiden: Sexual Grade Up Kaiteiban*; lit. *Dragon Knight Side Story: Sexual Upgrade Revised Edition*), Takeru saves the pickpocket Jody from the thugs she has just robbed, only to eventually discover that the young "boy" is actually a woman, Jodis, who duly seduces him, shortly before she is kidnapped by an evil bishop in search of a magic potion (well, powder, although the cast do not seem to know the difference).

In 1998 Pink Pineapple produced a four-episode sequel, *Dragon Knight: Wheel of Time* (*Dragon Knight 4*), based on the fourth game in the series. Not to be confused with the unrelated **LORD OF LORDS: DRAGON KNIGHT** or with **YAMATO TAKERU**, which is slightly less unfaithful to Japanese myth. ⓃⓋ

DRAGON LEAGUE *

1993. TV series. DIR: Nobuhiro Takamoto, Takashi Yamaguchi. SCR: Hideki Mitsui, Kenichi Araki. DES: Kazuyuki Kobayashi. ANI: Kazuyuki Kobayashi, Hideo Kudasaka, Junichi Shoji. MUS: N/C. PRD: Studio Gallop, Fuji TV. 25

mins. x 39 eps.

In a fantasy world populated by humans, animals, and dinosaurs, religion is based on soccer. Amon boasts that he is the greatest player in the world and trains his son, Tokio, in the forest until the boy is good enough to be considered "the second-greatest." Amon takes his son to the kingdom of Elevenia, whose soccer team has won the Dragon League five years in a row. Settling an old rivalry, Amon is challenged to a rematch by Elevenia's star player, Leon Legacius, who defeats him with the Golden Ball and turns him into a small dragon. If Tokio is ever to see his father in human form again, he must take over the local junior team and transform its players into winners, in a bizarre combination of **DRAGON BALL** and **CAPTAIN TSUBASA**. Tokio's relationship with Leon undergoes a transformation after Tokio defeats him in sudden-death overtime playoffs—Leon becomes Tokio's mentor and later team coach when they are called upon to play against the hellspawn Warriors of Darkness. A similar angle on sports-as-worship appears in **GALACTIC PIRATES**, though later episodes take a far darker turn. Presaging **BATTLE ATHLETES**, the entire religion is revealed as an attempt to hold off invasion—*real* dragons from an alternate dimension have given King Win of Elevenia a single generation to train a team that can hold off their champion players. The grand finale features a literal death match, as stone "Death Dragons" destroy a city every time the dragon-team scores a goal, while Tokio's team desperately fights a losing battle.

DRAGON PINK *

1994. Video. DIR: Wataru Fujii, Hitoshi Takai. SCR: Itoyoko. DES: Ayako Uchimi. ANI: N/C. MUS: N/C. PRD: Pink Pineapple, AIC. 25 mins. x 3 eps.

A fantasy sex romp parodying contemporary computer role-playing games, about slave girl Pink, who put on the cursed Panties of Torajima and literally became a sex kitten. Pink and her master Santa, along with sorceress Pierce and barbarian Bobo, make up an adventuring party à la *Dungeons and Dragons*. In episode 1, Santa and company must investigate the disappearances of young girls from the North Forest of Tajif. Episode 2 finds the party pawning Pink at an inn as insurance on their tab, only to have to rescue her from being sacrificed by a cult to their demon goddess when the innkeeper sells her prematurely. The final part introduces a Mink look-alike (see **DRAGON HALF**), whose friends are in need of rescuing from the dungeon of evil snake-woman Nymphomania.

Based on the Itoyoko manga, serialized in *Penguin Club* and *Hot Shake* magazines, that quickly spawned a computer game, a garage kit, this inevitable anime adaptation, and the question on everyone's lips—was "dragon" '90s Japanese slang for "soft-core"? **LNV**

DRAGON RIDER *

1995. Video. DIR: Katsuma Kanazawa. SCR: Tetsuya Taiseki. DES: Tomo Kino. ANI: N/C. MUS: N/C. PRD: Pink Pineapple. 30 mins. x 2 eps.

In Carnus village, the beautiful Callis is powerless to prevent the death of her mother, though she herself is saved by Ryke, a would-be dragon rider searching for a suitable mount. In this porno anime based on a manga in *Comic Papipo*, Callis transforms into a Red Dragon when she gets passionate or angry, and a different kind of mounting soon ensues. **NV**

DRAGON SLAYER *

1992. JPN: *Dragon Slayer: Eiyu Densetsu: Oji no Tabitachi*. AKA: *Dragon Slayer: Legend of Heroes: Voyages of the Prince*. Video. DIR: Tadayuki Nakamura. SCR: Kenichi Matsuzaki. DES: Ken Ishikawa, Hisashi Hirai. ANI: Hisashi Hirai. MUS: Fujio Sakai. PRD: Amuse Video. 30 mins. x 2 eps.

Faaren is a peaceful and happy realm ruled by a wise king, until the Demon Lord Ackdam invades with his black legions and terrifying dragon, killing the king and capturing the queen. Aswel's last brave old knight, Rias, spirits young Prince Sirius to safety. Ten years later, the teenaged Sirius returns to help Faaren's peasants overthrow Ackdam, slaying Ackdam's demon-baron Zanji at a mine. In revenge, Ackdam sends his chief henchman, Zagi, who transforms into a giant fire-breathing dragon. Zagi slays Rias and captures Sirius. But Sirius is rescued from Ackdam's dungeon by Ryunan, a brave knight from a neighboring kingdom, who is organizing

Faaren's peasant rebellion. Sirius is taken to the rebellion's headquarters under the command of Rias's twin brother, Aaron (a good way to have a tragic death scene without losing the character). Aaron's granddaughter, the tomboyish Sonya (combination comic relief and love interest), a wizard-in-training, nurses Sirius back to health and demands to join the boys in slaying Ackdam's orcish minions. The rebellion grows so serious that Ackdam threatens to execute Queen Felicia the next day if Sirius does not surrender. This sets the deadline for the final attack on Ackdam's castle. In preparation, Sonya has Sirius escort her to "the abandoned Temple of the Old Ones" (apparently copied from photos of Mayan temple ruins) where she can get a mystic weapon that will ensure Ackdam's defeat. She does not tell Sirius that the weapon is a dragon which she will animate with her soul, giving up her human form forever.

At the grand climactic battle, supporting-character wizard Roe reveals that he and Ackdam were classmates in magic school, and it is his duty to personally destroy Ackdam for betraying his vows to use his powers for good. The Sonya-dragon kills the Zagi-dragon, and the strength of Sirius's love for Sonya restores her human body. At the last minute, Ackdam breaks free of Roe and flees. While the rest of the party sets off in pursuit, leading-man Sirius elects to stay behind with his mother and help rule the kingdom, in the only unexpected twist to a standard fantasy template. Based on a game in the *Legend of the Heroes* franchise from Nihon Falcom; see also LEGEND OF THE HEROES: TRAILS IN THE SKY.

An early release for the U.S. company Urban Vision, *DS* features an early example of so-bad-it's-good dialogue, with priceless gems such as "Your reign of terror is nearing its end, you dog!" and the unforgettable "Now you die, hellspawn creature!"

DRAGON WARRIOR *

1989. JPN: *Dragon Quest*. TV series, movie. DIR: Rintaro, Takayuki Kanda, Katsuhisa Yamada, Nobutaka Nishizawa. SCR: Takashi Yamada, Sukehiro Tomita, Nobuaki Kishima. DES: Akira Toriyama, Yasushi Nagaoka. ANI: Takeyuki Kanda, Hiroshi Kanazawa. MUS: Koichi Sugiyama. PRD: Studio Comet, Toei,

Fuji TV. 25 mins. x 42 eps. (TV1), 25 mins. x 46 eps. (TV1), 40 mins. (m1), 40 mins. (m2), 45 mins. (m3).

Sixteen-year-old Abel, sorcerer Janac, and Daisy the swordswoman are in search of eternal life, for which they will have to drink a dragon's blood. Baramos is their enemy, a creature from the undersea kingdom of Estarkh so accustomed to pollution that it is unable to tolerate clean water. Seeking to summon the Great Dragon to lay waste to the world, Baramos kidnaps Abel's childhood sweetheart, Tiala, who is the guardian of the summoning jewel "the Red Stone."

Based on the 1985 *Dragon Quest* computer game created for the MSX computer and NES console, several games and the first part of the anime, *DQ: Legend of Abel*, were released in the U.S. by Saban but sank without a trace. In Japan, anime and game were far more successful, kicking off the vogue for computerized "role-playing games" that would culminate in FINAL FANTASY and POKÉMON. The U.S. dub by Saban ended after 13 shuffled episodes, with the party reaching the Tower of Najimi. It also replaced the soundtrack and some of the series' more adult elements: a scene in Port Myla where Abel is propositioned by a whore is altered to an unconvincing conversation about bullfighting.

The series went much further in Japan, following the *Legend of Abel* story arc in 1991 with the *Adventure of Dai*. Set, like LODOSS WAR, suitably long after an earlier legend, it features Dai, a young boy raised on the island of Demurin, where many monsters were said to have been banished by an ancient hero. The sorcerer Aban and his apprentice Poppu arrive on the island, looking for the demon lord Hadora, who is coming back from the dead. Aban sacrifices himself to save Dai and Poppu, and the boys continue Aban's quest. Dai's adventures were much longer-running than his predecessor's and also spun off into Yoshiki Shibata's 40-minute feature version *DQ: Disciple of Aban* (1992). Much later, the manga published to explain the plot of another *DQ* game was also made into a feature, *DQ: Crest of Roto* (1996), directed by Tsukasa Sunaga.

DRAGON'S HEAVEN

1988. Video. DIR: Makoto Kobayashi, Shigeru

Fukumoto. scr: N/C. des: Makoto Kobayashi, Toshiyuki Hirano, Kimitoshi Yamane. ani: Itaru Saito. mus: Yasunori Iwasaki. prd: Artmic, AIC. 45 mins.

A great war in 3195 destroys most of civilization when the robot servants of human armies run out of control. The robot Shaian lies dormant for a thousand years after the death of its operator but is accidentally reactivated by a girl, Ikaru, while she scavenges for a living after her family's death at the hands of the Brazilian army. Shaian wishes to avenge himself on the Brazilians' leader, Elmedyne, and enlists the help of the human in order to ensure he operates at top capacity. The victorious couple go off into the ruins together, in an anime with the weirdest robot designs until **EVANGELION**.

DRAGONAR

1987. jpn: *Kiko Senki Dragonar*. aka: *Armored Chronicle Dragonar; Metal Armor Dragonar*. TV series. dir: Takeyuki Kanda. scr: Fuyunori Gobu. des: Kenichi Onuki, Kunio Okawara. ani: Hirokazu Endo, Masami Obari. mus: Toshiyuki Watanabe, Kentaro Haneda. prd: Sunrise, Nagoya TV (TV Asahi). 25 mins. x 48 eps.

The Imperial Giganos Empire is invading planet Earth, and the multiethnic Kain, Tapp, and Lyte, with their female foils, Linda and Rose, steal the Dragonar Metalli-Armor from the enemy and turn it against them. The pesky kids are then "bonded" to their weapons, and the Earth military is forced to work with them, in this series which Sunrise hoped would be the "new **GUNDAM**." It wasn't, though it was certainly an improvement on *Double Zeta Gundam*, which it immediately followed on Japanese TV.

DRAGONAUT: THE RESONANCE *

2007. TV series. dir: Manabu Ono. scr: Atsushi Maekawa. des: Makoto Uno, Junya Ishigaki, Kei Ichikura. ani: Tadashi Sakazaki. mus: Kosuke Yamashita. prd: Gonzo, Konami, NAS. 25 mins. x 25 eps. (TV), 25 mins. (v).

Twenty years ago, Earth was almost destroyed by Thanatos, the asteroid that took out Pluto. The International Solar System Development Agency used a dragon egg found under the ocean to avert the danger, and now dragons are popping up all over the planet and their appetites are

deadly. But mankind has been breeding genetically engineered dragons ever since the destruction of Pluto, and specially selected humans are paired with these dragons to fight the attackers. Ordinary teenager Jin is is saved from death in the shuttle disaster that kills his family, and becomes a Dragonaut, one of the elites who pilot Earth's artificial dragons.

Humans and dragons in partnership have inspired some amazing science fiction, from Anne McCaffrey's *Dragonflight* to Naomi Novik's *Temeraire* series, but Gonzo's show just isn't on that level. The art is lovely, although the CG doesn't work so well—a pity because this detracts from the battle scenes. It looks like a step back from a studio that has proved it can do a great deal better in this area (see **LAST EXILE**.) The characters are less interesting: when every female, even a little girl, is presented as boobs on legs, it's a sign that no other kind of development is likely. The plot is entirely predictable, slowed down to a distracting extent by flashbacks that break the number one rule of narrative by *telling* us why the characters are the way they are, rather than letting them show us. Jin is the most slappable hero in a decade. A 26th episode appeared on the DVD release. **N**

DRAGOON *

1997. jpn: *Ryuki Dengyo*. aka: *Legend of the Dragon Machine*. Video. dir: Kenichi Maejima. scr: Ryota Dezaki. des: Shino Takada, Satoshi Nishimura. ani: Masami Nagata. mus: Harukichi Yamamoto. prd: KSS. 30 mins. x 3 eps.

May has blue hair, red eyes, a corpse-like pallor, and is the key to a powerful military device controlled by her father. She escapes from her captors and bumps into Sedon Calibre, a noble squire who takes up his father's sword and leads her to her destiny. This, it would seem, involves giving her an incongruous stripey hat to wear and some low-rent swashbuckling as they run away from Incompetent Soldiers and The Man Who Almost Killed His Father, while an Annoying Little Sister tags along for comic relief. Characters say things like, "He destroyed my village. He murdered my entire family. He's evil incarnate," and there's a bit of sub-Jedi bullshit about wielding a sword with your heart.

Harmless hokum, marred only by stingy

cost-cutting that renders almost all the battle sequences as freeze-frames or close-ups (presumably the savings were used to throw in a little more fan-service nudity since it seems May has a magical ability that causes her clothes to fall off). Sadly, it only ends with a partial resolution, revealing its origins as a marketing tool designed to drum up interest in the sequel to the original PC game. While the Japanese audience was able to enjoy the spin-off novel, both PC adventures, *and* a radio drama based on the story, U.S. fans are left with a bum deal, though distributor ADV wisely crammed all three episodes onto a single tape. The virtual absence of the titular "dragon machine" artifact is also rather disappointing, as if **AKIRA** had failed to make an appearance in the film that bears his name. Not much better than **PANZER DRAGOON**, but three times as long. **N**

DREAM CRAYON KINGDOM

1997. jpn: *Yume no Crayon Okoku*. TV series. dir: Junichi Sato. scr: Takashi Yamada, Yumi Kageyama. des: Akira Inagami. ani: N/C. mus: N/C. prd: Toei, TV Asahi. 25 mins. x 65 eps.

Princess Crayon must journey to 12 magical points to help her parents from the mountains to the seaside. She meets queens in different kingdoms, all the while traveling through space and time. Each four or five episodes constitute a "month" of both show and broadcast time, and Crayon's adventures are timed to coincide with real events, such as Christmas, New Year's, and the arrival of spring. Based on a children's book by Reimi Fukunaga and drawn by *Moon Bunny Egg Princess*–manga artist Michiru Kataoka. Not to be confused with **CRAYON SHIN-CHAN**!

DREAM DIMENSION HUNTER FANDORA *

1985. jpn: *Mu Jigen Hunter Fandora*. Video. dir: Kazuyuki Okaseko, Shigenori Kageyama. scr: Hirokazu Mizude, Takashi Yamada. des: Hideki Tamura, Eiko Yamauchi. ani: Masahiro Shita, Hiroyuki Ikegami. mus: Nozomu Aoki. prd: Hero Media, Kaname Pro. 45 mins. x 3 eps.

In dimensional year 2002, the ability to warp between new dimensions has created new customs and new criminals. The overworked Dimensional Police Force turns to bounty hunters for help, including Fandora and her partner, Quest (a shape-shifting dragon), who go to the oppressed dimension of Lem in search of rogue crook Red-Eye Geran. Later episodes center on lovers Soto and Fontaine, who are separated when galactic criminal Yog Sothoth destroys the Deadlander dimension. Desiring Fandora's Red Rupee gem, Sothoth tricks Soto into stealing it by telling him that balance can be restored if it is brought to him. Fandora stops Soto before he can unite the Red Rupee with the "Blue God's" Blue Rupee, but she is trapped in Sothoth's lair. Created by **DEVIL-MAN**'s Go Nagai specifically for video. Yog Sothoth is a sly nod to the works of H.P. Lovecraft, also referenced in **ICZER-ONE** and **ARMITAGE III**.

Using many crew members from Go Nagai's Dynamic Productions (hence the Nagai-esque look), *DDHF* was released in an English-dubbed version, by **BAVI STOCK**–producer Hiromasa Shibazaki, who hoped to jump-start an American commercial anime video market by selling an English dub by mail order *from* Japan. The lack of advertising, paucity of U.S. fans at the time, and the high price killed that experiment. However, *DDHF* was not particularly helped by the horrible quality of the dub itself—Fandora and Quest have very artificial, haughty English accents; a medieval innkeeper's voice is a bad W. C. Fields imitation; and the Chief of the Dimensional Police talks like a rural cop from the American South. Compare to **CIPHER**, which was also released in English in Japan but with no intention of reaching the U.S. market.

DREAM EATER MERRY *
2011. JPN: *Yumekui Merry*. TV series. DIR: Shigeyasu Yamauchi. SCR: Hideki Shirane. DES: Masahiro Fujii, Kenji Matsumoto, Yukie Yuki. ANI: Yukie Hiyamizu, Akiko Kumada, Atsushi Saito, Emiko Kobayashi. MUS: Keiichi Oku. PRD: JC Staff, TBS. 30 mins. x 13 eps.
Yumeji Fujiwara can see auras and predict the dreams of others, but his own dreams are getting stranger by the night. The leader of a cat army wants to possess his body to cross from the Dream World to the human realm, and sends his forces after Yumeji every night. Then a cute girl literally falls on top of him. Merry Nightmare is a Dream Demon who's tumbled

out of the Dream World and wants to get back. So far she's been fighting dream monsters in the hope that when they flee back to the Dream World she can follow them, but without success. How is Yumeji going to help her get home again without opening up the way for the forces of evil—especially since they can send him into a dream state at any time? The idea of infiltrating dreams is a well-worn but interesting plot device with many possibilities, few of which are used here. Watch **PAPRIKA** if you want to see it done superbly. JC Staff provides pretty pictures, but the animation is quite limited. At times the script moves at a frantic pace, at other points you may nod off. **N**

DREAM EATER: TSURUMIKU STYLE GAMES PRODUCTION
2011. JPN: *Yume Kui: Tsurumiku Shiki Game Seisaku*. Video. DIR: Hiromi Yokoyama. SCR: Kentaro Mizuno. DES: No'otto Shosakai. ANI: No'otto Shosakai. MUS: N/C. PRD: Toshiyuki Yamamoto, Tsurumiku, Suzuki Mirano. 30 mins. x 2 eps.
The male staff of a porn game company start acting out their products—and during office hours, which, in a Japanese office, is actually rather more shocking than any form of sexual depravity. The sex is nonconsensual, involving either rape or blackmail or both. A well-drawn and designed example of the genre, but very nasty. **NV**

DREAM HUNTER REM
1985. Video. DIR: Satoru Kumazaki, Kiyoshi Nagao, Shinji Okuda. SCR: Shinji Okuda. DES: Kazuaki Mori, Masami Aisakata, Akira Inoue. ANI: Moriyasu Taniguchi, Masahide Yanasawa. MUS: Heitaro Manabe. PRD: Project Team Nagahisa Kikan, Studio Zain. 45 mins. x 3 eps. (v1), 45 mins. x 2 eps. (v2).
The insomniac little girl Rem develops the power to enter other people's dreams and earns a living as a private investigator, accompanied by her dog, Alpha, and cat, Beta, who appear as a puppy and kitten in the real world but transform into a fierce giant wolf and cougar when Rem enters people's dreams. Her first mission is against the "Death God" who appears to be possessing a young girl's dreams and driving Rem to commit murder. In episode 2, she investigates a series of murders at a

high school rumored to be the work of the ghost of a girl who was held prisoner and died in the clock tower. The first series ends with a traditional ghost story, as Rem must fight the jealous spirit of a Taira warrior executed there many centuries earlier. Two further episodes that were pastiches of famous horror novels, *New DHR*, followed in 1990 and 1992, with Okuda writing *and* directing. In the first, a *Dracula* rip-off, Rem must discover why the pretty young Mina has developed sleeping-sickness. In the second, she journeys to the small Alpine city-state of Franken, where a Dr. Victor is troubled by dreams of a robot man called Julian. The sequels had their own subtitles, *The Knights Around Her Bed* (1990, *Yume no Kishi-tachi*) and *Massacre in the Phantasmic Labyrinth* (1992, *Satsuriku no Mugen Meikyu*).

Like **PROJECT A-KO**, *DHR* was originally planned as an erotic video series but released into the mainstream without undue nudity as the creative climate changed during the 1980s. She gets her name from the acronym for "rapid eye movement," a phenomenon of light sleepers. A combination of the magical girl and teen ghost-hunter genres.

DREAM NOTE
2009. Video. DIR: Tomi Tatsuyoshi, Takashi Kondo. SCR: Chibi Eguchi, Akira Nintai (V2). DES: Hayate. ANI: Hayate. MUS: N/C. PRD: schoolzone. 30 mins. x 2 eps.
Imagine if **DEATH NOTE** were *Lust Note*. Undermoon Studio's porn game, with original character designs by the delightfully named Jentoru (or Gentle) Sasaki, inspired this two-part video. Part one revolves around young teacher Masaya and a notebook that turns two unusually well-endowed schoolgirls and their mother into his sex slaves. **N**

DREAM USER
2006. JPN: *Yume Tsukai*. TV series. DIR: Kazuo Yamazaki. SCR: Yasuko Kobayashi. DES: Kiyotaka Nakahara, Shuichi Shimamura, Chikara Nishikura. ANI: Akemi Kobayashi, Noriyuki Fukuda. MUS: Tamiya Terashima. PRD: Madhouse, Pony Canyon. 25 mins. x 12 eps.
Misako and her nieces, 17-year-old Toko and 10-year-old Rinko, have a family store full of cool old toys. They also lead an

organization known as the Dream Users, fighting nightmares that have escaped from human dreams to cause havoc in the world. They can transform toys into weapons and monsters to help their work. The girls' father, Misako's brother, was killed in a dream battle, and now Toko wears his fox mask and is reluctant to go outside the shop except for work. **MYSTERIOUS GIRLFRIEND X**–creator Riichi Ueshiba's original manga is considerably darker and more explicit than the anime, playing up the incestuous attraction between the sisters and Lolita elements, but the TV version aims for a younger audience. It is, unfortunately, not especially memorable, even for the idea of a group of shrine maidens with a toyshop as their shrine, and the glimpses of Thunderbird One and several familiar robots and figurines in the backgrounds.

DREAM-STAR BUTTON NOSE

1985. JPN: *Yume no Hoshi Button Nose*. TV series. DIR: Masami Hata, Toshio Takeuchi, Katsuhisa Yamada, Kazuyuki Hirokawa. SCR: Tomoko Konparu, Hideo Takayashiki, Kenji Terada. DES: Akiyo Hirose, Masami Hata. ANI: Maya Matsuyama, Kazuyuki Omori. MUS: Kohei Tanaka. PRD: Sanrio, TV Asahi. 25 mins. x 26 eps.

The first TV series from the merchandise-led Sanrio studio, *Button Nose* was two years in the making. Button is an eight-year-old girl who lives at the Ichigo research institute. Her father invites space travelers from Hookland on planet Kalinto, but they arrive while he is away, so Button takes his place, accompanied by her pet, Franklyn (a pink kangaroo/mouse). With King Fastener of Hookland, Button sets off on the long journey to Kalinto.

DREAMY URASHIMA

1925. JPN: *Nonki na Tosan Ryugu Mairi*. AKA: *Carefree Father in the Palace of the Dragon King*. Movie. DIR: Hakusan Kimura. SCR: N/C. DES: N/C. ANI: N/C. MUS: N/C. PRD: N/C. ca. 5 mins.

Carefree Father is an old, bespectacled man in a bowler hat, patterned kimono, and black haori overcoat, who loves having fun and shirks work whenever he can. One day he finds himself in a turtle taxi, which takes him underwater to the palace of the Dragon King. There, he is feted and entertained by the Dragon King's beautiful

daughter and her geisha-like serving girls, but the allure soon fades, and he asks to be allowed to return home. As he leaves, the Dragon King's daughter gives him a casket that he should not open, but once home the curious old man is unable to resist peering inside. A demon jumps out and demands that he pay his palace bill. Realizing it was only a dream, Carefree Father resolves to work harder, in a modern refashioning of *Urashima Taro* (see **JAPANESE FOLK TALES**).

"Carefree Father" was the first true manga icon, a comedy figure created by Yutaka Aso for the *Hochi Shinbun* newspaper in January 1924. He enjoyed immense success in a Japan struggling to recover from the catastrophic Great Kanto Earthquake. Carefree Father's popularity was aided greatly by the absence of any copyright enforcement on cartoon characters at the time, spinning off into dolls, character goods, and this one-reel movie, none of which appear to have involved the character's original creator, either creatively or in the sharing of the profits. However, such issues only applied in the world of comics—music copyright enforcement was already much stricter, as the makers of **MADAME BUTTERFLY** would discover to their cost. Our choice of title reflects that used in the English-language program notes to a 21st-century screening at Tokyo's Metropolitan Art Museum.

DRIFTING CLOUDS

1982. JPN: *Haguregumo*. Movie. DIR: Mori Masaki. SCR: Chiku Yamatoya. DES: George Akiyama. ANI: Kazuo Tomisawa, Kuni Tomita, Nobuko Yuasa. MUS: Seiji Yokoyama. PRD: Madhouse, Toei. 91 mins.

A period-drama with real historical figures, in the style of the later **TREE IN THE SUN**. Haguregumo, a merchant in old-time Tokyo, leaves the running of his company to his wife and assistant and drifts "free as a cloud." He saves Ryoma Sakamoto (see **OI! RYOMA**) from an attack in the street, and Sakamoto entertains Haguregumo's family with his vision of a future Japan. Haguregumo's son, Shinnosuke, is inspired by Ryoma. Ryoma's attacker is inspired by Haguregumo, and announces that he plans to renounce his way of life and leave the Shinsengumi organization. Later that year, Haguregumo hears that Ryoma

has been assassinated. Based on George Akiyama's monstrously long-running 1973 manga, still going in *Big Comic*, and placed incongruously on a double bill with the **GOSHOGUN** movie.

DRILAND

2012. JPN: *Tanken Driland*. AKA: *Investigation Driland*. TV series. DIR: Toshinori Fukuzawa. SCR: Miyuki Kurei, Yoichi Takahashi. DES: Yuki Hayashi. ANI: Koji Nashizawa. MUS: Yoshihisa Hirano. PRD: Dentsu, Gree, Toei Animation, TV Tokyo. 25 mins. x 37 eps. (TV1), 25 mins. x 51 eps. (TV2).

In the fantasy realm of Driland, the bored princess Mikoto finally succumbs to temptation and leaves the safety of her palace to participate in treasure hunts. Cute designs are all that really distinguish this from any other generic dungeon crawl (**FANTASY AND FAIRY TALES**), in part because the source material is a cell-phone game that involves exploring a series of generic dungeons.

DROP OF DEW, A

2006. JPN: *Tsuyu no Hito Shizuku: Ueda Shoji no Shashin Sekai o Samayo*. AKA: *A Drop of Dew: Shoji Ueda's Photographs that Woke the World*. Video. DIR: Shiro Sano. SCR: Koizumi Yakumo. DES: N/C. ANI: N/C. MUS: Kazuhiko Kato. PRD: Toei, Gentosha. 36 mins.

This short video looks into the world of photographer Shoji Ueda, who began making photomontages and photocollages before World War II and continued until his death in 2000. Images of prewar and modern Japan bring a whole culture back to haunting life. The words of Koizumi Yakumo—i.e., Lafcadio Hearn, see **ANIMATED CLASSICS OF JAPANESE LITERATURE**—are used as narration. Kato's musical career embraces movie scores, stage music, kabuki, and the Sadistic Mika Band. Part of Toei's *ga-nime* series (**ARGOT AND JARGON**).

DT EIGHTRON

1998. TV series. DIR: Tetsuro Amino. SCR: Hideki Kakinuma, Toshimitsu Himeno. DES: Yoshi Tanaka. ANI: Yoshi Tanaka. MUS: Hiroyuki Nanba. PRD: Sunrise, Fuji TV. 25 mins. x 26 eps.

In the computer-controlled state of Datania, schoolboy Shu resolves to escape from the oppressive city life and joins the resistance movement known as the Returners. He fights Datania with the super-android

Eightron, which was created by applying powerful energies to a pile of junk. *Logan's Run* meets **EVANGELION** in this earnest but hackneyed replay.

DU ZIQUN

1981. JPN: *To Shishun*. TV special. DIR: Hideo Nishimaki. SCR: Takeshi Shudo. DES: Yoshio Kabashima. ANI: Yoshio Kabashima. MUS: Naoki Yamamoto. PRD: Tohoku, TBS. 84 mins.

In late Tang-dynasty China, Du Ziqun's mother, Bailian, is abducted by robbers. Twelve years later, the teenage Ziqun is leading a gang of thieves in nearby Luoyang, but he despairs of humanity and decides to become a hermit, putting himself through trials, including a vow of utter silence. Based on the 1920 short story by Ryunosuke Akutagawa, the story was animated a second time for the *Classic Children's Tales* series (1992) as a 30-minute stop-motion short released straight to video.

DUAL *

1999. JPN: *Dual! Parallel Trouble [Runrun] Adventure*. TV series, video. DIR: Katsuhito Akiyama. SCR: Yosuke Kuroda. DES: Atsushi Okuda, Kenji Teraoka, Yasushi Muraki. ANI: Atsushi Okuda. MUS: Seiko Nagaoka. PRD: AIC, Pioneer, WOWOW. 25 mins. x 13 eps. (TV), 25 mins. x 1 ep (v).

When he uncovers a strange artifact at a construction site, a worker accidentally splits the universe into two parallel continua. In one universe, the artifact is used to develop human technology in strange and new directions; in the other, life continues as normal. Twenty-two years later in the everyday world, Professor Sanada tries to prove the existence of a parallel universe. His daughter, Mitsuki, tells him about the visions of schoolboy Kazuki, who claims to see giant robots fighting in the streets. Accidentally triggering the professor's device, Kazuki finds himself in the parallel universe where the evil Rara is trying to conquer the world. Kazuki also learns that the parallel Prof. Sanada has gotten the UN's backing to create an Earth Defense Command to stop Rara, and that Mitsuki transported to this world the month before. She has had time to introduce herself to the parallel of her father, who is a bachelor in this world and has been too

busy fighting evil to develop a similar parallel world technology to send her home. Sanada accepts the obligation of adopting Mitsuki, also making her a robot pilot in the EDC. When they find that Kazuki has arrived and can also fly a robot, they enlist him, too.

Dual was Pioneer's entry in the race to duplicate **EVANGELION**, stealing plots, moods, characters, shots, and even set designs from the 1995 smash and adding half a dozen pretty girls straight out of their own **TENCHI MUYO!** franchise. The show adds some clever identity crises—Kazuki is the only person who does not exist in the parallel world that includes evil versions of love interest Mitsuki and her mother. With a passionless, suicidal girl (the cyborg D, last remnant of a lost civilization), young pilots forced to share a house, and *Eva*-like robots, its reverse-engineered origins are clear, but the slick marketing savvy of producers Toru Miura and Kazuaki Morijiri ensure that nothing gets taken *too* far. People don't get killed (at least not permanently), jokiness often takes precedence over drama, and a happy ending restores everything to *almost* normal, with Kazuki surrounded by adoring girls. Careful integration of computer graphics makes for some good robot battles, but much of the design in *Dual* seems a little too sparse; the scenes often seem too uncluttered, giving the show a sanitized look to match its sanitized plot. Thankfully, it also lacks *Evangelion*'s messy ending, though after a denouement seemingly shot on the same road-bridge that closes **SERIAL EXPERIMENTS LAIN**, a final episode on video threatens an as-yet-unmade sequel.

DUEL MASTERS *

2002. TV series, movie. DIR: Haruro Suzuki. SCR: Satoru Nishizono, Kenichi Kanemaki, Masanao Akahoshi. DES: N/C. ANI: N/C. MUS: Junichi Igarashi. PRD: Shogakukan. 25 mins. x 48 eps. (TV), ca. 80 mins. (m).

Shobu Kirifuda is a fan of a card game called Duel Masters, in which the monsters on the cards actually come to life and fight. He hopes one day to become as good at the game as his father, who is missing, presumed dead. He is educated in his gaming skills by a mystery man known only as "Knight," and attends big matches in the company of his friends, Rekuta the

eternal loser and Mimi the sparky girl. In the American release of the series, their ability was termed *kaijudo*, the "way of the monster," although this term does not exist in the Japanese original. Remarkable for the enthusiastic way it attempts to make the sight of children playing cards interesting, although the authors dread the day when someone tries to animate paint drying. A manga by Shigenobu Matsumoto was serialized in *Coro Coro Comic*, and a movie version followed in 2005. Compare to **YU-GI-OH**.

DUMPLING BROTHERS, THE

1999. JPN: *Dango San Kyodai*. AKA: *Three Dumpling Brothers*. TV series. DIR: Masahiko Sato. SCR: Masahiko Sato. DES: Masahiko Sato. ANI: Masahiko Sato, Masanobu Uchino, Noriko Akiho. MUS: N/C. PRD: NHK. 3 mins. x ca. 50 eps.

Ichiro Kushidango, middle brother Jiro, and youngest brother Saburo are dumplings who first appeared in a popular song in 1999, inspired by commercial director Masahiko Sato, who wondered which of the three dumplings on his lunchtime skewer was the oldest. It first aired as the "January song" on the children's show *Okaasan to Issho* (*With Mama*), which often uses animation to provide visuals to accompany its tunes. Something in it caught the attention of parents and children; quite possibly a postmodern nostalgia on the part of parents from larger families who knew that their own smaller family units would never boast three siblings—compare to **BUBU CHACHA**, which similarly yearned for the days when children had someone to play with. After the song became a runaway hit, selling more than three million copies in Japan, the brothers were brought back for a series of inserts in the show from October 1999 to March 2004. They sometimes shared the screen with their female friend Mochiyo Sakura (rice cake wrapped in a cherry leaf) and their buddies the Teacup Brothers. Their enemy is the double-flavored ice cream Vanilla and Mocha, while they are occasionally supported by dumpling shop owners as backing dancers. Each episode was very short and implied very limited animation, with basic repetitions easily forgiven by a young audience, although when released out of context on two compilation DVDs, it often simply looked cheap. Some producers believed that it was the food theme that made the difference, leading to imitators like **KAPPAMAKI AND THE SUSHI KIDS**, although such things are nothing new in Japanese animation. Compare to **TOMATO-MAN**.

DUNBINE *

1983. JPN: *Seisenshi Dunbine*. AKA: *Holy Warrior Dunbine, Aura Battler Dunbine*. TV series, video. DIR: Yoshiyuki Tomino, Toshifumi Takizawa. SCR: Yoshiyuki Tomino, Sukehiro Tomita, Yuji Watanabe. DES: Yukien Hirogawa, Yutaka Izubuchi. ANI: Hiroyuki Kitazume. MUS: Katsuyuki Ono, Tatsumi Yano. PRD: Sunrise, Nagoya TV (TV Asahi). 25 mins. x 49 eps. (TV), 75 mins. x 3 eps. (*Tales*), 25 mins. x 3 eps. (*Garzey*), 30 mins. x 6 eps. (*Wings*).

Japanese boy Sho Zama is transported to the alternate world of Byston Well because his human "aura" will make him a powerful robot pilot in Drake Luft's quest to rule the planet. However, Sho defects to the other side and leads the resistance, until his former employers, fighting a rearguard action, open a gateway through to our world and begin a second conquest.

Inspired by *Wings of Lin*, an earlier novel by **GUNDAM**-creator Yoshiyuki Tomino, *Dunbine* shares its stablemate's concentration on big robots (a studio addition not in the original) and heavy character development. It was soon remade by Toshifumi Takizawa as a three-part video series incorporating designs from **PATLABOR**'s Yutaka Izubuchi. The new series, *Aura Battler Dunbine: Tale of Neo Byston Well* (1987), featured more expensive animation and robots with literally scintillating armor. The original Dunbine designer Shott Weapon is thrown through a time warp at the end of the TV series to arrive in Byston Well 700 years later. He brings with him a veritable battalion of Earth weaponry, including a fully laden aircraft carrier, and the locals must form a new resistance to stop him. Although the video series only consisted of 75 minutes of footage, the series was stretched out three times as long with the aid of digest versions of the previous TV episodes.

Much later, in the wake of the similar **ESCAFLOWNE**, Tomino would adapt the robot-free *Wings of Lin* itself into a video anime, the truly awful three-parter *Garzey's*

Wing (1996). Chris, a Japanese teenager, loses half his soul when he is summoned to Byston Well by the priestess Hassan. The Meitomias tribe wishes to escape from Ashigaba slavers, and Chris is to be their champion. He guides them through their flight to their promised land, fighting off Roman-armored, dinosaur-riding Ashigabas, while the Tokyo half of his soul sends telepathic messages about such topics as how to make gunpowder. This show is very cheaply animated and shoddily written, and, though this was the only part of the series to be released in the U.S., the poor quality of the dub makes it almost unwatchable. A further sequel, *Wings of Rean* (2005), was premiered on the Internet in six parts.

DURARARA!! *

2008. AKA: *DRRR*. TV series, video. DIR: Takahiro Omori. SCR: Noboru Takagi, Toshizo Nemoto, Aya Yoshinaga, Ai Ota, Sadayuki Murai. DES: Takahiro Kishida, Tatsuo Yamada, Akira Ito. ANI: Akira Takata. MUS: Makoto Yoshimori. PRD: Brains Base, Aniplex, ASCII Media Works, Hakuhodo DY Media Partners, MBS, MOVIC, Square Enix. 25 mins. x 24 eps. (TV), 25 mins. x 2 eps. (v).

Country boy Mikado Ryugamine moves to the big city and winds up in the heart of more action than he ever imagined. There are the local punks and bullies you get anywhere, the gangs, the human traffickers, the dubious foreigners, the homeless people, the psychopath with a samurai sword—so far, so Tokyo. Then there's the Headless Rider, an Irish biker chick who has a heart of pure gold, but no head. And Anri, his classmate, the target of a mammoth crush for both him and his friend Masaomi. What's a country boy to do? What about facing down a gang, keeping the supernatural in check and trying to keep his new hometown from total meltdown?

Durarara!! resembles **BACCANO**. That can hardly be avoided—both are based on books by Ryogo Narita with illustrations by Suzuhito Yasuda, both have the same director and writer, and both have crazy, jazzy scores. The mad-jazz idiom fits *Durarara!!*'s storyline less easily, but works well with the similar animation style. There's a laid-back feel to the show that contrasts oddly with its darkness. The To-

kyo district of Ikebukuro seen through its eyes is a fascinating urban zoo (compare to **PARANOIA AGENT**), but not somewhere you would want to be after the lights go out. There's also a major shift in emphasis halfway through the show, from a slice-of-life plot that juggles its cast of oddballs with ease and charm, to a tightly focused three-strand emphasis on the points of its teen romance triangle. Overall it feels less coherent and satisfyingly resolved than its sibling, but still enjoyable in its own right. Two unaired episodes from the same team are presented as extras on the DVD release. **V**

DUSK MAIDEN OF AMNESIA *

2012. JPN: *Tasogare Otome*. AKA: *Dusk Maiden*. TV series. DIR: Shin Onuma, Takashi Sakamoto. SCR: Katsuhiko Takayama, Ayumi Sekine. DES: Yukiko Ban. ANI: Yukiko Ban, Yuko Kusumoto. MUS: Keigo Hoashi, Ryuichi Takada. PRD: Silver Link, Media Factory, Square Enix, TO Entertainment. 24 mins. x 13 eps.

Student Teiichi Niya comes to believe classroom myths about a student left for dead several decades earlier in the school's abandoned, derelict wing. This is largely because he meets her ghost, a beautiful girl called Yuko, who cannot remember the date or cause of her death. Inspired to investigate, Teiichi forms a Paranormal Club with Yuko as the "ghost" president, and soon attracts a cabal of schoolgirls who bicker among themselves and compete for his attention. As this synopsis might indicate, a moody and rather stylish take on the hoary clichés of school **GHOST STORIES** is periodically ruined by the injection of tedious teenage flirting. Based on a manga of the same name by "Maybe," serialized in 2009 in the magazine *Gangan Joker*. See also **SANKAREA: UNDYING LOVE**, which ran on television in the same year, and took the "dead girlfriend" idea to questionable extremes.

DVINE [LUV] *

2001. JPN: *D+Vine [Luv]*. Video. DIR: N/C. SCR: N/C. DES: N/C. ANI: N/C. MUS: N/C. PRD: Pink Pineapple. 27 mins. x 4 eps.

Treasure hunter Hyde and his sidekick Sakura go in search of "the treasures of the old world," the first turning out to be a naked girl encased in ice not unlike the one to be found in KAMA SUTRA. Cursed during his misadventures, Hyde is forced to seek an exorcism from local priestess Manatee, who becomes uncontrollably lustful as a result of the spell, and has sex with him in order to calm down. A series of other picaresque encounters soon follow, as Hyde rescues, is rescued, kidnaps, or is kidnapped by a series of women and ends up having sex with them as payment, or as atonement, or as punishment, or simply because they feel like it. Hyde saves a girl from a life-threatening disease, and then eases the side effects of the potion by having sex with her. He is then able to fight the evil wizard Slaine, take his mighty sword Stormbringer (no, really), and find the legacy of the old world. **LNV**

DYNAGIGA

1998. JPN: *Chokido Densetsu Dynagiga*. AKA: *Super Robot Legend Dynagiga*. Video. DIR: Naoyuki Yoshinaga. SCR: N/C. DES: Tada Miura. ANI: Yoshiko Sugai. MUS: N/C. PRD: Studio Deen. 30 mins. x 2 eps.

An anime series that began life on the TV variety program *What's Up, Shibuya?*, it's set in a near future when robots are commonplace and follows the lives and loves of a group of high school girls as they try to get their robot licenses—driving school with giant robots. Allegedly an experiment to discover new talent in voice acting and design, though cynics might suggest that amateur nights always have cheaper staff.

DYOGRAMMATON *

2006. Video. DIR: Junin Machida. SCR: Junin Machida. DES: Kazumitsu Murakami. ANI: Kazumitsu Murakami. MUS: N/C. PRD: Discovery. 30 mins. x 2 eps

Monsters attack Japan, or rather an international organization based in Odaiba in Tokyo—though the enemy seems more interested in disrobing than disarming them. Even over 30 minutes this can get repetitive, although with English, French, and German subtitles you could learn to talk dirty in four languages. If you're buying this for the visual references to EVANGELION on the sleeve of Act 1 (and we've heard feebler excuses), save your money. The 3D-rendered mecha are as clichéd as the frame layouts, designs, and multinational force of cuties hovering around one boy. The action sequences appear lifted directly from a console game; not wholly improbable, given that it's based on a game by CLOCKUP.

Dyogrammaton is "a combination of TRANSFORMERS meets the Galaxy's hottest babes"—or so it says on the sleeve for both volumes. Adult Source Media acquired *Dyogrammaton* on its Japanese release, a few months after they picked up the catalogue lost by NuTech Digital in its dispute with its Japanese licensor; but it wasn't released on U.S. DVD until nine months after its home debut. EROTICA AND PORNOGRAPHY often have short running times in Japan and home buyers don't seem to feel short-changed, but for the overseas market these two episodes have been bulked out with two "bonus trailers" enabling them to be spread over two 60-minute releases. **LN**

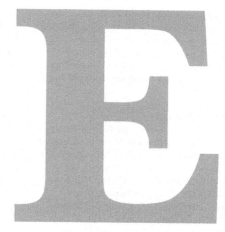

E-CHAN THE NINJA

1971. JPN: *Sarutobi Etchan*. AKA: *Monkey-style Jumper E-chan*. TV series. DIR: Yugo Serikawa, Mineo Fujita, Minoru Okazaki, Yoshio Takami, Masayuki Akehi, Hiroshi Ikeda. SCR: Shotaro Ishinomori, Shunichi Yukimuro, Tadao Yamazaki, Tatsuo Kasai. DES: Shotaro Ishinomori. ANI: Shinya Takahashi, Funahito Nagaki, Hideo Yoshizawa, Katsuya Oda. MUS: Seiichiro Uno. PRD: Toei, TV Asahi (NET). 25 mins. x 26 eps.

Average Japanese girl Miko gets a strange playmate in the form of Etsuko Sarutobi, an exceptionally athletic girl who has the ability to talk to animals. With her pet Buku, a dog that speaks with an Osaka accent, and Taihei Tenka, a confused crusader for justice, Etsuko helps Miko deal with problems in her neighborhood, particularly Takeshi Oyama, the local bully.

These humorous exploits of a psychic ninja girl and her talking dog were animated as a series of two-part stories, each segment occupying half the broadcast. The series was broadcast on Mondays in the slot vacated by the long-running SECRET AKKO-CHAN, which has led many Japanese sources to classify it as a "magical girl" story, although Etsuko never actually uses magic. Based on Shotaro Ishinomori's 1964 *Shojo Friend* manga *Okashina Okashina Anoko* (*There's Something Strange About That Girl*), *E-chan* was an early animation job for a young Hayao Miyazaki, who worked on episode 6. The show also inspired Katsuhiro Otomo, who wrote several manga for adults, each conceived as a modernized update of a children's classic. Consequently, *E-chan* was transformed into Etsuko, the psychic schoolgirl of *Domu* (1980). See also NINJA NONSENSE.

E'S OTHERWISE *

2003. TV series. DIR: Masami Shimoda. SCR: Katsuhiko Chiba. DES: Takehiro Hamatsu. ANI: N/C. MUS: Kazunori Miyake, Hajime Hyakkoku. PRD: Studio Pierrot, TV Tokyo. 25 mins. x 26 eps.

After a terrible war in the near future, a dozen corporations run the world. The public is deeply suspicious of the emergent race of psychics—a common anime set-up from GUNDAM onward. Enter the ASHRAM organization, which claims to offer sanctuary to those with psychic powers and to train them in methods of putting their skills to use for the common good. Two such foundlings are brother and sister Kai and Hikaru, brought into the fold by ASHRAM agent Eiji. Within a year of working for an ASHRAM subdivision, Kai has made great progress but his sister has yet to recover from recent trauma, and Kai must still face the daily hatred of "normal" humans. Before long, he also discovers that neither ASHRAM nor the quasi-governmental corporations are necessarily acting for the general good of humanity (who guessed?), in a show that begins well but soon begins to limp through the familiar tropes of science fiction anime. In the parlance of the show, "E's" (pronounced as is the letter "s") is a person with extrasensory powers that are too strong for conventional humans to defeat; all rather too close for comfort to the "X" of *X-Men* (2000), to which this show owes much of its inspiration. Based on the manga *E's* by Satoru Yuiga, serialized in *G-Fantasy Comics* since 1997. **Ⓥ**

E&G FILMS

Formed in 1988 by the merger of EG World and Luckymore, notable members include Takashi Abe, Rei Nakahara, and Makoto Sokuza. Representative works include FORTUNE QUEST and LOST UNIVERSE.

EAGLE SAM

1983. TV series. DIR: Hideo Nishimaki, Kanetsugu Kodama. SCR: Masaaki Sakurai, Tetsu Hirata, Kazunobu Hamada, Kazuo Yoshioka. DES: Yoshio Kabashima. ANI: Yoshio Kabashima, Yukio Otaku. MUS: Harumi Ibe. PRD: DAX, TBS. 25 mins. x 51 eps.

All-American private investigator Sam is transformed into an eagle one day as he prepares to open for business. With his shapely assistant, Miss Canary, and her little brother, Gooselan, he must fight the corrupt Chief of Police Albatross and somehow regain his true form. He travels all around the world and solves problems with his Eagle Hat, which contains many useful items à la DORAEMON, chiefly the glowing Olympic Rings that give Sam the extra confidence he needs to save the day. Other members of the mostly human cast included Pelican the hippie, Thunderbird the weightlifter, and dim-witted, donut-eating cop Bogie (presumably a Humphrey Bogart reference amid all the avian names). Though set in "Olympic City," the location is clearly modeled on Los Angeles, even down to Los Angeles County Sheriff's Department uniforms with distinctive six-pointed star badges. When not fighting corruption within the force itself, Eagle Sam chases Gokiburi, a skateboarding, jive-talking cockroach in shades. Made to cash in on the "Eagle Sam" mascot of the 1984 Los Angeles Olympics—compare to the Moscow equivalent, MISHA THE BEAR CUB.

EAGLE TALON *

2007. JPN: *Himitsu Kessha Taka no Tsume THE MOVIE—Soto wa Nido Shinu*. AKA: *Secret Society Eagle Talon THE MOVIE—Chancellor Only Lives Twice*. Movie, TV series. DIR: FROGMAN. SCR: FROGMAN. DES: FROGMAN. ANI: FROGMAN, Kotaro Yamawaki. MUS: manzo (all). PRD: DLE, Kaeruotoko Shokai, Dentsu, TV Asahi. 80 mins. (m1), 90 mins. (m2), 25 mins. x 12 eps. (TV1), ?? mins. (m3), ?? mins. x 39 eps. (TV2), ?? mins. x 38 eps. (TV3), ?? mins. x 38 eps. (TV4). Eagle Talon is a secret society based in the Tokyo suburb of Kojimachi. They plot world dominion but are constantly foiled by corrupt superhero Deluxe Fighter, who has his own villainous plans. Led by Chancellor, a 55-year-old guy with no real interests outside world domination, Eagle Talon has its own scientific genius in Dr. Leonardo, who goes crazy and attacks anyone who points out that he looks like a teddy bear. Four-year-old psychic Bodhisattva Boy and two guest characters from an earlier FROGMAN animation, Yoshida and Phillip, make up the rest of Eagle Talon.

This was billed as the first theatrically released Flash animation in the world. It was created by one-man Flash animation house Ryo Ono, AKA FROGMAN, as 11 shorts for his 2006 TV series *The Frogman Show*, then edited together as a movie. He also dubbed the voice roles and opened the movie with a sequence spoofing GHOST IN THE SHELL, a movie he worked on.

A second movie, *Eagle Talon The Movie II—My Love for Black Oolong Tea* (*Himitsu Kessha Taka no Tsume THE MOVIE II—Watashi o Aishita Kuro Oolong-cha*) was released in 2008, featuring a particularly striking giant-robot sequence. The first Eagle Talon TV series, *Eagle Talon Countdown*, followed in 2009, with a third movie, *Eagle Talon THE MOVIE 3—http:// takanotsume. jp Until Eternity* (*Himitsu Kessha Taka no Tsume THE MOVIE 3—http: //takanotsume. jp wa Eien ni*). The opening theme chosen by FROGMAN for this movie was Susan

Boyle's "I Dreamed a Dream," although the production is likely to be remembered for breaking new ground by giving away a limited edition DVD of the movie during its theatrical run in Japan. A location-based social networking game, *Eagle Talon Operation Apologize* (*Taka no Tsume Dan no Ayamaru Daisakusen*) was released in Japan in 2011, along with several smartphone apps based on the characters. **NV**

EAR OF THE YELLOW DRAGON

1995. JPN: *Koryu no Mimi*. Video. DIR: Kunihiko Yuyama. SCR: Kenji Terada. DES: Arimasa Ozawa. ANI: Masayuki Goto. MUS: Hiroki Nakajima. PRD: Vap. 25 mins. x 2 eps. An SF tale of intrigue in which agent Kiro, who can call on the mystic powers of "the yellow dragon" through his earring, falls in love with Kanako, daughter of the mob family he is trying to bring down. Based on just one story arc in a manga from *Young Jump* that won the coveted Naoki Prize for its creator Arimasa Ozawa. **NV**

EARLY ANIME

Controversy continues to haunt discussions of the first anime in Japan, particularly after Natsuki Matsumoto's discovery in 2005 of a scrap of film; barely three seconds long, stenciled straight onto blank film, and possibly never even screened. Depicting a boy drawing the characters for "moving pictures" on a blackboard, the Matsumoto fragment is undeniably a piece of early Japanese animation, but is little help in establishing a date for the beginning of the medium—we still do not know who drew it, or when. It is not impossible that it might date from as early as 1907, when, as the German scholar Frederick Litten points out, Japanese film magazines were advertising the sale of (mainly foreign) small-gauge film reels for use in home-movie projectors. However, the Japanese press and overeager Western fans immediately began assigning dates of "before 1915," "around 1907," and "in the early years of the 20th century," so that within a few days it was being reported as an anime from "shortly after 1900." Litten suggests that, for technical reasons to do with its quality of registration and fluctuations in the price of celluloid, the Matsumoto fragment is unlikely to have been made "before 1905 or after 1912."

In other words, the centenary of Japanese animation has probably passed us by, unnoticed and uncelebrated, at some point before 2012.

While such confusion may seem wholly innocent, some pundits may have political motives. A 1907 date would allow Japan to claim to have developed animation concurrent with the first known screening of a foreign cartoon *in* Japan that same year, and a pre-1907 date would allow Japan to claim to be the pioneer of the entire animated medium—the first example of which is currently acknowledged as J. Stuart Blackton's *Humorous Phases of Funny Faces* (1906).

The first completed Japanese animated film was probably a short by Oten Shimokawa, a 26-year-old amateur filmmaker who had previously been an editorial assistant for *Tokyo Puck* magazine. Sources including his cameraman claim that he worked using the "chalkboard" method, pointing a camera directly at a blackboard and then erasing and redrawing one frame at a time in order to create animation. Shimokawa himself claimed in 1934 that this film was *Mukuzo Imokawa the Doorman* (*Imokawa Mukuzo Genkanban no Maki*, 1917), although Frederick Litten has uncovered evidence that suggests *Mukuzo Imokawa the Doorman* was actually the *third* of Shimokawa's films to be screened, albeit possibly the first using the chalkboard method, hence the confusion. Two other Shimokawa shorts seem to have preceded it. Although the name of the first is not known, the second appears to have been *Dekobo Shingacho: Meian no Shippai* (1917, *Kid Deko's New Picture Book: Failure of a Great Plan*). Shimokawa may also have worked by drawing directly onto film, one frame at a time. His experiments lasted for six months and five short films before he gave up and returned to newspaper illustration. This, at least, is what is believed by Japanese sources, although none of Shimokawa's anime work survives.

Rivalry and one-upmanship lurk behind the scenes of early anime, as competing studios strove to be the "first"—similar claims and counter-claims have hounded the advent of digital animation almost a century later. Where Shimokawa was supposedly working for Tenkatsu, his fellow *Tokyo Puck*–illustrator Junichi Kouchi worked for Kobayashi Shokai (formed by former Tenkatsu employees), and both competed with Seitaro Kitayama, a watercolor artist who, it is said, proactively approached the Nikkatsu studio himself and offered to create its first cartoons.

Junichi Kouchi's first work was *Sword of Hanawa Hekonai* (*Hanawa Hekonai, Meito no Maki*, 1917), with artwork drawn directly onto paper. However, he was soon experimenting with paper cutouts, which were easier to manipulate and allowed, for example, for backgrounds to be reused. The animation cel, a transparent piece of nitrocellulose that would become the default material for most anime until the 1990s, had been invented in 1915, but had not yet made it to Japan. As with his fellow pioneers, little of Kouchi's work survives, and he gave up on anime in the 1930s.

Seitaro Kitayama preferred fairy tales and legends to Shimokawa's vaudeville humor, producing early versions of THE MONKEY AND THE CRAB (1917), MOMOTARO (1917), and *Taro the Guardsman* (*Taro no Banpei*, 1918). Kitayama displayed an early aptitude for applied animation, producing anime's first commercials and also anime's first documentary, *What to Do with Your Postal Savings* (*Chokin no Susume*, 1917, see DOCUMENTARIES AND HISTORY). He also founded Japan's first animation studio, largely specializing in subtitles, intertitles, and special effects for live-action film, although by 1930 he, too, had left the medium behind and moved into live-action newsreels.

So little of the work of these early animators survives, in part because of the low number of their prints and the relative ease with which a single-reel movie might be mislaid. The main culprit, however, is the Great Kanto Earthquake of 1923 and the subsequent fires that destroyed much of Tokyo, including almost all early anime materials.

One of Kitayama's protégés, Sanae Yamamoto, continued in the aftermath and arguably became the founder of modern anime. Crucially, when Kitayama fled to work in Osaka, the younger Yamamoto stayed behind in Tokyo. His works included *The Mountain Where Old Women Are Abandoned* (*Obasuteyama*, 1924) and another *Tortoise and the Hare* (1924)—both still extant, although we have less of an idea of

how they were presented. As silent movies, they were expected to be performed not just with live musical accompaniment but with a live narrator, or *benshi*. The *benshi* were holdovers from Japan's puppetry tradition and the magic lantern shows of the late 19th century, but their days were numbered with the introduction of movies with sound. Today, their last redoubt is the predominance of frankly unnecessary voice-over narration in Japanese audio dramas. But in the 1920s, their presence was vital and definitive—apparent lacunae, for example, in the onscreen images of DREAMY URASHIMA, would have been intended for a *benshi*'s commentary, without which the film is "incomplete."

Soon after the American movie *The Jazz Singer* (1927) featured a talkie section, Japanese animators were similarly experimenting with sound. The first was Noburo Ofuji's *Whale* (*Kujira*, 1927), a silhouette animation synchronized to the *William Tell Overture*. He followed this up with the cutout animation *Kuro Nyago* (1930), using the Tojo company's Eastphone sound system—anime's first genuine "talkie," albeit only 90 seconds long. The first talkie to use an optic track (as with modern films) was Kenzo Masaoka's THE WORLD OF POWER AND WOMEN (1933), the tale of a henpecked husband accused of having an affair with a younger woman.

The dying days of silent movies also encouraged new animators to enter into filmmaking. Yasuji Murata, whose first job had been cutting Japanese intertitles into silent movies from America to make the "dialogue" comprehensible to local audiences, was inspired by some of the cartoons he saw to make his own. His *Animal Olympics* (1928) refined the themes of comedic competition, essentially becoming the first in the new subgenre of SPORTS ANIME.

Anime of the period were not only screened in cinemas. Those sponsored by commercial concerns often preferred to screen them at shopping areas in order to increase the immediate possibility of sales. Early anime were also screened at schools, particularly if they were of a didactic nature. Murata's *Taro's Steamtrain* (*Taro-san no Kisha*, 1929) was an object lesson in consideration for others, as a lone Japanese boy tries to maintain order in a carriage packed with anthropomorphic

animals that fight over seating, throw litter, and become increasingly rowdy. Anime's first "sequel" was *The Pirate Ship* (*Kaizoku-bune*, 1931), a continuation of the previous year's *Monkey Island* (*Sarugashima*), in which a young child cast adrift has adventures on the high seas.

Amid such marvels, however, JAPANESE FOLK TALES continued to exercise a strong influence. *Tanuki*, Japan's indigenous "raccoon-dogs," appear in several early anime, where their fun-loving nature, their naughtiness, and their constant rivalry with snooty foxes made them an eternal hit with young audiences. In one such example, Murata's *Bunbuku Teapot* (*Bunbuku Chagama*, 1927) a kind-hearted man rescues a *tanuki* from a trap. The grateful animal turns itself into a teapot, which the man then donates to a Buddhist temple, whereupon the *tanuki* reverts to its previous form to cause chaos.

Similar transformations came with Ikuo Oishi's *Moving Picture Fight of the Fox and the Possum* (*Ugoki-e Kori no Tatehiki*, 1931) in which a fox disguised as a samurai is tormented by *tanuki* disguised as monks, who transform themselves into grotesque demonic phantoms—compare to like antagonisms in POM POKO.

Similar creatures would feature in another Japanese first, Kenzo Masaoka's *Dance of the Teapots* (*Chagama Ondo*, 1934), in which a group of *tanuki* break into a Japanese temple to steal the new-fangled gramophone records played by the monks. This was the first anime to be made wholly with animation cels, as opposed to earlier methods that utilized translucent papers.

Color took longer to arrive in anime's early years, although since the schoolboy in the Matsumoto fragment had a dot of red on his cap, one might equally argue that the first identifiable Japanese cartoon was *already* in color. There were many tinted or toned Japanese films in the early part of the 20th century, and several private experiments—Noburo Ofuji supposedly pioneered a two-color version of his *Golden Flower* (*Ogon no Hana*, 1929), for example, although the version released to the public was in monochrome. The first color anime to be actually released was Megumi Asano's *My Baseball* (*Boku no Yakyu*, 1948), but there are many quibbles and exceptions that might be raised, not the least moving-picture toys sold for home use, many of which count, in some sense, as color animation, albeit never screened in theaters.

Before the advent of recorded sound, it is arguable that anime were merely part of live dramatic entertainment, like LITTLE NEMO–creator Winsor McCay's *Gertie the Dinosaur* (1914), whose performance required her creator to interact, *benshi*-style, in front of the screen. However, such hybrid performances were increasingly uncommon by the late 1920s, as anime began to exist as single artworks in their own right, integrating sound, story, and image in a unified whole. During the 1930s, the anime medium continued to grow in size and accomplishment, although it also became largely subsumed into the propaganda machine of an imperialist government, with Yasushi Murata's *Aerial Momotaro* (1931) being the first of the WARTIME ANIME.

EARTH STORY: TELEPATH 2500

1984. JPN: *Chikyu Monogatari Telepath 2500*. Movie. DIR: Nariyuki Yamane. SCR: Yoshimi Shinozaki. DES: Ammonite, Yoshitaka Amano, Masashi Sato. ANI: Ippei Kuri, Sadao Miyamoto. MUS: Hiroshi Ogasawara. PRD: Tatsunoko. 105 mins.
On the fifth world of the Tolphan system in the year 2500, a supercomputer chooses marriage partners to find the best matches. Eighteen-year-old Will flies to an orbital facility to discuss his fate with his elders but receives telepathic SOS messages from the winged Flora. He deviates from his course and goes to help this damsel in distress, slowly coming to realize that he has fallen in love with her before they have even met. A star-crossed love story with an SF twist. **N**

EARTHIAN *

1989. Video. DIR: Nobuyasu Furukawa, Kenichi Onuki. SCR: Hiroyuki Kawasaki. DES: Kenichi Onuki. ANI: Kenichi Onuki. MUS: Shinnosuke Uesugi. PRD: JC Staff. 40 mins. x 4 eps.
Optimistic Chihaya and pessimistic Kagetsuya are two angels sent from Planet Eden to walk among mankind (the "Earthians") and determine whether the race deserves to survive. This interesting premise is then stretched in all kinds of hack directions by a crew that seems unable to decide what to do with it. The boys bicker constantly about humanity, though since both have been chosen for their good-cop/bad-cop attitudes, each is unlikely to convert the other. Like a fey version of *Highway to Heaven*, they simply wander in and out of what could almost be episodes from other shows—a London music biz soap opera, for example (featuring a dark angel), or an SF tale of psychics (when Chihaya rescues a runaway psionic in Hong Kong). Yun Koga's original 1987 pretty-boy manga was given a considerable amount of screen time for a video release, and the whistle-stop international setting would have been very difficult to achieve in a live-action budget. However, matters were not helped in the U.S. market by a distributor that coquettishly refused to number the tapes, forcing many potential fans to watch episodes in a random order.

EASY COOKING ANIMATION

1989. JPN: *Seishun no Shokutaku*. AKA: *Youth's Dining Table*. Video. DIR: Toshio Hirata. SCR: N/C. DES: N/C. ANI: N/C. MUS: N/C. PRD: Kitty Films, Madhouse. 30 mins. x 5 eps.
A set of handy hints for basic cooking, including advice on preparing noodles, salad, hot-pots, and pizza. From the studio that gave you WICKED CITY.

EAT-MAN *

1997. TV series. DIR: Koichi Mashimo, Toshifumi Kawase. SCR: Akemi Omode, Aya Matsui, Hiroshi Nomoto. DES: Satoshi Murata. ANI: Masaaki Kannan. MUS: Taifu Kamigami. PRD: Studio Deen, TV Tokyo. 25 mins. x 12 eps. (TV1), 25 mins. x 12 eps. (TV2).
Bolt Crank, a mercenary who can eat metal objects and then rematerialize them in times of need, wanders from city to city in a futuristic wasteland helping people in trouble.

Based on a manga by Akihito Yoshitomi that is similarly high in concept and low in plot, *E-M* takes the raw material of pulp TV and remolds the wandering heroes of *The Incredible Hulk* and *The Running Man*, adding a dash of Clint Eastwood and Ken from FIST OF THE NORTH STAR. However, it lacks the believable background of its similarly pulp-inspired contemporary COWBOY BEBOP—the world it creates is little more than a desert backlot, and it soon sinks into a quagmire of episodic set-ups and showdowns.

E-M shows both the good and bad aspects of a limited budget. Art director Jiro Kono deliberately uses flat, uniform colors (like TENCHI MUYO! without the shine) to exploit the talents of his Chinese animators, and it works well. There are some neat compositions (a face in a cracked mirror, the sky in a puddle), but also some blatant corner-cutting. A cheap loop of a girl's running silhouette is used for a total of three and half minutes. A staring match reaches ridiculous levels of stillness, which may be fine for free on late-night TV, but stretches the patience of video buyers.

Paramount among the series' problems is Bolt's peculiar ability itself, mystifying a succession of writers who push the titular "eating" into the background. Set-ups are drawn from the staples of U.S. law shows (a would-be dancer is forced to work as a stripper), SF (a clone hunts down all her sisters), and fantasy (a feisty young lady is a lost heiress), but Bolt merely watches the action unfold before producing a gun out of thin air instead of a holster for the finale. As *Manga Max* observed, "he could have pulled it out of his ass for all the difference it made."

The second season, *Eat-Man '98*, replaces director Mashimo with EHRGEIZ's Kawase and injects hints about Bolt Crank's past. In rip-offs from GENOCYBER, GHOST IN THE SHELL, and AKIRA, it suggests that Bolt was somehow involved in a genetic experiment, and that the titular "98" (despite the apostrophe in the titles of both Japanese and American editions) actually refers to the percentile of subjects who did not survive the process. Though the new direction is at least a plot of sorts, Bolt's habit of munching on metal objects is still little more than a display of macho toughness—you'd get the same effect if he regularly smashed a bottle over his own head. Though the animation is still limited, *E-M98* at least duplicates the look of Bolt's powers from the manga, but much of the storytelling remains shoddy and illogical despite a high-quality TRANSLATION in the English-language version far better than this show really deserves. **NV**

EDEN OF THE EAST *

2009. JPN: *Higashi no Eden*. TV, movie. DIR: Kenji Kamiyama. SCR: Kenji Kamiyama. DES: Chika Umino, Satoko Morikawa, Yusuke Takada. ANI: Satoru Nakamura. MUS: Kenji Kawai. PRD: Production I.G, Asmik Ace, Dentsu, Fuji TV, Sony Music Entertainment; Reelvision (OP). 22 mins. x 11 eps. (TV), 123 mins. (compilation), 82 mins. (m1), 93 mins. (m2).

Suppose they dropped a bomb and nobody died? On November 22, 2010, ten missiles strike Japan in an apparent act of terror. But nobody seems to be hurt and everyone soon forgets about this unexplained bit of weirdness. Three months later, Saki is on her graduation trip to the U.S.A. She runs into a spot of trouble in front of the White House and is saved by a fellow Japanese. The naked Akira Takizawa can't remember anything except his name. All he has on him—literally—is a handgun and a mobile phone charged with a ludicrous amount of digital cash. So is he linked to the mysterious entities who dumped missiles on Japan? And how does Eden, the augmented reality website created by Saki's college pals, tie in to all this?

Eden of the East the Movie I: The King of Eden (Higashi no Eden Gekijoban I: The King of Eden) premiered in November 2009, over five months after the series ended, with nothing but creator Kenji Kamiyama's personally edited compilation movie *Eden of the East Compilation: Air Communication (Higashi no Eden Soshuhen Air Communication)* and novelization to keep fans going. Then they had to wait until March 2010 for the second and final movie, *Eden of the East The Movie II: Paradise Lost (Higashi no Eden Gekijoban II: Paradise Lost)*, and its novelization.

So what kept fans watching? Humor, charm, good character development, and a plot derived largely from popular blockbuster novels and movies like *The Bourne Identity*, but given a contemporary Japanese twist by the inclusion of an oddball serial genital mutilator and 20,000 missing jobless young people. Kamiyama's storyline highlights the plight, or rather, choices of Japan's generation of NEETs—those "not in employment, education or training." The same crew stayed in charge throughout, avoiding the other major risk of loss of consistency. Kamiyama's trade-mark frame composition is so precisely crafted that it frequently attains the level of both poetry and engineering, every shot carefully selected, every expression magnificently effective. A lovely Kenji Kawai score is the icing on the cake and a clever ending is the juicy cherry. **NV**

EDEN'S BOWY *

1999. TV series. DIR: Tsukasa Sunaga. SCR: Masashi Sogo. DES: Hiroko Kazui. ANI: Hiroko Kazui, Yoshiaki Tsuhata. MUS: N/C. PRD: Studio Deen. 25 mins. x 26 eps.

On a world where a floating city rules over groundling farmers, humble peasant boy Yorn becomes the target of a group of assassins. He is protected by Ellissis, a girl with healing powers, who can also transform into a warrior version of herself called Seida. She reveals that Yorn is a "god-hunter" in hiding, a human with the ability to destroy unruly deities such as the one who now rules over the floating city of Eden. Based on a manga from *Shonen Ace* by Kitsune Tennoji, who was previously known for the adult story *Rape + 2πr*, *EB* soon transforms into a bizarre love triangle in the spirit of CREAMY MAMI, with Yorn falling for Seida while Ellissis falls for Yorn.

EDUCATIONAL TRAINING

2010. JPN: *Kyoiku Shido the Animation*. Video. DIR: Tsuyoshi Kimura. SCR: N/C. DES: Tsuyoshi Kimura. ANI: N/C. MUS: N/C. PRD: Milky, MS Pictures. 30 mins.

Yoshiyuki has always loved having sex with girls, so now that he's a teacher he takes every opportunity to have sex with his students. Unfortunately, he's now had almost all the girls at his current school so he has to change jobs. Naturally he lands a job at a famous girls' school with no difficulty and soon starts giving "educational guidance" to his pupils and tricking or coercing them into sex with him and each other. Based on a porn game by BISHOP. **NV**

EF: A TALE OF MEMORIES *

2007. Video, TV series. DIR: Shin Onuma. SCR: Katsuhiko Takayama. DES: Nobuhiro Sugiyama, Megumi Kato. ANI: Nobuhiro Sugiyama, Yoshiaki Ito, Shingo Tamaki, Shuji Miyazaki. MUS: Eiichiro Yanagi, Tenmon. PRD: SHAFT, Frontier Works, Geneon Universal Entertainment, Kitty, minori, MOVIC, Rondo Robe. ?? mins. (OV), 24 mins. x 12 eps. (TV1), 24 mins. x 12 eps. (TV2).

Christmas Eve: the most special night of the year for lovers in Japan, and the night when three romances begin. Wannabe filmmaker Kyosuke is out with his camera when he sees Kei as she races across the street. He finds she's the childhood friend of his pal Hiro, and so stuck on him that at first she can't see the chance of love offered by Kyosuke. Hiro has already met a girl that day, but only because she stole his bike. Miyako is chasing a purse snatcher, and when she returns his broken bike the two find they go to the same school. Their developing friendship makes Kei feel abandoned, and so she creates a love triangle with Hiro and Miyako. Meanwhile Renji meets a strange girl at an abandoned railway station. She's Kei's younger twin sister Chihiro, partially blinded in an accident and left with brain damage which means her memory only lasts for 13 hours. Renji decides to help her make her dream of writing a novel come true.

Two stories of love and the set-up for a third asks a lot of a single series, and partly explains why the first episode of *ef: a tale of memories* feels slow and crowded with seemingly unconnected people. Its origin as a "visual novel" (ARGOT AND JARGON) by Minori partly explains this: a wide range of characters is needed for the player/reader to choose from. The original game, *ef: a fairy tale of the two*, was released on December 22, 2006, just in time for Christmas Eve and is notable largely for a staff that had found greater fame on VOICES FROM A DISTANT STAR, including Makoto Shinkai as the animator of the opening sequence, and music from Tenmon. The game was itself based on a manga by Mikage which commenced publishing in 2005 and spun off a light novel and an Internet radio show in July 2006, with a set of four drama CDs commencing in October. The web of market-building added another strand when a short prologue DVD was released as a teaser for the TV series in August 2007, six weeks before it aired.

As the series progresses, the stories continue to interweave, and a character or two from the visual novel slips in without apparent purpose, but the main trace of its origin is that it's heavy on dialogue and light on action of any kind other than romance and some sex. The design is attractive, with some lovely visual effects, especially the stained glass metaphor for Chihiro's tragic existence, but the animation is extremely limited. Akiyuki Shinbo (BAKEMONOGATARI) was on the crew as a supervisor, as well as storyboarding under the alias Soji Homura, and his distinctive visual style may have had an influence here. Its popularity with fans may be explained by its solid sense of realism (EVERYDAY ANIME), with believable characters and stories. The positive presentation of a disabled character as a completely normal teenage girl in a terrible situation is a strong point in its favor.

A further book and more games followed the TV series, and a second series, *ef: a tale of melodies*, made by the same crew, aired in 2008. The format is the same—interlaced stories of young lovers, some introduced in series one. Both shows introduced themes using the same initials: Tenmon's "Euphoric Field" in the first, and his "Ebullient Future" in the second. This continued a tradition set in the game, where titles included *Eternal Feather, Emotional Flutter, Ever Forever,* and *Echt Forgather.* **◎**

EFFICUS

1998. Video. JPN: *Efficus: Kono Omoi o Kimi ni.* AKA: *Efficus: This Thought for You.* DIR: Shigeru Motomiya. SCR: Shigeru Motomiya. DES: Hideaki Shimada. ANI: Hideaki Shimada. MUS: N/C. PRD: Magic Bus. 40 mins. x 2 eps. Sisters Maply, Sucre, and Parte live in the magical kingdom of Efficus. In a cash-in of the video game of the same name, the girls are forced to find other sources of income after sales of buns go into decline. The second episode takes the girls to a haunted house to face an old adversary.

EHRGEIZ *

1997. JPN: *Next Senki: Ehrgeiz.* AKA: *Next Chronicle: Ehrgeiz.* TV series. DIR: Toshifumi Kawase. SCR: Atsuhiro Tomioka, Koji Miura, Toshiyasu Nagata, Chika Hojo. DES: Isamu Imakake, Tetsuya Yanasawa, Takahiro Yamada. ANI: Naoki Hishikawa. MUS: Kazuhiro Wakabayashi. PRD: BeStack, TV Tokyo. 25 mins. x 12 eps.
The Next orbital colony declares independence from Earth, starting a war of secession fought with giant robots called Metal Vehicles. Meanwhile, the terrorist organization Tera, led by the telepathic boy Hal, fights the Earth government from within, as the Next forces search desperately for the legendary "S" superweapon that will turn the tide of the war. On a wrecked colony satellite, a group of part-time pirates turn out to be the best pilots of the lot, and the scene is set for a blatant GUNDAM rip-off. Originally broadcast on Japanese late-night TV, the production may well have been dumped in the graveyard shift as a cheaper alternative to video; certainly, there is no "adult" content to otherwise justify its broadcast time. Though the English-language TRANSLATION tries to spice up the language somewhat, it is a perfectly mundane children's robot show with animation so cheap that the robots slide everywhere instead of walking. And no matter how old the original target audience, it was bound to be bewildered by the baffling array of sides in the war, with two nations, two freelance groups, and, as the plot advances, a newly arrived alien civilization to boot. Supposedly amusingly referential and parodic but really just plain daft, the series is best remembered for spawning a PlayStation game in which characters from *Final Fantasy VII* made cameo appearances, which is hardly a recommendation.

EIGHT CLOUDS RISING *

1997. Video. DIR: Tomomi Mochizuki. SCR: Go Sakamoto. DES: Yukiko Kusumoto. ANI: Yukiko Kusumoto. MUS: Hajime Mizoguchi. PRD: Studio Pierrot. 30 mins. x 2 eps.
Kuraki Fuzuchi and Takeo Nanichi are not only Japanese schoolboys, but also the reincarnations of an ancient shrine-maiden and a swordsmith. They fight off evil spirits and unwelcome female attention as they attempt to collect sacred swords and preserve them from evil. Based on a manga by Natsumi Itsuki (OZ), the anime covers only the first collected volume of the manga, originally published in *Hana to Yume* magazine. It also comes complete with moody evocations of Japan's past (see DARK MYTH) and a homoerotically charged buddy-relationship, deliberately aimed at Japan's large female audience of pretty-boy aficionados.

808 DISTRICTS

1990. JPN: *Ishinomori Shotaro no 808 Hyori.* AKA: *Shotaro Ishinomori's 808 Districts.* TV special, TV series. DIR: Hiroshi Fukutomi. SCR: Kaneto Shirasu. DES: Shotaro Ishinomori. ANI: Masuji Kinoue. MUS: N/C. PRD: Shinei, TBS. 30 mins. (special), 10 mins. x 15 eps. (TV).
A series of costume-dramas in which CYBORG 009–creator Shotaro Ishinomori plays out modern situations against the backdrop of samurai-era Japan. Linked by the wandering character, Kosanma, the stories include a man's desire to light up the sky with fireworks, a battle between a freelancer and a large company, a girl growing up in the Edo-period version of a massage parlor, and a man searching for a way to get a girl to love him.

The first episode was a 30-minute special, with subsequent parts screened irregularly as part of the *Gimme a Break* show on TBS. For an SF update of the same mean city streets, see CYBER CITY OEDO 808, which also takes its name from the 808 city blocks of old-time Tokyo.

8TH MAN *

1963. JPN: *8 Man* [sic]. AKA: *Tobor the Eighth Man.* TV series, video. DIR: Haruyuki Kawajima. SCR: Kazumasa Hirai, Ryo Hanmura, Tsunehisa Tomita, Tetsuyoshi Onuki, Masaki Tsuji. DES: Jiro Kuwata. ANI: Yukizo Takagaki, Kazuhide Fujiwara. MUS: Tetsuaki Akibara. PRD: Eiken, TBS. 25 mins. x 56 eps. (TV), 30 mins. x 4 eps. (v).
Police officer Hachiro Azuma (Peter Brady) is murdered by a criminal gang, but Professor Tani (Genius) installs his memories in a robot body, the 008 military prototype model from the Republic of Amarco. With his new body, he takes on the cyborgs and mutants of an international crime syndicate in a show partly inspired by James Bond 007 but way ahead of its spiritual descendants CYBORG 009 and *Robocop.*

Based on a story by HARMAGEDON-author Kazumasa Hirai that was previously adapted into a manga in *Shonen Magazine* by Jiro Kuwata, the TV series was notable for the script contribution of real SF authors such as Hirai himself and Ryo Hanmura, though much of the original impact was lost in the U.S. dub *Tobor the Eighth Man* (1965), in which our hero must defeat such creatively named adversaries as

Saucer Lips (the man who "killed" Peter Brady), as well as Armored Man, Baron Stormy, Dr. Spectra, the Satan Brothers, and the Intercrime spy ring. The TV series has since been rereleased on video in the U.S., though the later video compilations downplay Azuma's novel way of recharging his batteries—smoking nuclear isotope cigarettes.

After the success of the *Robocop* films, the story was remade as the live-action *8 Man* (1992, AKA *8 Man Returns*). Nobuyasu Furukawa's belated anime video sequel, *Eight Man After* (1993) plays up the drug subculture, as gangsters receive cybernetic prostheses with built-in weapons. Cybernetic implants, however, require stimulants, and the criminal fraternity is soon fighting a new turf war over control of its own drugs. Detective Azuma is sent to investigate the disappearance of a scientist from the Biotech Corp, but he is killed trying to save pretty Sachiko. He is brought back to life by Dr. Tobor, who makes him the new "Eight Man." The video series was also released in the U.S. in a dubbed version from Streamline Pictures.

EIJI
1990. Movie. DIR: Mizuho Nishikubo. SCR: Kazuya Miyashita, Yasuyuki Suzuki. DES: Takayuki Goto. ANI: Satoshi Murata. MUS: Rogue, Go-Bangs, Passengers, Rabbit, Mari Iwata, J-Bloods. PRD: Animate Film. 50 mins.
Legendary boxer Keijiro Akagi's second son, Eiji, is a high school dropout and the world's worst rock guitarist. Though his father and elder brother are both boxers, he hates the sport but suddenly takes an interest in it when he meets the local champion's little sister. This movie was based on a one-volume 1984 manga from *Fresh Jump* magazine by Hisashi Eguchi and features a rock soundtrack by the bands of the moment. Two other works by the same author were animated straight to video soon after—*Something's Going to Happen* (1990) and *The Hisagoro Show* (1991), directed by Rintaro and Osamu Nabeshima, and both consisting of several short comedy pieces.

EIKEN ★
2003. Video. DIR: Kiyotaka Ohata. SCR: Tomoyasu Okubo. DES: Masashi Ishihama. ANI: Masashi Ishihama, Yasuo Namaguro.

MUS: Sho Goshima. PRD: JC Staff, Genco. 30 mins. x 2 eps.
Densuke Mifune has just started at the exclusive Zashono High School when he's invited to join one of the school's top clubs, Eiken. He has no idea why, and is puzzled when every other member is a well-developed young woman—especially since the girl he really loves is the retiring, modest Chiharu. Most of the girls have large breasts (some *very* large), and then they do sports. No, really, that's about it. Based on the manga by Seiji Matsuyama serialized in *Shonen Champion* weekly. Eiken is also the name of an anime studio best known for SAZAE-SAN (see below).

EIKEN (STUDIO)
Animation company officially founded in 1969, although its assets pre-existed as the animation division of TCJ (Television Corporation of Japan), founded in 1953, making over 1,400 animated commercials and some 800 graphic inserts within "live" commercials throughout the 1950s. As budgets and expectations made actual animated TV series possible in the 1960s (ASTRO BOY), many Eiken staffers repurposed their advertising skills for entertainment; the business was instrumental to many early TV anime such as GIGANTOR and incorporated as a separate limited company in 1973. Eiken continues to work in animation but rarely attracts the attention of foreign viewers because its most enduring and lucrative work since 1969 has been anime's longest-running serial, SAZAE-SAN.

EKO EKO AZARAK GA-NIME
2007. Video. DIR: Toshikazu Nagae. SCR: Toshikazu Nagae, Shinichi Koga. DES: Shinichi Koga. ANI: N/C. MUS: N/C. PRD: Toei Animation, Gentosha. 27 mins.
Two stories in one volume from Toei's *ga-nime* limited animation series (ARGOT AND JARGON). In *Exorcism* a schoolgirl arrives at an inn only to find that the owner has hanged himself. The garden of the inn was a former execution ground where criminals were beheaded. A black mass is proposed to exorcise the spirits, but is it just a scam? *Metamorphosis* merges the Japanese schoolboy passion for stag beetles with the problems of school bullying and teen shoplifting to create a bloody tale

of death. Director Nagae has a successful career directing live movies and TV variety shows. Koga is riffing the hit manga and anime franchise of the same name (see, for example, *Wizard of Darkness*, ★DE).

EL ★
2001. AKA: *él*. Video. DIR: Katsuma Kanazawa. SCR: Katsuma Kanazawa. DES: Masaki Kawai, Takeo Takahashi, Yukio Segami. ANI: N/C. MUS: N/C. PRD: ARMS, Green Bunny. 30 mins. x 2 eps.
In 2030, humanity struggles for survival in the aftermath of a nuclear war. The conflict escalated from arguments about environmental pollution—the filmmakers make a big deal about this, so we're just passing the information on. A handful of survivors start the Megaro Earth Project, a city built under a dome to preserve what was left of human civilization. Life in the city is, however, totalitarian, with police known as Sniper Control keeping the citizens in line, along with high-tech floating "eyes" to observe everything. El is a member of the Snipers, engaged in an ongoing case against the secretive Black Widow organization and its leader, Gimmick. She also has to serve as a bodyguard for the pretty blue-haired pop idol Parsley, who likes her so much that lesbian sex is called for. Meanwhile, the ongoing police investigation presents some excuses for torturing female suspects. Based on a game created for elf by Masato Hiruda, the original version of which was titled *Elle*. ❶ ⓝ ⓥ

EL HAZARD ★
1995. JPN: *Shinpi no Sekai El Hazard*. AKA: *The Magnificent World of El Hazard*. Video, TV series. DIR: Hiroki Hayashi, Katsuhito Akiyama. SCR: Ryoei Tsukimura. DES: Kazuto Nakazawa. ANI: Jun Okuda. MUS: Seiko Nagaoka. PRD: AIC, Pioneer. 45 mins., 30 mins. x 6 eps., 50 mins. (v1), 25 mins. x 26 eps. (TV1), 45 mins. x 4 eps. (v2), 25 mins. x 12 eps. (TV2), 25 mins. (v3).
Whisked off to a faraway world, schoolboy Makoto has to impersonate a princess and fight the forces of evil. Spunky love interest Nanami and schoolteacher Mr. Fujisawa, a booze-swilling chain-smoker who inexplicably develops superhuman powers, are also dragged along. They must save the world from attacking insect armies led by Nanami's brother, school bully Jinnai,

who has taught the locals how to lie, cheat, and steal.

Two TENCHI MUYO! staffers, Marx Brothers fan Hayashi and *Edgar Rice Burroughs* fan Tsukimura, decided to combine their interests to create a screwball pulp adventure series, rooting their comedy in the culture clash of 20th-century people and fantasy characters. With a teacher trying to maintain school discipline in an Arabesque paradise, a cross-dressing hero, an evil general who names all his soldiers after his favorite film stars, and Mr. Fujisawa's eternal quest for more cigarettes, *El Hazard* is a masterly comedy. With fish-out-of-water characters in a world inspired by A THOUSAND AND ONE NIGHTS, it remains more popular outside Japan than some of Pioneer's more ethnocentric productions such as HAKKENDEN and KISHIN CORPS. Arguably one of the most seamless anime translations ever, the English-language dub by Jenny Haniver and John Pierce is a perfect TRANSLATION of the original Japanese version, even down to the background improvisations by talented voice actors.

The video series was remade for TV Tokyo in a version known abroad as *El Hazard: The Wanderers* (1996), which stretched the material of the original video series thinly over a longer time frame. A video sequel to the original *video* series, *El Hazard 2* (1997), was similarly disappointing as it merely replayed some of the old gags, though, typically for the series' sense of humor, even the production team inserted "here-we-go-again" jokes. A final incarnation of the series *El Hazard: The Alternative World* (1997), directed by Yasunori Kikuchi, reunited the video characters in a new adventure, shipping them off to the Kingdom of Creteria to fight Ajrah, the self-proclaimed ruler of the universe. The newly crowned priestess of water, Qawool, falls for Makoto with leaden predictability, and the old set-ups are rehashed once more with a few new characters and slight tweaks—in other words, a slow decline into hackery that mirrors the disappointing performance of the same studio's TENCHI MUYO! The 13th version and final episode of the *Alternate* series was never broadcast but was included as a "bonus" with the video release.

ELEC-KING THE ANIMATION

2007. TV series. DIR: Kenjiro Yoshida. ANI: Shohei Murai, Yasuyuki Toda, Itsuki Taniguchi. MUS: Kungo Teinaru. PRD: Gonzo. 5 mins. x 13 eps.
Wacky CGI animation smashing the slice-of-suburban-life approach of SAZAE-SAN into the surreal humor of GENIUS IDIOT BAKA-BON. Based on a four-panel gag strip, by Tsuyoshi Ohashi, first published in 2002.

ELECTRIC GIRL AND THE YOUTH

2011. JPN: *Denpa Onna to Seishun Otoko*. AKA: *Ground Control to Psychoelectric Girl*. TV series. DIR: Akiyuki Shinbo. SCR: Yuniko Ayana. DES: Asako Nishida, Koji Azuma. ANI: Asako Nishida, Nobuhiro Sugiyama. MUS: Franz Maxwell I. PRD: SHAFT, Starchild Records. 25 mins. x 13 eps.
Makoto lives with his aunt and her family while his parents are working away from home. Aunt Meme is a single mother who calls herself Jojo, owns a sweetshop, and is absurdly flirtatious. His cousin Erio lives on pizza, goes around wrapped in a futon, and says she's an alien. She actually did disappear for six months and claims that she was abducted by aliens who made her one of them and wiped her memory. And the whole city is famous for alien encounters. So what's really going on here, and what can Makoto do about it?

The term *denpa*—electromagnetic waves—is sometimes applied to people who imagine they're under the influence of aliens through rays from outer space (there's even a little nod to *E.T. The Extra-Terrestrial* in case you forget the alien aspects of Erio's character). This anime, based on a 2009 book series by Hitoma Iruma with art by Buriki, is an *X-Files* take on the harem show (ROMANCE AND DRAMA), a gentle and slow-moving look at how people fail to fit into society and what they do, or don't do, to conform—compare to PRINCESS JELLYFISH. The combination of Shinbo and SHAFT is virtually a guarantee of good looks, and the pretty designs, beautiful backgrounds, and quirky characters give this show a fey charm.

ELECTROMAGNETIC GIRLFRIEND

2009. JPN: *Denpa-teki na kanojo*. AKA: *Psychotic Girlfriend*. Video. DIR: Mamoru Kanbe. SCR: Hiroyuki Yoshino. DES: Chiyuki Tanaka, Akira Ito. ANI: Hironori Tanaka, Noriyuki Fukuda. MUS: kaji:m. PRD: Brains Base. 42 mins. x 2 eps.
Ju Juzawa is a lonely teenage delinquent with a problem—Ame Ochibana, a tiny girl from another class, is stalking him, claiming to be his loyal retainer from a previous life when he was a king. Ju has no idea if she's obsessed, crazy, or schizophrenic, but when one of their friends becomes the latest victim in a spate of horrific murders he decides to go along with her delusion so they can solve the mystery. A competently animated show that uses its limited resources intelligently to build atmosphere and interest, and doesn't go overboard on the gory action, preferring to draw you in to its story through character development. **OV**

ELEMENTALORS

1994. JPN: *Seirei Tsukai*. AKA: *Elemental Master*. Video. DIR: Katsuhito Akiyama. SCR: Takeshi Okazaki. DES: Hidenori Matsubara. ANI: Hidenori Matsubara. MUS: Masanori Sasamichi. PRD: Sony. 48 mins.
Kagura fails to save his brother-in-law in an accident. His sister accuses him of deliberately allowing the accident to happen because he harbors secret incestuous desires for her. She commits suicide, and Kagura is consoled by his neighbor, Asami, but *then* the world is invaded by "elementalors." Shiki, the leader of the water elementals, freezes most of the inhabitants of Earth, kidnaps Asami, and kills Kagura. However, Kagura is an elementalor himself, and he rises from the dead with help from Tsuyuha, the elemental of wood who resembles Kagura's sister, and Koimura, the elemental of metal. Shiki, only wanting to save his own daughter, leads an assault on Kagura's base, where Kagura's elementalor powers reach their full levels during a fight with Shizuku, the elemental of ice. Based on a 1989 manga by Takeshi Okazaki, serialized in *Newtype* magazine.

ELEMENTAR GELADE *

2005. JPN: *Erementar Gerad*. TV series. DIR: Shigeru Ueda. SCR: Naruhisa Arakawa. DES: Taeko Hori. ANI: N/C. MUS: N/C. PRD: Xebec, Sotsu Agency, TV Tokyo. 25 mins. x 26 eps.
In the distant future, the Adilraid tribe members are able to fuse with humans, ULTRAMAN-style, in order to create living weapons. Sky pirate Coud van Gillette

accidentally awakens Adilraid girl Reverie Metherlance, who announces that she will head off in search of Adilraid Glu Erden, the paradise of the Adilraid people. Coud decides to accompany her, and the pair initially evade the three agents sent to bring Reverie back to the ARC AILE organization that polices Adilraid activity. Eventually, however, they join forces with the agents Cisqua, Rowan, and fellow Adilraid Kuea, in an adaptation of Mayumi Azuma's manga from *Comic Blade* magazine.

ELEMENT HUNTERS

2009. TV series. DIR: Yoshiaki Okumura, Han Pyo Hong. SCR: Naruhisa Arakawa. DES: Bong Hyeon Yoo, Apuo Reino. ANI: Ju Hee Shin. MUS: Toshihiko Sahashi. PRD: NHK, Heewon Entertainment. 25 mins. x 39 eps.

It is 2029: the elements are literally vanishing from Earth, and as the gold, carbon, molybdenum, and others disappear, so do buildings, cities, and countries. Research shows that the elements are leaching into another dimension, to a planet called Nega Earth, stolen by monsters called Q-Exes. Specially gifted preteens are chosen, raised, and trained to cross the dimensional barrier and do battle with the Q-Exes as Element Hunters. However, three ordinary kids also band together to help to save the planet, causing an uneasy collaboration between the elite Colony Team and the entirely average Earth Team.

This is a Japanese-Korean coproduction with serious intent. According to the show's website, PATLABOR's Kazunori Ito created the series concept to teach children about chemical elements, while *Yumeria* game designer Daigo Okumura designed the characters and RAHXEPHON's Ryuichi Kaneko helped to develop the "science fiction concepts." A manga by Yuki Nakashima began its run a week after the anime, and a Nintendo DS game followed. Korean and Spanish versions are also available.

ELEPHANT TRAIN ARRIVED, THE

1992. JPN: *Zo Ressha ga Yattekita.* TV special. DIR: Mei Kato. SCR: Mei Kato. DES: Masashi Kitazaki. ANI: Takashi Ikemi. MUS: N/C. PRD: Mushi Pro, T&K Film, Bandai, Radio Tampo, TV Aichi. 90 mins.

Five-year-old Popo-chan is the zookeeper's daughter at Nagoya's Toyama Zoo. She plays every day with Sabu, an elephant who is the same age. When World War II breaks out, the zoo remains a popular tourist attraction, with the elephants at the top of the bill. Four more elephants arrive from the Kinoshita Circus, but a year later there is an order from the Japanese military to slaughter all the zoo animals. Twenty elephants are killed all over Japan, but two, Makani and Eldo from the Kinoshita Circus, are kept alive in Nagoya. After the war is over, children in Japan pester their parents to see the last remaining elephants, until a special train is supplied to take them to the zoo. As if ZOO WITHOUT AN ELEPHANT and GOODBYE LITTLE HIPPO were not enough, Japan gained yet another tale that mixes the pathos of war movies with the perennial crowdpleaser of cute animals. Based on a book by Takashi Koide.

ELEVEN CATS

1981. JPN: *Juippiki no Neko.* Movie. DIR: Shiro Fujimoto. SCR: Yoshitake Suzuki. DES: Noboru Baba. ANI: Akihito Kamiguchi. MUS: Hitoshi Komuro. PRD: Tac. 83 mins. (m1), 90 mins. (m2).

Eleven naughty cats on the run from the neighborhood police chief hear that a "giant fish" is nearby for the taking. They go on a hazardous quest to find it, learning that they must work as a team to reach their goal. Based on a children's book by Noboru Baba, this movie was followed by a 90-minute sequel, *Eleven Cats and an Albatross* (1986), directed by Tameo Ogawa, in which the cats set up a potato croquette restaurant, lose all their customers, and agree to provide croquettes for a kingdom of albatrosses, while secretly hoping that albatross drumsticks will be on the menu.

11-EYES *

2009. TV series. DIR: Masami Shimoda. SCR: Kenichi Kanemaki, Mayori Sekijima, Mie Kagi. DES: Shoji Hara, Yutaka Miya, Hirotsugu Kakoi. ANI: Shoji Hara. MUS: N/C. PRD: feng, Lass, Marvelous Entertainment, Pony Canyon, Russell. 25 mins. x 12 eps.

Kakeru and his friend Yuka are both orphans. Kakeru's beloved older sister committed suicide ten years ago. One night the pair are thrown into another dimension full of terrible monsters and powerful beings. Luckily they meet another girl from their school who turns out to be adept with a sword. Others from their school are also being pulled in and out of the Red Night—as they name the alternate dimension—but they have no idea why, except that each of them seems to have strange and hitherto unsuspected powers. Why do the monsters call them "fragments"? Who's the mysterious cutie trapped inside a crystal?

Based on a visual novel (i.e., a text-based computer adventure game) by Lass, *11 Eyes* is an interesting premise let down by abuse of game tropes and some truly awful writing. Cliché is layered on cliché: the girl with glasses whose personality changes when she takes them off is also a compulsive breast-groper. There's a pervy "bonus" episode. The dialogue is repetitive, and major plot points are signaled so explicitly and shamelessly that it's almost funny. The graphic violence and (mostly) mild sexual content make this a bad choice for younger viewers, but they're just as likely to be scarred by the incompetent plotting. A series part-written by the great Mayori Sekijima should have been better. 🆖

ELF 17

1987. Video. DIR: Junichi Sakata. SCR: Sukehiro Tomita, Toshimichi Suzuki. DES: Takumi Tsukasa. ANI: Takumi Tsukasa. MUS: Kohei Tanaka. PRD: JC Staff, Agent 21. 30 mins.

Mascat Tyler (Masakado Taira, see DOOMED MEGALOPOLIS), the 108th Galactic Emperor, holds a competition to determine who will accompany him on a secret mission. After some comedic mishaps, soldier KK and the beautiful elfin Lu win the contest and set off on their quest. Based on one part of a long-running manga by Masahide Yamamoto in *Comi Comi* magazine.

ELF PRINCESS NINA

2010. JPN: *Elf Hime Nina.* Video. DIR: Ahiru Koike. SCR: ZEQU. DES: Cho Oto, Masaru Sato. ANI: Cho Oto, Hisashi Tomii. MUS: N/C. PRD: Pixy. 30 mins. x 3 eps.

Kyle is one of seven heroes who recently defeated an evil overlord. His younger brother Syll and Syll's lover Nina were also among the band of heroes. Now Kyle has stolen Syll's throne and means to steal his lover with the help of infeasibly well-endowed dark elf Miria, who will also get her comeuppance at the hands of humans, ogres, and demons. Based on an erotic game by Black Lilith. We're guessing that the director, Ahiru Koike, is a pseudonym, unless Mr. and Mrs. Pond really did call their son Duck for a joke. **NV**

ELF PRINCESS RANE *

1995. JPN: *Yosei Hime Rane*. AKA: *Fairy Princess Rane*. Video. DIR: Akitaro Daichi. SCR: Hitoshi Yamazaki. DES: Toshihide Sotodate. ANI: Toshihide Sotodate. MUS: Harukichi Yamamoto. PRD: KSS. 30 mins. x 2 eps.
Teen slacker Go Takarada wants to be an archeologist like his parents. He meets the titular Rane, who is on a quest for magical objects to save her homeland. Meanwhile, in this genuinely funny comedy from the director of **CARDCAPTORS**, Go's sisters (just three of a veritable army of siblings, who even have their own rock band) are taking sibling rivalry to extremes of collateral damage, and corporate plans for a local theme park threaten everything. Though loaded with anime sight gags (such as a pretty-boy baddie whose hair keeps getting in his eyes), the show's real strength lies in its script, which has multiple onscreen speakers yelling abuse at each other in several Japanese dialects. Despite these hellish complexities, Anime Works' English-language dub artfully captures the spirit of the original and preserves much of the show's wacky humor. Sadly, however, this was just one of many mid-1990s video comedies that never made it past episode 2.

ELFEN LAID *

2005. JPN: *Daishikkin Helena*. AKA: *Incontinent Helena*. Video. DIR: Daifuku Suginami. SCR: Sekiro Kamatsuchi. DES: Daifuku Suginami. ANI: Daifuku Suginami. MUS: Yoshi. PRD: YOUC, Digital Works (Vanilla Series). 30 mins. x 2 eps.
In the 5th century A.D., sisters Theodora and Helena of the Burgundian tribe see their homeland invaded by soldiers of the Merovingians. Fleeing the mass rape of the Burgundian women after the Merovingian victory, warrior-princess Theodora plans to commit suicide, but upon hearing that the demure Helena is still alive resolves to help her. Julianus, the Merovingian commander, is impressed by Theodora's haughty bearing and alabaster beauty, but

he is the sort of person (because this is *that* sort of anime) who wants to see beautiful women degraded and conquered.

However, his methods of achieving this are, at least for this genre of anime, remarkably original. He makes her the leader of his armies and sends her out to conquer other lands in the Merovingian name, but cruelly neglects to mention that all the while he is using her sister Helena as his sex toy. She discovers the truth upon her return, whereupon a series of further abuses ensues. Considering the title, it's a fair guess that enemas may be involved. Our rendering of the proper names in this Dark Age erotic anime are mere guesswork—they might be Merovingians, but they might equally be Melvins … historical accuracy is not really a deal-breaker in this sort of show. Part of the **VANILLA SERIES**. The U.S. title is, of course, a punning reference to **ELFEN LIED**. **LNV**

ELFEN LIED *

2004. AKA: *Elfen Song*. TV series, video. DIR: Mamoru Kanbe. SCR: Takao Yoshioka. DES: Seiji Kishimoto. ANI: Seiji Kishimoto. MUS: Kayo Konishi, Moka, Yukio Kondoo. PRD: Genco, VAP, ARMS, AT-X. 25 mins. x 13 eps. (TV), 30 mins. (v).
The Diclonius mutants look like normal humans, but are prophesied to be "chosen by God to destroy mankind." Despite no actual proof of this, the authorities decide to lock them up and experiment on them just to be on the safe side, until the inevitable day when a laboratory accident frees a Diclonius called Lucy. Her escape bid results in the deaths of 20 guards, but a head wound causes her to lose her memory. By the time she is found washed up on a Kamakura beach by teens Kota and Yuka, the only word she can say is *Nyu*, and this is what they call her.

The two kindly Japanese are initially unaware that Lucy has invisible psychic arms that can destroy anything in a two-meter radius—the only thing that is notably different about her is the two little horns that resemble **CHOBITS** attachments or cat ears. As one might expect with a show that could be described as **MAHOROMATIC** with mutants, the government soon dispatches a SWAT team to deal with the escaped lifeform, causing Lucy to periodically lapse into berserk fits of **GENOCYBER**-like rage. A

2005 video sequel appears on the seventh Japanese DVD and is widely considered as the 14th episode. It focuses around a flashback to Lucy's past and a domestic chore for one of the team. Based on Lynn Okamoto's manga in *Young Jump* weekly, billed as an "action comedyromance," although there was never all that much comedy in *Dr. Jekyll and Mr. Hyde*, or indeed in Guantanamo Bay. The anime also makes several links to German themes, most notably in an opening sequence that refers to the artwork of Gustav Klimt and allusions to Eduard Mörike's 19th-century poem *Elfenlied*. *Elfen Lied* is nonetheless an intriguing update of old anime themes— in the bipolar behaviors and looks of Nyu/ Lucy we have an action movie variant on the dichotomy found in the transforming "magical girl" sagas like **MARVELOUS MELMO**, or indeed the **LOLITA ANIME**. **NV**

ELFY

1986. JPN: *Aoi Umi no Elfy*. AKA: *Elfie of the Blue Seas, Legend of Coral Island*. TV special. DIR: Yoshihide Terai, Yoshio Kuroda. SCR: Nobuyuki Fujimoto. DES: Yoichi Kotabe. ANI: Takao Kogawa. MUS: Toshiyuki Watanabe. PRD: Nippon Animation, OH Pro, Fuji TV. 75 mins.
Four hundred years after a catastrophic rise in sea levels, the inhabitants of Earth live in giant floating cities. Twelve-year-old Elfy is raised by Nereus, one of the Seven Sages who rule over the city of Neptune. She discovers that her own black hair turns green when she swims and that she can breathe underwater. Expansion of Neptune's undersea farms meets with resistance from the local dolphins, among whom Elfy sees a merman with a strange shell necklace like her own. Investigating with Nereus and her brother, Alcus, Elfy discovers that the dolphins were responding to warning signals from the undersea empire of Mu (see **SUPER ATRAGON**), and that the expansionist plans of the Sage Charisma will be Neptune's doom. Nereus confesses that Elfy is adopted, and the distraught girl is arrested for releasing captured dolphins. Charisma leads a force from Neptune out against the merpeople, but Elfy intervenes and forms a psychic link between the two cultures. In a TV movie that cynics might call a marine replay of **NAUSICAÄ**, Elfy saves the day, but the

strain proves too much, and she becomes one with the waters.

ELLCIA *

1992. JPN: *Genso Jodan Ellcia*. AKA: *Fantastic Tales of Ellcia*. Video. DIR: Noriyasu Furukawa. SCR: Noriyasu Furukawa. DES: Yasuomi Umezu. ANI: Yasuomi Umezu. MUS: Tatsumi Yano. PRD: JC Staff. 45 mins. x 4 eps.

In a pseudo-medieval society, the people of Megaronia stumble on the relics of a lost civilization and leap ahead of their neighbors. Soon, the nation has conquered all the surrounding kingdoms, and the king's evil daughter, Crystel, sets out to find Ellcia, the legendary Ship of God, before the prophesied Fall of Megaronia can come to pass. In doing so, she inadvertently rouses the Chosen One who will destroy her kingdom, a young pirate girl called Eira.

The only remarkable thing about this tedious fantasy is that all aspects of production are uniformly poor, from lackluster designs by the famous Umezu to Yano's sub–*Raiders of the Lost Ark* music. The dub similarly disappoints with risible attempts at British dialogue, riddled with pronunciation howlers and remedial grammar. But who can blame the crews on both sides of the Pacific for merely cashing their paychecks? With its unconvincing pirates, pretentious philosophizing, and hackneyed plot, *Ellcia* was doomed from the scripting stage. **V**

ELVEN BRIDE, THE *

1995. JPN: *Elf no Waka Okusama*. Video. DIR: Hiroshi Yamakawa. SCR: N/C. DES: Kazuma G-version. ANI: Inaji Shimizu. MUS: N/C. PRD: KSS, Pink Pineapple. 27 mins. x 2 eps.

Town guardsman Kenji marries the elfin Milfa despite hostility from their families and friends. On their wedding night, Milfa reveals that although she may look 18, in elf years she is only five and too underdeveloped for full sexual intercourse. Kenji resolves to go on a quest for Harpy Ooze, said to be the ultimate sexual lubricant. He discovers that harpies cannot breed with other harpies and is "forced" to sire triplets with the angelic Pyully before he can obtain any Ooze. Milfa goes to see the local gynecologist, who attempts to molest her, but she is saved in the nick of time by Kenji and his grandmother.

Mixing magic with the mundane in the style of BELOVED BETTY, this sex comedy is set in a pseudo-medieval world that recalls DRAGON HALF, where there are faucets in the kitchen, but characters still brush their teeth outside at a well. But while it and the original manga by "Kazuma G-Version" on which it was based may contain subtextual musings on miscegenation and the perils of modern marriage, ultimately it is simply an excuse to see what LODOSS WAR's Deedlit would look like with her clothes off. **NL**

ELVES OF THE FOREST

1984. JPN: *Mori no Tontotachi*. TV series. DIR: Masakazu Higuchi, Norio Yazawa, Osamu Inoue. SCR: Yoshiaki Yoshida, Ryoko Takagi. DES: Susumu Shiraume. ANI: Akihito Kato. MUS: Takeo Watanabe. PRD: Zuiyo, Fuji TV. 25 mins. x 23 eps.

Deep in the forests of Finland live the "little people," or Tonttus, the elves who work all year round to keep Joulupukki (Santa Claus) supplied with toys for Christmas Eve. Based on the Finnish book *The Story of Santa Claus* and featuring a very Western look in the animation, *Elves of the Forest* also features one of anime's youngest actresses—one character was played by the designer's four-year-old daughter.

EMBLEM TAKE TWO

1993. Video. DIR: Tetsu Imazawa. SCR: Tatsuhiko Urahata. DES: Hideyuki Motohashi. ANI: Hideyuki Motohashi. MUS: Kazuhiko Sotoyama. PRD: Toei. 50 mins. x 2 eps.

Gangster Susumu is betrayed in the backstreets and lies dying in a pool of his own blood. He wakes up to find a time warp has transported him ten years back into the past, returning him to a younger, healthier version of his former self who is ready to take on the world once more. In a tale of time travel revisionism similar to DEEP BLUE FLEET, Susumu is equipped with indelible memories of the people who will fall into and out of favor, who will rise to power in the organization, and who will betray him, and he begins a revenge vendetta before his opponents realize he's there. Based on the 1990 manga from *Young Magazine*, written by Kazumasa Kiuchi and drawn by Jun Watanabe, that cleverly combines nostalgia with modern savvy and gangster chic, the anime version was made to cash in on the success of a 1993

live-action film and TV series, directed by the creators.

EMBRACING LOVE: A CICADA IN WINTER *

2007. JPN: *Fuyu no Semi*. Video. DIR: Yoshihisa Matsumoto. SCR: Mutsumi Nakano. DES: Takako Onishi, Satoru Nosaka. ANI: Tomoyuki Kitamura. MUS: N/C. PRD: VENET. 30 mins. x 3 eps.

The Meiji period: as Japan struggles to decide how to deal with the modern world beyond its shores, two young men on opposite sides of the political divide meet and fall in love. When family, honor, and duty conspire to keep them apart, how can something as fragile as an insect's wing survive the pressure? A beautiful and moving story with real emotional impact, enhanced by Hitomi Sano's lovely color design, this anime is related to Yuka Nitta's 1999 manga and its spin-off anime EMBRACING LOVE: CHERISHED SPRING. **N**

EMBRACING LOVE: CHERISHED SPRING *

2005. JPN: *Haru o Daite Ita*. Video. DIR: Yoshikata Nitta. SCR: Mami Watanabe. DES: Hirotaka Marufuji, Noboru Numai, Mitsuharu Miyamae. ANI: Hirotaka Marufuji. MUS: Sosaku Sasaki. PRD: Trinet Entertainment. 28 mins. x 2 eps.

Two young gay actors are climbing the ladder of success, escaping from adult video in the hope of becoming better performers and moving into mainstream productions. One wins a role in a major movie, but it's only when the other gets a role costarring with an actor just returned from working overseas that they both acknowledge the love between them. This anime is based on Yuka Nitta's 1999 manga *Embracing Love*. Elements of the manga were left out or reduced in the animation process, making the plot rather random and difficult to follow, and overall the story is less coherent than EMBRACING LOVE: A CICADA IN WINTER, but there's plenty of eye candy. Creator Nitta made her manga debut in 1995, but gave up creating comics for a while after a scandal involving allegations that she traced some of her work from other artists. She's now created over a dozen titles setting gay love stories in milieux ranging from politics and the nobility to yakuza life, police work, and host clubs.

EMERALD PRINCESS

1992. JPN: *Ruri-iro Princess*. Video. DIR: Takeshi Mori. SCR: Jiyu Watanabe. DES: Tetsuhito Saito. ANI: Tetsuhito Saito. MUS: Yoshiaki Matsuzawa. PRD: Studio Pierrot. 28 mins. x 2 eps.

High school girl Ruri is dragged into a battle over the fate of the Pulsean Moon when the princess Leila sends assassins to dispense with her. Ruri's lover, Toru, is wounded protecting her, and Ruri must leave the real world behind and journey to the Pulsean Moon to save him. Based on the manga in *Omajinai Comic* by Mito Orihara, who also wrote the theme song.

EMILY OF NEW MOON

2007. JPN: *Kaze no Shojo Emily*. AKA: *Emily, Girl of the Wind*. TV series. DIR: Harume Kosaka. SCR: Michiru Shimada. DES: Kanae Komatsu, Keizo Shimizu, Mayumi Okabe. ANI: N/C. MUS: Akira Miyagawa. PRD: TMS Entertainment, NHK. 25 mins. x 26 eps.

Orphaned at ten, Emily is sent to live on Prince Edward Island in the home town of the mother who died giving birth to her. Her two aunts have very different standards of behavior than her carefree father, and they expect her to do well in school and be a credit to the family. But with the help of her cousin Jimmy and the new friends she makes, Emily adjusts to life on the island and finds happiness in her new world. Based on the novel of the same name, written in 1923 by Lucie Maude Montgomery, this has many similarities with Montgomery's better-known ANNE OF GREEN GABLES. The story is gently paced and laced with warm, light-hearted humor, but the serious issues of bereavement, loss, and learning to fit in while remaining yourself are well handled. Beautiful, simple animation and exquisite backgrounds showcasing Canada's fabled rural charms make this family show a breath of fresh air, with nothing to offend and much to delight.

EMMA: A VICTORIAN ROMANCE *

2005. JPN: *Eikoku Koi Monogatari Emma*. AKA: *British Love Story Emma, Victorian Romance Emma*. TV series. DIR: Tsuneo Kobayashi. SCR: Mamiko Ikeda, Shinya Kawabata, Minoru Hirami, Reiko Yoshida. DES: Keiko Shimizu, Yuko Kusumoto. ANI: Akemi Kobayashi, Hiroto Tanaka, Keiko

Shimizu. MUS: Kunihiko Ryo. PRD: Studio Pierrot, TV Kanagawa, Ajia-do. 25 mins. x 12 eps. (TV1), 23 mins. (v), 25 mins. x 12 eps. (TV2).

Emma is a housemaid in late-19th-century England, devoted to her employer Kelly Stownar, a retired governess. Mrs. Stownar was unable to stay idle and on her retirement took in Emma, who was a homeless beggar girl, teaching her reading, writing, and the ways of polite society as an experiment in education. Emma's life is thrown into turmoil when the house is visited by William Jones, a handsome man who was once one of Kelly's pupils. What began as a simple courtesy call takes on new meaning as William and Emma feel an instant attraction, although the path to true love is unlikely to be smooth—William is a member of one of the wealthiest merchant families in England, whereas Emma is a mere maid. As such, the couple might as well be from different worlds, and that's before William's friend Hakim, a bona fide Indian prince, arrives and falls for Emma himself. In season two Emma finds employment with the Mölders, an expatriate German merchant family, who live in Haworth, West Yorkshire, former home of the Brontë sisters.

Emma is a gorgeous, refreshing anime for the 21st century, a Victorian CINDERELLA invested with a truly rare quality—the people who made it actually seem to like what they are doing, working with Kaoru Mori's beautifully observed manga from *Comic Beam*. The sights and sounds of 19th-century England are lovingly recreated in a quiet, understated drama that recalls LITTLE PRINCESS and the better productions of the WORLD MASTERPIECE THEATER. At a time when the word "maid" in an anime synopsis normally heralds something like MAIDS IN DREAM or ANOTHER LADY INNOCENT, *Emma* is a sign that while corporate raiders and carpetbaggers are doing everything they can to ruin the medium, anime still has rare gems that can surprise and entertain. It is also another example of the curious Japanese love affair with Englishness, most notable in recent years in STEAMBOY and HERCULE POIROT AND MISS MARPLE. Note that, in a piece of period stunt-casting, lead actress Yumi Toma was also the Japanese voice of Kate Winslet in *Titanic*. Season two includes

an "episode 0," a recap episode for season one, which may have been a TV special or a direct-to-video release.

EMPEROR OF THE PLUM PLANET

1969. JPN: *Umeboshi Denka*. AKA: *Emperor of the Plum World*. TV series, movie. DIR: Shinichi Suzuki, Hiroshi Hatasenji. SCR: Koji Tanaka, Shima Namie, Takao Niinuma. DES: Fujiko-Fujio. ANI: Masuji Kigami. MUS: Hajme Hayashi. PRD: Studio Zero, Shinei Animation, Tokyo Movie Shinsha. 25 mins. x 27 eps. (TV), ca. 80 mins. (m).

When their homeworld is destroyed, the emperor, empress, and crown prince of Ume escape to Earth in a bottle. Forced to lodge with average Earth boy Taro Nakamura, they attempt to reestablish their empire on Earth with little success, even when their loyal retainer Benishoga arrives to "help." DORAEMON–creators Fujiko-Fujio conceived this story for *Shonen Sunday* in the style of their earlier Q-TARO THE GHOST. Originally broadcast on a Sunday to help promote its manga incarnation, it was moved to Tuesdays and then taken off-air completely. Compare to SERGEANT FROG, which similarly features a benignly incompetent alien invader. To mark its 35th "anniversary" (not that anyone cared, but modern producers love their meaningless celebrations), a new movie version, *EPP: Paro-paro-pan! From the Ends of the Universe*, brought Denka to the big screen in 1994.

EMPEROR OF THE SOUTH SIDE

1993. JPN: *Nanba Kinyu Den: Minami no Teio*. JPN: *The Story of Nanba Credit: Emperor of the South*. Video. DIR: Yoshitaka Fujimoto. SCR: Yoshitaka Fujimoto. DES: Masayuki Watanabe. ANI: Masayuki Watanabe. MUS: N/C. PRD: SHS Project, KSS. 45 mins. x 2 eps.

Ginjiro is a gangster in South Central Osaka who has just ten days to get back a massive debt. This hard-hitting yakuza tale was based on the 1992 manga by Dai Tennoji (pseud. for THERE GOES SHURA–author Yu Kawanabe) and Rikiya Go in *Manga Goraku* magazine and was also adapted into a live-action video movie. **Ⓥ**

ENCHANTED JOURNEY *

1981. JPN: *Glikko no Boken*. AKA: *Glikko's Adventure*. Movie. DIR: Hideo Nishimaki. SCR: Yasuo Tanami. DES: Yoshio Kabashima. ANI:

Takeshi Yamazaki. MUS: Reijiro Koroku. PRD: Studio Koryumi. 82 mins.

On the advice of Pippo the pigeon, Glikko the chipmunk leaves his urban home with his friend Nonnon (in the English dub, Nono), in search of a legendary forest where the animals run free, meeting Gamba the vole on the way. After many hardships, Glikko gives up and collapses in the snow, only to be rescued by his friends and arrive in the forest safely. Based on a story by Atsushi Saito that won a Best Newcomer award from the Association for the Study of Japanese Children's Books. Five years later, it was dubbed for U.S. TV by SPEED RACER's Peter Fernandez, featuring Lionel "Tom Terrific" Wilson in the title role, Jim "Mr Magoo" Backus as Gamba, and, we can't believe we're saying this, Orson Welles as Pippo the pigeon. Compare to BANNERTAIL THE SQUIRREL.

ENCOURAGEMENT OF CLIMB *

2013. JPN: Yama no Susume. TV series, video. DIR: Yusuke Yamamoto. SCR: Yusuke Yamamoto. DES: Yusuke Matsuo. ANI: N/C. MUS: Flying Pan et al. PRD: Earth Star Entertainment, 8-Bit, AT-X. 5 mins. x 12 eps. (TV1), 5 mins. (v), 5 mins. x ? eps. (TV2).

Old friends Aoi and Hinata form the unlikely nucleus of a group of would-be mountaineers, with Hinata dragging her agoraphobic friend into a hill-walking exercise in the hope of reliving the magical sight of a mountain-top sunrise in their childhood. The teenage girls and their friends are soon bickering over the rights and wrongs of camping and climbing, discovering the lore and legends of Japan's mountains, and getting back to nature with varying degrees of success. Empowered by their newfound love of the great outdoors, they return in a second season for further adventures, with the aim of tackling Mount Fuji itself.

Taking the perky girl hobbyists of K-ON and many another show, and throwing them into a celebration of outdoorsy life, this is another of those EVERYDAY ANIME that celebrates the Japanese hinterland as some sort of unspoiled wilderness, as indeed it may well be for the average couch-potato teen (SILVER SPOON). Based on the comic by "Shiro" that ran in Comic Earth Star.

END OF SUMMER *

1994. JPN: Dokyusei Natsu no Owari ni. AKA: Classmates until the End of Summer. Video. DIR: Kinji Yoshimoto. SCR: Sukehiro Tomita. DES: Masaki Takei, Ryunosuke Otonashi. ANI: Yoshiyuki Okuno. MUS: Tomas Unit. PRD: KSS, Pink Pineapple. 45 mins. x 1 eps. (v1 version 1), 30 mins. x 4 eps. (v1 version 2), 30 mins. x 2 eps. (Climax), 30 mins. x 12 eps. (Classmates 2), 30 mins. x 3 eps. (Graduation), 20 mins. x 1 eps. (Special: Love Special Lesson—Ren'ai Senka).

Wataru really loves Mai, but there's temptation all around and he just can't resist. The typical teenage-boy dream: lots of gorgeous women just throwing themselves at you, and a girl-next-door who believes you when you say you couldn't help yourself. The artwork, under the direction of PLASTIC LITTLE's Yoshimoto, is really lovely, and you can observe the artists' skill with flesh tones in some detail. This series was based on the computer game Classmates by DRAGON KNIGHT–creator "elf" (Masato Hiruda), and seems to be the first "dating sim" to be adapted into an anime, thereby initiating a significant subgenre within the medium. The original 45-minute one-shot was expanded with additional footage into two 30-minute episodes (less two seconds of footage inexplicably deleted from the original) plus two more episodes, for a total of four. The direct sequel of two episodes, Classmates: Climax, followed in 1995. A further 12-part sequel, Classmates 2 (1997), was released in Japan on video and later cut into two toned-down TV movies. The Classmates 2 video series was edited into a nine-part television drama and broadcast in summer 1998, followed by Classmates 2: Graduation Special, a three-part video that, we suspect, may have included the bits missing from the TV version. It was then released as an LD box set with the bonus disc Classmates:Love Special Lesson—Ren'ai Senka, which featured the leads in original anime form, super-deformed cartoon versions, and then in a live-action segment, played by their voice actors, in which they have to fight against two super-villainous girls. As seems traditional with such spin-offs, the 20-minute running time was augmented with a 20-minute "Making Of" recycling the scenery and collecting statements from those involved. Just to confuse things, an

unrelated live-action series with a similar theme and the same title, based on a manga by Fumi Saimon, was broadcast the same year; see Classmates (*DE).

As with its related title FIRST LOVES, Classmates presents a truly bewildering array of alternate versions for the encyclopedist. Many of these alternates were never rereleased on DVD, and are consequently uncatalogued on the filmmakers' websites and lost to the anime historian, until the inevitable giant anniversary box set of all variants in the style of CREAM LEMON. Ⓝ

ENDLESS SERENADE *

2000. Video. DIR: Rokurota Makabe. SCR: N/C. DES: Teruaki Murakami. ANI: Natsu Motoki. MUS: Yoshi. PRD: Digital Works (Vanilla Series), YOUC. 35 mins.

Yuji struggles with his feelings for his dead brother Ryoji's beautiful fiancée Satsuki, as the pair of them cooperate on setting up the store that was Ryoji's lifelong ambition. But Satsuki is still mourning her dearly departed, while the pretty young Miki has a crush on Yuji that the lovelorn boy has yet to notice. While the art and animation are mediocre, the character development is surprisingly intense for a pornographic anime. Compare with WIFE WITH WIFE episode 1; part of the VANILLA SERIES. ⒷⓃ

ENDO, SHIGEO

1949–. Born in Fukushima Prefecture, Endo joined Nippon Animation, where he worked in production for Hayao Miyazaki's FUTURE BOY CONAN, and subsequent WORLD MASTERPIECE THEATER serials, including ANNE OF GREEN GABLES and PETER PAN. In later years, he became the producer of CHIBI MARUKO-CHAN.

ENGAGE PLANET KISS DUM *

2007. JPN: kiss dum—ENGAGE planet. TV series. DIR: Yasuchika Nagaoka, Eiichi Sato. SCR: Yasuchika Nagaoka, Katsuhiko Takayama. DES: Sushio, Shoji Kawamori, Seo Gu Lee, Thomas Romain. ANI: Hiromi Okazaki, Kazuya Miyoshi, Kei Tsuchiya. MUS: II Mix Delta. PRD: Satelight, Bandai Visual, Project NES. 25 mins. x 26 eps.

In 2031, monstrous bug-like life-forms called Hardians commence a series of attacks on human beings. The Neo International Defense Force, or NIDF, is organized to investigate them and fight them.

Fighter pilot Shu and his amnesiac lover, scientist Yuno, are part of the fight, and when they hear rumors about a mysterious Book of the Dead, they set out to find if it can help them. They learn that one person will be chosen by the Book as its messenger, the Necrodiver, with the potential to save humankind.

Despite a slow start—an entire recap episode after just three weeks isn't the ideal way to maintain pace—and a chaotic plot, the show has a good deal to offer in visual terms. The deliberate confusion of similarly named characters is resolved by paying a little attention, and the character designs are distinctive enough to help out with that. Shoji Kawamori's machinery is gorgeous, the best part of the package, and his regular collaborator Thomas Romain gets a credit for art design. The show might have enjoyed wider success in the English-speaking market, but for the fact that it was licensed to Bandai Visual USA shortly before Bandai Namco Holdings announced the liquidation of the company's holdings.

ENGAGED TO THE UNIDENTIFIED *

2014. JPN: *Mikakunin de Shinkokei.* TV series. DIR: Yoshiyuki Fujiwara. SCR: Fumihiko Shimo. DES: Ai Kikuchi. ANI: Ai Kikuchi. MUS: Jun Ichikawa. PRD: Dogakobo, Dax, McRay, Toho. 24 mins. x 12 eps. (TV), 12 mins. (v1), 10 mins. (v2).

Achingly average schoolgirl Kobeni gets a surprise on her 16th birthday, when she is told that her late grandfather had promised her hand in marriage to a boy from her ancestral village, and that said boy, Hakuya, will now be coming to stay with them in the city. Hakuya arrives with his precocious little sister in tow, much to the excitement of Kobeni's ethically questionable Lolita-obsessed elder sister Benio. But while *Engaged to the Unidentified* is objectively bland and unassuming, its matter-of-fact treatment of a lodger who is also a fiancé is an interesting allusion to what was once a relatively common custom in old Japan. Hakuya's presence in Kobeni's life isn't merely a foil for misunderstandings and bickering, but also a reminder that so many Japanese city dwellers are themselves only one or two generations removed from the rural traditions from which Kobeni recoils in

horror. Additional weight is added to this town-country divide through revelations about Hakuya's origins, which turn out to be more supernatural than expected, as if the countryside is the place where magic can still happen (FANTASY AND FAIRY TALES). Unfortunately, later episodes drag up the tiresome specter of *osana-najimi* (ROMANCE AND DRAMA), revealing that Hakuya is not quite the stranger he first appears, and that he and Kobeni might truly be made for each other after all. Based on a 2009 four-panel strip by Cherry-Arai in *Manga 4-Koma Palette* magazine; two later compilation volumes of the manga were bundled with short bonus DVD episodes.

EQUATION OF THE ROTTEN TEACHER

1994. JPN: *Kusatta Kyoshi no Hoteishiki.* AKA: *Fish in the Trap, Bad Teacher's Equation.* Video. DIR: Nanako Shimazaki. SCR: Hiromi Akino. DES: Akira Koguro. ANI: Yumi Nakayama. MUS: N/C. PRD: Daiei, Tokuma Japan Communications. 30 mins. x 2 eps.

In this adaptation of another gay-love manga from Kazuma Kadoka, the creator of KIZUNA, ten years after being forced to suppress his feelings for the beautiful boy next door, a young man meets the object of his desires and gets a second chance. But Atsushi, whose unrequited love still burns, now finds himself in a classroom where Ma-chan, the object of his youthful affections, is now the teacher. A humorous homosexual variant on the school shenanigans of HOMEROOM AFFAIRS. **Ⓝ**

ERGO PROXY *

2006. TV series. DIR: Shuko Murase. SCR: Dai Sato. DES: Naoyuki Onda, Michiaki Sato. ANI: N/C. MUS: Yoshihiro Ike. PRD: Manglobe, Geneon. 25 mins. x 23 eps.

Lil Mayor is an agent in the Civil Intelligence Organization, charged with investigating crime in the dome city of Lando. Supposedly an emotionless utopia where humans and robots coexist in harmony, Lando has been troubled by a series of murders, although Lil herself is also troubled by a series of hauntings and attacks by phantoms that urge her to notice that an "awakening" is in progress. A series of psychological dramas soon reveal "an unimaginable truth," related to the world outside the dome, it says here. We don't

know, but we can imagine quite a bit. Compare to HEAT GUY J and the BIG O.

EROTIC TEMPTRESS, THE *

1994. JPN: *Inma Yojo.* AKA: *Lust-Beast Fairies; Imma youjo: The Erotic Temptress* Video. DIR: Yukiyoshi Makino. SCR: Tsukasa Tomii. DES: Kazushi Iwakura. ANI: Kazushi Iwakura. MUS: Takeo Nakazawa. PRD: Pink Pineapple, KSS. 45 mins. x 5 eps.

Witchery and bondage as a variety of women, all named Maya, wander a landscape inhabited by depraved rapists. One enters a town where the ruling tyrant dwells in a "tower of pleasures" and sends out young ruffians to procure women, whose juices he requires in the manufacture of a dangerous drug. Before long, Maya is captured and abused by a gang of men before the stories go on to depict several more episodes of assault, including one at the hands of robot women, the seduction of an unsuspecting knight, and even a retelling of one of the oldest JAPANESE FOLK TALES, as two witches lure passers-by to their deaths on a haunted mountain pass. Not to be confused with the COOL DEVICES story *Slave Warrior Maya*, or indeed with ROSE OF VERSAILLES, with which it shares some look-alike characters and costumes, though the costumes don't stay on for long. Previously released in the U.S. as *Imma Youjo: The Erotic Temptress.* **ⒸⓃⓋ**

EROTIC TORTURE CHAMBER *

1994. JPN: *Princess Lord: Bara to Dokuro no Monsho.* AKA: *Princess Lord: The Mark of Rose and Skull, Princess Road.* Video. DIR: Yoshitaka Fujimoto. SCR: Akira Oketani. DES: Masakatsu Sasaki. ANI: Masakatsu Sasaki. MUS: Torsten Rasch. PRD: Taki Corporation. 45 mins.

After 30 happy years, the twin kingdoms of Asronia and Gostania are awaiting the wedding of Prince Elias and Princess Yurie when the royal family is torn apart by the army of Maryuo, the "Demon Dragon Lord." Elias is captured, Yurie is enslaved, and while the two supporting players who will save the day in the as-yet-unavailable second episode mooch around in their own subplot, the princess is taught the meaning of submission and obedience. The dark armor of Maryuo hides a well-spoken young man called Andreas, who wears half a bathrobe for no apparent reason and is exactly the kind of Bad Boy we know that Yurie has been waiting for. Yurie "reluctantly" offers her body to her captor in order to save her people.

A roster of well-known voice talents but with animation and design of a poor quality one has come to expect from a production crew just trying to pay the bills. The in-betweening often falters and the characters are lifted from other shows. The ninja bodyguard Maya borrows elements from both Ayanosuke of **Yotoden** and Oscar of **Rose of Versailles**, while the other leads are a standard cluster of anime archetypes.

The story's origin in Pierce Hoshino's erotic novel is betrayed in a languorous pacing that takes a good 20 minutes to get down to the nitty-gritty and so much back story that you can feel the original straining to squeeze itself into the format. Sex was clearly not the be-all and end-all of the original story, resulting in an anime version that takes too long to get going and then ends on a cliffhanger just when it does. Note that the alternate title *Princess Road* is a mis-transliteration of the original title by the distributor, Five Ways. ◐

EROTICA AND PORNOGRAPHY

The first pornographic anime should have been Hakusan Kimura's *Cool Ship* (*Suzumi-bune*, 1932), the first part of an erotic two-reeler, seized by the police when only half complete; the remnants of this movie were eventually uncovered as part of a police archive donated to the National Film Center in the early 21st century, when Tokyo's police impounds tried to divest themselves of all the dangerously flammable silver nitrate film they had acquired over the years. After Kimura's film, anime avoided erotica until a slump in TV profits led Osamu Tezuka to produce **A Thousand and One Nights** (1969) and **Cleopatra: Queen of Sex** (1970) for cinema theaters. History records that these movies failed to revitalize the fortunes of Tezuka's Mushi Production, but at the time of its release the hype associated with the former impressed other animators enough to inspire the rival Nishimura Productions to make *Secret Movie: A Thousand and One Nights in the Floating World* (*Hi-eiga: Ukiyoe Sen-ichi Ya*, 1969). Deliberately drawn in an evocation of woodblock prints, the film also ran into

trouble with the authorities and only went onto general release after the removal of six scenes deemed obscene. But cartoons were still regarded as a children's medium, and making animation that would be invisible to its chief audience must have seemed silly. The last gasp of erotic anime in cinemas was **Yasuji's Pornorama** (1971), a comedy that ended with the frustrated leading man's attempt to commit ritual suicide—a perilous pastiche of the recent demise of novelist Yukio Mishima. Thereafter, all erotica—comedic, satiric, or otherwise—faded from cinemas, as Japan's soft-core "pink" live-action movies took over.

Erotica in any medium is beholden to censorship restrictions in the country that hosts it. Consequently, even live-action erotic cinema in Japan developed along lines that can seem strange to outside observers—proscriptions on visible genitalia and (until 1991) pubic hair often leading to ludicrously over-artistic camerawork, depilated characters who appear underage, or fetishes such as sexualized bondage. Pornography is also often the first part of any media culture to experiment with new means of distribution or access, and anime was no exception. Absent from animation as a genre for over a decade, pornography swiftly returned with the arrival of the video cassette recorder and the laserdisc player, with the infamous **Lolita Anime** and **Cream Lemon** (both 1984). Ever since, anime pornography has remained a constant blue-chip area in the video business, since the titles can be short, easily produced, and retail at high prices. Sales of anime porn to private consumers were less common—the tapes often seemed designed to be watched once and returned, and only gained a "collector's" cachet with the coming of laserdiscs and DVDs. Amid the frenzied couplings of everyday pornographic anime, two titles are worthy of special attention. Hideki Takayama's anime adaptation of Toshio Maeda's **Urotsuki-doji** (1987) pioneered the new subgenre of "erotic horror," incorporating sexual acts into fantasy scenarios and violence, and is particularly noted for popularizing the tentacle as a phallus substitute in order to evade censorship. Its polar opposite was Yukio Abe's **The Sensualist** (1990), a masterpiece of old-world geisha charm

and symbolic eroticism, based on Saikaku Ihara's 17th-century novel, *The Life of an Amorous Man.*

Video anime also introduced the new *sub*-subgenre of gay erotica, supposedly sold to a female audience, although evidence from the filmmakers' choices of advertising venues suggest that such titles have a far larger male audience than some Japanese sources acknowledge. Titles such as **Zetsuai** (1992), **My Sexual Harrassment** (1994), and **Legend of the Blue Wolves** (1996) are tales in which strong, predatory older men seduce young, virginal victims. Others, such as **Fake** (1996), attempt to introduce homosexual characters to mainstream genres such as the cop show.

The first lesbian activity in anime was in Tezuka's **A Thousand and One Nights**, when Aladdin's daughter, disguised as a young man, makes a marriage of convenience with a princess who finds the arrangement more convenient than expected. Overt lesbianism doesn't appear to have been referenced again until the erotic video boom of the 1980s. When it reappeared in 1984, in two **Lolita Anime** segments, lesbianism was in its usual mass media guise as entertainment for heterosexual men. The lackluster **Lolicon Angel** (1985) crashed school lesbianism into the mystery story but didn't escape the accident unscathed. Girls' schools and convents have always been prime territory for pornography, providing a secret space outside "normal" experience where exploration won't impinge on the outside world. In 1986, the **Cream Lemon** segment *Escalation* provided a dark view of exploitative lesbian S&M in—surprise, surprise—an exclusive girls' school. But *CL* also opened up new porn genres—fantasy and science fiction. *Pop Chaser* presented a lesbian biker heroine and a ditzy little damsel in distress happy to switch orientation depending on the situation, while *Star Trap* showed the lively lesbian crew of a vessel not entirely unlike the USS Enterprise. The intense sexuality of the girls' school got a less explicit, but much darker and more serious, treatment in **Brother Dearest** (1991) before reverting to type for 1995's **Angel of Darkness**. Meanwhile, **Hanappe Bazooka** poked tasteless and energetic fun at most forms of sexuality in 1992.

The authors are unable to think of many anime made *for* lesbians, as opposed to those likely to be targeting males in search of girl-on-girl titillation, although there are a few possible contenders such as SWEET BLUE FLOWERS and WHISPERED WORDS (both 2009). The cross-dressing traditions of the Takarazuka theater, as evoked in PRINCESS KNIGHT, and the regular use of female voice actors to play leading male roles in everything from DRAGON BALL to EVANGELION, suggest that some mainstream titles may have an unintended appeal to a lesbian audience. Certainly, the UTENA movie was regarded as sapphic enough in its outlook to play at the London Lesbian and Gay Film Festival—it should also be noticed that same-sex crushes are often a feature of mainstream school anime such as THE VIRGIN MARY IS WATCHING (2004), and lesbian activity, or its implication, remains a common feature of many erotica aimed at men.

Another strand of anime makes no explicit reference to sexuality at all, but is loaded with homoerotic potential—boy team shows. From the heroic teenagers of SAINT SEIYA fighting epic battles with the gods in 1986, via the Hong Kong hothouse of VIRUS (1997), to the sporting action of PRINCE OF TENNIS (2001), it seems that female FANDOM only needs good-looking guys in tense, emotionally charged situations, like saving the world, winning the match, or luring a best friend/older brother back from the Dark Side, to start producing fantasies that would make experienced porn writers blush. If this proves anything, it is that the principal sexual organ in humans is the brain, with its imagination, and—sometimes—sense of the ridiculous.

The rise of computer games saw a heavy concentration on the anime art-style, initially because anime-style images did not require the high resolution of real photographs. With the release of Studio Gainax's *Princess Maker* (1991) and its imitators, Japan also saw a rise in the "gamification" of female characters, reducing their motives and behavior to a series of customizable and manipulable variables. Romance itself (ROMANCE AND DRAMA), in many games, came to assume the form less of human interaction than of a series of database entries and ticked boxes, as male players tried to "win" the affections of their quarries, or even passively waited while their responses to certain situations sifted the ideal mate for them from a population of possibles. It was only a matter of time before many such games were adapted into fully animated versions, particularly in the "dating simulation" subgenre where lonely male protagonists searched for their ideal Girl Next Door among a group of carefully designed archetypes. Not all such games had an overt erotic subject, but GRADUATION (1994; original game, June 1992), END OF SUMMER (1994, original game released as *Dokyusei* in December 1992), and TOKIMEKI MEMORI-AL (1999; original game May 1994) still led to the establishment of a new paradigm. Erotic or not, the "harem show" took the premise of the dating sims and adapted it for a mainstream audience, resulting in a slew of chaste quests for love—the most famous examples being TENCHI MUYO! (1992) and LOVE HINA (2000). There also remains a thriving subgenre in erotic anime that parodies mainstream titles, such as BALTHUS: TIA'S RADIANCE, TOKIO PRIVATE POLICE, and VENUS FIVE. In a wider sense of the pornographic, delivering to audiences exactly what the audience demands, and *only* that, the 21st-century culture of *moe* presents a subset of anime fans with a series of archetypal little girls inviting adoration and protection, playing up to the arrested development implied in both watcher and watched (KIDS' ANIME). *Moe* has become a powerful commodity in the modern anime world, where its miniscule audience numbers, rarely above four figures for any particular show, are offset by the immense dedication and relative wealth of the audience. As a result, a disproportionate number of minor anime serials in the 21st century are little more than mood pieces serving as hooks for merchandise or spin-offs from software, pandering to the fetishes of a small circle of single men with disposable incomes and a professed interest in unthreatening, nonexistent female "characters." While apologists for *moe* often claim an asexual purity of intent, the authors choose to file it here with erotica, as it undoubtedly fills that function for many of its adherents.

During the 1990s, anime erotica found a new and unexpected audience outside Japan, where it became the secret cash cow of the foreign anime business. In some territories, teen titillation and erotic horror were used to manufacture controversy, leading to the popular public misconception that *all* anime is pornographic. In fact, most pornographic anime is available in small one- and two-episode formats; a book such as this is forced to use an unrepresentative amount of space discussing the genre, since it would take literally a thousand titles like EROTIC TORTURE CHAMBER to fill the running time of a single SAZAE-SAN. Nevertheless, pornographic anime was particularly likely to be translated for the English-language market in the late 20th and early 21st centuries, with franchises such as the D3 SERIES, DISCOVERY SERIES, SECRET ANIMA, and VANILLA SERIES reaching American video stores more rapidly than many mainstream works. Often in quantities far exceeding their original Japanese duplication runs, and retailing far more cheaply than Japanese titles (most of which were destined for the rental market), these titles focus on fetishes that can prove to be more problematic for live-action porn, such as the sexualized violence of BIBLE BLACK or the scatology of NIGHT SHIFT NURSES. Many viewers' first encounter with Japanese culture is hence with niche-area pornography aimed at a tiny subset of the Japanese population. Foreign journalists, in particular, are often eager to assume that Japanese are fervent fans of titles such as ANGEL CORE or WIFE EATER, whereas sales comparisons would suggest the exact opposite, and that many such titles reach larger audiences outside Japan than inside it.

ESCAFLOWNE *

1996. JPN: *Tenku no Escaflowne.* AKA: *Heavenly Escaflowne, The Vision of Escaflowne.* TV series, movie. DIR: Kazuki Akane, Shin-ichiro Watanabe, Takeshi Yoshimoto, Hiroshi Osaka, Takuro Shinbo, Tetsuya Yanasawa, Hiroyuki Takeuchi. SCR: Shoji Kawamori, Ryota Yamaguchi, Akihiko Inari, Hiroaki Kitajima. DES: Nobuteru Yuki, Kimitoshi Yamane, Mahiro Maeda. ANI: Shigeki Kobara, Yuki Kanno, Takahiro Omori, Yoshiyuki Takei. MUS: Yoko Kanno, Hajime Mizoguchi. PRD: Sunrise, TV Tokyo. 25 mins. x 26 eps. (TV), 98 mins. (m).

Hitomi Kanzaki is transported to an alternate Earth when a dragon appears on her school's running track. On Gaea, Earth is called the Mystic Moon, beast-men rub shoulders with knights in giant robots, and Earth girls are respected and feared for their sorcerous powers. Her companion, Van, is the disinherited prince of Fanelia and owner of the robot-armor Escaflowne, with which he resists the evil Zaibach Empire. Hitomi is witness to the uneasy alliance between Van and another nobleman, Asturia's roguish ladykiller Allen, but she is also the object of their competing affections. Tortured family ties writhe beneath the surface, with missing or disinherited siblings galore and revelations of dark or forgotten pasts. In only the first of several major plot twists, it is revealed that one of the leaders of the Zaibach armies is Folken, Van's disgraced brother. As war sweeps Gaea, Hitomi is revealed as the crucial key to victory, a role she is tempted to swap for a simple, carefree life back on Earth.

Deliberately designed to appeal to male and female viewers in equal measure, *Escaflowne* is genuine family entertainment, both in and out of the anime world, and arguably the best TV anime of the 1990s. Its ambiguous nature is reflected in *two* spin-off manga, Katsu-Aki's *The Vision of Escaflowne* for the male readership of *Comics A*, and Yuzuru Yashiro's *Messiah Knight* for the female readership of *Asuka Fantasy DX*.

Five years in the planning, with something of a debt to Secret of Blue Water, it and Utena were the two highly romantic shows that flourished in the morbid vacuum left by Evangelion. In retaining its coherence throughout, and its earnest devotion to fantasy ideals instead of arch irony, posterity may well decide that *Escaflowne* is the best of them all. Reputedly passed over by Manga Entertainment for being "too childish," it starts off looking like a school romance or girls' Sports Anime before transforming into high fantasy adventure. As with Gunbuster, its first episode is a red herring, a school soap opera where Hitomi pines for her handsome senior Amano. In a steal from the stage version of Peter Pan and Wendy, the actors of Earth scenes also play doubles in the fantasy world—Shinichiro Miki provides the voice of both Amano and *real* prince charming Allen. One of the few shows to continually outdo

itself, *Escaflowne* is a triumph—though the dub sadly missed the opportunity to differentiate between accents on the two worlds by making all the Gaeans British.

Though it was reduced in size from a planned 39-episode run partway through production, the only evidence is the absence of opening credits from the first episode in order to allow the crew time to cram in extra exposition. This was remedied in the Japanese video release, the retail version of which also restored deleted scenes to the first seven episodes. As the inevitable consequence of its popularity, it exists in bastardized versions, including the incoherent three-part *Best Collection* that unsuccessfully crams the entire story into just 180 minutes. The series was further bowdlerized for the American TV market, with Yoko Kanno's beautiful music torn out in favor of humdrum techno, and the first episode removed in a version that, with bitter irony, was taken off the air after 10 episodes because of "low ratings."

The movie version *Escaflowne: A Girl in Gaea* (2000) is a complete remake that redesigns the characters for the big screen and plays up the Asian feel of the series— the earlier TV version allowed elements of European fantasy to creep in.

ESPER MAMI

1987. AKA: *Malicieuse/Mischievous Kiki.* TV series, movie. DIR: Pak Kyon Sun, Keiichi Hara, Tsukasa Sunaga, Atsuhide Tsukata, Osamu Inoue, Mitsuru Honma, Shinya Sadamitsu, Tomomi Mochizuki. SCR: Sukehiro Tomita, Ryo Motohira, Akira Higuchi. DES: Fujiko-Fujio. ANI: Sadao Tominaga, Chuji Nakajima. MUS: Kohei Tanaka. PRD: Shinei, TV Asahi. 25 mins. x 119 eps., 40 mins. (m).
Schoolgirl Mami Sagura discovers that she has superpowers. She can sense other people in trouble and teleport to help them, but she keeps her secret double-life hidden from her parents with the help of her schoolfriend, Kazuo Takahata. Based on the 1977 manga in *Corocoro Comic* by Doraemon–creators Fujiko-Fujio, the series also spawned a short film, *EM: Midnight Dancing Doll* (1988), featuring Mami using her powers to make a puppet show for deprived children.

ETCHIIS

1997. Video. DIR: Kazunari Kume. SCR: Yokihi.

DES: Yokihi. ANI: Toshimitsu Kobayashi. MUS: N/C. PRD: Pink Pineapple, KSS. 30 mins. x 2 eps.
Two short comedies, *Unio Familia* and *Normal Human Relations*, reputedly praised for "realistic female characterization" and lots of sex scenes. Based on the 1995 manga anthology by Yokihi, though *2x1*, the original's most popular story, was animated as part of the Secret Anima series the following year and released in the U.S. as *Four Play.* **N**

ETERNAL FILENA

1992. JPN: *Eien no Filena.* Video. DIR: Naoto Hashimoto, Yoshikata Nitta. SCR: Takeshi Shudo, Yasuko Hoshigawa. DES: Akemi Takada, Akiyuki Shinbo. ANI: Chuji Nakajima. MUS: Jinmo, Noriyoshi Matsuura. PRD: Pierrot Project. 30 mins. x 4 eps.
The Devis Empire offers gladiatorial games to keep the masses happy. It's the only way for a commoner to make any kind of living, and the lucky few who last long enough are made citizens. Filena poses as a man to enter the arena and fight to support her ailing mother, but as time passes, she begins to prefer the life of a poor revolutionary to that of a rich slave. Based on a novel serialized in *Animage* by Pokémon–writer Shudo. Compare to Grey: Digital Target.

EUPHORIA

2011. Video. DIR: Kunio Ayano, Oji Hakudaku. SCR: ROMko Hachite. DES: Citizen. ANI: Lee Min Bae. MUS: N/C. PRD: Majin. 29 mins. x 2 eps.
Six students and a teacher wake in a mysterious white room, with no idea of how they got there. Keisuke Takato is the only male. A mysterious voice tells them that Keisuke is now the "unlocker" and one of the girls is the "keyhole." In order to escape the room, of course, Keisuke must commit certain immoral acts and unlock the keyhole. When one of the girls reacts angrily she is bound to a torture device and told that anyone who quits the game will die. As she defecates and pees in terror, Keisuke finds himself turned on. His dark secret, his wish to dominate and humiliate women, is coming into the open. This story of ciphers forced to obey the rules of a sadistic computer game is, appropriately enough, based on a sadistic

porn game by CLOCKUP, but has a basic premise curiously close to that of **GANTZ**. Or if you are Hollywood-minded, the *Saw* movies. **NV**

EUREKA 7 *

2005. JPN: *Kokyoshihen Eureka Seven*. AKA: *Symphonic Poem Eureka Seven*. TV series, movie. DIR: Tomomi Kyoda, Masayuki Miyaji, Kazuya Murata, Takeshi Yoshimoto. SCR: Chiaki Konaka, Dai Sato, Hiroshi Onogi, Shotaro Suga, Yuichi Nomura. DES: Kenichi Yoshida, Shoji Kawamori, Kazutaka Miyatake. ANI: Eiji Nakata, Seiichi Hashimoto. MUS: Naoki Sato. PRD: BONES, Bandai Entertainment, MBS. 25 mins. x 50 eps. (TV1), 115 mins. (m), 25 mins. x 24 eps. (TV2). Human colonists on an alien world utilize "trapars," strange airborne particles in the local atmosphere to allow them to surf through the skies in the manner of *the Silver Surfer*. This has led to the colonial sport of Ref, or aerial surfing, although former champion Holland has turned to politics, and formed the guerrilla organization known as the Gekkostate. His battles against the oppressive Federation are fought with LFOs, futuristic cars that can transform into giant robots, all based on alien technology that the early colonists found lying around—so, nothing to do with **MACROSS**, then. Fourteen-year-old Renton is dragged into the revolution when attractive female pilot Eureka crashes her LFO near his house and asks his mechanic grandfather for help. Before long, Renton has joined the rebels, although his motivation initially seems based more on heroworship of Holland the former sportsman than Holland the freedom fighter. It's all a remarkable coincidence, but not as remarkable as the fact that the Japanese title manages to look a little like that of **EVANGELION** and a little like that of the **ULTRAMAN** spin-off *Ultra Seven*. There is a certain Evangelic resemblance in the robots, too. Created as part of a multimedia project that included a PS2 game, *Eureka 7* lasted for far longer on TV screens than many similar shows and was resurrected as a film, *E7: Goodnight, Sleep Tight Young Lovers* (2009), that completely retold the story and refashioned character relationships. *E7: Astral Ocean* (2012) was a TV series reboot.

EVANGELION *

1995. JPN: *Shinseiki Evangelion*. AKA: *Neon Genesis Evangelion*; *New Century Evangelion*. TV series, movie. DIR: Hideaki Anno, Kazuya Tsurumaki. SCR: Hideaki Anno, Akio Satsugawa. DES: Yoshiyuki Sadamoto, Ikuto Yamashita. ANI: Masayuki, Kazuya Tsurumaki, Tadashi Hiramatsu. MUS: Shiro Sagisu. PRD: Tatsunoko, Gainax, TV Tokyo. 25 mins. x 26 eps. (TV), 102 mins. (m1), 97 mins. (m2), ca. 3 mins. x 24 eps. (v), 101 mins. (m 1.0), 108 mins. (m 2.0), 96 mins. (m 3.0). At the turn of the millennium, a "meteorite strike" on Antarctica wipes out half of Earth's population. The NERV project fights the real danger—aliens called the Angels who are sending bioengineered weapons to destroy the rest of humanity. The experimental Evangelion project fights the outsized invaders with giant cybernetic organisms, but only children born after the Antarctica incident can pilot the machines. With Rei, the original test pilot, critically ill after an accident, head scientist Gendo Ikari summons his estranged son, Shinji, to take the first mission. Shinji is taken in by the sisterly Misato, an alcoholic burnout with a passionate hatred for the Angels, and the arrival of the hot-headed pilot Asuka Langley creates a dysfunctional surrogate family.

With this novel excuse for young, audience-friendly protagonists and giant fighting robots, Gainax incorporates many of its favorite staples from classic anime and monster movies—the Evas themselves even have a five-minute timer in homage to **ULTRAMAN**. A deeply personal, psychological odyssey that allowed Anno to remake his earlier **GUNBUSTER** at a slower pace, *Eva* similarly replayed the Pacific War from the Japanese point of view, specifically the apocalyptic final events. Cosmetic use of Western religious imagery, such as Angel weaponry exploding in cruciform patterns, may appear to suggest that Western beliefs themselves are an alien invasion, but this owes more to Anno's own readings in Jungian psychology and archetypes as he coped with creative doldrums post-*Gunbuster*.

Like *Gunbuster*, *Eva* also piles on the parodies, beginning with its very title, which is a sly reference to the "proclamation of a new century" (*shinseiki sengen*), a 1981 publicity event for the **GUNDAM** movies, now widely regarded by Japanese **FANDOM** as the tipping point that marked the beginning of the otaku era. Within the series itself there are multiple references to fan-favorite shows, particularly from Gerry Anderson (see **THUNDERBIRDS 2086**), with hidden fortresses launching superweapons and uniforms lifted from Anderson's live-action *UFO* (1969). It also features innovative casting, allowing famous voice actors to shine in unusual roles, especially **RANMA** ½'s Megumi Hayashibara as the schizoid Rei and **SAILOR MOON**'s Kotono Mitsuishi as the tragic Misato.

Ultimately, however, *Eva* ended in a series of disappointments. Gainax was criticized for later scenes broadcast without network approval, indirectly causing the more censorious climate that hurt **COWBOY BEBOP**. Later episodes ran visibly low on funds, with overlong pauses to stretch the animation budget and two concluding episodes that were glorified radio plays. Rumors abounded that Gainax had run out of money and/or time, and that the final chapters were thrown together in just two weeks when Anno's hard-hitting original finale was disallowed. However, *Gunbuster* similarly ended with a montage of stills rather than the promised climactic battle, leading some to suggest Anno had always planned it this way and that the violent nature of the theatrical sequels reflected his annoyance that his more cerebral original ending was unappreciated by the audience. A succession of *Eva* movies followed, seemingly designed to leach the last cash and goodwill from remaining fans. An audio drama, *The Conclusion Continues* (1996), joked that having saved the world, the *Eva* cast would consider placing it in fake peril to get their old jobs back; though the gag was ironically close to the mark. The promised "real" finale turned out to be a double bill—*Death and Rebirth* (1997), a recap of the first 24 episodes with the first reel of the true ending. Audience patience was tested a second time with *Death (True)2*, which added tantalizing scraps of extra footage, including the moment of "Second Impact" and bonus sequences that also appeared in the Japanese (but not U.S.) video releases of the TV episodes. The genuine movie edition, *End of Evangelion* (1997), was a truly shocking apocalypse, taking the themes of the original to their logical conclusion presented as the two "missing" episodes that should have closed the series in the first place. These multiple endings have since been repackaged in another edition, *Revival of Evangelion*.

Despite this confused denouement, *Eva* was the most critically successful TV anime of the 1990s, drawing back many fans who had given up on the medium, and even inspiring *Newtype* to test market a new magazine for "intellectual" anime viewers. But like another of Anno's 1960s favorites, *The Prisoner*, it teased viewers with the illusion of hidden depths that weren't necessarily there, and though designed to be the last word on the giant-robot genre, its success merely ushered in a succession of imitations. Its influence, however, can also be seen in some of the better shows of the years that followed, BLUE SUBMARINE No. SIX's Japan fighting a morally superior foe, NADESICO's tongue-in-cheek homage to old shows, and GASARAKI's mixture of militarism and theatrical passion. In the wake of *Eva*, TV became the growth medium for anime, in turn altering the U.S. anime market, with distributors forced to risk more money for longer series when they would prefer shorter movies or video productions. However, this was eventually beneficial in the long-term, allowing American TV channels to scoop up these serials for broadcast during the boom in anime fandom that followed the POKÉMON generation into their teens.

In the aftermath of *Eva*, Anno reused many of its stylistic conceits (such as multiple onscreen titles) in the live-action *Love and Pop* (1999) and the anime romance HIS AND HER CIRCUMSTANCES. Sagisu's score was also recycled when parts of it were lifted for Katsuyuki Motohiro's live-action TV series *Bayside Shakedown*. In a final irony, two members of the Gainax studio were indicted for tax evasion over the films' profits—the impoverished filmmakers who finished on a shoestring were now the new fat cats. In 2004 a DVD box set entitled *Neon Genesis Evangelion: Renewal* (AKA *Renewal of Evangelion*, also the name of the 10th-anniversary project) was issued, containing reauthored versions of the television show (both broadcast and director's cut releases) and both of the movies, all using restored film prints. The TV com-ponents were released in North America as *NGE: Platinum* (or *Platinum Edition*). Themes and images from *Evangelion* were used by the British pop group Fightstar for the album *Grand Unification* (2005).

Evangelion's artistic heritage has endured for an entire generation, kept alive in the last instance by the continued existence of further manga and game tie-ins, and also by the 2007 comedy video series *Petit Eva: Evangelion@School*, featuring a super deformed version of the cast, including a *bancho* gang-leader-style Eva. The same year saw the inauguration of a four-part movie retelling, beginning with *Evangelion 1.0: You Are (Not) Alone* (2007). Appearing on the surface as little more than a clip-show from previous episodes, *1.0* nevertheless inserted tantalizing moments of new footage and also subtly switched around several character motivations. *Evangelion 2.0: You Can (Not) Advance* (2009) added a new character, Mari Illustrious Makinami, literally parachuted into the story in what seemed like a cynical exercise in justifying new action figures, but also making it clear that this story was diverging far from the original. This perhaps represents the high point of *Evangelion*'s 21st-century popularity, reaching a wide audience in Japan. It even became part of the mass media when a nationwide power-saving measure after the 2011 Great East Japan Earthquake became characterized by a Twitter hashtag referencing "Operation Yashima," an event in the original series when the Eva units co-opted the electricity from all the power plants in Japan. Subsequently, the *Eva* movies veered away from their popular appeal, focusing once more on a narrower otaku audience, with *Evangelion 3.0: You Can (Not) Redo* (2012), which moved the action 14 years into the future on a post-apocalyptic Earth. A "final" *Evangelion 4.0* is forthcoming at time of writing. Note that video releases in some territories add fractional subcategories to the numbering in order to denote yet more tinkering. There is, for example, a full 12 minutes difference in the running times between the videos *Evangelion 1.01* and *Evangelion 1.11*. **◐**

EVEN MORE GHOST STORIES

1995. JPN: *Zokuzoku Mura no Obaketachi*. AKA: *Even More Village Ghosts*. Video. DIR: Tameo Ogawa. SCR: Masatoshi Kimura. DES: Konomi Sakurai. ANI: Konomi Sakurai. MUS: Koichi Hiro. PRD: Toei. 40 mins. x 6 eps.

A succession of tales taken from the 1.3-million-selling children's books by Akiko Sueyoshi and Mako Taruishi, including *Ram the Mummy*, *Obatan the Witch*, *The Childish Goblin*, and *Kitten Ghosts Goo, Soo and Pea*.

EVEN THEN I LOVE MY WIFE

2011. JPN: *Sore demo Tsuma o Aishiteru*. Video. DIR: N/C. SCR: Ryu Terano. DES: Gentle Sasaki. ANI: N/C. MUS: N/C. PRD: T-Rex. 30 mins. x 2 eps.

Nanami is happily married, but unfortunately there's some indiscreet video footage in her past. Somehow the landlord of their building gets hold of it and uses it to blackmail her. Either she becomes his sex slave or he'll show it to her husband. This naturally leads Nanami, her kid sister, and her friend into much more embarrassing situations. Based on a porn game by Lune Team Bitters. **◐**

EVERY DAY'S A SUNDAY

1990. JPN: *Mainichi ga Nichiyobi*. Video. DIR: Hidehito Ueda. SCR: Hidehito Ueda, Kazuko Ueda. DES: Kazuya Ose. ANI: Kazuya Ose. MUS: Hiroya Watanabe. PRD: Animate Film. 30 mins. x 6 eps.

Yumi Takeshita is saved from a car accident but her rescuer is injured. When she meets him again a year later, she's a rookie police officer with the twin aims of working for justice and finding a boyfriend. His name is Toru Ichidai, and he's a conjuror. He would have gone to Hollywood by now, but the accident has held him back. And now that he's met her again, he may as well stay in Japan to form half of an unusual crime-fighting team. Based on an manga by 3x3 EYES–creator Yuzo Takada.

EVERYBODY'S SONGS

1961. JPN: *Minna no Uta*. TV series. DIR: Various. SCR: N/A. DES: Various. ANI: Various. MUS: Various. PRD: NHK. 5 mins. approx. x 1300+ eps.

Japan's national broadcaster NHK is a canny operator, as demonstrated by its long-running mini-show *Minna no Uta*. Presenting popular songs in five-minute slots on radio and TV for kids and families, it fills daily gaps in the schedule, promotes musicians and new releases, and keeps many anime studios and independent practitioners in work.

Not every song in *Minna no Uta* is animated—there are also montages and live-action episodes, disqualifying it from consideration as Japan's earliest or longest-running animated TV series (INSTANT HISTORY; SAZAE-SAN). Until the 1980s, the split between live action and animation or illustration was roughly 50:50; since then, animation has come to predominate. It is, however, likely to be one of the first cartoon works ever seen by many Japanese children, and forms an extensive, interactive element of MUSIC IN ANIME, with sing-along subtitles.

Not all of it has survived—as with other TV shows worldwide, many early episodes have been lost; a mere 500 are extant in NHK's own archives from the first two decades of broadcast. Although an online database exists of known performances and animators, it is difficult to accurately assess the exact number of episodes because of the number of repeats. Since 2006, the rebroadcast of earlier episodes has been marked with the logo *Minna no Uta Request*, and an onscreen title giving the original broadcast date. However, previous episodes were often broadcast several times a year (and day), without indication as to their original airing. The average five-year-old viewer, of course, would often be oblivious to such recycling, or even welcome it.

Minna no Uta has brought world music—and world animation styles—to Japan, reversioned in the local language. "Chim Chim Cheree," Dick Van Dyke's faux-Cockney hit from *Mary Poppins*, was translated and animated in black and white by Yoko Tadanori for a 1966 show. A Japanese version of the Italian hit "44 Cats" was charmingly animated in 1969, as was the very different "Donna Donna," a 1969 Japanese version of a Yiddish folk song about a calf going to a new home. Another European classic was animated in 1970: "Sur le Pont d'Avignon" with Japanese lyrics. In 1981 Dougal Dixon's book *After Man: An Ecology of the Future* inspired the *MnU* segment "After Man," sung by Akemi Okamura, later the voice of Fio in PORCO ROSSO.

Many vocal and animation superstars have taken part over the years, including Godiego (GANDHARA), whose 1979 song "Beautiful Name" was animated for *MnU*, and Pizzicato Five, whose "Message Song" was turned into a Christmas tune in a perky parade of teddy-bear-clutching Santas in 1996. "Akai Boshi" had Satoko Shimonari singing about two children enraptured by the flight of a red hat blown off in the wind in 1984. Also in 1984, the great animator Tadanari Okamoto brought "Metropolitan Museum," sung by Taeko Onuki, to life. Sumo wrestler Konishiki provided the vocals for 2002's bouncy, colorful "Happy Weekend." NHK got Makoto Shinkai (VOICES OF A DISTANT STAR) to tell the story of a cute hamster in 2003's "Egao," sung by 1970s musical actress Hiromi Iwasaki. A year later they scored an even bigger coup with a five-minute musical epic from the Studio Ghibli superstar team of Tomoki Mochizuki, Katsuya Kondo, and Naoya Tanaka. Madhouse director Atsuko Ishizuka did her first professional work for the show, animating and directing 2004's "Tsuki no Waltz (Moon Waltz)" sung by Mio Isayama. Independent animator Jun Aoki, director of 2005's hilarious KOTATSU CAT, directed "Winner" for *MnU* in 2007.

Cute or funny animals are perennially popular topics. 1974's "Higenashi Gogejabaru" is an animation about a naughty boy who cuts the whiskers off a sleeping cat, changing the view of everyone who sees it, while "Dracula no Uta" presented the Count as a mosquito in 1975's comical animation. In 2009 Ayaka Wilson warbled "Hiyoko Gumo" ("The Chick Cloud Song"), the tale of a cheerful chick-cloud hybrid who flits through the sky playing with friends. Few kids could resist 2007's "Oshiri Kajiri Mushi" ("The Bottom Biting Bug"), but more serious ecological and social concerns also have their place. 2009 saw Mimori Yusa performing the eco-ballad "I'm Here With You" over a simply drawn and touchingly beautiful crayon animation.

Romantic music is always a favorite. In 1997 former J-Pop idol Yoko Nagayama gave a touching performance of "Ano Koro no Namida Wa." Kiyoshi Nakajima animated Mio Isamiya's "Koi Hanabi" ("Love's Fireworks") in 2002. FRUITS BASKET-creator Natsuki Takaya provided the art and design for Angela Aki's "Tegami: Haikei 15 no Kimi e" ("A Letter: Dear 15-Year-Old You") in 2007.

All the available technologies and styles of anime have also been displayed, including cut-outs, sand-animation, and pixillation. Most, however, are in traditional TECHNOLOGY AND FORMATS, on cels and more recently digital (GAMING AND DIGITAL ANIMATION). 1987 saw Taku Furukawa animating dancing umbrellas for Etsuko Sai's vocals in "Kumo ga Haretara," in a style that many Western animators would feel at home with. Shigeru Tamura's stylishly blue "Itsumademo Tabibito" ("Eternal Travelers") was a highlight of the December 1988 shows. Taku Furukawa's 1996 animation for Kazuo Zaitsu's "A Gift with No Stamp" ("Kitte no nai Okurimono") is classically simple. In 2004 a CGI comedy showed two aliens arriving in Earth's orbit and fleeing after they are bombarded with our communications, singing "Arigato."

PUPPETRY AND STOP MOTION is also a popular choice; the Sylvanian Families toy line was brought to life in 1989 for "Fuyu no Yoru no Ohanashi," a song about a busy day in the forest. Kuniko Yamada's "Saboten ga Nikui," a song about a scorpion and dung beetle mercilessly teased by cheeky cacti, was animated in plasticine stop motion in 1988. "Boku wa Kuma" ("I'm a Bear") was the first children's song by pop star Hikaru Utada, animated in stop motion in 2006. Another stop-motion mini-epic popped up in 2007: "Kaiju no Ballad" ("Monsters' Ballad"). In 2010, though, the show returned to delicate simplicity for a fairytale interpretation of Juri Ueno's song "Egao no Hana."

MnU's family tree is hence a veritable all-pervading kudzu weed of Japanese popular culture, its roots feeding on every kind of music and its tendrils stretching out to cover all forms of animation and embrace every era of talent in TV anime.

EVERYDAY ANIME

From anime's earliest days, it has favored storylines that would be difficult to film in live action, be they the flights of fancy of SCIENCE FICTION AND ROBOTS or the odd niches of animated EROTICA AND PORNOGRAPHY. Reality itself was often of only minor consideration in shows and movies that focused on impressionistic representations of **Fantasy and Fairy Tales** or cartoon **Comedy**.

Some foreign critics in the late 1990s identified a group within **Fandom** that found Japan itself to be as intriguing a subject as the fantasies that took place there in an anime context. Video liner notes, particularly from AnimEigo, took great pains to explain elements of modern Japanese culture as revealed in shows such as **Urusei Yatsura** and **Ranma ½**, while some producers within Japan began to identify the particular "Japanese-ness" of, say, chairless dining rooms in **Sailor Moon**, as a barrier to mainstream international acceptance. The critic Koichi Iwabuchi suggested that unique cultural elements were often regarded as an unwelcome cultural "odor" that needed to be excised (see, for example, **Astro Boy**), but as Japan's global soft power grew, this was converted into a welcome cultural "fragrance" in which a Japanese origin and setting became part of the appeal.

The quotidian world has never been entirely absent from anime—it is, after all, the location for the long-running **Sazae-san** and many other dramas and comedies. In the 21st century, as media stories proliferated about the large number of *hikikomori* "shut-ins" represented within anime fandom, it became apparent that the last frontier for modern Japanese animation might be the real world itself, with a deep sense of ready nostalgia for hazy school days, mawkish classroom flirting, or the exotic appeal of old-fashioned friendships and hobbies. While **Colorful: The Motion Picture** was ostensibly a fantasy about the afterlife, much of its creative effort was expended in images of *reality*, and a story that treated mundane events and relationships with the breathless excitement of a wide-eyed tourist. "Everyday" Japan, as depicted in the glorious sunsets and summer days of Makoto Shinkai, often gained an aspect of hyper-real, romanticized beauty. Studio Ghibli movies since **My Neighbor Totoro** have valorized the technologies and etiquette of the Good Old Days; in a comparable attempt to appeal to a broader age-range, more recent films such as **Summer Wars** similarly developed a sense of nostalgia toward the recent past. Several modern anime, most conspicuously **Aesthetica of a Rogue Hero**, also

allude to a shared sense among the PlayStation generation—that today's children genuinely do spend their evenings leading armies, fighting crime, or casting spells on their consoles in their bedrooms, turning what's going on outside their windows into the new undiscovered country. Izumi Kizara, the writer of **Hal**, has suggested that this crosses over into the media mix offered by the news itself, and that our modern lives are so beset by images of disaster, terrorism and world-threatening crises that a humdrum, relatively carefree existence has attained new value as a form of escapism.

The term *nichijo* ("everyday" or "mundane") entered anime production slang in the early 21st century, as a term used to describe this sense of nostalgia applied with immediate effect, usually to a high-school life regarded by 20-something otaku with rose-tinted spectacles. In particular, the "everyday" sought out by such shows presented an opportunity to eavesdrop on the lives of attractive, single young ladies—offering not the pornography of their physical bodies, but a more intimate invasion of their inner lives. The subgenre was enough of a phenomenon for *Kinema Junpo* to publish a guide to it, as *Nichijo-kei Anime Hit no Hosoku* (*The Rules for Making a Hit Everyday Anime*, 2011). This identified the earliest successes in the field as **Azumanga Daioh** (2002) and **Lucky Star** (2007), but also the genre's key points as a "*moe*" concentration on the concerns of cute, and usually comedic schoolgirls. Its arguable apotheosis was **K-On**, similarly based on a four-panel gag comic strip, aimed at males, favoring characterization over incident in the lives of unattainable girls. One hence gets the sense that "everyday" anime have slightly different applications in Japan and abroad—to Japanese viewers, they can be a glimpse of the familiar; to foreign fans, they can offer a window on the many petty differences to be encountered in Japanese culture, from coffee in cans to school uniforms. In both cases, they offer a view of the greatest mystery of all—the private life, thoughts, and conversations of women, or at least as it is imagined by largely male anime and manga creators.

EVERYDAY TALES OF A CAT GOD, THE *

2011. JPN: *Nekogami Yaoyorozu*. AKA: *Cat God Myriads; Cat God*. TV series, video. DIR: Hiroaki Sakurai. SCR: Toko Machida, Tomoko Konparu, Tatsuya Takahashi, Masahiro Yokotani. DES: Atsuko Watanabe. ANI: Atsuko Watanabe. MUS: N/C. PRD: AIC PLUS+, Akita Shoten, AT-X, Lantis, Marvelous Entertainment, Pony Canyon, Sotsu Agency. 30 mins. x 12 eps. (TV), 48 mins. (v).

Cat god Mayu is kicked out of Heaven and moves in with human girl Yuzu, who runs the Yaoyorozu antique shop. Lots of Mayu's god-friends drop in on them, and between them and Yuzu's many cute girlfriends, much fluffy and harmless fun occurs. Based on the 2007 manga by FLIPFLOPs, the cute-styled characters and lightweight situations are pleasantly undemanding—compare with **Kamichu!** A video, *Nekogami Yaoyorozu Ohanami Ghostbusters*, about fun with a cherry tree possessed by a mischievous ghost, was released in March 2012 from the same team.

EVIL WOMAN EXECUTIVE

2011. JPN: *Aku no Onna Kanbu—Kono Watashi ni Oshioki Da to!? Fuzakeru na!* AKA: *Evil Woman Ruler—You Want to Punish Me!? You're Kidding!* Video. DIR: Ken Raika. SCR: Ryu Terano. DES: Ryu Terano, Gentle Sasaki, P-san Honda, Michihito Amagi, Dan Yoshii. ANI: Ryu Terano, Tomoaki Doshida. MUS: N/C. PRD: T-Rex. 30 mins. x 2 eps. (v1), 30 mins. x 2 eps. (v2).

Princess Lunartemis is put under a spell by her servant Katsuma, forcing her to obey his every command. He wants to claim her throne, but first he wants to make her have sex in front of him. The warrior princess Kaguya also gets her armor off and practices using dildos with the princess, and there's a bunny girl who literally goes like a rabbit. This anime based on an erotic game by Lune is set in a fantasy world. Two further episodes were released in 2012 under the title *Aku no Onna Kanbu Full Moon Night* with more fantasy domination from Katsuma, this time involving a pirate girl with blue skin, one with orange skin and a blonde dressed as an office lady. It's all because his bosses are so nasty to him. ⓝ

EXCEL SAGA *

1999. JPN: *Heppoko [Silly] Animation Excel*

Saga. AKA: *Quack Experimental Anime Excel Saga, Weird Anime Excel Saga*. TV series. DIR: Shinichi Watanabe, Akihiko Nishiyama, Jun Fukuda, Takafumi Hoshikawa, Ken Ando, Masahiko Murata. SCR: Kumi Jigoku, Yosuke Kuroda. DES: Satoshi Ishino. ANI: Satoshi Ishino. MUS: Toshio Masuda. PRD: JC Staff, TV Tokyo. 25 mins. x 25 eps. (TV), 25 mins. (v).

In the fortified section of a heavily fortified underground fortress (he's taking no chances), Across company boss Il Palazzo continues his ongoing attempt to conquer the world. Working for him are the two beautiful agents Excel and Hyatt, but conquering the world isn't a well-paying job, and the girls have to share a flat and travel to work on the subway. They also have to work part-time as bounty hunters to make ends meet, accompanied by their pet dog, Menchi (JPN: mince), who is also an emergency food supply. A truly insane comedy in the spirit of DRAGON HALF (featuring the same voice actress, Kotono Mitsuishi), with time out for cameo appearances from director Watanabe (as "Nabeshin") in his trademark giant afro, assassination attempts on the author of the original manga, Rikdo Koshi, a theme song barked by a dog with Japanese subtitles, and a "flexible" attitude toward the deaths of main characters, perhaps inspired by the tribulations of Kenny from *South Park*. *Excel Saga* is so fast-paced and energetic that watching it can be exhausting—famously, the English-language voice actress Jessica Calvello had to quit after straining her voice and was replaced partway through the run by Larissa Wolcott. The final episode was intentionally made too violent and obscene for television, ensuring that only 25 episodes would be broadcast and that fans would have to fork out for the DVD. PUNI PUNI POEMI is a spin-off from the show, and its influence can be felt long afterward in PANTY AND STOCKING WITH GARTERBELT.

EX-DRIVER *

2000. AKA: *éX-D*. Video. DIR: Jun Kawagoe. SCR: Shinzo Fujita. DES: Kenichi Hamazaki, Kosuke Fujishima, Hidefumi Kimura, Takeshi Takakura, Shunji Murata. ANI: N/C. MUS: N/C. PRD: Sunrise. 30 mins. x 6 eps. (v1), 63 mins. (m), 27 mins. (v2).

A century in the future, travel has been made perfectly safe by the introduction of fully automated AI cars. But when these electrically powered, computer-controlled cars run amok, it's the mission of the Ex-Driver team to rev up their engines and give chase. It takes a particular kind of person to drive one of the temperamental gasoline cars, and the perky Lisa and laid-back Lorna think they have what it takes, in a predictable rehash of Fujishima's earlier YOU'RE UNDER ARREST!, with a sop to younger viewers in the form of 13-year-old driver prodigy Soichi.

The movie (2002) featured Lorna, Lisa, and Soichi traveling to Santa Monica, California to take part in the eX-Driver World Meet, as the members of Team Japan. There they encounter Angela Gambino, the alienated daughter of ex-mob boss Rico Gambino, now the head of a supermarket chain, who in turn is the sponsor of Team USA—the bickering couple David and Kelly. Faced with sabotage and an apparent plot to gamble on the outcome of the World Meet's final race, they must work through the layers of intrigue and track down the true villain to bring him to justice. Of course, many car chases ensue.

When the movie was released on DVD (also in 2002) it came with a 27-minute extra, *eX-Driver: Nina & Rei Danger Zone*, a quasi-prequel in which the heroines must stop a miniature AI car with a tiny replica of Nina inside before it shuts down the whole of Tokyo's transport grid. There's a plot against the eX-Drivers lurking in the background somewhere, but once again the chases are the thing. This time the crew throws in a car/airplane chase down a runway, just for a change.

EXILE GENERATION

2009. JPN: *Examurai Sengoku*. TV series. DIR: N/C. SCR: Koji Miura. DES: Hiroshi Takahashi. ANI: N/C. MUS: N/C. PRD: TMS Entertainment. 12 mins. x 24 eps.

Seven masterless men, each using a different type of combat, join forces to navigate a fantasy world that mixes ancient and modern, but lives by the old laws of brute strength and deception. They live by their own code, doing their best to avoid anything resembling authority, but are finally forced to fight evil and corruption—which, as in most post-apocalyptic anime, has dressed for a glam metal gig

(HIGHLANDER: THE SEARCH FOR VENGEANCE). The animation is very pretty, with interesting use of single-color tones, shifts of viewpoint, and artful lighting to distract from limited movement. The timing and framing of the action sequences are all the more impressive when you notice how little actual animation takes place, but some of the CGI elements merge awkwardly with the 2D animation. Based on the phone game by HIRO (EXILE) and Makoto Matsuda, and the 2009 manga by Hiroshi Takahashi, creator of the macho high school battle manga *Worst*, in which more young men live by their own violent code and disdain authority, but this time inside the Japanese education system. Compare with SAMURAI 7 and FIST OF THE NORTH STAR. ●

EXPER ZENON

1991. Video. DIR: Yuji Moriyama, Hiroaki Hayase. SCR: Yuji Moriyama, Yasushi Hirano, Shigeru Yamamoto. DES: Yuji Moriyama, Satoshi Hashimoto. ANI: Yuji Moriyama. MUS: Kenji Kawai. PRD: Studio Fantasia. 60 mins.

Tadashi is a high school student and computer-game addict. After a long day spent playing the game *Zenon*, he is visited in a dream by the heroine, Sartova. In an anime replay of *The Last Starfighter*, she takes him to the world of Zenon, where the game is played with human lives at stake.

EXPLODING CAMPUS GUARDRESS

1994. JPN: *Bakuen Campus Guardress*. AKA: *Combustible Campus Guardress*. Video. DIR: Toshihiko Nishikubo. SCR: Satoru Akahori, Kazushi Hagiwara. DES: Kazuya Kose. ANI: Kazuya Kose. MUS: Fumitaka Anzai. PRD: Production I.G. 30 mins. x 4 eps.

Thirty thousand years ago, Takumi, Hasumi, and Kasumi were tragic lovers who vowed to finalize their romance in another life. Thirty thousand years after these heroic Guardians defeated the evil Remnant invaders from the Dark World and sealed them behind an interdimensional Gateway, their reincarnations return once more to save the world. The site of the ancient battle is now in downtown Tokyo, hidden under the somewhat conspicuously named Gateway High School. When the cosmic moment comes for the Guardians and the Remnants to do battle once more, the reincarnations create some confusing blends of ancient and modern personalities and priorities, as our noble warriors are forced to choose between Armageddon and the senior prom, and they must fight enemies who were their friendly teachers only the day before. To make matters *incredibly* complicated, the Guardians have been reincarnated as brother, sister, and mother. Mom and Sis do not see any problems with trying to get into Takumi's pants when they are not battling the Remnants. However, Takumi seems to be more attached to his girlfriend from this life, Hime-chan, a total airhead who may fatally distract him from his duty. Based on a manga in *V Jump* magazine by KNIGHTS OF RAMUNE's Akahori and BASTARD-creator Kazushi Hagiwara, this anime combines the gags and sauciness of the two.

EXPLORER WOMAN RAY *

1989. AKA: *The Explorer*. Video. DIR: Yasuo Hasegawa, Hiroki Hayashi. SCR: Mayori Sekijima. DES: Hiroyuki Ochi. ANI: Hiroyuki Ochi. MUS: Norimasa Yamanaka. PRD: Animate Film, AIC. 29 mins. x 2 eps.
Ray Kizuki is an archeology student and a black-belt martial artist, bequeathed a mysterious mirror by her father that turns out to be the key to a newly discovered temple. She sets off to find it, accompanied by twins Mai and Maki and pursued by the mysterious "Rig Veda," who eventually reveals himself as her late father's assistant. Based on a manga in *Comic Nora* by ELEMENTALORS-creator Takeshi Okazaki. **V**

EYESHIELD 21

2004. TV series, movie. DIR: Masayoshi Nishida, Tamaki Nakatsu. SCR: Daisuke Habara, Nobuaki Kishima, Rika Nakase, Toshifumi Kawase, Yoshio Takeuchi (TV), Riichiro Inagaki (m). DES: Hirotoshi Takaya (TV), Minoru Ueda, Miyoko Tanitsuna (m). ANI: Chiyomi Koyama, Hajime Watanabe, Hisashi Mitsui, Kazunori Takahashi (TV), Eiko Kato, Kazuyo Hasegawa (m). MUS: Ko Otani (TV), Kenji Kawai, Shin Iwashina (m). PRD: Frontline, Production I.G., TV Tokyo. 30 mins. (m), 25 mins. x 145 eps. (TV).
Sena Kobayashi is a little kid who has developed super-fast running skills in order to avoid the school bullies in the style of HARRIS'S WIND. Eventually, his skills are put to use by the school's (American-style) football team, when he is encased in armor and given the nickname "Eyeshield 21" to hide his identity from the rival schools, in this adaptation of the manga written by Riichiro Inagaki and drawn by Yusuke Murata.

While the TV series proper aired in 2005, in the previous year's one-shot theatrical prequel *Eyeshield 21: Maboroshi no Golden Bowl* (*Phantom Golden Bowl*), the Off Harajuku Boarders believe that they have lost their last chance to get into the Kanto district finals. That is, until the district leader Mr. Hatohara makes a Faustian pact—the Boarders will be permitted to play in the previously unknown Golden Bowl tournament, the winner of which will be admitted as a late entry into the championship. It is only when the Boarders take the field that they realize they are playing the Demon Devilbats, a team not of this world, in a story that combines the clichés of a sports tale with the traditions of a summertime ghost story. The episode of the TV series broadcast on 7 September 2005 was an hour-long special. Compare to MACHINE HAYABUSA.

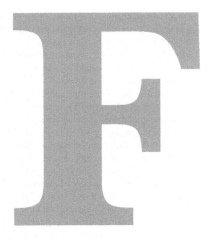

F
1988. TV series. DIR: Koichi Mashimo, Katsuyoshi Yatabe, Kunihisa Sugishima, Nobuyasu Furukawa. SCR: Hideo Takayashiki. DES: Masamitsu Kudo, Tomohiko Sato. ANI: Masamitsu Kudo, Ryunosuke Otonashi. MUS: Wataru Yahagi, Masaru Hoshi. PRD: Kitty, Fuji TV. 25 mins. x 31 eps.
After the death of his mother, Gunma Akagi discovers his real father is a professional racer. After befriending pit boss Tamotsu, Gunma is inspired to join his father's world and becomes a driver himself, staying at his grandmother's place in Tokyo. The "F" stands for "formula," and with a fish out of water, a surrogate family, and a sporting quest, formula is exactly what you get.

F-FORCE *
2001. JPN: *Asgaldh: Waikyoku no Testament*. AKA: *Asgard: The Torture Testament*. Video. DIR: Yusaku Aoi. SCR: Hajime Yamaguchi. DES: Naoki Yamauchi. ANI: Motokazu Murakami, Naoki Yamauchi. MUS: Hiroaki Sano. PRD: Discovery. 30 mins. x 3 eps.
Wandering knight Ash saves a young damsel from violation at the hands/tentacles of some evil monsters. Accompanying her back to her home village of Tylling, he discovers that she is the chief's daughter, and the last fair maiden left after successive attacks and kidnappings by the creatures of Demon Mountain—who not only steal local girls, but also local girls' underwear. Hearing that similar creatures have already caused a distant continent to sink beneath the waves (presumably not through the weight of panties alone), Ash

calls in favors from fellow adventurers to defend the village. When they arrive, they unsurprisingly turn out to be a bunch of girls, differentiated and attired with all the stereotypical predictability of a computer game, including one in a school uniform, another dolled up as a Chinese waitress, and a potty-mouthed cowgirl with an inappropriate New Jersey accent in the English dub. Any resemblance to *Seven Samurai* soon passes. Based on the computer game *Asgaldh*, by Zone, and one of the **DISCOVERY SERIES**. ●NV

F-ZERO FALCON LEGEND *
2003. JPN: *F-Zero Falcon Densetsu*. AKA: *F-0, F-Zero GP Legend*. TV series. DIR: Ayumi Tomobuki. SCR: Akiyoshi Sakai. DES: Toyoo Ashida, Shohei Kohara. ANI: Daisuke Yoshida. MUS: Takayuki Negishi. PRD: Ashi Pro, Dentsu, TV Tokyo, Nintendo. 23 mins. x 51 eps.
Set in 2201, this racing game tie-in tips its hat to *Demolition Man*, but owes more to Japanese live-action hero shows, whose madlynamed supervillains and heroes have gifts handed down through time by magical mentors. An evil overlord, Emperor Black Shadow, leads the Dark Million organization and plans to use the Dark Matter Reactor, which grants the wishes of anyone who activates it, to take over the universe and devote it to evil. Ryu Suzaku (Rick Wheeler) is awakened from a 150-year cryogenic sleep to oppose him and fulfill the ancient Legend of the Falcon. He has become a member of the Elite Mobile Taskforce of the Galactic Space Federation, a group of pilots who compete

in the F-Zero grand prix races popular throughout the Galaxy. He is not alone—his old girlfriend Haruka (Jody) was also in cryosleep and has also been awakened, but she is part of Dark Million, and now goes under the name of Miss Killer. Ryu's nemesis, arch-criminal Zoda, has also been resurrected from his cryo-prison by Black Shadow. The stage is set for a final confrontation, but not before various other characters, like fighting cyborg Mighty Gazelle and 97-year-old race pilot Ironman Neelson, have their cameos. A spin-off from Nintendo's 1990 video game of the same name, screened on Fox's 4Kids channel, whose audience was too young to remember **CYBERFORMULA GPX**.

F³: FRANTIC, FRUSTRATED AND FEMALE *
1994. JPN: *Nageki no Kenko Yuryoji*. AKA: *The Lament of an Otherwise Perfectly Healthy Girl*. Video. DIR: Masakazu Akan. SCR: N/C. DES: Koji Hamaguchi. ANI: Koji Hamaguchi. MUS: Bang Heads. PRD: Pink Pineapple, KSS. 30 mins. x 3 eps.
A sapphic satire about Hiroe, who is unable to achieve orgasm with her boyfriend and seeks a remedy for her teenage frustrations. Her sister, Mayaka, helps with Chinese medicine, scientific inventions, and even a lesbian BDSM orgy. The trilogy ends with a haunted-house spoof in which demonic possession allows Mayaka to grow a penis for a replay of the hermaphroditic sex of **LA BLUE GIRL**. The script backtracks on the incestuous characters of episode 1, later claiming that they only *look* as if they are related. Based on the manga by

Wan Yan A Gu Da, published in *Penguin Club*. ⓝⓛ

FABLES OF THE GREEN FOREST *

1973. JPN: *Yamanezumi Rocky Chuck*. AKA: *Rocky Chuck the Woodchuck; Chuck the Beaver*. TV series. DIR: Tadamichi Koga, Seiji Endo. SCR: Keiji Kubota, Takako Shigemori, Hikaru Mori, Hiroshi Yamanaka, Hiroshi Saito. DES: Nobuhiro Okaseko. ANI: Nobuhiro Okaseko, Toshio Hirata, Yasuji Mori. MUS: Morihisa Yamamoto, Seiichiro Uno. PRD: Zuiyo, Fuji TV. 25 mins. x 52 eps.

Rocky the adventurous woodchuck is separated from his family and wanders the forests meeting many different animals, including Polly, another woodchuck, Peter Cottontail the rabbit, and the avuncular jaybird Sammy. Based on the output of the prolific Thornton W. Burgess (1874–1965), who wrote a syndicated *Bedtime Story* newspaper column for daily newspapers and was said to have penned 15,000 stories in his lifetime. Many of these involved the adventures of forest animals such as Chatterer the Red Squirrel, Danny the Meadow Mouse, Grandfather Frog, Reddy Fox, and Buster Bear, though it is his ninth book, *The Adventures of Johnny Chuck* (1913), that was used as a framing device for these anime adaptations. Compare to SETON'S ANIMAL TALES. Sold at rights fairs as *Johnny Chuck*, but released in English by ZIV International under the title *Fables of the Green Forest* in 1978—hence its retitling here. Although technically made before Zuiyo became Nippon Animation and churned out the long running WORLD MASTERPIECE THEATER franchise, as an adaptation of a foreign children's story, this is often retrofitted into the WMT history in the same manner as HEIDI.

FAFNER *

2004 JPN: *Sokyu no Fafner*. AKA: *Fafner of the Blue Sky, Dead Aggressor, Fafner in the Azure*. TV series. DIR: Nobuyoshi Habara, Junki Honma. SCR: Kazuki Yamanobe. DES: Hisashi Hirai, Naohiro Washio. ANI: Akio Takami, Akira Takahashi, Akitoshi Maeda, Atsushi Hasebe, Genichiro Kondo, Hideyuki Motohashi, Satotake Kikuchi, Shinichi Yamaoka, Sunao Shiomi, Taeko Hori, Takuya Matsumura, Toru Kitago. MUS: Tsuneyoshi Saito. PRD: King Records, Xebec, TV Tokyo. 25 mins. x 26 eps. (TV), 50 mins. (v), 88

mins. (m1).

The peaceful lives of the people of Tatsumiya Island are shattered when they hear a voice echoing from the sky and a mysterious ray of light opens the sky, allowing an invading Festum alien army to arrive. A subterranean command center springs into action and the citizens take shelter as fighter planes and missile defense systems deploy on the apparently sleepy island. A giant robot weapon, Fafner, has been concealed on the island and could be deployed to fight the Festum forces, but its schoolgirl pilot, Karin Kurumae, is missing. Doctor Makabe wants his son, diffident teenager Kazuki, to take her place. Kazuki's childhood friend Soshi Minashiro, son of the island's chief citizen, is also drawn into the war, which has been raging for some time in the outside world and has decimated the population. Japan is already gone, and Tatsumiya Island is a rogue nation, continually under threat from attack, since the "new" UN wants the Fafner for itself at any cost. The result is a show that takes the transforming city of Gerry Anderson's *Stingray* (1964) and asks what life would be like for the inhabitants, particularly if they discovered that the outside world was a lie in the style of THE ANIMATRIX or MEGAZONE 23 and that they had been bred specifically for saving the world from alien attack. There are also shades here of John Wyndham's *Midwich Cuckoos*, later filmed as *Village of the Damned*. Meanwhile, a ragtag band of impromptu defenders of the Earth is forced to jury-rig a battle plan à la MACROSS, while the combatants wonder if there are other defensive islands out there shrouded in equal secrecy, and if there are, whether they plan on helping out any time soon. The Fafner, named after a giant who transformed into a dragon in Richard Wagner's *Das Rheingold* (1862), is dark and neutral-colored, while the aliens are golden and gorgeous, hammering home the message that "not everything beautiful is a friend to man." You've seen EVANGELION, right?

A prequel, *Fafner: Single Program—Right of Left* (2005), was released, as well as the film *Fafner: Heaven and Earth* (2010), set two years after the end of the TV show. ⓥ

FAIRGROUND IN THE STARS

1989. JPN: *Hoshi no Yuenchi*. Video. DIR:

Nobuhiro Aihara. SCR: Nobuhiro Aihara. DES: Ryutaro Nakamura. ANI: Junichi Shoji. MUS: Koichi Hirai. PRD: Gakken. 18 mins.

A kindly teacher demonstrates origami to his elementary class, but when he gives a paper crane to a child, it is stolen from him by Takeshi, the class bully. Takeshi discovers that the crane is really a talking spaceship that takes him and his friends to visit a fairground in the stars. A girl falls through a hole into Space Hell, and the children cooperate to rescue her. Takeshi wakes up, wondering if it was all a dream. The next day, he returns the magic crane to its rightful owner. This tale is from RAINBOW ACROSS THE PACIFIC's Daisaku Ikeda, the leader of the Buddhist Soka Gakkai organization, although it lacks a particularly religious or moral message, playing like a sanitized version of NIGHT ON THE GALACTIC RAILROAD. Note the presence of future SERIAL EXPERIMENTS LAIN–director Nakamura as a character designer. Ikeda also wrote PRINCE OF SNOW COUNTRY.

FAIRY KING

1988. JPN: *Yosei O*. Video. DIR: Katsuhisa Yamada. SCR: Tomoko Konparu. DES: Atsuo Noda. ANI: Atsuo Noda. MUS: Yuriko Nakamura. PRD: Madhouse. 60 mins.

Sickly high school student Taka journeys to Hokkaido in search of a magical cure and falls in with Khoo Fu-Ling, the king of the fairies. Ninfidia, the land of the fairies, is under attack from the evil Queen Mab, and Taka must save it. Based on the 1978 girls' manga by Ryoko Yamagishi, which incorporated elements of legends of KING ARTHUR AND THE KNIGHTS OF THE ROUND TABLE, as well as scraps of Celtic, Greek, and Ainu myth.

FAIRY TAIL *

2009. TV series, video, movie. DIR: Shinji Ishihara, Masaya Fujimori, Hiro Mashima. SCR: Masashi Sogo, Fumihiko Shimo, Shoji Yonemura, Atsuhiro Tomioka. DES: Aoi Yamamoto, Junko Shimizu. ANI: Takao Sano, Akio Watanabe, Minako Shiba, Satoru Kobayashi, Takafumi Hori. MUS: Yasuharu Takanashi. PRD: A-1 Pictures, Satelight, Dentsu, Pony Canyon, TV Tokyo, Kodansha (v/m), Shochiku. 24 mins. x 175 eps. (TV), 24 mins. x 3 eps. (v1–3), 90 mins. (m), 24 mins. (v4).

Lucy Heartfilia runs away from home to join the guild of fighting mages known as Fairy Tail. These are not just mages, they're cool mages, with a rambunctious attitude and famously destructive methods—a magically aided **DIRTY PAIR**, if you will, or a hot-blooded Bruce Lee–style dojo where they sling magic instead of blocks, kicks, and punches. She meets a boy named Natsu and his flying blue cat Happy, on a quest to find Natsu's foster parent, a dragon who disappeared seven years ago. Lucy is abducted by a wizard who claims to be the famous Salamander, a leading light of Fairy Tail, and Natsu has to reveal his true identity as the real Salamander and rescue her. He invites her to join Fairy Tail and they set out on a series of magical adventures, breaking rules and causing comical mayhem wherever they go.

A get-out-of-jail-free card for breaking rules and causing mayhem is the Holy Grail of preteen and teenage life. Wizards/ninja/**POKÉMON** trainers do whatever they like and escape the consequences, right? Wrong … but repackaging the fantasy in the latest craze is still a road to success for many a TV director, writer, and production house. Done properly, TV anime is a mighty economic engine that can turn even a standard plot and formulaic characters into something highly productive. With worldwide releases in English, French, Spanish, Portuguese, Chinese, and Tagalog, *Fairy Tail* is a solid achievement, arguably one of the quiet international success stories of anime in the second decade of the 21st century—dwarfed by **BLEACH** and **NARUTO**, but still running a close third in many territories. Its storyline veers from slight to passable, its animation is inconsistent, and like all anime based on still-running manga it has to pad itself out with additional material from time to time, to let the original creator catch up. None of this matters, because it has tapped into the audience's heads and won their loyalty. The 175 episodes equate with over three and a half years' work for hundreds of people in the anime business, to say nothing of manga, novels, radio, music, merchandise, and games.

Hiro Mashima's manga commenced publication in 2006 and is still going strong. Although the original anime series ended in March 2013, reruns began in April. and Mashima made a Twitter announcement that the anime itself would not end yet. There is more already—three video spin-offs, bundled with manga volumes released in 2011 and 2012. *Fairy Tail: Welcome to Fairy Hills! (Yokoso Fairy Hills!)*, *Fairy Academy: Yankee-kun & Yankee-chan (Yosei Gakuen Yankee-kun to Yankee-chan)*, and *Memory Days* showed three alternate universes for the characters. In the summer of 2012 the feature film *Fairy Tail The Movie: The Phoenix Priestess (Gekijoban FAIRY TALE Ho-o no Miko)* sent the team on a quest with a mysterious girl, bird, and stone. Creator Mashima himself directed a fourth video to be bundled with a manga volume in 2012. *Fairy Tale: Fairies' Training Camp (Yoseitachi no Gasshuku)* shows the team at a beach training camp and asks: what would happen if the girls got drunk? What indeed.

FAIRYTALE WARRIOR LITTLE RED RIDING HOOD

2005. JPN: *Otogi Jushi Akazukin*. Video, TV series. DIR: Tetsuro Araki. SCR: Shoji Yonemura. DES: Satoshi Tazaki. ANI: N/C. MUS: Toshio Masuda. PRD: Konami, Madhouse. 30 mins. x 3 eps. (v), 24 mins. x 39 eps. (TV).
After a sleep of a thousand years, Cendrillon the evil witch wakes once more and embarks on a quest for power that leads her to Sota Suzukaze, an otherwise normal Japanese boy who "holds the power to the seal"—whatever it means, it's catnip for evil sorceresses. In order to thwart Cendrillon's schemes, Little Red Riding Hood and Val the silver wolf are sent from the world of fairy tales to our own time. **CARDCAPTORS**-like high jinks soon ensue. The name of the antagonist also reflects fairy tales, using antiquated terms for the characters better known today as **CINDERELLA** and also Hansel, from *Hansel and Gretel*, the Pied Piper of Hamelin, and others from **GRIMM'S FAIRY TALES**.

Although the video version was not released in English, the 2006 TV retelling, directed by Takaaki Ishiyama, was streamed on Crunchyroll under the title *Fairytale Musketeers*.

FAKE *

1996. Video. DIR: Iku Suzuki. SCR: Akinori Endo. DES: Nagisa Miyazaki. ANI: Nagisa Miyazaki, Tomo Omota. MUS: Kix-S. PRD: Nippon Columbia. 60 mins.

Sanami Mato's original manga is a *Lethal Weapon* pastiche about fey New York cop Ryo being forced to partner up with Dee, a streetwise macho detective who wants to bed him. For this anime teaser to drag in new readers, Dee and Ryo are packed off to a British country hotel where guests are being murdered, and the supporting cast of the original manga drop by when they're least needed. While Dee's trying to seduce Ryo and idly mulling over the details of unsolved local killings, their teenage sidekicks serve little purpose except to play happy families with Ryo and Dee as mommy and daddy. The children turn what could have been a queer case of Agatha Christie into a pointless holiday farce, with much swapping of rooms and indoor roller-blading—because it's raining outside.

Ryo and Dee are the world's worst detectives, for whom solving a case involves gossiping for a while and waiting for the criminals to reveal themselves. Faced with a murder case that the *real* police would solve in roughly ten seconds, *Fake* throws in more cameos from the manga to pad out its running time, including the detectives' future boss, Berkley Rose, and Dee's unrequited admirer, JJ, who waste a few more minutes with comedy business before the script reluctantly returns to the murders at hand.

Fake often walks an uneasy line between comedy and tragedy. A bit of cop-on-cop banter fits fine with mayhem and chaos, but not when people are watching their friends die from multiple stab wounds. As one might expect from a story with its pedigree, it ultimately has too many characters and too little time, making the murder mystery unengaging and turning an original romantic farce into humdrum formula. Far from breaking new ground in gay characterization, Ryo is simply a man playing a stereotypical female role; he gets to be an intuitive sidekick, a maternal figure, an unattainable romantic prize, and, as the show rushes to an insane conclusion, even a damsel in distress.

FALSE FRIENDS

False Friends (French: *faux amis*) are **TRANSLATION** problems where words in two different languages appear to be alike, but have different meanings. We use the term in reference to the growing number of animated works that look like anime, but aren't.

Our definition of anime (ARGOT AND JARGON) is culturally inspired. We count a work as anime if it can reasonably be described as animation from Japan, with a high number of Japanese creatives working in the upper echelons of production: director, writer, designers, key animators, and music. That this is even an issue is not recognized among the general Japanese public, where *anime* usually refers to all animation. It is only within the industry itself that creators distinguish between animation from Japan and animation that is not. Some unscrupulous distributors choose to ignore the distinction, hoping instead that fans are stupid enough to buy literally anything if it has the word anime daubed on it.

Outside Japan, the ethnic origin of anime creators has been an issue of some importance. In the first waves of anime abroad between the 1950s and 1970s, anime's Japanese origins were often deliberately occluded—Japanese credit listings were replaced with the names of "writers" and "directors" who had merely adapted preexisting Japanese material. Tokyo landmarks regularly appeared in GIGANTOR, but were renamed—a Japanese origin in the early days of TV often seems like something to be ashamed of, with evidence that should be removed as carefully and completely as possible (CENSORSHIP AND LOCALIZATION). It is for this reason that one still meets French people who do not realize that ULYSSES 31 was made in Japan and Koreans who think that DORAEMON is a Seoul native.

However, the rise of anime on video in the 1980s brought a radical change to this perception. In the science fiction of William Gibson and Bruce Sterling, Japanesquerie became the new cool, and in the wake of the subsequent anime video boom, a Japanese origin became an actual selling point. It is at this juncture that False Friends become an issue—the authors recall a dozen different meetings over the last decade with companies keen to get involved in "anime," which inevitably lead to the big question: "Does it *have* to be Japanese?" The rationale being, among the world's shallower producers,

that if they can persuade a local artist to draw them a picture of a girl with big eyes who carries a gun, this will make something immediately "anime," and save them the messy business of having to deal with the Japanese.

Japanese companies, of course, have long farmed out their work to foreign companies in Korea, China, Thailand, and the Philippines—countries that not only have animation industries of their own, but also hope to profit from the sudden popularity of Asian animation abroad. So it is that several Korean cartoons have been released in the West by anime labels hoping that their ethnic origin would pass the average consumer by. Lee Hyun-se's *Armageddon* (*Amagaedun Uzu*, 1996) seemed deliberately designed to fool rightsbuyers at film festivals—presenting what was for the time an impressive CG opening, that fast collapsed into a dull sci-fi conflict. Similarly, Sang Il-sim's *Red Hawk: Weapon of Death* (1995) was a crass and derivative FIST OF THE NORTH STAR pastiche. Other False Friends are built on connections and resources established by people in anime, such as Andy Orjuela's *Lady Death* (2004), written by Carl Macek, or Andy Chan and Tsui Hark's *A Chinese Ghost Story: The Animation* (*Xiao Qian*, 1997), which featured a lead animator poached from the bona fide anime business: Tetsuya Endo, director of MOJACKO.

It is, of course, only natural that an artform as commercially successful as anime should inspire others. When hired to direct *Grandma and Her Ghosts* (*Mofa Ama*, 1998), Taiwanese director Wang Shaudi went shopping for inspiration, and did so at a time when several Studio Ghibli works had been released into the Taiwanese market, resulting not only in story elements but also a mood and an elegiac quality seemingly lifted from MY NEIGHBOR TOTORO and KIKI'S DELIVERY SERVICE. A similar aspiration toward a Studio Ghibli style can be discerned in Lee Syong-kang's Korean movie, *My Beautiful Marie* (*Mari Iyagi*, 2002), particularly in its depiction of a modern world ignorant of nearby numinous nature.

Mainland China has its own strong animation tradition, particularly stemming from the Shanghai Animation Studio, the foundation of which can be at least partly

accredited to the Japanese expat Tadahito Mochinaga. Recent years have seen Chinese attempts to learn from the commercial success not only of anime, but also of Disney cartoons, as demonstrated by such experiments as Chang Guang-xi's *Lotus Lantern* (*Baolian Deng*, 1999). The acquisition of Hong Kong in 1997 also brought the vast labor market of the Mainland into more direct contact with the advanced technology of the former colony, leading to such hybrids as Toe Yuen's *My Life as McDull* (*McDull Gushi*, 2001), an avowedly Cantonese movie that still managed to recall HELLO KITTY and MY NEIGHBORS THE YAMADAS. Meanwhile, Korean animation continues to aspire toward anime's status abroad, with movies such as Kim Moon-saeng's extended CGI pastiche of AKIRA, *Sky Blue* (AKA *Wonderful Days*, 2003).

False Friendship can also extend both ways. Serials such as *The Powerpuff Girls* (1998), *Hi Hi Puffy AmiYumi* (2004), and *Kappa Mikey* (2006) were conceived in imitation of anime, but then exported *back* to Japan. Nowhere is this more apparent than in THE ANIMATRIX, in which the work of genuine anime creators rubs shoulders with high quality works in an anime style, by creators such as Peter Chung, whose earlier *Aeon Flux* (1995) was itself a homage to Japanese animation.

Ultimately, a good film is a good film, regardless of where it came from. We hope that English-language distributors will accord non-Japanese creators the respect they are due, and hype them for what they are, and not for what they aren't—a "Korean anime" is an oxymoron. The debate over False Friends is likely to continue, as skill levels rise in non-Japanese countries, and increasingly larger amounts of animation work on supposedly "Japanese" films is farmed out abroad: even acknowledged "Japanese" classics like GHOST IN THE SHELL feature extensive contributions from non-Japanese animators.

FAMILIAR OF ZERO, THE *

2006. JPN: *Zero no Tsukaima*. AKA. TV series, video. DIR: Yoshiaki Iwasaki, Yu Ko. SCR: Takao Yoshioka, Yuji Kawahara, Mayu Suguira, Chinatsu Hojo, Nahoko Hasegawa, Shogo Yasukawa, Mariko Kunisawa. DES: Masahiro Fujii, Yoshinori Hirose. ANI: Masahiro Fujii, Toshiaki Miki, Osamu Sakata, Hiroyuki

Horiuchi. mus: Shinkichi Mitsumine. prd: JC Staff, GENCO, Media Factory, Matsutake, Shochiku, AT-X, Bushiroad, Columbia mus Entertainment, Cospa, Showgate, TO Entertainment. 24 mins. x 13 eps. (TV1), 24 mins. x 12 eps. (TV2), 24 mins. x 12 eps. (TV3), 24 mins. (v), 24 mins. x 12 eps. (TV4).

Louise is the least successful student at the Tristein Academy of magic. Her classmates call her "Zero Louise" because not a single one of her spells has worked. To pass a test, she has to summon a familiar: so she puts all her heart into summoning a "devoted, beautiful, powerful" being—and gets Saito, an ordinary Japanese schoolboy. How will he cope with a bad-tempered, arrogant, and completely incompetent wannabe magician? In true harem anime style (**Romance and Drama**), by showing he has hidden and hitherto unsuspected powers and charming other girls into the bargain.

Eiji Usatsuka's art and Noboru Yamaguchi's writing made a hit book series out of *Zero's Familiar* in 2004 and a manga spin-off began publishing a month before the first TV series. Three more spin-off manga and three more TV series followed, showing that, like **Fairy Tail**, giving an audience exactly what it wants is a formula for success. 2007's *Familiar of Zero: Knight of the Twin Moons (Zero no Tsukaima Futatsuki no Kishi)* picks up the story of Louise and Saito after the previous season, as the pair are developing a better relationship and Louise is beginning to appreciate what he has given up to stay with her. 2008's *Familiar of Zero: Princess Rondo (Princess no Rondo)* shows the pair rebuilding their relationship when Saito's powers, and the magical bonds that tied them together, mysteriously vanish. A "13th episode," *The Alluring Beach (Miwaku no Sunahama)*, was released on DVD only. 2012 saw the release of *Familiar of Zero F.* Author Yamaguchi passed away partway through the broadcast of the series, with the final chapters only partly completed. **ⓝ**

FAMILY OF DEBAUCHERY *

2002. jpn: *Haitoku no Shojo.* aka: *Corruption of a Girl.* Video. dir: Mikan Furukawa. scr: Jinmu. des: Gen Takase. ani: N/C. mus: N/C. prd: Five Ways. 29 mins. x 2 eps.

Hiroko is going to work for a rich family as tutor to a young girl named Yuki—compare to **Blue Experience**. When Hiroko reaches their beautiful mansion, Yuki's elder sister Shizuka drugs her tea, causing her to lose consciousness. When she wakes, she is naked and tied to a bed, and Yuki and Shizuka are trying out various sex toys on her. Just as Hiroko starts to enjoy this, it's revealed that Yuki is not, in fact, a girl, but a very pretty young boy. Only the second of the two episodes was released in English, as the first featured a sequence in which a bound mother was raped in a steel cage by a dog, which was considered too risky even for the jaded audience of Japanese animated erotica (**Censorship and Localization**). **ⓛⓝⓥ**

FAMOUS WORLD FAIRY TALES

1976. jpn: *Manga Sekai Mukashi Banashi.* TV series. dir: Osamu Dezaki, Hideo Nishimaki, Tatsuya Matano, Sadao Nozaki, Tadashi Shirakawa. scr: Teru Kataoka, Keiji Kubota, Takeo Ono, Takeshi Shudo, Shina Matsuoka. des: N/C. ani: Akio Sugino, Yoshiaki Kawajiri. mus: Harumi Ibe. prd: Dax International, TBS Brittanica, World Television Ltd., Madhouse. 25 mins. x 127 eps.

Usually divided into two stories per episode, this long-running children's series narrated by Mariko Miyagi managed to crank through a vast number of folk tales and fables from all around the world. Its early episodes favored **Aesop's Fables**, the **Tales of Hans Christian Andersen**, and **Grimm's Fairy Tales**, but by the second season it was also broadening its remit to cover many other kinds of stories, including adaptations of *Frankenstein*, *Robin Hood*, and the opera *Carmen*. By 1978, the filmmakers also experimented with the form of the show, sometimes matching a 12-minute short in the former part of each episode with an ongoing serial in the latter, as when an adaptation of Jules Verne's **Adrift in the Pacific** was spread across five episodes, shared with several incongruous one-shots. By 1979, the serial was arguably scraping the bottom of the barrel, repeating several stories, sometimes as remakes, sometimes as simple rebroadcasts, but also exploring some rewardingly obscure mythologies, such as fairy tales from Russia and Mongolia and an "Indian" variant of **Cinderella**. Its longest sub-story seems to have been a remake of **A Little Princess**, which ran for ten half-episodes toward the end of the series.

FANCY LALA

1998. jpn: *Maho no Stage Fancy Lala.* aka: *Magical Stage Fancy Lala.* TV series. dir: Masahiro Omori, Takeshi Yamazaki, Miko Shima. scr: Tomomi Mochizuki. des: Akemi Takada. ani: Masako Onishi, Kazuhiro Sasaki. mus: Michiru Oshima. prd: Studio Pierrot, TV Tokyo. 25 mins. x 26 eps.

Miho is an eight-year-old girl with a secret: using her two magical pets, Pig and Mog, and her magical sketchpad, she can turn into the beautiful teenage fashion model known as Fancy Lala. As might be expected in a rehash of **Creamy Mami**, she attracts the attention of 19-year-old local wiseguy Hiroya, who falls in love with her adult version, not realizing she is only a child underneath. See also **Harbor Lights**, which functions as an early try at the same material.

FANDOM

The presence of a mature audience for Japanese animation has been implicit since the days of **Early Anime**, many of which comprised instructional material (**Documentaries and History**) clearly aimed at an audience of adults. The existence of aficionados, appreciating animation for animation's sake, first arose in 1923 as a subset of the hobbyist groups and magazine readers associated with newly available small-gauge cameras, the Pathé Baby and the Eastman Kodascope. Among such individuals, Shigeji Ogino (1899–1991) became one of Japan's most prolific amateur animated filmmakers, producing works such as *One Day 100 Years Hence* (*Hyakunen-go aru Hi*, 1932); he was active until the 1970s. The accompanying technology of small-gauge projection also encouraged a small but influential group of film owners among the hobbyists, such as Yutaka Tezuka, whose son Osamu (q.v.) might be reasonably described as a fan of foreign animation and would eventually create Japanese work in imitation. The presence of a setting on the Pathé Baby projector that would show a single frame every ten seconds may have even formed a partial inspiration for Tezuka's later experiments in limited animation (**Technology and Formats**).

Although it would be anachronistic to use the term "fandom" during the Fifteen Years War (1931–45), the enthusiastic consumption and reception of **WARTIME ANIME** was mandated by the establishment, particularly in the compulsory school outings arranged for screenings of **MOMO-TARO'S SEA EAGLES**. However, the growth of true fandom, as we know it, rather than simple *fanaticism*, does not arise until the postwar period.

The critic Nobuyuki Tsugata ties the development of "anime" itself to two technologies and the culture that they created—television (from 1953), creating a boom in animation production (from 1963), and video (from the late 1970s), creating a means of storing and exchanging animation and eventually creating new products (from 1983) specifically for an audience of older viewers. The presence of an audience beyond that of children has also long been understood by anime producers, particularly in terms of **ADVERTISING AND SPONSORSHIP**, such as the Oronamin C vitamin drink that backed **STAR OF THE GIANTS**. **RATINGS AND BOX OFFICE** have long accepted the presence of adults among viewers—indeed, the requirement for an adult parental figure to accompany a child to a cinema has usually been part of the calculations for likely ticket receipts. With the arrival of television, primetime shows such as **SAZAE-SAN** and late-night programming such as **HERMIT VILLAGE** openly courted mature viewers, while the audiences for **HEIDI** and **STAR BLAZERS** scored ratings too high to be watched merely by children.

Hence, although it has always been widely understood that any animated film was aimed at an implied audience of enthusiastic viewers, and that any sequel played to an assumed audience of viewers keen enough about a franchise to return for more of it, the concept of "fandom" required the development of a viewable archive of materials about which to be fannish, and a forum where such passions could be discussed and transmitted. Its growth in Japan is usually tied to the maturation of the **ASTRO BOY** audience, which is to say, those viewers who grew up with homegrown Japanese cartoons since 1963, entering their teens in the 1970s and 1980s, and creating a new potential market for cartoons aimed at older consumers. The director Tadao Nagahama recognized the presence of an audience of teenage viewers in the 1970s that was not being served by **KIDS' ANIME**, but it was arguably Yoshiyuki Tomino, with shows such as **ZAMBOT 3**, who pushed the envelope of "children's entertainment" sufficient to cater to older viewers.

The existence of a growing, teenage or college-age audience of anime "fans" had been explicit since the guerrilla marketing campaigns designed to push the movies based on **STAR BLAZERS**, but the rise of the video cassette truly allowed fandom to flourish as a permanent phenomenon. It was to serve this audience that the first dedicated subcultural magazines began publication, including *OUT* (1977–95), *Animage* (since 1978), and *Newtype* (since 1985). Video permitted self-identified fans not only to save and savor their favorite shows, but also to share them with others, creating a culture of viewing and potential recruitment allowing for the maintenance of a core fandom. Video cassettes allowed anime, initially from television, to seep into Japan's SF convention culture, and were soon hailed as the ideal medium with which to test mature themes unsuitable for TV animation's implied audience of children.

The 1980s saw the rise of video-based anime, including "after-mono" that continued TV storylines into more mature areas (see, for example, **MACROSS**) and "Original Animation Videos" (**ARGOT AND JARGON**) that offered all-new stories. The private viewing venues afforded by videos allowed for the rise of **EROTICA AND PORNOGRAPHY**, but also for a boom in SF, fantasy, and horror titles that helped spearhead anime's export to the West in the 1990s. Western fandom differs from country to country, but largely follows the Japanese model in miniature. In North America, for example, video recordings formed an archive, seeped into SF conventions and Internet message board discussions, and eventually became the subject of early magazines such as *Animag* (1987–ca.1992) and *Protoculture Addicts* (1988–2008).

Anime fandom, as affectionately lampooned in **OTAKU NO VIDEO**, is a self-aware interest group of proud geeks and nerds, once associated simply with the consumption of anime and its attendant merchandise and spin-offs, now more likely to be more actively involved in a culture that merely includes anime as its inspiration.

Large enough to have formed its own community, history, and archive, it has itself become a subject of study and enquiry, in works such as Yasuo Nagayama's *Sengo SF Jiken Shi: Nihonteki Sozoryoku no 70-nen* (*An Event History of Postwar SF: 70 Years of Japanese Imaginative Power*, 2012), consigning its supposed subject to the margins. Indeed, we might even point to a prevailing trend in international scholarship in which the localizing and solipsistic gaze of anime fandom has become a more popular subject of enquiry than anime itself.

Fandom also forms a substantial and self-referential audience for those anime that glorify the activities of fandom itself, such as **THE MELANCHOLY OF HARUHI SUZUMIYA** and **COSPLAY COMPLEX**. Its average age in Japan is gradually rising, leading some commentators to wryly comment on the possible approach of a demographic bubble of Silver Otaku—men in their 40s and 50s, clinging to their teenage love of **GUNDAM** and similar shows, but served by an industry of ever more expensive, tailor-made products. Its average age in the West has plummeted, from 18–22 during the video boom post-**AKIRA**, to a sudden wash of 13-to-15-year-olds in the wake of **POKÉMON**, whose approach of legal drinking age in the mid-noughties was viewed and endured with some trepidation by older convention-goers.

A modern issue, among professional watchers of fandom, is concern with the lifespan of a notional fan; although individuals are apt to claim in the heat of their fannish passions that their love of a medium is a lifelong commitment, few fans are truly so devoted. Circumstantial evidence from the peripheries of fandom, such as return visits to annual conventions and the implied institutional memories of magazines such as *Newtype*, suggest that the half-life of the average fan is a mere 18–24 months (six to eight TV seasons), before he or she moves on, perhaps to a different kind of fandom, but perhaps out of fandom altogether. In particular, the aging, retention, and dissipation of the *Pokémon* audience, as played out in the boom and sudden bust of anime sales in the first decade of the 21st century, is one of the primary influences on the foreign anime business in recent times.

Demographically, fandom in Japan is

split 88:12 male/female. In one of the remarkable counter-intuitive statistics of the medium, this division is not reflected in the English-speaking world, where a 55:45 gender parity is usually noticeable. This leads to many odd appropriations and negotiations, as fan-friendly TV shows supposedly aimed at single 30-something Japanese males form part of the viewing culture of, say, teenage American girls. Some Japanese critics, most notably Takamasa Sakurai, have observed that the representative titles, audience, and reception of Japanese animation is often radically different outside Japan. This has led not only to several tardy continuations, such as TRIGUN, dragged back into production to serve an audience abroad a decade after ending in Japan, but also to OUTBREAK COMPANY, an anime satire concerning a soft-power initiative to push fan products onto an alternate fantasy world.

Anime conventions, gatherings of like-minded fans, are now frequent events all around the world, and often form platforms for movie premieres and marketing junkets, as well as the expression of amateur activities such as costuming ("cosplay"), fanzines, and AMVs (anime music videos, juxtaposing anime footage with music lifted from elsewhere). Some commentators have noticed that much modern convention activity does not directly monetize for the creators of anime. Indeed, many conventions, particularly in America, seem more likely to serve the business needs of pseudomanga artists, hucksters, and craft spin-offs, furthering anime fandom's self-identification as a new culture independent of its original purpose. Worldwide, the most crucial technological component of modern fandom is the Internet, with the former magazine subcultures now largely migrating to websites such as Anime News Network, and online discussions forming a community that can often feel, for good or ill, like a permanent convention.

Fandom remains the implied audience for all anime but the most mainstream of titles, the investment population for most crowd-sourcing initiatives, and the source of most Internet discussions. It has also served as a recruiting ground for the staff of anime distributors, with many a professional admitting to a misspent youth

as a fansubber (**OVERSEAS DISTRIBUTION AND PIRACY**) or costumer.

The size of fandom remains a contentious issue, since the catch-all term has always contained several overlapping groups. Fandom is certainly the most vocal of groups within the consumption of anime, and might reasonably be termed the tail that wags the dog in cases of small-interest products that might be expected to monetize solely through mail order or convention retail. However, fandom is demonstrably not the entirety of the audience for anime, and is outnumbered by a youthful audience of casual viewers (many of whom might become "true" fans), and the channel-surfers who bolster TV ratings. Unwary investors, led by incautious hype, have often assumed that the **RATINGS AND BOX OFFICE** for the biggest anime franchises equates with a potential market for all anime, regardless of genre or quality. In fact, it is a fallacy to believe that ten thousand Californians dressed as **NARUTO** for a single weekend will directly translate into sales, or that an Internet poster's professed "love" of any given franchise will ever monetize. Modern technology, which has inadvertently allowed the innocent tape-swapping and lending of early fandom to transform into an informal distribution network of permanent, perfect copies, has placed many fans in the ironic position of being blamed for the collapse of the very medium they profess to love. Fandom has also been blamed, somewhat unfairly, for a mindset among producers that equates any tropes in shows aimed at the lowest common denominator to be intended for "fans." Hence, the concept of "fan service" (**ARGOT AND JARGON**), in which the most puerile excesses and panderings of certain shows are excused as being the result of audience demand—itself mistakenly implying that fandom is a single-minded entity that can be appeased by such one-size-fits-all concessions.

FANTASCOPE - TYLOSTOMA

2006. Video. DIR: Soichi Kimura. SCR: Yoshitaka Amano. DES: Yoshitaka Amano. ANI: N/C. MUS: N/C. PRD: Toei Animation, Gentosha. 33 mins.
A man returns every 700 years to a dead city in a dust-covered world. Then a mysterious prostitute changes everything.

Auteur-illustrator Amano made over 200 new Indian ink paintings for this story, based on a scenario from his website, for Toei's *ga-nime* (Glam Art Anime) series; compare with **BIRD SONG**, also created by Amano for the series, and with **YO SHOMEI MUSEUM LINE** which takes a completely different, non-narrative approach to the concept.

FANTASISTA DOLL *

2013. TV series. DIR: Hisashi Saito. SCR: Yuko Kakihara, Noboru Kimura, Sadayuki Murai, Kiyoko Yoshimura, Hiroaki Jinno, Goro Taniguchi. DES: Anmi. ANI: Hiromi Kato, Yoshiko Takimoto. MUS: Yasuharu Takanashi. PRD: Hoods Entertainment, Toho, Studio Create, Studio Cj, Hebaraki. 24 mins. x 12 eps.
Prize-winning tournament card player Uzume Uno acquires a device which allows her to summon android warrior-women with her cards. A bunch of card masters challenge her to card-based combat in order to win the chance to have a wish granted. She fights them off with one or more of her five "fantasista dolls."

FANTASTIC CHILDREN *

2005. TV series. DIR: Takashi Nakamura. SCR: Hideki Mitsui, Takashi Nakamura. DES: Takashi Nakamura. ANI: Miyuki Nakamura, Koichi Maruyama, Shingo Ishikawa et al. MUS: Koji Ueno. PRD: Nippon Animation. 25 mins. x 26 eps.
For 500 years, there have been legends all over Europe about sightings of mysterious white-haired children, often alleged to have a maturity beyond their years as well as magical powers. They are the "children of Vefoele," for whom a pallid look like mutants from **AKIRA** is the price of immortality, since they are reborn time and again until one, a boy named Palza, grows tired of the cosmic circle of life and decides he just wants one rebirth as a human. Meanwhile, on Papan Island, orphans Chito and Helga are on a quest to find a mysterious crystal that they need in order to regain their fading memories. Helga has drawn a place she doesn't know; the pair leave their orphanage to look for it, but they are hunted and Helga is captured. They are rescued by another boy called Thoma, who takes the pair to a secret island only he knows of. Helga is beginning to fall for Thoma, but she is confused by feelings

for a fantasy man. She doesn't know she is really the incarnation of Princess Tina of planet Girishia, 200 million light years from Earth. The fantasy man is her lover from an earlier life. When Tarlant, one of the Vefoele, comes to the island, she begins to remember. A story created by writer/director Nakamura in search of "an old-fashioned adventure," with more than a few nods to the reincarnation romance of SAILOR MOON, and publicity materials that push its parent studio's earlier involvement with FUTURE BOY CONAN.

FANTASY AND FAIRY TALES

As early cartoons were regarded solely as a children's medium, fairy tales have formed a natural part of their repertoire—often with a discernible tension between local stories that have domestic sales potential and "international" ones that offer better profit, but also higher risks. All information about animation development before the 1923 Great Kanto Earthquake is necessarily vague, but the best contender for the "first" folk tale anime is Seitaro Kitayama's early version of MONKEY AND THE CRAB (1917). The following year saw anime's first use of ancient folklore for commercial ends, with the *Tortoise and the Hare* (one of AESOP'S FABLES) adapted into a one-reel children's entertainment by Ikuo Oishi, and sponsored by Morinaga Chocolate.

Anime has often fought its childish reputation with choices of worthy adaptations, such as the Chinese JOURNEY TO THE WEST, first appearing as Noburo Ofuji's *Songoku Monogatari* (1926), and A THOUSAND AND ONE NIGHTS, from which the tale of *Ali Baba and the 40 Thieves* (*Yonjunin no Tozoku*, 1928) became a 17-minute epic in the hands of Takeo Ueno. The film's producer, one Toshio Suzuki, is no relation to the man of the same name who produced so many Ghibli films half a century later.

During the rise of Japanese nationalism in the prewar years, there was an increased concentration on JAPANESE FOLK TALES, along with tales of piracy and anthropomorphic animals. In the midst of postwar deprivation, a notable early fantasy is Masao Kumagawa's *Magic Pen* (*Maho no Pen*, 1946), in which Su-chan, an impoverished boy in the ruins of Tokyo, dreams that the blue-eyed doll he finds (it is a black-and-white film, but the synopsis is keen to

stress that the doll has blue eyes) comes to life and draws him an apple with a magic pen. The pen's magic causes the apple to become real, prompting the pair to take the pen and draw a new building amid the postwar desolation, in a touching allegory of hope and reconstruction.

As Japan rebuilt, anime suffered an infestation of cute animals, including Kenzo Masaoka's *Tora the Stray Cat* (*Suteneko Tora-chan*, 1947) and its sequel *Tora's Bride* (*Tora-chan to Hanayome*, 1948), the Kindai Company's *Fox Circus* (*Kitsune no Circus*, 1948), and Hideo Furusawa's *Sports Tanuki* (*Sports Kotanuki*, 1949). Anime's first major postwar works drew on Asian inspirations, with *Princess of Baghdad* (*Baghdad-hime*, 1948), followed by PANDA AND THE MAGIC SERPENT (1958). With a return to relative prosperity, the anime movie world continued to avoid non-Asian fairy tales, presumably preferring to supply local demand rather than compete with more lavish Disney imports. This period saw another JOURNEY TO THE WEST (1960), alongside THE LITTLEST WARRIOR (1961), WOOF WOOF 47 RONIN (1963), and LITTLE PRINCE AND THE EIGHT-HEADED DRAGON (1963).

It was only with the coming of TV, and the realization that foreign subjects could lead to foreign sales, that anime turned once more to European sources, including movies of the TALES OF HANS CHRISTIAN ANDERSEN (1968) and PUSS IN BOOTS (1969). The sheer amount of material generated for television ensured that fairy tale anime enjoyed much greater variety. "Mundane" fiction was given a more fantastic look with anthropomorphic animals, as in TREASURE ISLAND (1965), while Japanese fairy tales, now dismissed as old hat, were given a new lease on life through their use as inspirations in shows such as LITTLE GOBLIN (1968) and SPOOKY KITARO (1968). But fantasy remained a difficult genre to spot in the 1970s, as anime fought against the eternal onslaught of sci-fi toy tie-ins. Only the "magical girl shows," such as LITTLE WITCH SALLY (1966) and MARVELOUS MELMO (1971), might reasonably be regarded as "fantasy," although fantastic elements formed part of almost all anime by this point.

Despite being often regarded as a fairy tale franchise, surprisingly few of the stories in the WORLD MASTERPIECE THEATER

(1975) actually are. Genuine fairy tales of Japanese origin made it to the screen in HEART OF THE RED BIRD (1979). But in a period in which Disney animation was widely regarded to be in a creative slump, anime began to make bold forays back into Western material, with GRIMM'S FAIRY TALES (1987).

By the time Disney had reclaimed the fairy tale high ground with *Beauty and the Beast* (1991), Japanese animators were confident enough to compete with full-length serials of SNOW WHITE (1994) and CINDERELLA (1996). Meanwhile, new fantasy anime developed a narrative style inspired not by myths or novels, but by the set-ups of role-playing games, as seen in RECORD OF LODOSS WAR (1990) and SLAYERS (1995).

Hayao Miyazaki's MY NEIGHBOR TOTORO (1988) and KIKI'S DELIVERY SERVICE (1989) reestablished a modernized fairy tale style in cinema theaters, while elsewhere the subtexts of fantasy were exploited for different ends in UROTSUKIDOJI (1987) and its imitators. Taking their lead from a recurring theme in the works of Shigeru Mizuki (SPOOKY OOKY KITARO), that modernity (and in particular, electric light) dispels the ability of traditional spirits and magical creatures to exist, many anime have explored a theme of numinous nature and the supernatural in a state of prolonged retreat from the onset of urban life. This can take many forms, from the relatively throwaway idea of modern construction projects awakening ancient ghosts (DEVIL HUNTER YOHKO) to broader ecological treatments in which the dwindling of the spirit world functions as an allegory for the ebb of humanity's own culture and respect for the natural world (POM POKO).

In the last 20 years movie theaters have continued to offer genuine family entertainment, with the most noteworthy works of recent times being Studio Ghibli's PRINCESS MONONOKE (1997), SPIRITED AWAY (2001), and PONYO (2008) revisiting and refashioning old stories with a personal touch that is pure Miyazaki. Fantasy on television often includes liminal dramas that transport youthful protagonists to new worlds, such as ESCAFLOWNE (1996) or TWEENY WITCHES (2004). Shows such as PETITE PRINCESS YUCIE (2002) combine the "magical girl" set-ups of recent times with the sumptuousness of old-school fairy tales, while **LOVELESS** (2005) cleverly uses anthropomorphic characteristics, or rather their disappearance, as an allegory of the loss of childhood innocence. In economically straitened times, even Japan's gods have been affected by the two-decade Japanese recession, as demonstrated by the leading man of **NORAGAMI** (2014), a god without any followers, obliged to take on mundane tasks in return for low-intensity worship.

Meanwhile, fantasy on video comprises rereleases of both the TV and movie media discussed above, but also a predictable concentration on private titillation. The sexual subtexts of fairy tales, with their allegories of taboos and fears, are often presented as physical plot elements in straight-to-video anime—it is only a short step from dungeons-and-dragons to tits-and-tentacles.

FAR EAST OF EDEN

1990. JPN: *Tengai Makyo.* AKA: *Evil World beyond Heaven.* Video. DIR: Oji Hiroi, Toshio Takeuchi. SCR: Toshio Takeuchi. DES: Kotaro Tsujino. ANI: Yasuo Otsuka. MUS: Kohei Tanaka. PRD: TMS. 50 mins. x 2 eps.
In the alternate world of Xipangu, hero Jiraiya defeats local pirates and heads off in search of the fabled treasure of the death god, Hiruko, but Jiraiya is opposed by an equally evil sorcerer. Joining forces with the beautiful princess, Yuki (who has the power to seal Hiruko away), Jiraiya must confront a gang of renegades, led by a female impersonator, that intends to conquer the entire kingdom. Based on a game for the PC Engine console, designed by Red Company, who would eventually make **SAKURA WARS** with director Hiroi. Though the vampiric Hiruko is defeated at the climax, in the original, the end-of-game boss was Masakado—see **DOOMED MEGALOPOLIS**. Note the presence of **CASTLE OF CAGLIOSTRO**'s Yasuo Otsuka as animation director and a crew roster that brought a great look to an otherwise forgettable cash-in.

FAST BREAK *

2011. JPN: *Ro-Kyu-Byu!* AKA: *Ro-Kyu-Bu—Fast Break!* TV series. DIR: Keizo Kusakawa. SCR: Michiko Ito, Taizo Yoshida, Takao Yoshioka. DES: Takayuki Noguchi. ANI: Takayuki Noguchi. MUS: Takeshi Watanabe. PRD: Barnum Studio, Studio Planc, Project No. 9, ASCII Media Works, AT-X, Klockworx, Warner Bros. 24 mins. x 12 eps. (TV1), 24 mins. x 12 eps. (TV2), ?? mins. (v).
Subaru joins his high school basketball team as a freshman, only to find out it has been dormant since the captain was suspected of taking too much interest in little girls—specifically, the coach's daughter. Then his aunt asks him to coach a basketball team in a girls' elementary school. His five little pupils are eager to do well and as he gets to know each of them individually he wants to help them win big. But they need six for a competition team, and the only way he can ensure enough players is to get on court with them as part of the team.

Lolicon, or Lolita Complex, as the Japanese describe it after Vladimir Nabokov's novel *Lolita*, is a regularly recurring thread in many anime, not merely in overt **EROTICA AND PORNOGRAPHY**. Are those cute girls popular with fans because they're cute and fans like cute art, or because they're childlike and fans are perverts? It's disturbing to see images of girls aged 6 to 12 in a sexualized context, whether that happens in anime, in manga, or in fashion, all the more so when the male gaze is directed at them from the point of view of someone who is supposedly *in loco parentis*—compare this with similar themes in **SLOW STEP** and **BAMBOO BLADE**, where the students were at least barely legal. The series has been praised in Japan for raising *lolicon* as an issue, and for the charm of the art and story despite the erotic elements.

This anime is based on a 2010 book series by Sagu Aoyama with art by Tinkle. The series has spun off two manga series and several video games. A second TV season, *Ro-Kyu-Bu! SS*, aired in July 2013. *SS* has two meanings, according to creator Aoyama: either "second season" or "*shogakusei wa saiko da ze*—primary school girls are great." A new video entitled *Tomoka's Strawberry Sundae (Tomoka no Ichigo Sundae)* was bundled with the PSP video game and released in June 2013.

FATAL FURY *

1992. JPN: *Battle Fighters: Garo Densetsu.* AKA: *Battle Fighters: Legend of the Hungry Wolf; Mark of the Wolf.* Movie, TV special. DIR: Kazuhiro Furuhashi, Masami Obari, Hiroshi Fukutomi. SCR: Takashi Yamada. DES: Masami Obari. ANI: Masami Obari. MUS: Toshihiko Sato, Toshiro Masuda. PRD: Asahi International, Pony Canyon, Fuji TV, NAS. 45 mins. (TVm), 73 mins. (TVm), 90 mins. (m).
As with its contemporary **STREET FIGHTER II**, this adaptation of a beat-'em-up console game struggles and ultimately fails to make the jump to non-interactive media, though not without some incidental pleasures on the way. Viz's dub is perfectly serviceable, albeit with some unplaceably alien accents from the supporting cast that only add to the fun as one tries to guess whether someone is supposed to come from Oirland or Scutlund. With overmuscled men meeting, greeting, indulging in strange acts, and then parting, it has a strangely homoerotic charge, peppered with sanctimonious moral messages about the nobility of fighting for what is right but without questioning whether anyone should be fighting at all.

FF: Legend of the Hungry Wolf (1992) sets up the original backstory to the game, in which Terry and Andy Bogard witness their father's murder and become bareknuckle fighters, in a tournament plot not unlike **TEKKEN**, eventually avenging him by defeating his murderer Geese Howard. Mere months later in *FF: The New Battle* (1993), Howard's half-brother, Wolfgang Krauser, returns to challenge Terry. With time out to reunite a street urchin with his mother in a halfhearted subplot, Terry soon hunts Krauser down to a showdown in a German castle, while other characters pop out of the woodwork for a few rounds to please their fans. The franchise reached theaters at its peak with *FF: The Motion Picture* (1994), which dumped at least part of the "you killed my father" plotting in favor of an Indiana Jones rip-off. Laocoön Gaudeamus is searching for the legendary Armor of Mars (compare to Jackie Chan's *Armor of God*, 1987), lost by his ancestors during the Crusades. His estranged sister, Sulia, hires Terry to stop him before he can use the armor's magical powers, in a plot that presages **SPRIGGAN**, though it was too late to save the tired and formulaic *FF* franchise. **Ⓥ**

FATE/ZERO *

2011. TV series. DIR: Ei Aoki. SCR: Akira Hiyama, Akihiro Yoshida, Kazuharu Sato, Takumi Miyajima. DES: Atsushi Ikariya, Tomonori Sudo, Koji Eto. ANI: Atsushi Ikariya,

Tomonori Sudo, Takayuki Mogi. MUS: Yuki Kajiura. PRD: ufotable, Aniplex, Nitroplus, Notes, Seikaisha. 23 mins. x 12 eps. + 45 mins. x 1 ep. (TV1), 23 mins. x 12 eps. (TV2).

The ancient Einzbern family has made three attempts over two centuries to take the Holy Grail, in a contest in which seven mages summon heroic spirits. The winner, it is said, will be granted a miracle. This time, they mean to succeed, and have hired famous mercenary mage-killer Kiritsugu as their representative. A man previously weary of life, but now with a new purpose in the love of his wife and daughter, Kiritsugu is conflicted. When he faces a man as empty and loveless as he once was, he fears he may lose everything in the Fourth Grail War.

Type-Moon's *Fate/Stay Night* franchise has had enormous success all over the world. The series is spun off the book series Gen Urobuchi wrote in 2006, with art by Type-Moon cofounder Takeshi Takeuchi. The light novels were adapted as four CD dramas between 2008 and 2010, and as a manga by Shinjiro in 2011. This is still ongoing. The story is set ten years before the events of *Fate/Stay Night*, but shares its epic scope and its Arthurian trappings used in almost unrecognizable ways. It's so big and complex that the writers (all from ufotable) and director felt they needed a 45-minute opening episode just to set the scene. Unsurprisingly, its scope and grandeur are hampered by what feels like eons of talking. It's like one of those historical novels where you need three pages of tables to keep the characters straight in your head, whereas in real life—or in good writing—you ought to be able to pick that up by observation. Exposition is the enemy of pace, and the magnificent action scenes that stud this show like flaming jewels are at grave risk of being extinguished in the morass of arcane power names, tactical talk, and similar pretentious twaddle.

The designs and music suffer from a similar dichotomy. Marvelous armor and weaponry, using historic and mythic inspiration to great effect, are set against largely substandard backgrounds. Battles get the full-on orchestral treatment but everything else is reduced to pop pap, with one or two tunes fit for little but breaking the silence in an elevator. It all comes back to the writing: too much of it, and

the wrong sort, make this a series only a diehard fan could love.

A second series in 2012, unsurprisingly entitled *Fate/Zero 2nd Season*, continues the Fourth Grail War to its conclusion, and the inevitable puzzle: did anyone really win? However, with the exposition out of the way, the plot and writing are stronger and the series' strongest point, its battle sequences, can shine as they deserve. There is much better and stronger character writing in this series, leavening the excess of tactical discussion. Some scenes may confuse those who have not read the novels or manga, and the pacing is still far from perfect, but the series finishes strongly and may well entice those who haven't seen *Fate/Stay Night* to give it a look. **N**

FAULT!!
2009. Video. DIR: Ken Raika. SCR: Shinichiro Sawayama. DES: Akane Aki. ANI: Akane Aki. MUS: N/C. PRD: T-Rex, Marigold/Cottondoll. 30 mins. x 3 eps.

Shuichi is having an incestuous relationship with his younger stepsister Mio. So that's not really incest, is it? They both belong to a tennis club and Shuichi's regular tennis partner, Saeki, has a crush on him. When she sees Mio and Shuichi kissing at the tennis club, she plucks up courage to tell him how she feels and they have sex on the tennis court. But Shuichi's teacher and his *senpai*, or older schoolmate—who is usually a guy, unless it's a straight porn anime—are also club members. Nobody gets coerced, the art is pretty and the female characters have more naturalistic body shapes than is usual in anime **EROTICA AND PORNOGRAPHY**. Based on an erotic game by Space Project's Ciel label with original character designs by Tony, which was also released in 2009. **N**

FEATHER STARES AT THE DARK, A ★
2003. JPN: *Yami o Mitsumeru Hane*. Movie DIR: Naoyuki Tsuji. SCR: N/C. DES: Naoyuki Tsuji. ANI: Naoyuki Tsuji. MUS: N/C. PRD: N/C. 17 mins.

Screened in Cannes in 2004 and at several North American festivals, this independent short film is made by a "charcoal anime process"—a single charcoal drawing is photographed, partly erased, and reworked for the next frame, much as many **EARLY ANIME** were made. It took the direc-

tor eight years to make 17 minutes of black and white film by erasing and reworking his first image over 13,500 times. He started making his own films in 1992, at age 20. Other works include 1994's *For the Lost Legend* (9 mins.), 1995's *Law of Dream* (6 mins.), and 2005's 13-minute *Trilogy About Clouds (Mittsu no Kumo)*, screened in London and out on DVD with four of his other short films.

FEMALE STUDENT
2010. JPN: *Seitokai Yakuindomo*. AKA: *Student Council Officers*. TV series, video. DIR: Hiromitsu Kanazawa. SCR: Makoto Nakamura, Hiromitsu Kanazawa et al. DES: Makoto Furuta, Masanobu Nomura. ANI: Makoto Furuta. MUS: Yuya Mori. PRD: GoHands, Starchild Records. 24 mins. x 13 eps. (TV), 27 mins. x 5 eps. (v), 24 mins. x 13 eps. (TV2)

Osai Academy used to be a girls' high school, but has just gone co-ed. Takatoshi Tsuda signs up for the school because it's the nearest to his home, but finds himself surrounded by girls everywhere—on the train, in class, and on the student council, where he's co-opted as a token male. Albeit a perfect setting for a harem anime (**ROMANCE AND DRAMA**), the main purpose of this anime is to provide a setting for a stream of rapid-fire smut gags and double-entendres. The same crew made five video episodes in 2011 to provide more of the same, as Tsuda enters his second year and his younger sister joins the school. Based on the 2007 manga by Tozen Ujiie. **LN**

FENCER OF MINERVA ★
1995. JPN: *Minerva no Kenshi*. AKA: *Knight of Minerva*. Video. DIR: Takahiro Okao, Tadayoshi Kusaka. SCR: Sukehiro Tomita, Yuji Kishino. DES: Takashi Wada. ANI: Tadashi Hirota, Nobuaki Shirai. MUS: Kanae Wada. PRD: All Products, Beam Entertainment. 45 mins. x 5 eps.

The beautiful, willful Princess Diana is betrothed to a handsome prince but is captured by nomads, who refuse to believe her royal protestations because out of her clothes she looks just like any other wench. After a brief initiation in the amatory arts, she is rescued from a gang bang by a masked man, her childhood sweetheart Prince Sho, who is returning to claim his rightful kingdom from the man who usurped it, Princess Diana's evil father.

Believe it or not, from the tacky designs that replace original ideas with two-legged horses and flying piranhas (sorry, water lizards) to U.S. Manga Corps' faithfully camp **TRANSLATION** of some of the world's worst dialogue, *Fencer of Minerva* genuinely is so bad that it's good. But what do you expect when the **CREAM LEMON** team try to imitate B-movie sword-and-sandal fantasy, complete with lost kingdoms, lovably chauvinist heroes, and breathless slave-girls in diaphanous veils? A guilty pleasure, as if John Norman had written an episode of **RECORD OF LODOSS WAR**. Compare to the similarly risible **EROTIC TORTURE CHAMBER**. In order to achieve a lower rating on its American release, *Fencer of Minerva* was stripped of some of its racier elements (**CENSORSHIP AND LOCALIZATION**). **NV**

FIFTH ICE AGE
1967. JPN: *Subarashii Sekai Ryoko: Alaska no Tabi: Daigo Hyogaki*. AKA: *Wonderful World Travel: Alaskan Journey: Fifth Ice Age*. TV special. DIR: Masahiro Mori. SCR: Mamoru Sasaki. DES: Hiroshi Manabe. ANI: N/C. MUS: Kiyoshi Iwami. PRD: Mushi Pro. 30 mins. x 2 eps.
In the near future, Earth is engulfed in a new ice age as snow falls ceaselessly in summer and glaciers advance with uncharacteristic speed. In this SF spin-off of the live-action *Wonderful World Travel* series, humanity must decide whether to use science to fight the ice or to adapt to it. The same team also peers into the future in **COMPUTOPIA**.

FIGHT: SPIRIT OF THE SWORD *
1993. JPN: *Fight!!* Video. DIR: Akira Koson. SCR: Ryo Yasumura. DES: Kenichi Onuki. ANI: Masanori Nishii. MUS: Taikai Hayakawa. PRD: Pony Canyon. 45 mins.
High school student Yonosuke Hikura is the latest in his family to protect the harmony between Heaven and Earth. With the help of the magical sword Chitentai, and Tsukinojo Inbe, a Protector sent to him by the High Priests of Earth, he courageously battles the demons, sending them back to the Earth World from which they have escaped. Another tale in the tradition of **DEVIL HUNTER YOHKO**, but it's played disappointingly straight.

FIGHT! OSPA
1965. JPN: *Tatakae! Ospa*. TV series. DIR: Masami Aragura, Nobuhiro Okaseko, Yoshiyuki Tomino. SCR: Koichi Yamano, Teru Nagashima. DES: N/C. ANI: Mami Murano, Nobuhiro Okaseko. MUS: Isao Tomita. PRD: NTV. 25 mins. x 52 eps.
The inhabitants of the sunken Pacific continent of Mu (see **SUPER ATRAGON**) yearn to leave their undersea dome and return to the surface world. After many centuries beneath the waves, they are threatened with destruction by the power-hungry Dorome. The good people of Mu send Ospa, their finest man, to find help on the surface world, where he assembles an international team to fight for justice. Based on an idea by **TAKE THE X TRAIN**–author Koichi Yamano, this series is a combination of the *Dolphin Prince* (see **MARINE BOY**) and **PRINCE PLANET**.

FIGHT! PUTER
1968. JPN: *Fight Da!! Pyu-ta*. TV series. DIR: Hiroyoshi Mitsunobu, Jun Nagasawa, Kunitoshi Shiraishi. SCR: Yoshitake Suzuki, Kenichi Ogawa, Kuniaki Hata-naka. DES: Tsunezo Murotani. ANI: Tameo Ogawa. MUS: Tetsuaki Hagiwara. PRD: MBS. 25 mins. x 26 eps.
Pyuta Imano helps his grandfather, Professor Tsulury, with his experiments. The evil Walther VII and his sidekick, Glocky, try to seize control of the world. While trying to stop them, an accident gives Pyuta a supercomputer for a brain. Airing the day after the first episode of **CYBORG 009**, this younger version was based on a manga in *Shonen Sunday* by Tsunezo Murotani, whose *Piccory Bee* (the tales of a "Thunder Child" who falls from the sky) had also been animated in 1967.

FIGHTER
1990. JPN: *Kentoshi*. Video. DIR: Yoichiro Shimatani. SCR: Ranko Ono. DES: Kuniaki Tsuji. ANI: Kuniaki Tsuji. MUS: Takahiko Kanemaru. PRD: Apple, Miyuki Pro. 45 mins. x 3 eps.
Kenji is a heavyweight boxer who wants to learn from the legendary Tokyo trainer Eddie Williams and win the American championships. In New York, he takes on the heavyweight Joe Roman, before fighting another American, George MacGregor, for the title at Madison Square Garden. In this predictable adaptation of

Takashi Tsukasa's series from *Manga Club*, it is needless to say that, in the tradition of innumerable **SPORTS ANIME** from **TOMORROW'S JOE** to **AIM FOR THE ACE**, by the time of the big fight, coach Eddie is on his deathbed. **V**

FIGHTING FOODONS *
2001. JPN: *Kakuto Ryori Densetsu Bistro Recipe*. AKA: *Legend of Grappling Cook Bistro Recipe; Bistro Recipe*. TV series. DIR: Tetsuo Yasumi. SCR: Taku Kadoya. DES: Naoko Shimada. ANI: Group TAC. MUS: Daisuke Asakura. PRD: NHK, Kodansha, Group Tac, Red Entertainment. 25 mins. x 26 eps.
Aspiring Chinese chef Chase (Zen)'s master chef father Jack (Tsukuji) is kidnapped by evil chef King Gorge (Don Cook) and his minions, the Gluttons (Four Big Gourmets). Chase, sister Karin, and their associates use the "strength" in food to fight magical combats by producing powerful creatures known as Foodons from the recipes they create. In a **POKÉMON**-like scenario, aspiring chefs cook a meal, stick it on a magical Recipe Card, and providing the cook has enough "heart" to power the transformation, his creation turns into a monster and goes into battle. A series of food fights follow, which are not as much fun as you might think. From the manga by Naoto Tsushima which first appeared, appropriately enough, in *Comic BonBon*. Compare to **CHINA NUMBER ONE**.

FIGHTING OF ECSTASY
2011. AKA. Video. DIR: Nana Tamaki. SCR: Hajime Shiba. DES: Nana Tamaki. ANI: Nana Tamaki, Dosan Saito. MUS: N/C. PRD: Pink Pineapple. 22 mins. x 2 eps.
Young women fight genetically enhanced monsters and warriors to entertain crowds of fans. The winners get to have sex with the losers in the ring in any way they choose. The girls lose, because this is based on a 2009 porn game by Crimson. It's also remarkably poor value even for **EROTICA AND PORNOGRAPHY**, with drastic changes to the original character design and very limited animation, full of loops and reused frames. **NV**

FIGHTING SPIRIT *
2000. JPN: *Hajime no Ippo, Hajime no Ippo: The Fighting!* AKA: *First for Ippo*. TV series, TV special, movie. DIR: Satoshi Nishimura,

Nanako Shimazaki. scr: Tatsuhiko Urahata, Shoji Sugiwara, Hiroshi Mori. des: Koji Sugiura. ani: Noriyuki Fukuda. mus: Tsuneo Imahori. prd: Madhouse, TV Tokyo. 25 mins. x 76 eps. (TV), 92 mins. (special), 60 mins. (v).

Highschool student Ippo Marunouchi is alienated from his classmates due to his need to help his widowed mother with the family business after school, and is furthermore the target of the school bullies. When a passing boxer, Mamoru Takamura, saves him from a beating, Ippo is inspired to take up boxing, begins a tough training regime, and eventually convinces the dubious Takamura to help him join Takamura's gym. From there Ippo's nascent talent begins to shine through, as he starts up the ranks of professional boxing, along the way earning the respect of not only his gym-mates but also his opponents—by his humility, dedication to the sport, and drive to succeed—and inspiring them to be both better boxers and better men. Based on the ongoing 1989 manga by Joji Morikawa, this is a lighter-hearted take on the sports drama genre that stretches right back to TOMORROW'S JOE (SPORTS ANIME). ⓥ

FIGURE 17: TSUBASA AND HIKARU *

2001. TV series. dir: Naohito Takahashi. scr: Yasuhiro Imagawa, Shoji Yonemura. des: Yuriko Chiba. ani: Yuriko Chiba. mus: Toshihiko Takamizawa. prd: Genco, OLM, Anime Theater X. 46 mins. x 13 eps.

Interstellar traveler "DD" is transporting the Magure energy source when he crashlands on Earth. He enlists the help of Hokkaido ten-year-old Tsubasa in getting it back, which requires her to merge with the newly formed robot Hikaru to form the superheroine Figure 17. When not fighting aliens, the two girls must pose as sisters. A predictable rerun of the transforming superhero of ULTRAMAN and BIRDY THE MIGHTY, pretentiously billed in Japan as "smashing the broadcast paradigm" just because the episodes were twice as long as usual and only broadcast monthly. Interviews at the time have the cast claiming that the running time offers them better opportunities to pursue a character-based drama, without the need to suddenly wrap everything up for the next episode. But this "innovation" was found to be more distracting than anything else, with complaints from some viewers that the gap between episiodes was so long that they often forgot what had happened previously.

FINAL APPROACH

2005. TV series. dir: Takashi Yamamoto. scr: Katsumi Hasegawa. des: Aoi Nishimata, Noriko Shimazawa. ani: N/C. mus: Angel Note. prd: Trinet Entertainment, ZEXCS. 13 mins. x 13 eps.

Japan's falling birthrate forces the government to consider drastic steps, institutionalizing dating services to ensure that all healthy young men get the fertile woman they so richly deserve. Consequently, ordinary teen Ryo Mizuhara, who lives with his younger sister Akane and works in cousin Harumi's café, is surprised one day when the strangely pushy Shizuka barges into his apartment, complete with government bodyguard, and claims to be his fiancée. She is part of the pilot scheme to test the new policy, and Ryo is the lucky recipient. Before you can say RIZELMINE, she has moved in with him and transfers to his school, although Ryo is suddenly also very popular among his school friends, and a harem of TENCHI MUYO! proportions soon ensues. Based on the so-called "original" creation from Princess Soft, and screened on TV Kanagawa as part of "Princess Hour," along with DOUBLE WISH, FA is hobbled by its origins: it is as leadenly predictable as a computer game, while any erotic potential is killed off by the need to keep it tame for television. Our anime crystal ball predicts that before long there will be an anime porn show about a fascist breeding program with none of Final Approach's attempt to play for laughs. The series' title in Japan used the Greek letter "phi" for its opening syllable, just to make things difficult for encyclopedists unsure where to file it.

FINAL FANTASY *

1993. aka: Legend of the Crystals: Based on Final Fantasy. Video. dir: Rintaro, Naoto Kanda. scr: Satoru Akahori, Mayori Sekijima. des: Yoshinori Kanemori, Kunihiko Sakurai. ani: Naoto Kanda, et al. mus: Masahiko Sato. prd: Madhouse. 30 mins. x 4 eps. (TV1), 106 mins. (m1), 25 mins. x 25 eps. (Unlimited), 25 mins. (Last Order), 101 mins. (Advent Children).

Two hundred years after the elimination of the evil Exdeath, reckless swordsman Prettz and the summoner Linaly are the youngsters who must save their world from Ra Devil, a bio-mechanical being from the dark moon. Set several centuries after the end of the game, this series is a distant spin-off from Final Fantasy V, whose character Batts is supposedly Linaly's ancestor.

The plot is similar to a computer game—after a few random encounters with wandering monsters, the leads must unite two warring parties to create a suitably mismatched party of fearless heroes. Pirate queen Rouge, the whip-wielding mistress of an airship crewed by leather-clad fat girls, falls in love with her sworn enemy, Valcus, leader of the Iron Wing squadron. After some mild tortures (Prettz is tickled and Linaly has to drink prune juice), the former enemies unite to fight Ra Devil, destroying both him and his Bond-villain hideout.

FF's hackneyed quest to save four elemental crystals is upstaged by its backgrounds. As in the games, a good image wins out over the practicalities of physics or geography. With a large number of Chinese and Korean staffers, FF lifts design ideas from all over the Orient, with the tall, thin mountains of Guilin forming a backdrop for klong canals from Thailand, and old-world Chinese houses from Canton providing hangars for pseudo-Miyazaki giant airplanes.

As later FF games achieved fame abroad, this anime was dusted off and released in English with undue prominence given to the words Final and Fantasy and rather less to its origins as a spin-off from an untranslated prequel.

Hironobu Sakaguchi's later, fully computer animated Final Fantasy: The Spirits Within (2001) features a quest to obtain eight organic specimens, whose "spirit signatures" will cancel out the energies of alien ghosts. Made in Hawaii, it boasts an all-star cast and the anime version's voice director, Jack Fletcher. Presumably intended as an attempt to make a truly international FF movie, The Spirits Within boasted so many foreign staff members that it does not strictly qualify as "anime" within our own criteria. It was also a box office flop, although Hollywood accountancy excels at making anything look like a box office flop—it remains likely that the code and development used on *Spirits Within* was paid for out of the movie budget, and could be reinvested in the next game.

Mahiro Maeda's TV Tokyo series *FF: Unlimited* (2001) was a return to old-fashioned anime stylings, brashly announced as a 52-episode series, but cut back to a cheaper 25, supposedly after low ratings, but largely because Square had lost its taste for investment after the failure of *Spirits Within* was plain on the balance sheets. It featured two children Ai and Yu, whose search for a lost parent draws them into an "Inner World" where they become the latest champions to fight against the onset of chaos, utilizing many items and references to earlier games in the *FF* series.

As with **STREET FIGHTER II**, numerals on the titles of films in the franchise do not refer to chapter numbers in a story, but to the incarnation of the game from which the anime is adapted. Hence Tetsuya Nomura's *FF VII: Advent Children* (2004) is a movie whose title refers to the *FF VII* game. Set two years after the events of the game, the CG *Advent Children* features Cloud Strife and Tifa, who have set up a delivery service after their heroic activities in the game, drawn into a new conflict to prevent their enemy Sephiroth from returning, aspiring to a messianic climax that has elements of **NAUSICAÄ OF THE VALLEY OF THE WIND**, at least in terms of its inspiration.

A further release, Morio Asaka and Tetsuya Nomura's video *FF VII: Last Order* (2005), serves as a prequel to the game, revisiting several incidents only remembered in flashbacks in the original, but also ties in to later game spin-offs for the PSP and mobile phones.

FIRE EMBLEM *

1995. JPN: *Fire Emblem: Aritia no Oji*. AKA: *Fire Emblem: Prince of Aritia*. Video. DIR: Shin Misawa. SCR: Yosuke Kuroda. DES: Yuji Moriyama. ANI: Yuji Moriyama. MUS: Hiroyuki Kozu. PRD: KSS, Studio Fantasia. 30 mins. x 2 eps.

Pacifist prince Mars reluctantly tools up when his homeland, Aritia, is conquered by the evil Druans. On the run with his faithful knights and a reformed mercenary in the neighboring kingdom of Taris, he enlists the aid of the king's only daughter, the Pegasus-riding Princess Cedar. Originating in a "Fantasy Simulation Game" for

the Nintendo Famicom (NES) console, this is a predictable spin-off—just enough episodes to drag back hard-core game fans then rerelease as a one-shot for rental and the export market, which cannot be expected to be as forgiving.

FIRE TRIPPER *

1985. JPN: *Rumic World: Fire Tripper*. Video. DIR: Motosuke Takahashi. SCR: Tomoko Konparu. DES: Katsumi Aoshima. ANI: Junko Yamamoto, Mami Endo. MUS: Keiichi Oku. PRD: Production Ai, OB. 47 mins.

Modern Japanese girl Suzuko and a neighbor's child are thrown back in time by a gas explosion. Meeting the handsome Shukumaru, Suzuko searches for the lost neighbor boy, not realizing that Shukumaru is the adult version of the 20th-century child who accompanied her, and that she herself is an exile from the 15th century. This adaptation of one of Rumiko Takahashi's *Rumic World* manga shorts (which also include **MERMAID'S FOREST**, **MARIS THE CHOJO**, and **LAUGHING TARGET**) cleverly exploits the conventions of time-travel stories as well as the shifting age boundaries put to more lascivious effect in **CREAM LEMON**. Released on a theatrical double bill with **THE HUMANOID**. Takahashi would return to medieval time travel in her later **INU YASHA**.

FIREBALL

2008. TV series. DIR: Wataru Arakawa. SCR: Wataru Arakawa. DES: Hitoshi Fukuchi, Asato Mifune, Rie Tanaka. ANI: Shigeyuki Watanabe. MUS: Yoshiyuki Usui. PRD: Jinni's Animation Studios, Walt Disney TV International Japan. 2 mins. x 13 eps.

There's a war on between humans and robots, but it doesn't bother Drossel von Flugel, a member of robot royalty, who lives at Tempest Tower with her servant Gedachtnis. This stylish series of shorts presents snippets of their wacky life together, and it's sheer delight from the bombastic Aryan opening theme to the surprise ending, when Disney's name shoots up in the end credits. Watch for sly sight gags including ruby slippers and a distinctive cream-puff hairstyle. The lighting and sound are especially crisp and fine, although the animation is extremely limited at times. Animation house Jinni's was involved in *Appleseed XIII* (**APPLESEED**) and the 2011 **REIDEEN**.

FIREFIGHTER! DAIGO OF FIRE COMPANY M

1999. JPN: *Megumi no Daigo*. Video. DIR: Susumu Nishizawa. SCR: Akihiko Inari. DES: Hideyuki Motohashi. ANI: Hideyuki Motohashi. MUS: Shiro Hamaguchi. PRD: Sunrise. 45 mins.

Maverick fireman Daigo Asahina risks disciplinary action by bodily throwing civilians from a high window, but he's exonerated when the building blows up seconds later. Running a gauntlet of girlfriend trouble, he is caught in a fire at a local concert hall and is forced to leave people behind. Outside, he steals a fire engine and rams through a wall, carrying the victims out to public acclaim.

Despite a five-minute closing credit sequence with only three minutes of credits, and under-animated moments pretending to be dramatic slow-mo, *FD* overcomes its low budget thanks to a stirring orchestral score and clever design. Fire and water surround Daigo, even in humdrum scenes of everyday life, with the camera zooming in on a hose at a car wash or a scarlet sunset that looks as if the sky itself is aflame. The fire-fighting scenes themselves are similarly well observed, with incongruous pillars of water falling down through an inferno, and a no-win scenario that finds Daigo knee-deep in water inside a burning building, dodging falling debris and sparking electric cables. Based on the 1995 *Shonen Sunday* manga by Masahito Soda that was itself doubtlessly inspired by Naoto Takenaka's 1994 live-action fire-fighting film *119*, this video traces a thematic line back to the 1991 Hollywood movie *Backdraft*. The manga was later released in English by Viz Media—our title here reflects that of the 2003 manga **TRANSLATION**, and not the one previously used in international rights solicitations. The story was also adapted into a live-action series on Fuji TV in 2004.

FIRESTORM

2003. AKA: *Gerry Anderson's Firestorm*. TV series. DIR: Kenji Terada. SCR: Kenji Terada. DES: Kenichi Onuki. ANI: Transarts. MUS: Fumitaka Anzai. PRD: Madhouse, TV Tokyo, Itochu Fashion Systems, AT-X. 25 mins. x 26 eps.

In the year 2104, Carlo Morelli's international crime organization Black Orchid is building a network of weapons and bases as strong as any government's. Nations band together to create an answer to the new threat: Storm Force. Sam Scott is the leader of Storm Force 9, a team tasked specifically with "Operation Firestorm," to unmask Black Orchid's motives. Scott is a clean-cut U.S. military hero, leading an international crew. African-American Wesley Grant, sarcastic blond Brit James Brady, green-haired Australian explosives expert Laura Hope, and feisty Japanese pilot ace Nagisa Kisaragi are based with Scott on the mighty submarine base Ocean Storm (a distant cousin of *Captain Scarlet*'s Cloudbase), commanded by the stern but heroic Drew McAllister. The team learns that Black Orchid is more dangerous than anyone ever imagined—they are in league with the Zolion, aliens who use advanced technology to mimic any living being. The fight is not just against crime, but for the survival of humanity, since a 5,000-vessel invasion fleet is just weeks away from Earth. Hence a multi-arc story structure that begins as a simple tale of fighting crime, before escalating into an operation to prevent the distribution of alien technology, and a seven-episode climax as the cast oppose the Zolion fleet.

Firestorm tries to cover too many conventional bases, and its best elements are underplayed—the evil masterminds aren't quite evil enough, the heroes are just too gung-ho and not undercut with irony. British creator Gerry Anderson enjoys immense popularity in Japan; shows such as his *Thunderbirds*, *Captain Scarlet*, and *UFO* were heavy influences on the generations that made both **ULTRAMAN** and **EVANGELION**, and he was an uncredited catalyst for the show that would become **MOSPEADA**. *Firestorm*, however, is a failure engendered by lack of communication between its coproducers—something of a sore point, considering Anderson's treatment a generation earlier on **THUNDERBIRDS 2086**. Anderson and his *Space Precinct* collaborator John Needham came up with the storyline, but the series was put together in Tokyo by people who seemed to value Anderson's name on their logo more than his actual contribution. Tellingly, a show originally billed as *Gerry Anderson's Firestorm* appeared after a delay of many months, as just plain *Firestorm*, while production details were removed at Anderson's own

request from a contemporary chronicle of his work. Also absent, even during production, were the names of the British designers who had actually worked on the concept—compare to similar shenanigans on **DRACULA: SOVEREIGN OF THE DAMNED.** Although acknowledged in the U.K., machine designer Steven Begg was nowhere to be seen on the promotional materials published in the Japanese *Newtype*, a fact of which Anderson and his U.K. cohorts may not have been aware. Similar obstruction hid the contribution of Steve Kyte, whose character concepts were specifically commissioned to look as realistic as possible in order to meet the parameters of the original production plans to use 3D CG. In fact, the only CG animation to be found in the final version is on the machines after budgetary issues led other aspects to be more cheaply rendered as conventional 2D, although many of Kyte's designs for uniforms, equipment, and logos, as well as the chilling alien mask transformation sequence he storyboarded, are unchanged in the finished series. ⓥ

FIRST KISS STORY

2000. JPN: *First Kiss Monogatari*. Video. DIR: Kan Fukumoto. SCR: Gaku Hoshino. DES: Hiroki Mizugami, Tatsuo Yanagino. ANI: Tatsuo Yanagino. MUS: N/C. PRD: Yaryu, Broccoli. 30 mins.

Yoshihiko is in his busy sophomore year at college while love-interest Kana is stuck back in high school. Her life takes a turn for the surreal when a new teacher at her school turns out to be the spitting image of her dead father. Set two years after the end of its PlayStation origins, Gaku Hoshino's screen adaptation of his game was released on Valentine's Day in a futile attempt to drum up business. The presence of **LA BLUE GIRL**'s Fukumoto as director invites the question: Is he trying to disentangle himself from tentacle porn or is the name an "Alan Smithee" credit used by others on titles of questionable value? Although four episodes were planned, only one seems to have seen the light of day.

FIRST LOVES *

1995. JPN: *Kakyusei, Kakyusei: My Petty Class Student, elf-ban Kakyusei, Anata-dake wo Mitsumete*. AKA: *First Loves, Under-*

classmates. Video. DIR: Koichi Yoshida, Kan Fukumoto. SCR: Masaru Yamamoto. DES: Yuji Takahashi. ANI: Yuji Takahashi. MUS: N/C. PRD: Pink Pineapple, KSS. 30 mins. x 4 eps. (*First Loves*), 30 mins. x 4 eps. (elf), 25 mins. x 13 eps. (TV1), ca. 30 mins. (*Special*), 30 mins. (*Music Graffiti*), 25 mins. x 13 eps. (TV2), 30 mins. x 2 eps. (*Kakyusei 2* v4), 30 mins. x 2 eps. (*Kakyusei 2* v5).

The protagonists in this quasi-sequel (originally titled *Kakyusei: My Pretty Class Student*) to **END OF SUMMER** (unrelated except for themes and atmosphere) are younger teenagers, though of course the U.S. version is at pains to assure us that they're not legally minors. Kakeru follows Wataru's lead, trying to make it with his dream girl, Urara, but getting distracted here and there, through no fault of his own of course, when love blooms at a tennis club and another student reveals that she has a sideline as a nude model. Only the first two episodes were released in America, under the title *First Loves*. These teen titillations were followed in 1997 by a four-part sequel, the special "elf" edition (*elf-ban Kakyusei Anata-dake wo Mitsumete*, or *elf-Edition Kakyusei: I Only Have Eyes For You*), named for the **DRAGON KNIGHT** creator involved in the original game; this because, unlike *First Loves*, the plot follows the game. Set once again in the high school dreamtime of a final summer vacation, it depicts new-boy Toru's attempts to bed girl-next-door Miho and featured an alternate ending for the final episode. *First Loves* also gained a 13-part TV remake with a spin-off video episode (*Kakyusei Bangaihen; Classmates Special*), and a TV sequel *Kakyusei 2: Girls in My Eyes* (2004, *Hitomi no Naka no Shojotachi*), directed by Yosei Morino. There was also a *Music Graffiti* spin-off featuring music from the series with both recycled footage and live-action performances. The latest additions are the erotic *Kakyusei 2: Kika Shishu* (2006, *Anthology*) and *Kakyusei 2: Sketchbook* (2007) video series.

The *Classmates* series is also distantly related to the *Transfer Student* series (1996, *Tenkosei*), which revisits many of the themes with a story of love between two childhood friends who are reunited when the girl moves back into town—the girl, Aoi, being played by the same voice actress who played Ai in the original. ⓝ

FIRST SQUAD *

2009. AKA: *First Squad: The Moment of Truth; Perviy Otryad.* Video. DIR: Yoshiharu Ashino. SCR: Aljosha Klimov, Misha Shprits. DES: Hirofumi Nakata, Masanobu Nomura, Tomoyasu Fujise. ANI: Hirofumi Nakata, Yusuke Tannawa. MUS: DJ Krush. PRD: Studio 4°C. 57 mins. (animated), 73 mins. (with extra footage).

Winter 1941: World War II is at a standstill on the Eastern Front. A Nazi occult group within the SS summons a long-dead German aristocrat to counter a perceived threat from an unknown Russian—a "moment of truth" at which one otherwise insignificant person's action can change everything. But the Soviets have a paranormal division, too, and to counter the Nazi threat the Sixth Division sends its best agent: the 14-year-old Nadya, sole survivor of her unit's last engagement.

A Russo-Japanese coproduction masterminded by Misha Shprits and Aljosha Klimov, *First Squad* playfully positions itself as a distaff horror-movie sequel to Sergei Einstein's *Alexander Nevsky* (1938) in which Russia is threatened by an all-new German menace with supernatural overtones (HORROR AND MONSTERS). In a cunning move that has met with mixed reception, it is bulked up to feature length by the insertion of several live-action sequences, impeccably shot in a documentary style, as old soldiers struggle to "remember" the supernatural events of World War II. As a result, *First Squad* has been seen in various territories in two versions—one as a shorter all-anime cut that simply tells the story, the other a longer hybrid that persuasively frames it as a Fortean mystery. Made with a nostalgia for Soviet pomp and iconography, but also with a sly reverence for classics of Russian propaganda, it is a B-movie that is oddly more than the sum of its parts, helped greatly by its Russian-language voice actors. The ending hints at more to come, although sadly this was all there was on screen. ◐

FIRST TRAM IN HIROSHIMA

1993. JPN: *Hiroshima ni Ichiban Densha ga Hashitta: 300-tsu no Hibaku Taiken Shuki kara.* AKA: *The First Tram Runs in Hiroshima: From the Experiences of 300 Bomb Victims; Best Tram in Hiroshima.* TV special. DIR: Toshio Hirata. SCR: Keiko Nobumoto. DES: Akio Sugino. ANI: Kyuma Oshita. MUS: Kosuke Onozaki. PRD: Madhouse, NHK. 32 mins.

Due to wartime labor shortages, 15-year-old Yayoi Harukawa is recruited as a tram conductor in her home town of Hiroshima. Losing her mother and many friends in the atomic bombing, she is a witness to the postwar reconstruction of the town, as symbolized by the recommencement of a regular tram service. This TV special is based on oral histories from 300 Hiroshima residents, with a heavy-hitting crew and studio behind the scenes—compare to GIRLS IN SUMMER DRESSES. Note that Leiji Matsumoto was similarly inspired by the experience of trains still running in the aftermath of the war, in his case to create GALAXY EXPRESS 999. Director Toshio Hirata also made a 15-minute short animation associated with a Hiroshima landmark. *The Story of the Atomic Dome* (*Genbaku Dome Monogatari*, 1990), as well as the sequel to the most famous Hiroshima story, BAREFOOT GEN.

FIST OF THE BLUE SKY

2006. JPN: *Soten no Ken.* TV series, video. DIR: Yoshihiro Yamaguchi. SCR: Yasuhiro Imagawa. DES: Yoshiaki Tsubata. ANI: Yoshiaki Tsubata. MUS: Marco d'Ambrosio. PRD: Studio A.P.P.P., Shueisha, TV Asahi. 25 mins. x 26 eps. (TV), 25 mins. x 4 eps. (v).

Asia is in turmoil in the 1930s (compare to NIGHT RAID 1931). Kenshiro Kasumi, also known as Yan Wang, is a Japanese professor. He has a more sinister alias—the King of Death, 62nd successor in direct line to the martial art of Hokuto Shinken. When he hears that his old friend Pan Guang-Yin, and his sister Pan Yu-Ling, have problems in Shanghai, he gives up his job in Tokyo and heads west to help them, not only because of his links of friendship with Pan's Qing Bang triad, but because he and Yu-Ling love each other. In Shanghai he must fight the other three Hokuto schools: Sonkaken, Sokaken, and Ryukaken. He must also take down the corrupt Hong Hua triad, sworn enemies of his Qing Bang friends. As the darkness of war and militarism spreads, expatriate French, Jews, Britons, and Germans are caught up in the struggles between Japan and the rest of Asia, and real-life figures like the "Last Emperor" Aisin-Goro Puyi become part of the story. Yes, it's a battle for love

and honor just like FIST OF THE NORTH STAR, with impossibly manly men and epic martial arts action. Manga creator Buronson (Yoshiyuki Okamura) and artist Tetsuo Hara both get due credit for this series based on their 2001 manga; Buronson is credited as a supervisor on the anime. The DVD version contains several unbroadcast episodes and sexual or violent footage deemed too hot for television. ◐◑

FIST OF THE NORTH STAR *

1984. JPN: *Hokuto no Ken.* AKA: *Ken the Great Bear Fist: Legend of a Karate Warrior.* TV series, movie. DIR: Toyoo Ashida, Hiromichi Matano, Hideo Watanabe, Masahisa Ishida. SCR: Susumu Takaku. DES: Masami Suda. ANI: Masami Suda. MUS: Katsuhisa Hattori, Nozomu Aoki. PRD: Toei, Fuji TV. 25 mins. x 109 eps. (TV1), 25 mins. x 43 eps. (TV2), 110 mins. (m), 55 mins. x 3 eps. (v), 4 mins. x 12 eps. (DD-TV1).

Rival gangs fight for supremacy in a postholocaust wasteland. Out of the dust walks Kenshiro, a young martial artist in search of his fiancée, Julia, who has been kidnapped by his brother Shin. In the opening story arc (complete in the U.S., truncated in the U.K.), Ken must hunt down the disparate members of his estranged martial-arts family before he defeats Shin and finds, and then loses, the love of his life.

Thrilling a teen audience with its hyper-violence and repetitive menace-of-the-week, the 1983 *Shonen Jump* manga by Tetsu Hara and Buronson was a timely re-tread of *Mad Max 2: The Road Warrior.* Continuing long after the initial "Julia" story was resolved, the series became a staple of 1980s Japanese pop culture, with Ken lampooned as the hulking Mari in PROJECT A-KO, and his booming voice actor Akira Kamiya becoming a star in his own right. But as the series wore on, drastic budget cuts forced the animators to improvise, sometimes with mind-boggling results. The crew constantly found creative new ways to dispatch villains, such as smearing wet paint on a cel between two pieces of glass, or shooting in real-time through the churning waters of a half-empty fish-tank. The show similarly exploited surreal perspectives—everyone seems giant and impossibly muscled seen through the eyes of children Bart and Lynn, but appear smaller from Ken's point of view. The show's star waned even in Japan, and though the second series ended sooner than expected, the franchise was kept alive by foreign sales. A movie-length remake of series one encompasses Ken's search for and defeat of Shin, Shin's admission that the more powerful Raoh has already kidnapped Julia to be *his* bride, a battle between Ken and Raoh, and the revelation that Julia has disappeared once more. Though Julia had committed suicide by this point in the original series, the movie edition leaves it open-ended, with Ken wandering into the desert in search of her again, believing her to be still alive. The movie version of series one, dubbed in the U.S. by Streamline, was Manga Entertainment's first U.K. release and became the cornerstone of their martial-arts-fueled "beer-and-curry" marketing plan. Riding the coattails of **AKIRA**, it became one of the U.K.'s best-selling anime videos, though more through its length of tenure in stores than its overt quality. A later Japanese DVD release included both the original, downbeat ending and the "international" finale that made Ken the victor. It also re-stored some gory elements that had been previously edged out of the international release.

In 1998, the company tried to capitalize on the anime's "success" by releasing the full 15-year-old TV series. This version featured a good actor as Ken, but it was clumsily cut together with no appreciation of story breaks and mixed so shoddily that Bart ends up playing a silent harmonica. The series was also "augmented" with a drum & bass music track, which, to be fair, couldn't have made it any worse. After predictably disappointing sales, the distributor pulled the TV edit only partway into the schedule, though by this time its "foreign popularity" had inspired a Japanese satellite network to rerun it every day. Like its hero, *Fist of the North Star* simply refuses to die. The series is more likely to be known in the mainstream for its 1995 live-action remake, directed by Tony Randall and starring Gary Daniels. A manga prequel, **FIST OF THE BLUE SKY** (2001), features the adventures of Ken's namesake uncle in 1930s Asia and was also adapted into an anime.

Takashi Watanabe's three-part "new" *Fist of the North Star* video series (2003) claimed to be based on a 1996 novel by the original creators, thereby avoiding ownership conflict with the copyright holders of the original TV series and the Hollywood remake. Motorcycles and backgrounds were much more impressive, occasionally evoking the draftsman-like architecture and vehicle representations of Otomo's **AKIRA**, but the foreground cast were still the same tired 1980s musclemen.

In the 21st century, ironically long after the date when the original manga claimed we were all going to die in a fiery apocalypse, *Fist of the North Star* continues to lurch onward, the literal embodiment of its original theme song, the boast of which to be "Living in the Eighties" no longer has the same implication of cutting-edge modernity. Its name recognition among businessmen of a certain age seems to make it periodically recur as part of the conversation among new investors in media, leading to odd repurposings such as a series of six feature-length movie edits of the original TV series, cut together by William Winckler Productions in 2009 and distributed through Japanese broadband services. A series of short Flash animations, *DD Fist of the North Star* (2011), plays with the comedic potential of Ken as an icon left behind by the march of progress, scowling manfully and over-reacting heroically among the shelves of a Tokyo convenience store after the real world has failed to provide him with a nuclear holocaust and suitably operatic angst. This self-parody, attributed to the pseudonymous artist "Kajio," was renewed in 2013. **LV**

FIVE CARD *

2003. Video. DIR: Akebi Haruno. SCR: Akebi Haruno. DES: Yukiho. ANI: Shigeru Kino, Hiroshi Sakagami. MUS: N/C. PRD: Five Ways. 29 mins. x 4 eps.
Young English teacher Nariyuki Daina is popular with his students and plans to get four of the hottest—Lisa, Fumiko, Naoki, and Mimiko—into bed. So does school principal, sorry, college dean Onikuma, though his tastes are rather more perverted and include chains, vibrators, and such. Daina also has a pretty assistant, Mayu, a former college buddy of his, who attempts to police his lecherous behavior. The girls have a few tricks of their own,

including aphrodisiac-laced lunchboxes for Teacher, although before long they are co-opted into the dean's satanic rituals, for a change. Based on a computer game by Crossnet. **LNV**

FIVE CENTIMETERS PER SECOND *

2007. JPN: *Byosoku 5 Centimeters*. AKA: *Byosoku 5cm*. Movie. DIR: Makoto Shinkai. SCR: Makoto Shinkai. DES: Takayo Nishimura, Makoto Shinkai. ANI: Takayo Nishimura. MUS: Tenmon. PRD: CoMix Wave. 62 mins.
Two best friends in elementary school have to separate because one family relocates for work. Takaki says goodbye to his friend Akari, but nobody ever replaces her for him. They exchange letters, but as time goes on they gradually lose touch. Yet Takaki does not seek out other close relationships, keeping Akari's place in his heart vacant. He composes emails that are never sent, and his distracted air puts off at least one potential teenage girlfriend. Moving from childhood into adult life, Takaki yearns for Akari so strongly that other romantic relationships have no chance. Meanwhile, Akari is getting ready to get married. On the verge of a breakdown, Takaki leaves his job and wanders the streets of Tokyo, stopping at a train crossing where he and Akari once agreed to meet and watch cherry blossoms together.

Makoto Shinkai is the master of allusion, never stating intent or clarifying emotions, allowing feelings to emerge through downcast eyes, sidelong glances, minimal and seemingly inconsequential dialogue. His passion is for exploring, and exposing, the tenuous, dreamlike quality of every connection that is not face-to-face. In **VOICES OF A DISTANT STAR**—still his most coherent work—the love of a teenage couple is defeated by the hard facts of relativity. Here, smaller, prosaic distances are shown to be just as effective in separating children (see also his later **GARDEN OF WORDS**), and he leaves us to make up our own ending from a fleeting smile, a glance, an evanescent shift in the air, but an ever-present hope that is the quintessence of that modern anime subgenre, the reunited childhood friends or *osana-najimi* (**ROMANCE AND DRAMA**).

Five centimeters per second is, allegedly, the speed at which cherry blossoms fall. Symbolic for the Japanese of the transience of life and beauty, this is only one such symbol in the movie. The young friends' last meeting is delayed by a snowstorm, a fall of delicate particles transformed into an irresistible force by sheer weight, like time itself. Takaki's teen years are spent close to the sea, where the constant shifting of wave and sand speak of inevitable, inexorable change. And although Shinkai stated that this movie, unlike his previous work, would have no science fiction elements, he still sets one of the three story segments near the Tanegashima Space Center, unable to resist the allegory of the "distance" between the lovers as symbolized by the ever-onward passage of a space probe.

There is a hint, in the truncated running time and the collapse of the final act into a pop video, that Shinkai was thwarted in plans to produce a longer work, although the novelization of the film sticks doggedly to what is seen on screen, and makes no attempt to add other vignettes that might have been dropped in production. However, even in its short span, *5cm/sec* shows a masterful grasp of romance and yearning, strongly influenced by the works of Haruki Murakami, particularly his twice-adapted, much-anthologized short story "On Meeting My 100% Woman One Fine April Morning." Shinkai also nimbly challenges the self-involved tropes of anime romance for boys, choosing to depict much of Takaki's life through the eyes of the women who do not quite measure up to Akari, rather than through Takaki himself—he is as absent from their lives as Akari is from his.

Takaki's dilemma is the same as Shinkai's, or any creator's: to let go of the perfect piece of art in your head, to expose it to the world that may not know how to interpret every silent glance, is to take a terrible risk. If that fragile and beautiful thing is destroyed, will there be another? And if you make another, will you forget the first? Better, perhaps, to do nothing further, but to endlessly rerun the one beloved movie in your heart.

Shinkai's art is oblique—literally as well as emotionally. Characters' eyes rarely meet, and many frames are composed of things in their line of sight, as if they were looking anywhere but at each other. Such mundane objects—building blocks of **EVERYDAY ANIME** like the school bike shed, the trail of a plane overhead, the snow, the grass—are minutely observed, as if by focusing so intently on the real, the absolute, fear and uncertainty can be kept at bay. Takaki is not apathetic like **EVANGELION**'s Shinji, but indifferent to everything but the object of his desire, because wanting that and that alone is the only way to keep it in perfect focus in his heart.

Considering the bloated, ambling aspects of **CHILDREN WHO CHASE LOST VOICES FROM DEEP BELOW** and **THE PLACE PROMISED IN OUR EARLY DAYS**, Shinkai seems to struggle with long-form narrative. So far, his most perfect creations have been miniatures. *5cm/sec* is a string of shining moments, like raindrops on a washing line, beautiful in themselves but also in the fact of their fragility. When there is no point in going forward, and nowhere to retreat, there is nothing to do but to focus absolutely on the beauty of the moment. How you feel about that defines whether you think this film is exultant or tragic, but you cannot deny its compelling commitment to beauty. Shinkai himself would eventually compromise on the anime's ending, writing a sequence in the later manga version that combined elements of both the anime and the novel, and implied that Takaki does eventually find happiness with one of the women in the story, albeit not his childhood sweetheart Akari.

FIVE NUMBERS! *

2011. JPN: *Norageki!* Video. DIR: Hiroaki Ando. SCR: Dai Sato. DES: Masaru Gotsubo, Kimitoshi Yamane, Yusuke Takeda. ANI: Hiroyuki Horiuchi. MUS: Yasutaka Nakata (capsule). PRD: Sunrise, Bandai Visual, Showgate. 25 mins.
Strangers in an isolated future prison wake from a drugged sleep to find that they can get out of their cells. The power has gone. So, it seems, have all other living things—no guards, nothing to stop them leaving, just a cat who tags along. But as they make their way through the featureless maze of corridors, they find something far more sinister than guards and locked doors. And one of the five may know more than he or she is telling. Film fans are hearing echoes of *Alien* and *Cube*, anime addicts may think back to **THEY WERE ELEVEN**. The

animation is not especially striking, but the design is strong and the writing is just as good, with some interesting twists of plot and character. If nothing else, the fact that Ando, Sato, and Horiuchi worked on **FREEDOM** should help to show it's worth your attention.

When home video first entered the anime market, a whole wave of new short series and one-shots was unleashed: pilots to test the water for TV, shows that couldn't have made it on TV, shows for niche audiences, ideas that couldn't get funding as movies, or ideas that were quirky and fun but couldn't be padded out into a whole series; shows like **BIRTH** and **DRAGON'S HEAVEN**. The one-shot trend continued in Japan, where the fans are used to paying what Western audiences consider absurdly high prices for anime, but this hampered them from Western release until companies began to bundle one-shots together. *Five Numbers!* is available on one disc bundled with another Sunrise-created title, **COICENT**. ●

FIVE STAR STORIES, THE *

1989. JPN: *Five Star Monogatari*. Video. DIR: Kazuo Yamazaki. SCR: Akinori Endo. DES: Mamoru Nagano, Nobuteru Yuki, Mika Akitaka. ANI: Nobuteru Yuki. MUS: Tomoyuki Asagawa. PRD: Sunrise. 60 mins.
The Joker Cluster consists of five star systems in close proximity, where human pilots (Headliners) are bonded with sentient androids (Fatimas) to control giant robots (Mortar Heads). Dr. Chrome Ballanche, the greatest of the genetic engineers, completes his two most perfect creations, the Fatimas Lachesis and Clotho. Their sister, Atropos, has vanished. The fatimas go to the castle of the local lord Uber to be "impressed," a ceremony at which they select their future partners from among the ranks of headliners. Most pilots have to make do with "Etrimls," low-grade subhuman versions, so the beautiful Fatimas are highly prized, not only by the assembled pilots, but also by several notables who are attending the ceremony in disguise.

Condensed from just one segment of Mamoru Nagano's sprawling 1986 manga that's still occasionally serialized in *Newtype*, *FSS* duplicates the original's baroque feel, as well as its near impenetrability. With mount-rider relationships that presage **Brain Powered** and sumptuous science-fantasy conceits, the look of the characters and machinery is as marvelous as one might expect from a fashion-designer-turned-rock-musician such as Nagano. **N**

FIVE WAYS

Erotic anime company whose subsidiaries include Wide Road, Honnybit, Blue Moon, and Creamy Doll. Notable for its generally low budget productions, and for abruptly declaring bankruptcy in mid-2003, causing the release of the (already completed) second and third episodes of *Handmaid Mai* (for which it was producer and distributor; sequel to **Handmaid May**) to be put on hold until the subsequent litigation could be settled.

FLAG *

2006. TV series. DIR: Ryosuke Takahashi, Kazuo Terada. SCR: Toru Nozaki. DES: Kazuyoshi Takeuchi, Shunsuke Suzuki. ANI: Kazuyoshi Takeuchi. MUS: Yoshihiro Ike. PRD: Ansa Studio (aka The Answer Studio), Aniplex. 24 mins. x 13 eps.

The near future: Japanese photojournalist Saeko is on the frontlines of one of those annoying regional wars, and takes a picture of civilians raising a makeshift U.N. flag. Like the famous photo of the American flag rising over Iwo Jima, it becomes an icon, a symbol of the yearning for peace, and makes her a celebrity. Just before a truce is finally signed, the flag is stolen by extremists seeking to keep the conflict alive. When U.N. peacekeepers decide to send in a special unit in a heavily armored mecha to rescue the flag, they offer Saeko the chance to go along. The other side has heavyweight backing and an armory to match, setting the stage for the kind of realistic, compelling animation of conflict that Ryosuke Takahashi helped to pioneer in **Votoms**.

There are many kinds of "robots" in anime and you can classify them in many ways, but Japanese **Fandom** recognizes two basic styles: fantasy robots, such as Go Nagai's magnificent machines forged from the superalloy Chogokin and fired by the passion of their pilots, and "Real Robots," machines based on sternly credible technology (**Science Fiction and Robots**). Takahashi is one of the guiding

lights of the Real Robot genre, and *Flag* is his creation. Paced and shot like a documentary, unshowy but overwhelmingly impressive, the slow-burning story builds through a series of escalating encounters to a satisfying climax. Like **Gundam**, *Flag* demonstrates that humanity creates its own monsters and its own heroes, though the ratio may be seriously out of balance at times. The feisty Saeko may stir memories of Sybel in **Black Magic M-66** but the realism of the situation is closer to **Yugo the Negotiator**, with added mecha. And while the machinery is terrific, Takahashi's finest achievement is in other areas, such as the well-realized characters, and a recurring obsession with the power of *still* images. Not to be confused with the 1994 racing anime *Flag!*, which has a separate entry in this encyclopedia. **LV**

FLAG!

1994. JPN: *Sakidama Hassai Saizen Sen Flag*. AKA: *Sakidama Racing Pole Position Flag*. Video. DIR: Satoshi Dezaki. SCR: Machiko Kondo. DES: Mutsumi Inomata. ANI: Hideki Takahashi. MUS: N/C. PRD: Vap, Magic Bus. 45 mins.

Sixteen-year-old Noboru Yamazaki and Akira Maruyama join the Moonlight bike gang at the Sakidama Biker Meet, although they don't actually own any motorcycles. A rival gang, the Asian Tigers, uses its gangster connections to take out a hit on the Moonlight gang's leader. Noboru inherits his leader's motorcycle, and also the attentions of biker chick Hisami. Based on Akio Hotta's manga in *Young King*, this is a latecomer to the anime subgenre established by **Bomber Bikers of Shonan**. **V**

FLAME OF RECCA *

1997. JPN: *Recca no En*. TV series. DIR: Noriyuki Abe, Kazunori Mizuno. SCR: Hiroshi Hashimoto, Satoru Nishizono. DES: Mari Kitayama, Atsushi Wakabayashi. ANI: Hiroyuki Kanbe, Minoru Yamazawa. MUS: Yusaku Honma. PRD: Studio Pierrot, Fuji TV. 25 mins. x 42 eps.

Contemporary teenage ninja fan Recca Hanabishi becomes embroiled in the activities of real-life ninja. The beautiful Yanagi is targeted by an evil industrialist who wants to use the girl's power to become immortal, and Recca must team up with his school friends to learn the secrets

of the martial arts before it is too late. Adapting Nobuyuki Anzai's 1995 manga from *Shonen Sunday*, this series owes a great debt to **Poltergeist Report**, with plenty of fighting, some off-color humor, and acrobatics to rival **Ninja Scroll**'s. However, despite early promise, a low animation budget takes its toll, as does the series' disappointing decline into endless martial-arts bouts. The character of Joker, wounded and cast into a black hole during the story, bears such a close resemblance to the amnesiac Nanashi in Anzai's later **Mär** that it is widely assumed that the latter is an oblique sequel to the former. **NV**

FLASHBACK *

2002. JPN: *Flashback Game*. Video. DIR: Shinsuke Terasawa. SCR: Bankyu Mizoguchi. DES: Shinsuke Terasawa. ANI: Go Yasumoto. MUS: N/C. PRD: Blue Cat, Five Ways. 30 mins. x 3 eps.

Yuri Honjo wins a beauty spa vacation, and arrives with her friends Mizuho and Noriko excitedly expecting a fun-packed experience rather than a vicious psychological trap. All three girls, it transpires, have repressed memories of sexual trauma, which the nefarious staff at the spa is determined to get them to admit. In the spa's isolation pod Mizuho relives her gang rape by schoolmates, while Yuri recalls the sexual abuse she suffered from friends. Then Mizuho goes to the beach and has lesbian sex with Ayame and heads back to the hotel to try it out with Noriko. Meanwhile, Noriko recalls what it was like to come home from school one day to find her mother sexually servicing two strangers. Once cured of their traumas, the girls are auctioned off as sex slaves. **LNV**

FLAT BROKE SISTERS

2006. JPN: *Binbo Shimai Monogatari*. AKA: *Poor Sisters Story*. TV series. DIR: Yukio Kaizawa. SCR: Tsuru Izumi. DES: Kazuhiro Takamura, Makoto Suwada, Shoichiro Sugiura, Yumi Hosaka, Yuri Sunami. ANI: Akiko Nakano, Konomi Sakurai. MUS: Akiko Kosaka. PRD: Toei Animation, Frontier Works. 24 mins. x 10 eps.

After the death of their mother, 15-year-old Kyo Yamada and her 9-year-old sister Asu are abandoned by their father, who runs away to escape his gambling debts, leaving them alone in their rundown Tokyo apartment. The sisters are determined to stay together and build a good life for themselves, so Kyo takes on part-time jobs like tutoring and delivering newspapers while her sister looks after the cooking and housework and manages the family finances. Luckily, they live in a community that looks out for each other, so their lady novelist neighbor and the lady who runs the public bath-house watch out for them, and they find happiness in being together and managing their own lives despite the problems they face. Based on Izumi Kato's manga, which first appeared in 2004, this charming story has not been released in English—which is a great pity, since so few shows depict children as effective and capable.

FLCL *

2000. JPN: *Furi Kuri*. Video. DIR: Kazuya Tsurumaki. SCR: Yoji Enokido. DES: Yoshiyuki Sadamoto. ANI: Tadashi Hiramatsu, Hiroyuki Imaishi. MUS: The Pillows. PRD: Gainax, Production I.G. 25 mins. x 6 eps.
Left alone in the house with his older brother's 17-year-old girlfriend, Mamimi, Naota Nandaba is concerned that her flirting ways will place him in a difficult situation. The arrival of the scooter-riding, guitar-swinging tomboy Haruko Haruhara swaps one set of problems for another, as Naota is forced to share his life with an alien, a grumpy robot, and the uncontrollable Mamimi. Mixing a narrative inspired by the same studio's HIS AND HER CIRCUMSTANCES with characterization and designs influenced by their earlier EVANGELION, *FLCL* represents a determined effort by Gainax to both supersede its successes of the late 1990s and incorporate elements of the one title that competed with them in fans' polls as the show of the moment. UTENA-writer Enokido brings a surreal tinge to the whole operation. All but episode 1 were released in Japan with English subtitles on DVD.

FLESHDANCE

2007. JPN: *Shimaizuma: Shimai Tsuma 3*. AKA: *Beautiful Wives*. Video. DIR: Shigenori Awai. SCR: Shigenori Awai. DES: AZMH, Osamu Honda. ANI: Michitaka Yamamoto. MUS: N/C. PRD: MS Pictures, Milky. 27 mins. x 2 eps.
Art student Kenta is the pupil of a successful painter and finds his Muse in his

mentor's beautiful wife. Or any attractive female he meets, really. Soon his painting skills are taking a back seat to other forms of activity. Based on a successful porn game series (hence the "3" in the title) by 13cm (which is five inches, for those who think size matters) with original character designs by Soka Ishihara. **N**

FLIGHT OF THE WHITE WOLF

1990. JPN: *Hashire! Shiroi Okami*. AKA: *Run! White Wolf*. Movie. DIR: Tsuneo Maeda, Masuji Harada. SCR: Wataru Kenmochi. DES: Isao Kumata, Marisuke Eguchi, Satoshi Matsuoka. ANI: Marisuke Eguchi. MUS: Antonín Dvořák. PRD: Tac, Toho. 84 mins.
Lasset has grown up with a wolf called Gray since they were both babies. Lasset's father found the cub and reared it, but, as he grows, the neighbors become understandably concerned. Gray kills a local dog that belongs to the sheriff, and his days seem numbered. Lasset sets out with Gray, determined to get him to a wolf sanctuary where he can live in peace. Unfortunately, it's several hundred miles away, so the pair face a long road and many adventures in the tradition of BELLE AND SEBASTIAN. Based on the novel by Mel Ellis. Just to confuse matters, this movie appears to have later been released in the U.S. under the title *White Fang*.

FLINT THE TIME DETECTIVE *

1998. JPN: *Jiku Tantei Genshi Kun*. AKA: *Time Detective Genshi*. TV series. DIR: Hiroshi Fukutomi, Koichi Takada, Shinji Okuda. SCR: Hideki Sonoda. DES: Yoshiko Ohashi. ANI: Takashi Yamazaki, Munekatsu Fujita. MUS: Tadashi Nanba. PRD: Pioneer, Tac, TV Tokyo. 25 mins. x 43 eps.
Petrafina Dagmar (accompanied by her two stooges, Might and Dyno) wants to loot the past so that the Dark Lord can destroy the Land of Time. Each period contains a special critter called a time-shifter, each of which possesses a magical power. To coin a phrase, Petra wants to "catch 'em all." Time-shifters keep the very fabric of time together, and their theft is policed by the Bureau of Time & Space Investigations. In one million B.C., Petra demands that caveboy triceratops-herder Flint Hammerhead (Genshi) and his father hand over Getalong (a penguin-like time-shifter whose power is to ensure that everyone

gets along). When they refuse, she turns her fossilizer ray on them then returns to the 25th century to dig them up. Using her modern-day disguise as schoolteacher Miss Aino (pronounced and spelled "Iknow"), she encourages her class to go out and find fossils for her. However, twins Sarah and Tony take their fossil to their uncle, Bernie Goodman, at the Bureau. Bernie, with a little behind-the-scenes help from the Dark Lord's adversary the Old-Timer, defossilizes Flint with one of his gizmos. The process has given Flint superhuman strength, so he is enlisted in the Bureau. Flint's father remains a talking rock, so Bernie carves him into a stone axe for Flint and installs a fossilizer/defossilizer ray in the haft. Each week, Flint is called upon to foil Petra's latest scheme in a different time period. Some of her temporal interferences include imprisoning and taking the place of Japan's ancient queen Himiko (see DARK MYTH) and instilling a lust for gold into the Conquistadors. A rehash of the successful TIME BOKAN series but with a monster-collecting angle bolted on for the 1990s, *Flint* was snatched up in the tidal wave of post-POKÉMON anime interest and brought to the U.S. in record time by DIGIMON-producers Saban Entertainment.

FLOATING MATERIAL

2011. Video. DIR: Do Ichimotsu. SCR: PON. DES: Hikaru Kinohara. ANI: N/C. MUS: N/C. PRD: PoRO. 30 mins. x 2 eps.
A schoolgirl finds out that her best friend is having sex with their homeroom teacher. Naturally, she tries to blackmail him into sex with her, but when he refuses she confesses all to her friend and they decide to share him: which of course makes it all right. Based on an erotic game by Biscotti. When a company named after food makes games devoted to sex, there's likely to be altogether too much oral gratification and not a great deal of nutritional content (EROTICA AND PORNOGRAPHY). **N**

FLOP-CAT

2011. JPN: *Pu-Neko: Pu-Neko Sho Gekijo*. AKA: *Pu-Neko: Pu-Neko Little Playhouse*. TV series. DIR: N/C. SCR: Makoto Yasaku. DES: N/C. ANI: Takashi Suzuki. MUS: N/C. PRD: FROGMAN Co., DLE, NTV. 3? Mins. x 22 eps.
Part of NTV's YURUANI? gag anthology

show created by DLE, based on the manga *Pu-neko* by Masayuki Kitamichi.

FLOWER AND SNAKE THE ANIMATION *

2006. JPN: *Hana to Hebi*. Video. DIR: Masahiko Takeda, Akira Shiba. SCR: Kenichi Nakahara. DES: James Hayashi, Reikai Endo. ANI: Junin Machida, O Yugi. MUS: N/C. PRD: Sumomo Film. 29 mins. x 3 eps.
Shizuko's stepdaughter is kidnapped by a gang in a truly absurd plot that has the CEO of a company hatching the whole thing to make Shizuko his sex slave. Because this is based on Elf's porn game, which in turn comes from a series of bondage novels by Oniroku Dan that started in 1969, the premise is hallowed by time and already has a fanbase. You could watch a movie in the time it takes to see this. Just saying. **◯**

FLOWER ANGEL *

1979. JPN: *Hana no Ko Lunlun*. AKA: *Lunlun the Flowergirl*. TV series/special, movie. DIR: Yuji Endo. SCR: Noboru Shiroyama. DES: Michi Himeno. ANI: Tatsuhiro Nagaki. MUS: Hiroshi Tsutsui. PRD: Toei, TV Asahi. 25 mins. x 50 eps. (TV), ca. 15 mins. (m).
Lunlun is the 12-year-old daughter of a flower seller in the French countryside. Nouveau, her talking dog, and a cat called Cateau are emissaries from the king of the floral planet Flowern. The bad queen, Toginicia, has seized control of the kingdom and sent her servant Yaboki (a disguised *tanuki*, see **POM POKO**) to seize the seven colors of magical flowers found on Earth. Lunlun, who can transform into a girl with special powers with her flower key, must travel the world with Nouveau and Cateau to collect the plants before Yaboki. Flower lore, a magical girl à la **CREAMY MAMI**, and an early collector's quest that presaged **CARDCAPTORS**, all dressed up in a European setting variously described by distributors as Switzerland or France, depending on their mood. There was also a short 15-minute movie version screened in Japanese theaters in 1980, *Flower Angel: Hello Kingdom of Cherries (Konnichi wa Sakura no Kuni)*.

FLOWER KAPPA

2010. JPN: *Hana Kappa*. TV series, movie. DIR: Kazumi Nonaka. SCR: Tetsuo Yasumi. DES:

Kazuya Hayashi, Yumi Matsumiya, Natsuki Takemura. ANI: Shin Koyama, Kazuchika Kise. MUS: Miki Kasamatsu. PRD: group TAC, Oriental Light & Magic, Xebec, Dentsu, GAGA Communications, Media Factory, Shogakukan, Sony PCL, Toho. 10 mins. x 80 eps. (TV), ?? mins. (m).
In a fantasy world where insects and *kappa* water spirits live together, Hana Kappa is one of a family of Flower Kappas. But unlike the rest of his family, the flower on his head keeps changing instead of settling into one form. Hana Kappa is impatient to find out what his adult flower will be, even though his wise old Grandpa tells him to wait until he's older. But an evil overlord wants to steal Hana Kappa's priceless flower. Based on a picture book for preschool and elementary school children by Tadashi Akiyama, this series spun off a movie *Eiga Hana Kappa Hana-sake! Pakkaan cho no Kuni no Daiboken (Hana Kappa the Movie Pakkaan's Great Adventure in Butterfly Land*, or *Hana Kappa the Movie* for short) that premiered in April 2013. Longtime fans may be surprised to see Kazuchika Kise's name on the animation credits—the creator of the series' ending animation is better known for work on **GHOST IN THE SHELL** and **BLOOD: THE LAST VAMPIRE**.

FLOWER WITCH MARYBELL

1992. JPN: *Hana no Maho Tsukai Marybell*. AKA: *Floral Magician Mary Bell*. TV series, movie. DIR: Tetsuya Endo. SCR: Yasunori Yamada. DES: Kenichi Onuki, Shigenori Kanatsu. ANI: Tadashi Hirota, Yuriko Chiba. MUS: Takako Ishiguro. PRD: Ashi Pro, TV Tokyo. 25 mins. x 39 eps., ca. 40 mins. (m).
The adventures of a girl with a magical tambourine who works in her parents' flower shop but rights wrongs in her superheroine disguise, often with the help of her friends, Julia and Ribbon. Magic and music in the everytown of Sunnybell, this was also released as a 40-minute theatrical short, *Marybell: The Movie* (1992), in which Marybell is transported to a fantasy world after reading the story of the phoenix in her aunt's book.

FLOWERING YOUTH *

2009. JPN: *Hanasakeru Seishonen*. TV series, TV special. DIR: Chiaki Kon, Hajime Kamegaki. SCR: Mamiko Ikeda. DES: Yuko Kusumoto, Mie Kasai. ANI: Ryunosuke Tsuno.

MUS: Tetsuya Saito, Tsuyoshi Saito. PRD: Studio Pierrot, NHK, Sogo Vision. 24 mins. x 39 eps. (TV), 24 mins. X 2 eps. (special).
Fourteen-year-old Kajika has been raised on a remote island, with her pet snow leopard Mustafa and an old Creole shaman for company, by order of her fabulously wealthy father. Then she briefly attended a Japanese middle school. Now the unlikely threesome are summoned back to her father's world, but only to play a game of his choosing. She has to meet three men he has chosen and decide which one to marry. If she picks the right one, he will reveal her true destiny. All three are older than her. One is an angst-ridden European nobleman, one is heir to the throne of an oil-rich country, and one is the woman-hating son of a competitor.
Dysfunctional families, political turmoil, and economic machinations form the backdrop for jealousy and overblown romance in a story that ends with the heroine choosing her own happiness. It all sounds too overblown and old-fashioned for words, but Kajika is a sparky, impulsive heroine whose choices are her own and who dives into life with gusto. Sadly, the animation and art don't show Studio Pierrot working at the top of its game, making this a show that fails to fulfill its promise. The manga by **OZ**-creator Natsumi Itsuki ran from 1987 to 1994 and has also inspired two stage plays. The anime also had two "specials" aired during the run, numbered as episodes 12.5 and 25.5, compilations of previous episodes to enable newcomers to catch up with the story so far.

FLOWERS OF EVIL *

2013. JPN: *Aku no Hana*. TV series. DIR: Hiroshi Nagahama. SCR: Aki Itami. DES: Hidekazu Shimamura. ANI: Hidekazu Shimamura, Yasunari Nitta, Noriko Shimazawa. MUS: Hideyuki Fukasawa. PRD: Animax, Gansis, Kodansha, Starchild Records, Klockworx. 24 mins. x 13 eps.
Mild-mannered teenager Takao Kusaga is a nerd who adores the class beauty Nanako Saeki from afar. Realizing that she has left her gymwear behind after school, he picks it up, intending to hand it back to her as an excuse to talk to her. Instead, he overhears her telling her friends that a "pervert" has stolen her stuff, and slinks

away. However, the manipulative outsider Sawa Nakamura realizes Takao's secret, and uses the threat of publicly shaming him to blackmail him into an increasingly sinister set of tasks and favors (compare to PET LIFE).

Shuzo Oshimi's original 2009 manga in *Bessatsu Shonen Magazine* was already a masterpiece of sadistic tension and ever-descending circles of a private, teenage hell. Nagahama's anime version ups the effect by plumping for rotoscoped animation—drawing the imagery over source footage of live actors to impart a true sense of realism and uneasy body-language to the plot. Rotoscoping is nothing new in anime—not since Yoshiko Sakuma provided reference footage for PANDA AND THE MAGIC SERPENT in 1958, and Shinichi "Sonny" Chiba supplied martial-arts reference footage for SINDBAD THE SAILOR in 1962—but anime stylistics have drifted away from realism and naturalism ever since the 1960s, particularly since Tezuka's experiments in limited animation with ASTRO BOY and the TV boom it kicked off. This makes *Flowers of Evil* stand out all the more in the crowd, aligning it closer to performance-capture like VEXILLE than to the more spartan animation of its fellow anime in the schedules.

FLY! MACHINE HIRYU

1977. JPN: *Tobidase! Machine Hiryu.* TV series. DIR: Seitaro Hara, Mizuho Nishikubo, Yuji Fukawa, Hidehito Ueda. SCR: Jiro Yoshino, Akiyoshi Sakai, Yu Yamamoto. DES: Yoshitaka Amano, Kunio Okawara. ANI: Tetsu Honda, Norio Hirayama, Masatoshi Fukuyama. MUS: Hiroshi Tsutsui. PRD: Tatsunoko, Tokyo 12 Channel (TV Tokyo). 25 mins. x 21 eps.

The bosses of rival car companies decide to fight each other in the sporting arena by backing different race car teams. Chairman Gapporin hires Okkanabichi the supreme racer, while Chairman Misaki hires Riki Kazama, a relatively untried driver for the flying car known as Machine Hiryu. Mixing elements of SPEED RACER with TIME BOKAN, this Tatsunoko production ticks the same boxes, with Riki's cute girlfriend Nana, mini-mechanic Chuta, the cute ape and pooch, and the comic and glamorous villains lurking in the background. Early work from many big names, including

Yoshitaka Amano and Kunio Okawara, is strictly in the studio mold. Manga versions of the story ran in several magazines, such as *Terebi Magazine* and *Terebi Land*. Racing fever seemed to have struck the Japanese animation business at this time: compare to the same year's ARROW EMBLEM.

FLY PEEK! *

1992. JPN: *Tobe! Kujira no Peek.* AKA: *Fly! Peek the Whale; Peek the Baby Whale; The Boy and the White Whale Calf.* Movie. DIR: Koji Morimoto. SCR: Keiko Nobumoto, Koji Morimoto. DES: Satoru Utsunomiya. ANI: Satoru Utsunomiya, Hideo Okazaki. MUS: Yoshihisa Tomabechi. PRD: Toho. 80 mins.

After a storm, two young brothers find a baby white whale, the titular Peek, trapped by a rock in a shallow inlet in the Spanish coast. The boys decide to help it return to its mother on the open sea, but one of the boys, Kei, is tormented by older children until he lets the secret out. The whale is taken away by circus owner Odeon, and Kei journeys to the big city to set Peek free. Based on an original story by Hidehito Hara and predating the 1993 Hollywood movie *Free Willy*, beautiful settings and charmingly retro-styled character designs combined in a high-quality children's film that was badly served in the U.K. market, where distributors Kiseki only released a subtitled print.

FLY PEGASUS!

1995. JPN: *Tobe! Pegasus: Kokoro ni Goal ni Shoot.* AKA: *Fly! Pegasus: Shoot for the Goal of the Heart.* Movie. DIR: Shinji Okuda. SCR: Hideki Sonoda. DES: N/C. ANI: Junji Aoki. MUS: Masahito Suzuki. PRD: EG, Victor. 74 mins.

A high school for blind children fields a soccer team using a ball that emits a noise so it can be located. The potential for accidental fouls is mind-boggling, but only in anime could you find such a bizarre combination of HELEN KELLER and CAPTAIN TSUBASA.

FLYING FISH IS TAKEN ILL, THE

1982. JPN: *Tobiuo no Boya wa Byoki Desu.* AKA: *The Young Flying Fish Is Taken Ill.* Movie. DIR: Kazuya Miyazaki. SCR: Tomiko Inui. DES: Renzo Kinoshita. ANI: Tatsuhiro Nagaki. MUS: Chuji Kinoshita. PRD: Mushi. 19 mins.

A young flying fish is happily frolicking in the waters of the Pacific when there is a

bright flash in the sky and white ash starts to rain down on him. He dives for cover beneath the sea, but that night, he goes to his mother complaining of feeling very ill indeed. An anthropomorphic parable based on a story by Tomiko Inui, set on March 1, 1954—the day of the infamous Bikini Bomb Test. The same event prompted producer Ishiro Honda to wonder if the test could do so much damage to fish, what would it do to other animals? The result of his speculation was released as *Godzilla* (1954).

FLYING GHOST SHIP

1969. JPN: *Soratobu Yureisen.* Movie. DIR: Hiroshi Ikeda. SCR: Masaki Tsuji, Hiroshi Ikeda. DES: Shotaro Ishi(no)mori. ANI: Yoichi Kotabe, Hayao Miyazaki, Hideki Hayashi. MUS: Takasuke Onosaki. PRD: Toei. 60 mins.

A ship carrying a load of the prized "BOA Juice" soft drink is attacked by a flying ghost. At the same time, the 12-year-old Hayato saves the Kuroshio drinks company president and his wife from a car accident and experiences a vision of the ship's skeletal captain. Hayato soon discovers that Kuroshio is concealing secrets in the basement, and, as Golem the giant robot, lays waste to the city center, Hayato confronts the company about the truth behind its popular drink. Golem causes the deaths of Hayato's parents, although his father confesses on his deathbed that Hayato's real father is … (drumroll) the captain of the ghost ship. Another cautionary tale from the creator of CYBORG 009, with animation and design work on the giant robot by Hayao Miyazaki, *Flying Ghost Ship* was also one of the first anime to be dubbed into Russian. Possibly, the film's most enduring legacy might be found elsewhere, since Hayato's faithful but cowardly dog is suspiciously similar to Scooby-Doo, an enduring icon that would first appear in America some four months later, although the designer Iwao Takamoto makes no mention of this connection in his memoirs. "BOA Beer," seemingly a reference to this film, would also crop up in *Rebuild of Evangelion* (EVANGELION) along with a "Kuroshio" company logo.

FOBIA *

1995. JPN: *Mirai Choju Fobia.* AKA: *Future Superbeast Fobia.* Video. DIR: Shigenori Awai.

SCR: Narihiko Tatsumiya. DES: Yoshinobu Yamakawa. ANI: Yoshinobu Yamakawa. MUS: Arcadia Studio. PRD: Tec, Gaga. 45 mins. x 2 eps.

Replinoids, creatures who thrive on human blood and have a preference for young girls, exhaust the supply in 2112 and come back to 1990s Japan to harvest more female flesh. They are pursued by Megumi, a time-traveling agent instructed to find a hero who can wield a magic sword of justice to destroy them. Replinoids murder several members of Enoshima College's drama group, and Megumi teams up with class geek Mutsumi, who inevitably turns out to be the Chosen One.

With a heroine resembling a younger version of Urara from his SAKURA DIARIES and a school background redolent of ANGEL, manga creator U-Jin makes a rare foray into SF for a tits-and-tentacles storyline that combines the story of *Terminator* with the facehuggers and adult beasts of *Aliens*. However, the attempts at both murder mystery and questing subplots are somewhat stillborn. Time and cast are so limited that there is only one suspect for the murders and only one candidate for hero, while the contemporary setting is underused in favor of a school that is conveniently deserted by all but the central cast every time something interesting happens. The overuse of flashbacks cleverly, but also obviously, recycles footage to save money. Compare to DEMON BEAST INVASION. 🅝🅛🅥

FOOLISH TEST SLAVE

2011. JPN: *Ijo Chitai Jikken Dorei*. AKA: *Silly Strangeness Slavery Experiment*. Video. DIR: Uketamawa Kan. SCR: Shiro Nakata. DES: Uketamawa Kan. ANI: Hisashi Tomii. MUS: N/C. PRD: MediaBank, Studio9MAiami. 15 mins. x 2 eps.

Schoolgirl Azusa, who has oversized breasts, inherits her parents' inn when they die. All the guests leave except for one pervert, so instead of selling the place she decides to cater to his every desire. Based on a porn game by Pin-Point—compare, if you must, to SWALLOWTAIL INN. 🅝🅥

FOR REAL

1990. JPN: *Maji!* Video. DIR: Kazuya Miyazaki. SCR: Shigeo Nakakura. DES: Ayumi Tachihara.

ANI: Chuji Nakajima. MUS: Hideo Shimazu. PRD: Creative Bridge, Transarts, Nippon Animation. 50 mins. x 2 eps.

Maji is a young punk in the Nagisa criminal organization whose name is synonymous with loyalty and truth. He falls for a local high school girl, Kumiko, but their affair is as doomed as any meeting of different worlds—when the tattooed boy and his moll go out on the town, they run into the rival Kikuchi gang looking for trouble. A gangster story based on the first two volumes of the 50-part 1986 *Shonen Champion* manga by JUSTICE–creator Ayumi Tachihara. The first episode was screened theatrically. 🅝🅥

FORBIDDEN LOVE *

2003. JPN: *Imoto de Iko!* AKA: *Let's Go with Sister*. Video. DIR: Hiroaki Nakajima. SCR: Makoto Nakamura. DES: Nishi Eta, Yuji Yoshimoto. ANI: Yuji Yoshimoto. MUS: N/C. PRD: Green Bunny. 30 mins. x 2 eps.

Mayuka is a princess from a faraway planet who comes to Earth on a good-hearted quest to save her mother's life. However, there any resemblance to LITTLE WITCH SALLY ends, since Mayuka is so distracted by the sight of the human couple Yoshizumi and Iori copulating that she crashes into their apartment. For reasons not all that clear, Yoshizumi uses Mayuka's perceptual alteration gun to convince the new arrival that he is her elder brother, thereby helping to set up another not-quite-incest story, as Mayuka joins a predictable gaggle of adoring alien girls trying to get into Yoshizumi's bed. Based on a 2002 computer game by Overflow. The U.S. release includes a bonus 20-minute audio drama, *Sex Tutor: Cute Boy Hunter*, that runs while still images play on screen—compare to GIRL'S LOCKER ROOM LUST. These additions seem to have been part of a move by Adult Source Media to add value to several releases that would otherwise run too short. 🅝

FORCE FIVE *

1980. TV series. DIR: Kenneth Feuerman. SCR: Mike Haller. DES: N/C. ANI: N/C. MUS: N/C. PRD: Toei, Jim Terry Productions. 25 mins. x 74 eps. (*Grandizer*), 44 eps. (*Gaiking*), 39 eps. (*Starvengers*), 56 eps. (*Dangard Ace*), 64 eps. (*Spaceketeers*).

Five separate anime serials bought and re-

packaged for U.S. syndication by Jim Terry so that each could be shown on a different day of the week, every week. The separate series have their own entries in this book as DANGARD ACE (Mondays), *Starvengers* (i.e., GETTER ROBO, Tuesdays), SPACEKETEERS (Wednesdays), GRANDIZER (Thursdays), and GAIKING (Fridays). Though many of the *FF* serials had figures that were included in the SHOGUN WARRIORS line, Mattel had lost its license for the toys by the time *FF* was broadcast. Jim Terry Productions also tried to sell a feature-length edit of each series, some of which made their way to U.K. video as the *Krypton Force* line.

FOREIGN INFLUENCES

EARLY ANIME often bears a resemblance to *Felix the Cat*, both in its use of animals and in the animation techniques employed. Ikuo Oishi's *Moving Picture Fight of the Fox and Possum* (*Ugoki-e Kori no Tatehiki*, 1931) drew on the comical deformation of reality in *Felix* to create a style we would now define as "cartoonish"—in particular the caricatured and exaggerated facial expressions that would eventually lead to the large-eyed figures of Osamu Tezuka.

The influence of the Fleischer brothers' Betty Boop, who was redesigned in *Stopping the Show* (1932) into a submissive, dark-haired, big-eyed heroine with a littlegirl voice, can be seen in Kenzo Masaoka's *The Gang and the Dancing Girl* (*Gang to Odoriko*, 1933) and the kidnapped geisha (really a *tanuki* in disguise) who bats her eyelashes at the hero of Yoshitaro Kataoka's *Bandanemon the Monster Exterminator* (*Bandanemon: Bakemono Taiji no Maki*, 1935). Although Betty's guest star Popeye stole the show in *Popeye the Sailor* (1933), sailors in anime remained behind the scenes, with the Japanese Navy exerting greater influence on production budgets. Both Popeye and his nemesis Bluto made appearances in WARTIME ANIME, fighting for the Allied enemy.

It was a Chinese film, however, the Wan brothers' *Princess Iron Fan* (1943), a Chinese adaptation of JOURNEY TO THE WEST, that shook up the wartime anime industry. A remarkable achievement using heavy amounts of rotoscoping, it appears to have shamed the Japanese Navy into commissioning a feature film of equivalent length, MOMOTARO'S DIVINE SEA WARRIORS (1945).

Either *MDSW*, or *Princess Iron Fan*, or both (depending on which source one believes) can also be credited with inspiring a young Osamu Tezuka to become an artist—possibly the most important influence of all! It is also noteworthy that stop-motion animation in Japan was pioneered by *MDSW*'s producer, Tadahito Mochinaga, who left Japan for a decade after 1945 and pioneered the techniques during his years in Manchuria and at the Shanghai Animation Studio.

Funding for lavish animated movies was in short supply after World War II, with Japan laid low by military defeat and bombarded by messages of consumerism and scientific progress. Consequently, with little local competition, Disney films descended en masse, including the all-important *Pinocchio* (1940, released in Japan in 1952), while newer releases also arrived with little delay. *Peter Pan* (1953), *Lady and the Tramp* (as *Woof-Woof Story/Wanwan Monogatari*, 1955), and *Sleeping Beauty* (as *Beauty of the Sleeping Forest/Nemureru Mori no Bijo*, 1959) packed theaters, while the burgeoning world of television had no hesitation in shoving American cartoons onto the airwaves. The first cartoon to be seen on Japanese TV was the Fleischer brothers' *Superman*, also airing in 1955—it was joined the same year by both *Betty Boop* (as *Betty-chan*) and *Popeye*, his wartime collaboration forgiven. Conspicuously, the guest stars of the Fleischers' *Popeye Color Specials*, Ali Baba, Sindbad the Sailor, and Aladdin, all became the subjects of early color anime productions.

During the rise of television, anime aspired to imitate foreign live-action shows, not foreign cartoons. It was the George Reeves *Adventures of Superman*, not the Fleischer version, that was one of the highest-rated TV shows ever in Japan, inspiring broadcasters to attempt both live and animated reworkings. One of the most successful was Osamu Tezuka's **ASTRO BOY**, which combined the power and duty of *Superman* with the yearning and pathos of *Pinocchio*. But an equal effect was felt in the girls' market, where the hidden heroic identity of Clark Kent was reworked for **PRINCESS KNIGHT** (1967).

Bewitched (as *My Wife Is a Witch/Okusan wa Majo*) and *I Dream of Jeannie* (as *Cute*

Witch Jeannie/Kawaii Majo Jeannie) both inspired imitations, including the landmark **LITTLE WITCH SALLY** (1966) and the live/anime mixture of the first **COMET-SAN** (1967). Later seasons saw refinements to these ideas, in which plucky Japanese modern girls would transform, not necessarily into superheroines like **CUTEY HONEY** (1973), but into older, more sophisticated versions of themselves, such as **MARVELOUS MELMO** (1971). As the cute-but-maternal, houseproud-but-ditzy Samantha in *Bewitched*, Elizabeth Montgomery enjoyed unprecedented fame in Japan, becoming one of the first foreigners to grace Japanese commercials (for Lotte Mother biscuits). Her onscreen husband's name, "Darrin," would eventually transform into the prolonged "Daaah-ling!" that became a catchphrase for another magical wife, Lum in **URUSEI YATSURA** (1981); successive generations have come to associate the word with approaching spousal trouble. Meanwhile, the allure of *I Dream of Jeannie*, a Tinkerbell figure who becomes a boy's secret companion, can be seen to this day in shows such as **BOTTLE FAIRY** (2003) and **MIDORI DAYS** (2004).

Other influences have yet to be proved. It is our belief, for example, that the American TV show *The Gallery of Madame Liu Tsong* (1951), featuring early screen star Anna May Wong as a Chinese sleuth and antiques dealer, may also have been a major influence. So obscure that it is no longer even extant in America, Wong's contemporary fame and ethnic origin would have made the show a sure-fire purchase for early Japanese TV, ultimately leading to the art-related action of **CAT'S EYE**, **PETSHOP OF HORRORS**, and **GALLERY FAKE**. To date, however, we can find no evidence of its Japanese broadcast.

In order to convey a show's high concept, even in a TV listings magazine that has only space for the titles, it became customary for many import shows to proclaim their origins with a large foreign name in Japan's *katakana* syllabary, qualified with a much smaller Japanese-language explanation to help bewildered viewers. This led to strange mouthfuls such as *Famous Dog LASSIE*, *Undersea King NELSON* (i.e., *Sea Hunt*), and *SAINT Heaven Guy* (i.e., *The Saint*), a style later parodied for its exoticism to create terms such as *Mobile*

Suit **GUNDAM** and *Neon Genesis* **EVANGELION**, which persist to this day in the orthography of anime titles.

The cheaper, more limited animation style of Hanna-Barbera cartoons was a blessed relief to the Japanese, who no longer faced expensive movie animation on TV, but cheaper productions that they could emulate more easily. *Deputy Dawg* (as *Woof-Woof Sheriff/Wanwan Hoankan*), but most notably *The Flintstones* (as *Prehistoric Family/Genshi Kazoku*), made it clear that cartoons should not be kept in a children's ghetto and encouraged the Japanese to offer their own alternatives. Felix the Cat returned as a TV character in 1960 with *The Adventures of Felix/Felix no Boken*, notably in a redesign by Joe Oriolo in which the titular feline had a "magic bag of tricks"—compare to **DORAEMON**.

The year of the Tokyo Olympics, 1964, saw the culmination of many local and national initiatives in technology and infrastructure, and the first stirrings of **SPORTS ANIME**. By the time of the Olympics opening ceremony, Japan had become a nation of color TV set owners, a fact not lost on Osamu Tezuka, whose **KIMBA THE WHITE LION** (1965) was partly funded by the American company NBC Enterprises, enabling color production. The first color TV anime to test this new format was **A MOLE'S ADVENTURE** (1958, *Mogura no Adventure*), a nine-minute short shown on NTV. In the late 1960s, both the Japanese and the Americans were claiming to be the "makers" of coproductions like **THE KING KONG SHOW** and **TOM OF T.H.U.M.B.**, but tastes were diverging. Anime were made in reaction to, not in imitation of, foreign works. While entertainment for boys was often so universal that shows like **MARINE BOY** and **SPEED RACER** were readily exported, anime sought other niches not taken up by foreign broadcasters, most notably in the sector of the "magical girl shows."

The late 1960s and early 1970s saw Japanese TV influenced in turn by Cold War paranoia and spy capers, particularly the James Bond movies, and *The Man from U.N.C.L.E.* (1964). Anime heroes fought increasing numbers of evil empires and shadowy organizations, until the 1970s when, whatever the motive for a conflict, sponsorship deals ensured that a toy tie-in was mandatory—"my father gave me a robot" becoming not merely a plotpoint, but a slogan for children to internalize, ready to use to full effect on harassed parents.

The greatest foreign influence in this spirit was kept hidden for many years, but came in the form of direct investment. Many supposedly "American" cartoons in this period were largely made in Japan where the Rankin/Bass company was subcontracting much of its work since THE NEW ADVENTURES OF PINOCCHIO (1960). In particular, stop-motion from Tadahito Mochinaga's MOM Films and cel animation from Toru Hara's Topcraft made a major contribution to foreign works in this period, including *'Twas the Night Before Christmas* (1974), *The Hobbit* (1977), and *The Last Unicorn* (1981). Meanwhile, a more obvious foreign influence came in the form of the WORLD MASTERPIECE THEATER (1975), a highly regarded domestic franchise that relied solely on foreign stories for its inspiration. Staff from Topcraft formed the foundation of the substantially more famous Studio Ghibli, but also of the more obscure Pacific Animation Corporation, which was eventually bought out and renamed Walt Disney Animation Japan (q.v.). Such works are usually excluded from chronicles of "Japanese" animation but could often form a substantial component of the workload at some Japanese studios.

Japanese animators remained a common choice as laborers on supposedly "foreign" cartoons in the 1980s, sometimes comprising most or all of the actual creative staff. Shows such as ULYSSES 31 (1981), DOGTANIANAND THE THREE MUSKE-HOUNDS (1981), and THE MYSTERIOUS CITIES OF GOLD (1982) were made with foreign money, while others, such as ROBIN HOOD (1990), relied on markets abroad for their success. However, this success was short-lived, chiefly through the rising costs of Japanese labor. As Japanese studios increasingly subcontracted their own work abroad in the 1990s, it was just as likely for their foreign clients to do the same—later seasons of *The Simpsons* (1989), which would probably have been farmed out to Japan if the show had been made a decade earlier, were instead animated in Korea.

The home video market, which many in the anime business seem to have regarded as a wholly domestic, bargain-basement operation, was to prove anime's savior. However, many foreign buyers developed false expectations based on their first experience of the medium. Although anime were sold abroad in the 1990s as a video medium, many of the video buyers were comparing their purchases with AKIRA (1988)—a feature film. Its success abroad, greeted with elation and bewilderment by its own over-stretched producers, ushered in the age of Japanese video exports—the beginning of "anime" as we know it in the West. Japanese sources, often unlikely to use the word "anime" as distinct from any other cartoon in preceding periods, often call the modern period the age of "Japanimation," deliberately using a foreign word to demonstrate that anime has come to be defined by foreign consumers, based on a criterion that largely rests on its place of origin.

As increasing numbers of foreign distributors fought over the rights to anime, foreigners began investing directly in Japanese productions in order to snatch the rights early. GHOST IN THE SHELL (1995) featured investment from Manga Entertainment, while many modern productions often involve foreign coproducers as benefactors. Indeed, by the middle of the first decade of the 21st century, some anime companies refused to even commence production without foreign backing. Instead of being offered as completed packages, many anime in the period were instead presented as concepts or works-in-progress. Many modern productions were now touted at rights fairs in the hope of attracting foreign investment, while ever-increasing numbers of both anime and FALSE FRIENDS are put into production at the instigation of Western producers. In KALEIDO STAR (2003), the lavish performance sequences were only possible with investment from ADV Films, while KILL BILL: THE ORIGIN OF O-REN (2003), was made by the Japanese in imitation of what foreign producers thought Japanese animation ought to be. This reliance on overseas investment, taking its significance from a belated 10% to a preemptive 50% of anime's value, created a brief and lucrative bubble in the Japanese market, and a production peak in 2006 that has yet to be matched, but also innumerable shows

purchased at costs significantly above their eventual value. The subsequent slump, as promising concepts like HEAT GUY J failed to live up to the expectations of their investors, caused considerable disruption in the overseas anime business. Today (2014), foreign sales once more amount to roughly 10% of most anime's value, restoring conditions from 1995, although foreign *potential* remains far higher. Based on experiments in digital fingerprinting and informal access (OVERSEAS DISTRIBUTION AND PIRACY), and the realities of simple demographics, the possible value of foreign markets has been assessed at up to 30 times the value of the domestic market for anime. It is this tantalizing prospect that keeps at least some eyes in the industry focused outside Japan, on emerging markets in China and Africa, and on the long tail of anime FANDOM in the developed world.

FOREIGN LOVE AFFAIR, A

2007. JPN: *Ikoku Irokoi Romantan*. Video. DIR: Hajime Otani. SCR: Kai Koishikawa. DES: Shuhei Tamura, Nobuyuki Shiogama, Miho Takematsu. ANI: N/C. MUS: N/C. PRD: Imajin, PRIMETIME, ANIK. 30 mins. x 2 eps. Ranmaru is the heir of a powerful gangster family, forced into a dynastic marriage. His new wife is just as unwilling and kicks him out on their wedding night after a shipboard ceremony in Italy. He meets a shipmate, the hunky Italian Alberto, and the pair develop a relationship that turns to romance. Ayano Yamane's manga came out in 2003 in *Core* magazine. There's also a drama CD for those who want more. The anime follows the manga reasonably closely, both in plot and design terms, but the animation is no better than adequate. Ⓝ

FOREST WARRIOR BONOLON

2007. JPN: *Mori no Senshi Bonolon*. AKA: *Bonolon Fushigi na Mori no Iitsutae; Bonolon, Message of the Mysterious Forest*. TV series. DIR: Hidehito Ueda. SCR: N/C. DES: Go Nagayama, Yutaka Kawasuji. ANI: N/C. MUS: Ken Kaidu, Hiroshiiro Takahashi. PRD: ACTAS Inc., North Stars Pictures, Kids Station. 5 mins. x 26 eps.
The tears of those who are sad or troubled flow into the earth and pass through the roots of the great oaks of the Tasuman

forest, summoning a huge orange-colored giant: Bonolon. Bonolon is a child of the forest, and despite his huge body, befitting the mighty oaks from which he was born, he is only nine years old. He has a child's strong sense of justice and is determined to grow up honest and loyal, and to do all he can to help those in trouble. This sweet, sincere, short series for children was produced by Tetsuo Hara, co-creator of FIST OF THE NORTH STAR—not so surprising when you consider that it's all about laying the foundations for children to grow up in a just and honest world. It's based on a story by children's author Nobuhiko Horie, working under the pen name Seibo Kitahara.

FORTUNE ARTERIAL *

2010. JPN: *Fortune Arterial: Akai Yakusoku.* AKA: *Fortune Arterial: Red Promise.* TV series. DIR: Munenori Nawa. SCR: Katsumi Hasegawa. DES: Megumi Ishihara, Yukie Abe. ANI: Kyoko Kotani, Satoshi Isono, Megumi Ishihara. MUS: Takaaki Anzai. PRD: feel., ZEXCS, SMG Entertainment, Kadokawa, NTT Docomo, Klockworx, TV Tokyo. 25 mins. x 12 eps. (TV), 30 mins. x 6 eps. (v).
Kohei's parents have moved around a lot during his childhood, so they finally decide to send him to boarding school. They pick a Christian school on the island where they once lived, and Kohei looks forward to a tranquil school life with normal friends. But in a harem anime (ROMANCE AND DRAMA) set in a high school where vampires form part of the student body, and the humans are crazy, this is unlikely. Based on an "adult" visual novel by August, this anime also has two manga adaptations, the first (2007) by Akane Sasaki and the second later in the same year by Miki Kodama. A four-panel gag strip compilation devoted to the show ran for ten volumes between 2008 and 2010. Six novels appeared in 2008–9, with five audio drama CDs and an Internet radio show in the same period. Artbooks and music CDs also embedded the franchise further into fans' consciousness, but it's a work of marginal interest to others, with nothing to distinguish it from other prettily designed lightweight bits of fluff. **N**

FORTUNE QUEST

1994. Video, TV series. DIR: Takeshi Yama-guchi, Takashi Watanabe. SCR: Keiko Maruo, Yumi Kageyama, Reiko Yoshida. DES: Yumi Nakayama. ANI: Nobuhiro Okaseko, Susumu Ishizaki. MUS: N/C. PRD: Victor, Beam Entertainment, MBS. 30 mins. x 4 eps. (v), 25 mins. x 26 eps. (TV).
A group of adventurers on a parallel world seek their fortunes in a story whose debt to role-playing games is so great that the press notes even describe the characters as "low-level." Teenage "mapper" Pastel leads a party comprising young swordsman Clay, bandit chieftain's son Trapp, blue-blood "walking dictionary" Kitton, gentle giant Knoll, baby dragon Shiro, and infant elf sorceress Rumy. After their latest quest, they call in at the Adventurers Support Group, which stamps their ID cards and evaluates their experience, both pastiching and predicting the inevitable console game version of the story.

Originally based on a best-selling 1991 novel by Michio Fukuzawa, who also wrote the *Duan Surk* prequel set in the same universe, the story was also adapted into a manga by Natsumi Mukai, in turn adapted into the sequel anime TV series *Fortune Quest L* by Eiichi Sato and SLAYERS-director Takeshi Watanabe. The series added the gaming experience by featuring hidden items and monsters, as well as unexpected dialogue from certain characters. Though hardly anything new, it prepared the ground for the success of POKÉMON, for which exploiting the game tie-in was the sole raison d'être.

FORZA! HIDEMARU

2002. TV series. DIR: Nobuhiro Takamoto. SCR: Hideo Takayashiki. DES: Masami Esaka. ANI: N/C. MUS: Yuko Fujishima. PRD: TV Tokyo, NAS, Gallop. 25 mins. x 26 eps.
A soccer anime with a cast of wacky animals in sports getup seems far out of its time in the early 21st century, but it was the year of the World Cup in Japan and South Korea, and the very young audience sees these tropes with fresh eyes. Hidemaru is a feisty fox; his friends include bunnies, dogs, horses, and a couple of hefty hippo girls. Based on a manga by "Sunny Side Up," in *Corocoro Comic.*

FOUR LEAF CLOVER

2008. JPN: *Yotsunoha.* Video. DIR: Hiroshi Nishikiori. SCR: Hiroshi Nishikiori. DES: Koichi Motomura, Hisaharu Iijima. ANI: Koichi Motomura. MUS: N/C. PRD: Hal Film Maker, Rondo Robe. 37 mins. x 2 eps.
Four little girls are separated when their school is closed down. Before they leave for the last time, they bury a box with mementoes under a tree and agree to meet again three years later under the same tree. When the time comes, they find one of their old teachers has turned their capsule into a treasure hunt. Prettily animated, very lightweight harem anime (ROMANCE AND DRAMA) based on a more explicit 2006 erotic video game by higo-soft. **N**

FOXES OF CHIRONUP

1987. JPN: *Chironup no Kitsune.* Movie. DIR: Tetsuo Imazawa. SCR: Fukuo Matsuyama. DES: Yoshinao Yamamoto. ANI: Noriko Imazawa. MUS: Etsujiro Sato. PRD: Tac, Herald. 72 mins.
Foxes Ken and Chin become the proud parents of cubs, Koro and Kan, who enjoy a carefree life on the northern Japanese island of Chironup. They befriend a fisherman and his wife but are forced to run for their lives when soldiers on a military exercise decide to take home some fox pelts as souvenirs. A sweet little film that obliquely symbolizes the plight of Japan's aboriginal Ainu people and the northern islands that have been contested with Russia since they were occupied by Stalin's soldiers in 1945. Based on a book by Yoshiyuki Takahashi.

FOXWOOD TALES

1991. Video. JPN: *Foxwood no Monogatari.* AKA: *Fox Wood Tales.* DIR: Seiji Endo. SCR: Seiji Endo. DES: Brian Paterson. ANI: Maya Matsuyama. MUS: Osamu Tezuka (mus). PRD: Grouper Productions. 25 mins. x 3 eps.
Harvey, Rue, and Willie are a hedgehog, rabbit, and mouse who live in a windmill in the peaceful town of Foxwood, where they have several adventures in this short-lived series based on the children's picture books by the British creators Cynthia and Brian Paterson.

FRACTALE *

2011. TV series. DIR: Yutaka Yamamoto. SCR: Mari Okada, Shinsuke Onishi, Hiroyuki Yoshino. DES: Masako Tashiro, Emi Kesamaru. ANI: Masako Tashiro. MUS: Sohei Kano. PRD: A-1 Pictures, Asmik Ace, Dentsu, Fuji TV, SME, Toho. 23 mins. x 11 eps.

Mankind's digital engagement has evolved to the extent where all humanity's needs are taken care of by the unseen engines of the Fractale system. This frees everyone to pursue their own individual passions, and has changed society to the extent that almost everyone now relates through digital avatars called doppels. When Clain, an antiques-crazy boy, meets a real girl for the first time ever, he's impressed by more than the fact that Phryne shows up in a glider with a crew of machine-gun-toting honchos in pursuit—shades here not only of SECRET OF BLUE WATER but also of TIME BOKAN. His perfect world isn't as perfect as it seems. Soon Clain is caught up in the terrifying conflicts between anti-Fractale activists and Fractale cultists, not knowing whether life as he knows it is about to end, whether that might be a good thing, or whether he'll survive long enough to make up his mind one way or the other.

Director Yutaka Yamamoto gives the show an almost archaically rustic, domestic feel, with echoes of the Studio Ghibli aesthetic in both the visuals and the relationships, not only between Clain and Phryne, but the maniacally merry preteen girl Nessa. Scriptwriter Mari Okada is renowned for punchy, powerful dramas like RED GARDEN and BLACK BUTLER. Scholar and critic Hiroki Azuma, creator of the original *Fractale* concept, is known in Japan for asking big, serious questions about where society is heading. Sohei Kano's music is richly beautiful, and any show with an ending theme whose lyrics were written in 1889 by Irish poet William Butler Yeats gets our vote on grounds of poetic daring alone. It all makes for a charming, intriguing package. And then it stops, with plot threads still unwoven and questions unanswered. If you can deal with that frustration, *Fractale* will reward you.

A TV series that runs for 11 episodes isn't usually considered the success of the year in any medium. *Fractale* was attractive enough to win over the hard-headed buyers at Funimation, although controversy dogged its U.S. simulcast debut in 2011, with the Japanese owners putting it on U.S. hiatus after just one episode, initially claiming that they would not release further episodes until Funimation could end piracy on the Internet—a Herculean requirement that was soon discreetly re-

voked. The manga adaptation also caused some controversy when director Yamamoto asked for it to be discontinued, soon after artist Mutsumi Akazaki blogged that she found the story "uninteresting." That seems unfair: cute as it looks and sounds, *Fractale* has a core of science underlying its fiction. True, there are plot holes aplenty, but there are also intriguing concepts. The series raises questions that our own world is struggling to answer, and the manga adaptation continued with the same artist—seemingly in a reminder to Yamamoto that the concept was not his to control either, but belonged to the production committee. ◐

FRANCESCA

2014. JPN: *Francesca: Girls, Be Ambitious*. TV series. DIR: Hitoshi Kumagai, Yuichiro Yano. SCR: Toshimitsu Takeuchi. DES: Hitoshi Kumagai. ANI: Rurina Igami, Akira Kishida. MUS: Shuji Katayama, Yasuharu Takanashi. PRD: Amuse, Daiichi Kosho, HeART-BIT, Hokkaido Azmasy, Hokkaido Cultural Broadcasting, Bandai Namco, Pony Canyon, Teichiku. 12 mins. x 2 eps.

An exorcist hoping to rid Hokkaido of the undead must face the revenant spirits of the Shinsengumi vigilante movement (SHINSENGUMI FARCE), and so hires the services of the undead demon-hunter and part-time idol singer Francesca. Francesca herself was invented as a "*moe* mascot" in 2012, seemingly as part of the same trend in domestic tourism promotion that propelled SILVER SPOON into bestseller-dom after the Great East Japan Earthquake. Consequently, the show comes loaded with identifiably Hokkaido food and cultural products, not the least the allusion in its subtitle "Be Ambitious." The quote "Boys Be Ambitious" was first rolled out by William S. Clark, foreign advisor and co-founder of what would become Hokkaido University, in 1876. It has since become something of a motto of Hokkaido and specifically Sapporo, even though it was seemingly blurted out as a kind of departing afterthought. One wonders what manner of brainstorming meeting identified the need to lure people to Hokkaido by suggesting it was the haunted domain of a lace-clad, big-chested, one-eyed undead crime-fighter, but then again, somebody greenlit CUTTA'S STORY.

FRANKENSTEIN *

1981. JPN: *Kyofu Densetsu Kaiki! Frankenstein*. AKA: *Mystery! Frankenstein Legend of Terror*. TV special. DIR: Yugo Serikawa. SCR: Akiyoshi Sakai. DES: Toyoo Ashida. ANI: Toyoo Ashida. MUS: Kentaro Haneda. PRD: Aoi Productions, Toei Animation, TV Asahi. 111 mins.

After the success of DRACULA: SOVEREIGN OF THE DAMNED, the same team made this bewildering version of Mary Shelley's novel. For reasons unknown, the setting was moved to North Wales, where Frankenstein conducts his experiments amid the mountainous splendor of Snowdonia. His creature, Franken, is brought to life by a lightning bolt and runs for Switzerland, where he is pursued by police inspector Belbeau. Franken befriends a little girl called Emily and her blind father, saving Emily from a wild bear before succumbing to his fate and committing suicide.

FRANZ KAFKA'S A COUNTRY DOCTOR *

2007. JPN: *Kafka Inaka Isha*. Movie. DIR: Koji Yamamura. SCR: Koji Yamamura. DES: Koji Yamamura. ANI: Koji Yamamura. MUS: Hitomi Shimizu. PRD: Yamamura Animation, Shochiku. 21 mins.

A young doctor retells the story of a terrible winter night when he failed to save a young patient. Events take on a surreal turn and soon he is plunged into a nightmare. This is Yamamura's take on a short story by the renowned Czech-Jewish writer. His individual approach to anime has brought him a clutch of awards and an Oscar nomination for MOUNT HEAD.

FRECKLES POOCH

1969. JPN: *Sobakasu Putchi*. AKA: *Freckled Butch*. TV series. DIR: Fumio Ikeno. SCR: Noboru Ishiguro, Tomohiro Ando. DES: Shozo Kubota. ANI: Tadao Wakabayashi. MUS: Asao Kasai. PRD: Shinsei, Fuji TV. 5 mins. x 162 eps.

Short comedy films about a cheeky little dog, Pooch, who is unable to let any evil deed go unchallenged. He flies in a vehicle shaped like a milk jug, powered by milk itself, and fights against the evil genius Walgie, using a yo-yo as a weapon, accompanied by his associates the lumbering monster Netaro and Ganko the impetuous parrot. *FP* was made by the remaining staff members of TV Doga, the company behind **MARINE BOY**, which lost much of its anime staff after it was rebranded Fuji TV Enterprises. With more emphasis on live-action television, many of the staff left, and the few animators remaining worked on this, farming out the actual animation to Shinsei Sekai Eigasha. The show was eventually replaced by **PINCH AND PUNCH**, with which it shares a large number of crewmembers.

FREE KICK FOR TOMORROW

1992. JPN: *Ashita e no Free Kick*. TV series. DIR: Tetsuro Amino, Toshiaki Suzuki. SCR: Masaru Yamamoto, Nobuaki Kishima, Akira Oketani. DES: Noboyushi Habara. ANI: Takahiro Omori, Masami Suda. MUS: Satoshi Tozuka. PRD: Ashi Pro, Nippon TV, Shizuoka TV. 25 mins. x 50 eps.

Shun arrives in Italy with his disabled friend, Roberto, to live with his rich grandfather who also emigrated from Japan many years ago. He becomes passionate about soccer, but Grandfather wants him to take over the family business and resents the time he devotes to sports. Eventually, though, he has to accept that Shun will become a professional player. Roberto, meanwhile, succeeds as an architect and wants to build a great stadium in their town, a project that Shun's grandfather very much opposes. The series has an open ending—a big competition with top teams comes to the town, but we never know if Shun's team wins. A series that reflects the reality of a modern sports business, where few players were born anywhere near the town they represent, and corporate interests can make or break a team.

FREEDOM *

2006. AKA: *Freedom Project*. Video. DIR: Shuhei Morita. SCR: Dai Sato, Katsuhiko Chiba, Yuichi Nomura. DES: Atsushi Irie, Daisuke Sanbu, Katsuhiro Otomo, Yasumitsu Suetake, Kei Ichikura. ANI: Atsushi Irie, Hiroyuki Horiuchi. Koichi Arai, Takao Maki. MUS: Yoshihiro Ike. PRD: Sunrise, Bandai Visual, Dentsu. 30 mins. x 7 eps.

In the middle of the 21st century, Earth establishes a colony on the Moon. Soon after, the planet is devastated by a climate shift and contact is lost. Cities with millions of people now thrive on the Moon, mankind's new home—calling itself the Republic of Eden. Over a century later, 15-year-old Takeru completes his education and embarks on his society's equivalent of the gap year, a short period of freedom to do whatever he likes before he's integrated into adult society. But a series of chances forces him to confront the sinister side of his society and get in touch with those who don't agree with its rigid controls. He and his best friend start a journey to Earth, a journey from which there may be no return.

A project with Katsuhiro Otomo's name attached to it (even when not directing) invariably attracts attention; after all, at the start of the 1990s his **AKIRA** was the crossover movie that took anime into the mainstream. Even though none of Otomo's later work has matched it for impact or achievement, his trademark design aesthetic, his well-known themes, and his narrative drive are still worth seeing in any form—even if it is a form that he has barely brushed against, in much the same manner as some of Masamune Shirow's lesser "consultancies" like **LANDLOCK**. In *Freedom*, it's true that the narrative drive veers slightly off track and slows down midstory, but it pulls itself back on track for a satisfying climax. This is a class act, well designed and well animated, with CGI that integrates magnificently into the 2D animation: there's more than enough to keep an audience happy despite the uneven pace. All the more surprising, then, that this is an extended commercial (**ADVERTISING AND SPONSORSHIP**) for snack food. The makers of Nissin Cup Noodles decided to celebrate their 35th anniversary by funding this series. It was money well spent, and the shots of characters eating from Nissin packages are a small price to pay for a taste of *Freedom*.

FREEZING *

2011. TV series. DIR: Takashi Watanabe. SCR: Masanao Akahoshi, Takao Yoshioka. DES: Mayumi Watanabe, Tomohiro Kawahara, Satoru Kuwabara. ANI: Mayumi Watanabe. MUS: Masaru Yokoyama. PRD: A.C.G.T., AT-X, Dax Production, Kill Time Communication, Media Factory, T.O. Entertainment, Inc. 30 mins. x 12 eps.

Once again, only high school girls can save the world from alien invasion. This time, the high school girls are genetically engineered beings called Pandoras. Their power is enormous, but they must still be assisted and controlled by an outside force. Enter the all-male Limiters. To be a Limiter one must have an inborn ability called "freezing." This limits the enemy's movement when a Pandora is fighting. Limiter Kazuya Aoi, whose late sister was a Pandora, decides to become the partner of a powerful but cold-hearted Pandora with a horror of being touched.

Imagine the old-school genetic-supremacist whimsy of Mamoru Nagano's **FIVE STAR STORIES** and the alien threat of **EVANGELION** crashed into the violent fan-service ethic of **IKKI TOUSEN**. The arcanely named techniques, ranks, and titles rework Nagano's concepts for a new generation. The less pleasant aspects are reworked too: exploitation under the guise of seeking "soulmates," slavery, disposable lower orders, and genetic experimentation on children. The neo-Victorian costume elements are symbolic as well as decorative; in this version of the world, the true power of women can only be exercised through men. But it's the slam-bang action and the absurdly overdeveloped bosoms that give *Freezing* its unique appeal. Nagano draws his girls slim to the point of etiolation. Kwang-Hyun Kim, the artist on *Freezing*, doesn't.

Creator Dall-Young Lim has had success both as a comics artist in his ancestral South Korea, with *Unbalance Unbalance*, *Zero* and *Aflame Inferno*, and as a manga creator with *Black God* (animated in 2008 by Sunrise as **KUROKAMI THE ANIMATION**) and *Freezing*. Artist Kim worked with him on *Aflame Inferno* before signing up for *Freezing*. South Korea has become increasingly important in the animation world over the past two decades, both in its own right as a creative force, and as a major contributor to the making of anime. There is a sizable Korean population within Japan; talent-hungry Japanese publishers and production houses have begun to hire artists of Korean descent as well as outsourcing work to Korea. The *Freezing* manga was launched in Kill Time Communication's *Comic Valkyrie* in 2006, and had clocked up seven collected volumes by the time production house Media Factory announced that the anime would make its Japanese TV debut in 2011. Funimation signed an online simulcast deal for the show, making it available to fans across America on whiplash turnaround designed to head off piracy and impatient **FANDOM**. Girls kick alien ass, let off steam with the odd cat-fight for rank and supremacy, and are, ultimately, just looking for love in a harsh universe: same old ideas dressed in new and skimpier outfits.

FRIED OCTOPUS MAN

1998. JPN: *Takoyaki Manto Man*. AKA: *Fried Octopus Cloak Man*. TV series. DIR: Masami Anno. SCR: Yoshio Urasawa. DES: Midori Nagaoka. ANI: Tsugenobu Kuma. MUS: N/C. PRD: Studio Pierrot, TV Tokyo. 25 mins. x 12 eps.

Evil priest Baobao is intent on ruling Earth, and a lone woman in a *takoyaki* (fried octopus dumplings) diner prays for a savior to protect the planet. In a series that owes a lot of its comedy and inspiration to the earlier **ANPANMAN**, the woman's request is answered, sort of, when a hero arrives draped in an edible cloak.

FRIGHTFUL NEWS

1991. JPN: *Kyofu Shinbun*. Video. DIR: Takashi Anno. SCR: Masaaki Sakurai. DES: Koji Uemura. ANI: Koji Uemura. MUS: Takashi Tsunoda. PRD: Pierrot Project. 50 mins. x 3 eps.

Junior high school student Rei Onigata finds a newspaper, *The Frightful News*, that cuts one's life short by a hundred days whenever it is read. It also, however, contains much interesting information about the spirit world and future events, and Rei is the only one who can read it. Realizing he has been tricked by an evil spirit, he offers his services to psychic Jo-un Hoshi. Rei, his love interest, Midoriko, and her sister are stalked by the ghost of an old man in a dark cloak. This short series is based on the 1973 *Shonen Champion* manga by Jiro Tsunoda, who also drew **HYAKUTARO** and **KARATE-CRAZY LIFE**. In 1996, the story was remade as a live-action movie, directed by Teruyoshi Ishii. Perhaps in the wake of the not-dissimilar live-action film *Ring* (1998), it was brought back in 2000 for a one-shot "manga video," in which voice actors narrated the story over still images from the manga onscreen.

FRISKY GIRL

2008. JPN: *Shishunki Shojo*. Video. DIR:

Hiromi Yokoyama. SCR: Ren Soto. DES: Sho Sakai. ANI: N/C. MUS: N/C. PRD: Suzuki Mirano, Hitoshi Oda. 30 mins. x 2 eps.

Two high school friends think they're tough enough to handle any trouble at school. Then they face the school punks and find they're not as tough as they thought, in this porn anime based on Shun Shirataki's 2006 manga. ⓃⓋ

FRITEN-KUN

1981. Movie, video. DIR: Taku Sugiyama, Kazuyuki Okaseko. SCR: Noboru Shiroyama, Tsunehisa Ito, Haruya Yamazaki. DES: Takamitsu Mitsunori. ANI: Takamitsu Mitsunori, Haruo Takahashi, Keiji Morishita. MUS: Haruo Matsushita. PRD: Knack. 75 mins. (m), 30 mins. X 2 eps. (v).

Gambling japes from Friten, a Tokyo gangster whose sense of humor was screened on a double bill with the diametrically opposed Osaka-based comedy of **JARINKO CHIE**. Based on the manga by Masashi Ueda, serialized in both *Modern Mahjong* and *Gamble Punch* magazines, the seven vignettes here include Friten demonstrating his winning gambling tactic and the wrong way to play mahjong. Among the stories are more far-fetched incidents such as his trip back in time to Edo-period Japan, his attempts to get involved in real sports, and his hapless tries at seducing the pretty Ikue-chan.

FROM THE APENNINES TO THE ANDES

1976. JPN: *Haha o Tazunete Sanzan Ri*. AKA: *3,000 Leagues in Search of Mother*. TV series, movie. DIR: Isao Takahata, Hajime Okayasu. SCR: Kazuo Fukuzawa. DES: Yoichi Kotabe. ANI: Yoichi Kotabe. MUS: Koichi Sakata. PRD: Nippon Animation, Fuji TV. 21 mins. x 51 eps. (TV1), 107 mins. (m1), 98 mins. (m2).

Italian boy Marco lives in the town of Genoa, which has been hard hit by heavy taxes and recession. His mother leaves for Argentina, where her husband runs a clinic for the poor, but Marco cannot bear to be parted from her and pursues her ship. So begins a long quest that will ultimately take him to Bolivia, in the company of the Peppino puppet theater, and Fiorina, the daughter of a local chieftain. The story was reedited into a 107-minute movie version in 1980 by Hajime Okayasu and complete-

ly remade by director Kozo Kusuba as the film *Marco* (1999). Based on part of the novel *Cuore* by Edmondo de Amicis, which was also adapted in its entirety as **HEART: AN ITALIAN SCHOOLBOY'S JOURNAL**. The moving story was also mercilessly lampooned in the 1991 **GENIUS IDIOT BAKABON**–movie *3,000 Leagues in Search of Osomatsu's Curry* (1991), directed by Akira Saito, in which the quest for Mother was replaced by a zany search for a decent meal.

FROM TODAY ON, THIS IS ME

1992. JPN: *Kyo kara, Ore wa!* Video. DIR: Takeshi Mori. SCR: Yukiyoshi Ohashi. DES: Masaya Onishi. ANI: Masaya Onishi. MUS: Kimio Morihari. PRD: Studio Pierrot. 61 mins.

Teenagers Takashi Mitsubashi and Shinji Ito move to a new high school in "C" Prefecture near Tokyo and resolve to pretend to be the toughest kids around, dyeing their hair into threatening tough-guy blond hairdos. Forced to cooperate simply because each could rat out the other, they outwit genuine tough guys with elaborate bluffs and deceits. This movie is based on a comedy in the 1988 manga in *Shonen Sunday* by Hiroyuki Nishimori. Compare to **BITE ME! CHAMELEON**.

FROM UP ON POPPY HILL ∗

2011. JPN: *Kokuriko-zaka Kara*. AKA: *Coquelicot-zaka Kara; From Up on Coquelicot Hill*. Movie. DIR: Goro Miyazaki. SCR: Hayao Miyazaki, Keiko Niwa. DES: Katsuya Kondo. ANI: Akihiko Yamashita, Atsushi Yamagata, Kitaro Kosaka. MUS: Satoshi Takebe. PRD: Studio Ghibli, Buena Vista Home Entertainment/Disney, Dentsu, Hakuhodo DY Media Partners, Kadokawa, Kodansha, Mitsubishi Corporation, NTV, Toho. 91 mins.

It is 1963: Umi Matsuzaka, oldest child in a loving family of five, raises signal flags every day outside the family home in a Yokohama boarding house, in honor of her father, missing in action in the Korean War. At school, she gets involved in a campaign to preserve the venerable clubhouse, and in the process starts to fall in love with fellow student Shun Kazama.

Poppy Hill marks a very public and publicized healing of the similarly public and publicized breach between animation auteur Hayao Miyazaki and his eldest son Goro, who was hauled into the family business just short of his 40th birthday to direct TALES FROM EARTHSEA. On this, his second movie, his own fingerprints have been wiped clean away. Gone are the oversaturated colors and overwrought black-and-white relationships, along with infidelity to the original that made *Tales from Earthsea* such a missed opportunity. Instead we have a discreet, delicately restrained piece of Showa-period nostalgia that does Tetsuro Sayama and Chizuru Takahashi's 1980 manga the honor of not trying to overdress it. Miyazaki senior's script allows the darkness at the heart of the story, the darkness still lurking in Japan after the terrible years of defeat, starvation, and occupation, to slither along in the shadows.

As one might expect from a multi-generational production, retelling a 1980s manga that itself recalled the after-effects of the 1950s on the 1960s, the film contains nostalgias within nostalgias, redolent of similar commemorations of the Japanese past such as MAI MAI MIRACLE and the hit series of live-action movies that began with *Always: Sunset on Third Street* (2005). This is made manifest in particular through the song "Ue o Muite" (1961), which, renamed "Sukiyaki" in 1963, was the first Japanese tune to reach number one on the American hit parade. The song plays in the background of one sequence, and its singer, Kyu Sakamoto, appears at one point on a grainy TV screen. The year 1963 is a moment of considerable importance, not only for Japan, but also for the elder Miyazaki who wrote the script—the success of "Sukiyaki" is but one feature of a triumphal period in the months before the following year's Tokyo Olympics, when Japan was full of hope and excitement over its impending return to the international community after wartime and postwar reversals. For Hayao Miyazaki, of course, 1963 was also the year when he left behind university life and commenced a career in Japanese animation. Japanese animation was itself transformed in 1963 with the release of ASTRO BOY, cited by the elder Miyazaki as a disastrous development in the history of the artform.

Themes and plot threads link this film more closely to Miyazaki senior's work than to the work of his son, who was not born until 1967, and who hence some-times seems merely a tourist in his father's

remembrances. We have the metaphorical return of a dead father like that of *Earthsea*, along with the male-female engagement of PONYO, PRINCESS MONONOKE, and PORCO ROSSO. Boys and girls, however attracted to each other, just don't understand what makes the other gang tick. Watch the girls' reaction to the rowdy mob of boys, fighting one minute and then best of friends the next, mirrored as the boys see the girls arrive with their own armory of cleaning materials to reclaim the old house. Yokohama becomes the backdrop for a community reclaiming its sense of self and a group of young people setting out to change the world. It's a charming, moving vision. It's not a great Ghibli movie, or a great Hayao Miyazaki movie, but it's the best movie that Goro Miyazaki has given us to date. On the evidence of these two works, the one thing he has yet to develop is a strong sense of himself as a director and an artist. Like the heroine of LA CORDA D'ORO, he was handed one of the world's most magical instruments on a plate, but has yet to show the world he can dance to his own tune.

FRUITS BASKET *

2001. TV series. DIR: Akitaro Daichi. SCR: Rika Nakase. DES: Akimi Hayashi. ANI: N/C. MUS: N/C. PRD: Studio Deen, Fuji TV. 25 mins. x 26 eps.
Happy-go-lucky orphan Toru Honda has to move in with the family of Yuki Soma, the high school boy she secretly adores. However, she is not expecting to discover that they are a family of sorcerers and shapeshifters, cursed to transform into animals (largely from the Chinese zodiac) if hugged by a member of the opposite sex. Fluffy animals, magic, and schoolgirl crushes, based on the manga by Natsuki Takaya in *Hana to Yume* magazine, develop into harder-hitting drama as the story investigates the implications of magical afflictions that many similar shows have previously simply played for laughs. Realizing that the curse has already had tragic consequences in her own life and in those of the Soma family, Toru sets out to find a way to break it.

FRUITS CUP *

2004. JPN: *Yugu Settai: Koto no Gokuraku e Yokoso*. Video. DIR: Yoshio Usuda. SCR:

Tsunekazu Murakami. DES: Waffle. ANI: Yoshio Usuda. MUS: Beeline. PRD: Waffle, Milky. 22 mins. x 2 eps.
After saving the life of his friend in a car accident, Riku temporarily inherits the convalescing man's job as a caretaker for a girls' dormitory on one of Japan's southern islands. Riku secretly films the girls in various lesbian couplings and then uses the footage to blackmail Yoshino, the most demure, into giving up her virginity. But Riku wants to seduce the other girls at the boarding house he runs, and so forces Yoshino to help him get what he wants. "The worst sexual humiliation" is assured by the press release. **CNV**

FUJI TV (FUJI TELECASTING)

Founded in 1959 by a consortium of radio companies, movie companies, and the *Sankei Shinbun* newspaper, Fuji was an early adopter of the anime medium and the channel that screened both ASTRO BOY and KIMBA THE WHITE LION. The channel's flagship anime is SAZAE-SAN, the longest-running cartoon series in the world, now over 44 years old. The broadcast company acquired the studio TV Doga in the 1960s, renaming it Fuji TV Enterprises. The station enjoys a particularly strong relationship with the magazine *Shonen Jump*, whose DRAGONBALL and ONE PIECE manga have both been adapted for its schedules.

FUJIKO F. FUJIO'S LITTLE WEIRDNESS THEATER

1990. JPN: *Fujiko F. Fujio no Sukoshi Fushigi (SF) Tanben Theatre*. Video. DIR: Satoshi Dezaki, Tomomi Mochizuki. SCR: Toshiaki Imaizumi. DES: Keizo Shimizu. ANI: Keizo Shimizu. MUS: N/C. PRD: Studio Gallop. 50 mins. x 5 eps.
A series of SF short stories by the cocreator of DORAEMON made for adults but in the spirit of fondly remembered shows from childhood. The punchy one-shots include *Tomorrow in the Letterbox*, in which a man receives a message from the future warning of impending danger for his friends; *A Dish for the Minotaur*, about a crash-landed astronaut who finds himself on a planet where the roles of men and cows are reversed, and finds that he is to be eaten at a royal banquet; *Green Guardian*, a pastiche of *Day of the Triffids* in which Tokyo is overrun by man-eating plants; *Island of*

Extinction, about the population of Earth being all but wiped out by invading aliens; and the lighthearted superhero pastiche, *Ultra Super Deluxe Man*.

FUJILOG

2011. TV series. DIR: Shigeo Shichiji. SCR: Shigeo Shichiji. DES: Shigeo Shichiji. ANI: Shigeo Shichiji, Ryo Shibata. MUS: Yoshihiko Oshiro. PRD: Team Fujilog, Kadokawa, ROONETS, uzupiyo Graphics. 4 mins. x 13 eps. (TV1), 4 mins. x 13 eps. (TV2).

An EVERYDAY ANIME slice of life in Saitama Prefecture, where extended families still live together, and where unmarried, unemployed 33-year-old virgin Osamu Fujiyama tries to survive life with his mother and 90-something grandfather. SAZAE-SAN it isn't, but none the worse for that—a wry, funny shot of CGI-animated irreverence about life in Japan with the gloss and fantasy stripped away.

FUKUBIKI! TRIANGLE - MIHARU AFTER

2010. Video. DIR: Do Ichimotsu. SCR: PON. DES: Hikaru Kinohara. ANI: N/C. MUS: N/C. PRD: PoRO. 30 mins. x 2 eps.

Ushio and Miharu are a couple with a healthy sex life until Miharu has a bad fall on the way to school and is hospitalized. Ushio and her sister Futaba stay with her until she awakes, but she doesn't remember Ushio and has changed completely from the girl he knew. Futaba reveals that Miharu was a miserable, moody sort before she met Ushio and the accident has simply made her revert to type. Meanwhile, she obviously wants her sister's devoted boyfriend for herself. While Miharu suffers the after-effects of her accident, her boyfriend and sister get together, making the sex the least objectionable part of this anime based on Blue Gale porn game *Fukubiki! Triangle*. ⬤⬤

FUKU-CHAN

1982. JPN: *Fuku-chan: Yokoyama Ryuichi no Kessaku Anime*. AKA: *Fuku-chan: Ryuichi Yokoyama's Anime Masterpiece*. TV series. DIR: Mineo Fuji. SCR: Masaki Tsuji, Toshiyuki Kashiwakura, Noboru Shiroyama, Hiroko Naka. DES: Ryuichi Yokoyama. ANI: Michishiro Yamada. MUS: Hiroshi Tsutsui. PRD: Shinei, TV Asahi. 25 mins. x 71 eps.

Childish goings-on for Fukuo Fuchida (also known as Fuku-chan), a small boy who attends nursery school with his "girl-friend," Kumi, and hangs out with his playmates Namiko (whose parents own a china shop), her younger brother, Kiyo, naughty twins Doshako and Garako, and school bully Ganchan. Based on the manga character created by Ryuichi Yokoyama for the *Asahi Shinbun*, Fuku-chan first appeared in 1936 as a supporting cast member in Yokoyama's strip *Edokko Ken-chan* (*Ken the Edo Boy*). He had previously appeared in anime form in the lost WARTIME ANIME *Fuku-chan's Surprise Attack* (1941, *Fuku-chan no Kishu*), and the extant *Fuku-chan's Submarine* (1944, *Fuku-chan no Sensuikan*).

FUKUTOMI, HIROSHI

1950–. Born in Kochi, he studied animation at the Tokyo Design Academy before joining A Productions (now Shin'ei) and the company's subsidiary Animaru-ya. After early storyboarding duties, became a director on IKKYU and LITTLE GOBLIN.

FUKUYAMA THEATER: SUMMER SECRETS

1990. JPN: *Fukuyama Gekijo: Natsu no Himitsu*. Video. DIR: Michiyo Sakurai. SCR: Michiyo Sakurai. DES: Keiko Fukuyama. ANI: N/C. MUS: N/C. PRD: Urban Project. 60 mins.

Several short animated films based on the short stories and four-panel manga of Keiko Fukuyama, including *My Father the Mouse*, *The Rabbit Brothers*, *Summer Secret*, *The Mysterious Fairy*, *How Very Strange*, and *Kuro*.

FULL METAL PANIC *

2001. TV series. DIR: Koichi Chigira, Akihiro Nishiyama, Yasuhiro Takemoto. SCR: Koichi Chigira, Fumihiko Shimo, Yasuhiro Takemoto. DES: Osamu Horiuchi, Kanetake Ebikawa, Toshiaki Ihara, Koji Ito, Masayuki Takano. ANI: Osamu Horiuchi. MUS: Toshihiko Sahashi. PRD: Gonzo, Mithril. 23 mins. x 24 eps. (TV1), 24 mins. x 12 eps. (*Fumoffu*), 24 mins. x 13 eps. (*Second Raid*), 30 mins. (v).

In a world where the Cold War continues into the 21st century, Russian scientists are gathering "the Whispered"—people with unique and special powers. The international troubleshooting agency Mithril is employed to prevent such acquisitions, a task it usually performs with military-grade giant robots called Arm Slaves, but which occasionally involves undercover assignments. Hence the arrival of Mithril agent Sosuke Sagara at a Japanese high school, where he is charged with maintaining undercover surveillance and protection for Kaname Chidori, a beautiful and intelligent 16-year-old girl, from enemies of Mithril and, regrettably, high school panty thieves. Kaname has been born with Black Technology, an innate and latent knowledge that makes her capable of producing formidable weaponry.

Transported swiftly from a world like GASARAKI to a world like SUKEBAN DEKA, Sosuke is written off as a weapons-obsessed geek by many of the other students. He "befriends" Kaname, wreaking appalling havoc on anyone he thinks may threaten her—teachers, friends, classmates—but when she is kidnapped by the forces of evil, he shows more than just professional concern and risks everything to save her.

Despite a bunch of predictable stereotypes, *FMP* somehow manages to retain a sense of fun lacking from so many other anime—as if SPRIGGAN were not all about global conspiracies, but focused instead on what its hero did on his days off. The "romantic" lead has a dark past and is so tied up in his work that he takes a long while to realize the full range of his story functions. The villains are really nasty and the robots are simply stunning, ensuring *FMP* a place as one of the best offerings of its year.

Based on a series of novels by Shoji Gato, *FMP* was originally slated for release in the fall season of 2001, but kept off-air by the terrorist attacks of 9/11—which found nobody in the mood for a wacky tale of anti-terrorist high jinks. Similar issues delayed the American release of METROPOLIS and caused rethinks in content for several U.S. TV shows, including the first season of *24*. When it did finally reach Japanese networks in early 2002, it was successful enough to get a second series right away, animated by Kyoto Animation instead of Gonzo. Screened from January 2002, sequel *FMP: Fumoffu* is based on several spin-off stories from the original and has a more comedic and/or lecherous outlook. It concentrates solely on life at the school, while Sosuke continues to cause mayhem, and his commanding officer Testarossa decides to try high school life for a few weeks. A third series, *FMP: The Second*

Raid (2005), is based on the two *Owaru Day by Day* novels that followed and takes a much grimmer tone. This time a secret organization wants to eliminate Mithril and the teenagers have to stop them. This was followed by a one-shot video, which features Captain Teresa Testarossa attempting to remember the previous day's events, after an alcohol-induced blackout. There is also a spin-off manga by Shikidoji in *Dragon Comics Age*, released under the unwieldy title *Full Metal Panic! The Anime Mission (Resource Book Manga)*. ◑

FULL MOON

2002. JPN: *Full Moon o Sagashite*. AKA: *Searching for the Full Moon; Furumyu; Until the Full Moon*. TV series, TV special. DIR: Toshiyuki Kato, Bob Shirahata. SCR: Genki Yoshimura. Hiro Masaki, Mayu Sugiura, Mushi Hirohira, Rika Nakase, Ryu Tamura, Shizuma Aozora. DES: Yuka Kudo. ANI: Studio Deen. MUS: Yoshiaki Muto, Keita Shiina. PRD: NAS, Studio Deen. 25 mins. x 52 eps. (TV), 10 mins. (special).

Mitsuki Koyama is 12, in love with her childhood friend Eichi, and dreams of becoming a singer. Then she finds she has throat cancer—a malignant tumor that prevents her from singing above a whisper. Two strange beings show up and inform her that they are angels of death and she has one year to live. But Takuto and Meroko are moved by her passionate desire to become a famous singer before her time runs out and decide to help her. Disguising themselves as a bunny and a cat in the best tradition of magical girl shows, they enable her to transform into a 16-year-old idol singer so that she can try for stardom before her last year elapses.

This is by no means the first show in which a pretty girl comes with a time limit attached, nor the first in which an idol singer's desperation for attention gains a life or death element—consider LIMIT THE MIRACLE GIRL and KEY THE METAL IDOL. Nor is its gloomy premise unfamiliar on Japanese television, since every TV season sees at least one youthful protagonist staring death in the face, particularly in imitation of another combination of death and pop music, 1998's *Please God! Just a Little More Time* (*DE). This could have been another thoroughly depressing show, since it never tries to fudge the fact that its perky

heroine is going to die, but the bickering between hunky Takuto and besotted Meroko provide comic relief and Mitsuki's determination to make the most of what she has keeps the tone upbeat. The series is based on the manga by Arina Tanemura, creator of KAMIKAZE THIEF JEANNE, and spun off a "special" *Cute Cute Adventure* (2002), a gift to *Ribon* magazine readers. This comic snippet shows Takuto and Meroko getting left behind as Mitsuki rushes to a photo shoot and the obstacles they have to overcome to catch up with her.

FULLMETAL ALCHEMIST *

2003. JPN: *Hagane no Renkin Jutsushi; Hagaren*. TV series, movie, video. DIR: Seiji Mizushima. SCR: Seiji Mizushima, Sho Aikawa. DES: Yoshiyuki Ito, Shinji Aramaki, Junya Ishigaki. ANI: Koji Sugiura. MUS: Michiru Oshima. PRD: Aniplex, BONES, MBS, Square-Enix, Shochiku Film. 24 mins. x 51 eps. (TV), ca. 80 mins. (m1), 24 mins. x 64 eps. (TV, _Brotherhood_), 30 mins. x 4 eps. (v), 110 mins. (m2).

Alchemy is a process by which ordinary, non-living material can be transmuted into other forms. The Elric brothers, Edward and Alphonse, live with their mother in the quiet little town of Resembool while their father, famous alchemist Hohenheim Elric, is helping the military in a war. Edward, the older brother by a year, is a precocious alchemist, and when their mother falls ill and dies, he and Alphonse break every law to perform a forbidden ritual to resurrect her. The attempt goes horribly wrong, and Edward manages to save his soul by transferring it to a suit of armor—although it literally costs him an arm and a leg. The only way to return themselves to their former state and have a chance of bringing back their mother, is to find the alchemical MacGuffin, the Philosopher's Stone.

Three years later, the 15-year-old Edward is a bad-tempered alchemist working for the military. Alphonse is still trapped in his armor, and Edward has gained mechanical limbs, fitted by the grandmother of their childhood friend Winry Rockbell. Winry is a tomboy who has inherited her grandmother's mechanical and technical skills. Colonel Mustang, also known as the "Flame Alchemist" because of his skill with

fire magic, is their commanding officer. Most alchemists are in the army because the general public distrusts and fears them, even though their skills are needed to fight fearsome enemies. The brothers and their friends battle foes based on the seven deadly sins, using symbols from the works of real-life medieval alchemist Nicholas Flamel. In a surprise twist, they are reunited with their father but become embroiled in the rise of Nazism, and Edward himself is transported to a terrifying other world—our own.

Uniting the quest narrative of DORORO with the militarized European sorcery of HOWL'S MOVING CASTLE, *FMA* rode the wave of *Harry Potter*'s success to become one of the fan-favorite anime of the early 21st century. In a way, it takes the robotbuddy sci-fi of HEAT GUY J and simply places it into a magical world. Edward is like a magical girl whose transformation has gotten seriously out of hand; without the help of a guiding angel or animal, he's overreached himself and now has to try and retrieve normal life. Necromancy and forbidden powers are drawn into the context of galloping scientific progress in the 19th century in the style of FRANKENSTEIN; the age of steam was a time of dark and wonderful magic for those driving it, and this adaptation of Hiromu Arakawa's manga catches that atmosphere, before turning in its later chapters to chills that foreshadow MONSTER. The Japanese screening saw multiple promo tie-ins including many video games and a theme song by rock group L'Arc-en-Ciel.

The movie, *FMA: The Conqueror of Shambhala* (*HNR: Shanbara o iku mono*, 2005), is set in our world in 1923, with a powerless Edward living in Munich with Alphonse Heiderich, a doppelgänger of his missing brother. The pair are researching rocketry and trying to find a way to send Edward home when Edward encounters an old enemy who may offer a clue to the way back, but at a terrible price to both worlds.

This, however, might have presented a chronological end, but was far away from being the end of the franchise. An all-new team, directed by Yasuhiro Irie, would reboot the franchise as *Fullmetal Alchemist: Brotherhood* (2009), arguing, as with their colleagues on HELLSING, that this new version adhered more closely to the original manga. A second movie, *Fullmetal Alchemist: The Sacred Star of Milos* (2011, *FMA: Milos no Sei Naru Hoshi*) was interpolated within the continuity of the *Brotherhood* series. **Ⓥ**

FUMOON *

1980. TV special. DIR: Hisashi Sakaguchi. SCR: Hisashi Sakaguchi. DES: Hitoshi Nishimura, Hisashi Sakaguchi. ANI: Hitoshi Nishimura. MUS: Yuji Ono. PRD: Tezuka Pro, Nippon TV. 91 mins.

Nuclear-bomb tests near Horseshoe Island have mutated the locals, creating a new breed of psychic humans called the Fumoon. Dr. Yamadono reports on the new species at an international conference attended by representatives from the nuclear superpowers, Star and Uran (a thinly disguised U.S. and U.S.S.R.), but nobody listens to his dire warnings. Star and Uran go to war, while the Fumoons constitute a third front, attacking all humans while a cloud of dark gas closes in around Earth. By the end, as the Fumoons flee into space, the warring nations join forces to save the planet and discover that the dark gas is a benign phenomenon that turns into harmless oxygen—though who is to say that next time the human race will be so lucky? A cautionary tale from **ASTRO BOY**–creator Osamu Tezuka based on his 1951 manga *Next World*, itself inspired in equal parts by the Korean War and nuclear testing in the Pacific. As with other TV specials from Tezuka, many characters from his other stories appear in cameo roles. See also **METROPOLIS**, to which *Fumoon* is a distant sequel. The original manga was itself a sequel of sorts to Tezuka's **METROPOLIS**.

FUNNY PETS

2006. TV series. DIR: Ryuji Masuda. SCR: Ryuji Masuda. DES: N/C. ANI: Ryuji Masuda. MUS: Shizuo Karahashi. PRD: KBS Kyoto, Rentrak Japan, Rumble Fish, TV Kanagawa. 6 mins. x 12 eps.

Moody, bubble-brained showgirl Funny finds two aliens when their UFO crashes on Earth. Moon-shaped Crescent and sun-like Corona find it hard to adjust to life as the pets of a red-headed airhead. Each episode contains two self-contained three-minute stories modeled in bright, candy-colored 3D. Masuda created **MR. STAIN ON**

JUNK ALLEY and led the students of Kyoto University of Art art Design in making **CHARADY'S DAILY JOKE**, which also stars a kooky redhead with two strange pets.

FURUHASHI, KAZUHIRO

1960–. A prime figure at Studio Deen, Furuhashi studied at an animation college before finding work as a key animator on **URUSEI YATSURA**. Storyboarding and directing jobs soon followed on a wide range of work, including **RURONI KENSHIN**, **VIRGIN MARY IS WATCHING**, and **ZIPANG**. He was "series" director on **HUNTER X HUNTER**—a "show runner" in American terms.

FURUSE, NOBORU

1955–. Key animator and character designer on **URUSEI YATSURA**, **CONFUCIUS**, and many of the later **LUPIN III** TV specials.

FUSE: MEMOIRS OF A HUNTER GIRL *

2012. JPN: *Fuse Teppo Musume no Torimono-cho*. AKA: *Fuse Memoirs of a Rifle Girl*; *Fuse: Memoirs of a Huntress*. Movie. DIR: Masayuki Miyaji. SCR: Masayuki Miyaji, Ichiro Okochi. DES: Okama, Seiichi Hashimoto. ANI: N/C. MUS: Michiru Oshima. PRD: Tokyo Movie Shinsha. 110 mins.

Raised by her late grandfather in the mountains, Hamaji is summoned to Edo to stay with her brother Dosetsu, a down-at-the-heels drunk trying and failing to become a samurai in the dying days of the Tokugawa period. The shogun Iesada resorts to prayer in an attempt to hold back foreigners, but also offers rich rewards to anyone who can hunt down the eight half-dog "*fuse*" monsters who have been plaguing the city. With Hamaji's help, Dosetsu kills the seventh, unaware that the eighth is already known to his sister.

GOSICK creator Kazuki Sakuraba's original novel wore its influences on its sleeve, functioning as a retelling of, but also sequel to the 19th-century tale already adapted into anime as the **HAKKENDEN**. Masayuki Miyaji's anime adaptation dives directly into a deftly postmodern consideration of reality and fiction, readable at one level as a romance in which a hunter is captured by her prey, and at another as a wild, occasionally surreal retelling of the *Hakkenden* as imagined by Meido, a bespectacled character who is later revealed as the grand-daughter of the *Hak-*

kenden's author Kyokutei Bakin. But Bakin, too, appears in this story, and is even seen writing a scene we have just witnessed "for real." One-hundred-eighty-degree swings of camera-angles mirror similar reversals in plot and motivation as hunters become the game, bullies become the bullied, and low-ranking characters assert newfound authority over their superiors. The imagery is similarly multi-layered, drawing on a rich evocation of woodblock prints not seen since **THE SENSUALIST**, abundant with period detail and glimpses of life in the "floating world" culture of kabuki actors, potboiler novelists, pedlars, and geisha. But like the story itself, it often wheels into wild flights of obvious fancy, false colors, and unlikely anachronisms, as if this loving re-creation of Edo-period Japan is itself being imagined by the haphazard, over-eager rookie Meido. Nowhere is this deliberately slippery grasp on reality more obvious than in the film's depiction of the Yoshiwara pleasure quarter, which remarkably manages to present it not only as the "men's paradise" of Edo popular myth, but also as a dingy, melancholy red-light district ringed by a sewer, and *also* as an impossible fantasy realm, centered on a wondrous clock tower that spins to reveal the effigy of a naked female torso.

While it might at first seem odd that something so bawdy and cartoonish should be commissioned to mark the 90th anniversary of the literary magazine *Bungei Shunju*, *Fuse* beautifully captures and reconciles half a dozen radically different modes of Japanese storytelling, from documentary to fantasy, from "counterfeit" penny-dreadfuls to modern anime like the director's previous **XAM'D: LOST MEMORIES**. Multilayered mind-games are to be expected in a film in which a group of actors present a pseudo-kabuki retelling of the *Hakkenden*, attended by the author's grand-daughter who is herself writing a retelling of the same story, and comments during the action on the bold liberties taken with the plot. This is a world where the plot itself is part of recorded history, but followed by a moment in which everything we have seen is revealed to have been just set down on paper by Bakin himself. *Fuse* is a gleefully subversive text with abyssal depths beneath its seemingly shallow surface. See also **HAKKENDEN: EIGHT**

DOGS OF THE EAST, for yet another take on the same material. ◐

FUSHIGI YUGI: THE MYSTERIOUS PLAY *

1995. JPN: *Fushigi Yugi*. AKA: *Mysterious Game*. TV series/special, video. DIR: Hajime Kamegaki, Nanako Shimazaki, Akira Shigeno. SCR: Yoshio Urasawa, Kazuhisa Sakaguchi. DES: Hideyuki Motohashi. ANI: Hideyuki Motohashi, Hisatoshi Motoki, Mayumi Hiroda. MUS: Tatsumi Yano. PRD: Studio Pierrot, TV Tokyo. 25 mins. x 52 eps. (TV), 56 mins. x 2 eps. (TVm), 30 mins. x 3 eps. (v1), 45 mins. x 6 eps. (v2), 30 mins. x 4 eps. (*Eikoden*).

Fifteen-year-old Miaka accompanies her friend Yui to Tokyo's national library, where the girls find an ancient Chinese book called *The Universe of the Four Gods*. They are transported to the world of the book, though Yui is soon thrown back to Earth, leaving Miaka temporarily stranded. Miaka finds herself in a fantasy version of ancient China, where she is rescued from slavers by the handsome Tamahome and becomes a ward of the emperor. The land of Konan ("Southern Scarlet," as it is called) is threatened by invaders from Kotuo, and Miaka volunteers to be the long-awaited priestess of Suzaku ("Vermilion Sparrow"), who will assemble the legendary heroes known as the Seven Stars of Suzaku and save the world.

Though Yu Watase's original manga in *Flower* magazine dated back to 1992, *Fushigi Yugi* was swamped by the later success of the superior **ESCAFLOWNE**, making *FY* look like a lackluster copy. This anime's problems include an intensely irritating heroine, Miaka, with all the charm of a spoiled child, conspicuously cheap animation that often has to resort to static pans, and a forgettable plot assembled from off-the-peg clichés. The Emperor Hotohori falls in love with Miaka, but she loves Tamahome, a predictable love triangle which causes a falling-out with her friend Yui. Nevertheless, *FY* clearly struck a chord with an audience too young to remember *The Neverending Story* or **THE WIZARD OF OZ**, and the series gained an enthusiastic fan following in both Japan and the U.S. The second season (episodes 27–52) changes slightly, with the death of one of Miaka's guardians, the removal of some of the

risqué humor that occasionally lightened the first season, and an endless succession of arbitrary magical obstacles to stretch out Miaka's journey.

Two TV specials were little more than clip shows of the highlights of the first 33 episodes, but a true sequel soon continued the series on video. The first video series was set a month after the close of the TV version, with the events in Konan returning to haunt the cast back on Earth in both serious and parody versions on the same tapes. Looking suspiciously like a third TV season consigned to video after falling ratings, 1997's second "video" series plunged the cast into a new conflict over the mystic Jewel of Memory. A later Yu Watase work, **CERES: CELESTIAL LEGEND**, soon followed in both Japan and the U.S.

A four-part video sequel, *FY: Universe of the Four Gods* (*FY: Eikoden*, 2001), was directed by Nanako Shimazaki, which threatens the happily-ever-after of the original by introducing a love-rival for Miaka, who enters the fantasy world determined to overthrow her and win her man for herself.

FUTURE BOY CONAN

1978. JPN: *Mirai Shonen Conan*. AKA: *Conan the Boy in Future*. TV series, movie. DIR: Hayao Miyazaki, Isao Takahata, Keiji Hayakawa. SCR: Takaaki Nakano, Soji Yoshikawa. DES: Hayao Miyazaki, Yasuo Otsuka. ANI: Yoshiaki Kawajiri, Hideo Kawauchi. MUS: Kenichiro Ikehama. PRD: Nippon Animation, NHK. 25mins. x 26 eps. (TV1), 123 mins. (m), 30 mins. x 24 eps. (TV2).

Twenty years after a devastating nuclear war in 2008, only scattered communities of humans are left living on the small islands that were once mountaintops. Conan grows up on his island with his grandfather, believing themselves to be the last survivors of their race until a young girl, Lana, is washed up on their shore. She is a refugee from the evil military kingdom of Industria, which is trying to revive the use of dangerous energy sources. A first-time directing job for Hayao Miyazaki that incorporated elements he would later reuse in his **NAUSICAÄ** and **CASTLE IN THE SKY** (though the original genesis of *FBC* lay in the novel *The Incredible Tide* (1970), by Alexander Key). The series was also edited into *FBC: The Movie*, which was released

three months before **CASTLE OF CAGLIOSTRO** and, hence, could be argued on a technicality to be Miyazaki's first "movie."

The franchise was revived as *FBC 2: Taiga Adventure* (1999), directed by Miyazaki's former assistant Keiji Hayakawa, though its relationship to the original is extremely tenuous. The eponymous Taiga and his archeologist father, Professor Dyno, are searching for ancient artifacts in South America, where there was supposedly a mysterious culture that could build great metallic birds 20 thousand years before. As he fights with treasure hunters for control of the ancient power-stones, Taiga discovers that the ancient O-Parts devices can power land, sea, and air machines that are each designed to look like a giant animal. In other words, it's a rehash of **BABEL II** and **MYSTERIOUS CITIES OF GOLD** with a name designed to promise more than it actually delivers.

FUTURE CARD BUDDYFIGHT *

2014. TV series. DIR: Shigetaka Ikeda. SCR: Masanao Akahoshi. DES: Kazumi Ono. ANI: Kazumi Ono. MUS: Hiroaki Hayama, Kazushi Miyakoda. PRD: OLM, Xebec, TV Tokyo. 24 mins. x 32 eps.

In the year 2030, humans are able to pair up with monsters from other worlds and participate in "buddy fights." Earth boy Gao Mikado befriends Drum Bunker Dragon, and then attempts to get on with a rather humdrum teenage existence, as if everyone were able to bring their **POKÉMON** and/or magical familiars to school.

As you might have guessed, this oxymoronically named show, rather desperately shoehorning the word "buddy" into "fight" as some sort of sop to the PTA, began as a collectible card game from the Bushiroad company. What makes it interesting is not the entirely derivative setting or plot, but the fact that its owners have largely bypassed television networks, distributing it in the English language straight to YouTube and similar platforms. Is this a sign that the cool kids can't be bothered to watch television any more, or that television has better things to do than screen long-running exercises in **ADVERTISING AND PROMOTION**? The authors suspect a little of both, and that toy companies simply don't need television channels quite as much as they used to. Although *Future Card Buddy-*

fight looks like business as usual on the surface, its means of distribution might make it one of a whole new generation of innovators.

FUTURE COP URASHIMAN

1983. JPN: *Mirai Keisatsu Urashiman*. AKA: *Rock'n Cop*. TV series. DIR: Koichi Mashimo, Shinya Sadamitsu, Takaaki Ishiyama. SCR: Hirohisa Soda, Haruya Yamazaki, Kenji Terada. DES: Takashi Nakamura, Shigeru Kato, Chuichi Iguchi. ANI: Takashi Nakamura, Kunihiko Yuyama. MUS: Shinsuke Kazato. PRD: Tatsunoko Pro. 25 mins. x 50 eps.

An SF adaptation of *Urashima Taro* (see **JAPANESE FOLK TALES**) about Ryo Urashima, a young private investigator from 1983 Tokyo who is whisked to the year 2050 by Professor Q, a mad scientist working for the evil, blue-skinned Führer. The trip into the future subjects Ryo to the "Urashima Effect"—he loses his memory and develops superhuman powers. Führer plans to use Ryo for his own ends, but Ryo is found by the police, who enlist him in their robot police unit, Magnapolice 88, along with a handsome wiseguy, Claude Mizusawa, and token girl Sophia Nina Rose. A witty sci-fi spectacle, it begins with comedy business (as Ryo insists on using his 1983 Volkswagen Beetle instead of a 2050 police car) that soon takes a more serious turn as Ryu tracks down Führer's Necrime group and becomes involved in the power struggle between Führer and his assistant, Adolph von Ludovich. Released in several language territories abroad, it was picked up by Saban Entertainment as *Rock'n Cop*, although the mooted English-language version seems to have been canceled before release.

FUTURE DIARY, THE ∗

2010. JPN: *Mirai Nikki*. Video, TV series. DIR: Naoto Hosoda. SCR: Katsuhiko Takayama, Rie Koshika, Shoichi Sato. DES: Hidetsugu Hirayama, Toshiyuki Tokuda. ANI: Tomoka Kojima, Hidetsugu Hirayama, Maiko Okada. MUS: Tatsuya Kato. PRD: asread, Dwango, Kadokawa, Lantis, Klockworx, chara-ani. com, MOVIC. 9 mins. (v), 24 mins. x 26 eps. (TV).

Imaginary friends can be dangerous. Yuki is a loner who spends most of his time writing a cellphone diary, or talking to his imaginary friends Deus Ex Machina, Lord of Time and Space, and his servant Murmur. Then Deus actually gives Yuki a gift—a diary with entries for the next 90 days. To Yuki's surprise, all these entries come true. Then he learns that he is one of 12 friends of Deus, and each of the others also has a diary—shades here of the twists of fate of **DEATH NOTE**. Deus is setting them up to kill each other so that only one is left. If they don't do this before Day 90, the Apocalypse will take the world apart. If they do, the world survives and the winner becomes the next Lord of Time and Space. At first he's reluctant: but then his parents are murdered. If he wins, he can bring them back. He must become the thing he hates to save those he loves.

Sakae Esuno's 2006 manga has spun off three further manga, a "visual novel" game and an 11-episode live-action TV drama as well as the anime. The reason: a plot packed with twists, tensions, and mistrust where little is as it seems. The design and color palette support the premise well, with interesting lighting and tonal shifts to add atmosphere and attractive characters with a kooky edge that can warp into something quite terrifying. A "pilot episode" was bundled with a limited-edition manga volume a full year before the anime aired in December 2011. **NV**

FUTURE WAR 198X ∗

1982. Movie. DIR: Toshio Masuda, Tomohiro Katsumata. SCR: Yuji Takada. DES: Masami Suda. ANI: Masami Suda. MUS: Seiji Yokoyama. PRD: Tokyu Agency, Toei. 125 mins.

American scientist Bart, a specialist in Star Wars orbital antimissile lasers, defects on a Russian submarine, which is sunk by the U.S. Navy. His best friend, Mikumo, is ordered to come out of mourning to finish Bart's work, while U.S. president Gibson tries to calm the volatile diplomatic situation. His efforts fail, and border troubles between East and West Germany escalate into full-scale war. When American Secretary of Defense Bugarlin murders Chief Secretary Orlof of the Soviet Union, all negotiations break down, and atomic war breaks out.

A controversial anime production inspired in part by the best-selling *The Third World War, August 1985* by General Sir John Hackett, *FW198X* was based on actual projections from contemporary government reports and statistics. During production, there were protests about the "aggressive content" of the story, creating something of a media stir in Japan. *Future War 198X* was released on video in Australia, not in a "full" dub but in an original language version with explicatory English narration.

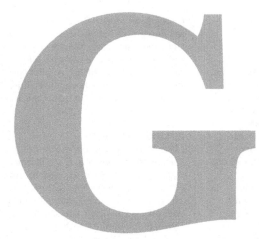

G-9

2006. AKA: *G-Nine*. Video. DIR: Keita Amemi-ya. SCR: Keita Amemiya. DES: Keita Amemiya. ANI: Keita Amemiya. MUS: DUSTZ. PRD: Toei Animation, Gentosha. 17 mins. x 1 ep.

Monstermeister Amemiya is renowned for his work in fantasy movies such as *Moon Over Tao: Makaraga* and **IRIA**. Here he's making his own story into a limited animation for Toei's *ga-nime* series (**ARGOT AND JARGON**). The story is pure Amemiya—a young girl waking alone in a strange city. She is a great mage, but to fight the evil creature threatening the world, she must manipulate the links between reality and memory and achieve self-knowledge. It's set to music by trilingual actor Rei Fujita's band DUSTZ.

G-ON RIDERS

2002. TV series, video. DIR: Shinichiro Kimura. SCR: N/C. DES: Katsuzo Hirata, Yasumasa Moriki. ANI: Hideo Okazaki. MUS: Norimasa Yamanaka. PRD: Katsuzo, TNK, WOWOW. 23 mins. x 13 eps. (TV), 23 mins. (v).

Brilliant Japanese scientist Mio Sanada develops a superweapon called G-On to defend Earth from attacking aliens—who eventually turn out to be cute, klutzy girls working as subcontractors to the real baddies. The weapon reacts to the energy of adolescent girls' minds, as long as they wear special glasses to enable the G-On to adapt their energies. The school of Saint Hoshikawa's is set up as a front to recruit "sensitive and beautiful girls" from all over Japan to help in the defense effort. Yuki Kurama becomes the latest chosen one and prepares to defend her homeworld

with the aid of fellow girls Sarah and Yayoi. A bonus 14th episode appeared on the DVD. The titles give the year as Showa 119—in other words, A.D. 2044.

G-SPOT EXPRESS *

2005. JPN: *Akugi: Itazura The Animation*. AKA: *Tease Tease*. Video. DIR: Katsuma Kanaza-wa. SCR: Katsuma Kanazawa. DES: Hiroya Iijima. ANI: Hiroya Iijima. MUS: N/C. PRD: ARMS, MUSE, Studio9MAiami. 26 mins. x 2 eps.

Katsuhiko gropes women on trains. He's so good at it that, even though they may not want his attentions, they soon melt under his skillful fingers. When an older pervert, Gin, sets him a challenge to grope a sexy TV anchorwoman, Katsuhiko is tempted—but will he also be cheated? This porn anime is based on a long-running PC game series by Interheart. This DVD is one of a list of titles banned in Canada, along with **COOL DEVICES**, **WORDS WORTH** and others. ⓛⓝ

G-TASTE *

1999. Video. DIR: Shunsuke Harada. SCR: Yoshiki Imamura. DES: Masaki Yamada. ANI: Masaki Yamada. MUS: N/C. PRD: Beam Entertainment, Mybic, AIC. 30 mins. x 7 eps.

A fun-filled day in the life of alleged real-life office lady Moe, from the moment she wakes up from a cozy dream about having sex, through her train-journey fantasies about having sex, to her office activities, which involve a lot of sex. Based on an erotic manga by Hiroki Yagami, who also created *Dear Boys* (see **HOOP DAYS**). Successive episodes detailed the erotic inner lives of a different large-breasted girl per

episode, including Nana the maid, Mai the manageress, Sayuka the schoolteacher, and Misuzu the over-proportioned swimming star. Only five of the seven Japanese episodes were released in America, depriving the U.S. public of whatever delights awaited in the stories of nurse Asuka and newscaster Yuna. ⓛⓝⓥ

G.A.: ART DESIGN CLASS *

2009. JPN: *GA: Geijutsuka Art Design Class*. TV series. DIR: Hiroaki Sakurai. SCR: Toko Machida. DES: Atsuko Watanabe, Reiji Kasuga. ANI: Atsuko Watanabe, Ryoko Nakano, Hideki Furukawa. MUS: Jun Abe, Seiji Muto. PRD: AIC PLUS. 24 mins. x 12 eps.

Five girls in their first year at high school take an art and design class. They learn about art, life, and each other in a series of cute vignettes. Although the characters look and sound much more childlike than most 13-year-old schoolgirls, the show is not just about presenting cute character icons and silly gags. It's more focused on the topic than **HIDAMARI SKETCH** or **SKETCHBOOK: FULL COLOR**. To call it educational is stretching things, but it has aspirations in that direction. Fans of creator Satoku Kidoyuki's four-panel manga strip will enjoy spotting homages to characters from her earlier work, and may also note that *G.A.* doesn't follow the classic formula of introduction/conflict/resolution/realization common to many of these strips. It often skips conflict, in the interests of making the world a fluffier place through art.

GA-REI ZERO *

2007. TV series. DIR: Ei Aoki. SCR: Katsuhiko

Takayama. DES: Osamu Horiuchi, Shinichi Kurita, Yoshimi Umino. ANI: Shinichi Kurita, Osamu Horiuchi. MUS: Noriyasu Agematsu. PRD: AIC Spirits, asread, Kadokawa, Lantis, Klockworx. 24 mins. x 12 eps.

Governments take the paranormal seriously, even if they don't admit it. Sometimes they even have interdepartmental conflicts over it. Japan's elite Ministry of Defense team is the Paranormal Disaster Countermeasure Headquarters, or PCDH. When they have a mission failure, the Ministry of Environment's Supernatural Disaster Countermeasure Division steps in to clean up the mess. But most Government spooks are nameless, faceless men in black who wouldn't hesitate to gun down their grannies for the greater good. The talents required for this kind of work tend to show up in a different type of person. Yomi and Kagura are two of the SDCD's top operatives—teenage girls who are as close as any blood-sisters, and both terrifyingly talented at the bloody, deadly work of slaying monsters. But what happens if the monster to be slain is someone the slayer loves?

Ga-Rei Zero hasn't often been compared with CLANNAD, but they have much in common. Both are perfect of their kind, and both are precisely calculated manipulations of audience expectation that deliver on their promises so magnificently it's chilling. Hajime Segawa's 2005 manga ran until January 2010. The anime is supposedly a prequel to it and begins with a two-episode flash-forward in which Yomi and Kagura are at each other's throats. Hence, the bulk of the narrative, telling the story of their friendship and cooperation, builds to a disaster that the audience already knows is coming, although its resolution is saved for the finale.

Ga-Rei Zero is all about violence: the violence of combat, the slice of blade or bullet through flesh, the impact of fists and feet; but it's also about the other kind of violence, the pure sadism of building relationships and plucking heartstrings with the clear intent of tearing them apart. As transparently honest in its approach as Quentin Tarantino, and just as capable of the cheap tricks you didn't think he'd risk, Aoki (purveyor of candy on GIRLS BRAVO) uses imagery, music, and pace to signal the tension to come—a high-risk strategy

that works only because he and his crew deliver on it so well. It's not subtle, but it is beautiful in many ways, all of them nasty. The horror and pity of love in a world of violence has rarely been so well imagined. 🅥

GAD GUARD *

2003. TV series. DIR: Hiroshi Nishikiori, Yoshikazu Miyao, Akihiko Nishiyama, Hideki Hashimoto, Yuichiro Miyake, Yutaka Hirata. SCR: Mayori Sekijima, Reiko Yoshida, Sadayuki Murai. DES: Masahiro Aizawa, Yoshitsune Izuna. ANI: Masahiro Aizawa. MUS: Kazuhiro Sawaguchi, Kohei Tanaka. PRD: Gonzo, Animax, Fuji TV. 25 mins. x 26 eps.

In the not-too-distant future, power shortages and energy crises force humanity to take drastic measures. Hajiki Sanada grows up on a planet divided into class-oriented enclaves or "units," where all power is shut off in his town at a regular midnight curfew. While working part-time as a delivery boy for a courier service, he touches the contents of the package he is supposed to be ferrying around and finds himself bonding with a robot made out of a special material. This "GAD-made" robot can reconstitute matter for him, making it a combination of the magical cat of DORAEMON and the fighting toys of POKÉMON.

Despite such derivative beginnings, *Gad Guard* has an undeniable style, informed more by the noirish look of recent fan favorites, with stark allegories of class struggle in the contrast between the poor Night Town and the privileged Gold Town. It also struggles to hang onto its PG rating, thanks to vampish female characters at odds with the squat, cartoony character designs inspired by late Tezuka productions.

Its hustlers, street kids, and lowlifes are distinctly occidental—*Gad Guard* is another anime hymn to life in the exotic, inscrutable West, where people have different hair colors, big noses, and, so the animators believe, more adventurous lives.

In this age of painfully cheap productions, Gonzo Digimation clearly had a little more money than usual from Fuji TV for this one. They pull out all the available stops to keep the show interesting, with impressive CG flashiness used on marble floors, lighting effects, and saturated colors. The crew also works harder than average, with nice little touches like a cat

disturbing birds in the background, or the detailed clutter of the Sanada family kitchen. The music is a self-consciously jazzy respray of COWBOY BEBOP, courtesy of GUNBUSTER-composer Kohei Tanaka. The plot is BRAIN POWERED wearing a retro cloak, via THE BIG O and a touch of *Dark City*. In other words, it's a shameless collection of well-worn clichés, but creatively assembled and entertainingly presented. However, the initial run of 19 episodes on Fuji TV was bulked out with seven extras to complete the full run on AT-X; a piecemeal form of assembly that often results in episodes that merely seem to be marking time.

GAG MANGA WEATHER

2005. JPN: *Masuda Kosuke Theater Gag Manga Biyori*. AKA: *Gag Manga Days*. TV series. DIR: Akitaro Daichi. SCR: N/C. DES: N/C. ANI: Masayoshi Tanaka. MUS: Harukichi Yamamoto. PRD: Artland, Dax Production, Studio DEEN, Bandai Visual, Kids Station, Sky Perfect Well Think. 5 mins. x 12 eps. (TV1), 5 mins. x 12 eps. (TV2), 5 mins. x 12 eps. (TV3), 5 mins. x 26 eps. (TV4).

A surreal series using a mix of live film, still images and 2D animation with parody, gags, Japanese culture both ancient and modern, and urban myths. Creator Masuda's original gag manga is renowned for its bizarre plot set-ups and crazily twisted humor, also specialities of director Daichi. This is probably why he stayed with the show through four series of this *Monty Python*-esque weirdness, in 2005, 2006, 2008, and 2010.

GAIKING *

1976. JPN: *Ozora Maryu Gaiking*. AKA: *Great Sky Dragon Gaiking; Daiking; The Protectors*. TV series. DIR: Tomoharu Katsumata, Takeshi Shirato, Masamune Ochiai, Hideo Takayashiki. SCR: Kunio Nakatani, Masao Murayama, Masaru Yamamoto, Soji Yoshikawa. DES: Takeshi Shirato, Akio Sugino, Dan Kobayashi. ANI: Takeshi Shirato, Moriyasu Taniguchi, Akio Sugino. MUS: Shunsuke Kikuchi. PRD: Toei, Fuji TV. 25 mins. x 44 eps. (TV1), 25 mins. x 39 eps. (TV2).

Sanshiro Tsuwabuki's dream of becoming a professional baseball player is crushed by an invasion of mysterious bird-men, the Dark Horror Army, sent by Prince Darius of Planet Zera (Zala) to kill any psychics who could be obstacles to their plans of world conquest. Zera needs Earth because Zera is just about to be engulfed by a black hole. In Toei Animation's first robot animation not to be based on a manga, Sanshiro is invited by Dr. Daimonji (Professor Hightech) to join the Great Sky Magic Dragon (Gaiking Space Dragon) combat force to fight back, and he duly does so. Shown as part of the FORCE FIVE series on U.S. television, for which Sanshiro's name was changed to Ares Astronopolis, which the producers must have deemed nicely inconspicuous. A sequel was broadcast in 2005 on TV Asahi, directed by Masahiro Hosoda.

GAINAX

Formed originally in 1982 as Daicon ("Radish") Films by a group of student fans intending to make an opening animation sequence for the Daicon III science fiction convention. Founder members included Hideaki Anno, Yoshiyuki Sadamoto, Takami Akai, and Shinji Higuchi. Subsequently renamed Gainax (from *gaina*, a local dialect word for "huge") during preproduction on WINGS OF HONNEAMISE. Representative works include THE SECRET OF BLUE WATER, GUNBUSTER, EVANGELION, and MAHOROMATIC, but also numerous landmark games in the history of Japanese computing, particularly *Princess Maker*.

GAKKATSU!

2012. TV series. DIR: Rareko. SCR: Rareko, Kota Fukihara. DES: N/C. ANI: N/C. MUS: Rareko. PRD: Fanworks, NHK. 5 mins. x 12 eps. (TV1), 5 mins. x 12 eps. (TV2).
This surreal "debate comedy" set in a high school with a feisty, outspoken student body is another short creation by the director of CHI-SUI MARU. NHK liked it enough to commission a second series in 2013. The production company Fanworks started out in online anime, on Livedoor's *Net Anime* area. It first came to international attention through a Flash anime series about an Osaka teashop, *From Osaka With Cheer*, commissioned by the Osaka Convention and Visitors Bureau in 2007—their website proudly proclaims their commitment to local enterprise.

GAKUEN HEAVEN *

2006. JPN: Gakuen Heaven. AKA: Boys' Love

Scramble. TV series. DIR: Yukina Hiiro. SCR: Natsuko Takahashi, Daisuke Watanabe, Yoshifumi Fukushima, Yukina Hiiro. DES: Yumi Nakayama. ANI: Akiko Kawashima, Hisami Teshima, Junko Abe. MUS: Kazuya Nishioka. PRD: Tokyo Kids. 25 mins. x 13 eps.
Keita is just an average high school boy from an ordinary family, so he's amazed when he is given a place at the exclusive Bell Liberty Academy. He believes that he has nothing in common with these handsome, high-achieving, well-connected rich boys, but is inexplicably inundated with attention from his classmates. What he doesn't know is that a childhood friend has engineered the invitation for a very special reason. Plenty of innuendo, but no explicit action in this sweet, slow-paced boys'-love show based on Yo Higuri's 2004 manga. Compare with the massively more successful OURAN HIGH SCHOOL HOST CLUB, where a girl is put into a similar situation, and the much more realistic depiction of nice guys at high school in YOU AND ME. Listen out for Jun Fukuyama, voice of Lelouche Lamperouge in CODE GEASS, using a completely different vocal range: impressively flexible.

GALACTIC PIRATES *

1989. JPN: Teki wa Kaizoku: Neko no Kyoen. AKA: The Enemy Is the Pirate: Banquet of Cats. TV series. DIR: Shinya Sadamitsu, Kazuo Yamazaki. SCR: Akinori Endo. DES: Takayuki Goto. ANI: Takayuki Goto, Hiroshi Hamazaki. MUS: Air Pavilion. PRD: Madhouse, Kitty Films, Mitaka Studio, NHK2. 30 mins. x 6 eps.
Apollo the jive-talking cat and his human sidekick, Latell, are working in the Anti-Pirate Division of the police force sent to Mars to put a stop to the activities of the space raider Yomei. The officers are intent on convincing each other to resign but eventually manage to solve a case involving piracy, double-cross, people turning into cats all around them, and an interlude in which they discover that the Martians have built up a militaristic religion that practices ritual games of hyperviolent baseball. Based on a comedy SF novel by YUKIKAZE–creator Chohei Kanbayashi, this is one of the earliest video serials to be given a satellite TV broadcast to recoup costs, a practice that would become commonplace in the late 1990s. "Air Pavilion," who provides

the soundtrack, is a supergroup comprising former members of Whitesnake, Iron Maiden, and Motorhead.

GALAXY ADVENTURES OF SPACE OZ *

1992. JPN: Space Oz no Boken. TV series. DIR: Soji Yoshikawa, Yoshiaki Okumura, Katsumata Kanezawa, Shinichi Suzuki. SCR: Soji Yoshikawa, Yasuko Hoshikawa, Seiji Matsuoka, Hirokazu Mizude. DES: Yoshiaki Okumura. ANI: Ichiro Hattori, Osamu Kamijo, Seiji Kikuchi. MUS: Ryuichi Katsumasa. PRD: E&G, Enoki, TV Tokyo. 25 mins. x 26 eps.
Eight-year-old blonde Dorothy Gale and her genetically enhanced dog, Talk-Talk, are swept off planet New Kansas and land in the distant galaxy of Oz. There, she joins forces with Dr. Oz, Mosey (a boy companion), Chopper (the Tin Man as a C-3PO rip-off), Lionman (the Cowardly Lion posing as Rambo), and Plantman (the Scarecrow) in order to defeat the evil witch Gloomhilda. This involves a race to obtain the three magic crystals of Love, Wisdom, and Courage, before Gloomhilda's minions Bungle, Skumm, and Sludge. A rehash of THE WIZARD OF OZ that ends with the acquisition of the Rainbow Crystal, allowing Dorothy to return home (there being no place like it). Released in the U.S. as *The Wonderful Galaxy of Oz*.

GALAXY ANGEL *

2001. TV series. DIR: Morio Asaka, Ryo Mizuno. SCR: N/C. DES: Kanan, Kikaku Design Kobo Sensen. ANI: Kunihiko Hamada, Masaru Kitao. MUS: Hikaru Nanase. PRD: Madhouse, Animax. 12 mins. x 26 eps. (TV1), 12 mins. x 19 eps. (TV2), 12 mins. x 54 eps. (TV3), 12 mins. x 26 eps. (TV4), 24 mins. x 13 eps. (TV5).
A century after the fall of the Galactic Network, the Transvaal Empire has risen on the ruins. However, the "lost technology" of the GN, looked after by priestesses called Moon Maidens, appears semimagical to the people of the Transvaal. Exiled prince Eonia kills King Gerrare and seizes control of the empire, but he is opposed by five pretty girls, the Angel Troopers, who steal a spaceship and team up with the young commander of the local militia. A sequel series, *Galaxy Angel Z* (2002), aired in nine half-hour slots, although each slot was split into two episodes. It was followed by *Galaxy Angel AA* (2002), *Galaxy*

Angel X (2004), and *Galaxy Angel Rune* (2006). *Galaxy Angel* was one of the first shows to achieve an unexpected online presence—its short episode length, sci-fi leanings, extremely limited animation, and cute female cast conspiring to make it an ideal commodity in Japan in the early days of Internet file-sharing and encouraging disproportionately wide merchandising tie-ins.

GALAXY EXPRESS 999 *

1978. JPN: *Ginga Tetsudo 999.* TV series, movie. DIR: Nobutaka Nishizawa, Masayuki Akehi, Kunihiko Yuyama. SCR: Hiroshi Yamaura, Keisuke Fujikawa, Yoshiaki Yoshida. DES: Leiji Matsumoto. ANI: Kazuo Matsubara. MUS: Nozomu Aoki, Godiego. PRD: Toei, Fuji TV. 25 mins. x 113 eps. (TV), 114 mins. (TVm1), 129 mins. (m1), 17 mins. (m2), 60 mins. (TVm2), 130 mins. (m3), 114 mins. (TVm3), 54 mins. (m4), 25 mins. x 6 eps. (Internet), 40 mins. x 4 eps. (*Maetel Legend*), 25 mins. x 26 eps. (*Railways*), 25 mins. x 26 eps. (*Crossroads*).

After his mother is killed by the evil count Kikai (Count Mecca), Tetsuro Hoshino (Joey) resolves to get an immortal metal body. Impossibly expensive on Earth, they are reputedly given away free to anyone who reaches Megalopolis, the last stop on the Galaxy Express. A ticket on the GE is also impossibly expensive, but the ethereal beauty Maetel (who looks uncannily like his mother) offers him one for free. She helps him to board the Galaxy Express 999 on the understanding that he must accompany her on her travels. In a long-running series based on Leiji Matsumoto's 1977 manga (distantly and occasionally related to the same author's CAPTAIN HARLOCK series continuity), after killing the Count to avenge his mother, Tetsuro sets off with Maetel on a journey across the galaxy. After the movie edition, *Galaxy Express* (1979), the second movie was the super-short featurette *GE999: Through a Glass Clearly* (1980, *Gurasu no Clear*), a partial remake of the third TV episode. A third movie, *GE999: Last Stop Andromeda* (1981, *Andromeda no Shuchakueki*), is set two years after the series, when Tetsuro, now a freedom fighter on Earth, receives a distress call from Maetel and heads out to help her one last time. Fuji TV also broadcast three specials, beginning with *GE999:*

Can You Live Like a Warrior (1979, *Senshi no Yo ni Ikirareru ka*), which combined scenes from episodes 12 and 13. *GE999: Emeraldas the Eternal Wanderer* (1980, *Endo no Tabibito Emeraldas*) expanded episode 22, which featured Maetel's sister, QUEEN EMERALDAS. The final TV movie, *GE999: Can You Love Like a Mother* (1980, *Kimi wa Haha no Yo ni Aiseru ka*), adapted parts of episodes 51 and 52, adding 47 minutes of all-new footage. The series received a very limited partial broadcast on local New York TV for the Japanese community with English subtitles. The first movie was released in the U.S. by Roger Corman's New World, which incurred the wrath of fans by renaming Harlock "Warlock" and giving him a John Wayne accent for his cameo appearance. He would also claim that Joey was searching the universe for revenge, that being a little easier to take than an upgraded cybernetic body, at least back then. Maetel would return for the video series *Maetel the Legend* (2000). The series would be remade to mark the 50th anniversary of Matsumoto's career as *The Galaxy Railways* (2003). Notes to this rerelease emphasized Matsumoto's original inspiration, that when he came up to Tokyo as a young man, the railway network seemed to be the only part of postwar Japan that was still functioning, and hence the only symbol of hope for survival and renewal. See, however, NIGHT ON THE GALACTIC RAILROAD, which draws on a much older source for spacefaring expresses.

Shinichi Masaki's *Space Symphonic Poem Maetel* (*GE: Wasurareta Toki no Wakusei*, i.e., *The Planet That Time Forgot*, 2004), is a sequel to the *Maetel Legend* series, issued as a TV series on the Japanese digital channels SKY PerfecTV and Animax, all of which would serve as a new home for the franchise in the 21st century with yet another series, *GE: Crossroads to Eternity* (2006, *Eien no Bunkiten*).

GALAXY FRAULEIN YUNA *

1995. JPN: *Ginga Ojosama Densetsu Yuna.* Video. DIR: Yorifusa Yamaguchi, Akiyuki Shinbo. SCR: Satoru Akahori, Masashi Kubota, Fumio Uetaki. DES: Katsumi Shimazaki, Mika Akitaka, Makoto Yamada. ANI: Ryoichi Oki. MUS: Takanori Arisawa. PRD: Animate Film, JC Staff. 30 mins. x 2 eps. (v1), 30 mins. x 2 eps. (v2).

A beauty contest is staged in present-day Tokyo with ulterior motives—as with BATTLE ATHLETES, it is really a front for choosing a champion to save the world. Yuna, the blond winner, is informed that, long ago, the Queen of Light fought the Queen of Darkness and lost the battle. All the remaining goodness of Light was concentrated in one of the android survivors, Elna, whose duty it was to carry the Light forward for the next battle. As Elna's successor, Yuna has three android doubles for use on land, sea, and air, as well as a supertransformation ability that allows them to turn into the mighty El-Line robot.

Based on a 1992 game for the PC Engine, the combination of giant war machines and cloyingly cute girls was resurrected for *GFY: Fairy of Darkness* (*Ginga Ojosama Densetsu Yuna: Shinkai no Fairy*; 1996, released in the U.S. as *GFY Returns*), in which the evil Princess Mirage spreads false rumors that Yuna is fighting on the wrong side, sending the mysterious Fraulein D to ravage a few cities in Yuna's name just to make sure that GP Officer Misaki will find lots of incriminating evidence. Yuna and her orally fixated friend Yuri must then fight off "D" and several of Mirage's minions. Yuna turns one of the three evil Apparition Sisters to the side of good by introducing her to the joys of shopping, and then the stage is set for a final, noisy showdown. Sold to the Japanese as "the last word in girls' anime," though thankfully that was a complete lie.

GALAXY SEARCH 2100

1986. JPN: *Ginga Tanken 2100: Border Planet.* TV special. DIR: Osamu Uemura, Mamoru Hamatsu. SCR: Osamu Tezuka. DES: Shinpei Ohara. ANI: Shinya Takahashi, Nobuhiro Okaseko. MUS: Ryotaro Haneda. PRD: Tezuka Pro, NTV. 79 mins.

A doomed romance from ASTRO BOY–creator Osamu Tezuka about sworn friends Subaru and Procyon almost falling out over their love for the pretty Mira. Eventually, Subaru steps aside, but Procyon contracts a deadly space disease soon after his wedding. Subaru discovers that the widow, whom he still loves, has contracted the disease that killed her husband. Subaru sets off across the galaxy in search of a cure, while Mira remains back on Earth in suspended animation. His quest takes him to a world of automated agricultural machinery, where humans are being turned into planet fertilizer. The next world he finds is ruled by "the Boss," who maroons travelers so he can salvage their spaceships. With the help of local girl Michelle, Subaru organizes a revolt and builds an escape vessel from salvaged parts. Further adventures follow on a planet of humanoids that go through a chrysalis stage, but Subaru finally returns with a cure for Mira. She is restored to life, but, though she is still young, Subaru's journey has aged him 50 years. Mira falls in love with the doctor who woke her, who is the spitting image of his father, Subaru. The aged Subaru comments to his wife, Michelle, that they make a lovely couple. A bittersweet romance from Tezuka—compare to the similar BANDAR BOOK: ONE MILLION A.D.

GALERIANS: RION *

2004. Video. DIR: Masahiko Maesawa. SCR: Kang Chinfa. DES: Sho-U Tajima. ANI: N/C. MUS: Masahiko Hagio. PRD: Enterbrain Inc., Polygon Magic Inc. 73 mins.
It's 2156, and an insane supercomputer called Dorothy has taken control of the Earth after a devastating war. Dorothy has created powerful artifical beings to wipe out the human race. Vulnerable but incredibly powerful teenager Rion escapes from a hospital and eventually realizes that he is carrying part of the computer virus in his own head that can shut down Dorothy for good, if he can only track down Lilia, the daughter of Dorothy's designer Doctor Pascalle, who has the other part of the code. The result is a plodding sub-*Terminator* digital cartoon that often feels unsurprisingly as if one is simply watching someone else play the computer games *Galerians* and *Galerians: Ash* on which it was based—compare to A.LI.CE. The soundtrack of the English language release features music from 2004 from Slipknot, Skinny Puppy, Fear Factory et al. ●○

GALILEI DONNA *

2013. JPN: Galilei Donna: Storia di tre sorelle a caccia di un mistero. TV series. DIR: Yasuomi Umetsu. SCR: Atsushi Oka, Hideyuki Kurata, Jun Kumagai, Toko Machida. DES: Shingo Adachi. ANI: Shingo Adachi, Shingo Ogiso. MUS: Shiro Hamaguchi. PRD: Studio Wanpack, A-1 Pictures, Aniplex, Dentsu, Fuji TV. 24 mins. x 11 eps.
In the year 2061, three sisters descended from the famous astronomer Galileo Galilei are thrown into a madcap quest. Their ancestor has supposedly hidden clues to a priceless treasure, but the girls know nothing about it until criminal elements come after them in search of it. Luckily, like the similarly sparky outlaw heroines of CAT'S EYE, they have plenty of well-matched skills to find it themselves, in a chase around the world, on the run from the Black Ganymede pirates, but also in search of their own heritage. A mostly harmless, pointlessly sci-fi retread of *The DaVinci Code*, this series starts out strong, but seems to lose its way after initial splashes of powerful animation and vibrant action.

GALL FORCE *

1986. Movie, video. DIR: Katsuhito Akiyama, Jun Fukuda, Koji Fukushima. SCR: Sukehiro Tomita, Kenichi Matsuzaki, Hideki Kakinuma. DES: Kenichi Sonoda, Jun Okada, Kimitoshi Yamane. ANI: Nobuyuki Kitajima, Masaki Kajishima. MUS: Ichizo Seo, Etsuko Yamakawa, Takehito Nakazawa. PRD: Animate, Artmic, AIC. 86 mins. (m), 45 mins. (Destruction), 60 mins. (Stardust), 60 mins. (Rhea), 45 mins. x 3 eps. (Earth Chapter), 45 mins. x 2 eps. (New Era), 30 mins. x 4 eps. (Revolution).
Elsa, Catty, Rabby, Pony, Patty, and Rumy are the crew of the Starleaf, a spaceship in the Solnoid Navy, at war with the alien Paranoids. Unknown to any but the highest-ranking officers, the Solnoid leaders have decided that the two species must unite to preserve the best qualities of both—the Solnoids are all female clones, so their gene-pool is self-limiting (compare to VANDREAD). Fighter pilot Lufy joins the Starleaf when her ship crashes onto the flight deck. Though she is a hostile, hot-tempered loner, the real source of danger is elsewhere. When Patty is injured in an encounter with the enemy, her "injury" is revealed as an accelerated pregnancy. She is about to become mother to a new race, providing they survive long enough to get her and her child to safety.

Based on a series of model features in *Model Graphix* magazine and illustrated with photos of the plastic cuties that inspired the characters, the original story for *GF* was accompanied by a manga from Hideki Kakinuma. Replaying both the sci-fi HORROR AND MONSTERS of *Alien* and its use of conspiratorial androids (Catty), the U.S. movie audience had Sigourney Weaver in a role written for a man, but the Japanese had an all-female crew whose heroism was counterbalanced by dollops of fluffiness. GUNSMITH CATS–creator Sonoda's designs for *GF* would establish him as a fan favorite. Subsequent parts of the saga were released on video, starting with *GFII: Destruction* (1987). Years after the violent conclusion of the movie, Lufy is found floating in space by the crew of the Solnoid ship Lorelei—as in *Aliens*. Most of the crew are androids, and one is identical to Catty. Lufy learns that the original Catty is the prime mover of the plan to interbreed the species, and her rescuers are en route to see if the plan is working. On Terra, Patty's half-Solnoid, half-Paranoid child and his mate, Starleaf-survivor Rumy, are starting a new race, but the war is still raging, and not everyone wants the plan to succeed. By *GFIII: Stardust War* (1988), the last remnants of both armies are still determined to annihilate each other and thwart the Unification Plan. A new *GF* team is set up, with *another* android Catty joining Lufy and some old friends to try and avert the final conflict. The plots were stuck in a rut by this time, but the theme of heroically cute young women fighting military bone-headedness and political machinations still had mileage in it.

Rhea Gall Force (1989) moves the action aeons into the future, when Patty's descendants have repopulated the ruined wasteland of Earth. On Earth's moon, an ancient crashed Paranoid spacecraft has "bred" cybernetic MMEs (Man-Made Existences). These cybernetic creatures turn on their creators and, à la *Terminator*, force a nuclear war. The only hope is to evacuate the survivors to Mars, regroup, and plan the repopulating of Earth. A small group led by Sandy Newman and her best friend Melodi resolves to save Earth's population. Though conceived as the first of a four-part series, the "Rhea" prefix was a victim of the same acrimonious split between the producers that plagued BUBBLEGUM CRISIS. Consequently, episodes 2–4 were released under a new title, renumbered 1–3 as the *GF: Earth Chapter* (1989) videos. The war machines led by computer entity

Gorn, who wants to eliminate humankind, are opposed by Sandy and her comrades, while Catty is still pulling all the strings behind the scenes. Once again, two different species must come together if the best of both is to survive, and once again military forces are conspiring to annihilate everything in a vain quest for victory. Later episodes of the franchise hint further at the series' cleverest conceit—it is implied that the narrative is completely cyclical (a true "eternal story"), with look-alikes of the original cast continually reappearing, and Catty living through the entire process. Asides in the original reveal that the Solnoids' homeworld was planet "Marsus," whence they had fled to avoid a catastrophe on their real homeworld—the similarity to *Earth Chapter*'s "Mars" likely to be more than mere coincidence. By *GF New Era* (1991), the action moves to 2291, when the humans live in peace on Earth with the machine entities now called Yuman, but Yuman leader Gorn is not convinced it's over and plans a preemptive strike. Android Catty, still planning for survival, selects six young women for a dangerous mission. Catty still has a few secrets in store—she's been around the human race for longer than anyone knows and has always worked to prevent its extinction. But if this last remnant of humanity is wiped out, the galaxy will be left to the machines.

A final lackluster outing came in the form of *Gall Force: Revolution* (1996), a flashback to the time of the original *Gall Force*, with the crew (now played by different actresses, with new character designs) caught in the crossfire between the East and West Solnoids. However, it could be argued that this final chapter is not an inexact remake, but instead the beginning of another cycle—compare to the similarly mind-bending continuity of **Urotsukidoji**. See also **Super-Deformed Double Feature**. 🅛🅝🅥

GALLERY FAKE

2005. TV series. DIR: Akira Nishimori, Osamu Yamasaki. SCR: Masashi Sogo. DES: Toshiko Sasaki. ANI: N/C. MUS: Face 2 Fake. PRD: TV Tokyo. 25 mins. x 37 eps.
After he loses his job and reputation in a public scandal over a Monet painting, Reiji Fujita finds a new career as the curator of a gallery that specializes in forgeries of masterpieces. As a result, he is soon dragged into a world of international theft and double-crossing in an inadvertently educational refashioning of the artworld crime stories of **Cat's Eye**. Later episodes feature plotlines based on other artistic deceptions, the theft of the Hope Diamond, and the search for Eldorado. The original manga, by **Judge**–creator Fujihiko Hosono, is distinguished by its older target audience (it originally ran in the mature manga anthology *Big Comic Spirits*) and also the long time it took to come to the screen, taking 13 years from first publication to the broadcast of the first episode. But good things come to those who wait, and *Gallery Fake* is a welcome change in contemporary TV schedules crowded with dysfunctional love stories and fighting monsters. Similar adventures featured in the live-action TV series *Mona Lisa's Smile* (*DE).

GALLOP

A smaller animation studio founded in 1979 by a former employee of Tokyo Animation Film. Its first conspicuous role was on **Auntie Spoon**, and it continues today on productions such as **Transformers** and **Yu-gi-oh**.

GALVION

1984. JPN: *Cho-kosoku Galvion*. AKA: *Superfast Galvion*. TV series. DIR: Akira Kamano. SCR: Tsunehisa Ito, Yoshihisa Araki, Yoshiyuki Suga, Haruya Yamazaki. DES: Yoshihisa Tagami. ANI: Hiroshi Negishi, Yoshinobu Shigeno. MUS: Masao Nakajima. PRD: Kokusai Eiga, TV Asahi. 25 mins. x 22 eps.
In the 23rd century, aliens seal off Earth with the impenetrable Sigma Barrier, ready to begin their conquest. United Nations police chief Ray Midoriyama sets up Circus, a team of robot pilots charged with fighting off the would-be world rulers of the Shadow Society. Unable to find anyone foolhardy enough to take the job, he offers it to convicted criminals Mu and Maya on the understanding that each task they perform will earn them days off their sentences. A similar set-up to the later **Cyber City Oedo 808**, and just as truncated, it was pulled off the air at short notice, with the rest of the plot hastily reported in a voice-over at the end of episode 22. A rare

anime job for **Grey: Digital Target**–creator Yoshihisa Tagami, whose distinctive snub-nosed style can be seen in all the main character designs.

GAMBA'S ADVENTURE

1975. JPN: *Gamba no Boken*. TV series, movie. DIR: Osamu Dezaki, Kyosuke Mikuriya, Mochitsugu Yoshida, Nobuo Takeuchi. SCR: Michiru Majima, Yutaka Kaneko, Atsushi Yamatoya, Soji Yoshikawa, Hideo Takayashiki. DES: Osamu Dezaki. ANI: Yoshio Kabashima. MUS: Takeo Yamashita. PRD: Kyodo Eiga, NTV, Tokyo Movie Shinsha. 25 mins. x 26 eps. (TV), 100 mins. (m1), 75 mins. (m2).
When Chuta, a badly injured mouse, staggers off a ship in Tokyo Harbor, he bumps into out-of-towners Gamba and Bobo, who are at a party being given by Yoisho, the sailor-mouse. Chuta tells the local mice that he has escaped from Devil's Island, where Norio the evil ermine (white stoat—see **Happy Ermine**) has crushed the mice with his reign of terror. Local tough-mouse Gamba rashly promises to help and leads a group of rodents on a long odyssey that eventually brings them to the island—they are hampered in the early stages by not actually knowing where it is.

Based on the novel *Bokensha-tachi (The Adventurers)* by Atsuo Saito, four 13-episode seasons were originally planned but only two were produced, leading to some frantic replanning after episode 14. In 1984, the TV series was edited into a movie for theatrical release, as *Theatrical Version Gamba: The Adventurers: Gamba and his Friends (Gekijoban Gamba Bokensha-tachi Gamba to Nanahiki no Nakama.)* Cutting out the subplots, Dezaki focused on the Noroi storyline. A new movie, *The Adventure of Gamba and the Otter (Gamba no Kawauso no Boken)* was released in theaters by TMS in 1991. Directed by Shunji Oga, written by Nobuaki Kishida, and with music by Hiroaki Kondo, the designs and Shunichi Suzuki's animation direction are faithful to the original. Manga tie-ins appeared in *Yoiko* and *Shogaku 123* magazines.

GAMBLER LEGEND TETSUYA

2000. JPN: *Shobushi Densetsu Tetsuya*. TV series. DIR: Nobutaka Nishizawa, Yuji Endo, Satoshi Nakamura. SCR: Yoshiyuki Suga. DES: Hidemi Kubo. ANI: Junichiro Taniguchi. MUS: Kuniaki Haishima. PRD: Toei, TV Asahi. 25

mins. x 20 eps.

In 1946, in a Shinjuku still reeling from the effects of the Pacific War, young Tetsuya Asada learns the secrets of mahjong from an old man. He meets his mentor Boshu and becomes a famous mahjong player and novelist, eventually earning the title Jong Sei (Jong Saint) and becoming the subject of a manga in *ShonenMagazine*, which goes on to win the Kodansha Manga Award. Then his life story is adapted into an anime, shown in the graveyard slot on Japanese TV.

GAME CENTER ARASHI

1982. TV series. DIR: Tameo Ogawa. SCR: Soji Yoshikawa. DES: Mitsuru Sugiyama. ANI: Nobuhiro Okaseko. MUS: Koji Makaino. PRD: Shinei, Nippon TV. 25 mins. x 26 eps.

An early spin-off of the craze for computer games, as Japan's national Invader Game champion Arashi ("Storm") Ishii discovers that while he is bottom of the class at school, he is unmatched with a joystick. Slowly developing a friendship with his rivals Satoru and Ippeita, he treats computer games with the reverence of martial arts, developing special attacks such as the Blazed Top, Vacuum Hurricane Shot, and Fish Stance. In other words, AIM FOR THE ACE, but less athletic.

GAMING AND DIGITAL ANIMATION

In the last three decades, graphics and computer gaming have exerted a growing influence on anime TECHNOLOGY AND FORMATS, until the concerns of gaming companies largely achieved dominance over those of filmmakers. As Asia's postwar industries rebuilt their economies through consumer durables and electronics, children traded their balls and skipping ropes for plastic boxes capable of generating fantasy worlds. From playing with each other, children have shifted over four decades to watching TV shows *about* playing with each other. Developments in computing gave them something even more seductive than television, the ability to step into the fantasy and exert some control, while the rise of the Internet meant that they could build themselves an entire fantasy existence online. Where children would once reenact their favorite TV episodes on the school playground, they are now just as likely to join an online game version, and

are encouraged to do so by a corporate marketing machine out to foster brand identity.

Early computer games in Japan swiftly made use of the graphic abilities of anime and manga artists. The pixels available on-screen might have been limited, but box art and storylines could still exploit the look and style of anime. With the greater memory available in coin-operated games using solid-state electronics, game companies were also able to use more advanced graphics. The strip game *Mah Jong Pai Pai* tried to titillate players with the addition of photographs of scantily clad girls, but lack of memory made the use of anime-style illustrations far more effective, as first used in *Mah Jong Game* (1978). Anime and gaming, particularly erotic gaming, have been inextricably linked ever since, with many anime staff and production companies moonlighting on game productions through the 1980s.

In the early 1980s, a crash in the American console games market coincided with the rise of Nintendo, Sony, and Sega as games producers in Japan and with falling prices of computer power worldwide. Home computers, however, were slow to catch on in Japan—as late as the early 1990s, word processors were still unpopular, and anime scripts were being written by hand. A few directors realized that the growing power of computers would allow them to cut certain corners, but even at the beginning of the era, amateurs were often more swift to adopt the tools and put them to use. *Daicon IV* (1983), an introductory animation for the convention of the same name, made by the animators who would go on to form the Gainax company, included brief sequences of wire-frame graphics, rendered with a shop-bought PC-9800. The first demonstrable use of computer graphics in professionally made anime was in Osamu Dezaki's GOLGO 13: THE PROFESSIONAL (1983), in a helicopter assault sequence. This, however, was purely for show—the scene gained nothing from the use of digital animation and was instead a mere gimmick. The limitations of computer graphics at the time restricted Dezaki to using animation for his vehicles, and not for the more complex polygons that would have been required for people.

Before the advent of high memory

capacity sufficient to make an entire anime by digital methods, computer graphics remained a showy special effect, best utilized where it was cheapest and most visible. It appeared in panels, viewscreens, and, in LENSMAN (1984), in the opening credits, where a single piece of footage could be reused for maximum impact over many episodes.

In 1986, RUNNING BOY and SUPER MARIO BROTHERS tied in the race to become the first gaming tie-in anime. Digital animation was not a feature of either—instead, their relation to the gaming world was one of investment and sponsorship. Toy tie-ins such as GUNDAM and the *Mighty Morphin' Power Rangers* (*DE) had already shown the influence that sponsors could have on television production; now it was gaming companies that found their profits increasing, along with their desire to promote their products through an anime spin-off. GREY: DIGITAL TARGET, the ultimate satire of the eternal escalation of game-based plotting, appeared in anime form in the same year.

Many games suffer in their anime adaptation from an overly simplified quest- or combat-based narrative. Shoot-em-ups like *Gradius*, adapted into anime form as SALAMANDER (1988), present problematic material, particularly outside the undemanding children's field. Gisaburo Sugii's masterful attempt to make something interesting out of STREET FIGHTER II (1994) helped create a series of new traditions and clichés for game adaptations, many based loosely on the conventions found in the SPORTS ANIME of the past—such as the plucky outsider, evil rivals, and doomed mentors of TOSHINDEN and TEKKEN.

The short, limited "cut scenes" of gaming, like advertising before it, presented the ideal platform for experimenting with new filming techniques, many of which were later incorporated into anime. MACROSS PLUS (1994) and, most significantly, Mamoru Oshii's GHOST IN THE SHELL (1995), used computers as tools for recreating realistic flaws in film—lens flares and moments of fuzzy focus, designed to accentuate the feeling of watching a live-action movie. Oshii dispensed with the rostrum camera of cel animation, instead scanning images directly into a computer. This allowed not only the integration of digital special effects, but made 2D (cel) animation elements for the first time as easy to manipulate as 3D elements. It also spelled the beginning of the end for cel animation, which was simply no longer necessary if everything could be digitized. Before long, the price of computer power had fallen to the point where Toei Animation regarded the purchase of a number of computers to be economical—1997 saw episodes of DOCTOR SLUMP and SPOOKY KITARO made wholly inside a computer, resembling cel animation but actually fully "digital" in their construction.

The large unit costs of games means that a successful gaming company has much higher budgets to play with, work for which would often trickle down into anime spin-offs or piece work for anime companies (QUO VADIS). Gaming capital hence became a major feature of the 1990s in anime, even in those works that were not immediately apparent as gaming tie-ins. By the late 1990s, with anime budgets squeezed ever tighter, many of the talents who might have previously worked in TV animation instead migrated to the higher returns of computing. The game *Scandal* (2000), animated by Production I.G, contained three hours of animation, ironically assembled at a higher budget than many "real" anime on television. Those anime that flourished on television often did so with the heavy backing of games concerns—POKÉMON, BOMBERMAN, and DIGIMON, to name a few. Their emphasis is often based on the collecting of cards, toys, or other cheaply mass-produced items that can be marketed to young consumers during the commercial breaks.

Animators' careers had followed roughly the same pattern since the 1950s, with artists taking low-paid jobs as inbetweeners, learning their trade as they rose through the ranks to key animator and perhaps director. Such career paths became rarer, as much low-ranking work was farmed out abroad, and computers were increasingly dominant in the local industry. Hayao Miyazaki once even seriously suggested setting up a "living museum" of old-school animators, who would continue to work using cel methods, lest skills completely atrophy. By 1998, SERIAL EXPERIMENTS LAIN took a bleak but clear-eyed view of the fascination of the Internet, reflecting the mindset of a generation for whom the postwar social ethic had no further relevance, and posing the question: does the physical world have anything to offer young people that can match what they find online?

The new generation of animators has grown up divorced from the former apprenticeship skills of cel animation. Where once there were inbetweeners and key artists using pencils, there were now graphic designers and computer animators used to working directly with machines, and often for bosses whose background was not in art but in marketing or production. The first signs of this group's very different working methods appeared at the end of the 20th century with several animated works that seemed more inspired by the look of polygon-based games than cel-based animation. VISITOR (1998) and A.LI.CE (1999) fought to be identified as anime's "first" 3D animated feature, their rudimentary puppet-style animation soon trumped by that in AURORA (2000) and BLUE REMAINS (2000). Notably, many CG anime from this period take place underwater—as with BLUESUBMARINE No. SIX, the reduced depth perception, limited underwater color schemes, and heightened interference from bubbles all helped obscure any joins between 2D and 3D animation. Also, "floating" characters, whether in zero gravity or underwater, were not obliged to touch the ground, and thereby saved on more expensive animation of feet.

Anime at the turn of the century initially aspired to imitate live action itself—audiences often expected to marvel not at the story, but at the latest feats of animation. FINAL FANTASY: *The Spirits Within* (2001), made in America but with Japanese money, was derided as an expensive flop, although the authors continue to suspect that its "failure" was a handy way of writing off the development costs of important new software that continues to be applied in the Japanese games industry. However, in the wake of its poor box office performance animators turned aside from any direct attempts to emulate reality. Digital animation was employed on live-action films such as *Casshern* (2004, see CASSHAN: ROBOT HUNTER) as a special effect, but within animation itself, animators returned to a more cartoonish look in works such as KAI DOH MARU (2001). APPLESEED (2004) employed a method called "toon shading" to make 3D animation look more like old-fashioned cels. Modern Japanese animation is often characterized by a hybrid animation style that spreads the workload by integrating the output of both 2D and 3D animators, which can now be conflated within the same frame. It has resulted in numerous anime in which mechanical work is the purview of 3D, or partitions of labor such as those seen in the BERSERK movies (2011–13), in which artifacts and armor are 3D while many other elements are not. Oddly, despite persuasive numbers worldwide for Pixar and DreamWorks, Japanese animators still seem reluctant or financially unable to embrace full-scale 3D (i.e., stereoscopic) film-making, although the most recent experiments in that regard have come from Kenji Kamiyama, whose *009 RE: Cyborg* (2012, see CYBORG 009) was released in a three-dimensional movie version as well as a more traditional film that didn't leap out of the screen at the audience.

The prominence of gaming companies has become most obvious in a series of takeovers and acquisitions since 2005, with the formation of the Bandai-Namco conglomerate and its ownership of Sunrise, Sega's acquisition of a controlling share in the anime studio Tokyo Movie Shinsha, and Takara's buyout of anime studio Tatsunoko. Particularly when one considers the number of anime based on dating-simulation or erotic games, it is fair to claim that the majority of anime are now no longer based on manga, but on software. The experience of gaming (both as players and as adaptors of games into other media) has also started to influence anime screenwriters' narrative form, with alternate endings, respawnings, and branching storylines incorporated into stories such as GANTZ and TATAMI GALAXY.

However, although the history of digital animation is normally told through the framework of games and 3D computer graphics, it is only part of the story. The Toei studio had been experimenting with computers in the animation process since as early as 1974 (TECHNOLOGY AND FORMATS) and would eventually adopt a completely digital production process, even though its output usually appeared to the uninitiated to continue to use old-fashioned cels. In 1992, animators at Toei working on a game based on FIST OF THE NORTH STAR were the first to use digital software from the Celsys company, which would come to dominate the Japanese animation industry. The Revolution Engineering Total Animation System (or RETAS) was widely adopted by Toei and its affiliates in 1997 and swiftly became a 2D industry default, offering an immediate 20% saving on coloring costs, and easy integration of domestic studios with offshore facilities linked by high-speed Internet. This, in turn, has drastically accelerated the overseas drift of the anime industry labor pool, some 66% of which is now understood to work outside Japan, in China, Vietnam, Korea, and Taiwan. In 1998, a full RETAS Pro animation suite would cost a prohibitive ¥540,000, making it solely accessible to corporations and eccentric millionaires. However, standard devolutions in price in the software market reduced the consumer cost, until 2008 when the price had dropped to a mere ¥30,000, easily placing it within the reach of any committed amateur.

Even as the conglomerates accrete into larger behemoths, the digital age also offers more opportunities for independents. Digital images can easily be put to other uses, for example in manga (Celsys also produces Japan's bestselling manga-making software) or merchandise. COBRA–creator Buichi Terasawa has long championed the creative freedom and control the computer gives to artists, and makes all his work on an Apple Macintosh for multimedia export. As the possibilities of Internet and mobile network distribution expand, the niche for those who want to make and present their own work in their own way will widen.

In a virtual repeat of the limits and demands of early arcade games, the modern vogue for mobile phone distribution favors similar materials—the simpler the better, leading to titles such as BLACK JACKFlash and LEGEND OF DUO making a virtue of their cheap animation. The advent of the mobile phone has also brought a new lease on life to older series, such as ROBOTECH, reborn on mobile phones where the lines and crackles of old age in its images are less visible on a smaller screen.

Distribution is key to success in anime, as in most mass media. Creators whose vision is hard to package for mass sales (like Bak Ikeda, director of PINMEN) have traditionally languished on the arts festival circuit, or done private work alongside a more conventional career. The turn of the millennium has seen individual creators able to work with little or no outside intervention, particularly now that the kind of software that the animators of the 1980s could not have even imagined is available off the shelf to private individuals. VOICES OF A DISTANT STAR (2002) and PALE COCOON (2005) are two of the most noticeable of these new "home-grown" works, ironically returning the medium to its EARLY ANIME roots of lone hobbyists tinkering in their bedrooms with a new art form.

GANBALIST SHUN

1996. AKA: *"Persevere-ist" Shun*. TV series. DIR: Hajime Kamegaki, Shinichi Watanabe. SCR: Katsuhiko Chiba. DES: Hideyuki Motohashi. ANI: Hideyuki Motohashi. MUS: Hiroaki Arisawa. PRD: Sunrise, Yomiuri TV. 25 mins. x 30 eps.

Shun, a boy in the first year of junior high decides to become an Olympic-class gymnast despite having no clue about the amount of effort and hard work involved. An uninspired retread of AIM FOR THE ACE and other SPORTS ANIME, given extra clout because the author of the original *Shonen Sunday* manga was Shinji Morisue, himself a former Olympic gymnast.

GANBARUGAR

1991. JPN: *Genki Bakuhatsu Ganbarugar*. AKA: *Happy Explosion Ganbarugar*. TV series, video. DIR: Toshifumi Kawase. SCR: Kenichi Kanemaki, Manabu Nakamura. DES: Takamitsu Kondo, Akira Kikuchi, Takahiro Yamada. ANI: Masamitsu Hidaka. MUS: N/C. PRD: Sunrise, TV Tokyo. 25 mins. x 47 eps. (TV), ca. 25–29 mins. (v).

Eldoran, the Knight of Light, gives teenage Torio a giant robot as long as he promises to use it to defend the Earth from alien invaders. In this typical Sunrise robot show, he luckily gets his chance, as flying space-whales, magical dimension holes, and time-slips test his mettle and his ability to persevere (*ganbaru* in Japanese).

The *Ganbarugar Encyclopedia* (1992) was a parody episode released straight to video, directed by Kunio Ozawa.

GANDHARA

1998. JPN: *Nessa no Ha-o: Gandhara*. AKA: *Lord of the Desert: Gandhara; Gandalla*. Video. DIR: Hidehito Ueda, Toshifumi Kawase. SCR: Akiyoshi Sakai, Kazuhiko Godo. DES: Haruhiko Mikimoto, Junichi Hayama, Yasushi Moriki. ANI: Masami Nagata. MUS: Toshiyuki Watanabe. PRD: Ashi Pro, Yoyogi Animation Gakuin, WOWOW. 25 mins. x 26 eps.

A group of teenagers struggles to make the big time with their amateur band, though their fortunes improve considerably when they take on a new lead vocalist, Emma Branton. As the group ducks and dives through seedy agents and dangerous deals in the media world, lead guitarist Yuki begins to wish he had never agreed to support Emma, but he reluctantly helps her career out of his own feelings of responsibility for her missing brother, presumed dead. Meanwhile, deep in the sand dunes, the people known as the Sunlight are busily resurrecting an ancient demon, the titular Lord of the Desert, master of Lovecraftian horrors, who may be supplicated and partly controlled by music. The band is drawn into the conflict, in a desperate attempt to create a new music-led anime franchise defeated by cheapskate 1990s production values. "Superior to MACROSS," was the unfounded claim of the ads at the time, a boast as risible as the characters' own comparison of themselves with the early Doors. Though looking suspiciously like a retread of Clive Smith's *Rock and Rule* (1983), the anime was supposedly inspired by the song "Gandhara," a 1980s favorite that closed the live-action series *Monkey* (see JOURNEY TO THE WEST), though this impoverished anime sadly lacks any other relation.

GANKUTSUOU *

2004. JPN: *Gankutsu-o*. AKA: *King of the Cave; The Count of Monte Cristo*. TV series. DIR: Mahiro Maeda. SCR: Shiuchi Kamiyama. DES: Hidenori Matsubara, Anna Sui. ANI: Gonzo Digimation. MUS: Jean Jacques Burnel. PRD: Mahiro Maeda, Gonzo, Media Factory. 25 mins. x 24 eps.

Bored aristocrat Albert de Morcerf sets out on an interplanetary Grand Tour with his friend Franz d'Epinay. In the city of Luna on the Moon, they are rescued from bandits and drawn into the pomp and circumstance that surrounds a blue-skinned, pointy-eared, fabulously wealthy man of mystery known as the Count of Monte Cristo. The ostentatious Count has style, wit, and an undeniable mean streak. In spite of rumors that the Count may be a vampire, Albert is dazzled and flattered by him but Franz is suspicious. Neither knows that Albert's mother was once the fiancée of Edmond Dantes—the Count's personal name. The families of Albert, Franz, and Albert's fiancée Eugine were all involved in a terrible injustice; the Count has spent years hatching his revenge and Albert is about to become part of his scheme. Increasingly isolated from his friends by his fascination with the Count, Albert loses his whole world. Yet even as the Count sees his plans come to fruition and he returns the evil done to him to the child of his enemy, he is moved by Albert's similarity to himself when young.

Maeda originally wanted to animate an existing SF story based on the 1844 novel by Alexandre Dumas, creator of the Three Musketeers, published in Japanese as King of the Cave. When he was unable to secure the rights to the adaptation, Maeda returned to the original novel to create his own SF version, which would also run in a manga version in Comic Afternoon. Dumas' story of a man unjustly outlawed from society and his plot to take revenge on the three men who wronged him forms the basis for dazzling artistic reinvention. This version not only adds sci-fi elements like Ulysses 31 or Alexander, but also tells the story from the point of view of a relatively minor character in the original. The result is a gripping anime that is one of the gems of the early 21st-century medium, helped considerably by the passion of Dumas' original. Maeda is renowned as a master at combining 2D cel animation and 3D models, as he did in Blue Submarine No. Six and the Second Renaissance sequences in Animatrix. The crew supposedly built a complete 3D CGI model of their future Paris so that Maeda could set his scenes anywhere in the city. The use of outlines filled with flat pattern to represent body and clothing elements produces images of baroque extravagance, filling the screen

with a visual richness rare in animation. For anyone interested in pure, dynamic style, this is a series to treasure. Burnel, bass player with The Stranglers, is an interesting choice as composer; this is his first anime score. Renowned fashion designer Anna Sui worked her way into the credits for some costumes sported by the female characters in the show's grand finale. Other sources imply that she designed all the costumes, although that makes us wonder why it would be news that she did so in the final episode. Note that the King of the Cave alternate title is not always applied even in Japan. A black-and-white live-action TV series based on the original Dumas source was broadcast on Kansai TV from 1955 to 57, under the title Kenshi Monte Cristo (Fencer Monte Cristo).

GANTZ *

2004. TV series. DIR: Ichiro Itano. SCR: Masashi Sogo, Seishi Togawa. DES: Naoyuki Onda, Toshihiro Nakajima. ANI: Hidemasa Arai. MUS: Natsuki Togawa. PRD: Gonzo, Fuji TV, Shochiku, GDH. 24 mins. x 26 eps.

Sullen, resentful teenager Kei and his estranged buddy Masaru die in a train accident, only to be apparently resurrected in a mismatched team of similarly unfortunate individuals, including a suicidal beauty, luckless gangsters, a baffled teacher, and a creepy schoolboy. Subject to draconian control by the Gantz, a mysterious black sphere, they are handed X-ray guns and told to hunt onion-based alien life-forms or die again.

Like Battle Royale crashed into Wings of Desire with courtesy breasts, Gantz throws everyday people into a life-or-death conflict, but focuses on their humdrum musings—what to wear, how to impress girls, who gets the rocket launcher. Based on a manga by Hiroya Oku, the brains behind the soft-core jailbait fantasy Strange Love, Gantz is a black comedy of manners. Its leading men have learned how to be heroes from anime, comparing themselves to characters from Dragon Ball and Fist of the North Star—"Oh wait! I'm already dead!" proclaims a joyous Kei as he attempts a death-defying leap. It also reveals internal thoughts, affording snatches of personal inner monologues, warts and all. Nowhere is this more apparent than in the early train scene, where commuters studi-

ously ignore a drunken tramp who has fallen on the railway track. Kei only offers to help because he is shamed into action by peer pressure, a rather British form of control through embarrassment that also afflicts his bickering, lustful associates in the afterlife. The voice-over exposition is also a handy aid in getting around primitive lip-sync in a cash-strapped animation budget.

The agents are also made to wear fetishistic skintight collars specially reinforced to protect the neck—if the aliens break an agent's neck, death is real and permanent. When the chosen agents return from each mission, Gantz displays another message showing their "score," as if Tokyo was a vast arcade and the battle was some grotesque shoot-'em-up. They pass the time between missions watching TV, which is how Kei and Masaru learn their bodies have never been found. They've been registered as missing ever since the subway accident. They decide to try and get their ordinary, boring, problem-filled high school lives back, leaving the battle to save the Earth to others.

Gantz seems to be one of the first TV anime to have been intended less for a broadcast experience than for binge viewing on TiVo or DVD. The ticking time limit on missions extends across several 25-minute episodes, and the content was something that even director Ichiro Itano, no stranger to controversy after Angel Cop and Violence Jack, did not expect to make it onto TV. In a candid interview included in the DVD extras, he reminisces about the good old days when bones snapped on prime time in Tiger Mask, and intelligently identifies Gantz, nihilism, lack of affect, voyeurism, and all as a touchstone for understanding modern youth's obsessions; in that regard it is worthy of comparison with Paranoia Agent. Episodes 1–11 were broadcast, heavily censored, on Fuji TV beginning in April 2004. The so-called Gantz: Second Stage began with episode 14 and aired uncut on satellite TV network AT-X. Episodes 12 and 13 only appeared on the DVD release, for a total of 26 episodes. Gantz becomes increasingly erotic in the second half, as the agents start to take advantage of their virtually indestructible status, although Kei remains frustrated with his feelings for a girl who does not realize that he has saved her "life." Two live-action movies followed. 🅛🅝🅥

GARAGA *

1989. JPN: *Hyper Psychic Geo Garaga*. Movie. DIR: Hidemi Kubo. SCR: Hidemi Kubo. DES: Moriyasu Taniguchi. ANI: N/C. MUS: Tatsumi Yano. PRD: AVN, Asmic. 100 mins.

The year is 2755, and humanity has traveled out to the stars with the aid of the jump-gate known as God's Ring. The starship Xebec is forced to crash-land on a world inhabited by psychics who use intelligent apes as warriors. Based on a manga by Satomi Mikuriya, whose other SF works include *Legend of Darkness*, NORA, and *Broken Passport*, as well as the manga that inspired KING ARTHUR AND THE KNIGHTS OF THE ROUND TABLE.

GARDEN OF SINNERS, THE *

2007. JPN: *Kara no Kyokai*. AKA: *Heaven's Limits*. Movie. DIR: Ei Aoki, Takuya Nonaka, Mitsuru Obunai, Teiichi Takiguchi, Takayuki Hirao, Takahiro Miura, Shinsuke Takizawa, Hikaru Kondo. SCR: Masaki Hiramatsu. DES: Takuro Takahashi, Mitsuru Obunai, Atsushi Ogasawara, Tomonori Sudo, Nobutaka Ike, Kazuo Ogura, Koji Ito. ANI: Takuro Takahashi, Mitsuru Obunai, Atsushi Ogasawara, Teiichi Takiguchi, Tomonori Sudo, Shintaro Naka-mura. MUS: Yuki Kajiura. PRD: ufotable, Anim-plex, Kodansha, Notes. 48 mins., 58 mins., 56 mins., 46 mins., 112 mins., 60 mins., 61 mins. (compilation), 119 mins.

Shiki has two outstanding talents. One is unique: she can see when you're going to die. The other is less so: she can use a knife to make sure you do. She may look like an ordinary teenage girl, and her strangeness might come from the fact that she's just spent two years in a coma after a traffic accident. Or maybe it's her weird background: children born into her family are usually raised with two distinct personalities, male and female. Sorcer-ess and puppetmaker Toko is especially interested in Shiki—so much so that she gave Shiki's childhood friend Mikiya a job in the paranormal investigation agency she runs. And there are plenty of paranormal cases to investigate in this ambitious series of movies based on an original novel by Kinoko Nasu of Type-Moon. It's often considered as being set in the same world as LUNAR LEGEND TSUKIHIME.

If you're ready to take a walk on the dark side, this is the series for you: seven movies from the same team that twist chro-nologies and narrative arcs like pretzels and mix magic, gore, and human cruelty for an intense and violent journey through the terrors of urban life and deathless love. They were released in Japan between December 2007 and August 2009, with a compilation "remix" released in March 2009. Ufotable's Hiramatsu wrote all the scripts.

The movies might as well be stand-alone tales in one sense, because the only way you can get any kind of grasp of the time sequence is to watch them attentively; but the hard work—and it feels like very hard going at times—is rewarded with an unusually complex story. The path may be stony, but the scenery helps—ufotable have never produced more beautiful design and work. The palette is uniformly gloomy and menacing but the art is superb, even though it's not for the faint-hearted. This series will stay in your memory long after you've watched it, and the stunningly beautiful soundtracks will haunt you. Controversially, and surpris-ingly successfully released in America as a high-end limited-edition box set, retailing at a few cents shy of $600, the expensive, bespoke distribution for this title may be a harbinger of the overseas anime business in the future.

GARDEN OF WORDS, THE *

2013. JPN: *Kotonoha no Niwa*. Movie. DIR: Makoto Shinkai. SCR: Makoto Shinkai. DES: Kenichi Tsuchiya. ANI: Makoto Shinkai, Kenichi Tsuchiya. MUS: Daisuke Kashiwa. PRD: CoMix Wave. 46 mins.

Playing truant in the park on rainy morn-ings, teenager Takao attempts to forget his broken home and failing grades, prefer-ring instead to doodle shoe designs in his notepad. He meets Yukari, an elegant, troubled 27-year-old woman sipping beer in the mornings, and the two begin a halt-ing dialogue.

After the bloated, fantastic extravaganza of CHILDREN WHO CHASE LOST VOICES FROM DEEP BELOW, Makoto Shinkai returns to his comfort zones and areas of proven accom-plishment, concentrating on romance and yearning in an EVERYDAY ANIME that lovingly recreates photo-real representations of

Shinjuku Park. Vegetation and water-modeling, particularly the ubiquitous rain, are well-realized, and the film's imagery revisits Shinkai's recurring preoccupation with the distances, both figurative and literal, between people. Precisely where someone sits on a park bench might be a tiny fraction of the detachment of VOICES OF A DISTANT STAR, but sometimes can seem no less far away.

Like FIVE CENTIMETERS PER SECOND, this film falls bravely short of the running time required to hold up a full-length feature—a sure sign of Shinkai's confi-dence in attracting a dedicated audience within FANDOM. It also presents much of its action as a montage, and ends with a golden-oldie romantic song that sum-marizes and anchors the action. As with his earlier romance, Shinkai offers hope but no closure—the film ends with the couple's love unconsummated and largely unconfirmed, but with signs that both have supported each other's growth. Seen from one angle, he is a high-school drop-out and she is a burnt-out (and ethically unsound) teacher; from another, she has recovered from her trauma and sought a new life, and he has boldly taken an alternate career path, completing a pair of intricate hand-made shoes in her size. The title seems deliberately archaic, using the term *kotonoha* rather than *kotoba,* in allusion to poetic couplets from the classi-cal *Manyoshu* collection, with which Yukari first reaches out to Takao, and to which, many months later, he finally supplies the correct response—that come rain or shine, he'll wait for her. A novel, also by Shinkai, was serialized in *Da Vinci* magazine, and offered a few new perspectives and expan-sions on the events of the movie, such as a larger concentration on the viewpoint of Takao's brother.

GARDLES, THE

1974. JPN: *Hajime Ningen Gardles*. AKA:*First People Gardles, First Human Giatrus*. TV series. DIR: Osamu Dezaki (as Makura Saki), Eiji Okabe, Kyosuke Mikuriya, Ryu Saka-moto, Masami Hata. SCR: Haruya Yamazaki, Noboru Shiroyama, Tsunehisa Ito, Hideo Kuju, Seiji Matsuoka, Yu Yamamoto, Yoshi-hisa Araki. DES: Shunji Sonoyama. ANI: Tatsuo Kasai. MUS: Hiroshi Kamayatsu, Mamoru Fujisawa (i.e., Joe Hisaishi). PRD: TMS. 25

mins. x 77 eps.

Created by Shunji Sonoyama, this is a comedy of everyday life in prehistoric times, an anime *Flintstones*—with each episode split into two, and hence sometimes listed as a 154-episode series. "Dad," the caveman protagonist lives with his wife, "Mom," and children in a cave, and makes rudimentary inventions and discoveries. They are often joined by the extremely stupid gorilla pal Dotekin. Dad's brews are a little less palatable than Fred Flintstone's—he drinks monkey juice, made by eating and regurgitating monkeys—and his black-haired wife wears her hair like Wilma's, with a bone through her chignon, but with one ample breast usually displayed outside her bearskin. As GON THE FIRST MAN, the eldest son of the Gardles family starred in his own anime in 1994. Compare to KUM-KUM. **N**

GARGANTIA ON THE VERDUROUS PLANET *

2013. JPN: *Suisei no Gargantia*. TV series. DIR: Kazuya Murata. SCR: Gen Uroboshi, Kazuya Murata, Daishiro Tanimura, Norimitsu Kaiho, Toriko Nanashino. DES: Hanaharu Naruko. ANI: Atsuko Sasaki, Masako Tashiro. MUS: Taro Iwashiro. PRD: Production I.G, Tokyo TV, Yomiuri TV, CTV, BS11. 24 mins. x 13 eps. (TV1).

In the far future, the Galactic Alliance of Humankind is in the midst of a long war against the Hideauze, a space-faring civilization that uses organic ships. Ensign Ledo, the teenage pilot of a "pilot-assisted A.I. battle suit" (all right, a giant robot), is flung through a space warp while on a mission to destroy an enemy superweapon, waking up six months later on a water-covered world. Soon realizing that he is on Earth, the legendary homeworld of humanity, he joins forces with some of the human scavengers who ply the great oceans on fleets of ships, but is soon plunged into local intrigues and a continuation of the self-same war he thought he had left behind.

Gen Uroboshi's story winningly recycles a number of traits from many similar sci-fi anime, gaining extra credit for its confrontation of its stranger in a strange land with a culture that serves to remind him of what the space-faring humans have lost. Ledo's space-faring humans are soon revealed as belonging to a fascistic, martial state, causing him to question many of the rationales he has been given for the war that has dominated his life, and ultimately, whether or not he was fighting on the right side at all (compare to GUNBUSTER).

GARGOYLE OF YOSHINAGA FAMILY

2006. JPN: *Yoshinaga-san'chi no Gargoyle*. AKA: The Gargoyle of the Yoshinagas. TV series. DIR: Iku Suzuki. SCR: Takao Yoshioka. DES: Mayumi Watanabe, Shigemi Ikeda, Shuichi Okubo. ANI: Mayumi Watanabe. MUS: Ko Otani. PRD: Studio Hibari, Trinet Entertainment. 23 mins. x 13 eps.

Futaba Yoshinaga is thrilled to win a runner-up prize in a local lottery. The prize is a stone gargoyle of a winged dog … which turns out to be alive. Gargoyle was created by an alchemist and can speak to any animals or statues that have enough sensibility and devotion. He can't move any part of his body, but he can shoot laser beams, electric bolts, and freezing rays and can teleport, so he's well equipped to carry out Futaba's orders to keep her family and the neighborhood safe and peaceful. This bright-colored, light-hearted family comedy is based on a book by Sennendo Taguchi illustrated by Yuji Himukai, and is pleasant but undistinguished except for the voice of Gargoyle, legendary voice-actor Norio Wakamoto.

GASARAKI *

1997. TV series. DIR: Ryosuke Takahashi. SCR: Toru Nozaki, Chiaki Konaka. DES: Shuko Murase, Shinji Aramaki, Yutaka Izubuchi, Atsushi Yamagata. ANI: Tatsuya Suzuki, Takuya Suzuki. MUS: Kuniaki Haishima. PRD: Sunrise, TV Osaka. 25 mins. x 25 eps.

As NATO forces fight a minor war against the new Middle Eastern nuclear power of Belgistan, the ancient Japanese Gowa arms-trading dynasty makes preparations to sneak its new humanoid combat robots (Tactical Armor) into the conflict as a "live" testing ground. In cahoots with the black operations division of the Japanese Self-Defense Forces, the Gowas have a secret of their own—they also intend to road-test their private top secret weapon. Family scion Yushiro Gowa is a psychic warrior who displaces his energies through a form of enhanced noh performance. However, as the weapons go into action, Yushiro encounters Miharu, a beautiful, mysterious psychic, working for the tip-top-secret organization Symbol.

One of the best of the EVANGELION clones of the late 1990s, *Gasaraki* successfully duplicates its predecessor's confused kids, military conspiracy, and electrifying action. Miharu is an obvious respray of Rei Ayanami (the words "mysterious girl" appearing depressingly often on 1990s press releases), while Yushiro's peculiarly dramatic powers are a welcome change from nebulous "natural" abilities. Director Takahashi, formerly a thespian but renowned since VOTOMS as the father of realistic robot shows, does not stint on the gritty action, a tactic aided greatly by the script's use of actual Gulf War events and news reports with the names changed, which adds a subtle note of realism.

GATE KEEPERS *

2000. TV series. DIR: Junichi Sato, Koichi Chiaki, Yasuhiro Takemoto. SCR: Hiroshi Yamaguchi, Hideki Mitsui, Aya Matsui. DES: Keiji Goto, Mahiro Maeda. ANI: Inao Takahashi. MUS: Kohei Tanaka. PRD: Gonzo, WOWOW. 25 mins. x 24 eps. (TV), 30 mins. x 6 eps. (v).

In 1969, Japanese schoolboy Shun Ukiya is co-opted into AEGIS (Alien Exterminating Global Intercept System), an international organization founded to hold off invading aliens. These creatures feed on human selfishness, possessing human hosts and transforming them into rampaging monsters. They can only be held off by operatives with "Gate" powers, young psychics whose latent abilities are awakened by trauma or powerful emotions. *GK* is an artful combination of the Cold War paranoia of *The Invaders* with the desperate battle and psychological angst of EVANGELION and the large female supporting cast of TENCHI MUYO! The show was previewed in a manga version by NADESICO–designer Keiji Goto. The six-part video series *Gate Keepers 21* (2003) picks up the action 32 years after the original, with the AEGIS organization largely out of action, surviving only as a forgotten underground group. Invaders, however, still present a threat, and one that gains extra power as old enemies are resurrected. Ayane Isuzu is an AEGIS member who gains the assistance of a ghostly helper in a quest to reform the remnants of AEGIS and to save the world, again.

GAZULA THE AMICABLE MONSTER *

1967. JPN: *Oraa, Gudzulla da do*. AKA: *Gudzulla; I'm Gudzulla; So It's Gudzulla, Is It?* TV series. DIR: Hiroshi Sasagawa. SCR: Ryohei Suzuki, Yugo Serikawa, Tsunehisa Ito, Satoshi Dezaki, Yoshiaki Yoshida. DES: Tatsuo Yoshida, Hiroshi Sasagawa. ANI: Yusaku Sakamoto. MUS: Takasuke Onozaki. PRD: Tatsunoko, Fuji TV. 25 mins. x 52 eps. (TV1), 25 mins. x 44 eps. (TV2).

After hatching from an egg on the volcanic island of Bikkura, the man-sized saurian monster Gazula comes to live in human society, where his predeliction for eating iron objects causes problems for the long-suffering Professor Nugeta and his family.

A lovable monster show designed to capitalize on the concurrent kiddification of the *Godzilla* movie series, *Gazula* bears a strong thematic resemblance to the live-action Tsuburaya show *Buska* (*DE), broadcast the previous year. Gazula befriends the professor's son Oshio and becomes a companion who combines the conjuring mischief of DORAEMON with the metabolism of EAT-MAN—since he, too, ingests metal to transform it into useful devices. Gazula wears a comical bowler hat, bow tie, and a diaper and lives in perpetual fear of the local veterinarian, who yearns to stick a hypodermic needle in his tail.

The original black-and-white series, which was split into two tales per episode, was screened in Australia in the early 1970s, although this version does not seem to have made it to any other English-speaking countries. A color version followed in 1987, directed by Seitaro Hara, but recycling many of the old scripts.

GDGD FAIRIES *

2011. JPN: *gdgd Yosei s* [sic]. TV series. DIR: Kotaro Ishidate. SCR: Kotaro Ishidate. DES: Sota Sugahara. ANI: Sota Sugahara. MUS: Junichi Inoue. PRD: Strawberry Meets Pictures, AT-X. 15 mins. x 12 eps. (TV1), 15 mins. x 12 eps. (TV2).

Three quirky fairies discuss the meaning of life, the universe, and everything, with occasional cutaways to footage or photographs that illustrate their ponderings, in a show that appears to have been largely improved by the voice actors and then synched to picture by the animators. Animator Sota Sugahara took over as director for the second season in 2013.

GDLEEN

1990. Video. JPN: *Gardurin*. DIR: Toyoo Ashida, Takao Kado. SCR: Michiru Shimada. DES: Mari Toyonaga. ANI: Kenichi Endo. MUS: N/C. PRD: Ashi Pro. 45 mins.

Ryu, an intergalactic trader, and his robot sidekick, MOS, are forced to make an emergency landing on planet Gardurin. Initially keen on repairing his ship and returning home, Ryu adopts the new world as his own and becomes a hero by righting wrongs among the locals. Based on a computer game.

GEAR FIGHTER DENDO

2000. JPN: *Gear Senshi Dendo*. TV series. DIR: Mitsuo Fukuda. SCR: Chiaki Akizawa. DES: Hirokazu Hisayuki, Masaharu Amiya, Hiroyuki Yoshino. ANI: Akira Takahashi. MUS: Toshihiko Sahashi. PRD: Sunrise, TV Tokyo. 25 mins. x 38 eps.

In a peaceful 21st-century Earth, it has been 17 years since humanity first learned of the spacefaring alien race of the Galfar Machine Empire. GEAR is the name of the organization to fight off the Galfar with specially adapted giant robots (oh, that's a change). Computer geek Hokuto and gung ho scrapper Ginga both want to pilot the Dendo robot, but with fading powers, the robot needs to feed on the boys' friendship to keep going. Strangely parasitic goings-on, directed by former CYBERFORMULAGPX–artist Fukuda.

GEISTERS: FRACTIONS OF THE EARTH *

2001. TV series. DIR: Sumio Watanabe, Koji Ito, Jang Jong-Geun. SCR: Tokiko Inoue, Naruhiko Adachi. DES: Masayuki Goto. ANI:. MUS: Kenji Kawai. PRD: Frame Entertainment, Groove Corporation, TV Osaka. 24 mins. x 26 eps.

Earth is threatened by an oncoming asteroid, leading the population to divide into two factions, burrowers who wait it out beneath the surface, and space-farers who run to the stars. Four hundred years later, both groups have returned to the surface, only to find it overrun with Siliconians—hostile life-forms that populate an unwelcome third faction in the struggle for limited resources and supplies. Based on a game from Frame Entertainment, this Japanese-Korean coproduction split the labors in a time-honored fashion, with the Japanese handling the character design and 2D, and the Koreans stuck with the backgrounds and computer graphics. Ironically, considering the plot, the two production teams are supposed to be working on the same side, but often seem to be pursuing entirely different agendas, with highly uneven animation, and little consideration for integration of the two differing working methods.

GEMINI PROPHECIES *

1982. JPN: *Andromeda Stories*. TV special. DIR: Masamitsu Sasaki. SCR: Masaki Tsuji. DES: Keiko Takemiya. ANI: Shigetaka Kiyoyama. MUS: Yuji Ono. PRD: Toei. 105 mins. (U.S. version 85 mins.).

A sentient computer disrupts the lives of the inhabitants of planet Lodorian (Geminix in the U.S. version) in its attempts to create a machine world. The young queen, Lilia, flees with the help of a small band of survivors including the warrior-princess Il, who hails from another planet destroyed by the same entity. Lilia gives birth to telepathic twins, Gimsa and Afl, who are fated to return with Il's people to avenge the death of their father the king.

Based on a manga by TOWARD THE TERRA–artist Keiko Takemiya and SF author Ryu Mitsuse, *Andromeda Stories* was rushed into production before the story had even finished running in its magazine incarnation. The big twist is the final revelation that the wanderings of the Lodorians were over when they finally settled on a new world—planet Earth. In the wake of *Battlestar Galactica*, this was unlikely to be too much of a surprise for a Japanese audience—the bulk of Mitsuse's work formed a far more serious, long-running "future history," though only this short story was ever adapted for the screen.

GENEDIVER

1996. TV series. DIR: Masami Furukawa, Takuo Suzuki, Akira Natsuki, Masakazu Amiya. SCR: Masami Furukawa, Riko Hinokuma, Yoshi Nowata, Toshiaki Komura. DES: Akihiro Taniguchi, Michio Mihara. ANI: Keiyo Nagamori. MUS: Masaaki Igawa. PRD: Juno, NHKEP2. 25 mins. x 56 eps.

Sneaker is an evil entity from a time

before the Big Bang, but currently it can only manifest itself in the virtual world. The peace-loving inhabitants need help, but the "heroine" they get to save them is nothing more than average schoolgirl Tada. Falling into the virtual world like ALICE IN WONDERLAND, Tada fights evil in the style of the later CORRECTOR YUI. This is one of the first 1990s TV series to combine cheaper cel animation with flashy computer graphics—a mixture much imitated by the end of the century.

GENERATOR GAWL *

1998. TV series. DIR: Seiji Mizushima. SCR: Hidefumi Kimura. DES: Yasushi Moriki, Takashi Tomioka, Kenji Teraoka. ANI: Akira Ogura. MUS: N/C. PRD: Tatsunoko, Victor, TV Tokyo. 25 mins. x 12 eps.

In 2007, new students Koji, Ryo, and Gawl arrive at Oju Academy Town in Japan, but they are not like the other students at this elite institution. They are time travelers from a future in which humanity has been enslaved by GUYVER-esque mutants called the Generators. After a hellish training program, the resistance movement has sent them back in time to prevent Professor Nekasa from inventing the Generator process at the Academy. However, the professor proves elusive, while the trio is opposed by agents from its own era, sent back to ensure Nekasa's activities are not interrupted. Their one hope in their struggle is Gawl himself, who has reluctantly submitted to the monstrous Generator process, allowing him to transform into a creature that can fight their enemies on their own terms. A mixture of the chronological espionage of *Terminator* and the unwilling, angst-ridden hero of CYBORG 009, Tatsunoko's first TV series since TEKKAMAN replaced the short-lived video outings of the 1990s with a *slightly* longer series, which featured themed monsters-of-the-week just like the same studio's BATTLE OF THE PLANETS and an ambiguous, conspiratorial secret society inspired by EVANGELION's NERV.

GENESHAFT *

2001. TV series. DIR: Kazuki Akane. SCR: Kazuki Akane, Hisashi Tokimura, Miya Asakawa. DES: Yasuhiro Oshima, Takeyuki Takeya. ANI: Junji Takeuchi. MUS: N/C. PRD: Satellite, WOWOW. 25 mins. x 13 eps.

In the 23rd century, human gene therapy is incredibly advanced, but a population imbalance has resulted in nine women to every man (blame TENCHI MUYO!). Life is discovered on Ganymede, but Earth is encircled by a mysterious ring, perhaps of alien manufacture. Terrorists blow up the survey team sent to investigate, and the incident triggers a weapon on the ring that devastates Earth. Terran girl Mika Seido is the planet's last hope, with only the incomplete robot prototype Shaft to help her. Director Akane's follow-up to ESCAFLOWNE, preceded by the tie-in manga *Lunar Shaft* in *Ace Next* magazine.

GENESIS SURVIVOR GAIARTH *

1992. JPN: *Sosei Kishi Gaiarth*. AKA: *Genesis Machine-Warrior Gaiarth*, *Genesis Surviver* [sic] *Gaiarth*.Video. DIR: Hiroyuki Kitazume, Shinji Aramaki, Hideaki Oba. SCR: Shinji Aramaki, "REM." DES: Hiroyuki Kitazume, Hiroyuki Ochi. ANI: Jun Okuda. MUS: Kazunori Ashizawa, Takehito Nakazawa. PRD: Artmic, Kuma, AIC. ca. 45 mins. x 3 eps.

In the aftermath of a cataclysmic war, one of the last Imperial cyborgs trains a young boy, Ital, among the ruins of an old military base. Republican forces kill Ital's mentor, and the boy's quest for vengeance leads him to team up with Sahari, the pretty female leader of the Junk-hunters, and an amnesiac war robot called Zaxon. The attacking Republicans are looking for the dormant Sakuya, a young girl who is the central intelligence system of a doomsday device. Ital kills the evil "General" who wishes to use Sakuya for his own ends, and Sakuya drives the device into the desert where she self-destructs. Ital, Sahari, and Zaxon set off into further adventures, although none were forthcoming for this competent but unremarkable science fantasy saga by future big names including ARMITAGE III's Ochi.

This postholocaust plot in the style of GREY: DIGITAL TARGET collapses in the face of humdrum pop-video interludes, and two pointless animal sidekicks. But despite massive steals from *Return of the Jedi*, *Beast Master*, and *Star Wars*, there are still moments when the world of Gaiarth shows true promise, particularly in technology so ancient it is treated as magical by its operators/summoners. The bright, flat colors were an early example

of the simpler anime shading popularized by outsourced Korean animation studios during the 1990s that would eventually define the look of TENCHI MUYO! and other AIC shows.

GENIUS IDIOT BAKABON

1971. JPN: *Tensai Bakabon*. AKA: *Genius Bakabon*. TV series. DIR: Hiroshi Saito. SCR: Yoshiaki Yoshida, Chikara Matsumoto, Yukinobu Komori, Masaki Tsuji, Shunichi Yukimuro. DES: Fujio Akatsuka. ANI: Tsutomu Shibayama. MUS: Takeo Watanabe. PRD: Fujio Pro, TMS. 25 mins. x 40 eps. (TV), 25 mins. x 103 eps. (TV2), 25 mins. x 10 eps. (TV3), 10 mins. x 88 eps. (TV4).

The insane Bakabon family—eccentric Papa, gentle Mama, genius Hajime, and absentminded Junior—are constantly trying to outdo each other with wacky schemes, but with the exception of the baby, they're all stupid. Shown after STAR OF THE GIANTS in a prime slot, the series soon deviated from the original as sponsor pressure increased—with Father getting a respectable job and the introduction of previously unseen characters to fill out the otherwise small cast.

Fujio Akatsuka, who wrote the original 1967 gag manga on which all the series were based, also created the comedy OSOMATSU-KUN and the girls' series SECRET AKKO-CHAN. The series returned in 1975 with *Original Genius Idiot Bakabon*, a title chosen by its creator to demonstrate that it was truer to the manga from which it came. The new version included the manga favorite Eel-Dog (whose mother is an eel and father is a dog), and Lelele, the Bakabons' next-door neighbor who is obsessed with sweeping, and several crazy classmates from Bakada University.

It came back once more in 1990 with *Heisei-era Genius Idiot Bakabon* and an all-new cast except for Mother, played by Junko Yamazawa. The series was brought back yet again in 2000 in a version from Studio Pierrot, reuniting the family with old favorites like the trigger-happy policeman and the grumbling old man Wanagin. The *Genius Idiot* cast would also team up with Akatsuka's other creations for the 1991 movie spoof *3,000 Leagues in Search of Osomatsu's Curry*, directed by Akira Saito. Father and son Bakabon go on a quest for the most delicious curry in the world in a spoof of both **FROM THE APENNINES TO THE ANDES** and **JOURNEY TO THE WEST**.

GENIUS PARTY *

2007. Movie. DIR: Atsuko Fukushima, Nicolas de Crecy, Shoji Kawamori, Shinji Kimura, Yoji Fukuyama, Hideki Futamura, Masaaki Yuasa, Shinichiro Watanabe, Mahiro Maeda, Kazuto Nakazawa, Shinya Ohira, Tatsuyuki Tanaka, Koji Morimoto. SCR: Yoji Fukuyama, Hideki Futamura, Shoji Kawamori, Mitsuyoshi Takasu, Masaaki Yuasa. DES: Shingo Suzuki, Hiroshi Okubo, Masaaki Yuasa, Eiji Abiko, Yusuke Takeda, Mahiro Maeda, Kazuto Nakazawa, Minoru Nishida, Tatsuyuki Tanaka, Shinya Ohira, Katsu Nozaki, Koji Morimoto, Marefumi Niibashi, Takahiro Tanaka. ANI: Atsuko Fukushima, Shoji Kawamori, Shinji Kimura, Takahiro Tanaka, Takayuki Hamada, Masaaki Yuasa, Shinichiro Watanabe, Mahiro Maeda, Toshiyuki Kubooka, Kazuto Nakazawa, Shinya Ohira, Tatsuyuki Tanaka, Koji Morimoto. MUS: Joe Hisaishi, Kaoru Inoue, Warsaw Village Band, Minami Nozaki, Juno Reactor. PRD: Studio 4°C. 5–20 mins. approx. x 7 eps. (m1), 15–20 mins. approx. x 5 eps. (m2).

An anthology movie showcasing talents associated with or admired by Studio 4°C, given free rein to explore what they could do with about 15 minutes of animation. Unlike, say, **ROBOT CARNIVAL** there is no linking or unifying theme, presenting a huge diversity of style and subject matter. Fukushima, who also worked on *Robot Carnival*, contributes some of her best ever work on the title segment, *Genius Party*, cocredited to Nicolas de Crecy. Kawamori is in humorous mode on *Shanghai Dragon*. Kimura's skill with 3D graphics, so evident on **STEAM BOY**, shows through on *Deathtic 4*, while *Doorbell* has Fukuyama exploring the themes of **PARANOIA AGENT** on a tiny scale. Futamura goes philosophical on *Limit Cycle* and Yuasa delivers a beautifully rounded, punchy piece in *Happy Machine*. High school romance with a twist wraps up the whole in Watanabe's *Baby Blue*—perhaps his strongest work since **COWBOY BEBOP**.

Genius Party Beyond followed in 2008, collecting works that couldn't be added to the first anthology for reasons of timing. Maeda, one of anime's most intriguing talents, echoes *Robot Carnival*'s opening and closing sequences with *Gala*, a story about a mysterious object arriving in a small village and the reactions of the inhabitants. Nakazawa, of *Kill Bill* fame (**KILL BILL: THE LEGEND OF O-REN ISHII**), contributes a tale of delinquent treasure hunters in *Moondrive*. Ohira's delicate piece *Wanwa the Puppy* harks back even further in time, to the fearless innocence of childhood. Tanaka's *Tojin Kit* presents an intriguing and scary world, remarkably well developed in such a short span, and Morimoto's *Dimension Bomb* finishes the party with a dreamlike, almost drugged vibe.

As variable in tone as one might expect from any anthology (see also **GLASSY OCEAN**), *Genius Party* seems to have been a difficult sell overseas, with neither its producers nor foreign distributors able to agree how much it is actually worth. Several pieces intended for *Genius Party* were, as far as we can tell, never released, perhaps never finished. Nicolas de Crecy's *Le Manchot Mélomane* and Tadashi Hiromatsu's *Tuoni* plus an untitled piece by Hiro Yamagata were widely discussed during production but have not appeared anywhere. Shinji Hashimoto worked on Ohira's segment as an animator, but did not contribute a piece as director although he was widely expected to do so.

GENIUS? DR. HAMAX

2007. JPN: *Tensai? Dr. Hamax*. TV series. DIR: Kazuyoshi Fuseki. SCR: Kei Tanaka. DES: Kenji Shinohara, Nobuhiko Genma (mecha), Masamichi Takano. ANI: N/C. MUS: N/C. PRD: Trans Arts, Digital Studio Japan, Tohoku Shinsha. 23 mins. x 12 eps.

A wacky show for elementary schoolchildren introducing them to environmental issues through Dr. Hamax and his pal Dodoarino, a talking dodo.

GENJI

1992. Video. DIR: Ryo Yasumura. SCR: Ryo Yasumura. DES: Michitaka Kikuchi, Masafumi Yamamoto. ANI: Masafumi Yamamoto. MUS: Kentaro Haneda. PRD: Somi, Tee-Up, JC Staff. 45 mins. x 2 eps.

Time-traveling lovers Katsumi and Sakura are thrown into the midst of Japan's medieval Heike-Genji civil war, which is not quite as the history books remember it, complete with sorcerers and unearthly beasts. Based on the manga in *Wings* magazine by **EARTHIAN**-creator Yun Koga, and not to be confused with the **TALE OF GENJI**.

GENMUKAN *

2003. JPN: *Genmukan Aiyoku to Ryojoku no Intsumi*; *Genmukan: The Sin of Desire and Shame*. AKA: *Phantom Mansion: The Sin of Desire and Shame*. Video. DIR: Hiroya Iijima, Hisashi Tomii. SCR: N/C. DES: Hiroya Iijima. ANI: Yasuhiro Okuda. MUS: N/C. PRD: Studio Kuma, Green Bunny. 30 mins. x 2 eps.

Private eye Satoru Kido is summoned to a remote island, where the butler of a lavish mansion wants him to investigate the theft of a ruby ring. He finds the country house occupied by Ayano, a young and beautiful orphan heiress, and her suspicious staff—a governess, a maid, and a groundsman. Satoru doesn't rule out any one of them as the potential thief, although his investigations into life at the mansion soon collapse into a series of set-ups for sex scenes. Based on a computer game, which featured designs by "Tony." ●

GENOCYBER *

1993. Video. DIR: Koichi Ohata. SCR: Sho Aikawa, "REM." DES: Atsushi Yamagata, Kimitoshi Yamane. ANI: Kenji Kamiyama. MUS: Michinori Matsuoka. PRD: C.Moon, Artmic. ca. 46 mins., 23 mins., 24 mins., 27 mins., 30 mins.

Diane is a cripple who relies on a cybernetic body. She lost her limbs in the same accident that killed her father, maimed her mother, and permanently altered her unborn sister, Elaine, a feral child with incredible psychic powers. Not content with stealing the credit for his work, Professor Kenneth adopts his dead friend's children and uses them in his experiments. Elaine goes on the run in Hong Kong, and the evil Kowloon corporation (misnamed "Kuron" in the Manga Entertainment dub) goes after her. She befriends Shorty, a street kid, but is then forced to fight Kowloon's minions and her own sister. Eventually, the two girls combine to form the terrifying Genocyber creature, and Hong Kong is destroyed.

An incoherent mishmash of **UROTSUKIDOJI**'s demon apocalypse and the psychic weapons of **AKIRA** held together with technobabble about "qi" energy and "vajra" force amid blatant steals from *Robocop* and *Aliens*. Beyond the idea of military experimentation on children, *Genocyber* also plunders later chapters of the *Akira* manga, in which Tetsuo's biomechanics take over a U.S. aircraft carrier. Though there are some nice ideas here (a science based on Hindu myth and a demonic machine that looks like the praying hands of a Hindu priest), *Genocyber* is far too derivative for its own good. Matters aren't helped by English dialogue like "You stupid, ignorant fucking piece of shit," which, needless to say, is a rather free **TRANSLATION** of the original.

The idea of bitter sibling rivalry and a retarded girl with godlike powers has much potential, but *Genocyber* does little with it. With bone-snappingly horrific fights and incredibly gory splashes of violence, it plays like **GUYVER** with girls, trying and failing to use many of the same ideas as the later **MACROSS PLUS**. It throws in computer graphics and icky live-action shots of offal, but these experimentations, along with several pans that use genuine photographs instead of artwork, just make the series look cheaper than it really is. Similarly, Elaine is a telepath, but *Genocyber* just makes it look like a cheap excuse for not moving her lips.

Later episodes are barely connected, as the action jumps a decade to the Middle Eastern republic of Karain, where the ageless Elaine is mistaken for a refugee by the UN. Taken to an aircraft carrier, where everyone decides to confuse things by calling her Laura, she witnesses the arrival of Kowloon's latest machine, a cyborg plane that uses vajra technology. She fights it and destroys Kowloon's latest plans, but not before she drives a woman insane by revealing that the child who saved her life is also the monster who killed her parents in Hong Kong.

The finale (released as two "episodes" on a single tape in both the U.S. and Japan, and not released at all in the U.K.), featured Genocyber laying waste to the world before falling dormant. The Kowloon group puts a doomsday device into orbit to await the creature's return. A hundred years later (or 300 in the U.S. version), the post-apocalyptic world develops a religion that worships Genocyber as a god and prays for its return, which eventually occurs with predictably gory results. **ⒷNⓋ**

GENSHIKEN *
2004. JPN: *Gendai Shikaku Bunka Kenkyukai*. AKA: *Society for the Study of Modern Visual Culture*. TV series, video. DIR: Takashi Ikehata et al. SCR: Michiko Yokote, Kokeshi Hanamura, Mamiko Ikeda, Miharu Hirami, Natsuko Takahashi, Reiko Yoshida, Roika Nakase, Yasuko Kobayashi. DES: Hirotaka Kinoshita. ANI: Hirotaka Kinoshita. MUS: Masanori Takumi. PRD: Palm Studio, GENCO, Kid's Station, Media Factory, Tora no Ana, Toshiba. 25 mins. x 12 eps. (TV1), 25 mins. x 12 eps. (TV2), 25 mins. (v, *Kujibiki*), 25 mins. x 12 eps. (TV, *Kujibiki*), 25 mins. x 13 eps. (TV, *Nidaime*).

Kanji Sasahara has a secret passion for manga, anime, and all related items. When he starts college, he's drawn to the titular club, but too proud to join at first, fearing that the other members are even bigger nerds than he—Madarame is into everything military, Kuragame is a wannabe illustrator, and Tanaka loves to dress up. Kosaka, a dreamboat with model looks and charm, seems an unlikely fan but is the most obsessive of them all. He even ignores the overt pursuit of a real girl in favor of getting to store openings and voice artist events. In an arch reference to the contrived reunion of **LOVE HINA**, Kosaka's childhood friend Saki runs into him at the beginning of school and begins to date him, only to find herself dragged into a world of fannish things. Based on Shimoku Kio's strip in *Comic Afternoon* monthly, this is an affectionate parody of geekdom. Aimed at an audience older than that of many similar titles and keen to stress that fans are people, too, it deliberately evokes some of the set-ups of live-action TV drama for 20-somethings such as *In the Name of Love* (*DE), many of which revolve around the reunions of college clubs for more "acceptable" pursuits such as sports or literature. *Genshiken* resembles **OTAKU NO VIDEO** in its empathy for those who refuse to put away childish things, but it's gentler and less confrontational than the early Gainax classic. *Kujibiki Unbalance* (2004) is a 25-minute spin-off video that purports to be episodes 1, 21, and 25 of the anime series that the club members watch in the show, itself later upgraded to a 12-part TV series in 2006. In it, orphan Chihiro lives with his sister and has just started a new high school. He's fallen

madly in love with classmate Ritsuko, while his childhood friend Tokino is madly in love with him. Once a year, their school elects new Student Council members by lottery. Chihiro and Tokino are chosen—but any mistake in their first year will result in expulsion from school. As befits the humor of the show that spawned it, it is a catalogue of daft stereotypes; compare to **NADESICO** and **SPACE TRAVELERS**, which similarly gave birth to their own shows-within-a-show, and **THE MELANCHOLY OF HARUHI SUZUMIYA**, which took fannish obsessions to much madder heights.

Because life is not difficult enough for encyclopedists, there is a *second* "second" *Genshiken* series, in the form of *Genshiken Nidaime* (*Genshiken the Second Time Around*, 2013), a late-night TV show based on the sequel to the original manga, impressively extending its artistic heritage for a whole decade after the appearance of the first issue. This latter version is sometimes filed as *Genshiken II*, with roman numerals, in a vain attempt to distinguish it from *Genshiken 2*.

GENTLEMAN MUGEN
1987. JPN: *Mugen Shinshi: Boken Katsugeki Hen*. AKA: *Dreaming/Mugen Gentleman: The Adventure Begins*. Video. DIR: Hatsuki Tsuji. SCR: Izo Hashimoto. DES: Hatsuki Tsuji. ANI: Hatsuki Tsuji. MUS: N/C. PRD: Studio Gallop. 49 mins.

In this one-shot video based on the 1981 *Shonen Captain* manga by Yosuke Takahashi and set in the 1920s, 15-year-old boy detective Mamiya Mugen gets involved with beautiful girls and solves fantastic mysteries. On this occasion, the case involves the kidnapping of a ballerina and several other girls by a criminal organization. Mamoru deduces that a beautiful concert pianist will be next, but not that the criminals need young girls' energy to power a resurrection machine. In replaying the classic murder mysteries of Ranpo Edogawa and injecting a hard-edged sense of humor, it was a forerunner for **CONAN THE BOY DETECTIVE**.

GEOBREEDERS *
1998. JPN: *Geobreeders: File X: Chibi Neko no Dakkan*. AKA: *Geobreeders: File X: Get Back the Kitty*. Video. DIR: Yuji Moriyama. SCR: Yosuke Kuroda, Yuji Moriyama. DES:

Yasuhiro Oshima. ANI: Yasuhiro Oshima. MUS: Motoyoshi Iwasaki. PRD: Victor. 30 mins. x 3 eps. (v1), 30 mins. x 4 eps. (v2).

A disastrously incompetent supernatural security agency is called in to stop an epidemic of feline ghosts in this anime adaptation of Akihiro Ito's manga. Perhaps for legal reasons, the original "File X" prefix was dropped from the title for the U.S. release, though *Geobreeders* owes just as great a debt to *Scooby-Doo* as it does to Mulder and Scully. Five feisty females in a dilapidated mystery machine run rings around the show's squashed-down Duchovny-clone, facing off against sulking military "allies" and a secret conspiracy.

A predictably madcap mix of ghostbusting tomfoolery in the spirit of **PHANTOM QUEST CORP** and **GHOST SWEEPER MIKAMI**, complete with lightheartedly gratuitous nudity, snappy dialogue, and some really big guns. Even distributors U.S. Manga Corps rise to the occasion for the U.S. dub. Considering the output of their sister-brand Anime 18, it must be a refreshing change for a voice actress to shout "Get on your knees, pussies" to an audience that genuinely does consist of cats.

Sight-gags show a return of the **PROJECT A-KO** spirit from chief director Moriyama: fake ads separate the episodes, characters must play soccer with hand grenades, and in one scene someone backs into a giant poster for *Geobreeders: The Movie*. Though the series wasn't quite *that* successful, it did spawn the four-part *Geobreeders 02* on video in 2000, reuniting the staff under new director Shin Misawa. **◐**

GESTALT *

1996. JPN: *Choju Densetsu Gestalt*. AKA: *Superbestial Legend Gestalt*. Video. DIR: Osamu Yamasaki. SCR: Mamiya Fujimura. DES: Takashi Kobayashi. ANI: Kazuhiro Ochi, Takashi Kobayashi. MUS: Toshiyuki Omori. PRD: SMEJ, TV Tokyo. 30 mins. x 2 eps. Father Olivier, a young priest, learns of a god that will grant a wish to anyone who can find him on his hidden island of "G." Teaming up with the mute Oli, Olivier sets out to find "G" but is thwarted by his old enemy, Suzu the Dark Elf. A comedy manga serialized in *G Fantasy* magazine by **EARTHIAN**–creator Yun Koga, *Gestalt* includes many jokes at the expense of fantasy role-playing games, including

moments of dialogue done deliberately in the non-sequitur style of console RPGs. Though clearly an attempt to capitalize on the success of the similar **SLAYERS**, *Gestalt* foundered after only two episodes, despite flashy computer graphics and the contemporary selling point of being made completely inside a computer.

GET A GRIP TSUYOSHI

1993. JPN: *Tsuyoshi Shikkari Shinasai*. AKA: *Get a Grip, Tsuyoshi*. Movie, TV series. DIR: Shin Misawa. SCR: Takashi Yamada. DES: Kiyoshi Nagamatsu. ANI: Takahisa Kazukawa. MUS: Kuniaki Haishima. PRD: Toei, Fuji TV. 30 mins. (m), 25 mins. x 112 eps. (TV). Kiyoshi Nagamatsu's original 1993 manga in *Comic Afternoon* and the TV series that followed were critically acclaimed for their "American-style humor," whatever that may be. Tsuyoshi is a typical high school student, good at sports but bad at studying, victimized at home by two sisters who hide their evil natures behind their angelic exteriors. The short cinema release removes him from the eternal feud with his mother and sisters, sending him back 12 years in time for a replay of *Back to the Future*.

GET ME PREGNANT, SEIRYU!

2011. JPN: *Haramasete Seiryu-kun*. Video. DIR: Hiro Asano. SCR: Hiro Asano. DES: Hiro Asano, Hideo Okazaki. ANI: Hiro Asano. MUS: N/C. PRD: Horannavi, Pixy. 28 mins. x 2 eps. Four mischievous spirits possess four high school students—three girls and one guy, Seiryu. The unsuspecting girls decide that they have to get pregnant and Seiryu is the one to do it. Of course, it's all up to the spirits in this anime based on a porn game by Lilith. **◐**

GET RIDE! AMDRIVER

2004. TV series. DIR: Isamu Torada. SCR: Satoshi Namiki. DES: Kenji Teraoka, Shinichi Miyazaki, Eiji Suganuma, Shinobu Tsuneki. ANI: N/C. MUS: Kazunori Maruyama. PRD: Studio Deen, TV Tokyo, NAS. 24 mins. x 51 eps. AmDrivers are an elite group of pilots who defend mankind. In their Baizer suits, powered by AmEnergy, they fight the Bugchines, minions of the mysterious Diguraz and his Justice Army. An ultrapowerful AmEnergy source called Zeam could render our heroes invincible and end the

fighting. Inexperienced AmDriver Jenus Dira teams up with top AmDrivers Shin Pierce and Regna Lauraria, but becomes annoyed by what he sees as their wish for personal glory before the good of mankind. Another newcomer, Sara May, feels the same, and the two start out on their own to try and find Zeam. This is standard action adventure fare for older children, not likely to offer much to the over-12s despite Konami's energetic ad campaign for the multifarious card game packs.

GETBACKERS *

2002. JPN: *Getbackers Dakkanya*. AKA: *Getbackers Recoverers*. TV series. DIR: Kazuhiro Furuhashi, Keitaro Motonaga, Makoto Sokuza, Masami Furukawa, Osamu Sekita, Shunji Yoshida, Tomoko Hiramuki, Toshiyuki Kato. SCR: Akemi Omode, Jun Maekawa, Masashi Kojima, Reiko Yoshida, Saizo Nemoto. DES: Atsuko Nakajima, Toshiharu Murata. ANI: Atsuko Nakajima, Akira Matsushima, Hirofumi Morimoto. MUS: Taku Iwasaki. PRD: Kodansha, Rondo Robe, TBS. 26 mins. x 49 eps. Hard-up heroes Ginji and Ban specialize in *getting stuff back*, from a lost lucky charm to a missing teenager, in a Japan where everyone is hustling for a dime. They are aided in this by their superpowers—Ban can exert 200 kilos of grip in his fist and also has the Evil Eye, the ability to project terrifying hallucinations into the mind of anyone who meets his gaze. Ginji can generate thousands of volts of electricity from his body at will. The pair claim a 100% recovery rate for their clients, but the goods aren't always returned in the original condition. Drawing not only on the ongoing *Shonen Magazine* manga by Yuya Aoki and Rando Ayamine but also on the classic TV series *Detective Story* (*DE), *Getbackers* refashions hard-boiled traditions as light comedy. **COWBOY BEBOP** may have emulated the look, but *Getbackers* emulates the plots—its heroes are loners with a dark past, co-opted by a vampish woman (the sultry Hevn) for missions above and below the law. In attitude, it often sails very close to *Magnum P.I.* (1980) or a righteous **LUPIN III**, until a long arc that returns the characters to their clandestine roots, fighting similarly superpowered individuals who were once their allies.

Cleverly recycling many of the issues and threats of Marvel superheroes into an everyday setting (compare to the later TIGER AND BUNNY), *Getbackers* features two protagonists who may have amazing powers but lack costumes or kit. Instead, they hang out at a restaurant called the Honky Tonk, where they lean on manager Paul for free food. Ban and Ginji's Shinjuku is dominated by the bold architectural statements of Japan's boom era, set on the steps of train stations empty of commuters and on the building sites of abandoned skyscrapers. What begins as a stylistic conceit is later revealed as an important plot point—the boys have a past association with the gangs who have occupied the Limitless Fortress, a massive complex in downtown Tokyo, left incomplete by the recession and subsequently inhabited by invincible squatters who terrorize anyone who tries to evict them.

The anime story diverges from the manga after episode 25, returning to investigative stories with a twist: an amnesiac car crash survivor who wants them to somehow retrieve his memory and the obligatory hot springs episode, where the boys mix business and pleasure while hunting for an old lady's diamond ring. Other plots drift into the artworld genre of GALLERY FAKE, with a woman who claims to have the lost arms of the Venus de Milo statue, while others drift further toward sci-fi territory—a super drug, a missing sample of real blood, and a revolutionary superalloy. Paul's own past as a thief is revealed when he hires the boys to retrieve a vase stolen by one of his old gang members before the Limitless Fortress storyline returns for a final showdown.

Like the cursed yuppies in PETSHOP OF HORRORS, the Getbackers' clients symbolically sell their souls for material possessions; most notably, a teenage girl prepared to whore herself to a gangster if he gives her "bags, clothes, and shoes." Sadly, it's not just the cast who are impoverished—the show itself is a victim of the Japanese recession, with extremely limited animation. When the boys agree to take a job that involves an extended pastiche of the CASTLE OF CAGLIOSTRO car chase, their fee is ¥2 million, which a contemporary newspaper article reported as the shockingly meager budget of a modern-day TV episode. Despite this, *Getbackers* had an impressively long run on TV, extending across an entire year when most similar shows barely last a season. Part of this endurance feat may be down to the flexibility of its storyline and pace, mixing long quests with short vignettes without losing sight of its big themes.

GETTER ROBO *

1974 AKA: *Starvengers*. TV series, movie, video. DIR: Tomoharu Katsumata, Yasuo Yamaguchi, Takeshi Tamiya, Takeshi Shirato. SCR: Shunichi Yukimuro, Seiji Matsuoka. DES: Kazuo Komatsubara. ANI: Kazuo Komatsubara, Atsuo Noda, Kazuo Nakamura, Takeshi Shirato. MUS: Shunsuke Kikuchi. PRD: Dynamic Planning, Fuji TV, Toei. 25 mins. x 51 eps. (TV1), 25 mins. x 39 eps. (G), 30 mins. (m1), 25 mins. (m2), 25 mins. x 50 eps. (Go), 25 mins. x 13 eps. (Change), 25 mins. x 4 eps. (Neo).

Professor Saotome creates the fearsome Getter Machine series of war robots and hires the nobly named Ryoma (see OI! RYOMA), Musashi (see YOUNG MIYAMOTO MUSASHI), and Benkei (see BENKEI VS. USHIWAKA) to pilot the three vehicles, the aerial Getter-1, land-based Getter-2, and seafaring Getter-3, that can be combined to form a giant humanoid robot—the first "transformer."

Based on a collaboration between DEVILMAN's Go Nagai and DEMON-BEAST PHALANX–creator Ken Ishikawa, the show returned in 1975 as *Getter Robo G*. The destruction of the evil Dinosaur Empire left the way open for a new enemy, the Clan of 100 Devils, and since the original machinery had been destroyed in the climactic fight of the previous series, it was also time for new vehicles: Getters Dragon, Rygar, and Poseidon (Star Dragon, Star Arrow, and Star Poseidon). Along with the other anime in the FORCE FIVE interlinked shows, *Getter Robo G* was redubbed for the U.S. market as *Starvengers*, and several of the vehicles were also included in the SHOGUN WARRIORS line. For the English-language version, the horned enemies were renamed the Pandemonium Empire, led by Emperor Ramzorch and his Hitler-look-alike commander, Captain Fuhrer. Back in Japan, *Getter Robo G* also appeared in short theatrical outings alongside other Go Nagai creations including *Great Mazinger vs. Getter Robo G* (1975) and *Great Mazinger / Grandizer / Getter Robo G: Battle the Great Monster* (1976).

After a long hiatus, the franchise hit a low point in 1991 with *Getter Robo Go!* directed by Yoshiki Shibata, featuring the same machines but an all-new team. Though long-running by modern standards, the series was considered a non-canonical flop. The original, however, remained a favorite among fans and professionals, demonstrated by the NADESICO staff in their spoof show-within-a-show *Gekiganger 3*. For most of the 1990s, the franchise was kept alive by computer games, and eventually the redesigned machines as used in the *Getter Robo* and *Super Robot Battle* games were resurrected for a new series. Poaching staff from the successful retro series GIANT ROBO, Jun Kawagoe's straight-to-video *Change Getter Robo* (1998) presented itself as the "true" sequel to the original 1974–75 serials, beginning with the death of Professor Saotome and Ryoma's arrest for his murder. Three years later, the two remaining team members are forced to contend with a cloned "evil" Saotome, hell-bent on avenging his own death and leading an army of Getter Dragons. In a sequel that exploited the limited budgets of late-1990s video productions to recreate the rough-edged look of 1970s television animation, Ryoma is recalled from prison to resist the invasion. This version was scheduled for release in the U.S. in 2001 as *Getter Robot: The Last Day*. The same staff returned for the four-part video sequel *Change Getter Robo vs. Neo Getter Robo* (2000), clearly made with an eye to foreign sales, in which another madman, Emperor Gaul, sends an army of robotic dinosaurs to destroy New York, and Professor Saotome's new lantern-jawed protégé, former wrestler Tetsuhito, leads the underground resistance. See also MAZINGER Z.

GHIBLIES

2000. TV special, movie. DIR: Yoshiyuki Momose. SCR: Yoshiyuki Momose. DES: Toshio Kawaguchi. ANI: N/C. MUS: Manto Watanobe. PRD: Studio Ghibli. 20 mins. (special), 20 mins. (m).

A series of short, comedic vignettes about life in an animation studio, doodled by the Studio Ghibli team to practice techniques on their new workstations around the time MY NEIGHBORS THE YAMADAS was being filmed. These slices of life developed into two short films, the first airing on Japanese

TV in 2000 as part of a Studio Ghibli documentary, the second released on the same theatrical bill as **THE CAT RETURNS** in 2002. Note that, just to confuse matters, the title of this show is pronounced with a hard G, whereas in real life, the name of the studio is pronounced with a soft G, sounding like *jibli*. Only the second set of animations is currently available on DVD.

GHOST HOUND *

2007. JPN: *Shinreigari*. AKA: *Spirit Hunting*. TV series. DIR: Ryutaro Nakamura. SCR: Chiaki Konaka, Daishiro Tanimura. DES: Mariko Oka, Hiromasa Ogura. ANI: Mariko Oka. MUS: TENG. PRD: Production I.G, WOWOW, AIC, Studio Jungle Gym, Studio Kuma. 25 mins. x 22 eps.

In a small town deep in the Kyushu countryside, three boys with traumatic pasts have found a way to let their souls cross over into another world. Taro, Makoto, and Masayuki can float between the Unseen World of ghosts and the Apparent World of reality. But until now, the ghosts from the Unseen World have not been able to cross over with them. Now the souls of the dead are coming back to the land of the living, and three young misfits must try to solve the mystery with the help of a girl who can see ghosts.

This was Production I.G's 20th anniversary project. Such enterprises tend to be a mixed bag—designed to showcase what a studio feels it does best, and celebrate its history while looking to its future; they don't always end up showing off the classic skills and storytelling styles that fans know and love. Consider **KARAS**, an interesting project in itself but not necessarily the first thing that springs to mind when one considers the legacy of the mighty Tatsunoko Pro.

There are several interesting issues raised in the course of the story—one of the protagonists is a former bully who forced another student to commit suicide, another survived a kidnap that killed his sister, and the third was indirectly involved in the kidnap and his father's suicide through a family cult. They all carry their ghosts with them, chained by unresolved feelings and unexpressed fears. This quiet, understated presentation, effectively but unflashily animated, carefully designed, supports a story that has no need to show

off its strength. Plot and character emerge gradually, developing at an unforced pace, and this too builds suspense like a distant rumble of thunder. The music is superb and the lighting and color design are masterful, but perhaps the most interesting element is the way the landscape itself becomes part of the story, a character in its own right, with its own secrets. **GHOST IN THE SHELL**–creator Masamune Shirow is credited as "original creator," although the extent of his actual involvement is unclear.

GHOST HUNT *

2006. TV series. DIR: Rei Mano. SCR: Reiko Yoshida, Rika Nakase. DES: Satoshi Iwataki, Mie Kasai. ANI: Ayako Tauchi, Koji Ogawa, Minami Tsuruakari. MUS: Toshio Masuda. PRD: JC Staff, Avex Entertainment, Marvelous Entertainment, TV Tokyo. 25 mins. x 25 eps.

Mai and her high school friends love to tell each other ghost stories, but she never expected to wind up investigating them. One of their sessions is interrupted by psychic researcher Kazuya, investigating an abandoned school building. Next day, nosing around in the building, she accidentally breaks a camera and injures Kazuya's assistant. He insists she helps him out to pay for the camera and cover for his assistant.

This story started as a series of novels by Fuyumi Ono, appearing in 1994, before being published as a manga by Shiho Inada in 1998. It's suspenseful without being too scary, the pace is varied and lively, and the art department does an excellent job of building a credibly normal universe that turns spooky at the right moments through tricks of light and well handled color shifts. Sound director Yasunori Ebina does a fine job helping to build the tension, and creates an atmosphere of spine-tingling creepiness when required.

There's also plenty of educational material in here: information on mythology, **RELIGION AND BELIEF**, and attitudes to the spirit world. But unlike, say, **GHOST SLAYERS AYASHI**, *Ghost Hunt* doesn't give you the feeling that there's a test coming up at the end of the session. It's interesting to compare this with teen investigator series like **YOUNG KINDAICHI FILES** or even **CONAN THE BOY DETECTIVE**, as well as with the more obvious psychic shows like **TOKYO BABYLON**. ▼

GHOST IN THE SHELL *

1995. JPN: *Kokaku Kidotai*. AKA: *Armored Riot Police/Ghost in the Shell*. Movie, TV series, video. DIR: Mamoru Oshii. SCR: Kazunori Ito. DES: Satoshi Okiura, Shoji Kawamori. ANI: Hiroyuki Okiura, Tensai Okamura, Toshihiko Nishikubo. MUS: Kenji Kawai. PRD: Studio IG. 83 mins. (m1), 25 mins. x 26 eps. (TV1), ca. 1 min. x 26 eps. (Tachikomatic 1), 25 mins. x 26 eps. (TV2), ca. 1 min. x 26 eps. (Tachikomatic 2), 100 mins. (m2), 159 mins. (Laughing Man), 161 mins. (Individual Eleven), 105 mins. (Solid State Society), 60 mins. x 6 eps. (Arise).

A top secret military project goes horribly wrong, and a sentient computer virus runs out of control. Its creators disperse in search of political asylum before the mistake is spotted, while the program itself tries to defect to the other side. Calling itself the Puppet Master, it hacks into government systems to gain extra leverage in negotiations. It takes control of gun-freaks, robot bodies, and even a tank, but what it really wants is a permanent, physical home. Meanwhile, Section Nine, agents for the Ministry of Internal Affairs, are forced to clear up after the mess left behind by Section Six (Foreign Affairs), even as the two departments contest jurisdiction in the case. Major Motoko Kusanagi is an angst-ridden platoon leader in Section Nine who can't leave the service because, like the original *Bionic Woman*, parts of her are government property. Her body is just a mass-produced "shell" (note the scene where she sees a twin working as a secretary) and the only part of her that is real is her "ghost," her soul. When seemingly random events all over the city turn out to be crimes committed by the Puppet Master's unwitting accomplices, Motoko realizes that there is a pattern, and that it eventually leads to her.

GitS is one of the best anime available in English, and one of the few that could reasonably claim to be a true cyberpunk film. It is a superb action film with marvelous moments, such as Motoko's final duel with a robot tank, and accomplished use of computer graphics, especially for Motoko's cloaking device. Unlike the many anime "movies" that are really nothing of the sort, it was genuinely made for the big screen, and the budget and dedication really show. It was also a coproduction partly funded by Manga Entertainment, and it kept the company's reputation afloat in the search for a new **AKIRA**, though at the time it was regarded by many as a money pit for ME's beleaguered boss Andy Frain.

While **APPLESEED**–creator Masamune Shirow set his original 1991 *Young Magazine* manga in a sprawling but plainly Japanese future metropolis, director Oshii deliberately relocated to Hong Kong for the film to create a lived-in, exotic look with Chinese-language street signs. This was a perfect film for the idiosyncratic Oshii, allowing him to replay **PATLABOR** with clueless "little people" dwarfed by events beyond their ken.

The original manga's intense philosophizing is artfully simplified by screenwriter Ito, who streamlines it into a perverse "romance" between Motoko and the Puppet Master, their final marriage eventually producing a new life form. Kenji Kawai's music is a haunting ceremony in arcane Japanese ("A god descends for a wedding and dawn approaches while the night bird sings"), two separate musical themes that slowly advance on each other during the film, until they marry to form a completely new synergy over the closing credits, adding a final coda to Ito's plot. Or rather, they did—the English-language version replaced the closing music with a mediocre effort from the Passengers CD. Such a gimmick may well have gained *Ghost in the Shell* more mainstream interest, but it wasn't necessary. This is a film that needed no marketing spin. A manga sequel, *Man-Machine Interface*, ran intermittently for several years in *Young Magazine*, regularly prompting rumors of an anime follow-up.

This eventually arrived in the form of Kenji Kamiyama's TV series *GitS:Stand Alone Complex* (2002) which was billed not as a sequel to the movie, but a "reimagining" of the same story. *Stand Alone Complex* drops the Puppet Master in favor of a new enemy and a broader, deeper introduction to Shirow's future world and his Niihama ("New Port") city. It uses Shirow's work as a foundation, but is a collaboration among a team of writers led by director Kenji Kamiyama—that same "KK" whose initials can be seen inside a cybernetic eye in the first episode. It also offers tantalizing scraps of new information about the characters from *Ghost in the Shell*, including the

revelation that Motoko was only six years old when unspecified events caused her to swap her original body for a shell. This, then, is what must make her so good; she must have been one of the first humans to undergo full cyborg remodeling, not out of choice, but necessity. When we see a hand unable to hold a doll in the opening credits, we are watching one of Motoko's oldest memories, as she struggled to control her new body. The *fuchikoma* robots from the original comic are remodeled here as the *tachikomas*, intelligent tanks with the firepower of a helicopter gunship and the minds of ditzy schoolgirls. They are given their own *Tachikomatic Days (Kokaku Kidotai: Section 9 Science File Tachikoma na Hibi)* gag reel, which closed each episode when the TV series was released on video.

Many of the episodes "Stand Alone"—that is, they are weekly installments of a futuristic cop show in which Section Nine fights crime in New Port City. However, in the style of **COWBOY BEBOP**, 12 episodes, #4–6, #9, #11, and #20–26, are "Complex," part of the main story arc, the tale of the entity or entities known as the Laughing Man. *Stand Alone Complex* makes recurring references to the work of legendary American recluse J.D. Salinger, whose judgmental Holden Caulfield in the novel *Catcher in the Rye* bears some similarity to the Laughing Man and even supplies the quote for his logo. "The Laughing Man" (1949) is also the title of a Salinger short story printed in *TheNew Yorker*, while the tune, "Comin' Through the Rye," is a regular feature of daily life in Japan in everything from elevator doors to pedestrian crossings and has been heard before in the anime **VAMPIRE HUNTER D** and **GREY: DIGITAL TARGET**. There are other tips of the hat to pop culture, including references to a Disney theme park ride in "Jungle Cruise" (#10), and a character modeled on Nurse Ratched from *One Flew Over the Cuckoo's Nest* in "Portraitz" (#11). Episode #3, "Android and I," is an extended homage to the works of Jean-Luc Godard, whose *Alphaville* (1965) also featured an investigator taking on an artificial intelligence over the control of a future society.

But beyond such name-checking, *Stand Alone Complex* is a compelling cyberpunk drama, concerned with medical espionage,

corruption, and consumer's rights in an increasingly globalized and corporate economy. Its success led in part to interest among the producers of the original film in commissioning an actual sequel to the original movie, which appeared as *GitS 2: Innocence* (JPN: *Innocence*, 2004). *Innocence* draws heavily on a single chapter of the original manga ("Robot Rondo"), but while it uses characters and situations created by Masamune Shirow, it is largely the work of Mamoru Oshii. With Motoko Kusanagi still absent following events at the end of the movie, *Innocence* concentrates on her former lieutenant Batou as he investigates a series of crimes in which robot sex-dolls have turned on their owners. Plot, however, is of secondary concern to Oshii's usual existentialist dialogues, and extended shots of the city, including a Chinese carnival scene that supposedly took a full year to animate. The effort and expense show, in a film that does much to enhance anime's reputation both for high-quality CG and impenetrably obtuse philosophical debates.

Despite *Ghost in the Shell*'s relatively obscure profile in Japan, where it is not particularly well known outside SF fan circles, it has enjoyed continued foreign success as a flagship for post-**AKIRA** anime. A second TV series, *GitS: 2nd Gig* (2004) continues the fine topical satire of its predecessor, focusing on a refugee crisis within Japan. It also reveals long-awaited details about Shirow's world, suggesting that "New Port City" is actually somewhere near Nagasaki Bay—or at least, might be if the real-world Deshima Island, the historical quarantine/ghetto for foreign traders, is the same place as the Deshima refugee camp in the series. Note that this geographical background, along with many other "facts" revealed in the TV series, contradicts information stated or implied in earlier versions of the franchise. Fans are thus at a loss as to how much of the TV continuity is "canon"—*2nd Gig* in particular is vastly more forthcoming with background details of the franchise world, its military conflicts, and the political troubles this has generated in New Port City. Meanwhile, in an exercise of somewhat pointless over-complexity, *2ndGig* develops the "Stand Alone/Complex" split of the first series even further, into episodes that can be classified as DI ("Dividual"), IN ("Individual"), or DU ("Dual")—a labored gimmick imparting unwarranted significance to story elements that can be found in many other episodic dramas we have, it seems, already forgotten *The X-Files*), but are trumpeted here as if someone has reinvented the wheel. Nevertheless, the overreaching story arc of *2nd Gig* is another excellent series, allegorizing modern terrorism and nuclear espionage in sci-fi clothes, as the reconstituted Section Nine fights against a terrorist group calling itself the Individual Eleven.

The other "film" releases *GitS: The Laughing Man* (2005) and *GitS: Individual Eleven* (2006) are video releases consisting of extended movie-length edits of the relevant episodes from seasons one and two of the TV series, with additional footage. Officially a video, but premiered on a satellite TV channel, ostensibly because it was "movie" quality, *GitS: Solid State Society* (2006), is set in 2034, two years after the events in *2nd Gig,* focusing on an environment in which children are in short supply and a population of sedentary, cybernetically nursed old-timers is becoming an increasing burden on the state. As in the thematically similar **ROUJIN-Z**, it asks if the aged population (which in 2034 will be us) has the right to set the agenda of the younger generation. In successfully steering the franchise away from Oshii and parking it in a lucrative TV slot that lasted for several years, Kenji Kamiyama proved his merit as one of the promising new show-runners of the 21st century, soon putting this promise into practice on **EDEN OF THE EAST**, which obliquely refers to several characters and situations from *GitS*, to the extent that some fans consider it to be a prequel by other hands. He would seemingly hand over the responsibility to a new team, including director Kazuchika Kise and writer Tow Ubukata, for the video prequel *GitS Arise* (2013), set in 2027 and filling in some of the backstory of the young Motoko Kusanagi. **LNV**

GHOST SLAYERS AYASHI
2006. JPN: *Ayakashi Ayashi*. TV series, video. DIR: Hiroshi Nishikiori. SCR: Sho Aikawa. DES: Toshihiro Kawamoto, Takeshi Sato. ANI: Hiroshi Osaka, Hisashi Yamamoto, Osamu Kamei. MUS: Ko Otani. PRD: BONES, Aniplex,

MBS. 25 mins. x 25 eps. (TV), 25 mins. x 5 eps. (v).
Feudal Japan is being ravaged by mystical beasts called *youi*. Middle-aged bath-house employee Yukiatsu may look just like any other peasant down on his luck, but he has a few mysterious powers of his own, which is why the *youi*-fighting group known as Ayashi are looking for him to join their ranks. Yukiatsu has the power to turn any object's or being's name into a weapon. He can fight with words, and Ayashi offer him all the monster flesh he can eat in return.

Sho Aikawa, who created this series, has spent years turning words into anime on shows like **RAH XEPHON, SORCERER HUNTERS,** and **NADESICO**. Here his passion for words, for explaining the origin of *kanji* and using them to illuminate social and historical issues, tends to slow the story down quite a bit. Viewers may also sometimes feel as though they're being educated whether they want it or not. The fights, though, are a huge compensation: BONES' trademark slick style mixes gore and slapstick, *Tom and Jerry*-style idiocy with unsettling images of starvation and gluttony. And while the fighters aren't quite in the **FIST OF THE NORTH STAR** class for mountainous muscles, they strip down and oil up quite nicely. The series wobbles on the line between macho and camp, but usually manages to stay on the side of entertainment.

The video series *Ayakashi Ayashi: Ayashi Divine Comedy* (*Tempo Ibun Ayakashi Ayashi: Ayashi Shinkyoku*) was made by the same crew and appeared in 2007. It takes up the story six months after the series ends with a new threat for the Ayashi team. Not to be confused with **AYAKASHI: SAMURAI HORROR TALES**, which has a similar Japanese title.

GHOST STORIES *
2000. JPN: *Gakko no Kaidan*. AKA: *School Ghost Stories*. TV series. DIR: Noriyuki Abe. SCR: Hiroshi Hashimoto. DES: Masaya Onishi, Mari Kitayama. ANI: N/C. MUS: Kaoru Wada. PRD: Pierrot, Fuji TV. 25 mins. x 20 eps.
Satsuki and her brother move into a new town, where their dead mother was once the principal of the now abandoned school. Their mother's diary reveals that the school was once haunted; hardly a surprise, considering **HERE COMES HANAKO** and **HAUNTED JUNCTION**—one wonders if there

is a school in anime that isn't. Not unlike the demonic figures in **TENCHI MUYO!** and **USHIO & TORA**, the spirit Amanojaku was trapped by Satsuki's mother in the forests behind the school, but has been released once more with the cutting down of the trees—unsurprisingly like some of those in **DEVIL HUNTER YOHKO**. Satsuki manages to trap Amanojaku's spirit inside her cat (compare to **CARDCAPTORS**), but there are other spirits on the loose requiring her attention, in a highly derivative show that only seems to have reached the schedules because the producers were not expecting any viewers old enough to remember any of its predecessors, particularly **REAL SCHOOL GHOST STORIES**, with which it shares a writer and director. Perhaps realizing that they didn't have a whole lot to work with and nobody would really care that much, ADV Films allowed the voice actors considerably freer rein than usual on the U.S. release—the Englishlanguage dub often seems less translated than "improvised," quite possibly to the show's betterment, although such a last-ditch attempt to make it interesting might also be a potentially troubling throwback to the non-translations of **ROBOTECH** and **SAMURAI PIZZA CATS**. The anime forms part of a long-running *School Ghost Stories* franchise that includes four theatrical live-action movies, five live-action TV movies, two live-action TV series, and 19 novels.

GHOST SWEEPER MIKAMI *
1993. AKA: *GS Mikami*. TV series, movie. DIR: Atsutoshi Umezawa. SCR: Aya Matsui, Nobuaki Kishima, Masaharu Amiya. DES: Takashi Shiina. ANI: Mitsuru Aoyama, Kenji Yokoyama, Yoshiyuki Kawano, Masayuki Uchiyama. MUS: Toshihiko Sahashi. PRD: Toei, TV Asahi. 25 mins. x 45 eps. (TV), 60 mins. (m).
Reiko Mikami is a sexy penny-pinching exorcist who forces her adoring assistant, Tadao, to work for a pittance. While the snobbish, self-regarding Reiko spars with the lecherous Tadao, Okinu the gentle ex-ghost tries to keep them calm enough to do their ghostbusting job. With an unlikable heroine who persists in selling out her friends, the show spoofs the mercenary do-gooder of Osamu Tezuka's **BLACK JACK**, as well as the miniskirted, "body-conscious" girls of Tokyo's 1990s club scene. There

are also occasional moments of social commentary, as it is revealed that Tokyo's ghost epidemic has been caused by urban sprawl pushing previously unseen spirits into the open (POM POKO). The chief emphasis, however, is on comedy, with a subsidiary cast including Pietro the shy half-vampire, impoverished Father Karasu, sexy voodoo ghost-sweeper Emiko, mad scientist Dr. Chaos, and his robot assistant, Maria (see METAL ANGEL MARIE). Reiko and her gang also appeared in Atsutoshi Umezawa's anime movie *GS Mikami: War in Heaven* (1994, *Gokuraku Taisen*).

The time *GS Mikami* took to reach the U.S. is a real mystery. Based on a long-running manga by Takashi Shiina in *Shonen Sunday*, it has all the lighthearted adventure and sex appeal of URUSEI YATSURA, and in the hands of Viz Communications, it might have even outperformed the same publisher's RANMA ½. In the Japanese market, where it peaked at a 14.6% TV rating, it swiftly sent the look-alike video anime PHANTOM QUEST CORP packing and outlasted most of its contemporaries in the harsh mid-1990s market. Rumors abound that it was picked up by a well-known distributor as part of a bulk deal then left to fester because the lighthearted banter didn't sit well with the company's more action-based titles. This may have damaged it irreparably, as its cheap animation style will probably lead it to date faster than other anime from the same period—it already looks slightly older than its years.

GHOST TALKER'S DAYDREAM *

2004. JPN: *Teizokurei Daydream*. AKA: *Vulgar Spirit Daydream*. Video. DIR: Osamu Sekita. SCR: Katsuma Kanazawa. DES: Akemi Kobayashi. ANI: N/C. MUS: Takayuki Negishi. PRD: Geneon, HAL Filmmaker. 25 mins. x 4 eps. Psychic investigator Misaki Saiki helps solve crimes in Tokyo while working at her regular job as an S/M dominatrix at an exclusive gentleman's club. Her powers are limited to seeing and conversing with the dead (see also THE TOP SECRET), but that appears to be all she needs, along with some gratuitous nudity and several misguided attempts to inject comedy. Her first case is that of Ai, a young woman whose sister and niece have supposedly committed double suicide. Somehow gaining an ability of her own to see the

dead, Ai stays with Misaki for later cases. There is something of a twisted genius in the concept of a psychic dominatrix, as if Chuck Palahniuk were let loose on *The Sixth Sense* (1999) or VAMPIRE PRINCESS MIYU, but *GTD* does very little with the idea of a psychic who puts her powers of empathy to such controversial use out of office hours. Instead, it plays out in the manner of PHANTOM QUEST CORP, another psychic investigation tale that stalled on video when it really should have been on TV, where the ghost-of-the-week formula has longer to grow. Mystifyingly, the story has barely started before Misaki is heading off on vacation in two episodes scripted specifically for the anime by the author of the manga, something that anime series really should only do when they're sure they have the audience's attention and indulgence. This turns out to be an excuse for a series of jokes about Misaki's lack of pubic hair, for which she is seeking a spiritual remedy. Based on the 2001 manga by Sankichi Meguro, itself based on a "concept" by Saki Okuse, whatever that means. Presumably, Okuse was the one who ran into the first meeting and shouted: "Two words! Bondage Investigator!" **Ⓝ**

GHOSTS

1982. JPN: *Obake*. TV special. DIR: Yasunori Kawauchi, Tameo Ogawa, Gisaburo Sugii, Tsutomu Shibayama. SCR: Yasunori Kawauchi. DES: N/C. ANI: N/C. MUS: N/C. PRD: Ai Planning Center, Tac, TBS. ca. 85 mins. An omnibus of four ghost stories from famous directors, beginning with *Comparing Transformations*, set at a ghoulish convention somewhere in the Japanese mountains. The scene moves to a seaside cave for *The Two-Eyed Goblin*, in which a family of cyclopes adopts a human child. A villager at a local festival meets a beautiful girl who suddenly disappears in *Divine Secret*, and in the final story, *Amulet*, Buddha punishes the behavior of Taira no Kiyomori by releasing evil spirits into the world.

GIANT GORG

1984. JPN: *Kyoshin/Giant Gorg*. TV series. DIR: Yoshikazu Yasuhiko, Norio Kashima. SCR: Masaki Tsuji, Sumiko Tsukamoto. DES: Yoshikazu Yasuhiko. ANI: Mayumi Ishigaki. MUS: Mitsuo Hagiwara. PRD: Sunrise, TV Tokyo. 25

mins. x 26 eps. Tectonic activity on the Pacific island of Austral reveals highly advanced technology. The Gail Corporation, an immensely powerful conglomerate that has been carefully manipulating the Cold War, wants the technology for itself and sends its chief executive's grandson, Rod Balboa, to get it. Opposing Balboa is Yu Tagami, the son of a Japanese researcher murdered by the Gail Corporation, who has teamed up with his father's associate, Doctor Wave. Pursued from New York across America and down to the South Seas by Gail's henchmen (and by other interested parties, including the soldier of fortune known as the "Captain," and Lady Lynx, queen of the Las Vegas casinos and underworld), Yu, Wave, and Wave's pretty sister Doris finally reach Austral. There, they discover that the island is a time capsule of artifacts from a lost civilization, and that Gorg, the "fearsome sea monster" that terrorizes shipping in the area, is actually a giant robot protecting its creator from interference. Manon, the pilot of a second guardian, is awakened from cryogenic slumber but cannot bear the thought that his civilization has been supplanted by humanity. Instead, he plans to destroy the world. Ronald Reagan and Yuri Andropov decide to launch a joint nuclear attack on Austral before Manon's doomsday device can go off; unfortunately for Yu's gang and the other treasure hunters, they are trapped on the island by Manon's forcefield and have only seven days to escape. Foreshadowing both SPRIGGAN, with its corporate conflict over ancient artifacts, and the antediluvian adventure of SECRET OF BLUE WATER, *GG* is also renowned for its comic-relief Professor Wave, who looks uncannily like Woody Allen.

GIANT KILLING

2010. TV series. DIR: Yu Ko. SCR: Toshifumi Kawase, Tatsushi Moriya, Kenichi Takeshita. DES: Tetsuya Kumagai, Junichi Higashi. ANI: Shosuke Shimizu, Akihito Asai, Daisuke Takemoto. MUS: Hideharu Mori. PRD: Studio DEEN, NHK. 24 mins. x 26 eps. East Tokyo United is struggling to stay in the top Japanese league. After several years of bad results, with their fans starting to drift away, they hire a guy who has recently had spectacular success in England, taking an amateur team to the top 32 of the FA Cup. Unfortunately, this wonderboss is former ETU player Takeshi Tatsumi, who left the club at the height of his powers as a player for overseas glory. Facing fan distrust, player resentment, limited budgets, and a squad that needs work, Tatsumi is unfazed. He knows he was born to be a giant killer.

Like CAPTAIN TSUBASA and KICKERS and all the other SPORTS ANIME before it, this isn't actually about the sport. It's about the psychological drama and the interplay between the disparate characters as they struggle to bond in a common cause. That's lucky, because the soccer in *Giant Killing* is hampered by a limited budget that robs it of the motion and gameplay that would make it great. That said, the animation and design are attractive and work fine off the pitch, but it's in the characters and their stories that this show's charm lies. These are all adults, but in many ways it is reminiscent of GTO, with Tatsumi learning as much from his homecoming as his team does from him in this refreshingly unpretentious version of Tsujitomo's 2007 manga.

GIANT ROBO *

1992. Video. DIR: Yasuhiro Imagawa. SCR: Yasuhiro Imagawa, Eiichi Sato. DES: Makoto Kobayashi, Toshiyuki Kubooka, Akihiko Yamashita, Takashi Watabe. ANI: Akihiko Yamashita. MUS: Masamichi Amano. PRD: Mu Film. 56 mins., 42 mins., 40 mins., 46 mins., 45 mins., 49 mins., 59 mins. (v1), 30 mins. x 3 eps. (v2 *Ginrei*).

The Shizuma drive, a clean energy source that has revolutionized world energy and eliminated pollution, has a fatal flaw. The evil Professor Franken von Folger and his associates, would-be world dictators Big Fire, dispatch a black orb to float across the world, draining the energy from all major cities and causing global chaos. Fearing a replay of the Tragedy of Bashtarlle, when faulty Shizuma prototypes wiped out an entire city, the Experts of Justice set out to stop Big Fire. Their members include martial artists, scientific geniuses, secret agents, Folger's own estranged daughter, Ginrei, and a young boy called Daisaku Kusama. Only the voice of Daisaku, the son of a scientist murdered by Big Fire, can control Giant

Robo, a 90-foot-tall war machine originally designed for Big Fire but now devoted to fighting crime.

GR began life as a short-lived 1967 manga by GIGANTOR's Mitsuteru Yokoyama and was also adapted into a live-action TV series known in the U.S. as *Johnny Sokko and His Flying Robot* (1968). Director Imagawa's *GR* was the first of the 1990s "retro" boom, a number of anime made in a deliberately old-fashioned style that recalls the imagery of the Golden Age of sci-fi and also reminds baby boomers of their carefree childhoods during Japan's economic miracle, before the oil shocks of the 1970s. Its style was copied in other shows, including SUPER ATRAGON, KISHIN CORPS, SAKURA WARS, and AMBASSADOR MAGMA, and also created the environment that allowed Tezuka Pro to seriously consider new versions of previously "dated" classics such as BLACK JACK. Imagawa himself became so involved in the development work for another retro anime, GETTER ROBO, that the final episode of *GR* only appeared in 1997, when most of the voice actors had forgotten their roles and needed a refresher course.

In addition to changing the manga's Franken to Franken von Folger (his own homage to *The Rocky Horror Picture Show*'s Frank-N-Furter), Imagawa pastiched characters from many of Yokoyama's other works, including GODMARS, BABEL II, and even LITTLE WITCH SALLY. Most notable among these is the presence of characters dressed like medieval Chinese rebels and an HQ in "Ryozanpaku," which *GR*'s U.S. translators failed to note was Japanese for Liang Shan Po, the famous marshes of the *Water Margin* (see SUIKODEN). Yokoyama's *Water Margin* was never animated but was turned into an extremely popular live-action TV series during the 1970s—however, many of its main characters were lifted wholesale for *GR*.

As implied by its Japanese subtitle, *The Day the Earth Stood Still*, *GR* also carries a subtle antinuclear message nestled amid the robot combat and gunfights, with a "safe" energy source put to evil use, ironically against all the major cities of Japan's enemies in WWII, including London, New York, San Francisco, and Shanghai. Featuring great music from UROTSUKIDOJI– composer Amano, it also has the recurring theme, "A Furtive Tear," taken from Doni-

zetti's comic opera *The Love Potion* (1832), which tells a similar tale of mankind putting too much faith in technology, albeit of a different kind!

The show also spun off into three videos featuring the undisputed microminiskirted star of the show, starting with *Barefoot Ginrei* (1993, *Hadashi no Ginrei*). This depicted the morning after the first episode of *Giant Robo*, showing a day in the life of Ginrei and Big Fire's Shockwave Alberto; at least, until Ginrei discovers that her combat China dress is missing. *Mighty Ginrei* (1994, *Tetsuwan Ginrei*) finds the Experts of Justice having a joint company party with "Blue Flower," and Daisaku defecting to the latter because of their better pay and benefits package. Since Giant Robo is in the shop for repairs, he takes with him GR's improved successor, Ginrei Robo. Both episodes are played tongue-in-cheek, with shots parodying LUPIN III and CUTEY HONEY. The third, *Blue-Eyed Ginrei* (1995, *Aoi Hitomi no Ginrei*) is played straight. Ginrei and Tetsugyu are sent undercover to investigate the disappearance of a research team in the desert, and (of course) Big Fire turns out to be involved. The three were released in English on one DVD as *Ginrei Special*.

GIFT: ETERNAL RAINBOW

2006. TV series, video. DIR: Shigeru Kimiya. SCR: Masashi Suzuki. DES: Motoki Tanaka, Hisayoshi Takahashi. ANI: N/C. MUS: Hikaru Nanase. PRD: Oriental Light & Magic. 25 mins. x 12 eps.

Haruhiko lives under a magic rainbow that promises to grant one wish, known as a "Gift," to those whose hearts are truly one. But a wrongly used Gift, between those whose feelings are not mutual, can wreak magical meteorological havoc. Haruhiko was close to his friend Kirino in childhood, but then developed a much stronger relationship with his foster sister Riko. Then, his father could no longer afford to support both children and Riko had to leave. Kirino resumed her old role as Haruhiko's best friend and remains in love with him, although he teases her constantly. Then Riko comes back to town and Haruhiko's old feelings for her resurface, while other girls circle him in the traditional harem dance (ROMANCE AND DRAMA). It turns out that the whole

Gift system was set up by Haruhiko's dead mother.

This adaptation of a "visual novel" porn game by CIRCUS and Moonstone has many similarities to CIRCUS' better known work DA CAPO—and, we observe wearily, to a huge number of other games for boys too scared to get to know girls outside their immediate family. There's a spin-off manga, story by Moonstone and art by Yukiwo, but we'd rather you take time to compare this to the less mawkish and far deeper FIVE CENTIMETERS PER SECOND. An unaired "13th episode" appeared in the DVD release, giving Kirino's family an inn and getting everyone from school to work there: yes, even without associated hot springs you may treat this as a cliché alert. **O**

GIGANTIC FORMULA

2007. JPN: Kishin Taisen Gigantic Formula. AKA: Apo Mekhanes Theos Giantic Formula; Mechanical Divine War Gigantic Formula. TV series. DIR: Keiji Goto. SCR: Hidefumi Kimura. DES: Koji Yabuno, Katsufumi Hariu. ANI: Koji Yabuno, Hiroyuki Shimizu, Noriyuki Fukuda, Ryosuke Tanigawa. MUS: Hiroyuki Sawano. PRD: Brains Base, Bandai Visual, TV Tokyo. 25 mins. x 26 eps.

In 2035, colossal stone heads resembling the Greek gods are found in different parts of the world. Shortly afterward, a huge belt of the Earth around the equator is engulfed in flames, devastating Africa, South America and the Middle East. The "Equatorial Winter" is followed by a huge energy surge, like a gigantic wall cutting off all contact between nations. Each nation finds special representatives who could communicate with the stone heads. Back came the order—build armor for the heads so they can fight, and provide human pilots for them. So begins the great war to unify the world.

This is a wonderful concept, although for older sci-fi fans, giant stone heads wielding huge power are forever Zardoz (1974). The design is nice, the mecha are interesting and there is very real jeopardy. But an action anime is about the action or it might as well go home, and GF commits the cardinal sin of interrupting the flow of battles for character flashbacks and plot exposition. Makoto Shinkai did something similar in VOICES OF A DISTANT STAR, but in

the context of a one-shot video that was mostly about emotional turmoil, that was logical. Prioritizing musing over mecha is a high risk strategy, and in a 26-episode series it gets tedious very quickly. Kimura created the story, with original character designs by Megumi Kadonosono, and it was adapted as a manga by Shohei Oka in 2007. Untranslated into English, perhaps because it was made right after the big slump in production, but also possibly because flinging around a name like "gigantic formula" is unlikely to impress fans and distributors who tire of cookie-cutter stories. **O**

GIGANTOR *

1963. JPN: Tetsujin 28-go. AKA: Ironman Number 28. TV series. DIR: Yonehiko Watanabe, Tadao Wakabayashi. SCR: Yoshikazu Okamoto. DES: Mitsuteru Yokoyama. ANI: Tadao Wakabayashi, Kazuo Nobara. MUS: Hidehiko Arashino. PRD: Eiken (TCJ), TMS. 25 mins. x 96 eps., 25 mins. x 51 eps. (New), 25 mins. x 24 eps. (FX).

Before Japan's experimental robot weapon project can be used against the Allies, U.S. bombers destroy the laboratory, killing its creator, Dr. Kaneda. A decade after the war, several crimes are found to have been committed by remote-controlled giant robots, the 26th and 27th prototypes of a long-forgotten military project. Kaneda's detective son, Shotaro (Jimmy Sparks), discovers that the syndicates are searching for a mythical 28th prototype, rumored to be even more powerful. He beats them in figuring out its whereabouts, finding both it and Professor Shikashima (Bob Brilliant), another researcher thought dead in the same attack that killed his father. Shikashima and Shotaro decide to use Ironman #28 for peace, not war. The final 13 episodes, broadcast after a hiatus of several months in which the Eiken team concentrated on PRINCE PLANET, featured a change of direction, with Shotaro having a vision that aliens from Planet Magma are about to invade and piloting Ironman against the Magmans' robot champions Magma X and Gold Wolf.

Based on a 1956 Shonen Magazine serial by GIANT ROBO–creator Mitsuteru Yokoyama, and thereby predating Osamu Tezuka's similar BIG X in both anime and manga forms, Ironman's design is not dis-

similar to that of Ryuichi Yokoyama's propaganda manga The Science Warrior Appears in New York (1943), suggesting perhaps this is indeed the way that WARTIME ANIME might have turned out if the war had gone on any longer! However, the postwar Ironman was considered peaceful enough for 52 of the early episodes to get a U.S. release courtesy of Fred Ladd, who toned down some of the death and violence and ensured that almost every villain in the show sounded like a Nazi or a Chicago mobster. In his memoirs published in 2009, Ladd revealed that the entire WWII subplot had been kept from him by canny licensors, who lied at the time that the animation of the show's first 26 episodes was of too poor quality for the U.S. and not even worth looking at. In answer to American concerns over CENSORSHIP AND LOCALIZATION, Ladd was obliged to ensure that no episodes ended on a cliffhanger, which required rehiring Japanese animators TCJ to make new endings for many episodes that had previously formed parts of ongoing two- and three-part story arcs. The old show is probably best remembered for its classic theme tune from Lou Singer and Gene Raskin redundantly announcing that our hero was "ready to fight for right against wrong." There was also a short-lived 1960 live-action series in Japan (*DE).

The franchise was revived for New Ironman28 (1980), directed by Tetsuo Imazawa, in which Interpol agent Shotaro works for the antirobot crime division, Branch Robo, and occasionally repels alien invaders, too. The new series removed the wartime angle by beginning in the 1990s with the death of Professor Kaneda and did not appear in the U.S. as New Gigantor until 1993, after the "future year" in which it was originally set.

Super-Electric Robo Ironman 28 FX (1992) was another, less successful TV series from Imazawa that moved the action to 2030 and starred the grandson of the original Professor Kaneda, fighting adversaries such as the "Pink Mafia" and the evil Franken organization, as well as the office politics within Interpol that find him arrested at one point by his own staff. Gigantor also supplied inspiration for creator Katsuhiro Otomo, who wrote a trilogy of adult manga designed to be modern retellings of old classics. They were *Fireball*, featuring a supercomputer modeled on **ASTRO BOY**; *Domu*, featuring a psychic schoolgirl modeled on **E-CHAN THE NINJA**; and **AKIRA**, in which a Shotaro *Kaneda* and a Colonel Shikashima who is the son of an inventor, fight over a classified weapon left over from an old war, known as Number 28.

Gigantor was remade yet again by **GIANT ROBO**–director Yasuhiro Imagawa in 2004, in a TV series that restored much of the dark seriousness of the original manga, bringing it fullcircle to its militaristic origins. There was also a live-action remake, *Tetsujin 28* (2005).

GIGI AND THE FOUNTAIN OF YOUTH *

1982. JPN: *Maho no Princess Minky Momo*. AKA: *Magical Princess Minky Momo; Fairy Princess Minky Momo*. TV series, video. DIR: Kunihiko Yuyama, Junji Nishiyama, Kenjiro Yoshida, Hiroshi Watanabe. SCR: Takeshi Shudo, Tomomi Tsutsui, Jiyu Watanabe. DES: Toyoo Ashida, Noa Misaki, Ayumi Hattori. ANI: Mamoru Tanaka, Hiroshi Watanabe, Kazuo Imura. MUS: Hiroshi Takada. PRD: Ashi Pro, TV Tokyo. 25 mins. x 61 eps. (TV1), 3 mins. (v1), 80 mins. (v2), 25 mins. x 62 eps. (TV2), 25 mins. x 3 eps. (v3).

Minky Momo (Gigi) is a princess from the magical dreamland of Fenalinasa who has been sent to Earth where she poses as the daughter of two veterinarians, albeit one who can transform (in the style of **CREAMY MAMI**) into a grown-up magical heroine, accompanied by her magical companions, Sindbook the dog, Mocha the monkey, and Pipil the bird. Perhaps unnaturally popular in the midst of the "Lolita complex" fad that also produced **CREAM LEMON**, she returned on several occasions, including the three-minute short *Creamy Mami vs. Minky Momo* (1985) and *Minky Momo: La Ronde in My Dream* (1985), released in the U.S. as *Gigi and the Fountain of Youth*. In this 80-minute video, also screened theatrically, her human parents' plane crashes in the sea, and Momo discovers a tropical island, above which floats a children's paradise where nobody ever ages. The island's ruler Peter (an obvious reference to **PETER PAN AND WENDY**) enlists Momo's help in holding off unsavory outsiders, including the original master thief Lupin (not his grandson **LUPIN III**).

After the original's apparent death and the destruction of Fenalinasa, a new Momo appeared in the 1991 TV series about a princess from the undersea kingdom of Marinnasa taking up the previous Momo's mantle and masquerading on Earth as the daughter of archeologists searching for the ruins of Fenalinasa. Though the new Momo lost her powers in episode 62, she had three extra unbroadcast adventures that were included when the TV series was released on video in 1993, comprising *SOS Marinnasa, Momo Goes to School*, and *A Favor from the Stars*.

GIGOLO *

1993. JPN: *Dochinpira: Onna Daisuki*. AKA: *Vulgar Punk: I Love Women*. Video. DIR: Hiromitsu Ota. SCR: Wataru Amano. DES: Hironobu Saito. ANI: Shigetaka Kiyoyama. MUS: Beyond Two. PRD: Pink Pineapple, KSS. 45 mins.

Jin drops out of college to become a gigolo, selling his favors to bored rich women in Tokyo while still living with his true love, the long-suffering Ranko. After some disastrous jobs that bring him into contact with the Hazakura gang, he is propositioned by Ai, a female contract killer. After he is the first man to "take her to heaven and back" (naturally), she reveals that she works for the rival Konatsu syndicate, whose boss adopted her after her original parents were killed in gangland cross fire. After also losing her stepfather to criminal intrigue, she has sworn revenge on Mr. Hazakura himself, who is in hiding after the last attempt on his life. Realizing that Jin has serviced Hazakura's mistress, Ai forces him to take her there, where both she and Hazakura die in a shootout. Jin buries her at sea in her beloved Shelby Cobra automobile, then returns to Ranko, who reveals that it is their anniversary, and takes him to bed.

Considering the liberal tastes of the Japanese video porn market, it is bizarre that *Gigolo* wasn't made as a gay anime like **FAKE**. If the lead characters had been male, the macho posturings and pompous codes of honor would be more believable, as would the appetites and attitudes of the "female" characters, but presumably such a narrative switch wouldn't have pleased the authors of the original manga, Makio Hara and Tetsumi Doko. Better plotted than

most porn anime, if only because there is a semblance of story that bolts together the halfhearted (and half-animated) sex scenes, *Gigolo* rivals **GOLGO 13** in both its contemptuous attitude toward women and its juvenile take on sex and crime. It also contains the cheesiest of dialogue, played absolutely straight in the U.K. dub. To add insult to injury, the initial British release even managed to misspell the title, calling it *Gigalo* on the video box. **LNV**

GILGAMESH *

2003. TV series. DIR: Masahiko Murata. SCR: Akio Satsugawa, Sadayuki Murai, Yasuko Kobayashi. DES: Masahiro Sato, Saki Okuse. ANI: Group TAC, Japan Vistec. MUS: Kaoru Wada. PRD: Group TAC, Japan Vistec, Kansai TV. 23 mins. x 26 eps.

The near future, two decades after a mysterious apocalyptic event in the Middle East that wiped out magnetic fields, disabled computers, and caused the "Sheltering Sky effect" that shut out the stars—perhaps an out-of-place reference to the film by Bernardo Bertolucci, or the novel by Paul Bowles that inspired it, although its closest analogue can be found in **THE ANIMATRIX**. Twins Tatsuya and Kiyoko are on the run from debt collectors when they are captured by a group called Orga and asked by the mysterious Countess von Werdenburg to join her child superheroes to fight a group of half-divine psychics called Gilgamesh. She claims their leader, Enkidu, was responsible for the apocalyptic incident and offers to pay the debts left by the twins' late mother in return for their assistance. The Countess is working with Dr. Enuma of the Midlight Corporation, who has developed a huge device to reverse the abnormal magnetic field and restore the world to its former state. It is contained in the tower of Turangalila—compare to **BABEL II**.

When Kiyoko is kidnapped by a Gilgamesh group, Tatsuya and his Orga associates chase after her, in the course of which Tatsuya realizes that he is developing paranormal powers of his own. Kiyoko, however, shelters Novem, her injured captor, becomes pregnant with his child, and begins to question the motives of her former boss the Countess. In a "twist," we discover that the twins are the children of Terumichi Madoka, the infamous Enkidu, who met their mother on an archeological dig in the ruins of Babylon shortly before he set off the Sheltering Sky disaster. Now, in a twisted echo of ancient myth, he is trying to destroy the world in a final cleansing flood (see SPRIGGAN) to enable the planet to recover from the errors of mankind and thrive for a new, pure race of humans.

Gilgamesh is another of the-21st century anime like DEMON LORD DANTE, based on forgotten works from the 20th century after all the best-known titles had been snapped up. It first appeared as a 1976 manga in *Shonen King* magazine by Shotaro Ishinomori, mixing ancient myth with UFO lore in the manner of NAZCA. Ishinomori's original is suffused here with a darker subtext, largely in the wake of the 9/11 terrorist attacks in 2001 that culminated in the fall of the twin towers of the World Trade Center. The disaster in *Gilgamesh* takes place on 10th October, and hence becomes known as "Twin X," a clever reference to the protagonists, although likely to cause some confusion in Taiwan, where the same day is known as "Double Tenth," and is a public holiday to celebrate the foundation of the Republic of China.

GINBAN KALEIDOSCOPE

2005. TV series. DIR: Shinji Takamatsu, Hazuki Mizumoto. SCR: Akatsuki Yamatoya, Michiko Yokote, Natsuko Takahashi, Rika Nakase. DES: Momoko Makiuchi. ANI: Tatsuo Miura. MUS: Koichiro Kamiyama. PRD: arp Japan, QEN, Studio B2, TV Tokyo. 25 mins. x 12 eps.
World-class figure skater Sakurano suffers a cataclysmic fall from favor, incurring the wrath of the media and other skaters. Such public troubles only serve to exacerbate her typical teen angst and school pressures. One day, she gains a ghostly companion, Pete, the ghost of a handsome blond skater, the cause of whose death is initially unknown to Sakurano. He becomes her companion and sometime ally, in an ice-skating rerun of HIKARU'S GO. Based on a manga by Rei Kaibara.

GINGUISER

1977. JPN: *Chogattai Majutsu Robo Ginguiser.* AKA: *Ultra-transforming Magical Robot Ginguiser.* TV series. DIR: Masami Anno. SCR: Rei Yada, Yu Yamamoto, Doki Kan. DES: Yasuo Kainai, Studio Nue. ANI: Hitoshi Tanaka. MUS: Seiji Yokoyama. PRD: Ashi Pro, Nippon Animation, TV Asahi. 25 mins. x 26 eps.
Emperor Kaindark of the Sazorian Empire wants three powerful energy sources, the spheres of Antares. They are hidden on Earth, so he sends his mighty monsters (awakened after 20,000 years in suspended animation) to bring them back. They are opposed by Doctor Godo, the scion of the Sazorian's rival Plasman clan, who had foreseen such a danger, but inexplicably decides that Earth's best line of defense should be a pair of teenagers with a traveling magic show and a pile of slick card tricks. Goro Shiroishi and Michi Ushio drive a truck that can transform into a fighting robot; their comrades Torajiro Aranami and Santa Minami each have another transforming vehicle. Ginguiser is formed when the three robots Grandfighter, Spinlancer, and Bullgaiter combine with the jet fighter Arrow Wing. When the enemy attacks, the plane takes off from its secret base under Luna Park and the other three robots gather to unite. Armed with a sword, a shield, and a rotary saw, Ginguiser fights to save the world from the monsters—it is no coincidence that it replicates the plotlines and attitudes of the early battle-team shows from live-action television, *Goranger* (*DE) and *Jaqk* (*DE).

GINNAGASHI

1992. JPN: *Terajima-cho Kidan: Ginnagashi.* AKA: *Ginnagashi: Strange Tales of Terajima District.* Video. DIR: Osamu Kobayashi. SCR: Yu Takita. DES: Masaya Fujimori. ANI: Takaichiro Nakamura. MUS: Hiroshi Ogasawara. PRD: Toei, Tac. 41 mins.
Ten-year-old Kiyoshi watches as a tramp transforms himself into a rich imposter at a stand-up bar in the Tamanoi district. Amusing tales from prewar Tokyo based on the 1968 autobiographical manga *Strange Tales of Terajima* and written by Yu Takita for the alternative magazine *Garo*.

GINTAMA *

2005. JPN: *Gin Tama.* AKA: *Silver Soul.* Video, TV series, movie. DIR: Shinji Takamatsu, Yoichi Fujita. SCR: Akatsuki Yamatoya, Michiko Yokote, Taketo Shimoyama. DES: Shinji Takeuchi, Yuki Nomura. ANI: Hitomi Tsuruta, Shinji Takeuchi, Akio Sugino, Akira Sotoya, Dai Imaoka. MUS: Audio Highs. PRD: Sunrise, Aniplex, Bandai, Dentsu, Shueisha, TV Tokyo, Warner Bros. 33 mins. (v1), 25 mins. x 201 eps. (TV1), 25 mins. x 51 eps. (TV2), 25 mins. x 64 eps. (TV3), 95 mins. (m1), 14 mins. (v3), ?? mins. (m2).
Edo hasn't been the same since the aliens arrived. The Amanto have taken over the planet and turned Japan into a sweatshop owned and managed by their own, with the natives as labor. They've even taken away the swords of the samurai. Those who don't want to toe the line have to fend for themselves, although the Amanto have introduced a great new healthcare plan. Silver-haired samurai Gintoki, swordsman Shinpachi, and alien girl Kagura team up to form an agency, Yorozuya, or "We do everything"—offering to take any job if the price is right. Unfortunately, things rarely go according to plan....

This delightful farrago of nonsense is based on Hideaki Sorachi's 2004 manga *Gin Tama*. Sorachi wanted to write a gag manga, only adding drama and character development later as the fans warmed to his motley crew of characters and their world—hence the *Monty Python*–esque absurdity and iconoclasm in the *Simpsons* mode. Frequently breaking the fourth wall, the manga and the anime steal many targets and themes from contemporary Japanese society, parodying the round of festivals and rituals that have endured since the Edo period and referring to historical figures. This allowed Sorachi to indulge his passion for the Shinsengumi (SHINSENGUMI FARCE), the shogun's fanatical supporters who have inspired so many writers and artists. The alien invasion also enables him to look at issues of social equality and the Allied Occupation.

The cross-references don't stop with history. Alien heroine Kagura looks like a cross between Chun Li of STREET FIGHTER II and the male form of RANMA ½. Anime parodies, nods, and winks abound, and one entire episode is a parody of *Slumdog Millionaire*. Characters from Kenta Shinhara's SKET DANCE guest-starred in an episode of series two. Some fans have criticized the series' humor for being hard to understand if you're not Japanese—which, frankly, is about as constructive as criticizing the French for speaking French, especially in these Internet days when everyone and their dog expounds on Japanese culture online. In any event, as far as gags go the series has plenty of fanboy in-jokes that anime fans of any nationality will enjoy.

Its life in animation began in 2005, as a short film made for the Jump Festa Anime Tour. The first series aired from April 2006. It ran for 201 episodes—four years, around a hundred hours of animation. A switch of directors halfway through didn't break the flow of silliness at all. During its run, a second video, *White Demon's Birth (Shiroyasha Kotan)* appeared in 2008, again for Jump Festa. This turned out to be a practical joke—a trailer for an imaginary *Gintama* movie. A theatrical film was finally released in 2010. *Gintama The Movie (Gintama: Shinyaku Benizakurahen,* or *A New Retelling Benizakura Arc)* put Shinji Takamatsu, veteran of **GUNDAM** and *Might Gine* (**BRAVE SAGA**) into the director's chair, retelling some of the events of series one. A 14-minute special, in which the characters reflect on events since the series began, was also put together by Sunrise for a special *Gintama* event in summer 2010. This was *Gintama Big Retrospective Meeting (Anime Ginatama dai hanseikai)*. Meanwhile episodes of the anime were aired on TV Tokyo in HD under yet another title, *The Very Best of Gintama (Yorinuki Gintama)*.

The second series, *Gintama'*, commenced in 2011 and ran for 51 episodes—note the apostrophe that appears after the *kanji* in the original Japanese title. Confusingly, there are also 60 titles for those 51 episodes because some contain two stories. Series three, *Gintama' Enchosen*, also known as *Kintama'* for its first four episodes for comedic reasons, began its run in 2012 and ended in March 2013 after 64 episodes. A second movie in 2012 was called *Gintama The Final Chapter, Be Forever Yorozuya (Gintama Kanketsu-hen Yorozuya yo Eien Nare)*, though *Gintama The Movie 2* will probably work just as well.

GIOVANNI'S ISLAND *
2014. JPN: *Giovanni no Shima*. Movie. DIR: Mizuho Nishikubo. SCR: Shigemichi Sugita, Yoshimi Sakurai. DES: Atsuko Fukushima, Nobutake Ito. ANI: Nobutake Ito. MUS: Masashi Sada. PRD: Production I.G. 102 mins.
In the tense aftermath of World War Two, the Kuril Islands in northernmost Japan are handed over to the Soviet Union. A Japanese father assures his family that all will be well, although the postwar Soviet Occupation ironically brings tension and fear to an island that has previously been relatively untouched by the conflict. Young boy Junpei develops a halting, international friendship with the newly arrived blonde beauty Tanya, but her countrymen prove to be less accommodating, shipping Junpei's father off to Siberia.

Ever willing to poke around in the interstices of history for children's stories of the war, the Japanese animation industry alights here on the true story of Hiroshi Tokuno, on whose life story this film is partly based. Director Nishikubo spoke in interviews of heartfelt drama and documentary realism, using Russian voice-actors in the style of **FIRST SQUAD**, and employing the same tactic as Hayao Miyazaki in **SPIRITED AWAY**, by refusing to depict anything beyond the understanding of his child protagonist. However, using such a perspective in a wartime theme arguably plays into Japan's ongoing amnesia about the war, once again depicting the Japanese as guileless innocents, caught up in determinist historical events not of their making (**WARTIME ANIME**). We might also point to *Giovanni's Island* as another iteration of a *sub-*subgenre in Japanese animation about the end of WW2, sitting alongside other films such as **RAIL OF THE STAR**, **MEMORIES OF YOUTH**, **STORY OF THE TSUSHIMA**, and **KIKU AND THE WOLF** in their focus on the Japanese imperial subjects who found themselves in "foreign" territory after the surrender. It is difficult to accept the giddy internationalism and pacifism of the film itself out of the political context—in 2006, the then-president of Russia Vladimir Putin offered to return Shikotan and the Habomai rocks, as long as Japan accepted that the larger disputed islands of Iturup and Kunashir were Russian ever more. Japanese school textbooks continue to refer to the islands as Japanese territory, but then again, Japanese school textbooks continue to downplay the Rape of Nanjing.

GIRL DETECTIVES' CLUB
1986. JPN: *Katsugeki Shojo Tanteidan*. Video. DIR: Masaharu Okuwaki. SCR: Yuho Hanazono. DES: Isamu Eguchi. ANI: Masako Goto. MUS: "The Girl Detectives' Club." PRD: Tokyo Movie Shinsha. 30 mins.
Yuriko Edogawa, Midori Ichinotani, and Ingrid Shizuka Gruber are ordinary students at the high-class Gautama School for Girls who moonlight as supersleuths. Midori disappears soon after discovering that her scientist father is working on a weapon, and the other girls track her down. They discover that she has been kidnapped by Akiko Jitsusoji, a bad-girl with her own gang working for the school principal, who is planning to conquer the world with Dr. Ichinotani's doomsday device. This very early multimedia offensive, including a tie-in manga in *OUT* magazine, ended with a very early disappointed audience, as *GDC* turned out to be a lackluster affair. Compare to the suspiciously similar **DEBUTANTE DETECTIVES**.

GIRL FROM PHANTASIA *
1993. JPN: *Fantasia*. Video. DIR: Jun Kamiya. SCR: Katsuyuki Sumisawa. DES: Kazuya Kise. ANI: Kazuya Kise. MUS: Toshiyuki Watanabe. PRD: Production I.G. 30 mins.
College boy Akihiro's girlfriend, Michiko, doesn't like his apartment enough to come over, and that seriously reduces his chances of getting her into bed. Finding a rug among some trash on the sidewalk, he takes it home to improve the decor, only to discover that it is a magical gateway to the fantasyland of Phantasia. Akihiko becomes the object of attention from the feisty sprite Malon. This video is a replay of a dozen other magical-girlfriend tales from **URUSEI YATSURA** to **OH MY GODDESS!**, this time with an eye on the soft-core porn market. Based on Akane Nagano's manga in *Comic Gamma*. **Ⓝ**

GIRL IN A BOX: VIRGIN TERRITORY
2011. JPN: *Hakoiri Shojo: Virgin Territory*. Video. DIR: Sado. SCR: Hanbe Anato. DES: Sado. ANI: Sado. MUS: N/C. PRD: Seven, Mary Jane. 20 mins. x 2 eps.
Sakuraya Academy screens its prospective pupils carefully, selecting only the elite. They're less careful about their teachers—Mr. Kannari is such a favorite with the girls that he's screwing many of them. Now he's set his sights on an innocent new pupil. Based on a 2010 porn game by Jiro of Dojin Soft. **Ⓝ**

GIRL MADE TO COME BY LUSTFUL OTAKU

2011. JPN: *Inshitsu Otaku ni Ikareru Kanojo.* Video. DIR: Hisashi Tomii. SCR: Shingatana Ikari. DES: Banana Milk. ANI: Banana Milk. MUS: N/C. PRD: Studio9MAiami, MediaBank. 30 mins. x 3 eps.

Shun desires his absurdly voluptuous younger sister Saki. When she tells him she feels the same way, their lust runs riot. Then Saki gets an email from a stalker, threatening to reveal all her sexual secrets and attaching a photo of her masturbating. He orders her to commit various sex acts to avoid exposure (though that would seem to be rather beside the point now) and she gradually starts enjoying it, in this anime based on a porn game by Pin-Point. **N**

GIRL NEXT DOOR *

2000. JPN: *Tonari no Oneesan.* Video. DIR: Teruaki Murakami, Sotsuki Mitsumura. SCR: Rokurota Makabe. DES: Bijin Happo. ANI: Takeshi Okamura. MUS: Yoshi. PRD: YOUC, Digital Works (Vanilla Series). 30 mins. x 2 eps.

Masahiko is a shy young man, who believes that he has already met his ideal woman, a Girl Next Door who is somewhere out there waiting for him. But as he tries to remember where he has seen her before, a series of other women in his life clamor for his attention, including his boss, his school teacher, and an old friend from his childhood. In other words, **LOVE HINA** with sex scenes, based on a game by the company Nikukyu. **N**

GIRL SUMMER

2011. JPN: *Nee Summer!* AKA: *Ane Summer; Sister Summer.* Video. DIR: Fumi Suedamube. SCR: Kaoru Takahashi. DES: Gen, baidoku. ANI: Fumi Suedamube. MUS: N/C. PRD: Rabbit Getto, Mary Jane. 15 mins. x 2 eps.

Yuta spends the summer vacation at home alone with his curvy cousin Kei. The two horny teenagers are supposed to be studying, but this anime is based on a porn game by Mary Jane so that flimsy pretence at a plot doesn't hold up the action for long. **N**

GIRL WEAPON SOUL EATER

2010. JPN: *Shojo Senki Soul Eater.* Video. DIR:

Tatsukichi Tomi. SCR: Akira Nintai. DES: Yuji Ushijima. ANI: Tatsukichi Tomi. MUS: N/C. PRD: schoolzone, Marigold. 26 mins.

The vengeful Mikoto joins a team hunting the beastmen who captured and raped her mother. But when she makes a mistake, she falls into the hands of the very same foes who are determined to treat her in the same way. Beastmen and tentacles (with attached suckers) are imported straight from the original porn game by Lune, which came out in 2009. Not to be confused with **SOUL EATER**, and actually a prequel to **BRAIN JACKER**. **NV**

GIRL WHO LEAPT THROUGH SPACE, THE *

2009. JPN: *Sora o Kakeru Shojo.* AKA: *Sora Kake.* TV series. DIR: Masakazu Obara. SCR: Jukki Hanada. DES: Yosuke Kabashima, Hiroyuki Taiga, Tomoyuki Aoki, Junichi Akatsu, Kazutaka Miyatake, Noriyuki Jinguji. ANI: Yosuke Kabashima. MUS: Hikaru Nanase, Kenichi Sudo, Tomoki Kikuya. PRD: Sunrise, Bandai Visual. 24 mins. x 26 eps.

The future—Earth has seeded the galaxy with colony clusters and reset the calendar. It's now year 311 of the new era. Teenager Akiha accidentally discovers a malevolent artificial intelligence on a colony. It calls itself Leopard and it's a raging megalomaniac with family issues. She joins forces with a cute robogirl, an InterColony Police chick, and a subdued moppet with a high IQ to defeat Leopard's plans.

There is actually a story here, but it's heavily derivative and Obara and Hanada simply forget about it most of the time. The idea of teens and adults boxed in by technology, infantilized by our electronic devices, is a lovely one and it would have been fun to see it go somewhere, but that never happens. The plot takes several episodes to get going, then jumps and spins like a flea on speed, starting this or that thread, then losing interest, then batting at it again until you're almost cross-eyed from trying to untangle it. Borrowing a title from **THE GIRL WHO LEAPT THROUGH TIME**, throwing in stereotyped characters and the odd giant robot show reference, and then doing everything fast, doesn't necessarily make it funny. Sunrise house name Hajime Yadate, tagged with numerous and often successful attempts to recycle old plot threads into new sponsor-

ship returns, is credited as creator, and original character designs are by Kazuyuki Yoshizumi.

GIRL WHO LEAPT THROUGH TIME, THE *

2006. JPN: *Toki o Kakeru Shojo.* Movie. DIR: Mamoru Hosoda. SCR: Satoko Okudera. DES: Yoshiyuki Sadamoto. ANI: Tomohiko Ito, Shigeru Fujita, Yasuhiro Nakura, Chikashi Kubota, Hiroyuki Aoyama, Masashi Ishihama. MUS: Kiyoshi Yoshida. PRD: Madhouse, Fuji TV. 98 mins.

Teenager Makoto narrowly avoids a fatal accident, only to discover that she has somehow gained the ability to travel back in time. She uses her newfound power to fix her life, ensuring that she is always early for class, ready for "surprise" tests, and kept out of trouble. With the school vacation approaching, she lives one glorious summer Friday 13th repeatedly, only to discover that her meddling has had unforeseen side effects on the people around her. With only a limited number of time leaps remaining, Makoto tries to put her world back on track, and fights to avoid an approaching tragedy.

The Girl Who Leapt Through Time is one of the classics of Japanese science fiction. First serialized in prose form in 1965, it has been novelized, rewritten, and adapted into five live-action variants over the last 40 years. It has a story that lent itself well to low-budget filmmaking, utilizing everyday settings to tell a time-travel story set largely in the present day. The very first incarnation of *The Girl Who Leapt Through Time* ran in a magazine for 15- and 16-year-old students, and its heroine prominently displayed the passive, diligent virtues required by the Japanese educational establishment. Hosoda's reworking includes the original protagonist as a middle-aged aunt, focusing instead on a more assertive, but also clumsier modern girl.

Satoko Okudera's anime script is fascinated with those moments in time where life could go either way. The lost painting that Aunt Kazuko is restoring at the museum resembles *Our Lady of the Snows*, a religious relic of a bygone era when samurai Japan flirted with Christianity—a period that could have entirely transformed the country. The lead characters say their farewells at a literal fork in the road, at which the filmmakers have playfully placed a prominent road sign pointing in two directions, and the Japanese phrase: "From this point on …"

Minor decisions can have dramatic consequences, even off-screen. In a subtle subplot, some students volunteer to help at a local old peoples' home, entirely unseen in the film, even though this radically affects the lives of two characters in at least one time-stream. Makoto's apparently minor decisions, often made for purely selfish reasons, soon swing out of control. There is a Pinter-esque moment when she tries desperately to change the subject in a conversation before it drifts onto an unwelcome track. Grown-up concerns are impinging on Makoto's life, and much of her time-travel efforts are aimed at holding back the years.

Hosoda's film is suffused with an elegiac quality found in many school anime. The summer vacation is looming, and after graduation the class is sure to be scattered to high schools and speciality institutions. Voices from the future, from the adult filmmakers, draw the audience's attention to things that children take for granted. As seen in many EVERYDAY ANIME, the simple delights of riding a bicycle, of seeing a cicada, of living in our own time, are regarded with the elation of a tourist from a time that, it is implied, lacks many modern pleasures.

Despite its subject matter, the story is ironically timeless. As the anime version seems to acknowledge, the passing decades have done little to age its central themes. Japanese school uniforms have remained largely unchanged for a century. Makoto's school is carefully shot so that we only see those areas that would resonate with all generations. There is no language lab, no computer room; instead we have the sports hall, the baseball field, the library, and the classrooms. Hosoda chooses to keep all automobiles indistinct in the distance, so that nothing except a brief appearance of mobile phones ties the setting to a particular era. With its pedestrian shopping precinct and its small-town atmosphere, the Kuranose setting could almost be one of the nostalgic low-tech towns that dot the works of Hayao Miyazaki.

Unlike his predecessors in the live-action world, Hosoda can count on perfect weather, perfect timing, and perfect framing. The cartoonish sequences of antics on the playing fields or Makoto's kitchen mishaps would have been unfilmable in the low-budget, fast-scheduled TV versions of the past. In one scene, Makoto momentarily breaks the fourth wall, and addresses the audience directly. In another, the camera tracks inexorably ahead of her as she runs desperately to stop time in its tracks. It is as if the film itself threatens to run ahead without her, just as time itself resists her interference. *The Girl Who Leapt Through Time* was a remarkable achievement in anime, but its makers were always likely to be unsure whether their acclaim belonged to them or to the original story's already-iconic place in Japanese pop culture. To prove this was not a one-off, the crew were obliged to return with an all-new idea of their own for their next project, SUMMER WARS.

GIRL WITH THE WHITE FLAG, THE

1988. JPN: *Shirahata no Shojo Ryuko*. Movie. DIR: Satoshi Dezaki. SCR: Satoshi Dezaki. DES: Yukari Kobayashi. ANI: Reizo Kiyomizu. MUS: Yuse Nakajima. PRD: Magic Bus. ca. 80 mins. In 1945, American troops land on the island of Okinawa. The Japanese fight a guerrilla war against the invaders, and little Ryuko is forced to leave her grandparents behind and flee with her mother and younger sister, who are eventually killed. Ryuko heads on alone across the war-torn island. Eventually she reaches safety in Japanese-occupied caves, only to witness the Japanese troops committing suicide with hand grenades. Based on a children's book by Akira Aratagawa and Hikuji Norima, itself inspired by real American footage of an Okinawan girl, Tomiko Higa, waving a white flag at the island's surrender. Shown in some theaters on a double bill with MY NEIGHBOR TOTORO instead of the similar GRAVE OF THE FIREFLIES. Another Okinawan war story was filmed as VOYAGE OF THE TSUSHIMA.

GIRLFRIEND IN A SWIMSUIT

2009. JPN: *Mizugi Kanojo: The Animation*. AKA: *Mizuho! Exercise!* Video. DIR: Ken Raika. SCR: Shinichiro Sawayama. DES: Mamoru Sakisaka. ANI: Mamoru Sakisaka, Tatsumi. MUS: N/C. PRD: T-Rex, Milky, Pink Pineapple. 30 mins. x 4 eps.

Short stories about girls who like to have sex on the beach, or at the swimming pool, in fact anywhere they can wear suits that leave nothing to the imagination and are shiny, or see-through, when wet. The curvaceous Mizuho and her well-endowed boyfriend Hiro devise new ways to work out in the pool. What Hiro doesn't know is that Mizuho is a descendant of ninja girls, and hundreds of years ago her ancestor and his had some pointed arguments—compare to LA BLUE GIRL. Reawakening the rage of the ninja could lead to disaster. Meanwhile Takuya offers to teach his cute but clumsy neighbor Sayaka to swim, which leads them across Hiro and Mizuho's path, along with a couple more curvy local girls from Bosshi's erotic manga, on which this is based. The main point of EROTICA AND PORNOGRAPHY is animated sex, but when director Raika and write Sawayama get together they usually try and deliver some semblance of a plot, and if possible a few laughs, which is what they aim for here—that is, insofar as one can add laughs alongside a rape scene. **NV**

GIRLFRIENDS IN GLASSES

2010. JPN: *Megane na Kanojo*. Video. DIR: Koji Ito. SCR: Koji Ito. DES: Yukiko Ishibashi, Hiroshi Kato. ANI: Yukiko Ishibashi. MUS: N/C. PRD: AIC. 14 mins. x 4 eps. Four short stories about schoolgirls who wear glasses, and how their glasses form part of their everyday lives and their romantic adventures. The old saying that men don't make passes at girls who wear glasses is untrue in Japan, certainly for girls of high school and college age—a fetish for glasses is one of the established tropes of both porn and harem anime. This, however, isn't porn. Adapted from Tobi's 2008 manga, it's just the thing when you're in the mood for some sweet, pretty, undemanding teenage romance.

GIRLS BRAVO *

2004. TV series. DIR: Ei Aoki. SCR: Hiroshi Watanabe. DES: Ryuichi Makino. ANI: Yoshiyuki Matsuzaki. MUS: Noriyasu Uematsu. PRD: AIC, Spirits, Fuji TV. 25 mins. x 11 eps. (TV1), 25 mins. x 13 eps. (TV2). Wimpy teen Yukinari Sasaki suffers so much teasing at the hands of the girls of Mizuno High that he develops girl-phobia—he breaks out in hives if a girl so much as touches him, much like the leads of DNA² and HANAUKYO MAID TEAM. The only girl he can be around is his childhood friend Kirie Kojima, a beautiful, brilliant student and a sports star, and comparing himself to her just makes him feel even more inadequate. Kirie really cares for him and is constantly trying to nag him into a more positive frame of mind, but his whole life changes when she throws him into a bathtub and he surfaces in another world. In Seilen, there are nine girls to every boy, and Seilenite Miharu Sena Kanaka decides to grab the gift Fate has sent her. She's very cute, with pink hair, curious, trusting, and best of all, she doesn't trigger Yukinari's hives, so when she decides to go back to his world and live with him, he's delighted. Although Kirie is jealous at first, the three become friends. But Nanae, manager of Seilen's version of the OH MY GODDESS! agency of divine intervention, the Inter-Dimensional Office, sends two cute girl agents to bring Miharu back. Koyumi and Tomoka pop out of Yukinari's bathtub and bring even more mayhem into his life. To vary the pace, Yukinari meets a girl who doesn't use bathtubs as interdimensional portals—dizzy blonde Risa Fukuyama, who immediately decides he's her Mr. Right. Meanwhile, there's a nod to URUSEI YATSURA in the shape of handsome rich kid Kazuharu Fukuyama, who decides Miharu is going to be his and enrolls her at Mizuno High. The series is based on a *Shonen Ace* manga by Mario Kaneda, and to judge from the number of clone geek-gets-girls stories being turned out year after year, the target audience doesn't mind it being just a tad derivative. Bath scenes in the first season were censored with the aid of digitally added steam to obscure nudity. A second season followed in 2005, reveling in its risqué honor of being "the first TV anime to earn an R15+ rating in Japan." However, this was nonsensical hype; Japanese TV has seen a lot worse, from TIGER MASK to GANTZ, and the fact that a few flashes of nudity should cause such a censorious honor is yet another sign of the current conservatism in Japanese television. The authors fear that if they encounter one more TENCHI MUYO! wannabe, they too will come out in hives. **N**

GIRLS FIGHT

2009. JPN: *Shojo Fight: Nora Inu-tachi no Odekake*. AKA: *Girl Fight: Stray Dogs Go All Out*. Video. DIR: Shunsuke Tada. SCR: Yoko Nihonbashi. DES: Hideki Takahashi, Masanobu Nomura. ANI: Hideki Takahashi. MUS: N/C. PRD: Production I.G, Kodansha. 30 mins.

Neri is a talented volleyball player who has spent some time on the sidelines in middle school. Entering high school, she's determined to get back in the game. Based on screenwriter Nihonbashi's manga, this video was made to ship with a special edition of the sixth volume: it's a very simply animated piece, a gently humorous highlighting of characters and relationships from the manga. Cute-style talking heads speak to the camera, figures make minimal movements against backgrounds so simple they might as well be made of Lego. The designs have considerable charm, but it's a present for Nihonbashi's fans rather than a standalone show.

GIRLS HIGH *

2006. JPN: *Joshi Kosei*. TV series. DIR: Yoshitaka Fujimoto, Yasuomi Umezu (ED). SCR: Hideki Shirane, Michiko Ito. DES: Seiji Kishimoto, Kazusuke Yoshihara. ANI: Yasuomi Umezu (ED, 5 eps.). MUS: Angel Note. PRD: ARMS, Futabasha, GENCO, Geneon Universal Entertainment, Showgate. 24 mins. x 12 eps.

Three friends entering an elite high school meet three girls moving up from an associated middle school. Despite some antagonism at first, the six soon become good friends and explore the rude, crude, and sometimes hilarious world of growing up. Towa Oshima's 2001 manga *High School Girls* set out to debunk the myths about teenage girls and present them as creatures just as wild and scary as boys, but a good deal more devious and intelligent. The series follows the same plan, stringing together events and experiences from school life with occasional diversions into comedy and drama. The writing can be uneven and not all the gags are successful, but this is a frank and often very funny attempt to smash the soft focus filter and show the other side of an all-girls' school. **LN**

GIRLS IN SAILOR SUITS

2005. JPN: *Seifuku Shojo*. Video. DIR: Teruaki Murakami. SCR: Osamu Momoi. DES: Teruaki Murakami. ANI: Teruaki Murakami. MUS: Kosaku Sasaki. PRD: Pink Pineapple, KSS. 30 mins. x 2 eps.

Schoolgirls are molested and abused by a lecherous principal in the classroom, backstage at the school play, and so on. Based on a manga in *Core* magazine by Oninojin. **LNV**

GIRLS IN SUMMER DRESSES

1988. JPN: *Natsufuku no Shojotachi*. TV special. DIR: Keiko Sugiura. SCR: Makiko Uchidate. DES: Yoshiyuki Momose. ANI: Toshio Hirata, Masao Murayama. MUS: N/C. PRD: Madhouse. 50 mins.

In 1945, the second- and third-year students of a Hiroshima girls' school are taken away to work in war factories. The remaining 220 girls of the first year try to make the best of their new-found status as the only teenagers in an almost deserted town, even amid the deprivations of wartime. On the 6th of August, an American bomber changes their lives forever. Broadcast on the 43rd anniversary of Hiroshima in memory of "the girls who lost their lives to the atom bomb," this is in the spirit of the earlier BAREFOOT GEN. This TV movie was a rare anime outing for the screenwriter Makiko Uchidate, better known for her many live-action drama serials.

GIRL'S LOCKER ROOM LUST *

2003. JPN: *Miniskirt Gakuen*. AKA: *Miniskirt College*. Video. DIR: N/C. SCR: N/C. DES: N/C. ANI: N/C. MUS: N/C. PRD: Obtain. 30 mins.

Madoka is underperforming on the girls' volleyball team, and so is put through a harsh training regime by her teamleader Yoko. This involves her fighting off a series of increasingly stronger attacks in the style of *The Sign Is V* (*DE), although whereas in the live-action inspiration such an ordeal killed its subject, in *GLRL* it merely leaves her lying exhausted on the floor and primed for "comforting" at the hands of her tormentor. Meanwhile, Madoka's boyfriend Noboru is feeling left out, until he realizes that classmate Yuna has a crush on him. Sexual complications ensue. The U.S. release includes a bonus 20-minute audio drama that runs while still images play on screen—compare to FORBIDDEN LOVE. **LNV**

GIRLS UND PANZER *

2012. TV series. DIR: Tsutomu Mizushima. SCR: Reiko Yoshida. DES: Fumikane Shimane, Isao Sugimoto, Takeshi Nogami. ANI: Isao Sugimoto. MUS: Shiro Hamaguchi. PRD: Bandai Visual, Lantis, Movic, Q-tec, Showgate, Hakuhodo. 24 mins. x 12 eps. (TV), 24 mins. x 2 eps. (recaps).

In an alternate reality where schoolgirls participate in a combat sport using reconditioned tanks, Miho Nishizumi is one of the leading stars of *sensha-do*, or "tankery," until the fateful day where she ditches her winning place in order to come to the rescue of an opponent in trouble. Discredited and disheartened, she quits the sport and transfers to a tank-free school, only to find herself swept up in its new initiative to field a team of tank girls. Loaded with in-jokes for anime fans and tank nerds, this odd tale recycles the clichés of SPORTS ANIME with an off-the-peg roster of anime ingénues, juddering around a battlefield launching shells at each other. A manga adaptation by Ryuichi Saitanya was also serialized in *Comic Flapper* magazine, Yu Hibiki wrote a novel, and there was a computer game.

Nothing surprises an anime encyclopedist any more, although *Girls und Panzer* was regarded as a step too far in the People's Republic of China, where in 2013 the *China Defense National Newspaper* published a stinging rebuke of its "promotion of military sentiments behind the guise of cute characters," thereby co-opting it into ongoing arguments over the disputed Senkaku Islands and Japan's continuing refusal to engage with its own wartime past. Perhaps it is also worth mentioning that *Girls und Panzer* wasn't legally available in China at the time, which only goes to highlight the long reach of OVERSEAS DISTRIBUTION AND PIRACY. For similar Chinese whispers, see DEATH NOTE.

GJ CLUB *

2013. JPN: *GJ-bu*. TV series. DIR: Yoshiyuki Fujiwara. SCR: Hideaki Koyasu. DES: Miwa Oshima. ANI: Atsushi Soga, Miwa Oshima. MUS: Hajime Hyakkoku (Fukai MUS Factory). PRD: Dogakobo, Studio Live, Studio Wanpack, NTV, VAP. 23 mins. x 12 eps.

Kyoya Shinomiya is "kidnapped" by the four girls of the Good Job Club, a nebulously defined collective at his school, whose members are apparently cute and supposedly zany, and whose activities include Twister, manga-reading. and awkward flirting. Based on the books by Shin Araki, who somehow spun multiple volumes out of such excitements.

GLASS FLEET *

2006. JPN: *Garasu no Kantai*. AKA: *Garasu no kantai—la legende du vent de l'univers; Glass Fleet—The Legend of the Wind of the Universe*. TV series. DIR: Minoru Ohara. SCR: Shoji Yonemura, Atsuhiro Tomioka. DES: Okama, Yuko Watabe, Kazutaka Miyatake, Shoji Kawamori, Takeshi Waki. ANI: N/C. MUS: Kosuke Yamashita. PRD: Gonzo, Satelight, Asahi Broadcasting Corp., G.D.H., Sony Pictures Entertainment, Sotsu Agency. 23 mins. x 26 eps.

In the far future, humanity has expanded into space, and some regard being stuck on the home planet as a curse. The galactic hierarchy is still split between nobles and commoners and one noble, Vetti Sforza, has claimed supreme power and formed an oppressive government. The leader of the opposition, Michel, is rescued after a terrible defeat by self-proclaimed lost prince Cleo in a glass battleship. She sees Cleo as a possible savior of the people, but they gradually learn that there is an even greater threat to mankind than Vetti.

A Renaissance-derived culture with SF elements, a conflict with more than one strand, a big cast of characters, and those beautiful ships: this series has a fascinating concept, but it's let down by uneven and dull execution. The main character conflict in the plot, between Cleo and Vetti, is stolen directly from LEGEND OF GALACTIC HEROES, where it was done so well that this version couldn't possibly meet its standards. It would have been good to see them try a little harder, but the characters are shallow and underpowered—and these are the leads. The most apt comparison is with ODIN—a show with some wonderful design, including an astonishing starship, and not much else. **NO**

GLASS MAIDEN *

2008. JPN: *Crystal Blaze*. AKA: *CryBla*. TV series. DIR: Mitsuko Kaze. SCR: Atsuhiro Tomioka, Masashi Tsukino. DES: Hisashi Kagawa, Tomohiro Kawahara, Yong Il Park. ANI: Hisashi Kagawa. MUS: Ryo Sakai. PRD: Studio Fantasia, FCC, Happinet, Toei Video. 25 mins. x 12 eps.

The city slums, the near future. Shun is a young detective working for a maverick agency when he stumbles upon a mystery: a beautiful girl who's lost her memory. And she's hot, and not just in the usual sense. Shun and his pals nose deeper and find a Government cover-up. Teenage girls are developing abnormally high temperatures and turning to glass. A determined reporter and the local cops are also on the trail. And the trail is getting hotter....

Take the ELFEN LIED trope of using a teenage girl as a weapon, mix it with the noir-ish hardboiled aura of, say, SPEED GRAPHER and the cool of COWBOY BEBOP and you have the show that *Crystal Blaze* wants to be. Sadly, it just doesn't try hard enough. The animation and character design are attractive but not especially distinguished, the plot is hackneyed, and the character development is shallow.

GLASS RABBIT

2005. JPN: *Garasu no Usagi*. Movie. DIR: Setsuko Shibuichi. SCR: Kazumi Koide, Mitsuyo Suenaga. DES: Setsuko Shibuichi. ANI: Kazunori Tanahashi, Yukari Kobayashi. MUS: Michiru Oshima. PRD: Magic Bus, Tokyo Metropolitan TV. ca. 80 mins.

Toshiko Takagi is safely evacuated to Ninomiya ahead of American air raids, but her mother and sisters are caught in the firebombing of Tokyo in March 1945—the same attack dramatized in KAYOKO'S DIARY. Rightly believing them to be dead, she endures a five-month wait until her father (a glassmaker conscripted to make syringes for the war effort) arrives to collect her. As the reunited parent and child wait for the train to Niigata where they intend to start a new life, the station is strafed by an American plane, and Toshiko's father is killed. Later that night, she walks into the sea, and it is only when she is bowled over by a wave that she realizes she cannot swim and has been inadvertently succumbing to thoughts of suicide. Back in Tokyo, she finds the ruins of her old house and the remains of a glass rabbit that her father had made, melted almost beyond recognition by the heat of the Tokyo firestorm. The traumatized 13-year-old girl waits for her brothers to return from the war.

Takagi's autobiography had already been a successful book, both on its original 1970s publication and in a more recent annotated edition to help modern readers with the more obscure words. Although the story had already been adapted for film and TV, Takagi reportedly resisted the idea of an animated version until her grandchildren convinced her that her antiwar message could reach a younger audience. Presumably in the wake of Japan's renewed involvement in foreign conflicts since the first Gulf War, the animated version adds a new emphasis at the author's insistence: a stark realism to the scenes of aerial bombardment and the highlighting of the book's final chapter, in which the youthful Toshiko greets Japan's postwar pacifist constitution with elation. Compare to CHOCCHAN'S STORY. **V**

GLASSY OCEAN *

1998. JPN: *Kujira no Choyaku*. AKA: *The Whale's Leap*. Movie. DIR: Shigeru Tamura. SCR: Shigeru Tamura. DES: Shigeru Tamura. ANI: Masaya Sato. MUS: Yutoro Teshiume. PRD: Bandai. 23 mins.
On another world where time works differently, the ocean has turned to glass. In an impressive feat of digital animation shown at several film festivals and broadcast on the U.K.'s Channel Four, people gather on the shore at a particular place to watch the group of whales that has arrived preparing to leap out of the water. Creator Shigeru Tamura also made the earlier *Galactic Fish* (1993), which also played with watery themes, this time visualizing a dimension where our world appears to be at the bottom of someone else's sea. He was also associated with Akiyuki Terajima's Japanese DVD compilation *A Piece of Phantasmagoria* (1995), which comprised 15 short animated films of a similar nature.

GLORIA *

1998. JPN: *Glo.ri.a: Kindan no Ketsuzoku*. AKA: *Gloria: Private Lessons; Gloria: House of Forbidden Fruit; Gloria: Forbidden Relations*. Video. DIR: Yasuhiro Kuroda. SCR: Akira Yokusuga. DES: Yasuaki Yoshino. ANI: Yasuaki Yoshino. MUS: N/C. PRD: Pink Pineapple, KSS. 30 mins. x 3 eps.
Kira and Gyorg (Beowulf in the U.S. dub) are selected to be personal tutors to the super-rich Gloria family in the U.S., whose five daughters turn out to be in need of an unexpected kind of "education." The tutors settle into the easy life, cosseted by servants and servicing their pupils, only to discover that the family hides a dark secret, and that the teachers will be in deadly danger if they do not leave immediately. Based on the C's Ware computer game of the same name. **N**

GLORIOUS ANGELS

1978. JPN: *Pink Lady Monogatari Eiko no Tenshitachi*. AKA: *Glorious Angels: The Pink Lady Story*. TV series. DIR: Katsuhiko Taguchi. SCR: Masaru Yamamoto. DES: Yuji Hosoi. ANI: Ichiro Dannohara. MUS: Kyosuke Onosaki, Pink Lady. PRD: T&C, Toei, Tokyo 12 Channel. 25 mins. x 35 eps.
Mitsuyo Nemoto and Keiko Masuda, two girls from the backwoods of Shizuoka, meet at school, share the same dream of becoming pop stars, and win the district talent contest. They specialize in the performing arts at school, persevering at ballet and music. One day, they hope they'll make it to the top. This schooldays biography of the singers who would eventually become Pink Lady, Japan's most famous duo in the late 1970s, was made at the height of their fame and a clever means of keeping the pair in the public eye without occupying their precious time—other actresses provided the girls' voices. An animated pop star tie-in similar to CAROL and HUMANE SOCIETY, in aims if not execution.

GLORIOUS SUBSECTION CHIEF

1976. JPN: *Hana no Kakaricho*. AKA: *Flower of Subsection Chiefs*. TV series. DIR: Minoru Okazaki, Kazunori Tanahashi. SCR: Noboru Shiroyama, Tsunehisa Ito, Haruya Yamazaki, Shinichi Matsuoka. DES: Shunji Sonoyama. ANI: Takeo Kasai. MUS: Hiroki Tamaki, Hiroshi Kamayatsu. PRD: TMS, TV Asahi. 25 mins. x 26 eps.
Mashumaro Ayanoroji has an insanely ostentatious name, but that is only to be expected from a former aristocrat, forced to slum it as a humble bureaucrat. Baffled by modern times, he puts a brave face on office life, hoping to claw his way back up to the top for the sake of his wife and son. The second anime to be based on the work of GARDLES–creator Shunji Sonoyama, in this case a manga in the *Post*

weekly, this show was broadcast relatively late at night (22:30), and so did not shy away from more adult humor. The first 16 episodes each contained two chapters, but this was later shortened to three 7-minute mini-stories per "half-hour" episode. Kazutaka Nishikawa, who was then popular in the role of Daigoro in *Lone Wolf and Cub* (*DE), provided the voice of Mashumaro's young son.

GLORIOUS TALES OF OLD EDO

1989. JPN: *Manga Edo Erobanashi*. AKA: *Glorious Manga Tales of Edo*. Video. DIR: Tsutomu Shibayama, Hajime Oedo, Hideo Kawauchi. SCR: N/C. DES: N/C. ANI: N/C. MUS: N/C. PRD: Group Tac, Studio Jump. 44 mins. x 5 eps.
Several tales of old-time Tokyo from well-known directors, mainly concentrating on the courtesans of the Yoshiwara and prostitutes in premodern Shinjuku but also on the merchants and the impoverished samurai class of the period, with star-crossed lovers, chirpy artisans, and human-interest stories. Compare to the altogether more accomplished SENSUALIST. Other olde-worlde porn preceded the series with the three-episode *Classical Sex-Zone* (1988), featuring erotic moments from the wars of the Heike and the Genji, and from the TALE OF GENJI itself. **N**

GLORY TO THE ANCESTORS

1989. JPN: *Gosenzo-sama Banbanzai*. Video. DIR: Mamoru Oshii. SCR: Mamoru Oshii. DES: Satoru Utsunomiya. ANI: Satoru Utsunomiya. MUS: Kenji Kawai. PRD: Studio Pierrot. 30 mins. x 6 eps.
Maroko, a girl from the future, decides to learn more about her ancestors and travels back in time to modern Japan, only to discover that they are a sorry single-parent family, struggling to make ends meet without Mother around. She tries to help out and soon runs afoul of the Time Police. A show that mixes homespun situation comedy with the chrononautical goings-on of DORAEMON, it was reedited with some extra footage and released as the 90-minute movie *Maroko* (1990).

GO FOR IT, GENKI

1980. JPN: *Ganbare Genki*. TV series. DIR: Rintaro, Masahiro Sasaki, Akinori Nagaoka. SCR: Shunichi Yukimuro. DES: Shigetaka Kiyoyama. ANI: Kazuo Komatsubara, Masami

Suda, Kazuo Mori, Tsukasa Abe. mus: Koichi Morita. prd: Fuji TV, Toei. 25 mins. x 35 eps.
When young Genki expresses an interest in boxing, his father decides to stage a comeback to regain his own featherweight title. Genki becomes a trainer for his own father, and the two take on the world as they struggle to relive past glories and create future ones. Based on a 1976 *Shonen Sunday* manga by Yu Koyama, who also created **Oi! Ryoma**.

GO FOR IT, GOEMON!

1991. jpn: *Anime Ganbare Goemon*. Video, movie, TV series. dir: Shigeru Omachi, Katsuyoshi Yatabe. scr: Shigeru Omachi. des: Masayuki Hiraoka. ani: Katsuyoshi Kobayashi. mus: Yasuo Tsuchida. prd: Public & Basic, TBS. 30 mins. (v), 25 mins. x 26 eps. (TV), 30 mins. (m).
Goemon, the hero of a fantasy computer game from Konami, is transported from his magical medieval world to become a superhero on Earth. First appearing in Yasunori Iguchi's video *GFIG: Nightmare Dimension* (1991), Goemon returned in earnest for a 1997 TV series, fighting enemy Seppuku-Maru and his army of computer beasts. The series soon followed the standard plotting of many others: Goemon saves the day at a sports stadium, fights on a train, thwarts a forest fire at a summer camp, meets Santa Claus, helps out an idol singer, etc. For the short movie version *GFIG: Battle to Rescue Earth* (1998), Japan is threatened by a growing mountain of trash, which duly turns out to be the work of evildoers, not humanity in general.

GO FOR IT, GONBE

1980. jpn: *Ganbare Gonbe*. TV series. dir: Hiroyoshi Mitsunobu, Hidenori Kondo, Susumu Ishizaki, Noboru Ishiguro, Tameo Ogawa. scr: Yukio Izumi. des: Shunji Sonoyama. ani: Kenjiro Yoshida. mus: Kenjiro Hirose. prd: Production Roots, Anime City, Tokyo 12 Channel. 15 mins. x 56 eps.
Believing himself to be a descendant of Sun Wu-Kong, the hero of **Journey to the West**, mountain monkey Gonbe and his sister, Monko, run away from school. Pursued by their schoolmates Sanjiro, Benkei, Gataro the bird, and frog couple Mr. and Mrs. Kerosuke, Konbe soon finds that there is much to learn out in the big wide world. Based on an educational

eight-panel manga strip from the *Mainichi Shogaku Shinbun* by Shunji Sonoyama, who also created **Gon the First Man**.

GO FOR IT, TABUCHI

1979. jpn: *Ganbare Tabuchi-kun*. Movie. dir: Tsutomu Shibayama. scr: Hideo Takayashiki, Masaki Tsuji, Tomoko Konparu. des: Michishiro Yamada. ani: Osamu Kobayashi, Minoru Maeda. mus: Hidenori Mori, Hiroki Inui, Kensuke Kyo. prd: TMS, Kitty Films. 95 mins. (m1), 94 mins. (m2), 96 mins. (m3).
An episodic **Sports Anime**, patched together from the work of five directors and five writers, about the hapless lunk Tabuchi, unlikely star player of the Seibu Lions, and his ongoing attempts to fake it till he makes it on the field and impress the disinterested Miyoko during a playoff against the Yakult Swallows, when Tabuchi has eaten too much takoyaki.
Six months later in the sequel *GfiT: Violent Pennant Race* (*GT: Gekito Pennant Race*, 1980), the Seibu Lions make it to the next round of a baseball tournament, but the next stage will involve hard work and cooperation. In a **Sports Anime** that pitches caricatures of real-life players against cartoon characters, the Lions (whose real-life mascot is the grown-up **Kimba the White Lion**), keep losing games due to Tabuchi's poor condition—his shadow is getting paler. A group of fellow players turns up at the stadium, accompanied by **Dokaben**, and they encourage Tabuchi to pull through. They organize a Tabuchi Day to show him how appreciated he is, but it is a miserable failure. Eventually, he is brought out of his depression by the arrival Miyoko, who obliges by dressing up as a cheerleader.
Before the year was out, Tabuchi was back again in *GfiT: Aa Tsuppari Jinsei* (*GT: What a Life*, 1980), incongruously running on a double bill with the live-action nature film *Tarka the Otter* (1979), facing the threat of being traded and attempting to get fit in an Arizona training camp before his playoff against the Nippon Ham Fighters. Based on the best-selling 1979 *Action* four-panel gag manga by Hisaichi Ishii, who also created **My Neighbors the Yamadas**, *Tabuchi* somehow caught the zeitgeist at the beginning of the 1980s, as demonstrated by the appearance of its second and third installments in the same

year. Plans were also raised for a TV show, although leading man Toshiyuki Nishida claimed that his schedule would not allow it. Behind the scenes, the project was more likely to have been defeated by a growing awareness of the value of sportsmen's images in merchandise—as an affectionate magazine parody or one-shot movie, it was fair comment and all in good fun, but players were already becoming agitated at the use of their images without compensation in a series that was threatening to turn into a franchise.

GO GOSHOGAWARA

1991. jpn: *Utchare Goshogawara*. Video. dir: Kazuyoshi Kozawa. scr: Noboru Hirose. des: Mitsuharu Kajiya. ani: Mitsuharu Kajiya. mus: N/C. prd: Nippon Eizo, JC Staff. 50 mins.
Kaku Goshogawara is the only dedicated martial artist at his high school, so he is forced to represent the school at the intercollegiate championships in both wrestling and judo. He tries to enlist help from his schoolmates, scouting among the local fat kids for a possible wrestling buddy, eventually deciding he's probably going to have to make it on his own. Based on the 1988 *Shonen Sunday* manga by Ben Nakajima.

GOAL FIELD HUNTER

1994. aka: *Goal FH*. TV series. dir: Masakazu Higuchi, Shinichi Watanabe, Akira Kiyomizu. scr: Hiroshi Terajima. des: Yuki Iwai. ani: Yuki Iwai, Akihiro Kaneyama. mus: N/C. prd: Dog Fight, NHK2. 25 mins. x 39 eps.
A standard tale of a soccer team overcoming the odds to become the champions of the J-League. Concentrating on an adult, professional cast instead of the amateurs of **Captain Tsubasa**, this series also boasts professional "soccer advisers" among the crew to ensure realism.

GOD FAMILY

2006. jpn: *Kamisama Kazoku*. aka: *Kamikazo*. TV series. dir: Kimitoshi Chioka. scr: Reiko Yoshida, Tomoko Konparu, Yasuko Kobayashi, Yoshimi Narita, Yumi Kageyama. des: Hideaki Maniwa, Michiyo Miki. ani: Hideaki Maniwa. mus: Hiroyuki Takei. prd: Toei Animation. 25 mins. x 13 eps.
Samataro is the child of a god and a goddess (**Religion and Belief**). His mother, love goddess Venus, is a gorgeous babe with a tendency to embarrass her children

by dressing inappropriately and acting outrageously. His father, Osamu, is a god of granting wishes, which can make him embarrassingly over-generous to his only son. His sisters Misa and Meme are goddess candidates. The whole family lives in the human world so that the children can learn about humans and be better divinities when they finally join the family business. Tenko, an angel who was born on the same day as Samataro and is his oldest friend, lives with them to keep an eye on him; naturally she's in love with him but he doesn't know it. Complications start when Samataro falls in love with a new girl at school and decides to get her to love him without using his powers. This is a charming little family comedy based on Yoshikazu Kuwashima's 2005 manga. The original character design is by Suzuhito Yasuda but the manga art is by Tapari. Brightly colored, cheerful, and ultimately optimistic, it's a teenage deity's version of My NEIGHBORS THE YAMADAS.

GOD SIGMA

1980. JPN: *Uchu Taitei God Sigma*. AKA: *Space Emperor God Sigma*. TV series. DIR: Takeyuki Kanda, Katsuhiko Taguchi. SCR: Masaki Tsuji. DES: Kaoru Shintani, Kazuhiko Udagawa, Yutaka Izubuchi. ANI: Kazuhiko Udagawa, Akira Saijo. MUS: Hiroshi Tsutsui. PRD: Toei, Tokyo 12 Channel. 25 mins. x 50 eps.

In the year 2050, the alien Eldar finally complete their 2,300-year journey to a new world, only to find it occupied by human colonists. Second-generation colonists Toshiya and Kensaku see their homeworld of Io destroyed but are recruited by Professor Kazumi to pilot one of the two "Thunder God" war robots in order to stop the Eldar general Teral reaching Earth. The robots also have a secret (can you possibly guess? …): the Earth and Sky Thunder robots can combine with the Sea Thunder Robot piloted by the professor's beautiful assistant, Julie, to form the invincible robot God Sigma.

GODAIKIN *

1982.

This is not an anime show. It is the name for the U.S. release (or rerelease) of a line of diecast and plastic toys from Bandai and its subsidiary company, Popy. In Japan the toy line was known as *DX Chogokin(De luXe Super Alloy)*, *Chogokin* being a term coined by Go Nagai to describe the metal used to build MAZINGER Z. The *Godaikin/Chogokin* range consisted of a mix of robots from both live-action *sentai* and anime shows, but only the anime robots included are listed here. The Godaikin range included Tetsujin 28 (see GIGANTOR), GOD SIGMA, Gardian (see CHAMPION OF GORDIAN), Daltanias (DARTANIUS), Golion (see VOLTRON), Combattra (COMBATTLER V), Voltes V (VOLTUS), DANCOUGAR, LASERION, and Abega (LIGHTSPEED ELECTRON ARBEGAS). The range enjoyed a Japanese revival in the late 1990s with a range of high-end diecast toys for the collector market entitled *Soul of Chogokin*.

GODANNAR *

2003. JPN: *Shinkon Gattai Godannar*. AKA: *God and Spirit Combination Godannar*. TV series. DIR: Yasushi Nagaoka. SCR: Hiroyuki Kawasaki, Yasushi Nagaoka, Tetsuya Endo. DES: Takahiro Kimura, Masahiro Yamane, Tsukasa Kotobuki, Kyoma Aki, Seiji Tanda. ANI: N/C. MUS: Michiaki Watanabe. PRD: AIC, ITT, OLM, Taki Corp., Klockworx, AT-X. 25 mins. x 13 eps. (TV1), 25 mins. x 13 eps. (TV2).

In 2047 humanity is threatened by Mimetic Beasts, savage creatures from the depths of the Earth that spread a virus turning people into similar monsters. Earth's last hope is the Dannars, symbiotic robots that have fought the Mimetic Beasts to a temporary standstill. Since the Dannars require dual pilots with close emotional contact, they are often piloted by siblings, relatives, or teams comprising husbands and wives. Consequently, tragedy is inevitable. Dannar pilot Go Saruwatani loses his wife in the early days of the assault, but is finally preparing to walk down the aisle again, this time with Anna, a girl he rescued as a child, but who is now 16. When a surprise attack threatens the wedding, Anna rushes to Go's aid in the top secret Neo-Okusaer robot, demonstrating an aptitude for Dannar piloting much to her husband's annoyance—Earth needs pilots, but Go doesn't want another dead wife.

Godannar has the best of both worlds: romance applied to military sci-fi (with the eye candy that is liable to bring): a giant robot drama with crossover potential for the aging fan, who can believe that even if he is no longer the age of the stereotypical "hot-headed protagonist" of other shows, fate might still bring him a barely legal spouse with an interest in robots. *Godannar* acknowledges this appeal to the more mature fan with a reference that will only make sense to men in their 40s (or *serious* fans)—a character named Tetsuya Koji, named in homage to Tsurugi Tetsuya and Kabuto Koji, two pilots from the MAZINGER Z franchise. Meanwhile, in a combination of the age-swaps of MARVELOUS MELMO or its mundane equivalent *My Wife Is 18* (*DE), Anna gets to flip between the role of competent adult and hapless ingenue, depending on what she wants out of her husband—LOLITA ANIME without the psychological or erotic subtext. However, it also contains fairy-tale elements lifted from *Beauty and the Beast* and *Sleeping Beauty*, since Go is infected with the Mimetic virus and put in cryogenic storage while his wife searches for a cure, before the final race against time to win a battle in Tokyo against the Ultimate Evolution Beast, the product of all existing Mimetic Beasts merging into one huge creature. A second season followed in 2004. ◆

GODDAM

1990. Video. DIR: Noboru Furuse. SCR: Tomo Fujikawa. DES: Noboru Furuse. ANI: Noboru Furuse. MUS: Eri Kani. PRD: Signal. 47 mins. x 2 eps.

The Seiyo racing team enters the world-famous Safari Rally, led by Japanese hero Todohara and his American navigator Rob Lowe(!). Based on the 1988 *Big Comic* manga by AREA 88–creator Kaoru Shintani. The two-part series was unnumbered, but *G: Survival Chaser* is the first, followed by *G: Go Ahead*.

GODDESS KARIN

2007. JPN: *Kamichama Karin*. TV series. DIR: Takashi Anno. SCR: Yuko Kakihara. DES: Kenji Shinohara, Reiji Kasuga. ANI: Takayuki Noguchi, Yukiko Ishibashi. MUS: Yo Tsuji. PRD: Satelight, NAS, Pony Canyon, TV Tokyo. 25 mins. x 26 eps.

Karin is an orphan living a miserable life. Her only treasures are a ring left to her by her mother and her beloved pet cat Shii-chan. Then Shii-chan dies. As she mourns him, she meets a strange boy called Kazune. Although they don't get on at first, it's through him that she learns her mother's ring has the magical power to turn her into a Greek goddess and bring Shii-chan back to her in another form. Kazune and his sister Himeka are on hand to help her, and Karin is determined to overcome her past troubles and become a strong and kind goddess. But her ring is only one of a number of God Rings, and someone is trying to control them.

Koge Donbo's 2003 manga started out as a parody of the magical girl genre. It ended up parodying itself through its 2006 sequel, *Kamichama Karin Chu* (not to be confused with **KAMICHU**), in which Karin and her gang of god-chums (maybe they should be the God Gang, like *Buffy the Vampire Slayer's* Scooby Gang) all acquire cat ears to fight a new evil. But before that, the manga turned serious, using the motif of Greek myths (**RELIGION AND BELIEF**) in a magical girl story that talks about why people want power and what they'll do to get it, all wrapped up in a wide-eyed, cute bundle. It's more interesting than usual, but the girls' voices are still squeaky enough to burst your eardrums.

GODMARS *

1981. JPN: *Rokushin Gattai Godmars.* AKA: *Hexademonic Symbiote Godmars; Six-God Union Godmars.* TV series, movie, video. DIR: Tetsuo Imazawa, Hideyuki Motohashi, Satoshi Dezaki, Junji Nishimura. SCR: Keisuke Fujikawa, Noboru Shiroyama. DES: Hajime Kamegaki. ANI: Hideyuki Motohashi. MUS: Kei Wakakusa, Reijiro Koroku. PRD: Hikari Pro, TMS. 25 mins. x 64 eps. (TV1), 97 mins. (m), 56 mins. (v), 30 mins. x 2 eps. (v2), 25 mins. x 13 eps. (TV2).

In the year 1999, humanity starts to advance beyond the confines of the solar system, encountering the evil Emperor Zaul of Planet Gishin. Takeru Akigami of the Earth Defense Force "Cosmocrushers" discovers that he was sent from Gishin as a sleeper agent 17 years previously. He is forced to choose between his two homes, deciding to defend Earth as one of the pilots of the six-part Godmars robot, which forces him into a tragic conflict with his elder brother Mark, who has chosen the other side.

This series was very loosely based on Mitsuteru Yokoyama's 1976 *Mars* manga

from *Shonen Champion* magazine, itself a retelling of Yokoyama's earlier **BABEL II**. The shows were recut to make a 1982 movie (released in the U.S. as *Godmars*), and Masakazu Iijima also directed *GM: Legend of Seventeen* (1988), a one-shot video retelling the life of the doomed Mark.

After the success of "retro" series like **GIANT ROBO**, the story was remade on video with greater faith to Yokoyama's original as *Mars* (1994) by Junji Nishimura, who had also worked on *Godmars*. It restored the original manga's storyline of a young boy in suspended animation inside a South Sea volcano who awakens a century before his alien masters planned to use his powers to reduce human civilization to a manageable low-tech level. As with his *Godmars* counterpart, however, he chooses to adopt the human race as his own and fight the invaders. This story, closer in attitude to the original manga, was remade a second time as *New Century Mars* (*Shinseikiden Mars*, 2002), a 13-episode TV series broadcast on AT-X.

GOING STEADY WITH A WITCH

1986. JPN: *Majo de mo Steady.* Video. DIR: Hiroshi Kobayashi. SCR: Reiko Nakada. DES: Tori Miki. ANI: Hideo Kawauchi. MUS: Hiroshi Ogasawara. PRD: Tokyo Media Connections, Ajia-do. 42 mins.

Hisashi Seki lives a gray, dull salaryman's life, living alone in an old apartment building that happens to be built over a dimensional warp. He wakes up to find the nude girl Mami in his room. They fall in love and decide to stay in Hisashi's world, but then an accident shoots Hisashi into another world: one occupied by everyone's ideal partners. Compare to **OH MY GODDESS!**, **URUSEI YATSURA**, and a zillion other stories in which a passive man gets a gorgeous girl just by loafing. **N**

GOKU: MIDNIGHT EYE *

1989. Video. DIR: Yoshiaki Kawajiri. SCR: Buichi Terasawa, Ryuzo Nakanishi. DES: Yoshiaki Kawajiri, Hirotoshi Sano. ANI: Hiroshi Hamazaki, Hirotoshi Sano. MUS: Yukihide Takekawa, Kazz Toyama. PRD: Madhouse, Toei. 50 mins. x 2 eps.

In the year 2014, private investigator Goku Furinji is contacted by former associates on the police force who are being picked off by a mysterious assailant. Left for dead

after an encounter with a female hypnotist, a mysterious force gives him a high-tech stick that can change sizes and a link to every computer on the globe through his left ("midnight") eye. He uses both devices in his ongoing fight against crime. But apart from the magic staff, the name ("Goku" being Japanese for "Wu Kong"), and some luxuriant sideburns, the story bears little resemblance to the Monkey King of **JOURNEY TO THE WEST**, which supposedly inspired it. It owes more to James Bond films, with the plush locations, silly plots, and breathless girls in tight dresses looking for a Real Man to sort out their problems. With the concentration on that super-duper eye of his, it also recalls *The Six Million Dollar Man.*

Based on a 1988 manga in *Comic Burger*, *GME* is a typical work from Buichi Terasawa, who gave us **SPACE ADVENTURE COBRA**, **KABUTO**, and the as-yet-untranslated *Red Brand Takeru.* It was the babes that really appealed to his audience, and the anime doesn't scrimp on regularly wheeling out a beautiful, scantily clad, eye-candy girl, normally with some incredibly theatrical shtick like peacock feathers or a pair of motorcycle handlebars on her back. Other designs are similarly impressive, from flying metal devil-dogs to motorized unicycles. It's not every day you get to see a fully robed Mandarin tycoon roller-skating down the side of a skyscraper, either. **LNV**

GOKUDO

1999. JPN: *Gokudo no Manyuki.* AKA: *Gokudo's Dissolute Wanderings; Jester the Adventurer.* TV series. DIR: Kunihisa Sugishima, Akihiko Nishiyama. SCR: Koji Miura, Sumihiro Tomioka, Masamichi Sugawara, Hirokazu Mizude. DES: Miho Shimokasa. ANI: Masayuki Hiraoka, Michiaki Sugimoto. MUS: N/C. PRD: Trans Arts, Pioneer, TV Tokyo. 25 mins. x 26 eps.

Gokudo is reckless, greedy, and ambitious, the crown prince of Esharott, and self-proclaimed treasure hunter. Exiled after Satan, Emperor of the Darkside, usurps his father's throne, he is saved by Satan's wife, Mora. Disguised as an old fortune-teller, she turns him into two people—Jester and Justice, wielders of the swords of Fire and Ice. After they overthrow Satan and his puppet king, Jester realizes that Justice would make the best ruler, leaves the kingdom to him, and sets out in search of adventure with tomboy Roubett and Mora's son, Prince—banished from the Darkside Empire and ordered to learn the ways of the world. This series, based on a novel by Usagi Nakamura, is part JOURNEY TO THE WEST, part RANMA ½.

GOKUSEN, THE *

2004. JPN: Gokusen. TV series. DIR: Yuzo Sato. SCR: Yasuko Kobayashi. DES: Yoshinori Kanemori. ANI: Yoshinori Kanemori. MUS: Takamitsu Gotoh. PRD: Madhouse, VAP, NTV. 25 mins. x 13 eps.
Shirogane High is renowned for the delinquency of its pupils, and Kumiko Yamaguchi, a teacher fresh out of training, draws the short straw and gets the worst class. Her colleagues feel sorry for her, but if they knew her background they might be more worried for the juvenile troublemakers, for she is the heiress of the dreaded Oedo yakuza family and currently acting as clan head. Linguists should note that her name in Japanese order is a pun on Yamaguchi-gumi, the largest crime syndicate in Japan, and that her pupils soon start calling her Yankume, a bad-girl reference equivalent to SUKEBAN DEKA, with which Gokusen has some similarities. The title is a contraction of Gokudo Sensei, literally "Gangster Teacher."

The only person who suspects there's anything out of the ordinary about the new teacher is Shin Sawada, ringleader of her class of troublemakers, but he can't uncover her secret despite organizing a class boycott and trying to force her to fight him. Nobody knows that the school's chairman of the board of trustees is looking for an excuse to shut the place down and redevelop the land for a huge profit (a plot device so common in live-action TV as to be its equivalent of anime's boy-gets-robot), but when the viceprincipal learns about Kumiko's background it gives the superintendent an excuse to act. Determined to save the school she's come to love, Yankume resigns; her class believe she's abandoned them, but soon rally round when her other life catches up with her and she is kidnapped.

Gokusen (see also *DE) began as a 2002 manga in You Comics by Kozueko Morimoto, a female-oriented pastiche of GTO that

began just as Kinpachi Sensei (*DE), one of Japan's most enduring teacher-pupil series, came to the end of its sixth season. The Gokusen manga was snapped up the same year for live-action TV for its handy combination of the omnipresent school subgenre with the postmodern gangsters of The Sopranos (1999). As with GTO, Gokusen was then kept on-air by its parent channel in an anime adaptation that kept the look and feel of the series, without the need to pay for its live-action star Yukie Nakama, who was replaced by voice actress Risa Hayamizu for the anime. Both seasons of the live-action TV serial (a second came after the anime) have also been broadcast in America on KSCI. Another orphaned female gangster boss would appear in the following year's KILL BILL: THE ORIGIN OF O-REN. ❶❸❷❷

GOLD LIGHTAN

1981. JPN: Ogon Senshi Gold Lightan. AKA: Golden Warrior Gold Lightan. TV series. DIR: Koichi Mashimo, Mizuho Nishikubo. SCR: Akiyoshi Sakai, Takeshi Shudo, Masaaki Sakurai, Tomomi Tsutsui. DES: Ippei Kuri. ANI: Sadao Miyamoto, Takashi Nakamura. MUS: Masaaki Shinbo, Masayuki Yamamoto. PRD: Tatsunoko, Tokyo 12 Channel. 25 mins. x 52 eps.
King Ibaldar of the Mecha Dimension sends alien invaders to attack Earth, not realizing that his enemies have already sent a champion to defend it. The invincible mecha superhero has joined forces with the 12-year-old boy Hiro, hiding unobtrusively inside his cigarette lighter. In times of trouble, he can use the lighter as a dimensional gate to call upon Gold Lightan's power to transform into a giant robot. With a heavy debt to the early UL-TRAMAN shows, Lightan and his five-robot team, who hide inside lighters carried by other members of Hiro's Naughty Rangers (a Bic, a Zippo, etc.), fight off the alien invaders in a mind-bogglingly inappropriate series that must have inspired teenage smokers and pyromaniacs all over Japan. A fine example of what can happen if a show's high concept is decided solely by the contents of the animators' pockets.

GOLD MOSAIC *

2013. JPN: Kin-iro Mosaic. AKA: Kinmoza. TV series. DIR: Tensho. SCR: Yuniko Ayana,

Tatsuhiko Urahata, Tatsuya Takahashi. DES: Kazuyuki Ueda. ANI: Haruo Ogawara, Eisuke Matsubara. MUS: Ruka Kawada. PRD: Media Factory, Showgate, Movic, AT-X, Flying Dog, Studio Gokumi. 24 mins. x 12 eps.
Shinobu, a Japanese teenager, gets the unexpected message that Alice, the British girl at whose home she once stayed, is not only coming to visit, but will be transferring to her school. Based on Yui Ohara's four-panel strip. A touching early episode, in which the two leads attempt to communicate with only a single word of each other's language, is soon displaced by the usual high-school comedy hijinks.

GOLDEN BAT

1967. JPN: Ogon Bat. AKA: The Phanta Man, Phantaman. TV series. DIR: Kujiro Yanagida, Seiji Sasaki, Tadao Wakabayashi. SCR: Mitsuhide Shimauchi. DES: Tatsuo Nagamatsu. ANI: Nobuhide Morikawa. MUS: Masashi Tanaka. PRD: Daiichi, Yomiuri TV (Nippon TV). 25 mins. x 52 eps.
Golden Bat is the warrior who looks like a golden skeleton, sent from ancient Atlantis to protect the people of our own time. He appears whenever his presence is requested by the Japanese girl Mari, with her associates Professor Yamatone and schoolboy Takeru, in their ongoing fight against attacking robots and monsters. Based on Tatsuo Nagamatsu's manga, although that itself has a long pedigree. Golden Bat first appeared in 1930 and became a popular character in kamishibai street theater before appearing in manga (including one by Osamu Tezuka), in live-action movies, and on TV. The story was remade again in 2007 as SKULL MAN.

GOLDEN BOY *

1995. Video. DIR: Hiroyuki Kitakubo. SCR: Tatsuya Egawa. DES: Toshihiro Kawamoto. ANI: Toshihiro Kawamoto. MUS: Joyo Katayanagi. PRD: KSS. 30 mins. x 6 eps.
The wanderings of a Tokyo University dropout (he completed the coursework, but has yet to graduate) who prefers to learn at the university of life, as Kintaro bicycles from job to job, charming the local lovelies as he goes—though it often takes time for them to see past his bad habits (such as worshiping the toilets said lovelies use and sketching everything that catches his eye). Seducing the hard-shelled-but-

sexy boss of a software company in the first episode, only to dodge the advances of the daughter of a small-town machine politician whose campaign he is supposed to be managing, Kintaro never gives up learning. Other jobs where Kintaro worms his way into female hearts include noodle chef; swimming instructor; housekeeper for a wealthy, traditional young woman; and, finally, working in an animation studio. Whatever trouble Kintaro gets into, he gets out of with his cheerfulness, dedicated work ethic, and phenomenal ability to learn new skills in record time, though unlike his manga incarnation, the anime Kintaro never manages to go all the way with his objects of desire. Based on the manga by Tatsuya Egawa, better known for MAGICAL TALULUTO, and the manga for TOKYO UNIVERSITY STORY and *Be Free*, featuring character designs by COWBOY BEBOP's Toshihiro Kawamoto. ◐

GOLDEN LAWS, THE *

2003. JPN: *Ogon no Ho: El Cantare no Rekishikan*. AKA: *Golden Laws: El Cantare's History*. Movie. DIR: Takaaki Ishiyama. SCR: Golden Laws Scenario Project. DES: Isamu Imakake. ANI: Masami Suda, Keizo Shimizu, Yukiyoshi Hane, Marisuke Eguchi. MUS: Yuichi Misuzawa. PRD: Toei, Group TAC, Visual Magic Nice and Day, Colorado FX, Sim EX. 110 mins.

Satoru, a schoolboy in the 25th century, is leafing through a copy of the religious classic *The Golden Laws*, which he has found in the New Atlantis library. He is disturbed by the crashing arrival of Alisa, a time-traveling teenager from the 30th century. The couple decide to travel back in time to 21st-century Japan, where the great religious renaissance was said to have begun. However, they end up far off course in 2300, where they are rescued from a sea serpent by the Greek hero HERMES. Then they journey through several notable points in history, witnessing the growth of human culture in Greece, Egypt, India, Palestine, and China.

Famous names on the crew and even in the cast (such as voice star Takehito Koyasu in a lead role) help distract from this anime's true colors. Although made by the Toei Studio, it is best regarded as work-for-hire in the services of a religious organization, as it is yet another publicity vehicle for the same Institute for Research in Human Happiness that gave us LAWS OF THE SUN. As with its predecessor, IRH leader Ryuho Okawa is credited with the original inspiration (the self-same religious book mentioned above), an anonymous committee provides a script mixing a cocktail of rival religions, and an impressive amount is squandered on digital effects and showy animation. An English dub was prepared for screenings on the west coast of America and Canada, and also made it to the U.K., where it was shown in a small London cinema with little mention of its original raison d'être. IRH subsequently changed its name to Happy Science and continued to make such works as REBIRTH OF BUDDHA. Compare to SUPERBOOK: VIDEO BIBLE.

GOLDEN TIME *

2013. TV series. DIR: Chiaki Kon. SCR: Fumihiko Shimo. DES: Shinya Hasegawa. ANI: Atsushi Komori, Masahiro Fujii. MUS: Yukari Hashimoto. PRD: JC Staff, Genco, Starchild Records. 25 mins. x 24 eps.

College nostalgia and benevolent stalking characterize this series based on the light novels by Yuyuko Takemiya, in which Banri, an amnesiac freshman, and Mitsuo, a confused law student, are pursued at their private academy by two girls to whom they swore undying love as children. With a weary sigh, the seasoned anime watcher anticipates another return of the clichés of *osana-najimi* (ROMANCE AND DRAMA), but the characters of Koko and Linda are far more rounded than that, and often demonstrate a certain maturity and ease with their initially one-dimensional traits—compare to a similar sense of more mature themes in SAKURA DIARIES. Later episodes take a turn for the surreal, with out-of-body experiences, hauntings, and other magic-realist occurrences that serve to allegorize the way that young people can reinvent themselves at a new institution of learning, for good or ill. This is one of those EVERYDAY ANIME that rely so heavily on mundane situations (or easily staged special effects), that one cannot help but wonder if it really should not have been turned into a live-action drama.

GOLDFISH WARNING

1991. JPN: *Kingyo Chuiho*. TV series. DIR: Junichi Sato, Atsutoshi Umezawa, Kunihiko Ikuhara. SCR: Keiko Maruo, Yumi Kageyama, Hiroko Naka, Aya Matsuyama. DES: Satoru Irizuki. ANI: Satoru Irizuki, Tomoyoshi Koyama. MUS: Takanori Arisawa. PRD: Toei, TV Asahi. 25 mins. x 54 eps.

Snooty rich girl Chitose Fujinomiya is left in poverty after the death of her father. Thrown out of the elite City Academy with nothing but her valuable pink goldfish, Gyopi, for company, she is found on the premises of the run-down Country High School where children and animals attend classes together. Regaining some of her inheritance from an embezzling family lawyer, Chitose uses some of the money to rebuild the struggling school, making herself chairperson of the school board *and* student-body president. With completely selfish motives, she tries to improve her new school in order to bring a little "urban sophistication," and, she hopes, trounce the feckless City Academy and its prissy student president, Yurika. Her classmates are less keen, with the likable redhead Wapiko mediating between Chitose and the irate animals, while simultaneously fending off the advances of Yurika's assistant, Takapi. A madcap comedy and long-term fan favorite, incorporating meditations on how CANDY CANDY would have worked out if its heroine were a bitch, coupled with surreal visuals and designs that presaged the more abstract moments of director Ikuhara's later UTENA. Based on Neko Nekobe's 1989 manga in the magazine *Nakayoshi*.

GOLGO 13: THE PROFESSIONAL *

1983. JPN: *Golgo 13*. Movie, video, TV series. DIR: Osamu Dezaki. SCR: Hideyoshi Nagasaka. DES: Shichiro Kobayashi. ANI: Shichiro Kobayashi. MUS: Toshiyuki Omori. PRD: TMS. 94 mins. (m), 60 mins. (v), 25 mins. x 50 eps. (TV), 94 mins. (m), 60 mins. (v), 25 mins. x 50 eps. (TV).

Golgo 13, one of Japan's longest-running manga series, has been drawn by Takao Saito since 1969. Its unsmiling hero, Duke Togo, has never revealed anything about his past. Instead, he wanders the world and kills people for a living, a modern *ronin* with a code name constructed from purest evil: the unlucky number 13 and the first two syllables of "Golgotha." An immense hit with middle-aged businessmen, Duke gets to travel the world, screw foreign chicks, and shoot unpleasant people. Although inspired by the James Bond films, he doesn't even pretend to be working for good. He is totally amoral.

In the 1983 film, Duke is hired by a mystery client to kill the heir of a wealthy businessman. The businessman offers the sexual favors of his newly widowed daughter-in-law to a psychotic killer on the understanding that the son's death will be avenged. And so begins a series of tit-for-tat escalations, risible dialogue, embarrassing characterizations, and a ludicrous procession of gunfights, as the two assassins kill and shag their way toward a final confrontation.

Director Dezaki treats Duke's quest as a modern samurai adventure, with improbable leaps and slices replaced by improbable marksmanship and set-ups (watch the moment Duke shoots someone through a building). He also experimented with computer graphics (**Gaming and Digital Animation**) in a helicopter assault scene, inserting now-dated CG that makes it not unlike watching an old Atari console, that was nevertheless groundbreaking at the time. But Dezaki would retain his obsession with out-of-place CG, using it once again in his later **Black Jack**. Duke would return in a video sequel, *Golgo 13: Queen Bee* (1998), in which Duke is assigned to kill Sonia, the titular South American nymphomaniac drug baroness, before she can carry out her own threat to murder a presidential candidate running on a Just-Say-No platform.

One of the few Japanese comic characters to appear in a magazine that actually bears his name, Golgo remains a popular icon with a Japanese salaryman audience, like a comfortable pair of murderous slippers. It should hence come as little surprise that, in straitened times, as producers fretted that the only real audience for anime was getting steadily older, he returned in a 50-part series on TV Tokyo, *Golgo 13* (2009), directed by Shunji Oga. Unfortunately, the sheer length of the series seemed to only accentuate the predictable and unchanging nature of Golgo's story arcs: with an unstoppable, unkillable, unchanging leading man who *always* wins, it offered little in the way of dramatic development and clung to Saito's

art style in a fashion that makes this anime series look considerably more dated than it actually is.

Before his lower budget anime outings, the assassin also appeared in two live-action incarnations, *Golgo 13* (1973), starring Ken Takakura, and *Golgo 13: Assignment Kowloon* (1977), starring Shinichi "Sonny" Chiba. **LNV**

GON THE FIRST MAN

1996. JPN: *Hajime Ningen Gon*. TV series. DIR: Yutaka Kagawa, Takashi Yamazaki, Hiroyuki Yokoyama. SCR: Yoshio Urasawa, Megumi Sugiwara. DES: Shunji Sonoyama. ANI: Masaaki Iwane. MUS: Yusuke Honma. PRD: KSS, NHK2. 25 mins. x 39 eps. (each ep. has 3 stories).

The wacky adventures of Gon the little caveman, as his family tries to cope with prehistoric life. Beginning as a simple comedy featuring Gon and his gang trying to hunt mammoths, running from saber-toothed tigers, and cowering from thunder, later episodes became more satirical of modern times, with Gon's trip to the prehistoric equivalent of summer camp. In the final stage, it developed an SF angle not unlike Shotaro Ishinomori's **Age of the Great Dinosaurs**, with the arrival of aliens in a flying saucer. Based on a manga by **Go for It Konbe**'s Shunji Sonoyama, who also created an earlier caveman anime, **The Gardles**. Gon's adventures made it to the screen in the wake of the live-action Hollywood *Flintstones* (1994) and were of no relation to the diminutive *dinosaur* hero of Masashi Tanaka's 1991 manga *Gon*. Compare to **Kum Kum**.

GON THE FOX

1989. JPN: *Gongitsune*. Movie. DIR: Yasunari Maeda. SCR: Tsunehisa Ito. DES: Shoji Ikehara. ANI: Nobukazu Otake, Tsukasa Abe, Yoko Tsukada. MUS: Yasuo Tsuchida. PRD: Ai Planning Center, Magic Bus, Orions, Radical Party. 76 mins.

Gon the orphaned fox cub is washed downstream into a small village in Aichi Prefecture. Making his home there, he steals some fish intended for the sick mother of a local villager. After the mother dies, an apologetic Gon brings offerings of mushrooms and fruit to the bereaved villager. One night, thinking Gon is an intruder, the villager kills him as he ap-

proaches the house. A Japanese tragedy rich in karmic misery, based on a story by Nankichi Nimi, though the early scenes depicting the death of Gon's mother were added by screenwriter Ito. Made to celebrate the tenth anniversary of the **Japanese Folk Tales** series.

GONZO

Also Gonzo Digimation Company or Gonzo Digimation Holdings (GDH). Influential modern anime company, particularly in the new field of digital animation. Gonzo was founded in 1992 by a small group of former Gainax employees. Its output includes animation for both anime and computer/console games and many landmark experiments in the integration of cel and digital animation techniques. Notable employees include Mahiro Maeda, Takeshi Mori, and Umanosuke Iida—representative works include **Last Exile**, **Blue Submarine No. Six**, and **Vandread**. The company also made the opening animation sequence for the otherwise live-action TV series *Densha Otoko*—incorporating homages to two earlier Gainax works in the process. Arguably, the company's most well-known work is actually a pop promo, "Breaking the Habit" (2005) for the band Linkin Park. In the 21st century, Gonzo was at the forefront of international coproductions, giving it a high profile in the boom times but making it the first and most conspicuous victim of the contraction of the anime market post-2006. With much of its capital tied up in foreign deals that would take years to monetize, it dwindled to a mere skeleton staff and was delisted from the Tokyo Stock Exchange, where it had previously been a high-profile emerging share opportunity. However, it weathered the financial storm, returning to profitability and a more cautious production regime in 2010.

GOOD EVENING MY ONLY DARLING

2009. JPN: *Anata dake Konban wa*. AKA: *Good Evening to You Alone*. Video. DIR: Masaki Kajishima, Ryu Maiami, Shinichi Shimizu. DES: Kujira Akishima. ANI: Kujira Akishima. MUS: N/C. PRD: Studio Eromatik, AIC, BOSS, MS Pictures. 30 mins. x 5 eps.

Shogo's grandfather dies, leaving a mansion and lots of money. His parents are very busy at work so they send him down to take possession of the house, since he's to inherit all the family assets. On arrival he finds a beautiful maid, Yoko, who's extremely enthusiastic about her duties and makes him very welcome. That night he has a strange dream, about a girl he doesn't know, but whose face seems very familiar. Next day he starts at his new school and finds that he has a fiancée, an arrangement made by their parents when they were babies. Not only does Ayane not want him, but the whole school is against him because she's the most popular girl there and every guy has the hots for her. Luckily, a beautiful teacher consoles him for his terrible reception, and he meets the Mizuchi twins, Mone and Mocha, who are also very friendly. And then he sees a ghost—the girl from his dream. Where has he seen her before? How friendly can a ghost get? This porn anime is an uneasy mix of sex, comedy, and the occult—which is more a device for setting up sex scenes than a real plot element. See also MASQUERADE and its sequel, to which this anime is allegedly related. **N**

GOOD LUCK GIRL *

2012. JPN: *Binbo-gami ga.* TV series. DIR: Tomoyuki Kawamura, Yoichi Fujita. SCR: Kento Shimoyama. DES: Kenji Tanabe, Yukihiro Shibutani. ANI: Kenji Tanabe. MUS: Masashi Hamauzu. PRD: Sunrise, Bandai Visual, TV Tokyo, Dentsu, Kodansha, Shueisha, Sun MUS. 23 mins. x 13 eps.
Momiji Binboda is no normal teenage girl but a Goddess of Misfortune sent to the human world to correct a dangerous imbalance in the flow of good fortune and happiness. Far too much of that positive energy has been flowing one way—to brilliant, beautiful high school girl Ichiko Sakura. Ichiko's power to absorb happiness energy is the source of her beauty, brains, money, radiant good health, and well-developed chest. Unfortunately this has made her snobbish, self-centered, and lazy. She also pulls happiness energy away from others, making them poor, plain, and jealous. If Momiji gets her way, Ichiko will stop absorbing all the world's happiness, restoring the balance by losing some of her own gifts. And maybe Momiji will stop being so depressed about her flat chest and stop picking her nose.

Slapstick fantasy love comedy is such an established genre that it takes skill to find a fresh spin. Clever writers, like Yoshiaki Sukeno, who created the *Binbo-gami ga!* manga on which the series is based, make the boy-girl connections a subplot underlying the exploration of a different kind of relationship, one in which a reluctant odd couple, thrown together by fate, bring out something new and precious in each other. In BEEZLEBUB the relationship is between a tough teen and an even tougher toddler; here it's between the spoiled prom queen, idolized by the guys and hated by the girls, and the kooky loner. Their common ground is one of past disappointment and hurt, and the serious thread of their opening up of each other's hearts, while not allowed to interfere with the jolly japes and crazy goings-on, is the core of the show. Meanwhile, there is also something of the numinous underpinnings of THE MELANCHOLY OF HARUHI SUZUMIYA, as the trials and tribulations of a supposedly EVERYDAY ANIME cloak a tense god-game over the hidden powers of a beautiful muse.

Sukeno and the animators invoke other classic tropes—Momiji's nose-picking is a direct homage to the equally eccentric Haruko of **FLCL**, and the transformative effects of bathing on her personality and appearance play as a sly dig at the fetishistic transformations of the magical girl genre. There's a butch girl named Ranmaru who is heir to a karate dojo and yearns to get in touch with her feminine side (RANMA ½). There are two butlers, one a pervert serving a childlike ninja brat and one a loyal and devoted friend. There's even a depressing magical sidekick to Momiji's depressing magical girl—Kumagai, a demonic stuffed bear who cannot talk but communicates by writing messages in a notebook. The staff piles in so much craziness that you almost expect to see Shinichi Watanabe's name on the crew list—the transforming grunge plushie sidekicks, the masochistic chihuahua god, the god with a head like a poop. The show may a have heart but it's not going to let that get in the way of any of the jokes.

The literal TRANSLATION of the title is "This God of Poverty"—poverty of heart and spirit, the meanness that closes our hearts to others. Wrapping its message in slapstick and sauce, this sweet show sets out the proposition that happiness is better shared. **N**

GOOD LUCK, NINOMIYA-KUN *

2007. JPN: *Goshusho-sama Ninomiya-kun.* AKA: *My Heartfelt Sympathy Ninomiya-kun.* TV series. DIR: Koji Yoshikawa. SCR: Akira Watanabe. DES: Haruo Ogawara, Minoru Maeda. ANI: Masakazu Sunagawa. MUS: Koichiro Kameyama. PRD: AIC. 25 mins. x 12 eps.
Mayu is a succubus and so she draws men to her like moths to a flame, needing them to stay alive. But she's terrified of men—except for one. Shungo Ninomiya, a talented martial artist and all-round nice guy, is hugely popular at school with all the girls trying to have sex with him, but he seems to have no interest in them except for Mayu and Reika, the snooty student council president. What he doesn't know is that he met both girls when they were all very young—he has no memory at all of his childhood, although you could have guessed if you'd heard of *osana-najimi* (ROMANCE AND DRAMA). Then his sister, who has been helping Mayu's sister to defend her from her unwanted suitors, proposes a solution: Mayu and her sister will move in with Shungo. He's more than capable of beating away importunate males. Mayu will sleep with him and share his bath so she can always feel safe. Yes, despite the idea of a girl with enormous powers who needs to be protected from them (coming to you from an anime near THE MELANCHOLY OF HARUHI SUZUMIYA) and despite a competent and capable un-klutzy hero, this is a harem show (ROMANCE AND DRAMA). It's a small harem—just Reika and Mayu—but it has all the necessary elements. Girls throwing themselves at a guy who isn't interested? Check. Maid costumes? Check. Accidental groping? Check. From the books by Daisuke Suzuki, illustrated by Kyorin Takanae, via AIC Spirits, who brought you GIRLS BRAVO. **N**

GOOD MORNING ALTHEA

1987. Video. DIR: Hideki Tonokatsu. SCR: N/C. DES: Michitaka Kikuchi. ANI: Moriyasu Taniguchi. MUS: Nobuhiko Kashiwara. PRD: Animate, Studio Pierrot. 50 mins.
Far in the future, the galaxy is ruled by a race of warrior-mages who have cast aside much of humankind's earlier follies in

cybernetics. However, the infamous "Automaton" robot that defended humanity from the Stemma Empire is rumored to be still operational, and three brave young teenagers go on a quest to shut it down … or perhaps steal it for themselves. For this they will require Althea of the Seal, a human symbiont. Based on a manga from *C-Live* magazine written by a collective of fans called "Black Point," this video begs the question, "It took more than one person to come up with that plot?"

GOOD MORNING CALL
2001. Movie. DIR: N/C. SCR: N/C. DES: N/C. ANI: Transarts. MUS: N/C. PRD: NAS, Shueisha. 19 mins.
Based on the 1997 *Ribon Mascot* manga by Yue Takasuka, this is a day in the life of Hisashi Uehara and Nao Yoshikawa, two teenagers accidentally forced to share an apartment but who conceal this fact from their classmates. With Hisashi's 16th birthday coming up, Nao goes in search of gift for him, only to become distracted by the attentions of a hunky hairstylist who wants her to model for his latest creation. The platonic friendship that eternally threatens to become something more, in the style of MARMALADE BOY, meets a glorified ad to stimulate manga sales similar to that employed by CIPHER THE VIDEO. This short work featured as part of a *Ribon*-sponsored touring cinema anthology along with TIME STRANGER KYOKO, hence its official "movie" status rather than the video that it really ought to be.

GOOD WITCH OF THE WEST, THE
2006. JPN: *Nishi no Yoki Majo: Astraea Testament.* TV series. DIR: Katsuichi Nakayama. SCR: Atsuhiro Tomioka, Yuji Kawahara, Mayu Sugiura, Chinatsu Hojo. DES: Masahiro Aizawa, Hisaharu Iijima, Stanislas Brunet. ANI: N/C. MUS: Hikaru Nanase. PRD: Hal Film Maker, Geneon Universal Entertainment, Imagica, Mag Garden, On The Run, Tablier Communications. 25 mins. x 13 eps.
Firiel Dee has lived with her foster parents for as long as she can remember. Her father, an astronomer, lives nearby but is too busy to take care of a child. Her main link with him is his apprentice, her childhood friend Rune. When she's 15, her father sends her a necklace that used to belong to her mother. She causes a stir by wearing

it at a local nobleman's party, and finds out that it proves her noble bloodline. Not only is she a member of the royal line, she could even be eligible to be queen. Her ordinary life is changed forever, and exciting new adventures await her—but this isn't an unmixed blessing. She also faces spite, envy, and danger, as she is drawn into political intrigue and conspiracy not because of anything she does, but simply because of her ancestry.

Noriko Ogiwara's 11-volume book series, which became a pretty 2004 manga with art from Haruhiko Momokawa, is a treat for anyone who enjoys well-riffed FANTASY AND FAIRY TALES with insights into adolescence. The main problem with the anime version is the usual one of trying to cram in far too much into a very short run. The first half of the show howls by like a whirlwind, and although it slows down a little after that, the final two episodes are rushed and crowded, leaving some issues unresolved and some wrapped up a little too miraculously. But this aside, the show has a lot of offer. It looks beautiful, and Hal Film Maker animates it well, integrating CG with 2D elements into an attractive whole. The story and the romance are character driven and credible, and the world in which the characters move is convincing. It's a little too short and rushed to be wholly satisfying but for those who want more, the manga is available in English.

GOODBYE LITTLE HIPPO
1989. JPN: *Sayonara Kaba-kun.* Movie. DIR: Yutaka Ozawa. SCR: Yoko Yamamoto. DES: Katsumoto Saotome. ANI: Shiro Nakagawa, Toshiki Saida. MUS: N/C. PRD: Asmik, OH Production. 25 mins.
A mixture of live action and animation telling the true story of the animals of Tokyo's Ueno Zoo during the harsh days of bombing raids and shortages that took their toll during World War II. *Newtype* called the story, "a study of the tragedy of war and a prayer for peace." No hippos were available for comment. See also ZOO WITHOUT AN ELEPHANT and THE ELEPHANT TRAIN ARRIVES.

GOODFELLA
1990. JPN: *Otokoki.* Video. DIR: Osamu Yamasaki. SCR: Noboru Hirose. DES: Masami Suda. ANI: Masami Suda, Masafumi Yamamoto.

MUS: N/C. PRD: Nichiei, JC Staff. 50 mins. x 3 eps. (v1), 40 mins. x 2 eps. (v2).
After his father leaves when he is very young, Kyosuke Murata grows up under the thumb of his overprotective mother, Shizuko. When he reaches adulthood, he is thrown into the harsh, violent world of Japanese gangland when his mother becomes involved in a gang-related crime. He goes up against the Murata-gumi organization, only to find that his estranged father is its head. Rising up through the ranks, Kyosuke eventually unites half the gangs in Japan beneath his own leadership, only to find that the other half have also combined to resist his new power, starting the greatest gang war in Japanese history. Based on a 1979 manga in *Big Comic Spirits* by Hiroshi Motomiya, who also created CLIMBING ON A CLOUD and MY SKY. The first episode was also screened theatrically.

Shigeru Ueda directed a two-part sequel, *New Goodfella* (1998), in which gang members attempt to arrange a jailbreak by infiltrating a prison disguised as guards. **NV**

GORILLAMAN
1992. Video. DIR: Yoshinori Nakamura. SCR: Noboru Hirose. DES: Koichi Endo. ANI: Mitsuharu Kajiya, Koichi Endo. MUS: N/C. PRD: JC Staff. 50 mins.
A school comedy about a mute transfer student, Tadashi Iketo, who is constantly shuffled from school to school for his "violent nature," though he really is a mild-mannered boy constantly taunted into fights over his simian appearance. Based on a 1989 manga in *Young Magazine* by Harold Sakuishi. Compare with the more dramatic ANGEL LEGEND.

GORSCH THE CELLIST *
1982. JPN: *Cello Hiki no Gorsch.* AKA: *Gauche the Cellist.* Movie, video. DIR: Isao Takahata. SCR: Isao Takahata. DES: Shunji Saita. ANI: Shunji Saita, Suemi Nishida, Mariko Nomura, Kumiko Tsukada, Yoko Tomizawa, Takashi Namiki, Taeko Otsuka, Nobuhiro Aihara, Kazuhide Tomonaga. MUS: Yoshio Mamiya, Beethoven. PRD: OH Productions. 19 mins. (m1), 63 mins. (m2), 30 mins. (v).
A mediocre cellist is forced to practice late at night and "dreams" that he is visited by talking animals. A cat, cuckoo, badger, and

field mouse each offer their opinions on his music and keep him company during the lonely sessions, but later on Gorsch discovers that his music, while terrible to human ears, has been healing sick animals all around the neighborhood. The knowledge that even his ability does *some* good brings heart and soul to his music and improves his performance the next time he faces a human audience. Released with English subtitles on DVD in Japan.

Though most likely to be known in the West through this striking 1982 film, the story was first animated in 1949 as a 19-minute short directed by Yoshitsugu Tanaka, and based originally on a short story by **NIGHT ON THE GALACTIC RAILROAD**–creator Kenji Miyazawa. The story was animated a third time for the *Classic Children's Tales* series (1992) as a 30-minute stop-motion short released straight to video.

GOSHOGUN *

1981. JPN: *Sengoku Majin Goshogun.* AKA: *Civil War Devil-God Goshogun.* TV series, movie, video. DIR: Kunihiko Yuyama, Tetsuro Amino, Junji Nishimura. SCR: Takeshi Shudo, Jiyu Watanabe, Sukehiro Tomita. DES: Studio Z-5, Mutsumi Inomata, Shunsuke Kasahara. ANI: Hiroshi Tanaka, Etsuko Tomita, Hideaki Matsuoka. MUS: Tachio Akano. PRD: Ashi Pro, Tokyo 12 Channel. 25 mins. x 26 eps. (TV), 65 mins. (m1), 90 mins. (m2).
Professor Masada is killed by the evil Docougar organization, which wants to steal the secrets of his latest invention, the Super Energy Vimra. His son Kenta takes the research to the mobile secret base of the God Thunder organization, assembling the "Goshogun" team of warriors to fight against the minions of Docougar.

Kunihiko Yuyama's movie *Goshogun* (1982) takes the cast to the South American republic of Felcona, where president Santos requires their assistance against Docougar agents. A reedit of episodes 17 and 20 of the TV series, the "movie" adds scraps of extra footage, including an introductory sequence and false interstitial advertisements for nonexistent products endorsed by the cast—Kernagul's Fried Chicken, Kutnall's Tranquilizers, Gitter's 35-section Combining Robot, and Docougar Total Training. The film also used images of characters' previously unseen

childhood years in the closing credits, a device that foreshadowed the subplot of the final *Goshogun* release (see below).

In 1985, the *Goshogun* series was combined with **SRUNGLE** and released in the U.S. as *Macron One.* As with its contemporary **ROBOTECH**, the series was given a completely new storyline, in this case about a teleportation experiment that hurls test pilot David Jance into a parallel universe, where he leads the Beta Command robot team against alien menaces. Meanwhile, the evil overlord Dark Star has been transported by the same experiment into our own universe, where another team must hold back his army of robotic warriors. With the U.S. market interest in SF buoyant after *Return of the Jedi* (1983), *Macron One* boasted a successful mix of alien crew, prattling robots, and enemies who looked suspiciously like Imperial Storm Troopers. The show's appeal was augmented further with contemporary pop music, not just Duran Duran's "The Reflex" over the opening titles, but other chart-toppers strewn around the battle scenes. These additions gave the show a feel not unlike an MTV pop video but inadvertently damaged its long-term salability, since rights were not cleared for the same tunes to be used on video (**MUSIC IN ANIME**).

Back in Japan, the original had a last hurrah in the video *Goshogun: Time Étranger* (1985), often confused with the unrelated **TIME STRANGER**. Also shown in Japanese theaters, this is the incarnation of the series best known today through the dub made by Manga Entertainment. Recycling the plot from the *Goshogun* novels, *Time Étranger* added a framing device set 40 years later in a world that looks like Chicago with taller buildings and hovercars. Much of the footage is wasted on a pointless car chase, leaving little time for anything but a few shots of beeping machines and hand-wringing bedside vigils. The strangely ageless Remi, infamous for refusing her medals, is mortally injured in a crash and looks back on her life while the rest of the old team (including three of her former foes, now pals with their one-time enemies) bickers around her comatose form. Using the world's most irritating French accent, Remi recalls an incident when she fell down a well as a child, and she also hallucinates a

surreal "mission" involving those who are assembled around her bed. The film then cuts to the team trapped in a city of confused religious fundamentalists (they worship like Muslims but have crucifixes in their graveyard), who are convinced that the God Thunder team's day of destiny has arrived, and that Remi will be the first of them to die. Remi and her friends fight off the seething locals in quietly racist scenes of the God Thunder team, with vastly superior firepower, shooting into wave after wave of stick-waving towelheads. They steal a tram (yes, a tram, driving it off its rails, not unlike the plot), mess around with hang gliders, and have a fight in a bar while pontificating about destiny and fate. All this, it transpires, is a metaphor for Remi's critical condition in the present day, since she must confront the demons of her childhood and psyche if she is to awaken from her coma. However, her fate is left unclear in an ending that is either a ham-fisted metaphor for her death or a reunion scene riddled with continuity errors and poor writing. So Remi either makes a miraculous recovery, springs out of bed, and chases after her comrades, or dies, recovers, and dies again, depending on your interpretation. To add to everybody's confusion, the movie was rereleased in the U.S. in 2003 under the title *Time Stranger*.

GOSICK *

2011. AKA: *Gothic.* TV series. DIR: Hitoshi Nanba. SCR: Mari Okada, Toshizo Nemoto, Shinichi Inotsume. DES: Takashi Tomioka, Toshihiro Kawamoto, Toshinari Tanaka, Yumiko Kondo. ANI: Takashi Tomioka. MUS: Kotaro Nakagawa. PRD: BONES, Kadokawa Shoten, Memory Tech, NTT Docomo, Klockworx, TV Tokyo. 24 mins. x 24 eps. (TV), 24 mins. (special).
It is1924: Kazuya Kujo is a long way from home. Third son of a soldier in the Japanese Imperial Army, he is a transfer student at the St. Marguerite Academy, an old school in a small European nation. The entire student body is crazy about horror stories and urban myths: this is unfortunate for Kazuya, whose black Japanese hair and eyes lead the students to label him "the Reaper" and decide he's a black magic master. To understand them, he decides to read up on their obsession with **HORROR AND MONSTERS**. In the library

he meets a strange girl named Victorique, with long golden hair, a razor-sharp brain, and a penchant for "Gothic" Lolita clothes to which the anime title alludes in a mangled fashion. She never goes to class, but spends all day reading and solving mysteries. She and Kazuya bicker, hit it off, and form a formidable mystery-smashing team in the mold of Holmes and Watson. At first they seem to be cracking a series of individual cases, but gradually they begin to wonder what the Ministry of the Occult's agenda is. Victorique's father is the Minister, but it seems her connections won't save them.

As a mystery series there are many, many better bets; but as an exercise in visual style and charm *Gosick* has few peers. BONES makes it look gorgeous, and animates it nicely, though there isn't much action for them to show off the dazzling fluidity of SWORD OF THE STRANGER. The music is attractive, though not particularly memorable, and the plots are very weak in places, especially early in the series before the main story arc emerges, but the character writing in the central relationship is strong enough to carry the plot forward over its weak points. Kazuya and Victorique are a clichéd teenage anime couple—she is bossy, arrogant, and conflicted; he is kind, understanding, supportive, and reliable—yet they make a convincing pair and their romance is heartwarming.

The book series by Kazuki Sakuraba (FUSE: MEMOIRS OF A HUNTER GIRL) with art by Hinata Takeda began in 2003, and the pair produced 13 volumes before wrapping the tale in 2011. It has also spun off three manga by the creators, a collection of shorts called *GosickS*, in 2004, a manga retelling of the novels in 2007, and *Gosick Win* in 2011. The anime also has a 24-minute "recap" episode, editing the story and featuring interviews with the cast. *Coming Spring GOSICK Special: Beautiful Monster Look Back In Chaos* (*Haru Kitaru GOSICK Special: Utsukushiki Kaibutsu wa Konton no Saki o Miru*) appeared in March 2011. **NV**

GOTO, KEIJI

1968–. Character designer on THOSE WHO HUNT ELVES and NADESICO, moving into animation with GATEKEEPERS. A member of a three-man production team called "gimik" that created KIDDY GRADE and UTA

KATA—the other members are Hidefumi Kimura and Megumi Kadonosono.

GOTTAMAN

1994. JPN: *Dengeki Oshioki Musume Gottaman*. AKA: *Electro Punisher Girl Gottaman; Butt Attack Punisher Girl Gotaman*. Video. DIR: Iku Suzuki, Hiroshi Kishida. SCR: Masaru Yamamoto. DES: Toyomi Sugiyama, Eisaku Inoue. ANI: Toyomi Sugiyama, Eisaku Inoue. MUS: N/C. PRD: Movic, Hero, Animate, All Products. 45 mins. x 2 eps.

A normal high school girl moonlights as the superhero Gottaman, who battles the lusty minions of the sinister Black Buddha organization while wearing little more than a skimpy top, turban, and loincloth. Tits and tentacles in the style of LA BLUE GIRL, based on the manga in *Shonen Champion* by Masakazu Yamaguchi. **NV**

GOVERNMENT CRIME INVESTIGATION AGENT Z. JOTARO

2006. JPN: *Naikaku Kenryoku Hanzai Kyosei Torishimarikan Zaizen Jotaro*. TV series. DIR: Hidetoshi Omori. SCR: Hideki Mitsui, Atsuko Terasaki. DES: Masami Suda, Takehiko Matsumoto. ANI: Yoshitsugu Hatano, Chuichi Iguchi, Kanji Isobe. MUS: Kan Takagi. PRD: Trans Arts, TV Asahi, Universal Pictures. 25 mins. x 11 eps.

Japan's economic bubble burst at the beginning of the 1990s, leading to a long, slow stagnation. The country began to recover, but corruption and political chicanery were still endemic. Japan needed a special kind of deep-cover investigator. Enter Jotaro Zaizen, who's been officially dead for three years—or so the CIA thinks. Armed with an ultra-high-grade credit card, connections in the military, broad shoulders, and lots of luck, Jotaro should be able to buy, shoot, slug, or charm his way out of a mess that involves the yakuza, big business, and government, all with someone out to get him.

Ken Kitashiba's hardboiled manga story and Yasuhiro Watanabe's art are in the manly tradition of GOLGO 13 and FIST OF THE NORTH STAR—Watanabe started out as an assistant to FOTNS artist Tetsuo Hara. The manga ended in 2007 and the anime wasn't extended, perhaps because the target audience is more likely to switch on the baseball game or a Steven Seagal movie when they get home from the office. It

may also have had something to do with the show's infamously cheap and limited animation, which was so bad that Trans Arts not only upgraded all 11 episodes for the DVD release, but also included the original TV transmission version of the first episode for comparison.

GOWAPPER 5 GO-DAM

1976. JPN: *Go Wappa 5 Go Dam*. TV series. DIR: Hisayuki Toriumi, Masami Suda, Tsuneo Ninomiya. SCR: Toshio Nagata, Saburo Taki. DES: Yoshitaka Amano. ANI: Yoshihisa Okuno, Chuichi Iguchi. MUS: Bob Sakuma. PRD: Tatsunoko, NET (TV Asahi). 25 mins. x 36 eps.

Go Tsunami, Yoko Misaki, Daikichi Kameyama, Goemon Koishikawa, and Norisuke Kawaguchi are friends who live in the same apartment block. Exploring an uninhabited island off Tokyo Bay, they discover a concealed complex, deserted for years. A hologram of the builder, Dr. Hoarai, tells them how nobody would believe his theory that the world would be invaded by the inhabitants of a demonic subterranean civilization. He worked alone until he died to create a base for space battle as the core of a defense system built around the mighty robot Godam. The friends pledge themselves to carry on his work and fly Godam into battle against Emperor Yokoyuda and his demon minions, in the style of the same studio's earlier BATTLE OF THE PLANETS—although the protagonists in this show were deliberately made to look younger than their predecessors in order to aid identification with a kids' audience. Despite such an attempt to appeal to younger viewers, the show was unafraid of piling on shocks, particularly in the form of the enemy's seemingly unstoppable suicide bomber androids, the Nendroids—compare to similar dangers in GUYSLUGGER.

Because the friends work from a deserted island without official sanction, they are both pirates and gamblers, carrying the skull and crossbones motif on their belts like CAPTAIN HARLOCK, and the insignia of spades, clubs, hearts, and diamonds emblazoned on their uniforms—an idea that would be shamelessly purloined by the following year's live-action superhero show *Jaqk* (*DE). They're joined by token kid Seitaro Shima and two cute dogs. Notable for the presence of Yoshitaka Amano as character designer and for the performance of Kayumi Iemasa, who both narrated the series and voiced the heroic robot. As with its predecessors **MAGNOS** and **STEEL JEEG**, the show was tied into a merchandise line whose distinguishing feature was that the robots' joints were held together by magnets.

GRADUATION *

1994. JPN: *Sotsugyo*. Video. DIR: Katsuhiko Nishijima. SCR: Mami Watanabe, Kenichi Kanemaki. DES: Kazuko Tadano, Kazuaki Mori. ANI: Kazuko Tadano. MUS: Kingo Hamada. PRD: Head Room, Animate. 30 mins. x 4 eps., 30 mins. x 2 eps. (*Marriage*), 30 mins. (*MVP*), 30 mins. x 2 eps. (*M*).

Mami, Reiko, Kiyomi, Shizuka, and Mika are five girls who have mixed feelings about their high school graduation day. They decide to hold a final celebration, but the clumsy Mami gets lost buying food, and the rest of the girls have to look for her. In a surprisingly heartfelt spin-off from a computer game, the girls decide on their future careers and say farewell as their school days come to a close. In the PC version, the player took the role of a career guidance counselor, steering the girls through their school days and into the right careers—the anime dramatizes a situation in which Mami and Reiko are undecided and need the advice of their fellows.

Exhausting the potential of the original, the series changed direction for the third and fourth episodes, renamed *Sailor Victory* (no relation to the proto-**SAILOR MOON**). A spoof that placed the archetypal women of *Graduation* in an SF setting, it features the girls as a team of superheroes in "hard suits," battling not only cybernetic criminals and invading creatures from another dimension (à la **BUBBLEGUM CRISIS** or **SILENT MÖBIUS**), but also the entire police force (à la **AD POLICE** or **PATLABOR**).

In a cleaner satire than the naughty **BATTLE TEAM LAKERS EX**, the girls take all of the familiar tropes of SF anime to their logical extremes, forgetting to use their secret identities, spending so long delivering pompous speeches that the crime scene is already secure, and even transforming in scenes of comedically gratuitous nudity.

The original game spawned several sequels and spin-offs, some of which were also adapted into anime. Kazuhiro Ozawa's *Marriage* (1996), also available in the U.S., is set several years after the original, with the same characters replacing their quest for the right grades with the search for the right man. This time, they are recast as five sisters, each one a year younger than the next. With the release of an all-male spin-off featuring a prefabricated pop group, Akiyuki Shinbo directed the one-shot pop promo *MVP EMU Music Video* (1996). In Hajime Kamegaki's inevitable two-part follow-up *Graduation M* (1998), the story of the game itself was retold, with a group of pretty young boys deciding to form a band and play at their school's 50th-anniversary celebrations. **Ⓝ**

GRANDAR

1998. JPN: *Grandar Musashi RV*. AKA: *Grandar Armory Revolution*. TV series. DIR: Takayoshi Suzuki. SCR: Nobuyuki Fujimoto, Machiko Ikeda. DES: Masayuki Hiraoka. ANI: Masamitsu Kudo, Masami Abe. MUS: Goro Omi. PRD: Nippon Animation, TV Tokyo. 25 mins. x 39 eps.

In order to stop seven legendary lures scattered around the world from falling into evil hands, teenager Musashi and his best friends, Suguru and Mio, set out to save the world, defeating their opponents in a series of martial angling competitions. Based on a manga by Takashi Teshirogi and Hajime Murata, who was once, predictably, a champion angler. Just when you thought you'd seen it all.

GRANDEEK

2000. JPN: *Grandeek Gaiden*. Video. DIR: Shige Sotoyama. SCR: Shige Sotoyama. DES: Toshiko Baba. ANI: Yoko Furumiya. MUS: Taku Iwasaki. PRD: Tac, Movic, SPE Visual Works, Animate Film. 45 mins.

Swords and sorcery as the young warrior-woman Tia Allbright and her hapless assistant, Luke, battle demon assassins in a fantasyland. Based on a manga by the pseudonymous Koki Ose, the story arguably is less about its putative heroine than it is about the sword she carries, the sentient Aihorn blade that wishes to find a wielder so that it can avenge the death of its former owner some 50 years earlier.

GRANDIZER *

1975. JPN: *UFO Robo Grendizer* [sic]. AKA: *Goldorak; Goldrake*. Movie, TV series. DIR: Tomoharu Katsumata, Masamune Ochiai, Masayuki Akehi, Kazuya Yamazaki. SCR: Shozo Uehara, Keisuke Fujikawa, Tomohiro Ando. DES: Kazuo Komatsubara, Shingo Araki. ANI: Kazuo Komatsubara, Keisuke Morishita. MUS: Shunsuke Kikuchi. PRD: Dynamic Planning, Toei. 30 mins. (m1), 25 mins. x 74 eps. (TV), 25 mins. (m2), 27 mins. (m3).

Young Duke Fleed (Orion Quest) of Planet Fleed (Antares) is forced to leave his homeworld when it is attacked by the forces of the evil King Vega. Fleed, together with his Grendizer spacecraft that can transform into a giant robot, reaches planet Earth, where he hides from Vega's forces and is adopted by the kindly Professor Umon (Bryant), who calls him Daisuke (Johnny). "Daisuke" works happily on a local farm, until the arrival of Vega's forces on Earth forces him to take a stand, together with his friends Koji Kabuto, Hikaru Makiba, and Duke's sister, Maria Grace.

The 30-minute anime movie *War of the Flying Saucers* (1975) introduced the character of Fleed alongside other creations of Go Nagai, such as Danbei from the same author's **CUTEY HONEY**, and pilot Koji Kabuto, whose inclusion effectively makes *Grandizer* another sequel to **MAZINGER Z**. The pilot movie features the same basic plot, with the mild-mannered Daisuke Umon appearing as the only son of Dr. Umon of the Umon Space Science Laboratory. To capture him, his flying saucer, and his combining robot Gattaidar, Princess Teronna from Planet Yarban attacks Earth with the Yarban Flying Saucer Unit.

In the series proper, before Fleed and Maria returned in triumph to their homeworld, *Grandizer* also appeared in two short Go Nagai crossover movies: *Great Mazinger / Grandizer / Getter Robo G: Battle the Great Monster* (1976) and *UFO Robo Grandizer vs. Great Mazinger* (1976). Twenty-six episodes were released as part of the **FORCE FIVE** series on American TV.

Grandizer's artistic heritage has arguably been far more enduring outside Japan. As *Goldrake*, it was the center of a media storm in Italy in 1975, aimed at unwelcome "Japanese" imports—an odd ethnic distinction, when the equally "Japanese" **HEIDI** was also appearing at the time on Italian television without a word of complaint. In France, as *Goldorak*, it was screened during the summer vacation when only children were watching, thereby possibly becoming, in some statistical sense, the "most watched anime" in history, with an estimated audience share of 100%. By becoming popular with French children, it also attracted parental concerns over its supposed violence and became the subject of Liliane Lurçat's landmark study *Five Years Old and Left Alone with Goldorak: The Young Child and TV* (*Cinq Ans, Seul Avec Goldorak: Le Jeune Enfant et la Télévision*, 1981). As a reflection of this immense popularity with viewers born around 1970, it has become a recurring topic in contemporary European academic discourse on anime, often referred to by those same children, now grown up and polishing their doctorates.

GRANDOLL ∗

1997. JPN: *Chokosoku Grandoll*. AKA: *Supralight Grandolls; Hyperspeed Grandoll*. Video. DIR: Hideki Tonokatsu. SCR: Katsumi Hasegawa, Yuko Nakada. DES: Toshinari Yamashita, Yoshinori Sayama. ANI: Toshinari Yamashita. MUS: N/C. PRD: Zero-G Room, Bandai. 30 mins. x 3 eps.
Sixteen-year-old anime fan-girl Hikaru has a mad scientist for a father, a crush on a high school senior, and a passionate obsession with the anime hero Rockin' Dorger. She dreams of becoming a real-life anime heroine, only to discover that she already is. Recovering her memories of her childhood, she realizes that she is the Crown Princess of Planet Gran, sent away during a civil war to live a life in exile on Earth. However, the evil alien Lord Friedshalf plans to use her Grandoll Armor for himself, sending minions to fight her for it, including his own lover, Sigil, who comes to Hikaru's school disguised as a transfer student. Switching in the style of **DRAGON HALF** from normal to squasheddown cartoon mode in the blink of an eye, *Grandoll* is either a lighthearted spoof of anime clichés or a cynical trawl through them, depending on how charitable you feel today.

GRANDZORT

1989. JPN: *Mado-o Grandzort*. AKA: *Sorcerer King Grandzort*. TV series, TV special, video, movie. DIR: Hideji Iguchi. SCR: Hideji Iguchi, Hiroko Naka, Takashi Yamada, Ryosuke

Takahashi. DES: Toyoo Ashida, Kunio Okawara. ANI: Takahiro Yoshimatsu. MUS: Kohei Tanaka. PRD: Sunrise, Nippon TV. 25 mins. x 41 eps. (TV), 30 mins. (TVm), 30 mins. x 2 eps. (v1), 30 mins. x 3 eps. (v2), 110 mins. (m).
Twelve-year-olds Daichi, Gus, and Rabi are heading off for a lunar holiday but get dragged into an ancient conflict between two forgotten tribes on the moon, who are trying to resurrect ancient evil powers to seize control of Earth itself. A popular giant-robot show whose robots were powered by "magic," it was created in part by **SAKURA WARS**' Oji Hiroi. The final episode was celebrated with a 30-minute TV special, *Grandzort: Nonstop Rabi* (1990). The series continued on video with the two-part *Final Magical War* (1990), in which the children fight off Grunwald, their most powerful enemy. It clearly wasn't final enough for the producers, who came back again with Nobuhiro Kondo's three-part *Grandzort: Adventure* (1992), in which the world turned out to be not quite saved enough. A magical stone in an ancient lunar monument begins emitting energy pulses toward Earth, attracting the attention of the Norman Bates space pirates, who steal it and decide to blow up a lunar city. The story was also released in a 110-minute feature-length edition under the same title.

GRAPPLER BAKI ∗

1994. AKA: *Baki the Grappler*. TV series, video. DIR: Hirokazu Ikeda. SCR: Yoshihisa Araki. DES: Keisuke Itagaki. ANI: Yoshihiko Umakoshi. MUS: N/C. PRD: Toei. 45 mins. (v), 25 mins. x 24 eps. (TV1), 25 mins. x 24 eps. (TV2).
Baki Hanma is the youngest martial artist to enter an underground free-for-all fighting tournament. He bests a karate opponent, then fights in the ring against someone whose specialty is ripping out opponents' nerves. The end. Devoid of even the merest hint of plot, Baki simply fights; instead of a damsel in distress to rescue or evil bad guy to defeat, Baki hits people until the ending credits roll. This anime takes the action-oriented plotting of **STREET FIGHTER II** and gruesome acts of **STORY OF RICKY** to extremes. Baki even comes across as something of a sadomasochist, grinning his way through nasty beatings. Based

on Keisuke Itagaki's long-running 1991 manga in *Shonen Champion*, whose *actual* plot was Baki's quest to find who genuinely is the toughest person on the planet. His quest takes him to gangsters, biker gangs, and mercenaries, and the karate sequence in this anime represents just a fraction of his search. The story was brought back for a 2001 TV series, directed by Hitoshi Nanba, beginning with a 13-year-old Baki fighting a hundred men at once, but only beating 37 of them. He trains at a number of martial arts, hoping to eventually become the best of the best, all so that he can beat Yujiro Hanma, his own father. The TV series adds extra material not in the manga, particularly concerning Baki's relationship with his mother, Emi, who keeps on finding new trainers to teach her little rugrat how to kick ass. A second television series, *Grappler Baki: Maximum Tournament* (*Grappler Baki: Saidai Tournament*; also 2001) followed the first. ◧◪

GRASSHOPPA ∗

2001. Video. DIR: Katsuhito Ishii, Takashi "Ken" Koike, Osamu Kobayashi, Sadamune Takenaka, Hajime Ishimine, Takei Goodman, Hideyuki Tanaka et al. SCR: N/C. DES: N/C. ANI: N/C. MUS: N/C. PRD: Madhouse, Studio 4°C. ca. 80 mins. x 4 eps.
A series of short animated and live-action independent films released on DVD. The animated *Trava—Fist Planet* (2001) is a film made in short episodes from Ishii and Koike, divided across several discs and forming a distaff prequel to their later **REDLINE**. **HAL AND BONS** is a four-episode CG media spoof by Ishii and Takenaka, in which two dogs are interviewed by a rice cake but are unimpressed by its style and technique. Kobayashi's *End of the World* mixes traditional and 3D animation. Ishimine's live-action *Frog River* featured in several collections before getting a solo release on the label in 2005, as did *Fist Planet* and *Hal and Bons*. An outlet for more personal, experimental work from animators better known for their mainstream anime, some of these shorts have been shown at festivals and the DVDs in the series are available with English subtitles, so *Grasshoppa* qualifies as an English-language release. Each of the four DVDs included one of the four "Sweat Punch" shorts from Studio 4°C: *Professor Dan Petory's Blues, Com-*

edy, End of the World, and *Higen.* The amazing *Comedy* short has two different audio tracks on the DVD, a "normal" version and a "comedy" version. The second DVD also includes an episode of SUPER MILK-CHAN. The third DVD includes a live-action short directed by Hideaki Anno.

GRAVE OF THE FIREFLIES *

1988. JPN: *Hotaru no Haka.* Movie. DIR: Isao Takahata. SCR: Isao Takahata. DES: Yoshifumi Kondo. ANI: Nobuo Koyama. MUS: Yoshio Mamiya. PRD: Shinchosha, Ghibli. 85 mins.
Seita and his little sister Setsuko are left homeless by the firebombing of Kobe in 1945, which claims their mother's life. Unable to contact their father in the navy and knowing of no other place to turn, they move in with a shrewish aunt who constantly upbraids Seita for not contributing to the war effort. Eventually, they move to an air-raid shelter in the country, begging and stealing what food they can, but both starve to death.

Based on a semiautobiographical novel by Akiyuki Nosaka, who lost his own sister to malnutrition during the war, this is an eerily quiet, sepia-toned apocalypse, accompanied by powerful subliminal messages. Throughout the entire film, we regularly return to the ghosts of Seita and Setsuko, lit in red, as they gaze accusingly at the countrymen who let them die, though these scenes are so fleeting as to pass most viewers by. Similarly, director Takahata loads on subtle guilt as to what might have been "if only" the slightest chance had been taken to make a difference. The firebombs seem almost laughable at their first appearance: tiny sputtering flames, leaning against a water trough and a fire bucket, but Seita doesn't stay to fight them. Instead, he runs to safety with his sister, only to see his old home burn from a distance, like the heroine of KAYOKO'S DIARY. He doesn't mumble a simple apology to the shrewish aunt who has taken him in, forcing his own exile. And as his sister dies, he turns to nobody for help, since he has given up hope that help would be forthcoming. This crushingly sad story begins by revealing both characters will die and then dares the viewer to hope they won't. Tragic in the truest sense of the word, every moment of Takahata's masterpiece is loaded with

portents of the suffering to come.

Much imitated in anime about World War II, most noticeably in RAIL OF THE STAR and RAINING FIRE, the film shows a very normal life wiped out by the horrors of war, however indirect. There are no frontline heroics here, merely two innocent children wasting away before our eyes, while an elder brother dutifully tries to assure his sister that everything will be all right. It is all the more effective for being animated, not only because the ruin and deprivation appears so insanely unreal, but because Seita and Setsuko destroy a raft of anime stereotypes. No perky victory in the face of overwhelming odds for these two; instead, they are crushed and left to gaze down on the lights of modern Kobe, expressionless, but ultimately condemnatory of something. Perhaps it is the Allies who defeated Japan (as with so many other anime of its ilk, it makes no mention of the reasons Japan is being bombed), perhaps the Japanese people who, as in BAREFOOT GEN, refused to see the light. More likely it is warfare itself, roundly rejected by just two of its many victims.

Producer Toshio Suzuki reputedly used the original novel's educational value to sell theater tickets to schools, thereby allowing him to also release a second film of doubtful potential as part of the same double bill: MY NEIGHBOR TOTORO. Some of Nosaka's other works would also form the basis for the ten-episode anime TV series *Akiyuki Nosaka's Tales of Wartime That Cannot Be Forgotten* (1997, *Nosaka Akiyuki Senso Dowashu: Wasurete wa Ikenai Monogatari*).

In 2005, the story was adapted into a live-action TV movie as part of the 60th anniversary of World War II—a year that also saw GLASS RABBIT and a remake of KAYOKO'S DIARY. The TV version shifts the focus from Seita and Setsuko onto their aunt (played by Nanako Matsushima). To bring the story up to date, a framing device depicts their cousin Natsu as an old woman, recounting the story to her own granddaughter, and a closing montage shows children in the Middle East, who continue to suffer the effects of war. See also MY AIR RAID SHELTER.

GRAVION *

2002. JPN: *Chojushi Gravion.* AKA: *Super*

Heavyweight God Gravion. TV series. DIR: Masami Obari. SCR: Fumihiko Shimo, Atsuhiro Tomioka, Kiyoko Yoshimura, Yuji Hosono. DES: Junichi Takaoka, Masato Uno, Masami Obari, Kunio Okawara, Yasuhiro Moriki, Yosuke Kabashima. ANI: Hiroki Mutaguchi, Ken Otsuka, Mikan Ehime, Yosuke Kabashima. MUS: Hikaru Nanase. PRD: Gonzo, Fuji TV, Imagica, Lantis, Media Factory. 24 mins. x 13 eps. (TV1), 24 mins. x 12 eps. (TV2).
Earth is attacked by an alien menace, but an eccentric millionaire has somehow learned of this in advance and prepared a private army of giant robots to fight the invaders. Their ultimate weapon is Gravion, a robot formed by the combination of a bunch of other super-vehicles, and piloted by the usual group of bickering teenagers.

GRAVITATION *

1999. Video, TV series. DIR: Shinichi Watanabe, Bob Shirahata. SCR: Hiroyuki Kawasaki, Michiko Yokote, Akemi Omote, Mamiko Ikeda. DES: Hiroya Iijima, Miho Shimokasa. ANI: Hiroya Iijima. MUS: Daisuke Asakura. PRD: Studio Deen, SPE Visual Works. 26 mins. x 2 eps. (v), 26 mins. x 13 eps. (TV).
The ups and downs of a band of pretty-boy musicians called Bad Luck, who spend less time rehearsing than they do indulging in moody stares and doomed loves. This anime was run-of-the-mill on video but somewhat risqué on evening TV. Based on a manga by Maki Murakami that ran in *You and Me* magazine, the original video production was upgraded to TV status after the success of similar boy-band adventures in WEISS KREUZ.

GREAT COMPOSERS

1989. JPN: *Meikyoku to Daisakkyokuka Monogatari.* AKA: *Great Composers and Their Compositions.* Video. DIR: Yasuaki Ebihara. SCR: Madoka Hino. DES: Kumiko Shishido. ANI: Masahito Sato. MUS: Various. PRD: Mushi Pro, Big Bang. 22 mins. x 9 eps.
Brief lives of some of the Western world's most famous composers, including Beethoven, Schubert, Mozart, Chopin, Vivaldi, Johann Strauss, and Tchaikovsky. Bizarrely, the obscure Stephen Foster, composer of "Beautiful Dreamer" (see URUSEI YATSURA) and JEANIE WITH THE LIGHT-BROWN HAIR, gets a whole episode to himself, probably thanks to being top of

the hit parade when Commodore Perry's gunboat diplomacy opened Japan in 1853, while Bach and Handel are forced to share. Several composers would also feature in **GREAT PEOPLE**.

GREAT CONQUEST: ROMANCE OF THE THREE KINGDOMS *

1982. JPN: *Sangokushi*. AKA: *Romance of the Three Kingdoms*. TV special, TV series, movie. DIR: Masaaki Sugatani, Hideo Watanabe (TVm), Seiji Okuda (TV), Tomoharu Katsumata (m). SCR: Masaaki Sugatani (TVm), Jinzo Toriumi (TV), Kazuo Kasahara (m). DES: Hiroshi Wagatsuma (TVm), Shingo Araki (TV), Koichi Tsunoda (m). ANI: Keishiro Kimura (TVm), Moriyasu Taniguchi (TV), Koichi Tsunoda (m). MUS: Seiji Yokoyama. PRD: Shinei Doga (m), Enoki Films, Toei, TV Asahi. 85 mins. x 3 eps. (TVm), 25 mins. x 47 eps. (TV), 90 mins. (m).

It's A.D. 220 as the Han Dynasty of China disintegrates into three warring states. The last Han emperor hands his throne over to the son of his protector, Cao-cao, who becomes the ruler of a fragment of the former empire known as the Kingdom of Wei. Two other former generals set up their own states in the West (Shu-Han) and South (Wu). Liu Bei, who claims to be a descendant of an early Han emperor, fights to bring a measure of liberty and justice to the people and ensure good government.

Based on Luo Guanzhong's novel, itself relatively faithful to actual historical events and one of the most important texts of Chinese literature, along with **JOURNEY TO THE WEST** and **SUIKODEN**. The story was given the full fantasy-legend treatment by Shinei Doga in an effort to grab audience share with lots of battle action, while doing its best to present costumes, architecture, and known historical fact as accurately as possible. It was so popular that they made a new version in 1985, and followed it up with *Romance of Three Kingdoms II: Heroes Crowned in Heaven* (1986). *Mitsuteru Yokoyama's Romance of Three Kingdoms* (1991) retold the story as a TV series, drawing on the manga retelling of the original by Mitsuteru Yokoyama, also known for **GIANT ROBO** and a manga *Suikoden*. The 1992 movie version by Toei was released in the U.S. as *Great Conquest: The Romance of the Three Kingdoms*, with narration by Pat

"Karate Kid" Morita. Once again the producers made much of their return to the historical record for details of design and architecture, while focusing on the battles in order to capture theater and video audiences. See also the later adaptation of the same material, **BEYOND THE HEAVENS**.

GREAT PEOPLE

1977. JPN: *Manga Ijin Monogatari*. AKA: *Manga Tales of Greatness*. TV series. DIR: Masakazu Higuchi, Kenjiro Yoshida, Ryosuke Takahashi, Hitoshi Sakaguchi. SCR: Ryohei Suzuki. DES: Susumu Shiraume. ANI: Toshiyasu Okada. MUS: Osamu Shoji. PRD: Tac, TBS. 25 mins. x 46 eps.

A similarly educational sequel to **JAPANESE FOLK TALES**, introducing famous people from history, bundled two to an episode. Classes of greatness include inventors and scientists such as Darwin, Copernicus, Galileo, the Wright Brothers, Bell, Newton, Curie, and Nobel; **GREAT COMPOSERS** Beethoven and Mozart, as well as Schumann and Foster (again! **JEANIE WITH THE LIGHT-BROWN HAIR**); explorers Livingstone, **MARCO POLO**, Scott, Amundsen, and Cook; several writers also covered in **ANIMATED CLASSICS OF JAPANESE LITERATURE**, including Hearn and Soseki, as well as the creators of **HUCKLEBERRY FINN**, **DON QUIXOTE**, **THE TALE OF GENJI**, and **TREASURE ISLAND**; poets Li Bo, Du Fu, Ryokan, and Basho; artists Hokusai, Hiroshige, Rodin, Millet, Gauguin, Leonardo da Vinci, and Michelangelo. There is space for baseball legend Babe Ruth, though surprisingly few religious figures beyond Shotoku Taishi. Military heroes are limited to the safely distant **ALEXANDER** and Genghis Khan, while political greats reflect an inevitable bias toward American and Japanese statesmen, such as Washington and Ryoma Sakamoto (see **OI! RYOMA**), or the philosopher of the Japanese Enlightenment, Yukichi Fukuzawa. Though such lists can rarely please everybody, one can only wonder at a series of historical giants that includes **IKKYU** but not **CONFUCIUS**, or that deems Ernest Seton, creator of **SETON'S ANIMAL TALES**, as somehow more noteworthy than Shakespeare.

An unrelated six-part video series, *Stories of Greatness* (1989), was directed by Yasuaki Ebihara and featured **COLUMBUS**, **HELEN KELLER**, Edison, Hideyo Noguchi, Lincoln,

and Marie Curie, all of whom had already been showcased in the earlier series.

GREED

1985. Video. DIR: Tomonori Kogawa. SCR: Tomonori Kogawa, Aiko Hanai. DES: Yukien Kogawa. ANI: Tomonori Kogawa, Hidetoshi Omori. MUS: N/C. PRD: Film Link, Be Bo. 57 mins.

Upstanding youngster Rid and his four friends stand up against the evil Vai, who wishes to seize control of the world, even though Rid's father tried and failed to resist Vai many years before. A sci-fi action one-shot from the designer of **SPACE RUNAWAY IDEON**.

GREEK MYTHOLOGY

2008. JPN: *Zettai Yareru Greece Shinwa*. AKA: *Absolutely Possible Greek Myths*. TV series. DIR: Junpei Miyazaki. SCR: Hirokazu Yamana. DES: Hoichoi Productions. ANI: Ken Ushikusa. MUS: Eiji Mori. PRD: A-1 Pictures, noside, NTV, VAP, D.N. Dream Partners. 25 mins. x 13 eps.

A mix of live-action drama and animation in which a professor of Greek history, reasoning that because the Greek gods were such a lusty lot they can teach anyone how to succeed at seduction, tests his theory on the number one hostess of a Tokyo cabaret club. Live-action sequences starring Ikkei Watanabe and Mayuko Iwasa frame basic but cheerful animation by A-1 and noside. This late-night show aimed at adult comedy fans is trailered as *etchi* (slightly perverted) but actually has little to offend, though plenty to amuse (**RELIGION AND BELIEF**). **Ⓝ**

GREEN GREEN *

2002. TV series, video. DIR: Chisaku Matsumoto, Yuji Muto, Noboru Yamaguchi, Yoshikazu Kawashima. DES: Kiyotaka Nakahara, Shinji Katakura. ANI: Katsuya Shirai, Studio Matrix. MUS: Shinkichi Mitsumune. PRD: Tetsuya Ishikuro, Pony Canyon, Sakamoto, Memory Tech. 26 mins. (v1), 24 mins. x 12 eps. (TV), 8–10 mins. x 3 eps. (v2), 31 mins. (v3).

The first *Green Green* video was based on the erotic game of the same name. Rural boys' school Kanenone High is going coed with a girls' school and the two student bodies meet on a getting-to-know-you visit to the Kanenone campus. Kanenone 10th grade stalwarts Bacchi-Gu, Tenjin, Ichiban, and Yusuke are caught peeping at the girls, so when they are accused of panty-theft they have to find the real thief to salvage what remains of their reputation. A year later, the TV series picks up Yusuke's story as the girls transfer in to the peaceful country school and cause all manner of romantic disruption. Predictably, for a series that so openly embraces boys' obsession with girls (and some might say, why not?), the cast actually starts the credits sequence naked, acquiring clothes during the opening theme (in a parody of Japanese erotic stripping games, even the hand-shaped cursor is present). Half-hearted mention is occasionally made that Yusuke and coed Midori were lovers in a past life, which is a thin attempt to put a spiritual gloss on the childhood betrothals of LOVE HINA and its ilk (ROMANCE AND DRAMA). The *GG Character DVD* spin-off came out the same year, with three short stories starring the main characters, plus music videos and TV clips. In 2004 another video one-shot, *GG 13: Erolutions,* was an erotic love story between Yusuke and classmate Futaba. **Ⓝ**

GREEN LEGEND RAN *

1992. Video. DIR: Satoshi Saga, Kengo Inagaki, Junichi Watanabe. SCR: Masaru Yamamoto. DES: Yoshimitsu Ohashi. ANI: Yoshimitsu Ohashi. MUS: Yoichiro Yoshikawa. PRD: MTV, AIC, Pioneer. 45 mins. x 2 eps., 60 mins. x 1 ep.
As natural resources on Earth become scarcer, the six alien "Holy Mothers" land from space and drain the world of most of its water and plants. Earth becomes a desert, forcing people to huddle in the small oases of greenery at the base of the Holy Mothers. The Lodo, a religion worshiping the Holy Mothers, becomes the new government, opposed by the Hazzard, a group of freedom fighters. Meanwhile, Earth-boy Ran is determined to find the man who killed his mother. He rescues the silver-haired girl Aira, a servant of the Holy Mothers. In a final showdown, the Holy Mothers release all the life force they have hoarded, the Earth returns to green again, and water falls from the sky.

An above-average video anime, well-served in the U.S. release by Pioneer's usual high-quality dubbing, though ultimately *Green Legend Ran* never does

anything that Hayao Miyazaki hasn't done earlier and better. There are moments of simply awesome design, as if Frank Herbert's *Dune* were illustrated by artists of the Golden Age of science fiction, but other parts simply play like low-rent versions of NAUSICAÄ or CASTLE IN THE SKY and aren't helped by a confused plot that has trouble deciding whether the Holy Mothers are alien invaders or avuncular saviors. Whatever they are, both their policy of making things worse on the offchance they feel like making things better one day and Aira's baseless faith that humanity, if given a second chance, won't ruin things again, display a naïveté of plotting that sits badly with the accomplished artwork (compare to WIND OF AMNESIA).

GREEN MAKIBAO

1996. JPN: *Midori no Makibao.* TV series. DIR: Noriyuki Abe. SCR: Satoshi Hashimoto. DES: Hidekazu Ohara. ANI: N/C. MUS: N/C. PRD: Studio Pierrot, Fuji TV. 25 mins. x 61 eps.
Two prize-winning racehorses, Midoriko and Tamakeen, become the proud parents of a white foal called Makibao, who is determined to live up to their achievements. With a rat for a trainer, he perseveres in this spoof SPORTS ANIME based on Tsunomaru's 1995 manga in *Shonen Jump* that used funny animals to tell a story of human trials. As with CAPTAIN TSUBASA and CYBERFORMULA GPX, the nature of Makibao's sport allows for a permanent underdog status: it takes him 20 episodes of struggle to qualify for his first race, but winning that merely places him in a more challenging arena with more experienced horses. Makibao develops a deadly rivalry with the Mongolian horse Tourdevil that occupies the later episodes as they compete in France and America, before Makibao finally becomes the world's fastest horse.

GREGORY HORROR SHOW *

2001. TV series. DIR: Kazumi Minagawa. SCR: Naomi Iwata. DES: N/C. ANI: Mihoko Niikura, Shiho Sugiyama, Takumi Kitagawa. MUS: N/C. PRD: Milky Cartoon, TV Asahi. 3 mins. x 25 eps.
A lone traveler checks in for the night at the remote hotel Gregory House, only to come face-to-face with a series of bizarre occupants. In a sequence of short vignettes, often only long enough to

introduce spooky characters and engage them in brief conversation, this all-CGI anime often looks more like cut scenes from a computer game—particularly since the first person perspective of the camera often likes to imply that it is the viewer who is the imprisoned traveler. Gregory himself is a rodent with a square head but Mickey Mouse ears, while his hotel guests sometimes look like the collection of a disturbed child's toy box: a pink lizard with a hypodermic needle, a zombie cat, and so on.

GRENADIER *

2004. JPN: *Grenadier: Hohoemi no Senshi.* AKA: *Grenadier: Smiling Soldier.* TV series. DIR: Hiroshi Kojima. SCR: Akira Okeya. DES: Hideki Inoue. ANI: Toshiyuki Kanno. MUS: Yasunori Iwasaki. PRD: Studio Live. 25 mins. x 12 eps.
In a world ravaged by war, *senshi* (warriors) are the only defense against evil—although we are tempted to point out that they are the source of it as well. Large-breasted blonde gunslinger Rushuna Tendo is so effective with her chosen weapon, the six-gun, that she has been given the even grander title of Grenadier. But Rushuna doesn't want to fight—she'd much rather smile at people and make friends. Only when they remain resolutely armed and grouchy does she use her sharpshooting skills. With her sidekicks, including sword-wielding samurai Yajiro Kojima and "cute" girl Mikan Kurenai, she sets out for the capital Tento on the far side of the ocean, seeking her childhood home. Rushuna is a complete airhead, but she's a nice girl with goodwill to spare for everyone. Her ditziness produces plenty of comical moments and her bathing scenes provide ample voyeuristic value for those viewers who care. Meanwhile, she embarks upon a half-hearted quest to defeat her enemies the "ten sages" in an opponent-of-the-week quest like that of FIST OF THE NORTH STAR, although even she seems to lose interest halfway. The climax of the final gunfight owes an extremely obvious debt to the end of the American movie *Equilibrium,* which was released in Japan under the name *Rebellion* earlier the same year. A manga by Sosuke Kaise preceded the show in *Shonen Ace* monthly. TRIGUN with tits. **ⒷⓋ**

GREY: DIGITAL TARGET *

1986. Movie. DIR: Satoshi Dezaki. SCR: Yasushi Hirano, Kazumi Koide, Satoshi Dezaki, Toshiaki Imaizumi. DES: Setsuko Shibuichi, Kenichi Maejima. ANI: Yukari Kobayashi. MUS: Goro Omi. PRD: Magic Bus. 73 mins.

On a desolate future Earth, isolated communities fight a ritualized war, scoring points with every confirmed kill. Survivors are allowed to advance through the ranks from class F to A, with the aim of eventually becoming a Citizen. Grey's lover, Lips, joins the forces after being raped by soldiers but dies on her first mission. A distraught Grey joins up himself and gets a formidable reputation as the "God of Death" for being the sole survivor of several missions. When his mentor Red goes missing in action, Grey steals a plane with his new-found accomplice, Nova, and goes to look for him. Red has joined the Resistance, a group fighting the Big Mama computer that, it transpires, pits human towns against each other because it believes the human race wants to die. Grey discovers that the Resistance itself is just another front for Big Mama, and he destroys its floating citadel, which crashes in the supposed location of the Citizens' paradise, itself nothing but a ruin. Determined to destroy Big Mama, Grey and Nova march on the computer's Tower complex in the distance, as countless robots come out to stop them.

Despite antique animation that has forever condemned it to the B-list, *Grey* is still an excellent film, a nihilistic romance in the spirit of COCKPIT, satirizing the unwinnable rules of computer games with ever-multiplying enemies. It also features some truly nutty designs, from traditional giant robots to flying knights' helmets and a city inside a giant floating statue of the Goddess of Mercy. Keeping closely to KARUIZAWA SYNDROME–creator Yoshihisa Tagami's original manga in *Shonen Captain*, the anime only changes one major plot point, keeping Nova alive to the end. In the style of GUNBUSTER, it also shies away from showing the cataclysmic final battle, leaving the viewer to fill in the gap between the final shot and the epilogue that follows the closing credits. Like the ant that is stepped on in the opening scene, only to struggle out of the footprint and continue on its way, life itself refuses to give up without a fight, even though the seas are red and the planet is dying. In its thesis that life is a sick computer game, it is a forerunner of *The Matrix*, though its actual roots extend back into Tagami's own love of Westerns, with Grey as a lone gunslinger righting wrongs because he has nothing better to do. **LNV**

GRIMMS' FAIRY TALES

1987. JPN: *Grimm Dowa*. TV series. DIR: Hiroshi Saito, Takayoshi Suzuki, Shigeru Omachi. SCR: Masaru Yamamoto, Nobuyuki Fujimoto, Akira Miyazaki. DES: Shuichi Seki. ANI: Hidekazu Ishii. MUS: Hideo Shimazu. PRD: Nippon Animation, TV Asahi. 25 mins. x 48 eps.

A selection of just a few of the 200 stories collected by the German brothers in their compendium of fairy tales, some of which have also been animated as stand-alone anime in their own right. Stories include CINDERELLA, SNOW WHITE, *Blue Beard, The Princess and the Frog, Hansel and Gretel*, PUSS IN BOOTS, *Rapunzel*, and many others, sometimes two or three to an episode, and sometimes serialized across two to do the longer stories justice. The Brothers Grimm were also profiled in GREAT PEOPLE, unlike their Danish colleague, who had to settle for TALES OF HANS CHRISTIAN ANDERSEN. See also VIDEO PICTURE BOOK.

GROIZER X

1976. AKA: *Gloyzer X*. TV series. DIR: Hiroshi Taisenji. SCR: Toyohiro Ando. DES: Takeo Suzuki. ANI: Eiji Tanaka. MUS: Hiroshi Koenji. PRD: Dynamic Animation, Knack, TV Tokyo. 25 mins. x 36 eps.

Far away from human civilization in the Arctic, the alien Emperor Gerdon from planet Gailer has built a secret base to seize control of the world. The Earth's last, best hope is Doctor Jan, a Gailer defector devoted to peace, who has created the flying robot Groizer X, and given it to his daughter Rita. Rita, however, soon does the proper female thing, handing over the robot to Jo Kaijan, a member of the Terran professor Hideki Asuka's elite pilot team. Jo becomes the pilot of Groizer X, with Rita as his assistant, in the continuing war against the Gailer invaders.

Groizer X is actually only the "plane" form of the titular machine. Like Nagai's X-Bomber in *Star Fleet* (*DE), it can also transform into a Groizer Robot configuration, although it does so very rarely. Although often credited to Go Nagai, this series was created by Nagai in collusion with Tagosaku Sakura, the suspiciously pseudonymous artist behind some of the MAZINGER Z manga. This minor series was overshadowed by the more successful Toei series GRANDIZER, with which its images and merchandise are often confused.

GROPE

2007. JPN: *Grope: Yami no Naka no Kotoritachi*. AKA: *Grope: Little Birds in Darkness*. Video. DIR: Hiromi Yokoyama. SCR: Sono Man, PON. DES: Noritomo Hattori, Takashi Tenteketen. ANI: Noritomo Hattori. MUS: Toshiyuki Yamamoto. PRD: May-Be Soft, Suzuki Mirano. 30 mins. x 2 eps.

An earthquake on campus kills everyone except four students—childhood friends Fukubi and Shinichi, their friend Takahaki, and a junior girl, Mizuha. Fubuki and Shinichi admit their love to each other, Takahaki rapes both girls, Shinichi has conflicted feelings. Although they are the only four survivors of a quake so devastating it has killed everyone else, none of them has so much as a grazed knee or mussed hair until the shagging starts, because this is a porn anime based on the 2003 game by May-Be SOFT (EROTICA AND PORNOGRAPHY). Damage to the school, which has allegedly collapsed, is also only visible when dramatically necessary. The authors cannot help but notice the superficial similarity to *Long Love Letter* (2002, *DE), a live-action drama series based on a manga by Kazuo Umezu. **OV**

GROUP TAC

Animation company formed in 1968 by a number of big names in the animation world, including director Gisaburo Sugii and composer Isao Tomita. Its first known production was the TV series ROAD TO MUNICH (1972). After early work in sound production on anime, the company moved in 1973 into animation itself. Contemporary works include FLINT THE TIME DETECTIVE and TEXHNOLYZE. The company suffered considerable cashflow issues after the sudden cutback in new anime productions post-2006, and filed for bankruptcy mere months after the death of its founder, Atsumi Tashiro, in 2010.

The once-great production house went to its grave owing more than $7 million to some 167 creditors.

GRRL POWER *

2004. JPN: *Makasete Iruka*. AKA: *Leave It to Dolphin*. Video. DIR: Akitaro Daichi. SCR: Mamiko Ikeda. DES: Yuka Shibata. ANI: Yuka Shibata. MUS: Jun Abe, Seiji Muto. PRD: GA-Pro, CoMix Wave Inc. 25 mins.

Three abandoned children band together as sisters. Their parents have gone into hiding for reasons not entirely clear. They should be in sixth grade but they have to make a living, so they set up an odd-job agency on Shonan Beach, near Kamakura, and are soon so busy that they don't have time to go to school. Umi, Sora, and Ao take on tasks ranging from delivery to cheerleading in this perky comedy, although FRUITS BASKET–director Daichi claims he has a serious aim—to raise social issues for his fans to ponder. Green-haired Ao, the youngest of the trio, is deaf and uses sign language; this was hyped at the time as an anime first, by people who had never heard of HOUSE OF ACORNS. Tanned redhead Sora is an athletic tomboy who tackles the more physical jobs, making her deliveries on a Jet Ski, while blonde Umi does her utmost to avoid being labeled an airhead and is actually the brains of the group. All three girls study hard in their free time, of course, since to imply otherwise would mean that the creators were encouraging truancy. This is hammered home *ad nauseam* by the arrival of 11-year-old boy Riku, who thinks they have an easy life, only to be continually told that they are reading very difficult books every day. They're intensely ambitious—they want to make enough money to buy an island and create their own country. Daichi seems to be seeking the same level of independence; he assembled his own team and produced the anime himself. The style is ultra-cute, a Japanese take on the *Powerpuff Girls*.

GTO *

1999. AKA: *Great Teacher Onizuka, Bad Company*. Video, TV series. DIR: Noriyuki Abe, Hiroyuki Ishido. SCR: Masashi Sogo, Yoshiyuki Suga. DES: Koichi Usami, Mari Kitayama. ANI: Kumiko Rokunohe. MUS: Yusuke Homma. PRD: SPE, Studio Pierrot, Fuji TV. 49 mins. x 1 ep., 25 mins. x 42 eps.

Twenty-two-year-old former biker Eikichi Onizuka decides to go straight and become a schoolteacher, though his old life often comes back to haunt him. He uses his criminal smarts to pass the entrance exams but ends up at a school for no-hopers where teenage pregnancies, drugs, and crime are rife. Despite his hard exterior, he genuinely cares about his students, and he uses his streetwise past to put them on the right track.

With a teacher who is little older than his charges, *GTO* traces a line through SLOW STEP to Soseki Natsume's BOTCHAN, though its true success lies in the conservative media's need to sanitize subculture thuggery—and what better way than by showing that even gangsters and bikers can rejoin the system? *GTO* has a convoluted pedigree that also stretches back to the meteoric success of BOMBER BIKERS OF SHONAN, which inspired manga author Toru Fujisawa to create his own version, the *Shonan Pure Love Gang* (*Shonan Junai Gumi*, 1990). Featuring the school and biker gang activities of Onizuka and Danma, it was adapted into a five-part anime series starting in 1994 by Katsumi Minoguchi, as well as a five-part live-action series of direct-to-video movies. A second prequel, *Bad Company* (1996), detailed the first meeting of Onizuka and Danma and also received the live-action treatment, as *Shonan Junai Gumi: Bad Company* (1998).

In 1997, Fujisawa began *GTO* as a sequel in *Shonen Magazine*, with Onizuka announcing his intention of becoming a teacher so he can chase girls. The series also spun off into a live-action TV version and theatrical outings, starring heartthrob Takashi Sorimachi as Onizuka. It is this live version that is the quintessential *GTO*, with its handsome loner fighting injustices on his motorcycle like an educational lawman, but the anime incarnation still has considerable bite, mainly because its cartoon origins allowed for slightly more violence and menace than its prime-time live-action counterpart. It also features unobtrusive use of computer graphics that add realistic cloud and water effects to lead the viewer's eye away from the cheap TV animation, and a moody monochrome opening sequence that sums up the series' sardonic attitude, playing the sound of a revving motorcycle while showing the handle of a toilet. Inevitably, the series was also lampooned in an erotic pastiche, *GTR* (*G-cup Teacher Rei*), a four-DVD set about a schoolteacher with unfeasibly large breasts and her adventures with her similarly well-endowed colleagues and pupils.

GUARDIAN HEARTS

2003. Video. DIR: Yasuhiro Kuroda. SCR: Kanata Tanaka, Takeshi Sakamoto. DES: Norikazu Nakano. ANI: Norikazu Nakano. MUS: N/C. PRD: Soft Garage, VENET, KSS. 30 mins. x 3 eps. (v1), 30 mins. x 2 eps. (v2).

The Guardian Hearts are girls from the Realm of Light who are sent on interplanetary missions to preserve peace and justice, in Ryo Amatsu's manga from monthly *Shonen Ace*. However, heroine Hina is a careless, ineffectual bungler whose first action on getting to Earth is to accidentally transform in front of astounded high school boy Kazuya. She then insists that his family take her in as an adopted daughter, so at least she has a base. Kazuya's family home is soon swarming with cute strangers, which will come as no surprise to anime viewers who remember URUSEI YATSURA or LITTLE WITCH SALLY. Girl uniform thief Kurusu, space ninja Maya, catgirl Daisy, magical princess Chelsea, and demure maiden Kotono are just a few of the babes who find this ordinary human strangely attractive and want nothing more than to hang around under the bemused eyes of his family, like well-behaved groupies who can be relied on to help with the chores. A second video series, *Guardian Hearts: Power Up* followed in 2005.

GUDE CREST *

1990. JPN: *Onna Senshi Efe and Jeila: Goude no Monsho*. AKA: *Female Soldiers Efe and Jeila: Crest of Gude; Jun and Sarah*. Video. DIR: Kazusane Kikuchi. SCR: Isao Seiya. DES: Tsukasa Dokite. ANI: Masamitsu Kudo. MUS: Shoji Honda. PRD: JC Staff. 45 mins.

In a one-shot based on Reiko Hikawa's fantasy novel in the spirit of the later SLAYERS, a pair of sexy, sassy swordswomen, modeled rather obviously on the DIRTY PAIR, must rescue a royal orphan, overthrow a cruel tyrant, and destroy an evil goddess. The leads were renamed Efera and Jiliora for ADV's U.S. dub.

GU-GU GUNMO

1984. TV series, movie. DIR: Akinori Naga-oka, Takenori Kawada, Shigeru Yanagawa. SCR: Keisuke Fujikawa. DES: Takao Kasai. ANI: Takao Kasai. MUS: Hiroshi Ogasawara. PRD: Toei, Fuji TV. 25 mins. x 50 eps. (TV), 45 mins. (m).

A tale of school high jinks from the *Shonen Sunday* manga by the versatile Fujihiko Hosono, who also created the more adult stories that became **BIOHUNTER** and **JUDGE**. Gunmo the giant pink bird hatches and befriends Japanese schoolboy Heita. A movie version was released in 1985 that lampooned several **JAPANESE FOLK TALES**, including that of the Princess Kaguya, which was also spoofed in **REI REI**.

GUILTY CROWN *

2011. TV series, video. DIR: Tetsuro Araki, Toshiaki Yamashita. SCR: Hiroyuki Yoshino, Ichiro Okochi. DES: redjuice, Atsushi Takeuchi, Shinobu Tsuneki, Takuma Ebisu, Yusuke Takeda. ANI: Toshiyuki Yahagi, Satoshi Kadowaki. MUS: Hiroyuki Sawano, Ryo. PRD: Production I.G, Aniplex, Dentsu, Fuji TV, MOVIC. 25 mins. x 22 eps.

The future. The Japanese government has surrendered the nation's independence after the outbreak of a devastating alien virus threatened the country with total collapse. Now the provisional government, GHQ, is in the hands of a man who wants to use the virus to take over the world—after drastically reducing its population. Teenager loner Shu lost his father in the epidemic in Japan; now he and a resistance group calling itself Funeral Parlor have to try and prevent the biggest funeral in the history of the planet, and reclaim Japan in the process.

Guilty Crown has many faults but lack of ambition isn't among them. The show constantly morphs into new shapes, from conspiracy theory to political drama to high school horror show to right-wing social engineering treatise to teen love story. These cataclysmic shifts are often heralded or accompanied by, or result in, major shifts in character—from meek to maniacal from sympathetic to scary, from alive to dead. Nothing is exempt from the show's constant sense of flux and turmoil, with weapons being morphed out of people as well as fired into them, robots getting sliced, diced and lasered, and

interesting uses of antigravity and prisms, as well as old-fashioned shoot-em-ups and knife fights.

Director Araki is never scared to think the unthinkable and then act it out: he has an unerring feel for suspense and a willingness to do anything to maintain it. Production I.G provides fluid animation, powerful action, and interesting design. Cliché-ridden, formulaic, and weak on character development though this show is, it delivers its dystopian rage with style and verve. It is surely a complete coincidence that "GHQ," as in General Head Quarters, was also the name of the U.S. Occupation authorities in the immediate postwar period, 1945–52.

GUIN SAGA *

2009. TV series. DIR: Atsushi Wakabayashi. SCR: Shoji Yonemura. DES: Toshiharu Murata, Junichi Higashi. ANI: Toshiharu Murata. MUS: Nobuo Uematsu. PRD: Satelight, Aniplex. 24 mins. x 26 eps.

The ancient, peaceful kingdom of Parro is invaded by the evil warlord Mongaul and his army. The king and queen are dead, but their heirs, Prince Remus and Princess Rinda, the "twin pearls of Parro," have escaped the capital. Alone and unprotected, facing a troop of the invading soldiers, they are rescued by a strange warrior with the head of a leopard. He knows his name is Guin, but his only other memory is a single word—"Aurra." To protect the twins and the motley group of allies they attract, and to stay ahead of a warrior princess who is hot on their trail, Guin will need to use all his strength and courage—but will this help him to answer the mystery of his own life?

Making a huge, long-running, award-winning book series story into an anime TV series is fraught with pitfalls. *Guin Saga* is a 130-volume fantasy novel series by Kaoru Kurimoto, with art by Natsuki Sumeragi, published between 1979 and 2009, the last four volumes after the author's death. Japanese publisher Jive began to adapt the work to comic form in 2006. This huge franchise shows how much there is to explore in Japanese fantasy, but the anime series gives only a tiny glimpse of its scope. The design is good, with some strikingly beautiful characters, and the animation and color

design are generally impeccable, with only a few points where character animation is weaker than normal.

Writer Yonemura has merged several of the novels into one narrative for his screenplay, and handles the pace and timing of events well. His quest-style adventure has a more coherent structure than **RECORD OF LODOSS WAR** and allows creator Kurimoto's passion for the novels of Edgar Rice Burroughs and Robert E. Howard, with their high adventure and derring-do, to shine through as it does in her own work. This series may only be the hors d'oeuvre to the epic banquet of the novels, but it's tasty in its own right.

GULKEEVA

1995. JPN: *Jusenshi Gulkeeva*. AKA: *Beast-Warrior Gulkeeva; Wild Knights Gulkeeva; Galkiba; Galkiva*. TV series. DIR: Masamitsu Hidaka. SCR: Kenichi Kanemaki, Sho Aikawa, Hiroyuki Kawasaki. DES: Hisashi Hirai, Takahiro Yamada. ANI: Hisashi Hirai, Satoshi Yoshida, Takuro Shinbo. MUS: Kenji Kawai. PRD: Sunrise, TV Tokyo. 25 mins. x 26 eps.

Adaptation of a manga originally serialized in *Shonen Sunday Super*, in which demonic Darknoid invaders from Nosfertia are held off by a group of pretty young boys, who inexplicably work in a noodle bar during their time off. Japanese teenager Toya Shinjo is told by his parents that he is not from Earth at all, but rather he is a Humanoid from the parallel dimension of Eternaliya, reincarnation of an ancient hero, and fated to work together with transforming Animanoid knights from Heaventsia in order to thwart the Darknoids. Unsurprisingly, the Animanoids are a wolf (Greyfas), a hawk (Beakwood), and a gorilla (Gariel), uniting speed, flight, and strength, like so many other shows since **BABEL II**. A series in the tradition of shows like **SAINT SEIYA**, although its attempt to integrate boys' and girls' TV anime genres was easily outclassed by **ESCAFLOWNE** the following year.

GULLIVER'S SPACE TRAVELS: BEYOND THE MOON *

1965. JPN: *Gulliver no Uchu Ryoko*. Movie. DIR: Yoshio Kuroda. SCR: Shinichi Sekizawa. DES: Hideo Furusawa. ANI: Hideo Furusawa, Takashi Abe, Hayao Miyazaki. MUS: Isao Tomita (Milton and Anne Delugg, U.S. version).

PRD: Toei. 80 mins.

Ted (Ricky in the U.S. dub) meets the aged Professor Gulliver in a deep, dark forest. Accompanied by Mack the dog, a toy soldier called The General, and the unimaginatively named Crow the crow (see CORAL INVESTIGATES), the two set off on a journey to the Planet of Blue Hope in their spaceship the Gulliver. After adventures in the Reverse Time Nebula, which transforms them all into younger versions of themselves, they finally meet the inhabitants of the Planet of Blue Hope, though they have been thrown off their homeworld by the evil Queen of Purple Planet and her robot soldiers. However, Ted and the professor discover that water disintegrates matter in this part of space, and they are able to lead a successful assault on the enemy, armed only with water pistols and water balloons. The doll-like princess of Blue Hope is transformed into a real girl by the victory, and she thanks them for saving her world.

A very remote sci-fi sequel to Jonathan Swift's classic satire *Gulliver's Travels*, which was itself adapted in 1983 as part of the FAMOUS WORLD FAIRY TALES series, featuring Yoshiaki Kawajiri as art director. The original novel would also inspire in-betweener Hayao Miyazaki's CASTLE IN THE SKY.

GUN FRONTIER *

2002. TV series. DIR: Soichiro Zen. SCR: Mugi Kamio. DES: Keisuke Masunaga, Miho Nakata, Katsumi Itabashi. ANI: Ikuo Shimazu. MUS: Hiroshi Motokura. PRD: AT-X, Maczam, Pronto, Tsuburaya Eizo, TV Tokyo, Vega Entertainment. 25 mins. x 13 eps.

Leiji Matsumoto never tires of finding new ways to present his concept of heroic manhood through his cast of character archetypes. It saves having to draw anything new, after all. In *GF* Frank Harlock Jr., a former pirate with a predictable resemblance to CAPTAIN HARLOCK, arrives with short samurai sidekick Tochiro in the lawless Wild West. They are looking for a missing clan of Japanese immigrants and a traitor, Wild Utamaru, who betrayed the settlement of Samurai Creek and with it Tochiro's family. Facing sex slavers, bandits, corrupt lawmen, and the unfair contempt of a world that is happy to rate tall, elegant, drop-dead-sexy men like Harlock as heroes, but mocks short, fat, miserable heaps

like Tochiro however brave and clever they are, the two friends team up with a lovely mystery woman and blaze a dangerous trail along the Gun Frontier. Notable from other Harlock universe stories insofar that Harlock often seems more like Tochiro's sidekick than vice versa. **V**

GUN X SWORD

2005. AKA: *Gun Sword*. TV series. DIR: Goro Taniguchi. SCR: Hideyuki Kurata. DES: Takahiro Kimura, Seiji Tanda. ANI: Asako Nishida, Seiichi Nakatani, Hisashi Saito, Masanori Aoyama. MUS: Shuntaro Okino. PRD: AIC, ASTA, Studio Tulip, TV Tokyo. 25 mins. x 26 eps.

Van is a swordsman hell-bent on avenging the death of his fiancée. Wendy Garrett is a pretty young girl with an arsenal of antique guns who belives her brother has been kidnapped by the same criminal. She joins forces with Van in a picaresque quest mixing the Western attitudes of TRIGUN with the town-of-the-week conceit of KINO'S JOURNEY. Their quarry is "the Claws," a serial killer intent on killing young brides—perhaps a little nod to *Kill Bill* (2003)—see KILL BILL: THE ORIGIN OF O-REN.

GUNBUSTER *

1988. JPN: *Top o Nerae! GunBuster*. AKA: *Aim for the Top!: GunBuster*. Video. DIR: Hideaki Anno. SCR: Toshio Okada. DES: Haruhiko Mikimoto, Koichi Ohata, Kazuki Miyatake. ANI: Yuji Moriyama, Toshiyuki Kubooka. MUS: Kohei Tanaka. PRD: Studio Fantasia, Gainax. 30 mins. x 6 eps. (v1), ? mins. x 2 eps. (*Science Lessons*), 25 mins. x 6 eps. (v3).

Noriko's father dies in space in the first encounter with an alien race that is preparing for an all-out assault on Earth. Noriko overcomes great difficulties at her school in Okinawa and qualifies as one of the pilots sent to defend the planet. She falls out with her partner, "Big Sister" Kazumi Amano, and teams up with Smith Toren, a handsome American pilot who soon dies in action. The predicament of the human race looks bleak: the "aliens" are really the galaxy's natural defense mechanisms, and humanity is merely a virus on the face of the universe. Coach Ota devises the Buster Machines to help the reunited girls turn the tables, and the first major assault is held off with heavy losses. Though only a few weeks have passed for the girls, the effects of relativity mean that several years

have passed on Earth. Kazumi marries the dying Ota, and Noriko goes on another tour of duty. Six months later (for Noriko, whereas 15 years have passed on Earth), an older Kazumi rejoins her with Buster Machine Three, a super-bomb designed to wipe out the heart of the galaxy in the final conflict.

Beginning as a sci-fi parody of AIM FOR THE ACE, *Gunbuster* eventually transforms into an homage to Kihachi Okamoto's live-action war film *Battle of Okinawa* (1971), complete with onscreen notes detailing the numbers of "ships sunk" and a background cast of dozens of generals, each only gaining the merest moment of screen-time. Foregrounded through all this is the spunky Noriko, who only ages a year as her friends near retirement age and is eternally in a world of childish things, much like the semiautobiographical heroes of the same producers' OTAKU NO VIDEO. Wartime allusions abound: the human race (i.e., Japan) is fighting on the wrong side in a war it cannot win, while the last-ditch attempt to hold the home islands launches from Okinawa, and schoolchildren age before the viewer's eyes in a variant of the "time travel" of 24 EYES. *Gunbuster* is also a loving pastiche of the anime serials of its creators' formative years, from the martial heroism of STAR BLAZERS (seen on one of the posters in Noriko's quarters) to the super-robots of GIGANTOR. The in-jokes reach staggering levels: Smith Toren was, for example, a tip of the hat to future Studio Proteus boss Toren Smith (see DIRTY PAIR), who was staying with the Gainax animators at the time, while shots of spacecraft under construction often show breakaway sprues as if they were model kits. Played deadly straight no matter how silly the onscreen visuals, it is the ultimate video anime, and, though outlines existed for a full 26-episode series, the story seems perfectly suited to its humble three-hour running time. It also set the pace for many 1990s anime, from the jiggling bosoms of PLASTIC LITTLE to the tongue-in-cheek posturing of BATTLE ATHLETES, though none of its imitators came close. Sadly, it never quite achieved its potential abroad, despite an excellent subtitled version. It was never dubbed, hence losing the large audience it truly deserved, a feat achieved by the same studio's later EVANGELION. The

1994 laserdisc box set included two new "Science Lessons" for episodes 5 and 6 (the humorous short segments attached to the episodes that provided explanations about the *Gunbuster* world), which had not been in the original releases.

Gainax chose to mark the company's 20th anniversary with Kazuya Tsurumaki's six-part video series, *Aim for the Top 2* (AKA *Diebuster*, 2004), focusing on Nono, a hapless waitress on Earth who is co-opted into a psychic anti-alien squadron called the Topless. As with the original, early episodes appear trite and shallow, only to take a turn toward the dramatic and gripping later on, most notably in a fourth episode storyboarded by Hideaki Anno himself. The series was then screened on Japanese TV after Gainax's more famous follow-up, released on Japanese DVD in 2000 (including the new Science Lessons), and ultimately remastered and rereleased on Japanese DVD in 2004. *Gunbuster Perfect Guide*, containing interviews and other ""Making Of"" information, was also released on DVD in 2004. **NV**

GUNDAM *

1979. JPN: *Kido Senshi Gundam*. AKA: *Mobile Suit Gundam*. TV series, movie, video. DIR: Yoshiyuki Tomino, Shinya Sadamitsu, Ryoji Fujiwara, Fumihiko Takayama, Takeyuki Kanda, Takashi Imanishi. SCR: Hiroyuki Hoshiyama, Kenichi Matsuzaki, Masaru Yamamoto, Yoshihisa Araki, Katsuyuki Sumisawa. DES: Yoshikazu Yasuhiko, Kunio Okawara, Kazumi Fujita, Mamoru Nagano, Hiroyuki Kitazume, Mika Akitaka, Haruhiko Mikimoto, Yutaka Izubuchi, Gainax, Yoshinori Sayama, Toshihiro Kawamoto, Hajime Katoki, Kimitoshi Yamane, Shuko Murase. ANI: Yoshikazu Yasuhiko, Kazuo Tomizawa, Kazuo Nakamura, Kazuo Yamazaki. MUS: Takeo Watanabe, Yuji Matsuyama, Shigeaki Saegusa, Tetsuro Kashibuchi, Yoko Kanno, Kohei Tanaka (G Gundam), Yasuo Uragami (Gundam W). PRD: Sotsu Agency, Sunrise, Nagoya TV (TV Asahi). 25 mins. x 43 eps. (*First Gundam*), 25 mins. x 50 eps. (*Zeta*), 25 mins. x 47 eps. (*Double Zeta*), 120 mins. (m, *Char's Counterattack*), 30 mins. x 10 eps. (*SD*), 30 mins. (m, *SD*), 30 mins. x 4 eps. (v, *SD ii–iv*); (30 mins. m2, *SD*), 40 mins. x 4 eps. (*SD Side Story*), 30 mins. x 6 eps. (*War in the Pocket*), 30 mins. x 12 eps. (*Stardust Memory*), 115 mins. (m, *F91*, also 120 mins. special edition), 25 mins. x 51 eps. (*Victory*), 30 mins. x 11 eps. (v, *08th Team*), 25 mins. x 49 eps. (*G Gundam*), 25 mins. x 49 eps. (*Wing*), 30 mins. x 3 eps. (*Endless Waltz*), 25 mins. x 39 eps. (*Gundam X*), 25 mins. x 50 eps. (*Turn-A*), ca. 3 mins. (*Gundam: Mission*), 24 mins. (*Neo Experience*), 128 mins. (*Turn A*, m1), 128 mins. (*Turn A*, m2), ? mins. x 15 eps. (*Evolve*), 25 mins. x 50 eps. (*Seed*), 94 mins. x 3 eps. (*Seed, Sp. Ed.*), 25 mins. x 50 eps. + 2 sp. (*Seed Destiny*), 95 mins. (*Zeta*, m1), 98 mins. (*Zeta*, m2), 90 mins. x 1+ eps. (*Seed Destiny*, Sp. Ed.), 15 mins. x 3 eps. (*Seed: Stargazer*), ca. 95 mins. (*Zeta*, m3). 25 mins. x 50 eps. (TV, *00*), 5 mins. (m, *Ring*), 120 mins. (m, *00*), 4 mins. x 2 eps. (v, *Frag*), 7 mins. (v, *Avant Title*), 60 mins. x 7 eps. (v, *Unicorn*).

In the "Universal Century" Year 0079, Earth and its space colonies are split between the democratic Federation and the Principality of Zeon. The Earth ship White Base arrives at the Side 7 research facility to pick up some prototype "mobile suits" (humanoid piloted robots), but it is ambushed by Zeon attackers with orders to destroy them. Fifteen-year-old Earth boy Amuro Ray climbs into the cockpit of his father's prototype RX-78 Gundam unit and fights them off. With most of the original military crew dead, the White Base is commandeered by young Side 7 evacuees—as they head for Earth, they are hounded by Zeon forces led by the dashing enemy officer Char Aznable. Touching down in enemy territory, they fight their way out to their own forces, who reveal that they are "newtypes," a new breed of human with nascent psionic powers. Eventually, they lead a final assault on the asteroid fortress of A Baoa Qu, the Zeon forces are riven by internal struggles (Char himself kills one of their leaders as part of a family feud), and the One Year War is over.

Along with STAR BLAZERS and MACROSS, *Gundam* is a cornerstone of anime SF, an ever-present franchise and sprawling saga, still active three decades after its premiere. This is somewhat ironic when the original series was initially regarded as a failure, scraping only 5% in the ratings and shifting nowhere near the desired amount of toys. *Gundam*, however, proved itself far more popular in reruns and flourished among an unexpectedly older fanbase, not of boys, but of teenagers and young adults with an interest in model-making. *Gundam*'s distinguishing features are firmly rooted in merchandising and its own longevity—a vast taxonomy of robot types ready for exploitation in model kits and action figures (compare to POKÉMON) and a long-running future saga that has often collapsed under its own weight only to be brought back with several attempts to reset the continuity. As with other successful franchises like *Star Trek*, keeping track of the characters themselves also requires a sizable concordance. It's bad enough that they often seem named after random words picked from a Scrabble bag, let alone that they switch sides and identities. Matters are not helped by "joke" names that seem like a great idea to the Japanese but have caused endless difficulties to English translators trying to keep romanizations consistent. Most infamously, Char Aznable is named after the French singer Charles Aznavour, which would have been a poor enough gag in a shallow comedy like SORCERER HUNTERS, but is quite damaging to the tone of an otherwise serious SF saga. *Gundam* combines elements of *Star Wars* with space-colony politics and a subtle metaphor for Japan's postwar "new breed" baby boomers—the "newtype" name was appropriated for Japan's most popular anime magazine.

The original series was rereleased in three movie editions—*Mobile Suit Gundam* (1981), *MSG 2: Soldiers of Sorrow* (1981), and *MSG 3: Encounters in Space* (1982). It was the launch event for the first movie that was billed as the "proclamation of a new century" (*shinseiki sengen*) and that found 15,000 people turning up to a cinema that could never hope to hold that many ticket-holders. In subsequent decades, this event has been mythologized, in the words of the *Asahi Shinbun*, as "the day anime changed"—an indicator that FANDOM for Japanese cartoons was substantially older than had been previously thought, and that there was an implied audience for video spin-offs. The latter two films comprised roughly 50% new material between them, with the bulk of it concentrated in the third movie. Part of the new footage showed Char escaping from A Baoa Qu, setting up the sequel series *Zeta*

Gundam (1985—the seventh year of the franchise named for the seventh letter of the Greek alphabet). *Zeta* kept surviving members of the original cast but reorganized their allegiances, with Char and the White Base now on the same side, resisting the Earth Federation's attempts to wipe out remaining rebels. The series' ambiguity toward enemies has come to be another of its distinguishing marks, though much of it may originate less in a desire for foes with feelings, and more from Tomino's own ambiguous attitude toward the series for which he has come to be known. *Zeta* was followed by a second season, *Double Zeta* (1986), with an all-new cast, while the "conclusion" to the long feud between Char Aznable and Amuro Ray came in the movie edition *Char's Counterattack* (1988, *Char no Gyakushu*). Determined that all humankind will join the colonists in space, Char plans to drop the Axis asteroid on Earth but is finally persuaded to work with Amuro to prevent the tragedy both sides have created.

The series was parodied in Tetsuro Amino's 1988 *SD Gundam* video series, which featured "super-deformed" squashed-down cartoon versions of the characters and machines in unlikely comedic situations. The original ten-part video series was followed by two short movies, and video sequels numbered *Mark II–IV*. There was also the two-part video series *SD Warrior Gundam* (1989), and a spin-off of the spin-off—*SD Gundam Side Story* (1990).

Gaps in the continuity of the original, serious *Gundam* were plugged by two video series, Fumihiko Takayama's *MSG 0080: War in the Pocket* (1989), which observed the One Year War from the new viewpoint of a very young child learning the real meaning of war, and *MSG 0083: Stardust Memory* which bridged the gap between *Gundam 0080* and the same year's movie *Zeta Gundam*. Following a template no less predictable than that of **TIME BOKAN**, *Stardust Memory* features a rehashed Char character, Anavel Gato, and a brash young Amuro clone, Ko Uraki. Three years after A Baoa Qu, as the Earth Federation struggles to rebuild its shattered fleet and Zeon plots revenge, the enemy ace once again tries to steal a Gundam. Drawn unwittingly into a conspiracy to wipe out the Earth Federation HQ by crashing a colony

onto it, Ko does his utmost to prevent disaster but is still court-martialed and jailed, set free only because further political machinations require that the whole affair be forgotten. *F91* was a stalled attempt to start again with a clean slate, moving the action 30 years into the future with an all-new cast—teenagers Seabrook Arno and love-interest Cecily Fairchild, who discover that Cecily is, like Char before her, a scion of a powerful noble family (in this case the Ronah dynasty), determined to impose a thousand-year Reich on the solar system. Though the story was continued in novel form with the *Crossbone Gundam* follow-up, it did not last as an anime. Aiming itself, like the same studio's successful **BRAVE SAGA** franchise, at a younger audience, the franchise returned as the TV series *Victory Gundam* (1993), though the director (who had gained the nickname "Kill 'em All" Tomino after **ZAMBOT 3**) soon asserted his trademark angst and tragedy. Set another 30 years on (in the year U.C. 0153), it featured yet another all-new cast, headed by the 13-year-old wonder-pilot Usso Ebbing. Takeyuki Kanda's video series *MSG: 08th M[obile] S[uit] Team* (1996) returns to the events of the first year in the saga (0079) and the activities of yet another group of characters in and around the events already established in the continuity.

The gap between *Victory* and *08th MS Team* saw several unrelated series that sought to capitalize on the *Gundam* brand without adhering to the future history continuity. Depending on your point of view, these are either interesting speculations on alternate universes or a cavalier attempt to jettison everything from the series except those all-important robot merchandise tie-ins. Released in the same year as **STREET FIGHTER II**, Yasuhiro Imagawa's completely unhinged *G Gundam* TV series was redolent of Stuart Gordon's *Robot Jox* (1989), with gladiatorial bouts between giant robots used to settle quarrels between nations (culturally stereotyped to ludicrous degrees with an elephant Gundam for India, a windmill Gundam for the Netherlands, and a Viking Gundam complete with its own rowing boat). No one is entirely sure why Neo-Sweden's Nobel Gundam looks like a character out of **SAILOR MOON**. The kids-in-combat premise was rehashed in another "alternate

universe," Masashi Ikeda's *Gundam Wing* (1995), in which five 15-year-old teenagers, inspired by the pretty-boys of **SAINT SEIYA**, are mobile-suit pilots in a new war between Earth and its colonies in space. Once more, political and economic machinations are out to crush the colonists' desire for self-determination. *Wing* was also reedited into the four-part *Operation Meteor* clip-shows and is arguably the most successful alternative universe adventure so far, though its sudden cancellation forced an ending on video as *MSG Wing: Endless Waltz* (1997), itself reissued with extra footage as the *Endless Waltz Special Edition* movie. A third alternate saga, Shinji Takamatsu's *Gundam X* (1996), did not flourish in the post-**EVANGELION** climate and was ignominiously dragged off the air. The series' next major outing after *Wing* was *Turn-A Gundam* (1999), yet another attempt to encompass as many previous serials as possible into one overarching continuity (compare to similar problems that dogged the *Macross* saga, especially post-**ROBOTECH**). Leaping two millennia into the future (a period guaranteed to make most continuity errors irrelevant), it depicts Earth people who have forgotten about their spacefaring past, rudely awakened into relearning about the mythical Gundam robots (refer to Tomino's **DUNBINE**) after they are invaded by a highly advanced society that has languished forgotten on the moon.

Featuring new music from Yoko Kanno, controversially bizarre robot designs by American futurist Syd Mead (see **STAR BLAZERS**), and a move to the Fuji TV network, *Turn-A Gundam* also appeared in compilation movie editions in 2002: *Earth Light* and *Moonlight Butterfly*. In case people weren't confused enough, there was also a spin-off of *Zeta Gundam* around this time, in the form of the movie *Gundam Neo Experience 0087 Green Divers* (2001), the "neo experience" element being the fact that the movie was screened in IMAX theaters, and hence offered virtual wraparound immersion in the events onscreen.

The next TV series in the franchise was Mitsuo Fukuda's *Gundam Seed* (2002) and its sequel *Gundam Seed Destiny* (2004), set in yet another continuity, termed the "Cosmic Era." Much of the intrigue, however, is the same old story, with Earth squaring off against ZAFT (the Zodiac Alliance of Freedom Treaty) using prototype pilotable robots. *Gundam Seed* made it swiftly to America, but in a format that led to the controversial kiddifying of some elements—as with *Case Closed* (see CONAN THE BOY DETECTIVE), the show was squeezed into slots aimed at a younger audience than it really warranted, causing producers to alter sequences of brief nudity and to add laserlight effects to weapons, a move lampooned by irate fans as the creation of "disco guns." The *Seed* titles also gained several spin-offs, including a compilation of key moments in *Special Edition*, as well as several manga side-stories under the *Astray* label, and the spin-off *GS: Stargazer* (2006), directed by Susumu Nishizawa, which premiered online in three 15-minute bursts.

The story continues to be constantly revised through novels, manga, games, and other spin-offs. These have included the live-action game *Gundam 0079: War for Earth*, the live-action movie *G-Saviour* (2000), and Katsuhiro Otomo's CG short *Mission to the Rise* (1998). As part of *Gundam*'s 20th-anniversary celebrations (which seemed to the authors to go on for about five years!), Sunrise also released a series of short anime called *Gundam Evolve* (2002), presenting vignettes from the many earlier franchises. The movie *MS Igloo* (2004), set during the *original* continuity and not the more recent Cosmic Era nonsense, was initially shown exclusively at the Bandai Museum in Matsudo, but has been revamped as a three-part video series under the subtitle *Apocalypse 0079* (2006). *Zeta Gundam* was also revamped as *MS Z Gundam: A New Translation* in the form of three movies (2004–6), blending old and new animation, and with a revised story.

Other variants of *Gundam* include the *A Baoa Qu* ride at the Fuji Express Highland amusement park (featuring original animation designs by *War in the Pocket*–designer Haruhiko Mikimoto), and Gichi Otsuka's novel and manga *For the Barrel* (2000), which refashioned Tomino's own *Gundam* novels. In an abortive attempt to adapt *For the Barrel* for English readers, *Newtype USA* also published a single chapter of an English-language prologue to *FTB* that was never seen in the original Japanese. Although *Newtype USA*'s staff

translated the entirety of *FTB*, the novel itself never appeared in the magazine.

As with the works of Leiji Matsumoto, particularly STAR BLAZERS, the *Gundam* franchise suffers from an identity crisis of sorts. Its continuity is a mess of remakes and restarts, its owner a conglomerate keen to make good an investment in earlier incarnations that now appear dated. Its original fans have children of their own; but newer aficionados often latch onto later incarnations contradicted by their predecessors. In a world of grown-up sci-fi fans, its mature moments and dramatic scenes are too often lost beneath the crushing weight of merchandising concerns. The tension between the desire to create something new and the desire to replicate proven successes in characters and situations has led much of *Gundam* to have a cyclical, repetitive nature. One of its best hopes in the 21st century lies in distribution to mobile phones and other portable devices where, as with ROBOTECH, the age of the earlier versions is less obvious on a smaller screen. It is difficult, however, to imagine its owners ever giving up on such a proven cash cow, despite the headaches it may cause encyclopedists.

Gundam's owners saw the sense in rebooting the series from scratch yet again, retelling it with more modern sensibilities, in the vain hope of tapping into anime's huge potential global audience. Seiji Mizushima's *Gundam 00* (2007) literally reset the series to zero, now set in the year 2307 amid an energy crisis that has been met with three competing superstates, each building an orbital elevator to massive solar energy platforms. The basic elements, however, remained the same, amid new concentrations on terrorism and religious extremism. A film, *A Wakening of the Trailblazer* (2010), continues the story two years after the finale, as the survivors face a new cybernetic menace from the outer planets. However, even as new creators fiddled with the franchise, its initiator Tomino was still on hand to reassert the old continuity, most prominently with *Ring of Gundam* (2009), a five-minute film premiered at a Gundam convention in celebration of the serial's 30th anniversary, in which a pilot goes in search of an archive that explains the original story. Good luck with that! Similarly, Kou Matsuo's seven-

minute video short *Battlefield Record: Avant Title* (2009) also remained in the original continuity, attached to a PS3 game, as did the two *Gundam Frag* (2009) shorts, which featured a small number of sequences of testing and maneuvers of vehicles from *Double Zeta*.

Because it really isn't confusing enough already, Kazuhiro Furuhashi's video series *Gundam UC* (2010), also known as *Gundam Unicorn*, was released in celebration of the 30th anniversary of the original and was set within the original continuity, in the Universal Century year 0096. This only goes to indicate the multi-generational nature of *Gundam*'s implied viewership, with the "normal" audience of young kids watching the latest new TV series, often subordinate to vestigial pockets of former fandoms. A nine-year-old boy who watched the first series in 1979 would be 44 in 2014, which perhaps explains the origin of super-merchandise like the full-sized, fully working Char Aznable–themed motor car, seemingly designed to feed the desires of an aging fan with surplus wealth and a mid-life crisis. It has been suggested by some pundits that such "silver otaku" are a non-renewable cash-cow resource for anime in the next two decades, which is sure to keep *Gundam* rebooting itself eternally, like a malfunctioning computer.

GUNDRESS *

1999. Video. DIR: Katsuyoshi Yatabe. SCR: Kentaro Isaki, Junichi Sakai, Kazumasa Fujiie. DES: Tetsuro Aoki, Koji Watanabe. ANI: Taro Yamada, Mikio Tsuchiya, Hideo Maru, Masahiko Okumasa. MUS: Yutaka Tominaga. PRD: Sanctuary, Nikkatsu. 82 mins.

In the year 2100, in Japan's newly constructed port of Bayside City, the all-female "Bouncer" task force is founded as an anti-crime unit but soon finds itself guarding the crime lord Hassan, in the hope that he will reveal vital information to bring down a terrorist ring, in a disappointing one-shot anime from the people who brought you LANDLOCK, which similarly cashes in on the alleged involvement of "planning assistant" Masamune Shirow. With a high concept tantalizingly close to an episode of the later GHOST IN THE SHELL spin-off *Stand Alone Complex*, a multiracial "Bayside City" that was once Yokohama like that in DOMINION, and robot suits like something out of **APPLESEED**, this confection is substantially less than the sum of its Shirow-designed parts. Early press hype talked up the use of "real" voice actresses instead of ones who specialized in anime, but it sank without a trace in the Japanese market, partly because not even Shirow can wave a magic wand and make something interesting out of four stereotypical girls conceived for a computer game, but largely because it was released unfinished. The premiere date of the film was immovable, since it relied upon block-booked theaters for which fans had bought tickets in advance. Rather than risk refunds and disaster, the producers elected to show the incomplete film with the promise of a later exclusive for the faithful. At the time, it was a fiasco; 15 years later, all too many anime seem half-finished, and **FANDOM** hardly seems to notice.

GUNGRAVE *

2004. TV series. DIR: Toshiyuki Tsuru. SCR: Yosuke Kuroda. DES: Yasuhiro Nightow. ANI: Cindy Yamauchi, Shino Masanori. MUS: Tsuneo Imahori. PRD: Red Entertainment, Madhouse, TV Tokyo, AT-X. 25 mins. x 26 eps.

Falsely implicated in a gangland shootout that caused the death of his putative father-in-law, mild-mannered Brandon Heat is on the run with his old orphanage buddy Harry McDowell. When love interest Maria becomes a ward of the Millennium underworld syndicate, Brandon joins them, hoping to get closer to her. Brandon and Harry rise up in the organization, until the ambitious Harry turns on his former ally, betraying and killing his best friend to become head of Millennium, with so much power he even has national politicians in his pocket. However, Brandon is brought back to life in the style of *Robocop* by the mysterious Lightning organization, whose secret Necrolyze project transforms him from a clumsy simpleton into the invincible assassin known as Beyond The Grave. His mighty handguns (named after Cerberus, three-headed guarddog of Hell) can mow down any opposition, and he is identified by his burning desire for revenge and the giant coffin he carries on his back. Years after they first clawed their way out of the ghetto, the pair return to face each other on their old stamping

ground—Harry abandoned by his own men, with a price on his head, Grave with his reanimated body starting to shut down.

Based on the PS2 game featuring designs by **TRIGUN**–creator Yasuhiro Nightow, *Gungrave* throws in so many influences and genre ideas that the authors would not be surprised to see a character somewhere with a kitchen sink on his back as well. The script admirably concentrates on fleshing out the character conflicts and plot, arguably at the expense of the action sequences. A tale of gangster careerism à la *Once Upon a Time in America* (1984), told chiefly in flashback like *The Godfather-Part II*, is also made to share the screen with redundant references to Westerns, particularly Nightow's beloved *They Call Me Trinity* (1971), and Sergio Corbucci's *Django* (1966), which similarly features a lone gun of venegeance intent on rescuing a damsel in distress. Meanwhile, the run-down urban gothic setting plays to the strengths of the Madhouse studio. In smart application of contemporary fads, it also mixes the resurrectionscience of **KIKAIDER** and **CASSHAN** with the evil undead menace of a zombie movie. The flashbacks catch up with the "present day" two thirds of the way through the series, ready for the final showdown. **ⓛⓝⓥ**

GUNPARADE MARCH *

2003. JPN: *GunParade March Aratanaru Kyogunka*. AKA: *GunParade March: A New Anthem*. TV series, video. DIR: Katsushi Sakurabi. SCR: Fumihiko Takayama, Junichi Shintaku, Yasushi Minakami. DES: Yasuhiro Irie, Kazunori Iwakura, Kunihiro Abe, Junko Kimura. ANI: Yoshio Okochi. MUS: Hikaru Nanase, Masayoshi Yoshikawa. PRD: Brains Base, JC Staff, SCEI, MBS. 25 mins. x 12 eps. (TV1), 25 mins. x 24 eps. (TV2), 30 mins. x 3 eps. (v).

In 1945, World War II was abruptly ended by the arrival of invading alien entities called Phantom Beasts. In the ensuing years, the Phantom Beasts occupy most of the world, until by 1999 one of the last lines of defense is on Japan's southern island of Kyushu. Severe losses on the human side led in 1978 to the reduction of the draft age to 16 and its expansion to include females. Now, in 1999, the teenage soldiers' main weapon against the Phantom Beasts is the HWT (Human-

oid War Tank), a single-seater robot that can grapple with the oversized aliens in the hope of destroying their vulnerable brain-spot. In death, the Phantom Beasts unleash poisonous residue that renders the surrounding area uninhabitable and threatens to kill any pilots unable to make it out of the war zone in time.

Like **SAKURA WARS**, *Gunparade* is based on a historically revisionist game for the PlayStation, although this one won an award at the 2001 Japanese national science fiction convention—the first game to do so. It is, perhaps, worth mentioning that if one really wanted to allegorize the defense of Japan in 1945 from evil invaders (that's us), **GUNBUSTER** did it far better and did so before most of *Gunparade*'s intended audience were born, but that, of course, is how people can get away with it. Unit 5121 has four Shikon units, and the concentration on the everyday lives and relationships of its pilots and their backup crew bears a strong resemblance to that depicted in **PATLABOR**. Nowhere is this more obvious than in the sudden arrival of Mai Shibamura, a cool, ruthlessly efficient transfer who is the sole survivor of a frontline unit which 5121 has been assigned to replace. Mixing elements of *Patlabor*'s Kanuka with Asuka from **EVANGELION**, Mai is a privileged rich girl whose father worked on the original HWT project, inexplicably forced to fight on the front alongside our point-of-view protagonist Atsushi, with whom she must practice to ensure that her moves are properly "synchronized."

Story editor Fumihiko Takayama, a native of the unit's hometown of Kumamoto and a veteran of many **GUNDAM** episodes, was on hand to ensure mechanical "authenticity," although making such a big deal about how the robots work might seem facetious considering the Japanese education system's obstructive policy on telling students what really happened in WWII (**DOCUMENTARIES AND HISTORY**). The show's Japanese subtitle might proclaim that it is a "new anthem," but really this is the same old song we've heard before in **KISHIN CORPS** and **DEEP BLUE FLEET**. However, *Gunparade* is an irresistible addition to the alternate universe subgenre in Japanese science fiction, if only for little touches like *Wicked Wizard*, wartime propaganda dressed up as a fairy tale, with which the childpilots are indoctrinated. There are also allegories of more modern conflicts in the style of GASARAKI and HEAT GUY J, particularly with cutaways to life away from the frontline, in which citizens enjoy relative levels of comfort and luxury, while their children sacrifice themselves to hold off a seemingly unstoppable menace—literally, since infants are required as operators for the PBE bombs that are the best weapons against the Phantom Beasts. With the first season leaving the plot unresolved, a sequel involving a new cast in Aomori, *Gunparade Orchestra*, followed in fall 2005.

GUNSLINGER GIRL *

2004. TV series, video. DIR: Morio Asaka. SCR: Junki Takegami, Kazuyuki Fudeyasu, Keiko Ueno, Kurasumi Sunayama. DES: Hisashi Abe. ANI: Fumie Muroi, Hajime Matsuzaki, Kazuo Watanabe, Kumi Ishii, Yasuhide Maruyama. MUS: Toshihiko Sahashi. PRD: Media Works, Madhouse, Animax, Fuji TV. 25 mins. x 13 eps. (TV1), 25 mins. x 13 eps. (TV2), 24 mins. x 2 eps. (v).

A trio of sweet young girls suffer childhood traumas that bring them to the attention of the Social Welfare Agency, an Italian secret service program that trains them as secret agents, complete with cybernetic enhancements that risk drastically shortening their lifespans. Yu Aida's original manga takes elements of the undercover agents of SPRIGGAN and SUKEBAN DEKA and blends them with the glamorous female agents of *La Femme Nikita* (1990) and *Alias* (2001). The series also revisits many of the tried-and-tested character clichés of modern anime, including Rico, a consumptive girl whose trauma was constant hospitalization, and Henrietta, an innocent whose childhood was brought to a brutal end by the murder of her family. Mental trauma also provides a foundation for subplots that present the girls as submissive blank slates in the style of CHOBITS—some of their handlers treat them like machines to be dispatched to perform tasks, while others try to befriend them, taking them on outings that, to the cynical might bear a close resemblance to the seduction of "damaged goods" in less mainstream works such as the LOLITA ANIME. Beethoven's Ninth Symphony, an anime favorite since EVANGELION, looms

large as a musical factor at the end of the show. Preceded by a manga by Yu Aida in *Dengeki Gao* monthly, and followed by a second season, *GG: Il Teatrino* (2008). **V**

GUNSMITH CATS *

1995. Video. DIR: Takeshi Mori. SCR: Atsuji Kaneko. DES: Kenichi Sonoda, Tokuhiro Matsubara. ANI: Tokuhiro Matsubara. MUS: Peter Erskine. PRD: Vap, TBS. 30 mins. x 3 eps.

Rally Vincent is a gun seller and bounty hunter in Chicago who works with her bomb-throwing sidekick Minnie-May Hopkins and straitlaced researcher Becky Farrah. She is blackmailed by an ATF agent into meeting with a gunrunner, whose main contact turns out to be a Russian assassin, Radinov. A local candidate for mayor decides to reward Rally's vigilante acts as a campaign gimmick, but the assassin is hiding out in the crowd for the final showdown.

A sparky adaptation of Kenichi Sonoda's 1991 manga from *Comic Afternoon* that steps outside the continuity of the original series, giving Rally the roguish ATF agent Bill Collins as her new "boss," and a new enemy in the form of Radinov. There are, however, several references to the manga, including the appearance of prosthetic limbs owned by Rally's manga enemies and a cameo by her Chicago PD contact Roy Coleman. Supporting character Becky becomes a stronger "part of the team" chiefly to satisfy the filmmakers' desire to reprise *Charlie's Angels*—a gambit that works particularly well in the bright, pop-art tones of the opening credits. Despite a setting in a fantasy Chicago like the urban war zone of MAD BULL 34's New York, *GSC* is remarkably lighthearted, complete with gratuitous underwear flashes, myopic bad guys who never shoot straight, and no sign of the manga's forays into drug addiction and child prostitution. The filmmakers made much of their research trips to the real Chicago, but, although intense effort is expended on the right noises for guns and cars, less thought was devoted to more important plot elements, such as how gunsmiths stow dangerous weapons, and what the police might think of an underage girl who collects hand grenades. But, apart from the holes, this is good fun, helped greatly in TRANSLATION by a streetwise U.S. dub from ADV.

Asides about May's boyfriend, Ken, imply the show was intended to go further, and if anything deserved a TV replay, it was this. *Gunsmith Cats* was presumably hobbled by its contemporary look; there wasn't much call for pulp crime in 1990s anime unless it had a sci-fi sheen like COWBOY BEBOP. A very different, earlier version of Rally Vincent also appeared in Sonoda's RIDING BEAN. **LNV**

GURREN LAGANN *

2008. JPN: *Tengen Toppa Gurren Lagann*. AKA: *Heaven-Piercing Gurren Lagann*. TV series, movie, video. DIR: Hiroyuki Imaishi, Osamu Kobayashi. SCR: Kazuki Nakashima, Kurasumi Sunayama. DES: Atsushi Nishigori, Imaitoonz, Yo Yoshinari, Yuka Hirama. ANI: Atsushi Nishigori, Katsuzo Hirata, Akira Amemiya. MUS: Taku Iwasaki. PRD: Gainax, Aniplex, Konami, Dentsu, Kadokawa, TV Tokyo. 25 mins. x 27 eps. (TV), 112 mins. (m1), 126 mins. (m2).

In the far future, Earth is ruled by Lordgenome and his army of beastmen. They force communities to live underground, tunneling ever deeper, isolated from their neighbors, and unable to make contact or combine forces. It looks as if nothing will ever change, until Simon, a quiet young miner, teams up with the brash, eccentric Kamina and joins his plan to drill through to the surface of the upper world. Adventure and tragedy await them, as does love—in the shape of Lordgenome's beautiful daughter Nia. But everything happens for a reason, and sometimes the evil overlords turn out to be the least of a hero's worries.

Gurenn Lagann is not nearly so acclaimed as the same studio's EVANGELION, yet in almost every way it's a far more lovable series. The production team seem to take their cue from their characters, a bunch of losers who throw their hearts and souls into their quest and give their best efforts to making good old-fashioned heartstring-plucking entertainment. The design and animation, the music and the script are all rock-solid: they display no Messianic or philosophical pretensions, but they do the job. Nobody could call the show and its characters deep, but nobody could call them pretentious or tedious either. If you want a mecha show that will give you a good time and leave you with a lump in your throat, Gainax's **GUNBUSTER** is still a great choice, but for those times when you want a more macho slant without losing the emotional impact, *Gurenn Lagann* fits the bill.

The 2008 movie *Gurren Lagann the Movie: Childhood's End* (*Tengen Toppa Gurren Lagann Guren Hen* or *Crimson Chapter*) and 2011's *Gurren Lagann the Movie: The Lights in the Sky Are Stars* (*Tengen Toppa Gurren Lagann Ragan Hen* or *Spiral Stone Chapter*) were directed by Imanishi and made by the same senior team. The first is a compilation of the first half of the series with about 20 minutes of new animation; the second compiles the second half, with a higher proportion of new material. The two *Gurren Lagann Parallel Works Videos* consist of short films exploring the theme of "multiple universes" spun off from the series by some of the animators.

Gurren Lagann has had manga, music, game, and merchandise spin-offs and was also the subject of an online scandal, when Takami Akai, one of the founders of Gainax, commented that reading fan criticism of the show was akin to breathing in farts. In a public chastisement, for voicing an opinion that is surely more common among anime creators than many viewers may think, he was publicly forced to resign his position at the time, although he still appears to be a part of the Gainax collective.

GURU-GURU

1994. JPN: *Maho Jin Guruguru*. AKA: *Magical Treasury Guru-guru*. TV series, movie. DIR: Nobuaki Nakanishi. SCR: N/C. DES: Masahiro Kase. ANI: Nobuhiro Okaseko. MUS: N/C. PRD: Nippon Animation, TV Asahi. 25 mins. x 45 eps.

The adventures of the heroic preteens Nike and friend Kukuri the witch deliberately told in a style that mimics the cartoony questing of computer role-playing games, as they defeat wandering monsters, liberate treasure from dungeons, and eternally seek to better themselves through "level-ups." Based on a manga by Hiroyuki Morifuji, serialized in *Shonen Gungun* magazine.

GUTSY FROG, THE

1972. JPN: *Dokonjo Gaeru*. TV series, movie. DIR: Eiji Okabe, Tadao Nagahama, Tsutomu

Shibayama. SCR: Masaki Tsuji, Haruya Yamazaki, Yoshiaki Yoshida, Noboru Shiroyama, Tsunehisa Ito, Masaru Yamamoto, Hideo Takayashiki, Tomoko Konparu, Masaaki Sakurai. DES: A-Pro, Yasumi Yoshizawa. ANI: Osamu Kobayashi, Tsutomu Shibayama, Osamu Kobayashi. MUS: Kenjiro Hirose, Reijiro Koroku. PRD: Tokyo Movie Shinsha, TBS; TMS, Nippon TV. 25 mins. x 103 eps. (TV1), 25 mins. x 30 eps. (TV2), 40 mins. (m).

Noisy, unruly middle school boy Hiroshi is walking home from school one day when he falls over, landing on top of a frog. The frog, whose name is Pyonyoshi, is flattened and imprinted onto the front of Hiroshi's shirt—and insists on commenting on everything he does, with humorous results. A wacky variation on the boy-and-his-dog theme based on the 1970 *Shonen Jump* manga by Yasumi Yoshizawa. Many of the original crew were reunited for *New [Shin] Gutsy Frog* (1981), a shorter-lived series that played up the cartoon slapstick even more than the original. Several episodes were also cut together to make the movie *GF: Gutsy Dreaming* (1982, *Dokonjo Yumemakura*) that was shown on a double bill with **HELLO SPANK**.

GUY *

1988. JPN: *Guy: Yoma Kakusei; Second Target*. AKA: *Guy: Awakening of the Devil; Second Target*. Video. DIR: Yorihisa Uchida. SCR: Hiroyuki Kawasaki, Kunihisa Sugishima, Masami Obari. DES: Yorihisa Uchida, Yasuhiko Makino, Yukio Tomimatsu. ANI: Yorihisa Uchida. MUS: Nobuhiko Kashiwara. PRD: Humming, AIC. 40 mins. x 2 eps.

Guy and his sexy female sidekick Raina, mercenaries out to make a quick buck, discover that a revolutionary youth drug is being developed on the prison planet of Geo. Prison warden Helga runs a white slavery operation out of her penal colony, where the victims are also sexually abused in a violent, tits-and-tentacles SF extravaganza in the fashion of **ADVANCER TINA**. Guy saves the day by transforming into a superviolent beast, as he does once again in the belated sequel, in which he and Raina discover that the Golden Goddess religious cult is really a corrupt front. The second episode, however, attempted to lighten the poker-faced sex and violence with a few in-jokes about earlier giant-robot shows and

a visual reference to the **DIRTY PAIR** movie. In the U.S., after the individual episodes were released separately, they were combined on a single tape and rereleased as *Guy: Double Target* in 1992. ●ⓃⓋ

GUYSLUGGER

1977. JPN: *Hyoga Senshi Guy Slugger*. AKA: *Glacial Warrior Guy Slugger*. TV series. DIR: Noboru Ishiguro, Kenjiro Yoshida. SCR: Shunichi Yukimuro. DES: Shotaro Ishinomori. ANI: Sadayoshi Tominaga. MUS: Toshinori Kikuchi. PRD: Toei, TV Asahi, Ishinomori Pro. 25 mins. x 26 eps.

Created by the ancient Solon civilization and left for 30,000 years in suspended animation somewhere in the Antarctic, the battle robots Shiki Ken, Mito Kaya, Tani Mari, Ono Riki, and Ii Taro wake to fight the invading Imbem from Eridanus 28, combining their vehicles to form the giant robot Guyslugger. Based on an idea by Shotaro Ishinomori, whose *Goranger* (*DE) had revolutionized children's entertainment only a couple of years earlier, *Guyslugger* represents an attempt to replicate the live-action battle-team shows in anime—compare to the same year's **GINGUISER**. The story also included many references to ancient mysteries such as Stonehenge, like the later **SPRIGGAN**, as well as conflicted postmodern *Pinocchio* angst in the style of Ishinomori's **KIKAIDER**. Nor did the show shy away from the harshness of war—the halfway mark was characterized by suicide bomber attacks like those of **GOWAPPER 5 GO-DAM**. The show ended with a last-ditch kamikaze run on the Imbem homeworld, much to the surprise of audiences at the time, although in retrospect it could be seen as a more gung ho variant on the final tragedy of **ASTRO BOY**, among other earlier shows. Tie-in manga ran in *Terebi* magazine, *Terebi-kun*, and *Terebi Land*.

GUYVER *

1989. JPN: *Kyoshoku Soko Guyver*. AKA: *Bio-Booster Armor Guyver*. Video, movie, TV series. DIR: Koichi Ishiguro, Masahiro Otani, Naoto Hashimoto. SCR: Riku Sanjo. DES: Hidetoshi Omori. ANI: Sumio Watanabe, Takaaki Ishiyama. MUS: Reijiro Koroku. PRD: Takaya Pro. 30 mins. x 12 eps. (v), 55 mins. (m), 24 mins. x 26 eps. (TV).

In ancient times, an alien race tinkered

with human DNA to create the ultimate warrior, or Zoanoid. Though these creatures were intended for battlefields on distant worlds, the Creators left before the experiment was complete. Zoanoids interbred with the human race in a number of incidents that survive today as stories of demons, vampires, and werewolves. The "bio-booster" suit was an advanced Creator armor that augmented its wearer's strength. Three such units are stolen in the present day by an agent of the Chronos corporation and scattered in an explosion. One ends up in the hands of Japanese schoolboy Sho, who activates it and becomes its designated wearer. Another is activated by Chronos' agent Lisker, whose power module malfunctions during a fight with Sho. Chronos' Commander Gyro arrives in Japan to recover the third Guyver unit and kidnaps Sho's friend, Mizuki, to draw him out of hiding. He also creates a Hyper-Zoanoid to fight the Guyver unit on equal terms. Agito Makishima, the son of the former head of Chronos Japan, becomes the third Guyver symbiont, and Sho's school is destroyed as Chronos' minions attack it in search of his control medallion. Though Chronos Japan is defeated, Sho learns that there are many other outposts, and he is forced to fight Dr. Valcus, who creates several new Zoanoids and even works on "Enzyme," the anti-Guyver. Sho's father is transformed into a monster and Sho is forced to kill him. Losing the ability to bio-boost, Sho regains it by asking the spirit of his father for help in a time of dire need. Though the evil is defeated for now, Sho must face several more of the Zoanoids' "Zoalord" controllers … one day.

Based on the 1985 *Shonen Captain* manga by Yoshiki Takaya, which continued the story long past the non-ending of the anime, this unremarkable sci-fi series remains a recognizable brand in the U.K. market, chiefly due to Manga Entertainment's policy of releasing it at an insanely discounted price that made it affordable for the young boys for whom it was originally made, though if they bought all *12* tapes, it would still cost them a pretty penny. An earlier version of the same story was animated as the 55-minute movie *Guyver: Out of Control* (1986), directed by Hiroshi Watanabe and also released in the

U.S. It has the same basic plot but a female owner of Guyver Two, and it possesses a brevity that leaves less room for the pointless repetitions of its straight-to-video successor. But neither anime version really does justice to the material—humanity as the descendants of abandoned military experiments may be a clever idea, but it is used as little more than an excuse for visceral transformations and predictable fights against monsters-of-the-week. Two live-action movies retold the same early chapters of the story, Screaming Mad George's *Guyver* (1991, AKA *Mutronics*) and Steve Wang's *Guyver: Dark Hero* (1994).

Katsuhito Akiyama's TV series *Guyver: The Biobooster Armor* (2005) seemingly went into production as a result of rose-tinted memories about the series and possibly misreading the sales figures of volumes sold rather than money accrued. Although it was faithful to the original, it suffered from a change in expectations among foreign audiences. Where *Guyver* had once been a standard-bearer of edgy, exotic sci-fi among the cool kids, its remake came after a decade of other, better anime and the long-running success of the *Mighty Morphin' Power Rangers* (*DE), which only made it look far tamer and less original.

GYO: TOKYO FISH ATTACK *

2012. JPN: *Gyo: Ugomeku Bukimi*. AKA: *Gyo: Creepy Crawly*. Video. DIR: Takayuki Hirao. SCR: Akihiro Yoshida, Takayuki Hirao. DES: Takuro Takahashi, Kazuo Ebisawa, Satoru Kuwahara, Takamasa Nakakuki. ANI: Makoto Nakamura, Takuro Takahashi. MUS: Go Shiina. PRD: ufotable, Aniplex, Shogakukan, Klockworx. 70 mins.

Okinawa is swamped by an influx of bizarre fish that walk out of the ocean on metal legs and head for the cities. Kaori, in Okinawa on a pre-graduation, prenuptial vacation, has lost contact with her boyfriend Tadashi, who's living in Tokyo, and heads to the capital to find him. Junji Ito's horror manga *Gyo* inspired this video, and although it makes major changes to the characters and the plot, it keeps the atmosphere of insanely grandiose mayhem pervaded with nihilistic despair.

The title has a double meaning in Japanese, meaning *fish* but also *catch/prey*, mixing the sense of hunter and hunted very much in the spirit of a Hollywood

B-movie. In addition, there is a periodic concentration on documentation—the seeing and the seen, as camera-touting rubber-neckers film the misfortunes of others, seemingly at a distance, but with an ever-nearing threat that soon overwhelms the viewer. *Gyo* embraces many of the tropes of Western HORROR AND MONSTERS— a fear of and obsession with sex, gratuitous jiggling boobies, and pointless, misogynistic fan service. This is a disaster movie, but it is also both a creature feature *and* a zombie movie, with multiple homages to the work of Roger Corman and George Romero, and a spiritual resemblance to the later, infamous schlock horror movie *Sharknado* (2013).

Common to many 21st-century anime, *Gyo* also exploits the availability of darkness—once an expensive indulgence in cel animation, now relatively easy to arrange thanks to new technology (GAMING AND DIGITAL ANIMATION). *Gyo* also alludes, perhaps inadvertently, to the previous year's Great East Japan Earthquake that was surely a major influence on its production. Despite a manga original that predated the disaster, there is often a sense of that real-world crisis as it played out in the word's media—the sea rushing inland and waterborne death at the door, and repeated references to the stench of fish and the heat of summer, both far more prominent in 2011 Japan due to austerity measures on power consumption. Those are all hidden depths, if you want to look for them. But *Gyo* is not a film that welcomes study of its hidden depths. This is a film that wants to shock you and disgust you, and hopefully entertain you. Beer will help, and certainly appears to have helped the subtitlers, whose English TRANSLATION is occasionally wonky. Director Hirao would refashion his bawdy apocalypse for a younger audience with remarkably softer edges in LITTLE WITCHES YOYO AND NENE. **NO**

GYROZETTER

2012. JPN: *Cho Soku Henkei Gyrozetter*. AKA: *Super High-speed Transforming Gyrozetter*. TV series. DIR: Shinji Takamatsu, Kunihiro Mori. SCR: Dai Sato, Megumi Shimizu, Toshimitsu Takeuchi. DES: Yoshinori Yumoto, Hiroshi Kaieda, Shoji Kawamori, Kanetaka Ebikawa, Yasuhiko Mori, Koki Nagayoshi, Masahiro Sato. ANI: Yoshinori Yumoto. MUS:

Naoki Sato. PRD: A-1 Pictures, Dentsu, Square Enix, TV Tokyo. 25 mins. x 31 eps.

So-called "A.I. cars" with artificial intelligence features for safety have revolutionized the Japanese car industry, and now even schoolchildren are learning to drive in special schools. Kakeru is a fifth grader in Arcadia Academy in New Yokohama. One day his head teacher tells him he has been specially chosen to drive a new type of car, a Gyrozetter, which is also capable of transforming into a robot. He and a few other chosen drivers will be Earth's defense against a mysterious threat—Xenon.

This formulaic childrens' TV show based on an arcade game by Square Enix has a truly astonishing array of talent and support lined up behind it. Eight car manufacturers—Daihatsu, Mazda, Mitsubishi, Mitsuoka, Nissan, Subaru, Suzuki, and Toyota—are partnering with the production of the anime, manga, cards, toys, and gadgets spun off from the game (ADVERTISING AND SPONSORSHIP). Sony, Bandai, and McDonalds are also on board as sponsors. Shoji Kawamori and his European cohorts Thomas Romain and Stanislas Brunet, FULLMETAL ALCHEMIST's Katagawa, Mori, whose CV runs from SABER RIDER AND THE STAR SHERIFFS to D.GRAY MAN, are less than half the team of 14 machinery designers, and the CG and animation teams are enormous by TV standards.

What they've produced is a show not dissimilar to BEAST WARRIORS—the same food-fixated guys, bubble-headed but good-hearted girls, impressively named spells and skills—but themed around TRANSFORMERS, a tried and tested marketing concept. The modern cars change into curiously old-fashioned robots, with girls piloting "feminine" mechs, and the critical transformation sequences largely obscured by flashes of light. The CGI action scenes, though pacy, are not especially well integrated into the 2D animation. The third-episode fight by the dockside would like to be the iconic Ingram-Griffin face-off from PATLABOR, and luckily none of its target audience is old enough to make comparisons.

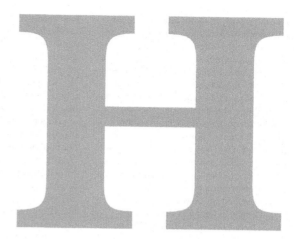

H TOGETHER

2010. JPN: *Issho ni Etchi*. Video. DIR: Saku, Masaaki Susobun. SCR: Shinichiro Sawanuma. DES: Asatsukasa Yamainu. ANI: Tatsukichi Tomi. MUS: N/C. PRD: Gramme, Pink Pineapple. 30 mins.

A schoolboy is called to the school nurse's office, and voluptuous redheaded Nurse Momoka assists his sexual development. Later he catches her blonde schoolgirl sister Maron masturbating in the same office. Despite being a virgin, at least at the start of their encounter, Maron proves to be just as demanding as her sister. Then Momoka walks in on them, so all three go to a public bath-house for more uninhibited sex. This kind of thing actually happens less often than anime might lead you to imagine, because (a) it's illegal and (b) not many sisters are close in quite this way.

.HACK//SIGN *

2002. AKA: *dot hack sign*. TV series, video, movie. DIR: Koichi Mashimo, Nobuhiro Takagi, Yuki Arie. SCR: Kazunori Ito, Akemi Omode, Koichi Mashimo, Kirin Mori, Michiko Yokote, Mitsuhiko Sawamura. DES: Yoshiyuki Sadamoto, Akira Osawa, Minako Shiba, Satoshi Osawa, Yukiko Ban, Yuko Iwaoka, Kenji Teraoka, Tatsuya Oka. ANI: Koichi Mashimo. MUS: Yuki Kajiura. PRD: Bee Train, TNK, Bandai Visual, Yomiko Advertising Inc. 25 mins. x 26 eps. (TV1), 30 mins. x 4 eps. (v1), 20 mins. (v2), 25 mins. (v3), 24 mins. x 12 eps. (TV2), 27 mins. (v4), 25 mins. x 26 eps. (TV, ROOTS), 93 mins. (m, G.U. Trilogy)

The near future: those with time on their hands while away the day in an online role-playing game called The World whose monsters and player characters present them with goals and challenges missing in the real one. Tsukasa is a teenage introvert whose online character has a certain mystique; but he finds himself in even more mysterious circumstances inside the game. He can't log out, and the Crimson Knights, the self-appointed gameworld police, corner him and accuse him of using an illegally modified character. As their game selves search for the secret of the Key and the solution to Tsukasa's log-out problem, their real-life counterparts BT, Mimiru, and Bear—the friends Tsukasa has never met in real life—try to help him return to the world outside The World, a world in which, it is later hinted, "he" may even be a "she." The game artifact known as the Key of Twilight might hold the answers.

Presenting the Internet as an alternate world in the manner of SERIAL EXPERIMENTS LAIN or *The Matrix* (1999), but with a pretentious title that removes it from alphabetical listings altogether, *.hack* (pronounced "Dot Hack") is a multimedia franchise—an anime about a game that looks like an anime, which has several realworld game tie-ins, as well as spin-off manga, novels, and even an American trading-card game. It is also aimed firmly at the aging POKÉMON generation, positing a future world where the entire Internet is crashed on Christmas Eve 2005 by a succession of viral attacks, most notably a supervirus called Pluto's Kiss. Subsequently, all of the world's computers begin running on a system called Altimit, hence the ability of the whole planet to partake in the online gaming that is The World. None of that helps much with the franchise's complex taxonomy, with prequels, sequels, and spin-offs creating an arcane, detailed universe that only fans of the game can really appreciate—exactly the kind of exclusivity and "in-crowd" sensibility that modern game companies hope to create among fickle teenage consumers.

Two months after *.hack* started running on television, in June 2002, a video series appeared to fill in the backstory. The prequel *.hack//Liminality* was directed by Mashimo and Ito with characters by Toshiya Washida and was given away free with the PlayStation 2 incarnations of the franchise. In its storyline, the multiplayer game The World becomes an international phenomenon on its U.S. release in 2007, but monsters inside the game start displaying strange abilities and players can't develop their characters. Concerned that this makes the game unplayable, player Kite decides to get to the bottom of it—the separate episodes had their own *sub*-subtitles, *Infection, Mutation, Outbreak*, and *Quarantine*.

2002's next video, *.hack//INTERMEZZO* (AKA *.hack// Episode 27*, or *Another Story*) gives Bear and Mimiru starring roles as they visit a newly reopened dungeon, and Mimiru looks back to her early experiencesin The World and the players she met there. This approach was successful, so a 2003 video, *.hack//Unison* (AKA *.hack// Episode 28*) appeared.Set after the end of the original series and the video game, it has Helba inviting Tsukasa, Bear, Mimiru, and a host of other familiar characters to an online party in Cyber Slum where fan favorites reunite or meet for the first time.

The Key of Twilight turns up again in 2003 in a second series, *.hack//Legend of the Twilight* (*.hack//Tasogare no Udewa Densetsu*, AKA *.hack//Udeden*), along with some semblance of a plot, in which two new players, twins Shugo and Rena, enter The World and find that characters who meet monsters in the game fall into a coma in the real world. They play a pair of legendary characters, Kite and Black Rose, who must use the bracelet's power to find out who or what is controlling events and stop them.

This second series was based on an original manga, based in the TV series world, by Rei Izumi and Tatsuya Hamazaki. Comedy enters the mix and the art style changes to accommodate a new angular, squashed-down look with 2003's *.hack// GIFT*, a parody of the series which was originally only available to players who mailed in tokens from all four spin-off games. In it, character Helba creates an in-game spa, the Twilight Hot Springs, and characters race to find it first—and solve some player murders along the way. A third TV series, *.hack//ROOTS* (2006), and its movie sequel *.hack//G.U. Trilogy* (2008), features Haseo, a new arrival in the game world, who is soon embroiled in a conflict between rival guilds. This latest incarnation attempts to make more of the fact that The World is not a fantasy realm but an online game, and consequently features more jargon and references to the real world outside.

Online gaming offers the possibility of entering a whole new world in cyberspace, creating a new self-defined persona and meeting others in circumstances you can choose and control—paradise for an insecure teenager. This is an ultimately lighthearted look at the new world, directed, scripted, and designed by a skilled team with enough TV experience to guarantee a quality product; but it plays along with the theory that the Web is a safe place to live the significant bits of your life and form your most important relationships. Which is fine, as long as you remember to log out occasionally.

H2

1995. TV series. DIR: Hidehito Ueda. SCR: Akira Oketani, Hisato Yamashita, Nobuaki

Kishima. DES: Tomoyoshi Hirata. ANI: Hiroki Takagi, Tadashi Hirota. MUS: Taro Iwashiro. PRD: TV Asahi. 25 mins. x 41 eps.

The lives and loves of four young people, all of whose names begin with the letter "H," set against a background of high school baseball. Pitching ace Hiro shatters his elbow, seemingly ending a promising career in baseball and throwing all his choices (school, friends, career) into doubt. Power hitter Hideo continues to train in baseball, while the boys' concerned friend Hikari frets over Hiro's future, and Hideo slowly falls for Haruka, a girl at his new school who is not only the daughter of his father's boss, but also the new manager of the school baseball club. Hiro and his friend Noda (who has also been placed on the injured list by a bad back) destroy the opposition from Haruka's club and suggest that she turn it into a proper competing team. Based on a 1992 manga in *Shonen Sunday* by Mitsuru Adachi, who used baseball and love polygons before in **NINE** and **SLOW STEP**. The story was also adapted into a live-action TV drama series for TBS in 2005.

H2O: FOOTPRINTS IN THE SAND *

2008. TV series. DIR: Hideki Tachibana. SCR: Jukki Hanada. DES: Atsushi Okada, Kazuhiro Takahashi. ANI: Fumiaki Kota, Hideki Tachibana. MUS: Junpei Fujita. PRD: ZEXCS, Broccoli, Kadokawa, NTT Docomo, Klockworx. 24 mins. x 12 eps.

Nobody knows why Takuma is blind, but when his mother dies suddenly he feels he must leave the city to escape his loneliness. He moves to the countryside and enrolls in a new high school where he makes friends, especially three girls: Hayami, Hinata, and Otoha. Through their friendship, he gradually begins to recover his sight in this harem anime (**ROMANCE AND DRAMA**) based on a dating simulation game and book series.

HAIBANE RENMEI *

2002. AKA: *League of Ashen Wings*; *Charcoal Feathers Federation*. TV series. DIR: Hiroshi Negishi, Tomokazu Tokoro, Hiroshi Kimura, Itsuki Imazaki, Jun Takada, Kenichiro Watanabe, Koji Yoshikawa, Masatsugu Arakawa, Takahiro Omori. SCR: Yoshitoshi Abe. DES: Akira Takada. ANI: Akio Ujie, Akira Takata, Chuichi Iguchi, Hideo Shimosaka, Masaki

Kudo, Mayumi Hidaka, Shinichi Yoshino, Takako Shimizu, Takuji Mogi, Toshinari Yamashita, Toshiyuki Abe, Yoshiaki Saito, Yuichi Tanaka. MUS: Ko Otani. PRD: Production I.G., Tatsunoko, Pioneer, Fuji TV. 25 mins. x 13 eps.

This is the story of a tribe of gentle winged humanoids called Haibane, who live alongside but not with ordinary humans in the mysterious walled city of Glie, which similarly has very little contact with the world that surrounds it. The Haibane are beings who emerge from waterfilled, womblike cocoons at various ages, with no memories or knowledge, and sprout beautiful but useless wings and halos soon after waking. Every Haibane has a dream before emerging from the cocoon; they tell it, and are given a name based on it, but nobody knows what the dreams mean. Heroine Rakka dreams of falling from the sky—*rakka* is Japanese for falling—while Reki dreamed of walking a path of pebbles (*reki*) and Kana dreamed of swimming in a river, so is named with the characters for river and fish.

The Haibane all live in the Old House on the outskirts of the city, their "nest," going out to work among humans during the day and returning home to housemother Reki and a few younger ones. Forbidden to use money or to own or wear anything that has not been used by a human, they live a life suspended between the closely supervised "integration"of those with learning difficulties and the segregation of religious sects like the Amish, allowed little self-determination and treated by most humans as curiosities rather than as people. Their backstory is all cryptic utterances and meaningful looks, including the mystery of why Reki was considered "born sin-bound" and what happened to Kuramori, the older Haibane who cared for Reki when she first arrived, but who never explained "the day of flight" to her, leaving Reki heartbroken when she disappeared without any warning.

The Haibane Renmei is the organization that watches over the Haibane. Comprising people in grand robes and masked faces, it is based in a temple on the outskirts of the city and functions like a fantasy Social Services Department. Haibane aren't allowed to speak inside the temple, but must communicate using bells attached to their wings. The Renmei tell their charges that at some unknown time in the future, if they work hard and prepare themselves, their wings will awaken and they will fly over the walls and leave the city—this is "the day of flight." Until then, the Haibane live in a state of limbo, taking each day as it comes and finding what happiness they can in their work and their relationships with each other.

Created and self-published by Yoshitoshi Abe, of SERIAL EXPERIMENTS LAIN and NIEA_7 fame, the manga *Old House no Haibane-tachi* forms the basis for a strange, slow-paced anime with very little action but delicate manipulation of emotion. Abe claims his initial inspiration came from the walled, placeless dream city of Haruki Murakami's novel *Hard-Boiled Wonderland and the End of the World* (1985), and it shares themes of fate in limbo with NIGHT ON THE GALACTIC RAILROAD, Hirokazu Kore-eda's masterpiece *After Life* (1998), and the children's show *Yuta and His Wondrous Friends* (*DE). Atmosphere, not event, makes for a drifting story bordering on daydream. It has many potential interpretations—the need to control the unknown, the restrictions of life dissolving in the flight of death, the purposelessness of the rules we impose, and the gradual surrender of curiosity to apathy. Whereas *Lain* was about a young girl seeing the pointlessness of her existence and actively pursuing a challenge that leads to another place altogether, *Haibane Renmei* is about regretting the pointlessness of existence while waiting to be rescued—by a legend, maturity, or death, but certainly not by self-determination.

HAIRY TALE

2007. JPN: *Asience: Hairy Tale*. TV series. DIR: Kazuto Nakazawa. SCR: Kazuto Nakazawa. DES: Kazuto Nakazawa. ANI: Kazuto Nakazawa. MUS: Yoshihiro Ike. PRD: Production I.G. 1 min.

Heian-period Japan—a princess lets down her long hair so that her samurai lover can climb the castle walls. But when her father discovers their secret trysts, he cuts her hair, and she and her lover fall to their deaths in a shower of blood-red maple leaves. Her death poem, written in blood, reads "Hair is the heart of a woman." Because this bloody, historical

tragedy is a TV commercial for shampoo.

ADVERTISING AND SPONSORSHIP, like video game work, enables both young animators and established studios to earn money to fund other projects. This beautifully shot and composed film blends elegantly contemporary graphics with 18th-century painting techniques, as refined and simple as a Japanese screen. It was created in 2D, with old-school pencil sketches linking Nakamura's key frames, animated onto Shuichi Hirata's beautifully textured backgrounds. It won Gold at the 22nd London International Advertising Awards in 2007. How well it did for Kao Corporation in selling their Asience line of shampoos is another matter.

HAITAI NANAFA

2012. TV series. DIR: Hiroshi Kimura. SCR: Takeshi Konuta. DES: POP, Kazuyuki Ueda. ANI: Sayaka Koiso. MUS: Rie Ayase. PRD: Passhone, Ryukyu Asahi Broadcasting. 2 mins. x 13eps. (TV1), 2 mins. x 13 eps. (TV2). Okinawan teenager Nanafa and her two sisters are dragged into the world of island mythology (RELIGION AND BELIEF), as they develop hereditary abilities to see spirits of plants, animals, and statues. The title of the show reflects its passionate interest in the subtle differences of Okinawan life and culture—the Ryukyu Islands historically paid tribute to both China and Japan, turning them into a liminal environment where both cultures mixed. Nanafa's own name means "Seven Leaves" but is pronounced counter-intuitively to Japanese ears. "Haitai" is a simple greeting in Okinawan, used exclusively as "women's language."

The authors suspect that a sudden tourism-fueled interest in Okinawan culture in 2012 might be parsed in relation to a similar obsession with Hokkaido (SILVER SPOON), as a means of distracting domestic tourists from the no-go zone of post-tsunami Tohoku.

HAIYORU! NYARUANI

2010. TV series. DIR: Azuma Tani, Tsuyoshi Nagasawa. SCR: Manta Aisora, Mamoru Nakano, Azuma Tani, Susumu Kobayakawa, Noboru Kimura, Toko Machida, Kazuho Hyodo, Takeyuki Ishida. DES: Koin, Shintetsu Takiyama, Keito Watanabe. ANI: Takasuke Suzuki, Ryusuke Suzuki, Tsukasa Nishi-

yama, Shintetsu Takiyama. MUS: Yuki Sudo, SLF!!, monaca. PRD: DLE Inc., Xebec, SoftBank Creative Corp, avex entertainment, Cospa, Klockworx, TV Tokyo. 2 mins. x 9 eps. (online), 5 mins. x 12 eps. (TV1), 25 mins. x 12 eps. (TV2), 25 mins. x 12 eps. (TV3). Nyaruko is a deity of chaos who has chosen to take the form of a silver-haired high school girl. She saves hapless teen Mahiro Yasaka from a gang of pursuing aliens one night, and makes it her mission to keep protecting him when her kindergarten pals Cthuko and Hasta show up.

H. P. Lovecraft must be spinning, creepily, in his grave. That wacky Manta Aisora has turned Cthulhu and Nyarlathotep into a pair of wide-eyed, skimpily clad girls in a series of books, and Koin's illustrations were so cute that the stories made the leap to Net animation in 2010. TV series *Haiyoru! Nyaruani: Remember My Mr. Lovecraft* (*Haiyoru! Nyaruani: Remember My Mr. Love (Craft-Sensei)* followed in 2010 as an expanded retelling of the original shorts, with *Nyarko-san: Another Crawling Chaos* (*Haiyore! Nyaruko-san*) extending the story along with the running time by throwing in more creeping horrors in cute bodies on TV in 2012. This time everyone except Mahiro is desperate to procreate and his parents just happen to be out of town. Cue his house as Harem Central (ROMANCE AND DRAMA), transfer students from everywhere in the known and unknown worlds, beach parties, kidnaps, and aliens fixated on anime. A third TV series, *Haiyore! Nyaruko-san W*, aired in 2013, with Nagasawa once more at the helm.

The first Flash animation series revolves around short gags that assume familiarity with the books but don't require it—silly little situation-snippets to raise a smile as you surf the net. No familiarity with the Lovecraftian mythos is required, either. In the first TV series the randomness and disorientation caused by viewing fragments of a much larger world begin to emerge. The constant sexual references and fan service begin to throw some light on the relationships and characters: by the second TV series we know where we are, and where we are is in another harem comedy. Nobody has ever done this better than Rumiko Takahashi in URUSEI YATSURA, but by lacing its entirely conventional plot with sly nudges and winks to Lovecraft and pop culture, *Haiyoru!* gives it a solid try. For more references to unnameable horror, see ICZER-ONE and ARMITAGE III. ◐

HAKKENDEN, THE *

1990. AKA: *Legend of the Dog Warriors.* Video. DIR: Takashi Anno, Yukio Okamoto. SCR: Sho Aikawa, Hidemi Kamata. DES: Atsushi Yamagata. ANI: Kazuhiro Konishi. MUS: Takashi Kudo. PRD: AIC. 30 mins. x 13 eps. Fifteenth-century lord Satomi rashly promises his daughter Fuse's hand in marriage to whoever brings him the head of his enemy, Lord Anzai. But no one expects Yatsufusa, the family dog, to win the prize. Fuse and Yatsufusa are both killed, but their karma lives on in a group of "dog" warriors, each symbolizing a great virtue. A generation later, the dog warriors are united and begin their quest to restore the honor of the house of Satomi.

An adaptation of a multivolume popular serial written from 1814 to 1841 by Kyokutei Bakin, a samurai fallen on hard times who wished to retell *Water Margin* (see SUIKODEN) for a Japanese audience and instill some decency in his own merchant son by concentrating on the Eight Virtues of CONFUCIUS: Benevolence, Righteousness, Courtesy, Wisdom, Fidelity, Loyalty, Filial Piety, and Service to Elders. Bakin's original characters left nothing to the imagination, and were often ciphers for particular virtues or sins, spouting pompous mock Chinese dialogue. The animation crew preferred modern heroes who often doubt their roles and each other, particularly bad-guy Samojiro Aboshi who drips foppish charm, far removed from the one-note voice of evil in the book.

The 96-part novel had a large number of starting points to draw in new readers—an occasionally confusing policy that remains in the anime. Each of the heroes has an origin story of his or her own, thus delaying the "beginning" of their team adventures until episode 9! The first, Shino, must deliver a magic sword to a nobleman, while the second, Sosuke, is sworn to stop him. The third, Dosetsu, is the half-brother of Shino's betrothed, sworn to avenge her death, while the fourth, Genpachi, is a disgraced guardsman offered his freedom if only he kills Shino. And so on. Episode six was director Anno's last, and the remaining parts were originally released under a separate subtitle, *New Hakkenden* (1993), with changes in the crew that are particularly reflected in the character design. As with DARK MYTH, the heavy use of Japanese names often makes the dub a polysyllabic mess, but it is the look rather than the meaning of this series that appeals to its fans, and it is best watched in Japanese for that fully cultural experience.

More concerned with drama than with the impressive battle scenes of NINJA SCROLL, *Hakkenden* was sold abroad on the strength of its literary and cultural pedigree, although the original crew were less likely to have been inspired by the novel as by the 1973 *Hakkenden* (*DE) puppet TV show of their youth or the 1983 live-action film by Kinji Fukasaku. There are, however, references to the many woodblock prints inspired both by the original novel and the kabuki plays that drew on it, most obviously in the opening credits, in which the anime characters share the screen with their woodblock predecessors. See also the sci-fi remake SHIN HAKKENDEN and the postmodern retelling FUSE: MEMOIRS OF A HUNTER GIRL.

HAKKENDEN: EIGHT DOGS OF THE EAST *

2013. JPN: *Toho Hakken Ibun.* TV series. DIR: Osamu Yamazaki, Mitsue Yamazaki. SCR: Osamu Yamazaki, Mitsue Yamazaki. DES: Hiromi Kato. ANI: N/C. MUS: Hitomi Kuroishi. PRD: Bandai Visual, Dax, Frontier Works, Lantis, Movic, Sony PCL, Studio Deen, MBS, Tokyo MX TV, TV Aichi, BS11. 24 mins. x 13 eps. (TV1), 24 mins. x 13 eps. (TV2). Eight teenagers, all with tell-tale peony birthmarks on their bodies, are revealed as the latest incarnations of a group of warriors who once stood alongside the legendary Princess Fuse to fight evil in the "time of darkness." Now they and their magical beads are the target for a Church-backed group of sorcerous "Beast Houses"—the Fox, Wolf, Snake, and Cat—in a fantastical retelling of THE HAKKENDEN, based on a manga version by Miyuki Abe, and jammed with TROPES AND TRANSFORMATIONS from several decades of manga and anime storytelling.

FUSE: MEMOIRS OF A HUNTER GIRL took a postmodern angle on the original, choosing to present itself as a baroque refashioning of several different ways of telling the story, and arriving *very* late in the action, when the tale of the eight dog-warriors was almost done and unreliable witnesses are already twisting the facts. *Eight Dogs of the East* takes an alternate track, refashioning it as if it were dreamt up by modern anime hacks trying to excuse a team-based line of action figures and slam-bang magic-user game combat. Both approaches present fascinating versions of the original, and only serve to point to the strength of its primary source, that it can endure such transformations and still come out strong. Sadly, however, this version is let down by lackluster animation, with a lot of talking-head exposition, leavened by explosions of vivid computer-graphics as leading man Shino Inuzuka unleashes the living sword Murasame, that dwells within his arm.

HAKUGEI: LEGEND OF THE MOBY DICK *

1997. JPN: *Hakugei Densetsu.* AKA: *Legend of the White Whale.* TV series. DIR: Osamu Dezaki. SCR: Osamu Dezaki, Akio Sugino. DES: Hirotoshi Takaya. ANI: N/C. MUS: Masahiro Ando. PRD: Image K, Studio Junior, NHK2. 25 mins. x 26 eps. In the year 4699, deep in space out by the Nantucket Nebula, a group of salvage experts search for "whales"—the abandoned hulks of colony ships left over from humanity's massive expansion into the cosmos. Young teenager Lucky Luck has come to the area in search of Captain Ahab, ostensibly hoping to join the crew of his ship, the Lady Whisker. In fact, as later episodes reveal, he is actually hoping for Ahab's help against the Moby Dick, a predatory space vessel whose approach threatens to destroy Lucky's homeworld. The series aired across three calendar years on its original broadcast, after being temporarily suspended partway.

HAKUOKI *

2010. AKA: *Demon of the Fleeting Blossom.* TV series, video. DIR: Osamu Yamasaki. SCR: Yoshiko Nakamura, Mitsutaka Hirota, Megumi Sasano, Ryota Yamaguchi. DES: Atsuko Nakajima, Satoru Hirayanagi. ANI: Atsuko Nakajima, Yukiko Ban, Yuko Yamada, Minoru Morita. MUS: Ko Otani. PRD: Studio DEEN, AT-X, Frontier Works, Geneon. 24 mins. x 12 eps. (TV1), 23 mins. x 10 eps.

(TV2), 25 mins. x 6 eps. (v), 25 mins. x 12 eps. (TV3).

It's 1863. Chizuru comes to Kyoto looking for her missing father. She accidentally sees a fight between officers of the Shinsengumi, the shogunate's private police force, and a demon. Although at first suspicious, the officers discover that she's the daughter of the same doctor they're seeking, and gradually come to trust her. She gets involved in events on the historical record, but also has some dangerous encounters with powerful demons: it seems her father's disappearance isn't the only mystery about Chizuru.

Based on a successful video game series for Playstation and Nintendo, with manga to match, *Hakuoki* is packed with pretty boys in harem situations (**ROMANCE AND DRAMA**) to please female fans, bloodsoaked blade-slashing action for the guys, and history for the geeks. It's a good idea, and could have made an excellent show, but is let down by two factors. The first is a tendency to let the timeline tangle and drag, so that the audience loses track of Chizuru's personal quest amid the sweep of history and occasionally vice versa— we're in 1866 before the end of episode 9. The other is that Chizuru herself is such a wimp. The tradition that the focus of a harem must be a complete nonentity is one that could profitably have been shattered here, especially given the fascinating historical material provided by the Shinsengumi, a fighting force not known for being unable to resist hapless females.

Luckily the male characters, both historical and invented, are dynamic and attractive enough to carry the show. Designer Nakajima has strong form with pretty boys—see **TRINITY BLOOD**. Studio Easter does a good job on the backgrounds and Shinji Matsumoto's color design is fine. The show did well enough for a second series the same year: the crew was largely unchanged except that Masami Obari did the storyboards for *Hakuoki: Record of the Jade Blood (Hakuoki Hekketsuroku)* in which Chizuru and her gang of bloodthirsty boys face a challenge they may not survive on the northern island of Ezo (present-day Hokkaido).

The 2011 video *Hakuoki: A Memory of Snow Flowers (Hakuoki Sekkaroku)* told a story set in the first season's timeframe to provide an excuse for shenanigans in the floating world as Chizuru goes undercover as a young geisha. A third TV series, *Hakuoki Dawn Record (Hakuoki Reimeiroku),* is a prequel to the main story, and a movie, *Hakuoki Number One Chapter Kyoto Revel (Hakuoki Dai-issho Kyoto Ranbu)* followed in August 2013. For more Edo-period fantasy, see **FUSE: MEMOIRS OF A HUNTER GIRL.** ◐

HAL *
2013. Movie. DIR: Ryotaro Makihara. SCR: Izumi Kizara. DES: Katsuhiko Kitada. ANI: Katsuhiko Kitada. MUS: Michiru Oshima. PRD: WIT Studio, Pony Canyon, Production I.G, Shochiku. 50 mins.

A robot is refitted and programmed to help a bereaved person recover from the loss of a beloved in a plane crash. However, all is not as it seems, as the couple's past is slowly revealed.

Designed as a showcase and shingle for WIT Studio, the Production I.G subsidiary that would also make **ATTACK ON TITAN,** *Hal* is a moving emotional exploration of love and loss, inspired in part by the writer's own experience of spousal illness. Izumi Kizara, whose live-action robot-romance TV script *Q10* (2010) led to the approach of the producers in the first place, has characterized the story not as science fiction but as an iteration of **EVERYDAY ANIME,** suggesting that modern media expose audiences to so much conflict, worldthreatening crises, and terror that the new form of "escapism" demands a sedate and slow-paced, comfortable world. Seemingly a direct reference to Kubrick's *2001: A Space Odyssey* (1968), the lead character's name evokes an almost autistic confusion at the contradictions of life and the real world, in which the rules and expectations he has internalized still prove to be confounded by grim fate.

HAL AND BONS
2002. Video. DIR: Katsuhito Ishii. SCR: Katsuhito Ishii. DES: N/C. ANI: N/C. MUS: N/C. PRD: Grasshoppa!, Kanaban Graphics. 8 mins. x 4 eps. (v1), 6 mins. x 9 eps. (v2).

Hal and Bons are a pair of beer-swilling slacker dogs who agree to be interviewed by a talking rice cake named Mochi. It seems like a lark at the time, but despite their disrespect for his interviewing technique, Mochi decides he likes them and moves in. There's no real story, just a sit-down sequence of jokes and satire, in which director Ishii lends audio credibility with his deeply sonorous voice, alongside Ikki Todoroki and Shunichiro Miki, who would also play the leads in **MOLE BROTHERS: FULL THROTTLE.** *Hal and Bons* was first released as part of the **GRASSHOPPA** anthology series in 2001. *New Hal and Bons* followed in 2006, with Mochi now a permanent fixture on the sofa, not smelling so good, and our heroes trying to think of ways to get rid of him while keeping up their satirical comments on life. The characters periodically recur in other stories set in the "Ishii-verse," which is to say, they are habitual doodles by the director, liable to crop up elsewhere in his work, such as in cameos in his later **REDLINE.**

HAL'S FLUTE
2011. JPN: *Hal no Fue.* Video. DIR: Hiroshi Kawamata. SCR: Michiru Shimada. DES: Toshiharu Mizutani. ANI: Genta Chiba. MUS: Akihiro Komori. PRD: TMS Entertainment. 48 mins.

A *tanuki* (raccoon-dog) named Hal finds a human baby in the forest. *Tanuki* are famous in Japanese legend as shapeshifters (see **POM POKO**) and Hal decides to change into a human woman and raise the baby as a mother should. The boy grows up to be a gifted young musician. This charming story was based on a picture book by Takashi Yanase, the creator of **ANPANMAN**, published in 2009 when he was 90 years old. It premiered at the 24th Tokyo International Film Festival in 2011, before opening in Japanese cinemas in 2012 with two other Yanase-inspired short films under the surtitle *Yanase Takashi Theater.* A new ten-minute *Anpanman* short, *The Day Anpanman was Born (Anpanman ga Umareta Hi),* retells the first episode of the TV series in musical form, and *Robo-Pal and the Little Bird (Robo-kun to Kotori)* is another ten-minute tale about a desert journey that forges a friendship between a robot and a bird.

HALO LEGENDS *
2010. Video. DIR: Frank O'Connor, Hideki Futamura, Daisuke Nishio, Hiroshi Yamazaki, Koichi Mashimo, Koji Sawai, Mamoru Oshii, Shinji Aramaki, Tomoki Kyoda, Toshiyuki Kanno, Yasushi Murai. SCR: Daisuke Nishio, Eiji Umehara, Hiroshi Yamazaki, Hiroyuki

Kawasaki, Megumi Shimizu, Naruki Naka-gawa, Ryan Morris, Dai Sato. DES: Hideki Futamura, Katsuyoshi Nakatsuru, Kazuchika Kise, Shinji Aramaki, Naruhito Sekikawa, Manamu Amasaki, Shuko Murase, Atsuki Takeuchi, Hiro Ui, Tomoaki Kado, Toshiyuki Kanno, Tsunenori Saito, Shiho Takeuchi. ANI: Katsuyoshi Nakatsuru, Tatsuhiko Tachibe, Tomoaki Kado, Tsunenori Saito, Yuji Haka-mada, Atsuki Sato, Teruaki Shiraishi. MUS: Eiko Konoo, Tetsuya Takahashi, Yasuharu Takanashi, Martin O'Donnell, Michael Sal-vatori. PRD: 343 Industries, Warner Brothers, Studio 4°C (*Origins I & II, The Babysitter*), BONES (*Prototype*), Bee Train, Production I.G (*The Duel, Homecoming*), Toei Animation (*Odd One Out*), Casio Entertainment (*The Package I & II*). 10–15 mins. approx. x 8 eps.

The world of *Halo* is a science-fiction universe based on a hugely successful game and toy franchise. *Halo Legends* is a seven-part anthology telling various stories set in its world, from historical background to cultural examination and old-fashioned fights. It succeeds better than most anime versions of Western pop culture by sticking closely to its source and simply making the world of *Halo* look as cool as possible.

The project was originated by Frank O'Connor of 343 Industries, a division created by Microsoft to manage its multimedia, multimillion-dollar franchise. O'Connor spent several years developing the *Halo Legends* project and felt that Japan's approach to animation would be a good fit for the universe and the target audience. He already had story outlines when he approached the chosen animation houses, and Microsoft was heavily involved in the stories and scripts, but the look and style of the segments were open to interpretation by each studio. Production I.G took this freedom furthest, creating a fluid, intriguing watercolor look (reminiscent of Studio Ghibli's ground-breaking work on **MY NEIGHBORS THE YAMADAS**) for the segment *The Duel*.

Studio 4°C had already been involved in two anime projects for Warner Brothers: **ANIMATRIX** and **BATMAN: GOTHAM KNIGHT**. All the studios involved do a decent job on the animation, with some interesting effects, and the writers and directors keep up a brisk pace throughout. The script gets a little wordy and portentous at times,

though never to the same extent as in *The Spirits Within* (**FINAL FANTASY**). Although it doesn't reach the heights of **BLACK AND WHITE**, this is a more enjoyable blend of Eastern and Western creativity than many other recent collaborations: more **ULYSSES 31**, less **WOLVERINE** or **DANTE'S INFERNO**.

HAMTARO TALES *

2000. JPN: *Tottoko Hamtaro*. AKA: *Hamtaro the Hamster*. TV series, movie, video. DIR: Kazuo Nogami, Koichi Sasaki, Yusaku Saotome. SCR: Michiru Shimada, Miho Maruo, Yoshiyuki Suga. DES: Ritsuko Kawai. ANI: Masaaki Sudo, Junko Yamanaka, Yukari Kobayashi. MUS: N/C. PRD: SMDE, TV Tokyo. 23 mins. x 296 eps. (TV), 50 mins. (m1), 55 mins. (m2), 53 mins. (m3), 41 mins. (m4), 45 mins. (v1), 45 mins. (v2), 40 mins. (v3), 40 mins. (v4).

Hamtaro is a happy hamster who lives with his owner, a five-year-old girl called Hiroko (5th-*grader* Laura in the company's foreign sales sheets). He sleeps in a little home kept on the buffet counter in the kitchen of a house on a quiet suburban street. But in the park, across the street, under the roots of the old tree, there is a hideout where the local hamsters go for secret meetings of the "Ham-Ham Friends." Sappy rodent goings-on based on a manga by Ritsuko Kawai.

Movie spin-offs duly followed. In *Big Adventure in Hamhamland* (2001), Hamtaro feels neglected on owner Laura's birthday, heads off with his friends in a magic flying basket over the rainbow to HamHam-land to find the magic sunflower seeds, for which he has to face Ma-O-Ham, the Hamster Demon Lord. The movie took in excess of $20 million at the Japanese box office. *Ham Ham Ham Jya: Mysterious Princess* (2002) has an exotic **A THOUSAND AND ONE NIGHTS** theme, with flying carpets and a beautiful hamster princess, Shera, living in a golden desert palace with a hamster handmaid harem of cute musicians and dancers. More than one and a half million people bought tickets for it. *Ham Ham Grand Prix* (2003) involves a sled race through an Alpine valley and a hamster pirate captain on a flying galleon. It was similarly huge at the box office, although the authors feel they should point out that all three were sharing double bills with each year's *Godzilla* movie! *Ham Ham and*

the Mysterious Demon's Picture Book Tower (2004) capitalizes on the rise of *Harry Potter*, with the rodent friends adventuring through magical storybooks.

The franchise also produced several video incarnations, including a parody of **FROM THE APENNINES TO THE ANDES**, *Hamtaro's Birthday: 3000 Skitters in Search of Mama* (2002, *Hamutaro no Otanjobi: Mama o Tazunete 3000 Techitechi*), *Hamtaro's Race for the Summer Seaside Vacation Treasure* (2003, *Hamu-chanzu no Takara Sagashi Daisakusen: Hamu wa Suteki na Umi no Natsuyasumi*), and, in time for the Athens Olympics, *Hamtaro's Gold Medal* (2004, *Hamuchanzu no Mezase Hamuhamu Kin Medal*), as well as several educational videos on trains, learning the *hiragana* syllabary, and school life.

HANAICHI MONME

1990. Video. DIR: Toshihiko Arimasa. SCR: Norio Hayashi, Hiroshi Kitano, Junichi Sato, Kazuki Hirada. DES: N/C. ANI: Koichi Arai, Satoshi Kushibuchi. MUS: Toshihiro Nakanishi. PRD: Toei. 30 mins. x 6 eps.

Animated versions of tales that won the Short Story Prize in the *Hanaichi Monme* bulletin, including *Noboru and the Wildcat*, *The Misleading Friends*, *Sanma's March*, *Red Mail-Box on the Mountain-Top*, and *One Sunday Morning at the Beginning of May*. The title is taken from a traditional Japanese children's game, similar to the Western game Red Rover.

HANAMARU KINDERGARTEN

2010. JPN: *Hanamaru Yochien*. TV series. DIR: Seiji Mizushima. SCR: Yuichiro Oguro, Shoji Saeki. DES: Mai Otsuka, Hiroki Matsumoto, Mina Nagaoka. ANI: Koichi Motomura, Mai Otsuka. MUS: NARASAKI. PRD: GAINAX, GANSIS, Hanamaru Yochien Hogoshakai, Starchild records, Klockworx. 24 mins. x 12 eps.

Anzu, Hiiragi, and Koume are three girls attending kindergarten. Their teacher, Mr. Tsuchida, is just out of school himself and a great favorite with the class—in fact, Anzu wants to marry him when she grows up—but he's desperate for a date with the beautiful Miss Yamamoto who teaches the class next door. The fun and games the girls have together and their crushes on their teachers are not so different from the relationships of the teachers themselves—it's just that the children are far more open and innocent than their elders.

Although written about a kindergarten, Yuto's manga originally ran in *Young Gangan*, a magazine for 20-something guys, in 2006. Each TV "episode" consists of two stories (three in episode 9) showing how age has no relationship to the depth of feeling, and how small children are deeply affected by the adults around them, even though those adults may be thinking of themselves more than the children. Parallels with Gainax's more famous EVANGELION are not entirely unjustified, or indeed with CHITOSE GET YOU, which would rip off much of the plot two years later.

HANAPPE BAZOOKA *

1992. Video. DIR: Yoyu Ikegami. SCR: Fumio Saikiji. DES: Fujio Oda. ANI: Fujio Oda. MUS: Nozomu Aoki. PRD: Studio Signal. 45 mins. Hapless teenager Hanappe is masturbating in front of a porno film when two demons appear from his TV. The brusque Ophisto Bazooka and his sexy female sidekick, Mephisto Dance, reveal that they can be summoned once a millennium by particular penile jerking. Charged with turning Hanappe into the new messiah, they give him superhuman powers, allowing him to kill the local bullies. Bazooka, however, falls for Hanappe's mother, while Dance develops an unhealthy interest in Hanappe's sister. They pay off his father and turn his house into a party zone for devils, hoping to fob Hanappe off with the power to charm any woman. Hanappe is not convinced, chiefly because his power backfires and he is chased by the inhabitants of a geriatric ward and a transvestite. He also refuses to use the power on the girl he loves because compulsion would make the love they shared meaningless. Discovering that the girl he adores is sleeping with her professor to get good grades, a distraught Hanappe takes his own life, and his soul is sent to the Fairy of the World's Forest to be judged. She determines that he is well-loved by his acquaintances, and he is rescued at the last minute by Dance and taken back to Earth to be reincarnated.

A forgettable sex romp from Kazuo Koike and Go Nagai, originally published as a manga in *Young Jump*, *HB* tries to compensate for its flimsiness by piling on the parodies—split-second cameos exist for many other Nagai characters, including KEKKO KAMEN, DEVILMAN, and GETTER ROBO, while Nagai himself has a voice cameo as an irritated priest. A 15-minute ""Making Of"" documentary, showing the momentous occasion when Nagai reads out a single line, pads out the running time of the video to 60 minutes. Groping vaguely for a romantic message then giving up and simply groping for hooters, it is a minor Nagai work and nowhere near his best. **CN**

HANASAKU IROHA: BLOSSOMS OF TOMORROW *

2011. JPN: *Hanasaku Iroha*. AKA: *Hanairo*; *Blooming Iroha*; *The ABCs of Blooming*. TV series, movie. DIR: Masahiro Ando. SCR: Mari Okada. DES: Mel Kishida; Kanami Sekiguchi; Kazuki Higashiji. ANI: Kanami Sekiguchi. MUS: Shiro Hamaguchi. PRD: P.A. Works, Bandai Visual, KIDS STATION, Lantis, Pony Canyon, Showgate, Sotsu Agency, Yomiuri TV. 25 mins. x 26 eps. (TV), 66 mins. (m). Sixteen-year-old Ohana Matsumae's mother has run away with her latest boyfriend, leaving behind a pile of debt. Ohana is sent off without warning to live with her grandmother, whom she's never met and who is not at all happy to find a strange girl on her doorstep. Grandmother owns a hot springs inn called Kissuiso, dating from the Taisho period, a beautiful old building full of tradition, where Ohana is expected to pitch in to earn her keep.

Saddled with poor customer manner and low self-esteem, Ohana fixates on the friends she has left behind, including the lovestruck young man who might have been boyfriend material. But she soon realizes that she is the only person who can change her life for the better, and throws herself into her unexpected new profession and duties.

The real charm of this show is the presentation of teenage girls in all their shouty, conflicted, annoying, self-doubting glory. The girls are not unbelievably cute, and their personalities, concerns, and behaviors ring true. The adults around them are not all-kind, all-wise, and all-loving; they are flawed people doing their best with the hands life has dealt them. The issues of how to love your mother while not turning into her and how to confront your fears with better weapons than noise and bluster are presented with honesty as well as charm. Even the fan service (ARGOT AND JARGON) isn't too annoying. It's easy to claim that a script requires nudity when you set it at a hot springs—one reason why almost every harem show has a hot springs episode—but *HanaIro* justifies the claim more than most. Teen drama queen Mari Okada, also known for BLACK BUTLER, writes a credible script packed with humor and emotion; some of the plot threads remain unresolved, and the three-episode story arcs within the series makes for occasionally awkward pacing. But the underlying subtext of how adult relationships shape the lives of children is beautifully and subtly developed. Good-looking animation from P. A. Works and an attractive score from Hamaguchi make this series one of the finds of 2011. It was simulcast across the English-speaking world, in Scandinavia, Europe, and South America, and was well-enough received to spin off a movie, while rumors of a second series abound.

The movie *Hanasaku Iroha: Home Sweet Home* (2013), again directed by Ando and written by Okada with music by Hamaguchi, pushes a new angle, as Ohana discovers documents relating to her mother's life when she was Ohana's age, offering a glimpse into the distant days of the semi-mythical 20th century. Eito Chida's manga ran for two years from December 2010, and there is also a spin-off manga, *Hanasaku Iroha: Green Girls Graffiti*, with art by Jun Sasameyuki, which ran from July 2011 to July 2012. **N**

HANAUKYO MAID TEAM *

2001. JPN: *Hanaukyo Maid Tai*. AKA: *Maid in Hanaukyo*. TV series, video. DIR: Yasunori Ide. SCR: Yasunori Ide. DES: Takaharu Okuma. ANI: Takaharu Okuma. MUS: Tamiya Terashima. PRD: Domu, m.o.e., TVK. 15 mins. x 12 eps. (TV1), 17 mins. x 3 eps. (v), 25 mins. x 12 eps. (TV2). An insipid TENCHI MUYO! clone about the pathologically shy Taro Hanaukyo becoming the leader of his powerful political family, even though he cannot bear to be touched by women (shades here of DNA² and GIRLS BRAVO). And guess what, there are loads of them, all dressed as French maids—and only Marielle seems to have the magic touch. The Maid Team consists of four units: the Domestic Unit mothers him, bathes him, dresses him, and sleeps with him; the Security Unit protects him with high-powered military hardware; the Technical Unit develops new robots for him; and the Intelligence Unit runs Memol, the world's fastest supercomputer. An Oedipally suspect farce with added gadgetry based on Morishige's manga in *Shonen Champion*. Whereas the first series was produced by the notorious "fan service" company M.O.E. ("Master of Entertainment") and consequently featured much nudity, the second season, Takuya Nonaka's *HMT: La Verité* (2004), was made by Geneon and was significantly tamer. *La Verité* is not a sequel but a comprehensive remake, with a different order of episodes and a storyline that reaches further into the manga source. To tell at a glance which version you're looking at, Marielle has lavender hair in the original and light blue hair in *La Verité*; the subtitles also bafflingly render her name as "Margarate Yale." It is this version that was released in the U.S., while the original went unlicensed. ◐

HAND MAID MAY *

2000. AKA: *Handmaid Mei*. TV series. DIR: Junichiro Kimura, Tetsuya Yanasawa. SCR: Kazuki Matsui. DES: Yuzo Hirata. ANI: Tetsuya Yanasawa. MUS: Toshio Masuda. PRD: TNK, Pioneer, WOWOW. 25 mins. x 10 eps. (TV), 25 mins. x 1 ep. (v1), 30 mins. x 1 ep. (v2).
Nineteen-year-old student Kazuya Saotome is determined to build a robot of his own. Facing fierce competition from college rival Nanbara, a nasty prank goes wrong when a virus sends Kazuya's PC into a spin and (in a weak *Terminator* homage) he accidentally accesses Cyberdyne Systems' latest project, a "cyberdoll" a sixth the size of normal human being. Stuck with a cute little girl who can literally fit in his hand, Kazuya gets a frilly pink friend to help with his housework, but he also becomes the target of Cyberdyne's later models, determined to steal back the prototype at any cost. An OH MY GODDESS! retread for the new millennium, based on an idea by Juzo Mutsuki, creator of DEVIL HUNTER YOHKO.

The series spawned a video sequel, *Hand Maid Mai* (2003), of which the planned three episodes were made, but only the first and a mostly live-action preview episode ("number 0") were released before the distributor Five Ways went bankrupt, putting the project's concluding releases on indefinite hold. Some sources have subsequently filed the only publicly extant episode as an "11th" TV episode—a victimless confusion liable to continue now that the series is more easily obtained on video than TV broadcast. *HM Mai* depicts Hideo Ozu, who works as an editor and assistant at the "adult video" studio Yamamoto Project, but who has aspirations as a director and has worked since his grade school years on making a movie about his childhood friend, Mai Kurosawa. However, she is about to make her professional movie debut and demands all of his footage of her back. He goes on a drunken binge and wakes the next morning to find he has signed for the delivery of three Cyberdolls. Mai, Ai, and Mii (a joke also used in POPOTAN and the title of STRAWBERRY EGGS) are "twins" to the original Mai, but at three different ages. Conveniently, they are also equipped as a mobile digital filming/editing suite, something that Hideo puts to full use.

HANDLE WITH CARE

2002. Video. DIR: Shigenori Kurii. SCR: Hideo Ura. DES: Shigenori Kurii. ANI: Jiro Oiwa. MUS: N/C. PRD: Shindeban Film, Museum Pictures, Milky. 30 mins.
Embittered and bored with a series of one-night stands, a musician finds his passions stimulated by the arrival of Sion, a beautiful singer who inspires him to form a new band. Both struggle to place high in the local Wild Jam contest, but their secret pasts are soon exposed. This is an anime from Milky, so sex duly follows. ◐

HANDSOME DETECTIVE LABYRINTH

2007. JPN: *Suteki Tantei Labyrinth*. AKA: *Fantastic Detective Labyrinth*; *Lovely Detective Labyrinth*. TV series. DIR: Hiroshi Watanabe. SCR: Natsuko Takahashi. DES: Yukiko Akiyama, Koki Nagayoshi. ANI: Yukiko Akiyama, Yoichi Ishikawa, Yukiko Ban. MUS: Kei Haneoka. PRD: Studio DEEN. 25 mins. x 25 eps.
Thirty years ago, Tokyo was destroyed by a huge earthquake. From the ruins, the new city of Kyuto arose. But other things came up from the ruins: supernatural occurrences are increasing and the situation is getting out of hand. Twelve-year-old Hyuga Mayuki is a genius detective, with psychic powers and an amazing intelligence, even though he's never been to school until the series begins. His background is shrouded in mystery and he's protected by a devoted butler and maid. Not even the police can find out anything about him, yet he can solve mysteries that leave them baffled.

Part of a long line of youthful sleuth tales from GIGANTOR to CONAN THE BOY DETECTIVE, *HDL* has much in common with STEAM DETECTIVES, with abandoned heroes who must penetrate different kinds of smoke-screens to uncover truth. Director Watanabe, an anime veteran who worked for Studio Live on the animation crew of 1978's *The Mystery of Mamo* (LUPIN III), is not above stepping into the voice actors' booth when required. In the same year he directed *HDL* he also played a role in the live-action movie *Crows Zero*.

HANDSOME GIRLFRIEND

1991. JPN: *Handsome na Kanojo*. Video. DIR: Shunji Oga. SCR: Megumi Hiyoshi. DES: Yumi Nakayama. ANI: Mitsuharu Kajiya. MUS: Marika Haneda. PRD: JC Staff. 35 mins.
Teenage pop star Mie Hagiwara and gifted film director Kazuya Kumagai get off to a bad start when they fight in rehearsals. Selected as the main actress in Kazuya's film, Mie hates him at first but is attracted by Kazuya's passion toward filmmaking. Meanwhile, at a meeting just before shooting commences, the production is called off, and Kazuya decides to fund it with his own money. In this adaptation of Wataru Yoshizumi's manga from *Ribon* magazine, tragedy looms as he prepares to perform the final stunt himself.

HANE, YOSHIYUKI

1940–. Concept artist and key animator on many famous anime of the 1960s and beyond, including LITTLE WITCH SALLY and NAUSICAÄ OF THE VALLEY OF THE WIND.

HANOKA

2006. JPN: *HANOKA—ha no ko*. AKA: *Hanoka—Leaf's Incense*. TV series. DIR: Aruji Morino. SCR: Aruji Morino. DES: N/C. ANI: N/C. MUS: Jun Fujimoto. PRD: Fanworks, RAMS, Lantis. 5 mins. x 12 eps.
Humanity has polluted the planets with

machinery, but uses technology to survive. Another civilization, known as the Inhabitants of the Star, attacks humans on planet Tokinea because of their destructive ways. But humans have powerful war machines, known as Demon Gods. Yuji and his Demon God, Hanoka, are sent to destroy the Inhabitants of the Star.

Created by director Morino, the first TV anime made entirely in Flash is an early work from animation house Fanworks and RAMS, which aired on KIDS STATION in 2006. It's always difficult being a pioneer, in that your efforts to break new ground will look dated and amateurish against those who follow in your footsteps with the advantage of your example and newer, shinier technology: Flash is still not the best choice for TV animation and *Hanoka* doesn't shine technically. The best way around that is to write something brilliant, but the story is a revamp of plot tropes and stock characters from decades of giant robot anime. The studio would go on to produce more original work in CHI-SUI MARU and GAKKATSU.

HAPPINESS!

2006. TV series, video. DIR: Hiroshi Hara. SCR: Satoru Nishizono, Ryota Yamaguchi. DES: Miyabi Ozeki, Mitsuharu Miyamae. ANI: Miyabi Ozeki. MUS: Toshimichi Isoe. PRD: Artland, Happiness! Production Committee, Marvelous Entertainment. 24 mins. x 12 eps. (TV), 24 mins. (v).

Haruhi Kamizaka was rescued from bullies by a boy mage when she was just a child. She longed to become a mage herself (just as UTENA longed to become a prince like the prince who comforted her at her parents' grave) and so she enrolls in a school for magic along with her regular classes. Haruhi studies hard to outdo Anri and dreams that one day she'll give her rescuer chocolate on Valentine's Day as a thank-you. Then she meets a boy she thinks may be her long-ago rescuer—but he says he can't use magic. How will she get her man?

Based on an erotic visual novel by Windmill, which spun off a series of seven novels and a manga with art by Rino Fujii, the anime contains mild fan service (ARGOT AND JARGON) but is more strongly focused on romance and school comedy.

HAPPINET

Established in 1969, Happinet is a manufacturer of toys, games, and software, with a wide portfolio of other businesses—although for our purposes the two most important are its subsidiaries Green Bunny and Beam Entertainment, the people who brought you CREAM LEMON, KITE, and WORDS WORTH. The Bandai Namco conglomerate is currently a major shareholder. Beam Entertainment was renamed Happinet Pictures Corporation in 2002.

HAPPY ERMINE

2002. JPN: *Shiawase-so no Okojo-san*. AKA: *Happy Mr. Ermine*. TV series. DIR: Yusuke Yamamoto, Kenichiro Watanabe, Matsuo Asami, Ryuichi Kimura, Kiyoko Sayama, Takahiro Omori, Toshinori Fukushima, Yasuhito Kikuchi, Yuki Hayashi. SCR: Hiroko Naka, Katsuhiko Takayama, Kazuharu Sato, Yoshio Urasawa. DES: Takahiro Kishida. ANI: Motoki Ueda. MUS: Masamichi Amano. PRD: Eigasha Kyoritsu, Radix, Sotsu Agency, TV Tokyo. 25 mins. x 51 eps.

Captured in Japan's northern mountains and brought to an urban pet shop, a white ermine escapes, only to meet with an accident on the mean streets of Tokyo. College student Haruka Tsuchiya finds him in the street and takes him to the vet, while Haruka's kid brother names the creature Kojopii. The wild creature sticks around for the sake of the fried chicken the humans offer but finds human life, and his own human, quite a puzzle. Among the wacky characters in this day-to-day sitcom, where animals figure as strongly as humans, there's a cute mouse whom our hero sees as a meal, and a beautiful girl—but will Tsuchiya ever notice her?

Based on a manga in the spirit of I AM A CAT from *ComicLaLa* by Ayumi Uno. The title recalls Misako Ichikawa's manga *Mr. Happy* (*Shiawase-san*) which featured a cat as a major character and spun off the anime OYO MY HUGGABLE CAT. A strangely high proportion of stoat, weasel, and ferret-related FANDOM arguments appear to surround all anime featuring such creatures, which obliges the authors to point out that although he may look like a ferret, Kojopii is more likely to be a Hongo or Ezo stoat.

HAPPY FRIENDS

1990. JPN: *Shiawase no Katachi*. Video. DIR: Shinya Sadamitsu. SCR: Takao Koyama. DES: Takayuki Goto. ANI: Takayuki Goto. MUS: Kenji Kawai. PRD: IG Tatsunoko. 30 mins. x 4 eps.

The comedy adventures of a series of squashed-down characters who live in a world that functions on the rules of role-playing games, based on a manga that was originally serialized in the Nintendo gaming magazine *Famicom Tsushin*. The stories incorporate many game themes, from attacking monsters to tennis tournaments, with character designs that presage the later U.S. cartoon *Powerpuff Girls*.

HAPPY HAPPY CLOVER

2007. TV series. DIR: Tetsuo Yasumi, Kazumi Nonaka. SCR: Tetsuo Yasumi. DES: Kazuya Hayashi, Kimiko Kubo. ANI: Kazuya Hayashi. MUS: Akihisa Matsuura, Shinichiro Fukuda, Sosaku Sasaki. PRD: Group TAC, KIDS STATION, Shogakukan. 11 mins. x 26 eps.

Happy rabbit Chima lives in the Mikazuki Forest with her friends Haru, Gaku, and Meru. Their adventures are based on Sayuri Tatsuyama's manga. Covering the familiar ground of friendships, festivals, food, school, and childhood fears, the stories also inspired a Nintendo DS game of the same name, while the characters made guest appearances in another DS game. The art, design, and animation are charmingly simple and the color design is bright and sweet.

HAPPY HUMPING! BOING BOING

1992. JPN: *Etchi (H) de Happy Pin! Pin! Pin!* Video. DIR: Katsuma Kanazawa. SCR: Hidemi Kamata. DES: Takeshi Oshima. ANI: Yutaka Arai. MUS: N/C. PRD: E&G Film. 45 mins.

Tokio is an assistant director at TV Aoyama, while his father is an archeologist. When Dad marries Karuri, a beautiful woman of easy virtue, and then heads off to Peru on a research trip, Tokio is stuck back at home with Karuri and her nubile schoolgirl daughter Miki. Matters are soon complicated by the introduction of Karuri's rival, porn actress Kazuka Kurodawara (who, in an imitation of the real life porn star Kaoru Kuroki, advocates the sexiness of armpit hair), by Tokio's crush on his coworker, the newscaster Noriko, and by Miki's own rival, Reiko. All of this leads Tokio to a series of lighthearted sexual encounters, some of which would have gotten a real Japanese television station prosecuted for violating the anti-obscenity law. Based on a manga by Takeshi Oshima in the spirit of WEATHER REPORT GIRL. Compare also with NINE O'CLOCK WOMAN and *Foxy Nudes* in the DISCOVERY SERIES. ◐

HAPPY KAPPY

2011. TV series. DIR: Takuya Minezawa. SCR: Tomoko Konparu. DES: Masumi Hibino, Mitsuru Kuwabata. ANI: N/C. MUS: Cher Watanabe. PRD: Shogakukan Music & Digital Entertainment, ShoPro, TV Tokyo. 5 mins. x 26 eps.

Suguri Kinoshita is nine years old, in the third grade at school, and she loves animals. She also makes fashion accessories. One day she finds an attractive rock and picks it up thinking it would look good on a bracelet. It turns out that the rock is really a cute little creature named Kappy. He's three years old and he's the Prince of the land of Kapimeshia. Not only does he have magical powers to help Suguri and her friends, but he has lots of mischievous magical friends of his own. This bright, sweet series based on Rino Mizuho's 2007 manga revolves around simple themes—helping in the home, playing and fighting with friends, doing everyday tasks with the help, or hindrance, of a little magic. Compare with DORAEMON.

HAPPY LESSON *

2001. Video, TV series. DIR: Takafumi Hoshikawa, Takeshi Yamaguchi, Iku Suzuki. SCR: Yoshio Takaoka. DES: Yasuhisa Kato. ANI: Yasuhisa Kato, Yukiko Ban, Satoru Minowa. MUS: N/C. PRD: KSS. 30 mins. x 5 eps. (v), 25 mins. x 14 eps. (TV1), 25 mins. x 13 eps. (TV2), 24 mins. x 3 eps. (v2).

Predictable classroom high jinks, based on the Dreamcast game in which a group of female teachers must nurture a group of female students, while dwelling at the house of a shy Japanese boy, Hitotose Chitose, who plays the TENCHI MUYO! role in this harem comedy. Catching the zeitgeist of foreign attention and early *moe* (ARGOT AND JARGON) the story jumped to a TV version in 2002. As with many such harem shows (ROMANCE AND DRAMA), the drama revolves around a rotating, fluctuating concept of who is the leading man's ideal mate, matters not resolved until the

closing 2004 video spin-off, in which the old school building is threatened with demolition and the characters reunite to oppose the plan, in honor of all their happy memories.

HAPPY PRINCE, THE

1975. JPN: *Shiawase no Oji*. Movie. DIR: Yoshiyuki Tomino. SCR: Zensuke Oshima. DES: Jack. ANI: Shinichi Tsuji. MUS: Mahiko Nishiyama. PRD: Kyoritsu. 19 mins.

High above a nameless city, the gilded, jeweled statue of a prince looks down on the population. He befriends a lone swallow and urges him to pilfer his jewels and distribute them among the needy of the town. The swallow duly does so, although few of the recipients appreciate the gifts, and lingers so long that winter commences and he is killed by the cold. The dead bird and the despoiled statue's lead heart end up on the town garbage heap, where angels pronounce them to be the most precious things in the entire city.

A short film made for screening in schools, based on Oscar Wilde's 1888 parable that love is nothing if it does not act, and we are nothing if we do not love—noble sentiments with fatalistic meditations that also recall director Tomino's anime career, particularly ZAMBOT 3 and GUNDAM. Considering that Wilde's original had a hostile attitude toward officialdom, depicting a math professor as a pompous fool who does not approve of children dreaming, the authors would probably have been amused by such a screening for the benefit of the teachers rather than the students. The story is referenced in TAMALA 2010: A PUNK CAT IN SPACE, in which a bird is shown trying to peck out a statue's eyes.

HAPPY WORLD!

2002. Video. DIR: Takashi Ikehata. SCR: Tomofumi Nobe. DES: Hirotaka Kinoshita. ANI: N/C. MUS: N/C. PRD: KSS, Shueisha. 27 mins. x 3 eps.

Takeshi Omura's mother ran away from home when he was a little boy, and his distraught father abandoned Takeshi to look for her, leaving his son alone in a cheap apartment which then burnt down. All he owns is the school uniform he still wears, until the day a girl with wings falls out of the sky and introduces herself as Elle. She says she's come to cure his bad luck. She

reveals that Takeshi's father nominated him as the family scapegoat to inherit all the bad luck they were due. She tells Takeshi that he has a choice reminiscent of that presented in the following year's TV series *Sky High* (*DE)—he can transfer his bad luck to someone else, just by saying the word; or he can deal with it alone. But the "someone else" Takeshi could transfer his bad luck to is an innocent young girl, and he can't bring himself to put her through the kind of life he has already had, so he opts to deal with his life as it is. Elle finds this very touching and becomes human, moving in with Takeshi to protect him from the curse. Though he objects at first, he finds that spending lots of time with her makes him far less likely to run into bad luck. Based on a manga by Kenjiro Takeshita in monthly *Ultra Jump* that mixed the badluck protagonist of URUSEI YATSURA (Ataru Moroboshi was supposedly the unluckiest boy on Earth) with the divine intervention of OH MY GODDESS! ◐

HARA, KEIICHI

1959–. Animator at Shinei Doga on shows including ESPER MAMI. Subsequently became a writer and director on CRAYON SHIN-CHAN which occupied him for a decade before he broke out as the acclaimed director of the life-after-death feature COLORFUL: THE MOTION PICTURE (2010).

HARA, TORU

1935–. Born in Fukuoka Prefecture, Hara graduated from Tokyo's Waseda University and joined Toei Animation in 1959, where he was a production assistant on LITTLE NORSE PRINCE and manager of the studio's Rankin/Bass work-for-hire for many years. He left Toei in 1972 to found Topcraft, a company that specialized in coproductions with American and European studios, including Rankin/Bass, on shows such as THE STINGIEST MAN IN TOWN, *The Hobbit* (1977), and *The Last Unicorn* (1982). The company also farmed its services out on domestic animation, in movies such as NAUSICAÄ OF THE VALLEY OF THE WIND, after which Topcraft was effectively dissolved—its staffers forming the bulk of the animation team on CASTLE IN THE SKY and subsequent Studio Ghibli productions.

HARADA, MASUJI

1947–. Joined Mushi Production and worked as an animator on *Vicky the Viking*. Later a director on **HATTORI THE NINJA** and **ULTRA GRAN**.

HARBOR LIGHTS

1988. JPN: *Harbor Light Monogatari Fashion Lala Yori*. AKA: *Harbor Light Story from Fashion Lala; Fashion Lala*. Video. DIR: Tadamasa Takahashi. SCR: Kenji Terada. DES: Yoshiyuki Kishi. ANI: Tadamasa Takahashi. MUS: N/C. PRD: Studio Pierrot. 50 mins.
Eleven-year-old Miho wants to be a fashion designer and is eager to make a dress for her little sister, Shuri, to help her win the Dancing Queen contest. When Miho's stupid aunt ruins the dress, the Fairies of Fanland hear her prayer and transform her into the 16-year-old Lala, a top designer. And in the end, it was all a dream: a cop-out that probably helps to explain why this attempt to create a new magical girl in the tradition of **CREAMY MAMI** never came back for a repeat performance. A prequel of sorts to **FANCY LALA**.

HARD AND LOOSE

1992. JPN: *Shiritsu Tantei Doki Seizo Trouble Note Hard and Loose*. AKA: *Private Investigators Down But Not Out: Trouble Notes Hard and Loose*. Video. DIR: Noboru Ishiguro. SCR: Noboru Ishiguro. DES: Noboru Sugimitsu. ANI: Noboru Sugimitsu. MUS: Masaru Watanabe. PRD: Artland. 45 mins.
A detective thriller in which former boxer Shozo is thrown into a web of intrigue when he picks up a ringing phone in a room whose occupant he is supposed to be following. Based on a manga by **SILENT SERVICE**–creator Kaiji Kawaguchi and **BORDER**'s Karibu Marai and boasting the distinctive square-jawed characters found in Kawaguchi's other work.

HARDCORE HOSPITAL *

2002. JPN: *Shiroki Tenshitachi no Rondo*. AKA: *Ring of Bright Angels*. Video. DIR: Go Yasumoto. SCR: Shinji Rannai. DES: Go Yasumoto. ANI: Go Yasumoto. MUS: Yoshi. PRD: YOUC, Digital Works (Vanilla Series). 30 mins. x 2 eps.
Date Hospital is sited at the edge of a rich suburb and has a ward that doubles as a brothel. Afraid that the secret will surface, the hospital owner puts his son Ryuichi in charge of training new nurses in the "spe-

cial skills" required of them. In a combination of the medical drama of **BLACK JACK** with the coercion of **NIGHT SHIFT NURSES**, Ryuichi is a brilliant surgeon, who allegedly saves the life of new nurse Sayaka's biker boyfriend Masahiko, and then uses that as leverage in order to force Sayaka to accept training as one of the "special nurses"—said training including the usual domination, humiliation, and in this case, serial enemas. Ryuichi is also involved with a Ritsuko Akagi look-alike (see **EVANGELION**) who is researching (what else?) the ultimate aphrodisiac. In the second episode, lonely widow Miyako Kisaragi also joins the hospital, and Ryuichi uses aphrodisiacs and the usual "special" methods to help her overcome her grief. This entry in the **VANILLA SERIES** is rife with a lack of cut-to-cut continuity—the (alleged) animators seem to have been barely awake while working on this, and it shows. For a look at their better work, see **STORY OF LITTLE MONICA**. 🔞

HARÉ + GUU *

2001. JPN: *Jungle wa Itsumo Hare nochi Guu*. AKA: *It Was Nice in the Jungle Then Along Came Guu*. TV series, video. DIR: Tsutomu Mizushima, Hiroshi Yamamoto, Wataru Takahashi. SCR: Yasuhiro Takemoto, Michiko Yokote, Hiroko Hagita. DES: Hiroshi Kugimiya. ANI: Yuichiro Sueyoshi, Kanami Sekiguchi, Kazumi Ikeda. MUS: Akifumi Tada. PRD: Shinei Doga, Bandai Visual, TV Tokyo. 25 mins. x 26 eps. (TV), 30 mins. x 7 eps. (v1), 20 mins. x 6 eps. (v2).
Ten-year-old Haré lives in a jungle village with his pretty mother, Weda, who is something of a hippie—she had Haré out of wedlock, and left her well-to-do home in the big city because the carefree jungle life suited her better. Weda adopts a little blonde orphan girl named Guu, who seems like a sweet, innocent little sister for dark-skinned, blue-haired Haré, though she is short-tempered and has a voracious appetite. Then he learns that she's really a glutinous mind-reading alien with an interdimensional portal in her stomach through which weird creatures and objects emerge to cause trouble for him. She's also a typical kid sister—she teases and tyrannizes Haré mercilessly but is fiercely loyal to him and seems to feel it's her duty to teach him about life

outside the jungle and help him grow up. An old suitor of Weda's, Dr. Clive, shows up to disturb the balance of Haré's peaceful life even further, in a new variation on the **DORAEMON** premise, based on the long-running *Shonen GanGan* manga by Renjuro Kindaichi. The TV series spun off two video series: *Haré + Guu Deluxe* (2002) in which Haré deals with a wacky substitute teacher and Weda gets pregnant again; and *Haré + Guu Final* (2002), in which Weda takes the children to visit her mother in the city. Haré goes to school there and falls for a pretty girl named Rita, but what are kid sisters for if not to mess up a budding romance? Presumably the two video serials were originally intended as a third 13-episode TV season, but the show was taken off-air early.

HARELUYA II BOY

1997. TV series. DIR: Kiyoshi Egami. SCR: Yasuhiro Imagawa. DES: Takahiro Kishida. ANI: N/C. MUS: Shingo Kobayashi. PRD: Triangle Staff, TV Tokyo. 25 mins. x 25 eps.
When tough-guy Hibino saves wannabe-artist Kyoshiro from a gang of bullies, the two become firm friends. They also befriend Makoto, who wants to be the lead singer of the Fire Guns rock band and find superstardom, and Michiru, a young girl who wants to be a jewelry designer. Each member of the group seeks to find success in his or her chosen field, though Hibino's only wish is to stay out of trouble long enough to graduate from school. Then he wants to conquer the world.
A comedy anime that looks askance on Hareluya Hibino's burgeoning relationship with Michiru, *HB*'s message is that friends, however mismatched, should always help each other strive for their dreams, especially when one of them is the prodigal son of God. Like a modern-day **DORAEMON**, Hibino can pull useful objects from a seemingly bottomless backpack, including baseball bats, frying pans, and lobsters, as the occasion demands. Based on a 1992 *Shonen Jump* manga by Haruto Umezawa, who began his career as an assistant to **CITY HUNTER**'s Tsukasa Hojo.

HARLEY SPINY

1996. JPN: *Harimogu Hari*. TV series. DIR: Satoshi Nakamura. SCR: Satoshi Nakamura, Hideki Mitsui, Yumi Kageyama. DES: Takashi

Murakami. ANI: Mitsuo Shindo, Masaaki Iwane, Yoshihiro Nagamori, Kiyoko Sayama. MUS: Kenji Yamamoto. PRD: NHK, Image K, Studio Junio. 10 mins. x 80 eps. (TV1), 10 mins. x 60 eps. (TV2).

The adventures of the eponymous hedgehog and his fellow animal friends, who observe humans in the wild in the manner of cute anthropologists and attempt to get local hardware store owner Mr. McCraw to explain mankind's odd artifacts, usually with comedic results. This is only the beginning of a series of KIDS' ANIME adventures featuring the group of brightly colored animals, whose mismatched color schemes and counter-intuitive alliances make them seem winningly like a randomly assembled group of children's toys.

HARMAGEDON *

1983. JPN: Genma Taisen. AKA: Great War with Genma; Ghenma Wars. Movie, TV series. DIR: Rintaro. SCR: Chiho Katsura, Makoto Naito, Masaki Mori. DES: Katsuhiro Otomo. ANI: Mukuo Takamura, Yoshiaki Kawajiri, Takashi Nakamura, Iwao Yamaki. MUS: Keith Emerson, Nozomu Aoki. PRD: Madhouse, Magic Capsule. 131 mins. (m), 25 mins. x 13 eps. (TV).

An awkwardly paced and overlong film adapted from a long series of books by WOLF GUY's Kazumasa Hirai and filtered through their manga incarnation by Shotaro Ishinomori. Genma ("Phantom Demon"), the personification of entropy, has eaten half the universe and intends to destroy Earth. Its nemesis, good interdimensional being Floy, who has an intensely annoying voice, contacts Princess Luna of Transylvania and warns her of impending doom. Luna is already aware of it, since the plane carrying her on a diplomatic mission has just been struck by a meteor bearing Vega, a cyborg from a world destroyed by Genma in the distant past (compare to Andro in TEKKAMAN). Luna and Vega set about recruiting a multinational army of psionics (including Sonny Rinks, a black kid from the New York ghetto), specifically Japanese schoolboy Jo Azuma, who is the most powerful. As Genma's powers lay waste to Earth, his comic sidekicks, Zombi and Samedi, kill his friends and loved ones. They attack Jo's sister Michiko, who reveals her own psychic powers, only to die seconds before Jo

can save her. A distraught Jo is saved from an earthquake by Tao, a Chinese psionic, who leads him to Genma's hideaway amid the boiling lava of a newly active Mount Fuji. Jo and several other psionic warriors, who arrive as an afterthought, then defeat Genma, who comes back in a predictable twist and is defeated again in a final battle. Vega dies in the final conflict but commends his friends on their victory as he prepares for rebirth, along with life on Earth itself.

This first anime film from Newtype publishers Kadokawa boasts a fatuous pseudo-religious message, a truly awful English-language song, a cameo appearance by director Rintaro as a flustered artist, and much-hyped character designs from Katsuhiro Otomo. It also features an interesting choice from the animators, who concentrate on drawing high-quality still images at the expense of actual animation and lip sync. Trying and failing, like DARKSIDE BLUES, to cram a complex text into the running time of a mere movie, it nevertheless contained the seeds of the anime business as we know it today. Designer Otomo was so disillusioned by his experience of working on Harmagedon that he resolved to do things differently five years later with AKIRA. Not to be confused with Lee Hyunse's Armageddon (1995), which was distributed by Manga Entertainment as "anime," but actually made in Korea. Genma Wars (2002) is a 13-part TV remake also released in America.

HARRIS'S WIND

1966. JPN: Harris no Kaze. TV series. DIR: Yoshiyuki Shindo. SCR: Keisuke Fujikawa, Shunichi Yukimuro, Haruya Yamazaki, Tadaaki Yamazaki. DES: Tetsuya Chiba. ANI: Fukuo Watanabe. MUS: Gatchatorian. PRD: B Pro, Fuji TV. 25 mins. x 25 eps. (TV1), 22 mins. x 46 eps. (TV2).

Kunimatsu Ishida is a regular wild-child, thrown out of every school in his area for fighting. One day he meets the principal of Harris Academy, where he drifts from club to club trying his hand at sports, mainly contact sports like boxing and kendo, though he also brings his own hands-on style to soccer and baseball. Eventually, he becomes a hero of the school by channeling his aggression into improving the school's athletic reputa-

tion. Based on a Shonen Magazine manga by TOMORROW'S JOE–creator Tetsuya Chiba, the same story was remade by Tezuka Productions as Kunimatsu's Got It Right (1971, Kunimatsu-sama no Otoridai), directed by Masami Hata.

HARUKA *

2002. JPN: Harukanaru Toki no Naka de: Hachiyo Sho. AKA: HaruToki; In A Distant Time: Hachiyo Chapter, In a Distant Time. Video, TV series, movie, TV special. DIR: IKU SUZUKI, NAGISA MIYAZAKI, Aki Tsunaki, Toshiya Shinohara, Shigeru Kimiya. SCR: Junko Okazaki, Yuka Yamada, Koji Takamura, Ritsuko Hayasaka. DES: Akemi Hayashi, Kenichi Onuki, Kyoko Kotani, Chikako Shibata. ANI: Noriko Otake, Akemi Hayashi, Nanae Morita. MUS: YASUNORI HONDA, YOSHIHISA HIRANO, Masanori Sato. PRD: Yumeta Company, Hakusensha, KOEI, TV Tokyo, Aniplex (m) cinequanon (m). 30 mins. x 2 eps. (V, Ajisai Yumegatari), 30 mins. x 3 eps. (V2, Shiroki Ryu no Miko), 24 mins. x 26 eps. (TV, Hachiyo Sho), 30 mins. x 2 eps. (V3, Hachiyo Sho), 60 mins. (m, Maihitoyo), 60 mins. (TVm1, Kurenai no Tsuki), 60 mins. (TVm2, Owari Naki Unmei), 90 mins. (V4, Owari Naki Unmei).

Akane Motomiya is 16, with red hair and a generous heart. She's popular but has two particular friends, both boys—14-year-old blond cutie Shimon Nagareyama, a junior-high student who looks up to her, and fellow redhead Tenma Morimura, aged 17 but in her grade at school; compare to similar tensions in ESCAFLOWNE. She lives an ordinary life until, on the way to high school with her friends, she hears voices coming from nowhere and is suddenly dragged down an old well. She finds herself alone in a strange world that resembles the Japan she's seen in history books. This is the land of Kyo, and she is recognized by its people as the Priestess of the Guardian Dragon, whose special powers can protect Kyo in its hour of need. Kyo is under attack from demons led by Akram, a rather charming devil despite the mask he always wears and his virulent hatred of the people of Kyo.

Before long, Akane has acquired a bodyguard of eight handsome men, the Hachiyo, each with his own talents, hair color, and backstory, and each totally devoted to the well-being of the Maiden of the Guardian Dragon—compare to THE

HAKKENDEN. Although Akane is worried about her friends, scared, and not at all sure how she can help, she begins to influence events just by being herself. Her bravery and compassion change the hearts of those around her—even the demons, and especially Akram. Created by KOEI and based on a manga by Toko Mizuno from monthly *Comic Lala* magazine, the anime's real roots are in a dating sim game for girls launched in 1999. The makers claim it "may be" the first anime based on a girls' dating sim, obviously hoping this element of originality will gloss over any perceived similarities with **FUSHIGI YUGI**, **INU YASHA**, or the manga *Red River*. The 2004 TV series (released in English) followed on from two direct-to-DVD releases, the two-part *Ajisai Yumegatari* in 2002 and three-parter *Priestess of the White Dragon* (*Shiroki Ryu no Miko*) in 2003. The series was followed up with a *Hachiyo Sho* DVD in 2005 and a movie, *Maihitoyo* (*Dance of Night*) in 2006. An hour-long TV special *Harukanaru Toki no Naka de 3—Kurenai no Tsuki* (*Red Moon*) was aired in December 2007, and another, *Harukanaru Toki no Naka de 3—Owari Naki Unmei* (*Endless Destiny*), in January 2010. This last edition, rewriting the historical Battle of Dannoura, was extended by a further 30 minutes for the DVD release, and was also given ies with sion ng of the Maiden of the Guardian Dragoning the historical Battle of Dannoura, was extended by a further 30 minutes for the DVD release, and was also given "multiple love endings" featuring ten characters. The manga also ended in 2010, and despite the franchise's decade-long popularity, at the time of writing there is no indication of a further anime revival.

HARUKA NOGIZAKA'S SECRET

2008. JPN: *Nogizaka Haruka no Himitsu*. TV series, video. DIR: Munenori Nawa. SCR: Tsuyoshi Tamai. DES: Satoshi Ishino, Reiji Kasuga. ANI: Masakazu Ishikawa, Mitsuru Ohara, Satoshi Ishino, Takehiro Hamatsu. MUS: Takeshi Watanabe. PRD: Studio Barcelona, ASCII Media Works, Geneon, Kadokawa Mobile, Studio Mausu, Klockworx, Yomiko Advertising, Yomiuri TV. 25 mins. x 12 eps. (TV1), 25 mins. x 12 eps. (TV2), 24 mins. x 12 eps. (v).
Haruka Nogizaka is beautiful, gifted, clever, and rich, hailing from an old fam-

ily. She's idolized at school and waited on by servants and retainers at home. An ordinary guy like Yuto Ayase would seem to have no chance of getting into her circle. One day in the library, he discovers her most shameful secret: she's an otaku, a dyed-in-the-wool manga and anime fan. He's a nice guy, so he keeps her secret, and becomes a friend and confidant. He accompanies her to anime events and encourages her to draw manga, but there's a downside to his newfound friendship: jealous classmates.

This sweet TV anime, offering a more **EVERYDAY ANIME** take on the fanboy Muse of **THE MELANCHOLY OF HARUHI SUZUMIYA** and based on the books by Yusaku Igarashi, is part of a whole raft of merchandise and media including manga and games, with numerous guest appearances and references to and from other anime and manga. The second series, *Nogizaka Haruka no Himitsu: Purezza*, made by the same team and first aired in 2009, contains nods to **TORADORA**, **CAT'S EYE**, **HAYATE THE COMBAT BUTLER**, **MARIA IS WATCHING OVER US**, **PLEASE TEACHER**, *Star Wars*, and more. The story was wrapped up in a four-part video, *Nogizaka Haruka no Himitsu: Finale*, in 2012.

HARUMI'S BAD PLAY *

2001? JPN: *Harumi-chan no Oita*. AKA: *Naughty Harumi; Harumi's Mischief*. Video. DIR: N/C. SCR: N/C. DES: N/C. ANI: N/C. MUS: N/C. PRD: Obtain, Onmitsudo. 30 mins.
Wafaru wakes up one morning to find Harumi, a virginal young girl, hiding out in his room and begging to stay. He takes pity on her, if sexually molesting her can be regarded as pity, in a story that drifts perilously close to the pedophile interests of **LOLITA ANIME**, only to turn the tables when Harumi turns out to be more than she seems—compare to a similar bait-and-switch maneuver in **SEE IN AO**. Submitted to the Australian film censor in 2002 under the title *Naughty Harumi*, but refused certification. **◯◯**

HARVEST NIGHT, THE *

2002. JPN: *Shukaku no Yoru*. Video. DIR: Katsuma Kanazawa. SCR: Katsuma Kanazawa. DES: Kiichiro Yoshida. ANI: Hiroya Iijima. MUS: N/C. PRD: Blue Eyes, Studio Kuma, Triple X. 30 mins. x 2 eps.

Ryoko crosses the bridge that divides the nice side of town from the mean streets to try and persuade her childhood friends Masato and Honoka to come back with her. Masato has become a gang leader and Honoka is seriously ill, but refuses to seek treatment on the clean, healthy side of the bridge. Emi, Masato's moll, lures the pure, romantically inclined Ryoko into group sex, and the other girls try to get her under contract as a hooker. Gang fights, murder by sexual abuse, and beating old men to death are just some of the signs of social degradation on offer before the ailing Honoka is gang-raped to death and her brother goes crazy and kills everyone except Ryoko, who finally goes back where she belongs, leaving Honoka's corpse on the bridge. The age-old notion that it's possible to keep all the nasty things on the wrong side of the tracks is perpetuated in two episodes of pornographic melodrama. **◯◯◯**

HATA, MASAMI

1942–. Born in what was then the Japanese colony of Taiwan, Masami Hata "returned" as a child to a homeland he had never seen in 1945. He briefly studied at the Tama College of Arts but dropped out to work full-time for Mushi Production, where he worked on **PRINCESS KNIGHT**, among others. With the collapse of Mushi Pro in the 1973 recession, Hata freelanced for Tokyo Movie Shinsha and Madhouse, before finding a new home at the newly established animation wing of the merchandise company Sanrio. With Sanrio's brief move into full-length features, he was thus able to become a feature director at the relatively young age of 30. He directed the disturbing children's parable **RINGING BELL**, the lavish feature **LEGEND OF SIRIUS**, which he also wrote, and **JOURNEY THROUGH FAIRYLAND**. The latter was the last full-length feature to be produced by Sanrio, which moved into smaller, lower-budget works in the late 1980s. He returned to Tokyo Movie Shinsha in 1985 to direct **SUPER MARIO BROTHERS**, one of the first anime to be based on a computer game. Despite his role at TMS, Hata is credited on many Sanrio productions of the 1990s as a supervising director or scenarist, notably on spin-off films featuring the merchandising icons Keroppi and Hello Kitty. His most recent work includees *Stitch!* (2008), the Japanese spin-off from Disney's *Lilo & Stitch*.

HATARAKIDS MY HAM GUMI

2007. JPN: *Hatara Kids Maiham Gumi*. AKA: *Working Kids, Meister Hamster Team*. TV series. DIR: Tetsuo Imazawa. SCR: Takashi Yamada. DES: Tadashi Yamamuro, Takashi Honda. ANI: Takashi Nashisawa, Tatsuzo Nishida. MUS: Yoshichika Inomata. PRD: Toei Animation. 25 mins. x 50 eps.

A group of young hamster pals hold down a series of demanding jobs, from firefighting to patisserie, Grand Prix driving to babysitting. Credited to Izumi Todo, the house pseudonym for Toei, this action-adventure series for elementary school children has been screened in France, Spain, and the Phillipines but is unknown in English. Compare with **HAMTARO TALES**.

HATARAKI MAN

2006. TV series. DIR: Katsumi Ono. SCR: Yuka Yamada. DES: Hisashi Kagawa, Hiroshi Kato. ANI: Kazuyuki Kobayashi, Makoto Sawazaki, Mieko Seki. MUS: Yugo Kanno. PRD: GALLOP, Dentsu, Fuji TV, Hataraki Man Production Team, Kodansha, SME. 23 mins. x 11 eps.

Hiroko is a hardworking woman who puts her all into her career as an editor with a magazine company. She's respected by her colleagues as someone who can put herself into *hataraki* (working) man mode. Her boyfriend is an even bigger workaholic than she is. No wonder the romance is missing from Hiroko's life. Manga creator Moyoco Anno's 2004 manga was also turned into a TV drama in 2007. Famous for the international hit movie *Sakuran* (2007), directed by Mika Ninagawa, she is arguably even better known as the wife of Hideaki Anno (**EVANGELION**). Her manga **SUGAR SUGAR RUNE** was animated in 2005.

HATSUINU

2007. JPN: *Hatsuinu the Animation*. AKA: *First Dog*. Video. DIR: Toshiro Watase, Nodame Ichigo. SCR: Yamakichi Hana, Milk Ichigo. DES: Yu Kizaki, Shun Manuwame. ANI: Yu Kizaki, Candy Ichigo. MUS: N/C. PRD: Café de Jeilhouse, office Take Off, Pink Pineapple. 30 mins. x 2 eps. (v1), 30 mins. x 2 eps. (v2).

On the train to school, Fukaya accidentally crashes into Fujino, causing her vibrator to skip to a higher setting. She can't turn it off discreetly so she asks him to satisfy her sexual cravings. We have no idea how he manages to do that discreetly, but when they get off the train Fujino is so grateful that she gives him a remote control for her vibrator as a thank you gift. Based on the manga of the same name by Inu, which focuses on the sex triangle between Fujino, Fukaya, and their classmate Mita, who has a crush on Fukaya. The second video, *Hatsuinu 2 the Animation—Strange Kind of Woman—Again*, appeared in 2008 and continues their story. **Ⓝ**

HATSUKOI LIMITED *

2009. AKA: *First Love Limited*. TV series, TV special. DIR: Yoshiki Yamakawa. SCR: Mariko Kunisawa. DES: Tomoyuki Shitaya, Hirotsugi Kakoi. ANI: Koji Yamakawa, Tomoyuki Shitaya, Shinya Hasegawa. MUS: Nijine. PRD: JC Staff, Geneon, Lantis, Shueisha, Klockworx. 24 mins. x 12 eps. (TV), 4 mins. x 6 eps. (special).

For eight girls in middle school and high school, their friendships and love lives weave together to create one story with many strands in this TV series based on Mizuki Kawashita's manga. Gentle comedy and slice-of-life storytelling make for a prettily animated show told from the female viewpoint. Fan service (**ARGOT AND JARGON**) is relatively low-level and inoffensive. The six short specials were extras on the DVD release.

HATSUNE MIKU LIVE PARTY

2011. AKA: *Miku Pa!* Video. DIR: Arden, Jambo. SCR: N/C. DES: Kei Garo. ANI: N/C. MUS: Minato, Noboru. PRD: Crypton Future Media, Marza, 5pb. 103 mins.

"Live" from Tokyo, the virtual idol Hatsune Miku performs along with her band and with several special guests who are also animated characters. Later followed by similar concerts from Sapporo (2011) and Kansai (2013), among others, Miku represents the apotheosis of 21st-century animation. A DIY "Vocaloid" creation that can be programmed to sing songs, her motion-captured performance is displayed on a clear glass sheet that seems to integrate her with the human band who accompany her. The concert video puts on a performance on several layers, of a 3D holographic idol singer, and an enthusiastic capacity crowd that cheers her on.

The framing makes it all seem incredibly realistic, but to be sure, you would have to go there yourself, making such hybrid events one of the unpiratable golden tickets of the modern industry. It helps as well that, to an even greater extent than the voice-actress singers of **BUBBLEGUM CRISIS** and its spin-off concerts, Miku is a digitally generated idol reliant on the whims and caprices of no single performer (**MUSIC IN ANIME**).

As producers increasingly search for a way to thwart pirates and monetize "live" events, concerts like Miku's, partly generated by fan programmers, openly referencing Internet memes and monetized in both ticket sales and in concert DVD sales (largely to the same ticket buyers), may present a vision of the future, alongside other "4D" tricks like smell-o-vision, vibrating seats, and similar gimmicks. It also bears an inadvertent resemblance to some of the earliest cartoons, which were similarly presented as hybrid theatrical events requiring interaction with a live human host. It's not all that far from Winsor McCay's *Gertie the Dinosaur* (1914) to Miku's concert a century later. To be sure, part of the mystique lies in the *performance* of popularity; the camera angles show the show only at its best, the audience reaction seems carefully managed, and one concert in Los Angeles was billed in Japan as being part of a "sell-out tour," when it was actually presented to a largely captive audience at an anime convention. The enthusiasm of the Japanese crowd, at least, in this first DVD is a substantial part of the performance, from their exuberant chanting and dancing, to their yells of encouragement when Miku feigns stagefright.

The "Hatsune Miku Movement" is an interesting phenomenon: fans can create their own Hatsune Miku songs and videos using the synthesizer software developed for Windows with the voice of Japanese actress Saki Fujita. Many such creations are shared on YouTube and other streaming sites, with over 100,000 songs to her name, of which over 20,000 are supposedly original songs written for her. Miku has made a number of appearances on record, in anime, manga and games. She teamed up with Louis Vuitton and director Toshiki Okada to create the "Vocaloid opera" *The End*, premiering at the Theatre du

Chatelet in Paris in the autumn of 2013. A similar Vocaloid creation became the online origins of another anime story: **MEKAKUCITY ACTORS**.

HATTORI THE NINJA

1981. JPN: *Ninja Hattori-kun.* TV series, movie. DIR: Hiroshi Sasagawa, Fumio Ikeno. SCR: Masaaki Sakurai, Noboru Shiroyama. DES: Fujio-Fujiko. ANI: Hiromichi Matano. MUS: Shunsuke Kikuchi. PRD: Shinei, Pan Media, TV Asahi. 10 mins. x 694 eps. (TV), 53 mins. (m).

The everyday Sanyo family gets an unexpected surprise in the shape of a new lodger—Hattori is a ninja boy who has come down from the Iga mountains to attend normal school. Befriending Kenichi Sanyo, who is the same age as he, Hattori starts attending school undercover, occasionally accompanied by his brother, Shinzo, Shishimaru the ninja dog, and Kenichi's girlfriend, Yumeko. The gang is also threatened by the rival Koga ninja, Kemumaki, and his evil sidekick, Kagechiyo the Shadow-cat.

Hattori, the lead character in this long-running work from **DORAEMON**-creators Fujiko-Fujio, also appeared in an anime movie, *Hattori and the War of the Little Ninja Villages* (1983), directed by Shinichi Suzuki, in which the evil Dr. Mekamaro, wishing to be the best ninja in the world, kidnaps Hattori's parents, leaving the little assassin and his friends to save the world. He teamed up with **PER-MAN** for a movie.

HAUNTED JUNCTION *

1997. TV series. DIR: Yuji Muto. SCR: Kazuhisa Sakaguchi, Satoru Nishizono, Yuji Hashimoto. DES: Atsuko Nakajima. ANI: Ryoko Hata, Atsuko Nakajima, Satoshi Inoue. MUS: Hayato Matsuo. PRD: Studio Deen, BeStack. 25 mins. x 12 eps.

Haruto, the son of a Christian minister, becomes the president of his high school's Saints Club, where he, Buddhist acolyte Kazuo, and wannabe Shinto shrine maiden Mutsuki must somehow keep their school's epidemic of ghosts under control.

Based on a manga by Nemu Mukudori first serialized in *Monthly Electric Comic GAO*, *HJ* is a genuinely funny look at what school life might be like with fish-monsters in the swimming pool, statues that come to life, and biology lab skeletons that

dance like Cossacks. With a Christian who just wants a mundane, boring life and a Buddhist who is easily possessed, there are hilarious set-ups for cross-dressing and animal impersonations. Mutsuki's "Shouta Complex," however, is an unhealthy obsession with little boys, which may well have appeared like an ironic inversion of **CREAM LEMON**'s Lolita complex to the Japanese crew, but is likely to keep *HJ* forever off U.S. TV. As it was, the show was only shown on Japanese TV very late at night, and elements remain too risqué for children. As for the ghostbusting, Mutsuki has a sideline in Shinto exorcisms, while Kazuo can write Buddhist charms. Haruto, however, is neglected by a writing team that knows nothing of Christianity, coming across as little more than a blond dummy in a smock who regularly yells "Oh my God!" in exasperation.

Like the later **JUBEI-CHAN THE NINJA GIRL**, elements of *HJ* rely on ethnocentric jokes liable to fly over the heads of a U.S. audience. Throwaway lines about a girl in the toilets (see **HERE COMES HANAKO**) are left initially unexplained, as is an anatomical doll named after novelist Haruo Sato and a talking statue based on a legendarily hard-working student Kinjiro Ninomiya, whose effigy can be found in many Japanese schools. Nonetheless, a fine, fun parody of school spook stories.

HAUNTED SLUTS

2000. JPN: *Hyakki Yako: Warashi.* AKA: *100 Nights of Happiness: Haunted House; Pandemonium.* Video. DIR: Yoshiteru Takeda. SCR: N/C. DES: N/C. ANI: N/C. MUS: N/C. PRD: St. Lilia. 30 mins.

Systems engineer Shuichi grows tired of life in the city and moves out to the countryside, where he soon finds himself a new sexual partner in the form of a bored local housewife. However, he also finds himself haunted by a *warashi*: either an innocent girl or a local spirit, depending on what one believes. As with other modern treatments of spirits from **SPOOKY KITARO** to **POM POKO**, *warashi* are unable to live in human cities. In this erotic variant, however, they are able to become homeless wanderers who subsist like succubi on male "energy." **Ⓝ**

HAWAIIAN BREEZE

1992. JPN: *Shin Dosei Jidai: Hawaiian Breeze.* AKA: *New Age of Cohabitation: Hawaiian Breeze.* Video. DIR: Hiroshi Fukutomi. SCR: Takashi Yamada. DES: Fumi Shibama. ANI: Masuji Kinoue. MUS: King Biscuit Time. PRD: Japan Home Video. 45 mins.

In this adaptation of a manga by Fumi Shibama, itself a retelling of a 1972 manga by Kazuo Kamimura (the original *Age of Cohabitation* whose existence is implied by the "new" in this title), Honda has been living with Eri for two years and debates whether or not he should ask her to marry him.

HAYAKAWA, KEIJI

1950–. Born in Aomori Prefecture, he worked briefly at Toei Animation and Tokyo Movie Shinsha before joining Nippon Animation. He was the supervising director on **ISABELLE OF PARIS** before running the production of **BELLE & SEBASTIAN**. He joined Studio Pierrot, and played a role in the animation of shows including **SHERLOCK HOUND** and **TOUCH** before moving to Studio Gallop, where he worked on numerous video productions, including **MAPS**.

HAYATE THE COMBAT BUTLER *

2007. JPN: *Hayate no Gotoku.* TV series, video, movie. DIR: Keiichiro Kawaguchi, Yoshiaki Iwasaki, Hideto Komori, Yoichi Ueda, Masashi Kudo. SCR: Junki Takegami, Shinichi Inotsume, Taku Sato, Hideki Shirane, Hiroko Fukuda, Yosuke Kuroda, Yasuko Kobayashi, Rie Koshika, Natsuko Takahashi, Masashi Suzuki. DES: Osamu Horiuchi, Masahiro Fujii, Makoto Shiraishi, Hideto Komori, Takashi Aoi, Masashi Kudo, Norifumi Nakamura. ANI: Masaaki Sakurai, Masahiro Fujii, Ryoichi Oki, Hideto Komori, Chiyoko Sakamoto, Masashi Kudo, Taketomo Ishikawa, Keiko Sasaki, Kumiko Shishido, Mutsumi Kadekaru, Yoshinori Izuno. MUS: Kotaro Nakagawa, Wataru Maeguchi. PRD: SynergySP, J.C.Staff, Manglobe, Shogakukan, TV Tokyo, Geneon, MOVIC. 25 mins. x 52 eps. (TV1), 27 mins. (v), 25 mins. x 25 eps. (TV2), 59 mins. (m), 24 mins. x 12 eps. (TV3), 25 mins. x 12 eps. (TV4).

Life has dealt Hayate Ayasaki a rough hand. His parents, chronic gamblers, have no jobs and no assets. He's worked part-time throughout school to help keep the family going. Yet on his 16th Christmas his no-good folks sell him to the mob as an organ donor to wipe out their gambling debts. Desperate, he decides to kidnap a rich kid and hopes the ransom will save his bacon, or at least his liver and kidneys. Somehow, his victim Nagi mistakes this as a declaration of love. When his true nature reasserts itself and he rescues her, she gives him a job as her family butler.

This was never going to be a heart-rending Christmas tale to rival DOG OF FLANDERS. Instead, director Kawaguchi and writers Inotsume and Takegami very sensibly focus on the most insane elements of Kenjiro Hata's 2005 manga, letting gags, parody, and strangeness drive the show into comic orbit. Winking at almost every major anime hit of the last decade and scattering more Easter eggs than the eponymous bunny, it's a fan trivia championship in itself. The standard harem plot (ROMANCE AND DRAMA) is nothing special, and the same applies to the design and animation, but for verve, nerve, and whip-fast editing this show has few rivals. When it lets its focus stray from broad comedy it sinks faster than an underdone cupcake, but that hasn't happened often enough to put off its legion of fans.

A change of animation studio and director for the 2009 video and TV series, both called *Hayate the Combat Butler!! (Hayate no Gotoku!!)*, changed nothing about the basic formula. It was all change again on the staff front for the 2011 movie, *HtCB: Heaven Is a Place on Earth* (the producers chose to give the movie an English subtitle rendered in Japanese script.) Kotaro Nakagawa (of PLANETES fame), whose score had been the one constant of the previous anime versions, was replaced by comparative rookie Maeguchi. *HtCB: Can't Take My Eyes off You* once again had an English subtitle rendered in Japanese script, and this time it has a sci-fi comedy plot completely unrelated to the manga, although creator Hata was still involved in its genesis. A further TV series, *HtCB: Cuties*, aired in spring 2013.

HAZEDON

1972. TV series. DIR: Makura Saki (pseud. for Osamu Dezaki), Fumio Ikeno. SCR: Haruya Yamazaki, Yoshitake Suzuki, Toshiaki Matsushima, Hiroyuki Hoshiyama. DES: Toshiyasu Okada. ANI: Kazuhiko Udagawa, Keisuke Morishita, Satoshi Dezaki. MUS: Hiroshi Tsutsui. PRD: Fuji TV. 25 mins. x 26 eps. Young fishboy Hazedon wants to be the "strongest fish in the world," fighting against the evil Ankoragon and Samegills, who eternally plague the undersea kingdom with crab attacks, shark thieves, and kidnappers sent to steal away Hazedon's love interest, the mermaid girl Sealan.

HE IS MY MASTER *

2005. JPN: *Kore ga Watashi no Goshujin-sama*. AKA: *That's My Master; This Is My Master*. TV series. DIR: Shoji Saeki. SCR: Jukki Hanada, Natsue Yoguchi, Shoji Saeki, Takashi Aoshima. DES: Kazuhiro Takamura. ANI: Bow Ditama, Kazuhiko Takamura. MUS: Seiko Nagaoka. PRD: Gainax, Shaft, BS-i. 24 mins. x 12 eps.
Teenage runaway sisters Izumi and Mitsuki need somewhere to stay, not the least because Mitsuki's pet alligator Pochi cannot stay in conventional lodgings. Luckily for them, they run into Yoshitaka Nakabayashi, a 14-year-old orphan who has inherited a fortune from his millionaire parents. Yoshitaka employs the girls as servants, on the condition that they dress up in revealing maids' outfits and address him at all times as "master." Based on an allegedly "ultra-racy" manga by Mattsu and Asa Tsubaki and screened on satellite TV in Japan, this lightweight work is loaded with in-jokes at the expense of other anime, particularly other Gainax products like EVANGELION, HIS AND HER CIRCUMSTANCES, GUNBUSTER, and MAHOROMATIC.

HEADGEAR

A collective of five creators, whose early coffeeshop discussions about science fiction eventually led to the writing and production of PATLABOR and TWILIGHT Q. The members are: manga author Masami Yuki, designer Yutaka Izubuchi, screenwriter Kazunori Ito, designer Akemi Takada, and director Mamoru Oshii. Works credited to Headgear split all profits five ways, regardless of the extent of involvement of any one member.

HEART: AN ITALIAN SCHOOLBOY'S JOURNAL

1981. JPN: *Ai no Gakko Cuore*. AKA: *Beloved School Cuore*. TV series. DIR: Eiji Okabe. SCR: Ryuzo Nakanishi. DES: Yu Noda. ANI: Fumio Kurokawa, Iku Suzuki. MUS: Katsuhisa Hattori. PRD: Nippon Animation, TBS. 25 mins. x 26 eps.
Enrico Pocchini is a kindhearted fourth-grader with a strong sense of justice who lives in the picturesque Italian town of Torino. But as he starts the new semester at school, he loses his adored teacher, Miss Delcacci, who is replaced by the stern Mr. Pelboni. After some misunderstandings, the boys in Enrico's class come to respect Mr. Pelboni, and learn about love, life, and human kindness.

Though financed by Calpis, original sponsors of the WORLD MASTERPIECE THEATER, and made by Nippon Animation, *Heart* is not one of the *WMT* series, though it could easily pass for one. Two episodes of the series focus on one boy's quest to be reunited with his mother in South America, a chapter from the original novel by Edmondo de Amicis that was already animated in 1976 as the famous FROM THE APENNINES TO THE ANDES.

HEART COCKTAIL

1986. TV series. DIR: Yoshimitsu Morita, Shinpei Wada, Osamu Kobayashi, Akio Hayashi. SCR: Seizo Watase. DES: Seizo Watase. ANI: Yasuko Yamazaki. MUS: Naoya Matsuoka. PRD: Kodansha, Nippon TV. 5 mins. x 77 eps. (TV), 45 mins. (v).
CHALK-COLORED PEOPLE–creator Seizo Watase's 1983 series of short manga in *Comic Morning* is adapted into dozens of romantic vignettes, each designed to tell a simple love story in "no more time than it would take to smoke a cigarette," which often means that there is little time for even revealing people's names; many tales simply star "Me" and "Her." Stories include *Emblem of My Father, Two in the Beer Garden, Old Hawaii Corner, My Brother's Zippo*, and *Takeru's Love of Two and a Half Millennia*. The tobacco analogy may sound strange in these politically correct times, but it is better than the alternative, remembering that such short manga stories are *actually* designed to take no longer to read than the average dump. A one-shot video sequel, containing nine further stories, was released in time for the 25th anniversary in 2003.

HEART OF THE RED BIRD

1979. JPN: *Nihon Meisaku Dowa Series: Akai Tori no Kokoro.* AKA: *Japanese Masterpiece Fairytale Series: Heart of the Red Bird.* TV series. DIR: Yoshio Hanajima, Kenzo Koizumi, Tsutomu Shibayama, Daikichiro Kusunobe, Osamu Kobayashi, Kimio Yabuki, Shigetsugu Yoshida, Hideo Nishimaki, Shingo Araki. SCR: Shingo Araki, Mitsuo Wakasugi, Hamakichi Hirose, Taichi Yamada, Rena Kukisawa, Keisuke Kinoshita, Osamu Kagami, Zenzo Matsuyama, Taku Warabi, Kazuo Yoshida. DES: N/C. ANI: Shingo Araki, Daikichiro Kusunobe. MUS: Chuji Kinoshita. PRD: Studio Korumi, Ajia-do, Studio Junio, Tomi Production, Araki Production, TV Asahi. 25 mins. x 26 eps.

Trawling through the children's story magazine *Akai Tori* (*Red Bird*), composer Chuji Kinoshita resolved to organize the adaptations of its best stories as children's animation for a new generation and to mark the 20th anniversary of the channel TV Asahi. The result is this series of literary adaptations like a kiddified ANIMATED CLASSICS OF JAPANESE LITERATURE, including *Reach to the Heaven* (Kojiro Yoshida), *The Cow Tethered to a Camellia Tree* (Nankichi Niimi), *Mysterious Window* (Yaso Saijo), *Weeping Red Devil* (Kosuke Hamada), *A Story about Ascending to Heaven* (Shohei Hino), *Devil's Horn* (Kyoka Izumi), *The Spider's Thread* (Ryunosuke Akutagawa), and *The Mermaid and the Red Candles* (Mimei Ogawa). Early negotiations at the planning stage suggest that Kinoshita was being even more ambitious, hoping to lure in big-name directors like Akira Kurosawa to run particular episodes, but that does not seem to have actually happened. Compare to WORLD MASTERPIECE THEATER, with which it has certain similarities of aim, if not execution.

HEARTBROKEN ANGELS

1990. JPN: *Kizudarake no Tenshitachi.* Video. DIR: Tsuyoshi Sasakawa. SCR: Tsuyoshi Sasakawa, Takeshi Saito. DES: Masahiko Kikuni. ANI: N/C. MUS: Toshiyuki Ebihara, Masaya. PRD: Studio M. 70 mins.

Thirty-one stories based on the four-panel manga strips drawn by Masahiko Kikuni for *Young Sunday* magazine make up this anime that mixes animation and live action. Possibly intended for TV broadcast like HEART COCKTAIL, though the rude na-

ture of Kikuni's humor may have prevented that part of the plan. *Tetsuo*'s Tomoro Taguchi was among the live-action actors. See also MOST SPIRITED MAN IN JAPAN.

HEART-COLORED KILLER TICKET

1989. JPN: *Satsujin Kippu wa Heart Iro.* AKA: *Killer Ticket Is Heart-Colored.* Video. DIR: Taku Sugiyama. SCR: Akira Miyazaki. DES: Hiroyasu Yamaura. ANI: Tomoko Kobayashi. MUS: N/C. PRD: Nippon Eizo. 50 mins.

A "soft-boiled" detective comedy based on a series of young adult novels by Hiroyasu Yamaura, in which sweet, unassuming, bullying victim Seiko is suspended from school and takes the opportunity to go to Nagasaki, where she becomes embroiled in a murder mystery. In keeping with the originals' focus on the female market, sleuthing à la YOUNG KINDAICHI FILES becomes less important in the story than cats and ghosts.

HEARTFUL CAFÉ

2002. JPN: *Mune Kyun! Heartful Café.* AKA: *Heart Skips! Heartful Café.* Video. DIR: Hirohide Shikishima. SCR: Tsunekazu Murakami. DES: Mochizuki. ANI: Mochizuki. MUS: Kennosuke Matsumura. PRD: Uni Soft, Museum Pictures, Milky. 30 mins. x 2 eps.

Shinya is the manager of a small coffee house staffed by his twin stepsisters Chiyori and Chika. When a franchise for a large café chain opens across the street, the siblings are forced to improvise to hang onto their business. The girls start wearing revealing costumes to attract more clientele, although when regular customer Aya becomes close to Shinya, it inspires feelings of jealousy in Chika. Chika decides to seduce Shinya herself, although this soon causes problems for her twin, whose feelings toward him remain purely platonic. Erotic high jinks ensue. ⓝ

HEARTWORK: LOVE GUNS *

2003. JPN: *Heartwork: Symphony of Destruction.* AKA: *Heartwork: Love Guns.* Video. DIR: Hitoshi Kawaguchi. SCR: Hitoshi Kawaguchi. DES: Tomohiro Koyama, Bucifer. ANI: Tomohiro Koyama. MUS: Artistic Concepts, Kishow Yamanaka. PRD: Active Soft, Kyushyu Animation Network. 30 mins., 29 mins., 29 mins.

Detective Yukari Morikawa has a problem—a Colt Government Model pistol that she had assumed was properly destroyed

has disappeared from police custody and is wreaking havoc again with its curse, one that allegedly drives the possessor murderously insane. Meanwhile, high school student Yuu Asakura has accidentally exchanged briefcases with a stranger and discovered that he is now the owner of the gun, a video tape, and ¥2 million in cash. The video tape has instructions for an assassination, and out of curiosity Yuu decides to follow them, leading him to a beautiful blonde partner with the codename of "Angel," and a hot night in a hotel while waiting for their target. In a change of pace, the second episode depicts a school day focusing on two of Yuu's classmates—his childhood friend Nami Kumagai and her friend, bad girl Hozumi Sakatsu, their declarations of love for Yuu, and the gun working its tragic curse on another classmate. However, ignoring its immediate predecessor entirely, in episode 3 Yuu's widowed stepmother Misako seduces him and keeps him home to satisfy needs left wanting since her husband died.

Given the incompatibility of the last two episodes with each other (and the first with the third; the first two may be shoehorned together), it seems likely that two—or even three—different plot lines from Active Soft's original erotic game are shown here, one per episode. This, along with an uneven mixture of 2D cel-style animation and 3D CG backgrounds, leads to a jarringly flawed whole, though one which is not without its merits. ⓛⓝⓥ

HEAT GUY J *

2002. TV series. DIR: Kazuki Akane. SCR: Akihiko Takadera, Hiroshi Onogi, Kazuki Akane, Miya Asakawa. DES: Nobuteru Yuki, Takahiro Kishida, Takayuki Takeya, Takeshi Takakura, Akihiko Takadera. ANI: Nobuteru Yuki, Haruo Sotozaki, Osamu Kobayashi, Shinji Takeuchi, Yuko Watabe. MUS: Try Force. PRD: Magic Capsule, Omnibus Japan, Bandai, BS-I, TBS. 25 mins. x 26 eps.

In the far future, the nations of today have collapsed and have been replaced by a number of giant city-states. In the city of Judoh, which still retains some architectural vestiges of its former existence as New York, young cop Daisuke Aurora and his cyborg partner Jay work for the Special Services Division of the Bureau of Urban Safety, a small department charged with preventing crimes before they happen, in the style of the same year's *Minority Report*. As with **PATLABOR**, the agency with the interesting job is also the one that all the other cops look down on, leaving third teammember Kyoko to police their ammo supply and break up fights between them and angry plaintiffs. They also have to deal with prejudice against Jay; cyborgs aren't normally allowed to enter major cities for fear they will go on a rampage of destruction, so his robot identity has to be kept secret. But prejudice begins at home—Daisuke doesn't much care for cyborgs. They're fighting some heavy-duty organized crime; the Vampire mob recently lost its godfather, Leonelli, but his insane son Claire (and you'd be insane if you were a boy called Claire) is more than capable of keeping crime on the streets of Judoh.

There is a *Heat Guy J* manga, written and drawn by Chiaki Ogishima and serialized in *Magazine Z*, but this anime has a much longer pedigree. From **ASTRO BOY** onward, Japanese science fiction has owed a great debt to Isaac Asimov, and nowhere is it more obvious than in this pastiche of *The Caves of Steel* (1954), which similarly featured an unlikely robot-human detective alliance on a prejudiced Earth. It also featured a race of snooty superior beings whose technology and lifestyle was far beyond Terran understanding—the Spacers in the original, and the Celestials in this "homage." If the plot was not enough of a clue, Daisuke even appears to have been named after Asimov's Spacer homeworld Aurora. Compare to **THE BIG O**, which similarly lifted elements of Asimov's work.

Heat Guy J was also influenced by the same 9/11 terrorism fallout that affected **FULL METAL PANIC** and **METROPOLIS**. The pseudo–New York City lends itself to numerous references inspired by post 9/11 rumors about civilization under siege. It is easy to forget that over a hundred Japanese were killed in the 9/11 attacks, and that in the ensuing months the Japanese government controversially urged its citizens to stay at home. Elements of this paranoia can be pursued in the hermetic world of *Heat Guy J*'s city-state; there may be other nations, but it is implied that Judoh is a place one must either love or leave, and once one quits there is no going back. The

Vampire syndicate attempts to manipulate the stock market in order to make the ultimate killing, although they do so in a humble product like tomatoes, leading to an in-depth look at the city's food supply: a refreshing change in a genre where all too often everyday commodities just appear as if by magic. Other elements of the 21st-century zeitgeist can be discerned in the stranglehold the Celestials have on Judoh's waterpurification technology. They return once each generation to collect their fee and overhaul the machines, otherwise they automatically grind to a halt—a pattern that meets with disaster when a Celestial murder case causes the engineers to boycott Judoh, leaving Daisuke with a limited time to solve the case before the city goes into meltdown.

Later episodes return to the crime subplot and introduce the community of Siberbia, a harsh existence beyond the city limits whose populace take self-reliance to such extremes that they have become completely callous and self-interested—a social parable like those found in **KINO'S JOURNEY**. The home video release included revised and improved animation quality over the initial Japanese TV broadcast. **🎬📼**

HEAVEN'S LOST PROPERTY *

2009. JPN: *Sora no Otoshimono*. AKA: *The Sky's Lost Property; Misplaced by Heaven*. TV series, video, movie. DIR: Hisashi Saito, Tetsuya Yanagisawa. SCR: Yuko Kakihara. DES: Yoshihiro Watanabe, Hiromasa Ogura, Mutsumi Kadekaru, Satoshi Ishino, Hiroshi Goroku. ANI: Yoshihiro Watanabe, Kosuke Kawamura. MUS: Motoyoshi Iwasaki. PRD: AIC A.S.T.A., AIC, Kadokawa, NTT Docomo, Klockworx, Glovision. 24 mins. x 13 eps. (TV1), 25 mins. (v), 24 mins. x 12 eps. (TV2), 90 mins. (m).

Sex-mad Tomoki is an average teenage boy whose mantra is "anything for a quiet life." For years, ever since he was a child, he has dreamed about a strange girl and has woken in tears. Then, an angel falls into his ordinary world of sadistic neighbors and classmates, devoted childhood friends, and mad scientists. Ikaros is a huge-breasted, submissive "Angeloid" who declares herself Tomoki's servant and will do anything for him. She introduces him to a world of busty, powerful girls wearing collars and chains and longing only to

serve their masters, flying panties in attack formation, and the lechery potential of gender-switching.

There's no nudity in this show based on Suu Minazuki's 2007 manga, but there is a childishly obsessive interest in underwear. There's also no sexual violence, despite the offensiveness of the idea that absolute submission to a pervert enables him to reveal his inner nice guy. The animation is uneven and the music unremarkable, apart from a series of closing songs whose elements of parody and fun would have made for a much better series had they been unleashed throughout the episodes.

The first TV series was followed in 2010 by the video *Heaven's Lost Property: Project Pink*, released with the limited edition of volume 9 of the manga. In the same year a second TV series, *Heaven's Lost Property: Forte*, introduces some more serious plot elements to the fan service (**ARGOT AND JARGON**) without in any way improving on the tastelessness of the first series. Tomoki gets to have conversations with his penis and finds new uses for panties.

Heaven's Lost Property the Movie: Clockwork Angeloid (Sora no Otoshimono: Tokei-jikake no Angeloid) appeared in 2011. The first half summarizes the events of the two TV series from another viewpoint, using new animation mixed with TV clips. The second half resolves one of the dangling plot threads from the second series in predictably crass fashion. If you think a restaurant that serves edible panties sounds like your kind of place, this is your kind of show. At the time of writing, a third TV series has allegedly been greenlit in Japan, proof that few companies lose money underestimating audience taste.

HEAVEN'S MEMO PAD *

2011. JPN: *Kamisama no Memo-cho*. TV series. DIR: Katsushi Sakurabi. SCR: Seishi Minakami, Takayo Ikami. DES: Keiichi Sano, Yutaka Onishi. ANI: Keiichi Sano. MUS: Taku Iwasaki. PRD: JC Staff, AT-X, Lantis, Klockworx, Warner Bros, ASCII Media Works. 25 mins. x 12 eps.

Narumi has moved around a lot because of his father's job. He doesn't make lasting friendships, he just tries to not stand out at each new school. But in his latest school, in Tokyo, two girls start to change all that. His classmate Ayaka drafts him into her

Garden Club—just the two of them—and introduces him to the crowd at the ramen shop where she works after school. They're a strange group of NEETS—people "not in employment, education, or training"—with no apparent purpose in life (EDEN OF THE EAST). But it turns out that this gang of misfits actually work for an agency run by Alice, a childlike weirdo who claims to be an advocate for the dead. After a lifetime of non-involvement, Narumi is suddenly up to his ears in the strangeness of life, thanks to Ayaka.

Hikaru Sugii's book series began its run in 2007 and was adapted for manga in 2010 before making the leap to TV. Sakurabi and Minakami adapt freely, changing the story sequence to create a series of short arcs that compensate to some extent for the episodic problem-of-the-week nature of the story, altering key characters and leaving many questions unanswered. The kooky Lolita detective, her bumbling but heroic assistant, and the strong overtones of *moe* fan service may recall GOSICK, but there are some interesting plot elements and a fascinating assembly of characters. A loli-girl show with a yakuza baseball episode is worth seeing just for its cheek.

HEAVY

1990. Movie. DIR: Shinya Hanai. SCR: Noboru Ishiguro, Shoji Imai. DES: Masao Nakada. ANI: Masao Nakada. MUS: N/C. PRD: Artland. 50 mins.

Yet another boxing anime, this time based on SWORD OF MUSASHI–creator Motoka Murakami's 1989 manga from *Shonen Sunday* magazine about an impressionable man taking his father's advice to heart and "fighting for as long as he is still breathing." This takes on a double meaning when Dad needs a life-saving operation, and our hero enters the boxing ring to win the money. ●

HEAVY METAL L-GAIM

1984. JPN: *Jusenki L-Gaim*. AKA: *Heavy War Machine L-Gaim*. TV series, video. DIR: Yoshiyuki Tomino, Minoru Onotani, Yasuhiro Imagawa, Toshifumi Kawase, Osamu Sekita, Iku Suzuki, Toshifumi Takizawa, Kunihisa Sugishima, Hideji Iguchi. SCR: Jiyu Watanabe, Sukehiro Tomita, Mami Watanabe. DES: Mamoru Nagano, Kunio Okawara, Toshifumi

Nagasawa. ANI: Hiroyuki Kitazume. MUS: Kei Wakakusa. PRD: Sotsu Agency, Sunrise, Nagoya TV (TV Asahi). 25 mins. x 54 eps. (TV), 60 mins. x 3 eps. (v).

The immortal Poseidal of Gustgal leads his 24 elite Temple Knights to subdue the Pentagonia System, proclaiming himself Star Emperor. His "second crusade" ends in the year 3975, when he defeats King Camon Wallha V, but Camon hides his heir on the forgotten planet Coam, with a single giant white battle-robot. Fifteen years later, *Prince* Camon, using the name Daba Myroad, leads a revolt on Coam, backed by the arms dealer Amandara Kamanadara, unaware that his supporter is in fact Poseidal himself, supplying weaponry to both sides while a doppelgänger sits on his throne.

A giant-robot show that functioned as a dry run for designer Nagano's later FIVE STAR STORIES, *L-G* boasts the creator's trademark mixture of far-future and fantasy-medieval designs, and many look-alikes of characters from his more famous work. A three-part video series followed, with the initial two parts comprising edited footage from the series, and the third, *L-G: Full Metal Soldier,* adding a coda to the series proper.

HEIDI

1974. JPN: *Alps no Shojo Heidi*. AKA: *Alpine Girl Heidi*. TV series, movie. DIR: Isao Takahata. SCR: Yoshiaki Yoshida. DES: Yoichi Kotabe, Hayao Miyazaki. ANI: Toshiyasu Okada. MUS: Takeo Watanabe. PRD: Zuiyo, Fuji TV. 25 mins. x 52 eps. (TV), 107 mins. (m).

Eight-year-old orphan Adelheid (or Heidi, for short) is taken in by her aunt Dete, who soon packs her off to stay with her old grandfather on Alm mountain in the Swiss Alps. Heidi befriends local goatherder Peter, only to be spirited away once more by Aunt Dete, who takes her to Frankfurt, where she is to be a playmate for the disabled Klara. Pining for her alpine happiness, Heidi heads back to Alm in this famous anime based on the 1881 children's book by Johanna Spyri.

An early masterpiece from GRAVE OF THE FIREFLIES–director Takahata, featuring storyboard contributions from his long-term associate Miyazaki and from future GUNDAM-director Yoshiyuki Tomino, *Heidi* began as an earnest creative experiment

by animators at Zuiyo: a classy animated series in a world of television corner-cutting. Consequently, the *Heidi* production ran far over budget, with cel counts of up to 8,000 per episode and an artistic attention to detail that made it visibly superior to its rivals. As Miyazaki bitterly recounted in his book *Starting Point*, the animators finished the production with palpable relief, only to discover that producers now expected them to output work of equivalent quality all the time. Quality won out, however, in the public arena, where *Heidi* ran against *Space Battleship Yamato* (STAR BLAZERS) in the schedules and drew an equal share of the TV ratings. Famously, the combined figures for *Heidi* and *Yamato* were so high that it was literally impossible for the audience to solely comprise Japanese children. Animators and producers came to understand that there was a bonus audience of interested adults who would sometimes tune in with their children. The success of *Heidi* would lead to a concerted effort to match it, in turn a major influence on the rise of WORLD MASTERPIECE THEATER.

Much-loved across Europe, the anime version is less well-known in English. In Japan, its CINDERELLA qualities and Alpine pastorals would lead to many similar children's shows, such as JULIE THE WILD ROSE, TREASURES OF THE SNOW, and the very odd NETTI'S MARVELOUS STORY. A 1979 movie-edit consists primarily of footage from the Frankfurt episodes with Klara. Of the many live-action adaptations available in English, the most recent is Disney's 1993 version featuring Jason Robards and Jane Seymour. See also VIDEO PICTURE BOOK. Although still largely unknown in its anime version in the U.S., *Heidi* was screened in Spanish in Costa Rica.

HELEN KELLER

1981. JPN: *Helen Keller Monogatari: Ai to Hikari no Tenshi*. AKA: *Story of Helen Keller: Angel of Love and Light*. TV special. DIR: Fumio Ikeno. SCR: Hiroshi Kitahara. DES: Michiyo Sakurai. ANI: Seiji Yamashita. MUS: Hiroshi Ogasawara. PRD: NOW Planning. 81 mins.

At 19 months, baby Helen succumbs to a fever that leaves her deaf and blind. Refusing to believe her case is hopeless, her parents seek help from all quarters, eventually finding "Miracle Worker" Annie Sullivan. Arriving in Helen's native Tuscumbia,

Alabama when the child is seven, Sullivan teaches Helen to communicate purely through touch and the sensation of writing on the palm of the hand. An anime made for broadcast on Japan's National Day for the Disabled, *HK* celebrates the early life of a remarkable woman (1880–1968) who would eventually graduate from Radcliffe College, champion the causes of the disadvantaged, and win many international honors, including Japan's Order of the Sacred Treasure. Thanks to biographies in the **GREAT PEOPLE** series, Keller shares with **COLUMBUS** the distinction of having her life turned into anime on three separate occasions.

HELL GIRL

2005. JPN: *Jigoku Shojo*. TV series. DIR: Hiroshi Watanabe. SCR: N/C. DES: Mariko Oka. ANI: N/C. MUS: Yasuharu Takanashi. PRD: Studio Deen. 25 mins. x 26 eps. (TV1), 25 mins. x 26 eps. (TV2), 25 mins. x 26 eps. (TV3).

It was only a matter of time before someone mated the internet zeitgeist of **SERIAL EXPERIMENTS LAIN** with the Faustian chills of **PETSHOP OF HORRORS**. Kiyoshi Kurosawa tried it in the live-action world with the influential *Kairo* (2001), and anime's take on the same material is *Jigoku Tsushin* ("Hell Dispatches"), an Internet billboard which only appears at midnight, and where disgruntled people can post details of who has wronged them, in the hope that the Hell Girl Ai and her straw dolls will appear to drag sinners into limbo. There is a catch, of course. Anyone wishing evil upon another will sacrifice his or her own soul in the process—compare to similarly devilish small print in the live-action series *Sky High* (*DE). The show was preceded by a manga running in *Nakayoshi* magazine. Since the Internet crosses all time zones, we wonder if the site is only limited to a Japanese midnight, or if it manifests 24 times a day all around the world.

The third season, *Hell Girl: Three Vessels* (2008, *Jigoku Shojo Mitsuganae*), features a somewhat penitent Ai possessing the body of schoolgirl Yuzuki Mikage, and attempting to use this new venue to dissuade others from wasting their eternal souls over often trivial grievances. New characters are introduced and old ones return, providing an ongoing framework to support the episodic grudge-of-the-week plot structure

and helping Watanabe to wrap up his story with an emotional climax. Animation support credits include some names not featured on the first two series, including AIC Digital, Brains Base, and Production I.G, and backgrounds come from Beijing Golden Pinasters Animation Company instead of Green, but the look of the show stays consistent with its precursors.

HELL TARGET

1986. Video. DIR: Yoshinori Nakamura. SCR: Kenichi Matsuzaki. DES: Hiroshi Yokoyama. ANI: Teruyoshi Nakamura. MUS: Rosa Bianca. PRD: Nakamura Pro. 50 mins.

A spaceship is lost near the forbidding planet of Inferno II. Some years later, a second ship with a crew of nine gets there and encounters a monster that rapidly makes mincemeat of most of them. In an obvious anime retread of James Cameron's *Aliens* (1986), the sole survivor, Makuro Kitazato, must destroy the monster before it can surprise a third ship that is already en route.

HELL TEACHER NUBE

1996. JPN: *Jigoku Sensei Nube*. TV series, TV special, movie, video. DIR: Yoshio Misawa. SCR: Takao Koyama. DES: Yoichi Onishi. ANI: Masami Suda, Ken Ueno. MUS: BMF. PRD: Toei, TV Asahi. 25 mins. x 48 eps. (TV), 25 mins. (TVm).

Meisuke Nueno, otherwise known as Nube, is a grade-school teacher whose left hand is possessed by demonic forces, and whose school is constantly beset by apparitions. This anime lightheartedly retells old **JAPANESE FOLK TALES** updated for modern times in much the same tongue-in-cheek fashion as **HAUNTED JUNCTION** and **GHOST SWEEPER MIKAMI**. So it is that Nube is stalked by besotted snow maiden Yukime, must evict a "Hanako" from the toilets (see **HERE COMES HANAKO**), finds a cursed samurai sword in the lost-and-found, and generally busts ghosts in every conceivable part of his school, from the library to the swimming pool. At the height of Japan's 1990s ghost-story trend, *HTN* made it to theaters with the short anime films *HTN: The Movie* (1996), *HTN: Nube Dies at Midnight* (1997), and *HTN's Scary Summer Vacation: Tale of the Sea Phantom* (1997); each replaying the formula of a TV episode, but with a slightly longer running time. In

1998, a readers' survey chose three previously unfilmed chapters from the original 1993 *Shonen Jump* manga by Sho Masakura and Takeshi Okano to be adapted straight to video as *HTN: Sun God vs. the Wall Man*, *HTN: Bukimi-chan of the Seven Mysteries*, and *HTN: Biggest Battle in History—Attack of the Relentless Demon*.

HELLO KITTY *

1989. Video, movie, TV series. DIR: Tameo Ogawa, Yasuo Ishikawa, Masami Hata, Yuji Nichimaki, et al. SCR: Tomoko Konparu. DES: N/C. ANI: Kanji Akabori, Maya Matsuyama. MUS: Toyomi Kojima. PRD: Sanrio. ca. 30 mins. x 50+ eps.

A simply drawn icon, Hello Kitty is the most successful image created by the merchandising corporation Sanrio to sell toys, toasters, luggage, dolls, stickers, and just about anything else. Her fellow brands include **KERO KERO KEROPPI** and **PEKKLE THE DUCK**, but Kitty has a bigger international fan base than the rest put together. A complete rundown of her screen appearances, including all the compilations and recombinations of the last 21 years, would require substantially more space than this book allows, but these are the highlights of her anime resume.

A Hello Kitty version of **CINDERELLA** (1989) was originally shown theatrically before initiating the franchise of *Hello Kitty's Fairy Tale Theater*, where the mouthless icon appeared in many adaptations of famous stories, including her own versions of **SNOW WHITE**, **HEIDI**, *Sleeping Beauty*, **ALICE IN WONDERLAND**, *The Dream Thief*, *Kitty and the Beast*, and the **WIZARD OF OZ** pastiche *Wizard of Paws*. Sensibly realizing that the U.S. market would not bear a single episode to a tape, these were bundled into compilation volumes in America, where they were well received as children's entertainment, and *Santa's Missing Hat* was combined with *Keroppi* crossover *The Christmas Eve Gift*.

Meanwhile, Kitty's popularity continued in Japan—1990 saw a theatrical retelling of **THUMBELINA**, and the Japanese audience was treated to several successive video outings that never made it to the West, including a second *Heidi* pastiche in 1994 and a ten-part series of **JAPANESE FOLK TALES**, including adaptations of *The Hidden Tengu*, **MOMOTARO**, *Kintaro*, *The Snow Maiden*, **THE**

MONKEY AND THE CRAB, *Princess Kaguya* (see REI REI), and HERE COMES THE MOUSE BRIDE. Kitty also featured in several video specials with fellow Sanrio character BAD BATZ MARU (see same) and the old-time Japanese adventures *Ratboy* and *Return of the Tanuki* (both 1989).

Other stories were more original, including some set in Kitty's hometown of London, such as *The Day the Clock Stopped* (1992), in which Kitty and sister Mimi have to restart Big Ben, and *HK: Aliens in London* (1992), in which the gullible sisters are convinced that two jewel thieves are visitors from outer space. Other outbreaks of the Kitty virus were aimed squarely at impressing parents. *HK: Mom Loves Me After All* (1992) deals with a child's jealousy for a newborn sibling, telling the tale of Kitty's mother babysitting for someone else. *We Love Hello Kitty* (1993) ex-plained the wonders that await good little kittens on their birthdays, when they get presents from all their friends and the chance to eat their favorite food. The franchise jumped on the eco-bandwagon in 1994, the same year as POM POKO, with *HK: Everyone Must Protect the Forest*. In 1997, the parental propaganda machine began rolling in earnest with a succession of short informational videos including *Trying Hard, Cleaning up the House, Going to the Toilet Alone, Sleeping Alone, Being Careful Outdoors, Saying Sorry, Table Manners,* and *Enjoying the Bath,* all followed by the winning subtitle *"… with Hello Kitty."* The late 1990s saw the Kitty team animate a six-part video series of AESOP'S FABLES in their own inimitable style. The *"… with Hello Kitty"* series, combined with *"Kitty Parody Theater"* (possibly a new name for the fables or fairy tales above) was rebroadcast on Japanese TV as the 39-episode *Kitty's Paradise* (1999), which was swiftly snapped up for the U.S. market by Saban Entertainment during the mad rush to option Japanese children's animation post-POKÉMON. This was particularly ironic, since it was now sought after because "anime sells," whereas it had clearly been selling rather well without the "anime" tag for several years already.

In 2014, a spokesman for Sanrio caused an international stir by asserting that Hello Kitty was "not a cat" but actually a British schoolgirl, briefly exposing fans all over the world to the kind of intricate and picky semantic micromanaging that periodically drives anime encyclopedists mad. We get such memos all the time, about hair colors, release dates, spelling of characters' names … you name it. In other news, you are not reading an encyclopedia, but a small squirrel called Dave.

HELLO SANDYBELL

1981. AKA: *Sandy Jonquille.* TV series. DIR: Hiroshi Shidara, Kazumi Fukushima, Hideo Kozawa. SCR: Noboru Shiroyama. DES: Makoto Sakurai. ANI: Shoji Yanagise. MUS: Takeo Watanabe. PRD: TV Asahi, Toei. 25 mins. x 47 eps.

Sandybell is a happy-go-lucky Scottish girl who lives in the highlands and adores local nobleman Mark Wellington, though he is betrothed to Kitty Shearer, a rich heiress. Sandybell cherishes a dream of becoming an artist, but when her father, Leslie Christie, falls ill, she discovers that she is adopted. Sensing her real parents are still alive somewhere, she heads for London, where she stays with Can-Can, an old family friend. She becomes a cub newspaper reporter, traveling all over Europe in search of clues about her own past, while the venal Kitty plots to ruin her future. Like its more melancholy predecessor CANDY CANDY, *HS* may look European, but has an all-Japanese origin: it is based on a book by Shiro Jinbo, whose illustrator Makoto Sakurai also provided basic designs for the animated version.

HELLO SPANK

1981. JPN: *Ohayo Spank.* TV series, movie. DIR: Shigetsugu Yoshida, Susumu Ishizaki, Satoshi Dezaki, Naoto Hashimoto. SCR: Satoshi Kaneko, Masaaki Sakurai. DES: Shizue Takanishi, Yukari Kobayashi. ANI: Takao Kasai. MUS: Koji Makaino. PRD: TMS, TV Asahi. 10 mins. x 10 eps. (TV), 50 mins. (m).

When teenage Aiko Morimura's father disappears on his yacht, her mother gets a lucrative hat-designing job in Paris. Instead of going with her, Aiko stays with her uncle and his dog, Pappy. With predictable Japanese pathos, Pappy is soon killed in a road accident. The arrival of a new dog, Spank, brings a smile back to Aiko's face, even if Spank is constantly getting her and her friends into trouble. *Spank* began as a 1978 manga in the girls' magazine *Nakayoshi,* drawn by Shizue Takanashi from a script by Shunichi Yukimuro, the writer of dozens of anime including CANDY CANDY, but curiously not this one. In 1982, Spank returned for an all-new movie outing about his falling for the mongrel puppy Anna, whose handsome male owner has newly transferred to Aiko's school.

HELLS *

2008. AKA: *Hells Angels.* Movie. DIR: Yoshiki Yamakawa. SCR: Yoshiki Yamakawa, Kazuyuki Fudeyasu. DES: Kazuto Nakazawa, Hiroshi Ono. ANI: Kazuto Nakazawa. MUS: edison. PRD: Madhouse Studios, Hells Production Committee, Nippan, Q-Tec. 117 mins.

Rushing to a new school with a lot on her mind, Linne Amagane doesn't even realize she's been hit by a truck and killed. She just thinks her new classmates are rather strange. But the Destinyland high school has more surprises in store for Linne. It's the scene of a battle between good and evil that stretches all the way back to the Bible, and people from the world of the living can be sucked into its nightmare reality.

Shinichi Hiromoto's 2002 manga inspired Madhouse's movie, which we have filed as an "English-language release" on account of its appearance at several film festivals and on English-subtitled Blu-ray in Japan. It's a mess of a movie with a preachy, didactic plot, uneven pace, too much exposition and a casual appropriation of Western culture, from Cain and Abel to Minnie Mouse. It never misses a chance to pound the audience over the head with hidden meaning: yes, Disneyland and Destinyland sound pointedly similar pronounced by Japanese speakers, and the principal is called Helvis for the most obvious reason. Yet its sketchy, apparently casual visual style looks enticingly cool, as if Tim Burton at his best had gone over to work at Madhouse. The characters could be dolls from the Monster High line. Visually, there's nothing to dislike. It's also hard to dislike Madhouse's sheer daring in making movies with no real commercial potential just to let their directors have a chance to develop. *Hells* might have been a great movie instead of an interesting curiosity if Yamakawa had been instructed to develop a relationship with a strict and experienced editor.

HELLSING *

2001. TV series, video. DIR: Umanosuke Iida, Yasunori Urata. SCR: Chiaki Konaka. DES: Toshiharu Murata, Yoshitaka Kohno. ANI: Tomoaki Kado, Toshiharu Murata. MUS: Yasushi Ishii. PRD: Gonzo, Pioneer, Fuji TV. 23 mins. x 13 eps. (TV), 50 mins. x 10 eps. (v).

Vampires stalk the shadowy streets of a London bathed in permanent fog. A secret society fights an infestation of the undead as irresponsible bloodsuckers allow the ghoulish survivors of vampire feasts to proliferate. There are zombies in Cheddar, ghouls in the Home Counties, and werewolves in London. As for the good guys, the Royal Order of Religious Knights, also known as Hellsing, their chief agent is a vampire himself, known only as Alucard (spell it backward …).

Night-time sequences were usually avoided in anime pre-digital, as it always works out to be more expensive to get the lighting and shading right, but *Hellsing* bucked the trend with stark contrasts and blood-red evening skies. Chiaki Konaka, creator of **MALICE DOLL**, provides a script that recalls some of the better horror of recent years (**HORROR AND MONSTERS**). With its crack teams of military paranormal investigators thrown into chaos by creatures of the night and a secret organization devoted to defeating an infestation of vampires, it is best described as the anime incarnation of *Ultraviolet*, incorporating a number of motifs common to vampire legends and popular folktales of the 20th century. These include a growing number of allusions to an ancient "dark continent," implying, in the process, that the vampire known in *Hellsing* as Incognito may have once ruled Egypt in the guise of the god Set.

Hellsing is also another anime to add to that small but growing list that chooses the British Isles as an exotic, inscrutable location. Kohta Hirano's original manga in *Young King Ours* magazine played up the spires and buttresses of old London, and the anime incarnation keeps locations including the Tower of London, the British Museum, and Waterloo Station. There is an equally impressive attention to linguistic detail, as demonstrated by a dubbing script carefully polished by Taliesin Jaffe, which rips out all Japanese exposition that would only come across as pedantic in English. The majority of the leads also sport flawless British accents, an adherence to the author's original intention that makes *Hellsing* one of those true rarities, a dub like **GUNSMITH CATS** or **LICENSED BY ROYALTY** that often plays better in English than the Japanese original.

The series was subsequently remade on video as *Hellsing Ultimate* (2005), a deliberate attempt to revisit the storyline of the original manga and to adhere to it far more closely than the TV version, with a script by Hideyuki Kurata and Yosuke Kuroda. Note that there is considerable argument over nomenclature in *Hellsing*, since manga and anime translations disagree on the best way to render some of the names, and several errors have crept in. In a typical example, a *baobhan sith* (a type of Scottish vampire) infiltrates the *Hellsing* base, using the alias Laura, itself a reference to Sheridan Le Fanu's vampire novel *Carmilla* (1872). The English dub, however, does not spot the Scottish folklore reference, and instead renders the creature as a *bubbancy*. **LNV**

HELTER SKELTER: HAKUDAKA NO MURA

2009. AKA: *Helter Skelter! Clouded Village; Turbid Village*. Video. DIR: Hitomi Yokoyama. SCR: Ren Soto. DES: Furubayashi. ANI: Furubayashi. MUS: N/C. PRD: Suzuki Mirano. 29 mins. x 2 eps.

Three model-girl sisters go to the country for a photo shoot. While there, they learn that a local religious ritual known as the Hunter Festival is about to take place. Curiosity leads them to participate, and wild sexual activity ensues in this porn anime based on a game by Guilty. **N**

HENNEKO *

2013. JPN: *Hentai Oji to Warawanai Neko*. AKA: *Hentai Prince and the Stony Cat*. TV series. DIR: Yohei Suzuki, Tomoaki Ota. SCR: Michiko Ito. DES: Haruko Iizuka. ANI: Yukako Tsuzuki, Sumie Kinoshita. MUS: Tomoki Kikuya. PRD: JC Staff, Bushiroad, Frontier Works, Furyu Corporation, Media Factory. 24 mins. x 12 eps.

Prize pervert Yoto Yokodera discovers the existence of a magical stone cat that can remove personality traits from people unhappy with their characters. He tracks it down and wishes to be more truthful with his expression of his feelings, thereby hoping to get through his shyness and get some action. Tsukiko is a girl who wishes to be more discreet in her dealings with people. Both their wishes are granted after a fashion, with Yoto now physically unable to lie, and Tsukiko entirely unable to show any emotions.

Based on the book series by Sou Sagara, *Henneko* plumbs the depths of teenage introspection, offering its characters the tempting chance to reinvent themselves, only to discover that they preferred the way things were. Personality traits are not destroyed in this series, so much as they are reassigned to others, causing Yoto and Tsukiko to search their school for pupils who might be behaving differently, for whom their discarded character traits might be perceived as a benefit. The result could have been an intriguing psychological drama, embraced by the creative staff on this show, with Tsukiko's true feelings conveyed solely by actions and body language, and Yoto's truth-overdose playing havoc with Japanese etiquette and social norms. However, far too much effort is devoted to establishing the usual bawdy objectifications of a harem show (**ROMANCE AND DRAMA**), while the ease of swapping and blending character traits only serves to highlight the essential shorthand of so many anime, that "characters" are often little more than a short list of box-ticking *characteristics*, rather than believable beings invested with true personalities.

HENTAI EXPRESS *

2007. JPN: *Inyoku Tokkyu Zetsurin'o*. AKA: *Hentai Express: Lust Train*. Video. DIR: Kenji Taru. SCR: Haruhi Sakura. DES: Samurai Gomon, Hiroshiro Shigeta, Atamadochichi Tan. ANI: N/C. MUS: PolyphonicBranch. PRD: schoolzone. 24 mins.

The Oraga Stone is a powerful energy source activated by female orgasm. It can power cyborgs or trains. When an evil professor steals the M-77 express, the only way to stop him is with a very special service—the Lust Train. A few brave women must save the world in this piece of porn for trainspotters. Not to be confused with **LUSTFUL TRAIN**. **N**

HER AND HER AND HER

2009. JPN: *Kanojo x Kanojo x Kanojo—San*

Shimai to no Dokidoki Kyodo Seikatsu. AKA: *Her and Her and Her: Three Sisters and the Heartbeat of Daily Life.* Video. DIR: Ko Murayama. SCR: N/C. DES: Ko Murayama. ANI: Ko Murayama. MUS: N/C. PRD: Studio Eromatick, MS Pictures/Milky. 30 mins. x 3 eps.
Haruomi Shiki used to play with the three Orifushi sisters when he was a child. Now he's staying at their home, so all four of them are going to get much closer. Based on a 2008 porn game by Crossnet. **N**

HER NEED FOR EMBRACE

1989. JPN: *Dakaretai Onna.* Video. DIR: Yoshihisa Matsumoto, Akane Yamada. SCR: Milk Morizono. DES: Milk Morizono. ANI: N/C. MUS: N/C. PRD: Toei. 45 mins. x 2 eps.
Several erotic short stories taken from a manga of the same name by the controversial erotic creator Milk Morizono, featuring high-quality animation and vignettes along such themes as *Hold Me Harder, Hold Me Lustier,* and *Sunday Ecstasy.* See also **MILKY PASSION.** This release is notable for being one of those rare erotic anime that flirts with live-action content—risky because much of the appeal of erotic anime seems founded on its audience's lack of access to "real" pornography. Cutaway sequences show real women going about their daily lives (such as taking a shower, of course), and confessing their sexual histories to add a note of realism. **N**

HERCULE POIROT AND MISS MARPLE

2004. JPN: *Agatha Christie no Meitantei Poirot to Marple/Mabel.* AKA: *Agatha Christie's Famous Detectives Poirot and Mabel.* TV series. DIR: Naohito Takahashi. SCR: Hiroshi Shimokawa. DES: Sayuri Ichiishi. ANI: Takaya Mizutani. MUS: Toshiyuki Watanabe. PRD: OLM, NHK. 28 mins. x 39 eps.
Adaptations of Agatha Christie stories are tweaked to accommodate young Mabel West and Arthur Hastings as points of identification for a teen audience. Sixteen-year-old Mabel is Miss Jane Marple's great-niece, and when she finds herself working for Belgian detective Hercule Poirot she has a great opportunity to learn about life as well as detection methods. Poirot's assistant Arthur Hastings, transformed from a middle-aged chap into a handsome youth, is Mabel's love interest in anime versions of *The Mysterious Affair at Styles, The ABC Murders,* and *The 4.50 from Pad-*

dington, all licensed from Christie's estate, with bonus historical consultancy provided by a Tokyo University professor. Compare to **EMMA** and **THE CASEBOOK OF CHARLOTTE HOLMES.** The 1989 BBC live-action series *Poirot,* starring David Suchet as the detective, previously aired on NHK in 1991 as *Meitantei Poirot (Famous Detective Poirot).* Note the chance homophony of "Marple" and "Mabel" in Japanese allowing to imply rather more involvement of one than the other—a similar trick was tried in **THUNDERBIRDS 2086.**

HERE COMES HANAKO

1994. JPN: *Gakko no Kowai Uwasa: Hanako-san ga Kita.* AKA: *Scary Stories of Your School: Here Comes Hanako; Phantom of the Toilet.* Video. DIR: Tetsuo Yasumi. SCR: Yukiko Matsui, Nobuyuki Hori. DES: Tac. ANI: N/C. MUS: Ko Suzuki. PRD: Tac. 10 mins. x 10 eps.
The granddaddy of all children's anime ghouls remains Shigeru Mizuki's **SPOOKY KITARO.** However, the 1990s were dominated by "Hanako," an iconic figure that came out of nowhere. The indisputable hit of Toru Tsunemitsu's urban myth collection *School Ghost Stories* was the short story "*Ghost Toilet,*" set in an elementary school in Nagano Prefecture (**HORROR AND MONSTERS**). In the dark, dank toilet on the north side, the fourth stall was said to be permanently locked. Students forcing the door discover the corpse of a girl in a red dress, presumed to have committed suicide, whose ghost is said to haunt the restrooms, eternally trying to lead schoolboys into hell with the temptation "Shall we play?" This tall tale has become the defining spooky story for the Japanese children who grew up in the 1990s, creating a subgenre in children's books beginning with *Hanako in the Toilet: Scary Stories of Your School* (1993). This in turn was adapted into the *Here Comes Hanako* manga by several artists, most of whom also wrote the anime version that was broadcast as part of the TV program *Ponkikki Kids* in 1994. In that special, Hanako, with a deathly pallor like a juvenile Elvira, introduces episodes such as *The Haunted Cinema* and *The Cursed Promise Ring.*
Hanako also appeared in her own 50-minute anime movie, *Hanako of the Toilet* (1996), directed by Akitaro Daichi,

which recast the wild-child as a ghostbuster keeping evil spirits at bay. The franchise reached live-action cinema with Joji Matsuoka's 1996 film of the same name and *New Hanako* (1998), which returned to the original story by featuring a group of high school sleuths contacting Hanako through a Ouija board and saving another classmate from a homeless pervert who is the true cause of all the strange happenings. The phenomenon and its exploitation are parodied in **HAUNTED JUNCTION,** where Buddhist Kazuo wishes to collect "all the Hanakos" from every school in Japan; **DIRTY PAIR** *Flash,* which features a Hanako hologram; and **HELL TEACHER NUBE,** which features a more "traditional" Hanako apparition. **REAL SCHOOL GHOST STORIES** and **SCHOOL SPIRITS** are among its many distant relatives. The generation that grew up watching *Hanako* swelled box office receipts for modern horror such as *Ring* and **ANOTHER** and kept on consuming her appearances in older shows such as **ALIGNMENT YOU! YOU!**

HERE COMES THE MOUSE BRIDE

1979. JPN: *Nezumi no Yomeiri.* Movie. DIR: Daisaku Shirokawa. SCR: Daisaku Shirokawa. DES: N/C. ANI: Sadao Tsukioka. MUS: Shingo Asano. PRD: Toei. 13 mins.
A mouse father seeks the ideal husband for his beloved daughter, but the sun refuses on the grounds that he is not the most powerful thing in the universe. A humble cloud blocks his rays, but the cloud concedes defeat to the wind, who can blow it away. The wind, however, is unable to budge a little girl's house, but the house is unable to rid itself of a troublesome mouse. The lucky mouse marries the bride, and they all live happily ever after. Also adapted as one of the many **HELLO KITTY** retellings of classic folk tales.

HERE IS GREENWOOD *

1991. JPN: *Koko wa Greenwood.* Video. DIR: Tomomi Mochizuki. SCR: Tomomi Mochizuki. DES: Masako Goto. ANI: Masako Goto. MUS: Shigeru Nagata. PRD: Pierrot Project. 30 mins. x 6 eps.
When his brother marries the woman *he* secretly adores, Kazuya moves out of the family home and into the student dorm of Greenwood. There, the heart-broken loner gains the friendship and support he

needs, including his androgynously pretty roommate, Shun Kisaragi, and a gang of sweet-natured but mildly zany boys. With obvious parallels to **MAISON IKKOKU**, the show also incorporates occasional supernatural moments, such as a ghostly haunting that brings out people's true feelings for each other (compare to similar events in **KIMAGURE ORANGE ROAD**). In the group's occasional involvement in sports championships, wacky pranks, and personal problems, it also recalls the more sedate installments of **PATLABOR**. In one episode, Shun's younger brother is kidnapped by the sister of one of the upperclassmen, while in *Here Is Devilwood*, the characters make a fantasy film about wandering swordsman Lemon Herb having to defeat the evil overlord Clorettes. The final episodes involve the arrival of a gangland bad-girl who replaces Kazuya's sister-in-law in his affections, but each of these episodes are merely brief moments from the original 11-volume run of the 1986 manga by Yukie Nasu, serialized in *Hana to Yume* magazine. In a mere six episodes, there is little chance of anything but a general survey of the original's content and themes, which was, of course, exactly what the producers wanted in order to encourage people to go out and buy the manga.

HERITAGE FROM FATHER *

2001. JPN: *Tsubaki-iro no Prisione* [sic]. AKA: *Camellia Prisoner*. Video. DIR: Jiro Fujimoto. SCR: Jiro Fujimoto. DES: Hideki Hashimoto. ANI: Noboru Sanehara. MUS: N/C. PRD: Green Bunny. 30 mins. x 3 eps.
After the death of his father, Akitsugu is contacted by Susan, the pert young secretary in charge of the estate, and asked to take charge of the family affairs. Akitsugu has nursed resentment toward his father for some time, but agrees as long as the secretary remains in her post. He arrives at the family's mountain mansion to discover it occupied by a group of maids that his father kept on the payroll for his own sexual gratification. He is initially angry, although he is eventually won over by the erotic opportunities, but not before an overzealous maid has tried to dispatch him with an ice pick and been raped for her troubles. Additional revelations are not long in arriving, as Susan discovers that she is actually the daughter of the previous owner, and consequently that she has been in an incestuous relationship with both her father and half-brother. The show was confusingly released in the U.S. with haphazard subtitles that localized all names to either English or Chinese, but not the original Japanese. Suspiciously close in plotting to *Mama Mia* in the **SECRET ANIMA** series and based on a game. **ⒸⓃⓋ**

HERMES *

1997. JPN: *Hermes: Ai wa Kaze no Gotoku*. AKA: *Hermes: Winds of Love*. Movie. DIR: Tetsuo Imazawa. SCR: Hermes Scenario Project. DES: Yoshiaki Yokota. ANI: Yoshiaki Yanagida. MUS: Yuichi Mizusawa. PRD: Toei. 114 mins.
Hermes, a youth who it is said will one day overthrow the evil King Minos of Crete, falls in love with the beautiful Princess Aphrodite. After two pointless musical interludes, he rescues her from the tower where she is imprisoned and decides it's time to defeat Minos. To do this, he enlists the help of the Athenian Theseus and Minos' daughter, Ariadne, "the only one who is sane and religious." After a straightforward run through the events of the tale of Theseus and the Minotaur, Hermes turns up at the last moment to kill Minos himself, at which point Theseus and Ariadne sail off into the sunset and out of the story. Hermes is told that he is a reincarnation of the great god Ophealis—though he is told this *by* Ophealis, meaning he spends part of the film talking to himself. He is given a magic staff and does great deeds all over Greece, before rescuing Aphrodite's blind mother from prison and descending into Hell to kill Minos … again. Meanwhile, the childless Aphrodite muses that she wouldn't mind if Hermes took a mistress, only to find that her selfless thoughts have reached the ears of the Goddess of Love. The Goddess shoots her with a magic arrow to make her give birth to an heir. After chatting with some fairies, Hermes resolves to unite Greece, but he suspects it might take a while. Then he defeats his enemies through peaceful means by setting up a trade confederacy which they all want to join.

A lavish but clumsily written combination of Greek myth and half-remembered fairy tales, though occasional scenes of contradictory preaching show its true colors as a publicity vehicle for a religious organization. Based on a book by Ryuho Okawa, the founder of the Institute for Research in Human Happiness (since renamed Happy Science), who claims to be a reincarnation of the same alien being who was once Hermes and Ophealis. As with the later **LAWS OF THE SUN**, it received a very limited theatrical release in the U.S., chiefly at screenings for the faithful, though perhaps a few mystified anime fans were also present and guessing just which scenarists wisely declined to be credited for this one. The film limped out onto video in 2001, amid hype that preferred to emphasize the director's previous work on **DIGIMON** rather than the story's origins.

HERMIT VILLAGE

1963. JPN: *Sennin Buraku*. AKA: *Village of Immortals*. TV series. DIR: Fumiaki Kamigami. SCR: Akira Hayasaka. DES: Tsutomu Kojima. ANI: Susumu Nojima. MUS: N/C. PRD: Eiken. 15 mins. x 23 eps.
The ancient Chinese village of Taoyuan is populated solely by Taoist ascetics. The eldest, Lao Shi, conducts research into the mysteries of magic and alchemy, while his disciple Zhi Huang remains more interested in pleasures of the flesh. He has fallen for three pretty sisters who live nearby, much to Lao Shi's annoyance. Based on a manga serialized in *Asahi Geino* magazine by Tsutomu Kojima, this naughty comedy was the first-ever late-night anime, broadcast just before midnight. Its producers reported that this seemed like a bright idea at the time, although the market for **ADVERTISING AND SPONSORSHIP** was not yet developed enough for any advertisers to willingly support it. The graveyard slot would continue to run erotica such as **LEMON ANGEL**, though by the late 1990s it would also be used to premier serials like **AWOL** that would formerly have gone straight to video in an attempt to amortize rising production costs.

HERO TALES *

2007. JPN: *Jushin Enbu*. TV series. DIR: Osamu Sekita. SCR: Mayori Sekijima. DES: Naoki Aisaka, Kuniaki Nemoto, Iho Narita. ANI: Naoki Aisaka. MUS: Tamiya Terashima. PRD: Studio Flag, GENCO, TV Tokyo, Media Factory, Jushin Enbu Hero Tales Production Committee. 25 mins. x 26 eps.
Taito is a teenager training at the Lian

Tong temple when Imperial General Keiro attacks the temple in search a legendary sword. When Taito tries to rescue the sword it calls forth a mysterious mark on his shoulder, revealing him as one of the Celestial Deities, the seven stars of the Great Bear. Another is Keiro—he and Taito are fated to fight for the sacred sword, and when Keiro carries it off, Taito must find the other star warriors and rescue it.

This is a hero tale by the numbers, with little in the way of tension, unpredictability, or excitement and an unsatisfying ending. Visually attractive, with vivid period costumes and architecture, it's also let down by the animation, which only comes to life in the fight scenes. Sekijima has written better, more involving scripts for shows as varied as PETITE COSSETTE and PLASTIC LITTLE, and Sekita won his spurs as a director on episodes of RONIN WARRIORS and URUSEI YATSURA, but they fail to make this story based on Hiromu Arakawa's 2006 manga fly—it is likely that it wouldn't even have gone into production were it not for Arakawa's high-flying profile in the wake of the anime success of her FULLMETAL ALCHEMIST.

HEROIC AGE *

2007. TV series. DIR: Takashi Noto, Toshimasa Suzuki. SCR: Tow Ubukata. DES: Hisashi Hirai, Ken Otsuka, Naohiro Washio, Yoshiki Kuga, Yoshinori Shiozawa. ANI: Hisashi Hirai. MUS: Naoki Sato. PRD: Xebec, Starchild Records. 25 mins. x 26 eps.

The Golden Tribe once ruled the galaxy, but they departed long ago for the farthest stars. They left their knowledge and technology to the humanoid Silver Tribe, the insectoid Bronze Tribe, and the gigantic Heroic Tribe. The humans of Earth became the Iron Tribe, but were attacked by the Bronze and Silver hordes and scattered across the stars. Many years later, the starship *Argonaut* carries Princess Dhianeila, a human psychic, on a mission of peace, seeking the mythical savior of the human race. The ship's crew find a boy called Age on a devastated planet, not knowing that by rescuing him they are changing the fate of the Universe.

It's Hercules in space, with giant cyberoids. Greek myths (RELIGION AND BELIEF) have long been fertile hunting grounds for studios in search of a story—

look at ULYSSES 31 or SAINT SEIYA. Unfortunately a mythic backdrop only works with compelling characters and good plotting, and here an impressive backstory goes to waste for want of anything driving the front end. There is some stunningly beautiful design and art going on in the background, and the score is dramatic, creating a sense of wonder that flies out the window as soon as the script kicks in. This is something of a surprise, since Tow Ubukata is not only an award-winning novelist in his own right, but a published author of how-to manuals on writing anime. Not like this, we hope.

HEROIC LEGEND OF ARSLAN, THE *

1991. JPN: *Arslan Senki*. AKA: *Arslan; Chronicle of Arislan*. Video. DIR: Mamoru Hamatsu, Tetsuro Amino. SCR: Tomoya Miyashita, Kaori Takada. DES: Sachiko Kamimura. ANI: Kazuya Kise. MUS: Norihiro Tsuru, Yasuo Urakami. PRD: Animate Film. 60 mins. x 2 eps., 30 mins. x 4 eps.

King Andragoras of Persia (or Parthia, or Parse, or Palse) wars against the invading Lusitanian army, while his son, Arslan, gathers a band of adventurers about him, including the disgraced officer Daryoon. Andragoras is defeated with sorcerous fog and imprisoned by the enigmatic usurper Silver Mask. Meanwhile, Hermes, agent of Silver Mask, searches for the legendary sword of Ruknabard, which once belonged to Kai Hoslo, the first King of Kings. Arslan assembles an army of a hundred thousand and marches on Silver Mask, while a second party tries to stop Hermes, lest he awake the evil snake-king Zahak.

Arslan began as a series of novels by LEGEND OF GALACTIC HEROES–creator Yoshiki Tanaka. It was very loosely inspired by several genuine medieval Arslans, most notably the one taken hostage after leading a hundred thousand archers against Mahmud of Ghazna, and whose nephews founded the Seljuk Empire. Other models include Ali Arslan, who founded the Qarak-hânid dynasty in modern-day Turkestan, and Alp Arslan, who captured the Byzantine Emperor Romanus IV at the battle of Manzikert in 1071. Tanaka's dates do not match any single historical event (even if we count by the Muslim system), but the maps in the novels are clearly based on historical Persia, stretching from

contemporary Baghdad to Kashmir and bordered by the Caspian Sea and the Persian Gulf. Like Robert E. Howard's *Conan* series, *Arslan* mixes history and fantasy with impunity, with the Romanesque "Lusitanians" to the west and Rajendra's "Sind" kingdom to the east—for all the effort, Tanaka might as well have set it in the far future and be done with it, à la ALEXANDER. To an uneducated Japanese audience however, it all looks equally exotic, much as Western moviegoers rarely concern themselves with the difference between, say, kung fu and karate.

From its early heyday when the videos were premiered in movie theaters, the *Arslan* series soon declined. Later episodes show a fall in budget, with a different production team, simplified designs, slashed running times, low-quality animation, and the ditching of the earlier diplomacy for a simplistic quest modeled on KING ARTHUR AND THE KNIGHTS OF THE ROUND TABLE. The first two parts were translated in the early days of Manga Entertainment, which altered the name to *Arislan* in a futile attempt to avoid "ass" jokes. The company elected to use British voices in an unremarkable dub that nonetheless seems to have impressed a U.S. audience inured to everyone sounding like they attend the same Californian high school (see ESCAFLOWNE). However, the British dub takes considerable liberties with the TRANSLATION, claiming that Andragoras is dead (even though he is later found to be very much alive!) and missing some lines that explain otherwise incomprehensible events. The inferior later episodes passed to Central Park Media, which released them bundled two to a tape. As with UROTSUKIDOJI, the different dub location led CPM to hire a completely different set of actors, as well as altering many of the already-confusing names at the request of the Japanese producers, whose whimsical spelling has been completely ignored in this encyclopedia entry. As with many other anime, *Arslan* exists chiefly to promote the novels and their manga spin-off to a Japanese audience, whose access to the textual continuations of the story leaves them less baffled than English-speakers, who are left with a cliff-hanger but little hope of a sequel.

HEROMAN *

2010. TV series. DIR: Hitoshi Nanba. SCR: Akatsuki Yamatoya, Megumi Shimizu. DES: Shigeto Koyama, Toshinari Tanaka, Yoshihiro Ishimoto, Yumiko Kondo. ANI: Toshihiro Kawamoto, Osamu Kamei, Hisashi Yamamoto, Kazuhiro Miwa. MUS: Metalchicks, MUSIC HEROES. PRD: BONES, BVHE/Disney Dentsu, Bandai Namco Games, Square Enix, TV Tokyo, Wowmax Media. 25 mins. x 26 eps.

Joey is an orphan who lives with his grandmother and works in a restaurant after school. He dreams of owning the latest toy robot, the Heybo, but can't afford one. When he picks up a broken Heybo and names it Heroman, a mysterious flash of lightning transforms it into a giant robot and gives Joey the chance to be the hero he's always dreamed of being. And it's not a moment too soon—his high school science teacher has accidentally summoned the ferocious insectoid Skrugg and they have Earth in their sights.

Marvel frontman Stan Lee came up with the basic plot and is credited with BONES as writer of the 2009 manga illustrated by Tamon Ota. The series was broadcast in Japan in 2010, but although it has streamed on the Internet in subtitled format it has yet to have a U.S. television broadcast. This is a pity, since the show makes good use of Lee's years of experience in seasoning overblown epic plots with heart-tugging human moments, and BONES's ability to render action sequences fluidly and thrillingly, all handled with a restraint in the depiction of gore and death that makes it suitable for nervous parents. The pompous lectures on the nature of heroism and the waste of several dramatic possibilities are disappointing. But overall, even if anime and giant robots aren't usually your thing, this is a series that's easy to enjoy. Compare with **BLADE**, which isn't.

HETALIA *

2009. JPN: Hetalia Axis Powers. TV, movie. DIR: Bob Shirohata, Hiroshi Watanabe. SCR: Takuya Hiramitsu, Kazuyuki Fudeyasu. DES: Masaaki Kannan, Mariko Oka. ANI: Keiichi Matsuda. MUS: Frontier Works. PRD: Studio DEEN, Frontier Works, Media Factory, MOVIC. 5 mins. x 52 eps. (TV1), 80 mins. (m), 5 mins. x 48 eps. (TV2).

Italia is a cute and helpless boy, a pasta-gobbling slacker unworthy of the mighty heritage of his Imperial ancestors. He's not at all sure what to do in a world where America is brash and pushy, Japan is naïve and nervous, Britain is sarcastic and stubborn, Canada is sweetly shy, and Germany fancies the pants off him. So how are the boys going to reduce conflict among themselves and get along together? World peace through racial stereotyping and boys' love, that's how.

Hidekazu Himaruya's four-panel gag strip Axis Powers Hetalia (Hetalia Axis Powers) struck gold online in 2006 by making conflict cuddly. Economic, military, political, and cultural events around World War II (**DOCUMENTARIES AND HISTORY**) are reframed as social and romantic interactions between nations personified as pretty boys. Like most other Japanese romantic comedies (**ROMANCE AND DRAMA**), the story also involves modern holidays and events, so the timeline is not historically accurate. A number of American fans have got hot under the collar about anti-American racism, but Hetalia is equal-opportunity racist; it coats everyone with the same marshmallow. There's a subplot where Chibitalia stays over at Austria's place and a further farrago of nonsense involving the Holy Roman Empire, all rendered in bright colors and basic animation. And as the series progresses, some of the minor nations are even personified as girls; compare with **STRIKE WITCHES** which also deals with World War II via personification, and Timaking's manga Afghanis-tan, which personifies the history of the titular region through cute girls.

Despite this, the series contains nuggets of fact under its frothy coating and has succeeded where generations of educators have failed in making over a century of world politics a topic of fascination to a small but significant proportion of the rich world's teenagers. For those who look beyond its pastel colors and soft lines, it's also often satirical, obligatory when your storyline revolves around a cutely militaristic Germany babysitting the cutely helpless Italy and Japan and trying to turn them into a force for world domination. Print publication commenced in March 2008. The web anime directed by Shirohata led to TV anime. An anime movie, more TV, a game, armies of cosplayers, tons of plushies, and U.S. publication followed. Since 2009 fans have held a yearly "Hetalia Day" in various locations on the weekend closest to United Nations Day (October 24).

The 2010 movie, Axis Powers Hetalia: Paint It, White (Ginmaku Hetalia Axis Powers: Shiroku Nure!), has the boys trying to stop arguing long enough to prevent aliens invading Earth and painting everything white, turning our cuties into faceless blobs in the process. Think Independence Day (1996) with all the disaster-movie tropes but without the eventual unity of purpose. In the same year, the second TV series Hetalia World Series explored the wilder shores of 20th-century history with a detour through the Baltic states and the medieval period. The show also threw in Nekotalia, a series of shorts about all the countries of the world as cats. Hetalia The Beautiful World introduced a new director, writer, and character designer in 2013, but kept to the same jokes and tropes.

HHH TRIPLE H

2010. JPN: HHH Triple Ecchi. Video. DIR: Makoto Kasahara. SCR: Taifu Sekimachi. DES: Toshihide Masutate. ANI: N/C. MUS: N/C. PRD: Mary Jane, Studio Eromatik. 20 mins. x 4 eps.

High school senior and straight-A student Shigure Takashima is considered an idol by her classmates, but she has a dark secret. After school she masturbates in empty classrooms fantasizing about what would happen if someone walked in. One day she chooses a classroom with someone already in it: Kita Komatsu, her junior classmate, who is supposed to be cleaning. They agree to share the secret, and Kita now has to satisfy a sex-addicted girlfriend. The second episode introduces the sex-mad Konami and her stepbrother, episode 3 has a father getting his wildly overdeveloped daughter pregnant, and episode 4 wraps up the tale of lust-crazed Shigure and the hapless Kita. Based on the 2009 manga by DISTANCE, all the sex in this story is consensual and the title leaves viewers in no doubt as to the content—provided of course they're not so new to anime that they have yet to identify the terms hentai, its initial H, and the initial's Japanese pronunciation "ecchi" (**ARGOT AND JARGON**). The cover, however, should leave them in little doubt. **Ⓝ**

HIDAMARI SKETCH *
2007. AKA: *Sunshine Sketch*. TV series, video. DIR: Akiyuki Shinbo, Ryoki Kamitsubo, Kenichi Ishikura, Yuki Yase. SCR: Nahoko Hasegawa, Natsue Yoguchi, Masashi Kubota, Rima Kitaki, Miku Oshima. DES: Yoshiaki Ito, Hisaharu Iijima. ANI: Yoshiaki Ito. MUS: Tomoki Kikuya. PRD: SHAFT, TBS, Aniplex, Hobunsha, MOVIC. 24 mins. x 12 eps. (TV1), 24 mins. x 2 eps. (v1), 25 mins. x 13 eps. (TV2), 25 mins. x 3 eps. (v3), 25 mins. x 12 eps. (TV3), 25 mins. x 2 eps. (v3), 25 mins. x 2 eps. (v4), 25 mins. x 12 eps. (TV4).
Yuno has been accepted into the high school of her dreams, a specialist arts institution. She'll have to live away from home, but she's looking forward to an interesting new life packed with fascinating people. Just how fascinating she has no idea until she moves into Hidamari Apartments. The ups and downs of looking after oneself, as well as dealing with school life, are made much easier by her new friends.

Based on Ume Aoki's 2005 four-panel manga strip, this well-worn theme could have been just another *moe* moment but for the intervention of Akiyuki Shinbo. He first directed anime in 1990, on Studio Pierrot's romantic comedy MUSASHI ROAD. He's often been associated with SHAFT, where he also directed the surreal PETITE COSSETTE. Here the surreality is less disturbing and more entertaining, as he and his gifted team break each flat frame into stylized shapes, happy colors, whip-snappy visual gags, and abstract images.

The first TV series was released on DVD with two bonus episodes, and quickly followed in 2008 by another TV series, *Hidamari Sketch x 365*. This had a bonus DVD-only episode and two further video releases under the same title in 2009. Kamitsubo, who had assisted Shinbo on the first series, is credited as unit director for the title sequence. In 2010 a third TV series, *Hidamari Sketch Three Stars (Hidamari Sketch Hoshimittsu)*, took us into Yuno's second year at high school, with new students moving into Hidamari Apartments for more of the same EVERYDAY ANIME fun. Shinbo stepped down from the top slot to allow Ishikura to take over as series director, but the core writing team of Hasegawa and Yoguchi remained unchanged. Once again, there were two video-only special episodes in the same year. In 2011 two

more videos were released under the title *Hidamari Sketch x SP*, and a fourth TV series, *Hidamari Sketch Honeycomb*, was aired in 2012 with Yuki Yase in the series director's seat. Yase's career began as a production runner on NOEIN, and has included episode director credits on six other series including DURARARA and WHITE ALBUM, so Shinbo's experienced hands stayed on the reins. The consistent level of directing and writing continuity has resulted in a series far superior to most of its genre.

HIGEPIYO THE BEARDED CHICK
2009. JPN: *Higepiyo*. TV series. DIR: Atsushi Takeyama. SCR: Natsuko Takahashi. DES: Hiroko Okugi, Mika Nakajima. ANI: N/C. MUS: Toshio Masuda. PRD: Kinema Citrus, NHK. 5 mins. x 39 eps.
Higepiyo is a feisty little chick with a moustache and a talent for picking fights. He's the pet of third-grader Hiroshi and lives with him and his family. His constant quest to define his own masculinity leads to gently humorous antics. This series is based on Risa Ito's 2007 manga and was successful enough to inspire a further manga in *Ribon* magazine in 2009. Ito's earlier work *Ebichu Minds The House* was animated for a more adult audience as part of MODERN LOVE'S SILLINESS.

HIGH SCHOOL AGENT
1988. Video. DIR: Junichi Sakata. SCR: Izo Hashimoto. DES: Takumi Tsukasa. ANI: Takumi Tsukasa. MUS: Scrap. PRD: JC Staff, Agent 21. 30 mins. x 2 eps.
Teenager Kosuke Kanemori is a secret agent for the international "VN" spy network. Using his computer hacking skills, he tracks international criminals all the way from New York to Spain. In his second outing, he is packed off to the Arctic Circle, where Neo-Nazis are trying to raise a sunken U-boat that holds a sinister WWII secret onboard. Based on a manga by Satoshi Tanimura in *Comic Burger*, this anime foreshadows similar Bond-style adventures in SPRIGGAN. **Ⓥ**

HIGH SCHOOL DXD *
2012. TV series, video, Special. DIR: Tetsuya Yanagisawa. SCR: Takao Yoshioka. DES: Junji Goto, Shigemi Ikeda. ANI: Junji Goto, Maki Fujii, Masahiko Yoda. MUS: Ryosuke Nakanishi. PRD: TNK, AT-X, Fujimi Shobo, GENCO,

Lantis, Media Factory, Showgate. 25 mins. x 12 eps. (TV1), 25 mins. x 2 eps. (v), 3 mins. approx. x 6 eps. (special), 25 mins. x 12 eps. (TV2).
Issei Hyodo is an average second year high school boy—not too bright and sex-obsessed, with a reputation for being a complete creep at school. On his first date, he is killed by the girl he's dating. Turns out she's a fallen angel with a vicious streak. But this isn't the end of Issei—he is reborn as a demon thanks to the intervention of one of the hottest senior girls at his school, also a devil and now his master. A war between angels and demons is coming, and Issei has powers he never even suspected. Both sides want to control him—he just wants to grab as much female flesh as possible.

High school harem anime with nudity and fan service galore are not exactly uncommon (see HIGHSCHOOL OF THE DEAD) but the angels-and-demons plotline and digs at organized religion give this one more of a plot to punctuate the leering. Ichiei Ishibumi's book series bundled an unaired episode from the first series with volume 13 of the novel in September 2012, and bundled a further episode with volume 15 in May 2013. These episodes have been numbered 13 and 14, but as they remain unaired on TV, they are listed as videos here. Six standalone three-minute specials packed with even more fan service were bundled with the DVD and Blu-ray releases. A second TV series, *High School DxD New*, followed in 2013 from the same team. **Ⓝ**

HIGH SCHOOL GIRLS AND THE LEWD TEACHER 4
2011. JPN: *JK to Inkyo Kyoshi 4*. Video. DIR: N/C. SCR: PON. DES: Hikaru Kinohara. ANI: N/C. MUS: N/C. PRD: PoRO. 30 mins. x 2 eps.
Two busty babes named Satsuki and Shizuka transfer to a new high school. The head teacher allows them to keep working as models outside school hours, on condition they take a teacher along as a chaperone. Shizuka is a selfish, egotistical bitch and forces Satsuki to join her in making fun of the hapless teacher—until he turns the tables. The second episode is mostly him having sex with both girls. Based on an erotic PC game by Blue Gale's Blue Gale Light label, one of a whole raft

of game-based anime involving schoolgirls having sex with men in different professions—convenience store clerks, hotel staff, nightwatchmen, doctors—including a 2012 storyline involving new lead character Hatsune and fictional politicians from the Japanese parliament, *JK to Ero Giin Sensei (JK and the Sex-mad Politican),* which was also scripted by PON and designed by Kinohara. **Ⓝ**

HIGH SCHOOL HONOR

1992. JPN: *High School Jingi.* Video. DIR: Tetsuro Amino. SCR: Keiji Michiyoshi. DES: Hisashi Abe. ANI: Hisashi Abe. MUS: N/C. PRD: JC Staff, Nippon Eizo. 50 mins.
Hiroshima gangster Seiji goes undercover in a Tokyo high school to set up a front for moving large quantities of drugs. However, he falls in love with both his attractive fellow teacher Reiko and with the city of Tokyo itself. Local Shinjuku mobsters, however, want him out of town. An adaptation of Shushi Mizuho's manga in *Young Jump* magazine. Not to be confused with Justice, which has a similar Japanese title. **ⓃⓋ**

HIGH SCHOOL KIMENGUMI

1985. Movie, TV series. DIR: Hiroshi Fukutomi, Shin Misawa. SCR: Takao Koyama, Shigeru Yanagawa. DES: Hiroshi Kanazawa. ANI: Hiroshi Kanazawa, Kenichi Chikanaga. MUS: Shunsuke Kikuchi. PRD: Studio Comet, NAS, Fuji TV. 51 mins. (m), 25 mins. x 86 eps. (TV), 25 mins. x 51 eps. (*Tonchinkan*).
A Japanese high school is divided into rigid gangs, including Jocks, Seducers, Bad Girls, and Brains. Paramount among them is the Kimengumi, the "Strange Faces," a five-man team with punning names and strange quirks, who lord it over all the other students. Two summer-vacation episodes were also cut together and shown in theaters as a "movie" version before broadcast. The same crew returned with *Regarding Tonchinkan* (1987, *Tsuide ni Tonchinkan*), a similar series about one particular gang deciding to play at burglary without the knowledge of their schoolmates, each masquerading at different times as the master thief Tonchinkan.

HIGH SCORE

2011. TV series, video. DIR: Hajime Kurihara. SCR: Kazumi Ishizuka. DES: Yuko Kanai. ANI:

N/C. MUS: SLF!! PRD: DLE Inc. 4 mins. approx. x 8 eps. (TV), 4 mins. approx. x 2 eps. (v).
Megumi is a high school girl with a strong personality and a selfish streak, and this short series highlights comical snippets from her everyday life. It was adapted from Chinami Tsuyama's four-panel gag manga, 17 years after its 1994 debut in *Ribon* magazine, focusing on jokes and character tropes with very basic animation. Eight episodes were aired on TV, and two more were added to the DVD release, making them technically videos.

HIGH SPEED JECY

1989. AKA: *Hi-Speed Jecy.* Video. DIR: Shigenori Kageyama. SCR: Sukehiro Tomita, Yukiyoshi Ohashi. ANI: Hidetoshi Omori, Akinobu Takahashi. MUS: Kei Wakakusa. PRD: Studio Pierrot. 30 mins. x 12 eps.
Jecy is an incredibly fast runner who detests all forms of violence but has vowed to avenge the deaths of his parents. He wanders the galaxy in the "living ship" Paolon, which can transform into an elderly gentleman for convenience, accompanied by the love-struck Tiana and a priest from a cult of sadists, searching all the while for the trail of the man who killed his parents. Based on a novel by Eiichiro Saito in the spirit of CRUSHER JOE, this series boasts illustrations from Haruhiko Mikimoto, who also worked as a designer on the adaptation.

HIGH STEP JUN

1985. TV series. DIR: Junichi Sato, Hiroshi Shidara, Yukio Misawa. SCR: Akiyoshi Sakai, Tadaaki Yamazaki, Shunichi Yukimuro. DES: Kazuo Komatsubara. ANI: Kazuo Komatsubara, Michi Himeno, Mitsuru Aoyama, Hirokazu Ishino. MUS: Nozomu Aoki. PRD: Toei, TV Asahi. 25 mins. x 45 eps.
Jun Nonomiya is a child prodigy who loves tinkering with machines and has even invented some robot companions for herself. The real companion she desires is Rei ("Zero"), the class biker boy, but Yoko, another girl in her class, claims to be Rei's fiancée. Beginning in an early Sunday morning slot, this love comedy based on a manga by Yasuichi Oshima changed radically in its latter half. Thrown into a new late Wednesday morning slot, presumably where most of its original audience

wouldn't see it, it ditched the love triangle, packing Rei off to boarding school in England, and transforming into a robot comedy centered on Jun's inventions.

HIGHLANDER: THE SEARCH FOR VENGEANCE *

2007. AKA: *Highlander: Vengeance.* Movie. DIR: Yoshiaki Kawajiri, Hiroshi Hamasaki. SCR: David Abramowitz. DES: Hisashi Abe. ANI: Hisashi Abe, Satoshi Tasaki. MUS: N/C. PRD: Madhouse, Studios, Imagi, Davis-Panzer Productions. 80 mins. (m), 96 mins. (director's cut).
Colin McLeod is an Immortal, fated to survive agelessly unless killed by another Immortal. One such killed his beloved wife, and now Colin is on the trail of revenge in the ruined New York of the 22nd century.

This is that strange hybrid class of animation made in Japan but based on an American product and designed specifically for American consumption (compare to DANTE'S INFERNO). In this case, the product is the franchise that began with the 1986 movie *Highlander* and moved on to the small screen and games with the tagline "there can be only one"—which, sadly, proved untrue. Despite the potential on offer from the infinite options of the *Highlander* franchise, *Search for Vengeance* plumps for a half-hearted post-apocalyptic scenario with actionable similarities to FIST OF THE NORTH STAR—even down to the pantomime villains, plucky street kid, and permanently under-dressed damsels. The narrative also has trouble working out where the Highlands even are, suggesting at one point that Colin McLeod of the clan McLeod comes from northern *England*—those are fighting words in a Glasgow pub. Occasional flashbacks, particularly to the samurai era in Japan, demonstrate just how well this could have gone, but Kawajiri seems to have put little effort into this work-for-hire. Although he is a master at producing scale, action, and tension out of sex and violence, not even a wizard like Kawajiri can do much without a decent script. His brilliant fight set-pieces and chase sequences are floating islands in a swamp of sticky plotting, appalling dialogue and nonexistent character development. Despite the script's shortcomings, the movie's pace and scale are impressive, and the quality of the animation and spectacle puts it closer to the original live-action movie than any of its sequels.

The American producers removed "seven or eight" scenes from the original U.S. release; these were largely restored in the 2008 *Director's Cut* rerelease in Japan. Coproduced by Imagi, the studio that remade ASTRO BOY in 2009 as a CGI movie before folding. **OW**

HIGHSCHOOL OF THE DEAD *

2010. JPN: *Gakuen Mokushiroku High-school of the Dead*. TV series, video. DIR: Tetsuro Araki. SCR: Yosuke Kuroda, Tatsuya Takahashi. DES: Masayoshi Tanaka, Ayu Kawamoto. ANI: Masayoshi Tanaka, Hitomi Ochiai. MUS: Takafumi Wada. PRD: Madhouse, AT-X, Geneon, Showgate. 24 mins. x 12 eps. (TV), 20 mins. (v).

An infection breaks out worldwide, turning people into zombies. Takashi Komuro is determined that he and his friends will survive. Aided by the school nurse, they escape their high school in Japan and set out to discover exactly what happened to turn the world into zombieland. Daisuke Sato's manga with art by Shoji Sato is intensely graphic, and the anime follows suit with a slap and jiggle factor almost equal to the legendary PLASTIC LITTLE and grotesquely gory zombie action along the lines of Yohei Fukuda's live-action 2008 zombie-slasher *Onechanbara*. It's mindless, brain-eating fun, and it continued in 2011 with a one-shot video, *HOTD: Drifters of the Dead*. Notably, the 21st-century zombie trend was so pronounced in the West that Manga Entertainment went looking for the English-language video rights before this show even went into production, based solely on the look of the manga and the fan-bait prospect of the title. **OW**

HIGHWAY JENNY

2006. Video. DIR: Masaaki Fukushi. SCR: N/C. DES: N/C. ANI: N/C. MUS: Blankey Jet City, Kenichi Asai. PRD: Toei Animation, Gentosha. 28 mins.

A rock 'n' roll tragedy, the story of a boy who leaves home for the big city of the future at 16, lives amid turmoil and terrorism, and dies a useless death at 18. The *ga-nime* series (ARGOT AND JARGON) mixes artistic and literary work with themes plucked from mainstream anime and manga, such as this one.

HIIRO NO KAKERA: THE TAMAYORI PRINCESS SAGA *

2012. JPN: *Hi-iro no Kakera*. AKA: *Fragments of Scarlet*. TV series. DIR: Bob Shirohata. SCR: Michiko Yokote, Yoshiko Nakamura, Rika Nakase. DES: Naoyuki Onda. ANI: Naoyuki Onda. MUS: Hikaru Nanase. PRD: Bandai Visual, Enterbrain, Kids Station, Lantis, Movic, Studio Deen, Yomiuri TV. 24 mins. x 13 eps. (TV1), 24 mins. x 13 eps. (TV2).

Tamaki Kasuga is reluctant to take up her family's monster-hunting mantle, when she is told that it is her destiny to save the world. There might be a few perks, though, such as the prospect of being guarded and cosseted by six fiercely pretty boys. As if you couldn't guess, this forgettable reverse-harem (ROMANCE AND DRAMA) is based on a computer game, in which a female lead shuffles her preferences among a bunch of identikit clothes horses. A small sop is thrown to the implied female viewer at the end of each episode, with one of the boys addressing the camera as if he has just come back from a date with (gasp) *you*. Anime encyclopedists are left far more breathless and flustered at the prospect of a production committee so lazy that they cannot even be bothered to translate their own title.

HIKA RYOUJOKU: THE LUST OF SHAME *

2003. JPN: *Hika Ryojoku*. AKA: *Lust of Shame*. Video. DIR: Tokuma Shinohara. SCR: Yasuyuki Muto. DES: Takumi Nishino. ANI: Hiroshi Muneta. MUS: N/C. PRD: Potato House, Five Ways. 30 mins.

Shinichi and Megumi become step-siblings after their parents marry; no great surprise in any anime made since MARMALADE BOY. Shinichi suppresses his growing feelings for his stepsister, but is forced by school bullies to embark on a series of perverse missions. These range from stealing her underwear to taking photographs of her, until he stands up for himself and is punished by being forced to watch as they sexually assault her. **OOW**

HIKARIAN

1997. JPN: *Chotokkyu Hikarian*. AKA: *Super Express Hikarian; Hikarian: Great Railroad Protector*. TV series. DIR: Kazuyuki Hirokawa. SCR: Kazuyuki Hirokawa, Toshiki Inoue, Shunichi Yukimuro. DES: Takeshi Miyao. ANI:

N/C. MUS: N/C. PRD: Tomy. 7 mins. x 154 eps. (TV1), 8 mins. x 52 eps. (TV2).

In a bizarre cross between TRANSFORMERS and *Thomas the Tank Engine*, Hikari the bullet train and his robot allies are struck by a "mysterious light" from the heavens that gives them transforming robot powers to defend Earth from the invading Bratcher Force. Broadcast as part of the children's TV show BUBU CHACHA and tied into a line of toys from Tomy, the series was also edited into 51 half-hour episodes. A second TV series ran in 2002, directed by Hideaki Oba.

HIKARU'S GO *

2001. JPN: *Hikaru no Go*. TV series, TV special. DIR: Shin Nishizawa, Jun Kamiya, Tetsuya Endo. SCR: Yukiyoshi Ohashi. DES: Hideyuki Motohashi, Kanami Sekiguchi, Miyuki Ueda. ANI: Hideyuki Motohashi, Shinichi Miyamae, Takako Onishi, Yoshinori Tokiya. MUS: Kei Wakakusa. PRD: Studio Pierrot, TV Tokyo. 23 mins. x 75 eps. (TV), ca. 80 mins. (TVm1), ca. 80 mins. (TVm2).

Sixth-grader Hikaru Shindo is rummaging in his grandfather's attic when he uncovers a *go* board possessed by the spirit of an ancient champion, Fujiwara no Sai. Sai was once the instructor to a medieval emperor, who committed suicide after being falsely accused of cheating. At first refusing to accept that he's been possessed, especially by something as uncool as an ancient board game champion when he could have been ULTRAMAN or BIRDY THE MIGHTY, Hikaru goes to a *go* parlor to try his and Sai's luck and trashes Akira Toya, a gifted player of his own age, to the astonishment of the old guys who make up the rest of the clientele. As time passes Hikaru comes to understand the complexity of the game and to respect Sai's intelligence and commitment. *Hikaru's Go* cleverly mixes the traditions of the sports genre such as YAWARA! with that buddysubgenre of anime that bestows teens with spirits of the past to help them grow—compare to similar arrangements in USHIO AND TORA and PUPPET MASTER SAKON. A fittingly sedentary game for the couchpotato generation, and easier to comprehend at a basic level than Japan's other national boardgame obsession, *shogi* (which is preferred by all rational individuals, including the anime's bad-guy Tetsuo Kaga, and most anime encyclopedists), *go* may seem at first like a strange choice. But it is precisely the kind of anime one might expect the aging **YU-GI-OH** generation to enjoy, exchanging getting excited about cards for getting excited about little black and white pebbles. It survived for an impressive three seasons on Japanese television, as well as two feature-length New Year's specials that continue Hikaru's career into the international championships. It also contains a subtle commentary on pulling one's own weight—since Hikaru's victories are actually Sai's, Sai eventually leaves him to win games on his own. This leads to Hikaru's temporary withdrawal from the game, and his eventual return with a newfound respect for his long-term rival Akira Toya. Based on the manga in *Shonen Jump* by Takeshi Obata and Yumi Hotta.

HIMAWARI! *

2006. AKA: *Sunflower.* TV series. DIR: Shigenori Kageyama. SCR: Mamiko Ikeda, Yuka Yamada, Masahiro Yokotani, Megumi Sasano. DES: Seiji Kishimoto, Maho Takahashi. ANI: Seiji Kishimoto. MUS: Kei Haneoka, Takeshi Seno. PRD: ARMS, GENCO, Starchild Records, Tohoku Shinsha. 25 mins. x 13 eps. (TV1), 25 mins. x 3 eps. (TV2). Himawari has wanted be a ninja ever since she was rescued by one as a child. On her first day at Ninja High she meets a new teacher, Hayato. He's not a ninja—he teaches social studies—but he still saves her life, and she notices that he has the same marks on his neck as the man who saved her long ago. Little does she know she'll end up saving *him*, and again, and again, in this light-hearted, silly, and highly entertaining ninja comedy. Ever wondered what it would be like to date a *kappa*? If so, this is the show for you. Adapted from GoDo's manga *Himawariden!* with art by Okama; the second series, *Himawari Too!! (Himawaritsu!!),* followed in 2007 from the same team.

HIME-CHAN'S RIBBON

1993. JPN: *Hime-chan no Ribon.* TV series. DIR: Hatsuki Tsuji, Hiroaki Sakurai, Shinji Sakai, Tomohiro Takamoto, Masato Namiki. SCR: Takashi Yamada, Shunichi Yukimuro, Tomoko Konparu, Hiroshi Koda, Shigeru Yanagawa. DES: Hajime Watanabe. ANI: Hajime Watanabe, Masayuki Onchi, Yoko

Konishi. MUS: N/C. PRD: Victor, TV Tokyo. 25 mins. x 61 eps.
A princess from a magical world appears before Himeko and offers her a deal. As part of her magical training, she must observe the behavior of a human girl who resembles her for a whole year. In exchange, Hime-chan (lit.: "little princess") is given a magical ribbon that allows her to transform. A magical-girl story packed full of magic items, talking toys, and problem-solving resolutions in the mold of **CREAMY MAMI**, this anime was based on the 1991 *Ribon* magazine manga by Megumi Mizusawa and actually ran longer than the original, magically defined time limit.

HININDEN

2005. JPN: *Hininden Gausu.* AKA: *Legend of Red Ninja.* Video. DIR: Kan Fukumoto. SCR: Yoshio Takaoka. DES: Rin Shin. ANI: Rin Shin. MUS: N/C. PRD: ARMS, Pink Pineapple. 30 mins.
The beautiful princess Kurama has been imprisoned with her ninja associates Momoka and Kaede in a castle dungeon. The girls attempt to escape but are cornered by a party of soldiers sent to retrieve them. Refusing to be taken back, Kurama calls out to the Moon to answer her plea, and hurls herself from a nearby cliff. Flash forward to the present day, where average boy Daisuke is just about to lose his virginity to his first love Hazuki. Imagine, then, his frustration, as a birthmark on his neck suddenly glows with the light of the Moon, and he is whisked away to Kurama's time, where he inadvertently saves her, is soon seduced by the approachable ladies of the past, and imprisoned in the dungeon himself. Kurama resolves to rescue him, in an erotic anime that mixes ninja lore with the usual sex scenes. ⓁⓃⓥ

HIPPO AND THOMAS *

1971. JPN: *Kabatotto.* TV series. DIR: Hiroshi Sasagawa. SCR: Jinzo Toriumi, Takao Koyama. DES: N/C. ANI: N/C. MUS: Koba Hayashi. PRD: Tatsunoko, Fuji TV. 5 mins. x 560 eps.
A daily breakfast-time treat for the tinies, and five minutes' peace for busy mothers, this long-running micro-series starred good-natured and fairly dim hippo Kaba and big-mouthed bird Totto. Characterized as a good-natured but gullible landlord who indulges the foibles of

his bragging, deceitful tenant, the pair would often be led into trouble by Totto's schemes, but only Totto would suffer the consequences. The result is a cunning object lesson in tolerance and cooperation for the young viewers, who might be expected to see themselves in the naughty Totto and their parents in the long-suffering Kaba. Voice actors Toru Taihei and Machiko Soga were credited, though there were hardly any actual lines, with much of the story being told through expressions and noises. Broadcast as part of a Saban umbrella show called *Tic Tac Toons,* the series also made it into some U.S. territories in a Spanish-language version, hence our decision to file it under the title by which it is most likely to have been seen by American viewers, if they have seen it at all.

HIPPO-KEEPER: A ZOO DIARY

1981. JPN: *Kaba-Encho no Dobutsuen Nikki.* TV special. DIR: Masayuki Akehi. SCR: Makoto Naito, Ryuzo Nakanishi. DES: Kozo Masanobu. ANI: Kozo Masanobu. MUS: Nozomu Aoki. PRD: Toei. 75 mins.
Aging zoo keeper Toshio Nishiyama acquires two young trainees: short-tempered former chef Takeshi Ishizawa and gentle vet Ichiro Hasegawa. Both are surprised by the difficulties they face in a deceptively easy job but persevere through troubles such as an escaped pelican, a dying camel, and the birth of a hippo.
A semiautobiographical series of anecdotes from real-life Tobu Animal Park zookeeper Toshio Nishiyama, who appears at the beginning and end of the film to talk about his love for animals—and to reveal that Ishizawa is in fact a projection of his younger self. Blatant self-promotion for Nishiyama's place of employment, to be contrasted with **GOODBYE LITTLE HIPPO**, which presents a far more negative view of bad times at the rival Ueno Zoo.

HIRANO, TOSHIHIRO

1956–. Sometimes credited, by his own choice, as Toshiki Hirano. Born in Tokyo, Hirano showed a strong aptitude for graphic design and was still a college student in that discipline when he began working part-time at Studios Wombat and Number One. He found full-time employment at Studio Io after showing his skills as an animator on an episode of **DOCTOR SLUMP**. He soon moved to Artland and then AIC, working as an animator on **MACROSS** and **URUSEI YATSURA**. However, it was in the video world that his talents for the horrific truly came to the fore, on shows such as **ICZER-ONE** and **VAMPIRE PRINCESS MIYU** (the latter based on a manga by Hirano's wife, Narumi Kakinouchi).

HIRATA, TOSHIO

1938–2014. Born in Yamagata Prefecture, Hirata graduated from the Department of Western Art at Musashino Fine Arts University in 1961, immediately finding work at Toei Animation as an animator on **THE LITTLEST WARRIOR** and **LITTLE PRINCE AND THE EIGHT-HEADED DRAGON**. He worked for a number of companies, including Mushi Production, Zuiyo (now Nippon Animation), Group Tac, and Sanrio. His directorial debut came with **UNICO**, and later works included the second of the **BAREFOOT GEN** movies and **RAIL OF THE STAR**. In addition to his impressively prolific resumé under his own name, and work such as **AZUKI-CHAN** for which he went entirely uncredited at his own request, he is also sometimes credited under the pseudonym Sumiko Chiba. In later years he continued to work in anime, directing the opening and ending sequences for **CATNAPPED** and working as a key animation supervisor on **METROPOLIS**. He also created the oil painting that forms a major fulcrum of the plot of **THE GIRL WHO LEAPT THROUGH TIME**. His last credited work was as a storyboarder on **SPACE DANDY** in the year of his death, thereby spanning an impressive six decades of anime history.

HIS AND HER CIRCUMSTANCES *

1998. JPN: *Kareshi Kanojo no Jijo*. AKA: *Tales at North Hills High; Secret Diary; KareKano*. TV series. DIR: Hideaki Anno, Kazuya Tsurumaki. SCR: Hideaki Anno. DES: Tadashi Hiramatsu. ANI: N/C. MUS: Shiro Sagisu. PRD: Gainax, JC Staff, TV Tokyo. 25 mins. x 26 eps.

Yukino Miyazawa is the most popular girl at school and a permanent straight-A student, her frantic home life hidden to preserve her seemingly effortless perfection. Her classroom kingdom is invaded by a newcomer, the handsome Soichiro Arima, who competes with her for every

prize and accolade. Both are appointed as class reps and forced to work together. Behind icy masks of politeness, the pair fight a private battle of wills and slowly begin to fall in love.

Based on a 1996 manga by Masami Tsuda in *Hana to Yume* magazine, *H&HC* effortlessly outclasses its look-alike U.S. cousin *Ally McBeal* in its dramatic innovation and use of surreal "cartoon" effects in a contemporary sitcom. In Japan, it owes a debt to earlier comedies of manners such as **GOLDFISH WARNING** and **REIKO SHIRATORI I PRESUME**, throwing in Greek choruses of cynical siblings, split-screens, and squashed-down cartoon versions of the lead characters. In terms of off-the-wall experimentation, it rivals the earlier **FIST OF THE NORTH STAR**—not just stop-motion and live action, but one episode features a character whose head is a photograph of a Gainax staff member, while another is animated with paper cutouts, until Yukino bursts into real flames. As with director Anno's earlier **EVANGELION**, onscreen captions and subtitles comment on the action and warp the characters' meanings, perfectly capturing the adolescent power struggles and hypocrisies of the original. A very funny satire about unlikable people who are nevertheless sympathetic characters.

HISAICHI ISHII'S WHATEVER THEATER

1989. JPN: *Ishii Hisaichi no Nandakanda Gekijo*. Video. DIR: Kazuyoshi Hirose. SCR: Hisaichi Ishii. DES: Hisaichi Ishii. ANI: Kazumi Nonaka. MUS: Yukadan. PRD: Balk. 30 mins. x 2 eps.

In this spin-off from the *Action Comics* manga by **MY NEIGHBORS THE YAMADAS**–creator Hisaichi Ishii's serial, the Underground People desire to leave their overcrowded cavern and seize control of the surface world, but they never quite succeed. A second episode, *Christmas Aid*, soon followed, in which the brainless Undergrounders' second futile escape attempt is set to music by the popular group Yukadan. The first volume also included two unrelated stories by Ishii: *101 Ninja* and *Ken-chan's Space Exploration Adventure*.

HISAISHI, JOE

1950–. Pseudonym for Mamoru Fujisawa.

Born in Nagano Prefecture, he was a childhood violin prodigy who went on to study composition at Kunitachi College of Music. His first work in anime comprised short pieces for **THE GARDLES**, under his real name. He subsequently adopted a pseudonym loosely based on the Japanese pronunciation of "Quincy Jones." Although he has composed music for over 100 productions, shows, and events, including the Nagano Winter Olympics, he is best known for his association with Hayao Miyazaki, which began with **NAUSICAÄ OF THE VALLEY OF THE WIND**, and has continued throughout Studio Ghibli's production history.

HIT AND RUN

1979. JPN: *Ganbare! Bokura no Hit and Run*. AKA: *Go for It! Our Hit and Run!* TV special. DIR: Hiroyoshi Mitsunobu. SCR: Fumi Takahashi. DES: Hiroshi Kanazawa. ANI: Hiroshi Kanazawa. MUS: Kensuke Kyo. PRD: Nippon Animation, Fuji TV. 75 mins.

Baseball captain Ran leads his team to victory in another tale of athletes overcoming adversity, this one based on a manga by Hideo Aya originally serialized in *Shonen Sunday* magazine.

HIT HARD, DREAMERS!

1994. JPN: *Kattobase! DREAMERS! Carp no Tanjo Monogatari* JPN: *Kattobase! Dreamers! Story of the Birth of the Carp*. Movie. DIR: Yoshinori Kanemori, Morio Asaka. SCR: Hideo Takayashiki. DES: Yuzo Sato. ANI: Yuzo Sato. MUS: N/C. PRD: Hiroshima Film Center, Madhouse. 86 mins.

In an original story by **BAREFOOT GEN**–creator Keiji Nakazawa, a group of children orphaned by the bombing of Hiroshima fulfill their dream of playing with the professional baseball players of the Hiroshima Carp. We've plumped for "Hit Hard" as a **TRANSLATION** of *kattobase*, even though there are dozens of other possible exclamations that might be used to convey excitement at an impressive hit—possibly a better summary of its meaning is an exhortation to "Knock it out of the park!"

HITOHIRA *

2007. TV series. DIR: Akira Nishimori. SCR: Megumi Sasano, Rima Kitaki, Tatsuto Higuchi. DES: Junko Yamanaka, Masatomo Sudo, Yukiko Ijima. ANI: Hideyuki Motohashi.

MUS: Conisch. PRD: XEBEC M2, ASCII Media Works, AT-X, Futabasha, GENCO, Gigno Systems, NEC Interchannel. 23 mins. x 12 eps.
A painfully shy girl who literally becomes speechless in the spotlight is forced by seniors in her new school to join the drama club. The story of how she finds new friends and builds her confidence is sweetly told in this anime version of Izumi Kirihara's manga (compare to MASK OF GLASS). The story is a straightforward school narrative, although it's refreshing to see friendship rather than romance take center stage in changing the heroine's life. Good character development and some lovely melodies in the score make up for average animation.

HITORIGA THE ANIMATION

2009. Video. DIR: Toshihiro Watase. SCR: Shinichi Sawayama. DES: Shun Manuwame, Tatsukichi Tomi. ANI: Milk Ichigo, Candy Ichigo. MUS: N/C. PRD: Café de Jeilhouse, Pink Pineapple. 28 mins. x 4 eps.
On the train to school one day, Sumire is molested. She tells her teacher, Mr. Takahashi, but she's confided in the wrong person and soon finds herself in a nightmare of drugs and abuse under the guise of counseling, in this nasty anime based on Hiroki Tsukiyoshi's 2008 porn manga. Another Tsukiyoshi manga featuring Sumire was animated as NATSUMUSHI THE ANIMATION. ❶❷

HIYOKOI

2010. TV special. DIR: Norihiro Naganuma. SCR: Tomoko Konparu. DES: Yuka Shibata. ANI: Yuka Shibata. MUS: N/C. PRD: Production I.G, Shueisha. 23 mins.
Little and large, tall and short—the contrast is hilarious when teeny tiny shy schoolgirl Hiyori comes back to school after an absence in hospital, and finds herself sitting next to a guy who's almost two feet taller than she is. That's the basic idea behind Moe Yukimaru's manga, which began in 2009 in *Ribon* magazine, and was animated as a special for screening at an event in the summer of 2010 to celebrate the magazine's 55th year of publication. The publishers certainly went all out, getting Production I.G to animate this simple high school love comedy in between high-profile gigs working with Studio Ghibli and making ads for Mercedes-Benz,

which just goes to show how titles we've never heard of in the West are often highly regarded in Japan.

HOLEY PANTS: DESIRE ON A STROLL

1987. JPN: *Pants no Ana: Manbo de Ganbo!* Video. DIR: Nobuyuki Kitajima. SCR: (see below). DES: N/C. ANI: Noboru Furuse. MUS: Seiko Ito. PRD: Gahosha. 25 mins.
The ad blurb claims that this is a sweet, humorous look at teen worries, born from the real-life concerns of correspondents for *Bomb!* magazine. An excellent excuse to blame the audience if a project is unsuccessful. Since there were no follow-ups, we can assume that the experiment was a failure. ❶

HOLMES THE TORTOISESHELL CAT

1992. JPN: *Mikeneko Holmes no Yurei Joshu.* AKA: *Holmes the Tortoiseshell Cat and the Haunted Castle.* Video. DIR: Nobuyuki Kitajima, Takeshi Aoki. SCR: Emu Arii. DES: Neko Shijisha. ANI: Noboru Furuse, Jun Okuda. MUS: Kentaro Haneda. PRD: AIC. 45 mins.
A tortoiseshell cat (who solves mysteries on the side) decides to question whether or not the police really have solved a murder case at a castle on an uninhabited island. Based on the best-selling novel *Holmes the Tortoiseshell Cat and the Bouquet of Flowers* by Jiro Akagawa.

HOLY KNIGHT

2012. Video. DIR: Jiro Fujimoto. SCR: Hiroyuki Shimazu. DES: Mai Toda, Ayumi Sugimoto. ANI: Mai Toda. MUS: N/C. PRD: Lilix, ammot. 30 mins. x 2 eps.
Shinta Mizumura is at a mission school in Tokyo with his best friend from childhood. A half-Romanian girl named Lilith Kishimoto transfers to his class and inexplicably starts coming on to the shy boy. But when he discovers he's a vampire hunter from an ancient family, things become clearer—Lilith is a vampire and will do anything, including seducing or killing her hunter, to keep her secret hidden. This adaptation of Maya Miyazaki's 2011 manga may recall DANCE IN THE VAMPIRE BUND in its basic premise of vampires wanting to integrate in human society but the love triangle is pure high school romance in the mode of VAMPIRE KNIGHT. ❶

HOLY THE GHOST

1991. JPN: *Obake no Hori.* TV series. DIR: Minoru Okazaki, Rikuko Yoshida, Masami Furukawa. SCR: Osamu Nakamura, Riko Hinokuma, Megumi Sugiwara, Minori Ikeno. DES: Megumi Watanabe. ANI: Noriko Imazawa. MUS: N/C. PRD: Apollon Create. 10 mins. x 200 eps. (TV), ? mins. x 3 eps. (v).
Humorous stories about a weak-willed ghost made of chocolate, whose mild adventures take him to a birthday party, a carnival, a fight with a bullying witch, and so on. In 1992, his best adventures were released on video as the three-part *Holy the Ghost: Special.* Based on *The Cowardly Ghost,* a children's book by Megumi Watanabe.

HOLY VIRGINS *

2001. JPN: *Tres Marias: Sannin no Sei Shojo.* AKA: *Three Marias: Three Holy Girls.* Video. DIR: Kanzaburo Oda. SCR: Rokurota Makabe. DES: Ken Raika. ANI: Shinichi Omata. MUS: Yoshi. PRD: YOUC, Digital Works (Vanilla Series). 30 mins. (v1), 29 mins. (v2).
Despite his skill as a doctor, Fuwa is fired from a hospital over justifiable allegations of sexual harassment. Down on his luck, he accepts an offer from an old university buddy to investigate the case of Makoto, a novice nun who falls into a state of catatonia every night. He takes a trip to her home island and encounters other religious ladies, who are soon stripping off for a series of erotic scenes. Makoto herself "lacks experience," although she certainly doesn't by the end of this porn anime, in which Fuwa provides a predictable hands-on cure. Fuwa discovers that two women, including a nun, have gone missing in the last five years and ultimately a more sinister cause for the disease than he expected, as is often the case with isolated movie islands. Based on the game by Nikukyu, this VANILLA SERIES release is typical of that company's generally mediocre production values (including plot holes and hanging threads), though at least Fuwa shows something that his fellow doctors in INTERNAL MEDICINE and HARDCORE HOSPITAL don't: some restraint. ❶❷

HOMEROOM AFFAIRS *

1994. JPN: *Tanin no Kankei.* AKA: *Human Relations.* Video. DIR: Osamu Sekita. SCR: Hiroyuki Kawasaki. DES: Minoru Yamazawa. ANI: Minoru Yamazawa. MUS: Hiroyuki Takei. PRD:

Jam Creation, JC Staff. 45 mins. x 2 eps. Young minx Miyako teases older man Tokiro Ebara with views of her underwear at a train station, but both are in for a shock. She is a student at Mitsuba Girls' School, and he is her new homeroom teacher. To make matters worse, Miyako's father then asks the flustered Mr. Ebara to babysit while he is away, forcing the couple to live together. Coy soft-core high jinks ensue, as our teacher nobly resists Miyako's charms, while fantasizing about her all the time. Eventually, she points out that if they were married, they could have sex as often as they liked, and nobody would care—though it is somewhat presumptuous of her to assume that anyone does anyway. Based on the 1992 manga by Ichiro Arima published in *Young Animal* magazine, the most amusing thing about this "comedy" is the distributor's hysterical insistence, at every available occasion, that Miyako is over the age of consent. Quote of the week: "Not to be viewed by minors under 18." As opposed to what? Compare with the very similar VERY PRIVATE LESSON. **N**

HONEY AND CLOVER *

2005. JPN: *Hachimitsu to Clover*. TV series, video. DIR: Kenichi Kasai, Tatsuyuki Nagai. SCR: Yosuke Kuroda. DES: Hidekazu Shimamura. ANI: N/C. MUS: Yumi Hayashi and Salon 68. PRD: JC Staff, Fuji TV. 25 mins. x 24 eps. (TV1), 25 mins. x 2 eps. (v), 25 mins. x 12 eps. (TV2).

Three young arts students live a poor but happy existence in the same apartment. Their balanced life is disrupted by the arrival of Hagumi Hanamoto, the daughter of their instructor. One boy, Shinobu Morita, attempts to show his feelings for her, but only ends up scaring her. His love-rival Yuta Takemoto tries an alternate tactic, hiding his true feelings and trying to be a conspicuously good friend to her. The final roommate, Takumi Mayama, has other problems, since he is being pursued by Ayumi Yamada, a beautiful potter also known as Tetsujin, "The Iron Lady," adored by all the young men in the district, but who has eyes only for him. He, meanwhile, has eyes only for his employer, who is a pretty widow. Based on the manga by Chika Umino serialized in *Young You* magazine, this was commissioned by Fuji TV as the first of several "Noitamina"

series—"animation" spelled backward. These series were aimed at a nighttime, mainstream audience distinct from the usual fans to which evening anime so often pander, with the expectation that many viewers would be women in their 20s. PARADISE KISS was another outing in the experiment. The two final "episodes" were specials not broadcast on TV but included as bonuses to the Japanese DVD, although a second season then followed on TV in 2006.

HONEY HONEY *

1981. JPN: *Honey Honey no Suteki na Boken*. AKA: *Honey Honey's Wonderful Adventure*. TV series. DIR: Takeshi Shirato, Masakazu Yasumura, Minoru Hamada. SCR: Masaki Tsuji, Shunichi Yukimuro, Tomohiro Ando. DES: Yoshiyuki Yamamoto, Kozo Masanobu. ANI: Takeshi Shirato, Akira Daikuhara. MUS: Akihiro Komori. PRD: Toei, Fuji TV. 25 mins. x 29 eps.

Teenage Austrian orphan Honey is a waitress in 1907 Vienna whose pet cat, Lily, swallows Princess Florel's precious gemstone, the "Smile of the Amazon." Honey is forced to go on the run with Phoenix the gentleman jewel thief, pursued by Florel's angry suitors. Equal parts LUPIN III and THREE MUSKETEERS, the story eventually transforms into a fairy tale worthy of CINDERELLA, when Honey is revealed to be Florel's long-lost twin and marries Phoenix so they can all live happily ever after. Based on a 1966 manga by Hideko Mizuno and given a partial release on an obscure U.S. video label.

HONEY THE BUG

1986. JPN: *Bug-tte Honey*. AKA: *Honey the Bug Dance Megarom Girl 4622*. TV series, movie. DIR: Akinori Nagaoka, Minoru Okazaki, Toshio Takeuchi, Yutaka Sato, Kanetsugu Kodama. SCR: Kasumi Oka, Hideki Sonoda, Shunichi Yukimuro, Yasushi Hirano. DES: Minoru Maeda. ANI: Takao Kasai. MUS: Hiroshi Tsutsui. PRD: TMS, Nippon TV. 51 mins. x 51 eps. (TV), 48 mins. (m).

Computer-gaming prodigy Harahito Takahashi is whisked off to Game World by Honey the insect girl and her friends, who need his help in a quest that takes them through several different sectors, each suspiciously similar to several Nintendo games, including *The Adventures of Morihito*

Takahashi and *Xanadu*. Fast on the heels of the theatrical success of SUPER MARIO BROTHERS, this mixture of *Tron* and *The Last Starfighter* also appeared in a movie version, *Honey the Bug: Mai the Megarom Girl 4622* (1987), featuring Leo, a scientist from Toycom World whose lover, Mai, has been brainwashed by evil forces. A rather quaint relic of the early days of product placement before the hard-sell of more recent series such as POKÉMON.

HONEY X HONEY DROPS

2006. JPN: *Mitsu x Mitsu Drops*. Video. DIR: Mitsuhiro Togo. SCR: Junko Komura. DES: Koji Murai, Yutaka Mukumoto. ANI: Koji Murai. MUS: Shoichi Kasuya, Melonest. PRD: Radix, Shogakukan, Soft Garage. 27 mins. x 2 eps.

Yuzuru is an ordinary 15-year-old girl who gets a summer job and runs into rich, spoiled playboy Renge Kai, who's in an elite stream at her school called the Kuge class. Renge decides he wants her for his Honey—ordinary students who agree to act as a kind of general servant and companion to the Masters of the Kuge class. Honeys have all their tuition paid, and Yuzuru knows it would help her hard-up family if she agreed, but how can she tolerate this brat's commands? Quite happily, once she gets used to a girl's place in the scheme of things, as it eventually turns out in this "romantic" story based on Kanan Minami's 2004 manga. Compare with MOMIJI. **N**

HONGO, MITSURU

1959–. Sometimes miscredited as Mitsuru Honma. Animator at Shin'ei Doga who subsequently became a director on shows including CRAYON SHIN-CHAN and PILOT CANDIDATE. Now associated with Production I.G.

HOOP DAYS *

2003. JPN: *Dear Boys*. TV series. DIR: Susumu Kudo. SCR: Nobuaki Kishima, Takao Yoshioka. DES: Akira Kano. ANI: N/C. MUS: Nittoku Inoue. PRD: OB Planning, Avex Trax, TV Tokyo. 25 mins. x 26 eps.

Transfer student Kazuhiko rediscovers his love of basketball, when he leaves behind the harsh sport-oriented regime of his old school for the more relaxed attitudes of Mizuho High—so relaxed in fact, that the school doesn't even have a basketball team any more. The previous coach bowed out in spectacular fashion when he was punched on court (and on camera) by one of his team, thereby ensuring that the remaining players were banned from playing for the rest of the season. Kazuhiko tries to drag them back into the game through his own love of it, while other bonds develop between some of the boys and their opposite numbers on the girls' basketball team. A predictable but endearing rerun of SLAM DUNK with a little of the cheesy faux-tough attitude of INITIAL D, this show was based on a 1989 manga by Hiroki Yagami in monthly *Shonen Magazine*. Although it is a title aimed at male teens and based on a manga with considerably more risqué content, *Dear Boys* sounded a little too girly for the American audience, hence the renaming in the U.S. release, but not even that seemed to stop the serial's English-language release foundering partway, presumably due to lack of interest.

HORIZON ON THE MIDDLE OF NOWHERE *

2011. JPN: *Kyokai Senjo no Horizon*. TV series. DIR: Manabu Ono. SCR: Tatsuhiko Urata, Kurasumi Sunayama, Yoriko Tomita, Seishi Minakami. DES: Kanta Suzuki, Shinya Nishizawa, Tomoyuki Fujii, Yukiko Aikei, Hiroyuki Taiga, Takumi Sakura, Tomohiko Kawahara, Kazuo Nagai. ANI: Takoro Shinbi, Kanta Suzuki, Noriko Ogura. MUS: Tatsuya Kato. PRD: Sunrise, ASCII Media works, Bandai Visual, Lantis, Sony PCL. 25 mins. x 13 eps. (TV1), 23 mins. x 13 eps. (TV2).

In Japan's distant future, the nation returns to its feudal past, divided into territories ruled by overlords. But many are foreigners: Japan has been divided up following a disastrous collision of parallel worlds that left it the only inhabitable land on the planet. Unable to travel into space, mankind divides Japan and a flying city-ship, the *Musashi*, holds the last remnants of the refugee Japanese people. Meanwhile history is reenacted according to a Holy Book known as Testament under the control of the powerful Testament Union. But rumors start to circulate that history will run out after year 1648 of the Testament Era. Can the young people aboard help to save the day? Pervert student leader Aoi Tori and his obsession with the android girl Horizon may be the

key to saving their homeship, Japan, and the world.

If you think this reenactment of the occupation of Japan crashed into *End of Days* sounds wacky, wait for the 2012 TV sequel, where the *Musashi* and her crew go to "England" and survive a reenactment of the invasion by the Spanish Armada. This show based on a series of books by Minoru Kawakami, with illustrations by Satoyasu, is like a hotpot in a student house—everyone throws in bits of what they like, stirs it up, and hopes that something amazing will come out. This creates a chaotic muddle where nobody's quite sure whom this is supposed to please, but the intriguing basic ideas, the attractive design, and the goofy humor compensate for much of the chaos. There's nothing original here except the basic premise, and we frequently caught ourselves wondering (rather wistfully) what a great SF writer—say, Chiaki Konaka—might have made of it; even the clichés piled on top of the story can't quite bury its originality. In a depressingly common own-goal, certain foreign language distributors were obliged by the Japanese rightsholders to use the Engrish title, even though it doesn't actually make any sense to native speakers. **NV**

HORROR AND MONSTERS

The earliest chills in anime came from ghost stories and scary fairy tales, such as Noburo Ofuji's *Kujira* (1927) and *Ghost Ship* (1956), but it was a children's medium, and as such didn't initially attempt anything designed to give anyone goosebumps. Osamu Tezuka's DORORO (1968), made as the creator's Mushi Production began to spiral into bankruptcy, was one of the first anime to be genuinely disturbing, filled with ghosts, nightmares, and bloodshed, and with a central character whose father's pact with devils leaves him scarred, eyeless, and maimed. That didn't stop some kids' cartoons from being downright disturbing anyway, with the lamb-turned-killer of Sanrio's RINGING BELL (1978) reputedly giving a number of *adult* fans nightmares.

Children's entertainment often recognized the appeal of the horrific. SPOOKY KITARO (1968) suggested that cutting class to hang out with zombies was a fun thing to do, while DEVILMAN (1972) dressed up

the traditions of a superhero show with the accoutrements of demonology. But not even *Devilman* was "horror" as we know it; that was a foreign concept, and arguably its first appearance was Minoru Okazaki's TV movie DRACULA: SOVEREIGN OF THE DAMNED (1980), based on the Marvel comic.

True horror reached Japan by an unexpected route, in the depictions of radiation burns and traumatized war victims of BAREFOOT GEN (1983). The 1980s saw the widespread arrival of the home video player, permitting anime producers to make shows for an older audience. Horror met science fiction in VAMPIRE HUNTER D (1985), but it was the Madhouse studio that appeared to perfect its use in modern animation. WICKED CITY (1987) and DEMON CITY SHINJUKU (1988) established Madhouse and director Yoshiaki Kawajiri as the kings of urban gothic. A slew of imitators followed, in which demons broke through into our everyday world, and fought on the streets of Tokyo. But everyone's thunder was stolen by UROTSUKIDOJI (1987), the first in a series of "erotic-horror" stories based on the work of Toshio Maeda that, while it might not have *scared* its audience, certainly shocked them with its scenes of depravity and excess—its monsters externalized the chaos in the pubescent mind, to devastating effect.

Ultimately, horror usually scares us by persuading us that something terrible really might happen—both PERFECT BLUE (1997) and MONSTER (2004) successfully instill fear with their application of *reality*, not the fantastic. Anime, by its nature, is already one step from reality, making it harder to scare a cartoon audience. Modern-day incarnations of anime "horror" continue to coquettishly avoid making an audience scream in terror. Instead they hope to titillate, amuse, or otherwise behave in a non-horrific way. VAMPIRE PRINCESS MIYU (1988) preferred mood and imagery to actual scares—style over substance, if you like. Western horror is often concerned with subtexts, but erotic-horror anime like DARK SHELL (2003) or ONI-TENSEI (2001) can put all the subtext right in the foreground. No sublimated desires here, no Victorian prudery repressing thoughts of sex with stories of men who drink virgins' blood—horror is a permanent feature of anime erotica, but whether such shows are scary *because* of their horror content is open to debate.

Japanese folklore has a rich tradition of monsters, some of which have built successful second careers in animation. In 1955's PIGGYBACK GHOST, a green-eyed elemental befriends a village blacksmith and his neighbors. GOLDEN BAT (1967) was a skeletal superhero from ancient Atlantis who fought monsters and robots at the request of Japanese schoolgirl Mari. SPOOKY KITARO (1968) gave supporting roles, as friends or adversaries of the young hero, to a host of traditional ghouls like the one-legged, one-eyed Umbrella Man and the ghostly Piece of Paper, a tradition which continued in shows like DORORON ENMA (1973) with its Japanese Monster Patrol, GHOSTS (1981), and USHIO & TORA (1992). Oni, Japan's native ogres, are generally represented as powerful but stupid, extremely violent, and with nasty eating habits. They feature in anime such as OGRE SLAYER and SHUTENDOJI, and have inspired many other creations like Rumiko Takahashi's alien Oni in URUSEI YATSURA.

American TV's fascination with the supernatural in the 1960s inspired a number of monstrous tales, like the 1968 Korean coproduction MONSTER MAN BEM in which a trio from the world of monsters strive to bring good to the Dark Realm in the hope that this will enable them to become human. The generic Western vampire became a popular stock character from 1968, when Mushi Production mixed live action and anime in VAMPIRE. LITTLE GOBLIN (1968), the story of a monster prince sent to live on Earth, gave supporting roles to the Hollywood stars who inspired Forrest J. Ackerman's long-running magazine *Famous Monsters of Filmland*: Dracula, the Wolfman, and a young Frankenstein's monster. All three also featured in the SPOOKY KITARO movie *Great Ghost Wars* (1986).

Mary Shelley's tragic creation FRANKENSTEIN (mystifyingly relocated to North Wales for the Toei TV special) has also influenced a long line of anime dealing with the dangers of genetic experiment, from thoughtful works like Tezuka's BAGHI (1981) to 1998's POKÉMON movie and BLUE SUBMARINE NO. SIX. The Wolfman's descendants have starred in shows including WOLF GUY (1992), alongside other werecreatures in MIDNIGHT PANTHER (1998). Strangely, the Mummy has yet to star in his own anime; bit-part appearances in shows like 1971's LUPIN III have reduced him to the level of an extra in *Scooby-Doo*.

THE KING KONG SHOW (1966) was made specifically for the American market. The elemental ape became a small child's friend in a TV movie and series of eight-minute adventures. Japan's own giant monster, Godzilla, appeared as a comical parody of himself in 1967's GAZULA THE AMICABLE MONSTER, a gentle but clumsy creature invading the life of a typical Japanese family.

Gross, misshapen monsters that would equally be at home in medieval Buddhist or Western Hells are found in anime such as 1985's ICZER-ONE and 1991's SILENT MÖBIUS where they are the shock troops of alien forces bent on world domination. In most Japanese movies humanity tries to fight monsters with iron determination and heavy weaponry, but many anime play with the idea that to beat monsters you must join them, by taking on some of their physical or magical powers, as in DEVILMAN (1972) and later pastiches such as HELLSING. Nagai's series suggests that ordinary-looking people can be possessed by or transformed into monsters, simply by unleashing their own inner demons. Some of the most magnificently silly monsters ever to grace an enduring franchise threaten mankind in ULTRAMAN (1979), an animation spun off the live-action hit of the same name. To defeat them, our hero must achieve monstrous size and strength by borrowing the magical-girl technique of assisted transformation.

Other monstrous transformations in anime range from the comical-but-threatening to the stomach churning. When neglected pet dog Papadoll is changed to a monster in CATNAPPED (1995), he still drools and looks amiably stupid, but he can eat people. AKIRA (1988) transforms all its protagonists, but Tetsuo's shifts from scrawny runt to drug-crazed god to overflowing river of flesh are truly monstrous, giving visceral impact to his final moment of self-awareness and self-acceptance, and hope of redemption for all monsters, even the human kind.

In the 21st century, anime seemed to rediscover horror, most notably in a series of variations on the themes of zombies and the undead, from HIGHSCHOOL OF THE DEAD to GYO: TOKYO FISH ATTACK. This new trend can be ascribed in part to the international success of *The Walking Dead* (2010), but also to a general interest in zombies replacing the noughties vampire fad. Ickiness reached undreamt-of heights with the necrophiliac subtexts of SANKAREA: UNDYING LOVE and the incestuous feedback-loop of PUPA. Meanwhile, monsters continued to stand in for anything non-Japanese, such as the creatures of the night reluctantly granted immigration and assimilation in DANCE IN THE VAMPIRE BUND.

HOSODA, MAMORU

1967–. A director who studied oil painting at the Kanazawa University of Arts and Crafts before becoming an animator on shows such as CRYING FREEMAN and SLAM DUNK. He moved into storyboards in the mid-1990s before gaining his first directorial positions at the turn of the century. After well-received work on DIGIMON and SPOOKY OOKY KITARO, Hosoda collaborated with the artist Takashi Murakami on *Superflat Monogram*, a short piece screened exclusively in Louis Vuitton stores, and was initially commissioned by Studio Ghibli to direct HOWL'S MOVING CASTLE. Hosoda left Ghibli under a cloud—*Howl's Moving Castle* was taken over by its famous director Hayao Miyazaki (coming out of retirement a second time), while Hosoda went off to make the ONE PIECE movie *Baron Omatsuri and the Secret Island*. The story of a team given inadequate resources to complete an impossible task, *Baron Omatsuri* is reputed to be Hosoda's very personal comment on his time at Ghibli. His directorial work on GIRL WHO LEAPT THROUGH TIME earned him the 2007 Tokyo Anime Award for Best Director, and he subsequently moved from adaptations of others' works into original movies such as SUMMER WARS and WOLF CHILDREN. The authors are tempted to observe that Hosoda's ejection from Ghibli amid its well-chronicled handover throes was a far greater indicator of potential and originality than being allowed to stay there. His subsequent work has established him as one of anime's few, true original voices.

HOT FOR TEACHER *

2003. JPN: *Jokyoshi: Yumi Hokago*. AKA: *Female Teacher: Yumi After Class*. Video. DIR: Haruo Okawara. SCR: Yuta Takahashi. DES: Haruo Okawara. ANI: Haruo Okawara. MUS: Yoshi. PRD: YOUC, Digital Works (Vanilla Series). 30 mins. x 2 eps.
Busty, raven-haired school teacher Yumi has split up with her fiancé, and now faces sexual harassment from the vice-principal in yet another escapee from the VANILLA SERIES. Although she tries to thwart his advances, he lies in wait for her with a group of her own students and subjects her to a series of sexual torments. After she is forced to agree to service her entire class, she looks to two students for rescue, although they are both quite timid, and just as likely to be "forced" to rape her themselves in an anime unsurprisingly similar to PROFESSOR PAIN. ●N●

HOT JUICY TEACHER *

2002. JPN: *Onna Kyoshi*. Video. DIR: Sosuke Kokubunji. SCR: Sosuke Kokubunji. DES: Jun Papaya. ANI: Jun Papaya. MUS: Yoshitaka Jo. PRD: Milky. 30 mins. x 3 eps.
When Yuichiro runs into a group of rich kids raping their teacher, he is framed for the offence and forced to transfer schools. The experience causes him to swear revenge on all women (why not on rich bullies?), and the prime candidate presents herself at his next school, where the principal's daughter is seducing some of her students after class. Meanwhile, shyboy Hiromi is also bullied by a group of classmates who sexually humiliate him and persuade local bad girls to tease him. He develops a crush on the sexually predatory teacher, which turns him into her protector when Yuichiro tries to have his wicked way. Predictable anime erotica, with slightly more bodily fluids than usual in evidence. As with many of Milky's popular series, a video subtitled "The Best," compiling the highlights of the show, was also released. Based on an erotic computer game created by Atelier Kaguya. ●N●

HOURGLASS OF SUMMER COLORS

2008. JPN: *Natsuiro no Sunadokei*. Video. DIR: Takahiro Okao. SCR: N/C. DES: Yasunari Nitta, Mitsuharu Miyamae. ANI: N/C. MUS: N/C. PRD: Picture Magic, Rikuentai, Lantis. 30 mins. x 2 eps.
Kotaro is in love with the aloof and seemingly unattainable Kaho. He's made up his mind that at some point before summer vacation is over, he's going to tell her how he feels. But the night before he plans to take the plunge, he's thrown into his own future after meeting a strange girl. And the future is the worst of all possible worlds—Kaho *did* agree to go out with him, and they became a couple, but she died in a terrible accident. Kotaro has to go back to his own time to change the future. Oddly enough, this seems to involve him in misdemeanors with a number of other girls, some of them appearing rather too old or much too young for him, in this porn anime based on a game by Princess Soft. Compare to KIRARA, which similarly introduces a dream-girl, only to kill her off to make room for others. ●

HOUSE HUNTING

2006. JPN: *Yado Sagashi*. Movie. DIR: Hayao Miyazaki. SCR: Hayao Miyazaki. DES: Katsuya Kondo, Sayaka Hirahara. ANI: Katsuya Kondo. MUS: N/C. PRD: Studio Ghibli. 12 mins.
A short film made by Japan's leading animation director for screening at the Ghibli Museum in the suburbs of Tokyo. Featuring a red-haired heroine with pigtails in a classically heartwarming story, the film has been screened with WATER SPIDER MONMON at Carnegie Hall in New York, but this can't really be counted as an English release.

HOUSE OF 100 TONGUES *

2003. JPN: *Mozu no Nie*. AKA: *Sacrifice of Birds*. Video. DIR: Keitaro Motonaga. SCR: Toshizo Nemoto. DES: Yoshitaka Kono. ANI: Yoshitaka Kono. MUS: N/C. PRD: Discovery. 30 mins.
The tragic tale of an ancient noble family gone bad through the lusts of its women, from virginal Nanako who means to change her state as soon as possible, to her mother bravely surrendering herself to a gang of bandits. This porn anime got a 2010 rerelease on the Japanese market. Interestingly, director and screenwriter have done more mainstream work, with Nemoto writing on STEINS;GATE and Motonaga an episode director on LEGEND OF GALACTIC HEROES. They worked together again in 2005 on the temple harem show AH! MY BUDDHA. ●N●

HOUSE OF ACORNS

1997. JPN: *Donguri no Ie*. Movie. DIR: Takashi Anno, Osamu Yamamoto. SCR: N/C. DES: N/C. ANI: Hideo Kawauchi, Yoshiaki Yanagida, Masaya Fujimori, Yuko Ikino, Hiroshi Kawaguchi, Masayuki Sekine. MUS: N/C. PRD: Saitama Association for the Disabled. 110 mins.
Keiko Tazaki is born deaf and mentally handicapped, but her loving parents fight to give her the best possible start in life. Keiko and her parents meet many other deaf and handicapped children and their families as she attends a special school and grows up. After graduation, Keiko throws herself heart and soul into opening a workshop where handicapped people can participate in the modern world, earning their own money, and with it some respect and independence. Although commissioned by an association for the disabled, this production also capitalized on a fad within Japanese entertainment. The previous two years had seen a deaf character central to the live-action TV series *Heaven's Coins* (*DE) and the immense ratings success of the autism drama *Pure* (*DE), both of which helped establish token disability as one more element to be shuffled around dramatic plotlines. *House of Acorns* can be seen as an attempt to return to the issue at hand—the plight of the disabled—rather than another glossy attempt to glamorize it. Compare to MY SISTER MOMOKO.

HOUSE OF FIVE LEAVES *

2010. JPN: *Sarai-ya Goyo*. TV series. DIR: Tomomi Mochizuki. SCR: Tomomi Mochizuki. DES: Kazuto Nakazawa, Michie Watanabe. ANI: Kazuto Nakazawa, Yoshimitsu Yamashita. MUS: Kayo Konishi, Yukio Kondo. PRD: Manglobe, Dentsu, Fuji TV, Media Factory, MOVIC, Shogakukan. 23 mins. x 12 eps.
Edo-period Japan: timid country boy Masanosuke, a samurai without a master or clan, is heading to the capital when he runs into Yaichi, a playboy who hires him as a bodyguard. It's just a ruse to lure the unsophisticated warrior into Yaichi's bandit gang, the Five Leaves. Although he's the world's worst bodyguard, inclined to run away in the face of trouble, Masanosuke is a good-hearted soul and deplores their kidnapping and robbery, but he's been fired so often he's desperate. He

gradually becomes aware that Yaichi's motives aren't what they seem, and the band's grim camaraderie helps him learn about life at the bottom of the pile in samurai-era Japan, as well as giving him plenty of chances to practice his already outstanding sword skills.

Based on Natsume Ono's 2006 manga of the same name, this is a strikingly stylish series from the studio that brought us **SAMURAI CHAMPLOO**, but much more reflective and demanding greater audience attention. The pace and structure recall **RISTORANTE PARADISO**, also based on an Ono manga. Its dark, intense color palette with dramatic splashes of red emphasizes an understated drama that reveals its source with tantalizing slowness. Director Mochizuki said that he wanted "to make a period drama that looked and felt like the real thing," and he succeeds admirably. As the drama unfolds, he often uses a device employed by Osamu Tezuka—the unthreatening comic-relief character that pops up to defuse tension or misdirect attention with a gag or a smile—in this case, a calico cat from the manga. Otherwise, the imagery of blood-red maple leaves falling and of flowing water conveys a sense of fatalism, of the inevitability of change in a world where the only choice is how you deal with it. This is the opposite of feel-good anime, but its flashes of humor and beauty in a dark world make it, despite the darkness, an enjoyable one.

HOWL'S MOVING CASTLE *

2004. JPN: *Howl no Ugoku Shiro*. Movie. DIR: Hayao Miyazaki. SCR: Hayao Miyazaki. DES: Hayao Miyazaki. ANI: Akihiro Yamashita, Takeshi Inamura, Kitaro Kosaka. MUS: Joe Hisaishi. PRD: Studio Ghibli, Gonzo, T2, Production IG, Madhouse. 119 mins.
Plain, shy hat maker Sophie is cursed by the Witch of the Waste to turn prematurely into an old woman. In search of a remedy, she works as a cleaner for Howl, a handsome wizard who, it is rumored, steals the hearts of young girls. Sophie brings a woman's touch to a ramshackle bachelor household, edging her way into the antagonistic world of Howl, his boy apprentice Markl, and Calcifer, the fire demon, whom Howl has bound to the castle's machinery to keep the power flowing. Meanwhile, Howl and several of his pseudonyms are

resisting a king's order to fight against the wizards of a rival state. He contends with two women with whom he seems to have a past, the Wicked Witch, whose fading spells cause her to age and collapse into dementia, and Madame Suliman, a government sorcerer who urges Howl to enter royal service.

Hayao Miyazaki's adaptation of the novel by Diana Wynne Jones adds several personal touches, starting with a wheezing comic relief lapdog. The wholly magical realm of the original novel is given a more modern, steam-based technology and a new subplot about a distant war, fraught with mixed feelings that appear rooted in Japan's role as bystander and beneficiary of the invasion of Iraq. War breaks out over the search for an important artifact—the infamous real-world "weapons of mass destruction" transformed here into a missing prince, demands for whose return lead to the background conflict. *HMC* wrestles with the ideas of duty and obligation, and how best to do the right thing in a world gone wrong.

Flushed with international approbation for **SPIRITED AWAY** and Miyazaki's long-deserved Academy Award, *HMC* was less a movie than a national celebration. On its opening weekend 1.1 million Japanese spent over $14 million—an opening surpassed only by *Harry Potter and the Sorcerer's Stone* (2001). Buena Vista invested reverently in the English language adaptation, casting the new *Batman*, Christian Bale, as the selfish Howl and Billy Crystal in a comic turn as Calcifer. The dub is also tied firmly into America's film heritage with Jean Simmons as the aged Sophie, and Lauren Bacall as the Witch of the Waste.

HMC is a charming film, visually inventive and magnificently crafted. The castle itself is a fabulous creation, like a magic mechanical version of Baba Yaga's Hut from Russian folklore, and the settings are beautifully realized, with the wild mountains and uplands handled particularly well. However, there is a difference between an excellent film and an excellent Miyazaki film. All film is a collaborative process, but in the best films of a genius one finds a unique creative soul, a way of seeing and showing that can be imitated but not replicated. Other great Japanese directors, given Ghibli's unrivaled re-

sources, could have made a movie very like *HMC*; but no one else could have made anything approaching **NAUSICAÄ**.

HMC was originally intended for another director until Miyazaki stepped in, the legendary perfectionist seemingly unable to let a good idea go to waste, even though he had supposedly retired. The film's hidden message is Miyazaki's love letter to Akemi Ota, the young, hard-working animator girl he married so long ago, a plucky heroine who woke up one day to find herself a glorified scullery maid to a self-absorbed creative, obsessed with distant battles and otherworldly sorceries.

HMC sometimes appears more like the product of a committee rehashing Miyazaki's glory days: heroines confronted by outsized obstacles, contending witches, and lead characters unwittingly transformed (**TROPES AND TRANSFORMATIONS**). Absolute simplicity and innocence are hard to handle realistically—in **MY NEIGHBOR TOTORO** they work sublime wonders, but in *HMC* it leaves the characters alienated from the events around them, like preoccupied children or the "little people" of **PATLABOR**, ignorant of a big picture that is only apparent on repeat viewings.

It may be a tribute to the original novel character, who fed on the souls of besotted young girls, that Howl is Miyazaki's first consciously beautiful male hero who gets to have Miyazaki's first full-on screen kiss, but he's also the first Miyazaki hero to turn into a conventional father figure by the end of the movie. By the close of the film, the wild, magical creatures are tamed into an image of a nuclear family. The magnificently depraved Witch is a gentle granny mumbling in a sunny garden, the resourceful Markl a kid teasing an old dog, and the fire elemental a lovably grouchy Disney domestic appliance, as the irresistible wizard steers his companion and the domesticated castle into the happily-ever-after. Compare this with the ending of **PRINCESS MONONOKE**, where San and Ashitaka agree to accept each other's separate needs without compromising their love.

The major Miyazaki themes are still there—integrity, consideration for others, the destructive power of war and greed, ecological awareness, the synergy of true teamwork. What is lacking is a spark so unique it seems churlish to expect Miyazaki to produce it on demand, movie after movie; and the supernaturally sure-footed sense of pace and timing that informs his greatest works. *HMC* is a detailed and generous answer, but so caught up in its own complexity that it seems to have misheard the question.

HOZUKI NO REITETSU *

2014. AKA: *Hozuki Keeps His Cool*. TV series. DIR: Hiro Kaburaki. SCR: Midori Goto. DES: Hirotaka Kato. ANI: Hirotaka Kato. MUS: Tomisiro. PRD: WIT Studio, Kodansha, MBS, Starchild Records. 24 mins. x 13 eps.
Hozuki is an ogre, assistant to Enma the ruler of Hell, and tasked with troubleshooting numerous problems of logistics, staffing, and fulfillment in his strange workplace. Seemingly made in the hope that viewers would find it to be a COMEDY, this odd, visually striking series seems to rely far too heavily on sight gags derived from Japanese RELIGION AND BELIEF, as numerous mythological characters are shunted around a Hell reconceived as some terrible variant of working in a Japanese corporation. There is some absurdist humor to be found, after the fashion of THE DEVIL IS A PART-TIMER, in demons and mythical figures having to negotiate mundane irritations like factory inspections and airport security, but actual gags are few and far between.

HUCKLEBERRY FINN

1976. TV series, movie. DIR: Hiroyoshi Mitsunobu, Tameo Ogawa, Keiichi Abe. SCR: Mamoru Sasaki. DES: N/C. ANI: Eisuke Kondo, Teruhito Kamiguchi. MUS: Nobuyoshi Koshibe. PRD: Tac, Nippon Herald, Fuji TV. 25 mins. x 26 eps. (TV1), 86 mins. (m), 25 mins. x 26 eps. (TV2).
Huckleberry Finn and his friend Jim, a black slave, make a bid for freedom by floating down the Mississippi River on a raft. Huck is faced with the perilous choice of damnation or saving his friend, choosing friendship. This WORLD MASTERPIECE THEATER adaptation of Mark Twain's 1885 sequel to TOM SAWYER was cut into an 86-minute "movie" version in 1991. A second TV version, *The Story of Huckleberry* (*Huckleberry Monogatari*), was made by Norio Kashima for Enoki Films and an NHK satellite channel in 1994. This second series was released in English in a feature-length edit as *Huck & Tom's Mississippi Adventure* (1996).

HUMAN CROSSING *

2003. JPN: *Ningen Kosaten*. AKA: *Human Scramble*. TV series. DIR: Kazunari Kume. SCR: Nobuaki Kishima, Seitaro Shimizu, Toshio Okabe. DES: Sachiko Kamimura. ANI: Shojiro Abe. MUS: Norihiro Nomura, Yusuke Hayashi. PRD: TV Tokyo, Shogakukan, To Max. 24 mins. x 13 eps.
A series of unrelated stories about people reaching turning points in their lives, using the animated medium to tell tales that often seem more suited to live-action drama. A privileged youth, nursing a long-term grudge against his mother, strives to become a championship boxer in a reversal of the rags-to-riches tradition of TOMORROW'S JOE. An idealistic young lawyer, helping a woman regain custody of her baby from its grandparents, rediscovers the true meaning of justice. A father tries to make up for his workaholic ways by giving his disinterested son an expensive bike. An academic who has left his working-class roots behind comes to terms with his orgins when his brother asks for a favor. A star and his manager, who have been lifelong friends, suffer strains in their relationship as the luster of fame begins to wear off. An adult brother and sister must cope with their old father, a man neither of them has much liked, whose house they have sold but whose care they are still obliged to maintain. A snooty reporter is forced to reconsider his attitude toward the news, and seek it through human contact when he is demoted to a regional newspaper. A rookie guard in a women's prison must confront an inmate who has lied to her. A married couple is torn between an impoverished life of creative fulfillment in Paris or commercial drudgery in Tokyo. A nuclear family find themelves inheriting an old "relative" who turns out to be their late father's mistress. A teenager endures bullying at school because his mother is a hostess in a bar. A male employee at a girls' reformatory agonizes about the 10% of girls that offend again upon release and frets over the best way to deal with a runaway.

It is a symptom of anime that they are so often unreal—when all one is paying for is paint, it is only logical for producers and creators to aim for the fantastic as often as possible in order to make virtues of their production's shortcomings. Anime rooted in reality (EVERYDAY ANIME) are few and far between, but *Human Crossing* is one of them—every element of its production suggests that it began life as a live-action TV series, including resemblances to drama serials such as *Tabloid* (*DE), *Unmarried Family* (*DE), and particularly the prison drama *Lipstick* (*DE), since two of the *HC* tales revolve around female offenders. For some reason, perhaps budgetary issues, perhaps a change in the broadcast climate toward short stories, it appears to have been downgraded to anime status, in the manner of PERFECT BLUE. Its origin is a series of manga vignettes by Masao Yajima, the creator of *Big Wing* (*DE), and Kenshi Hirokane, the creator of DOMAIN OF MURDER. Both are giants of the manga world who specialize in realistic stories of everyday folk, which has naturally led them to enjoy far greater success in the world of live-action TV drama than they could ever hope for in anime. Hirokane in particular is famed for *Shooting Stars in the Twilight*, a manga series written for aging readers, so it is perhaps no surprise that one story concentrates directly on the plight of the elderly in an uncaring modern society, while several others allude to it.

The honest and realistic storytelling demonstrates that anime doesn't have to rely on ninja battles and magic babe harems to create sympathetic, understandable characters. The animation is very limited, the storyboarding and camera work is pedestrian, and the use of live-action footage in the opening and ending sections only highlights its inadequacy. However, music is used very intelligently, that is, only when required to enhance a scene or move the story along, rather than being an inescapable irritation. Despite its deficiencies, this is an unusual and worthwhile addition to any anime collection.

HUMANE SOCIETY

1992. JPN: *Humane Society: Jinrui Ai ni Michita Shakai*. AKA: *Humane Society: A Society in Which Humanity Is Loving*. Video. DIR: Jun Kamiya. SCR: Mayori Sekijima, from an idea by Demon Kogure. DES: Kazuchika Kise. ANI: Kazuchika Kise. MUS: Yokai Matsuzakisama (Yuichi Matsuzaki). PRD: Animate

Film. 57 mins.

In an anime adventure featuring one of Japan's most eccentric pop groups as themselves, the five members of the rock band Seikima-II must save the world from the demonic forces of the Tower of Babel. Claiming to be demons from the other side of the universe, the KISS-look-alikes announced that the apocalypse was coming in 1999 and that ownership of a ticket stub from one of their "Black Masses" would entitle the holder to salvation. Despite a slightly incoherent message (as in **DEVILMAN**, how were demons supposed to save us from Satan?), Seikima-II gained many fans, particularly among young Office Ladies who thought they were cute, with some of their best songs including "Pinky Dinosaur," "Frightful Restaurant," and "Stainless Night" (the latter used in a **BEAST WARRIORS** spin-off CD). They also sang themes to **WANNA-BE'S**, **MAZE**, and one of the **CONAN THE BOY DETECTIVE** movies, while lead singer Demon Kogure was the voice of Munchausen in **UROTSUKIDOJI**. The band's apocalyptic message became more subdued as the 1990s wore on, and they played a farewell concert on New Year's Eve 1999. The music in *Humane Society* is credited to their producer and sometime keyboardist, but it's derived from many of their most famous songs, including "Rosa," the name of their evil adversary.

HUMANITY HAS DECLINED *

2012. JPN: *Jinrui wa Suitai Shimashita*. TV series. DIR: Seiji Kishi. SCR: Makoto Uezu, Yuniko Ayana, Jun Kumagai. DES: Kyuta Sakai. ANI: Kyuta Sakai. MUS: Ko Otani. PRD: AIC ASTA, Lantis, Marvelous AOL, Movic, Pony Canyon, Sotsu. 24 mins. x 12 eps.

Far in the future, the human race is facing the real prospect of extinction. The nameless heroine plays in the ruins and cares for her aging grandfather, in a picaresque series of encounters with sentient chickens, the "fairies" who somehow have inhabited niches left behind by humanity's decline and several failed experiments in prolonging the human race.

Uneven but often wildly inventive, this bitter-sweet comedy plays to an interesting trend within Japan's modern zeitgeist—a sense of managed decline as the population ages (**ROUJIN Z**) and the number of children dwindles (**BUBU CHACHA**). The

nameless heroine's misadventures play to a sense of modern ennui: a melancholy sense among certain teenagers that they are already witnessing the end of the world, and that it comes accompanied by absurdities, oddities, and the glimmerings of new species coming to fill the vacuum (compare to **KINO'S JOURNEY**). Based on a series of novels by Romeo Tanaka, and with several thematic similarities to the later and far more serious **SUNDAY WITHOUT GOD**.

HUMANOID, THE *

1986. JPN: *The Humanoid: Ai no Wakusei Lazeria*. AKA: *The Humanoid: Laseria the Planet of Love*. Video. DIR: Shinichi Masaki. SCR: Koichi Minade. DES: Hajime Sorayama, Jinpei Kohara. ANI: Takuya Wada, Osamu Kamijo. MUS: Masao Nakajima. PRD: Toshiba EMI, Hero Media. 45 mins.

A truly awful *Star Wars* rip-off, written solely to showcase the "Sexy Robot" art style of illustrator Hajime Sorayama. After a crash-landing, two hotshot pilots seek help from Professor Watson, unaware that they are stumbling into an evil man's attempt to rule the world. Pilot Eric falls for the android Antoinette, who sacrifices herself to save him, but only after pathologically obsessive dialogue about coffee, a couple of chase scenes, and painfully geeky flirtation. A dire reprise of Tezuka's **SPACE FIREBIRD** or an amateurish rehearsal for the infinitely superior **ARMITAGE III**, however you look at it, it is a sure contender for one of the worst anime ever made. Also shown theatrically in Japan as part of a triple bill.

HUMILIATED WIVES *

2007. JPN: *Joku Tsuma*. Video. DIR: Kentaro Shigeta. SCR: Akio Uitsuki. DES: Ryosuke Morimura, Seiho-do. ANI: Ryosuke Morimura. MUS: Yoshi. PRD: YOUC, Digital Works, Love Juice. 2 eps. x 30 mins.

A debt collector picking up payments from housewives forces anyone who's short of cash—and even some who aren't—to pay in kind instead, by threatening to let their husbands know about the extent of their debts. Created by LiLiM Nama and Shupil, part of the **VANILLA SERIES**. **NV**

HUMMINGBIRDS *

1993. JPN: *Idol Boetai Hummingbird*. AKA:

Idol Defense Band Hummingbird. Video. DIR: Kiyoshi Murayama. SCR: Kiyoshi Murayama. DES: Masahide Yanasawa. ANI: Kenichi Katsura. MUS: Kazuo Otani. PRD: Youmex. 50 mins. x 1 ep., 30 mins. x 3 eps.

Starstruck mother Hazuki Toriishi pushes her five daughters into careers as pop idols in a Japan "the day after tomorrow" that has privatized the armed forces. With only media companies having the finances to invest, the air force has become an entertainment industry, as prefabricated pop groups sing songs and fly jets in bizarre competitions, occasionally breaking off to defend the country from foreign invaders.

A silly spoof of the media from **IRRESPONSIBLE CAPTAIN TYLOR**–creator Hitoshi Yoshioka, combining the siblings and super-vehicles of *Thunderbirds*, from whose Tracy family the Toriishis get their name (see **THUNDERBIRDS 2086**), with pop-song interludes in the style of **MACROSS** to promote the singing careers of the five lead voice actresses. Though the quality of the songs never declined, later episodes lost their satirical edge, with middle sister Satsuki developing a crush on her trainer and competing against the feisty foreign Fever Girls, in a predictable run-through of clichés from **SPORTS ANIME**.

The first two volumes were released in the U.K. by Western Connection with rhyming song subtitles. However, they were clumsily cut together in order to avoid paying the BBFC classification authority for two separate releases. The British version is consequently missing two songs and any proper credits—its short "closing credits" actually being the *opening* credits from episode 2. The series was never released in the U.S.

HUNDREDTH MONKEY, THE

1986. JPN: *Hyakubanme no Saru*. Movie. DIR: Kazuo Anzai. SCR: Masaaki Sakurai. DES: Shingo Ozaki. ANI: Shingo Ozaki. MUS: Yuki Takamura. PRD: Tokyo Media Communications, Cinework. 20 mins.

A short cartoon of the 1981 book of the same name by New Age guru Ken Keyes, Jr., based on the story of a 1952 experiment on the southern Japanese island of Kojima. Once one monkey has learned how to wash its food, it is able to teach others the same skill. When a certain number have learned (and Keyes suggests an arbitrary figure of 100), not only do the remaining monkeys suddenly appear to know how to do it, but so too does a completely different group of apes on a completely separate island. Keyes uses this apocryphal tale as a parable for the antinuclear movement, as "proof" that change would come if enough people joined forces. The story has a triple appeal to the Japanese: not only is it "local," it is also antinuclear in the tradition of **BAREFOOT GEN**, and, best of all, copyright-free in accordance with Keyes's wish for it to reach as many people as possible.

HUNTER X HUNTER

1999. TV series, video, movie. DIR: Kazuhiro Furuhashi. SCR: Nobuaki Kishima. DES: Yoshihiro Togashi. ANI: Masaaki Kannan. MUS: Toshihiko Sato. PRD: Nippon Animation, Fuji TV. 25 mins. x 62 eps. (TV1), 25 mins. x 8 eps. (v1), 25 mins. x 8 eps. (v2), 23 mins. x 14 eps. (v3), 25 mins. x 110+ eps. (TV1), 96 mins. (m1), ? mins. (m2).

Twelve-year-old orphan Gon lives on Whale Island with his Aunt Mito. A chance forest meeting with Kyte the Hunter reveals that his father is actually still alive and is known throughout the world as the greatest hunter who ever lived. Gon decides to be just like his dad (the all-purpose job description encompassing monster-killing, bounty-taking, treasure-troving, and tomb-raiding), setting off to take the tests of manhood. In this anime based on a manga by **POLTERGEIST REPORT**–creator Yoshihiro Togashi, however, only one in ten thousand makes it through the tough trials. The television series was followed by three video series—*Hunter X Hunter* (2002), *Hunter X Hunter: Greed Island* (2003), and *Hunter X Hunter: G.I. [Greed Island] Final* (2004), which continued the episode numbering of the television series. The franchise also spun off two live-action stage musicals, a television remake (2011), and the 2013 movies *Hunter x Hunter: Phantom Rouge* (directed by Yuzo Sato) and *Hunter x Hunter: The Last Mission*. Note that in a bizarre convention that also affects shows such as **GUN X SWORD** the "x" in the title is supposed to be silent—the title is thus pronounced "Hunter Hunter."

HURDLE

2005. JPN: *Hurdle Shinjitsu to Yuki no Aida de*. AKA: *Hurdle: Between Truth and Heroism*. Movie. DIR: Satoshi Dezaki. SCR: Kazumi Koide, Mitsuyo Suenaga. DES: Setsuko Shibuichi, Shichiro Kobayashi. ANI: Yukari Kobayashi, Keiko Yamamoto, Shun Matsusada. MUS: Yuki Nakajima. PRD: Magic Bus, Cinema Tohoku, T&K Telefilm. 90 mins.

Did he fall or was he pushed? When a student is thrown off a flight of stairs in middle school, everybody agrees it's a tragedy: but was it really bullying, or attempted suicide? Maybe it was just carelessnessness? His brother and friends decide to lift the lid on the truth in this anime based on Kazuo Aoki's 1999 novel, illustrated by Yoshitomi Tani.

HURRICANE POLYMAR *

1974. JPN: *Hariken Polymar*. AKA: *Inner Destruction Fist Polymar*. TV series, video. DIR: Eiko Toriumi, Hideo Nishimaki, Yoshiyuki Tomino. SCR: Jinzo Toriumi, Akiyoshi Sakai, Masaru Yamamoto, Junichi Shima. DES: Tatsuo Yoshida. ANI: Tsuneo Ninomiya. MUS: Shunsuke Kikuchi. PRD: Tatsunoko, NET. 25 mins. x 26 eps. (TV), 30 mins. x 2 eps. (v).

Mild-mannered police chief Takeshi works for the International Crime Division in Washinkyo City (Washington + Tokyo). One night, he is set upon by four thugs and, despite being an expert at karate, is severely injured. In a replay of **8TH MAN**, kindly Professor Oregar gives him the Polymar suit, an experimental project that could save his life. Takeshi becomes a supercop with a voice-activated suit that fits him like a second skin but can also transform into a plane, a boat, a submarine, and a tank.

A lighthearted and popular superhero show that rode the wave of interest in Bruce Lee and martial arts, with time out for a few in-jokes at the expense of the same studio's earlier **BATTLE OF THE PLANETS**, the series was remade by Akiyuki Shinbo (with designs by Yasuomi Umezu, who would work on a number of other updates of classic Tatsunoko properties) as *New HP* (1996), which is the version available in the U.S. Tatsunoko's remake simplified the original somewhat, moving the action to the man-made island of Tokyo Plus, where Oregar's lab is attacked

by the Catshark Squad. The professor is killed, but his beautiful assistant, Ryoko, manages to get the prototype Polymar Helmet to detective Takeshi before her own death.

HUSTLE PUNCH

1965. TV series. DIR: Hiroshi Ikeda, Kazuya Miyazaki, Hiroshi Shidara. SCR: Hiroshi Ikeda, Hiroaki Hayashi. DES: Yasuji Mori. ANI: Yasuji Mori. MUS: Asei Kobayashi. PRD: Toei, NET. 25 mins. x 26 eps.

Three orphaned animals, Punch the Bear, Touch the Mouse, and Bun the Weasel, try to live a carefree life in a seaside town despite the efforts of their evil enemies, the lupine Professor Garigari and his hench-creatures, Black the Cat and Nu the Pig. Based on a manga in *Manga-O* by prolific animator Yasuji Mori.

HUTCH THE HONEYBEE

1970. JPN: *Mitsubachi Monogatari: Minashigo Hutch*. AKA: *Bee Story: Hutch the Orphan*. TV series. DIR: Ippei Kuri, Seitaro Hara. SCR: Jinzo Toriumi, Saburo Taki, Masaaki Yoshida. DES: Tatsuo Yoshida. ANI: Eiji Tanaka. MUS: Nobuyoshi Koshibe. PRD: Tatsunoko, Fuji TV. 25 mins. x 91 eps. (TV1), 25 mins. x 26 eps. (*New*), 25 mins. x 55 eps. (TV3).

Life in the peaceful Bee Kingdom is disrupted by an invasion of wasps, who destroy the eggs and force the queen to flee with her subjects. A single remaining egg hatches, and young Hutch grows up in an environment where his bee-like looks lead to bullying and persecution. In a mixture of **FROM THE APENNINES TO THE ANDES** with the "Ugly Duckling" from the **TALES OF HANS CHRISTIAN ANDERSEN**, Hutch realizes he is really a bee and sets off with his insect companions to find others of his race. This award-winning tale of a bug's life was so successful that it returned for a second series, *New Hutch* (1974), featuring new designs from the Tatsunoko studio's teenage prodigy, Yoshitaka Amano. For the sequel, the wasps return, and Hutch and his sister are exiled and hear that their mother has perished. With nowhere else to go, they search for a mythical "Beautiful Hill," along with insect companions including a firefly, butterflies, and a ladybug. In 1989, the story was completely remade for Tatsunoko by Iku Suzuki using many of the original scripts from the 1970 version but with all-new animation.

HYAKKI: THE SECRET OF DEVIL'S ISLAND *

2003. AKA: *Pandemonium*. Video. DIR: Yoshitaka Fujimoto. SCR: Yo Tachibana. DES: Minoru Murao. ANI: Jiro Hirakata. MUS: N/C. PRD: Pink Pineapple, ARMS. 30 mins. x 3 eps.
Young visitors on an apparently deserted island find themselves overtaken by uncontrollable lusts and fear that their lives, souls, and, unsurprisingly, bodies may be in danger of demonic invasion. ⓛⓝⓥ

HYAKKO

2008. TV series, video. DIR: Michio Fukuda. SCR: Yoshihiko Tomizawa. DES: Keiko Ota, Megumi Kato. ANI: Keiko Ota, Tetsuya Ishikawa. MUS: Hiromi Mizutani, Kenji Fujisawa. PRD: Nippon Animation, Flex Comics, Hakuhodo DY Media Partners, Media Factory. 25 mins. x 13 eps. (TV), 10 mins. (v).
A huge high school campus can be an intimidating place, but when new girls Ayumi and Tatsuki meet the irrepressible Torako and her best friend Suzume they find allies in the confusing world of high school and adolescence. Haruaki Kato's 2007 manga is a slice of school life leavened with some comedy and mild fan service. A ten-minute video from the same crew, *Hyakko Extra*, was included on the DVD release in 2009.

HYAKUTARO

1991. JPN: *Ushiro no Hyakutaro*. AKA: *Hyakutaro by My Side*. Video. DIR: Seitaro Hara. SCR: Jiro Tsunoda, Isao Shizudani, Masaaki Sakurai. DES: Koji Uemura. ANI: Seiji Kikuchi. MUS: Hiro Tsunoda. PRD: Pierrot Project. 50 mins. x 2 eps.
Occult researcher's son Kazutaro Ushiro and his guardian spirit, Hyakutaro, investigate paranormal activity. Based on the 1973 manga in *Shonen Magazine* by FRIGHTFUL NEWS–creator Jiro Tsunoda, this anime is said to be the indirect inspiration for most of the ghostbusting genre, from PHANTOM QUEST CORP to POLTERGEIST REPORT.

HYOUKA

2012. AKA: *Frozen Dessert*. TV series. DIR: Yasuhiro Takemoto. SCR: Maiko Nishioka, Miyuki Egami, Katsuhiko Muramoto, Sugihiko

Ashida. DES: Futoshi Nishiya. ANI: Miku Kadowaki, Kazuya Sakamoto, Hiroko Utsumi. MUS: Kohei Tanaka. PRD: Kyoto Animation, Kadokawa, Lantis, Klockworx. 26 mins. x 22 eps. (TV), 26 mins. (v).
Reluctant teenager Hotaro Oreki joins his high school's Classical Literature Club at the insistence of his elder sister, who needs members for her member-free society. But, surprise-surprise, the memberless club soon attracts a bunch of oddballs, while the members' interest in "classical literature" begins to focus on solving mysteries both criminal and cultural. Although this series takes its name from the first of Honobu Yonezawa's series of books about the teen sleuths of the Classical Literature Club, the episodes encompass a further three volumes of the print version. Creator Yonezawa was a relatively minor author of young adult fiction for Kadokawa in the noughties, whose output was subject to reconsideration after one of his later standalone works won an award from the Mystery Writers of Japan, perhaps explaining why this series was suddenly dusted off again. A single bonus episode was packaged on DVD and given away with the manga.

HYPER POLICE *

1997. TV series. DIR: Masahiro Omori, Shinya Sadamitsu, Koichi Chiaki. SCR: Sukehiro Tomita, Shigeru Yanagawa. DES: Keiji Goto. ANI: Keiji Goto, Hiroyuki Kanbe, Kazumi Ikeda. MUS: N/C. PRD: Studio Pierrot, TV Tokyo. 25 mins. x 25 eps.
Natsuki Sasahara is a human-feline cross-breed, her associate Sakura is an eight-tailed fox-girl (a sure sign she cannot be trusted, since she needs to swindle Natsuki to gain her ninth tail), and both use their magical powers to hunt criminals in a Tokyo crawling with animal hybrids, ghosts, and goblins. Other major cast members are Batanen Fujioka, Natsuki's lycanthrope senior, Batanen's cousin and partner Tommy, stationchief Mudagami (a minor deity), and the single flustered human: the (initially) beast-hating patrolwoman Naoko Kondo. As befits ensemble cop shows like PATLABOR and YOU'RE UNDER ARREST!, downtime is as important to the show as crime-fighting, and the cast spends an inordinate amount of time at Makoto and Ayami Tachibana's friendly Ranpo

Coffee Shop. *HP* has the supernatural urban feel of SILENT MÖBIUS, but it's played for laughs and features a considerable dose of anthropomorphic titillation. Based on a manga by "MEE," who also created ADVENTURES OF KOTETSU. ⓝ

HYPERDOLL *

1995. JPN: *Rakusho Hyperdoll*. AKA: *Happy Victory Hyperdoll; Hyper-Doll: Mew and Mica the Easy Fighters*. Video. DIR: Makoto Moriwaki. SCR: Ryo Motohira. DES: Satoru Nakamura. ANI: Satoru Nakamura. MUS: Hiroshi Nakano, Masayuki Negishi. PRD: Pioneer, AIC. 40 mins. x 2 eps.
Mica (the cool, sensible one) and Mew (the hotheaded, impulsive one) are two beautiful aliens sent to defend Earth from monsters. Disguised as typical Japanese high school girls, they befriend Earth girl Shoko and hapless boy Hideo, taking time off (when their boss tracks them down) to fight alien invaders with the aid of an orbiting power converter that harnesses the energy of "zero-space" and beams it to them via their earrings. Unfairly termed "hyperdull" in FANDOM, this lighthearted superhero comedy features high-quality animation, a good dub, and spoofs of monster shows stretching back to ULTRAMAN, though its dim-witted girls in skimpy costumes accidentally causing massive collateral damage owe a further debt to the DIRTY PAIR. There are also bonus live-action sections in which the petrified voice actresses stammer their way through some minor comedy business, demonstrating why so many Japanese scripts are better performed as anime. Based on a manga from *Shonen Captain* by Shinpei Ito, who also wrote the manga adaptation of MOLDIVER. The live-action sections were written and directed by the Konaka brothers, ARMITAGE III's Chiaki and BLACK JACK's Kazuya.

HYPNOTIC DISGRACE ACADEMY

2008. JPN: *Saimin Ryojoku Gakuen*. Video. DIR: N/C. SCR: N/C. DES: Hifumi. ANI: N/C. MUS: N/C. PRD: Studio9MAiami, MediaBank. 30 mins. x 3 eps.
A student gets hold of a mysterious device that allows him to command the will of any female he chooses, turning them into lust machines and amplifying any feeling they may be concealing. Guess how he uses it?

This premise from the game by Liquid was also used in **Hypnotized College Slaves** because **Erotica and Pornography**, like mainstream material, doesn't always need to be original. Our usual sources are silent on the identity of most of the crew, even their pseudonyms. **Ⓝ**

HYPNOTIZED COLLEGE SLAVES
2010. JPN: *Gakuen Saimin Reido*. Video. DIR: Tsuyoshi Kimura. SCR: Taifu Sekimachi. DES: Tsuyoshi Kimura. ANI: Tsuyoshi Kimura. MUS: N/C. PRD: Milky, MS Pictures, Gakuen Saimin Reido Production Committee. 28 mins. x 3 eps.

Mr. Sato is an ugly, awkward teacher despised by all the females in school … until he gets his hands on a magical cellphone that enables him to hypnotize anyone just by taking a photo. When they're in a trance he can make them do anything. Now, not only the students but the head teacher and the faculty will bend to his will. The McGuffin of Absolute Power Without Responsibility (as seen in **Death Note**) turns up again in this anime based on a porn game by Silky's. They're wearing school uniforms, but we just know that if this is ever translated, the U.S. release will insist that a *gakuen* is a college. **ⓃⓋ**

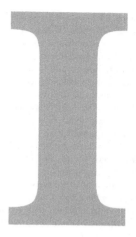

I AM A CAT

1982. JPN: *Wagahai wa Neko de Aru*. TV special. DIR: Rintaro. SCR: Kiyohide Ohara. DES: Kazuo Komatsubara, Etsumi Haruki. ANI: Kazuo Komatsubara. MUS: Antonio Vivaldi. PRD: Toei, Fuji TV. 73 mins.

"I" is a cat without a name who lives with an English teacher, Mr. Kushami (Mr. Sneeze). "I" can't believe how stupid human beings are and chronicles some of their more incredible foibles. In particular, he is fascinated by Kushami's pupil Mizushima, who falls in love with Haruko, only daughter of war profiteer Kaneda. Based on the 1905 novel by BOTCHAN–author Soseki Natsume, this adaptation gained a huge 27.8% rating when broadcast. The feline character designs were by JARINKO CHIE's Etsumi Haruki.

I AM A DOG

1983. JPN: *Wagahai wa Inu de Aru: Don Matsugoro no Monogatari*. AKA: *I Am a Dog: The Story of Don Matsugoro*. TV special. DIR: Kimio Yabuki. SCR: Kiyohide Ohara. DES: Etsumi Haruki. ANI: Takashi Abe. MUS: Hiroki Tamaki. PRD: Toei, Fuji TV. 73 mins.

Mr. Matsuzawa is a novelist who lives in Chiba Prefecture. Only his daughter Kazuko knows that the family dog, Don Matsugoro, can talk. Don is wounded in a fight with the neighbors' dog, King, a nouveau-riche mongrel with ideas above his station. At the vet, however, he falls in love with a little patchwork puppy called Chotaro. A less successful follow-up to the previous year's I AM A CAT; some of the same team from that show adapted Hisashi Inoue's novel *The Life of Don Matsugoro*,

changing the title to imply a connection that simply wasn't there.

I BELIEVE HER

2011. JPN: *Ore wa Kanojo o Shinjiteru*. AKA: *Second Virgin*. Video. DIR: N/C. SCR: N/C. DES: N/C. ANI: Genki Satsumaya. MUS: N/C. PRD: Silver. 27 mins.

Porn isn't just porn (EROTICA AND POR-NOGRAPHY). To its aficionados it has as many classifications and subdivisions as any other genre, and this anime falls into the *netorare* division: stories about sluts who cheat on their oblivious boyfriends. Salesman Kensuke is posted to a branch office of his company. The commute from his home would be really difficult, so he moves into closer digs and leaves the gorgeous Ayumu behind. Kensuke isn't exactly a go-getter so he does as he's told, even though he feels sure that a girl like Ayumu could do better. And guess what? On her first night out after he leaves, she does. Soon she's having a full-on affair with a handsome guy. Meanwhile Kensuke is also being pursued by several women in his new location. Based on a 2007 video game, *Ore wa Kanojo o Shinjiteru! ~ Enkyori Renai no Susume ~ Genteiban (I Believe Her! Susume's Long Distance Love Affair: Restricted Edition)*, by Lune Team Bitters, which was popular enough to have a further release in 2009 minus the "restricted" tag. This video version was billed as the "first" on its Japanese release, in such a way as to imply being part of a two- or three-part series, but this appears to be the only story that made it to market. **N**

I CAN

2010. JPN: *Ai Kyan*. Video. DIR: N/C. SCR: N/C. DES: Motohiko Kurihara, Pink Kanemetai. ANI: Pink Kanemetai. MUS: Masaya Koike. PRD: PoRO. 30 mins. x 2 eps.

In an anime based on a porn game by LiLiM, the magical creature Kupu helps and watches over wannabe idol singer Miyu in time-honored magical-girl anime style. When they meet average teenager Ryota, it turns out he's not so average after all, since he has mysterious powers. But Miyu's ambition leads her into the path of a rapacious manager, perverse photographers, and all the other perils of stardom. Since one of the functions of magical girl anime is to enable small girls to fantasize about the gorgeous older girls they will one day transform into, it's a trope much loved by porn game and anime creators and their customers. It's not unusual for credit listings on such anime to be thin, or pseudonymous, but Motohiko Kurihara has a resumé that goes beyond porn, with a solid list of key animator credits and animation direction on shows including BEN-TO. **N**

I DON'T HAVE MANY FRIENDS *

2011. JPN: *Haganai*. AKA: *Boku wa Tomodachi ga Sukunai*. TV series, video. DIR: Hisashi Saito, Toru Kitahara. SCR: Tatsuhiko Urahata, Kurasumi Sunayama. DES: Yoshihiro Watanabe, Yuka Hirama, Aya Kuginuki, Toshihiro Koyama. ANI: Maki Fujii, Naoko Nakamura, Yoshihiro Watanabe, Hong Shen, Yuka Takashina. MUS: Tom-H@ck. PRD: AIC, TBS, Bushiroad Inc., Media Factory, Bandai Namco Games, Good Smile Company. 25

mins. x 12 eps. (TV1), 24 mins. x 12 eps. (TV2), 25 mins. x 2 eps. (v).

Kodaka Hasegawa is an accidental misfit. His blond hair, inherited from his dead British mother, and his glaring eyes make his classmates decide he's some kind of hoodlum, and they avoid him. So instead of having the usual high school friends and allies, he has to start over when he joins a Catholic high school. One day he finds classmate Yozora talking to her imaginary friend, and after some embarrassment they decide to form a club in the hope of attracting new friends. But as tennis clubs attract tennis players, misfit clubs attract misfits, with comical results. That most of them are female proves the thesis of all harem shows in anime ROMANCE AND DRAMA: you may be too weird to have friends, but somewhere there's a whole group of girls who will fall for you. Not to mention the casual racism that immediately equates a foreign hair color with criminality—thanks, Japan.

This comedy of cliché is based on the 2009 light-novel series *Boku wa Tomodachi ga Sukunai* by Yomi Hirasaka with art by Buriki, which spun off two manga in 2010: *Haganai: I Don't Have Many Friends* written by Hirasaka with art by Itachi, and *Boku wa Tomodachi Ga Sukunai+* by Misaki Harukawa with art by Shoichi Taguchi. There have been two videos at the time of writing. The first, bundled with the seventh volume of the light novel in September 2011, to generate interest in the series' TV debut two weeks later, is a dream sequence episode. The second, released a year later, emphasizes the series' harem show allegiances, with all the club members writing a chapter of a novel in which Kodaka is the protagonist. The success of the franchise extended into gaming in 2012.

The original TV production team made a further 12-episode TV series, which commenced screening in 2013. *Haganai NEXT* was directed by Toru Kitahara, with original creator Hirasaka joining Urahata on the planning team and Kurasumi Sunayama scripting several episodes.

I DREAM OF MIMI *
1997. JPN: *Buttobi!! CPU*. Video. DIR: Masamitsu Hidaka. SCR: Atsuhiro Tomioka. DES: Yuriko Chiba. ANI: Yuriko Chiba. MUS: N/C. PRD: Pink Pineapple, KSS. 30 mins. x 3 eps.

In this erotic comedy based on the *Young Animal* strip from AREA 88–creator Kaoru Shintani, a hapless boy finds himself in possession of Mimi, a new model of "sexy computer." Biocomputer Mimi must fend off romantic rivals such as the Nac sisters and the superpowered Performa Girl, while her man Akira looks on shyly like the hero of HANDMAID MAY, METAL ANGEL MARIE, and any number of similar geek-meets-love-toy shows. **N**

I GIVE MY ALL
1987. JPN: *Minna Agechau*. AKA: *I'll Do It with Anyone; Everybody's Doing It*. Video. DIR: Osamu Uemura. SCR: Yutaka Takahashi. DES: Takumi Tsukasa. ANI: Takafumi Hayashi. MUS: Hiromoto Tobisawa. PRD: Animate Film, JC Staff. 45 mins.

Mutsuro has been forced to take a "ronin" year off to study for retaking his university entrance exams. Resorting to self-abuse in his lonely room, he attracts the attentions of lonely neighbor Yuno, the bored daughter of a rich corporate magnate. The two are soon in bed together, though Yuno's interfering grandmother decides that she should make an honest man out of Mutsuro and give him a job in Daddy's company. Based on the 1982 manga by Hikari Yuzuki, serialized in *Young Jump*, this well-animated soft-core story premiered on a double bill with DIGITAL DEVIL STORY. **N**

I LIKE THE NANIWABUSHI
1982. JPN: *Naniwabushi Daisuki*. TV series. DIR: Takashi Sawada. SCR: Kiyohiro Yamamoto. DES: N/C. ANI: Norio Takahashi. MUS: N/C. PRD: Kansai TV, Tohan Planning, Fuji TV. 54 mins.

Two stories that mix animation with *naniwabushi* (storytelling accompanied by shamisen playing). One is a tale of General Nogi, the famous suicide, visiting the shrines at Ise on his way to Nagoya, while his wife is mistaken for a commoner as she books into a hotel. The second story is of a sumo wrestling trainee, ridiculed by his fellows, who trains hard and avenges himself—the standard clichés of a SPORTS ANIME, just with plink-plonky music on top of it.

I LOVE YOU *
2001. JPN: *Suki da yo*. Video. DIR: Haruo

Okawara. SCR: Rokurota Makabe. DES: Aoi Kimizuka. ANI: Haruo Okawara. MUS: Yoshi. PRD: YOUC, Digital Works (Vanilla Series). 30 mins. x 2 eps.

Jun and Hijiri are enjoying themselves in bed when Jun realizes that he wants more to life than casual encounters. He yearns for true romance, and anime tradition dictates that likely candidates will arise in the form of his childhood friends, Ren and her sister Rina. He is mistaken for a pervert on a train by Mina, a third girl who turns out to be the younger sister of the others, who was separated from them by the conditions of their parents' divorce. Sub–LOVE HINA romantic entanglements ensue, with plenty of sex, until Jun eventually ends up in bed with Mina—all antagonism between them is dispelled when she is helping out in her mother's coffee shop and is consequently dressed as a waitress. However, their relationship begins to turn sour when old photos reveal that Mina may not be who she says she is—she looks far too young in the old pictures to be the person that she claims to be. Another entry in the VANILLA SERIES. **LNV**

I SAW THE LAZYBONES
1988. JPN: *Namakemono ga Miteta*. Video. DIR: Akinori Nagaoka, Masami Furukawa. SCR: Takashi Murakami. DES: Takashi Murakami. ANI: Kinichiro Suzuki. MUS: N/C. PRD: Toei, Agent 21. 30 mins. x 2 eps.

In this short comedy based on a gag manga by Takashi Murakami originally serialized in *Young Jump*, a koala robs a bank to help poverty-stricken pandas. Listed as a "movie" in some Japanese sources, even though the package clearly states "original video anime."

I SHALL NEVER RETURN *
2006. JPN: *Boku wa Konomama Kaeranai*. AKA: *Our Road of No Return*. Video. DIR: Katsumi Minokuchi. SCR: N/C. DES: Yumi Nakayama, Yoshinobu Hirose. ANI: Yumi Nakayama. MUS: Harukichi Yamamoto. PRD: JC Staff, Soft Garage. 30 mins.

Ken Amafuji is crazy about his best friend Ritsuro Yoshinari, despite the fact that Ritsuro seems happy with his girlfriend Moeko. After his mother divorces and asks him to move out for a while, Ken drops out of school, gets a job in a host club, and moonlights as a rent boy. Ritsuro, keen to help his friend, helps him fix up his apartment and eventually moves in with him. Despite their close friendship, Ken can't confide in him, but he does steal his girlfriends, including Moeko, hoping that somehow this will bring them together. Based on a 1992 manga by Kazuna Uchida, this video can't hope to condense four years of manga stories into its running time. That didn't matter to the intended audience of *yaoi* fangirls (ARGOT AND JARGON), who bought it to add another dimension to their passion for the manga, but it makes for limited plot and character development. Most such one-shot spin-offs have relatively low budgets, so animation and design are not outstanding. On the plus side, the manga was also published in English by the now-defunct Aurora Publishing, which meant that it was possible for U.S. fans to replicate the Japanese experience and get the anime after reading the manga.

I'LL/CKBC *

2002. JPN: *I'll Generation Basket.* AKA: *I'll / Crazy KOUZO Basketball Club.* Video. DIR: Itsuro Kawasaki. SCR: Miyuki Takahashi. DES: Kaname Sekiguchi. ANI: Kaname Sekiguchi. MUS: N/C. PRD: Mamiko Namazue, Aniplex, SME Visual Works. 30 mins. x 2 eps. Akane Tachibana and Hitonari Hiiragi are two former basketball rivals forced to cooperate when Hitonari is transferred to Akane's school in order to play on its basketball team. However, Hitonari's parents expect better things for their son and hope to move him to an even better team, threatening to turn them into rivals once more. Based on the 14-volume manga by Hiroyuki Asada, which ran for nine years, from the time when SLAM DUNK and HOOP DAYS were new, until 2004, this is yet another of those short-lived anime releases designed to reawaken interest in a franchise as it nears the end of its days. As so often occurs with such ventures, the story suffers from being compressed into an hour, despite attractive design work.

I'M GONNA BE AN ANGEL *

1999. JPN: *Tenshi ni Naru Mon.* AKA: *Let Me Be an Angel; Make Me an Angel.* TV series. DIR: Hiroshi Nishikiori. SCR: Mamiko Ikeda, Masashi Sogo. DES: Hiromi Kato. ANI: Hiromi Kato. MUS: Yoshikazu Suo. PRD: Studio Pierrot, TV Tokyo. 25 mins. x 26 eps. As is the way with so many anime children, Yusuke's father goes away on business and leaves him at home alone (there is no sign of his mother). En route to school, he lands on top of a naked girl with a halo. The "accidental kiss" she receives makes him her husband in her eyes—for similar inadvertent betrothals see URUSEI YATSURA and PHOTON. Yusuke runs a mile but is shocked to discover that his new "wife" Noelle is a new transfer student at his school. Unable to shake her off, he gains a new extended family of supernatural creatures, including a father modeled on FRANKENSTEIN, vampiric elder brother Gabriel, dark-elf sister Ruka, and invisible older sister Sara. The grandmother matriarch, even more opposed to the marriage than Yusuke himself, tries to oppose his presence, though since they have moved into and converted his own house into a supernatural dwelling, this is not so easy. Meanwhile, Noelle is at the center of another anime love polygon with Despair, who wants her for himself, Yusuke, still lusting after girl-next-door Natsume, and the enigmatic Michael, whose book of dreams writes the closure of each episode. A hyper-cute, hyper-silly TV series that crashes together innumerable clichés of unwelcome-guest and magical-girlfriend shows, along with the traditions of school dramas and a brighter, breezier rip-off of *The Addams Family.*

I'M TEPPEI

1977. JPN: *Ore wa Teppei.* TV series. DIR: Tadao Nagahama, Shigetsugu Yoshida, Yoshifumi Kondo, Hiroshi Fukutomi, Tsutomu Shibayama. SCR: Seiji Matsuoka, Shunichi Yukimuro, Soji Yoshikawa, Hirokazu Mizude. DES: Tetsuya Chiba. ANI: Daikichiro Kusunobe. MUS: Michiaki Watanabe. PRD: Shin'Ei, Nippon Animation, Fuji TV. 25 mins. x 28 eps. Fortune hunters Hiromi Uesugi and his son Teppei are arrested for damaging a field in the Shinshu mountains, though they claim they are only following the directions to buried treasure from an ancient map. Teppei blows up the police station to aid his father's escape, and the case reaches the local newspaper, where it is read by estranged members of the Uesugi clan. The prodigal clan members return, and Teppei, who has grown up in the wild in the company of animals and his semicivilized father, has trouble adjusting to the genteel culture of the Rin Academy school where he is sent.

Based on a 1973 manga in *Shonen Magazine* by TOMORROW'S JOE–creator Tetsuya Chiba, *I'm Teppei* was soon taken off the air due to low ratings, despite featuring storyboards from future WHISPER OF THE HEART–director Yoshifumi Kondo.

I'S *

2002. JPN: *From I's—Mo Hitotsu no Natsu no Monogatari.* AKA: *From I's: Another Summer Story.* Video. DIR: Yosei Morino. SCR: Shigenori Kageya. DES: Rin Shin. ANI: Studio Pierrot. MUS: N/C. PRD: Studio Pierrot, DigiCube. 29 mins. x 2 eps. (v1), 30 mins. x 6 eps. (v2). Ichitaka Seto is a high school sophomore, not very confident or forthcoming and madly in love with Iori Ashizuki, the class babe, who is working hard toward a career as an actress. He turns into a total dork around her but begins to build a friendship that may go further with his dream girl, until his other childhood friend Itsuki Akiba, a perky tomboy with an open, freeandeasy attitude, comes back from America. Her family moved over to the States years ago, but when she wants to graduate high school in her old hometown, it's only natural that she should room with old friends the Setos.

Masazaku Katsura's manga *I's* is a rerun of his VIDEO GIRL AI without the magic video store, a gentle romance whose three main characters are childhood friends whose names all begin with I. The girls are no mere eye candy, but bright, ambitious young women. Iori is serious enough about her career to question whether she wants a romantic relationship with anyone for a while, and Itsuki wants to be a sculptor and is working hard toward her dream. Teen romance is beautifully rendered both visually and psychologically in all Katsura's love stories, and he understands but rarely overplays the importance of the jiggles, giggles, and wiggles of "fan service." A remake, *I's Pure* (2005), was directed by Mamoru Kanbe. **N**

IBLARD TIME

2007. JPN: *Iblard Jikan.* Video. DIR: Naohisa Inoue. SCR: N/C. DES: Mitsuki Nakamura. ANI: Kenichi Konishi. MUS: Kiyonori Matsuo, Kazuyuki Komuro. PRD: Studio Ghibli. 30 mins. The fantasy realm of Iblard, created by Inoue (and previously glimpsed in the dream sequences of **WHISPER OF THE HEART**), is explored through digitally manipulated shots of his fantasy paintings, so that trees and grass move in the wind, people walk, and the scenery unfolds around the viewer, drawing him or her into this otherworld. There's no dialogue, just soft, relaxing music. This is a beautifully made piece of moving art, but its elegance can't completely mask the echo of those old screensavers showing a tankful of tropical fish. Iblard looks like an interesting place; it deserves to be a setting for stories, not a piece of extremely high-end wallpaper.

ICE *
2007. AKA: *ICE—The Last Generation; ICE—Yesterday, Today, and No Future.* Video, movie. DIR: Makoto Kobayashi. SCR: Yasushi Hirano, Makoto Kobayashi. DES: Masaya Onishi, Makoto Kobayashi. ANI: N/C. MUS: Il Won. PRD: PPM, E-Net Frontier, Eleven Arts. 30 mins. x 3 eps. (v), 102 mins. (m). It's 2012. Most of the human race has been wiped out by an environmental disaster. The last man died almost 20 years ago. Nothing that grows can be eaten, so all that sustains the remnant of humanity is the dwindling stock of processed food. The remaining women are divided between two ideologies. One group is busy accepting its fate and grabbing as much pleasure as possible before the end; the others are using the science of "vicious men" to try and find a solution. In Tokyo, one of the world's last inhabited areas, the two sides come into a conflict over a hidden sample of ICE, a mysterious substance that could save them all.

There are some strong ideas in *ICE*, but unfortunately they are hampered by lazy writing. Why is there a conflict in the first place? Surely women interested only in pleasure would just shrug and let the geek girls get on with it? Why do the geeks constantly condemn "vicious" male toys like guns while making gleeful use of any armaments that come their way? If the world was dragged to the edge of destruction less than 20 years ago, how have they managed to find the time and resources to create new fashions? If there's no food growing any more, how do you explain the still

well-stocked convenience store? Why does the bad-ass fighting broad have a high-tech artificial hand and an old-school peg leg? Both plot and design are incoherent: society teeters on the brink of extinction, but the arts of the hairdresser and the lingerie designer are flourishing (see also **HIGHLANDER: THE SEARCH FOR VENGEANCE**, **FIST OF THE NORTH STAR**, etc. etc.). The animation too is inconsistent, veering from fluid and graphic action scenes to clunky scenes low on frame-counts.

Creator and director Makoto Kobayashi has been active in anime for over three decades. In 1983 he designed the mecha for **BIRTH**, one of the earliest anime made for video. In 1988 he created and directed **DRAGON'S HEAVEN**, one of the most intriguing mecha-combat videos ever made. Although he's worked on a solid list of titles since, his only other directing gig was the overlooked **6 ANGELS**. Hirano and Akimoto both worked on *6 Angels*, but Akimoto is better known as the producer behind girl idol army AKB48 (**AKB0048**) and its many spin-offs. Five members of AKB48 have voice roles in *ICE*. That indicates the target audience for this anime, who are obviously not expected to be concerned about character development, plot, structure, or logical consistency. A movie-length edit of the videos appeared in Japanese theaters, and Hirano wrote a novelization that was published in 2007. **V**

ICHI THE KILLER *
2002. JPN: *Koroshiya Ichi.* AKA: *Ichi The Killer the Animation: Episode Zero.* Video. DIR: Shinji Ishidaira. SCR: Sakichi Sato. DES: Tsuneo Ninomiya. ANI: Masanori Ohara. MUS: Yu Takase. PRD: Shogakukan, Amuse. 50 mins. Quiet schoolboy Ichi must put up with constant abuse from his classmates, but never does anything to stand up to them. Beaten and attacked at school, he then returns home to a tongue lashing from his parents who criticize him harshly before running off to their bedroom for another noisy sex session with ropes and whips. Ichi stoically endures such torments until the night he finds a wounded animal in the road. He goes to help it, but the confused creature bites him, causing Ichi to snap. Years of pent-up aggression come to the fore as he literally kicks the animal inside out, discovering in the process that

he gets a thrill out of dealing death.

Some years later, an amnesiac Ichi is being cared for in a mental asylum. All memories of his earlier life having been blocked out, he has been forced to start again from scratch and has the mind of a six-year-old in an adult body. His parole officer Kakihara finds him work placement at a karate hall, hoping that the discipline of a martial art will help bring Ichi back into society. Instead, it sets him on a series of encounters that reawaken the psychopath within, setting him up for a life as a brutal assassin.

A prequel spin-off of Takashi Miike's violent movie *Ichi the Killer* (2001), itself based on a manga by Hideo Yamamoto, *Ichi* refashions the tropes of teen revenge for a new generation who has never heard of **UROTSUKIDOJI** or, for that matter, the original *Count of Monte Cristo* that informed **GANKUTSUOU**. However, this story ditches fantastic or science fictional trappings in favor of the methods of live-action cinema: shaky-cam effects and moments of surreal magic realism to illustrate Ichi's inner torment. Limited animation is compensated by the liberal use of red paint; there is a great deal of violence. Miike himself voices the pivotal role of Kakihara. **○NV**

ICZER-ONE *
1985. JPN: *Tatakae! Iczer-1; Boken! Ic-zer-3; Iczer Gal Iczelion.* AKA: *Fight! Iczer-1; Adventure! Iczer-3; Iczelion; Iczer Saga.* Video. DIR: Toshihiro Hirano, Hideaki Hisashi. SCR: Toshihiro Hirano, Arii Emu ("REM"). DES: Toshihiro Hirano, Junichi Watanabe, Masanori Nishii, Hiroaki Motoigi, Shinji Aramaki, Yasuhiro Moriki, Takashi Hashimoto. ANI: Narumi Kakinouchi, Masami Obari, Hiroaki Ogami, Masanori Nishii, Takafumi Hashimoto. MUS: Michiaki Watanabe, Takashi Kudo. PRD: AIC, KSS. 30 mins. x 2 eps., 48 mins. (v1), 60 mins. x 3 eps. (v2, *Iczer-3*), 30 mins. x 2 eps. (v3, *Iczelion*). An alien ship carrying the survivors of the Cthulhu, a race of female clones, is taken over by the sinister entity Big Gold and heads for Earth. The Cthulhu (hastily and ineptly disguised as "Cutowolf" in early Western publicity to avoid possible copyright problems) seek a new home, and with Big Gold's malign energy driving them, they decide that Earth will suit them nicely once they kick out the current oc-

cupants. One of the Cthulhu, Iczer-One, is willing to fight for Earth but must link up with the right human to help her power her mighty fighting machine, Iczer-Robo. The "right human" is Nagisa Kano, an ordinary Japanese schoolgirl who is so terrified by seeing her parents transformed into alien monsters and her world falling to pieces around her that she can do very little apart from quake in terror. Only when she unleashes the full force of her anger can she power the huge robot, but then she and Iczer-One are an unstoppable combination. The Cthulhu call on all their powers to warp dimensions, transform familiar objects and places into nightmarish threats, and send in gross, drooling monsters. At last, they even throw in Iczer-One's nasty red-haired clone sister, Iczer-Two; but they can't win against the love and trust between Nagisa and Iczer-One, since both are willing to make the ultimate sacrifice to save Earth.

Hirano's dark, dank otherworld was based on a story by Rei Aran, with nightmarish references to the work of H. P. Lovecraft (see ARMITAGE III). However, nameless terrors (HORROR AND MONSTERS) are hampered by the fact that the "unimaginable," once animated, looks merely nasty, but Watanabe's monsters are as well crafted as Aramaki's fabulous robots. The script is loaded with homoerotic subtexts and sexualized cruelty, all the more effective for being less than completely explicit. Nagisa's helpless terror is an understandable reaction to an extreme situation, rather than being an annoying character trait played up by writer and actress in the mistaken belief that helplessness is cute, and Iczer-One is the ideal heroine—brave, understanding, and determined. A shameless steal from the ending of *Superman II* doesn't jibe but makes for a rather touching finale in which Nagisa, having given her all to save the world, is rewarded by getting her old life back and forgetting everything else, including the friend who would have died to save her.

Hirano returned to the concept with *Iczer-3* (1990), toning down the violence but keeping the fan-service nudity. Big Gold was defeated but left many of her progeny still at large in the galaxy. Iczer-One has tracked them down and destroyed all but one, Neos Gold. After a terrible battle,

both are wounded and agree to a truce to heal, after which they'll settle things with a final fight. As Iczer-One withdraws to recoup her strength, Neos Gold cheats by sending her cohorts to soften up Earth for her attack, so the Cthulhu send prepubescent Iczer-3 to defend the planet until "big sister" recovers. With a descendant of Nagisa Kano and the crew of an Earth battle cruiser, Iczer-3 attempts to hold off the enemy with the Power of Cute. A helium-powered performance from wrestler Cuty Suzuki in the leading role took what had been a tale of nameless horrors into the realms of high camp, grounded by the reappearance of the two older Iczer clones for the final battle.

Hirano reworked the concept again as an armored-girl-team show in the manner of BUBBLEGUM CRISIS, first as a manga and then for the two-part video *Iczelion* (1994). For this resurrection, production moved to KSS, with Hashimoto and Masanori Nishii joining Hirano for design work. Nagisa Kai is an ordinary teenager until fate intervenes and makes her the chosen combat partner of an intelligent battlesuit. Iczel robots, useful entities in their own right, become Iczelion battlesuits when "fused" with their girl operatives in a nude transformation sequence. Together with three other young women, Nagisa must save Earth from subjugation by an invading alien army headed by Chaos and Cross, who have so far swept across the galaxy defeating all in their path. At first Nagisa is too terrified to fight and even separates from her Iczel in an attempt to escape, but when her friends at school are threatened, she decides she must save them. Once more, affection between girls wins the day, though the explicit lesbian overtones of the first series have been edged into the background. The two later incarnations lack the dark power of the first, moving the original concept in less adventurous directions, but the series remains a firm favorite with older fans. *Iczer-3* was subsequently renamed *Iczer Reborn* in a 2003 U.S. DVD release—a smart move that helped offset some of the numerical confusion. **○Ⓝ♡**

IDOL ANGEL WELCOME YOKO
1990. JPN: *Idol Tenshi Yokoso Yoko*. AKA: *Hello Yoko*. TV series. DIR: Tetsuro Amino.

SCR: Takeshi Shudo. DES: Studio Live. ANI: Sanae Kobayashi. MUS: Hideyuki Tanaka. PRD: TSC, Quest, Ashi Pro, TV Tokyo. 25 mins. x 43 eps.
A unique addition to the magical-girl genre of CREAMY MAMI and its ilk, in which real-life idol Yoko Tanaka, along with her anime alter ego (also called Yoko Tanaka, but with different Chinese characters spelling out the name), must solve problems and get to the concerts on time.

IDOL FIGHTER SU-CHI-PAI *
1996. AKA: *Idolfight Sweetypie II*. Video. DIR: Yasunori Ide. SCR: Yasunori Ide. DES: Hiroko Kazui. ANI: Hiroko Kazui. MUS: Fumitaka Anzai. PRD: Darts, Domu. 30 mins.
Once a century, ten magical mahjong tiles (the "Legendary Pais") appear, and once collected are capable of granting the possessor a wish. Heroine Suchi Pai ("Sweetypie"), S/M queen Cherry Pai, cyborg warrior Lemon Pai, erstwhile emissary from Peachyland and singing idol Peach Pai, and alien bunny(girl) Milky Pai are all magical girls (as in SAILOR MOON) who are competing to obtain the tiles, which take the form of feral catgirls ("Monsters"). One of many computer-game spinoffs (such as GRADUATION or BATTLE TEAM LAKERS EX) that, perhaps wisely, dumped the gameplay and merely reassigned the characters to a more interesting situation. In this case, it was the stars of the second iteration of a popular strip computer game franchise, *Idol Janshi Su-chi-pai*, notable for designs by GUNSMITH CATS' Kenichi Sonoda. As with the STREET FIGHTer II franchise, there was no *Su-chi-pai "I"* in anime form, a fact lampooned in the show's subtitle: "Somehow this feels like the first episode." Nor was there a sequel, despite the set-up for an ongoing plot, although a largely live-action making-of video, *Clear the Su-chi-pai*, was also released. "Su-chi-pai" is the collective name in mahjong of the tiles representing the four winds (east, south, west, and north). The American release was notable for editing out the nudity present in both the original and in the making-of.

IDOL OF DARKNESS *
1997. JPN: *Inju Nerawareta Idol*. Video. DIR: Susumu Aran. SCR: N/C. DES: N/C. ANI: Lion Ginan. MUS: N/C. PRD: Pink Pineapple. 45 mins.

Lesbian goings-on as famous idol singer Rie initiates newcomer Ikumi in the pleasures of the flesh, much to the annoyance of her boyfriend, who always suspected the media was a corrupt world. Soon, onstage jealousies lead to the activation of a cursed wooden idol, which leads to more sex. **◐**

IDOL PROJECT *

1995. Video. DIR: Yasushi Nagaoka. SCR: Toshimitsu Amano. DES: Noritaka Suzuki. ANI: Masahiko Murata. MUS: Kanji Saito. PRD: KSS. 30 mins. x 4 eps.

Fourteen-year-old Mimu Emilton wants to be an idol singer and applies for the Starland Festival, where the people's next idol will be chosen. Inspired by her hologram pendant, which carries a pep talk from the last idol, Mimu learns from a number of other aspirants the various secrets of being an idol, including the power of a smile and the value of dance. A silly, perky anime based on a computer game in which the player's job was to become the top idol singer.

IDOLMASTER *

2007. JPN: IDOLM@STER. AKA: The IdolM@ster. TV series. DIR: Tatsuyuki Nagai. SCR: Jukki Yamada, Sumio Uetake. DES: Hiroshi Takeuchi, Junichi Akutsu, Toshiyuki Tokuda. ANI: Hiroshi Takeuchi. MUS: Tsuneyoshi Saito. PRD: Bandai Visual, Sunrise. 24 mins. x 26 eps. (TV), 17 mins. (v), 25 mins. x 25 eps. (TV2), 25 mins. (v2), ?? mins. x 64 eps. (TV3, Puchimas), ?? mins. (m).

In 2005 Namco launched an arcade game called The Idolmaster. The concept was simple: a nurturing game in which the player guides and trains a young girl to success as an idol singer. One of a popular genre at the time, it went on to become a huge franchise, spinning off a number of anime along the way. The first TV series, IdolM@ster Xenoglossia, came a year before before its biggest game success on the Xbox. It was set in an alternate world from the manga, which preceded it by a month, a world in which the ten cute idol wannabes are actually pilots fighting to save the planet a century after the destruction of the Moon. In the tradition of the best mecha-girl anime, like **GUNBUSTER**, the one with little apparent natural talent and all the odds against her is the one who wins through in the end. The anime has

no relationship to the story of the games, except in its ten cute idol characters. A 17-minute video, IdolM@ster—Live For You, was released as an extra to the game of the same name in 2008. Aside from the games, and numerous homage appearances, and references in other games, there are 11 manga, including Puchimas! Petit IdolMaster, a four-panel gag strip that gives the idols cute, compressed versions of themselves, like the magical companions who often guide and direct magical girls and make such marketable plushies. This, in turn, was adapted into an online series in 2013, ahead of a 2014 movie. So the characters become their own cuddly toys. There's something profoundly disturbing about the neatness with which this closes the franchise-into-fantasy circle.

IF HER FLAG BREAKS *

2014. JPN: Kanojo ga Flag o Oraretara. AKA: Gaworare. TV series. DIR: Ayumu Watanabe. SCR: Takashi Aoshima. DES: Shizue Kaneko. ANI: Shizue Kaneko. MUS: Ruka Kawada, Yukari Hashimoto. PRD: Hoods Entertainment, Flying Dog, Kodansha, Klockworx. 24 mins. x 13 eps.

Traumatized by his experience of a shipwreck (no, really), Sota Hatate is withdrawn and a loner at his high school, despite a unique ability to tell people's immediate fates through being able to see the spiritual "flags" they inadvertently fly from their heads. The sight of a flag marks a moment in someone's life when they are facing a critical juncture: perhaps a romantic encounter or sudden career change. Hatate's own flag is flying deathly colors, leading him to realize that he must somehow assemble a group of friends with particular complementary abilities in order to save himself. It helps, sort of, that he has to live in a dormitory full of pretty girls.

Flags and tags have been a feature of visual novels (**ARGOT AND JARGON**) since the 1990s, and represent the breakdown of what used to be characters into a set of hinges, motivations, and tickable boxes that define how a player gets through a dating simulation (**GAMING AND DIGITAL ANIMATION**). By reimagining them as literal flags on people's heads, Toka Takei's original series of light novels hence makes the formula part of the fun and plays into

a very modern form of wish fulfillment, affording the leading man the ability to essentially see the "programming code" affecting the positions of his fellow characters in the plot threads surrounding him, like some moe version of The Matrix. But this in itself amounts to an amusing and entertaining commentary on the world of the clichés of an anime harem (**ROMANCE AND DRAMA**), since merely because Sota can see unspoken emotions and oncoming twists, they are not necessarily twists in his story, or to his benefit. However, after the initial shock of the new, the show soon settles down into yet another bunch of self-consciously quirky, color-coded clothes horses bickering about who loves the lead the most.

IF I CALL YOUR NAME

2008. JPN: Kimi no Na o Yobeba. Video. DIR: Hiromi Yokoyama. SCR: N/C. DES: N/C. ANI: Yuki Tatejima. MUS: Reijiro Koroku. PRD: Suzuki Mirano. 27 mins. x 2 eps.

A school for the sons of the privileged keeps girls on campus for another kind of educational purpose. They're sex slaves for the use of the boys, known only by their assigned numbers. Then one of the boys, Nakagawa, realizes that he knows number 3's name—Mitsuko, a childhood friend (**ROMANCE AND DRAMA**), fallen on hard times after the failure of her family business. Nakagawa dreams of saving her from constant (and rather repetitive) gang rape, but all he manages to do is get beaten up and make her situation worse. Her number gave her a cloak of anonymity; once the other students find out her name, she can no longer ignore the reality of her situation. This is a particularly disturbing and nasty example of the genre, encouraging the viewer to take pleasure in mental as well as physical abuse. It's based on a 2003 manga by Ryuta Amazume. Director Yokoyama, if it is a real name, is also credited as an animator on the U.S. series Inspector Gadget and a number of well-known anime including **LUPIN III** and **GUNDAM** before seemingly moving into the director's chair on **EROTICA AND PORNOGRAPHY**. **◐Ⓝ♡**

IF I SEE YOU IN MY DREAMS

1998. JPN: Yume de Aetara. AKA: If I See You in My Dream [sic]. Video, TV series. DIR:

Hiroshi Watanabe. scr: Nao Tokimura. des: Hiroshi Watanabe, Ryoichi Oki. ani: Ryoichi Oki. mus: Shigesato Kanasumi. prd: JC Staff, Shueisha, TBS, Tokuma Japan Communications. 30 mins. x 3 eps. (v), 8 mins. x 16 eps. (TV).

Twenty-four-year-old Masuo has never really talked to a girl, until the fateful day he meets the pretty Nagisa. As he begins a faltering attempt at seduction, illness finds him in a hospital bed on Christmas Eve, the traditional time for shy Japanese boys to pop the question. Nagisa makes it easier for him by visiting and staying till he confesses his love. The original videos were also made into a TV series. Based on Noriyuki Yamahana's manga, serialized in *Business Jump*.

IGANO KABAMARU

1983. TV series. dir: Tameo Ogawa, Akinori Nagaoka, Tsutomu Shibayama, Keiji Hayakawa, Naoto Hashimoto. scr: Tokio Tsuchiya, Rei Akimoto, Shigeru Yanagawa, Tomomi Tsutsui. Hirokazu Kobayashi. des: Akio Hosoya. ani: Akio Hosoya, Kaworu Hirata, Keiko Yoshimoto. mus: Toshiyuki Omori. prd: Tohoku, NTV. 25 mins. x 24 eps.

Kabamaru is a new boy at high school, who cannot reveal to anyone that he is really the scion of an infamous ninja clan. He helps the kindly Mrs. Okubo, falls in love with her granddaughter, and is forced against his will to use his ninja skills in struggles against other schools, and his own corrupt principal. Yu Azuki, creator of AKANUKE ICHIBAN, wrote this 1983 manga for *Margaret* magazine as a spoof of Mitsuteru Yokoyama's 1961 ninja story *Kagemaru the Ninja* (*Iga no Kagemaru*).

IGPX *

2003. aka: *Immortal Grand Prix*. TV series. dir: Koichi Mashimo. scr: Koichi Mashimo, Yuki Arie. des: Tomoaki Kado. ani: Hiroshi Morioka, Shinya Kawatsura, Tomoyuki Kurokawa, Yuki Arie. mus: Fat Jon, Amon Tobin, Hint, Neotropic, Funki Porcini, Arata Iwashina. prd: Production I.G, Cartoon Network. 5 mins. x 5 eps. (TV1), 25 mins. x 24 eps. (TV2), 25 mins. x 2 eps. (v).

Conceived as a coproduction between the Cartoon Network in America and the Japanese studio Production I.G, this international collaboration led first to a series of short cartoons about robotic arena combat, replaying many traditions of SPORTS ANIME with the arrival of a team of rookies who must somehow fight their way to the top.

A second series, directed by Mitsuru Hongo, kept to a traditional half-hour running time, but seemed only loosely related to the original, moving the action to 2049, when the gladiatorial nature of the original *IGPX* has somehow transformed into something more like a car race, taking place in a purpose-built city, surrounded by a 60km track. *IGPX* thus incorporates many elements known to be a success in the merchandising-led world of children's cartoons—the emphasis is on teamwork, but in a sport involving high-tech items, personal robots, and a gameplay that usually revolves around a combat lap, followed by a more traditional race to the finish.

IIDA, UMANOSUKE

1961–2010. Pseudoym of Tsutomu Iida, ultimately deriving from his apparent resemblance to a character in the manga series *1, 2, Sanshiro*. Born in Hokkaido, Iida entered the anime business as both a writer and animator. He wrote scripts for the video version of DEVILMAN and MIGHTY SPACE MINERS, transposing his name for the latter into English as "Horceman Lunchfield." After the death of Takeyuki Kanda midway through *Mobile Suit Gundam: The 08th MS Team* in 1996 (GUNDAM), he took over the work, with later directorial appointments including HELLSING. He directed TIDE-LINE BLUE in 2005 but was already spending increasing amounts of time back on storyboarding. His last directorial work was TOWANOQUON, which was released posthumously and dedicated to him.

IIZUKA, MASANORI

1965–. Animator and illustrator who debuted on HIGH SCHOOL KIMENGUMI, before becoming an animator and animation checker on many other works, including MAMA IS A FOURTH GRADER and CYBERFORMULA GPX.

IKEDA, HIROSHI

1934–. Born in Tokyo, Ikeda graduated in art from Nihon University in 1959, joining Toei Animation that same year and rising to director within 12 months. His first major work, however, did not appear for almost a decade, with the release of his feature-length adaptation of Shotaro Ishinomori's FLYING GHOST SHIP. He also worked on a number of popular TV shows, including LITTLE WITCH SALLY and SECRET AKKO-CHAN. He became head of Toei's Animation Research Department (a training division) and later became a lecturer in animation at both the Tokyo Polytechnic University and Nihon University Graduate School of Art.

IKENAI BOY

1990. aka: *The Boy Who Couldn't*. Video. dir: Hiroshi Uchida. scr: Satoichi Moriyasu. des: Toshio Takahashi. ani: Toshio Takahashi. mus: N/C. prd: JC Staff. 50 mins. x 2 eps.

College boy Shinichi Kamigawa moonlights as the master masseur Doctor K, popular with many young women all around Tokyo for his sexily soothing hands. This anime was based on Yoshihiro Suma's erotic manga in *Business Jump* and features a live-action epilogue from real-life adult video star Ayami Kida, in a futile attempt to make up for the low quality of the rest of the production. ◐

IKKI TOUSEN *

2003. jpn: *Bakunyu Hyper Battle Ikki Tosen*. aka: *Battle Vixens; Strength of a Thousand; Dragon Girls*. TV series. dir: Takashi Watanabe, Koichi Ohata, Rion Kujo. scr: Takao Yoshioka, Masanao Akahoshi, Koichi Ohata, Hideyuki Kurata. des: Shinya Hasegawa, Shigemi Ikeda, Rin-Sin (Rin Shin), Jiro Kono, Minoru Maeda. ani: Takashi Wada, Masayoshi Nakaya, Junji Goto, Yukiko Ishibashi. mus: Hiroshi Motokura, Yasuharu Takanishi. prd: Geneon, AT-X, GENCO, JC Staff, Wani Books. 24 mins. x 13 eps. (TV1), 25 mins. x 12 eps. (TV2), 45 mins. (v1), 25 mins. x 12 eps. (TV3), 45 mins. (v2), 25 mins. x 12 eps. (TV4), 45 mins. (v3).

Eighteen hundred years after his youthful demise in a Chinese civil war, the legendary warrior Shou Hao is reborn in Japan as Hakufu Sonsaku, a girl with large breasts and a ditzy attitude. She carries her predecessor's soul sealed away in a *magatama*, a comma-shaped jewel of ancient significance, also seen in BLUE SEED (as *mitama*) and *Gamera*. Nor is she the only one— many of her high school associates have also come into possession of sealed souls of Chinese warriors, resulting in a long and convoluted series of brawls and feuds between Tokyo high schools. The fighters are destined to relive the struggles and fates of their ancient counterparts unless they can find a way to break the bonds of history.

The events of GREAT CONQUEST: ROMANCE OF THE THREE KINGDOMS are re-enacted in modern-day Tokyo, as ancient heroes of Chinese legend are reincarnated as Japanese schoolgirls—but as with Takashi Miike's live-action *Tennen Shojo Mann* (*DE), there is something ineffably silly about watching the pompous macho feuds and vendettas of old played out by scrapping schoolgirls. Where the warriors of old had heralds and imperial messengers, we have e-mail circulars and mobile phones. Unlike most of their viewers, they also seem aware of the histories and backgrounds associated with their names, in a postmodern touch that adds an old-fashioned sense of inevitable destiny. Some embrace the fate of their former incarnations, while others fight against it. They attend seven different high schools in the Kanto area, allowing for an endless round of plot, counterplot, alliance, betrayal, double-, triple-, and quadruple-cross, and of course a school uniform to suit every preference, because there are actually those who care whether panties flash from under a sailor suit or a tartan skirt—this is a big deal in an anime which cares about underpants as much as AGENT AIKA. There are guys who fight as well, because the Japanese state school system is coeducational and the target audience needs an identification point. Yuji Shiokaze's manga, originally serialized in monthly *Comic Gamu*, was published in English as *Battle Vixens*, leading to the release of this show under that title in several territories.

Three Kingdoms is a big novel, so it shouldn't come as a surprise that there were sequels, in the form of the TV series *IT: Dragon Destiny* (2007), *IT: Great Guardians* (2008), and *IT: Xtreme Xecutor* (2010). Each later iteration also came accompanied by a one-shot video release. *Dragon Destiny* continues the *Three Kingdoms* story thread with a fight against a divine dragon. Koichi Ohata, mecha designer on GUNBUSTER and creator of CYBERNETICS GUARDIAN, directed, though the six short

videos that appeared as extras on the DVD release were directed by Katsuma Kanazawa, with Korean art director Park Minsyok and animation director Joung Soon An. They feature the female cast at a hot springs under the title *Dragon Destiny: Great Battle at the Red Cliffs Hot Springs* (*Dragon Destiny Sekiheki Onsen Daikessen*), itself a punning reference to the Battle of the Red Cliffs that forms a pivotal moment in *Three Kingdoms*.

Great Guardians veered away from the *Three Kingdoms* story to focus on the central female character Hakufu and her friends, and involves significantly less combat than the previous two seasons. It also throws in a subplot that compels good characters to become evil under the influence of dark magic. That said, the combats still involve over-endowed girls in escalating states of undress. Six short videos, collectively entitled *Battle Tour Club: Sexy Cosplay/Dangerous Jobs*, were featured on each of the six Japanese DVDs. After a year's hiatus, 2010's TV outing *XTREME XECUTOR* featured a plot to take over all the fighting clans through a tournament. The 2011 video release features a class trip to Kyoto for the rival schools, where they not only fight each other but also rumble with the teen fighters of Kyoto's education system.

Even in times past, the *Three Kingdoms* story contained subtexts of reincarnation and retribution. Although set at the close of the Han dynasty (3rd century a.d.), elements of the tale suggested that the last Han emperor was actually the reincarnation of the *first* Han emperor, getting his just desserts for executing three loyal generals four hundred years earlier. Compare to SUIKODEN. **LNV**

IKKIMAN

1986. JPN: *Hagane Q Choji Ikkiman*. AKA: *Steel Q Armored Child Ikkiman*. TV series. DIR: Nobutaka Nishizawa. SCR: Haruya Yamazaki, Kenji Terada, Yoshiyuki Suga. DES: Takashi Saijo. ANI: Masahiko Imai, Michio Shindo. MUS: Seiji Yokoyama. PRD: Toei, NTV. 25 mins. x 32 eps.

A bizarre combination of SPORTS ANIME and martial arts, as Ikki leaves behind the woman who broke his heart in Hokkaido, and comes to 21st-century Tokyo to seek his fortune at the violent baseball-fighting

game Battle Ball. Gate-crashing a game between the Terran team, the Blue Planets, and the off-world team, the Satano Blackies, he steps up to bat and is soon the star player. Based on a manga by Yasuo Tanami and Kazuo Takahashi, serialized in *Shonen Magazine*, among others.

IKKYU

1975. JPN: *Ikkyu-san*. TV series. DIR: Kimio Yabuki, Tetsuo Imazawa, Hideo Furusawa, Shinya Miyazaki. SCR: Masaki Tsuji, Satoshi Ishida, Tatsuo Tamura, Keisuke Fujikawa, Tomoko Konparu, Hiroshi Yamaura, Tomomi Tsutsui. DES: Hiroshi Wagatsuma. ANI: Yasu Ishiguro, Shinya Miyazaki, Takeshi Shirato. MUS: Seiichiro Uno. PRD: TV Asahi, Toei. 25 mins. x 296 eps. (TV), 15 mins. (m1), 15 mins. (m2), 25 mins. x 26 eps. (*Ikkyu-san*).

After the Ashikaga shogun unifies Japan, the emperor's son Sengikumaru is sent to the Yasukuni Shrine by family politics—his maternal grandfather opposed the Ashikaga in the conflict. Shaving his head and changing his name to Ikkyu, he tries to live as a good monk, though taking any opportunity he can to outwit the greedy merchant Kikyoya, his daughter Yayoi, and even Yoshimitsu Ashikaga himself.

The series received a very limited partial broadcast, as *Ikkyu the Little Monk*, on U.S. local TV for the Japanese community, with English subtitles. The character had two short theatrical outings: *Ikkyu and Princess Yancha* (1978), in which Ikkyu must talk a tomboy into behaving in a more ladylike manner before her habit of calling herself by the boy's name Tsuyumaru and attacking shogun Yoshimitsu Ashikaga with a wooden sword gets her into trouble. This was followed by *Ikkyu: It's Spring!* (1981), in which further feudal fun ensued.

An unrelated 26-episode series, *Ikkyu-san* (1978), was a baseball drama on the rival Fuji TV directed by Toshifumi Takizawa, based on a STAR OF THE GIANTS–influenced manga by Shinji Mizushima.

IKUHARA, KUNIHIKO

1964–. Born in Tokushima Prefecture, he joined Toei Animation after graduating in graphic design from Komatsu City College. Served as an assistant to Junichi Sato on shows such as MAPLE TOWN before achieving renown as the show runner for later seasons of SAILOR MOON. Left Toei in 1996 to form Be-Papas, a small production team whose most famous creation is UTENA. Spent two years in California at the American Film Institute, while continuing to work on non-anime output for Be-Papas.

IMAZAWA, TETSUO

1940–. Born in Oita Prefecture, he graduated from Nakazu High School and went to Tokyo to work in publishing as a graphic designer. Part-time work for animation companies soon helped pay the bills, and his name appears on the credits for IKKYU and the new series of STAR OF THE GIANTS (1977). He subsequently joined Studio Juno full-time, and his works as director include GODMARS, HERMES, and COO OF THE FAR SEAS.

IMMORAL SISTERS *

2001. JPN: Ai Shimai. Video. DIR: Roku Iwata, Hideo Ura. SCR: Osamu Kudo, Momoi Sakura. DES: Rin Shin. ANI: Yuki Iwai. MUS: Chikutaru Roman. PRD: Elf, Office Take Off, Pink Pineapple. 30 mins. x 3 eps. (v1), 30 mins. x 2 eps. (v2), 30 mins. x 2 eps. (v3, Blossoming). The president of the Nogawa Estate Agency sends his son Taketo to negotiate a compensation claim by Yukie Kitazawa. Yukie was the driver in a traffic accident, and Nogawa hopes to settle out of court before Yukie's husband returns home from a business posting abroad. However, Taketo's method of negotiating involves drugging Yukie and then photographing himself molesting her unconscious form. Using the photographs as blackmail, he demands an impossibly high settlement from her, forcing her to become his sex slave by way of payment in lieu. His father then approaches Yukie's daughters Rumi and Tomoko and has them for himself. Eventually, with the help of the president's private secretary Yumi, who has been one of the principal engineers of the situation, Yukie and the girls turn the tables on both the father and son, and Taketo moves in with all four women.

In the sequel, Immoral Sisters 2, when Yukie's husband Kunihiko returns, there are mixed feelings in the household. Taketo and Yukie try to keep their affair secret, Tomoko wants everyone to be one big happy family, while Rumi tries to engineer her "real" father's departure (although the story implies she may be

a stepdaughter, once again pandering to the not-quite-incest subgenre of so much porn anime) so she can return to the only "norm" she knows. On discovering his family members' secret, Kunihiko confesses that he has harbored a secret lust for his own daughter Tomoko for some time, and Tomoko duly offers herself to him to preserve order. These two serials, Ai Shimai 1: Coupling's Fruit (three parts), and Ai Shimai 2 (two parts), were later reedited to make the compilation two-parter Ai Shimai: Coupling's Fruit Juice (2004).

For the third series, released in 2004 as Ai Shimai Tsubomi, AKA Ai Shimai 3, AKA Ai Shimai: Make Me Wet, AKA Immoral Sisters: Blossoming, the title remains but the characters change. This time the "immoral sisters" are Kotono and Suzue Miyatsuji, students at a school where their mother is the principal. They both yearn for fellow student Shoichi, who will be expelled from the school if he fails his exams again. Shoichi, however, is more interested in the school nurse, Maiko. Maiko suggests that he cheat in the exams by stealing a disc containing the questions. But while he is trying to do so, he is caught by Kotono and duly rapes her in order to ensure her silence. When did it get to be so hard just to study? Based on a series of computer games by Elf. **LNV**

IMMORALITY *

2004. JPN: In no Hoteishiki. AKA: Equation of the Immoral. Video. DIR: Kanzaburo Oda. SCR: Sosoro Masaoka. DES: Eri Kohagura. ANI: Eri Kohagura. MUS: N/C. PRD: Milky. 30 mins. x 2 eps.
New school nurse Sayoko Saeki has an innocent face and a voluptuous body. She begins as an object of fantasy for the boys at the school, but is later revealed as a succubus who drains men dry. Based on an erotic thriller by Azuki Kurenai. The series was also released (along with the first two episodes of AKIBA GIRLS) in North America as part of Hentaipalooza. **LNV**

IMMORALS, THE *

2006. JPN: Jokei: Kazoku Inbo. AKA: Female Family Lusts. Video. DIR: Ken Raika, Masato Kitagawa. SCR: N/C. DES: Takuya Matsumoto. ANI: Takuya Matsumoto, Hayato Nakaya, Kazunori Higuchi. MUS: Salad. PRD: T-Rex, Milky. 29 mins. x 2 eps.

Local politician Arimiya had 40 years of power, influence, and all the pretty women he wanted. Now he's dead. His most recent wife and their three beautiful daughters are set to inherit his money and his power. But he wronged many people in his lifetime, and now the son of one of his former victims is out for revenge. An interesting set-up and attractive character design are let down by poor pacing and a hurried resolution. This is especially disappointing for fans of the EROTICA AND PORNOGRAPHY genre because both directors have shown they can deliver something better. Ken Raika (which probably isn't his real name, since the kanji roughly translate as "lightning blade") is a hentai stalwart, with a score of titles on his rap sheet. Back in the 1990s, Kitagawa was directing episodes of shows including TOPSTRIKER and Turn-A Gundam (GUNDAM). He's sticking with boys' toys in this video based on an erotic video game by Silky's. **LN**

IN PRAISE OF JUDO

1974. JPN: Judo Sanka. TV series. DIR: Shigetsugu Yoshida, Masami Hata, Tetsuo Imazawa, Hiroshi Fukutomi, Hideo Takayashiki. SCR: Haruya Yamazaki, Tsunehisa Ito, Akio Matsuzaki. DES: Hiroshi Kaizuka. ANI: Takao Kasai, Yoshiaki Kawajiri. MUS: Yukio Takai. PRD: Nippon TV, Tokyo Movie Shinsha, Madhouse. 25 mins. x 27 eps.
This was the last of the original TMS SPORTS ANIME, ending a line that began with STAR OF THE GIANTS. Tosshinta Tomoe grows up by the rough seas of Sotobo in Chiba Prefecture. He goes to high school where he decides to follow in the footsteps of his divorced mother, Teruko, a former judo champion. As with every other sports story, our hero is trained by a tough but kind coach who only wants the best for him, and he eventually faces up to an opponent who has sworn revenge on the previous generation—in this case, a male judoist defeated by Tomoe's mother in her fighting days. The series was taken off the air due to low ratings before the more touching later episodes of Hiroshi Kaizuka's manga could be adapted. Compare to YAWARA!

IN THE BEGINNING *

1992. JPN: Tezuka Osamu no Kyuyaku Seisho Monogatari. AKA: Osamu Tezuka's Old

Testament. TV series. DIR: Osamu Dezaki. SCR: Osamu Tezuka. DES: Osamu Tezuka, Shinji Seya. ANI: Masaki Yoshimura, Akio Sugino, Junji Kobayashi, Hideaki Shimada. MUS: Katsuhisa Hattori. PRD: NTW, RAI, Tezuka Pro. 25 mins. x 26 eps.

In 1984, the Italian RAI channel approached **ASTRO BOY**–creator Tezuka and asked him to make a series of Bible stories (**RELIGION AND BELIEF**) for this international coproduction that were closer to the originals than the apocryphal **SUPERBOOK: VIDEO BIBLE**. Tezuka threw himself into adapting his earlier manga version of the *Old Testament,* even to the extent of working as a humble animator on the *Noah's Ark* episode. The series was not completed until 1992, long after the death of its creator, and though it was soon screened in Italy, Germany, and the U.S., it did not receive a Japanese broadcast until 1997, when it was dumped on the WOWOW satellite channel. Coro, a sloe-eyed fox, acts as the viewpoint character for the entire series, witnessing the Fall of Man, the Flood, the rise of King David, and other major events. There was simply no time to allow for the many minor stories included in *Superbook.*

IN THE FOREST OF THE FIREFLIES' LIGHT *

2011. JPN: *Hotarubi no Mori e.* AKA: *The Light of a Firefly Forest.* Movie. DIR: Takahiro Omori. SCR: Takahiro Omori. DES: Akira Takada, Yukihiro Shibutani. ANI: Akira Takada. MUS: Makoto Yoshimori. PRD: Brains Base, Aniplex, Hakusensha, NAS, TV Tokyo. 45 mins.
Hotaru spends every summer at her uncle's place in the country. Once, when she was a little girl, she got lost and was rescued by a young man wearing a fox mask with strange eyes. Gin never changes and hardly ages: he is a mountain spirit, and she can never touch him or he will vanish forever. Yet, every summer, they meet again, and as Hotaru grows up, she and Gin both struggle with the limitations on their relationship.

Yuki Midorikawa's 2003 manga is brought to beautiful life in this short film, which some critics compared to the work of Hayao Miyazaki and Makoto Shinkai. The concept of a human friendship with a tragic phantom is nothing new in Japanese children's fiction, and appeared in the Japanese media at least as early as the

live-action series *Yuta and His Wondrous Friends* (1974, *DE). But Omori's short film, screened as an independent theatrical event for many weeks in a small Tokyo cinema, adroitly repurposes the clichés for an otaku audience as an allegory of the impetus to put away childish things, offering a subtle challenge to the optimistic desire of the *osana-najimi* ("childhood friends") subgenre in much anime **ROMANCE AND DRAMA**. Notably, this short, sweet film beat the very similar **A LETTER TO MOMO** to a Judges' Award at the 2011 Scotland Loves Anime film festival, with its relative brevity cited as one of the deciding factors. Much of the scenery is drawn from Kumamoto Prefecture, the home of Midorikawa, who is better known in the anime world as the creator of **NATSUME'S BOOK OF FRIENDS**.

INARI KON KON *

2014. JPN: *Inari, Kon Kon, Koi Iroha.* TV series. DIR: Toru Takahashi. SCR: Toko Machida, Ayumi Sekine, Tomoko Konparu. DES: Yuka Takashina. ANI: Masami Inomata, Hiroaki Ikeda, Shinpei Kobayashi. MUS: Takeshi Seno. PRD: Production IMS. 24 mins. x 10 eps.
Average Japanese girl Inari comes to the aid of a fox cub at her local shrine, and is granted a wish by Uka, the incarnate form of the shrine's presiding goddess. Awash with hormones and giddy with teenage self-regard, Inari rashly wishes to be as beautiful as Sumizome, the most popular girl in school. She soon realizes the error of her ways, but Uka is merely able to twist the wish a little once it has been granted. Inari thereby gains the power to transform into the image of *anyone* she has seen—an ancient power from Japanese **RELIGION AND BELIEF**, accorded new uses in an everyday school setting.

Of course, teenage life is all about transformations, and this supernatural anime merely allegorizes such real-world shape-shifting as Inari tries to find her place in adult society. Meanwhile, the story comes with deep resonances to Japanese myth and folklore, beginning with Inari's full name, Fushimi Inari, which she shares with one of Japan's most photogenic shrines, long associated with fox spirits and their mischievous ways. The presence in the credits of both the shrine itself and the Keihan Railway (which can take you there) suggests a tourist-promotion

tie-up behind the scenes (**ADVERTISING AND SPONSORSHIP**).

Kon kon in Japanese onomatopoeia is the sound of stamping feet that precedes a vulpine transformation, while *iroha* comprises the first three letters of the Japanese kana syllabary, using an archaic mnemonic device that reorders the complete set into a poem. In other words, while the title is impossible to translate precisely into English, its meaning amounts to something like "Inari Hocus-Pocus: An ABC of Love."

INAZUMA ELEVEN *

2008. AKA: *Lightning Eleven.* TV series, movie. DIR: Katsuhiro Akiyama, Yoshikazu Miyao. SCR: Atsuhiro Tomioka. DES: Yuji Ikeda, Yuko Inoue, Chikara Nishikura. ANI: Yuji Ikeda, Yuko Inoue. MUS: Yasunori Mitsuda. PRD: Oriental Light & Magic, TV Tokyo, Dentsu. 25 mins. x 127 eps. (TV1), 25 mins. x 51 eps. (TV2), 90 mins. (m1), 90 mins. (m2), 90 mins. (m3), 25 mins. x 13 eps. (TV3).
Mamoru Endo is a gifted goalkeeper and the grandson of one of Japan's soccer greats. But the Raimon Junior High soccer club only has six members and they're not interested in training. When a hotshot player moves into town and the top local soccer school issues a challenge to Raimon, Mamoru sets out to find a team and lead them to victory from the goal-line. Based on a 2008 soccer game for the Nintendo DS, with a curtain-raiser manga that started running in *CoroCoro Comic* in May 2008 to build the market, this **SPORTS ANIME** has also spun off a collectible card game and a pop idol group, Twe'lv. The manga ran until 2011, and the anime has aired across Asia and Australasia, in South America, and in ten European countries including the U.K. In 2011 it spun off another series, the 47-episode *Inazuma Eleven GO,* set some years later and featuring a new young protagonist. In 2012 this was followed by *Inazuma Eleven GO Chrono Stone,* and in 2013 by the shorter run of *Inazuma Eleven GO Galaxy.* There have also been three movies. In December 2010 a movie version of the game, *Inazuma Eleven 3 Ogre (Gekijoban Inazuma Eleven Saikyo Gundan Ogre Shurai),* appeared, followed by *Inazuma Eleven GO Ultimate Bond: Griffon (Gekijoban Inazuma Eleven GO Kyukyoku no Kizuna Griffon)* in December 2011. The 2012 movie *Inazuma Eleven GO vs Danball*

Senki W (Gekijoban Inazuma Eleven GO vs Little Battlers Experience W) is a crossover story between these two popular game-based anime (**LITTLE BATTLERS EXPERIENCE**).

INDIAN SUMMER *

2007. JPN: *Koharu Biyori*. Video. DIR: Takayuki Inagaki. SCR: Takashi Aoshima. DES: Nariyuki Ogi. ANI: N/C. MUS: Takeshi Watanabe. PRD: Daume, ASCII Media works, AT-X, Geneon, Showgate. 25 mins. x 3 eps.

An Indian summer is a heatwave in autumn. Hard to see what that has to do with a near-future story about a robot maid bought by a young guy who names her Yui. She's programmed to cook, clean, and look after the house, but he just wants to dress her up in skimpy outfits and get naked with her and other maid robots, plus a few real girls for variety. It's silly, it's clichéd, and it's based on the manga by Takehiko Mizuki, which doesn't have anything to do with meteorology either. **Ⓝ**

INFINITE RYVIUS *

1999. JPN: *Mugen no Ryvius*. TV series, video. DIR: Goro Taniguchi, Akihiko Nishiyama. SCR: Yosuke Kuroda. DES: Hisashi Hirai. ANI: Yoichi Ueda, Asako Nishida. MUS: Katsuhisa Hattori. PRD: Sunrise, TV Tokyo. 25 mins. x 26 eps. (TV), ca. 6 mins. x 6 eps. (Internet).

An **EVANGELION** clone set in a solar system 80 years after a solar flare has immersed the system in a massive plasma field that links all the planets like a nervous system. Troubled youth Koji Aibo (who looks just like *Evangelion*'s Shinji) is lured into a quest by the enigmatic Neya (a girl who looks like *Evangelion*'s Rei) to sail to the heart of the plasma field in the titular ship. The series was also an early pioneer in the spread of Internet downloads, when six Flash animation shorts—entitled *Infinite Ryvius Illusion* (JPN: *Mugen no Ryvius Illusion*, aka *Ryvius Illusion*)—parodying the series were put online for fans. Each was divided into four subepisodes (six for the last episode) which were selectable from within the main episode, and which generally featured ongoing storylines. These were subsequently included as extras in the DVD releases.

INFINITE STRATOS *

2011. TV series, video. DIR: Yasuhito Kikuchi. SCR: Atsuhiro Tomioka, Chinatsu Hojo,

Fumihiko Shimo. DES: Tomoyasu Kurashima, Takeshi Takakura, Shunichiro Yoshihara. ANI: Tomoyasu Kurashima. MUS: Hikaru Nanase. PRD: 8-bit, Project IS, TBS. 30 mins. x 12 eps. (TV), 30 mins. (v).

Infinite Stratos (IS) is the name of an exoskeleton weapons system which has become the dominant combat choice. With very few exceptions, only females can operate IS systems. Orphan Ichika is one of those exceptions, raised by his older sister who is a top IS pilot. Aged 15, he is enrolled in a specialist training school where the shy, quiet boy is surrounded by beautiful girls. Yes, it's a mecha harem anime (**ROMANCE AND DRAMA**). All the girls are secretly in love with Ichika, and despite their intelligence and capability they think it's fun to sit around at mealtimes with their mouths open like baby birds, waiting for him to spoon-feed them. *IS* checks all the cliché boxes—childhood friends with unresolved emotional fixations, a girl dressing as a boy, girls beaten by our hero who then go all gooey over him, and girl-on-girl crushes. The only thing that saves it from complete and total tedium is the rather good mecha animation—designer Takakura worked on **EVANGELION** and **APPLESEED**, though animation director Kurashima has less experience with action anime than with cute girls like **MAGICAL KANAN**. Basing a light novel by Izuru Yumizuru, the same team delivered a half-hour video, *Infinite Stratos Encore: Sextet of Burning Love (Koi no Kogareru Rokujuso)*, in November 2011. It's set during summer vacation at a shrine festival and is much more about the harem than about the mecha.

INITIAL D *

1998. TV series, movie, video. DIR: Shin Misawa. SCR: Hiroshi Ashida, Nobuaki Kishima. DES: Noboru Furuse. ANI: Noboru Furuse. MUS: Ryuichi Katsumata. PRD: Fuji TV, Prime Direction, OB. 25 mins. x 26 eps. (TV1), 25 mins. x 13 eps. (TV2), 114 mins. (m), 25 mins. x 24 eps. (TV3), 40 mins. (v1), 27 mins. x 2 eps. (v2), 45 mins. (v3), 45 mins. (v4).

In a blighted, soulless town north of Tokyo in mountainous Gunma Prefecture, disaffected youths rev souped-up cars in illegal downhill races. Seventeen-year-old gasoline pump attendant Itsuki dreams of saving up enough to buy his own set

of wheels and join the Akina Speed Stars gang, fellow garage worker Iketani boasts of his prowess, and their manager occasionally regales them with tall tales about the fastest man on the mountain. This shadowy figure is actually their shy friend Takumi, who breaks the speed limit each dawn to keep the deliveries fresh for his father's tofu shop, enjoying the beginnings of a romance with Natsuki, a local girl who has a secret—she has an older man as a lover, one who gives her expensive gifts in an instance of "subsidized dating."

Replaying the semifantastic road mythologies of **BOMBER BIKERS OF SHONAN** and his own earlier **LEGEND OF ROLLING WHEELS**, Shuichi Shigeno's human interest manga in *Young Magazine* about boys and their toys was snapped up on the cusp of the revolution in digital animation. Featuring car magazine test-driver Keiichi Tsuchiya as a technical adviser, the anime version plays up an anal attention to detail with lectures on driving skill and interior shots of engine activity. Meanwhile the traditional cel animation of the non-racing scenes contrasts jarringly with the computer-animated racing sequences in the style of the PlayStation game *Gran Turismo*. The second season, unsurprisingly rebranded as *Initial D: Second Stage*, begins with Takumi's car trashed by the rival Akagi Red Suns—a challenge if ever there was for a new duel over who owns the road. When the series gained a 24.5% TV rating, a movie, *Third Stage* (2001), was produced, focusing on the characters' graduation from high school and opportunities to leave the dead-end town of their birth behind. A third season, the confusingly titled *Fourth Stage* (2004), features the boys going professional, forming a Project D in order to challenge rivals outside their home region.

Initial D was an immense success not just in Japan, where such ratings for anime are rare indeed in modern times (**RATINGS AND BOX OFFICE**), but across Asia. It was thus not much of a surprise that when the inevitable 2005 live-action remake followed, it was a Cantonese production, starring Taiwan popstar Jay Chou as Takumi, with Natsuki (Ann Suzuki) the only major cast member played by a Japanese performer. Despite the strange sight, sound, and body-language of Chinese actors pretending to be Japanese—a subject of greater controversy in the same year's *Memoirs of a Geisha*—the movie is a remarkably fair and faithful adaptation of the spirit of the original.

The video *Battle Stage* (2002) simply collects some of the best moments from the racing sequences in the TV series. The two-part *Extra Stage* (2005) was sold as a bonus with the final volume of the *Initial D* manga and features two female characters taking on the infamous Emperor team whose activities caused so much trouble for the boys in earlier volumes. *Battle Stage 2* (2007) summarized the movie in video form, while *Extra Stage 2* (2008) was a new chapter, subtitled *Travelers of Green* (*Tabidachi no Green*). Compare to **WANGAN MIDNIGHT**.

INMU *

2001. JPN: *Inmu: Ikenie no Utage*. AKA: *Lustful Dream, Inmu: Feast of Victims; Banquet of Sacrifice*. Video. DIR: Ran Misumi. SCR: N/C. DES: N/C. ANI: N/C. MUS: N/C. PRD: Pink Pineapple. 29 mins. x 2 eps. (v1), 31 mins. x 2 eps. (v2).
The "mysterious witch," voiced in the American release by porn actress Asia Carrera, is a masked figure who is the living embodiment of the maxim that people should be careful what they wish for. In a vengeful, rapacious variant on the initiatress of **REI REI** or the Faustian owner of the **PETSHOP OF HORRORS**, she narrates a series of short pornographic vignettes, including a schoolgirl who thinks she is being stalked by a fellow train passenger, a snooty fashion designer publicly humiliated by the assistant she spurned, tentacle rape on the school swim team, and a girl obsessed with dolls. Each story is barely 15 minutes long, hence the presence of four "stories" in only two "episodes," although they are called "nights" here, doubtless intended to give a dreamlike **A THOUSAND AND ONE NIGHTS** quality to the whole sordid mess. As with many other releases from Nu-Tech, Carrera is joined by fellow stars of adult entertainment on the voice track, and lends her real-life image to the box art—compare to similar gimmicks tried in Japan with the likes of **ADVENTURE KID**.

A second two-parter, *Inmu 2*, features similar tales. In one, a teenage virgin discovers that her would-be boyfriend has been having sex with a prostitute who looks just like her. In another, a peeping tom finds his fantasies coming to life when he is hospitalized in the care of the nurse he has been stalking. A man becomes possessed by the sexy succubi that inhabit a cursed deck of playing cards. And finally, in what seems to be a compulsory not-quite-incest tale, a man struggles with his confused memories of an affair with his widowed stepmother. ●Ⓝⓥ

INNOCENT VENUS

2006. TV series. DIR: Jun Kawagoe. SCR: Shinsuke Onishi, Takahiko Masuda. DES: Hideki Nagamachi, Hiroshi Ogawa (mecha), Katsuhiro Hashi. ANI: Atsuo Tobe, Fujio Oda, Hideki Nagamachi, Mariko Emori. MUS: Tomohisa Ishikawa. PRD: Brains Base, Bandai Visual. 24 mins. x 12 eps.
In 2010 the world was ravaged by huge Hyper Hurricanes. Five billion people died, with only three billion survivors. The map of the world was completely altered, not just with the fall of nations but with the obliteration of land masses under ice and water. A few wealthy people managed to isolate themselves in special enclaves and hold onto power by force. They called themselves Logos and set up a secret police force, Phantom, to suppress internal dissent and keep the poor in the wastelands, outside their circles of privilege, subservient and quiet. But a change is coming, signaled by the arrival of a mysterious girl—the set-up may remind older fans of **AI CITY**. Art director Hashi was on the background team for **SWORD OF THE STRANGER**, and although this is Nagamachi's first animation director gig, you'd expect a team including his highly experienced colleagues to deliver slick, solid animation and interesting design. They don't disappoint. The problem is the uneven script and direction. A classy first episode fizzing with ideas and interest is let down by a leaden second part. The series regains its poise in episode 3, and the rest delivers a punchy, satisfying narrative that almost makes up for its undercooked center. ⓥ

INOMATA, MUTSUMI

1960–. An illustrator with many credits as an in-betweener and key animator on 1970s shows such as **URUSEI YATSURA**, Inomata moved into character design on **CITY HUNTER**. Her work adds a feminine touch to otherwise male-oriented shows such as **BRAIN POWERED**.

INOUE, TOSHIYUKI

1961–. An animator and concept artist on **ONLY YESTERDAY**, among others.

INSATIABLE *

2005. JPN: *Haitokuzuma*. AKA: *Immoral Wife: Woman's Hidden Sexual Nature*. Video. DIR: Linda, Tsubasa Kazamatsuri. SCR: Jiro Muramatsu. DES: Linda. ANI: Hikaru Tojo. MUS: N/C. PRD: Sunny Side Up, SS Studio, T&B, Milky. 30 mins. x 2 eps.
Natsumi has tired of her promiscuous life of multiple partners and sexual experiments and settled down into a quiet marriage. But when she encounters an old lover, it's not long before she finds herself secretly yearning for the good old days. Based on an erotic manga by "Linda," and released on Christmas Day 2005: ho ho ho. ●Ⓝⓥ

INSTANT HISTORY

1961. JPN: *Instant History; Otogi Manga Calendar*. AKA: *Manga Fairy Tales*. TV series. DIR: Ryuichi Yokoyama, Shinichi Suzuki, Michihiro Matsuyama. SCR: Ryuichi Yokoyama, Shinichi Suzuki, Michihiro Matsuyama. DES: Ryuichi Yokoyama, Shinichi Suzuki, Michihiro Matsuyama. ANI: Ryuichi Yokoyama, Shinichi Suzuki, Michihiro Matsuyama. MUS: N/C. PRD: Otogi Pro, Fuji TV, TBS. 3 mins. x 312 eps. (as *Instant History*), 5 mins. x 54 eps. (as *Otogi Manga Calendar*).
Anime's very first TV series. This black-and-white series of shorts explains various historical events and notable occasions, normally through a framing device of a character who is not aware "what happened on this day in history," discovering firsthand for themselves. Explanations did not always take a cartoon form, but sometimes included photographs and film footage, often taken from the research archives of the *Mainichi Shinbun* newspaper, where director Ryuichi Yokoyama's **FUKU-CHAN** manga was running at the time. The series began as *Instant History* on Fuji TV but appears to have migrated to TBS in 1962 under the title of *Otogi Manga Calendar*. Chunks of it may have also later

turned up on MBS in 1966 as episodes of *Knowledgeable University: Future Calendar* (1966, *Monoshiri Daigaku: Ashita no Calendar*), also incorporating PUPPETRY AND STOP MOTION. This odd and promiscuous broadcast history is a likely reflection of the early days of television, when the content that filled the slots was deemed less worthy of notice than the sponsors that provided it. *Instant History* was sponsored by Meiji Seika (the candy company that would later part-fund ASTRO BOY), whereas *Otogi Manga Calendar* was paid for by Kirin Beer. In the days before video, it was unlikely indeed that anyone would notice if Ryuichi Yokoyama's studio Otogi Pro recycled the occasional three-minute piece a few years later or that anime encyclopedists 50 years in the future would have access to enough footage to confirm any of this.

Note: though *IH* was the first TV *series*, it was still not the first anime broadcast on TV. It was preceded by several one-shots, including the color, paper cut-out short A MOLE'S ADVENTURE (1958, *Mogura no Aventure*), and *Three Tales* (1960, *Mittsu no Hanashi*), an experimental anthology broadcast on the NHK channel, comprising adaptations of famous stories—*Oppel and the Elephant* by Kenji Miyazawa (see NIGHT ON THE GALACTIC RAILROAD), *Sleepy Town* by Mia Ogawa, *The Third Blood* by Kosuke Hamada, directed by Keiko Osonoe. Those determined to find a "first" for TV animation are urged to also consider the many hundreds of animated advertisements (ADVERTISING AND SPONSORSHIP).

INTERLUDE *

2004. Video. DIR: Tatsuya Nagamine. SCR: Akemi Omode. DES: Eisaku Inoue, Hideo Horibe, Yukitoshi Hotani. ANI: Eisaku Inoue. MUS: Koichiro Kameyama. PRD: Toei Animation, Happinet Pictures, Sky PerfecTV. 40 mins. x 3 eps.
A nameless protagonist wakes up in a world empty of people, though his solitude is occasionally interrupted by attacks from unexplained demonic creatures. He eventually meets Aya, a dark-haired girl waiting silently at one of the deserted railway stations, driven by an intense state of denial into living each day perfectly normally, as if the rest of the population of the world has not disappeared. In fact, he and Aya are both part of the Pandora

Project, a secret plan that is supposed to allow the human race to survive the end of the world, although it currently has some major flaws, one of which is the existence of Aya herself. An intriguing update of WIND OF AMNESIA for the ANIMATRIX generation, focusing on just one of the three heroines from the original game for the Dreamcast and PS2.

INTERNAL MEDICINE *

2004. JPN: *Shuchu Chiryoshitsu*. AKA: *Examination in Progress / Sick Bay of Domination*. Video. DIR: Aim. SCR: American Pie. DES: Mario Yaguchi. ANI: Mario Yaguchi. MUS: Yoshi. PRD: YOUC, Digital Works (Vanilla Series). 30 mins. x 2 eps.
Makoto is a man on a mission, a doctor-in-training who has sworn vengeance on the doctor whose negligence caused the death of his sister. All he knows is that the doctor in question has a scalpel scar on the back of his hand and has a peculiar handshake. He finds the right hospital and takes a job there in order to investigate further (since simply asking or checking his sister's medical records would have made this a short story), uncovering another conspiracy even greater than he previously thought, involving sexual liaisons among the other staff members. In order to investigate the mystery, he sleeps his way to the top, in yet another hospital porn anime—compare to NIGHT SHIFT NURSES. Based on a game created by MBS Truth. ❶❿❾

INTERSTELLA 5555 *

2003. AKA: *Interstella 5555: The 5tory of the 5ecret 5tar 5ystem*. Movie. DIR: Kazuhisa Takenouchi, Yushun Tatsusen, Daisuke Nishio. SCR: Thomas Bangalter, Cedric Hervert, Guy-Manuel de Homen-Christo. DES: Masaki Sato. ANI: Katsumi Tamegai, Keiichi Ichikawa. MUS: Daft Punk. PRD: Toei. 68 mins.
A band of four blue-skinned alien musicians is kidnapped by the Earl of Darkwood, a sinister figure who has leeched off musical talent since at least the time of Mozart—his previous captives include Jimi Hendrix. The band members are taken to Earth and put into disguises to enable them to perform as the "Crescendolls," Darkwood's latest signing. However, a fan from their homeworld has followed them to Earth, and manages to break the spell on the three male members of the band by

shining a light into their eyes. The men escape and later rescue the bass player who remained behind, although their faithful fan dies during the process. Defeating Darkwood and retrieving the discs that contain their original memories, the band returns home.

Electronic pop group Daft Punk comprises writers Bangalter and de Homen-Christo, whose French-speaking childhoods exposed them to the work of Leiji Matsumoto, most obviously his CAPTAIN HARLOCK in its *Albator* incarnation. Hiring Matsumoto to supervise the animation of several songs in order to make video promos for their album *Discovery* (2001), the pair later returned with new songs and bridging footage in order to make this dialogue-free musical movie, which gets to recycle Matsumoto's stock beautiful, enigmatic woman; tall, slender hero; and short, squat sidekick one more time, with stunning visuals, lush color, and an attitude charmingly goofy enough to give anime its first pure rock opera. It also sits happily within the tradition of Franco-Japanese coproductions ushered in by ULYSSES 31 a generation earlier.

INTRIGUE IN THE BAKUMATSU *

2006. JPN: *Bakumatsu Kikansetsu Irohanihoheto*. TV series. DIR: Yoshimitsu Ohashi, Ryosuke Takahashi. SCR: Junichi Miyashita, Shin Yoshida, Yasuyuki Suzuki. DES: Yusuke Kozaki, Etsuno Iwanaga, Takayuki Yanase, Masumi Narita, Emi Suzuki, Jiro Kono. ANI: Atsushi Okuda, Atsushi Shigeta, Naoyuki Onda, Tatsuya Suzuki. MUS: Hideyuki Fukasawa. PRD: Bandai Visual, Sunrise. 24 mins. x 26 eps.
Japan in the mid-1800s: the final days of the shogunate loom, and the government that has ruled the country in isolation for over 250 years will soon have to fight for its supremacy. Mercenaries like Yojiro Akizuki are waiting on events. But Yojiro isn't just another sword for hire: he has strange powers that guide him in unexpected directions. He meets a mysterious playwright who likes to secretly adjust the flow of history, and a traveling theater troupe after revenge. Together they face conspiracy, danger, and romance, meeting famous real-life figures including Ryoma Sakamoto (OI RYOMA), Army Chief of Staff Saigo Takamori, and Sir Harry Smith

Parkes, formerly Britain's envoy to the Chinese Emperor, then the consul-general in Japan.

To old-school mecha fans, Ryosuke Takahashi is a god, one of the shining lights of the Real Robot movement (VOTOMS), when 1980s animators decided to strip away the transforming-toy accretions of mystic mumbo-jumbo and make mecha serious and credible as machinery for grown-ups. He's created some fascinating shows in the past (see GASARAKI, for example), and cocreated this with Sunrise's house pseudonym Hajime Yadate. That attention to detail shows in the credits for a calligraphy specialist and props designers, as well as the heavyweight talent in the rest of the crew list. Takahashi embraces the concept of the supernatural for this story, but integrates it credibly and well with history, although he takes some liberties with facts that may annoy students of the era. He also nods to several Japanese and Western pop culture tropes—the theater troupe out for revenge for the murdered parents of one of its stars recalls Robin's origin story in *Batman*, and there are several moments from *Indiana Jones* (and *Seven Samurai*) where the beautiful art of the sword is defeated by the crude mechanism of the bullet.

There are also issues with the animation in mid-series, where the quality drops. This is a common experience in anime—directors frontload the early episodes with special effects and strong animation to attract audiences and encourage them to commit to the series, then allow their overstretched budget some slack. Some of the action scenes have very skimpy work on the backgrounds, perhaps expecting that strong fight choreography would distract attention from weaker artwork. The quality improves again as the series moves to its conclusion. Overall, this is a classy package, comparable in many ways with DAGGER OF KAMUI.

INU X BOKU SECRET SERVICE *

2012. TV series. DIR: Naokatsu Tsuda. SCR: Toshizo Nemoto, Cocoa Fujiwara. DES: Haruko Iizuka. ANI: Haruko Iizuka, Satoru Kiyomaru. MUS: Kotaro Nakagawa. PRD: David Production, Aniplex, Dentsu, MBS, Movic, Square Enix. 24 mins. x 12 eps.
Abrasive, sarcastic rich girl Ririchiyo Shirakiin is just misunderstood, or at least *partly* misunderstood, since her half-demon heritage probably doesn't help. She moves into a house populated by similar hybrids and half-breeds, regarded by the locals as haunted and mysterious, but actually little more than a refuge for people who do not conform to the norm. There, she finds herself saddled with Miketsukami, a submissive, uncomplaining secret service bodyguard who is immune to her wit because he never supplies her with any feedlines for her put-downs. And then she … goes to school, in a show that sets up moody, atmospheric situations and then largely forgets it should do something with them. The budding romance between Ririchiyo and her bodyguard turns out to be a damp squib until the final couple of episodes, when Miketsukami's own backstory is suddenly revealed to add new and interesting dimensions.

INU YASHA *

2000. TV series, TV special, movie. DIR: Masashi Ikeda, Akira Nishimori. SCR: Masashi Ikeda, Katsuyuki Sumisawa, Takashi Yamada, Akinori Endo. DES: Eiji Suganuma. ANI: Kazuhiro Soeta, Eiji Suganuma, Shinichi Sakuma. MUS: Kaoru Wada. PRD: Nippon TV, Sunrise, Yomiuri TV. 25 mins. x 167 eps. (TV1), 25 mins. x 26 eps. (TV2), 60 mins. (TVm), 100 mins. (m1), 99 mins. (m2), 98 mins. (m3), 86 mins. (m4).
Japanese schoolgirl Kagome is pulled into a well by a centipede monster and through a 500-year time tunnel to Japan's civil-war era. She escapes from the well to discover Inu Yasha, a half-dog demon, pinned to a nearby tree by the priestess Kikyo. The local villagers believe Kagome to be the reincarnation of Kikyo, and she must reluctantly team up with her predecessor's enemy to hunt down the many shards of the "Jewel of Four Souls," which Inu Yasha originally came to steal.

In the unsure economic climate that began the 21st century, with the POKÉMON tide ebbing and their BRAVE SAGA on hiatus, Sunrise bought into the success of a long-running, best-selling creator, optioning this recent manga from RANMA ½'s Rumiko Takahashi. A buddy-story in the tradition of USHIO AND TORA, with a time-traveling element that bears a close relationship to the creator's earlier FIRE TRIPPER. Movie editions followed, including *IY: Love Across Time* (*Jidai o Koeru Omoi*, 2001), *IY: The Castle Beyond the Looking Glass* (*Kagami no Naka no Mugenjo*, 2002), *IY: Swords of an Honorable Ruler* (*Tenka Hado no Ken*, 2003), and *IY: Fire on the Mystic Island* (*Guren no Horaijima*, 2004). The TV special *IY: The Love Song Before We Met* is a prequel, detailing the reasons why Inu Yasha and Kikyo hate each other at the start of the series.

INUKAMI!

2006. AKA: *Dog Gods*. TV series, movie. DIR: Keizo Kusakawa. SCR: Tasaharu Amiya, Tomoyasu Okubo, Tsuyoshi Tamai. DES: Shinpei Tomooka, Shinji Katahira. ANI: Atsushi Komori, Chiyuki Tanaka, Isao Yoshida, Takayoshi Hashimoto, Yuki Iwai. MUS: N/C. PRD: Seven Arcs, ASCII Media Works, Inukami Production Team, Starchild Records, Yomiko Advertising, Inc. 30 mins. x 26 eps. (TV), 30 mins. (m).
Inukami are dog-demons who protect humans from other demons. Keita comes from a famous family of inukami-tamers, but he has absolutely no talent for the work. This is made even more evident when he meets Yoko, an inukami that no trainer, however talented, has been able to control. In fact, she treats Keita like a dog, in this perverted rom-com whose male protagonist is exposed and embarrassed as often as any female (which may explain why it has yet to get an English-language release). This is based on a light novel by Mamizu Arisawa, illustrated by Kanna Wakatsuki, and released in 2003. Mari Matsuzawa took over art duties for the 2005 manga that preceded this series. There was a short movie spin-off in 2007, released on a triple bill for the *Dengeki Bunko 2007 Movie Festival* with SHAKUGAN NO SHANA and KINO'S JOURNEY movies, accompanied by a nine-minute short film featuring all three female leads. The elephant graphic that covers Keita's privates at key moments, and the child who keeps telling his mother that he's just seen an elephant, recall CRAYON SHIN-CHAN. **N**

INVASION OF THE BOOBY SNATCHERS *

2005. JPN: *Bakunyu Shimai*. AKA: *Wetnurse Sisters*. Video. DIR: Aim. SCR: N/C. DES: Benk, Michitaka Yamamoto. ANI: Aim, Michitaka Yamamoto. MUS: Yoshi. PRD: YOUC, Digital Works (Vanilla Series). 30 mins. x 2 eps.

College student Shinji wakes up one morning to find himself sleeping alongside Yuria, a sexy alien catgirl who has come to learn all about Earth culture. He teaches her all about sex with him, which is a start, we suppose. Her sister Alissa arrives later on. The girls have large breasts. If nothing else, the authors greatly enjoyed the English release title—another entry in the **VANILLA SERIES**. **ONV**

INYOCHU

2006. JPN: *Inyochu the Animation*. Video. DIR: BanzoTokita, Yoshitaka Higuchi. SCR: Kaoru Takahashi, Katzen Hamburg. DES: Hikokai, Aojiru. ANI: Noritomo Hattori. MUS: Toshiyuki Yamamoto. PRD: Amour, Suzuki Mirano, Studio Fantasia, MS Pictures. 29 mins. x 2 eps. (v1), 27 mins. x 2 eps., 10 mins. x 1 ep. (v2), 29 mins. x 2 eps. (v3).

Mikoto, Sui, and Yamato are classmates at a high school for demon-slayers and work in its demon-busting agency after class. They meet their match in a horse-demon who imprisons them in his world of tentacle sex. Coproducers Amour are famous among *hentai* fans for the quality of their animation: it's worth reflecting how much serious talent often goes into anime **EROTICA AND PORNOGRAPHY**. Hattori is on the animation credits for **DIRTY PAIR** and **HAIBANE RENMEI**. Director Tokita worked with character designer Hikokai on **LUSTFUL TRAIN**, and lifting the veil of their pseudonyms (and that of Katzen Hamburg) might reveal more varied resumés. This is based on an erotic game by TinkerBell with character designs by Aojiru, and has a following in Japan, with two games, books, and fan manga; so it's not surprising that two further two-part videos followed. *Inyochu Shoku: Ryoshokujima Taimaroku* in 2008, featured Mikoto, her little sister Takeru, Sui, and a very large monster on an island during summer vacation. The compilation edition added a short film as a bonus. In 2011 Studio Fantasia and MS Pictures released *Inyochu Etsu: Kairaku Henka Taimaroku*. Mikoto, Takeru, and Yamato visit a quiet village for the final stage of their training, and discover that their mother has sealed a demon within Yamato—think **NARUTO**'s nine-tailed fox, but with tentacles. **ONV**

IRIA *

1994. JPN: *Iria: Zeiram the Animation*. Video. DIR: Tetsuro Amino. SCR: Tsunehisa Arakawa, Tetsuro Amino. DES: Ryunosuke Otonashi, Masakazu Katsura. ANI: Ryunosuke Otonashi. MUS: Yoichiro Yoshikawa. PRD: Bandai. 35 mins. x 6 eps.

Bounty hunter Iria and her associates are charged with rescuing hostages from a deep-space cargo vessel, only to discover that they are already dead. Her brother Gren dies defending her from Zeiram, an unstoppable bioweapon with a carnivorous noh mask built into his head. As the vengeful Iria chases Zeiram across a marvelously well-realized alien planet, she sees that she has been framed in a conspiracy and has accidentally obtained a pendant containing an incriminating data chip.

Featuring excellent music, wonderful designs inspired by Terry Gilliam films such as *The Adventures of Baron Munchausen* (1988), and a rare anime character design job for **VIDEO GIRL AI**–creator Masakazu Katsura, *Iria* is an excellent science-fantasy adventure with a truly alien feel, let down only by a mediocre English-language dub.

The series is a prequel to Keita Amemiya's live-action movie *Zeiram* (1991), in which Iria, played by Yuko Moriyama instead of the anime's Aya Hisakawa, pursues Zeiram to Earth. Set three years earlier, the anime is mercifully free of the mundane constraints of the live version (which primarily took place in deserted Japanese streets), leaping from vast space freighters to alien worlds and cities full of bizarre technologies. More characters are introduced, and the handful of rubber monsters in the original are replaced by an army of clones, causing a degree of carnage that would bankrupt a live-action studio. The franchise continued in its live-action format with *Zeiram 2* (1994) and *Zeiram 3* (1997), directed once more by Amemiya. He would also direct *Moon Over Tao* (1997), also starring Moriyama, which moved the general look and feel of *Zeiram* to an unconnected historical-fantasy setting.

IRON LEAGUER

1993. JPN: *Shippu Iron Leaguer*. AKA: *Whirlwind Iron Leaguer*. TV series, video. DIR: Tetsuro Amino. SCR: Fuyunori Gobu, Akihiko Inari, Noboru Sonekawa. DES: Tsuneo Ninomiya, Kunio Okawara. ANI: Hideyuki Motohashi. MUS: Kaoru Wada. PRD: Sunrise, Studio Nue, TV Tokyo. 25 mins. x 52 eps. (TV), 25 mins. x 5 eps. (v).

An inevitable combination of the sports-anime plotting of **CAPTAIN TSUBASA** with the giant-robot combat of **GUNDAM**, as a team of cartoonish armored super-soldiers plays a fusion of soccer and street basketball against cybernetically augmented rivals. With secret attacks, absentee parents, struggles against adversity, and the usual rash of off-the-peg formulae, credited as usual to house pseudonym "Hajime Yadate," the *Iron Leaguer* series survived on video for another handful of episodes but never attained the popularity of its predecessor **CYBERFORMULA GPX**, in whose sci-fi **SPORTS ANIME** image it was clearly made.

IRON MAN *

2010. TV series, video. DIR: Takeshi Koike, Yuzo Sato. SCR: Toshiki Inoue, Naoki Tozuka, Kazuhiko Inukai. DES: Takahiro Umehara, Hideyuki Ueno. ANI: Takahiro Umehara, Kim Dong Sik, Ai Kikuchi, Haruhito Takada. MUS: Tetsuya Takahashi. PRD: Madhouse, Sony Pictures Entertainment. 25 mins. x 12 eps. (TV), 88 mins. (v).

Tony Stark, ambassador for world peace, in this alternate take on the Marvel Comics hero's origin story, saves his own life by creating the original Iron Man suit and escaping terrorists, but on his return home he decides to move to Japan and devote his life to the peace and well-being of the world. He will mass-produce Iron Man suits to take over his role as guardian of peace and will turn his brilliant mind to work on a new power station that doesn't run on fossil fuels. But, as ever in the world of superhero stories, evil lurks in the wings. Only this time it's armored, Japanese-style, and ready for action.

There's no doubt that Madhouse is a classy studio—polished, slick, and tailored to Western tastes. Previous adapted Western texts, such as **WITCHBLADE** and **HIGHLANDER: THE SEARCH FOR VENGEANCE**, have not quite succeeded, but the studio's technical skill and fan credibility have made them the go-to guys for Western studios wanting to dip a toe into action adventure anime. They've made three other TV series for the Superhero Anime Partners committee—**BLADE**, **WOLVERINE**, and **X-MEN**—and they all share the same slick production values and the same deal-breaking central dichotomy. Japanese studios can't make convincing American comic-book movies, any more than American studios can make convincing Japanese comic-book movies. When Batman and Spider-Man made their Japanese comic debuts they became something other than their all-American selves, and while that something other has its own good qualities, it isn't the same. The pilot episode was directed by **REDLINE**'s Takeshi Koike, although he is conspicuously absent from the subsequent episodes.

Unfortunately, the same problems of poor plotting and one-dimensional characters that plagued Marvel's earlier Western-based work reappear in *Iron Man*. The action sequences are fast and powerful, but they could have come from any Japanese mecha show of the past decade. Don't expect anything other than a passing resemblance to the Iron Man of the U.S. comics and movies, or even the amusing novelty that was the U.S. cartoon series. Don't expect anything more than a passing resemblance to Madhouse at the top of its game. As a good-looking, forgettably generic action series, this is OK, but as a marriage of titans?

Iron Man: Rise of Technovore was a one-shot video follow-up released in 2013, directed by Hiroshi Hamasaki with a screenplay from **WOLVERINE**'s Kengo Kagi, character designs by Masanori Shino, and music from Marvel stalwart Tetsuya Takahashi (who, incidentally, also provided the score for the second **TIES OF LOVE** video). It features a fight between Iron Man and Ezekiel Stane, terrorist supporter and owner of an armor that could outclass him. Stark is framed for Stane's terrorist activity and has to evade a S.H.I.E.L.D. manhunt, clear his name, and stop Stane.

IRON VIRGIN JUN *

1992. JPN: *Tetsu no Otome (Shojo) Jun*. Video. DIR: Fumio Maezono. SCR: Fumio Maezono, Tsukasa Sunaga, Akihiko Takadera. DES: Mitsuyoshi Munesaki. ANI: Mitsuyoshi Munesaki. MUS: Hiroki Ishikawa. PRD: Triangle Staff, Animaruya. 46 mins.
A sword-and-sorcery romp from **DEVILMAN**–creator Go Nagai about spunky teenager Jun refusing to accept an arranged

marriage and fighting to save her honor. Her mother makes this difficult for her by sending a gang to bring her back and teach her that sex isn't something to be afraid of. After watching the way this show handles it, you might disagree. **NV**

IRONFIST CHINMI

1988. JPN: *Tekken Chinmi*. AKA: *Ironfist*. TV series, video. DIR: Toshitaro Oba, Kazuhiro Mori. SCR: Junji Takegami, Yukiyoshi Ohashi. DES: Kenichi Onuki. ANI: Kenichi Onuki, Hideyuki Motohashi, Osamu Tsuruyama. MUS: Kei Wakakusa. PRD: Tohoku, TV Asahi. 25 mins. x 12 eps. (TV), 32 mins. (v).
Chinmi is a kung-fu protégé brought to the Dailin temple by the Old Master. There, he learns at the feet of the teacher Ryukai, befriends fellow student Jintan, and plays in the forest with his pet monkey, Goku (see **JOURNEY TO THE WEST**). He runs errands for the temple, learning all the while about the nature of strength, both physical and mental. This short-lived adaptation of Takeshi Maekawa's 1983 *Shonen Magazine* manga, faithfully depicted the first 12 volumes (all that were available at the time, though the manga itself is still ongoing today) but introduced new characters, kung-fu aspirant Laochu and female foil Lychee, to even out Maekawa's original boy-heavy cast. Chinmi was back the same year with the straight-to-video *Ironfist Chinmi's Kung-fu Picture Book (Tekken Chinmi Kenpo Daizukan)*, a clip-show of his eight best bouts, which, with an emphasis on fighting, outlasted the series that spawned it by a mile.

IRRESPONSIBLE CAPTAIN TYLOR, THE *

1992. JPN: *Musukenin Kancho Tylor*. TV series, video. DIR: Koichi Mashimo. SCR: Hiroyuki Kawasaki, Kenichi Kanemaki, Mami Watanabe. DES: Tomoyuki Hirata. ANI: Tomoyuki Hirata. MUS: Kenji Kawai. PRD: Big West, Tatsunoko Pro, TV Setouchi. 25 mins. x 26 eps. (TV), 40 mins. x 2 eps. (v1), 35 mins. x 6 eps. (v2), 30 mins. x 2 eps. (v3).
Justy Ueki Tylor is the ultimate slacker, a lazy good-for-nothing who joins the galactic military because he thinks it is the passport to an easy life. Put in charge of a battered hulk called the Soyokaze (Slight Wind), the former captain of which committed suicide due to depression, Tylor

finds himself commanding a gang of thugs led by two stuffy officers (named after martial icons Mifune and Fuji) who would like nothing better than to throw him out of the airlock. Tylor, however, continually falls on his feet, accidentally thwarting an enemy double cross by giving them a parcel bomb meant for him, haphazardly steering his way through a battle so that alien warships shoot each other, and even unknowingly volunteering for a suicide mission only to escape from danger by leading his would-be destroyers right into the middle of the Terran fleet. In the tradition of Tylor's contemporary **TENCHI MUYO!**, our loser hero is also surrounded by a bevy of beauties, including girl-next-door Lieutenant Yuriko Star, adoring alien ruler Queen Azalyn Goza (who likes Tylor, even though her ministers want her to invade his planet), pretty and vacant twins Eimi and Yumi, and alien spy Harumi, who is planted on the Soyokaze to assassinate Tylor but never quite gets around to it.

The character is a cartoon version of Hitoshi Taira, the lazy protagonist of the 1962 live-action movie *Japan's Irresponsible Age* who was played by comedian Hitoshi Ueki. This popular satire on Japan's salaryman culture featured a feckless individual who always managed to come out on top, advancing up promotional ladders when accidents befell his superiors, or lucking into important business information simply by malingering and goofing off. The series and its theatrical spin-offs were revived in 1990, suspiciously close to the time when **HUMMINGBIRDS**–creator Hitoshi Yoshioka would have begun work on this anime version.

The series returned in several video outings starting with the two-parter *Tylor: An Exceptional Episode* (1994), followed in 1995 by a six-part series that concentrated in turn on some of the supporting cast—Azalyn, for example, given an episode of her own, followed by one in which the star is Tylor's mad-dog pilot, KB Andressen. The series was rounded off by the two-part video series *Tylor: From Earth to Eternity* (1996), in which the lazy captain once again saves Earth from an alien menace by hoping the problem will go away. However, he is not permitted a tidy happy end—the series finishes with the Ralgon

Empire on the brink of civil war, Earth and the Ralgon Empire in a confused state of relations, and the nature of a third-party enemy revealed.

IS THIS A ZOMBIE? *

2011. JPN: *Kore wa Zombie Desuka?* TV series. DIR: Takaomi Kanasaki. SCR: Makoto Uezu, Shigeru Morita, Toko Machida, Satoko Sekine. DES: Shinobu Tagashira, Kei Ichikura. ANI: Hirofumi Morimoto, Yuko Yahiro. MUS: Shinji Kakijima. PRD: Studio DEEN, AT-X, Flying Dog, Kadokawa Pictures, Kadokawa Shoten, Klockworx. 25 mins. x 13 eps. (TV1), 30 mins. x 10 eps. (TV2).
Eucliwood Hellscythe, known as Eu to her friends, is a necromancer. When teenager Ayumu Aikawa is murdered by a serial killer, she revives him as her zombie bodyguard. But when Ayumu accidentally removes the powers of the chainsaw-wielding magical girl Haruna, Haruna orders him to take her place in a battle against evil animal-like monsters who wear schoolboy uniforms—which naturally requires him to dress as a magical girl. A surreal harem comedy show that overdoes absolutely everything, including the fan service, this is based on Shinichi Kimura's book series, illustrated by Kobuichi and Muririn. The series has spawned three manga set in its universe; the anime is related to the 2010 manga, with art by Sacchi. Its mix of absurdity and underwear was powerful enough to support a second series, *Is This a Zombie? Of the Dead (Kore wa Zombie Desuka? Of the Dead)*. with Satoko Sekine joining the original script team and the rest of the key players unchanged. Compare to CORPSE PRINCESS.

ISABELLE OF PARIS

1979. JPN: *Paris no Isabelle.* TV series. DIR: Keiji Hayakawa. SCR: Takeshi Shudo. DES: Nobuyuki Kitajima. ANI: Yoshiyuki Sugawara, Tadayuki Hayashi. MUS: Tsutomu Matsushita. PRD: DAX, TV Tokyo. 25 mins. x 13 eps.
Romance, cross-dressing, and intrigue in 1870s France, which could conveniently imply a relationship (of sorts) to ROSE OF VERSAILLES. Fifteen-year-old Isabelle Laustin is the daughter of a wealthy landlord, Leon, and his wife, Marie. She has spent a happy childhood with her friend Jean and sister Genevieve, and she has a suitor in the person of Captain Victor of the French army. However, her life changes when Napoleon III's army is beaten by the Prussians, and Paris is besieged. When the city is sold to the enemy by the feckless Louis Adolphe Thiers, it falls to Isabelle to save France by disguising herself as a boy and heading for London on a secret mission. A short-lived tale of French whimsy drawing on LES MISÉRABLES and THREE MUSKETEERS, but a solo scripting project for future POKÉMON–writer Takeshi Shudo that made little use of the rich historical potential, looked just like every other adventure anime, and sank without a trace. Compare to STAR OF THE SEINE.

ISAKU *

1997. JPN: *Isaku.* AKA: *Written Clues; Posthumous Works.* Video. DIR: Katsuma Kanazawa. SCR: Sakura Momoi. DES: Hiroya Iijima. ANI: N/C. MUS: N/C. PRD: Pink Pineapple, KSS. 30 mins. x 4 eps. (v1), 30 mins. x 3 eps. (v2).
An everyday school is found to have dark secrets—a hidden torture chamber, secret passages, and an insane janitor who has trapped several schoolgirls in the deserted hallways. Five girls, their attractive female teacher, and some token boys star in a schlocky slasher-thriller, with plenty of time out for sexual assault, as befits an anime adapted from an unpleasant computer game. The aim of the original was reputedly to escort the female cast safely off the premises, though many of the players preferred to watch them succumb to the janitor's lust. A similar mindset seems to have dominated the filmmakers. The series was remade as *Isaku Respect* (2001), and the franchise continued in SHUSAKU and KISAKU THE LETCH, which each feature one of Isaku's similarly nasty brothers. **NV**

ISHIGURO, NOBORU

1938–2012. Born in Tokyo, Ishiguro graduated from the film department of Nihon University, before becoming an animator on ASTRO BOY. He joined TV Doga in 1964, but went freelance in 1965, his first independent job being directorial work on MARINE BOY. Work on WANSA-KUN and LITTLE GOBLIN led to his bestknown work on STAR BLAZERS, a franchise that has dominated his career ever since. He was also the director of the MACROSS movie *Do You Remember Love?*, MEGAZONE 23, and many other anime of the 1980s. Less well known is his crucial role in documenting the history of Japanese animation, with his coauthorship of the 1980 Japanese-language book *The Frontline of Television Animation* (see Bibliography). In an unprecedented move, Ishiguro divided the workload with his colleague, the voice actress Noriko Ohara, with the couple alternating chapters to present different angles on familiar stories from the world of anime. He ended his part of the book by lamenting the absurd, self-defeating glut of anime on the market and saying no good could come of an era in which there were more than 30 titles a week on television screens. However, Ishiguro would live and work in anime for another 32 years and see the number of shows climb to several times that figure.

ISHINOMORI, SHOTARO

1938–98. Pseudonym for Shotaro Onodera; credited before 1986 as Shotaro Ishimori. Born in Miyagi Prefecture, Ishinomori made his first manga sale while still in high school. Like CLAMP and Rumiko Takahashi, his influence on the anime world is huge, but largely through being the original creator of many important manga.

As the creator of CYBORG 009 and 8TH MAN, he established many of the traditions of later Japanese espionage and superheroes, whereas in the live-action world, his involvement with *Masked Rider* (*DE) and the original KIKAIDER, not to mention the long running team show franchises that led to *Mighty Morphin' Power Rangers* (*DE), have made his work a vital component in understanding the last 50 years of Japanese popular entertainment.

IT'S A FAMILY AFFAIR *

2005. JPN: *Ane to Boin.* AKA: *Older Sisters and Boobs.* Video. DIR: Hideki Araki. SCR: Osamu Momoi. DES: Hideki Araki. ANI: Hideki Araki. MUS: N/C. PRD: Milky. 30 mins. x 2 eps.
Keisuke has ten older stepsisters, all absurdly well-endowed. He lusts after all of them, and eventually succeeds in his gropey quest. There's no plot, just ten short scenes in ten different locations—train, car, fast food restaurant, office, bath, and so on—each catering to a different fetish with a different girl. No story, no humor, just exactly what it says on the cover,

which boasts "From the creators of **AKIBA GIRLS**." It started life as an erotic computer game from G.J? with character designs by Toshihide Sano. **N**

ITANO, ICHIRO

1959–. After an early career designing machinery for shows such as **MEGAZONE 23** and **MACROSS**, Itano moved into action direction, gaining fame on such explosive works as **ANGEL COP** and **VIOLENCE JACK**. In particular, Itano was revered for his super-abundant, multi-angled shots of aerial battles, culminating in the "Itano Circus," a huge eruption of dozens of warheads and missiles, contrails going in multiple directions, shot from the point-of-view of a camera in the very center of the action. His reputation continued in the 21st century with **GANTZ**, the anime considered "too tough for TV." Although he lacks the celebrity name-recognition of many of his colleagues as a show-runner, his realist camera-use and application of real-world physics to unreal or science-fictional situations has made him an immensely influential figure in the look of modern anime, much imitated by animators of the last 30 years. He remains an important figure behind the scenes, having embraced the digital age with alacrity, credited with CG direction on such recent successes as the third rebooted **EVANGELION** movie.

ITO, IKUKO

1961–. A freelance animator whose character design work has made her name a regular appearance on the rosters of popular TV anime, including **SAILOR MOON** and **MAISON IKKOKU**. Specializing as a designer of pretty girls, Ito has also worked as a lead animator.

ITO, KAZUNORI

1954–. Born in Yamagata Prefecture, Ito sold his first script to the **URUSEI YATSURA** TV series. As a member of the Headgear collective, he began a long-term collaboration with Mamoru Oshii, leading to their association with the **PATLABOR** series, for which Ito wrote many of the best episodes—Ito's wife Akemi Takada was a character designer on the same show. Ito is one of the best writers working in anime; his arguable masterpiece being the **GHOST IN THE SHELL** movie, for which he artfully translated Masamune Shirow's complex manga to the screen. He has subsequently moved into live-action films, scripting a *Gamera* movie and also Mamoru Oshii's *Avalon*, which, the director ominously commented in interviews, has been their last collaboration. Oshii's subsequent work has been demonstrably poorer for the absence of Ito's contribution at the scripting stage.

ITO, TSUNEHISA

1941–. Born in Kochi Prefecture, Ito sold his first animation script while still studying law and politics in college. His subsequent work has included episodes of **GUNDAM**, **NOBODY'S BOY REMI**, and **FRITEN-KUN**.

IUCHI, SHUJI

1950–. Born in Kanagawa Prefecture, Iuchi graduated from Design College of Tokyo before finding work as an animator on **MICROID S** and **DEVILMAN**. His directorial debut was an episode of the TV series **GALAXY EXPRESS 999**. Iuchi also has a number of script credits, billed as a writer and director on episodes of **MAMA IS A FOURTH GRADER** and **YAMATO TAKERU**.

IXION SAGA DT *

2011. AKA: *Ixion Saga Dimension Transfer*. TV series. DIR: Shinji Takamatsu. SCR: Akatsuki Yamatoya. DES: Shinji Takeuchi, Hiroshi Ogawa, Kaoru Aoki. ANI: Ai Yoshimura, Yoshinari Saito. MUS: Elements Garden. PRD: Pony Canyon, CAPCOM, TV Tokyo, TO Entertainment. 24 mins. x 25 eps.
Teenage online role-player Kon answers a call to adventure from a character in a computer game, only to find himself whisked away to the world of the game, where he becomes an unlikely addition to a party of adventurers. Bawdy humor, including many gags about testicles, soon follows, with much parodic humor at the expense of other anime shows, particularly **SAILOR MOON** and **FIST OF THE NORTH STAR**.

IZUBUCHI, YUTAKA

1950–. Born in Tokyo, Izubuchi is a popular and prolific designer of robots and machinery in many landmark anime. His debut work was on **STARBIRDS**, where he was a protégé of director Tadao Nagahama, but his big break came with his involvement in the Headgear collective, which led to **PATLABOR**. He is also fortunate enough to be a member of another, nameless, clique—attending the same high school as Shoji Kawamori and fellow designer Haruhiko Mikimoto. He has demonstrated that his work is not limited to robots alone, both with the organic and, literally, fantastic character designs in **RECORD OF LODOSS WAR** and with his role as supervising director on **RAHXEPHON**.

IZUMO

1991. Video. DIR: Eiichi Yamamoto, Takaya Mizutani. SCR: Yoshihiko Tsuzuki. DES: Takaya Mizutani. ANI: N/C. MUS: Reijiro Koroku. PRD: Kove, Studio Kumosuzu. 45 mins. x 2 eps.
Izumo, a prince of Nakatsu, hates old-fashioned custom and befriends Sanae, a girl from the rival kingdom of Yamatai. Meanwhile, neighboring countries Asuka and Yamato are plotting to steal the Amenomukumo Sword, a sacred treasure of Nakatsu. The warrior **YAMATO TAKERU** kidnaps Sanae, and Izumo takes up the sword to regain her, but he must first defeat Orochi, a serpent with eight heads and eight tails. This adventure anime combines the Japanese myth of **LITTLE PRINCE AND THE EIGHT-HEADED DRAGON** with a prehistorical meeting of cultures that would be revisited in **PRINCESS MONONOKE**. Based on Yoshihiko Tsuzuki's manga in *Comic Nora*.

IZUMO (B)

2003. JPN: *Izumo*. Video, TV series. DIR: Takefumi Goda. SCR: Yasuyuki Muto. DES: Yoshi Ten. ANI: Tao Min. MUS: Pyonmo. PRD: Studio E-go!, Museum Pictures, Milky. 30 mins. x 5 eps. (v), 25 mins. x 12 eps. (TV).
Teenager Hikaru is plagued by dreams of a naked priestess praying by a spring who addresses him as her Savior. He also dreams of a secret room at his school and eventually cannot resist the temptation to seek it out, discovering a gateway to what at first appears to be another world, but may in fact be ancient Japan during the time of legends. Undertaking a quest to return to their own world by releasing four mythical beasts from captivity, Hikaru and his companion Ayaka soon discover that their fairy-tale world is underpinned by traumas in their own world—Ayaka has been suppressing memories of childhood sexual abuse; an intriguing decision to

drag some of the subtexts of fairy tales into the open in the style of **Urotsukidoji**. A TV series without the nudity, *Izumo: Flash of a Bold Blade* (*Takeki Tsurugi no Senki*, 2005), features a new cast of Japanese schoolchildren, transported to the world of Izumo by an earthquake at their school, in the style of the earlier *Long Love Letter* (*DE). We have added a (b) to the title in order to distinguish this franchise from the earlier **Izumo** (1991), which has its own entry. ●Ⓝ🅥

J

JACK AND THE BEANSTALK *

1974. JPN: *Jack to Mame no Ki.* Movie. DIR: Gisaburo Sugii, Naoto Hashimoto. SCR: Kenji Hirami. DES: Shigeru Yamamoto. ANI: Shigeru Yamamoto, Kazuko Nakamura. MUS: Morihisa Shibuya. PRD: Herald, Tac. 98 mins. Farmer's son Jack believes a traveling salesman (similar to the portrayal of THE WIZARD OF OZ back in Kansas) when he tells him that his beans are magical. Willingly exchanging his cow for them, Jack is chastised by his mother and throws the beans away. The beans grow into a massive stalk overnight, and Jack's dog, Crosby, is approached by a mouse, who entreats them to climb up. The beanstalk leads up through the bottom of the well into the courtyard of a castle in the sky that is occupied by the witch Mrs. Noire (Hecuba). Keen on stealing treasure, Jack is eventually convinced by Crosby that he should rescue the imprisoned Princess Margaret (whom Mrs. Noire intends to marry to her ogreish son, Tulip) and break Noire's spell that has turned all the castle's former occupants into mice. After a final confrontation with Tulip, Jack saves the day, though it becomes patently obvious that Margaret is a clearheaded girl of 18, determined to get on with restoring her people's fortunes, while Jack is merely a child in love with the idea of being a hero. In an original and poignant twist on happy-ever-after, Margaret stays on in her castle while Jack returns home (happily) to his farm, where he soon forgets all about her. This feature debut of future TALE OF GENJI–director Gisaburo Sugii is an excellent musical anime that could easily have given Disney's films of the day a run for their money, but one which sank without a trace on a very limited U.S. release.

JACK AND THE WITCH *

1967. JPN: *Shonen Jack to Mahotsukai.* AKA: *Boy Jack and the Sorcerer.* Movie. DIR: Taiji Yabushita. SCR: Shinichi Sekizawa, Susumu Takaku. DES: Reiji Koyama. ANI: Akira Daikuhara. MUS: Seiichiro Uno. PRD: Toei. 80 mins. The mischievous Jack and his friends are racing through the forest when they meet Kiki (Allegra), a girl on a mini-helicopter. With Chuko (Squeaker) the mouse and several other companions, he is taken to the Devil's Castle. Kiki is revealed as a Devil-child, working for Grendel (Queen Iliana), the master of Devil's Castle, who uses a Devilization Machine to turn children into monsters (or "harpies," in the U.S. dub). Chuko is turned into a devil, but Jack escapes. Kiki is sent after him but falls out of the sky, where she is nursed back to health by Jack. Accompanied by bear, fox, and dog companions, Jack returns to the castle to confront the witch. Grendel captures the animals and leaves them imprisoned to watch through her crystal ball as she kills Jack. The animals are keen to watch events unfold, but seeing that they are anxious to see what is happening, the spiteful Chuko (who is still devilized) smashes the crystal ball. This breaks Grendel's spell, and she dies trying to escape in a balloon. Chuko, Kiki, and all the other occupants of the castle are restored to normalcy and pile into Jack's car for the journey back to his place.

A bizarre updating of the Old English poem *Beowulf*, originally entitled *Adventure in the Wonder World*, *JatW* was originally commissioned to mark the tenth anniversary of Toei Animation. Pushing the envelope at the time for Japanese animation, it features a striking change in style after Jack enters the "witch-world" and was the first anime work to win a Mainichi Film Award for best score.

JAKOBUS NIMMERSAT *

1980. JPN: *Nodoka Mori no Dobutsu Daisakusen.* AKA: *Great War of the Animals of Placid Forest.* TV special. DIR: Yoshio Kuroda. SCR: Toshiyuki Kashiwakura. DES: Yasuji Mori. ANI: Kazuko Hirose. MUS: Tatsumi Yano. PRD: Nippon Animation, Fuji TV. 70 mins. When people from a nearby village discover a hole in their church roof, they unthinkingly rush into the forest to cut down trees to repair it. Agreeing that they should warn the humans off, Peter the Root Fairy and his animal friends attempt to shoo them from the forest, and when this tactic fails, they embark on a campaign of careful resistance and nuisance— compare to POM POKO. Based on the book by Boy Lornsen, this TV special reduced the age of the original Peter to make him more appealing to young viewers and dropped all child characters in order to allow the young audience to enjoy watching little people avenge themselves on the folly of grown-ups. Released in English under differing titles, including *Peter of Placid Forest* and *Back to the Forest.*

JANKEN MAN

1991. AKA: *Scissors-Paper-Stone Man.* TV

series. DIR: Toshiya Endo, Hiroshi Yoshida, Naohito Takahashi. SCR: Satoru Akahori, Yoshiaki Takahashi, Tsunehisa Arakawa, Takao Oyama. DES: Nobuyoshi Habara. ANI: Nobuhiro Ando, Naoyuki Matsuura. MUS: N/C. PRD: Ashi Pro, TV Tokyo. 20 mins. x 51 eps.

A superhero who defeats adversaries by playing games of scissors-paper-stone with them hardly seems like a pitch for a successful show, but Janken Man's fight against the evil Osodashi Mask kept young viewers hooked for a year.

JAPAN INC.

1987. JPN: *Manga Nihon Keizai Nyumon*. AKA: *Manga Introduction to Japanese Economics*. TV series. DIR: Takenori Kawata, Masamune Ochiai, Yoshimasa Yamazaki, Teruo Kogure. SCR: Takashi Yamada, Shunichi Yukimuro, Miho Maruo. DES: Shotaro Ishinomori. ANI: Nobuhiro Soda. MUS: Sunset Hills Hotel. PRD: Knack, TV Tokyo. 25 mins. x 25 eps.

In the middle of the 1980s, yuppie career girl Sawako Matsumoto graduates from Harvard Business School and returns to Japan. As the country struggles under the export pressures brought by the high yen, she works through the night to produce a business plan that will drag her company out of its rut. Based on the manga by **CYBORG 009**–creator Shotaro Ishinomori that was originally serialized in the high-class business paper *Nihon Keizai Shinbun* and even published as an economics textbook by the University of California. The anime version was broadcast in a ten-o'clock evening slot when hard-working salarymen stood a better chance of seeing it.

JAPAN, OUR HOMELAND

2007. JPN: *Furusato Japan*. AKA: *Little Heart Songs*. Movie. DIR: Akio Nishizawa. SCR: Akio Nishizawa. DES: Hiroshi Kugimiya, Tadashi Kudo. ANI: Hiroshi Kugimiya. MUS: Makoto Kuriya. PRD: WAO! WORLD Co. Ltd., WAO Corporation. 96 mins.

It is 1956: a decade after the surrender of Japan, the nation is still poor and many are struggling for survival. But the Occupation is over, and recovery has begun. Japan has joined the United Nations, a sign of acceptance in the international community. Young teacher Rieko Sakamoto joins an elementary school in downtown Tokyo. Spurred on by the last message from her kamikaze pilot brother, she wants to pass down the traditional songs of Japan to the children in her class. Even though war has been over for a decade, families are still grieving and many of the old traditions are dying. Can this teacher inspire her young pupils with an old song, even in the face of new tragedy?

Seemingly capitalizing on the same postwar nostalgia that propelled the live-action film series *Always: Sunset on Third Street* (2005) to the top of the Japanese box office (see also **FROM UP ON POPPY HILL**), this animated movie also has a more earnest desire to cling to Japanese culture in the face of foreign cultural colonization and domestic amnesia. Director/screenwriter Nishizawa, a founder of the WAO Corporation, works in media education and has directed two other anime, **NITABOH** and **SYMPHONY IN AUGUST**. Kugimiya, Kudo, and Kuriya have all worked with him on one or the other of these. *Japan: Our Homeland* has been released in French, Italian, German, Chinese, Russian, and Polish, but not into English, presumably because there are neither boobs nor robots in it. A website, in four languages including English, gives an idea of what Anglophone audiences are missing. Even though it lacks the imaginative breadth of **MAI MAI MIRACLE** and the transcendent beauty of **MY NEIGHBOR TOTORO**, its loving, respectful, and humane depiction of a way of life now lost has a great deal of charm.

JAPANESE FOLK TALES

1975. JPN: *Manga Nihon Mukashi-banashi*. AKA: *Manga Japanese Folk Tales*. TV series. DIR: Rintaro, Norio Hikone, Hidenori Kondo, Gisaburo Sugii, Hiroyuki Hoshiyama, Hiroyoshi Mitsunobu, Isao Okishima. SCR: Isao Okishima, Hiroyuki Hoshiyama, Tsunehisa Ito, Ryohei Suzuki. DES: Tsutomu Shibayama. ANI: Masakazu Higuchi. MUS: Jun Kitahara. PRD: Ai Planning Center, Tac, TBS. 25 mins. x 1467 eps.

Crammed two to an episode, the original *Japanese Folk Tales* series retold many old stories for a children's audience. Some were old anime staples, such as **MOMOTARO** and **THE MONKEY AND THE CRAB**. Others were commonly pastiched in anime but rarely seen in their original form, such as *Snow Woman*, the tale of a sultry siren who lures unsuspecting travelers to their deaths on a snowbound mountain pass. This was first animated as Noburo Ofuji's *Dream of a Snowy Night* (1947), but snow princesses often appear as characters in diverse anime from **DORORON ENMA** to **URUSEI YATSURA**. Similarly, *Princess Kaguya*, the story of a beautiful woman found inside a strip of bamboo who cannot find a husband on Earth and eventually returns to her home on the moon, was first animated in 1942 by Goro Araiwa and also appears here, but this tale is most likely to be known through oblique references to it in anime such as **REI REI** and **GU-GU GUNMO**. In *Urashima Taro*, first filmed as Noburo Ofuji's *Cut-Out Urashima* (1928), a Japanese fisherman is carried away to an underwater castle where he lives happily with the daughter of the Dragon King, only to discover that centuries have passed back on the surface when he returns. This early time-travel tale is often referenced in modern anime, including **FUTURE COP URASHIMAN** and **GUNBUSTER**, where time dilation is called the "Urashima Taro Effect."

Shown on several occasions in movie theaters, the series also inspired the **FAMOUS WORLD FAIRY TALES** and **JAPANESE HISTORY** serials, as well as imitators such as Hajime Koedo's 28 theatrical shorts *Japanese Fairy Tales* (1988) and Takashi Kurahashi's adult video spin-off *Flirting Japanese Fairy Tales* (1989). Although new tales ceased after 1994, the series continued in reruns long afterward, and was remastered and rebroadcast for a whole new generation in 2005. It is one of the longest-running series in the anime world, after the unstoppable **SAZAE-SAN**. Screened for a new generation in 2010, it beat many more modern shows in the ratings, leading to the modern imitator **JAPAN'S INTERESTING FOLK TALES**.

JAPANESE HISTORY

1976. JPN: *Manga Nihon-shi Series*. AKA: *Manga Japanese History Series*. TV series. DIR: Hidenori Kondo, Norio Yazawa. SCR: Junji Tada. DES: Oji Yutabe. ANI: Oji Yutabe. MUS: Takeshi Sato. PRD: Nippon TV. 25 mins. x 52 eps.

A trawl through the centuries of Japanese history, beginning in myth with the **BIRTH OF JAPAN** then speeding through the early cultures, the rise of the Yamatai nation, the Heian period, the civil war, and finishing with the Meiji Restoration in the 19th century. The series' look was deliberately haphazard, with character designs changing with each historical period in order to give a sense of the passage of time. Ironically, for treatment of Japan's more modern history, the anime medium descends once more into myth-making. Apart from the dramatized historical events of ANIMENTARY, Japan's descent into fascism in the 1920s and 1930s is rarely shown in anime except in revisionist shows like KISHIN CORPS and SAKURA WARS that try to play down the harsh realities in favor of fantastic whimsy. Japanese history was also covered in the MANGA PICTURES OF JAPAN series. A series with the same title later ran on NHK in 1992–93, largely focusing on particular historical characters for several episodes at a time, later slightly shifted in format so that characters deemed illustrative of a particular era narrated the periods before and after their lifetimes, such as Hideyoshi describing Japan's long century of civil war, even though he was only around for the end of it.

JAPAN'S INTERESTING FOLKTALES

2011. JPN: *Nihon Omoshiro Mukashi Banashi*. TV series. DIR: Katsunari Mochizuki. SCR: Go-gatsu-byo Mario. DES: Go-gatsu-byo Mario. ANI: Moscow Mule Shisho, Namazukun. MUS: Akiba Kobo. PRD: Akiba Kobo, CROSSPHERE, Moscow Mule Shisho. 12 mins. x 12 eps.

When the 1975 anime series JAPANESE FOLK TALES was rescreened in autumn 2010 and spring 2011, it beat many first-run anime in the ratings. Part of that was undoubtedly the nostalgia premium—people love to catch snippets of shows they remember from childhood; but part of it was also a fondness for genuine family entertainment. Of course, the nostalgia may also be for a time when families would still watch TV together instead of tuning in on their handheld devices while rushing through increasingly crowded lives. In November 2011, this charming series of paper-cut animations appeared on Japanese TV. Apparently inspired by the earlier show, it's a very contemporary take on timeless folktales, animated at the most basic level and proving that less can be so much more.

JARINKO CHIE

1981. AKA: *Chie the Brat*. Movie, TV series. DIR: Isao Takahata, Masahiro Sasaki, Tetsu Takemoto, Takashi Anno, Katsuhito Akiyama. SCR: Noboru Shiroyama, Hideo Takayashiki, Kazuyoshi Yokota. DES: Yoichi Kotabe. ANI: Kazuhiko Udagawa, Yuki Kishimo, Kazuyuki Kobayashi. MUS: Kiyoshi Suzuki. PRD: Tokyo Movie Shinsha, MBS. 45 mins. (m), 25 mins. x 64 eps. (TV).

Eleven-year-old Chie Takemoto runs a restaurant for her father, until the fateful day that the local gang boss comes around to collect her father's gambling debts. In an attempt to scare the girl, the gangster sets his cat Antonio on Chie's cat Kotetsu, but Chie's pet is the tougher, killing the gangster's. The distraught gangster decides to go straight, opening an *okonomiyaki* restaurant and hiring Chie's father Tetsu as a bodyguard. Everything goes well until Tetsu sees Chie having a secret meeting with his estranged wife.

Based on the manga by Etsumi Haruki who also worked on I AM A CAT, the *Jarinko Chie* film is a loving look at life in Osaka, a city with a very different attitude from the more famous Tokyo (see COMPILER). Featuring actor-turned-Diet-politician Chinatsu Nakayama as Chie and the anime debuts of a number of Kansai comedians in other roles, the movie was promoted with a second anime sequence shown as part of the *Kao Master Theater TV* program as the 84-minute TV special *Jarinko Chie: Anime Stand-Up*. The *manzai* comedy tradition of an abusive straight man and an eternally stupid joker is popular in Japan, and it's mixed with anime here in several scenes of live-action comedians spliced with footage from the anime. The best part is the dream sequence between the anime character Tetsu and his real-life voice actor, the *manzai* comedian Norio Nishikawa. Following the success of the film, *JC* returned to television on the TBS channel, where it survived until 1983.

JC STAFF

Originally "Japan Creative" Staff, although the full title is rarely used. Founded in 1986 by former employees of Tatsunoko as an outsourcing studio for Kitty Films, some of its notable directors include Hiroaki Sakurai, Iku Suzuki, Yasuhisa Kato. A major contributor to the modern anime

scene, often to be found on the credits of the kinds of anime that get picked up for foreign release—representative works include AI YORI AOSHI, MABURAHO, and SLAYERS.

JEANIE WITH THE LIGHT-BROWN HAIR

1979. JPN: *Kinpatsu no Jeanie*. AKA: *Golden-Haired Jeanie; Girl in the Wind*. TV series. DIR: Keinosuke Tsuchiya. SCR: Iwao Yamazaki, Kenji Terada, Yasuo Yamayoshi. DES: Masami Abe. ANI: Masami Abe, Masahiro Kase. MUS: Harumi Ibe. PRD: Dax, Tokyo 12 Channel. 25 mins. x 13 eps. (TV1), 25 mins. x 52 eps. (TV2).

Fifteen-year-old Jeanie Reed has grown up on a farm in Agarta, Virginia, and is disgusted at the outbreak of the American Civil War, when her father uses his position to profit from both sides. Turning her back on her profiteering family, she volunteers to care for orphans and becomes a nurse for the soldiers of the Union army, fretting all the time about the whereabouts of her soldier boyfriend, Robert.

A drama from the same era as LITTLE WOMEN, though this original work owes more to *Gone with the Wind* in its depiction of the Civil War. Popular tunes of the time were interwoven into the scenario, including "Oh, Susanna," "Camptown Races," and the titular "Jeanie with the Light-Brown Hair," all by the American Stephen Foster (see GREAT COMPOSERS).

The title would return in a 52-episode run of *Girl in the Wind: Jeanie with the Light-Brown Hair* (1992, *Kaze no Naka no Shojo Kinpatsu no Jeanie*), directed by Makoto Yasumura for Nippon Animation. The new version has nothing to do with the previous incarnation, and is instead set in Pennsylvania as a fanciful and largely speculative account of the musical exploits, young love, and romance between Stephen Foster and Jane "Jeanie" McDowell, the girl who was the original inspiration for the song. The anime subjects her to a series of hardships and setbacks akin to those of any other anime orphan (CANDY CANDY) but ends with the marriage of Jane the newly qualified doctor to Stephen the composer in 1850, and the announcement of the birth of their daughter. No mention is made in the anime of the real-world epilogue, in which Jane dumped her impoverished husband in 1853 after his music failed to pay the bills—the famous song about her was actually written in 1854 in a vain attempt to win her back. Foster died ten years later, aged 37, alone and penniless, after a fall at his Manhattan hotel. New Jeanie actress Mitsuko Horie would also star in the ill-fated final remake of NOBODY'S BOY REMI. Note that in accordance with the TRANSLATION of Foster's original into Japanese as referring to a girl with *kinpatsu* ("golden hair"), both anime incarnations depict a Jeanie that doesn't have light-brown hair at all.

JESTER

2011. JPN: *Hyouge Mono.* AKA: *A Jest; Tea for Universe, Tea for Life.* TV series. DIR: Koichi Mashimo. SCR: Hiroyuki Kawasaki. DES: Yoshiaki Tsubata, Yoshimitsu Yamashita, Yoshimi Umino. ANI: Yoshiaki Tsubata, Yoshimitsu Yamashita. MUS: cro-magnon, Ko Otani. PRD: Bee Train, NHK, Sogo Vision. 25 mins. x 39 eps.

Civil war rages in 1582, as Nobunaga Oda's influence grows. Sasuke Furuta, an unscrupulous, ambitious samurai, aesthete, and art lover, falls under the spell of the tea ceremony, its peace and harmony completely at odds with the violence all around him. Yet his desire for promotion is as fierce as his passion for art.

Slow, talky, and packed with cultural and historical references, this is a fascinating piece of television, not least in the way the opening credits specifically interweave Japan's past with its present, folds of the same screen. It views its characters in the round—not only fighting, but also talking about pottery, remembering the beauty of autumn, worrying about the next promotion, and admitting that not every samurai welcomes death. And there are moments of understated comedy, as when the guardswoman just about to slice Furuta with her polearm spots that his offered bribe is a fake, and he reluctantly recognizes her connoisseurship. The production didn't run as tranquilly as a tea ceremony. A month after the show began airing, cocomposers cro-magnon split up after a band member was arrested on suspicion of cannabis control law violations. Three months into its run, the show's official website changed the credit for manga creator Yoshihiro Yamada from "original

story" to "original concept" although, with discretion that would do a samurai credit, no reason was given. For other tall tales of Nobunaga's ambition, see BLACK LION, YOTODEN, and PEACOCK KING, among others.

JETTER MARS

1977. AKA: *Jet Mars.* TV series. DIR: Rintaro, Sumiko Chiba (pseud. for Toshio Hirata), Noboru Ishiguro, Wataru Mizusawa, Masami Hata, Katsuyoshi Sasaki, Yugo Serikawa. SCR: Masao Maruyama, Masaki Tsuji, Shunichi Yukimuro, Ryohei Suzuki, Hiroshi Yamamoto. DES: Akio Sugino. ANI: Akio Suzuki, Kazuo Mori, Akira Daikuhara, Wataru Mibu. MUS: Nobuyoshi Koshibe. PRD: Madhouse, Tezuka Pro, Fuji TV. 25 mins. x 27 eps.

In 2015, Dr. Yamanoue, chief researcher at the Ministry of Science, creates the boy-robot Jetter Mars and prepares to teach him how to fight as a super-soldier. However, he is opposed by the cybernetic specialist Dr. Kawashimo, who is responsible for Jetter's brain. When a storm threatens his island home, Jetter saves the day by cooperating with Kawashimo's robot daughter, Miri. Soon, he becomes a superhero saving the world from harm, though his two mentors war constantly about his true purpose.

A lackluster copy of ASTRO BOY (if Astro was 10–12 years old, Jetter is 6–8) bluntly commissioned by Toei from creator Osamu Tezuka as just that, though the studio's interference would lead him to lose all interest in the project and claim that they had chipped away everything that made it anything other than a poor imitation. Early episodes involved a will-he-won't-he crisis, as Jetter decided whether to do the altruistic thing as advised by Kawashimo or to follow Yamanoue's more mercenary advice. However, Yamanoue was soon edged out, and the show became an almost carbon-copy of the relationship between Astro and Ochanomizu in *AB*. To compound the resemblance, *JM* featured *AB* voice actors Mari Shimizu and Hisashi Katsuta, and even lifted *AB* scripts wholesale, pausing only to change the names.

JEWEL BEM HUNTER LIME *

1996. JPN: *Takara Ma Hunter Lime.* AKA: *Treasure Demon Hunter Lime; Jewel BEM Hunter Lime; Homa Hunter Lime.* Video. DIR:

Tetsuro Amino. SCR: Kenichi Nakamura. DES: Atsuko Nakajima. ANI: Atsuko Nakajima. MUS: N/C. PRD: Asmik. 30 mins. x 3 eps.

Self-explanatory adventures, as the pretty, scantily clad Lime busts ghosts and steals valuables; based on a computer game but bolstered by designs from RANMA ½'s Nakajima.

JEWELPET *

2009. TV series, movie. DIR: Nanako Sasaki, Hiroaki Sakurai, Takashi Yamamoto, Takayuki Inagaki, Makoto Moriwaki. SCR: Takashi Yamada, Yuko Kakihara, Takashi Yamada. DES: Tomoko Miyakawa, Kazuya Fukuda, Wakumi Takagi; Hitomi Odajima, Tomoko Miyakawa, Masatoshi Muto, Sumiko Aihara; Tomoko Miyakawa, Yukiko Ibe, Reiji Kasuga; Tomoko Miyakawa, Mariko Fujita, Mayumi Yokoda, Manami Koyama; Tomoko Miyakawa, Masatoshi Muto, Tomoko Miyakawa, Hitomi Odajima, Keisuke Nagai. ANI: Akihiro Sekiyama, Takahisa Ichikawa, Daisuke Matsumoto, Hiromichi Mogaki. MUS: Shiro Hamaguchi, Wataru Maeguchi, Cher Watanabe. PRD: Studio Comet, TV Osaka, We've, Inc., TV Tokyo, AT-X, Bandai, Furyu Corp., Sanrio, Sega Toys, Sotsu Agency, TV Aichi, Universal MUS, Toho. 24 mins. x 52 eps. (TV1), ?? mins. (m), 25 mins. x 52 eps. (TV2), 25 mins. x 52 eps. (TV3), 25 mins. x 52 eps. (TV4), 25 mins. x 52 eps. (TV5), 25 mins. x 52 eps. (TV6).

The Jewel Land is a magical world where sweet little animals called Jewelpets can be made into Jewels to be carried by a stork to the magic forest. The Jewelpets are creatures of magic, and in partnership with a human they can achieve great powers. When the stork is blown off-course, some of the Jewels spill to Earth, looking like shooting stars. Schoolgirl Rinko accidentally catches one of them and awakens its Jewelpet form, Ruby the white hare. Next day she and her friend Minami are rescued from a jewel robbery by a boy named Keigo, who tells them he is working for a secret organization linked with Jewel Land. Can the trio save the Jewelpets from an evil force and return them home?

Sanrio and Sega's Jewelpet franchise is perfectly calculated for its intended audience. There are a number of themes that rarely fail with little girls—school with its familiar settings, routines, friendships, and rivalries; pets, the cuter and more magical the better; and bright-colored sparkly things, preferably wearable. Starting with character toys and merchandise in 2008, the first anime series was developed for airing the following year. Joined by the Sweetspets, cute creatures that turn into sweets, they have sold enormous quantities of merchandise in Sanrio's stores, theme parks, and beyond. A 2009 manga by Sayuri Tatsuyama in *Ciao* magazine let fans read along. There have also been three Jewelpet musicals staged in Sanrio Puroland, six video games, and a number of books.

The careful groundwork and integrated merchandising approach has kept the franchise running, with four more TV series and a movie. *Jewelpet Twinkle* (2010) sees Jewelpet Ruby linking up with a new human friend, schoolgirl Sakura Akari. Takashi Yamamoto directs. In 2011 *Jewelpet Sunshine* takes viewers to school with the Jewelpets as Ruby and her classmates aim to graduate with the help of new human friends. Takayuki Inagaki directs and Yuko Kakihara leads the eight-strong scriptwriting team. The 2012 series *Jewelpet KiraPDeco!* turns cute Ruby the hare into a shop owner in Jewel Land. She hears a legend about a magical Mirror Ball, shattered long ago, and she and her friends set off to collect the fragments to protect the human world from evil.

Also released in 2012, *Jewelpet the Movie: Sweets Dance Princess (Eiga Jewelpet Sweets Dance Princess)* is a child's wish-fulfillment dream about saving the world through eating lots of sweets, turned into a feature-length movie. A fifth series, *Jewelpet Happiness*, aired in April 2013, with Ruby and her human friends opening a café. The sixth series, *Lady Jewelpet*, followed in 2014. The only two constants on the *Jewelpets* crew, character designer Miyazawa and animation house Studio Comet, are back on duty for this latest installment in a successful tale of knowing your audience and giving it exactly what it wants (see also **POKÉMON**).

JIBAKU-KUN

1999. AKA: *Bucky the Incredible Kid.* TV series. DIR: Naoyoshi Kusaka, Atsuko Nakajima. SCR: Atsuhiro Tomioka. DES: Miyuki Shimabukuro. ANI: Masashi Hirota. MUS: Kan Sawada. PRD: Ashi Pro, TBS. 25 mins. x 26 eps.

In this madcap **POKÉMON** clone, nasty exploding pink balls called "Trouble Monsters" fall into the hands of spiky-haired hero Baku ("Explosion"), who has his life turned upside down when he bumps into Great-Child Dan—a traveler through the Twelve Worlds. Featuring a love interest called Pink, a cameo appearance from Ali Baba, and more cute mascots than you can shake a stick at (who also happen to explode). Based on a manga by popular **PAPUWA-KUN**–creator Ami Shibata.

JIBURIRU: THE DEVIL ANGEL *

2004. JPN: *Makai Tenshi Jibril.* AKA: *Hell Angel Jibril.* Video. DIR: Ao Amamoto. SCR: Kazunari Kume. DES: Shinichiro Kajiura. ANI: N/C. MUS: N/C. PRD: Studio Ten, Animac. 30 mins. x 4 eps. (v1), 30 mins. x 4 eps. (v2), 30 mins. x 2 eps. (v3).

The magical-girl genre gets another pornographic twist, as average Japanese girl Rika is told by the angel Loveriel that she can transform into Jibril, a powerful angel, but only if she charges up her magical powers through sexual intercourse. Different acts, positions, and orifices lead to different "special attacks." Meanwhile, Rika's bespectacled love rival Miss Otonashi gives herself to the demon lord Asumo as a means of getting enough power to transform into her own superheroine, Misty May; cue tentacle rape and abuse as she powers up with abilities from the Dark Side.

Although modern viewers would probably find it most similar to **BEAT ANGEL ESCALAYER** or **MAGICAL KANAN**, *Jiburiru* follows the lead of **UROTSUKIDOJI** in taking the anxieties of teen life and extrapolating them into demonic conflict. It borrows the tropes of superhero shows in order to mix its fantasy sex with more everyday tensions when the cast are all wearing their secret identities and doing mundane things like going to the movies. It's a long way from **LITTLE WITCH SALLY**, but the signposts are still there. Jibril is the pronunciation of Gabriel favored in the Quran, although the English-language release steadfastly refuses to acknowledge that and clings to the lumpen "Jiburiru," presumably to avoid any religious protests. We do not believe there is any connection between this Misty May and the heroine of **OTAKU NO VIDEO**. A sequel, *Hell Angel Jibril 2*

(Makai Tenshi Jibril 2), followed in 2007, released in the U.S. as *Jiburiru: The Second Coming.* In it, the forces of good seek a new champion, choosing a girl who loves her stepbrother. Hero Naoto's stepsister Hikaru, who was studying away from home, has come back, and his girlfriend Rika, alter ego of sex angel Misty May, is a little jealous. This is all based on a series of erotic computer games by FrontWing, with characters designed by Yosai Kuchi, so (as you've probably already realized) the combined powers of Misty May, the angel Lovriel, and Naoto won't save Hikaru from sex with her brother in order to save Rika from various tentacled monsters. The opening credits are perky and cute enough for a magical girl show, which makes the tentacle sex all the more incongruous, as if someone remade **UROTSUKIDOJI** for elementary schoolgirls. *Devil Angel Jiburiru 3* followed in 2009, with more perky magical girl and tentacle sex action plus an android with huge breasts and the return of popular Devil Angel Aries from episode 2. **NV**

JIM BUTTON

1974. JPN: *Jimubotan.* TV series. DIR: Rintaro, Katsuhisa Yamada. SCR: Masaki Tsuji, Seiji Matsuoka, Noboru Shiroyama. DES: Katsutoshi Kobayashi. ANI: Toshimichi Kadota. MUS: N/C. PRD: Eiken, Top Craft, Imamura Pro, Yoyogi Studio, NET (TV Asahi). 25 mins. x 26 eps.

Adventure series for young children, in which the naïve and unworldly darkskinned boy Jim Button and his best friend Luke the engine driver leave their peaceful island home and travel the world in Luke's amphibious steam railway engine. On the way they learn that a beautiful princess named Lisi has been kidnapped by pirates and handed over to the evil dragon Grindtooth (Drinka), ruler of Sorrowland, so of course they decide to rescue her. The characters are heavily inspired by Western, rather than Japanese, children's graphics; they are based on the 1960 German children's book *Jim Button and Luke the Train Driver (Jim Knopf und Lukas der Lokomotivführer)* and its 1962 sequel *Jim Button and the Wild 13 (Jim Knopf und die Wilde 13)* by *Never Ending Story* author Michael Ende, illustrated by Franz Josef Tripp.

By a strange coincidence, a decade after the anime appeared, the shareware revolution was founded by two Americans, one of whom had the same name as the German edition of this show—Jim Knopf. He has trademarked the name and its English TRANSLATION *Jim Button* in the U.S., so web searches will return a high percentage of fascinating but unhelpful results unless you include the term "anime." Two puppet versions of the original story were issued on DVD in 2004 by the Augsburg Puppet Theater.

JINKI: EXTEND ✱

2005. TV series. DIR: Masahiko Murata. SCR: Naruhisa Arakawa. DES: Naoto Hosoda, Katsuyuki Tamura. ANI: N/C. MUS: Kenji Kawai. PRD: feel, Gansis, Mag Garden, TV Asahi. 25 mins. x 12 eps.

When hostile robotweapons known as Jinki are uncovered in Venezuela in the 1980s, their initial attacks are held off by Angel, a secret government organization. All seems calm, but a generation later the world is rocked by a series of city-leveling explosions, revealing that the aftereffects are greater than previously realized. Meanwhile, amnesiac Japanese shrine maiden Akao Hiiragi tries to remember the point of her existence and finds a new purpose in life when an encounter with a Jinki robot turns her into a pilot for a new counterattack, utilizing Moribito, a "guardian" Jinki that can be turned against the rest of its race. We would like to say that this is an intriguing allegory for the effects of U.S. foreign policy since the Reagan administration, but actually it is just an excuse for girls in giant robots. Based on two manga by Shiro Tsunashima, *Jinki: Extend* and its plain *Jinki* prequel, tracing a long line back through EVANGELION to GIANT GORG. The poses and shots in the credits sequences are made in distinct homage to two other shows: MAZINGER Z and the original GUNDAM.

JIN-ROH: THE WOLF BRIGADE ✱

1999. Movie. DIR: Hiroyuki Okiura. SCR: Mamoru Oshii. DES: Hiroyuki Okiura, Tadashi Hiramatsu. ANI: Kenji Kamiyama. MUS: Hajime Mizoguchi. PRD: Production I.G. 98 mins.

In a Japan torn apart by riots, an officer from the paramilitary Third Force is almost killed by a suicide bomber from the fanatical Sect. He begins an affair with the bomber's sister, not realizing that they are both pawns in a power game played out by opposing factions in the government.

Scenarist Oshii has tackled this subject several times before—not only in his manga *Hellhounds*, but also in the live-action spin-offs *The Red Spectacles* and *Stray Dog*. However, it is notable that the acclaimed director of GHOST IN THE SHELL should have avoided seeing this particular project through, instead handing it over to the younger Okiura. Although this is Oshii's fourth pass at the same material, it jettisons the authorial input of his PATLABOR–cohort Kazunori Ito, leaving a script with a hollow heart. *Hellhounds* had Inui ("Dog"), an officer who is almost killed by a sly female terrorist. It ended with Inui facing the same foe a second time and losing his life. *Jin-Roh* replays this story with Fuse (equally punning, since it is made up of the characters for "man" and "dog") unable to shoot one of the Little Red Riding Hood activist girls who transport satchelcharges to the rioters.

Oshii's original script employed the Red Riding Hood analogy throughout, retelling the story sympathetically from the wolf's point of view. Elements of this remain in carefully composed shots of Fuse beneath a full moon, and a meeting-place in front of the wolf-pack display at the museum. Fuse himself has a lupine cast to his features, and, in the finale, the fairy tale's use of disguises as bluff and counterbluff assumes PERFECT BLUE proportions—within the government, the paramilitary, the elite brigade, and, ultimately, the group that masterminds the whole affair.

Director Okiura, however, does not use the lupine imagery as much as Oshii intended, opting instead for a doomed romance between the softness of the impressionable girl Kei and the impenetrable steel of Fuse's armor. His nightsights are literal rose-tinted glasses through which everything is reduced to straightforward good and evil. In his armor, he can fight the rebels without a thought; out of it, he is a whirl of contradictions. Unfortunately, so is the script, which presents an alternate Japan of the late 1950s, but like *Hellhounds* and *The Red Spectacles* before it, fails to explain why. Is it a Japan that was not economically rejuvenated by the Korean War? Or simply a Japan with a few more riots? What do the rioters and the wolf-brigade vigilantes want? What is the mysterious Sect fighting for? Advanced technologies like nightsights and tracers jostle with 1940s gear like Volkswagens and German antitank guns, but why? *Jin-roh* was premiered abroad long before its Japanese release in early 2000, possibly to drum up "foreign interest" among audiences who would assume that their failure to comprehend the backstory was a cultural problem and not simply lazy plotting—an issue that could be said to haunt the same studio's later BLOOD. The end result is a skillfully animated but aimless film, with a desperate opening voice-over that tries to explain the foundation of the Third Force, in a failed attempt to convince that this is anything more than a Cold War thriller with a respray. ❶❷

JM ANIMATION

Based in Seoul the JM corporation takes its name from its founder and CEO Jung Mee. Originally formed as a multimedia company in 1997, it set up a dedicated animation arm in 2003, and formed strong connections with nearby animation academies. It is also a prominent player behind the scenes in the "Japanese" animation world, contributing to the production of anime shows and foreign animation including *Avatar: The Last Airbender*, Gonzo's GANKUTSU-O, *Macross Zero*, *Wonderful Days*, NOEIN, AQUARION, and *New* FIST OF THE NORTH STAR. JM pursues its own projects in Korea, such as the TV serials TAI CHI CHASERS and *The Little Mom*. The investment in young potential paid off in 2007 when Yu Jae-Myoung's short film *Adventure Time* was nominated for a primetime Emmy and won a coveted "Annie" award for character animation. The studio continues to work as a subcontractor on American productions, such as *The Boondocks* and *GI Joe: Resolute*.

JOHNNY CYPHER IN DIMENSION ZERO ✱

1968. TV series. DIR: Joe Oriolo. SCR: N/C. DES: N/C. ANI: Tadakatsu Yoshida, Akinori Kubo, Kaori Izumiguchi, Isao Kumada, Fumio Ikeno, Akira Maeda, Takashi Aoki, Kenichi Sugiura, Akira Iino, Jiro Tsuno, Masaharu Endo. MUS: N/C. PRD: Warner, Seven

Arts, Terebi Doga, Children's Corner. 5 mins. x 138 eps.

Square-jawed superagent Johnny can travel through inner space, Dimension Zero, and uses his superpowers to combat evil all over the universe. He is helped by the beautiful blonde Zena and tiny alien Rhom from the Black Star. An early Japanese-American coproduction by former Disney animator Joe Oriolo for Warner/Seven—a company formed by the merging of Seven Arts production after its merger with Warner Bros. Always intended for screening in both markets, *Johnny Cypher* appeared in short segments six nights a week for 23 weeks in Japan, and in various combinations and compilations in the U.S. and Australia.

JOJO'S BIZARRE ADVENTURES *

1993. JPN: *Jojo no Kimyo na Boken*. Video, movie, TV series. DIR: Hiroyuki Kitakubo. SCR: Hiroyuki Kitakubo. DES: Junichi Hayama. ANI: Junichi Hayama. MUS: Marco D'Ambrosio. PRD: APPP. 40 mins. x 6 eps. (v1), 40 mins. x 7 eps. (v2), 90 mins. (m), 25 mins. x 26 eps. (TV).

Joseph Joestar and his Japanese grandson, Jotaro, fight an ongoing blood feud against Dio Brando, an immortal vampire who caused the death of their ancestor Jonathan. Using the magical powers of the Stands, psychic attributes inspired by tarot cards, the Joestar clan and Brando's minions face off in a violent battle that plays like FIST OF THE NORTH STAR at its most surreal.

With its warring secret elites and magical trumps, *Jojo* owes a considerable debt to Roger Zelazny's *Nine Princes in Amber* (1972), particularly considering the "immortal" undertones of its hero. There are several Jojos stretching from the 19th to the 21st century—a more correct TRANSLATION of the title might be to put the apostrophe *after* the "s." BAOH–creator Hirohiko Araki's 1987 manga in *Shonen Jump* begins in the 1880s, when an Aztec death mask causes trouble for all who come into contact with it. Archaeologist Jonathan Joestar begins a vendetta against Dio, who tries to steal his inheritance and kills his dog. Dio eventually dons the mask and becomes a vampire, causing Jonathan's death as his family flees for the U.S. The story jumps to New York in the 1930s,

where Jonathan's descendant Joseph continues the battle through the Second World War, before the story moves into the 1980s with Jotaro Kujo, Joseph's half-Japanese grandson. The anime version deals primarily with the 1980s incarnation, as he and Joseph fight Dio, while he tries to heal his terrible wounds (his disembodied head has been sewn onto the body of Jonathan Joestar) and activate his ultimate trump card—the ability to stop time.

Following the series, the manga moved into the 1990s with Joseph's illegitimate Japanese son, Josuke Higashikata, then the 21st century with the Italian Giorno Giovanna, who, though officially the son of Dio, had been sired using the genitals of Jonathan and is hence the uncle of Joseph. The most recent member of the family to take the Jojo mantle is Jolyne Kujo, Jotaro's daughter, who uses her powers to escape from a Florida prison.

Gripping despite low-grade animation, the 1993 *Jojo* series was overlooked during the anime boom of the 1990s reputedly because of a prohibitively high asking price for the rights. The original *Jojo* remained unreleased in English for a decade, perhaps because the anime was always intended to sell the 87-plus-volume manga, and one could not be sold without the other. Another possibility is that the license had been considered by U.S. companies but turned down because of the surreal in-jokery of the characters' names—in the style of BASTARD, the series is full of musical references, including psychic warriors Mariah [Carey], [Bette] Midler, [Ronnie James] Dio, Cream, the psychic dog Iggy [Pop], and even the titular character himself ("Jojo was a man who thought he was a loner"), who hails from the Beatles song "Get Back."

In the wake of a Capcom computer game released in the U.S. as *Jojo's Venture* (1998), the series began to reach the American market, released by the original production company, although episodes were reordered to make the chronology easier for viewers to comprehend if they had not seen the manga. This also handily ensured that the American release "began" with much more modern episodes dating from the year 2000 instead of the 1993 chapters. Perhaps in recognition of this, Junichi Hayama's animated movie *Phantom*

Blood (2007) returned to the beginning of the story, retelling its first arc. The story was rebooted again in Kenichi Suzuki's TV series *Jojo's Bizarre Adventures* (2012), which returned to the first two generations covered. **V**

JOKER MARGINAL CITY

1992. Video. DIR: Osamu Yamasaki. SCR: Junichi Watanabe, Hiroyuki Onuma. DES: Chuichi Iguchi. ANI: Taeko Sato, Takaaki Ishiyama. MUS: N/C. PRD: Studio Zyn. 45 mins.

Jokers are genetically engineered beings who can switch sex at will, among other, more powerful psychic abilities. A young man escapes from a secret research facility and goes on the run. He is befriended by a reporter, who then has to call on the help of other Jokers to keep the boy safe from his pursuer—a wanted killer known only as the Heartless Assassin. This stylish, well-paced science-fiction video plays with the notions of gender and genetic tinkering, combining the themes of BAGHI with images from the pretty-boy subgenre of gay anime such as FAKE. Based on the manga in *Wings* magazine by ARCHA LYRA–creator Katsumi Michihara. **N**

JORMUNGAND *

2012. TV series. DIR: Keitaro Motonaga. SCR: Yosuke Kuroda. DES: Kazuhisa Nakamura, Yoshito Takamine. ANI: Kazuhisa Nakamura, Masahiko Nakata, Taro Ikegami. MUS: Taku Iwasaki. PRD: WHITE FOX, MADBOX, Geneon Universal Entertainment, Shogakukan. 25 mins. x 12 eps. (TV1), 25 mins. x 12 eps. (TV2).

Teenage arms dealer Koko Hekmatyar travels the world selling weapons in her work as an unofficial subcontractor for international shipping company HCLI. Under the cloak of its main activities, the company has a lucrative and illegal network of dealers in death. Constantly surrounded by her team of ex-military bodyguards, Koko has a new travel companion—a withdrawn, seemingly motionless but very skilled child soldier named Jonah. Jonah actually hates arms dealers, and has joined Koko's crew to find the arms dealer responsible for his family's deaths.

If you can't see what's coming, you haven't watched enough anime, or enough war movies. But if you're after a show that gives you gallons of blood and flocks of flying artillery, thick and fast enough to level buildings, without a single preachy precept to leaven its amoral revelry in death, but with real character development and plotting strung so tight you could play a guitar riff on it, this is your show. Opening with a running fight down a freeway where anti-tank missiles and heavy vehicles are tossed around like party favors, the first episode never lets up, setting a standard that the show maintains throughout.

As you'd expect, the military hardware is depicted with fanatical attention to detail, but the rest of the design is good. It's not always well executed—some of the drawing is shoddy and facial expressions can be basic—but the washed-out postmodern color palette makes up for a lot. Taku Iwasaki's score is his usual clever, polished mix of styles that adds the right note to every scene, however bloodsoaked or frenetic.

Unsurprisingly, the success of this show based on Keitaro Takahashi's 2006 manga spawned a second series in the same year, but here the action sags a little. *Jormungand: Perfect Order* lacks the precision of series one. There are more shortcuts, more speed-blurs and rapid edits. The explosions of violence are still there, and there's a more complex plot. Koko becomes the target of dangerous machinations by her own side as she takes on the CIA, develops her character in risky ad intriguing ways. How does someone who has lived through the willful destruction of others resolve the basic contradictions of her own human weakness—loves, loyalties, vulnerability?

There are echoes of the premise of GUNSMITH CATS—a deadly killer girl with actionably young sidekick, hiding behind a hail of bullets from a lifetime of abuse. *Jormungand* doesn't quite live up to that perfectly polished artifact but it's good, and dangerously seductive in its embrace of action as its own justification. It reminds us how good it can feel when the bullets and bazooka rounds fly, the choppers explode and cannon fodder shreds in a red storm, how admirable it is to see a group of professionals get the job done effectively. The moral issues are given more room in the second series, but the scales come down on the side of making mayhem fun. ●

JOSEPHINA THE WHALE

1979. JPN: *Kujira no Josephina*. TV series. DIR: Kazuyuki Hirokawa, Kazuo Yamazaki, Kazuo Tomizawa. SCR: Hiroshi Yamamoto, Hirohisa Soda. DES: Kazuo Tomizawa. ANI: Satoshi Hirayama. MUS: Kunihiro Kawano. PRD: Ashi Pro, Tokyo 12 Channel. 25 mins. x 22 eps.

Madrid schoolboy Sante Costas keeps a tiny whale in a bowl, invisible to everyone except him. Josephina takes him on many dreamlike adventures, but when Sante starts taking an interest in the outside world and gets to know his distant father, Josephina herself fades away like the dream she was. However, the final two episodes were unbroadcast in the show's original run. Excerpts were shown in an extended version to rush the plot to a conclusion, but viewers had to wait for repeats in syndication to watch the friends' final farewell.

JOURNEY THROUGH FAIRYLAND, A ∗

1985. JPN: *Yosei Florence*. AKA: *Florence the Fairy*. Movie. DIR: Masami Hata, Kazuyuki Hirokawa. SCR: Tamanobu Takamasa. DES: Sadao Miyamoto, Noma Sabear. ANI: Sadao Miyamoto, Shigeru Yamamoto. MUS: Naozumi Yamamoto (arranger). PRD: Sanrio. 92 mins.

Michael, a struggling music student not unlike GORSCH THE CELLIST, loves flowers more than he loves music itself. Replacing a begonia in a broken pot, he is visited that night by Florence the flower fairy, who thanks him for his kindness. In this musical fantasy four years in the making, a depressed Michael, cut from the orchestra for the next concert, is whisked away to Flower World by Florence. Naozumi Yamamoto, a conductor with the Tokyo Philharmonic, selected 20 pieces of classical music, which were used in the film itself and, in an imitation of Disney's *Fantasia* (1940), to inspire the surreal storyboards for the animators. Michael was played by Masaki Ichimura, a leading figure in Japan's leading musical performance troupe, Theater Shiki. Released in the U.S. by Celebrity Home Entertainment.

JOURNEY TO THE WEST ∗

1967. JPN: *Saiyuki*. AKA: *Xiyouji; Monkey; My Son Goku; Alakazam the Great; Spaceketeers; Paradise Raiders*. Movie, video, TV series, TV special. DIR: Gisaburo Sugii, Osamu Dezaki, Hideo Makino, Ryosuke Takahashi, Masami Hata. SCR: Akihiko Kanno, Morihisa Yamamoto, Michio Sano, Michiaki Ichiwa. DES: Osamu Tezuka, Gisaburo Sugii. ANI: Shigeru Yamamoto. MUS: Seiichiro Uno. PRD: Tezuka Pro, Fuji TV. 25 mins. x 39 eps. (1967).

Stone Monkey is born from a rock by the ocean. His boastful, irrepressible nature soon causes a stir on Earth as he makes himself king of all the monkeys. In search of the secret of immortality, he learns martial arts and magic from the Buddhist monk Subhuti, who renames him Sun Wu Kong (in Japanese, Son Goku), meaning "Awakened to Emptiness." Back on his mountain, he finds that demons have taken over his cave, but the skills he has learned from Subhuti enable him to throw them out. The Demon King's brothers trick him into sneaking into the Dragon King's palace and stealing a famous weapon, a miraculous iron staff that can change size on command. Sun Wu Kong is brought before the Jade Emperor for punishment. Wu Kong eats the Peaches of Immortality and is chased from Heaven, only to lose a bet with Buddha. Immured beneath a mountain for 500 years, he is saved by the Buddhist Priest Xuanzang (AKA Tripitaka), who invites Wu Kong to accompany him on a pilgrimage to Gandhara in India, the modern Punjab. En route, the pair meet a pig-changeling called Pigze and Monk Sand, a river spirit who was once a Heavenly guard. After Wu Kong defeats them, they both join the pilgrimage.

Possibly inspired by travelers' garbled tales of the Hindu monkey-god Hanuman, Wu Cheng-En's 16th-century novel *Xiyouji* is the Chinese story most often animated in Japan, perhaps because its trickster hero is more appealing to the children's audience than the dour generals of GREAT CONQUEST or the hotheaded revolutionaries of SUIKODEN. Noburo Ofuji's EARLY ANIME *Legend of Son Goku* (1926) used cut-out figures animated by stop-motion and was soon remade as the two-reel *Son Goku* (1928), directed by Takahiro Ishikawa. However, Wu Kong's real push into the Japanese market came through foreign influences. Amid the many propaganda WARTIME ANIME, the Wan brothers' Chinese cartoon *Xiyouji* (1941) was screened in

Japan under the title *Princess Iron Fan*. Featuring one chapter from the legend, when Wu Kong and friends steal a magic fan from Mount Inferno, the film inspired the 16-year-old Osamu Tezuka to write his manga *My Son Goku* (1952), based on the same Mount Inferno episodes.

Japan's animation business was in ruins after the war, though Taiji Yabushita's *New Adventures of Hanuman* (1957) was a 14-minute PR exercise funded with American money. Hanuman was chosen over Wu Kong as a subject, presumably because the former Occupying Forces of Japan felt that a character whose main aim in life is revolt against authority was not the most suitable folk hero for the times; for similar reasons during the war, the Japanese censor had lopped 20 minutes off the running time of *Princess Iron Fan*.

Yabushita returned to the story in 1960 when he directed the anime remake of Tezuka's *My Son Goku*. Retitled *Journey to the West (Saiyuki)* in Japan and *Alakazam the Great* in the U.S., Yabushita's film featured many similarities to the Chinese film that inspired Tezuka. Not only did it keep to the Mount Inferno scenes, but it also played up the moment when Wu Kong, Pigze, and Monk Sand decide to cooperate for the first time and featured a final aerial battle when the characters' feet are surrounded by airbrushed clouds. Substantial name changes were made for the U.S. version, which is set in "Majutsoland," ruled by His Majesty King Amo (Buddha), his wife, Queen Amas, and his son, Prince Amat (Tripitaka). King Alakazam (Wu Kong) tricks Merlin the magician (the Emperor of Heaven) into revealing his secrets and fights past palace guardsman Hercules to confront King Amo, who imprisons Alakazam until he is released to protect Prince Amat's quest to India. Joined by Sir Quigley (Pigze) and reformed cannibal Lulipopo (Sandy), Alakazam defeats King Gruesome (ruler of Mount Inferno) and his wife (Princess Iron Fan), is reunited with his beloved Dee Dee (a new creation in the anime), and all live happily ever after. The film's Japanese origins were further occluded by a big-name voice cast including Dodie Stevens, Jonathan Winters, Arnold Stang, and Sterling Holloway, music by Les Baxter, and the voice of Frankie Avalon whenever Alakazam sang. Released

in the summer of 1961, coincidentally alongside fellow postwar anime **MAGIC BOY** and **PANDA AND THE MAGIC SERPENT**, it was *Alakazam*'s commercial failure that led to the perception in the entertainment industry that Americans would not accept Japanese animation at all.

Back in Japan, the experience of making the film further inspired Tezuka to consider repeating the process for TV, indirectly giving birth to **ASTRO BOY** and the inevitable TV remake of the Wu Kong story, *Goku's Great Adventure* (1967, *Goku no Daiboken*). The first three episodes of this series stay close to the legend, but it soon becomes a gag free-for-all filled with surrealistic and adult humor. Viewers were puzzled or irate; the PTA complained about the level of bad language and the series ended after 39 episodes instead of the intended 52.

Leiji Matsumoto's *Starzingers* (1978) was a science-fiction version that moved the events into outer space; redubbed as **SPACEKETEERS**, it was shown in the U.S. alongside the other anime in the **FORCE FIVE** series. The next incarnation was the live-action series *Monkey* (1978, *DE), featuring scripts from **JAPANESE FOLK TALES**–scenarist Isao Okishima. The music was from the group Godiego, who also provided the theme to Matsumoto's **GALAXY EXPRESS 999**—their mournful song about Son Goku's final destination became a hit in its own right, in turn inspiring the otherwise unrelated anime **GANDHARA**. The live-action series became well known in the U.K. and Australia through the BBC dub, supervised by future Manga Entertainment voice director Michael Bakewell, but the period following it produced only one TV movie in Japan, Gisaburo Sugii and Hideo Takayashiki's anime musical *Son Goku Flies the Silk Road* (1982), and a number of SF pastiches, including **DRAGON BALL** (1986), the **DORAEMON** movie *Parallel Journey to the West* (1988), and Buichi Terasawa's **GOKU: MIDNIGHT EYE** (1989). Even **HELLO KITTY**–creators Sanrio got into the act with *Raccoon Fun Journey to the West* (1991, *Pokopon no Yukai Saiyuki*). At the close of the 20th century, the character reappeared in several new incarnations, including the *very* loose adaptation **ONE PIECE**. Another series, *Monkey Magic* (1999), was released on video and then recommissioned for TV.

Based on a computer game, the 13-episode series retells the early part of the legend relatively faithfully, with a hero now named Kongo, though the actual *journey* to the west only begins in the penultimate episode. The same year saw a new *Saiyuki* (*Gensomaden Saiyuki*, a pun on the characters for *Chronicle of Total Fun*, AKA *Paradise Raiders*), a two-part video based on Kazuya Minekura's *G-Fantasy* manga that also graduated to a full-fledged 50-episode TV series. The Minekura *Saiyuki* is set long after the evil demon Gyumao is buried by the god of Heaven. After magic and science are mixed by parties unknown, Gyumao is brought back, and the monk Genjo Sanzo, accompanied by the usual suspects in updated form, is charged with heading west to determine the cause of the trouble. The movie *GS: Requiem* appeared in 2001 from the same crew. In 2002 came made-for-video *Saiyuki Interactive* (*Saiyuki: Kibou no Zaika*);second series *Saiyuki Reload* appeared in 2003, directed by Tetsuya Endo with characters designed by Noriko Otake and music from Daisuke Ikeda; third series *Saiyuki Gunlock* (*Saiyuki Reload Gunlock* in Japan, just to confuse matters) appeared in 2004 from the same team.

The legend shows no sign of letting up in the 21st century, with a Tezuka Production movie remake of *Boku no Son Goku* (2003), along with modern reversionings such as **ONE PIECE**, one of the **MILMO DE PON** TV specials, and **ASOBOT CHRONICLE GOKU**. The story is also referenced or parodied often in other serials, such as an episode of **LOVE HINA** in which the cast put on a play version of it at a resort. The *Journey to the West* story also returned to live-action television in 2006 with a season on Fuji TV.

JUBEI-CHAN THE NINJA GIRL *

1999. JPN: *Jubei-chan: Lovely Gantai no Himitsu*. AKA: *Jubei-chan: Secret of the Lovely Eyepatch*. TV series. DIR: Hiroaki Sakurai. SCR: Akitaro Daichi. DES: Mutthuri Moony, Takahiro Yoshimatsu. ANI: Takahiro Yoshimatsu. MUS: Toshio Masuda. PRD: Madhouse, Bandai, TV Tokyo. 25 mins. x 13 eps. (TV1), 26 mins. x 13 eps. (TV2).
Seventeenth-century warrior hero Jubei fights his last battle, and with his dying breath entrusts his servant Koinosuke with the task of finding his true spiritual heir.

Three hundred years later, the magically sustained Koinosuke finds a suitable candidate, the Japanese schoolgirl Jiyu "Jubei" Nanohana, who has the large breasts and pert buttocks that mark her as the Chosen One. Koinosuke must convince Jubei to don the heart-shaped eyepatch that will call forth her spiritual ancestor, but the insufferably perky girl (who has paroxysms of joy if she manages to fry an egg) is a reluctant recruit. Transferring to a new school populated by the descendants of samurai, she is adored by all, even Shiro Ryujoji, whose family, wronged by the original Jubei, insists on sending evil substitute teachers to challenge her to duels.

Jubei-chan must have looked great on paper—a samurai spoof from the same Madhouse studio that produced the kinetic **Ninja Scroll**, featuring school gags, unwelcome guests, historical references, mawkish romance, transformations, and fighting. In other words, reheated **Ranma** ½, further damaged by a succession of befuddling ethnocentric in-jokes for the benefit of Japanese parents who remember the 1950s samurai swashbucklers, which also inspired the same scenarist's **Carried by the Wind: Tsukikage Ran**.

Without the presence of other Jubei stories in English (the aforementioned *Ninja Scroll*, its illegitimate sibling **Ninja Resurrection**, and the live-action movie *Samurai Armageddon*), there is little chance that this would have even been considered for **Translation**. Its historical roots are too deeply buried; some, like the prissy Sachi Toyama's relationship to Toyama no Kinsan (also parodied in **Samurai Gold**), would be difficult even for a Japanese audience (**Documentaries and History**). Others, like the simian Ozaru and Kozaru getting their names from Big Monkey and Little Monkey, could really do with explanatory sleeve notes, sadly lacking in the Bandai English-language release. The result is a nonsensical dub in which a mystified cast and crew hope that the audience will laugh at jokes that they plainly do not find funny themselves. Amid a cynical challenger-of-the-week formula, creator Akitaro Daichi has the temerity to write himself into the story as Jubei-chan's narcoleptic father—somehow appropriate since he could well have written this in his sleep.

The sequel series, *Revenge of the Siberian Yagyu (Siberia Yagyu no Gyakushu,* 2004) finds Jiyu and her friends Maro and Satchin now in the ninth grade. A transfer student named Freesia Yagyu joins their class, and around the same time the Siberian Yagyu clan launch an all out attack to kill Jiyu, as a descendant of Jubei, the man who killed their ancestor Kitaretsusai Yagyu 300 years ago. But then Freesia claims to be the legitimate heir to the Yagyu line and demands that Jiyu hand over the Lovely Eyepatch. The true heir of the Lovely Eyepatch, the Siberian clan's quest for revenge, the fraught relationship between Jiyu and her father Sai, and the role of Mikage, a former enemy turned Dad's editor, are all resolved in a final battle between the two girls.

JUDGE *

1991. JPN: *Yami no Shihokan Judge.* AKA: *Magistrate of Darkness: Judge.* Video. DIR: Hiroshi Negishi. SCR: Katsuhiko Chiba. DES: Shin Matsuo. ANI: Shin Matsuo. MUS: Toshiro Imaizumi. PRD: Animate Film. 45 mins. Hoichiro Oma is an everyday salaryman who is really Enma, the Judge of Hell (see **Dororon Enma**), meting out nightly justice for those who are wronged back in our world. His first case involves a ruthless executive who has committed murder on his route to the top—with ironic cruelty, Oma makes his punishment fit his crime. The second involves a conflict with Oma's own boss back in the real world, who has hired a supernatural lawyer to get him off a murder charge. Faced with weasly tactics at the bench, Oma appeals to the Court of Ten Kings, presided over by the rulers of Hell. Short tales of the unexpected in a similar style to **Pet Shop of Horrors**, based on a manga by sometime **Crusher Joe**-artist Fujihiko Hosono.

JUDO STORY

1991. JPN: *Judo-bu Monogatari.* Video. DIR: Shinichi Shoji. SCR: Daiki Ike. DES: Shinichi Shoji. ANI: Shinichi Shoji. MUS: Goro Omi. PRD: Nippon Animation. 50 mins. x 2 eps. Mochi, a novice, decides to join the judo club when he begins high school. He must endure many trials before he is accepted—shaving his head, cleaning up after his elders, and enduring their bullying. Eventually, after much blood, sweat, and tears,

his fellows select him as a team member for the local championships. Based on the 1985 *Young Magazine* manga by Makoto Kobayashi, creator of **What's Michael?**

JULIE THE WILD ROSE

1979. JPN: *Nobara no Julie.* TV series. DIR: Keiji Hayakawa, Masami Kizuu. SCR: Akira Saiga, Shina Matsuoka, Tomomi Tsutsui. DES: Masami Abe. ANI: Masami Abe. MUS: Isao Matsushita (arranger). PRD: Dax, Tokyo 12 Channel. 25 mins. x 13 eps. Eleven-year-old Julie Braun lives in the lush green mountain pastures of Austria's Southern Tyrol. Her parents are killed by Italian soldiers, and she is sent to Vienna to live with her relatives, the Clementes. She befriends cousins Johan and Tanya but has trouble adjusting to life with Uncle Karl and Aunt Klara. As Austria is plunged into World War I, Karl is fired from his job at a glass factory, and Julie's new family is forced into a life of hardship.

A short-lived **Heidi** clone made with the assistance of the Austrian Tourist Board, though sources are unclear as to whether this was a full-fledged cooperation or merely the provision of a few holiday brochures. The music keeps the Austrian motif, selected from the works of Franz Schubert and Johann Strauss, who had their own anime appearance in **Great Composers**.

JULIET

1998. Video. DIR: Tsukasa Tomii. SCR: Masaru Yamamoto. DES: Kazutoshi Kobayashi. ANI: Akira Takeuchi. MUS: N/C. PRD: Adobe Pictures. 30 mins. In this adaptation of a minor work by **Sakura Diaries**-creator U-Jin, the pretty, young Reina enjoys the advances of her lusty stepbrother and a mysterious stranger. Sold to the Japanese as their one chance to hear Kae Araki, the baby-faced voice of Minnie-May in **Gunsmith Cats** and Rini (Chibi-Usa) in **Sailor Moon**, behaving in a more erotic manner than that to which her public was accustomed. Episode #10 of the **Secret Anime** series. **Ⓝ**

JUMPING *

1988. Video. DIR: Osamu Tezuka, Eiichi Yamamoto, Taku Sugiyama, Shingo Matsuo, Takamitsu Mitsunori. SCR: Osamu Tezuka. DES: N/C. ANI: N/C. MUS: N/C. PRD: Various.

100 mins.
A video compendium of several short films released in Japan to coincide with the Second Image Software Awards. The centerpiece is Tezuka's *Jumping*, a six-minute 1984 short in which a character takes successively higher and higher leaps until he (or is it she?) eventually bounds across the ocean to the middle of a war zone, where an explosion blasts him/her down to Hell. From there, s/he is thrown back out to the beginning of the film, ready to start jumping again. This exercise in perspective is accompanied by another Tezuka short, *Broken Down Film* (1985, *Onboro Film*), a playfully postmodern joke showing a supposedly rare print of an old silent cartoon Western in which the condition of the film itself affects the action onscreen. The characters have trouble seeing because the film is so dirty, are confused by abrupt jumps in continuity due to missing footage, and even have to climb to the next frame when the projector jams—compare to Chuck Jones's *Duck Amuck* (1951). These famous but rarely seen anime were accompanied by several other experimental shorts from other animators for an audience who lacked the resources to travel to the film festivals where they were usually only to be seen. Another experimental Tezuka film, the longer **LEGEND OF THE FORESTS**, was released on video the previous year. It and the films in the *Jumping* collection were released together on U.S. DVD as *The Astonishing Work of Tezuka Osamu* (2009).

JUNGLE BOOK, THE *
1989. JPN: *Jungle Book Shonen Mowgli*. AKA: *Jungle Book Boy Mowgli*. TV series. DIR: Fumio Kurokawa, Shinji Takahashi, Akira Kiyomizu, Kazuya Miyazaki, Shigeru Yamazaki, Tatsuya Hirakawa. SCR: Nobuyuki Fujimoto, Kenichi Yoshida, Saburo Sekiguchi, Mami Watanabe. DES: Sadahiko Sakamaki. ANI: Masashi Kojima, Sadahiko Sakamaki, Kazuya Hayashi. MUS: Hideo Shimazu. PRD: Nippon Animation, TV Tokyo. 25 mins. x 52 eps.
An explorer and his wife are killed in the jungle. Their baby son, Mowgli, is raised by wolves, and befriends Baloo the bear and Bagheera the panther, who teach him the Laws of the Jungle. Rejected by local humans, who see him as a demon, Mowgli prefers to dwell in the forest, where he must outwit the evil tiger Shere Khan.

Eventually, after conflict between the humans and the animals, Mowgli defeats Shere Khan and gets to meet the beautiful human girl he has worshiped from afar for so long, leaving behind his jungle friends as he returns to the world from which he came. An anime adaptation likely to remain dwarfed by the earlier Disney classic, this version updates Rudyard Kipling's novel for the 20th century—including planes, for example, understandably absent from the original. Another old story of a human boy reared by animals was adapted as **TA-CHAN: KING OF THE JUNGLE**.

JUNGLE DE IKOU! *
1997. JPN: *Jungle de Iko!* AKA: *Let's Go with Jungle; Let's Get Jungly*. Video. DIR: Yuji Moriyama, Osamu Mikasa. SCR: Jiro Takayama. DES: Yuji Moriyama. ANI: Yuji Moriyama. MUS: N/C. PRD: Studio Fantasia, Movic, King Records, J Project. 30 mins. x 3 eps.
Ten-year-old Natsumi's father gives her a necklace from the ruins of the Myuginian jungle. Soon afterward, Natsumi dreams that a jungle god is teaching her a powerful ritual dance. Discovering that her father's researchers have also awakened an ancient forest devil, Natsumi must deal with jungle spirits, gigantic whales, and armed fighter pilots. She performs the jungle dance and transforms into Mii, a large-breasted fertility goddess. A cynical combination of the jiggling bosoms of **PLASTIC LITTLE** and the magical transformations of **CREAMY MAMI**, *Jungle de Ikou!* comes complete with a childhood pal for Natsumi, who naturally develops a crush on Mii, as well as comic-relief devil-child Ongo and his fiancée, Rongo. Originally based on a segment of voice actress Megumi Hayashibara's *Boogie Woogie Night* radio show, the series was memorably described by *Manga Mania* magazine as a "Boogie Woogie Congo Ongo Bongo Jungle Bungle."

JUNGLE KUROBE
1973. TV series. DIR: Osamu Dezaki. SCR: Yoshitake Suzuki, Toshiaki Matsushima, Yoshiaki Yoshida, Haruya Yamazaki, Chikara Matsumoto, Shinji Tahara, Noboru Shiroyama, Yu Yamamoto. DES: Fujiko-Fujio. ANI: Yasuo Kitahara, Sadayoshi Tominaga, Yoshiaki Kawajiri. MUS: Goro Misawa. PRD: Tokyo Movie Shinsha, NET (TV Asahi). 25

mins. x 61 eps.
Kurobe, the son of the chieftain of the Pilimy jungle tribe, rashly tries to catch what he believes to be an "iron bird," and ends up dangling from what is actually an airplane until he drops into the garden of unsuspecting Japanese boy Shishio Sarari. Believing himself to be in debt to his "rescuer," Kurobe insists on repaying him in the "jungle way," which means hanging around in modern Tokyo and using his imperfect jungle magic to help his newfound friend. Further complications ensue with the arrival of Paopao the elephant, Kurobe's brother Akabei, and Gakku the lion.

This blackface comedy, which has since been gently edged out of the public eye, began as an idea by lowly staffer Hayao Miyazaki, who proposed a comedy about the hobbit-like Korobokkle creature from Ainu folklore (**ADVENTURES OF KOROBOKKLE**), although he subsequently left to make **HEIDI** at Nippon Animation. Quite possibly to preserve the feelings of the Ainu, the idea transformed in the hands of **DORAEMON** cocreator Fujiko F. Fujio to become the tale of an African pygmy, transported to modern Tokyo, reversing the plot of the Hanna-Barbera cartoon *Dino Boy* (1966), which had a child of our own time fall out of a plane into a primitive lost valley. However, civil rights groups, even in the notoriously racist Japan, complained about the depiction of the lead character, and the show was quietly dropped. While not suppressed or censored, it has not been released on video, and the spin-off manga was not reprinted. It is not mentioned in the text of the official 1998 TMS studio history, although its episode listing is included, without comment or explanation, along with all the other broadcast lists in the book's index.

JUNGLE WARS
1990. Video. DIR: Yoshio Kuroda. SCR: Mayumi Koyama, Akira Sakuma. DES: Moriyasu Taniguchi, Takayuki Doi. ANI: Moriyasu Taniguchi. MUS: N/C. PRD: Nippon Animation. 25 mins. x 2 eps.
An evil syndicate of hunters attacks a jungle village where animals and humans coexist peacefully. With his parents out of action and his way of life in jeopardy, the imaginatively named "Boy" swings through

the creepers to save the day. Based on the game of the same name for the Nintendo Gameboy.

JUNJO ROMANTICA *
2008. AKA: *Junjo Romantica; Pure Romance; Pure Hearted Romance.* TV series. DIR: Chiaki Kon. SCR: Rika Nakase, Yoshiko Nakamura, Michio Yokote. DES: Yoko Kikuchi, Junko Shimizu. ANI: N/C. MUS: MOKA. PRD: Studio DEEN, Frontier Works, Kadokawa Pictures, Kadokawa Shoten, Memory Tech, Klockworx. 30 mins. x 12 eps.

Usami is an overgrown, over-indulged child, a successful novelist who fills his room with giant teddy bears and toys. He also writes steamy boys'-love novels as a sideline. His latest sex-filled story has a new protagonist: his best friend's kid brother Misaki. Tutoring Misaki for college entrance exams is doing his friend a favor and has enlivened Usami's fantasy life considerably. But how to bring his fantasies to life?

Based on Shungiku Nakamura's 2008 manga, this anime tells a story that was old when Abelard stalked his teenage pupil Heloise in 12th-century Paris. And while boys' love and male erotic anime used to be a very specialized niche, without much chance of sales outside Japan, this title has sold in China, Korea, Russia, and the Arab world as well as in English-speaking territories. Compare with ANTIQUE BAKERY.

JUNK BOY *
1987. AKA: *The Incredible Gyôkai [Industrial] Video.* Video. DIR: Katsuhisa Yamada. SCR: Tatsuhiko Urahata, Hiroyuki Fukushima. DES: Hiroshi Hamazaki. ANI: Hiroshi Hamasaki. MUS: Takashi Kudo. PRD: Madhouse. 44 mins.

A charmless "comedy" in which sex-crazed Ryohei Yamazaki gets a job at the seedy *Potato Boy* magazine, chiefly because his uncontrollable erection allows the staff to evaluate nude photographs before going to press. He is sent to assist at a fading starlet's photo shoot, where he talks her into baring all by confessing that he spent many happy hours masturbating over pictures of her younger self. Sinking to new depths, he volunteers to conduct an "investigative report" at a local brothel, to which his superiors agree somewhat illogically, since they already have an undercover reporter, the pretty Aki, working there as

one of the girls. Ryohei is rebuffed by Aki, and he takes it as a personal challenge that she has never had an orgasm. The way to any woman's heart, it would appear, is to throw on a tuxedo, take her on a bicycle ride through the red-light district, put her into a stolen ballgown, and then get her drunk on your office rooftop. Ryohei then leaves the sexually sated Aki behind so he can file a new story with the treacly moral message of "treating women right." He almost impresses his tough female editor with this change of heart, until she finds him snuffling through her underwear drawer and realizes that he's still a jerk. The authors wonder why she ever doubted it.

Based on a 1985 manga in *Manga Action* magazine by Yasuyuki Kunitomo, *JB* would like to think it is a media satire, and occasionally attempts to balance its priapic hero's infantile nature by letting a female character slap him. But since this is hardly a redeeming feature, it also boasts a brief fake commercial interlude made by NINJA SCROLL–director Yoshiaki Kawajiri, as well as a bizarre moment when Ryohei attempts to mate with a plastic effigy of fast-food mascot Colonel Sanders. ●◍

JUNKERS COME HERE *
1994. JPN: *Junkers Come Here: Memories of You.* Video. DIR: Junichi Sato. SCR: Naoto Kine, Ai Morinaga. DES: Kazuo Komatsubara, Shinya Ohira. ANI: Keiichi Sato, Mahiro Maeda. MUS: N/C. PRD: Gaga, Triangle Staff. 103 mins.

Sixth-grader Hiromi has a relatively carefree life; with her rich professional parents often out of the house, she is often left in the care of the housekeeper. She also has a friend in Keisuke, the college boy who rents a room at the house, and sometimes supplements his income by tutoring her in school subjects. Her best friend is her dog Junkers, a talking animal in the style of I AM A CAT, who has a comedic obsession with bad samurai dramas, and who attempts to offer Hiromi advice on life, although he is often as unsure about things as she is. Based on two books by former pop guitarist Naoto Kine (see CAROL), *JCH* is a gentle slice-of-life story employing similar misdirectional techniques to the works of Hayao Miyazaki, presenting magical distractions from the actual plot,

which is one of a marriage breakup and its potential effects on the heroine. Originally screened in segments as part of the TV Asahi show *Kuni Sanchi Witches*, the anime was given a theatrical showing the following year, although it was officially sold in Japan as a "movie."

JURA TRIPPER
1995. JPN: *Kyoryu Boken Ki Jura Tripper.* AKA: *Dinosaur Chronicle Jura Tripper.* TV series. DIR: Kunihiko Yuyama, Yoshitaka Fujimoto, Naohito Takahashi, Shigeru Omachi, Kunihisa Sugishima. SCR: Isao Shizuya, Yasushi Hirano, Sukehiro Tomita, Katsuyoshi Yutabe. DES: Kenichi Chikanaga, Mari Tomonaga. ANI: Seiji Kikuchi, Kenichi Chikanaga. MUS: Toshiyuki Omori. PRD: NAS, Ashi Pro, TV Tokyo. 25 mins. x 39 eps.

In a conflation of ADRIFT IN THE PACIFIC and *Jurassic Park* (1993), 15 boys and girls are thrown into an alternate world where dinosaurs and humans live alongside each other. Later episodes developed a distant similarity to EL HAZARD, with the adventurers spending more time flirting than fighting, as they pick their way across a desert on the run from a newly awakened golem monster.

JUST ANOTHER FAMILY
1976. JPN: *Hoka Hoka Kazoku.* TV series. SCR: Noboru Shiroyama, Satoshi Murayama. DES: Katsutoshi Kobayashi. ANI: Kazutaka Kadota, Isao Kaneko. MUS: Kunio Miyauchi. PRD: Eiken, Fuji TV. 5 mins. x 1428 eps.

The Yamano family, including wise granny Yone, know-it-all father Yutaka, caring mother Sachiko, and children Makoto and Midori, learn about life in modern Japan, in a live-action show that often switches to simple animation to illustrate key points or technical information. Conceived in the style of KOTOWAZA HOUSE or OUTSIDE THE LAW as a series of public information films sponsored by the office of the Japanese Prime Minister, the show utilized extensive input from former crewmembers of the long-running SAZAE-SAN series. The show ran until March 1982—compare to BOTTLE FAIRY, which tries something similar with a radically shorter running time.

JUSTICE
1991. JPN: *Jingi.* AKA: *Humanity and Justice.* Video. DIR: Kiyoshi Murayama. SCR: Hideo

Nanba. DES: Toshi Kawamura. ANI: Katsushi Matsumoto. MUS: N/C. PRD: JC Staff. 50 mins. x 2 eps.

A kindhearted gangster tries to live by rules of kindness and justice even though he is on the wrong side of the law. When he meets a former college left-winger who has also become a street punk, the two form an unlikely team, bringing their own peculiar code of ethics to the underworld. Based on the 1988 manga in *Young Champion* magazine, this is widely regarded as the masterwork of Ayumi Tachihara, who also created **FOR REAL**. Not to be confused with **HIGH SCHOOL HONOR**, which has a similar Japanese title. **NV**

JUSTY

1985. JPN: *Cosmo Police Justy*. Video. DIR: Osamu Uemura. SCR: Hiroyuki Hoshiyama. DES: Tsuguo Okazaki. ANI: Kazuya Iwata. MUS: Hiroya Watanabe. PRD: Studio Pierrot. 44 mins.

Justy Kaizard is a Cosmo Police Hunter—his job is to track down rogue psychics and exterminate them before they can harm others. He and his partner, Borba Len, track down the criminal psychic Magnamam Vega, and Justy kills him in front of his six-year-old daughter, Asteris. The distraught child swears that she would kill Justy herself if she were bigger, and her own psychic powers, triggered by the tragedy, transform her into a 16-year-old, though the shock leaves her with amnesia. Growing up at Cosmo Police headquarters under the care of Justy's friend Jilna Star, she treats him as an adored big brother.

But then the Crimina Esper, a group of malicious psychics, decide to dispose of Justy by awakening her memory and her hatred of the man who killed her father. Based on the 1981 manga by Tsuguo Okazaki serialized in *Shonen Sunday* magazine, *Justy* was one of the more popular of the 1980s videos in early overseas anime **FANDOM**, chiefly because of the short running time and easy-to-follow plot that did not really require subtitles. However, it was not brought to the U.S. as one might have expected, reputedly because the rights were prohibitively expensive.

JVC

Japan Victor Company (i.e., Nippon Victor locally) was founded in 1927 as a subsidiary of the American company Victor Records. The company was a pioneer in radio and television development, but cut off from its parent company during World War II. By 1953, ownership had been transferred to Matsushita. The company is also credited with the invention of the VHS cassette, a major catalyst in the rise of adult-oriented anime in the 1980s and beyond. Subsidiaries include Victor Entertainment (Japan), a major distributor of anime-related soundtracks and itself the owner of the Victor Entertainment Animation Network.

JYU-OH-SEI *

2006. JPN: *Ju-o-sei*. AKA: *Planet of the Beast King*. TV series. DIR: Hiroshi Nishikiori. SCR: Reiko Yoshida, Natsuko Takahashi, Michihiro Tsuchiya. DES: Hiroshi Osaka, Takeshi Sato. ANI: Hiroshi Osaka, Koichi Horikawa, Tetsuya Kawakami. MUS: Hajime Mizoguchi. PRD: BONES, Asmik-Ace Entertainment, Dentsu, Fuji TV, SKY Perfect Well Think, Sony Music Entertainment. 23 mins. x 11 eps.

The far future: with Earth dying, mankind migrates to the Balkan System, but the departure from Earth brings its own social and political tensions. Brothers Thor and Rai are dumped on prison planet Chimera after their parents are murdered. In a place where only the strongest survive and mankind reverts to its bestial roots, they must escape and bring their parents' killers to justice, although Rai soon meets an untimely demise. Thor decides that the only way is for him to become the Beast King, the ruler of Chimera. Based on a 1993 manga by **OZ**-creator Natsumi Itsuki, this is a fast-paced, exciting science fantasy whose flaws come from cramming a big, multi-threaded, character-packed plot into too few episodes. Many plot elements recall classics from the golden age of science fiction, so your reaction to the story is likely to depend on whether you consider *Day of the Triffids* and **SPACE FIREBIRD 2772** brilliant or boring. The animation quality is not at the level of BONES's superb movie **SWORD OF THE STRANGER** but it's not at all bad, the design is pleasing, and the central concept—becoming top dog in a vicious arena—is strong enough to hold the viewer's attention despite having so little time to flesh out its main concepts.

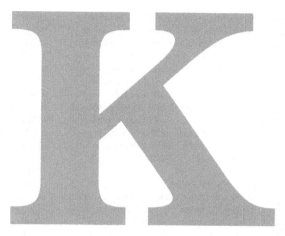

K THE ANIME *

2012. AKA: *K Project; K-anime*. TV series, movie. DIR: Hiromitsu Kanazawa, Susumu Kudo, Shingo Suzuki. SCR: Gora, Tatsuki Miyazawa, Hideyuki Furuhashi, Kohei Azano, Rei Rairaku, Suzu Suzuki, Tatsuki Miyazawa, Yashichiro Takahashi, Yukako Kabei. DES: Shingo Suzuki. ANI: Makoto Furuta, Hiroshi Okubo. MUS: Mikio Endo. PRD: GoHands, Sanzigen, MBS, TBS, AT-X, BS-TBS, CBC, Starchild Records, Klockworx. 25 mins. x 13 eps. (TV), ?? mins. (m).

An overpopulated cast in an island school seek to solve a murder mystery and duel with psychic powers, in an immensely confusing series that posits undercover color-coded "kings" in a battle for supremacy. Notable in the history of anime because its *oh-so-edgy* single-letter title has made it almost impossible to dig up with search engines to either buy or rent, hence the "K the Anime" or "K-anime" designation used for it in several language territories. A movie followed in 2014.

K-ON! *

2009. JPN: *Kei-On*. AKA: *Light* MUS. TV series, video, movie, TV special. DIR: Naoko Yamada. SCR: Reiko Yoshida, Jukki Hanada, Katsuhiko Muramoto, Masahiro Yokotani. DES: Yukiko Horiguchi, Seiki Tamura. ANI: Yukiko Horiguchi, Miku Kadowaki, Shoko Ikeda. MUS: Hajime Hyakkoku. PRD: Kyoto Animation, MOVIC, Pony Canyon, TBS. 24 mins. x 13 eps. (TV1), 24 mins. (v1), 2 mins. x 7 eps. (v2), 24 mins. x 26 eps. (TV2), 24 mins. (v2), 3 mins. x 9 eps. (special), 110 mins. (m), 23 mins. (v3).

New to high school, Yui is recruited into the school's light music club by Ritsu and Mio, who are desperate to save the club from closing down. With Tsumugi on keyboards they have a viable band, especially with guitar prodigy Yui. Only she isn't—in fact she can hardly even play the castanets. She's a natural, though, and in no time at all she's producing effortlessly cool guitar solos.

Four-panel gag manga strips are popular sources for anime, but many of the shows rely so strongly on local humor that they never make it out of Asia. One of the strengths and drawbacks of such strips is their reliance on running gags and recurring characters: easy to understand and digest, not so easy to turn into an unmissable weekly date with the TV screen. Director Yamada does a good job of packaging the invitation, offering a sweet slice of high school life with gentle humor, occasional wackiness, parodies (watch out for the homages to DETROIT METAL CITY), visual puns, and pretty animation.

Kyoto Animation is going a long way toward out-cuting all others, with shows like KANON and THE MELANCHOLY OF HARUHI SUZUMIYA on its rap sheet. And someone at Kyoto Animation loves their instruments. This may not be a hard-hitting, edgy rock chronicle like BECK, but the gear is all hugely credible. How schoolgirls have the money and connections to get such fabulous instruments is another matter; this is EVERYDAY ANIME as wish fulfillment for the intended 20-something male audience, many of whom can be expected to know AKG k701 cans and a Korg RK-100 when they see them. Cute girls and hot gear: a

boys' dream series. Don't be fooled into quoting this or similar shows as evidence of the feisty independent young women of anime. These girls, and *Haruhi* and all their *moe* classmates (ARGOT AND JARGON) are as objectified as any porn victim. They were constructed for the male gaze, but because they were constructed very cleverly, they can attract and deceive their own kind: decoy ducks for the patriarchy, and with such fine feathers.

The construction of the broadcast schedule was fluid, responding to the show's huge success: 13 episodes aired on TV on 2009 with a 14th, *K-ON! Live House* (described as a video), exclusive to Animax Asia for the 2010 rebroadcast made up series one. Then there were seven extra shorts, *K-ON!! Ura-On*, released on DVD in 2009–10, with the Animax Asia extra episode also tagging along. The second TV series *K-ON!! Season 2* (note the doubled exclamation points, sure to send encyclopedists into conniptions) aired in 2010, taking the four girls into their final year of high school. It also had an original video episode tagged onto the DVD, plus 9 more *K-ON!! Ura-on!!* "DVD Extras."

The 2010 *K-ON!* movie takes the girls to London for their graduation trip, wrapping up the story before they head to university. It functions as an intriguing, often inadvertent study of the Japanese abroad, from the impossibly tight schedule for a once-in-a-lifetime trip, to the oddly parochial mindset that packs a suitcase of Japanese food "for emergencies." London itself comes to life as a character in its own right, with beautifully observed moments of tourist encounters and a denouement like something out of CINDERELLA, as the girls play their final concert on the South Bank, with the clockface of Big Ben looming before them, counting down not only the time until their flight, but until the likely end of their youth and community.

The video K-ON!! Keikaku—the story of how the girls went to the passport office to get their passports for the London trip—was released in Japan on the ninth volume of DVD and Blu-ray in 2011.

KAASAN: MOM'S LIFE *

2009. JPN: Mainichi Kaasan. AKA: Everyday Mother. TV series. DIR: Mitsuru Hongo. SCR: Natsuko Takahashi. DES: Kenta Mizutani, Nobuaki Minegishi. ANI: Takaaki Wada. MUS: Masaki Kurihara. PRD: Gallop, NAS, AT-X, TV Tokyo. 25 mins. x 142 eps.

Mom is a manga artist with deadlines to meet, but that doesn't save her from having to look after two infuriatingly dopey children, a house, and a demanding husband who drinks too much. A bittersweet EVERYDAY ANIME comedy about family life from the point of view of a Japanese housewife and mother, this long-running show is based on Rieko Saibara's manga about her own life as a mother of two. The manga isn't for children, despite the childlike naïveté of its art style, although the anime softens the harsh realities a little. Saibara began her manga in 2002, and hit the headlines in a disagreement with her children's school, which features extensively and not always flatteringly in the story, in 2004. This was the first of her manga to be animated, though Bokunchi was made into a live-action movie in 2003. Mainichi Kaasan got its own live-action movie in 2011.

KABUTO *

1990. JPN: Karasu Tengu Kabuto. AKA: Raven Tengu Kabuto. TV series, TV special, video. DIR: Takashi Watabe, Kazuya Miyazaki, Akira Kiyomizu, Mamoru Yamamoto, Taku Sugiyama. SCR: Hiroyuki Hoshiyama, Satoru Akahori. DES: Satoshi Urushihara, Buichi Terasawa. ANI: Kinji Yoshimoto, Hideaki Matsuoka. MUS: Seiko Nagaoka. PRD: Hiro Communications. 25 mins. x 39 eps. (TV), 45 mins. (v).

Dohki, the ruler of hell, is summoned to our world by the "evil mood of the age" and sets out to rule the universe with the help of his cronies. Raven Tengu Kabuto, a warrior-mage with the power of flight, magical runes, and a deadly blade, assembles a party of stock characters (a giant warrior, a loyal samurai, a cunning rogue, and the usual token blonde) in order to fight back. He rounds up the old members of his clan, who have been scattered to the four corners of Japan by an undisclosed disaster. Dohki in turn has assembled a group of baddies that represent the "dark halves" of Kabuto's little band, and the battle begins, with plenty of strange techno-fantastic machinery, most notably a flying metal dragon in the shape of a giant swastika.

After GOKU: MIDNIGHT EYE–creator Buichi Terasawa rejected the science-fiction medium for a while, he chose to work on the ALICE IN WONDERLAND-inspired Black Knight Bat manga and this decidedly unhistorical fantasy, which began as a 1985 manga in Fresh Jump magazine. Kabuto seems permanently unsure of whether it wants to be steampunk science fiction or fantastic adventure, with a madly anachronistic clutter of design goofs that polite critics would call eclectic. Kabuto's sword is a double-edged blade, yet he wields it like a single-edged katana, for example (as do the "Greek" warriors of ARION), while any sense of period is compromised by the hard-rock guitar music throughout. Kabuto is a tengu warrior, although whether this is a reference to the supernatural crow-demons of JAPANESE FOLK TALES or merely a particular martial arts school is unclear. Kabuto himself claims the latter, but at several points in the story also sprouts wings to fly out of dangerous situations. Suzaku, Kabuto's love interest, wears fishnet tights for no discernible reason, someone uses a semiautomatic musket, and characters can speak and breathe underwater without any effort or explanation. Nevertheless, elements creep in from actual Japanese folklore, including the notorious Fuma clan, also seen in LUPIN III and KOJIRO, as well as Kabuto's giant halberd-wielding companion Genbu, a respray of the Little John of Japanese legend, the super-monk Benkei.

The TV series was later edited down into two feature-length videos, Kabuto: The Warrior (compiling episodes 1–13) and Kabuto: The Visitation (compiling episodes 27–39). The hero returned in the one-shot original video Kabuto: The Golden-Eyed Beast (1992), the only incarnation of the series to be released commercially in English. For this story, the beautiful princess Ran is kidnapped by the evil vampiress Tamamushi. Kabuto must then rescue the princess, fighting off typically anachronistic threats such as muskets and medieval helicopters, as well as face-hugging spiders—an arachnid take on the Heike crabs, real-life creatures from Japan's Inland Sea whose shells bear shockingly accurate pictures of samurai warriors' faces. Eventually, Tamamushi turns out to be a machine herself, which begs the question: If she really is an android, why does she need to sacrifice the souls of young women to keep herself young?

As before, the plot is heavily laden with inconsistencies—dialogue in both language versions switches from ancient idiom ("verily thou art a knave") to modern vernacular ("outta my way, bitch") and back again, while background scenery switches from that of northern Japan to that of southern China. Compare to Terasawa's other big success, SPACE ADVENTURE COBRA.

KAGIROHI: SHAKU KEI

2009. Video. DIR: Hiromi Yokoyama. SCR: Tomy. DES: Hideki Arai. ANI: Hadaka Nishikiha. MUS: N/C. PRD: PoRO, Eiwanshi. 30 mins. x 2 eps.

In a remote village in Japan, the ancient practice of sacrificing virgins to the tentacled god Izanami endures into modern times. Schoolboy Aoi, his friends, cute schoolgirl angel Kusano and diffident new-girl-in-town Ajisai, are caught up in these ancient rituals. Based on a porn game by Shelf, proof of the enduring power of the tentacle (EROTICA AND PORNOGRAPHY). ❿Ⓥ

KAI DOH MARU *

2001. JPN: Kaidoumaru. Video. DIR: Kanji Wakabayashi. SCR: Nobuhisa Terado. DES: Sho-u Tajima. ANI: Kyoji Asano. MUS: Yoshihiro Ike, Yutaka Fukuoka. PRD: Production I.G, SME Visual Works. 46 mins.

After her uncle causes the death of her parents, Kintoki is raised as a boy, fighting off the advances of her brother's disturbed ex-girlfriend and struggling with her own feelings for Raiko, the handsome knight who is her guardian. Old enmities come back to life in the middle of a smallpox epidemic, as Raiko's group, the Four Knights, hunts down its enemies in an evocative and original anime from Production I.G, seemingly conceived as a means of testing new toon shading and oversaturation technologies.

Kai Doh Maru's greatest achievement is the washed-out watercolor style that makes the whole thing seem like gazing at a fragile ancient painting. Color designer Nagisa Abe gets top billing alongside the distinctive character designs of **Otogi Zoshi**'s Sho-u Tajima, and he deserves it. Make no mistake, someone spent a *lot* of money integrating the traditional and CG artwork in this, and some scenes, like the prolonged tracking shot across Heian palaces, are plain and simple showing off.

The pallid color scheme is not merely a deliberate contrast to the same team's earlier **Blood: The Last Vampire**, but also a bold subversion of much of what anime stands for, sacrificing the kid-friendly strengths of primary colors for a watercolor look reminiscent of Studio Ghibli's **My Neighbors the Yamadas**. But part of the glamor of the Heian period is precisely that we tend to view it through a historic haze. While violent moments may recall the samurai savagery of Yoshiaki Kawajiri's **Ninja Scroll**, *Kai Doh Maru* recreates a fantasy ideal of the Japanese past and does it so well that it belongs on the shelf with the classical anime **The Sensualist** and **The Tale of Genji**.

Its story is less coherent—a rushed jumble of fights and shots, great on a showreel but almost incomprehensible as a movie. Our lead is a girl who takes on a man's mission, like the cross-dressing heroines of **Yotoden** and **Dororo**. Our creepy bad guy behind the scenes is a *girl* called **Shutendoji**. The bad guys want to bring back the same Masakado demigod who haunts **Doomed Megalopolis**. A "healer character" with a couple of cameos is addressed as "Mr. Seimei"—in yet another sly reference to the manga and movie phenomenon *Onmyoji* (see *DE, as *The Yin-Yang Master*). But *Kai Doh Maru* is more than the sum of its parts, a careful re-creation of the famously languid pace of Japan's medieval capital, put into production at the turn of

the 21st century, when Japanese popular culture developed a minor fetish for the turn of the 11th.

The Japanese titles clearly state that the year is A.D. 995, although some characters and events seem to originate from a century earlier (i.e., 889), causing some confusion for the translators. Then again, Seimei died ten years *after* the events shown here—*Kai Doh Maru* might imply a sense of historical accuracy, but it's still prepared to play fast and loose with the actual facts. That, however, is part of director Wakabayashi's plan. It should not be lost on the viewer, for example, that the magical, fantastical Kyoto depicted here experiences four complete seasons in just 35 minutes. The box blurb in some territories disingenuously counts the DVD extras as part of the main feature, in an attempt to claim a running time of "80 mins. approx." In fact, the main feature only lasts for 46 minutes, and 7 of those comprise the plodding ending credits. **Ⓥ**

KAIBA *

2008. TV series. DIR: Masaaki Yuasa. SCR: Akitoshi Yokoyama, Eun-Yong Choi, Michio Mihara, Tomoya Takahashi, Masaaki Yuasa. DES: Nobutake Ito. ANI: Nobutake Ito, Akira Honma, Jamie Vickers, Eun-Yong Choi. MUS: Kiyoshi Yoshida. PRD: Madhouse, Sony, VAP, WOWOW. 25 mins. x 12 eps.

A man wakes in a ruined room. He has no memory, just a hole through the center of his chest, a strange tattoo around his navel, and a pendant with a picture of a woman he doesn't recognize. Then he meets a man named Popo who tells him that the social order has fallen apart, with the rich and powerful living above the electrical stormclouds that surround the Earth, and the poor trapped below. The cause: a technological leap that made it possible to trade bodies and memories and extend life almost indefinitely. Popo belongs to an organization fighting to rid the world of this evil technology, but is he really just out for his own ends?

Yuasa is one of the most consistently interesting director/writers of his generation, and he's at his best when he ignores the conventional and flies in the face of marketing advice. He created this "sci-fi love story" and it's filled with invention, both in terms of the wonderful visuals

and the idea-packed plot. With characters and costumes that nod to an earlier era, overtones of Osamu Tezuka and Shotaro Ishinomori also inhabit the morality tale at the heart of this story of memory, sorrow, and loss. Anime is at its absolute best as a medium for unique visions such as this.

KAIJI *

2007. JPN: *Gyakkyo Burai Kaiji: Ultimate Survivor*. AKA: *Gambling Apocalypse Kaiji; Tobaku Mokushiroku Kaiji*. TV series. DIR: Yuzo Sato. SCR: Hideo Takayashiki, Mitsutaka Hirota, Kazuyuki Fudeyasu, Tadao Iwaki, Tomomi Yoshino. DES: Haruhito Takada, Norihiko Yokomatsu, Hideyuki Ueno. ANI: Dong Joon Kim, Jang Hee Kyu, Kunihiko Hamada, Haruhito Takada, Takahiro Umehara. MUS: Hideki Taniuchi. PRD: Madhouse Studios, D. N. Dream Partners, NTV, VAP. 23 mins. x 26 eps. (TV1), 23 mins. x 26 eps. (TV2).

Kaiji Ito is a small-time gambler, but karma bites him when he signs a loan for a workmate who then disappears. The interest on the loan is astronomical and the only way to clear it is to gamble some more—but this time Kaiji is gambling with his life. Anime inspired by pachinko games are less numerous than those based on video games, but they throw a light on a whole other area of Japanese society, where men and women sit for hours, silent and focused, pulling the handles of the rows upon rows of pachinko machines in the din of brightly lit downtown halls. That was the target audience for *Kaiji*, based on a 1996 manga by Nobuyuki Fukumoto, who also devised the fiendishly simple games of choice embedded in the series. The simple, highly stylized animation and the hardboiled noir-ish story make this a show for those whose fathers brought them up on **Golgo 13**, set in a world where an ordinary guy has few choices except ducking and diving and no faith except in his own skills and schemes.

Fukumoto and director Sato kept faith with their audience, and it paid off with a second TV series. *Kaiji: Transgression Transcript* (*Gyakku Burai Kaiji Hakairoku-hen*), made in 2011 by a largely unchanged team, took our bad boy into a yet worse situation, thrown into an underground forced labor camp for debt. An episode of this series showing Kaiji drawn into a torrent of floodwater was changed after the Great East Japan Earthquake and tsunami, out of consideration for audiences who had been devastated by similar events. There have also been two *Kaiji* live-action movies, in 2009 and 2011, with the gambling man played by Tatsuya Fujiwara, better known as Light Yagami in the live-action **DEATH NOTE**.

KAIKAN PHRASE

1999. AKA: *Sensual Phrase.* TV series. DIR: Hiroko Tokita. SCR: Katsuhiko Koide, Reiko Yoshida, Satoru Tsuchiya. DES: Yumi Nakayama. ANI: Hiroaki Shimizu, Kazuhiro Sada. MUS: Takeshi Tsuji, Lucifer. PRD: Studio Unsa, TV Tokyo. 25 mins. x 44 eps.
Realizing that their pop group, Climb, is going nowhere, guitarist Yuki and drummer Santa decide to split and form a new combo. Calling themselves Lucifer, they discover their new vocalist in the form of pretty-boy Sakuya, who takes the job over playing the piano in a hotel bar. Sakuya, however, harbors some dark secrets of his own. This series was based on a manga by Mayu Shinjo serialized in *Shojo Comic* and rushed onto TV to cash in on the success of the earlier boy-band extravaganza **WEISS KREUZ**. Toning down the sensual original for an early-evening audience, the show nevertheless concentrates on the broody, moody male stars, emphasizing music and drama over the animation itself, which is of a rather cheap digital nature (**MUSIC IN ANIME**).

KAITO REINYA

2010. AKA: *Phantom Thief Reinya.* TV series. DIR: "Something" Yoshimatsu (aka Takahiro Yoshimatsu), Hideaki Iwami. SCR: Kenichi Kanemaki. DES: Mr A. ANI: Hideaki Iwami. MUS: N/C. PRD: Stingray, Kyushu Asahi TV. 3 mins. x 12 eps.
Reinya is just another girl working in a convenience store—except that she's half-cat and half-human, and after hours she transforms into a master bullion thief. She and her assistant Chutaro have a hideout under the store where they hatch their daring plans. Their nemesis lives at the police station right next door: a pervert police inspector, a bubble-headed policewoman, and a detective who's hopelessly in love with Reinya. Reinya greatly resembles her voice actress and inspiration, redheaded Reina Tanaka of

TV supergroup Morning Musume, but the plot of this short anime has an even closer resemblance to that of **CAT'S EYE**. The art style, too, is reassuringly retro, with clear, clean lines, disarmingly rounded forms, and a perky color palette.

KAJISHIMA, MASAKI

1952–. Born in Okayama, Kajishima became a freelance animator whose name is most often found on the production credits of works by the AIC studio, including **GALL FORCE** and **TENCHI MUYO!** It was in the latter series that he achieved his most iconic success, with a narrative that he deliberately pitched to an implied audience of frustrated, lonely, virginal boys between the ages of 13 and 18, establishing many of the tropes of "harem anime" (**ROMANCE AND DRAMA**).

KAKINUMA, HIDEKI

1958–. Born in Tokyo, Kakinuma's early work saw him as a mechanical designer on **MOSPEADA** and **MEGAZONE 23**. He subsequently created, storyboarded, and scripted the **GALL FORCE** series.

KAKKUN CAFÉ

1984. Movie. DIR: Osamu Kobayashi. SCR: N/C. DES: Tsutomu Shibayama. ANI: Tsutomu Shibayama, Hideo Kawauchi, Mitsuru Hongo, Michishiro Yamada, Tomomi Mochizuki. MUS: Takashi Fukui. PRD: Tokio MC, Ajia-do, Tokyo Communications. 86 mins.
Kakuei "Kakkun" Tanaka is a superhero who hangs out with his friends Yasuhiro Nakasone (who agrees with everything anyone says), Tokushima yokel Takeo Miki, stingy Takeo Fukuda, and Masayoshi Ohira, who says nothing except "ooh" and "ah." Kakkun's misadventures begin with playing rugby at school, though after graduation he accidentally becomes prime minister of Japan. He visits New York, where he literally causes a stink by grilling dried mackerel, before preventing a nuclear war between hapless superpowers America and Russia. A political satire featuring anime caricatures of several Japanese politicians.

KAKURENBO: HIDE AND SEEK *

2005. JPN: *Kakurenbo.* AKA: *Hide and Seek.* Movie. DIR: Shuhei Morita. SCR: Shuhei Morita, Shiro Kuro. DES: Daisuke Sajiki.

ANI: Shuhei Morita, Shiro Kuro. MUS: Karin Nakano, Reiji Kitasato. PRD: Yamatoworks, D.A.C. 25 mins.
Hikora's sister Sorincha is missing. At night in the Demon City the lamps flare of their own accord and dangerous beings stalk the shadows. Masked children play "otokoyo," or hide-and-seek, and every child who has ever played has vanished forever. Hikora and his best friend Yaimao don fox masks and join the gang waiting outside the city gate to reach the seven players required before the gate opens and the game begins. The seekers are monsters, half-machine and half-animal, and the clever ending reveals why the game is played. The short run-time doesn't allow much time for characterization, and this is echoed in the animation, with the characters showing no emotion in their faces or movements; the voice actors have to work extra hard.

Director Morita also makes clever use of dim backgrounds, atmospheric lighting and fade-outs to save on actual animation without losing too much impact. He is well supported by the music, which uses unusual sounds to enhance the eerie atmosphere, and employs that rarest of soundtrack elements, silence, very skillfully. Creator-writer-director-producer Morita also did storyboards, CGI animation, and editing, although he shares several credits with the obviously pseudonymous Kuro (*Shiro/Kuro* = White/Black). Morita wanted to make a movie merging the old traditions of ghosts and ghouls stalking the darkness with the cities of modern Asia, where children play outside in dark, maze-like streets under flickering neon lights without a second thought, and reinstill that ancient fear of the dark. He succeeds very well, but his influences are just as much from older anime as from tradition. Hikora dresses like **DRAGON BALL**'s Son Goku with the addition of a priest's beads, Sorincha is a funky shrine maiden, and the atmosphere of fashionable ennui shares much with **BOOGIEPOP PHANTOM**. An intriguing and rewarding exploration of the dark side of **JAPANESE FAIRY TALES**, taking the eery elements of **SPIRITED AWAY** much further toward the horrific. The result is a short but often chilling showcase for modern computer graphics, seemingly informed by Japanese folklorist Kunio

Yanagita's claim (quoted at its beginning) that one should never play hide-and-seek at night, lest it awaken demons in the shadows. Morita also spun off a manga from the movie in the quarterly *Magazine Zero*. ⓥ

KALEIDO STAR *

2003. AKA: *Kaleidostar*. TV series. DIR: Junichi Sato, Yoshimasa Hiraike, Tadashi Hiramatsu. SCR: Reiko Yoshida, Miharu Hirami, Rika Nakase, Tsukasa Nakase. DES: Hajime Watanabe, Fumitoshi Oizaki. ANI: Hajime Watanabe, Fumitoshi Oizaki. MUS: Mina Kubota. PRD: Gonzo, TV Tokyo, Medianet, Hori Pro. 25 mins. x 26 eps. (TV1), 25 mins. x 25 eps. (TV2), 30 mins. x 2 eps. (v).
Kaleido Stage is a combination of circus, theater, and magic show, based in its own waterside complex in California—a fantastical version of the Cirque de Soleil. Fans the world over dream of standing in its spotlight thanks to world TV syndication and tours. Sixteen-year-old Sora Naegino has had her sights set on becoming Queen of the Kaleido Stage since childhood. She travels from Japan to America to take the entrance exam for the KS training school, and succeeds in getting into the show despite arriving late, missing the audition, and irritating the current leading lady, blonde Layla Hamilton. In the dressing room and later in her room at the school dorm, she finds a talking clown doll named Fool. Fool is really the "stage fairy," whom only a chosen few can see, and he tells Sora she has been chosen by the spirit of the stage to become a Kaleido Star. She has some talent and athletic ability, but her performance and dancing skills are woefully underdeveloped and she lacks confidence—all traits designed to encourage identification from wallflower viewers and put to their best effect in director/creator Junichi Sato's earlier SAILOR MOON.

The stage is set for a series of performances of the week, taking the cast through rehearsals, backstage intrigues, and productions of works that include their own versions of *Romeo and Juliet*, LITTLE MERMAID, and A THOUSAND AND ONE NIGHTS. Sora acquires several friends, including fellow performers Anna and Mia, who become her occasional allies in the battle of wits with Layla, as well as a performing seal called Jonathan. Typical

to all such anime rites of passage, she also gains an affable, avuncular patron (Kalos, the owner of Kaleido Stage), a love-struck boy nextdoor (lowly stage manager Ken), and potentially dangerous prospective suitor (Layla's associate Yuri).

In a welcome change in the fast-paced 21st century, *KS* often takes its time with its plots and remains unafraid to shake things up. Later episodes find Sora packed off to Theatrical Camp and Marine Park, affiliated entertainment centers where she must hone new skills and deal with new problems. She must also wrestle with family issues and the growing realization that while she and Layla may be at each other's throats, they are also superb performers who are likely to end up having to share the stage. Layla believes in cold professionalism and is prepared to discard anything and anyone in the service of her talent, while Sora wants the stage to be a warm, friendly world where there's no conflict between players, and the audience is drawn in to a circle of happiness. After much conflict, the ingenue and the star become friends, and pull off a trick considered impossible, the Legendary Maneuver, in a show to save the Kaleido Stage—a theatrical apocalypse averted by a synchronized performance, something pastiched long before in EVANGELION.

The adherence to performance clichés even extends to the anime's surprise twist (look away now), in which Layla is injured and forced to retire, but not before entrusting Sora with the stewardship of the Kaleido Stage. In the second season, *KS Kanon 2*, released in the U.S. as *KS: New Wings*, the conflict between the warm camaraderie of a dream team and the tooth-and-claw struggle for stardom continues, as a new leading man arrives, and a new ingenue, talented and uberconfident May Wong, decides to take the crown Sora hasn't even claimed yet.

Even without real-world parallels like Japan's own Takarazuka troupe, whose young actresses must pass a strict entrance exam and live in a company dormitory, there are plenty of anime and manga inspired by the performing arts, most notably MASK OF GLASS, to which the plot of *KS* is often actionably similar. Creator Sato layers elements of many live-action and animated dreams of stardom, as well

as throwing in the TROPES AND TRANSFORMATIONS, spirit guide, and cute animal sidekick so beloved of magical-girl shows, but he also asks: does the performer serve the audience, or vice versa? In these times of celebrity without talent and fame without effort, it's a valid question.

Kaleido Star is silly and lightweight on the surface, but with powerful truths about the vanity, insubstantiality, and basic nastiness of many performers; the physical tyranny of performance; and the temporary nature of fame, at its heart. Most of its "stars" are shallow and self-centered. Yet Sato is as spellbound by the roar of the crowd and the smell of the greasepaint as any old vaudeville hack, and he gives his fantasy a full-on, top-quality staging. In a sign of the times, he was actually unable to produce the show to his own specifications in Japan—it took the injection of foreign funding from ADV Films and a Korean backer to ensure that the performance scenes had the necessary pizzazz. The stage sets and effects are gorgeous, and color planner Kunio Tsujita does a stunning job; the depiction of the sunset and the lighting of the end of the first episode, a true work of art, sets the tone. In Sato's hands, foreign lands and rites of passage are exciting but safe—so much so that the natives, from the police to chance-met passers-by, are uniformly friendly, everyone speaks your language and wills you on to succeed.

Two later videos, *KS: New Wings Extra Stage* (2004) and *KS: It's Good! Goood!! / Layla Hamilton Story* (2005), introduce Rosetta, a new performer with the same endearing clumsiness and innocence that once defined Sora.

KAMA SUTRA *

1991. JPN: *Kama Sutra Kyukyoku no Sex Adventure*. AKA: *Kama Sutra: The Ultimate Sex Adventure*. Video. DIR: Masayuki Ozeki. SCR: Seiji Matsuoka. DES: Shinsuke Terasawa. ANI: Shinsuke Terasawa. MUS: Ken Yashima. PRD: Animate Film. 44 mins.
In 6th-century India, the brave knight Gopal is slain by the Naga cult. His bride Surya is saved from a fate worse than death by the Hindu gods, who transport her to a cavern of ice in the Himalayas. She is found in the 20th century by a team of archeologists, who thaw her out in a

Calcutta hospital by feeding her a mixture of male and female bodily fluids from an ancient relic called the Spermatic Cup. Surya immediately falls for the professor's handsome Japanese grandson, Ryu, who is a reincarnation of her beloved Gopal. However, she is kidnapped by the Naga cult's present-day leader, Rudracin, who whisks her away to the underground paradise of Shambhala. Realizing that Rudracin intends to take Surya as his bride, drink from the Spermatic Cup, and return to the surface world as an immortal, Ryu pursues them. After pleasuring 48 nymphs in midair, he is allowed to enter Shambhala's temple, where he defeats Rudracin in a trial by combat. Ryu has sex with Surya but must leave her behind in Shambhala—the small print in the immortality contract. Back on the surface, he is reunited with his adoring Japanese girlfriend, Yukari.

A very different take on Hindu myth from the pious RAMAYANA, KS mixes the lovers-across-time theme of ADVENTURE KID with the playful smuttiness that has come to characterize Go Nagai's erotica. Based on an idea by Nagai and Kunio Nagatani, KS is the DEVILMAN-creator's answer to the *Indiana Jones* films, complete with an adventurous archeologist who is scared of snakes, rooms with crushing walls (which the lovers must halt by taking off their clothes and jamming them in the cracks), chases through Third World marketplaces, and a holy grail whose powers are not all they seem. As if that wasn't enough of a hint, our hero also has an irritating sidekick, seemingly modeled on Nagai himself, who asks to be called Indy. Surprisingly little is made of the central lovers Ryu and Surya, who only get to do the deed once as the closing credits roll, or indeed of Ryu and Yukari, who hardly even meet during the story. Instead, Ryu is educated in the techniques of the *Kama Sutra* by his father's red-haired Indian assistant Shakti, who escorts him through an elaborate maze of enclosed rooms from which the occupants can only escape by assuming the correct sexual position. Mostly harmless, with some nice sitar music, but not a patch on the oriental eroticism of Tezuka's A THOUSAND AND ONE NIGHTS. ⓁⓃⓋ

KAMEARI PARK PRECINCT
1985. JPN: *Kochira Katsushika-ku Kameari Koen-mae Hashutsujo*. AKA: *This Is the Police Station in Front of Kameari Park in Katsushika Ward; "Kochikame"*. Video, TV series, movie. DIR: Hiroshi Sasakawa (v), Shinji Takamatsu, Shinichi Tabe, Shinichiro Watanabe (TV). SCR: Takao Koyama (v), Takashi Yamada, Satoru Nishizono, Nobuaki Kishima (TV). DES: Ammonite (v), Tsukasa Fusanai (TV). ANI: Tsukasa Fusanai, Akitaro Daichi, Shunji Yoshida. MUS: N/C. PRD: Tatsunoko (v), Studio Gallop, Fuji TV. 30 mins. x 2 eps. (v), 15 mins. x 373 eps. (TV), 90 mins. (m).
The gently humorous antics of a group of police officers responsible for a sleepy area near a large park. High jinks redolent of YOU'RE UNDER ARREST!, based on a 1976 manga from *Shonen Jump* magazine by Osamu Akimoto. Mild-mannered cop Kankichi Ryotsu is forever having to apologize for his behavior—as a shop assistant's son, he's a friendly neighborhood cop but eternally at odds with his avuncular boss Chief Ohara. The salt-of-the-earth Kankichi is forced to share his duties with supercompetent officer Reiko Akimoto and rich dandy Keiichi Nakagawa (a set-up not unlike that of Goto, Shinobu, and Azuma in the later PATLABOR). The 2000 movie broadened the plot to encompass a bombing campaign by a disguised explosive expert named Benten (refer to CYBER CITY OEDO 808), with the Japanese police forced to cooperate with prissy FBI agent Lisa Hoshino. At over 100 volumes, Akimoto's manga is one of the longest-running in Japan. The anime's similar success, like that of SAZAE-SAN, is a mark of its popularity beyond the standard anime audience—the video versions were made to mark the 10th anniversary of the manga, and the first of the TV broadcasts marked the 20th.

KAMEGAKI, HAJIME
1957–. Popular designer of robots on the GODMARS series who established Studio Z-5 with his sometime collaborator Hideyuki Motohashi. After several animation jobs, he became chief director on RESCUE KIDS and moved on to greater things with NARUTO.

KAMICHU! *
2005. JPN: *Kamisama de Chugakusei*. AKA: *Junior High School God*. TV series, video. DIR: Koji Masunari. SCR: Hideyuki Kurata. DES: Takahiro Chiba. ANI: Koji Yabuno, Takahiro Chiba, Hideaki Shimada, Katsuya Asano. MUS: Yoshihiro Ike. PRD: Aniplex, Brains Base. 25 mins. x 12 eps. (TV), 25 mins. x 4 eps. (v).
In a sleepy, hilly town on the edge of Japan's Inland Sea, shy, good-hearted eighth-grader Yurie Hitotsubashi suddenly becomes a *kami*—but she has no knowledge of what kind and what powers she now possesses. She's acknowledged as a god by both other Japanese gods and normal humans, especially her classmate Matsuri Saegusa, who hopes to resurrect the fortunes of her family's bankrupt shrine. But any thoughts she may have of living the life of a superhero are regularly thwarted—her powers desert her at critical moments, forcing her to grow up fast and embrace new levels of self-reliance.

In many ways, all magical-girl shows are about the same thing; based on a manga in *Dengeki Gao* by the pseudonymous Besame Mucho (a trio combining the director, screenwriter, and producer Tomonori Ochikoshi, who would later reunite on WELCOME TO THE SPACE SHOW), *Kamichu* is played for laughs and yet contains within it some thoughtful musings on why magical girls ever gain the ability to transform at all. It's all about growing up—compare to MARVELOUS MELMO and a similar tale of teen godhood, HARELUYA II BOY. The show exhibits tremendous creativity and Japanesquerie in illustrating *kami* and depicting a Japan in which the mundane and spiritual cohabitate, in a similar fashion to POM POKO. The wide variety of supernatural creatures also recalls those depicted in SPIRITED AWAY and SPOOKY KITARO. Four extra episodes were released on video, and constitute the renumbered #8, #11, #13, and #16.

KAMIKAZE THIEF JEANNE
1999. JPN: *Kamikaze Kaito Jeanne*. AKA: *Jeanne de la Cambriole*. TV series. DIR: Atsutoshi Umezawa. SCR: Sukehiro Tomita. DES: Hisashi Kagawa. ANI: Katsumi Tamegai. MUS: Michiaki Kato. PRD: Toei, TV Asahi. 25 mins. x 44 eps.
Alienated child-of-divorce Marron Kusakabe puts on her brave face and tries not to think about being left alone in Tokyo while her parents work abroad. She is visited by the angel Fin Fish, who reveals that she is the reincarnation of Saint Joan

of Arc (known in the French fashion as Jeanne D'Arc in Japan). As the Day of Judgment approaches, it's Marron's job to retrieve important magical items to use in the battle against Satan. In her way stand transfer student Chiaki (who is really the rival angel Sindbad) and his dark angel assistant, Access Time. Meanwhile, since Marron's mission is to steal artifacts, she must keep her secret from her best friend, whose father is the chief of police. Owing more to **Cat's Eye** and **Saint Tail** than the legendary liberator of Orleans also depicted in **Tragedy of Belladonna**, this adaptation of Arina Tanemura's manga for *Ribon* magazine is set in a strange conflation of France and Japan, with European buildings but Oriental lifestyles.

KAMISAMA DOLLS *
2011. TV series. DIR: Seiji Kishi. SCR: Makoto Ueno. DES: Kazuaki Morita, Ayumi Miyakoshi. ANI: Hideyuki Motohashi. MUS: Chiaki Ishikawa, Masara Nishida. PRD: Brains Base, AT-X, Flying Dog, Media Factory, Shogakukan, Sony Music Communications, TV Tokyo. 25 mins. x 13 eps.
In Kyohei Kuga's home village, ancient wooden figures can perform amazing feats when controlled by a *seki*. Kyohei was once a *seki*, but fled to Tokyo to try and build a new life as a university student. But other *seki* are on his trail, determined to bring him back to his ancestral home, where the wooden gods wait to play out the old hatred between his family and the Hyuga.

Based on Hajime Yamamura's 2007 manga, the series is too short to give a satisfying account of its complex backstory; despite a hint that another series would follow, it wasn't commissioned. This may be because too much was revealed too fast in the TV series, leaving the audience with little incentive to invest emotion in the characters, or simply because only Kyohei and his rival Aki were properly fleshed out. You can get away with ciphers in *pornography* but it's much more difficult to win over a TV audience, and sadly the interesting basic idea wasn't enough to keep them coming back for more, despite the success of the manga. **V**

KAMPFER *
2009. TV series. DIR: Yasuhiro Kuroda. SCR: Kazuyuki Fudeyasu, Hiroko Fukuda, Takashi

Aoshima. DES: Mariko Fujita, Yoshinori Hirose. ANI: Mariko Fujita, Kenji Ota, Eri Baba, Akatsuki Koshiishi. MUS: Tatsuya Kato. PRD: Nomad, Bowel Familiars, Dax Production, Lantis, McRAY, Media Factory, Starchild Records, TBS. 24 mins. x 12 eps. (TV), 25 mins. x 2 eps. (special).
Natsuru Seno is just an ordinary high school boy. He likes girls, but not enough to want to turn into one. But he doesn't have any choice. A tiger plushie tells him he's been chosen as a Kampfer, a member of a fighting elite whose sole purpose is to battle other Kampfers with guns, swords, or magic. Nobody can refuse when chosen, and a Kampfer can only use its powers when in the body of a girl. Luckily, the clothes also switch gender when a Kampfer changes, since this can happen without warning. Based on the book series by Toshihiko Tsujiki, with illustrations by Senmu, this show's high concept—the hero forming part of *his own* harem—can't entirely conceal its borrowing from **Ranma ½** and **Utena**. It's distinctly average all round—the art is acceptable, the animation OK, the violence isn't very violent, and even the fan service (**Argot and Jargon**) is mild. Still, the belligerence-controlling plushies are cute. Two further episodes from the same crew, *Kampfer: Fighter for Love (Kampfer fur die Liebe)*, were screened at a cinema event in Tokyo in 2011 and later released on DVD.

KAMYLA *
2001. Video. DIR: Shinichi Shimizu. SCR: Dansu Ban. DES: Makoto Urawa. ANI: Makoto Urawa. MUS: N/C. PRD: Five Ways, Studio March, Studio Tulip. 29 mins. x 3 eps.
Agatha, Lily, and Koyomi are three female police officers whose skirts are way too short for regulation attire. They are members of a crack squad set up by the Japanese government to combat sex trafficking. During a warehouse raid to rescue a female hostage, Agatha is captured herself by the criminal mastermind Lead Suits (Led Suits in the original Japanese notes). She's taken to a small apartment and forced to watch as Lead plies the hostage with the forbidden drug Kamyla, which turns humans into mindless slaves. After the victim is sexually assaulted, Lead orders her to kill herself before forcing Agatha to take the drug as well.

Even after she escapes his clutches, she finds the effects of Kamyla interfering with her work—code words set her off, and a side effect of the drug makes her feel uncontrollable lust at inappropriate moments. This eventually causes her to have sex with a suspect she is supposed to be interrogating, allowing her and Koyomi to locate Lead's hideout, where both girls are swiftly captured. Meanwhile, Lily is leading another group of agents to the rescue, but they get captured too, thanks to their drugged-up lust-crazed colleagues. An orgy duly ensues while Koyomi and Agatha half-heartedly try to fight off the effects of the drug. The protagonists make a brief appearance in the second series of **The Venus Files**, which shares the same creator. **CNV**

KANAMEMO
2009. TV series. DIR: Shigehito Takayanagi. SCR: Rika Nanase, Michiko Yokote, Yasuko Kamo. DES: Shinichi Tatsuta, Hisayoshi Takahashi. ANI: Go Suzuki, Kuniaki Masuda, Shinchi Tatsuta. MUS: Yukari Hashimoto. PRD: feel, Starchild Records. 24 mins. x 13 eps.
Kana Nakamichi is only 13 and still in middle school when she loses her last surviving relative, her grandmother. Repossession men turn up to take away her grandmother's belongings, and she runs away. With nowhere to go and nobody to turn to, she gets a live-in job at a newspaper delivery office. To her delight, she finds a whole community of charming, pretty girls who are glad to welcome a new friend. Based on Shoko Iwami's four-panel manga strip, this is a never-never land of parentless and completely capable girls who are all holding down jobs, despite the fact that one of them is still in elementary school. The older ones drink and gamble, they all worry about their weight and their crushes on past and present members of the team, and it's all prettily inconsequential except for the constant sexual overtones. Molestation and sexual grooming are just as tasteless within one gender as across both.

KANADA, YOSHINORI
1952–2009. Concept artist and animator on many anime movies, including later installments of the **Star Blazers** series and **Galaxy Express 999**. His art style was of radical importance in anime involved with

SCIENCE FICTION AND ROBOTS, for which he experimented with wide-angle and fish-eye lens effects and in which he pioneered the use of points-of-view entirely divorced from the upright, horizon-based perspective of standard filming. This "Kanada Perspective," acknowledging that in space there is no such thing as "up" or "down," achieved an almost viral spread of influence in the 1980s, caused in part by the ready access of the video generation to recordings of his earlier work. He hence became something of an icon in SF anime, imitated so often that critics even began referring to *Kanada-modoki* ("mock-Kanada") stylings among lesser animators. In the 1980s he became associated with the output of Hayao Miyazaki, as an animator on NAUSICAÄ OF THE VALLEY OF THE WIND and subsequent Studio Ghibli productions such as CASTLE IN THE SKY, KIKI'S DELIVERY SERVICE, PORCO ROSSO, and SPIRITED AWAY.

KANDA, TAKEYUKI

1965–96. Born in Fukushima Prefecture, Kanda joined Mushi Production in 1965 and worked on shows including TALES OF HANS CHRISTIAN ANDERSEN. He went freelance in 1972 and worked as an animator on LITTLE PRINCE and DORAEMON. Later works were largely for the Sunrise studio, including DRAGONAR and VIFAM, for which he has a cocreation credit.

KANEMORI, YOSHINORI

1949–. Born in Hiroshima Prefecture, Kanemori joined the animation department of Asahi Films in 1971, before establishing Studio Bird in 1974. He worked as a key animator on such productions as SPOOKY KITARO and PENGUINS MEMORY, before subcontracting his services as a character designer to the Madhouse studio for YAWARA! and BARK! BUNBUN. He also worked as a character designer and key animator, respectively, on the war anime RAIL OF THE STAR and the DIARY OF ANNE FRANK. His directorial credits include HIT HARD, DREAMERS!

KANNAGI: CRAZY SHRINE MAIDENS *

2008. TV series, video. DIR: Yutaka Yamammoto. SCR: Hideyuki Kurata, Tatsuya Takahashi, Toru Honda. DES: Kakeru Mima, Atsushi Morikawa. ANI: Satoshi Kadowaki. MUS: Satoru Kosaki. PRD: A-1 Pictures, Aniplex, Ichijinsha. 24 mins. x 13 eps. (TV), 24 mins. (v).

Jin Mikuriya saw a tree spirit when he was just a child. Now a teenager, he chops down an old tree to get wood for a sculpture of the spirit for his art class project. Amazingly, the sculpture changes into a Nagi, a cute teenage tree spirit who has nowhere to go because her sacred tree has been cut down. She moves in with Jin, her sister shows up, his childhood friend has a secret crush on him, and it's OH MY GODDESS! with a less interesting story and much poorer art. If you're addicted to goofy teenage love comedies you may enjoy this, but the plot (based on Eri Takenashi's 2006 manga) is unevenly paced and poorly developed, with the noble idea of Nagi and Jin removing "impurities" gathering in people's souls left to play a distant second fiddle to the same old harem tropes (ROMANCE AND DRAMA). A 14th episode was released only on DVD, and the characters make a guest appearance in the Playstation game *Nendoroid Generation*.

KANNAZUKI NO MIKO *

2004. AKA: *Priestess of the Godless Month*; *Witch of the New Moon*. DIR: Tetsuya Yanagisawa. SCR: Jukki Hanada, Sumio Uetake. DES: Maki Fujii, Goro Murata. ANI: Akihiro Saito, Hideki Fukushima, Masanori Nishii. MUS: Mina Kubota. PRD: TNK, Rondo Robe. 25 mins. x 12 eps.

Two Japanese schoolgirls become the priestesses of the Sun and the Moon in a battle against ancient evils. Chikane is classy and aloof, while her friend Himeko is chattier and friendlier—a reprise of the oddcouple pairings of innumerable buddy movies all over the globe, but most notably YOU'RE UNDER ARREST in recent times. Based on a manga serialized in *Shonen Ace*, which was created by Kaishaku, the pseudonymous creator of UFO PRINCESS VALKYRIE. Note that some Japanese sources wrote the title as *Kannaduki no Miko*, using an unorthodox romanization that has survived into some Western sources and fan discussions.

KANNO, YOKO

1964–. One of anime's most prominent and best-loved composers, Kanno was born in Miyagi Prefecture and first found fame as the keyboard player with the band TETSU100%. She subsequently moved into composing for television dramas, commercials and, ultimately anime—at first guesting on PLEASE SAVE MY EARTH. A "representative" work is a difficult thing to find for Kanno, since her talent often lies in seamless imitations of whatever music styles are presented to her by producers, creating note-perfect pastiches of pop, classical, rock, and folk music from any other composer or musician. She excels at using obscure instruments, eclectic mixtures of styles, and mass orchestrations. Her work embraces the classical scoring of MACROSS *Plus* and ESCAFLOWNE and the dance-influenced tracks of GHOST IN THE SHELL: *Stand-Alone Complex*. She often works with a team of collaborators, sharing the credit for some work with her husband Hajime Mizoguchi, and occasional collaborators such as Akino Arai, Tim Jensen, and Steve Conte. She formed the jazz band Seatbelts as part of the composing process for COWBOY BEBOP. It is widely believed that "Gabriela Robin," who sings on some of Kanno's albums, is a pseudonym for the composer herself.

KANOKON: THE GIRL WHO CRIED FOX

2008. TV series, video. DIR: Atsushi Otsuki. SCR: Rie Koshika. DES: Akio Takami, Toshihiro Kohama. ANI: Shin Tosaka. MUS: Tsuyoshi Ito. PRD: Xebec, 5pb., AT-X, Media Factory, MOVIC. 25 mins. x 12 eps. (TV), 26 mins. x 2 eps. (v).

Country boy Kota is orphaned and transfers to a new school in the city. On his first day, a gorgeous older girl asks him to meet her alone in the music room where she reveals that she is a fox spirit and madly in love with him. Chizuru doesn't hesitate to demonstrate her affection, which draws attention to Kota at school, and also unsettles the other local animal spirits. It seems the school has quite a few of these, and all have agreed to keep their true identities a secret (POM POKO); Chizuru is rocking the boat. Soon wolf spirit Nozomu, another new student, falls for Kota. Sadly neither girl can cook but otherwise they're absolutely lovely and completely devoted to him. With enough flashes of nudity and extensive sexual aggression to make you wonder how it got on TV, but not enough to make this reheated mess of harem leftovers interesting (**ROMANCE AND DRAMA**), this show based on Katsumi Nishino's book series with art by Koin is neither foxy nor sexy. Yet it drew enough interest to have a straight-to-video sequel, *Kanokon Big Midsummer Carnival (Kanokon Manatsu no Taishanikusai),* over a year after the TV series ended, in autumn 2009. The crew was unchanged, as was the result—a predictable rehash-by-the-numbers of harem festival tropes. **N**

KANON *

2002. TV series, TV special. DIR: Naoyuki Ito, Tatsuya Ishihara. SCR: Hiroaki Sotoyama, Michiko Yokote, Makoto Nakamura. DES: Yoichi Onishi, Itaru Hinoue. ANI: Masahiro Okamura, Nobuhiro Masuda, Nahomi Miyata, Haruo Ogawara. MUS: Hiroyuki Kozo. PRD: Toei Animation, Visual Art's/Key, Fuji TV. 23 mins. x 13 eps. (TV1), 20 mins. (TVm), 24 mins. x 24 eps. (TV2).

Sixteen-year-old Yuichi is, like so many other anime latchkey kids, effectively abandoned by his parents when they head off to Africa on business. He is ordered to move to his aunt's place, where he hasn't been for seven years, and finds himself living with his attractive cousin Nayuki. Although his memories of the time are hazy, it seems that he and Nayuki were once very close. As if that were not enough of a nod to **LOVE HINA,** Yuichi soon finds himself befriending and flirting with several other girls in the town, many of whom claim to have been friends with him in the past and may be interested in being more than friends now that they are teenagers.

Anime appears to excel at depicting, revisiting, analyzing, and fantasizing the desperate teenage stage where a boy will consider dating anything that moves. As with so many others, *Kanon* is based on an erotic dating simulation game (released in 1999), the only distinguishing feature of which was a series of supernatural subplots and some quite tragic endings for some of the girls, in the style of **DIAMOND DAYDREAMS**. However, the impact of the sad endings is lessened considerably in this anime version through some softening of the plots and an over-large cast of characters that make it difficult to care what happens to any of them.

The special, *Kanon Kazahana,* a 20-minute "bonus episode" directed by Ito and with character concepts by Itaru Higami, came out the following year and reveals a little more background about events that occurred before the final scene of the TV series. Although originally released in the U.S. by ADV Films, *Kanon* was left unfinished by the demise of that company, and was completed by Funimation in a rescue similar to that instituted for **PUMPKIN SCISSORS** and **WELCOME TO THE NHK**. Funimation also released the 2006 follow-up series, set seven years later, with an amnesiac Yuichi returning to town and slowly recovering his memories.

KAPPAMAKI AND THE SUSHI KIDS

2003. JPN: *Kappamaki*. TV series. DIR: Saburo Hashimoto, Youn Sun-Kyu, Kim Dae-Jong, Lim Young-Bea, Lim Moon-Ki. SCR: Ikki Yamanobe, Tsunekazu Baba. DES: Takashi Saijo. ANI: Takashi Saijo, Kim Dae-Jung. MUS: Keiichiro Suzuki. PRD: Dream Eggs, Trans Arts, TV Tokyo. 3 mins. x 130 eps.

The adventures of a band of talking sushi people, all friends of Kappamaki, a playful cucumber roll. Sent off to school by octopus dad and tuna mom, they dodge trouble from Mr. Wasabi the school principal and play under the watchful eye of the policeman Mr. Aoyagi, in a world that appears at a distance to be like our own, but is revealed in close-up to comprise the accoutrements, sauces, and tools to be found behind a sushi chef's counter. Conceived as a merchandising opportunity in the style of **TAREPANDA**, the *Kappamaki* world was initially modeled in clay by designer Eri Okamoto. A *kappa* is a Japanese water sprite familiar from **JAPANESE FOLK TALES**, who must keep wet at all times, and maintains this quasi-amphibian lifestyle thanks to a natural bowl-shaped depression on the top of his head that allows him to carry water with him. Cucumbers are supposedly the favorite food of *kappa*, hence the loan of their name to the cheap cucumber sushi known as *kappamaki*.

The series is not available in English, although the English title we use here is derived from the rightsholder's English Web site, which urges us earnestly: "Please enjoy the mind-healing tales in this fantasy land." Until someone eats your protagonist. Compare to **TOMATO-MAN** and **DOGTATO**.

KARAKURI NINJA GIRL *

1996. JPN: *Ninpo Midare Karakuri*. AKA: *Sowing Disorder the Ninja Way; Ninja Trickery*. Video. DIR: N/C. SCR: Miyasuke Ran. DES: Miyasuke Ran. ANI: N/C. MUS: N/C. PRD: Pink Pineapple, KSS. 30 mins. x 2 eps.

Reirei the sex ninja (Fawn Bell in the U.S. **TRANSLATION**) and her companion Tsukimaru (Moon Shadow) attempt to escape from their hard life in Ninja Country so they can settle down together. After several sexual humiliations at the hands of their pursuers, they eventually reach our own world (compare to **BEWITCHED AGNÈS**), where Reirei becomes a housewife, and Tsukimaru puts his climbing skills to use as a construction worker. However, their married bliss is interrupted by the arrival of Reirei's former lesbian lover Asagiri (Morning Mist), who demands that she return to her homeland. When initial entreaties fail, she attempts to remind her what she's been missing, immobilizes her by attaching a sacred card to her privates (difficult to do unnoticed, even with ninja skills), and tries to carry off Tsukimaru. However, true love conquers, and then it's Asagiri's turn for a bit of erotic punishment from Tsukimaru. A light-hearted erotic anime based on a manga by Ryo Ramiya (wife of Hiroyuki Utatane), lampooning many of the traditions of both other erotica and the magical-girl genre itself. **ONV**

KARAS *

2003. JPN: *Karas*. AKA: *Karasu, Crow; The Karas*. TV special, video. DIR: Keiichi Sato. SCR: Shin Yoshida, Masaya Honda. DES: Keiichi Sato, Kenji Hayama, Kenji Ando. ANI: Kenji Hayama. MUS: Yoshihiro Ike. PRD: Tatsunoko. 30 mins. (TVm), 30 mins. x 5 eps. (v).

In a near future Tokyo, humans go about their business unaware that they coexist with a spirit world. Japan's traditional ghosts and goblins are all around, but invisible to most. In order to keep things that way, every city has a priestess, a creature from the spirit world who takes on the form of a human girl, and chooses a supernatural aide or *karas* to help preserve the balance between the two worlds. However, Tokyo's guardian *karas*, the handsome blond warrior Echo, who has watched over it since it was called Edo, has gone rogue. Realizing that humans still have an atavistic fear of the spirit world, he aims to use an army of cybernetically engineered supernatural creatures to seize control of Tokyo, then Japan, then the world.

Mixing elements of the supernatural Cold War of WICKED CITY with the disappearing folklore of SPIRITED AWAY, *Karas* was designed as an anniversary event for the Tatsunoko studio's 40th birthday. Its storyline has heavy echoes of both DOOMED MEGALOPOLIS, with its concentration on a secret battle rooted in Tokyo's history and local lore—a *karasu* [sic] is a crow, one of the many black birds that can be seen and heard flocking around real-life Tokyo.

As in UROTSUKIDOJI, which *K*'s plot also vaguely resembles, Echo's nemesis is a spirit creature in human disguise, in this case his former boss Yurine, who looks like a trendy Shinjuku teen, but is really a long-lived sorceress. Yurine dispatches a number of opponents to deal with Echo, but when all fails she turns in desperation to Otoha, a young doctor running a spirit world hospital in Tokyo. He becomes the city's newest *karas*. He can fight like a ninja, and has spiky black armor that's a cross between bird and crustacean. He can fly; he can transform into various guises. He'll need all of this and more if he is to stop the course of destiny and limit the collateral damage to innocent parties on both sides.

Meanwhile, trendy young detective Narumi Kure has been assigned to a special unit dealing with spirit crime in Tokyo. Pretty, feisty Hinaru is investigating a series of strange killings in the city. And Nue the ski-bum wields a pair of infeasibly large and very arcane handguns, sounds like a country bumpkin, but is really a supernatural hunter, older and much more dangerous than he seems.

Director Sato brings an otherworldy look to the streets of Shinjuku, unsettling with tiny details such as incongruous European gargoyles and Singapore's famous Merlion statue in the background, and street signs in Korean and Chinese, so that at a glance street signs and writing look Japanese, but aren't. Sato describes the overall look as "Asian Gothic"—compare to a similar attempt to wrong-foot the audience in both GHOST IN THE SHELL and SPIRITED AWAY. The first episode was shown on pay-per-view TV before being released on DVD. ❶❷❸

KARATE-CRAZY LIFE, A

1973. JPN: *Karate Baka Ichidai*. AKA: *Life of a Karate Idiot*. TV series. DIR: Eiji Okabe, Osamu Dezaki, Hideo Takayashiki. SCR: Yoshiaki Yoshida, Akinori Matsumoto. DES: Jiro Tsunoda. ANI: Okichiro Nanbu, Keijiro Kimura, Kazuhiko Udagawa. MUS: Mitsuru Kotani. PRD: TMS, MBS. 25 mins. x 47 eps. Failed kamikaze pilot Ken Asuka becomes a rough, tough hooligan who settles all of his problems with karate, until he learns about the legendary swordsman Musashi Miyamoto in the novels of Eiji Yoshikawa. Resolving to live his life like Musashi, he begins to take karate more seriously. Based on a manga by Ikki Kajiwara and Jiro Tsunoda, itself inspired by the real life of Yasunobu Oyama, the founder of the "hard-knock" Kyokushin Karate school. The manga was also adapted into a trilogy of films starring Shinichi "Sonny" Chiba: *Champion of Death, Karate Bear Fighter,* and *Karate for Life*. Compare to KICK FIEND, which is similarly based on a real-life sportsman.

KAREN *

2002. Video. DIR: Shinichi Shimizu. SCR: Dansu Ban. DES: TAKA. ANI: Akira Nakamura. MUS: N/C. PRD: Studio March, Five Ways, T.I. Net. 26 mins.
Ryo Ogawa is the captain of the ToAi high school male cheer squad, and one of the first female members in its 90-year history. In an apparent power play, she is threatened with the walkout of the four male members in the middle of a soccer match, one where the club's district supervisor is in attendance. Desperate to avoid the appearance of weakness, Ryo agrees to a series of "challenges." These are all designed around sexual humiliation, including pantyless cheerleading and, inevitably, having sex with the (previously winless) rugby team. Despite her initial reluctance she winds up liking it, in an anime that seems jointly inspired by the campery of *Water Boys* (2001) and the cheerleading comedy of *Bring It On* (2000). ❶❷❸

KARIN

2005. TV series. DIR: Shinichiro Kimura, Hideaki Uehara, Takeshi Yoshimoto. SCR: Junichi Shintaku, Masaharu Amiya, Sumio Uetake, Takashi Aoshima, Yasunori Yamada. DES: Yumi Nakayama. ANI: Yumi Nakayama,

Haruko Iizuka, Hiroyuki Shimizu, Osamu Sugimoto. MUS: Masaru Nishida. PRD: JC Staff, Garan, Studio Mark, WOWOW. 25 mins. x 24 eps.
Karin Maaka is the daughter in a family of vampires, who are supposed to be living in Japan without attracting the notice of the population. However, unlike her relatives, Karin does not suffer from a chronic lack of blood requiring donations from victims. Instead, she has too much blood and must somehow find ways of transfusing it into victims, lest she suddenly develop the ubiquitous nosebleeds common to so many school anime. A high school anime that tastefully allegorizes the obsession of teenage girls with blood and its loss—compare to BLUE SONNET and the manga *Red River*. Based on the manga *Chibi Vampire* in *Comic Dragon Age,* by Yuna Kagesaki.

KARL AND THE CURIOUS TOWER

2010. JPN: *Karl to Fushigi na To*. TV series. DIR: Jun Takagi. SCR: Miho Maruo. DES: Junzo Terada. ANI: Yuji Umoto. MUS: Cher Watanabe, Tetsuya Kuwayama. PRD: Nippon Animation, KIDS STATION, Horipro, Nippon Columbia. 25 mins. x 26 eps.
Catboy Karl and his friends Punett the bunny and Lolo the squirrel live in a small town with a rickety bell-tower made of the strangest collection of blocks, bits, and pieces. Three times a day, an old man rings the bell in the tower and keeps the life of the town on track. When he fails to ring one day, nobody knows when to eat lunch. Karl decides to go and find out what's happened, and opens the door to adventures. Illustrator Junzo Terada created the concept and provided the delightfully simple designs for this anthropomorphic KIDS' ANIME fantasy. The characters are reminiscent of anime of the 1940s and 1950s, flattened out to two dimensions with no attempt at shading; the complete lack of depth of field in the picture frame gives the air of an old storybook and suits the gently surreal tale—as if some illustrator of children's books from the 1920s were to reimagine *Yellow Submarine*. Terada has created a picture book, fabrics, and stationery based on his designs.

KARMA SAIYUKI, THE *

2007. JPN: *Iyashite Agerun Saiyuki*. AKA: *Doing the Naughty Journey to the West*. Video.

DIR: Tsuyoshi Yoshimoto, Yorihisa Uchida. SCR: Tsuyoshi Yoshimoto, Tatsuya Suzuki. DES: Tatsuya Suzuki, Yorihisa Uchida. ANI: Tatsuya Suzuki. MUS: Takashi Nagakawa. PRD: OZ Ink, Studio Max. 40 mins.

Three cute girls use their magical powers to work as electronics repair persons, but their secret is known to local lad Tsutomu whose price for silence is sex with all three. Suddenly, the four of them are transported to another time in China, replaying the JOURNEY TO THE WEST but with more sex in the style of KAMA SUTRA—the American TRANSLATION seems to have introduced the misspelling of *Karma*, but its heart is in the right place. They get very friendly with some of the locals and Tsutomu learns that the girls have more secrets than he knows—including the reason why they have such an affinity for electronics.

This is one of the silliest pieces of anime EROTICA AND PORNOGRAPHY, and one of the happiest. Everyone's having a good time, everyone wants everyone *else* to have a good time, and it's clear that if Tsutomu wasn't pressing the girls to have sex it would be the other way round. Even the tentacles are happy. Given the joyously cheesy content, it's irresistible to point out that the touch-up animation was done in China at the Changzhou New Star Art Company. **N**

KARUIZAWA SYNDROME

1985. Video. DIR: Mizuho Nishikubo. SCR: Tokio Tsuchiya. DES: Yoshihisa Tagami. ANI: Chuichi Iguchi. MUS: Shinsuke Kazato. PRD: Kitty Films. 76 mins.

In an adaptation of the manga that made a name for creator Yoshihisa Tagami, though radically different in every way from his more famous GREY: DIGITAL TARGET, the sex life of a young man is portrayed in graphic detail, occasionally lapsing into moments of super-deformed silliness. Sections are also shot in live action, directed by Tatsuo Moriyasu. **N**

KARULA DANCES

1989. JPN: Hengen Taima Yako Karula Mau. AKA: Karula Dances! Nocturnal Phantasm Warders; Garuda Dances. Movie, video. DIR: Takaaki Ishiyama. SCR: Masaru Yamamoto. DES: Chuichi Iguchi. ANI: Chuichi Iguchi. MUS: Makoto Mitsui. PRD: Agent 21, Picture Kobo. 80 mins. (m), 30 mins. x 6 eps. (v).

Teenage twins Maiko and Shoko Ogi are the 38th generation to inherit the mystic warrior mantle of the holy Karula Shinyo line. They can also switch minds and combine their powers for greater strength against evil. Raised and trained by their grandmother, herself a psychic warrior of awesome powers, they fight the ancient spirits that lurk beneath the surface of modern Japan. Based on Masakazu Nagakubo's manga in *Halloween* magazine, the girls were just two of several anime "inheritors of ancient tradition" from the early 1990s, and they could be said to have inspired DEVIL HUNTER YOHKO and TWIN DOLLS, at least in part. They returned on video in 1990, finishing off demons in Japan's old capital of Nara, before heading up north to the city of Sendai to investigate cases of merpeople, amnesia, and crimes of demonic passion.

KASAI, OSAMU

1941–. Born on Hokkaido, Kasai graduated in fine art from the Japan University of Fine Art, becoming an animator at Toei Animation. His first animation work was on SECRET AKKO-CHAN, and he went on to work on shows including CUTEY HONEY and the DRAGON BALL spin-off *GT*.

KASIMASI ∗

2006. AKA: Kashimashi: Girl Meets Girl. TV series. DIR: Nobuaki Nakanishi. SCR: Jukki Hanada. DES: Sukune Inugami. ANI: Tomoko Iwasa. MUS: Hitoshi Fujima, Soshi Hosoi, Toshimichi Isoe. PRD: Studio Hibari, JC Staff, AT-X. 25 mins. x 13 eps.

Teenage boy Hazumu Osaragi attempts to confess his feelings for his classmate Yasuna Kamiizumi, but is told that she isn't interested. This is because Yasuna suffers from a strange condition that finds her unable to "see" the faces of boys. Imagine, then, how lucky Hazumu must feel when he is killed that night by a crash-landing alien spaceship, only to be resurrected by apologetic aliens in the body of a girl. This is good news for his chances with Yasuna, who suddenly finds him/her much more attractive, but causes friction with his/her childhood friend Tomari, who harbored a secret heterosexual crush on him, and has trouble accepting the fact that genders have switched. As if one's teens were not confusing enough, this anime based on

an idea by Satoru Akahori was also turned into a manga in *Comic Dengeki Dai-oh* magazine. The term "*kashimashi*" literally refers to a cacophony of female voices, and is written with a character that uses three "woman" radicals—a visual pun in this case, since one of the women is actually a man ... sort of.

KASUMIN

2001. JPN: Soideyo! Henamon Sekai Kasumin. TV series. DIR: Mitsuru Hongo. SCR: Reiko Yoshida. DES: Yoshihiko Umakoshi, Masaaki Yuasa. ANI: N/C. MUS: Yoshikazu Suo. PRD: NHK, OLM. 25 mins. x 26 eps. (TV1), 25 mins. x 26 eps. (TV2), 25 mins. x 26 eps. (TV3).

Fourth-grader Kasumi Haruno is left by her Africa-bound parents in the care of the Kasumi family, whose huge mansion sits in a heavily forested park in Kasumi town. Kasumi is expected to help out with household chores at the strange house, but she soon befriends the appliances who, in a Disneyesque take on TONDE MONPE, are talking, interfering creatures called *Henamon* ("Weirdlings") by the family. Slapstick, candy-colored fun ensues, with highly stylized characters that often look more like POKÉMON than people.

KATOKI, HAJIME

1963–. The designer of many of the "mobile suits" in GUNDAM, Katoki also has a strong track record in games design.

KATRI THE MILKMAID ∗

1984. JPN: Makiba no Shojo Katri. AKA: Katri the Girl of the Pastures; Nathalie. TV series. DIR: Hiroshi Saito, Hiromi Sugimura. SCR: Akira Miyazaki. DES: Noboru Takano. ANI: Noboru Takano, Noriko Moriyoshi. MUS: Toru Fuyuki. PRD: Nippon Animation, Fuji TV. 25 mins. x 49 eps.

When her mother remains in 1915 Germany, little Katri is sent to stay with her grandfather in Finland. Life is hard for the nine-year-old girl as war breaks out, and she is forced to earn money by working as a maid in the Raikola household. She meets various people, including Akki, a campaigner for Finnish independence, and Emilia, a doctor who inspires her to seek a better life for herself. This is another WORLD MASTERPIECE THEATER anime that mines the seemingly limitless vein of stories about little European country girls facing hardships, this one based on the Finnish novel *Paimen, Piika ja Emäntä* (*Shepherd, Maid, and Mistress*) by Auni Nuoliwaara. The first and last episodes were broadcast on Channel 4 in the U.K. in 1987 as part of a local Japan season, dubbed into English under the title *Little Girl on the Farm*. Like many *WMT* stories, it was a success in the export market, appearing under various names in German, Italian, Dutch, Spanish, Portuguese, and Arabic. Oddly, the series was never released in its native land, quite possibly because a live-action film of the same name, albeit based on *Isäntä ja Emäntä*, the sequel to the original, was a box office disaster in Finland. Compare to **HEIDI**.

KATSUMATA, TOMOHARU

1938–. Born in Shizuoka Prefecture, Katsumata graduated from the film department of Nihon University in 1960. He found work the same year with the Kyoto branch of Toei, working as an assistant director to Masahiro Makino on numerous samurai dramas. Transferring to Toei Animation in Tokyo, he worked as a director on the anime **KEN THE WOLF BOY** and **CYBORG 009**. During the 1970s he became strongly associated with Toei studio's output of anime based on the works of creator Go Nagai, most notably **DEVILMAN** and **MAZINGER Z**. He also worked on many of Toei's action-based anime, including **FIST OF THE NORTH STAR** and **SAINT SEIYA**.

KATTE NI KAIZO

2011. Video. DIR: Akiyuki Shinbo, Naoyuki Tatsuwa. SCR: Katsuhiko Takayama. DES: Hiroki Yamamura, Hisaharu Iijima. ANI: Hiroki Yamamura. MUS: Ruka Kawada. PRD: SHAFT, Starchild Records. 23 mins. x 6 eps. (v), 7 mins. x 3 eps. (special).

Ever since the disaster that destroyed his old school, 17-year-old boy genius Kaizo Katsu hasn't been the same. Nor have any of the others from his specialist academy for genius-level brains, now going to ordinary schools. Kaizo's childhood friend Umi, who actually kicked him off the jungle gym in childhood, is indirectly responsible for him blowing up the school in a daze. She feels very guilty about it but can't bring herself to admit responsibility

for his belief that he's a cyborg at constant risk of alien abduction. When he joins the school Science Club he makes new friends, but also comes into contact with ghosts, living dolls, killer sushi, and more new and interesting ways to get hurt.

Koji Kumeta's original manga ran from 1999 to 2004. He's something of a specialist in strange goings-on at school, as he went on from this to create **SAYONARA ZETSUBO-SENSEI**. Packed with unsubtle underwear jokes and a constant barrage of gags traded by the wacky cast, it's reminiscent of **PING PONG CLUB** but with prettier characters. SHAFT also animated Shinbo's **ARAKAWA UNDER THE BRIDGE** and it's interesting to compare the two works. ◎

KAWAI, KENJI

1957–. Born in Shinagawa, Tokyo, this composer is best known for his scores to the live-action *Ring* movies and in anime for his collaborations with Mamoru Oshii, notably **GHOST IN THE SHELL** and **PATLABOR**. He dropped out of a nuclear engineering course to study music at Shobi Music Academy, only to drop out again 18 months later to form the rock fusion band Muse. Aged 29, he worked on his first anime scores for the largely forgotten **COSMOS PINK SHOCK** and the popular romance **MAISON IKKOKU**. He continues to specialize in incidental music that favors a driving, minimalist menace, put to use not only on later anime such as **SKY CRAWLERS** but also on numerous live-action films more likely to be better known in the foreign mainstream, including Oshii's *Avalon*, Hideo Nakata's *Ring* series, and several films for directors outside Japan, including Tsui Hark's *Seven Swords*, Julien Magnat's *Bloody Mallory*, and Wilson Yip's *Ip Man*.

KAWAII!! JENNY

2007. AKA: *Cute!! JeNny*. TV series. DIR: Koichi Kawakita. SCR: Yoshio Urasawa, Katsuhiko Chiba. DES: N/C. ANI: Tomoaki Miwa (VFX). MUS: Koji Takanashi. PRD: Toho, Takara Tomy. 30 mins. x 13 eps.

Jenny and her friends Akira and Nadeshiko are three schoolgirls granted the power to transform into the Sweets Angels, superheroes who fight to defend the world from the evil Sister B. Aided and abetted by three bears in uniform, Sister B plans to steal all the fashions and sweets in the

world, leaving it a bleak and joyless place for girls everywhere.

"Dolls + Diorama + Drama" is the formula for this series, with its overtones of the more conventionally animated **SAILOR MOON**. Unlike **LICCA-CHAN**, it's not aimed solely at the 6- to 11-year-olds who are the prime customers for fashion dolls. The episodes, each containing two stories, ran far past bedtime. Adults watch TV at 1:40 a.m., when little girls are fast asleep, basking in the warm glow of nostalgia milked by shows like **CHIBI MARUKO-CHAN**.

The stories sited actual dolls from the JeNny line, with doll's accessories and outfits you could go out and buy the next day, in wonderfully detailed scenes of everyday life, employing effects from CGI to the rubber-suited actors familiar from Japanese life-action science fiction TV–*Ultraman* monster actor Shinya Iwasaki plays a giant robot in the opening episode. Previously, doll fans could only imagine a playtime like this, choreographed by one of Japan's leading effects masters. Director Kawakita is a former visual effects director for some of Toho's biggest productions, including all the *Godzilla* films between 1989 and 1995. On retirement in 2003, he set up his own VFX company, Dream Planet Japan. The company worked on a number of live-action projects with Toho before *Kawaii!! JeNny*. The creators insist that the name should be spelled JeNny with a median capital N, for no clear reason.

KAWAJIRI, YOSHIAKI

1950–. Born in Yokohama, he found work with Mushi Production after leaving high school, where he soon rejected his previous obsession with "full" animation in the Disney style in favor of an impressionistic, staccato representation of comic art style made possible by the advent of xerography "machine tracing" (**TECHNOLOGY AND FORMATS**). With the demise of Mushi in 1973, he was one of the early employees of Madhouse, and had his directorial debut with **LENSMAN** (1984). His **WICKED CITY** was upgraded to full-length movie status after initial commission as a 35-minute video, leading to Kawajiri's association with several other adaptations of the work of novelist Hideyuki Kikuchi, and with the incorporation of erotic and violent tropes within the mainstream of video animation.

His work is often distinguished by careful juxtapositions of the colors red and blue and by sudden outbreaks of bounding, speedy action, separated by moments of iconic stillness, as if the thing that interests him most is the moment when movement begins or ends, rather than the movement itself. Kawajiri was the most conspicuous proponent of the "urban gothic" style that characterized many of the most successful anime abroad in the 1990s (such as CYBER CITY OEDO 808 and DEMON CITY SHINJUKU) and also with the fast cutting of NINJA SCROLL. A combination of these influences is thought to have led to his commission to provide one of the works in THE ANIMATRIX.

KAWAMORI, SHOJI

1960–. Born in Toyama Prefecture, he began studying mechanical engineering at Keio University, but dropped out when his aptitude for realistic fantasy machines led to offers in anime. His first design sale, a "guest" robot in CAPTAIN HARLOCK in 1978, led to work with the design studio Studio Nue, and to major contributions to the look of MACROSS and DANGAIOH. Moving into animation direction and writing, he demonstrated a grasp of mature themes as a show-runner on MACROSS *Plus* (1994), leading to his innovative attempt to reach a dual male/female audience in ESCAFLOWNE (1996). Kawamori has been acquainted since high school with Haruhiko Mikimoto, Yutaka Izubuchi, and writer Hiroshi Onogi through their association with the science fiction event Kuri Con, and the group has often worked together since.

KAWAMOTO, KIHACHIRO

1925–2010. Born in Shibuya, Tokyo, and graduating from Yokohama National University, Kawamoto worked briefly as an art department assistant at Toho Studios before being fired in 1950 during a labor dispute. He supported himself by making dolls of famous stars, both for sale as novelty items and as part of a column on doll making, which ran from 1949 to 1952 in *Asahi Graph* magazine. Commissioned by *Asahi Shinbun* journalist Tadasu Iizawa to make and pose dolls in photographic tableaux for children's books, Kawamoto was eventually persuaded to make puppet animation in imitation of Jirí Trnka's *The Emperor's Nightingale* (1948). After early

work in commercials, for which he was trained by Tadahito Mochinaga, Kawamoto studied in Prague with Trnka himself, before returning to Japan to make *Breaking of Branches Is Forbidden* (1968, *Hanaori*)— the first of what was originally intended to be a series of tales by both Kawamoto and Trnka, set along the stages of the "Silk Road" between Europe and Asia. As well as puppet work, Kawamoto was one of the few Japanese animators to continue working with paper cutouts, in both *Travel* (1973, *Tabi*) and the semiautobiographical *A Poet's Life* (1974, *Shijin no Shosai*), the latter inspired by the labor disputes that followed the cancellation of THE KING'S TAIL. Although famed on the arthouse circuit for his shorts (for which see KIHACHIRO KAWAMOTO FILM WORKS), Kawamoto's work is better known to the Japanese public through television, most notably the 400 puppets he made for the 1982 NHK series *Romance of the Three Kingdoms* (*DE), and his later *Tale of the Heike* (1993). His later work reflects Buddhist and pacifist sensibilities, including Shinobu Orikichi's *Book of the Dead* (*Shisha no Sho*) and the anthology movie *Winter Days* (*Fuyu no Hi*, 2003), based on the poetry of Basho. Following the death of Osamu Tezuka, Kawamoto assumed the role of president of the Japan Animation Association in 1989.

KAYOE CHUGAKU

2011. AKA: *Kayochu*. TV series. DIR: Taketo Shinkai. SCR: Taketo Shinkai, Umenomago, Midorinomago. DES: Jun Oson. ANI: N/C. MUS: N/C. PRD: DLE, King Records, Tokai TV, Gentosha. 1 min. approx. x 36 eps.
The manic tale of a transfer student named Wada in a wacky Kansai school where his classmates include an immaculately dressed bear, a transvestite, a black guy and a posse of sassy girls, brought to life by a cast including comedian Shigeki Nakanishi, originally broadcast online and on late-night TV. DLE are among the stars of the new wave of short-short animation, with shows like EAGLE TALON and HAIYORU NYARUANI on their rap sheet.

KAYOKO'S DIARY ∗

1991. JPN: *Ushiro no Shomen Daaaare*. AKA: *Someone at My Shoulder*. Movie. DIR: Seiji Arihara. SCR: Seiji Arihara, Tetsuaki Imaizumi. DES: Takaya Ono. ANI: Takaya Ono. MUS: Reijiro

Koroku. PRD: Mushi Pro. 90 mins. (m1), 90 mins. (m2).
Kayoko is a nine-year-old girl in 1940 Tokyo, with a poor extended family that includes three brothers and a grandmother. She plays in her neighborhood but is bullied by other children, though she is protected by her kindly big brother Kisaburo. By 1944, Kayoko is caring for another brother, the newest addition to the family, while fear of air raids eventually results in her evacuation to live with her aunt in rural Numazu. From the hilltop, she can see the distant lights of Tokyo, until the night of March 10, 1945, when the city glows with the fires of an American bombing. All Kayoko's family are killed except Kisaburo, and the now-teenage girl returns to her old home one last time to say farewell to her childhood. Based on the autobiography of Kayoko Ebina, who also wrote the novel *Wolf of Downtown*, this tale follows the lead of GRAVE OF THE FIREFLIES, telling a war story through the eyes of a child. It also bears an uncanny resemblance to director Arihara's earlier RAINING FIRE. Shown on a double bill with the short ON A PAPER CRANE and given a limited foreign release through subtitled showings at film festivals. In 2005, the story was remade as the anime feature film *A Brighter Tomorrow: Half a Sweet Potato* (*Ashita Genki ni Naare: Hanbun no Satsumaimo*), directed by Shinichi Nakata, whichconcentrated more on the horror of the air raids and Kayoko's search for her brother in the ruins. The remake was one of several movies, including GLASS RABBIT and *Nagasaki 1945: The Angelus Bell*, put into production to mark the 60th anniversary of the end of World War II.

KAZE NO STIGMA ∗

2007. AKA: *Stigma of the Wind*. TV series. DIR: Junichi Sakata. SCR: Mayori Sekijima, Kiyoko Yoshimuea. DES: Yasunari Nitta, Yasutada Kato, Yohei Kodama. ANI: Kan Ogawa. MUS: Yutaka Fukuoka. PRD: Gonzo. 24 mins. x 24 eps.
Kazuma Kannagi was cast out of his clan after being defeated by his cousin Ayano for control of the family's sacred sword and its powers of fire-magic. Four years on, he has a new name and a new skill as a master of wind magic. He also has unfinished business at home, where his

antagonism for his beautiful cousin is soon compromised by a growing attraction that her family seems only too eager to encourage.

Kaze no Stigma is an unfinished sequence of six novels and five short-story collections by Takihiro Yamato, who passed away in 2009. The anime version is is unsatisfying, despite attractive animation and some funny moments in the second half, which also contains an interesting story arc where an evil schemer has the cast playing a battle game for real as part of his plot. The spacing is very uneven; the first half starts well then sags like a soggy pancake and the better-written second half leaves a number of plot threads dangling. Characterization is inconsistent and plot often illogical, while the fan service (**ARGOT AND JARGON**) is so overt as to be tedious. Too weak to be really awful, and too serious about itself to be really funny, this is a missed opportunity of a show. **NV**

KAZE NO YOJIMBO *

2001. AKA: *Bodyguard of the Wind; Yojimbo of the Wind.* TV series. DIR: Hayato Date. SCR: Atsushi Yamatoya, Daisuke Yajima, Michiko Yokote, Satoru Nishizono. DES: Takeshi Ito. ANI: Choi Hoon-chul, Motosuke Takahashi, Tatsuo Yanagino, Yukimaro Otsubo. MUS: Tsuneyoshi Saito. PRD: Bandai, Studio Pierrot, Nippon TV. 25 mins. x 25 eps.

Lone investigator George Kodama comes to the small coastal town of Kimujuku, looking for a man called Genzo Araki. The townsfolk, however, are reluctant to offer much support, since they are deeply suspicious of outsiders and of each other—a strange building pattern has caused Kimujuku to be literally cut in two by the railway tracks, with different architecture and attitudes on either side. George's investigations drag him deeper into a 15-year-old mystery about a disappearing train carriage, its contents a perennial subject of rumor and gossip.

Like **SAMURAI 7**, this anime relocates and refashions the action of a Kurosawa movie, in this case the divided town of *Yojimbo* (1961). However, the running time of a TV series offers the potential for a much slower pace and far more depth than the movie's simple parable, introducing local legends about "demons" that may refer to forgotten contacts with foreigners, and an

ever-widening conspiracy with ties to the top that has more in common, not with the movie, but with the 1961 *Yojimbo* TV series (*DE). Considering that it is set in modern times and runs six times as long, one wonders why anyone should bother to play up the connections to Kurosawa at all.

KEEP IT UP! GUIDE DOG SAAB

1988. JPN: *Ganbare! Modoken Saab.* TV special. DIR: Seiji Okuda. SCR: Fujio Takizawa. DES: Shuichi Seki. ANI: Takashi Saijo. MUS: Hisashi Miyazaki. PRD: Tama Pro, NHK. 27 mins.

The true story of a seeing-eye dog that brings hope to a blind child, based on a novel by Yuichi Tejima. Lifting several tropes from **SPORTS ANIME** such as **AIM FOR THE ACE**, a well-loved puppy's life is turned upside down as he is put through a tough training regime, until he triumphs and makes the world a better place.

KEKKAI *

2002. JPN: *Kekkai.* AKA: *Nature of the Heart; Clinical Interrogation.* Video. DIR: Shigenori Kurii. SCR: Hideo Ura. DES: Tettechi. ANI: Shigenori Kurii. MUS: N/C. PRD: Studio Foglio, Milky. 30 mins.

Chief inspector Kaoru is investigating a grisly murder; her sole clue is Kyoko, an amnesiac girl found at the scene of the crime. She calls in her old flame Junichi, a consultant psychologist who only agrees to help if she performs sexual favors for him. When Junichi does eventually get around to examining Kyoko, he pronounces her as suffering from multiple personality disorder and entertains the possibility that among her sexuallymotivated personalities there may be a murderous one that committed the crime. Psychological investigation was big on Japanese live-action TV at the turn of the 21st century, with shows such as *Hypnosis* (*DE) and *MPD Psycho* (*DE), so it is perhaps no surprise that someone should put a sexualized spin on the proceedings in anime. Compare to **PRIVATE PSYCHO LESSON** and **ONI-TENSEI**. At time of writing, only the first "report" is available in English of what is clearly intended as a series. However, the Japanese website for the production company conspicuously files the *Kekkai* episode among its "completed serials," implying that there is not currently a plan to produce a sequel. **LNV**

KEKKAISHI *

2006. AKA: *Barrier Master.* TV series. DIR: Kenji Kodama. SCR: Yoichi Kato, Miyuki Kishimoto, Hiroshi Onogi. DES: Hirotoshi Takaya, Shigemi Ikeda, Shuichi Okubo. ANI: Hirotoshi Takaya, Rie Nakajima, Atsuo Tobe. MUS: Taku Iwasaki. PRD: Sunrise, Yomiuri TV. 24 mins. x 52 eps.

Many teens have an after-school job. Fourteen-year-old Yoshimori Sumimura has one with a lot of satisfaction and opportunities for personal growth—if he survives. He's a *kekkaishi*, a monster killer. His childhood friend Tokine Yumimura, a year his senior, is also a *kekkaishi*. In fact, she's his main rival for promotion as heir of the Sumimura clan. But in his secret heart, Yoshimori has a different dream—he wants to make pastry.

Based on Yellow Tanabe's 2003 manga, this is a by-the-numbers boys' show of the kind Sunrise has been doing for years. The studio's competence at this kind of show is so practiced it looks almost casual, but is far from it. To make a successful boys' show—not necessarily a mega-hit, but one that pulls in the sponsors and earns back its money plus—requires a balance between the entirely predictable and just enough of the new, a difficult act to pull off, let alone to repeat. To old anime hands, *Kekkaishi* has moments of interest—some nice ideas, some good moments of characterization, and some intriguing family relationships—but nothing exceptional. To its target audience, boys longing for a hero they can really identify with and a world that can take them away from dull reality, it's pure magic.

KEKKO KAMEN *

1991. JPN: *Kekko Kamen.* Video. DIR: Chuji Iguchi, Nobuyoshi Kondo, Jun Kawagoe, Kinji Yoshimoto. SCR: Masashi Sogo. DES: Satoshi Hirayama. ANI: Masayoshi Sudo, Koji Morimoto. MUS: Keiji Ishikawa. PRD: Studio Signal, Dynamic, Bee Media. 45 mins. x 2 eps.

The students of Sparta College are terrorized by the perverse regime of the principal, Great Toenail of Satan (AKA Satan Tochiz), and his lecherous assistant, Ben. Regularly appointing new teachers to abuse and humiliate the girls (the boys are let off because Tochiz only wants to see the girls with their clothes off), they are thwarted on every occasion by Kekko Kamen, the "naked avenger."

A smutty, saucy adventure based on the 1974 *Shonen Jump* manga from **SHAMELESS SCHOOL**'s Go Nagai, lampooning **MOON-LIGHT MASK** (*Gekko Kamen*) and the sappiest formulae of girls' school dramas, with liberal doses of female nudity. Though occasionally pushing the boundaries of good taste (the first substitute teacher, S/M queen Gestapa, has just transferred from Auschwitz College), the idea of a superheroine wearing nothing but boots and a mask so that "we see her dumplings, but her face remains a mystery," has plenty of comic potential. The hapless student Mayumi is whipped, tickled, and tortured, while her "big sister" Chigusa tries to offer helpful advice on escaping the teachers' notice. Superpowered opponents sent to take care of Kekko Kamen include the muscle-bound Austrian PE teacher, Taro Schwarzenegger, and a samurai camera-man with a hilarious Sean Connery accent in the U.K. dub. Mayumi must also fend off the advances of the Paradicer Mark One, a lesbian android sent to break up her friendship with Chigusa—Kekko Kamen must find Paradicer's off-button, which inventor Ben has put in a pre-dictably sensitive spot. Though never explained in the anime version, the manga reveals that Kekko Kamen is actually Chi-gusa's twin, allowing the sisters to switch places and keep the superheroine's iden-tity hidden. The story exists in U.S. and U.K. versions, though the British one did not survive the British censor unscathed—a scene in which Gestapa strips Mayumi by throwing knives at her while she is strapped to a giant rotating swastika was just one of the casualties. The story was also adapted into a live-action film, *Kekko Mask: The Birth* (1991), directed by Yutaka Akiyama, and two sequels, *Kekko Mask* (1993) and *Kekko Mask in Love* (1995). But the live versions, which feature cameos from **MAZINGER Z** and **CUTEY HONEY**, suffer from a heroine who is understandably coy about revealing all and lack the slapstick verve of the anime. ●**ⓁⓃⓋ**

KEN THE WOLF BOY *

1963. JPN: *Okami Shonen Ken*. TV series. DIR: Sadao Tsukioka, Kimio Yabuki, Yugo Serikawa, Hiroshi Ikeda, Yoshio Kuroda,

Isao Takahata, Taiji Yabushita, Takeshi Tamiya, Masayuki Akehi, Kazuya Miyazaki. SCR: Satoshi Iijima, Yugo Serikawa, Kuniaki Oshikawa, Daisaku Shirokawa, Minoru Hamada, Jiro Yoshino, Aya Suzuki. DES: Sadao Tsukioka. ANI: Takeshi Kitamasa. MUS: Asei Kobayashi. PRD: Toei, NET. 25 mins. x 86 eps.

Climate changes brought on by a passing comet plunge Africa into chaos, and a group of wolves struggle to survive. Howev-er, they have a trump card, the "two-legged wolf" Ken, a boy who lives with them in the jungle. Learning from Jack the wolf-hero and Boss the wolf-elder, Ken protects wolf cubs Chichi and Poppo. Put into produc-tion by Toei in answer to the challenge presented by Osamu Tezuka's **ASTRO BOY**, this variant on Kipling's *Jungle Book* was broadcast in Australia but is otherwise unknown in the English-speaking world. Director Sadao Tsukioka was still in his 20s at the time, accepting the job after several older, more experienced animation hands had turned it down on the grounds that producing 25 minutes a week of animation was impossible.

KENICHI THE MIGHTIEST DISCIPLE *

2006. JPN: *Shijo Saikyo no Deshi Kenichi*. AKA: *History's Strongest Disciple Kenichi*. TV series, video. DIR: Hajime Kamegaki, Hiroshi Ishiodori. SCR: Yoshiyuki Suga, Hideki Shirane, Koichi Taki, Eizo Kobayashi. DES: Junko Yamanaka, Masatomo Sudo, Nobuto Sakamoto, Hideyuki Motohashi. ANI: Shinichi Suzuki, Nobuharu Ishido, Junko Yamanaka. MUS: Joe Rinoie, Keiji Inai. PRD: TMS, TV Tokyo, Brains Base, Flying Dog. 25 mins. x 50 eps. (TV), 30 mins. x 3 eps. (v).

Kenichi is constantly getting picked on at school. When he meets a mysterious girl named Miu, she encourages him to start training at the *dojo* where she lives. Tackling martial arts of all kinds, Kenichi learns from great masters in an effort to become strong enough to beat the bul-lies. But his newly acquired and growing skills make him even more of a target, not just for his classmates but for some much nastier characters. This is the third incarnation of Kenichi's adventures—the anime is based on a 2002 manga by Shun Matsuena, itself a reversioning of a manga that first appeared in 2002 under the title *Fight!! Ryozanpaku, History's Strongest Dis-*

ciple (*Tatakae! Ryozanpaku, Shijo Saikyo no Deshi*). Three videos with the same title as the TV series followed five years after the series ended, in 2012, picking up the story where the series left off with a new raft of enemies to fight. Sharp-eyed linguists may notice the loaded term *Ryozanpaku*, the Japanese pronunciation for the Chinese *Liang Shan Po*, revealing Kenichi to be the latest inheritor of the literary mantle of the classical Chinese novel *The Water Margin*, also referenced in **GIANT ROBO** and **SUIKODEN**, among others.

KENNEL TOKOROZAWA

1992. Video. DIR: Hiroshi Sasakawa, Seitaro Hara. SCR: Yukiyoshi Ohashi. DES: Katsumi Hashimoto. ANI: Katsumi Hashimoto. MUS: Ma-ri-ko. PRD: Animation 21. 44 mins.

Pet shop owner's daughter Chika Tokoro-zawa spends every waking hour with her dog, Rin Tin Tin, who repays her love by watching over her while she sleeps. Based on the manga in *Young Sunday* magazine by Maki Otsubo, who is better known in the manga world for *Mr. Cinema*.

KENYA BOY

1984. Movie. DIR: Norihiko Obayashi, Tetsuo Imazawa. SCR: Chiho Katsura. DES: N/C. ANI: Hiroshi Wagatsuma, Masami Suda, Kazuo Mori, Shingo Araki, Michi Himeno, Kenji Yo-koyama, Hirohide Yashikijima. MUS: Tatsuzo Usaki. PRD: Kadokawa, Toei. 109 mins.

In late 1941, textile trader Mr. Murakami takes his son Wataru on a business trip out of his home base in Nairobi, Kenya. They are attacked by a rampaging rhinoceros and separate to escape it, but Murakami is found by the British. After the attack on Pearl Harbor, the British and Japanese are now at war, so Murakami is arrested. Wataru is taken in by Masai tribesmen and goes native, heading off in search of his father, with time out for *Indiana Jones*–style adventures with lions, elephants, a lost valley of dinosaurs, a giant snake, and a slimy Nazi spy. Based on Soji Yamakawa's novel *The Boy King*, this movie uses heavy rotoscoping techniques from former live-action director Obayashi to impart a more realistic look to many of the scenes. Com-pare to **KEN THE WOLF BOY** and **BUSHBABY**.

KERAKU NO OH: KING OF PLEASURE *

2002. JPN: *Keraku no O*. Video. DIR:

Katsuyoshi Yatabe, Taro. scr: Rokurota Makabe. des: Berrys. ani: Hyoei Tadokoro. mus: N/C. prd: Five Ways, K-Production, Imagehouse, Tamanegi Studio. 30 mins. x 3 eps.

After he suffers a brain injury in a childhood playground accident, Ryuichi Sashima is a hopeless case: he's bullied at school, he has no friends, and he is so passive even his parents have given up. Then the childhood friend who caused the accident transfers to his high school after ten years in America. Chihiro Himenoki had no idea he was so severely injured, and she is guilt-stricken. Naïvely, she offers to do anything she can to make it up to him, and when he asks for sex she doesn't feel she can refuse. Ryuichi learns that he has one ability that really is outstanding and decides to use his unsuspected sexual prowess to get revenge on all the females who have ever scorned or bullied him. The rest of the series shows him working his way down the scale of his (female) tormentors (real and imagined)—Miyuki, the upper crust bully; Kanata, the judo club captain; Miyako, the school nurse; and Tamana the student council president—while using Chihiro as a combination spy, bait, and sex slave. Based on a PC game from Fusen Club, with a nasty taste for revenge that echoes **Ichi the Killer** and an insidious attempt to excuse it with disability, in the style of **Nanaka 6/17**. Compare to **Sextra Credit**. Not to be confused with the similarly titled **Kokudoh Oh: Black-Eyed King**, also by Five Ways, who are responsible for this series' cut-rate production values (following their usual practice of not spending any more than is necessary to get it out the door). Based on a game by the Merlot (sic) label of Gensakuza. **⬤🅝Ⓥ**

KEROPPI *

1989. jpn: *Kerokero Keroppi*. Video. dir: Masami Hata, Masahito Kitagawa. scr: Mami Watanabe, Yukiyoshi Ohashi, Satoru Nishizono. des: N/C. ani: Tsuchiaki Noma. mus: Yoshihisa Shirokawa, Richard Niels, Takeshi Ike, Katsuyoshi Kobayashi. prd: Sanrio. ca. 30 mins. x 15 eps.

Kerokero ("Ribbit") Keroppi is a friendly green frog with huge eyes and stripy pants, designed on the same Sanrio merchandising production line that created **Pekkle**, **Pochacco**, and **Bad Badtz-maru**. As do

his stablemates, he appears in a series of cash-in videos designed to burn brand identity into the retinas of impressionable young children, commencing with cameo spots in other Sanrio videos in 1989. He appeared in the anthology title *KK Adventures* (1990), comprising his adventures in *In Search of the Pink Mushroom*, *Everybody Say Hello to the Priest*, and *Secrets at the Plum Shop*. Since then, *KK* has flitted between the staple formulae of Sanrio adaptations, including fairy-tale pastiches of *Three Musketeers* (1991), the theatrically shown "movie" *Jack and the Beanstalk* (1991), *Robin Hood* (1993), and *Gulliver's Travels*—these last two released in the U.S. He has also appeared in two moral tales, *Friends Are Fun* (1992) and *Let's Be Friends* (1994), though his educational aspirations never became quite so all-encompassing as those of his brand sister **Hello Kitty**. Other *KK* outings are more "original," featuring several adventures for the frog and his friends, including *K's Christmas Eve Gift* (1992), the baseball adventure *Go for It! Keroppies!* (1993), the ghostly *Secrets of KK House* (1993), and the haunted museum chiller *That Dinosaur's Alive!* (1993). More wistful outings came in the form of *K's Flying Dream Ship* (1992) and *If I Could Fly …* (1994). In recent years, his anime appearances have waned—his last outing was in *Adventures of the Cowardly Prince* (1997), which was released combined on a tape with the earlier *KK's Flying Ghost Ship*. *Go for It! Keroppies* and *Let's Be Friends* were also released in the U.S., under the title *K: Let's Play Baseball*.

KETSU-INU

2010. aka: *Butt Dog*. TV series. dir: Haruki Kasugamori. scr: Haruki Kasugamori. des: Lifestyle Tsunoda. ani: Inushige, Jun Mita. mus: 1869-iwarock-. prd: THINK Corporation, Toei Animation. 3 mins. x 13 eps.

There's an old saying that dog owners end up looking like their pets. A strange dog with a face like a very unattractive backside turns up in town. But is it really a dog, or something more sinister? Suddenly dogs just like it seem to be all over town and people's faces start to change. Based on the web manga of the same name by Lifestyle Tsunoda, this series of Flash-animated comedy shorts was aired on the AT-X network (starting on April Fools' Day)

before going to mobile phone and online distribution. The manga's scratchy, naïve art style is almost, but not entirely, subsumed in Toei's classic rounded, colorful TV anime look; Ketsu-Inu itself stays much as in the manga but the other characters are rendered very differently. The gags, though, still come thick and fast. Look for an ass-faced homage to James Cameron's *Titanic* amid a barrage of other jokes.

KEY THE METAL IDOL *

1994. Video. dir: Hiroaki Sato. scr: Hiroaki Sato. des: Kunihiko Tanaka. ani: Keiichi Ishikura. mus: Tamiya Terajima. prd: Studio Pierrot. 25 mins. x 13 eps., 90 mins. x 2 eps.

A dying professor leaves a message for his granddaughter Tokiko "Key" Mima. She is an android, but she is dying, too, and her battery is irreplaceable. If, however, she can make 30,000 friends, their love will rejuvenate her and turn her into a real girl. Realizing there are not too many ways to reach that many people in a limited time, Key heads for Tokyo, where her friend Sakura helps her begin a career as a pop singer. But she soon discovers that there is more to her destiny than the simplistic quest outlined by her grandfather—Key's predicament and its solution are tied up in the dark secrets of her own family. The adoration of the crowd can literally free her soul for a moment, but it can also unleash other, more effective powers that other interested parties are keen on gaining for themselves. An uneven but engrossing anime that flips between the attention-hungry desperation of a performance artist and a vampiric military conspiracy, with time out for a number of superior musical interludes. And with a lead character who thinks she is a dying robot but whose friends merely think she is a traumatized, abused little girl, it contains a subtle identity crisis that would be used to greater effect by another Mima, played by the same actress Junko Iwao, in **Perfect Blue**.

KHRONOS GEAR

2012. jpn: *Katayoku Khronos Gear*. Video. dir: Hiroki Hayashi. scr: JR Eki Sakurajima. des: Ryuichi Makino, Ayu Kawamoto. ani: Ryuichi Makino, Shigemi Ikeda. mus: G-Mode. prd: AIC, G-Mode. 25? mins. x 5 eps.

Humanity has finally completed an orbital

elevator and developed the outer planets of the solar system, only to find that another species has its eye on Terran real estate. Little is known about the Obliqus except that they're alien and have far superior technology. To counteract this, the Khronos Foundation assembles a gang of wide-eyed moppets descended from every nation's heroes, from Musashi Miyamoto and Ryoma Sakamoto to Britain's Florence Nightingale and France's Napoleon and Joan of Arc. These victims of their genetic heritage are then fused to battlesuits known as "Gear" to become bioweapons: Khronos Gear. This collaboration between anime studio AIC and games company G-Mode was designed as a franchise from the beginning, with anime, game, and manga versions carefully planned and timed. The Japanese publicity for the manga puts blonde, blue-eyed heroine Jeanne Saya's apparently naked bottom front and center, a clue that this isn't all about the gear and has little to do with history.

KIBA *

2006. AKA: *Fang*. TV series. DIR: Hiroshi Kojina. SCR: Michiko Yokote, Toshiki Inoue. DES: Susumu Matsushita, Takahiro Yoshimatsu. ANI: Takahiro Harada, Toru Shigeta. MUS: Jun Miyake. PRD: Madhouse, Mook, Dr Movie, Asahi Pro, Dogakobo, Studio Wombat, Kyung Kang Ania, AT-X, TV Tokyo, Aniplex, Dentsu, Upper Deck Japan. 24 mins. x 51 eps.
Zed, a young outlaw in a dystopian urban future, stumbles into a gateway to the verdant, natural world of Templar where he nurtures his new-found abilities as a Shard Caster, using his magical spirit to protect his new home from the invading hordes of the dark Zymot empire. His friend Noah also arrives in this new world, but chooses a different and more forbidding path for his own nascent sorcerous powers.

Conceived as an advert for a collectible card game, this cliché-ridden boys' show would have come and gone without incident, were it not for its commissioning and impressive 51-episode run right on the cusp of the mid-noughties slump in anime revenues. While the series came to an uncelebrated end after a single calendar year, it erupted into a far more exciting legal battle between two of the producers, with Aniplex suing the American card company Upper Deck over non-payment of funds.

Upper Deck counter-claimed that Aniplex had disregarded many production directives, delivering an "age-inappropriate" violent cartoon unsuitable for the target audience of preteen boys. Notably, none of this dispute arose publicly until after the series had finished, suggesting that matters might have been self-solving if the franchise had proved to be a runaway hit, and not yet another also-ran in the year of anime's historic production peak.

The conflict, eventually resolved in Aniplex's favor, led to a public disclosure of the kinds of figures and considerations that go into creating a multimedia anime franchise, making the finger-pointing after *Kiba*'s finale far more long-running, entertaining, educational, and gripping than the series itself—to anime encyclopedists, at least. Arguably, it also marked the true end of the late-20-century boom in foreign funding for anime, confronting overseas investors with the true difficulties of whipping up a new **POKÉMON** out of thin air, and the Japanese with the litigious nature of the American entertainment business when producers feel they have been gypped. A different kind of legal tangle, just as interesting, arose around the same time on **RGB ADVENTURE**.

KIBUN²

2003. AKA: *Kibun x Kibun*; *Feeling x Feeling*. Video. DIR: Ryu. SCR: Aruto Raiga. DES: Ryu. ANI: Ryu. MUS: AC Sound. PRD: Museum Pictures, Milky. 30 mins. x 2 eps.
Kenji is a hard-working man, to the extent that by the time he comes home he is too tired to romance his girlfriend, who is tiring of his lack of interest in anything but sex. But after she inadvertently causes him to have an accident, they are stuck together at home, and must learn how to be intimate once more. Before long, however, she is suspecting him of having an affair and sends her friend to follow him in secret, in an adaptation of the manga by **MAHOROMATIC** cocreator Bow Ditama. **Ⓝ**

KICK FIEND

1970. JPN: *Kick no Oni*. AKA: *Devil Kick*; *Kick-Boxing Demon*; *Kick Fiend*. TV series. DIR: Yoshio Kuroda, Yasuo Yamaguchi, Nobutaka Nishizawa. SCR: Masaki Tsuji, Toyohiro Ando, Kuniaki Oshikawa. DES: N/C. ANI: N/C. MUS: Asei Kobayashi. PRD: Toei, Noguchi Pro,

Kajiwara Pro, TBS. 25 mins. x 26 eps.
After Osamu Noguchi, a Japanese fight promoter, brings traditional Muay Thai boxers to Japan in December 1959, karate champion Hideki Shihara takes the stage name Tadashi Sawamura in order to compete against them in the new sport of kickboxing. However, when he first goes into the ring, he is knocked out after 13 close calls. Determined to learn from his mistakes, he trains with Coach Endo and promoter Noguchi, hoping to improve his martial arts skills and popularize the new sport. The Japan Kickboxing Association sets out its new rules in 1966, and the first World Kickboxing Championship is held in Tokyo in 1968, in a rags-to-riches tale that may seem to be a fictional account like YAWARA!, but is actually based on a true story. Sawamura also appeared live in an ULTRAMAN (*DE) episode, training with "Ultraman Jack" Hideki Go. The anime was preceded in 1969 by a manga in *Shonen Gaho*, presented as a biography by KARATE-CRAZY LIFE's Ikki Kajiwara and Kentaro Nakashiro. ●

KICKERS

1986. JPN: *Ganbare Kickers*. AKA: *Go for It! Kickers!* TV series. DIR: Akira Shigino, Mutsu Iwata, Shigeru Morikawa. SCR: Sukehiro Tomita, Isao Shizuya, MitsuoAimono. DES: Takeshi Osaka. ANI: Takeshi Osaka, Takeshi Nagai. MUS: Jun Irigawa. PRD: Studio Pierrot, Nippon TV. 25 mins. x 23 eps.
The soccer team Kitahara Kickers have lost 22 matches in a row, but all that changes when Sho Oji transfers to the team's school and imbues it with his hot-headed spirit. He inspires the team members to aim to win just a single match to regain their self-esteem. This short-lived series was based on a 1984 *Corocoro Comic* manga by Noriaki Nagai and is uncannily similar to OFFSIDE.

KICK-HEART *

2013. Movie. DIR: Masaaki Yuasa. SCR: Masaaki Yuasa. DES: Michio Mihara. ANI: Michio Mihara, Yasunori Miyazawa, Eunyoung Choi. MUS: Oorutaichi. PRD: Production I.G. 12 mins.
Romeo and Juliet is reimagined in a wrestling ring, as two well-matched brawlers go up against each other in a high-stakes bout, each unaware that the other is secretly seeking to use the prize money for the same noble cause. Romeo Maki (Maskman M) is a hero cast in the same mold as TIGER MASK, but then again, so is Sister Juliet (Sister S)—both will fight to save their orphanage, but neither can back down. Perversion saves the day, when the combination of "S and M" turns out to have a double meaning, and Maskman M discovers that he enjoys having Sister S beat him up.

This light-hearted SPORTS ANIME would be otherwise unremarkable, were it not for the groundbreaking, possibly even game-changing logistics behind its production. Although many anime already pander to a dwindling handful of otaku that pay far over the odds for essentially tailor-made entertainment, *Kick-Heart* was the first to be officially crowd-sourced, with Production I.G passing round a digital hat on the Kickstarter service before animation commenced. With funding secured ahead of production, this was a win-win move for the animation company, with its surreal, often-psychedelic short, well-stuffed with cash that would normally suffice to make a 45-minute video. Time alone will tell whether *Kick-Heart* was a one-off experiment or the shape of anime productions to come. The financially minded reader is likely to ask if everyone is now a producer, does this mean that everyone gets to share in the profits? The realistic Japanese money-man is liable to reply: what profits? While the authors welcome the idea of getting fans to back up their clamorings with hard cash, they dread the likely implications for what gets put into production. Nobody in the anime business thought that MY NEIGHBOR TOTORO would be a success, but people threw money by the shovelful at KIBA.

KIDDY GRADE *

2002. JPN: *Kiddie Grade*. TV series. DIR: Keiji Goto. SCR: Hidefumi Kimura. DES: Megumi Kadonosono. ANI: Masanori Ishioka, Megumi Kadonosono. MUS: Shiro Hamaguchi. PRD: gimik, Gonzo, GOTT, Kyoto Animation. 25 mins. x 24 eps. (TV1), ca. 80 mins. x 3 eps. (m), 25 mins. x 24 eps. (TV2, and).
The galaxy has suffered interstellar war and has finally formed the Globe-Governments' Union to bring peace and stability. But disputes persist over jurisdiction, eventually leading to the establishment of GOTT, the Galactic Organization of Trades and Tariffs, particularly its Encounter of Shadow-Work Member (ES) force, a group of agents who tend to work in pairs. Amid the slew of similarly unnecessary acronyms that makes a plot synopsis look like a government manual, the important part is this: there are pretty girl agents, and they tend to work in pairs.

Hoping that the modern generation's attention span is short enough not to notice a darker, less exuberant take on DIRTY PAIR (and probably right in that assumption), Keiji Goto's "original" story concerns Éclair, a teenage agent whose secret weapon is a tube of lipstick made of a high-tech substance that actualizes on contact with air—thus when she draws a whip or a rope, she will have one for real. Her preteen cohort Lumiere has the power to control machines with her thoughts. These abilities, we are told, are what allow them to be agents at such a young age.

Mixing the girl-buddy crime fighters of GUNSMITH CATS with a sexy sci-fi setting out of AGENT AIKA, *KG* unsurprisingly introduces a forgotten past for one of its protagonists like something out of GUNSLINGER GIRL, causing Éclair and Lumiere to go on the run from their former associates. A feature of Éclair's trauma is that she seems unable to prevent herself from endlessly repeating the same pattern of events, which is somewhat ironic from an anime series that relentlessly reversions dozens of clichés from earlier shows. However, instead of being one more off-the-peg quirk, this revelation leads to a major shift in the show's priorities after the ninth episode, dumping the planet-of-the-week crime fighting of the early chapters in favor of a long arc in which the hunters become the hunted. As the characters recall their past lives, it also introduces elements of amnesia and reincarnation more familiar from GALL FORCE (or indeed, the final moments of the first GHOST IN THE SHELL movie), and more serious science fiction in the form of the Nouvlesse (an Engrish mangling of *Noblesse*), the wealthy, privileged elite of the GOTT universe who regard themselves as the last true humans in a galaxy of hybrids and mongrels. This ultimately leads to a full-on apocalypse as the fate of the Earth itself is threatened by a master race's master plan.

The Gonzo studio doesn't appear able to make anime that looks less than glorious; but here it faces what might be called the Ghibli problem—we have this fantastic technical ability, can we marry it to the same level of script and storytelling every time? *KG* is a thing of beauty, but not an earth-shaker, and the dark undertow of sensuality never quite comes good—or should that be bad? A manga spin-off also appeared in *Dragon Junior* magazine, and the end of the series led to its repurposing as three feature-length recaps, *KG Ignition, Maelstrom,* and *Truth Dawn* (all 2007). Keiji Goto's 24-episode TV series *Kiddy Girl-and* (2009) picks up the story 25 years later, with new heroines Ascoeur and Q-feuille.

KIDS' ANIME

Despite the breathless boasts of foreign pundits that anime is "not just kids' stuff," the bulk of the medium is still made for an audience of high school age or below. Fairy tales and folklore comprise most EARLY ANIME, with animals and children pressed into allegorical service in WARTIME ANIME.

In the years after World War II and before television ownership spread through urban Japan, movie theaters and comics were the major sources of children's entertainment outside the playground. Toei's PANDA AND THE MAGIC SERPENT premiered in 1958 and went on to win international honors a year later, marking an important step in the rehabilitation of Japanese culture in the eyes of the Western world. Of the six children's movies made by the studio in the next five years, five were also sold in the U.S.A. MAGIC BOY (1959), JOURNEY TO THE WEST (as *Alakazam the Great*, 1960), THE LITTLEST WARRIOR (1961), and LITTLE PRINCE AND THE EIGHT HEADED DRAGON (1963) drew on Chinese and Japanese sources, while 1962's SINDBAD THE SAILOR later inspired scriptwriter Osamu Tezuka to produce a children's TV series and a movie for adult audiences. WOOF WOOF 47 RONIN (1962), an anthropomorphic take on Japanese history, was unseen in the West, though rookie animator Hayao Miyazaki was to enjoy greater success overseas in later years. Interestingly, Miyazaki has claimed that he still believes that one movie a year is all the anime children should be allowed to watch, and that they

should spend the rest of the time reading, playing with friends, and having their own adventures out of doors. We're guessing that the single mandatory film, in his eyes, should be one by Studio Ghibli.

These three themes—local legend, foreign literature, and animal antics— became staples of the children's anime market as television gained dominance. JAPANESE FOLK TALES got their own TV series in 1975. Classic European stories were retold in the WORLD MASTERPIECE THEATER series, as well as in big and small screen adaptations from "Jonathan Swift's" GULLIVER'S SPACE TRAVELS (1965) to Agatha Christie's HERCULE POIROT AND MISS MARPLE (2004).

Anime has continued to use animals as mirrors for the human condition in three distinct subgenres, reflecting the changes in 20th century Japanese society: semirealistic stories of animal life and human interaction with other species, like 1981's TAOTAO THE PANDA or 1994's TICO OF THE SEVEN SEAS; anthropomorphic stories, often comedies such as SAMURAI PIZZA CATS (1990), in which animals reflect aspects of human behavior; and stories where animals provide companionship for an isolated child, like DOG OF FLANDERS (1975) or SECRET OF THE SEAL (1991).

The year 1963 also marked the first wave of science fiction in TV anime. After Tezuka's ASTRO BOY appeared on both Japanese and U.S. screens, the giant robot genre was born with Mitsuteru Yokoyama's GIGANTOR, while human-android hybrid 8TH MAN foreshadowed *The Six Million Dollar Man,* and *RoboCop,* as well as 1966's CYBORG 009. Anime did not buy into the team shows popular in live action until SKYERS 5 joined forces to fight evil in 1967. The show was revived in 1971, and a year later came perhaps the greatest of anime's contributions to the team show genre, BATTLE OF THE PLANETS. The show brought new levels of emotion and involvement to the rather simplistic monster-of-the-week formula established by live-action equivalents and generated such successors as SAINT SEIYA (1986) and RONIN WARRIORS (1989). Its influence persisted for more than a decade on shows such as GUNDAM *Wing* (1995's "boy band *Gundam*") and WEISS KREUZ (1998).

SCIENCE FICTION AND ROBOTS remain

popular themes for children's anime, but females were subsidiary characters in most of these tales; it was 1966 before TV had its first true heroine, LITTLE WITCH SALLY, whose *Bewitched*-inspired trip to Earth to live as an ordinary girl and study humans became a prototype for a long line of magical girls; her thematic descendants include SAILOR MOON. The following year, Osamu Tezuka produced his first TV series for girls, the romantic yet powerful PRINCESS KNIGHT, a veiled comment on the roles and aspirations of girls in modern Japan wrapped up in a classic story of hidden identity and adventure that would inspire shows from ROSE OF VERSAILLES (1979) to UTENA (1997).

All these exotic fantasies should not obscure the numerous anime made about the events of children's day-to-day lives. Ordinary girls like AKANE-CHAN relocated to new lives more often than little witches; in Akane's case, her family moved from the country to Tokyo in Toei's 1968 series, mirroring a huge shift in a country whose prewar population was largely rural to a modern world where most live in cities. Twenty years later, Hayao Miyazaki was to look back with love and longing at a country childhood like the one Akane left behind in his movie MY NEIGHBOR TOTORO.

WANDERING SUN looked at two teenagers longing for a singing career, like many of its young viewers, in 1971. Children thrilled to SPEED RACER (1967), STAR OF THE GIANTS (1968), and RED-BLOODED ELEVEN (1970), dreaming of sporting success while parked in front of the TV set, a pattern which was to grow more pronounced across the developed world in the next 20 years. Even when they outgrew the comical antics of animals and cute spacemen, viewers could enjoy the outrageous behavior of Machiko Hasegawa's NASTY OLD LADY (1970), who may have reminded them of their own granny or aunt at a time when extended families still lived together. The real world was also present in titles focusing on children's experiences of war. Often made as movies or video "specials" to commemorate anniversaries, these avoided awkward questions by recounting events from the standpoint of the truly innocent, as in BAREFOOT GEN (1983), but also acknowledged the struggles of the young and the tragic waste of their lives, as in Isao Takahata's powerful **GRAVE OF THE FIREFLIES** (1988).

Television acts as a mirror to everyday life, a babysitter, and a wish fulfillment mechanism, but all of these functions can also be afforded by movies. Television's two biggest selling points were cheapness and availability. Its status as the trusted visitor in the corner of the livingroom soon highlighted another function, one it filled far better than movies ever could; its ability to trade on pester power, to sell large amounts of merchandise to children.

The need to secure **ADVERTISING AND SPONSORSHIP**, and the likelihood it would be coming from toy companies, has eternally steered the priorities of anime production. So, too, have the relatively low demands of the juvenile audience. The plotlines of early television anime are less stories than paradigms, blueprints for success to be tweaked and remodeled every couple of seasons, ready to impress a new group of youngsters who have never seen such a show before. Advertising on popular shows commands high prices, and production companies began to insist on merchandising potential before they would sponsor a show, while popular toy lines like the **ZOIDS** (1999) and fashion doll **LICCA-CHAN** (1990) got their own TV shows and videos.

Home video brought the possibility of buying movies to be repeated endlessly, or time shifting so that youngsters with heavy school schedules need not miss their TV favorites. This move away from a programming schedule is accelerating in the new millennium as children in the developed world spend more time on personal delivery devices. Anime is being developed into bite-sized, attention grabbing segments that can be delivered cheaply on demand over a mobile phone. This reflects a social shift as massive as the one that moved Japan from a rural economy to an industrial and then a virtual one, or that which moved women out of the home and into the world of men. Its impact on children's anime will be enormous; no longer shared with family and friends, no longer delivered to set schedules, no longer requiring much investment of time or attention, but still, no doubt, an effective mechanism for selling to the young and impressionable.

In Japan as across the world in the latter half of the 20th century, adults began to hang on to childhood pleasures such as comics and trading cards. As **FANDOM** grew up and looked for an older version of their teatime and Saturday morning viewing, anime became a multigenerational medium, the origins of the "retro boom" in nostalgia shows since the 1980s. Regardless of the growth of the market for erotica, which remains negligible in size compared to children's shows, the themes which appealed to children in the early years of anime still predominate today, often in anime aimed at far older audiences—a fact lampooned in shows such as **NANAKA 6/17**. In deference to the old sci-fi truism that "the golden age of science fiction is 12," the Gainax producer Hiroki Sato has parsed the modern otaku customer base as "forever 14 years old," either *actually* being 14, or *choosing* to remember the golden years of their teens in shows that recall it, or being *arrested* at a stage of teenage development and continuing to obsess over teen issues long into adulthood. Nor does he regard the latter two market sectors as anything but benign, noting that with a declining population in Japan of actual 14-year-olds, the presence of the other sectors helps take up the shortfall.

KIDS ON THE SLOPE *

2012. JPN: *Sakamichi no Apollon*. AKA: *Apollo on the Hill*. TV series. DIR: Shinichiro Watanabe. SCR: Ayako Kato, Yuko Kakihara. DES: Nobuteru Yuki. ANI: Katsuya Yamada, Yoshimitsu Yamashita. MUS: Yoko Kanno. PRD: Mappa, Tezuka Pro, Dentsu, Fuji TV, SME, Toho. 24 mins. x 12 eps.

Mild-mannered intellectual Kaoru moves to his uncle's home in the port town of Sasebo on the southern island of Kyushu in 1966. There, he strikes up an unlikely friendship with the troubled, brawling teenager Sentaro (you know he's a fighter because his father is *American*). The oddly matched couple are united through their friendship with Ritsuko, whose father owns a record shop. Despite initial tension, the boys bond over music, with budding jazz drummer Sentaro inspiring the pianist Kaoru to set aside classical pieces in the face of something more modern.

This adaptation of Yuki Kodama's 2007 manga from *Flowers* magazine takes the original's girl-oriented love-polygons of **ROMANCE AND DRAMA** (everyone has an unrequited crush on everybody else, not just in the main cast but in several subsidiary triangles) and injects a powerful new audio component (**MUSIC IN ANIME**). As one might expect from collaborators whose previous successes have included **MACROSS PLUS** and **COWBOY BEBOP**, the music itself is a powerful part of this serial's overall effect, and the animation itself seems to focus much of its energies on faithfully recreating the *sight* of music as it is made. Like **FROM UP ON POPPY HILL**, its 1960s setting allows for consideration of generational change and adolescent pressures, not the least the threat presented to the cast's new-found love of jazz by the arrival in Japan of rock and roll. It also buries some meditations about race (Sentaro's *gaijin* genes, and jazz's black roots) as well as **RELIGION AND BELIEF**—both Sentaro and Ritsuko are Catholics, rare in Japan but more common in the south, which was the heartland of the religious conversions and persecutions of the samurai era.

Kids on the Slope is one of those anime whose very animated existence might arguably seem forced—one wonders why it was not put into production as a live-action TV drama, since every season on Japanese television seems to have some sort of similar show. Perhaps it is a matter of special effects: as with **SCIENCE FICTION AND ROBOTS**, the ability of animation to cover up who is really playing the instruments in any given shot permits a greater level of realism than if we were watching another bunch of witless, live-action idols miming. In particular, the use of digital animation allows for what appears to be an immense amount of real-world reference, making parts of the show seem less animated than shot live and then heavily treated (compare to **FLOWERS OF EVIL**). Perhaps it is a matter of setting, since animation finds it much easier to recreate the 1960s in exacting period detail. Or perhaps it is a matter of time-scale—most live-action shows in a similar vein are set up as *reunions* of adults, in which their original shared college years are implied but usually unseen. In that regard, *Kids on the Slope* forms the preamble to a later story that is only glimpsed in its final episode, in scenes set eight years later. ◐

KIGURUMIKKU V3 *

2009. Video. DIR: Hisashi Saito. SCR: Hisashi Saito. DES: Hisashi Saito, Michiko Morokuma. ANI: Hisashi Saito. MUS: Atsushi Hirasawa. PRD: AIC A.S.T.A., IC. 12 mins. x 3 eps.

Kigurumi is a mode of cosplay that involves dressing up as a giant plushie or doll. Three little girls who share the hobby gain the power to protect their peaceful little town when their cosplay outfits transform them into magical heroines: Kigurumikki-Swan, Kigurumikki-Swallow and Kiguru-mikki-Falcon. Created by Saito, who also directed **BAMBOO BLADE**, this is a parody of two genres in one: magical girls and hero teams. Random events, excruciatingly bad gags, and perverted cuteness abound.

KIHACHIRO KAWAMOTO FILM WORKS *

2002. JPN: *Kawamoto Kihachiro Sakuhin-shu*. Video. DIR: Kihachiro Kawamoto. SCR: Kihachiro Kawamoto. DES: Kihachiro Kawa-moto. ANI: Kihachiro Kawamoto, Takeichi Sugawa, Yasushi Araki. MUS: Akihiro Komori, Goro Yamaguchi, Seiji Tsurusawa. PRD: Echo Studio. 14 mins. (*Breaking Branches*), 8 mins. (*Anthropo-cynical Farce*), 8 mins. (*Demon*), 12 mins. (*Travel*), 4 mins. (*Travel—short version*), 19 mins. (*Poet's Life*), 19 mins. (*Dojoji*), 19 mins. (*House of Flame*), 1 min. (*Self-Portrait*), 25 mins. (*Shooting*), 22 mins. (*Briar Rose*).

A DVD compilation of stop-motion and pa-per-cut animation by Kihachiro Kawamoto, released with English subtitles in the Japanese market—although many of the works on the DVD require no subtitles at all, with the action and drama conveyed through sign language and emotive expressions. Kawamoto's work impressively bridges East and West, with some films relying heavily on the conventions of kabuki and noh—such as the stylized backgrounds and movements of *Breaking of Branches Is Forbidden* and *Demon*. His *Self-Portrait* is very short indeed and largely comprises a film loop of a plasticine Kawamoto alternately squashing and being squashed by a plasti-cine demon.

Breaking of Branches Is Forbidden (1968, *Hanaori*) features a classic set-up from Japanese drama, in which a young appren-tice, left to pray and contemplate blossoms in a temple precinct, is persuaded to let a drunken samurai and his squire into the garden. In scenes of earthy comedy, the apprentice steals alcohol from the drinkers by dipping his prayer beads into the bowl and wringing out the sake. In one moment, the apprentice's head is drawn to the smell of fresh sake poured by the samurai, the head drifting several paces ahead of the body in a set-up that owes more to the cartoonish deformations of Warner Bros. cartoons than puppetry.

Based on a story by Riichi Yoshimitsu, *Anthropo-cynical Farce* (1970) mixes paper cut-outs and stop motion for the tale of a betting man. It is not the only Kawa-moto animation to use paper cut-outs on the disc; once a major component of all Japanese animation in the days before cels, cut-out animation now finds its last repose in some of Kawamoto's other work, most notably *Travel* (1973, *Tabi*), which can be found in two versions on this DVD. Using a collage style most likely to evoke Monty Python in modern audiences, *Travel* seems rooted in Kawamoto's own experi-ences of foreign countries. Its protagonist, a Japanese girl, heads away from home and experiences a Europe that is both museum and inner monologue, until the arrival of tanks symbolizes the upheavals in Czechoslovakia that so shocked Kawamoto after his happy experiences there. The final message, however, reflects a burgeon-ing sense of Buddhist struggle that would become ever stronger in Kawamoto's work—here, it is the journey itself, not the destination, which makes the titular travel worthwhile.

In *Demon* (1972, *Oni*), two Japanese brothers go out hunting for deer, only to be attacked by a demon in the forests. They cut off its arm and report home to their mother, but discover that the old woman's arm has itself been cut off, in a Japanese fairy tale adapted from the *Kon-jaku Monogatari*—the same "Tales of Past and Present" collection that also supplied the inspiration for **NAUSICAÄ OF THE VALLEY OF THE WIND**. A similarly Japanese theme can be found in *Dojoji Temple* (1976, *Dojoji*), in which a young monk's love for a fair maiden is thwarted when she transforms into a sea monster, all told in a scrolling form with a watercolor background. Com-parable warnings about the fair sex can be found in *House of Flames* (1979, *Kataku*), in which the ghost of a young girl tells a fear-ful traveler about her torment in hell—having allowed two men to fight and die for her love, she suffers eternal agony for having given herself to neither of them.

Kawamoto's *A Poet's Life* (1974, *Shijin no Shogai*) is supposedly based on a story by Kobo Abe, although Kawamoto himself has suggested in interviews that its origins lie with his own experience of being fired from the Toho studio in his youth, shortly after the collapse of the production of **THE KING'S TAIL**. In it, a sleepy old woman factory worker accidentally weaves herself into the fabric of a jacket. When her son attempts to sell the jacket, old lady and all, he is fired and reduced to accosting his former workmates at the gate. Another strange career path can be found in *Shoot-ing Without Shooting* (1988, *Bushe zhi She*), made by Kawamoto as a Chinese copro-duction and set in an idealized ancient China, in which an expert archer seeks to learn from a master even better than his own, only to be told that he should put down his bow and shoot without shooting.

In *Briar Rose or the Sleeping Beauty* (1990, *Ibara-hime mata wa Nemuri-hime*) a princess in an unspecified European country is shocked to discover that a prophecy pre-dicts she will prick herself on a spindle and die, but that the action of good fairies has altered the curse so that she will merely fall asleep. Despite beginning like one of **GRIMM'S FAIRY TALES**, the story soon takes a new direction, when Briar Rose reads a secret diary, revealing that her mother the queen inadvertently broke a betrothal in order to marry her father the king. Wish-ing to break the curse, Briar Rose tracks down her mother's jilted lover, finding him living alone in the forest, bitterly lamenting that the queen did not wait for him when he went to fight in a war. Briar Rose offers herself in her mother's place, only to be abandoned in turn by the name-less old soldier once he has taken her vir-ginity. Back at the palace, she is bereaved by her mother's death and lives in a daze, leading some gossips to refer to her as the "Sleeping Beauty." Eventually, she agrees to a loveless marriage with a handsome prince, in a sinister retelling of the fairy tale that highlights its Freudian subtexts.

The *Film Works* DVD is not exhaus-tive—it does not, for example, include Kawamoto's feature-length puppet animations *Rennyo and His Mother* (1983, *Rennyo to Sono Haha*) and *The Book of the Dead* (2003, *Shisha no Sho*). But it is a vital part of any core collection of Japanese animation—it may be Japanese and animated, but it is often a world away from what the mainstream often conceives as "anime" (ARGOT AND JARGON).

KIKAIDER

2000. JPN: *Jinzo Ningen Kikaider*. AKA: *Android Kikaider*. TV series, video. DIR: Tensai Okamura. SCR: Akemi Omode, Shinsuke Ohashi, Masashi Sogo. DES: Naoyuki Konno. ANI: Naoyuki Konno. MUS: N/C. PRD: Radix, Studio OX, Kid's Station. 25 mins. x 13 eps. (TV), 4 eps. (v1), 25 mins. (v2).

When he is mortally wounded in an accident, Professor Koakishi is restored to life in an android body, believing that a good heart does not deserve to die before its time. But Koakishi's laboratory is attacked one stormy night by an unknown assailant. As his daughter Mitsuko escapes the flames, the whole incident is being watched by a young boy, Jiro, from a vantage point in the forest. Jiro is the last of Koakishi's creations, a robot created to save humankind, Mitsuko in particular. Fighting off the robot minions of the "dark professor" Gill, Jiro transforms into Kikaider, a superpowerful android ready to fight for good. One of CYBORG 009–creator Shotaro Ishinomori's most popular live-action creations, *Kikaider* was a relative latecomer to anime, not animated until after its creator's death. The box set of the DVD came with a 25-minute bonus episode, *Kikaider 01: The Boy with a Guitar* (*Guitar o Motta Shonen*, 2003), directed by Naoyuki Konno.

KIKI AND LARA ...

1989. JPN: *Kiki to Lara*. Video. DIR: Masami Hata. SCR: Mami Watanabe, Kenji Terada. DES: Yukio Abe. ANI: Maya Matsuyama. MUS: Takanori Arisawa. PRD: Sanrio. 30 mins. x 8 eps.

The HELLO KITTY team returns for another onslaught of stories based around Sanrio-themed merchandise, on this occasion featuring the loving twins Kiki and Lara. First appearing in a 1989 remake of Maeterlinck's BLUE BIRD, they got their own short-lived series of videos in the early 1990s. The children play house, chase after a Pegasus foal, decide they want to be princesses for a day, and try out some magical dance shoes. They also appeared in their own version of the *Hansel and Gretel* story from GRIMMS' FAIRY TALES.

KIKI'S DELIVERY SERVICE *

1989. JPN: *Majo no Takkyubin*. AKA: *Witch's Special Express Delivery*. Movie. DIR: Hayao Miyazaki. SCR: Hayao Miyazaki. DES: Katsuya Kondo. ANI: Shinji Otsuka, Yoshifumi Kondo. MUS: Joe Hisaishi. PRD: Studio Ghibli. 102 mins.

Thirteen-year-old Kiki decides to follow in her mother's footsteps and become a witch, meaning she has to fly away from home and live for a year in a strange town. Accompanied only by her irascible black cat, Jiji, she heads for the seaside and finds the bustling harbor town of Koriko without its own witch. Finding a room at a kindly baker's, she discovers that her ability to fly on a broomstick is a marketable skill and begins delivering packages and messages. Despite minor mishaps and an often-ungrateful clientele, the freelance witch wins hearts all over town, particularly that of would-be pilot Tombo (a forerunner for the lead of THE WIND RISES), who is smitten with her. A crisis of confidence causes Kiki to lose her ability to fly, but she regains it in time to save Tombo, who is trapped on a runaway airship. Writing to her mother, Kiki proudly calls Koriko her home.

Like MY NEIGHBOR TOTORO, *Kiki* is a world without definable enemies or evil—prissy rich girls may sulk when they get a fish pie for their birthday, but it's hardly an offense, and the only crime the police investigate in the course of the film is a fake one (Tombo pretends he has been robbed). Everyone creates value in their own ways, from the silent baker who melts Kiki's heart with a witch-themed bread sculpture, to the kindly old dog who protects Jiji from a bratty child. Venerable oldsters sigh about how times have changed, but the young generation shouldn't cause them to despair—like Kiki and her artist friend Ursula, they are simply finding their way in their own lives and times.

Miyazaki's follow-up to *Totoro* leaves childhood behind and steps into the early teens in one of the most wonderful films ever made about growing up. Set in a neverwhere Europe that combines the look of Stockholm and Visby (where Miyazaki had been location hunting for the canceled 1971 Tokyo Movie Shinsha anime *Pippi Longstocking*) with the light of the Mediterranean, this utterly charming story is based on a book by Eiko Kadono, who also wrote the less well-known CHOBI THE CUTE LITTLE CAT. The original *Kiki* novel lacked both the crisis of faith and the airborne resolution, which were added for the screen adaptation, initially against the author's wishes. Miyazaki films his witch with the same love of flight that characterizes NAUSICAÄ, with views and perspectives impossible from the ground. He imbues her with the independent spirit of Fio from PORCO ROSSO but does not shy from having a heroine who can catch cold, feel sorry for herself, and worry about her food budget. The result is arguably one of his best films, the seventh highest-grossing animated film at the Japanese box office, and a character who deserves to be the patron saint of freelancers, students, and motorcycle messengers.

Picked up by Buena Vista for U.S. distribution but not given a theatrical release, *Kiki* became one of the best-selling anime videos in America, trouncing AKIRA with sales topping a million. The U.S. dub featured Kirsten Dunst, Janeane Garofalo, and Phil Hartman freely improvising as Jiji in one of his last film roles. An earlier English dub, prepared by Carl Macek's Streamline Pictures for in-flight screenings on JAL trans-Pacific flights, was included on the Japanese LaserDisc but never released in the U.S. The original title was pastiched in the live-action Japanese bicycle courier movie *Messengers* (2001), which went by the suspiciously similar name of *Majo no Sokutei*, or *Witch's Courier Service*, in its home country. A live-action movie adaptation of the original book of *Kiki*, with a script from Jeff Stockwell, was rumored to be forthcoming from Walt Disney Pictures, although nothing appears to have come of this. Instead, a Japanese live-action adaptation was announced in 2013, pointedly based on the first *two* books in the six-volume series, rather than related in any direct way with the anime.

KIKO-CHAN'S SMILE

1996. JPN: *Kiko-chan Smile*. TV series. DIR:

Setsuko Shibuichi. scr: Tsubasa Yoshiura. des: Yukari Kobayashi. ani: Yukari Kobayashi. mus: So-Fi. prd: Magic Bus, TBS. 7 mins. x 51 eps.

In this adaptation of Tsubasa Yoshiura's comedy manga, a sullen, cynical child is born to a pair of lovestruck parents who truly adore each other. Arch comments on the folly of adulthood, in what some might describe as a junior version of *Daria*. Two episodes of *Kiko* bracketed a single episode featuring her pet cat and his feline friends, who develop the power of speech in their own shows, but become mute once more for Kiko's.

KIKU AND THE WOLF

2008. jpn: *Kiku-chan to Okami*. TV Special. dir: Tetsuo Yasumi. scr: Tetsuo Yasumi. des: Junichi Seki (aka Shuichi Seki), Minoru Nishida. ani: Masae Otake. mus: Masae Sagara. prd: Shin-Ei Animation. 45 mins.

It's wartime in Manchuria, and the defeated Japanese occupiers are forced to flee. When the bombers come, little Kiku's family and their neighbors have no option but to trek through the woods and mountains. Kiku falls ill and is left behind, but she finds the strangest of allies—one prepared to risk everything to help her, against all reason. This animation of a short story by Akiyuki Nosaka, creator of THE BOY AND THE SEA TURTLE and GRAVE OF THE FIREFLIES, was originally screened in Japan on August 15, 2008, the 63rd anniversary of the surrender of Japan to the Allies. Compare to RAIL OF THE STAR.

KIKUCHI, MICHITAKA

1963–. Born in Iwate Prefecture, Kikuchi graduated from Tokyo Design College and first worked in animation as a concept artist on one of the later seasons of LUPIN III. His subsequent animation credits included some of the "magical girl" output of Studio Pierrot, sketch work on FIST OF THE NORTH STAR, and character designs on ZEOR-YMER HADES PROJECT. However, Kikuchi is far better known by his manga creator pseudonym "Kia Asamiya," in which role he is credited with the original stories for many popular franchises, including SILENT MÖBIUS, NADESICO, and STEAM DETECTIVES. He is the founder of the design outfit Studio Tron.

KILL BILL: THE ORIGIN OF O-REN *

2003. Movie. dir: Kazuto Nakazawa, Toshihiko Nishikubo. scr: Quentin Tarantino. des: Sho-u Tajima, Katsuhito Ishii. ani: Yasunori Miyazawa, Mitsuo Iso, Hideki Takahashi, Eiji Ishimoto, Naoyuki Onda, Mahiro Maeda. mus: Luis Enrique Bacalov. prd: Production I.G. 8 mins.

At nine years of age, O-Ren Ishii cowers unseen beneath the bed while mobsters attack her parents. Her father, a U.S. army officer of Asian descent, kills two of them but is mortally wounded by a third. Her mother is thrown onto the bed and stabbed by Boss Matsumoto, a ruthless yakuza. Two years later, O-Ren capitalizes on Matsumoto's love of little girls by seducing him in a school uniform and murdering him in bed. Before long, she is one of the world's top assassins, although she makes a fatal mistake when she and some of her fellow killers leave a former associate, "The Bride," comatose but still alive.

Although not a film in itself, this brief sequence appears as part of Quentin Tarantino's *Kill Bill: Volume One*. Tarantino's movie is a pastiche of Asian pulp genres and his anime sequence is no exception, conceived in apparent homage to the ultraviolence of GOLGO 13 and Madhouse urban gothic like WICKED CITY. Its influences are thus restricted largely to a handful of exploitationers released in the 1980s, when Tarantino presumably caught the beginnings of the U.S. anime video business: eviscerations, stabbings, and all, while any similarity to the original story of TheGokusen is purely coincidental. The use of animation to present this particular part of the film may have also been a cunning ruse to avoid an NC-17 rating for the most controversial scenes—if he had used real actors for this sequence, would Tarantino have been able to show a preteen assassin murdering the pedophile who has just raped her? Nevertheless, the anime sequence was still slightly censored for its American release. In the uncut Japanese DVD release, O-Ren does not merely stab Matsumoto, but draws the knife lengthwise up his torso in graphic detail.

There are moments when *The Origin of O-Ren* seems to quote tropes and ideas from manga rather than anime—the spattering blood is inky rather than bloody, and in one notable moment O-Ren has

the word "whimper" literally issue from her mouth like a manga sound effect. Production I.G, which must have come to this job shortly after completing BLOOD: THE LAST VAMPIRE, puts a heroic amount of effort into replicating cel animation battles with early 21st century technology—the sequence is largely motion-captured and then treated to look as if it were made in the old-fashioned way. Along with THE ANIMATRIX and the works of Hayao Miyazaki, this piece of footage was one of the anime most likely to reach a mainstream audience in the early 21st-century, although considering its origins in the writer's *idea* of what anime should be and its dated adherence to video-nasty shock tactics, some might prefer to file it among the FALSE FRIENDS. ⓁⓃⓋ

KILL LA KILL *

2013. TV series. dir: Hiroyuki Imanishi, Hisatoshi Shimizu. scr: Kazuki Nakashima, Hiromi Wakabayashi, Hiroshi Seko. des: Sushio. ani: Sushio, Shota Iwasaki, Masaru Sakamoto, Mai Yoneyama. mus: Hiroyuki Sawano. prd: Trigger, Aniplex, Dentsu, Lucent, MBS, Movic, Ultra Super Pictures. 25 mins x 24 eps. (TV) 25 mins. (v).

Ryuko Matoi comes to Honnoji Academy in search of the woman who killed her father, imparting a degree of samurai vendetta to this over-the-top school-fighting drama. Honnoji takes the posturings and pretentions of high-school life to ludicrous lengths, with sentient school uniforms made from mystical "Life Fibers" that can impart super powers to their wearers, at a vampiric price. Ryuko, meanwhile, lugs around a weapon shaped like one half of a giant pair of scissors—her father's last and greatest invention, the other half of which she believes to be in the possession of his murderer.

Unlike so many other anime, *Kill La Kill* does not rest happily on whatever laurels it can rustle up in its first episode. Although on the surface it seems assembled from a standard bucket of familiar anime clichés, it's made with real heart, and a love of those same traditions. Escalating its conflict in exponential levels of mayhem and danger, its latter half transforms into a battle for supremacy of the Earth itself in the face of alien invasion, with revelations galore about the characters' pasts, switching sides and changing allegiances, and a final battle that stretches across five explosive episodes. From the people who brought you **GURREN LAGANN**. An unaired 25th episode was bundled with the video release and previewed in selected cinemas in 2014. **NV**

KILLIFISH SCHOOL

2001. JPN: *Medaka no Gakko*. Video. DIR: Hiroyuki Takagi, Ryoji Fujiwara. SCR: Miho Maruo. DES: Yukie Mori. ANI: Kiyotaka Ki-yoyama. MUS: N/C. PRD: Office Ao. 30 mins. x 1 ep. and 10 mins. x 4 eps.

Japanese teenage girl Medaka transfers to a new school, where her homeroom teacher, Mr. Tanaka, has a fish for a head. This series is based on the surreal four-panel strip in *Ribon* magazine by Yukie Mori and supposedly sold exclusively through the Internet (though since you could also phone, you'd be forgiven for just calling it mail order).

KILLING STONE

1968. JPN: *Sessho Seki: Kyubi no Kitsune to Tobimaru*. AKA: *The Nine-Tailed Flying Fox*. Movie. DIR: Shinichi Yagi. SCR: Michio Yoshioka, Hideo Suzuki, Yasuzo Masumura. DES: Isamu Kageyama. ANI: Makoto Nagasawa. MUS: Shigeru Ikeno. PRD: Nihon Doga. 81 mins.

In Heian-period Japan, a beautiful 17-year-old girl named Tamamo comes to Kyoto and quickly attracts the attention of many powerful political figures, including high-ranking Minister Tadanaga. They don't know that she is really a fox spirit, mischievous and malicious. She seduces the emperor and causes havoc, and when she is finally umasked and killed she transforms into a poisonous stone. The Kido Okamoto novel that inspired this film, *Tamamo no Mae*, was such a favorite with producer Gentaro Nakajima, one of the founding members of Daiei, that he wanted to make a live-action version, starring one of Daiei's most beautiful stars, former Miss Japan Fujiko Yamamoto. It never happened, and Nakajima went on to become Japan's Minister of Education. Others on the crew stayed with anime—Masami Hata, who would direct **STITCH!** for Disney Japan 40 years later, and **WORLD MASTERPIECE THEATER**–regular Shuichi Seki were among the key animators on the project.

KIMAGURE ORANGE ROAD *

1987. AKA: *Orange Road Follies*. TV series, movie, video. DIR: Osamu Kobayashi, Kazuhiko Kobayashi, Hiroyuki Yokoyama, Kazuhiko Ikegami. SCR: Kenji Terada, Sukehiro Tomita, Yukiyoshi Ohashi. DES: Akemi Takada. ANI: Masako Goto, Toyomi Sugiyama. MUS: Shiro Sagisu. PRD: Studio Pierrot, Nippon TV. 26 mins. (pilot), 25 mins. x 48 eps. (TV), 40 mins. (special), 25 mins. x 8 eps. (v), 34 mins. (music), 69 mins. (m1), 94 mins. (m2).

Kyosuke Kasuga falls for the pretty Madoka when her hat blows away in the wind, but the attractive, musically minded girl often seems aloof. To complicate matters, Madoka's bubbly friend Hikaru has fallen for Kyosuke, and although he likes her as a friend, he truly has eyes only for Madoka. Meanwhile, the junior champion of the karate club, who wants Hikaru for himself, is mad at Kyosuke, while Kyosuke's irritating sisters do everything within their power to make him realize that Hikaru is the girl for him.

A standard anime love polygon is exacerbated by a superfluous subplot revealing that Kyosuke and the rest of his family have psychic powers. Here, then, is the reason that Kyosuke is an eternal transfer student, as his family tries to outrun public suspicion. Terminally underused in many episodes, these optional extras merely allow for some easy getaways from difficult situations, though they are more often likely to backfire, like **DORAEMON**'s inventions, and get him into still greater trouble. They also provide occasions for comedies of manners and social observations, such as Kyosuke's mind-reading cousin, who periodically blurts out people's secret inner thoughts for comedic effect.

KOR began as a manga in *Shonen Jump* by Izumi Matsumoto, its 1983 premiere imbuing the entire series with a deep sense of 1980s nostalgia by the time it reached foreign audiences. Its TV run was contemporary with **MAISON IKKOKU**, another drama-comedy about unsuitable friends becoming unexpected lovers, both made for the **URUSEI YATSURA** viewing audience as it aged and found comedy less exciting than romance. Retained in the anime version is a plethora of 1980s cultural references, chiefly musical, but also extending

to films of the moment such as *Top Gun*.

In 1988, the manga was jettisoned by its publisher and ended early in *Shonen Jump*, though the anime continued straight to video for several more episodes. Studiously tiptoeing around the TV series continuity, the videos packed the characters off for stand-alone episodes including a trip to Hawaii and a winter skiing trip in the Japanese Alps. The uneven TV series, which often flitted from romance to comedy to sci-fi pranks, was compartmentalized into several "specials" designed to bury the lackluster episodes and polish the undeniable jewels in each genre. A 34-minute music video, *KOR: Music Version*, comprised 12 tunes from the series played over a clip-show of best scenes. The story proper ended with the movie *KOR: I Want to Return to That Day* (1988). Directed by Tomomi Mochizuki and told chiefly in flashback, it discards all thought of comedy or psychic powers and concentrates instead on Kyosuke making a tough decision and breaking Hikaru's heart. Compare this to the coy attitudes of its spiritual successor **TENCHI MUYO!**, which remains permanently undecided in order to save everyone's focus-group feelings. Several more video episodes limped along afterward, two misleadingly premiered in theaters for those fans who couldn't accept that there would be no more—*KOR: Shapeshifting Akane, KOR: I Am a Cat/I Am a Fish*, and *KOR: Heart on Fire/Love Stage*. *KOR*, however, found a new lease on life in the U.S., where it was one of the cornerstones of early overseas video anime **FANDOM**, many members of which were of an age to savor the 1980s nostalgia. It remained a fan favorite in Japan, too, and eventually returned for a second ending in *New KOR: Summer's Beginning* (1996), directed by Kunihiko Yuyama. This version flings the 19-year-old Kyosuke three years into the future, where his newly graduated adult self is a cameraman in Bosnia. With his relationship with Madoka in trouble, and the return of Hikaru, the final *KOR* film presents an opportunity for everyone to live happily ever after—and for the viewers to say a final farewell by seeing their characters do the same, in much the same way as the final **PATLABOR** send-off.

KOR was preceded by a pilot episode, which was refashioned into a regular episode, and which was then released on laserdisc as *KOR: Weekly Shonen Jump Video*. A 40-minute "*Tanabata Special*" seems to also have been made in 1987, but we have little information about it.

KIMBA THE WHITE LION *

1965. JPN: *Jungle Taitei*. AKA: *Jungle Emperor*. TV series, movie. DIR: Eiichi Yamamoto, Junji Nagashima, Toshio Hirata, Chikao Katsui, Hideaki Kitano. SCR: Masaki Tsuji, Shunichi Yukimuro, Eiichi Yamamoto. DES: Osamu Tezuka. ANI: Chikao Katsui, Hiroshi Saito. MUS: Isao Tomita. PRD: Mushi Pro, Tezuka Pro, Fuji TV. 25 mins. x 52 eps. (TV1), 75 mins. (m1), 25 mins. x 26 eps. (TV2), 25 mins. x 52 eps. (TV3), 98 mins. (m2).

Panja (Caesar), the white lion king of the jungle, is killed by the human hunter Hamegg (Viper Snakely), who captures his mate Eliza (Snowene) alive. Caged on a ship en route to an overseas zoo, Eliza gives birth to their son Leo (Kimba), who escapes by jumping overboard. Eventually returning to the jungle, Leo befriends Mandy (Dan'l Baboon), a wise mandrill counselor, Coco (Pauley Cracker) the parrot, and Tommy (Bucky) the chronically shy deer. They revere him as Panja II, and Leo resolves to keep the jungle forever peaceful by ridding it of Bubu (Claw), his evil, scarred lion adversary, and bumbling hyena minions.

Paid for in part with money from the American company NBC Enterprises (not, as many Japanese sources claim, the NBC *network*), *Kimba* was made with the demands of the foreign market in mind. Hence, **ASTRO BOY**–creator Tezuka was forced to make the story in bite-sized chunks that could be screened out of order without overreaching story arcs. This restriction has severely damaged **DRAGON BALL** and certain other more recent anime that are often shown in a jumbled order by TV channels who can't count. On the bonus side, foreign money secured a high enough budget to leave monochrome behind, and *Kimba* became the first full-color anime TV series. Several episodes were cut together to make the movie *Jungle Emperor* (1966, *Jungle Taitei*), which was nominated for a Golden Lion for animation at the Venice Film Festival. The name Leo was regarded as unacceptable in the American market, where it

was the name of the famous MGM lion; instead, the translators originally intended to name their hero *Simba*, Swahili for "lion." However, this was also rejected on account of a number of African-American trademark applications using the Simba name, which the producers could not be bothered to sort through in search of loopholes and potential infringements. The coincidence would return to haunt the franchise in the 1990s.

Tezuka's original 1950 manga *Jungle Emperor*, serialized in *Manga Shonen*, took the story of Leo much further along, with the white lion growing up, siring his own heir, and eventually laying down his life to save his realm. However, the concept of characters aging was another casualty of the stand-alone episode structure, and the anime Kimba remained permanently a cub. Tezuka redressed this balance with *New Jungle Emperor: Onward, Leo!* (1966, *Shin Jungle Taitei, Susumu Leo!*), a second series that took Leo to adulthood, which was initially intended solely for the Japanese audience. *Onward, Leo!* featured character designs from a young Rintaro and an involving subplot about Mount Moon and a fabled gem—a plot that would later be ripped off for episode 6 of **POKÉMON**. The adult Kimba/Leo was popular enough to become the mascot of the Seibu Lions baseball team in Japan (see **GO FOR IT, TABUCHI!**), and eventually made it to the States on the Christian Broadcasting Network under the title *Leo the Lion* (1984). By that time, however, Tezuka's studio Mushi Production had filed for bankruptcy, and a litigation tangle had taken the original *Kimba* series off the air.

The series was remade by Tezuka Productions as *New Adventures of Kimba the White Lion* (1989, *Shinsaku Jungle Taitei*), directed by Takashi Ui, taking Leo from his birth up to the moment when he brings some semblance of order to the jungle. This version was also eventually released in the U.S., but not until after an unexpected brush with controversy in the mid-1990s.

The series had slowly faded from public perception until the release of Disney's *The Lion King* (1994), the tale of a lion called Simba, whose father dies, who just can't wait to be king, who has a mandrill for a counselor, an argumentative parrot-like bird (a hornbill) for a friend, and an

evil, scarred lion adversary (plus bumbling hyena minions). Like Kimba, Disney's Simba is also haunted by his father's face in the clouds, a fact lampooned in an episode of *The Simpsons*, when the ghostly apparition of Disney's Mufasa appears to Lisa and mixes up the Simba-Kimba names. Disney representatives made the unlikely assertion that the *entire* production staff of *The Lion King* was unaware of the Tezuka original (including codirector Roger Allers, who, by Disney's own admission, had spent *two years* in Tokyo working on **LITTLE NEMO: ADVENTURES IN SLUMBERLAND**). The controversy was given further fuel when Fumio Suzuki, a creditor who claimed partial ownership of the original 1965 series, authorized the rerelease of eight episodes on video as *Kimba the Lion Prince* (1996), with a new dub that seemed deliberately calculated to imply further, previously nonexistent parallels with the Disney production.

Ironically, the controversy over the Disney film may have pushed Tezuka Productions into making yet another version of its own work, the movie *Kimba the White Lion* (1997, AKA, much to the annoyance of encyclopedia compilers, *Jungle Emperor Leo*), released just a little too late to warrant the filmmakers' claims that it was in honor of the original's 30th anniversary. This time directed by Toshio Takeuchi and with character designs by Akio Sugino, the big-budget *Kimba* anime is the last incarnation of the series to date. Disney would inadvertently antagonize the anime audience again with *Atlantis: The Lost Empire* (2001)—see **SECRET OF BLUE WATER**.

KIMERA *

1996. JPN: *Ki-Me-Ra*. Video. DIR: Kazu Yokota. SCR: Kenichi Kanemaki. DES: Kazuma Kodaka. ANI: N/C. MUS: Shiro Sagisu. PRD: Toho. 48 mins.

Legends about vampires and vampirism are finally explained, as strange "lifepods" from space crash in the Western mountains. Their occupants are alien creatures who need humanity to help them propagate their species. A war begins between the space-vampires and their earthly prey, but Terran boy Osamu begins to have feelings for the androgynous Kimera, the vampire sent to kill him. An erotic thriller, based on a manga by Kazuma Kodaka, creator of KIZUNA, not to be confused with CHIMERA. **NV**

KIMIHAGU

2009. Video. DIR: Jiro Nakano. SCR: Shigeto Sunaga. DES:. ANI: Shiro Shibata. MUS: N/C. PRD: MS Pictures, Milky, Frontwing. 29 mins. x 2 eps.

Emily Yuki is the school principal's bossy daughter. When she becomes president of the disciplinary committee she decides to ban all romantic activity on school premises. So the Love Club—interested in all forms of romantic behavior—has to meet in secret in the basement of the school church. When Emily learns she's been defied, she decides to take action, but she doesn't expect the reaction she gets. We, however, could have warned her what would happen, because this anime is based on a porn game by Frontwing, so the outcome is lots of sex between five hot girls and the blank cipher protagonist. **N**

KIMIKISS: PURE ROUGE *

2007. TV series, video. DIR: Kenichi Kasai. SCR: Michihiro Tsuchiya, Michiko Ito. DES: Kazunori Iwakura, Shichiro Kobayashi. ANI: Tsuyoshi Kawada, Masaru Hyodo, Tomoyuki Shitaya. MUS: Hikaru Nanase, Masaru Yokoyama, Noriyuki Iwadare. PRD: JC Staff, Bandai Visual, Enterbrain, Hakuhodo DY Media Partners. 25 mins. x 24 eps. (TV), 25 mins. (V).

Mao has been living in France for several years with her parents, but now they've sent her home alone for her senior year in high school. She moves in with the family of her childhood friend Koichi. He and their other childhood friend Kazuki attend Mao's new school and the three agree to help each other deal with the problems of life, love, and high school (ROMANCE AND DRAMA).

The original (2006) dating sim game by Enterbrain had Koichi as the sole hero. Thankfully, perhaps because the producers realized that a dating show with only one guy gets tedious very fast, the anime splits him into two characters and throws in another major male player, creating a geometric tangle of love possibilities. But this doesn't actually add much depth to the plot. The cookie-cutter characters get into cookie-cutter situations, and unless you're addicted to the game, or to high

school romance in general, there isn't much to hold your attention. The animation is fairly basic, and a high point of the plot is a love story between two of the characters' plushies. The ninth DVD release carried a bonus video from the same team, listed in many sources as episode 25. There are also five different manga and a light-novel series.

KING ARTHUR AND THE KNIGHTS OF THE ROUND TABLE *

1979. JPN: Entaku no Kishi Monogatari Moero Arthur. AKA: Rage of Arthur; Tales of the Knights of the Round Table. TV series. DIR: Masayuki Akehi, Tomoharu Katsumata, Masamune Ochiai, Kazumi Fukushima, Teppei Matsuura, Shigeru Omachi. SCR: Mitsuru Majima, Akira Nakano, Tsunehisa Ito. DES: Takuo Noda. ANI: Takuo Noda, Yasuhiko Suzuki, Seiji Kikuchi. MUS: Shinichi Tanabe, Shunsuke Kikuchi. PRD: Toei, Fuji TV. 25 mins. x 30 eps. (TV1), 25 mins. x 22 eps. (TV2).

When his parents are killed by the evil King Lavic, the three-year-old Arthur is spirited away from Camelot castle by the sorcerer Merlin. Becoming a squire to Sir Ector, at the age of 15 he is able to pull the sword Excalibur from a stone, thus becoming the rightful ruler of the Britons.

A lackluster series that manages to make Arthurian legend look like just another cartoon, it compares unfavorably with anime such as ESCAFLOWNE that can make cartoons look like Arthurian legend. Based on Thomas Malory's Morte D'Arthur, but only indirectly, through a manga adaptation by GARAGA-creator Satomi Mikuriya, it was serialized in several children's publications, including Terebiland and Terebi magazine. The second series, Prince on a White Horse (1980, Moero Arthur Hakuba no Oji), sinks almost completely into anime cliché, dumping earlier talk of Lancelot, Morgan le Fay, and a Leiji Matsumoto–influenced Lady of the Lake. Instead, it seems to confuse legends of King Arthur with legends of King Alfred and a heavy dose of 1970s pulp fantasy, pitting the prince against an invasion of flying Norse longships crewed by the "Zaikings." Accompanied by a young boy with the suitably Old English name of Pete, Arthur must travel undercover, find some secret treasure, and defeat the evil Baron

Damiane. In the final episodes, the story reintroduces the Knights of the Round Table and Princess Guinevere, but not before Arthur has met some mermaids, fought off some pirates, and had an encounter with a snow princess straight out of JAPANESE FOLK TALES.

Some of the more recognizable episodes were released in a U.S. dub in the 1980s by Family Home Entertainment in a version that provides additional unintentional hilarity as voice actors attempt English accents with varying degrees of failure. Further dolorous strokes were dealt to British heritage in MARINA THE MANGA ARTIST GOES TO CAMELOT.

KING FANG

1978. JPN: Oyukiyama no Yusha Ha-o. AKA: King Fang, Hero of Snowy Mountain. TV special. DIR: Eiji Okabe. SCR: Ryuzo Nakanishi. DES: Takao Kasai. ANI: Susumu Shiraume. MUS: Ryusuke Onosaki. PRD: Nippon Animation, Fuji TV. 75 mins.

A European wolf and a Sakhalin dog sire five puppies in the wild north of Japan. One day, the canine family is attacked by Gon, the man-eating bear, and the mother is killed. One of the puppies is found by a human girl under a waterfall. She adopts him and names him Taki (Japanese for waterfall), rearing him as a domesticated dog. However, as in CALL OF THE WILD, doubtlessly the inspiration for the Tatsuo Edogawa novel on which this anime is based, Taki's true nature eventually comes out, and he heads for the mountains to return to his own kind. Compare with SILVER FANG.

KING KONG SHOW, THE *

1966. JPN: Sekai no Osha King Kong Daikai. AKA: King Kong Ruler of the World. TV special, TV series. DIR: Hiroshi Ikeda. SCR: Noboshiro Ueno (trans.). DES: Jack Davis, Rod Willis. ANI: Sakei Kitamasa, Tsutomu Shibayama, Osamu Kobayashi, Midori Kusube, Yasuo Maeda, Norio Fukuda. MUS: Asei Kobayashi. PRD: Toei, Videocraft, Rankin/Bass, NET. 56 mins. (TVm), 8 mins. x 52 eps. (TV), 56 mins. (TVm), 8 mins. x 52 eps. (TV).

King Kong is a giant ape who lives on an island in the Java Sea. Bobby Bond, whose father is a professor studying the island, meets King Kong and befriends him. Bond father and son cooperate to protect King Kong from the evil Dr. Who, although the large creature can more than hold his own in a fight.

Commissioned by Rankin/Bass (Videocraft) from Toei in Japan, *King Kong* was the first cel-based anime to be made specifically for the American market. Though Toei was funding part of it themselves and eventually showed it in Japan, the designs, scripts, storyboards, and voice track were all supplied ready-made from the U.S. As with the American version, episodes of *KK* bookended a single episode of TOM OF T.H.U.M.B. to comprise a half-hour show.

KING OF BANDIT JING *

2002. JPN: *O Dorobo Jing.* AKA: *Bandit King Jing.* TV series, video. DIR: Hiroshi Watanabe. SCR: Reiko Yoshida, Chinatsu Hojo. DES: Mariko Oka. ANI: Mariko Oka, Studio Deen. MUS: Fumiko Harada, Scudelia Electro. PRD: Aniplex. 23 mins. x 13 eps. (TV), 27 mins. x 3 eps. (v).

Jing looks like an ordinary kid, but in fact he's a master thief. He and his lecherous bird partner, Kir, can steal anything, whatever security measures are taken. And if Jing ever finds himself in a tight spot, Kir can bond with his arm to form a supergun.Yuichi Kumakura's manga was animated for TV to show some of Jing's criminal triumphs, resulting in a series of capers like a kiddified LUPIN III, with just a touch of a SLAYERS-style cynic's attitude toward the genre. Nowhere is this more apparent than in the opening sequence, when the camera focuses on a lone figure, only be told it's got the wrong guy. Just as with Jing's antecedents in anime and manga, the masterthief is soon stealing more than just trinkets; he rescues a girl from a slave market and becomes embroiled in a search for perfect paint colors. Later episodes take a leaf from the YOUNG KINDAICHI FILES, stretching across two- and three-part story arcs. One focuses on a collection of astrologically themed gems that is almost complete and only requires Jing to acquire the Sun- and Moon-stones. The final sequence finds Jing forced to endure gladiatorial combat in an arena, where, like all masterthieves before him, he hopes to win the love of a noble beauty. A three-part video sequel, *King of Bandit Jing in Seventh Heaven,* followed in 2004,

again directed by Watanabe with design and animation by Oka. Jing and Kir get into Seventh Heaven, the most notorious and most ironicallynamed prison in the world, to try and steal the Dream Orb from convict Campari.

KING OF BOOBS 48

2010. JPN: *Oppai no Oja 48.* Video. DIR: Ken Raika. SCR: N/C. DES: N/C. ANI: N/C. MUS: Aruhito Chichisan, PaPa's Pleasure, Lisa Tutti. PRD: T-Rex, MS Pictures (Milky). 30 mins. x 2 eps.

Once upon a time there was a boy who loved to look at picture books about big-breasted ladies. Then one day he received a letter with a bunch of tickets, each showing a woman's breasts on the reverse. He's clueless until a sexy girl suddenly materializes and explains to him that he's been invited to take part in a game. The challenge is to find all the owners of those breasts. Then, naturally, he has sex with all of them. You may or may not be relieved to hear that "48" is just part of the title and not a series number. **N**

KING OF THORN *

2009. JPN: *Ibara no O.* Movie. DIR: Kazuyoshi Katayama. SCR: Kazuyoshi Katayama, Hiroshi Yamaguchi. DES: Hidenori Matsubara, Goki Nakamura. ANI: Naoyuki Onda. MUS: Toshihiko Sahashi. PRD: Sunrise, Bandai Visual, Dentsu, Enterbrain, Kadokawa, Sony PCL, TV Tokyo. 120 mins.

A hundred and sixty people awake from suspended animation in a remote Scottish castle, to a world very different from the one they remember. They went into cryosleep to try and ensure humanity would survive the deadly Medusa virus; they wake to find themselves under attack from strange creatures, not knowing whether or not they are the last remnants of human civilization. Japanese teenager Kazumi Ishiki, separated from her beloved twin sister Shizuku, is determined to find out what happened while she was sleeping. But unless she and her fellow survivors can band together and fight, their world will end within these walls.

Yuji Iwahara's original manga began running in *Monthly Comic Beam* in 2002—a rather mature venue for the story, and a commencement date that seems to owe something to the previous year's

September 11 terrorist attacks. Compare the opening scene of this film with the opening scene of M. Night Shyamalan's *The Happening,* and you may see a similar sense of a world about to change, and to change for the worse, as well as the sense of an international coalition, struggling to deal with a worldwide disaster like an ideological plague.

Yuji Iwahara's manga was successful and profitable, though not a runaway hit. Creator Iwahara was already working on characters for the sequel to Studio Bones' DARKER THAN BLACK anime series when the anime of his own work was announced, so he wasn't involved. Instead, director Katayama cowrote the script with Yamaguchi, reframing the manga within the *Sleeping Beauty* story (see also GODANNAR and KIHACHIRO KAWAMOTO FILM WORKS). The crossovers with Greek RELIGION AND BELIEF in the Medusa myth, European FANTASY AND FAIRY TALES with *Sleeping Beauty* and Hollywood mythology in the visual references to *Alien* offer promising territory, and the story is packed with ideas. Katayama and Yamaguchi also cut one of the manga's leading characters down to cameo size. A climactic twist ending picks up on clues seeded early in the story and resolves them in a way you may not expect. The weakest area of the movie is the interface between CGI and traditional animation, but the atmospheric design, well-paced action, and sharp writing more than make up for this. *King of Thorn* deserved to be more successful that it was. **NV**

KING'S TAIL, THE

1949. JPN: *Osama no Shippo.* Movie. DIR: Mitsuyo Seo. SCR: Taro Iwasaki, Mitsuyo Seo. DES: Mitsuyo Seo. ANI: Hidekazu Fukui, Hideo Furusawa. MUS: N/C. PRD: Toho, Nihon Manga-Eiga-sha. 47/33 mins.

In the Kingdom of Foxes, a prince is born without a tail, in this heavily allegorical retelling of "The Emperor's New Clothes" from the TALES OF HANS CHRISTIAN ANDERSEN. This obscure title was planned as the grand renaissance of the Japanese animation business in the deprived 1940s. Clocking in at a 47-minute running time, sufficient to form the main "feature" in a program of all-Japanese cartoons, *The King's Tail* was intended to present local competition for an oncoming tidal wave of Disney films, which had been kept from the Japanese public during the war years. The production employed 40 animators—the bulk of the surviving creatives from **WARTIME ANIME**—and supposedly used 100,000 cels, which would have made it a work of abundantly "full" animation. However, it went into production during a time of extreme tensions and Cold War witch-hunts at the Toho studio, whose new union-busting chairman Tetsuzo Watanabe proclaimed it to be "riddled with redness." The film was cut down to 33 minutes in an attempt to remove its alleged left-wing leanings, but Watanabe still refused to release it. His decision bankrupted the production studio Nihon Manga-Eiga-sha and ruined the chances of Japan mounting an effective opposition to American animation imports for almost a decade. Mitsuyo Seo, the former director of **MOMOTARO'S DIVINE SEA WARRIORS**, left the animation business in disgust. As a result of the colossal prerelease failure of *The King's Tail*, the Japanese animation industry struggled to complete a feature film, with only the 25-minute **PIGGY-BACK GHOST** (1955) coming remotely close before the release of **PANDA AND THE MAGIC SERPENT** (1958).

KINNIKUMAN: ULTIMATE MUSCLE *

1983 AKA: *Muscleman*. TV series, movie. DIR: Yasuo Yamayoshi, Tetsuo Imazawa, Takenori Kawata, Takeshi Shirato. SCR: Haruya Yamazaki, Kenji Terada. DES: Toshio Mori. ANI: Eikichi Takahashi. MUS: Shinsuke Kazato. PRD: Toei, Nippon TV. 25 mins. x 137 eps. (TV1), 48 mins. (m1), 48 mins. (m2), 45 mins. (m3), 39 mins. (m4), 60 mins. (m5), 45 mins. (m6), 51 mins. (m7), 25 mins. (*Ramen Man*), 25 mins. x 35 eps. (*Ramen Man*), 23 mins. x 41 eps. (TV2), 26 mins. (*K2* m1), 60? mins. (*K2* m2).
Superhero Suguru Kinniku, the overmuscled Prince of Planet Kinniku, wrestles against numerous outlandish opponents, including the Texan Terryman, British lord Robin Mask, and legendary Chinese brawler Ramen Man. The most popular anime superhero of the 1980s, based on the manga in *Shonen Jump* magazine by Tamago Yude, Muscleman also wrestled on the big screen in seven anime features between 1984 and 1988. When his reign in the ring was over, he was replaced by *Fight! Ramen Man* (1988), first as a 26-minute

"feature," then as a 35-episode spin-off TV series, directed by Masayuki Akehi, in which the Chinese superwrestler Mien-Nan hunts down the Poison Snake gang who killed his wrestler parents, employing comedy kung fu in the style of **RANMA ½**. Though unknown for a decade in the West, the wrestlemania appeal of *Muscleman* was too great to resist in the wake of the **POKÉMON** boom, and a U.S. broadcast was announced as forthcoming in 2001. The toys, however, sneaked abroad long before, released from Mattel as M.U.S.C.L.E. (Millions of Unusual Small Creatures Lurking Everywhere). Kinnikuman's son, Kinnikuman II, appeared in his own short anime movie in 2001. A new series, *Ultimate Muscle: Kinnikuman II* (2002) was followed by a third commissioned specifically for the American market—i.e., with toned down violence, ironically causing it not to be broadcast in Japan.

KINO'S JOURNEY *

2003. JPN: *Kino no Tabi*. AKA: *The Beautiful World*. Video, TV series, movie. DIR: Ryutaro Nakamura. SCR: Sadayuki Murai. DES: Shigeyuki Suga, Kohaku Kuroboshi, Takamitsu Kondo. ANI: Fumio Matsumoto, Takuya Matsumoto. MUS: Ryo Sakai. PRD: ACGT, GENCO, Media Works, WOWOW. 12 mins. (preview), 24 mins. x 13 eps. (TV), 30 mins. (m).
Kino is a teen on a talking motorcycle called Hermes, in a picaresque set of new places-of-the-week, drawing on stories from *Pilgrim's Progress* to *The Littlest Hobo*. Kino's encounters are surreal fables, loaded with repetition and allegory. Encounters often involve experiments with utopia that have gone strangely awry (compare to **WIND OF AMNESIA**), such as a society where telepathy has been enforced upon the populace to foster harmony, but instead causes the opposite effect. Other meetings are framed as fables, such as three men, each unaware of the others' existence—one polishing railway tracks, the other ripping them up, and a third laying new tracks down, in a satire of corporate waste. A state adopts total democracy, only to collapse into mob rule; another gets robots to do all the work, leaving its populace idle. A nation declares itself to be the repository of all the world's books, but then censors its publications so mercilessly that there is

little in the library but technical manuals and children's books. Two rival countries sublimate their warring impulses into sporting matches instead of war, but sporting matches with deathly consequences.
Some storylines stretch across more than one episode, such as the "Coliseum" arc, in which Kino must escape a gladiatorial arena where citizens fight for the right to make laws. In any other anime this would be an excuse for prolonged combat, but while Kino does eventually start shooting, the plot remains thoughtful. In any other anime, this would also be pretentious, obfuscating nonsense, but *Kino*'s symbolism has an ultimate purpose. Based on a series of novels by Keiichi Sigsawa, with art by Kuroboshi, originally serialized in *Dengeki* magazine, it is difficult to discuss the story of *KJ* without giving away one of its secrets: Kino is actually a girl. Although not a plot point of major importance, not referenced in many episodes, and less of an issue in non-gender-specific Japanese dialogue, this fact had a palpably damaging effect on the way the show could be sold abroad. On DVD in English, *KJ* has struggled to reach new audiences with carefully noncommittal press releases and box blurbs.
The surprise is deadened somewhat by Kino's androgynous look, and by the fact that the voice is provided, like so many anime boys, by a female actress. She is traveling in imitation of Hermes' previous owner, the original Kino, a male traveler who stopped briefly in her homeland. Like the many utopias through which she passes, it was a flawed paradise, a country where children receive a neural modification before puberty that turns them into contented, compliant adults. Our Kino takes up the questing mantle of the original after he dies protecting her from her parents, who wanted her to undergo the same operation.
Screened on late-night television in Japan, *KJ* seems designed to provoke thought and debate, its surreal encounters often scripted by **PERFECT BLUE**'s Murai, its sparse direction often by **SERIAL EXPERIMENTS LAIN**'s Nakamura. The pale colors are so painterly that the screen frequently gains canvas textures, the images so superfluous at times it's practically radio rather than animation. Its wandering protagonist

is an everyman for the teenage audience, a living symbol of their own search for meaning and belonging in an inner world whose rules are eternally shifting. Many, if not most, anime are about the trauma of growing up and finding one's place, but *KJ* breaks new ground in its use of magic realism to convey the idea. That's not to say it does not have its inspirations, but it seems rooted in the "soft" SF of the New Wave, such as J.G. Ballard, or the poetic allegories of Ray Bradbury, rather than the "hard" SF that informs so many other anime storylines. The result is beautiful and remarkably restful after the frantic attentiongrabbing of some contemporary shows with their excess of flash and bounce, but it's more like meditation than entertainment.

A short prequel disc, *Kino's Journey: Totteoki no Hanashi*, was issued with a booklet in Japan in 2003, which included a "visual version of the novel" entitled *To no Kuni: Freelance*, and trailers for the then-upcoming series. The 2005 movie, *Kino's Journey: Life Goes On (Kino no Tabi: Nanika o Suru Tame ni)* is a prequel which shows the protagonist, wracked with guilt about the death of the real Kino, being trained by her teacher. After being directed to seek out Kino's mother, she sets off on her journey, framing the rest of the season of *KJ* as an homage to **FROM THE APENNINES TO THE ANDES**—"3000 leagues in search of *someone else's* mother."

KINOSHITA, RENZO

1936–97. Born in Osaka, Kinoshita graduated from the Electrics department of Daitetsu High School before finding work making commercials in Osaka. He moved to Mainichi Broadcasting, after which he founded his own company, Peppe Productions, in 1963. Under the Peppe aegis, he worked on early TV anime such as **BIG X** and **QTARO THE GHOST**. He joined Mushi Production in 1966, where he worked on **CLEOPATRA: QUEEN OF SEX**, before forming his own Studio Lotus in 1970. His later work, often made in collaboration with his wife Sayoko (1945–), is characterized by short animated films exhibited at film festivals. Before the post-**AKIRA** boom of the 1990s, Kinoshita was arguably the "official" face of Japanese animation abroad, and as the founder of the Hiroshima

International Animation Festival was often seen in Japan as the proponent of arthouse animation in opposition to all that "anime" stuff that was on television (**ARGOT AND JARGON**). His *Made in Japan* (1972) won the Grand Prix of the inaugural New York Animation Festival, while later shorts such as *Men Who Did Something First* and *Pikadon* won similar accolades elsewhere. In recent times, his work has reflected a pacifist, internationalist, antinuclear stance, as shown in **THE FLYING FISH IS TAKEN ILL** and his unfinished *Okinawa*.

KIRA KIRA MELODY ACADEMY

2001. JPN: *Kirakira Melody Gakuen*. AKA: *Twinkling Melody Academy*. Video. DIR: Nobuo Tominaga. SCR: Toshimichi Ogawa. DES: N/C. ANI: Narimitsu Tanaka. MUS: N/C. PRD: Media Factory, AIC. 30 mins.

A mystery drama centering on four would-be singer-actresses, students at the Kira Kira Melody Academy and top of a class of 22 who have agreed to intrusive media attention during their studies. The twist lies in the fact that all 22 are based on real girls who volunteered for the "Kira-Melo" talent contest and its subsequent radio, merchandise, and gaming spin-offs. The girls are students at the Melody Academy, a nonexistent drama school on the outskirts of Yokohama, who have been whittled down from the original 2,000 applicants to a reception class of 56 through a year of "exam failures" and "transfers" to 22, and then thinned still further to determine the stars of the anime. In other words, a kind of staged reality TV—the logical, marketing-led conclusion of a long tradition that ran from the animated biography of a pop group in **GLORIOUS ANGELS**, through artificially engineered singing groups based on anime casts in **HUMMINGBIRDS**, and up to anime shows built entirely around prefabricated groups such as **DEBUTANTE DETECTIVES**. The point being that producers can now effectively market-test future stars *while* they train them, which is either very clever or shamelessly exploitative, depending on how seriously you take **PERFECT BLUE**. As with reality TV itself, throwing two dozen amateurs at an audience may indeed be more entertaining than a lot of fictional drama, but such a situation is an indictment of the depths to which fictional drama has sunk.

Compare also to the "real-life" drama of the earlier **LEMON ANGEL**.

KIRAMEKI PROJECT *

2005. Video. DIR: Katsuhiko Nishijima. SCR: Hiroshi Yamaguchi. DES: Yoko Kikuchi. ANI: Yoko Kikuchi. MUS: Koichiro Kameyama. PRD: Studio Fantasia. 30 mins. x 5 eps.

Three pretty sisters are the rulers of the Jeunesse kingdom, where the eldest, Krone, is head of the military. Middle sister Kana is a bespectacled scientist who, for reasons not all that clear, has spent a lot of time working on a robot handmaid called Lincle. Youngest sister Nene simply hangs around, until the kingdom is attacked by a giant robot called Big Mighty. So what? You may well ask. One of the show's major attractions is that Kana owns and controls a super powerful remote-controlled giant robot of her own, which looks exactly like a blonde girl, complete with a frilly dress and a purse. Shades of **ARIEL**, only with a parody attitude instead of sci-fi action.

KIRARA

2000. Video. DIR: Kiyoshi Murayama. SCR: Noriko Hayasaka. DES: Shinya Takahashi. ANI: Shinya Takahashi. MUS: N/C. PRD: Ashi Pro, Toho. 39 mins.

Teenager Konpei daydreams about how his future wife might look, only to find her ghost sitting by his bedside. Kirara Imai has traveled back in time from her own death, hoping to rewrite history to keep her and her beloved Konpei together forever. Sure enough, as the apparition predicts, Konpei meets a girl called Kirara Imai and falls in love with her, but he is reluctant to tell her that they are destined to marry in seven years, or that she will be killed in an accident shortly afterward.

A clever variation on the quintessential time-travel story, this video was based on a 1993 *Young Jump* manga by **CREAM LEMON**'s Toshiki Yui. With an older, experienced woman initiating her husband-to-be into romance, and aiding in the seduction of her own younger self, it is a truly mind-bending set of paradoxes, not unlike the teen years it so subtly surveys. Beyond the story itself, the anime version increased the level of cheesecake and swimwear from the original manga—artful sci-fi or not, teenage boys will never complain about female nudity.

Also available in an extended edition that includes footage of the open casting call in 1998 where amateur actresses read for the part of the young Kirara. Though hyped at the time as a great way of obtaining raw young voices (a tactic also employed in HIS AND HER CIRCUMSTANCES), the *Kirara* production was so delayed that sweet-16 actress Chiaki Ozawa was a strapping 18-year-old by the time the anime was released. Compare to HOURGLASS OF SUMMER COLORS, which takes a more pornographic approach to similar material, and NATSUYUKI RENDEZVOUS, which offers a more mature perspective. **Ⓝ**

KIRARIN REVOLUTION

2006. TV series. DIR: Masaharu Okawari. SCR: Michihiro Tsuchiya. DES: Yoshihiro Nagamori, Sun Geun Han. ANI: Hiroshi Wagatsuma. MUS: Bice. PRD: G*G Entertainment, SynergySP, Sho-Pro, TV Tokyo, TV Tokyo Media Net. 23 mins. x 153 eps.

While all around her are into idol singers, especially the dishy guys from SHIPS, 14-year-old Kirari is only interested in food. She's also soft-hearted about animals, and one day she rescues a lost turtle. She falls head over heels in love with his owner, the gentle Seiji, and when she learns he's part of SHIPS decides to get closer to him by becoming an idol herself. Determined to bridge the gap between their worlds, she embarks on a career in entertainment.

An Nakahara's 2004 manga ran for five years, and the anime has been screened in France, Spain, Italy, Portugal, Poland, Hungary, the Philippines, and China, though it has yet to appear in the English-speaking world. Its success is not due to originality, clever plotting, good writing, or fast-paced action, but there's always a market for fluffy musical romances packed with wish fulfillment—and not only among little girls. This kind of undemanding show has the same nostalgia value as CHIBI MARUKO-CHAN because it reminds harassed wives and mothers of a time when sugar rushes, pop idols, and accessories were the only things they had to worry about.

KIREPAPA

2008. AKA: *Pretty Daddy*. Video. DIR: Ai Guchi. SCR: Kai Koishikawa. DES: Shuhei Tamura, Miho Takematsu. ANI: Ai Guchi. MUS:

Nobuyuki Abe. PRD: ANIK, Primetime. 29 mins. x 2 eps.

Chisato is still a stunner, even though he's now 35 and father to a teenage boy. Riju is turning out just as handsome as his father. Remembering his own youth, Chisato is determined to protect his boy from every predatory male who tries to take advantage of him. Every suitor, or even friend, that Riju brings home is chased off. Writer Shunsuke and actor Kakeru are both interested in Riju, but Shunsuke seems just as keen on Chisato. What secrets are all three concealing from the boy they all love? Based on Ryo Takagi's 2003 manga, which combines mystery and boys' love, and has been published in English by Deux Press. **Ⓝ**

KISAKU THE LETCH *

2002. AKA: *The Letch*. Video. DIR: Hiromi Yokoyama. SCR: N/C. DES: Hidero Horibe. ANI: Shinichi Furukawa. MUS: N/C. PRD: elf, Pink Pineapple. 30 mins. x 6 eps. (v1), 60 mins. (v2), 30 mins. x 3 eps. (v3).

A janitor holds keys to every door in the building and has a reason to go into every room, any time. The opportunities for a lecher are boundless—especially when the building he's responsible for is a girls' high school … er, college. He doesn't just confine his activities to the workplace, either—he's soon out and about tying up hotel chambermaids, getting heated at a spa, partying with a salaryman at the Playboy Club, and checking out the nurse's office. The one hour *Kisaku Ultimate Sirudaku* AKA *Kisaku Revival* (2004) was a reedit of the highlights of the first six episodes, to prepare the audience for the sequel *Kisaku Spirit: The Letch Lives* (*Kisaku: Tamashii*) in which Kusaki, a lawyer, concludes a large contract with Sugimoto Pharmaceuticals, but feels too shy to go to the celebration party. However, he is possessed by the soul of Kisaku, who steers his body toward following some pretty girls into the party, where predictable high jinks ensue. Compare to ISAKU and SHUSAKU, which are spun off from the same constellation of computer games, and LOVE IS THE NUMBER OF KEYS, which has a much lighter take on sex and building management. Based on a computer game by Elf. **ⒸⓃⓋ**

KISHIN CORPS *

1993. JPN: *Kishin Heidan*. AKA: *Machine-God Corps; Geo-Armor*. Video. DIR: Takaaki Ishiyama. SCR: Takaaki Ishiyama. DES: Masayuki Goto. ANI: Masayuki Goto. MUS: Kaoru Wada. PRD: AIC, Pioneer. 60 mins. x 1 ep., 30 mins. x 6 eps.

An alternate World War II history even more insidious than DEEP BLUE FLEET, suggesting that Japan only invaded Manchuria to protect the world from aliens! Japanese scientists have reverse-engineered some of the captured alien technology to create the Kishin Corps, a group of giant robots who travel in trains, start with hand cranks, and then pummel the opposition into submission—the opposition being not only the invaders, but also those misguided Japanese who have sided with the Nazis.

Based on a series of novels by Masaki Yamada, the story is pure 1940s matinee adventure, with wonderful character stereotypes—the good woman, the femme fatale, the goofy scientist, the dashing flying ace, the dastardly general, and his obedient minions. Real people crop up, or rather have their names borrowed; Eva Braun is included as a top scientist prepared to do anything in the pursuit of knowledge, though in this reality she has an angelic twin sister, Maria. Superb robot action spread throughout an excellent story and some particularly great chase sequences make up for pacing that is at times painfully slow. One of several retro anime that try to rewrite the lead-up to Pearl Harbor, to be filed with SAKURA WARS and VIRGIN FLEET—doubtless intended as innocent hokum, but somehow distasteful in a country that still avoids telling its schoolchildren the truth about the war, however entertaining the fictions (DOCUMENTARIES AND HISTORY). Pointlessly retitled *Alien Defender Geo-Armor* in a later video rerelease.

KISS FOR THOSE LIPS, A

2010. JPN: *Sono Hanabira ni Kuchizuke o— Anata to Koibito Tsunagi*. AKA: *A Kiss to the Lips—Joined in Love with You*. Video. DIR: Masayuki Sakoi. SCR: Masayuki Sakoi. DES: Kyuta Sakai, Takashi Tenshumo. ANI: Kyuta Sakai. MUS: N/C. PRD: chuchu, Fuguriya. 23 mins.

Reo catches a cold, so her friend Mai moves in to take care of her; romance blossoms between them. Based on a visual novel (**ARGOT AND JARGON**) about the gentle romance that blossoms between two schoolgirls, it's a curiously old-fashioned tale despite the sex scenes. Flashbacks give hints about the girls' previous relationship and life at Saint Michael's School for Girls without too much interruption in the cuddling, caressing, and sex that are the main content of the story. Fan collective Fuguriya struck gold with this game series and its attendant drama CDs, books, and anime. The anime sticks closely both to the original art by Peco and the mood and atmosphere of the game, and benefits from excluding most of the game's characters and focusing on romantic sex between one couple. **N**

KISS X SIS

2008. JPN: *Kisssis*. TV series, video. DIR: Munenori Nawa. SCR: Katsumi Hasegawa, Masashi Suzuki, Sumio Uetake. DES: Naoko Kosakabe, Tomoyuki Shitaya. ANI: Kuniaki Masuda, Tomoyuki Shitaya, Go Suzuki, Motoaki Sato, Takashi Maruyama. MUS: Mizuki Ueki. PRD: feel, Starchild Records. 22 mins. x 10 eps. (v), 24 mins. x 12 eps. (TV).
Fifteen-year-old Keita has two older twin stepsisters. They lust after him and since they're not related that's apparently okay (**EROTICA AND PORNOGRAPHY**). When Keita moves up to the same junior high school as his sisters, he also becomes attracted to them. The anime follows Bow Ditama's original manga in that Keita's father and stepmother are all for the idea: despite his initial reluctance he eventually goes for it, then ends up dating his home-room teacher, an anime and manga fan who seems to have no idea of the appropriate boundaries for dealing with pupils. The TV series is an "alternate retelling" of the video and manga with no visible sex. **N**

KISS XXXX

1991. Video. DIR: N/C. SCR: Maki Kusumoto. DES: Maki Kusumoto. ANI: N/C. MUS: Yurei, Sakana. PRD: Victor Entertainment. 25 mins.
Kanon, the lead vocalist in a band, falls for the doll-like charms of the pretty Kameno-chan. She inspires him to write a love song every day but brings trouble into his life along with the happiness. An image video of scenes from Maki Kusumoto's 1988 manga in *Comic Margaret* magazine

set to music from several popular bands of the day.

KITAKUBO, HIROYUKI

1963–. Kitakubo was a true prodigy in the anime world, working on **URUSEI YATSURA** while still a teenager. After a directorial debut with **CREAM LEMON**, he went on to design and direct landmark works including **BLACK MAGIC M-66**, a segment of **ROBOT CARNIVAL**, and **ROUJIN Z**. Credited with part of the early computer graphics work seen in **AKIRA**, he would subsequently direct **BLOOD: THE LAST VAMPIRE** for Production I.G. He also pastiched the dystopian style of many 1980s Madhouse anime in "Last Orders" (1997), an animated commercial for Murphy's Stout, screened in the U.K. (**ADVERTISING AND SPONSORSHIP**).

KITAYAMA, SEITARO

1888–1945. Born in Wakayama, former watercolor artist Kitayama founded the Japan Association of Western Art in 1912 and published its bulletin *Gendai no Yoga* (*Contemporary Western Art*). Seeing French and American animated shorts in Japanese cinemas in 1916, he persuaded the Nikkatsu company to fund his first work, the earliest **MONKEY AND THE CRAB** (1917), drawn directly onto paper. Kitayama was the most prolific of the early animators, largely thanks to his ability to delegate to a staff of half a dozen underlings. His *Momotaro* (1917—see **EARLY ANIME**) was the first anime to go abroad, screened in Paris three months before its Tokyo premiere. He established the Kitayama Eiga studio in 1921, acquiring lucrative contracts in commercials and documentaries. Relocating to Osaka after the Great Kanto Earthquake, his animated output gradually dwindled as he became more involved with producing live-action newsreels. Despite his comparatively large output, his only extant work is *Guardsman Taro and His Submarine* (1918, *Taro no Banpei: Sensuitei no Maki*).

KITAZUME, HIROYUKI

1961–. Found fame as a character designer with Studio Vivo on the "Zeta" **GUNDAM** series and **L-GAIM**. One of the animators selected to contribute to the anthology **ROBOT CARNIVAL**.

KITE *

1998. JPN: *A Kite*. Video. DIR: Yasuomi Umezu. SCR: Yasuomi Umezu. DES: Yasuomi Umezu. ANI: Yuki Iwai. MUS: An Fu. PRD: Beam Entertainment. 30 mins. x 2 eps. (v1), 57 mins. (v2, *Liberator*).
Sawa is a teenage girl and an agent for an underground ring of vigilantes who has been traumatized by the deaths of her parents. Kept in line by drugs and sexual abuse at the hands of corrupt cop Akai, she is sent out armed with explosive bullets to assassinate criminals the law cannot touch. She starts to fall for a boy on a mission with her, but she also comes to realize that the man she now calls father (and lover) is the man who killed her parents.

Excessively violent and featuring scenes of child abuse and underage sex that had to be cut even for the liberal American market, *Kite* draws on several live-action movies for its inspiration. Most notable is John Badham's *Point of No Return* (1993, itself a remake of Luc Besson's earlier *La Femme Nikita*), in which a pretty killer is trapped within the organization that has made her. There are also tips of the hat to Takashi Miike's *Fudoh* (1996), particularly a vicious restroom shootout. Umezu had formerly treated the same themes and ideas in *Yellow Star*, one of the entries in the **COOL DEVICES** erotica series. Remade with a longer running time and high-quality animation, he concentrates on balletic, graceful fight choreography amid utter mayhem, and a poignant tale of doomed love between two damaged souls. But as the video-cover panty shots of Sawa attest, *Kite* is far more interested in titillating its audience with sex and violence than it is with condemning them. Owing to the hard-hitting nature of the original, its complete release in the U.S. only arrived in a single 45-minute episode from Anime Works in 2000, a "director's cut" totaling 51 minutes released by Kitty Media (the erotic subsidiary of the same Media Blasters that also owns Anime Works) in 2002, and finally Kitty Media's *Kite Uncut* in 2004. The 57-minute *Kite Liberator* (2008) is set several years later and features another female vigilante, Monaka, whose astronaut father has been transformed into a bone-monster by eating irradiated space curry. We didn't believe our eyes, either. **LNV**

KITERETSU ENCYCLOPEDIA

1987. JPN: *Kiteretsu Daihyakka*. TV special, TV series. DIR: Takashi Watanabe, Keiji Hayakawa. SCR: Shunichi Yukimuro, Takashi Yamada. DES: Fujiko-Fujio. ANI: Tsukasa Fusanai, Kunihiko Yuyama. MUS: Katsunori Ishida. PRD: Shinei, Fuji TV. 75 mins. (TVm), 25 mins. x 331 eps. (TV).

Kiteretsu and Eiichi love inventing things, but they only ever show their latest creations to Eiichi's girlfriend, Miyoko. Kiteretsu discovers that he is a descendant of the 19th-century inventor Kiteretsu Sai, receiving a copy of Sai's legendary *Encyclopedia of Inventions* from his father. The story returned in 1988 as a full-fledged series, overseen by Hiroshi Kuzuoka. Based on a Fujiko-Fujio manga in *Corocoro Comic* but with its concentration on a group of children getting in and out of trouble with a selection of magical toys, *KE* is little more than a respray of the same creators' earlier and far more successful DORAEMON.

KIZUNA *

1994. AKA: *Bonds*. Video. DIR: Rin Hiro. SCR: Miyo Morita. DES: Ayako Mihashi. ANI: Ayako Mihashi. MUS: Fujio Takano. PRD: Seiji Biblos, Daiei. 30 mins. x 2 eps. (v1), 30 mins. (v2).

Handsome young man Ranmaru "Ran" Samejima is involved in a hit-and-run "accident" that was really a failed attempt on the life of his friend Enjoji. As he recovers, the care and attention lavished upon him by Enjoji make him fall deeper in love with him, and the couple move in together. Their friendship is strained by the attentions of a college professor, who tries to seduce Ran. But Enjoji's family are gangsters, his half-brother also wants Ran, and the lothario professor has bitten off more than he can chew. This video was based on the manga created for *Be-Boy* magazine by Kazuma Kodaka, who also created KIMERA. In 2001, a one-shot sequel, *Kizuna: Much Ado About Nothing* (*Kizuna: Koi no Kara Sawagi*) was released. Despite being let down by poor subtitling on the part of the original distributor, this was one of the very first openly gay anime available in English, to be filed alongside the more humorous FAKE. It has since been joined by a rising tide of similar (and more hardcore) titles, such as MY SEXUAL HARASSMENT. ❶ⓃⓋ

KNIGHT IN THE AREA, THE *

2012. JPN: *Area no Kishi*. TV series. DIR: Hirofumi Ogura. SCR: Hirofumi Ogura. DES: Hitomi Tsuruta, Akira Suzuki. ANI: Sachie Tanaka. MUS: Keiji Inai, Yasunori Iwasaki. PRD: Shin-Ei Animation, TV Asahi. 25 mins. x 37 eps.

Kakeru Aizawa thinks he's useless at soccer. His beloved brother Suguru, the school team's ace striker, disagrees but can't persuade him to give it a try. He manages the school soccer team instead, and never forgets the time he accidentally shattered another player's knee with one kick. Then his old friend Nana comes back to town, and a terrible tragedy changes his life forever. Will coming back to soccer help him to heal?

We've seen this SPORTS ANIME story long before Hiroaki Igano and Kaya Tsukiyama's manga made its 2006 debut. It's TOUCH, set in a different sport, and not nearly as good as the original. One of the big issues for any such series is how well it presents the action, and here director Ogura uses recycled frames, blurred stills, and every possible cheap trick, including commentary as a substitute for action. This is a pity, because the script sets up some tight gameplay and wonderful interaction between the team-mates. There are a few moments that feel lifelike, like the running gag over a player's battle with the bulges of excess indulgence. However, when it comes to non-team relationships the show is clichéd, predictable and sometimes downright embarrassing, with the relationship between Kakeru and Suguru its most spectacular own goal.

KNIGHTS OF RAMUNE *

1990. JPN: *NG Knight Lamune and 40; NG Knight Lamune and 40 EX; NG Knight Lamune and 40 DX*. TV series, video. DIR: Hiroshi Negishi. SCR: Brother Anoppo, Satoru Akahori. DES: Takehiko Ito, Rei Nakahara, Takuya Saito. ANI: N/C. MUS: Tadashige Matsui. PRD: Ashi Pro, TV Tokyo. 25 mins. x 39 eps. (TV1), 30 mins. x 3 eps. (v1, EX), 30 mins. x 3 eps. (v2, DX), 25 mins. x 26 eps. (TV2, Fire), 30 mins. x 6 eps. (v3, Fresh).

Japanese schoolboy Ramune is a big fan of the computer game *King Sccasher*, until one day the beautiful Princess Milk jumps out of his screen and drags him back to the game-world of A'lala. There, he is hailed as the legendary hero Ramuness, come to save the world from the evil overlord Don Harumage. *N[o] G[ood] Knight Ramune and 40* made a name for Satoru Akahori, who would reprise the formula ad infinitum throughout the decade. Resprays of the same set-ups and gags would dominate BEAST WARRIORS, MAZE, SORCERER HUNTERS, and many others, while the bold, unshaded splashes of bright color, originally an attempt to simplify designs for less experienced animators in Korea, would appear in many other shows of the 1990s.

The series returned straight to video as *NG Knight Ramune and 40 EX* (1991), directed by Koji Masunari, in which Ramune, now at middle school, is approached by Milk once more in search of his aid because her world has been attacked by a mysterious giant robot. Before long, the series was back again as *NGR&40 DX* (1993), in which "Ramuness" and his band travel back 5,000 years in time. Adopting a TENCHI MUYO!–style formula of throwing in new cheesecake whenever it ran out of ideas, the series returned to TV as *V[ersu]s Knight Ramune and 40 Fire* (1996). In this incarnation, Ramune's help is solicited by three beautiful androids named Drum, Trumpet, and Cello. By this point, he is a full-grown adult, who Turns To The Dark Side, remaining there for the video sequel *VS Knight Ramune and 40 Fresh* (1997). The only part of the series to be released in English, under the title *Knights of Ramune*, it features busty babes Parfait and Cacao on a quest to bring back the legendary knight Ramuness, only to discover that he's at the helm of the lead ship in an invading alien fleet. With a poverty of ideas typical to late 1990s anime, many of which persist in believing that "zany" means "amateurish," this involves a bit of espionage, spell-casting, and a few gags about how underwear interferes with the power of magic, as they run around a big spaceship in the company of a mascot that resembles a talking tumor, waiting for the enemy to bring the plot to them.

However, despite being the fifth series in the franchise, *KoR* contains little to confuse audiences—the hours of backstory prove to be utterly inconsequential. New director Yoshitaka Fujimoto papers over gaping holes in the plot and action with perfunctory T&A and a few incidences of halfhearted sauciness—because more "mature" viewers can apparently be appeased by a couple of nipples and a bit of suggestive panting. There are some frames of **Gunbuster**-inspired space warfare, and tantalizingly short bursts of excellent animation, but *KoR* is the kind of anime that leads first-time viewers to assume the entire medium is nothing but big eyes, explosions, and weary plot-by-numbers. The U.S. voice cast seem to think so too, contemptuously indulging in over-the-top pseudonyms like Ruby Seedless and Autumn Harvest. **Ⓝ**

KNIGHTS OF SIDONIA *

2014. JPN: *Sidonia no Kishi*. TV series. DIR: Kobun Shizuno. SCR: Sadayuki Murai, Shigeru Murakoshi, Tetsuya Yamada. DES: Yuki Moriyama. ANI: Hiroaki Ando. MUS: Noriyuki Asakura. PRD: Polygon Pictures, Kodansha, MBS, Starchild Records, Klockworx. 24 mins. x 12 eps. (TV1), 24 mins. x 12 eps. (TV2).

The asteroid-ship Sidonia is a piece of the lost planet Earth, destroyed many centuries ago in an attack by the all-devouring alien Gauna. For all its inhabitants know, they are the last of humanity, since there has been no contact with other refugees for generations. Although much of the Sidonia's culture and history is rooted in ethnically Japanese origins for its inhabitants, several catastrophic encounters with Gauna have led to some severe transformations. The most valued members of the crew are effectively immortal, while their lower-ranking subjects endure harsh austerity measures and martial law under a permanent war footing of vigilance and tension. Clones are commonplace in a critically small gene pool, reproduction is now largely asexual, and genetic engineering has led to some weird hybrids.

Nagate is raised apart from other Sidonians by his eccentric grandfather, inadvertently developing a talent for piloting the Guardian machines used to repel Gauna attacks. Drafted into the Sidonian military after breaking cover in search of food, he soon becomes the fulcrum of a new line of defense, when the first Gauna attack in a century threatens the half-million Sidonians once more with extinction.

We've been here before many times, not only in the space-war genre of **Gundam** and its imitators, but also in the desperate resistance of **Evangelion**. So while *Knights of Sidonia* offers nothing new, it is at least a competent and well-crafted entry in the genre, very much in the terror-beset spirit of its near-contemporary **Attack on Titan**, and with strong roots in the rebooted *Battlestar Galactica* (2003). Sadayuki Murai, best known in these pages as the screenwriter of **Perfect Blue**, provides many of the episodes, although the long-term impact of the show is not necessarily in its writing, but in its distribution. *Knights of Sidonia* was the first show to be picked up by Netflix for exclusive release; it was then released all at once, in that channel's particular binge-enabling style, with English and Spanish subs already in place. Its acquisition and release suggested the opening shots of a new rights-rush among Western distributors, repeating the price-inflation and infighting that typified similar bubbles in the mid-1990s and mid-2000s. Anime plots aren't the only things that repeat themselves.

KOBATO.

2009. JPN: *Kobato*. [sic]. TV series. DIR: Mitsuyuki Masuhara. SCR: Michio Yokote, Nanase Ohkawa. DES: Hiromi Kato, Hideyuki Ueno. ANI: Hisashi Abe, Satoshi Tasaki. MUS: Takeshi Hama. PRD: Madhouse, D.N. Dream partners, Flying Dog, Kadokawa, Memory Tech, NHK Enterprises, Klockworx. 25 mins. x 24 eps.

Kobato is a delicate, beautiful creature who has come to earth to fill a mysterious flask with the suffering released from the hearts of people she heals. She cares deeply for everyone whose pain she feels, but she is not permitted to fall in love with any of them. If she fulfills her task, she will be able to go to a place that's very important to her. Her guardian and guide is Ioryogi, a spirit in the form of a dog plushie. He and his friends are being punished for a terrible sin, but if he helps Kobato to succeed they will return to their true forms. In a kindergarten in a Japanese suburb, they both find a way to come closer to their dream, but there will be a heavy price to pay.

Mixing things up has worked for CLAMP throughout their career. Following the rule established by Osamu Tezuka (never let an idea go to waste and recycle it whenever you can), they've made hit after hit by mixing and matching characters from their personal universe. *Kobato* the series is based on *Kobato* the 2005 manga and *Wish*, a manga that dates back to 1996, but has remained un-animated apart from a six-minute music video in 1997. Kobato and Ioryogi made their first animated appearance in *Clamp in Wonderland 2* (**Miyuki-chan in Wonderland**).

CLAMP's real business is the construction of **Fantasy and Fairy Tales**. Like all builders of such (see **Princess Tutu**) they pick from a collection of archetypes, changing the dress and decoration to suit the audience on the day, filling their plots with fantastical folderol, but underneath it all preserving the same pure, simple, unsettling outlines of love and loss, desire and greed, death and redemption. In *Kobato* the animation by Madhouse is utterly gorgeous, setting the scene for the archetypal tale in breathtaking style. The gently goofy humor balances the poignant moments and helps us brace for the heartbreak no good fairy tale can avoid. *Kobato* may be a minor work in a mighty canon, but its sweetness and life-affirming belief in the power of love—not just romantic love, but the relationships that sustain us all—make it worthy of attention. Similar themes, approached from an older perspective, can be discerned in **Colorful the Motion Picture**.

KOBO-CHAN

1990. AKA: *Kobo the Little Rascal*. TV series. DIR: Hiroyuki Torii, Tameo Ogawa. SCR: Noboru Shiroyama. DES: Joji Yanagise. ANI: Hiroyuki Torii, Joji Yanagise, Hisatoshi Motoki. MUS: Noriko Sakai. PRD: Eiken, Yomiuri TV. 12 mins. x 15 eps.

The adventures of a five-year-old boy in the tradition of *Peanuts*, based on Masashi Ueda's four-panel cartoon strip in *Yomiuri Shinbun* newspaper.

KOGEPAN

2001. AKA: *Burnt Bread*. TV series. DIR: Shuichi Ohara. SCR: Masako Hagino. DES: Miki Takahashi. ANI: Shuichi Ohara, Yoshiki Hanaoka. MUS: Takeshi Yasuda. PRD: Studio Pierrot, Pony Canyon, Sony Magazines, Animax. 4 mins. x 10 eps.

In a Hokkaido bakery, a little red bean bun looks forward to being one of the 20 most delicious buns in the shop. However, the baker accidentally drops him, and the bun is burned. Overcooked for 30 minutes, he is eventually retrieved from the oven, but now with a blackened crust that will render him forever unable to enter the ranks of the elite buns. Bullied and mocked by the other buns, he gains the nickname *Kogepan*, or Burned Bread. He runs away from home and takes up smoking and heavy drinking (of milk), but eventually returns to the bakery, where he reads a book on self-improvement, hoping one day to be as perfect as the other buns. His friends include the similarly fire-damaged Cream Bread and Charcoal Bread (who is even worse off), and the Pretty Breads, who are always happy and perfect, and do not understand the poignancy of Kogepan's life. Wildean pathos ensues, in a tale that takes the bakery-themed children's entertainment of ANPANMAN and introduces a note of irredeemable tragedy. Kogepan is doomed to languish unsold while his perky golden-crusted companions fulfill their destiny and fly off the racks into the wide world, although perhaps it is best that he doesn't see his friends getting eaten alive each week—compare to KAPPAMAKI AND THE SUSHI KIDS. Stationery, accessories, and other merchandise featuring the characters created by Miki Takahashi enjoyed some popularity but didn't attain the heights of TAREPANDA, let alone HELLO KITTY.

KOI KAZE *

2004. AKA: *Love's Zephyr; Love's Wind*. TV series. DIR: Takahiro Omori. SCR: Noboru Takagi. DES: Takahiro Kishida. ANI: Naoyuki Oba. MUS: Masanori Takumi, Makoto Yoshimori. PRD: ACGT, Geneon, TV Asahi, Rondo Robe. 25 mins. x 13 eps.

Wedding planner Koshiro Saeki is dumped by his girlfriend over commitment issues and ends up on a date with 15-year-old schoolgirl Nanoka. He finds himself falling for her, only to discover, to his horror, that she is his sister. Estranged from his mother for the 14 years following his parents' divorce, Koshiro has all but forgotten about his sibling, but now he is forced to pretend that nothing has happened between them when Nanoka moves in with him and his father.

As Koshiro and Nanoka struggle to behave like "normal" brother and sister once more, Koshiro is filled with self-loathing. He even goes to visit his mother for the first time in years to see if she can help him find answers, though there are no answers he wants to hear. He and Nanoka are brother and sister, and that's how they must love each other, if their story is not to have a tragic and sinful end. Meanwhile, Koshiro's state of mind leads to overreactions to otherwise everyday events. His lecherous work colleague Odagiri asks if Koshiro can set him up with his sister, while a female coworker Chidori sometimes appears like an older, more socially acceptable clone of his sister.

Despite sounding like the set-up for a hundred erotic anime, *Koi Kaze* is nothing of the sort. It's a serious, well-written TV show about forbidden love, drawing for inspiration not on anime but on several recent live-action dramas—*High School Teacher* (*DE), *Strawberry on the Shortcake* (*DE), and, at a more superficial level, *Wedding Planner* (*DE). It deals, of course, with many of the subliminal themes and rationalizations of LOLITA ANIME, but also with the impossible relationship that has been a staple of TV anime since URUSEI YATSURA and MARMALADE BOY. Based on a manga by Motoi Yoshida.

KOI KOI SEVEN *

2005. TV series. DIR: Yoshitaka Fujimoto. SCR: Tamotsu Mitsukoshi. DES: Koji Watanabe. ANI: Masafumi Yamamoto. MUS: N/C. PRD: Trinet, Studio Flag. 25 mins. x 13 eps.

TENCHI MUYO! crashed into SAILOR MOON, as average teenager Tetsuro Tanaka transfers to a new school, where he foolishly refuses to believe that the largely female classroom population will make much trouble. Instead, he finds himself on the run from a series of military attacks and defended by a mystical group of schoolgirl warriors called the Koi Koi Seven, although there are initially only six of them. Based on a manga by the pseudonymous Morishige, which ran in *Champion RED* magazine, and featuring terrible animation quality, made barely tolerable by a constant barrage of anime parodies and clichés including references to, most notably, EVANGELION and GUNDAM.

KOIHIME *

2000. AKA: *Love Princess*. Video. DIR: Shinichi

Masaki. SCR: Takao Yoshioka. DES: Mayumi Watanabe. ANI: Mayumi Watanabe. MUS: N/C. PRD: Pink Pineapple. 30 mins. x 2 eps. (v1), 30 mins. x 2 eps. (v2).

Musashi comes to his old home in a tiny remote village to stay with his grandmother for summer vacation. He's been away for 15 years and has very few remembrances of childhood, but on the way he recalls vague memories of a strange, intensely emotional game-ritual when he and four local girls pricked their skin and tasted each other's blood. Once he gets to the village, hot local cuties Nami, Anzu, Suzaku, and Mayuki remember him very well, and their intentions toward him are anything but childish. As he sleeps his way back through his lost memories, a story from his childhood unfolds. He actually promised to marry all four girls, who are not really girls at all but nature spirits, whose father is a dragon and whose love for Musashi almost caused the end of their world last time he left, when the grief of Nami the snow princess caused the entire region to ice up. LOVE HINA meets CRIMSON CLIMAX, although at the softer end of the scale—despite being billed as a production by KSS's erotic label Pink Pineapple, many crewmembers have retained their real names, including designer Watanabe, who worked on TENCHI MUYO! A sequel, *More Koihime* (*Zoku Koihime*), followed in 2001, while Nobuaki Nakanishi's TV series KOIHIME MUSO (2009), was such a departure from the original that we have filed it as a separate entry. **N**

KOIHIME MUSO *

2008. AKA: *Peerless Princess*. TV series, video. DIR: Nobuaki Nakanishi. SCR: Go Zappa. DES: Miwa Oshima, Tomoya Hiratsuka, Shinji Takasuga. ANI: Miwa Oshima, Tomoya Hiratsuka. MUS: N/C. PRD: Dogakobo, AT-X, Marvelous Entertainment, Pony Canyon. 23 mins. x 12 eps. (TV1), 30 mins. (v1), 30 mins. x 2 eps. (v2), 23 mins. x 12 eps. (TV2), 23 mins. x 12 eps. (TV3).

Orphaned by bandits in the dying days of China's Han dynasty, Kan'u becomes a feared bounty hunter, not for revenge but to prevent others suffering from similar terrible loss and pain. Rin Rin has had similar experiences, so naturally the girls join forces. As the empire crumbles around them, the pair travel the open road, fighting for fun and profit and meeting other fighting women—and guys—along the way.

The anime is based on a 2008 adult visual novel (ARGOT AND JARGON) but should not be confused with a porn video of similar name related in gaming terms albeit not in plot—for which see KOIHIME. The game is a SLAYERS-type spin on the great Chinese historical novel *Romance of the Three Kingdoms* (GREAT CONQUEST), so events and characters are loosely based on, or at least named from, the novel. The exception is the 2009 video of the same title, and its 2010 two-part follow-up *New (Shin) KM,* in which the cast is transported to a modern-day girls' boarding school. A second TV series, also called *New KM,* aired in 2009 continuing the Chinese story where the first series left off, and *New KM: Virgin Rebellion (Shin KM: Otome Tairan)* continued the small-screen story in 2010.

If three TV series and three videos sounds like big success, bear in mind that this is actually just 39 episodes in total—less than a quarter of the run of, say, KIRARIN REVOLUTION, which has yet to see an English-language release despite its multilingual worldwide broadcast credentials. In the English market, the tropes that sell are frequently related to fan service. The sweep of history is merely a backdrop for girls fighting, girls drinking, girls dressing and undressing, girls getting it on with each other. Girls of all ages and sizes from very small to very grown-up feature throughout, and Dogakobo render them in such cute, bright vivacity that the relatively limited animation is less annoying than it might have been. 🅝🅥

KOIKEN

2012. *Koiken! Watashi-tachi wa Anime ni Natchatta.* AKA: *Koiken! Now We've Become an Anime!* TV series. DIR/s: kamisiro. SCR/s: Deko Akao. DES/s: refeia, Yasuyuki. ANI/s: Takeyuki Yanase, Shigenori Kageyama, Masahiro Sonoda. MUS: Takahiro Ando. PRD: Marvy Jack. 4 mins. x 12 eps.
Kaede, the chairman of the Love Research Club (Koiken) rashly observes that becoming an idol singer must be easy, thereby insulting hard-working idol singer Nagisa. She challenges Kaede and the other girls to experience an idol singer's tough life first-hand, in this forgettable Internet-

based series for mobile phones: K-ON with idol singers (MUSIC IN ANIME).

KOIKO'S DAILY LIFE

1989. JPN: *Koiko no Mainichi.* Video. DIR: Noboru Ishiguro. SCR: Akira Miyazaki. DES: Joji Akiyama. ANI: Kiyotoshi Aoi. MUS: N/C. PRD: Nippon Animation. 50 mins. x 2 eps.
In a story that flits between serious drama and comedic farce, Shinjuku gangster Sabu and his young wife Koiko try to live a normal life, despite the interferences of gang politics and criminal deals. After she saves his life, Sabu's gangboss, Tominaga, falls in love with Koiko, and sends Sabu into increasingly more dangerous situations, hoping to cause his arrest, and thus obligate himself to "take care" of Koiko while Sabu is in prison. Based on a manga in *Manga Action* magazine by PINK CURTAIN–creator Joji Akiyama, this was also adapted into a TV drama starring Beat Takeshi—years ahead of *The Sopranos.* 🅝🅥

KOJIRO OF THE FUMA CLAN *

1989. JPN: *Fuma no Kojiro.* Video. DIR: Hidehito Ueda. SCR: Takao Koyama. DES: Shingo Araki, Michi Himeno. ANI: Takeshi Tsukasa. MUS: Toshiro Imaizumi. PRD: Animate Film, JC Staff. 30 mins. x 13 eps.
Five young boys are the reincarnations of elemental spirits and replay old tales and enmities from Japanese history in a modern setting. Teenager Kojiro receives a letter from Himeko, the young owner of Hakuo (White Phoenix) High School, who needs help dealing with gang intimidation. Kojiro decides to help her because she's very cute, but gang intimidation is the least of her worries—a rival clan is planning a takeover, and Kojiro must face their champion, Nibu, before dealing with another adversary, Oscar Musashi (see SWORD OF MUSASHI). The interclan school struggle is just a cover for the powers of evil, who wish to collect the ten magical swords that determine the balance of power in the universe. It's pretty boys at a ninja high school but with a surprisingly old-fashioned look to the designs and animation. This video was based on a 1982 manga in *Shonen Jump* by Masami Kurumada, who would recycle the same ideas in SAINT SEIYA, though the anime adaptation of the latter preceded this to Japanese screens. 🅝🅥

KOKORO LIBRARY

2001. JPN: *Kokoro Toshokan.* AKA: *Heart Library.* TV series. DIR: Koji Masunari. SCR: Yosuke Kuroda. DES: Hideki Tachibana. ANI: Studio DEEN. MUS: Hisaaki Hogari. PRD: Media Works, Studio DEEN, Victor Entertainment, TV Tokyo. 30 mins. x 13 eps.
Sisters Iina, Aruto, and Kokoro inherit a library in the middle of the mountains and fret that they will never get enough customers. Youngest sister Kokoro is pleased that someone takes out a book on her first day, but when it isn't returned she discovers that the customer has moved away. She decides to take a bus to a faraway town in search of the errant borrower, only to be prevented by her sisters Iina and Aruto, who reveal that the book has just been returned by mail—only the first of a series of prosaic miracles in the style of TOKYO GODFATHERS. *Kokoro Library* is a bizarre mixture of the maid's clothing fad with the bookish goings-on of WHISPER OF THE HEART or HAIBANE RENMEI, complete with a sappy, soporifically soothing soundtrack. A later episode introduces a robot librarian, but otherwise the show is relentlessly slow—compare to the excitement of director Masunari's earlier R.O.D. Somewhere in *Kokoro Library*'s past is a creator's decision that anime don't need to be about conflict and danger to be interesting, but this is neither HUMAN CROSSING nor MY NEIGHBOR TOTORO. Pretty the girls may be, but it is difficult to warm to characters who get excited about holding committee meetings to discuss their outreach strategy. Based on a manga by Nobuyuki Takagi in *Dengeki Daioh* magazine. The video "special" *Kokoro Library Communication Clips* is not so much a sequel as a series of short segments from the first episode interspersed with title cards and explanatory comments by Kokoro.

KOKUDO-OH: BLACK EYE KING *

2000. JPN: *Kokudo-O.* AKA: *Black Eyed King; Charmstone; Legend of the Black Eye: Koku-dohoh.* Video. DIR: Mikan Fuyuno. SCR: Manka Sen. DES: Studio Jikkenshitsu. ANI: Kazuo Takeuchi. MUS: N/C. PRD: Alice Pro, Five Ways. 30 mins. x 5 eps.
Isildur (Isiodore in the U.S. dub) inherits the throne of the small mountain kingdom of Bothal (Bosarre), sandwiched in between the mighty empires of Rohan

and Geld. Hoping to maintain his kingdom's independence, the new ruler is faced with a difficult choice—since each empire has sent him a prospective bride, whom should he choose? Princess Belciel (Bellecher) is feisty and proud, a former classmate of Isildur when he studied in the Rohan empire. Princess Ariel is demure and kind, a Geld childhood playmate of Isildur who once treated him as a brother. Unable to choose, Isildur suggests a series of prenuptial trials for the girls, in order for Isildur and his maid Irene to instruct the princesses in the correct modes of behavior for Isildur's future queen. Predictably, this starts innocently enough before devolving into sexual abuse, bondage, toilet games, and the girls' imprisonment in a cage; compare to **Erotic Torture Chamber** and **Blood Royale**. Nor does Isildur seem to give much thought to what may happen when he is eventually forced to choose one of them, since the other one will have endured four weeks of sexual humiliation, likely grounds for an invasion by her homeland! As the month progresses, Isildur receives the troubling news that the king of Geld, Ariel's father, is dying. If Ariel is still unmarried at the time of her father's death, then the princess is fated to be betrothed to Herum, the heir to the Rohan empire, depriving Isildur of both his sex games and his chances of diplomatic independence. Despite a more modern setting than this synopsis implies (a quasi-Victorian world), the series can't help alluding to *The Lord of the Rings*. The result is an anime that is immensely entertaining, not so much for its content, but for imagining the looks on the faces of Tolkien's literary executors if they ever see it. For some reason, the fifth episode was not part of the initial release in America, although it did eventually arrive after Nu Tech's license passed to new distributors JapanAnime. 🄲🄽🄾

KON, SATOSHI

1963–2010. A protégé and former art assistant to Katsuhiro Otomo, Kon was catapulted into films in the wake of Otomo's **Akira**, as Otomo delegated art, scripting and design duties on several lesser follow-ups. Kon first worked in animation on **Roujin Z**, for which he lovingly created trash-strewn backgrounds in a sci-fi future.

It was Otomo who recommended Kon as the director of **Perfect Blue**, for which he refused to anchor the images in a trustworthy reality, taunting the audience with dreams within flashbacks within dreams: a mode to which he returned in his later **Paprika**, and which some have credited as an influence on Christopher Nolan's *Inception*. Kon was enthralled by the artificiality of animation, and used it to actualize internal monologues, dreams, and memories, as best seen in his signature work, **Millennium Actress**. Never quite losing his outsider's-eye view of Tokyo, the Hokkaido-born Kon's films exulted in the re-creation of antiseptic shopping malls and grungy backstreets, and in a filmmaker's power to find beauty and drama even in such mundane environments. The Tokyo suburb of Musashino was the focal point of Kon's life; it was where he studied at Musashino Art University, where he made his home for the next decade, and where he set his animated TV series **Paranoia Agent**. His underrated John Ford pastiche **Tokyo Godfathers** was a secular Christmas movie in which Tokyo was an active participant, from the opening credits inserted into billboards and construction site fences, to a closing sequence in which the buildings come to life and dance. In a posthumously published diary of his last days, Kon expressed his hope that his staff would complete his last film project, *The Dream Machine*. However, the degree to which this film might be said to be "in progress" seems to have been a matter of some conjecture—it is thought that at the time he died, much of it was still irretrievably in his head.

KONAKA, CHIAKI

1961–. Born in Tokyo, Konaka is a novelist and influential screenwriter in anime and live-action since the late 1980s. A film school graduate who joined the Eizo company as a director in 1986, he left to become a freelance writer the following year. He founded the production company Kyodai ("Brothers") in 1992 with his director sibling Kazuya, for whom he has written several later *Ultraman* scripts (*DE). His most notable works in anime include **Armitage III**, the **Bubblegum Crisis** remake *BGC Tokyo 2040*, **Devilman** *Lady*, and **Serial Experiments Lain**. His works often acknowl-

edge his interest in H. P. Lovecraft, **Alice in Wonderland**, and dolls, all of which come together in **Malice Doll**. Sometimes credited, for no good reason, as Chiaki J. Konaka.

KONDO, YOSHIFUMI

1950–98. Sometimes miscredited as Toshinobu Kondo or Yoshifumi Kindo. Born in Niigata Prefecture he attended Design College of Tokyo after high school, but began working for A Pro (now Shin'ei Doga) within six months of arriving in Tokyo. He met Hayao Miyazaki while working on **Lupin III**, beginning a lifelong association. He moved to Nippon Animation in 1977 and served as an animation director on **Anne of Green Gables** and **Future Boy Conan**. In this period, he also wrote a textbook on animation methods. He moved to Telecom in 1980, where he worked as a character designer on **Sherlock Hound**, although he was to resign from Telecom in 1985 due to illness, possibly caused by overwork. He freelanced for Nippon Animation for another year before quitting for good in order to take up a post at Studio Ghibli. He was a key animator and character designer on many of Ghibli's classic movies of the late 1980s and early 1990s, and had his directorial debut with **Whisper of the Heart**. Groomed as Hayao Miyazaki's successor at Ghibli, Kondo was a key animator on **Princess Mononoke**, but succumbed to an aneurysm in 1998. His death was not only a tragic loss to Ghibli and the anime world but also a reminder of the terrifyingly long hours and stressful labor involved in creating Japanese animation.

KONPORA KID

1985. TV series, TV special. DIR: Juzo Morishita, Yuji Endo, Tatsuo Higashino, Yoshikata Nitta, Shigeyasu Yamauchi. SCR: Takao Koyama, Shigeru Yanagawa, Kenji Yoshida. DES: Yasuhiro Yamaguchi. ANI: Yasuhiro Yamaguchi, Tatsuhiro Nagaki, Masami Shimoda. MUS: Kohei Tanaka. PRD: Toei, TV Asahi. 25 mins. x 26 eps. (TV), 57 mins. (TVm).

In the distant future, merely because someone is eight years old, it doesn't follow that they will have to go to school. In fact, little Daigoro Harumi JR (AKA JR) is a teacher at Torad Academy in charge of educating Class Five, whose ages range from a newborn baby to a crusty old grandfather. Partway through the TV series, JR and his class also appeared in a summer TV special, where the flustered eight-year-old plans on taking a summer vacation with his family in space but ends up chaperoning half his class as well. Based on the manga by Masahide Motohashi, serialized in *Shonen Magazine*, among others.

KOSUKE AND RIKIMARU: DRAGON OF KONPEI ISLAND

1990. JPN: *Kosukesama Rikimarusama: Konpeijima no Ryu*. Video. DIR: Tooyo Ashida. SCR: Tooyo Ashida, Akira Toriyama. DES: Akira Toriyama. ANI: N/C. MUS: N/C. PRD: JC Staff. 45 mins.

Squashed-down samurai Kosuke and Rikimaru must save the world from an evil dragon who wants to rule it for all eternity. This one-off anime, based on an idea by **DRAGON BALL** and **DOCTOR SLUMP**–creator Akira Toriyama, was preceded by a 1990 manga in a special issue of *Shonen Jump* but written originally for the screen.

KOTATSU CAT

2009. JPN: *Kotatsu Neko*. AKA: *Cat Under the Table*. TV series, video. DIR: Oji Ogawa, Jun Aoki. SCR: N/C. DES: N/C. ANI: N/C. MUS: N/C. PRD: Iyasakado Film, Aoki Film. 5 mins. x 26 eps. (TV), 1 min. x 2 eps. (online).

Two cats live in a Tokyo apartment under a *kotatsu*—a Japanese table with a heater below it, necessary in unheated homes in winter. Their human, whom everybody calls Junior, is a third-year middle-schooler who's obsessed with games and doesn't get out much. He likes a girl in his class but can't bring himself to tell her. The same situation applies to one of his cats, Zero. Their sci-fi fantasy romance is played out in wryly humorous papercut animation.

Kotatsu-neko was already a character in manga and anime, having appeared in Rumiko Takahashi's **URUSEI YATSURA** as the ghost of a huge cat who was thrown out in the cold centuries ago and decided to haunt those who brought about his death by freezing. Director Ogawa had made the same story as a live-action movie, which he also cowrote, in 2006. Before that, in 2005, another *Kotatsu-Neko*, a far more in-your-face feline, starred in two ultra-short online animations by Jun Aoki.

Shot in stop motion and claymation in a wonderful room set, they're action-packed and hilarious. Aoki has made a number of wryly funny short films in a variety of styles, from the hand-drawn animation of *Shogi Hour* (2004) and *Nara Deer Story (Nara Shika Monogatari*, 2008) to rotoscoping in *Red Bean Soup (Oshiruko*, 2005) and a mix of techniques in 2008's *Space Neko Theater*.

KOTOURA-SAN *

2013. TV series. DIR: Masahiko Ota. SCR: Takashi Aoshima. DES: Takaharu Okuma. ANI: Takaharu Okuma, Hayato Hashiguchi, Tomoko Tsuji, Rika Kato. MUS: Yasuhiro Misawa. PRD: AIC, Studio Tulip, AT-X, Tokyo MX TV, Sun TV, Echo, CISSE. 24 mins. x 12 eps.

Secret telepath Haruka has become withdrawn and timid after seeing a little too much of the insides of the heads of people around her, particularly when she so often forgets that people's *thoughts* may not match their deeds or promises. Only an idiot would welcome the prospect of a girlfriend who knows exactly what he is thinking, but Manabe fits the bill perfectly, teasing her with lascivious thoughts but also welcoming her ability to see that his intentions toward her are ultimately honorable.

Despite being based on the usually shallow concepts of a four-panel gag manga, Kotoura-san surprises the viewer with a hard-hitting opening act that explains some of Haruka's childhood traumas, and focuses in later episodes on character-driven drama as the leads investigate her powers, hang out with the school ESP Club, and eventually, inevitably, fight crime. Compare to **TELEPATHY GIRL RAN**.

KOTOWAZA HOUSE

1987. TV series. DIR: Hiroshi Yoshida. SCR: Motoko Misawa, Hiroshi Yoshida. DES: Tadao Wakabayashi. ANI: Tadao Wakabayashi. MUS: N/C. PRD: Eiken, Fuji TV. 5 mins. x 338 eps.

Peter the salaryman lives a very unhealthy lifestyle, starving then bingeing until he feels sick, or slobbing around the house until badgered into taking up exercise, during which he invariably pulls a muscle. In this public-service proverb-of-the-week anime from the same team who made **DOTANBA'S MODERN MANNERS**, Peter's caring boss and the beautiful Office Lady Sueko drag in a straight-talking doctor and a

sprightly granny to educate him about physical and mental health. For the series' first year on air, the title was simply *KH: Health Edition*, but this was dropped in 1988 to reflect the move toward more general tips and proverbs for well-being.

KOUCHI, JUNICHI

1886–1970. Sometimes also transliterated Sumikazu Kouchi. Born in Okayama Prefecture, Kouichi relocated with his family to Tokyo, where he eventually studied watercolor painting at the Pacific Art Institute. His illustrations first appeared in *Tokyo Puck* magazine around 1908, and by 1912 he was drawing political cartoons for a newspaper. He was approached by the Kobayashi Shokai Company (formed by defectors from the production company Tenkatsu), for whom he produced his first animation, the *Sword of Hanawa Hekonai (Hanawa Hekonai, Meito no Maki*—see **EARLY ANIME**) in June 1917. Soon afterward, he enjoyed the doubtful honor of being the first Japanese animator to have a film banned when his short comedy *Playful Boy's Air Gun* (1917, *Chamebo: Kukiju no Maki*) ran afoul of the state censor. With Kobayashi experiencing financial difficulties, Kouchi set up his own animation company, Sumikazu Eiga, and began producing political propaganda, commencing with a commercial for the politician Shinpei Goto in 1924. The anime talkie *Chopped Snake* (1930, *Chongire Hebi*), was his last before he returned to straightforward illustration.

KOWAKU NO TOKI

2011. AKA: *Hour of Enchantment*. Video. DIR: N/C. SCR: PON. DES: Hikaru Kinohara. ANI: N/C. MUS: N/C. PRD: PoRO. 30 mins. x 2 eps.

Detective Mibu gets lost in the mountains and falls asleep. After a dark dream about a beautiful girl ritually abused by old men and a bull, he wakes and walks until he comes across a house. The girl who opens the door is the girl in his dream. He wants to save her, but she begs him to leave because the place is dangerous for outsiders. Will he go before he gets caught up in the family's nightly ritual of obscenity and torture? Of course not, because this is based on a porn game by TinkerBell with original designs by Aojiru. If you like the idea of climaxing in orifices not designed for the purpose and watching girls have sex with animals, this is for you. **NV**

KOYAMA, TAKAO

1948–. Born in Tokyo, Koyama studied literature at Waseda University and joined Tatsunoko Productions after graduation. His debut work was an episode of RURAL LEADER, which he followed with scripts for CASSHAN and SONG OF THE LADYBUGS, before going freelance in 1975. He subsequently wrote for the TIME BOKAN series and DRAGON BALL. As a guest at American conventions, Koyama has made some controversial (and to the authors, highly welcome) comments about the state of the anime business, decrying the outsourcing of talent and production, and criticizing the "glorified advertisements" that comprise much of the video market. He has also explained why so much of *Dragon Ball* seems like a prolonged fight scene, since on occasion he had been asked to turn a single panel from the manga into a 25-minute episode.

KSS

A Japanese record and animation firm made famous by many of the lighter-hearted video anime of the 1990s, including BEAST WARRIORS. Its place in anime has largely been superseded by that of its erotic subsidiary Pink Pineapple, which seems to have a far greater output in modern times, including IMMORAL SISTERS, MOONLIGHT LADY, and WIFE EATER.

KUM-KUM *

1975. JPN: *Wanpaku Omukashi Kum-Kum.* AKA: *Naughty Ancient Kum-Kum; Kum-Kum the Caveman.* TV series. DIR: Rintaro, Noboru Ishiguro, Wataru Mizusawa. SCR: Eiichi Tachi, Keisuke Fujikawa, Yoshiaki Yoshida. DES: Yoshikazu Yasuhiko. ANI: Rintaro, Noboru Ishiguro, Minoru Tajima, Akio Sakai. MUS: Masami Uno. PRD: ITC Japan, Mainichi Broadcasting (TBS). 25 mins. x 26 eps.
Kum-kum is a small cave boy living in the prehistoric mountains that will one day be Japan, where he, his sister Furu-furu, and tag-along companions Chil-chil, Mochi-mochi, and Aron behave the way that their distant descendants would if only modern Japanese children had access to mammoth rides, troublesome dinosaurs, and the opportunity to throw rocks at each other.

Kum-kum was an unexpected success on British children's TV in the early 1980s, not for being the first English-language broadcast of work by original creator Yasuhiko, or indeed as an early example of Rintaro's direction, but because its hero didn't wear any pants.

KUNOICHI SAKUYA

2011. AKA: *Girl Ninja Sakuya.* Video. DIR: Tatsuhiko Yoshiwara. SCR: Akira Nintai. DES: Ken Nishimura. ANI: Ken Nishimura. MUS: N/C. PRD: schoolzone, Marigold (Girls Talk). 30 mins. x 2 eps.
Based on a porn game by Lune in which innocent female ninja Sakuya undergoes "sex training." **NV**

KUPU! MAMEGOMA

2009. TV series. DIR: Hidekazu Oka. SCR: Hiroyuki Onoda. DES: Masayuki Sekine, Maki Morio. ANI: Masayuki Sekine. MUS: Megumi Ohashi. PRD: TMS Entertainment, Columbia MUS Entertainment, Creative Core, San-X, Sotsu Agency, TV Kanagawa. 12 mins. x 51 eps.
Adorable little Mameta, a "bean seal" tiny enough to fit in a person's palm, lives with Mama and Papa Mamekawa, big sister Akane, and little sister Yui. The Mamekawa family look after him and his pals Cherry-san, Soda-kun, Lemon-chan, and Candy-chan. Together they have happy adventures in this series aired as part of the *Chibi Anime Gekijo* anthology show. Created by San-X to decorate accessories and stationery, Mamegoma is a stablemate for KOGEPAN and AFRO KEN and has already starred with his pals in a range of Nintendo DS games. *Mame* is Japanese for "bean" and *goma* is an abbreviation of the Japanese name for a mottled seal.

KURAU PHANTOM MEMORY *

2004. TV series. DIR: Yasuhiro Irie. SCR: Aya Yoshinaga, Tsuyoshi Tamai, Yasuyuki Suzuki, Yasuhiro Irie, Shin Yoshida. DES: Tomomi Ozaki, Masahisa Suzuki, Shingo Takeba. ANI: Atsuko Sasaki, Hiroyuki Kanbe. MUS: Yukari Katsuki (S.E.N.S.). PRD: BONES, Kurau Project, TV Asahi, Victor Entertainment. 24 mins. x 24 eps.
By the year 2100, humans have colonized the Moon and appear to have solved most of their problems on Earth, too. Mankind even seems to have the ecology issue

licked, with Earth divided into inhabited areas called METROPOLIS and green "support" areas known as ECOLOGIA. But every Eden breeds its serpents, and despite there being no poverty, there's still crime. A group of special agents is tasked to deal with crimes that the Global Police Organization can't handle. Twenty-two-year-old Kurau Amami is a highly skilled and successful agent, but still lonely and emotionally immature. She has good reason—she's a rare being, a human-alien hybrid created by accident. In her case, the accident happened in her father's lab ten years before when her body was possessed by a transdimensional life form called Rynax, making her a Ryna-Sapien. Rynaxes live in the microscopic spaces between their partner's atoms. If they can escape into our world, they can make anything they touch decompose. They bestow superhuman physical abilities: Kurau can fly, make solids decompose, and defeat giant robots without even wearing armor. But there's a price to be paid in the style of ELFEN LIED: normal people fear her and she's lonely and friendless. Then, on Christmas Day, Kurau gets her best ever present. Light pours from her body, and a girl who is the image of her 12-year-old self materializes before her eyes. She seems completely ordinary. Kurau names her Christmas and enjoys having a younger "sister" around to ease her loneliness. Then other Rynaxes try to emerge from her body, and the Government decides she's becomes a destructive virus who must be exterminated along with her Rynax other self. Determined to protect Christmas from mankind, and mankind from the destructive abilities of the Rynax, Kurau has a fight on her hands. The girls flee around the world, and even to the Moon, and on the way they meet other Ryna-Sapiens and other Rynaxes. It seems the two species can coexist, even though not everyone on either side wants to. Director Irie, who also directed ALIEN 9, another show about symbiotic relationships between humans and aliens, says the theme of the show is communication—between different life-forms or just people with totally different perspectives. By getting others to see that Christmas isn't a threat and that she isn't to be feared, Kurau can overcome her own loneliness and finally become a mature, happy woman. Compare to **BIRDY THE MIGHTY** and its ultimate inspiration, **ULTRAMAN**. ⬤ⓃⓋ

KURENAI *

2008. AKA: *Crimson*. TV series, video. DIR: Ko Matsuo. SCR: Ko Matsuo, Sotaro Hayashi, Sumino Kawashima, Osamu Morikawa, Hideaki Koyasu. DES: Kumi Ishii, Kazuhiro Arai. ANI: Kumi Ishii. MUS: Ken Muramatsu. PRD: Brains Base, Shueisha. 25 mins. x 12 eps. (TV), 30 mins. x 2 eps. (v).

Sixteen-year-old Shinkuro Kurenai lost his parents in a terrorist attack years ago. He was raised by a family of martial artists and now lives alone and works for the man who saved his life as a "problem fixer" of shady or dangerous situations. He's good at his job and wants to prove himself even further, so he volunteers to look after and protect a precocious seven-year-old girl whose mother's dying wish was to get her out of her wealthy father's family clutches. Although surrounded by beautiful girls who are very interested in him, Shinkuro finds himself bonding with his young charge in a much deeper way. The little girl, dazzled by her kindhearted mentor, naturally wants to grow up to marry him. This martial arts action harem romance is a well-made, very convincing show with little traditional fan service: instead it focuses on incest and grooming. Based on Kentaro Katayama and Yamato Yamamoto's manga, this story also has two videos bundled with manga releases in 2010, anthologies containing short stories about each cast member. ⓃⓋ

KURI, YOJI

1928–. Pseudonym of Hideo Kurihara. Born in Fukui Prefecture, he graduated from middle school in 1945 and went to Tokyo in 1950 to study at the Tokyo Art School. His early work in comics led to his selection for the Bungei Shunju Manga Prize in 1958, but his work was always more avant-garde than his peers'. Whereas others like Osamu Tezuka were embracing the commercialism of television, Kuri was drawn to the experimental animation of the Canadian Norman McLaren. He began making his own animated works, in deliberate reaction to the mainstream attitudes of other Japanese animators and the Disney empire. Proclaiming that he wanted to make "animation for adults," he pursued a solitary route, leading to a large number of solo (or at least, independent) works, many of them very short—the *Yoji Kuri Film Works* DVD released in Japan contains 18 alone. He was also, along with Ryohei Yanagihara and Hiroshi Manabe, one of the "Animation Group of Three," annual displays of whose work eventually became the basis for a series of animation film festivals in Japan from 1960 to 1971. However, despite Kuri's relative obscurity from the mainstream, his animated opening sequence to *Madcap Island* (**PUPPETRY AND STOP MOTION**) was seen more times, and for more episodes than Tezuka's **ASTRO BOY**. His early arthouse works include *Fashion* (1960), *Two Pikes* (1961, *Nihiki no Sanma*), *Human Zoo* (1963, *Ningen Dobutsuen*), and *The Discovery of Zero* (1964, *Zero no Hakken*), in a body of work stretching up to *Manga* (1977), *The Imagination of Trousers* (1981, *Zubon no Naka no Imagination*), and *The War of Men and Women* (1983, *Otoko to Onna no Senso*). His creations have been exhibited at many international film festivals, and he has received accolades in New York, Amsterdam, and Venice, among others.

KUROGANE COMMUNICATIONS *

1998. JPN: *Kurogane Communication*. TV series. DIR: Yasuji Kikuchi. SCR: Mitsuhiro Yamada. DES: Shinya Takahashi. ANI: Toshimitsu Kobayashi, Hideaki Shimada. MUS: Kenji Kawai. PRD: APPP, WOWOW. 10 mins. x 24 eps.

Earth has been ravaged by a devastating war, while one-time robot servants fight in the ruins over spare parts. Haruka, a human girl who might be the last survivor of her race, is found by some kindly robots, who protect her from war machines hellbent on carrying out their programming to wipe humanity off the face of the Earth. Haruka and her new friends set off in search of other survivors in, if you can believe such a thing, a lighthearted tale of surviving the apocalypse. This series was based on the manga in *Dengeki King* by Yoshimasa Takuma and Hideo Kato and broadcast as part of the satellite TV strip *Anime Complex*.

KUROKAMI THE ANIMATION *

2008. AKA: *Black God*. TV series. DIR: Tsuneo Kobayashi. SCR: Reiko Yoshida. DES: Hiroyuki Nishimura. ANI: Hiroyuki Nishimura. MUS: Tomohisa Ishikawa. PRD: Sunrise, Bandai Visual. 25 mins. x 23 eps. (TV), 25 mins. (v).

The Terra Guardians are beings who work to keep the world's Luck, or life-force, in balance. Luck is shared out between three identical individuals: if you meet your doppelgängers, the one with the strongest luck will absorb the luck of the weaker ones, who die. The Guardians normally stay out of human sight but one of them, Kuro, accidentally involves a young Japanese guy in an attack by another Guardian. When he loses an arm, she swaps it for one of hers—she has enhanced healing powers. This creates a bond between them that cannot be broken and greatly enhances her power, but requires them to stay together (compare to **BIRDY THE MIGHTY**, and its ultimate inspiration, **ULTRAMAN**). Previously, Keita's worst problem was surviving daily life as a student. Now, it's preventing the world from sliding into chaos.

This was the first anime to be broadcast *dubbed* into English within 24 hours of the first Japanese broadcast. It's based on *Black God* (*Kurokami*) a Japanese-Korean comic, written by **FREEZING**'s Dall-Young Lim and illustrated by Sang-Woo Park for Square Enix's *Young Gangan* magazine. Created entirely by a non-Japanese team who would joke with their readers about their lack of fluency in the language, published in Japan for a local audience, it ran from 2005 to 2012, so only a small section of the plot was animated.

This may explain the unevenness of pacing—some fight sequences last less than a minute, other elements drag on, essential details are missing, characters turn up and vanish without warning or explanation. It's hard to tell whether the plot is twisting or simply unraveling, so it's hard to care. This is a pity, since there are some really interesting ideas, along with a moving sibling feud and a bittersweet ending. The animation is mostly good, and the fluid, well-choreographed battles stand out. Where some shows rely on editing and still frame effects, *Kurokami* has characters moving dynamically. Even though most of the fights are brief, they make a real impact, which makes the show seem even more of a missed opportunity. An unaired "special" episode was added to the final DVD and Blu-ray volume. ◐

KUROKO'S BASKETBALL *
2012. JPN: *Kuroko no Basuke*. TV series. DIR: Shunsuke Tada, Shingo Irie, Toshizo Nemoto. SCR: Noboru Takagi. DES: Yoko Kikuchi. ANI: Takayuki Goto, Yoko Kikuchi. MUS: Ryosuke Nakanishi, R.O.N., Alpha Eastman. PRD: Production I.G, Bandai Visual, Lantis, NAS, Banpresto, Shueisha. 25 mins. x 25 eps. (TV1), 25 mins. x 25 eps. (TV2), 25 mins. x 25 eps. (TV3),

Tetsuya Kuroko was the secret weapon of his middle school's basketball team, an unassuming, often invisible player with a ninja-like ability to blend in and be unseen, until the crucial moment when he could pass the ball to one of the team's champion scorers. Everybody remembers the five boys of the "Miracle Generation" and their multiple winning streak, but nobody, it seems realizes that the stand-out players could only shine when Kuroko (lit.: the "black child") was able to sneak through as the mystery sixth man and pass them the ball at the right moment.

A fine player with no record or following, Tetsuya sees raw talent in high school player Taiga Kagami. Through Kagami, and through his own well-honed skills of being the power behind the throne, he aims to turn his new school's team into champions of high school basketball. Based on a 2008 *Weekly Shonen Jump* manga by Tadatoshi Fujimaki, *Kuroko's Basketball* was a runaway success with a generation that welcomed its shy, wallflower take on the standard tropes of SPORTS ANIME. There is something ineffably austere and Japanese about a hero whose particular talent is *not* being noticed while others take the credit, and indeed in the subversive potential of a team of handsome pretty boys in the girl-magnet style of SLAM DUNK.

However, *Kuroko's Basketball* is liable to be remembered not for its diffident take on time-worn clichés, but for the prolonged terror campaign waged on its author and fans by Hirofumi Watanabe, a troubled, suicidal 30-something determined to drag the manga and anime into his personal vortex of drama. Poisoned packages and death threats, combined with hundreds of abusive letters, ensured that *Kuroko's Basketball* DVDs and manga

were removed from shelves by jumpy shopkeepers and that several fan events refused to allow fanzines based on the show to be sold on the premises. Watanabe was caught in 2013 and sentenced to four-and-a-half years in prison, and went to jail still bragging that his acts were a fine revenge against his parents and against a creator of whose success he was resentfully jealous. Compare to DEATH NOTE, which similarly achieved both fame and infamy on account of its more avid and deluded fans (LAW AND DISORDER).

KUROZUKA
2008. AKA: *Black Hill*. TV series. DIR: Tetsuro Araki. SCR: Tetsuro Araki, Osamu Morikawa. DES: Masanori Shino. ANI: Masanori Shino, Gi Du Kim. MUS: Kiyoshi Yoshida. PRD: Madhouse, Sony Pictures Entertainment. 23 mins. x 12 eps.

History records that Japanese hero Minamoto no Yoshitsune, brother of Japan's first shogun, died in the 12th century. Instead, he assumed the name of Kuro and fled into the mountains, where he met a strange and beautiful woman in a lonely hermitage. He fell in love with her before he learned her dark secret. Now, unable to die, he observes as his country develops into a very different society from the one he knew (compare to DOOMED MEGALOPOLIS, which similarly framed modern Japan through the gaze of a famous historical figure).

Based on Baku Yumemakura's novel, which became a manga with art by Takashi Noguchi in 2003, this dark and gory vampire tale whirls the audience giddily through the ages like a debutante at a ball, allowing glimpses of the world spinning around in apparent wild disorder. The suspense and action are beautifully animated. Director Araki, who handled DEATH NOTE with such style and humor, cuts Madhouse loose to do what they do best: paint the screen any color you want as long as it's red and black. There are faults with the pacing and the script, but overall this is a classy-looking piece of mind candy that isn't unworthy to be shelved alongside the studio's earlier WICKED CITY. ◐

KURUNEKO
2009. AKA:. TV series. DIR: Akitaro Daichi. SCR: N/C. DES: N/C. ANI: Rie Oshima. MUS: N/C. PRD:

Studio DEE, Dax Production. 3 mins. x 50 eps. (TV1), 5 mins. x 37 eps. (TV2). Once a catlover, always a catlover. A 30-something Japanese designer sharing her life with just one cat finds that she can't resist welcoming new furry friends into her home. She relates the stories of their everyday antics and even provides voiceover for their dialogue. She also reveals her fondness for *sake*. This simple EVERYDAY ANIME is based on Yamato Kuruneko's blog, which, according to publisher Enterbrain, was the most popular manga blog in Japan in 2009—conclusive proof that it's impossible to have too many cat stories on the Internet. Also in 2009, Kuruneko launched online manga *Tonosama to Tora*, starring a tiger-striped cat named Tora and his human in Edo-period Japan.

KUTTSUKIBOSHI
2009. Video. DIR: Naoya Ishikawa. SCR: Naoya Ishikawa. DES: N/C. ANI: Naoya Ishikawa. MUS: Shunsuke Morita. PRD: Primastea, Dax Production. 22 mins. x 2 eps.

Kiiko is an ordinary girl, and she's completely recovered from the accident that left her concussed a while ago. She doesn't ever mention the fact that, since the accident, she can move objects with her mind—she just wants to fit in. She falls in love with Aaya, but a dark secret in Aaya's family threatens to tear them apart. This girls'-love anime has a few plot twists that old anime hands may see coming—especially those who remember the CREAM LEMON *Ami* episodes—and is rather more shocking and less gentle than KISS FOR THOSE LIPS. ◑

KYO KARA MA-O *
2004. AKA: *From Now On, I'm a Demon King!* TV series. DIR: Junji Nishimura. SCR: Akemi Omode. DES: Yuka Kudo. ANI: Kazuki Noguchi. MUS: Yoichiro Yoshikawa. PRD: Yuji Shibata, Studio DEEN, NHK. 25 mins. x 78 eps.

Yuri Shibuya is an ordinary guy, baseball fan, and loyal friend. When he tries to help a pal being beaten up by a gang of bullies, he ends up having his head flushed in a public toilet. Much to his surprise, he emerges in another world—Shinmakoku, a world populated by magic-using demons and the humans they despise. Humans have no magic powers in Shinmakoku and are considered a lower species, but there have been some intermarriages, and Yuri meets one of the human/demon hybrids right away. Lord Conrad ("Call Me Conrad," he suggests, in a reference to Roger Zelazny's *This Immortal*) Weller treats him like a younger brother and helps him find his way around this quasi-medieval European setting. Yuri's black eyes and hair, and his school uniform, attract a lot of attention, and soon he's told that he is not just some inferior human, but the reincarnated spirit of the 27th King of the Mazoku, or to use his formal title, the Maoh. Black is the royal family color, as it was for the historical first emperor of China. Royal aide Lord Gunter von Christ takes over from Conrad in tutoring the new King. A purple-haired exquisite, the archetypal European aristocrat, he's part scholar, part soldier—and part mother hen, fussing over his young monarch and treating him like an infant. The Mazoku tribe was rather hoping for a belligerent monarch who would help them drive their enemies before them, but instead they get a nice, quiet guy who likes to sort things out by negotiation and get a fair outcome for all sides.

A satire of the otherwordly conflicts of ESCAFLOWNE and FUSHIGI YUGI with the irreverent attitude of SLAYERS, *KKM* flits back and forth between the worlds of demons and humans as its hapless protagonist tries to do his duty by going on quests and saving distant kingdoms. Like so many other anime heroes, including PHOTON, whose desert storyline *KKM* echoes for several episodes, he is accidentally betrothed in the first couple of episodes, although in his case to a man. Based on the eight-part series of *Ma no Tsuku* novels by Tomo Takabayashi. Kadokawa also published two volumes of spin-off stories set in the same universe.

KYOSOGIGA

2011. TV Series (online). DIR: Rie Matsumoto. SCR: Miho Maruo. DES: Yuki Hayashi, Hiroshi Kato, Hirotsugo Kakoi. ANI: Yuki Hayashi. MUS: Hiroshi Takaki, Go Shiina. PRD: Toei Animation, Banpresto. 25 mins. (special), 25 mins. x 5 eps. (TV).

Kyoto, but not as we know it: a strange alternate dimension where a monk, a demon, and a priest hold sway. Koto and her two little brothers are stuck in this strange place. To get home, they have to find and follow the rabbit. A storyline of almost hallucinogenic obscurity (easier to follow if you have a copy of *Alice in Wonderland* at hand) is decorated with frenetically bright animation and design—imagine FLCL crashed into SOUL EATER with elements of CATNAPPED. Based on a 2011 manga credited to Izumi Todo, Toei's house pseudonym, this single online episode was really only the appetizer for 2012's *Kyosogiga Dainidan (Kyosogisa Part 2)*, five stories about the characters introduced in the first episode. If these were the first few episodes of a TV series, they would be intriguing, but with no sign of anything further to come they're ultimately frustrating—one of those charming curiosities with much unfulfilled potential.

KYOTO ANIMATION

Formed by former employees of Mushi Production in 1981 and incorporated in 1985, becoming a public company in 1999, the studio takes its name from its prefecture of location, not the ancient capital of Japan that the name evokes; in fact, it is sited in Uji, a nondescript town half an hour by train from all the temples and cherry blossoms. It also owns a subsidiary, Animation-do (Anido), in nearby Osaka. Representative works included GATEKEEPERS and the "Turn A" sequence of the GUNDAM franchise, before the company became known in the 21st century for numerous serials that tapped into the otaku audience, particularly THE MELANCHOLY OF HARUHI SUZUMIYA and K-ON. The company has run an annual new talent contest, although at time of writing (2014) it has pointedly refused to give out a grand prize since 2010. The authors note that this means those "honorable mentions" that the studio has put into production anyway have hence *failed* to meet its own criteria for excellence.

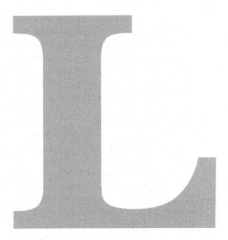

LA BLUE GIRL *

1992. JPN: *Inju Gakuen La Blue Girl.* AKA: *Lust-Beast Academy La Blue Girl.* Video. DIR: Raizo Kitazawa, Kan Fukumoto. SCR: Megumi Ichiyanagi. DES: Kinji Yoshimoto. ANI: Miki Bibanba, Rin Shin. MUS: Teruo Takahama. PRD: Daiei, Green Bunny. 45 mins. x 6 eps. (v1), 30 mins. x 4 eps. (v2), 30 mins. x 4 eps. (v3).

Not unlike **DEVIL HUNTER YOHKO**, high school girl Miko Mido and her sister are the heirs to the secrets of an ancient ninja clan. When they become embroiled in an interdimensional war with rapacious demons, they reveal their secret powers— they are sex-ninja who cast spells with the power of orgasm and, hence, cannot get enough of their enemies' lusty attentions. Based on an idea by **UROTSUKIDOJI**-creator Toshio Maeda, *LBG* continues his obsession with hormonal chaos, as demons kidnap the high school volleyball team, and Miko can only rescue them (from sexual degradation, naturally) by submitting to the wanton desires of her demonic enemies. The series was also released in compiled feature-length editions and an *Ecstasy* collection that included only the sex scenes.

After the first four episodes in Japan, the series was followed by *Shin* ("True") *Inju Gakuen La Blue Girl,* comprising a 45-minute part one, and a " part two" comprising two 30-minute episodes (there always being more money to be made in splitting a show in half and bulking it out with synopses of the story so far!). We believe these three videos to comprise "episodes five and six" of the American release.

The franchise was rebranded as *La Blue Girl EX* (1996, released in the U.S. as *Lady Blue*) for a further four episodes, taking Miko off to college, where her crush on a fellow classmate turns out to be part of a conspiracy, as her jilted immortal aunt seeks to bring her ancient lover back from the dead, predictably by raping Miko. Notorious in the U.K. market for being refused a release point-blank by the British censor, *LBG* also caused some controversy in the U.S., where the Japanese censorship dots were removed prior to release, revealing half-drawn genitals which the animators never intended to be seen, giving the impression that some of the participants were underage. The franchise was also made as three live-action films, starting with *Sex Beast on Campus* (1994), directed by Kaname Kobayashi, and continuing with *SBoC: Birth of the Daughter with Dark Spirit* (1995) and *SBoC: Female Ninja Hunting* (1996), both directed by Kaoru Kuramoto. Compare to **ANGEL OF DARKNESS**. A further series, the four part *La Blue Girl Returns* (2001, *Inju Gakuen La Blue Girl Fukkatsu-hen; Lust Beast Academy La Blue Girl: Revival Chapter*) produced by Green Bunny, featured the Shikima realm invaded by a race of butterfly demons, resisted in a predictable manner by the denizens, although the art style was remarkably different from earlier incarnations, with more of a cutesy, pastel look. **LNV**

LABYRINTH OF FLAMES *

2000. JPN: *Honoo no Labyrinth.* Video. DIR: Katsuhiko Nishijima. SCR: Kenichi Kanemaki. DES: Noriyasu Yamauchi, Hidefumi Kimura. ANI: Noriyasu Yamauchi. MUS: Koichi Fujino. PRD: Studio Fantasia, Bandai Visual. 30 mins. x 2 eps.

The secret city of Labyrinth Four was founded by Japanese citizens of the Aoi Shigemasa domain, who were either exiled after the fall of the shogunate, or perhaps deliberately sent there in order to plot the shogun's restoration. Years later, Labyrinth Four is a forgotten village in what is now Russia, where the inhabitants still cling to a samurai lifestyle. Imagine, then, the glee with which Russian samurai-fan Galan flings himself into his life in the newfound village, where he befriends Japanese princess Natsu, in an often incoherent comedy from the people who brought you **AGENT AIKA**. **NV**

LADIES VERSUS BUTLERS *

2009. JPN: *Lady x Bato.* TV series. DIR: Atsushi Otsuki. SCR: Tsuyoshi Tamai. DES: Akio Takami, Ryoka Kinoshita, Kaoru Aoki. ANI: Kazuchika Kise, Beom Seok Hong, Sunao Chikaoka. MUS: Kei Haneoka. PRD: Xebec, AT-X, ASCII Media Works, Lantis, BIGLOBE, Geneon, Klockworx. 24 mins. x 12 eps.

Akiharu Hino was orphaned as a child and adopted by his uncle. He looks like a delinquent (in other words, he gels his hair and scowls) but is really a nice guy. He doesn't want to be a burden on the family, and he's also worried that his uncle might be after his inheritance. So he decides to go to a specialist school where he can be trained for his future career. He wants to be a butler. At the school he meets an old girlfriend, the manipulative Tomomi, and runs into trouble with a girl who takes an instant dislike to him; but over time, he settles in and makes friends.

An upstairs-downstairs set-up, where the upper crust lives cheek-by-jowl with those trained to serve them, is a story concept of enormous flexibility. *Downton Abbey* and *Spartacus: Blood and Sand* both start from that point. Here it's repurposed as a harem (**ROMANCE AND DRAMA**) hooked into the trend for maids and butlers, alongside the very worthy concept that you can't judge a person by their looks (unless of course they're a girl, when the options are cute or invisible). Taken from Tsukasa Kozuki's book series of the same title, the show aired three years after the story began. It lasted just 12 episodes, but the problem wasn't the concept—the books carried on until 2012 and had other spin-offs. Having relied on fan service to bridge gaps throughout, director Otsuki hasn't built up enough emotional investment in the characters to sweeten the letdown of the unresolved ending. Yes, blatantly ignoring structure worked for **BACCANO**, but not here. **◐**

LADIUS *
1987. JPN: *Makyo Gaiden Le Deus*. AKA: *Demon Frontier Legend Le Deus; Le Deus*. Video. DIR: Hiroshi Negishi. SCR: Hideki Sonoda, Hiroyuki Kitakubo. DES: Rei Aran. ANI: Hideyuki Motohashi. MUS: Hiroyuki Nanba. PRD: Ashi Pro. 48 mins.
GUNDAM-meets-*Indiana Jones* as treasure-hunting archeologists fight over an ancient energy source. Spunky hero Riot Geenas travels a post-apocalyptic world accompanied by his dim but well-intentioned twin-girl companions, Sulpica and Seneca. He needs the mystic energy Lidorium that's found in the artifact known as the Eye of Zalem, but so too do his competitors, the evil Dempsters. When he finally locates the Eye, it's being worn around the pretty neck of bar owner Yuta la Carradine, who insists on accompanying him on his quest until such time as he can pay for the damages done to the establishment in a brawl with his enemies. Needless to say, Yuta is the last inheritor of the ancient Kingdom of Quall who holds the key to unlocking its powers, which are unleashed in a grand finale involving massive collateral damage amid ancient ruins, the defeat

of the bad guy, and the arrival of the titular war machine, a giant robot hidden inside a transforming humpback whale. Derivative hokum, repeated five years later in the suspiciously similar **BEAST WARRIORS**, with which it shares a director. The last anime **TRANSLATION** to be made in the U.K. by Western Connection and subtitled in that low-budget company's inimitable randomly timed style.

LADY GEORGIE
1983. TV series. DIR: Shigetsugu Yoshida, Naoto Hashimoto, Satoshi Dezaki, Kenjiro Yoshida, Tsuneo Tominaga. SCR: Hiroshi Kaneko, Noboru Shiroyama. DES: Junsaburo Takahata. ANI: Junsaburo Takahata, Yoshiaki Kawajiri. MUS: Takeo Watanabe. PRD: IU, TMS, TV Asahi. 25 mins. x 45 eps.
In the Australian forest, the Batoman family finds a dying woman who begs them to take care of her newborn daughter, Georgie. Despite the opposition of Mrs. Batoman, the father agrees, and the girl is raised as their own, with no mention of her true parents or that her father was a British convict. Mr. Batoman dies rescuing Georgie from a river, and his two sons, Abel and Arthur, keep their promise to look after their "sister," though they are both falling in love with her themselves. When Georgie falls in love with the Englishman Dowell Gray, Abel confesses his feelings to his mother, who in her fury blurts out Georgie's true origins. Georgie goes to England to find her birth father, and her arrival causes Dowell to dump his fiancée Elise, the daughter of the powerful Duke Dunkelin. With little evidence but the bracelet that is the sole memento of her real mother, Georgie eventually tracks down her father, who is, of course, not exactly a convict but the noble Earl Gerald. Meanwhile, however, the evil Dunkelin has captured Arthur, who has followed Georgie to England and accidentally witnessed the duke's drug-smuggling operation. Arthur nearly dies from the drugs fed to him by Dunkelin's men, while Abel is thrown into the dungeons of the Tower of London for killing one of Dunkelin's relatives.

With a Victorian setting, a foundling heroine, and a long quest for love, *LG* closely resembles the landmark **CANDY CANDY**, all the more for being based on a manga in *Shojo Comic* by the same artist,

Yumiko Igarashi, though originally written as a novel by Michiru Isawa. Eventually, everything ends happily with Georgie and her "brothers" returning to their native Australia, though the original novel was far more tragic. As with the same year's **TREASURES OF THE SNOW**, the anime adaptation builds on the original story, chiefly with early scenes of the heroine's childhood not in the novel or manga versions. These were perhaps inserted as an afterthought to justify scenes of playtime with koala bears, a ubiquitous feature of early 1980s anime—see **NOOZLES**.

LADY LADY
1987. TV series, movie. DIR: Hiroshi Shidara, Yugo Serikawa, Yasuo Yamayoshi, Yuji Endo, Masahisa Ishida. SCR: Mitsuru Majima, Tomoko Konparu, Shigeru Yanagawa. DES: Takao Sawata, Yoko Hanabusa. ANI: Kazuya Koshibe. MUS: Kohei Tanaka. PRD: Toei, TBS, TV Tokyo. 25 mins. x 21 eps. (TV1), 27 mins. (m), 25 mins. x 36 eps. (TV2).
Five-year-old Lynn Midorigawa sets off for England to meet her Japanese mother for the first time she can remember but discovers that her mother has been killed in a car accident. Her British father remarries, and Lynn must endure bullying at the hands of her stepmother, Vivianne, and her stepsiblings, Mary and Thomas. Her only friend is the kindly boy Arthur, who promises to help her become a true lady. It's another syrupy romance in the spirit of **CANDY CANDY**, based on the manga *Hitomi* by Yoko Hanabusa. The short 1988 *LL* movie is set a year after the series and focuses on the heroine's misery at the mansion of Marquis Bourbon, where she is forced to work as a maid to help repay her father's debts.

The movie bridges the gap between *LL* and its sequel, *Hello Lady Lynn* (1988), for which the franchise moved to TV Tokyo from TBS. Set three years after Lynn's original arrival in England, *HLL* packs her off to stay with Countess Isabelle and attend Saint Patrick's College for young girls, where she joins the equestrian club and gets involved in genteel high jinks in the spirit of **TWINS AT ST CLARE'S**. There was also a live-action movie, *Ready! Lady!* (1989), directed by Kei Ota.

LAGRANGE: THE FLOWER OF RIN-NE *

2012. TV series. DIR: Tatsuo Sato. SCR: Shotaro Suga. DES: Haruyuki Morisawa, Chizuru Kobayashi, Takushige Norita. ANI: Takushige Norita. MUS: Saeko Suzuki, Tomisiro. PRD: Xebec, Bandai Visual, Flying Dog, Production I.G, Sammy, Yomiuri TV. 25 mins. x 12eps. (TV1), 25 mins. x 12 eps. (TV2), 44 mins. (v).

Kind-hearted schoolgirl Madoka helps out around her seaside hometown, and seems destined for a humdrum existence, until she discovers that she has somehow bonded with a robotic combat aircraft called a Vox Aura. Weapons like Madoka's are being employed in a clandestine war against aliens, in which the Japanese government is already involved. So, too, is the alien princess Lan, sent to Earth to protect Madoka, and integrating into Earth culture with something of a lack of success.

Sub-EVANGELION hijinx soon ensue, in a teens-piloting-robots-to-save-the-planet show that will only seem new if you have never watched any Japanese animation before. That's not to say that *Lagrange* doesn't approach its time-worn clichés with a degree of heart and passion, not the least in the form of Lan, who is gullible to the extreme, and has already been persuaded that "Woof!" is Japanese for hello. Later episodes drag the conflict into a typical anime time abyss, suggesting that events now playing out were set in motion some 20,000 years earlier, for reasons that finally go some way toward explaining why the future of the entire planet should be played out in skirmishes over an anonymous seaside resort. The denouement of the second season owes something to a crucial moment of truth in the earlier MACROSS—or more exactly, *Do You Remember Love?*—in which homespun, mundane Earthling *niceness* turns out to have unexpected applications when weaponized.

LANDLOCK *

1996. Video. DIR: Yasuhiro Matsumura. SCR: ORCA. DES: Kazuto Nakazawa, Masamune Shirow. ANI: Koji Matsuyama. MUS: N/C. PRD: Sega Enterprises. 50 mins. x 2 eps.

In the Aztec-like fantasy-land of Zer'lue, Chairman San'aku leads an invading army of seemingly unstoppable Zul'earth warriors. A lone boy, Lue'der, can stop him, but the chairman's daughter Aga'lee has been sent to hunt him down before his powers (a nebulous ability to control the wind) can truly awaken. Luckily for Lue'der, who has one normal eye and one red eye as a mark of the chosen one, Aga'lee's sister Ansa has a normal eye and a *blue* eye. He takes this to be some sort of sign that she should help him escape, which she duly does. Accompanied by a friendly entomologist, Lue'der reaches an ancient temple where he discovers the nature of his destiny, and that the man Aga'lee killed was not his real father. He combines the fabled Red and Blue Flows to become an avatar of the power of the wind, and then he wins the day.

A horrific mess of an anime, complete with pretentious apostrophes in people's names (inserted for the English version, to be fair), and a *you killed my father, prepare to die* plot unsurprisingly thought up by a committee. This turgid two-parter was rushed out to cash in on the recent success of GHOST IN THE SHELL by producers banking on the star power of Masamune Shirow's name, even though the famous artist's involvement was limited to mere "design assistance." This was enough for distributors in some territories, who eagerly snatched up the chance to release another anime from the successful creator of BLACK MAGIC and APPLESEED—though they, and their consumers, were to be very disappointed. Four years later, the same criminals would strike again with GUNDRESS, another low-rent sci-fi thriller with slight Shirow involvement, even worse than *Landlock*.

LASERION

1984. JPN: *Video Senshi Laserion*. AKA: *Video Warrior Laserion; Rezarion*. TV series. DIR: Kozo Morishita, Hideki Takayama, Masao Ito, Hiromichi Matano, Shigeyasu Yamauchi. SCR: Kozo Morishita, Akiyoshi Sakai, Takeshi Shudo, Keiji Kubota, Haruya Yamazaki. DES: Hideyuki Motohashi, Koichi Ohata, Akira Hio. ANI: Hideyuki Motohashi, Daisuke Shiozawa, Seiji Kikuchi, Hajime Kaneko. MUS: Michiaki Watanabe. PRD: Toei, Tabac, TBS. 25 mins. x 45 eps.

Laserion, a program created by game-crazed boy Satoshi, is brought to life by an accident that sends the data to Professor Blueheim's teleportation experiment. Luckily, Satoshi soon finds a use for a giant war robot, which, GIANT ROBO–style, will only obey his commands, when Earth is invaded by evil lunar-based minions of the evil scientist God Haid, and Satoshi joins the Secret Force to stop them, accompanied by token girl Olivia. Also part of the GODAIKIN toy line.

LASSIE

1996. JPN: *Meiken Lassie*. AKA: *Famous Dog Lassie*. TV series. DIR: Sunao Katabuchi, Jiro Fujimoto, Kenichi Nishida. SCR: Aya Matsui, Hideki Mitsui. DES: Satoko Morikawa. ANI: N/C. MUS: N/C. PRD: Nippon Animation, Fuji TV. 25 mins. x 26 eps.

Country-boy John finds a young puppy by the roadside and nurses her back to health. Lassie grows into a fine collie, blessed with almost human intelligence, though her early years are not without their share of odd mishaps, scoldings, and discoveries.

This WORLD MASTERPIECE THEATER anime displays all the hallmarks of the series' 1990s decline, most notably a cavalier disregard for the original classic that inspired it, Eric Mowbray Knight's 1940 novel that was expanded from his 1938 short story "*Lassie Come Home.*" As with HEIDI and TREASURES OF THE SNOW, the characters' early years, not seen in the original, were used to bulk up the running time, so when the series was ignominiously yanked off the air after just 25 episodes, the novel's central plot had barely begun. Consequently, the extant *Lassie* anime takes its time with the minutiae of Lassie's upbringing, only to rush through her famous long journey home in just three episodes. The unbroadcast final episode, "*Run to the Place of Dreams,*" was included in the later video release. In a final irony, Knight never lived to see any of the TV or movie incarnations of his much-loved dog—he died in a wartime air crash in Dutch Guiana (modern Surinam).

LAST EXILE *

2003. TV series. DIR: Koichi Chigira. SCR: Koichi Chigira. DES: Range Murata, Minoru Murao, Osamu Horiuchi, Yuichi Tanaka, Mahiro Maeda, Makoto Kobayashi. ANI: Hiroyuki Okuno, Yasufumi Soejima. MUS: Dolci Triade, Hitomi Kuroishi. PRD: Gonzo, Victor Entertainment, TV Tokyo. 25 mins. x 26 eps. (TV1),

25 mins. x 21 eps. (TV2).

Claus Valca (or Barca) and his friend Lavie are orphans whose only asset apart from determination and courage is Claus's inheritance from his late father Hamilcar—a small two-man flier called a vanship. It's enough to make a living as couriers on their homeworld, Prester, and keep them comfortably out of the gutter, but they both dream of going further. Prester is made up of two warring countries on either side of a permanently raging storm called the Grand Stream, but the war has been conducted with honor and policed by the Guild for years; it doesn't much affect ordinary people like them. They rescue a sweet-faced little girl named Alvis Hamilton from a killing machine and are asked to deliver her to the legendary warship Silvana, but are shocked by the attitude of the commander, Alex Row, who simply accepts the girl as a piece of cargo. They go back to rescue her, and so they are drawn into the war and their lives are changed forever.

Like CHOBITS, *LE* is a fascinating example of the anime business in the early 21st century—quite literally state-of-the-art, good and bad. Its design work is utterly superb, particularly the washed-out, drained color of its characters, seemingly taking inspiration from GHOST IN THE SHELL. Made to celebrate the tenth anniversary of the Gonzo studio and blessed with the longer running length of television, it takes half the series for the action on-screen to start making sense. With its Georgian and Victorian costumes and influences, Morse-code mirrors, Napoleonic riflemen, and Nazi uniform chic that resembles LEGEND OF GALACTIC HEROES, designers are credited for everything from computer graphics to color keys, but the opening credits point the finger for the story itself at an anonymous committee. Literary influences include the multiple pointsofview of Leo Tolstoy's Napoleonic conflict in *War and Peace* (1865) and the battle over limited resources of Frank Herbert's *Dune* (1965), which shares with *LE* a "Guild" that controls the means of transport. Later episodes draw further on Herbert's ecological interests, introducing an environmental subplot about climate changes that have forced the population movement behind some of the conflict. The result often

resembles NAUSICAÄ crossed with the *Phantom Menace* Pod Race—although designer Maeda cites Miyazaki's CASTLE IN THE SKY as his chief influence.

But *LE* also makes the mistakes of many an ill-thought fantasy, introducing oodles of impressive technology, and then refusing to apply it to its obvious uses. *LE* is happy to let the computer graphics do the grandstanding while the characters mug, squabble, and behave in the childish ways that anime producers expect anime fans to expect of anime characters. Lavie, in particular, is the latest in a line of outstandingly infantile ingenues, fretting about her weight (for plot-related reasons, of course; anime wouldn't *dream* of clichés), and enthusing inanely about the fact that the water in a fountain is so clear "you can see right through it." Meanwhile, Alvis is the archetypal anime "mysterious girl," who can provide changes of messianic proportions to the world of *LE*, making her a vital commodity for all sides in the conflict.

Despite onscreen homages to Victoriana in the style of STEAMBOY, *LE* finds innovative ways to cut corners using digital processes. With artwork such a vital part of its success, still images from the series were previewed far ahead of the broadcast premiere, ensuring that everyone had fallen in love with its look before they ever had to see it move. Not that *LE* is poorly animated, but its use of CG is cunning to the extreme. Once rendered for the first time in the computer, it is easy and relatively cheap to keep a giant CG vanship lumbering past the camera. The overlong shots of ships in flight are modern anime's version of the cost-cutting "static pan" of old. Although *LE* has a love of flight and pilots to rival PORCO ROSSO, its fighters are not subject to the laws of aerodynamics. Instead, they are darting, wingless lumps in the sky, ignoring the laws of physics and saving much money in the process.

The TV sequel *Last Exile: Fam, the Silver Wing* (2011) was a reunion both behind the scenes and within the story, as the trouble-struck Gonzo studio pulled itself out of its mid-noughties doldrums and turned to one of its golden age successes in an attempt to kickstart its finances. *Fam, the Silver Wing* picks up the story two years after the end of the first season and depicts a stand-off between the original

inhabitants of planet Earth and the somewhat unwelcome colonists who have returned from their "exile" elsewhere. Writer Kiyoko Yoshimura caroms between several intersecting plots much as the planes of the series dart all over the place in the air, before settling into a succession of epic battles, revolutionary turnabouts, and pivotal politics. The seven-year gap between the sequel and the original, albeit less pronounced overseas where the original did not necessarily appear at the same time as the Japanese broadcasts, was nevertheless a long time in anime—enough time for the *Last Exile* license to lapse in many territories or even for its licence holders to go under. In the U.K., *Fam, the Silver Wing* was not only picked up by a new distributor, but with a rerelease for the first season in a rare rescue, demonstrating just how much faith this series engenders among those who sell anime.

LAST KUNOICHI, THE *

2003. JPN: *Kunoichi Bakumatsu Kitan*. AKA: *Tale of Female Ninja at the End of the Bakufu Period*. Video. DIR: Sosuke Kokubunji, Kenjiro Nakano. SCR: Sosuke Kokubunji. DES: Taka Hiro, Miyuki Abe. ANI: Taka Hiro. MUS: N/C. PRD: Studio Machi, FAI International, Milky. 30 mins. x 2 eps.

The long reign of the Tokugawa shogunate is coming to an end. In the capital, revolution stirs. Three girl ninja are doomed by fate—either they betray their ninja code, or their love for each other and the men they are destined to betray. Kyoto is the setting for this tale of rape and violence: pornography, not history.
🔞

LAST WALTZ

2010. JPN: *Last Waltz—Hakudaku Mamire no Natsu Gasshuku*. AKA: *Last Waltz—Summer Camp Wreathed in White Clouds*. Video. DIR: Hiromi Yokoyama. SCR: Ren Soto. DES: N/C. ANI: Satan Ototoro. MUS: N/C. PRD: Suzuki Mirano. 30 mins. x 2 eps.

Yuki's high school baseball club is at a summer camp on a remote island when civil war breaks out. Some of the male teachers leave to find out what's happening, but their ship is attacked and sunk. As time passes those left behind lose all self-control. In return for the boys' protection, the girls have to pay in kind. Yes, it's another porn story based on a PC game by Guilty, seemingly with distant inspiration in **ADRIFT IN THE PACIFIC** or *Lord of the Flies*, and breaking new ground with orifices you've probably never even considered using. **NV**

LAUGHING SALESMAN

1989. JPN: *Warau Salesman*. TV series, TV special. DIR: Toshiro Kuni, Ryoshi Yonetani. SCR: Ichiro Yoshiaki, Kazuya Miyazaki, Kaoru Umeno. DES: Fujiko-Fujio "A." ANI: Nobuhiro Okaseko. MUS: N/C. PRD: Shinei, TBS. 10 mins. x 44 eps. (TV1), 60 mins. (TVm1), 10 mins. x 47 eps. (TV2), 10 mins. x 12 eps. (TV3), ? mins. x 9 eps. (TVm), 10? mins. x 14 eps. (v).

The miserable life of a salesman whose wife only cares about golf is played for laughs in this long-running series, based on the manga *Black Salesman* by Motoo Abiko, one half of the Fujiko-Fujio duo who created **DORAEMON**. Splitting from his working partner Hiroshi Fujimoto in the 1980s, he produced several titles under the name Fujiko-Fujio "A," including **PARASOL HENBE**, **LITTLE GOBLIN**, **PROGOLFER SARU**, and **BILLY DOG**. Broadcast as part of the *Gimme a Break* variety show on the TBS channel, which occasionally also showed episodes of Shotaro Ishinomori's **808 DISTRICTS**. Several episodes were also edited into the feature-length TV movie *LS Special* (1990), concentrating on the cheerful way that the psychotic salesman took out his midlife crisis on his coworkers with an extensive campaign of blackmail and extortion. From episode 41 onward, the series was rebranded as *New LS* (1991).

LAUGHING TARGET *

1987. JPN: *Rumic World: Warau Mokuteki*. Video. DIR: Yukihiro Takahashi. SCR: Tomoko Konparu, Hideo Takayashiki. DES: Hidekazu Obara. ANI: N/C. MUS: Kuni Kawauchi. PRD: Studio Pierrot. 50 mins.

Azusa is a girl from a traditional Japanese family, who, through an old-fashioned arranged marriage, has been "promised" to her cousin Yuzuru since the age of five. Growing up in an isolated country mansion, she undergoes several bizarre experiences, culminating in the death of her mother. She sets off to snag her long-term betrothed but is shocked to discover that Yuzuru already loves Satomi,

a more modern urban girl, and that not even Azusa's beauty is enough to shake his resolve to break the family's pacts. In a sorcerous revenge straight out of **JAPANESE FOLK TALES**, Azusa then reveals that there is more to her family's traditional beliefs than straightforward marriages. The third in the *Rumic World* series based on short manga tales by **URUSEI YATSURA**–creator Rumiko Takahashi. Other entries included **FIRE TRIPPER**, **MERMAID'S FOREST**, and **MARIS THE CHOJO**. **V**

LAW AND DISORDER

Japanese animation had been part of the ongoing discourse over media influences and harmful content since its first appearance. **EARLY ANIME** were released shortly after the Tokyo Moving Pictures Entertainment Industry Control Regulations (1917), which divided all films into those that were suitable for children and those that were not, severely discouraging animators from pushing the available boundaries. Cartoons were included in the Film Recommendation System (1921) as an area of potential growth, not just as children's entertainment, but for their use in education (**DOCUMENTARIES AND HISTORY**). The banning of the import of foreign films under the wartime Film Law (1939) created a huge vacuum in Japanese entertainment and permitted animators to flourish in unprecedented numbers on military and propaganda contracts (**WARTIME ANIME**)—an increase in investment not seen again until the 1960s.

Postwar purges, such as those that ruined the chances of **THE KING'S TAIL**, often employed legal smokescreens to settle entirely mundane scores and rivalries within the film industry as animators fought over the available work. Legal matters returned to the fore with the inauguration of television animation after **ASTRO BOY**, leading to several conflicts in localization (**CENSORSHIP AND LOCALIZATION**), but also over the allegedly harmful content of children's cartoons. The debate, as ever, centered on "imitable violence"—it was deemed unlikely that parents needed to worry about invading aliens with laser guns, but the more prosaic misbehaviors to be found in shows such as **OSOMATSU-KUN** and **SHAME ON MISS MACHIKO**, which any viewer might conceivably be able to

reenact with everyday items. Similar PTA complaints have hounded such edgy shows as **CRAYON SHIN-CHAN**, usually in that liminal area where children might be expected to be able to access racier material aimed at adults. The issue rarely troubles the video sector in Japan, where it is widely understood and accepted that adult videos are for adults, although there are occasional scares in other countries where **EROTICA AND PORNOGRAPHY** such as **BIBLE BLACK** and **ADVENTURE KID** are mistaken for children's entertainment.

Legal matters also affect anime's reception and heritage among its audience, from spats over intellectual property (**CANDY CANDY**) to allegations of copycat crimes (**DEATH NOTE**) and hate campaigns by vengeful fans (**KUROKO'S BASKETBALL**). The most notorious cases within Japan were those of the serial killer pedophile Tsutomu Miyazaki in the late 1980s, publically derided as an "otaku," and members of the Aum Shinrikyo death cult, masterminds of the 1995 sarin gas attack on the Tokyo subway and embarrassingly vocal fans of **NAUSICAÄ OF THE VALLEY OF THE WIND**. Such lunatic fringes, however, are not unique to Japan—San Diego's Heaven's Gate religious cult was supposedly found to be in possession of a stack of VHS tapes of **EVANGELION** at the time of its mass suicide in 1997.

In years to come, particularly as Japanese corporations fight for a share of the lucrative Chinese market, *business* law may come to the fore, as companies wheel and deal to ensure that a production is somehow 51% Chinese-owned and hence not subject to import quotas in the People's Republic.

In terms of subject matter, anime for children often places emphasis on law and discipline, either through enforcement by parental figures or as the object of cathartic defiance by naughty protagonists, beginning with the notorious *Playful Boy's Air Gun* (1917), the first anime to be banned (**CENSORSHIP AND LOCALIZATION**). Yasuji Murata's *Taro's Steamtrain* (*Taro-san no Kisha*, 1929) showed its protagonist desperately, and largely unsuccessfully, attempting to keep control of an unruly group of passengers, allegorizing an adult's plight by putting a child in a parent's position for comedic effect.

Many children's anime protagonists exist in a dreamworld without parents, adopting an orphan status that may initially be played as tragedy, but can also be exploited as an excuse for an unsupervised existence. Many enjoy an officially "free" orphan status but with parental figures somewhere closeathand, such as the numerous professor-mentors in anime from **ASTRO BOY** to **CONAN THE BOY DETECTIVE** (AKA *Case Closed*), the mysterious stranger who offers help in **CANDY CANDY**, the latchkey children whose parents work long hours away from home—even in a different city—or the impossibly accommodating bases to be found in every **POKÉMON** town, where children are welcomed, fed, and cared for, and then sent back out into the world to have more fun. This condition in anime has not always been used without comment—**HIPPO AND THOMAS** allegorized the parent-child relationship as that of a kindly, indulgent giant and a constantly scheming, ungrateful freeloader, much to the amusement of any parents who found the time to look in.

Not all anime iconoclasm is as obvious as that found in the bratty behavior of **CRAYON SHIN-CHAN**. Bad guys in cartoons the world over are often given dialogue with a vocabulary at least a couple of years older than of the target audience, thereby giving the subliminal impression of a bullying elder sibling or evil parent. However, in anime made specifically for children, it would be counterproductive for producers to sanction bad behavior without retribution. Consequently, many anime protagonists are heroes working to enforce a greater good—employees or heirs of an individual or organization dedicated to the defeat of evil.

Such trends have led to many crime-related serials, in which protagonists hunt down evildoers, or solve crimes by means of deduction. The **NAUGHTY DETECTIVES** (1968) may not have appeared in anime until relatively late in the 20th century, but drew on a tradition of crime-solving kids dating back to the early 20th-century works of Ranpo Edogawa. The works of Arthur Conan Doyle have been as influential on anime crimefighters as those of his contemporary Jules Verne were on science fiction—we not only have the adventures of **SHERLOCK HOUND**, but also the Doyle-inspired *Conan the Boy Detective*. Note, however, that the **CASEBOOK OF CHARLOTTE HOLMES**, in its original Japanese form, was far less closely related to the works of Doyle than its English title implies.

Japan's own detective tradition, the *torimono-cho*, entertained readers with tales of samurai-era detectives, like those found in **808 DISTRICTS**. Some of these, such as the undercover authority figures of **MANGA MITO KOMON** and **SAMURAI GOLD**, were remade for the anime audience in a fantasy or science fiction format. Three of the most famous were controversially remodeled for an anime audience without the consent of the original creators' estates—a descendant of the superefficient *Heiji Zenigata* (*DE) was cast as a dogged, incompetent detective in the long-running **LUPIN III**, whose title character was descended from famous fictional French thief Arsène Lupin, while the grandson of Kosuke Kindaichi would chase criminals in the **YOUNG KINDAICHI FILES** (see also *DE).

Anime detective dramas and cop shows often search for a gimmick designed to separate them from the "mainstream," although with the occasional rare exception of one-shots like **DOMAIN OF MURDER**, there is no crime "mainstream" within the anime medium itself—anime is instead competing directly with live-action. Consequently, crime anime will search, in much the same way as **EROTICA AND PORNOGRAPHY**, for areas within the live-action genre that can be more easily served by animation. Science fiction is perhaps the most obvious, with the Knight Sabers in **BUBBLEGUM CRISIS** and the **AD POLICE**, although anime also offers fantasy crimefighters, such as the cast of **SAILOR MOON**. Shows like **SUKEBAN DEKA** (see also *DE) flirt with the erotic potential of "bad girls," in which a fallen heroine is offered the chance of redemption through working for the police; **CYBER CITY OEDO 808** plays the same redemptive game without the gender-loaded subtext. **YOU'RE UNDER ARREST** had little "new" to offer except a self-conscious cuteness, perhaps explaining why it was so easily adapted for live-action (*DE). Rarer explorations within the detective genre include **FAKE**, which replays the clichés of the detective drama with a homosexual cast.

Anime criminals have also functioned as protagonists rather than antagonists, ever since the adventures of **PRIDE THE MASTER THIEF** in 1965. **LUPIN III** remains the most famous thief, and many of his fellow burglars, such as the heroines of **CAT'S EYE** or **SAINT TAIL**, turned to crime only in the service of a higher and ultimately noble purpose, such as stealing back something that is rightfully theirs. With the coming of the video age, such thieves with hearts of gold began to share the line up with far more unusual suspects, as stories for mature audiences chose to focus on, or even valorize other forms of criminal. Critics of the early video era characterized a subgenre of *bike-mono* ("biker stories") such as the **BOMBER BIKERS OF SHONAN**, in which gang life among boy racers often drifted over to the wrong side of the law. Organized crime also appeared in anime, such as the **THE ABASHIRI FAMILY** or **THE QUIET DON**, while a subset of criminal dramas romanticized the life of the assassin—characters such as **ICHI THE KILLER** and **GOLGO 13** making killing their business, while the likes of **PHANTOM OF INFERNO** and **NOIR** tried to have their cake and eat it too, by traveling the world, killing people, and then feeling very *bad* about it.

Japanese live-action police dramas are reluctant to deal with the issue of a cop on the edge or the wrong side of the law—the hard-bitten, borderline criminal cop of *The Shield* (2002) all too often mutating in Japan into the sanitized rule-benders of live-action serials like *Unfair* (2006). However, while the Japanese mainstream generally insists that its cops are good-hearted, anime can push the envelope in new directions, either with science fictional satire of bad policing like **DOMINION** or **ANGEL COP**, or by pinning all the blame on foreigners, as with **MAD BULL 34**.

The perennial emphasis on science fiction in anime often puts it several years ahead of live-action cop shows in its treatment of new crimes. Hacking, identity theft, and computer viruses are old news in the anime world and continue to be innovatively explored in **GHOST IN THE SHELL** and its spin-offs (see also **PSYCHO-PASS** and **THE TOP SECRET** for more recent iterations). Perhaps the best crime show in anime, however, remains **PATLABOR**, whose robotic supporting cast represents an excellent use of the animated medium over its live-action competitors, while its TV running time permitted long story arcs in which petty infractions gradually escalate into major felonies, and eventually massive governmental conspiracies. For those who want a more traditional sleuthing, there is always **HERCULE POIROT AND MISS MARPLE**, continuing the long tradition in Japanese television of detectives hunting down the truth to make us all feel safer.

LAW OF UEKI, THE *

2005. JPN: *Ueki no Hosoku*. AKA: *Ueki's Laws*. TV series. DIR: Hiroshi Watanabe, Chiaki Kon, Ryoji Fujiwara, Shigeru Kimiya, Shigeru Ueda, Shogo Mitsui. SCR: Kenichi Araki, Masashi Kubota, Masashi Suzuki, Toshifumi Kawase. DES: Shinobu Tagashira. ANI: Maki Murakami, Nozomu Watanabe. MUS: Akifumi Tada. PRD: Echo, Studio Deen, Studio Tulip, TV Tokyo. 25 mins. x 51+ eps.

Life for eighth grader Ueki changes radically when his homeroom teacher is revealed to be a god in training. Ueki becomes the lucky student in the class who is permitted to receive special powers—although his is the rather silly ability to transmute trash into plants, not unlike the ability enjoyed by **EAT-MAN**. He is then sent out to do battle with similarly powered humans, but also expected to live life in an officially sanctioned manner. Every time he commits a sin, he loses one of his mundane abilities as penance and soon finds himself unattractive to girls. Ultimately, if his sponsor attains godhood, he'll win a prize of his own—a blank-slate talent the nature of which he can decide for himself. Compare to *Bruce Almighty* (2003), but also **KAMICHU!** and **MABURAHO**. Based on a manga in *Shonen Sunday* weekly by Tsubasa Fukuchi.

LAWS OF DIVORCE AND INHERITANCE, THE

1989. JPN: *The Horitsu, Rikon, Sozoku*. Video. DIR: Kazuki Sakaguchi. SCR: N/C. DES: N/C. ANI: Keiichiro Okamoto. MUS: N/C. PRD: Koh Planning, Yang Corporation. 60 mins. x 2 eps.

An unusual public-information series in which helpful lawyer Taro Bengoshi talks the viewer through the fascinating world of divorce relating to marital violence, adultery, and irreconcilable differences, as well as methods for dealing with a partner unwilling to consent to divorce, general procedure, division of assets, compensation, parental rights, and child support. The second episode concentrates on inheritance, planning a will, the rights of legitimate children, rights of children from a former marriage, renouncing the right to inherit, finding missing fortunes, intestate wills, and procedures for dividing assets. One to remember next time someone suggests that anime is nothing but **POKÉMON** and porn.

LAWS OF ETERNITY, THE *

2006. JPN: *Eien no Ho*. Movie. DIR: Isamu Imakake. SCR: Ryuho Okawa. DES: Yoshiyuki Hane, Hiroshi Kato. ANI: Keizo Shimizu. MUS: N/C. PRD: Group TAC, Toei Animation. 114 mins.

Ryuta is on a museum trip with his high school science club when he learns about Thomas Edison's efforts to construct a phone that would allow communication with the dead. Later he meets a shaman who claims to have a message from Edison. Suddenly, Ryuta has the knowledge to build Edison's device and set off on a spiritual adventure.

Scientologists aren't the only sect to make films, although you'd think that anyone forced to sit through Roger Christian's *Battlefield Earth* (2000) would realize that tedious movies are not necessarily the best recruiting tool for **RELIGION AND BELIEF**. *The Laws of Eternity* is another anime based on a book by Ryuho Okawa, founder of the religious organization Happy Science, for which see also **THE LAWS OF THE SUN**, **THE MYSTICAL LAWS**, and **HERMES**.

LAWS OF THE SUN, THE *

2000. Movie. DIR: Takaaki Ishiyama. SCR: Laws of the Sun Scenario Project. DES: Don Davis. ANI: Keizo Shimizu. MUS: MIZ Music Inc. PRD: Group Tac. 101 mins.

The Cosmic Consciousness creates the human race on planet Venus, a paradise of wisdom, love, and learning. However, the absence of struggle prevents humanity from striving for perfection, so the entire species is moved to the less hospitable world of Earth, where it is encouraged to seek enlightenment through a process of reincarnation. The early human civilization is smashed up by the dinosaurs, which are luckily killed off by cruel big-game hunters from outer space. Humanity continues to struggle amid several alien assaults. Satan is variously described as leading a revolution against the gods in heaven, leading a revolution in hell, or simply as being an invading alien from the Greater Magellanic Cloud. Mu, Atlantis, Greece, and the Inca civilization all represent peaks of achievement, but are all too soon destroyed by human folly—after, in the case of the Incas, defeating reptilian space invaders with the power of love. Throughout history, however, the same souls are constantly reincarnated, including the wisest humans, such as Jesus, Moses, Confucius, Zoroaster, Buddha, Newton, Thoth, Archimedes, and Hermes. It has now been 2,500 years since Buddha, and the time is right for a new cycle of redemption, handily offered to the audience by the Institute for Research in Human Happiness (now known as Happy Science), the religious cult that funded the film.

Based on a book by Ryuho Okawa (AKA "El Cantare"), the leader of the IRH and supposed reincarnation of several notable historical figures. As with his earlier **HERMES**, the plot is risibly incoherent, mixing myths and pulp sci-fi with such impunity that no writer seems prepared to take responsibility for it. There are, however, some spots of cleverness—particularly the use of reincarnation to ensure that the same point-of-view characters can lead the dumbstruck audience through the 40 *billion* years covered in the feature. As well as doing respectable boxoffice in Japan, where the IRH faithful flocked to see their leader's latest cinematic outpouring, *Laws of the Sun* was also given a very limited screening in the U.S., chiefly in California, a state not unknown for its readiness to embrace new religions. Director Ishiyama filmed similarly revisionist histories in **SAKURA WARS** and **KISHIN CORPS**, while art director Don Davis won an Emmy for his work on Carl Sagan's landmark science *fact* documentary, *Cosmos*. Readers will be pleased to hear that Okawa no longer claims, as he did in the early 1990s, that the end of the world is nigh. One hopes this means that more of his 400 books will be animated soon. **THE GOLDEN LAWS** soon followed.

LEARNING THE HARD WAY *

2007. JPN: *Doki Doki Oyako Lesson: Oshiete H na Obenkyo*. AKA: *Heartbeat Mother/ Daughter Lesson—Sex Instruction*. Video. DIR: Ken Raika. SCR: Ha'Kei Kunfu. DES: Shibafu Karakuri. ANI: Mamoru Sakisaka, Yushi Ueshino. MUS: N/C. PRD: ANI FACTORY, Milky. 30 mins. x 2 eps.

College student Atsushi takes on a part-time job tutoring a cute teenage girl, but things quickly get hot and heavy as she and her sexy mother fight over his attentions. The poor boy has even more problems when another mother and daughter join in the way of the wrestling match. Not much in the way of higher education goes on in this porn anime based on an erotic game by Tinker Bell, though you may find some new uses for sink plungers. Pornmeister Ken Raika's sense of the ridiculous must be stoked by wacky pseudonyms like that of character designer Karakuri, whose name could be read as "old lawnmower." Ⓝ

LEATHERMAN *

2001. Video. DIR: Hideo Ura. SCR: Hideo Ura. DES: Junichi Tanaka. ANI: N/C. MUS: N/C. PRD: Aiti, Five Ways. 30 mins. x 5 eps.

Bad boy biker Cruz is the titular Leatherman. After sex with beautiful but dumb Shisui at her research institute workplace, he robs the safe and makes off on his bike, meeting and bowling over women from a shy nun to a UFO fanatic. Shisui's boss is furious, not just about sex on company time but because the safe contained material that would damage "the organization" if made public. Shisui sets out to find her naughty biker boy and get the bag back, and she's under orders to kill him if he doesn't cooperate. All the women he romps with en route are hostages for his final cooperation in an operation that's bigger than he knows. ⒸⓃⓋ

LEAVE IT TO SCRAPPERS

1994. JPN: *Omakase Scrappers*. TV series. DIR: Hideaki Oba. SCR: Hiroyuki Hoshiyama. DES: Satomi Aoki. ANI: Satomi Aoki. MUS: Nagayoshi Yazawa. PRD: ACC Pro, Beam Entertainment, NHK. 25 mins. x 9 eps.

A children's SF series from LUPIN III–creator Monkey Punch, this anime features a boy and his diminutive robot assistants (think *Silent Running*, but played for laughs) attempting to do the right thing, but often creating more trouble for themselves when they take on deceptively easy jobs, such as guarding an idol singer or running a summer camp.

LEDA: THE FANTASTIC ADVENTURE OF YOHKO *

1985. JPN: *Genmu Senki Leda*. AKA: *Dream-war Chronicle Leda*. Video. DIR: Kunihiko Yuyama. SCR: Junji Takegami, Kunihiko Yuyama. DES: Mutsumi Inomata. ANI: Shigenori Kageyama, Mutsumi Inomata, Mayumi Watanabe. MUS: Shiro Sagisu. PRD: Toho, Kaname Pro. 70 mins.

Yohko Asagiri is a shy teenager who is secretly in love with a schoolmate. She writes a song to express her feelings, only to find that the tune is a bridge to the fantasy world of Ashanti (Leda in the English version). There, the former high priest is making plans to lead his army across to Earth and rule it for all eternity. Aided by warrior-priestess Yoni, a talking dog called Lingam, and a tin man reminiscent of THE WIZARD OF OZ, Yohko must overcome her fears to become Leda's Warrior and pilot the Wings of Leda into the enemy's floating citadel. Here, her ability to tell between true love and falsehood will be tested to the utmost. A high point of early video anime also shown in theaters in Japan, this video combines many anime staples, including large robots, pilot heroines, battle bikinis, and even a love song to save the world. Fifteen years later, the main crew members would still be in the public eye, directing POKÉMON, designing BRAIN POWERED, and composing the music to EVANGELION.

LEFT OF O'CLOCK

1989. JPN: *Hidari no O'Clock*. Video. DIR: Satoshi Inoue, Hiroaki Sakurai. SCR: Yugo Serikawa. DES: Osamu Kamijo. ANI: Masami Suda. MUS: N/C. PRD: Toei. 50 mins. x 2 eps.

Disenchanted with life ruled by other people's timekeeping, Yu gets on a motorcycle and rides down the length of Japan from his northern home. While his sister Megumi and girlfriend Aoi fret about him at home, he becomes a different person during his journey, helping out people he meets on the way and falling in love with the pretty Tomo after an accident. A knight-of-the-road tale based on the manga by AREA 88–creator Kaoru Shintani and presented as four TV-length "episodes," though these two video incarnations were its only appearance.

LEGEND OF CENTAURUS

1987. JPN: *Centaurus no Densetsu*. Video. DIR: Teruo Ishii. SCR: Junzo Toriumi. DES: Osamu Otake. ANI: Hidemi Kama. MUS: Hatanori Fusayama. PRD: Jin Pro. 95 mins.

The Centaurs are a racing team of 93 bikers from the port city of Yokohama who are named after the legendary Greek horse/men. Arthur and Ken fall out over their love for the same lady, who is unhelpfully called Lady, deciding to settle their competition with a race. Based on a manga by Osamu Otake.

LEGEND OF DUO

2005. TV series. DIR: Koichi Kikuchi. SCR: Daisuke Ishibashi, Toshiki Inoue. DES: Project DUO. ANI: N/C. MUS: N/C. PRD: Marine Entertainment, Mobanimation. 5 mins. x 12 eps.

In the 21st century, humanity begins to lose its vitality, or *prana* energy—some might say the same thing of the anime business, particularly if they compare this plotline to the same year's AQUARION. As the human race faces extinction, the last hope lies in the vampires, a race whose blood may supply the muchneeded *prana* that humanity requires. An incredibly short and incredibly cheap animation style, often little better than radio, does little to help this complicated story with an over-large cast of characters better suited to a full-length TV series, not these rapid shorts in the style of BLAME. However, the authors suspect that *LoD* had less to do with television anyway, and more with an experiment in order to create material ahead of the boom in direct downloads to mobile phones, where many of *LoD*'s vices would become virtues.

LEGEND OF GALACTIC HEROES

1988. JPN: *Ginga Eiyu Densetsu*. AKA: *Heldensagen von Kosmosinsel*. Video. DIR: Noboru Ishiguro, Akio Sakai, Akihiko Nishimura, Kenichi Imaizumi. SCR: Takeshi Shudo, Shimao Kawanaka, Kazumi Koide. DES: Matsuri Okuda, Masayuki Kato, Studio Nue. ANI: Matsuri Okuda, Keizo Shimizu. MUS: Michiyoshi Inoue (arranger). PRD: Kitty Films. 60 mins., 100 mins. x 28 eps. (109 "episodes" on 28 tapes), 90 mins. (m), 60 mins. (v/GW), 100 mins. (v/Vows), 100 mins. (v/Dom, Son), 100 mins. (Disgrace), 100 mins. x 3 eps. (v/TSTPL), 100 mins. x 3 eps. (v/SL).

In the year A.D. 3597, 150 years into the conflict between the Alliance of Independent Worlds and the Galactic Empire, both forces claim victory at the Battle of Astarte. On the Alliance side, the strategic genius Yang Wenli, a former historian dragged into a military life. Fighting for the empire, Reinhardt von Lohengramm, the estranged son of a provincial nobleman, determined to rise through the ranks until he can overthrow the ruling dynasty, whose kaiser bought Reinhardt's sister, Annerose, as a concubine from his dishonorable father. Lohengramm's childhood friend, Kircheis, loves Annerose in a different way.

Yoshiki Tanaka's *magnum opus*, the 18 novels of *LGH* are far superior to his other works, which include APPLELAND STORY, HEROIC LEGEND OF ARSLAN, and LEGEND OF THE FOUR KINGS. *LGH* is a tragic far-future epic, in which two heroes, who would probably have been the best of friends, find themselves on opposing sides in a galactic war. *LGH* has a pathos redolent of Leiji Matsumoto's COCKPIT or CAPTAIN HARLOCK, and a sympathetic treatment of both sides—though it is also renowned for truly vast space battles with thousands of ships, set to classical music. The imperial forces are part-Nazi, part-stuffy, decadent European aristocracy, while the Alliance is an American-style melting pot. As in WWII itself, which inspires much of the sci-fi, the imperial forces have the best uniforms and the nastiest schemers, but the other side has its fair share of machinations behind the scenes.

The first two episodes were screened as a movie-edit in at least one theater, with the grossly inferior ULTIMATE TEACHER on the same double bill. Released in TV-episodic form but straight to video, *LGH* is one of anime's silent successes, sold chiefly by mail order to a dedicated audience large enough to keep the series running for a whole decade. Ishiguro shoots the anime version like a disaster movie or a Kihachi Okamoto war film (see EVANGELION), retaining the novel's cast of thousands and many onscreen titles to remind us who is who. Though the sci-fi trappings are occasionally halfhearted and hokey (there are, mercifully, no transforming robots, although there are hackneyed hovercars and similarly redressed contemporary technology), the execution is still brilliant. If FIST OF THE NORTH STAR was animation taken in interesting directions by lack of time and budget, then *LGH*'s need to continuously find new ways to depress its audience has encouraged some masterful writing, most notable in the early episodes. In a scene in which Jessica Edwards is elated to hear of her fiancé's promotion, it takes several seconds for her to register the implication of *posthumous*. But despite the stirring music, gripping plots, and doomed pretty-boy heroes, *LGH* can be too smart for its own good—whereas the anime LENSMAN chose the pulp, kiddified sci-fi route, *LGH* keeps to cerebral plotting likely to doom it in the modern anime market.

Another film, *LGH: Overture for a New Conflict* (1993), flashed back to Reinhardt's first great victory at Astarte during the Tiamat War. Promoted to senior admiral, he decides to accept the Lohengramm family title of Count and retire from the military, but he is thwarted by the actions of other officers, who redeploy his efficient subordinates. Sent to Astarte in the company of his adjutant Kircheis, Reinhardt proves himself against the odds.

As befits a series whose sprawling plot makes *Dune* look like *The Cat in the Hat*, there are plenty of other opportunities for video spin-offs. *LGH: Golden Wings* (1992) is adapted from one of the eight flashback novels set apart from the main series continuity, set four years before the beginning of the story proper. Reinhardt and Annerose meet Kircheis for the first time and fight off a group of assassins sent by the court. Similar intrigues await in *LGH: Valley of White Silver* (1997), depicting Reinhardt and Kircheis's first mission after leaving the military academy. They are sent to the front line on the icy planet of Kapturanka and placed under a commander who hates Annerose because she is favored by the kaiser. Once again, they must deal with assassins without upsetting the status quo. *LGH: Dream of the Morning, Song of the Night* (1997) finds Reinhardt seconded to the military police and sent to investigate a murder at his old school. He undertakes the job, though he is fully aware that he is being framed. The focus shifts to Kircheis for *LGH: Disgrace* (1997), in which the vacationing adjutant rescues an old man, who turns out to be a retired general, forced out of military service after losing a battle. Alliance hero Yang Wenli features in *LGH: A Trillion Stars, A Trillion Points of Light* (1997), in which Schoenkopp, the new commander of the Rosenritter regiment (Knights of the Rose), leads his forces into battle against Runeberg, the *old* commander and his former boss, who has defected to the imperial side and been made a commodore. In the most recent video series to date, *LGH: Spiral Labyrinth* (1999), young Lieutenant Yang Wenli saves the lives of millions of people from an imperial attack and becomes a hero. Soon afterward, he is sent to investigate the murder of Ashby, a retired general. One more tape, the *LGH: Season Four Preview* (1996), is a "making-of …" documentary featuring shots of the crew at work and interviews with the voice actors.

LEGEND OF GUSCO BUDORI

1996. JPN: *Gusco Budori no Densetsu.* Movie. DIR: Ryutaro Nakamura. SCR: Ryutaro Nakamura. DES: Shinichi Suzuki. ANI: Shinichi Suzuki. MUS: Yoshihiro Kanno. PRD: Bandai Visual. 85 mins.

Another children's story by NIGHT ON THE GALACTIC RAILROAD–creator Kenji Miyazawa, adapted into an anime as part of the anniversary of the author's birth (see SPRING AND CHAOS). Gusco is driven from his home and family by a series of natural disasters but fights back by joining the Iihatov Volcano Department. Science brings improvement to the local people, but also causes Gusco's tragic death.

The story was remade by Gisaburo Sugii with something of a steampunk feel as the tedious 106-minute film *Biography of Gusco Budori* (2012, *Gusco Budori no Denki*). In keeping with the anime versions of *Night on the Galactic Railroad* and *Spring and Chaos*, this later film version recast all the main characters as cats, a conceit not present in the original story. The central message, a combination of technophilia and Buddhist charity that sees Gusco "paying it forward" on countless kindnesses from others, is marred somewhat by a hero that appears almost pathologically passive, a muddled finale that does not make it clear how exactly his death occurs, and our own changing sense of scientific achievement and ethics, which no longer regards the release of a massive carbon footprint as anything to really celebrate.

LEGEND OF HIMIKO *

1999. JPN: *Himiko-Den*. TV series. DIR: Ami Tomobuki. SCR: Saburo Kurimoto. DES: Megumi Kadonosono. ANI: Hiroto Kato. MUS: Kuniaki Haishima. PRD: Tac. 25 mins. x 12 eps.

A Japanese teenager discovers that she is the daughter of shrine guardians from the ancient land of Yamatai, flung centuries into the future by an incident that occurred during an invasion of forces from the neighboring kingdom of Kune. Accompanied by her classmate Masahiko, she is dragged back to her original era, where they join forces with the rebels who are still holding out against the undead soldiers born of the Black Mist.

Yet another girl-transported-to-different-world/time anime, tracing its ancestry to THE WIZARD OF OZ, but with more immediate antecedents in MAZE, ESCAFLOWNE, and FUSHIGI YUGI. However, considering that *Himiko-den* originated in a 1999 PlayStation RPG, it is remarkably coherent and well plotted, superior to many other game-based anime. The slightly longer running time afforded by the TV airing is a considerable help, as is the effective opening animation and music. Produced by SAKURA WARS' Oji Hiroi.

LEGEND OF KAMUI

1969. JPN: *Ninpu Kamui Gaiden*. AKA: *Extra Tales of Kamui the Wind Ninja; Search of the Ninja*. TV series, movie. DIR: Yonehiko Watanabe, Satoshi Murayama, Keisuke Kondo, Kiyoshi Onishi. SCR: Junji Tashiro, Hiroyuki Torii. DES: Sanpei Shirato. ANI: Yoshihide Yamauchi, Toyoo Ashida, Tadashi Maeda, Takashi Oyama. MUS: Ryoichi Mizutani. PRD: Akame Pro, Eiken, Fuji TV. 25 mins. x 26 eps. (TV), 88 mins. (m).

Kamui is a new initiate into the world of the ninja, a young boy who wants a normal life, thrown into a society of assassins. He learns the secret tricks of the trade and tries to fight for what he believes in, but the beliefs of his fellow ninja are more mercenary, and liable to cause fatal friction.

Hot on the heels of MANUAL OF NINJA MARTIAL ARTS, a 1964 manga by Sanpei Shirato was also adapted, this time for the small screen. Shirato's original ran out with two episodes to go, so the author wrote two further chapters in order to round off the series. The same creator also wrote SASUKE. Several TV episodes were also recut into the anime film of the same name, released in 1971. Not to be confused with the unrelated DAGGER OF KAMUI.

LEGEND OF KOIZUMI, THE

2010. JPN: *Mudazumo Naki Kaikaku*. AKA: *Reform with No Wasted Draws*. Video. DIR: Tsutomu Mizushima. SCR: Tsutomu Mizushima, Hideki Owada. DES: Junichiro Taniguchi. ANI: Kazunori Hashimoto. MUS: Ryuji Takagi. PRD: TYO Animations, Geneon, Studio Mausu, Klockworx. 8 mins. x 3 eps.

World leaders have found a new arena to resolve political disputes—one requiring all their wiliness, ruthlessness, and brainpower. The fate of the world now hangs on the turn of a tile as presidents, popes, prime ministers, and dictators face each other across the mahjong board.

Hideki Okawa's satirical mahjong manga started its run in 2006. The idea of settling international disputes on the mahjong table is a masterstroke. Fictional characters, who appear very much like real-life politicians despite the opening disclaimer that it's all fictional, are shown as mahjong champions. This connection to real politics is carried through even in the Japanese title, a parody of Prime Minister Junichiro Koizumi's slogan "Reform With No Sanctuary." Both U.S. Presidents Bush, Chairman Mao, and Russia's President Putin make appearances, though Margaret Thatcher is only an onlooker. If you think HETALIA is great political satire, watch this show take it to a whole new level.

LEGEND OF LEMNEAR *

1989. JPN: *Kyokuguro no Tsubasa Barukisasu*. AKA: *Jet Black Wings of Valkisas*. Video. DIR: Kinji Yoshimoto. SCR: Kinji Yoshimoto. DES: Satoshi Urushihara. ANI: Kinji Yoshimoto. MUS: Norimasa Yamanaka. PRD: AIC, Nippon Cine TV Corp. 45 mins.

Lemnear, the sole survivor of her village, is a beautiful girl whose destiny is to become the Champion of Silver, the warrior who will lead the people against the invading

Dark Lord and his evil minion, the wizard Gardein.

A girl out for revenge, a harem, wobbly breasts, escape, massive fight, bigger fight, the end. Like the same creators' later PLASTIC LITTLE, *LoL* suffers from an oversimplification of audience demands—realistically bouncing breasts and massive collateral damage will not make an anime work. They can add to its appeal (see GUNBUSTER), but more discerning fans demand plot and characterization. Urushihara and Yoshimoto are clearly masters of their craft, but masters to the extent that, when given control of a production, they ignore many important aspects in order to concentrate on their beloved designs. The result is a hodgepodge of incongruities commonplace today in such game-based fantasy anime such as FINAL FANTASY—a honky-tonk piano playing in a medieval tavern and a plot so thin that the credits start rolling before the baddie's even cold. There are probably a lot of animators who are using five-second segments from *Lemnear* in their resumés, particularly the highly realistic fire-modeling, but the anime itself is no more than a series of such apprentices' showpieces connected by a halfhearted plot and lovingly drawn cheesecake. The story was also published in manga form, also drawn by Urushihara, while two decades later, Yoshimoto would be back at the helm with QUEEN'S BLADE. Ⓝ Ⓥ

LEGEND OF LYON *

1986. JPN: *Riyon Densetsu Flare*. Video. DIR: Yukihiro Makino. SCR: N/C. DES: Yorihisa Uchida. ANI: Yorihisa Uchida. MUS: Nobuhiko Kajiwara. PRD: Hayama Art, Media Station. 30 mins. x 2 eps. (v1), 30 mins. x 2 eps. (v2).

Claude leads an army of demons in an invasion of the peaceful kingdom of Lyon, but he is held back by the martial (and marital) powers of the beautiful Flare, mixing the alien rapists of DEMON BEAST INVASION with the hokey fantasy plot of EROTIC TORTURE CHAMBER. After dispatching the invaders in episode 1, the pretty Flare and her sidekick, Neris, discover more of them lurking in the woods, and the tentacled menace is once again dealt with after several scenes of clothes-ripping and high-pitched screams. It was followed by the similarly titled *Legend of Reyon: God of Darkness*, a pastiche in the spirit of **TOURNAMENT OF THE GODS**, in which the hackneyed conventions of beat-'em-up game adaptations (a secret fight arranged to destroy all the bad guy's opponents at once) are adapted for the erotic market. Though *Reyon* was not an actual sequel to *Lyon*, it did recycle the same character designs. **❶❷❸**

LEGEND OF ROLLING WHEELS

1987. JPN: *Baribari Densetsu*. Video. DIR: Nagayuki Toriumi, Satoshi Uemura. SCR: Jiyu Watanabe, Mami Watanabe. DES: Shuichi Shigeno. ANI: Noboru Furuse. MUS: Ichiro Nitta. PRD: Studio Pierrot. 30 mins. x 2 eps.
Miyuki Ichinose sees something remarkable—a kid on a 50cc moped outracing a man on a 750cc bike. Since she is the daughter of a motorcycle racing team chief, she wastes no time in inviting the kid, Gun, onto the team. Gun finds it hard to fit in at first, and the rivalry between him and successful rider Hideyoshi makes things even harder. Gun gains confidence, and he and his friends accept Hideyoshi's challenge to enter their team in the world championship. Their team wins, but Hideyoshi's career is interrupted by a tragic accident.

Based on a 1983 manga in *Shonen Magazine* by Shuichi Shigeno, whose need for speed would find a greater outlet in the later **INITIAL D**. This was made for video but shown in some theaters in its year of release.

LEGEND OF THE BLUE WOLVES *

1996. JPN: *Aoki Okamitachi no Densetsu*. AKA: *Legend of the Four Horsemen of the Apocalypse; Hot Space Cowboys*. Video. DIR: Yasunori Urata. SCR: N/C. DES: Makoto Kobayashi. ANI: N/C. MUS: Masamichi Amano. PRD: Beam Entertainment. 45 mins.
In the year 2199, humans have spread out across the solar system, until the unfortunate day when they encounter the alien enemies known only as the Apocalypse. Assimilating human victims and transforming them into new members of their invading army, the Apocalypse represent the worst threat humanity has ever faced. Meanwhile, at a training camp for robot pilots, new recruit Jonathan Tiberius finds himself developing inappropriate feelings

of lust toward his roommate, the older, wiser soldier Leonard Schteinberg. Meanwhile, both are victimized by the camp commander, a fat, ugly man who uses his position of authority to have his wicked way with attractive young cadets. Despite science fictional trappings that seem inspired at least in part by the previous year's **EVANGELION**, the appeal of this gay porn anime rested chiefly on its explicit sex scenes—in addition to the 45-minute full version, there is an R-rated edit with ten minutes missing. It was later released in the U.S. under the fantastic title *Hot Space Cowboys*. **❶❷❸**

LEGEND OF THE CONDOR HERO *

2001. JPN: *Shinkyo Kyoro: Condor Hero*. TV series. DIR: Akira Miyata, Atsushi Nigorikawa, Hiromitsu Morita, Jun Takagi, Kazuya Miyazaki, Keiji Hayakawa, Kenichi Nishida, Masami Anno, Takayoshi Suzuki. SCR: Mayumi Koyama. DES: Noboru Sugimitsu. ANI: Hironobu Saito. MUS: Kanae Shinozuka. PRD: Jade Animation, Nippon Animation, Taiseng Entertainment, BS Fuji. 25 mins. x 26 eps. (TV1), 25 mins. x 26 eps. (TV2).
Yang Guo (Youka) is an orphaned martial arts student in 13th-century China. Seeking revenge for the death of his father whom he never knew, Yang studies under the Taoist Quan Zhen sect in Zhong Nan Mountain, and under crazy kung fu master Ou Yang Feng, nicknamed "Western Poison" for his oddity and lethal skills. On leaving the Taoist temple he meets another kung fu master with a temple on the mountain—Xiao Long Nü (Shoryujo). The beautiful heiress of the Gumu Bai school, she is compelled to accept him as a student by a friend's dying wish. The pair are so naïve that they don't realize the love which grows between them is forbidden until it's too late, and Xiao Long Nü leaves the mountain to get away from her feelings for Yang. But away from the mountain, the tide of history is moving. The Mongols have conquered the northern Chinese kingdom of Jin and their next target is the Southern Song empire. The region has many great martial artists who band together to fight the invaders, but in the end they will be defeated at the historic battle of Xiang Yang, and China will fall under Mongol rule.

The 1959 novel by Jin Yong (AKA Louis

Cha), *Return of the Condor Heroes* (*Shendiao Xialu*), on which the anime is based, is actually a sequel. The first book, *Eagle-Shooting Heroes*, had a number of spin-offs of its own, including a 1994 live-action Chinese TV series and a live-action movie filmed by Wong Kar-wai as *Ashes of Time* (1994). A third novel followed. The anime series was a Japanese–Hong Kong coproduction, conceived partly in anticipation of import restrictions that would shut out the lucrative Chinese broadcast market to some "foreign" imports. Showing up on official records as a "coproduction" with a heavy Chinese staff presence, the show was thus deemed enough of a local production to evade any import restrictions, one of many such anime in the early 21st century as Japanese producers set their sights on the last and biggest market remaining, China itself. Two seasons were produced, but only the first season was dubbed into Japanese and shown on late-night Japanese satellite television, in such an obscure slot that it escaped the notice of all but the most scrupulous scrutineers of the anime magazines. The show didn't prove as successful in Japan as in mainland China (nor did it need to), and season two was only shown in Cantonese, with Mandarin subtitles. The first half (i.e., the Japanese half) was eventually released in the U.S. with English subtitles, although the U.S. version does not contain Japanese language tracks, only Cantonese and Mandarin ones. **❸**

LEGEND OF THE FOREST *

1987. Movie. DIR: Osamu Tezuka. SCR: Osamu Tezuka. DES: Osamu Tezuka. ANI: Takashi Okamura, Yoshiaki Kawajiri. MUS: Peter Tchaikovsky. PRD: Mushi Pro. 23 mins.
In the forest, in the valley, by the river that will eventually flow to the sea, insects buzz among the flowers. Two squirrels fall in love, but the forest is threatened by property developers. The innovation is not in the story, but in the way in which it is told. As with his *Broken Down Film* (see **JUMPING**), Tezuka experiments with the film medium itself, starting with the still frames and limited camera movement on still pictures, before progressing through early monochrome, color, limited TV animation, and Disney-style full animation. In other words, *LotF* takes the viewer through several decades of animation history in just

a few minutes. A second, unrelated film follows, in which forest spirits, shown in lush, *Fantasia*-quality animation and coloring, fight off the human building developers (led by a Hitler-look-alike construction boss), who are shown in limited animation with jagged, angular art design and bright, garish colors. Compare to **POM POKO**, in message if not execution. Released in the U.S. on DVD as part of *The Astonishing Work of Tezuka Osamu* (2009).

LEGEND OF THE FOUR KINGS *

1991. JPN: *Soryuden*. AKA: *Sohryuden; The Endragonning; Legend of the Dragon Kings*. Video. DIR: Norio Kashima. SCR: Akinori Endo. DES: Shunji Murata. ANI: Moriyasu Taniguchi, Nobuaki Nagano, Makura Saki (pseud. for Osamu Dezaki). MUS: Hiroyuki Nanba. PRD: Kitty Films. 45 mins. x 12 eps.
Three thousand years in the past, there was a war in the heavenly realm. Betrayed by their allies, the Go clan are banished from heaven and forced to wander Earth as mortals for 117 generations, until the dragons contained within them burst forth once more to begin the battle anew.

Fast forward to the present, where the four Ryudo brothers live in Tokyo but have recently been the subject of several kidnapping attempts. While the brothers are plagued by kidnappers and dreams of dragons, they have to cope with a takeover bid at the family academy and dynastic machinations as a mobster tries to marry his son to their cousin Matsuri. As if a surname that is Chinese for "Dragon Pavilion" is not enough of a hint, the brothers are the earthly incarnations of the four Dragon Kings of legend, and the powers of their former lives still dwell within them, bestowing superhuman strength and speed. These powers are desired by the "Old Man of Kamakura," who lures them to a firing range by kidnapping Matsuri. The Old Man is not the only one who wishes to possess the magical powers of the Ryudos—the mad Dr. Tomosawa, famed for live vivisections, and the U.S. military are both keen to kidnap the brothers themselves. The doctor sends cybernetic soldiers in to obtain the brothers, but, as with all the previous assailants, his minions are seen off by the brothers' powers of transformation. One Ryudo, however, is caged and taken to Yokota Air Force Base

(see **BLOOD**). The others must rescue him before the cruel experiments awaken the dragon within him and turn him into a monster of awesome destructive capabilities. You can guess the rest.

Dense without being engaging, *LotFK* is based on a series of novels by **LEGEND OF GALACTIC HEROES**–creator Yoshiki Tanaka, but it has none of the virtues of its more illustrious counterpart. A failed attempt to recreate the monthly "video comic" feel of the U.K. distributor's previous **GUYVER**, the dub is particularly poor, with the "Weirdo" brothers speaking a mixture of English and American, and for all their supposed genius, not being able to pronounce each other's names properly. The plot development is confused by the intercutting of disparate scenes from the eight-volume series of novels, patched together with unhelpful voice-overs. The animation itself is often mediocre, barely above the level of later **CRYING FREEMAN** episodes, but the design has a certain special something. From the opening credits that depict the brothers in Chinese dress through to the uncommonly "Asian" features of the characters, *LotFK* is steeped in oriental myth and culture, particularly legends of the hero Nezha and the four dragon kings of Chinese lore, shamefully occluded by the English-language dubbers, who do not bother to rewrite the Japanese pronunciations of Chinese proper nouns and bungle a whole succession of historical and geographical references. These, however, are minor issues unlikely to rescue an already doomed production. The U.S. subtitled version, released as *Legend of the Dragon Kings*, demonstrates all too clearly that the dub is a surprisingly faithful rendition of the original's tepid tone, with the exception of the story's single funny line ("Don't step in the custard"), which was not present in the Japanese version. Dubbed at the height of Manga Entertainment's beer-and-curry era, *LotFK* even managed to disappoint the lowest-common denominator audience with its failed leap of faith toward hidden depths—the same company would return many years later with a much better version of similar material: its adaptation of CLAMP's **X: THE MOVIE**.

In addition to the *Four Kings* novels, the brothers also appear in the Japanese audio drama *Mirage City* (1995), released on CD

with an accompanying manga drawn by CLAMP, who also contributed to the earlier anime adaptation of Tanaka's **HEROIC LEGEND OF ARSLAN**. ⓥ

LEGEND OF THE HEROES: TRAILS IN THE SKY *

2011. JPN: *Eiyu Densetsu: Sora no Kiseki the Animation*. Video. DIR: Masaki Tachibana. SCR: Makoto Uezu. DES: Atsuko Nozaki, Kiroku Ataru, Yusuke Takeda. ANI: Atsuko Nozaki. MUS: N/C. PRD: Kinema Citrus, Bandai Visual, Bushiroad, Chara Ani, Swango, Kaga Hitech, Lantis, Showgate. 43 mins.
In a small kingdom with aggressive neighbors, war is a constant threat. Cassius Bright, a hero of the last conflict and a master Craftsman, has raised two children alone in this uneasy peace. Craft is a blend of magic and high technology wielded by the Bracer's Guild: Cassius is a member and his daughter Estelle and adopted son Joshua are apprentices. When he's called away on business, Cassius is not concerned because Estelle and Joshua are bright, capable teens who can fend for themselves. But they become worried for his safety when they are given notice that his airship has gone missing. They gear up and set off to rescue their father.

There are problems inherent in animating a tiny slice of a huge universe: anyone unfamiliar with the world and setting will be lost unless the work is a beautifully written masterpiece of compressed exposition, or crafted to be so independent that only the trappings of the original world remain. With 11 games in Nihon Falcom's series since 1989, there's a lot of backstory, and those who are not already familiar with the world of the games have to accept much of it without explanation. That said, Kinema Citrus does a good job, showing their prowess with attractive backgrounds, plenty of detail, and solid, serviceable animation. Essentially a commercial for the games rereleased in HD, this looks good, but the story and characters are not strong enough to stand alone. **DRAGON SLAYER** is based on an earlier game from the same series.

LEGEND OF THE LEGENDARY HEROES, THE *

2010. JPN: *Densetsu no Yusha no Densetsu*. TV series. DIR: Itsuro Iwasaki. SCR: Kiyoko Yoshimura. DES: Noriko Shimazawa. ANI: Erukin Kawabata. MUS: Miyu Nakamura. PRD: ZEXCS, Fujimi Shobo, Kadokawa Contents Gate, Lantis, Media factory, SK Independence, T.O. Entertainment. 25 mins. x 24 eps.

Ryner Lute is a student at the Royal Magician's Academy. He's an orphan who can't remember anything about his childhood, even his parents' names. He's naturally gifted, but lazy and unmotivated until his country goes to war and most of his classmates are slaughtered. He and the ruler, his former classmate Sion, share a number of secrets. When Sion asks him to seek out the relics of a legendary hero he sets out on the quest, only to find a deadly curse spreading across the entire continent.

Takaya Kagami's book series ran for four years from 2006, with 11 volumes published showcasing Saori Toyota's art. Three more book series, a manga, a podcast, a drama CD, and video game have spun off it to create a small but solid franchise. More to the point for our purposes, this large and highly evolved world has a level of complexity that's difficult to contain in 24 TV episodes. Alliances, impressively named powers and factions, kingdoms, and histories are cut to shreds or left out altogether. The variations of tone, from comical to dark, from graphic to goofy, that can be explored across a wide canvas look inexplicable or downright silly when crammed into a smaller container.

Many of the people in this shrunken saga have grim stories—parental rape, family murder, the terrible responsibility of power—and the show has a high level of violence, yet most characters remain relentlessly perky, and harem comedy tropes (**ARGOT AND JARGON**) are scattered through the plot like snacks at a party. Sometimes it's like watching one of the bloodier episodes of *Game of Thrones* reframed as a 25-minute sitcom and directed by a comedian. The intelligence and pathos are there, but there's such a load of camp tat on top that it's hard to find them. The "bonus" recap episode on the second U.S. DVD may help you pick up some of the loose ends, but on the whole this show offers more frustration than fascination. **ⓥ**

LEGEND OF THE MILLENNIUM DRAGON *

2011. JPN: *Onigamiden*. AKA: *Legend of the Devil-God*. Movie. DIR: Hirotsugu Kawasaki. SCR: Hirotsugu Kawasaki, Naruhisa Arakawa. DES: Tetsuya Nishio, Tatsuya Tomaru, Mutsuo Koseki, Satoshi Matsuoka. ANI: Tatsuya Tomaru, Shinji Hashimoto. MUS: Ryudo Uzaki, Eitetsu Hayashi. PRD: Studio Pierrot, SME, TV Tokyo, Sony Pictures Entertainment (Japan). 98 mins.

In the Heian period, monks and samurai battle *oni*, the demons seeking to ravage Japan. Modern boy Jun Tendo is hauled 1,200 years back in time to persuade legendary eight-headed dragon Orochi (**LITTLE PRINCE AND THE EIGHT-HEADED DRAGON**) to help humankind in their battle with the demons. Bullied, confused, and terrified, Jun must gather all his courage, befriend the dragon, cut through deceit and sorcery, and somehow find a reason to fight. Inconsistencies in the plot, characterization, and design turn what could have been a fascinating movie into a tedious chore to watch. Kawasaki did a much better job on **SPRIGGAN** than on this adaptation of Takafumi Takada's novel series. Although the CGI animation of the dragon, *oni,* and armor shine, and the 2D frames are allegedly all hand-drawn, the legendary Studio Pierrot has better work on its animation resumé.

LEGEND OF THE WOLF WOMAN *

2003. JPN: *Megami Kyoju*. AKA: *Wolf Woman*. Video. DIR: Katsuma Kanazawa, Shunsuke Harada. SCR: N/C. DES: Masaki Yamada, Yuji Ushijima. ANI: N/C. MUS: N/C. PRD: Cherry Lips, Kuma. 28 mins. (v1), 25 mins. (v2).

Shortly after successfully apprehending a childmurderer, sexy New York SWAT team member Linda tries to blow off steam by hitting a strip club with her boyfriend Brian. But Kata, one of the strippers, is infected with a deadly lycanthropy virus and is soon infecting other people around the city. Linda tries unsuccessfully to contain outbreaks of werewolf violence, while her friend Mary from Forensics gets to work on a cure. Since this is an erotic anime, there is also considerable concentration on the more violent aspects of sexual perversion, including a woman linked up to a car battery for impromptu shock treatment and Linda's idea of foreplay with her boyfriend, which involves a condom and a loaded gun. Compare to **ONI-TENSEI** and **P.I.: PERVERSE INVESTIGATIONS** (which

similarly tries to capitalize on the success of the television series *CSI*), although considering some of the insane things the cast try in a New York minute, this strange porn anime owes a certain additional debt to **MAD BULL 34**. **ⒸⓁⓃⓋ**

LEGENDARY IDOL ERIKO

1989. JPN: *Idol Densetsu Eriko*. TV series, video. DIR: Tetsuro Amino. SCR: Brother Anoppo. DES: N/C. ANI: Noriyasu Yamauchi. MUS: N/C. PRD: Bandai, TV Tokyo. 25 mins. x 51 eps. (TV), 30 mins. (V).

In this popular TV series with a star whose look presaged the girl of the 1990s, **SAILOR MOON** herself, 14-year-old Eriko Tamura wants to be a pop star but must compete against her prissy rival, Rei Asagiri. It's scandal and high-pressure performances, as the tropes of **SPORTS ANIME** (e.g., **AIM FOR THE ACE**) are adapted for a show about a hothouse for wannabe stars—the lighter-hearted flipside of artistic pressures that would be so heavily criticized a decade later in **PERFECT BLUE**. *LIE: Music Video* (1989) was, predictably, a ten-song compilation of some of the serial's best tunes, released straight to video.

LEGENDZ

2004. JPN: *Legendz Yomigaeru Ryu-o Densetsu*. AKA: *Legendz: Tale of the Dragon Kings*. TV series. DIR: Akitaro Daichi. SCR: Aki Itami, Yuki Enatsu, Kinuko Kuwabatake, Yuka Yamada. DES: Nagisa Miyazaki, Kazuyuki Kobayashi. ANI: Nom Jong Sik. MUS: Jun Abe, Seiji Muto. PRD: Studio Gallop, Wiz, Bandai, Pony Canyon, Fuji TV. 24 mins. x 50 eps.

New York, the present: Shu gets a game machine called a Talispod, developed by his father. It doesn't play the game it was designed for, so Shu thinks it's broken, until Shiron the white Wind Dragon emerges, an event that will come as no surprise to anyone who remembers **DRAGON DRIVE** two years earlier. The Talispod is a device that can revive ancient myths. Soon it will be needed to protect the world from new evil. The Dark Wiz company is planning to take over the world, and Shiron's enemy the black-winged dragon Ranshin plans to restart an old war. Long ago, the Earth was ruled by strange creatures worshiped as gods or feared as demons. The Four Dragon Kings (compare to **LEGEND**

OF THE FOUR KINGS) ruled over each of four species of monsters commanded by the four elements—Volcano monsters (fire), Tornado monsters (wind), Earthquake monsters (earth), and Storm monsters (water). Then the Dragon Kings fought, and their monster armies were turned into crystals, known as Soul Dolls. Forgotten except in folklore, they became known as "Legendz." These are the creatures Shu's device can revive.

POKÉMON with dragons, anyone? Director Daichi helms another comical, cutely designed childrens' story, this time adapted by Hiroshi Nagahama from Kenji Watanabe's original manga in *Shonen Jump* monthly, but with some stylistic similarities to his own GRRL POWER.

LEISURE CLUB

1992. JPN: *Yukan Club*. Video. DIR: Satoshi Dezaki. SCR: Machiko Kondo. DES: Yukari Kobayashi. ANI: Yukari Kobayashi. MUS: Toy-Boys. PRD: Pioneer. 35 mins. x 2 eps.
Filthy-rich boys and girls occasionally take time out of their luxurious lifestyle to solve crimes in this short-lived series based on the 1981 manga in *Ribon* by Yukari Ichijo. For the second episode, the cast relocates to the exotic foreign destination of Hong Kong, where they are dragged into a gangland conspiracy over a stolen microfilm. Compare to DEBUTANTE DETECTIVES.

LEMON ANGEL

1987. JPN: *Midnight Anime Lemon Angel*. TV series, video. DIR: Yasunori Ide, Takashi Akimoto, Susumu Aki, Osamu Yamasaki, Yukio Okazaki, Satoru Namekawa. SCR: Yasunori Ide, Osamu Yamasaki. DES: Kurahito Miyazaki. ANI: Katsu Oyama, Osamu Yamasaki. MUS: Human Company. PRD: Fairy Dust, AIC, Fuji TV. 5 mins. x 37 eps. (TV1), 5 mins. x 9 eps. (TV2), 30 mins. x 2 eps. (v), 25 mins. x 13 eps. (TV3).
Three lovely teenagers—and the three actresses who provide their voices—share their midnight confidences and fantasies with the TV audience, as Erika Shima, Miki Emoto, and Tomo Sakurai play "themselves" in a sanitized late-night TV incarnation of the CREAM LEMON franchise. Purporting to be studying at the fictitious Lemon Academy (compare to KIRA KIRA MELODY ACADEMY), the girls returned the following year for a second season, though

it was soon taken off the air. Sakurai's career did not suffer, and she was soon a popular voice actress in mainstream anime such as EL HAZARD. The other actresses no longer show up on lists of big names. *Lemon Angel Y[oung] J[unior]* (1990) comprised two toned-down videos made for more censorious times, with Sakurai directed by Tetsuro Amino, who would make her a star in MACROSS 7. *Lemon Angel Project* (2006) is a 13-part TV series in which a producer attempts to assemble a group of young performers to form a new Lemon Angel, in imitation of a girlband from the past. Innocent starstruck schoolgirl Tomo Minaguchi signs up for the auditions, unaware of the more salacious side of the previous Lemon Angels.

LEMON CHUHAI LOVE 30'S

1985. JPN: *Chuhairemon Love 30's*. Video. DIR: Kozo Koizumi. SCR: Ryochi Yagi. DES: Sho Shimura. ANI: Kozo Koizumi. MUS: Yoshikazu Sano, Rob Bird. PRD: Tsuchida Pro. 45 mins.
Bug-eyed Katsumi (known as Chuhai to his friends) is a muscle-bound detective determined to use his strength and pig-headed stupidity to rescue his teenage girlfriend from a succession of embarrassing situations. Based on a manga by Sho Shimura and heavily seeded with background music from the 1960s U.S. hit parade. Note that *chuhai* is a Japanese fruit-flavored alcoholic beverage, associated in the 1980s with hard-drinking tramps, but since rehabilitated as a more refined, even lady-like tipple. The title of this anime hence implies a degree of macho masculinity that has already faded in Japanese slang. ⓃⓋ

LENSMAN *

1984. JPN: *Galactic Patrol: Lensman*. TV series, movie. DIR: Hiroshi Fukutomi, Yoshiaki Kawajiri, Kazuyuki Hirokawa. SCR: Soji Yoshikawa, Masaki Tsuji, Ha-ruya Yamazaki, Mitsuru Majima. DES: Kazuo Tomizawa. ANI: Nobuyuki Kitajima. MUS: Akira Inoue, The Alfee. PRD: MK, Madhouse, TV Asahi. 25 mins. x 25 eps. (TV), 107 mins. (m).
In A.D. 2742, during a fight to the death in space, the decimated survivors of the Galactic Patrol obtain vital details that could help defeat the evil Boskone Empire. The warship Brittania crashes on the peaceful farm world of M'queie, where the dying pilot passes his lens (a techno-

magical power amplifier) to local boy Kim Kinnison. Kim's father, a former Patrolman, sacrifices his life to allow Kim to get off-planet, throwing the young farmer into a life of adventure, as he joins forces with the Patrol to defeat evil throughout the galaxy.

E. E. "Doc" Smith's *Galactic Patrol* (1937), along with its prequels and sequels, was one of the landmark series in the history of U.S. pulp sci-fi. Shortly after Edmond Hamilton's CAPTAIN FUTURE (1940) was turned into an anime in 1978, Smith's classic series was also adapted into the 25-episode *Galactic Patrol: Lensman* TV series, directed by BATTLE ANGEL's Hiroshi Fukutomi and introducing several new elements in the wake of *Star Wars*. The anime turns Kim Kinnison, originally the superhuman product of a eugenics project dating back to Atlantis, into nothing but a humble farm boy who wants to be a pilot. Nurse Clarissa "Chris" MacDougall, the fiery red-haired product of another breeding program, who eventually becomes the fearsome Red Lensman and gives birth to the immortal *Children of the Lens*, becomes yet another simpering damsel in the anime.

Carl Macek, of ROBOTECH fame, picked up the series and dubbed a couple of episodes in a failed attempt to interest U.S. networks. The episodes were eventually cut into the English-language video *Power of the Lens*, while Macek bought the feature-length Japanese theatrical edition instead to release in the U.S. as *Lensman*. As suggested by the 25-minute acts, the film version takes several episodes of the TV series and stitches them together. This makes the "movie" seem strangely paced, with fast action interspersed with overlong *gee-whiz* beauty-passes of the spaceships to allow us to gawp at the incredibly expensive computer graphics, made with the same mega-powerful Cray computers used to animate Jupiter in *2010: Odyssey Two*. Still vaguely recognizable from the book are the Overlords of Delgon, evil creatures whom Kim defeats in the company of the "Dragon Lensman" Worsel, and van Buskirk, a Dutch giant (inexplicably half-bison in the anime). Later scenes set on the "drug planet" Radelix start to go off the rails. Whereas Kim goes deep undercover posing as the drug addict

"Wild Bill" in the book *Gray Lensman*, Wild Bill is a character in his own right in the anime, DJ-ing in a dated 1980s disco. By the end, we're in a ho-hum world of final showdown and lighthearted coda, with the baddie predictably still alive; a great disappointment if you've read the books, which feature crashing worlds, maimings, and dismemberments, a revolution on a planet of lesbians, mind-blowing psychic powers, double-, triple-, and quadruple-crossing conspiracies, and gunplay that makes *The Matrix* look like a puppet show.

Instead of reproducing such joys, the anime takes only the characters and most basic of plot outlines, adding the off-the-peg elements that are supposed to guarantee success in the George Lucas mode. The "comic relief" robot Sol, whose appearances are never comic and seldom a relief, is another pointless homage. Ironically, the end result makes *Lensman* look like a cheap knockoff of *Star Wars*, whereas it was original literally decades ahead of it.

LES MISÉRABLES *

1979. JPN: *Jean Valjean Monogatari*. AKA: *Story of Jean Valjean*. TV special, TV series. DIR: Keiji Hisaoka. SCR: Masaki Tsuji. DES: Masami Suda. ANI: Masami Suda. MUS: Yasuo Minami. PRD: Toei, Fuji TV. 75 mins. (m), 25 mins. x 52 eps. (TV).

Jean Valjean is thrown into prison for stealing a single loaf of bread. Returning to his hometown after several years away, he steals from the kindly bishop Myriel, who tells him that he is "buying his soul" by letting him get away with the silver candlesticks from the altar. Eventually, he becomes a wealthy man and a local philanthropist, only for his past to come back to haunt him in the form of Inspector Javert, who catches him. Once more, Valjean escapes and flees to the big city, where tragedy awaits. An adaptation of the 1862 novel by Victor Hugo, it was released in the U.K. on the Kids Cartoon Collection label and Quebec in a French dub, but this version is unavailable in the U.S.

A later iteration of the WORLD MASTERPIECE THEATER franchise produced a longer-running version of the story, focusing on the second section of Hugo's five-part original, as *Les Misérables: Shojo Cosette* (2009, *LM: Petite Cossette*), lasting for 52 episodes and directed by Hiroaki

Sakurai. This version had some 25 hours to tell the story, beginning with Valjean as the mayor of a French town, but was criticized in some quarters for fetishizing Cosette, Valjean's surrogate daughter, as a "*moe*" heroine (ARGOT AND JARGON), regarded by some as an unnecessary sop to a fad that was likely to date the series faster than some others. Although this version has a number of changes from the original novel to render it suitable for children's TV, it's still harsher than most Western TV channels would consider acceptable for young viewers. Cosette's mother is no longer a prostitute, and there's no sexual content, but death, cruelty, political indifference, and the grinding terror of poverty are an integral part of the story. Parents who prefer their children to believe that the world functions like a Disney Princess movie should preview this before they decide to share it. The story was also twice adapted as part of the FAMOUS WORLD FAIRY TALES series, a children's anthology show that ran in the late 1970s.

LESBIAN WARD *

2001. JPN: *Les' Byoto*. Video. DIR: Kenji Matsuda, Kaoru Tomioka. SCR: N/C. DES: N/C. ANI: N/C. MUS: N/C. PRD: Soft on Demand, DEEPS. 30 mins. x 2 eps.

While the director is away on business from Ryoka University Hospital, his sexy daughter Yuka is in charge. She manages everything normally during the day, but at night turns the hospital into a den of sin, where nurses provide personal services to their VIP patients who are encouraged to watch closed-circuit TV footage of girl-on-girl action, while their personal nurse attends to more immediate needs. The men's nocturnal emissions are then gathered up and put to unexpected uses—compare to HOT JUICY TEACHER and NURSE ME. ❶❷

LESSON OF DARKNESS *

1996. JPN: *Inju Kateikyoshi*. Video. DIR: Tsutomu Ono, Tsutomu Yabuki. SCR: N/C. DES: N/C. ANI: N/C. MUS: N/C. PRD: Pink Pineapple. 45 mins.

In Tokyo at the turn of the Showa period (1920s), a number of young women are found dead, their bodies shriveled like mummies. Two Tokyo college girls, Miho and Azusa, are drawn into the mystery.

Miho has a weird stalker, while Azusa tried seducing her professor only to find that he was really a tentacled beast in mild-mannered academic clothing. Now he, or it, is determined to stop his secret being revealed, and the friends are on the run. Combining two kinds of action isn't easy, and this erotic thriller focuses on the erotic stuff its target audience expects, leaving the other kind of action predictable and formulaic. It does at least gain a few marks for its period setting; compare to ARISA. ❶❷❸

LESSON XX

1994. Video. DIR: Rin Hiro. SCR: Ei Onagi. DES: Sanae Chikanaga. ANI: Sanae Chikanaga. MUS: N/C. PRD: Tokuma Japan Communications. 50 mins.

Teenager Shizuka is finishing up school and staying at a boardinghouse, but he is confused by his romantic feelings toward another man called Sakura. In a rash moment, he confesses his feelings, though both boys are concerned that once they take the first steps on the road to male love, there may be no going back. A gay-love drama without the gut-wrenching angst that seems almost obligatory with the rest of the genre, based on a manga by Ei Onagi. ❸

LET THE DREAMS NEVER END

1987. JPN: *Yume kara Samenai*. Video. DIR: Satoshi Inoue. SCR: Ran Kawanishi. DES: Yumi Shirakura. ANI: Kazuo Tomizawa. MUS: Kazuhiko Matsuo. PRD: Shaft. 40 mins.

Student Tako is inexorably drawn toward Sao despite class rumors that she has appeared in a porno film. If this were an anime for boys, he wouldn't mind so much, but this is based on a girls' manga by Yumi Shirakura, so it's all dreadfully scandalous. Sao was played by idol singer Ryoko Sano, who also provided the theme tune.

LET'S ARBEIT

2008. JPN: *Arbeit Shiyo!* Video. DIR: Tatsukichi Tomi. SCR:. DES: ari, Shizu Mukaihara. ANI: ari, Shizu Mukaihara. MUS: N/C. PRD: ChiChi No Ya. 8 mins. x 3 eps.

Three short porn stories about working women—a window cleaner who enjoys teasing office workers behind the glass, a waitress getting hot and steamy with the maitre d', and an office lady who prefers a management role when it comes to sex. All adult, all consensual, although you may never feel comfortable ordering carrots in a restaurant again. **Ⓝ**

LET'S DO IT WITH SISTER!
2005. JPN: *Ne-chan to Shiyo yo; Ne, chanto Shiyo yo*. Video. DIR: Katsuma Kanazawa. SCR: Katsuma Kanazawa. DES: Hiroya Iijima. ANI: Yuji Ushijima. MUS: N/C. PRD: D3. 30 mins. x 5 eps.

Unceasingly spoiled by his sisters as a child, Kuya is sent away to his distant relatives the Hiiragi family in the hope that he will learn self-reliance. Instead, he forgets about his sisters until ten years later, when he moves back in with the family and must deal with the presence of six beautiful girls. Since this is an erotic anime, he finds a way of coping. The title is a pun, which can either mean "Hey, do it right!" or "Sister, do it right!," or our more abrupt choice as listed above. It's all in the punctuation. Based on a PC game, and a release in the **D3 SERIES**. **Ⓝ**

LET'S FALL IN LOVE THE ERO-MANGA
2008. JPN: *Eromanga Mitai na Koi Shiyo*. Video. DIR: Hyogo Kusunoki. SCR: N/C. DES: Takehiro Hamatsu, Kazushi Tashiro. ANI: Takehiro Hamatsu. MUS: N/C. PRD: Flavours Soft, Pink Pineapple. 28 mins. x 2 eps.

Four short stories, two per episode, based on the manga of the same title by Yasuiriosuke. Two arrogant girls finally admit their love for the protagonist; two younger brothers get it on with their airheaded older sisters. The breasts and buttocks have the usual unfeasible proportions, exploited by the animation that's above average for the genre. Although the score is the usual elevator-muzak-with-climaxes, the use of liquid noises on the soundtrack is better handled than usual. **Ⓝ**

LET'S GO TAFFY!
2006. JPN: *Wanwan Celeb Soreyuke! Tetsunoshin*. TV series. DIR: Kiyoshi Fukumoto. SCR: Yoshimi Narita, Mitsutaka Hirota, Takashi Yamada. DES: Junichi Seki, Tadashi Shida, Yasutoshi Kawai. ANI: Jung-Duk Seo. MUS: Kazumi Kitashiro. PRD: Studio Comet, TV Aichi. 25 mins. x 51 eps.

Ten-year-old Rumi and her family lose all their money and move into an apartment in Tokyo. Celebrities and their dogs enjoy a luxurious lifestyle here, while others are strays with nobody to look out for them. Rumi's dog Taffy can actually transform into a superhero, and together with a group of stray dogs in the neighborhood he helps Rumi find the gateway to a magical fantasy land where dogs can talk and act like humans. But can he help her family to thrive in their new life? This gentle, prettily designed reflection on how we invest our pets with the qualities we wish we had ourselves uses the twin hooks of pets and celebrity lifestyles to engage the intended little-girl audience. A comparison with **THE CAT RETURNS** might be just as apt as one with **HELLO SPANK!** or **WHAT'S MICHAEL?**

LET'S HAVE SEX
2009. JPN: *Issho ni H Shiyo*. AKA: *Let's Do Hentai Together*. Video. DIR: Kentaro Mizuno, Saburo Miura. SCR: Toshihiro Watase. DES: Ryuten Shishi, Me Bin. ANI: Ryuten Shishi. MUS: 10 Gemini. PRD: ChiChi no Ya. 17 mins. x 6 eps. (v1), 20 mins. (v2).

A young man whose face we don't see has six encounters with hot babes. A drunken female friend crashes at his place overnight after celebrating long and late when her team wins the big game. A classmate comes over and brings him lunch. Our guy hires a maid, who turns out to have cat ears and tail and is very clumsy. He just wants to finish his homework but his sister and her girlfriend are making too much noise. His stepsister comes to town for a visit and stays at his place. He heads for a farm to stay with his cousin and see if farm life would suit him. It's predictable porn that proves you can always make money from old ideas—even with cucumbers. Compare to **LET'S ARBEIT** and wonder why ChiChi no Ya is on a mission to spread distrust of vegetables.

Porn fans can also check out the related 2010 video *Akina to Onsen de H Shiyo* (*Let's Have Sex with Akina at the Hot Springs*). College softball captain Akina—the female friend in the first story of *Let's Have Sex*—celebrates a string of victories by taking some quality time at a hot springs resort with her new boyfriend, the guy she stayed with after her drunken night out. **Ⓝ**

LET'S NUPUNUPU
1998. TV series. DIR: Kazuyoshi Hisakome. SCR: Ko Nanbu. DES: Hiroko Seino. ANI: Yasuto Kaya. MUS: N/C. PRD: Ajia-do. 4 mins. x 16 eps.

Schoolteacher Mr. Shidara has trouble keeping his male and female students apart in this comedy broadcast as part of the *Wonderful* slot on TBS, along with shows such as **COLORFUL** and **COOL COUPLE**. It was originally based on a four-panel strip in *Shonen Magazine* by Akira Mitsumori. **Ⓝ**

LETTER BEE *
2008. JPN: *Tegami-bachi*. TV series, video. DIR: Mamoru Kanbe, Akira Iwanaga. SCR: Tetsuya Oishi, Masanao Akahoshi, Sho Aikawa. DES: Minako Shiba, Maho Takahashi. ANI: Minako Shiba. MUS: Kunihiko Ryo. PRD: Pierrot Plus, Studio Pierrot, TV Tokyo, Shueisha. 30 mins. (v1), 21 mins. x 25 eps. (TV1), 25 mins. x 25 eps. (TV2), 3 mins. x 25 eps. (v2).

AmberGround is a land of night, only partly illuminated by an artificial sun. Only the rich live in its full light. Letter Bees deliver packages and mail to towns across AmberGround, accompanied by a "dingo" or personal bodyguard. It's a risky job—giant armored insects attack in an effort to steal the mail and feed off the "heart," the emotion that resides in communication between people. Twelve-year-old Lag Seeing has become a Letter Bee to emulate the man who saved his life after his mother was kidnapped; but he learns that his hero Gauche has vanished, and that an insurrectionist movement known as Reverse is stealing mail. Helped by his dingo, the childlike being Niche whose long blonde hair is a deadly weapon, Lag sets out to find Gauche and save the world.

Crash *Postman Pat* into *Pony Express* and the result would be nothing like *Letter Bee*. To build the anime based on Hiroyuki Asada's 2006 manga you'd also need industrial quantities of cuteness and a collection of strangely named characters with equally strangely named arcane powers. The series also has lots of musical references—characters named Aria, Largo, Gauche, and Sunny, a town named Blue Note Blues, weapons called Crimson Melody, Nocturne, and Gymnopedie. The major play on words, though, is embedded throughout the script—the notion of delivery as deliverance, of the communication between individuals as the key that unlocks their hearts.

This makes for an adventure series that's longer on monologue and introspection than most, although there's insect-battling action and political intrigue to balance the melancholy melodrama. The often overwrought script is all of a piece with the fancy naming system—unnecessary decoration for a set-up that could hold its own without bells and whistles. It would be easy to care for these characters without the constant throb of overstrung violins emphasizing the tears, and those who stick with the series (perhaps by gritting teeth or gnawing on fingers to keep from laughing out loud through the truly sappy bits) will find a rewardingly warm heart beneath the absurdity. Composer Ryo is overfond of wailing strings and plinky-tinkly harpsichord, but despite the aural emo-overload he's crafted a varied score with plenty of interest, reminiscent in some ways of Yoko Kanno's mighty music for ESCAFLOWNE. Similarly, while the animation is no great shakes and the CGI can be downright clumsy, the artistry of the backgrounds is stunning and the design creates an intriguing, convincing proto-industrial world. Overall, it's a show worth watching providing you can stand the schmaltz.

A second series, *Tegami Bachi Reverse*, followed in 2010. The 3-minute videos entitled *Tegami Bachi Academy* are DVD extras. A 30-minute video by Studio Pierrot was screened to promote the series during the Jump Super Anime Tour in autumn 2008, entitled *Tegami Bachi Hikari to Ao no Genso Yawa* (*Letter Bee Light and Blue Night Fantasy*) and released on DVD in 2009.

LETTER TO MOMO, A *
2011. JPN: *Momo e no Tegami*. Movie. DIR: Hiroyuki Okiura. SCR: Hiroyuki Okiura. DES: Hiroyuki Okiura, Masashi Ando. ANI: Masashi Ando. MUS: Mina Kubota. PRD: Production I.G, Oh! Production, Pierrot, Studio MAT. 120 mins.
Relocating to Shio Island on Japan's Inland Sea after her father's death, 11-year-old city girl Momo has trouble adjusting to life in the sleepy seaside community. She fixates on her father's last letter to her, in which only the words "Dear Momo"

were completed, and comes to believe that a spate of vandalism and petty thefts around the island is the work of mischievous spirits. These are later revealed to be somewhat incompetent agents of an unspecified higher power, termed "Above" in a pun on the Japanese word for god.

Legendarily occupying the director of JIN-ROH for seven years (and hence being beaten to the thematic punch by TAMAYURA in 2010), this gentle pastoral also seems inspired by the work of his uncle Kazuteru Okiura, a folklorist who has written an entire book on the legends of the Inland Sea, the waterway between the main Japanese islands of Kyushu, Shikoku, and Honshu. *Letter to Momo* draws heavily on the spirit of MY NEIGHBOR TOTORO, but is also admirably readable from the adults' point of view as the idle fantasies of a troubled preteen, acting up in reaction to her bereavement. The earthy, bawdy humor of her supernatural friends creates moments of fine wit and entertainment for the film's midsection, only for the final reel to collapse in a vague jeopardy and formulaic resolution, as if control had been wrested from the director by a committee demanding a predictable finish.

While very much an enjoyable imitation of Studio Ghibli movies from POM POKO to PONYO, *Letter to Momo* ultimately falls short in its lack of faith toward its audience. The payoff to a recurring trope, in which Momo is asked to make a literal leap of faith from a bridge, would have been left without comment in a Ghibli film, but is deconstructed here in a closing scene in which the characters discuss what has just happened, as if they think the audience are idiots.

Much more prosaic, earthbound matters kept this film out of the international limelight. It was first premiered in Toronto in 2011, several months ahead of its official Japanese release in 2012. However, it was held back from a wider international release until late in 2013, seemingly in a pragmatic attempt to clear the Academy Awards longlist of any potential Ghibli competition. Nobody can seriously believe that *A Letter to Momo* stood a chance against Hollywood rivals, but the opportunity to secure even a nomination in a Ghibli-free year seems to have been a legitimate consideration in order to

help this worthy film find an appreciative market.

LEVEL C
1996. JPN: *Level C: Gokuraku no Hoteishiki*. AKA: *Level C: Paradise Equation*. Video. DIR: Yorifusa Yamaguchi. SCR: N/C. DES: Yumi Nakayama. ANI: Yumi Nakayama. MUS: N/C. PRD: Pink Pineapple, KSS. 40 mins.
A story of forbidden love between men, based on a manga by the pseudonymous Futaba Aoi and Mitsuba Kurenai. Not to be confused with EQUATION OF THE ROTTEN TEACHER. ❶

LEVEL E *
2011. TV series. DIR: Toshiyuki Kato. SCR: Jukki Hanada, Kazuyuki Fudeyasu, Masashi Suzuki. DES: Itsuko Takeda, Toshihiro Kohama, Yuta Chimoto. ANI: Itsuko Takeda. MUS: Kunihiko Ryo. PRD: David Production, Studio Pierrot, TV Tokyo. 24 mins. x 13 eps.
High school freshman Yukitaka Tsutsui has been recruited to a new school because of his talent for baseball, and moves out of his parents' home to live alone in the north. But he arrives to find his new apartment occupied by a stunning blond guy who claims to be an alien amnesiac. It turns out that the world is full of aliens, and Tsutsui's unexpected roommate is a Prince with an attitude as bad as PATALIRO and a devoted sidekick as bullied as D in PROJECT A-KO. A series of comedy vignettes along the lines of *Men in Black* without the insect-splatting, or the plot, follows, although there are serious moments— one plot thread involves a transgender character, another explores how children deal with separation. Purposely terrible folk-singing, some interesting tunes on the theremin—surely the ultimate sci-fi instrument, one of the few that looks as magical in play as it sounds—and a wonderful evocation of the exploitative power of celebrity. ❶❷

LEVIATHAN: THE LAST DEFENSE *
2013. JPN: *Zettai Boei Leviathan*. AKA: *Total Protector Leviathan*. TV series. DIR: Kenichi Yatani. SCR: Yasunori Ide, Go Zappa. DES: Takaharu Okuma. ANI: Satoru Kiyomaru. MUS: Shiho Terada, Tomoki Kikuya. PRD: Gonzo, TV Tokyo, Domerica. 23 mins. x 13 eps.
Meteorites crash onto the peaceful fantasy realm of Aquafall, causing the local fairy

population to enlist pretty girls and dragons to come to the world's defense. Syrup the fairy finds herself in command of three color-coded ladies with well-matched beasts—Leviathan the water dragon, fire-controlling Bahamut, and the mighty strength of Jormungandr. Relentlessly, cloyingly cute, this RPG-adaptation ignores much of the potential drama of an alien attack in favor of bickering about the food supply and searching for soft cushions, as if Anne McCaffrey were serializing her Pern books in *Good Housekeeping*.

LIBRARY WAR

2008. JPN: *Toshokan Senso*. TV series, video, movie. DIR: Takayuki Hamana. SCR: Kenji Konuta, Ikuko Takahashi, Sayaka Harada, Taishiro Tanimura. DES: Satoru Nakamura, Shigemi Ikeda, Naoki Arakawa. ANI: Satoru Nakamura, Hiroyuki Shimizu. MUS: Yugo Kanno. PRD: Production I.G, ASCII Media Works, ASMIK, Dentsu, Fuji TV, SME, LWPF 2012, Kadokawa. 23 mins. x 12 eps. (TV), 24 mins. (v), 105 mins. (m).

In an alternate world not so very unlike our own, the mass expansion of information in the public domain was a threat to social stability as potent as any terrorist bomb. With both truth and deception out there in ever greater quantities, available to anyone who wanted to read it, the Japanese Government passed a law allowing the censorship of any media considered harmful to Japanese society, with its own stormtroopers, the Media Betterment Committee, to enforce it. Local governments band together under the Freedom of Libraries Law to stand against MBC raids on libraries; they, too, have their own "library soldiers." Thirty years after the enactment of the law, in 2019, Iku Kasahara joins the Kanto Library Base. At first she doesn't seem like the most promising recruit, and her coach really has to push her to bring out her abilities, but she and her colleagues are fighting for freedom and she's determined to persevere.

Any bit of popular culture pointing gets our vote if it points out that knowledge is power and access to information is a right worth defending. This contemporary take on Ray Bradbury's *Fahreinheit 451* is based on a 2006 book series by Hiro Arikawa with art by Sukumo Adabana and includes a couple of nods to its mighty precursor. In a world of media manipulation by politicians and corporations, libraries and their contents—whether physical or electronic—may actually be the last line of defense against slavery to the drugs and devices of consumption culture. Compare with **READ OR DIE**, **A CERTAIN MAGICAL INDEX**, and **BOOK OF BANTORRA**.

You may also hear echoes of **GUNBUSTER** or **PATLABOR** in the timeworn klutz-made-good scenario, but here are two more interesting facts to ponder. From 1945 to 1952 the occupying forces in Japan (that's us) rigidly censored all media, whether locally produced or imported from the West, to present all manifestations of Japanese militarism as destructive and all forms of American civilization as ideal. In 1954, Japan published the Statement on Intellectual Freedoms in Libraries, declaring the responsibility of libraries to support the right to knowledge as a fundamental human right and the duty of librarians to secure the freedom of libraries. *Library War* is based on this legislation: its fictional Freedom of Library Law differs in some detail, but the inspiration is the same.

A show with a solid intellectual and historical foundation can easily turn worthy and preach itself free of entertainment value, but not this one. Production I.G's animation team and its cohort of supporting studios are on good form throughout, delivering fluid dynamic action, convincing fights, and beautifully lit atmospheric moments. The characters are engaging and develop through the story in a credible way. Whether or not you believe that control of information is this century's major battleground, you can't help but root for them.

Two manga adaptations and podcast shows followed the books. A video appeared on the TV series DVD release, and a movie *Library War: The Wings of Revolution* (*Toshokan Senso Kakumei no Tsubasa*) premiered in 2012. The same core team stayed in charge of both.

LICCA-CHAN *

1990. JPN: *Licca-chan Fushigina Fushigina Unia Monogatari; Licca-chan Fushigina Maho no Ring; Licca-chan no Nichiyobi; Licca-chan the Movie: Licca-chan to Yamaneko, Hoshi no Tabi*. AKA: *Licca and the Mystery of Mysterious Unia; Licca and the Mysterious Magic Ring; Licca's Sunday; Licca the Movie: Licca and the Wildcat: Journey of Dreams; Superdoll Licca-chan*. Video, TV series, movie. DIR: Tomomi Mochizuki, Fumiko Ishii, Tatsuo Sato, Tsutomu Shibayama. SCR: Kazunori Ito, Mami Watanabe. DES: Akemi Takada, Yoshiyuki Kato. ANI: Masako Kato, Takuya Saito. MUS: Mineo Maeda, Kenji Kawai. PRD: Asia-do, Madhouse, TV Asahi. 28 mins. x 2 eps. (v1), 60 mins. (v2), 25 mins. (v3), 78 mins. (v4), 25 mins. x 32 eps. (TV), 10 mins. (m).

Licca is playing the piano when she notices that one of the keys doesn't work. Opening it up to see why, she is transported to the world of Unia with her stuffed toy bird Dodo and Ine the cat. Trying to find her way out of a world that is equal parts **ALICE IN WONDERLAND** and **THE WIZARD OF OZ**, she meets the craftsman who makes dreams and wanders through the Square Pole forest of doppelgängers. A dragon tells her to seek the Amaranth flower at the Tower of Beginning, but Ine has become spoiled by all the fuss he gets and wants to stay. Licca and Dodo are almost trapped in the Maze of Anger by their bad-tempered arguments, but they eventually find their way to the Sky Garden and the Rainbow Bridge that takes them home.

Licca-chan is the Japanese equivalent of Barbie, a child's doll designed in 1967 by Miyako Maki, the wife of **CAPTAIN HARLOCK**–creator Leiji Matsumoto. Her first video adventure was followed by *Licca and the Magic Bracelet* (1991), in which the titular item falls out of the sky into Licca's playground, where she discovers that it can unlock the three seals of Dreams, Shadows, and Death. It was this video, under the title *Licca*, that was released in English by Anime Cartoon International. Less scary antics occupied the third video, *Licca's Sunday* (1992), about her traveling to her auntie's house to play with her cousins. As her 30th birthday grew near, the doll returned to adventure in the video misleadingly and clumsily entitled *Licca the Movie: Licca and the Wildcat: Journey of Dreams* (1994), in which she goes on a country holiday with her father, dreams that she is attending a school for the stone cats that populate the town, and heads off on a journey through the sky with the largest. The film was also repackaged the same year in a *Special Collection*, including the movie, a selection from 30 years of Licca TV commercials, and an exclusive Licca doll dressed in the uniform of a video-store clerk.

The franchise was revamped for a new generation as *Superdoll Licca-chan* (1998), a TV series featuring new designs from Tetsuya Kumatani and direction from **Street Fighter II**'s Gisaburo Sugii. For the TV version, there are *two* Liccas—the first is a third-grader at St. Therese's School, attacked without warning by Scarecrow, Pul, and Wahya. She discovers that she is the heir to the Doll Kingdom, a human dreamland where dolls live and breathe, though they can become human if loved and cherished for 100 years. Licca is the child of a union between French musician Pierre and "normal human" Orie, who is really the Doll Queen in disguise. Licca's grandmother gives her the magical Call Ring that can summon help and three dolls named Licca, Izumi, and Isamu, the spirits of wisdom, courage, and life. Since it is a fundamental problem with shows based on dolls that children often have duplicates of the same ones, this is a clever means of encouraging play with duplicate Liccas, as the child begins her quest to regain her rightful kingdom from the usurper Queen Yaë, her greataunt. The doll returned again for *Licca-chan: Tale of the Mysterious Sea* (2001), a fully computer-animated short film shown in department stores and amusement parks. For similar doll-inspired action, see **Rainbow Across the Pacific** and, frankly, the entire **Gundam** series.

LICENSED BY ROYALTY *

2003. JPN: *L/R*. AKA: *Licensed by Royal*. TV series. DIR: Itsuro Kawasaki. SCR: Kazuki Matsui. DES: Kenji Teraoka, Kayoko Nabeta. ANI: Masahiro Sato. MUS: Keiichi Nozaki. PRD: Pioneer (Geneon), Fuji TV. 25 mins. x 13 eps.

Cool, calm, quick-witted Rowe Rickenbacker and action-hero Jack Hofner are agents for Cloud Seven, the secret service of the royal state of Ishtar. This quasi-British enclave, seemingly designed by someone channeling the '60s chic of Sean Connery-era 007 along with its modern pastiche, *Austin Powers* (1997), is under threat from numerous enemies, including the shadow organization known only as Hornet.

The stage is set for a retro espionage thriller played like a straight version of **Pataliro**, as our heroes strive to ensure that the name of the royal family remains unimpeachable. When the royal name is used to authenticate fake antiques, it's Jack and Rowe who make sure the truth is known, but discreetly and with style. They also thwart assassination attempts and terrorist bombers, some aimed at Ishtar's biggest corporation, DTI—supposedly Digital Terra Incorporated, although connoisseurs of the show's Anglophile references will know of the Department of Trade and Industry in real life.

Amid the sub-Bond antics (they take their orders from "Mister," clearly intended as a substitute for Ian Fleming's "M"), there is a continuing story arc that initially seems to owe more to the fairy tale foundling traditions of girls' entertainment like **Candy Candy**. A royal baby has been missing for 15 years, and a local beauty contest is actually a thinlyveiled attempt by the government to search for her. A prime candidate is presented in the form of Noelle, a girl who has been raised on a remote Ishtar outpost and whom the team soon find themselves obliged to guard. But not everything is as it seems, and a series of reversals of fortune in the later episodes give *Licensed by Royalty* an impressive bite. Although at heart it is a humble action series, its use of an imaginary kingdom and heavy insistence on British imagery allow it to do something more subversive. No anime series would dare to comment directly on the Japanese Imperial family, which at the time of broadcast, faced a succession crisis if Japanese law were not changed to allow Princess Aiko (born 2001) to ascend the throne on the death of her father, the current Crown Prince Naruhito. Those in search of subtextual meanings for *L/R* might like to speculate on the fact that in our own world, an entire generation had passed without the birth of a male heir to the Japanese throne, and that as a result, the old order of Japan faced similar upheavals to those experienced by the fictional Ishtar, until the birth of a male heir in 2006 rendered such discussion irrelevant.

Ishtar (1987) was also a comedy in which Warren Beatty and Dustin Hoffman become involved in a coup in a fictional country, but on the surface at least, the country in *L/R* seems as British as that in **Master Keaton** or **Emma**. This is well handled in an American dub from the people who worked on **Hellsing**, which ensures similar attention to detail on the accents. Many shots look just like London, and with an opening theme sung by Billy "Get Back" Preston, the show is packed with nods to British pop. The two leads are named after Lennon and McCartney's guitars, while the Moneypenny role is taken by another Beatles reference, one Claire Pennylane.

LIGHT OF THE RIVER

2009. JPN: *Kawa no Hikari*. Movie. DIR: Tetsuo Hirakawa. SCR: Takao Yoshioka. DES: Tsukasa Tannai, Nizo Yamamoto, Kazuo Oga. ANI: N/C. MUS: Masaki Kurihara. PRD: GALLOP, NHK. 70 mins.

A family is forced out of its home by redevelopment. They have to find a new place in a world which is ever more crowded and less and less tolerant of the poor and marginalized. We could be talking about the Brazilian slum dwellers whose homes are being bulldozed to make a nice shiny setting for the 2016 Olympics, or the Amazon tribes displaced by logging and redevelopment in the rainforest, or the Syrians displaced by the demolition of their country, but we're actually talking about a family of rats displaced by a Japanese building consortium, trekking along a riverbank in the hope of finding somewhere to call home before winter sinks its teeth into them.

This beautiful, gentle adaptation of Hikaru Matsuura's ecological novel has background art by a stellar team including Kazuo Oga, who has long worked his magic at Studio Ghibli, and Masato Yokoi, whose color design is unobtrusively beautiful. The Ghibli movie closest to this one in spirit is not **Pom Poko** but **Arrietty**: the *tanuki* of Isao Takahata's movie have more options than the rats and Borrowers, who cannot hope to "blend in" to the human world and must live in hiding or flee.

LIGHTSPEED ELECTROID ARBEGAS

1983. JPN: *Kosoku Denshin Arbegas*. TV series. DIR: Kozo Morishita, Masamitsu Sasaki, Masao Ito, Noriyasu Yamauchi, Keiji Hisaoka, Takao Yoshizawa, Masayuki Akehi. SCR: Akiyoshi Sakai. DES: Shigenori Kageyama,

Koichi Ohata. ANI: Shigenori Kageyama, Hajime Kaneko, Toshio Mori. MUS: Michiaki Watanabe. PRD: Toei, TV Tokyo. 25 mins. x 45 eps.

Earth is invaded by the evil Derringer aliens, who are held off repeatedly by a group of Japanese schoolchildren that have "won the robot prize." These children have inexplicably managed to knock together a giant war machine formed from three combining sub-machines that can transform in turn into six separate configurations for different missions—electron, magma, space, marine, guard, and sky. Obviously, kids were better at science in the 1980s. Far-fetched, but nothing can surprise an anime viewer after GOLD LIGHTAN. The toys also appeared in the GODAIKIN range and as part of Matchbox's VOLTRON line, though *Arbegas* was completely unrelated.

LIKE A CLOUD, LIKE A BREEZE

1990. JPN: *Kumo no yo ni, Kaze no yo ni.* AKA: *Kumokaze; Fly, Little Bird, Fly; Like the Clouds, Like the Wind.* TV special. DIR: Hisayuki Toriumi. SCR: Akira Miyazaki. DES: Katsuya Kondo. ANI: Katsuya Kondo. MUS: Haruhiko Maruya. PRD: Studio Pierrot, Yomiko Advertising Inc., NHK. 80 mins.

In Imperial China, energetic and outspoken teenager Ginga (more properly in Chinese, Yinhe) decides to enter the harem because of the rumors she hears of the comfortable life and plentiful food. But when she arrives at the palace, there are accusations over the death of the previous emperor, which may have been murder, while there are stories of a revolt in the countryside that threatens the dynasty itself. Her fellow new arrivals in the harem include the snooty Ceshamin and the withdrawn Tamyun, and the girls must take lessons in deportment from the stern teacher Kakute, whom Ginga defies and eventually befriends. Meanwhile, her own position becomes more precarious as she manuevers to become the first wife of the new emperor, which places her in considerable and unexpected danger. As former acquaintances of Ginga's march on the capital in revolt, it is Ginga who organizes the women of the harem into an impromptu defensive force.

Like a Cloud originates in *Tale of the Harem* (*Kokyu Shosetsu*, 1989), a book by

Kenichi Sakemi that won the first Japan Fantasy Novel Award, much to the embarrassment of sponsors who had promised to turn the winner into an anime. Instead of a tale of elves and dragons, the producers were handed a book devoted to detailed descriptions of sexual techniques. If this were a video production like EROTIC TORTURE CHAMBER, it might not have bothered anyone, but writer Akira Miyazaki had the seemingly impossible task of making the story palatable for a television audience. In a sense, he performs admirably, concentrating not on the content of the lessons, but on the existence of the lessons themselves. Accordingly, life in the Forbidden City is framed as a boarding school drama like TWINS AT ST. CLARES in period costume. Ginga must deal with rivals, a crush on a handsome authority figure (the guardsman Koryun), and classroom conflict, although at times the parallels become ludicrous—one scene features the trainee concubines exercising in the schoolyard, accompanied by anachronistic piano music.

The show stumbles with stylistic issues related to the original source material. Sakemi's novel, written with a love of Chinese pomp inspired by *The Last Emperor* (1987), is patently not based on historical fact—if it were, it would never have won a *fantasy* award. Although the anime production attempts to set its fashions and hairstyles in the closing years of the Ming dynasty (around 1630), the Beijing scenery seems to date from the later Qing era (the 1800s), while the reign title of the incumbent emperor is actually only found in the semi-legendary Xia dynasty, in the 17th century B.C., not A.D. This is a China without footbinding, where Ginga is permitted to behave like a willful, confident heroine in the style of designer Kondo's earlier KIKI'S DELIVERY SERVICE, the only Chinese quality to her seemingly manifested in her slanted eyes—an exotic and ironically orientalist decision from Japanese artists. *Like a Cloud* appears to lift several events from Chinese history, including the organization of a female demonstration platoon by Sun Zi, author of the *Art of War*, and tales from both the Ming and Tang dynasties. The nature of Ginga's education, that she is, in modern parlance, an underage girl being primed for sexual slavery, is swept

far under the lavish, beautifully embroidered but anachronistic carpet. Compare to GREAT CONQUEST: ROMANCE OF THREE KINGDOMS and THE STORY OF SAIUNKOKU.

LIKE MOTHER, LIKE DAUGHTER *

2006. JPN: *Donburi Kazoku.* AKA: *Family Dinner.* Video. DIR: Hayate Goto. SCR: Tenkei Fujimiya. DES: Jiro Okada, Seihodo. ANI: Jiro Okada. MUS: Yoshi. PRD: YOUC, Digital Works. 27 mins. x 2 eps.

Yukiko is a wife and mother, but still attractive; not that her husband notices these days. She's found pictures of another woman on his phone and she's seen her son and daughter in bed together. Although she seems to have the perfect family on the surface, underneath it's falling apart. Then her husband's father catches her satisfying her sexual needs alone. Before long the whole family is sharing its secret desires. Part of that long-running pornfest the VANILLA SERIES, and based on *Carnal Family: Bonds of Other* (*Tanin Kazoku: Nikuyoku no Kizuna*). **🅝**

LILPRI *

2010. JPN: *Hime Chen! Otogi Chikku Idol Lilpri.* AKA: *Spellbound! Magical Princess Idol Lilpri.* TV series. DIR: Makoto Moriwaki. SCR: Yuka Yamada, Megumi Sasano. DES: Atsuko Watanabe, Hiroshi Nitta, Yasuhiro Yamako. ANI: Atsuko Watanabe. MUS: Takatsugu Muramatsu. PRD: Telecom Animation Film, TMS, TV Tokyo, ShoPro. 25 mins. x 51 eps.

Ringo (Apple) is the daughter of bakers, and her parents' apple pie is renowned as the best in the world. She has seven identical brothers, named for the days of the week but nicknamed "the seven dwarfs." One day she is approached by Sei, a being that looks like a talking parrot, who tells her that Fairyland is in trouble. Its princesses and their worlds are vanishing, causing havoc on Earth where their stories inspire girls to be good and kind. To save two worlds, Earth and Fairyland, Sei and two more magical pets have been sent to find three human girls to transform into Super Miracle Idols. Ringo and her comrades must collect the power of happiness created by music. This sweet anime for little girls is adapted from the Sega arcade game of the same name, which also inspired two manga by Mai Jinna.

LILY C.A.T. *

1987. Video. DIR: Hisayuki Toriumi. SCR: Hiroyuki Hoshiyama. DES: Yasuomi Umezu, Yasuhiro Moriki, Yoshitaka Amano. ANI: Toshiyasu Okada. MUS: Akira Inoue. PRD: Studio Pierrot. 70 mins.

It's A.D. 2264 and the exploration vessel Saldes is on a 20-year mission to planet L.A.O.3, carrying seven passengers. Not all of them are on the right side of the law, or totally open about their background and motives—but all of them, and the six-person crew, are in deadly danger. In a blatant rip-off of the first *Alien* movie, death is stalking the ship, picking off the occupants one by one, though the titular cat is revealed to be more than just an excuse to go back out into danger, since it is really the key to the mother computer that will save the day. **⓵ⓃⓋ**

LIME WARS

2002. JPN: *Lime-iro Senkitan*. AKA: *Lime Colored Fleet; Lime-Colored Military Chronicle*. TV series, video. DIR: Iku Suzuki (TV1, v) Tsuneo Tominaga (TV2). SCR: Satoru Akahori (TV1, 2, v), Takao Yoshioka (TV1), Hideaki Koyasu (v). DES: Mayumi Watanabe (TV1, v), Naoki Honda (TV1), Yoshiten (TV2). ANI: Soft Garage (TV1), A.C.G.T. (TV2), Studio Hibari (v). MUS: Toshiyuki Omori (TV1), Kazuhiro Sawaguchi (TV2). PRD: KSS, Soft Garage. 25 mins. x 13 eps. (TV1), 28 mins. x 2 eps. (v), 25 mins. x 13 eps. (TV2).

In 1904, Russian-Japanese diplomat Shintaro Umakai has been hired to teach at the Amanohara School for Girls, which naturally enough is sited on a battleship—Russia and Japan are currently at war. He's on the run from a failed romance with a Russian girl and, again naturally enough, a girls' school will be the best place to get over it. The five archetypal girls he is to teach (unsurprisingly, as this is based on an erotic computer game) can summon up and control elemental superpowers that might just save Japan, in the style of **VIRGIN FLEET**. Needless to say, each of the girls is an embodiment of a particular wish-fulfillment stereotype, be it tomboy, girl next door, or prissy princess, and each of them will of course find the shy, inept young teacher quite irresistible. The enemy also has a supernatural unit, and by pure chance Shintaro has a past link with one of the girls in that unit, too.

No amount of historical set dressing can disguise the formulaic plot and characterization, in yet another example of the eternal quest for a harem show with a difference, refusing to admit that with harem shows there is no difference. Nevertheless, *Lime Wars* was still successful enough to spin off a 2004 two-part video, *Lime Wars: The South Sea Island Dream Romantic Adventure (Lime-iro Senkitan: Nankoku Yume Roman)*, whose main purpose seems to be to give the characters an opportunity to lounge about in beachwear, and a 2005 TV sequel, *Lime Wars X: Love, Please (Lime-iro Ryukitan X: Koi Oshiete Kudasai)*, in which, *Newtype* proudly reported, "the girls were all-new, but the uniforms were the same." The home video release of the first TV series included nudity not found in the TV broadcast version.

LIMIT THE MIRACLE GIRL

1973. JPN: *Miracle Shojo Limit-chan*. TV series. DIR: Takeshi Tamiya, Masayuki Akehi, Hideo Furusawa. SCR: Shunichi Yukimuro, Masaki Tsuji, Makio Hara, Toyohiro Ando. DES: Kazuo Komatsubara. ANI: Kazuo Komatsubara, Reiko Okayama, Teruo Kogure, Minoru Tajima. MUS: Shunsuke Kikuchi, Tokiko Iwatani. PRD: TV Asahi, Toei Animation, Studio Cosmos, NET (TV Asahi.) 25 mins. x 25 eps.

After gifted scientist Dr. Nishiyama loses his teenage daughter in an airplane accident, the bereaved father makes a robot exactly like her with her personality impressed on its cybernetic brain. Limit stands in for the dead girl, not telling her closest friends that she has a computer in place of a heart; she yearns for human happiness like **KEY THE METAL IDOL**. However, in a foreshadowing of many, many later artificial heroines, Limit only has a year to live—compare to **VIDEO GIRL AI**.

The studio obviously thought it was onto a winner with an anime based on a proposal from Hiromi Productions, which was then transformed into a manga by Shinji Nagashima, combining the magical girl with the **ASTRO BOY** concept. Twelve days later saw the first broadcast of Go Nagai's **CUTEY HONEY**, which does the same thing, but with more action and bigger breasts, decisively stealing its thunder. Aimed at a very different audience than Nagai's heroine, Limit may not have

registered as powerfully on the public consciousness, but she had a successful career in Italy, where she has many fans under the name *Cybernella*. Manga tie-ins were published in *Shojo* weekly and *Terebi Land* magazines.

Although the "girl with a time limit" concept is enough to assure Limit her place in history, the show was also one of the first to save costs by using overseas labor—the last five episodes were prepared in collaboration with Toki Doga, a South Korean company.

LINEBARRELS OF IRON *

2008. JPN: *Kurogane no Linebarrel*. TV series, video. DIR: Masamitsu Hidaka. SCR: Kiyoko Yoshimura, Shigeru Morita. DES: Hisashi Hirai, Tsutomu Suzuki. ANI: Hisashi Hirai. MUS: Conisch. PRD: Gonzo., Akita Shoten, CBC, Flying Dog. 24 mins. x 26 eps. (TV), 30 mins. x 2 eps. (v).

Koichi escapes from being bullied at school through daydreams of being a hero. A freak accident during a class trip leaves him in a coma when a falling satellite hits him on the head. Months later he wakes up with strange powers, including superhuman strength, becoming a gang leader himself and straining relationships with old friends. Three years later, a giant robot turns up and he learns that this robot, Linebarrel, was the real cause of his "accident." He's been chosen as a Factor, one of the few who can pilot the giant Machina robots. A mixed-up, arrogant, resentful kid in charge of a giant superweapon is supposed to save the world.

Linebarrels of Iron is what would really happen if you gave a downtrodden teen the power to save the world. He'd only save the bits he liked, and he might even trash those in his determination to get even with everyone who'd ever made him feel small—including his protective friends. There's a fascination in watching this trail of havoc, especially with big punchy mecha as the weapons, but when the point of identification for the intended audience is so unappealingly ugly it's not exactly fun. When a vicious plot twist turns Koichi around, he gets tedious very quickly. His behavior is entirely credible in both phases, but that doesn't make it entertaining in either.

Characters are always pulled and

pushed by life. It's how they push *back* that defines them; but this show revels in turmoil to the extent where how characters develop is irrelevant because there's another change coming along in a minute. It's a show with huge ambition in both plot and character, but it never draws breath for long enough to actually deliver. This may because it's so seduced by slam-bang heavy-metal action, which is by far the best choreographed and animated part of the whole enterprise.

Based on the manga by Eiichi Shimizu and Tomohiro Shimoguchi, who were both involved in creating the TV version, the anime departs from the original in several respects. It has a new plot strand, a parallel universe of machine-humans with some characteristics similar to *The Matrix* (1999). Interestingly, after adapting their comic for animation, the original manga creators then adapted the first episode of the anime series into a manga one-shot for a younger audience than the original. Two videos made in 2009 are comical slice-of-life takes on the characters. **Ⓥ**

LINKED HOSPITAL WARD

2007. JPN: *Rensa Byoto*. Video. DIR: Masapuku. SCR: N/C. DES: hidehide. ANI: Masapuku. MUS: I've. PRD: Milky, GP Museum Soft. 30 mins. x 2 eps.

Shuji works in a hospital just outside Tokyo—the very hospital where his father died on the operating table while he was still in college, ten years ago. He became a doctor to find out exactly why his father died. Dr. Takao, who operated on Shuji's father, is now the assistant director of the hospital, and Shuji's old girlfriend Misako is now Mrs. Takao. Shuji is determined to get revenge and win her back, but that doesn't mean he won't have some fun playing doctor along the way in this porn anime based on a computer game by Selen. **Ⓝ**

LION BOOKS

1983. JPN: *Midori no Neko; Amefuri Kozo; Lunn wa Kaze no Naka; Yamataro Kaeru; Adachigahara; Akuemon*. AKA: (see below). TV specials, movies. DIR: Hitoshi Nishimura, Masamitsu Yoshimura, Hisashi Sakaguchi, Makoto Tezuka. SCR: Hitoshi Nishimura, Masamitsu Yoshimura, Hisashi Sakaguchi. DES: Hitoshi Nishimura, Osamu Tezuka,

Hisashi Sakaguchi. ANI: Hitoshi Nishimura, Masamitsu Yoshimura, Hisashi Sakaguchi. MUS: Reijiro Koroku. PRD: Tezuka Pro. 24 mins. x 6 eps.

Twenty-four episodes were planned for this series of one-shots, but the hope of **ASTRO BOY**–creator Osamu Tezuka to animate many of his early short manga was soon dashed by lack of interest. Instead, several were shown as TV "specials," while two more were made for theaters, then collected under the *Lion Books* umbrella for release to video in 1997.

In *The Green Cat* (1983), the titular feline is thought to be a good-luck charm but soon brings misfortune to all who come into contact with it. In the second tale, *Rain Boy* (1983), Mouta is on his way home during a storm when a boy asks if he can have his shoes. The boy is a magical creature who can grant him three wishes after the fashion of **ALADDIN**'s jinni.

Lunn Flies into the Wind (1985) features a boy who falls in love with the girl he sees in an advertisement poster on a wall and goes searching for the original model— in hindsight it seems like a forerunner of many of the artificial or blank-slate girlfriends of subsequent 1990s anime **ROMANCE AND DRAMA**. *Yamataro Comes Back* (1989) is an *Incredible Journey*–themed adventure about a young bear cub losing his parents and having to survive in the wild. *Adachigahara* (1991) was shown in theaters as a second feature and based on one of the **JAPANESE FOLK TALES**, though the action is moved into the near future. An old woman meets the young space pilot Jes, exiled for trying to overthrow Earth's pro-independence president Phippo and pining for his girlfriend, Anny. The final story, *Akuemon* (1993), was directed by Tezuka's own son Makoto and shown at the Hong Kong film festival instead of broadcast on Japanese TV. A tale set in old-time Japan, it portrays a fox outwitting a hunter and choosing to live out his life in the shadow of the titular temple gate with his newfound squirrel companion.

LISTEN TO ME, GIRLS, I'M YOUR FATHER *

2012. JPN: *Papa no Iu Koto o Kikinasai*. TV series. DIR: Itsuro Kawasaki. SCR: Naruhisa Arakawa, Keiichiro Ochi, Masaharu Amiya, Yoshimi Narita. DES: Takashi Mamezuka.

ANI:. MUS: Hiroshi Uesugi. PRD: feel, Starchild Records, PPP, Bandai Namco, Klockworx, Shueisha, Studio Mausu. 24 mins. x 12 eps. (TV), 24 mins. (v).

College boy Yuta Segawa becomes a reluctant guardian when an accident leaves him in charge of his three nieces. But despite the chaos caused by four people sharing a pokey little apartment, he realizes that the girls might be the secret weapon he needs to win the heart of Raika, the college girl with a love of cute.

Surrogate parenting is a common theme in live-action Japanese TV drama, in which a devil-may-care singleton is somehow lumbered with a sullen but transformative child, learning in the process the values of responsibility and the importance of family. This anime, based on the book series by Tomohiro Matsu and illustrated by Yuka Nakajima, regretfully plays to the odder elements of the otaku crowd by fetishizing the underage sex appeal of its leads in early episodes, before dropping this conceit in favor of a story more in keeping with the mainstream televisual precedents. Needless to say, like the protagonist of **MY WIFE IS A HIGH-SCHOOL STUDENT**, Yuta is obliged to keep his guests secret, and misunderstandings duly ensue, but alongside the comedy is a recurring sense of pathos, not the least because someone has to tell the girls what has happened to their parents. A bonus episode was released on disc to accompany the DVDs of the TV show and is filed as a phantom "13th" TV episode in some sources.

LITTL' BITS *

1980. JPN: *Belfy to Lilibet*. AKA: *Belfy and Lillibit*. TV series. DIR: Masayuki Hayashi, Mizuho Nishikubo, Hiroshi Iwata. SCR: Masaru Yamamoto, Kazuo Sato, Takao Oyama, Akiyoshi Sakai, Isao Okishima, Leo Nishimura. DES: Hiromitsu Morita, Akiko Shimomoto. ANI: Hiromitsu Morita. MUS: Takeo Watanabe. PRD: Tatsunoko. 30 mins. x 26 eps.

The Fanitt family of fairies protects the forest, even though they are only a few inches tall. Lilibet is a male fairy, happy-go-lucky and always willing to help out. Though the other fairies make fun of him, he never lets it get him down, getting into all manner of adventures in the company of his girlfriend, Belfy, and pals Napoleon,

Dokkurin, and Chuchuna. Later episodes of this Tatsunoko fairy story included early jobs for future **VIDEO GIRL AI**–director Nishikubo and writer Okishima, who also scripted episodes of the live-action *Monkey* TV series.

These *Smurf*-alikes were translated into English and shown on Nickelodeon in 1984, with the location changed to "Foothill Forest." The names were also altered, to a roster including Lillabit, Williebit, Snoozabit, Browniebit, Snagglebit, and the old-timer Elderbit.

LITTLE BATTLERS EXPERIENCE *

2011. JPN: *Danboru Senki*. AKA: *LBX*. TV series, movie. DIR: Naohito Takahashi, Yoshikazu Miyao. SCR: Atsuhiro Tomioka, Kenichi Yamada, Tatsuto Higuchi, Akihiro Hino. DES: Hiroyuki Nishimura, Jun Sonobe, Toshihiro Kohama, Yoshio Tanioka, Tazuko Nagano. ANI: Hiroyuki Nishimura, Toshiaki Ohashi, Kii Tanaka. MUS: Rei Kondo, Natsumi Kameoka, Yasunori Mitsuda. PRD: Oriental Light and Magic (Team Inoue), Dentsu, TV Tokyo. 25 mins. x 44 eps. (TV1), 25 mins. x 58 eps. (TV2), 25 mins. x ?? eps. (TV3).

Yamano Ban isn't allowed to have the big-hit toy LBX—Little Battlers Experience, small fighting robots loved by children everywhere. His father was taken from him in an LBX-related accident four years ago in 2046, when the revolutionary shock-absorbing cardboard that forms the basis of LBX was invented. Now his mother refuses to allow him to have his own LBX, and he has to borrow others' toys to play. A mysterious woman gives him a case containing a completely new LBX robot. Now he's the target for the many organizations that want the data and technology it carries, and he and his friends are dragged into a corporate war that stretches all the way to the top and could even change Japanese politics. That's a tall order for a series that is, essentially, an extended toy commercial, but *Little Battlers Experience* has enough character interplay, goofy comedy, plot twists, and mecha battle action to keep viewers glued to the screen. A manga by Hideaki Fujii started its run in *Coro Coro Comic* in February 2011 and is still going.

A second series, *Danball Senki W*, brings Ban and friends back one year on, to battle a new menace: a terrorist organization threatening the world using LBX technology. It began airing in 2012, immediately after the first series finished, and the third series *Danball Senki Wars* commenced immediately after that. In a similar fashion to **BAKUGAN BATTLE BRAWLERS**, the story brings in a new lead character and a change in emphasis. Arata is a 14-year-old student at a special school for gifted LBX players: he and his friends find secrets lurking in the academy. Before this, a movie in Japanese theaters in December 2012 combined the worlds of *Danball Senki* and future soccer show **INAZUMA ELEVEN**. Akihiro Hino of Level 5, creator of the original PSP games on which both shows are based, wrote the movie screenplay.

LITTLE BUSTERS *

2012. TV series. DIR: Yoshiki Yamakawa. SCR: Michiru Shimada, Yuniko Ayana. DES: Na-Ga, Itaru Hinoe, Haruko Iizuka. ANI: Haruko Iizuka, Masayuki Onchi. MUS: Jun Maeda, PMMK, Magome Togoshi, Manabu Miwa. PRD: Key, JC Staff, Big Owl, AT-X, BS11 Digital, Tokyo MX TV, TV Aichi. 24 mins. x 26 eps.

Riki Naoe is an orphan, who slowly overcomes his trauma through the friendship of a new-found gang of friends, the self-styled "Little Busters." Now a high-school sophomore, facing the prospect that his old group of friends will be dispersed by the end of their education, he proposes one last adventure: the formation of a baseball team. Based on a "visual novel" computer game (**ARGOT AND JARGON**) from Key, the creators of **CLANNAD** and **KANON**, this **EVERYDAY ANIME** remains perpetually obsessed with the need to treasure childhood friends—compare to **COLORFUL THE MOTION PICTURE**. However, although it makes a play for both tragedy and mawkish, clumsy social interactions, it seems to suffer from the absence of Key's usual collaborators, Kyoto Animation on the production side, and never quite manages to rise above the pedestrian confines of its "high" concept.

LITTLE DEVIL

1989. JPN: *Akuma-kun*. TV series, movie. DIR: Junichi Sato, Shigeyasu Yamauchi, Masayuki Akehi. SCR: Yoshiyuki Suga, Takao Koyama, Nobuaki Kishima. DES: Ginichiro Suzuki. ANI: Fujio Yamamoto, Masami Abe. MUS: Nozomu Aoki. PRD: Toei, TV Asahi. 25 mins. x 42 eps.

(TV), 40 mins., 26 mins. (m).

A minor work based on a 1966 manga by **SPOOKY KITARO**–creator Shigeru Mizuki, in which the Little Devil appears once every ten thousand years (in this case, as Japanese schoolboy Shingo Yamada) to save the world, although his reasons are not too clear considering that he is supposed to be on the side of evil and has 12 "dark apostles" to contend with. Similarly confused renditions of Christian apocalypse turn up for adult audiences in **DEVILMAN**, **UROTSUKIDOJI**, and **HUMANE SOCIETY**, though this anime is most definitely aimed at children. The second "movie," a glorified episode screened as part of the traditional vacation moviegoing season, packs Shingo off to Devil-Land, a Satanic theme park. Come on, Disney, you know you want to.

LITTLE EL CID

1979. JPN: *Little El Cid no Boken*. AKA: *Adventures of Little El Cid*. TV series. DIR: Fumio Kurokawa. SCR: Toshiyuki Kashiwakura. DES: Shuichi Seki. ANI: Takao Kogawa, Akio Sakai. MUS: N/C. PRD: Nippon Animation, TV Tokyo. 25 mins. x 26 eps.

In 10th-century Spain, the Christian inhabitants are fighting a losing battle against the invading Muslim Moors. The young Luis Díaz de Bivar decides to become a knight, but it will be a long time before he becomes the legendary warrior El Cid. A fictitious dramatization of a famous character's youth (compare to **ROBIN HOOD**), commissioned as a Spanish coproduction but not broadcast in Japan until 1984, long after its Spanish premiere. Curiously, in the original 12th-century *Poema di Mio Cid*, El Cid's name is Rodrigo, not Luis.

LITTLE GHOSTS: ATCHI, KOTCHI, AND SOTCHI

1991. JPN: *Chiisana Obake: Atchi, Kotchi, Sotchi*. AKA: *Little Ghosts: Thither, Hither, and Yon*. TV series. DIR: Osamu Kobayashi. SCR: Yoshio Urasawa, Kazuhiko Godo. DES: N/C. ANI: Hideo Kawauchi. MUS: Takeshi Ike. PRD: Pastel House, Studio Pierrot, Nippon TV. 11 mins. x 100 eps.

Three friendly ghosts play around, make friends, and become involved in mildly surreal adventures, such as delivering donuts to aliens from Venus. Their prime concern, however, is getting lots of lovely food, an orally fixated quest of some appeal to their audience of toddlers.

LITTLE GOBLIN

1968. JPN: *Kaibutsu-kun*. AKA: *Li'l Monster Prince*. TV series, movie. DIR: Masaaki Osumi, Eiji Okabe, Shinichi Suzuki, Hiroshi Fukutomi, Shinji Okuda, Makoto Nakahara. SCR: Haruya Yamazaki, Tsunehisa Ito, Takashi Hayakawa, Takashi Yamada, Hirokazu Mizude, Yoshio Urasawa. DES: Fujiko-Fujio, Tsutomu Shibata. ANI: Norio Kubii, Sadao Tominaga. MUS: Michio Okamoto, Asei Kobayashi. PRD: Tokyo Movie Shinsha, TBS. 25 mins. x 49 eps. (TV1), 25 mins. x 49 eps. (TV2), 75 mins. (m1), 51 mins. (m2). Kaibutsu the little goblin appears one day in the apartment next door to average Japanese schoolboy Hiroshi's. He is the prince of Monster Land, sent to Earth to keep him out of trouble, accompanied on occasion by his associates Franken (a junior **FRANKENSTEIN**'s monster), **DRACULA**, and the Wolfman.

Ghostly goings-on in the tradition of **DORORON ENMA**, **SPOOKY KITARO**, and **LITTLE DEVIL**, based on a 1965 manga by **DORAEMON**-creator Hiroshi Fujimoto, though credited to the Fujiko-Fujio team of which he was a member. The franchise was brought back in color as the TV series *New Little Goblin* (1980), this time on the TV Asahi channel. The remake graduated to movie status with *LG in Monster Land* (1981), on a double bill with the *Doraemon* film *Nobita the Space Colonist*. The character returned for a second film outing with *LG: Sword of the Devil* (1982), set in the rival kingdom of Devil Land, which Kaibutsu is forced to invade in order to save his father's life.

LITTLE HOUSE ON THE PRAIRIE

1975. JPN: *Sogen no Shojo Laura*. AKA: *Laura the Girl of the Grasslands*. TV series. DIR: Mitsuo Sawazaki, Masaharu Endo. SCR: Iwao Yamazaki, Fumi Takahashi. DES: Yasuji Mori. ANI: Megumi Mizuta. MUS: Akihiko Takashima. PRD: Nippon Animation, TBS. 25 mins. x 26 eps.
Young Laura lives a happy life in Wisconsin but is forced to move west, out of the woods with her family, when a harsh winter makes it impossible to stay in her old home. After encountering American Indians and settling on the Dakota prairie,

she has a happy time (again) with her loving family, particularly her sisters, Mary and Carrie.

Not a **WORLD MASTERPIECE THEATER** production, though made by the WMT studio Nippon Animation, the anime was commissioned and filmed in Japan following the success of the anime **HEIDI** and the popularity of the U.S. live-action TV series of *LHotP* in Japan. As with the live-action series, the anime version concentrates on adapting the early books in the long sequence of novels by Laura Ingalls Wilder—later volumes would take the child characters into adulthood, way beyond the 1953 volume from which the series takes its name.

LITTLE JUMBO

1977. JPN: *Chiisana Jumbo*. Movie. DIR: Toshio Hirata, Masami Hata. SCR: Takashi Yanase. DES: Takashi Yanase. ANI: Kazuko Nakamura, Shigeru Yamamoto. MUS: Taku Izumi. PRD: Madhouse, Sanrio. 28 mins.
Jumbo the kindhearted elephant arrives at Red Rose Island after floating across the sea in a big red box, accompanied by his friend Baloo the elephant-trainer. The pair immediately leap out of the box and begin a series of supposedly cute song-and-dance numbers to entertain the king and his three subjects, although clearly not cute enough for Sanrio, which kept this minor offering from **ANPANMAN**-creator Yanase on the shelf for two years before allowing it to sneak into theaters in 1977.

LITTLE KOALA

1984. JPN: *Koala Boy Kokki*. AKA: *Adventures of the Little Koala*. TV series. DIR: Takashi Tanasawa, Katsuhisa Yamada, Masamitsu Sasaki, Shigeru Omachi. SCR: Toshiro Ueno, Nanako Watanabe, Yoshiaki Yoshida, Toshiaki Imaizumi, Kiichi Takayama, Mamoru Kanbe. DES: Kazuyuki Kobayashi. ANI: Kazuyuki Kobayashi, Hidekazu Obara, Yoichi Kotabe, Masahiro Yoshida, Megumi Kagawa, Masayuki Uchiyama. MUS: Tsuyoshi Kawano. PRD: Nagata, TV Tokyo. 25 mins. x 26 eps.
Kokki and his twin sister Laura are baby koalas who live in Yukari Village in the countryside. They play with their other animal friends, including Panny the Penguin, but often have to fight to preserve the peace of their village from the predations of the three evil Kangaroo Brothers.

Other troubles include a sick whale, invading UFOs, an attacking witch, and other incidents that only go to demonstrate that if your highconcept is so thin as to be nothing more than "Let's do something with koalas," the end result is a mishmash of everything else on TV at the time. Commissioned during the same koala fever that brought us **NOOZLES**.

LITTLE KONISHIKI

2000. JPN: *Dotto Koni-chan*. AKA: *Kaboom Koni-chan*. TV series. DIR: Shinichi Watanabe. SCR: Satoru Akahori, Masaharu Amiya. DES: Mitsuhiro Yoneda. ANI: Shinichi Watanabe. MUS: N/C. PRD: Sky PerfecTV. 5 mins. x 26 eps.
Spoof SF, adventure, and fantasy drama featuring squashed-down child-versions of the sumo wrestler Konishiki, along with his cartoon companions High, Moro, and Nari. Based on a cartoon strip in *The Television* magazine, the series premiered on pay-per-view television before moving to regular broadcasts. Screened within the *Animax* anime-themed schedule strip.

LITTLE LORD FAUNTLEROY ★

1988. JPN: *Shokoshi Ceddie*. AKA: *Young Noble Ceddie; Adventures of the Little Prince*. TV series. DIR: Kozo Kusuba, Fumio Ike. SCR: Shiro Ishimori. DES: Michiyo Sakurai. ANI: Michiyo Sakurai, Hideaki Shimada, Hisatoshi Motoki, Eimi Maeda, Megumi Kagawa, Toshiki Yamazaki. MUS: Koichi Morita. PRD: Nippon Animation, Fuji TV. 25 mins. x 43 eps.
Young American boy Cedric Errol discovers that his late father was English and that he is being deprived of his true inheritance by anti-American relatives. Captain Errol, sent away to the U.S. by his resentful father, incurred the wrath of his family by falling in love with a girl in the colonies, and the other Errol family members are determined to keep Cedric out of their lives. Eventually, he returns to his English homeland and the stewardship of Dorincourt Castle. This rags-to-riches tale was based on the 1886 children's book by Frances Hodgson Burnett, who also wrote **A LITTLE PRINCESS** and **THE SECRET GARDEN**. As befits its trans-Atlantic tone, it was released in both British and American dubs, although with a title that has often led to confusion with the unrelated **LITTLE PRINCE**. See also **VIDEO PICTURE BOOK**.

LITTLE LOVE LETTER, A

1981. JPN: *Chiisana Love Letter: Mariko to Nemunoki no Kodomotachi.* AKA: *A Little Love Letter: Mariko and the Children of the Silk Tree.* TV special. DIR: Yuzo Ishida. SCR: Sachiko Akita. DES: Kenzo Koizumi. ANI: Swan Pro. MUS: Nozomu Aoki. PRD: TV Asahi, NOW Planning. 65 mins.

A follow-up to the same studio's **HELEN KELLER** anime, *A Little Love Letter* kept the handicapped theme but focused on a wholly Japanese story. During the 1970s, actress Mariko Miyagi became heavily involved in the Silk Tree Academy, a rehabilitation center for disabled children. She appeared in several live-action films to promote the project, including *The Silk Tree Ballad, Mariko-Mother,* and *Children Drawing Rainbows.* This anime charts the 14-year period of Miyagi's stewardship of the academy and her relationships with several of the children. Divided into four seasonal chapters, the film uses highly realistic character designs based on the actual people involved and features storyboarding from the versatile **STAR BLAZERS**–director Noboru Ishiguro.

LITTLE LULU AND THE GANG

1976. JPN: *Little Lulu to Chitchai Nakama.* AKA: *Little Lulu and her Cute Friends.* TV series, movie. DIR: Fumio Kurokawa. SCR: Juzo Takahashi. DES: Shuichi Seki. ANI: Shinichi Tsuji, Tatsuo Maeda. MUS: Nobuyoshi Okabe. PRD: Nippon Animation, Trans Arts, TV Asahi. 25 mins. x 26 eps. (TV), 87 mins. (m1), 88 mins. (m2).

Everyday family situations with lots of gentle humor and sight gags for the heroine of the American comic by Marge Henderson Buell. Her friends include Wilbur, the good-natured son of a wealthy family, Annie, the daring girl, and chubby Tubby, all of whom collaborate in making mischief in the fashion of **PINCH AND PUNCH**. Note that this *Little Lulu* is wholly different from the Fleischer brothers cartoon of the same name, which was originated in the U.S., but was exported to Japan at roughly the same time, and aired on a rival channel. Two feature-length edits were made from the series.

LITTLE MERMAID

1975. JPN: *Andersen Dowa Ningyo Hime.* AKA: *Andersen Story Mermaid Princess.*
Movie. DIR: Tomoharu Katsumata. SCR: Ikuko Ooyabu, Mieko Osanai. DES: Takashi Abe, Shingo Araki, Kazuo Komatsubara. ANI: Reiko Okuyama. MUS: Takekuni Hirayoshi. PRD: Toei. 68 mins. (m1), 21 mins. (m2).

Blonde Marina, the youngest of six mermaid sisters, falls in love with the handsome human Prince Fritz when she sees him one night passing overhead in a boat. The boat is swamped by a large wave, and Marina rescues the man she adores, nursing Fritz back to health with an array of magical potions. He falls in love with her, but if she is to be with him on land, she must lose her tail and her beautiful voice.

The most famous of the **TALES OF HANS CHRISTIAN ANDERSEN**, *LM* was animated to celebrate the centenary of its author's death—bracketed at both ends by live-action footage of Denmark shot by Henning Christiansen. The story was remade in 1995 as a 21-minute fully computer-animated version based on a retelling published by the children's illustrator Chihiro Iwasaki. *Little Mermaid Series* was also the umbrella title to the unrelated four-part collection of pornographic vignettes in the tradition of **LOLITA ANIME**, filed elsewhere in this encyclopedia as **SYMPHONY DREAM STORY**. See also **VIDEO PICTURE BOOK** and the radical reimagining that is Miyazaki's **PONYO**.

LITTLE MRS. PEPPERPOT

1983. JPN: *Spoon Obasan.* AKA: *Auntie Spoon.* TV series. DIR: Keiji Hayakawa. SCR: Maki Nakahara, Tomoko Kawasaki, Keiko Maruo, Masaaki Sakurai, Mamoru Oshii. DES: Koji Nanke. ANI: Noboru Furuse, Toshio Hirata, Kenjiro Yoshida, Naoto Hashimoto, Satoshi Dezaki, Teruo Kogure, Mamoru Oshii. MUS: Koji Nanke, Tachio Akano. PRD: Pierrot, NHK. 10 mins. x 130 eps.

Auntie Spoon (so called because of the strange pendant she wears around her neck) is an old lady loved by everybody. Only local girl Ruri knows Auntie's secret—that she can use her magic pendant to shrink herself to the *size* of a spoon, bringing a whole new perspective to the everyday world. Originally based on a Norwegian folk tale, then filtered through Alf Prøysen's retelling of the story as *Little Mrs. Pepperpot* before reaching Japan, this was the first anime series to be serialized on Japan's state channel, NHK.

LITTLE NEMO: ADVENTURES IN SLUMBERLAND *

1989. Movie. DIR: Masami Hata, William Hurtz. SCR: Chris Columbus, Richard Outten, Bruce Schaefer. DES: Jean Giraud, Brian Froud, Paul Julian, Kazuhide Tominaga. ANI: Yasuo Otsuka, Kazuaki Yoshinaga, Nobuo Tominaga. MUS: Richard Sherman, Robert Sherman. PRD: Tokyo Movie Shinsha. 95 mins.

Nemo is a little boy who lives in 1905 New York City. A blimp approaches his house, and the clown who steps out of it informs him that he has been requested as a playmate by the princess of Slumberland. Traveling to Slumberland, the boy is soon involved in a mission to rescue its ruler, who has been kidnapped by the Nightmare King. A tiresome and condescending attempt to reverse-engineer Disney by a studio that reputedly removed members of staff who refused to toe the party line—one of whom was Hayao Miyazaki, whose version of *LN* might well have been vastly superior if he had only been allowed to complete it. As it is, the film is a confusion of good-intentioned but insincere clichés, including halfhearted musical numbers, far removed from the original 1905 comic strip by Winsor McCay on which it is based. The production features a large number of famous names, including voice actors Mickey Rooney (Flip the Clown) and René Auberjonois (Professor Genius). Disney's Frank Thomas, Roger Allers, and Ollie Johnson were among the animators, the songs were written by the Sherman brothers (*Chitty Chitty Bang Bang*), while Jean "Moebius" Giraud provided "conceptual design." However, many of the crew are "ghost" credits symptomatic of a long and troubled production—Ray Bradbury is credited with the "screen concept" but seems to have left the production early on, while the press notes carelessly trumpet the involvement of *Chinatown* scenarist Robert Towne as a "story consultant," a likely sign that Towne had been called in to rescue a failing premise. Both Hayao Miyazaki and Isao Takahata split from the production at an early stage due to "creative differences," while Yoshifumi Kondo stayed to work on the first (1984) pilot. A second (1987) pilot, credited to Osamu Dezaki, also exists, and both are included as bonus items on the LaserDisc release.

LITTLE NORSE PRINCE *

1968. JPN: *Taiyo no Ko Hols no Daiboken.* AKA: *Prince of the Sun: Hols's Great Adventure; The Great Adventure of Little Prince Valiant; Little Norse Prince Valiant.* Movie. DIR: Isao Takahata. SCR: Isao Takahata. DES: Hayao Miyazaki. ANI: Yasuo Otsuka. MUS: Tsuneo Mamiya. PRD: Toei. 82 mins.

Fisherman's son Hols is a brave boy, but when we first meet him, surrounded by a pack of hungry wolves and armed only with an axe, his chances don't look good. He is saved by the intervention of Rockor, a giant of earth and stone awakened from centuries of sleep by the noise of the fight. Hols thanks his new friend by removing a sword wedged deep into the rock of his shoulder; it is the Sword of the Sun, and Rockor predicts that it will help him to defeat the evil of Frost King Grunwald. Then Hols's father dies, but on his deathbed he tells his son how they originally came from a fishing village far to the north, and how they were the only survivors when it was destroyed by Grunwald's sorcery. He begs Hols to return to his birthplace and find out what has happened to the other villages. Armed with his axe and his new sword, and accompanied by his pet bear, Coro, Hols heads north.

He is attacked on the way by Grunwald and is almost killed falling off a cliff, but the people of a fishing village find him and care for him. They too are suffering from Grunwald's magic: a giant pike under his dominion is eating all the fish in the area and threatening the village's livelihood. Hols goes after the fish-monster alone and kills it after a titanic battle. This brings him great popularity, and some jealousy, but it further provokes Grunwald, who is determined to destroy all life in the region and sends in another, more stealthy attack. In a deserted village, Hols meets a young girl named Hilda. When he takes her back to the village, she is welcomed for her gentle nature and beautiful singing voice, but as Grunwald's dark sorcery continues to threaten the village, she is revealed as his sister.

Isao Takahata's feature debut shows fluid animation of movement, well-paced action scenes, and a charming style of character design that would become synonymous with the work of the studio he was later to found with his young colleague Hayao Miyazaki, who also assisted on this production. The film received unusually sympathetic treatment from its Western adapters, director Fred Ladd and editor Eli Haviv, who kept the tragic elements of the story intact, including the death of a loved one and the grief that follows. There is no connection with *Prince Valiant*, but the popularity of the comic in Europe led *LNP's* Italian licensees to try and piggyback the film to success, hence the alternate title.

LITTLE PRINCE *

1978. JPN: *Hoshi no Ojisama Puchi Prince.* AKA: *Prince of the Stars: Petit Prince; Adventures of the Little Prince.* TV series. DIR: Takeyuki Kanda, Yoshikazu Yasuhiko, Osamu Sekita, Norio Kashima. SCR: Eiichi Tachi, Susumu Yoshida, Tsunehisa Ito, Takero Kaneko, Yoshiaki Yoshida, Masaaki Sakurai. DES: Yasuji Mori, Yoshikazu Yasuhiko, Eiji Tanaka. ANI: Shinnosuke Mina. MUS: Tsuyoshi Kawano. PRD: Knack, TV Asahi. 25 mins. x 35 eps. (TV), 25 mins. x 4 eps. (v).

The Little Prince is the ruler of a very small planet, but he is also its sole human occupant, so he must sweep the volcano clean and control the roots of the overgrown baobab tree. He talks to springs and butterflies, but his only real friend is the selfish human-shaped Star Rose. One day, the prince has an argument with the rose and sets off to Earth to search for his real friends.

Based on the 1943 novella by Antoine de Saint-Exupéry, though little of the French original remains—instead, it is lost almost completely beneath the prince's wanderings after the first episode, concealed still further in the English-language version by a dub that gives Saint-Exupéry a risible French accent, seemingly modeled on Inspector Clouseau. The series was only broadcast as far as episode 35—the remaining four sneaked out onto video when it was reissued.

LITTLE PRINCE AND THE EIGHT-HEADED DRAGON *

1963. JPN: *Wanpaku Oji no Orochi Taiji.* AKA: *Naughty Prince and the Giant Snake.* Movie. DIR: Yugo Serikawa, Isao Takahata, Kimio Yabuki. SCR: Ichiro Ikeda, Kei Iijima. DES: Yasuji Mori. ANI: Sanae Yamamoto, Yasuji Mori, Hideo Furusawa. MUS: Akira Ifukube.

PRD: Toei. 76 mins.

Susanoo (see TAKEGAMI), son of the creators of Japan, Izanami and Izanagi, sets off accompanied by his rabbit assistant Akahana (Red-Nose) to rescue his dead mother, who has gone to the Underworld. After defeating a giant fish and a fire monster, he then witnesses the story of the Sun Goddess Amaterasu, who hides in a cave and needs to be lured out. Falling in love with the earthly princess Kushinada, he discovers that she is to be sacrificed to Orochi, an eight-headed serpent that returns once each year to raid her parents' village until placated by a human sacrifice. All three of these tales are adapted from chapters of the *Nihon Shoki*, an 8th-century chronicle that links the historical emperors with the Japanese gods and demigods, though much of the mythical meaning was lost in the transition to the American kiddiefilm. Orochi would also appear in BLUE SEED and YAMATO TAKERU. Note also a rare anime score for Ifukube, better known as the composer for the *Godzilla* films.

Director Yugo Serikawa has somewhat controversially claimed in modern interviews that the stripped-down, impressionistic art-style of the film represented the end of the old "full animation" style of Toei, and the beginning of a new strand of limited animation more suitable for television. Obliquely, this implies that he, or his staff, came up with the ASTRO BOY look at roughly the same time as Osamu Tezuka was poaching staff from Toei to work at his own studio. While it is widely understood that Tezuka's limited TV animation style was the product of many animators working under him, the idea that those animators were themselves repeating ideas already established by Serikawa has not really taken off.

LITTLE PRINCESS, A

1985. JPN: *Shokojo Sara.* AKA: *Young Noblewoman Sara; Princess Sarah.* TV series. DIR: Fumio Kurokawa, Takeshi Yamaguchi, Jiro Saito. SCR: Ryuzo Nakanishi, Keiko Mukuroji. DES: Shunji Saita. ANI: Toshiki Yamazaki, Shunji Saita, Kuniyuki Ishii. MUS: Yasuo Higuchi. PRD: Nippon Animation, Fuji TV. 25 mins. x 46 eps.

Fearing that the Indian climate and environment will do more harm than good, Sara Crewe's father sends her away to boarding school in England, where she diligently attends Miss Minchin's academy and dreams that she is a princess. However, her life is shattered when her father dies, and his will reveals that he had no money. Sara is forced to become a servant at her school, reduced to the lowest rung of the social scale, though, as the title already implies, a CINDERELLA-like transformation eventually awaits. The 16th entry in the WORLD MASTERPIECE THEATER series was adapted from the 1888 children's novel *Sarah Crewe* by Frances Hodgson Burnett, who also wrote LITTLE LORD FAUNTLEROY and THE SECRET GARDEN. See also VIDEO PICTURE BOOK and compare with CANDY CANDY.

LITTLE RED [RIDING] HOOD CHA CHA

1995. JPN: *Akazukin Chacha*. Video, TV series. DIR: Yuji Moriyama, Hiroaki Sakurai, Tatsuo Sato, Akitaro Daichi, Kazuhiro Sasaki. SCR: Hiroshi Koda, Takashi Yamada, Shigeru Yanagawa, Hideki Mitsui, Tomoko Kaneko, Ryosuke Takahashi, Hiroshi Yamaguchi. DES: Hajime Watanabe. ANI: Masayuki Onchi, Yoko Konishi. MUS: Toshihiko Sahashi, Osamu Tezuka (mus). PRD: Studio Gallop, TV Tokyo. 30 mins. x 3 eps. (v), 25 mins. x 74 eps. (TV).
Twelve-year-old Cha Cha lives in the Mochi-mochi mountains, where she is studying to be a magician. A clumsy student, Cha Cha's spells often backfire on her, though she has the support of her friends Riya (a young werewolf) and Shine, who can help her undergo the magical transformation of Love, Heroism, and Hope. Meanwhile, the great Devil King wants Cha Cha dead in order to lift the curse her grandfather put on his castle, while other rivals include Black Hood and Marine, a competitive mermaid. A spirited SAILOR MOON clone that is more than the sum of its parts, taking much-appreciated time to explore the geography and history of its fantasy world, and thereby making the school/magical-girl antics of its cast all that more appealing. Based on a 1992 manga in *Ribon* magazine by Min Ayahana.

LITTLE TWINS

1992. Video, movie. DIR: Toshio Hirata, Satoshi Inoue, Yorifusa Yamaguchi. SCR: Junji Takegami. DES: Kazuo Komatsubara.

ANI: Shunji Saida, Hiroki Takahashi, Yasuyuki Hirata. MUS: Mash Morse. PRD: Bandai. 25 mins. x 3 eps. (v), 25 mins. (m1).
In these adaptations of Isamu Tsuchida's picture books for children, Tiffle and Tuffle are two little twins in pointed hats who live on Coracle Island and have a few lighthearted adventures. The "movie" release, *How Our Summer Flew Past*, is of a length and quality to suggest it was merely the fourth video installment, dumped on theaters as a promotional exercise for the tapes.

LITTLE WITCH CHAPPY

1972. JPN: *Mahotsukai Chappi*. TV series. DIR: Yugo Serikawa, Hiroshi Ikeda, Katsutoshi Sasaki, Masayuki Akehi, Osamu Kasai, Keiji Hisaoka, Hideo Furusawa. SCR: Masaki Tsuji, Saburo Taki, Shunichi Yukimuro, Noboru Shiroyama, Jiro Yoshino, Kuniaki Oshikawa. DES: N/C. ANI: Shinya Takahashi, Fusahito Nagaki. MUS: Hiroshi Tsutsui. PRD: Toei, NET. 25 mins. x 39 eps.
Chappy the little witch is sent from her magic kingdom to solve problems on Earth, accompanied by her little brother, Jun, and wielding her family heirloom, a magical baton to help her make the world a better place. A magical-girl tale following on from LITTLE WITCH SALLY and featuring the late addition of the mascot character Don-chan, a cuddly panda that easily dates the show to the panda hysteria of the early 1970s—see PANDA GO PANDA.

LITTLE WITCH SALLY

1966. JPN: *Mahotsukai Sally*. TV series, movie, TV special. DIR: Osamu Kasai. SCR: Akiyoshi Sakai. DES: Yoshiyuki Hane. ANI: Takashi Kasai, Minoru Tajima, Katsuya Koda, Hideo Furusawa. MUS: Asei Kobayashi. PRD: Toei, Hikari Pro. 25 mins. x 109 eps. (TV1—1st 18 episodes in b/w), 25 mins. x 88 eps. (TV2), 27 mins. (m), 50 mins. (TVm).
Sally is a trainee witch sent to Earth to study humans and learn how to blend in among them, though she does not always succeed. She befriends Earth children Yotchan and Sumire and fights the corrupt Kabu, who steals from department stores. This was the first of the "magical girl" genre that would extend to the present day through look-alike titles such as CREAMY MAMI, GIGI, and SECRET AKKO-CHAN. Originating in a 1966 manga for

Ribon magazine by GIANT ROBO–creator Mitsuteru Yokoyama, the character was originally called Sunny but had her name changed to avoid protests from the car manufacturer Nissan.
Sally returned for a new series in 1989 on TV Asahi, directed by Osamu Kasai, with character designs by Yasuhiro Yamaguchi. In 1990, the new incarnation also appeared in a short 1990 movie and a TV special, *LWS: Mother's Love Is Eternal*, which ended the series with Sally's dream that she is to become the new queen of the magical land of Astria and must bid farewell to her friends. Yokoyama's witch, like Tezuka's ASTRO BOY, was one of the defining archetypes of anime, and it is still much imitated to this day—see also his less successful follow-up, COMET-SAN.

LITTLE WITCHES YOYO AND NENE *

2013. JPN: *Majocco Shimai Yoyo to Nene*. AKA: *Witch Sisters Yoyo and Nene*. Movie. DIR: Takayuki Hirao. SCR: N/C. DES: Yuka Shibata. ANI: N/C. MUS: Go Shina. PRD: ufotable, King Record, T-Joy. 100 mins.
Yoyo, a young witch who specializes in lifting curses, is transported through a portal into a world that, for her, is exotic and magical—modern Yokohama. While her sister Nene tries to find a solution back home in Sorceria, she works with a pair of disbelieving Japanese brothers to contain an outbreak of curses, searching for the source of the contagion before higher powers take brutal, extreme action.
Evoking and replaying many of the tropes of a genre that dates back to LITTLE WITCH SALLY, Takayuki Hirao offers a clumsy magical girl with a job to do in our world, and an infestation of sorcery gradually spiraling out of control into a completely fluffy, cuddly reimagining of the director's earlier, schlocky GYO: TOKYO FISH ATTACK. But this film also plays like a cynical reverse-engineering of many recent anime hits, with a young girl struggling to overcome a parental transformation like that in SPIRITED AWAY, a sorcerous matriarch and gentle apocalypse straight out of PONYO, and a technological plot device that transforms personal, family tensions into global danger, as if a producer has glibly ordered a fantasy reworking of SUMMER WARS.
At one point, Yoyo bursts into song,

suggesting the discarded prospect of a magical musical in the style of *Enchanted* (2007), particularly when the lyrics turn increasingly, obliviously sinister. She also arrives on Earth entirely unphased by the revelation that she is the star of a line of children's books in our world, merrily reading a bedtime story about her own activities to a toddler already at home with the idea of extreme interactivity (KIDS' ANIME). Based on the manga *Witch Sisters* (*Noroi Shimai*) by Hirarin, which ran in *Comic Ryu*.

LITTLE WOMEN *

1980. JPN: *Wakakusa no Yon Shimai*. AKA: *Four Sisters of Young Grass*. TV special, TV series. DIR: Yugo Serikawa, Kazumi Fukushima, Fumio Kurokawa, Kozo Kusuba. SCR: Eiichi Imato, Akira Miyazaki, Michiru Shimada. DES: Yasuhiro Yamaguchi, Tadaumi Shimogawa, Seiji Kikuchi, Yoshifumi Kondo, Kiharu Sato. ANI: Yasuhiro Yamaguchi, Takeshi Shirato, Akira Daikuhara. MUS: Nozomu Aoki, Takeo Watanabe; Kazuo Otani, David Silvers. PRD: Toei, Fuji TV, Kokusai Eiga, Toei, Tokyo Channel 12, Nippon Animation. 68 mins. (TVm), 25 mins. x 26 eps. (TV1), 25 mins. x 48 eps. (TV2), 25 mins. x 40 eps. (TV3).

In the 1860s, Frederick March goes to serve as a chaplain in the American Civil War, leaving his family behind in Concord, Massachusetts. His daughters, Jo, Meg, Beth, and Amy, help out their mother and try to get along with the Lawrence family next door. The 1868 novel by Louisa May Alcott has appeared in several anime incarnations (all of which are at least partially available in English), the first being a 1980 TV special directed by Yugo Serikawa that seems to rely more on movie versions for its plot than the book itself. The first scene is a case in point when we see Jo fooling around in the snow before throwing a snowball at the window from which her sisters are laughing at her—the same sequence opens the 1949 movie adaptation featuring June Allyson as Jo and Elizabeth Taylor as Amy.

The TV special's true role as a dry run for a series became plain in 1981, when many of the same crew returned with a TV series version. The design for the girls remained the same, but the quality of animation fell considerably, as one might expect from the more limited budgets of TV (especially a TV series that cannot make the cost-cutting economies of recycling transformation footage for robots and superheroes). Alcott's original, however, is subsumed in this version to a patronizing tone that insists on imparting a prepackaged moral to each episode. The series was dubbed in the 1980s and a small number of episodes released on video, featuring new music from usual suspects Haim Saban and Shuki Levy.

The story returned to Fuji TV in 1987 as an all-new TV series, made as the 18th in the WORLD MASTERPIECE THEATER franchise, and featuring character designs by future WHISPER OF THE HEART–director Kondo. Though rather pointlessly setting the action in the new town of "Newcord," the *WMT* version remains the best anime adaptation of Alcott, despite, or perhaps because of, writer Miyazaki's ruthless reordering of the narrative at the scripting stage. The first incident from the novel proper does not arise until episode 18 of the anime, whereas the first line from the novel does not appear until episode 21—instead, this *LW* begins with the Pennsylvania countryside-dwelling Marches forced to flee their burning home, heading for Massachusetts to live with their aunt Marte. An introduction seemingly designed to educate the Japanese audience about the events of the Civil War, while simultaneously extending the possible run of the series in the same manner as the later CINDERELLA, the extra sequences eventually click back onto track with the stories of the girls' hopes, dreams, and mild mishaps. Perhaps inspired by similar events in HUCKLEBERRY FINN (a book Alcott detested!), this *LW* also features Jim, an escaped slave whom the Marches hide from soldiers, while the female-heavy cast is evened up with David, an extra nephew, and Newcord reporter Anthony. Though the scenes may be cut up and rearranged, the anime remains studiously faithful to the events within them, with the exception of an incident where one of the girls is struck at school—a cause for scandal in the novel, but accepted with traditional Japanese resignation in the anime. One of the few *WMT* serials to be translated for the U.S. market, it was bought by Saban and broadcast on HBO in the 1990s.

A third series was commissioned as a sequel to the second, adapting Alcott's 1871 *Little Men: Life at Plumfield with Jo's Boys* under the title *Story of Young Grasses: Nan and Teacher Jo* (1993, *Wakakusa Monogatari: Nan to Jo Sensei*). However, since the *WMT LW* only adapted the first part of Alcott's original, there is something of a gap between the stories—*LM* takes place ten years later, after Jo has departed for New York, met and married a German professor, and given birth to two children. Inheriting Aunt March's house in Concord (note that it's not Newcord this time, despite this being a sequel to the second series), Jo sets up a school with her husband, turning both the book and its anime version into a different, more schooling-oriented slice-of-life than the familial predecessor. *LM* features new, softer character designs from another Studio Ghibli collaborator, MY NEIGHBOR TOTORO's Sato, though its approach to the cast seems designed not to disturb the sensibilities of a conservative audience—two disabled characters are mysteriously absent from the anime.

Not to be confused with the unrelated CHARLOTTE, whose Japanese title is similar to *LW*'s, or with the *Little Women in Love* broadcast as part of the MODERN LOVE'S SILLINESS anthology show. See also VIDEO PICTURE BOOK.

LITTLEST WARRIOR, THE *

1961. JPN: *Anju to Zushio-Maru*. AKA: *Anju and Zushio; Orphan Brother*. Movie. DIR: Taiji Yabushita, Yugo Serikawa, Isao Takahata. SCR: Sumie Tanaka. DES: Akira Daikuhara, Yasuji Mori. ANI: Sanae Yamamoto, Akira Daikuhara, Yasuji Mori, Taku Sugiyama, Reiko Okuyama. MUS: Chuji Kinoshita, Hajime Kaburagi. PRD: Toei. 83 mins. (70 mins. U.S.). After their father quarrels with local military men, Anju (Anjue) and Zushio (Zooshio) are forced to flee, but they are captured and sold into slavery. When their mother dies, they are sold to Sansho the Bailiff (or Dayu in the U.S. version, which would translate as Bailiff the Bailiff!), a cruel man who subjects them to hideous torments—though his son Saburo secretly shows kindness to the orphans. Anju falls into a lake and is transformed into a swan. Zushio escapes to a nearby temple, is adopted by a nobleman, and, after many trials, grows into a handsome young man.

He defeats the Giant Blue Widow Spider that has been terrorizing the village and is appointed to his father's former post as governor. His first act is to subjugate the evil Dayu and his followers then free all the slaves. Reunited with his mother, he then rules wisely and well.

Based on Ogai Mori's novel *Sansho the Bailiff* (*Sansho Dayu*), which was also made into a 1954 live-action film by Kenji Mizoguchi. The original folk tale that inspired the novel was also adapted as one of the **MANGA PICTURES OF JAPAN**.

LIVE ON CARDLIVER KAKERU *

2008. TV series. DIR: Hatsuki Tsuji. SCR: Tatsuhiko Urahata, Tomoyasu Okubo. DES: Toshihiko Masuda, Seiko Akashi. ANI: Masaki Inada, Masaru Hamada, Toshihiko Masuda. MUS: Kazunori Miyake. PRD: TMS Entertainment, AIM Entertainment, AT-X, BTO, Window. 25 mins. x 51 eps.
Eleven-year-old Kakeru loves the Live On card game, the latest craze for kids. He wants to be his school's top player but cute red-haired Ai always beats him, even though she's a year younger. One day he saves a small dog from a strange gang of people—only it's not a dog but a Create Monster. To help Kakeru save its hide, it gives him a Live Change Card from the game, which enables him to transform and win the battle. Kakeru learns that there's far more at stake than beating Ai and being top player in school. The world is under threat from the mysterious Q.B.—*Kyube*, the nine-tailed fox of Japanese mythology—who wants to drown it in despair. Can Kakeru and his friends harness the power of positive teamwork to save the world for fun and games? There are numerous similarities with other collecting-game shows, such as **POKÉMON**, in this anime adapted from the 2007 manga by Choji Yoshikawa with art by AIYAH-BALL.

LIVING FOR THE DAY AFTER TOMORROW *

2006. JPN: *Asatte no Hoko*. AKA: *Direction of the Day After Tomorrow*. TV series. DIR: Katsushi Sakurabi. SCR: Seishi Minakami, Tatsuhiko Urahata. DES: Ikuko Ito, J-ta Yamada, Shichiro Kobayashi. ANI: Ikuko Ito, Shinya Hasegawa. MUS: Shinkichi Mitsumune. PRD: JC Staff, Bandai Visual, GENCO, Lantis, Mag Garden, MOVIC, TBS. 25 mins. x 12 eps.
Karada can't wait to grow up. Her big brother has looked after her ever since their parents died; he had to come back from college in Boston to look after her. One day she prays at a roadside shrine that she can grow up fast and stop being a burden to him. As she prays, Shoko stops at the same shrine. She's just come back from America, unhappy, alone, and hoping for a fresh start. Her boyfriend suddenly left her behind in Boston and she never heard from him again. The shrine grants their wishes and they suddenly find themselves in each other's shoes. Be careful what you wish for: now Karada knows exactly what her big brother gave up for her sake, while Shoko knows that her bitterness and resentment was misplaced. Meanwhile, both can see that the man they love in different ways didn't handle the situation very well.

This jewel of a series is one of the best anime of its year in terms of heartfelt, truthful, unflashy emotion. The point of fantasy, from fairytale to sitcom, is to tell us truths about ourselves that would otherwise be too painful or difficult to face, and this gorgeous little body-swap story does exactly that, riffing on the two sides of puberty in a manner that anime has often explored since the days of **MARVELOUS MELMO**. The art and animation are no better than serviceable, but the writing is more than enough to carry the show.

LIVING SEX TOY DELIVERY *

2002. JPN: *Nikuyoku Gangu Takuhainin*. AKA: *The Boxed Woman*. Video. DIR: Shigeki Awai. SCR: Rinsei Kure. DES: N/C. ANI: N/C. MUS: N/C. PRD: Five Ways. 30 mins. x 3 eps.
Young removal man Shoji is invited to a party by pretty Yuika, then drugged and used as a sex toy by multiple women. He wakes up to find himself dumped on a railway line in a cardboard box with a suicide note. Understandably annoyed, he vows revenge. He goes back to Yuika's place, tricks his way in by pretending to be a delivery man, and takes her prisoner. He forces Yuika to take incriminating photographs of each of the girls in secret and then convinces each that the only way to dispose of the pictures is to climb into a box and agree to be delivered to its destination—a secluded warehouse where he assaults them. Since he already knows their secret fetishes, his chosen method in each case ensures that they begin by resisting, but are then forced to admit that they actually enjoy his attentions. He then subjects them to an additional humiliation by boxing his victims back up and mailing them to their places of work, thus ensuring that everyone knows their secrets. The final episode finds Shoji having to avoid, and then abuse, the two ringleaders, who discover that he was not killed in a train accident as originally planned. Based on a game by the Merlot (*sic*) label of Gensakuza. ●🅝🅥

LOCKE THE SUPERMAN *

1984. JPN: *Chojin Locke*. AKA: *Locke the Superpower; Star Warriors*. Movie, video. DIR: Hiroshi Fukutomi, Noboru Ishiguro, Takeshi Hirota. SCR: Atsushi Yamatoya, Takeshi Hirota. DES: Yuki Hijiri, Keizo Kobayashi, Susumu Shiraume, Masahiro Sekino. ANI: Susumu Shiraume, Yuji Moriyama, Seiji Okuda, Eimi Maeda, Hideki Tamura, Masahiko Imai, Noboru Takano, Yutaka Kubota. MUS: Goro Omi, Toshiki Ishikawa, Toshiki Hasegawa. PRD: Nippon Animation. 10 mins. (m1), 120 mins. (m2), 30 mins. x 3 eps. (v1), 50 mins. x 2 eps. (v2), 60 mins. (v3).
Former federation supersoldier Locke is a pacifist psychic who has willed himself to stay eternally young in order to avoid becoming a bellicose man (see **PETER PAN AND WENDY**). He is dragged out of retirement by agent Ryu Yamaki to thwart Lady Cahn, an industrialist secretly training a group of psychics to form the Millennium, a thousand-year dominion over mundane humans.

Surprisingly little of the film centers on its titular hero. Instead, much of it is taken up with Cahn's school for psychics—a bizarre Nazi convent, where Jessica Olin is completing her training. A girl who falsely believes that Locke killed her parents, Jessica is the most powerful of Cahn's new breed, and, after successfully destroying her opponents, she is drafted into a sabotage mission against a government outpost. When her psychic cohorts destroy the base, Cahn's agents start revolts on five outlying planets; the first steps in the foundation of a new order. They then delay Ryu's attempts to return home (though God knows why) by crashing the ship sent to take him home. Ryu rescues Jessica from the wreck, but she has amnesia. Now calling herself Amelia, she follows him back to Earth, confessing her love for him. Eventually, after all this padding, Locke appears and defeats Cahn. Amelia stays in the arms of her beloved Ryu, while Locke finds love in the form of Cahn's alter ego, schoolmistress Cornelia Prim, only to discover that her personality was removed as punishment for her crime. Alone but satisfied he has saved the universe, he returns home.

Based on the 1979 manga in *Shonen King* by Yuki Hijiri, *Locke* was rushed into production during the post–*Star Wars* boom in sci-fi that also created **Captain Future** and **Lensman**—the ten-minute *Cosmic Game* pilot film for the project was made as early as 1980. It was the first Nippon Animation film made directly for theaters and boasts technical experiments to rival **Fist of the North Star**, including some subtle early computer graphics and actual "live" footage of flames, static, and bubbles. An earnest spectacle that crashes Frank Herbert's *Dune* (Cahn wants to use Holy Mothers to breed a master race) into the thousand-year empire of Isaac Asimov's *Foundation*, with reviled psychic warriors lifted from *The X-Men*, *LtS* is let down by amateurishly clunky dialogue, as twee British-accented voices mispronounce "esper" and "combatant" throughout, confuse planets with stars, and intone priceless lines such as "a small man-made planet in this universe." This appears to be the result of a low-rent dub made somewhere in East Asia and released in some quarters under the name *Star Warriors*. Ryu Yamaki suffers worst at the hands of Japanese *and* English scripts—a man so outstandingly stupid that he lectures Locke on care of "sheeps," tries to break down a steel door with his own head, and insists on having sex with his ladylove while she is still recuperating in a hospital bed. Released in English with the original names still in place, presumably in a Japan-commissioned **Translation** that explains the poor-quality dub, the "superman" part was dropped in some territories to avoid conflict with DC comics—similar wrangles dogged **Maris the Chojo**.

With plenty more of Hijiri's manga left to adapt, the "industrialist-seeks-power,

Locke-leaves-retirement, Locke-loses-girl" plot was rehashed straight to video with *LtS: Lord Leon*, in which the titular cyborg pirate kills the grandson of Great Jugo, a wealthy industrialist whose starship-building project is in financial difficulty. Locke is once more unwillingly pressed into service by Federation Security, only to discover that Leon is the wayward brother of his new girlfriend, Flora, who has sworn vengeance on Jugo for killing the rest of his family. Jugo is responsible for the terrible injuries that caused Leon to have cybernetic augmentation and for the loss of Flora's eyesight. Fearing for his own life, he kidnaps Flora, and Leon sails into a trap while Locke rescues her.

A third incarnation was released as *LtS: New World Battle Team* (1991, *Shin Sekai Sentai*), in which Elena, the leader of the Galactic Alliance, decides to begin an Esper Elimination Project. Locke and four other psychics go on the run but lose their memories. To regain them, they must hunt down the creature known as the Tsar, unless the agents of the Galactic Alliance catch them first.

A sequel, *LtS: Mirroring* (2000), followed after a long hiatus and features new character designs by Junichi Hayama. Elena's "backed-up" cyber-successor Cassandra mutates on the "Galactic" Internet and returns as the mighty "Neon." Locke must round up his old cohorts once more (and why not, the writers just rounded up the old plot, after all). **NV**

LOLICON ANGEL

1985. JPN: *Lolicon Angel: Bishojo Comic: Himitsu no Mi*. AKA: *Loli[ta] Co[mplex] Angel: Pretty Girls' Comic: Secret Honey*. Video. DIR: N/C. SCR: N/C. DES: N/C. ANI: N/C. MUS: N/C. PRD: Pumpkin Pie. 25 mins.

While Yuka, Nami, and Aiko are in the shower together, somebody steals Yuka's wallet. The three lesbians set out to investigate at their exclusive girls' school, where everyone seems to harbor secret desires. The anime may seem to be a pale imitation of **Cream Lemon**'s *Escalation* arc—even the normally timid *Newtype* comments that, "While there may be hard lesbian action, the animation and story line are considerably below standard." **N**

LOLITA ANIME

1984. AKA: *Wonder Magazine Series*. Video. DIR: Kuni Toniro, R. Ching, Mickey Soda, Mickey Masuda. SCR: Fumio Nakajima. DES: Fumio Nakajima. ANI: Tatsushi Kurahashi. MUS: N/C. PRD: Wonder Kids. 15 mins. x 4 eps. (1–4), 30 mins. x 3 eps. (5–7), 60 mins. (8), 3 x 30 mins. (Uchiyama).

A collection of underage porn, which, with its cheerful incitement to abuse children, is in its own way far more offensive than **Urotsukidoji**. Based on manga by Fumio Nakajima, the stories range from risqué but unremarkable dramas of sexual awakening to full-blown pedophile rape scenes, with the questionable distinction of being the first erotic anime video release. So it was that after the relative excitement of theatrical outings such as **A Thousand and One Nights** and **Cleopatra: Queen of Sex**, anime entered a tawdry phase with the sickening gang rape of "The Reddening Snow" (#1), in which a group of boys sexually assault a schoolgirl, while the boy who secretly adores her is "forced" to join in. "Girls Tortured with Roses" (#2) is no less shocking—a bondage fable in which older men abuse and assault very young girls—though it pales into insignificance when compared to "Dying for a Girl" (#3), in which the assault of a girl in a playground is offered for the audience's titillation, only to have the neighborhood pervert's intentions thwarted by the timely arrival of a younger man. He then takes the girl back to his place, where, after a shower, she gratefully offers her body to her savior.

The next entry in the series, the lesbian-awakening story "Altar of Sacrifice" (#4), was successful enough to create its own subseries within the *Lolita Anime* franchise—a form of brand identity that was repeated with greater success within the **Cream Lemon** series. "Variations" (#5) was a direct sequel, double the normal length, about one of the girls becoming an artist's model and being invited to a postsession dinner where she is drugged and raped.

Another mini-franchise began with "House of Kittens" (#6), in which several schoolgirls are inspired to experiment sexually with each other after witnessing their teacher in the act. However, their friend Miyu prefers to fantasize about having sex with a man. A character whose popularity prefigured that of *Cream Lemon*'s Ami,

Miyu returned for "Surfside Dreaming" (#7), about an innocent encounter between two consenting teenagers, and consequently far less disturbing than many of the other *LA* entries. The character returned for the finale, "Seaside Angel Miyu" (#8), a clip-show of earlier episodes, presented as a radio show conducted from orbit, as Earthbound callers telephone Miyu's spaceship and discuss their sexual experiences. The running time is bulked out with four minutes of still images of Miyu at the beach and ends with the "bonus" scene of Miyu having sex with the captain of her spaceship.

Later in 1984, an unrelated *Lolita Anime* was released by Nikkatsu. Directed by Naosuke Kurosawa, it comprised "Aki Feels Ill," "Milk-Drinking Doll," and "Gokko Plays Nurse," all adapted from manga by Aki Uchiyama, an artist who once took *lolicon* imagery so far as to eroticize infants in diapers for *Shonen Magazine*. **NV**

LONE WOLF IS THE KID BOSS

1969. JPN: *Otoko Ippiki Gaki Daisho*. TV series. DIR: Tadao Wakabayashi. SCR: Shunichi Yukimuro, Susumu Yoshida, Tadaaki Yamazaki. DES: Shingo Araki. ANI: Takao Yamazaki, Saburo Sakamoto, Takashi Saijo, Soji Mizumura. MUS: Mitsuhiro Oyama. PRD: NTV, Tokyo TV Doga. 10 mins. x 156 eps. Ever since beating 180 other kids in single combat, Mankichi Togawa of Seikai Junior High is the acknowledged "boss" of a gang of a thousand tough children. Still dissatisfied with his achievement, he heads for Tokyo with his sidekick Ginji, where he decides to become rich in order to battle social evils in Tokyo—his encounters including old financial bigwig Mito (see **Manga Mito Komon**) and Daisaburo no Kasumi, the good-natured leader of the local tramps. Based on a manga by **Salaryman Kintaro**-creator Hiroshi Motomiya, this daily show has been cited as a major influence by Masami Kurumada, creator of **Saint Seiya**. Yoshiyuki Okamura (AKA Sho Fumimura or Buronson), creator of **Fist of the North Star**, started his manga career as Motomiya's assistant.

LORD OF LORDS: DRAGON KNIGHT

1994. JPN: *Ha-o Taikei Ryu Knight*. AKA: *Adeu's Legend*. TV series, video. DIR: Makoto Ikeda, Toshifumi Kawase. SCR: Katsuyuki

Sumisawa, Hiroyuki Hoshiyama. DES: Kazuhiro Soeta. ANI: Kazuhiro Soeta, Tetsuya Yanagawa, Chuichi Iguchi. MUS: Junichi Kanezaki, Michiru Oshima. PRD: Sunrise, TV Tokyo. 25 mins. x 52 eps. (TV), 25 mins. x 13 eps. (v1), 25? mins. x 3 eps. (v2), 120 mins. (v3). A popular show in its day, mixing the role-playing-game feel of **Record of Lodoss War** with the giant-robot combat familiar to so many other Sunrise shows. **Outlaw Star**-creator Takehiko Ito, in collaboration with Sunrise's house pseudonym "Hajime Yadate," posited a standard quest narrative of young Adeu, who sets out to become a knight and ends up saving the universe. When the TV series was released on video, each tape contained at least one unbroadcast episode as a bonus, which is a clever way of dragging in extra customers.

LOST UNIVERSE *

1998. TV series. DIR: Takashi Watanabe, Eiichi Sato, Hideki Takayama. SCR: Mayori Sekijima, Jiro Takayama, Sumio Uetake. DES: Shoko Yoshinaka, Tsutomu Suzuki. ANI: Kazuaki Mori, Hikaru Maejima. MUS: Osamu Tezuka (mus). PRD: IG Film, TV Tokyo. 25 mins. x 26 eps. Galactic troubleshooter Kane Blueriver wanders the stars in his sentient ship Sword Breaker, whose artificial intelligence, Canal, is his eternal sparring partner and confidante. A chance meeting forces them to team up with Milly Nocturne the private eye, an irritating girl determined to be the world's best, though world's best *what* is open to debate.

A lighthearted space opera based on a sequence of novels by **Slayers**-creator Hajime Kanzaka (which were illustrated by designer Yoshinaka) and featuring many of the same cast and crew as the *Slayers* anime. After predictable early beginnings not unlike **Outlaw Star**, the bounty-of-the-week angle falls away to be replaced with a more gripping quest angle as the trio search for the fabled Lost Ships. Despite being written off in its early stages as shallow comedy, the final chapter of *LU* won *Animage*'s Best Individual Episode Award in a year otherwise dominated by **Nadesico**. Like many other shows of the late 1990s, *LU* featured incongruous amounts of computer graphics designed to distract the viewer from the low-rent cel animation. However, *LU*'s CG, such as the

Sword Breaker itself, is consistently below-par—an example of a gimmick backfiring, though the same tactics were used to far greater effect in **Cowboy Bebop**. Broadcast on U.S. TV in Spanish and Turkish!

LOUPS=GAROUS *

2010. Movie. DIR: Junichi Fujisaki. SCR: Midori Goto, Sayaka Harada. DES: Akiharu Ishii. ANI: Akiharu Ishii. MUS: SCANDAL. PRD: Production I.G, TransArts. 98 mins. A terrifying virus has spread throughout the world. The threat is still so strong that people have to eat synthetic food and avoid all contact, communicating only online. The only places people ever meet are the schools—now called "community centers." But there's still some contact of a very violent kind, as brutal murders take place. Five young girls who have defied all the rules of society to meet as friends begin to investigate. Soon they become targets, not just for the murderer but for the whole of their frightened society.

Production I.G's work is always interesting, and this film based on a novel by Natsuhiko Kyogoku (**Requiem from the Darkness**) is no exception. It presents a fascinating world of totalitarian control disguised as benevolence, where people with money are rigidly separated from the underclass, homes have internal security, robots watch the streets at night, and life is lived via handheld personal monitors. Sounds familiar? Looks familiar too, as Fujisaki and his team employ angles we recognize from security camera footage, distort frames like low-res video feed, and show us exactly how our addiction to cellphones could be a useful means of control. Compare to **Denno Coil**, which similarly uses science fictional imagery to examine the present.

The studio usually serves up exquisite feasts of art and animation, but in this case both fall flat, lacking technical razzle-dazzle and appearing basic. There are also a few major holes in the plot. Overall, though, this take on the werewolf legend (and if you think that's a spoiler you obviously didn't read the title) has enough interest to be worth watching. The pilot film and an eight-minute "picture drama" were included as extras on the Blu-ray and DVD releases. To add to the mystery, the U.S. dub inexplicably insists that one of the girls is a boy, even to the extent of giving her a male voice actor. **V**

LOVE BITCH

2011. JPN: *Love Bitch: Yasashii Onna.* AKA: *Love Bitch: Kindhearted Woman.* Video. DIR: Ken Raika. SCR: Ryu Terano. DES: N/C. ANI: Yumei Aoi. MUS: N/C. PRD: T-Rex, MS Pictures (Bootleg). 17 mins.

Chisato is a horny young woman who's having hot sex with her lover at an inn when his friend joins in. Based on a porn manga by Linda. **O**

LOVE CADETS

1998. JPN: *Ren'ai Kohosei.* AKA: *Starlight Scramble.* Video. DIR: Hideki Tonokatsu. SCR: Hideki Tonokatsu, Osamu Kudo, Katsuhiko Koide. DES: Kenji Hattori, Masahiro Koyama. ANI: Kenji Hattori. MUS: N/C. PRD: KSS. 30 mins. x 2 eps.

In a love comedy set in 2149 but rooted very much in the dork-gets-harem spirit of **TENCHI MUYO!** and its 1990s imitators, orphaned Megumi struggles hard at school to qualify as a space pilot, leave behind the space colony, and visit Earth.

LOVE DOLL *

1997. JPN: *Ai Doru.* AKA: *Melancholy Slave.* Video. DIR: Raizo Kitagawa. SCR: Yuri Kanai, Naomi Hayakawa. DES: Aidoru Project. ANI: Kazumasa Muraki. MUS: Yoshi. PRD: YOUC, Digital Works. 30 mins. x 4 eps.

Bereft at her mother's death, Rachel goes into a convent, only to discover that the contemplative life is not quite as she imagined when she is bound, gagged, and sexually assaulted by lust-crazed lesbian nuns. Based on a story by **BEAST CITY**–creator Naomi Hayakawa. The first release in the notorious **VANILLA SERIES**. **ONV**

LOVE GET CHU

2006. JPN: *Love Ge CHU—Miracle Seiyu Hakusho.* AKA: *Love Get You; Love Ge CHU—Miracle Voice Actress Report.* TV series. DIR: Mitsuhiro Togo. SCR: Naruhisa Arakawa, Yasutomo Yamada, Kurasumi Sunayama, Michiko Ito. DES: Naruse Takahashi, Shinji Katahara. ANI: Takashi Tsuda, Ryuta Nakahara, Hideyuki Motohashi. MUS: Yuki Matsuura. PRD: Radix, ARiKO System. 24 mins. x 25 eps.

Five girls all want to become voice actresses, and attend a training school to learn the skills they'll need. There's an anime fan, a failed live actress, a tomboy who wants to live out her fantasy of boyhood, a shy girl who has little voice of her own, and an überfan who's doing this to get to meet and marry her favorite star. This series based on a visual novel (**ARGOT AND JARGON**) by ARiKO System for mobile phones has romance (a love triangle between two of the girls and a young anime artist) and tries for realism with its stories centered on humiliating interviews, intrusive fans, and the embarrassment of messing up a job. Don't expect too much realism though; this is pure wish fulfillment for wannabes. Compare to **REC**.

LOVE HINA *

2000. TV series, TV special. DIR: Shigeru Ueda, Takashi Sudo, Koichi Sugitani. SCR: Kuro Hatsuki, Manabu Ishikawa, Hiroyuki Kawasaki. DES: Makoto Uno, Eiji Yasuhiko. ANI: Makoto Uno, Akio Takami. MUS: N/C. PRD: Xebec, TV Tokyo. 25 mins. x 24 eps. (TV), 44 mins. (TVm, *Silent Eve*), 30 mins. (v1, *Final*), 45 mins. (v2, *I Wish Your Dream*), 30 mins. x 3 eps. (v3, *Again*).

As a child, Keitaro makes a vow with his sweetheart that they will meet at Japan's prestigious Tokyo University (Todai) when they are older. He doesn't, however, count on failing the exams, or indeed on forgetting his sweetheart's name in the decade that follows. Now in his late teens, he is left by his grandmother to look after a student dorm and meets two students, one of whom he suspects is the long-lost love. As Keitaro attempts to regain his memories of his one true love, he becomes an object of attention among the other girls at the dorm, who are "characterized" by a standard rack of female anime **STEREOTYPES AND ARCHETYPES**.

The culmination of a decade of geek-centered anime **ROMANCE AND DRAMA**, *Love Hina* is based on a manga in *Shonen Magazine* by Ken Akamatsu, but it plays like a combination of **TENCHI MUYO!**, the ronin romance of **SAKURA DIARIES**, and the occasional filmic experimentation inspired by **HIS AND HER CIRCUMSTANCES**. The franchise returned on several occasions to remind the consumers to keep consuming, firstly for a one-shot TV special, *Silent Eve*, in Christmas 2000. The series compilation *Love Hina Final* (2001), which, by compressing the entire story into 30 minutes, rather implied that much of the running time had been unnecessary filler. Keitaro finally sits his exams in *Spring Special: I Wish Your Dream* (2001), only to believe that he has failed and runs away to a deserted island, whence his harem must drag him back to civilization. The franchise ended with both bangs and whimpers, in the contrived and unnecessary video series *Love Hina Again* (2002). Supposedly adhering more closely to the character designs from the original manga, *Again* sees Keitaro happy in love and about to start university, only to break his leg and get packed off to recuperate at a magical inn run by his crazy sister. The course of true love is hence thwarted by a series of arbitrary and increasingly unlikely obstacles, until the various problems are largely solved by the aid of explosives.

LOVE IS THE NUMBER OF KEYS *

2002. JPN: *Ai wa Kagi no Kazu Dake.* Video. DIR: Ichiro Watari. SCR: N/C. DES: Yoko Murasaka. ANI: Yoko Murasaka. MUS: N/C. PRD: Milky, Concept Films. 28 mins.

When her father moves abroad to work, Jun promises to finish high school back in Japan. He gets himself a room at an apartment building, which conveniently turns out to be a brothel, or rather a "sex service apartment" where goodtime girls forget about their dayjobs and act out their sexual fantasies. Before long, Jun is servicing the owner Sumire and collecting freebies from other tenants, including waitress Marina and nurse Miki. An erotic variant of **MAISON IKKOKU**, with an unexpectedly jazzy soundtrack. **ON**

LOVE LAB *

2013. JPN: *Ren'ai Labo.* TV series. DIR: Masahiko Ota. SCR: Takashi Aoshima, Hideaki Koyasu, Kenji Sugihara, Takamitsu Kono. DES: Chiaki Nakajima. ANI: Aya Takano. MUS: Yasuhiro Misawa. PRD: Dogakobo, MBS, AT-X, Aniplex, MOVIC, Dentsu. 24 mins. x 13 eps.

At an all-girls school for elegant young ladies, the local tomboy Riko agrees to be a boy-chasing consultant (see **SUMMER WARS**) so the class president can experiment with her yearnings for passion and love. Slapstick humor and occasional pathos intrude, in what, despite the summary above, is not a lesbian drama in any way, but an innocent comedy about heterosexual confusions—Riko is nowhere near as qualified for her post as the others presume, and much of the comedy issues from her own cluelessness. Not to be confused with Love Labo, which is the name of one of the backers of THE BIHADA TRIBE.

LOVE LESSONS *

2001. JPN: *Jinshin Yugi.* AKA: *Games of the Heart.* Video. DIR: Shin Fujisaki. SCR: Reiji Izumo. DES: Masayoshi Sekiguchi. ANI: Masayoshi Sekiguchi. MUS: N/C. PRD: EVE, Milky, Museum Pictures. 30 mins. x 2 eps.
Kusanagi is deep in debt to the Mob, but discovers that even loan sharks are people. Instead of breaking his legs, his old acquaintance, gangster Takamori, offers to find him a job so he can work off his debt. The task he is given involves "training" tasks on a yacht, where bondage mistress Sakura Matsura encourages Kusanagi to help her break in four girls, who are working off their own debts by working as prostitutes. The "fun" side of coerced sex work, although unusually for anime porn, the female characters don't look particularly young, the sex is fairly mild, the fetishes non-challenging, and beyond their need to earn money, the girls are relatively free from coercion (though not from manipulation). The production quality is even quite good and shows signs that it could have been even better if the staff had been given a larger budget. As with so many other pornographic anime, the second episode ends without completing the story; no further volume has been released. Based on a PC game from EVE. **LNV**

LOVE LIVE: SCHOOL IDOL PROJECT *

2013. TV series. DIR: Takahiko Kyogoku. SCR: Jukki Hanada, Hideaki Koyasu. DES: Asako Nishida, Yuhei Murota. ANI: Mitsuaki Takabe, Minami Yoshida, Tomoyuki Fujii. MUS: Yoshiaki Fujisawa. PRD: Sunrise, Studio Easter, BS11 Digital, Tokyo MX TV, TV Aichi, Yomiuri TV. 23 mins. x 13 eps.
In a Japan with an ever-declining population (BUBU CHACHA) teenager Honoka is informed that her school is due to be shut down due to lack of children. Determined to drum up support and new transfers, she starts an idol group. **K-ON** meets **MASK OF GLASS** as the new pop project "μ's" face

rehearsals, brainstorming, and an embittered rival determined to see them fail. In an attempt to beef up their performances, the production team make the interesting decision to use 3D motion capture for the dance sequences, which unfortunately jars with the rest of the 2D animation.

LOVE POSITION: THE LEGEND OF HALLEY

1985. JPN: *Love Position Halley Densetsu.* AKA: *Legend of Love Position Halley; Love Position: Legend of Halley.* Video. DIR: Hideharu Iuchi. SCR: Masaki Tsuji. DES: Hiromi Matsushita, Kunio Aoi, Indori-Koya. ANI: Shinya Takahashi, Isao Kaneko, Kazutoshi Kobayashi, Masashi Maruyama. MUS: Kei Wakakusa. PRD: Tezuka Pro. 93 mins.
A crippled old man recounts his wartime experiences in Vietnam to his son Subaru, telling of his encounter with the young elfin girl Lamina in a temple. He takes a fatherly interest in her after she saves him from the Viet Cong, but she refuses to reveal to him any details about her past. Fifteen years after he is sent home and leaves her behind, he receives a letter from her announcing that she is coming to the U.S. and desperately needs his help. Since he owes her his life but cannot help her himself, he begs his son to take his place, and a very surprised Subaru discovers that the "teenage" Lamina does not appear to have aged a day. Subaru escorts Lamina across the U.S., where they are pursued by a former vagrant who has been possessed by a killer entity that escaped from a crashing meteorite. Eventually, after a series of escalating battles, Lamina is revealed to be the spirit of Halley's Comet, a messenger sent from the planet/goddess Venus to the sun/goddess Amaterasu, but she is pursued by agents sent by Venus's enemy, Mars. This movie was based on an original idea by **ASTRO BOY**–creator Osamu Tezuka and released to cash in on the real-life reappearance of Halley's Comet in the skies. Compare to **WIND OF AMNESIA**, a similar road movie with a mystery girl.

LOVE, ELECTION AND CHOCOLATE *

2012. JPN: *Koi to Senkyo to Chocolate.* TV series. DIR: Toru Kitahata. SCR: Katsuhiko Takayama. DES: Hiroaki Goda. ANI: Masami Inomata, Seiji Tachikawa. MUS: Elements Garden. PRD: AIC Build, BS-TBS, Movic, ASCII

Media Works. 24 mins. x 12 eps. (TV) 24 mins. (v).
Amid a flurry of useless high school activities, Yuki Ojima's Food Research Club has to be one of the most pragmatic, spending most of its budget on snacks. But when a would-be class president runs on a platform of abolishing pointless clubs, Yuki is put forward by his members as a rival candidate.
Love, Election and Chocolate has its origins in a 2010 "visual novel" (**ARGOT AND JARGON**), in which the player took on the role of Yuki and tried to win the affections of one of five cookie-cutter female characters while also garnering a popular vote. Despite such generic beginnings, it has a premise with real promise, as long as one accepts the suspension of disbelief required for the cast's *alma mater* to be a self-subsistent, autonomous polity of 6,000 students, thereby allowing Yuki's political issues to take on real power and effect. Particularly interesting are (perhaps) inadvertent allusions to the political economy of real-world Japan, with shadowy elder statesmen manipulating fresh-faced young candidates from behind the scenes, and earnest campaign promises swiftly ditched in favor of whatever makes the numbers work.
Unfortunately, the show soon squanders this potential with yet another humdrum collective of bickering soubrettes, while the bite and possible debate of Yuki's manifesto is soon reduced to *let's-do-the-show-right-here* fund-raising, more flirting, and some revelations of off-the-shelf trauma in place of character depth. Long-term viewers may discern elements of **HIS AND HER CIRCUMSTANCES** in the dueling leads with unspoken feelings for each other; there's nothing awful about this show, but the *idea* was so good that your average encyclopedist is let down by merely adequate execution. An unaired "13th" episode was included in the DVD.

LOVE, CHUNIBYO AND OTHER DELUSIONS *

2012. JPN: *Chunibyo demo Koi ga Shitai.* AKA: *Even Someone with Eighth-Grader Syndrome Wants Love.* TV series. DIR: Tatsuya Ishihara. SCR: Jukki Hanada. DES: Kazumi Ikeda. ANI: Kazumi Ikeda. MUS: Nijine. PRD: Kyoto Animation, Lantis, Studio Blue,

Animax, TV Aichi, Tokyo MX TV, KBS, Sun TV, BS11 Digital. 24 mins. x 13 eps. (TV1), 24 mins. x 12 eps. (TV2), 4 mins. x 7 eps. (v).

Yuta Togashi was a self-obsessed, delusional eighth-grader in middle school, hoping to put his "syndrome" behind him at high school, only to discover himself surrounded by similarly odd people, including Rikka, the spunky heroine who believes that one of her eyes has deadly magic powers. Channeling an almost actionable amount of THE MELANCHOLY OF HARUHI SUZUMIYA, this anime has its origins in a couple of books by "Torako" that failed to win the Kyoto Animation talent competition, but went into production anyway. It pokes lovingly at the otaku mindset and the sense of make-believe and suspension of disbelief that we are supposed to leave behind as children (*chunibyo* = eighth-grader syndrome), but which still offers a degree of emotional armor for the troubled teens in Yuta's new circle of friends.

A series of shorts, subtitled *Depth of Field*, takes Yuta and Rikka's playtime seriously enough to imagine them transported to a world torn apart by robot combat. The movie edit, *Takanishi Rikka Kai Gekijo-ban* (*Rikka Takanishi Renewed: Theatrical Version*, 2013) rearranges elements of the first season, as a prequel to the second, *Chunibyo: Heart Throb*, which came along in 2014. Compare to WATAMOTE, which similarly confronts a deluded teen with the harsh realities of high school.

LOVEDOL: LOVELY IDOL

2006. TV series. DIR: Keitaro Motonaga. SCR: Makoto Uezu, Shoichi Sato. DES: Kumi Horii, Madoka Hiroyama, Minoru Maeda. ANI: N/C. MUS: Hirotake Fukui. PRD: AIC, TNK, AT-X, Sun TV, TV Saitama, Chiba TV. 25 mins. x 12 eps.

Lovedol is a contraction of "lovely idol" and this series tells the story of a group of six girls who are striving for success in the J-pop business (MUSIC IN ANIME). The Lovely Idols have been popular through two changes of line-up, but just as their manager is about to debut the third generation the company president stops him in his tracks. Maybe a young street musician could be the "something extra" they're lacking? The franchise had its origin in a series of short stories in Enterbrain's *Magical Cute Premium* magazine between 2001

and 2004, illustrated by Aoi Nishimata. Radio shows, CD dramas, a dating sim game for the PlayStation 2, and a book series followed, along with the usual raft of character merchandise. AKB48 (**AKB0048**) had already made their debut when the show appeared, and *Morning Musume* had been storming Japan's charts since 1997, but the idol-singer concept goes back before even CREAMY MAMI, so this show has nothing new in concept terms; its primary sin is that its music is among the most unmemorable in anime history. What's the point of a show dedicated to the world of catchy bubblegum pop if none of the tunes is catchy?

LOVELESS *

2005. TV series, video. DIR: Yuh Koh. SCR: Yuji Kawahara. DES: Kazunori Iwakura. ANI: Yumi Nakayama. MUS: Masanori Sasaji. PRD: JC Staff. 25 mins. x 12 eps. (TV), ? mins x 3 eps. (v).

New transfer student Ritsuka Aoyagi keeps quiet about his past: his mother is dead, his brother has been murdered, and the shadowy figure of Sobi is offering to avenge his death, at a price. Sobi is a warrior, or "fighter," and as in UTENA, fighters have passive counterparts or "sacrifices," whose job is to cast spells that ward away attackers during combat. Sobi wants Ritsuka to take his late brother's place as his sacrifice, a request to which Ritsuka eventually agrees, hoping that by doing so he will find the culprit of his brother's death, which has something to do with an organization called the Septimal Moon. Each pairing of fighter and sacrifice has a name, and since his brother and Sobi were the Beloved, the new Ritsuka-Sobi pairing is the Loveless.

This adaptation of EARTHIAN creator Yun Koga's manga from *Zero Sum* magazine cleverly retains its conceit that the characters live in a surreal world where children grow up with cat's ears and tails. These attributes slowly fade away as they lose their innocence and turn into adults, sublimating many sexual tensions into concerns over whether someone still has his feline characteristics—BROTHER DEAREST with a series of opponents of the week. The DVD releases contained three bonus shorts.

LOVELY COMPLEX *

2007. JPN: *LoveCom*. TV series. DIR: Konosuke Uda. SCR: Midori Kuriyama, Mio Inoue, Takashi Yamada, Yumi Kageyama. DES: Hideaki Maniwa, Yukiko Iijima. ANI: Hideaki Maniwa. MUS: Hironosuke Sato. PRD: Toei Animation, Shueisha, TBS. 24 mins. x 24 eps.

A tall girl and a short guy—the odd couple in any high school, but in Osaka, where the humor is sharp as a whip, Risa Koizumi and Atsushi Otani need a survival strategy fast. Nicknamed after a popular comedy duo with the same height difference, the pair agree to band together as friends and try and help each other out with their romantic difficulties; but their best efforts fail when the only guy who's as tall as Risa falls for the girl Atsushi has a crush on. As they get to know each other better, the pair find their own relationship is getting more complicated. Meanwhile, Atsushi, who's only just over five feet tall, is also a gifted basketball player who dreams of making the game his career—even if he'll only ever be able to teach elementary school players. A sweet, funny love comedy based on Aya Nakahara's 2001 manga, *LoveCom* also spun off a live-action movie directed by Kitaji Ishikawa in 2006. Most of the characters in the anime speak Osaka's local dialect, or Kansai-ben, unusual in a show made for a national audience (JARINKO CHIE). Kansai-ben is the language of comedy but not normally the top choice for a teen romance.

LOVER-IN-LAW *

2008. JPN: *Aniyome wa Ijippari*. AKA: *Messing With Big Brother's Wife*. Video. DIR: Tsukasa Kaido. SCR: Akimi Kuroda. DES: Tatsuya Suzuki. ANI: Tatsuya Suzuki. MUS: N/C. PRD: Discovery. 27 mins. x 2 eps.

Tsutomu's older brother and his wife Mai take over the family flower shop after the death of their parents, while Tsutomu stays with them so he can attend a local college. When Tsutomu's brother gets transferred to another city for work, Tsutomu notices how lonely and unfulfilled his beautiful, busty sister-in-law has become. But it's not just her—her friend Kozue also has a husband who works long hours and is rarely home. You can probably guess what happens next in this anime based on a porn game by Tinker Bell. **Ⓝ**

LOVE'S FORM: DO YOU HATE PERVY GIRLS?

2008. JPN: *Ai no Katachi: Etchi na Onna wa Kirai ... Desu ka?* Video. DIR: Ken Raika. SCR: Shinichiro Sawayama. DES: Mamoru Sakisaka. ANI: Mamoru Sakisaka. MUS: N/C. PRD: MS Pictures (Milky). 30 mins. x 2 eps.
Amateur porn magazines offer easy money for young girls who are willing to get down and dirty for the cameras. They can indulge their wildest fantasies and get paid for it. Thinking of the many readers who will go wild over their pictures, some of the girls become completely uncontrollable and the staff and photographers step in. Based on a porn game by Silky's. ⓃⓋ

LUCKY MAN

1994. JPN: *Tottemo Lucky Man.* AKA: *Really Lucky Man.* TV series. DIR: Hajime Kamegaki, Akira Shigino, Masami Shimoda, Osamu Nabeshima. SCR: Yoshio Urasawa, Kazuhisa Sakaguchi, Yukichi Hashimoto. DES: Hiroshi Kamo. ANI: Hideyuki Motohashi, Tsuneo Ninomiya. MUS: Yusuke Honma. PRD: Studio Pierrot, TV Tokyo. 25 mins. x 50 eps.
Yoichi is an unpleasant teenager, but one who can transform at will into the luckiest man in the world—a superpower that he uses freely to get himself out of embarrassing situations. Based on a *Shonen Jump* manga by Hiroshi Kamo and featuring a lead character who resembles a mohawked version of *South Park*'s yammering Canadians, Terrence and Phillip.

LUCKY STAR *

2007. TV series, video. DIR: Yutaka Yamamoto, Yasuhiro Takemoto. SCR: Toko Machida, Shoji Gato, Tomoe Aratani. DES: Yukiko Horiguchi, Seiki Tamura. ANI: Yukiko Horiguchi. MUS: Satoru Kosaki (MoNACA). PRD: Kyoto Animation, Lucky Paradise. 24 mins. x 24 eps. (TV), 42 mins. (v).
Konata Izumi is both athletic and intelligent, yet she's not in a sports club and her grades are low. She doesn't want to waste time studying or playing sports when she could be watching anime, reading manga, or playing video games. Her friends, ultra-cute Miyuki and twins Tsukasa and Kagami, feel the same way—they just want to slack their way through high school having fun.

This is a pointless show, one that wouldn't know a story arc if it was hit over the head with one, shunning plot and character development in favor of a barrage of puns, goofy gags, and reference to anime, manga, and games—all seemingly designed to test the **FANDOM** of the proudest otaku, in what is regarded as one of the successes of the **EVERYDAY ANIME** subgenre.

Unless you get the point of being able to list every hot springs episode ever made or recall every obscure 1980s video game, this show will leave you cold, hungry, and bored. Even the scraps of fan service are played as gags. You don't even have Kyoto Animation's usual lush visuals to look at, since *Lucky Star* is purposely kept flat, simplistic, and cartoony, although the studio keeps things moving fluidly and its production values are high as usual. Luckily, the nature of the show makes it easy to dip in and out if you decide you just want a few minutes' mindless fun.

LULLABY FOR WEDNESDAY'S CINDERELLA

1987. JPN: *Aitsu to Lullaby: Suiyobi no Cinderella.* Video. DIR: Yukihiro Takahashi. SCR: Yuji Watanabe. DES: Joji Yanase, Masayoshi Sato. ANI: N/C. MUS: Satoshi Kadokura, Takashi Kudo. PRD: Studio Pierrot, Nippon Herald. 50 mins.
Kenji is a motorbike-mad teenager in Yokohama, who just loves his ZII machine, and likes nothing better than grabbing his girl Yumi, skipping school, and motoring down the coast. Hearing from fellow biker Hayase about a fabled racer called Wednesday's Cinderella, Kenji witnesses Hayase on his SRX, squaring off against Cinderella on her Porsche cycle (the synopsis spends more time on the brands than the characters!). Concerned for his friend's safety, Kenji sets off after him, borrowing his friend Kyosuke's Ducati. Based on a *Shonen Magazine* manga by Michiharu Kusunoki, who also created **SHAKOTAN BOOGIE**. Made for video, but screened on a double bill in cinemas with **LEGEND OF ROLLING WHEELS**, which must have made the day as exciting as changing an oil sump.

LUNA VARGA *

1991. JPN: *Maju Senshi Luna Varga.* AKA: *Demon/Beast Warrior Luna Varga.* Video. DIR: Shigenori Kiyoyama. SCR: Aki Tomato, Yumiko Tsukamoto. DES: Yuji Moriyama. ANI: Kazuhiro Konishi. MUS: Kenji Kawai. PRD: AIC, Studio Hakk. 30 mins. x 4 eps.
The Dunbas Empire tries to conquer a world where humans and beasts have lived in medieval-fantasy harmony for centuries. The three princesses of Rimbell are determined to fight the invaders, but middle sister Luna (the "tomboy princess") does so in a very strange way. Engulfed in a ray of light, the accomplished swordswoman recovers to find herself embedded in the head of a giant tyrannosaur-like beast that communicates with her telepathically, calling her its "brain." To save her land, she has been granted control of the legendary dragon Varga, and even when not in dragon form, she has a reptilian tail. She manages to fight off the Dunban troops but must rescue her sister Vena, who has been kidnapped by the invaders. From the high concept that posits a princess with a dragon sticking out of her ass (or a dragon with a princess stuck to its forehead, depending on your perspective) to the insanely overblown theme song, *LV* is a madcap comedy to file with **DRAGON HALF**.

LUNAR LEGEND TSUKIHIME *

2003. JPN: *Shingetsutan Tsukihime.* AKA: *Lunar Legend Moon Princess; Moon Princess.* TV series. DIR: Katsushi Sakurabi. SCR: Hiroko Tokita. DES: Takashi Takeuchi, Kaoru Ozawa. ANI: Kaoru Ozawa. MUS: Toshiyuki Omori. PRD: Geneon, JC Staff, MOVIC, Rondo Robe, TBS. 30 mins. x 12 eps. (TV).
Injured in a mysterious childhood accident, Shiki Tono suffers bizarre after-effects. These include his belief that he can see strange lines emanating from objects around him, which can only be repressed with the aid of special spectacles. He is sent away to stay with relatives until eight years later when his father dies and he is ordered home by his older sister Akiha, the new head of the family.

On his first day back he dices up a woman in a murderous rage—seen in graphic detail on the home video release, but not in the original TV broadcast. He is, however, still understandably disconcerted when she shows up later, alive and well, and asks him to be her bodyguard. Strange things are going on in Shiki's very traditional family—the revenant woman turns out to be a vampire, one of the True Ancestors, who is charged with eliminating their bastard offspring, the Dead Apostles, the result of True Ancestors feeding on humans. And it seems that his big sister Akiha may not be entirely human. And then there is the new girl at school, who is stalking him. Shiki has to find out where his past is leading him. It turns out that the things he can see are "deathlines," the threads that bind all life together, which he can manipulate to cause destruction.

This story originated in a fan-produced game made by Type-Moon, which generated considerable merchandise since its creation in 2000, and allowed its inventors to turn professional (see also **Garden of Sinners**). Unfortunately the atmospheric design and well-created undercurrent of tension can't hide the erratic pacing—the original game contained over 5,000 pages of text, condensed here into a mere 12 episodes, and leading to the production of major plot points like rabbits from a hat and blind alleys caused by inclusion of game elements which the story allows no time to resolve. Compare to **Hellsing** and **Vampire Princess Miyu**. ❶❶❸

LUNAR RABBIT WEAPON MINA

2007. jpn: *Getsumento Heiki Mina*. TV series. dir: Keiichiro Kawaguchi. scr: Junki Takegami. des: Takashi Kumazen, Yutaka Mukumoto. ani: Takahiro Sakagami. mus: Kosuke Yamashita. prd: Gonzo, Fuji TV. GDH., Pony Canyon, Getsumento Heiki Mina Production Team. 25 mins. x 11 eps.

Humanity's big contribution to the aliens who inhabit the rest of the galaxy is sport, a concept that our alien colleagues find completely odd and that they embrace with alacrity. In fact, the aliens get so keen that they harass stadiums and teams to get good seats, play in games, overrule refereeing decisions, and generally cause mayhem. Finally, a treaty is agreed on ruling all interference in other cultures illegal. To police the treaty, Earth has the Rabbit Force—a group of flying bunny girls responsible for dealing with any offenders.

LRWM originated as a fictitious show in the live-action TV show *Train Man* (2005, *Densha Otoko*), for which the Gonzo studio lovingly pastiched early Gainax animation in a fake credits sequence. This extremely silly comedy was popular enough to support a manga by Nylon, which ran for

over a year from February 2007. Compare with **Kujibiki Unbalance** and with **Space Travelers: The Animation**, which similarly struggled to turn an off-hand visual gag into an actual narrative.

LUNATIC NIGHT *

1996. Video. dir: Shinji Nishiyama, Fuyumi Shirakawa, Teruo Kogure. scr: Shinji Nishiyama, Haruka Kaio. des: Kiginmaru Oi. ani: Taiichi Kitagawa. mus: Hideyuki Tanaka. prd: Knack. 35 mins. x 3 eps.

College boy Kanzaki gets a sex-crazed girl for a pet on a moonlit night. She's come to remind him he's the lord of Atlantis and final incarnation of Krishna, forced to fight his satanic schoolmate Mutsuki for control of the world amid innumerable jokey references to classic anime like **Giant Robo** and **Babel II** (on which director Kigure worked as an animator) as well as porn-like appearances by characters more familiar from **Sailor Moon**. In part two, overindulgence has turned all Atlantean men into penises, and incredible power awaits the man who can pass the trials and give Queen Estelle the orgasm of a lifetime. Kanzaki also has to pleasure a giant Amazon who drowns him with her breasts and prompts the meaningful quote, "She's huge! I could stick my whole head in there." The authors would like to apologize for making this sound a lot more interesting than it is. Based on a manga by Akira Mii that was serialized in *Comic Lies*, mercifully only the first two parts of this anime appear to have been released in the U.S. ❶❸

LUNCH FROM A BUCKET

1996. jpn: *Baketsu de Gohan*. aka: *Meal in a Bucket*. TV series. dir: Satoshi Dezaki. scr: Kiriko Kubo. des: Yukari Kobayashi. ani: Yukari Kobayashi. mus: Shinichi Kyoda. prd: Magic Bus, Yomiuri TV. 25 mins. x 20 eps.

The animals at Uenohara Zoo love their jobs, and their jobs involve acting like animals when the human beings are watching and getting on with very human lives when they're not. Paramount among them is Ginpei the penguin, who is eternally getting into trouble with the giraffes, lions, and pandas. Based on a manga by *Cynical Hystery Hour*–creator Kiriko Kubo.

LUPIN III *

1971. jpn: *Lupin Sansei*. aka: (see below). TV series, movie, video, TV specials. dir: Masaaki Osumi, Isao Takahata, Hayao Miyazaki. scr: Tadaaki Yamazaki, Atsushi Yamatoya, Yoshio Urasawa, Yuki Miyata, Yoshio Urasawa, Soji Yoshikawa, Tohru Sawaki. des: Monkey Punch. ani: Yasuo Otsuka, Osamu Kobayashi, Hideo Kawauchi, Yoshifumi Kondo, Tameo Ogawa, Norio Yazawa, Minoru Okazaki, Satoshi Dezaki, Tetsuo Imazawa, Yasuhiro Yamaguchi, Koichi Murata. mus: Takeo Yamashita, Yuji Ono. prd: Tokyo Movie Shinsha, Nippon TV. 25 mins. x 23 eps. (TV1), 25 mins. x 155 eps. (TV2), 102 mins. (m, *Mamo*), 100 mins. (m, *Cagliostro*), 25 mins. x 50 eps. (TV3), 100 mins. (m, *Babylon*), 74 mins. (m, *Fuma*), 97 mins. (TVm, *Liberty*), 92 mins. (TVm, *Hemingway*), 90 mins. (TVm, *Napoleon*), 90 mins. (TVm, *Russia*), 90 mins. (*Sword*), 90 mins. (TVm, *Nostradamus*), 90 mins. (TVm, *Harimao*), 90 mins. (*Dead*), 90 mins. (*Twilight*), 90 mins. (TVm, *Walther*), 90 mins. (TVm, *Crisis*), 90 mins. (TVm, *Money*), 90 mins. (TVm, *Alcatraz*), 50 mins. (v, *Magician Lives*), 90 mins. (TVm, *First Contact*), 90 mins. (TVm, *Return the Treasure*), 90 mins. (TVm, *Stolen Lupin*), 90 mins. (TVm, *Angel's Tactics*), 90 mins. (TVm, *Seven Days Rhapsody*), 90 mins. (TVm, *Elusive*), 90 mins. (TVm, *Green vs Red*), 90 mins. (TVm, *Sweet Lost Night*), 104 mins. (TVm, *vs Conan*), 92 mins. (TVm, *Last Job*), 90 mins. (TVm, *Blood Seal*), 25 mins. x 13 eps. (TV, *Fujiko Mine*), 92 mins. (TVm, *Another Page*), 90 mins. (m, *vs Conan*).

Lupin is a Japanese criminal with a heart of gold, grandson of the infamous French burglar Arsène Lupin (see **Lupin the Master Thief and the Enigma of 813**). His gang includes Lee Marvin–look-alike Jigen, a sharpshooter with a 0.3-second quick draw, and Goemon Ishikawa XIII, descendant of the samurai thief first immortalized in the puppet play *Ishikawa Goemon* (ca. 1680). Together with Lupin's occasional girlfriend and frequent rival, the flame-haired Fujiko Mine, they travel the world stealing great treasures while Lupin charms the ladies, Jigen is suspicious of them, and Goemon tries in vain to hold them at arm's length lest they taint his samurai honor. They are pursued all the while by Inspector Zenigata of Interpol (a descendant of Kodo Nomura's samurai-era sleuth Heiji Zenigata, who was the subject of nearly 400 stories and a long-running TV series).

Longer running than GUNDAM and with a pedigree beaten by few anime except perhaps SAZAE-SAN, *Lupin III* began as a 1967 *Manga Action* publication by SCOOPERS-creator Monkey Punch (pseudonym for Kazuhiko Kato). Adapted by the TMS studio, the series still makes regular appearances in the fifth decade after its debut—largely due to its dogged faith to the camp original, which has endured so long that some of its stories (such as *Mamo*, see below) now outgroove the self-consciously groovy COWBOY BEBOP with their *original* kitsch. Yuji Ono's theme music remains one of Japan's best-selling musical exports. *L3* also has many hidden attributes, such as the casting of "famous voices" to draw unseen parallels for the Japanese audience—among the original voice cast, late Lupin actor Yasuo Yamada used to dub all Clint Eastwood's Japanese dialogue, Jigen actor Kiyoshi Komori "was" the Japanese voice of Lee Marvin, and Goemon's Makio Inoue normally played the gruff anime hero CAPTAIN HARLOCK. There is a certain irony in sharpshooter Jigen getting the "voice of" Lee Marvin, since the actor was a Marine sniper in the Pacific War credited with a number of kills on Japanese soldiers.

After the manga and anime finished their first runs, the franchise continued in the form of the live-action film *L3: Strange Psychokinetic Strategy* (1974, *Nenriki Chin Sakusen*) reuniting all the characters except Goemon. After the original anime series was rebroadcast to popular acclaim, it was revived as the longer-running *New L3* (1977)—as a rule of thumb, the hero's jacket is green in series one, and red in series two, though its pigment varies in the later movies and specials. Monkey Punch claims that only the first series captured the true spirit of his manga, but fan favorites were episodes #145 and #155, written and directed by Tsutomu Teruki (pseudonym for Hayao Miyazaki). In the wake of Miyazaki's later popularity with foreign anime fans, the episodes were released in the U.S. as *L3: Albatross Wings of Death* and *L3: Aloha, Lupin*. The Lupin name, however, was edged from the credits after a legal dispute—the estate of Maurice

Leblanc, creator of the original Lupin, discovered the existence of the series when dubbed episodes were broadcast in Australia, and challenged the producers' rights to the name Lupin. Eventually, the courts ruled that, since *L3* had existed uncontested for more than a decade, Leblanc had no right to it in Japan. Such mitigating circumstances, however, do not apply in the rest of the world, and some anime distributors have avoided the wrath of the Leblanc estate by removing all reference to Lupin from the films—the aforementioned episodes renamed *Tales of the Wolf*, with their lead now "Wolf" throughout the script itself. AnimEigo, which subtitled some of the films (see below) instead opted for the safely facetious transliteration of *Rupan III*. The major casualty of the legal upheaval was Rintaro's 22nd-century sci-fi remake, *Lupin VIII*, planned as a Franco-Japanese follow-up to ULYSSES 31 and regrettably mothballed by TMS and Jean Chalopin's Studio DIC in 1982. Intellectual property issues are likely to haunt the franchise until 2016, when Leblanc's work finally comes out of copyright under current European law.

Meanwhile, the franchise reached theaters with Soji Yoshikawa's *Mystery of Mamo* (1978, *Lupin tai Fukusei Ningen*, AKA *Lupin vs. Clone*). At a time when the rest of the world was desperately trying to cash in on *Star Wars*, *Mamo* was a burst of 1960s nostalgia. Fujiko cons Lupin into stealing the Egyptian "Philosopher's Stone" for her without revealing that she is working for the shadowy would-be dictator Mamo—originally Mameux, though the distributors felt obliged to bring the spelling into line with the inferior transliteration already common in U.S. FANDOM. As befits its "clone" subplot, *Mamo* plays up the similarities between Lupin and Zenigata. Without his trademark trenchcoat in the Egyptian scenes, Zenigata looks almost identical to Lupin, and the idea reaches its logical conclusion in the final reel, when the two enemies are cuffed together and forced to cooperate to save their skins. The film exists in *three* different dubs—the earliest, made by TMS in 1978 for screenings on Pacific flights, changes Jigen's name to Dan Dunn, Goemon's to simply Samurai, and Mamo's henchman Frenchy to Flinch. As a symptom of its time, it

also gives the U.S. president the voice of Jimmy Carter. The second, made in 1995 by Streamline shortly before European legal reforms brought Leblanc back into copyright, calls the hero "Lupin." A third, made in 1996 by Manga Entertainment under the title *Secret of Mamo*, calls him "Wolf" once more, and modernizes some of the dialogue with effective, if anachronistic, rewrites. It leaves in a parody of Henry Kissinger, but lines like "Okay, so I'm not Keanu Reeves" and an in-joke about *Dynasty* can be reasonably expected not to hail from the original Japanese script.

The best-known *L3* film, CASTLE OF CAGLIOSTRO, followed in 1979, and though it was an immense success for director Hayao Miyazaki, the aforementioned legal troubles kept a third TV season off the air until *L3: Part III* (1984). Famous live-action director Seijun Suzuki helmed Lupin's last *true* anime movie outing *Gold of Babylon* (1985, *Babylon no Ogon Densetsu*), in which the gang is pursued by the New York mafia, the police, and the elderly bag-lady Rosetta. The trail leads from a hilarious bike chase through Madison Square Garden to the Middle East and back again to New York, pastiching the *Indiana Jones* films, Erich von Däniken, and gangster films, as Lupin searches for buried gold under New York, hidden inside an alien spaceship. Rosetta eventually reveals her true form and Lupin misses out on sex with a space goddess, though the ever-pragmatic Fujiko is simply concerned with getting as much of the gold as possible.

Masayuki Ozeki's superb *L3: Fuma Conspiracy* (1988, *Fuma Ichizoku no Inbo*, AKA *Secret Plot of the Fuma Clan*) was originally made for video but given a theatrical release at the last moment. Distinctive for returning the globe-trotting thief to his native Japan, it begins at Goemon's long-delayed wedding, interrupted by the kidnapping of the bride. The mysterious Fuma clan want the Suminawa clan's treasure as a ransom, and Lupin helps out, with an eye on the girl and the chances of loot. Inspector Zenigata, who has abandoned the world and entered a monastery believing Lupin to be dead, soon regains his old lust for life and dogged pursuit of his nemesis. *Fuma Conspiracy* is available in two foreign versions—a very good one from AnimEigo (U.S.) and a very bad one from Western Connection with *manually* timed subtitles (U.K.).

All successive *L3* outings have been made for TV as one-shot specials, though some foreign distributors still like to imply that they are "movies," despite a marked drop in animation budget and great variations in quality. In *Bye Bye Liberty* (1989, AKA *Goodbye Lady Liberty*), an Interpol computer has predicted Lupin/Wolf's every movement, so he hangs up his cat-burglar suit and settles down in unwedded bliss with a French floozy, until Jigen drags him back out in search of a treasure hidden inside the Statue of Liberty. Director Osamu Dezaki returned with *Mystery of theHemingway Papers* (1990, *Hemingway Papers no Nazo*), in which Lupin tracks down a treasure described in clues left in the diaries of Ernest Hemingway that lead him to the tiny Mediterranean island of Colcaca just in time for a coup d'état led by the evil Carlos. Current affairs broke into the series for Dezaki's *Steal Napoleon's Dictionary* (1991, *Napoleon no Jisho o Ubae*), which begins at a G7 conference in New York after the Gulf War, in which delegates blame Lupin for the loss of $2 trillion from the world economy. Lupin, however, is in Europe for a classic car race, for the prize of the long-lost dictionary used by Napoleon himself, in which the original Arsène Lupin hid a map to his own treasure house. Matters are complicated by the agents of the G7 nations, all intent on avenging their depressed economies on the man who has removed so much money from them.

Dezaki's *From Russia with Love* (1992, *Russia yori Ai o Komete*) concerns Lupin's search for the treasure of the Russian Czars, supposedly lost forever after the murder of the Romanovs in 1917. Only two people can conceivably find the treasure—Princess Anastasia, long rumored to have escaped death, and the mad monk Rasputin (see also MASTER OF MOSQUITON), who has been in hiding for decades and is now seeking the treasure himself by using his powers of telepathy and persuasion.

Masaaki Osumi took over as director for *Voyage to Danger* (1993, *Lupin Ansatsu Shirei*, originally *Order to Assassinate Lupin*), an original departure in which the discredited Zenigata is taken off the case and reassigned. The cold-blooded assassin Keith

Hayton is set on Lupin's trail, and the thief realizes that the only way to stay alive is to salvage Zenigata's shattered career. Using the stolen Russian nuclear sub Ivanov to infiltrate the criminal gang Shot Shell, Lupin maneuvers them into a position where they can be exposed to Interpol, Zenigata can take the credit, and he can relax without a hit man on his tail. He is not the only one, since the Russian scientist Karen still holds a grudge against Jigen for killing her father, and she is determined to extract her own revenge.

Masaharu Okuwaki's *Dragon of Doom* (1994 *Moeyo Zantetsuken*, originally *Burning Zantetsuken*) features a race to find a mysterious dragon statue said to contain the secrets of making weapons like Goemon's sword, a blade that effortlessly cuts through steel. In a story that deliberately concentrates on Goemon, in honor of the fourth centenary of his illustrious ancestor's death in 1594, Chinese gangster Mr. Chan reveals that the statue was last seen setting sail on the Titanic in 1912, and the quest begins.

The following year saw the death of main Lupin voice actor Yasuo Yamada and *two* TV specials. Nobuo Fujisawa's *Farewell to Nostradamus* (1995, *Kutabare Nostradamus*, originally *To Hell with Nostradamus!*) finds Lupin and Jigen posing as Brazilian soccer players when they are hijacked by a cult, whose leader, Lisely, is determined to bring all of the predictions of Nostradamus to pass. Needless to say, a hunt for treas-ure soon begins, though it means climbing to the top of a 200-story skyscraper. Barely six months later in Dezaki's *The Pursuit of Harimao's Treasure* (1995, *Harimao no Zaiho o Oe*, originally *Treasure of Harimao*), after a mysterious explosion in the English Channel Tunnel, Lloyd's Insurance investigator Archer (see MASTER KEATON) and his beautiful archeologist daughter, Diana, go in search of three statues said to contain clues to the location of the fabled treasure of Harimao. Archer must race a group of neo-Nazis to find them—but, of course, Lupin and Jigen already have plans of their own. *Dead or Alive* (1996), supposedly directed by author Monkey Punch, features Lupin searching for a fabled "drifting island," while simultaneously running from a gang of bounty hunters each after the million-

dollar price on his head. It was succeeded in the same year by Gisa-buro Sugii's *The Secret of Twilight Gemini* (1996, *Twilight Gemini no Himitsu*), which sends Lupin to Morocco in search of a diamond to match the titular stone bequeathed to him by dying mobster Don Dorune. It was a return to the annual schedule with Hiroyuki Yano's *Island of Assassins* (1997, *Walther P –38*), in which Lupin's pistol of choice becomes a crucial key in the race to unlock the mysteries of the Tarantula Seal and find the Golden Ghost. Lupin made a rare stop back in his native Japan for Toshiya Shinohara's *Crisis in Tokyo* (1998, *Honoo no Kioku: Tokyo Crisis, Burning Memories: Tokyo Crisis*), in a quest to find the legacy of the last shogun, racing against a psychokinetic treasure hunter employed by theme-park millionaire Michael Suzaku. In Shinichi Watanabe's *The Columbus Files* (1999, *Ai no Da Capo: Fujiko's Unlucky Days, Love's Da Capo: Fujiko's Unlucky Days*), Fujiko lets Lupin get away with the loot from a Swiss bank job because she is more interested in the Columbus File, a document that can direct her to a 15th-century gem, supposedly connected to COLUMBUS himself. The last *Lupin* of the 20th century was *Missed by a Dollar* (2000, *$1 Money Wars*), in which a disguised Lupin completes the swindle of his life, buying a priceless ring at a rigged auction in New York for a single dollar, though the ring's rightful owner, St. Cyr, is prepared to use any means necessary to get it back. Lupin himself soon returned in Hideki Tonokatsu's TV movie *Alcatraz Connection* (2001), in which he battles the Mob for a treasure to be found somewhere in San Francisco Bay. He also appeared in a video spin-off, *L3: The Magician Lives* (2002), AKA *The Return of the Magician*, AKA *The Return of Pycal*, in which Lupin races against his archenemy Pycal to steal one of seven "magic" crystals.

With the advent of the 21st century came several attempts to reinvigorate the franchise with some new directions. *L3: Episode 0: First Contact* (2002) returns to the masterthief's early days, when he is just starting out as a thief, in a move presumably designed to reset the chronology of the series and serve as an introduction to the older Lupin for new viewers—of which there are a lot, following the serial's TRANSLATION and release in English by Funimation. *L3: Operation: Return the Treasure!!* (2003, *Otakara Henkyaku Dai-sakusen!!*) is another TV movie which finds Lupin on the trail of the Trick diamond, but sucked into a scheme by rival thief Mark Williams, whose dying wish is for his lifetime's haul of stolen objects to be returned to their rightful owners—in other words, Lupin is turned from a masterthief into a stealthy benefactor. The new thief Becky is introduced in *L3:Stolen Lupin: Copy Cat's Midsummer Butterfly* (2004, *Nusumareta Lupin: Copy Cat wa Manatsu no Cho*), in which Lupin and his gang must steal a gem in order to ransom the kidnapped Fujiko from Malkovich, her evil captor. *L3: Angel's Tactics: Dream Fragment's Scent of Murder* (2005, *Tenshi no Sakuryaku: Yume no Kakera wa Koroshi no Kaori*) also bestows a new female assistant on Inspector Zenigata, in the form of his sidekick Emily. The story introduces science fictional elements, as Lupin breaks into America's legendary Area 51 to steal an alien artifact known as the Original Metal, thereby incurring the wrath of an all-female assassins group called the Bloody Angels.

Further specials continued throughout the noughties, as the franchise thrashed around in search of some means of keeping fresh. In some cases, this led to a jarring focus on fantasy or the paranormal, such as time travel, which arrived as a mercifully short-lived device in *L3: Elusiveness of the Fog* (2007, *Kiri no Elusive*), or the attentions of a wish-granting genie in *L3: Sweet Lost Night* (2008). More traditional Lupin adventures in the period included *L3: Seven Days Rhapsody* (2006), combining a diamond heist with a rigged horse race, and *L3: Record of Observations of the East, Another Page* (2012, *Toho Kenbunroku Another Page*), in which Lupin tracks down a priceless manuscript of the *Travels* of **MARCO POLO**.

The series also experimented with several metatextual diversions, slyly alluding to design differences in its original TV incarnation in *L3: Green vs Red* (2008), in which Lupin squares off against a Lupin impersonator, and pitting Lupin against another ratings-winning detective, **CONAN THE BOY DETECTIVE** in the TV special *L3: Lupin vs Detective Conan* (2009) and *L3: Lupin vs Detective Conan the Movie* (2013), which was technically the first genuine

Lupin movie in 17 years. In *L3: The Last Job* (2010), the titular caper seems at first to allude to a far-fetched heist in which Lupin bamboozles ninja over a priceless antique in Germany, but actually refers to the swansong of much of the main voice cast, who retired after this installment. An all-new supporting cast began with the following special, *L3 Blood Seal, the Eternal Mermaid* (2011, *Chi no Kokuin, Eien no Mermaid*).

However, the franchise's most powerful iteration in recent times is arguably Sayo Yamamoto's 13-episode TV series *Lupin III: The Woman Called Fujiko Mine* (2012, *Mine Fujiko to Iu Onna*), which finally put Lupin's smarter, sexier colleague front and center and returns to the story's adult-oriented roots, telling the story of Fujiko's activities before she fell in with the more famous master-thief. Lupin III and Zenigata both appear, but as supporting characters in a story that claims to be Fujiko's yet insistently views her with the male gaze of her implied fanbase, in a narrative that usually feels incredibly 1970s but occasionally drops a jarring moment of modernity to remind the viewer that this is a contemporary reboot and not a period piece.

LUPIN THE MASTER THIEF AND THE ENIGMA OF 813

1979. JPN: *Kaito Lupin: 813 no Nazo*. TV special. DIR: Hiroshi Sasakawa, Masayuki Akehi. SCR: Akira Miyazaki, N/C. DES: Ippei Kuri, Yoshitaka Amano, N/C. ANI: Sadao Miyamoto, Nobuyuki Kishi. MUS: Nobuyoshi Koshibe, Yoshiki Takaragi. PRD: Herald Enterprises, Tatsunoko, Fuji TV; Toei. 84 mins. (TVm1), 84 mins. (TVm2).

Four years after the gentleman thief Arsène Lupin was last seen on the streets of Paris, diamond dealer Kesselbach is found stabbed to death in his hotel room. The police decide that Lupin is the chief suspect, but the master thief himself retrieves a message from Kesselbach containing the mysterious phrase "Napoleon 813." Lupin is forced to team up with Kesselbach's widow to solve the crime before Inspector Lunolman arrests him for the one crime he *hasn't* committed. An adaptation of one of Maurice Leblanc's best-loved Lupin stories, possibly made in a deliberate attempt to annoy Tatsunoko's

rival studio TMS, which was experiencing legal difficulties with its **LUPIN III** franchise at the time. This Lupin fable is particularly well known in Japan, where it was also adapted into the live-action Kenji Mizoguchi film *813: The Adventures of Arsène Lupin* (1923).

Just to rub salt into the wounds, a second Leblanc adaptation followed, this time from another big studio, Toei. In *Lupin vs. Holmes* (1981), the famous English detective Sherlock Holmes is sent to France to track Lupin at the instigation of Baron Autrech, though the baron soon turns up dead, and his priceless blue diamond is missing. *LvH* was based on Leblanc's 1907 series of original stories featuring Holmes, and even includes a famous scene from *The Jewish Lamp* in which the two well-matched rivals face each other on a sinking boat, each daring the other to show the first sign of weakness. In a final karmic irony, the original stories brought protests from Arthur Conan Doyle that Leblanc was using his character without permission, though Leblanc's estate would be just as unforgiving toward Monkey Punch's *Lupin III* many decades later. Leblanc's Lupin has been the subject of dozens of radio dramas, TV series, and movies both in English and French, and even a rumored live-action Hong Kong version, in development from **WICKED CITY**'s Tsui Hark. One of his most recent incarnations was in François Bresson's *Les Aventures de Arsène Lupin* (1996), a French cartoon series dubbed into English as *Nighthood*. Lupin also appeared in **GIGI AND THE FOUNTAIN OF YOUTH**.

LUSTFUL COLLEGE

2010. JPN: *Inmu Gakuen: Dame Konnani Na'chau no wa Yume no Naka Dake na no?* AKA: *Lustful College: Can This Really be Nothing but a Dream?* Video. DIR: Futoshi Yone. SCR: Futoshi Yone. DES: hayate. ANI: Futoshi Yone. MUS: N/C. PRD: schoolzone, Marigold (Girl's Talk). 30 mins.

High school student Shinji lusts after his classmate Mayuri. He's getting so stressed that the school nurse gives him a pendant, telling him it will bring him good dreams. When he takes the pendant to bed with him, he wakes up in Mayuri's bed and has sex with her, but next day it seems nothing has changed. The pendant lets him enter alternate realities, and he goes on to use it with other girls in his school, in this porn anime based on a game by Lune with art by SkyHouse. **N**

LUSTFUL NIGHTS AT THE CUCKOLD VILLAGE

2013. JPN: *Kagachisama O-nagusame Tatematsurimasu—Netoraremura Inyu Hanashi THE ANIMATION*. Video. DIR: Takashi Nishikawa, Shinpei Nagai. SCR: N/C. DES: Takashi Nishikawa. ANI: Takahiro Mizuno, Shinpei Nagai. MUS: N/C. PRD: Pink Pineapple. 25 mins.

A guy about to marry his voluptuous childhood friend abandons her in his home village when she is forced to succumb to local custom, i.e., raped and trained as a sex slave by his family. Moving to Tokyo to put it all behind him, he finds another voluptuous girl—but when his father summons him back home, he takes his new love with him so that history can repeat itself in this porn based on a game by OrcSoft, with original character designs by Kohaku Sumeragi. **NV**

LUSTFUL NURSE

2007. JPN: *Warau Kangofu The Animation*. AKA: *Lustful Laughing Nurse*. Video. DIR: Hideki Araki. SCR: N/C. DES: Takashi Uchida, Kenichi Kurata. ANI: Takashi Uchida. MUS: N/C. PRD: Pink Pineapple. 28 mins. x 2 eps.

Three short stories based on Kengo Yonekura's porn manga, first published in 2005. A nurse has sex with a patient and his childhood friend, who has come to visit; a brother catches his sister watching porn and they have sex; a mother and daughter can't keep their urges hidden from a friend and have a threesome. **N**

LUSTFUL TRAIN

2005. JPN: *Man'in Densha*. Video. DIR: Banzo Tokita, Hiromi Yokoyama, Kuro Kawasaki. SCR: Taifu Sekimachi, Hiro Hide. DES: Tase Muzushima, Kase Okiyumi. ANI: Noritomo Hattori. MUS: N/C. PRD: Bishop, Himajin. 29 mins. x 3 eps.

Train gropers find sexual release on crowded public transport, even managing to infiltrate the "Women Only" carriage in disguise. The story's Japanese title capitalizes on a pun—*man'in densha* is a crowded train, but change the "*in*" from "people" to

"lust," and suddenly it's all very different. Based on a computer game by Bishop. **N**

LUV WAVE *

2000. Video. DIR: Nobutaka Kondo. SCR: Takao Yoshioka. DES: Hiroya Iijima. ANI: Hiroya Iijima. MUS: Eric Satei. PRD: Triple X, Pink Pineapple. 27 mins. x 3 eps.

In the year 2039, special agent Kaoru Mikogami is saddled with an unwanted partner—American-made military cyborg Alice, who looks like a cute girl, and has been sent to Kaoru in order to gain better experience. The reluctant allies set out on the trail of a dangerous new drug called Nine Heavens and a computer virus that once shut down international networks and has now been reactivated in a new, stronger form. Kaoru has also been ordered to terminate Mercy Specter, a dead hacker whose undead persona now travels the Net and invades the minds of those who use Nine Heavens. When Kaoru's sister Mamoru is threatened, he sets off to rescue her, while Mercy invades Alice's mind and awakens a new, more human alter ego. She has the memories of Kaoru's childhood sweetheart Mayumi, put there by the girl's scientist father who is involved in a plot to control the global network and create a new digital deity. Sci-fi porn that wants to be **SERIAL EXPERIMENTS LAIN** but spoils it with some very violent sex, *LW* nevertheless manages to both pastiche **GHOST IN THE SHELL** and foreshadow *Ghost in the Shell: Stand Alone Complex*. Based on a 1998 adult PC game from C's ware. **CNV**

LYCHEE LIGHT CLUB

2012. JPN: *Litchi DE Hikari Club*. TV series. DIR: Masahiro Takada. SCR: Motoichi Adachi. DES: Sao Tamado. ANI: Sao Tamado. MUS: N/C. PRD: Bellz Whistles, Kachidoki Studio, Tokyo MX TV. 10 mins. x 8 eps.

Nine boys at a school construct a machine that runs on lychees, supposedly with the intention of seeking out the beautiful women of the world. But the machine has a life of its own, unlike this short-lived anime series, based on Usamaru Furuya's one-volume **COMEDY** manga originally serialized in *Manga Erotics F* magazine in 2005.

LYRICAL NANOHA *

2004. JPN: *Maho Shojo Lyrical Nanoha*. AKA: *Magical Girl Lyrical Nanoha*. TV series, movie. DIR: Akiyuki Shinbo. SCR: Masaki Tsuzuki. DES: Yasuhiro Okuda. ANI: Yasuhiro Okuda. MUS: Hiroaki Sano. PRD: Seven Arcs, King Records, Echo, Shanghai Xinyang Animation, Studio Elle, Hanjin Animation, Studio Gomez, Studio Mu, White Line. 24 mins. x 13 eps. (TV1), 25 mins. x 26 eps. (TV2), 130 mins. (m1), 150 mins. (m2).

After he causes a terrible accident with the magical Jewel Seeds, archeologist Yuno Scryer comes to Earth to fix the problem. Transformed into a ferret, he enlists the help of latent telepath Nanoha, a nine-year-old Japanese girl who can transform into the superheroine Lyrical Nanoha with the aid of Scryer's Raising Heart pearl. The 21 Jewel Seeds can confer magical powers upon anyone who finds them, or turn them into beasts, leading into many monster-of-the-week confrontations to be resolved. By episode 6, Nanoha has also gained a nemesis, the rival magical-girl Fate Testarossa, who is really the clone of the dead daughter of a woman fleeing the Time Police. Abused by her guilt-ridden mother Precia, Fate eventually joins forces with Nanoha to prevent Precia from using the remaining Jewel Seeds for evil.

Spun off from the forgotten video **TRIANGLE HEART—SWEET SONGS FOREVER**, itself based on an erotic game as part of the **DISCOVERY SERIES**, *Lyrical Nanoha* has been appreciably more successful than the story that spawned it, particularly with its appeal-by-design to an audience not of nine-year-old girls but of older male fans who can appreciate the references to other anime. As a result, it included a number of elements that separated it from shows for preteen girls, not the least combat sequences in which the protagonists physically grappled rather than waving wands at each other from a safe and inimitable distance. The "triangle" of the original has its last vestiges in the tripartite structure of its teams, in which two girls are usually paired with a single lucky boy.

Seemingly in recognition of this alternate audience (hardly much of a surprise in this sector, ever since **CUTEY HONEY**), the sequel series *Lyrical Nanoha StrikerS* (2007) moved the action forward ten years, with a significantly more adult Nanoha forming a crime-busting trio with her fellow magical girl Fate and boy love-interest Hayate, now actively in the employ of the Time-Space Administration Bureau.

Nanoha's origin story was retold in a parallel movie version, *The First* (2010) and continued in *Second A's* (2010), both of which generated impressive Blu-ray returns in Japan, and reminding foreign critics that the implied viewer of a "girl's show" is not always necessarily a girl (see also PUELLA MAGI MADOKA MAGICA).

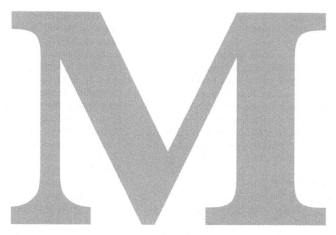

M3 THE DARK METAL *

2014. JPN: *M3: Sono Kuroki Hagane*. TV series. DIR: Junichi Sato. SCR: Mari Okada. DES: Hideki Inoue. ANI: Hideki Inoue, Norie Tanaka, Toru Imanishi. MUS: Hajime Sakita. PRD: C2C, Satelight, Happinet Pictures, Bandai Namco Games, Sotsu. 24 mins. x 24 eps.

Near-future Japan suffers from a specific and creepy form of pollution, in the form of the Lightless Realm—a massive chunk of slowly expanding darkness from which creepy monsters occasionally issue forth. A coeducational team of teenagers is selected to explore the Lightless Realm in specially constructed war machines.

Ten years of the War on Terror and climate change has led to an entire subgenre within anime of late-capitalist musings on what it is to live in a society that relies on distant conflicts and a drain on unrenewable resources, coupled with a constant concern that peace today might be shattered by an atrocity tomorrow—the world of ATTACK ON TITAN and KNIGHTS OF SIDONIA. *M3 the Dark Metal* offers a shadowy allegory of the elephant in the room of modern Japanese politics—*something* horrible is going on at the periphery of everybody's vision, and whatever the problem is, it will probably be a problem that the kids have to clear up—compare to GANTZ. A military-industrial complex offers training and materials for managing the threat, but does not admit it might be part of the problem itself.

Darkness itself is also a product of technological changes that have only been possible since the advent of GAMING AND DIGI-TAL ANIMATION. Whereas Katsuhiro Otomo once sweated blood to get the night right in AKIRA, the problems of animating dark scenes using cels that relied on light to be seen have been dispelled by a generation of animation inside computers. *M3* is only possible today—the darkness at its center, and through which its characters move, would have been almost impossible to depict in animation 20 years previously.

MABURAHO *

2003. TV series. DIR: Shinichiro Kimura. SCR: Koichi Taki. DES: Yasunari Nitta, Eiji Komatsu. ANI: N/C. MUS: Koichi Korenaga, Ryo Sakai. PRD: JC Staff, Klockworx, WOWOW. 24 mins. x 24 eps.

Teenage Kazuki Shikimori attends Aoi Academy, a school for witches and wizards. But magic is a finite resource, everyone has a limited number of spells they can cast in their lifetime, and Kazuki's limit is a fraction of most other's. With only eight "charges," he has to carefully conserve his spell-casting energy lest he crumble into dust, a plan that falls to pieces when he attracts the lustful attentions of several girls. Another harem show with magical overtones like NEGIMA, *Maburaho* takes the *Harry Potter* analogies a little further by making its hero a descendant of famous sorcerers, and hence prime marriage material. Meanwhile, Kazuki ends up wasting a number of his precious charges keeping Yuna, his self-styled "wife," out of trouble, and dodging the attentions of samurai throwback Rin Kamishiro and large-breasted heiress Kuriko Kazetsubaki. Meanwhile, the girls do everything in their power to win him over, or failing that, to get his parents' approval, in an anime that could be taken as a satire of materialist dating customs were it not such a blatant case of cliché reassembly—DNA² meets TENCHI MUYO!

However, *Maburaho* does attempt to do something new with such outrageously hackneyed raw material. Many situations from the geek-gets-girls subgenre are deliberately inverted, such as the time-limit lifespan of MAHOROMATIC or VIDEO GIRL AI, here given to the male protagonist. Nor does the series shy away from following its own internal logic—it establishes that ghosts are part of everyday life, and consequently has no qualms about killing off its hero midway. The inversions of traditional formulae become increasingly obvious, since it is now Kazuki who is the untouchable, unattainable love object, forced to continue school in a phantom state, in the hope that his death can be somehow reversed and his magical mojo recharged. Based on the manga by Toshihiko Tsukiji in *Dragon Magazine* and *Dragon Age* monthlies.

MACADEMI *

2008. JPN: *Macademy Wasshoi*. AKA: *Magician's Academy*. TV series. DIR: Takaomi Kanasaki. SCR: Katsumi Hasegawa, Takashi Aoshima. DES: Takaharu Okuma, Shinobu Tsuneki, Shinichi Tanimura. ANI: Takaharu Okuma, Hiroki Mutaguchi. MUS: Tomoki Hasegawa. PRD: ZEXCS, Enterbrain, Kadokawa, MA Project, Media Factory, T.O. Entertainment. 24 mins. x 12 eps.

Student magician Takuto accidentally creates a girl with enough power to destroy his entire country. Luckily she professes absolute devotion to her creator. A dog-girl maid, dwarves, and a pretty male teacher lusting after his pupils, plus a barrage of gags, are not enough to disguise the harem stereotypes (ROMANCE AND DRAMA) and tropes that replace plot in this not especially well-animated series based on the 2003 books by Ichiro Sakaki, illustrated by Blade. Other series spin-offs include games and manga. **N**

MACHINE HAYABUSA

1976. AKA: *Machine Peregrine*. TV series. DIR: Yugo Serikawa, Hidenori Yamaguchi, Minoru Okazaki, Seiji Okada, Yoshikata Nitta. SCR: Shunichi Yukimura, Keiji Kubota, Masaki Tsuji. DES: Takao Kasai, Hideji Ito. ANI: Junzo Koizumi, Yutaka Tanizawa. MUS: Koichi Sugiyama. PRD: Matsuji Kishimoto, Toei, TV Asahi. 25 mins. x 21 eps.

The world of Formula One racing has become a lawless battlefield after the victories of the Black Shadow team and their leader Ahab the Devil King. Only the Nishionji racing team is prepared to make a sporting stand with their star driver, the vengeful Ken Hayabusa, whose brother was killed by Black Shadow. Ken's car, the Hayabusa Special, enables him to beat all opponents, however treacherous. Luckily he's part of a supportive team of drivers, mechanics, and administrative staff, who will willingly give their all to see their leader head the field. Created by Mikiya Mochizuki and directed by Yugo Serikawa, this story walks a different line between sci-fi sports like EYESHIELD 21 and a fascination with technology à la INITIAL D, albeit technology that is yet to exist. Manga tie-ins were published in *Shonen Jump* monthly, *Terebi-kun*, and *Terebi Land*. The authors are unsure whether the "Devil King" part of Ahab's name should be translated or simply left as Ma-O—itself a popular baddie's monicker in the 1970s, courtesy of Chairman Mao, the leader of the People's Republic of China, who died the year this was made. Followed by RUBENKAISER, which was more of the same. The series might have faded entirely from memory were it not for its influence on a young Katsuhito Ishii, who would cite it 30 years later as a primary inspiration for REDLINE.

MACHINE ROBO *

1986. JPN: *Machine Robo: Chronos no Dai Gyakushu; MR: Butchigiri Battle Hackers*. AKA: *Machine Robo: Revenge of Chronos; MR: Go for It Battle Hackers*. TV series, video, TV special. DIR: Hiroshi Yoshida, Yoshitaka Fujimoto, Yasuo Hasegawa, Hiroshi Negishi, Yoshinori Nakamura, Kiyoshi Murayama, Yasunori Urata. SCR: Hideki Sonoda, Nobuaki Kishima, Yasushi Hirano, Toshimichi Okawa, Mami Watanabe, Hiroko Naka. DES: Nobuyoshi Habara. ANI: Masami Obari, Norio Hirayama, Yoshiaki Akutagawa, Hajime Inai, Shigeru Omachi, Hiroaki Aida. MUS: Tachio Okano. PRD: Ashi Pro, Plex, TV Tokyo. 25 mins. x 47 eps. (TV1), 25 mins. x 31 eps. (TV2), 30 mins. x 3 eps. (v1), 30 mins. (v2, *Lightning Trap*), 30 mins. (v3), 5 mins. (v4, *Leina Music*), 24 mins. x 52 eps. (TV3), 25 mins. (TVm).

Gandler space pirates attack Planet Chronos in search of the super-element Hiliveed, but their plans are thwarted by the death of the noble Kirai. His son, Rom Stol, acquires Kirai's "Wolfblade," the key to the secrets of Hiliveed. Accompanied by his sister, Leina, and his friends Rod Drill and Blue Jet, Rom sets out in search of his destiny, finding along the way his ability to transform into the giant robot Vikung-fu.

Conceived by Bandai to promote its Machine Robo toy line, *MR* was nevertheless a success in its own right. The first series was immediately followed by *MR: Battle Hackers* (1987), in which a ship crewed by Earthlings crashes on Chronos. Believing themselves stranded, the crew volunteers to fight alongside the Machine Robos. The second season, however, did not quite live up to the popularity of its predecessor. Realizing that one of the serial's most popular attributes was not the robots at all but the miniskirted Leina, the series was revived straight to video with a spin-off, *Leina Stol: Legend of the Wolfblade* (1988, *LS: Kenro Densetsu*). In this story, Rom's sister disguises herself as an Earth girl and goes undercover to a typical Japanese school to investigate a series of disappearances. Demonstrating surprising tenacity, the character returned for a last hurrah in a one-shot, *Lightning Trap: Leina and Laika* (1990), about the well-traveled sister on a hijacked plane teaming up with the cyborg Interpol agent Laika to save the day. The songs from the series were also rereleased

as "image videos" *MR: Revenge of Chronos Battlefield Memory* (*Senjo no Kioku*, 1987) and *Leina Music Video: Thank You for You* (1989).

Some of the original toys were released in the U.S. under the brand name Robo Machine along with the unrelated "Future Machine" from the DX Robo Machine line, which was actually a spin-off model of Cobra's car from SPACE ADVENTURE COBRA.

A second TV series, *Machine Robo Rescue* (*Shutsugeki! Machine Robo Rescue*, 2003), features the titular organization, which uses machines based on many of the original *MR* concepts such as the Drill Robo and Shuttle Robo, but "research has shown" that the machines are most effectively piloted by people aged between 10 and 12 years. Young hero Taiyo Ozora (lit.: Sun Sky), pilot of HyperJetRobo, and his 11 teammates are split into three divisions, Red Wings, Blue Sirens, and Yellow Gears, and rescue people from advanced airplanes, ships, trains, submarines, and other vehicles or installations that run out of control or collide with the wrong thing. Each team has a LeaderRobo and SupporterRobos, which can combine to form a HyperRobo. The pilot of each Hyper-Robo is referred to as the RoboMaster. Like International Rescue (THUNDERBIRDS 2086), they are hampered in their operations by a mysterious mastermind, Colonel Hazard, and his Disaster organization. The first opponent Disaster sends against them is a mysterious dark-skinned boy called Jey, strongly reminiscent of a similar subplot in PATLABOR. They also have to contend with the press, in the shape of a boy TV reporter who will do anything for a scoop and intends to find out the secrets of their organization. When Disaster decides to crash the planetoid Tartaros into Earth using an electromagnetic induction wave, Taiyo and company have their work cut out to save the planet. The final "special" episode shows the team a few years later, no longer working together, but all still working to protect the world—compare to GOSHOGUN.

MACROSS *

1982. JPN: *Chojiku Yosai Macross*. AKA: *Superdimensional Fortress Macross*. TV series, movie, video. DIR: Noboru Ishiguro, Fumihiko Takayama, Masakazu Yasumura, Hiroyuki

Yamaga, Kazushi Akiyama, Hiroshi Yoshida, Kazuhito Akiyama. scr: Kenichi Matsuzaki, Sukehiro Tomita, Hiroyuki Hoshiyama, Shoji Kawamori, Noboru Ishiguro, Hiroshi Onogi, Tatsuya Kasahara. des: Haruhiko Mikimoto, Kazumasa Miyabe, Shoji Kawamori, Ichiro Itano, Toshihiro Hirano, Eiji Suzuki, Hideaki Shimada. ani: Noboru Ishiguro, Fumihiko Takayama, Hiroyuki Yamaga, Taro Yamada, Katsuhisa Yamada, Akina Nishimori. mus: Kentaro Haneda; Yoko Kanno. prd: Big West, TBS. 25 mins. x 36 eps. (*Macross*), 115 mins. (m), 30 mins. x 6 eps. (*Mac2*), 40 mins. x 4 eps. (*Mac+*), 115 mins. (*Mac+ Movie*), 25 mins. x 49 eps. (*Mac7*), 55 mins. (*Mac7 Encore*), 30 mins. (*Mac7 Galaxy*), 30 mins. x 4 eps. (*Mac7 Dynamite*), 30 mins. x 5 eps. (*Zero*), 25 mins. x 25 eps. (*Frontier*), ca. 90 mins. (m1, *Frontier*), 120 mins. (m2, *Frontier*), 90 mins. (m3, *Hear My Song*). In 1999, a giant space fortress crashes on Earth. Technology salvaged from it changes the face of Terran science, but the military is painfully aware that it is a warship, and that somewhere out in space is the race who built it. Sure enough, the giant Zentraedi arrive to reclaim their errant spacecraft. Attacking just as the recommissioned fortress, now named SDF-1, prepares for takeoff, they are thwarted by the brave people on board, who include spunky young pilot Hikaru Ichijo, heroic veteran Roy Fokker, and a ragtag crew of outnumbered Earthlings. During the ensuing conflict out at the edge of the solar system (where SDF-1 has been trapped by a malfunctioning warp engine), the invaders reveal their fatal flaw. Themselves the creations of a far older civilization, the Protoculture, their society knows nothing but war. Zentraedi spies are deeply confused by the concepts of friendship and romance, and entire fleets are driven insane by their first encounter with the dreaded "culture," as transmitted through the love songs of Chinese pop star, Lin Minmei. The fighting is long and hard, with several false truces and partial victories, but eventually humanity wins the day. The Zentraedi volunteer for "micronization" and are reduced in size to interbreed with the human race. It is eventually learned that humans are the descendants of a long-forgotten Protoculture terraforming experiment and, consequently, are just as much children of the Protoculture as the

Zentraedi, who were genetically engineered to fight the Protoculture's battles.

Released in the U.S. in a substantially altered form as **Robotech**, *Macross*, along with **Star Blazers** and **Gundam**, is one of the three unassailable pillars of anime sci-fi, pioneering the tripartite winning formula of songs, battling robot-planes (the show's famous "Valkyries"), and tense relationships. The series was a success across all media—designer Kawamori insisted on beautiful but practical machinery that was nevertheless exploitable as toys, while the numerous record spin-offs made a star of Minmei's voice actress, Mari Iijima.

After several false starts (see below) the franchise was finally revived in earnest with *Plus* (1994), set in 2040 on the colony world of Eden. Like his spiritual predecessor Ichijo, Isamu Dyson is a maverick pilot, in this case sent back to his homeworld to be a test pilot for a new generation of Valkyries, competing with his former friend Guld Bowman. *M Plus* turns its predecessor on its head, introducing a *broken* love triangle with the return of Myung Fan Lone, a girl over whom the pilots fell out in their teens. A failed singer turned record producer, Myung is in town with the virtual idol Sharon Apple, and studiously trying to avoid dredging up old memories. In their own way, they all face the unemployment line; the pilots because the military is developing an unmanned fighter, and Myung because her artificial songstress (who formerly needed to leech off Myung's talent) can now run on autopilot. *M Plus* concerns itself with the very human fear that machines will take over; ironic considering that much of the hype surrounding its Japanese release concentrated on extensive computer graphics. Impressive digital effects make regular appearances, though the old-fashioned cinematography of *M Plus* is of very high quality indeed, needing no flashy distractions. Directed by **Escaflowne**'s Shoji Kawamori, and with a script from **Cowboy Bebop**'s Keiko Nobumoto, *M Plus* is another excellent example of what anime sci-fi has to offer. The original videos were reedited into *MP: The Movie* (1995), which added some intriguing extra scenes but also removed a substantial portion of the breathtaking battles.

M Plus was released in Japan at the

same time as a TV follow-up, *Macross 7* (1994), directed by Tetsuro Amino and incorporating elements of a rejected plot for the original *Macross* series that were to have taken place on a colony ship. Set in a colony fleet heading for the galactic core in 2045, *M7* features Max and Miria Jenius, supporting characters from the original series, as the parents of the love interest Mylene. The fleet is attacked by the soul-vampire race of Protodevlin, eventually revealed to be a race of super-Zentraedi, genetically engineered by the Protoculture and imprisoned for millennia on the distant world of Varauta. Despite a backstory that artfully ties upearlier continuity issues in the series, *M7* is still a mixed bag, let down somewhat by cheap, oft-recycled animation, formulaic menaces-of-the-week, and an overconcentration on hotheaded pilot Basara Nekki and his pop group, Fire Bomber, which seems a little too cynically market-oriented. Whereas the original series actually made the audience believe that a love song could save the world, *M7* featured bizarre sequences of pilots strumming guitars in their cockpits to create weapons. Played for laughs, as in the later **Black Heaven**, it can work, but not in a show that occasionally wants to be taken seriously. As yet unreleased in English, *M7* was nevertheless popular enough in Japan to spawn several spin-offs, including Haruhiko Mikimoto's manga *M7: Trash* (an excellent study of Max Jenius's illegitimate son, Shiba), and the spin-off "movie" *M7: The Galaxy Is Calling Me* (1995), in which Basara, now a journeyman musician, is imprisoned on an ice-planet by mysterious forces. There are also two sets of straight-to-video ephemera. The first, *M7: Encore*, simply consists of two unbroadcast TV episodes. *Macross Dynamite 7* (1997) was a new story about Basara going to the isolated planet of Zora, where he meets the elfin alien Elma. Although they have little in common, they communicate through the universal language of song, and Elma's older sister Liza enlists Basara's help in attempting to decode the songs of the interstellar whales that have come to Zora. True to form, Liza is an ace pilot in the *Macross* mold, and there is an all-new love trian-gle to keep fans of the formula happy.

A fully digital sequel, with the working title of *Macross 3D*, was announced for

2001 as a directorial project for Takeshi Mori. This project, however, seems to have been canceled in favor of *Macross Zero* (see below). Early reports include a scarred, embittered veteran who goes by the name Redline, a traditional *Macross* heroine in the shape of the red-haired Lorin, and the "mysterious silver-haired" Karno, who seems heavily inspired by EVANGELION's Rei Ayanami. There are several other spin-offs from the *Macross* series apart from the central plot discussed above. These include the music video *Flashback 2012* (1987), Minmei's "farewell concert," which included bonus epilogue footage of the characters' lives after the show. The theatrical feature *Macross: Do You Remember Love?* (1984, AKA *Clash of the Bionoids*) retells much of the original series but with several deviations. The official explanation for this is that it is actually a film made *in* the *Macross* universe *about* the events of the series, taking artistic license with several events. Seen in 2031 by the 15-year-old Myung Fan Lone, it inspires her to become a singer and hence the events of *Macross Plus*! Max's eldest daughter, Comiria, starred in the video game *Macross 2036*, which was followed by another, *Eternal Love Story*. There is also the noncanonical video *Macross II: Lovers Again* (1992), an inferior sequel to the original series, now disowned by its creators. Set 80 years after the original series, this guilty rehash features hotshot journalist Hibiki Kanzaki, who is sent to interview Valkyrie ace Silvie Gena but gets caught up in the action on Earth. A new alien enemy has attacked—the Marduk, who are encouraged in battle by the singing voice of Ishtar, a beautiful girl who switches sides when she falls for Hibiki. A live-action movie version of the original series, *Macross: Final Outpost—Earth*, was planned as a U.S.-Japanese coproduction and reputedly scripted by *Superman*-writer David Newman, but it has been stuck in turnaround for several years.

Macross Zero (2002) is a video series set before the arrival of the Zentraedi and at the time of the creation of the first Valkyrie prototype, in the final days of an Earthbound conflict between the United Nations and anti-UN factions. Previewed in the last days of 2007, in order to justify its claims of being a 25th-anniversary commemoration, but not fully screened until

several months later, Shoji Kawamori and Yasuhito Kikuchi's TV series *Macross Frontier* (2008) functions as a sequel to both the original series and *M7*, screened in a graveyard slot suggesting it was entirely aimed, again, at the audience of "silver otaku." Set 14 years after *M7*, it replays all the old saws once again—colony fleet, unknown enemy (this time the insectoid Vajra), idol singer, and love triangle. Music, and love, conquers all, although not before the movie sequels *Diva of Lies* (*Itsuwari no Utahime*, 2009) and *Wings of Goodbye* (*Sayonara no Tsubasa*, 2011). However, *Macross Frontier* does seem to possess a sensibility born of real-world issues, with allusions to a hawkish conspiracy within the fleet to both seize power and steal the Vajra homeworld, through a hate campaign aimed at dehumanizing the enemy (well, they *aren't* human, but that's not the point). Another film, Tetsuro Amino's *Macross FB7: Hear My Song* (*Ore no Uta o Kike*, 2012) seems to have been intended as a theatrical advert for the rerelease of the *M7* TV series, retelling the story through "found footage" as the cast of *Frontier* spool through an archive of old videos about the legendary Fire Bomber.

MAD BULL 34 *
1990. Video. DIR: Satoshi Dezaki. SCR: Toshiaki Imaizumi. DES: Keizo Shimizu. ANI: Keizo Shimizu, Hideo Okazaki, Kazunori Iwakura. MUS: Curio, John Michael, James Brown. PRD: Magic Bus. 45 mins. x 4 eps.
America, as we all know, is a land of happy blonde hookers, gun-toting schoolchildren, and roller-skating hoodlums, where self-defense teachers use their classes to scout for potential rape victims, pretty journalists use their bodies as bait to trap molesters, and kindly police get freebies from "high-class" whores. One such hero is "Sleepy," a vast hulk of a police officer also known as Mad Bull. In a series of astoundingly misconceived set-ups lifted from the worst of U.S. cop shows, Japanese-American rookie Daizaburo is assigned to Mad Bull in New York's 34th precinct, and the older cop shows him the ropes.

While *MB34* is one of the most puerile anime ever made, it is at least partly inspired by American TV itself—a diet of murder and crime shows genuinely does make America look like this to many

foreigners, who could be forgiven for assuming that the U.S. jumped straight from the genteel LITTLE WOMEN to the killing fields of GOLGO 13. Lacking any of the redeeming qualities of the lighterhearted GUNSMITH CATS, *MB34* presents a stunningly infantile story in which "not doing things by the book" means shooting all suspected perps on sight and the way to snap a traumatized hostage out of shock is to "stick your finger up her ass." Based on a 1985 *Young Jump* manga by Kazuo Koike and Noriyoshi Inoue, the English dub features a new hip-hop music track, which, frankly, is one of the high points of this odious show—the mind boggles at James Brown lending his name to a show that features an episode called "Hit and Rape." The credits thank the *real-life* 34th precinct of the NYPD for unspecified assistance, though the public relations officer must have had a baby when he saw the final result—a ruthless cop hunting down the assassin who has already tried to kill him with poisoned soap, in revenge for the death of the prostitute they share on alternate weekdays. Listen, too, for the British-made dub, which seems to think that referring to civic *dooty* at irregular intervals means you've got a New York accent. A generation after its release, *MB34* has assumed something of the status of a cult classic, on the understanding that nobody can possibly take it seriously. **ⓁⓃⓋ**

MAD OLD BAG
1990. JPN: *O-Batarian*. TV series. DIR: Tetsuro Amino. SCR: Shunichi Yukimuro, Toshiki Inoue. DES: Yoshinobu Shigeno. ANI: N/C. MUS: Yasuo Urakami, Katsuyoshi Kobayashi. PRD: TV Asahi/SPO. 25 mins. x 7 eps.
The misadventures of an unpleasant old woman (compare to NASTY OLD LADY) who embarrasses her family at a school open house, makes a nuisance of herself during a vacation to a hot spring, and lusts after nice young men. Based on the 1984 manga by Katsuhiko Hotta.

MADAME BUTTERFLY
1940. JPN: *Ocho Fujin no Genso*. AKA: *Fantasy of Madame Butterfly*. Movie. DIR: Wagoro Arai, Chuya Tobiishi. SCR: N/C. DES: N/C. ANI: N/C. MUS: Tamaki Miura. PRD: Asahi Eiga. 12 mins.
Butterfly, a faithful Japanese wife, waits

patiently in Nagasaki for the return of her American husband, Pinkerton. She sees the Stars and Stripes fluttering atop an approaching ship and rightly surmises that Pinkerton is onboard. However, the feckless foreigner is arriving in the company of his "real" Caucasian wife, causing the heartbroken Butterfly to commit suicide.

This masterpiece of Japanese silhouette animation makes the best of its source material. Giacomo Puccini's 1904 opera must have seemed like an obvious choice for adaptation for a Japanese audience, particularly in the rising tide of the WARTIME ANIME that favored any opportunity to cast aspersions at Americans. Puccini's opera famously ends with Butterfly's suicide in silhouette behind a screen, making the use of all-shadow animation particularly poignant—the animated version ends just like any "live" one. However, since Puccini had only died in 1924, his opera was still in copyright, a fact that had escaped the animators until they began preparing to lay down the audio track, 18,000 frames into production. Faced with a prohibitively high demand for royalties from Puccini's estate, the producers were forced to commission new music and lyrics, thereby rather defeating the point of this "adaptation." Compare to DREAMY URASHIMA, which got away with arguably cheekier copyright infringement, and MEMORIES, which put Puccini's legacy to use after a safe time had elapsed.

MADARA
1991. JPN: Moryo Senki Madara. Video. DIR: Yuji Moriyama. SCR: Akinori Endo. DES: Yuji Moriyama, Junichi Watanabe. ANI: Yuji Moriyama. MUS: The Great Riches. PRD: Animate Film. 30 mins. x 4 eps.
Madara is disowned by his father, King Miroku, who steals his "chakra power" and banishes him to planet Earth, where he is saved by the old man Tatara. Attacked in the forest by Miroku's evil tree-spirits, Madara swears to get back at his father, but he must contend with his brother, sent to Earth to kill him first.

Based on the 1987 manga written by Eiji Otsuka and drawn by Sho-u Tajima, published in Maru Sho Famicon magazine. Episode two contains the 36-page Madara Special Edition, a sequel to the fourth volume of the manga. Tajima also provided designs for KAI DOH MARU and drew the original manga of Otsuka's MPD Psycho (*DE).

MADCAP ISLAND
1967. JPN: Hyokkori Hyotanjima. AKA: Pop-up Gourd Island. Movie. DIR: Taiji Yabushita. SCR: Hisashi Inoue, Morihisa Yamamoto. DES: N/C. ANI: N/C. MUS: N/C. PRD: Toei Animation. 61 mins.
After a volcanic explosion, Madcap Island is set adrift and eventually runs aground on a continent governed by man-hating dogs. The dogs of Madcap Island mount an artillery attack on the island's town, and top dog Commander Pitz takes town chief Don Gavacho prisoner. Gavacho is rescued and sets to work hatching a plot, which involves hatching fleas. The hatching flea eggs, inside balloons, are set off on a fair wind to burst over the enemy, and the plan is that nature will do the rest. But biological warfare fails, and in the end there is a gunfight between Commander Pitz and Don Gavacho's ally Machine Gun Dandy. Shown at some film festivals with English subtitles, this short movie was a spin-off from the 1964 children's puppet show Madcap Island (*DE), a show of immense influence during the 1960s, but which has been largely forgotten in modern times—only eight episodes of the original now survive. Creator Hisashi Inoue would later become one of the writers on MOOMINS. Disenchanted with the reaction to the film, director Taiji Yabushita would turn his back on anime production in the 1970s, instead going into teaching.

MADHOUSE
Sometimes credited as Studio Madhouse, Madhouse Studios, or Madhouse Productions, the studio does not have one single location, but is scattered across several buildings in a Tokyo suburb. An animation studio founded in 1972 by several former employees of Mushi Production, including Masao Murayama, Rintaro, Yoshiaki Kawajiri, and Osamu Dezaki. Notable staffers include Toshio Hirata, Yoshinori Kanemori, Tatsuhiko Urahata, and Kunihiko Sakurai. After its first job on AIM FOR THE ACE, Madhouse has become one of the most influential studios in anime, particularly abroad in the 1990s, where its concentration on adult-oriented horror and sci-fi made its works some of the better-known anime of the video boom—particularly Kawajiri's own WICKED CITY and NINJA SCROLL. Although the studio has a long track record in video releases, it did not limit itself solely to them, ensuring that there were plenty of high profile cinema titles on its resumé—including BAREFOOT GEN, LENSMAN, and METROPOLIS. In addition to Kawajiri, Madhouse also enjoyed a long association with Satoshi Kon, whose PERFECT BLUE and MILLENNIUM ACTRESS were critically acclaimed. Nor has the studio shied away from TV production, benefiting greatly from the success of CHOBITS in the early 21st century. As of 2014, the company is 95% owned by the TV channel NTV.

MADLAX *
2004. TV series. DIR: Koichi Mashimo. SCR: Yosuke Kuroda. DES: Minako Shiba, Satoko Miyachi, Satoshi Osawa, Kenji Teraoka. ANI: Satoshi Osawa, Yasuhiro Saiki. MUS: Yuki Kajiura. PRD: Bee Train, Victor Entertainment, TV Tokyo. 25 mins. x 26 eps.
Gazth-Sonica is a small country in Asia, torn by civil war and almost ignored by the rest of the world. Young noblewoman Margaret Barton lives in the little European state of Nafrece with her maid Eleanor Baker, seemingly a world away. Margaret lost her memory in a plane crash 12 years ago, and is plagued by terrifying dreams and hallucinations. Her only link with her past is a damaged, bloodstained foreign book that her missing father left for her. Margaret doesn't know that it is a holy book, sought by secret organization Enfant and its weird masked leader, Friday Monday; but she is convinced that she must try to find her father and resolve the mystery of her past. She hires Madlax, a mercenary willing to do anything from assassination to intelligence gathering, to take her into Gazth-Sonica and find her father. The two girls seem very different—a lonely, confused teenager from a privileged background and a tough, self-reliant mercenary—but they have more in common than they know, not the least an uncanny resemblance to the lead characters of creator/director Mashimo's earlier NOIR, the first entry in the "girls-with-guns" trilogy. However, Madlax has a distinct change of pace from its predeces-

sor in the girls-with-guns genre, telling its leads' stories in two completely separate arcs that slowly converge on each other in the course of the story. It thus takes almost half the series for the actual plotline to turn up in anything more than hints and rumors—compare to **GUNSLINGER GIRL** and **EL CAZADOR DE LA BRUJA**, the third entry in the "girls-with-guns" trilogy.

MADONNA *

1988. JPN: *Madonna: Honoo no Teacher*. AKA: *Madonna: Fiery Teacher*. Video. DIR: Akinori Nagaoka. SCR: Kaori Okamura. DES: Minoru Maeda. ANI: Minoru Maeda. MUS: N/C. PRD: Studio Junio, Toei Video, Aomi Planning. 52 mins. x 2 eps.

Well-bred young lady Mako Domon decides to be a teacher but is sent to the rough Gyunabe Technical High School, where she is put in charge of a class of juvenile delinquents. She becomes the coach for the school rugby team, which allows this **SPORTS ANIME** to repeat the standard clichés of shows in the tradition of **AIM FOR THE ACE**, but with the added frisson of a female coach. Based on the popular manga by Ikuko Kujirai, published in *Big Comics Spirits*, and featuring Norio Wakamoto reprising his role in **GUNBUSTER** (also 1988) almost exactly as the male coach who is introduced in episode 2. Also compare to **THE GOKUSEN**, another show about reforming delinquents.

MADOX-01 *

1987 AKA: *Metal Skin Panic Madox 01*. Video. DIR: Shinji Aramaki. SCR: Shinji Aramaki. DES: Hideki Tamura. ANI: Hiroaki Goda. MUS: Ken Yashima. PRD: AIC. 45 mins.

Overworked (but pretty) scientist Miss Kuzumoto sends the new MADOX-01 military robot off for more tests, but she carelessly forgets to turn it off. The robot is lost in a crash, falling into the hands of lovable college boy Koji, who tries it on for size. Trapped inside, Koji tries to sneak across Tokyo for a midnight tryst with his estranged girlfriend, Shiori, though he has trouble looking inconspicuous. Realizing that the jealous officer Kilgore will do anything to destroy the MADOX, Kuzumoto suits up in another model and tries to find out what Koji wants. All Koji wants, of course, is to get out of the suit, but he conveniently forgets to mention

this until large swathes of Tokyo have been turned into smoldering rubble by the ensuing battle.

A weapon-goes-haywire story inferior to its contemporary **BLACK MAGIC**, *Madox* features a robot design also used in the same studio's **BUBBLEGUM CRISIS** but is otherwise unrelated. Tiresomely attempting to compensate for lackluster production with idle moments of "humor" and a couple of references to *Apocalypse Now*, *Madox* also makes some avoidable bloopers in its depiction of the real world—watch for military alarms that go from DEFCON Three to DEFCON *Four* when trouble escalates. Political types may enjoy the show's shameless characterization of Americans as belligerent morons who revel in destruction with war machines they do not fully comprehend, whereas the Japanese are all mechanically minded innocents with no interest in fighting. "You'd better not turn Tokyo into another Vietnam," Kuzumoto archly warns Kilgore, while neglecting to mention that none of this would have happened in the first place if she'd bothered to switch the MADOX unit off.

MAEDA, MAHIRO

1963–. Born in Tottori. A former Studio Ghibli animator who found fame as a designer on **EVANGELION** and **ESCAFLOWNE**, before an association with the Gonzo company that led to leading roles on **BLUE SUBMARINE NO. SIX**, **LAST EXILE**, and **GANKUTSUOU**. He also enjoyed considerable foreign recognition, thanks to his contributions to **THE ANIMATRIX** and **KILL BILL: THE ORIGIN OF O-REN**, for which he was a key animator.

MAEDA, TSUNEO

1946–. Born on Hokkaido, he found work at Mushi Production after leaving high school. He left Mushi to go freelance, and worked on children's programming such as **JAPANESE FOLK TALES**. He inadvertently became one of the pioneers of CG animation, when he served as technical director on **BIT THE CUPID**. He has also been a key animator on titles ranging from **ZOO WITHOUT AN ELEPHANT** to **THE TALE OF GENJI**.

MAGI: THE LABYRINTH OF MAGIC *

2012. TV series. DIR: Koji Masunari. SCR: Hiroyuki Yoshino, Isana Kakimura, Masahiro

Yokotani, Yoichi Kato. DES: Toshifumi Akai. ANI: Toshifumi Akai, Koichi Usami, Chie Nishizawa, Tomofumi Sakai. MUS: Shiro Sagisu. PRD: Aniplex, Dentsu, GyaO, MBS, Movic, Shogakukan. 25 mins. x 25 eps. (TV1), 25 mins. x 13 eps. (TV2).

In a fantasy Middle East like something out of the **1001 NIGHTS**, Alibaba and Aladdin resolve to drag themselves out of poverty by the most dangerous but lucrative means. For the last 14 years, large towers known as Dungeons have been appearing all over the realm. Anyone who can enter a Dungeon, conquer its guardians, and steal its treasure can live for the rest of his life like a king.

Despite a promising opening, suffused with orientalist charm and adventurous tropes, and a stirring soundtrack to rival that of **EL HAZARD**, *Magi* soon devolves into clichés derived from role-playing games. That, however, still puts it head-and-shoulders above many other anime shows for young boys. Later episodes, introducing Central Asian nomads, are in keeping with the spirit of the original Persian-influenced *Arabian Nights* (which often told tales from Central Asia rather than the Middle East), but separate Alibaba and Aladdin for much of the storyline, before broader story arcs involve them in political intrigues and wars beyond the borders of their homeland. Literary historians may have already noticed that despite their worldwide fame, neither Alibaba nor Aladdin appear in the original *Arabian Nights* as brought to the West—both are "orphan tales" of uncertain origin, possibly interpolated by French retellers. The 2013 second season changed the subtitle to *The Kingdom of Magic*. Based on the manga by Shinobu Ohtaka, which began in *Weekly Shonen Sunday* in 2009.

MAGIC BOOBS SECRET SWORD SCROLL

2011. JPN: *Manyu Hikencho*. TV series. DIR: Hiraku Kaneko. SCR: Seishi Minakami, Fumihiko Takayama, Yasutomo Yamada, Yuniko Ayana. DES: Jun Takagi, Shigemi Ikeda. ANI: Jun Takagi. MUS: Miyu Nakamura. PRD: Hoods Entertainment, Enterbrain, Happinet Pictures, Lantis, Memory Tech, TV Tokyo. 24 mins. x 12 eps.

In a parallel universe, the Edo period is dominated by big breasts. Those possessing them are guaranteed fame and fortune. Those without them are not considered human (we mean the women, of course, because *nobody* would be stupid enough to judge a man by the size of his chest). The Manyu clan possesses a secret scroll said to contain the techniques that give them the ability to raise so many women with enormous assets. Unfortunately the next heir of the clan is a tomboy with a breast fixation that makes her an easy target for busty assassins. But Chifusa's heart is in the right place—she wants to end the cruel system her clan perpetuates.

This series based on Hideki Yamada's manga for Enterbrain has also spun off a drama CD and an Internet radio show, seemingly unlikely venues for a premise that relies heavily on the visual. So far there is no game spin-off, preventing fans from trying Chifusa's trademark Breast Flow technique for themselves. She can enlarge and reduce breasts at will and intends to use this technique to give every woman in Japan a decent-sized bust. However, her costume makes an appearance in the *Lollipop Chainsaw* game. And we thought **QUEEN'S BLADE** was pushing it.... **N**

MAGIC BOY *

1959. JPN: *Shonen Sarutobi Sasuke*. Movie. DIR: Taiji Yabushita, Akira Daikuhara. SCR: Toppei Matsumura. DES: Akira Daikuhara, Hideo Furusawa. ANI: Taku Sugiyama, Gisaburo Sugii, Norio Hikone. MUS: Satoshi Funemura. PRD: Toei. 83 mins.

When his pet deer is killed by Princess Yasha, mountain boy Sasuke resolves to go away to Mount Togakushi and study the art of *ninjutsu* under the master Hatsuunsai Tozawa. Bidding farewell to his elder sister Oyu, he heads off, leaving his village prone to attacks from Princess Yasha's agent, Gonkuro, and his gangs of bandits. The local lord, Yukimura Sanada, is unable to deal with the bandit problem because of a spell cast by Yasha, but he teams up with the returning Sasuke to defeat the menace. A flawed film that mixes ninja action with highly idiosyncratic work by several artists who had never worked in anime before. Compare to **SASUGA NO SARUTOBI**.

MAGIC OF CHOCOLATE, THE

2011. JPN: *Chocolat no Maho*. Video. DIR:

Shinichiro Kimura, Toshiki Fukushima, Katsumi Ono. SCR: Yuko Fukuda, Tomoko Konparu. DES: Takayo Mitsuwaka, Takao Sano, Natsuko Tosugi, Natsumi Sakamoto. ANI: Takayo Mitsuwaka, Junko Nakamura, Chao Kobayashi. MUS: tenten. PRD: SynergySP, Studio Hibari, Shogakukan. 14 mins. x 13 eps.

Chocolat Aikawa seems very young to manage a shop, but the pretty little Gothic-Lolita is a skilled *chocolatiere*, and runs the exclusive Chocolat Noir store. It's deep in a forest and not everyone finds their way there, but those with troubles often end up trying one of Chocolat's expensive confections—the price is the most precious thing in your life. Chocolat comes from a long line of magical confectioners, and her flavors have a meaning in a titanic battle between the forces of light and dark. Based on the 2009 manga by Rino Mizuho, the first part was on an anthology DVD bundled with *Ciao* magazine, in which the comics appeared, in April 2011. A second episode was circulated in the same way in May 2011, before the series began streaming free on the magazine's online channel in August that year. A complete change of crew after episode 9 signaled a "second video series."

The premise is similar to that of **PET-SHOP OF HORRORS** or **xxxHOLIC**, but also bears a resemblance to the eight-minute 2001 video *Magical Chocolate* (*Maho no Chocolate*), animated using Photoshop 5.0 and Premiere 4.2 by one-man studio Ishikawa Pro. Mami-chan has a crush on her school's star soccer player and wants to give him chocolate on Valentine's Day. Her friend Koko-chan tells her about the mysterious magic chocolate that can grant a wish, but will it make her dreams come true? Rather than fantasy, this is a story about finding courage within yourself to make your dreams come true. The animation and design are far more basic than the 2011 work, but it's a bold attempt.

MAGIC THIEF

2010. JPN: *Magic Kaito: Kid the Phantom Thief*. TV specials. DIR: Toshiki Hirano. SCR: Junichi Miyashita. DES: Masaki Sato, Shuzo Ueda. ANI: Shingo Ishikawa, Toshimitsu Kobayashi. MUS: Atsushi Umebori. PRD: TMS Entertainment, Dream Force. 24 mins. x 12 eps.

Kaito Kuroba is a young magician with a secret. His late father was the legendary thief Kaito Kid. Now Kaito moonlights as the new Kaito Kid, using his skills to pull off daring heists. The origin of this story is a manga by Gosho Aoyama (**CONAN THE BOY DETECTIVE**), and Kaito has crossed over to appear in Aoyama's better-known work as one of Detective Conan's most formidable opponents.

MAGIC TREE HOUSE *

2012. Movie. DIR: Hiroshi Nishikiori. SCR: Ichiro Okuji. DES: Yoshiaki Yanagida, Toshiharu Mizutani. ANI: Yoshiaki Yanagida. MUS: Akira Senju. PRD: Ajia-do, Dentsu, Yahoo! Japan, TV Aichi, TV Osaka, TV Tokyo, GAGA Communications, Media Factory, Asahi Shinbun, TSUTAYA. 105 mins.

Jack and his little sister Annie find a magic tree house in the woods near their home. The books inside enable them to travel through time. The magician Morgan le Fay needs help to find four medallions, each hidden in a different epoch of history, and the children set out to help her. Mary Pope Osborne's children's book series had the distinction of eclipsing Harry Potter at the top of the *New York Times* bestseller list in 2006. Since the publication of *Dinosaurs Before Dark* in 1992, the *Magic Tree House* series has become a successful **KIDS' ANIME** franchise, with fact books, a planetarium show, and two musicals.

MAGIC USER'S CLUB *

1996. JPN: *Maho Tsukaitai*. AKA: *Witches' Club; I Wanna Do Magic*. Video, TV series. DIR: Junichi Sato. SCR: Akinori Endo, Chiaki Konaka, Michiko Yokote, Sadayuki Murai. DES: Ikuko Ito, Mahiro Maeda. ANI: Ikuko Ito. MUS: Michiru Oshima. PRD: Madhouse, WOWOW. 30 mins. x 6 eps. (v), 25 mins. x 13 eps. (TV).

Earth has been invaded *again*, by ugly high-performance robots powerful enough to destroy the UN forces with a single blast. Is it the end of the world? Actually, no. The invaders just roam around observing life, don't attack unless provoked, and are very polite. Most people have gotten used to just living around them. But they're still invaders, so somebody obviously has to fight them and save Earth. Cue the members of the Kitanohashi High School Magic Club. The president, Takeo, is always trying to impress pretty (but clumsy) new recruit Sae. Androgynous vice-president Aburatsubo (who, the titles very carefully inform us, *is* a boy) is devoted to Takeo. Sae's best friend, Nanaka, has a crush on Aburatsubo … and remember they're supposed to be fighting the aliens. Takeo is just hoping to impress the girls by leading an attack on the invaders. So far, however, their magic isn't all that good, and with the school's Manga Club taking over their room space, he needs a project to hold the Magic Club together before all the members quit. Then things start to get serious when journalist Minowa begins finding out who these magical kids really are, and Sae finds she feels a bit more for Takeo than the respect of a junior classmate for a senior club leader.

The video series was followed in 1997 by 13 TV episodes focusing on the huge cherry tree Sae creates in the center of town in the final battle to get rid of the aliens. Its petals, far from being a nostalgic seasonal pleasure, are snowing up the roads and causing chaos. In the process of trying to get rid of the tree, the club members discover that it isn't the only unsuitable magical object plaguing the city, and they have a new mission. The video series spun off a manga version by Tami Ota, which ran in *Fantasy DX* magazine. We can think of no reason why the U.S. release title implies there is only one "Magic User," except perhaps a lack of familiarity with English grammar.

MAGIC WOMAN M *

1996. JPN: *Maho Shojo Meryl*. AKA: *Magical Girl Meryl*. Video. DIR: Tougenan, Ahiru Koike. SCR: Hiroshi Ishii. DES: Nekoshita Pong. ANI: Hoichi Hirade. MUS: N/C. PRD: Beam Entertainment. 30 mins. x 2 eps.
This video was based on a manga by Nekoshita Pong that was originally serialized in *Monthly Fantazine*. Sexy young witch Meryl Shelk wanders a forest full of rapacious beasts—her only defense, the sorcerous powers she unleashes at the moment of orgasm. ●NV

MAGICAL CANAN

2005. TV series. DIR: Masashi Abe. SCR: Mitsuhiro Yamada. DES: Akio Watanabe, Masaki Yamada, Yoshitaka Kono, Mamoru Yokota,

Hiroshi Ogawa. ANI: Keiichi Ishikura, Michio Sato, Masaki Yamada, Yoshitaka Kono, Tetsuya Watanabe, Masanori Nishii. MUS:N/C. PRD: AIC, Terios, AT-X. 25 mins. x 13 eps.
Chihaya Hiiragi is a junior high school girl at Meiho Academy. She finds an injured fluffy purple-and-white creature and takes him home to tend him. As soon as he's recovered, he runs away. Following him, she sees him square off against a terrifying monster and instinctively grabs him and tries to protect him. The medallion around his neck blinks, a wand emerges, she grasps it, and suddenly transforms into a brave, athletic magical warrior called Carmine, with a pneumatic chest about seven years older than she is—compare to **MARVELOUS MELMO**. She's even more surprised when cute critter Natsuki also transforms into a hunky, spiky-haired teenage boy. After that, hearing about his homeworld of Evergreen, where creatures are born from seeds, seems reasonable enough. The seeds are getting into the human world and turning people into monsters, and Natsuki is on a mission from the Queen of Evergreen to help prevent this. Chihaya urges him to recruit her shy friend Sayaka Mizuki, who also gets a confidence boost, plus blonde hair, a French maid outfit, and an inflated chest, along with her ability to transform into magical warrior Cerulean Blue. But the villain of the piece, Evergreen renegade Bergamot, also has his agents in the human world—his magical winged warrior Septem seems to have a link to transfer student Emi Kojima.

One of the important elements of the magical-girl series format is that magic can bestow the illusion of maturity, status, and power, and this usually involves sexualizing the heroine to some degree. Even so, the old and cynical among us, who remember when magical-girl series featured characters with chest measurements in which the letter D played no part, may be saddened to know that this is a repackaging of an earlier porn anime—filed here as **MAGICAL KANAN**.

MAGICAL DOREMI *

1999. JPN: *Ojamajo Doremi*. AKA: *Bothersome Witch Doremi*. TV series, video. DIR: Junichi Sato, Takuya Igarashi, Akinori Yabe. SCR: Reiko Yoshida, Yumi Kageyama, Atsushi

Yamatoya, Midori Kuriyama. DES: Yoshihiko Umakoshi. ANI: Yoshihiko Umakoshi, Chuji Nakajima. MUS: Keiichi Oku. PRD: Toei, TV Asahi. 25 mins. x 51 eps. (TV1), 25 mins. x 49 eps. (TV2), 26 mins. (m1), 25 mins. x 50 eps. (TV3), 25 mins. x 51 eps. (TV4), 25 mins. x 13 eps. (v), 27 mins. (m2).
Doremi is an average third-grade girl who wishes she could be a witch. She meets Lika, the owner of a magic shop, and correctly guesses that she is a genuine witch. Unfortunately, the lucky guess transforms Lika into a frog, and Doremi can only transform her back by becoming a qualified witch herself. Doremi minds the store with her schoolmates Hazuki and Aiko, beginning her adventures in witchery. This child-oriented variant on **SAILOR MOON** features innovative crayon and watercolor backgrounds in the style of children's books. The third season, which began in 2001, transforms the girls' magic shop into a bakery and introduces a "funny" American, Momoko, who only speaks halting Japanese. The show was created by Toei house pseudonym Izumi Todo, who is also credited with the similar **PRECURE**. Although the series finished in 2004 with a shorter video spin-off, it continued in prose form with Midori Kuriyama's novella *Ojamajo Doremi 16* (2011), charting the lead's progress at high school.

MAGICAL EMI

1985. JPN: *Maho no Star Magical Emi*. AKA: *Magical Star Magical Emi*; *Magical Emi the Star*. TV series. DIR: Nobuyasu Furukawa, Kazuyoshi Katayama, Tomomi Mochizuki, Mizuho Nishikubo, Michiru Hongo, Tadayuki Hayashi, Takashi Anno, Fumihiko Takayama. SCR: Hiroshi Kobayakawa, Mami Watanabe, Akinori Endo, Hideki Sonoda, Sukehiro Tomita. DES: Yoshiyuki Kishi, Kazuhiko Kobayashi. ANI: Yoshiyuki Kishi, Yuji Motoyama. MUS: Keiichi Oku. PRD: Studio Pierrot, NTV. 25 mins. x 38 eps.
Would-be conjuror Mai Kazuki is playing with her brother Misaki when the fairy Topo offers to grant her a wish. She transforms herself into Magical Emi, a magical girl in the tradition of **CREAMY MAMI**, but who prefers to concentrate on more mundane concerns than her crime-fighting sisters—much of *ME*'s plot concerns her performances at her grandmother's Magicarrot Theater. As with the other magical-

girl stories, Mai loses her powers as she leaves childhood behind and becomes an adult in the final episodes. Many of the crew would go on from this obscure work to make some of the best-known anime of the late 1980s and beyond.

MAGICAL FAIRY PERSIA

1984. JPN: *Maho Shojo Persia*. AKA: *Magic Fairy Pelsh; Magic Girl Pelsha*. TV series, video. DIR: Takashi Anno, Kazuyoshi Katayama, Tsuneo Tominaga. SCR: Junki Takegami, Keiko Maruo, Sukehiro Tomita, Yoshiyuki Kishi, Taeko Aonuma, Mami Watanabe, Sukehiro Tomita. DES: Akemi Takada, Yoshiyuki Kishi, Mitsuki Nakamura, Satoshi Miura, Hiroki Takago, Eiko Hamada. ANI: Yumiko Horazawa, Yoshiyuki Kishi, Hiroki Takago. MUS: Koji Makino. PRD: Pierrot, NTV, Shueisha. 25 mins. x 48 eps. (TV), 30 mins. (v1), 45 mins. (v2).

Eleven-year-old Persia lives on the Serengeti plains in Africa, wearing a leopardskin and surrounded by wild animals, until local storekeeper Goken and his hunky twin teenage grandsons Gaku and Riki take her to live in Japan. On the way, Persia finds herself in the magical land of Lovely Dream, where dreams are born. But the land is frozen and the dreams can't get out into the human world. The Fairy Queen gives Persia a special mission: to collect Love Energy in the human world and allow springtime to return to Lovely Dream. If she fails, or if humans see her using her magical powers, the important men in her life—Goken, Gaku, and Riki—will be transformed into women.

The Queen sends Persia back to the human world with a magic headband, which connects her to Lovely Dream and turns her into a teenager. Three magical companions accompany her in the form of *kappa*, named Gera Gera, Meso Meso, and Puri Puri (onomatopoeia in Japanese for Guffaw, Whimper, and Huff.) Using her magic, she transforms her beloved lion Simba into a cat so she can bring him along from Africa to Japan.

This series is usually ranked below CREAMY MAMI in the magical girl canon, but it was popular enough in its day to attract a cameo appearance from *Creamy Mami* characters in episode 3 and to form part of two video spin-offs, 1986's *Three Enchanting Magical Girls (Adesugata Maho no Sannin Musume)* and 1987's *Magic Girl Club Foursome—Alien X from A Zone (Majokko Club Yoningumi—A Kukan Kara no Alien X)*. In the first video, Persia, Mami, and MAGICAL EMI get stuck in their alter egos and have to go to a hot spring and recite tongue twisters to change back. In the second, the trio and PASTEL YUMI have to save the world from a terrible monster assaulting cute young girls and changing them into ugly hags. Unsurprisingly for a series so rooted in sexual subtext, there was also a porn parody, *Maho no Rouge Lipstick*, created in 1985 by critic and novelist Eiji Otsuka.

A manga version by Takako Aonuma commenced publication in October 1984. In September 1985 Persia (renamed Evelyn) was on Italian TV, and made her French debut (renamed Vanessa) in 1988. Saban Entertainment, of *Mighty Morphin' Power Rangers* fame, are said to have planned an English version, based on the Italian dub, but this never materialized.

MAGICAL GIRL ELENA

2011. JPN: *Maho Shojo Elena*. Video. DIR: Katsuhiko Nishijima. SCR: Inochi Kado. DES: Masaaki Sakurai, Akira Itoman. ANI: Masaaki Sakurai, PN Egota, Kyoichi Daihiryu. MUS: Tatsuhito Nakagawa. PRD: Studio Fantasia, Anime Antenna Iinkai, Valhalla. 27 mins. x 3 eps.

When a tentacle monster threatens her sister Emile, a mysterious creature helps Elena change into a magical girl to fight it. Ever since then, to protect Emile and keep the planet safe from monsters, Elena fights these ugly creatures despite constant humiliation and immorality. Then her sister is drawn into the fight, and even her dead mother gets involved in this anime based on a porn game by Valkyria. **NV**

MAGICAL GIRL ISUKA *

2010. JPN: *Maho Shojo Isuka*. Video. DIR: Takashi Kondo. SCR: ZEQU. DES: Yuji Ushijima, Hifumi. ANI: Yuji Ushijima. MUS: Saisho Chikuzen. PRD: Lilith, Pixy. 30 mins. x 3 eps.

The powers of the King of Hell are sealed into a magic stone. To prevent the king's revival, the stone is placed inside the body of a pure and innocent magical girl. The clans of Hell track her down, eager to recover the stone, but discover that they can't get it back just by killing her—they have to destroy her purity and innocence.

Based on a porn game by Black Lilith; there's also a spin-off manga by SASAYUKi entitled *Maho Shojo Isuka: After School*. **NV**

MAGICAL GIRL LALABEL

1980. JPN: *Maho Shojo Lalabelle*. TV series, movie. DIR: Hiroshi Shidara, Hideo Furusawa, Masahiro Sasaki, Yuji Endo. SCR: Masaki Tsuji, Hirohisa Soda, Noboru Shiroyama, Tomoko Konparu, Tomohiro Ando. DES: Michio Shindo, Eiji Ito. ANI: Hideaki Oshika, Kiyoshi Matsumoto, Masami Abe. MUS: Taku Izumi. PRD: TV Asahi, 25 mins. x 49 eps. (TV), 15 mins. (m).

Lalabel is a magical girl (see LITTLE WITCH SALLY) accidentally sent down to the human world. Finding a place to live with old couple Sakuzo and Ume Tachibana, she promises not to use her magic and tries to fit into the human world. She befriends two local children, Toko and Teko, but is continually forced to bend her own self-imposed rules when her town is placed in jeopardy by Viscous, a fame-obsessed conjuror, and his sidekick, Tsumio. Yet another juvenile rehash of *Bewitched*, attached to a heavy-handed moralizing tone, with each episode ending with Lalabel's Proverb of the Week. Based on a manga by Eiko Fujiwara, better known as the author of *The Infamous Himeko*. Lalabel also appeared in the theatrical short *MGL: The Sea Calls for a Summer Vacation* (1980).

MAGICAL GIRL SAE

2006. JPN: *Maho Shojo Sae*. Video. DIR: Yu Koishikawa. SCR: Yu Koishikawa. DES: Kimiko Mitsui. ANI: Noritomo Hattori. MUS: N/C. PRD: Himajin Planning. 30 mins. x 2 eps.

Evil from another dimension threatens Earth. Encouraged by a magical creature, popular schoolgirl Sae steps in to protect the planet, but even she can't stand against the invaders' obscene magic. Based on a porn game by millefeuille, which also spun off a manga by Isami Higuchi and a book. **NV**

MAGICAL GIRL TICKLE

1978. JPN: *Majokko Chickle*. AKA: *Little Witch Chickle*. TV series. DIR: Takashi Hisaoka. SCR: Tatsuo Tamura, Akiyoshi Sakai, Mitsuru Majima. DES: Osamu Motohara, Hiroshi Takahisa. ANI: Takeshi Tamazawa, Kanji Hara. MUS: Takeo Watanabe. PRD: Neomedia, Nippon Sunrise, Toei, TV Asahi. 25 mins. x 48 eps.

Shy girl Chiko opens an illustrated book, only to be confronted by Tickle, a magical girl who has been sealed inside for her naughty behavior. Deciding to stay with her rescuer, Tickle uses her magic to transform herself into Chiko's twin, lives with her in her house, and attends school, hoping to study the mysteries of human behavior. Go Nagai's career as a purveyor of exposed flesh, extreme gore, and heavy metal also includes this magical-girl show for small children.

MAGICAL KANAN *

2000. AKA: *Septem Charm: Magical Kanan*. Video. DIR: Yasuhiro Matsumura. SCR: Hideki Mitsui. DES: Mamoru Yokota, Shoji Dodai. ANI: Masanobu Aoshima, Takeyasu Kurashima. MUS: N/C. PRD: Lemon Heart, Triple X. 30 mins. x 4 eps. (v1), 28 mins. x 2 eps. (v2).
"Seeds" of unmade creatures are breaking through into our world from the distant world of Evergreen, turning innocent human beings into rapacious betentacled rapists. Luckily, schoolgirl Chihaya can transform into a superheroine to fight off the menace, although she needs to do so by kissing and fondling her male associate Natsuki, a handsome teenager who can also transform into a fluffy creature that looks like a bunny. This is a pornographic anime in the style of JIBURIRU THE DEVIL ANGEL, based on the *Septem Charm: Magical Kanan* PC game. Since it has the same staff, plot, characters, and origin as the more innocent TV series MAGICAL CANAN, you would be forgiven for confusing the two. This, however, is the version with exposed T&A, and (predictably) reworks the relationships to some degree. It makes us wonder which is more revealing, that there is another porn version of an innocent Japanese TV series in the style of MASQUERADE, or that *only* the porn version is available in English. The authors have long suspected that many of the most familiar names from the VANILLA SERIES and other erotic anime staff lists are pseudonyms for more established industry personnel—*Magical Kanan* may finally offer some clues. A further adventure, *Magical Kanan: Palpitating Summer Camp*, featured a trip to the beach, where Chihaya and Natsuki's love story reaches a "surprising" conclusion. **Ⓝ**

MAGICAL MAKO-CHAN

1970. JPN: *Maho no Mako-chan*. TV series. DIR: Yugo Serikawa, Yoshio Takami, Minoru Okazaki, Tadaaki Yamazaki. SCR: Masaki Tsuji, Shunichi Yukimuro, Kazuko Yamamoto, Hide Ogawa, Moritada Matsumoto, Kuniaki Oshikawa. DES: N/C. ANI: Toshiyasu Okada, Shinya Takahashi, Fumi Kudo, Nobutaka Nishizawa. MUS: Takeo Watanabe. PRD: TV Asahi, Toei. 25 mins. x 48 eps.
Mako, the youngest daughter of the undersea Dragon King, defies her father and comes to the surface world. There, she falls in love with Akira, the first man she has ever seen. She asks a wise old woman to transform her into a human, knowing that she can never go back to being a mermaid. Then she goes to live with the animal-loving Mr. Urashima, longing all the while for another meeting with her beloved Akira. A mixture of LITTLE MERMAID and JAPANESE FOLK TALES, created for the screen by Masaki Tsuji under the pen name Shinobu Urakawa.

MAGICAL MEG

1974. JPN: *Majokko Meg-chan*. AKA: *Meg the Witch*. TV series. DIR: Yugo Serikawa, Minoru Okazaki, Hiroshi Shidara, Teruo Kogure, Satoshi Dezaki, Norio Suzuki, Kazuya Miyazaki. SCR: Hiroyasu Yamaura, Shunichi Yukimuro, Masaki Tsuji, Tomohiro Ando, Fumihito Imamura, Kiyoshi Matsuoka. DES: Isamu Tsuchida. ANI: Shingo Araki, Shinya Takahashi, Minoru Maeda. MUS: Takeo Watanabe. PRD: TV Asahi, Toei. 25 mins. x 72 eps.
Meg, the oldest child in the Kanzaki family, is forever separating her quarreling brother and sister. She cannot reveal that she is really a witch, sent from Witchland to help the human world fight demons. This magical-girl anime has a distinctly European look, particularly in the streets and houses.

MAGICAL MEOW MEOW TARUTO *

2001. JPN: *Maho Shojo Neko Taruto*. TV series. DIR: Tsukasa Sunaga. SCR: Koji Naota, Koji Ueda, Akihiko Takadera. DES: Hikaru Nanase. ANI: Hikaru Nanase. MUS: Jun Watanabe. PRD: Bandai Visual, Dentsu, TNK, Madhouse. 25 mins. x 12 eps.
Taruto, one of three cat-eared girls, believes she is the long-lost princess of the Nekomata tribe of feline sorcerers. This cynical mixture of anthropomorphic anime females, the "magical-girl" genre, and a dash of TENCHI MUYO! (since she has a shy young master, of course) is based on the manga in *Ultra Jump* magazine by the creators of STEEL ANGEL KURUMI.

MAGICAL PLAY *

2001. JPN: *Maho Yugi*. AKA: *Magical Witchland*. Video. DIR: Hiroki Hayashi. SCR: Hideyuki Kurata. DES: Kiyohiko Azuma. ANI: Yukinori Umetsu, Chizuko Kusakabe. MUS: Seiko Nagaoka. PRD: AIC. 5 mins. x 24 eps. (2D), 29 mins. (3D).
Twelve-year-old girls from different towns in Majokko Land are sent to the central castle to take part in magical duels. The coastal port of Seahaven sends Padudu, a luckless girl who falls into a river and is washed up in the party town of Dancevalley, where she is imprisoned by the mayor, who wants to increase the chances of his own candidate winning the contest. A dejected Padudu shares her cell with Nononon, a former magical-girl candidate defeated by the current incumbent Purilun. In this combination of magical-girl genre with game-based fighting anime, Nononon encourages Padudu to persevere and win for the sake of all underdogs. The first fully digital animation from the people who brought you TENCHI MUYO!, which similarly combined two disparate genres—can lightning strike twice? The series was also remade in 2001 as a 3D one-shot, the original being in the traditional two dimensional cel-style.

MAGICAL SHOPPING ARCADE ABENOBASHI *

2001. JPN: *Abenobashi Maho Shotengai*. TV series. DIR: Hiroyuki Yamaga. SCR: Hiroyuki Yamaga, Satoru Akahori, Jukki Hanada. DES: Kenji Tsuruta, Kazuhiro Takamura, Tadashi Hiramatsu. ANI: Fumie Muroi, Hiroyuki Imaishi, Hideaki Anno, Shinji Takeuchi. MUS: Shiro Sagisu. PRD: Gainax, Madhouse, Dentsu, Imagica, Starchild Records, AIC, Dr Movie, Studio Fantasia. 24 mins. x 13 eps.
Satoshi Imamiya has grown up in the seedy but friendly shopping arcade of Abenobashi in Osaka, but faces a series of modern ills as his childhood friend prepares to move away to Hokkaido and bulldozers line up to demolish the shabby but much-loved bath house. Soon, he is propelled through a series of alternate-universe

Abenobashi arcades, each repurposing his family and friends through the framework of particular stories, legends, or mythologies. That in itself might be fun enough, as Satoshi and his love-interest attempt to navigate back to their home dimension, but the narrative hides oodles of in-jokes at the expense of fan-favorite anime and Hollywood movies, as one might expect from the people who gave us OTAKU NO VIDEO. Satoshi, in fact, has very little interest in getting home, wallowing in a series of ever-more-exciting fantasy environments and finding them far preferable to the traumatic changes just about to beset him in the real world.

A far deeper backstory draws, like POM POKO, on the erosion of traditional Japanese life by modernity, eventually revealing one of the characters to be the famous medieval sorcerer Abe no Seimei (OTOGI ZOSHI) who transports out of a love scandal to a distant world, finding himself now just plain "Mr. Abe" in modern Osaka, where the reincarnations of two star-crossed lovers are just about to replay the tragic events that led to their deaths in his hometime, resulting in the birth of his modern son, our hero's father. Abenobashi is hence reframed not as a simple place name, but as "Abe's Bridge"—a relic in a place name that beautifully encapsulates this good-hearted TV show's celebration of tradition, even as it pastiches it. A manga adaptation ran in *Afternoon*, with somewhat more adult themes befitting the magazine's likely readership.

MAGICAL TALULUTO

1979. JPN: *Magical Talruto-kun*. TV, movie. DIR: Hiroyuki Kadono. SCR: Yoshiyuki Suga. DES: Tatsuya Egawa. ANI: Hisashi Eguchi. MUS: Seiji Yokoyama. PRD: Toei. 25 mins. x 87 eps. (TV), 51 mins. (m1), 41 mins. (m2), 30 mins. (m3).
Taluluto escapes a nursery school in the magical dimension and comes to the human world, pursued by teacher Teichianu. In order to save the mother of his friend in the human world, Taluluto decides to go back to the magical world. Then, a huge robot appears from hell. Based on a manga by Tatsuya Egawa from *Shonen Jump*.

MAGICAL TRAVELERS

2006. JPN: *Rakugo Tennyo Oyui*. TV Series. DIR: Nobuhiro Takamoto. SCR: Yasushi Yoritsune. DES: Miwa Oshima, Yutaka Miya, Takashi Miyano. ANI: Miwa Oshima. MUS: Jun Ichikawa. PRD: TNK, Three Fat Samurai. 24 mins. x 12 eps.
Evil threatens Edo-period Japan, but the spirits summon six girls from the future through the power of mystic stones. These girls will protect cities from evil using different powers bestowed by their stones. Yui's power is words. Can she give the people hope and dispel evil through her positive, cheerful words? *Rakugo* is traditional Japanese storytelling, and is still a popular performance art. This show was created by renowned *rakugo* performer Utawaka Katsura.

MAGICAL TWILIGHT *

1994. AKA: *The HeX Files*. Video. DIR: Toshiaki Kobayashi, Toshiaki Komura. SCR: "Hisashi Yuki." DES: Junichi Mihara. ANI: Akinobu Takahashi, Toshiaki Komura. MUS: N/C. PRD: Pink Pineapple. 30 mins. x 3 eps.
Tsukasa Tachibana is a student with problems. His exam failures are giving him nightmares; he's dreaming he's about to die. But he's not the only one with exams on his mind. Three young witches have to go to Earth to pass their final exam, and they all have the same project—Tsukasa. They'll affect his life in a weird variety of ways, though black witch Liv fails in her project to kill him after horrendous tortures. This leaves Tsukasa with two young witches on his hands. Guess who's up for hands-on tuition? A cleaned-up U.S. version was released for people who want porn with the porn removed. During the peak of mania for *The X-Files*, the U.S. distributor gave this series a "HeX Files" suffix, which was then featured far more prominently on the box art than the actual title. **N**

MAGICAL WARFARE *

2014. JPN: *Maho Senso*. TV series. DIR: Yuzo Sato. SCR: Kazuyuki Fudeyasu. DES: Ryoma Ebata. ANI: Ryoma Ebata. MUS: Masato Koda. PRD: Madhouse, Flying Dog, BS-TBS, Kadokawa Shoten, Sony Music Communications. 24 mins. x 12 eps.
Kendo club member Takeshi is inadvertently exposed to magic when he runs into a sorcerous battle. Along with his younger brother and childhood friend (**ROMANCE AND DRAMA**), he chooses not to stay in the mundane world, but to enroll in Subaru Magic Academy. Because if you've grown up without any books in the house, you'll never have heard of Harry Potter. Based on a series of books by Hisashi Suzuki.

MAGICAL WITCH ACADEMY

2007. JPN: *Magical Witch Academy Boku to Sensei no Magical Lesson: The Animation*. AKA: *Magical Witch Academy My Teacher's Magical Lesson the Animation*. Video. DIR: Eiyu Ura. SCR: Shinichiro Sawayama. DES: Kenchi Hattori, Shanghai Fukuoka. ANI: Kenchi Hattori. MUS: Haruka Takimoto. PRD: Atelier Kaguya, Pink Pineapple. 28 mins. x 2 eps.
In a world where magic is common, Tsukasa Strobilanthus has a big problem—Mystic Eyes. He only has to take off his glasses and look at a girl for her to turn into a raging lust-crazed creature. So he's sent to a special magic school to learn to control this power. He's the only boy at the school, and as soon as he takes off his glasses he's molested by his classmates and teacher. The principal is concerned that she might have to kill him to protect the other students, but when he overhears this, it triggers his transformation into a tentacle monster and mass rape ensues. Based on a porn game by Atelier Kaguya. **NV**

MAGICAL WITCH PUNIE-CHAN *

2006. JPN: *Dai Maho Toge*. AKA: *Great Magical Gap*. Video. DIR: Tsutomu Mizushima. SCR: Tsutomu Mizushima. DES: Satoshi Isono, Toru Koga, Yuya Kusumoto. ANI: Satoshi Isono, Shigeru Ishii, Naoki Yamauchi, et al. MUS: Ryuji Takagi. PRD: Studio Barcelona. 12 mins. x 8 eps., 1 min. x 4 eps.
Punie-chan is next in line to the throne of the Magical Land. To inherit, she has to successfully complete a year on Earth, so she transfers to a high school in Japan. Although she may appear to be a sweet, charming girl, she's really a vicious and cruel creature who won't hesitate to wreak violence both physical and magical on anyone who displeases her. Not surprisingly, there are plenty of opponents who want her dead, including local punks, her older sisters, and her magical mascot sidekick,

forcibly abducted from Mascot Village.

Adapted from Hideki Owada's 2002 manga, this story's ruthless *realpolitik* would give that renowned right-winger Robert Heinlein pause and makes the political machinations of *Game of Thrones* look almost fluffy. The low budget and short running time don't stop director Mizushima from packing this utterly heartless show with ideas, nudges, nods, and winks to mainstream movies and magical girl shows alike. If you've never before seen the connection between the iron-willed Fairy Queen in **MAGICAL FAIRY PERSIA** and the insane Colonel Kurtz in Francis Ford Coppola's *Apocalypse Now* (1979), be prepared to find out. Four clips of between one and two minutes were added to the original DVD release in Japan, though not in the U.S., and are collectively titled *Dai Maho Toge Omake.* **V**

MAGIKANO *
2006. TV series. DIR: Seiji Kishi. SCR: Hideki Mitsui. DES: Takashi Kobayashi. ANI: Takashi Kobayashi. MUS: Katsuyuki Harada. PRD: Tokyo Kids, AT-X. 25 mins. x 13 eps.
Cynically but successfully rehashing almost every cliché in modern anime in one giant pudding, *Magikano* stars the geeky Haruo Yoshikawa, a clueless boy unaware that his three cute sisters are witches. They have shielded him from all knowledge of magic and the sorcerous realm, which becomes increasingly difficult when Ayumi Mamiya, yet another witch, arrives at their house to be a maid. Ever since looking into an old mirror as a child, Ayumi has suffered from a curse that only Haruo can lift, and she has been ordered to work in his house until she can awaken his own latent powers and get him to dispel it. His sisters, however, are deeply suspicious of her motives. Crushingly predictable geek-girl-witch-maid-harem high jinks ensue.

MAGIPOKA
2006. JPN: *Renkin 3-kyu Magical? Pokahn*. TV Video. DIR: Kenichi Yagatai. SCR: Yasunori Ide. DES: Katsuzo Hirata, Ayu Kawamoto. ANI: Katsuzo Hirata. MUS: Noriyasu Agematsu. PRD: REMIC, Magipoka Group, Media Factory, GENCO, Nippon Shuppan Hanbai. 24 mins. x 12 eps. (TV), 24 mins. x 3 eps. (v).
A plotless porn comedy depicting the adventures of four princesses from the

World Below—witch, vampire, werewolf, and android. We weren't sure how androids became creatures of the night, but then we remembered the lyrics from *The Rocky Horror Picture Show* that tie them in to the late-night horror movie mythology. The girls live in Garakuta House, which is a homage to the author of the same name, and have the usual adventures while adapting to the human world—stripping in overheated elevators, visiting the beach, going to a hot springs resort where *tanuki* steal their clothes, discussing **HORROR AND MONSTERS**, and so on. Three video episodes were added to the DVD release. Garakuta House wrote the eponymous manga, with art by Jacky Dorei. **O**

MAGNOS *
1976. JPN: *Magne Robo Ga[thering] Keen*. TV series. DIR: Tomoharu Katsumata, Masayuki Akehi, Teppei Matsuura. SCR: Hiroyasu Yamaura, Tomohiro Ando, Keisuke Fujikawa, Hiroyuki Hoshiyama. DES: Kazuo Komatsubara. ANI: Kazuo Komatsubara, Toshio Nitta, Yoshinori Kanemori. MUS: Michiaki Watanabe. PRD: Japad, Toei, TV Asahi. 25 mins. x 39 eps.
The alien Izzard, former rulers of Earth, have been sleeping beneath its surface for the last two million years. Now they have awakened, and only Professor Hanatsuki of the Earth Research Institute can stop them. Luckily, he has the required teen assistants, including his daughter, Mai, and a square-jawed man named Takeru, who pilot the combining robot Ga Keen. Though Takeru is the nominal hero, the robot cannot move without Mai's presence—that's nepotism for you. A follow-up to the similar **STEEL JEEG**, reputedly released in the U.S. in a feature-length dub under the *Magnos* title around 1984.

MAHJONG QUEST
1992. Video. DIR: Maru-chan Program Suru. SCR: Kaneyama 6800. DES: ARG, Gekitsuio, Tattakatta. ANI: N/C. MUS: Pinch Pinch. PRD: Kaneyama 6800. 43 mins.
Animated sequences as part of a how-to guide to completing the simulation game *Mahjong Quest*, in which the player gets to see all 25 nubile opponents as well as the ending of the game, for those who weren't good enough to finish it by themselves. Bonus footage of the girls only just qualifies

this release as an anime, as opposed to a rather futile spin-off from a video game.

MAHORABA
2005. AKA: *Heartful Days*. TV series. DIR: Shinichiro Kimura. SCR: Yasutomo Yamada, Junichi Shintaku, Koichi Taki, Masaharu Amiya, Shoichi Sato. DES: Masahiro Fujii. ANI: Masahiro Fujii, Hidetoshi Sano, Ryoichi Oki. MUS: Anne. PRD: JC Staff, TV Tokyo, Square Enix, Starchild Records. 24 mins. x 26 eps.
Ryushi Shiratori moves into an apartment complex when he comes to Tokyo to learn how to be a children's book illustrator. There, he finds himself commuting between the two communities of his art school and his dorm, as an unexpected link between the two very different groups. He also finds himself falling for his landlady Kozue, whose multiple personality disorder means that she functions as a one-woman harem (**ROMANCE AND DRAMA**). Not to be confused with **MABORAHO** or **MAHOROMATIC**, or indeed with **MAISON IKKOKU**, with which it has many obvious similarities. Based on the manga by Akira Kojima, which ran in *Gangan Wings* from 2000 to 2006.

MAHOROMATIC *
2001. TV series, TV special. DIR: Hiroyuki Yamaga. SCR: Hiroyuki Yamaga. DES: Kazuhiro Takamura. ANI: Kazuhiro Takamura. MUS: Toshio Masuda. PRD: Gainax, Shaft, BS-i. 25 mins. x 12 eps., (TV1), 25 mins. x 14 eps. (TV2), 24 mins. (special).
After long and faithful service as a Vesper Hyper Soldier fighting alien invaders in outer space, android Mahoro V1046 is permitted to choose her retirement posting. In a triumph for female subservience, she elects to live at her former commanding officer's house and work as a maid for his teenage son. However, her retirement is short-lived, not only because she is told to expect only 350 remaining operational days, but also because menaces keep on arriving and forcing her to blow her mundane cover. *Mahoromatic* channels chunks of the same studio's **GUNBUSTER**, with bawdy gags about breasts, self-consciously silly poetry, and the constant threat of alien attack forcing Mahoro to come out of retirement, its heroine a disposable girlfriend with a ticking time limit, like the famous **LIMIT THE MIRACLE GIRL**.

When Japanese boys are Suguru's age, a "350-day" deadline isn't the time limit on a robot girlfriend; it's a reminder that college exams and the adult responsibilities that follow are less than a year away. Deep down, with its schooldays nostalgia and its ticking time limit, *Mahoromatic* is *really* about that other perennial Gainax subject—staying forever young.

In a "twist" reminiscent of TENCHI MUYO!, a second robot companion arrived for the sequel series *M: Something More Beautiful* (2002). The one-shot *Mahoromatic Summer Special* (2003) features a decision by the "girls" to hunt down and destroy every one of the boys' pornographic magazines, leading to a light-hearted variant on the themes of treasurehunting and saving the world. Based on the manga in *Comic Gamu* by Monjuro Nakayama and Bow Ditama.

MAHYA THE SERVANT *

2001. JPN: *Maid Meshimase Mahya*. Video. DIR: N/C. SCR: N/C. DES: N/C. ANI: N/C. MUS: N/C. PRD: Princess Productions, Obtain. 30 mins.

Embittered, hard-up college student Takahata realizes it's his lucky day when Mahya turns up at his door. She is a new hireling of an erotic maid service, commissioned by a Professor *Takada* to come and clean the place while not wearing any underwear. Takahata neglects to tell her that she's got the wrong house and proceeds to put her in a series of humiliating situations in order to get an eyeful, while trying to come up with insidious and frankly puerile ways to get around the No Touching clause in her contract. This anime is also inadvisable viewing for anyone who likes eels, since it depicts these poor creatures going where no eels have gone before; compare to BLOOD ROYALE, which tries similar tricks with an octopus. 🅛🅝

MAI MAI MIRACLE *

2009. JPN: *Mai Mai Shinko to Sennen no Maho*. AKA: *Mai Mai Shinko and the Millennium-Old Magic*. Movie. DIR: Sunao Katabuchi. SCR: Sunao Katabuchi. DES: Shigeto Tsuji, Shinichi Uehara. ANI: Shigeto Tsuji, Chie Uratani, Kazutaka Ozaki. MUS: Minako Obata, Shusei Murai. PRD: Madhouse Studios, avex entertainment, KRY Yamaguchi, Shochiku. 93 mins.

Feisty nine-year-old Shinko believes that her cowlick of hair—which she called "maimai"—enables her to connect with the past. She believes that she can see what happened a thousand years ago on the land her family still farms. It's 1955. Change is spreading from the big cities into rural Japan, but the pace is slow. When shy city girl Kiko moves to the remote village with her doctor father, she and Shinko forge a friendship over one magical summer that helps them face the changing future; but not even a child's ability to morph reality into magic can shield them from the harshness of life.

This enchanting film based on Nobuko Takagi's novel was directed and written by Studio Ghibli collaborator Sunao Katabuchi. It stands firmly on turf that Ghibli's founder directors have staked out as their own: nostalgia for a remembered childhood and a half-imagined history, a leap of faith across the gap between everyday life and true magic, the small joys and sorrows of a country childhood, the darkness that lurks at the heart of life.

Director Katabuchi is no mere imitator. He brings his own vision and voice to this story. His sensitivity, ability to ground magic in reality without reducing it to tinsel, and sheer sense of fun make it unique. For all the gilding, softening effect of present-day nostalgia (FROM UP ON POPPY HILL, SHOWA STORY), the Showa period was a difficult time of change, challenge, and contrast. Japan was still recovering from a terrible war and the devastating poverty it created. Shinko and her friends are now Japan's sprightly present-day 60-somethings, the generation born in the last years of war and the Occupation, who have lived through Japan's resurgence from atomic devastation to see this film with their own grandchildren. Today, a real-life Shinko would look back to her nine-year-old self and reflect on how far both she and Japan have come since 1955. So the film is both a historical adventure for modern nine-year-olds, and an exercise in nostalgia for their grandparents. It succeeds admirably in both areas, and it's beautiful.

MAI'S MAGIC AND FAMILY DAYS

2011. JPN: *Mai no Maho to Katei no Hi*. TV Special. DIR: Masayuki Yoshihara. SCR:

Shotaro Suga. DES: Hiromi Makino, Masayuki Yoshihara. ANI: N/C. MUS: eufonius. PRD: T2 Studio, P.A. Works. 29 mins.

Mai Tatsumi has magical powers, but she doesn't use them for fighting; instead the second-grader uses them to understand others' feelings. Her mother (voiced by Sumi Shimamoto, who played NAUSICAÄ OF THE VALLEY OF THE WIND) and grandmother (Mami Koyama, the voice of Minky Momo—see GIGI AND THE FOUNTAIN OF YOUTH) help her to understand the importance of family ties in this TV special made with funding from the local authorities in Toyama Prefecture.

MAICO 2010

1998. AKA: *Androidana Maico 2010; Android Announcer*. TV series. DIR: Kozo Masanari. SCR: Toshimitsu Shimizu. DES: Keiichi Ishiguro. ANI: Keiichi Ishiguro. MUS: N/C. PRD: Pony Canyon, WOWOW. 8 mins. x 24 eps.

In 2010, Nippon Broadcasting tries to increase its ratings by employing Maico the android as a broadcaster. An adaptation of a popular story also made into a radio drama and manga, based on an idea by AIRBATS-creator Toshimitsu Shimizu.

MAID IN HEAVEN SUPER S *

2005. Video. DIR: Kurige Katsura. SCR: Kurige Katsura. DES: Masahide Yanasawa. ANI: Masahide Yanasawa. MUS: N/C. PRD: Green Bunny. 30 mins. x 2 eps.

A Japanese boy is very surprised by the sudden appearance of a maid at his messy apartment. She sets about servicing both the apartment and its owner, and eventually turns out to have been a childhood friend of his, conditioned by something he once said into a career choice that would allow her to seduce him once she was old enough. LOVE HINA meets MAHYA THE SERVANT, in an erotic anime based on the remake version of a computer game by Pil/Stone Heads, the creators of SEXFRIEND. In an interesting experiment, the single story has two language tracks, one standard and one incorporating the inner monologue of one of the characters. This technique was employed in both the Japanese and English editions. 🅝🅥

MAID SAMA *

2010. JPN: *Kaicho wa Maid-Sama*. AKA: *The Boss Is a Maid*. TV series. DIR: Hiroaki

Sakurai. scr: Mamiko Ikeda, Reiko Yoshida, Masahiro Yokotani, Masaharu Amiya. des: Yuki Imoto. ani: Yuki Imoto, Shuichi Hara, Masayuki Onchi. mus: Wataru Maeguchi. prd: JC Staff. Geneon, Hakuensha. 24 mins. x 26 eps.

Misaki Ayuzawa has worked her way to the top—she's the first female student council president at a former boys' school, now co-educational. It hasn't been easy winning the respect of the whole student body and she rules the school with an iron hand. But she has a secret. Her mother barely has enough money to make ends meet for Misaki and her younger sister. Misaki only enrolled at the school because the fees were cheap. To make ends meet, she works part-time at a maid café. Naturally this would completely wreck her image at school, so when her hunky classmate Takami Usui finds out, she's open to blackmail. But he finds her really intriguing, despite her stern demeanor, and the price of his silence is just spending some time with him. Through him and her classmates, as well as her coworkers at the café, Misaki begins to learn better ways to deal with people in this slight but charming romantic comedy based on Hiro Fujiwara's 2005 manga.

MAIDEN INFRINGEMENT PLAY

2010. jpn: Otome Jurin Yugi: Disgrace Return Play. Video. dir: Hiromi Yokoyama. scr: Ren Soto. des: Si Min Lee. ani: Satan Ototoro. mus: N/C. prd: Suzuki Mirano. 30 mins. x 2 eps.

Two pretty young friends think they've won a prize—a week at a summer resort. But Ibuki and Akira are the victims of a cruel trick by their fellow students, led by wealthy Shuji. They end up prisoners and he has a week to turn them into sex slaves. Based on a porn game by Guilty, and part of the same franchise as MAIDEN SHAME GAME. **ⓝⓥ**

MAIDEN OF ... *

1998. jpn: Kai no Naka no Kotori. aka: Little Bird in the Shell; The Maiden Diaries. Video. dir: Hideki Takayama. scr: Masateru Tsuruoka. des: N/C. ani: Hirota Shindo, Makoto Yoshizaki. mus: N/C. prd: Discovery, Seven Eight. 35 mins. x 5 eps. (v1), 30 mins. x 2 eps. (v2).

An original take on the anime porn genre, set in 19th-century Europe, where a secret society exerts political power, controlling important figures by using a ring of professionally trained prostitutes. The ring is eventually disbanded, but Foster, the man in charge, is approached some time later by Dread Burton, a railroad tycoon who wants him to train maids to perform very particular duties—cooking, cleaning, and *submitting*. A surprisingly old-fashioned and distinctly British tale of poor waifs abused by rich cads, based on a computer game.

In the tradition of the TALES OF ... series Kitty Films renamed the separate episodes *Maiden of Deception, ... Desire, ... Decadence,* and *... Destruction*. The second episode was not released in the U.S. due to the appearance of an underage character. The series was subsequently rereleased under the umbrella title *The Maiden Diaries*, although its final episodes, *Maiden of Deliverance* (released as a separate DVD), had no relation to the franchise in Japan. Instead, it was a retitling of *Song of the Baby Bird* (2000, *Hinadori no Saezuri*), another entry from the DISCOVERY SERIES, of which the original *Maiden Diaries* are also a part. Although the original mansion was seen burning to the ground in the original series, it has now been fully rebuilt, just in time for the arrival of Carol, a spoiled railway tycoon's daughter who is accompanied by her "friend" Liz. Liz is in fact the anime's CINDERELLA figure, a girl pressed into service to Carol's family to pay off her own debts, and whose flirting with Foster the manservant causes Carol to order her degradation. Dungeon domination duly develops. **ⓛⓝⓥ**

MAIDEN ROSE

2009. jpn: Hyakujitsu no Bara. Video. dir: Hidefumi Takagi. scr: Hajime Otani, Yukari Enatsu. des: Mayuko Nakano, Kazuo Watanabe. ani: Mayuko Nakano. mus: Masaaki Mori. prd: Prime Time, Amumo. 30 mins x 5 eps. (v), 5 mins. x 2 eps.

The world has been at peace for a hundred years when the European empire breaks the truce and begins to invade its neighbors. Taki and Klaus are officers fighting the Empire, even though Klaus was born European. But he's bound to Taki by passion, and the price of his continued loyalty is Taki's body. Based on the manga by Fusanosuke Inariya, and suffering like most short series from restrictions of time and budget. Two five-minute bonuses on the DVD feature the protagonists as cute furries—Taki a cat and Klaus a dog. **ⓝⓥ**

MAIDEN SHAME GAME

2010. jpn: Otome Chibaku Yugi. Video. dir: Hitomi Yokoyama. scr: Ahiru Koike. des: Kimiko Mitsui. ani: Katsuyu Shimizu. mus: N/C. prd: Suzuki Mirano. 28 mins. X 2 eps.

Elite students at a high school are raped by a fellow-student—or at least, by someone wearing their school uniform. He threatens to put the videos online if they don't help him get his next victim, and they all agree. Based on a porn game by Guilty. **ⓝⓥ**

MAIDS IN DREAM *

2003. Video. dir: Genzo Sugiyama, Yoshikazu Yabe, Naomi Hayakawa. scr: Rokutaro Makabe. des: Okami Asaoki. ani: Mizuho Haku. mus: N/C. prd: Lemon Heart, Picol. 30 mins. x 2 eps.

A nameless man, later calling himself Akio, wakes up in a bed in a secluded mansion, unaware of who he is or how he got there. He is told by pretty head maid Suzuran that he is in a place beyond the boundaries of the real world and that he must remain there until he has worked through his personal issues, although since he can't remember anything, he must wait for his memory to return. He is haunted by dreams of a girl with purple hair, but soon begins fantasizing about the maids who work at the house. Before long, he is putting his fantasies into action and "punishing" the maids for a series of misdeeds, real and imagined (much to the maids' pleasure, and to his guilt). TENCHI MUYO! with bondage, based on the PC game by Lune. **ⓛⓝⓥ**

MAID-SISTER

2011. jpn: Maid-Ane. Video. dir: Onijima. scr: Hideo Kobayashi. des: N/C. ani: Heki nei. mus: N/C. prd: Digital Works. 27 mins. x 2 eps.

Aki comes back to her home in the country after working in Tokyo as a maid. Her childhood friend Yuta is glad to see her again, but begins thinking of her in a whole different light, probably because he's watched too many porn anime and thinks all maids are easy. Based on the manga by Tuna Empire—and we didn't make that up, it's a proper TRANSLATION for Maguro Mikuni. Part of the VANILLA SERIES. Ⓝ

MAIL ORDER MAIDEN 28 *

1995. JPN: *Nankyoku 28-go.* AKA: *South Pole #28; Dutch Wife 28.* Video. DIR: Hiroshi Midoriyama. SCR: Hogara Hatta. DES: Hachi-ko. ANI: Shinya Sasaki, Genichi Murakami. MUS: N/C. PRD: Sente Studio. 38 mins.
Based on a manga by TALES OF ...–creator U-jin and pastiching GIGANTOR (i.e., *Tetsujin 28*), this obscure porn title features Aiwa, a typical anime geek, who orders a sex doll and gets more than he bargained for. He opens the package to discover Satomi, a lifelike, sex-crazy android, whose being a robot is a thin excuse for portraying a character who would be otherwise underage. Wild sex ensues, though Aiwa still yearns for his "real" ladylove, the innocent Kozue, who will surely never speak to him again unless he can find Satomi's off-button before she arrives. A predictable rehash of VIDEO GIRL AI, with the flimsy plot papered over, as in ADVENTURE KID, by the hiring of a famous starlet to provide a voice, in this case Mika Yoshino of the "Giri Giri Girls." Ⓝ

MAISON EN PETITS CUBES, LA *

2008. JPN: *Tsumiki no Ie.* Movie. DIR: Kunio Kato. SCR: Kenya Hirata. DES: Kunio Kato. ANI: Kunio Kato, Yoshie Fujiwara, Kohei Morikawa, Yu Maeda, Maya Asakura. MUS: Kenji Kondo. PRD: Oh! Production, Robot. 12 mins.
An old man lives in a town which is gradually vanishing under water. He builds more and more floors onto his home to stay above the rising tide. When he accidentally drops his favorite pipe, he decides to rent scuba diving gear to search for it—but as he sinks into the water and through his past, he uncovers submerged memories. Kunio Kato's melancholy meditation on time and memory won the 2009 Oscar for Best Animated Short Film, but since it was made on company time at his day job at the production company Robot, if he wants to visit his Academy Award, he has to book an appointment with his boss.

MAISON IKKOKU *

1986. TV series, movie, TV special, video.

DIR: Kazuo Yamazaki, Naoyuki Yoshinaga, Osamu Sekita, Setsuko Shibuichi. SCR: Tokio Tsuchiya, Shigeru Yanagawa, Kazunori Ito, Hideo Takayashiki, Tomoko Konparu. DES: Yuji Moriyama, Akemi Takada. ANI: Masaaki Kannan, Keiko Hattori, Ryunosuke Otonashi. MUS: Takuo Sugiyama. PRD: Kitty, Fuji TV. 25 mins. x 96 eps., 90 mins. (m1), 25 mins. x 96 eps. (TV), 65 mins. (m2), 91 mins. (v1), 30 mins. (v2), 27 mins. (v3), 27 mins. (v4).
While he waits for the chance to retake his university entrance exams, Yusaku Godai lives in the Maison Ikkoku dormitory, a strange place peopled by the party-loving Hanae Ichinose, perverse Yotsuya, and free-spirited club hostess Akemi. But Godai soon falls for the new apartment manager, the pretty widow Kyoko Otonashi—a courtship dogged by troubles from the other tenants and from the pressure brought by Godai's rival for her affections, Mitaka.

A popular manga from URUSEI YATSURA–creator Rumiko Takahashi, the story is highly regarded among her works, not the least because it has a beginning, a middle, and an end, and not the interminable repetition of RANMA ½. *MI* was troubled by early problems—the character designs were changed twice before it truly got underway. It is worth the wait, however, and is an attractive, touching EVERYDAY ANIME drama that shares a special place in fans' hearts alongside KIMAGURE ORANGE ROAD, a similar tale of almost-unattainable love. The series eventually ends with the movie version *MI: Final Chapter* (*MI: Kanketsuhen*), in which plans for the long-awaited wedding are thwarted by whispered rumors that have Godai believing that Kyoko is hiding an incriminating letter from him. Capping the story while the TV series was still running, the movie also featured a cameo from the mystery inhabitant of Room Two, unseen in the TV series.

This was followed by several video outings. Later in 1988 *MI: Through the Passing of the Seasons* (*MI: Utsuriyuku Kisetsu no Naka de*) was released, recapping the TV series with recycled footage plus some new animation, and concentrating on Godai and Kyoko's relationship. A music video compilation, *MI Karaoke Music Parade* (1989), collected all of the opening and ending songs. Two years would pass before a vacation special, Setsuko

Shibuichi's *MI: Side Story* (*MI: Ikkoku-to Nanpa Shimatsu Ki*), while 1992 would see *Prelude MI: When the Cherry Blossoms in the Springtime Return* (*Prelude MI: Meguru Haru no Sakura no yo ni*). The series was also adapted into a 1986 live-action film and two live-action TV specials (2007 and 2008), as well as parodied in the live-action erotic video *Maison Akiho* (2006), featuring video starlet Akiho Yoshizawa.

MAISON PLAISIR *

2002. JPN: *Gekka Bijin.* AKA: *Moon, Flower, Beauty.* Video. DIR: Hisashi Okezawa. SCR: Joichi Michigami. DES: Takanari Hijo. ANI: Yuki Kinoshita. MUS: Sentaro. PRD: Discovery. 30 mins. x 2 eps.
When Seiichi's father discovers him training his stepmother in bondage and submission instead of studying, he throws his wayward son out of the house. Seiji moves into the Kazenaha boarding house and soon discovers that there is a secret crawlspace that allows him to peek in on the other rooms and their attractive occupants. This in turn leads to the discovery that his widowed landlady Miyuki misses the bondage sessions she experienced at the hands of her late husband. Seiichi assists her in getting over her grief to the extent that she can urinate on a picture of her late husband while tied up—it's hardly MAISON IKKOKU! Then Seiichi's stepmother finds his new address and comes to visit him with her nubile daughter Kiriko. Scatology and more urine are involved in another entry in the DISCOVERY SERIES. Ⓝ

MAJIKOI! OH SAMURAI GIRLS *

2011. JPN: *Maji de Watashi ni Koi Shinasai!!* AKA: *Majikoi; Seriously, Fall in Love With Me!* TV Series. DIR: Keitaro Motonaga. SCR: Katsuhiko Takayama. DES: Mayumi Watanabe, Yasuhiro Moriki, Hiroshi Ito. ANI: Mayumi Watanabe. MUS: Ryosuke Nakanishi. PRD: lerche, AT-X, GENCO, Lantis, Pony Canyon, T.O. Entertainment, Klockworx. 25 mins. x 12 eps.
The people of Kawakami City don't just revere their samurai ancestors—they want to keep that fighting spirit alive, even in their schools. Yamato and his six friends are a tight-knit, inseparable group who have known each other from childhood and even have their own "secret base," but when they welcome two new girls into the

second year, things start to change. The secret perversions hidden under the samurai ethic begin to emerge—well, in a town with a penis festival you have to expect it—and the established relationships between the original guys and girls are challenged. Based on a porn video game (or adult visual novel, if you prefer, see ARGOT AND JARGON) by Minato Soft. **N**

MAJOR

2004. TV series, video. DIR: Kenichi Kasai. SCR: Michihiro Tsuchiya. DES: Masaru Oshiro. ANI: Taro Sato. MUS: Noriyuki Asakura. PRD: Studio Hibari, NHK Enterprise 21, NHK. 25 mins. x 154 eps. (TV), 28 mins. (v1), 28 mins. x 2 eps. (v2).

Widowed pro baseball player Shigeharu Honda struggles to raise his son Goro on his own. Goro aspires to be a baseball player like his father; meanwhile, Goro's school teacher Momoko finds herself falling for Shigeharu, in a baseball romance along the lines of TOUCH or SLOW STEP. Based on the manga in *Shonen Sunday* magazine by Takuya Mitsuda.

MAKAI OJI: DEVILS AND REALIST *

2013. AKA: *Prince of Hell: Devils and Realist.* TV series. DIR: Chiaki Kon. SCR: Chiaki Kon, Michiko Yokote. DES: Kikuko Sadakata. ANI: Hiromi Okazaki, Atsushi Soga, Kikuko Sadakata, Hiroaki Ikeda, Maria Ichino. MUS: Hiroshi Takaki. PRD: Pony Canyon, Sotsu Agency, TV Tokyo, Studio Tulip, Dogakobo. 24 mins. x 12 eps.

Impoverished nobleman William Twining accidentally summons the demon Dantalion (MYSTIC ARCHIVES OF DANTALIAN), who realizes that his new master is a descendant of Solomon, and hence likely to become the Elector—the man who chooses the successor to Satan. A somewhat demonic variation of the harem genre ensues (ROMANCE AND DRAMA), as Heaven tries to get his soul back, while a series of Hellspawn try to get his attention and support in the prospective election, just in case Lucifer fancies a rest. **LNV**

MAKEN-KI BATTLING VENUS *

2011. JPN: *Maken-ki.* TV series, video. DIR: Koichi Ohata, Hiraku Kaneko. SCR: Yosuke Kuroda. DES: Nobuteru Yuki, Tadashi Abiru, Kyo Inoue, Akio Takami. ANI: Nobuteru Yuki, Akatsuki Koshiishi, Masakazu Sunagawa.

MUS: Cher Watanabe. PRD: AIC Spirits, AT-X, Kadokawa Pictures, Klockworx, Xebec. 24 mins. x 12 eps. (TV1), 10 mins. x 6 eps. (v1), ?? mins. x 2 eps. (v2), 24 mins. x 10 eps. (TV2), 5 mins. x 5 eps. (v3).

Takeru Oyama, an average high school pervert, doesn't know that the school he has signed up for specializes in combat and magic. Nor is he expecting three girls to come into his life on day one: the childhood friend he hasn't seen in years (ROMANCE AND DRAMA), the fiancée he never knew he had, and the blonde who wants to exterminate him. In fact, it's really strange how many girls just don't like him. If he could use a Maken, a magical weapon, he'd be fine, but he's the only person in the school who doesn't seem to have any magic ability at all. This show based on Hiromitsu Takeda's manga *Maken-Ki!* was followed with a beach trip video in autumn 2013 and with a second TV series *Maken-Ki Tsu (Two)* in 2014.

MAKI PRODUCTIONS

Often credited as Maki Pro. A titling house that performs a relatively simple process, adding credits to animation or blank screens to make the opening or closing titles. Since all anime have credits, Maki Pro's name appears in a huge number of titles, although its role is limited. We presume that Maki Pro's role may have extended to other forms of effects, known in Japanese as "Ris Work" (ARGOT AND JARGON), such as the addition of mist or fog effects to preexisting film. These jobs, however, are few and far between since the advent of digital animation, allowing most studios to add such effects in-house.

MAKI-CHAN ENTWINED

2012. JPN: *Maki-chan to Nau.* [sic, with period]. AKA:. Video. DIR: Oji Hakudaku. SCR: Takashi Kishitsu. DES: citizen 08. ANI: citizen 08. MUS:. PRD: Collaboration Works, TY Network, Ryuzo Matano. 30 mins. x 3 eps. Maki lives next door to Seiichi. He's always assumed she is very well-bred until he catches her masturbating on the veranda. She admits she's a dirty girl and jokingly suggests to Seiichi that she needs to be blackmailed into being his sex slave. If you have a similar sense of humor you may enjoy this anime based on a porn game by WAFFLE. **N**

MAKOTO-CHAN

1980. Movie. DIR: Tsutomu Shibayama. SCR: Noboru Shiroyama, Masaki Tsuji, Tsunehisa Ito, Tomoko Konparu. DES: Osamu Kobayashi. ANI: Osamu Kobayashi. MUS: Ryo Kawakami. PRD: Tohoku, TMS. 85 mins. Kindergarten kid Makoto tries hard to be a good boy but is dumped by his nursery-school sweetheart, Anko-chan. Walking through the park feeling sorry for himself, he meets Yuko Daiyu, a grown-up who has also just had her heart broken. They get along well with each other, but for Yuko, flirting with a little boy is just a game, and Makoto is soon left heartbroken again. Recovering from the experience, he performs a mini-play for his mother on Mother's Day, looks after some sparrow's eggs, and attempts to win the "Good Child" award at his nursery. An unusual comedy based on the short manga *Small Sweetheart, Mother's Day Present, Love Lunch Pack, Sparrow's Eggs*, and *Good Child Award* by BOY WITH CAT'S EYES–creator Kazuo Umezu, who also sings the theme song with his backing group, the Super Police.

MALICE@DOLL *

2001. Video. DIR: Keitaro Motonaga. SCR: Chiaki Konaka. DES: Shinobu Nishioka, Yasuhiro Moriki. ANI: N/C. MUS: N/C. PRD: @ Entertainment. 30 mins. x 3 eps. In an indeterminate underground realm, robot prostitute Malice goes in search of repairs. Instead, she is ravished by a tentacled beast, and wakes to discover that her previous dollform has been replaced with a living, breathing, feeling body. Initially shunned by her former associates, she soon converts her fellow prostitutes into a similar life-state by kissing them, though the transformation process often leaves them hideously malformed. When even the cynical Doris asks her for a kiss, Malice worries about the aftereffects of the transformation, and goes in search of some way of undoing the spell. In the repair shop, she is told that this is all a dream—a doll dreaming of being human, or a human dreaming of being a doll? Whatever the answer, Malice's spirit escapes from bondage, leaving her former colleagues behind.

Malice Doll cleverly makes virtues out of its many vices. Whereas many late-20th-century anime augmented their cel work with computer graphics, *MD* improves its *digital* animation with the addition of old-fashioned cels, neatly papering over the cracks between the polished yet static images of the dolls—supposedly in a studied jerkiness inspired by the puppet animations of Jan Svankmajer. Chiaki Konaka's script cunningly calls for a virtually expressionless cast, and the animators conceal the shortcomings of their work in copious shadows and montages seemingly inspired by the work of French filmmaker Chris Marker.

Depending on one's point of view, *MD* is either a fairy-tale allegory of the end of childhood, or a misogynist fantasy of redemption through rape—*Pinocchio* for perverts. Its heroine is an unfeeling sextoy, seeking "repair" as oil trickles down her shapely legs; she is haunted by the image of an angelic child and molested by an ithyphallic menace. She wakes after her ordeal to discover that it has made her warmer, more sensitive, and sassy—she is now clad in revealing bad-girl garb, and targeted by a succession of other lustful monsters.

This is not the first time that Konaka has dealt with fetishes and gender issues—*MD* shares several tropes with the writer's earlier work on BUBBLEGUM CRISIS and ARMITAGE III, along with rich pickings for psychiatrists, who will be intrigued to observe the depiction of life itself as a sexual disease.

Missing its original release date, *MD* was crucially delayed just a moment too long. By the time its first episode reached video stores in 2001, Japan was already swept up in hype over the flashier (and immensely more costly) FINAL FANTASY: *The Spirits Within*, and *MD* sank without a trace. That was an unfortunate fate, as *MD*'s artful exploitation of its own limitations makes it an interesting object lesson in low-budget filmmaking. It was eventually released as a single feature, with a misleading "2003" copyright date that only really referred to the date of the feature-length compilation and concealed the fact that, in the fast-moving world of computer animation, *Malice Doll* was already two years behind the times. Note: the "at" symbol in the title is merely a typographical adornment; it was never intended to be pronounced. **NV**

MAMA LOVES POYOPOYOSAURS

1995. JPN: *Mama wa Poyopoyosaurus ga Daisuki*. AKA: *Mom Loves Poyopoyosaurs*. TV series. DIR: Hiroshi Nishikiori, Futa Morita, Shinya Hanai, Masahiro Hosoda, Teppei Matsuura. SCR: Mamiko Ikeda, Minori Ikeno, Tomoko Ishizuka. DES: Takako Aonuma. ANI: Tatsuo Miura, Hiroshi Oikawa, Kenichi Imaizumi, Hirokazu Ishino, Masayuki Hiraoka. MUS: N/C. PRD: TBS, Nippon Animation. 25 mins. x 52 eps.

Cute but high-strung two-year-old Jura Poyota and her elder brother, stolid four-year-old Hyoga, are spoiled rotten by their doting grandparents and often drive their parents crazy, simply by being normal kids. Mom Miki struggles to keep her career as a writer of children's books alongside taking care of her family; husband Gendai does his best to help, but sometimes he drives her as crazy as the children. A modern SAZAE-SAN, based on the best-selling manga by Takako Aonuma, this comedy of family life focuses on raising two children of kindergarten age in modern day Tokyo. Each episode is split into two mini-stories, hence leading to some broadcast lists filing this as a 104-episode show.

MAMA'S A FOURTH GRADER

1992. JPN: *Mama wa Shogaku Yonensei*. TV series. DIR: Chuichi Iguchi, Kazuki Akane, Nobuyuki Kondo, Nana Harada. SCR: Satoshi Nakamura, Tetsuko Watanabe. DES: Sachiko Kamimura. ANI: Yuichi Endo, Kisaraka Yamada, Atsushi Aono. MUS: Hayato Kanbayashi. PRD: Sunrise, Nippon TV. 25 mins. x 36 eps.

Japanese schoolgirl Natsumi gets the fright of her life when her own baby daughter Mirai ("Future") falls through a time warp from 15 years ahead in time. A comedy with elements of the future offspring of SAILOR MOON and the unwilling babysitter of BABY AND ME, but also owing something of a debt to the sequels to *Back to the Future*, which reached Japan around the time of its production. Later episodes veer away from a teen-unwed-mother farce and into science fiction, as Natsumi attempts to return Mirai to her rightful time. Originally intended as a children's series, this thoughtful comedy soon attracted an unexpected adult audience sufficient for it to be nominated for, and subsequently win a Seiun Award. In accepting his prize, director Iguchi pleaded that the work was

not really science fiction, but a comedy that used time paradox as a narrative device, but nobody was going to let him get away with that.

MAMEUSHI-KUN

2007. AKA: *Bean Cow*. TV series. DIR: Kazumi Nonaka. SCR: Hideki Shirane. DES: Momoko Makeuchi, Jiro Kawano. ANI: Momoko Makeuchi, Keiko Yamamoto, Shinichi Suzuki. MUS: Motoyoshi Iwasaki. PRD: TMS. 11 mins. x 52 eps.

A KID'S ANIME series in which a calf as small as a speck of dust and a host of other tiny creatures bounce around the Japanese countryside having adventures. Based on the books by Tadashi Akiyama and originally shown as part of the *Chibi Anime Gekijo* (*Tiny Animation Theater*) anthology show.

MAN WHO CREATED THE FUTURE, THE

2003. JPN: *Asu o Tsukutta Otoko: Tanabe Sakuro to Biwako Sosui*. AKA: *The Man Who Created Tomorrow: Sakuro Tanabe and Biwa Lake Incline*. Movie. DIR: Shinichi Ushiyama. SCR: Jun Sekiguchi. DES: Shungiku Uchida. ANI: Seiji Arihara. MUS: N/C. PRD: Mushi Production. 86 mins.

In 1869, the capital of Japan is relocated to Tokyo, leaving Kyoto as something of a backwater. Concerned over the city's imminent decline, the council proposes to deal with a recurring seasonal water shortage by building a canal to bring fresh water and provide a transport route from Lake Biwa to Kyoto. This was the first domestically run civil engineering project in modern Japan, and thus a suitable subject for educational anime. Twenty-one-year-old engineering student Sakuro Tanabe (1861–1944) outlines the project in his undergraduate thesis, and the president of his college puts his name forward to Governor Kitagaki. Despite strong opposition from local politicians and foreign engineers, the Governor and the young engineer persuade the Meiji government to go ahead, and work commences in 1885. Tanabe and his colleague Bunpei Takagi visit the U.S.A. in 1888 to study the world's first hydroelectric power plant in Colorado, and Tanabe adds such a plant to the canal project. Keage Power Plant is completed in 1891 and still supplies power to Kyoto. The canal, which runs partly underground and partly on a brick aqueduct, is finally completed in 1912. Tanabe later becomes professor of engineering at Kyoto Imperial University. Based on the snappily titled book, *Kyoto Incline Story*, by Yoshiko Tamura, the project obviously pushed all the right buttons—heritage, human interest, a good role model, and national pride. Note the presence of manga artist Uchida, creator of *Minami's Sweetheart* (*DE), in a rare anime staff role—animation being used for all the big-budget Meiji period scenes, while other elements used live actors in taking the history of the canal forward to the present day. Compare to the **STORY OF SUPERCONDUCTORS**.

MANABI STRAIGHT

2007. JPN: *Gakuen Utopia Manabi Straight*. AKA: *High School Utopia Manabi Straight*. TV series, video. DIR: Takayuki Hirao, Takuro Takahashi. SCR: Ryunosuke Kingetsu. DES: Atsushi Ogasawara, Miyuki Onodera. ANI: Atsushi Ogasawara, Takuro Takahashi. MUS: Yasuhiro Misawa. PRD: ufotable, ASCII Media Works, Klockworx, Starchild Records. 24 mins. x 12 eps. (TV), 24 mins. (v).
It's 2035. Japan's birthrate is still falling (**BUBU CHACHA**) and many schools are being closed. Morale among pupils and teachers is low. When Manami Amamiya, nicknamed Manabi, transfers to a new school, she's determined to improve things for everyone and create a livelier atmosphere. She makes a good impression and wins the post of student council president, then realizes she has no idea how to even run a meeting. Luckily she has made good friends who help her out. Oddly enough, all four of them also have names beginning with M. A slice-of-life high school show for people who wish all teenage girls looked as if they were ten years old. It also has a 2007 video release, the obligatory resort-trip story said to be set between episodes six and seven.

MANGA MITO KOMON

1981. TV series. DIR: Kazuyuki Okaseko, Yoshio Nitta, Hiroshi Yoshida. SCR: Tsunehisa Ito, Yoshiaki Yoshida, Masatoshi Fuji. DES: Keisuke Morishita. ANI: Emiko Minowa. MUS: Kentaro Haneda. PRD: Knack, TV Tokyo. 25 mins. x 46 eps.
Though he looks like a humble traveler,

this old man is really Mitsukuni Tokugawa, the shogun's uncle, traveling Japan incognito in the company of some feisty young heroes—sword master Sasaki, mountain-of-a-man Atsumi, ninja-boy Sutemaru (with Junpei his faithful hound), and pretty maiden Okoto. The group wanders the land in search of trouble, cowing its opponents into submission by brandishing Mito's *inro*, a lacquered case bearing the shogun's crest. A remake of a popular live-action TV series, originally based on the novels of Sanjugo Naoki (1891–1934). The story reached its widest audience through a live-action NTV series in 1954, and its incredibly long-running successor on TBS, which lasted from 1969 to 2000 and wore out three leading men (this anime version was made shortly before Eijiro Higashino was replaced by Hikaru Nishimura in the live version). Budgets kept the live-action version to human-interest stories such as corrupt merchants and samurai, but the anime production was able to introduce more fantastic elements from **JAPANESE FOLK TALES**. The same set of legends was a distant inspiration for **SPACE PIRATE MITO** and **ROBOT KING DAIOJA**. See also **SAMURAI GOLD**, another popular story retold in anime form.

MANGA PICTURES OF JAPAN

1977. JPN: *Manga Nihon Emaki*. TV series. DIR: Noboru Ishiguro, Kazuhiko Udagawa, Yasuo Hasegawa. SCR: Kenji Terada, Tomomi Tsutsui. DES: Tsuneo Ninomiya, Kazuo Imura, Takashi Nakamura. ANI: Osamu Kamijo. MUS: Yutaka Masuda. PRD: World Television, Anime Room, TBS. 25 mins. x 46 eps.
Deliberately less faithful to fact than **JAPANESE HISTORY**, this series happily throws in apocryphal anecdotes and legends about the figures it portrays, normally two to an episode. Suitable subjects, famous in Japan though not always famous enough for the internationally minded **GREAT PEOPLE** series, include many figures from the Heike-Genji War, such as woman warrior Tomoe Gozen, doomed samurai flautist Taira no Atsumori, and Nasu no Yoichi, who shot a fan off a pole to preserve Minamoto honor at the battle of Yashima. Other stories depict Anju and Zushio (see **LITTLEST WARRIOR**), Iwami no Jutaro's victory against a giant baboon, and the tale, oft-referenced in anime from **INU YASHA** to

USHIO AND TORA, of Fujita no Tawara's fight with a giant centipede.

MANGIRL *

2013. TV series, video. DIR: Nobuaki Nakanishi. SCR: Reiko Yoshida, Masahiro Yokotani. DES: Yasu. ANI: Shinya Ojiri. MUS: N/C. PRD: Dogakobo, Earth Star Entertainment, AT-X, Sun TV, Tokyo MX TV. 5 mins. x 13 eps. (TV), 8 mins. (v).
Three girls who have never edited a manga magazine before decide that guts and cuteness will be all it takes, in a series of short gag-based observational skits, as if **BAKUMAN** had been squashed down into cute form and hosed with maple syrup. Writer Yoshida blows the dust off a few situations from her earlier work on **K-ON**, as the trio cluelessly blunder through the manga business, and somehow make it. The Blu-ray release included a previously unaired episode. Imagine our surprise when it turned out to be a story that levered the girls into swimsuits.

MANGLOBE

The Manglobe company was formed in 2002 by two producers from the Sunrise corporation (best known for **GUNDAM**). Like Production I.G, Manglobe comprised a team from a larger studio working in an experimental medium—their first work was the net cartoon *Trip Trek* in 2003, before their landmark **SAMURAI CHAMPLOO**, which retold old sword-fighting clichés with a sarcastic, sassy modern touch. The studio followed this with works such as **ERGO PROXY** and **SACRED BLACKSMITH**. The company has often collaborated with the studios Bones and Xebec—the former a spin-off from Sunrise, the latter a spin-off from Production I.G, forming just one of many invisible connections within the Japanese animation business.

MAN-MAID

2011. JPN: *Otoko no Ko Ojosama—Hikaru to Ayana no Himitsu Collection*. AKA: *Boy Young Lady—Hikaru and Ayana's Secret Collection*. Video. DIR: Tsuyoshi, Akira Onoda. SCR: N/C. DES: Takumi Torikoshi. ANI: Eiichi Tokura. MUS: Mizuki Tomoeta. PRD: ChiChi no Ya. 16 mins.
Hikaru is a young servant in Ayana's household. He looks about ten years old and very feminine, so Ayana enjoys dressing him up as a girl. She also enjoys using

him as a sex toy because one part of his anatomy is neither girly nor childlike. ⦿

MANMARU THE NINJA PENGUIN
1997. JPN: *Ninpen Manmaru*. TV series. DIR: Tetsuo Yasumi. SCR: Haruya Yamazaki, Ayako Okina, Masaaki Sakurai. DES: Yuichiro Miyoshi. ANI: Nobuhiro Okaseko, Yoshio Kabashima. MUS: N/C. PRD: Shinei, TV Asahi. 10 mins. x 48 eps.
Manmaru goes to ninja school at Nenga, where foxes and raccoons study the art of assassination under a bear ninja master. He is soon thrown into local rivalry between the Nenga school, the Koga (monkeys), and the Iga (dogs), as well as facing temptations from the Dobe, a group of dropouts from the Nenga. A lighthearted adaptation of ninja folktales, based on a manga by Mikio Igarashi, creator of **BONOBONO**.

MAN'S AN IDIOT!
1970. JPN: *Otoko do Aho Koshien*. AKA: *Koshien's an Idiot*. TV series. DIR: Akira Nono. SCR: Tatsuo Tamura, Tadaaki Yamazaki. DES: Shiro Tamura. ANI: Shiro Tamura. MUS: Mamoru Sasaki. PRD: Nippon TV. 25 mins. x 26 eps.
Koshien Fujimura is named after the semiannual high school baseball championship, so it's only natural that he grows up to be absolutely crazy about the sport. Failing a school entrance exam because he has been training too hard, he ends up at party-school Nanba High. Befriending ace catcher Mametan, he decides to join his new school's baseball team but faces opposition from the bad boys of the school. Based on a manga by **DOKABEN**-creator Shinji Mizushima, working with Mamoru Sasaki. The original manga has more space to tell the story of Koshien's family and school life; the anime leaves his parents out altogether and ends with his first year in high school. The anime was originally shown in short segments, every night but Sunday.

MANUAL OF NINJA MARTIAL ARTS
1967. JPN: *Ninja Bugeicho*. Movie. DIR: Nagisa Oshima. SCR: Nagisa Oshima, Mamoru Sasaki. DES: Sanpei Shirato. ANI: Akira Takada (photography). MUS: Hikaru Hayashi. PRD: Sozosha. 117 mins.
A barely animated adaptation of Sanpei

Shirato's long-running manga tale retelling the life of Kagemaru, a charismatic ninja leader in Muromachi period Japan. Shirato's art is shown in still montages shot by a rostrum camera. The film was directed by Nagisa Oshima, also known for *Merry Christmas, Mr. Lawrence, Gohatto*, and *In the Realm of the Senses*, and its use of "inanimate animation" was later parodied in the opening sequence to Yoichi Sai's live-action movie *Kamui* (2009).

MANXMOUSE ∗
1979. JPN: *Tondemonezumi Dai Katsu-yaku*. AKA: *Overactive Mouse; Legend of Manxmouse; Adventures of Manxmouse*. TV special. DIR: Hiroshi Saito. SCR: Hiroshi Saito. DES: Yasuji Mori, Yoshiyuki Momose. ANI: Yoshiyuki Momose, Noriko Moritomo. MUS: Akira Nakagawa. PRD: Nippon Animation, Fuji TV. 84 mins.
Meyer the English village potter creates a mouse when drunk one night, but the blue, long-eared, tailless Manxmouse comes to life. Setting out to see the world, he leaves Buntingdowndale and is warned on several occasions to beware of the Manx Cat. After helping rescue a friendly circus tiger, Burra Khan, from crooked London pet shop owner Mr. Petman, Manxmouse confronts the fearsome Manx Cat, who turns out to be a gentlemanly creature who invites him to tea. The two decide to stay friends, in contravention of the traditional antagonism between their species as set down in the ancient Book of Destiny. Based on the book by Paul Gallico, written to entertain the late Grace Kelly (Princess Grace of Monaco, see **CASTLE OF CAGLIOSTRO**) after she gave him one of the first model mice she made in pottery class.

MANY DREAM JOURNEYS OF MEME, THE
1983. JPN: *Meme Iroiro Yume no Tabi*. TV series. DIR: Yoshio Kuroda, Kazuyoshi Yokota, Takayoshi Suzuki. SCR: Yoshio Kuroda, Nobuyuki Isshiki. DES: Shuichi Seki. ANI: Sadahiko Sakamaki. MUS: Takeo Watanabe. PRD: Nippon Animation, TBS. 25 mins. x 127 eps.
Daisuke and Sayaka explore the world of science, accompanied by Meme the pixie, who has popped out of their computer screen. In the second season, starting with episode 51, they were replaced by a coterie

of seven children who spend more time solving mysteries, but the series still had a heavily educational angle, as one might expect for something originally designed to promote the Tsukuba Science Expo.

MAO-CHAN ∗
2002. JPN: *Rikujo Boeitai Mao-chan*. AKA: *Land Defense Force Mao-chan*. TV series. DIR: Yoshiaki Iwasaki. SCR: Yosuke Kuroda. DES: Masahide Yanagisawa. ANI: Yoshio Suzuki. MUS: Takayuki Hattori. PRD: Pioneer, Xebec, TV Tokyo. 12 mins. x 26 eps.
Japan's Self-Defense Forces have often been rolled out in anime and science fiction, instructed to save the world from all kinds of dangers, from Godzilla to the attacking angels of **EVANGELION**. But not all alien menaces require the SDF's full level of firepower. Mao Onigawara, AKA Mao-chan, is a cute preteen girl whose grandfather happens to be the Chief of Staff for the Land Defense Unit. Dressed inexplicably like drum majorettes, she and her fellow girls deal with the cuter forms of alien invasion. As insanely over-privileged military brats, they get to do so by flying 1:1-scale model kits into battle, although their foes often turn out to be incredibly cute, fluffy aliens, which can often be dealt with by the simple expedient of tapping them on the head with a baton.

Each comes down from space in a toy capsule, which breaks open once safely in the atmosphere; then the being inside floats down to Earth on a candy-colored parachute. So far, the invaders haven't actually done anything more evil than crowd out tourist spots, and there is minimal public support for the use of force against these endearing aliens; the authorities have to fight cute with cute. As in certain other shows that take themselves a little more seriously, the answer lies in using the aliens' own weaponry against them, mainly through badges made of retrieved alien material. Shaped like clovers with smiley faces, these "chibi SMA" items react to the power of the universe and the fighting spirit of the wearer, enabling her to transform.

A cheerful parody of anime's alien invasion excesses, this show also includes several walk-on cameos for cast members from creator Ken Akamatsu's earlier **LOVE HINA**, although their identity is often masked for copyright reasons. Where once anime sought to allegorize the trauma of Japan's defeat in a terrible war, it now sanitizes and homogenizes it all to look like a glorified treasure hunt out of **POKÉMON**. The aliens, however, are smarter than they look and have infiltrated major positions of power and influence, like the student council presidency of Mao-chan's high school. However, when the aliens' reaction when found out and told how naughty it is to invade is to apologize and go away, a bloodbath is never in the cards. Even their supposedly evil emperor, Galaxy King, is a Pillsbury doughboy who just says "Oh!" and steams gently when defeated. Silly and sweet.

MAPLE COLORS *

2005. Video. DIR: Ryo Kanda. SCR: Yasuyuki Muto. DES: Shiro Shibata. ANI: Shiro Shibata. MUS: N/C. PRD: Cross Net, Image House, Milky, GP Museum Soft. 30 mins. x 2 eps.
Transfer student Ryojiro Saku gets off to a bad start when he is caught committing a violent crime with pretty Mirao Aoi in front of the head of the drama club. In order to save Class 2-B from indefinite suspension, Ryojiro agrees to a contest against the drama club, which somehow means he has to cajole his reluctant classmates into a series of porn performances. Based on a computer game of the same name. ●⚫⚫

MAPLE TOWN STORIES *

1986. JPN: Maple Town Monogatari. TV series, movie. DIR: Junichi Sato, Keiji Hisaoka, Yukio Misawa, Hiroyuki Kadono. SCR: Chifude Asakura, Shigeru Yanagawa, Tomoko Konparu, Keiji Kubota, Keiko Maruo. DES: Tsuneo Ninomiya. ANI: Kazuo Komatsubara, Hiroshi Shidara, Shingo Araki. MUS: Akiko Kosaka. PRD: Toei, TV Asahi. 25 mins. x 52 eps. (TV1), 25 mins. x 44 eps. (TV2, New), 24 mins. (m1), 30 mins. (m2).
Maple Town is a peaceful community of talking animals, where the Hoprabbit family opens a post office. Middle daughter Patty is an innocent female but often caught up in the schemes of the evil Gretel the Wolf. However, Patty is able to triumph with the help of her friends, Bobby the Bear, Diana the Fox, and shy genius Johnny the Dog. A second series, New MS (1987), directed by former lead animator

Hiroshi Shidara, dumped all the characters except Patty and her sister Lolly, who set off on a journey to the southern resort of Palmtown to live with the kindly Nurse Jane. Each of the series also had a movie spin–off, though on available evidence, both "movies" appear to have been TV episodes shown in theaters as part of holiday season multiple bills. The series was a very early job for future **SAILOR MOON**–director Junichi Sato. Shown on Nickelodeon in the U.S.

MAPLESTORY

2007. TV series. DIR: Takaaki Ishiyama, Min Hee Joo. SCR: Toshiki Inoue. DES: Yoshinori Kanemori, Hideyuki Ueno. ANI: Yoshinori Kanemori, Kunihiko Sakurai. MUS: Tomoji Sogawa. PRD: Madhouse Studios, Dentsu, Nexon, TV Tokyo. 25 mins. x 25 eps.
The World Tree protected peace and order for centuries, but ten years ago it self-destructed during an attack by an evil organization called Zakum. Other races blamed the humans for this disaster, and now all the survivors are crammed together on Maple Island. Resources are running low and the various races are constantly fighting one another. Ten-year-old Al, son of a great human warrior, is tired of dressing like a monster to avoid the hatred directed toward humans. With his friend Kino (a mushroom-like monster), magician Nina, and thief Anji, he sets out to find the legendary seeds of the World Tree and revive it. But the evil Zakum have the same idea. Based on the popular South Korean online game of the same name by Nexon, this is a fascinating example of cross-cultural fertilization, but as a game-based quest anime for children it does nothing new. Compare with **BLUE DRAGON**. The authors are unsure as to why leaving out the space between *Maple* and *Story* is really necessary, but that's what the creators have done.

MAPS *

1987. Movie, video. DIR: Keiji Hayakawa. SCR: Kenji Terada. DES: Hatsuki Tsuji. ANI: Hatsuki Tsuji. MUS: Kohei Tanaka. PRD: Studio Gallop (m), KSS (v). 51 mins. (m), 30 mins. x 4 eps. (v).
Teenager Gen Tokishima is abducted with his girlfriend, Hoshimi Kimizuka, by the huge spaceship Lipmira that's shaped

like the body of a beautiful woman. Gen is a "map-man," the last descendant of an ancient tribe, on whose body there is a map of a secret route, the Flowing Light of the Nomad Star Tribe. Accompanied by Lipmira, the female space pirate and electronic brain of the ship, Gen begins a search for the Flowing Light, though the galaxy's treasure hunters are soon hunting him, hoping to swipe his birthright.

An incoherent and badly plotted story, supposedly based on a manga by Yuichi Hasegawa but with characters looking quite different from the original. Lipmira's spaceship, however, is a design triumph—a giant flying statue, inspired by the Spirit of Ecstasy found on the hood of every Rolls Royce automobile. A 1994 video remake, directed by Susumu Nishizawa, was the incarnation released in the U.S.

MÄR *

2005. AKA: Marchen Awakens Romance. TV series. DIR: Masaharu Okuwaki. SCR: Junji Takegami. DES: Toshiyuki Komaru. ANI: Toshiyuki Komaru. MUS: Daisuke Ikeda. PRD: Shogakukan, TV Tokyo. 25 mins. x 102 eps.
Ginta is a loser in our own world who never seems to get anything right, but when he travels through the magical portal into the world Mâr Heaven he discovers that he has incredible powers in a world under threat from the Chess enemy. Although supposedly "based on a manga" by Nobuyuki Anzai in *Shonen Sunday* weekly, *Mâr* has all the hallmarks of a show conceived by a committee, designed to halfheartedly rehash all the standard clichés and create a new franchise for Shogakukan, the publisher who not only owns *Shonen Sunday*, but also the studio behind the 3D CGI transformation sequences and the Business Center credited with arcane "Planning Assistance."

MARCO POLO

1979. JPN: Anime Kiko Marco Polo no Boken. AKA: Anime Journey Adventures of Marco Polo. TV series. DIR: Katsuhiko Fujita, Masami Hata, Kazuyuki Sakai. SCR: Masao Maruyama, Michiru Kaneko, Hideo Takeuchi, Soji Yoshikawa. DES: Akio Sugino. ANI: Masaki Mori, Yoshiaki Kawajiri, Toshio Hirata, Hideo Nishimaki, Hideo Takayanagi. MUS: Takanori Onosaki, Kei Ogura. PRD: MK, NHK Promote Service, NHK. 25 mins. x 43 eps.

When his mother dies in Venice, young Marco must accompany his merchant father Niccolo and uncle Maffeo on a trip along the Silk Road to the mysterious East. Years later, when the travelers' wanderings bring them to China, an older, wiser Marco becomes a trusted adviser to the Great Khan, Kublai. An early collaboration by many of the names who would go on to form the Madhouse Studio, this series depicts the man whose writings on the famous "Land of the Rising Sun" would inspire COLUMBUS to set out in search of it and form the treasure stolen by the master-thief LUPIN III in one of his later TV specials.

MARDOCK SCRAMBLE *
2010. Video. DIR: Susumu Kudo. SCR: Tow Ubukata. DES: Jun Nakai, Shingo Suzuki. ANI: Jun Nakai, Shingo Suzuki. MUS: Conisch. PRD: GoHands, Aniplex. 65 mins., 61 mins., 66 mins.
In the crime-ridden city of Mardock, the shocking murder of a young girl leads the city authorities to pass the law "Scramble 09," permitting the use of previously forbidden techniques and technologies in the apprehension of the killer. The murder victim, Balut, is brought back from the dead with the new ability to manipulate electricity and goes in search of her killer, who is soon revealed as Shell, her former lover, who uses his periodic memory losses as the perfect alibi to shield himself from ever confessing, even inadvertently, to a series of grisly crimes. Based on a novel by author Tow Ubukata, and loaded with a series of egg-related puns that only serve to distract from the hard-boiled (sorry) story. ❤

MARGARET VIDEO SERIES
1993. JPN: Shueisha Margaret Video Series. Video. DIR: Takuji Endo, Tsukasa Abe, Mami Watanabe, Tomihiko Okubo. SCR: Akinori Endo, Kenichi Araki, Tatsuhiko Urahata. DES: Tomihiko Okubo. ANI: Kazuhiro Soeta, Masaru Kitao. MUS: Satoshi Okada. PRD: Madhouse. 40 mins. x 6 eps.
A series of romantic tales, all adapted from manga originally serialized in the girls' magazine Margaret. The first, A-Plus for the Fashion Boy (O-Share Koso wa Hana Maru), based on a manga by Tsueko Ansei, features Hodaka, a successful young businessman whose life is turned upside down when he falls in love with a 14-year-old schoolgirl. Singles, based on a manga by Mari Fujimura, moves the setting to a university, where student Saki is torn with guilt over her feelings for her sister's boyfriend, Yo. She joins the same club to be close to him but is selected to work on a project with another boy, Daichi. Though she feels herself drawn to Daichi, she cannot put thoughts of Yo from her mind. Pops, based on a manga by Aya Ikuemi, is an even simpler tale of teenage angst, as two young students fall in love but must endure the pressures of their studies, the opposition of their parents, and the teasing of their classmates. Sleepless Edo (Oedo wa Nemuranai), based on Moonlit Night: Starry Dawn by Noriko Honda, is a period drama set in the Yoshiwara pleasure district of old Tokyo, where a courtesan, a thief, and a doctor become involved in a love triangle. In Kiss My Eyes (Kiss wa Me ni Shite), based on an original by Noriko Ueda, average schoolgirl Ibuki falls for a handsome exchange student newly arrived from the U.S. For the final episode, A-Girl, based on a manga by Fusako Kuramochi, sisters Mariko and May, along with Mariko's bad-tempered boyfriend, become involved with Ichiro, an arrogant, womanizing male model. At the artist's request, A-Girl was shown with subtitles, but no dialogue.

MARGINAL PRINCE
2006. JPN: Marginal Prince—Gekkeiju no Ojitachi. AKA: Marginal Prince—Princes' Laurels. TV series, video. DIR: Takayuki Inagaki. SCR: Ritsuko Hayasaka. DES: Toshiko Sasaki. ANI: N/C. MUS: Yasunori Iwasaki. PRD: Studo T&B, Tokyo Kids. 24 mins. x 13 eps. (TV), 24 mins. (V).
Yuta transfers to a new school on the beautiful Pacific island of St. Alfonso. At first it's hard for him to fit in with his stunningly good-looking dorm-mates, who are all children of celebrities, but his perseverance and good humor win them over. The curriculum is a puzzle, too, because all the classes seem to be about imperial rule and magic. As students progress they become "marginal princes" and aspire to be kings.

There's a lot of singing in this show—every main character has a song, because it's based on NTT Docomo's 2005 dating sim game, whose main purpose was to allow players to hear romantic songs by successfully forming relationships with the characters. The shock of a beautiful young man suddenly bursting into song for no apparent reason is one of the more comical elements in an otherwise wit-free plot (MUSIC IN ANIME). The original story had homosexual elements which were softened for broadcast animation. An additional episode subtitled Tokyo Merry-Go-Round was released on DVD in summer 2007; it may have been intended for TV, but as it's a standalone story set in the city it could just as easily have been put together as a DVD extra.

MARIA IS WATCHING OVER US *
2004. JPN: Maria-sama ga Miteru. AKA: Maria Is Watching; Marimite. TV series, special. DIR: Yukihiro Matsushita. SCR: Chiaki Manabe, Genki Yoshimura, Na-tsuko Takahashi, Reiko Yoshida. DES: Reine Hibiki, Akira Matsushima. ANI: Hirofumi Morimoto, Akira Matsushima, Yukiko Akiyama, Miyako Tsuji et al. MUS: Mikiya Katakura. PRD: Rondo Robe. 25 mins. x 13 eps. (TV1), 24 mins. x 13 eps. (TV2), 2 mins. x 13 eps. (special).
Elite Catholic girls' school Lillian Academy has a system whereby senior students adopt freshmen as their "little sisters," signifying the relationship by giving their chosen freshman a rosary. The two are then known as soeurs—French for sisters. Yumi Fukuzawa is asked by junior Sachiko Ogasawara to be her soeur, and is drawn into the inner circle of the Roses, the name given to members of the student council, setting the stage for a whole hothouse of blooming passions, rivalries, and non-incidents. Getting elected to the council, giving Valentine's Day chocolate (normally only given to men), and buying jeans all assume massive significance. Based on a series of novels by Oyuki Konno, the 13-episode series spun off a sequel, VMiW: Spring (MSgM: Haru). Spring is the season of change, covering New Year parties, graduation ceremonies, and the start of the Japanese school year in April, but despite this, nothing much happens in the second series, either. Humorous "outtakes" from the series were added to the DVD in 2004, as the two-minute "specials" Don't Tell the Virgin Mary (Maria-sama ni wa Naisho). A video series followed in 2006.

MARIA+HOLIC *

2008. TV series. DIR: Yukihiro Miyamoto, Akiyuki Shinbo, Tomokazu Tokoro. SCR: Masahiro Yokotani, Miku Oshima. DES: Hideyuki Morioka, Hisaharu Iijima. ANI: Hideyuki Morioka, Hiroki Yamamura, Noriyasu Yamauchi. MUS: Tatsuya Nishiwaki. PRD: SHAFT, AT-X, GENCO, Media Factory, Frontier Works, Hakuhodo DY Media Partners. 24 mins. x 12 eps. (TV1), 24 mins. x 12 eps. (TV2).

Kanako enrolls in an exclusive all-girls' academy at the start of her second year in high school. She doesn't choose it only because it was her late mother's old school, but because she hates men. She hopes to find her dream girlfriend. Mariya seems to fit the bill—an adorable younger girl just starting at the school—but Mariya has a dark secret: she's really a boy in disguise. And he's a nasty, manipulative piece of work who sets out to blackmail Kanako into keeping his secret. He and his outspoken maid Matsurika have a reason somewhere—but what can it be?

Mixing the high-concept weirdness of CROMARTIE HIGH with the dorm secrets of HERE IS GREENWOOD, this anime adapted from Minari Endo's manga works best when it concentrates on comedy rather than drama. The animation and fan service (ARGOT AND JARGON) are both limited. Tokyo Animator Institute gets a cooperation credit, providing both an opportunity for student animators to gain professional experience and a useful pool of cheap labor for cash-strapped producers. A second series followed in 2011, from the same crew except for a change of animation director, but without TAI input.

MARIE AND GALI

2009. JPN: Mari to Gari. TV series. DIR: Takashi Yamada. SCR: Rie Matsumoto. DES: Yoshihiko Umakoshi, Ryutaro Masuda. ANI: N/C. MUS: Yuji Yoshino. PRD: Toei Animation, NHK. 5 mins. x 40 eps. (TV1), 5 mins. x 30 eps. (TV2).

Marika is a cute middle schooler whose fashion sense is Gothic Lolita to the core. She always carries a cute stuffed toy that she calls Pet, and starts to yawn at the slightest mention of boring stuff; science actually sends her to sleep. Then, one day, she's taking an ordinary train ride when Pet comes to life, and they end up in a strange town called Galihabara. Some of history's greatest scientists live here, including the astronomer Galileo, Marie Curie, Hertz, Archimedes, Newton, and that perennial anime favorite Leonardo da Vinci. But they're not a bit like Marika imagined them—they're a whole lot funkier. Galileo is a rumpled loser along the lines of DOCTOR SLUMP. Newton's a hot romantic hero with flowing locks, Hertz is a high school thug, Fleming is groovily spaced out, and Curie is a foxy big sister in 19th-century schoolmarm's clothing. Created by Toei's house name Izumi Todo, this is a fun way of introducing great scientists and their discoveries to middle schoolers. A second series followed in 2010, introducing a rival for Marika, the terrifyingly pink-clad Lolita Norika and her pink stuffed bear Kuma. See also GREAT PEOPLE, which tried to introduce historic figures in a more documentary fashion.

MARINA THE MANGA ARTIST GOES TO CAMELOT

1990. JPN: Ai to Ken no Camelot: Mangaka Marina Time Slip Jiken. AKA: Marina the Manga Artist's Time Slip Incident: Love and Swords of Camelot. Video. DIR: Fumiko Ishii. SCR: Hitomi Fujimoto, Mami Watanabe. DES: Ayume Taniguchi. ANI: Masahiro Koyama. MUS: Kazz Toyama. PRD: Ashi Pro. 45 mins.

Marina and her adoring circle of gorgeous young boys are transported back in time to England in the Middle Ages (sic), where they help a young King Arthur acquire his sword, Excalibur. Cashing in on the success of Hitomi Fujimoto's popular Marina the Manga Artist series of novels for teenage girls, this one-shot was also shown theatrically. Camelot would also appear in the longer-running KING ARTHUR AND THE KNIGHTS OF THE ROUND TABLE.

MARINE A GO GO *

2001. JPN: Soreyuke Marin-chan. AKA: Go! Marin. Video. DIR: Masami Obari. SCR: N/C. DES: N/C. ANI: N/C. MUS: N/C. PRD: KSS, Pink Pineapple. 30 mins. x 3 eps.

Japan is facing a population crisis, and Catholic schoolgirl Marin is out to do her best to save her country. Enlisted into "Project Preservation of Japan" by a professor concerned that the birthrate will fall so low that the Japanese race will die out, she must take part in an attempt to collect sperm samples from 100 Japanese men in the style of DNA HUNTER. But there's opposition to the plan from the diabolically cute Marilyn, who even builds a sex android, the blonde and bounteously endowed South Pole One, designed to look like the Japanese idea of an American porn star, to exterminate Marin's targets through exhausting sex. Corny but consensual is the keynote here. Based on a porn comedy manga by Hideki Nonomura and Sanae Komiya. ●○

MARINE BOY *

1966. JPN: Ganbare Marine Kid. AKA: Go for It, Marine Kid. TV series. DIR: Haruo Osanai, Masaharu Endo, Yoshiyuki Tomino, Suguru Sugiyama. SCR: Hiroshi Yamauchi, Masaki Tsuji, Morimasa Matsumoto, Tomohiro Ando. DES: N/C. ANI: Masaharu Endo. MUS: Tetsuo Tsukahara. PRD: Toei, TBS. 25 mins. x 3 eps. (TV1), 25 mins. x 12 eps. (TV2), 25 mins. x 78 eps. (TV3, combined series).

Inspired in part by the novel Deep Range by Arthur C. Clarke, the Toei Studio made three pilot episodes of Dolphin Prince, the tale of an undersea boy with a pet dolphin, who swam in a wetsuit with a built-in jetpack and stunned his enemies with an aqua-boomerang. An experiment in color anime that predated KIMBA THE WHITE LION (the first broadcast color anime), Suguru Sugiyama's DP was shelved but then remade the following year as Marine Boy. Marine, whose father, Dr. Mariner, is an oceanographer with the Ocean Patrol, has been genetically altered to have superior underwater swimming abilities and chews Oxygum to supply himself with air underwater. Along with his companion, Whitey the white dolphin (Splasher in the U.S. version), Marine helps his father keep the sea safe. Though originally intended for broadcast on Fuji TV and subsequent sales overseas, the production was dogged by difficulties, and taken off the air after just 13 episodes.

The series returned with the same crew in 1969, retitled Undersea Boy Marin (Kaitei Shonen Marin), for further adventures about Marine, now equipped with an underwater boomerang, a hydrojet, and a mermaid girlfriend Neptuna (Neptina in the U.S. version). It lasted for a total of 78 episodes, including some recycled from the previous series. Broadcast on TBS, the entire run was not seen until

1971, when it was shown on Nippon TV.

During all this confusion, the series was already doing well in the U.S., where it premiered in 1966. With three episodes dropped for violence, *Marine Boy* still incurred the wrath of the National Association for Better Broadcasting, which claimed it was "one of the very worst animated shows. Child characters in extreme peril. Expresses a relish for torture and destruction of evil characters." Strangely, no mention was made of Neptuna's strategically placed hair, which obscured the fact that she spent the entire series topless, or that the three "violent" episodes were considered harmless enough to be screened when the series was rerun during the 1970s. Though obscure today, *Marine Boy* was a popular anime in its time, outperformed in the 1960s only by SPEED RACER in the U.S. and the first anime to achieve any degree of success in the U.K., though its Japanese origins were occluded. According to popular myth, decades later, the same BBC that screened *Marine Boy* in the 1970s would turn down POKÉMON, claiming that "nobody was interested in Japanese cartoons." In another spurious assertion, the father of the five-year-old Jonathan Clements claimed that "Marine Boy always eats his greens," though none of our Japanese sources support this.

MARINE EXPRESS *

1979. JPN: *Kaitei Cho Tokkyu Marine Express.* AKA: *Undersea Super Express: Marine Express.* TV special. DIR: Osamu Dezaki, Satoshi Dezaki. SCR: Osamu Tezuka. DES: Keizo Shimizu. ANI: Shigetaka Kiyoyama, Hitoshi Nishimura. MUS: Yuji Ono. PRD: Tezuka Pro, Nippon TV. 93 mins.

Murder on the Transpacific Express, as private investigator Shunsaku Ban boards an undersea train on its inaugural trip from California to Japan in 2002, tracking the killer of the director of the Public Construction Corporation. Meanwhile, architect Dr. Nasenkopf, much-praised designer of the train, has had a change of heart and now decides he should destroy his creation before it forever changes life in the Pacific. As if that wasn't enough, the feckless Mr. Credit, U.S. Secretary of State, is using fake passenger dummies to smuggle laser weapons, and the train's engineer is convinced that he can

see visions of the legendary queen of the undersea empire of Mu (see SUPER ATRAGON). Confused? You will be, because then the train falls through a time tunnel, traveling ten thousand years back to a time before Mu sank beneath the waves. Widely regarded as one of Osamu Tezuka's best works, this TV movie manages to mix Easter Island, invading aliens, time travel, and murder mystery—which just goes to show that not every complex story line needs to be as messy as LAWS OF THE SUN. As seems traditional for Tezuka TV movies, several of his other characters make cameo appearances, including ASTRO BOY (as Adam, robot "son" of Nasenkopf, who is "played" by Dr. Ochanomizu), BLACK JACK, and the THREE-EYED PRINCE, all voiced by their original voice actors. *ME*, however, crams cameos in to insane levels (Queen Sapphire, Empress of Mu, is actually PRINCESS KNIGHT, who arrives riding on the adult KIMBA THE WHITE LION), and also casts against type, with many of Tezuka's traditional good-guys playing evil roles. To Japanese audiences who would have experienced this as the sole annual appearance onscreen of much-loved characters, it must have been a joyous sight in the 1970s; in more jaded modern times when so many anime are available to view on demand, it just seems trite and glib. The theme tune features vocals from Tommy Snyder of the pop group Godiego, who also contributed to GALAXY EXPRESS 999.

MARINE SNOW

1980. JPN: *Marine Snow Densetsu.* TV special. DIR: Leiji Matsumoto, Fumio Ikeno. SCR: Keisuke Fujikawa. DES: Leiji Matsumoto, Katsumi Sakahashi. ANI: Seiji Yamashita. MUS: Hiroshi Ogasawara. PRD: Studio Uni, Mini Art, Now Planning. 81 mins.

Another tale of underwater expansion, suspiciously similar to the previous year's MARINE EXPRESS. Once again, there is a conflict between the land and sea people, this time caused by a series of underwater cities constructed by the surface-dwellers to ease overcrowding on a future Earth. Construction worker Hiroshi Umino notices that his colleague Nami Shimaoka is behaving suspiciously—shortly afterward, construction is halted by a saboteur's bomb. Someone (no prizes for guessing who) claiming to be Izanami, the Queen

of the Sea People, challenges the surface-appointed ruler Zerbert, demanding that the sea people be left in peace. Written and directed by CAPTAIN HARLOCK–creator Leiji Matsumoto.

MARIS THE CHOJO *

1986. JPN: *Rumic World: The Supergal.* AKA: *Supergal; Maris the Wondergirl* (U.K.). Video. DIR: Tadamasa Takahashi. SCR: Tomoko Konparu. DES: Katsumi Aoshima. ANI: Tadamasa Takahashi. MUS: Ichiro Arata. PRD: Studio Pierrot. 48 mins.

Space Police Officer Maris comes from Thanatos, a world of incredibly high gravity, so she has to wear a harness to prevent her superhuman strength from damaging people and objects around her—she often causes massive collateral damage nevertheless. She jumps at the chance to wipe out her debts by rescuing Koganemaru Matsushita, a handsome kidnap victim. Her mission forces her (and her alien sidekick, Murphy, the Irish-accented, nine-tailed fox) into a wrestling ring with her old rival, Zombie Sue. The harness comes off for a no-holds-barred showdown, though the entire affair is revealed to have been orchestrated by the bored Matsushita (a cop-out plot twist as unimaginative as "it was all a dream"). Combining the intergalactic crime-busting of the DIRTY PAIR with a martial arts comedy from manga creator Rumiko Takahashi, this is one of her weakest offerings. Part of the *Rumic World* series that also brought us FIRE TRIPPER, LAUGHING TARGET, and MERMAID'S FOREST. As with IRONFIST CHINMI and LOCKE THE SUPERMAN, the original U.S. title was altered in the English-language market to avoid legal conflict with the owners of a U.S. comic character. The production was noted at the time for including fake "outtakes" along with the closing credits—an idea later adopted by Pixar for *A Bug's Life*.

MARMALADE BOY *

1994. TV series, movie. DIR: Akinori Yabe, Atsutoshi Umezawa, Yasuo Yamayoshi, Satoshi Yamada. SCR: Aya Matsui, Yumi Kageyama, Motoki Yoshimura. DES: Yoshihiko Umakoshi. ANI: Yoshihiko Umakoshi, Hiroyuki Kawano, Michio Sato. MUS: Keiichi Oku. PRD: Toei, TV Asahi. 25 mins. x 76 eps. (TV), 30 mins. (m).

A bizarre wife-swapping variant on *The Brady Bunch*, as two married couples decide to exchange partners and live together in an extended family, with their children Miki Koshikawa and Yu Matsuura becoming stepsiblings and inevitably falling for each other. Love triangles extend into love polygons, as more male and female characters are introduced, each trying to tempt the lovers from their true desires. The initial premise, however, is stretched to absurd lengths by the series' long broadcast run, with the initial humor of the strange family set-up soon fading before seemingly endless rivals in love, breakups over nothing, and reconciliations. The show's quite unexpected success caused it to run ahead of the manga, with new characters and situations not present in the original, causing the plots to diverge. In the spirit of **CHILD'S TOY**, a genuinely quirky set-up whose quiet success far exceeded that of its more famous contemporaries—it ran for three times longer than the "mega-hit" **EVANGELION**. The story was cleverly completed in a 1995 "movie" that functions as both a prologue and epilogue. Flashing back to the day Yu is first told his parents are to divorce, it reveals that he has worshiped Miki from afar since before the beginning of the series and helps to explain exactly what he really sees in Miki, a mystery that had befuddled many fans for the duration of the series. Based on the 1992 manga by Wataru Yoshizumi. Following the earlier success of the romance **HANA YORI DANGO** as a Mandarin live-action TV series, *MB* was similarly adapted with real human actors and broadcast in Taiwan (2002, *Juzi Jiang Nanhai*).

MARS DAYBREAK *

2004. JPN: *Kenran Butosai: The Mars Daybreak*. AKA: *Gorgeous Tango: The Mars Daybreak*. TV series. DIR: Kunihiro Mori. SCR: Miya Asakawa, Jiro Takayama, Yuichi Nomura. DES: Koji Osaka, Yoshinori Sayama, Michiaki Sato, Kenji Mizuhata. ANI: Koji Osaka. MUS: Kaoru Wada. PRD: TV Tokyo, BONES, Dentsu. 23 mins. x 26 eps.

Mars now has oceans, but the end of an interstellar war has thrust the planet's economy into deep recession. Frustration and deprivation have led to riots among the colonists, separatist movements, and widespread looting and piracy. The Earth government means to suppress the trou-

ble—a combination of the revolution of **GUNDAM** and the human flotsam of **COWBOY BEBOP**, both of which were earlier production credits for first-time director Mori.

Gram River lives from hand to mouth, drifting through a variety of temporary and casual jobs in one of Mars' floating cities. By chance he is asked to pilot a Round Buckler, a humanoid mobile suit, "The Vector of Hope." The suit's almost obsolete—the older models were used to fight the interstellar war and most are remote-controlled nowadays—but Gram finds he has a knack for handling it. When this leads to another offer of work with the same machine at a higher rate of pay than he's used to, he's just too tempted to weigh the risks. He finds himself on the pirate submarine The Ship of Aurora, under the command of the tough and scary Captain Elizabeth Liati. They're on the run from a Round Buckler squadron from Earth, and by coincidence the squadron leader is Gram's childhood friend Vestemona (AKA Ves, but surely an Engrish mangling of Desdemona) Lauren. She was adopted years ago by a rich Earth family and now commands the Mars Division of the Sol Global Forces. When the two old friends reunite, they are on opposite sides of the law—she's the hunter and he's the hunted.

The fancy names of the suits and the romantic undersea settings, plus the talking cat and dolphin, which can get around in its own humanoid-shaped environment suit, all betray a fascination with pirate tales and submarine yarns. The story, based on a computer game by Sony, owes as much to *Seaquest DSV* (1993) and *Pirates of the Caribbean* (2003) as to anything else; yet there's something irresistibly appealing about oceans and glaciers on Mars and a butch dyke and a crew of talking beasts and deadbeats taking on the might of the Empire. The anime world, never one to ignore a good idea that was not yet wholly wrung of all saleability, flooded Mars again the following year in **ARIA**.

MARVELOUS MELMO

1971. JPN: *Fushigina Melmo*. AKA: *Mysterious Melmo*. TV series. DIR: Osamu Tezuka, Yoshiyuki Tomino, Fusahito Nagaki. SCR: Osamu Tezuka, Morimasa Matsumoto, Tatsuo Shibayama, Ran Seki. DES: Osamu Tezuka. ANI: Shigeru Yamamoto, Toshiyasu Okada.

MUS: Seiichiro Uno. PRD: Tezuka Pro, TBS. 25 mins. x 26 eps.

When her mother "goes to Heaven" after a traffic accident, young Melmo receives a jar of red and blue candy that allows her to magically age ten years and turn into a young woman and also return to her normal age. In **ASTRO BOY**–creator Tezuka's take on the popular magical-girl genre typified by **CREAMY MAMI** and **LITTLE WITCH SALLY**, Melmo decides to use the candy, which was intended to allow her to survive her childhood without an adult protector, for the greater good. As the series progressed, Melmo's age swings became more pronounced—she comes close to dying of old age or regressing back to "prehuman" fetal states. This allowed her to reorder her cells as she regrew to gain temporary animal characteristics like fur or a strong sense of smell in order to aid her with the task at hand. On the 70th anniversary of Tezuka's birth, the series was rereleased on video as *Melmo: Renewal,* with an all-new voice and music track and Maria Kawamura replacing Reiko Fujita as Melmo. The story was remade again as part of a trilogy of live-action TV specials, *Osamu Tezuka Theater* (2000), along with Tezuka's *Canon* and *Lunn Flies into the Wind* (see **LION BOOKS**).

MASAKI, MORI

1941–. Pseudonym for Masaru Mori. Sometimes miscredited as Mori Masaki. A sometime manga artist who also works as an animator, Masaki joined Mushi Production in 1963 and worked on **KIMBA THE WHITE LION**, among other shows. He left in 1968 to devote himself to manga, but was tempted back in 1979 to direct **DRIFTING CLOUDS** for Madhouse. He has also scripted several anime, including **DAGGER OF KAMUI** and **HARMAGEDON**.

MASAOKA, KENZO

1898–1988. Born in Osaka, he moved to Tokyo to study Western art. His first anime was Nikkatsu's *Monkey Island* (1931, *Sarugashima*), which he soon followed with the groundbreaking talkie **THE WORLD OF POWER AND WOMEN** (1934) for Shochiku. He moved miniatures one frame at a time to create special effects on the live-action *Princess Kaguya* (*Kaguya-hime*, 1935), inadvertently becoming a pioneer in **PUPPETRY**

AND STOP MOTION. His World War II output included the now-lost *Fuku-chan's Surprise Attack* and the allegorical fairy tale *The Spider and the Tulip* (1943), an advanced integration of animation and live action. After the war, he made SAKURA (1946), although it was not distributed. He was subsequently summoned to Toho, where he presented a series of lectures on animation technique that would form the basis of the skills of the Toho animators, who would go on to form Nihon Doga, which would in turn form the basis of Toei Animation. A generation later, dog-eared copies of his notes were still in circulation in certain anime companies, where his ideas on explosive effects and water-modeling had not been surpassed. His best known postwar works were *Tora the Stray Cat* (1947, *Suteneko Tora-chan*) and its sequel *Tora's Bride* (1948, *Tora-chan to Hanayome*), made under intensely restrictive conditions and lack of materials. Citing lack of financial returns in the animation business, but secretly incensed at the reneging on financial promises during the production of *Poppoya: Carefree Stationmaster* (1948, *Poppoya: Nonki Ekicho*), Masaoka officially retired to illustrate children's books, although animators' memoirs refer to encounters with him behind the scenes at many anime companies as late as the 1970s. Even in "retirement" he remained focused on animation, and was last seen in the 1980s still drawing storyboards for his unrealized lifelong ambition, an adaptation of the fairy tales of Hans Christian Andersen.

MASHIMO, KOICHI

1952–. Sometimes miscredited as Koichi Mashita. Born in Tokyo, he began his media career in TV documentaries and commercials, before joining Tatsunoko in 1975. He went freelance in 1984, subsequently setting up the company Office Free Hands and becoming one of the founders of Bee-Train in 1997. He is the long-serving director of anime from DIRTY PAIR through AI CITY, to modern works such as NOIR and .HACK.

MASHIROIRO SYMPHONY *

2011. JPN: *Mashiroiro Symphony: The Color of Lovers*. AKA: *Pure White Symphony*. TV series, video. DIR: Eiji Suganuma. SCR: Team RIKKA, Tomomi Mochizuki. DES:

Toshie Kawamura, Ayumi Sato. ANI: Toshie Kawamura. MUS: Nijine. PRD: Manglobe, Frontier Works, Lantis, Media Factory. 25 mins. x 12 eps. (TV), 7 mins. x 2 eps. (v), 14 mins. (v).

Girls' private school Yuihime Academy is considering turning co-ed, and invites some students from a neighboring mixed private school to join the student body on a temporary basis. Shingo Iryu and some of his friends are transferred to the Academy for ten months. They're impressed by the facilities on campus but the girls aren't pleased with the nasty, noisy, uncouth boys. Can Shingo win them over with a little help from his friends? Will they be able to help the sheltered princesses of the Academy deal with the troubles hidden under their polished exteriors? Based on a porn game by Palette, this is a typical softcore harem anime (ROMANCE AND DRAMA) with more emphasis on romance than sex. Two 7-minute "picture dramas" were added to the 2012 disc release in Japan, with a 14-minute "special" providing an alternative ending; as indicated by the title *Mashiroiro Symphony: Airi ga Anata no Kanojo ni!? (MS: Airi Is Your Girlfriend!?)*, this features a different chosen harem princess who wins our hero's heart. 🄝

MASK OF GLASS

1984. JPN: *Gurasu no Kamen*. TV series, video. DIR: Gisaburo Sugii, Hideo Makino, Seiji Okuda, Tsuneo Tominaga. SCR: Keisuke Fujikawa, Tomoko Konparu, Tomoko Misawa, Yukifude Asakura. DES: Makoto Kuniho. ANI: Keizo Shimizu, Jiro Tsujino, Masami Abe. MUS: Kazuo Otani. PRD: Eiken, Nippon TV. 25 mins. x 23 eps. (TV1), 45 mins. x 3 eps. (v), 25 mins. x 51 eps. (TV2).

Inspired by Chigusa Tsukikage, a star who retires due to injury, Maya Kitajima resolves to become an actress and joins her idol's theater troupe. Pushed to the limit by Chigusa, who turns out to be a tough taskmistress, Maya trains to perform the infamous Red Angel role solo, all the while repudiating the adoring advances of boy-next-door Masami Hayami and competing with her fierce rival from the Theater Undine, Ayumi Himekawa. Based on the ongoing 1976 *Hana to Yume* manga by Suzue Miuchi, *MoG* is Sugii's tribute to *Flashdance*, but it slips easily into the clichés of SPORTS ANIME such as AIM FOR

THE ACE, even with the sport removed. The titular "mask of glass" is the invisible dramatic energy an actress wears in front of her audience. A three-episode video series *GM: The Girl of a Thousand Masks* (*Glass no Kamen: Sen no Kamen wo Motsu Shojo*) was released in 1998, and the television series was remade in 2005 under the original title, released in English as *Glass Mask*. There have also been numerous theatrical productions, and a two-season live-action TV adaptation beginning in 1997 (*DE). *Mask of Glass* has become a keystone of the dramatic traditions of anime about performers and performing and has been referenced in many subsequent shows about acting or singing, from KALEIDOSTAR to PRETTY RHYTHM.

MASKED MAID GUY

2008. JPN: *Kamen no Maid Guy*. AKA:. TV, video. DIR: Masayuki Sakoi. SCR: Kazuyuki Fudeyasu. DES: Yuka Okamoto. ANI: Yeong Beom Kim. MUS: Kaoru Okubo. PRD: Madhouse Studios, AT-X, Frontier Works, Rondo Robe, Geneon, Klockworx. 23 mins. x 12 eps. (TV), 19 mins. (v).

Naeka is heiress to her billionaire grandfather's fortune. When she comes of age at 18, she and her younger brother will inherit it. To protect her from predators, agent Koharashi is sent to guard her. Despite his huge muscles and shark-like teeth, it's decided that he will try to blend in to the background as her maid, complete with frilly outfit. This, and his arrogance, upsets Naeka's real maid, the competent and devoted Fubuki, and much would-be comical mayhem follows. Based on the 2005 manga by Maruboru Akai, and burdened with more comedy breasts than any show could be reasonably expected to carry. The video (same year, same crew) is an unaired episode set at the beach. Allegedly, it could not be aired for "ethical reasons." Draw your own conclusions. 🄝🄥

MASQUERADE *

1998. JPN: *Gosenzo Sane*. AKA: *Ancestor's Glory*. Video. DIR: Yusuke Yamamoto. SCR: Ryota Yamaguchi. DES: Masaki Kajishima, Kazunori Takahashi. ANI: Kazunori Takahashi. MUS: T. K. Crow. PRD: AIC. 30 mins. x 4 eps. (v1), 30 mins. x 4 eps. (v2).

When his mother dies, Gen Hiraga goes to live with his grandmother, the rich chancellor of an exclusive college. Pursued by Jennifer Collins, a feisty foreign PhD student, he discovers that one of his ancestors discovered the alchemical secrets of immortality. A woman who sleeps with Gen and receives his golden sperm (or "aqua-permanence") can prolong her lifespan for a considerable time. Needless to say, this makes Gen popular with the ladies, starting with Beth, a nubile woman who claims to be over 400 years old, though she strangely still works as a maid for his grandmother.

As the TENCHI MUYO! audience *finally* reached puberty, the franchise had its last gasp in a couple of pornographic pastiches. SPACESHIP AGGA RUTER handled the sci-fi end, while *Masquerade* takes the same stereotypes and dumps them in a horror setting. After a suspenseful, artistic beginning that toys with the viewer's expectations for almost a quarter of an hour, the story turns to the requisite sex, falling to pieces in a ludicrous series of assignations as a set of desperate women try to milk Gen for his particular elixir of life. Laughable hokum, helped not a bit by a listless dub spoken by actors who understandably cannot believe what they are saying. In Japan, the franchise continued for two more series, *More Ancestor's Glory* (2000, *Zoku Gosenzo Sane*) and GOOD EVENING MY ONLY DARLING (2009, *Anata dake Konban wa*), in which other men, presumably related to the original Gen, were similarly beset by women in search of their life-prolonging elixir. ◐

MASS EFFECT: PARAGON LOST *
2012. Movie. DIR: Atsushi Takeuchi. SCR: Henry Gilroy. DES: Henry Gilroy. ANI: Akihiro Saito, Hwang Il-jim, Hiroyuki Hashimoto. MUS: David Kates, Joshua R. Mosely. PRD: Production I.G, Bioware, EA Games, Funimation, TO Entertainment. 94 mins.
In the year 2183, several Marines are dispatched to the remote colony of Fehl Prime to hold off an attack by Blood Pack mercenaries. Shot down before they can land, only a few of the Delta team under Lieutenant James Vega survive the insertion and successfully repel the assault. Two years later, the Marines remain embedded on Fehl Prime, and are there to witness an attack by a Collector ship, intent on harvesting the human colonists.

Given a limited cinema release ahead of a multiple-platform roll-out, this prequel to *Mass Effect 2* features an incident alluded to in the games by James Vega. It is, however, somewhat disappointing in its hand-waving lack of attention to tactical detail, featuring a bunch of supposedly trained soldiers who seem entirely unprepared for actual combat against enemies with brains. Fortunately, very few of the Blood Pack can shoot straight. ◐◑

MASTER KEATON *
1998. TV series, video. DIR: Masayuki Kojima. SCR: Tatsuhiko Urahata, Tomoko Konparu, Hideo Takayashiki. DES: Kitaro Takasaka. ANI: N/C. MUS: Kuniaki Haishima. PRD: Madhouse, Nippon TV. 25 mins. x 24 eps. (TV), 25 mins. x 15 eps. (v).
Half-English, half-Japanese ex-soldier Taichi Keaton is a divorced university lecturer and a part-time private investigator on behalf of the Lloyd's insurance syndicate. His investigations take him into many dangerous situations, but his survivalist training always helps him out, as does his plucky daughter, Yuriko. Bravely concentrating on the more cerebral elements of the original 1988 manga by Hokusei Katsushika and Naoki Urasawa, the anime version takes Keaton all around the world, with stops at London's Chinatown (looking suspiciously like Yokohama's, which must have been closer for the studio's picture researchers), Stonehenge, the Middle East, and all over Europe. Combining the wandering, supersmart troubleshooter of *Indiana Jones* or LUPIN III with an introverted investigator in the mold of Sherlock Holmes (even to the extent of a Baker Street office address), *MK* is also a product of its time, ditching the original Keaton's Falklands War experience in favor of more up-to-date activities in the Persian Gulf. Seemingly influenced by the popularity of *Riverdance*, *Braveheart*, and *Titanic*, the anime production also comes heavily smeared with misplaced Celtic whimsy, particularly in Haishima's folksy musical score.

MASTER OF EPIC *
2007. JPN: *Master of Epic: The Animation Age*. TV series. DIR: Tetsuya Endo. SCR: Tetsuya Endo. DES: Sayuri Sugito, Hiromi Sato. ANI: N/C. MUS: For-EVER. PRD: Gonzo,

Palm Company, GDH, TV Tokyo. 25 mins. x 12 eps.
Master of Epic is a Japanese online role-playing game from Hudson Soft. It must be popular because it's managed to get a show consisting of parodies, skits, and comedy vignettes on TV, themed around a specific game element in each episode. Loaded with in-jokes, this is a treat for fans of the game as well as a cunning plan to lure the casual viewer into the role-playing commuity.

MASTER OF MARTIAL HEARTS *
2008. JPN: *Zettai Shogeki: Platonic Heart*. Video. DIR: Yoshitaka Fujimoto. SCR: Hideki Shirane. DES: Naomi Mitaya, Yoshihiro Hiramure. ANI: Naomi Mitaya. MUS: Masaru Kuba. PRD: ARMS, BROSTA TV, Futabasha, Lantis, Pony Canyon, Shochiku, Studio Kikan, T.O. Entertainment. 30 mins. x 5 eps.
Martial artist Aya Iseshima accidentally gets drawn in to the contest for possession of the wish-granting Platonic Heart when she steps in to break up a brutal fight. High school girls, nurses, office ladies, air hostesses, shrine maidens, maids—in fact, every fanboy fantasy stereotype you can imagine—are fighting for the Platonic Heart in a high-stakes match where the losers vanish into the realm of darkness. Essentially, it's a series of costume fights with fan service (ARGOT AND JARGON) galore and an ugly, selfish ethic at its heart. Apart from fans of the original video game and those who honestly believe that possession of a hot fashion accessory can change your life and make all your wishes come true, it's hard to imagine who would get anything out of this. ◐◑

MASTER OF MOSQUITON *
1996. JPN: *Master Mosquiton*. Video, TV series. DIR: Hiroshi Negishi, Satoru Akahori. SCR: Satoru Akahori. DES: Takahiro Kishida, Kazuya Kuroda. ANI: Hideki Watanabe. MUS: Osamu Tezuka (mus). PRD: Zero-G Room, TV Tokyo. 30 mins. x 6 eps. (v), 25 mins. x 26 eps. (TV).
Tomb-raiding hokum as spunky red-haired Transylvanian schoolgirl Inaho raises the mild-mannered vampire Mosquiton as part of her quest for immortality. Eschewing the simple option of simply letting him suck on her neck, she drags him off on a treasure hunt for the legendary life-

prolonging "O-part," in a madcap version of 1920s Europe that soon includes alien invaders in a giant pyramid and battles with Rasputin and the Count de Saint Germaine for control of London. With undertones of a controlling yet adoring parent and angrily dependent child who wants everything to be the same forever, *Mosquiton* shows early promise but soon buries it beneath weak humor (signposted, in typical Satoru Akahori style, by pratfalls from a writer who doubts that the audience will notice it otherwise) and strident bickering from an Inaho voice actress who may once have had depth but comes across in the dub as nothing more than a spoiled brat. The English-language script also seems ignorant of the many historical characters and references, though it does inject some genuinely funny gags, many of which were not present in the original. In Japan, the series was brought back from the dead after its video run as the TV series *Mosquiton '99*—though it was taken off the air in 1998, not surviving to reach the year for which it optimistically named itself.

MASUDA, TOSHIO

1927–. Born in Kobe, he graduated in 1949 from the Osaka Foreign Languages University, and studied screenwriting with the New Toho script division. He began working as a scenarist and assistant director for Toho and then Nikkatsu, solely in the live-action field, with his best-known contribution being that to *Tora! Tora! Tora!* In the anime world, he played a major staff role in **STAR BLAZERS**. "Toshio Masuda," credited with several anime scores in this book, is a different individual.

MATASABURO THE WIND IMP

1988. JPN: *Kaze no Matasaburo*. Video. DIR: Rintaro. SCR: N/C. DES: Yoshinori Kanemori. ANI: Yoshinori Kanemori. MUS: Fujio Miyashita. PRD: Argos, Madhouse. 30 mins.
Heartrending tale of new student Saburo Takada, who comes to a ramshackle school with only one classroom in a remote valley. By the time he has befriended the shy village children, it is time for a sad farewell. Based on the children's story by Kenji Miyazawa, who also created **NIGHT ON THE GALACTIC RAILROAD**. The same author's *Wildcat and the Acorns* was animated the

same year by Toshio Hirata as a 25-minute video.

MATSUGORO THE WOLF

1989. JPN: *Ogami Matsugoro*. Video. DIR: Hidetoshi Omori. SCR: Norio Soda. DES: Hidetoshi Omori. ANI: Hidetoshi Omori. MUS: N/C. PRD: Nippon Animation. 50 mins.
Schoolboy gang-leader Matsugoro swears revenge when his lieutenant Koume's house is burned down by a land speculator in an insurance scam. In this unlikely adaptation of the *Shonen Magazine* manga by Minoru Ito, Matsugoro takes on the local gangsters by himself. ◐

MATSUMOTO, LEIJI

1938–. Pseudonym for Akira Matsumoto; sometimes credited as Reiji Matsumoto, the "Leiji" is his preferred romanization. Born in Fukuoka Prefecture, Matsumoto was still a 15-year-old high school student when he published his first manga. He went to Tokyo in 1958, where he continued to pursue a manga career, although he worked chiefly in girls' comics for many years—his adoption of the Leiji Matsumoto pseudonym signifying his eventual break with previous work drawn under his own name. He took a direct hand in the production of anime adaptations of his work, contributing to **STAR BLAZERS** as a director and designer and elements of the **CAPTAIN HARLOCK** franchise as a designer and screenwriter. The bulk of his anime credits, however, are as the creator of the original manga on which an anime happens to be based. He was involved for some years in a legal dispute with producer Yoshinobu Nishizaki over who is the creator and hence controller of *Star Blazers* (i.e., *Space Battleship Yamato*), which remains a lucrative source of merchandising, spin-off, and remake revenue. The dispute was considered resolved by the latter's death, albeit only because Matsumoto was the last man standing.

MAYA MIYAZAKI COMPENDIUM

2010. JPN: *Miyazaki Maya Daizukan*. Video. DIR: N/C. SCR: N/C. DES: N/C. ANI: N/C. MUS: N/C. PRD: AniMan, MS Pictures (Milky), Max. 17 mins. x 2 eps.
Three short stories based on Maya Miyazaki's porn manga. *Legend of Oedo's 800 Holes* is a timeslip story where a guy

falls down a manhole and emerges in old-time Tokyo, where he has his way with a reluctant Tokugawa princess. *Bicycle* has a pervert watching an infeasibly well-endowed schoolgirl ride downhill on her bicycle every morning; he plans to get involved with her obvious enjoyment of the ride. *Winter Love* is the story of science teacher Jinpachi's lust for 22-year-old music teacher Aiko; he decides that her disrespectful attitude to him has to be dealt with, so he drugs her and uses a pen and various lab implements for purposes for which they were not designed before raping her. ◐◑

MAYA THE BEE *

1975. JPN: *Mitsubachi Maya no Boken*. AKA: *Adventures of Maya the Honeybee*. TV series. DIR: Hiroshi Saito. SCR: Fumi Takahashi. DES: Susumu Shiraume. ANI: Toshio Nobe, Takao Ogawa. MUS: Takashi Ogaki. PRD: Nippon Animation, Peter Film, TV Asahi. 25 mins. x 52 eps. (TV1), 25 mins. x 52 eps. (TV2).
Flighty young honeybee Maya learns from her teacher, Cassandra, how to fly and collect pollen. But she is so good at her job that she exhausts the supply in the area surrounding her hive and must head out to find a new field of flowers—whereupon she has many adventures with beetles, grasshoppers, and her friend Willy, who is sent by the Queen Bee to find her. It's another tale of a bug's life, similar to **HUTCH THE HONEY BEE** but based on the 1929 children's book by Waldemar Bonsels and made as a coproduction with the German company Peter Films. The series was shown on Nickelodeon back in the days before a Japanese origin was something to boast of, and, consequently, it is not generally known as "anime." A sequel, *New Maya* (*Shin Mitsubachi Maya no Boken*), made soon after but not screened until 1982, featured a new crew and was chiefly animated by the inferior Wako Production. It centers on Maya waking from hibernation and discovering that her friend Phillip the Grasshopper's house has been burned during the winter. Meeting Phillip's savior, Mousey the mouse, they begin a series of new adventures.

MAYO CHIKI! *

2011. TV series. DIR: Keiichiro Kawaguchi.

SCR: Reiko Yoshida. DES: Kosuke Kawamura. ANI: Kosuke Kawamura. MUS: Yukari Hashimoto. PRD: feel., Dax Production, McRAY, Media Factory, MOVIC, Starchild Records, TBS. 25 mins. x 13 eps.

Kinjiro's violent mother and sister have left him terrified of women. His classmate Kanade decides to cure his fear but this means he has to keep the secret he's just uncovered about Kanade's butler—"he" is really a girl in disguise. Based on the book series by Hajime Asano illustrated by Seiji Kikuchi, this show is full of visual and verbal double entendres and dirty jokes plus some nudity and violence, but apart from that is lightweight and mostly harmless. **ⓛ**Ⓥ**Ⓝ**

MAZE *

1996. JPN: *Maze Bakunetsu Jiku*. AKA: *Maze: Exploding Dimension*. Video, TV series. DIR: Iku Suzuki. SCR: Katsumi Hasegawa, Satoru Akahori. DES: Eiji Suganuma, Masayuki Goto. ANI: N/C. MUS: N/C, Seikima-II. PRD: JC Staff, TV Tokyo. 30 mins. x 2 eps. (v), 25 mins. x 25 eps. (TV).

By day, Maze is a girl who wanders the countryside protecting exiled princess Mill of Bartonia, whose kingdom has been overrun by the Jaina Holy Group. But by night, she transforms into a brash, annoying, sex-obsessed boy. A lighthearted (and lightweight) cross of **RANMA ½** with **THE WIZARD OF OZ**, featuring the same look, plot, and often gags as Satoru Akahori's earlier **BEAST WARRIORS** and a stereotypical supporting cast that includes ninja Solude, the demi-hunter (barbarian warrior) Aster, the female knight Rapier, and the old wizard Woll. Their opponent is a pretty-boy cast from the same mold as **ESCAFLOWNE**'s Dilandau and is unabashedly named Gorgeous. The original video series was designed for an audience that had already read the books and listened to the radio show, so it consequently dumps the viewer right into the middle of the action without any explanation, expecting them to thrill to the self-indulgent quips and breakneck pace, all designed to hide the fact that nothing new is happening. For the older video audience, it is also considerably more risqué, loaded with erotic humor and innuendo. The later TV series takes things a little more slowly and conservatively, opening with Maze's origi-

nal arrival in this never-never land of giant robots and dueling princes, but even this introduction does little to hide the show's off-the-peg origins, so typical of so many 1990s video anime, although this one did at least survive to reach television. **Ⓝ**

MAZINGER Z *

1972. AKA: *TranZor Z*. TV series, movie. DIR: Yugo Serikawa, Tomoharu Katsumata, Fusahito Nagaki, Yasuo Yamayoshi, Takeshi Shirato, Masayuki Akehi, Nobutaka Nishizawa (TV1-2), Yoshio Hayakawa, Hideharu Iuchi (TV3). SCR: Susumu Takaku, Keisuke Fujikawa (TV1-2), Hiroyuki Onoda, Masaki Tsuji (TV3). DES: Go Nagai (TV1-2), Satoshi Hirayama (TV3). ANI: Koji Uemura, Masamune Ochiai, Keisuke Morishita (TV1-2), Hideyuki Motohashi, Tsutomu Shibayama (TV3). MUS: Hiroaki Watanabe (TV1-2), Kentaro Haneda (TV3). PRD: Dynamic Planning, Toei, Fuji TV (TV1-2), TMS, Nippon TV (TV3). 25 mins. x 92 eps. (TV1, *Mazinger*), 25 mins. x 56 eps. (TV2, *Great Mazinger*), 25 mins. x 23 eps. (TV3, *God Mazinger*).

Robot inventor Dr. Hell (Dr. Demon) wants to control the world with his MachineBeasts, who are led into battle by his minions, Baron Ashler/Ashura (Devleen, "half man, half woman, and the worst of both"), whose body is literally split down the middle, left side male and right side female, and Count Broken (Count Decapito), a cyborg who carries his head tucked underneath his arm. His attacks are resisted by the Photon Research Institute (Volcanic Research Institute). Photon inventor Dr. Kabuto's grandson, Koji (Tommy Davis), works out how to operate Mazinger Z, Kabuto's giant superalloy robot (see **GODAIKIN** and **SHOGUN WARRIORS**), climbing inside its head and using it to fight back against Hell, aided by his stepsister, Yumi Sayaka (Jessica), her robot Aphrodite A (later upgraded to Diana Alpha 1), and Boss Borot (Bobo-bot), a comic-relief machine driven by the local tough-guy, Boss. Based on a 1972 *Shonen Jump* manga by Go Nagai, *Mazinger Z* (*TranZor Z* in the U.S.) was the first "pilotable" robot, not a sentient being like **ASTRO BOY** or a remote-controlled toy like **GIGANTOR**. This changes the relationship between the young hero (and therefore the viewer) and the robot; instead of merely observing its actions, the viewer wears it like a suit of armor

and controls it as if he and the robot were one. Secondly, the robot bristled with cool weapons that were all activated by the hero calling out their names ("Rocket Punch!"), which added to the viewer's involvement in the show as well as the play value of the toys. The "gadgets 'n' gimmicks" approach was to have a long life in robot merchandising—see **GUNDAM**, **EVANGELION**, et al.

After the 43-minute crossover movie *Mazinger Z vs.***DEVILMAN** (1973), the show returned as *Great Mazinger* (1974). With Koji absent in South America, the pilot of the new, improved prototype is Tetsuya Tsurugi, with new token girl Jun Hono (and her token girl robot Venus Ace) and Boss Borot retained from the old series. They were fighting the subterranean army of Mikene and its mechanical monsters, led by Jigoku Daisensei, the reincarnation of Dr. Hell. Koji returned for the grand finale and would also appear in the Nagai robot-series **GRANDIZER** along with Boss Borot. The robots appeared again in short cinema outings alongside other Go Nagai creations including *Mazinger Z vs. the General of Darkness* (1974), *Great Mazinger vs.* **GETTER ROBO** G (1975), and *Great Mazinger/Grandizer/Getter Robo G: Battle the Great Monster* (1976).

The concept was also rehashed as the short-lived *God Mazinger* (1983). Japanese teen Yamato Hibino is sucked through a time warp into the past, where the dinosaur army of the Dragonia Empire threatens the world, and Queen Aira of Mu (see **SUPER ATRAGON**) needs Yamato to help her fight back with the aid of the guardian God Mazinger, which looks suspiciously like a giant robot. Their chief opponent is the evil Emperor Dorado of Dragonia and his golden-haired son, Prince Eldo, whose vendetta against the dark-haired Yamato was only just beginning when the series was canceled. Though Nagai still drew the tie-in manga, the anime robot was designed in "the Nagai style" by Satoshi Hirayama. More remote tie-ins were the 1988 *Mazinger* manga Nagai wrote and Ken Ishikawa painted for First Comics (the first manga done specifically for U.S. release) and the Mazin Kaiser robot created for Banpresto's *Super Robo Wars* multiplatform game in 1991, which subsequently featured in the video anime *Mazinkaiser* (2001) and its spin-offs. The lead robot in

Nagai's PSYCHO ARMOR GOBARIAN bears a staggering resemblance to Mazinger Z, as does the eponymous PANDA Z: THE ROBOMINATION (2004).

The series was rebooted for Yasuhiro Imagawa's 26-episode TV series *New Mazinger Shock Z-edition* (*Shin Mazinger Shogeki Z-hen*, 2009).

MD GEIST *

1986. JPN: *Sokihei MD Geist*. AKA: *Armored Devil-Soldier MD Geist*. Video. DIR: Hayato Ikeda. SCR: Riku Sanjo. DES: Tsuneo Ninomiya, Koichi Ohata. ANI: Hiroshi Negishi, Kenichi Onuki, Hirotoshi Sano. MUS: Yoichi Takahashi. PRD: Hero Media. 45 mins. (v1), 48 mins. (*Director's Cut*), 47 mins. (v2). Humankind leaves Earth behind and spreads out among the stars. On the distant world of Jerra, a group of rebels called the Nexrum begin a war of attrition, demanding that Jerra split from Earth's authority and seek its own independence. In the bloody war that ensues, the military devises a series of genetically enhanced superwarriors, the Most Dangerous Soldiers. Combined with their powerful armored exoskeletons, they are unstoppable. For reasons that aren't terribly clear, one particular Most Dangerous Soldier is imprisoned on a satellite, even though the war is still raging. An indeterminate number of years later, he falls back to the surface into a ravaged post-apocalyptic wasteland. After killing the leader of a biker gang, Geist (for it is he) decides to lead his new followers to save a beleaguered mobile fortress, which is coincidentally commanded by his old boss, Colonel Krups. The assassination of the president activates a Doomsday machine called Death Force, and the soldiers are on a mission to stop it, lest the world be overrun with legions of robot berserkers. Geist signs up for the final assault, lots of people get killed, and then there's an ending with several twists in it, the last of which makes the whole race-against-time of the previous hour utterly pointless.

With 1980s fashions, squealing guitar music, and simplistic post-holocaust bikers-in-a-desert, Geist is a product of the era that gave us *Mad Max*, FIST OF THE NORTH STAR, and VIOLENCE JACK. And there it might have stayed were it not for the U.S. company Central Park Media,

which uses Geist in its corporate logo, throwing money at the Japanese to blow the dust off this 1986 stinker and produce the previously canceled *Death Force* sequel (1996)—today, these two awful offerings are most likely to be found conjoined in a full-length "director's cut."

MD Geist is cheap and nasty, featuring some of the world's most halfhearted dialogue and plotting, including a seduction scene where a female character strips solely for the benefit of the camera—not even Geist can be bothered to watch her. The plot is riddled with holes. Why is Krups still alive when Geist returns from suspended animation? Why hasn't the supposedly oppressive Earth government sent reinforcements? Why is Death Force triggered by so inconsequential an event as the death of a president when the world has already been nuked almost to oblivion? There are tiny moments of interest, including a pastiche of *Easy Rider* (1969) when Geist destroys a pocket watch. There are the vaguest hints of subtlety as Krups and Geist duel for the men's respect; Krups by giving them halfhearted pep talks (though that could be the dub, of course), while Geist just "is" the ultimate warrior. And Jason Beck, who plays Geist in the U.S. dub, has a great voice. But these virtues are few and far between in an anime that, despite some respected names in the credits, is one of the medium's more brain-dead offerings. It was, however, the first time that U.S. interest and money resulted in the commissioning of a sequel to an anime video, and hence marks an important milestone in the narrative of the tail of overseas interest wagging the anime dog, which would arguably grow in influence until the production peak of 2006. ⒸⓃⓋ

ME AND I: THE TWO LOTTES

1991. JPN: *Watashi to Watashi: Futari no Lotte*. TV series. DIR: Kanetsugu Kodama, Yukio Okazaki. SCR: Michiru Shimada. DES: Shuichi Seki. ANI: Hisatoshi Motoki, Toyomi Sugiyama. MUS: Kazuo Otani. PRD: Tokyo Movie Shinsha, Nippon TV. 25 mins. x 29 eps.
During summer school, Louise meets Lotte, a girl who looks uncannily like her. Though they initially avoid each other, they eventually become friends and discover that they are twin sisters, raised

separately by their divorced parents. Resolving to get their parents back together, they swap families for a while and begin a series of deceptions in order to engineer a reunion that means the chance to live as one family. Adding several new plot threads but remaining ultimately faithful to the original, *Me and I* was based on Erich Kastner's novel *Das Doppelte Lottchen* (1949), which was also adapted into the British film *Twice upon a Time* (1954) and two Hollywood versions, both titled *The Parent Trap* (1961 and 1998). In Japan, it was also turned into a musical as well as a live-action film (1951), which starred Hibari Misora as both girls.

MECCANO

1995. JPN: *Mechano Scientific Attack Force*. Video. DIR: Hideyuki Tanaka, Nick Phillip, Yasuaki Matsumoto. SCR: N/C. DES: N/C. ANI: Takeshi Hirota. MUS: Pierre Taki. PRD: Sun Electronics. 29 mins.
A short animated collection produced by Pierre Taki of the musical group Denki Groove. It includes the CG Western *Plastic Gun Man*, *World Meccano Triangle*, for which he wrote the music, and the cel animation *Prime Minister of Gray Hill* (*Hai-irogaoka no Soridaijin*). The last sequence is a parody of a famous 1977 manga by Akira Mochizuki.

MECHA AFRO-KUN

2010. JPN: *Cyborg Salaryman Mecha Afro-kun*. Video. DIR: Yusaku Hanakuma. SCR: Yusaku Hanakuma. DES: Yusaku Hanakuma. ANI: Yusaku Hanakuma. MUS: N/C. PRD: Happinet Pictures. 32 mins.
Japan, the near future. Robots are becoming more common, and one company gets the latest model—the Afro-kun mechanism. Because he doesn't understand the real intentions behind people's actions, the cyborg is very bad at office politics: he views the vain and vulgar managers, the other robots, the strident office ladies, and the rest of the staff with innocent eyes in this wacky but heartwarming show. If you like watching cyborgs wrestle bears or seeing the zombie apocalypse reenacted in the park, this is for you. Hanakuma is also the creator of *Tokyo Zombie* which was filmed in 2009 by Sakichi Sato, starring Tadanobu Asano and Sho Aikawa. He wrote, directed, and animated this

one-shot based on his 2002 manga *Cyborg Salaryman Mecha Afro-kun.*

MECHA MOTE

2009. JPN: *Gokujo Mecha Mote Iincho.* TV series. DIR: Harume Kosaka, Masatsugu Arakawa. SCR: Natsuko Takahashi. DES: Madoka Katto, Shoko Hagiwara, Masami Hagiwara, Maki Morio. ANI: Isamu Abe, Munehiro Nishiyama. MUS: Junichi Igarashi, Kotaro Nakagawa. PRD: Shogakukan, SynergySP, TV Tokyo. 25 mins. x 51 eps. (TV1), 25 mins. x 51 eps. (TV2).

Kind-hearted Mimi Kitagawa is president of her class student council, and she likes everyone to get along. She only has one problem—the three bad boys who just won't obey the rules. Unfortunately she has a huge crush on one of them, and it's not the one who has a crush on her. If she only knew it, she has a source of help and advice close at hand—her beloved pet hamster Temotemo can speak and empathize with her feelings, but Mimi just can't understand its squeaks. Adapted from Tomoko Nishimura's 2006 high school romance manga, this was successful enough that a second series. *Mecha Mote Iincho Second Collection* was televised in 2010. The animation makes some annoying—and seemingly irrational—switches from 2D to 3D and back, and both it and the writing are not very original or striking.

MEDABOTS *

1999. JPN: *Medalot Damashii.* AKA: *Medarot Spirits, Techno-Robot Battle Adventure.* TV series. DIR: Katsuhisa Yamada. SCR: Akihiko Inari, Takashi Yamada. DES: N/C. ANI: Hiroyoshi Iida. MUS: N/C. PRD: NAS, TV Tokyo. 25 mins. x 52 eps. (TV1), "25 mins. x 39 eps. (TV2).

In A.D. 2022, children use their "Medabot" robot toys to fight in "robattles." Young boy Ikki finds a medal (a Medabot CPU) that has been stolen by the phantom thief Retort. Installing it in a beat-up, second-hand medalot unit, he discovers that it is a rare kind of medallion that imparts superhuman strength to its Medabot. With his friends Metabee, Rokusho, Koji, and Arika, he fights off the "bad guys" Fishface, Calamari, Gillguy, and Squidguts in a succession of robot battles. This series is a cash-in on a 1997 Imagineer computer game, with robot combat indebted to

PLAWRES SANSHIRO, doubtlessly brought back from the dead in the wake of POKÉMON because there are 222 basic Medalots, and merchandise beckons. A second series, *Medabots Spirits* (*Medalot Damashii*), followed in 2000.

MEDAKA BOX *

2012. TV series. DIR: Shoji Saeki. SCR: Shoji Saeki, Nisio Isin. DES: Ikuo Kawana. ANI: Sumie Kinoshita. MUS: Tatsuya Kato. PRD: AT-X, Media Factory, Gainax, Dentsu, Lantis. 24 mins. x 13 eps. (TV1), 24 mins. x 12 eps. (TV2).

Super-efficient, super-confident, massive-breasted Medaka Kurokami wins the race to be class president with a boggling 98% of the vote, and determines to right all wrongs in her school with the aid of her meek-mannered childhood friend Zenkichi and a suggestion box. Memorably described by Anime News Network as "SKET DANCE with boobs" this forgettable school comedy was followed by a second season, *Medaka Box Abnormal* (2012), in which the titular chesty heroine is co-opted into a dastardly scheme to create a master race by sacrificing her fellow students. Based on a manga by Nisio Isin and illustrated by Akira Akatsuki, which ran in *Weekly Shonen Jump.*

MEDICAL HUMILIATION *

2006. JPN: *Ijoku.* Video. DIR: Kentaro Shigeta. SCR: Tenkei Fujimiya. DES: Ryosuke Morimura. ANI: Ryosuke Morimura. MUS: Yoshi. PRD: Digital Works, Vanilla, YOUC. 27 mins. (v1), 28 mins. (v2).

A man, "Ryuuki Sakuma," is picked up outside a hospital by the police and interrogated, although he claims to remember nothing of his past. He escapes, and bursts into the same hospital, where he begs for succor and sanctuary from the all-female staff. They hire him as janitor and give him in a shed on the hospital's roof for living quarters. He then proceeds to his real purpose—the domination and sexual submission in turn of each of the nurses and the director, making them into his sex slaves. The art and animation are at the usual serviceable, but not outstanding, level of the Vanilla Series. Based on the game by corporate partners LiLiM Nama and Love Juice, as part of a thematic series whose other anime adaptations include

SEXTRA CREDIT and *Horny Ladies and the News* (VANILLA SERIES). For more medical mischief, see the much better SEX WARD and THE MYSTERY OF NONOMURA HOSPITAL, and compare with the much nastier NIGHT SHIFT NURSES. ❶🅛🅥🅝

MEGAMAN *

2002. JPN: *Rockman.EXE.* AKA: *Megaman Battle Network; Megaman: NT Warrior.* TV series. DIR: Takao Kato. SCR: Keiichi Hasegawa, Kenichi Yamada, Masaharu Amiya, Mayori Sekijima. DES: Mitsuru Ishihara, Koji Watanabe. ANI: Xebec. MUS: Katsumi Hori. PRD: TV Tokyo, Capcom, NAS, Shogakukan, Xebec. 24 mins. x 56 eps. (TV1), 24 mins. x 51 eps. (TV2), 24 mins. x 51 eps. (TV3), 30 mins. x 3 eps. (v), 24 mins. x 26 eps. (TV4, *Beast+*).

Hikari Netto and his NetNavi Megaman (Rockman in Japan) set out to become the best NetBattlers, defending the Net from evil Operators like the sinister World 3, the DarkLoids, and the alien NetNavi Duo, in the process. Beginning life as the Capcom video game *Rockman* in 1987, back at the beginning of the gaming boom that would bring STREET FIGHTER II, this show's protagonist was created as a lab assistant to doctors Thomas Light and Albert Wily, but following Wily's turn to the dark side, Megaman/Rockman is turned into a battle android to protect the world.

The original platform game was later converted into a cartoon series by American animation company Ruby-Spears, which does not qualify it as anime. The Capcom website also claims that a Japanese-made straight-to-video *Rockman* two-parter was released in 1993 and 1994. Following the cancellation of the American series at the beginning of its third season, the franchise was revived in its anime form as *Rockman.EXE*, a series based loosely on the contents and plots of the first two games. This was followed by later seasons: *Rockman.EXEAxess* (2003, based on the fourth game), *Rockman.EXE Stream* (2004, not directly linked to any one game), *Rockman.EXE Beast* (2005), and *Rockman.EXE Beast+* (2006). An edited version of *Rockman.EXE* airs in America as *MegaMan NT.*

Protagonist Rock, paired with his canine assistant Rush, has a certain superficial resemblance to the superhero and wonderdog combination of **CASSHAN: ROBOT HUNTER**. Their world and adventures, however, are very different. Set in the year 200X (and therefore firmly rooting the show's continuity in the early *Rockman* games and not in the later episodes set centuries later), the series posits a world where electronic communication is universal, and all electronic devices are connected—so far, so **GHOST IN THE SHELL**. Everyone has a personal terminal or PET, a helpmate that can delete viruses and other network threats, as well as functioning, as the name implies, as electronic pets. Many manga spin-offs also exist, including titles by Hitoshi Ariga and Ryo Takamisaki.

Takao Kato's *Rockman.EXE: Program of Light and Dark* (2005) is a theatrical movie release in which Rockman must journey underground to defeat a new enemy, Nebula Grey.

MEGAMI PARADISE *

1995. JPN: *Megami Tengoku.* AKA: *Goddess Paradise.* Video. DIR: Katsuhiko Nishijima. SCR: Katsuhiko Chiba, Mayori Sekijima. DES: Noriyasu Yamauchi. ANI: Noriyasu Yamauchi. MUS: Toshiro Yabuki. PRD: King Record. 30 mins. x 2 eps.
The Megami Paradise is a world of beauty and purity, ruled by the Mother Goddess whose protective influence shields the inhabitants from the corrupt and cruel universe. The reigning Mother Megami is due to step down soon, but her replacement has already been found in the form of the beautiful Lilith. The forces of Darkness, however, are keen on ending the blissful Megami existence once and for all, and it falls to Lilith and her Amazonian cohorts to save her world from destruction. Lilith's friends Lulubell, Juliana, and Stasia set out to foil the evil plotters and keep the world safe for lingerie and fan service. Any excuse to show acres of female flesh, from the people who would go on to give us **AGENT AIKA**. Based on a PC game with distinctly un-PC aims. **◐**

MEGAZONE 23 *

1985. Video. DIR: Yasuo Hasegawa, Hiroyuki Kitazume, Ichiro Itano. SCR: Hiroyuki Hoshiyama, Arii Emu ("REM"). DES: Toshihiro Hirano, Haruhiko Mikimoto, Shinji Aramaki, Yasuomi Umezu. ANI: Toshihiro Hirano, Masami Obari, Nobuyuki Kitajima. MUS: Shiro Sagisu. PRD:

Aidoru, Artmic. 107 mins. (v1), 80 mins. (v2), 50 mins. x 2 eps. (v3).
Bike-loving Shogo Yahagi obtains the transformable motorcycle-weapon Garland and is soon hotly pursued by the military. While location-hunting for a film he plans to make with his girlfriend's roommate, he wanders into the underground world beneath Tokyo and realizes that he is not in Tokyo at all but a facsimile built inside a spaceship, controlled by the master computer Bahamut. He is in a Megazone, a ship built to hold a billion people, one of many that fled Earth in 2331 as the planet faced imminent environmental collapse. In order to reeducate humankind to avoid making previous mistakes, the Megazones are completely virtual worlds. The occupants are convinced that they are really living in the 20th century, and the central computer, Bahamut, is programmed to maintain the illusion until such time as humankind is ready to repopulate the slowly recovering Earth. However, alien vessels are preparing to attack, and Eve, a virtual idol constructed by Bahamut, contacts Shogo through Garland and begs him to help.

A video anime given a theatrical release in Japan, *Megazone 23* shared many of the same staff as the earlier **MACROSS**, a fact exploited in the U.S., where it was edited into the unrelated **ROBOTECH** series as *Robotech: The Movie.*

The sequel, *M23: Tell Me the Secret,* features radically different artwork from new designer Umezu. Set six months later, Shogo collaborates with the Trash motorcycle gang in an attempt to regain Garland from the military. The alien Desarg are causing considerable damage to the technologically inferior crew of *Megazone 23,* but amid the battle, Shogo is reunited with his girlfriend, Yui, in a series of bed scenes cut from the video but left in the theatrical release. Eventually, Shogo saves the day, and it is revealed that *Megazone 23*'s journey has come full circle, and the time is right for humanity to return to Earth.

As the *Megazone* series drew to a graceful close, the anime business was thrown into upheaval by the runaway success of **AKIRA**. Mere moments after they laid their original story to rest, successfully delivering their characters from a gritty, urban nightmare, the producers turned

right around and jammed them back in for the two-part finale *M23: Return of Eve* and *M23: Freedom Day.* Typically, these episodes were released abroad as *Megazone 23* with no reference to the two earlier installments. Instead of the pastoral idyll promised by the end of the original, the story restores the characters to a *Blade Runner*–esque future. Amid mock religious musings about Eve, a virtual idol who shall redeem us all from our sins, life isn't all it's cut out to be in Eden, and new hero Eiji Tanaka is a motorcycle-riding hacker who gets recruited by the government to fight computer terrorism. Except that the terrorists are the good guys, and when Eiji discovers this, he switches sides and leads a revolution from the inside.

News broadcasts make it obvious that the government is lying. People ride around on bikes. There's a conspiracy within a conspiracy. The bad guys aren't necessarily all that bad. But while these elements worked well enough in *Akira,* they leave a nasty taste in the mouth when you know that they're being deliberately swiped in a cynical cash-in—annoying enough for the screenwriter himself to use the Arii Emu pseudonym also seen in the lackluster **BUBBLEGUM CRISIS** spin-off *Bubblegum Crash.*

MEINE LIEBE

2004. JPN: *Ginyu Mokushiroku Meine Liebe.* AKA: *Minstrel Apocalypse Meine Liebe.* TV series. DIR: Koichi Mashimo, Shinya Kawamo. SCR: Akemi Omode, Hiroyuki Kawasaki. DES: Minako Shiba, Yoshimitsu Yamashita. ANI: Minako Shiba, Hiroshi Morioka, Masayuki Kurosawa, Shinya Kawamo, Tomoyuki Kurokawa, Yuki Arie, Yoshimitsu Yamashita, Tomomi Ishikawa. MUS: Yoshihisa Hirano, Yutaka Minobe. PRD: Bee Train, Animax, Rondo Robe, Geneon Marvelous Entertainment. 25 mins. x 13 eps. (TV1), 25 mins. x 13 eps. (TV2).
The king of the pretty little European island kingdom of Kuchen is advised by five magistrates, almost always drawn from the Strahls, the elite graduates of the Rosenstolz Boarding School. One has to be well connected, intelligent, and talented to even get into the school, let alone strive for Strahl status. In 1935, five young noblemen aim to become Strahls and achieve magistrate status and political

power. They are Orpherus, Ludwig, Eduard, Camus, and Naoji. Their friendships and rivalries form the plot of this anime for girls based on dating sim games *Tanbi Muso Meine Liebe*, released by Konami for the Game Boy Advance in 2001 and PS2 in 2004, and its follow-up *Meine Liebe Yubi Naru Kioku*. The handsome young men in the game were designed by androgynous glamour specialist Kaori Yuki, author of **ANGEL SANCTUARY** and *Count Cain*. A manga version of the anime entitled *Meine Liebe* (German for *My Love*) also ran in *Bessatsu Hana to Yume*, and yearningly elegant merchandise includes a trading card game and CD dramas.

In 2006 a second TV series with a new director brought a new headmaster to the elite Rosenstolz Academy. *GRML wieder* brings our five heroes from the first series face to face with a plot to sell their beloved homeland into foreign hands, a plot that naturally they alone can foil. Is the aristocratic English spy Sir Isaac Cavendish friend, foe, or both? Is the world of title, privilege, and duty about to end? The German subtitle *wieder* implies both afresh and against—new beginnings, but not welcomed by all—and the overall tone of the series is somber.

MEKAKUCITY ACTORS *

2014. AKA: *Blindfold City Actors*. TV series. DIR: Akiyuki Shinbo, Yuki Yase. SCR: Jin. DES: Genichiro Abe. ANI: Naoto Nakamura, Haruka Tanaka. MUS: Jin et al. PRD: Shaft, 1st Place, Aniplex, Mages, Tokyo MX TV. 23 mins. x 12 eps.
Shintaro, a boy who has barely left his bedroom for two years, haplessly ventures out after spilling a drink on his keyboard, only to get tied up in a terrorist attack on a department store, foiled by the coincidental presence of several superpowered teenagers.

Released out of order, online, a series of Vocaloid songs by the artist "Jin" soon developed a narrative quality of their own, transforming into a canon of ballad-like celebrations of the activities of a gang of misfit teens, each with strange powers revolving around sight and seeing, on the rampage in Tokyo. Don't take our word for it—search for them on YouTube and you'll soon be dragged into a cycle of boppy songs (**MUSIC IN ANIME**) that first appear to

be banal and blundering, but soon reveal themselves as subversive and cynical, as if someone were trying to tell the story of *Batman* through the medium of a Hatsune Miku musical (**HATSUNE MIKU LIVE PARTY**).

Like **SERIAL EXPERIMENTS LAIN** crashed into **THE MELANCHOLY OF HARUHI SUZUMIYA**, *Mekakucity Actors* keeps on shunting new prequels onto pre-existing narratives, as if a confused storyteller keeps saying: "Oh, did I forget to mention … ?" Character motivations are regularly turned on their heads by revelations about their pasts—simple actions suddenly take on sublime depth when we realize what they relate to, and each chapter changes one's perspective on everything that has gone on before. Throughout, there is a recurring sense of being special in a world that doesn't even notice you—these invisible, everyday teens have crazy abilities that they can't even control, like a girl whose very presence commands everybody's attention, or a Medusa woman who can turn people into stone by simply meeting their gaze. Meanwhile, director Akiyuki Shinbo piles on dozens of stylish shots, visual experiments, and iconic moments, making this anime as much of a feast for the eyes as it is a tangle for the brain.

MEKANDER *

1977. JPN: *Gasshin Sentai Mekander Robo*. AKA: *Combiner Battle Team Mekander Robot*. TV series. DIR: Yoshitaka Nitta, Takashi Anno, Yasuo Hasegawa, Masayuki Hayashi. SCR: Haruhiko Kaido. DES: Nobuhiro Okasako, Tsuneo Ninomiya. ANI: Tsuneo Ninomiya, Masayuki Hayashi, Satoshi Tozan, Takeshi Honda. MUS: Michiaki Watanabe. PRD: Wako, Telescreen, TV Tokyo. 25 mins. x 35 eps.
The evil general Edron (in Japanese: Hedoron) overthrows good Queen Medusa of Ganymede in the Magellan star cluster. Like many other mothers, most obviously that of *Superman*, she puts her only son Jimi into a space capsule and fires it into the void, and it eventually crash-lands on Earth. With Ganymede destroyed, Edron sends his fearless Kongister Corps to conquer Earth, all of which is defeated. All? Not all, for in the northeast corner of Asia sits a small island of indomitable warriors—the Japanese, who have placed their trust in Dr. Shikishima's revolutionary new Mekander Robo battle-robot. His son

Ryusuke and friend Kojiro are the nominated pilots, alongside Ryusuke's adopted brother Jimi, unaware that his mother, or a cybernetically remodeled version of her, is now a prominent leader in Edron's army who remembers her son only in confused flashbacks. However, when he and his colleagues are in terrible danger, her memory returns, and she sacrifices herself to save her son and his new home planet.

Beginning with Earth already defeated, *Mekander* had no qualms about piling on even more disasters—as soon as Mekander activates, the enemy launches Omega missiles to wipe it out! Unfortunately, similar troubles plagued the production, and the bankruptcy of a main sponsor forced the creators to cobble together new episodes from old footage with very limited new animation. Dubbed into English for screening in the Philippines. Manga tie-ins were published in several magazines, including *Terebi-kun* and *Yoiko*.

MELANCHOLY OF HARUHI SUZUMIYA, THE *

2006. JPN: *Suzumiya Haruhi no Yuutsu*. TV series. DIR: Hiroshi Yamamoto, Seiji Watanabe. SCR: Hiroshi Yamamoto, Tatsuya Ishihara. DES: Akiko Ikeda. ANI: Akiko Ikeda, Mitsuyoshi Yoneda, Satoshi Kadowaki. MUS: Satoru Kosaki. PRD: Kyoto Animation. 25 mins. x 14 eps. (TV1), 25 mins. x 28 eps. (TV2), 163 mins. (m).
Sassy schoolgirl Haruhi Suzumiya is the leading light of the Spreading Excitement All Over the World with Haruhi Suzumiya Brigade (the SOS Club), an association formed to befriend, attract, and generally hang out with time travelers, visiting aliens, and anyone with superpowers. She finds mundane humans terribly boring, which is bad news for Kyon, the local boy who sits in front of her in class and is unwittingly dragged into her science fictional adventures. For Haruhi is more than the girl next door; unknown to herself, she is also a godlike being with a control over reality itself, whose expectations and obsessions must be carefully managed in order to protect the fabric of the universe.

The result is a fearsome parody of fans, **FANDOM**, and the otaku world's obsession with unattainable muses, marrying the affectionate teasing of **GENSHIKEN** to the surreal satire of **EXCEL SAGA**. Based on the series of novels in *Sneaker* magazine by Nagaru Tanigawa, the series begins with an episode "00" that features the SOS Club's student movie, a ridiculously silly anime pastiche about a "combat waitress from the future" that is all too accurate—for instance, compare to VARIABLE GEO. However, the series then unspools at a cunning, postmodern level, broadcast out of chronological order and hence viewable as an expanding investigation of character, or reordered as a simple chronicle of events. The second series in 2009 arguably took such experimentation a little too far, with its notorious "Endless Eight" sequence, repeating some, but mercifully not all, of the 15,532 iterations of a time loop, from which the cast can only escape by observing minute changes in detail—a conceit perhaps used to better effect in TATAMI GALAXY. The ponderous movie spin-off, *The Disappearance of Haruhi Suzumiya* (2010), is another narrative experiment, long enough to be considered a "third season" in one lump, suddenly confronting the characters with a world in which Haruhi does not exist, and daring Kyon to determine the nature of her sudden removal, or if his memories of her are a hallucination.

MELLOW

1993. JPN: *Mero*. AKA: *Girl-Boy*. Video. DIR: Teruo Kogure. SCR: Rin Kasahara. DES: Rin Kasahara. ANI: Teruo Kogure. MUS: N/C. PRD: KSS. 45 mins.
Trouble in the classroom when the new teacher turns out to be a transvestite. Based on the 1991 manga by Rin Kasahara, published in *Shonen Champion*.

MELODY OF OBLIVION, THE *

2004. JPN: *Bokyaku no Senritsu: The Melody of Oblivion*. TV series. DIR: Hiroshi Nishikiori, Atsushi Takeyama. SCR: Yoji Enokido. DES: Shinya Hasegawa, Yutaka Izubuchi, Yo Yoshinari, Yoshikazu Miyao, Yoshiyuki Sadamoto. ANI: Takashi Wada, Daisuke Takashima, Hiroaki Nishimura, Hiroyuki Ishido, Koji Ogawa, Yoshihisa Matsumoto, Katsushi Sakurabi, Matsuo Asami. MUS: Hijiri Kuwano, Yoshikazu Suo. PRD: Gainax, TBS, Ken Media, Kadokawa. 24 mins. x 24 eps.
In the far future, a war breaks out between humans and monsters, and humans lose—see WARTIME ANIME for details! After many

years, the defeat has almost been forgotten and humans have accepted subordinate status because the monsters keep largely out of sight and rule the world through fear. A few Melos warriors like Kurofune still keep up the fight in the mighty Aiba Machines. High school boy Bokka has always been fascinated by the legends of the brave Melos Warriors; he meets Kurofune and hears the legend of the Melody of Oblivion. This is a legendary girl, seen and heard only by Warriors, who is waiting to be rescued so that she in turn can save mankind. Bokka finds he too can hear her and joins the fight to bring the beauty of melody back to the world. Based on the manga written by GJK and illustrated by Shinji Katakura, *MoO* is an often surreal show that recalls some of the strange transformations of UTENA or JOJO'S BIZARRE ADVENTURES, with the motorcycle road trip of KINO'S JOURNEY. In a plot point seemingly ripped wholesale from Pete Docter's *Monsters Inc.* (2001), the monsters feed on the life energy of children in order to create mayhem, leading to some strange contrasts of everyday life and alien attack. Sound plays an important part in the show—there is a conspicuous amount of voice-over and inner monologue which removes the need for lip sync, and the score, as befits a show that foregrounds music itself, is one of the most impressive elements. ●

MELTY LANCER *

1999. AKA: *Melty Lancer: The Animation*. Video. DIR: Takeshi Mori. SCR: Hiroshi Yamaguchi. DES: Tomohiro Hirata, Shoichi Masuo, Kanetake Ebigawa. ANI: Shoichi Masuo. MUS: Masamichi Amano. PRD: Gonzo. 30 mins. x 6 eps.
Earth has joined the galactic federation, and humanity has changed beyond all recognition. A religion that sees God in the Internet, alien technology indistinguishable from magic, and a huge Earthbound crime wave of alien crooks. Luckily, we have the Lancers on our side, Galactapol's elite crime-fighting corps, led by a man who's just served a five-year prison sentence and staffed by a gang of dangerous girlies. Sylvie Nimrod is a martial artist, Melvina McGarren only got her job because she's the boss's daughter, and cute little Angela is really an eight-year-

old bioweapon. Nana (full name Nanai Nataletion Neinhalten) learned sorcery on her adopted homeworld of Promised Land, and Sakuya is a high priestess of the Arcanest Temple. Jun Kamijo, the team mecha specialist, suspects that Earth's new attackers are her old schoolgirl enemies, a team of women warriors from Mad Scientist College, called the Vanessas. And she's right.

A standard team template, stamped out originally for a PC game before jumping to the Sony PlayStation for *Melty Lancer: Galactic Girl Cops 2086* and the later tie-in game *ML: Third Planet*. A manga spin-off, *ML: Can We Return to Tomorrow?* (1998), was drawn by Akira Matsubara for *Anime V* magazine. The manga, like the anime, preferred to concentrate on gratuitous angles that ogled the female form, rather than attempting to get on with a story.

MEMBERS OF THE STUDENT COUNCIL

2010. JPN: *Seitokai Yakuindomo*. TV series, video. DIR: Hiromitsu Kanazawa. SCR: Makoto Nakamura, Tomoko Koyama (v). DES: Makoto Furuta, Masanobu Nomura, Tomoko Koyama (v). ANI: Makoto Furuta. MUS: Yuya Mori. PRD: GoHands, Starchild Records, Kodansha (v). 24 mins. x 13 eps. (TV), 30 mins. x 8 eps. (v).
Takatoshi has just started a new school, which has recently become co-ed. He's asked to join the student council and finds himself in a harem, sorry, a group of three girls (ROMANCE AND DRAMA). This makes him the target of perversion, dirty jokes, and all manner of indignities. It seems the writers set themselves a target of an innuendo a minute or more, and they work very hard to keep up to speed. Based on the 2007 manga in *Weekly Shonen Magazine* by Tozen Ujiie, the team and the premise stayed unchanged, except for the addition of writer/artist Koyama, for the 2011 video series of the same title. Takatoshi's younger sister joins the school as his second year starts, but this doesn't help his situation at all. ●

MEMORIES *

1995. Movie. DIR: Koji Morimoto, Tensai Okamura, Katsuhiro Otomo. SCR: Katsuhiro Otomo, Satoshi Kon. DES: Toshiyuki Inoue, Takashi Watanabe, Hirotsuge Kawasaki,

Hidekazu Ohara. ANI: Yoshiaki Kawajiri. MUS: Takuya Ishino, Yoko Kanno, Jun Miyake, Hiroyuki Nagashima. PRD: Madhouse. 115 mins.

An anthology film in the tradition of **ROBOT CARNIVAL** and **NEO-TOKYO**, hyped further for comprising three stories based on works by Katsuhiro Otomo. For *Magnetic Rose* (*Kanojo no Omoide*, JPN: *Her Memories*, hence the title for the film), a group of space salvage operators find a gravity well in the center of the "Sargasso" area of space. Sensing booty, they investigate, to find that the giant metal rose is the mausoleum of a famous opera singer from the 20th century. Robots and holograms on the ship recreate the events of her life and her bitterness over her rejection by her lover, Carlo; though as the visitors dig deeper, they not only discover more sinister aspects of her past, but also that the mausoleum wants to drag them into the illusions forever. For astronaut Heintz Beckner, haunted by his daughter Emily's death on Earth, this is a tempting prospect, and Morimoto's direction juxtaposes ultramodern sci-fi designs with the stately baroque interiors of the space station and the homespun farmhouse of Beckner's family. Redolent at times of Tarkovsky's *Solaris* (1971) and the post-stargate scenes from *2001: A Space Odyssey* (1968), the *Magnetic Rose* sequence is one of the triumphs of anime, helped all the more by liberal extracts of Puccini's *Madame Butterfly* and *Tosca*, which manage to dwarf the other music by Yoko Kanno.

The second sequence, *Stink Bomb*, reprises the runaway-weapon theme of Otomo's **ROUJIN Z**. Hapless scientific researcher Nobuo takes an antihistamine, unaware it is an experimental bioweapon that generates a fatal odor. Not realizing there are any ill effects, he heads for Tokyo to report to his bosses, while the military throw every weapon it has at him, and passers-by drop dead in his tracks. Eventually, the task is left to foreign soldiers (thinly disguised Americans) whom the canny Japanese everyman effortlessly outwits. A well-made but lightweight comedy.

The final part, *Cannon Fodder*, was the first anime Otomo directed after **AKIRA**. Originally planned as a five-minute sequence, it ran well over time and budget, eventually reaching the 15-minute form

shown. Set in a steam-punk world that recalls the animation sequences of Pink Floyd's *The Wall* (1982), it features a nameless boy living in a town whose entire existence revolves around an unexplained war with a distant foe. He goes to school to learn about gunnery, while his father goes to work on one of the giant cannons, shooting an immense shell over the horizon. Shot in a drained, drab color scheme, *Cannon Fodder* is a stinging indictment of war—the boy knows nothing except fighting and dreams of cartoon soldiers. It is also a masterpiece from Otomo, planned as a single, continuous tracking shot (though this is not sustained for the entire film) and utilizing digital effects and scoring, reputedly as an experiment for **STEAMBOY**.

MEMORIES OF ...

2001. AKA: *Memories Off* [sic]. Video. DIR: Kazu Yokota, Takahiro Okao, Toshikatsu Tokoro. SCR: Masashi Takimoto. DES: Mutsumi Sasaki. ANI: N/C. MUS: Chiyomaru Shikura. PRD: Scitron. 30 mins. x 3 eps. (v1), 30 mins. x 3 eps. (v2), 30 mins. (v3).

Teenager Tomoya Mikami is so traumatized by the death of his girlfriend Ayaka in a car accident that he is unable to form any new relationships. He alienates his friends, and although he attempts to find love anew, he is unable to forget Ayaka and keeps on "seeing her" whenever he is with his new girlfriends—compare to **THE ETERNITY YOU DESIRE**. Based on a 1999 dating sim, released by KID Corporation.

Based on a follow-up game in the franchise, the 2001 sequel features a completely different couple. This time, there is no car accident; instead, the inane Ken Inami lends his umbrella to a stranger and immediately gets thrown into paroxysms of self-doubt about whether his girlfriend really is the one. Luckily, a series of stereotypical girls are around to help him make his decision. A third installment, *Memories Of... 3.5* (2003), presumably featured plot elements of the third and fourth games in the series by KID Corp., the most recent installment of which, *Memories Of... Again*, is the sixth in the franchise.

MEMORIES OF YOUTH

1993. JPN: *Aoi Kioku: Manmo Kaitaku to Shonen-tachi*. AKA: *Blue Memory: The Recla-*

mation of Manchuria and the Boys. Movie. DIR: Satoshi Dezaki. SCR: Kazumi Koide. DES: Setsuko Shibuichi. ANI: Keizo Shimizu, Yukari Kobayashi. MUS: Yuki Nakajima. PRD: Magic Bus, Mushi Pro, Ashi Pro. 90 mins.

In 1932, Japanese farmers are encouraged to emigrate to the state of Manchukuo, a country newly carved out of sovereign Chinese territory by the Japanese army. More than a million Japanese colonists arrive, buying into the government's claims for the country as an untamed wilderness and a bountiful frontier. As the clouds of war gather, teenage boys sign up for the youth volunteer development "army" on land reclamation projects deep in the interior. Kyota goes to help reclaim land in Manchuria, but his best friend Kenji isn't sure if this will really be good for Japan. Kenji decides to stay at school and become a teacher, while Kyota witnesses the invasion of the Soviets. Many boys flee back to Japan as refugees, although a substantial number of orphans are caught behind enemy lines and raised by Chinese families as their own.

Despite its role in the lives of many Japanese families, with 1.7 million refugees returning to Japan after the war, Japan's decade running the Manchurian puppet state is one of anime's least-tackled subjects, although it has been occasionally mined for spy thrillers such as **NIGHT RAID 1931** and **KISHIN HEIDAN**. As is common for antiwar anime, Satoshi Dezaki's obscure feature emphasizes the brutalization of innocent youth, in the form of clueless teenage boys who sign up for an "adventure" in the spirit of many **WARTIME ANIME**. At least part of Manchukuo's appeal to Japanese in WW2 came from its relative calm—Manchukuo was largely spared the food shortages and Allied bombings of the Japanese mainland, only to be plunged into the war in earnest when the Russian and Chinese armies suddenly converged on it in 1945. This movie was planned as the first of a series based on wartime youth comics published by Sodo Bunka.

MENAGE A TWINS *

2003. JPN: *Futago no Haha-sei Honno*. AKA: *Twin Moms Maternal Instinct*. Video. DIR: N/C. SCR: N/C. DES: Jiro Oiwa. ANI: Jiro Oiwa. MUS: N/C. PRD: Milky. 29 mins. x 2 eps.

Minoru has been raised by a very protective mother. He never gets the chance to talk to girls, so when he gets an email from an older woman named Akane, he's more than ready to start an online relationship. They start to meet regularly and have sex. Encouraged by this success, he also starts having sex with his lonely older neighbor Yuko. Then, he and his mother Tomoe run into Akane while out shopping, and seeing them together, he sees how closely they resemble each other. What's more, they know each other. When next Minoru meets Akane for sex he tortures her until she reveals the relationship. Minoru uncovers a family secret that shocks him to the core, and naturally he reacts by having nonconsensual sex with both his mother and his aunt. Based on the porn game by G.J? with original characters by Toshihide Sano. The *haha-sei* of the title would normally be read *bosei* (i.e., "maternal instinct"), but is pointedly glossed on the box with an alternate reading that instead implies "maternal sex." **NV**

MENKUI!
2011. Video. DIR: Runa Shirafuji. SCR: Shinichiro Sawayama. DES: Tomomi Kiryu, Red S H. ANI: Tomomi Kiryu. MUS: Koichi Kobe. PRD: Office Takeout, Pink Pineapple. 30 mins. x 2 eps.
Four stories about young couples and their sex lives. Mitarai loves the beautiful Manami, a student at his college, but is terrified by her very high standards—she turns down every man who asks her out. Reiko and her partner are both working long hours and their sex life has taken a back seat, so she decides to spice things up with some dressing up. Masaru's childhood friend Akina learns that not only does he have a maid fetish but he keeps a sex doll named Number Two as his girlfriend. Nevertheless, she enters into a love triangle with him and his doll, which compounds matters by coming to life. *Menkui!* has a slightly confusing origin: it's based on a porn manga by Tosh, not to be confused with the boys'-love manga of the same name by Suzuki Tanaka. This one is heterosexual and consensual. **N**

MEREMANOID
1997. JPN: *Shinkai Densetsu Meremanoid*. AKA: *Deep-Sea Legend Meremanoid*. TV series. DIR: Shigeru Morikawa. SCR: Kenji Terada, Nobuaki Kishima. DES: Akehiro Yamada. ANI: Akehiro Yamada, Shigeo Akahori. MUS: N/C. PRD: Triangle Staff, TV Asahi. 25 mins. x 24 eps.
Life has evolved very differently on the distant world of Mere. With the planet's surface almost totally covered by water, human beings have turned themselves into sea-dwellers. The males are called mermen, and the females, for some reason, are now referred to as meremanoids. Queen Ruthmilla broods over evil plans from within the Dark Reef, and Kings Moslem and Akkadia try to thwart her. But only sorceress Misty Jo and her little brother Oz hold the key to stopping Ruthmilla's dark designs. Writer Terada previously used the name "Ruth Miller" for an evil character in **BAVI STOCK**—his ex-girlfriend, perhaps?

MERMAID MELODY
2003. JPN: *Mermaid Melody Pichi Pichi Pitchi*. TV series. DIR: Yoshitaka Fujimoto. SCR: Michiko Yokote. DES: Kazuaki Makida. ANI: N/C. MUS: Masaki Tsurugi. PRD: Synergy Japan, PPP Production Commission, We've Inc., TV Aichi. 25 mins. x 52 eps. (TV1); 25 mins. x 39 eps. (TV2).
Lucia Nanami is a mermaid princess who lives in the North Pacific Ocean. She is the designated Bearer of the Pink Pearl, but she's lost it. Seven years ago she rescued a boy from a sinking ship, lost the pearl, but also lost her heart. She missed her coming-of-age ceremony last year because she didn't have her pearl, so she needs to find it in order to become officially adult; but she also wants to find the boy, so she heads for a city on the coast. Passing for human, she soon meets her first love, but he's such a cocky, flirtatious guy that at first she doesn't recognize him. Kaito Domoto is a surfer, all-round athlete and babe magnet, but with a very arrogant attitude. Lucia registers at his school to be closer to him, but if she falls in love with a human and tells him how she feels, she'll die.
This modern take on **LITTLE MERMAID** has another twist. Sea monsters led by the evil Gaito are attacking the mermaid kingdoms. The magical power of the colored pearls can transform the princesses into Singing Divas with enough power to defeat the sea monsters. If Lucia stays in the human world to be with Kaito, she can't join in the battle.

Supposedly based on a manga by screenwriter Michiko Yokote and Pink Hanamori in *Nakayoshi* magazine, some of *MM*'s comic situations are a little obvious—for instance, Lucia is chosen to play the lead in a class performance of *Little Mermaid*, only to have water imps threaten to expose her as a real mermaid. But, as with the original, there's pathos in this story. The idea that a cute girl with a heartfelt song can save the world, or that you can love someone enough to give him up or die for him, is still as corny and as touching as it was when **MACROSS** premiered. The second series, *MMPPP Pure*, followed straight on in 2004.

MERMAID'S FOREST *
1991. JPN: *Rumic World: Ningyo no Mori*. Video. DIR: Takaya Mizutani, Morio Asaka. SCR: Masaichiro Okubo, Tatsuhiko Urahata. DES: Sayuri Isseki, Kumiko Takahashi. ANI: Sayuri Isseki, Kumiko Takahashi. MUS: Kenji Kawai, Norihiro Tsuru. PRD: Madhouse. 56 mins. (v1), 46 mins. (v2), 25 mins. x 11 eps. (TV), 25 mins. x 2 eps. (v3).
Yuta is over 500 years old, a former Japanese fisherman who caught and ate the immortality-bestowing flesh of a mermaid. Though it killed his fellow sailors or turned them into feral "Lost Soul" mutants, Yuta has stayed forever young, and now he wanders modern Japan in search of others like him. One such person is Mana, a girl whom Yuta rescues from mermaid crones who intend to restore their own youth by eating *her*. However, she is also kidnapped by a human woman who has been deformed by ingesting mermaid's blood in an attempt to cure an illness.
Mixing **JAPANESE FOLK TALES** with a modern vampire analogy seemingly informed by *Highlander* (1985), the original 1988 *Mermaid's Forest* manga is one of the darker works from **URUSEI YATSURA**–creator Rumiko Takahashi. Though parts of the original manga concentrated on Yuta's early wanderings, the anime sequel, *Mermaid's Scar* (1993, *Ningyo no Kizu*), opted for another modern tale. This time, Yuta and Mana arrive in another seaside town where they suspect that another woman living in another secluded mansion (coastal Japan being littered with them, it would seem; see also the **COOL DEVICES** episode "Bind-

ing") is another eater of mermaid flesh. In this they are not mistaken, since the slightly crazed Misa has recovered her beautiful looks with suspicious rapidity after the boating accident that killed her husband. Though at first believing her to be abusing her young son Masato, the pair discover that Masato is the 800-year-old manipulator of a succession of adult foils—Misa, a bereaved mother to whom he fed mermaid flesh during the WWII bombing of Tokyo, is only the latest. However, as happened in its predecessor, *Mermaid's Scar*'s brooding Gothic soon collapses into a succession of gory fights. Its chilling premise is reduced to the straightforward rescue of a damsel in distress, and it suffers somewhat from the same inconsistencies that dog **VAMPIRE PRINCESS MIYU**—Masato's supply of 800-year-old mermaid flesh seems both inexhaustible and unperishable. Furthermore, the blurb on the box claims that Yuta is tired of immortality and searching for a way to die, though everyone already seems agreed that decapitation or immolation would both do the job nicely. One of the *Rumic World* series based on Takahashi's short manga tales; other entries included **FIRE TRIPPER, LAUGHING TARGET**, and **MARIS THE CHOJO**. Compare to its contemporary **3x3 EYES**.

The story was resurrected for the 13-part *Rumiko Takahashi Theater: Mermaid's Forest* (2004), directed by Masaharu Okuwari—11 episodes screened on TV, and the two final ones available only on video. This follows Yuta's wanderings through the world seeking a mermaid who can set him free to live as a normal human again. He finds a companion, Mana, who was kept prisoner by mermaids who intended to eat her—this is how mermaids, like *Countess Dracula*, keep their youthful looks. Mana, too, has eaten mermaid flesh and joins Yuta on his quest. Although they do not age, they can still feel pain and can be killed. They can never stay in one place for long or risk drawing too much attention to themselves, but Yuta's memories and past experiences draw them back to his old haunts and bring them in touch with a few survivors of those experiences. Many of the stories refer back to events in the manga and video release. Although a well-crafted, well-written series, the TV *MF* doesn't really give the viewer anything

different from the original. Yuta's mixed feelings about his own immortality and his constant need to reaffirm himself and his humanity, and the easygoing adaptability that has enabled him to survive 500 years of change and turmoil, remain the same, so it's one for Takahashi completists. **ONV**

MERMAIDS IN BRINE

2010. JPN: *Shiofuki Mermaid*. Video. DIR: Narumi Kuroguchi. SCR: Akira Nintai. DES: Futoshi Yone. ANI: Futoshi Yone. MUS: N/C. PRD: schoolzone, Marigold (Girls School). 28 mins.
University student Makoto hangs around the swimming pool to ogle girls in swimsuits. He gets a job as a part-time coach, and is asked to teach a young married woman, Marina, to swim. Unknown to him she's had the hots for him from the start, and soon unleashes his hidden talent: he can bring any woman to noisy orgasm with his fingers. So he does. Based on a porn game by Marine. *Shiofuki*, by the way, is Japanese for both the spouting of a whale and female ejaculate, so be very careful how you use the word in mixed company. **ON**

METAL ANGEL MARIE *

1995. JPN: *Boku no Marie*. AKA: *My Dear Marie*. Video. DIR: Tomomi Mochizuki. SCR: Go Sakamoto. DES: Hiroto Tanaka. ANI: Hiroto Tanaka. MUS: Hisaaki Yasukari. PRD: Victor Entertainment. 30 mins. x 3 eps.
Orphaned techno-geek Hiroshi sublimates his love for unattainable schoolgirl Marie, creating a "surrogate sister" robot who is her exact duplicate. Hiroshi has to keep his "sister's" robot nature secret while chasing the real Marie and trying to fight off all the neighborhood bad girls—who naturally find him incredibly attractive. Robot Marie isn't just a talking blow-up doll with pink hair; her affinity with machines gives her a certain power over electrical objects. She can put cars into spins, track pagers, and open doors—a kind of low-rent superpower that is very handy for keeping your "brother" away from femmes fatales. Despite her robotic limitations, she can do something that Hiroshi never can, and that's have a conversation with the real Marie without blowing a fuse. The two girls become firm friends, much to Hiroshi's chagrin, and his "sister" gets

to hear all sorts of inside gossip that he would kill for. In the privacy of the girls' locker room (private, that is, except for the anime cameramen filming fan-service underwear footage), it's the robot who finds out that her twin is still available—rumors that she's dating the high school hunk are unfounded. Hiroshi discovers that a sure-fire way of standing a better chance with girls is actually *talking* to them, and with his sister's help, he starts to take his first unsteady steps into the adult world. But, like the similar **VIDEO GIRL AI**, Marie isn't all that keen on helping him attain the love of his life. She'd rather *be* the love of his life, and another anime love triangle is born.

Based on a manga by Sakura Takeuchi in *Young Jump*, *MAM* mixes sports, romantic intrigue, and a slight superheroic twist, coupled with the mid-1990s craze for rearing your own creation, which peaked with **TAMAGOTCHI VIDEO ADVENTURES** and **POKÉMON**. But while popular as a manga, its video incarnation died an early death, swamped by the runaway success of the **TENCHI MUYO!** marketing machine. Renamed *My Dear Marie* for the subtitled version from AD Vision, presumably simply to annoy people compiling encyclopedias. Like Maria in **GHOST SWEEPER MIKAMI**, the robot's name is a distant homage to the robot girl in Fritz Lang's *Metropolis* (1926).

METAL FIGHTERS MIKU *

1994. JPN: *Metal Fighter Miku*. Video. DIR: Akiyuki Shinbo. SCR: Yasushi Hirano. DES: Takeshi Honda. ANI: Sadahiko Sakamaki. MUS: Kenji Kawai. PRD: JC Staff, TV Tokyo. 25 mins. x 13 eps.
In 2061 the latest fad is Women's Neo Pro Wrestling—"neo" because the combatants' natural fighting abilities are augmented with high-tech metal suits. Miku, Ginko, Sayaka, and Nana team up as the Pretty Four, but when they enter a championship tournament, they seek out the help of coach Eiichi Suo, a discredited drunk. After intrigues backstage, Coach Suo rules that the Pretty Four should fight each other in a one-off match. Only a weakling would try to destroy the team by dishonorable means; therefore (obviously!) the guilty party can be hunted down through trial by combat. After this very tongue-in-cheek tale of female fascism, the team gets

ready for the next match, but Miku sprains her shoulder. Miku has to overcome her injuries in order to save her team from the invincible Beauties of Nature. Realizing that the Pretty Four are undefeatable in the ring, the father-and-son baddies Shibano and Naoya resolve to destroy the team spirit by making them fight among themselves. Naoya pretends to fall in love with the hapless Miku while simultaneously encouraging Ginko to dump her teammates and head off for new pastures in America.

Wrestling has always been popular in Japan, from the quasi-religious sumo to the adoption of American-style staged matches. *MFM* belongs firmly in the latter camp; although sharp-eyed fans might be able to see more bubbling beneath the surface than straightforward babes in battlesuits. A whole generation of Japanese creators grew up watching wrestling tournaments, and there are many homages within anime (see CRUSHER JOE). One of Japan's most popular wrestling teams was an all-girl combo called the Beauty Pair, hence *MFM*'s Pretty Four, who are, logically speaking, twice as good, and the much more famous DIRTY PAIR, whom we all know to be twice as bad.

METAL JACK

1991. JPN: *Kiko Keisatsu Metal Jack.* AKA: *Armored Police Metal Jack.* TV series. DIR: Ko Matsuzono, Akihiko Nishiyama, Jun Kamiya, Hideki Tonokatsu. SCR: Hiroyuki Kawasaki, Katsuhiko Chiba, Tsunehisa Arakawa, Ryoei Tsukimura. DES: Yorihisa Uchida, Yukihiro Makino. ANI: Hideyuki Motohashi. MUS: Fuminori Iwasaki. PRD: Sunrise, TV Tokyo. 25 mins. x 37 eps.

In 2015, Tokyo is a high-tech "intelligent city," which just means that criminals also have access to even better weapons and equipment to carry out their schemes. When three young men die saving a little boy's life, they become the core of the Tokyo Police's top secret Metal Project as cyborgs who can even the score for the good guys in the fight against crime and, in particular, the criminal network known as Ido. Former police marksman Ken and his cybermutt, F-1 driver Ryo, and wrestler Go are aided and abetted by the mysterious Shadow Jack, survivor of an earlier foreign scheme to use cyborgs

in police work, who escaped to Japan and now lives undercover, desperately seeking the human memories his transformation wiped out. Their powerful transforming armor and weaponry achieved its main aim of selling toys for the show's sponsors in this derivative Sunrise show that marries parts of PATLABOR and 8TH MAN to *Robocop* (1987).

METAMORPHOSES/WINDS OF CHANGE *

1978. JPN: *Hoshi no Orpheus.* AKA: *Star of Orpheus; Orpheus of the Stars.* Movie. DIR: "Takashi," Gerry Eisenberg, Richard Hubner, Sadao Miyamoto. SCR: "Takashi". DES: Yukio Abe, et al. ANI: Masami Hata, Shigeru Yamamoto, et al. MUS: Billy Goldenberg, Jim Studer, Steve Tosh, Michael Young (*Meta*), Alec Costandinos (*Winds*). PRD: Sanrio. 95 mins. (U.S. edition, 80 mins.).

An animated version of five of Ovid's Roman versions of Greek myths, this film gives the stories of Actaeon, Orpheus and Eurydice, Herse and Aglauros, Perseus and Medusa, and Phaethon. Originally planned as a modern *Fantasia* in 70mm, *Metamorphoses* featured original pop music "starring musical performances by Joan Baez, Mick Jagger & The Rolling Stones, [and] The Pointer Sisters." The music and images, however, rarely matched, and the dialogue-free action was simply mystifying to audiences. Matters were not helped by the literary device of having the hero in each of the stories played by the same character, misleading some into thinking the anthology was one long story with a plot too incoherent to follow. The *Winds of Change* version followed in 1979, with music by a single composer and a sardonic narration by Peter Ustinov (Juzo Itami in the Japanese release) explaining the adventures of "Wondermaker" as he wanders through the five tales and takes the leading role in each. A product of Sanrio's short-lived Hollywood animation studio, which made the similarly unsuccessful *The Mouse and His Child.*

METROPOLIS *

2001. Movie. DIR: Rintaro. SCR: Katsuhiro Otomo. DES: Yasuhiro Nakura. ANI: Yasuhiro Nakura. MUS: Toshiyuki Honda. PRD: Madhouse, Tezuka Pro. 107 mins.

Japanese detective Shunsaku Ban arrives

in the mega-city Metropolis, accompanied by his nephew Kenichi—their mission, to arrest renegade scientist Dr. Laughton. But Laughton has friends in high places; he has been hidden away by the industrialist Duke Red, who wants him to create the final part of his Ziggurat super-skyscraper—a living robot who can rule the world from the throne secretly installed in its heights. While the Japanese visitors look for Laughton, Red's embittered stepson Rock hunts him for his own reasons, while Red's agents encourage the impoverished human citydwellers to revolt against their masters. When Dr. Laughton is killed, his robot creation Tima goes on the run through the warrens of the city, unaware of who—or what—she really is.

Osamu Tezuka began work on *Metropolis* when he was 15, and when it was published in 1949 he was only just out of his teens. Although he had not seen Fritz Lang's movie of the same name, he was inspired by a magazine article about it, including an image of the movie's famous robotwoman, Maria. He wondered what life would be like in a city of the future where robots would do all of the work (compare to the similar ARMITAGE III), postulating a disaffected underclass of jobless humans, open to suggestion from anarchist agitators.

Metropolis was the middle part of a sci-fi manga trilogy, beginning with Tezuka's manga *Lost World* (1948), in which Shunsaku and Kenichi were searching for energy-bearing meteorites and stranded on Earth's rogue twin planet. After *Metropolis*, they would return in the Cold War thriller *Next World* (1951, see FUMOON), in which the Earth is threatened by a giant dust cloud. The character of Tima (named Michy in the original) was an early try-out for Tezuka's most famous creation, the super-robot ASTRO BOY.

Mixing elegant computer graphics with the squat, cartoony characters of Tezuka's original, *Metropolis* is an excellent introduction, not only to Japan's greatest manga artist, but also the latest developments in anime. The crew is simply stellar, with direction by X: THE MOVIE's Rintaro, and other jobs filled by Hiroyuki Okiura (JINROH), Yoshiaki Kawajiri (NINJA SCROLL), and Kunihiko Sakurai (FINAL FANTASY). Almost everyone who is anyone in the anime business seems to have been involved—the film even credits **DEVILMAN**-creator Go Nagai as a guest voice actor, and the director himself moonlights as a bass clarinetist in the jazz band!

Of particular note is screenwriter Katsuhiro Otomo, who, like all manga artists, owes an incredible debt to Tezuka, and one which he openly acknowledged with a dedication that closed the **AKIRA** manga (dropped from the English release). In *Metropolis* we see many similarities—a city held for ransom by a terrorist group secretly funded by a corrupt politician, a great construction venture with a hidden purpose, and a child unaware it has the power to destroy the world. *Metropolis* also shares *Akira*'s explosive finale, involving the destruction of a considerable amount of urban real estate—the film was originally scheduled for an American release in late 2001, but was delayed several months after the September 11th terrorist attacks. Added for this movie version is a tip of the hat to *Blade Runner*, in the form of Duke Red's Ziggurat skyscraper—in the original manga, the secret project was to control the proliferation of sunspots and solar flares, of which only a small vestige remains in the movie.

Metropolis is a sumptuous film, loaded with homages to Fritz Lang and Tezuka himself—best displayed by a title sequence of an airship flying over a fireworks display in the city, while a jazz party gets into full swing. It is an evocative window into the work of manga's greatest artist, retaining both his child-like character designs and his bitingly serious plotting—even in Tezuka's own lifetime, many anime adaptations of his work tried to have one without the other. Suspiciously, it also contains a lot of CG work similar to early footage from Otomo's long-delayed **STEAMBOY** project—was this a way of realizing some of the costs for that other movie? Ironically, some of the computer graphics seem to come at the expense of more traditional techniques— certain painted cel backgrounds lack the three-dimensional immediacy of their CG counterparts and end up looking just like, well, paintings. In 1949, Tezuka closed his *Metropolis* manga with a question—"Will mankind destroy itself by developing technology too far?" One could well ask the same of the anime industry—as in the

earlier **MACROSS PLUS**, there is something ironic in a film that questions the value of new technology, when so much of its production rests upon it.

MEW MEW POWER *

2002. JPN: *Tokyo Mew Mew*. AKA: *Tokyo Myu Myu*; *Mew Mew*; *Mew Mew Power*. TV series. DIR: Noriyuki Abe. SCR: N/C. DES: Mari Kitayama, Koichi Usami. ANI: Studio Pierrot. MUS: Takayuki Negishi. PRD: Kodansha, TV Aichi, Studio Pierrot. 25 mins. x 52 eps.
Thirteen-year-old Ichigo Momomiya gets a hot date—school dreamboat Masaya Aoyama. Unfortunately during the date she's zapped by a strange ray that scrambles her DNA with that of an endangered species. When you think how many endangered species there are, she was lucky—instead of an Amazonian insect or fish, she was mixed with the Iriomote wildcat, giving her great agility, cute ears, and a tail. She can now transform into pink-haired superheroine Mew Mew Ichigo. It turns out that (as in **SAILOR MOON**) she's one of a team of five girls selected to protect the Earth from the mysterious alien known as Deep Blue, each endowed with color coding, special powers, and the cutest attributes of an animal from the "Red Data" list (see **RED DATA GIRL**). Ichigo (whose name means strawberry) and her colleagues Mew Mint, Mew Lettuce, Mew Pudding, and Mew Zakuro (pomegranate) each get individual transformation sequences, magical weapons, and special powers. Guided by their magical companion, cute pink robot Masha, they set out to help save the Earth and its endangered creatures in a show based on the manga by Mia Ikumi and Reiko Yoshida.

MEZZO *

2001. JPN: *Mezzo Forte; Mezzo: Danger Service Agency*. AKA: *Mezzo: DSA*. Video, TV series. DIR: Yasuomi Umezu. SCR: Yasuomi Umezu, Takao Yoshioka. DES: Yasuomi Umezu. ANI: Yasuomi Umezu. MUS: Toru Shura. PRD: Studio ARMS, Green Bunny, Hanjin Animation, Jiwoo Production. 29 mins. x 2 eps. (v), 25 mins. x 13 eps. (TV).
Teenage killer Mikura is hired to kidnap a wealthy baseball-team owner, but she finds herself facing two major-league problems. One is that rich man Momokichi Momoi made his money with the Mob and his

underworld connections are still active; the other is that his daughter Momomi is no terrified little rich girl but a feisty, arrogant bitch and a crack shot into the bargain. Such was the plot for *Mezzo Forte*, a short erotic video series that was spun off into *Mezzo*, a longer, less risqué TV sequel featuring Mikura and her surrogate family, the nerdy Harada and embittered ex-cop Pops Kurokawa, carrying out various commissions that show their softer, funnier side as well as action-packed mayhem. Yasuomi Umezu, who created the similar **KITE**, was also responsible for the most heartrending segment of **ROBOT CARNIVAL** and the sexiest introduction ever for a **PROJECT A-KO** movie. He knows about pace, he knows about style, and he gives good cute, though his bewildered little girls and gutsy, hard-headed, big-hearted teens get repetitive after a while. **LV**

MIAMI GUNS *

2000. TV series. DIR: Yoshitaka Koyama. SCR: Yutaka Hirata. DES: Shinichi Masaki. ANI: Yuka Kudo. MUS: Takashi Nakagawa. PRD: Toei, Group Tac, TBS. 25 mins. x 13 eps.
Unlikely adventures in a fantasy version of Miami, a "stateless town" populated almost entirely by Japanese people, as schoolgirl cop Yao Sakurakoji takes on evil power barons with her sharpshooting skills and superhuman athletic abilities. Or so she thinks—like the self-centered beauties of **DEBUTANTE DETECTIVES**, she is actually a spoiled rich girl who is prepared to do anything to impress, even to the extent of stunning a hostage negotiator so she can force a firefight. In a template stamped straight out of the buddy-movie production line, the maverick Yao is assigned a new partner, police commissioner Amano's daughter Ru, who is cool-headed and always does everything by the book. A series with all the depth of **YOU'RE UNDER ARREST!**, all the originality of **EHRGEIZ**, and all the realism of **MAD BULL 34**. Based on the manga by Takeaki Momose.

MICHIKO AND HATCHIN *

2008. JPN: *Michiko to Hatchin*. TV series. DIR: Sayo Yamamoto. SCR: Takashi Ujita. DES: Hiroshi Shimizu, Shigeto Koyama, Seiki Tamura. ANI: Hiroshi Shimizu. MUS: Kassin. PRD: Manglobe, Caliente Latino, Fuji TV, Hakuhodo DY Media Partners, Media Factory, Shochiku,

Yomiko Advertising. 23 mins. x 22 eps. Hana, known as Hatchin, is an orphan with abusive foster parents. They force her to slave for them and their two children, who are just as abusive. Then sexy criminal Michiko blitzes into her life, straight from prison and carrying the same tattoo as Hatchin in the same place. Hatchin doesn't trust anyone, but she's desperate to escape her life—and Michiko claims to know her father. Together they take off in search of the man who means so much to them both. Hatchin's honesty and determination and Michiko's daring and criminal connections carry them through a series of adventures as they learn to trust one another and uncover the mystery of Hana's past.

Debut director Yamamoto brings freshness and sincerity to this story. The South American–inspired borderland setting may recall Manglobe's earlier hit **COWBOY BEBOP** and the road movie/odd couple format will no doubt awaken echoes of **SAMURAI CHAMPLOO**, but old-school fans will see earlier parallels with **CANDY CANDY**. The settings look gorgeous, the Latin-inspired music adds to the freshness of the concept, and they're both matched by almost addictive character development and pacing. The writing isn't perfect—the links between the story arcs are sometimes weak or nonexistent—but the charm of the leading characters and the aural and visual delights make this a show worth seeing: no franchise-building, no high-concept selling, just a straightforwardly enjoyable action-adventure with plenty of heart.

MICROID S

1973. TV series. DIR: Masayuki Akehi, Hiroshi Shidara, Osamu Kasai, Minoru Okazaki, Masamune Ochiai. SCR: Masaki Tsuji. DES: Osamu Tezuka. ANI: Hiroshi Wagatsuma, Kazuo Komatsubara, Takeshi Shirato. MUS: Ko Misawa. PRD: Tezuka Pro, Toei, TV Asahi. 25 mins. x 26 eps.
Little does the human race realize that it is under threat from the Gidoron, a race of superintelligent ants who have developed powerful weapons. Butterfly-like Yamma, Ageha, and Mamezo escape from a Gidoron base and convince humans Dr. Mishiji and his son, Manabu, to help them. In a combination of **WONDERBEAT SCRAMBLE** and the later **MICROMAN**, the microids continue

the war against the ants with full-sized human assistance. Osamu Tezuka's original *Shonen Champion* manga was called *Microid Z*, but the initial letter was changed to "S" at the insistence of the show's sponsor, Seiko watches.

MICROMAN

1999. JPN: *Chiisana Kyojin Microman*. AKA: *Tiny Titan Microman; Micronauts*. TV series. DIR: Noriyuki Abe. SCR: Hiroshi Hashimoto, Yoshio Urasawa. DES: Takashi Wakabayashi. ANI: Hideo Shimosaka. MUS: Seiko Nagaoka. PRD: Studio Pierrot, TV Tokyo. 25 mins. x 52 eps.
Japanese schoolboy Kohei Kuji is understandably surprised when five of his action figures come to life and claim to be Micromen from the planet Micro-Earth, sent on a 30,000-light-year mission to save Earth from the Acroyears—"bad" Micromen who have crashed in Earth's polluted oceans and been transformed into mutants. Bold leader Arthur, blond pretty-boy Isamu, big lunk Walt, bespectacled brain Edison, and veteran tough-guy Odin enlist Kohei's help in their secret battle against the demonic invaders.

A 1980s toy sensation like **ZOIDS**, *Microman* figures began life as an economic design decision at former *GI Joe* manufacturer Takara—8-cm action figures meant smaller vehicles and lower production costs than their 30-cm counterparts. With distinctive chrome-colored heads, mounted on top of colored bodies, the toys had interchangeable parts—limbs and attachments could be swapped around by creative kids, one of whom was the young Yukito Kishiro, who cited his childhood Micromen as the inspiration for his own **BATTLE ANGEL**. Released in the U.S. in 1976 as the "Micronauts," the *Microman* line enjoyed a brief popularity before being swamped by the popularity of *Star Wars* action figures, and, as the 1980s wore on, by another Takara line, the **TRANSFORMERS**. Memorable tie-ins include Michael Golden's U.S. comic *Micronauts* (1979), as well as a 1984 *X-Men* crossover in which the X-Men were shrunk to micro-size, and the *Micronauts: New Adventures* (also 1984). Though an anime series was planned in the 1980s by the Artmic studio, it was shelved because the fad of the moment changed. Revived as part of a multimedia promotion for Gameboy and PlayStation releases,

Microman finally returned over a decade after it was considered finished. Not only did the new line feature some fabulous gimmicks, like a transforming base that looked like a PlayStation, all the figures were upgraded to "magnepower" status, so they could not only "use a table as a base," but also stick to the fridge and explore the rest of the kitchen, to infinity and beyond.

MIDNIGHT MILK PARTY *

1999. JPN: *Pikkoman no Oni Chikudo: Midnight Milk Party*. AKA: *Pikkoman's Way of Devil Taming; Pikkoman's Devil Taming*. Video. DIR: Rion Kushiro. SCR: Tedokoro Imaike. DES: Piko Fujikatsu (Pikkoman). ANI: Ken Raibi. MUS: N/C. PRD: Tsuyusha, Akatonbo. 30 mins.
Teenager Akiho Chino wants to have an adventure before she leaves her school days behind, so she auditions for a role in a schoolgirl porn video, believing that her performance will be of a wholly solo nature. However, when she reaches the set, she is raped on camera. Her travails do not end there—four months later her boss at the restaurant where she now works as a waitress has discovered the video and is blackmailing her to be a sex slave for himself and his friend. Another of anime's more distasteful offerings, this one based on a manga by Piko Fujikatsu. **NV**

MIDNIGHT PANTHER *

1998. Video. DIR: Yosei Morino, Hiroshi Ogawa. SCR: Yosei Morino. DES: Rin Shin. ANI: Yosei Morino. MUS: Yosei Morino. PRD: Beam Entertainment. 30 mins. x 2 eps.
During the interdimensional apocalypse of 1999, Kate Sinclair is killed by a dragon from a parallel world. Her biotechnician lover, David Owen, tries to restore her to life, conferring a kind of immortality on himself by continual cloning. Two centuries later, an Owen clone finally finds a way. Inspired by his muse, the exotic dancer "Panther," he combines Kate's DNA with a wildcat's. The experiment is a success, but the Kate-creature kills her former lover. Panther, however, falls in love with the new her and begins murdering humans to bring her fresh meat. A hundred years later, the aged Panther runs her own cartel of assassins, one of whom is the pretty granddaughter of the long-dead Kate. But very little of the above

backstory is included in the anime, confusing the hell out of many U.S. viewers. Meanwhile …

Only boys may rule the Blue Dragon kingdom, which is why Princess Loukish's gender is kept secret, even from Crown Prince Bad. But Bad fears that Loukish will become the royal favorite and plots to kill his "brother" anyway. Thrown from the battlements and left for dead, Loukish is found by an old witch and soon becomes part of her traveling minstrel troupe, the Pussycats. She loses all memories of her previous life and of her brother's evil deeds—he now exists only as an idolized figure in her dreams.

In fact, the Pussycats are a trio of assassins who use their musical talents as a cover. The spells woven to nurse the half-drowned Lou back to health have wrought some strange side effects. While she may look like a sexy young wench, her exposure to dragon's blood has left her with superhuman strength and virtual invulnerability—though nothing has prepared her for the shocks she will have in her next mission, which is to assassinate Prince Bad himself.

Yu Asagiri's complex manga tale of incestuous family ties across generations is compressed into a 60-minute sword-and-sorcery sex romp. Without the long back story, viewers of the anime are instead thrown into the deep end with the story of little Lou—the titular Panther is actually the nameless, zany old crone who saves her young life. This is a pity, because *MP*, despite all appearances to the contrary, is not the bastard offspring of a short-lived erotic computer game, but the culmination of an artist's lifelong obsession with love, desire, and obsession itself. A terrible adaptation of a lighthearted sex-manga, unleashed upon the English-language market with little attempt to explain its origins, and an awful dub to boot. ❶❸❷

MIDNIGHT SLEAZY TRAIN *

2003. JPN: *Saishu Chikan Densha*. AKA: *Molester on the Last Train*. Video. DIR: Raikaken. SCR: Rokurota Makabe. DES: P-zo Honda. ANI: P-zo Honda, Yuya Soma. MUS: Salad. PRD: Milky. 30 mins. x 3 eps. (v1), 30 mins. x 3 eps. (v2), 30 mins. x 2 eps. (v3).

With Kankyu Railroad on the verge of bankruptcy and its imminent demise threatening to shut down the sole lifeline to the town of Momogawa, three train operators come up with a plan to save the company and their hometown. By instituting the last trip of each night as a rolling orgy, catering to men who like to molest female passengers, they intend to up the ridership to profitable levels. One of them, Tetsuo (who is scion of the family that owns the company), has a secret which is key to recruiting women for their campaign—he is a master molester, whose touch can seduce a woman in seconds, turning them to his will. However, this power has a flaw in that the victims become nymphomaniacs forever after—not much of a handicap in this case.

Meanwhile, as Tetsuo gropes and seduces his way to success, his childhood friend Sana reveals that her grandfather is working on an alternative scheme, digging down through local rock in search of a hot spring that could turn the town into a tourist destination. The series was also rereleased in a condensed movie version titled *SCD the Best* and was followed by a three-episode second series titled *Midnight Sleazy Train Track 2* (*Shin SCD*), and a further sequel, *SCD Next*. Compare to **XPRESS TRAIN** and, in the live-action world, the Ken Takakura vehicle *Poppoya* (1999), which similarly featured a town threatened by the closure of its rail link, but mercifully did not include any perverts. ❶❸❷

MIDNIGHT STRIKE FORCE *

2001. JPN: *Yosho*. AKA: *Phantom Whispers*. Video. DIR: Katsuma Kanazawa. SCR: Juzo Rokutanda. DES: Masayaki Yamada, Shunsuke Harada. ANI: Ken Matsugaoka. MUS: N/C. PRD: D3, Studio Kuma. 26 mins. x 2 eps.

A team of three female investigators in the style of Charlie's Angels and DNA Hunter—martial arts champion Yuka, fortune-teller and *onmyoji* (see Yin-Yang Master) Sakura, and hacker Miharu—are sent undercover to investigate the disappearance of patients' bodies at a remote hospital, which (not coincidentally) happens to be located next to the headquarters of a mysterious cult. The cult is unsurprisingly revealed to be the secret owner of the hospital and is attempting to transplant the mind of its real founder—millennium-old Rikurei Ochi—into a new body. Unfortunately for everyone, the corpses keep turning into out-of-control tentacle monsters who rape the oh-so-conveniently near-naked female acolytes. Pretty art does not cover the clichés and plot holes in this entry in the **D3 SERIES**—e.g., the cult inexplicably allows the heroines to escape not once, but twice, back to the hospital it controls after they have discovered some of its secrets, and lets them continue to work as nurses. ❶❸❷

MIDORI DAYS *

2004. JPN: *Midori no Hibi*. AKA: *Days with Midori*. TV series. DIR: Tsuneo Kobayashi. SCR: Mamiko Ikeda, Takuya Sato et al. DES: Yuko Kusumoto. ANI: Pierrot. MUS: Yoshihisa Hirano. PRD: Studio Pierrot, Toho, Bandai Visual. 24 mins. x 13 eps.

High school boy Seiji Sawamura is really quite a nice guy, but he's got a bad reputation and the nickname Mad Dog, earned by copious streetfighting, often in pursuit of justice. His right hook is so deadly that it's got its own nickname—The Devil's Right Hand. Other students avoid him and he can't get a girlfriend. In fact, 20 girls have turned him down. But unknown to him, he has had a secret admirer for the past three years—quiet goody-two-shoes Midori Kasugano, who is so paralyzed by her shyness that she couldn't possibly tell him how she feels. Then, in the tradition of *Minami's Sweetheart* (*DE) and **THE ETERNITY YOU DESIRE**, Midori falls into a coma, while Seiji finds that instead of a right hand, he now has a living glove puppet—compare to **PUPPET MASTER SAKON**. A tiny, living and speaking Midori is attached to the end of his arm and reveling in his undivided attention. The situation is awkward and embarrassing but the pair find they really do like each other, even when things are switched for an episode and Seiji becomes Midori's left hand. The result is a very silly show that still manages to convey how paralyzing shyness can be and how enforced intimacy can reveal unsuspected aspects of a person's character. Based on the manga by Kazuro Inoue in *Shonen Sunday*, itself a surreal cartoon version of the perennial surrogateparenting and reluctantroommates genres of live-action Japanese television.

MIDORIYAMA HIGH

1989. JPN: *Midoriyama Koko: Koshien Hen*.

AKA: *Midoriyama High: Koshien Chapter.* Video, movie. DIR: Shigeru Ikeda. SCR: Shigeru Ikeda. DES: Atsuo Kurisawa. ANI: Shinichi Suzuki. MUS: Michiya Katakura. PRD: Balk, Onimaruya. 50 mins. x 10 eps. (TV), 81 mins. (m).

The slow route to success of a school baseball team that doesn't know the meaning of the word "teamwork," adapted from the manga in *Young Jump* by Atsui Kurisawa. Over time, the power-hitter Inushima loses his desire to hit everything and concentrates on hitting the ball, while ladies' man Hanaoka devotes just enough time to helping his teammates win before chasing after more skirt. In the same vein as STAR OF THE GIANTS.

MIGHTY ORBOTS *

1985. TV series. DIR: Osamu Dezaki. SCR: Michael Reaves, Hideo Takayashiki. DES: Ron Maidenberg, Akio Sugino, Katsuya Kondo. ANI: Hirokata Takahashi, Satoshi Dezaki, Kazuyuki Hirokawa. MUS: Yuji Ono. PRD: Intermedia, Tokyo Movie Shinsha. 25 mins. x 13 eps.

In the 23rd century, the evil Umbra, ruling computer of the Shadow World, tries to conquer Earth, only to be held off by the brave agents of the Galactic Patrol. Though there are humanoid operatives, including the elfin commander Rondu and his beautiful daughter Dia, the GP's last line of defense is the Orbots, a group of android warriors created and led by human cybernetics genius Rob Simmons. Simmons rides in his Beam Car with his flustered robo-assistant, Ono—the other Orbots can function separately or combine to form a mighty superrobot (somehow suddenly 50 feet tall), comprising Tor (torso), Bolt and Crunch (left and right leg), and Bo and Boo (left and right arm). Additionally each of the robots (except Crunch, for some reason) has a special ability—strength, customizable gadgets, energy beams, and teleportation/invisibility, which the whole of the group can access in Mighty Orbot mode.

A U.S.-Japan coproduction, blown out of the water by the runaway success of TRANSFORMERS and limited to a single season. With the same team's *Galaxy High School*, it was part of a concerted effort by TMS to break into the U.S. market in coalition with producer Fred Silverman. The

inept Bolt and Crunch were added to the lineup purely for "comic" relief, though fans' most frequently asked question was why superinventor Rob built two bumbling incompetents.

MIGHTY SPACE MINERS *

1994. JPN: *Oira Uchu no Tankofu.* Video. DIR: Umanosuke Iida. SCR: Ritsuko Hayasaka, Tsutomu Iida. DES: Toshihiro Kawamoto, Isamu Imakake. ANI: Toshihiro Kawamoto. MUS: Kenji Kawai. PRD: Triangle Staff, KSS. 30 mins. x 2 eps.

In A.D. 2060, an accident at the Toutatis asteroid mine forces the colonists to survive on their wits alone in the deadly environment of space. A supposedly realistic "hard SF" study of the dangers of zero-gravity life, based on a story by "Horceman Lunchfield." However, such a noble claim is somewhat ruined by having a character who survives exposure to vacuum and another with Big Anime Hair, hardly suitable for tough life in the asteroid belt. These problems may have influenced the buying public, as the story remains unfinished, with the planned additional four episodes not forthcoming. Sharp-eyed linguists may notice that "Horse-Man Lunch-Field" could be written in Japanese as "Uma no Suke Ii Da."

MIJA *

2003. JPN: *Bi Indoshi Miija.* AKA: *Mija: School of Insult Video.* DIR: Jun Fukuda. SCR: Saki Hosen. DES: Akira Kano. ANI: N/C. MUS: N/C. PRD: FAI International, Five Ways. 30 mins. x 2 eps.

Something strange is going on at Saint Moses Academy, and Sara Tadeshina has been sent by the Church to investigate undercover. Posing as a teacher, she soon discovers that the Academy was designed as an emergency shelter for the surrounding area, so it's unusual in design but also a powerful occult site. Unknown to Sara, an exiled demon has settled on the Academy as her Earthly home. Mija is a lust demon, and is drawing the students to her and teaching them the pleasures of the flesh, starting with attractive young Mayu and her would-be boyfriend Kotaro. When Sara finds the gate to Mija's domain, there are monster battles and demonic orgies before the two face off against each other. Some online sellers appear to think

that the episode subtitles, *Beautiful Demon* and *Demon of Lust*, are part of the main title. **⬤Ⓝⓥ**

MIKAN'S DIARY

1994. JPN: *Mikan E-nikki.* AKA: *Mikan Picture Diary.* TV series, video. DIR: Noboru Ishiguro. SCR: Mayumi Koyama. DES: Noboru Sugimitsu. ANI: N/C. MUS: Toshiki Hasegawa. PRD: Bandai. 25 mins. x 31 eps. (TV), 5 mins. (v).

A cute kitten keeps a diary about life in the human world. A set-up in the style of the more famous I AM A CAT, though this adaptation of Mimei Ogawa's manga in *Lala* magazine is aimed at a far younger audience, with trips to the seaside, Christmas parties, and even a vacation in America. Presumably, a trip to the U.K. was ruled out because "Mikan's Six-Month Quarantine Diary" wasn't catchy enough. When released on video, the final installment included the five-minute pilot film.

MIKIMOTO, HARUHIKO

1959–. Pseudonym for Haruhiko Sato, also sometimes billed as "Hal," particularly in his signatures on illustrations. Born in Tokyo, he dropped out of college to become a character designer on such shows as MACROSS and ORGUSS. His distinctive, feather-haired females have made him one of the most popular designers in anime, and his later works have included GUNBUSTER and the computer-animated BLUE REMAINS (on which his designs were recognizable but misused). He remains a popular illustrator, to the extent that, as with Masamune Shirow, his involvement on some productions is sometimes hyped beyond his actual role.

MILADY LOVES SEX

2010. JPN: *Ojosama wa H ga Osuki the Animation.* Video. DIR: Tatsumi. SCR: Shinichiro Sawayama. DES: Akane Aki. ANI: Garyu. MUS: N/C. PRD: T-Rex, Pink Pineapple. 29 mins. x 2 eps.

Two stories of two princesses, each very different in her approach to sex. One is a nymphomaniac switching dominant and submissive roles with her male sex slave; the other is a more conservative type who goes in for foursomes with her more experienced friend and her maids. Based on the 2009 porn manga of the same title by Bosshi. **Ⓝ**

MILF MANSION *

2007. JPN: *Yakata Jukujo*. AKA: *Immoral House*. Video. DIR: Terurin. SCR: Uitsuki Satoshi. DES: Taro Fuwaku, Seihodo. ANI: Taro Fuwaku. MUS: Yoshi. PRD: YOUC, Digital Works. 28 mins. x 2 eps.

Ryo lives with his stepmother Madoka. She's young and hot and they lust after each other, but do nothing about it. Then Ryo finds out that Madoka owes money to the Yotsuya family. He offers to work off the debt, and moves into the Yotsuya mansion where he soon finds himself working night shifts with Akie Yotsuya, the head of the family, and her maid Fumi. Then two more babes move in—Reiko, Akie's sister, and his stepmother. It turns out she's connected to the family by more than debt. A VANILLA SERIES entry based on a porn game by Guilty, and with a title change in the English language that brings great joy to the lonely anime encyclopedist, halfway through the M's. ●ⓃⓋ

MILK HOUSE DREAMING

1987. JPN: *Milk House Dreaming: Ai no Shiki*. Video. DIR: Hiroyuki Torii. SCR: Mami Watanabe. DES: Yumiko Kawahara. ANI: Yoshiyuki Momose. MUS: Taeko Onuki. PRD: Kadono Superstation. 43 mins.

An "image video" in the tradition of CIPHER, setting watercolors from Yumiko Kawahara's 1983 manga to a series of 11 pop songs. Made to cash in on the artist winning the Shogakukan Best Young Female Artist Award.

MILK MONEY *

2004. JPN: *Uba*. Video. DIR: Norihiko Nagahama. SCR: Norihiko Nagahama. DES: Daifuku Sugiya. ANI: Norihiko Nagahama. MUS: Yoshi. PRD: Digital Works (Vanilla Series), YOUC. 30 mins. x 2 eps.

After losing her unborn baby in a car accident, Kyoko takes a job as a wet nurse in order to ease the strain on her still lactating breasts. Many years later, she realizes that the baby she nursed was Toji, who is now a classmate of her teenage daughter Marika. Before long, Toji is invited to the house for a taste of days gone by—part of the VANILLA SERIES. ●ⓁⓃⓋ

MILKY HOLMES *

2010. JPN: *Tantei Opera Milky Holmes*. AKA: *Detective Opera Milky Holmes*. TV series, video. DIR: Makoto Moriwaki, Yoshiaki Iwasaki, Hiroshi Nishikiori. SCR: Kazuyuki Fudeyasu, Takayo Ikami, Hideki Shirane. DES: Seiya Numata, Shichiro Kobayashi, Toshiharu Mizutani, Mariko Fujita. ANI: Seiya Numata, Shosuke Shimizu, Shoko Takimoto, Miyabi Ozeki, Mariko Fujita. MUS: Katsumichi Harada (Angel Note), Satoru Kosaki, Satoru Inohara (Angel Note), monaca, Jun Ichikawa. PRD: JC Staff, Artland, Bushiroad, emotion, Bandai Visual, Dwango, Good Smile Company, Lantis, Pony Canyon, Sotsu Agency, Chronogear Creative. 25 mins. x 12 eps. (TV1), 25 mins. x 2 eps. (v1), 24 mins. x 12 eps. (TV2), 24 mins. x 2 eps. (V2/3), 12 mins. x 12 eps. (TV3).

The future: people use electronic toys to give them superhuman abilities, enabling them to commit crimes. Most of the crimes are minor, but it takes a Toy-savvy detective to track down the perpetrators, and the average police officer doesn't have the necessary skills. This has ushered in a new Great Age of Detectives, when anyone with the right Toys can play. Enter schoolgirl entrepreneur Opera Kobayashi and her team of Gothic Lolita–dressing, hair-ribboned schoolgirl sleuths known as Milky Holmes. How can they solve cases and cope with schoolwork and looking cute at the same time? Well, it helps that their school is the Holmes Detective Academy—but when will they realize that their greatest criminal opponent is very close to home?

There's no explicit sexual activity or nudity but this show is loaded with both verbal and visual innuendo. We all know what sea cucumbers stand for, and projectile nipples have been around since MAZINGER Z. But that doesn't mean this show is entirely without wit or a sense of irony. It's loaded with references to detective fiction and anime: Sherlock Holmes, Arsène Lupin (LUPIN VS SHERLOCK HOLMES), Nero Wolfe, Hercule Poirot (HERCULE POIROT AND MISS MARPLE), Cordelia Grey, GOLGO 13, SQUID GIRL, and more. There's even an homage to Frances Hodgson Burnett's classic novel A LITTLE PRINCESS in the second series storyline, where the girls lose their Toys to the villains and are flung into an attic in poverty, facing expulsion from the Academy unless they can get them back.

This is part of a carefully crafted media franchise owned by Japanese trading card game company Bushiroad. These franchises generally start with a character, or better a group of characters, geared to cover most bases of male fannish taste. Images and snippets of story are released across various media to test the water and build the market. *MH* started with an Internet radio drama and publicity pictures in December 2009. The anime series was phase two, and anime releases continued on TV and DVD alongside a manga, a visual novel, a light-novel series, plus of course a trading card game and merchandise.

A two-part video from the same crew followed in the winter of 2011, with a beach theme providing the opportunity to see all the characters in swimwear. Although the titles of both episodes were all about final farewells, the sleuths in frilly skirts were back on TV in January 2012 in *Milky Holmes 2 (Tantei Opera Milky Holmes Dai Ni Maku*, or *Big 2nd Act)*. Two specials followed: *Tantei Opera Milky Holmes Alternative One—Kobayashi Opera to Gomai no Kaiga (Opera Kobayashi and Five Pictures)* in summer 2012, and *Tantei Opera Milky Holmes Alternative Two—Kobayashi Opera to Koku ni Ogarasu (Opera Kobayashi and A Big Crow in an Empty Sky)* in January 2013. A third TV series, *Futari wa Milky Holmes (We Two Are Milky Holmes)*, commenced in July 2013. For sleuthing from an earlier and more innocent generation, see THE CASEBOOK OF CHARLOTTE HOLMES.

MILKY PASSION

1990. JPN: *Milky Passion: Dogenzaka, Ai no Shiro*. Video. DIR: Takashi Imanishi. SCR: Takashi Imanishi. DES: Moriyasu Taniguchi. ANI: Moriyasu Taniguchi. MUS: Keiko Senda. PRD: Animation 501. 30 mins.

In this sexy tale based on a manga by Milk Morizono, one of the shining stars of women's erotica, the attractive owner of a love hotel falls in love with her handsome manager. Their different class backgrounds come between them, and she is tempted by the arrival of a rich American hotel magnate; though she eventually returns to the arms of her Motel Mellors. See also HER NEED FOR EMBRACE. Ⓝ

MILLENNIUM ACTRESS *

2001. JPN: *Sennen Joyu*. Movie. DIR: Satoshi Kon. SCR: Sadayuki Murai, Satoshi Kon. DES:

Takeshi Honda, Satoshi Kon. ANI: Takeshi Honda, Toshiyuki Inoue, Hideki Hamazu, Kenichi Konishi, Shogo Furuya. MUS: Susumu Hirasawa. PRD: Genco, Madhouse. 87 mins.

Small-time film producer Genya Tachibana is hired to make a documentary commemorating the 70th anniversary of Gin Ei film Studios. He chooses to interview Chiyoko Fujiwara, a one-time superstar actress who has lived as a recluse for 30 years—a story that has certain resonances with the plot of Kon Ichikawa's live-action *Film Actress* (1987, *Eiga Joyu*). Fujiwara's life story combines fragments of 20th-century history (compare to **OSHIN**) with dramatic incidents from her acting career, blurring the boundaries between reality and fiction in a similar fashion to the same staff's earlier **PERFECT BLUE**. Director Kon and his staff shoot the whole thing as a collaboration between two unreliable narrators, with numerous surreal and impressionistic tours de force, such as a physical journey that begins in the late Tokugawa era and traverses the succeeding decades, changing art-styles and technology as it progresses in the style of Tezuka's **LEGEND OF THE FOREST**. The film also discloses the events behind Fujiwara's fall from favor, leading to inevitable comparisons with the desolate opera star of Katsuhiro Otomo's **MEMORIES**. Though completed in January 2001 and premiered in Montreal that July, the film was not actually given a general release in Japan until September 2002.

MILMO DE PON

2002. JPN: *Wagamama Fairy Milmo de Pon.* AKA: *Naughty Fairy Milmo de Pon; Mirmo Zibang!* TV series, TV special. DIR: Kenichi Kasai. SCR: Michihiro Tsuchiya. ANI: Masayuki Onchi. MUS: Takayuki Negishi. PRD: TV Tokyo, Shogakukan. 25 mins. x 81 eps. (TV1), 25 mins. x 26 eps. (TV2), 25 mins. x 42 eps. (TV3), 60 mins. x 4 eps. (TVm).

Kaede, aged 14, has a crush on her classmate Yuki. Daydreaming about him while she makes herself a cup of cocoa in her new mug, she makes a wish, and out pops baby-faced blond cutie Milmo, prince of the fairy kingdom, love specialist, and chocolate addict, to help her in her quest to win his heart. Milmo is just one of a whole fairy kingdom that invades Kaede's life and the lives of her friends,

aiming to bring them joy through music, fun, and extreme silliness. The little fairy's adventures, based on the manga by Hiromu Shinozuka, continued in 2003 with *NFMdP: Golden* and in 2004 with *NFMdP: Wonderful.* Two one-hour specials, *How's the Squid?* (*Ika wa Ikaga?*) and *Cake Crumbles,* were also screened in June and July 2004; a third, *Journey to the West* (*Saiyuki*), at the end of December 2004; and a fourth, *Hole of Asaze,* as part of the Anime Festival in March 2005—all on the same evening as regular 25-minute episodes. Compare to **WONDERFUL GENIE FAMILY**, whose method of summoning was, upon reflection, not all that much sillier.

MINA SMILES

1993. JPN: *Mina no Egao.* Video. DIR: Shinichi Suzuki. SCR: Mohammed Nor Khalid. DES: Mohammed Nor Khalid. ANI: N/C. MUS: N/C. PRD: UNESCO. 8 mins. (v1), 20 mins. x 2 eps. (v2).

Directed by former Studio Zero and Otogi Pro stalwart Shinichi Suzuki (subsequently the curator of the Suginami Anime Museum), and based on the series of educational books by Suzuki and the Malaysian artist Mohammed Nor Khalid (AKA Lat), the *Mina Smiles* animation is a short, punchy advertisement for the joys of literacy, demonstrating to third-world mothers and elders the immediate bonuses in safety, health, and wealth that learning to read can bring.

Paid for by a Tokyo insurance company as part of a charitable tax write-off, the *Mina Smiles* film featured a dark-haired, dusky mother-of-five, and was translated into a succession of languages, firstly on VHS. When the DVD of *Mina Smiles* and its sequels eventually came out in 2007, it contained an impressive 37 language tracks, including Mongol, Uzbek, Kiswahili, Wolof, and Lao, not to mention Portuguese (for Mozambique) and Spanish (for everywhere else).

Mina soon returned in other books designed to teach remote communities about ecological issues: *Mina's Village and Waste Management, Mina's Village and the Forest,* and the later, longer animation productions *Mina's Village and the River* and *Mina's Village and Fire Prevention.* The simple Mina comic has reached an audience of millions, and the cartoon that accompanied it

might be, for some, the only cartoon they have ever seen. Mina is an international star to rival Pikachu (**POKÉMON**), recognized in classrooms over half the planet, but you're unlikely to have heard of her unless you work for UNESCO or learned to read in the Vietnamese jungle. Not to be confused with UNICEF educational products featuring "Meena," a young Southeast Asian girl, although possibly both organizations had the same rationale for choosing the name—it sounds "local" in a remarkable number of languages covered.

MINAMI-KE

2007. AKA: *The Minami Family.* TV series, video. DIR: Masahiko Ota, Naoto Hosoda, Kei Oikawa, Keiichiro Kawaguchi. SCR: Hideaki Koyasu, Kenji Sugihara, Masashi Suzuki, Rie Koshika, Kosuke Kobayashi, Takamitsu Kono. DES: Shinji Ochi, Yoshihiro Watanabe, Shunsuke Suzuki, Seiki Tanaka, Toshiyuki Tokuda, Go Suzuki, Kenta Shimizu. ANI: Ryuchi Murakami, Seiki Tanaka, Go Suzuki. MUS: Yasuhiro Misawa. PRD: Daume, asread, feel, Yomiko Advertising, Kodansha, Starchild Records. 23 mins. x 13 eps. (TV1), 24 mins. x 13 eps. (TV2), 24 mins. x 13 eps. (TV3), 25 mins. (v1), 25 mins. x 5 eps. (V2), 24 mins. x 13 eps. (TV4).

The Minami sisters live alone while their workaholic parents are off pursuing their careers. Haruka keeps house for Kana and Chiaki while attending high school. Their cousin Takeru drops by occasionally with a cheque from their parents for living expenses. Classmates and pals, each with their own quirks and foibles, come to visit. And then, to make this life of housework, schoolwork, secret crushes, boob obsession, panty shots, and cross-dressing elementary schoolboys even more complicated, the girls meet *another* Minami family, completely unrelated to them and mostly male.

This clichéd show's main strength is its character interactions: most of the main cast get even-handed treatment, with their comeuppance exploited for comedic purposes and nobody escaping the retribution they earn. Otherwise the anime based on Coharu Sakuraba's manga is same-old same-old, especially the show-in-show *Sensei and Ninomoya-kun* (which has not been animated in its own right—yet).

Minami-ke has, however, spun off more sequels than one would imagine such a slight premise could bear. Starchild Records and composer Misawa are the only link between the crews of the first series and 2008's *Minami-Ke Okawari* (*The Minami Family: Seconds*) and while asread stays in charge of the animation on 2009's *Minami-Ke Okaeri* (*Minami Family: Thirds*) there's a new director and writer charting the sisters' growing up. Director Oikawa stayed in charge for the 2009 video *Minami-Ke: Betsubara* (*Minami Family: Another Rose*), a Valentine's Day story, but 2012 saw Keiichiro Kawaguchi at the helm for the video series *Minami-Ke Omatase* (*Minami Family: Please Wait*). In 2013, Kawaguchi directed another TV series, *Minami-Ke Tadaima* (*Minami Family: I'm Home!*). **◐**

MIND GAME *

2004. Movie. DIR: Masaaki Yuasa. SCR: Masaaki Yuasa. DES: Yuichiro Sueyoshi. ANI: Yuichiro Sueyoshi, Koji Morimoto, Masahiko Kubo. MUS: Seiichi Yamamoto, Yoko Kanno. PRD: Studio 4°C, Beyond C, Rentrack Japan, Asmik-Ace Entertainment. 104 mins.
Loser manga artist Nishi has a chance encounter with his childhood sweetheart Myun, although even that proves to be bad luck for him. Myun and her family are being pursued by an irate moneylender who shoots and kills Nishi. Finding himself in the afterlife, the regretful Nishi rails against not only a meaningless death, but also the meaningless life that preceded it. As he promises to try harder next time, he finds himself back in his original body, still alive—shades here of EMBLEM TAKE TWO.

Back in Osaka, Nishi turns the tables on his attackers before evading their pursuit by jumping off a bridge. Finding themselves literally in the belly of a whale, Nishi and his two female companions set up house with a man they meet who has been there for some time (recalling the Jonah story, see SUPERBOOK), telling stories about far away places. Based on a manga by Robin Nishi, and with characters designed to look like the famous actors who play them, *Mind Game* has been loaded with awards—the prestigious Noburo Ofuji prize at Japan's 59th Mainichi Film Festival, four awards at Montreal's Fantasia, a ranking above that of HOWL'S MOVING CASTLE at the 2004 Japan Media Arts Festival, and two

subtitled New York screenings at the NYC Asian Film Festival and the Museum of Modern Art's *Anime!!* exhibit.

MINORI SCRAMBLE

2012. Video. DIR: Takuya Nonaka. SCR: Masaki Hiramatsu. DES: Takayuki Mogi, Kazuo Ebisawa. ANI: Takayuki Mogi, Masato Nagamori. MUS: Akiyama-uni. PRD: ufotable, Aniplex, Klockworx. 39 mins.
Tamaki is in the fifth grade at school and has a problem. Her father is a scientist and his research topic is penguins. He brings his work home all the time, and Tamaki is sick and tired of having her life dominated by penguins. Instead of realizing that no girl should have to compete with a flock of incredibly cute birds for her father's attention, Dad decides to cure her hatred of penguins by giving her a penguin robot, or *penguinoid*, as a friend. Minori has the body of a penguin and the head of a small child, and looks disturbing enough to reinforce anyone's loathing for penguins. This may lead you to suspect that Tamaki's father has very little consideration for anyone else's views, and you'd be right; Tamaki and Minori spend most of their time racing round the neighborhood trying to put right the problems he's caused. Chihaya Mikage's 2007 manga ran for just eight months, but in 2010 ufotable announced they were making an anime series. So far this video is the only release.

MIRACLE GIANTS

1989. JPN: *Miracle Giants Domu-kun*. TV series. DIR: Takashi Watanabe, Koichi Chiaki, Masahito Sato, Masao Ito. SCR: Haruya Yamazaki, Michiru Shimada, Tsunehisa Ito. DES: Hatsuki Tsuji. ANI: Hatsuki Tsuji. MUS: N/C. PRD: Studio Gallop. 25 mins. x 10 eps.
Short-lived baseball story based on a manga by Shotaro Ishinomori, in which fifth-grade baseball prodigy Domu joins his late father's team and plays against anime versions of many real-life stars of Japanese baseball.

MIRACLE GIRLS

1993. TV series. DIR: Takashi Anno, Satoshi Kimura, Hiroyuki Kuzumoto, Akitaro Daichi, Kazuhiro Sasaki. SCR: Hirokazu Kobayashi, Mami Watanabe, Takashi Waguri, Miho Maruo. DES: Masayuki Sekigane. ANI: Ryoko Hata, Mariko Fujita. MUS: Michiru Oshima.

PRD: Japan Taps, NAS, Nippon TV. 25 mins. x 51 eps.
The 15-year-old Matsunaga girls are identical twins with very different personalities—the tomboyish Tomomi and the feminine Mikage. Both, however, have the paranormal powers of telepathic communication, limited telekinesis, and teleportation (but only if they both concentrate). The girls are brought closer together when Mikage's boyfriend Kurashige leaves to study in faraway England. They teleport to foil a hijack attempt on his plane, but after this semi-superheroic beginning, the series soon settles into a much more mundane story line. The twins occasionally swap identities, sometimes as a prank, sometimes to help each other out of difficult situations, and use their powers to cheat on the occasional exam or win the occasional sporting event. But as in the similar KIMAGURE ORANGE ROAD, the paranormal elements are swamped by more everyday teenage concerns. Based on the feel-good manga by Nami Akimoto in *Nakayoshi* magazine, *MG* is a sideways look at love and growing up, with occasional detours through time travel, ghost stories, and postmodern japery—in one episode, the voice actresses find other jobs and the twins must get them back to the studio! Episodes also steal from JAPANESE FOLK TALES, and even pastiche *The Red Shoes*, but the characters are so endearing that they more than compensate for the patchwork series of plots. The final episodes add a CINDERELLA twist, where the twins are revealed to be the prophesied saviors of the kingdom of Diamas and must fight the evil Mr. X for control of the country. By the end, everything has returned to normal, the girls are back home, and Mikage continues her chaste epistolary relationship with her absent boyfriend.

MIRACLE IN THE STARRY SKY *

2006. JPN: *Hoshizora Kiseki*. Video. DIR: Akio Watanabe, Toshikazu Matsubara. SCR: Akio Watanabe, Koichiro Ito, Toshikazu Matsubara. DES: Akio Watanabe, Toshikazu Matsubara. ANI: Akio Watanabe, Toshikazu Matsubara. MUS: Jun Abe, Seiji Muto. PRD: CoMix Wave. 27 mins.
Kozue loves stargazing. She's a keen amateur astronomer, and she even wears a piece of meteorite from her backyard

on a bracelet. When a class trip into the mountains to see a meteorite falls through, she goes alone, and meets a strange boy in a space suit. His mysterious abilities are somehow connected with the stars, but his life is far more restricted by reality than hers. From an original idea by codirector Matsubara, and from the studio that brought you the far stronger VOICES OF A DISTANT STAR, this is Shinkai-lite; a prettily designed show with slow pacing, limited animation, low-key music, and an air of gentle melancholy. Bundled with the Korean animation *Coffee Samurai* for U.S. release, because a half-hour DVD is a really hard sell in America.

MIRACLE OF LOVE

1982. JPN: *Ai no Kiseki: Dr. Norman Monogatari*. AKA: *Miracle of Love: The Story of Dr. Norman*. TV special. DIR: Masami Anno, Yasuo Hasegawa. SCR: Toshi Nagasaki. DES: Yoshitaka Amano. ANI: Hiroshi Yamane, Kazutoshi Kobayashi, Noriko Yazawa, Noboru Furuse. MUS: Chikara Ueda. PRD: Kokusai Eiga, Studio Gallop, TV Asahi. 85 mins.
Dr. Oppenheimer ruins a promising medical career when he kills a small child in a car accident. Hiding from the police, he changes his name to Norman and lives among the people of the slums. When property developers try to clear away the slum-dwellers to build a theme park, Norman defends their rights, though his public good deeds allow Detective Gavan to finally catch up with him. A tale of sin and redemption, screened on Christmas Eve.

MIRACLE! MIMIKA

2006. JPN: *Mirakuru! Mimika*. AKA: *Taste Made Easy! Mimika*. TV series. DIR: Shotaro Terada, Seijun Nagata, Miho Nikura. SCR: Masuo Kameda. DES: Akane Kasuga, Goma. ANI: N/C. MUS: Atsushi Ike, HARCO. PRD: Digital Media Lab, NHK. 10 mins. x 225 eps.
Mimika Himeno is the daughter of a famous chef, descended from a long line of cooks. She attends a magical cookery academy with other would-be cooks from all over the world. A show devoted to teaching children about food and cooking, *MM* mixes animation and live action, with Mimika supported by adorable elementary schooler Miracle Nana-chan, who wields a knife with disturbing competence. The

show even got a guest appearance by three members of AKB48's Team B (**AKB0048**) dressed as desserts, singing the ending theme. Seiko Ogawa is credited as cooking consultant for the 2006–7 shows, with Shino Oda taking over in 2008. Created by Akane Kasuga, the show also spun off a manga illustrated by anime storyboard artist Yumi Tsukirino, a Nintendo DS game, and merchandise.

MIRAGE OF BLAZE *

2002. JPN: *Honoo no Shinkiro; Honoo no Mirage*. AKA: *Blazing Mirage; Mirage of Flame*. TV series, video. DIR: Toshio Hirata, Fumie Muroi. SCR: Hiroko Tokita, Kazuyuki Fudeyasu, Ryosuke Nakamura, Yuki Enatsu. DES: Itsuko Takeda, Fumie Muroi. ANI: SME Visual Works. MUS: Koichiro Kameyama. PRD: Madhouse, Kid's Station, SME Visual Works. 25 mins. x 13 eps. (TV), 31 mins. x 3 eps. (v).
Takaya Oge believes himself to be haunted by the ghosts of ancient warriors and keeps seeing people surrounded by a strange aura of purplish flames. A mysterious man, Nobutsuna Naoe, appears in his room and saves him from the visions; he claims to be a reincarnated warlord from Japan's civil war era, and says that Takaya and others like him are warrior spirits reborn in modern Tokyo—like IKKI TOUSEN, but not as silly. The Feudal Underworld is seeping into the modern world and threatens to repeat ancient clan battles and devastate the present; Takaya is one of those who can use his ancient powers to prevent this. Takaya doesn't remember his past life at first, but as his powers return he begins to recall the passionate and sometimes abusive relationship that he and Naoe once shared. This series is based on the popular novel series by Mizuna Kuwahara and 32-volume manga series by Shoko Hamada, which was stuffed with beautiful young men brooding mysteriously while calling up purple flames (the "blaze" of the title) that give them power to destroy objects and people by thought. It was followed in 2004 by the video series *MoB: Rebels of the River Edge* (*HnS: Minagiwa no Hangyakusha*) in which Takaya hunts down a rebel in Kyoto who deserted the clan and uncovers a 400-year-old tale of love and betrayal. **Ⓥ**

MIRATSU, TAKEO

1960–. Born in Oita Prefecture, Miratsu was only 19 when he formed a band to compete in the Yamaha Popular Music Contest, although he would later find fame as a composer rather than a performer. He released albums of his own in 1992 and 1996, before turning to jingles and "image music" (compositions on spinoff CDs) for such anime as HUMMINGBIRDS and USHIO AND TORA. He subsequently became a composer for actual anime, scoring shows including SAIKANO, NINJA CADETS, and DETATOKO PRINCESS. His work has also appeared in games such as *Jumping Flash*.

MIREI

1995. JPN: *Kotoyoshi Yumisuke Mirei*. AKA: *Yumisuke Kotoyoshi [presents] Mirei*. Video. DIR: Akira Nishimori, Takashi Yoshida. SCR: Yumisuke Kotoyoshi, Nana Okatsu, Masao Oji. DES: Yumisuke Kotoyoshi, Naoki Ohei. ANI: Mitsuharu Miyamae. MUS: N/C. PRD: Reed, TDK Core. 30 mins.
In this adaptation of Yumisuke Kotoyoshi's manga, two beautiful girls are washed ashore on a South Sea island paradise, where they proceed to take their clothes off. **Ⓞ**

MIROKU

1989. JPN: *Kyomu Senshi Miroku*. AKA: *Expunged Chronicle of Miroku*. Video. DIR: Toshio Takeuchi, Junichi Watanabe. SCR: Hideo Takayashiki, Megumi Hiyoshi. DES: Hideyuki Motohashi. ANI: Hideyuki Motohashi. MUS: Michiaki Kato. PRD: Animate Film, Dynamic Planning, JC Staff. 30 mins. x 6 eps.
Psychic ninja fantasy suggesting that the assassins did not die out during the early modern period but burrowed under Japan, where they fought a new war against the alien occupants of a crashed spaceship that has lain undisturbed for several millennia. The shogun Ieyasu is just one of the historical figures who wander into this decidedly unhistorical plot that was based on a story written for *Shonen Captain* magazine by GETTER ROBO–cocreator Ken Ishikawa.

MIRROR OF HALLEY

1985. JPN: *Arei no Kagami*. AKA: *Mirror of Arei*. Movie. DIR: Kozo Morishita. SCR: Mitsuru Majima. DES: Leiji Matsumoto. ANI: Kazuo

Komatsubara. mus: Yuri Nishimura. prd: Toei. 25 mins.

Meguru and Mayu are two future-wanderers hoping to find the mythical Mirror of Arei that is said to allow all who glimpse it to pass beyond the edge of the universe. Hijacked by renegade android Zero, the trio joins forces when they realize that they are all searching for the same thing. At the edge of our universe they encounter the ethereal being Rin'ne (Japanese for transmigration) and a council of spirits who judge those who wish to enter a new universe. The gatekeeper, Arei, is not impressed with what the travelers' memories tell her of human history. Though the humans try to argue their case, Arei decides to destroy the mirror. Though it will strand them for eternity, the humans use their gravity generator to hold the mirror together so that others may not be denied the opportunity to see it. Arei is impressed by their noble sacrifice and reveals that the mirror was not really destroyed. She sends them home but first permits them a fleeting glimpse of the wonders of the world beyond our universe. Based on a manga by **GALAXY EXPRESS 999**–creator Leiji Matsumoto, this film was originally screened at the 1985 World Expo in Tsukuba.

MISCHIEVOUS KISS

2008. jpn: *Itazura na Kiss.* aka: *Itakisu.* TV series. dir: Osamu Yamazaki. scr: Yukako Shimizu, Mitsutaka Hirota, Naruo Kobayashi, Eriko Matsuda. des: Kazuhiru Soeta, Maki Fujioka, Hiroki Matsumoto. ani: Shuichi Okubo, Kazuma Uike, Nobuhiro Watanabe. mus: Yasuharu Takanashi. prd: BMG Japan, TMS Entertainment, TBS, Sun TV, Chubu Broadcasting. 24 mins. x 25 eps.

Naoki Irie is wealthy, gorgeous, clever, and a gifted athlete. He's also snooty and arrogant. When his classmate Kotoko Aihara tells him that she's carried a torch for him since their first day in high school, he lets her know that he's just not interested. She's in the lowest class at school, and he doesn't like stupid girls. Then Kotoko and her father, one of his father's oldest friends, move in with the Irie family when their own house is damaged in an earthquake. Naoki's mother warms to Kotoko right away, but with or without help, Kotoko is determined to get her man.

This romance based on Kaoru Tada's

1990 manga is one of the few shows to credit a medical consultant, Toshitaka Takeshita, who also consulted on the **BLACK JACK** videos and movie. Both leads move into the medical world after school. Tada's story develops over a period of years, showing the relationship changing as both characters mature and creating a believable real-world romance. Sadly the manga was cut short by Tada's sudden death in 1999; the anime is said to conclude with her intended ending.

MISHA THE BEAR CUB

1979. jpn: *Koguma no Misha.* TV series. dir: Yoshikata Nitta. scr: Shunichi Yukimuro, Yoshiaki Yoshida, Ryuzo Nakanishi. des: Isamu Noda. ani: Yutaka Oka, Sadao Tominaga, Takashi Saijo, Yoshiyuki Kishi. mus: Shunsuke Kikuchi. prd: Trans Arts, Nippon Animation, TV Asahi. 25 mins. x 26 eps.

Misha the Russian bear cub comes with his parents to a peaceful mountain village full of different kinds of animals. The animals come out to see the train, but Misha's father believes they are a welcoming committee and decides to stay. Misha befriends Natasha (another bear cub) but must avoid the evil local tiger (unimaginatively named Tiger). It's a simple children's series made to cash in on the 1980 Moscow Olympics' Misha mascot. Not quite as successful as the later Olympic anime **EAGLE SAM**.

MISS HORI AND MR. MIYAMURA

2012. jpn: *Hori-san to Miyamura-kun.* aka: *Horimiya.* Video. dir: Shingo Natsume. scr: Yuniko Ayana. des: Kenichi Kutsuna, Yukai Takeda, Harumi Okamoto. ani: Kenichi Kutsuna. mus: Shinta Yoda. prd: Hoods Entertainment, OOZ Inc. 21 mins.

The story of a bubbly, popular girl who gets good grades, and a quiet guy who's labeled an otaku at school. Both of have complete different lives out of school: she works hard at home to look after her little brother and keep house for her two working parents, while he has a tattoo, piercings, and a full social life. When they find out about each other's life outside school, a sweet love story blossoms. Based on the manga by HERO, which started life in 2007 as a web comic before going into print, the anime sensibly focuses on just one incident: the point at which Miyamura

helps Hori's little brother get home after he's hurt, and the classmates realize for the first time that there's another side to both of them.

MISS MONOCHROME *

2013. jpn: *Miss Monochrome the Animation.* TV series. dir: Yoshiaki Iwasaki. scr: Kazuyuki Fudeyasu. des: Yuki Morimoto. ani: Naoto Nakamura. mus: Shigenobu Okawa. prd: Liden, Sanzigen, Ameba, TV Tokyo. 5 mins. x 13 eps.

Two-tone android Miss Monochrome (voiced by singer Yui Horie) aspires to be an idol singer like her heroine, Kikuko (played, with a degree of self-referentiality, by Kikuko Inoue). She embarks upon a haphazard career in the creative arts (**MUSIC IN ANIME**), with time out for alien invasions and a convoluted subplot that suggests the two ladies were friends in a distant past life. Shades here of **KEY THE METAL IDOL**, although Miss Monochrome was originally an artificial pop star cut from the same cloth as Hatsune Miku (**HATSUNE MIKU LIVE PARTY**).

MISS MORITA KEEPS SILENT *

2011. jpn: *Morita-san wa Mukuchi.* aka: *Miss Morita Is Taciturn.* TV, video. dir: Naotaka Hayashi. scr: Hiroshi Sato, Ryo Karasuma. des: Takashi Kumazen, Hirofune Hane, Toshinari Yamashita, Shinji Katahira. ani: N/C. mus: Shinji Kakijima. prd: Studio Gram, Dream Creation, Seven. 30 mins. (v1), 24 mins. (v2), 3 mins. x 13 eps. (TV1), 3 mins. x 13 eps. (TV2).

Schoolgirl Mayu Morita may look blank when she looks into your eyes without speaking. That doesn't mean she's stupid, or has nothing to say. She just spends so long thinking how to say it that the moment passes, and so she says nothing. Despite this, she has friends who understand her and lives a normal, happy life at high school, and her best friend Miki talks so much that they balance each other out.

The TV series based on Sae Tano's 2007 four-panel gag manga had two earlier versions, designed to build sales for the collected volumes of the manga as well as alert fans to the anime. Publisher Takeshobo set the ball rolling with a two-minute animated trailer on its website in January 2011. A preview DVD was bundled with the third collected volume of the manga in February, and a 24-minute video was released in March with narration by Rika Matsumoto. The TV series was streamed worldwide on the day it made its Japanese debut. It sticks closely to the form of the original, plotless and without character development, with simple backgrounds and basic animation, devoted exclusively to providing a quick smile or a warm fuzzy glow. The formula was successful enough to get a second series aired straight after the first. Watch out for Mayu's cameo in the first episode of RECORDER AND RANDSELL.

MISSION OF DARKNESS *
1998. JPN: Inju Dai Kessen. AKA: Immorality Wars, Lust-Beast Great Battle. Video. DIR: Iwao Zumen, Tai Kikumoto. SCR: Atsuhito Sugita. DES: Shimendoji. ANI: N/C. MUS: N/C. PRD: KSS, Pink Pineapple. 47 mins.
A demonic rapist plagues Japan (for a change), repeatedly dividing itself and reforming in different places. In order to stop Japan becoming "a hell of mad sex," the government initiates a sex sting operation, predictably encouraging attractive young agents to submit to the rapist for the benefit of world peace and the pornographic consumer. ⓁⓃⓋ

MISTER AJIKKO
1987. AKA: Mr. Flavor. TV series. DIR: Yasuhiro Imagawa, Makoto Ikeda, Akihiko Nishiyama, Kunihisa Sugishima, Akio Yamadera, Tatsuo Suzuki, Junichi Sakata, Tetsuro Amino. SCR: Noboru Shiroyama, Akinori Endo, Sho Aikawa, Yoshikazu Sakata, Ryoei Tsukimura, Yoshinori Watanabe, Toshifumi Kawase. DES: Masahiro Kato. ANI: Nobuhiro Okaseko, Kazuko Yano. MUS: Daito Fujita. PRD: Sunrise, TV Tokyo. 25 mins. x 99 eps.
They call him "Mr. Flavor" because middle school boy Yoichi is one of the best chefs around, taking on and learning from masters in the many subsets of cooking, including spaghetti, sushi, steak, sardine gratin, ramen, omelets, hamburgers, okonomiyaki, bento boxes, curry, hotpot, and donburi. And that's just in the first season. Mr. Flavor returned for two more, until he walked off into the sunset on a quest for even better recipes with a final episode entitled "Gochiso-sama, Mr. Ajikko," the traditional Japanese thanks for a hearty feast. A gourmet anime aimed at a younger audience than the following

year's OISHINBO, based on the 1986 King of Sushi (*DE) manga by Daisuke Terasawa, who wrote the similarly foody Ryota's Sushi.

MISTER HAPPY *
1989. JPN: Yarukimanman. AKA: Ready-to-get-it-on Man; Mad-for-it-man. Video. DIR: Teruo Kogure, Masamune Ochiai. SCR: Masahito Nishio. DES: Masamichi Yokoyama. ANI: Jiro Sayama. MUS: N/C. PRD: Knack. 26 mins., 45 mins., 40 mins.
Kazua Jinno is the scion of Japan's oldest and most accomplished family of brothel keepers. In preparation for Kazua's taking over the family business, his father, Sopetuen, sends him out into the world to have sex with as many women as possible while always ensuring that the ladies come first (how this is training for running a brothel, Lord knows). He is aided in his erotic misadventures by "Mr. Happy," his talking penis, who provides advice and commentary at relevant moments. The Japanese sales sheet thoughtfully adds, "The ultimate sex battles developed by his proud penis together with women's juicy vaginas never stop making the lower half of men's bodies hot." Based on the 1977 manga in Daily Gendai by "Gyujiro" and AGEMAN AND FUKU-CHAN–creator Masamichi Yokoyama and reputedly screened on a U.S. adult cable channel in the 1990s. ⓁⓃ

MISTER PEN-PEN
1986. TV special. DIR: Ken Baba, Tsukasa Sunaga, Yuzo Yamada, Hiroshi Watanabe. SCR: Kenji Terada. DES: Mayumi Muroyama. ANI: Takahisa Kazukawa. MUS: Takeo Watanabe. PRD: Shinei, TV Asahi. 60 mins. x 2 eps.
Pen-Pen, the hat-and-tie-wearing prince of Penguin Land, turns up unexpectedly on little Mika's doorstep and invites himself and his zany penguin friends to stay. Based on a manga written by ASARI-CHAN–creator Mayumi Muroyama for Shogakukan's Second Grader magazine and comprising eight 15-minute mini-episodes, these two TV "specials" may be a salvage job from a canceled TV series. It had friends in high places, however—Hideaki Anno would incorporate a genetically engineered penguin called Mr. Pen-Pen into his own EVANGELION.

MISTREATED BRIDE *
2008. JPN: Nikuyome: Takayanagi-ke no Hitobito. AKA: Mistreated Bride: People of the House of Takayanagi. Video. DIR: Corrida. SCR: Taketo Watarai, Takehito Watari. DES: Jiro Nakano. ANI: Shiro Shibata. MUS: N/C. PRD: Image House, Milky, Studio Tamashii. 30 mins. x 4 eps.
Ichiro and Mitsuko have been married for several years and have a child when they move in with his family. Mitsuko starts out by helping her aged father-in-law to relieve his sexual tensions, then Ichiro's brother gets in on the action, then the pair find Ichiro's stepmother Sumie having sex with the gardeners because her elderly husband isn't satisfying her, then Sumie's daughter gets involved. This family has no idea of appropriate boundaries and their sexual tastes are extremely eclectic. Based on the porn manga by Tsuruzu Miyabi. ⓄⓋ

MITSUDOMOE *
2010. TV series, video. DIR: Masahiko Ota. SCR: Takashi Aoshima, Takamitsu Kono, Kenji Sugihara, Hideaki Koyasu, Masahiko Ota. DES: Takaharu Okuma, Shunsuke Suzuki. ANI: Takaharu Okuma. MUS: Yasuhiro Misawa. PRD: Bridge, Akita Shoten, Aniplex, Cospa, AT-X, Lantis. 24 mins. x 13 eps. (TV1), 23 mins. (V), 24 mins. x 13 eps. (TV2).
Satoshi Yabe is a newly qualified teacher starting his first job in elementary school. On day one, he falls for the bubble-brained school nurse and encounters his nemeses, the three teeny terrors known as the Marui triplets. They're just 11 but have more guile and ruthlessness than any grown criminal, plus assorted obsessions like most girls their age, including toilet humor, breasts, and pornography. Based on an adult gag manga by Norio Sakurai, and definitely not child-friendly, the story focuses on everyday situations and on the triplets' constant attempts to get Yabe-sensei to declare his love for the nurse. An unaired episode was bundled with the DVD and Blu-ray release in 2011, before the same crew produced a second series, Mitsudomoe 2 (Mitsudomoe Zoryochu), in 2012. Ⓛ

MIYAZAKI, HAYAO
1941–. Born in Tokyo, he graduated from the Politics and Economics department of the prestigious Gakushuin University

in 1963. He joined Toei Animation the following year and found work on **KEN THE WOLF BOY** and Isao Takahata's **LITTLE NORSE PRINCE**, for which he drew literally thousands of images. A shop steward and union leader at the company, he also demonstrated early aptitude for storylining, famously persuading the director of **GULLIVER'S SPACE TRAVELS** to allow him to rewrite the ending. The first example of his distinctive style came in **PANDA GO PANDA** (1972), released shortly before he and his long-time collaborator Isao Takahata moved to the Zuiyo company, later known as Nippon Animation. Had Miyazaki only stayed in TV animation, he would still have enjoyed a reputation as one of anime's most internationally minded directors, adapting children's stories for the screen from British, American, French, German, Italian, and Japanese originals, including **SHERLOCK HOUND**, **HEIDI**, and **ANNE OF GREEN GABLES**.

After a long apprenticeship in TV, his directorial debut came with **THE CASTLE OF CAGLIOSTRO** (1978), although it was **NAUSICAÄ OF THE VALLEY OF THE WIND** that truly established him as an original voice in the medium. The establishment of Miyazaki's own Studio Ghibli followed, which led to some of the most renowned films of the anime medium, including **CASTLE IN THE SKY**, **MY NEIGHBOR TOTORO**, **KIKI'S DELIVERY SERVICE**, and **PORCO ROSSO**. Notably, these films also generated good box office returns, as opposed to many other anime movies, which are only exhibited in theaters in order to gain review coverage in cinema magazines and to generate publicity for a video release. Although he supposedly intended to retire after **PRINCESS MONONOKE**, the death of Yoshifumi Kondo (q.v.) caused him to return to direct **SPIRITED AWAY**, which won the first Feature Animation Academy Award. His last official film as director was **THE WIND RISES**, accompanied in 2013 by the announcement of his retirement from full-length features—front-page news in Japan, where so many of his films had significantly impacted the soft-power economy. In 2014 he received a Governors Award from the Academy of Motion Picture Arts and Sciences honoring his lifetime contribution to animation films. His legacy to Studio Ghibli included a raft of blue-chip

titles that continue to generate income, as well as a recommended reading list of 50 children's books, seemingly adopted by his successors as an outline of worthy projects to undertake in imitation of the **WORLD MASTERPIECE THEATER**, including **ARRIETTY** and a 2014 adaptation of Joan G. Robinson's *When Marnie Was There*.

Miyazaki is often termed "Japan's Disney" by the foreign press—a faintly patronizing title that downplays his true originality. As he once sourly noted in an interview, Disney was a producer, whereas Miyazaki was a writer, artist, and director. His modern acclaim has also largely eclipsed his groundbreaking work in anime criticism, particularly during the 1980s, when he was a perceptive and often dissenting voice on matters such as the rise of hyper-realism and the threat presented by television toward true artistry. Although many of his articles are untranslated, a representative English sample can be found in his collected essays *Starting Point: 1976–96* and *Turning Point: 1997–2008*.

MIYORI'S FOREST

2007. JPN: *Miyori no Mori*. TV special. DIR: Nizo Yamamoto. SCR: Satoko Okudera. DES: Shunji Saida, Tetsuya Ishikawa, Nizo Yamamoto, Osamu Masuyama. ANI: Tetsuya Ishikawa, Yasuko Sakuma, Shono Saegusa, Hideki Ito. MUS: Takeshi Umoda. PRD: Nippon Animation, Fuji TV. 107 mins.

Ten-year-old Miyori has been abandoned by her parents. Her mother has left home and her father has taken her to live with his parents because he can't work and look after her at the same time. She had a strange experience in the forest near her grandparents' home when she was a baby, where the forest spirits seemed to reach out and embrace her, but now she's a thoroughly modern city girl, cynical, bored, and convinced that life stops at the end of the Tokyo subway. Her grandparents are kind but she encounters a bully in school and finds even the nice kids hard to get on with. But gradually, the spirits of the forest reach out to her again. Even though they're no fairytale and can be even harder to deal with than people, Miyori finally commits wholeheartedly to her new home, and begins to decide how she wants to live her life and where she belongs.

Hideji Oda's 2004 manga has spun off

two sequels as well as this TV movie. It marks Nizo Yamamoto's debut as director, although he's already known for his art direction at Studio Ghibli and on **THE GIRL WHO LEAPT THROUGH TIME**, which also featured a script from *Miyori's Forest*'s Satoko Okudera. Working with Okudera, he directs with an artist's eye, bringing out both the beauty and the strangeness of the forest and its inhabitants, and also provides some of the background art. To say that the movie hints at what might happen if Chihiro from **SPIRITED AWAY** were to end up in the forest from **MY NEIGHBOR TOTORO** is not mere flattery; this is a very fine piece of work. But there are other influences at play: the forest spirits draw on the rich traditions cherished by Shigeru Mizuki (**SPOOKY OOKY KITARO**). And Miyori, as awkward and conflicted as the young Taeko in **ONLY YESTERDAY**, is a lovable, believable protagonist. Compare to **A LETTER TO MOMO** and **IN THE FOREST OF THE FIREFLIES' LIGHT**, with which this story shares some thematic similarities.

MIYUKI

1983. TV series. DIR: Mizuho Nishikubo, Hiroko Tokita, Shigeru Omachi, Shigeru Yanagawa, Junichi Sakata. SCR: Michiru Shimada, Yukiyoshi Ohashi. DES: Mitsuru Adachi. ANI: Hayao Nobe, Kazuhiro Oga. MUS: Ryan Merry, Masamichi Amano. PRD: Kitty Films, Fuji TV. 25 mins. x 37 eps.

Two high school students discover they have the same name and become friends, but both fall in love with Masato, a boy who is forced to choose just one. Based on the 1980 *Shonen Sunday* manga by Mitsuru Adachi and the first of his many works to be adapted into anime. Others would include **TOUCH**, **H2**, **NINE**, and **SLOW STEP**.

MIYUKI-CHAN IN WONDERLAND *

1995. JPN: *Fushigi no Kuni no Miyuki-chan*. AKA: *Miyuki-chan in the Strange Kingdom*. Video. DIR: Kiyoko Sayama, Mamoru Hamazu. SCR: Nanase Okawa. DES: Tetsuro Aoki. ANI: Makoto Koga. MUS: Toshiyuki Honda. PRD: Animate Film. 29 mins.

A pointlessly kinky retelling of **ALICE IN WONDERLAND** in which all the characters are sapphically inclined females. Japanese schoolgirl Miyuki is late for school when she is distracted by a bunny-girl on a skateboard. She is dragged into a sex-obsessed

Wonderland, complete with strip chess, Humpty Dumpty as a svelte diva, a bondage Queen, and a Cheshire cat resembling a blonde, stockinged Lum from **URUSEI YATSURA**. Based on the manga by the all-girl collective CLAMP, *MiW* appeared intermittently in *Newtype* over several years, and its absent plot is explained with the age-old get-out clause of it all being a dream. A one-note gag that falls crushingly flat when the clever designs are forced to do more than look good on paper. **Ⓝ**

MIZUIRO

2002. AKA: *Water-Color*. Video. DIR: Kiyotaka Isako. SCR: Ryota Yamaguchi, Makoto Nakamura. DES: Takeyasu Kurashima. ANI: Takeyasu Kurashima. MUS: N/C. PRD: Movic, Pink Pineapple. 30 mins. x 2 eps. (v1), 30 mins. x 2 eps. (v2).

Lonely teenage boy Kenji finds first two, then three, fantasy females hiding in his closet. They reappear each night, but only he seems to be able to see them, in a predictably risqué respray of **URUSEI YATSURA**, based on a PS2 computer game. *Mizuiro 2003* (2003), the "second series," is a remake with the sex scenes greatly toned down. Not to be confused with **AQUA AGE**, which has a similar title in Japanese, or **AQUARIAN AGE**, which doesn't.

MM! *

2010. JPN: *Mad Masochist*. TV series. DIR: Tsuyoshi Nagasawa. SCR: Rie Koshika, Naoko Marukawa. DES: Kazumi Ono, Natsuko Fujiwara, Taeko Hori, Keito Watanabe. ANI: Taeko Hori, Shintetsu Takiyama. MUS: Yukari Hashimoto. PRD: Xebec, AT-X, Lantis, Media Factory, T.O. Entertainment. 25 mins. x 12 eps.

High school boy Taro Sado is an extreme masochist. It's not the sort of thing most girls find irresistible, and made him something of an outcast in middle school. Luckily there's a club for almost everything at the average Japanese high school, and Sado's school has the Second Volunteer Club, a group set up to help all those in need. Club president and confirmed sadist Mio and her happy band may not be able to cure him, but they'll do their level best. Despite the fact that they are the sweetest, most well-meaning perverts you are ever likely to see on a TV screen, these characters have no limits.

Nor do the writers, who attack the premise with gusto, looking for comic potential in the most unlikely places: one episode gives our hero amnesia to set up a porn parody in which he believes he's raped his best friend and impregnated his mother, sister, and girlfriend. The animation crew join the fun with as many sight gags as they can squeeze onscreen, especially favoring those that save on animation. Xebec called on over 30 studios and a Tokyo animation college to help out; it still wasn't enough. Too chaotic and noisy to be clever and too focused on pace to be involving, this show grabs you by the hair and drags you across the room whether you like it or not. Based on a manga by Akinari Matsuno with art by QP:flapper. **ⒺⓃ**

MOCHI MOCHI TREE, THE

1992. JPN: *Mochi Mochi no Ki*. Video. DIR: Isamu Noda. SCR: Takasuke Saito. DES: N/C. ANI: Susumu Shiraume, Hidekazu Ohara. MUS: Keiichiro Hirano. PRD: Ask Kodansha. 20 mins.

In this adaptation of a lyrical children's best-seller by Ryusuke Saito and Jiro Takihira, an ailing old man talks about the meaning of life with the shy little boy who keeps him company. The same crew followed with *The Mountain in Full Bloom* (1992, *Hanasaki Yama*), based on another story by the same authors, in which an old woman tells a young girl that a flower opens every time someone does a good deed.

MOCHINAGA, TADAHITO

1919–99. AKA Fang Ming; AKA Tad Mochinaga. Born in Tokyo, Mochinaga grew up in Japanese-occupied Manchuria, where his father worked for the railway company. Inspired by early Disney cartoons to seek a career in animation, he studied art in Tokyo before finding work with Mitsuyo Seo as a background artist. For Seo's *Ant Boy* (1941, *Ari-chan*), Mochinaga designed and built Japan's first multiplane camera, a rostrum device allowing for simultaneous action on four different overlaid levels of cels. He was the lead animator on the acclaimed **MOMOTARO'S SEA EAGLES** (1943) before getting his directorial debut on the **WARTIME ANIME** *Fuku-chan's Submarine* (1944). Exhausted by the effort and left homeless by an air raid, he returned to

Manchuria to recuperate, only to find himself conscripted to produce documentary animation for Man-Ei (Manchurian Film Studios). With Japan's defeat, Man-Ei's assets were handed over to China and renamed Dong Bei (North East) Animation, under which Mochinaga continued to work on graphics, animated maps, and satirical puppetry for Chinese Communist newsreels. Electing to stay in China, Mochinaga adopted the name Fang Ming and was instrumental in the foundation and early output of the Shanghai Animation Studio, where he befriended the Chinese master animator De Wei.

With the end of the U.S. Occupation of Japan, Mochinaga returned home in 1953, in time for the early rise of television and the new opportunities it presented. He was able to put his Chinese experience of **STOP-MOTION AND PUPPETRY** to use on the Asahi commercial *Beer Through the Ages* (1956), and his *Little Black Sambo* (1956) won an award at the Vancouver Film Festival, leading to an approach from the American producer Arthur Rankin, Jr. Mochinaga's newly formed MOM Films produced several Videocraft (Rankin/Bass) coproductions, beginning with the **NEW ADVENTURES OF PINOCCHIO** (1960), which proved it was possible to make an animated TV show on a weekly schedule. He later focused on TV specials, including *Rudolph the Red-Nosed Reindeer* (1964), although he neither wanted nor welcomed the treadmill of TV work and walked away from MOM Films to return to China, where he worked for several years in TV journalism and as a teacher. He taught at the Beijing Film Academy for two years in the 1980s and funded his final movie, *Boy and the Badger/Tanuki* (1992, *Shonen to Kotanuki*), with his own money, thereby spanning six decades of Japanese animation. Mochinaga is one of anime's real originals, the only man in history who can claim to have produced a Japanese World War II propaganda film, founded a Chinese animation studio, *and* made an American Christmas TV classic. His wife Ayako salvaged his memoirs in progress, which were published, tantalizingly incomplete, in 2006.

MOCHIZUKI, TOMOMI

1958–. Born on Hokkaido, he became

involved with the Tokyo anime scene when he joined the Animation Society at Waseda University. Hired by the Ajia-do company after graduation, he shared directing credit for **Creamy Mami** (1983) with Osamu Kobayashi before moving into romance and comedy with **Maison Ikkoku** (1987) and **Ranma ½** (1989)—his feature debut was the *Maison Ikkoku* movie. Subsequently hired by Studio Ghibli to direct the TV movie **Ocean Waves** (1993).

MODERN DEAF RECORD OF STRANGENESS

2006. JPN: *Gendai Kibunroku Kaii Monogatari*. AKA: *Modern Deaf Record of Weird Tales*. Video. DIR: Toshiyuki Kimura. SCR: Saruta Yu. DES: N/C. ANI: N/C. MUS: Akira Sudo, Leilani. PRD: Toei Animation, Gentosha. 46 mins.

A flea-market purchase leads to horror, a summer vacation in the idyllic countryside leads to horror, a refrigerator abandoned in a dry riverbed leads to horror, and as for crossing a long bridge in the middle of the night ... Japanese literature has a long tradition of ghost stories, expressed in the centuries-old anthology *Hyaku Monogatari* (**Requiem from the Darkness**) that presented tales of ghouls and monsters in familiar, everyday settings. This modern six-story anthology inspired by the Edo-period classic has another source nearer the present day. Writer Yu spent several years delivering a new ghost story in his email newsletter every Sunday evening and has published three books of horror tales, the first with the same title as this anime. Director Kimura is better known as a VFX designer on games and movies including the live-action version *Casshern*.

MODERN DOG TALES BOW

1993. JPN: *Heisei Inu Monogatari Bow*. TV series, movie. DIR: Takeshi Kaga. SCR: Yasuhiro Komatsuzaki, Shunichi Yukimura. DES: Terry Yamamoto. ANI: N/C. MUS: N/C. PRD: Nippon Animation. 25 mins. x 40 eps. (TV), 25 mins. (m).

Based on the manga by Terry Yamamoto in *Big Comic Superior*, here are the comic misadventures of a lovable stray mongrel called Bow and his little-girl owner. The situations are a standard list of food-related story lines, a few interfering cats, and a trawl through the various seasonal events

of the Japanese and Western calendar. For the short "movie" version, however, the story sends the couple back to prehistoric times, where they must save a friendly mammoth from an erupting volcano.

MODERN LOVE'S SILLINESS

1999. JPN: *Anime Ai no Awa Awa Hour*. AKA: *Anime Lovers' Awa-Awa Hour*. TV series. DIR: Makoto Moriwaki, Kume Issei. SCR: Chika Hojo, Motoki Yoshimura. DES: Yukiko Ohashi, Wataru Yamaguchi, Shuri Nakamura. ANI: N/C. MUS: Minami Toriyama. PRD: Gainax, Pioneer, Tac, DirecTV. 22 mins. x 12 eps.

Three short gag anime presented in a late-night anthology show, aimed at adult women instead of the usual male or fan audiences for anime and produced by Hideaki Anno in the midst of his work on **His and Her Circumstances**. The first, *Ebichu Minds the House* (*Oruchuban Ebichu*), based on the *Manga Action Pizazz* manga by Risa Ito, portrays modern life from the viewpoint of a hamster, Ebichu, who observes her Tokyo Office Lady owner's kinky relationship with her slacker boyfriend. Some of the show's controversial sex scenes were cut from the original digital TV broadcast but reinstated in the DVD release.

Little Women in Love (*Ai no Wakakusayama Monogatari*), based on the manga in *Manga Club* by Reiko Terashima, concentrates on unmarried Shizuka, still living with her parents, who fear she will be left perpetually on the shelf.

The final story, based on Mitsue Aoki's manga *Here Comes Koume* (*Koume-chan ga Iku*), switches location to the distinctive accents and attitudes of Osaka (see **Compiler**), where Koume works as a designer for the Caramel Ribbon company with a fey boss, an assistant who used to be a bad-girl biker, and a tough-guy boyfriend. **LN**

MODERN MAGIC MADE SIMPLE *

2009. JPN: *Yoku Wakaru Gendai Maho*. TV series, video. DIR: Yasuhiro Kuroda. SCR: Michiko Ito, Yuichi Monda, Naoki Tozuka. DES: Makoto Koga. ANI: Masafumi Tamura. MUS: Yukari Hashimoto. PRD: Nomad, Lantis, Klockworx, Shueisha, Geneon. 24 mins. x 13 eps.

Koyomi is a short, clumsy high school freshman who is often mistaken for someone much younger. She wants to be

a magician, and becomes a disciple of one of the most powerful Modern Mages, graduate student Misa Anehara, who can cast spells in computer code. She's soon drawn into the rivalry between Modern Mages and Classical Mages, and their battle for possession of a great magical library. This potentially intriguing plot is based on a book series by Hiroshi Sakurazaka, better known as the author of *All You Need Is Kill*, which was famously optioned by Tom Cruise as the basis for *Edge of Tomorrow* (2014). It's attractively animated, but its potential is wasted by lapses in continuity and a complete failure to make the characters engaging. In many sources the episodes are numbered 0 to 12, since the first episode was a promotional DVD release, creating much confusion for anime encyclopedists. **N**

MOEGAKU*5 *

2008. TV series. DIR: Nobuhiro Takamoto. SCR: Akira Watanabe. DES: Koji Watanabe, Kazuhiro Takahashi. ANI: N/C. MUS: Katsuryo Kobayashi. PRD: AIC Spirits, BS Fuji. 13 mins. x 8 eps.

Magical girl Moe and her cute companion RuRu wander round Akihabara, helping foreign fans find and purchase that rare anime collectible they've always wanted, while learning the basics of English, Korean, Spanish, French, and Chinese. Their main purpose, though, is to prevent Akihabara from falling into evil hands; they were chosen by the Goddess Megami-sama to protect the sacred source of *moe* energy. The show originated as a series of English-language study adventure games for the PC and PSP, based on the same concept as **Moetan**: lure kids into basic language study by presenting it through cute characters and a geek-friendly setting. The show was made in two parts, an animated adventure and a live-action segment in which hostess Aya Hirano and the anime cast join in language tutorials.

MOEKAN

2004. AKA: *Moekko Company The Animation*. Video. DIR: Kazuhisa Ono. SCR: Mayori Sekishima, Masashi Kubota. DES: Konomi Noguchi. ANI: Konomi Noguchi. MUS: N/C. PRD: Axis, KSS. 30 mins. x 3 eps.

AC Company is a corporation that makes android "escort maids"—beautiful girl-like robots to serve its clients' every whim. The androids are sent for finishing and communication training to Moekko Island, which functions as an independent state, with more financial and military muscle than any nation. Takahiro Kanzaki, head of the training facility, lives in a huge mansion on the island. He was once an extremely powerful man within the organization, despite his youth, but has been demoted; he is depressed and has lost many of his memories. New maid Rinia, who has also lost her memories, arrives for training; an obsolete type of android, she's very clumsy but tries very hard, and her well-meaning attempts to improve endear her to Takahiro. A predictable piece of fluff, based on the PC, PS2, and Dreamcast "love adventure game" *Moekan.*

MOETAN

2007. TV series, video. DIR: Keiichiro Kawaguchi. SCR: Saki Jasemi. DES: Kohaku Nishio, Takashi Kiruma. ANI: Kohaku Nishio. MUS: Takeshi Watanabe. PRD: Actas, Bandai Visual, Hakuhodo D.Y. Media Partners, Planet. 25 mins. x 12 eps. (TV), 25 mins. x 2 eps. (v).

Ink Nijihara, a very short high school girl, is madly in love with a boy who barely even notices her. A chance encounter with a magical duck changes her into a magical girl, and in this guise she decides to get closer to her beloved by helping him to study English. It may sound like an unusual plot for a magical girl show, but *Moetan* had an unusual origin. It was inspired by a series of English teaching guides, with manga-style illustrations by POP. The title is short for *Moe Ei-Tango (Moe English Vocabulary)* and the books have been hugely successful, with artbooks, manga, CDs, and a mobile phone language teaching app. They have been translated into Korean and Chinese—compare to MOEGAKU*5.

The levels of fan service (ARGOT AND JARGON) in this anime seem to have outweighed its potential educational benefits, at least in the eyes of its Japanese broadcaster. Episode six was pulled off the air at a week's notice and replaced with a compilation of highlights from the first five shows, for unspecified reasons. Both prior to this and later, the broadcaster had faded the screen to white on several occasions while the show was airing. The final episode also went unscreened. Both unaired episodes were later released on DVD. **O**

MOEYO KEN *

2004. JPN: *Kido Shinsengumi Moeyo Ken.* AKA: *Robot Shinsengumi Flashing Sword.* Video, TV series. DIR: Hideki Tonokatsu. SCR: Junji Takegami. DES: Kazuo Takegawa, Rumiko Takahashi. ANI: Magic Picture. MUS: N/C. PRD: Magic Picture, Enterbrain, Trinet Entertainment. 30 mins. x 4 eps. (v), 25 mins. x 13 eps. (TV).

Kyoto, 1882: statesman Kaishu Katsu asks Oryu, widow of the great patriot Ryoma Sakamoto, to form a new division of the Kyoto Prefectural Police to protect the city from robot and demon crimes. Her recruits are all girls, the daughters of famous figures of the Edo period. Alas, they take their lead not from their famous fathers but from their senior officer, Yuko, daughter of Isami Kondo, a clumsy, sentimental glutton; they waste their time on love and sword fighting instead of getting down to the serious business of defending Kyoto.

The heroes of the later Tokugawa and early Meiji period have been thoroughly examined in anime, providing material for shows like OI! RYOMA and PEACEMAKER KUROGANE. But *MK* is based on a PlayStation 2 game, and a game from Oji Hiroi, the man behind SAKURA WARS, at that. It takes a similarly cavalier attitude toward history, using historical events as a springboard into the realms of fighting-female fantasy. It aims to attract the widest possible range of fans by crashing RURONI KENSHIN into SAILOR MOON and throwing in historical figures, robots, and cars. Rumiko Takahashi, the creator of RANMA ½, is credited for her work designing the characters from the original game, in the same manner as Masamune Shirow on LANDLOCK and Kosuke Fujishima on *Sakura Wars*—it looks good on the box, but doesn't actually lend all that much to the quality of the production. Meanwhile, evil characters attempt to bring SHUTENDOJI back from the dead in order to plunge Kyoto into an age of darkness.

It would be kind to describe this show as an action parody, but the running gags about small breasts, wholly unnecessary bath scenes, and monster-of-the-week idiocy make kindness difficult. The producers have employed stellar talent and spent serious money to prove that what works in a game doesn't necessarily make great anime. **O**

MOJACKO

1995. TV series, TV special. DIR: Tetsuya Endo, Norihiko Sudo, Satoshi Inoue, Masamitsu Hidaka, Masashi Abe. SCR: Raita Okura, Yukiyoshi Ohashi, Hiroshi Koda, Yasuhiro Komatsuzaki, Chika Hojo, Atsuhiro Tomioka. DES: Hidetoshi Owase. ANI: Hidetoshi Owase. MUS: Kei Wakakusa. PRD: OLM, Shogakukan Pro, Tokyo TV. 25 mins. x 73 eps. (TV), 60 mins. (TVm).

Ghost-hunting schoolchildren Sorao, Miki, and Wu-Tang find a crashed spaceship belonging to Mojacko, an alien from the planet Mojamoja, and his robot, Donnoh. He takes them on a journey to the moon (with the aid of handy "air pills"), which is only one of many great adventures—though in exchange, he wants to learn about wacky Earth pursuits like rollerblading, golf, and scuba diving. He also enlists his new friends in a battle against the fearsome Maharaja Moja clan of space pirates.

An unremarkable children's anime based on a manga by DORAEMON-cocreator Fujiko F. Fujio, though it was an early voice-acting job for PERFECT BLUE's Junko Iwao. The series would eventually lose its animation director, Endo, to Hong Kong, where he would work on Tsui Hark's *Chinese Ghost Story* animation. Episodes 60 and 61 were rebroadcast as a one-hour TV movie with the title *Fujio F. Fujiko's Mojacko Christmas Present.*

MOKKE

2007. TV series, video. DIR: Masayoshi Nishida. SCR: Seiko Nagatsu. DES: Toshio Kawaguchi, Masato Shiba, Minoru Nishida. ANI: Toshio Kawaguchi, Akio Sugino. MUS: Yoshihiro Ike. PRD: Madhouse Studios, Tezuka Pro, avex entertainment, Kodansha. 25 mins. x 24 eps. (TV), 25 mins. x 2 eps. (v).

It's tough having children who are gifted. They need more time and attention than busy parents working to keep them clothed and fed can provide. Shizuru and Mizuki are gifted: Shizuru can see ghosts, while little sister Mizuki is often possessed by them. Their grandfather is an expert on ghosts, so their parents send them to live in the country with their grandparents. In the peace of rural life, and guided by their elders, the sisters begin to understand the importance of learning to live with other forms of life, whether natural or supernatural.

Adapted from Takatoshi Kumakura's 2002 manga, this is an episodic series of tales, each with its own lesson, a ghost story of charm and sweetness rather than one of gritty, gory horror. The lovely backgrounds are rich in natural detail and the attractive character designs complement them, creating an aura of high quality. Occasional lapses into oversimplified facial expression imply comedy where none was intended, but overall the animation is good and the didactic element of the story is kept under control. MUSHI-SHI takes a very different approach to the same topic, both stylistically and in story terms, but both shows are interesting and rewarding, making comparison worthwhile. Two unaired episodes were added to the DVD release, rendering them technically videos.

MOLDIVER *
1993. Video. DIR: Hiroyuki Kitazume. SCR: Ryoei Tsukimura, Manabu Nakamura. DES: Hiroyuki Kitazume. ANI: Hiroyuki Kitazume, Masashi Handa. MUS: Kei Wakakusa. PRD: AIC, Pioneer. 30 mins. x 6 eps.
Tokyo, 2045. Superhero Moldiver rights wrongs and strikes poses all over the city, and pretty Mirai Ozora discovers that Moldiver is actually her brother, Hiroshi. Hiroshi's suit allows the user to repel and defy all laws of physics, which makes flight, bullet-proofing, and incredible strength easy. Mirai decides to be a superhero herself, and Hiroshi gets a shock and a half when he finds himself wearing his sister's revealing costume!

Bright, colorful, and fun, *Moldiver* is packed with gentle jibes at the superhero phenomenon and very aware that the only crime in this kind of anime is taking oneself too seriously. With plotlines and characters from a KIDS' ANIME, but a tongue-in-cheek self-awareness aimed at a far older audience, it's also another excellent example of how good English-language TRANSLATION can be. The humor in Pioneer's dub crosses international borders with deceptive ease. Neophytes might be a little confused by Professor Amagi's attempt to raise the Yamato from

the seabed in episode 4, but they should be told that this old battleship has many resonances for a slightly older anime audience. It's as famous in Japan as the Titanic in the English-speaking world, with extra baggage brought by its place in military history. For anime fans, of course, it's also the star of STAR BLAZERS, and its appearance here is a tip of the hat from Pioneer's next generation to the classic creators who inspired them to pursue their careers in the first place.

The initial letters of the episode titles ("Metamorforce," "Overzone," "Longing," "Destruction," "Intruder") spell the name of the series, right up until the final episode ("Verity"), which crams the rest of the title in one go—possibly a sign of an early cancellation.

MOLE BROTHERS: FULL THROTTLE
2007. JPN: *Hokuro Kyodai Full Throttle!!!!* AKA: *Hokuro Brothers the Origin.* TV series. DIR: Katsuhito Ishii. SCR: Katsuhito Ishii. DES: N/C. ANI: N/C. MUS: N/C. PRD: Nice Rainbow, Geneon. 5 mins. x 7 eps.
The comedy duo Mole Brothers—played by Shunichiro Miki and Ikki Todoroki—are characters created by director Ishii for his live-action movie *Funky Forest* (2005, *Nice no Mori*). He had already used both actors as voices on HAL AND BONS, and he liked the new characters so much that he made this 3D web animation series of seven short episodes to provide them with a backstory. Being Ishii, the backstory he creates is surreal and any narrative has to be extracted from a forest of quickfire gags, physical abuse, giant monster/railway action, comic-making, science fiction, yakuza, and even a rival comedy duo. The quality of the animation is unusually high for web anime, but few will buy or watch this for technical merit—it stands or falls on whether you get the gonzo comedy style of Japanese standup. All the violence is comedic, but if you don't like grown men hitting each other while screaming abuse you should avoid *Mole Brothers* and never go into a Japanese comedy club. The Mole Brothers would also return in a cameo in REDLINE, as the representatives of planet Earth.

MOLE'S ADVENTURE, A
1958. JPN: *Mogura no Adventure.* TV special.

DIR: Hiroshi Washizumi. SCR: N/C. DES: N/C. ANI: N/C. MUS: N/C. PRD: NTV. 8 mins. 53 secs.
Kuro-chan is a mole who hides from the sun underground, and dreams of traveling into space. He's a reluctant hero, literally falling into a spacesuit at the behest of an insistent rocket ship, terrifying the clouds with his erratic flying while his girlfriend waves farewell. On landing, he almost falls down a crater, and dons skis to cross the alien landscape. He collides with one of the locals but wins the resulting fight. After encountering many strange plants, animals, and people, he has to hide from three purple aliens and comes close to losing his head, but then wakes safely on Earth.

The mole's story aired on NTV on October 15—Osamu Tezuka was almost 30 years old when it was screened; Hayao Miyazaki was 17. Then it vanished. Almost 55 years later, in February 2013, researcher Masahiro Haraguchi discovered a forgotten print in an NTV warehouse and rewrote the history of anime yet again. Previously, the oldest surviving TV anime was 1960's black-and-white anthology show *Three Tales*, or, if you want to be picky, the many hundreds of commercials (ADVERTISING AND SPONSORSHIP) that have fallen through the cracks in the archives.

In 1958, black and white TV was still the norm in Japan—the general population did not upgrade to color TV sets until the eve of the 1964 Tokyo Olympics. This only serves to illustrate the bold, experimental nature of *A Mole's Adventure*. The colors are rich—a bright sun lights the Earth, space is a deep, vibrant blue, and the surface of the alien world is red and gold, with gray rocks and mountains, even a hint of green. Kuro-chan's blue spacesuit tucked into bright red boots is a more colorful version of Marco's flying suit in PORCO ROSSO, and his long-snouted golden helmet and curvaceous, shiny spaceship, emblazoned with his name, were sure to impress young audiences. Narration, dialogue, and theme song were provided by 22-year-old actress Sonomi Nakajima, then at the beginning of a career that would include films for Kihachi Okamoto, Kengo Furusawa, and Hiroshi Inagaki.

The animation was made using paper cut-outs, a technique from the earliest days of animation, against its brightly painted backgrounds. It will take further research in NTV's archives to find out who was involved in its creation—the surviving print has no end credits—but they knew their anime and manga. Elements of the animation, including Kuro-chan's energetic arm and leg movements piloting the spaceship, recall Noboru Ofuji's EARLY ANIME *Haru no Uta (Song of Spring)* made in 1931, while the sequence where Kuro-chan evades three purple aliens in underground tunnels echoes panels from Osamu Tezuka's 1948 manga *Tuberculoses*, remade in 1953 as *The Monster of the 38th Parallel*.

MOMIJI *

2003. Video. DIR: Toshiaki Kanbara. SCR: Taifu Kancho. DES: Masaki Kawai. ANI: Hideki Araki. MUS: N/C. PRD: Marigold, Shura, Blue Eyes. 30 mins. x 4 eps.

Momiji is a ridiculously passive teenage girl who is pressured by her classmate Kazuto to work as a maid for his wealthy family. As soon as she moves in, he takes her virginity, then has sex with her whenever he chooses, in school and in public places as well as at home. He is also having sex with a classmate and the other maids, one of whom is in love with him, who have sex with him and with each other whenever he commands. Despite episode 4's suggestion that Kazuto is a poor tortured soul who had almost given up on life until he found Momiji, he is one of the nastiest protagonists of this type of anime porn, getting his kicks out of refusing to give his women what they want and abusing them with vibrators and hot wax, which naturally makes them even more eager to serve his every whim. **ⒸⓃⓋ**

MOMO: THE GIRL GOD OF DEATH *

2006. JPN: *Shinigami no Ballad*. AKA: *Ballad of the God of Death; Momo the God of Death*. TV series. DIR: Tomomi Mochizuki, Ryuichi Kimura. SCR: Reiko Yoshida. DES: Hiroyuki Horiuchi. ANI: Hiroyuki Horiuchi. MUS: Moka. PRD: Gingaya, Group Tac, WOWOW. 25mins. x 6 eps.

Momo, an attractive girl clad in gothic clothes, is a classier, prettier version of the Grim Reaper. Assisted by her talking cat Daniel, she interferes in the lives of humans—her mission is supposedly only to do so at the times of their deaths, when she collects their souls, but Momo is

often tempted to other duties, including helping people. *Highway to Heaven*, but with a scythe, based on a novel by Keisuke Hasegawa.

MOMOKO

1989. Video. DIR: Hideo Norei. SCR: Masahito Nishio. DES: Haru Hosokawa. ANI: N/C. MUS: N/C. PRD: Clion Soft. 45 mins. x 2 eps.

The life of "fashion model and masseuse" Momoko is detailed in this saucy adaptation of Haru Hosokawa's manga in *Comic Be* told in a combination of animated images on live backgrounds. With little else to recommend it, the marketing for this tape declared itself to be a "CVP," a "Comic Video Picture." Compare to MY FAIR MASSEUSE. **Ⓝ**

MOMOTARO

1989. JPN: *Momotaro Densetsu*. AKA: *Legend of Momotaro*. TV series. DIR: Masamune Ochiai, Yuji Ikeno, Koichi Fujiwara, Teruo Kogure, Akinori Yabe. SCR: Tadaaki Yamazaki, Shunichi Yukimuro. DES: Kazuo Mori, Hideo Okamoto. ANI: Kazuo Mori. MUS: The Peach Boys. PRD: Knack, TV Tokyo. 25 mins. x 51 eps. (TV1), 25 mins. x 24 eps. (TV2).

A childless woodcutter and his wife adopt Momotaro, a foundling child who springs from the inside of a peach. The superstrong child defeats Lord Brindled Dog, Lord Monkey of the Mountain, and Lord Pheasant of the Moor, who agree to become his traveling companions as he sets out to defeat all the ogres on the nearby island of Onigashima. Perhaps distantly inspired by JOURNEY TO THE WEST, one of the most famous of the JAPANESE FAIRY TALES, and a perennial children's favorite, the story of Momotaro is retold here with some science-fictional elements and a pastiche of Kurosawa's *Seven Samurai*. Pheasant Keeko, dog Pochi, and monkey Monta are asked by harassed villagers to find a hero who can save them—they approach Momotaro, who is famed far and wide for his naughtiness (guaranteed to annoy ogres everywhere). For the latter half of the series it was rebranded as *New Momotaro (P[each] C[ommand] Shin Momotaro Densetsu)*, in which the stout Japanese boy and his companions head off into space for a more fantastical sequel. See also VIDEO PICTURE BOOK.

MOMOTARO'S DIVINE SEA WARRIORS

1945. JPN: *Momotaro Umi no Shinpei*. Movie. DIR: Mitsuyo Seo. SCR: Kiichiro Kumaki. DES: Mitsuyo Seo. ANI: Mitsuyo Seo, Ichiro Takagi. MUS: Yuji Koseki. PRD: Shochiku, Geijutsu Eiga-sha, Japanese Imperial Navy Department of Information. 74 mins. (b/w).

After completing their naval training, a bear cub, a monkey, a puppy, and a pheasant say goodbye to their families. The monkey's young brother plays with his sailor's cap and falls into a river trying to retrieve it. He is rescued by the other animals in the nick of time, before falling over a waterfall. The scene jumps to a South Pacific island, where the rabbit sailors of the Imperial Navy are clearing the jungle to build an airfield. Watched in fascination by the native creatures (who, rather strangely for the South Pacific, include kangaroos, elephants, tigers, leopards, and rhinos), they complete it just in time for the arrival of a fleet of transport planes, bringing the animals from the former sequence, as well as a human boy, Commander MOMOTARO. While the military creatures get acclimated, the puppy teaches the local child-animals a nursery rhyme about the Rising Sun. Training takes a more meaningful turn when recon planes bring pictures of the British base on the other side of the island. The monkey, bear, and puppy begin parachute training, while the pheasant becomes a pilot. Presenting a history lesson using silhouette animation, Momotaro explains that Europeans have stolen Asia from its rightful rulers, and that the time has come to fight back (WARTIME ANIME). The animals attack the British base in a jarringly violent change of tone from the previous sequences, and the cowardly British ogres each try to get the other to take the responsibility for signing the surrender. Back home in Japan, the animals rejoice at the defeat of the British, while children play at parachuting ... onto a map of the United States.

A sequel of sorts to MOMOTARO'S SEA EAGLES (1943), and named in an apparent pastiche of the live-action propaganda film *Divine Sky Warriors* (*Sora no Shinpei*, 1942), *MDSW* was Japan's first full-length animated feature, released on April 12, 1945, scant months before the end of the war. It singularly failed to find an audience, not merely because the people of Japan had other priorities, but because children by this point had been largely evacuated from the cities, and teenagers had been conscripted to work in factories (**GIRLS IN SUMMER DRESSES**). In a coincidental similarity to many later anime "movies," it has a disjointed quality, seemingly resulting from the output of separate teams; one on the opening pastoral, one on the island sequences, and another on the "why-we-fight" exposition. Inspired by Japanese screenings of *Princess Iron Fan* (a Chinese adaptation of **JOURNEY TO THE WEST**), Seo keeps to a slow pacing, with time out for comparisons such as paratroopers or falling dandelions. He also appears to have found native English-speakers to play the British in the surrender scene—perhaps prisoners of war?

In 1983 (ironically, a year dominated by the pacifist **BAREFOOT GEN**), the lost film was rediscovered in Shochiku's Ofuna warehouse and rereleased in 1984. It eventually made it to video, bundled on the same tape as *The Spider and the Tulip* (1943), an unrelated 16-minute short in which a black-faced spider, seemingly modeled on Al Jolson in *The Jazz Singer*, tries to tempt a ladybug into his web. The inclusion of Kenzo Masaoka's film seemed calculated, as in its original year of release, to distract audiences from wartime realities, albeit for different reasons. After the war, director Seo tried to make a comeback with the disastrous production of **THE KING'S TAIL** (1947), before retiring from anime and becoming a children's author and illustrator.

MOMOTARO'S SEA EAGLES *

1943. JPN: *Momotaro no Umiwashi*. AKA: *Momotaro's Sea Eagle*. DIR: Mitsuyo Seo. SCR: N/C. DES: N/C. ANI: Tadahito Mochinaga, Toshihiko Tanabe, Tamako Hashimoto, Shizuyo Tsukamoto. MUS: Noboru Ito. PRD: Japanese Imperial Navy Department of Information, Geijutsu Eiga-sha. 37 mins. (b/w).

After a moodily shot dawn launch from a carrier, the hero Momotaro's animal warriors set off on a bombing mission against "Demon Island" (Oahu). They save a lost eagle chick en route, and are rewarded for their kindness on the return journey, when the eagle's grateful mother rescues three

downed pilots and returns them to their waiting shipmates.

Momotaro's Sea Eagles was the state of the art in Japanese animation in 1943 and remains a richly layered historical document. Despite anthropomorphized "funny" animals, its scenes of navy life often have a documentary edginess, while the soundtrack contains samples from propaganda hits of its day. There are coded messages in everything from the Morse flashes from ships, to the semaphore signal-ears of a rabbit technician, to the battle flag of Admiral Togo, a "Z" signal raised to signify that "the fate of the Empire rests upon this battle." Seo and his assistant Mochinaga blew much of their production budget on the detailed take-off and landing sequences, leaving little time for the central narrative of the film itself and making it somewhat oddly paced. The attack on "Demon Island" begins with a Pacific idyll, accompanied by a slide-guitar rendition of "Aloha Oe," before Momotaro's planes scream out of the sky, panicking groups of sailors seemingly modeled on Popeye and Bluto. Exceeding the achievements of the real-life attackers of Pearl Harbor, Momotaro's squadron lands a bunch of monkey saboteurs, who destroy planes on the ground to the tune of "Come on, Come on, Light Your Match." There remains something deeply chilling about the jaunty, joyous songs that accompany shots of fleeing "demons," yet also something equally melancholy about the long, tense wait on the carrier for all the planes to come home.

Seemingly named in a knowing pastiche of the live-action propaganda film *Sea Eagles* (*Umiwashi*, 1942), and supposedly the **WARTIME ANIME** hit of the decade, this film's popularity was largely a foregone conclusion, since attendances were block-booked for compulsory school outings. It has often been misleadingly described as a "feature," seemingly in recognition that it was a stand-alone work, although it usually came accompanied by a rousing speech from a Navy officer warm-up man. Although director Seo's later **MOMOTARO'S DIVINE SEA WARRIORS** was a longer and more accomplished film, it is *Momotaro's Sea Eagles* that was the most widely seen throughout the 1940s Japanese Empire, and hence foggy memories from the wartime generation

often confuse one with the other. Released on English-language DVD as *Momotaro's Sea Eagle*, singular, even though there are demonstrably two of them.

MON CHERIE COCO

1972. AKA: *Coco My Darling*. TV series. DIR: Kozo Masanobu, Nobuo Onuki. SCR: Jiro Saito. DES: Koei Yoshihara. ANI: Takekazu Kuchida. MUS: N/C. PRD: Nihon TV Doga, NTV. 25 mins. x 13 eps.

French-Japanese Coco Marchand is a scatterbrained girl with design talent, whose playful, dressed-down designs all but ruin a stuffy show by the famous Madame Elle. However, her innovative attitude impresses Madame Cheryl, the kindly editor of *Mode* magazine, who takes her under her wing and offers to help her become a fashion designer. Based on a 1972 manga by **SMART-SAN**-creator Waki Yamato, this rags-to-better-rags tale might at first seem like a strange follow-up to the TV Doga studio's **ROAD TO MUNICH**. But the tropes and trials of the fashion world have many similarities to those of **SPORTS ANIME**, and *Mon Cherie Coco* sits in the tradition of other girls' stories like **MASK OF GLASS**, just with more sewing. Strictly speaking, the bilingual title probably should have been *Ma Cherie Koko*, but we have kept with both the creator's deliberate evocation of Coco Chanel and her hazy grasp of French grammar. In modern times, compare to **PARADISE KISS**. Fashion designer Miyako Kawamura helped out with some of the artwork.

MONARCH: THE BIG BEAR OF TALLAC

1977. JPN: *Seton Dobutsu Monogatari: Kuma no Ko Jacky*. AKA: *Seton's Animal Tale: Jacky the Bear Cub*. TV series. DIR: Yoshio Kuroda. SCR: Ryuzo Nakanishi, Michio Sato. DES: Yasuji Mori. ANI: Takao Ogawa, Shinichi Tsuji, Koichi Murata, Seiji Okuda, Isao Takahata. MUS: Akehiro Omori. PRD: Nippon Animation, TV Asahi. 25 mins. x 22 eps.

Ran the Native American boy lives high in the Sierra Nevada mountains of California, where he cares for a brother-bear and sister-bear he found as cubs in a cave. Calling them Jacky and Jill, he plays with them and their mother, until the mother bear is killed by Ran's father. Adopting Jacky and Jill as his own, Ran takes them back to his house. An adaptation of one of Ernest

SETON'S ANIMAL TALES that was soon to be followed by BANNERTAIL THE SQUIRREL.

MONCHICHI TWINS, THE

1980. JPN: *Futago no Monchichi*. TV series. DIR: Tetsuro Amino, Mariko Oizumi, Ryoji Fujiwara, Tatsuya Matano. SCR: Akiyoshi Sakai, Masaaki Sakurai, Tomomi Tsutsui. DES: N/C. ANI: Mamoru Tanaka, Minoru Tajima. MUS: N/C. PRD: Ashi Pro, Tokyo 12 Channel. 6 mins. x 130 eps.

Monchichi-kun and Monchichi-chan are simian twins who live in the forest. He "likes to play and she likes to be cute," and they get up to many fairy-tale-inspired adventures in the countryside. A long-running cartoon series made to cash in on the dolls made by the Sekiguchi corporation, which were also released by Mattel for the U.S., where they were accompanied by the less successful all-American cartoon series *The Monchichis*.

MONCOLLÉ KNIGHTS *

2000. JPN: *Rokumon no Moncollé Knight*. AKA: *Mon[ster] Colle[ction] Knight of Rokumon*. TV series. DIR: Yasunaga Aoki, Akitaro Daichi, Akira Shimizu, Shunji Yoshida, Akio Sato. SCR: Katsumi Hasegawa, Satoru Akahori, Reiko Yoshida. DES: Atsuko Nakajima. ANI: Hiroko Sugii, Tetsuhito Saito. MUS: N/C. PRD: Studio Deen, TV Tokyo. 25 mins. x 51 eps. (TV), 25 mins. (m).

Mondo Oya is a hotheaded 12-year-old schoolboy who just loves playing with his Monster Collection Collectable Card Game. One day, Mondo discovers that Rokumon, the world of the CCG, is actually a real place, when he is co-opted to defend the planet from the predations of mad scientist Duke Collection—described in *Newtype*, rather mysteriously, as "a straightforward homosexual."

A pointless addition to the game cash-in phenomenon of POKÉMON and DIGIMON, artlessly setting itself in the Rokumon "World of Six Gates" to imply a nonexistent connection to its more successful predecessors and tellingly crediting MAZE's Satoru Akahori as a "story generalizer." A theatrical short would pit Mondo against a Fire Dragon and a Lava Chimaera in the magical world of Rokumon, as if anyone cared.

MONEY WARS

1991. JPN: *Money Wars: Nerawareta Waterfront Keikaku*. AKA: *Money Wars: Waterfront Project in Peril*. Video. DIR: Yusaku Saotome. SCR: Shuichi Miyashita. DES: Chuji Nakajima. ANI: Chuji Nakajima. MUS: N/C. PRD: Gainax. 45 mins.

Everyday life at a finance company is upset when a client turns up murdered, and his death is connected to land ownership after the upcoming handover of Hong Kong to the Chinese in 1997. A financial thriller in an exotic Chinese setting that soon relocates to Japan for further conspiratorial investigations, this anime was based on the manga serialized in *Business Jump* by Soichiro Miyagawa, though the animated story was completely original and did not appear in the print version. **NV**

MONKEY AND THE CRAB, THE

1988. JPN: *Saru Kani Gassen*. AKA: *Fight Between the Monkey and the Crab*. TV special. DIR: Yoshikazu Fujita, Minoru Okazaki. SCR: N/C. DES: Minoru Maeda. ANI: Minoru Maeda. MUS: Bimoth. PRD: Studio Juno, Fuji TV. 25 mins.

The monkey agrees to swap his persimmon seed for the crab's rice ball. The monkey eats the rice ball and is soon hungry again, but the crab plants the seed and grows an entire tree. The monkey steals some of the fruit but refuses to bring any down for the crab, and so the two fight until the crab holds the monkey's tail in his pincers. The monkey promises that, if the crab lets him go, he will give him three hairs from his tail, which is why crabs have three hairs on their claws.

The version listed here, screened as part of the *Ponkikki Kids* children's show, is only one of the more recent appearances of the better-known of the JAPANESE FOLK TALES. An early *Saru Kani Gassen* (1917) by Seitaro Kitayama was the second EARLY ANIME ever to be made, and the tale is often referenced—e.g., in MY NEIGHBOR TOTORO, when Satsuki draws Mei as a crab because she is waiting so intently for her seeds to grow.

MONKEY PUNCH'S WORLD: ALICE

1991. JPN: *Monkey Punch no Sekai: Alice*. Video. DIR: Yuzo Aoki. SCR: Juttoku Yoshida. DES: Monkey Punch. ANI: Tatsuo Yanagimachi, Etsuji Yamada. MUS: N/C. PRD: Takahashi

Studio. 45 mins.

Doctor Stein, a mad scientist, falls in love with his own creation, the female android Alice, though Alice has feelings for the scientist's handsome young son Jiro. In this one-shot adaptation of a minor manga by LUPIN III–creator Monkey Punch, Alice flees the doctor's castle but is pursued by Jiro, either to avenge his father's descent into madness or to have her for himself, or perhaps both.

MONKEY TURN

2004. TV series. DIR: Katsuhito Akiyama. SCR: Atsuhiro Tomioka. DES: Jun Okuda. ANI: PLM. MUS: Daisuke Ikeda. PRD: VAP, Shogakukan, BS Japan. 23 mins. x 25 eps. (TV1), 23 mins. x 25 eps. (TV2).

The Monkey Turn is a cornering technique that shaves seconds off your time in a powerboat race—but it's tricky to pull off and requires skill and daring. Kenji Hatano gets into powerboat racing in high school and promises his would-be girlfriend Sumi Ubukata that he'll be a champion in three years. He gets himself a top coach, Kanichi Koike; the tough and unyielding man puts him through a harsh regimen of training but he's determined to get to the top. His main rival is Takehiro Doguchi, son of a famous man, but there are many others with more experience, and Kenji has to work hard to make good on his promise to Sumi. Based on the manga by Katsutoshi Kawai; the second season was called *Monkey Turn V*.

MONOCHROME FACTOR

2008. AKA: TV series. DIR: Yu Ko. SCR: Yuji Kawahara. DES: Shigeyuki Suga, Satoru Kuwabara. ANI: N/C. MUS: Takeshi Abo. PRD: A.C.G.T., d-rights, GENCO. 25 mins. x 24 eps.

Akira is an ordinary, lazy 16-year-old until he meets a mysterious stranger called Shirogane and gets attacked by a shadow monster. The balance between the human world and the shadow world has been destroyed, and he can put it right—by becoming a *shin*, a creature of the shadow world. But as so often happens with magical guardians, Shirogane has his own motives: he may be telling the truth, but not necessarily all of it. Kaili Sorano's 2004 manga differs from the anime version, both in some details of plot and character—including an entirely new character who does not appear in the manga—and in the boys'-love themes which are far more prominent in the anime. **N**

MONONOKE *

2007. TV series. DIR: Kenji Nakamura. SCR: Chiaki Konaka, Ikuko Takahashi, Manabu Ishikawa, Michiko Yokote. DES: Takashi Hashimoto, Takashi Kurahashi, Yumi Hosaka. ANI: Takashi Hashimoto. MUS: Yasuharu Takanashi. PRD: Toei Animation, Mononoke Production Team, Sky Perfect Well Think Co., Ltd., Asmik Ace Entertainment, Inc., Dentsu, Fuji TV, SME. 23 mins. x 12 eps.

A medicine seller in old Japan has skills beyond his patients' expectations. Having already witnessed a demon cat stalking a family for revenge and emerged alive, he finds himself in many strange situations facing unnatural spirits that have lingered too long in the human world and been lured or forced to vengeance by human folly. He carries a magic sword to dispatch them, but before he can do that he must use his intelligence to learn their shape, their true purpose, and their reasoning. Only then can he destroy them. Stylistically related to the same team's *Bakeneko* segment of AYAKASHI SAMURAI HORROR TALES, this is one of the most beautiful anime of the decade, its stylish design and breathtaking execution putting it on a level with rarities like THE SENSUALIST.

The use of traditional motifs such as framing *shoji* screens alongside strongly textured papers and watercolor styling is dazzling, and the color range is warmly seductive, giving the show the aura of ancient Japanese scroll painting alongside an Art Deco feel for sinuous line and strong shapes. The digital animation techniques serve the art and story well, keeping the action flowing without intruding onto the audience's consciousness. Despite the sensuality of line and color that wouldn't feel out of place in **1001 NIGHTS**, the characters and situations have enough historical credibility to keep us anchored in Edo, spirits notwithstanding: the shock people feel at seeing a mere tradesman wearing a sword, and human vanity and frailty that would be at home in a film by Akira Kurosawa. The writing, from a stellar team including one of Japan's best SF screenwriters, is another exotically beautiful hybrid, blending murder and mystery with supernatural and historical elements to produce a bold and stylish work that doesn't even try to be like other anime. For intelligent, entertaining writing and visual beauty, this series has few equals.

MONSTER *

2004. TV series. DIR: Masayuki Kojima. DES: Kitaro Takasaka, Shigeru Fujita. ANI: Madhouse. MUS: Kuniaki Haishima. PRD: VAP, NTV, Madhouse, Shogakukan. 24 mins. x 74 eps.

Kenzo Tenma, a Japanese brain surgeon working at a top hospital in Germany, is handsome, brilliant, and engaged to a beautiful girl. One night, he faces a terrible decision. A young boy arrives at the hospital after a mysterious shooting, needing surgery; shortly after, the city's mayor is also brought in. Sickened by hospital politics, Kenzo insists on saving the boy because he came in first, despite pressure from his boss. He loses the support of his director, his rank at the hospital, and his fiancée. It seems his career is over; then a series of grisly murders removes the director and the doctors who were promoted over him. Kenzo discovers that the boy he saved was more than he seemed to be, and his life becomes ever darker and more dangerous as he follows a trail of murders and political machinations, trying to clear his name and understand why doing the right thing has had such terrible consequences. Based on the manga by creator Naoki Urasawa, with each TV episode corresponding to two chapters, this compelling story takes a man who has it all and throws it away, and asks what it takes to make a monster.

A superior anime series that doesn't demand viewers suspend their intelligence in order to be entertained, *Monster* reunites a number of staff from the earlier Urasawa adaptation MASTER KEATON, including composer Haishima, whose ending theme for the first 33 episodes is sung by David Sylvian, late of British New Romantic band "Japan." In spring 2005 New Line Cinema licensed the *Monster* movie rights for a proposed live-action coproduction with Shogakukan; although nothing came of this, the torch was passed on to Guillermo del Toro and HBO, who announced their intention in 2013 to turn it into a live-action mini-series. **V**

MONSTER HUNTER DIARIES

2010. JPN: *MonHun Nikki Girigiri Airu-Mura Kiki Ippatsu.* AKA: *Monster Hunter Diary Last Minute Felyne Village—Felyne in the Nick of Time.* TV series. DIR: Benpineko, Kotaro Yamawaki. SCR: N/C. DES: Benpineko, Kotaro Yamawaki. ANI: N/C. MUS: N/C. PRD: DLE, CAPCOM, Geneon. 3 mins. x 10 eps. (TV1), 3 mins. x 13 eps. (TV2).

Airu are a race of Felynes, feline creatures that walk on two legs and are naturally nurturing. They love to look after hunters, adventurers, and heroes, carry all the necessary equipment, rustle up meals, and generally be supportive. Hero Nyaito has a good heart, but an unlucky fate: he's part of a team that frequently goofs off without completing its missions. Maybe, with the help of the Professor, they'll finally finish one task: land that giant fish, or learn how to escape from rampaging monsters while carrying eggs for supper. This madcap show spun off the CAPCOM game *Monster Hunter* in which the Airu played a support role. They soon qualified for their own game, charming gamers very much as **DIGIMON** did, and this Flash-animated series was made to promote it. Two unaired episodes were added as extras on the Blu-ray release, before the second series was commissioned. *MonHun Nikki Girigiri Airu-mura G* aired in July 2011.

MONSTER MAN BEM

1968. JPN: *Yokai Ningen Bem.* AKA: *Humanoid Monster Bem.* TV series, video. DIR: Kujiro Yanagida, Seiji Sasaki, Tadao Wakabayashi. SCR: Akira Adachi. DES: N/C. ANI: Nobuhide Morikawa. MUS: Masahiro Uno. PRD: Daiichi, Fuji TV. 25 mins. x 26 eps. (TV1), 25 mins. x 2 eps. (v), 25 mins. x 26 eps. (TV2).

Bem, a gangster with pupil-less eyes, Bero, a young boy, and Bera, a dark, almond-eyed witch, are not humans but creatures from the world of monsters. They wander the Dark Realm as agents of justice, hoping that, by bringing Good into the monster realm, they will eventually be granted the opportunity to become human themselves.

A follow-up to Daiichi's earlier GOLDEN BAT, *MMB* was one of the first Korean coproductions in anime, and an early example of the horror genre that would come to be so popular in the medium. Bero's constant catchphrase of "I just can't wait to be human" resulted in chuckles from audience members of a certain age at Simba's "I just can't wait to be King" in Disney's *The Lion King*. Two pilots produced in 1986 for an abortive "second season" which was never broadcast were released on video with the first television show in 2001. In 2006, the story was resurrected as a projected 26-part TV series, animated by Studio Comet.

MONSTER RANCHER *

1999. JPN: *Monster Farm*. TV series. DIR: Hiroyuki Yano, Yuichiro Yano, Fujio Yamauchi. SCR: Shoji Yonemura, Osamu Nakamura, Shinzo Fujita. DES: Minoru Maeda. ANI: Masahiro Sekiguchi. MUS: BMF. PRD: TMS, TBS. 25 mins. x 48 eps. (TV1), 25 mins. x 25 eps. (TV2), ? mins. (v).

Eleven-year-old Genki is an expert at the video-game *Monster Battle*. When he wins a video game tournament, he's rewarded with a 200x CD-ROM. But the game transports him from the real world to Monster Rancher Land. There, he meets Holly and her own personal monster, Suezo, and together they team up to fight Moo, accompanied by monsters Mocchi (a large, live personification of the Japanese dessert of the same name), Golem (a giant golem), Tiger of the Wind (a talking horned wolf), and Hamm (called Hare in the American dub, presumably because he is one). The personification of evil, Moo is misbehaving by corrupting all the otherwise good monsters. So Genki and his new friends set off on a quest to find the Phoenix, a mysterious creature with the power to change bad monsters into good ones. A hackneyed rip-off of POKÉMON and its ilk but swiftly snapped up for U.S. broadcast as a partner to DIGIMON on Fox Kids, in spite of poor ratings in Japan. A "special episode," *MR: Circus Caravan*, was bundled with a release of the game in Japan.

MONSTER TAMAGON

1972. JPN: *Kaiketsu Tamagon; Eggzilla*. AKA: *Tamagon the Monster*. TV series. DIR: Hiroshi Sasagawa. SCR: Takao Oyama. DES: N/C. ANI: Yuji Nonokawa. MUS: Koba Hayashi. PRD: Tatsunoko, Fuji TV. 5 mins. x 193 eps.

Tamagon helps anyone with a problem to solve it by producing a huge egg that contains exactly the right creature to provide whatever assistance is needed, from cleaning out the bathtub to finding missing objects. For the people who need a babysitter, he creates babysitting monster Peekaboo, for the kid who is falling behind at school, he comes up with Nininger the homework monster, and so on. However, as with the magical remedies of DORAEMON, comedic complications invariably ensue. Made to fill the same daily slot vacated by HIPPO & THOMAS, this show generated immense success for its producers, largely because of the theoretically infinite potential for spin-off toys. A *tamago*, of course, is an egg—for more egg-based monsters see TAMAGOTCHI VIDEO ADVENTURES. Compare to the same team's earlier GAZULA THE AMICABLE MONSTER. Note that some Japanese sources claim a much higher episode count of 308, although the Tatsunoko studio's own records only show 193—it is presumed that many of the "phantom" episodes are misfiled repeat broadcasts.

MONSUNO *

2012. JPN: *Jusen Battle Monsuno*. AKA: *Monster Flag Battle Monsuno*. TV series. DIR: Yoshiaki Okumura. SCR: Jeremy Padawer, Jared Wolfson. DES: Yuichiro Hayashi. ANI: Ichiro Ogawa, Kenji Matsuoka. MUS: Shinnosuke, Michael Tavera. PRD: Larx Entertainment, Dentsu, TV Tokyo, Fremantle. 25 mins. x 26 eps. (TV1), 25 mins. x 26 eps. (TV2).

Sub-POKÉMON monster-hunting antics ensue, as a bunch of teenagers somehow acquire and control a number of collectable hybrids of Earth creatures, cybernetic thingies, and similar mascot critters. They run away from the evil Strategic Tactical Operatives for Recovery of Monsuno (S.T.O.R.M.), in this Japanese-American coproduction that harks back to the good old days of animation made-to-order for foreign clients. After "peak anime" in 2006 (KIBA), it seems that everybody and his dog was ready and able to work on this juvenile show, with over 50 animation studios credited for inbetweening work, seemingly tying up every animator from Seoul to Shanghai and back, as well as many Japanese outfits. The Japanese premiere on TV Tokyo came three seasons behind the first U.S. broadcast.

MONTANA JONES

1994. TV series. DIR: Tetsuo Imazawa. SCR: Marco Pagot, Satoshi Nakamura, Megumi Sugiwara. DES: Marco Pagot. ANI: Yoshiaki Okumura, Masamitsu Kudo, Norio Kaneko. MUS: Mario Pagano, Gianni Bobino, The Alfee. PRD: Studio Juno, NHK. 25 mins. x 52 eps.

It's the 1930s, and Montana Jones, bored with life as a pilot for Onboro Sea-Air Freight, sets off in search of fortune and adventure. His cousin Alfred would prefer a family life, complete with quiet contemplation, decent music, and copious amounts of spaghetti. They couldn't be more dissimilar, which is exactly why they have been thrown together by the sacred fates of buddy-movie plotting. Accompanying the Jones boys is their talkative interpreter, Melissa Sohn, an annoying girl who is obsessed with shopping but is endured by the Joneses because she speaks a zillion languages.

The team travels the world in search of treasure on behalf of Baron Gilt, hounded all the way by the evil Lord Zero, who, with the help of the mad scientist Baron Nitro and his idiot assistants, Slim and Slam, aims to steal all the Jones boys' hard-won treasure. Starting in the Mayan jungles, the globe-trotting fortune-seekers head to the Caribbean for a pastiche of *20,000 Leagues under the Sea*, tour Prague in search of an antique bell, search for a hidden chamber in the Taj Mahal, hunt yetis in Tibet, and raid tombs in Egypt.

A fast, furious, and funny Italian anthropomorphic coproduction in the spirit of SHERLOCK HOUND but with such a blatant pastiche of the *Indiana Jones* series that we can only assume the series was unreleasable in the U.S. "Homages" go both ways, however, and Marco Pagot was the inspiration for a character created by his former collaborator Hayao Miyazaki: PORCO ROSSO. Compare to Disney's similar pulp-serial homage *TaleSpin*.

MOOMINS *

1969. JPN: *Moomin*. TV series, movie. DIR: Masaaki Osumi, Moribi Murano, Masayuki Hayashi, Wataru Mizusawa, Seiji Okuda, Rintaro, Ryosuke Takahashi, Noboru Ishiguro, Toshio Hirata. SCR: Tadaaki Yamazaki, Hisashi Inoue, Yoshiaki Yoshida, Shunichi Yukimuro, Chikara Matsumoto, Keisuke Fujikawa, Kuni Miyajima, Hiroyuki Hoshiyama. DES: Tove Jansson. ANI: Yasuo Otsuka,

Tsutomu Shibayama, Toyoo Ashida. MUS: Seiichiro Uno. PRD: Tokyo Movie Shinsha, Mushi Pro, Telescreen, Fuji TV, TV Tokyo. 25 mins. x 65 eps. (TV1), 25 mins. x 52 eps. (TV2, *New*), 25 mins. x 104 eps. (TV3, *Happy*), 62 mins.

The adventures of a cute little hippo-like troll and his friends and family, based on the series of children's books written between 1945 and 1971 by the Finnish author Tove Jansson (1914–2001) and Jansson's comic versions of the same characters, written for the *London Evening News*. The relationship of the anime series to Jansson's original, however, has been the subject of some controversy, since the original anime adaptation from Tokyo Movie Shinsha introduced anachronisms such as motorcars, much to the author's annoyance, and leading to her stern directive: "No money! No cars! No fights!" Consequently, production was moved to Zuiyo (later known as Nippon Animation) for the second season, *New Moomins* (*Shin Moomin*, 1972).

While the author was reportedly more satisfied with the designs and stories of the new series, it is the TMS version that remains preferred by most of the Japanese audience. Jansson famously complained about the sight of a military vehicle in one episode, which turned out to have been designed by a lowly animator called Hayao Miyazaki. The authors believe, although they cannot prove it, that Jansson's experience with the Japanese somehow made it back to Astrid Lindgren, the creator of *Pippi Longstocking*, leading in turn to Lindgren's refusal to sell the rights of that series to Miyazaki (**KIKI'S DELIVERY SERVICE**). Episode 7 of the first *Moomins* series and episode 2 of the second were also screened in cinemas as part of Toei anthology events in 1971 and 1972 respectively. Hence, they also show up as 25-minute "movies" in some sources.

Tove Jansson's brother Lars, who was responsible for drawing and writing much of the *Moomins* comic strip in the 1960s and 1970s, became one of the producers of a third anime version, *Happy Moomin Family* (*Tanoshii Moomin Ikka*, 1990), in a remake by Hiroshi Saito screened on TV Tokyo. It is this version, made during the heyday of the video era and with far closer ties to merchandising, that established the

"Moomin Boom" in Japan—an obsession with plush hippo-troll toys that endures to this day and ensures surprising numbers of Japanese tourists in Finland. The directors changed to Takeyuki Kanda and Tsuneo Tominaga, and the series was renamed *Happy Moomin Family Adventure Diary* (*Tanoshii Moomin Ikka Boken Nikki*, 1991) for episodes 79–104. Jansson's *Comet in Moominland* was brought to the screen as Hiroshi Saito and Masayuki Kojima's *Moomin Tani Suisei* (1992), a movie edition that was later released on video with ten minutes of extra footage. Twenty-eight episodes of the most recent series were dubbed in the U.K. market by the BBC, and subsequently broadcast on Hawaii's K5 channel as *Tales of Moomin Valley*.

Although Jansson had Finnish nationality, she was one of a large ethnic minority of Swedish-speaking Finns, and wrote all her original books in a dialect still sometimes called "Moomin-Swedish," as it invariably reminds native Swedish listeners of Jansson's characters. *The Moomins* is often erroneously listed as one of the **WORLD MASTERPIECE THEATER** anime, since it is based on a foreign work and made by the studio that would become known as Nippon Animation.

MOON PHASE *

2005. JPN: *Tsukuyomi Moon Phase*. AKA: *Lunar Chant Moon Phase*. TV series. DIR: Akiyuki Shinbo. SCR: Mayori Sekijima. DES: Masahiro Aizawa. ANI: Masahiro Aizawa; Nobuyuki Takeuchi. MUS: Daisaku Kume. PRD: SHAFT, Victor Entertainment, TV Tokyo. 25 mins. x 26 eps.

Luna Hazuki is a young German girl of Japanese descent, raised as an old-fashioned European lady. She is obsessed with wearing fake cat ears, and although she can be headstrong and selfish she's basically a nice person who just happens to be a vampire—compare to **VAMPIRE PRINCESS MIYU**. Photographer Kohei Morioka runs into her when out taking pictures on assignment in an old castle in Germany; it's not a total surprise, as he is descended from a line of psychics and has always had a strange talent for including ghosts and supernatural beings in his shots. Desperate to escape the castle, Luna tries to make Kohei her servant by sucking his blood and fails, but he has managed to set her

free of the barriers keeping her within the castle; so, naturally, she follows him to Japan and moves in with him. Unfortunately his cousin Seiji is a demon hunter, and another vampire is hot in her trail. Of all the things the world needs, another magical girlfriend story isn't top of the list, but this one at least looks cute in a slightly different way. Hazuki's late mother soon arrives in the reincarnated form of a cat, which then transforms into a flying cat-like creature. Based on a manga by Keitaro Arima, who simply adds Gothic Lolita fashions (see also the previous year's **PETITE COSSETTE**) to the usual clichés of a magical girlfriend story—**URUSEI YATSURA** with extra teeth. Part of the relatively recent "Gothic Lolita" subgenre of anime, based on the fashion fad of the same name and also found in **PETITE COSSETTE** and **MOON PHASE**.

MOONLIGHT LADY *

2001. JPN: *Kao no Nai Tsuki*. AKA: *Faceless Moon; No Surface Moon: The Animation*. Video. DIR: Toshiharu Saito. SCR: Masanobu Arakawa. DES: Megumi Ishihara, Carnelian. ANI: Megumi Ishihara, Noritomo Hattori. MUS: N/C. PRD: Pink Pineapple. 30 mins. x 5 eps.

Suzuna—proud, prissy, mercurial, and needy—is the latest in a long line of hereditary temple priestesses, whose assumption of her duties is a matter of considerable importance for her family, coming as it does at the time of the long-awaited Expectant Moon Ceremony. When she finds that the (orgasmic) preparations have raised her previously suppressed lust, her maids Tomomi and Sayaka (who bears an uncanny resemblance to the recently missing young television actress Ruri) engage her in various sex acts, much to her embarrassment (and pleasure).

Suzuna is additionally haunted by a shadowy dream lover, who makes free with her body—and who is realized in the flesh by the arrival of Koichi, a young man, also endowed with great magical power, who must become her husband as part of the Expectant Moon Ceremony. She is greatly disappointed to find out that he is not her longed-for knight in shining armor, but coarse-mannered and very human. Despite this (and her rape at his hands on the night of his arrival), she begins to fall for him, and he for her.

However, this is all orchestrated by

Suzuna's "mother," Yuriko (who has her own liaisons with Tomomi, Koichi, and the gardener Gohei), actually the ghost of a former priestess, in a plot to resurrect herself from her watery grave.She has supplanted Suzuna's family and is using Tomomi's power of forgetfulness as well as the mystical aphrodisiac qualities of a camellia tree to control the other characters and to raise the necessary magical energy from them to bring the ceremony to her desired conclusion. The result is an increasing atmosphere of eroticism, where the boundaries of dream and reality become almost indistinguishable to those caught in Yuriko's web.

Unfortunately, the last episode discards various subplots—Koichi's university instructor Chikako, who has been using Koichi as her mystical tool, penetrates the barrier which now surrounds the mansion in order to investigate; Suzuna's mute identical twin Mizuna, hidden in a cave behind a waterfall; Suzuna's childhood cousin and childhood friend Io—in order to concentrate on the erotic final ceremony, losing in the process a great deal of the coherence which makes up much of the serial's appeal. The result, though it could have been more, is still an above average erotic anime, which features particularly good art thanks to the designs from Carnelian, who created the original game for the company Root. See also **TOKA GETTAN**, a distaff spin-off made several years later. 🄝🄥

MOONLIGHT MASK

1972. JPN: *Gekko Kamen*. TV series. DIR: Nobuhiro Okaseko. SCR: Tsunehisa Ito, Haruya Yamazaki. DES: Sadayoshi Tominaga, Nobuhiro Okaseko. ANI: Tadashi Yamashita. MUS: Goro Misawa. PRD: Ai Planning Center, Knack, Nippon TV. 25 mins. x 39 eps. (TV1), 25 mins. x 25 eps. (TV2).
Shavanan, the good king of Paradai, is murdered by the man-monster Great Claw of Satan, an evil figure intent on stealing the fabled treasure hidden somewhere in the small country. He only has one of the three golden keys required to reach the treasure, so he hunts down Shavanan's daughter, Fujiko Kuwata, believing her to have another. However, Fujiko is protected by a group of noble detectives and by the "warrior of love and justice," the

mysterious motorcycle-riding superhero Moonlight Mask.

Originating in a 1957 live-action TV series that spun off into four live-action movies, the first two seasons of the anime kept close to the continuity of the TV original, adapting the *Claw of Satan* and *Mammoth Kong* story lines, while the final part was the *Dragon's Tooth* plot. Curiously, the fourth live *MM* movie, *Last of the Devil* (1957, *Akuma no Saigo*), was to feature a plot very similar to that of **PATLABOR** 2, in which an abandoned soldier decides to avenge himself on the country that betrayed him. Fiercely lampooned in Go Nagai's saucy pastiche **KEKKO KAMEN** (which featured a Great *Toenail* of Satan as a school principal), in 1981, *MM* returned to the live-action theater screens with a new high-kicking female sidekick—martial arts star Etsuko Shiomi. In 2000, it was also remade as a comedy anime designed to hook the original fans and their own very young children. Directed by Toshio Takeuchi and written by Yoshio Urasawa, *Look! It's Little Moonlight Mask!* (*Gozonji! Gekko Kamen-chan*) featured Naoto, who was a humble schoolboy by day and the nemesis of Satan's Claw in the evenings (before bedtime).

MOONLIGHT MILE *

2007. TV series. DIR: Iku Suzuki. SCR: Akinori Endo. DES: Isao Sugimoto, Takao Takegami, Takashi Miyano. ANI: Isao Sugimoto. MUS: Kan Sawada. PRD: Studio Hibari, Amuse Soft Entertainment, Inc., Imagica, Klockworx, WOWOW. 25 mins. x 12 eps.
Two men climb Mount Everest together and see the International Space Station overhead. Goro Saruwatari and Jack Woodbridge vow that their next adventure will be a trek into outer space. Years later, when a new energy source is found on the Moon, they have a chance to make that dream come true. By now Jack is a pilot and Goro knows all there is to know about heavy construction—both have acquired quite a reputation, not only for work but for play.

Staking a claim on space for Real Men, this is a testosterone-fueled hymn to the old-fashioned alpha male that makes *Star Trek* (2009) and *X-Men Origins: Wolverine* (2009) look like they've donned schoolgirl outfits and picked up a book of poetry.

Masculine on a level unseen outside **MAD BULL 34,** Goro and Jack are just too macho for the intelligent story about man's return to space that could have otherwise fought its way out of this show.

MOONLIGHT PIERCE YUMEMI AND THE KNIGHTS OF THE SILVER ROSE

1991. JPN: *Gekko no Pierce: Yumemi to Gin no Bara no Kishi-dan*. Movie. DIR: Takeshi Mori. SCR: Yukiyoshi Ohashi. DES: Katsumi Aoshima. ANI: N/C. MUS: Kyosuke Himuro. PRD: Studio Pierrot. 70 mins.
Seventeen-year-old Yumemi Sato is dragged into an interdimensional conspiracy when her handsome upperclassman Masaki Suzukaga reveals that he is a German were-creature who can use magical powers to change shape at will. Hate it when that happens. A pretty-boy anime based on the best-selling novel of the same name by Hitomi Fujimoto.

MOONLIGHT SONATA

2001. Video. DIR: Hayato Nakamura. SCR: Renmu. DES: Shinsuke Terasawa. ANI: Shinsuke Terasawa. MUS: N/C. PRD: Éclair, Museum Pictures, Milky. 30 mins.
The sacred city of Aerial is torn apart by a civil war, in which swordmaster Lian is overcome with lust for his sister, the queen. He kills her husband King Eril and runs for the hills, where the couple live briefly in unwedded, incestuous bliss, before being attacked by the agents of justice. Based on an erotic computer game by Éclair. 🄛🄝🄥

MORAL HAZARD *

2001. JPN: *Changing Moral Hazard*. Video. DIR: N/C. SCR: N/C. DES: N/C. ANI: N/C. MUS: N/C. PRD: Obtain, Onmitsudo. 30 mins.
A nameless young girl is walking home through a park at night, where she is set upon by a would-be rapist. However, she is saved by a nameless man wielding a baseball bat, who confesses to her that he is a businessman facing bankruptcy and is so depressed that he might as well rape her himself. However, the former thug then fights him off, and the pair of them chase her around the park. Compare to *Dying for a Girl* in the **LOLITA ANIME** series. 🄛🄝🄥

MORI, YASUJI

1925–92. Born in Taipei, Taiwan (at the

time, part of the Japanese Empire), Mori was inspired to become an animator by seeing Kenzo Masaoka's *Spider and the Tulip* and graduated from the design department of the Tokyo University of the Arts in 1949. By 1951, he had joined Nippon Doga (Nichido), where he was instrumental in many 1950s cartoons, and survived straitened circumstances that saw him forced to take on an additional job in the advertising department for the Seibu department store. Clinging to animation as a career, he endured the tough times, and was hence a high-ranking staffer at the time of the studio's acquisition by Toei and rebranding as Toei Animation. Under the new management, he worked on PANDA AND THE MAGIC SERPENT as a concept artist and JOURNEY TO THE WEST as a key animator. Along with Akira Daikuhara (q.v.), Mori trained a new group of key animators, who would then train further groups of key animators in turn, gradually expanding Toei in increments until it not only had enough staff to meet its founders' production aims, but sufficient surplus to allow for poaching by many of the start-up companies of the TV era. As a man who remembered the era before television, Mori was quick to voice his concerns about overwork in the modern anime business, coining the term "Anime Syndrome" for the combination of overwork, poor diet, exhaustion, and diminished immunities that affects the health of so many animators. He left for Zuiyo (now Nippon Animation) in 1973, and his last prominent roles in the anime business were on NOOZLES and FUTURE BOY CONAN.

MORIBITO: GUARDIAN OF THE SPIRIT *

2007. JPN: *Seirei no Moribito*. TV series. DIR: Kenji Kamiyama. SCR: Kenji Kamiyama, Shunpei Okada. DES: Gato Aso, Yusuke Takeda. ANI: Takayuki Goto. MUS: Kenji Kawai. PRD: Production I.G, Dentsu, Geneon, NHK. 25 mins. x 26 eps.
Warrior woman Balsa's skill with a spear wasn't enough to save the eight people she held dear. To make amends for her part in their deaths, she has vowed to save eight lives. She has just one more life to save to fulfill her vow when she rescues a young man from a suspicious accident: Chagum, a prince on the run from his imperial

father's attempts to kill him. Balsa must call on the help of friends to keep them both alive and finally fulfill her vow, while Chagum's old tutor tries to unravel the mystery of why the prince is allegedly so dangerous that his father wants him dead.

Production I.G puts its considerable artistic talents on display to bring to life a beautifully realized and well designed world peopled by capable, convincingly grown-up characters. Based on a novel by Nahoko Uehashi, the stock fantasy plot is intelligently written and the characters beautifully developed. The writing is of a generally high standard, with good pace and balance, and the animation is almost as good as the design, with few visible short-cuts. The result is a show that looks almost as good as a movie, and plays far better than many.

MORIMOTO, KOJI

1959–. Born in Wakayama Prefecture, he graduated from the Osaka School of Design and worked briefly as a lowly animator for Annapuru on TOMORROW'S JOE. Inspired by the sight of Takashi Nakamura's work on GOLD LIGHTAN, he went freelance, first achieving fame as one of the animators on NEO TOKYO. Subsequent works have included segments in ROBOT CARNIVAL and MEMORIES (1995), by which time he had founded the Studio 4°C with Eiko Tanaka and Yoshiharu Sato. His involvement in anime has since been largely uncredited, apart from two distinctive Morimoto moments—the concert sequence in MACROSS *Plus* (1994) and the pop promo NOISEMAN (1997). His best-known work today is probably his contribution to THE ANIMATRIX (2002).

MORIYAMA, YUJI

1960–. Graduating high school in 1978, Moriyama found work as an animator on the STAR BLAZERS movie of the same year. He subsequently worked as a key animator on MACROSS and art director on URUSEI YATSURA. His work was also a major feature of the video anime of the early 1980s with highenough quality work to get away with a cinema screening, such as PROJECT A-KO. He sometimes uses the pseudonym Yuji Motoyama.

MOSAICA

1991. JPN: *Eiyu Gaiden Mosaica*. AKA: *Heroic Tale Mosaica*. Video. DIR: Ryosuke Takahashi. SCR: Ryoei Tsukimura. DES: Norio Shioyama. ANI: Hidetoshi Omori, Hideyuki Motohashi. MUS: Kaoru Wada. PRD: Studio Deen. 30 mins. x 4 eps.
The kingdom of Mosaica is on the verge of being overrun by King Sazara when the great warrior Lee Wu Dante is executed for questioning the King of Mosaica's judgment. His son, Lee Wu Talma, decides to save Mosaica in his father's memory, using ancient giant robots that lie dormant in a forgotten valley. Taking the advice of the hermit Ritish, Talma gathers an army but must first rescue Princess Menoza, who has been taken prisoner by his enemies. An SF fantasy deliberately designed to evoke memories of the crewmembers' earlier VOTOMS and RONIN WARRIORS.

MOSPEADA *

1983. JPN: *Kiko Soseiki Mospeada*. AKA: *Armored Genesis Mospeada; Genesis Climber Mospeada*. TV series, video. DIR: Katsuhisa Yamada, Tatsuya Kasahara, Masayuki Kojima, Kazuhito Akiyama, Norio Yazawa. SCR: Sukehiro Tomita, Ryo Yasumura, Kenji Terada. DES: Yoshitaka Amano, Shinji Aramaki, Hideki Kakinuma. ANI: Kazuhiko Udagawa. MUS: Joe Hisaishi, Hiroshi Ogasawara. PRD: Tatsunoko, Fuji TV. 25 mins. x 25 eps. (TV), 49? mins. (v).
In the year 2083, the last remnants of the human race on Mars send a military mission to recapture Earth from the Invid, who overran it a generation before. However, all but young fighter pilot Stick Bernard are wiped out. Crash-landing in the Amazon jungle, he resolves to head north and attack the Invid base single-handed, even though this is sure to be a suicide mission. En route, he meets Rei, an inexperienced kid with a natural talent for piloting robots, and the pair hone their skills with the Legioss and Mospeada Ride Armor transforming motorcycles. Slowly, the duo gather other revolutionaries around them in order to fight a guerrilla war against the Invid, though their struggle was curtailed by poor ratings in Japan. A famous SF anime featuring several famous designers, whose plot was supposedly based on writer Tomita's interpretation of the medieval standoff between

Christianity and Islam! However, it also bears an uncanny resemblance to his unproduced story outline for *Terrahawks* (see **THUNDERBIRDS 2086**). The series was cut together with **MACROSS** and **SOUTHERN CROSS** to form the basis for the English-language **ROBOTECH**, long before it was released subtitled in its unadulterated form as part of the *Robotech Perfect Collection*.

Yellow Dancer (Yellow Belmont), a cross-dressing singer from the series, lived on after its cancellation to record an album, *Live from the Pit Inn*, and the *Love, Live, Alive* music video (chiefly comprising recycled footage, as with *Macross Flashback 2012*).

MOST SPIRITED MAN IN JAPAN

1999. JPN: *Nihon-ichi no Otoko no Tamashii*. TV series. DIR: Toshio Yoshida. SCR: Masashi Sogo. DES: Masaaki Kannan. ANI: Bob Shirahata. MUS: N/C. PRD: Studio Deen, TBS. 5 mins. x 48 eps.
Tales of sex and sadomasochism, based on the manga in *Young Sunday* by Masahiko Kikuni, creator of **HEARTBROKEN ANGELS**. Japan's highest-ever-rated late-night anime, with a TV share of 9.1% in the graveyard slot, it was broadcast as part of the *Wonderful* anthology program. ❶❷❸

MOTHER *

1993. JPN: *Mother: Saigo no Shojo Eve*. AKA: *Mother: Eve, the Last Girl*. Movie. DIR: Iku Suzuki. SCR: Soji Yoshikawa. DES: Shuichi Seki. ANI: N/C. MUS: Naoki Nishimura. PRD: Nippon Skyway. 75 mins.
Amnesiac boy Dew and pretty girl Eve set out on a quest to find out how the human race came to die out. An "international version" was reputedly released, dubbed into English with Japanese subtitles.

MOTHER AND CHILD

2012. JPN: *Oyakodon: Oppai Tokumori Bonyu Tsuyudaku de*. AKA: *Mother and Child: Boobs Overflowing with Breast Milk Juice*. Video. DIR: N/C. SCR: N/C. DES: N/C. ANI: N/C. MUS: N/C. PRD: Tora no Ana. 30 mins.
"Innocent daughter and chaste mother, both of them have big tits. Squeeze them like fruit and the milk overflows without stopping." That's all the box tells us about Sakie and her daughter Rumi, in what appears to be an adaptation of a game

by Yukke Ani. Available footage largely presents the action with the ladies breaking the fourth wall, addressing the viewer directly in the style of many first-person erotic games. The authors' attention is drawn to the super-abundant Japanese title, which manages to use two words for breasts and also two terms for fluids, as if every aspect of the creators' minds is focused on matters of double vision. Our sole pleasure in writing this entry is contemplating what mainstream movie will get its title punningly altered to supply the inevitable English-language release, along the lines of **MOTHER KNOWS BREAST**. ❸

MOUNT HEAD

2002. JPN: *Atamayama*. Movie. DIR: Koji Yamamura. SCR: Shoji Yonemura. DES: Koji Yamamura. ANI: Chie Arai. MUS: Takeharu Kunimoto. PRD: Yamamura Animation. 10 mins.
A miserly old man eats a cherry pit, only to discover a cherry tree growing out of his head. When the tree begins to blossom, people throw parties beneath it, much to the old man's annoyance, in a stop-motion adaptation of one of the **JAPANESE FOLK TALES**, which achieved great fame when it was nominated for a Best Short Animation Oscar in 2002. Despite being an impressive achievement liable to set newsgroups alight for weeks (the authors still remember the excitement in **FANDOM** when **POM POKO** was *almost nominated* for an Academy Award), its thunder was rather stolen by the success of **SPIRITED AWAY**, which won Best Animated Feature the same year.

MOURETSU ATARO

1969. AKA: *Exaggerator Ataro; Extraordinary Ataro; Furious Ataro*. TV series. DIR: Isao Takahata (TV1), Kunihiko Ikuhara (asst TV1, dir TV2). SCR: Shunichi Yukimuro (TV1). DES: Fujiko-Fujio. MUS: Taku Izumi. PRD: Toei, TV Asahi (TV1). 8 mins. x 90 eps. (TV1), 25 mins. x 34 eps. (TV2).
Batsugoro is an idle father whose hobby is telling fortunes. After his death, his young son Ataro runs the local grocery store, only to discover that the ghost of his father has missed out on his chance to get into heaven and is now obliged to hang around offering unwelcome advice. Based on a manga by **DORAEMON** cocreator Fujio Akatsuka, the first half of this series

adhered to the set-ups of the original story. Later episodes veered away in favor of the supporting cast, such as Nyarome the cat, resulting in a series of stories far removed from Akatsuka's original manga. The show was remade in 1990 under the helmsmanship of Kunihiko Ikuhara, who, it was claimed, directed two episodes of the original, although he was only five years old at the time.

MOUSE *

2003. JPN: *Møuse*. TV series. DIR: Yorifusa Yamaguchi. SCR: Hiroyuki Kawasaki. DES: Toshiharu Murata. ANI: Studio Deen. MUS: Naoki Sato, Shigeru Chiba. PRD: Media Factory, Studio DEEN, Broccoli. 14 mins. x 12 eps.
Young teacher Sorata Muon has a secret identity. Following centuries of family tradition, he moonlights as master thief Mouse. Since the original manga was written by **SORCERER HUNTERS**–creator Satoru Akahori and drawn by Hiroshi Itaba, he is assisted by three nubile and scantily dressed young ladies who abuse him and teach by day and wear revealing costumes by night, willingly submitting to (and encouraging) his lecherous advances. Similarly interested in his hide, though for different reasons, is a secret society of art lovers who have recruited a former ally of Mouse to trap him once and for all. A short, lightweight piece in every sense, but you don't go to the man who gave the world **SABER MARIONETTES** for deep social significance. ❸

MOUSE STORY: THE ADVENTURES OF GEORGE AND GERALD

2007. JPN: *Nezumi Monogatari: George to Gerald no Boken*. Movie. DIR: Masami Hata. SCR: Seishi Minakami. DES: Toshio Hirata, Yukio Abe. ANI: Shinji Seya. MUS: Takayuki Hattori. PRD: Madhouse Studios, Sanrio. 52 mins.
George and Gerald are two feisty young mouse friends who set out on an adventure under orders from their clan leader Leopold. He sends them to find the legendary Dragon of Light in an effort to decide who will become his successor. Aided by three friends, the pair set out on a quest that will test their friendship and their courage to the limit. This movie for small children is based on a picture book

by Sanrio's founder and president Shintaro Tsuji, with art by Kazumi Fukasawa, published by Sanrio in April 2007. It showed on a double bill with another Sanrio film, **CINNAMON THE MOVIE**. The art and animation styles are very different, *CtM* being softer and flatter, while *MS* is rendered in the faux-naturalistic manner of a book of **FANTASY AND FAIRY TALES** from the 1940s: the characters are rounded, solid, and childlike. Tezuka Pro gets a production cooperation credit, and the great Chikao Otsuka, father of Akio, still working in his 80s, plays wise old patriarch Leopold.

MOYASHIMON *

2007. AKA: *Tales of Agriculture*. TV series.
DIR: Yuichiro Yano. SCR: Natsuko Takahashi.
DES: Junchi Takaoka, Satomi Higuchi, Hiroshi Nitta. ANI: Masayuki Sekine, Taichi Furumata, Yutaro Kishigawa. MUS: Naoki Sato, Takefumi Haketa. PRD: Telecom Animation Film, Shirogumi Inc., Dentsu, Fuji TV, Kodansha, SME, ASMIK, Aniplex. 25 mins. x 11 eps. (TV1), 25 mins. x 12 eps. (TV2).
Tadayasu Sawaki has a really odd gift: he can actually see microbes. It's a bit like seeing ghosts, but microbes are real; in just the same way, it gets you ostracized and ridiculed at school, so he's kept his mouth shut about it ever since. Then he and his best friend Yuki go to Tokyo to an agricultural college, and suddenly he's in a world where his unique skills are prized by his prof. And his prof's hot leather-wearing graduate student. Fun with yeast and yogurt is about to become even more fun.

Masayuki Ishikawa's 2004 manga spun off a live-action TV drama series, *Moyashimon*, in 2010 and a second animated series, *Moyashimon Returns*, in 2012. There's an obvious demand for TV shows about people over 16; not everyone abandons anime completely once they're out of high school. Yes, these audiences want to be taken somewhere they wouldn't normally go, but their fantasy life has progressed beyond the school uniform.

Under all the silliness, the cute renderings of bacteria as flights of super-deformed plushies, and the jokes about stinky substances and fermentation, this is a show about science. Fermentation isn't just God's gift to bakers and boozers, it's a process driven by living things and their reactions to circumstance and resources—our own life in miniature. The "Microbe Theater" segments at the end of each episode are fabulous little showcases for creatures most of us will never see in any other way. That said, there are numerous incidents that may give the weak-stomached pause. Few anime can compete with the sight of a character sucking a dead seagull's fermented insides out through its anus and then talking to you through a smear of animated seagull poo. Compare to the similarly odd **STORY OF SUPERCONDUCTORS**. **ꆤ**

MR. STAIN ON JUNK ALLEY *

2003. JPN: *Garakuta-dori no Stein*. AKA: *Stain in Trash Street*. TV series. DIR: Ryuji Masuda. SCR: Ryuji Masuda. DES: Wakako Masuda. ANI: Daisuke Suzuki. MUS: Meina Co. PRD: Kid's Station. 7 mins. x 13 eps. (TV1), 7 mins. (sequel).
The adventures of society dropout Stein and his cat Balban, who find themselves living on a forgotten, trash-strewn street in the middle of an unforgiving city. The trash, however, has a life of its own; like him, it ends up cast away for a reason, leading Stein to discover the tales associated with it—compare to **TOKYO GODFATHERS**. As with **VOICES OF A DISTANT STAR**, this CGI animation, created by Masuda and designed by his wife, demonstrates how technology has enabled anime to go back to cottage-industry roots, with individual creators in far greater control. The design is quirky and charming, with more than a touch of antique British children's series like *The Flowerpot Men* (1952) about the hero and his fat cat friend, and displays a deep, unsettling color and lighting palette. A one-shot sequel, *GnS: Epilogue*, followed later in 2003.

MS PICTURES

A powerful player in the field of anime **EROTICA AND PORNOGRAPHY**, MS (Museum Soft) Pictures began as a subsidiary of All In Entertainment, an educational video label formed as Sophia in 1987. Renamed Museum in 1994, the company moved into animation with its entry into the DVD market in the year 2000, establishing Milky Animation Label (Milky for short) in 2001 and debuting with the first episode of **NINE O'CLOCK WOMAN**. As so often happens with developers in this lucrative but tawdry sector, the precise name of the parent company has shifted and mutated under numerous liability shields and shells, known as Museum until April 2002, GP Museum ("GP" stood for "Grand Prix") for 13 months, then GP Museum Soft until October 2011. Operating under the MS Pictures umbrella are its flagship anime porn label Milky and its sisters AniMan, BOOTLEG, Celeb, HiLLS (*sic*), Jam, Mitsu, Pashmina, and Platinum Milky, as well as the erotic DVD player game labels Mints and Virgin Cream. It also reissues other anime porn studios' back catalogues, cooperating with the **DISCOVERY SERIES**, Digital Works' **VANILLA SERIES**, Cherry Lips, and Happinet for its Beam Entertainment (under the MAX label) and Green Bunny offerings. MS Pictures' best-known works include **BIBLE BLACK**, **BOIN**, **ANAL SANCTUARY**, and the second and third **INYOCHU** series. Its parent company continues to function as a legitimate video label, releasing such worthy works as a guide to the Japanese Maritime Self-Defense Force.

MUCHABEI

1971. JPN: *Chingo Muchabei*. AKA: *Glorious Muchabei; Extravagant Muchabei*. TV series. DIR: Tadao Nagahama. SCR: Hideko Yoshida, Masaki Tsuji. DES: Kenji Morita. ANI: Daikichiro Kusakabe, Shingo Araki. MUS: N/C. PRD: Tokyo Movie Shinsha, TBS. 25 mins. x 46 eps.
In the early days of the Edo period, masterless samurai Muchabei is forced to eke out a living making umbrellas. He is the sworn guardian of Bokemaru, a disinherited prince, who is the rightful heir to the riches of the Toyotomi family. They dream of reviving the family's fortunes, but Bokemaru is not the smartest of men and is often outwitted by Kaburezukin, a government spy, in a comedy period piece.

Originally conceived as a standard anime series, the show was broken up into smaller chunks for daily screening when it was discovered that the production was ahead of schedule! The story seems inspired by kabuki dramas about Matajuro Yagyu, the outcast brother of Jubei Yagyu (see **NINJA SCROLL**), who famously bested an opponent by fighting with twin umbrellas instead of swords. There, however, any classical allusions end, since the rest of the show is clogged with anachronisms—there are road signs on the streets of Edo, and Muchabei fights with modern umbrellas seemingly inspired by John Steed in *The Avengers* (itself broadcast in Japan in 1967 under the title *Oshare Mitsu Tantei—Dandy Secret Detectives*). Created by Kenji Morita.

MUKA-MUKA PARADISE

1993. JPN: *Nauseous/Angry Paradise*. TV series. DIR: Katsuyoshi Yatabe, Kunihisa Sugishima. SCR: Yasushi Hirano, Yukiyoshi Ohashi, Miho Maruo, Mayumi Koyama. DES: Hiromitsu Morita, Masayuki Hiraoka. ANI: Masayuki Hiraoka, Akio Watanabe. MUS: N/C. PRD: Nippon Animation, Mainichi Broadcasting. 25 mins. x 51 eps.

Thanks to a messy accident with the professor's time machine, little Eiba arrives in a world where humans never evolved and cutesy talking dinosaurs still walk Earth. He befriends the baby dinosaur Nikanika, tries to avoid provoking the wrath of Nikanika's father Gojigoji, and is (sort of) adopted by long-lashed brontosaurus mother Dosudosu. Based on a manga by **BONOBONO**-creator Mikio Igarashi.

MUNTO *

2003. Video. DIR: Yoshiji Kigami, Tomoe Aratani. SCR: Yoshiji Kigami. DES: Tomoe Aratani. ANI: Yoshiji Kigami. Tomoe Aratani. MUS: N/C. PRD: Kyoto Animation. 52 mins. (v1), 57 mins. (v2).

Two kingdoms beyond our world are fighting over an energy source known as *akuto*. To save the Kingdom of the Heavens and the Magical Kingdom, Magical King Munto must find a human girl, Yumemi, whom a prophetic vision has suggested will save the universe. Yumemi is just an ordinary schoolgirl, but she's the only human who can see the islands of the Heavens floating above us. As a result, she's not even certain she's sane, and persuading her to find the courage to believe Munto and save his people will be a tough task. A sub-**ESCAFLOWNE** or **BRIGADOON** fantasy, which feels curiously old-fashioned, this also harks back to the remarkable **LEDA: THE FANTASTIC ADVENTURE OF YOHKO**, though without its powerful sexual and emotional tension. A sequel, *M2: Toki no Kabe o Koete*, followed in 2004.

MURAKAMI, "JIMMY" TERUAKI

1933–2014. Also credited as Jimmy T.

Murakami. Born in San Jose to first- and second-generation Japanese immigrant parents, Murakami and his family were sent to an internment camp in Oregon when the U.S. entered World War II. He subsequently studied Fine Arts at the Chouinard Institute in Los Angeles (now part of CalArts) and worked as a commercial artist before becoming an animator on the American series *Gerald McBoing Boing*. He worked briefly for Toei Animation in Japan, returning to America and cofounding the animation studio Murakami-Wolf, with Fred Wolf. Later moving to Ireland, he worked with Roger Corman as an executive producer on the live-action *Battle Beyond the Stars* (1980) before founding another animation studio, Quateru, working chiefly in the European market. His most recognizable works are arguably the two cartoons he made based on the works of cartoonist Raymond Briggs—Dianne Jackson's Christmas classic *The Snowman* (1982), for which he was supervisor, and the nuclear satire *When the Wind Blows* (1986), which he directed himself. He subsequently directed the feature-length cartoon *Christmas Carol: The Movie* (2001). With a career path rivaled only by Tadahito Mochinaga's for sheer variety, Murakami does not technically qualify for inclusion in an encyclopedia of *Japanese* animation. We include him here in anticipation of questions arising from his name.

MURATA, YASUJI

1896–1966. Sometimes Yasushi Murata. Born in Yokohama as the son of a sake seller, Murata left school in his mid-teens and began his career drawing film posters. Joining Yokohama Cinema in 1923, he moved on to drawing the intertitles for silent movies. Inspired by the sight of foreign cartoons imported by Yokohama Cinema, he set up his own animation company, debuting with the **EARLY ANIME** *Why Is the Giraffe's Neck So Long?* (1927, *Giraffe no Kubi wa Naze Nagai?*). Murata used paper-cut animation, but used his paper like anime cels, in anticipation of later developments in animation, his most famous work arguably being *Animal Olympics* (1928, *Dobutsu Olympic Taikai*). He joined the Nippon Manga Eiga company after World War II, but retired soon after due to illness.

MURDER PRINCESS *

2007. Video. DIR: Tomoyuki Kurokawa. SCR: Tatsuhiko Urahata. DES: Yoshimitsu Yamashita, Shin Watanabe, Yoshimi Umino. ANI: Yoshimitsu Yamashita, Yukiko Ban. MUS: Yasufumi Fukuda. PRD: Bee Train, avex mode, Marvelous Entertainment. 23 mins. x 6 eps.

On the run after the murder of her father in a bloody coup, Princess Alita accidentally switches souls with bounty hunter Falis, known for her ferocity as the "Murder Princess." Alita persuades Falis to act the Princess, foil the coup, and reclaim the throne, while she acts as her maid. And as the pair get to know each other better, a bond forms between them that has nothing to do with status. This is a good idea, and if it had been backed by a single other idea, good or middling, that wasn't recycled from some other show it might have made a really enjoyable anime. Note to producers: saying "it's fantasy" is not sufficient justification for inserting robots into a feudal scenario. Nor is "this is technology left from the old world." If there was enough technology left from the old world to be repaired and kept running, people would be reproducing it. ❻❼

MUSASHI

2006. JPN: *Gundo Musashi*. AKA: *Musashi Gun Road*. TV series. DIR: Yuki Kinoshita. SCR: Naoyuki Sakai. DES: Masami Suda, Hideto Nakahara. ANI: N/C. MUS: Norio Ishiguro. PRD: C&S, ACC Production Studio. 25 mins. x 26 eps. (TV), 25 mins. x 4 eps. (recaps).

The war to unify and control Japan is over. Victorious warlord Hideyoshi Toyotomi has allowed his rival Ieyasu Tokugawa to live and thus unwittingly put his own achievements and the future of Japan in danger. An *ayakashi*, a monster sealed in subspace hundreds of years ago by the mighty Heian-period magician Abe no Seimei (**YIN-YANG MASTER**), has emerged in human form and is urging Ieyasu to claim power for himself. Calling himself Yasha, this monster urges Ieyasu to kill Hideyoshi's stepdaughter Kaguya, princess of Osaka Castle. If he does so, the whole of history will change and he will be master of Japan. Standing in his way: just one brash, loud-mouthed teenager, a brilliant swordsman who has learned a new way of fighting with a gun and electro-sword from an old priest in Daitokuji temple. With a little help from Leonardo da Vinci, maybe they can prevent the death of the princess.

This fascinating train-wreck of a series is based on a manga by Monkey Punch, creator of LUPIN III. It is infamous in FANDOM for truly appalling animation and poor production quality overall. Many of the backgrounds are uncropped and unretouched photographs, the dubbing crew laughed at the mere notion of lipsync and even if they hadn't, the audio usually comes in too late to give them any chance of making it work. There are rumors of persons unknown absconding with the animation budget and making it necessary to run the show on a frayed shoestring. Four recap episodes were also made, which displays little faith in either the audience's ability to recall six episodes or the director's ability to keep things coherent. Three of them were then not screened until after the show had finished airing, while the recap of episodes 1–9 was aired between episodes 11 and 12. And the only way you can currently own the whole show is by buying the 2008 French DVD set from Kaze Animation.

Somewhere inside this show there are a ton of wonderful ideas fighting to get into your head. This truly awful anime is an order of magnitude better in terms of story and ambition than dozens of tediously competent shows available now from a harem supplier near you (ROMANCE AND DRAMA). It crashes and burns because it refuses to stop trying to fly, even when everything is against it.

MUSASHI LORD

1990. JPN: *Karakuri Kengoden Musashi Lord*. AKA: *Tales of the Trickster Swordsmaster Musashi Lord*. TV series. DIR: Akira Shigino, Satoshi Nishimura, Noriyuki Abe, Akiyuki Shinbo, Yoshitaka Fujimoto. SCR: Akira Shigino, Tsunehisa Ito, Isao Shizuya, Yoshihisa Araki, Yukiyoshi Ohashi. DES: Tsuneo Tominaga, Kunio Okawara. ANI: N/C. MUS: Kenji Kawai. PRD: Studio Pierrot, Nippon TV. 25 mins. x 50 eps.
Musashi and Kojiro are two squasheddown robots in the spoof sci-fi samurai world of Edotopia. This anime car-crashes plots from JAPANESE FOLK TALES, historical events and legends, including Empress Himiko (see ZEGUY), the Japanese civil war, and the tale of YAMATO TAKERU. See also YOUNG MIYAMOTO MUSASHI.

MUSASHI: THE DREAM OF THE LAST SAMURAI *

2009. JPN: *Miyamoto Musashi Soken ni Haseru Yume*. Movie. DIR: Mizuho Nishikubo. SCR: Mamoru Oshii. DES: Kazuto Nakazawa, Shuichi Hirata. ANI: Kazuchika Kise. MUS: N/C. PRD: Production I.G, Pony Canyon. 72 mins.
The legendary swordsman Musashi Miyamoto (1584–1645) is so much a part of Japanese legend and culture that his true story has become an agglomeration of legend and romance, with many facts obscured or lost in time. One question that has obsessed many Musashi scholars is what motivated him to develop his trademark dual-blade style. In this anime, combat geek Mamoru Oshii, director of SKY CRAWLERS and a sometime martial artist himself, attempts to unravel the answer to that question.

Supposedly born from the remnants of footage for an abortive History Channel documentary, *Musashi: The Dream of the Last Samurai* is a nonfiction piece (DOCUMENTARIES AND HISTORY) mixing animated combat, live-action footage of ancient battle sites, and animated hypertexts telling the history of mounted knights across Eurasia. Director Mizuho Nishikubo throws in graphic demonstrations of sword techniques and notes on the history of the samurai, from the brawlers of the middle ages to the military ideals of the 20th century. The film's narrator looks suspiciously like a cartoon version of its celebrity screenwriter—aided at times by a hapless doll-like assistant and, for reasons that defy explanation, an incontinent robot pig. His story comes accompanied by a whirl of musical styles, including old-school Japanese songs that relate the deeds of Musashi in a clash of shamisen and electric guitar.

For Oshii, it's all about the money, which makes all noblemen worth more alive for the ransom, and the geography, which makes traditional Chinese weapons and tactics practically useless in mountainous Japan. These factors combine to create the unique appearance of Japan's own mounted warriors: a class to which, according to Oshii, Musashi aspired in vain.

Oshii's vision is deeply personal—a class-based, left-wing armchair general's approach to samurai history that glares unswervingly at issues of wealth and power

in medieval Japan. For Oshii, Musashi was haunted all his life by a thwarted desire to become one of the horsemen he so admired. Born as Japan's violent centuries of civil war came to a close, but still too early to take advantage of the peaceful samurai life of the Tokugawa period, Oshii's Musashi is caught between the careers of a thug and an artist. According to Oshii, Musashi developed his famous two-sword technique in imitation of the way he would fight *if he ever had a horse*, discovering in the process that it worked well against unmounted opponents.

Oshii delves impressively deep into matters of historiography—the history of history itself. The two-sword technique never really caught on despite Musashi's own attempts to highlight its value. Oshii puzzles over why Musashi himself never bragged about the battle that made him most famous, and offers a scathing analysis of the uses of samurai legends for state propaganda in the 20th century.

The gorgeous battle animation from Production I.G, and the fascinating discussion of the development of sword styles and the role of the horse in combat, make it worth watching if you have any interest in history or swordsmanship, but those who come mainly for the fights may find the lecture format annoying, particularly when complex arguments are occasionally interrupted by pratfalls and comedy business. In a back-handed compliment from Manga Entertainment, *Anime Encyclopedia* coauthor Jonathan Clements (billed as Julian Cheng) was hired to supply the voice-over in the English-language release, because "You can pronounce all the foreign words, and you already sound like a mad professor."

MUSHI PRODUCTION

Studio founded by Osamu Tezuka in direct competition with Toei Animation, its most notable successes being the 1963–65 boom in television animation started by ASTRO BOY. The company stumbled in the climate of the late 1960s and collapsed in the early 1970s, declaring bankruptcy in 1973. The dispersal of its staff led to the foundation of many of the independent studios of today, such as Madhouse. In 1975, the company's works were the subject of a "masterpiece" retrospective in Yoyogi. Tezuka's work is represented today by Tezuka Productions, a different company.

MUSHI-SHI *

2005. TV series, TV special. DIR: Hiroshi Nagahama, Shinpei Miyashita, Tatsuyuki Nagai. SCR: Kinuko Kuwabata, Aki Itami, Yuka Yamada. DES: Yoshihiko Umakoshi. ANI: Yoshihiko Umakoshi, Noboru Sugimitsu, Masayoshi Tanaka. MUS: Toshio Masuda. PRD: ARP Japan, Fuji TV. 25 mins. x 24 eps. (TV), ca. 60 mins. (TVm1), 25 mins. x 10 eps. (TV2), c.60 mins. (TVm2).

Ginko is a wandering expert in *mushi*, the most basic life-forms in the universe, representing primal energy. Their manifestations often appear to the uninitiated to be supernatural, in the form of hauntings or unexplained phenomena. In other words, a pseudo-scientific gloss on everyday GHOST STORIES, based on the manga by Yuki Urushibara, which began running in *Comic Afternoon* in 2000. A live-action movie adaptation directed by Katsuhiro Otomo, was released in 2006—a fitting job for the man whose own term for "primal energy" was AKIRA. This was followed in 2014 by an anime TV special, *Mushi-shi Special Chapter: Shadow to Undermine the Sun* (*Mushi-shi Tokubetsu Hen: Hihamukage*), and a second series *Mushi-shi Zoku-sho* (*M: The Next Chapter*).

MUSHI-UTA

2007. AKA: *Insect Song*. TV series. DIR: Kazuo Sakai. SCR: Reiko Yoshida, Takaomi Kanasaki. DES: Kanetoshi Kamemoto, Koji Azuma. ANI: Chikashi Kadekaru. MUS: Junpei Fujita. PRD: Beat Frog, Broccoli, D.N. Dream Partners, Kadokawa, Sony PCL, ZEXCS. 24 mins. x 12 eps.

The near future: strange insect-like creatures known as Mushi have been around for ten years, consuming people's dreams and granting them supernatural powers in return. Naturally, governments want to control this unexpected resource, although they prefer to do so in secret. Those possessed by Mushi are held in a prison known as GARDEN whose soldier-warders masquerade as a conservation force. Teenager Daisuke meets a girl on the run from GARDEN, and through her, the resistance organization known as Mushibane. The Mushi are powerful weapons, but their power comes at a high

price. As Daisuke learns more about their secrets, he begins to reveal his own. Based on the 2003 book series by Kyohei Iwai, with illustrations by LLO, the series was also preceded by a manga and followed by a further light-novel series. You may wish to compare with AI CITY as well as MUSHI-SHI.

MUSHKA AND MISHKA

1979. JPN: *Hokkyoku no Mushka Mishka*. AKA: *Mushka and Mishka of the Arctic*. Movie. DIR: Chikao Katsui. SCR: Akira Kato. DES: Shinichi Tsuji. ANI: N/C. MUS: Reijiro Koroku. PRD: Mushi Pro, Nikkatsu. 80 mins.

Two polar bears and their friendly seal acquaintance share adventures in this film supervised by Osamu Tezuka and based on the children's book by Tomiko Inui, also known as the writer of *The Tedious Penguin* and *We Are Kangaroos*.

MUSIC IN ANIME

From the early days of silent film, when theater owners paid a pianist to provide appropriate accompaniment, sound has heightened the impact of the image onscreen. For many Japanese children since 1961, their first encounter with animation has been in the sing-along tunes of EVERYBODY'S SONGS, which has often incorporated animation into its episodes.

Anime is supported by a phalanx of talented composers, many of whom also work on live-action or game soundtracks and a few with distinguished careers outside the motion picture industry in classical, jazz, or other musical forms. The leader of the pack is Yoko Kanno, whose scores cover every musical angle from the jazz of COWBOY BEBOP to the church-influenced chorals of ESCAFLOWNE. Joe Hisaishi, who has been Studio Ghibli's house composer since he scored 1984's NAUSICAÄ OF THE VALLEY OF THE WIND, started out as a minimalist. LUPIN III–composer Yuji Ono is a leading purveyor of lounge jazz, and one of the main reasons why the series' reputation as one of the coolest shows ever is still intact after more than three decades. Kohei Tanaka excels at martial themes and variations on Mozart, most notably in his score to GUNBUSTER. Kenji Kawai's pulsing compositions have added extra menace to the scores of GHOST IN THE SHELL and PATLABOR; and

Shiro Sagisu's multiple variations on both Beethoven and Burt Bacharach add a distinctive tone to EVANGELION.

Composers from other musical areas also dip into anime. Some of Osamu Tezuka's works were scored by famous mainstream composers Isao Tomita and Kaoru Wada. Ryuichi Sakamoto, formerly of pop trio Yellow Magic Orchestra, and best known to moviegoers for *Merry Christmas, Mr. Lawrence* and *The Last Emperor*, was one of the three composers for WINGS OF HONNEAMISE while his Yellow Magic Orchestra colleague Haruomi Hosono scored THE TALE OF GENJI. Some of these "guests" in the anime world are notable for their distinctively different voices—particularly Shoji Yamashiro, whose thumping, south-Asian influenced score for AKIRA was later reclaimed by the composer as the middle sequence of a symphonic trilogy beginning with *Reincarnated Orchestra* and ending with *Ecophony Rinne*.

Foreign pop luminaries who have scored anime include Jean-Jacques Burnel of the Stranglers, composer for the elegant and original GANKUTSUOU, and Glenn Danzig, whose music formed the basis of the obscure SATANIKA, while Western singers who have sung themes include David Sylvian, of the New Romantic band Japan, on MONSTER. *Babylon 5* composer Christopher Franke provided the music for the first TENCHI MUYO! movie. In imitation of Japanese live-action drama, some modern opening and closing themes are deliberately designed as advertisements for music tie-ins. Whereas American serials often reduce their opening themes to mere musical stings—e.g., *Will & Grace* or *Frasier*—in order to lessen the temptation to switch channels, anime capitalizes both on the ritual quality of viewing for younger audiences and on the fact that a recyclable opening sequence saves on animation budgets, and is hence preferably extended for as long as possible. This has led to unexpected appearances by pop stars on the credit listings for anime—such as the use of a Franz Ferdinand track on PARADISE KISS, the surprise showing by the Backstreet Boys on YOUNG HANADA, or the appearance of Radiohead's "Paranoid Android" on ERGO PROXY. Real-life performers also crop up in anime, including a cameo by the boy-band Tokio in CHILD'S

Toy and a similar appearance by SMAP in **Hime-chan's Ribbon**.

Anime scores are complemented by so-called image albums: CDs with music "inspired by" popular titles abound in Japan. Sometimes the music is composed after the event to cash in on a strong market; sometimes it includes material that didn't make it into the show's final cut, or additional songs by whichever popular singer or composer is working on the rest of the project. Occasionally a composer and director will build up a special relationship: Joe Hisaishi works closely with Hayao Miyazaki from the early stages of a new project, providing sketches of possible themes which the director also uses for inspiration and which are amended and expanded as the movie grows. With a number of shows getting their own spin-off CD and radio dramas, each needing some kind of soundtrack, there's a whole other strand of releases, both with and without the accompanying dialogue.

The music attached to anime in its native land doesn't necessarily travel overseas. Foreign releases quite often get their own theme songs or even soundtracks, whether they be the borrowed 1980s pop on *Macron One*, the U.S. release of **Goshogun**, or songstress Chantal Goya, who provided the French theme for **Monarch: The Big Bear of Tallac**. Claude Lombard sang themes for over 40 animated shows in France, from **Queen of a Thousand Years** and **Star of the Seine** to American cartoons like *The Adventures of Teddy Ruxpin*. Italy has its own anime theme stars, like the Micronauts of **Daitarn 3**, Christina D'Avena of **Three Musketeers**, or Massimo Dorati, whose energetic performance of the Italian **Dirty Pair** opening theme *Kate & Julie* deserves immortality. Popular local themes are treasured by their fans, but using current chart hits or locally popular styles is not always the best strategy. Excessive use of popular music dates and places a show with great precision, which can work to create an instant identification point for audiences at the time, but usually shortens the shelf life of the product—for which see, or rather, hear **Bubblegum Crisis** and **Samurai Champloo**. Of course, as the French, Italian, Spanish, and other importers of anime have demonstrated, a soundtrack isn't all that hard to replace,

either wholly or in part; but hiring composers like Kanno and Sakamoto is likely to produce a more interesting result than using hand-me-down songs based on transient fads. Sometimes, however, the inspiration can travel both ways—it was the French group Daft Punk who hired Leiji Matsumoto to create pop promos for them, which eventually led to the movie **Interstella 5555**. Similarly, the musicians of the British group Boa were to use their performance of the opening theme to **Serial Experiments Lain** as a means to break into the American market that had previously eluded them.

Music in anime can also be a story element in itself. Stories inspired by or themed around music include lives of famous musicians or **Great Composers**, wish-fulfillment tales of wannabe musicians, and stories where the role of music or sound in our lives is the central idea (**Detroit Metal City**). The concept of stealing sound is the focus of shows from the highly traditional **Carol** to the experimental **Noiseman**. The struggle to become a performer is depicted in so many shows it could form a book in itself, covering all musical genres from pop musicians like those in **Black Heaven**, **Wandering Sun**, or **Beck**, classical artists like **Kanon**, or wannabe idols like **Creamy Mami**. Real-life performers also crop up in anime like **Nit-aboh**, the story of a Japanese folk musician, while virtual idols reached their arguable apotheoses with software that allowed users to control their own singer (**Hatsune Miku Live Party**). Perhaps anime music's finest moment of inspiration was when **Macross** floated the idea that a pretty girl could save humanity from alien annihilation with the power of a heartfelt love song—such a simple and beautiful idea that it still brings a tear to the eye, even for cynical old anime historians.

MUSICAL WANDERINGS OF JIROCHO OF SHIMIZU
2000. JPN: *Anime Rokyoku Kiko Shimizu no Jirocho Den*. TV series. DIR: Mitsuo Kobayashi, Tatsuo Suzuki. SCR: Kazuo Kosuge. DES: Mitsuo Kobayashi. ANI: Michishiro Yamada, Nanpei Mitsunori. MUS: N/C. PRD: Piman House, Mainichi Broadcasting. 25 mins. x 10 eps.
Tales of samurai derring-do, set to old-time

tunes for the entertainment of the elderly. The target audience for this anime was the over-60s, though since it was shown at 5:45 a.m., it's difficult to imagine that *anyone* saw it at all. Composed of ten episodes of three stories each.

MUTANT TURTLES: SUPERMUTANTS
1996. JPN: *Mutant Turtles Chojin Densetsu Hen*. AKA: *Mutant Turtles Legend of the Supermutants*. Video. DIR: Shunji Oga. SCR: N/C. DES: Minoru Maeda. ANI: Minoru Maeda. MUS: Takeshi Ike. PRD: Ashi Pro, Bee Media, Nippon Columbia. 25 mins. x 2 eps.
The Teenage Mutant Ninja Turtles have acquired crystals that allow them to become Super Turtles—but only for three minutes at a time. Unfortunately their opponents, the evil Shredder and his minions, have something similar. But the four friends have another weapon born of their unity and loyalty—they can combine to become Turtle Saint, a fighting giant. This Japan-only sequel to the U.S. TV cartoon incorporated elements from giant robot anime and live-action SF shows such as *Ultraman* and the shows that inspired *Mighty Morphin' Power Rangers*. The voice cast was the same as for the TV Tokyo dub of the original U.S. cartoon whose 102 episodes screened from 1993 to 1995.

MUTEKING
1980. JPN: *Tondemo Senshi Muteking*. AKA: *Invincible Warrior Muteking*. TV series. DIR: Seitaro Hara, Koichi Mashimo, Hiroshi Sasagawa, Shinya Sadamitsu, Kenjiro Yoshida, Kazuo Yamazaki, Yutaka Kagawa. SCR: Kazuo Sato, Akiyoshi Sakai, Haruya Yamazaki, Takeshi Shudo, Masaru Yamamoto. DES: Ippei Kuri, Kunio Okawara. ANI: Shizuo Kawai. MUS: Koba Hayashi. PRD: Tatsunoko, Fuji TV. 25 mins. x 56 eps.
Law enforcement officer Takoro leaves planet Tako in pursuit of the fugitive Kurodako (Black Octopus) crime family: Takokichi, Takomaro, Takosaku, and Takomi. Arriving on Earth, the octopoid gang disguise themselves as humans and prepare to conquer the planet with their transforming minions. Takoro enlists Earth boy Rin Yuki as his deputy. Rin can now transform into the dashing warrior MuteKing, a superhero (on roller skates) who both fights off the bad guys and wins the heart of Takomi, the female octopus

invader who finds his charms irresistible. He also has Takoro's seemingly endless supply of TIME BOKAN–inspired robots at his disposal. Transforming robot vehicles, Las Vegas–inspired musical interludes, and roller-skating superhero action from the usual suspects at the Tatsunoko studio, whose most popular chapter was the "MuteQueen" incident in which Takoro's transformation ray accidentally misses Rin and makes his girlfriend the hero of the hour—compare to MOLDIVER.

MY AIR RAID SHELTER

2005. JPN: Boku no Bokugo. TV special. DIR: Toshio Takeuchi. SCR: Toshio Takeuchi. DES: Seitaro Kuroda. ANI: Ryutaro Hirai. MUS: N/C. PRD: Shinei Doga, TV Asahi. ca. 80 mins.
An old man remembers the time 60 years earlier when he huddled with his mother Yuko in the family's air raid shelter, while American B-29 bombers flew overhead. Based on a story by Akiyuki Nosaka, better known for GRAVE OF THE FIREFLIES, it deals with similar issues of death and trauma, beginning with young Yusuke's pride that his father is going away to war to fight the Americans. His father Tetsuo, however, is concerned for his family's well-being, and devotes his last days before marching off to building a suitably secure air raid shelter for his family. Some time after all the neighborhood families assembled to wave off their menfolk (in the style of CHOC-CHAN'S STORY), Yusuke hears chilling news on the radio of the fall of Saipan. When the war eventually, inevitably comes to Japan in the form of bombing raids, Yusuke is left alone in the shelter when his mother inexplicably walks out into danger. Alone in the dark, he begins to believe that his father's soul inhabits the shelter and is talking to him. Compare to GLASS RABBIT, which was similarly released in the 60th-anniversary year of the end of the war.

MY ALL-DAY ALL-COLOR

1987. JPN: Boku no All-Day All-Color. Video. DIR: Yoji Takatsuki. SCR: Seizo Watase. DES: Seizo Watase. ANI: Seizo Watase, Mikie Maeda. MUS: Tyrone Hashimoto. PRD: Tatsunoko. 30 mins.
Five short manga stories from HEART COCKTAIL–creator Seizo Watase, set to musical standards such as "Fly Me to the Moon" and "Love Me Tender." The tales adapted include Riding the Wave for Ten Miles, 20 Minutes till Princess Kaguya, 250 Km, A Couple Requesting Gentle Rain, and Long-Distance Call from the West Side. The experiment was repeated the following year with CHALK-COLORED PEOPLE.

MY BRIDE IS A MERMAID *

2007. JPN: Seto no Hanayome. AKA: The Bride of Seto; The Inland Sea Bride. TV series, video. DIR: Seiji Kishi. SCR: Makoto Uezu. DES: Kazuaki Morita, Maho Takahashi. ANI: Kazuaki Morita, Shuichi Hara, Kumi Horii, Masahiro Kogure, Takehiko Matsumoto. MUS: Yasuharu Takanashi. PRD: AIC, avex mode, GONZO, Set Project, Sotsu Agency, Square Enix, TV Tokyo. 24 mins. x 26 eps. (TV), 30 mins. x 2 eps. (v).
It's definitely not good to be saved from drowning by a mermaid. According to mermaid law, if a human sees a mermaid's true form, both must be killed—unless, of course, they get married. Nagasumi's holiday in the beautiful Seto countryside where his grandmother lives would have been cut short if the lovely San hadn't rescued him from drowning. Now he's dead if he doesn't marry her, but most certainly dead if he does—because her relatives are a marine Mafia who would rather see him fry than let him marry their precious princess. What's worse, she's not the only girl with an overprotective father and her sights set on Nagasumi: enter Luna Edomae, mermaid and idol singer, who is also determined to marry him—or maybe keep him as her butler.
Tahiko Kimura's 2002 manga ran for eight years in Square Enix's Shonen Gan-Gan magazine. The anime kept going for a full six months on TV by dint of a constant barrage of cheerful, if not very original, humor, and by borrowing from romantic comedies including HARE + GUU and URUSEI YATSURA, as well as less predictable sources like James Cameron's The Terminator (1984) and FIST OF THE NORTH STAR. 2008's videos are two standalone stories from the same team, featuring Luna and San and their overprotective fathers, but also providing new girls for Nagasumi to rescue. There's less overt pervery than in CAST AWAY: BLUE LOTUS ISLAND, though not everyone will regard this as a good thing.
The original song, "Seto no Hana-yome," about a bride on a boat heading off for a new life on a new island, was a hit in 1972 for Rumiko Koyanagi and has become something of a karaoke staple. On the north coast of Shikoku, it can often also be heard in many station announcements as express trains approach. It achieved a certain notoriety in anime FANDOM when someone with too much time on his hands realized that the lyrics could also be sung to the STAR BLAZERS theme tune.

MY FAIR MASSEUSE *

1996. JPN: Soap no Moko-chan. AKA: Moko the Soap Girl. Video. DIR: Shunji Yoshida. SCR: Naruo Kusugawa. DES: Naruo Kususgawa. ANI: Kawase Toshine. MUS: N/C. PRD: Sente Studio. 40 mins.
The perky, horny Moko takes a job in a "soapland" massage parlor, where she cheerfully helps the clientele fulfill their fantasies. This involves sex with old men, helping a nebbish who is being taken advantage of, and the need to tactfully brush off a priapic man who wants to "save her" from a life she fully enjoys. A porno anime remarkable only for the consensual nature of its sex scenes—a welcome change from the rape and domination that seems to occupy so much space on anime shelves. Based on the manga by Naruo Kusugawa in Young Champion magazine. The story was also adapted into live-action, as the 64-minute TV "movie" in 1992, and an 86-minute video release, Leave It to Moko (1994, Moko ni Omakase). ◐

MY FATHER'S DRAGON

1993. JPN: Elmer no Boken. AKA: Elmer's Adventure. Movie. DIR: Masami Hata. SCR: N/C. DES: Shuichi Seki. ANI: N/C. MUS: Naoto Kine. PRD: Shochiku. 98 mins.
Elmer Elevator runs away with an old alley cat to rescue Boris, a young dragon imprisoned on the faraway Wild Island. The everyday items he needs to help himself include some pink lollipops, rubber bands, chewing gum, and a comb. Based on the children's book by Ruth Stiles Gannett, whose title reflected the original premise that the heroic youngster Elmer is actually the narrator's father as a boy.

MY LIFE AS ... *

1999. AKA: My Life As ... Stage 1: A Chicken. Video. DIR: Akebi Haruno. SCR: Ippei Taira. DES:

Akira Ina. ANI: Akira Ina. MUS: N/C. PRD: Five Ways. 35 mins.

Teenager Yasunari runs away from a broken home and is saved from sinking into a life of prostitution by two women, Fumi and Rino. They take him in, along with his friend Chie, and make him their pet. When he publishes the story of his new life of bondage, domination, and group sex in a magazine, it is read by his brother Tomoyasu, who has been searching for him ever since he left home. Tomoyasu is devastated to find his brother loves his new life, so much so that he forces himself on his new tutor, Serina, without knowing that she is a good friend of his brother's new owners. A much more toned down version of the same themes could be found on live-action Japanese television in *You Are My Pet* (*DE). ❶❷❸

MY MY MAI *

1993. JPN: *Sono Ki ni Sasete yo*. AKA: *Get Me in the Mood*. Video. DIR: Osamu Sekita. SCR: Yumi Nakamura, Osamu Sekita. DES: Masakazu Yamaguchi. ANI: N/C. MUS: Koichi Ota, Koji Tajima. PRD: Apple, Beam Entertainment. 44 mins. x 2 eps.

Mai is a psychic investigator who specializes in consultancy jobs—putting members of the public together with the right healer, surgeon, or cure for strange phobias. As with the heroine of the similar **PRIVATE PSYCHO LESSON**, she prefers hands-on treatment, which she administers with a mix of psychobabble, flashes of her lingerie, and as a common last resort, her bounteous nude charms. Based on the *Shonen Champion* manga by *Heart Boiled Papa*-creator Masakazu Yamaguchi and presented as four stories, two per episode. Similar psychosexual investigations turn up in **REI REI**. ❶

MY NEIGHBOR TAMAGETA

1974. JPN: *Tonari no Tamageta-kun*. AKA: *Little Traveler Tamageta*. TV series. DIR: Shotaro Ishinomori, Noboru Ishiguro. SCR: Shotaro Ishinomori, Shinichi Suzuki. DES: Shotaro Ishinomori. ANI: Nobuyoshi Sohara. MUS: N/C. PRD: Studio Zero, Studio Uni, Tohoku Shinsha. 5 mins. x 60 eps.

Yasushi is an average Japanese boy who gains a series of weird new playmates when his new neighbors turn out to be Mr. Gyoten, a time-traveler from the future,

Gyoten's son Tamageta, and the family pet Pochi (i.e., Pooch) the dinosaur. Whenever Tamageta switches on the time machine, trouble inevitably ensues in the style of the "help" offered by **DORAEMON**. Quite often, the playmates are forced to undo other problems created by Yasushi's would-be girlfriend, local girl Yotchan, and her occasional associates Gorilla, Racoon (i.e., Tanuki), and Fox. Based on a manga by Shotaro Ishinomori, this kids' show was put into production by Tohoku Shinsha, but ultimately animated wholly in-house by Studio Zeo. It sat around on the shelf for almost five years before its broadcast, in small chunks on the *Ohayo Kodomo Show* (*Good Morning Kids Show*). *Tamageta* literally means "Astonished."

MY NEIGHBOR TOKORO

1990. JPN: *Tonari no Tokoro*. TV series. DIR: Haruya Mizutani. SCR: Joji Tokoro. DES: Joji Tokoro. ANI: Tokuhiro Matsubara. MUS: Hiroaki Nakamura. PRD: Pasteoinc. 40 mins.

Parodies of several **JAPANESE FOLK TALES** and others, starring an animated version of star-of-the-moment Joji Tokoro, whose bright idea this was. Originally broadcast as part of the *Not the Real Mr. Tokoro* (*Tokoro-san no Tadamono dewa Nai*) show, these feeble pastiches of *Urashima Taro*, *Little Red Riding Hood*, and several "comedy" skits were bulked out on video by a "making-of" documentary, starring the camera-hungry Mr. Tokoro. The name manages, not quite accidentally enough, to get the show filed next to **MY NEIGHBOR TOTORO** in both English and Japanese, as if somehow the greatness of the latter would improve its chances. The comedian returned in computerized form as *Mr. Digital Tokoro* (2001).

MY NEIGHBOR TOTORO *

1988. JPN: *Tonari no Totoro*. Movie. DIR: Hayao Miyazaki. SCR: Hayao Miyazaki. DES: Hayao Miyazaki. ANI: Yoshiharu Sato. MUS: Joe Hisaishi. PRD: Studio Ghibli. 86 mins. (m1), 10 mins. (m2).

While their mother is in the hospital convalescing from a long illness, Satsuki and her little sister, Mei, are taken by their father, Professor Kusakabe, to an old house in the country. They clean the house of lurking "soot sprites" and turn it into a home. Father takes the bus to the university where he lectures, Satsuki

attends the local school, and Mei gets lost in the undergrowth, where she discovers a family of round, fluffy woodland creatures. Mispronouncing "troll," from the *Three Billy-Goats Gruff*, she calls them Totoros. Adults cannot see these Totoros, who befriend the children when Satsuki lends one an umbrella. He returns the favor by growing them a tree with magic acorns and taking them on a magical ride through the countryside on the Catbus—a many-legged feline transport with a Cheshire Cat's grin straight out of **ALICE IN WONDERLAND**. Mei resolves to take her mother a gift but becomes lost on the way. Fearing the worst, the adults send out search parties, and a distraught Satsuki calls on the Totoros' aid.

Hayao Miyazaki's greatest work, and hence probably the best anime ever made, *MNT* is also a very personal film, set in the disappearing countryside of the creator's childhood and featuring a child's love for a bedridden parent—Miyazaki's own mother suffered from spinal tuberculosis. *MNT* has the widest appeal of any of Miyazaki's films, aimed as it is at an audience so young that it can genuinely be described as family entertainment, unlike his more adult-themed works such as **PORCO ROSSO** or teen adventures like **NAUSICAÄ**. *MNT* sees everything through the unquestioning, uncritical, undaunted eyes of a child, and it is an uplifting film of unadulterated hope, originally shown on a double bill with its heartrending opposite, **GRAVE OF THE FIREFLIES**, or in some theaters, **THE GIRL WITH THE WHITE FLAG**. There are many echoes of other productions from Studio Ghibli, particularly in *MNT*'s depiction of a disappearing pastoral existence, with a ghostly rural world superimposed on modern times, much like the studio's more serious **POM POKO**. Miyazaki's Japan is a nation very much rooted in its own past, with ancient local shrines overlooking the contemporary action, and the Totoros leading the girls in a stirringly primal fertility ritual. It also mixes the magical with the mundane in the charming style of **KIKI'S DELIVERY SERVICE** and, like the creator's much more downbeat **PRINCESS MONONOKE**, refuses to point a formulaic finger at a bad-guy scapegoat. This latter point was of particular importance to Miyazaki, exasperated at modern parents' willingness to use the TV as a babysitter and disgusted with the conflict-based story lines of most modern children's cartoons.

MNT's appeal has not diminished since its appearance. Now the center of a huge industry of tie-in products, it is that rare case of a film whose spin-offs were created *by audience demand* after the fact, instead of generated by the company as part of a publicity offensive. The most recent spin-off is a ten-minute short anime, *Mei and the Kittenbus*, which premiered at Tokyo's Studio Ghibli Museum in 2001.

At one critical point in the plot, the "next stop" sign on the Catbus revolves to reveal a destination of particular importance. Whereas modern anime distributors would have digitally replaced it with English letters in **TRANSLATION**, the dub released in the U.S. in 1994 was actually made in 1989 at a time when such technology was unavailable. Consequently, the Catbus has a warm, fluffy voice to announce the next stop in the English version—provided by Streamline Pictures' producer Carl Macek. The girls' house was re-created as a life-size mock-up as part of the 2005 Expo in Aichi. In recognition of Ghibli's later partnerships with Pixar, Totoro himself would get a supporting role as one of the cast in *Toy Story 3* (2010).

MY NEIGHBORS THE YAMADAS *

1980. JPN: *Ojamanga Yamada-kun; Hohokekyo Tonari no Yamada-kun*. AKA: *Troublesome Manga Yamadas*. TV series, movie. DIR: Hiroyoshi Mitsunobu (TV), Isao Takahata (m). SCR: Masaki Tsuji, Tomoko Konparu, Noboru Shiroyama (TV), Isao Takahata (m). DES: Hisaichi Ishii. ANI: Hiroshi Kanazawa (TV), Kenichi Konishi (m). MUS: Makoto Kawanabe (TV), Akiko Yano (m). PRD: Herald, Fuji TV, Studio Ghibli. 25 mins. x 102 eps. (TV1, 3 stories per ep.), 104 mins. (m), 25 mins. x 61 eps. (TV2, *Nono-chan*).

The Yamada family comprises retired couple Yoshio and Ine, their daughter Yoneko and her husband Komugi, eternal retake student Shigeru (who has failed to pass his university entrance exams three times), hapless high school baseball player Noboru, early teen Minoru, and toddler Sanae. In addition, the house is often visited by the occupants of the family's dormitory, several university students, and the local doctor—and soon the stork brings

Yoneko and Komugi a new baby of their own. Designer Hisaichi Ishii, who also created **GO FOR IT, TABUCHI**, and **HISAICHI ISHII'S WHATEVER THEATER**, deliberately used flat, two-dimensional artwork for *Meet the Yamadas* (1980, *Ojamanga Yamada-kun*). Scheduled straight after **SAZAE-SAN**, the show continued the slot of gentle humor, although leavened in this case with chunks of satire, parody, and even science-fiction adventures. Later remade for theaters by Studio Ghibli as *My Neighbors the Yamadas* (1999, *Hohokekyo Tonari no Yamada-kun*) in a deliberately washed-out sketch style. This version was released in Japan with English subtitles on the DVD.

In 1997, Ishii began serializing *Nono-chan*, a follow-up to the original manga. Featuring very similar comic situations but concentrating this time on the misadventures of a cheeky third-grader, *Nono-chan* was picked up for TV broadcast late in 2001. It was directed for Toei Animation by Nobutaka Nishizawa, using fully digital animation in imitation of the *Yamadas* movie, and shown on TV Asahi in 61 episodes.

MY ORDINARY LIFE *

2011. JPN: *Nichijo*. AKA: *Ordinary*. TV series. DIR: Tatsuya Ishihara. SCR: Jukki Hanada, Joe Ito, Keiichi Arawi. DES: Futoshi Nishiya, Joji Unoguchi. ANI: Futoshi Nishiya, Shoko Ikeda, Kazumi Ikeda. MUS: Yuji Nomi. PRD: Kyoto Animation, Kadokawa, Lantis, MOVIC Shinonome Lab, Klockworx. 24 mins. x 26 eps.

High-school friends Mio and Yuki live in a small town with some very strange neighbors—despite the implications of the title, this is not quite an **EVERYDAY ANIME**. There's the Professor, a five-year-old genius who has created a robot mother and just can't stop modifying it. There's Sakamoto the talking cat. There's goat-riding and voodoo. There's their crazy, stand-offish friend Mai. All in all, there's plenty in small town life to keep our heroines entertained through their ordinary days. Wacky anime centered around stereoptypically cute schoolgirls is not unusual, but not all such shows are animated with the devotion that Kyoto Animation brings to this one: character movements, camera angles, expressions, background fades, every trick to keep things moving is used to turn Keiichi Arawi's manga into a living thing of light and beauty.

MY PICO

2006. JPN: *Boku no Pico*. Video. DIR: Katsuyoshi Yatabe. SCR: Katsuhiko Takayama. DES: Yoshiten. ANI: Yoshiten. MUS: Shinobu. PRD: Blue Cats, Sugar Boy, Natural High. 33 mins. (v1), 34 mins. x 2 eps. (v2), 30 mins. (v3).

Pico Onedari is a lonely preteenager who loves to swim, often in the nude. One summer, hoping to make some new friends, he works part-time in his grandfather's beachside bar BeBe and meets office worker Tamotsu. Grandfather practically pushes him into Tamotsu's arms and Tamotsu seduces him and persuades him to crossdress as a girl. Described by the producers as the first *shotacon* anime—*shotacon* being the male equivalent of *lolicon* (**ARGOT AND JARGON; LOLITA ANIME**), a passion for young girls—this series is also a carefully targeted niche marketing product, which has spun off a short manga, a computer game, and a music video compilation CD.

It was never intended as a one-shot. In 2007 the same team produced *Pico & Chico* (*Pico to Chico*, AKA *Pico Series 2*) in which Pico meets a younger boy who loves to play out of doors naked. Chico has been watching his older sister masturbate and is curious about sex. Pico helps him to find out more, and the pair spy on big sister and make use of her collection of sex toys and fetish outfits. This second episode was also edited into a format more suitable for boy-loving under-18s, as *Pico: My Little Summer Story* (*Pico Boku no Chiisana Natsu Monogatari*).

For 2008's *Pico x CoCo x Chico*, AKA *Pico Series 3* (once again from the same team) the series introduces a mysterious girl who lives in a room off the subway, deep beneath Tokyo. Soon Pico is questioning both his own sexuality and his feelings for Chico, but as the "girl"'s true origins emerge they are soon engaged in a crossdressing threesome. It seems that CoCo is a "city fairy" who has a magical relationship with Tokyo, so it's entirely appropriate that after a rift in their relationship the three meet again at Tokyo Tower, scene of dramatic meetings in so many anime including **COWBOY BEBOP** and **RAYEARTH**.

MY PLACE

2002. JPN: *Atashi n' Chi*. AKA: *My Family*. TV series, movie. DIR: Akitaro Daichi, Tetsuo Yasumi. SCR: Kazuyuki Morosawa, Natsuko

Takahashi. DES: Eiko Kera. ANI: N/C. MUS: Motoi Sakuraba. PRD: TV Asahi, Yumeta, ADK, Media Factory, Shinei Animation, Toei Animation. 19 mins. x 123 eps. (TV), 95 mins. (m).

The Japanese title is short for "at my home," and this anime based on the comic strip by Eiko Kera is an everyday slice-of-life with the Tachibana family—mother, father, perky daughter Mikan, who tells the story, and son Yuzuhiko. Originally published in the Sunday edition of *Yomiuri Shimbun* newspaper and running since 1995, it has been described as the present-day SAZAE-SAN.

MY SEXUAL HARASSMENT *

1994. JPN: *Boku no Sexual Harassment*. Video. DIR: Yosei Morino. SCR: Yosei Morino. DES: Aki Tsunaki. ANI: Aki Tsunaki. MUS: Burnheads. PRD: Seiyo, KSS. 35 mins. x 3 eps.

Jun Mochizuki is one of the best salesmen for his computer company, a position he has achieved by seducing the bosses of the companies to which he sells. He travels Japan and, in a later episode, even heads off to Boston, bedding his colleagues, his superiors, and his clients in a gay pornographic anime. Based on the series of erotic novels by Sakura Momo. ◐

MY SISTER MOMOKO

2003. JPN: *Momoko, Kaeru no Uta ga Kikoeru yo*. AKA: *Momoko, Listen to the Frog Song*. Movie. DIR: Setsuko Shibuichi. SCR: Kazumi Koide, Mitsuyo Suenaga. DES: Setsuko Shibuichi, Shichiro Kobayashi. ANI: Kazunori Tanahashi, Yukari Kobayashi. MUS: Michiru Oshima. PRD: Magic Bus, GoGo Visual Planning. 80 mins.

Riki's twin sister isn't like other girls. Momoko needs help to breathe, and her body and brain aren't developing properly, so she can't go to the same school as her adored older brother. She gets upset when he leaves for school in the morning without her; her favorite song about frogs is the only thing that distracts her as he heads off for the day. All the attention she needs makes Riki wonder if their parents love her more than him, but he defends and protects her when one of his classmates is mean to her. Then an experiment in integrated education means that Momoko can finally join her brother in school. Both children and adults are challenged by her extreme disability and her loving nature.

Shibuichi, who directed GLASS RABBIT to commemorate the 60th anniversary of the atomic bombing of Hiroshima, also wrote and designed characters for Satoshi Dezaki's 1999 movie about child abuse and bullying, RE-BIRTHDAY; here Dezaki gets an executive producer credit. Credibly but not outstandingly animated, the heart of this film is its story; there are so few honest representations of disability in any medium and realistic disabled characters are largely airbrushed out of children's entertainment, making this film a rarity worth seeking out. See also HOUSE OF ACORNS and RUN.

MY SKY

1991. JPN: *Ore no Sora: Keiji Hen*. AKA: *My Sky: Cop Chapter*. Video. DIR: Takeshi Shirato. SCR: Hiroshi Motomiya. DES: Masami Suda. ANI: Masami Suda. MUS: Takeshi Yasuda, Chage and Aska. PRD: APPP. 45 mins. x 2 eps.

A thriller revolving around political connections with a multinational corporation as a lone cop, son of the company boss, tracks down the murderer of a female university student, finding that there is a conspiracy to prevent him from discovering the truth. Based on the manga in *Young Jump* magazine by GOODFELLA and CLIMBING ON A CLOUD–creator Hiroshi Motomiya. ◐

MY TEEN ROMANTIC COMEDY SNAFU *

2013. JPN: *Yahari Ore no Seishun Love Come wa Machigatteiru*. AKA: *My Youth Romantic Comedy Is Wrong as I Expected*. TV series, video. DIR: Ai Yoshimura. SCR: Shotaro Suga, Toko Machida, Katsuhiko Takayama, Wataru Watari. DES: Yu Shindo. ANI: Yu Shindo, Keiya Nakano. MUS: Kakeru Ishihama, monaca. PRD: Geneon, TBS, Marvelous AQL, MOVIC. 24 mins. x 13 eps.

Anti-social slacker Hachiman Hachigaya is forced to join his school's Service Club, which is obligated to solve any problems brought to it. With Hachiman's fellow problem-solver, the icy and forthright Yukino Yukinoshita, and more humane assistance from the perky Yui Yuigahama, the club members ignore the suspiciously contrived coincidence of their alliterative names and get to work, bickeringly, on a series of tasks-of-the-week. Despite its label as a romantic comedy, this is a show that devotes far more time to character, in a fashion that lesser shows like HENNEKO would have done well to emulate.

MY THREE DAUGHTERS

2008. JPN: *Uchi no San Shimai*. AKA: *Three Sisters Out*. TV series. DIR: Izumi Todo. SCR: N/C. DES: Satoru Iriyoshi, Joyeon Ju, Satomi Tanaka. ANI: Iku Ishiguro. MUS: Hiroyuki Takei. PRD: Toei Animation, Studio Animal. 25 mins. x 141 eps.

The EVERYDAY ANIME adventures of five-year-old Fu and three-year-old Sue, their baby sister Chi, their pets, their harassed mother, and their salaryman father, based on comic artist Pretz Matsumoto's 2005 manga blog of her own day-to-day life with three lively girls. These engaging and sometimes brutally honest little stories with their artfully basic style soon made the leap to print, anime, and even games for the Nintendo DS. They show the Japanese extended family (SAZAE-SAN) alive and well—both sets of grandparents live within half an hour by car—and the neighborhood ethos thriving, with the family on good terms with the people next door and their two lively little boys. Mama's editor, who looks scary but is really playful and friendly, is a regular visitor. Compare with KAA-SAN: MOM'S LIFE: the two manga mothers cooperated on a crossover comic in 2012.

MY WIFE IS A HIGH SCHOOL STUDENT

2005. JPN: *Okusama wa Joshi Kosei*. TV series. DIR: N/C. SCR: Hideo Takayashiki. DES: Kazuo Watanabe. ANI: N/C. MUS: Kei Wakakusa. PRD: Madhouse, TV Saitama, TVK. 25 mins. x 13 eps.

Teenage bride Asami Onohara is forced to keep her marriage secret when she is transferred to the high school where her husband Kyosuke is a teacher. High jinks ensue as the couple conceal their cohabitation from fellow students and staff, as colleagues try to set their "single" friend Kyosuke up with a date, and Asami dodges scandal in the classroom. An extra twist: Asami is not the only student with a relative on the staff—one of her classmates is the little brother of the haplessly single English teacher Miss Iwasaki. A late-night anime based on the manga by Hiyoko Kobayashi in *Young Jump* weekly, but part of a long tradition in Japanese TV that stretches back to the 1970 show *My Wife Is 18* (*DE), whose plot was virtually identical. Note that Japanese TV has a large number of "My Wife is a…" shows, most of which are translations of American sitcoms, including *My Wife Is a Big Star* (*Mona McCluskey*) and *My Wife Is a Witch* (*Bewitched*). **BEWITCHED AGNÈS**, AKA *My Wife Is a Magical Girl*, ended shortly after this knock-off began.

MY-HIME *

2004. JPN: *Mai-HiME*. AKA: *Mai Princess; Princess Mai; Mai-Otome*. TV series, video. DIR: Masakazu Obara, Tatsuyuki Nagai. SCR: Hiroyuki Yoshino, Noboru Kimura. DES: Hirokazu Hisayuki, Tomoyuki Aoki, Saori Naito, Mutsumi Inomata, Hisashi Hirai, Hiroyuki Okawa, Junichi Akutsu, Kazutaka Miyatake. MUS: Yuki Kajiura. PRD: Sunrise, TV Tokyo. 25 mins. x 26 eps. (TV1), 25 mins. x 26 eps. (TV2), 30 mins. x 4 eps. (v1), ca. 28 mins. x 3 eps. (v2).

Mai Tokiha and her younger brother Takumi have won scholarships to attend prestigious Fuka Academy. On the long journey, two girls start a supernatural battle on the ferry and Mai begins to learn that she has some of the same powers. Thirteen girls known as HiME—for the Highly Advanced Materializing Equipment power they wield—fight monsters and risk the lives of those they love most. Adapted from the manga written by Noboru Kimura with art by Kenetsu Sato, in which high school boy Yuichi Tate discovers that he is the "key," or essential fighting partner, of two HiME, the anime shifts the emphasis away from the boy-girl partnership of the manga into a less demanding fantasy for guys too lazy to read—**VIRGIN FLEET** meets **ALICE ACADEMY**. A second series, entitled *Mai-Otome* (2005), stars Arika, a minor character in series one, and is set in a European-style castle, with the uniforms inspired by French maids rather than Japanese schoolgirls.

A video follow-up, *My Otome Zwei* (2006), was not a sequel so much as a wholesale sci-fi revision in the style of later **TENCHI MUYO!** serials, relocating the original cast to almost completely different settings and situations; in this case,

the faraway land of Windbloom, where heroine Arika Yumemiya is searching for her mother, enrolling en route into the hothouse competitive environment of Garderobe Academy.

Hirokazu Hisayuki's 2008 prequel, weighed down in pretentious typography as *My-Otome 0-S.ifr-*, features 14-year-old orphan Sifr Fran, kidnapped because of her ties to the Royal Family of Windbloom and her own potential as a possible inheritor of the quasi-mystical power to operate lost technology. Rescued by the current Windbloom heir and his devoted female bodyguards, she is still the target of hostile forces who want to control her powers. All anime like to indulge in backfilling if they survive long enough: this one has survived two 26-episode TV series and a sequel, all based on the premise that females only exist in relation to males and their potential can only be fully achieved under masculine control. Yet another clichéd boys' series that flips the finger at the widely touted truism that anime is intrinsically feminist while actually saying that all a female needs to Fulfill Her Destiny is youth, revealing outfits, and the right boy.

MYSELF; YOURSELF *

2007. TV series. DIR: Tetsuaki Matsuda. SCR: Go Zappa. DES: Tomoya Hiratsuka, Shinji Takasuga. ANI: Tomoya Hiratsuka. MUS: Sho Fujimaru. PRD: Dogakobo, 5pb, Happinet Pictures, Marvelous Entertainment, Pony Canyon. 23 mins. x 13 eps.

Sana Hidaka has been in Tokyo with his family for five years. Having been bullied in middle school, he moves back to his hometown alone, aged 16. Visiting an old shrine, he notices a girl in a shrine maiden outfit watching him. Next day in school he realizes she's an old friend from his childhood (**ROMANCE AND DRAMA**). Since he left, she's lost her parents in a fire and now lives with her aunt and uncle. Other old friends and dramas emerge, because this show is based on the dating game by Yeti, with original design by Mutsumi Sasaki, which also inspired a 2007 book by Takumi Nakazawa.

MYSTERIES OF THE WORLD

1978. JPN: *Sekai no Fushigi Tanken Series*. AKA: *Investigating World Mysteries*. TV series. DIR: Masahiko Soga, Sadao Nozaki. SCR: Keiji

Kubota, Takeshi Shudo, Kyoko Tsuruyama, Junji Takegami. DES: N/C. ANI: N/C. MUS: N/C. PRD: Heart Media, TBS. 25 mins. x 10 eps.

Documentaries combining anime with live action, exploring a mixed bag of mysteries and historical topics, including the statues of Easter Island, the search for a lost continent, the Bermuda Triangle, the **NAZCA** Lines, the Sphinx and the Pyramids, the Greenwich Meridian, the Leaning Tower of Pisa, and the Great Buddha of Nara. Confusing in its inability to decide whether it wants to be history, geography, travelogue, or the titular "mysteries."

MYSTERIOUS CITIES OF GOLD, THE *

1982. JPN: *Taiyo no Ko Esteban*. AKA: *Esteban the Child of the Sun; Esteban and the Cities of Gold; Esteban the Sun-Kissed Boy*. TV series. DIR: Eiko Toriumi, Bernard Deyries, Kyosuke Mikuriya, Mizuho Nishikubo. SCR: Mitsuru Majima, Michiru Kaneko, Soji Yoshikawa, Jean Chalopin. DES: N/C. ANI: Toshiyasu Okada, Hiroshi Kawanami, Yutaka Oka, Norio Yazawa, Hajime Hasegawa, Mitsuki Nakamura, Shingo Araki, Kazutoshi Kobayashi, Yukihiro Takahashi, Toyoo Ashida, Takashi Nakamura. MUS: Nobuyoshi Koshibe (Haim Saban, Shuki Levy, Western version). PRD: MK, Studio Pierrot, NHK. 25 mins. x 39 eps.

In 1532, the orphan Esteban sets out from Barcelona in search of the fabled South American Cities of Gold. He's accompanied by the young Inca girl Zia, the adventurous Spaniard Mendoza, who found the baby Esteban adrift on the open sea, and (later) Tao, the last survivor of the sunken kingdom of Mu (Heva in the English dub).

Set in the time when Japan was "discovered" by the West but made at a time when old-fashioned adventure yarns were rediscovered by the *Indiana Jones* mob, *MCoG* was a Franco-Japanese coproduction undertaken after the completion of **ULYSSES 31**. There are a few concessions to kiddie programming, such as an infuriating parrot and some comic-relief bunglers, but there is also much in this series to recommend it. It was loosely based on the books *The King's Fifth* (1966) and *City of Seven Serpents* (so claim the producers, though no work of that name exists in the Library of Congress) by Scott O'Dell, better known in the U.S. as the award-winning author of *Island of the Blue Dolphins* (1961). According to O'Dell's widow, Elizabeth Hall, *City of the Seven Serpents* was briefly a working title of *The Captive* (1979), a book by O'Dell relating to Mayan civilization. Full of unexpected changes in gear, *MCoG* starts as a straightforward sea voyage, before giving the first indications of its sci-fi leanings in episode 9 when the crew of the Spanish galleon Esperanza jump ship onto the flying ship Solaris. Needless to say, as the quest begins in earnest in South America, Esteban discovers he is the offspring of an Inca princess (with an absent father who turns out to be not so absent)—hence, in true anime tradition, the perfect pilot for the show's supermachine, the solar-powered Golden Condor. Ancient technologies, lost cities, and warring tribes create an exciting mix, and though there are occasional anachronistic bloopers (a tribe of Amazons, *in* the Amazon, for example), the Japanese version closed each episode with a mini historical documentary explaining the actual events and personages that inspired the fictional characters—explaining the differences between Aztecs, Olmecs, Mayas, and Incas, or filling in the background about Pizarro or Magellan. However, these documentaries were dropped from many foreign-language territories, including the U.K. Though made primarily for the French market, *MCoG* was also popular with the Japanese audience, particularly with those who could spot the irony of staff members from **Gold Lightan** animating the flight of the Golden Condor using similar glare effects and shot compositions. Perhaps the most compelling element of *MCoG* is the way in which it genuinely conveys a feel for the age. There was, literally, a whole New World to conquer, and the sense of anticipation and adventure is gripping. Predating the similar **Secret of Blue Water** by several years, *MCoG* remains an original, not the least because it presented a positive, sympathetic view of Native American peoples unique to children's television. See also **Pepelo, Boy of the Andes**.

MYSTERY GIRLFRIEND X *

2012. JPN: *Nazo no Kanojo X*. TV series. DIR: Ayumu Watanabe. SCR: Deko Akao. DES: Kenichi Konishi. ANI: Shizue Kaneko. MUS: Tomoki Hasegawa. PRD: AT-X, Hoods Enter-

tainment, Kodansha, Starchild Records, Klockworx, Yomiko Advertising. DUR: 24 mins. x 13 eps.

Virginal teenager Akira Tsubaki experimentally licks some of the drool left behind by napping bad-girl Mikoto Ukabe, only to discover that her saliva allows her to transfer emotions, memories, and feelings. It also bonds him to her in a perverted relationship, as the pair begin exploring connections with other classmates. Riichi Ueshiba's manga in *Afternoon* magazine was already pretty weird, repurposing the allegorical teen awakenings of many a story for an older, more knowing audience. Ayumu Watanabe's anime plays up the allegory of the fluidic, hormonal chaos of puberty for all it's worth, with a whole bunch of saliva-swapping encounters that viewers should categorically not try at home.

One wonders, however, whether this tale is doomed to disappear into the dead-end sumps of search engines, since almost every teen anime can surely be summarized as "Mystery Girlfriend X" …

MYSTERY OF THE NECRONOMICON *

1999. JPN: *Kuro no Dansho*. AKA: *Black Fragment*. Video. DIR: Hideki Takayama, Yoshitaka Makino. SCR: Ryo Saga. DES: Yutaka Sunadori. ANI: Koichi Fuyukawa, Masaki Kaneko. MUS: Kazuhiko Izu, Hiroaki Sano. PRD: Discovery, Seven Eight. 35 mins. x 4 eps.

After a savage mass murder at a remote Nagano ski resort, most of the guests leave the mountain complex. As a storm brings down the phone lines and cuts off the hotel, vacationing private investigator Satoshi Suzusaki hunts down the killer as further murders occur. Accompanied by his foster-daughter Asuka Kashiwagi, he interviews a succession of suspects, discovering a web of intrigue that includes blackmail, sexual assault, black magic, and experimental gene therapies.

Despite the sex and gruesome violence one would usually expect from **Urot-sukidoji**-director Takayama, the first half of *MotN* is also a simplistic but engaging whodunit. Satoshi collects a number of carefully balanced clues and artifacts, interviewing suspects and collating information that regularly contradicts the viewers' expectations and even prompts suspicion that perhaps *he* is really the murderer.

However, with the arrival of his lover, Mina, the dramatic tension snaps. Bearing a satellite phone that allows Satoshi to reconnect to the outside world and the Internet, Mina throws in several extra variables, and the plot spins wildly out of control. Instead of a sedate unmasking in the drawing room, the second episode breaks the rules of detective fiction by keeping several last-minute surprises up its sleeve, setting up the plot for the second half, which moves firmly into the territory of **Horror and Monsters**. In the latter two episodes the action moves to the Half Acre Mansion in Maine, as Satoshi, Asuka, and several new characters, including someone writing a dissertation on the legendary Necronomicon, pursue the culprit (who has kidnapped the teenage Nozomi Fuyukawa) back to the scene of the murder of Asuka's parents—and Satoshi's girlfriend Nora—six years before, a crime about which Satoshi suffers amnesia, with only flashbacks as memory of the event.

In its continual return to computer-screen research, *MotN* betrays its origin as a game by Abogado Power for the PC-9801 (a version was later ported to the Sega Saturn). The characters and their quirks are meticulously distributed—on-screen titles give extra details about people's names and the times of critical events, while sudden revelations come accompanied by fast-forward flashbacks, which are cheap and easy with digital animation. Despite this being pornography, unusually the plot takes much greater precedence than the sex—even the gore rivals the sex for screen time, or at least impact. Part of the **Discovery Series**. **NV**

MYSTIC ARCHIVES OF DANTALIAN, THE *

2011. JPN: *Dantalian no Shoka*. TV series, video. DIR: Yutaka Uemura. SCR: Kurasumi Sunayama, Tatsuhiko Urata, Hiroyuki Yamaga. DES: Sumie Kinoshita, Hiroyuki Yamaga. ANI: Masaru Sakamoto, Sumie Kinoshita, Satoru Kiyomaru. MUS: Yo Tsuji. PRD: Gainax, Dwango, Kadokawa, NTT Docomo, Klockworx, TV Tokyo. 25 mins. x 12 eps. (TV), 24 mins. (v).

Hugh Anthony Disward, a pilot who survived the Great War, inherits his grandfather's title, mansion, and personal library. But that's not all: in the basement is a childlike girl-creature named Dalian, a living gateway to another library altogether. Dalian is a Biblioprincess, guardian of an archive of demonic books containing all the world's forbidden knowledge, and Disward succeeds his grandfather as her Keykeeper. Together they explore the world of hidden texts that lies below England's tranquil byways, showing the ordered calm of the society that survived the Great War as a palimpsest on pages of deep, dark HORROR AND MONSTERS. And they're not the only ones: there are other Keykeepers and Biblioprincesses out there, engaged on the same mission: an attempt to protect ordinary people from the terrible consequences of absolute power.

The opening credit sequence serves notice that this show makes style its substance: every classic horror movie you ever shivered over late at night on the sofa in your parents' house, captured in images as achingly beautiful as the music around them. Uemura displays a grasp of atmosphere almost on a par with Roger Corman in *Masque of the Red Death* and has a superb team to turn his creeping dream into reality. Some of Gainax's animation ranks with the best they've produced. Studio DEEN, Brains Base, Toei, and AIC were among the in-betweeners. Tatsunoko's and Xebec's photography teams helped to shoot the film. Lolita fashion houses Alice and the Pirates and Baby, the Stars Shine Bright are credited for costume design. Style and atmosphere can't conceal some uneven passages and ineffectual attempts at humor, but the frisson of darkness under the calm exterior, the hint of bruising on a perfect skin, is a refined thrill worth the occasional awkwardness.

The series numbering is deceptive: the 12 episodes have 14 titles, with episodes 3 and 8 containing two stories apiece. A second series didn't materialize and an unaired episode was bundled as a video with the fifth collected volume of the spin-off manga. Despite its brevity, this series based on Gakuto Mikumo's book series says three things dear to these authors' hearts. Firstly, words and books matter, and not only because they have transformative powers. Secondly, an intelligent grown-up with no harem makes a perfectly service-

able leading man. Thirdly, simple, formulaic stories, done with professionalism and commitment, can be very entertaining.

MYSTICAL LAWS, THE *

2013. Movie. DIR: Isamu Imakake. SCR: N/C. DES: N/C. ANI: Hideaki Shimada, Masami Suda, Riku Sato. MUS: Yuichi Mizusawa. PRD: Happy Science. ca. 90 mins.
In the 2020s, China transforms into the fascistic Godom Empire and soon expands its borders while the international community wrings its hands impotently. Sho Shishimaru is a doctor working for the international relief charity Hermes' Wings, who has a premonition that Japan will be next on the Godom Empire's hitlist. Rescued by a bunch of priests, he is informed that he might be a reincarnation of Buddha, in yet another anime based on the works of Ryuho Okawa, founder of the religious cult Happy Science (formerly the Institute for Research in Human Happiness—see also THE GOLDEN LAWS, LAWS OF THE SUN, and REBIRTH OF BUDDHA).

Long derided in anime FANDOM for their ludicrous plotting and hand-waving hokum, the films of Happy Science regularly pop up in the industry like moles on a lawn (RELIGION AND BELIEF). They remain expensively wrought, and plainly better-funded than many more lauded anime. The staff are usually recognizable names, even to the extent of recurring voice actor Takehito Koyasu, although the script and actual animation company are often anonymous. They get cinema releases not only in Japan, where they have no trouble entering the year's top ten at the box office, but also abroad, although the chance to be their local agent is often passed around anime companies like a hot potato. One distributor, offered the opportunity to put his company's logo on a Happy Science film in a European territory, infamously said he would only do it if the contract permitted him to run in front of the screen every ten minutes with a banner reading: "THEY REALLY BELIEVE THIS STUFF!"

The Mystical Laws, however, sits at odds with many of the organization's previous works, being so overtly science fictional, and drawing so obviously on the TROPES AND TRANSFORMATIONS of schlock fantasy,

that it comes across less as a hectoring recruitment drive, and more as a winningly bad B-movie. Tathagata Killer, the masked dictator who molests his minions with a whip, is a creation straight out of the nuttier team shows for kids, as is the movie's concluding *deus ex machina*, in which the whole planet unites in prayer for the hero's victory—compare to similar actions in, say, SUMMER WARS. Make no mistake, *The Mystical Laws* is an awful film, but like its stable-mate HERMES, it's often so bad it's good. One wonders at its likely power to influence an audience of the lunatic fringe of otaku—if you already believe that your imaginary girlfriend lives in your pillow, then perhaps Happy Science isn't such a huge leap of faith.

MYTHICAL DETECTIVE LOKI RAGNAROK *

2003. JPN: *Matantei Loki Ragnarok*. AKA: *Detective Loki; Demon Detective Loki*. TV series. DIR: Hiroshi Watanabe. SCR: Kenichi Kanemaki. DES: Mariko Oka. ANI: Studio Deen. MUS: Kei Haneoka. PRD: TV Tokyo. 25 mins. x 26 eps.
The Norse trickster Loki annoys the father of the gods Odin once too often and is banished from Heaven. Sent to Earth in the body of a child (shades of CONAN THE BOY DETECTIVE), he lives a comfortable enough life in a huge mansion but schemes to get back to his own world. Loki is the target of constant attacks by other gods whom he's teased and tricked in the past. To regain his powers and be readmitted to Heaven, he has to outwit them, collect the mischievous spirits that infest the human world, and use them to enhance his natural abilities. Consequently, he sets himself up as a detective with the help of his loyal assistant Ryusuke Yamino and cute, bespectacled schoolgirl mystery fan Mayuri Daidoji. Among the many Norse legends that show up to cause problems is Verdandi, better known to anime fans as Belldandy from OH MY GODDESS!, who crashes the wedding of one of Mayuri's friends to kill Loki. Also appearing are her Norn sisters Urd and Skuld, love goddess Freya and her older brother Frey, and Heimdall. Based on a manga by Sakura Kinoshita, and no relation to RAGNAROK: THE ANIMATION.

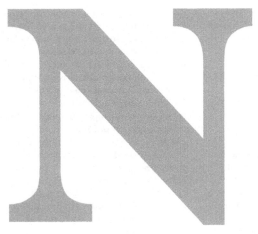

NABARI NO OU *

2008. AKA: *Ruler of Nabari*. TV series. DIR: Kunihisa Sugishima. SCR: Kiyoko Yoshimura. DES: Kazunori Iwakura, Yoshinori Hirose. ANI: Shigeki Kimoto, Yumi Nakayama, Shiro Shibata, et al. MUS: Michiru Oshima. PRD: J.C.Staff, d-rights, Geneon, KIDS STATION, Kinyosha, MOVIC, Square Enix. 24 mins. x 26 eps.

Secret ninja clans, hidden masters of elemental magic, have their own hidden world in modern Japan, the world of Nabari. They continue their clan warfare, but legend says that one day a ninja will possess the power to control all creation. He will become the ruler of Nabari and bring peace to the ninja world. The power is enshrined in a mystical scroll hidden within Rokujo Miharu, a teenager with no interest in ninja and no relationship whatsoever to any clan. He doesn't care about it—and even if he did, how could a skinny kid with no fight training whatsoever survive ninja warfare? His sarcasm and detachment aren't going to help him at all; but maybe recovering his memory of his mother's death will.

Based on Yuhki Kamatani's 2004 manga, this is an interesting reversal of the NARUTO scenario—instead of a kid with inner powers desperate to control them and become the best, Miharu is a kid who doesn't want to be a ninja and doesn't care about his inner powers until people try to kill him for them. Instead of a predictable boys' action show, we have a disaffected and mistrustful protagonist, an interesting set of evolving relationships, and an unusually low proportion of

action. When it happens, the action is well handled with fluid movement and some interesting effects: Yoshihide Mukai earns his font design credit with some beautiful work on the magical battle sequences. There are also some genuinely heart-wrenching moments, with deaths that devastate everyone involved. The character design is CLAMP-lite, with much attention to clothing and hair. Background art is beautiful, the soft watercolor effects a showcase for the work of Mika Funabashi and the rest of the color design team. The script is tedious in places thanks to an over-reliance on exposition, but this is an interesting show. **V**

NADESICO *

1996. JPN: *Kido Senkan Nadesico*. AKA: *Robot Warship Pink (Sweet William); Martian Successor Nadesico*. TV series, movie. DIR: Tatsuo Sato, Nobuyoshi Habara, Kenichi Hamasaki. SCR: Sho Aikawa, Takeshi Shudo, Hiroyuki Kawasaki. DES: Kia Asamiya, Keiji Goto, Takeshi Takakura, Takumi Sakura, Rei Nakahara, Yasuhiro Moriki. ANI: Keiji Goto, Natsuki Egami, Masayuki Hiraoka. MUS: Takayuki Hattori. PRD: Xebec, Studio Tron, TV Tokyo. 25 mins. x 26 eps. (TV), 30 mins. (*Gekiganger*), 90 mins. (m).

In the year 2195, while Earth prevaricates about sending troops to fight invaders from Jupiter, a brave civilian takes matters into her own hands and steals a privately owned warship. With a rogue captain straight out of SILENT SERVICE, an unwinnable war out of GUNBUSTER, and a plaster of irony over any cracks, Earth's last hope against the Jovian "lizards" is the ragtag crew of the Nadesico—a ship named after the *nadeshiko* flower that is said to represent Japanese womanly perfection. Captain Yurika and her mostly female crew are determined to meet the challenge, while their cook (and Yurika's childhood sweetheart) Akito is a former pilot ace on the run from his fears, pilot Jiro Yamada is an anime addict bent on living his favorite show, and the military is out to take control by fair means or foul.

Based on a manga in *Monthly Ace* magazine by Kia Asamiya and supposedly set in the same universe as his SILENT MÖBIUS, *Nadesico* is one of the better 1990s shows, particularly for a hard-core fan audience that can spot the in-jokes and identify the fine line between a *satire* of cheesy shows and the cheesy shows themselves. Parodies and homages are handled lightly, and the anime's characters and situations are cleverly scripted to avoid the repetitive tedium of TENCHI MUYO!, whose adoring-female-of-the-week policy it often imitates. The most striking example of this is cute moppet Ruri—a mixture of Wednesday Addams and *Tenchi*'s Sasami, marrying intelligence and competence with sullen cynicism.

Often playing like a superfast trailer for a much longer series, the viewer is left dazed by the compression of information, events, and background. Director Sato cuts conversations as if they were fight scenes; tone and mood change without a by-your-leave, and there's an incredible amount of shouting. The camp giant-robot show-within-the-show *Gekiganger Three* is more than mere comic-relief pastiche of GETTER ROBO and its ilk—a viewing experience that turns the crew into anime fans, it eventually becomes a cultural bridge between the warring worlds. Some might also detect a sly note in later episodes, in which the enemies' interest in *Gekiganger* serves as a commentary on the right-wing, militarist subtexts of so many SF shows. With a wink to the fan audience, anime saves the universe in much the same way as the power of song in the earlier MACROSS. The *Gekiganger* segments were compiled and released with extra footage straight to video in 1997.

The movie release *Nadesico: Prince of Darkness* (1998) closes the series with a flash-forward redolent of the second PATLABOR movie. Years after the original series, the two main leads are missing, presumed dead, and an older Ruri is now the commander of the Nadesico B, fighting an enemy that's not all it seems. The gap between the two stories is filled by a game, *Nadesico: The Blank of Three Years* (also 1998), one of several tie-in console products released by Sega and Nintendo.

NAGAHAMA, TADAO

1932–80. Born in Kagoshima, Nagahama graduated in drama from Nihon University, and found early work in puppetry (PUPPETRY AND STOP MOTION), such as on the TV series of MADCAP ISLAND (see also *DE). He joined the animation studio A Pro (later Shin'ei Doga) as an animator on QTARO THE GHOST, before spending a productive three years on such shows as STAR OF THE GIANTS and ROSE OF VERSAILLES, where he oversaw the former's landmark experiments in hyper-reality and artistic deformation (TECHNOLOGY AND FORMATS). At Tokyo Movie Shinsha, he was playfully known as "the Emperor of Tokyo Movie," an allusion to Akira Kurosawa's nickname as "the Emperor of Movies." By the late 1970s, he had achieved a reputation as the "fans' anime director," with an understanding that his shows had an appeal beyond the usual implied audience of children, to connoisseurs of the animated image. Along with his sometime rival Yoshiyuki Tomino, who was trying similar efforts in GUNDAM, he expressed an interest in maturing the presentation of anime in step with the aging of the audience. In 1978, he wrote that animation had a new and largely unserved audience of middle-

and high-school-age viewers who deserved shows aimed at their own interests and concerns. This has been taken, in hindsight, as one of the earliest recognitions of the advent of video FANDOM in the 1980s, although Nagahama was not around to see it himself, dying midway through the French coproduction ULYSSES 31.

NAGAI, GO

1945–. Born in Ishikawa Prefecture, Nagai became an assistant to the manga artist Shotaro Ishinomori after completing high school. He enjoyed early and controversial success as a manga artist, with titles such as SHAMELESS SCHOOL introducing nudity and crudity in abundance to young readers' great enjoyment and the eternal annoyance their parents. He subsequently copied the model of Osamu Tezuka's Mushi Production to set up his own company, Dynamic Planning, which has overseen Nagai's works in their anime forms, including DEVILMAN, CUTEY HONEY, and KEKKO KAMEN. His greatest influence, however, has been in the world of giant robots, including such important works as GETTER ROBO, GRANDIZER, and MAZINGER Z, anime's first pilotable robot. Although he does have an English-language following, his work still seems much better known in Europe and the Arab world. He was also notably a designer on the puppet series *X-Bomber* (*DE, as *Star Fleet*), including the impressive combining robot Dai-X.

NAGANO, MAMORU

1960–. Born in Kyoto, Nagano's anime debut was HEAVY METAL L-GAIM in 1984. Later design credits include BRAIN POWERED, although he is chiefly known as the creator of FIVE STAR STORIES.

NAGAOKA, AKINORI

1954–. Born in Nagasaki Prefecture, Nagaoka began studying literature at Chuo University, but dropped out and became an animator on THE GARDLES. He subsequently contributed as a key animator on shows such as TOUCH and DOCTOR SLUMP, before his directorial debut on the latter.

NAISHO NO TSUBOMI

2008. AKA: *Tsubomi's Secret; Enlightening Tsubomi*. Video. DIR: Akira Shigino. SCR: Naruhisa Arakawa. DES: Akira Takeuchi,

Kazuhiro Inoue. ANI: Akira Takeuchi, Isamu Utsugi. MUS: UbiQuinta. PRD: ARMS, Studio Kikan, Happinet Pictures. 30 mins. x 3 eps.
Tsubomi (whose name means flower bud) is a little girl learning about the world as she grows up. She experiences her first crush on a boy, learns where babies come from and how they get there when her mother is pregnant, and has her first period. This educational anime for young girls is based on an award-winning manga of the same title by Yu Yabuchi, which also deals with issues not featured in the video such as the risks of predation. See also MARVELOUS MELMO.

NAJICA *

2001. JPN: *Najica Dengeki Sakusen*. AKA: *Najica Explosion Battle; Najika Blitz Tactics*. TV series. DIR: Katsuhiko Nishijima, Takeshi Mori. SCR: Takeshi Mori, Kenichi Kanemaki, Kazunori Chiba, Mayori Sekijima. DES: Noriyasu Yamauchi. ANI: Noriyasu Yamauchi. MUS: N/C. PRD: Studio Fantasia, Amber Films. 25 mins. x 12 eps.
Thirty years after ecological disaster has sunk 17% of Earth's surface below rising seas, perfumer Najica Hiragi, age 27, moonlights as a secret agent, using her knowledge of 500 different scents to save the world from terrorism. Pretty girls, action, and unlikely plotting from the people who brought you AGENT AIKA.

NAKAMURA, TAKASHI

1955–. Born in Yamanashi Prefecture, Nakamura is one of the unsung heroes of modern anime, with a strong resumé of work that often seems to be better known and more highly respected by other animators than by the public at large. He performed key animation duties on both NAUSICAÄ OF THE VALLEY OF THE WIND and AKIRA, but his directorial work has remained limited to relatively obscure titles such as CATNAPPED and TREE OF PALME. He deserves to be considered alongside Mamoru Oshii (q.v.) as one of the distinctive creators in modern Japanese animation.

NAKAZAWA, KAZUTO

1968–. Animator and illustrator whose debut work was on the second of the FATAL FURY TV movies. Has subsequently been a character designer on shows including EL HAZARD and a popular choice as key animator. He is credited with a "unit director" role on **Kill Bill: The Origin of O-Ren**.

NANA *

2006. TV series. DIR: Morio Asaka. SCR: Tomoko Konparu, Ryosuke Nakamura. DES: Kunihiko Hamada. ANI: Kunihiko Hamada, Toshihiko Fujisawa. MUS: N/C. PRD: Madhouse, NTV. 25 mins. x 50 eps.

Two girls called Nana, one a naïve middle-class young woman, the other a streetwise punk rocker, meet on the train to Tokyo, and end up sharing an apartment. Based on the manga by Ai Yazawa serialized in both *Cookie* and *Shojo Beat* magazines, and also adapted into two live-action movies, *Nana* (2005) and *Nana 2* (2006).

NANA AND KAORU

2011. JPN: *Nana to Kaoru*. Video. DIR: Hideki Okamoto. SCR: Hideki Okamoto. DES: Atsuko Watanabe, Ryusuke Shiino, Satoshi Miura. ANI: Atsuko Watanabe. MUS: Shunichi Yuki. PRD: AIC PLUS+, Shiraizumi-sha. 24 mins. x 2 eps.

Nana is a beautiful, friendly straight-A student. Her next-door neighbor and childhood friend Kaoru is a low achiever, pervert, and social outcast at school. The pair have drifted apart in recent years, mainly due to Kaoru not taking his education seriously while Nana is constantly striving to keep her grades at the top. But when Nana discovers Kaoru's secret passion for S&M fetish play, she realizes she may have found the perfect way to unwind from her demanding student life. Based on Ryuta Amazume's 2008 manga, this fetish comedy is a more perverted take on **His and Her Circumstances**. ●❖

NANAKA 6/17 *

2003. TV series. DIR: Hiroaki Sakurai. SCR: Tomoko Konparu. DES: Masayuki Iimura, Yoshiki Yamagawa. ANI: Masayuki Iimura. MUS: Toshio Masuda. PRD: JC Staff, GENCO. 23 mins. x 12 eps. (TV), 25 mins. (v).

After suffering a brain injury, 17-year-old Nanaka Kirisato becomes convinced that she is a six-year-old trapped in an older body. From being an intelligent, serious young woman she becomes a cute little girl who just wants to watch anime all day, especially her favorite show, *Magical Domiko*. She believes that, just like her cartoon heroine, she's been placed under a magic

spell. Her best friend Renji Nagihara, who feels partly responsible for the action that caused this trouble, teams up with her father to help her grow up again and to keep her injury secret to keep her life as normal as possible. Japanese teenagers acting like six-year-olds.... Who's going to notice? Based on the *Shonen Champion* weekly manga by Ken Yagami, which artfully reverses many of the clichés of magical-girl shows, *N6/17* essentially plays **Petite Princess Yucie** or **Marvelous Melmo** in reverse. It also contains within it the seed of an arch commentary on **Fandom** itself in the style of **Genshiken**—so many anime tropes began as aspirational entertainment for children, only to become the chosen obsession of teenagers (**Kids' Anime**). The U.S. release included a bonus unaired episode, titled *Nanaka: The Distraction*.

NANAKO SOS

1983. AKA: *Nana the Supergirl*. TV series. DIR: Akira Shigino, Yoshihiko Yamatani, Yoshinobu Shigino, Tetsuro Amino, Tsukasa Sunaga. SCR: Masaru Yamamoto, Yukiyoshi Ohashi, Mami Watanabe, Tomoko Ishizuka. DES: Tsuneo Ninomiya. ANI: Geki Katsumata, Shiro Murata, Tsuneo Ninomiya, Yoshiyuki Kikuchi, Masami Abe. MUS: Ichiro Nitta. PRD: Kokusai Eiga, movie International, Fuji TV. 25 mins. x 39 eps.

An alien girl crash-lands on Earth, losing her memory in the process but keeping her superpowers. "Rescued" by a boy, who has a knack for making money, and his dopey friend, she agrees to work for them for room and board. They set up the Supergirl Company investigation agency, and Nana gets to work bringing villains to justice, solving love problems, and dodging the unwanted attentions of a mad scientist out to use her for his own ends. Based on an original *Just Comic* manga by **Pollon**-creator Hideo Azuma, this is one of the most neglected of the magical-girl series, eclipsed in its year of release by the more famous **Creamy Mami**. Mercifully, it has nothing whatsoever to do with **Amazing Nurse Nanako** or with the porno anime **Sexy Sailor Soldiers**, the Japanese title of which is *NamiSOS!*

NANIWA SPIRIT

1992. JPN: *Naniwa Yukyoden*. AKA: *Tales of Naniwa Heroism*. Video. DIR: Teruo Kogure.

SCR: Haruyuki Maeda. DES: Dokuman Pro. ANI: Teruo Kogure. MUS: Jiro Takemura. PRD: Knack. 58 mins. x 2 eps.

Taido Kaimon is the leader of the Kinshu Group gangster syndicate in Japan's Kansai region. His gang is a cluster of wisecracking madmen, eternally running into trouble with the law, each other, and the local girls who give as good as they get. It's a fast and furious Osaka comedy (see **Compiler**) in an adaptation of the gag manga in *Asahi Geino* magazine by Dokuman Pro. The same year saw the release of a three-part video series based on another Dokuman manga: the Osaka motorcycle gang comedy *Nanbono Monjai: Yankee Gurentai*, directed by Masamune Ochiai and written by Yoshihisa Araki. ●❖

NAOKO-SAN FROM PLANET LILY

2010. JPN: *Yuri Seijin Naoko-san*. AKA: *Lesbian Citizen Naoko-san; Yurian Naoko-san*. Video. DIR: Tetsuya Takeuchi. SCR: Tetsuya Takeuchi. DES: Tetsuya Takeuchi, Masakazu Miyake. ANI: Tetsuya Takeuchi. MUS: MOSAIC.WAV. PRD: ufotable, Aniplex, Klockworx. 6 mins. (v1), 30 mins. (v2).

Naoko is an alien from Planet Yuri, here to conquer Earth by turning it into a lesbian paradise. She lives in Misuzu's home and dresses as a maid. Together they do battle against a neighborhood pervert; this involves Naoko making phone calls from under little girls' skirts. This six-minute short based on the 2005 manga by Kashmir was the curtain-raiser for a half-hour video with the same title and crew, released in 2012. Here Naoko has taken the place of Misuzu's older sister, who is studying abroad. Misuzu's little brother Ryota and best friend Hii-chan help out with her deranged adventures. This string of surreal events may recall **FLCL** and, despite the pretty pastel art, lack of nudity, and nonviolence, is not suitable for the impressionable young. The tentacle-waving, child-chasing alien pervert with a camera should give you a clue. *Yuri*, of course, is a slang term for a lesbian (**Argot and Jargon**).

NARUTO *

2002. TV series, video, movie. DIR: Hayato Date, Tensai Okamura, Hirotsugu Kawasaki (m2). SCR: Katsuyuki Sumisawa, Akatsuki Yamatoya, Hirotsugu Kawasaki, Yuka Miyata. DES: Hirofumi Suzuki, Tetsuya Nishio,

Shinji Aramaki. ANI: Atsuho Matsumoto, Hiroto Tanaka, Tatsuya Tomaru, Tetsuya Nishio. MUS: Toshiro Masuda, Musashi Project. PRD: Studio Pierrot, TV Tokyo, Aniplex, Dentsu, Bandai, Shueisha, Toho. 23 mins. x 220 eps. (TV, original), 17 mins. (v1), 40 mins. (v2), 82 mins. (m1), ca. 80 mins. (m2), ? mins. (v3), 23 mins. x 315+ eps. (TV, *Shippuden*), 90 mins. (m3), 95 mins. (m4), 85 mins. (m5), 108 mins. (m6), 110 mins. (m7).

Before Naruto Uzumaki was born, a great fighter called Yondaime battled evil nine-tailed fox Kyuubi, and sealed him into a human body—Naruto's. The people of his home village of Konoha fear and distrust what is inside the boy, and as a result of this distrust—and of being orphaned—he's hot-headed and a bit of a troublemaker; but Naruto is determined to show them he is a human being who can be loved and trusted, not a demon. He plans to do this by succeeding to Yondaime's title of Hokage, given to the strongest ninja of the Fire Country. To reach this goal he has to travel, train, study, and fight many opponents, making enemies and allies along the way. This sets up an ongoing tournament/fight scenario with multiple opportunities to introduce new characters, and as with **DRAGONBALL** and **HATTORI THE NINJA**, this proved hugely popular. Based on the manga in *Shonen Jump* by Masashi Kishimoto.

Several "movies" toured as part of the *Jump Festa* cinema roadshow—a vacation diversion to keep kids off the streets. Their increasing length is a fair indicator of *Naruto*'s growing stature—strictly speaking these are video releases premiered in theaters rather than actual movies, a distinction which was once a big issue in 1980s anime, but now only really applies to the *Jump Festa*. *Find the Crimson Four-Leaf Clover* (2003) was only 17 minutes long and featured a story about the grandson of the third Hokage and his crush on a local girl. *Battle At Hidden Falls—I am the Hero!* (2004), occupied a more significant slot on the bill, at 40 minutes. *Naruto* became the top billed movie for that winter's *Naruto: It's the Snow Princess's Ninja Art Book!* (2004, *Naruto Dai Katsugeki!! Yuki Hime Shinobu Hojo Datte Bayo!*) in which our hero and friends are ordered to escort his favorite film actress to the Snow Country

to film a new movie. Its status was assured with the stand-alone *Naruto the Movie: The Great Clash! The Phantom Ruins in the Depths of the Earth* (2005, *Gekijoban Naruto Daigekitotsu! Maboroshi no Chiteiiseki Datte Bayo!*) in which our heroes get caught up in a huge battle with a moving castle while on the highly dangerous and significant errand of delivering a lost pet. If this sounds like the plots are increasingly an excuse for the battles, it could be because all ninja shows eventually face this problem—when you have to slot in the rumble-of-the-week, give the favorite characters screentime, and keep your audience happy, a good plot and tight writing are usually the first casualties.

Naruto faced up to this issue by aging with its original audience, rebranded as *Naruto Shippuden* (2007, lit.: "Hurricane Chronicles"), which begins two and a half years after the 220th episode that closed the original series. Although the basic structure of challenges, setbacks, training, and victories remained unchanged, the slightly older cast now faced a greater deal of angst and torment. This decision to go older proved to be a winning one, and the *Naruto* franchise has maintained its position in Japanese **RATINGS AND BOX OFFICE**, with a healthy 5% showing in TV ratings that is impressive in the multi-channel 21st century. Naruto films have continued to appear annually in Japanese cinemas, with *Naruto Shippuden the Movie* (2007), *NS: Bonds* (2008), *NS: The Will of Fire* (2009), *NS: The Lost Tower* (2010), *NS: Blood Prison* (2011), and *Road to Ninja: Naruto the Movie* (2012). Far from showing the usual pattern of declining viewership as the years go by, *Naruto* continues to remain buoyant, with *Road to Ninja* being the highest grossing film in the franchise so far. This is in part because even a low-seeming 5% rating still means literally millions of viewers (1.25 million of whom bought cinema tickets to *Naruto the Movie*), and also because *Naruto*'s cultural footprint extends to the ongoing manga serial and to a great number of video games, which periodically beckon former fans back into the fold.

NASTY OLD LADY

1970. JPN: *Ijiwaru Baasan.* AKA: *Bullying Old Woman.* TV series. DIR: Satoshi Murayama, Hiroshi Yamazaki, Yoshio Okamoto, Shoichi

Sugiyama. SCR: Susumu Yoshida. DES: Shoichi Hayashi. ANI: Sadayoshi Tominaga, Hiromitsu Morita. MUS: Yasuhiro Koyama. PRD: Knack, Nippon TV. 25 mins. x 40 eps. (TV1), 25 mins. x 46 eps. (TV2).

Based on a 1966 manga by **SAZAE-SAN**–creator Machiko Hasegawa, this is another slice-of-everyday-life tale, centered around a spiteful old woman who causes trouble for neighbors with her constant bumbling and grumbling. The first show from anime production house Knack, with a leading "lady" voiced in pantomime-dame fashion by gravelly male voice actor Shigeo Takamatsu to add to the horror. The story was brought back for a new generation as *New NOL* (1996), a TV remake directed by Yoshimitsu Morita.

NASU: SUMMER IN ANDALUSIA *

2003. JPN: *Nasu: Andalusia no Natsu.* Movie. DIR: Kitaro Kosaka. SCR: Kitaro Kosaka. DES: Naoya Tanaka. ANI: Hisao Shirai. MUS: Toshiyuki Honda. PRD: Madhouse. 45 mins. (m), 54 mins. (v).

Pepe is a minor competitor in a Spanish cycling race not unlike the Tour de France, charged with working as a support rider to ensure that the team's star rider gains maximum points on each leg. However, with his team threatening to drop him, Pepe must also face up to his past, as the race blows through his hometown, where his former girlfriend Carmen is preparing to marry his elder brother Angel. Based on the manga in *Comic Afternoon* by Io Kuroda, it was followed by a 54-minute straight-to-video sequel, *Nasu: A Migratory Bird with a Suitcase* (*Nasu: Suitcase no Wataridori*, 2007), focusing on Pepe's teammate Ciocco as bereavement threatens to tear apart the team during Japan-based training for another big race. Compare to **OVER DRIVE**.

NATSUKI CRISIS

1993. Video. DIR: Koichi Chiaki, Junichi Sakata. SCR: Mayori Sekijima. DES: Futoshi Fujikawa. ANI: Futoshi Fujikawa. MUS: Yasuhiko Shigemura. PRD: Madhouse. 30 mins. x 2 eps.

Natsuki is a karate ace in a private high school where martial arts are a major part of the curriculum. There's fierce rivalry between Natsuki's team and another local school's with an even better reputation for fighting skills. A transfer student from the rival school is attacked by her former classmates, the student president authorizes spying missions, and there are romantic complications, too. The designs are attractive, even though contemporary school stories can date fast because the background detail—what to wear, what bags and accessories are cool, how hair is styled—changes very quickly. This one, based on a 1990 manga from *Business Jump* by Hirohisa Tsuruta, has enough heart and punch to retain its charm.

NATSUME'S BOOK OF FRIENDS *

2008. JPN: *Natsume Yujincho*. TV series.
DIR: Takahiro Omori. SCR: Kenichi Kanemaki, Mayori Sekijima, Kenichi Araki, Sadayuki Murai, Jukki Hanada, Aya Yoshinaga, Hiroshi Onogi. DES: Akira Takata, Tatsuo Yamada, Yukihiro Shibutani. ANI: Akira Takata, Tatsuo Yamada. MUS: Makoto Yoshimori. PRD: Brains Base, NAS. 25 mins. x 13 eps. (TV1), 25 mins. x 13 eps. (TV2), 25 mins. x 13 eps. (TV3), 25 mins. x 13 eps. (TV4).
Takashi Natsume can see *yokai, ayakashi,* and other spirits, but now keeps it to himself. After he was orphaned, talking about his ability got him passed from family member to family member, shunned in school, and called a liar or an attention-seeker. He has no idea why spirits gravitate to him until he finds his dead grandmother's notebook. Grandmama Reiko made binding contracts with spirits by writing their names in her book. They all want to be free. Takashi decides to track down each spirit and return its name, thus dissolving Reiko's contract. With the help of a powerful spirit in cat form, he sets out on the road to freedom, learning how to trust and make friends in the human world along the way.

Yuki Midorikawa's charming 2005 manga examines the power inherent in true names in a very different way to that in DEATH NOTE or SPIRITED AWAY. This anime adaptation is also a rare instance of a production team working closely with a manga creator to produce a show that respects the original without being hamstrung by it. Brains Base and director Omori have made a beautiful, sometimes dark, but always engaging story. The episodic nature of the original makes it easy to dip in and out of the individual adventures, but the thread of Takashi's evolution from a reserved and remote young man hiding his painful childhood to the open, kindhearted person he always wanted to be ties the stories together and makes the series a rewarding whole.

The series packs a powerful emotional punch, without descending into mawkishness. In this, it's very like MUSHI-SHI. Spirits and humans have overlapping needs, which is where much of the conflict as well as the emotion arises. Some of the monsters are not the kind you want to imagine under the bed, making this an unsuitable show for easily frightened children. Choking and bloodsucking occur but gore is minimal and the occasional bath scenes are tastefully steamy. *Natsume's Book of Friends 2* (*Zoku Natsume Yujin-cho*) followed in 2009 from the same crew, but there was a change of writing team in 2011 for *Natsume's Book of Friends 3* (*Natsume Yujin-cho San*) that carried over to the fourth series *Natsume's Book of Friends 4* (*Natsume Yujin-cho Shi*) in 2012. The same creator was responsible for IN THE FOREST OF THE FIREFLIES' LIGHT, which was adapted into anime form with many of the same staff. **N✓**

NATSUMUSHI THE ANIMATION

2009. Video. DIR: Toshihiro Watase. SCR: Shinichiro Sawayama. DES: Nodame Ichigo, Shun Manuwame. ANI: Candy Ichigo. MUS: N/C. PRD: Café de Jeilhouse, Pink Pineapple. 30 mins. x 2 eps.
Tomoe is the schoolgirl victim of a groper who finds he has the ability to bring any female to orgasm with his touch. But it's not his fault: he was molested on a train by Sumire and became addicted to the thrill of illicit gropes. Rina looks like an innocent little girl but she gropes men of all ages on trains, until a group of them get together and get their own back. Based on Hiroki Tsukiyoshi's 2005 manga. See HITORIGA THE ANIMATION, which also features Sumire. **N✓**

NATSUYUKI RENDEZVOUS *

2012. TV series. DIR: Kou Matsuo. SCR: Kou Matsuo. DES: Junichiro Taniguchi. ANI: Junichiro Taniguchi, Mami Komatsu, Atsuko Sasaki. MUS: Ken Hiramatsu. PRD: Dentsu, Dogakobo, Fuji TV, Shodensha, Sony Music Entertainment, Toho. 24 mins. x 11 eps.
Part-time, short-sighted florist Ryosuke Hazuki nurses a secret crush on his widowed boss Rokka, who has foresworn all contact with men for eight years. Rokka's dead husband, Atsushi, is a ghost that only Ryosuke can see. The living pair embark on a reluctant, halting romance, rendered all the more awkward by Atsushi's despair, and Ryosuke's secret knowledge of it.

Ghost or *Truly, Madly, Deeply* (or for anime fans, KIRARA) are replayed here in a winning adaptation of Haruka Kawachi's manga. Discarding many of the shallower concerns of usual anime ROMANCE AND DRAMA, *Natsuyuki Rendezvous* offers a series of far meatier issues to resolve. Like the heroine of MAISON IKKOKU, Rokka is an older woman carrying a torch for a man who is perfect because he is too dead to ever let her down. No living man can compare with the idea of her husband, but Ryosuke tries anyway, only too aware that his every move is causing Atsushi pain, even as Atsushi is forced to admit that he wants his wife to be happy.

NAUGHTY DETECTIVES

1968. JPN: *Wanpaku Tanteidan*. TV series. DIR: Rintaro, Toshio Hirata, Masami Hata, Moribi Murano. SCR: Keiji Abe, Aritsune Kato, Masaki Tsuji. DES: Osamu Tezuka. ANI: Kiyomi Numamoto, Akihiro Kanayama. MUS: Takeo Yamashita. PRD: Mushi Pro, Fuji TV. 25 mins. x 35 eps.
A group of young boys (plus a token girl and her little brother, the obligatory brat) form a detective club, pooling their talents for brain, brawn, invention, and driving skills to solve crimes in Tokyo. Much to the consternation of police chief Nakamura, they often succeed where the professionals fail. The first show made by Tezuka's studio from a non-Tezuka work, this series adapts the juvenile *Boy Detectives Club* stories of Ranpo Edogawa, a 19th-century novelist better known today for his Poe-inspired tales of horror and suspense, some of which were adapted for the ANIMATED CLASSICS OF JAPANESE LITERATURE. A watershed show that transferred the literary penchant for amateur sleuthing into the anime market, setting up a formula that survives to this day in CONAN THE BOY DETECTIVE and the YOUNG KINDAICHI FILES.

NAUGHTY DOTAKON

1981. JPN: *Mechakko Dotakon*. AKA: *Robot Kid Dotakon*. TV series. DIR: Takeshi Shirato, Kazumi Fukushima. SCR: Masaru Yamamoto, Takao Yotsuji, Kenichi Matsuzaki, Tetsuya Michio. DES: Takeshi Shirato, Iwamitsu Ito, Mitsue Ito. ANI: Takeshi Shirato. MUS: Shunsuke Kikuchi. PRD: Kokusai Eiga, Toei, Fuji TV. 25 mins. x 28 eps.

Geeky genius Michiru has already got her PhD in atomic physics (from a California university) by the age of 11. But she still longs for a little brother, so she builds her own. Robot boy Dotakon is soon joined by their little robot sister, Chopiko, and the trio embarks on a series of fantastic adventures fueled by Michiru's inventions. Luckily for their little town, and the sanity of Michiru's bulky guardian Gorilla Capone, nothing ever gets too out of hand. Eclipsed in its year of release by a far more successful android child, Arale from **DOCTOR SLUMP**.

NAUGHTY NURSES *

2003. JPN: *Heisa Byoin*. AKA: *Closed Hospital*. Video. DIR: Ichiro Meiji. SCR: Naruhito Sunaga. DES: Ryosuke Morimura. ANI: Ryosuke Morimura. MUS: Yoshi. PRD: Digital Works, YOUC, Vanilla. 30 mins. x 2 eps.

Yusuke Nimura is a chronically shy boy, unable to bring himself to have sexual intercourse with his perky girlfriend Mayu Mizuno. The couple separate, only to discover that coincidence brings them back together when they both find work at Aoshima General Hospital. Before long, Yusuke is dodging the attentions of amorous patients, sex-crazed nurse Satsuki, and the lustful senior nurse Ryoko. Meanwhile, he continues to struggle with his feelings for Mayu, who herself is not immune from the attentions of the patients. Relatively everyday hospital high jinks in this erotic anime—though it suffers from excessive use of digital animation loops in the sex scenes, for which the moaning talents of the voice actresses cannot fully compensate; and somewhat oversimplified. Compare with less mainstream stuff in **NIGHT SHIFT NURSES** and **NURSE ME**. **🔞⊗**

NAUSICAÄ OF THE VALLEY OF THE WIND *

1984. JPN: *Kaze no Tani no Nausicaä*. AKA: *Warriors of the Wind*. Movie. DIR: Hayao Miyazaki. SCR: Hayao Miyazaki. DES: Hayao Miyazaki. ANI: Kazuo Komatsubara, Takashi Nakamura, Kazuyoshi Katayama, Hideaki Anno, Takashi Watanabe. MUS: Joe Hisaishi. PRD: Nibariki, Tokuma, Hakuhodo, Toei. 117 mins. (95 mins. as *Warriors of the Wind*).

A thousand years after a great war, in a world dominated by the pollution-induced Sea of Corruption, Princess Nausicaä grows up in a peaceful valley shielded from the devastation by its prevailing winds from the sea. These keep the deadly spores that spread the Sea of Corruption away from its fertile lands—survival by a combination of geographical and meteorological chance. Terrible insect-like creatures roam the Sea of Corruption and the desert lands around. Mightiest of all are the huge crustaceans, the Ohmu. One of these can wipe out most human threats, but in a herd, they are unstoppable. Outside the valley, while smaller communities struggle to survive, factions within the Tolmekian Empire are fighting for supremacy. Princess Kushana of Tolmekia finds one of the superweapons that made the ancient war so terrible, the last God Warrior embryo, and plans to use it to ensure that her people stay on top, even if it means upsetting the fragile balance Nature has struggled to regain after the long-ago war.

When the ship carrying her superweapon crashes in the valley, it brings Kushana's army down on the agrarian enclave to retrieve the terrible cargo. Nausicaä's father dies in the struggle, but she can't give herself up to the lust for vengeance—she is the only one with the vision to see that understanding, tolerance, and patience might give a better outcome than aggression, not only with the Tolmekians, but also with the Sea of Corruption and its giant denizens. Faced with the God Warrior's awakening, an Ohmu stampede, and even the failure of the wind that has protected her Valley for generations, she must also face up to her own fears and make the ultimate sacrifice to preserve everything she loves.

It would have been easy to make this a hero-villain tale in the Hollywood mold (something the woefully inferior 1986 U.S. edit *Warriors of the Wind* attempts), but what emerges is a far richer, more complex world. Shunning more conventional firepower, Nausicaä uses her brains, her heart, and her courage to find a solution with compassion for everyone involved. The result is a film that is superbly put together on all levels, with messianic and ecological subtexts that don't weigh down a story packed with action and adventure.

After his initial success as a director-for-hire on **CASTLE OF CAGLIOSTRO**, Hayao Miyazaki directed this short segment of his own epic 1982 manga, originally serialized in *Animage* magazine. Despite an ending that seems to owe a debt to David Lynch's movie of *Dune* (1984), *Nausicaä* draws on a variety of other sources, including *The Princess Who Loved Insects* (one of the **JAPANESE FOLK TALES**) and, for its scenes beneath the poisonous-yet-cleansing Sea of Corruption, the 1959 adaptation of Jules Verne's *Journey to the Center of the Earth*. It even pastiches *Bedknobs and Broomsticks* (1971) with an opening montage that ends with Nausicaä in flight where Disney has a witch. As with many of Miyazaki's later characters, there are powerful echoes of the work of British historical fantasy novelist Rosemary Sutcliffe, whose hero-kings are defined by the extent to which they willingly live and die for others. Nausicaä has much in common with Ashitaka, her spiritual heir in **PRINCESS MONONOKE**, and the art direction of both films spares no effort in the quest for perfection. *Nausicaä*'s access to cutting-edge technology, however, was more limited; the Ohmu were animated by a range of techniques which included cut-paper segments. Despite the notoriously short-lived attention spans of the anime-watching public (see **BRAVE SAGA**), *Nausicaä* polled high in Japanese top-ten lists for two decades after its original release. It influenced many imitators, particularly the incoherent eco-babbling of **GREEN LEGEND RAN**, and even films with little direct relation—**WIND OF AMNESIA** and **WINGS OF HONNEAMISE** both had their original titles altered to reflect the cadences of *Nausicaä* in an attempt to inspire Pavlovian ticket-buying in the Japanese audience.

NAYUTA

1986. Video. DIR: Masami Hata. SCR: Akiyoshi Sakai. DES: Akio Sugino. ANI: Akio Sugino. MUS: Masamichi Amano. PRD: Circus Production, Toshiba EMI. 75 mins.

Nayuta is on her way home from high

school when she saves a mother and son from an accident and takes them to the hospital. The son, Kiro, wears a strange metal headband and seems to have some extrasensory powers. Then his mother is abducted, and Nayuta finds her good deed has drawn her into conflict with a strange group of activists known as Jarna and aliens called Hazard. Based on Junko Sasaki's 1981 manga published by Flower Comics.

NAZCA *
1998. JPN: *Jiku Tensa Nazca*. AKA: *Time Reincarnation Nazca*. TV series. DIR: Hiroko Tokita. SCR: Tsunehiro Ito. DES: Hirotoshi Sano. ANI: N/C. MUS: Suneyoshi Saito. PRD: Pioneer, TV Tokyo. 25 mins. x 12 eps.
Kyoji is a high school student who loves kendo and adores his charismatic instructor, art teacher Masanare Tate. Kyoji and Tate's fiancée, Yuka, see him transform into an Incan warrior at a kendo match. Long ago they were all Incan nobles, and Kyoji's past self betrayed Tate's just before the conquistadors rolled in and destroyed their empire for good. As history seems set to repeat itself, the two meet again as deadly enemies, dressed in implausibly large feather headdresses and enough spandex to cover a chorus line. Not only this trio but everyone they know in modern Tokyo, right down to Kyoji's dog, has counterparts in 16th-century South America. Flashbacks retell the original fight between Bilka (lieutenant of the last Incan general, Huascar) and Yawaru (lieutenant of his usurper brother, Atahualpa) over both priestess Akulia and the Incan doomsday device Ilya Tesse. In a parallel story line, their reincarnations repeat their previous lives, loves, and conflicts in modern Tokyo, as Tate attempts to revive Ilya Tesse and destroy the modern world.

Amid this hokey plot, screenwriter Ito mixes Aztecan and Incan myths and history with impunity, throwing in a spaceship straight out of von Däniken (or **MYSTERIOUS CITIES OF GOLD**) and vague musings about the "close genetic ties" between the Incas and the Japanese. Sano's design work has all the edge he brought to **BOUNTY DOG**, but, as with that show, design alone won't make things work. Also adapted into manga form by the pseudonymous female duo "Akira Hinakawa." As

a historical footnote, the real Atahualpa's brother was actually called Manko, presumably omitted from the anime version because *manko* is Japanese for pussy. Alien Incas also appeared in the 1960 kids' TV show *National Kid* (*DE). In a dubious and rather obscure extension of its artistic heritage, two clips from *Nazca* appeared in the opening credits of the American sitcom *Malcolm in the Middle* (2000).

NECROMANCER *
2006. JPN: *Shimai Ningyo*. AKA: *Little Sister Death Doll*. Video. DIR: SCR: Kyokai Aoigatana. DES: Kinomi Noguchi, Mitsuharu Miyamae. ANI: Hotaru Kawano. MUS: N/C. PRD: Animac. 30 mins.
Set in the pseudo-medieval Paltia Kingdom, Lester Clieford, the son of a famous priest, cares for his sick sister Mith while both of them attend the local academy. Haughty Lady Pusel Rainzett, the daughter of a great general, arrives to attend the school and to seek a cure for her mother, who is also also suffering from an unnamed disease. When Mith dies unexpectedly, Lester and his mentor, the scholar Olphen, turn to the dark arts in an attempt to raise a demon who they hope will be able to place Mith's soul into a beautiful homunculus that Olphen has developed. But the wrong demon appears, and wants a "sacrifice" from not only Lester, but also the virginal Pusel, since this is that kind of anime. Mediocre porn from the makers of the much better **WIFE WITH WIFE**; based on a game by Amalgame's Nine Heads label. **❶❷❸**

NEEDLESS *
2009. TV series. DIR: Masayuki Sakoi. SCR: Satoru Nishizono, Yuki Enatsu. DES: Hiromi Kato, Yuka Okamoto. ANI: Yoshio Kosaki, Kazuo Watanabe. MUS: Masaaki Iizuka, Tatsuya Kato. PRD: Madhouse Studios, Avex Inc., Hakuhodo D.Y. Partners, Lantis, AT-X. 24 mins. x 24 eps.
The Needless: human survivors of the Third World War who have emerged from the chaos with superhuman powers. They work for the highest bidder, and for some that's the Simeon Megacorp. From the Black Spot, the nuclear blast crater at the heart of Tokyo (compare to **AKIRA**), Simeon sends out its Testament robots and hordes of Needless. Cruz Child, the sole

survivor of a resistance movement wiped out by Simeon's Needless troops, is out for revenge for his friends and his older sister, presumed dead in action. He and a motley gang of followers gather to beard the evil overlords of Simeon in their own den.

If **BUBBLEGUM CRISIS** were remade for an audience of beer-and-curry boys conditioned by years of fan service to prefer girls in school uniforms or maid outfits to girls in hardsuits and plots, it would be *Needless*. Escalating superpowers and battles in the **DRAGON BALL** mold, constant flirtation with nudity that wimps out at actual revelation, insanely overspecified weaponry, and bad jokes abound. Give your brain and your critical faculties an early night, and settle down for lots of mindless action based on Kami Imai's 2004 manga. **❶❷**

NEGADON: THE MONSTER FROM MARS *
2007. JPN: *Wakusei Daikaiju Negadon*. Movie. DIR: Jun Awazu. SCR: Jun Awazu. DES: Jun Awazu. ANI: Jun Awazu, Makoto Miyahara. MUS: Shingo Terasawa. PRD: CoMix Wave. 30 mins.
In the hundredth year of the Showa period (i.e., an alternate 2025), the overpopulated Earth is at its limits. Desperate, humanity decides to use nuclear weapons to terraform Mars. In so doing they wake an ancient terror: Negadon. The monster travels to Earth and attacks Tokyo. Only Dr. Narasaki and his giant robot Miroku 2 stand in Negadon's way. Can they save the city?

If you even think it's worth asking that question, or if you couldn't swallow the logical idiocy of using nuclear weapons to terraform a planet, you are not the target audience for this short film. It's a loving gift to fans of the giant monster movie genre that gave us *Godzilla*. Set in a dream of the 1950s, saturated with nostalgia for a Japan that never really existed, opening with a homage to Ishiro Honda's unforgettable anti-nuclear fable, this story was never about saving Tokyo. No monster movie is ever about *saving* the city. Trashing the city, helping the monsters to level it to ruin, is merely the process by which we learn that what matters is how we fail.

Director Awazu fails brilliantly. Allocating the second half of his mini-movie to an epic battle in Tokyo and a space battle, he stays short on plot and long on impact, with the CGI money concentrated where it can make the biggest splash; some elements and characters suffer as a result. Terasawa's music cleverly evokes Japan's great monster movie scores. This whole movie is fan service for *kaiju* lovers, a little box of monster chocs with all your favorite titbits.

NEGIMA! *

2004. JPN: *Maho Sensei Negima!* AKA: *Magister Negi Magi; Master Negi Magi.* TV series, video, movie. DIR: Hiroshi Nishikiori, Nobuyoshi Habara, Nagisa Miyazaki, Akiyuki Shinbo, Shin Onuma. SCR: Ichiro Okuchi, Kenichi Kanemaki. DES: Hatsue Kato, Yoshimi Umino, Kazuhiro Ota, Hiroshi Kato, Megumi Kato. ANI: Hatsue Kato, Hideyuki Motohashi, Mitsutoshi Kubota, Minoru Mihara, Noriyasu Yamauchi. MUS: Shinkichi Mitsumune, Kei Hanaoka. PRD: Xebec, Shaft, GANSIS, Studio Pastoral, TV Tokyo. 7 mins. x 3 eps. (v1), 25 mins. x 26 eps. (TV1), 25 mins. x 2 eps. (v2), 30 mins. x 3 eps. (v3), 30 mins. x 4 eps. (v4), 76 mins. (m).

Negi Springfield is a bespectacled ten-year-old Welsh orphan, highly intelligent, well-mannered, and quiet. He's already graduated as a teacher, but he has another ambition—to follow in the footsteps of his father, the legendary Nagi Springfield, as a great wizard. Nagi, known as the "Thousand Master" (allegedly because he was master of a thousand spells) has been missing, presumed dead, for many years. Negi has been studying at the Merdiana Academy in Wales, and has just one more test before he qualifies as a wizard. To pass, he has to prove that he can cope with everyday life and new relationships on his own, by becoming a class teacher at a girls' high school in Japan, while keeping his powers secret. His class consists of 31 14-year-old girls: challenging enough for someone three times his age, without the dangerously powerful opponents and magical challenges that come his way.

The harem show is a well-established trope in manga and anime (**ROMANCE AND DRAMA**). A hapless boy suddenly finds himself surrounded by a crowd of girls inexplicably but completely in love with him, and dithers over whether to do something about it. If the creator is clever enough and lucky enough to hit the right formula

for his girl characters, so as to attract the largest possible number of boy viewers, the process turns into a self-perpetuating franchise. *Negima* has clever girls, dumb girls, magicians, martial artists, an alien, a spirit, an idol, a vampire, a demi-demon, and a robot. The merchandising spin-offs—figures, posters, collectible cards—can be even more lucrative than the original work.

Negima! twists the formula by making the boy *much* younger than the girls. This is played for comedy, but creates some uncomfortable moments when the clichés of the harem genre (**ROMANCE AND DRAMA**) and the age of the boy collide. The idea of a group of teenage girls pursuing a ten-year-old boy is unsettling, whether they're cooing over him as if he were a cute fluffy toy, sharing his bedroom, or chasing after him for a kiss.

Perhaps to compensate for this disturbing subtext, the show parades concealment like a banner. Negi carries a highly conspicuous bandaged object resembling a magical staff. Where magical girls usually get naked as they grasp their magical baton, wand, or whatever and transform into their costumed selves, Negi's staff gets naked to cast a spell while he keeps his clothes on. The arrival of the magical boy's animal familiar, a cute but dirty-minded ermine gangster wannabe with an eye for the girls and an outrageous line in tall tales, moves the spotlight back onto sex. Meanwhile, *shotacon*, the male equivalent of *lolicon* (**ARGOT AND JARGON**), an unhealthy interest in little boys, is no mere subtext but one of *Negima*'s primary selling points.

The success of the *Harry Potter* franchise—the story of a bespectacled young orphan wizard at a boarding school with a powerful magical enemy—is an obvious point of reference, but transplanting it to the harem was a stroke of brilliance from Ken Akamatsu. The TV series is based on his best-selling 2003 manga *Magical Teacher Negima (Maho Sensei Negima)*, and its success was planned with great care. Three videos were produced solely to introduce the TV anime characters between August 2004 and March 2005. The first two, reenacting chapters of the manga, were bundled with CD dramas and one was sold separately.

The first series launched in January 2005. Its biggest problem is its compressed time span. The amount of editing needed to get 18 volumes of story into 12 hours of screen time means that story arcs from the manga are missed out or simplified. There are serious problems in the animation—for example, a scene where one character suddenly acquires an extra finger. After complaints from Japanese fans, a number of episodes were redrawn for the Japanese DVD release (the version released in the West). There were no storyline changes, but the redrawing managed to introduce a few new errors, probably due to a lack of continuity checking.

Fans are often willing to disregard problems like this if a TV adaptation gives them enough of what they loved in the manga original—favorite characters looking cute, a coherent storyline, and an atmosphere that reflects the original—and here *Negima* scores well. It's not as dark as the manga but that didn't hamper its success. Two videos, *Master Negi Magi: Spring* and *Summer (Maho Sensei Negima Haru/Natsu)*, appeared in 2006, and a second TV series, *Negima!?* (note different punctuation), aired in Japan the same year, an alternate story unseen in the manga, with new character designs, more action and comedy, and less fan service. A live-action drama series followed in 2007 and further videos were released with manga volumes in 2008, subtitled *White Wing (Shiroki Tsubasa Ala Alba,* "white wing" in both Japanese and Latin), and in 2009, subtitled *Another World (Mo Hitotsu no Sekai)*. The *Negima* anime story wrapped up in 2011 with a movie based on the final chapters of the manga, following on from *Another World*. *Maho Sensei Negima! Anime Final* aired on a double bill with the **HAYATE THE COMBAT BUTLER** movie *Heaven Is a Place On Earth* wrapping up a much-loved and highly successful series that put the harem into Hogwarts. ◐

NEIGHBORHOOD STORY

1995. JPN: *Gokinjo Monogatari.* TV series, movie. DIR: Atsutoshi Umezawa. SCR: Aya Matsui, Yumi Kageyama, Motoki Yoshimura. DES: Yoshihiko Umakoshi. ANI: Chuji Nakajima. MUS: Masahiro Kawasaki. PRD: Toei, TV Asahi. 25 mins. x 50 eps. (TV), 30 min (m).

One of the freshest and most stylish TV

shows of its season, *NS* goes back to the 1960s for its look and atmosphere. Childhood friends and neighbors Mikako and Tsutomu head off to art college (he for photography, she for fashion), where they slowly fall for each other. A bubbly adaptation of the 1995 manga in *Ribon* magazine by **I'M GONNA BE AN ANGEL**–creator Ai Yazawa, there was also a short theatrical release, *NS: The Movie* (1996). Compare to **HIS AND HER CIRCUMSTANCES**, which tells a similar story, but with a more negative slant. The manga sequel, **PARADISE KISS**, was also adapted into an anime in 2005.

NEKO RAHMEN *

2006. TV series. DIR: Haruki Kasumori, Ai Ohara, Ai Chiketani, Yoriko Yamazaki, Kenshiro Mori. SCR: N/C. DES: Kenji Sonishi. ANI: Haruki Kasumori, Ai Ohara, Ai Chiketani, Yoriko Yamazaki, Kenshiro Mori. MUS: Maruchikkuai. PRD: THINK Corp., Mag Garden. 3 mins. x 13 eps.
Salaryman Koichi Tanaka finds a new ramen store. It's weird, but he's compelled to come back every day to listen to the hopes and dreams of the proprietor, a cat named Taisho, who dreams of a chain of ramen shops serving his own recipes. Ambitious and scheming, with a hard life behind him and a complex and demanding family, Taisho has also diversified his business interests by opening a curry shop.

Simply and artfully animated, with odd stories and surreal treats embedded in each episode—the cute but useless part-timer who sleeps on the job and gets pregnant, the Japanese subtitles for cat dialogue, the Christmas shopping experience, the picture-frame credits, and crochet cat—this series is a tiny gem. It doesn't have much in the way of resources but it uses them with imagination. Kenji Sonishi's 2006 gag manga, which is also available in English, is playfully and lovingly brought to life with a different director for each episode. It gained a place in history as the first anime series to be licensed exclusively by

an Internet TV company and made available for unrestricted free download when Vuze released it in 2007.

NEO TOKYO *

1987. JPN: *Manie Manie Meikyu Monogatari.* AKA: *Labyrinth Tales.* Movie. DIR: Yoshiaki Kawajiri, Katsuhiro Otomo, Rintaro. SCR: Yoshiaki Kawajiri, Katsuhiro Otomo, Rintaro. DES: Rintaro, Katsuhiro Otomo, Yoshiaki Kawajiri, Takashi Watanabe, Atsuko Fukushima. ANI: Takashi Nakamura, Atsuko Fukushima, Koji Morimoto, Kunihiko Sakurai. MUS: Micky Yoshino. PRD: Project Team Argus, Kadokawa. 50 mins.
A slender anthology brackets two dark shorts by Kawajiri and Otomo inside the titular *Labyrinth,* a chiller by veteran Rintaro. Little Sachiko is warned by her mother about playing with strangers and staring into mirrors, but she ignores the warnings with results as predicted by the Brothers Grimm. She and her cat stray into a carnival straight out of a Ray Bradbury story—the kind where you don't want to stay after dark but can't find the exit. Otomo's story, *Order to Stop Construction,* is a classic SF essay on the possibilities of chaos inherent in the most efficient automated system. Kawajiri contributes *Running Man,* the tale of a top racing driver who finds he just can't quit. Despite its futuristic trappings, it's anime for the couch-potato audience, a warning against machine addiction that they'll forget while slavering over the gleaming, roaring engines, and the least interesting of the three plot premises. All three selections ooze dark, edgy style. See **ROBOT CARNIVAL** and **MEMORIES** for anthologies on a different theme.

NEORANGA *

1998. TV series. DIR: Jun Kamiya. SCR: Sho Aikawa. DES: Hiroto Tanaka. ANI: Hirofumi Suzuki. MUS: Kuniaki Haishima. PRD: Pierrot, Pony Canyon, Marubeni. 15 mins. x 48 eps. (#1–#24 1st series / #25–#48 2nd series)
A giant robot, a relic of an ancient

South Sea civilization, threatens to destroy Tokyo, but it can be controlled by the three teenage Shimabara sisters, who are descended from its makers. Despite their reservations about inheriting this relic of their previously unknown ancestry, the 18-foot-tall robot becomes "one of the family"—with sometimes comic consequences. Originated by Aikawa, with striking designs, backgrounds, and music, this show begins as a *Godzilla* pastiche but soon transforms into a slice-of-life drama with occasional city-stomping. The short and variable episode lengths stem from its original existence as just one of several anime shown on TV's *Anime Complex* anthology slot, though it is a measure of its quality that it was at least optioned for a follow-up season—few of its fellow short shows shared such success.

NERIMA DAIKON BROTHERS *

2006. JPN: *Oroshitate Musical Nerima Daikon Brothers.* AKA: *Freshly Grated Musical Nerima Daikon Brothers; Dress-Up Musical Nerima Daikon Brothers.* TV series. DIR: Shinichi Watanabe. SCR: Yoshio Urasawa. DES: Takamitsu Kondo, Satoshi Matsudaira. ANI: Daiki Yoshida. MUS: FCK. PRD: Studio Hibari, Aniplex. 24 mins. x 12 eps.
Brothers Hideki and Ichiro live with their sexy cousin Mako in a field where they grow *daikon*—Japanese radishes. As children they made a pact that one day they would perform in a concert in a dome built over the field. Now the boys do everything they can to make money to fund their dream, despite Mako spending it as fast as they can bring it home. A prominent local businessman has other ideas—he plans to build a baseball stadium on the field and will stoop to anything to get his way. Hideki loves Mako, who tells him that the Japanese constitution won't let them marry (even though it will). Mako is attracted to Ichiro, who works in a host club charming older ladies, but he is devoted to his pet seaweed

and Pandaikon, a strange bear/daikon hybrid who lives with them.

In true musical comedy style, the show breaks into song at every possible moment, but its main purpose is to be an insanely fast-paced parody of Japanese and foreign politicians, performers, and cultural institutions, with overtly sexual gags and references to homosexuality, crime, race, and moneylending. Director Watanabe loves to appear in his own shows, and here, as in EXCEL SAGA, his Nabeshin alter ego features as prominently as his passion for schoolboy humor. If you can't stand the idea of an anus-seeking enema rocket, this is not the show you're looking for. But if you want another anime featuring the prime minister who inspired LEGEND OF KOIZUMI or a mind-blowingly, grin-till-your-face-aches singalong funtime in the worst possible taste, it just might be.

A manga version, with art by Taka-mitsu Kondo and story by Aniplex and Studio Hibari, was published from December 2005 to May 2006. **◐**

NESTING CRANES
1971. JPN: *Tsuru no Sugomori*. AKA: *Cranes in their Nests*. Movie. DIR: Kazuo Saito (pseud-onym for Tsutomu Shibayama). SCR: Kazuo Saito. DES: Kazuo Saito. ANI: Kazuo Saito. MUS: Yasuji Kiyose. PRD: Japanese Film Collective. 17 mins.
An earnest tale of animal cooperation, as two out-of-place chickens try to make their home on an island inhabited by cranes. When they are attacked by an eagle, their adoptive parent cranes are killed, but the chickens organize a counterstrike. Eventually, peace is restored to the island. Based on a story by Teru Takakura, this anime was made over a three-year period by around 80 members of the Japan Film Broadcasting Industry Association under the pseudonymous lead of Shibayama.

NETORARE
2010. JPN: *Netorare: Tanabe Yuka no Doku-haku*. AKA: *Cuckoldry: Yuka Tanabe's Solilo-quy*. Video. DIR: Naomi Hayakawa. SCR: N/C. DES: Naomi Hayakawa. ANI: Naomi Hayakawa. MUS: N/C. PRD: ChiChi No Ya. 18 mins x 2 eps.
Yuka is happily married until she is raped, but she likes the experience and carries on seeing her rapist. Porn, if you hadn't guessed. **◐◑◒**

NETORARE FIGHTER YATCHINGU
2010. AKA: *Cuckoldry Fighter Yatchingu*. Video. DIR: P-san Honda, Shigeru Sawaguchi, Megumi Jiro. SCR: N/C. DES: LINDA, Reo Ka-mei. ANI: Reo Kamei. MUS: N/C. PRD: T-Rex, MS Pictures (BOOTLEG). 30 mins. x 3 eps
A drug that makes women sexually insatiable is being used by mobsters on a private pleasure boat where they have set up a ring for a very unusual kind of fight. Harry's girlfriend Ai has been captured and held hostage. He and his friends go to the rescue but are captured and he is forced to watch her and other girls being gang-raped, but the main event will be even worse. Porn based on a story and character designs by LINDA. **◐◑◒**

NETORARE ZUMA
2012. AKA: *Cuckold Wife*. Video. DIR: Yumei Aoi. SCR: Magnum Minamichatei. DES: LINDA, Yumei Aoi. ANI: Yumei Aoi. MUS: N/C. PRD: T-Rex, MS Pictures (BOOTLEG). 17 mins.
Reiko is a hot young housewife, yet her husband Hiroaki is obsessed with a teen-age idol singer. He even calls the singer's name when the couple have sex. She tells her troubles to Hiroaki's best friend Taniguchi, and he suggests that they be-come sex friends and release each other's frustrations in this porn anime based on LINDA's 2006 manga. **◐**

NETTI'S MARVELOUS STORY
1977. JPN: *Alps no Ongaku Shojo Netti no Fushigi na Monogatari*. AKA: *Musical Alpine Girl Netti's Marvelous Story; The Wonderful Story of Netti, Musical Girl of the Alps*. TV special. DIR: Hiroshi Shirai, Isao Takahata. SCR: N/C. DES: N/C. ANI: Isao Takahata, Ryo-suke Takahashi, Shinichi Tsuji. MUS: N/C. PRD: TV Man Union, Mushi Pro, Nippon Anima-tion, TV Asahi. ca. 80 mins.
Netti is the six-year-old daughter of a musi-cal family in an Austrian mountain village. Nervous at the thought of the town mayor coming to see her first performance, Netti makes many errors in rehearsals, before fleeing into the forest in anguish. Lost in the woods, she is rescued by a mysterious old man who calls himself a "snow wizard" and gives her a magic flute to practice on.

This frightfully obscure TV special, mix-ing live-action footage with animation, was screened in Japan to mark the imminent arrival of the Engel family, a group of performers from Reutte in Austria, best known today for their appearance in the German film *The Singing Angels of the Tirol* (1954, *Die singenden Engel von Tirol*). The Engels had been performing since the 1940s, but this tour was approaching their 1981 swansong, with the original family now nearing retirement and the focus inevitably switching to their four grand-daughters, one of whom we assume to be the titular Netti. The animation sequences comprised three folktales told by the snow wizard, directed in part by future Studio Ghibli giant Isao Takahata. One features a character study of the lonely old man Kar-zermandel and another features a boy who scares away devils with a magic flute. The final tale is one of chickens escaping from a henhouse and dancing, for some reason, in the farmyard to the pop song "SOS" by the Japanese pop duo Pink Lady (see GLORIOUS ANGELS). Although framed as an Alpine adventure in the style of TREASURES OF THE SNOW or HEIDI—or indeed, THE SOUND OF MUSIC—such similarities are only superficial. Compare to YOUNG PRINCESS DIANA, which was another bizarre attempt to educate the Japanese public about a real-life visitor to their country with the aid of fictional cartoon stories.

NEURO *
2007. JPN: *Majin Tantei Nogami Neuro*. AKA: *Demon Detective Nogami Neuro*. TV series. DIR: Hiroshi Kojina. SCR: Ryo Tamura, Satoshi Suzuki. DES: Mika Takahashi, Hidetoshi Kaneko. ANI: Mika Takahashi, Ai Kikuchi, Kyoko Takeuchi, Toyoo Ashida. MUS: Tomoki Hasegawa. PRD: Madhouse Studios, D/N/ Dream Partners, NTV, Shueisha, VAP. 25 mins. x 25 eps.
Yako Katsuragi wants to know who murdered her father, but no one can tell her. He was killed inside a locked room and everyone else thinks it was suicide. She needs someone to help her solve the mystery. Then she meets someone with an appetite for mystery and a secret that he has to hide: Neuro is a demon who feeds on mysteries and puzzles, and humans planning evil release the best, juiciest energy of all. But human/demon law says he mustn't make his presence known in the human world. So he makes a deal with Yako: he'll act as her "assistant" and do all the detective work if she provides a front

for his activity. In return he'll help her solve her father's murder.

Yusei Matsui's 2005 manga set up this odd couple and interesting premise, reminiscent of the deal between shrine kid and demon in USHIO AND TORA. Neuro is arrogant, self-centered, and completely amoral, while Yako is a typical 16-year old, unfocused and not overconfident. Neuro's constant urging of Yako to make something of herself is almost parental, though it sounds much cooler coming from a demon and contrasts strongly with the show's graphic violence. The characters are the charm of this series. The plots, while adequate detective stories, are not especially interesting, and the animation is of variable quality. The design, all points and angles, is interesting, and the color shows that you don't have to go down the DEATH NOTE route of monochrome and pallor to make demons look interesting. In fact, the first episode of *Neuro* pays tribute to a much perkier series: Gosho Aoyama's CONAN THE BOY DETECTIVE. It may have dark supernatural trappings, but it wants to be in the same room as Holmes and Watson and all the boy detectives when the mastermind reveals whodunnit.

NEW ADVENTURES OF PINOCCHIO, THE *

1960. JPN: *Pinocchio no Shin Boken*. TV Series. DIR: Tadahito Mochinaga. SCR: Arthur Rankin Jr. DES: Ichiro Komuro. ANI: Satoru Ota, Kunihiko Ide, Shigeru Omachi, Tadanari Okamoto. MUS: N/C. PRD: Dentsu Studios (MOM Production), Fuji TV, Videocraft (Rankin/Bass). 5 mins. x 130 eps.

Pinocchio the puppet travels the world in search of the Blue Fairy, a magical creature who can supposedly transform him into a real boy. The sly conman Foxy Q. Fibble takes advantage of the innocent wooden boy, enlisting him in numerous schemes such as a bank heist "movie" that turns out to be the real thing. But Pinocchio continues to search the globe (and history, thanks to a time-traveling closet), in a series of picaresque adventures described in the Rankin/Bass studio history as a "ten-and-a-half-hour road movie."

The New Adventures of Pinocchio was the first stop-motion (or "Animagic") deal struck between the American animators Arthur Rankin Jr and Jules Bass, and the Japanese animator Tadahito Mochinaga. A giant of WARTIME ANIME and early key figure in 1950s ADVERTISING AND SPONSORSHIP, Mochinaga was a specialist in PUPPETRY AND STOP MOTION who accepted the *New Adventures* contract with extreme reluctance in order to pay off some of his art-house debts. His MOM Production company would subsequently make many of the 1960s Rankin/Bass features, including the Christmas classic *Rudolph the Red-Nosed Reindeer* (1964).

The New Adventures was conceived as a series of 25-minute adventures, although each was shot and originally broadcast in 5-minute episodes. The series is rather obscure, not the least because it was often shown as an interior segment of other umbrella shows, both in America and its native Japan. As a result, it has often been confined to the shadows and footnotes of TV histories, despite its remarkable achievement. Of each episode's 300-second running time, a full 100 seconds would comprise recycled or repurposed footage, telling the "Story So Far," presenting Pinocchio's opening dance, or flashing up the end credits. Regardless, the acheivement of MOM Production in generating the entire run in a single calendar year, at a rate of just over 12 minutes a week, demonstrated the viability, or at least possibility, of producing animation on a weekly schedule, two whole years before Osamu Tezuka supposedly pioneered the idea with ASTRO BOY. In fact, *The New Adventures* episodes were not shown on Japanese television until they were included as part of the puppet show *Ciscon Oji* (1963) and hence may have appeared to viewers to have been following the innovation of Tezuka, rather than preceding it. The last five episodes featured stories of the new character "Willy Nilly," as told to Pinocchio by his father Gepetto, and effectively functioned as test footage for the stop-motion feature *Willy McBean and His Magic Machine* (1965). See also THE ADVENTURES OF PINOCCHIO.

NEW KARATE HELL

1990. JPN: *Shin Karate Jigoku Hen*. Video. DIR: Kozo Kusuba, Toshiyuki Sakurai. SCR: Hideo Nanbu. DES: Kenzo Koizumi, Shunji Saida. ANI: Kenzo Koizumi, Shunji Saida. MUS: Nobuyuki Nakamura. PRD: Nippon Animation. 50 mins. x 2 eps.

A single karate master is all that stands between beautiful women and a group of neo-Nazi rapists. Hellbent on revenge ever since the Gestapo murdered his father and sister, our hero pursues his quarry from the United States to the Amazon rainforests. Based on a manga by Ikki Kajiwara, creator of KARATE-CRAZY LIFE (with Jiro Tsunoda and Joya Kagemaru), this anime devotes equal screen time not only to the hero's flying fists of vengeance, but to questionable audience titillation in the form of the baddies' many crimes.

NEWMANOID CAM

2010. JPN: *Newmanoid CAM—Cam Castin*. Video. DIR: Heisaku Wada. SCR: ZEQU. DES: N/C. ANI: N/C. MUS: N/C. PRD: Pixy. 15 mins.
In 2030, crime is running rife and genetic technology is harnessed to combat it. Dr. Jubei Yanagisawa devises artificial humans with pneumatic solenoid technology. The first successful humanoid product of his labs is designed to look like a cute girl and named Cam Castin. Partnered with police officer Scott, she infiltrates a ring of perverts using cosplay as a cover. Based on the porn manga by Urotan, this short video, whose similarity to ARMITAGE III passes very quickly, was bundled with an issue of the manga.

NHK

Nippon Hoso Kyokai, or Japan Broadcasting Corporation. NHK is license funded—it derives its funding from a monthly fee charged to each household that possesses a television. As Japan's public broadcaster, it was formed in 1925 by the integration of three radio stations, and subsequently offering television broadcasting from 1953. Japan's first TV channel, the conservative NHK has a large number of anime shows, most clustered around the lower age group—for NHK, cartoons generally remain "kid's stuff," and are used to entertain preschoolers (EVERYBODY'S SONGS). There are, however, notable exceptions, such as THE SECRET OF BLUE WATER. NHK's sister channel NHK Educational often reaches older age groups, with shows such as KASUMIN.

NIEA_7 *

2000. AKA: *Nia Under Seven; NieA_7–Do-*

mestic *Poor @nimation*. TV series. DIR: Takuya Sato, Tomokazu Tokoro. SCR: Takuya Sato. DES: Yoshitoshi Abe, Yoshiaki Yanagida. ANI: Tsuneo Kobayashi. MUS: Yoshio Owa. PRD: Triangle Staff, WOWOW. 25 mins. x 13 eps. On an Earth still struggling to come to terms with making contact with aliens, failed college student Mayuko, forced to live in Tokyo while she retakes her exams, shares a flat with a zany alien girl (cat-ears and all) called Niea. Niea is an Under-7, one of the strange underclass of aliens that hasn't integrated into this neat near future. Made by the same studio as the surreal **SERIAL EXPERIMENTS LAIN** and intended as a "fantasy sitcom" by original creator Yoshitoshi Abe, *NieA_7* is a gentle examination of the immigrants' plight not unlike **DEARS**—rather than dealing with galaxy-spanning invasions or world-saving plots, the cast are more concerned with everyday life in Tokyo and how to keep their bathhouse from going bankrupt. A manga version in *Ace Next* magazine preceded the show, but was created as a promotional tool—it is not fair to say that *NieA_7* was "based on" the *AceNext* manga.

NIGHT FOR LOVING
1983. JPN: *Ai Shite Night*. AKA: *Kiss Me Licia*. TV series. DIR: Osamu Kasai, Kazumi Fukushima, Yugo Serikawa, Shigeo Koshi. SCR: Mitsuru Majima, Sukehiro Tomita, Tatsuo Tamura. DES: Yasuhiro Yamaguchi. ANI: Yasuhiro Yamaguchi, Akira Kasahara, Tsuneo Komuro. MUS: Nozomu Aoki. PRD: Toei, TV Asahi. 25 mins. x 42 eps. Cute schoolgirl Yaeko helps out in the family restaurant in the evenings. Dad disapproves of her friend Satomi, a big fan of the rock band Beehive, and when the pair meet Hashizo, little brother of Beehive's lead singer Takeshi, things get even worse. Yaeko falls for Takeshi and Satomi resents his friend's new infatuation, much to the annoyance of his *own* fiancée. Based on Kaoru Tada's 1981 manga in *Margaret*, and popular in Europe in its day, it has probably passed its sell-by date in the English language.

NIGHT HEAD GENESIS *
2006. TV series. DIR: Yoshio Takeuchi. SCR: George Iida. DES: Yo Higuri, Hiroshi Kato, Toshihiro Koyama. ANI: Noboru Furuse, Yasuyuki Ebara. MUS: Shigeru Umebayashi. PRD:

Bee Media, Foursome. 25 mins. x 24 eps. The Kirihara brothers are abandoned by their parents because of their terrifying psychic powers. Handed over to a research lab, they spend 15 years as guinea pigs in a series of psychic experiments, aimed at accessing the "Night Head," the 70% of human brain capacity that, in most of us, simply sleeps unused. Older brother Naoto is psychokinetic and Naoya, six years his junior, is a clairvoyant, telepath, and healer. When they finally break out of the lab and go on the run, they meet other paranormally gifted individuals and become more and more aware that a terrible plague threatens the world.

An interesting premise that looks back to 1980s classics **AKIRA**, **AI CITY**, and **BAOH**, with a solidly talented crew including the legendary Noboru Furuse from **LUPIN III**, this ticks all the boxes. *Night Head: Genesis* began as a live-action TV series conceived and directed by George Iida in 1992 (*DE). As a writer, Iida is solid, but slow. His people generally act and interact convincingly, his plots usually work out, and the characters who pop up briefly and then vanish from the storyline have valid reasons: but it takes a long, long time for anything to happen. To apply the glacial pace of a *yaoi* manga (**ARGOT AND JARGON**) to a boys' action series is a brave move, but not necessarily a clever one. There are compensations—this really is an intriguing story, packed with ideas, and Umebayashi, who has worked with such great directors as Wong Kar-Wai, provides a chillingly creepy score. It's a missed opportunity, but still worth seeing. Iida also made 2003's live-action *Dragon Head* based on Minato Mochizuki's manga. In 2007 he turned *Night Head: Genesis* into a manga with art by Yo Higuri.

NIGHT OF TANEYAMAGAHARA
2006. JPN: *Taneyamagahara no Yoru*. Movie. DIR: Kazuo Oga. SCR: Kazuo Oga. DES: N/C. ANI: N/C. MUS: Ensemble Planeta. PRD: Studio Ghibli. 27 mins. Camping out in the fields overnight so they can start cutting grass at dawn, four farmers chat over a campfire. They hear a horse nearby and three of them walk off to investigate. The fourth falls asleep and dreams he's talking to the plants and trees. When the others come back, the sun has

risen and they go on with their day.

This beautiful short film was released by Studio Ghibli to celebrate the 110th anniversary of the birth of Kenji Miyazawa, one of Japan's greatest 20th-century writers (**NIGHT ON THE GALACTIC RAILROAD**). It's a fabulous showcase both for Miyazawa's original story and for the art of Kazuo Oga, whose backgrounds have created such perfect worlds for the Ghibli directors. He has drawn every frame of this piece, and while the animation is extremely limited the whole work is breathtaking, with wonderful sound supporting the imagery. It's closer to such projects as *ga-nime* (**ARGOT AND JARGON**) or even **NEKO RAHMEN** than to fully animated Miyazawa adaptations such as **GORSCH THE CELLIST**.

NIGHT ON THE GALACTIC RAILROAD *
1985. JPN: *Ginga Tetsudo no Yoru*. AKA: *Night Train to the Stars*. Movie. DIR: Gisaburo Sugii. SCR: Minoru Betsuyaku. DES: Takao Kodama. ANI: Marisuke Eguchi, Koichi Mashimo, Yasunari Maeda. MUS: Haruomi Hosono. PRD: Hiroshi Masumura, Asahi, Herald, Tac. 115 mins. Based on Kenji Miyazawa's 1927 novel, this dark but gentle fantasy of life and death is a demanding, rewarding film with some dazzling animation and a script by avant-garde playwright Betsuyaku. Giovanni is a lonely child in unhappy circumstances. Late one night, he boards a strange steam train in a meadow on the outskirts of town. He has no plans or expectations; he's simply along for the ride, and finding his classmate and only friend, Campanella, on board is an unexpected bonus. The fantastic voyage takes them along the Milky Way, through landscapes symbolic of death and rebirth, based on Miyazawa's beliefs as a Nichiren Buddhist and student of Christianity and his background as a naturalist. Only when the train comes full circle and deposits him back at home does Giovanni understand that Campanella's journey had a different destination—in the real world he has drowned in a river while trying to save another boy's life.

Director Sugii isn't afraid to take things slowly or to take liberties with a text when necessary (see **TALE OF GENJI**). Here he turns almost all Miyazawa's characters into cats, creating a distancing effect that blurs the edges of the film's tragedy and helps us to accept its overriding sense of wonder and optimism. The imagery of the novel, using a railroad as a metaphor for life's journey, is interpreted with superb attention to detail. The steam train and the stations are as rich and credible as any real-world setting, and the poetic beauty of the imagery combines with this richness to give the long journey a powerful emotional weight. Yellow Magic Orchestra–cofounder Hosono's music perfectly fits this visually stunning film, with its imagery of almost hallucinogenic beauty and power, though even he takes a back seat for Handel's *Hallelujah* chorus. Compare to **GALAXY EXPRESS 999**, with a similar interstellar train, also pastiched in Tsui Hark's Hong Kong cartoon, *A Chinese Ghost Story* (1999). The story was also directed by Kazuki Omori as the live-action film *Night Train to the Stars* (1996). The original book forms a crucial component in the narrative of **GIOVANNI'S ISLAND**.

NIGHT RAID 1931 *

2010. JPN: *Senko no Night Raid*. AKA: *Night Raid in Flash*. TV series, video. DIR: Jun Matsumoto. SCR: Shinsuke Onishi. DES: Akimine Kamijo, Keigo Sasaki, Shinobu Tsuneki, Yoshio Tanioka. ANI: Keigo Sasaki. MUS: Satoshi Kadokura, Taro Hakase. PRD: A1 Pictures, Aniplex, AT-X, TV Tokyo. 23 mins. x 13 eps. (TV), 23 mins. x 3 eps. (v), 23 mins. (recap).

Shanghai, 1931: the Imperial Japanese Army is spreading the gospel of Pan-Asianism (compare to **FIST OF THE BLUE SKY**). In the shadows of this fractured city a military intrigue organization called Sakurai operates. Its officers will be forgotten by history, but their actions could change it. They possess paranormal talents and a range of other abilities that make them a formidable team.

This show is part of the TV Tokyo/Aniplex collaboration *Anime no Chikara*, set up to create original series. Following **SOUND OF THE SKY**, it starts with an attractive idea: superpowered spies operating in a real historical conflict. By choosing a place and time when Japan was heading for totalitarian control of Asia, an ambition that still sours relations with the neighbors it occupied over 70 years ago, the producers have taken a daring and ambitious step. Japan is not portrayed in a flattering light

here, and the refusal to ignore the treatment of the Chinese and the actions of the Japanese military is admirable.

But this is first and foremost a spy series, and on that score it delivers action and entertainment in a stylish and satisfactory fashion. The animation is uneven and the script sags when it tries to be funny, but the action is sharp and the style is snappy and enticing. Three unaired episodes were included on the Japanese DVD release, which also featured the "recap" episode aired instead of series episode 7. The actual episode, which featured the notorious Mukden Incident, a bombing engineered by Japan so that it could attack Manchuria in "self-defense," was too controversial for the TV network that collaborated on its creation to air—which is precisely the sort of blinkered refusal to engage with its past that annoys Japan's neighbors in the first place (**DOCUMENTARIES AND HISTORY**). An episode dealing with the attempted Tokyo coup of February 26, 1936 was another one of those kept back for video, lest it tweak the tender sensibilities of Japan's easily offended right wing.

NIGHT SHIFT NURSES *

2000. JPN: *Yakin Byoto*. AKA: *Night Shift Ward*. Video. DIR: Hisashi Okezawa. SCR: Ryo Saga. DES: Kuniyoshi Hino. ANI: Hiroya Iijima. MUS: Hiroaki Sano. PRD: Tatsuya Tanaka, Hiromi Chiba, Discovery, Mink, Studio9MAiami. 30 mins. x 10 eps. (v), 30 mins. (5.5), 30 mins. (10.5), 30 mins. x 3 eps. (*Kranke*), 30 mins. x 5 eps. (*YB2*), 30 mins. x 3 eps. (*YB3/Experiment*), 33 mins. (*Yu Yagami*), 31 mins. (*Kazama Mana*), 34 mins. (*Ren Nanase*).

Although he hasn't practiced medicine for a decade following an experiment that went wrong, Doctor Ryuji Hirasaka is put on call for a month at Saint Juliana's Hospital. He spends much of his time daydreaming about making the attractive, perky nurses his slaves but eventually meets the chief medical officer, who turns out to be the self-same woman that caused his career to stall all those years before. Blackmail, rape, and bondage duly ensue, in what would become the largest and most successful franchise in the **DISCOVERY SERIES**—representing roughly 20% of the label's entire output since 2000. Compare to **NURSE ME** and **LESBIAN WARD**, both of which attempt to emulate its success. Not

that erotic movie makers require a reason to write a show about nurses, but *NSN* was commissioned in the year when the long-running live-action serial *Leave it to the Nurses* (*DE) approached the height of its popularity. The show's actual origin can be traced to a 1999 computer game and its sequels, all by Mink. The taxonomy of the series is fiendishly complicated, not helped by different game-origins in Japan, leading in turn to different adaptations of the "same" material by separate production companies, sold in turn to different U.S. distributors, one of which has gone bust and sold its license to a third party (who retitled episodes 1–3 as *NSN: Head Nurse*).

Although not distinguished by a title of its own in the Japanese market, the fourth and fifth episodes were rebranded *NSN: RN's Revenge* (2001) in America, with Hirasaka using a nurse's hospitalized sister as leverage to blackmail her into doing his bidding. The American release also included several sequences of scatology and bodily insertions that had been cut from episodes 1–3, supposedly as a result of increased confidence in the show's more outré appeal after the early releases had been more successful than expected. Note that this installment appears to draw on the plot from the sequel to the original *NSN* game, but with the male protagonist from the original, a change in cast that would later be revoked in the remake *Yakin Byoto 2* (see below).

An "episode 5.5," a recap clip show of the previous five episodes, reintroduced the series to the Japanese audience for further adventures. Episodes 6–7 were released in America as *NSN: Clinical Confessions* (2003), as the series continued with Hirasaka's abuse of his compliant nurses, particularly Ren Nanase, a poor waif who only wants a normal romantic life with her would-be love object Naoya, only to be denied it by Hirasaka's "experiments," which continue to involve enemas, insertions, and scatology. However, the emphasis also adds a new voyeuristic element, told through the eyes of a detective investigating reports of "crimes" at the hospital. The detection angle continued with *NSN: Carnal Corruption* (2003), comprising episodes 8 and 9 of the Japanese series, in which the nurses are confronted with evidence of their crimes—a handy excuse for recycling footage from earlier shows. The story is retold of Ryuji's first-ever guinea pig, Narumi Shinguji, and how she discovered her love for him after he took her virginity by force, before introducing feelings of murderous intent. As the Japanese press release so earnestly put it: "The shudder that ran through the industry will come back again."

The series reached another turning point in 2004 with episode "10.5" in Japan, which revisited the "Golden Moments" (their words, not ours!) of episodes 6–10. According to a former employee of Central Park Media, episode 10 was never released in the U.S. due to a scene involving a vacuum cleaner. The three-episode spin-off series *NSN: Kranke* (2005) features nurse Hikaru inexplicably falling in love with Dr. Hirasaka and agreeing to marry him, before becoming his willing assistant in breaking in his latest victim, Nurse Ai, her stepsister. Hirasaka, however, married Ren Nanase, and the two of them set up a happily abusive home together at the Hirasaka Medical Clinic in the third episode.

A variant version of *NSN* exists in Japan, based on the sequel to the original game and distributed as part of the **D3 Series**. In a futile effort at avoiding confusion, we shall retain the Japanese title for this series, *Yakin Byoto 2* (2004), and note that it revisits the plot surrounding Ren Nanase from *Clinical Confessions*, but with a new protagonist, Dr. Kuwabara, whereas *Clinical Confessions* simply retained Dr. Hirasaka from the previous installment.

Yet another spin-off, this time as part of the *Discovery Series* once more, presumably based on the third game in the series, came in the form of *Yakin Byoto 3* (2005, released in the U.S. by Adult Source Media as *NSN: Experiment*), in which a critically injured homeless man is found dumped at the hospital entrance. He is saved by earnest young nurse Yu Yagami, but is then asked to participate in a "new experiment" run by beautiful hospital chief Reika Rikage. Miss Yagami, Mana Kazama, and Ren Nanase would get their own spin-offs, this time from Soft On Demand's 37°C Binetsu (*binetsu* is "fever" in Japanese) label: *Anime Ren Nanase*, *Anime Kazama Mana* (both 2005), and *Anime Yu Yagami* (2006), in which each thoughtful young nurse tries to do sexual favors for the most

hopeless patients, only to find herself having to try ever harder to please them. Episodes 1 and 3 were released by Kitty Media in the U.S. as *Night Shift Nurse*, singular, because the encyclopedist's life wasn't difficult enough already; episode 2 remains unavailable in the U.S., presumably due to content. These were followed by a variety of reissues and clip shows of the subseries. The authors would like to protest at the effort involved in making sense of a series whose most enduring memory is likely to be a DVD menu screen spattered with feces. **LNV**

NIGHT WALKER: MIDNIGHT DETECTIVE *

1998. JPN: *Night Walker: Mayonaka no Tantei*. TV series. DIR: Kiyotoshi Sasano, Yutaka Kagawa. SCR: Ryota Yamaguchi. DES: Miho Shimokasa, Ryoichi Makino, Satoshi Isono. ANI: Satoshi Isono, Ikuo Sato. MUS: Akifumi Tada. PRD: AIC, Studio Gazelle, TV Tokyo. 25 mins. x 12 eps.

Half-vampire detective Shido takes a job with Yayoi Matsunaga, a beautiful investigator from the secret NOS government organization, devoted to hunting down the evil "Nightbreed." His orphaned (and lovestruck) assistant, Riho, believes Yayoi and Shido are having an affair, but Yayoi only pays Shido by letting him drink her blood.

Though Buck-Tick's moody industrial rock opening theme disappointingly fades away to reveal yet another man surrounded by adoring girls, *NW* soon steers clear of the comedy path taken by **Master of Mosquiton**—with the possible exception of a pointless devil-Tinkerbell sidekick. A melting pot of contemporary horror influences, particularly *Nightbreed* (1990) and *Buffy the Vampire Slayer* (1992), it throws a demons-stalk-Tokyo plot out of **Wicked City** into a conspiracy inspired by *The X-Files*. Soon, Shido is on the run from the *good* guys, protecting a human woman bearing a Nightbreed child, facing off against the vampire who created him, and saving Riho's life in a predictable fashion that will link them for eternity.

Despite a short run on late-night TV like **Pet shop of Horrors**, *NW* still manages some original twists, particularly in the second episode that focuses on the suicide of an actress. Selling her soul for

fame, she eats human hearts to feed the demon within her and cannot bear to live without her possessor when it dumps her in favor of her understudy. *NW* has a pragmatic attitude toward the supernatural, running with Ayana Itsuki's original story for *Dengeki Comic Gao*, and suggesting that anyone who knew what was waiting in the afterlife would stoop to *any* level to avoid death. In this tale of addiction where life itself is the drug, Shido duels with a sword literally made of his own blood, all the while fighting the distrust of the NOS.

Such moments clash with less polished incidents, particularly Riho's naïve solo "investigation," in which she hitches a ride with two strangers, hoping to be attacked by a Nightbreed before they can molest her. Shido condescendingly tells Riho that her crucifix is "fake," even though it clearly satisfies the important criterion of being cross-shaped. On several occasions, most notably in a scene lifted from *Interview with the Vampire* (1994), Shido claims to be unable to endure the sun, even though we have already seen him wandering around in broad daylight. As in **Phantom Quest Corp**, it would seem that a simple pair of shades will protect modern-day vampires from burning alive. An above-average dub from U.S. Manga Corps completes the package, along with a closing theme by rockers Lacrima Christi, who inexplicably sing in Japanese with a Canadian accent. **NV**

NIGHT WARRIORS: DARKSTALKERS' REVENGE *

1997. JPN: *Vampire Hunter*. Video. DIR: Shigeru Ikeda. SCR: Tatsuhiko Urahata, Shigeru Ikeda. DES: Shuko Murase. ANI: Shuko Murase, Hiroyuki Tanaka, Hideki Takayama. MUS: Ko Otani. PRD: Madhouse. 40 mins. x 4 eps.

Demitri Maximoff, the most powerful and most feared of vampires, plots to use the psychic energy raised by his human followers to take over the power of the other Darkstalkers, who have always regarded him as an undesirable element. Given that his hair resembles a squeeze of toothpaste, it's hard to blame them completely, but the alternatives aren't so attractive. Meanwhile, the elderly band of advisers to luscious Darkstalker clan chief Morrigan, the girl who put the suck in succubus, is concerned about her general flightiness and the constant in-fighting between clans, which weakens their chances of retaining dominion. But their lady just wants to fight, seeking out Demitri for that purpose and turning the end of episode 1 into a duel with erotic overtones. Some of the other game characters put in cameo appearances—dour half-Darkstalker Donovan, tiny psychotic Anita, kitten-girl Felicia, and zombie serial killer/rock-star Raptor. Volume 2 sees Donovan fighting some cursed armor and meeting sisters Hsien-Ko and Ling-Ling, who have become Darkstalkers to help them free their late mother's soul from the dark powers she died fighting.

Amid all the rumbles (which recreate the original game's battles onscreen with real punch and conviction), there is the glimmer of a plot surrounding the Darkstalkers' removal of light from Earth. This has divided humankind into their servants and the rest, preventing the rest from growing much food or progressing against the faux religiosity that rules their lives. The mysterious Pyron seems to offer humankind the promise of renewed light from his artificial suns, but he's really out to destroy Earth. Things turn nasty as the Darkstalkers struggle to fight Pyron off before Donovan saves the day.

Films based on games have to overcome major structural problems before they can work as anything but cynical merchandising exercises. *Night Warriors* comes close to sustaining a narrative, but as with **STREET FIGHTER II**, the characters are too firmly embedded in the endless repetitions of gameplay to develop much. There are some interesting subplot possibilities—Donovan's self-hatred and his quest for enlightenment, Morrigan's *Gormenghast* ennui, Anita's shattered childhood, the spiritual and material impoverishment of humankind—but they're flagged rather than explored, relegated to the status of motivation for yet another rumble. **LNV**

NIGHT WHEN EVIL FALLS, THE *

2006. JPN: *Ma ga Ochiru Yoru*. Video. DIR: Sosuke Kokubunji. SCR: Sosuke Kokubunji. DES: Makoto Amamiya. ANI: Kimisuke Murayama. MUS: N/C. PRD: Cranberry. 30 mins. x 3 eps.
A magical being comes to the human world to track down an evil adversary. She

enlists the help of a sexy demonslayer, but finds herself betrayed to an evil mage who plans to use the sexual energy generated by demonic rape of women to give even more power to demons. Tentacles unfurl and bodily fluids flow in this porn tale based on a visual novel by Mille Feuille with art by Hiroshi Sasa. **NV**

NIGHT WIZARD

2007. JPN: *Night Wizard the Animation*. TV series. DIR: Yusuke Yamamoto. SCR: Kiyoko Yoshimura. DES: Tomoyuki Shitaya, Yukie Abe, Hiroki Matsumoto. ANI: Tomoyuki Shitaya. MUS: Tamayo. PRD: HAL Film Maker. 25 mins. x 13 eps.
Night wizards are those who protect the world from dark forces. Renji Hiiragi is a Night Wizard but he hates being called away for missions because it gets in the way of his true ambition—to graduate from high school (**SPRIGGAN**). A new transfer student at his school needs protection, and he and his childhood friend Kureha soon realize that Elis has the potential to be a Night Wizard, too. It seems that, no matter where you go in anime, you just can't take the high school out of the story. Based on Takeshi Kikuchi's fantasy role-playing game published by Enterbrain in 2002, and part of a franchise that includes manga, games, light novels, and drama CDs, this predictable series essentially fictionalizes the campaign the viewer might have played before his mother told him to go to bed so as to be ready for high school next day. A straightforward plot and basic characters make this much less demanding than the game itself.

NIGHTMARE CAMPUS *

1995. JPN: *Blackboard Jungle: Gedo Gaikuen*. AKA: *Blackboard Jungle: Outerway College*. Video. DIR: Koji Yoshikawa. SCR: Koji Yoshikawa. DES: Keiichi Sato, Kenji Hayama. ANI: Kenji Hayama. MUS: Masamichi Amano. PRD: Phoenix Entertainment. 50 mins. x 4 eps. (v1), 50 mins. x 1 ep. (v2).
Teenager Masao is visiting his father at an archeological dig in the Himalayas with his mother. When demonic creatures overrun the site, he shoots the one who kills his mother, only to see the corpse turn into his father. A huge earthquake shakes the area, and his school friends back in Japan believe Masao has been killed, but

his eventual reappearance is far from the strangest event in school. Masao and his best friend are the embodiment of powerful demonic beings. Other beings, seemingly angelic but in fact completely evil, are trying to take control of the school and the world by unleashing the "demon" in everyone and controlling the powers so released. It's up to the teenage demons to save the world.

Blood, pain, and sadism abound, and there is much nasty sexual content, with the depiction of genitals ranging from the absurdly absent, to suggestive shadows, to explicit realism. The design, art, and animation also vary wildly, with every kind of character style from an Adam Warren-type bimbette to gag-manga goons and retro-styled escapees from early Go Nagai series such as the similarly themed **DEVILMAN**. The unevenness may be partly blamed on budget problems (even Amano's music budget cuts corners with public-domain Beethoven), but it also indicates Yoshikawa's willingness to experiment with aspects of a genre that can simply be run by the numbers, so uncritical is its audience. This typical (but minor) Toshio Maeda offering has interesting possibilities but sadly never really gets off the ground. A sequel "series," known in Japanese as *Blackboard Jungle: Gedo Gakuen Z*, only lasted one episode and is now out of print in Japan, though it has been included in the American releases as "episode 5." The same creator's **UROTSUKIDOJI** was saved from an early finish by export sales (that means us), but this never took off to the same extent in the West, and so the series climaxed prematurely—a fate with which its target audience is probably in sympathy. **LNV**

NIKO NIKO PUN

1988. JPN: *Nikonikopun*. TV series, movie. DIR: Yasuo Kageyama. SCR: N/C. DES: Yoshishige Kosako. ANI: Takaaki Ishiyama, Kazuo Iimura, Mitsuo Kusakabe. MUS: Takao Ide. PRD: Visual 80, NHK. 23 mins. x 40 eps. (TV), 70 mins. (m).
Anime spin-off from a children's show that featured out-of-work actors dressed up as a giant mouse, penguin, and lion, itself part of the Japanese *Watch with Mother* TV strip for the preschool audience. With episode titles like "I Am a Pirate," "Let's Play," and

"The Picnic March," the show primed a generation for the later import *Teletubbies*.

NILS' MYSTERIOUS JOURNEY *

1980. JPN: *Nils no Fushigina Tabi*. AKA: *Nils Holgersson*. TV series. DIR: Hisayuki Toriumi, Mamoru Oshii, Yukimatsu Ito. SCR: Narumitsu Taguchi, Ryo Nakahara. DES: Toshiyasu Okada, Mitsuki Nakamura. ANI: Toshiyasu Okada, Noboru Furuse, Jun Tanaka. MUS: Chito Kawachi. PRD: Studio Pierrot, Gakken, NHK. 25 mins. x 52 eps.

A horrible little boy who torments animals is reduced to the size of a mouse. Rather than seeking revenge, a flock of wild geese take pity on him and ask him along on their migration. In an anime version of Nobel laureate Selma Lagerlof's classic Swedish novel, Nils is finally restored to his normal size a nicer person. Future **GHOST IN THE SHELL**–director Mamoru Oshii helmed several episodes. Toshiyasu Okada went on to greater things with **MYSTERIOUS CITIES OF GOLD**. The first production for Studio Pierrot.

NINE

1983. TV special, movie. DIR: Gisaburo Sugii, Hideaki Tsuruta. SCR: Hirokazu Nunose. DES: Mitsuru Adachi. ANI: Minoru Maeda, Hiroshi Wagatsuma. MUS: Hiroaki Serizawa, Yasuo Tsuchida. PRD: Group Tac, Toho, Fuji TV. 71 mins. (TVm1), 71 mins. (m), 67 mins. (TVm2), 73 mins. (TVm3).

Misfit middle-schoolers Karasawa and Katsuya, one a transfer student, sign up for the Seishu school baseball team chiefly because they think it will impress Yuri, the girl they both desire. Before long, their shallow initial reasons have transformed into a burning desire to win the All-Japan championships, in a predictable plotline based on a *Shonen Sunday* manga by Mitsuru Adachi, who also dramatized baseball stories in **H2**, **TOUCH**, **SLOW STEP**, and this show's immediate predecessor **MIYUKI**. The popular movie adaptation was followed by two TV movies the same year, *Nine* and *Nine 2: Declaration of Love*. In 1984, it all ended with *Nine: The Conclusion*, in which Katsuya and his teammates, now high school juniors, win the regional qualifying tests in an effort to meet Coach Nakao's expectations. However, Karasawa is suffering from a "hitter's block" and is lampooned by school reporter Yoko, who

secretly loves him. Inspired by her attention, Karasawa hits a home run just for her, and Katsuya becomes suspicious that his friend has scored with Yuri when he smells that both are using the same shampoo. However, as with all Adachi manga, such minor misunderstandings cannot stop the path of true love, and they all live happily ever after, ending with a double-date at the Koshien baseball stadium.

NINE LOVE STORIES

1992. JPN: *Ai Monogatari*. AKA: *Love Stories*. Video. DIR: Tomomi Mochizuki, Koji Morimoto, Mamoru Hamazu, Hiroshi Hamazaki, Hidetoshi Omori, Takashi Anno. SCR: Kaiji Kawaguchi. DES: Kaiji Kawaguchi. ANI: N/C. MUS: The Beatles. PRD: Toho. 92 mins.

A feature-length anthology of short romantic tales from the pen of **SILENT SERVICE**–creator Kaiji Kawaguchi, joined by an underlying theme of Beatles songs. The roster of famous directors is matched by a similarly high-ranking group of voice talents.

NINE O'CLOCK WOMAN *

2001. JPN: *21-ji no Newscaster Miki Katsuragi*. AKA: *Nine O'Clock Newscaster Miki Katsuragi*. Video. DIR: Yoshio Shirokuro. SCR: Reiji Izumo. DES: Sadaharu Nakamura, Midori Okuda. ANI: N/C. MUS: N/C. PRD: Milky, Museum Pictures. 30 mins. x 3 eps.

Miki Katsuragi has achieved her dream— she's landed the job as anchorwoman for the evening news. But despite the success, respect, and popularity this brings her, the young journalist can't beat her addiction to nonstop masturbation. When lowly cue card holder Satake catches her in the act in her dressing room, she agrees to do anything he wants if he'll keep her secret. With the massive success of reality TV, one would hardly imagine it would harm her career; but this is a porn anime, so "publish and be damned" was never a likely response. Only the first two episodes were released in the U.S. Based on the manga in *Core* magazine by Akira Goto. Miki's program, *News 9*, seems to have been conceived as a direct pastiche of NHK's *News 21*. **LN**

NINETEEN 19

1990. Video. DIR: Takaichi Chiba. SCR: Koji Kawahara. DES: Sho Kitagawa. ANI: N/C. MUS:

Toshiki Kadomatsu. PRD: Madhouse, Victor Music. 42 mins.

Kazushi, university student and football player, sees the girl of his dreams in an advertisement. She's really a medical student, who models as a sideline, and one day they meet. As love blossoms against a background of well-to-do student life, can their romance survive the pressures of the 1990s? A tale of yuppie love isn't what most Westerners expect from the Madhouse team, renowned abroad for horror like **WICKED CITY**, but this exudes quiet charm and elegance. Made for an audience of young, rich Tokyoites, this anime was based on the manga in *Young Jump* by **BLUE BUTTERFLY FISH**–creator Sho Kitagawa.

NINJA *

1999. JPN: *Kunoichi Gakuen Ninpocho*. AKA: *Female Ninja Academy Ninpocho*. Video. DIR: N/C. SCR: N/C. DES: N/C. ANI: N/C. MUS: N/C. PRD: D3, Onmitsudo. 30 mins. x 6 eps.

Three girls from the Koga ninja clan run into trouble when they spot boys from the rival Iga clan at a restaurant. Aya and then her friend Shinobu are captured, sexually assaulted, and infected with a parasite that causes them to lose control of their sexual lusts. Their friend Lena resolves to break in to the enemy stronghold to retrieve the antidote, whereupon she must fight her way through a series of sexually oriented traps and pitfalls. Legendary conflict between rival ninja clans has been a staple of anime for many years, from the innocuous fun of **HATTORI THE NINJA** and **NARUTO** through to the guiltier pleasures of **LA BLUE GIRL**. This porn release, however, is distinguished only by the surprisingly large amounts of recycled footage.

The term *kunoichi* ("female ninja"), is assembled from the three disassembled strokes that form the character for woman (*onna*) in Japanese: making the sounds *ku* in the *hiragana* syllabary, *no* in the *katakana* syllabary, and the *kanji* for *ichi*. The first and most successful release in the **D3 SERIES**. **LNV**

NINJA CADETS *

1996. JPN: *Ninja Mono*. Video. DIR: Eiji Suganuma. SCR: Mitsuhiro Yamada. DES: Nobuhito Sue, Keiji Goto. ANI: Fumitomo Kizaki. MUS: N/C. PRD: AIC. 30 mins. x 2 eps.

The Kabuso clan's seizure of Byakuro

Castle is marred by the disappearance of the infant princess, who is carried off into hiding by an honorable ninja. Years later, an energetic young group of ninja wannabes are about to be put through their final exam—a mission into the occupied Byakuro Castle to steal the MacGuffin Scrolls of Power. The evil Kabuso clan has hired highly skilled mercenaries to follow them, knowing that one of the young cadets is actually the missing princess.

Often looking like a spin-off of designer Sue's work on **EL HAZARD**, *Ninja Cadets* is a lazy afternoon's *Dungeons & Dragons* with a sushi flavor—wandering monsters, a bit of comedy business, and a satisfyingly big fight finale. There is a promising monochrome beginning as Byakuro Castle is stormed by evil hordes, but the story soon collapses into a pastoral idyll in which the life of an outcast assassin is presented as a summer camping trip, where you get to play with knives while a mommy ninjette cooks supper. Faced with innumerable foes and a map seemingly drawn by a bored teenage Dungeon Master (you can go any direction you want, as long as it's over the single bridge), the daftest ninja in the world decide it would be a good idea to split up. Then they wander listlessly around the countryside like bored kids on a school trip, which is probably the distant genesis of this whole story.

Luckily, when they reach the impregnable fortress, it's guarded by the daftest samurai in the world, and the scene is set for a walk through all the set pieces of chop-socky ninja films—tiger claws, throwing stars, singing floors, and reconnaissance kites. Our elite assassins try some really smart moves like throwing fire around in a room full of paper scrolls, and voice actress Maria Kawamura steals the show as a suicide-blonde evil minion with an electric-chair hairdo, seemingly inserted at the last minute to inject some much-needed evil into the proceedings. Armed with the Scrolls of Power, the ninja set off to depose the bad guys, just as the ending credits roll—further episodes were not forthcoming. Forgettable fun, but while this does indeed boast both scrolls and ninja, **NINJA SCROLL** it ain't. ◐

NINJA NONSENSE: THE LEGEND OF SHINOBU *

2004. JPN: *Ninin ga Shinobuden*. AKA: *2 x 2 = Shinobuden; 2 x 2 = Tale of Stealth; The Nonsense Kunoichi Fiction*. TV series DIR: Hitoyuki Matsui, Haruo Sotozaki. SCR: Ryunosuke Kingetsu. DES: Jun Shibata. ANI: Ufotable Zippers. MUS: Harukichi Yamamoto. PRD: Ufotable Zippers, Media Works. 24 mins. x 12 eps.

Girl ninja Shinobu attends a secret ninja school—no outsiders are allowed on campus. Like all good Japanese school story heroines, she has boundless enthusiasm but very little ability. She has a partner, a magical creature Onsokumaru, a bright yellow ball with arms, wings, and perverted tastes. The school principal Ninja Master is the same type of creature, but with a white beard. Shinobu is unfortunately too dim to realize that both are the same shapeshifting being—a fact of which Onsokumaru takes merciless advantage. Her other companions include talking alligator Devil and her genius younger sister Miyabe. Onsokumaru gives her a test of ninja skill as part of her exam—she has to steal an ordinary schoolgirl's underwear. The target is Kaede Shiranui, who coincidentally is also studying for an exam. But Shinobu is such an incompetent ninja that she's immediately spotted by her intended victim. When Kaede challenges her, she bursts into tears and the story of her total failure comes tumbling out. Kind-hearted Kaede gives her a pair of panties so she can pass, and a friendship is forged in vague imitation of that to be found in **E-CHAN THE NINJA GIRL**. But when Shinobu invites Kaede to look around the ninja academy campus as a thank-you for helping her to pass her test, the principal tells them that any non-ninja who sees the campus cannot be allowed to leave. Fortunately this doesn't apply to the audience. Based on a manga by Ryoichi Koga.

NINJA RESURRECTION: THE REVENGE OF JUBEI *

1997. JPN: *Makai Tensho*. AKA: *Reborn from Hell*. Video. DIR: Yasunori Urata. SCR: Kensei Date. DES: Kenji Hayama. ANI: Kenji Hayama. MUS: Masamichi Amano. PRD: Amuse Video, Phoenix Entertainment. 40 mins. x 2 eps. Out of favor, Jubei the ninja roams Japan alone. He believes that a new, dark menace is lurking, waiting to enter the world of men. The great swordsman Musashi, now retired to a monastery, senses the same evil. The Tokugawa shogunate has banned the Western fad of Christianity and is slaughtering its followers. The survivors believe that a new Messiah will be born among them, but the prophecy has a dark side—the Savior could turn bad and become Satan himself. Charismatic Christian leader Shiro Amakusa isn't all he seems, and the believers inside his stronghold are in as much danger from the evil forces within as from the shogun's armies. Jubei and his associates are sent to infiltrate the Christian citadel of Shimabara, where they find that the peaceful messiah Amakusa has turned to devilry.

Based on the popular novels that inspired **NINJA SCROLL** but misleadingly advertised abroad as a sequel to that film, *NR* is a ninja film for the post-**EVANGELION** generation, with cruciform explosions in the streets, aliens invading the minds of Japanese citizens, and the use of alien weaponry to fight an alien threat. The eerie, unworldly sight of samurai raising Christian banners and working their foreign magic is truly chilling in this context. Shiro Amakusa's ambiguous position as gentle messiah *and* tormented devil brings echoes of the **UROTSUKIDOJI** saga—a parallel aided by beautiful music from Masamichi Amano.

NR boasts some classy moments, but the running time is simply too short to contain such multitudes. The mix of fact and fiction is something that really warrants liner notes, and the intense compression of Futaro Yamada's story results in a messy rush of incidental characters. After a promising, portentous beginning with samurai huddling in a Kurosawa rainstorm and turning foreign guns on their convert countrymen, the film rushes headlong into a final battle with no time for a middle act. A completely unnecessary sex scene adds to the collapse of the latter half into substandard anime hackery—described by one of its own producers as "horrendous." The U.S. edition follows the Japanese pattern, with two separate releases, *TROJ* being followed by a second tape, *Hell's Spawn*. In the U.K., both were condensed onto one 80-minute tape. The character has a brief cameo in **JUBEI-CHAN THE NINJA**

GIRL, which purports to be a comedy about his modern-day reincarnation. **ⒸⓃⓋ**

NINJA ROBOTS ★

1985. JPN: *Ninja Senshi Tobikage*. AKA: *Ninja Warrior Flying Shadow; Tobikage; Flying Shadow*. TV series. DIR: Masami Anno, Hiroyuki Yokoyama, Takashi Akimoto, Kazuyoshi Katayama. SCR: Sukehiro Tomita, Hideki Sonoda, Hideo Takayashiki. DES: Shigeru Kato, Toshihiro Hirano, Yasushi Moriki, Koichi Ohata. ANI: Takeshi Osaka. MUS: Koji Kawamura. PRD: Studio Pierrot, Magic Bus, Nippon TV. 35 mins. x 43 eps.

Soldiers from the evil planet Zaboom invade the peace-loving world of Radorio, forcing princess Romina to flee on the starship Elshank in search of the fabled "ninja" warrior who can save her people. Arriving in the solar system, she recruits several Earthlings to become the ninja warriors of old—the Black Lion, Fiery Dragon, and Thunder Phoenix. They return to pilot the Flying Shadow giant robot against the minions of Zaboom, in spite of the distinctly ungrateful population of Radorio, who refuse to believe they can do it. A mix of a team show and giant-robot combat, with an alien starship whose interior is modeled on samurai-period Japan.

NINJA SCROLL ★

1993. JPN: *Jubei Ninpocho*. AKA: *Jubei the Wind Ninja; Wind Ninja Chronicles*. Movie, TV series. DIR: Yoshiaki Kawajiri. SCR: Yoshiaki Kawajiri. DES: Yutaka Minowa. ANI: Yutaka Minowa. MUS: Kaoru Wada. PRD: Madhouse, Toho, Movic. 94 mins. (m), 25 mins. x 13 eps. (TV).

After 1603, the people of Japan might as well have lived on another planet for two and a half centuries. Foreign barbarians (that's us) were expelled, along with their corrupting religious influences (Christianity) and their superpowerful, alien weaponry (guns). Under the rule of the Tokugawa family any uprising was ruthlessly suppressed, and stories began to spread about the ninja, a mythical class of superhuman peasants who could beat the samurai through trickery and cunning.

The ninja master Jubei Yagyu occupies a similar position in Japanese popular culture to Robin Hood in ours. A semihistorical figure who mysteriously disappeared, this sword master to the sho-gun has inspired many plays, novels, and films. It was Jubei's father, Mataemon, who founded the Yagyu school, and his brother Matajuro who became the hero of a kabuki play, *True Tale of Twin Umbrellas* (1887). It wasn't until the 20th century that his own fan base really grew, stirred up by Futaro Yamada's potboiler novels (**BASILISK**) and turned into anime that eventually made him better known abroad than the rest of his family. *Ninja Scroll*, ironically, has contributed significantly to this reputation, even though its own "Jubei" officially bears no relation to the Jubei Yagyu of popular legend. Matters were kept nicely vague in the first movie, but later incarnations were obliged to explain that he is actually "Jubei Kibagami," a generic wandering swordsman who just happens to have had a series of adventures and encounters remarkably similar to that of Futaro Yamada's *Jubei* novels. Hence, although *Ninja Scroll* has a title that recalls the various ninja novels of Yamada and a hero whose name recalls that of Yamada's own protagonist, it is not a direct adaptation. A true Yamada adaptation would require the insertion of ninja into real historical events, which director Kawajiri regarded as a stretch too far for many modern viewers. *Ninja Scroll* went into production during the rise of anime's foreign markets, and was, wisely it seems, written as a stand-alone work set in a more fantastical Japan. There are elements of the historical Tokugawa period and allusions to real-world events, but Japanese history in *Ninja Scroll* is merely a flavor. Kawajiri's script and story is far keener to introduce his stock-in-trade more familiar from **WICKED CITY**, a menagerie of iron-skinned, fang-toothed beast-men, each with a trademark schtick or combat style, more likely to be found in a superhero comic than a Japanese folktale. In *NS*, he has a set number of superpowered opponents (on this occasion, eight of them) to defeat on a quest for justice against an evil sorcerer. Jubei's ultimate aim is to stop Spanish muskets from reaching the shogun's enemy and toppling the fragile order.

Kawajiri's world embraces the "realism" of 1950s and 1960s pulp fiction, rather than the truth of Japanese history. The first time we see the Koga ninja receiving their orders, they are delivered by a portly official who has the shaven head and top-knot of a samurai, to a man who does not leave the shadows of the shrubbery where he is hiding. In other words, the ninja are working for the samurai, as an unseen force that investigates places where Tokugawa officialdom cannot or will not go. In a sentence that trails off with "If any of your people are infected…," there is also a faint echo of Kawajiri's secret inspiration, warnings delivered to the characters of *Mission: Impossible* (1966), that the establishment will disavow all knowledge of them if their attempt fails.

The same basic plotting can be found in Yamada's *Jubei* novels, the "real" Jubei anime **NINJA RESURRECTION**, Kinji Fukasaku's live-action Sonny Chiba vehicle *Darkside Reborn* (1981), and its remake, Masakazu Shirai's *Samurai Armageddon* (1996). *NS*, however, beats the cheap special effects of its live-action rivals hands-down and comes complete with a menagerie of flawed heroes, each with distinct magical abilities. The main love interest is one of anime's most interesting female characters, a woman whose very touch is poison. The set pieces are wonderful, from a duel in a bamboo grove to the explosive finale on a sinking ship. Made for a cinema release, *NS* boasts a coherent plot instead of, say, several TV episodes cut together, and a larger budget than many similar anime. The consequently higher production values have made it an enduring anime favorite in the English language, although it is relatively obscure in its native Japan. Kawajiri plumps for a color palette of dark, shadowy blues and juxtaposes them with vibrant, glowing reds, in turn accentuating night fights, flight into shadows, and sudden glints of light in a dark forest. Even the glints are part of the package, using "transmitted light," shining through the cel image (**TATSUNOKO PRODUCTION**). Most often used in modern anime for the glow of robot eyes or jet engines, here it is used not only for the flash of swords, but also for great washes of glare across half the screen, in order to suggest forbidding skies or blinding sun. Tatsuo Sato's 13-episode TV series *Ninja Scroll Dragon Stone Chapter* (*NS: Ryuhogoku-hen*, 2003, released in English as *Ninja Scroll: The Series*) features an older Jubei who acquires the titular artifact and becomes embroiled in a conflict between a rival ninja clan and demons. ❶❷❸

NINJAMAN IPPEI

1982. JPN: *Ninjaman Ippei*. TV series. DIR: Hideo Takayashiki, Saburo Hashimoto, Masakazu Yasumura, Yoshihiro Kowada. SCR: Hideo Takayashiki, Masaaki Sakurai, Tomoko Konparu. DES: Saburo Hashimoto, Naoto Hashimoto. ANI: Junsaburo Takahata. MUS: Kiyoshi Suzuki. PRD: Tokyo Movie Shinsha, Nippon TV. 25 mins. x 13 eps.
Way out in the sticks, the fourth-graders of the local school in Tokio village all come with their own superpowers of doubtful merit, including flying eyeballs and missile-hair. Ippei and his friends study hard at being ninja, but they are constantly under threat from the arrogant cheats over in the neighboring village of Techno. A strange mix of assassins and school comedy, based on a children's manga by Kazuyoshi Kawai in *100-ten Comics* magazine.

NINKU *

1995. JPN: *Ninku*. TV series, movie, video. DIR: Noriyuki Abe. SCR: Hiroshi Hashimoto, Ryu Tamura. DES: Tetsuya Nishio, Mari Kitayama, Shigenori Takada. ANI: Kazunori Mizuno. MUS: Yusuke Homma. PRD: Studio Pierrot, Fuji TV. 25 mins. x 55 eps. (TV), 27 mins. (m), 35 mins. (v).
Adapted from Koji Kiriyama's 1993 *Shonen Jump* manga, the anime follows the adventures of the Ninku ninja clan. Since the third year of the Edo period, the clan has brought about a fragile peace through its command of esoteric martial arts, but others are constantly trying to steal their techniques and take over the country. The primary target is Fusuke Ninku, a geeky-looking kid but one of the clan's most vital members; the kidnappers hope he will give them access to its secrets. In the summer "movie" *Ninku: Headstone of a Knife* (1995), screened while the series was still on the air and so separate from its continuity, a gang of impostors is traveling round the country pretending to be the Ninku clan, and the real clan members have to find out what they're up to. The *Ninku* characters also appeared in *Ninku Extra*, a 35-minute video released to popularize the series.

NIPPON ANIMATION

Formed in 1975 as Zuiyo Enterprises to create animation for HEIDI, the studio was split into two legal entities: plain Zuiyo, which retained the rights to the *Heidi* anime, and also its mounting debts; and "Nippon Animation," which continued to employ Zuiyo's staff on other projects. The studio is best known for the WORLD MASTERPIECE THEATER series, which adapted many foreign children's stories, including ANNE OF GREEN GABLES and FUTURE BOY CONAN. Local works include CHIBI MARUKO-CHAN. References to a "Nippon Animation" predating the 1970s are likely to be to the unrelated "Nippon Doga" (*doga*—animation, also known as Nichido), a company that was eventually absorbed by Toei.

NISEKOI: FALSE LOVE *

2014. JPN: *Nisekoi*. TV series. DIR: Akiyuki Shinbo, Naoyuki Tatsuwa. SCR: Akiyuki Shinbo, Fuyashi Tou. DES: Nobuhiro Sugiyama. ANI: Kazuya Shiotsuki. MUS: Monaca. PRD: Shaft, Aniplex, MBS, Shueisha. 23 mins. x 20 eps.
Teenager Raku Ichijo is obliged by his gangster father to feign a relationship with the bitter, bitchy, biracial Chitoge, daughter of the boss of the rival Beehive mob. They hate each other, of course, and Chitoge's arrival makes it difficult for Raku to pursue his search for the girl to whom he pledged his heart as a child (ROMANCE AND DRAMA). He still has a locket; somewhere in Tokyo is a lady who holds the key. Casual racism and benign criminals aside, *Nisekoi* acknowledges that it is reshuffling an entire pack of clichés and goes all-out in its references, to the extent of a play-within-a-play in which the cast members take roles in a production of *Romeo and Juliet* (ROMEO X JULIET). Director Akiyuki Shinbo arguably tries a little *too* hard to make this incredibly derivative show appear more interesting than it really is with camera tricks and other caprices—a curse on both their houses. Based on the manga in *Jump Next* by Naoshi Komi.

NISHIJIMA, KATSUHIKO

1960–. Cofounder of Studio Fantasia and one of the creators credited with PROJECT A-KO. Other work includes direction and key animation on URUSEI YATSURA and direction on AGENT AIKA, NAJICA, and LINGERIES.

NISHIKUBO, MIZUHO

1958–. Often credited as Toshihiko Nishikubo—Japanese sources cannot agree which is the pseudonym and which is the real name; he uses Mizuho on GHOST IN THE SHELL. After graduating in sociology from Waseda University in 1976, he became an animator at Tatsunoko. He went freelance in 1979 and worked as an animator on ROSE OF VERSAILLES and MYSTERIOUS CITIES OF GOLD. His directorial debut was STREET CORNER FAIRYTALES; he has also written scripts for anime.

NISHIMURA, JUNJI

1955–. Born in Saga Prefecture, Nishimura graduated in sociology from Meiji Gakuin University in 1980. At the studio Nishiko Pro, he learned animation from director Kazuyuki Hirokawa, working as a key animator on shows such as URUSEI YATSURA. He became the supervising director on PROGOLFER SARU and oversaw the video adaptation of SHUTENDOJI.

NISHIZAKI, YOSHINOBU

1934–2010. Pseudonym for Hirofumi Nishizaki. Sometimes credited as Yoshinori Nishizaki. Born in Tokyo to a family that specialized in ancient Japanese dancing traditions, Nishizaki rebelled by founding a jazz club in 1957, the year of his graduation from Nihon University. He moved into music production in 1962, setting up his own company, Office Academy, in 1963 and becoming a general manager for Osamu Tezuka's Mushi Production later in the decade. With the collapse of Mushi, Nishizaki was somehow able to wrest copyrights for WANSA-KUN and TRITON OF THE SEA from their creator, producing them under the auspices of his newly founded Anime Staff Room. His biggest hit, however, came with STAR BLAZERS—a franchise he continually revised in the decades since. In particular, Nishizaki infamously enlisted the first generation of adult anime FANDOM in a prolonged guerrilla marketing campaign to request the theme song on radio shows, flypost details of upcoming screenings, and badger cinemas into taking the film. His efforts paid off with media reports of a "grass roots" popularity that had been at least partly engineered, and the movie's rebooking into a vastly greater number of theaters. Its success, and that of its sequels, hence became something of a self-fulfilling prophecy and a lucrative franchise that soon led to spats at the top.

Prolonged legal action ensued between Nishizaki and Leiji Matsumoto over who has the right to claim to be the creator of the series. Nishizaki ended with the moral right to claim himself as the author of the series and the movies, but Matsumoto is free to make his own new versions. Office Academy was subsequently renamed Westcape Corporation, a direct calque of his surname into English, under which auspices Nishizaki was the executive producer of **ODIN** and **UROTSUKIDOJI**, before the company was declared bankrupt in 1997. Nishizaki was arrested in 1999 over drug and weapons charges and served five and a half years in prison. The authors submit that while Nishizaki's production career often makes him appear something of a one-hit wonder, perpetually refashioning his one cash cow into knock-offs such as **THUNDERSUB**, his greatest untold story remains his own autobiography, even to the events of his untimely death, when he fell from the deck of his own boat, which was called, of course, the Yamato.

NISHIZONO, SATORU

1962–. Born in Kagoshima Prefecture, Nishizono studied law at Waseda University. He worked briefly at an educational company before becoming a scriptwriter for anime including **CRAYON SHIN-CHAN** and **BONOBONO**.

NITABOH

2004. JPN: *Nitaboh: Tsugaru-jamisen Shisho Nitaboh Gaiden*. AKA: *Another Tale of Nitaboh, Father of Tsugaru Guitar*. TV special. DIR: Akio Nishizawa. SCR: Akio Nishizawa, Koji Tanaka. DES: N/C. ANI: N/C. MUS: N/C. PRD: WOW-World. 90 mins.
Born in 1857 to a poor family, Nitaro was orphaned early and lost his sight at the age of eight. He learns to play the *shamisen*, and his love of the instrument gives him the will to go on living. He becomes known as Nitaboh of Kambara, and he and his pupils forge the modern Tsugaru shamisen style before his death in 1928.

Tsugaru shamisen is a folk music style from Tsugaru in Aomori Prefecture in snowy Northern Japan. It's based on the traditional meter-long, three-string picked instrument, which came from China by way of Okinawa over 500 years ago. By the late Meiji period, the instrument was widely used by street entertainers and beggars. Many performers were blind, as music was one of the few ways open to blind people to make a living (see also the "Ghost Story" episode of **ANIMATED CLASSICS OF JAPANESE LITERATURE**). Nitaro Akimoto was such a player, and this movie tells his story.

The classical shamisen style is heavily formalized, but *tsugaru* encourages freeform jamming and is often compared to Western jazz. Nitaboh's influence was so central that two monuments to him were dedicated near his hometown in 1988 and 1993; this TV movie is another mark of respect. The animation style is traditional, and the backgrounds are particularly pretty, showing his hometown and its environs as a pastoral idyll unspoilt by the encroaching tide of modernity.

NO GOOD DADDY

1974. JPN: *Dame Oyaji*. TV series. DIR: Hisashi Sakaguchi, Fumio Ikeno. SCR: Tomohiro Ando, Susumu Yoshida. DES: Mitsutoshi Furuya. ANI: Fumio Ikeno. MUS: Amp. PRD: Family Planning, Knack, TV Tokyo. 26 mins. x 26 eps.
Poor salaryman Damesuke is married to Onibaba, the Demon-Wife from Hell, who rules him with an iron fist. Every time he tries to assert himself, his family turns on him and beats him up, for they think of him as the world's worst waste of space.

Though in the latter part of the original comic Dad eventually made good and became the boss of a small company, the anime version was canceled before reaching that point in the story. Created by Mitsutoshi Furuya in 1970 for *Shonen Sunday* magazine, this spiteful, violent series was toned down for an early evening TV audience, and each two-chapter episode involved a greater concentration on son Takobo and his school life. **V**

NO MONEY *

2007. JPN: *Okane ga nai*. Video. DIR: Makoto Sokuza. SCR: Hitoyo Shinozaki. DES: Sawako Yamamoto. ANI: Sawako Yamamoto. MUS: N/C. PRD: Lilix, Happinet Pictures, Klockworx. 24 mins. x 4 eps.
University student Yukiya Ayase is gentle, trusting, and very, very pretty. His one surviving relative decides to pay off his debts by auctioning Yukiya to the highest bidder, secure in the knowledge that Yukiya is far too nice to walk out and report him to the police. A rich, grumpy but rather hot loan shark with a forgotten past connection to Yukiya buys him to save him from a fate worse than death, then suggests a repayment plan: the ¥1.2 billion debt will go down by ¥500,000 every time Yukiya has sex with him. Although Yukiya is horrified, he soon begins to feel real affection for his owner: which is just as well, because even at 500K per shag, it will take a long time to work off ¥1.2 billion—go on, do the math. And that's before you factor in university fees. Based on Hitoyo Shinozaki and Toru Kosaka's 2009 porn manga and oddly similar in its basic plot to Jane Campion's *The Piano*. We just love pointing that out. **N**

NO-RIN *

2014. TV series. DIR: Shin Onuma. SCR: Michiko Yokote. DES: Masahito Onoda. ANI: Masahito Onoda, Hideki Furukawa. MUS: Tomoki Kikuya, Akito Matsuda. PRD: Silver Link, Frontier Works, Square Enix. 24 mins. x 12 eps.
Prominent pop idol Yuka Kusakabe suddenly announces her retirement from show business, devastating her number-one fan, country boy Kosaku. He is, however, much more surprised than we are when a new girl arrives at his agricultural college, looking just like the retired singer. Ringo Kinoshita (her real name) has decided to embrace the mundane life of **EVERYDAY ANIME**, electing to study land management in the little town from which an unknown admirer used to send her gifts of prize vegetables. This is greeted with predictable fury by Minori, the childhood friend (**ROMANCE AND DRAMA**) of Kosaku, who has always regarded him as prime marriage material. The title is a pun—it would usually mean "agriculture and forestry" but also combines characters from the names of Minori and Ringo, implying that this is their story, rather than that of the man who thinks he is choosing between them. Not that Kosaku does much choosing—there is remarkably little character development after these basic **COMEDY** templates are introduced, although by the end Kosaku does make a

plea for a polygamous resolution ... which he doesn't get. Based on the books by Shiro Shiratori, which were swiftly adapted into manga incarnations when the success of **Silver Spoon** became apparent.

NO. 6 *

2011. TV series. DIR: Kenji Nagasaki. SCR: Michiko Ito, Seishi Minakami, Hiroshi Onogi. DES: Satoshi Ishino, Kazushige Kanehira. ANI: Satoshi Ishino. MUS: Keiichi Suzuki. PRD: Bones, Aniplex, Dentsu, Fuji TV, Kodansha. 25 mins. x 11 eps.

After a devastating conflict leaves much of the world flooded, six city-states are created by the Babylon Treaty. Teenager Sion lives in No. 6, and never questions his comfortable life until he meets a runway called Rat on the eve of his 12th birthday. For helping an enemy of the State, Sion is stripped of all his privileges. He and his mother are downgraded as citizens and move to the lower-class district, where she has to work in a bakery. Sion has to leave his elite school program and go to work for the parks department. When he and Rat meet again four years later, he's ready to go even further into the depths to uncover the truth about No. 6.

For connoisseurs of dystopia it's hard to beat Patrick McGoohan's superb TV series *The Prisoner*, in which a character called Number Six constantly challenges and questions the workings of the authoritarian state that holds him prisoner. There are no explicit references to the British series in Nagasaki's show (or in Atsuko Nagano and Hinoki Kino's original manga), but there are exquisitely delicate literary references to Shakespeare, Ray Bradbury's *Fahreinheit 451*, and Oscar Wilde's **The Happy Prince**. Visual references could come from any war-torn tyranny: drab refuse-strewn streets with people scurrying along, anxious to get out of the way as fast as possible, flies on food stalls without much food to offer. Anywhere from Iraq to Turkey to Syria to Ethiopia could show us similar sights, and we watch them from our own well-fed, well-lit enclaves just as Sion did before he made his life-changing decision.

Governments and corporations believe that entertainment should keep you distracted. They would prefer you to be entertained rather than engaged because that makes you easier to manage. Entertainment that makes you think is overstepping its boundaries, heading for the territory of art and literature. Not enough anime does that without boring you or preaching at you; this is one of the few. Not to be confused with **Blue Submarine No. Six**, which also takes place in a drowned future.

NOBODY'S BOY REMI *

1970. JPN: *Chibikko Remi to Meiken Capi; Rittai Anime Ie Naki Ko; Ie Naki Ko*. AKA: *Little Remi and His Famous Dog Capi; 3D Animation: Child without a Family; Sans Famille; Homeless Child*. Movie, TV series. DIR: Yugo Serikawa. SCR: Masaharu Segawa. DES: Akira Daikuhara. ANI: Akira Daikuhara, Yasuji Mori, Katsuya Oda, Akihiro Ogawa. MUS: Chuji Kinoshita. PRD: Toei, TMS, Nippon TV. 81 mins. (m1), 25 mins. x 51 eps. (TV1), 96 mins. (m1), 25 mins. x 26 eps. (TV2).

Hector Malot's 1878 novel *Sans Famille* inspired veteran Serikawa to animate the story of little Remi and his search for his lost parents in the early 20th century as the film *Chibikko Remi to Meiken Kapi* (1970, Toei Animation). Accompanied by his faithful dog, Remi is forced to join a band of traveling players, but after many adventures he finally finds his mother, who thought he was dead, and is no longer a child without a family.

In 1977, a TV series, *3D Animation: Child Without a Home* (*Ie Naki Ko*), followed from Tokyo Movie Shinsha. Directed by Osamu Dezaki with character designs by Akio Sugino and a soundtrack by Takeo Watanabe, it covered the same story at much greater length. "3D" was a grandiose claim, but the characters are well designed, and the skill of the animation is considerable, making use of moving backgrounds to give a sense of depth. Another Malot adaptation, **Nobody's Girl**, followed the next year. In 1980, TMS edited the TV series into another movie, *Child Without a Home*, which genuinely appears to have been screened with a stereoscopic process that qualified it as Japan's first true "3D" anime. But the concept still had possibilities—perhaps an influence on the success of the live-action **Oshin** in 1983, the concept was revived once more, this time with a female lead, as another live-action series, again called *Child Without a Home* (1994). The story was brought back *again*

as *Remi: A Child Without a Home* (1996), a 26-episode series directed by Kozo Kusuba for Nippon Animation's **World Masterpiece Theater** franchise. However, the newest version introduced major changes to the story line, switching Remi's gender and transforming *her* into a child singer in order to showcase the talents of voice actress Mitsuko Horie, for whom the series was a glorified star vehicle. With a shorter running time and such major alterations contravening the worthy spirit of previous shows, the series received the lowest ratings ever for the *WMT* and was the death knell for the franchise. See also a further great boy-and-his-dog epic **Belle and Sebastian** and another oft-adapted tale of an orphan's quest, **From the Apennines to the Andes**.

NOBODY'S GIRL

1978. JPN: *Perrine Monogatari*. AKA: *En Famille; Her Own Folk; Story of Perrine*. TV series. DIR: Hiroshi Saito, Shigeo Koshi. SCR: Akira Miyazaki, Kasuke Sato. DES: Shuichi Seki. ANI: Takao Ogawa. MUS: Takeo Watanabe. PRD: Nippon Animation, Fuji TV. 25 mins. x 53 eps.

Young Perrine travels with her father around Bosnia, where he is a photographer. After his death, Perrine and her mother are forced to move to France, making ends meet with their own photo business, until Perrine's mother also dies. Perrine continues on the journey with only her dog, Baron, for company, heading for the mansion of her rich grandfather Bilfranc. He turns out to be a cruel man, and instead of announcing herself, Perrine takes a job as a humble worker in his string factory. After many trials of cruelty, he comes to trust Perrine, appointing her as his interpreter and awaiting a fairy-tale ending where she reveals that she has been his granddaughter all along.

Another entry in the **World Masterpiece Theater** series, this family anime was based on an 1893 novel by Hector Malot and is not to be confused with the 1996 sex-change remake of his earlier **Nobody's Boy Remi**. Since Malot's original begins with the death of Perrine's mother, all that precedes it in the above synopsis is the creation of scriptwriter Akira Miyazaki. This was a first-time collaboration between writer Miyazaki and Hiroshi Saito, who would become stalwarts of the *WMT* franchise in the absence of an "old guard," such as Hayao Miyazaki and Isao Takahata, who had gone on to better things. Their next entry in the series would be Tom Sawyer.

NOBUMOTO, KEIKO

1964–. Born on Hokkaido, Nobumoto graduated from the Asahikawa School of Nursing before attending the Third Anime Scenario House workshop in 1987; she won a Fuji TV new writer's prize two years later. She has written many live-action TV scripts, largely for the channel that first nurtured her talent, including *Give Me Good Love* (*DE) and *LxIxVxE* (*DE), and movies, including Tokyo Godfathers and the live-action *World Apartment Horror* (1991) and *Nurse Call* (1993). She has written many of the better anime scripts of recent years, justifying comparisons with Kazunori Ito. Her greatest achievements include the superb recycling of old themes in Macross *Plus*, and many crucial episodes of Cowboy Bebop. Her recent work includes Wolf's Rain and the live-action TV series *Backen Record* (2012), and she has also written novels, including the prose adaptation of her own *Macross Plus* scripts.

NOBUNAGA THE FOOL *

2014. TV series. DIR: Eiichi Sato. SCR: Shoji Kawamori, Jun Kumagai, Shigeru Morita, Toko Machida. DES: Hirotaka Marufuji. ANI: Takako Shimizu, Yosuke Kabashima, Hirotaka Marufuji. MUS: Masaru Yokoyama. PRD: Satelight, Media Factory, Sotsu, TV Tokyo. 23 mins. x 24 eps.

In an alternate world where the historical division of East and West has resulted in a literal splitting of the planet in two (compare to similar issues in Beast Warriors), the gap between the two halves is widened by the loss of the great Bridge of Heaven that once connected them. Leonardo da Vinci and Jeanne d'Arc arrive in Japan with new technologies, which they hope to use to bolster the military power of local warlord Nobunaga.

Nobunaga the Fool begins as a willfully anachronistic mash-up of Earth history, keeping with relative accuracy to the figures of Sengoku-period Japan, but confronting them with "European" figures that arrive pell-mell, from numerous points in history. Not unlike Samurai Champloo, it walks a difficult line between actual ignorance and ignorance as an artistic statement, feigning cluelessness about European figures, while cunningly allegorizing many true aspects of the attempted colonization of Japan by Europeans. There *was* a Nobunaga; there *were* European figures behind the scenes, attempting to puppet their chosen warlords into positions of authority. However, there was never an actual stand-off between King Arthur and Nobunaga as to the fate of the entire planet—later episodes of the show attempt to push this element of the narrative, and in taking themselves a little too seriously, arguably detract from the chaotic Comedy that made the first half more watchable.

NOBUNAGUN *

2014. TV series. DIR: Nobuhiro Kondo. SCR: Hiroshi Yamaguchi. DES: Hiromi Matsushita, Kazz Toyama. ANI: Takeshi Furuta. MUS: Yutaka Shinya. PRD: Bridge, Dax, Japan Narration Actor Institute, VAP, Yomiuri TV. 24 mins. x 12 eps.

Shio Ogura is on a class trip to Taiwan, disrupted by that most everyday of anime crises, an attack by monsters. She discovers a newfound ability to channel the powers and weapon of choice of a historical personage of whom she is the apparent reincarnation, leading to her co-option into an organization of similarly gifted individuals. Shio has somehow awoken or controlled the restless spirit of samurai warlord Nobunaga Oda, making her a trump card in the battles against invaders, alongside fellow agents, each of whom wields a weapon that similarly contains the spirit of a historical personage.

You can just imagine the pitch meeting for this, as enthusiastic producers presumably outlined the potential for online gaming spin-offs and pick-your-own celebrity character creation. And we'll bet you a buck that the words "It's educational!" were blurted out at least twice. One wonders, however, at the likely powers exhibited by some of the celebrities. You can see the action anime potential for an unhinged heroine channeling a samurai, but how exactly will someone help to save the world if they are possessed by, to quote just a few of the oddities from the manga: baseball legend Babe Ruth, notorious peacemonger Mahatma Gandhi, or loopy architect Antonin Gaudí? Based on the manga by Masato Hisa in *Comic Earth Star*.

NODAME CANTABILE *

2007. TV series, video. DIR: Kenichi Kasai, Chiaki Kon. SCR: Tomoko Konparu, Masahiro Yokotani, Miho Maruo, Yoji Enokido, Reiko Yoshida, Hiroshi Onogi. DES: Shuichi Shimamura, Shichiro Kobayashi. ANI: Shuichi Shimamura, Yukako Tsukichi, Mitsuharu Kajitani. MUS: Suguru Matsutani. PRD: JC Staff, Asmik Ace, Dentsu, Fuji TV, Kodansha, SME, GENCO. 24 mins. x 23 eps. (TV1), 23 mins. (v1), 23 mins. x 11 eps. (TV2), 23 mins. (v2), 24 mins. x 11 eps. (TV3), 24 mins. x 2 eps. (v3).

This is the story of an odd couple—an arrogant young pianist whose ambitions to become an international conductor are hampered by travel phobia and excessive perfectionism, and a messy, disorganized, laid-back glutton who prefers playing by ear to sticking to the score and wants to be a preschool teacher. Megumi Noda, or Nodame as she likes to be called, falls for Shinichi Chiaki almost right away, but it takes a long time for him to appreciate what she does for him. Her sheer joy in music and love of sharing it helps him to overcome his own prejudices and fears. Gradually they change each other for the better and their music blossoms.

Tomoko Ninomiya's *Nodame Cantabile* is probably the most famous music manga of recent years, and a justifiably lauded pinnacle of Music in Anime. Serialized in Kodansha's *Kiss* magazine from 2001 to 2009, and collected in 23 volumes, it has inspired two live TV drama series, and two feature films as well as this and two more anime series—2008's *Nodame Cantabile Paris* and *Nodame Cantabile Finale* in 2010. The videos listed are extra episodes on the series DVD release, made by the same crews as the series. The character of Megumi is based on a real person, and a later supporting character in the manga, James DePreist, is based on the conductor of the Tokyo Metropolitan Symphony Orchestra. He must have liked his manga portrayal because the Tokyo Met provide the classical music for both the live-action and anime versions. All the music on the soundtrack is performed well enough to be worth listening to in its own right, and the multiple CDs based on the series have all sold strongly.

A top-selling manga doesn't always get the treatment it deserves, but with Gainax and Tatsunoko among the key animation credits and a host of top names among the writing and animation credits, this show did. It's easy to see why: its appeal goes far beyond the usual anime and manga audience. It's a wonderful romance with plenty of humor and drama, an ideal family show, highlighting the way we all shape each other in the course of daily life. Its emphasis on the theme that all the natural talent in the world won't help you much without hard work and commitment echoes shows across a wide range of genres from GUNBUSTER to OISHINBO and sets it apart from those fantasies that offer magical McGuffins, like LA CORDA D'ORO. Heartwarming, spirit-lifting stuff.

NOEIN *

2005. JPN: Noein: Mo Hitori no Kimi e. AKA: Noein: To My One and Only. TV series. DIR: Kazuki Akane, Hiroyuki Tsuchiya, Kenji Yasuda, Kiyoshi Matsuda, Naoki Horiuchi, Mamoru Enomoto. SCR: Kazuki Akane, Hiroshi Onogi, Hiroaki Kitajima, Miya Asakawa, Kazuharu Sato. DES: Takahiro Kishida. ANI: Kensuke Ishikawa, Akira Takada, Haruo Sotozaki, Yukari Kobayashi. MUS: Hikaru Nanase. PRD: Satelight, Viewworks, Chiba TV. 25 mins. x 24 eps.
Preteen Haruka Kaminogi lives with her divorced mother in the Hokkaido port of Hakodate and frets over her lifelong friend Yu, a thoughtful boy who is studying hard to get into a private school in distant Tokyo. Their everyday existence is thrown into turmoil by Karasu, a shadowy man who claims to have traveled in time from the year 2020, when the rival dimensions of Lacrima and Shangri La are locked in conflict.

NOEL'S FANTASTIC TRIP *

1983. JPN: Noel no Fushigi na Boken. AKA: Noel's Mysterious Adventure. Movie. DIR: Tadao Takakuwa, Yasuo Maeda. SCR: Ryohei Suzuki. DES: Iruka. ANI: Nobukazu Otake, Chikao Katsui. MUS: Iruka. PRD: Iruka Office. 72 mins.
On a hot summer's day, Noel and his faithful dog, Kinnosuke, get into a plane to buy some ice cream for the sun. En route, they stop off at the planet Kikazari, where dressing up is compulsory. After meeting with the sun, Noel encounters the master of smog, and must wrestle a sludge monster on the bottom of the ocean.

A vehicle for the singer-songwriter Iruka, who wrote the original story and also provides the voice of Noel, while her three-year-old son plays the dog. The film was shown on a double bill with another of the musician's creations, the short film Iruka's Christmas: Jeremy's Tree, in which a lonely orphan finds a bird in the snow who tells him that she lost her home when her tree was cut down. Jeremy agrees to steal the tree from a family's living room but is shot in the process. As he loses consciousness, he has a vision of Santa Claus. This story of sub-Wildean pathos was made by Noel-assistant director Maeda—a seasonal outing somewhat ruined by being released in April. By the time it reached American shores as Noel's Fantastic Trip in 1985, the English dub completely stripped out Iruka's contribution, replacing it with performances by Charlotte Russe Music.

NOIR *

2001. TV series. DIR: Koichi Mashimo. SCR: Ryoei Tsukimura. DES: Yoko Kikuchi, Minako Shiba. ANI: N/C. MUS: Yuki Kajiura. PRD: Bee Train, TV Tokyo. 25 mins. x 26 eps.
Near-future replay of GUNSMITH CATS, as sexy hitwoman Mireille Bouquet, searching the Tokyo underworld for the assassin who killed her parents, teams up with traumatized Japanese girl Kirika Yumura. Neither can remember the full details of their pasts, but both are dragged into a conspiracy that shows that they are linked by more than mere amnesia. In a series of missions that take them to numerous 21st-century hotspots—the Middle East, gang-run cities, a collapsed former Soviet Republic—they establish themselves as the reliable "Noir" team, taking their name from a legendary assassin, only to discover that another assassin, Chloe, calls herself the "True Noir." A secret society called Les Soldats has tried to kill the women before, and seems intent on finishing the job, although both Mireille and Kirika will need their memories back if they are to fight them off. However, restoring a full set of memories may compromise their friendship, in a crime caper heavily redolent of other millennial thrillers like Alias (2001), which began broadcasting in America at roughly the same time.

In 2011, it was announced that the U.S. cable network Starz had bought the rights to Noir and would be adapting it into a live-action series. However, the project seems to have stalled. Compare to MADLAX and EL CAZADOR DE LA BRUJA, the first and third entries, respectively, in creator/director Mashimo's and Bee Train's "girls-with-guns" trilogy.

NOISEMAN

1997. JPN: Onkyo Seimeitai Noiseman. AKA: Noiseman Sound Insect. Movie. DIR: Koji Morimoto. SCR: Hideo Morinaka. DES: Koji Morimoto, Masaaki Yuasa. ANI: Masaaki Yuasa. MUS: Yoko Kanno. PRD: Bandai Visual, Studio 4°C. 16 mins.
The future, in the city of Camphon: a scientist has creatured a synthetic life-form called Noiseman, which can turn music into crystals, thus making it inaudible over the airwaves. A teenage biker gang decides to defeat the scientist and his "sound insect." Mixing 2D and 3D animation, the film was originally conceived as a 45-minute movie with an opening linear narrative sequence that could then open out into various interactive possibilities, along the lines of a game. The film has an arresting design that manages to be both wacky and edgy, a color palette of dusty pastels in the style of the studio's later MIND GAME, intense lighting, and steampunk visuals forshadowing STEAMBOY. Initially given away free to anyone who bought certain models of Pioneer DVD players in 1997, and only later released in 2003 as part of a Studio 4°C retrospective DVD.

NOITAMINA

Name derived from "Animation" in reverse, used as a brand for a late-night slot on Fuji TV, beginning in 2005 with HONEY AND CLOVER. Set up with the express intention of showing serials outside anime's "normal" demographic, Noitamina has been used as a testing bed for a number of eccentric or off-the-wall serials, many of which were initially intended for the audience of female fans estimated to comprise 12% of anime RATINGS AND BOX OFFICE. Such numbers might be small but take on new significance in the graveyard slot—

Noitamina broadcasts typically begin after one o'clock in the morning.

More recent releases have been less obviously "female," including standard sci-fi fare like PSYCHO-PASS, alongside shows like SILVER SPOON (fan-bait on account of its author's previous fame). Expanded to a one-hour slot sufficient to run two weekly serials since 2010, the *Noitamina* hour has become one of the crucial sources for smarter shows liable to appeal to overseas FANDOM, including such oddities as KIDS ON THE SLOPE. However, late-night anime are nothing new in themselves, and the name is arguably little more than a brand designed to make the graveyard slot seem less like a dumping ground for shows that couldn't possibly get high ratings elsewhere and more like a showcase for quality. Foreign viewers often assume that such anime are primetime hits, whereas in fact they are often watched by literally nobody at the time of their initial broadcast, time-shifted on video and TiVo to more civilized hours even by their most ardent fans.

NONOMURA HOSPITAL *

1996. JPN: *Nonomura Byoin no Hitobito*. AKA: *People of Nonomura Hospital*. Video. DIR: Nobuyoshi Ando. SCR: Oji Miyako. DES: Jun Sato. ANI: Jun Sato. MUS: The Pinks. PRD: Pink Pineapple, KSS. 30 mins. x 2 eps.
After breaking his leg, detective inspector Umihara is sent to Nonomura Hospital to recuperate. When the hospital owner dies, the convalescing Umihara goes to work. Unsure of whether the death was suicide or murder, Umihara questions the victim's beautiful wife, the three attractive nurses, and his charming fellow patient. An anime based on an erotic computer game, it consequently boasts more sex than suspense. Released in the U.S. as *The Mystery of Nonomura Hospital*. ◐

NONTAN

1992. JPN: *Genki! Genki! Nontan*. AKA: *Happy Happy Nontan*. TV series, video. DIR: Yutaka Kagawa. SCR: Kei Muto. DES: N/C. ANI: N/C. MUS: N/C. PRD: Itochu, Polygon Pictures, Columbia Music Entertainment. 5 mins. x 263 eps. (TV1), 5 mins. x 2 eps. (v1), ca. 6 mins. x 35 eps. (TV2), 6 mins. x ??? eps. (v2).
This digitally animated series for young children is based on the adventures of perky white kitten Nontan. With his friends, fun-loving Tanuki, strong Bear, and the pink Rabbit triplets, and his rival, Pig, he teaches children positive lessons about the beauty and wonder of life. Originally created as a picture-book series by Sachiko Kiyono, Nontan's adventures have sold a million copies in Japan and there are six volumes on DVD, each containing four episodes and a short educational segment.

NOOBOW: THE DISAPPEARING MEDAL

1990. JPN: *Nubo Kieta Medal*. Video, TV series. DIR: Hiromitsu Ota. SCR: N/C. DES: N/C. ANI: Hiromitsu Ota. MUS: Hiroaki Ran. PRD: Aubec. 25 mins. (v), 25 mins. x 26 eps. (TV), ? mins. x 52 eps. (web TV).
In the green and pleasant village of Noobow, the summer festival is ruined when a gold medal (first prize in the pie-eating contest) disappears. All the local inhabitants, who happen to be the mascot characters from the various types of Morinaga chocolate, go hunting for the missing medal. A cynical exercise in product placement, designed to sell chocolate to kids and, presumably, get them to eat more pies.

NOOZLES *

1984. JPN: *Fushigina Koala Blinky*. AKA: *Blinky the Mysterious Koala; Blinky and Printy*. TV series. DIR: Taku Sugiyama, Noboru Ishiguro. SCR: Taku Sugiyama, Michiru Tanabe. DES: Isamu Noda. ANI: Eimi Maeda. MUS: Reijiro Koroku. PRD: Nippon Animation, Nippon TV. 25 mins. x 26 eps.
Ten-year-old girl Sandy Brown stays with her grandmother while her archeologist father is away on a research trip. She is given a toy koala, only to discover that when she "noozles" her nose against it, it transforms into a real koala, Blinky, a refugee from Koalawalla Land. On the run from (literally) a kangaroo court with kangaroo cops, Blinky has come to Earth to hide, his only possession a magical watch that can stop time. His sister, Printy (Pinky in the U.S. dub), also arrives in search of her brother—Printy has a magical makeup compact that can open dimensional gateways. Blinky and Printy take Sandy on many adventures as they study Earth and pop back on occasion to Koalawalla Land, also hiding out from the two evil poachers Frankie and Spike.

Back in the real world, 1984 saw the arrival of six koalas in Japan, sent as goodwill ambassadors by Australia. Japan went into a koala frenzy, lapping up this otherwise unremarkable anime and its rival on TV Tokyo, LITTLE KOALA. The same production team specialized in animal cartoons, most notably DOGTANIAN AND THE THREE MUSKEHOUNDS. The series was broadcast on the U.S. children's channel Nickelodeon.

NORA

1985. Video. DIR: Satomi Mikuriya. SCR: Satomi Mikuriya, Reiko Nakada. DES: Satomi Mikuriya, Yuki Motonori. ANI: Masami Suda. MUS: Yuji Ono. PRD: Mik Mak Pro, Toyo Links, Pony Canyon. 56 mins., 45 mins.
In the year 2097, a beautiful girl and two scientists must prevent their frontier space-town's governing computer from going haywire and starting Armageddon. This adaptation differs considerably from the original 1980 manga from GARAGA-creator Mikuriya, but, since the creator performed so many tasks on the staff, we can assume the changes were made with his approval. A second episode, *Twinkle Nora Rock Me*, completed the story. Compare with MIGHTY SPACE MINERS.

NORAGAMI *

2014. AKA: *Stray God*. TV series, video. DIR: Kotaro Tamura. SCR: Deko Akao. DES: Toshihiro Kawamoto. ANI: Hideki Yamazaki, Toshihiro Kawamoto. MUS: Taku Iwasaki. PRD: Bones, A-sketch, Avex Entertainment, Dentsu, Kodansha, Lawson, Movic, Shochiku. 24 mins. x 12 eps. (TV), 24 mins. (v).
Yato is an obscure Japanese war god, fallen on hard times and lacking even a roadside shrine to call his own. In desperation, he scrawls a cell phone number on a wall, and offers to carry out tasks for the price of the average shrine donation, which in parsimonious times, turns out to be a mere ¥5. He begins working at a series of odd jobs hardly befitting a deity, such as finding a lost cat, all the while hoping to drag himself out of the doldrums by amassing enough worshipers to be a real god once more.

Positing an alluring, Gaimanesque world in which even Japanese deities are obliged to roll with the recessionary punches and conform to austerity measures, *Noragami* is an insightful allegory of modern Japan after two decades of economic stagnation. Yato is an arcane god forced to subsist among mundane humans (compare to **Ushio and Tora**), prepared to undertake odd jobs in the fashion of **Kiki's Delivery Service**, for a bargain-basement fee. As in Adachitoka's original manga in *Monthly Shonen Magazine*, today's gods are oddly narcissistic. With their powers waning in keeping with many **Fantasy and Fairy Tales**, rather than demand worship they plead for it—if humans stop believing in them, they will literally fade away. Yato needs to be needed, in an artful perspective on very human concerns. An unaired "13th" episode was bundled with the DVD release. Compare with **Kamichu**.

NORAKURO

1970. JPN: *Norakuro-kun*. AKA: *Black Stray*. Movie, TV series, movie. DIR: Yonehiko Watanabe, Satoshi Murayama. SCR: Masaki Tsuji, Ichiro Wakabayashi, Shunichi Yukimuro. DES: N/C. ANI: Tsuneo Komuro, Toshitaka Kadota. MUS: Hidehiko Arashino. PRD: TCJ, Fuji TV. 11 mins. (m), 25 mins. x 28 eps. (TV1), 25 mins. x 48 eps. (TV2).

Shiho Tagawa's *Norakuro* began as a 1931 manga in *Shonen Club* with the story of a brave stray dog's fight against oppressive monkeys. The popular character was soon put to use promoting Japan's militaristic expansion in the 11-minute short *Corporal Norakuro* (1934, *Norakuro Gocho*), a **Wartime Anime** directed by Yasuji Murata, in which the loyal doggy joins the army, beats his monkey allies at rifle practice, has some fun with fireworks, and then wakes up to discover it was all a dream.

The *Norakuro* manga enjoyed a new lease on life during the nostalgia boom that followed the 1968 centenary of the Meiji Restoration. Transferring to *Comic Bon-Bon*, where it ran for another decade, it was brought back for a young audience as the TV series *Norakuro* (1970), in which the low-ranking soldier returned once more, ever jostling for power within an army dominated by General Bull and kept strictly under control by Captain Mole. Playing up the military comedy angle in skits that were crammed two to each episode, Norakuro also had time to fall for Miko, a pretty nurse and troops' pinup.

Never one to admit defeat, the franchise jumped to *Comic Morning* in the 1980s to promote Norakuro's latest incarnation, making this one of the earliest retro anime. The original character's grandson was the lead character in *Norakuro-kun* (1987), a lighthearted Studio Pierrot series directed by future **Kishin Corps**–crew member Takaaki Ishiyama. The child of a poor family is visited by the titular canine, now resembling less a military cartoon than a man in a life-sized Mickey Mouse costume, courtesy of character designs by Yuji Moriyama. The children are soon enlisted in war games, as General Bull arrives and warns of the approaching pig forces of Jimmy Butagawa.

NORAMIMI

2008. TV series. DIR: Yoshitaka Koyama. SCR: Makoto Nakamura. DES: Toshihiko Masuda, Kenji Kato. ANI: N/C. MUS: Ko Nakagawa. PRD: TMS Entertainment. 20 mins. x 12 eps. (TV1), 20 mins. x 13 eps. (TV2).

Mascot characters are big in Japan—almost every town, company, and enterprise has a mascot. But what if they lived and worked among humans? Noramimi is a mascot who works for a childcare agency. Unfortunately nobody wants to hire a mascot based on a demon as a babysitter, so Noramimi can't move in with a family and become part of their lives; he's stuck living at the agency in this anime based on Kazuo Hara's comedy manga of the same title. A second series from the same crew, *Noramimi 2*, aired later in 2008. Each episode tells two short stories featuring Noramimi's mascot pals, their clients, and agency boss Handa-san.

NOSTRADAMUS THE PROPHECY *

1994. JPN: *Nostradamus Senritsu no Keiji*. AKA: *The Terrifying Revelations of Nostradamus*. Movie. DIR: Yumiko Awaya. SCR: Nostradamus, Hisao Maru. DES: Takeo Kimura, Koichi Takeuchi. ANI: Kazuto Kawagoe (SFX), Katsuyuki Sugimura, Takahiko Akiyama (CG). MUS: Yuichi Mizusawa. PRD: Planning Atsu, Animation Staff Room, Lynx. 103 mins. Despite the screenplay credit for Nostradamus himself, this sci-fi epic with ambitions way beyond its technological or writing capacity is based on a book by Ryuho Okawa, founder of the religious movement Happy Science (formerly known as the Institute

for Research in Human Happiness). It's made in live action with extensive CGI and some animation, and is included here for disambiguation: because the organization is responsible for half a dozen other anime movies, including **Laws of the Sun** and **Hermes**, it's often assumed that this movie is animated. Art director Kimura is currently the oldest director to make his debut in feature films, having written and directed *Dreaming Awake* aged 90.

NOTARI MATSUTARO

1990. Video, TV series. DIR: Toshio Takeuchi. SCR: Tadaaki Yamazaki, Seiji Matsuoka, Shunichi Yukimuro. DES: Akihiro Kanayama. ANI: Masayoshi Kitazaki. MUS: Masayoshi Kitazaki. PRD: Mushi Pro. 30 mins. x 10 eps. (v), 25 mins. x 15+ eps. (TV).

A teenage school dropout finds new meaning in his life when he discovers sumo wrestling, heading off to Tokyo for the bright lights and training with an aging master of the sport. Based on a 1973 *Big Comic* manga by **Tomorrow's Joe**–creator Tetsuya Chiba, *NM* packs two "episodes" into each 60-minute tape to give the impression that it is actually a 10-part TV series, even though it was never broadcast.

NOW AND THEN, HERE AND THERE *

1999. JPN: *Ima, Soko ni Iru Boku*. AKA: *Now I'm There*. TV series. DIR: Akitaro Daichi. SCR: Hideyuki Kurata. DES: Atsushi Oizumi. ANI: Michinori Nishino. MUS: Taku Iwasaki, Toshio Masuda. PRD: AIC, WOWOW. 25 mins. x 13 eps.

Schoolboy Shu Matsutani climbs a chimney to rescue a girl he sees sitting at its summit, but he falls into an alternate world. There, the damsel he tried to rescue is revealed as Lala Lu, the bearer of a magic pendant that can control the water element in this new world. The evil Hamdo needs Lala's pendant so that he can construct his fortress in a place called Hellywood—and now Shu isn't just visiting, he's the point man in a war against the forces of darkness. Despite a plot redolent of the comedy **El Hazard**, childish designs, and a sub-Miyazaki look, *N&TH&T* is a remarkably adult show that refuses to stint on images of violence and abuse. Shown on more forgiving satellite TV, this anime was compared to Alex Haley's epic *Roots* by screenwriter Kurata—a trifle optimistic from the man who wrote **Battle Athletes**. A later bonus disc contained 70 minutes of extras. **Ⓥ**

NTV, NIPPON TV, I.E., JAPAN TV
TV channel, formed in 1953 as Japan's first commercial broadcaster, and a direct competitor with the license-funded NHK. The TV channel has strong ties with the Yomiuri Group, including not only the Yomiuri TV channel affiliate in some outlying regions, but the *Yomiuri Shimbun* newspaper and the baseball team Yomiuri Giants. It is thus perhaps no surprise that one of the channel's biggest anime successes in early years was the baseball anime **Star of the Giants**. Anime on NTV remains in children's slots and clustered in the late-night graveyard shift; perhaps in reflection of this, the channel became a substantial investor in the animation studio Madhouse, taking an 84.5% stake in the company in 2011 and 95% in 2014.

NURA: RISE OF THE YOKAI CLAN *
2010. JPN: *Nurarihyon no Mago*. AKA: *Nurarihyon's Grandson*. TV series. DIR: Junji Nishimura, Michio Fukuda. SCR: Natsuko Takahashi, Mayumi Morita, Hideaki Koyasu. DES: Mariko Oka, Shinobu Tagashira. ANI: Hirofumi Morimoto, Masaaki Sakurai, Yu Hamanaka, Michio Fukuda, Shinya Takahashi. MUS: Kohei Tanaka, Keiji Inai, Kazuhiko Sawaguchi. PRD: Studio DEEN, Pony Canyon, Shueisha, Yomiuri TV, Hakuhodo D.Y. Media Partners, NBS, Toho, Yomiko Advertising, Animax, Animax Asia, BS11 Digital, NBS, Tokyo MX TV. 25 mins. x 26 eps. (TV1), 25 mins. x 26 eps. (TV2).
Rikuo Nura is three-quarters human, but the quarter demon blood in his veins is very grand indeed. His grandfather is currently head of the Nura clan of *yokai* (Japanese spirits), and Rikuo is his heir. Monsters follow him to school and get in the way of his desire to have a normal school life, and he also learns that if he doesn't do his duty by his heritage there may be serious consequences for his human friends. He decides to take up his duties as young master of his grandfather's household—but that only seems to get everyone, including himself, into even more trouble. He needs to unleash his demon side, Night Rikuo, an older and more powerful version of his 12-year-old daytime

self. Even that might not be enough to keep everyone safe.

Hiroshi Shiibashi's original manga gives us a hero straight from the Harry Potter mold—a bespectacled innocent with astonishing powers sealed inside him (**Negima**; **Conan the Boy Detective**). Rikuo is a much meatier proposition, long-haired, wild, cast from the same material as the transformed Ushio in **Ushio and Tora**. But while the attractive design promises a walk on the wild side, the show's gentle pace and likable characters position it more on the tame side. It's an easy watch, though, and attracted a big enough audience to get a second TV series, subtitled *Demon Capital* (*Sennen Makyo*) in 2011.

NURSE ANGEL LILIKA SOS
1995. TV series. DIR: Akitaro Daichi. SCR: Akitaro Daichi. DES: Koi Ikeno. ANI: Hajime Watanabe. MUS: Shinkichi Mitsumune. PRD: Studio Gallop, TV Tokyo. 25 mins. x 35 eps.
Ten-year-old Ririka is a typical Japanese elementary-school heroine—cute, sweet, kindhearted, and always willing to help others. When a very handsome older boy returning from his travels gives her a present from the exotic, mysterious realm of England, it turns out to be the device that transforms her into the latest of a long line of anime heroines dating back to **Little Witch Sally**. Earth is under threat from the playing-card-themed forces of Dark Joker (see also **Wild Cardz**), and whenever his minions, complete with ace-of-spades tattoos, threaten Earth, Ririka puts on her magic nurse's cap and becomes Lilika, the Nurse Angel. She uses the power bestowed on her to fight evil, extend her powers of healing to the world, and also to sell the many items of product-placement accessories that she wields in the commercially savvy post–**Sailor Moon** world. At the halfway point, the series suddenly becomes much darker and more unpredictable—heading for a tear-jerker ending with a real twist. A manga was published the same year by Yasushi Akimoto and Koi Ikeno, who also created **Tokimeki Tonight**.

NURSE ME! *
2002. JPN: *Seijun Kango Gakuen*. AKA: *Sexy Nurse Academy*. Video. DIR: Juhachi Minamisawa. SCR: Joichi Michigami. DES: Tetsuya. ANI: Tetsuya. MUS: Hiroaki Sano, Takeshi

Nishizawa. PRD: Discovery. 30 mins. x 3 eps.
Hospital manager Doctor Miura and head nurse Etsuko hit upon an innovative new way of avoiding malpractice suits; well, innovative if you haven't seen **Lesbian Ward** or **Doctor Shameless**. They decide to train their nubile young nurses to perform sexual services for the patients and each other, hoping to ensure a happy hospital. Not all the nurses are easily won over, particularly when they discover that part of their duties include whoring themselves to difficult patients in order to avoid legal action. Virginal new recruit Yumi's lifelong dream of being a nurse is soon shattered after she is broken in by the powers that be. A betterthan-average nurse-porn anime, if you like that sort of thing, with higher than usual production values that extend to generally decent animation, and a rare widescreen presentation. Another entry in the **Discovery Series**, conceived in an apparent attempt to replicate the success of the franchise's similar **Night Shift Nurses**, and based on an erotic novel by Domu Kitahara. **ⓁⓃⓋ**

NURSE WITCH KOMUGI *
2002. JPN: *Nurse Witch Komugi-chan; NWK Magical Te; NWK Magicarte Z*. AKA: *Nurse Witch Komugi-chan It's Magic*. Video. DIR: Yasuhiro Takemoto, Yoshitomo Yonetani, Toshihiro Ishikawa, Masato Tamagawa, Masatsugu Arakawa, Ko Matsuzono. SCR: Armstrong Takizawa, Tsuyoshi Tamai. DES: Akio Watanabe. ANI: Yoshinobu Ito. MUS: Ryuji Takagi. PRD: Kyoto Animation, Pioneer, Rondo Robe, Tatsunoko, Toshiba. 25 mins. x 5 eps. (v1), 30 mins. (v2), 30 mins. x 2 eps. (v3).
Komugi Nakahara is a hyperactive airhead whose main ambition in life is to wear costumes based on famous characters—compare to **Cosplay Complex**. When she gets a job at a café where she can dress up all day, she's in heaven. She doesn't even dream that there's such a place as Vaccine World, or that Ungrar the King of Viruses has escaped from prison there, but when the Goddess of Vaccine World sends cute critter Mugimaru to Earth to find a suitable candidate to accept the powers of the Nurse Witch and defend mankind (or at least Akihabara) from the Virus King, she's ready and willing, if not particularly able.

This parody offshoot of the **Soul Taker** anime series has its amusing moments.

In one episode Komugi dresses up as the whole **BATTLE OF THE PLANETS** team without even taking off her trademark rabbit ears, and Tokyo's Big Sight convention center turns into giant robot Big Sightron during Comic Market. Most of the *Soul Taker* cast turns up at some point, and throughout Komugi is tormented by her cosplay rival, Magical Maid Koyori. A half hour "special" *NWK Magical Te* (2002) appeared two weeks before the series was released, and just to confuse matters it's set between episodes 2 and 3 of the series. It is included on the English language DVD as episode 2.5, in which tortured hero Kyosuke, object of Komugi's obsessive desire, becomes a rock star. The two-part *NWK Magicarte Z* followed in 2004.

Parody can be a rewarding genre, but if the parody is the only thing the show has going for it the jokes need to be plentiful and broad enough for anyone to catch. As anyone who's ever been stuck in the middle of the row at a Worldcon Masquerade watching a group of Danes performing a skit on the complete works of Michael Moorcock can tell you, jokes which go down a storm to an audience of hardcore fans don't always play outside that narrow circle. A handful of nods and winks in the direction of industry giants is small reward for three hours of your life.

NYAN KOI! *

2009. AKA: *Meow Love*. TV series. DIR: Keiichiro Kawaguchi. SCR: Shinichi Inotsume. DES: Kazuaki Morita, Naoko Kosakabe. ANI: Yukie Sato. MUS: Manabu Miwa, Shigenobu Okawa. PRD: AIC, TBS. 24 mins. x 12 eps.
Junpei Kosaka is in his second year of high school, and has a huge crush on a girl who adores cats—creatures to which he is unluckily allergic. When he accidentally brings himself to the attention of the local cat god, he finds he can understand the language of cats. The downside is that, now he understands them, he must grant 100 wishes from cats or turn into a cat himself—which would probably kill him, since being allergic to oneself makes life difficult. Sato Fujiwara's 2007 manga is an unusual starting premise for a harem show (**ROMANCE AND DRAMA**), but in a harem as in a casino the house always wins. The formula that was so fresh and funny in **TENCHI MUYO!** is drained dry, in need of

a more inspired reinvention that anyone has so far managed. Most modern harem shows call on either zanier and zanier comedy or more and more extreme fan service to spice up the same-old same-old, while *Nyan Koi!* is almost charmingly old-fashioned in its restraint on both fronts.

NYANPIRE THE ANIMATION

2011. TV series. DIR: Takahiro Yoshimatsu. SCR: Natsuko Takahashi. DES: Takahiro Yoshimatsu. ANI: Takahiro Yoshimatsu. MUS: N/C. PRD: Gonzo. 4 mins. x 12 eps.
An abandoned kitten is saved when a vampire gives him a few drops of his blood. Now immortal, Nyanpire lives with a human girl, Misaki, and hangs out with his chums: Nyantenshi the fallen angel cat, Masamunya the Japanese warlord cat, and normal kitty Chachamaru. First appearing in 2009 in yukiusa's fan manga *The Gothic World of Nyanpire*, the cute little cat was brought to life by **TRIGUN** alumnus Yoshimatsu (also known as Something Yoshimatsu). The show can be read as a critique of the parlous state of the anime industry, constantly on the brink of death and saved only by the tainted blood of *moe*-polluted fans; or you can just watch it because it's fun.

NYMPHET

2007. JPN: *Kodomo no Jikan*. AKA: *Kojikan*. TV series, video. DIR: Seiya Numata, Eiji Suganuma. SCR: Mari Okada. DES: Masakazu Ishikawa, Ayu Katamoto. ANI: Seiya Numata, Masakazu Ishikawa. MUS: Masaru Nishida. PRD: Studio Barcelona. 23 mins. (v1), 25 mins. x 12 eps. (TV), 25 mins. x 4 eps. (v2), 25 mins. (v3).
Rin Kokonoe is in elementary school. Widely considered as "old beyond her years," she has a crush on her teacher Mr. Aoki and isn't ashamed to show it. He's 23, dedicated and idealistic, and really wants to help this troubled little girl, even though she's constantly coming on to him with sexual innuendo and threats that she will accuse him of molesting her if he refuses. He's also worried because she's 9 years old and any action that gets misinterpreted could lead to him losing his job, not to mention the damage to Rin. Her friends Kuro and Mimi are a weird contrast: spoiled rich brat Kuro is as apparently sexually precocious as Rin,

while Mimi, unusually well-developed for a 9-year-old, let alone a Japanese 9-year-old, is a complete innocent and has managed to preserve her childhood naïveté despite bullying and the precocity of her best friends. Aoki-sensei's struggle to do the right thing by his pupils and survive the experience with his reputation and job intact is just part of the tangled web surrounding all three girls.

The anime title translates as "A Child's Time." We have used the title of the manga on which it's based, Kaworu Watashiya's *Nymphet*, as better representing the central idea. The idea of Lolita as a fiction is dangerous; like all transgressive notions it can encourage extension into reality (**LOLITA ANIME**). Meanwhile changes in society and family life both sexualize and marginalize children.

Reality held back the TV series release for two years. Following the September 2007 release of the video *A Child's Time: Your Gift to Me* (*Kodomo no Jikan Anata ga Watashi ni Kureta Mono*) on the official anime website and bundled with the fourth volume of the manga, the anime was set to air in October that year. Two TV stations removed it from their broadcast schedules, one stating that their decision was informed by the arrest of self-described "pedophile superstar" and elementary school vice-principal Takayuki Hosoda. Two other stations aired the series heavily censored. It wasn't until December 2007 that the uncensored series commenced release on DVD. Two further videos, the four-part *A Child's Time 2: Second Term (Kodomo no Jikan Nigakki)* and *A Child's Summer Time* (*Kodomo no Natsu Jikan*), followed in 2009 and 2011. A book by Watashiya was published in 2012 in a comic magazine aimed at young men. ◐

NYMPHS OF THE STRATOSPHERE *

2002. JPN: *Stratosphere no Yosei*. AKA: *Fairies of the Stratosphere*. Video. DIR: Lan Misumi. SCR: Yuki Katayama, Ai Shibuya. DES: "Satuki". ANI: Hiro Asano. MUS: Hiroto Suzuki. PRD: Ypsilon. 39 mins., 30 mins., 23 mins.
Five young abuse victims turn out to be imperfect angels sent down to earth in order to bring pleasure to the human race—somehow, this is supposed to save the environment, although we are not sure how. One falls in love with a computer pro-

grammer and half-heartedly tries to avoid his advances before giving herself to him, in an anime whose plot only really makes sense when read off the box, since much of the early action comprises disparate sex scenes featuring the five girls before their angelic secret identity is known. Although these creatures have breasts and look feminine, like the original Biblical angels they have no sexual organs. Luckily for the animators, they *do* have fully operational digestive systems, leading to a predictable concentration on either end of same and a focus on nonconsensual sex. Compare to ANGELIUM. **⬤N⬤V**

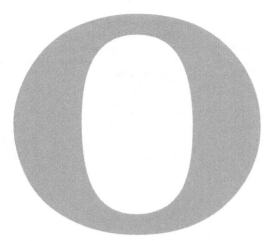

OBAN STAR-RACERS *

2006. TV series. DIR: Thomas Romain, Savin Yeatman-Eiffel. SCR: Savin Yeatman-Eiffel. DES: Thomas Romain, Stanislas Brunet, Isao Sugimoto. ANI: Tetsuya Kumagai. MUS: Taku Iwasaki. PRD: HAL Film Maker, Pumpkin 3D, JETIX Europe. 24 mins. x 26 eps.

In 2082, Earth is invited to send a team to the Great Race of Oban, an intergalactic event where the prize is any wish in the world—even bringing someone back to life. The race is organized by The Avatar, a mysterious force set on bringing peace and stability to the galaxy, as an excuse for a truce to end Earth's hostilities with another planet. When the Wei Racing team is chosen to represent Earth, rookie mechanic Molly stows away to joi n the race team—hiding her greatest secret, that she is really Eva, the Wei team owner's daughter. As sabotage and intrigue threaten the team's success, and even its survival, secrets emerge on all sides. Not even The Avatar is without a dark side.

Savin Yeatman-Eiffel's company, Sav! The World Production, released a two-minute short film called *Molly Star Racer* in 2001. Produced by Sparx Animation Studios, it contained drafts of many of the characters and ideas for *Oban Star-Racers*. It took Yeatman-Eiffel nine years to put together a deal to make the show as he wanted, largely in Tokyo, with Japanese animators. The inclusion of producers Katsunori Haruta and Minoru Takanashi and composer Iwasaki, plus episode directors Kiyoko Sayama and Masahiko Watanabe, was just enough to get the show into this book; we generally exclude any title without a predominantly Japanese creative team, but the intent to make a true Japanese-French hybrid persuaded us to bend the rules. Yoko Kanno's opening and closing songs didn't weigh as heavily as they might have done, since the opening theme was replaced by an inferior American tune for the English-language release.

The opening credit sequence nails its colors firmly to the mast, channeling several Studio Ghibli films, with nods to SECRET OF BLUE WATER, DRAGON BALL and the great SCIENCE FICTION AND ROBOTS of the 1970s and 1980s. Once you get used to the noseless character designs, the deliberately basic animation style and bright, clear color palette seem innocent and refreshing rather than clunky and old-fashioned. The story, an amalgam of anime tropes from classic shows—look for SPEED RACER, GUNBUSTER, and more—is put together with loving care and a respect for audience expectation, and hangs together as well as most Japanese kids' TV shows. The characters have solid backstories from which they develop and grow, and the emotional impact Yeatman-Eiffel hoped to deliver is there. We wouldn't want to see all anime made as Westernized hybrids, but when foreign creators bring this much love and enthusiasm to the table it can only be good for animation all over the world.

OBARI, MASAMI

1966–. Born in Hiroshima Prefecture, Obari went to Tokyo and joined Ashi Production after leaving high school. His early work included low-level animation on TRANSFORMERS and mechanical designs on DANCOUGAR, before he broke into directing when offered the opening sequence of DRAGONAR. He has subsequently become known for the large-breasted, vulpine look of his female characters, as seen in shows such as VIRUS and TOSHINDEN, as well as such pornographic anime as VIPER GTS and MARINE A GO GO, usually as the head of Studio G-1 Neo.

OBLIVION ISLAND: HARUKA AND THE MAGIC MIRROR *

2009. JPN: *Hottarake no Shima—Haruka to Maho no Kagami*. Movie. DIR: Shinsuke Sato. SCR: Shinsuke Sato, Hirotaka Adachi. DES: Ryo Hirata, Ren Ishimori, Masanobu Nomura. ANI: Akatsuki Watanabe, Fumie Anno, Tomohiko Takahashi. MUS: Tadashi Ueda. PRD: Production I.G, Dentsu, Fuji TV, Pony Canyon. 98 mins.

Haruka is an only child who lost her mother when she was very young. She lives with her father, but his absorption in his work has made them distant. She has lost a hand mirror, a gift from her mother, when they moved house after her death, and goes to a local shrine to pray for its return. At the shrine, a fox-creature called Teo opens the way into another world where everything is lost from this world is kept safe. But mirrors have magical powers there, and an evil nobleman has taken Haruka's mirror for his own ends.

Production I.G has gone down the 3D route for this movie, making it in full CGI rather than the classic 2D animation used for similar fairytales such as THE CAT RE-

TURNS. The animation is a little awkward in places but the backgrounds are glorious: the magic world is made entirely of lost items, giving rise to backgrounds reminiscent of CATNAPPED, KARL AND THE CURIOUS TOWER, or what might happen if you let Terry Gilliam and *The Borrowers* share the same playpen. The story isn't especially original, a mix of themes and morals from FANTASY AND FAIRY TALES, but the adventure sequences are well handled and will appeal to children without giving adults any cause for concern.

The DVD extras include a bizarre ceremony in which the director and lead actress visit Gunkanjima, the infamous "Battleship Island" off the coast of Nagasaki as a publicity stunt to link it with the oblivion island of the title.

OCEAN WAVES *

1993. JPN: *Umi ga Kikoeru*. AKA: *I Can Hear the Ocean*. TV special. DIR: Tomomi Mochizuki. SCR: N/C. DES: Yoshifumi Kondo. ANI: Katsuya Kondo. MUS: N/C. PRD: Studio Ghibli, Tokuma, Nippon TV. 72 mins.
En route to a high school reunion, Taku Morisaki reflects on his past. Ten years earlier, transfer student Rikako fell for Taku's friend Matsuno, perhaps to hide the alienation she felt at an unwelcoming school. On a trip to Hawaii, her money was stolen, and she surprisingly turned to Taku for help—a simple and possibly innocent act that changed the trio's relationships forever.

Based on a Saeko Himura novel originally serialized in *Animage* magazine (and hence presumably always intended for the screen), this is Studio Ghibli's only television drama and was made by the studio's younger members for a themed broadcast during the Golden Week holiday. The stress of making *OW* and HERE IS GREENWOOD simultaneously would leave director Mochizuki briefly hospitalized. The studio also made two animated shorts to celebrate the 40th anniversary of broadcaster Nippon TV.

OCCULT ACADEMY *

2010. JPN: *Seikimatsu Occult Gakuin*. AKA: *End of the Century Occult Academy*. TV series. DIR: Tomohiko Ito. SCR: Seishi Minakami, Hiroshi Onogi. DES: Takahiro Chiba, Yusuke Takeda. ANI: Takahiro Chiba, Kunihiko

Hamada. MUS: Junpei Fujita, Hitoshi Fujima, Noriyasu Agematsu. PRD: A-1 Pictures, Aniplex, TV Tokyo. 24 mins. x 13 eps.
It's 1999. Nostradamus prophesied doom for the year. Time agent Fumiaki Uchida is sent from the future to prevent this. The predictions say that the Waldstein Academy, a place devoted to paranormal studies, will be the starting point for alien invasion and the end of the world as we know it, so he goes there—only to meet Maya Kumashiro, a nonbeliever in the paranormal who's at the school for the funeral of her father, the former principal. She wants to know why he died: Uchida wants to know how to stop the apolcalypse. After some initial reluctance, they team up. If only Uchida can keep his mind off the girls and on the job, they might just save the world.

TV Tokyo and Aniplex teamed up for the *Anime no Chikara (Power of Anime)* project in 2010. The aim was to create original series animation, and this was one of three titles produced. The others were SOUND OF THE SKY and NIGHT RAID 1931. Mixing SF and the supernatural and leavening the whole with very silly humor, the team has produced a basic primer of weird stories and elements of strangeness, assembled from all kids of pop culture sources inside and outside Japan, with everything from spoon-bending to witches and dowsing to demons. Even the nudity is silly—one shower scene and a nod to *The Terminator*. The result is a good-hearted series with a lot of beautiful background art, charming design, and absolutely no focus. You may well chuckle while watching, but the tangled plot will trip you up somewhere.

ODA, KATSUYA

1932–. Born in Fukuoka Prefecture, he graduated in Western-style art from Musashino College of Fine Arts (now Musashino Art University) in 1961, but had already been working as an animator for two years at Toei on such titles as PANDA AND THE MAGIC SERPENT and TALES OF HANS CHRISTIAN ANDERSEN. Although he continued to work as an animator on TV shows such as CALIMERO, he drifted away from anime in the 1970s, organizing film festivals and writing film criticism. He subsequently wrote the book *How to Become an Animator (Animator ni Nareru Hon)*.

ODIN *

1985. JPN: *Odin: Koshi Hansen Starlight*. AKA: *Odin: Photon Ship Starlight; Odin: Photon Space Sailer Starlight; Odin: Starlight Mutiny*. Movie. DIR: Takeshi Shirato, Toshio Masuda, Eiichi Yamamoto. SCR: Kazuo Kasahara, Toshio Masuda, Eiichi Yamamoto. DES: Geki Katsumata, Shinya Takahashi. ANI: Eiichi Yamamoto, Kazuhito Udagawa. MUS: Hiroshi Miyagawa, Kentaro Haneda, Noboru Takahashi, Masamichi Amano, Fumitaka Anzai, Loudness. PRD: Westcape Corp. 139 mins. (93 mins., English-language version).
The photon ship Starlight sets sail from the orbital space colony City of Einstein, en route for Jupiter. Along the way, crew member Akira picks up Sarah, the last survivor of the spacewreck Alford. Sarah is receiving telepathic messages from what she believes to be an alien spacecraft near one of the moons of Uranus. Disobeying orders, the younger members of the crew change course for the alien craft's distant destination, planet Odin.

A beautifully designed film, its already shaky story line was dealt irreparable damage through the removal of 45 minutes of footage and a dire English-language script and dub (though the uncut version was also released in the U.S.). The story of a youthful crew and experienced skipper setting out in a spacegoing sailing ship on a dangerous mission inspired by a mysterious and beautiful girl had already been done with enormous success in STAR BLAZERS, and less so with THUNDERSUB. Either producer Yoshinobu Nishizaki wanted to prove that he could repeat that success without help from his former collaborators Leiji Matsumoto and Noboru Ishiguro, or else he is a one-trick pony when it comes to story-lining SF shows. Yet despite the gorgeous design and a skilled crew including Tezuka veteran Yamamoto and "advice" from NORA-creator Satomi Mikuriya, Nishizaki's new version never takes off.

OED48 *

2007. JPN: *Oedo Shijuhatte*. AKA: *48 Hands of Edo*. Video. DIR: Shigeki Awai. SCR: Shingatana Ikari. DES: Masaki Yamada. ANI: Shigenori Kurii. MUS: N/C. PRD: Studio9MAiami, MediaBank. 30 mins. x 3 eps.
Old Edo, where a girl could only get ahead on her back, whether by entering a geisha house as a servant or apprentice, or find-

ing a lover with money and connections. The capital was the way to, well, capital. This tale of a poor girl who comes to town to make her fortune ends each episode with a description of sexual positions. We haven't attempted to verify their historical accuracy, but this tale of Ushizu's adventures as she tries to make her fortune has some semblance of plot and some attractive backgrounds framing the sex scenes. We don't recommend you try the unorthodox use of chopsticks depicted here, on sanitary grounds. Nor should you assume, as the producers clearly hoped you would, that *OED48* was some sort of new addition to the idol-group franchise that also gave us **AKB0048**. ◐

OFFICE AFFAIRS *

1999. JPN: *Me Chi Ku*. AKA: *Female Animal, Bitch*. Video. DIR: Mitsuhiro Yoneda. SCR: Rokurota Marabe. DES: Mitsuhiro Yoneda. ANI: Toshiyuki Nishida, Mitsuhiro Yoneda. MUS: Yoshi. PRD: FAI International, YOUC. 30 mins. Ono is a new publishing recruit, assigned to one of the fastest-rising new titles under editor-in-chief Megumi Sugiyama. His girlfriend since college days, Rie, works at the same company, though she's "only in the administration department." Still the two have a good relationship until he gets the hots for his boss. As he gradually "learns the ropes" he is admitted to the department's elite corps of workers who put in overtime satisfying their editor-in-chief's need for sex and humiliation in the name of stress relief. Eventually Rie finds out and dumps him, and he leaves the company, rationalizing that his boss's kinky sexual needs are the inevitable result of giving women too much responsibility in the workplace.

The tawdry, predictable story line is the benchmark for the standard of work in every department. The most memorable images from this sad video are shots of the door of Ono's apartment, the rejection box into which his manager tosses most of his writing efforts, and the cigarettes and ashtray by his bed—memorable because these are the frames you see most often, with dialogue, orgasmic moans, or panting heard over them to indicate action that's too expensive to draw. Much of the "animation" consists of intercut stills. The characters appear catatonic because they

hardly move, even in the grip of passion. For the English dub, Kitty Video gave this lackluster effort as much attention as it deserves, with an undistinguished cast yawning through the tedious script under a director who can't be bothered. *Office Affairs* was later combined with the unrelated **CO-ED AFFAIRS** to make a one-hour video under the title *The Affairs*. The show was retroactively added to the **VANILLA SERIES**, because anime encyclopedists didn't have enough complication in their lives already. ◐

OFFICE LINGERIE *

2003. Video. JPN: *Lingeries*. DIR: Katsuhiko Nishijima. SCR: Hiroshi Morinaga. DES: Masaki Yamada. ANI: Masaki Yamada. MUS: N/C. PRD: Studio Fantasia, Green Bunny. 30 mins. x 3 eps.
Ace temp agency hireling Yusuke is brought in as an acting section chief at the intimate apparel maker Best Beauty Body Inc. However, he also has a secret mission, which is to dig into allegations that the vice-president is plotting against the company founder. While conducting his investigations, Yusuke pursues a new product line as part of his cover story, and backs rookie Mayumi's idea for a line of "seamless" lingerie. The project brings him into contact with workers from every aspect of the corporation—sexy blonde Alice, computer geek Chisa, and minx Rena, all of whom he has the onerous duty of seducing in turn in order to further his investigation—while coming up with a new design for the perfect panties and exposing corruption in middle management. The series is notable for art and plot superior to the general run of anime porn, in part due to the original erotic game by the company Mink and in part to the character designs and animation by Masaki Yamada, surprisingly working under his own name. One of the minor characters even bears an actionable resemblance to Linna Yamazaki from Yamada's earlier **BUBBLEGUM CRISIS** *2040*. ◐◐

OFFSIDE

1992. JPN: *Offside*. Video, TV series. DIR: Takao Yotsuji, Hisashi Abe. SCR: Takao Yotsuji. DES: Hisashi Abe. ANI: Hisashi Abe. MUS: Saburo Takada. PRD: Holly Production, Leona, Visual House Egg. 50 mins. (v), 25

mins. x 39 eps. (TV).
The world's worst soccer team has never won a single match despite being made up of eager young boys who desperately crave success. Their prayers are answered in the form of new manager Nagisa, who puts them through a sporting regimen punched out of the standard **AIM FOR THE ACE!** template. Based on Natsuko Heiuchi's "original" 1987 manga serialized in *Shonen Magazine*, this anime is from the same artist who created the tennis manga *Fifteen–Love*. Compare to **CAPTAIN TSUBASA** and the actionably similar **KICKERS**. As the 2002 World Cup approached, the series was revived on Japanese satellite TV in an anime series directed by Seiji Okuda.

OFFSIDE GIRL

2007. Video. DIR: Eimaru Yaguchi. SCR: Eimaru Yaguchi. DES: Susumu Komori. ANI: Eimaru Yaguchi. MUS: Ispring. PRD: Kyutibi, Animan MS Pictures. 17 mins. x 2 eps.
Soccer gets in the way of Nanami's attempts at romance with Akira. Unsurprisingly, she hates soccer, so when he asks her to manage the soccer team she's reluctant. But he insists, and their sex life moves to a whole new level. This soccer porn anime based on Ippon Nagare's 2006 manga takes cheap production to a whole new level too; made in Flash animation, it consists mainly of scrolling over still frames with a few seconds of animation repeatedly looped. Camera-shake is used as an animation technique, and backgrounds are largely dispensed with. Even porn should have higher standards than this. ◐

OFUJI, NOBURO

1900–1961. Pseudonym of Shinshichiro Ofuji. Born in Tokyo's Asakusa district as the seventh of eight children, Ofuji was raised by his eldest sister after their mother died in 1907. At age 18, he became an apprentice at Junichi Kouichi's Sumikazu Eiga. Ofuji's paper-cut fairy tales led to a series of innovative experiments at the periphery of the medium—he pioneered silhouette animation and sound in *Whale* (1927, *Kujira*) and made the brief but groundbreaking *Black Cat* (1929, *Kuroneko Nyago*), in which two cats dance in sync to a jazz tune. He also experimented with color in the unreleased *Golden Flower* (1929, *Ogon no Hana*) and stop-motion techniques in *Pinocchio* (1932). He enjoyed considerable success within the foreign arts community, with a 1952 remake of *Whale* placing second in competition at the Cannes Film Festival and his *Ghost Ship* (1956, *Yureisen*) exhibited in Venice. The Noburo Ofuji Prize, an annual award for achievement in animation, was inaugurated in his memory in 1962.

OGENKI CLINIC *

1991. AKA: *Welcome to the O-Genki Clinic; Come to Ogenki Clinic; Return to Ogenki Clinic*. Video. DIR: Takashi Watanabe. SCR: Haruka Inui. DES: Takashi Watanabe. ANI: N/C. MUS: N/C. PRD: AC Create. 45 mins. x 3 eps. (four stories per ep.).
Dr. Ogeguri and his pretty assistant, Nurse Tatase, run a clinic specializing in sexual problems. Ever ready to apply hands-on therapy, the doctor and his assistants help those who can't help themselves, with problems varying from the sexually dysfunctional to the just plain weird.

Based on Haruka Inui's manga from *Play Comic*, this somewhat dated tale of everyday working life in a sex clinic has one redeeming feature—everybody in it is obviously a consenting adult, even if their adulthood is signified by the disproportional body shapes in keeping with the art-style of the original manga. Humor plays a central part, leavening the sex scenes with moments of "comedy," such as Ogeguri's giant talking penis, and Nurse Tatase's ongoing attempts to convince her mother that Ogeguri would make a good husband. The stage is set for a series of smutty *Carry On*–style tales where the pair give their all to their professional duties while yearning for each other. Refused a release in the early 1990s by the British Board of Film Classification, it is hence only available in the U.S., where it was released by two different companies as *Welcome to the Ogenki Clinic* (episode 1) and *Ogenki Clinic Adventures* (episodes 2 and 3). The Japanese-language version allegedly features famous voice actors using pseudonyms (although this is true of numerous erotic anime, it seems to be a selling point here), but the English dub is poor quality. The live-action porn movie *The Ladies' Phone Sex Club*, also created by Haruka Inui, repeats many of the same jokes. **N**

OGRE SLAYER *

1994. JPN: *Onikirimaru*. Video. DIR: Yoshio Kato. SCR: Norifumi Terada. DES: Masayuki Goto. ANI: Masayuki Goto. MUS: Kazuhiko Sotoyama. PRD: KSS, TBS. 30 mins. x 4 eps.
A young man who is really the child of an ogre is destined to wander Earth slaying his own kind. When he has killed every ogre, he believes he will become fully human; until then, he is known only by the name of the sword he bears, Ogre Slayer. In each separate story, all set in modern Japan, he meets humans in trouble and deals death and destruction to ogres, but he isn't in the business of "happy endings." An episodic, melancholy quest with a resemblance to Tezuka's **DORORO** but actually inspired by scenes of sword-swinging schoolboys in Paul Schrader's *Mishima* (1985), *OS* has limited animation but attractive artwork and design. The ogres, superbly gross and amoral, are the best things in this short series based on Kei Kusunoki's 1988 manga in *Shonen Sunday* magazine. The same artist also created **YAGAMI'S FAMILY TROUBLES** and **YOMA: CURSE OF THE UNDEAD**. **NV**

OH! EDO ROCKET *

2007. TV series. DIR: Seiji Mizushima. SCR: Sho Aikawa, Akatsuki Yamatoya et al. DES: Takahiro Yoshimatsu, Junichi Higashi, Junko Sakurai. ANI: Takahiro Yoshimatsu. MUS: Yusuke Honma. PRD: Madhouse Studios, Hakuhodo DY Media Partners, Index, Universal Japan. 24 mins. x 26 eps.
Edo, the mid-1800s: summer in the city, the time for fireworks and festivals. Commoners like teenage firework-maker Seikichi Tamaya and his neighbors are struggling to make a living under the harsh rule of a city magistrate who has banned all luxuries, including fireworks. Then Seikichi meets an alien girl who wants him to make a rocket that will take her to the moon. Now he's in trouble with the magistrate, the local policeman, a crew of very dangerous aliens, and his neighbor.

Mixing period detail and modern popular culture for its look, and broad slapstick with serious intrigue for its plot, *Oh! Edo Rocket* is a romp that will take liberties with anything from history to the laws of physics, as long as the result is a good time (compare to **FUSE: MEMOIRS OF A HUNTER GIRL**). Based on a play by **GURREN LAGANN**'s

Kazuaki Nakashima, the anime uses Aikawa's solid writing skills and Mizushima's ability to ground action in real concerns and emotions to produce entertaining and sometimes moving results. True, the original material won't really stretch to 26 episodes without padding, including unwelcome doses of self-referentiality and self-indulgence in the last half-dozen chapters. But the fun still bubbles to the surface occasionally, and for most of the time the show looks like an exploding firework, the screen packed with event and energy. Japan's first rocket to the Moon fizzles out as it falls to Earth, but it dazzled on the way up.

OH! FAMILY

1986. TV series. DIR: Masamune Ochiai, Takashi Hisaoka, Hideki Tonokatsu. SCR: Shunichi Yukimuro, Yoshiaki Yoshida, Tsunehisa Ito, et al. DES: Fumio Sasaki. ANI: Mikio Tsuchiya, Isao Kaneko, Minoru Kibata. MUS: Tadanori Matsui. PRD: Knack, TV Tokyo. 25 mins. x 26 eps.
A comedy soap based on the everyday lives of the Andersons, a "typical" California household, as seen through the eyes of Taeko Watanabe, on whose 1981 Flower Comic manga *Family* it was based. Mom, Dad, and kids Kay, Tracey, and Fay, along with Fay's boyfriend, Rafe, get on with their lives, though much of the comedy arises from the fact that Kay displays every sign of being gay, and his efforts at concealment cause embarrassment to the family. Meanwhile, Dad starts receiving calls from Jonathan, a stranger who claims to be his long-lost son, much to the consternation of Mrs. Anderson. Shown in Italy, where it was much admired, though one episode was banned. **N**

OH! HARIMANADA

1992. JPN: *Aa Harimanada*. TV series. DIR: Yukio Okazaki. SCR: Shizuo Nonami, Shunichi Nakamura, Hitoshi Yasuhira. DES: Yutaka Arai. ANI: Ichiro Hattori, Katsuma Kanazawa, Yutaka Arai, Shunichi Nakamura. MUS: Masamichi Amano. PRD: Horman Office, EG Films, TV Tokyo. 25 mins. x 23 eps.
The unconventional adventures of Harimanada, a sumo wrestler who attains the top rank of *yokozuna* but fights in a ring that seems to owe a lot more to the masked wrestlers and strange tricks of

KINNIKUMAN. As with other SPORTS ANIME such as AIM FOR THE ACE! and TOMORROW'S JOE, the series progresses through hardships (an opponent undefeated through 26 bouts), conflicts outside the ring (the Masked Wrestler's fiancée), forbidden techniques (the Murder Mackerel Snap!), and mysterious challengers (the "Mysterious Wrestler," naturally). Based on the 1988 manga in *Comic Morning* by Kei Sadayasu.

OH MY GODDESS! *

1993. JPN: *Aa Megamisama*. AKA: *Ah! My Goddess*. Video, movie, TV series. DIR: Hiroaki Goda. SCR: Naoko Hasegawa, Kunihiko Kondo. DES: Hidenori Matsubara, Hiroshi Kato, Atsushi Takeuchi, Osamu Tsuruyama. ANI: Hidenori Matsubara, Nobuyuki Kitajima, Yoshimitsu Ohashi, Masanori Nishii. MUS: Takeshi Yasuda. PRD: AIC, WOWOW. 30 mins. x 4 eps. and 40 mins. x 1 ep. (v1), 8 mins. x 48 eps. (TV1), 106 mins. (m), 24 mins. x 2 eps. (v3), 29 mins. x 2 eps. (v4), 25 mins. x 24 eps. (TV3), 24 mins. x 2 (v3), 29 mins. x 2 eps. (v4).

Hapless student Keiichi phones for takeout and accidentally gets through to the Goddess Helpline. When Belldandy (Verthandi—the Norse embodiment of the concept of Being) turns up in his bedroom and offers to grant him a wish, he wishes for her to be his girlfriend, and they're stuck with each other. In the video series, she's a divine doormat who waits on him hand and foot, exerts her powers very discreetly and then only to make life easier for him, and includes both their siblings in the household without a murmur—a parody of ideal Japanese femininity. The 1988 *Comic Afternoon* manga by Kosuke Fujishima does more justice to all the characters, but the anime compresses the whole tale into a romance between the wettest pair of lovers since Noah, a wimp and a doormat whose excuse is that they were fated to be that way. A soft-soap rendition of alienspouse drama tradition that traces a line back through URUSEI YATSURA and BELOVED BETTY all the way to the American sitcom *Bewitched*, Kosuke Fujishima's story posits a boy who is pure of heart and gives him the perfect girlfriend, whose role seems to be to look pretty, cook, and clean. The story is sugary enough to rot teeth, but the animation and design are remarkably faithful to Fujishima's stunning original art.

Surprisingly, given the fad for mawkish romance à la TENCHI MUYO!, *OMG* did not immediately graduate to a TV series. While other shows jumped onto its formulaic bandwagon, it was Fujishima's other big manga, YOU'RE UNDER ARREST!, that got a TV broadcast. Instead, fans had to contend with a series of short, squashed-down comedy skits, *The Adventures of Mini-Goddess* (1998, *OMG: Chichaitte Koto wa Benri da ne!*, AKA *The Adventures of Mini-Goddesses in the Handy "Petite" Size*), directed by Yasuhiro Matsumura. Running as part of the *Anime Complex* anthology TV show, the series was a predictable rush of sight gags as cartoon versions of Belldandy's sisters Urd and Skuld, accompanied by Gan-chan the rat, rushed through comedy business seemingly inspired by old Warner Bros. cartoons. Belldandy's original voice actress, Kikuko Inoue, is conspicuously absent from the first 14 episodes. There were also, however, brief cameos by *OMG* manga characters not seen in the previous anime version, as well as parodies of contemporary anime, such as BERSERK.

After much hype and delays (reputedly occasioned at one point by a go-slow from animators convinced that the world would end according to the prophecies of Nostradamus, so there was little point in doing overtime!), the feature-length *OMG: The Movie* (2000) was finally released, reuniting director Goda and many of the video staff. Originally planned as an adaptation of the "Welsper" story arc from the manga, the film's plot changed through many rewrites into a simpler set-up in which Belldandy is approached by her mentor, Celestin, a one-time member of the Gods' Council. Discredited and imprisoned on the moon, Celestin seeks Belldandy's help, though Keiichi is initially suspicious of her association with the newcomer.

The issue of how to render the title, as *Oh My Goddess* or *Ah My Goddess*, is a thorny and tedious one. *Oh My Goddess* was the decision of Toren Smith when publishing the original manga in TRANSLATION. The Japanese "Aa" is unfortunately the very first syllable one learns in Japanese classes, thereby ensuring that a whole generation of self-appointed experts, with a whole one-hour lesson behind them, have tried to impress their friends by claiming that

"Ah" should be the "correct" translation. It usually takes another couple of years for would-be linguists to get to the lesson where they are told that "Aa" can be a contraction of "Anna ni," and hence is an expression of exasperation with transformed conditions, making Smith's original translation seem all the more apt. Original creator Kosuke Fujishima agrees, but has wisely excused himself from the ongoing argument, claiming that he is in no position to comment on how foreign territories might best render Japanese. As a result, many iterations of this franchise have indeed been released as *Ah My Goddess* abroad; compare to a similar unhappy compromise with the LUPIN III film *Secret of Mamo*.

The show was pastiched on many occasions, particularly in erotic variants such as TROUBLE EVOCATION and CAN CAN BUNNY. The *OMG* story itself did not receive a bona fide TV adaptation until 2005, with Hiroaki Goda's 24-episode TBS series, which included two bonus chapters on the DVD release. This was followed by another TV series, *OMG: Everyone Has Wings* (*Sorezore no Tsubasa*, 2006), released in the U.S. as *AMG: Flights of Fancy*) and a two-part video spin-off, *OMG: Fighting Wings* (2011, *OMG: Tatakau Tsubasa*). A different "Verdandi" would also appear in MYTHICAL DETECTIVE LOKI RAGNAROK.

OH! MY KONBU

1991. TV series. DIR: Tetsuo Imazawa, Mineo Fuji, Shingo Kaneko, Katsunori Kosuga. SCR: Riko Hinokuma, Tatsuhiko Muraame, Aki Tanioka, Shunsuke Suzuki, Yutaka Hayashi, Megumi Sugiwara. DES: Takahiro Kamiya. ANI: Yukio Otaku. MUS: N/C. PRD: Narumi, TBS. 12 mins. x 44 eps.

Fifth-grader Konbu Nabeyama is the son of a cook in a slice-of-life gourmet comedy that tries to add an element of adventure to slaving in the kitchen. Konbu helps his father solve problems in the world through the judicious use of seasonings, the right choice of menu, and the pleasing of fickle customers.

OH! MY SEX GODDESS *

2007. JPN: *Megachu!* AKA: *Megamisama Chuuiho the Animation*. Video. DIR: Tatsukichi Tomi. SCR: Ahiru Koike. DES: Yoshiten. ANI: Yoshiten, Wataru Yamaguchi. MUS: FUJI-

MOTO. PRD: Milky, Megachu! Anime Production Committeee. 33 mins. x 3 eps.
Kosuke is an ordinary guy who has a recurring nightmare in which he's a sex demon, an unstoppable force of lust. When a beautiful Goddess turns up to destroy him, he finds out the reason for his dreams: he has a demon trapped inside him. But there's another way out: taming the demon through lots of sex with the Goddess and her equally divine sister. And who's that naughty little demon girl trying to horn in on the fun? Based on a porn game by Frontwing, with a title and storyline that deliberately parodies OH MY GODDESS in both English and Japanese. **ⓝ**

OI RYOMA!
1992. AKA: *Hey Ryoma!; Rainbow Samurai.* TV series. DIR: Hiroshi Sasakawa, Yutaka Kagawa. SCR: Masao Ito, Michio Yoshida, Makoto Sokuza, Nobuaki Kishima. DES: Katsumi Hashimoto. ANI: Katsumi Hashimoto, Hideo Kawauchi, Takeshi Shirato. MUS: N/C. PRD: Animation 21, NHK. 25 mins. x 13 eps.
In the 19th century, Japan is in the grip of the shogunate, with the shogun wielding power in the name of a puppet emperor. Young Ryoma Sakamoto is growing up with dreams of being a samurai and doing heroic deeds for his country. He witnesses the arrival of Commodore Perry's black ships, and realizes that, although he is a samurai, the time has come to challenge the authority of the shogun, who wishes to keep Japan trapped in a feudal time warp. In this adaptation of a manga by Tetsuya Takeda and GO FOR IT, GENKI–creator Yu Koyama, after successfully completing his training, Ryoma leaves Chiba town for a life of adventure.

A famous figure in Japanese history, Ryoma brokered the fateful alliance between the rebel domains of Satsuma and Choshu, and he wrote an eight-point plan for modernizing Japan. His greatest moment was the coup of 1867, when he and his companions managed to negotiate the "return" of power to the emperor, which ended centuries of rule by the shogunate. Barely a month later, he was assassinated at age 33 without living to see the Japan he helped create. Three weeks after Ryoma's death, the emperor came to power in the Meiji Restoration, beginning Japan's modern era. Ryoma would appear in many

other anime, including DRIFTING CLOUDS and CLOCKWORK FIGHTERS.

OISHI, IKUO
1904–44. Working name of Iku Oishi, one of the founding fathers of Japanese animation, who died before the rise of postwar cartoons but whose pupils and colleagues went on to establish much of the anime industry as we know it today. Among his innovations was *The Hare and the Tortoise* (*Usagi to Kame*, 1918), which was screened as part of a promotional drive by the Morinaga chocolate company (ADVERTISING AND SPONSORSHIP). Among his many EARLY ANIME are *Hooray for Beer* (*Beer Banzai*, date unknown) and *Moving Picture Fight of the Fox and the Tanuki* (*Ugoki-e Kori no Tatehiki*, 1931). A key creator in the artistic foment of the 1930s, he also made *The Story of the Talkies* (*Talkie no Hanashi*, 1936), a hybrid of live action and animation showcasing the technology in use at the PCL film studio. During Japan's Fifteen Years War, he was drafted into the Shadow Staff making WARTIME ANIME for military personnel, such as *The Theory of Horizontal Bombardment* (*Suihei Bakugeki Ron*, 1941), claimed by his assistant Soji Ushio to have been used in the training of the pilots who bombed Pearl Harbor, and *Naval Aviation Combat for Base Personnel* (*Kaigun Kokusen Kuchi Butai-hen*, 1943). He was killed by enemy fire in December 1944, on his way back to Japan from a location hunt in the Caroline Islands. A sizable proportion of his professional output was classified and/or lost, causing much of his influence on anime to be forgotten until late in the 20th century, when some of his former colleagues retired from the anime business and wrote their own memoirs.

OISHINBO
1988. AKA: *Feast; Taste Quest.* TV series. DIR: Toshio Takeuchi, Kunihisa Sugishima, Masayuki Kojima. SCR: Ryuzo Nakanishi, Yasuo Tahada. DES: Masaaki Kannan. ANI: Masaaki Kannan, Shigetaka Kiyoyama. MUS: Kazuo Otani. PRD: Shin'ei, Nippon TV. 25 mins. x 136 eps. (TV), ?? mins. (TVm1), ?? mins. (TVm2), 90 mins. (TVm3).
The live-action TV show *Banzai! Oishinbo* started in 1975 and ran for 25 years. A short slot where celebrities sampled various regional delicacies, it started a craze

for gourmet food shows and the 1983 *Big Comic Spirits* manga *Oishinbo* by Tetsu Kariya and Akira Hamasaki. The anime version sticks close to the original, in which two young reporters go in search of the ultimate celebration menu for their newspaper's hundredth anniversary. A live-action movie version followed in 1996. After the resolution of the original quest, the anime story focuses on comedy and romance, as chef Jiro aims for the top in an elegant Tokyo restaurant. Despite Jiro's youth, his boss has put him in sole charge of the menu, and he works hard to ensure that he deserves such trust. As in the manga, as much care is given to the depiction of food as to Jiro, his lovely costar Yuko, and the other characters. Several interrelated episodes were also edited into the TV specials *Oishinbo: Jiro vs. Katsuyama* (#2, 10, 12, and 36) and *Oishinbo: The Ultimate Full Course* (#1, 6, 23, and 62). The characters also appeared in spin-offs, including *Oishinbo: Ultimate Shopping* (1992), which was an animated segment of the *Magical Brain Power* TV quiz game, and the topical TV special *Oishinbo: The U.S.-Japan Rice War* (1993). See also MISTER AJIKKO and the live-action series *Iron Chef* (1993). Original creator Kariya would also inadvertently cook up a giant robot show: UFO ROBOT DAI APOLLON. COOK DADDY's unorthodox ingredients put it in a different category despite the similarity of the Japanese title.

OJARUMARU
1999. JPN: *Ojarumaru.* AKA: *Prince Mackaroo.* TV series, movie. DIR: Akitaro Daichi. SCR: Rin Futomaru. DES: Hajime Watanabe. ANI: N/C. MUS: Harukichi Yamamoto. PRD: Adobe Pictures, Nippon Crown, NHK Educational, NHK. 8 mins. x 270 eps. (TV), 30 mins. (m).
A short series of short episodes for young children tells the story of a chirpy nobleman's child from Heian-period Japan who time-slips into the modern world. He has wacky adventures living with an ordinary Japanese family, whose son Kazuma becomes his special friend. References to 11th-century culture and modern aspirations mix with artwork that looks naïve but is calculated for comic effect. Like *Teletubbies*, it's paced slowly and simply for easy assimilation by the young. A short film, *Summer of Promises* (2000), introduces Semira, a strange boy who comes to play

with Ojaru and his chums and bears a marked resemblance to a boy of the same name who spent a summer with the village elders when they were boys, long ago. A very different blast from the past would characterize director Daichi's **Jubei-chan the Ninja Girl**.

OK!! EKODA *

2011. JPN: *Rinshi!! Ekoda-chan*. TV series. DIR: N/C. SCR: Shota Nishitani. DES: Junko Tokunaga. ANI: Ichi Domiki, Shinobu Ogawa, Itaru Kishikawa, Keiko Kitayama, Takashi Suzuki. MUS: sin. PRD: about 17, Studio Indigo, FROGMAN, DLE, NTV. 3? mins. x 22 eps.

Part of NTV's **Yuruani?** gag anthology show, created by DLE, based on the manga *Rinshi!! Ekoda-chan* by Yukari Taninami about an acquisitive girl's adventures in the nightlife of the big city.

OKADA, TOSHIO

1958–. Born in Osaka, Okada opened the General Products sci-fi store in 1982. The store would become a focal point for Gainax, the studio of which Okada would eventually became president. He subsequently became an adjunct professor of fan and audience studies at Tokyo University—his untranslated *Introduction to Otakuology* (*Otakugaku Nyumon*, 1996) remains one of the best studies of the anime world, while his later *Yuigon* (*Testament*, 2010) is a valuable eye-witness account of the development of the Gainax studio. He is often self-styled as the "Otaking," the King of Otaku.

OKAMA REPORT

1991. JPN: *Okama Hakusho*. AKA: *Homosexual Report; Homosexual White Paper*. Video. DIR: Teruo Kogure. SCR: Ippei Yamagami, Sheila Shimazaki. DES: Teruo Kogure. ANI: Jiro Sayama. MUS: Jiro Takemura. PRD: Knack. 45 mins. x 3 eps.

Shinya Okama (a surname that's a Japanese pun on "homosexual") is a university student who gets a part-time job in a gay bar. He puts on a dress (gay=transvestite here, apparently) and calls himself Catherine, then finds himself falling in love with a pretty customer, Miki. Miki is a real girl—and thinks "Catherine" is, too. The first video was followed by *Okama Report: Midsummer Happening* and a year later by

OR: Man's Decision, in which Shinya's high school pal Dan (who doesn't wear dresses) also falls for Miki, presenting Shinya with the dilemma of whether or not he should risk revealing his true nature and losing Miki altogether. Based on the *Young Sunday* manga by Hideo Yamamoto, another of whose sexually themed manga is available in English as *Voyeur*.

OKAMI-SAN AND HER SEVEN COMPANIONS *

2010. JPN: *Okamisan to Shichinin no Nakamatachi*. TV series. DIR: Yoshiaki Iwasaki. SCR: Michiko Ito. DES: Haruko Iizuka, Teruhiko Niida. ANI: Haruko Iizuka. MUS: Megumi Ohashi. PRD: JC Staff, AT-X, Flying Dog, GENCO, Marvelous Entertainment, Media Factory, MediaWorks. 24 mins. x 12 eps.

High school cutie Ryoko Okami acts as tough as her name, which means "wolf." But Ryoshi is so crazy for her that he joins her deranged after-school club to prove his love. The Otogi Bank pays it forward: they'll help you now, you pay back later. In such situations, the interest rate is always steep, but for the neurotically shy Ryoshi, no price is too high if the club enables him to win Ryoko's heart.

Based on a book series by Masashi Okita, with art by Unaji, *Okami and her Seven Companions* is a teenage fairytale. Anime references both Western and Japanese **Fantasy and Fairy Tales** frequently, but here transplants both to a high school setting, with all the characters signaling their origins: Ryoko's red-headed friend Ringo affects a red cape and basket (**Little Red Riding Hood Chacha**). But there are twists (like Tweedledum and Tweedledee mashed with the Three Little Pigs). Red Riding Hood is best friends with a wolf in **Snow White** clothing, and is also one of her seven dwarfs. There's another lupine villain in the story who couldn't be bigger or badder. There's another Snow White too, complete with cute dwarf babies. Delinquent teenage demons are part of a corporate fixation on image and branding.

The high-school world is brutally gender-specific and class-conscious, fixated on shadow not substance: outward appearance and external opinion matter more than anything. The show's takes on classic tales and the sly, wry commentary of its unseen narrator are cynically polished

reflections of real high-school fears and emotions. Few recent shows have played with the interface between truth and fiction, reality and fantasy, so well. Playing with such notions through fairytale opens up a huge range of possibilities, and while *Okami* misses opportunities, it has serious fun with those it picks up. The show doesn't just twist classic stories, including Japanese myths like *Momotaro* and *Urashima Taro* as well as fairytales. It refers slyly to classic TV (including **Project A-Ko** with its lesbian subtext, **Utena**, **Prince of Tennis**, even *The Monkees*) as well as more recent shows like **Black Butler** to reinforce its stereotypes. This creates a mythic visual/literary shorthand, flashing information straight to the subconscious inner child.

It's also visually polished and pretty. The end credits with their paper-theater characters are a delight. The backgrounds brim with invention: textured tarmac, light on water refracted as if by the eye, soapsuds smearing on a wet window, all beautifully rendered.

OKAMIKAKUSHI: MASQUE OF THE WOLF *

2010. JPN: *Okami Kakushi*. TV series. DIR: Nobuhiro Takamoto. SCR: Toko Machida, Atsushi Oka, Hideki Shirane. DES: Atsuko Watanabe, Junichi Higashi, Tomoya Asami. ANI: Atsuko Watanabe. MUS: Takumi Ozawa. PRD: AIC, Flying Dog, Dax Pro, Media Factory, MOVIC, Pony Canyon, Studio Fantasia. 24 mins. x 12 eps.

Hiroshi Kuzumi moves with his family to the remote little mountain town of Joga. His crippled sister and father are made welcome, and so is he—except by his aloof and beautiful class president. His next-door neighbor Isuzu even seems to want him. But why does she warn him to stay away from the old part of town? And why do so many students transfer away suddenly and without warning? There are legends of huge wolves roaming the mountains, and masked bands are roaming the streets after dark as if they're hunting for something. The town's Hassaku festival is approaching, and although a festival celebrating the local orange harvest seems innocuous enough, people are very edgy. Can Hiroshi and his new friends solve the mystery before something ancient and terrible runs riot?

This series is based on an adventure game for the PSP by Konami, which also spun off two manga in 2009. It was created by Ryukishi07, who also originated WHEN THEY CRY, and design team Peach-Pit, renowned for shows including ROZEN MAIDEN and DEARS. So we expect beautiful art, portentous set-ups, angst, and escalating levels of tension. But the tension is almost completely missing. The first half of the show is almost entirely devoted to character and set-up. When the plot finally gets going, the pace remains strikingly slow and the climax peaks low. Undeniably pretty, but so slow it could almost be enjoyed as an artbook.

OKAMOTO, TADANARI

1932–90. Born in Osaka, Okamoto graduated in law from Osaka University in 1955 and in film from Nihon University in 1961. He worked as one of the puppeteers at Tadahito Mochinaga's MOM Films on such works as THE NEW ADVENTURES OF PINOCCHIO until 1963, before founding Echo Productions in 1964 and working as a director on such titles as *The Mysterious Medicine* (*Fushigina Kusuri*), installments of EVERYBODY'S SONGS, and THE MOCHI MOCHI TREE. He also produced many TV commercials and won the Noburo Ofuji Prize in 1965, 1970, and 1975.

OKAWA, KOGI

1966–. Concept artist on works including VENUS WARS, GHOST IN THE SHELL, and EVANGELION. Often misread "Hiroyoshi Okawa."

OKAWARA, KUNIO

1947–. Sometimes miscredited as Kunio Daikawara. A designer on parts of the TIME BOKAN SERIES and VOTOMS, but best known as the founding father of "real robot design," which strives to make robots credible as real machines made by humans, instead of the quasi-magical creations of the 1970s. Okawara is hence credited with the trend for more scientifically plausible robots-as-vehicles—beginning with his own work on GUNDAM, and continuing with other "real robot" shows such as DOUGRAM: FANG OF THE SUN, VOTOMS, SPT LAYZNER, VIFAM, and DRAGONAR. Okawara also designed more traditional fantasy super-robots for the BRAVE SAGA.

OKAZAKI, MINORU

1942–. Okazaki left his native Osaka at the age of 20 with the hope of securing a job in the live-action film industry in Tokyo. Instead, he found work with the animation studio Hatena Pro, where he was assigned to drawing storyboards for the new production of ASTRO BOY. He soon moved from storyboarding into directing, mainly in the TV world. His resumé includes many famous shows of the 1960s and 1970s, including ROSE OF VERSAILLES, TIGER MASK, and DORORO. Okazaki became a prime mover in Studio Junio in the 1980s, presiding over a period in which the company once achieved the remarkable height of 120 staffers, producing 20 TV episodes in a single month. Much of the company's output continued to be for Toei Animation and Tokyo Movie Shinsha.

He directed many episodes of the 1980s hit DOCTOR SLUMP, an achievement that brought him his first feature credit for a movie spin-off from that series. However, his output remains largely confined to the world of the television series, where he continues to storyboard and direct. He also directed the TV special DRACULA: SOVEREIGN OF THE DAMNED, based on the Marvel comic.

In 1998, he joined forces with Hiroshi Wagatsuma and Minoru Maeda to found Synergy Japan, a "new" animation company largely comprising former staffers from Toei Animation. Synergy worked as one of many contributors to famous anime at the turn of the century, including the COWBOY BEBOP movie. However, by 2005, the company was better known as Synergy SP, associated with the ShoPro subsidiary of the Shogakukan publishing corporation. Synergy's first anime produced under this new deal was the adaptation of HAYATE THE COMBAT BUTLER.

OKIURA, HIROYUKI

1966–. After work as a character designer and key animator on both MEMORIES and GHOST IN THE SHELL, Okiura achieved directorial fame with JIN-ROH, based on a script by Mamoru Oshii (q.v.). Despite maintaining a relatively low profile in the anime business thereafter, he came back to public attention after a long hiatus with A LETTER TO MOMO (2011).

OKUDA, SEIJI

1943–. Born in Tokyo, he was one of the animators on the original GIGANTOR series, subsequently finding work at TCJ, Tatsunoko, and Art Fresh, before going freelance. His directorial debut came with PSYCHO ARMOR GOBARIAN.

OKUDERA, SATOKO

1966–. A writer who graduated from the Literature Department of Tokai University and was already working in a day job when she sold her first screenplay. Much of her work has been in the world of live-action Japanese television, including *Living Room*, about a woman who reluctantly shares an apartment with her boyfriend; *Don't Worry*, about a down-and-out who poses as the detective who formerly lived in his apartment; and the slice-of-life anime series HUMAN CROSSING. As a movie scenarist she has written several entries in the *High School Ghost Stories* series, as well as the 2003 remake of *Samurai Armageddon*. Her involvement in the anime world is limited but impactful, as the regular collaborator of Mamoru Hosoda, beginning with the adaptation of the novel GIRL WHO LEAPT THROUGH TIME and the subsequent original features SUMMER WARS and WOLF CHILDREN.

OLD CURIOSITY SHOP, THE

1979. JPN: *Sasurai no Shojo Nell*. AKA: *Wanderings of the Girl Nell*. TV series. DIR: Hideo Makino, Katsumi Kosuga, Hajime Sawa, Mineo Fuji, Keinosuke Tsuchiya. SCR: Keisuke Fujikawa, Kazumi Asakura. DES: Norio Kashima. ANI: Norio Kashima, Hiroshi Kuzuoka. MUS: Harumi Ibe. PRD: Dax, TV Tokyo. 25 mins. x 26 eps.

Nell is a perky girl in 19th-century London, who lives with her grandfather, Trent, above his antique shop, while her mother and brother live in a place evocatively named Paradise. When Grandfather loses all his money gambling and the principal creditor wants to marry Nell to his slimy nephew, she has to flee and try to reach her family. A less permanent abode than the Paradise of Charles Dickens's original novel, Nell's destination still takes some hardship to reach, pursued all the while by the feckless Quilp, who wants her for himself. Dickens's *A Christmas Carol* was also turned into anime as THE STINGIEST MAN IN TOWN.

OLD MAN'S SURVIVAL GUIDE, THE

1990. JPN: *Ojisan Kaizo Koza*. Movie. DIR: Tsutomu Shibayama. SCR: Chinami Shimizu. DES: Tsutomu Shibayama. ANI: Kuniyuki Ishii. MUS: Kazz Toyama. PRD: TMS. 92 mins.

In this anime adaptation of the popular *Weekly Bunshun* manga by Chinami Shimizu and Yoshi Furuya, an old man confesses his secrets of business success to an attentive Office Lady, imparting such gems of wisdom as How to Say the Right Thing, Better Commuting, and Etiquette for Meetings. Compare to the same idea from another angle—**SURVIVAL IN THE OFFICE**.

OLYNSSIS THE SILVER-COLORED

2006. JPN: *Gin-Iro no Olynssis*. TV series. DIR: Katsumi Tokoro. SCR: Yuichiro Takeda. DES: Hisashi Hirai, Ryuji Yoshiike. ANI: Hideaki Maniwa. MUS: Yugo Kanno. PRD: Toei Animation, ABC, Nagoya TV. 25 mins. x 12 eps.

In the far future, Earth is covered by an Olynssis barrier—a field that disrupts space and time. Within this barrier organic machines, or Gardeners, are out to exterminate all human life. A few small groups of hunters destroy the machines when they can and sell the scraps to survive. Tokito Aizawa is part of this subsistence economy-in-hiding until he meets a strange girl named Tea and her machine Silver. For some reason she calls him "Koichi" … Who does she think he is? And who is the real Koichi?

Striking resemblances in style and story to the mighty **GUNDAM** franchise—especially *Gundam Seed* and *After War Gundam X*—don't help this predictable series to be any less formulaic, but they do make it nicer to look at than the less than top-notch animation would normally allow. There are nods to **BLUE GENDER**, too, so you know where to go if you want the same plot elements with fewer plot holes. Based on a book series by Hitomi Amamiya, with art by designer Arai, this series was intended to run as a sales-booster for the serialization, which started a month later.

OME-1 *

1985. JPN: *SF Lolita Fantasy OME-1*. Video. DIR: Nobuyoshi Sugita. SCR: N/C. DES: N/C. ANI: Hajime Iwasaki. MUS: N/C. PRD: Towa Creation. 30 mins. x 2 eps.

Two science-fiction adventures attempting (and failing) to cash in on the earlier success of the **CREAM LEMON** and **LOLITA ANIME** releases. In the first, "Torture Chamber at Penius Base," pretty schoolgirl Momoko is found to be an interstellar spy and punished for her deception. In the second part, "The Model Is a Soap-Girl," Momoko goes to work at a "soapland" bathhouse/brothel in order to track down her missing friend, Yuko. A low-quality entry in an already low-rent genre. Both episodes were distributed in the U.S. as *Gonad the Barbarian* and *The Search for Uranus* in the Brothers Grime animation series. **NV**

ON A PAPER CRANE *

1993. JPN: *Tsuru ni Notte: Tomoko no Boken*. AKA: *Riding a Crane; On a Paper Crane: Tomoko's Adventure*. Movie. DIR: Seiji Arihara. SCR: Seiji Arihara. DES: Yoshio Kabashima. ANI: Takaya Ono. MUS: Reijiro Koroku. PRD: Mushi Pro. 30 mins.

Modern Japanese schoolgirl Tomoko visits the Hiroshima Peace Memorial Museum, where she has to write a report as part of a school assignment. The 12-year-old finds the museum's story so shocking that she has to leave, going into the nearby Peace Memorial Park, where children are playing happily. She meets a girl her own age, but when Sadako tells her story, Tomoko realizes she is a ghost. When she was two years old, Sadako Sasaki was exposed to radiation in the bombing of Hiroshima, and she contracted leukemia at the age of six. She folded a paper crane every day in the hope that it would help her recover, but the girl died before reaching her teens. Tomoko comes to understand that the bombings affected far more people than those who were killed and injured at the time, then she wakes up and sees the statue of Sadako. A short film shown on a double bill with **KAYOKO'S DIARY** and sharing much of its crew along with director Arihara, this Hiroshima anime in the spirit of **BAREFOOT GEN** dwells on the long-term effects of radiation poisoning in the fashion of **BENEATH THE BLACK RAIN**. The first part gives what is almost an animated tour of the museum and the last half is devoted to Sadako's flashback autobiography. The animation was inspired by the efforts of Miho Cibot-Shimma, a Japanese woman living in France, who decided to spread the word about the evils of nuclear war after seeing children in her adopted homeland playing "atomic war games." Her Japanese friends started raising funds to make *OAPC* in 1989. Given very limited exposure in the U.S. through subtitled screenings at film festivals.

ON A STORMY NIGHT

2005. JPN: *Arashi no Yoru ni*. AKA: *Stormy Night*. Movie. DIR: Gisaburo Sugii. SCR: Yuichi Kimura, Gisaburo Sugii. DES: Marisuke Eguchi. ANI: Yasuo Maeda. MUS: Keisuke Shinohara. PRD: Arayoru Committee, TBS. ca. 90 mins.

May the goat takes shelter in a mountain hut during a fierce storm, only to find himself sharing it with Gub, a wolf. Despite their differences, the two animals become friends and promise to meet again, using the phrase "on a stormy night" as a password. Gub wrestles with his in-built desires to eat May, but restrains himself at their successive meetings. However, both animals must deal with others of their kind; both wolves and goats are initially disapproving, and then slyly suggest that each spy on the other on future occasions. Realizing that their friendship is no longer a secret and that they risk ostracism by both species, the pair jump into a fast-moving river, hoping that they can meet each other safely "on the other side." A tale of a love that dare not speak its name in the style of the earlier **RINGING BELL**, based on the best-selling 1994 children's book by Yuichi Kimura.

ON YOUR MARK

1995. Video. DIR: Hayao Miyazaki. SCR: Hayao Miyazaki. DES: Hayao Miyazaki, Masashi Ando. ANI: Masashi Ando. MUS: Chage and Aska. PRD: Ghibli. 7 mins.

In a futuristic supercity, armed police raid the headquarters of a religious cult. One of them finds an angel chained in a corner, and the winged girl is rushed into quarantine. The officer who found her and his partner break into the science facility to rescue her, but the story then divides into one of two endings. In the first, the officers fall to their deaths as their stolen truck spins off a collapsing bridge. In the second version, the truck develops wings of its own and flies away from the city, revealed to be an oasis amid a desolate, postindustrial polluted landscape.

The angel flies free, and the cops return to face the music.

A short promo-video made by Miyazaki for the pop duo Chage and Aska (whose likenesses can be discerned in the police characters), it was eventually shown in theaters alongside WHISPER OF THE HEART and reputedly tested some of the digital techniques he would reuse in PRINCESS MONONOKE. It's prettily made, but the reduction of Miyazaki's standard ecological concerns to the time limit and formulae of a pop video makes the story line seem a trifle pretentious. The Japanese video release bulked out the running time with the storyboards and animatics used in production and the live-action video version of the same song.

ONA X 2
2011. Video. DIR: Ippei Taru. SCR: Hirotoshi Abi. DES: Manju Onsen. ANI: Manju Onsen. MUS: N/C. PRD: schoolzone, ChiChi No Ya. 15 mins.
Anri has just said goodnight to her date. In her bedroom she imagines all the risky situations that she might have got into if he had been unwilling to leave. This 15-minute title will cost you over ¥2,600 in Japan, around $20 or £13 at current rates of exchange, which seems like an unacceptably risky situation to us. **◐**

ONCE UPON A TIME ... MAN *
1978. AKA: Il était une fois ... l'homme. TV series. DIR: Albert Barillé. SCR: Albert Barillé. DES: Rene Borg, Phillipe Landrot. ANI: Bernard Fievre, Francois Fievre. MUS: Michel Legrand, Yasuo Sugiyama. PRD: Procidis, FR3, Societe Radio-Canada, RAI, SSR, BRT, KRO, NRK, RTVE, Sveriges Radio, Access Alberta, Tatsunoko Pro. 26 mins. x 26 eps.
In this series, the history of the world is summarized as almost wholly Eurocentric, with America presented as an offshoot and China seen through the eyes of MARCO POLO. A recurring cast, similar to Osamu Tezuka's "repertory company" of characters, plays different roles in each episode as they live their lives in each major historical period.

This Franco-Japanese coproduction with a predominantly French senior team qualifies for inclusion not because of the involvement of Tatsunoko, but because it shows how far anime has come in terms of attaining respect and influence as a distinct strand in world animation (FOREIGN INFLUENCES). Comparing this series, made in a style still familiar in France from comics and TV animation, with OBAN STAR-RACERS is instructive. *OSR* was made by a French director-producer who grew up watching anime dubbed into his mother tongue on TV—a process that began with MAZINGER Z's French debut in the year *Once Upon A Time ... Man* was first aired. It is saturated in the anime aesthetic, as far removed from Eurocentric as can be, but it could not have been made but for the bridge between Europe and Asia built by earlier collaboration and adaptation.

Barillé's company Procidis had huge international success with the *Once Upon A Time ...* concept. The follow-up show ONCE UPON A TIME ... SPACE (1982) was animated by another Japanese studio, Eiken, and released in Japan as *Galactic Patrol PJ* in 1984. Some English-language anime sites only mention Barillé and Procidis' involvement as creators of the show in passing amid a long list of Japanese names, creating the impression that the main impetus of the coproduction came from Japan. But Procidis does not mention Japanese staff or companies at all on its series webpages—a dismissal of talent that was also repeated in early credits for ULYSSES 31. No wonder readers and researchers get confused. Five more 26-episode series followed, covering topics such as exploration, life, and the history of the Americas. They have been screened in over 120 countries around the world. *Once Upon A Time ... Man* was released in English on DVD in Canada by Imavision in 2011.

ONCE UPON A TIME ... SPACE *
1981. JPN: *Ginga Patrol PJ*. AKA: *Galactic Patrol PJ*. TV series. DIR: Eiken Murata. SCR: Hideo Takayashiki, Masamichi Nomura. DES: Lune Valgue, Manchu. ANI: Tetsuo Shibuya, Jiro Tsuno. MUS: Koji Makaino, Michel Legrand. PRD: Eiken, Fuji TV. 27 mins. x 26 eps.
A Franco-Japanese coproduction that, like ULYSSES 31, was not shown in Japan until several years after it was made, *GPPJ* is virtually unknown in Japan, where it was buried in an early-morning TV slot. The story supplied by the French for the Japanese to animate involves Captain Jumbo and his loyal servants Jim, Putty, and Metro the robot, who work to keep law and order in the Omega Alliance of Peaceful Planets. Sworn to abstain from using deadly weapons, as befits the representatives of a multiracial coalition of spacefaring life-forms, they must solve every hazard they meet by negotiation and quick thinking. Perhaps the absence of much fighting might have also contributed to the series' swift disappearance.

Better known throughout Europe under local language translations of its French title, *Il Était Une Fois: Éspace*, the show was broadcast in English on *Irish* television, and we have unconfirmed reports that it was also shown on Nickelodeon in the U.S. Taking a leaf from Osamu Tezuka, the leads in the show were stock characters (or reincarnations) recycled from French director Albert Barille's first work for the French Studio Procidis, ONCE UPON A TIME ... MAN, an explicitly educational series.

ONE HIT KANTA
1977. JPN: *Ippatsu Kanta-kun*. AKA: *One Hit Kanta; Kanta the Batsman*. TV series. DIR: Hiroshi Sasagawa. SCR: Jinzo Toriumi. DES: Akiko Shimomoto. ANI: Mamoru Oshii. MUS: Akisuke Ichikawa, Koba Hayashi. PRD: Akira Inoue, Tatsunoko. 25 mins. x 53 eps.
Based on a manga by Tatsuo Yoshida, this is the story of how little monkey Kanta honors his dead father's memory. Because father was a baseball champion, Kanta forms a baseball squad in his memory with his numerous siblings. With his mother's help, he sets up games with other animal teams and eventually wins the inter-school championship in his father's name. This series featured debut work from Mamoru Oshii, who went on to become one of the most famous directors in anime, most notably for GHOST IN THE SHELL.

100%
1990. JPN: *Hyaku Percent*. Video. DIR: Yoshihisa Matsumoto. SCR: Daiki Ike. DES: Kazuo Iimura. ANI: Akio Takami. MUS: Yuki Nagasaka. PRD: JC Staff. 50 mins.
A pretty 22-year-old girl leaves university and gets her dream job as a TV newscaster, only to discover that life is tough at the top. In this adaptation of the *Young Action* manga by Michio Yanagisawa, she must juggle the demands of her career with her troubled love life. Compare with WEATHER

REPORT GIRL, which approaches the same idea, but for laughs.

ONE OFF
2012. Video. DIR: Junichi Sato, Shigeru Kimiya. SCR: Masashi Suzuki. DES: Kohaku Kuroboshi, Atsuko Watanabe. ANI: Kazunori Hashimoto. MUS: Takashi Harada. PRD: 1 or 8, Dentsu, Shochiku, TYO Animations. 15 mins. x 4 eps.

Small-town Japanese teenager Haruno Shiozaki realizes that the only thing stopping her from experiencing the world is her own lack of motivation, when her parents' boarding house is turned upside-down by the arrival of Australian motorcycle chick Cynthia. As if the cast of K-ON were suddenly confronted with a busty, brash, blonde on a motorbike.

ONE OUTS
2008. TV, video, movie. DIR: Yuzo Sato. SCR: Hideo Takayashiki, Mitsutaka Hirota. DES: Takahiro Umehara, Hideyuki Ueno. ANI: Haruhito Takada, Kunihiko Sakurai, Masaki Hyuga. MUS: Akihiko Matsumoto. PRD: Madhouse Studios, DN Dream Partners, NTV, VAP. 23 mins. x 25 eps.

Baseball star Hiromichi Kojima is in a slump. He heads for the southern island of Okinawa to train and hopefully regain his form. On the island he meets Toa Tokuchi, an inveterate gambler who can throw fast, accurate pitches and is currently using his talent in a gambling baseball game known as "One Outs" with some of the U.S. servicemen stationed on Okinawa. It's pitcher against batter for money, and Tokuchi strikes out almost every batter he faces. Kojima manages to win a bet against the odds and persuades Tokuchi to sign with his team, the Lycaons. Just to make it interesting, the contract is a gamble—¥5 million for every out Tokuchi pitches, and a ¥50 million penality for every run he gives up. That kind of contract is illegal, but the Lycaons' owner is greedy enough to go for it—and besides, he's plotting to make sure he comes out ahead. But Tokuchi's been a gambler for too long to miss a trick, and he has plans of his own to counter any crooked dealing.

Baseball is hugely popular in Japan, and gambling on the results is endemic. Shinobu Kaitani's baseball manga is one of dozens of similar SPORTS ANIME set on

the shadier side of the game, but the dimension of plot and counterplot gives it elements in common with tales of mystery and psychological battle like DEATH NOTE as well as other gambling stories like KAIJI (another Madhouse show). Simply animated in a semi-realistic style with careful attention paid to differentiating the main characters, it does justice to the baseball scenes, but its main purpose is the creation of suspense and the delivery of enjoyable entertainment. It does that, in spades, without a mystical name or giant robot in sight.

ONE PIECE *
1998. TV series, movie. DIR: Goro Taniguchi, Konosuke Uda. SCR: Michiru Shimada, Atsushi Takegami. DES: Noboru Koizumi. ANI: Hisashi Kagawa. MUS: Kohei Tanaka. PRD: Toei, Fuji TV. ? mins. x ? eps. (v), 25 mins. x 263+ eps. (TV), 50 mins. (m1), 55 mins. (m2, Clockwork), 6 mins. (Django's), 56 mins. (m3, Chopper's), 6 mins. (Dream), 95 mins. (m4, Dead End), ca.45 mins. (sp3, Open Upon), ca.45 mins. (sp4, Protect!), 90 mins. (m5, Curse), 5 mins. (Take Aim), 90 mins. (m6, Baron Omatsuri), 95 mins. (m7, Soldier), 90 mins. (m8, Alabasta), ca. 90 mins. (m9, Cherry), 30 mins. (v, Strong World), 113 mins. (m10, Strong World), 30 mins. (m, Mugiwara Chase), 30 mins. (TVm, Glorious Island), ca.90 mins. (m, Glorious Island).

Impetuous, headstrong 16-year-old Monkey D. Luffy eats a piece of magic fruit that renders his whole body elastic and almost invulnerable. Now he wants to be a pirate and find the fabled "One Piece" treasure of Gold Rogers. He saves the life of the red-haired Junx, who gives him his trademark lucky hat. He meets a motley crew of fortune hunters and misfits, and wacky adventures ensue as they hunt the treasure. A movie, also entitled One Piece, appeared in summer 2000, in which Luffy and Zorro are captured by the pirate El Dragon and have to escape. Based on Eiichiro Oda's Shonen Jump manga, with some debt to JOURNEY TO THE WEST in the lead character. Subsequent One Piece movies have included OP: Clockwork Island Adventure (Nejimaki-shima no Boken, 2001), which played in cinemas with a featurette, OP: Django's Dance Carnival; OP: Chopper's Kingdom of Strange Animals (Chinju-jima no

Chopper Okoku, 2002), which ran along with the featurette Dream Soccer King; OP: Dead End Adventure (Dead End no Boken, 2003); OP: Curse of the Sacred Sword (Norawareta Seiken, 2004), which ran with the featurette Take Aim! The Pirate Baseball King. OP: Baron Omatsuri and the Sacred Island (Omatsuri Danshaku to Himitsu no Shima, 2005) forms an interesting watershed in the franchise history, as it was directed by Mamoru Hosoda shortly after his exit from Studio Ghibli and seems to have a subtext of a team of heroes given insufficient resources to meet an impossible goal! Further iterations include OP: The Giant Mechanical Soldier of Karakuri Castle (Karakuri-jo no Mecha Kyohei, 2006), OP: The Desert Princess and the Pirates, Adventure in Alabasta (OP Episode of Alabaster: Sabaku no Ojo to Kaizokutachi, 2007), OP Episode of Chopper Mysterious Cherry Blooms in Winter (Fuyu ni Saku, Kiseki no Sakura, 2008).

The tenth movie, OP: Strong World (2009) was written by the original manga author Eiichiro Oda in recognition of the anime's tenth anniversary. It was preceded in April of the same year by OP: Strong World Episode 0, a video prequel that served as a teaser for the film itself. As might be reasonably said to befit a franchise searching for new ways to keep on rolling, the short film OP 3D: Mugiwara Chase (2011) was a 3D effort in which Luffy's rubberized limbs were able to fling themselves out into the audience. This not only served as a handy gimmick but made the film effectively unpiratable, although the authors confess we are unable to determine whether this is supposed to be filed as the "11th" OP film or simply as a tangential extra. But it was back to business as usual with the following year's OP Film Z (2012), in which the characters, animated in standard form, square off against the new enemy Zephyr. Seemingly following in a newly established teaser tradition, the TV special OP Glorious Island (2012) earlier in the year presented Zephyr's backstory in order to integrate it into the continuity in time for the theatrical rerelease. OP Episode of Luffy Hand Island Adventure (OP Episode of Luffy Hand Island no Boken, 2012) duly followed. There is also a relatively rare video series of OP, which preceded the original TV series as part of the Super Jump roadshow and which was available to readers who sent in a number of redeemable coupons to the magazine.

One Piece, along with **NARUTO**, is one of the defining children's anime of the early 21st century, with a remarkable following in Japan and abroad—it's difficult to go too wrong with pirates, particularly when Hollywood rediscovered this with the initiation of a movie franchise for *Pirates of the Caribbean* (2003). It is the top of the ratings for teenage anime, still beaten out by **SAZAE-SAN** for cartoons in general but continuing to run rings around its rival **NARUTO** in the teen market, with contemporary (2014) ratings healthily at the 8% mark (**RATINGS AND BOX OFFICE**). It is even one of the few anime to retain a publicly acknowledged following in the People's Republic of China, where the game spinoffs and manga are legally released. *One Piece* has been subject to the usual issues in **CENSORSHIP AND LOCALIZATION** in the U.S. market, including some scenes trimmed for length; the replacement of its original score with a synthesizer soundtrack; the removal of alcohol references, tobacco paraphernalia, blood, and many weapons; and the digital alteration of characters deemed to be unwelcome racial stereotypes. There is also an alternate English dub recorded and broadcast in Singapore, which is far more faithful to the intent of the Japanese original, although it lacks much of the American version's finesse and budget. See also **RAVE MASTER**, a pale imitation.

1+2=PARADISE

1989. Video. DIR: Junichi Watanabe. SCR: Nobuaki Kishima. DES: Akiyuki Serizawa. ANI: Keiichi Sato. MUS: Jun Watanabe. PRD: Uemura/Toei. 30 mins. x 2 eps.
A strange relationship develops between college-boy Yusuke and the beautiful twins, Yuika and Rika, he saves from a wild dog. The girls fall for their dauntless hero, but Yusuke is pathologically scared of women. The girls eventually help him overcome his fear, only to find that he's stopped fantasizing about them and has fallen for the new girl in the school—rich corporate heiress Barako.

A two-part erotic adaptation of Junko Uemura's *Shonen Magazine* series and an early directorial job for **SUPER ATRAGON**'s Watanabe. **◐**

ONE POUND GOSPEL *

1988. JPN: *Ichi Pondo no Fukuin*. Video. DIR: Makura Saki (Osamu Dezaki), Takaya Mizutani. SCR: Hideo Takayashiki, Tomoko Konparu. DES: Katsumi Aoshima. ANI: Shojuro Yamauchi. MUS: N/C. PRD: Studio Gallop. 55 mins.
Sister Angela is a novice nun. Kosuke Hatakana is a young boxer who has a problem keeping to his fighting weight, which means that he has never fulfilled his real potential. Angela's concern for Kosuke and his future goes beyond the detached compassion expected of a nun, and his determination to justify her faith in his ability makes him try to prove himself one more time. His despairing trainer can't believe he really means it this time, but Kosuke has another chance at success and seems ready to take it.

Manga creator Rumiko Takahashi is better known to American fans for her lighthearted romantic fantasies **URUSEI YATSURA** and **RANMA ½**, but her heart lies in exploring offbeat events and relationships in the real world, and this is a good example. The director of **GOLGO 13** turns in a crisp, professional job on this very different story.

ONE TERM, ONE CLUB KOIBANA TOMOBANA

2007. JPN: *Ichigo Ichie: Koibana Tomobana*. AKA: *Once-in-a-Lifetime Encounter: Love and Friends* TV series. DIR: Yukio Kawajima. SCR: Shin Umemura. DES: Yukio Kawajima, Atelier Roku. ANI: Ekura Animal. MUS: Include P.D. PRD: Four-Some, Mind Wave. 5 mins. x 13 eps. (TV1), 3 mins. x 13 eps. (TV2).
A series of short, bittersweet stories about friendship, missed chances, separation, and change in high school life. The cute, simply drawn characters are nameless schoolgirls, based on a line of stationery designed by Tomoko Katano for Mind Wave. The character creation industry is huge in Japan; characters created purely as visual icons to sell goods, such as **HELLO KITTY**, **TARE PANDA**, or **KOGEPAN**, step off the design into other media. A second series, *Ichigo Ichie: Kimi no Kotoba* (*Your Words*), followed in 2010 from the same team.

1001 NIGHTS *

1999. Video. DIR: Mike Smith. SCR: Yoshitaka Amano. DES: Yoshitaka Amano. ANI: N/C. MUS:

David Newman. PRD: 1001 Nights Prd Cttee, Bell System 24, Hyperion. 25 mins.
The Demon King Darnish plots to ruin the lives of mortals, engineering a meeting between Princess Budhu and Prince Kamahl solely to make the pair fall in love and to heighten the suffering when they are inevitably parted. The princess cannot bear the separation and throws herself from a tower, but is saved by the fairy Mamune. The angry Darnish chases the lovers, who escape forever when they are transformed into a shining star.

A film commissioned by the Los Angeles Philharmonic Orchestra, featuring music by *The Brave Little Toaster*–composer Newman and showcasing **ANGEL'S EGG**–creator Amano's artistic talents in the U.S.

ONE WEEK FRIENDS *

2014. JPN: *Isshukan Friends*. TV series. DIR: Taro Iwasaki. SCR: Shotaro Suga. DES: Eri Yamazaki. ANI: Eri Yamazaki. MUS: Irone Toda. PRD: Brains Base, Dax, NAS, Pony Canyon, SCSK Corporation, Toho. 24 mins. x 12 eps.
Yuki notices that his classmate Kaori seems permanently withdrawn. She eats lunch alone and she doesn't have any friends. Kaori has a good heart but a bad memory induced by the trauma of a car accident—every Sunday, she forgets any friendships established over the previous week, and she has come to shun human contact. Yuki determines to somehow work his way into Kaori's life, despite the risk that every Monday morning he will discover his friendship and good works have been reset to zero.

As with the film *50 First Dates* (2004), to which *One Week Friends* has obvious similarities, an intriguing premise also bears with it an unpleasant undertone of control and domination. The romantic viewer might see Yuki and Kaori as destined for each other; the cynic might instead read into her the latest iteration of many hundreds of lame-duck anime girlfriends who exist as blank slates craving a male signature. Beyond such concerns, the story makes some innovative uses of common anime tropes, starting with its central conceit that offers a weekly **EVERYDAY ANIME** version of the Endless Eight time-loop from **THE MELANCHOLY OF HARUHI SUZUMIYA**. Later episodes introduce an interesting, oblique twist on the *osana-najimi* cliché (**ROMANCE**

AND **DRAMA**) of reunited childhood friends, in which Yuki is not a participant but a helpless observer of someone else's story. Based on the 2012 manga series from *Gangan Joker* magazine, created by Matcha Hazuki.

ONE-CHOP MANTARO

1990. JPN: *Ippon Bocho Mantaro*. AKA: *One Knife-slice Mantaro*. Video. DIR: Toshio Takeuchi. SCR: Megumi Hikichi. DES: Hidetoshi Omori. ANI: Keiichi Sato. MUS: Kensuke Kyo. PRD: JC Staff, Animate Film. 45 mins. x 2 eps.

Downtown cook Ginpei's prodigal son Mantaro returns after several years traveling. When he offers to help out in the restaurant, Ginpei notices that the guests eagerly consume Mantaro's pork cutlets but leave his untouched. Mantaro teaches his old-town friends and family the many tricks he has learned on his travels, before setting off to Osaka for a repeat performance. An anime spin-off of the 1973 *Business Jump* manga *One-Chop Ajimei*, by an artist known as "Big Jo," this kitchen tale was based on an original book by **MISTER HAPPY**–creator "Gyujiro." The original manga was way ahead of **OISHINBO** but only made it to anime in the wake of its successor—perhaps this subtle irony is what led the production staff to concentrate on a "new generation."

ONE: TRUE STORIES *

2001. JPN: *One: Kagayaku Kisetsu e*. AKA: *One: To the Glorious Season*. Video. DIR: Yosei Morino (v1), Kan Fukumoto (v2). SCR: Tetsuro Oishi. DES: Jun Sato. ANI: N/C. MUS: Yoshiro Hara, Tomomi Nakamura. PRD: KSS, ARMS, Nexton, Cherry Lips. 27 mins. x 4 eps. (v1), 30 mins. x 3 eps. (v2).

Orphan Kohei Orihara lives with his aunt and suffers from memory loss, in particular with regard to a childhood friend who was a great help to him in a time of crisis (the death of his sister). Now, in the style of **LOVE HINA**, he is trying to work out which of several neighborhood girls is The One, although the prime candidate actually turns out to be Mizuka, the surrogate sister who has known him for so long that he has not realized she has become a beautiful teenager. So, that would make her a "childhood friend," then? Based on a 1998 game from Tactics, the anime version

constantly returns to Kohei's childhood—an interesting way of approaching the multiple routes of computer games, but also of recycling footage.

The action, such as it is, spreads out across the four seasons of a Japanese school year in the style of **SLOW STEP**, beginning with the rains that herald the end of summer vacation, and taking us through fall winds, winter snow, and the inevitable cherry blossoms that signify spring and **GRADUATION**. This sounds like a rerun of a number of other anime because it is. Director Morino has handled the premise of childhood friends separated for years in Masakazu Katsura's **I"s**. Note that there are two versions of this series—a mainstream one released by KSS in 2001 and the later Cherry Lips erotic variant released in 2003. Technically, the subtitle "True Stories" only applies to the second series, which is the one released in America. **Ⓝ**

ONEECHAN GA KITA *

2014. AKA: *My Big Sister Arrived*. TV series. DIR: Yoshihide Yuzumi. SCR: N/C. DES: Takeshi Oda. ANI: N/C. MUS: Fuga Hatori. PRD: C2C, Takeshobo. 3 mins. x 12 eps.

Thirteen-year-old Tomoya gets a 17-year-old stepsister when his father remarries, and Ichika is creepily interested in him. Great **COMEDY** entertainment if you think that stalkers are funny—we'd say it plumbed new lows in 2014, but then we saw **RECENTLY, MY SISTER IS UNUSUAL**.

ONEGAI MY MELODY *

2005. JPN: *Wish For My Melody, Please My Melody My-Melo*. TV series, movie. DIR: Makoto Moriwaki. SCR: Takashi Yamada, Atsushi Maekawa, Yasushi Hirano. DES: Tomoko Miyakawa, Kazuya Fukuda, Yukiko Mizuno. ANI: Yasuyuki Noda, Tsukasa Miyazaki. MUS: Cher Watanabe. PRD: Studio Comet, Sanrio, TV Osaka, TV Tokyo, We've, Inc., Yomiuri Advertising, AT-X, Bandai, Furyu, Showa Note, Sotsu Agency, Toho, Universal MUS. 25 mins. x 52 eps. (TV1), 25 mins. x 52 eps. (TV2), 25 mins. x 52 eps. (TV3), 25 mins. x 52 eps. (TV4).

My Melody is a cute little white rabbit in a pink hood. She lives in Mary Land, a place formed out of the music and dreams of humans. Its King isn't very bright, but he means well. When naughty Kuromi

and his sidekick, the dream-eater Baku, escape into the human world, they create a chance for the Spirit of Dark Power to revive and destroy all human dreams. The King sends My Melody to stop them. Along the way she meets a human girl named Uta Yumeno (lit.: "A Song of Dreams") and the two become friends and comrades in the fight to keep songs and dreams alive for everyone.

This sweet story for little girls was devised by Sanrio, creators of **HELLO KITTY** and scores of other icons of cute, to sell toys and accessories to little girls: the fluffy pink equivalent of **BEYBLADE** or **TRANSFORMERS**. It was very successful indeed, running to three more year-long series from the same team. *Onegai My Melody KuruKuru Shuffle* (2006) is set a year after the first series and more or less reprises its plot, with Kuromi and Baku escaping once again and setting up a chance for the Spirit of Dark Power to revive. This also provides another chance for Uta, who misses My Melody, to see her again. In 2007 *My Melody Sukkiri* sees My Melody and Kuromi going head to head as they battle to replace the deposed King. Their rivalry threatens both Earth and Mary Land by enabling the Spirit of Dark Power to rise again. *My Melody Kirara* (2008) was set before the main Uta Yumeno story arc, starring schoolgirl Kirara Hoshizuka. In 2012 the people of Mary Land and their human friends made their movie debut in *Onegai My Melody Yu & Ai*, screened on a double bill with the first **JEWELPET** film. Jewelpet was Sanrio's next big TV franchise, having taken over the *My Melody* TV timeslot in 2009. A *My Melody* novel was published in 2013: depending how many of the eight-year-olds who watched the first series buy it, *My Melody* may take another step towards achieving the same enduring iconic status as *Hello Kitty*.

ONI

1995. JPN: *Toma Kishinden Oni*. AKA: *Fighting Devil Divinity Oni*. TV series. DIR: Iku Suzuki. SCR: Natsuko Hayakawa. DES: Masayuki Goto. ANI: N/C. MUS: N/C. PRD: JC Staff, TV Tokyo. 8 mins. x 25 eps.

Human beings can transform into powerful creatures, at which point they fight each other. A series designed to cash in on the Gameboy game of the same name, it was broadcast during the early morning *Anime Asaichi* children's program. No relation to the more recent *Oni* PC game from Bungie, which featured anime-style cut-scenes outsourced to real-life anime studio AIC.

ONIAI *

2012. JPN: *Onii-chan da kedo Ai Sae Areba Kankei Nai yo ne.* AKA: *As Long as There's Love, It Doesn't Matter if He's My Brother, Right?* TV series. DIR: Keiichiro Kawaguchi. SCR: Kazuyuki Fudeyasu, Shogo Yasukawa, Mio Inoue. DES: Kosuke Kawamura. ANI: Kosuke Kawamura, Kazuya Hirata, Ikuko Matsushita. MUS: N/C. PRD: Silver Link, AT-X. 24 mins x 12 eps.

The "childhood friends" subplot common to anime ROMANCE AND DRAMA gets an incestuous twist here more common to EROTICA AND PORNOGRAPHY when siblings separated as children are reunited as adults. Akito is a building manager and sometime author who has been writing pseudonymous books of incest porn. Akiko is the long-lost sister who has not seen him for six years, moves in, and immediately commences trying to seduce him. Other girls turn up for a predictable harem set-up, almost as predictable as the eventual "revelation" that they are only adopted siblings, and that it's been the threat of *not-quite-incest* all along (MARMALADE BOY). Based on a book series by Daisuke Suzuki, illustrated by Gekka Uru. For a much more serious look at the same theme, see KOIKAZE. ◐

ONI-TENSEI *

2001. Video. DIR: Nobuhiro Kondo. SCR: Ryota Yamaguchi. DES: Jingi Miyafuji. ANI: Yuji Mukoyama. MUS: N/C. PRD: AIC, Studio Gazelle, Green Bunny. 30 mins. x 4 eps.

Sexy lady investigator Reiko is looking for the murderer responsible for the gruesome deaths of 13 gangsters—her only clue, the timid girl Ema Nozomi, who always seems to be somewhere near the scene of a crime. That would be suspicious even for people who had not seen KEKKAI, and Ema, whose name is shared with that of a king of hell, is soon revealed to have a demonic tattoo on her back that can come to life to wreak havoc on our world. The result is an intriguing horror anime in which the story takes second place to the obligatory sex, exploring the urban

myth that a perfect tattoo will come to life, and placing Reiko in the midst of a crime conspiracy that mixes elements of CRYING FREEMAN and JOJO'S BIZARRE ADVENTURES. ◐◑◒

ONIMARU

1990. JPN: *Onimaru: Senjo ni Kakeru Itsutsu no Seishun.* Video. DIR: Osamu Dezaki. SCR: Osamu Dezaki. DES: Setsuko Shibuichi. ANI: Yukari Kobayashi. MUS: Eimi Sakamoto. PRD: Magic Bus. 45 mins.

During the Onin wars in Japan's medieval Muromachi period, five superpowered warriors hire out their services to the highest bidder. Leader Onimaru can beat two hundred mercenaries singlehandedly, Bo handles demolitions, Saru is as agile as a monkey, Osamu is a cool tactician, and Kiri is the obligatory token swordswoman. This prefabricated group (who might as well be a group of superheroes like those in BATTLE OF THE PLANETS for all the difference the period setting makes) gain an extra unwelcome member when Onimaru rescues Princess Aya, who naturally falls in love with him and refuses to go away. Not to be confused with *Onikirimaru*, which was released in English as OGRE SLAYER.

ONLY YESTERDAY *

1991. JPN: *Omohide Poroporo.* AKA: *Tearful Thoughts.* Movie. DIR: Isao Takahata. SCR: Isao Takahata. DES: Yoshifumi Kondo, Yoshiharu Sato. ANI: Yoshifumi Kondo. MUS: Joe Hisaishi. PRD: Hayao Miyazaki, Studio Ghibli. 119 mins.

The action skips back and forth between 1966 and 1982 as Office Lady Taeko Okajima, visiting the country for a working sabbatical on a farm, recalls events from her childhood—achievements, embarrassments, hopes, dreams, and people. She's trying to decide whether to return to the city and go on with her career or to marry and settle in the countryside, and her reminiscences, at first seemingly aimless, help to shape her decision just as those events and people helped to shape the person she has become.

Hotaru Okamoto's and Yuko Tone's original 1987 story, serialized in *Myojo* weekly, concentrated on the misadventures of the 10-year-old Taeko—the 1982 framing device was conceived by Takahata solely for the film. Beautiful animation

and design are almost taken for granted in a Studio Ghibli production, and the script is excellent. The overall emphasis on the importance of marriage, and the assumption (still widespread in Japan at the time) that a real career and family life are mutually exclusive for women, may offend some viewers. Sexual politics aside, Takahata's tale of one woman's choice recreates everyday life in town and the Yamagata countryside with loving care and a marvelous eye for detail, imparting the weight of a historical document without overwhelming the delicate human story.

OPPAI HEART: SHE'S IN HEAT

2011. JPN: *Oppai Heart: Kanojo wa Kedamono Hatsujoki.* Video. DIR: N/C. SCR: PON. DES: Toru Hasegawa. ANI: N/C. MUS: N/C. PRD: Nikihime no Dozeu, A1C. 30 mins. x 2 eps.

A new medicine is invented that makes women develop massive breasts and become so horny that they have to seek sexual release. The onset of pregnancy turns a victim's blood into a vaccine, which leaves Ryuya as a little man with a big job to do, forced to inseminate all his friends and his sister after they accidentally drink the potion.

All the stupid misinformation teenagers have ever spouted about sex has been used to make this porn anime, based on a game by BISHOP. ◐

ORCHID EMBLEM *

1996. JPN: *Rei-Lan Orchid Emblem.* Video. DIR: Hideaki Kushi. SCR: Toshihiko Kudo, Jutaro Nanase. DES: Taro Taki, Shoichiro Sugiura. ANI: Makoto Fujisaki. MUS: Hajime Takakuwa. PRD: Dandelion, Beam Entertainment. 40 mins.

Rei-Lan is a virginal cop on a stakeout of a drug baron when her team is captured and her boyfriend, Doug, is forced to watch while she has wildly enthusiastic sex with crime lord Tojo. Then she stays on Tojo's ship and has more sex with him, naïvely accepting his word that Doug has "gone ashore." The pair get matching tattoos of great mystical force that make it impossible for either of them to attain ecstasy without the other. Then Rei-Lan finds Doug's body in a barrel on the ship, escapes, goes to live with a cute little lesbian, becomes a top martial artist, and plots revenge on Tojo. But the dragon tattoo is too powerful, and she ends up back with him, carrying on her martial arts career as a sideline.

Based on an erotic novel from the same Napoleon imprint that gave us **Erotic Torture Chamber**, you could drive a fleet of very large trucks through the holes in the plot, and the defects are in no way concealed by the average animation. As for the English dub, the pseudonymous actors turn in shamefully wooden work, though Rei-Lan's impressions of a Dalek having an orgasm have some comic value. In their defense, however, given the awful script, any cast picked at random from the greatest classical actors would have struggled to do better. **☯**

ORDIAN

2000. JPN: *Ginso Kido Ordian*. AKA: *Attack Armor Ordian; Silver Knight Ordian; Platinumhugen Ordian*. TV series. DIR: Masami Obari. SCR: Kengo Asai, Hiroyuki Kawasaki. DES: Fumihide Sai, Masami Obari, Tsukasa Kotobuki. ANI: Fumihide Sai. MUS: N/C. PRD: Prime, WOWOW. 25 mins. x 24 eps.
High school student Yu Kananase is crazy about combat, and even though he's never actually fought anything, he's recruited by the International Military Organization as a potential test pilot for new mobile armor. There are other young recruits in the running, and he has to prove he's the best to achieve his dream. Realizing that game-based anime such as his **Fatal Fury** and **Toshinden** were hardly rocket science, director Obari decided to create his own world, inspired by the mismatched design follies and action-heavy plotting of the genre. Sadly the story isn't hugely original; the low quality of Obari's inspiration causes him to throw his creative efforts behind a show that looks like a hundred other robot serials (see **Brave Saga**), whether inspired by computer games or not. However, the character designs have the pointy-nosed charm of **Virus**, albeit without sulky homoerotic pouts.

ORESHURA *

2013. JPN: *Ore no Kanojo to Osana-Najimi ga Shuraba Sugiru*. AKA: *My Girlfriend and My Childhood Friend Fight Too Much*. TV series. DIR: Kanta Kamei. SCR: Tatsuhiko Urahata. DES: Mai Otsuka. ANI: Mai Otsuka, Masaaki Yamano. MUS: Masatomo Ota. PRD: Aniplex,

Softbank, AT-X. 24 mins. x 13 eps.
Embittered child of divorce Eita Kaido throws himself into schoolwork in order to make life better for his ailing childhood friend Chiwa. However, he gains new attention at school from Masuzu Natsukawa, a silver-haired beauty newly returned from time abroad in exotic Sweden. She is just as cynically anti-romantic as him, but determined to throw off male suitors by entering into a sham relationship with Eita, a boy she considers safe. As the beginnings of yet another harem of breathless girls accretes around yet another troubled teen, this anime recycles a series of tropes from anime **Romance and Drama**, based on the novels by Yuji Yuji (so good they named him twice?), illustrated by Ruroo, and presumably read by absolutely nobody who can remember last season's anime shows. At heart, *OreShura* is more open than most about what all these shows are really about—teenagers' desire for acceptance by their peers and popularity at their school, with a hero who eventually decides to dispel his harem by annoying all but one of them, and snagging the last girl standing.

ORGUSS *

1983. JPN: *Chojiku Seiki Orguss*. AKA: *Superdimensional Century Orguss*. TV series. DIR: Noboru Ishiguro, Yasumi Mikamoto, Kazuhito Akiyama, Osamu Nabeshima, Hiroshi Yoshida, Masakazu Iijima. SCR: Kenichi Matsuzaki, Sukehiro Tomita, Hiroshi Nishimura. DES: Haruhiko Mikimoto, Yoshiyuki Yamamoto. ANI: Haruhiko Mikimoto, Akiyoshi Nishimori. MUS: Kentaro Haneda. PRD: Magic Bus, Big West, TBS. 25 mins. x 35 eps. (TV), 30 mins. x 6 eps. (v).
In 2062, Kei is an officer in one of the two forces fighting over the latest scientific-military advance, the Orbital Elevator, and he is sent to blow it up to avoid its capture by the enemy. Caught in the blast of his own time-oscillation bomb, he is flung into an alternate world, one of many created by the explosion. There he meets his daughter, conceived on a one-night stand just before his mission. She's now 18, fighting on the other side in a terrible war, and in love with his best friend. He also has problems with cute but not-at-all-disposable alien girlfriend Mimsy. Her species has to mate before they're 17 or not at all, and her ex-

boyfriend is still very much on the scene. The fate of the patchwork of worlds fragmented by the bomb, with all their diverse citizens and cultures, and the future of all his relationships hangs in the balance. By now Kei must have realized that casual sex brings its own complications.

One of the big SF series of its day, *Orguss* wasn't cut into **Robotech** (with **Macross**, **Mospeada**, and **Southern Cross**) because, coming from a different studio, it couldn't be bought in the same package. Its Mikimoto-designed characters would have fitted perfectly, and its ethos, a giant-robot show in which robots weren't the only item on the agenda, looks forward to **Patlabor**, as well as fitting the prevailing fashion for heavy mecha and heavy emotion.

The series returned straight to video as *Orguss 02* (1993), directed by Fumihiko Takayama, featuring character designs "inspired" by Mikimoto's originals from Toshihiro Kawamoto and a thumping industrial rock soundtrack from Torsten Rasch. Set 200 years after the close of the original series, in a steampunk world not dissimilar to that of **Wings of Honneamise**, the opposing nations of Zafrin and Revillia send archeologists to find "Decimators" (giant robots left over from the original series). Though the technology is half-forgotten, the reconditioned robots are important weapons in a fast-approaching war. Lean, a young officer on the Revillan side, is excavating a Decimator from the seabed when an ambush forces him into the machine to survive the attack and discover piloting skills he never suspected. He is sent behind enemy lines to destroy their Decimators, and he meets a girl (a distant descendant of Mimsy) who holds the key to a secret and is a target for all sides. As the conflict escalates, he learns that his own prince plans to use the most powerful Decimator ever discovered to subjugate the world, while an ancient stranger (the "General," the only surviving character from the original series) seeks to bring peace once more. There are byzantine court machinations—the queen poisons the ruler to allow her general to rule in the name of a retarded prince. There are even echoes of more recent Japanese history, as soldiers are forced to choose between their allegiance to the throne itself and the throne's current occupant. The script, from **SOL BIANCA**'s Mayori Sekijima and **BLUE SIX**'s Hiroshi Yamaguchi, manages to pull strong political overtones out of a story that would have been good enough if it were just a straightforward actioner. A superior giant-robot series.

ORIGIN: SPIRITS OF THE PAST *

2006. JPN: *Gin-iro no Kami no Agito*. AKA: *Silver-Haired Agito*. Movie. DIR: Keiichi Sugiyama. SCR: Umanosuke Iida. DES: Koji Ogata. ANI: Kenji Ando, Mahiro Maeda, Koji Ogata. MUS: Taku Iwasaki. PRD: Gonzo. 94 mins.

Three hundred years into our future, the world has been sharply divided between luxuriant forests and blasted wastelands. The woods are ruled by sentient plants, hostile to humans; the waste areas are home to what's left of the human race. Teenager Agito lives on the border between the two zones, and wanders too close to a forbidden pond, only to discover a young woman, Tuula, who has been sleeping for centuries inside a shining machine. When she was sealed into her shell the world thought itself civilized; her reaction to the changes that took place during her long sleep may threaten the new world order. Gonzo chairman Shoji Murahama claimed that the theme was the importance of the physical, concrete world, as the one thing that can be trusted in our meaningless modern culture. As to how he thought this might be conveyed through the appearance of a volcano on legs, attacking the remnants of humanity and thwarted by turning someone into a mutant tree, your guess is as good as ours.

ORPHANS OF SIMITRA, THE

2008. JPN: *Porphy no Nagai Tabi*. AKA: *Porphy's Long Journey*. TV series. DIR: Tomomi Mochizuki. SCR: Kei Kunii, Maria Yamamoto. DES: Shigeo Akahori, Noboru Sakamoto. ANI: Takafumi Hori. MUS: Moka. PRD: Nippon Animation, Bandai Visual. 25 mins. x 52 eps.

Brother and sister Porphyras (Porphy) and Mina are orphaned by a terrible earthquake in Greece, in the aftermath of World War II. They are separated, and neither knows if the other has survived, but they know their parents' gas station was completely destroyed and there is nothing left for them except an orphanage. Porphy sets out to look for his sister and a new life, while Mina travels with migrant workers. This beautifully crafted series chronicles their adventures, unfolding slowly as the pair travel across war-scarred Europe in the hope of a better tomorrow. Based on *The Orphans of Simitra*, a novel by Paul-Jacques Bonzon, this is the second in the revived **WORLD MASTERPIECE THEATER** series. Bonzon is almost unknown in the English-speaking world but respected in Japan, where his works have been translated by Kozo Sakakibara.

ORPHEN: SCION OF SORCERY *

1998. JPN: *Majutsushi Orphen*. AKA: *Orphen the Magician; Sorcerous Stabber Orphen*. TV series. DIR: Hiroshi Watanabe, Iku Suzuki. SCR: Mayori Sekijima, Masashi Kubota, Yasushi Yamada, Kenichi Araki, Kenichi Kanemaki. DES: Masahiro Aizawa. ANI: Masahiro Aizawa. MUS: Hatake, Sharan Q. PRD: JC Staff, TBS. 25 mins. x 24 eps. (TV1), 25 mins. x 23 eps. (TV2).

Growing up in an orphanage after losing his parents at a very young age, "Orphen" and his two adopted elder sisters, Azalea and Letitia, are selected to study sorcery under the famous Childman at the Tower of Fang. At age 15, Orphen becomes a sorcerer to the Royal Family, but his life is plunged into new difficulties when one of Azalea's spells backfires, transforming her into a monster. Even though he has fallen in love with Azalea, Childman is honor-bound to hunt down the beast that she has become, and Orphen decides to stop him.

Based on a series of over a dozen fantasy novels by Yoshinobu Akita, the *Orphen* TV series begins *in media res* with our hero already a powerful wizard, training a young boy called Majiku. As with **BERSERK**, the majority of the story is told in flashback, as Orphen is threatened by the return of the demon-dragon "Bloody August" only to reveal that it was once the girl he called his sister. Sharing much of the crew of the earlier **SLAYERS**, *Orphen* fortunately lacks much of its predecessor's comedy, opting instead for hard-core fantasy adventure. However, despite a rocking opening theme from pop group Sharan Q, much of the background music sounds like computer-game filler muzak. *Orphen: The Revenge* (1999) is simply the title for the second season. A game based on the series was the first incarnation to reach the U.S., preceding the anime version by several months.

ORUORANE THE CAT PLAYER

1992. JPN: *Nekohiki no Oruorane*. Video. DIR: Mizuho Nishikubo. SCR: Mayori Sekijima. DES: Shunji Murata. ANI: Shunji Murata. MUS: Gen Shiraishi, Kawaji Ishikawa. PRD: JC Staff. 30 mins.

An out-of-work musician mooching round the streets just before Christmas befriends a cat who is fond of good wine. The cat, Iruneido, is one of a feline trio owned by Oruorane, a mysterious old man who can "play" cats as if they were musical instruments. Our hero, always on the lookout for another string to his bow, decides he wants to learn cat-playing for himself. This surreal curio was based on the first novel written by successful writer Baku Yumemakura, who also created **AMON SAGA** and **BATTLE ROYAL HIGH SCHOOL**.

OSHII, MAMORU

1951–. Born in Tokyo's Ota district, Oshii graduated from the education department of Tokyo Gakugei University, where he experimented with his own moviemaking while still a student. With a passionate interest in film (he once claimed to have watched a thousand movies in a single year), he joined the Tatsunoko studio and debuted as an animator on **ONE-HIT KANTA**. Moving to Studio Pierrot (later just Pierrot) in 1980, he met Yoshitaka Amano and Kazunori Ito, who would become frequent collaborators with him on his landmark works of the 1980s and 1990s. Work as a storyboarder and episode director on **URUSEI YATSURA** secured him the chance to direct the *UY* movie *Only You* (1983). His next *UY* movie, *Beautiful Dreamer* (1984), was the first of many Oshii projects to divide critics with surreal imagery and unfocused plotting. He directed **DALLOS** (1983), the first anime made for home video, before going freelance. After **ANGEL'S EGG** (1985) and an abortive association with Hayao Miyazaki and Isao Takahata (whose views on plot and filmmaking seem ever to clash with Oshii's), he began his association with the Headgear collective, which would eventually collaborate on **PATLABOR** (1988). Oshii also began a series of live-action experiments, including *The Red Spectacles* (1987) and *Stray Dog* (1991), which would form the background to **JIN-ROH** (1991), for which he wrote the script. He achieved wider recognition with the superb *Patlabor* movies in the early 1990s, leading directly to his commission to direct **GHOST IN THE SHELL** (1995), for which he pioneered techniques in integrating cel and digital animation.

Oshii's work is characterized by more realistic characters, an aversion to the bright, flat colors of most anime, and an obsession with recreating reality, even down to its mistakes and imperfections, through lens flares, focus-pulls, and other trickery. Owing to the number of his theatrical features released during anime's diaspora abroad, Oshii has become one of the most recognizable directors in the medium, despite a relatively low output in recent years comparable to that of Katsuhiro Otomo. His recent work has included the Polish-language live-action *Avalon* (2001), the *Ghost in the Shell* sequel *Innocence* (2004), and the aerial combat anime **SKY CRAWLERS** (2008). His basset hound, Gabriel, appears in cameo roles in many of his films.

OSHIN

1984. JPN: *Oshin*. Movie. DIR: Eiichi Yamamoto. SCR: Sugako Hashida. DES: Akio Sugino. ANI: Nobuko Yuasa, Keizo Shimizu. MUS: Koichi Sakata. PRD: Sanrio. 122 mins.
Oshin is a young girl who lives in Japan's northern Yamagata Prefecture at the turn of the 20th century. She endures terrible hardships and poverty, eventually being sold into domestic service at the age of eight. Separated from her mother, she escapes from the timber merchant who treats her like a slave and briefly finds happiness working at a rice shop.

An anime spin-off from one of the landmark Japanese live-action melodramas (*DE), *Oshin* focuses on the early episodes of the 300-part 1983 TV drama, reusing both Sugako Hashida's scripts and the voice of child-star Ayako Kobayashi, who played the young Oshin in the TV version. Supposedly based on true stories, cut-and-pasted from hundreds of letters sent to a women's magazine, the live-action *Oshin* was an immense hit all around the world, screened in over 40 countries. After the events of the anime version, the character would continue to struggle for many more

on-screen decades, through two changes of actress. Accused of stealing from the rice shop, she would be cast out, rescued by a deserting soldier, married to a southern weakling, left penniless by the 1923 Tokyo earthquake, abused by her mother-in-law, and widowed by her husband's suicide caused by his shame at supplying Japan's military machine during the Pacific War. Eventually, she would become the rich boss of a grocery business, but that would not be until her 83rd year—the year in which the original series was screened. A different female experience of Yamagata can be seen in **ONLY YESTERDAY**, while a very different dramatization of the years around the 1923 earthquake can be found in **DOOMED MEGALOPOLIS**.

OSOMATSU-KUN

1966. AKA: *Young Sextuplets*. TV series. DIR: Makoto Nagasawa, Hiroyoshi Mitsunobu. SCR: Fujio Akatsuka, Kon Kitagawa. DES: Makoto Nagasawa. ANI: Jiro Murata, Kazuo Komatsubara. MUS: Urahito Watanabe. PRD: Fujio Pro, Studio Zero, Children's Corner, NET. 25 mins. x 57 eps. (TV1), 25 mins. x 86 eps. (TV2).
Osomatsu, Kazumatsu, Karamatsu, Choromatsu, Todomatsu, and Jushimatsu are six identical brothers who are continually making trouble in their town, chasing after the fishmonger's daughter Totoko, and harassing the local snob, Francophile Iyami. Based on a manga in *Shonen Sunday* by Fujio Akatsuka, who also created **GENIUS IDIOT**, *Osomatsu-kun* was derided by the Japanese PTA as "one of the worst programs ever made," and was consequently very popular with children; compare to the modern-day excesses of the similarly criticized **CRAYON SHIN-CHAN**. The issue, supposedly, was that the home-centered adventures presented far more opportunities for "imitable violence" and dangerous situations than more fantastical shows, as the sextuplets clambered out of high windows, rummaged in knife drawers, and played with matches (**LAW AND DISORDER**). It was remade in 1988 by Studio Pierrot into 86 episodes, retaining its former popularity and soon gaining a 20% audience rating.

OTAKU NO VIDEO *

1991. JPN: *1982 Otaku no Video; 1985 Zoku*

Otaku no Video. AKA: *Fan's Video; Thy Video*. Video. DIR: Takeshi Mori. SCR: Toshio Okada. DES: Kenichi Sonoda. ANI: Hidenori Matsubara. MUS: Kohei Tanaka. PRD: Studio Fantasia, Gainax. 50 and 45 mins.
This fan-favorite fantasy by the Gainax studio, which would also produce **WINGS OF HONNEAMISE** and **EVANGELION**, is wry and affectionate, self-parody and wish fulfillment. Inspired by events from the team's own real-life history, it recounts the story of one ordinary young man's efforts to follow the way of the true fan, or "otaku." He loses his girl, his social standing, and his business. His story is counterpointed by a series of spoof live-action "interviews" with **FANDOM** personalities such as a cel thief, a costume freak, and a pornography junkie. In the second video, merged with the first for Western release, our hero, his devotion undimmed by age, indignity, and failure, triumphs over the sordid cynicism of the world through the purity of the fanboy spirit, aspiring to become the Ota-King. An English **TRANSLATION** by Shin Kurokawa and the Ledoux/Yoshida team plus AnimEigo's excellent liner notes provide a wonderful snapshot of an era of fandom and allow us to laugh with and cry for the true otaku.

OTOBOKU: MAIDENS ARE FALLING FOR ME *

2006. JPN: *Otome wa Boku ni Koishiteru*. TV series, video. DIR: Munenori Nawa, Shinya Kawamo. SCR: Katsumi Hasegawa, Masaharu Amiya, Masashi Suzuki, Tomoyoshi Nagai, Michiko Yokote. DES: Noriko Shimazawa, Naoko Kusakabe, Keiichi Sano, Eiji Iwase. ANI: Noriko Shimazawa, Kuniaki Masuda, Takashi Maruyama, Keiichi Sano. MUS: Toshimichi Isoe, Ko Nagakawa. PRD: feel., GANSIS, Hobby Box, Kadokawa, Starchild Records, SILVER LINK, Frontier Works, Media Factory. 24 mins. x 12 eps. (TV), 24 mins. (v1), 25 mins. x 3 eps. (v2).
Mizuho's dying grandfather wants his grandson to graduate from an all-girls' private school because his mother was educated there. Mizuho dutifully cross-dresses with the help of two female friends and enters the school, where he rapidly becomes a much-loved friend and big sister to a horde of girls who firmly believe him to be a girl. You, the viewer, are supposed to find this charming and quirky and to

enjoy seeing the endearing interactions between these unsuspecting girls and our harem hero.

A single video subtitled *Big Boys and Girls Masterpiece Forest Tsunderella (Oki na Shonen Shojo no Sekai Meisaku no Mori—Tsunderella)*, a parody of the CINDERELLA story, spun off it in 2007. It was followed in 2012 by a three-part story, *Otoboku Futari no Elder*, in which another boy, Mizuho's cousin Chihaya, transfers to the same school at his mother's insistence. Chihaya's mother is sending him to the school to avoid his being bullied and hit on by guys. Once again, one of the girls knows his secret and keeps it, and he quickly becomes a much loved older sister and role model for the younger girls. The series is based on a porn video game by Caramel-Box with the porn removed. Unfortunately it's not been replaced by, say, a plot, interesting characters, or good art. Instead it's an amalgam of the girls-school tripe offered up in so many other places, and already very stale.

OTOGI ZOSHI *

2004. AKA: *Story Scroll; Otogi Zoshi: Legend of Magatama*. TV series. DIR: Mizuho Nishikubo, Toshiyasu Kogawa, Hideyo Yamamoto, Jun Takahashi, Junichi Sakata, Yu Ko, Yumi Kamakura, Hisashi Ezura. SCR: Yoshiki Sakurai, Yutaka Omatsu, Junichi Fujisaku, Midori Goto, Hidetoshi Kezuka. DES: Sho-u Tajima, Kazuchika Kise. ANI: Kazuchika Kise. MUS: Hideki Taniuchi, Kenji Kawai. PRD: NTV, VAP, Production I.G, Animax Asia. 23 mins. x 24 eps. (TV), 23 mins. x 2 eps. (TVm).

It is A.D. 972. With the capital Kyoto falling into a mire of corruption and sleaze, and both samurai and priests only looking after their own interests, the imperial court sends champion archer samurai Minamoto no Raiko on a mission to find the Magatama, a legendary gem (see BLUE SEED) reputed to contain the power to bring peace. When he succumbs to disease, his 17-year-old sister Hikaru has to step in to save the family honor and the capital, much as other girls took on men's roles in KAI DOH MARU and YOTODEN.

The story and characters of the first half of the series are loosely based on actual events—Minamoto really was a famous hero of old Kyoto, who slew the demon SHUTENDOJI. His four real-life retainers,

known as the Shitenno or Four Kings after the heavenly guardians of Buddhist mythology, all turn up in the anime to help Hikaru on her quest, and Abe no Seimei, one of Hikaru's advisers, really was a renowned priest and scholar and appears in numerous other anime and manga, as well as the *Onmyoji* movie series (see *DE, as *The Yin-Yang Master*).

The link to reality gets stronger from episode 14 when the action moves to present-day Tokyo for a series of stand-alone episodes, linked to local history and mythology in the style of DOOMED MEGA-LOPOLIS. In a bizarre mythic retelling of the boardinghouse stories of MAISON IKKOKU, Hikaru is recast as a teenage landlady, while many other cast members are reincarnated as some of her strange tenants, most notably Tsuna, a writer on occult subjects. Many anime feature modern incarnations of ancient warriors, but none spend several hours beforehand explaining who was who. Consequently *OZ* has the ancient resonances of SUIKODEN, KARAS, or IKKI TOUSEN, but much less of the confusion of those shows. We have already grown to love these characters in the opening half, making our emotional investment in them considerably stronger. If it is remembered for nothing else, *OZ* will go down in history as a story with a truly unexpected change in direction (compare to FULLMETAL ALCHEMIST), which puts the rehashes and more-of-the-sames of lesser shows to shame. In uniting ancient and modern so firmly and inextricably, it also plays into the urban mythologies made more famous by SPIRITED AWAY and POM POKO. The last two episodes were broadcast separately from the rest, more than two months after episode 24, and consequently are classified as TV specials.

OZ is based on a real story scroll, a 17th-century collection of myths and folktales, some of which predate their written versions by several hundred years. The *Comic Blade* manga spin-off series is not the first modern version; novelist Osamu Dazai rewrote some of the stories for his 1945 compilation released in English as *Crackling Mountain and Other Stories*.

OTOHIME CONNECTION

1991. Video. DIR: Takayuki Goto. SCR: Satoru Akahori. DES: Takayuki Goto. ANI: N/C. MUS:

Jun Watanabe. PRD: Animate Film, ING, Aniplex. 45 mins.

Schoolgirl Yuki finds a part-time job at a TV station, but while this might be glamor enough, she also latches on to handsome, pretty-boy private investigators Nagisa and Michio. Based on the manga in *Bessatsu Shojo Comic* by Kazumi Oya.

OTOME DORI

2012. Video. DIR: Takashi Nishikawa. SCR: N/C. DES: Takashi Nishikawa. ANI: Takashi Nishikawa. MUS: N/C. PRD: 44°C Baidoku, Seven, Mary Jane. 20 mins. x 2 eps.

Average schoolboy Kazuki has an ordinary life. He's happy to continue being friends with school dream girl Otome and looking out for his kid sister. He and Otome aren't a couple but they get on so well that he believes one day they'll just naturally fall into a relationship and maybe even marriage. Then someone sends him a DVD of Otome being raped by revolting old men. As more and more DVDs arrive, each with escalating levels of sexual depravity, he starts to question his own sanity. Is it all a bad dream, or some deep dark plot? Another animated tale of rape and violence was released a year later, based on the same porn manga by Carn. In *Bitch Stealing* (*Mesu Nochi Torare*) a couple of high school sweethearts working on the school festival committee are separated by a guy who plies her with drink and rapes her. We haven't found a director credit yet, but the script is credited to Kaoru Takahashi and it's another 44°C Baidoku/Mary Jane product. NV

OTOMO, KATSUHIRO

1954–. Born in Miyagi Prefecture, Otomo failed to get into the art college of his choice, and went to Tokyo after finishing high school in 1973, where he began selling comics professionally to *Manga Action*. Like many young manga artists, he found occasional work as a commercial designer, and on anime—notably as a designer on Rintaro's HARMAGEDON, which he did not enjoy. However, Otomo's realistic art style was enough to get him promoted off the shop floor and into direction, and he subsequently became one of the prodigies selected for the anthology movies ROBOT CARNIVAL and NEO-TOKYO. His true claim to fame, however, is his own adaptation of his landmark **AKIRA**. A notorious perfectionist, Otomo's creative control caused the production to run far over budget, although its subsequent foreign success has made him one of the posterboys of Japanese animation, particularly with foreign fans. However, in Japan, he retreated from the anime world, making a live-action low-budget movie of his own, *World Apartment Horror* (1990), and restricting himself to minor roles on a select few films—scripting duties on **ROUJIN Z** and **METROPOLIS**, a codirecting credit on **MEMORIES**, and the nebulous "supervising" role on **SPRIGGAN**. It was only with **STEAMBOY** that Otomo returned to full-length anime feature directing, over 15 years after his most famous success. He was subsequently hired to direct a live-action version of **MUSHI-SHI**.

OTSUKA, YASUO

1931–. Born in Shimane Prefecture, he went to Tokyo in 1951 to seek a career as a political cartoonist. Joining Toei Animation in 1957, he worked on a **JOURNEY TO THE WEST** anime and **LITTLE PRINCE AND THE EIGHT-HEADED DRAGON** as a concept artist before becoming a key animator on **LITTLE NORSE PRINCE**, where he was a mentor to Isao Takahata and Hayao Miyazaki. He left the company in 1969 and worked for A Production (now Shin'ei Doga), Nippon Animation, and Telecom. He remained a prominent key animator on works including **THE MOOMINS** and **LUPIN III**, but refused to direct, citing Takahata's disillusionment on *Little Norse Prince*, although own his experiences on **TENGRI THE BOY OF THE STEPPES** cannot have helped. However, in a training capacity, he became one of the guiding lights of Studio Ghibli. The studio honored him in 2004 with a documentary: *Yasuo Otsuka's Joy of Animating*. As the author of several insider memoirs of the anime business, he is also one of the main documentary sources for Japan's animation industry, particularly for the 1960s and 1970s.

OUR HOME'S FOX DEITY *

2008. JPN: *Wagaya no Oinari-sama*. AKA: *Ku: Our Guardian*. TV series. DIR: Yoshiaki Iwasaki. SCR: Reiko Yoshida. DES: Yasunari Nitta. ANI: Fumiaki Kota. MUS: Yasuharu Takanashi. PRD: ZEXCS, Kadokawa, NTT Docomo, Sony PCL, Klockworx. 25 mins. x 24 eps.

Noboru and his younger brother Toru are lured back to their ancestral home by their grandmother. They learn for the first time that their late mother was the clan priestess, and although Noboru is now head of the clan in her place, Toru has inherited her powers, making him the target for a horde of dark spirits. The brothers are assigned a clan bodyguard, a magic-wielding prestess named Ko, and given the help of the clan's powerful guardian deity, fox spirit Kugen. Kugen—Ku for short—is not only extremely cute but seems to bear no grudges for having been sealed inside a rock until needed. So the brothers move Ko and Ku into their household.

So far, so harem (**ROMANCE AND DRAMA**), but then things get more interesting. Ku can switch genders at will and is completely uninterested in romance. And the household the boys move their supernatural pals into isn't a typical adult-free home but one with a real family already in place. Noboru and Toru love their father and he loves them. He's also easygoing enough to accommodate a nervous, unworldly kid like Ko and a temperamental drama junkie like Ku.

The animation is sometimes poor, with the action scenes getting so much of the budget that other movement is at times unconvincing, but the design is pretty. The humor is light and not especially clever, and the plot isn't complex. The violence is minimal and so is the fan service (**ARGOT AND JARGON**)—a single bath scene and a few lingerie-type shots and tasteless but harmless jokes. The whole thing is just sweet. It proves that you can take the boy out of the harem and focus on the other relationships in his life, the ones that really matter: parents, brothers, friends, people he likes and trusts and respects.

The series isn't long enough to accommodate all the characters and situations from Jin Shibamura's original book series, first published in 2004 with illustrations by Eizo Hoden, but it presents the story charmingly.

OURAN HIGH SCHOOL HOST CLUB *

2006. JPN: *Oran Koko Host Club*. TV series. DIR: Takuya Igarashii. SCR: Yoji Enokido. DES: Kumiko Takahashi, Norifumi Nakamura. ANI: Kumiko Takahashi. MUS: Yoshihisa Hirano. PRD: BONES, Hakusensha, NTV, VAP. 24

mins. x 26 eps.

Haruhi is a student at an exclusive high school. She got a scholarship, so she's obviously bright, but her family are so poor she can't even afford a uniform. She just doesn't fit in to this moneyed, unfriendly world. One day she accidentally stumbles upon one of the school's more unusual after-school societies—a host club, where six rich and handsome guys play at being bar-fodder for customers who want to be distracted and amused. When she breaks a valuable vase the club's vice-president suggests she work off the cost: if she becomes a host, and attracts a hundred regular clients, that will wipe out the debt. They'll even get her a decent uniform. The only catch is that they haven't realized she's a girl—and by the time they do, she's such a hit with the Club's clientele that they decide to keep up the charade. As time goes on, fast friendships are forged and everybody realizes that money can't buy you love.

Bisco Hattori's 2003 manga had a long and successful run, 18 collected volumes in seven years, turning into a media franchise with a live-action movie and TV series, a mobile phone drama, and the usual torrent of merchandise. The anime series has the great good sense not to outstay its welcome. It's an insubstantial cockleshell full of froth and bubble, something both Shakespeare and Noel Coward would have recognized and felt quite at home with—a pleasant after-dinner diversion, like a visit to a host club or a drag cabaret.

With some of the creative team from **UTENA** onboard, it's no surprise that the design and color palette are exquisitely overdone, packed with visual nudges and winks and all in the best possible taste. The liberal use of parody saves the show from *Utena*'s tendency to portentousness. Nothing is serious, everything is postmodern, the fourth wall exists only to be demolished, and tropes and clichés are worn with knowing pride. This is absolutely not a series to watch for its emotional significance and character development. It knows that, and it isn't ashamed, although this confidence was not reflected in foreign sales. In the U.K., it was one of the worst-selling anime on record.

OUTBREAK COMPANY *

2013. JPN: *Outbreak Company: Moeru Shinryakusha*. AKA: *Outbreak Company: Fanboy Invader*. TV series. DIR: Kei Oikawa. SCR: Naruhisa Arakawa. DES: Takashi Mamezuka. ANI: Kosuke Murayama, Kuniaki Masuda, Masakazu Yamazaki, Yumi Shimizu. MUS: Keiji Inai. PRD: feel, Dax, Kodansha, Pony Canyon, TBS. 24 mins. x 12 eps.

Rejected by his childhood friend when he tries to become her boyfriend (ROMANCE AND DRAMA), Shinichi Kano loses himself in FANDOM, living a listless life as a consumer of anime, manga, and games. He is, then, fortunate indeed to discover that there is a job that only he can do, functioning as a cultural ambassador to a parallel universe where the Japanese government hopes to offload fannish products and other items from Earth. The Eldant Empire is a generic fantasy realm (FANTASY AND FAIRY TALES) with its own political problems, intrigues, and social ills (including slavery), plunging Shinichi into a heady combination of culture shock and fanboy glee.

In 2005, the Japanese prime minister Taro Aso began the opening gambit of a long-term effort to push "Cool Japan" at the rest of the world, and to recognize Japanese intellectual property, particularly cultural items like films and anime, as major exports. Not all these initiatives worked out, and some manifested as little more than pseudomanga competitions at Japanese embassies and the occasional martial arts demonstration. Others have spearheaded Japanese culture into many foreign territories, and, presumably, inspired Ichiro Sakaki to write the seven-volume book series on which this anime is based. Like the protagonists of EL HAZARD, Shinichi exults in being able to experience a fantasy realm for real, but also comes to appreciate the many comforts of home that he once ignored. His blinkered but enthusiastic grapplings with an alien culture reflect many aspects of the Japanese overseas experience, as well as the underlying absurdity of real-world soft power initiatives—Taro Aso wanted to make Japan rich by selling us anime like this, an idea that is both ridiculous and strangely endearing.

OUTLANDERS *

1986. JPN: *Outlanders*. Video. DIR: Katsuhisa Yamada. SCR: Kenji Terada. DES: Hiroshi Hamazaki. ANI: Hiroshi Hamazaki. MUS: Kei Wakakusa. PRD: Tatsunoko. 48 mins.

Earth is invaded by the galaxy-spanning Santovasku Empire in its organic spaceships. Princess Kahm first appears slicing up unsuspecting Earthmen as part of her imperial father's great invasion plan; then she falls into the arms of photographer Tetsuya and decides to save him from the destruction that the empire has planned for the rest of humankind. This puts both lovers and their friends in serious danger from Kahm's conquest-mad daddy and his nasty minions. Based on Johji Manabe's 1985 manga for Hakusensha, with affectionate nods to *Star Wars* and URUSEI YATSURA, the story has considerable charm despite a fairly high violence quotient. Manabe has done little except repeat it since (see RAI and CAPRICORN), but this doesn't detract from the original. ⓃⓋ

OUTLAW STAR *

1998. JPN: *Seiho Bukyo Outlaw Star*. AKA: *Stellar Chivalry Outlaw Star*. TV series. DIR: Mitsuru Hongo. SCR: Katsuhiko Chiba. DES: Takuya Saito, Junya Ishigaki. ANI: Takuya Saito, Hiroyuki Hataike. MUS: Ko Otani. PRD: Sunrise, Sotsu, TV Tokyo. 25 mins. x 26 eps.

Hajime Yadate (Sunrise's name for its in-house idea machine) and Takehiko Ito (ANGEL LINKS) adapted an alternate future from Ito's 1988 *Space Hero Tales* manga for the late-night slot on TV Tokyo. A loose and unstable galactic alliance is trying to bring order to the chaos of the expanding space frontier. Hot Ice Hilda is on the wrong side of the law, on the run, in disguise, and in search of a fabulous treasure when she runs across Gene Starwind, a Han Solo wannabe running a rather sleazy, jack-of-all-trades business with his 11-year-old "brother," Jim Hawking, who is definitely the brains of the outfit. Gene's career is severely hampered by space phobia; as a child he watched his father die in space, and by a weird coincidence he thinks one of the gangs chasing Hilda is responsible. Hilda hires the duo to help her with a nebulous "repair job," but before long they've gotten aboard a hidden prototype spaceship and its cybernetically engineered living navigation computer, a cute girl named Melfina. Then Hilda gets killed and Gene & Co. suddenly have more enemies than they ever expected. The Outlaw Star and Melfina are targets for every powerful group in the galaxy; it's widely believed that, aside from the value of the ship itself, it contains clues that will lead to the fabled treasure known as Galactic Leyline (refer to SOL BIANCA). As they struggle to survive, they run into comic tropes like Suzuka, a deadly Japanese assassin who's so friendly she joins the crew, and Aisha, a cat-girl who does likewise. The writers rely on such tropes to liven up a plot whose guidance is mostly inertial. Arms mounted on the "grappler" ships turn space combat into something more like a mechanized wrestling match, and, while there are some good flashes of humor (like the over-the-top opening narrations), this is no competition for COWBOY BEBOP in terms of style, content, or execution. When screened on the Cartoon Network, the anime was edited for nudity, violence, gambling, drinking, and lechery because those things don't happen in America.

OUTSIDE THE LAW

1969. JPN: *Roppo Yabure-kun*. AKA: *Yabure Roppo*. TV series. DIR: Eiji Okabe. SCR: Masaki Tsuji, Ichiro Wakabayashi, Haruya Yamazaki, Yoshiaki Yoshida, Hideko Yoshida, Tsunehisa Ito, Takashi Hayakawa, Shigeru Omachi, Seiji Matsuoka, Kinzo Okamoto. DES: N/C. ANI: Takeo Kitahara. MUS: Yasuhiro Koyama. PRD: Tokyo Movie Shinsha, NTV. 5 mins. x 110 eps.

Yabure Roppo is a perfectly average salaryman, remarkable only for his incredible run of bad luck—comparable only to that of Ataru Moroboshi in URUSEI YATSURA. He becomes the victim of a series of outrageous scams and accidents, many based on modern urban myths. A girl he sees socially suddenly demands that he marry her. A conman rips him off, and then attempts to blackmail him. He agrees to help out a friend by cosigning a contract, only to discover that his friend has absconded and he is now responsible for the debt. He endures all this torment in order to instruct the viewers on thorny problems within modern Japanese civil law, based on an idea by Sen Saga, who became a mystery novelist after 30 years as a lawyer. Compare to LAW OF DIVORCE AND INHERITANCE.

Mr. Roppo gets his name from two

Japanese concepts: *Happo Yabure*, meaning "without preventions," and *Roppo Zensho*, a "compendium of laws." His name thus translates as something like Outside the Law, with the emphasis on its inability to protect him, rather than criminal intent.

OVER DRIVE

2007. TV series. DIR: Takao Kato. SCR: Katsuhiko Koike. DES: Yuichi Oka, Keito Watanabe. ANI: Sunao Chikaoka. MUS: Ko Otani. PRD: Xebec, Pony Canyon. 25 mins. x 26 eps.
Fifteen-year-old Mikoto has a routine life and is bullied and picked on at school, until the girl he fancies suggests he might take up cycling. He's been scared of bikes since a childhood accident, but he really wants to impress her, so after a bit of private practice to get over his initial clumsiness, he joins the school cycle club. To everyone's surprise, he turns out to be a natural sprint cyclist with real potential. Even more surprising, he starts to love cycling for its own sake. Based on Tsuyoshi Yasuda's 2005 manga, the anime follows its format in that most of the story happens in flashback while Mikoto rides in the Tour de France. So the suspense of wondering if the hero will achieve his goal is dead from the start—a technique Isao Takahata used in GRAVE OF THE FIREFLIES, and one that takes some confidence for a director to pull off. Kato manages this with great charm, making his characters so engaging that their journey really does matter more than the destination. Compare to NASU: SUMMER IN ANDALUSIA.

OVERMAN KING GAINER *

2002. TV series. DIR: Yoshiyuki Tomino. SCR: Ichiro Okochi. DES: Kenichi Yoshida, Kinu Nishimura, Yoshihiro Nakamura, Akira Yasuda, Kimitoshi Yamane. ANI: Kenichi Yoshida. MUS: Kohei Tanaka. PRD: Bandai, Sunrise, WOWOW. 25 mins. x 26 eps.
In a distant future, mankind has wrecked the Earth's environment and retreated to domed cities, leaving the ecosystem to take its chances. The cities are run and supplied by private corporations, overseen by a worldwide authority based in London, but not everyone believes that these corporations are working for the public good. In any event, they have captive markets—any movement outside the cities must be authorized, and any unauthorized

excursions are severely punished—compare to similar set-ups in THE BIG O and HEAT GUY J. Teenage gamer Gainer Sanga is arrested in the Siberian dome on suspicion of being involved with the Exodus movement, a nebulous group wanting to leave the confines of the domes in search of a better life. In prison he meets mercenary Gain Bijou, and together they commandeer an Overman robot, take the daughter of the city's duke hostage, and lead an exodus out of the city under cover of a festival headlined by idol singer Meeya Laujin. Their destination is the fabled land of Yapan.

Gainer was such a hotshot at virtual combat that he was known in gaming circles as "King Gainer"—now he has to transfer his skills to the real world as he defends the group of travelers from the elite Saint Regan squad sent from London to stop them and the troops of the Siberian Railway.

Director Tomino takes his basic GUNDAM mix—gifted but disengaged young pilot, political conflict, and struggle for a promised land—and throws in elements from MACROSS: rakish big brother figure, idol singer, journey in constant jeopardy. Unfortunately, he also includes some of today's fashionable high school romance elements. Several members of Gainer's high school escaping the city with him is plausible enough, but stretches credibility to its limits when they continue classes while on the run and under fire. Tomino has had characters switch sides in earlier work, but having the enemy commander not only switch sides but also become the hero's teacher and roommate is a definite postmodern touch. The statutory cute child, Princess Ana, has statutory cute pets, in this case three ferrets. Although these unnecessary refinements don't slow things down too much, it seems a pity that the man who has led the field in robot anime with a serious human dimension for so long should borrow from less creative minds than his own to satisfy an industry which is increasingly less discerning and less interested in originality.

OVERSEAS DISTRIBUTION AND PIRACY

Although there was some international contact among filmmakers in the days of

EARLY ANIME, Japanese animation made its first major steps abroad after the Second World War. Toei Animation became involved at an early stage as part of a long-term company policy to make movies suitable for the export market. Its first feature film, PANDA AND THE MAGIC SERPENT, was a prizewinner at the 1959 Venice Film festival. It was followed by Osamu Tezuka's first feature *Alakazam the Great* (see JOURNEY TO THE WEST), in a dubbed version that had great longevity.

Television anime began its export drive early, with THE NEW ADVENTURES OF PINOCCHIO, made in Japan for American clients in 1961, and ASTRO BOY, screened in America mere months after its Japanese premiere in 1963. Few American viewers realized they were watching a Japanese show, and were indeed encouraged not to, through CENSORSHIP AND LOCALIZATION. Several more anime series were sold to U.S. TV in the 1960s—8TH MAN, GIGANTOR, PRINCE PLANET, MARINE BOY, KIMBA THE WHITE LION, SPEED RACER, and THE AMAZING THREE. Many were also screened in other English-speaking territories such as Australia and South Africa, although of all these early TV translations, only *Marine Boy* made it to Britain. The same period saw Japanese animators from the Topcraft studio and others working on "American" cartoons for Rankin/Bass. The 1970s saw only two major U.S. TV screenings of openly "Japanese" works, but STAR BLAZERS and BATTLE OF THE PLANETS achieved something new—winning fans in high schools and colleges all over the country.

Anime enjoyed similar paths to success in Europe. French TV screened children's series from the early 1970s, some of which later reappeared in North America on French-speaking channels in Canada. *Kimba the White Lion* aired in 1972 as *Le Roi Leo*, with PRINCESS KNIGHT (*Prince Saphir*) shown two years later alongside Italian-Japanese coproduction CALIMERO. Movies were also screened on television and theatrically, starting with the 1969 Toei PUSS IN BOOTS (*Le Chat Botté*) in 1978; but the major event in French anime history was the screening of GRANDIZER (*Goldorak*) in 1978. Summer vacation was considered a wasteland for children's programming in France, but by the time the schools reopened in September Go Nagai's robot show was a word-of-mouth hit, believed by some critics to have secured an audience share approaching 100%, since only children were presumed to be watching at that time of day. The series is still selling strongly today; Toei found it necessary to issue writs against pirate *Goldorak* DVD releases across French-speaking Europe in 2004.

Goldorak was part of an anime viewing schedule which consisted for the most part of retold fairy tales and innocuous series: **CANDY CANDY** (as *Candy*) made her French debut just two months after Nagai's epic, but was followed in 1979 by **CAPTAIN HARLOCK** (*Albator, le Corsaire de l'Espace*) on Antenne 2, and *Battle of the Planets* (*La Bataille des Planetes*) on TF1. Meanwhile, *Goldorak* was dubbed into Spanish as *Goldrake* and into Arabic as *Grandizer*. Go Nagai's giant robot shows became a staple of Spanish TV and created a strong demand for preteen and teenage animated shows, while in Italy they were so successful that Nagai set up an Italian company, Dynamic Italia, to manage his work there.

In 1979, *Spectreman* (*DE) became the first Japanese live-action show to hit French television, with Haim Saban and Shuki Levy on the crew list—15 years later, they would launch the *Mighty Morphin' Power Rangers* (*DE). Following on from **CALIMERO**, French studio DIC collaborated on **ULYSSES 31** and **MYSTERIOUS CITIES OF GOLD** (*Les Mysterieuses Cités d'Or*). Nippon Animation's coproduction with Spain's BRB International, **AROUND THE WORLD IN 80 DAYS** (*Le Tour de Monde en 80 Jours*), was shown in both France and Spain. The same studio's coproduction with Apollo Films, **ALICE IN WONDERLAND**, was screened in Europe in 1985, as was the French release of the Topcraft/Rankin/Bass fantasy *The Last Unicorn* (*La Derniere Licorne*). That year also saw the Western debut of *Rainbow Brite*, DIC's collaboration with U.S. and Japanese studios.

Classics of world literature have always attracted Japanese audiences, and created an interesting rebound market in which children watch their culture's stories, interpreted by foreign artists, then redubbed into their native tongues. **LITTLE EL CID** was shown in Spain and France in 1981, with **LES MISÉRABLES** in France the same year. Monkey Punch's **LUPIN III**

has enjoyed huge success in France and Italy since 1985, and **ROSE OF VERSAILLES** (*Lady Oscar*) sold the French Revolution back to France. Scandinavian stories have charmed European children in Japanese versions, including **NILS' MYSTERIOUS JOURNEY** (European debut 1983) and **AUNTY SPOON** (European debut 1984). Less success awaited in Finland, where **MOOMINS** met with criticism from its original author, and **KATRI THE MILKMAID**, based on a Finnish children's book, was never broadcast at all. Meanwhile, Hayao Miyazaki's fascination with all things exotically European, including Italian airplanes, Scandinavian cities, Welsh miners, and Welsh writers, has helped to make his work popular across the continent.

Anime also enjoyed success across East Asia, even in countries such as South Korea where Japanese associations and imports were discouraged. **DORAEMON** in particular became a local icon in Korea and Taiwan. Indonesian broadcasters feigned a complete lack of interest in Japanese television programming, only to find themselves screening it by proxy when they bought the supposedly "American" serials of *Robotech* and *G-Force*. Anime's popularity in East Asia also led to a rise in the piracy of animated titles; this was particularly prevalent in Taiwan, which was not a member of the United Nations, and hence not a signatory to several important copyright conventions. Pirate editions of both anime and manga built entire publishing industries in many East Asian countries, in a boom that ironically worked to the advantage of the Japanese. In Korea, where Japanese imports were banned until the 1990s, since anime and manga did not officially exist, they were not subjected to strict government censorship. For transgressive Korean youths, the best way to annoy their parents was to become an anime or manga fan. In other parts of Asia, most notably Taiwan and Hong Kong, the tsunami of cheap, unlicensed Japanese material, springing into the market as fully formed serials and tie-in comic stories, often with merchandise and gaming spin-offs already present, undercut and outperformed many local artists, stifling native talent and leaving local comics and animation industries far behind the Japanese. Although there are numerous

local talents and creators today, many East Asian creators find themselves pressured or steered into drawing "pseudomanga" in imitation of the now-legal Japanese titles which so dominate the medium.

In the 1980s, as the exponential expansion of TV channels created still more demand for cheap programming, American television saw Go Nagai's 1972 hit **MAZINGER Z** (screened in 1985 as *TranZor Z*) and **QUEEN OF A THOUSAND YEARS.** Two hybrid series were created by splicing several entirely unrelated Japanese originals into a new American entity. **FORCE FIVE** (1980) and **ROBOTECH** (1985) not only filled syndication schedules but also sold robot toys to American boys with great success.

Television before the general availability of the home video recorder had a captive audience. Viewers were unable to time-shift in order to follow their favorite programs, a limitation networks could exploit with repeat showings. Just as the video recorder put an end to cinema theater rescreenings of "favorite" anime episodes in Japan, it also made it possible for Japanese television to travel to America without the need to pass through a broadcaster. Legend has it that anime first entered America through science fiction **FANDOM** on the east and west coasts, where a large Japanese immigrant community, anime broadcasts on Japanese-language local television, and a strong science fiction audience combined to make convention screenings, with and without translations, a possibility. Behind the scenes, certain anime companies were active collaborators in this supposed "grassroots" movement. Some of the first convention screenings used VCR or even 16mm prints donated by Japanese agents.

The rise of the household VCR brought a new market into being, although some might argue that the combination of videocassette and personal computer was a deadly genie that the anime industry has been unable to stuff back into its bottle. Thanks to the Amiga (and much later to PCs and Macintoshes), it was now possible to add amateur subtitles, or "fansubs," to anime videos, rendered easier in America than in Europe through the fact that Japan and the U.S. shared the NTSC video format. Fansubs were soon circulating unofficially and helping to build demand for

Japanese animation in cult TV circles.

The 1990s saw the return in syndication of serials first screened in the previous three decades, most notably the early morning screening of *Speed Racer* on MTV, which would in turn lead to a prominent *Speed Racer* poster seen on the wall of the apartment in the sitcom *Friends*. Also screened in 1995 were *Battle of the Planets* (in new variants) and **RONIN WARRIORS**, a test for later screenings of **DRAGON BALL** and **SAILOR MOON** with the newer **TEKNO-MAN**. This did not result in spectacular ratings, but American licensing company Funimation persevered with a further series, **DRAGON BALL Z**. A new Cartoon Network slot, Toonami, aired in March 1997 bringing back old U.S. and Japanese shows like *Thundercats* and **VOLTRON**, and 1998 saw the arrival in America of Nintendo's latest Japanese merchandising gambit, **POKÉMON**. **POKÉMON** was followed by **DIGIMON** and **MONSTER RANCHER**, setting the scene for a new millennium of exploitation, not merely through television, but through merchandising and tie-ins, in imitation of the model already in place in Japan.

At first traded via the convention circuit and the existing network of anime fan clubs, copies of anime found even wider circulation as Americans accessed the Internet and created an unregulated, fast-moving market in information and goods. At a time in the 1990s when there might have been only 100 anime fans per *state*, Internet access helped establish virtual communities in order to encourage interest in the medium. As a predominantly young, tech-savvy interest group, many with access to computers at home or college, anime fans were also able to use the Internet for the preparation and distribution of fansubs in unprecedented quantities. The prevalence of unlicensed translations has been a subject of unending debate within the American anime business—many industry employees admit to an early interest fostered by fansubs and argue that fansubs often function as free samples that encourage a later purchase or rental. However, fansubbing is also undeniably open to extreme abuse, and regardless of the motives of many fansubbers to popularize a medium they love, the phenomenon creates ready-made materials for video pirates prepared to sell fansubs

for personal profit. Consequently, what was once deemed a harmless activity not unlike borrowing a book from a friend, has escalated into a multimillion-dollar copyright infringement industry, and one which has periodically led companies to litigate against persistent offenders. The arrival of BitTorrent and other peer-to-peer file-sharing systems has made it even easier to obtain anime without paying for it.

FANDOM itself, legal, illegal, or in the gray area of fansubbing (which is illegal but often overlooked), remains an influential informal distribution channel for anime. With weekend attendances often climbing into five figures, the convention circuit has formed its own micro-culture, effectively unionizing consumers. Some anime companies, particularly those whose sales rely on titles popular only in fandom rather than with the general public, often present a friendly brand identity at conventions by sending representatives to announce new releases and deflect criticism. Such trips can make or break smaller releases—they would have a negligible effect on a major distributor, like Buena Vista, but a thousand fans reaching for their wallets in a single weekend can make the difference between profit and a loss for titles aimed at the otaku market. The precise power of fandom is a paradox— some argue that fandom is small and insignificant, and that, for example, fansubbing consequently represents a negligible loss in business when set against its promotional value. Others claim that fandom's power is so great that companies should obey its every (contradictory) whim, which would suggest that fansubbing and Internet downloading represent a significant danger to anime's increased profitability abroad, and hence the future of the foreign language anime business itself. Since piracy is by its very nature shadowy, it is difficult to determine what difference it makes to the anime business. An experiment in late 2009 and early 2010, digitally fingerprinting 21 new anime titles and tracking their progress through informal distribution channels, revealed that the objects were copied 25,000 times and viewed 28.7 *million* times, suggesting that the potential overseas market for anime may be up to 20 to 30 times larger than it

currently is, so long as nobody has to pay for anything. The question of how many of these viewers would or could be transformed into paying customers remains a matter of prime discussion within the anime industry.

As anime moves into its seventh decade in the U.S., science fiction and fantasy remain the dominant genres, with animated pornography gaining a higher profile than in its home market. A Japanese origin is no longer hidden from viewers, but boldly (sometimes falsely) proclaimed, particularly in cases where American networks are involved directly with a Japanese studio. There is also a relatively small theatrical market, which was bolstered when **SPIRITED AWAY** won the Oscar for Best Feature Animation in 2002, but which remains a mere fraction of the kind of numbers commanded by Hollywood big-hitters such as Pixar and DreamWorks.

As we write in 2014, anime is screened regularly on TV and sold for home viewing not just in America but also in every part of Europe, including its Eastern borders: Poland and Russia have embraced Japanese cartoons with as much enthusiasm as their Western neighbors. With foreign companies now eagerly buying the rights to new anime, still often before they are even made, the new frontier for the Japanese industry is now China, a vast territory of one billion potential fans on the cusp of a digital switchover, many already acquainted with the medium through viewings of Sino-friendly anime like **RANMA ½** and **CHINA NUMBER ONE**. However, anime is currently largely absent from Chinese television, with import quotas now strictly legislating even against coproductions. **NARUTO** and **CONAN THE BOY DETECTIVE** might win slots among the paltry 35 foreign films permitted annually in Chinese theaters, but viewing their TV incarnations is often possible only through access to pirated material.

Broadcasting's increasing reliance on direct downloads and the Internet has presented many anime companies with the opportunity to cut out numerous middlemen. The future of anime may well rest on hard drives and mobile phones, with foreign language versions released simultaneously (or as near as makes no difference, in the case of **KUROKAMI THE**

ANIMATION) in order to minimize the potential losses through fansubbing and piracy. This, however, creates new issues in overseas distribution: the potential for increased revenue from direct sales may well be offset by the increased headache caused by the loss of the echelon of foreign middlemen, forcing anime's Japanese producers to confront issues such as localization in multiple languages or the expense and clearances of music rights in multiple territories. While a global day-date release for an anime is theoretically possible, the concerns of multiple cultures, multiple clearances, and multiple translations would be sure to radically skew it away from the anime it might otherwise have been if initially aimed solely at the Japanese market.

OYO MY HUGGABLE CAT

1984. JPN: *Oyoneko Bunyan*. TV series. DIR: Hiroshi Sasakawa, Hiroshi Fujioka, Kenjiro Yoshida, Teruo Kogure, Katsumi Kosuga. SCR: Hiroshi Kaneko, Hideki Sonoda, Tsunehisa Ito, Hideo Takayashiki, Yoshio Urasawa, Miho Maruo, Hiroko Naka. DES: Misako Ichikawa. ANI: Shinichi Suzuki. MUS: Takeo Watanabe. PRD: Shinei, TV Asahi. 25 mins. x 31 eps.

The comical adventures of bad-tempered fat cat Oyoyo who charms his idiot human family but fights an ongoing battle with other neighborhood pets. Based on the manga *Mr. Happy* (*Shiawase-san*) by Misako Ichikawa (no relation to **MISTER HAPPY**), serialized in several magazines, including *Shojo* and *Ciao*. Unmatched in anime for feline humor until **WHAT'S MICHAEL?** appeared a year later.

OZ

1992. Video. DIR: Katsuhisa Yamada. SCR: Mami Watanabe. DES: Toyomi Sugiyama. ANI: Toyomi Sugiyama. MUS: Yoichiro Yoshikawa. PRD: Madhouse. 35 mins. x 2 eps.

A nuclear war kills 60% of humanity and splits the U.S. into six warring states. By 2021, a legend has grown amid the hunger, chaos, and devastation—the fabled city of Oz, where high technology has survived to serve humankind, and hunger and war are unknown. Scientist Felicia sets out to find Oz with mercenary Muto and Droid #1019. At the end of the road they find a madman dreaming of world dominion in a military base with enough firepower to create a new nightmare for the world. Natsumi Itsuki's original 1988 manga in *Comic Lala* was based very loosely on **THE WIZARD OF OZ** but owed a greater debt to the same studio's **WIND OF AMNESIA** in this anime adaptation. For reasons known only to the distributor, the *Oz* soundtrack was released in the U.K., though the anime has never been translated.

OZEKI, MASAYUKI

1950–. Joined Studio Mates in 1970 to work on **COWBOY ISAMU**, before going freelance. His directorial debut was the **LUPIN III** "movie" *The Fuma Conspiracy* (1987).

OZMA *

2012. TV series. DIR: Ryosuke Takahashi, Takahiro Ikezoe. SCR: Junki Takegami. DES: Kenji Fujisaki, Kimimichi Nanko, Hideyuki Matsumoto, Keiichi Eda, Nao Kadoguchi, Kunihiko Inaba. ANI: Kenji Fujisaki, Kimimichi Nanko. MUS: Kosuke Yamashita. PRD: Gonzo, LandQ Studios, Equity Pictures Japan, Planet Entertainment, Pony Canyon, Slowcurve Co., Ltd., Viki, WOWOW. 23 mins. x 6 eps.

The far future: Earth is desolate, devastated by abnormal solar activity with very little water. Most of the planet is covered in deep seas of sand. In these deserts, according to legend, lives a great creature called Ozma, a sand whale. The survivors of humanity have split into two opposing ideological factions: the Children of Theseus, created by cloning and putting their faith in technology, and the Natura, who believe in reproducing the old-fashioned way. Sam Coyne is hunting Ozma, the cause of his brother's disappearance, when he sees a young woman in trouble. She's being chased by Theseus Army tanks. He rescues her, helped by the sudden appearance of Ozma, and they get safely back to the Natura sand submersible Baldanos, but the Theseus Army won't give up the chase. Helping out a damsel in distress has got Sam and his friends into a situation they didn't expect, and the fate of the world hangs in the balance.

When Leiji Matsumoto dreams, he dreams big. And the roots of his dreams go far outside anime: here his passion for World War II, huge submerged ships, impossible odds, motorbikes, and willowy blondes merge with another take on *Moby Dick* (**MOBY DICK IN SPACE**) to create a world that's at once familiar and intriguing. Familiar, because Matsumoto, a fan of Osamu Tezuka's work from early childhood, has followed his mentor in using the same character set in the same roles for decades; intriguing because the premise of a world with great red oceans of sand through which ships and creatures swim is beautiful. But this is too big a dream for the time available. Matsumoto's characters are primarily archetypes running along predictable tracks, but even those tracks are truncated because there isn't time to develop anything. The plot has little time or space to expand into the epic it could have been, with a couple of nice plot twists underplayed and no room to play with the political, ecological, and evolutionary subtexts.

Apparently, this script was 30 years in the making, one of Matsumoto's long-shelved projects finally brought to fruition. Chief director Takahashi is one of the legends of robot anime, renowned for "real robot" shows such as **VOTOMS**. Writer Takegami provided the story for the complex, intriguing **BIRTH**. But with far too much plot and far too many ideas to cram into the time they have, this remains Matsumoto's shorthand series; all his big ideas, themes, and characters are scribbled down, every corner is stuffed, and there's no room to do anything much with any of it. If only there had been another 20 episodes, we might have had another **CAPTAIN HARLOCK**.

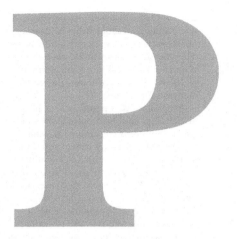

P.I.: PERVERSE INVESTIGATIONS *

2003. JPN: *Sei Sai*. AKA: *Sex Judge*. Video. DIR: Kanzaburo Oda. SCR: Shinji Rannai. DES: Ryosuke Morimura. ANI: Ryosuke Morimura. MUS: Yoshi. PRD: YOUC, Digital Works (Vanilla Series). 30 mins. x 2 eps.

When much-loved schoolteacher Yuko falls from the roof under suspicious circumstances, four of her favorite pupils form a team to investigate. Their most important clue is her diary, which shows meetings scheduled with seven female students on the night of her death. The boys duly start hunting for further clues among the girls and are prepared to use any methods at their disposal, soon transforming this anime into the usual cavalcade of rape and abuse, particularly over at the photography club and the swimming club. The U.S. release cunningly found a title and font that would recall the TV series *C.S.I.: Crime Scene Investigation*. Part of the VANILLA SERIES. ●◐Ⓥ

PACHISLO KIZOKU GIN

2001. JPN: *Pachisuro Kizoku Gin*. AKA: *Pachinko Slot Aristocrat Gin*. TV series. DIR: Hidehito Ueda. SCR: Hiroyuki Hoshiyama, Tsunehisa Ito. DES: Junichi Hayama. ANI: N/C. MUS: N/C. PRD: A Line, Atlas, Fuji TV. 25 mins. x 23 eps.

University student Ginya Otonashi writes articles for a pachinko magazine, but would really prefer to be a famous novelist. He discovers a new and unexpected skill when he finds himself taking part in a secret pachinko contest run by the "Slotium" pachinko consortium. The authors suspect that a "Pachislo Aristocrat" is something

similar to a "Pinball Wizard," but there is no direct connection to Ken Russell's rock musical *Tommy* (1975), which was released in Japan under its original title. The name *Gin*, however, literally means "silver," as in the silver balls of both pursuits.

PACIFIC ANIMATION CORPORATION

A short-lived animation company calved from the foundering Topcraft in the early 1980s; other staff members went off to form the core of what would eventually become Studio Ghibli. PAC's most noticeable work was on the original "American" series of *Thundercats* (THUNDERCATS). Its other works-for-hire for the American market included the TV movie *The Life and Adventures of Santa Claus* (1985), *SilverHawks* (1986), and *The Comic Strip* (1987). The company was bought by Disney in 1988, and renamed Walt Disney Animation Japan (q.v.), under Motoyoshi Tokunaga (formerly of Tokyo Movie Shinsha), in which capacity it animated action sequences for numerous straight-to-video Disney sequels in the 1990s and *The Tigger Movie* (2000).

PALE COCOON

2005. Video. DIR: Yasuhiro Yoshiura. SCR: Yasuhiro Yoshiura. DES: Yasuhiro Yoshiura. ANI: Yasuhiro Yoshiura. MUS: Toru Okada. PRD: Studio Rikka. 23 mins.

In a claustrophobic future world Ura reconstructs old images and archives from the past. His latest project turns out to be a music video, whose singer offers up a message from the Moon, where she has just arrived, to dwellers on "the rust-cov-

ered Earth." Realizing that the location of the recording seems familiar, the archivist resolves to climb through the abandoned upper levels of his underground home to see for himself, in an interesting, albeit derivative, sci-fi short. Made over a two-year period, and largely the work of a single creator, *Pale Cocoon*'s clearest debt is to VOICES FROM A DISTANT STAR, whose attitude, length, and tone it often mirrors. As with so many modern "homebrew" anime, it lifts plot elements from earlier fan favorites—in this case the COWBOY BEBOP episode "Speak Like a Child" and the underlying conceit of MEGAZONE 23. A singer's trip to the Moon is also the starting point of A.LI.CE, although this is probably a coincidence. The final moment refers, perhaps inadvertently, to the closing shot of the first-ever straight-to-video anime, Mamoru Oshii's DALLOS. *Pale Cocoon* is also a creation of its time—its action reflects the sedentary computer-bound life of modern teenagers (and of modern animators!), its setting a world in environmental crisis, and its ending, a note of mournful hope, with a noninterventionist tone familiar from many other ecological anime. The creator's website gives a 2005 copyright date, although the DVD only appeared in Japanese stores in the early weeks of 2006. ●◐Ⓥ

PANDA AND THE MAGIC SERPENT *

1958. JPN: *Hakujaden*. AKA: *Legend of the White Serpent; Tale of the White Serpent; The White Snake Enchantress*. Movie. DIR: Taiji Yabushita. SCR: Taiji Yabushita, Soichi Yashiro. DES: Akira Daikuhara, Yasuji Mori.

ANI: Yasuo Otsuka, Kazuko Nakamura, Reiko Okuyama, Taku Sugiyama, Gisaburo Sugii. MUS: Masayoshi Ikeda. PRD: Toei. 78 mins.

The beautiful snake princess Bai-Niang falls in love with the young boy Xu-Xian. His parents make him put the snake back in the fields where he found her, but he never stops missing his pet. Years later, magically transformed into a beautiful girl during a storm, the snake goddess changes a rainbow fish into her handmaid Xiao Chin, sets up house in the town, and seeks Xu-Xian out again. Both grown up, the two fall in love. Local wizard Fa Hai, convinced Bai-Niang is a vampire out to harm Xu-Xian, tries to break up their romance, and banishes Xu to hard labor in a distant city, reasoning that it's the only way to save him. Xu's two clever pets, Panda and Mimi, set out to follow him and become the leaders of the local animal Mafia, using the gang's skills to find him. Determined to save Xu from what he sees as a terrible supernatural evil, Fa whisks him off to his castle by the ocean, and the devoted Panda and Mimi follow him again through a terrible storm. Xiao has to intervene with the gods to save them, while Bai-Niang fights Fa for Xu's freedom. Even after saving Xu from death, she must give up her magical powers and become human before Fa accepts that her love is genuine. The two young lovers can finally marry, Xiao returns to her true form as a pretty fish, and Panda, Mimi, and their animal friends all live happily ever after.

Often regarded as the "first" modern anime, this variant on LITTLE MERMAID marked the maturation of several years of training at Toei to produce the critical mass of animators required to make a feature, as well as the final ebb of the flood of Disney cartoons that had dominated the Japanese domestic market since 1952 (FOREIGN INFLUENCES). It was originally adapted from Chinese mythology as a story by Shin Uehara, under the auspices of producers who deliberately sought a non-Japanese theme in an attempt to find exhibitors in mainland Asia. As the first color feature of the Toei animation studio, it casts a long shadow on the history of Japanese animation and is one of the twin "big bangs" of the modern business, rivaled only by Osamu Tezuka's later ASTRO BOY. Featuring uncharacteristically

"oriental" character designs and serious trials and hardships for the young lovers and their animal friends, it inspired many others to become animators, including the young Hayao Miyazaki, on whom it made a deep impression. It won honors at the Venice Children's Film Festival in 1959 but reaction to its U.S. release in 1961 was disappointing. Mimi, a small "red" panda, is mistakenly referred to as a cat in some sources.

PANDA GO PANDA *

1972. JPN: *Panda Kopanda*. AKA: *Panda; Panda Cub; Panda and Child*. Movie. DIR: Isao Takahata. SCR: Hayao Miyazaki. DES: Hayao Miyazaki. ANI: Yasuo Otsuka, Yoichi Kotabe, Yoshifumi Kondo, Seiji Kitara, Takao Kasai, Minoru Maeda. MUS: Teruhiko Sato. PRD: A-Pro, Tokyo Movie Shinsha. 33 mins. (m1), 38 mins. (m2).

Miyazaki's first original work as a screenwriter is a charming tale of a little girl who befriends a panda and his cub. Left home alone when her grandmother has to go away for a few days, little Mimiko is surprised to find a panda and his cub moving in. They very soon form a little family of their own, with Father Panda offering the fatherless Mimiko the paternal affection she's always wanted, and Mimiko mothering the motherless cub. Everything is going well until the local policeman discovers exactly who Mimiko's houseguests are. The father-bear, a model of good parenthood foreshadowing Miyazaki's ongoing concern with the parent/child relationship, can also be seen as one of the stages in the creation of MY NEIGHBOR TOTORO, and the young protagonist has much in common with the heroine Miyazaki had sketched for TMS's abortive *Pippi Longstocking* project. There are also substantial foreshadowings of Miyazaki's masterful grasp of a child's-eye view of the world, which would come to fruition in his later works such as SPIRITED AWAY and PONYO. Notably, street signs in the show make it clear that it is set in Kita Akitsu near Tokorozawa—in other words, Miyazaki's birthplace and the same area of countryside where a later movie would locate his Totoro spirits. In light of much later media coverage of the Miyazaki family, it is tempting to read extra levels of meaning into Mimiko's decision that all fathers have

to work, but not hers, because "every day is his day off"—Miyazaki's son Goro, the future director of TALES FROM EARTHSEA and FROM UP ON POPPY HILL, would have been five years old when this was in production. The sequel, *Panda Go Panda: Rainy Day Circus*, also directed by Takahata, followed a year later and is bundled with the first part on modern DVDs in order to approach "feature-length."

Pandas were big box office in the 1970s after the arrival of a Chinese panda at Tokyo Zoo, and other unrelated appearances during the period included Yugo Serikawa's *Panda's Great Adventure* (1973) and the Sino-Japanese coproduction TAOTAO THE PANDA. The following decade would see a similar obsession with koalas—see NOOZLES.

PANDA-Z THE ROBONIMATION *

2004. AKA: *Robonimal Panda-Z*. TV series. DIR: Mamoru Kanbe. SCR: N/C. DES: Shuichi Oshida. ANI: N/C. MUS: Panda-Z Band. PRD: Bandai Visual, Dynamic Planning, Megahouse Corp., Kid's Station. 5 mins. x 30 eps.

In Robonimal World, where robots are shaped like animals, seven-year-old Pan Taron finds a Super P-Z engine under the research facility headed by his grandfather Doctor Pan Ji, a mad scientist complete with lightbulb on his head to show when he has a really bright idea. The Doctor and Pan's father use it to build superrobot Panda Z, complete with flying fist to deliver a rocket punch, abdominal missiles for a really powerful six-pack, and a bright red jet-pack to fly with. Aimed at younger children, but also exploiting the retro interests of fans-turned-parents who yearn for the pre-GUNDAM days of mighty robot action, the characters are named in simple, picture-book fashion—Denwan the telephone dog gets his name by crashing the Japanese words for "phone" and "bark" together, Rabinna is a pink rabbitnurse, Etekki the monkey is named for the sound monkeys make in Japanese, lumbering Zoutank's name starts with the word for "elephant," and Moo-Gyuu's ends with the Japanese word for cow.

Taron, however, is the only one who can bond with Panda-Z to battle the evil machinations of SkullPanda. Like the Emperor in Go Nagai's puppet show *Star Fleet* (*DE), SkullPanda's body is entirely hidden under a long cloak; he commands his forces from a mobile floating fortress. His chief henchman is evil mustachioed Doctor Jangar, who leads the Warunimal forces in his deadly Black Ham Gear, a giant robot hamster. Warunimal is a hybrid of the Japanese word *warui* (bad) and animal.

Created by **MAZINGER Z** fan Shuichi Oshida when he was learning Adobe Illustrator on his Mac, this Go Nagai–inspired heroic robot and his cohorts were picked up by Megahouse when he went freelance, and appeared as a highly successful merchandise line before they were animated. Go Nagai's name appears on the show credited with "original concept," in reflection of the number of distinct Nagai ideas that Oshida lampoons.

PANDORA HEARTS *

2009. TV series. DIR: Takao Kato. SCR: Mayori Sekijima, Masashi Kubota, Kenichi Araki, Hiroaki Katajima. DES: Chizuru Kobayashi, Shinichi Yamaoka, Keito Watanabe. ANI: Chizuru Kobayashi, Shinichi Yamaoka, Taeko Hori. MUS: Yuki Kajiura. PRD: Xebec, TBS. 24 mins. x 25 eps.

Oz Vessalius is the son of a noble house. Apart from the absence of his father, his life is comfortable and carefree. Cast into prison when he comes of age, he is saved by a mysterious being who looks like a girl but is really a human transformed into a creature that consumes other humans' spirits. Threatened by toys that are symbols of horror rather than happiness, Oz must unravel the secret of events a century in the past and find the truth behind the weird organization known as "Pandora."

Saturated with Victorian fantasy from Lewis Carroll to Sherlock Holmes, from gaslamp fantasy to fairytale, Jun Mochizuki's 2006 manga *Pandora Hearts* spun off a successful game series and a wave of merchandise, all predicated on the same basic premise as **A LITTLE PRINCESS**—the story of a brave young innocent who has to grow up quickly and in cruel circumstances when the world falls apart around him, but is saved and enabled to thrive through the power of courage and friendship. The anime's problem is that it loses the purity of that simple outline under a dressing-up box of constantly changing frills and furbelows, with shadowy gothic gaslight

alternating with perky, flashy brightness and both fighting for screen time with super-deformed shenanigans, comic relief, and absurd anime tropes vying with gritty brutality and overwrought emotion. Xebec's animation doesn't help, sometimes looking old-fashioned and rather cheap. The plot is similarly chaotic. One feels for writers with an epic manga universe to cram into 25 episodes—to enjoy the style without the confusion, you might want to stick to the nine three-minute *Pandora Hearts Specials* released as DVD extras in 2009–10.

PANI PONI DASH

2005. TV series. DIR: Akiyuki Shinbo. SCR: Kenichi Kanemaki, Katsuhiko Takayama. DES: Kazuhiro Oda. ANI: Kazuhiro Oda. MUS: Kei Haneoka. PRD: Gansis, Shaft, TV Tokyo. 25 mins. x 26 eps.

Rebecca "Becky" Miyamoto is a diminutive 11-year-old genius shorter than the children she is supposed to teach at Momotsuki High School. Pretty girls and a rabbit, with occasional swimsuits. Suspiciously similar to **DOKI DOKI SCHOOL HOURS**, but why not just keep wringing that idea until it's totally dry?

PANTY AND STOCKING WITH GARTERBELT *

2008. TV series. DIR: Hiroyuki Imaishi. SCR: Hiromi Wakabayashi, Masahiko Otsuka. DES: Atsushi Nishigori, Masanobu Nomura. ANI: Atsushi Nishigori, Sushio, Shoko Nakamura. MUS: Taku Takahashi (m-flo), TCY Crew. PRD: GAINAX, AT-X, Flying Dog, Kadokawa, MOVIC, Klockworx. 23 mins x 13 eps.

A group of ghosts, made up of the regrets of the dead, has moved into Daten City. Two angels arrive from heaven, allegedly on a mission to exterminate the evil influences—but in reality the pair of avengers are slackers who were kicked out for bad language and worse behavior along with their sidekick, Garterbelt. If they can collect enough Heaven Coins the girls might just get their halos back, but earning that kind of bread in this kind of town is going to take some seriously un-angelic behavior.

You have to hand it to Gainax. The makers of the sublime **WINGS OF HONNEAMISE**, the adorable **SECRET OF BLUE WATER**, and the epic of negativity **EVANGELION** know two things better than almost anyone else in

the business: how to put their whole heart and soul into their work, and how to do potty humor. Whatever they do, they do to excess, and excess is the core of *PSG*. One could allege this story has a feminist subtext, since the protagonists do exactly what they want all the time and leave others, often men, to clean up after them: to which we counter that a feminist subtext which chimes so exactly with the patriarchal dream of the bad girl is very probably a tart in vicar's clothing.

You may have to leave aside the script, because the U.S. dub is even less sophisticated than the Japanese, and either you snigger every time someone says bra and poop and whore, or you don't; but the most puritanical critic can't deny the dazzling visual invention, or the saturation in the sticky fluids of pop culture that informs almost every frame. It looks as crude and cheap as it sounds, but it's as compulsive as a car crash and as clever as a perfectly timed pratfall into a pool of vomit. The title of the 2011 spin-off video, *Panty and Stocking in Sanitarybox*, is on the same level of sophistication as the rest of the writing. Remember, as the great Dolly Parton once remarked, it costs a fortune to look (and sound) this cheap: 7 writers and 18 animation directors for 13 episodes, double and triple-teaming to get every crap joke just right. **ⓛⓝ**

PANTY FLASH TEACHER *

2004. JPN: *Panchira Teacher*. Video. DIR: Hisashi Ozekawa, Nao Ozekawa. SCR: Joichi Michigami. DES: Kuniyoshi Hino, Kenichi Tatefuji. ANI: Kuniyoshi Hino, Yukke Ani, Hiraku Kaneko. MUS: Hiroaki Sano. PRD: Discovery. 28 mins. x 2 eps.

New teacher Machiko is seduced by Utsui, one of her students, who requests an autographed pair of her panties as a memento of their tryst. Unfortunately, he is the leader of the school's most notorious delinquents, who have been turning some of their fellow students into sex slaves for their own amusement. Utsui then uses the panties to blackmail her, threatening to expose her and ruin her politician father's campaign for local office. Rather than fighting back, Machiko allows Utsui to bully her into increasingly humiliating sexual situations, because this is porn and porn characters, by definition, don't behave sensibly. Kyomi Shibata claims credit for the "original" story—we wouldn't, but to each her own. The historically minded might like to consider the coincidence of names between the subject of this show and the infamous lead of SHAMING MISS MACHIKO.... Coincidence? **N**

PANZER DRAGOON *

1996. JPN: *Panzer Dragoon*. Video. DIR: Shinji Takagi. SCR: Yosuke Kuroda. DES: Atsushi Takeuchi, Kazuhiro Kishita. ANI: Atsushi Takeuchi. MUS: Azuma. PRD: Production I.G. 30 mins.

Kyle's girl is stolen from him by the Black Dragon, which also kills his obviously expendable fat friend. When he meets blue dragon Blau, Kyle is suspicious, but only Blau can help him save Alita, who will otherwise be enslaved by the Dark Tower and become the catalyst for the destruction of the entire world.

If a bored director and crew copied a few pages from the *Beginner's Book of Fantasy Gaming*, then lost the important bits like plot and characterization, this is what might emerge. The 1995 Sega Saturn game's distinctive look is matched by what, at the time of release, must have been a truly innovative combination of cel and digital animation. There are set pieces that recall the game itself and quirkily mismatched compositions of technology and magic, setting up a damsel in distress, cross-species buddy business, a rescue, and a big fight in just 30 minutes.

With a fallen empire, a blind sorceress, human/dragon symbiosis, and a quest to defeat the ultimate evil, *Panzer Dragoon* had truly epic potential. People have spun trilogies out of less, but the paltry running time isn't up to it. What little space there is for dialogue that doesn't advance the plot, writer Kuroda fills with poetic meditations on sight and seeing. The blind Alita cannot *see* the color red, instead she must *experience* it. "So this is what the sky feels like!" proclaims Kyle during his first dragon flight—a throwaway line that belongs in a much better story.

A.D. Vision's dub is far better than the spartan original deserves, but this remains a heroic rescue attempt by both Japanese and U.S. crews, fighting impossible odds of budget and (lack of) inspiration. **V**

PANZER WORLD GALIENT

1984. JPN: *Kikokai Galient*. AKA: *Mechanical Armor World Galient*. TV series, video. DIR: Ryosuke Takahashi. SCR: Ryosuke Takahashi, Hajime Yadate. DES: Norio Shioyama. ANI: Norio Shioyama. MUS: Toru Fuyuki. PRD: Sunrise, Nippon TV. 25 mins. x 26 eps. (TV), 55 mins. (v).

Young Jordy is fighting his father, Madar, who is bent on world domination using giant robots. His brother, Hai Shartart, is also fighting Madar, but not to save the people from dominion; instead he plans to take his father's place, and so he sees Jordy and their sister, Chururu, as rivals. Legend tells of a mysterious avenger, known only as the Iron Giant, who will come to overthrow the tyrant. The video, subtitled *Iron Emblem*, covered the same dramatic ground two years later: ruthless ambition, family conflict, and massively overspecified armor.

The golden age of the robot was in full swing in 1984; *God Mazinger*(see MAZINGER Z) and SOUTHERN CROSS among the multitude onscreen, MACROSS in the theaters, and toys everywhere. Takahashi is renowned as one of the prime movers of the "real robot" style spun off from Tomino's GUNDAM, but the introduction of more realistic elements into future fantasy didn't preclude designs of baroque splendor. The *Galient* robots are among the best—a magnificent fusion of futuristic technology, steampunk weightiness, and off-the-wall neoclassical design. Robot centaurs—you gotta love 'em. **V**

PAPA LOVE

2012. JPN: *Papa Love: Kyonyu Bishirikko Saime-chan no Kinshin Jodo Boso Boso Oppai*. AKA: *Papa Love: Busty and Pretty-Assed Girl Saime-chan's Close Relative Super-Wild-Wild Boobs*. Video. DIR: N/C. SCR: N/C. DES: N/C. ANI: N/C. MUS: N/C. PRD: Blue Gale, PoRO. 30 mins. x 2 eps.

Neither of the plot synopses available for this porn release make much sense, since both replicate the rushed, breathless jumble of sensations and exclamations to be found in the overlong and rather charmingly ungrammatical enthusiasm of the subtitle. We can but guess that not-quite-incest Lolita temptations are on offer, in yet another addition to the pile of anime EROTICA AND PORNOGRAPHY. Since

words for "wild/delusional" and "boobs" are repeated twice, we can only assume that everybody ends up with double vision. Based on a computer game. **N**

PAPA MAMA BYE-BYE

1980. JPN: *Papa Mama Bye-Bye*. Movie. DIR: Hiroshi Shidara. SCR: Atsushi Yamagata. DES: Katsumi Aoshima. ANI: Katsumi Aoshima. MUS: Tadahito Mori. PRD: Toei. 75 mins.

Dungaree-wearing teenage tomboy Kaori lives next door to the brothers Ko and Yasu. One day they find an injured pigeon and nurse it back to health. As Kaori is walking to school soon afterward, a U.S. Phantom jet screams overhead and crashes near the boys' house. A heavy-handed juxtaposition of animal hospital and international friendship, inspired by a real-life incident in 1977 when a U.S. jet did indeed make a forced landing in Yokohama. For another U.S. plane ending up where it shouldn't, see SEA OF THE TICONDEROGA.

PAPILLON ROSE *

2006. TV series, video. DIR: Yasuhiro Matsumura. SCR: Kazuharu Sato. DES: Takayuki Noguchi, Toshihide Matsudate, Koji Watanabe, Mitsuharu Miyamae. ANI: N/C. MUS: Masaya Koike. PRD: Kelmadick. 24 mins. (v), 25 mins. x 6 eps. (TV).

An evil group of transvestites who call themselves Gel Dynasty are spreading STDs around the sex industry in order to wipe out the existing managers and take over—because of course straight dressers don't give each other STDs, not ever. Tsubomi, the legendary lingerie warrior Papillon Rose, gathers together her fellow lingerie fighters to protect the sex trade from this hostile takeover. Allegedly parodying magical girl series like SAILOR MOON, this rather nasty little plot is an attempt at mainstream revival for fan writer-director Shinji Tobita's 2003 video *Lingerie Warrior Papillon Rose (Lingerie Senshi Papillon Rose)*. In this surreal extravaganza, horny high school girl Tsubomi works part-time at a lingerie hostess club, blackmailing her boss to keep the job she's not very good at. Then she's recruited as a magical warrior by a talking cat pervert with a butterfly on its head. This was the beginning of Tsubomi's career as a champion of the sex trade against hostile takeover, this time by an elf dominatrix and the Queen of the Bees. The concept was touted as a 25-episode net animation series but never got off the ground, yet Tobita persisted to sell it for TV. **Ⓝ**

PAPRIKA *

2006. Movie. DIR: Satoshi Kon. SCR: Satoshi Kon, Seishi Minakami. DES: Masashi Ando, Nobutaka Ike. ANI: Masashi Ando. MUS: Susumu Hirasawa. PRD: Madhouse Studios, Sony Pictures Entertainment (Japan) Inc. 86 mins.

The near future: a new psychotherapeutic technique has been developed using a cutting-edge device called the DC Mini. Through it, the therapist can enter patients' dreams and explore their unconscious. Then one of the prototypes is stolen, raising the terrifying possibility that untrained or unscrupulous users could enter anyone's brain and personality while they sleep and wreak havoc. Atsuko Chiba, a key member of the development team, enters the dream world as her sassy alter-ego Paprika to try and find out who is behind the theft and what they intend.

Approaching the source novel by THE GIRL WHO LEAPT THROUGH TIME's Yasutaka Tsutsui with "humility and respect," Kon invests somewhat more effort in remaining faithful to the original than he did with his earlier PERFECT BLUE. The main addition to the novel is the movie's recurring image of an oncoming parade, growing in intensity and surreality as a psychological storm risks breaking through into the real world—a touch very much in keeping with Tsutsui's own work, and likely to have contributed to the author's willingness to appear in a cameo with Kon himself as a pair of barmen.

But Paprika is also classic Kon territory. There's a mystery to solve, with dark and terrible deeds cloaked in fantasy yet affecting the real world. There's a protagonist whose dual life is rooted in fantasy. There's a cast of flawed, fallible characters. There's the city and the communications revolution, serving and shaping our ideas; and there's an otaku, a hapless geek whose chances of getting the girl and living the dream look remote. The whole movie is a perfect piece of science fiction: the science and technology cannot be separated from the story.

Kon tackles ideas of responsibility and

individuality, of what it means to be part of society in a nation where conformity and cooperation transform in the face of increased wealth, slackening family ties, and a cultural invasion that has been gathering pace ever since 1945. The fear of aging is the major underlying theme of urban culture, for men as well as women, with a particular resonance in a culture that traditionally reveres old age. The youthful, perky alter ego that dogged the protagonist's steps in *Perfect Blue* pops up again in *Paprika*, disguised as a useful piece of professional equipment, but really a key to the heroine's own secret dreams. Thirty-something professional Atsuko creates a perky, fearless teenage avatar to confront the mundanity of everyday life and the tyranny of time.

Paprika contains plenty of in-jokes to please film buffs and make them feel part of the director's own club—not just the references to *Roman Holiday* and *Tarzan of the Apes*, but a wonderful bit of blink-and-you'll-miss-it Kurosawa fan service. He also pays homage to Alfred Hitchcock in the movie's structure, a classic double-helix: a mystery, like *Rear Window* or PARANOIA AGENT, entwined with a clash between two worlds that seem entirely separate, but turn out to be not so very different after all, like PRINCESS MONONOKE. As in all his movies, Kon reminds us that the monsters in the closet turn out to be nothing but a few old clothes; it's the monsters in our heads we have to confront. **⒩Ⓥ**

PAPUWA-KUN

1992. JPN: *Nangoku no Shonen Papuwa-kun*. AKA: *Southern-Kingdom Boy Papuwa*. TV series, video. DIR: Jun Takagi, Masahiro Hosoda. SCR: Nobuyuki Fujimoto. DES: Hiroshi Takeuchi, Ken Kawai. ANI: Satoshi Takeuchi, Takao Osone. MUS: Nobuyuki Nakamura. PRD: Nippon Animation, TV Asahi. 25 mins. x 42 eps. (TV), 30 mins. x 2 eps. (v1), 25 mins. (v2).

Papuwa is a little boy living a quiet life with his dog Chappy on a small island in the South Pacific. Then Shintaro turns up. Not only is he carrying valuable jewelry, but he's being chased by gangsters. When Chappy steals the jewel, the stage is set for insane high jinks of a kind not normally associated with the creators of WORLD MASTERPIECE THEATER. This anime was based

on a 1991 manga by Ami Shibata, who also created JIBAKU-KUN, though a similar dogs-and-jewels caper can be found much earlier in HONEY HONEY. The series returned on video with the two-part *Papuwa-kun Encyclopedia* (1993, *Papuwa-kun Daihyakka*), which included an "extra" episode, the pilot film for a nonexistent sequel, and some interviews with the cast and crew. A final video release in 1994 comprised an unbroadcast "dream" episode, in which Papuwa-kun gets a fever and hallucinates a bizarre journey among the stars.

PARADE PARADE *

1996. Video. DIR: Motoaki Isshu. SCR: Hideyuki Kurata. DES: Toshimitsu Kobayashi. ANI: Toshimitsu Kobayashi, Yasuhito Kikuchi (opening animation). MUS: Kanji Saito. PRD: Pink Pineapple, AIC. 30 mins. x 2 eps.

Rising pop star Kaori Shiine has just finished the first concert of her first tour, a year after her debut. However, she has two secrets which, if revealed, would betray her squeaky clean image: her female manager, Yoko Imai, is her lover; and, in addition to a woman's "normal" sexual atttributes, she has a functioning penis. Things become even more complicated when her work schedule causes Kaori to cross paths with Saki Midorizawa. Saki is a talented veteran star, whose public image is Kaori's opposite—a bad girl who wears revealing outfits and uses her appearance and sex appeal to their full measure. She also has a penchant for seducing her sororal "idols" and adding them to her harem, and Kaori is her next target. But Yoko is not about to let her love go, so Saki offers to settle the matter with a duel, using the bodies of Kaori and Saki's current "pet" Sayaka Tamura as the battlegrounds: the duelist who makes the other's partner orgasm first wins (the contesting parties having swapped). The possibility of revenge also sweetens the pot for Saki, as it turns out that Yoko is her former lover, who abandoned her three years ago.... Based on the manga by Satoshi Akifuji, this is an entertaining and well-executed entry in the idol subgenre of anime porn; compare with SPOTLIGHT and COOL DEVICES' *Fallen Angel Rina*. **Ⓝ**

PARADISE KISS *

2005. TV series. DIR: Osamu Kobayashi. SCR: Osamu Kobayashi. DES: Nobuteru Yuki. ANI:

Nobuteru Yuki, Yuichi Tanaka, Akiko Asaki, Hiroyuki Hashimoto. MUS: Hiroaki Sano. PRD: Madhouse, Twinkle, Fuji TV. 25 mins. x 12 eps.

Teenager Yukari thinks that she spends her whole life trying to live up to the expectations of her pushy mother. Her life of books and constant studying is interrupted by the not entirely unwelcome attentions of a group of fashion students, who think that she would make an ideal model for their clothes label, the titular Paradise Kiss. She initially refuses their offer, although they are able to blackmail her into her first show by threatening to reveal the identity of her secret crush, which they have discovered by reading her mislaid notebook. With friends like these, who needs enemies?

Yukari begins to hang out at a bar with the bad boy, the pretty boy, the mysterious girl, and the one who is supposed to be cute. Before long, however, she begins to appreciate that these people are more than just another rack of off-the-peg schoolday archetypes, there is more to life than school, and that even if these misfits are not behaving conventionally, they are nevertheless choosing their own path. In becoming their muse, Yukari is inspired to become her own person. Combining the fashion obsessions of COSPLAY COMPLEX or MON CHERIE COCO with the questionable associates of BOYS OVER FLOWERS, this series is actually a sequel of sorts to TV Asahi's NEIGHBORHOOD STORY, and is similarly based on a manga by Ai Yazawa. The closing theme of the Japanese broadcast was "Do You Want To?" by Franz Ferdinand, liable to secure more interest from outside anime FANDOM than one might normally expect—compare to INTERSTELLA 5555.

PARADISE WITHOUT STARS

1991. JPN: Hoshikuzu Paradise. Video. DIR: Masato Namiki. SCR: Takuya Kubo. DES: Fumio Sasaki. ANI: Fumio Sasaki. MUS: Takeshi Kusao. PRD: OB Planning, Pastel. 55 mins.

A love comedy about Hiroshi, a normal teenage boy who discovers after his mother's death that his real father is a famous singer. Moving in with his new-found parent, Hiroshi must cope with having a stepmother who is closer in age to himself than her husband, and who until the previous week, he used to fantasize about when-

ever he saw her on TV. Based on a *Shonen Sunday* manga by Katsu-Aki, who would also draw one of the manga adaptations of ESCAFLOWNE several years later. Ⓝ

PARANOIA AGENT *

2004. JPN: Moso Dairinin. AKA: Paranoia. TV series. DIR: Satoshi Kon. SCR: Seishi Minakami, Tomomi Yoshino. DES: Masashi Ando. ANI: Akiko Asaki, Hideki Hamazu, Mamoru Sasaki, Toshiyuki Inoue, Satoru Utsunomiya, Hisashi Eguchi, Tadashi Hiramatsu. MUS: Susumu Hirasawa. PRD: Madhouse, WOWOW. 25 mins. x 13 eps.

Detectives Keiichi Ikari and Mitsuhiro Maniwa are assigned to the case of Tsukiko Saki, the designer of a popular cute animal character in the style of HELLO KITTY, who has been the victim of a vicious attack. They are not the only people on Tsukiko's trail; so, too, is tabloid journalist Akio, although he soon falls prey to the same criminal. The attacker is "Li'l Slugger," a shadowy vigilante wielding a battered metal bat (some might say, a GOLDEN BAT), who stalks a series of victims in a dark and forbidding Tokyo. What the investigators fail to realize is that they may not be hunting a single human at all, but a complex social malaise, starting with one small exaggeration that gets progressively larger until the victims' stories of a baseball bat and golden in-line skates feed an urban myth that rampages out of control. Is the kid real, or is he called into being by the stress, unease, and sheer paranoia of living in the big city?

The first TV project from Satoshi Kon is a masterpiece of urban legend, combining the psychological knots of Kon's earlier PERFECT BLUE and the perverted gamesmanship of David Fincher's Se7en (1995). Kon exploits the longer running time of TV for all it's worth, setting up supposedly disconnected events that soon reveal a mortifying ripple effect. What at first seems to be a simple police procedural soon gains new complexity. The viewer's attention is drawn first to clues in the background and script, such as the relationship of character names to phases of the moon or the names of animals hidden in their names. This, too, is a red herring, as later episodes reveal *PA* to be an involved meditation on the futility of false hopes and sanitized dreams. As with *Perfect Blue* and

MILLENNIUM ACTRESS, *PA* often makes the entertainment industry itself the subject of its ire, with suspicious deaths at an anime studio and later satirical references to superheroics. But Kon also homes in on more general modern issues, opening with crowds of commuters in the style of GANTZ, each studiously ignoring the other while yammering inanities on a mobile phone to a distant listener. Asides and moments in each episode point to a series of unseen connections between the characters in the style of HUMAN CROSSING, particularly with relation to an Internet chatroom in which three buddies make a suicide pact, only for one of them to turn out not to be a dying man, but a young girl—shades here of Hiroshi Shimizu's movie *Ikinai* (1998). Kon also loves postmodern angles on familiar clichés, focusing in one episode on a day in the life of a cop whose main contribution will be to apprehend a character later on. ⒺⓋ

PARAPPA THE RAPPER

2001. JPN: Para Parappa. TV series. DIR: Hiroaki Sakurai. SCR: Yoshio Urasawa. DES: Rodney Alan Greenblat, Takayuki Goto. ANI: N/C. MUS: Masaya Matsuura, Yoshihisa Suzuki, Yasushi Kurobane. PRD: JC Staff, Production I.G, Fuji TV. 25 mins. x 30 eps.

The adventures of a happy dancing dog in his ongoing attempts to impress a flower called Sunny. Based on the surreal 1996 PlayStation game, the series features new characters and music from the original designers.

PARASITE HEAVEN

1996. JPN: Isoro Tengoku. AKA: Home-stay Heaven; Heaven of a Hanger-on. Video. DIR: Teruo Kogure. SCR: Satoshi Aoyama. DES: Teru Aranaga. ANI: Kazuyoshi Ota. MUS: N/C. PRD: Beam Entertainment. 30 mins., 40 mins.

Eighteen-year-old Masahiko Kisugi is sent to stay with his Aunt Mizuhara so he can study at a nearby college. In an erotic anime based on the manga by Teru Aranaga in *Comic Lies* magazine, he soon begins an affair with his aunt, and with her three daughters. Ⓝ

PARASOL HENBE

1989. JPN: Parasol Henbe. TV series. DIR: Masakazu Higuchi, Takami Fujikawa, Shigeru Fujikawa, Takaya Mizutani, Yugo Serikawa. scr: Megumi Sugiwara, Aya Matsui, Satoru Akahori. des: Motoo Abiko. ani: Takao Yamazaki. mus: Reijiro Koroku. prd: Fujiko Studio, NHK. 8 mins. x 109 eps.

Japanese boy Megeru meets Henbe, a strange hippo-like creature from another world. Henbe and his trademark magical parasol have many adventures with Megeru in this series for the very young, with episode titles such as "*I Can't Stand the Rain*," "*A Broadcast from Parasol World*," "*A Butterfly from Another World*," and "*The Flying Bicycle*." Based on a manga by **BILLY DOG**–creator Fujiko-Fujio "A," and featuring the screenwriting debut of Satoru Akahori, whose "zany" output would dominate comedy anime for the coming decade.

PASTEL YUMI

1986. jpn: *Maho no Idol Pastel Yumi*. aka: *Magical Idol Pastel Yumi; Pastel Yumi the Magical Idol*. TV series. dir: Akira Shigino, Yutaka Kagawa, Hiroshi Yoshida, Mitsuru Hongo, Toshio Okabe, Miho Maruo, Kazuyoshi Katayama. scr: Shoji Imai, Azuma Tachibana, Yoshiyuki Suga, Yoshihisa Araki. des: Yumiko Hirosawa. ani: Yumiko Hirosawa. mus: Koji Makaino. prd: Studio Pierrot, Nippon TV. 25 mins. x 25 eps.

Schoolgirl Yumi Hanazono lives happily with her parents. She loves nature and all living things. On carnival day, two little imps called Keshimaru and Kakimaru give her a magic baton and a magic ring; anything she draws in the air now becomes real. Using their power, she can transform into the magical idol Pastel Yumi. Another magical-girl story from the people who brought you **CREAMY MAMI**.

PATALIRO

1982. jpn: *Pataliro! Boku Pataliro!* aka: *Pataliro! I'm Pataliro!* TV series, movie, video. dir: Nobutaka Nishizawa, Satoshi Hisaoka, Yugo Serikawa, Hiroshi Shidara, Yasuo Yamayoshi. scr: Masaki Tsuji, Akiyoshi Sakai, Tomomi Tsutsui, Tomoko Konparu. des: Mineo Maya. ani: Yasunori Kanemori. mus: Nozomu Aoki. prd: Toei, Fuji TV. 25 mins. x 49 eps. (TV1), 48 mins. (m), ca. 9 mins. x 24 eps. (TV2), ca. 9 mins. x 2 eps. (v).

Based on Mineo Maya's 1978 manga in *Hana to Yume* magazine, the series was the first to introduce homosexuality to TV anime audiences, and the nudity is reasonably tasteful (allowing for some floral backgrounds) and mostly male. A fantastical plot revolves around Jack Bankolan, a former British agent licensed to kill, who has somehow ended up working on the fabulously wealthy diamond-trading South Sea island of Marinera as a nursemaid to Pataliro VIII, the superpowered brat who is head of state. The joke is that this 007 is gay and the foes he faces are gorgeous men, transposing the machismo of the Bond mythos into lighthearted camp. Originally called just *Pataliro!*, the longer version of the title was used from episode 27 on. Nishizawa's movie, *Pataliro: Stardust Project* (1983), featured the titular plan by the international Tarantella crime syndicate to raid Marinera's diamond vaults. Typically, they send in an advance assassin to remove Bankolan, but the tall, handsome Andersen instead falls in love with his quarry.Kenichi Maejima's *Pataliro Saiyuki* (2005) remodeled the characters as the cast of **JOURNEY TO THE WEST**. ◐

PATEMA INVERTED *

2013. jpn: *Sakasama Patema*. Movie. dir: Yasuhiro Yoshiura. scr: Yasuhiro Yoshiura. des: N/C. ani: Ryo-timo. mus: Michiru Oshima. prd: Purple Cow, Asmik Ace, Good Directions, Good Smile, Kids Station. 99 mins.

Deep in an underground society, Patema defies her elders by exploring the forbidden levels, discovering a seemingly bottomless pit, into which she falls. On the surface, the disenchanted schoolboy Eiji (spelt Age in the Anglophone subtitles, for no reason we can comprehend) plays truant at the edge of a hole in the ground, out of which Patema "falls" upward. Her world is entirely upside down—she and her people are the descendants of the victims of an experiment gone wrong, who will fall into the sky unless they are anchored to the Earth.

Boy-meets-girl has never been so strange as in this feature, in which the leads must literally cling to each other or fall away to an uncertain fate. Originating, like the director's earlier **TIME OF EVE**, as an Internet animation upgraded to a feature, *Patema Inverted* winningly plays with matters of spatial awareness, perspective, and weight, regularly flipping its angles until the viewer literally can no longer remember which way is truly up. Its release a few scant months ahead of the similarly themed Hollywood movie *Upside Down* (2013) shows that Japanese storytelling can still be at the forefront of global competition.

Like the protagonist of Tezuka's classic **JUMPING**, Eiji and Patema swing up and down in increasingly far-reaching leaps, exploring the odd history of their world in the process, and also challenging the established order in both of their tribes. Eiji's is the better realized—an Orwellian state where even looking up is frowned upon. Patema's is more roughly delineated, with little consideration of how the "Inverts" might acquire clothes or food in their limited-resource underground hideaway.

Yoshiura playfully subverts a few filmic traditions, including a lead who interrupts her own swelling musical soundtrack to confirm her arrangements for meeting later, and a baddie's henchman who not only switches sides but charmingly offers comfort to a thwarted love interest. The film also features impressive penmanship from Michael Arias, who is credited with much of the contents of the English-language notebooks, to which the action occasionally cuts away for expository scenes. Ending, like **PONYO**, with the world explained but the central relationship still immensely unlikely to succeed, *Patema Inverted* is a massively ambitious movie that perhaps really should have been made in vertiginous 3D—given the treatment of, say, *Gravity* or *Inception*, it could have truly dragged Japanese animation to the forefront of experiments in Cartesian space. As it is, it is an intriguing exercise in reversals and rereversals, albeit one that falls short. Failing up, you might say.

PATLABOR *

1989. jpn: *Kido Keisatsu Patlabor*. aka: *Mobile Police Patlabor*. Video, TV series, movies. dir: Mamoru Oshii, Naoyuki Yoshinaga, Fumihiko Takayama, Yasunori Urata. scr: Kazunori Ito, Mamoru Oshii, Michiko Yokote. des: Akemi Takada, Yukata Izubuchi, Hiroki Takagi, Yoshinori Sayama. ani: Hiroki Takagi, Hiroyuki Kitakubo, Kisaraka Yamada. mus: Kenji Kawai. prd: Headgear, Sunrise, Nippon TV. 30 mins. x 7 eps., 30 mins. x 16 eps. (v), 25 mins. x 47 eps. (TV), 118 mins. (m1), 113 mins. (m2), 107 mins. (m, *WXIII*), 12 mins. x 3 eps. (*Mini Pato*).

At the close of the 20th century, a rise in global sea levels forces a massive building program in Japan, causing the creation of new "labor" construction robots. In a series that effortlessly incorporates human drama and comedy with hard science fiction, the police set up a Pat[rol] Labor division to deal with the new crime that the new technology brings.

The team behind *Patlabor* is arguably the finest assembly of talents in modern anime, rivaled only by Hayao Miyazaki's cohorts at Studio Ghibli and the erratic Gainax collective. Written in direct opposition to the gung ho conflicts of **GUNDAM** and the post-apocalyptic violence of *The Road Warrior*, *Patlabor*'s creators posit a future world where humanity muddles through regardless, and being a giant-robot pilot is just another job—taken, as with the space-force in **WINGS OF HON-NEAMISE**, by misfits unable to secure work in more glamorous sectors. The tribulations of Special Vehicle Division 2 are consequently dogged by idle bureaucrats, budget cuts, interfering R&D officers, and feuds within the group. Girlish rookie Noa Izumi, disaffected techno-millionaire's son Azuma Shinohara, and ultracool Captain Goto occupy central stage, though the other cast members are some of the most well-realized characters in anime. From bad-tempered gun-nut Ota to henpecked husband Shinshi, down to the gentle giant Hiromi and competent-but-snooty half-American visitor Kanuka Clancy (whose role was greatly expanded from the original manga), all contribute to a truly marvelous ensemble. The series is loaded with subplots that put many live-action shows to shame, including the unrequited love of Goto for his better-qualified opposite number Shinobu (hilariously telegraphed in a spoof episode that featured the pair forced to share a room in a love hotel), Ota's desperately lonely existence (in a *Blade Runner* pastiche scripted by Oshii), and Noa's deeply respectful love for her "pet" labor Alphonse. Made on video because **ADVERTISING AND SPONSORSHIP** was initially unavailable to make it for TV, the show was soon heading for broadcast and movie success. Some of the TV and video stories are downright goofy, like the white-alligator-in-the-sewers urban myth and a ghost story with spirits that need to be appeased; but there's also a long and carefully evolved story line about industrial espionage between rival labor manufacturers, the exploitation of children, and the lengths people go to for money.

Theatrical outings extend this dark agenda further. *Patlabor: The Movie* (1990), directed by Oshii, uses a threat of destruction by a suicidal visionary terrorist to examine the extent to which man depends on technology and the dangers involved in that dependency. Noa and the returning American labor captain Kanuka have to overcome their antagonism to save Tokyo from flood and disaster. *Patlabor 2* (1993) rounded off the series in a brilliantly contrived manner. Set in 2002, after the original team members have gone their separate ways, it features the attempt of a disaffected ex-soldier to orchestrate a military coup. The former members of the Patlabor team reunite one last time to stop him, and the film includes some real treats for long-term fans, including an explanation for Shinobu's eternal spinsterhood and the rare sight of Goto losing his temper. The unquestionable peak of the franchise, the second movie secured Oshii's chances of directing **GHOST IN THE SHELL** and shares with its successor a similar mood, pace, and political cynicism. It also features chilling images of a Japan returning all too swiftly to martial law, a topic that Oshii would approach again in **JIN-ROH**, as well as "guest" designs from Shoji Kawamori and Hajime Katoki.

Christophe Gans, who directed the live-action movie of **CRYING FREEMAN**, reportedly optioned *Patlabor 2* for a remake in the early 21st century, impressed with its ability to involve its cast in action to which they always seem to arrive a minute too late. This marginalization of the "little people" is a motif that runs through the entire series and adds to the realism. It is also a fundamental feature of the third *Patlabor* movie *WXIII* (2002), in which Tokyo is threatened by a mutant monster. With Oshii conspicuously absent as director (as he was from the inferior *Jin-Roh*), *WXIII* retells an early story from Masami Yuki's *Patlabor* manga but concentrates on the "guest stars," relegating the central cast almost completely to cameo roles. Seemingly recognizing the "malachro-nism" of catching up with the future date on which the original was set, *WXIII* also takes the interesting creative decision to depict its setting *as imagined in the 1980s*, with bulky computer terminals and chunky cellphones, acknowledging itself in an alternate timeline from our own world.

Sadly for *Patlabor*, accidents in rights acquisitions have had a similar effect on the series itself. The first two movies were well dubbed and promoted by Manga Entertainment but reached a far larger audience than the video and TV incarnations, which were sold to the smaller distributor U.S. Manga Corps. The series was also lampooned in the erotic pastiche **TOKIO PRIVATE POLICE**, although luckily only anime encyclopedists remember this. In theaters and on video, the *WXIII* movie was also accompanied by the *Minipato* shorts, humorous pastiches of *Patlabor* made in part by motion-capturing paper cut-out puppets and feeding the data into a computer, which then rendered them as 3D artifacts. No, we don't know why, either. The shorts were directed by Kenji Kamiyama, who would go on to take up Oshii's mantle on the *Ghost in the Shell* franchise.

The Next Generation -Patlabor- (2014–15) is a live-action series, shot in 45-minute episodes but premiered in Japanese cinemas in order to qualify as "films" rather than consigned to the amnesiac schedules of television. Mamoru Oshii is prominent in the credits as a writer and director of many of the sequences. Although billed as a sequel, with a new group taking over duties, with the exception of Shigeo Shiba, the former mechanic, now section leader (and played by his original voice-actor), so many elements of *TNG* repeat the formulae and conflicts of the original (klutzy but earnest new girl, cynical foreigner ...), even to the extent of soundalike names, that we might just as reasonably call it a remake. Arguably, much of the original *Patlabor*'s enduring strength lay in its animated form, and the independence it afforded from the failings of mainstream Japanese television. While there was certainly more to the original than the robot action, *TNG* must endure the twin indignities of low-budget CG and what passes for acting in the Japanese mainstream. Ironically for something that derives its name recognition from its past in animation, the labors in *TNG* look great until they actually have to move.

PAUL'S MIRACLE WAR

1976. JPN: *Paul no Miracle Daisakusen*. AKA: *Paul's Miraculous Adventures*. TV series. DIR: Hiroshi Sasakawa, Mizuho Nishikubo. SCR: Junzo Toriumi, Masaru Yamamoto. DES: Akiko Shimomoto. ANI: Hayao Nobe. MUS: Shunsuke Kikuchi. PRD: Tatsunoko Pro, Fuji TV. 25 mins. x 50 eps.

Little Paul has a very special cuddly toy— Pakkun is really a spirit from an alternate world under threat from the evil invader Belt Satan. Pakkun has come in search of help from Earth, and Paul is obliged to get involved when Belt Satan kidnaps his friend Nina. This charming series is hardly in the traditional science-fiction mold of the studio known as the "home of heroes," but for younger viewers, it's magic.

PEACE-HAME

2012. Video. DIR: Takashi Kondo. SCR: Takashi Kondo. DES: N/C. ANI: Takashi Kondo. MUS: N/C. PRD: Studio9MAiami, MediaBank (Queen Bee). 20 mins. x 6 eps.

A high school senior asks the yearbook executive committee to consider a slightly different approach for the next edition. Alongside the usual pictures of the *kendo* club and the cultural festival, why not have a few pages showing what the students really like to get up to between classes and after school? Considerable flexibility and unusual, even incredible, levels of physical endowment are on display in this porn story based on Shiwasu no Okina's erotic manga of high school life. ◐

PEACEMAKER KUROGANE *

2003. AKA: *Peacemaker; Peacemaker: Gunning for Trouble*. TV series. DIR: Tomohiro Hirata. SCR: Naoko Hasegawa, Hiroshi Yamaguchi. DES: Akemi Hayashi. ANI: Tadashi Hiramatsu. MUS: Keiichi Oku. PRD: Gonzo Digimation, Imagica, TV Asahi. 25 mins. x 24 eps.

In the 1860s, as disorder and unrest signify the imminent fall of the Tokugawa shogunate and the end of the Edo period, an elite military corps of skilled and ruthless swordsmen becomes a major force in Kyoto. When 15-year-old Tetsunosuke Ichimura's parents are killed by Choshu revolutionaries, he and his elder brother

Tatsunosuke join the Shinsengumi, the elite band of warriors in Kyoto. Employed as a page to Toshizo Hijikata, he vows to acquire the skills to avenge his parents' murder. ViceCommander Hijikata is a stern, seemingly cold leader. His underling, Captain Souji Okita is a complete contrast, a cheerful, laid-back type—until he unsheathes his sword, when he shows himself to be the deadliest fighter of them all. The diminutive Tetsunosuke is reckless, unsophisticated, and often mistaken for someone younger than his years. He befriends another orphan, Suzu Ichimura, not realizing that their lives mirror each other, since Suzu's parents were killed by the Shinsengumi. Ichimura senior was devoted to peace; the man who brought about his death was devoted to political reform, and in that cause he is willing to do anything, even burn Kyoto to the ground.

Drawing, like **SHINSENGUMI FARCE**, on real historical events, director Hirata focuses on a very minor character from history, using Tetsunosuke as a sort of everyman, in much the same way as **TREE IN THE SUN**, exemplifying the need to find one's own center in the confusion and danger of life in interesting times. A number of famous people play roles in the story—including Ryoma Sakamoto of **OI RYOMA!**, who appears under an alias and wearing dreadlocks in a manner more befitting **SAMURAI CHAMPLOO**, and Sanosuke Harada and Hajime Saito, who also show up in **RURONI KENSHIN**—but, just as in life, great events and political change occupy Tetsunosuke's mind far less than his personal concerns. A mix of broad comedy, violent action, and vivid characterization helps maintain interest in the journey of the sympathetic but not very original young hero, with his height hang-up, attitude problem, andthirst for revenge, allied to the perky klutziness of a magical-girl show heroine.

Based on the manga by Nanae Chrono, the anime's soft, earthy color palette gives a period feel without looking too much like a history lesson. After this show, the Gonzo studio stayed with the martial theme for **SAMURAI 7**. It represents a return to swordplay for designer and animation director Hayashi, whose resumé of gentler shows like **FRUITS BASKET** also includes a stint on **UTENA**. The DVD box in some

territories left the *Kurogane* part of the title in Japanese, leading many to assume that the title was simply *Peacemaker*, with an inscrutable squiggle next to it. ◑

PEACH-COLORED SISTERS

1998. JPN: *Momoiro Sisters*. TV series. DIR: Bob Shirahata. SCR: Satoru Akahori, Satoru Akahori Office. DES: Masaaki Kannan, Tomoko Kosaka. ANI: N/C. MUS: N/C. PRD: Studio Deen, TBS. 7 mins. x 24 eps.

A love comedy about Momoko ("peach girl"), a hapless 17-year-old who can't seem to snare herself a man, and whose Office Lady sister is very little help at all. Broadcast as part of the *Wonderful* program on TBS, this series of shorts was originally based on a 1993 manga by Tamami Momose. ◑

PEACOCK KING *

1988. JPN: *Kujaku-o; Shin Kujaku-o*. Video. AKA: *Spirit Warrior*. DIR: Katsuhito Akiyama, Ichiro Itano, Rintaro. SCR: Sho Aikawa, Hajime Inaba, Tatsuhiko Urahata. DES: Takuya Wada, Takahiro Kishida, Ken Koike. ANI: Masahiro Tanaka, Takahiro Kishida. MUS: Satoru Kogura, Kit Kat Club, Yas-Kaz, Toshiyuki Honda. PRD: AIC, Studio 88, Madhouse. 55 mins., 60 mins., and 50 mins. (v1). 45 mins. x 2 eps. (v2, *True PK*).

Kujaku is a young monk and an avatar, the incarnation of a god. His friend and cute blonde fellow-avatar Ashura, his teacher Ajari, and the leather-clad biker/magic master Onimaru band together to fight the demons released by Tatsuma from the ancient temple statues at Nara. Tatsuma is a powerful psychic, but he's never learned proper control of his abilities, and in seeking to test his powers, he puts humankind in terrible danger in the first episode, *Feast for Returning Demons*. In the second story, *Castle of Illusion*, Onimaru and graduate student Hatsuko are the sole survivors of a team digging up relics of medieval warlord and supposed black magician Nobunaga Oda (see **YOTODEN**). If the two scrolls found by the team are joined, Azuchi Castle will rise again and the warlord will unleash hell on Earth. For the third story, *Harvest of Cherry Blossoms*, the threat is undead shogun Ieyasu Tokugawa, who has joined forces with the restless ghost of an actress murdered during WWII and intends to sink Japan beneath the waves.

The story of Kujaku-myo'o (to some Buddhist sects, a manifestation of Gautama Buddha often depicted riding on a giant peacock) was updated by Makoto Ogino for his 1985 manga in *Young Jump*, using the idea of avatars of the gods as inspiration for a modern-day adventure. The franchise returned as *True PK* (1994, *Shin Kujaku-o*, released in the U.S. as *Spirit Warrior: Revival of Evil* and *Spirit Warrior: Regent of Darkness*), more faithful to Ogino's original, and it replaced the Madhouse-look-alike animation of AIC with *actual* animation from the Madhouse studio itself, under veteran director Rintaro. His versions throw much of their budget into the movie-quality opening scenes, creating impressive images that soon devolve into less expensive animation. Trawling outside Japan for villains, it features twin avatars, a boy and a girl, born to reincarnate god of light Kujaku-o and god of darkness Tenja-o. The boy, Akira, is a member of a Buddhist sect charged with guarding the Dragon Grail, a mystic vessel that has the power to release Tenja-o into the world. Power-crazed neo-Nazi Siegfried von Mittgard plans to steal the grail and reincarnate himself as Tenja-oh; this will prevent Akira's twin, Tomoko, from fulfilling her destiny, but Siegfried has another role in mind for her.

Like the director's earlier **DOOMED MEGALOPOLIS**, *PK* suffers in English simply through the weight of the original source material—American actors, working with the Japanese names for the Chinese versions of Buddhist takes on Hindu gods, create a predictably confusing roster, though translators Bill Flanagan and Yuko Sato make a heroic effort to incorporate the original Sanskrit. A live-action Japanese–Hong Kong coproduction, *PK: Legend of the Phoenix* (1988), was directed by **STORY OF RIKI**'s Nam Nai Choi and starred martial-arts legend Yuen Biao. Another Kujaku appears in CLAMP's **RG VEDA**. ●○●○

PEEP HOLE
2013. JPN: *Nozoki Ana*. Video. DIR: Katsuhiko Nishijima. SCR: Masahiro Okubo. DES: Masaaki Sakurai. ANI: N/C. MUS: predia. PRD: Studio Fantasia, Toho. 43 mins.
Tatsuhiko Kido, an art student newly relocated to the big city, discovers that a con-

venient hole in the wall allows him to see whatever's going on in the neighboring apartment, occupied by the lonely, pretty, and onanistic Emiru. Having witnessed her pleasuring herself, he visits her to warn her of the hole, but trips in predictable anime clumsiness, lands on top of her, and finds himself "blackmailed" with a photograph of the incident. Now he is not-particularly-reluctantly forced to let Emiru peep on him, and for him to peep on her. Based on a manga by Wako Honna, and originally bundled as a DVD with a volume of the comic. The later Blu-ray edition added a scrap of extra footage to make it a "Sexy Extended Edition." ○

PEEPING LIFE, THE *
2008. JPN: *Peeping Life ... The Perfect Edition*. TV series. DIR: Ryoichi Mori. SCR: N/C. DES: N/C. ANI: Hiroyoshi Wakamatsu, Mizuki Samejima, Ryoichi Mori, Shuichi Aso, Tatsuya Hoshimura. MUS: detune. PRD: CoMix Wave. 5 mins. x 10 eps. (TV1), 5 mins. x 10 eps. (TV2), 5 mins. x 10 eps. (TV3), 5 mins. x 10 eps. (TV4).
Featuring incidents from everyday life, capturing the sense of listlessness that pervades most people's days, this series of shorts was made in the computer using motion-capture from improvising live actors. Each five-minute episode features only one or two characters. Using the same "ennui-style" (*datsuryoku-kei*) comedy, director-producer Mori created a digital short called *Each Life* in 2007. It ran on NHK's premium channel and won a major award. He and CoMix Wave, the studio that produced **KAKURENBO: HIDE AND SEEK** and **VOICES OF A DISTANT STAR**, extended the concept for TV with such success that three more series followed: *Peeping Life ... The Perfect Emotion* in 2009, *Peeping Life ... The Perfect Evolution* in 2010, and *Peeping Life ... The Perfect Extension* in 2011.

PEKKLE *
1993. JPN: *Ahiru no Pekkle*. AKA: *Pekkle the Duck*. Video. DIR: Akira Shimizu. SCR: Mitsukuni Kumagai. DES: Toshikazu Ishiwatari. ANI: Takashi Asakura, Kennosuke Tokuda. MUS: Yasunori Honda. PRD: Sanrio. 30 mins. x 4 eps.
Another of Sanrio's cute kiddie characters, this time a sweet little duck, accompanied by his girlfriend, Ruby, reenacts tales from

A THOUSAND AND ONE NIGHTS for his U.S. video release—*PtD: Aladdin and the Magic Lamp* and *PtD: Sindbad the Sailor*. The final two adventures, unreleased in the U.S., were the shark-infested *PtD: Trouble at the Swimming Gala* and the *Indiana Jones* pastiche *PtD: In Search of the Secret Treasure*. The character, however, was a lame duck when compared to the successes of his Sanrio stablemate **HELLO KITTY**.

PELICAN ROAD CLUB CULTURE
1986. JPN: *Pelican Road Club Culture*. Video. DIR: Eiichi Yamamoto. SCR: Eiichi Yamamoto. DES: Koichi Igarashi. ANI: Kazuhiko Udagawa. MUS: Kazuo Kogure. PRD: Studio World, Nippon Columbia. 55 mins.
High school boy Kenichi Watanabe is crazy about his MBX50 motorcycle. He and his buddies organize a motorcycle club, which they call Culture. In among the engine oil and spark plugs, however, they begin to learn that there's more to life than bikes, chiefly when they are approached by reporter Kanako, who is interested in their stories ... particularly Kenichi's. Based on Koichi Igarashi's 1982 manga *Pelican Road*, which was a contemporary of **BOMBER BIKERS OF SHONAN**in the same *Shonen King* magazine.

PENDANT
1997. JPN: *Pendant*. Video. DIR: Yoshihiro Oka. SCR: Kaori Nakase, Takao Nitta. DES: Masaki Takei. ANI: Akio Watanabe. MUS: N/C. PRD: Beam Entertainment. 30 mins. x 3 eps.
Tales of young love, based on a computer game by Masaki Takei, creator of **END OF SUMMER**, starting with a lonely summer holiday enlivened by a chance meeting of an old flame and building up to a romantic "climax" on Christmas Eve. Unlike many adaptations of games that simply dump a male protagonist into a sea of women in the style of **TENCHI MUYO!**, this one separates the various female characters into separate stories with different male love interests, which is slightly more realistic, if no less boring. ○

PENELOPE *
2006. JPN: *Ukkari Penelope*. AKA: *Absent-minded Penelope; Penelope tete-en-l'air*. TV series, video. DIR: Michiru Shimada. DES: Mayumi Sato, Yumi Sano. ANI: N/C. MUS: Yuko Fukishima. PRD: Nippon Ani-

mation, NHK. 5 mins. x 26 eps. (TV1, TV2), 5 mins. x 2 eps. (v).

Little blue koala Penelope is rarely apart from her beloved stuffed rabbit pal Deudeu. The pair and their cuddly animal friends have all kinds of small adventures, many of them caused by Penelope's absent-mindedness and carelessness. This charming KIDS' ANIME series based on the picture books by Georg Hallensleben and Ann Gutman also inspired a two-part Christmas Video, *Merry Christmas Penelope/ Penelope's Christmas Tree* released in 2007, and a second TV series in 2009. Some sources list the video as two unscreened episodes of the first TV series, but the first series is confirmed at 26 episodes by TV listings and the Japanese book publishers announced the two five-minute Christmas broadcasts as a separate production in 2007.

PENGUIN'S MEMORY

1985. JPN: *Penguins Memory Shiawase Monogatari*. AKA: *Penguins Memory Happy Tale*. Movie. DIR: Satoshi Kimura. SCR: Hiroshi Kawano, Ryo Yamazaki, Rei Kuno, Dodekagon. DES: Ginjiro Suzuki. ANI: Norio Hikone, Akinori Nagaoka. MUS: Seiko Matsuda. PRD: Animation Staff Room, CM Land. 101 mins.

Mike, a traumatized penguin who once fought in the Delta War, returns to his hometown of Lake City and takes a job as a librarian. He falls in love with Jill, a would-be singing penguin who is the daughter of the owner of the local penguin hospital. Jill meets a record producer and embarks on a successful career, but Mike waddles away alone—he has discovered that she is engaged to marry Jack the penguin doctor, and he doesn't wish to get in the way.

A film made to cash in on the unexpected popularity of a 1984 series of Suntory Beer commercials that replayed famous American films such as *Casablanca* and *The Deer Hunter* but with a cast of cartoon penguins.

PENGUIN'S TROUBLES, A

2008. JPN: *Penguin no Mondai*. TV series, movie. DIR: Jun Kamiya. SCR: Kazuyuki Fudeyasu, Hiro Masami, Jun Kamiya et al. DES: Michiru Kuwabata. ANI: Maiko Nakata, Takehito Ueno. MUS: Shuhei Naruse. PRD: Shogakukan, ShoPro, TV Tokyo. 10 mins. x

100 eps. (TV1), 25 mins. x 50 eps. (TV2), 10 mins. x 52 eps. (TV3), 10 mins. x 51 eps. (TV4), 25 mins. (m).

Beckham Kinoshita goes to a regular elementary school and loves burgers and fries. His little friends treat him like every other kid, despite the fact that he's a round blue penguin with huge green eyes. Yuji Nagai's 2006 comedy manga has won a major award and been hugely successful, and the anime has followed in its footsteps, with director Kamiya and his team producing over 250 episodes in five years. The first series was followed in 2010 by *Penguin no Mondai MAX*, in 2011 by *Penguin no Mondai DX*, and in 2012 by *Penguin no Mondai POW*. A movie, *Geki-joban Penguin no Mondai: Shiawase no Aoi Tori de Go-Pen-nasai* (*A Penguin's Troubles Theatrical Version: Leave Your Pen With The Blue Bird of Happiness*), archly referencing Maeterlinck's BLUE BIRD, opened in Japan in autumn 2009 on a double bill with the DUEL MASTERS movie *Lunatic God Saga*, introducing several original characters to join the flood of games, toys, and other money-spinners—this is truly a penguin that lays golden eggs. Compare to MISTER PEN-PEN.

PENGUINDRUM *

2011. JPN: *Mawaru Penguindrum*. AKA: *Rotating Penguindrum*. TV series. DIR: Kunihiko Ikuhara. SCR: Kunihiko Ikuhara, Takayo Ikami. DES: Terumi Nishii. ANI: Terumi Nishii. MUS: Yukari Hashimoto. PRD: Brains Base, MBS, TBS, TVA, BS11. 24 mins. x 24 eps.

The terminally ill Himari Takakura appears to die during a visit to an aquarium, only to be resurrected (ULTRAMAN) through the intervention of a magical hat that transforms her into the Princess of the Crystal. In this new incarnation, she orders her two brothers, aided and abetted by three magical penguins, to go in search of the Penguindrum, an unidentified artifact that supposedly holds the key to her well-being.

Director Kunihiko Ikuhara has been one of the key figures in postmodern approaches to Japanese "magical girls" (TROPES AND TRANSFORMATIONS), ever since his landmark work in later episodes of SAILOR MOON. *Penguindrum* is a multi-layered text, readable on one level as yet another anime hokum about spell-casting

children, playing at petty theft and benign stalking in search of a vaguelydefined MacGuffin. However, its infantile surfaces serve a far deeper purpose, with later episodes that imply its wilder flights of fancy are part of the worldviews of damaged, deluded minds trying to come to terms with terrible trauma and unbearable memories (PERFECT BLUE). The second half of *Penguindrum* achieves this by veering far off the original apparent course into a realm of metaphor and magic-realism that will not surprise anyone who has seen Ikuhara's earlier UTENA. In this case, the allegories and allusions are plainly to an infamous event in 1995, the AUM Shinri-kyo sarin gas attack on the Tokyo subway perpetrated by cultists whose unwelcome self-identification as anime fans caused a long backlash against FANDOM in the Japanese media (RELIGION AND BELIEF; LAW AND DISORDER). Ikuhara's protagonists are hence recast, in terms that will be familiar to anime viewers, as the generation that has grown up since his defining Year Zero event—not merely the generation born since EVANGELION, but since the beginnings of modern-day, digitally interconnected FANDOM, and since the day when Japan suffered the consequences of human minds that were unable to see where fiction ended and reality began. *Penguindrum* deserves to be considered alongside PUELLA MAGI MADOKA MAGICA as a contemporary juxtaposition of the juvenile themes of early TV anime with the more mature interests of modern fandom, but also the ever-present concern that the latter is merely a thin veneer over the former, and vice versa.

PEPELO, BOY OF THE ANDES

1975. JPN: *Andes Shonen Pepelo no Boken*. AKA: *Adventures of Pepelo the Andes Boy*. TV series. DIR: Kazuhiko Udagawa, Yasuo Hasegawa, Seiji Okada, Takashi Anno, Fumio Ikeno. SCR: Shunichi Yukimuro, Soji Yoshikawa, Masaki Tsuji. DES: Nobuhiro Okaseko. ANI: Moriyasu Taniguchi, Nobuhiro Okaseko. MUS: Takeo Yamashita. PRD: Wako, Telescreen, NET (TV Asahi). 25 mins. x 26 eps.

In the 19th century, Pepelo's father sets off to find the mythical city of Eldorado and the Golden Condor, said to lie in Central America. When he hasn't returned a year later, Pepelo sets out to find him. On the way, Pepelo joins forces with Titicaca, an old man, Quena, a girl who has lost her memory, and an Aztecan boy called Azteco. They walk into the Andes using only a condor talisman as a guide. With a certain resemblance to FROM THE APENNINES TO THE ANDES, this series was a reasonable success in Europe, but largely eclipsed seven years later by MYSTERIOUS CITIES OF GOLD, which revisited many of its themes. Perhaps the strangest name on the credits, though, is lyricist Kazuo Umezu, who went on to fame as a creator of gory manga like THE BOY WITH CAT'S EYES.

PERFECT BLUE *

1997. Movie. DIR: Satoshi Kon. SCR: Sadayuki Murai. DES: Hisashi Eguchi, Hideki Hamazu, Satoshi Kon. ANI: Hideki Hamazu, Hisao Shirai. MUS: Masahiro Ikumi. PRD: Madhouse, Oniro. 82 mins.

Singer Mima Kirigoe leaves the pop trio Cham to become a serious actress. Her change in careers causes a decline into madness, as forces conspire to keep her from changing her public persona, to the extent of interfering directly in her private life. Matters aren't helped by a murderous stalker, egged on by e-mails from someone claiming to be the real Mima. Eventually, Mima's hold on reality is thoroughly undermined as she sinks into the mother of all neuroses. And she's not on her own—this film is told from the viewpoints of three characters, and each one of them is going slowly insane.

Based on a novel by Yoshikazu Takeuchi and originally planned as a live-action film, PB features obvious influences from Hitchcock's Vertigo (1958), Stage Fright (1950), and Dario Argento's Suspiria (1977), but it has ultimately a less bleak and more humane agenda. Murai's script, which adds the film-within-a-film Double Bind to really confuse matters, remains one of anime's best since Kazunori Ito's for PATLABOR. The obsessive fan stalker, who was merely a red herring in the novel, is given a succession of actual murders to perform in the anime version, though the blurred line between fantasy and reality is one of PB's greatest achievements—the director deliberately cut all transition shots that signified dream sequences or flashbacks, leaving the audience floundering in a confused world

cleverly matching the protagonists' own. Kon, the former animator on the surreal JOJO'S BIZARRE ADVENTURES who created environments full of faux-live-action clutter in ROUJIN Z, makes a virtue of a limited animation budget, depicting crowd scenes with empty faces and playing up the ghostly pallor of fluorescent lighting. The cinematography is gorgeous, as loving a rendition of real-life contemporary Tokyo as the dark, glittering forward-projection of the city in AKIRA (whose creator Katsuhiro Otomo has a production credit for introducing the producers to his protégé Kon, although some press releases implied his involvement in PB was far greater). The increasing influence of the Internet and cyber-reality on mass perceptions is seriously examined here (and further explored on TV in SERIAL EXPERIMENTS LAIN), but PB is also strong on traditional story values—beautifully paced plot development and a craftsman's ability to subvert the conventions of the medium. Most notable and controversial remains a scene in which Mima's character is raped, played out as a pastiche of The Accused (1988) but continually taunting the viewer with the question of whether this time it is really for real. The prosaic movements of lights and camera, and the whispered apologies of the actor playing one of the attackers who has to stay in position during a shooting break, heighten the surreality precisely because they remind us that Mima is being assaulted in a "respectable" professional context—later in the movie, she is assaulted for real.

The English version is excellent despite some inevitable losses in TRANSLATION. Japan may look like every other modern, industrialized, media-led country, but both language and social interaction are hugely important in this tale of fishes out of water. Some of the bowing, scraping, and statement of the obvious (culturally, an attempt to ingratiate oneself by appearing more clueless than the next person) just seems insincere with American voices. Mima's oft-repeated "Who are you?" loses some of its clout when lip-synching considerations force the actress to add a mitigating "Excuse me." The English dub also loses an extra level of emphasis—two scenes when Mima slips into her native dialect, demonstrating to the Japanese audience that not

even the girl we see in private is the real Mima. The city girl-next-door whom the fans worship is actually another mask—a pretty country maid who forgets her elocution lessons when Mom phones from back home. This shift is also heard in the film's final line, when Mima announces that she is "herself" at last (and uses her native accent, not the well-spoken Tokyo dialect she's been taught to use on TV). Despite these minor cavils, PB remains one of the best anime of the late 1990s. The remake rights were optioned by director Darren Aronofsky, who lifted a shot from the film (of Mima crouching in her bathtub) for his live-action movie Requiem for a Dream (2000) and returned to many of the film's thematic concerns and stylistic flourishes in Black Swan (2010). Director Kon and writer Murai would return with another peek behind dramatic masks: MILLENNIUM ACTRESS. Sequences from PB were shown onstage by Madonna as part of her Drowned World concerts in 2001. The live-action movie Perfect Blue: If This Is a Dream Wake Me Up (2002) is based on a later book in the series, and not the one that informed the anime production. **LNV**

PER-MAN

1967. JPN: Pa-man. TV series. DIR: Tadao Nagahama, Eiji Okabe, Shinichi Suzuki. SCR: Fujiko-Fujio, Tadao Nagahama, Masaki Tsuji, Koji Miharu, Tatsuo Tamura. DES: Fujiko-Fujio. ANI: Shinichi Suzuki, Tsutomu Shibayama. MUS: Hiroshi Tsutsui. PRD: Studio Zero, Tokyo Movie Shinsha, TBS. 25 mins. x 54 eps. (b/w; two stories per episode), 25 mins. (m1), 15 mins. x 526 eps. (TV2), 52 mins. (m2), 52 mins. (m3), 32 mins. (m4), 33 mins. (m5).

Four children and Boobie the chimpanzee are recruited to protect their hometown by a mysterious masked man. He gives them helmets that endow the wearers with superstrength and cloaks that let them fly at 91 kph; they derive their names from "Super" without the "Su." Lead male Per-man #1, chimp superhero Per-man #2, token female Per-ko, Osaka-born miser Per-yan, and baby Per-bo must try to solve the town's problems, great and small, and help its people. After a brief cameo in the final episode of the same creators' QTARO THE GHOST, Per-man got his own series in order to keep money rolling in from the

TBS sponsors. The franchise was revived many years later for a short film, *Per-Man: The Coming of Birdman* (1983), directed by Shinichi Suzuki, a former animator on the original series. Inevitably, the film was revealed as a preview of a coming series, the extremely long-running *New Per-man* that began soon after on TV Asahi. The update revealed Per-ko's real identity (she is really the pop star Sumi Hoshino) and introduced a new character, Yuki. To this was added more movies, in the form of two crossovers with **HATTORI THE NINJA**: *Hattori the Ninja + Per-man ESP Wars* (*Ninja Hattori-kun + Pa-man Cho-Noryoku Wars*, 1984) and *Hattori the Ninja + Per-man Ninja Giant Monster Jippo vs. Miracle Egg* (*Ninja Hattori-kun + Pa-man Ninja Kaiju Jippo VS Miracle Tamago*, 1985). Two decades later *Per-man the Movie* (*Pa-Pa-Pa the Movie Pa-man*, 2003) and *Per-man the Movie Octopus de Pop! Reed ha Pop!* (*Pa-Pa-Pa the Movie Pa-man Tako de Pon! Ashi ha Pon!*, 2004) followed.

PERSONA *

2011. JPN: *Persona 4 The Animation; Persona Trinity Soul, Persona 3*. TV series, movie. DIR: Yasuyuki Muto, Shinsuke Onishi, Shogo Yasukawa, Jun Kumagai, Jun Matsumoto, Noriaki Akitaya. SCR: Yuko Kakihara, Mitsukata Hirota, Jun Kumagai. DES: Yuriko Ishii, Shinobu Tsuneki, Michie Suzuki, Keisuke Watabe, Kazuaki Morita, Ayumi Miyakoshi, Shinji Nagaoka. ANI: Yuriko Ishii, Keisuke Watabe, Kiyotaka Nakahara. MUS: Taku Iwasaki, Shoji Meguro. PRD: A-1 Pictures, Aniplex, SPE, We've Inc., MOVIC, AIC, ASCII Media Works, Hakuhodo DY Media Partners, Index, MBS, MOVIC, Yomiko Advertising. 25 mins. x 25 eps. (TV, *Trinity*), 100 mins. (m, *Trinity*), 25 mins. x 26 eps. (TV2), 90 mins. (m2). The *Persona* role-playing game series is rooted in the same mythology and storyline that has already been adapted into anime form as **DIGITAL DEVIL STORY** and **TOKYO REVELATION**. It had, however, drifted far away from Aya Nishitani's original novels by the time the franchise was rebooted as the game *Revelations: Persona* in 1996, and still further when *Persona* itself was inevitably adapted into anime form, somewhat tardily, after the third iteration of the rebooted game (see **STREET FIGHTER II** for another franchise that began in one medium with a numerical title that referred to its origins in another). To the great

annoyance of the anime encyclopedist, its success has led to a series of sequels and spin-offs, released out of chronological order, and with an often tenuous continuity that only makes sense to people who have played the games. Despite this disordered narrative, we shall do our best to make sense of it, paying it the undeserved compliment of treating it like a standalone TV show even though, like **FINAL FANTASY**, the separate iterations of the story are often only vaguely connected.

The TV show *Persona: Trinity Soul* (2008) is based on the 2006 release *Shin Megami Tensei: Persona 3*, notably the first iteration to be translated in a non-bowdlerized form. It is set a decade after the events of the game, with the suggestion that a city has been plagued by dark supernatural forces ever since a great disaster that claimed the lives of Shin and Jun Kazato's parents and Jun's twin sister. The brothers are reunited with their significantly older sibling, Ryo, who is now the chief of police. Something about their hometown seems to create an environment that makes it possible for people to manifest their "Persona" inner selves as powerful spirit forces. Ryo is deep into an investigation of mysterious deaths and occurrences in the city, which he attributes to a criminal Persona group involved in the disaster that killed the boys' parents. An incident forces Shin's Persona to emerge, and he realizes that Ryo is aware of the supernatural events affecting the area. Others are manifesting Personas too, even at school.

It looks impressive, with Shigenori Soejima's designs for the game retaining their elegance when tweaked for animation. Combat sequences are good, too. Unfortunately the story is incoherent and confusing, with too many of the same old high school tropes and too much vague, mysterious dialogue, and it takes so long to get going that even die-hard fans of the game may snooze off. A *Persona 3* movie subtitled *Spring of Birth*, based on the *P3* manga was released in autumn 2013; it has an entirely new team at the helm.

In the TV series *Persona 4* (2011) Japanese teenager Yu Narukami (unnamed in the game, but identified here) moves from Tokyo to a quiet country town to stay with his police detective uncle and becomes entangled in a weird world of murders,

changing weather patterns, and a TV show that's trying to pull him into its universe. Yu and his new friends must find their Personas—their "other halves" inside the TV screen—and prevent more destruction in their own world.

The idea that in another reality you have special powers and a vital purpose has been exploited by shows from **SAILOR MOON** to **VISION OF ESCALOWNE**. The displaced teen hero is found in myriad places, from **PRINCESS MONONOKE**'s early Japan to **FULLMETAL ALCHEMIST**: *Conqueror of Shamballa*'s Nazi Europe. Where *P4: The Animation* scores is in spinning this handful of old tropes into an interesting pattern.

The opening credits play up one of the show's key features, the difference between the TV world and the real. The mix of 2D and 3D is a tricky one to pull off in anime, but lead 2D house D-Station was supported by some of the top names in the TV anime business, including AIC, Gainax, and Sunrise. There are a few problems with the animation, an occasional over-reliance on still frames, but not enough to spoil your enjoyment of an otherwise entertaining show. An unscreened 26th episode was included in the DVD and Blu-ray releases of the show; a compilation movie, *Persona 4 the Animation: The Factor of Hope*, was screened in Japan in summer 2012, and a spin-off manga from Satoshi Shiki followed that November. ◉

PERVERTED THOMAS *

2004. JPN: *Chikansha Thomas*. AKA: *Thomas the Pervert Train*. Video. DIR: Kenji Matsuda. SCR: Hiroshi Sasaki. DES: Hirotaka. ANI: Takashi Tsukamoto. MUS: N/C. PRD: Dream Entertainment, Studio March, Milky, Museum Soft. 30 mins.
A man with nothing better to do tries to "teach the women of the world about the pleasures of sex" by feeling them up on a crowded train. He has a special technique, it says here. Based on a computer game by Xuse. Compare to **MIDNIGHT SLEAZY TRAIN** and **XPRESS TRAIN**, but not to the children's books and TV shows of *Thomas the Tank Engine*, which is *Kikansha Thomas* in Japanese. ◉◐◉

PERVS ON A TRAIN *

2007. JPN: *Tsukin Kairaku Chikan de GO!!;*

Kaihoku. AKA: *Pleasure Commute: Go with the Pervert; Free Zone*. Video. DIR: Goro Yasunada, Shigenori Awai. SCR: Yasuyuki Muto, Akira Kishi. DES: Tao Min, Mai Shinata. ANI: Tao Min, Kusakai Kokubunji, Ryukichi Daihi, Shinjuro Yuki. MUS: FUJIMOTO. PRD: MS Pictures (Jam). 19 mins. x 2 eps.

On crowded trains, strangers become physically intimate for a short time. Some go beyond the necessity of accidental contact to become train gropers. It's a popular genre in anime porn, with titles such as MIDNIGHT SLEAZY TRAIN encouraging punters to dream of a more exciting commute. The trend for anime porn titles to get shorter and shorter, and the reluctance of American audiences to pay regular DVD prices for less than 20 minutes of screen time, has led to the creation of a completely new English-only title for two separate stories bundled together. This makes commercial sense for the U.S. distributor but leads to endless confusion for researchers and encyclopedists. Both from the same Japanese label, *Pleasure Commute* and 2008's *Free Zone* (*Kaihoku*) are made by different teams, related only by theme. Ⓝ

PET GIRL OF SAKURASOU *
2012. JPN: *Sakuraso no Pet na Kanojo*. TV series. DIR: Atsuko Ishizuka. SCR: Mari Okada. DES: Masahiro Fujii. ANI: Hiroshi Tomioka, Masahiro Fujii, Yukie Hiyamizu. MUS: N/C. PRD: Animax, ASCII Media Works, Frontier Works, GENCO, MBS, Media Factory, Sony Music Communications. 24 mins. x 24 eps.

Ejected from his no-pets accommodation for taking in stray cats, Sorata Kanda ends up in the shabby Sakura Hall, a dormitory for no-hopers. However, he soon discovers that despite their odd habits, questionable interpersonal skills, and hard-luck stories, many of the residents are masters or mistresses of their chosen craft, including a womanizing writer, a genius animator, and an idiot savant computer programmer. Mashiro Shiina is an artist newly returned from England and so self-absorbed and pampered that she cannot cook, clean, or care for herself (England can have that effect on people; just ask anyone who has written an encyclopedia of Japanese cartoons). Luckily, Sorata is available to care for her in a bizarre codependent arrangement, which soon becomes an even odder love triangle.

If you fed MAISON IKKOKU through a hypothetical modern-day Ruination Machine, that took good old ideas and turned them into crappy new ones, you might well end up with something like this, pandering without pause to what GUNDAM-creator Yoshiyuki Tomino has decried as "an autistic artistic consciousness." *Pet Girl of Sakurasou* is feel-good fiction for the *hikikomori* shut-in generation, suggesting that every group of losers and no-hopers has a redeeming feature or talent and that "quirkiness" now includes borderline mental illness. But it has ever been thus in anime romance (JUBEI-CHAN THE NINJA GIRL), and indeed, the idea of life in a fan-friendly hug-box has been approached in a far better manner in works such as PRINCESS JELLYFISH. The historically minded might detect in the title and character roster a questing hope that the inhabitants of the dorm are headed for greater things. Just as the real-life Tokiwa-so dormitory became a crucible for many talents of the 1950s manga business (WE'RE MANGA ARTISTS: TOKIWA VILLA), Sakura Hall has the potential to offer its inhabitants a community of their own, where the more traditional recruiting grounds of school and the office have let them down. The creative staff under Atsuko Ishizuka certainly put their hearts into this work, paying it the entirely unmerited compliment of taking it seriously and passionately, despite its frankly creepy overtones. Ishizuka and her team deserve better … but really, so do we all.

PET LIFE
2011. Video. DIR: Takuo Saki. SCR: Kaoru Takahashi. DES: Yukke Ani. ANI: Yukke Ani. MUS: N/C. PRD: Kanto Dogakai, Mary Jane. 25 mins.

For some reason, Shizumori's classmate puts away her underwear after Phys Ed class—and it's in the wrong locker. This means that Shizumori has to spend half the school day with no underwear until she can get back to the locker room. The lockers don't seem to work too well because she finds class creep Ozaki smelling her undies. He flings them on the ground and takes a photo of her leaning over to pick them up, then claims that he'll share the photo and everyone will think she's an exhibitionist—unless she has sex with him. Years of state education have obviously

failed to deliver any kind of reasoning capacity and so she goes along with it, in this porn anime based on Terunyo Kusatsu's 2008 manga of the same name. A similar situation has been handled with substantially more maturity in FLOWERS OF EVIL. Ⓝ

PET SHOP OF HORRORS *
1998. TV. DIR: Toshio Hirata, Norihiko Nagahama, Yoshiaki Kawajiri, Satoshi Nishimura. SCR: Yasuhiro Imagawa, Matsuri Akino. DES: Hisashi Abe, Hiroshi Kato. ANI: Hisashi Abe, Hiroshi Hamasaki, Hitoshi Sasaki. MUS: Mario Litwin. PRD: Madhouse, TBS. 25 mins. x 4 eps.

In Chinatown, in a generic U.S. city (on the Japanese release, *Newtype* magazine claimed it was New York, but *Animage* and *AX* both noted the visual references to Los Angeles), "Count D," a fey Faustian pet shop owner, sells personified desires as "pets" to society's misfits, including a mother who refuses to accept that her own weak will turned her daughter into a drug addict, a faithless husband who cannot admit he drove his bride to suicide, and a proud gangster who wants people to fear his power. Signing deceptively simple contracts, they discover that deals made with the supernatural should never be taken lightly. Leon, a loud-mouth cop who encapsulates several anime stereotypes of Americans, is convinced that the count is up to something, but the count is strangely welcoming and hospitable toward him. The "horrors" happen when purchasers ignore the strict instructions provided for the care of the unusual creatures they buy—*Gremlins* parallels are obvious. Old meets new and East meets West, not just in the mixture of mythologies, but in the mismatched central characters. Everyday laws cannot touch these criminals, but the count cuts through the red tape and delivers punishment where Leon cannot, without fear or favor toward a would-be president, or even a child star prepared to sell his soul for adult fame. Though our wiseacre policeman is too boneheaded to realize it, the count is on his side, transforming the story from a humdrum chiller into a moral *X-Files*, in which Hell's own angel teams up with an earthy cop to mete out peculiar justice.

Matsuri Akino's original 1990 manga ran for over a dozen volumes in *Mitzi*

Comics DX, and yet this 1999 TBS series was never planned as more than four episodes. Limited animation is bolstered by flashy effects (from some big names, including **DOOMED MEGALOPOLIS**–director Rintaro on the opening animation), but the biggest mystery is why there was no more. Perhaps wisely, the show canceled itself before the "sin of the week" angle could become too predictable. Compare to similar rough justice in **JUDGE**. **Ⓥ**

PETER PAN AND WENDY *

1989. JPN: *Peter Pan no Boken*. AKA: *Peter Pan's Adventure*. TV series. DIR: Yoshio Kuroda, Fumio Kurokawa, Kozo Kusuba. SCR: Shunichi Yukimuro, Michiru Shimada. DES: Takashi Nakamura, Shohei Kawamoto. ANI: Hirotsugu Kawasaki, Tomihiko Okubo, Moriyasu Taniguchi. MUS: Toshiyuki Watanabe. PRD: Nippon Animation, Fuji TV. 25 mins. x 41 eps.

J.M. Barrie's 1911 novel is given a new twist as Wendy, *not* wanting to grow up, travels with her two little brothers and Peter Pan to Never Land where he must fight the terrible pirate leader Captain Hook and face many other perils, including Darkness, an evil sorcerer who joins forces with Hook. Nakamura's presence may surprise those who know him only from **AKIRA** and **ROBOT CARNIVAL**, as would that of future **SPRIGGAN**-director Kawasaki. A compilation video of the first three episodes was released in the U.K. on an obscure children's label, featuring new music from Haim Saban and Shuki Levy.

PETITE COSSETTE *

2004. JPN: *Cossette no Shozo; Le Portrait de Petit [sic] Cossette*. AKA: *Portrait of Little Cossette*. Video. DIR: Akiyuki Shinbo. SCR: Mayori Sekijima. DES: Hirofumi Suzuki. ANI: Hirofumi Suzuki. MUS: Yuki Kajiura. PRD: Aniplex, Studio Hibari. 38 mins. x 3 eps.

Art student Eiri Kurahashi works part-time in his uncle's Tokyo antique shop, where he finds an antique Venetian glass goblet in which he can see visions of a beautiful young girl with long blonde hair. Her name is Cossette d'Auvergne and she's been dead for 250 years. She's looking for someone to help her—a man with the courage to risk everything, even his own life, to release her from her prison. Eiri's friends start to notice he's acting strangely;

previously his life has been bound up with his art, and though he has lots of female friends there hasn't been a special girl. He becomes completely absorbed by his visions and fantasies, losing track of where his life ends and Cossette's begins. His best friend Shoko Mataki is so concerned that her aunt, the local doctor, gets involved, along with tarot reader Michiru and priestess Shakodo. Meanwhile Yu, a young girl with latent talents and a secret crush on Eiri, is drawn into Cossette's dangerous web. Her sweet face hides a calculating heart and an insatiable lust for vengeance. Eiri can only free her by atoning for the betrayal of her former lover through a blood pact, swearing to love her and her alone and taking on another's soul—compare to similar entrapment in **MEMORIES**.

Putting a Gothic spin on both the harem show and the magical girlfriend theme reprised in **MOON PHASE** the following year, *PC* plays elegantly at darkness and foreboding. The three video episodes were edited together into a TV movie, *Le Portrait de Petit Cossette*, in 2005. Based on the manga by Asuka Katsura in *Magazine Z*. Part of the relatively recent "Gothic Lolita" subgenre of anime, based on the fashion fad of the same name, also found in **ROZEN MAIDEN** and **MOON PHASE**.

PETITE PRINCESS YUCIE *

2002. JPN: *Petit Puri[ncess] Yushi*. TV series. DIR: Masahiko Otsuka. SCR: Hiroyuki Yamaga. DES: Kazuko Tadano. ANI: Hideaki Anno, Mitsuru Obunai, Tadashi Hiramatsu. MUS: Seiko Nagaoka. PRD: Gainax, AIC, NHK. 25 mins. x 26 eps.

Yucie lives long ago and far away, in a Ruritanian magical land with her foster father and the family's young but fiercely loyal butler, Cube. She's 17 years old, but because of a magical curse, she looks like a 10-year-old girl—compare to **NANAKA 6/17**. Her positive attitude makes her seem even cuter and perkier—she never lets anything get her down, although she desperately wants to look her real age and become a beautiful, elegant lady with a handsome husband of her own. She has the chance to make her dreams come true when she's chosen as a Petite Princess, one of the elite girls from many different realms who will be trained in the ways of femininity and elegance. If she can defeat the competi-

tion, she may even become the Platinum Princess, and win the prize of a magic tiara that will grant her any wish—no prizes for guessing what Yucie's wish will be.

Takami Akai, who created the *Princess Maker* game series in which Cube first appeared, isn't about to let a winning concept drop. Crashing the countless fairy tales of enchanted princesses into every little girl's impatience to acquire those arcane skills that define a grown-up woman, he's produced the finishing school version of **DRAGON BALL**. Our heroine is trying to find her true self. Along the way, just like Toriyama's perky hero Son Goku, she makes loyal friends and converts former enemies to friendship.

PETOPETO-SAN

2005. TV series. DIR: Akira Nishimori, Tetsuya Endo, Tamaki Nakatsu, Yasuyuki Shinozaki, Toru Kitahata, Satomi Nakamura, Kenichi Ishikura. SCR: Megumi Ikeno. DES: Mari Tominaga. ANI: Mari Tominaga, Masakazu Iguchi, Hiroyuki Shimizu, Miwa Oshima. MUS: Masami Kurihara. PRD: Xebec M2, TV Saitama. 25 mins. x 13 eps.

After centuries of antagonism and misunderstanding, the Japanese finally welcome "monsters" into their community. In an attempt at species integration, normal children begin attending school with paranormal creatures—see similarly unlikely acceptance of foreigners, sorry, otherworldly creatures, in **DEARS**. Japanese boy Shingo Ohashi finds himself developing feelings for Hatoko "Petoko" Fujimura, a girl from the sorcerous realm whose main power appears to be the ability to make anything she regards as "cute" cling inescapably to her bare flesh until she falls asleep—compare to **URUSEI YATSURA**.

PHANTOM HEROES

1991. JPN: *Phantom Yusha Densetsu*. AKA: *Legend of the Phantom Heroes*. Video. DIR: Satoshi Dezaki. SCR: Kazumi Koide. DES: Keizo Shimizu. ANI: Toshifumi Takizawa. MUS: Kyan Marie with Medusa. PRD: Magic Bus. 45 mins.

Yazawa, a former navy F4 Phantom pilot, becomes embroiled in a South American coup when his lover is killed during a CIA operation in El Salvador. A violent thriller based on a best-selling novel by **DARK WARRIOR**–creator Sho Takejima, this video was rushed out in the year of his untimely death. **NV**

PHANTOM HUNTER MIKO

2000. JPN: *Reino Tantei Miko*. AKA: *Spirit Investigator Miko*. Video. DIR: Hiroshi Furuhashi. SCR: Tetsuo Tanaka. DES: Masashi Kojima. ANI: Waki Noguchi. MUS: N/C. PRD: Maxam. 30 mins.

This is a sexually charged variant of the ghostbusting anime typified by **PHANTOM QUEST CORP** or **GHOST SWEEPER MIKAMI**, as a sexy exorcist takes on the legions of hell. **N**

PHANTOM MASTER

2004. JPN: *Shin Angyo Onshi*. AKA: *Phantom Master—Dark Hero from a Ruined Empire; New History of the Dark Ways*. Movie. DIR: Joji Shimura. SCR: Joji Shimura, Mitsuru Hongo. DES: Hideki Takahashi. ANI: Hideki Takahashi. MUS: Ko Otani. PRD: Klockworx, Oriental Light & Magic, Character Plan. 87 mins.

A Korean-Japanese coproduction based on a Korean comic by author Youn In-Wan and artist Yang Kyung-Il, this is a reversioning of an ancient Asian folktale. In the fictional land of Jushin, the Angyo Onshi are secret agents who roam the land in disguise, rooting out and punishing corrupt officials. Agent Monsu wanders out of the desert into a town where the locals are losing their life forces to a cruel overlord. Justice ensues. The comic was printed in Japan in *Shonen Sunday GX*. **V**

PHANTOM QUEST CORP *

1994. JPN: *Yugen Kaisha*. AKA: *Phantom Company/Limited Company; Private Company*. Video. DIR: Koichi Chigira, Morio Asaka, Takuji Endo. SCR: Mami Watanabe, Tatsuhiko Urahata, Satoshi Kimura. DES: Hitoshi Ueda. ANI: Yasuhito Kikuchi. MUS: Junichi Kanezaki. PRD: Madhouse. 30 mins. x 4 eps.

Ayaka is a modern girl running her own successful business—a freelance psychic agency, supplying the power to deal with any problem. Ayaka is also a hopeless lush who can't stay ahead of her finances, blows all her money on designer clothes and karaoke bars, and relies on her child butler, Mamoru, to run her home and her life and to make sure she gets up in the morning. The police's own ghostbusting squad, Section U, headed up by a crumpled-but-cute detective with a soft spot for our heroine, causes even more complications. And as for her staff—she's stuck with a dropout priest, a twisted firestarter, a psychic who only works to enhance her meager pension, and her own rich family's hereditary butler.

Like its longer-running contemporary **GHOST SWEEPER MIKAMI**, *PQC* is packed with gentle digs at what has become of Japan. The money-culture of the late 1980s produced many unreal phenomena of its own (the bubble economy, Generation X) while simultaneously trying to forget the spiritual past. The title, with a double meaning in the real and ghostly worlds, sets the tone for a witty, wacky post-*X-Files* series, but it didn't get the success it deserved at home or abroad. Takuji Endo and Morio Asaka cram their episodes with innovative jerky camera effects to play up the feel of a horror B-movie, just one of the little touches that made *PQC* memorable, but somehow failed to ignite the audience. Other noticeable presences include Yoshiaki Kawajiri as a "guest" director for the striking opening credits and future **TENCHI MUYO!**–director Kimura as a humble scriptwriter. Creator Juzo Mutsuki has several other underrated series—the similar ancient-meets-modern clashes of **DEVIL HUNTER YOHKO** and **CYBER CITY OEDO 808**. The dub from Pioneer is of high quality, and even boasts a hilarious English-language version of one of Ayaka's excruciatingly melancholy karaoke sessions—the single 30-something modern girl singing a widow's song that likens herself to "a riderless horse."

PHANTOM: THE ANIMATION *

2004. AKA: *Phantom of Inferno*. Video, TV series. DIR: Keitaro Motonaga. SCR: Shoji Harimura. DES: Koji Watanabe. ANI: N/C. MUS: N/C. PRD: KSS, Earth Create. 30 mins. x 3 eps. (v), 25 mins. x 26 eps. (TV).

Teenage tourist Reiji Agatsuma accidentally runs across pretty girl assassin Ai (codenamed Ein, AKA Phantom) while out late at night on the streets of Los Angeles. He witnesses her at work, but when she attacks him he evades her. This makes the Inferno organization think he has the aptitude to join her. He is captured, has his memories erased, and is trained as an assassin in the style of **CRYING FREEMAN**.

Given the name Zwei, he struggles to regain his freedom and his memories. As he and Ein grow closer, she begins to look at her own life and question the emotions she has always suppressed—compare to **GUNSLINGER GIRL**. Initially released as the interactive title *Phantom of Inferno* (2001), the original involved the use of the DVD remote to steer the course of the game. This adaptation makes all the viewer's choices for them—if that's all that was necessary, what was the point of having "interactivity" in the first place? The original game was later bundled with the anime in a single release.

Five years later it returned in a far more sustained edition, remade as *Requiem for the Phantom* (2009), a 26-part TV series directed by Koichi Mashimo. Featuring a "second generation Phantom" assassin who recovers from amnesia to realize that he is not a tourist at all, but a highly trained killer, with the option of working as an assassin or being killed. The sheer length of running time allows for a far better sense of pace than the video series, particularly when an assassin's lifestyle is reasonably depicted as scenes of frenzied action, leavened with long, talky hiatuses.

PHAROAH'S SEAL

1988. JPN: *Oke no Monsho*. Movie. DIR: Daisuke Yasaku. SCR: Chieko Hosokawa. DES: Chieko Hosokawa. ANI: N/C. MUS: Joe Hisaishi. PRD: Toei. 40 mins.

Two lovers are caught up in civil unrest in 1000 B.C. Egypt. Based on Chieko Hosokawa's 1976 manga, which has been reprinted over 130 times by its publishers Princess Comics, this is best described as a "costume drama" since, while the setting is ancient Egypt, the characters' concerns speak to any modern schoolgirl, perhaps explaining the series' runaway success in manga form.

PHI BRAIN: PUZZLE OF GOD *

2011. JPN: *Phi Brain: Kami no Puzzle*. TV series. DIR: Hirotaka Endorse, Junichi Satao. SCR: Mayori Sekijima. DES: Yohei Sasaki, Norifumi Nakamura. ANI: Yohei Sasaki, Yuji Ito, Chiaki Nakamura et al. MUS: Akio Izutsu. PRD: Sunrise, NHK. 25 mins. x 25 eps. (TV1), 25 mins. x 25 eps. (TV2), 25 mins. x 25 eps. (TV3).

Kaito is a brilliant 16-year-old with a gift

for solving puzzles. He acquires a gadget called the Armband of Orpheus, which lets him access all his brainpower but leaves him exhausted afterwards. Using this extra boost of brainpower he's able to join a team of elite puzzle-solvers and is encouraged by his school principal to battle a secret organization named POG (short for Puzzle of God because secret organizations are rarely modest). POG creates fiendishly complicated puzzles to protect rare treasures. Kaito thinks puzzles should be about pure entertainment and intelligence rather than having any other purpose, but he plays the games anyway, discovering that three of his schoolmates are also in the elite league of top puzzlers known as Solvers.

Tapping into the popularity of Dan Brown's novels and movies like *National Treasure* (2004), this anime created by Sunrise enjoyed considerable popularity, with a second series *PB: PoG - The Orpheus Order* airing in 2012 and a third series in 2013. The idea of making complex puzzles the center of a boys' adventure series stretches the audience age bracket, encouraging the kids who traded cards and watched the related shows to carry on watching anime for another year or two. The puzzles themselves, usually mercifully unreliant on Japanese language, are often the stars of the show, prompting much true interactivity among viewers, many of whom are liable to be shouting at the screen as supposed geniuses take forever to realize the blindingly obvious.

PHOTO KANO *

2012. TV series. DIR: Akitoshi Yokoyama. SCR: Akitoshi Yokoyama, Sotaro Hayashi, Yoshitaka Shishido. DES: Masaharu Yamazaki, Mae Shimada. ANI: Mae Shimada. MUS: Mina Kubota. PRD: Dax, Enterbrain, Madhouse, McRay, Movic, Pony Canyon, TBS. 24 mins. x 13 eps.

Teenager Kazuya Maeda inherits his father's digital camera and immediately puts it to productive use at his school, where the girls are apparently lining up to have their self-esteem affirmed, looks appreciated, and bodies digitally preserved for later ogling. As in BAKEMONOGATARI, each girl-of-the-week has a problem that needs solving, which is somehow solved by letting Kazuya perve at them through his camera lens.

Never has the male gaze been quite so obvious, not only in the underlying rationale of this show but in the way it is shot, with unapologetic up-skirt and down-blouse camera angles, that continue Kazuya's obsession even in the way that his world is presented to the viewer. There is much to be said in anime about the power of the lens and the power of the visual image (FLAG), but *Photo Kano* disregards any such concerns, preferring instead to use its camera as a magic mask that presents the lead with a perfect excuse to stare at female bodies. The redemptive nature of the photo sessions betrays this tawdry show's origins in a dating sim game, where at least a surfeit of still images would have been part of the format. Compare to SKY COLOR WATER COLOR.

PHOTON *

1997. JPN: *Photon*. AKA: *The Idiot Adventures*. Video. DIR: Koji Masunari. SCR: Yosuke Kuroda. DES: Masaki Kajishima, Shinya Takahashi, Koji Watanabe. ANI: Shinya Takahashi. MUS: Haruhiko Nishioka. PRD: AIC. 45 mins. x 6 eps.

On Sandy Planet, where the locals are so stupid they worship Magic Markers, chieftain's daughter Aun goes AWOL because she's got a crush on a troubadour, and laconic local boy Photon is sent to find her before she causes trouble. But Photon discovers a crashed spaceship and wakes its beautiful pilot, Keyne, from her cryogenic slumber. Accidentally marrying her by writing the word "Idiot" on her forehead, Photon is forced to protect Keyne from the evil spacefaring prince Papacha.

Planned, like its stablemate TENCHI MUYO!, as a multimedia promotion involving animation, radio drama, novels, and a manga, *Photon* is distinguished by BATTLE ATHLETES–director Masunari allowing the designers free rein with their insane visual conceits, from a girl who can stop time in selected places, to levitation garters, windpowered landspeeders, and a girl trying to proclaim her love through a mouthful of sand. Sadly, the script doesn't live up to the visual promise, relying on puerile nudie gags and a charmless lead, though moments remain when it looks as if a mad scientist has combined DRAGON HALF and NAUSICAÄ in a secret laboratory. **Ø**

PIA CARROT *

1997. JPN: *Pia Carrot e Yokoso!!* AKA: *Welcome to Pia Carrot*. Video, movie. DIR: Kan Fukumoto, Nobuyoshi Ando. SCR: Katsuma Kanazawa. DES: Cocktail Soft. ANI: Katsuma Kanazawa. MUS: N/C. PRD: Pink Pineapple, KSS. 30 mins. x 3 eps. (v1), 30 mins. x 3 eps. (v2), 30 mins. x 6 eps. (v3, *DX*), 50 mins. (m).

In an anime based on a computer-dating simulation game, a lusty teenage boy gets a part-time job at a restaurant, where he is soon seducing the waitresses. By episode 3, even the crew tired of the setting, and the cast relocates to Okinawa. For the grand finale, manager Kyoko invites the girls back to her place, everyone gets drunk, and formulaic high jinks ensue. This was followed by a sequel, *PC2*, which features a whole new cast at another franchise of the Pia Carrot restaurant. After a manga adaptation appeared in *Comic Gao*, the franchise was renewed again for the non-erotic *Pia Carrot 2 DX* (1999), in which, predictably, a new branch of the restaurant opens up, a new boy gets a summer job, and a new rack of girls finds him irresistibly attractive. The first two series were released in the U.S. as *Welcome to Pia Carrot* and *Welcome to Pia Carrot 2* (both 2001), respectively. A short *Pia Carrot* "movie," *PC: Sayaka's Love Story* (*Sayaka no Koi Monogatari*, 2002), was directed by Yuji Muto. **Ø**

PIANO *

2002. TV series. AKA: *Piano: The Melody of a Young Girl's Heart*. DIR: Norihiko Sudo. SCR: Mami Watanabe, Ryunosuke Kingetsu. DES: Kosuke Fujishima, Yuji Ikeda. ANI: Yuji Ikeda. MUS: Hiroyuki Kozu, Ayako Kawasumi. PRD: Oriental Light and Magic (OLM), Marine Entertainment, Animate, Pioneer LDCE, Kid's Station. 24 mins. x 10 eps.

Eighth-grader Miu Nomura has been taking piano classes since she was small. Her parents, big sister Akiko, teachers, and best friend Yuki Matsubara know her as a shy, quiet girl, and she lacks self-confidence. Her music teacher Mr. Shirikawa feels that her playing, though almost note-perfect, lacks emotion. However, Miu is maturing in hesitant steps from a girl into a young woman, and her crush on handsome track team member Kazuya Takahashi is inspiring a change in her playing, opening the possibility that it may also mature as well—

if she can even gain the courage to make him notice her.

Guaranteed almost supernatural prettiness through the presence of **OH MY GODDESS!**–creator Kosuke Fujishima, this series also exploited the persona of its lead—voice actress Ayako Kawasumi supposedly started piano classes in childhood and both composed and performed the series' opening theme. The video release included four "Visual Monologues," supposed diary entries narrated by Miu about the preceding episodes (numbers 4, 6, 8, and 10), composed mostly of live-action footage of Kawasumi as well as some recycled animation. Not to be confused with *Pianist*, which is an episode of the erotic **SECRET ANIMA SERIES**.

PICCOLINO
1976. JPN: *Pinocchio Yori: Piccolino no Daiboken*. AKA: *The Adventures of Piccolino, after Pinocchio*. TV series. DIR: Hiroshi Saito, Masaharu Endo, Shigeo Koshi. SCR: Masao Maruyama. DES: Takao Ogawa, Michiyo Sakurai, Marty Murphy. ANI: Takao Kogawa, Michiyo Sakurai, Koichi Murata. MUS: Karel Svoboda. PRD: Nippon Animation, TV Asahi. 25 mins. x 52 eps.
Lonely toymaker Gepetto constructs a puppet son to keep him company and names him Piccolino. The boy lives as a normal child but yearns to be *real*. This German-Japanese coproduction of Carlo Collodi's 1881 tale involves one of Disney's stalwarts, Marty Murphy. Despite the renaming, the series remains close to the original, with sculpting by old Gepetto, the learning of worldly wisdom, and achieving real humanity—the story is the same. See also **ADVENTURES OF PINOCCHIO** and **NEW ADVENTURES OF PINOCCHIO**.

PICTURES AT AN EXHIBITION
1966. JPN: *Tenrankai no E*. Movie. DIR: Osamu Tezuka, Shingo Matsuo, Taku Sugiyama. SCR: Osamu Tezuka. DES: Osamu Tezuka. ANI: Akihiro Mori, Shigeru Yamazaki. MUS: Modest Mussorgsky. PRD: Mushi Pro. 34 mins.
This short film by **ASTRO BOY**'s Tezuka sets ten short vignettes of his own devising to music by Mussorgsky originally based on scenes created by a friend of the composer. The Tezuka stories, like the originals, are contemporary social satires:

The Critic, The Artificial Gardener, The Plastic Surgeon, The Factory Owner, The Tough Guy, The Champion, The TV Star, The Zen Funeral, The Soldier, and *The Finale*. The music is an original arrangement of Mussorgsky's score by Isao Tomita; he was later to make an arrangement of the same work for synthesizer, but this one is fully orchestrated, making for interesting comparisons. Definitely one to file in the "art house" section of Tezuka's output, here in an unmistakable homage to Disney's *Fantasia* (1940).

PIG HILL
2009. JPN: *Butazuka*. TV series. DIR: Akira Hodo, Miki Kobayashi. SCR: Yasunari Suda, Hiroki Takahagi. DES: N/C. ANI: N/C. MUS: Hirotaki Fukui. PRD: Milky Cartoon, Studio MC. 5 mins. x 13 eps.
Parodying the Takarazuka revue, the ecological movement, and modern society, this surreal show stars CGI pigs. In a remote South American nature reserve in the Republic of Panabia, there is a new species called Puchibuta—minipigs. A Queen rules a huge mound in which pigs just eight centimeters long live like termites. When a dedicated researcher discovers them, he sets out to make a documentary observing their strange society. A charming oddity, created by Furifuri Company.

PIG PRINCESS
2011. JPN: *Buta Hime-sama*. Video. DIR: Shinpei Nagai. SCR: Shinpei Nagai. DES: Yukari, Shigeru Tani. ANI: Yuki Tatsunotaka. MUS: N/C. PRD: Seven KK, Pink Pineapple. 24 mins.
A peaceful country is invaded by orcs. To keep her people safe, Queen Ilena agrees to marry the king of the invaders. He looks like a pig (although our research has not gone far enough to reveal if he shares the boar's most interesting sexual characteristic, a corkscrew penis), and he slobbers a lot. Does that really turn people on? Based on an erotic game by ORCSOFT. **NV**

PIGGYBACK GHOST
1955. JPN: *Onbu Obake*. AKA: *Knapsack Ghost; Ghost in a Knapsack*. Video, TV series. DIR: Ryuichi Yokoyama. SCR: Ryuichi Yokoyama. DES: Ryuichi Yokoyama. ANI: Mitsuhiro Machiyama. MUS: N/C. PRD: Fuji, Eastman Color, Yomiuri TV (Nippon TV). 25 mins. (m), 25 mins. x 54 eps. (TV).

Green-eyed spirit Onbu is created when lightning strikes jade in a river. He loves swimming through the air but is adopted by Ojie the village blacksmith, who carries him in a knapsack. Onbu plays with the cheeky Kanchan brothers, Ojo the gentle girl, Chinnen the young priest, and the other kindly villagers.

Although forgotten today, this obscure anime made by the manga-creator Ryuichi Yokoyama's do-it-yourself studio Otogi Pro was the landmark anime event of the year back in 1955. Premiered at an exclusive event before a celebrity audience, it was designed to establish this company as a name in the newly burgeoning field of anime, and did indeed lead to several other contracts, such as the TV series **INSTANT HISTORY**. However, Yokoyama, who also created **FUKU-CHAN**, lacked the financial clout to expand as fast as Toei, or the passion for animation that fired Osamu Tezuka, causing his studio to sink from view during the 1960s. Lifting many ideas from **JAPANESE FOLK TALES**, the later TV series shared many staff members with the more successful **SAZAE-SAN**, and was made by Hajime Watanabe at the Eiken Studio in 1966.

PILOT CANDIDATE *
1999. JPN: *Megami Kohosei*. AKA: *Candidate for Goddess*. TV series, video. DIR: Mitsuru Hongo. SCR: Akira Oketani, Miho Sakai. DES: Shinichi Yamaoka. ANI: N/C. MUS: N/C. PRD: Production I.G, Xebec. 25 mins. x 12 eps. (TV), 23 mins. (v).
Rei "Zero" Enna and a group of other teenagers from various space colonies must train together at an interstellar academy in order to protect Zion, the last human colony, from the devastating alien invaders known only as "Victim." In a setup that will be familiar to anyone who has followed **SPORTS ANIME** or military training movies, the teenage pilots soon bond, with the exception of a ruthless candidate determined to out-score everyone else. Typically, they idolize their tough, no-nonsense Coach (compare to **GUNBUSTER**) and the upperclassmen who are so good at the tasks which Zero and company are only just learning. Meanwhile, there are hints that something untoward is going on—as in *The Matrix* (1999), which featured a hero who was "The One," not a Zero, and

a bastion of freedom called Zion—what first appear to be design problems or story inconsistencies take on more sinister meanings. Zero's offhand comment that he can't remember his family turns out to be a statement of the literal truth. Meanwhile, the pilots get on with their pilot training, flying five (and only five—why not make more?) robots modeled on Greco-Roman goddesses, color-coded like the creations of a live-action team-show like *Goranger* (*DE).

This anime was based on a manga in *Comic Ga* by **DNAngel** creator Yukiru Sugisaki and influenced by the existential musings of **Evangelion**, but it features slapstick and a cat-girl thrown in for good measure. As with other anime made at the turn of the century (see **Dual**), the transition to digital animation makes for clever camerawork but a sanitized, "clean" feel to all the art. Note that the episodes are numbered "00" through "11," apparently in order to cause confusion to anime encyclopedists. A one-shot 2002 video spin-off retold the TV series story from the point of view of one of the other pilots.

PINCH AND PUNCH

1969. JPN: *Pinch to Punch*. TV series. DIR: Fumio Ikeno. SCR: Noboru Ishiguro, Toyohiro Ando. DES: N/C. ANI: Tadao Wakabayashi. MUS: N/C. PRD: Fuji TV Enterprise. 5 mins. x 162 eps.

Pinch and Punch are genius twins with a mean streak, easily annoyed with their associates, particularly with the hypocrisy of adults. Their main nemesis is Mamagon, their education-obsessed mother, against whom they soon form a rebel alliance, in the company of their friend Dotako, pet Ijibuta the pig, and little sister Chibigon—note that the *gon* suffix in Japan is usually only applied to dangerous creatures, such as **Monster Tamagon**.

Pinch and Punch is, quite literally, an anime that just happened—as **Freckles Pooch** came to an end, the staff slowly transferred to this new production, which briefly shared *FP*'s slot before taking it over. The story, so Japanese sources claimed, was not actually pitched to the network; it was simply assumed that a cartoon of equivalent value to *FP* would replace it, and that's what occurred, in an implementation of the "more of the same"

policy first instituted by money-men observing the decline of sales in merchandise from **Qtaro the Ghost**.

PING PONG CLUB *

1995. JPN: *Ike! Inachu Ping-Pong Club*. AKA: *Let's Go! Inachu Ping Pong Club; Make Way for the Ping Pong Club*. TV series. DIR: Masami Hata. SCR: Sukehiro Tomita, Tsunehisa Ito, Kenji Terada, Yoshihiro Sasa. DES: Minoru Furuya. ANI: Mamoru Tanaka. MUS: Katsuyoshi Kobayashi. PRD: Grouper Production, KSS, TBS. 25 mins. x 26 eps.

The boys' table-tennis club consists of earnest captain Takeda, school dreamboat Kinoshita, and four deadbeats who constantly goof off instead of practicing. Their coach, Mr. Shibazaki, is a pushover for all the other teachers. The girls' club is a large group of dedicated, gifted young athletes, whose coach, Mr. Tachikawa, despises the boys' club and covets its premises. But the clubroom is about more than just ping-pong; it's a refuge for a group of misfits, no-hopers, and adolescents trying to cope with the petty pains and embarrassments of growing up. To keep it, the boys will have to find that old fighting spirit they all seem to lack—a plan helped by the pretty Kyoko, who offers a personal "sex pass" to the highest scorer.

It's hard to describe this short series, based on Minoru Furuya's 1993 *Young Magazine* manga, as anything other than insane. The raging of teenage male hormones and the nonoperational status of the related brain cells is conveyed in a fractured visual and directorial style, complete with a **Lupin III** pastiche, mom-and-pop gags, enka and taiko, male impersonators, crossdressers, St. Francis Xavier, the legend of **Momotaro**, volcanic eruptions, smelly foreigners, feats of *Endurance*, and every conceivable offensive reference to sexual habits and bodily functions. There are more naked penises in this low-rent "buddy movie" series than in many erotic anime—falling out of shorts, stuffed into bird's heads for a **Swan Lake** ballet skit, accidentally revealed during exercise—and all the tropes normally used to peek at female nudity, but there's hardly a hint of any real possibility of sexual action. The overall effect is as directionless and futile as the average teenager's life, but it's hard not to feel a creeping sympathy for its

hopeless, dogged solidarity with those facing hormonal challenge and social failure.

The throwaway nature is so determinedly pursued as to obscure the solid track record of its crew. This isn't a team of young punks talking dirty to their peers (see **Bite Me!: Chameleon**), but a rack of seasoned professionals with an instinct for video sales. Their work is full of knowing nudges and winks, entirely unashamed of itself. Despite the multitude of monocultural references, the overall *Beavis and Butthead* atmosphere would have spoken loud and clear to legions of hormonally challenged males too young to get most of the cultural digs, but that's hardly the audience for the subtitled version that was released in the U.S. No relation to the 2002 live-action movie, written by Kankuro Kudo and directed by Fumihiko Sone, which was adapted from a different 1996 manga by Taiyo Matsumoto. **LNV**

PINK CURTAIN

1987. JPN: *Pink no Curtain*. JPN: *Curtain of the Pink*. Video. DIR: Yoshiharu Kurahashi. SCR: Masahito Nishio. DES: N/C. ANI: Minoru Kobata. MUS: Hikaru Onda. PRD: Bip. 30 mins.

Virgin boy Okuyama is a stocker at the supermarket who has no luck with women. His life is thrown upside down when his sister Noriko unexpectedly moves into his house. Okuyama is overcome with lustful thoughts for her, but she regards him simply as a brother. With more incest from the era that gave us **Cream Lemon**, this story was based on the strip in *Manga Action* magazine by George Akiyama, who also created **Koiko's Daily Life**. The animated video release was preceded by three *Pink Curtain* live-action movies, two in 1982 and one in 1983, from the notorious Nikkatsu studio. **N**

PINKY:ST.

2006. Video. DIR: Keiichiro Kawaguchi. SCR: Saki Hasemi. DES: Satoshi Shimada, Asao Takahashi. ANI: Satoshi Shimada. MUS: Hideaki Takatori, Hiroaki Kagoshima. PRD: Gonzo—Gonzino, Sofa Studio (3D) GDH, GSI Creos. 13 mins. x 2 eps.

Tomboy Mei is a skilled martial artist, a talent that comes in handy to deal with the hassle she and her friends get from guys at school. Her skill in dealing with harassment has earned her the nickname

"King Kong," but inside she yearns to dress in cute, girly frills. As a Pinky:st. otaku, collecting the cute dolls that are the latest craze, you might expect Keiichiro to get picked on, but he's more worried about a recent argument with a good friend. Help is at hand for the hapless pair when Pinky:st. figure Saki comes to life and takes them into a fantasy land where they learn to solve both their problems through the power of fashion and friendship.

Don't expect depth: these two anime, each bundled with a special Pinky:st. figure, are extended commercials for the toy line designed by Yuki Kanaya for GSI Creos and VANCE PROJECT (ADVERTISING AND SPONSORHIP). Asako Ohashi's color design is as bright and vibrant as the toys themselves. Pinky:st. has had a close relationship with anime from its inception: fans can get tiny versions of beloved anime characters from STREET FIGHTER II, SAKURA WARS, EVANGELION, THE MELANCHOLY OF HARUHI SUZUMIYA, THE GIRL WHO LEAPT THROUGH TIME, SKY CRAWLERS, and more.

PINMEN

2000. AKA: *PiNMEN: Workers From Space Video*. DIR: Bak Ikeda. SCR: Bak Ikeda. DES: Bak Ikeda. ANI: Bak Ikeda. MUS: Homo Sapiens Sapiens. PRD: Trilogy Future Studio, Pierrot, Animax, Dentsu. 7 mins. x 12 eps.
A group of superadvanced, superpeaceful aliens have locked away all knowledge of warfare deep in their distant past—the flipside of the Zentraedi from MACROSS. Learning of a distant blue-green planet where all kinds of "fun" are available, a group of them resolve to come to Earth. Since they are industrious, frugal aliens, they intend to work hard so that they can earn enough money to pay for the entertainment they bring back to their homeworld. An innocuous short animation by an artist calling himself Bakuhat-suro "Bak" Ikeda—a pseudonym meaning Explodey Ikeda.

PIPI THE ALIEN

1965. JPN: *Uchujin Pipi*. TV series. DIR: Yoichi-ro Konishi. SCR: Sakyo Komatsu, Kazumasa Hirai. DES: Toshikazu Fukuhara. ANI: N/C. MUS: Isao Tomita. PRD: NHK, TV Doga, NHK. 25 mins. x 52 eps.
Toshihiko and Ryoko meet the gnome-like alien Pipi and his friends, who have one year (the length of a lunch break on Pipi's world) to learn all they can about planet Earth. Since these two Japanese children are the first people they have met who are close to them in size, they tag along with them as they explore their neighborhood, repaying them by taking them on fantastic space journeys during their own school lunch breaks. A series that mixes live action and animation.

PIPI THE FLIGHTLESS FIREFLY

1995. JPN: *Pipi Tobenai Hotaru*. Movie. DIR: Shinichi Nakada. SCR: Yoshimi Kato. DES: Akimi Ozawa. ANI: Takaya Ono. MUS: N/C. PRD: Office CHK, Success Road, Mushi. 90 mins.
In a heavy-handed "educational" film that also finds the time to tackle environmental issues, a young firefly is bullied by his fellow insects because he cannot actually fly. Government approved, it says here.

PIPOPAPO PATROL

2000. JPN: *Pipopapo Patrol-kun*. AKA: *Pip Pop Pattle*. TV series. DIR: Mitsuo Hashimoto. SCR: Aya Matsui. DES: Birthday, Izumi Todo. ANI: N/C. MUS: Toshiyuki Takizawa. PRD: Toei Animation, BS Fuji. 25 mins. x 65 eps.
In Sunflower City, technology is so advanced that vehicles are able to think and speak. Perky little police patrol car Pattle (Patrol) and his driver Hajime are partners: both rookies, but eager to learn from more experienced officers and vehicles and determined to do their bit to keep the peace on their patch. A show that takes *Starsky and Hutch*, extracts the cardigans and comedy pimp, and whisks in a dash of *Bob the Builder*, or if you prefer, BUBU CHA-CHA meets YOU'RE UNDER ARREST! Created by Izumi Todo, the house pseudonym that was also responsible for MAGICAL DOREMI and PRECURE.

PIROPPO

2001. JPN: *Aibo*. TV series. DIR: Katsuhito Ishii. SCR: Katsuhito Ishii, Yumiko Fujimura. DES: Katsuhito Ishii. ANI: Yumi Chiba, Shigeko Sakuma, Rie Nishino. MUS: Eiko Sakurai. PRD: Studio 4°C, Sony, Fuji TV. 20 secs. x 54 eps.
A series based on Sony's hugely popular range of robot pets, *Piroppo* stars two new robots, Latte and Macaron, designed by Katsura Moshino, which went on sale in Japan two weeks before the October 11 series premiere. The series was planned as 54 episodes of 20 seconds each, but shown in 5-minute and 10-minute compilations. There's also a web comic on Sony's *AIBO-Life* site. It's hard to see 20-second animations as anything other than commercials, despite the PR claims of a "lavish anime staff." The design is deliberately wacky, with references to pop culture icons like masked wrestlers and cowboys, and a collar-and-tie wearing hammerhead shark. The Aibo appears to have been the inspiration a decade later for the Heybo in HEROMAN.

PITA-TEN

2002. TV series. DIR: Yoshiaki Okamura, Yuzo Ten. SCR: Akemi Menda, Yasuko Kobayashi. DES: Kyuta Sakai. ANI: Toshifumi Kawase, Shinichiro Minami. MUS: Hikaru Nanase. PRD: Madhouse, Broccoli, TV Osaka. 24 mins. x 26 eps.
Kotaro Higuchi has recently lost his mother, and his businessman father works long hours and is only around at breakfast. Kotaro is a quiet boy who looks after the house and hangs out with his best friends from childhood, Takashi Ayanokoji, AKA Ten-chan, and Koboshi Uematsu, who has been sweet on Kotaro ever since they were small and he comforted her after she hurt herself playing. Ten-chan is the boy with everything—looks, intelligence, great sporting ability, and a wealthy family—but Kotaro has his own special gift: he can see the supernatural. This leads him into a meeting with apprentice angel Misha, a clumsy, tactless but kind-hearted spirit who succumbs to a huge crush on him and invades his life. She moves in next door to him, starts at his school, and becomes his very own cute and perky stalker. When apprentice devil Shia, who is in big trouble because she's far too nice to succeed as a demon, gets a crush on Ten-chan and moves in with Misha, the stage is set for a comedy romance based on the manga by DIGI CHARAT author Koge Donbo. All this was done far better in URUSEI YATSURA two decades ago, but the twist of adding quasi-infantile cuteness to overt teen sexuality has hooked many fans.

PLACE PROMISED IN OUR EARLY DAYS, THE *

2004. JPN: *Kumo no Muko, Yakusoku no Basho*. AKA: *The Place of Promise in the*

Clouds; Beyond the Clouds, the Promised Place. Movie. DIR: Makoto Shinkai. SCR: Makoto Shinkai. DES: Ushio Tazawa. ANI: Ushio Tazawa. MUS: Tenmon. PRD: CoMix Wave. 91 mins.

In an alternate universe, Japan is partitioned after WWII. Hokkaido is annexed by the Soviet Union, while Honshu and the southern islands go to the USA. A huge tower is built on Hokkaido, rechristened with its old name of Ezo, which can be seen across the waters of the Tsugaru Strait from Aomori, the northernmost town on Honshu. Four decades later, in 1996, two teenagers vow to take the girl they both love to see the tower's mysteries in their homemade aircraft, the Bella Ciela. Then Sayuri Sawatari falls ill with a strange narcolepsy and is transferred to Tokyo for treatment by a specialist. Her friends Hiroshi Fujisawa and Takuya Shirakawa abandon their dream and get on with their lives, but when Hiroshi learns that Sayuri is still in a coma three years later, they decide to try and help her. The world is on the brink of war again, and Sayuri's dreams are the key to a mystery which will bring her two childhood friends in touch with parallel worlds and political tensions as she tries to dream herself back to a place where unfulfilled childhood promises can finally be kept.

Makoto Shinkai has developed greatly since he drafted VOICES OF A DISTANT STAR virtuallysingle-handed on his home computer. Mixing the Hokkaido quest of DIAMOND DAYDREAMS with the girlfriend-in-a-coma of THE ETERNITY YOU DESIRE and the alternate history of FULLMETAL ALCHEMIST, this project shows almost the same level of hands-on control—he created, wrote, directed, and storyboarded, and also handled art direction, color design, editing, postproduction, and sound direction. This, plus the use of elements such as flight and hand-built aircraft with Italian names, has led some critics to make comparisons with Hayao Miyazaki. Beautiful as this second work is, such comparisons are extremely premature. Shinkai the writer is still fixated on the theme of his early work—the agony of loss imposed by time, distance, and age. He creates beautiful characters, real and engaging, but they are entirely caught up in yearning and reminiscence, reluctant

to move in any direction except back. His promising plot is simply left to unravel, its threads unresolved. His assured handling of lighting, color, and music creates and sustains atmosphere so well that it seems almost unkind to highlight the deficiency, but this is not yet the output of a mature and rounded creator. Like its story, it's a youthful promise, a shining dream that still awaits fulfillment.

PLACE TO PLACE *

2012. JPN: *Atchi Kotchi.* AKA: *Here and There.* TV series. DIR: Fumitoshi Oizaki. SCR: Nobuhiko Tenkawa. DES: Atsuko Watanabe. ANI: Hideki Furukawa. MUS: Masaru Yokoyama. PRD: AIC, BS-TBS, Hobunsha, Pony Canyon. 25 mins. x 12 eps.

True love may or may not blossom between the capricious, sarcastic Tsumiki and Io, the boy she secretly adores, who is completely oblivious to her romantic interest. A four-panel gag manga by Ishiki, running in *Manga Time Kirara*, is arguably stretched a little too far in animated form. The original manga constantly dueled with the reader's assumptions, leaping into impressionistic moments of deformation in which Tsumiki would suddenly develop cat-ears or psionic powers. Repeatedly dragged out on television, these humorous moments take on a new tone, suggesting that she might really be an alien or transformed animal. Wish fulfillment for the lonely male viewer, meanwhile, pushes the usual elements of anime ROMANCE AND DRAMA, that even the most clueless of boys are unwittingly objects of admiration for besotted girls.

PLANE CABBY'S LUCKY DAY, THE *

1932. JPN: *O-atari Sora no Entaku.* Movie. DIR: Teizo Kato. SCR: N/C. DES: Teizo Kato. ANI: Teizo Kato, Kiyoji Nishikura. MUS: N/C. PRD: Marvel Graph, Kyoroku Eiga-sha. 10 mins.

In the future year of 1980, humans live atop towering skyscrapers while the surface of the world is populated by anthropomorphic animals. A lowly aerial cab-driver takes a fare on a long journey to the South Seas, where he stumbles upon a rich cache of treasure and happy natives willing to sell it to him.

Released in the same year as Shigeji Ogino's *One Day A Hundred Years Hence* (1932, *Hyakunen-go Aru Hi*), and display-

ing a fascination with future modernity, including aerial traffic control and food cooked in seconds, *The Plane Cabby's Lucky Day* is one of Japan's first SF anime (SCIENCE FICTION AND ROBOTS), a generation ahead of ASTRO BOY. However, its genre trappings soon fade, leaving it little different from numerous other WARTIME ANIME that repackaged fantasy as an allegory for Japanese imperialism. Despite resonances of Fritz Lang's *Metropolis* (1926, see METROPOLIS), it makes no attempt to engage with the political implications of the social Darwinism it depicts: the animal proles are all willing dupes. A human passenger's desire to be taken to "the South Seas" not only refers to Japan's colonial ambitions as a fait accompli, but also as an enduring, albeit distant and backward, addition to the Empire. Meanwhile, even the animal inhabitants of the new-found isle that the hero plunders are happy to offload their diamonds on him, to the greater benefit of his aged mother, and leading to the closing homily: "Charity is a good investment."

The film was included in the Digital Meme *Japanese Anime Classic Collection* box set, released on DVD in 2007.

PLANET BUSTERS *

1984. JPN: *Birth.* AKA: *World of the Talisman.* Video. DIR: Shinya Sadamitsu. SCR: "Kaname Pro." DES: Yoshinori Kanada, Makoto Kobayashi. ANI: Shinya Sadamitsu, Mutsumi Inomata, Shigenori Kageyama. MUS: Joe Hisaishi (Randy Miller in U.S. version). PRD: Idol, Kaname. 80 mins.

Namu Shurugi (Prince Talon) and his sister Rasa Jupiter (Princess Rasa) are descended from a race wiped out by the people of planet Aquaroid (Pandora), who are engaged in a devastating global war with the android Inorganics race. They fall into the company of Bao (Mo) and Kim (Keen), two treasure hunters in search of the mystic talisman. This planet, it seems, is a "testing ground" to reveal the one destined to become the leader of the Galactic Empire. In an arrangement similar to KING ARTHUR AND THE KNIGHTS OF THE ROUND TABLE, whoever gets the talisman will become the new ruler. The fight for the talisman is a conflict that begins *every* cycle of cosmic existence, as factions compete to determine whether the dominant life-form throughout the universe will be flesh or metallic.

Though the American dub unsurprisingly reduces this to the usual simplistic Good Humans vs. Evil Robots, this sci-fi story, which features lots of action, cool machines, and frequent shots of Rasa's rear end, is a paradoxical and densely layered parable of reincarnation. This makes it very unsuitable for the audience of under-fives at whom the U.K. video release was aimed. Even with the script revamped to minimize the spiritual dimension and make the goal of their quest the "Planet Buster," a secret weapon made by the creator of the universe (who would really need one, right?), it still makes no sense, but it's fun to watch. Ending with the destruction of this cycle of existence, and only the four main characters preserved in spirit form, it is liable to have befuddled many a preteen viewer, especially with the finale, when two alien superbeings sit down and start debating the transient nature of existence. Made for video but shown in Japanese theaters, a "Special Edition" on video includes the 22-minute *Making of Birth* documentary.

PLANET MASK
1966. JPN: *Yusei Kamen*. TV series. DIR: Yonehiko Watanabe, Tsutomu Yamamoto. SCR: Akira Adachi. DES: Takaji Kusunoki. ANI: Masakazu Tanokura. MUS: Hidehiko Arano. PRD: TCJ, Eiken, Fuji TV. 25 mins. x 39 eps.
In the 21st century, the discovery of the inhabited tenth planet, Pineron, out past Pluto, is happy news for the solar system. Earthman Johansen and Pineron girl Maria fall in love and become the proud parents of the first mixed-race child, Peter. Fifteen years later, Earth and Pineron are thrown into a state of war when Pineron warships mistake an Earth vessel in trouble for an attack ship. A lone masked figure riding on a rocket tries to keep the spacefaring powers apart. This Cold War superhero thriller was inspired in equal chunks by the troubles in Vietnam, Japan's conflicts with the U.S.S.R. over its northern islands, and the children of mixed-race parents after WWII—children who would shortly be entering their teens. With typical TV double standards, the theme song cried "stop the war," even as the show encouraged kids to go out and *fight* for peace.

PLANETES *
2003. TV series. DIR: Goro Taniguchi, Tatsuya Igarashi, Megumi Yamamoto, Hiroshi Ishiodori. SCR: Ichiro Okochi. DES: Yuriko Chiba, Seiichi Nakatani, Takeshi Takakura. ANI: Eiji Nakata, Hisashi Saito, Masashi Kudo, Yuriko Chiba. MUS: Kotaro Nakagawa. PRD: Sunrise, AD Cosmo, NARA Animation, Bandai, NHK. 25 mins. x 26 eps.
By the year 2075, decades of missions and projects have left Earth's orbit cluttered with space junk—bits of rocket, defunct satellites, and other debris. Such space garbage needs to be collected, a task farmed out to private corporations such as Technora. Hachirota "Hachimaki" Hoshino is a young employee who has always wanted to own his own spaceship, but now seems stuck in a workaday rut as little more than a glorified dumpster driver. To his annoyance, he is saddled with rookie recruit Ai Tanabe, who has yet to appreciate that life in space is fraught with dangers—the slightest mistake in a jet firing or the smallest tear in a space suit can spell instant death. Their fellow employees include American Fée Carmichael, a compulsive smoker whose habit is doubly dangerous in oxygen-rich environments, and Russian Yuri Mihalkov, a widower whose wife was killed when a tiny screw hit a low-orbit craft's window at highvelocity. Their troubles in orbit include confrontations with illegal dumpers, terrorists who want mankind to stay Earthbound, and lunar eccentrics who use the low gravity to imitate the flying leaps of ninja.

The idea behind *Planetes* is not new—it lifts elements of both STAR DUST and MIGHTY SPACE MINERS—but its execution is sublime. Its future is not the wish-fulfillment fantasy of GUNDAM, but a mundane, troubled place like something out of Larry Niven's *Known Space* series. Space travel is possible, but only within extremely limited confines—a trip to the Moon still takes several days, and later episodes include the immensely detailed preparations for the first manned flight to Jupiter; compare this to less realistic sci-fi shows like GUNBUSTER, which can happily encase Jupiter in a steel shell in a simple throwaway gag. Yes, it's true that anime's potential is infinite, and creators can show us whatever they can draw. But, like PATLABOR before it, *Planetes* gives equal weight to the science

and the fiction, and is all the better for it. Based on a manga by Makoto Yukimura in weekly *Comic Morning*.

PLANZET *
2010. Movie. DIR: Jun Awazu. SCR: Jun Awazu. DES: N/C. ANI: Kanji Kawai, Yoshitaka Takeuchi. MUS: Shingo Terasawa. PRD: CoMix Wave, Media Factory. 53 mins.
Taishi Akeshima lost his father in the alien attack that smashed the world's major cities in 2047. The planet was already on the edge of ecological disaster and humanity was about to colonize Mars, but defense became the priority. Six years on, the forces of Earth are finally in a position to fight back—although coming out from behind their defensive shield will leave them vulnerable, it's the only way they can attack, take revenge, and ensure their survival.

Apocalyptic anime has not always been a major strand in the medium. Before the war, Japan's experience of devastation was purely natural; like America, it had to imagine the apocalypse. Buddhist imagery of Hell was useful to some extent, but a childlike vision of war dominated WARTIME ANIME. The narrative of armed conflict was unexamined in anime until long after the Occupation ended, and even then was framed as science fiction or fantasy with the exception of a few unflinching visions such as BAREFOOT GEN. Alien invasion as a metaphor for war was easy to sell in Japan; to many Japanese, the invaders looked like aliens. As a result, the anime apocalypse covers a wide range of styles from FIST OF THE NORTH STAR to EVANGELION, and the style of the apocalypse is one of its most interesting features. It's easy for a director with a strong design team to create something that looks intriguing; less so for the writers to make the content as striking as the package. *Planzet* has some strong concepts and attractive designs, but it's let down by lackluster execution. It really is past time studios stopped expecting audiences to say "Wow, CGI!" and look no deeper (GAMING AND DIGITAL ANIMATION).

PLASTIC LITTLE *
1994. Video. DIR: Kinji Yoshimoto. SCR: Mayori Sekijima. DES: Satoshi Urushibara, Studio Nue. ANI: Satoshi Urushibara. MUS: Tamiya Terashima. PRD: Animate Film, SME.

45 mins.

Orphaned teenager Tita takes over her father's pet shop hunter business, collecting and selling exotic animals from all over the galaxy. In port on planet Yietta (where, to feebly justify the title, there's very *little plastic*) she rescues a young girl who is being pursued by the local authorities. Elysse Nalerov is in big trouble; her father designed a new weapon, she has the arming codes, and the government will stop at nothing to get them. Tita and her crew decide to help her out, and mayhem ensues.

A lightweight but enjoyable sci-fi adventure made, like its predecessor LEGEND OF LEMNEAR, solely to show off the artistic talents of Urushibara and Yoshimoto. While lacking a particularly strong story line, it succeeds most perfectly in the rendition of an individual artist's style into moving pictures. Unfortunately for the genre, Urushibara's style isn't SF illustration but cheesecake. The artist on numerous books of cutie-girl illustrations, he renders lush young flesh with glowing perfection. Yoshimoto transfers this perfection exactly to celluloid and puts a remarkable range of motions onto it, so before they take on the evil overlord, the girls can stop for a bath scene where they can compare their breasts. Not only every jiggle of every curve, but the characters' expressions and movements all give the impression of seeing the creator's original art come to life on the page. When one considers the violence often done to original design art in the cause of simplifying it enough to animate cheaply (see VAMPIRE HUNTER D), the achievement is all the more remarkable.

At the time of its release, the creators claimed that it was only a prequel to a set of other stories—though as time passed, the only evidence was a single-volume manga and a brief *PL* audio drama that described Elysse as a "guest star," thereby implying there was more to come. In 1999, Urushibara and Yoshimoto unveiled artwork from a new project, *Femme Femme Buccaneers*, charting the progress of Ann and Ricorne, a two-piece idol-singer act known collectively as Virginity. Though they promised that these two girls, along with the unshaven male pirates of the Yiettan isle of Espaniola, would soon grace anime screens alongside Tita and her crew,

the wait continues, making *PL2* the most delayed project in anime, beating even Otomo's STEAMBOY. Owing to accidents of international pricing and rights negotiation, *PL* is available in separate U.K. and U.S. translations. **NV**

PLATONIC CHAIN

2003. TV series. DIR: Takeshi Okazaki. SCR: Aki Itami. DES: Takeshi Okazaki. ANI: Takahiro Goto. MUS: I.S.O. PRD: AciD Films, TV Tokyo. 5 mins. x 25 eps.

The day after tomorrow, when videophones and constant Internet access are available to everyone. And where there's a network, there's a hacker. Someone has broken into the government's information archive and created the Platonic Chain website, through which anyone can discover anything about anyone else via his or her cellphone. You can find your double and try a life swap, or find the double of your secret crush and practice on him until you're confident enough to hit on your love. You can even find out where the cute guy you just passed on the escalator in the mall goes to school. Teenage friends Hitomi Tanaka, Rika Kagura, and Kanae Mizuhara use the site to help them deal with the problems of everyday life—a nicer attitude than that exhibited in the later HELL GIRL. Manga artist Okazaki makes his directorial debut on this version of Koji Watanabe's SF novel, and makes extensive use of CG and motion-capture to help give his characters and settings the Shibuya look. Okazaki and Watanabe have also collaborated on color manga *@Run-city*, which appeared in *Ikki* magazine. A decade onward, this prediction of the future seems strangely quaint and mundane—but sometimes it's worth remembering that there used to be a time without Facebook.

PLAWRES SANSHIRO

1983. TV series. DIR: Kunihiko Yuyama, Masahisa Ishida, Masamune Ochiai, Osamu Sekita, Katsumi Endo, Susumu Ishizaki. SCR: Keisuke Fujikawa, Kenji Terada, Junji Tagami. DES: Mutsumi Inomata, Shigenori Kageyama, Shigeru Katsumata. ANI: Mutsumi Inomata, Hitoshi Yoshinaga, Kazuhiro Ochi, Hirotoshi Sano, Takashi Sogabe, Satoshi Yamazaki. MUS: Yasunori Tsuchida. PRD: Kaname Productions, TBS. 25 mins. x 37 eps.

Pla[stic] wres[tlers] are miniature robot toys that can be operated to fight each other. Orphan Sanshiro Sugata (see SAN-SHIRO SUGATA) has inherited a superb plawres from his vanished father and wants to make it a champion, while his grandfather wants him to put away childish things and focus on becoming a judo champion.

The conflict between a child's and an adult's view of "achievement," the symbolism of inheritance, and the way in which toys provide an interface with a world that seems too big and scary to handle directly are interesting concepts for a series. Sadly, the need to keep things on a child's level restricts what Yuyama can do with his material. He can't have minded, though—14 years on, he made POKÉMON. Jiro Uma and Minoru Kamiya produced the spin-off manga in the same year, but strangely enough, the expected toy line didn't materialize.

PLAY BALL

2005. TV series. DIR: Satoshi Dezaki. SCR: Koji Ueda, Makoto Ohama, Mitsuya Suenaga. DES: Keizo Shimizu, Ryosuke Senbo. ANI: Ippei Masui. MUS: Kaoru Wada. PRD: Eiken. 25 mins. x 13 eps.

Junior-high baseball captain Takao Taniguchi ruins his sporting future when he heroically continues to play a game with broken fingers—compare to H2. Later, as a student at Sumitani High, he is approached by the captain of the soccer club, who sees him watching a baseball game with a sad look in his eye. Takao begins playing on the soccer team, but baseball remains his first love. Eventually, he decides to return to baseball, only to discover a lackluster club full of apathetic, uncaring players. A predictable tale of overcoming sporting odds then ensues. Based on a manga by Akio Chiba, and broadcast in Japan on a series of syndicated channels, including Kansai TV, Kumamoto TV, TV Miyazaki, and Sendai Broadcasting. **LNV**

PLEASE OPEN THE DOOR

1986. JPN: *Tobira o Akete*. Movie. DIR: Keizo Shimizu, Tsuneo Tominaga. SCR: Kazumi Koide, Satoshi Dezaki. DES: Setsuko Shibuichi. ANI: Toshihiro Kawamoto, Mayumi Hirota. MUS: Mark Goldenberg. PRD: Kitty Films, Magic Bus. 81 mins.

Miyako Negishi is a seemingly ordinary high school girl but has amazing powers of ESP, while her friend Keiichiro can transform into a were-lion, and her friend Kaori has the power of teleportation. On a night when the moon is full, they are transported to the alternate "Middle Kingdom," where Miyako is the fair princess Neryura, fighting a losing battle against the Western king Duran III. Forming an alliance with the Eastern king Dimida, Miyako and her friends use their powers to save the world, hoping eventually to return home. Based on an SF novel by Motoko Arai, better known in the English-speaking world for her story *Green Requiem.* Compare to FUSHIGI YUGI. Not to be confused with Studio 4°C's short film *Tobira o Akete*, written with different characters.

PLEASE SAVE MY EARTH *

1993. JPN: *Boku no Chikyu o Mamotte.* Video. DIR: Kazuo Yamazaki. SCR: Kazuo Yamazaki. DES: Takayuki Goto, Yuji Ikeda. ANI: Takayuki Goto. MUS: Hajime Mizoguchi. PRD: Victor Entertainment. 30 mins. x 6 eps. (v1), 100 mins. (v2), 30 mins. (v3).

Seven schoolchildren have a recurring collective dream in which a team of alien scientists on the moon gather data about Earth. Seeking each other's company, they begin to suspect that the dreams are really suppressed memories of their distant past lives. Past relationships replay themselves, as teenage Alice Sakaguchi is desired by eight-year-old Rin, while he in turn is pursued by the mature woman Mokuren. But love is not the only thing that survives reincarnation, as the members of the group discover that their former incarnations ended in tragedy—a tragedy fated to repeat itself.

One of a glut of mid-1990s lunar reincarnation stories, but it is far more mature than the populist SAILOR MOON and better executed than the shoddy BOUNTY DOG. This emotive tale of love, loss, and anger echoing through reincarnation was based on a manga serialized in *Hana to Yume* by Saki Hiwatari, whose other manga works include *A Favor of the Devil* and *Tower of the Future.* Only a fraction of the 21-volume original would fit into the anime, and the story was compressed further into a 100-minute "movie" edit concentrating on the Alice/Rin relationship. There was

also an animated music video, comprising eight tracks of the wonderful Mizoguchi music that featured guest contributions from his former wife Yoko Kanno. Though released before the series to publicize it, the video actually contained some footage of later chapters and the manga's conclusion, unseen in the anime series proper.

PLEASE TEACHER *

2002. JPN: *Onegai Teacher.* AKA: *Teacher, Please.* TV series. DIR: Yasunori Ide. SCR: Yosuke Kuroda. DES: Hiroaki Goda, Yasuhiro Moriki, Yoshihiro Watanabe, Taraku Uon. ANI: Dome. MUS: Kazuya Takase, Shinji Orita, Tomoyuki Nakazawa. PRD: Bandai, Studio Orphee. 22 mins. x 12 eps. (TV1), 21 mins. (v1), 22 mins. x 12 eps. (TV2), 26 mins. (v2).

High school boy Kei Kusanagi lives a quiet life with his feisty aunt and lecherous but kind-hearted uncle. He's 18, but looks a lot younger as a result of a rare disease that put him in a coma for three years and arrested his physical growth. He is prone to passing out anytime his spirits are low. His cute new schoolteacher is a redhead with glasses who is really an alien—Kei knows because they've already met by accident. Mizuho Kazami has a spaceship with a living control unit, a tiny yellow-clad gnome named Marie. Mizuho is an observer for the Galactic Federation but she's come to Earth on a private mission—to try and find out about her human father. Her mother Hatsuho met him when the 2009 expedition to Mars got lost and was rescued by a Galaxy Federation ship. Kei marries Mizuho, purely as a matter of form, to help conceal her secret; but as their families and friends cause endless complications the pair fall in love. Hatsuho, who turns out to be something of a minx, along with her interfering younger sister Maho (Mizuho's aunt), also make appearances, notably in the 2003 video sequel in which they attempt to engineer a situation so that Kei and Mizuho can finally consummate their marriage. Both the series and its manga adaption with art by Shizuru Hayashiya are out in English, from Bandai and ComicsOne, respectively. There is also an untranslated CD drama spin-off, *Onegai Friends.* A decade later, the same core team would reunite for the rather similar WAITING IN THE SUMMER.

A second TV series, *Please Twins* (2003, *Onegai Twins*), dumped its predecessor's dogged adherence to a TENCHI MUYO! paradigm in favor of one that owed more to LOVE HINA—a truly rarefied distinction in harem shows, if you care about that sort of thing. Its protagonist is Maiku Kamishiro, a student at the school where Mizuho teaches and classmate of characters from the previous series, who has no family and is supporting himself through high school by working as a freelance computer programmer. His only memento of his childhood is an old photograph showing two children, a boy and a girl, playing outside a blue house. He hopes that finding the house might help him find his family, so he tracks it down and moves in—the tracking down of a similar domicile forms an important plot point in POPOTAN. Then two cute girls turn up to visit, both with a copy of the same photograph, each with the same blue eyes as Maiku, and each claiming to be his twin sister. He decides they can both stay until they know for sure which one is his sister. Miina Miyafuji is a feisty redhead, given to saying exactly what she thinks and constantly bickering with Maiku; Karen Onodera is gentle, easily frightened, and ultra-dependent. She's also fond of a biscuit snack called Prech Salad (a pastiche of Japanese Pretz snacks, whereas Mizuho was obsessed with Pochy, a thinly disguised homage to the real-world Pocky snack), and this has led to a tiny little gnome-like creature dressed all in yellow (the first serial's Marie) following her everywhere hoping for titbits. Meanwhile, Maiku must also dodge the amorous intentions of Tsubaki Oribe, a girl, and Kosei Shimazaki, a boy. Fans of this type of anime will recognize the fantasy set-up where, without actually having to make any effort to woo a girl, a guy suddenly finds that there's always one around and she's always cute—like being a rock star, but without the need for drugs or talent. However, *Please Twins* is notably more "mature" than others of its ilk, and mercifully lacks much of the endemic male-character lechery or indignant female-induced slapstick of similar shows. Instead, Maiku conceals his interest in the female characters so well that some of them wonder if he might be gay, and then, of course, do everything they can to test the hypothesis. ◐

PLUSTER WORLD

2003. JPN: *Bouken Yuuki Pluster World*. AKA: *Adventure Bravery Pluster World; Journey of Adventure Pluster World*. TV series. DIR: Yuji Himaki. SCR: Sukehiro Tomita. DES: Hiroshi Kugimiya. ANI: N/C. MUS: Motoi Sakuraba. PRD: Nippon Animation, TV Tokyo, Takara. 25 mins. x 52 eps.

Pluster World is a magical realm in which tribes of strange creatures are at war. The tribes resemble various different Earth creatures and are further divided into those who want peace and justice, and those who don't. The Plusters, heroic creatures to whom legend attributes the power to "plus on," or merge with humans to create mighty warriors, battle the evil Minusters. Beetma, a Pluster of the Kabuto tribe, sets out to become the strongest Pluster in the world. On his journey he meets Wyburst, of the Grip tribe, who wants to find the legendary Gonggorah-gong, a being who can bring peace to Pluster World. Then he is badly beaten in a fight with a Minusbeast, and thrown down the fabled passage into the world of humans. There he meets 11-year-old Tohma and "plusses on" with him to become Plust Beetma. Returning to Pluster World, the pair meet Wyburst and join him in trying to find a power that can defeat the Minusters.

The legendary toy company name in the credits is a clue to the show's intent: to sell as many items of merchandise to children as possible. Like TRANSFORMERS and POKÉMON it's a 25-minute commercial. While Yoshiyuki Tomino used GUNDAM to show that a TV series can be something more, rookie director Himaki is not terribly ambitious.

POCHACCO *

1992. TV series. DIR: Masami Hata, Akira Kiyomizu, Katsuma Kanazawa, Seiichi Mitsuoka. SCR: Kyoko Kuribayashi. DES: Rie Oshima. ANI: N/C. MUS: N/C. PRD: Sanrio. 10 mins. x 4 eps.

Adventures of a cute little puppy and his animal friends from the team that gave you HELLO KITTY and PEKKLE. Pochacco rescues tiny chicks, hunts down a carrot thief, looks for a pink mushroom, and has other adventures to thrill the under-threes. Despite the mushrooms, *Magic Roundabout* fans must look elsewhere for drug references; this is pure, clean, and sweet.

POKÉMON *

1997. JPN: *Pocket Monster*. TV series, movie. DIR: Kunihiko Yuyama, Masamitsu Hidaka, Yoshitaka Fujimoto. SCR: Atsuhiro Tomioka, Takeshi Shudo, Hideki Sonoda, Junji Takegami. DES: Satoshi Tajiri. ANI: Shunya Yamada. MUS: Junji Miyazaki. PRD: SOFTX, TV Tokyo. 25 mins. x ca. 836+ eps. (TV), 75 mins. (m1, *Mew2*), 23 mins. (m1s, *Vacation*), 81 mins. (m2, *Lugia*), 24 mins. (m2s, *Rescue*), 74 mins. (m3, *Emperor*), 23 mins. (m3s, *Pichu*), 99 mins. (m4, *Encounter*), 23 mins. (m4s, *Hide & Seek*), 70 mins. (m5, *Heroes*), 23 mins. (m5s, *Pika Pika*), 81 mins. (m6, *Jirachi*), 23 mins. (m6s, *Dancing*), 100 mins. (m7, *Destiny*), 103 mins. (m8, *Mew*), ? mins. (m9, *Rangers*), 90 mins. (m10, *Darkrai*), 96 mins. (m11, *Giratina*), 94 mins. (m12, *Arceus*), 95 mins. (m13, *Zoroark*), 95 mins. (m14, *Black and White*), 94 mins. (m15, *Kyurem*), 96 mins. (m16, *Genesect*).

Ash (Satoshi) oversleeps and is late for the distribution of the trainers' manual giving details of how to capture and train wild Pocket Monsters (Pokémon), fighting-pets much coveted by children. Since the manual sets out which Pokémon are most desirable and how to find them, the other kids have all the "best" catches, and he is stuck with the only one he can find without help from the manual, an "electric mouse" called Pikachu. After a shaky start, the two soon become firm friends, as Pikachu helps Ash capture many more Pokémon and head toward his goal of becoming the world's greatest Pokémon trainer. However, at every turn, Ash and his friends are dogged by the evil Team Rocket, intent on stealing the best Pokémon for themselves. Officially let off school to hunt their Pokémon, they trek around a safe and supportive world, always finding a bed for the night, and a sisterly type to help out with meals and other necessities. It's a child's dream, with the joys of independence but without the tedium.

Pokémon is a perfectly average TV anime tied into the huge marketing machine of a successful game and, consequently, immeasurably more successful than its contemporaries. There have been many attempts to explain its success, including Joseph Tobin's edited collection of academic essays *Pikachu's Global Adventure* (2004), but if anybody really knew why it was such a hit, someone would have been able to match it. Giving children an ongoing adventure, the chance to pit their monsters against each other, and a vast menagerie of creatures guaranteed to befuddle their parents, the game certainly met the requirements for a modern media mix franchise, its cross-promotional anime and manga spin-offs reaching the West in record time, arguably creating the most important influence on the medium since AKIRA.

Though the stars of TAMAGOTCHI VIDEO ADVENTURES can claim to be the first "virtual pets," it was the interactive quality of Nintendo's *Pokémon* game that seized the high ground. First broadcast in Japan in April 1997, the *Pokémon* phenomenon came to the notice of the West that December in a news item about strobe-like effects in one episode that caused seizures among the Japanese audience (see also YAT BUDGET! SPACE TOURS). Popular myth accords the effects of this as a form of mass hysterics, although subsequent examination of medical records has suggested that perhaps less than a tenth of the alleged "800 cases" required medical attention. Others appear to be viewers who may have felt slightly queasy, jumping on the bandwagon to be part of a national event (and skip school), and whose experience made for entertaining tabloid journalism abroad, but may not have been quite the broadcasting disaster first reported. Despite this initial stumble, the *Pokémon* juggernaut descended on the Western world, with millions of dollars in advertising eventually generating billions of dollars in sales. Compare this investment with the desultory way SAILOR MOON was dumped on the U.S. Though *Pokémon* was undoubtedly a hit, it was also something of a self-fulfilling prophecy. The transition was not completely smooth—several episodes were "lost," chiefly for content comprising the womanizing antics of Ash's friend Brock, or cross-dressing by the zany Team Rocket.

Thanks to the runaway success of *Pokémon* in English, anime became relatively commonplace on American TV. After years of equating the medium with sex and violence, producers suddenly saw it as a cash cow in the children's market. Clone shows

DIGIMON and MONSTER RANCHER swiftly followed, along with unrelated serials such as CARDCAPTORS, GUNDAM W, and FLINT THE TIME DETECTIVE. Early attempts at selling anime for an older audience foundered, with ESCAFLOWNE flopping on American TV, but the early years of the 21st century were characterized by a rush to keep the Western *Pokémon*-boom generation watching anime as they grow up, a gravy train that only came crashing to a halt in 2006 with the sudden slump of the market, at least in part because the *Pokémon* generation was now leaving its teens.

The TV series went through several name changes to reflect the exact brand of game being promoted. After the initial 82 episodes, it became the more U.S.-friendly *Pokémon: Orange Island* until episode 118, when it returned to previous form in *Pokémon G[old &] S[ilver]*. Subsequent iterations have roughly matched the new versions of the *Pokémon* games, with such subtitle additions as *Diamond and Pearl* from 2006, *Best Wishes (Black and White)* from 2010, and *XY* from 2013.

The franchise also reached theaters in several film outings. *Pokémon the Movie: Mew vs. Mew-two* (1998) gained Japan's second-largest domestic box office for an animated film, at least for a while, until it was beaten by PRINCESS MONONOKE and then SPIRITED AWAY. It featured a fight against an embittered mutant monster, crazily flipping from promising, cautionary SF in the style of Tezuka's BAGHI, through cartoon comedy, to a patronizing moral ending that weakly argued against fighting all the time, even though such activities characterize the rest of the series! The 70-minute film was shown accompanied by the saccharine "let's cooperate" children's short, *Pikachu's Summer Vacation (Pikachu no Natsuyasumi)*. Despite a slow decline of interest, the film series continued with *Revelation Lugia* (1999, AKA *Power of One*), anime history's *third*-largest Japanese box-office draw, in which yet another very, *very* rare form of Pokémon is the object of the quest. This time, Lugia can only be called forth by bringing three sacred birds together in one spot. The show was accompanied by the short film *Pikachu's Rescue Adventure (Pikachu Tankentai)*. A year later, the *Pokémon* movie was *Emperor of the Crystal Tower* (2000, translated in 2001 as *Spell of*

the Unown [sic]), a fairy-tale variant of *Sleeping Beauty* about an imprisoned princess accidentally kidnapping Ash's mother when she wishes for one of her own. The film was accompanied by another short for toddlers, this time *Pichu and Pikachu*, displaying "baby" versions of some of the lead Pokémon. A fourth film, *Encounter Beyond Time* (AKA *Pokémon 4Ever*, 2001) features the very, very, *very* rare Pokémon Celebi from the GS game, accompanied by the short *Pikachu's Hide and Seek (Pikachu no Doki-doki Kakurenbo)*. *Pokémon Heroes Latias and Latios* (*Mizu no Miyako no Mamorigami*, i.e., *Guardian Spirits of the Water Capital*) accompanied by the short *Glittering Starlit Sky Camp (Pika Pika Hoshizora Camp*, both 2002); *Pokémon Jirachi Wish Maker (Nana-Yo no Negai Boshi Jiraachi)* and the short *The Dancing Pokémon Secret Base (Odoru Pokémon Himitsu Kichi*, both 2003); *Pokémon: Destiny Deoxys* (2004, *Rekku no Homonsha Deokishisu*, aka *Visitor from Above, Deoxys*), *Pokémon: Mew and the Wave Hero* (2005, *Myu to Hado no Yusha*), and *Pokémon Rangers and the Sea King* (2006, *Pokémon Ranger to Umi no Oji*) continue the franchise, while on television, the *Pokémon GS* season transformed into *Pokémon Ranger* and *Pokémon Advanced Generation*. And on it went, with *Pokémon: The Rise of Darkrai* (2007, *Diagia vs Palkia vs Darkrai*), *Pokémon: Giratina and the Sky Warrior* (2008, *Giratina to Sora no Hanatana Sheimi*), *Pokémon: Arceus and the Jewel of Life* (2009, *Arceus Chokoku no Jiku e*), *Pokémon: Zoroark Master of Illusions* (2010, *Gen'ei no Hasha Zoroark*), *Pokémon: Black Victini and Reshiram and White Victini and Zekrom* (2011), *Pokémon Kyurem vs the Sword of Justice* (2012, *Kyurem tai Seikenshi Kerudio*), and *Pokémon: Genesect and the Legend Awakened* (2013, *Shinsoku no Genesect: Mewtwo no Kakusei*).

Often held in snooty disregard by a hard-core anime FANDOM that would prefer its hobby to be forever outside the mainstream, *Pokémon* is nevertheless the most commercially important anime of the 1990s in terms of brand recognition and the investment it attracted to the medium—many more obscure anime and manga translations were, and still are, funded with Pikachu's profits. As befits a cultural icon, the series has been mercilessly lampooned in other media, most notably as the "Battling Seizure Robots"

in an episode of the *The Simpsons*, and the brainwashing Chinpokomon in *South Park*.

POKONYAN

1993. AKA: *Raccoon Miaow; Rocky Rackat*. TV series. DIR: Hiroshi Sasakawa, Seitaro Hara. SCR: N/C. DES: N/C. ANI: N/C. MUS: Man Brothers Band. PRD: Nippon Herald, NHK. 8 mins. x 170 eps.

A Japanese girl discovers a *tanuki* (a Japanese raccoon dog; see POM POKO) in her backpack during a camping trip. He proclaims that he is her sister and follows her everywhere. He can use his powers to turn Amy's dreams into real-life adventures, though his good intentions, like those of the creators' earlier DORAEMON, do not always work according to plan. Based on a manga by Fujiko F. Fujio, this anime was also spun off into the *Pokonyan Christmas* and *Pokonyan Summer Holiday* specials.

POLAR BEAR CAFÉ

2012. JPN: *Shirokuma Café*. TV series. DIR: Mitsuyuki Masuhara. SCR: Toru Hosokawa. DES: Aya Takano. ANI: N/C. MUS: Kenji Kondo. PRD: Studio Pierrot. 25 mins x 50 eps.

A lazy panda fails in his job application at a café, but befriends the polar bear owner and many of the chatty animal clientele, in a light-hearted slice-of-life story. Somewhat reminiscent of Miyazaki and Takahata's earlier PANDA GO PANDA, not the least for the lead's part-time job in a petting zoo and the presence of a human girl on the staff, *Polar Bear Café* was based on Aloha Higa's strip in *Flowers* magazine, running since 2006. It was plainly snapped up for animation on the expectation that the anthropomorphic characters heralded a potential gold mine in merchandise and spin-offs, although it is more likely to be remembered by anime historians for the glimpse it afforded of the production process behind the scenes. The show was several episodes into its broadcast run when the creator publicly complained about the lack of consultation—she was contractually permitted to sign off on designs and scripts, but had been presented with nothing from the animators at all. The angry Higa pulled her comic from the publisher for a month, seemingly blaming editorial liaisons for waving through design choices in her name without seeking her approval. She was particularly annoyed about the number of claws given to her polar bear protagonist, seemingly unaware of a long-standing debate in the animation world about the need to reduce actual finger counts in order to present cleaner images. However, that's not the point—Higa had the right of consultation, and argued that her right was being denied her by corporate busybodies. As the creator, she was perfectly entitled to throw her weight around, and undeniably did. *Polar Bear Café* lasted for many more episodes, but Higa's discord briefly shone a light on some of the shenanigans that can go on in the background of anime shows. It helps explain, at least to some extent, the controlling and invasive nature of some other creators.

POLLINIC GIRLS ATTACK, THE

2008. JPN: *Kafun Shojo Chuiho The Animation*. Video. DIR: Eiyu Ura. SCR: Shinichiro Sawayama. DES: Noritomo Hattori, Naomi Hayakawa. ANI: Noritomo Hattori. MUS: N/C. PRD: Space-X, Pink Pineapple. 29 mins. x 4 eps.

Men and women reproduce by pollination. Pollinic humanoids (male and female, though we see more of the girls, if you get the drift) just float through the air and fertilize anyone they find receptive, which pretty much means that everybody is at it all the time. Even those allergic to pollen find ways around it, in this story so weird it's almost gone beyond porn into science fiction, although it's hard to find a scientific reason why maid costumes, school uniforms, or lingerie are necessary for pollination. Based on Keito Koume's manga, contains a love gun impressive enough for American band KISS—or, come to that, the stars of Rob Reiner's *This Is Spinal Tap* (1984). ❶

POLLON

1982. JPN: *Ochamegami Monogatari Korokoro Polon*. AKA: *The Story of Little Goddess Roly-Poly Pollon; Roly-Poly Pollon: The Tallest Tales of the Gods; Little Pollon*. TV series. DIR: Takao Yotsuji. SCR: Masaru Yamamoto, Kenji Terada, Tomohiro Ando. DES: Toshio Takagi, Tsutomu Fujita. ANI: Hirokazu Ishiyuki, Toshio Takagi. MUS: Masayuki Yamamoto. PRD: Kokusai Eiga, movie International, Fuji TV. 25 mins. x 46 eps.

Pollon, the little daughter of the God

Apollo, wants to be a powerful and beautiful goddess when she grows up. Somewhat neglected by her single godly parent, she often assists him in his womanizing ways in the vain hope that she will get a new mommy. With her little friend Eros, she plagues the Olympians in various comical ways as she attempts to earn the trappings of godhood. Sadly (if predictably), her good deeds often backfire, leaving her in hot water with some deity or other and causing chaos for gods and humans alike. But, because she's a kindhearted girl, she will eventually achieve her aim and become a proper, respectable grown-up goddess. This sweet little series for children was the first to be produced in its entirety by Kokusai, based on the manga *Pollon of Olympus* by NANAKO SOS–creator Hideo Azuma, originally serialized in *100-ten Comic*. Combining stories about the Greek and Japanese sun gods (with Apollo taking the role of Japan's female Amaterasu for a few tales), the story also contained comic-relief characters absent from Greek mythology, such as the Hollywood-stereotype mad scientist Dr. Nya-ha-ah. Compare to BIT THE CUPID.

POLLYANNA

1986. JPN: *Ai Shojo Pollyanna Monogatari*. AKA: *The Story of Loving Child Pollyanna*. TV series. DIR: Kozo Kusuba, Norio Yazawa, Shigeo Koshi, Fumio Kurokawa, Harumi Sugimura. SCR: Saiko Kumasen, Tamao Kunihiro. DES: Yoshiharu Sato, Ken Kawai. ANI: Yoshiharu Sato. MUS: Reijiro Koroku. PRD: Nippon Animation, Fuji TV. 25 mins. x 51 eps.

Eleven-year-old pastor's daughter Pollyanna is sent to live with her aunt, Polly Harrington, after her father's death in 1920s America. Auntie doesn't like children at all and is brusque and distant, but Pollyanna is an irrepressibly buoyant child and softens her aunt's hard heart with her affectionate, gentle personality. Then she has a tragic accident and loses the use of her legs. After a dangerous operation, and with the help and encouragement of the friends she's made in her new life, Pollyanna recovers and is able to join the party for her aunt's wedding.

Based on the 1913 novel and its sequel by Eleanor Hodgman Porter, this is part of the WORLD MASTERPIECE THEATER series, and in the true *WMT* tradition, ends in happi-

ness all around after a touching, not to say tear-jerking, series of trials. Sato went on to work with Studio Ghibli and has built on his U.S. links, most recently with work for Disney on *The Tigger Movie* (2000).

POLTERGEIST REPORT *

1992. JPN: *Yu Yu Hakusho*. TV series, movie. DIR: Noriyuki Abe, Masakatsu Iijima, Shigeru Ueda, Katsunori Mizuno, Akiyuki Shinbo. SCR: Yoshiyuki Ohashi, Sukehiro Tomita, Katsuyuki Sumisawa, Yoshihiro Togashi. DES: Minoru Yamazawa, Yuji Ikeda. ANI: Saburo Soya, Yoshinori Kanno. MUS: Yusuke Honma. PRD: Studio Pierrot, Fuji TV. 25 mins. x 112 eps. (TV), 26 mins. (m1), 93 mins. (m2), 30 mins. x 2 eps. (v1), 30 mins. x 5 eps. (v2), 30 mins. x 3 eps. (v3).

Middle school tough-guy Yusuke Urameshi is killed trying to save a child in a car accident. In a fustily bureaucratic hell, his name is found to be missing from the Big Book of Dead People, and his "application" is rejected. The son of the ruler of hell (see DORORON ENMA) comes to his rescue and offers him a chance to return whence he came. Repatriated to Earth, he teams up with Death, two demons, and his former rival and becomes a psychic investigator, fighting battle after battle against evil spirits.

Based on the 1990 *Young Jump* manga by HUNTER x HUNTER–creator Yoshihiro Togashi, *PR* sets up a milieu not dissimilar to the background of UROTSUKIDOJI. The human, spirit, and demon worlds coexist, along with a more nebulous, barely glimpsed hell said to be worse than all the others combined. Like the "Wandering Child" Amano, Yusuke does good deeds in the human world, but there the resemblance ends, since *PR* is far more interested in fight-of-the-week standoffs in the manner of DRAGON BALL. A very successful series, particularly by the short runs of many 1990s anime, *PR* returned in the 30-minute short *PR: The Movie* (1993). Shown as part of a triple bill of TV tie-ins, it took the traditional summer-special route, as Yusuke's vacation is interrupted by the kidnapping of his boss, Koenma. The kidnappers demand the King of Hell's seal as ransom, and Yusuke is torn between his loyalty to his friend and savior and his fears of what will happen if the seal falls into the wrong hands.

A full-length feature, *PR: Fight for the Netherworld* (1994), featured the Lord of the Netherworld returning after several millennia to conquer Earth by seizing five power sites around Tokyo. The lush, rich, expensive animation was almost totally wasted on a tired plot, making the *PR* feature look remarkably like a bad remake of several other shows, some of which it actually predated—geomancy from SILENT MÖBIUS, a demon invasion à la SAILOR MOON, and modern-day ghostbusting straight out of USHIO AND TORA. Sadly, this suffered the usual flaws of movies released out of context: the overlarge, idle cast of TENCHI MUYO! and the missing backstory of PATLABOR. *PR* isn't an outstanding show of its type, but the TV series might well have fared better than the movie on English release.

There were also several half-hour spin-off videos, whose self-indulgence only goes to show just how popular *PR* was in Japan. The best fight scenes were excerpted on the two-part video compilation *PR: Image Report* (1994, *YYH: Eizo Hakusho*), followed swiftly by five themed clip-shows, compiled as *PR: Image Report II* (1995, *YYH: Eizo Hakusho II*), one for each of the leads. For the ultimate in futile nostalgia, the "next episode" bumpers that closed each episode were released in their own three-part set, *PR: In Next Week's Episode* (1992–94), allowing viewers to spend 90 minutes watching nothing but ads. ●

POLYPHONICA *

2007. JPN: *Shinkyoku Sokai Polyphonica*. AKA: *New Symphonic World Polyphonica*. TV series. DIR: Junichi Watanabe, Masami Shimoda, Toshimasa Suzuki. SCR: Ichiro Sakaki, Junichi Osako, Shinku Hidaka, Kenichi Kanemaki, Mayori Sekijima, Hiroyuki Kawasaki. DES: Hiroyuki Horiuchi, Rei Nakahara, Yuka Ohashi, Mitsuru Ohara, Yoshinori Shiozawa. ANI: Takahiro Goto, Ryo Haga, Hiroyuki Horiuchi, Shingo Tamaki. MUS: Hikaru Nanase. PRD: Ginga-ya, Fuji Creative, Memory-Tech, MOVIC, Office Tsuge, Pony Canyon, SoftBank, T.O. Entertainment, Inc., TBS, Diomedia. 25 mins. x 12 eps. (TV1), 25 mins. x 12 eps. (TV2).

On the continent of Polyphonica, creatures called Spirits live alongside humans, surviving on the music humans create (MUSIC IN ANIME). A few grow strong enough to take material form as humans or animals. The strongest are attracted to highly skilled musicians called Dantists who play a special kind of music called "Commandia" and become contracted to them. So music is about the summoning and command of spirits for power—and this power can be evil as well as good, since music can function as a drug to the spirits, making them dependent on their pushers. The story revolves around new Dantist Phoron Tatara, his beautiful Spirit Corticate and their fellow Dantists and Spirits.

It's based on a 2006 visual novel (ARGOT AND JARGON) by Ocelot, writer Sakaki's pseudonym, which has since spun off several games, light novels, and a manga, as well as a prequel TV series, *Polyphonica Crimson S*, in 2009. It's very pretty, and elements in the story echo great antecedents—the childhood contract recalls HOWL'S MOVING CASTLE, as well as the multitude of anime in which a boy and a girl meet as tiny children and vow eternal love (ROMANCE AND DRAMA), but that doesn't make the pet/master dynamic of the relationship much different than that of SABER MARIONETTES. With no discernible plot or character development, it is perhaps not altogether surprising that the advertising for the second series touts its all-new, all-different crew and prequel story with an insistence verging on desperation.

POM POKO *

1994. JPN: *Heisei Tanuki Gassen Pom Poko*. AKA: *Heisei [Modern-day] Raccoon Wars Pom Poko; Defenders of the Forest*. Movie. DIR: Isao Takahata. SCR: Isao Takahata. DES: Megumi Kagawa, Shinji Otsuka. ANI: Shinji Otsuka. MUS: Joe Hisaishi. PRD: Studio Ghibli. 119 mins.

A group of *tanuki* (Japanese raccoon dogs) finds its country life threatened by the construction of a human New Town. At the instigation of the town elder, these *tanuki* use their powers of transformation to oppose the human encroachment. Unwilling to declare all-out war on humans (they would miss human food), they fake ghostly hauntings, though the supply of human construction workers appears inexhaustible. An 800-year-old super-*tanuki* orchestrates a ghostly parade down the main street, but the humans are more intrigued than scared—possibly because some of the "ghosts" include cameo appearances from the stars of Hayao Miyazaki's PORCO ROSSO, MY NEIGHBOR TOTORO, and KIKI'S DELIVERY SERVICE. Any spooky effects are ruined when a local theme park takes credit for the parade, falsely claiming that it was a stunt to showcase its special effects technology. The horrified *tanuki* discover that the theme park is run by foxes, who have given up fighting humanity and instead live among them in disguise. After outwitting the foxes, the *tanuki* meet for one last trick, transforming the built-up landscape all too briefly into the virgin countryside it once was. Admitting defeat, they scatter among the human race, though sometimes they meet in secret to briefly walk once more in *tanuki* form.

Familiar characters from JAPANESE FOLK TALES, the mischievous *tanuki* are used here to tell a touching variant of Studio Ghibli's oft-repeated ecological message—supposedly inspired by the 1960s real-life construction of a suburb in Tama Hills, west of Tokyo. Lamenting the destruction of a way of life in much the same way as NAUSICAÄ and PRINCESS MONONOKE, it also recalls the happy pastorals of *Totoro*. *Tanuki* were certainly "in" at this point in the 1990s—the unrelated POKONYAN was a big hit at the same time. An English-subtitled print was shown in very limited release in American theaters in advance preparation for a failed attempt to gain the film an Oscar nomination. However, unlike the universal *Totoro*, *Pom Poko*'s appeal is, to some extent, ethnocentric. Gags come at the expense of Japanese history and folklore, and some of the humor is a little too earthy for the sanitized Disney market. The end result is often a foreign-language variant on *Watership Down* (1978), with time out for wacky satire, tear-jerking whimsy, and an unforgettable scene in which a *tanuki* distracts a driver by flattening his testicles against the windshield. Ghibli's usual standard-setting art direction and design are much in evidence. "Pom Poko," by the way, is the sound you get when you tap gently on a tummy stretched full of food, as opposed to "Poko-pom," which is the Japanese TRANSLATION of Winnie the Pooh's "Tiddle-pom." The Tama Hills development also featured in UNTIL THE UNDERSEA CITY and WHISPER OF THE HEART.

POMEGRANATE PAVILION

2006. JPN: *Zakuro Yashiki*. AKA: *La Grenadiere*. Video. DIR: Koji Fukada. SCR: Shigeru Kashima. DES: Ken Fukasawa. ANI: Ken Fukasawa. MUS: Naoki Ageo. PRD: Toei Animation, Gentosha. 48 mins.

Honore de Balzac's story of a mother and child in 19th-century France is brought to life through tempera paintings and video by CG artist and filmmaker Ken Fukasawa. Part of Toei's *ga-nime* series (ARGOT AND JARGON), which also includes CAT TOWN and FANTASCOPE: TYLOSTOMA.

PONY CANYON

Formed in 1966 as Nippon Broadcasting System Inc., a record label subsidiary of the radio station NBS, the company's name was changed to Pony in 1970 and, following a merger with the record company Canyon, to Pony Canyon in 1987. The company was an early innovator in the field of computer games, but its chief involvement in the anime world is as the music producer on many titles, contributing to such unlikely bedfellows as AIM FOR THE ACE, EMMA, and MAD BULL 34. As Pony Canyon Enterprises, it has also become more directly involved in anime production on titles including GREEN GREEN.

PONYO *

2008. JPN: *Gake no Ue no Ponyo*. AKA: *Ponyo on the Cliff by the Sea*. Movie. DIR: Hayao Miyazaki. SCR: Hayao Miyazaki. DES: Katsuya Kondo, Noboru Yoshida. ANI: Katsuya Kondo. MUS: Joe Hisaishi. PRD: Studio Ghibli, BVHE Japan, d-rights, Dentsu, Hakuhodo DY Media Partners, NTV, Toho. 101 mins.

Kindergarten boy Sosuke lives with his parents in a small fishing community. His father is away most of the time on his boat, and his mother works in a local old folks' center. One day Sosuke finds a strange-looking fish on the shore. He names her Ponyo, but unknown to him she's actually Brunhilde, daughter of the Goddess of the Sea and a mortal scientist. She wants to escape her father's suffocating love and see the world beyond the sea, and once she arrives, she wants to stay. But things are never quite as simple as they seem in FANTASY AND FAIRY TALES, and it will take some real magic—and sacrifice—for Ponyo's wish to be granted.

Ponyo grew out of a suggestion from producer Toshio Suzuki that Miyazaki should make a children's film set in a nursery school, based on Rieko Nakagawa's classic book *Iya Iya En* (*The No-No Nursery*). The resultant work, however, seems only distantly inspired by its kernel. The story of a nursery school under a cliff became *Ponyo*, with Sosuke's kindergarten and house set *on* cliffs amid thrilling flooded landscapes redolent of similar scenes in Miyazaki's FUTURE BOY CONAN, as boats fight through the waves and the sea comes absurdly, alarmingly inland to create lakes where once there was earth. Here, Miyazaki revisits the water-logged realm of his SPIRITED AWAY, along with his recurring interest in the world as viewed by a child. Ponyo is arguably the perfect pinnacle of this concern in his work, entirely conceived using the logic and ludic sense of a toddler, and with the children literally deaf to any concept or conversations that they might not be expected to understand—at a key moment of exposition, the adults' mouths flap but no sound comes out.

Ponyo draws on Hans Christian Andersen's LITTLE MERMAID and highlights Miyazaki's well-known ecological concerns. He also returns to his life-long practice of hand-drawn animation after using computers from PRINCESS MONONOKE onward. Choosing a simpler art style than in previous works, he creates a breathtakingly beautiful world, again as a child might see it—sometimes flat as a crayon drawing, sometimes magically rich and deep. Shapes can morph and shift, waves becoming fish, fish becoming girls. Yet there are unchanging verities, the kind that sustain his other movies. Women are powerful, mysterious, terrifying, even after the wild magic of their early years is contained in the cage of domesticity. Mothers are always reliable, fathers are often absent. Neither of the fathers in the book—Ponyo's mad scientist daddy Fujimoto and Sosuke's adored sailor father Keiichi—see their wives very often or take much active part in the daily lives of their children. Fujimoto keeps his legion of fish-daughters in a goldfish bowl at home; Keiichi signals to Sosuke from far across the waves.

When it comes to creating parents, Miyazaki seems to have lost the sureness of touch that created the close, loving family of KIKI'S DELIVERY SERVICE and the busy but devoted working fathers of NAUSICAÄ OF THE VALLEY OF THE WIND and MY NEIGHBOR TOTORO. It's as if his own perception of himself as a father has shifted, perhaps mirroring the public comments of his son during their much-reported feud during the making of TALES FROM EARTHSEA. Ponyo's and Sosuke's parents are mirrors of each other; one partner constantly fretting and one calm and remote, and in both cases the one doing all the fussing is the one left at home with the kids while the other does a *really* important job. Sosuke's mother Lisa is a strong character, accepting but not surrendering to her husband's absences and broken promises. Yet in one of the least convincing plot twists ever seen in a Ghibli movie, she does something both unconvincing and unnecessary, simply to get the story out of a hole and along to a gorgeous set-piece. Fujimoto is an interesting concept, a magician with something of the hero of HOWL'S MOVING CASTLE about him, choosing to exist in a world where humans should have no place and where their meddling can be dangerous, but his eccentricity is carried too far into comedy business, and his hesitation and uncertainty with the women in his life is overplayed. Ponyo's mother is all warm, benign distance; we never see her raging. Her anger has been externalized into nature. Where Fujimoto is forever trying to contain, to protect, to put right, she is eternally calm, eternally accepting.

The depictions of small children and the very old are precise and honest, rooted in close and affectionate observation. There's a moment where elderly ladies are magically released from their wheelchairs to sprint and jostle. Careful character-building and juxtaposition with the nursery school children have let us glimpse their inner five-year-olds; when they're finally let out to play, it's both joyous and poignant to watch. These are spiritual sisters to Ma Dola in CASTLE IN THE SKY, hemmed in by life and age, but with their inner fire undimmed.

Ponyo's depiction of a flooded Japan took on new meaning after the Great East Japan Earthquake and tsunami of 2011 (see also GYO: TOKYO FISH ATTACK)—its imagery both chillingly predictive and winningly unthreatening, with a cast that often does not acknowledge it is in danger.

It's a surprisingly bleak subtext—yet despite its plot holes and characterization problems, *Ponyo* is a deeply joyous film. It's all about suspending disbelief and reveling in the moment; about observing and accepting, not judging. Like Rintaro in **YONA YONA PENGUIN**, Miyazaki seems to be preaching the gospel of acceptance. Go with the flow, let the ocean carry you and you will rediscover the joyous irresponsibility of childhood, where logic cannot resist beauty and obstacles can be colored out of existence.

Ponyo also introduced a new scheme for title credits to Ghibli films, when Miyazaki decided to shove all 400 names of the staff into the 110 seconds that would pass in the first verse of the theme song. This led to a simple roll of names in AIUEO order (the Japanese equivalent of an alphabetical list), without job titles or ranking, which may appear to be, and may indeed have been intended to be, a statement of equality, with the studio cats and nursery staff getting the same level of attention as major investors and big-name actors. However, subsequent Ghibli movies have arguably exploited this tactic. The great statement of community has ironically the opposite effect, leading some viewers to associate the film not with everybody, but with *nobody*, except perhaps Miyazaki himself, even when, as in the case of **ARRIETTY**, he was not actually the director.

POPOTAN *

2003. TV series. DIR: Shinichiro Kimura. SCR: Jukki Hanada. DES: Rondo Mizukami, Poyoyon Rock, Haruka Sakurai. ANI: Haruka Sakurai. MUS: Osamu Tezuka (mus). PRD: SHAFT, Bandai, BS-I. 24 mins. x 12 eps.
Sisters Ai, Mai, and Mii and their android housekeeper Mea live in an old house which travels through time, jumping ahead on each occasion. The sisters are searching for someone, but the search means constantly having to leave the friends they make behind. Based on the erotic PC computer game of the same name, which is a play on *tanpopo,* the Japanese word for dandelion, *Popotan* features nudity in keeping with its original incarnation, but also an intriguing variant on a perennial anime theme. Whereas childhood memories of a beloved location or friend form background elements in many harem anime such as **LOVE HINA**, *Popotan*'s periodic temporal relocations allow shifts in relative ages and perspectives like those found in **GUNBUSTER** and **VOICES OF A DISTANT STAR**. At its heart, it reflects a yearning for a carefree childhood and a terror of creeping age that feature in many anime for an audience on the cusp of adulthood. **Ⓝ**

PORCO ROSSO *

1992. JPN: *Kurenai no Buta.* AKA: *The Crimson Pig.* Movie. DIR: Hayao Miyazaki. SCR: Hayao Miyazaki. DES: Hayao Miyazaki, Megumi Kagawa, Toshio Kawaguchi, Katsu Hisamura. ANI: Megumi Kagawa, Toshio Kawaguchi, Katsu Hisamura. MUS: Joe Hisaishi. PRD: Studio Ghibli. 93 mins.
The Adriatic, 1929—the Balkans may go up in flames at any moment, and the Fascists are on the rise in Italy. Mercenary pilots, survivors of the last Great War, work for hire defending transports from marauding pirates, and Marco is the best of them. But as his idealistic youth fades behind him, the former handsome flyer has undergone a strange transformation. He has literally turned into a humanoid pig, but nobody seems to mind, least of all him. His life is tranquil and simple; he owns a tiny island and when he isn't flying, he's dozing on the beach with his radio, a newspaper, and a cigarette, or he's meeting his childhood friend, Gina, now a beautiful widow. But Marco's own world is tipped out of balance by the arrival of an American cad, Curtis, who sets out to make his name by shooting down the Crimson Pig. Taking his beloved plane to Milan for repairs after their duel, Marco meets the irrepressible Fio, just 17 but already an aircraft designer of formidable talent. He also finds the secret police are on his tail, along with a gang of angry aerial pirates who want Marco out of the sky for good. Fio mollifies the pirates by appealing to their sense of pride, reminding them that it took an American to shoot down Marco. The pirates, mortified at this threat to their Italian spirit, wager on a rematch, with a victorious Marco winning the costs of his repairs, whereas a victorious Curtis (already rebuffed by Gina) would win the hand of Fio. As the Italian air force arrives to break up the illegal match, Marco and Curtis prepare to hold them off while the others escape. An epilogue implies that Marco has returned to human form, and that he and Gina live happily ever after.

Initially conceived for an audience of middle-aged men who had forgotten their youthful aspirations, *PR* is by turns touching, comic, romantic, and edge-of-the-seat gripping, it is a grown-up's fantasy with a child's directness and innocence. It reflects many of its creator's passions and obsessions and also restates many of his central themes, yet the film has its own freshness and originality. Based loosely on a three-part series Miyazaki wrote in 1990 for *Model Graphix* magazine, *PR* was originally planned as a 45-minute in-flight feature for Japan Air Lines. Eventually produced as a full-length movie, a dub was prepared for the English-language audio channel on JAL flights, and subsequently broadcast on British TV. The idea of porcine transformation would return in Miyazaki's **SPIRITED AWAY**, in which a girl must restore her parents to human form, while Miyazaki would revisit aircraft with **THE WIND RISES**.

PORTRISS

2003. JPN: *Mugen Senki Potriss.* AKA: *Tank Knights Portriss; Infinite Military History Portriss.* TV series. DIR: Akira Shigino, Nam Jong-sik. SCR: Shinzo Fujita, Junichi Iioka. DES: Yoshikazu Takaya. ANI: N/C. MUS: N/C. PRD: Bandai, NAS, Sunrise, TV Tokyo. 25 mins. x 52 eps.
Long ago, Portriss Planet was hit by a meteor, and its humanoid population was almost wiped out. To cope with the changed environment, the few survivors evolved into a race of beings with body chemistry based on heavy metallic elements. An elite fighting sect, the Portriss Knights, rose to fight a dictator, and several hundred years later they continue to protect freedom. They have evolved the Portriss Rise function, which enables them to convert their bodies into humanoid tanks during battle and incorporate more weapons. When another evil dictator, Dark Portriss, appears and sets out to construct the ultimate weapon, three Knights stand ready to thwart his plans. Dragon Blue, the leader, Tiger Barrel, the muscle, and birdlike female Rozze Kyaree, who can split into two separate beings with different weapon

functions, infiltrate the enemy headquarters at Babel Tower. Dragon Blue loses his Portriss Rise function after a direct hit from Dark Portriss' superweapon, but in Babel the team encounter a boy with no memories who can merge with Dragon Blue and restore his full functions. They name the boy Yue-ma. Dark Portriss is out to find four mythical ultimate weapons evolved by their ancient humanoid ancestors, and, analyzing Yue-ma's DNA, he uses the boy's strange powers to produce a new life-form with the same abilities as the Portriss Knights. He names it Black Dragon and sends it to destroy the Knights and their Resistance supporters.

A coproduction with South Korea, based on an online computer game, this has tank-tread robots and quasi-comical design aimed at a child audience. Codirector Nam has direction credits for the Korean animated SF TV series *BASToF Syndrome* and movie *Armageddon*. The **GUNDAM** and **TRANSFORMERS** influences are obvious in design and plot, with a love child of the Guntank leading a group of young people to change the world, but the nods to *Star Wars* are also unmissable.

POTECCO BABIES

2011. Video. DIR: Shinichi Kuniyasu, Yosuke Suzuki. SCR: Ippei Yokota, Yutaka Hiranuma. DES: Taizo Iwanaga. ANI: N/C. MUS: Tomoko Hyodo. PRD: Shin-Ei Animation. 3 mins. x 2 eps. (TV1), 2 mins. x 6 eps. (TV2).
Delicious, beautiful food that grows to its full potential ends up being eaten. Food that doesn't conform to human standards gets rejected. It's a fact of life, but the food doesn't have to like it, or cooperate. After all, they don't eat, or judge, humans. Five cute little vege-beings grown on a Japanese farm have comical adventures as they strive to "grow into delicious ingredients" in this simply but beautifully drawn series. Shin-Ei, the studio that helped to make **DORAEMON** and **CRAYON SHIN-CHAN**, took this Flash animation online as part of the *ShinEi Petit Ani Theater* Internet and YouTube channel, before moving onto TV when the second series appeared in 2011. Compare with **KOGEPAN** and **ANPANMAN**.

POTEMAYO

2007. TV series. DIR: Takashi Ikehata. SCR: Yasutomo Yamada, Hideki Shirane, Kazuaki Yamanobe, Masaharu Amiya. DES: Ryuichi Oki, Shichiro Kobayashi. ANI: Tetsuya Takeuchi. MUS: Tomoki Kikuya. PRD: JC Staff. 24 mins. x 12 eps.
Sunao is a junior high school student whose father's work takes him away frequently. His mundane and lonely life changes forever when he finds a baffling, but very cute, little creature in his fridge. It looks like a cute little girl with cat ears, a rabbit tail, and a vocabulary of one word; he adopts her and names her Potemayo. When he finds another strange, cute, much more disruptive child-creature in his fridge later that day, she's more than he can handle, largely thanks to her habit of slicing things up with her cute but deadly scythe and then putting them back together with sticky tape. His classmate Kyo helps him out by adopting her and naming her Gokuchu; her reward is a string of dead animals left on her desk. **CHI'S SWEET HOME** with little girls instead of kittens, based on Haruki Ogataya's 2005 manga; each episode consists of two short stories about the comically cute things pets/children get up to, and how they can transform a humdrum life through sheer silliness.

POTOMAS THE HIPPO

1988. JPN: *Kaba no Potomas*. Movie. DIR: Taku Sugiyama. SCR: Hitoshi Yokota. DES: N/C. ANI: Shunji Saita. MUS: Takeo Watanabe. PRD: OH Pro. 25 mins.
Potomas the Hippo has a secret—he can speak like a human being, but only the young kids Maki and Toshi realize it. He also wears a bright green T-shirt with a giant letter "P" on it, but this is supposed to be nicely inconspicuous. Momentarily forgetting to keep quiet, Potomas speaks to a child he has just saved from drowning. Rumors soon spread about a talking hippo, and Potomas is forced to go on the run.

POWER DOLLS *

1995. Video. DIR: Tsuneo Tominaga, Masamitsu Hidaka. SCR: Midori Uki, Atsuhiro Tomioka. DES: Masayuki Goto, Yasuhiro Nishinaka. ANI: Masayuki Goto. MUS: Hiroto Saito, Innerbrain. PRD: Kogado Studio, Artmic, VAP. 25 mins. x 2 eps.
It's A.D. 2540, and rebels on the colony world of Omni have been holding out against the Terran government for five years. Without a standing army, the breakaway colonists have fought back by adapting robotic Power Loaders. Originally used to unload spaceships, the machines have been turned into humanoid battle-tanks. A handful of young female pilots (who serve in the Detachment of Limited Line Service to justify the title acronym) is assigned to blow up the dam at Chatteau Village.

Based on a Japanese computer game of the same name, *PD* taps into many well-established conventions designed to appeal to male fans: girls in battledress, girls in robots, girls with guns, girls sniping at other girls. The characters and situations are all stolen stereotypes, and not especially well handled, with competent but limited animation. There's a heroic effort to establish character depth by delving into the parental relationships of one of the lead characters, and there's a passable fight toward the end, but since its appeal in Japan was predicated on a love of the game, it's difficult for a foreign audience to feel anything except cheated. None of them would stand a chance in a fight with Ripley from *Aliens*, however big their power loaders.

A sequel, *PD2*, reunited the girls in another adaptation of a game scenario, this time a mission to recapture a stolen prototype. This episode in particular was further damaged in the English-language version by an overdose of reverb effects in the dubbing studio, though the pointlessly flashy audio matched the halfhearted attempt by the original crew to polish the *visuals* with some unnecessary digital effects. In 1997, the series continued in Japan on CD-ROM with a story set after the war, as the newly free state starts to pick up the pieces. The Power Dolls unit is disbanded but antigovernment rebels start causing trouble, and former leader Hardy Newland starts gathering the old crew for one more mission as poachers-turned-gamekeepers.

POWER STONE *

1999. TV series. DIR: Masahiro Omori. SCR: Yukiyoshi Ohashi, Masashi Yokoyama, Kenichi Araki. DES: Tadashi Shida. ANI: Yuji Moriyama, Kazuya Miura, Hideyuki Motohashi. MUS: N/C. PRD: Kokusai Eiga, Studio Pierrot, TBS. 25 mins. x 26 eps.
Fokker is on a quest to retrieve the mystical power stones hidden by his father. In a

19th-century world modeled on the foggy London of **SHERLOCK HOUND** and an olde-worlde Tokyo populated by ninja, Fokker's quest brings him into contact with the British princess Julia, the ninja-girl Ayame, Ryoma the samurai (see **OI! RYOMA**), Wang Tang the Chinese brawler (actually Wonton in Japanese, but the jokey name was altered), Garuda the Red Indian (*sic*), and Rouge the belly-dancing dusky maiden. Then they fight.

Based on a popular game from CAPCOM, creators of **STREET FIGHTER II**, *PS* began as a launch title for the Sega Dreamcast, featuring a true 3D environment packed with useful items and a "power stone" collection theme that allowed the players to transform into more powerful versions of themselves. A few years earlier, such a concept might have barely made it straight to video, but in the late 1990s climate heavy with gaming money and short on options, *PS* became a TV series shown in the prime five-o'clock slot, with the characters regressed from the game to create a slightly younger look designed to appeal to children.

POWERPUFF GIRLS Z

2006. JPN: *Demashitaa Power Puff Girls Z*. AKA: *And They're Off! Powerpuff Girls Z*. TV series. DIR: Hiroyuki Kakudo, Megumi Ishiguro. SCR: Takashi Yamada. DES: Miho Shimogasa. ANI: Ryo Onishi. MUS: Hiroshi Nakamura, Taichi Master. PRD: SME, Aniplex, Cartoon Network, Toei Animation, TV Tokyo. 25 mins. x 52 eps.

A scientific experiment involving a mysterious chemical goes horribly wrong when a strange glacier appears in Tokyo Bay. Ken, dashing son of Professor Utonium, uses Chemical Z to break up the glacier but the fragments emit rays of black light that turn people into monsters throughout the city. However, three rays of white light also shoot out, hitting three ordinary schoolgirls who transform into the Powerpuff Girls Z—Hyper Blossom, Powered Buttercup, and Rolling Bubbles—and set out to help save Tokyo. This Japanese version of U.S. creator Craig McCracken's Japanese/Korean-animated TV hit *Powerpuff Girls* (1995) also inspired two spin-off manga.

PRECURE *

2004. JPN: *Futari wa Precure*. AKA: *Together We're Precure; Together We're Pretty Cure; Pretty Cure TV series*. Movie. DIR: Daisuke Nishio, Akinori Yabe, Takao Iwai, Takenori Kawada, Toru Yamada, Yasuo Yamayoshi. SCR: Ryo Kawasaki. DES: Akira Inagami. ANI: Hiroyuki Kawano, Masumi Hattori, Mitsuru Aoyama, Toshie Kawamura, Yasuhiro Namatame. MUS: Naoki Sato. PRD: ABC, Asatsu DK, Toei Animation, TV Asahi. 25 mins. x 49 eps. (TV1), 25 mins. x 37 eps. (TV2, *Max Heart*), ca.70 mins. (m1, 14), 25 mins. x 49 eps. (TV3, *Splash Star*), 25 mins. x 49 eps. (TV4, *Five*), 25 mins. x 48 eps. (TV5, *Gogo*), 25 mins. x 50 eps. (TV6, *Fresh*), 25 mins. x 49 eps. (TV7, *Heart Catch*), 25 mins. x 48 eps. (TV8, *Suite*), 25 mins. x 48 eps. (TV9, *Smile*), 25 mins. x 49 eps. (TV10, *Doki Doki*), 25 mins. x 28+ eps. (TV11, *HappinessCharge*).

Athletic, energetic Nagisa Misumi and her schoolmate, bookish Honoka Yukishiro have nothing in common until they see a shower of shooting stars, and find that two otherworldly visitors have invaded their lives. Pretty pink Mipple and heroic yellow Mepple are refugees from the Garden of Light, which has been overrun by the forces of darkness led by the wicked king Dusk Zone. But instead of a standard trawl through the tropes and clichés of magical-girl anime, this series owes a substantial debt to martial arts serials, such as director Nishio's earlier **AIR MASTER**. Dusk Zone wants to steal seven magical life-stones that will make him immortal, and the Queen of Light has sent the girls to find help from humankind, with special powers to transform into Cure Black and Cure White, defenders of light. Together, they are Pretty Cure, or Precure—compare to the Beauty Pair, the wrestlers who ultimately inspired the **DIRTY PAIR**. The forces of evil infiltrate their school disguised as student teachers and transfer students, but are no match for Precure, especially when one of them falls for Honoka. The second half of the first series was particularly influenced by **DRAGONBALL Z** (another Nishio production), with the appearance of muscle-bound warriors that could power-up with a glowing aura, just like Super Saiyajins.

At the end of the first season, the wicked King was defeated and the amnesiac Queen came to Earth in the shape of a 12-year-old girl named Hikari Kujo, or Shiny Luminous in her magical incarnation. The second season, *Pretty Cure Max Heart* (2005), featured the return of Nagisa and Honoka, complete with new powers and new costumes, to help her find 12 new magic artifacts. The show was created by **MAGICAL DOREMI**'s Izumi Todo—which is to say, by a Toei house pseudonym, perhaps explaining why this particular show has continued to soldier on right through the recession, since ownership and profits accrue direct to the studio rather than to any original creator. As a result, over the last decade, *Precure* has come to dominate the modern "magical girl" genre in prime-time, as **SAILOR MOON** did during much of the 1990s. Where other shows might have officially "ended" to be replaced by something very similar, *Precure* instead maintains its umbrella title over several essentially different stories, leading some to describe it as a "meta-series" like some witchcraft-oriented version of the Marvel superhero universe, or closer to home, the similarly long-running, same-but-different seasons of Japan's various live-action *sentai* superhero shows, beginning with *Goranger* (*DE).

Director Toshiaki Komura took over for the third series, *Precure: Splash Star* (2006), which introduced two new heroines. The fourth and fifth series confusingly called *Precure 5* (2007) and *Precure Gogo Go* (2008), introduced another set of new characters, focusing on a schoolgirl who must collect 55 "pinkies" that will allow her to restore a lost kingdom. She transforms into the superheroine Cure Dream and enlists her friends to also fight evil as Cure Rouge, Cure Lemonade, Cure Mint, and Cure Aqua.

Seemingly intent on aging with the *Gogo* audience, Junji Shimizu's *Fresh Pretty Cure* (2009) was aimed at a slightly older audience, with a 14-year-old would-be dancer as the protagonist Cure Peach, accompanied by her heroic assistants Cure Berry and Cure Pine. Tatsuya Nagamine's *Heart Catch Precure* (2010) introduces yet another set of heroines, this time associated with the high school fashion club, along with a series of recurring flower motifs. Munehisa Sakai's *Suite Precure* (2011) refashions the collecting theme once more, this time with a quest to recover the lost notes of a transformational tune that will restore peace and happiness to a troubled land. Takashi

Otsuka's *Smile Precure* (2012) adopts a somewhat baffling structure based on fairy stories, and *Doki Doki Precure* (2013) bases its character interactions and identities on a suit of playing cards to be found in the magical kingdom of Trump. The most recent iteration, *HappinessCharge* (2014), pits Pretty Cures against invading soldiers of the Phantom Empire, with the aid of a veritable beauty salon of mirrors, cards, compacts, and other clutter. The Phantom Empire is determined to ruin the world by sucking out the joy and replacing it with despair—a mission they swiftly achieved among encyclopedists by removing the space from between the words Happiness and Charge. Each iteration of the franchise also gets at least one outing in a theatrical movie, usually in the fall season.

PREFECTURAL EARTH DEFENSE FORCE *

1986. JPN: *Kenritsu Chikyu Bogyo Gun*. AKA: *Earth Defense Force*. Video. DIR: Keiji Hayakawa. SCR: Kazunori Ito. DES: Katsumi Aoshima. ANI: Katsumi Aoshima. MUS: Kentaro Haneda. PRD: Shogakukan. 49 mins.
A parody anime in the spirit of writer Ito's URUSEI YATSURA about schoolyard feuds being blown out of all proportion—compare to PROJECT A-KO. Realizing that the ominous-sounding Telegraph Pole Society (which wishes to conquer the world) are probably students at his school, Mr. Roberi forms a Defense Force. Students Shogi Morita (the handsome blond), Kuho Tasuke (his beefy dark-haired pal), and token girl Akiko Ifukube are ranged against an army of inept ninja. Meanwhile, the high school's mad scientist, Dr. Inogami, has turned local boy Kami Sanchin into a cyborg, and both sides try to recruit him. While the TPS boasts an army of ninja, as well as the pretty pink-haired Captain Baradaga, and "Scope" Tsuzaki, a hulking brute with many high-tech devices, the EDF is somewhat underfunded—after initial promises of super-vehicles and amazing gadgets, the best Roberi can rustle up for the fighters is a ramen cart. The two organizations attempt to steal each other's secrets and poach each other's members, while, amid much comic angst about his condition (see CASSHAN or CYBORG 009), Sanchin tentatively falls in love with the professor's daughter, Yuko, who has been similarly cyberized. Their romance is truncated by their unerring habit of setting off their built-in military hardware anytime they get angry. Once the TPG has been defeated, the professor reluctantly concedes that he can return the couple to human form, but the reversion process accidentally switches their genders. The couple get used to it, while Morita starts going out with his former enemy Baradaga. Based on the 1983 *Shonen Sunday* manga by Koichiro Yasunaga, this send-up was presented as three fake episodes and a fake preview for a nonexistent episode 4.

PRETEAR *

2001. JPN: *Shin Shirayuki Densetsu Preytia*. AKA: *New Snow White Legend Pretear*. TV series. DIR: Kenichi Tajiri, Kiyoko Sayama, Yoshitaka Fujimoto, Yoshimasa Hiraike, Takaaki Ishiyama, Yukio Nishimoto. SCR: Hiroyuki Kawasaki, Kenichi Kanemaki, Yoshimi Narita. DES: Akemi Kobayashi. ANI: Itsuko Takeda, Nobuhito Akada, Michinori Chiba, Megumi Kadonosono, Akemi Kobayashi. MUS: Toshiyuki Omori. PRD: Digimation, Group TAC, Anime R, Hal Filmmaker. 25 mins. x 13 eps.
The happy life of 16-year-old Himeno Awayuki is thrown into turmoil when her hard-drinking author father marries a wealthy fan who is so obsessed with his work that she has named her own daughters after characters in his books. Shunned by her snobbish new stepsisters, Himeno drifts into depression until she meets a group of seven young men on the grounds of the family mansion. They are the Leafe Knights, denizens of the land of Leafeania, here to save the world from the evil Princess of Disaster and her Demon Larva. The Princess has come to Earth to suck all the Leafe—the life-force of all living things—out of the world and use it for her own ends. The Knights are looking for a special girl, the Pretear, who has the ability to merge with any one of them and become a single, all-powerful defender of life. Although the leader of the Knights, hunky 18-year-old Hayate, doubts it, it seems Himeno is the Pretear. His six companions, cute guys aged from 17 down to 5, all take to Himeno; instead of two snooty sisters she suddenly has a band of brothers.
Based on a manga by Junichi Sato and Kaori Naruse, *Pretear* deliberately invokes fairy-tale antecedents, chiefly CINDERELLA and SNOW WHITE. The style is generic girl's fantasy, with absurdly nasty siblings and cookie-cutter guys, from the moody but fiercely loyal loner playing hard to get, to the adorable surrogate kid brothers for mothering practice. The show has a certain amount of charm, but not many outside its target audience of 10-year-old girls will find much to impress.

PRETTY RHYTHM *

2011. TV series. DIR: An Jai Ho, Masakazu Hishida. SCR: Shuji Iuchi, Fumi Tsubota. DES: Okama, Mai Matsuura, Sang Hoon Cha. ANI: Chan-Young Park. MUS: Seiko Nagaoka. PRD: Dongwoo Animation, Tatsunoko Pro, BS Japan TV Tokyo, Takara Tomy. 25 mins. x 51 eps. (TV1), 25 mins. x 51 eps. (TV2), 25 mins. x 51 eps. (TV3).
In a franchise based on the Tomy Takara arcade game of the same name, competitors fight for prizes in "Prism Shows," where they must combine the skills of singing, dancing, and ice skating. Prism Stones allow them to augment their costumes, and Prism Jumps are athletic feats that solicit audience acclaim. The first season, *Aurora Rising*, blatantly lifts its plot from MASK OF GLASS, with two rookie performers teamed with an older, more experienced Prism Star to form an idol group. One is the daughter of a former starlet, who hopes one day to be able to perform the "Aurora Rising" Prism Jump that eluded her mother.

Time moves fast in the entertainment world, and by the second season *Dear My Future* (2012), the achievements of the first season's girls are already semi-legendary and three whole years in the past—that's a century in pop time. An all-new group of girls attempt to inherit the crown and better the achievements of their barely-elders.

That's all *ancient* history by the time of the third season *Rainbow Live* (2013), in which seven even newer, even more numerous starlets form an idol platoon reminiscent of the unstoppable, teeming horde of AKB48 (**AKB0048**). The narrative progression of this brightly colored, incredibly enthusiastic show seems to contain a microcosm of the Japanese pop world's own evolving image of itself, with the smaller, more awkward idol groups of the early 21st century gradually replaced by the robotic marching columns of saccharine sameness of huge idol projects (MUSIC IN ANIME). It is also notable for a larger-than-usual number of Korean names conspicuously high up the staff roster, and a media-mix grasp of ADVERTISING AND SPONSORSHIP of truly military precision. Entire episodes were targeted to push action-figures and fast-food chain promotions of tie-in merchandise, timed to the nearest day. Now *that's* a Prism Jump.

PRIDE THE MASTER THIEF

1965. JPN: *Kaito Pride*. TV series. DIR: Yuichi Fujiwara. SCR: Takehiko Maeda. DES: Yuichi Fujiwara. ANI: Taku Sugiyama, Motoyoshi Matsumoto, Noboru Ishiguro. MUS: Seiichiro Uno. PRD: TV Doga, Fuji TV. 5 mins. x 115 eps.

Professor Pride and his faithful dog Dry are masters of crime who boast that they can steal anything from the Eiffel Tower to Mount Fuji itself. Pursued across the world by the hapless Detective Scope, Pride stars in the first-ever crime-caper anime, a distant ancestor of the later LUPIN III and CAT'S EYE. The first anime made by TV Doga, a company formed in 1963 by a coalition between the Tokyo advertising company Koei and Fuji TV. The black-and-white series was completely remade in color in 1967 but never broadcast.

PRIME ROSE

1983. JPN: *Time Slip 10,000-nen Prime Rose*. AKA: *10,000 Year Time Slip Prime Rose*. TV special. DIR: Osamu Dezaki, Naoto Hashimoto. SCR: Keisuke Fujikawa. DES: Osamu Tezuka. ANI: Keizo Shimizu, Yukari Kobayashi, Kenichi Onuki. MUS: Yuji Ono. PRD: Magic Bus, Tezuka Pro, Nippon TV. 98 mins.

An accident on the orbiting military satellite Death Mask wipes out cities in Japan and America, but the occupants have not been killed. Danbala Gai, a member of the time patrol, travels 10,000 years into the future, when Earth is ruled by strange creatures, and the occupants of the two cities have formed their own nations. Though he is not supposed to interfere, Gai becomes involved with Prime Rose, a girl who vows to avenge the murder of her fiancé by learning to fight and killing his murderer, Prince Pirar. But the time patrolman shares her ultimate goal—the

restoration of true peace to the world. Based loosely on his manga serial in *Shonen Champion*, creator Tezuka intended the title to refer to the "primrose" flower, though his pronunciation recalls the old English origins of the word, not its modern spelling.

PRINCE OF SNOW COUNTRY

1985. JPN: *Yukiguni no Ojisama*. Movie. DIR: Tomoharu Katsumata. SCR: Yugo Serikawa, Tadahiro Shimafuji. DES: Takao Kasai. ANI: Takao Kasai. MUS: Seiji Yokoyama. PRD: Shinano, Toei. 88 mins.

Koichi and his sister Yuki befriend Hanaguro, a swan who has flown to Japan from Siberia. Hanaguro is attacked by a dog, and the cowardly Koichi flees, but that night he has a dream in which he is whisked away to the Kingdom of the Snow Prince, where he finds the bravery to help the other swans. A moral fable from the Buddhist Soka Gakkai leader Daisaku Ikeda, who also created RAINBOW ACROSS THE PACIFIC and FAIRGROUND IN THE STARS.

PRINCE OF TENNIS, THE *

2001. JPN: *Tennis no Ojisama*. AKA: *TeniPuri* (short for *Tennis Prince*). TV series, movie. DIR: Takayuki Hamana. SCR: Jun Maekawa. DES: Akiharu Ishii. ANI: Trans Arts. MUS: Cheru Watanabe. PRD: NAS, Production I.G., JC Staff. 22 mins. x 178 eps. (TV), 40 mins. (v), 65 mins. (m).

Ryoma Echizen is a tennis prodigy, haunted by the fame of his father, a former top player who retired unexpectedly at the height of his career—compare to YAWARA! With four championships under his belt after several years in America, Ryoma returns to Japan to join Seishun Gakuen (Youth Academy) because of its reputation as one of the best junior high schools for tennis, but also because it was Dad's old school. Not everyone else in the school is as focused on the game or as driven by family rivalry, but there's plenty of competition, and he is the first freshman to make it onto the squad. Ryoma is ambidextrous and often switches hands during a game; he's also a loner, and can come across as arrogant, but his veneer of coolness is ignored by friendly Takeshi Momoshiro, who takes him under his wing, and wise-cracking Eiji Kikumaru. Most high school and SPORTS ANIME tropes make an appear-

ance, but the talented crew gives the show genuine freshness and charm.

Based on a manga by Takeshi Konomi in *Shonen Jump*, with a huge number of characters and the constant challenge of new teams to face, sports soap opera *PoT* replicated the success of basketball series SLAM DUNK for the female market. A video followed: *PoT: A Day on Survival Mountain (TnO: Sonzokuyama no Hi)*. In the movie *PoT: The Two Samurai: The First Game* (2005, *TnO: Futari no Samurai: The First Game*), Ryoma and his classmates play an exhibition game on a luxury cruise ship, only to learn that they're being used as pawns in a corrupt millionaire's web of gambling and deceit, while Ryoma meets his supposed brother. **LV**

PRINCE PIRATE

1966. JPN: *Kaizoku Oji*. TV series. DIR: Yoshio Kuroda, Kimio Yabuki, Kenji Araki. SCR: Jiro Yoshino, Minoru Hamada, Hiroyasu Yamaura, Yasuo Yamaguchi, Daikichi Harada, Ichiro Wakabayashi. DES: Shotaro Ishinomori. ANI: Tameo Ogawa, Eisuke Kondo, Shinichi Suzuki, Hiroshi Wagatsuma. MUS: Hisayuki Miyazaki. PRD: Toei, NET. 25 mins. x 31 eps.

Kidd's dying father tells him of Morgan, a pirate who yearns to rule the seven seas. Kidd tracks down Morgan's ship, the Hurricane, wins over its skipper, an old sailor called Crapp, and becomes the new captain. However, his dreams of a life on the open sea are soon scrapped by the arrival of the Barracuda and its nasty captain, Fugg Hook.

Mixing equal parts of PETER PAN AND WENDY with SINDBAD THE SAILOR, and adapted from CYBORG 009-creator Ishinomori's manga in *Shonen King*, *PP* also featured a genuine kid playing Kidd—the lead voice actor was the 13-year-old Satoshi Furuya, better known today as King Philip in ALEXANDER. Captain Kidd's treasure would also feature in DAGGER OF KAMUI.

PRINCE PLANET *

1965. JPN: *Yusei Shonen Papi*. AKA: *Planet Boy Papi*. TV series. DIR: Tsutomu Yamamoto, Yonehiko Watanabe, Tadao Wakabayashi, Takeshi Kawauchi. SCR: Ichiro Kanai, Jusaburo Futaba, Satoshi Ogura. ANI: Tadao Wakabayashi. MUS: Toriro Miki. PRD: TCJ, Eiken, Fuji TV. 25 mins. x 52 eps.

Unwilling to admit Earth into the Galactic

Council of Planets until its warlike ways are curbed, the council appoints a prince from the pacifist planet Radion as an Earth-based ambassador. Crash-landing in the American Southwest, he befriends local oil heiress Diana Worthy, who helps him blend in with Earth society. Before long, "Bobby," as he is now known, moves to the urban sprawl of New Metropolis, where his superpowered pendant from Radion bestows superhuman strength and the ability to fly. With his sometime associates Ajababa the magician and wrestler Dan Dynamo, he fights crime in a predictable but earnest cross of **AMAZING THREE** and **ASTRO BOY**. Based on a manga by Hideoki Inoue, a former assistant of Mitsuteru Yokoyama. As was customary in the American market at the time, the original Japanese theme was replaced with a new track, on this occasion by the Carol Lombard Singers.

PRINCE SHAMPOO

2007. JPN: *Shampoo Oji.* TV series. DIR: Yuki Kinoshita. SCR: Kyoko Sagiyama. DES: Fumiko Urawa, Hiromi Ishigami, Hideto Nakahara. ANI: Fumiko Urawa, Hiromi Ishigami. MUS: Hironobu Kageyama. PRD: Best Field Inc., Dax, TC Entertainment, TV Saitama. 5 mins. x 12 eps.
In the cleanest kingdom ever, Prince Shampoo lives with his mommy Queen Rinse and daddy King Soap. Grandpa Sponge can be scary—and funny—when he shouts and rages at the naughty little Prince, but life is full of happy adventures. This show for small children was created by Keiko Nagita, better known as **CANDY CANDY** writer Kyoko Mizuki. It first appeared in 2004, as a picture book illustrated by Makoto Kubota, while Mizuki's long and bitter lawsuit with her *Candy Candy* cocreator was still in progress. The suit wasn't settled until 2007, by which time the *Prince Shampoo* anime was in production.

PRINCESS 69 *

2002. JPN: *Shintaiso Kari.* AKA: *New Gymnastics Kari* (i.e., *Rhythmic Gymnastics Kari*). Video. DIR: Teruaki Murakami. SCR: Osamu Momoi. DES: Teruaki Murakami. ANI: N/C. MUS: N/C. PRD: Pink Pineapple. 30 mins. x 2 eps. (v1), 30 mins. x 2 eps. (v2).
In an erotic pastiche of the school sports genre of **AIM FOR THE ACE**, rich, privi-

leged Tomomi is the star of her school gymnastics club, determined to break the will of shy, innocent new arrival Miku by indoctrinating her in the sadistic rituals of the Gymnastics of Darkness. This involves torture and bondage after school, both at the hands of Tomomi and her sometime lover, the coach Nikasuke. Other girls are soon recruited, some willingly, some less so, such as Madoka, who confesses to her friend Wakana that she has seen the secret rituals, only to discover that Wakana is already an initiate. Later episodes collapse from the silly into the disturbing as the tortures get increasingly sadistic. For some reason, the sequel *Rhythmic Gymnastics Shin* (2005, titled in the U.S. *Princess 69: Midnight Gymnastics*) was released by a different company, as part of the **DISCOVERY SERIES. ○**🄽🅥

PRINCESS AND THE PILOT, THE *

2011. JPN: *Toaru Hikoshi e no Tsuioku.* movie, TV series. DIR: Jun Shishido. SCR: Satoko Okudera. DES: Hidenori Matsubara, Kazuyuki Hashimoto. ANI: Satoshi Tasaki, Geum-Soo Kim, Kazuo Watanabe. MUS: Shiro Hamaguchi. PRD: Madhouse, Bandai Visual, KIDS STATION, Medianet. MOVIC, Sammy, Shogakukan, TMS, Tokyo Theaters, TV Tokyo. 99 mins. (m), 24 mins. x 13 eps. (TV).
In the middle of a war, a future Imperial bride is a target for the enemy. Unfortunately the other side also has superior air power, making a strike on the Princess's island home a possibility. To get her to safety, her air force will run a decoy mission while she sets out in a fast scout plane with only a single pilot to get them both to safety. The pilot is a half-breed with enemy blood who has fought his way up the ranks against cruelty and prejudice to become the most skilled ace in the ranks. He also knew the Princess as a child (**ROMANCE AND DRAMA**). Together they set out over thousands of miles of open water, but detection and capture by the enemy is the least of the risks they run.
It's no shame to lose the sky-and-water contest and the unborn romance stakes to **PORCO ROSSO**; this is an attractive movie, told with heart and sensitivity. The animation, especially the aerial combat sequences, is nicely done and a rival to **SKY CRAWLERS**, the world is well realized in an understated, unfussy way, and the

characterizations are touchingly good. Without flinching from the ugly face of racism the script doesn't judge it; a German half-breed in Blitz-torn London might have faced similar discrimination, as many Japanese Americans did in the 1940s. Films about good people in bad circumstances are a dime a dozen, but this one neither preaches nor takes refuge in fantasy. Quality entertainment for grown-ups is rare: don't miss it.
Toshimasa Suzuki's later *The Pilot's Love Song* (*Toaru Hikushi no Koiuta,* 2014) is a TV series based on several follow-up novels set in the same universe.

PRINCESS ANMITSU

1986. JPN: *Anmitsu Hime.* TV series. DIR: Masami Anno, Rei Hidaka, Takaaki Ishiyama. SCR: Yoshio Urasawa, Tomoko Konparu, Hideo Takayashiki, Yoshiyuki Suga, Masaru Yamamoto. DES: Shosuke Kurogane. ANI: Yoshiyuki Kishi. MUS: Hiroshi Ogasawara. PRD: Studio Pierrot, Fuji TV. 25 mins. x 51 eps.
A cheeky, vivacious little medieval Japanese princess is bored with life in her father's castle of Amakara. With her best friend Takemaru in sometimes reluctant pursuit, she sets about livening things up. Luckily, as her father's sole heir, she's unlikely to get into real trouble, and since she really loves Takemaru, she'll try and make sure he doesn't either.
Shosuke Kurogane's original manga began in 1949 in *Shojo Comic* magazine, finished in 1955, and was first approached as an anime project in 1961. Abandoned by the inexperienced team because of soaring costs, it took Studio Pierrot to give it all the charm and energy the author hoped for 25 years later, presenting a sweetly fantasized picture of the ideal Japanese childhood, in which preschool- and kindergarten-age children are secure, loved, and much indulged, and their little naughtinesses always innocent and always forgiven.

PRINCESS ARETE

2001. JPN: *Arete Hime.* Movie. DIR: Sunao Katabuchi. SCR: Sunao Katabuchi. DES: Keiko Morikawa. ANI: Kazusane Ozaki. MUS: N/C. PRD: Studio 4°C, Omega Project. ca. 90 mins.
Princess Arite, a little girl who lives in a small room on top of a tower, yearns to

learn magic and escape to the town below. This fairy tale from Katabuchi, former assistant to Miyazaki on KIKI'S DELIVERY SERVICE, was made inside a computer, though it retains the appearance of traditional cel animation. Based on the novel *The Clever Princess* by Diana Coles.

PRINCESS ARMY

1992. Video. DIR: Osamu Sekita. SCR: Miyuki Kitagawa. DES: Yumi Yamada. ANI: Yumi Yamada. MUS: Yuichi Takahashi. PRD: Group Tac, Animate Film. 30 mins. x 2 eps.

Rescued from a drunken attacker by a judoist, Nonoka Aida resolves to become as good as her savior, hoping one day to recognize him by the scar on his back. Transferred to a new high school, she meets two older boys who could possibly be the person to whom she owes her life and wants to give her heart—see UTENA. Multiple unrequited yearnings as three judo girls and three judo boys fall in and out of love while they're supposed to be throwing each other around a room—with matters greatly exacerbated by the sudden arrival of a forgotten fiancé from Holland. Based on the manga in *Shojo* magazine by Miyuki Kitagawa, this is an even gentler judo soap opera than YAWARA!, whose earlier success it was doubtless trying to emulate.

PRINCESS BE CAREFUL *

2006. JPN: *Himesama Goyojin*. AKA: *Princess Beware*. TV series. DIR: Shigehito Takayanagi. SCR: Shigehito Takayanagi. DES: Makoto Koga, Kazuya Fukuda. ANI: N/C. MUS: Katsuyuki Harada. PRD: Nomad, Animax Asia. 25 mins. x 12 eps.

Schoolgirl Himeko accidentally takes a bag from a pair of thieves. The magic crown it contains turns her into a princess, but far from making all her wishes come true it just marks her as a target for more thieves. Wacky hijinks ensue, with a panty-thief monkey, a policeman who sleeps in the toilet so as to be ready to go on early duty, an assortment of crazy thieves, and our heroine's xenophobia creating semi-comic mayhem of a mildly entertaining kind. Director Takayanagi created the story. Aired in English on Animax Asia.

PRINCESS JELLYFISH *

2010. JPN: *Kurage-hime*. TV series. DIR: Taka-hiro Omori. SCR: Jukki Hanada, Yuki Enatsu, Toko Machida. DES: Kenji Hayama, Mio Isshiki. ANI: Kenji Hayama, Junko Abe, Natsuko Kondo. MUS: Makoto Yoshimori. PRD: Brains Base, Asmik Ace, Dentsu, Fuji TV, GENCO, SME. Toho, Kodansha. 25 mins. x 11 eps.

Imagine an apartment complex just for nerds—female nerds: a completely safe home territory where no guys are allowed and girls can indulge their favorite obsessions without fear of ridicule. Welcome to Amamizu-kan, home to jellyfish otaku Tsukimi and her friends. When a bossy, beautiful woman helps Tsukimi save one of her favorite jellyfish, she can't really refuse to let her sleep over. Except she is a *he*—the cross-dressing bastard son of a high-ranked politician. Add a few more misfits on the loose, a scheming, ruthless woman who wouldn't know sisterhood if she shot it and made its skin into shoes, and the threat of a safe haven vanishing, and you have a perfect recipe for a sweetly funny romantic comedy about being who you are, fighting for what you love, and never making the mistake of judging the contents by the label.

PJ's raindrops on roses and whiskers on kittens don't mask the harsh reality of life as a socially inept and determinedly unattractive girl with no job, no conversation, and no hope; instead the characters grit their teeth and survive, accommodating where they must and preserving what they can, resulting in a series with both a heart and a brain, a rarity that's pure pleasure from start to finish. Akiko Higashimura's manga was published in 2000 and inexplicably remains untranslated into English as we write. Compare to PET GIRL OF SAKURASOU, which tries the same essential storyline but depressingly fumbles it.

PRINCESS KNIGHT *

1967. JPN: *Ribon no Kishi*. AKA: *Knight of the Ribbon; Choppy and the Princess; The Adventures of Choppy and the Princess; Princesse Saphir*. TV series. DIR: Chikao Katsui, Nobuo Onuki, Yoshiyuki Tomino, Masami Hata, Ryosuke Takahashi, Hideo Makino, Seiji Okuda, Norio Hikone. SCR: Osamu Tezuka, Masaki Tsuji. DES: Kazuko Nakamura, Sadao Miyamoto, Minoru Nishida. ANI: Sadao Miyamoto. MUS: Isao Tomita. PRD: Tezuka Pro, Fuji TV. 25 mins. x 52 eps., 25 mins. (pilot).

Thanks to an accident in heaven, where the mischievous cherub Tink is responsible for giving out hearts to babies, Princess Sapphire of Silverland is born with two—a man's *and* a woman's. This is fortunate for her father the king, who proclaims to the populace that the new child is a boy, and, consequently, that any succession problems are over. The secret is kept, since if it becomes known that the heir is a girl, the succession will pass to the corrupt Duke Jeralmin. She grows up as a boy, learning all the masculine skills and doing her utmost to excel and make her father and her people proud. But when she falls in love with the charming prince Franz Charming, she faces a terrible dilemma. Revealing her womanhood would throw away her own achievements, her father's dreams, and the stability of her country—but staying a man means she must sacrifice her dream of love forever.

Beginning as a 1953 manga in *Nakayoshi*, Osamu Tezuka's *PK* was the ASTRO BOY–creator's tribute to the many Takarazuka musical revues he saw as a child, where the all-female cast made cross-dressing a narrative necessity. This gem of a series, much loved in Europe, is less well known in the English-speaking world despite several English-language releases, but its enduring influence can be seen in the massive success of its immediate heirs ROSE OF VERSAILLES and UTENA, as well as in the prevalence of cross-dressing battle-babes throughout anime. It also has powerful links with the magical-girl shows in the princess's masquerade under another identity, her fight against supernatural evil, and her friend and protector-sprite Tink. Its style and pace seem dated now, but the themes, ideas, and plots Tezuka generated are still being reexamined by modern directors and writers who were not even born when it was first broadcast. Versions of *PK* will probably go on being retold forever, but however modern the trappings, they will stand or fall on how they measure up to the power and simplicity of Tezuka's original.

It had a limited American TV release in 1972 under the title *Princess Knight*. Licensees Joe Oriolo and Burt Hecht did better with three episodes edited into a movie entitled *Choppy and the Princess*. With Tink renamed Choppy, this was shown frequently on syndicated TV throughout the U.S. in the 1970s and 1980s. The series also made it onto Australian screens under the *PK* title, and a number of 25-minute episodes were released on British video by two different distributors. Movie Makers released seven episodes under the general title *The Adventures of Choppy and the Princess* and at least three more under individual episode titles without the *AoCatP* surtitle. Tasley Leisure of Leeds released six episodes as *Choppy and the Princess, Adventures 1–6*. The English dubs lose one of Tezuka's beloved jokes—he named the good characters and countries in his fable after precious stones and metals, with the bad guys named after cheap synthetics like nylon and plastic, but the names have been mangled in TRANSLATION. Following Tezuka's death in 1989, the series was released on Japanese Laser-Disc in 1991, with the original unbroadcast pilot included as a bonus extra.

PRINCESS KNIGHT ANGELICA
2008. JPN: *Hime-kishi Angelica*. Video. DIR: Noritomo Hattori. SCR: Ryu Haru. DES: N/C. ANI: Shiro Shibata. MUS: N/C. PRD: GP Museum Soft. 30 mins. x 2 eps.
The evil Ernest kidnaps and rapes elf princess Angelica, but is believed by everyone to be her rescuer. Since Angelica doesn't enlighten her father the king, Ernest becomes a lord, heals the blind elf princess Flora, and gets engaged to her. Then he rapes dark elf Serafina. It's all a revenge plot because his beloved elf princess Christina rejected him and he wants revenge. So having raped all four elf girls he persuades them to help him murder the king, and becomes king in his place, because elves are all stupid rape addicts. That sound you hear is J. R. R. Tolkein spinning in his grave. There is no connection to Osamu Tezuka's PRINCESS KNIGHT—this is merely stunt TRANSLATION for an anime based on a porn game by Silky's. ⓃⓋ

PRINCESS KNIGHT CATUE
2008. Video. DIR: Yukihiro Makino, Tatsuhiko Yoshihara. SCR: Inochi Kado. DES: Hiroshi Iijima, Hifumi. ANI: Hiroshi Iijima, Shigenori Awai. MUS: Ruri Yakushi, Kazuhito Kiuchi. PRD: Studio9MAiami, Valhalla. 30 mins. x 3 eps.
Dragons, demons, pigs, ogres (but as far as we know no pig ogres, so no relationship to PIG PRINCESS) and multi-tentacled beings rape Dragon Knight Catue

Draguundaala, a princess of the Dragon Clan, and her loyal maid Anna. Catue's castle falls to a monstrous horde including hunky-looking Guignol, a captain in the Monster Battalion, and his allies in the Pig Clan. They were formerly enslaved by the Dragon Clan so they're looking for some payback in this porn anime based on a game by Valkyria. Oh look, by a mysterious coincidence it ends up getting filed close to PRINCESS KNIGHT, but not close enough because a bunch of other pornographers have had the same idea. ⓃⓋ

PRINCESS KNIGHT JANNE
2010. JPN: *Inda no Hime-kishi Janne the Animation*. AKA: *Princess Knight Janne's Degenerate Lewdness*. Video. DIR: Banzo Tokita. SCR: Kaoru Takahashi. DES: Noritomo Hattori. ANI: Noritomo Hattori. MUS: N/C. PRD: Himajin. 30 mins. x 2 eps.
Princess Janne's sword skills and magical abilities are widely admired, but turn out to be less than useless when her peaceful country is invaded by ogres and dark elves who kidnap her younger sister. She goes to the elves' fortress but is captured, raped, learns new uses for jewelry and everyday objects, and begins to like it. Based on a porn game by catwalkNERO. It's a remarkable coincidence that this gets filed so close to PRINCESS KNIGHT, isn't it? ⓋⓃ

PRINCESS KNIGHT LILIA
2006. JPN: *Hime-kishi Lilia*. Video. DIR: Hiro Asano. SCR: Hiro Asano. DES: Hiro Asano, Ichiro Kamoku. ANI: Hiro Asano. MUS: N/C. PRD: Pixy. 30 mins. x 6 eps.
Princess Lilia's bad brother Dirk means to get the kingdom for himself and will do anything to prevent his beautiful, innocent sister succeeding to the throne. He enlists the help of a demon, who tells him that by sending Lilia to the highest level of sexual ecstasy they will unleash and capture her hidden power. The obvious way to send a woman to the highest level of sexual ecstasy is to involve her in multiple rapes and fetish play. To be on the safe side Dirk also brings along their mother and Lilia's loyal Knights, because you can't have too much of that hidden power. Based on a porn game by Black Lilith, who had the remarkable and original idea of using the words for Princess and Knight, so it sounded a bit like PRINCESS KNIGHT. ⓃⓋ

PRINCESS LOVER!
2009. TV series, video. DIR: Hiromitsu Kanazawa. SCR: Makoto Nakamura. DES: Shingo Suzuki, Koichi Kikuta, Tomoyuki Niho, Masaru Sato. ANI: Shingo Suzuki, Hiromi Masuda, Kazuaki Imoto. MUS:. PRD: Go Hands, Frontier Works, Lantis, Media Factory, Public Enemies. 24 mins. x 12 eps. (TV), 30 mins. x 2 eps. (V).
Teppei's parents are killed in a tragic accident. His grandfather adopts him and forces him to become heir to the family business, the mighty Arima Group Corporation. He even forces poor Teppei to go to an elite high school where he's surrounded by beautiful, well-born girls. Oh, and he gives him an orphan maid whom he adopted years ago and who is absolutely delighted to be permitted to serve the heir of the Arima Clan. It's a hard life being the focus of a high school harem anime (ROMANCE AND DRAMA), but this one, based on Mura Midorigi and Ricotta's 2009 manga *Princess Lover! Pure My Heart*, goes even further with a two-part porn video of the same title in 2010. There were also six 30-second promo shorts for the TV series, aired in 2009, featuring one of the characters as a magical girl, under the title *Princess Lover! Magical Knight Maria-chan*. The *Princess Lover! Picture Drama* was a series of six nine-minute limited animation shorts included as an extra on the DVD releases in Japan.

PRINCESS MEMORY *
2001. Video. DIR: Ko Tomi. SCR: Mirin Muto. DES: Akira Kano. ANI: Yuji Ushijima. MUS: N/C. PRD: Lemon Heart. 30 mins. x 2 eps.
Collin is a serving boy in a tavern, haunted by dreams of a naked pink-haired damsel in distress, begging for him to rescue her. His fellow workers, pretty girls Pony and Sallion, refuse to take him seriously and force him to get on with his chores until flame-haired adventurer Lily arrives. She has come into town to explore a forbidden cave on its outskirts. Deciding to accompany her on her quest, Collin discovers that there was an element of truth in his dreams—one Felina is being held captive, but her soul has been split into separate personality shards, each of which must be collected like POKÉMON. If he is able to win them all over, then she shall be restored and accept him as her knight in shining

armor, but not before he has had sex with the other cast members—compare to **DVINE [LUV]**. Ⓝ

PRINCESS MINERVA *

1995. Video. DIR: Mihiro Yamaguchi. SCR: Hideki Sonoda. DES: Tokuhiro Matsubara. ANI: Tokuhiro Matsubara, Hanchi Rei, Hokukan Sen. MUS: Kenji Kawai. PRD: Pastel. 45 mins.
Without a male heir, the kingdom of Wisler has a girl for its next leader. Minerva is a vain, headstrong, selfish princess who's bored with her role and wants to excel at combat and spellcasting. Despite the best efforts of her chief guard, Blue Morris, to keep her safe (and keep her in check), she disguises herself to fight in a big tournament for girl fighters. Unfortunately, evil sorceress Dynastar hates Minerva and sets out to kidnap her, but grabs Blue Morris instead. The Princess realizes the error of her ways, gets the warrior girls to help her, and sets out to rescue her long-suffering bodyguard.

PM is sweetly predictable, signaling its next move so far ahead that suspense is not one of its outstanding qualities. Based on a computer game/manga/novel multimedia offensive by Ko Maisaka and Run Ishida, its origins are betrayed in an outsized cast to showcase everyone's favorite from the original. Gently poking fun at **PRINCESS KNIGHT** and other tomboy heroines (at one point, the narrator tries to explain how kindhearted Minerva is, only to choke on his own words), the result is a lackluster cousin to **DRAGON HALF** but without its predecessor's insane charm. The character designs are cute but not very original; ditto the story. Uncritical fans of babes in battle bikinis may be amused.

PRINCESS MONONOKE *

1997. JPN: *Mononoke Hime*. AKA: *Princess Ghost; Phantom Princess*. Movie. DIR: Hayao Miyazaki. SCR: Hayao Miyazaki. DES: Hayao Miyazaki. ANI: Masashi Ando, Kitaro Kosaka, Yoshifumi Kondo. MUS: Joe Hisaishi. PRD: Studio Ghibli. 133 mins.
Young Prince Ashitaka defeats a supernatural beast plaguing the remote Eastern lands in which his tribe dwells but is left with a wound that refuses to heal. Because its origin is supernatural, it has a strange effect that gives Ashitaka superhuman strength and accuracy, enabling his arrows to take the heads or arms off his enemies, but it will also kill him, slowly but surely. Finding that the beast was maddened by an iron ball in its flesh, he goes in search of the culprits, hoping they can provide some way of curing him. As he wanders through the Western forests, he finds a village of ironworkers, the source of the bullet. Tataraba, the ironworkers' fort, is in conflict with both the local overlord and the creatures of the forest, which are led by a wild girl who rides on a wolf. San, an abandoned child adopted by the wolf god Moro and raised as one of her own cubs, now hates the humans who abandoned her. All her loyalty and devotion is given to her new family, the ancient beast gods whose lands are threatened by the incursions of the growing human population. Eboshi, the tough, pragmatic leader of the ironworkers, is consumed with hatred for San, and Ashitaka, a natural peacemaker whose wish is to see everyone live in harmony, tries in vain to settle their differences. He has another agenda; apart from his hope that he may find healing in the forest, he is falling in love with San. The distant, unseen emperor, who claims to be the Son of Heaven, authorizes the death of Shishigami, the woodland god who is responsible for the natural (and supernatural) resistance to Tataraba. Stealthy humans massacre many of the forest creatures, but the wrath of Shishigami is unstoppable ... almost.

Purportedly set in medieval Japan but depicting a symbolic *neverwhen* clash of three proto-Japanese races (the Jomon, Yamato, and Emishi), *PM* is the ultimate prequel to Studio Ghibli's ecological concerns in films such as **NAUSICAÄ** and **POM POKO**. It is set at the very point in time when humankind pushed Nature into submission, toppling the old "natural" order and starting the long chain to the present day, when Nature itself seems under threat of extinction. Twenty years in conception and three in production, the highest-grossing Japanese *movie* in any genre at least until **SPIRITED AWAY** beat Miyazaki's own record, and the first of Miyazaki's films to be released theatrically in America through the Disney/Tokuma marketing deal, *PM* has built a cinematic legend of its own. Born from the creator's own dissat-isfaction with the end of *Nausicaä*, which required a miraculous *deus ex machina* to resolve the human/nature conflict, *PM* is consequently far more downbeat and melancholy. Though a minority of critics still regard it as a tedious harangue, even the many who call it Miyazaki's masterpiece agree it's a difficult film for U.S. movie audiences, who are simply unaccustomed either to animation as polemic, or to the level of violence depicted. Preview audiences, not expecting a Tarantino image in a Disney movie, reacted with nervous laughter to a sequence where a man gets his arm shot off. Producer Toshio Suzuki's strict and noble "no cuts" policy may have preserved Miyazaki's creative vision but made the film difficult to sell into markets that still believed cartoons were kids' stuff. Technically, *PM* is a remarkable achievement, especially on the level of art direction and design; the primeval forests of Japan and the first stirrings of industrial society are depicted with ravishing realism. The characters are well drawn in every sense, each with his or her own motivations and needs, not cardboard heroes and villains but humans struggling to get by in a hostile world. This is a grown-up fantasy, and unlike the vast run of anime that gives us stock figures in pretty clothes and wish-fulfillment situations, *PM* presents real people in a real world that is beautiful and fascinating but must be taken on its own terms.

The U.S. dub, which featured a script rewrite by *Sandman* author Neil Gaiman, was the first theatrical anime production since the **ARMITAGE III** movie to use "name" actors (**VOICE ACTING**), with a cast including Billy Crudup, Claire Danes, Minnie Driver, and Gillian Anderson. *PM* was widely reported as being Miyazaki's last film, but he managed to cram in a few more before **THE WIND RISES**. Ⓥ

PRINCESS NINE *

1998. TV series. DIR: Tomomi Mochizuki. SCR: Hiro Maruyama. DES: Akihiko Yamashita, Yoshimi Hashimoto. ANI: Yoshimi Hashimoto. MUS: Masamichi Amano. PRD: Phoenix/ NEP21, NHK2. 25 mins. x 26 eps.
Girls don't play baseball, they play softball. But 15-year-old Ryo Hayakawa is a natural ace pitcher, just about to finish junior high and leave so she can help her

widowed mother with the family noodle bar. Instead, Mrs. Himuro, Chairperson of the prestigious Kisaragi High School, persuades Ryo to continue her education by handing her a scholarship. Keiko Himuro plans to take on the male-dominated "hard" sports with an all-girl team, deliberately designed to irritate the snooty and chauvinistic male teachers and staff who think that a girl's education should only aspire to motherhood and housewifery. But sporty girls are competitive by nature, and Ryo is soon butting heads with Izumi Himuro, the prideful, overly competitive daughter of the chairwoman and the school's tennis champion. Despite her initial opposition, Izumi eventually joins the team, adding much-needed batting power. Rivalries soon break out on and off the field, as the girls fight over token boy Hiroki and corporate sponsorship comes attached to corporate scandal. This typical baseball anime in the fashion of **H2** was dumped onto satellite TV in the impecunious late 1990s as the post-**EVANGELION** anime TV boom turned into a slump.

PRINCESS PRINCESS *

2006. TV series. DIR: Keitaro Motonaga. SCR: Akemi Omode. DES: Atsuko Nakajima, Kunihiro Shinoda. ANI: Hirofumi Morimoto. MUS: Kaoru Mizuki. PRD: Studio DEEN, Pony Canyon, TV Asahi. 24 mins. x 12 eps.
Toru is a very pretty teenager who transfers to an all-boys' school with an unusual social set-up. The cutest new boys are nominated by their classmates to become part of the "Princess System," dressing up as Gothic Lolita girls at social events to lighten up the atmosphere (no, really). At first unconvinced and reluctant, Toru soon comes to realize that being a Princess isn't only about having to wear one rigid type of clothing and get hit on by other guys—well, OK, it is, but he rather likes it. This anime based on Mikiyo Tsuda's 2002 manga exploits the humor rather than the sexual angle. There's nothing explicit and nothing very deep, though there are some nice character touches as Toru and the other Princesses debate their relationships with girls and each other, and the role of clothing and presentation in sexuality. Loli guys will love it.

PRINCESS RESURRECTION *

2007. JPN: Kaibutsu Ojo. AKA: Monster Princess. TV series, video. DIR: Masayuki Sakoi, Keiichiro Kawaguchi. SCR: Keiichiro Kawaguchi. DES: Kazuya Kuroda, Si Min Lee, Yoshio Kosakai, Yuka Okamoto, Kikuko Sadakata, Yutaka Kuramoto. ANI: Kazuya Kuroda, Kikuko Sadakata. MUS: Mikiya Katakura, Makoto Takou. PRD: Madhouse, Index, Kodansha, Lantis, MOVIC, Shaft, TBS, Universal Pictures, Tatsunoko. 25 mins. x 25 eps. (TV), 23 mins. (v1), 25 mins. x 3 eps. (v2).
Orphan Hiro's sister Sawawa has a new live-in job as caretaker of an old house and asks him to move in with her. A bizarre accident involves him dying while saving the life of the girl who lives in the house. Luckily, or perhaps not, she's a princess of the monster realm and brings him back to life (**ULTRAMAN**), provided he stays by her side as her servant. Hime, as she calls herself, is a bona fide Princess engaged in a vicious struggle with her relatives over the order of succession. She doesn't actually want the throne herself, but doesn't want to be killed so someone else can get it either. Gathering together a motley army of helpers from the half-breeds and oddities at Hiro's new school, the unlikely pair fight off a range of threats both predictable and unusual, including classic movie monsters, enchanted boats and haunted villages.

The story varies slightly from Yasunori Mitsunaga's 2005 manga—Hiro is hit by a car in the original, rather than dying heroically, and Sawawa and other minor manga characters get bigger anime roles—and the overarching plot is often treated as an afterthought, while the animation doesn't live up to Madhouse's usual standards, let alone their best efforts. After 25 episodes (a 26th "special" showed up on the 2008 Japanese DVD release) the show went dark before reemerging in 2010 in an "alternate retelling" on video, with an all-new cast and crew, and more gore and sexual innuendo than the TV version—compare with *Hellsing Ultimate* (**HELLSING**). **V**

PRINCESS ROUGE *

1997. AKA: Legend of the Last Labyrinth. Video. DIR: Isato Date. SCR: Mamoru Takeuchi. DES: Minoru Yamazawa. ANI: Minoru Yamazawa. MUS: N/C. PRD: Beam Entertainment. 30 mins. x 2 eps.
Recently orphaned teenager Yusuke Mizuki struggles to live alone, until a dimensional portal opens while he is cycling to school, literally dumping a pretty girl in his lap. Reluctantly he takes care of the amnesiac green-haired girl who can only remember her name, Rouge. As a mawkish romance develops between them, **OH MY GODDESS!** comparisons become actionably obvious, as the couple is besieged by Rouge's supernatural sisters, Kaige and Meige. Discovering that Rouge is a princess of the underworld, the pair is forced to flee from other family members, chiefly a man called Raiga and his sword-wielding minions. Raiga wants Rouge to help him unseal Gaia's Sword, an artifact of great power. As with so many video anime, the cliffhanger ending and lack of follow-up aren't the fault of Western distributors. Six episodes were projected, but after poor sales, only the two on the American video release were ever made.

PRINCESS SLAVE

2008. JPN: Hime Dorei: Mesu e to Ochiyuku Futago no Ojo. Video. DIR: Shinpei Nagai. SCR: N/C. DES: Mamoru Kobayashi. ANI: Shinpei Nagai, Mamoru Kobayashi. MUS: N/C. PRD: MS Pictures (Milky). 30 mins. x 2 eps.
The king of the peaceful little kingdom of Luvence has two beautiful twin sisters, Tita and Liese. He decides to make Tita his heir. Despite these worthy intentions his other sister Liese is jealous and looks for a way to get rid of Tita. When she meets the magician Waldo, whose country was destroyed by the Luvence army and who seeks revenge, a plan begins to take shape. This is based on a porn game by BISHOP, so the plan involves rape, demonic rape, tentacle rape, mental domination, and the rest of the usual suspects. In the end, Waldo's sexuality is so powerful that Liese submits to him and he becomes king with both sisters as his playthings. It was never this easy for real medieval schemers, probably because they didn't have tentacle back-up. **Ⓝⓥ**

PRINCESS TUTU *

2002. JPN: Princess Tutu/Chuchu. TV series. DIR: Junichi Sato, Shogo Kawamoto, Ikuko Ito, Kiyoko Sayama, Osamu Sekita, Yu Ko. SCR: Chiaki Konaka, Mamiko Ikeda, Michiko

Yokote, Rika Nanase, Takuya Sato. DES: Ikuko Ito. ANI: Akemi Kobayashi, Takashi Shiokawa, Yuji Ushijima, Nobuto Akada, Shinichi Yoshikawa. MUS: Kaoru Wada. PRD: Hal Film Maker, Kid's Station, Imagica. 30 mins. x 13 eps. (TV1), 15 mins. x 26 eps. (TV2).

Gangly, clumsy but determined, Ahiru (whose name is Japanese for duck) studies ballet at Kinkan Academy—a duckling training to become a swan, just in case that wasn't obvious. She adores Mythos, the school's star male dancer, from afar, but he's so remote and passive that he hardly seems to notice anything. His sinister friend Fakir protects and bullies him in equal measure, and elegant and self-centered Rue, the school's star ballerina, wants him for herself.

This fairy tale redolent of TALES OF HANS CHRISTIAN ANDERSEN is also a magical-girl story, a high school romance in which the clumsiest but most determined and kind-hearted girl in the class struggles to win the school hunk; a drama fable along the lines of MASK OF GLASS (featuring much music from famous ballets), and the tale of a hero's fight against the forces of darkness seen through the eyes of the princess. The characters inhabit a reality not dissimilar to that of RANMA ½, in which an ordinary town can be populated with animal-human hybrids subject to strange enchantments.

The reason is supposedly rooted in an ancient fairy tale, in which a handsome, noble prince fought an evil raven. The story teller died before the story could be finished, and, determined to fulfill their destinies despite the death of their creator, the prince and the bird escaped from the story. In our own world, the prince sacrificed his heart to seal the raven's powers away and protect the world from her malice. But since a story demands an ending a duck is magically transformed into a human girl—with help and advice from mechanical doll musician Edel, Ahiru can use a magic pendant to transform herself into Princess Tutu. When she has retrieved every piece of the prince's lost heart, he will be free. But the raven princess is also free, and determined to fight the swan princess, and Ahiru has a hitherto unsuspected handicap. She transforms back into her duck self whenever she quacks, and she quacks when she's startled. It takes a

splash of water to get her back to normal.

The charm of *PT* is its attempt to subvert the formulae of its genres, such as allowing the princess to save the hero. The sensual yearning at the heart of all school romances mixes with the fear of the adult world, in which everything is unfamiliar and safety nets are few; but stronger than the powerful mix of fear and sex is a passion for stories and storytelling, for the magic of making a new world. Borrowing from European folklore already familiar to many Japanese through earlier anime, it deftly creates an internal reality where perception is just a medium for filtering dreams to find the one your heart holds dearest. Writer Konaka brings in a mechanical being wiser and more reliable than most organic ones, just as he did in ARMITAGE III and MALICE DOLL, and keeps the story closer to the terrifying undercurrents of SWAN LAKE than the sugarplum fairy tale of *The Nutcracker*. There's a wonderful echo of LITTLE MERMAID each time Tutu gives the Prince back a piece of his heart; with each piece he gains the power to express new emotions and ideas, but not always pleasant ones. The things she unleashes in him often tear at her own heart like knives. The series is divided into two parts, the first 13 half-hour episodes known as the Egg Chapter, and the following 26 15-minute episodes, shown two at a time, known as the Chick Chapter. ●

PRISM ARK

2007. TV series. DIR: Masami Obari. SCR: Yuji Hosono. DES: Risa Ebata, Kazuhiro Inoue. ANI: Risa Ebata, Megumi Noda, Yukihito Ogomori. MUS: Naruki Endo. PRD: Front Line, 5pb, Marvelous Entertainment, Media Factory, Studio G-1 Neo. 24 mins. x 12 eps. (TV), 30 mins. (v).

The Sablum Empire enlists mercenaries Sister Hell and Darkness Knight to take over the kingdom of Windland, using magical beings called Angels. Hyaweh and his friend Precia are studying swordsmanship and sorcery at the Windland Knights' Academy, and band together with their friends to defend the realm from invasion. Now if they could just find the lost princess and get the high school play and graduation ball together.... This conventional fantasy/high school hybrid isn't necessarily what one would expect from

the director of VIRUS BUSTER SERGE (who also directed the 2010 video *Prism Magical: Prism Generations!*). It's based on the erotic video game of the same name, by Pyjamas Soft, released in 2007 as a sequel to their successful *Prism Heart* game.

PRISM SEASON

1989. JPN: *Nagata Megumi Prism Season*. AKA: *Megumi Nagata's Prism Season*. Video. DIR: Yuichi Ito. SCR: Yuichi Ito. DES: Megumi Nagata. ANI: Yuichi Ito. MUS: Ami Osaki. PRD: Grouper Pro. 30 mins.

In a gentle adaptation of Megumi Nagata's book *Flowers Wait for the Moon*, a girl grows up, falls in love, and becomes a mother, realizing that her childhood is now forever behind her. The same illustrator's distinctive pastels, Victorian-style fairies, and falling flowers could also be seen in later follow-ups, 1994 Japanese-style adaptations of THUMBELINA, Mimei Ogawa's children's book *The Coloring Magician*, and *Mermaid and the Red Candles*, though, as a combination of still pictures and narration, none of them is technically anime.

PRISON BATTLESHIP

2009. JPN: *Kangoku Senkan*. Video. DIR: Teruaki Murakami. SCR: Shinichiro Sawayama. DES: Teruaki Murakami. ANI: Teruaki Murakami. MUS: Tomohiro Yoshida, Teruaki Murakami. PRD: Pixy, Shift R (3D). 30 mins. x 4 eps.

Commander Lieri Bishop and Major Naomi Evans of the Universal Federation board a battleship to Earth to report on the crimes of a group called the Neo Terrors. Unfortunately the ship they choose is commanded by a member of the Neo Terrors, Donny Bogan, who has been nursing a grudge since they got him arrested four years back. He brainwashes them and implants a personality change tied to the pattern of lighting on the ship. When the lights change, they become sexually insatiable. Based on an erotic game by Anime Lilith, this has uniforms cool enough for Gerry Anderson's *UFO* worn by heroines dumb enough for *Valley Girls*. ●●●

PRIVATE PSYCHO LESSON *

1996. JPN: *Kojin Jugyo*. AKA: *U-Jin's Personal Tuition*. Video. DIR: Tetsuro Amino. SCR: Ryusei. DES: Makoto Takahata. ANI: N/C. MUS: N/C. PRD: JC Staff, Blue Mantis. 35 mins. x

2 eps.

Sara Iijima of Stunford (*sic*) University is a psychotherapist working in the field of higher education—which means most of her patients are high school or college students, coincidentally the target audience for this video. The traditional watch-on-a-chain method is not for her; to hypnotize patients she whips her top off, gets into a state of sexual excitement, and rotates her breasts in opposite directions. Once the patients are under her hypnotic influence, she regresses them to the point of trauma and sorts it out with a bit of fan service. This sex-solves-everything school of analysis has made her very successful—she travels to assignments in her own helicopter gunship and disciplines inadequate teachers with a few hundred well-aimed bullets. A variant on the elder erotic initiatress also seen in **REI REI**, but the script's treatment of rape—a punishment for bad Japanese girls dealt out by foreign men—is particularly offensive. U-Jin, who wrote the original manga, knows what his audience wants, but he's capable of delivering it more cleverly; see the **TALES OF ...** series. ✪🅝🆅

PRIVATE SESSIONS *

2001. AKA: *Tokubetsu Jugyo. Video.* DIR: Hiroyuki Yanase. SCR: Rokurota Makabe. DES: Hiroyuki Yanase. ANI: Hiroyuki Yanase. MUS: Yoshi. PRD: YOUC Digital Works (Vanilla Series). 30 mins. x 2 eps. (v1), 30 mins. x 2 eps. (v2).

Takumi Mikami is unable to find full-time work as a teacher because he has a record for sexually abusing his pupils. However, such foibles are no bar to employment in the world of anime pornography, and so he is soon taking a temporary teaching job at a high-class girls' school famed for its discipline. By a remarkable coincidence, discipline is what Takumi is best at, and his sex slave Sahi Azuma is already working at the school in another teaching post. His first victim is Natsuki, the heroine of the basketball club, whom he rapes in his office after practice, while Sahi captures the incident on video. Meanwhile, the brother of one of Takumi's other victims decides that it is more important for his sister's honor for him to regain the tape of her rape than it is for him to report it to the police.

The seemingly unrelated *Private Sessions 2* (2003) features Juichiro Aoki, a famous painter who lives in a mansion in the leafy suburbs of Kyoto. His wife Reika is 30 years younger than he, and only married him in order to pay off the debts of her father, an *ikebana* master. Although the marriage is technically loveless, Juichiro's wife has come to enjoy their bondage games, as does Juichiro's new apprentice Kaoru, who witnesses their activities in secret.

For the second part of *PS2*, the scene changes once more to a school, where Tomoya Ishiguro realizes that he is the spitting image of one of the real teachers, and so is able to smuggle himself into the daily life of the school. His schoolgirl victims include computer geek Yumi, librarian Seira and art student Asuka. Based on a computer game by Bishop. Another entry in the **VANILLA SERIES**. ✪🅝🆅

PRO GOLFER SARU

1982. AKA: *Progolfer Monkey.* TV special, TV series, movie. DIR: Hiroshi Fukutomi, Junji Nishimura, Minoru Arai, Yasuhiro Imagawa, Tameo Ogawa, Tsukasa Sunaga. SCR: Noboru Shiroyama, Seiji Matsuoka. DES: Shinichi Suzuki. ANI: Toshiyuki Honda, Hideyuki Motohashi. MUS: Hiroshi Tsutsui. PRD: Shinei Doga, TV Asahi. 111 mins. (TVm1), 25 mins. x 147 eps. (TV), 96 mins. (TVm2), 44 mins. (m1), 75 mins. (m2).

Sarumaru Sarutani is a professional golfer, determined to defeat the shadowy Mr. X and his syndicate of evil golfers, including Dragon the kung-fu golf master. This TV special was based on the 1974 manga by Motoo Abiko, one half of the Fujiko-Fujio duo who created **DORAEMON**. Splitting from his working partner Hiroshi Fujimoto in the 1980s, he produced several titles under the name Fujiko-Fujio "A," including **PARASOL HENBE**, **LAUGHING SALESMAN**, and **BILLY DOG**—*PGS* is his longest and most successful creation. Serialized in publications for the very young, such as *Mommy, Baby Book*, and *Corocoro Comic*, the story was never intended for the adult audience, except perhaps as a way of making Dad's weekend hobby look more interesting to his children. The hero's much more akin to the Man with No Name than to the irrepressible Stone Monkey of **JOURNEY TO THE WEST**, but these games are played strictly for laughs.

Bringing new meaning to the term "crazy golf," *PGS* returned as a TV series in 1985, with a series of fantastical tournaments in which players used absurd special powers, and the simian Saru remained determined to triumph. Amid kung-fu masters, dragon warriors, and fairway fairies, his opponents include Death himself. In the midst of these adventures, he went to America in another TV movie *PGS: Saru in USA* (1985) for a duel against the Native American golf-shaman Hawkwild. The movies beckoned with *PGS: Challenge of Super Golf World* (1986), set in the eponymous theme park where our hero faced the world greats at a tournament run by the ever-present Mr. X. A second movie, *PGS: Koga's Secret Zone—the Shadow Ninja Golfer* (1987), took Saru to a hidden valley in the Japanese Alps, where Saru and his family must battle a trio of golf-assassins. More adult golfing activities would be the focus of **BEAT SHOT!!**

PRODUCTION I.G

Founded in 1987 by Mitsuhisa Ishikawa and Takayuki Goto as an offshoot of Tatsunoko Productions, the company was first known by a name that combined its founders' initials—IG Tatsunoko. Its first major role was as a production house on the first **PATLABOR** movie—the authors speculate that, had the movie been a failure, the existence of a separate company would have shielded the parent from liability. Renamed Production I.G, it was subsequently merged with ING, another of Ishikawa's companies, to form the entity as it is known today, with credits ranging from **GHOST IN THE SHELL** to **BLOOD: THE LAST VAMPIRE** and a prominent position as a subcontractor on Studio Ghibli's **PRINCESS MONONOKE**. Notable staffers include Ishikawa himself, Hiroyuki Kitakubo, Toshihiro Kawamoto, and computer animator Norifumi Kiyozumi. Production I.G has benefited greatly from its association with director Mamoru Oshii and also from its high profile in the Western fan community, bolstered by a U.S. office. The company is a major player in digital animation, and pioneered "screen architecture"—that is, the pre-visualizing of effects that will be applied to a scene, allowing animators to get a better idea of how their work will look when it is finally composited with multiple effects and filters. Production I.G also created the "anime" sequence of **KILL BILL: THE ORIGIN OF O-REN** and "Last Orders" (1997), a superb one-minute pastiche of Madhouse Studios' future dystopias as an animated commercial for Murphy's Stout in the U.K. Production I.G's advertising work for other companies includes commercials for Kirin Lemon, T-Mobile, and Samsung. The animation studio Xebec is a subsidiary of the company, while I.G merged in 2007 with the manga publishing company Mag Garden, placing both firms subordinate to a newly created holding company, IG Port. IG Port, in turn, has a 70% stake in Wit Studio, formed in 2012 and best known for **ATTACK ON TITAN**.

PROFESSOR LAYTON AND THE ETERNAL DIVA *

2009. JPN: *Layton Kyoju to Eien no Utahime*. Movie. DIR: Masakazu Hashimoto. SCR: Aya Matsui. DES: Noboru Sugimitsu. ANI: Noboru Sugimitsu. MUS: Tomohito Nishiura. PRD: Oriental Light and Magic, P.A. Works, MBS, Chubu-Nippon Broadcasting, Hokkaido Broadcasting, LEVEL-5 Inc., RKB Mainichi Broadcasting, TBS, Shogakukan. 95 mins.
Puzzle expert Professor Herschel Layton and his loyal assistant Luke are invited to a special night at the opera by a former student, Janice, now a singer. But this turns out to be a puzzle in itself, wrapped in a series of puzzles that must be solved before one lucky member of the audience is granted eternal life. It appears that Janice's friend died and was reincarnated in the body of a little girl, claiming that she has the secret of immortality.

This story of lost civilizations and lost loved ones is based on a successful series of Nintendo games, and intended as a family-friendly bit of fun with brain-teasers thrown in. The animation and design stick closely to the pattern of the games, as does the plot-driven style of storytelling and the richly detailed score with its operatic inserts. However, playing like a respray of **CASTLE OF CAGLIOSTRO**, made by a gaming company (which is effectively what it is), *Professor Layton* disappoints at the level of puzzle-making. Unlike **PHI BRAIN**, which often gives its audience the chance to solve the problems themselves, most of Layton's obstacles are far too complex for anyone

to do more than simply sit passively and wait for him to succeed. In other words, this film simply replicates the experience of watching *someone else* play the game, which is hardly fun. Despite this cavil, the production team pile on some nice touches, including leitmotifs redolent of both the James Bond movies and the musical of *The Phantom of the Opera*. Some elements do not ring true, however. As with many Tezuka productions from **ASTRO BOY** onward, the pathos and bathos of life-threatening situations is often dispelled or ruined by the sight of overly cartoonish characters, as if a bunch of Warner Brothers icons were forced to face the perils of **GANTZ**. Layton himself comes across as a cantankerous bore, repeatedly asserting that he is "an English gentleman," even though he wears his hat indoors and talks at the opera.

PROFESSOR PAIN *

1998. JPN: *Gakuen Sodom*. AKA: *Sodom Academy*. Video. DIR: Genkuro Shizuka. SCR: Genkuro Shizuka. DES: Saki Kuradama. ANI: Saki Kuradama. MUS: N/C. PRD: Beam Entertainment. 25 mins. x 2 eps.
Frustrated teacher Mr. Ohse plants high explosives all over the school (a *university* in the U.S. dub), locks his students in the chemistry lab, and subjects them to sexual torments. A female teacher tries to negotiate and becomes Ohse's next victim. Eventually, however, the secret behind Ohse's madness is revealed. Distraught at his sister's suicide after a gang rape and livid that the press assumed she led her assailants on, Ohse has been encouraged, in a pastiche of the previous year's **PERFECT BLUE**, to wire up the school and kill his pupils by anonymous e-mails sent by someone posing as his sister. His aim is to create an over-the-top circus of depravity for the media he so despises. In other words, *PP* wants the best of both worlds—a snide pop at media perversity as an excuse for an hour of orgiastic bondage.

Whereas the original computer game had one of the hapless boys ("forced" by Ohse to copulate with the girl he secretly adores) as a point-of-view character, Genkuro Shizuka's script concentrates on Ohse himself, though the result is still one of anime's most filthily degenerate videos. Merely summarizing the plot is pushing

the boundaries of decency—lowlights include grateful rape victims, sexual assault with a mop, a girl forced to evacuate her bowels at the front of the class, needles stuck into breasts, and a lactating teacher providing nourishment for her pupils. **LNV**

PROFESSOR POPPEN AND THE SWAMP OF NO RETURN

1982. JPN: *Poppen Sensei to Kaerazu no Numa*. TV special. DIR: Shiro Ii, Yoshimitsu Morita. SCR: Akiteru Yokomitsu. DES: Shinya Takahashi. ANI: Kazuyoshi Yoshida. MUS: Kuni Kawauchi. PRD: Heruhen, Mainichi, TBS. 90 mins.
The assistant professor of biology at Udo University is dispatched to the local marshes to write a paper on the food chain. However, he is unable to formulate a thesis and angrily decides to stop time. Transforming himself into an insect, he then changes shape into a fish, a kingfisher, and a weasel in order to experience the struggle for life firsthand. Based on the *Professor Poppen* series of stories by Katsuhiko Funahashi.

PROJECT A-KO *

1986. JPN: *Project A-Ko*. Movie, video. DIR: Katsuhiko Nishijima; Yuji Moriyama. SCR: Yuji Moriyama, Katsuhiko Nishijima, Tomoko Kawasaki, Takao Koyama. DES: Yuji Moriyama. ANI: Yuji Moriyama, Tomohiro Hirata. MUS: Richie Zito, Joey Carbone. PRD: APPP, Studio Fantasia. 80 mins. (m), 70 mins. (v2), 50 mins. (v3), 60 mins. (v4), 55 mins. x 2 eps. (v5, *Versus*).
An alien spaceship crashes on Graviton City. Nobody clears it away, people get used to it being there, and gradually the district is rebuilt on an island around the hulk. Years later, two new girls arrive in class—late, as they always will be—at the Graviton Institute for Girls. Eiko ("A-Ko") Magami is a normal Japanese schoolgirl hero, apart from superstrength and superspeed inherited from superparents who are only revealed at the end of the film—one of its many in-jokes. She's cheerful, loyal, and always tries her best. Her best friend, C-Ko Kotobuki, is very, very stupid but so unbelievably cute that she reawakens an intense crush in rich, clever, and beautiful B-Ko Daitokuji. B-Ko decides that she'll break up the friendship

between A-Ko and C-Ko, and then C-Ko will be *her* best friend.

Starting out looking like just another girls' school story in the tradition of **Twins at St. Clare's**, *PA* was actually named after Jackie Chan's *Project A* (1984), and the inspiration of the master of slapstick martial-arts mayhem is obvious. The film pokes fun at such anime staples as the heroic **Captain Harlock**, here transformed into a cross-dressing dipsomaniac, and the alien-princess-school-love-triangle so successful in **Urusei Yatsura**, as well as throwing in foreign jokes like the rotund American fast-food icon Colonel Sanders, in a parody of a scene from **Harmagedon** depicting a terrifying warrior emerging from a dark alley toward the hero. (Kentucky Fried Chicken had just opened its franchise in Japan and the lifesize statue of the colonel outside every restaurant became a target for comedians for years—see **Junk Boy** and **Compiler**) C-Ko isn't what she seems—she is really the princess of a lost alien civilization, and the captain was coming to find her when he accidentally crashed his ship.

In the video sequel *PA2: The Plot of the Daitokuji Corporation* (1987), directed by Moriyama from Koyama's script, B-Ko's millionaire industrialist father, from whom she inherited all her least charming characteristics, is plotting to acquire the alien technology for his own ends, but he reckons without his daughter's determination to win C-Ko's affection or A-Ko's loyalty to her annoying little friend. The pair unite to stop the aliens taking C-Ko home. Moriyama also directed the Kawasaki-scripted video *PA3: Cinderella Rhapsody* (1988), about an unusual love quadrangle forming when A-Ko and B-Ko fall for Kei, who loves C-Ko, who can't stand him because he's taking A-Ko's attention away from her. The whole thing culminates in a huge party on the crashed battleship, which the captain and his crew have converted into the best disco in town. Opening and closing sequences have stunning artwork by Yasuomi Umezu, and the ending reassures us that men come and go, but friends are always friends. Moriyama and Kawasaki teamed up again for *Project A-Ko: Final* (1989, AKA *PA4*), in which Kei's matrimonial negotiations with the girls' teacher, C-Ko's origins as an alien princess, and the captain's

continuing failure to complete his mission culminate in the arrival of C-Ko's mother in a spaceship modeled on a George Lucas Star Destroyer. But the world's cutest bubble-brain doesn't go home after all, and the video ends, as the first movie began, with our heroines late for school again.

Final wasn't so final after all. A video two-parter, *A-Ko the Versus* (1990, AKA *PA5*), took our heroines into an alternate universe to reprise their story with a new twist and new opponents but still the same theme—rivalries, friendships, love, and massive rumbles with bigger collateral damage than most medium-sized wars.

Nishijima and Moriyama (also known as **Cream Lemon**'s "Yuji Motoyama") wrote the story for *PA* with Kasumi Shirasaka reputedly as a pitch for the soft-core franchise, mercifully dropped. Allowed to flourish as comedy instead of erotica, *PA* throws in parodies of and references to just about every area of popular Japanese and American youth culture. Just like its pornographic precursor, *PA* is cunningly telling the same story with the same ingredients, spinning it just enough to hold the audience's attention. The team added two saving graces: good comic timing and a complete failure to comprehend the meaning of the word "excess." The whole canon—especially the first film and *Cinderella Rhapsody*—is still watchable, whether you have seen enough anime to get the in-jokes or just enjoy comedy that goes completely over the top. Nishijima would reprise the character relationships for the 1990s in the less successful **Agent Aika**.

PROJECT ARMS

2001. TV series. DIR: Hirotoshi Takaya. SCR: Aya Yoshinaga, Shuichi Miyashita. DES: Masaki Sato. ANI: Masako Shimizu, Hideyuki Motohashi. MUS: N/C. PRD: TMS, TV Tokyo. 25 mins. x 26 eps.
Teenager Ryo Takatsuki almost loses his left arm in an accident, only to discover his wounds taking on a life of their own—he hasn't lost an arm, so much as gained a symbiotic bioweapon. Sub-**Guyver** action based on the *Shonen Sunday* manga by **Spriggan**-cocreator Ryoji Minagawa. **O**

PROJECT BLUE EARTH SOS *

2006. JPN: *Project BLUE Chikyu SOS*. TV series. DIR: Tensai Okamura. SCR: Ryota

Yamaguchi. DES: Tokuyuki Matsutake. ANI: Fumio Matsumoto, Shigeyuki Suga, Takaaki Fukuyo, Tokuyuki Matsutake. MUS: Michiru Oshima. PRD: A.C.G.T., Amuse Soft, AT-X, GENCO, Imagica, Memory Tech, NAC, Showgate. 45 mins. x 6 eps.
A different 1995: the new G-Reactor plane vanishes in a rainbow flash of light on a test flight. Rumors of alien abduction are discredited. Five years later, zillionaire boy genius Billy Kimura's company is about to unveil a new train with a G-Reactor engine when fellow boy genius Penny Carter (yes, a boy called Penny) crashes the party and announces there's something wrong with the engine. The hostility this naturally generates from Billy is dissipated when the train vanishes in a rainbow flash of light. The youthful superbrains team up with a discredited alien theorist from 1995, Billy's young friend Lotta, and her tutor Emely to uncover the truth. It's out there, and yes, it involves an alien invasion of the big, splashy, 1950s kind.

Project Blue Earth SOS is an anime to file alongside **Metropolis**, offering a glimpse of a very different world and set of criteria for story-telling. It is based on an idea by Shigeru Komatsuzaki (1915–2001), an artist who was one of the greats of the postwar Japanese magazines but who refused to set aside his double-paged Golden Age splash spreads in favor of the newfangled manga artwork being pushed by the likes of Tezuka. Hence, despite being one of the greatest icons of the Japanese pulp SF world in the 1950s, Komatsuzaki's artistic heritage has largely faded away, remembered only in a footnote to the genesis of **Super Atragon**, and as a production designer on a few rubber-monster movies. Despite this, his career continued for decades, largely as the illustrator of the box art for model kits, contributing behind the scenes to the world impact of everything from *Thunderbirds* to *Metal Gear Solid*. A fire at his home in 1995 destroyed much of his personal archives, threatening to turn him into one of the lost ghosts of 20th-century entertainment.

Under its original title of *Earth SOS* (1948) the basis for this anime was an illustrated story published in his heyday, adapted here as an old-fashioned show with old-fashioned values. Director Okamura, better known for **Wolf's Rain**, gives out logical inconsistencies, hammy scenarios, and joyously overwritten characters lifted straight from B movies, with finny, superdetailed retrofuturist mecha to match.

PROJECT BOOBS *

2006. JPN: Kan Goku. AKA: No Way Out. Video. DIR: Sumito Machida. SCR: Yu Koishikawa. DES: N/C. ANI: Kazumitsu Murayama. MUS: enon. PRD: E-Shoku Honpo, Picoletta, Milky Pictures. 25 mins. x 2 eps.

Special agents Yuki, Reiko, and Kana are on a misson to infiltrate a company selling illegal drugs. They are caught and subjected to a series of perverted experiments by researchers who really just want to molest them, in this anime based on a porn game by Black Package Try. **NV**

PROMISE TO THIS BLUE SKY, A *

2007. JPN: Kono Aozora ni Yakusoku o: Yokoso Tsugumi Ryohei. AKA: A Promise to This Blue Sky: Welcome Ryohei Tsugumi. TV series. DIR: Ken Ando. SCR: Satoru Nishizono. DES: Hirokazu Hanai. ANI: Hirokazu Hanai. MUS: N/C. PRD: Artland, Marvelous Entertainment. 25 mins. x 13 eps.

Wataru finds a girl asleep in his room wearing only her undies. She wakes up, punches him in the face, and makes her escape via the window. It will be no surprise to seasoned anime fans that she turns out to be the new transfer student at Wataru's school and his new roommate. Why Rinna has been transferred to the school is a mystery, since it's set to close in a year's time when the major industry on their island shuts down and all the families are sent back to the mainland. She decides that she'd rather spend a year on a small island without making friends than face the pain of separation. Wataru—the only boy in the dorm—tries to convince her she's wrong, and naturally succeeds. Did we mention this is a harem show? It's based on an erotic visual novel (ARGOT AND JARGON) from 2006, for which the author is uncredited by developers Giga and TGL—and frankly we're not surprised. The saucy aspects were toned down for TV, leaving nothing to attract the attention. Not even Artland's professionalism can rescue this repetitive and tedious tale.

PROTECTING FROM THE SHADOWS

2006. JPN: Kage kara Mamoru. AKA: Mamoru from the Shadows; Ninja Next Door, TV series. DIR: Yoshitaka Fujimoto. SCR: Ryunosuke Kingetsu, Toshimitsu Takeuchi. DES: Sai Madara, Natsuki Watanabe. ANI: Ichiro Hattori. MUS: Tsuyoshi Watanabe. PRD: Group Tac, Studio Tulip, TV Tokyo, TV Osaka. 25 mins. x 12 eps.

Shy, unkempt, bespectacled teenager Mamoru is really the latest in a long line of ninja, who, for the last 400 years, have been sworn to protect the nearby Konyaku family from harm. The pretty Yuna Konyaku is thus safe from danger for as long as her benevolently geeky stalker is nearby. A harem comedy based on an idea by Taro Achi, the creator of DOKKOIDA, KKM is a less risqué rewrite of MOUSE for a slightly younger audience: a nerdy, hapless guy is actually a cool thief, surrounded by girls who want him—romantically, in this case, rather than sexually/romantically. Note that the last two episodes were broadcast in a single timeblock and so may be filed in some sources as a single double-length "11th" episode. Not to be confused with the similarly titled KYO KARA MA-O.

PROTECTIVE CHARM HIMARI *

2010. JPN: Omamori Himari. AKA: Himari. TV series. DIR: Shinji Ushiro. SCR: Masaharu Amiya, Masashi Suzuki. DES: Satoshi Isono, Naoko Kosakabe. ANI: N/C. MUS: Yukari Hashimoto. PRD: ZEXCS, Kadokawa, NTT Docomo, Sony PCL, Klockworx. 25 mins. x 12 eps.

It seems there is no such thing as an ordinary 16-year-old Japanese boy. Yuto Amakawa thinks he's one, but it turns out that he's descended from a line of demon slayers. He didn't know this because he has been protected by a powerful charm given to him by his grandmother, but it has run out of power because he's come of age; now the demons want payback. Luckily there's a backup system—beautiful cat-spirit Himari, who turns up wielding a sword in the nick of time. What a pity Yuto's allergic to cats; it's a close-run thing whether the demons or allergies will get him first. Milan Matra's 2006 manga (possibly the first by someone whose pen name combines the names of his favorite anti-tank missile and its manufacturer) is a harem mélange of catgirls, demons, maids,

and monsters. One might almost call it SPOOKY KITARO for the shut-in generation. **NV**

PSAMMEAD, THE

1985. JPN: Onegai, Samiadon! AKA: Samiadon, I Wish ...; Psammead the Sand Imp. TV series. DIR: Osamu Kobayashi, Hideharu Iuchi, Fumiko Ishii, Tomomi Mochizuki, Mitsuru Hongo, Kazuhiko Kobayashi. SCR: Toshiyuki Yamazaki, Eiichi Tachi, Haruya Yamazaki. DES: Tsutomu Shibayama. ANI: Hideo Kawauchi. MUS: Kentaro Haneda. PRD: Tokyo Movie Shinsha, NHK. 25 mins. x 39 eps. (TV, 2 stories per ep.), ? mins. (v), 30 mins. (m).

In a deserted English chalk quarry, the older siblings of the five Turner children—Jill, Robert, and Jean—find a strange creature buried in the sand and decide to "take care" of it. It looks like Pikachu in a pointy hat and is allergic to water, but the children have found the powerful and capricious Psammead in this adaptation of E. Nesbit's novel Five Children and It (1902). The sand-fairy can grant one wish every day, but the wish only lasts until sundown, and like many such magical "advantages" (see DORAEMON), it doesn't always work as the wishers intend. The children ask for all sorts of toys and adventures, including becoming a mermaid, going into space, and having a robot of their own. Despite the mishaps some of their wishes bring, they learn valuable lessons from their strange friend.

TMS relocated the story to the present-day "English countryside," a half-timbered neverland of green fields and friendly policemen. The sand-imp character was renamed Samiadon (a Japanese wind spirit) in order to bring an oriental association not present in the original. Several TV episodes were also cut into a feature-length edition for video, and a short movie was released in 1989.

PSYCHIC ACADEMY *

2002. JPN: Psychic Academy Ora Bansho. AKA: Aura Bansho. TV series. DIR: Shigeru Yamazaki. SCR: Mitsuhiro Yamada. DES: Miho Shimogasa. ANI: N/C. MUS: Michihiko Ota. PRD: E. G. Films, Gansis, Starchild Records. 9 mins. x 24 eps.

Ai Shiomi is an insecure teenager following his gifted older brother to a school for students with psychic abilities. All the female pupils seem to manifest their biggest talents at chest level, providing a clue that this is just another formulaic wish-fulfillment show. The love triangle between Ai, his sweet-and-pneumatic childhood friend Orina, and his tomboyish-but-pneumatic classmate Myu is interrupted by random psychic battles and rough-and-ready wisdom from his crusty psychic coach. Much eye candy, plus boys' uniforms shamelessly stolen from *Harry Potter,* may please the undiscerning. Based on a manga by Katsu Aki, who produced the boys' manga version of **ESCAFLOWNE**, this show's sole attempt at innovation was being released straight to the Internet, although in its American incarnation it was released on DVD. **N**

PSYCHIC DETECTIVE YAKUMO *

2010. JPN: *Shinrei Tantei Yakumo*. TV series. DIR: Tomoyuki Kurokawa. SCR: Hiroyuki Kawasaki. DES: Suzuka Oda, Manamu Amasaki, Yukiko Ban, Minako Shiba, Chitose Asakura. ANI: Manamu Amasaki, Yukiko Ban. MUS: R.O.N. PRD: Bee Train, NHK, Sogovision. 25 mins. x 13 eps.

Yakumo Saito is a loner who lives in the film club room at his college. Withdrawn and mistrustful, he has heterochromia—one eye, his left, is a different color. His red eye isn't just a color variation; it allows him to see ghosts and spirits. As in **NATSUME'S BOOK OF FRIENDS**, this ability has led to his being ostracized, and he also has dark secrets in his family. He believes most spirits are bound to earth by unresolved emotions and that he can help to free them by talking through this unfinished business. When fellow-student Haruka asks him to help save her friend from possession, his world begins to change because he's finally met someone who is not afraid of him.

Manabu Kaminaga's novel series, with illustrations by Kato Akatsuki, is still ongoing. It has spun off further novel series, and two manga, and was adapted into a live-action TV drama in 2006 as well as inspiring a stage play. Yakumo is an attractively awkward protagonist, not above exploiting his talent to play mean tricks, with a sly, sarcastic line in teasing that might explain why he has so few close friends. Like the sociopathic protagonist of the BBC's 2011 *Sherlock,* the moments when you want

to slap him almost outweigh sympathy or admiration. The story dodges the mystery-of-the-week problem with an overarching plot about Yakumo's family (watch out for excessively sentimental moments when his kindly uncle is on the scene) and subplots from the original novels linking several episodes. The mysteries are enjoyable if not exceptionally challenging, and there is considerable violence. **V**

PSYCHIC FORCE

1998. Video. DIR: Fujio Yamauchi. SCR: Hiroyuki Kawasaki, Kenichi Onuki, Katsuhiko Takayama. DES: Kenichi Onuki. ANI: Hideki Araki. MUS: N/C. PRD: Triangle Staff, Broccoli. 40 mins. x 2 eps.

In 2007, the world is under martial law. As telepathic powers manifest in the young, the army begins conducting its own experiments, hoping to create its own elite Psycorps, known as the Psychickers. One day, Keith Evans escapes from the American compound. Evans is taken in by the kindly Griffiths family, but he goes on the run with the Griffiths boy Verne when the family is attacked by soldiers. Griffiths and Evans then fall in with the international Noah cartel, led by the eccentric Richard Wong, and the fight for freedom begins. This anime was based on an arcade fighting game but bizarrely uses Welsh names for the lead characters.

PSYCHIC SCHOOL WARS *

2012. JPN: *Nerawareta Gakuen*. AKA: *School in Peril*. Movie. DIR: Ryosuke Nakamura. SCR: Ryosuke Nakamura, Yuko Naito. DES: Mieko Hosoi. ANI: Mieko Hosoi. MUS: Shusei Murai. PRD: Aniplex, Bandai Namco, Shochiku, Sony Music Entertainment, Sunrise. 110 mins.

A new transfer student arrives in the eighth grade at a Kamakura school, although he is soon revealed as the pointman for an attempt to take over the school with an army of psychic fascists.

Seemingly put into production in the wake of **THE GIRL WHO LEAPT THROUGH TIME**, this adaptation of Taku Mayumura's 1970s sci-fi novel must have seemed like a no-brainer to its producers. Revisit the original, which has been adapted multiple times as movies and live-action TV shows including *School in Peril* (*DE), add a few whistles and bells, and hey presto, an instant anime classic like Mamoru Hosoda's

runaway hit. At its heart, this could have been a film with a lot to say, finding new resonances for modern kids by depicting that most horrific of fascist clampdowns—a ban on mobile phones at school—and using that as a window into a study of how human beings connect, or fail to connect, with one another, in the manner of **GARDEN OF WORDS**.

Sadly, this is nothing of the sort, coming across as a muddled and bumbling mood piece, in which elements of the plot have been discarded in the apparent hope that audiences will already know what's going to happen. Digital effects are slapped on in a vain attempt to plaster over the gaps, creating scintillating, iridescent moments of sunbeams, lens flares, and light pouring through stained glass, over a bunch of talking heads fiddling with their cellphones, in an inadvertent homage to the films of Makoto Shinkai. A heroic attempt at distraction by animators who could clearly see that nothing could save the script, these super-abundant elements make for great stills from the movie, but are not much help when you are sitting in the cinema, waiting desperately for it to end. The script makes one rather bold decision in its finale, but then wimps out and reverses it in a post-credits coda.

PSYCHIC SQUAD *

2008. JPN: *Zettai Karen Children*. AKA: *Absolutely Lovely Children*. TV series, video. DIR: Keiichiro Kawaguchi. SCR: Satoru Nishizono, Kazuyuki Fudeyasu, Shinichi Inotsume. DES: Takahiro Kagami, Kimitake Nishio, Yutaka Mukumoto. ANI: Yuji Kondo, Kenji Fujisaki, Akihiro Tamagawa. MUS: Kotaro Nakagawa. PRD: SynergySP, Shogakukan, TV Tokyo. 25 mins. x 12 eps. (TV1), 30 mins. (v), 25 mins. x 12 eps. (TV2).

In an alternate world where extrasensory powers are common, there are still different levels of skill. Only three people in the world possess the highest level yet discovered—Level 7. They are three ten-year-old girls, collectively referred to as The Children. They work for **BABEL**, an organization committed to stopping crimes before they happen. Their handler is Koichi Minamoto, a young field agent who's going to need all his skills to keep tabs on three lively, mischievous psychic ten-year-olds.

Based on Takashi Shiina's manga, this is a rather awkward mash-up of Steven Spielberg's *Minority Report* (2002—how did he ever miss the trick of putting in three cute kids?) with a dash of the **POWERPUFF GIRLS Z**, a sprinkling of **AKIRA**, and a rather distasteful tang of lewdness. The main villain looks like a parody of Japanese fetish wrestler Hard Gay, one of the trio makes very off-color jokes that send her little friends into fits of laughter, and the boss of BABEL is creepy. The girls wear uniforms with fitted jackets that show off more curves than is normal for ten-year-old girls anywhere except in boys' anime and manga. Despite the lively, bouncy aura and happy colors, this is not a show for ten-year-old girls.

Two years after the series ended, in 2010, a video also entitled *Zettai Karen Children* (and also known as *ZKC Video*) brought the girls back to clear their handler of planting a bomb at BABEL HQ. Most of the original crew returned, with a change of scriptwriter and some extra design support from Nishio. Another TV series began airing in January 2013. *The Unlimited—Hyobu Kosuke* (*Courtesy of Zettai Karen Children: The Unlimited—Hyobu Kosuke*) focuses on the manga's main antagonist, leader of the pro-ESPer group PANDRA. It also has a new spin-off manga of its own.

PSYCHIC WARS *

1991. JPN: *Soju Senshi Psychic Wars*. AKA: *Bestial Warrior Psychic Wars*. Video. DIR: Tetsuo Imazawa. SCR: Yasushi Ishiguro. DES: Masami Suda. ANI: Masami Suda. MUS: Tetsuro Kashibuchi. PRD: Toei. 50 mins.
In this disappointingly trite adaptation of Yasuaki Kadota's SF novel, a recently qualified Kyoto doctor discovers that prehistoric Japan was the site of an ancient war between demons and ninja. Injecting Julian May's *Saga of the Exiles* with a Japanese attitude toward honor, obligation, and love, the *PW* novel was clearly optioned for its time-traveling messiah and prehistoric demon wars, as with **DARK MYTH**, hinging on a threat that Japan's ancient enemies are returning to continue a vendetta older than time. But its fascinating take on Japanese history is dumped in a mix of breakneck exposition and supposedly arty pauses. Director Imazawa

tries to jolly things along by playing up the rich historicity of the Kansai region and the (literally) many-colored land of the past, but he doesn't have the time or budget to do it properly. He is not helped in this by a particularly poor U.K. dub that has academics discussing the mysteries of Japan's lost Jomon culture (see **PRINCESS MONONOKE**) without being able to pronounce its name. **V**

PSYCHO ARMOR GOBARIAN

1983. TV series. DIR: Seiji Okuda, Satoru Kumazaki, Kazuya Miyazaki, Hiroshi Yoshida, Tatsuya Sasahara, Yasuo Ishikawa, Hiroshi Negishi, Kazuyuki Okaseko. SCR: Yoshihisa Araki, Hideki Sonoda, Katsuhiko Taguchi, Yuji Watanabe, Tsukasa Takahashi. DES: Kiyoshi Fukuda, Yuki Kinoshita. ANI: Kiyoshi Fukuda, Yuki Kinoshita. MUS: Tatsumi Yano. PRD: Knack, Dynamic, TV Tokyo. 25 mins. x 26 eps.
Sometime in the 21st century, Earth is threatened by the Galadine, evil psychics from another dimension. The world's last line of defense is the giant robot Gobarian and its teenage pilot, Isamu Napoto, who moves the huge weapon using his immense powers of ESP. He's aided in his fight by his companions Kult Buster and Hans in their robots Reido and Garom. If you think that the robot Gobarian and, indeed, the whole set-up are strongly reminiscent of **MAZINGER Z**, it won't surprise you to learn that this is another of Go Nagai's many robot tales—though not one of his best.

PSYCHO DIVER: SOUL SIREN *

1997. JPN: *Psycho Diver Masei Rakuryu*. Video. DIR: Mamoru Kanbe. SCR: Toshiaki Kawamura, Tatsuhiko Urahata. DES: Makoto Koga, Masafumi Yamamoto. ANI: Makoto Koga. MUS: Akihiko Hirama, SORMA, TA-1. PRD: Toei, AIC, APPP, Madhouse. 47 mins.
Yuki Kano has it all—fame, wealth, the world at her feet—but she's occasionally unable to sing (and for a pop star, this is probably bad). Enter Bosujima, a "psycho diver" with the capability to enter people's heads and straighten out what's wrong with them. Well, most of the time, anyway. Based on a novel by **AMON SAGA**–creator Baku Yumemakura, this production has a list of distinguished animation houses in its credits as long as your arm. The look

is urban-hard, cool, and savvy with just enough retro and pop-culture references; check out the psychodiving machine for echoes of the brain-swap apparatus from cult 1960s series *The Prisoner*. The voice cast is full of fan favorites headed by Junko Iwao as Yuki. **N V**

PSYCHO-PASS *

2012. TV series. DIR: Katsuyuki Motohiro, Naoyoshi Shiotani. SCR: Gen Urobuchi, Makoto Fukami, Aya Takaha. DES: Kyoji Asano. ANI: Kyoji Asano, Naoyuki Onda, NaO, Osamu Horiuchi. MUS: Yugo Kanno. PRD: Production I.G, Dentsu, Fuji TV, Sony Music Entertainment, Toho. 24 mins. x 22 eps. (TV1), 24 mins. x ?? eps. (TV2), ??? mins. (m).
Future cop Akane Tsunemori is a rookie with fast-growing doubts about a newfangled device that allows the police to determine the levels of criminality and *potential* criminality in a suspect (**LAW AND DISORDER**). As a result of the ability to read their "psycho-pass" remotely, guilt and suspicion have become, or seem to have become, much more clear-cut, leading to law enforcement that often takes the role of judge, jury, and executioner. This, however, has other implications in a society that is increasingly intrusive toward its citizens, demanding ever more invasive levels of scrutiny and access to their lives. Sound familiar? Gen Urobuchi, already riding high on his scripts for **PUELLA MAGI MADOKA MAGICA**, lifts elements of *Minority Report* and a textbook on social ethics for this dark, confrontational sci-fi thriller. **V**

PUELLA MAGI MADOKA MAGICA *

2011. JPN: *Maho Shojo Madoka Magica*. AKA: *Magical Girl Madoka of the Magus*. TV series, video, movie. DIR: Akiyuki Shinbo, Yukihiro Miyamoto. SCR: Gen Urobuchi. DES: Takahiro Kishida, Kunihiko Inaba. ANI: Junichiro Taniguchi, Mika Takahashi. MUS: Yuki Kajiura. PRD: SHAFT, Aniplex, Hakuhodo DY Media Partners, Houbunsha, MBS, MOVIC, Nitroplus. 25 mins. x 12 eps. (TV1), 130 mins. (m1), 109 mins. (m2), 116 mins. (m3).
Madoka Kaname is just an ordinary girl in middle school, with a happy home life, devoted family, and good friends. After being caught up in a surreal dream, she is informed by a cute animal familiar that

she can make a difference to others and save her beloved home and friends. All she has to do is become a Magical Girl and fight the witches who spread despair. The opening of the show, which resembles so many other magical girl shows, gives no clue that here we're witnessing a contract with no escape clause, a deal with forces that are not all they seem. The candy-store battles of brightly colored children with their transformation sequences and inappropriate lingerie are not a game; Madoka is playing for real, as are the existing magical girls in the series, including the frightening stranger Homura, who seems hellbent on stopping Madoka attaining magic powers. The cat-like familiar Kyubey isn't playing at all.

If you set out to find a director to turn the magical girl genre on its head, Akiyuki Shinbo would be high on your shortlist. An earlier step along that route, the Daliesque universe of faith and terror that he orchestrated for PORTRAIT OF PETITE COSSETTE was unforgettable, but even in more realistic settings like the modern Japan of ARAKAWA UNDER THE BRIDGE, he uses fantasy to underline the dark subtexts of modern life. Ume Aoki's original character designs for the promo film are beautifully reworked by Kishida, and the art team does a superb job, with animation and background assistance from companies including Tezuka Pro, Madhouse, Artland, Production Reed (formerly Ashi Pro), SynergySP, and David Production. Urobuchi's beautifully paced script rarely hits a wrong note. The entropy of ennui, so differently explored in PEEPING LIFE, and the persistence of hope may be equally crushing, equally terrible, but the fact that one persists despite the other is presented as a human triumph on a heartbreaking scale. It seems tragically appropriate that the transmission of the final two episodes was delayed when reality—in the form of the 2011 Great East Japan Earthquake—destroyed the world's TV schedules.

The TV series teased the audience with sequel prospects not once, but twice, in its final moments. The DVD release allowed the team to revise the original broadcast series, and this process continued in the three movies by the same team, reusing the original material with some new animation and an all-new voice track by

the TV actors. This could be the action of a team restricted by TV schedules and budgets finally able to give the work the space and time it merits, or it could be a pragmatic attempt to get as much mileage as possible out of an unexpectedly popular concept—see EVANGELION. *Puella Magi Madoka Magica The Movie Part 1: Beginnings* (*Gekijo-ban Maho Shojo Madoka Magica Zenpen: Hajimari no Monogatari*) and *PMMM The Movie Part 2: Eternal* (*G-b MSMM Kohen: Eien no Monogatari*) appeared in Japanese cinemas just a week apart, October 2012. The story continued with *PMMM The Movie Part 3: The Rebellion Story* (*G-b MSMM Shinpen: Hangyaku no Monogatari*) in October 2013. Meanwhile there is much interest to be had in comparing *PMMM* with THE MELANCHOLY OF HARUHI SUZUMIYA, another show that invests a school girl with superhuman significance. **NV**

PUGYURU

2004. TV series. DIR: Hajime Kurihara. SCR: Hiroyuki Nakaki. DES: Tohiro Konno. ANI: N/C. MUS: Yasunori Koda. PRD: 2000 Creators. com, Dex, Kids' Station, Kodansha, Media Factory, MOVIX. 3 mins. x 13 eps.
Not so much a series as a televised gag strip, Tohiro Konno's surreal manga was animated as part of the *Anime Paradise!* TV segment. High school girl Maa … (the rest of her name is inaudible) meets Cheko when her mother hires a maid so that Maa … won't be alone when she has to go away on a long trip. Cheko has allegedly come from the Maid Village, where real maids live and train, but she's not an ordinary maid; she can dissolve, grow roots, fly, and separate her head from her body. She's been sent to change Maa … 's life, and Maa … and her friends have wacky moments with their new little friend, water-gun toting gangsters, an overbearing American, and other strange creatures. Director Kurihara plays a character called Kurihara in episode 5, and the kind of food gag commonly found in juvenile shows like ANPANMAN is a staple of the story, with Cheko's head replaced with dumplings in one episode while in another she eats another appropriatelynamed character's head with syrup. Self-consciously strange, and made using limited animation techniques liable to make it easier to port into mobile phone delivery systems in future.

PUMPKIN SCISSORS *

2006. TV series. DIR: Katsuhito Akiyama. SCR: Yuji Hosono. DES: Chizuko Kusakabe, Shuichi Hara, Maho Takahashi. ANI: Chizuko Kusakabe, Toshiharu Murata, Eiji Suganuma. MUS: Ko Otani. PRD: Gonzo, AIC. 24 mins. x 24 eps.
A long and terrible conflict between Empire and Republic has left the war-torn lands in such a bad state that three years after, starvation and disease are still rife. Much of the Empire is in ruins and former soldiers have turned to banditry to survive. Idealistic, determined Alice Malvin is the rookie leader of the Pumpkin Scissors Platoon, an Imperial Army unit set up to lead the relief effort. It's considered by some to be no more than a propaganda exercise and by others a complete waste of money, but Alice believes passionately in her duty to make a difference. That seems a distant dream until she meets up with battle-damaged, taciturn Oland, a soldier with a mysterious past.

Based on Ryotaro Iwanaga's 2004 manga, *Pumpkin Scissors* is set in an alternate reality around the time of World War II, but the premise could just as easily fit Afghanistan or Iraq, two wars led by powerful forces with no exit strategy and no plans for post-conflict infrastructure support. It could also easily fit in FULLMETAL ALCHEMIST—just strip out the brothers and the magic.

Unfortunately you'd also have to strip out the coherent planning, because *PS* goes adrift in terms of pace, especially in the last four episodes, and leaves story elements hanging. (Who *was* that mysterious masked man?) The main source of power for the now-redundant State supersoldiers is just silly, but luckily almost nobody can shoot or throw a grenade straight, enabling them to stand in the midst of explosions, calmly certain that they won't be hurt until it's dramatically necessary. You may want to fling a grenade at every lame joke and redundant gag, but you'll miss, just as they do.

That said, the overriding theme of the inhumanely exploitative nature of war, the laziness and indifference of the powerful, and the courage and forbearance needed to be a true pacifist is compelling. There's some good character development, and recognition of the importance of idealism in a genre that too often falls back on slacker disengagement or bad-boy sass. The combat choreography won't win any major prizes but it gets the job done. This is a series that falls short of greatness, but at least it made some effort. **Ⓥ**

PUMPKIN WINE

1982. JPN: *The Kabocha Wine*. TV series, TV special, movie. DIR: Kimio Yabuki. SCR: Shunichi Yukimuro, Mitsuru Majima, Shinji Shimizu. DES: Megumu Ishiguro, Fumihiro Uchikawa. ANI: Megumu Ishiguro, Akira Shimizu. MUS: Osamu Shoji. PRD: Toei, TV Asahi. 25 mins. x 95 eps. (TV), 60 mins. (TVm), 24 mins. (m).

Shy teenager Shunsuke is terrified of girls. He's grown up surrounded by his sisters, and his mother owns a lingerie shop. When he moves to a new high school thinking it's for boys only but finds it's actually a coed establishment, he's in danger of letting his obsession ruin his schooldays. His fellow pupil, the lovely Natsumi "Call Me L" Asaoka, is a lot bigger than he is in every way. But despite being kindhearted, taller, and stronger, she falls in love with short, neurotic Shunsuke. And even though he feels he's being run over by a well-meaning bulldozer, he comes to appreciate her finer qualities.

Based on Mitsuru Miura's *Shonen Magazine* manga, the series jars modern audiences because of the dated design and Rubensesque physique of the heroine, but the story has charm, and the French dub was very successful. The TV movie *PW: Is She Really on a Honeymoon with Him!?* (1982) features predictable misunderstandings in a remote ski lodge, following a winter wonderland formula also found in KIMAGURE ORANGE ROAD and URUSEI YATSURA. A short movie, *PW: Nita's Love Story* (1984), ran on the Toei Manga Matsuri summer double bill alongside KINNIKUMAN: ULTIMATE MUSCLE. In it, the titular dog, who lives in the school dormitory at the Sunshine academy, has a puppy sired by the pet of the wealthy Takizawa family. Nita steals milk for her offspring but disappears. While searching for the dog, Natsumi is lured onto the Takizawas' yacht by their wayward son, who claims to have the dog on board but really has designs on Natsumi herself.

PUNI PUNI POEMY *

2001. Video. DIR: Shinichi Watanabe. SCR: Yosuke Kuroda. DES: Satoshi Ishino. ANI: Satoshi Ishino. MUS: Toshiro Soda. PRD: JC Staff. 30 mins. x 2 eps.

Poemi Watanabe is a cheerful student at Inunabe elementary school who lives happily with her parents until they are attacked and killed by mysterious aliens. Adopted by the parents of her classmate Futaba Memesu, she finds that the seven Memesu sisters have secret lives as the Earth Protect Unit, defending humankind against the aliens who killed her family and are now popping up in war machines all over the place. The snag is that, like *Thunderbirds'* International Rescue, they are sworn to save life, not threaten it—they can defend but not attack. But Poemi has no such scruples, and, with a bit of magical help, she transforms into Puni Puni Poemi, magical girl and enemy of Earth's attackers. A spin-off of EXCEL SAGA, with Poemi resembling Excel, and Futaba her associate Hyatt. **ⒸⓃⓋ**

PUNISHMENT: POSH SCHOOLGIRLS' SEXUALIZATION SCHOOL

2011. JPN: *Oshioki: Gakuen Reijo Kosei Keikaku*. Video. DIR: Hisashi Tomii. SCR: Shiro Nakata. DES: N/C. ANI: Dohyun Lim. MUS: N/C. PRD: MS Pictures (Celeb). 20 mins. x 3 eps.

A pervert insinuates himself into an elite girls' high school mid-term, alleging that he was sent by the director. Wearing a white coat and a benign expression, he sets out to find students and teachers who "break the rules" and makes it his business to punish them appropriately. This naturally involves sex with him and each other, in this porn anime based on a game by TinkerBell. **ⓃⓋ**

PUPA *

2014. TV series. DIR: Tomomi Mochizuki. SCR: Tomomi Mochizuki. DES: Maki Fujii. ANI: N/C. MUS: Moka. PRD: Studio Deen. 4 mins. x 12 eps.

A brother and sister with a creepily close relationship are forced to deal with the awful after-effects of a virus. Yume Hasegawa has been infected with the Pupa disease, which causes a hideous monster to emerge from her body if she ever gets hungry. And unfortunately for everybody else, the virus ensures that her hunger is a craving for *human* flesh. "Luckily," her brother Utsutsu has also been infected by the virus and can regenerate any limb loss he sustains. Whereas X-MEN used such a mutation as an excuse for Wolverine's indestructibility, Sayaka Mogi's 2011 manga in *Comic Earth Star* uses it to turn Utsutsu into a living food supply, forced to let his sister chow down on him on a regular basis in order to hold off an even worse fate. It's utterly horrible, exactly as edgy, gritty horror should be (HORROR AND MONSTERS), confronting the reader with an awful, recurring nightmare of cannibalism and decay, as its two leads are forced to feed on each other. Psychologists might determine an underlying subtext of incest, as the leads' codependent relationship is rationalized as some sort of sacrifice for the sake of others. Sociologists might see it as another addition to anime's growing selection of 21st-century zombie parables, in which an unsustainable society increasingly feeds on itself.

However, there are intimations of trouble behind the scenes—the production was delayed and the episodes eventually released at an unmanageably short running time, as if the producers were experiencing second thoughts about the likelihood of getting away with such grotesqueries, even in the relatively forgiving world of Japanese animation. As it is, the show still shows clear signs of censorship of some of its edgier moments. Truly repulsive, but in a good way for once. **Ⓥ**

PUPPET MASTER SAKON

1999. JPN: *Karakuri Soji Sakon*. AKA: *Sakon the Ventriloquist*. TV series. DIR: Hitoyuki Matsui, Hideki Tonokatsu, Kazuo Nogami. SCR: Chiho Katsura, Daisuke Habara. DES: Toshimitsu Kobayashi, Tetsu Koga. ANI: Toshimitsu Kobayashi. MUS: Norihiro Tsuru, Yuriko Nakamura. PRD: Kyoiku, Tokyo Movie Shinsha, WOWOW. 25 mins. x 26 eps.

Scooby-Doo meets *Child's Play*? Sakon is following in the footsteps of a master puppeteer who took the art of ventriloquism to undreamed-of levels centuries ago, but not even his studies in these ancient arts and his great talent can explain why his doll Ukon seems to have a life of its own. Realizing that his skills and Ukon's unexpected independence could be very useful in solving mysteries and crimes, Sakon starts to develop a new sideline as an investigator of unusual problems. Based on the 1995 *Shonen Jump* manga by Ken Obata and Maro Sharaku, with attractive designs and an evocative score, *PMS* nonetheless boasts one of the most unlikely premises in detective history. About as believable as Sherlock Holmes talking to a sock puppet, though sleuthing tales such as CONAN THE BOY DETECTIVE and YOUNG KINDAICHI FILES are hardly less strange. ◐

PUPPET PRINCESS *

2000. JPN: *Karakuri no Kimi*. Video. DIR: Hirotoshi Takaya. SCR: Junichi Miyashita. DES: Hirotoshi Takaya, Tsutomu Suzuki. ANI: Hirotoshi Takaya, Tsutomu Suzuki. MUS: Kaoru Wada. PRD: Shogakukan, Toho, TMS Entertainment. 42 mins.

Lord Ayawatari is not interested in governing his territory or in conflicts between the other warlords but instead only lives to create puppets. Knowing Ayawatari's nature, the evil warlord Sadayoshi Karimata invades Ayawatari's castle and kills almost all his family. Princess Rangiku, the daughter of Ayawatari, is forced to seek out the legendary ninja Danzo Kato to oppose the evil Karimata, but Danzo's assistance comes at a cost. Together these unlikely heroes must find a way to infiltrate Karimata's castle and restore the mysterious stolen puppet. Based on a *Shonen Sunday* manga by USHIO AND TORA–creator Kazuhiro Fujita.

PUPPETRY AND STOP-MOTION

True animation was preceded on Japanese television by puppetry and picture shows, which often used similar forms and materials. *Child Without a Home* (1955, *Ie Naki Ko*) was a TV series, presented in 26 episodes, each 25 minutes in length, in which the entire story was told "live" with shadow puppets, operated by the Kakashiza troupe. In its manipulation of flat characters against a painted background it bore many similarities with the process of cel animation but was significantly cheaper and faster.

The first stop-motion animation in Japan was *Princess Tsumeko and the Devil* (*Tsumeko-hime to Amanojaku*, 1955), produced by Tadahito Mochinaga, who had left cel-based anime behind after MOMOTARO'S DIVINE SEA WARRIORS. Mochinaga

learned the techniques of stop-motion animation in China during his sojourn at the Shanghai Animation Studio and took them back to Japan in 1953. He oversaw several other stop-motion shorts in the 1950s, his collaborators including Yoshikazu Inamura and Kiichi Tanaka. Their highest profile work was the German sequence in *Beer Through the Ages* (*Beer Mukashimukashi*, 1956), a 12-minute commercial commissioned by the Asahi brewing company to celebrate its 50th anniversary—compare to PENGUINS MEMORY. The authors presume that it was commissioned as several separate TV commercials, and only later edited together into its full running time as listed in Japanese sources. Beginning with dancing, drunken Babylonians, it traces the story of intoxicants through ancient Egypt and medieval Germany, before a depiction of Commodore Perry's ships bringing beer to Japan, comprising cut-cellophane animation from Noburo Ofuji. *Kinema Junpo* magazine voted it the ninth best cultural work of the year.

Other works included Mochinaga's *Little Black Sambo's Tiger Conquest* (*Chibikuro Sambo no Torataiji*, 1956), exhibited at the Vancouver International Film Festival, and *Five Little Monkeys* (*Gohiki no Kozarutachi*, 1956), which won an education award in the year of its release. Often funded by Dentsu Eigasha, early stop-motion appeared to reach the limit of its development with *Penguin Boys Lulu and Kiki* (*Penguin Boya Lulu to Kiki*, 1958) and *Removing the Lump* (*Kobutori*, 1958), the latter of which reached the heady heights of a 21-minute running time. Stop-motion, however, has all the labor intensive difficulties of cel animation, but few of its advantages. Sets must still be constructed, gravity still limits special effects, and the chances of mistakes ruining an entire scene are greatly increased. Furthermore, the success of the feature-length cel animation of PANDA AND THE MAGIC SERPENT in 1958 was a damaging blow to future investment in stop-motion.

The potential for production-line techniques allowed the output of cel animators to swiftly outstrip stop-motion animators, and cels soon took over. Stop-motion enjoyed limited success on Japanese television, with Tadahito Mochinaga's series *Prince Ciscon* (*Ciscon Oji*, 1963), based on a

manga by DORAEMON-creators Fujiko-Fujio and incorporating footage already made by Mochinaga for foreign export as THE NEW ADVENTURES OF PINOCCHIO. *Rudolph the Red-Nosed Reindeer* (*Akabana no Tonakai Rudolph Monogatari*, 1964), based on a script by Romeo Muller, was undertaken by Mochinaga's team as work-for-hire for Videocraft (later known as Rankin/Bass); this TV special remains a Yuletide regular in the English-speaking world, but like many other export works was little known in Japan. Mochinaga's MOM Production company turned out a number of other stop-motion works for Rankin/Bass, including *Willy McBean and His Magic Machine* (1963), *Andersen's Fairy Tales* (1966), *Ballad of Smokey the Bear* (1967, broadcast in Japan as *Smokey Bear no Uta*, 1970), and *Mad Monster Party* (1967), all animated to match prerecorded soundtracks and scripts supplied from America.

It is notable that MOM Production largely limited itself to TV specials, as serial stop-motion animation at 24 minutes a week was unworkable. A long-running stop-motion series was Ichiro Komuro's *Little Battles of the Salaryman* (*Salaryman Minimini Sakusen*, 1970), but even that only managed a 27-episode run by keeping the episodes at a manageable four minutes each. As Japanese children's television succumbed to the onslaught of live-action rubber-monster shows, there was some experimentation with the use of animation for effects work (for the cel variant of this, see BORN FREE). *Devil Hunter Mitsurugi* (*Majin Hunter Mitsurugi*, 1971), featured three live-action children, wielding ceremonial swords themed on Wisdom, Humanity, and Love, which allow them to combine into the stop-motion giant Mitsurugi, who can fight giant monster invaders from Scorpio. Made by the married animators Takeo Nakamura and Ayako Magiri, the show was innovative, but suffered from production processes that made it inevitably more time-consuming than cels. The TBS network tried something similar with *Transform! Pom Poko Jewels* (*Henshin! Pom Poko Tama*, 1973) a live-action series about two feuding Japanese families whose children were able to switch identities and genders—shades here of the gender-swapping comedy of RANMA ½. As with MARVELOUS MELMO, the engines of transformation were red and blue magic items (jewels here); as with **POM POKO**, *tanuki* were involved, although here they were regarded as interfering creatures from another world who happened to *resemble* Japanese raccoon dogs. As with *Mitsurugi*, the stop-motion elements were only employed very briefly, since the transformative powers of the magical jewels would only last for a maximum of ten minutes. Such an artificial time limit was common in special effects shows, whatever the medium, since it allowed the filmmakers to limit their effects budgets—similar excuses were tried in the live-action **ULTRAMAN** and later pastiched in the perilously short battery life of **EVANGELION**.

Stop-motion seemed fated to slip into the world of film festival awards for worthy effort, the prerogative of hobbyists and artists but unlikely to attract much interest from the money-minded producers of the rest of commercial animation. Kazuhiko Watanabe's *The Crane Returns a Favor* (*Tsuru no Ongaeshi*, 1966) won an educational prize at that year's Mainichi Film Concours, and Katsuo Takahashi's *Issun Boshi* (1967) was voted one of the top ten movies of the year by *Kinema Junpo*. However, many of the early pioneers in stop-motion found alternative employment in puppetry, a creative medium that never escaped from children's television but remained a lucrative field, largely on the license-funded channel NHK. The animator Tadanari Okamoto made TV's first marionette series, *Tamamo no Mae* (1953), a short-lived tale about a fox who is able to transform herself into a beautiful human girl.

The original puppet version of **CHIRORIN VILLAGE TALES** (1956, see also *DE) lasted for over a thousand episodes on television, its stars becoming familiar voices to an entire generation, including Tetsuko Kuroyanagi (see **CHOCCHAN'S STORY**). Other TV experiments in puppetry included the space-voyaging vessel *Silica* (*DE), created by science fiction author Shinichi Hoshi, and Osamu Tezuka's *Space Patrol* (*DE), which was chiefly a puppet show, but also used cel animation for certain special effects and its opening sequence. **MADCAP ISLAND** (see also *DE) ran for more than a thousand episodes and received that ultimate of TV accolades—complaints

about violence and bad language! As a mark of its fame to Japanese viewers of a certain age, it even appeared in a cameo role playing on a TV screen in **ONLY YESTERDAY**. Notably, its opening sequence was not puppetry but a piece of cel animation by the "art-house" creator Yoji Kuri; the sequence was shown every weekday for five years, arguably outlasting **ASTRO BOY** in its visibility to the Japanese public, despite not being part of an "animated" show.

Further discussion of the development of puppetry is beyond the scope of this book, except to note *Aerial City 008* (1969, see also *DE), *11 People of Nekojara City* (*Nekojara-shi no Juichinin*, 1970), and the samurai epic *Hakkenden* (*DE), widely acknowledged by the makers of the anime **HAKKENDEN** to have been a greater influence on them than the 19th-century original. Other puppet shows of the 1970s include the original of **SANADA'S TEN BRAVE WARRIORS** (see also *DE, as *Ten Brave Warriors of Sanada*), an adaptation of the radio drama *The Flutist* (*DE), and 1978's *Kujaku-o* (a Japanese retelling of the same myth that later became **PEACOCK KING**). The early 1980s saw the flourishing of both *Prin Prin* (*DE) and a puppet version of **GREAT CONQUEST** (see also *DE as *Romance of the Three Kingdoms*), for which the accomplished Kihachiro Kawamoto made over 400 puppets.

Regarded as a highly disposable medium, with many thousands of episodes lost or wiped soon after their original broadcast, TV puppetry foundered in the 1980s, particularly after the ill-fated attempt of the commercial channel Fuji TV to make its own puppet show, the sci-fi spectacular *X-Bomber* (1980). Despite creative input from **DEVILMAN**-creator Go Nagai and a truly gripping plot, *X-Bomber* was canceled partway through its run amid whispers of low ratings and enjoyed better success abroad under the title *Star Fleet* (*DE). Fuji TV's attitude also seemed to influence NHK, the home of TV puppetry, whose *Farewell Higeyo* (*Higeyo Saraba*, 1984) was the last puppet series to be shown on the channel for some years. The channel revived puppetry with *Tale of the Heike* (*Heike Monogatari*, 1993), which also featured puppets designed by Kihachiro Kawamoto, and *Drum Canna* (*DE), a significantly shorter puppet series broad-

cast in seven-minute segments as part of another program.

The traditions of puppetry found new relevance in the late 1990s in digital animation (**GAMING AND DIGITAL ANIMATION**), as an example to the manipulators of *virtual* 3D models in 3D environments. Early digital anime often borrowed from puppetry, particularly in attempts to depict realistic human movement. As with puppets in the physical world, virtual models often have difficulty interacting with the environment around them—figures are best filmed from the waist up to avoid notably unrealistic leg movements and foot placements, and characters in early digital animation such as **A.LI.CE** and **BLUE REMAINS** spend prolonged periods sitting in vehicles or floating in space, water, or cyberspace. **MALICE DOLL** took the links between puppetry and stop-motion to extremes, with a cast of puppets that comes to life.

Stop-motion continues to flourish outside the commercial world of cel or digital animation, particularly at film festivals. In particular, Kihachiro Kawamoto (see **KIHACHIRO KAWAMOTO FILM WORKS**) has continued to keep Japanese stop-motion in the eyes of festival crowds. While the majority of the Japanese animation in this book reflects Western preconceptions of what "anime" should be, it is worth noting that Kawamoto became the president of the Japan Animation Association, and that Koji Yamamura's **MOUNT HEAD** was nominated for a Best Short Animation Academy Award in the same year as Hayao Miyazaki's **SPIRITED AWAY**. For the average Western viewer, however, the most likely encounter with stop-motion animation is probably the special effects in Shinya Tsukamoto's surreal live-action movie *Tetsuo: The Iron Man* (1991) or the claymation credit sequences of **NINJA NONSENSE** and many **CRAYON SHIN-CHAN** movies.

PURE LOVE *
1998. JPN: *Rhythm*. Video. DIR: Miyo Morita. SCR: N/C. DES: N/C. ANI: Chuji Nakajima. MUS: N/C. PRD: Daiei. 30 mins. x 2 eps.
In a fantasy world modeled loosely on medieval Europe, knight Hiro sneaks into the king's secret chambers one evening to meet with the queen. Then, the two of them go at it like rabbits, because this is a porn anime, and she is a nymphomaniac.

An early example of CGI in anime erotica (**Gaming and Digital Animation**). **N**

PURE MAIL *

2001. Video. DIR: Shinichi Masaki, Yuji Yoshimoto. SCR: Yoshio Takaoka. DES: Nishieda. ANI: Yuji Yoshimoto. MUS: N/C. PRD: Green Bunny. 30 mins. x 2 eps.

Highschooler Kei Ogata is a loner who has constructed a different persona and life on the Internet, where he chats with girls as "A.W." He begins to suspect that his online friend Eve is also his classmate Midori Nagawa, someone he would love to get to know in real life. However, he fears he'll never be as attractive as A.W.; the other problem is that he once had a disastrous relationship with her friend Miki, behaved like a monster, and fears he can't control himself outside the safety of the Net. Meanwhile, Kei is caught using the school's servers to log into the chatroom, and is blackmailed into becoming the slave of the cruel tech support girl. **LN**

PURPLE EYES IN THE DARK

1988. JPN: Yami no Purple Eye. AKA: Purple Eye of Darkness. Video. DIR: Mizuho Nishikubo. SCR: Asami Watanabe. DES: Chie Shinohara. ANI: N/C. MUS: Derek Jackson, Purple Gar, Mayumi Seki. PRD: Youmex, Toei. 30 mins.

Rinko has always had a strange birthmark on her arm but discovers that it indicates she is *not like other girls*. The teenager's young body hides a murderous beast that threatens to transform her at any moment, manifesting itself as glowing, savage purple eyes. An "image video" consisting of images from Chie Shinohara's 1984 *Comic Margaret* manga set to seven musical interludes in the style of **Cipher the Video**. A full-blown anime, however, was not forthcoming, as instead the franchise was adapted for live-action television in 1996 (*DE). The same author also created **Sea's Darkness: Moon Shadow** and *Red River* (AKA *Anatolia Story*).

PURURUN! SHIZUKU-CHAN

2006. TV series. DIR: Atsushi Yano. SCR: Ryu Tamura, Osamu Nakamura, Koji Miura. DES: Toshihiko Masuda. ANI: Toshihiko Masuda. MUS: Koichiro Kameyama. PRD: TMS Entertainment. 24 mins. x 51 eps. (TV1), 24 mins. x 51 eps. (TV2, Aha), 24 mins. x 52 eps.

(TV3, *Pitchipichi*).

Shizuku-chan is a raindrop sprite, named after his home, the Shizuku Forest. *Shizuku* is also the Japanese word for raindrop. Rain makes Shizuku-chan so happy that rainbows sprout from his forehead, and he and his little friends have many cheerful adventures in this **Kids' Anime** series based on a manga for tinies by Q-LiA Planning, which was first published in 2003. All the sprites are liquid-inspired, and this generic origin is interpreted with a liberality that delights its target audience, since small children are generally fascinated by bodily functions and have not yet been taught to distance themselves from their own effluvia. (To judge from **Panty and Stocking with Garterbelt**, not all big children have either.) Characters include a snot sprite, a slobber sprite, a mud sprite who's mischievous and given to flinging dirt around, a nosebleed sprite, and a sweat sprite (the fat one of the gang). There are also sprites for red, green, and brown tea; don't cross them, they're sisters and vicious fighters with a pike, nunchaku, and frying pans. Then there are the sprites of tears, shampoo, conditioner, skin lotion, eau-de-cologne, milk, honey, mineral water, and alcohol of various sorts, including sake, red, white, and rosé wine. All alcohol sprites are, naturally, of legal drinking age. Shizuku also has a snail friend called Tsumurin. A flood of merchandise reflected the characters' popularity, including toys, stationery, CDs, DVDs, Nintendo DS games, and picture books. A second TV series *Pururun! Shizuku-chan Aha*, followed in 2007, and *Pitchipichi Shizuku-chan* commenced in October 2012. This series introduces a new character, human girl Miku-chan, who visits Shizuku-chan's world from Earth—yes, this is science fiction for small children, part of a lineage stretching back to Osamu Tezuka's recognition that blood cells and bacilli can be actors too.

PUSS IN BOOTS *

1969. JPN: Nagagutsu o Haita Neko. AKA: Wonderful World of Puss 'n Boots. Movie, TV series. DIR: Kimio Yabuki. SCR: Hisashi Inoue, Morihisa Yamamoto. DES: Yasuo Otsuka. ANI: Yasuji Mori, Reiko Okuyama, Takao Sakano, Hayao Miyazaki, Akio Hattori. MUS: Seiichiro Uno. PRD: Toei. 80 mins. (m1), 53 mins. (m2), 58 mins. (m3), 25 mins. x 26 eps. (TV).

Pierre, youngest of three brothers, befriends Perrault, a cat-musketeer in boots on the run from the henchmen of the evil, rat-loving Nekoboss. Perrault helps Pierre pose as the Marquis of Carabas in order to woo the beautiful Princess Rosa. She, however, is betrothed to the Demon King Lucifer, who kidnaps her on the night of the full moon. Perrault and Pierre set off to rescue Rosa from Lucifer's castle.

This delightful if freely adapted version of Charles Perrault's 18th-century fairy tale was given a limited U.S. release to the Saturday morning kids' market, along with several other Toei anime including **Jack and the Witch** and **Treasure Island**. Featuring nods to **Swan Lake** and *Beauty and the Beast*, it was such a success in Japan that the feline hero became Toei Animation's mascot. According to studio legend, and only partly in jest, he was regarded as "a cat that could devour the Disney mouse." The comic elements of the movie owe much to the characterization of the extremely stupid transforming ogre who gets all the best bits of slapstick business. Note the presence of a young Hayao Miyazaki in the lower ranks of the animators.

Tomoharu Katsumata's movie sequel *Three Musketeers in Boots* (1972) dispatched Perrault to the Wild West, where he accompanies the young Annie and Jimmy to Gogo Town, a frontier staging post. Annie's father is killed, and the characters' lives are all endangered when the town boss discovers they know about his counterfeiting operation that he runs out of the basement of the town saloon. Annie is kidnapped, and it is time for a replay of the rescue scenario from the first film, as Perrault and Sheriff Jimmy save her from the bad guys.

A third movie, *PiB: Around the World in 80 Days* (1976), was directed by Hiroshi Shidara for the same film studio—its feline version of Jules Verne a distant precursor of **Around the World with Willy Fogg**. Perrault bets Grumon the pig industrialist that he can travel around the world in 80 days but is pursued by cat assassins, Carter the obstructive hippo, and Grumon's sneaky lupine agent Professor Garigari.

The unrelated TV series *The Adventures of Puss in Boots* (1992) was directed by Susumu Ishizaki and broadcast on TV Tokyo, featuring young boy Hans and his cat Kusuto. Their adventures include cameos by characters from many other fairy tales and stories, including SNOW WHITE, DON QUIX-OTE, *Hansel and Gretel*, DRACULA, *The Little Match Girl*, and THE THREE MUSKETEERS. This series is currently being repromoted in the U.S. as *Puss 'n' Boots* along with a 75-minute feature, *The Journey of Puss 'n' Boots*, which is probably three episodes edited together. The original 1969 film was restored in 1998 and shown with GALAXY EXPRESS 999 as part of the regular Toei Anime Fair theater run. An adaptation of *Puss in Boots* was also included in the anime series GRIMMS' FAIRY TALES.

PUT IT ALL IN THE RING

2004. JPN: *Ring ni Kakero 1*. AKA: *Get in the Ring*. TV series. DIR: Toshiaki Komura, Shigeyasu Yamauchi et al. SCR: Yosuke Kuroda. DES: Michi Himeno, Shingo Araki. ANI: Eisaku Inoue, Keiichi Ichikawa, Shingo Araki, Hideji Ishimoto. MUS: Susumu Ueda. PRD: Toei Animation, Marvelous Entertainment, TV Asahi, Sammy. 25 mins. x 12 eps. (TV1), 25 mins. x 12 eps. (TV2), 25 mins. x 6 eps. (TV3), 24 mins. x 6 eps. (TV4).
The Takane siblings are determined to fulfill their late father's wish that a Takane should become a champion boxer. Ryuji sets out to develop special techniques that will make him unstoppable in the ring, trained by his sister Kiku and aiming for the national squad. But first he has to

take the junior high school championship against his archrival Jun Kenzaki. Based on the manga by Masami Kurumada, this old-fashioned saga of a boy's growth into manhood by way of extreme physical pain (see TOMORROW'S JOE) has a mix of old and new names on the crew, and a penchant for improbably flashy attack sequences that take it out of EVERYDAY ANIME and into DRAGON BALL territory. **Ⓥ**

PUTTSUN MAKE LOVE

1987. Video. DIR: Minoru Okazaki. SCR: Wataru Amano. DES: Masaki Kajishima. ANI: Masaki Kajishima. MUS: N/C. PRD: Agent 21, Toei. 25 mins. x 6 eps.
The fall and rise of a loving couple's fortunes, in which cute high school girl Saori begins barely speaking to Yuji, putting him through a series of trials as she slowly realizes that he's the boy for her. As her parents try to fix her up with a husband in an *omiai* ("arranged") marriage meeting, Saori convinces Yuji to impersonate her at the meal, with predictably comedic results. Realizing there is fun to be had in impersonating a girl, Yuji disguises himself again and sneaks into the girls' locker room with a camera, only to be waylaid by his teacher, Miss Akimoto, who confiscates his film. A traditional anime love triangle enters the plot, as Yuji schemes and matchmakes to ensure that Saori's new suitor and the girl who is chasing *him* are maneuvered safely

into each other's arms. Yuji and Saori head off to the seaside in the final episode but are kept from consummating their budding relationship by the attentions of their teacher and Yuji's unexpected heroism when he stops a suicidal girl from jumping in front of a train. Based on the manga by Jun Amemiya in *Scholar* magazine, this is an early work for TENCHI MUYO!'s Masaki Kajishima in the playful spirit of SLOW STEP and KIMAGURE ORANGE ROAD.

PYUNPYUNMARU

1967. TV series. DIR: Yugo Serikawa, Yasuo Yamaguchi, Kazuya Miyazaki. SCR: Jiro Yoshino, Tsuneaki Nakane, Kenji Urakawa, Enrico Dolizoni, Tomohiro Ando, Masashi Hayashi, Shunichi Yukimuro. DES: Jiro Tsunoda. ANI: Keijiro Kimura, Hiroshi Wagatsuma, Tetsuhiro Wakabayashi. MUS: Yoshioki Ogawa. PRD: Toei, Shin Production, NET. 25 mins. x 12 eps. (TV1), 25 mins. x 14 eps. (TV2).
Pyunpyun Maru is a ninja of the Iga clan, in charge of their Nandemo OK (Anything Goes) Office. Lumbered with the crybaby ninja Chibi Maru, downtrodden by his boss, and secretly enamored of the lady ninja Sayuri, Pyunpyun must also fend off the unwelcome advances of Kemeko, the office man-eater. This funny mix of office life and ninja japery was based on the manga *Ninja Awatemaru* by A KARATE-CRAZY LIFE–creator Jiro Tsunoda serialized in *Shonen King* magazine.

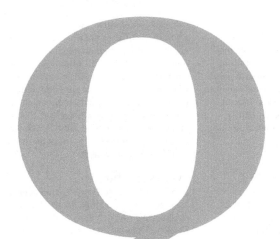

QTARO THE GHOST *

1965. JPN: *Obake no Qtaro*. TV series, movie. DIR: Eiji Okabe, Tadao Nagahama. SCR: Jiro Yoshida, Kunihiko Hanashima, Susumu Yoshida, Chikara Matsumoto, Hisashi Oi, Masaki Tsuji, Shichima Sakai, Seiji Matsuoka, Asako Shiozawa. DES: Fujiko-Fujio. ANI: Daikichiro Kusube, Tsutomu Shibayama, Yasuhiro Yamaguchi, Sadayoshi Tominaga, Moriyasu Taniguchi, Susumu Shiraume. MUS: Hiroshi Tsutsui. PRD: Tokyo Movie Shinsha, Shinei, Nippon TV. 25 mins. x 97 eps. (original), 25 mins. x 70 eps. (new), 25 mins. x 96 eps. (*new new*), 13 mins. (m).

Shota Ohara is a klutzy kid who finds an egg that hatches Qtaro, a large big-eyed blob. The Ohara family takes him in, and predictable misunderstandings ensue, with a normal Japanese household gaining an extra member who can fly, make things disappear, and has a whole host of supernatural friends who insist on dropping in. Qtaro's chums include General Godzilla (no relation to the giant monster), the rich Kizao, the Professor, and Doronpa, the comic-relief American ghost. *Qtaro* is a Fujiko-Fujio project that, like the same creators' more successful **DORAEMON**, features an otherworldly playmate foisted on a hapless boy.

Qtaro was notorious within the anime business for a number of swindles behind the scenes, as the puppeteers-turned-anime-producers of Tokyo Movie Shinsha were handed invoices for up to ten thousand animation cels per episode. Sneaky animators cheerily gamed the system, prioritizing all the simple jobs, leaving the complex ones until the last minute when

they could charge overtime, and partitioning simple frames into several unnecessary components in order to charge for multiple cels. However, cooler managerial heads eventually prevailed, not only bringing the production in at a more realistic budget, but also noticing that ratings above a notional 15% had no effect on merchandise sales. Until *Qtaro*, producers had assumed that an anime "success" needed to match **ASTRO BOY**'s ratings of 30% and up. After *Qtaro*, producers came to realize that anything above 15% was over-engineering, commencing anime's slow evolution into targeted niche programming. *Qtaro* was also the first series to be canceled because managers assessed its toy-selling potential as exhausted. Thereafter, it was widely understood in the anime business that no franchise could go on unaltered for more than two years, and that it was in the interests of most owners for it to be brought to an end and then resurrected in a slightly different format, with slightly different merchandise (**GUNDAM**).

The original monochrome series was remade in color as *New Qtaro* (1971) and moved to new production house Shinei after a long hiatus. The second remake, confusingly also called *New Qtaro* (1985), was directed by Shinichi Suzuki and represented a concerted effort to update the postwar character for a new generation. A few episodes of this version were translated by the Hawaiian Japanese-language station KIKU and shown subtitled in some U.S. TV areas with Japanese communities. In 1986, Qtaro starred in his first "movie," *Jump, Qtaro! BakeBake's Grand Strategem,*

which uses 3D technology. Another short film followed in 1987, *Go Qtaro! War at 100th Size*, in which Shota and the Professor try to enlarge a cake but only end up shrinking themselves, setting up a fantastic voyage across the new terrors of an oversized living room.

QUEEN AND SLAVE *

2002. JPN: *Jo-o Sama wa M Dorei*. AKA: *The Queen Is a Masochist*. Video. DIR: Hiei Tadokoro. SCR: Rokutaro Makabe. DES: Gekka. ANI: Raizo Kitagawa. MUS: N/C. PRD: Five Ways. 28 mins.

Yumi is a sweet and gentle nurse, who moonlights as a whip-wielding dominatrix. Traumatized in childhood by her parents' separation, she sees all men as copies of her womanizing father. Hiroyuki, one of her patients, falls in love with her, only to get annoyed when her darker side is revealed. Disappointed that she has more than one side to her character (how dare she!), he "teaches her a lesson" which, predictably, unleashes her inner masochist—compare to **RAPEMAN**. Based on a manga by Beauty Hair, also known for **ORGY TRAINING**. **ⒸⓃⓋ**

QUEEN EMERALDAS *

1998. JPN: *Queen Emeraldas*. Video. DIR: Yuji Asada. SCR: Baku Kamio. DES: Masahito Sawada, Katsumi Itabashi. ANI: Masahito Sawada. MUS: Michiru Oshima. PRD: OLM. 30 mins. x 4 eps.

In the distant future, the Afressians are out to dominate the galaxy, and humankind's only hope for freedom is the pirate known as Queen Emeraldas. Driven by the memory of a long-lost love, she sails the seas of space in her namesake ship, fighting evil on her own terms—more like Robin Hood than a traditional pirate. She is fiercely determined to protect the "good name" of her vocation, and when an Afressian crew flies the Skull and Crossbones she insists they cease, employing her usual forceful arguments when reason fails. In a remote corner of space she meets a young man who has no faith in humanity and a group of ordinary folk who do their best to revive that faith. When the Afressians under Captain Eldomain come looking for revenge, they take these ordinary folk hostage as bait for a trap for Emeraldas.

Leiji Matsumoto has spent most of his career constructing a huge personal universe in which to develop his notions of honor, justice, courage, and what it means to be a real human being. At the center are his two most glorious creations, the heroic pirate-knight CAPTAIN HARLOCK and his friend and ally Emeraldas. Around them revolve a huge cast of friends and foes, people who define their own place in the universe by their responses to its trials and hardships. The video series shows us a young boy with a hard, sad past setting out to make a hard, sad future for himself, until pirate queen Emeraldas and an unlikely crew of galactic deadbeats show him that an open heart is as vital as courage.

Emeraldas is the active facet of Matsumoto's ideal woman, most fully embodied in Maetel of GALAXY EXPRESS 999. In a sense, every Matsumoto story is the same story, and so the viewer always knows what to expect and is drawn into Matsumoto's world without any protest or difficulty. An enticing introduction to Matsumoto's old values and never-changing style, combined here with up-to-the-minute animation techniques. Though limited in places, the animation itself is stylish, and while the computer graphics vary in quality, they don't impede the flow of the story.

QUEEN OF A THOUSAND YEARS *
1981. JPN: Shin Taketori Monogatari Sennen Jo-o. AKA: Queen Millennia; Captain Harlock and the Queen of a Thousand Years. TV series, movie. DIR: Masayuki Akehi. SCR: Keisuke Fujikawa, Leiji Matsumoto. DES: Yasuhiro Yamaguchi, Yoshinori Kanemori, Geki Katsumata. ANI: Yasuhiro Yamaguchi.

MUS: Kitaro. PRD: Toei, Fuji TV. 25 mins. x 42 eps. (TV), 121 mins. (m).

Yayoi Yukino seems like any other young woman; she's secretary to the chief of Tsukuba Observatory, and her father owns a noodle bar. Then she commissions Hajime Amemori's father to construct a strange building for her, and Hajime's own house is blown up. The orphaned Hajime learns that she is actually an alien whose home planet is fated to crush Earth at nine minutes and nine seconds past midnight on the ninth day of the ninth month of 1999. She is the Queen of a Thousand Years, and she wants to ensure that Earth will survive into a new millennium. Just as Hajime is beginning to believe her, another alien arrives. Selen, the Thief of a Thousand Years, tells Hajime that Yayoi is really Earth's enemy, and he no longer knows who to believe. This being a Leiji Matsumoto film, the obvious answer is the one who most resembles Maetel of GALAXY EXPRESS 999, Matsumoto's archetype of perfect womanhood. Based on Matsumoto's manga serialized in the newspaper Sankei Shinbun, the TV series was also followed by an original movie production that was released in theaters as Queen of a Thousand Years (1982) and featured a theme song sung by Neil Sedaka's daughter Dara.

It was later acquired by U.S. company Harmony Gold and combined by ROBOTECH's Carl Macek with CAPTAIN HARLOCK to create the 65-episode U.S. series Captain Harlock and the Queen of a Thousand Years. Even though they were two different stories from two completely different studios, Macek welded them together by switching the action constantly between two war fronts separated by light-years, thus sidestepping the fact that the major characters could never appear together.

QUEEN'S BLADE *
2009. JPN: Queen's Blade: Ruro no Senshi. AKA: Queen's Blade: Exiled Warrior. TV, video. DIR: Kinji Yoshimoto, Yosei Morino, Shigenori Kageyama, Shin Itagaki, Kan Fukumoto. SCR: Kinji Yoshimoto, Takao Yoshioka, Michiko Ito, Toshimitsu Takeuchi, Hideki Shirane, Yosei Morino, Ryunosuke Kingetsu. DES: Rin-Shin, Takayuki Noguchi, Junichi Higashi, Takafumi Suzuki, Yukiko Ishibashi, Koichi Monma, Maho Takahashi, Yutaka Mukumoto. ANI: Rin-Shin, Takayuki Noguchi, Yukiko

Ishibashi, Chang Hwan Park, Ik Hyun Eum, Isamu Utsugi, Sang Min Lee, Satoshi Isono, Shunryo Yamamura. MUS: Masaru Yokoyama. PRD: ARMS, Hobby Japan, GENCO, AT-X, Media Factory, Comic Toranoana. 24 mins. x 12 eps. (TV1), 24 mins. x 12 eps. (TV2, QB2), 30 mins. x 6 eps. (v1, Beautiful Fighters), 25 mins. x 12 eps. (TV3, Rebellion), 40 mins. (v2, Premium Visual Book), 20 mins. x 2 eps. (v3, Rebellion Premium Visual Book), 30 mins. (v4, Vanquished Queens).

Every four years a new queen is chosen by combat from among the most beautiful young warriors of the land. The only rule is that combatants must be over 12 years of age. They need not be nationals of the country, human, or even intelligent. Any weapon can be chosen, killing is allowed, and the winner is the person still standing and not fleeing the field at the end of a bout. It is a convention of the world that women's armor is designed for attraction rather than protection, and the bloody, erotic spectacle is broadcast for all to see through the power of a wizard using a crystal sphere.

Readers may be thinking of Suzanne Collins' 2008 novel The Hunger Games, but the story of Queen's Blade began in the West, in 1983, when Nova Game Designs published a "combat picture book (or 'visual combat') game" called Lost Worlds. Designed by Alfred Leonardi, this paper-based fantasy role-playing game for two players became very popular and was published by a number of companies, including Flying Buffalo and 1% Inspiration Games. Between 2005 and 2008 Japanese publishers Hobby Japan licensed and published a series of ten visual combat books under the title Queen's Blade. The game plot similarly revolves around a tournament held once every four years to choose a queen.

The anime's purpose is mainly to provide fan service (ARGOT AND JARGON) for game geeks, and ARMS delivers on this in one of the most revealing non-porn anime franchises ever. LEGEND OF LEMNEAR's Yoshimoto does his utmost to supply a plot and characters with at least some pretensions to pace, interest, and motivation, though there are much better serials out there for fantasy fans who want more than girls swinging swords in skimpy outfits.

The game series evolved into a

multimedia franchise, with four manga adaptations, three novels, a video game, and three anime versions, along with three sequel games, figures, and memorabilia. The second anime TV series, *Queen's Blade 2: The Evil Eye (Gyokuza o Tsugumono)*, aired in 2009, with a video series, *Queen's Blade: Beautiful Fighters (Utsukushiki Toshitachi)*, in 2010. The 40-minute *Queens Blade Premium Visual Book* was bundled with an artbook in 2011. A third TV series based on the second game series, *Queen's Blade: Rebellion*, aired in 2012, with the ever-popular pirate motif (**ONE PIECE**) co-opted to spice up the fantasy armor. Also in 2012, two more 20-minute videos, *Queen's Blade Rebellion Premium Visual Book*, were bundled as an extra with an artbook for the Japanese market. A spin-off video from the *Queen's Blade Premium Visual Book* entitled *Vanquished Queens* was released in March 2013. **NV**

QUIET DON, THE

1990. JPN: *Shizukanaru Don: Yakuza Side Story*. AKA: *The Quietened Don: Yakuza Side Story*. Video. DIR: Hajime Kamegaki. SCR: Kuniaki Oshikawa. DES: Osamu Nabeshima. ANI: Osamu Nabeshima. MUS: Shinji Miyazaki. PRD: TMS. 40 mins.

Soft-spoken, mild-mannered Shizuya works by day at a respected underwear factory but at night leads a double life as the third most powerful gangster boss in the Tokyo region. Based on the 1988 manga serialized in *Shonen Sunday* magazine by Tatsuo Nitta, this story was also adapted into a live-action TV drama. The original manga did not end until its 108th volume in 2012, whereupon the creator noted that he felt he "had written more than enough."

QUILTIAN

1996. JPN: *Kigurumi Sentai Kildian*. AKA: *Dress-Up Battle-Team Kildian; Quiltian*. Video. DIR: N/C. SCR: Rei Nekojima. DES: Rei Nekojima. ANI: N/C. MUS: N/C. PRD: Pink Pineapple, KSS. 30 mins. x 2 eps.

Twin schoolgirls transform into their superhero aspects to save the world from an evil cabal of would-be dictators, but they can only fight for justice by having lots of sex. This short-lived porno anime was based on a manga by the pseudonymous Rei Nekojima—the only name of any sort attached to this show in our sources. **N**

QUINTUPLETS *

2001. JPN: *Go Go Itsutsugo Land*. AKA: *Go!Go! Quintuplets Land; Let's Go Quintuplets*. TV series. DIR: Setsuko Shibuichi, Yukari Komori. SCR: Michihiro Tsuchiya, Koji Ueda, Mitsuyo Suenaga. DES: Setsuko Shibuichi, Yukari Komori. ANI: Yukari Kobayashi. MUS: Taku Iwasaki. PRD: Eiken, TBS. 22 mins. x 50 eps.

A formulaic comedy for small children featuring five elementary school siblings (two girls, three boys) and their dog. The Kabuto quints are designed like a typical live-action team—there's the bespectacled smart one, the cute girl, the loner, the dashing hero, and the fat but good-hearted one—in this instance, also a girl. The show uses these stereotypes to emphasize that they have "totally different personalities" despite being born just a few minutes apart and focuses on everyday adventures with a fantasy twist at home and school. Broadcast in English in Europe, but more successful in Spanish as *Los Quintillizos*, it has also, sadly, been the subject of pervy fanzines. Nothing's sacred, not even infant stories.

QUIZ MAGIC ACADEMY

2008. AKA: *Quiz Magic Academy—The Original Animation*. Video. DIR: Keitaro Motonaga. SCR: Makoto Uezu. DES: Kumi Hori, Minoru Maeda. ANI: Yoichi Ueda. MUS: Tomoki Hasegawa. PRD: AIC PLUS, Konami. 29 mins. (v1), 30 mins. (v2).

Ruquia and her class are the worst dimwits in the Magical Academy. They may be extremely cute, but can they win a magic competition and improve their class's standing in the eyes of the teachers and the other students? Or will they bring their floating college right down to earth? This pretty, silly amalgam of catgirls, school uniforms, and magical boarding school tropes is based on a series of arcade games by Konami, so it had an existing fanbase to sell to. It was popular enough to get a second video, *Quiz Magic Academy The Original Animation 2*, made by the same team.

QUO VADIS

1996. JPN: *Quo Vadis: Visual Collection*. Video/Movie. DIR: N/C. SCR: N/C. DES: Haruhiko Mikimoto. ANI: N/C. MUS: N/C. PRD: Grams, Sony Records. 29 mins.

A hundred years after the establishment of a galactic peace treaty, a group of officers within the armed forces plot to seize power in a military coup. It is your job to stop them, without becoming implicated in the fake "rebellion" that they hope to use as their excuse.

The 1995 Sega Saturn game *Quo Vadis* has character designs from one of anime's best-known luminaries, Haruhiko Mikimoto of **MACROSS** fame. Shortly ahead of the 1997 release of a version of the game on the Sony PlayStation, *Quo Vadis: Visual Collection* compiled the animated opening sequence and all the cut scenes, along with an interview with Mikimoto, a selection of character sketches, and the usual "Making of" padding. It does not seem that the laserdisc contained any animation that was not already in the game itself. A video anime release was also promised, but canceled in production due to the bankruptcy of the Grams company.

QWASER OF STIGMATA, THE *

2010. JPN: *Seikon no Qwaser*. TV series, video. DIR: Hiraku Kaneko. SCR: Shigeru Morita, Makoto Uezu, Toko Machida, Hiroshi Sato, Hiro Akitsuki. DES: Makoto Uno, Isao Sugimoto, Takafumi Suzuki, Junichi Higashi, Koki Nagayoshi, Si Hyeong Lee. ANI: Hiroya Iijima, Isao Sugimoto. MUS: Tatsuya Kato. PRD: Hoods Entertainment, Flying Dog, Lantis, Showgate, Q Ent, Taki Corp. 24 mins. x 24 eps. (TV1), 25 mins. x 12 eps. (TV2), 25 mins. (v).

At St. Mikhailov Academy Mafuyu Oribe and her adopted sister Tomo rescue an injured boy named Alexander, or Sasha, who has a scar on his face. He turns out to be a Qwaser, a super-warrior who can manipulate a specific element into an immense array of weapons. Alexander can manipulate iron, but his power is drawn from breast milk. Qwasers need lactating female partners known as Marias—as many of them as possible—in order to fight and win. Even in a strange world of magical powers and mysteries, it's not exactly the relationship a teenage girl envisages finding at high school. This nursery-harem set-up is not exactly what the West envisages in a TV cartoon aimed at teens, either, even if it is intended for airing in a late-night slot. Hiroyuki Yoshino's 2006 manga with art by Kenetsu Sato was the inspiration for this series, which was heavily censored even in that late-night slot, but streamed with fewer cuts online, and made available uncut on Blu-ray and DVD.

A rather basic plot is counterbalanced by elegant background art from Studio Easter, whose work redeems many an otherwise flimsy show, and by some seriously graphic but well-animated action scenes. The character designs are pretty, and director Kaneko does his best to develop his cast, finding plenty of broad humor and even a little romance among the relentless waves of extreme fan service, sado-masochism, sex, and breast-feeding. A spin-off video, *The Qwaser of Stigmata: Portrait of the Empress (Jotei no Shozo)* appeared in 2010. The second TV series, *The Qwaser of Stigmata II*, aired in 2011 giving Sasha a new partner and a chance to cross-dress. **ⓃⓋ**

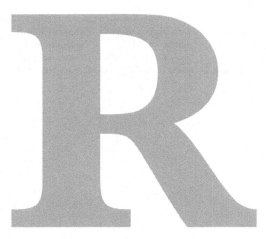

R-15 *

2011. TV series, video. DIR: Munenori Nawa. SCR: Sumio Uetake, Masashi Suzuki, Yasutomo Yamada, Takamitsu Kono. DES: Mariko Fujita, Naoko Kosakabe. ANI: Mariko Fujita, Hideki Furukawa, Takuya Tani. MUS: Yuichi Nonaka (HEAD OFF). PRD: AIC, AMG Entertainment, Kadokawa, Klockworx. 25 mins. x 12 eps. (TV), 31 mins. (v).

Taketo Akutagawa is a gifted young novelist whose chosen genre is pornography. He attends a high school for the specially gifted, where he accumulates a harem of "specially gifted" but otherwise absolutely stereotypical girls. In the video of the same name, released the same year, Taketo and company are accidentally stranded on an island without adult supervision. This happens all the time, at least in Japanese high school harem anime. All this nonsense is adapted from Hiroyuki Fushimi's 2009 book, illustrated by Takuya Fujima. **Ⓝ**

R.O.D. *

2000. JPN: R.O.D. AKA: Read or Die. Video. DIR: Koji Masunari. SCR: Hideyuki Kurata. DES: Taraku Uon, Shinji Ishihama, Noriyuki Jinguji. ANI: Shinji Ishihama. MUS: N/C. PRD: Studio Deen, Studio Orfee, SPE Visual Works. 30 mins. x 3 eps. (v), 25 mins. x 26 eps. (TV).

Bespectacled Yomiko Readman is a teacher whose passion is collecting books. She's also a secret agent for the Royal British Library's Division of Special Operations, a crack squad of bookhunters whose mission is to save literature for posterity. The two sides cross over when she has a run-in with a giant cricket and a strange old man out

to steal a book she's just acquired. It's very rare, and the division assigns her a partner to work on finding volume 2 before the alien bugs get her. We never expected to see the British Library in anime; there's no topic or setting too arcane for the Japanese fantasy romance. Based on a manga in *Ultra Jump* magazine by Hideyuki Kurata and Shutaro Yamada.

The later TV series drops the original cast in favor of sisters Michelle, Maggie, and Anita, who become rescuers and then bodyguards to author Nenene Sumiregawa—one of Yomiko's favorite authors, and a character in the first episode of the video series. Two years later, the author is trying to find Yomiko, but her path and that of the sisters keep crossing with other British Library agents from the Special Engineering Force and with their sinister assassins. A rogue agent is plotting to conquer first Japan, and then the world.

Recalling CAT'S EYE with its trio of sisters going undercover to steal artworks linked to their father's disappearance, the series uses the trio format to provide a range of types and ages, maximizing the chance of viewers finding a character to identify with. As in GRRL POWER and KOKORO LIBRARY, the producers try to cover all bases with the sisters—one quiet and standoffish, one extrovert and gossipy, one headstrong; one loving Hemingway, one into Harry Potter, and one not keen on books at all; teens, 20s, and prepubescent; brown, blonde, and pink hair.

RACING BROTHERS LETS AND GO

1996. JPN: Bakuso Kyodai Lets & Go!! TV

series, movie. DIR: Tetsuro Amino, Yoshio Kado. SCR: Hiroyuki Hoshiyama. DES: Akio Takami, Michiru Ishihara. ANI: Akio Takami. MUS: Goji Tsuno. PRD: Xebec, TV Tokyo. 25 mins. x 102 eps. (TV1), 25 mins. x 51 eps. (TV2), 81 mins. (m).

Lets and Go are a pair of preteen brothers obsessed with mini racing cars—half lawn mower, half Formula One. In this long-running series based on a manga by Tetsuhiro Koshita, the boys work for genius inventor Professor Tsuchiya to defeat the agents of his rival, Professor Inugami, both on and off the tracks. After the first 51 episodes, the series was rebranded as *L&G: WGP* (1997) and trailed with a feature-length theatrical release, *L&G: WGP: Runaway Mini Four Wheel Drive Follow-up!* (*L&G: WGP: Boso Mini Yon Ku Dai Tsuiseki!*, 1997). The series proper finished after 102 episodes, but it was brought back as *L&G: MAX* (1998), renumbered back to 1, and featured a new look courtesy of new designer Ishihara. A junior version of CYBERFORMULA GPX, whose sci-fi racing drama was still running when *L&G* began.

RAGNAROK THE ANIMATION

2004. TV series. DIR: Seiji Kishi, Lee Myung-jin. SCR: Hideki Mitsui. DES: Kenji Shinohara, Lee Myung-jin. ANI: N/C. MUS: Noriyuki Asakura. PRD: TV Tokyo, G&G Entertainment, Gonzo. 24 mins. x 26 eps.

Swordsman Roan is really a complete wimp, but he and his childhood friend the trainee priest Yufa are on a dangerous mission—a journey to the kingdom of Rune-Midgard to investigate a mysterious event. Yufa is very cute and Roan wants to impress her with his sophisticated talents, but she treats him like a moron. She's pretty naïve herself, but as the journey goes on her talents in healing and magic develop alongside her understanding of people. Along with stern female mage Takius, rough and rowdy female Hunter Judia, and little Maya, who is good at negotiating the best deals thanks to her upbringing with merchants and sailors, the pair travel through a world based on the online game *Ragnarok Online*, developed by the South Korean company Gravity Corp. and the enchantingly named Gungho Online Entertainment Inc. It is stuffed with a whole shopping basket of cultural and anime references from Egyptian gods and Crusaders to vanished older brothers, Dark Lords, and cute but cynical moppets. Seasoned fans and cynics will recognize elements of the classic gaming quest party crashed into the harem show, but director Kishi says it's all about "the drama of human interaction." The game also spun off into a Korean comic.

RAHXEPHON *

2002. TV series, movie. DIR: Yutaka Izubuchi. SCR: Chiaki Konaka, Hiroshi Onogi, Ichiro Okochi. DES: AkihiroYamada, Hiroki Kanno, Michiaki Sato, Yoshinori Sayama. ANI: Hiroki Kanno, Kenji Mizuhata, Takashi Tomioka, Tsunenori Saito, Shiho Takeuchi. MUS: Ichiko Hashimoto. PRD: Asatsu DK, BONES, Media Factory, Fuji TV, Victor Entertainment. 23 mins. x 26 eps. (TV), ca. 80 mins. (m), 15 mins. (v).

In the year 2027, teenager Ayato Kamina is living with his scientist mother in Tokyo Jupiter, the new name for the Japanese capital, which now exists under a huge protective dome after alien invaders destroyed the rest of civilization 15 years earlier. The danger from the alien Mu race and its Dolem monsters is still present, and would-be artist Ayato is caught up in an attack with a remote and mysterious girl, Reika Mishima. They witness the defense of Tokyo by huge, beautiful sonic weapons in female form, redolent of the gorgeous machines of MAPS. Haruka Shitow, an older woman and feisty fighter, tells him she has the answers to his many questions, but instead of fleeing the city with her, he follows Reika and witnesses the "hatching" of the godlike giant weapon RahXephon

from an egg in a great shrine. Climbing inside the creature, he becomes its perfect partner and pilot; but as he explores his new skills, he also learns that he and the citizens of Tokyo are living in a different time line to the rest of the world, which has not been completely destroyed, and that they are being ruled by the aliens—a revelation with elements of MEGAZONE 23, but more likely to have been inspired by *The Matrix* (1999). His own mother is caught up in the conspiracy, and Haruka is part of the Earth forces fighting the aliens. Another girl enters the equation when Quon Kisaragi appears to Ayato in a vision. Part of the anti-alien forces through her adopted family, she is also a vital part of the mystery.

Despite the efforts of EVANGELION to become the last word on the giant robot genre, it continued unabated with *RahXephon* as one of the better emulators. Where *Evangelion* had angels, *R* has "dolems," a name derived from the *do-re-mi* of a musical scale and the mythical clay *golem*, each named after elements of musical notation—*Arpeggio*, for example, or *Mezzo Forte*. While much of its influence may seem derived from modern shows, at heart it is a clever, atmospheric, and beautifully designed retread of the science fiction robot shows of the 1970s and 1980s, complete with an alien culture inspired by Mayan ruins (see SUPER ATRAGON), whose first attack occurs on December 21st, 2012, the end of the current 400-year Maya age, or *baktun*. Some may also like to see in it an allegorization of the relationship of the Meiji Restoration–era Japanese toward the West: vastly advanced invaders that force the local population to make incredible leaps in science and technology, ready for a rematch.

Go Nagai's "psychic linkage" between pilot and craft is crashed into Yoshiyuki Tomino's classic format of a boy's rite of passage through an unjust world in which war sets friend against friend and his own blood betrays the hero. Many TV shows simply leech from the past for a ragbag plot with poorly crafted design and script, relying on the fact that the current TV audience is too young to have seen its source material or developed much in the way of critical faculty; but this show doesn't disgrace its antecedents.

In 2003 the series was edited into a 116-minute movie version *R: Pluralitas Concentio* (*R: Tagen Hensokyo*), with Izubuchi as chief director and Tomoki Kyoda as director. The same year saw the video *R Interlude: Thatness and Thereness*, a 15-minute existential dialogue between Quon and a fragment of herself, also directed by Tomoki Kyoda, and given away free as a bonus extra with the RahXephon PS2 game. The 2002 manga tells a slightly different version of the story, starting in 2001 instead of 2012.

RAI: GALACTIC CIVIL WAR CHRONICLE

1994. JPN: *Ginga Sengoku Gunyu Den Rai*. AKA: *Galactic Civil War Rivalry Between Chiefs: Rai; Thunder Jet*. TV series. DIR: Seiji Okuda. SCR: Junzo Toriumi, Satoshi Fujimoto. DES: Makoto Takahoko, Takashi Watabe, Kenji Teraoka, Mitsuki Nakamura. ANI: Makoto Takahoko. MUS: Kaoru Wada. PRD: IG Film, TV Tokyo. 25 mins. x 52 eps.

The Galactic Empire is in shreds after the emperor's death, and the universe is consumed by conflict. Young warrior Rai Ryuga, descendant of an old samurai line, wants to bring peace to the warring clans and enlists the help of Shimon, daughter of the late emperor. A replay of Japan's civil war, but in space with fighting robots, *Rai* was a huge success in its original manga form. Serialized in *Dengeki Comic Gao* magazine by Johji Manabe, it shares character archetypes and graphic style with his earlier OUTLANDERS and sold over two million copies, making the anime adaptation a foregone conclusion. It has a martial feel courtesy of DANCOUGAR-director Okuda and oriental music from KISHIN CORPS' Wada.

RAIJIN-OH

1991. JPN: *Zettai Muteki Raijin-o*. AKA: *Completely Invincible Raijin-o*. TV series, video. DIR: Toshifumi Kawase, Nobuhiro Kondo, Takuya Sato. SCR: Hideki Sonoda, Noriko Hayasaka. DES: Satoshi Takeuchi, Takahiro Yamada, Shige Ikeda. ANI: Shinichi Sakuma, Satoshi Takeuchi. MUS: Kohei Tanaka. PRD: Sunrise, TV Tokyo. 25 mins. x 51 eps., 30 mins. x 3 eps. (v).

Earth is under threat of invasion from another dimension. Balzeb, Taldar, and their shapeshifting underlings, the Akudama

(Evil Orbs), create part-cyborg monsters based on problems humankind has created for itself, like pollution, litter, and noise. There is a solution—three robots stored in a secret hangar that can combine to form the mighty fighting machine Raijin-Oh. When a pilot crashes Raijin-oh into an elementary school and is too badly hurt to carry on, he asks the pupils to take his place and become the Earth Defense Group. Once again, the government has no alternative but to put the safety of Earth in the hands of its children. Although 3 of them will be pilots, all 18 classmates have tolearn to work together unselfishly for the good of all humanity. With such a large regular cast, one would expect most to be sidelined, but each of the regulars is featured strongly and has his or her own importance to the team and the story.

Another series created by Sunrise house pseudonym Hajime Yadate, *Raijin-Oh* follows in the tradition of giant-robot shows begun by Mitsuteru Yokoyama's **GIGANTOR** and Go Nagai's **MAZINGER Z**, which Sunrise raised to the level of an art form in the late 1970s with shows for a slightly older audience, like **GUNDAM**. Sunrise was also responsible in no small part for the use of very young children—the target audience for merchandising—as heroes in these shows, and the success of *Raijin-Oh* came shortly after the beginning of their long-running **BRAVE SAGA**.

RAIL OF THE STAR *

1993. JPN: *O-hoshisama no Rail*. Movie. DIR: Toshio Hirata. SCR: Tatsuhiko Urahata. DES: Yoshinori Kanemori. ANI: Katsutaka Iizuka. MUS: Koichi Saito. PRD: Madhouse. 79 mins.
As a Japanese national growing up in occupied Korea during World War II, young Chiko learns that soldiers on the battlefield are not the only casualties of armed conflict. As the Japanese Empire reaps the increasingly bitter harvest of a failing war effort, her well-to-do middle-class family is rocked by tragedy, losing friends and loved ones to the everyday domestic hazards of life in the 1940s, before peace brings the greatest danger of all. Korea is divided between the victors, and Chiko's family is in Pyongyang, in the northern half. The Soviet Army begins a search for Japanese veterans like her father, a factory manager

called up for military service. Chiko and her surviving relatives embark upon an epic journey to the U.S. Occupied Zone below the 38th parallel. They must rely on the help of the Korean people to get them to safety. Many Koreans suffered during the Japanese colonization, but in this sanitized true-life story (based on a book by Chitose "Chiko" Kobayashi), everything works out tidily. The threadbare but clean and perky-looking Japanese survivors manage to reach safety with the help of forgiving Korean villagers who put human life above race, nationality, or revenge, and Chiko grows up in modern, prosperous Japan, remembering the war through the eyes of a child.

It's not an exclusively Japanese tendency to present war stories in the best possible light—every nation talks about the suffering of its own civilians and the terrible impact of war on children, though sadly only after the event. For this approach, children make the ideal protagonists, since they can't be held responsible for any of the events they observe. A very similar story premise, also based on semiautobiographical memoirs, was transformed into something sublime by the artistry of Studio Ghibli in **GRAVE OF THE FIREFLIES**, whose success encouraged a number of imitators, of which *Rail of the Star* is perhaps the most blinkered. Compared to the deeply romanticized view of war presented in **THE COCKPIT** or the realistic yet humane outlook of **BAREFOOT GEN**, it's pap, used by the Japanese to assure themselves that World War II was some sort of unexpected natural disaster, and that Koreans don't hold much of a grudge for 50 years of colonial rule (**THE WIND RISES**). Ironically, *RotS*'s artificial worthiness made it more marketable abroad, where American distributors warmed to its deluded cultural relativism, the "bring me your poor" concept of the U.S. zone as refuge, and the opportunity to demonstrate that not all of their anime output was guns and hooters.

RAIL WARS *

2014. TV series. DIR: Yoshifumi Sueda. SCR: Masashi Suzuki, Masanobu Nozaki. DES: Makoto Uno. ANI: Makoto Uno, Sayaka Koiso. MUS: Yoshiaki Fujisawa. PRD: Passione, Docomo Anime Store, Lantis, Pony Canyon,

Q-tec, Sogeisha, Studio Maus, Klockworx. 24 mins. x 12 eps.
Charmless teen romantic **COMEDY**, as a bunch of school-leavers are placed on internships within Japan National Railways, whereupon hijinks duly ensue. JNR ceased to exist in 1987, which means that this exercise in train nerdery is set in an alternate universe where Japan's trains were never privatized—a nostalgic attempt, perhaps, to wind back the clock to the days before the country's current economic problems. Extremists want to privatize the railway system (which is apparently a bad thing) and keep threatening to blow stuff up, while the lead flails around in the middle of an off-the-shelf love triangle. The whole thing feels like an exercise in **ADVERTISING AND SPONSORSHIP** but seemingly does not involve secret cash from any railway company seeking to create train propaganda. Instead, cooperation behind the scenes is accredited to Tomytec, a toy company presumably with a lot of model trains to sell.

RAINBOW *

2010. JPN: *Rainbow Nisha Rokubo no Shichinin*. AKA: *The Seven Criminals from Compound Two, Cell Six*. TV series. DIR: Hiroshi Kojina. SCR: Hideo Takayashiki, Kazuyuki Fudeyasu, Mitsutaka Hirota. DES: Ai Kikuchi, Tomoyuki Shimizu. ANI: Ai Kikuchi, Mika Takahashi. MUS: N/C. PRD: Madhouse Studios, VAP. 23 mins. x 26 eps.
It's 1955. The Occupation of Japan has ended (**JAPAN OUR HOMELAND**), but there's still a heavy American military presence. The nation is struggling to live with cataclysmic social, moral, spiritual, and cultural upheaval. Teenage boys who were children during the war years, many fatherless or from broken families, run amok and are sent to reform schools. In one such school, with a pedophile doctor and a venal senior guard in command, seven boys band together to survive the brutality of daily life and get back to the outside world to create a better future for themselves and their friends. Meanwhile there's violence, rape, and brutality on a daily basis.

George Abe, who wrote the original *Rainbow* manga in 2001 with art by Masasumi Kakizaki, was 18 years old in 1955 and spent some time in a reformatory, giving his work a solid foundation in reality.

Just as *West Side Story* was a 1950s American version of Shakespeare's *Romeo and Juliet*, *Rainbow* is Akira Kurosawa's *Seven Samurai* reframed as a 1950s Japanese version of Frank Darabont's *The Shawshank Redemption* (1995). Madhouse's anime version is not flawless—the plots are predictable, and the inane female narrator is infuriatingly inappropriate—but this dark, tightly written, fast-paced show is packed with suspense and emotion, as well as extreme brutality. It should really be viewed as a prison camp drama rather than a reform school story, with the forces of the crumbling but mighty empire of adulthood facing off against their captives in humanity's oldest war. The central character is a tribute to men striving for humanity in a harsh and indifferent world—compare with TOMORROW'S JOE and TIGER MASK. It's a welcome antidote to the dime-a-dozen magical girls, candy-floss harems, and superpowered ninja that flood from Japan's TV screens. **◐◐**

RAINBOW ACROSS THE PACIFIC

1992. JPN: *Taiheiyo ni Kakeru Niji*. Video. DIR: Masayuki Akehi. SCR: Yugo Serikawa, Tadahiro Shimafuji. DES: N/C. ANI: Takao Kasai. MUS: Seiji Yokoyama. PRD: Toei. 30 mins.
Schoolgirl Mitsuko tries to protect half-Chinese transfer student Yu-Lian from bullies. That night, she discovers Emily, an old American doll. Given to a Japanese child during an exchange in 1921, it was hidden from the "doll burnings" of the anti-Western war period and saved by a brave young girl (Mitsuko's grandmother) from bayonet practice. At the next day's show-and-tell, Mitsuko tells the story of Emily and encourages Yu-Lian, who has brought her own doll, the beautiful Feng-Qun. When Feng-Qun's ribbon blows away and is caught in a tree, even the bullies cooperate in retrieving it.
Combining treacly internationalism with inadvertent comedy, especially when a girl donates her underwear to help make a rope, this story also suffers from flabby editing (why have a talking doll *and* a doll fairy?) characteristic of a creator with whom nobody dares argue, in this case Daisaku Ikeda, the leader of the Soka Gakkai Buddhist organization. But it is superior to his FAIRGROUND IN THE STARS, cleverly appealing to children by using

toys as allegories for human suffering and heroism.

RAINBOW BATTLETEAM ROBIN

1966. JPN: *Rainbow Sentai Robin*. TV series. DIR: Yugo Serikawa, Takeshi Tamiya, Tomoharu Katsumata, Michiru Takeda, Yasuo Yamaguchi. SCR: Kazuhiko Kojima, Hiroshi Ozawa, Minoru Hamada, Hiroaki Hayashi, Michio Suzuki. DES: Studio Zero. ANI: Yoichi Kotabe, Keishiro Kimura, Tetsuhiro Wakabayashi, Shinya Takahashi. MUS: Koichi Hattori. PRD: Toei, Studio Zero, NET. 25 mins. x 48 eps.
The people of the dying planet Palta choose Earth as their new home, much to the annoyance of the human race. In an animated pastiche of live-action shows such as ULTRAMAN, teenage Robin and his six color-coded friends (nurse-robot Lily, Wolf the werewolf, Benkei the warrior-mage, Bell the cat, the know-it-all Professor, and Pegasus the transforming rocket) form a heroic team to save the planet. Inspired in part by Edmond Hamilton's CAPTAIN FUTURE novels, the original concept was thought up by CYBORG 009–creator Shotaro Ishinomori, then calling himself Ishimori.

RAINBOW COLORED FIREFLIES

2012. JPN: *Niji-iro Hotaru: Eien no Natsu*. AKA: *Rainbow Colored Fireflies: Eternal Summer*. Movie. DIR: Konosuke Uda. SCR: Kei Kunii. DES: Hisashi Mori. ANI: Hisashi Mori. MUS: Masataka Matsutoya. PRD: Toei Animation. 105 mins.
Yuta visits the Hotarugaoka Dam on a hot summer's day, where he gives some water to an old man. The man repays his kindness by making it possible for him to leap backward in time to 1977, the year when the dam was built, and in which Yuta's father died. Based on a novel of the same name, serialized in 2004 on the website of author Masayuki Kawaguchi, this story comes with many possibly inadvertent signifiers of similar tales, from IN THE FOREST OF THE FIREFLIES' LIGHT, to LETTER TO MOMO, to *Yuta and His Wondrous Friends* (*DE), to Yukio Mishima's untranslated novel *The Drowned Waterfall*. Like all of them, it deals with matters of bereavement and healing, but also with a sense of melancholy for the loss of Japan's natural environment beneath a jumble

of storm drains and barricades—usually the prerogative of Studio Ghibli, and only superficially imitated here.

RAINBOW COLORED PRISM GIRL

2013. JPN: *Niji-iro Prism Girl*. Video. DIR: Yoshitaka Fujimoto. SCR: N/C. DES: Shoko Hagiwara. ANI: N/C. MUS: Tomoro Kudo. PRD: Synergy SP, APPP. 12 mins. x 4 eps.
The orphaned daughter of an actress resolves to become an entertainer of some description and to snag the coveted Rainbow Prism prize in her mother's memory. Released concurrently with the end of the four-year run of An Nakahara's 2010 manga in *Ciao* magazine, in the spirit of MASK OF GLASS, but with far cuter designs. Director Yoshitaka Fujimoto is credited as "coach"—possibly an acting in-joke, but more likely to be a reluctance to be blamed for the results. The four episodes were bundled on anthology DVDs and given away with issues of *Ciao*.

RAINBOW MAN

1982. JPN: *Ai no Senshi Rainbow Man*. AKA: *Love Warrior Rainbow Man*. TV series. DIR: Nobuhiro Okaseko. SCR: Tsunehisa Ito. DES: Yasunori Kawauchi, Nobuhiro Okaseko. ANI: Nobuhiro Okaseko. MUS: Jun Kitahara. PRD: Ai Planning, Hayama Art, Oscar Studio, Studio Pop, MBS. 25 mins. x 22 eps.
Takeshi Yamato has spent years as a student of yogic master Devadatta. He now has superpowers that allow him to transform himself in seven ways and operate seven kinds of machinery. By combining his powers with an organic V Armor, which he can call up at will, he becomes Rainbow Man. In this form, he fights to defend Japan against the evil machinations of the Death-Death Group. This animated adaptation of the live-action SFX series *Rainbow Man* (1972) recreates the feel of the original, even down to the theme song taken from the earlier series. Compare to ULTRAMAN, which also has both live-action and anime incarnations.

RAINING FIRE

1988. JPN: *Hi no Ame ga Furu*. Movie. DIR: Seiji Arihara. SCR: Toshiaki Imaizumi, Seiji Arihara. DES: Yoshitsuge Hasegawa. ANI: Takaya Ono. MUS: N/C. PRD: Space, Nikkatsu, Mushi Pro. 80 mins.
On the 19th of June 1945, 230 Ameri-

can B-29s bomb Fukuoka while two horror-struck Japanese children watch the incendiary devices make the night sky look as if it is "raining fire." Funded in part by the Kyushu Film Center, jealous at the attention lavished on other towns in anime such as **GRAVE OF THE FIREFLIES** (Kobe) and **BAREFOOT GEN** (Hiroshima), *RF* fatuously claims to be an antiwar film, though it conveniently neglects to mention that the sleepy harbor town of Fukuoka was actually a major military port. Conventional weaponry killed more Japanese during the war than the much-hyped A-Bombs at Hiroshima and Nagasaki—in addition to Arihara's look-alike follow-up **KAYOKO'S DIARY**, a similar study of the firebombing of civilian and industrial targets was directed by Tsuneharu Otani as *After the Unhealable Wounds: Osaka the Sea of Fire* (1991, *Kiesaranu Kizu Ato: Hi no Umi Osaka*).

RAMAYANA *

1998. AKA: *Ramayana: The Legend of Prince Rama, Prince of Light*. Movie. DIR: Ram Mohan, Yugo Sako. SCR: Krishna Shah. DES: N/C. ANI: Kazuyuki Kobayashi. MUS: N/C. PRD: Nippon Ramayana Film Co. 96 mins.
The God-King Rama and his devoted young wife, Sita, are exiled by political intrigue but determined to prove Rama's right to his ancestral throne. In the course of their long wanderings through the forests and kingdoms of ancient India, they meet many friends and allies, including an old friend of Japanese animation, the Monkey God Hanuman, who was the original template for Monkey King Sun Wu-Kong, hero of **JOURNEY TO THE WEST**. But the beautiful Sita also attracts unwelcome attention from the Demon King Ravana, who kidnaps her and holds her captive in his island fortress. Rama and their friends set out to rescue her and destroy Ravana; before he can recover his throne he must recover his bride. Shapeshifting vampires, flying fortresses, and epic battles provide plenty of action and interest in a film as stuffed with over-the-top weaponry, weird martial arts, and romance as any fantasy anime.

The story, one of the great religious texts of Hinduism, is credited to a half-mythical robber-poet who is said to have given it its present form around 300 B.C. Like the Greek poet Homer, unwitting originator of **ULYSSES 31**, Valmiki could scarcely have suspected where his tale would end up. This first Indian-Japanese coproduction took years of heroic effort on the part of Mohan and Japanese producer Yugo Sako. Licenses from the Hindu religious authorities were required before work on the animation could go ahead in India, and local artists and animators were trained to work to Japanese standards and methods. Every aspect of the story was carefully constructed to avoid any offense to Hindu religious sensibilities. The end result did not score the hoped-for success either in India or Japan or among film-fan Hindi communities overseas. Less faithful adherence to Hindu myth can be found in **RG VEDA**.

RAMEN FIGHTER MIKI *

2006. JPN: *Muteki Kanban Musume*. AKA: *Invincible Poster Girl*. TV series. DIR: Nobuo Tomizawa. SCR: Toko Machida, Toshimitsu Takeuchi, Mitsutaka Hirota. DES: Keiko Nakaji, Hiroshi Nitta. ANI: Keiko Nakaji. MUS: Ryuji Takagi. PRD: Telecom Animation Film, Geneon USA, Toshiba Entertainment, Yomiuri Advertising, Yomiuri TV. 25 mins. x 12 eps.
Miki is an angry 20-going-on-12-year-old who works part-time in her mother's ramen restaurant—although one wonders why her mother thought it was a good idea to make this cute homicidal maniac the poster girl for her business, because Miki spends most of her time picking fights. She's got a good heart and really wants to help people, but if the slightest thing annoys her she hits out at the nearest moving object and beats it to a pulp. The series repeats the same basic gag—Miki gets absurdly annoyed, levels the block in a comical fashion—on an endless loop, its dedication to mindless bone-crunching fun and stunningly choreographed fights concealing the fact that its episodes are quite neatly plotted. Jun Sadogawa's 2002 manga was published in English as *Noodle Fighter Miki*. ◐

RAN ® SEM

2011. JPN: *Ran ® Sem: Hakudaku Deimo Tsuma no Mirai*. AKA: *Ran ® Sem: A Steamy Wife's Future*. Video. DIR: Hiromi Yokoyama. SCR: Toshiyuki Yamamoto. DES: Si Min Lee. ANI: Si Min Lee. MUS: N/C. PRD: Suzuki Mirano.

30 mins. x 2 eps.
Riko used to be a legendary gravure idol—a Japanese pinup model who made her living from soft porn photobooks. Her younger sister Anna idolizes her and talks about her career with pride, although she's now retired. Then Anna disappears, and Riko discovers that she's joined a weird enlightenment cult and gone to one of their seminars. She signs up for the same group to investigate, and discovers that to attend the same seminar as Anna she'll have to rise through the ranks of the enlightened, and the only way to do that is to help others achieve enlightenment through sexual release. This may sound like an interesting exploration of cult scandals but it's based on a porn game by Guilty+, so don't get your hopes up. A cross-over with **RIN X SEN** followed in 2013. ◐◑◒

RANCE: GUARDIAN OF THE DESERT

1994. JPN: *Rance: Sabaku no Guardian*. Video. DIR: Hisashi Fujii. SCR: Satoru Akahori. DES: Kazuto Nakazawa. ANI: Kazuto Nakazawa, Koji Matsuyama. MUS: N/C. PRD: Alice Soft, Tokuma. 50 mins.
Lecherous knight Rance decides that all the women in the world belong to him, and that he should start claiming his rights by getting naked with as many of them as possible. This smutty spin-off from a fantasy role-playing computer game featured big names from the mainstream, including **BEAST WARRIORS**' Akahori and **EL HAZARD**'s Nakazawa. ◒

RANCOU CHOUKYO: ORGY TRAINING *

2001. JPN: *Ranko Chokyo Maid ni Natta Shojo*. AKA: *Orgy Training: The Girl Became a Maid Video*. DIR: N/C. SCR: N/C. DES: N/C. ANI: N/C. MUS: N/C. PRD: Five Ways, Wide Road. 30 mins.
A poor little rich boy is completely in thrall to his brutal, arrogant father, whose womanizing with the servants drove his mother away. When he finally plucks up the courage to date a girl from school, he tries to copy Dad and have his way with her, and she rejects him. Next day he's walking to school feeling sorry for himself when he meets a beautiful girl who's lost. When he gets home that night, he finds she's the new live-in maid. His father has

paid off her father's loanshark debts in exchange for the girl; she has to do whatever her master tells her to work off the debt. He means to challenge his father and "save" her, so as to make her his own sex slave. Based on a manga by Beauty Hair, author of QUEEN AND SLAVE, the show adds another layer to the depersonalization of characters in porn by not giving anyone a name. Curiously, it is also rather lacking in both the orgy and training departments, although it is extremely explicit in its depiction of rape. **ⒷⓃⓋ**

RANMA ½ *

1989. JPN: *Ranma Nibunnoichi*. TV series, movie, video. DIR: Tsutomu Shibayama, Hideharu Iuchi, Iku Suzuki, Junji Nishimura, Kazuhiro Furuhashi. SCR: Shigeru Yanagawa, Ryota Yamaguchi. DES: Atsuko Nakajima, Torao Arai. ANI: Tomomi Mochizuki, Takeshi Mori, Masako Sato, Masamitsu Kudo. MUS: Eiji Mori, Kenji Kawai. PRD: Kitty Films, Studio Deen, Fuji TV. 25 mins. x 18 eps. (TV1), 25 mins. x 143 eps. (TV2), 75 mins. (m1), 60 mins. (m2), 30 mins. x 6 eps. (v1), 25 mins. (m3), 30 mins. x 2 eps. (v2, *Special*), 30 mins. x 3 eps. (v3, *Super*).

Ranma (*luan ma*, Chinese for "wild horse") Saotome and his father, martial artist Genma, fall into magical pools while training in a region of China. Henceforth, Ranma will change into a girl whenever doused in cold water and back to a boy when doused in hot. Genma fares even worse—he becomes a giant panda. The pair leave exotic, dangerous China and return home to safe, familiar Japan, where years ago Saotome senior agreed with his old friend Tendo that Ranma would marry one of the Tendo daughters and take over the family dojo. The Tendo girls are underwhelmed by their prospective bridegroom. Youngest sister Akane, who draws the short straw, is a feisty young lady with formidable fighting skills and considerable contempt for the teenage boys who attempt to defeat and date her. She and boy-Ranma (Ranma-kun) strike antagonistic sparks off each other right away. Ranma tries to keep his inadvertent sex changes secret at school by posing as his/her own sibling, resulting in Akane and girl-Ranma (Ranma-chan) becoming rivals for supremacy among their classmates. Ranma-chan attracts unwelcome attention

from the guys in class, while Ranma-kun is a babe magnet. The stories revolve around a fight-of-the-week, flavored by the familiar world of teenage home and school life, with the magical element providing injections of fantasy and romance. Just about every stranger who wanders into town has fallen into some kind of magical pool, and the resulting transformations turn school and dojo into a veritable zoo. Meanwhile Ranma and Akane grow to love each other but can't admit it, their various friends and rivals start to pair off, often unwittingly, and the quest to find a cure for the curse goes on.

Based on a 1988 manga in *Shonen Sunday* from URUSEI YATSURA–creator Rumiko Takahashi, RANMA ½ duplicated her earlier success, but this time with a lead character that is both boy and girl and a strangeness that comes not from extraterrestrial origins but from magic. The story was soon picked up for TV, where it lasted for several years despite *Shonen Sunday's* sales sinking to their lowest-ever ebb while the manga was running in it. The TV series is available in the U.S. divided into "seasons" under the titles *Ranma ½ Digital Dojo* (the first series), *R: Anything Goes Martial Arts*, *R: Hard Battle*, *R: Outta Control*, *R: Martial Mayhem*, *R: Random Rhapsody*, and *R: Ranma Forever*. However, real success has come abroad, particularly in Asia, where the kung fu and comedy, dubbed into local languages, make it the most China-friendly anime series. It is even shown in the censorious People's Republic, where its repetitive, lighthearted obsessions with romance, food, fighting, and sibling rivalries are not regarded as much of a threat to Communism.

The first movie, directed by Iuchi, was not based on incidents from the manga but had a specially created story based on Chinese legend. In *Ranma ½ The Movie: Big Trouble In Nekonron, China* (1991), Akane is kidnapped by prince Kirin, who wants to marry her, Ranma and the gang rescue her (in a battle scene that pays open homage to SAINT SEIYA, reflecting the involvement of Arai in both movies), and everything ends as usual with the leads refusing to admit their love for each other. The second, *Nihao My Concubine* (1992), directed by Suzuki, has the girls shipwrecked in the South Seas with a crazed young illusionist

who forces them to compete in various skill tests to select his bride. To save Akane and the others from this fate worse than death, Ranma-chan has to compete in wacky activities such as survival flower arranging and obstacle-course cooking.

Several video releases also kept the series in the public eye throughout the 1990s, many of which have also been released in English. *Dead Heat Music Match* (1990) started a new "career" for the three Tendo girls, Ranma-chan, and Chinese interloper Shampoo; their voice actresses formed the band DoCo, acting in their character roles, and went on to release numerous *Ranma ½* music CDs and videos. These were followed in rapid succession by more videos, many of which have been released in English with desperately labored titles punning on famous Western films. Thus it was that the *R Special* video series (1993) was released in America as *Desperately Seeking Shampoo, Like Water for Ranma ½*, and *Akane and Her Sisters*. A second video series, *R Super* (1995), was similarly altered into *An Akane to Remember, One Flew Over the Kuno's Nest* (paired with a 30-minute "movie" *Ranma ½ Team vs. The Legendary Phoenix*), and *Faster, Kasumi! Kill! Kill!* Nishimura directed most of the videos.

With animation that has not aged as badly as *UY*'s and a seamless dub in the U.S., *Ranma ½* has attracted fanatical Western devotees, but Takahashi had already covered the territory thoroughly, and a huge amount of plot and character recycling goes on. She cleverly exploits the factors that made *UY* such a success but with less inventiveness and humor, eventually dumbing down to sheer predictability. Takahashi's talent is far greater than *Ranma ½* reveals; but her commercial success comes from giving her audiences exactly what they want, as often as they want it, and the *Ranma ½* franchise delivers honestly on that basis. This makes it popular with a young teenage audience, which doubtless appreciates a series so interchangeable that the episodes do not need to be numbered, making little difference whether one is watching a TV episode or a video special. For a better measure of Takahashi's work, see MAISON IKKOKU and ONE-POUND GOSPEL.

RANPO
1984. JPN: *Ranpo*. TV series. DIR: Ken Baba, Shin Misawa, Hirokazu Fukuhara. SCR: Yasushi Hirano, Keiko Maruo, Kenji Terada, Hideki Sonoda, Yoshio Urasawa. DES: Hiroshi Kanazawa, Masatoshi Uchizaki. ANI: Hiroshi Kanazawa, Toshiyuki Honda, Kaoru Ogawa, Masayuki, Moriyasu Taniguchi. MUS: Chito Kawachi. PRD: NAS, Fuji TV. 25 mins. x 20 eps.

Mild-mannered Japanese kid Ranpo is kidnapped by aliens whose UFO-based experiments turn him into a "warp boy" who truly believes that he can do anything. Back at school on Earth, he enlists his classmates in a number of wacky schemes, and comedic misunderstandings ensue. Based on a 1979 manga in *Shonen Champion* magazine by Masatoshi Uchizaki, *Ranpo* was swiftly yanked off the air—though the official excuse was that its slot was required for baseball games, the series never returned. Years after its original release, the only traces it left behind were praise for Hiroshi Watanabe's Beatles-pastiche opening credits and an unbroadcast 21st episode.

RANTARO
1993. JPN: *Nintama Rantaro*. AKA: *Rantaro the Little Ninja, Ninja Boys*. TV series. DIR: Tsutomu Shibayama. SCR: Yoshio Urasawa. DES: Sobei Amako. ANI: N/C. MUS: Koji Makaino. PRD: Ajia-do. 12 mins. x 91 eps. (TV1), 12 mins. x 72 eps., 20 mins. x 18 eps. (TV2), 45 mins. (m), 10 mins. x 120 eps. (TV3), 10 mins. x 120 eps. (TV4), 10 mins. x 100 eps. (TV5), 10 mins. x 60 eps. (TV6), 10 mins. x 80 eps. (TV7), 10 mins. x 80 eps. (TV8), 10 mins. x 80 eps. (TV9), 10 mins. x 80 eps. (TV10), 10 mins. x 80 eps. (TV11), 10 mins. x 80 eps. (TV12), 10 mins. x 56 eps. (TV13), 10 mins. x 50 eps. (TV14), 10 mins. x 50 eps. (TV15), 10 mins. x 100 eps. (TV16), 10 mins. x 90 eps. (TV17), 10 mins. x 90 eps. (TV18), 10 mins x 90 eps. (TV19), 10 mins. x 90 eps. (TV20)—total episodes to date (2014): 1660+.

Well, the ninja have to learn their trade *somewhere*. Rantaro is a little boy who wants to grow up to be a highly trained assassin. So he goes to a ninja school, where he gets to clown around and meet famous people from Japan's civil-war period. Featuring high-profile theme music from bands-of-the-moment Hikaru Genji and Super Monkeys, this lighthearted kids' comedy, based on a manga by Sobei Amako, returned after 91 episodes as *New Rantaro* (1994), which similarly featured ninja whose favorite food was mushrooms, a warrior forced to work part-time at a launderette, and time out from learning about poisons so the gang can go shopping. Several episodes of the second series were "specials" that ran for almost double the time, and the central cast's best moments were later rereleased in the four-part *Rantaro Masterworks* series (1996). The same year saw a short *Rantaro* movie, in which the little ninja, trained for cunning and deceit, must somehow convince his elders that he is not responsible for thefts at the school, and has been followed ever after by constant returns to the screen. Compare to HATTORI THE NINJA. Takashi Miike's live-action film *Ninja Kids* (2011) and its follow-up, Ryuta Tazaki's *Ninja Kids: Summer Mission Impossible* (2013), were also based on the franchise.

RAPE EXPRESS HIGH TIDE
2010. JPN: *Kan'in Tokkyu Michi Shio*. Video. DIR: Onijima. SCR: Onijima. DES: Onijima, Kuroneko, Seihodo. ANI: Onijima. MUS: N/C. PRD: YOUC, Digital Works. 30 mins. x 2 eps.

There's a rumor spreading around high schools that if you're unlucky enough to get on a certain train, you'll disappear. The rumor is true: a train that looks exactly like any other train is really a set-up to kidnaps girls and train them as sex slaves. Whether they're schoolgirls, commuters, or railway staff, conductor Seiji will make sure they don't get off the train until they're completely submissive and ready to be delivered to their new masters. Based on a porn game by Turumiku. ❶❷

RAPE GUERRILLA HUNT 3
2008. JPN: *Ryojoku Guerrilla Kari 3*. Video. DIR: Yoshitaka Fujimoto. SCR: PON, Taifu Sekimachi. DES: Norimoto Hattori, Takashi Tenshumo. ANI: Norimoto Hattori. MUS: Toshiyuki Yamamoto. PRD: Liquid, Suzuki Mirano. 30 mins. x 2 eps.

Invincible spaceship Victoire and its all-female crew have delivered a string of victories for their government. But when war is over, the ship and its secrets are sold to the enemy and the crew thrown into prison. They have no way to protect themselves from the men they defeated so often, and in space no one has heard of the Geneva Convention. Bondage, rape, and violence ensue. Production company Suzuki Mirano is one of a clutch of companies owned by A1C, the porn arm of IMAGIN, which is also involved in animation and production on titles including LUPIN III, ONE PIECE, and MAGIC KNIGHT RAYEARTH. Based on the third iteration of a series of porn games by NEXTON's label Liquid. ❶❷

RAPE! RAPE! RAPE!
2008. Video. DIR: Kobo Ryuren. SCR: Kobo Ryuren, Inochi Fudo. DES: Mikio Fushihara, Isao Shoji (color), hidehide. ANI: Mikio Fushihara. MUS: Mizuho Kitaura. PRD: Anime Antenna Production Committee, Odin. 27 mins. x 3 eps.

This anime based on Valkyria's porn game offers exactly what the title implies. A young man goes on a rape spree, attacking schoolgirls, pregnant women, in fact any attractive female he happens to meet. He threatens them with a knife and rapes them. ❶❷

RAPEMAN, THE
1994. JPN: *Za (The) Rapeman*. Video. DIR: Kinta Kunte, Kazuo Sawada, Hiroshi Ono. SCR: Shintaro Miyawaki. DES: Keiko Aizaki. ANI: Hidemi Kubo. MUS: N/C. PRD: Pink Pineapple, KSS. 45 mins.

Shotoku and his nephew Keisuke are vigilante rapists. With a company motto of "Righting Wrongs through Penetration," they will don black hockey masks and rape females who have somehow offended their clients by dumping them, refusing their advances, or otherwise treating them inappropriately. After teaching their victims a "good lesson," they donate the money they earn to Keisuke's former home at the Sunflower Orphanage. This deeply offensive series was based on the controversial manga by Shintaro Miyawaki and Keiko Aizaki. The anime version was released roughly halfway through the live-action video series, directed by Takao Nagaishi between 1990 and 1998. ❶❶❷

RASCAL RACCOON *
1977. JPN: *Araiguma Rascal*. TV series. DIR: Seiji Endo, Shigeo Koshi, Hiroshi Saito. SCR: Akira Miyazaki. DES: Seiji Endo. ANI: Seiji Oku-

da, Noboru Kameyama, Nobuo Fujisawa, Sadahiko Sakamaki, Yoichi Kotabe, Toshiko Nakagawa, Hayao Miyazaki, Hirokazu Ishino. MUS: Takeo Watanabe. PRD: Nippon Animation, Fuji TV. 25 mins. x 52 eps.

Young Sterling lives on a farm in Wisconsin with his parents in the early years of the 20th century. One day, he finds an abandoned baby raccoon in the forest and decides to take it home. The pair soon become inseparable. The raccoon's antics keep the neighborhood in quite a stir, but Sterling also finds his little companion a great comfort in the difficult times of his life, including his mother's illness and the terrible storm that devastates the farm and threatens the family's livelihood. Based on the writings of Sterling North about his own boyhood, this is part of Nippon Animation's WORLD MASTERPIECE THEATER series and includes Hayao Miyazaki among its animators. Just to show how much times can change, the "same" character was dusted off as *Famous Detective Rascal* (*Meitantei Rascal*, 2014) in a COMEDY cartoon for NHK—compare to SHERLOCK HOUND, as the makers were rather hoping you would.

RATINGS AND BOX OFFICE

In general, anime's ratings on Japanese television are not particularly high. Those anime regarded in the Western market as fan favorites are often broadcast in the late-night slots when literally nobody is watching—even the fans are expected to set their video recorders and get some sleep, as "How-to-Timeshift" articles in late 20th-century magazines implied. Japanese TV ratings are not precisely the same as America's Nielsen ratings, and are designed to show the percentage of televisions switched on in Japan, and tuned in to a particular channel at any given time. This has tended to grossly distort comparative ratings over time—since, for example, it was not all that difficult for the George Reeves *Adventures of Superman* to gain a rating of 73% in the 1950s, when there was only a handful of channels to choose from. ASTRO BOY's famous peak rating of 40.3% in early 1964 was generated less by the story and more by the fact that the episode in question was a test broadcast for color TV.

Arguably the biggest television program in Japanese history was the opening of the Tokyo Olympics in 1964, for which many consumers bought their first color television set, thereby helping to contribute to its massive 89.9% audience share. Live-action television continues to enjoy ratings vastly superior to animation on Japanese television, with notable peaks including the live-action OSHIN in 1983, with 62.9%. Popular primetime drama shows and NHK historical dramas regularly gain ratings around the 30% mark. Contrary to misleading publicity in America, the live-action GTO was never "the most watched TV program in Japan," since its peak ratings were a respectable 36.8%, an impressive figure, but one which is regularly trounced, and was in fact beaten by *Hero* (*DE) that same season.

Average anime tend to have ratings below the 7% mark, and it is not unusual for ratings to fall below 2%. The highest rating achieved by an anime in recent memory was for an episode of CHIBI MARUKO-CHAN in 1990, at 39.9%, beating the previous record of 39.4% that had been held by SAZAE-SAN since 1979. STAR OF THE GIANTS (in 1970) and DOCTOR SLUMP (in 1981) tie for third place with 36.9%. The television broadcast of PRINCESS MONONOKE secured a rating of 35.1%, while other shows with peaks in the 30s include THE GUTSY FROG, JAPANESE FOLK TALES, TIGER MASK, TOUCH, and TOMORROW'S JOE.

Unsurprisingly, anime's ratings are higher when adult viewers are discounted and analysis is restricted solely to the juvenile audience. Statistics compiled by NHK's Cultural Research Bureau suggest not only that very young viewers are encouraged by their parents to see shows such as *Watch with Mother* (*Okaasan to Issho*) and *Playing in English* (*Eigo de Asobo*), but also that they comprise a large viewing component of the audiences for primetime programming such as SAZAE-SAN at ages as young as two. In recent years, the only statistically noteworthy anime challenge to juvenile classics has been presented by POKÉMON, which still regularly snatches a large proportion of the young audience (around 5%). The contemporary high-rated shows include NARUTO (5%), CONAN THE BOY DETECTIVE (6%), and ONE PIECE (8%). Conversely, the critic Makoto Tada, in his book *Kore ga Anime Business da* (2002, *This Is the Anime Business*), estimated

the size of the dedicated anime otaku audience in Japan to be just 400,000, which suggests a maximum possible rating *among otaku*, of merely 0.4%. The Nomura Research Institute, in its study *Otaku Marketing* (2005), estimated this audience to be merely 112,000 people, which is to say, in audience share terms, a rating of 0.1%. This perhaps explains why so many anime for mature audiences congregate in the graveyard shifts—the only place where such a small audience is remotely acceptable to advertisers and broadcasters.

The picture of anime at cinemas is very different. Arguably, we are living in the Golden Age of anime cinema, since recent years have seen anime movies becoming the highest-grossing movies of any kind at the Japanese box office. However, until the coming of Studio Ghibli, anime's box office performance was significantly less impressive. Anime movies were aimed at children during seasonal vacations, and often took the form of "roadshow" anthologies in which popular TV anime characters of the moment would briefly shine in a theatrical release. The emphasis, as in children's movies around the world, is often a choice between pablum for a child-only market, in the hope that parents can earn a two-hour rest by leaving their offspring at a cinema, or a genuine "family" movie with cross-generational appeal, designed to ensure that the parents have to buy tickets for themselves along with those for their kids.

The Japanese cinema industry was in a notorious slump for many years, never quite recovering from the arrival of TV, with many "movie" releases simply taking the form of very limited theatrical runs for promotional purposes. The difference, in such cases, between a video release and a cinema release is that screening in a cinema anywhere, however brief, obligates dedicated cinema magazines to at least review a movie, and thereby helps gain additional press attention ahead of the inevitable video release. Sometimes, the difference can be quite astonishing—Mamoru Oshii's GHOST IN THE SHELL, hailed around the globe as a masterpiece of modern anime, played in Tokyo theaters for barely two weeks.

Japanese box office records were dominated for almost two decades by two live-action movies—Spielberg's *E.T.* (1982) and Koreyoshi Kurehara's *Antarctica* (*Nankyoku Monogatari*, 1983, see **STORY OF THE SOYA**). It is not until the late 1990s that a sudden rush of blockbusters leapt ahead—*A.I.*, *Mission Impossible 2*, *Independence Day*, *Star Wars Episode I: The Phantom Menace*, *Jurassic Park*, and *Armageddon*. The number one spot at the Japanese box office then fell in quick succession to **PRINCESS MONONOKE**, *Titanic*, and then **SPIRITED AWAY**. Hype for **HOWL'S MOVING CASTLE** tends to emphasize its record-breaking opening weekend, avoiding mention of the fact it failed to outperform its predecessors overall. Such high numbers for Ghibli movies are a relatively recent phenomenon, and only really date from 1997, when *Princess Mononoke*'s takings were four times that of its Miyazaki predecessor, **PORCO ROSSO**, which had until that point been the best performing Ghibli film in cinemas. Previously, Studio Ghibli's real strength had been in the home video market—its films performed reasonably at cinemas, breaking records for *anime* if not for movies in general, and were the only films that seriously competed for the cartoon market share of Buena Vista Japan's Disney videos and DVDs. Even in the 1990s, the best-selling non-Ghibli cartoons in Japan were works such as *Beauty and the Beast* and the *Lion King*, with only a handful of works such as **EVANGELION** and **OH MY GODDESS!** even scraping into top tens.

Anime movies for the otaku audience in Japan are increasingly likely to be screened as unique or limited-period "events" in a single theater or on a very small tour, in order to concentrate fans and marketing—there is no point in a 200-screen release and a nationwide marketing campaign for a franchise with only 5,000 dedicated followers. It is becoming increasingly common for such events to monetize through merchandise, on the understanding that venues will present the only opportunity to buy unique goods or limited-edition Blu-rays of the film just seen. Although this helps keep alive films for a small audience, it has also led to a drift away from feature-length works, with films such as **IN THE FOREST OF THE FIREFLIES' LIGHT** (2011) only running 44 minutes. Although this is harmless for specialized public events in Japan, it makes such works problematic to

release as "films" in cinemas abroad.

Ghibli encourages a certain brand loyalty in the Japanese public—a survey conducted for Toho discovered that the Studio Ghibli name enjoyed an impressive 43% trust rating from film-going respondents. The score rose to an even more impressive 64.2% if the name Miyazaki appeared on a movie, perhaps helping to explain Ghibli's controversial decision to hire Hayao Miyazaki's son Goro to direct **TALES FROM EARTHSEA**.

The Japanese successes of Ghibli, or indeed of any other anime, are not necessarily repeated abroad. At the American box office, three of the top four best-performing anime are **POKÉMON** films, with the number one spot going to the $85 million gross of *Pokémon: The First Movie* (1999). The **YU-GI-OH** movie is at number 3 with $19.8 million, and by the time we reach the highest-grossing Ghibli movie, **SPIRITED AWAY** at number five, takings have fallen to a more modest $10 million. The **COWBOY BEBOP** movie, at number 11, is the last American anime release to earn over a million dollars in theaters; takings in the lower half of the top 20 for movies such as **PERFECT BLUE** and **TOKYO GODFATHERS** barely break into six figures. To put such figures in their business context, DreamWorks spent over $30 million on prints and advertising alone for *Shrek* (2001), which went on to take more than a quarter of a *billion* dollars at the U.S. box office. Anime may be growing in popularity, but it still has a long way to go before it presents a serious challenge to big movie business. In fact, it is arguable that without Hayao Miyazaki and Pikachu, anime's standing in cinemas would be almost unnoticeable.

RAVE MASTER *

2001. JPN: *Rave*. AKA: *Groove Adventure Rave*. TV series. DIR: Takashi Watanabe. SCR: Nobuaki Kishima. DES: Akira Matsushima. ANI: Studio DEEN. MUS: Kenji Kawai. PRD: Kazunori Noguchi, RAVE Production Committee, Studio DEEN, TBS. 24 mins. x 51 eps. Teenager Haru Glory inherits the Rave Sword, a weapon wielded 50 years earlier by the legendary Rave Master Shiba. Shiba managed to forestall disaster by scattering the evil Shadow Stones throughout the world in a mighty explosion, but in the process also lost the "good" Rave

Stones. When Haru fishes a weird looking dog, Plue, out of the sea, he also inherits Shiba's faithful canine companion. Heading to the city of Hip Hop with Plue, Haru joins forces with the feisty Elie and soon finds himself on a quest to collect the scattered stones, while evading the Shadow Guards and their General Shuda. Can the pair and their allies succeed in their quest? Well, this is a strictly-by-the-numbers quest story so of course they can, but take our word for it rather than spending 24 hours of your life to find out. Despite quite attractive character design, this show is limited in both concept and animation; **POKÉMON**, **CARDCAPTORS**, and **ONE PIECE** were here long before. Using pseudo-cool references to music and pop culture instead of a decent script is *so* last century; nothing dates a weak show faster. In outbreaks of sub-Tezuka whimsy, there's a Punk Street and a Ska Village as well as Hip Hop City, and Haru's battle cry is "Rave-olution!" Need we go on? Viewers chained to a chair and forced to watch it, however, may pass the time by drawing Cold War analogies—50 years elapsing since the world was transformed by a large explosion, itself caused by the splitting of a magic stone. Based on the manga by Hiro Mashima.

RAY THE ANIMATION *

2006. TV series. DIR: Naohito Takahashi. SCR: Atsuhiro Tomioka, Shuichi Kamiyama, Yuji Hosono. DES: Hisashi Kagawa, Osamu Imai. ANI: Hisashi Kagawa. MUS: GodSpeed, Masami Okui. PRD: Oriental Light and Magic, Akita Shoten, Tezuka Pro. 25 mins. x 13 eps. Ray is a gifted surgeon who works outside the normal structures, saving lives for free, taking on cases that would be near-impossible for doctors more than twice her age. Ray has a special advantage; her X-ray eyes enable her to actually see inside patients' bodies, reducing the risks of surgery enormously. Her devoted team of nurses and aides is headed by the man who gave her her eyes and saved her life when she was just a child. For Ray was raised in a white room with a carefully selected group of children, raised like cattle to provide organs for wealthy buyers. As she works, she's constantly on the lookout for traces of her old friends, and the sinister man at the head of the organization that kept them as animals to be cut up for profit. One day she'll find the people who stole her own eyes, and then she will have justice.

Of all Japan's medical manga, the one that has inspired the most spin-offs across all media is Osamu Tezuka's **BLACK JACK**. *RtA* is open in its homage to Tezuka's scarred outcast surgical genius. The scarred outcast surgical genius who saves Ray's life and gives her back her sight is named B. J. and voiced by Akio Otsuka, voice of Black Jack. The story also flirts with other elements that interested Tezuka: telepathy, the paranormal, the link between humanity and ecology. There are other interesting parallels with **EVANGELION**, but any perceived similarities with the novel that inspired Mark Romanek's 2010 film *Never Let Me Go* must account for the fact that Kazuo Ishiguro's book was not published until 2005, while Akihito Yoshitomi's manga *Ray* commenced publication in 2003.

Like many very interesting anime ideas, this series is let down by its execution. The plot tends toward the episodic disease-of-the-week format, and some of the diseases are extremely unusual—human-tree hybridization and shellfish pathogens that must be operated on underwater, for example. The character development, particularly the romantic subplot, doesn't go very far for the first half of the series, but things pick up with some interesting plot twists, though minor characters remain visual ciphers included mostly for fan-service purposes. It's not that *RtA* is bad—it's just that it isn't amazing, when it could have been.

RAYCA

2002. AKA: *Reika*. Video. DIR: N/C. SCR: N/C. DES: Haruhiko Mikimoto. ANI: N/C. MUS: N/C. PRD: Digital Frontier, Bandai Visual. 30 mins. In the 31st century, individuals exist only as data in computer networks. Rayca, a beautiful young idol character, comes back one thousand years to our time to explore memories of ancient Tokyo and its subcultures. Created by Mikimoto and delicately lit and animated by Digital Frontier, who were also involved in **ZOIDS**, the 2004 remake of **APPLESEED**, and a whole clutch of games, this is a slight but pretty work divided into ten short chapters. The DVD package includes an artbook.

RAYEARTH *

1994. JPN: *Maho Kishi Rayearth*. AKA: *Magic Knight Rayearth*. TV series, video. DIR: Toshihiro Hirano, Keitaro Motonaga, Hajime Kamegaki, Koichi Chiaki, Hitoyuki Matsui. SCR: Keiko Maruo, Osamu Nakamura, Nanase Okawa. DES: Atsuko Ishida, Masahiro Yamane. ANI: Atsuko Ishida, Keiji Goto, Hideyuki Motohashi, Masahiro Yamane, Madoka Hiroyama. MUS: Hayato Matsuo. PRD: TMS, Yomiuri TV. 25 mins. x 49 eps., 45 mins. x 3 eps.

Hikaru Shido, Umi Ryuzaki, and Fu Ho-oji are three ordinary Japanese schoolgirls who suddenly find themselves transported to Cephiro, a world of magic and monsters in another dimension. Clef, a very youthful looking ancient wizard, tells them that they have been summoned by the guardian of Cephiro, Princess Emeraude. The princess is a "pillar" of Cephiro, the link that holds the magic kingdom together, but she has been kidnapped by the evil High Priest Zagato. In order to save this fragile world, the three girls must literally win their spurs and become Magic Knights, for only the combined powers of the Knights can hope to challenge Zagato and save the world. Clef helps them from time to time, and they have another friend, the rabbit-like Mokona, whose cuddly exterior hides many secrets. Nothing else is quite as it seems either; the sorcerer is in love with the princess, and each of the girls has her own secret strengths and weaknesses. If they are ever to see Tokyo again, they must work together to save Cephiro.

In the second season, the three girls are once again summoned to Cephiro, once again on the brink of oblivion. With Emeraude absent, the three kingdoms of Autozam, Farhen, and Cizeta begin an invasion of Cephiro to overthrow the pillar system. They must also contend with a girl called Nova, who seems to be Hikaru's nemesis and attacks everything she loves.

The three-part 1997 video series keeps the same basic premise but changes the story. To reflect the change, the title became simply *Rayearth*. Cephiro is slowly materializing in Tokyo and the meeting of two dimensions is causing huge earthquakes on Earth. To avert the impending disaster, Guru Clef and Lantis must find the Magic Knights whose powers can put things right. High school girl Hikaru is waiting for her friends Umi and Fu under a cherry tree with supposed magic connections when there's another strong quake, and a strangely cute rabbit-like creature, Mokona, falls out. As Hikaru chases the white rabbit and her friends follow, they are all whisked to the Tokyo Tower where they learn that they must summon the Mashin Gods, powerful sentient fighting machines, and use their powers to defeat the sorcerer Eagle Vision and his Mashin if both worlds are to be saved.

Based on a manga in *Nakayoshi* that combined elements of girls' manga with boys' action-adventure, this magical romance was a huge hit for its creators, manga collective CLAMP, whose work has not always been served well on video (see **RG VEDA**) and had considerable success in the U.S. The three heroines, linked specifically with the elements of fire, water, and air, are more "magical" in origin than anything on Cephiro, where many people and places are named for popular Japanese cars. There are references not only to anime tropes, such as destined heroes who alone can control powerful armor, and popular locations, like the Tokyo Tower that features in numerous shows, but also to Western classics—as in **ALICE IN WONDERLAND** and CLAMP's earlier **MIYUKI-CHAN IN WONDERLAND**, the girls are guided by a white rabbit.

READY FOR ADVENTURE

1989. JPN: *Boken Shite mo Ii Goro*. Video. DIR: Masamune Ochiai. SCR: Masaru Yamamoto. DES: Nami Saki. ANI: Akihiro Izumi. MUS: Toshiya Uchida. PRD: Knack. 45 mins. x 3 eps.

Forced to wait a year to retake his university exams, would-be film director Junpei jumps at the chance to leave Hokkaido and head for the big city for a job in the film business. But when he arrives, he discovers he's volunteered to work as a porn actor for the beautiful Apollo Productions director Mika. Rising through the ranks, he becomes a talent scout, "road-testing" would-be actresses in a Harajuku love hotel. Eventually, there is trouble on the set as new star Masako turns out to be understandably afraid of men. Luckily, Junpei is on hand to show her just how nice men can be. This smutty respray of

JUNK BOY was based on the 1986 manga in *Big Comic Spirits* by Nonki Miyasu. ◐

REAL BOUT HIGH SCHOOL *
2001. AKA: *Samurai Girl*. TV series. DIR: Shinichi Shoji. SCR: Aya Matsui. DES: Keiji Goto. ANI: Hiroyuki Kanbe. MUS: Takeshi Yasuda. PRD: Gonzo, Kid's Station. 25 mins. x 13 eps.
Ryoko Mitsurugi is a bubbly teenager who enjoys martial arts, both in practice and on TV in old samurai shows. The star of the school kendo team, she takes up the all-new K-Fight martial art, and soon beats all comers. Her training, however, is not as it seems and has a more practical use. One day, time stops, and the surprised Ryoko is forced to defend the frozen world from an attacking monster. Based on a manga in *Dragon* magazine by Reiji Shiga and Sora Inoue.

REAL DRIVE
2008. JPN: *RD Senno Chosashitsu*. AKA: *RD Potential Memory Investigation Room*. TV series. DIR: Kazuhiro Furuhashi. SCR: Junichi Fujisaki, Yasuyuki Muto et al. DES: Tetsuro Ueyama, Mio Ishiki, Shigenori Takada, Yusuke Takeda. ANI: Hideki Takahashi, Hiraku Kaneko, Hiroshi Yako. MUS: Hideki Taniuchi, Yoshihisa Hirano. PRD: Production I.G, D.N. Dream Partners, NTV, VAP. 23 mins. x 26 eps.
In 2061 a new way of sharing and securing information called the Meta-Real Network ("the Metal" for short) has taken over from the old-fashioned Internet. Fifty years ago Masamichi Haru was a highly specialized diver testing electronic implants for the Metal when he fell into a coma. Waking after a half century, he finds himself a paraplegic old man, in a wheelchair on an artificial island where the Metal is everywhere, with an android aide and a teenage care giver. He returns to the sea of information to search for answers to the mystery that robbed him of most of his life.
Given this outline, with its echoes of **GHOST IN THE SHELL**, it's no surprise to see Masamune Shirow's name alongside Production I.G as creator of the original story. There are plenty of other Shirowverse manifestations both in the design elements and in the story: androids made like sex dolls, including a scene that recalls the infamous lesbian boat orgy removed from the *GITS* manga abroad, questions about

consciousness, the origins of self, and the validity of memory, and issues around loyalty and friendship. However, the echoes of Shirow past resonate alongside concepts and imagery recalling **PAPRIKA** and **ROUJIN Z**—it is interesting to reflect that *Paprika's* director Satoshi Kon also worked on Otomo's film about militarizing the care of the elderly. Slip in some of Shirow's beloved real-world sci-tech references and a nod to Stanley Kubrick's 1968 masterpiece *2001: A Space Odyssey*, coat liberally with gorgeous artwork and imagery, and you have a show that is trying very hard to be the next *GITS*. It doesn't quite get there, but it's a journey worth watching.

REAL SCHOOL GHOST STORIES
1996. JPN: *Honto ni Atta Gakko Kaidan*. AKA: *School Ghost Stories That Really Happened*. Video. DIR: Moriyasu Taniguchi, Noriyuki Abe. SCR: Toshimitsu Himeno, Hiroshi Hashimoto. DES: Moriyasu Taniguchi, Masaya Onishi. ANI: Moriyasu Taniguchi. MUS: Satoshi Hirata. PRD: Shochiku Home Video, Studio Pierrot, SPE Special Works, Fuji TV. 30 mins. (v), 25 mins. x N/D eps.
A "true-life" variant of the school ghost stories that characterized the **HERE COMES HANAKO** phenomenon, the idea remained popular into the 21st century, where it was repackaged as simply **GHOST STORIES**, a TV series with a larger framing device. Heroic schoolgirl Satsuki must protect her cry-baby brother, Keiichiro, from ghosts at their new school while fending off the amorous advances of class lothario Hajime. The trio are accompanied by Momoko, a pallid, withdrawn girl who always attracts the attention of spirits, good and otherwise.

REALLY HAPPENED! SPIRIT MEDIUM TEACHER
2011. JPN: *Honto ni atta! Reibai-sensei*. TV series. DIR: Azuma Tani. SCR: N/C. DES: Masaki Hyuga. ANI: Ju Moji, Dream Force. MUS: SLF!!, sin. PRD: FROGMAN Co., DLE, NTV. 4 mins. x 22 eps.
Juri Kibayashi is a middle school history teacher with a very strange hobby: she can talk to the dead and she's a part-time exorcist. She's constantly causing problems for her class, introducing displaced ghosts, summoning the spirit of an ancient warlord into the body of a schoolgirl, fighting off invading cat aliens, and having wacky

adventures. The gags are mostly past their sell-by date and the Flash animation varies from passable to truly horrendous, but the characters have plenty of charm and their interactions are convincing enough to get you involved. It's part of NTV's **YURUANI?** gag anthology show created by DLE, based on the manga by Hidekichi Matsumoto and narrated by Shinya Takahashi.

REASON WHY SHE DOESN'T VISIT ME IN THE HOSPITAL, THE
2010. JPN: *Kanojo ga Mimai ni Konai Wake*. Video. DIR: Ken Raika. SCR: Shinichiro Sawayama, Ryu Terano. DES: Tatsumi, P-San Honda. ANI: MUS: N/C. PRD: Cotton Doll, T-Rex. 30 mins. x 2 eps.
Shinji is thinking about marrying Ai, his girlfriend of two years. Then he's involved in a traffic accident, breaks his leg, and has to stay in hospital. Ai promises to visit him every day, but when Seiji realizes that his nurse is actually his voluptuous ex-girlfriend, he starts to worry. And that's before the guy who ran him down, his roommate, his coworker, and the doctor looking after his case get involved. Based on a porn game by Lune Team Bitters. ◐

REBIRTH OF BUDDHA, THE
2009. JPN: *Buddha Saitan*. Movie. DIR: Takaaki Ishiyama. SCR: Hiroshi Okawa. DES: Masaru Sato. ANI: Masami Suda, Riku Sato. MUS: Yuichi Mizusawa. PRD: Group TAC. 115 mins.
Seventeen-year-old Sayako wants to be a journalist, following in the footsteps of a family friend she admires. Then, the friend commits suicide after the publication of a story that turns out to be wrong. Soon afterward Sayako starts to have paranormal experiences, and her little brother contracts a mysterious illness. Her boyfriend Yuki, who's at college, saves her from evil spirits and cultists and cures her brother with the help of the leader of his church. Sayako has a mission to help the world see the truth—the peaceful beliefs of the reborn Buddha who leads Yuki's church are far better than those of the evil powermongers and politicians who want to kill people. Any similarities with the Happy Science movement, whose founder Ryuho Okawa wrote the book on which this anime is based, are of course purely coincidental. No real powermongers or

politicians were harmed in the making of this anime.

RE-BIRTHDAY

1999. JPN: *Happy Birthday: Inochi Kagayaku Shunkan (Toki)*. AKA: *Happy Birthday: Life's Glittering Moment (Toki)*. Movie. DIR: Satoshi Dezaki. SCR: Setsuko Shibuichi. DES: Setsuko Shibuichi. ANI: N/C. MUS: Yuki Nakajima. PRD: Magic Bus, GoGo Visual Planning. 80 mins.

Asuka's mother doesn't like her. She seems to like Asuka's big brother Naoto, but she doesn't help Asuka deal with being bullied at school and deliberately ignores her birthday. When she tells Asuka that it would be better if she'd never been born, the little girl is so traumatized that she loses the ability to speak, and Naoto decides he has to intervene. He arranges for Asuka to go to stay with their grandparents in the country. The peaceful routines of rural life help Asuka to heal. Gradually, with the love and support of her grandparents and her best friend Megumi, she begins to understand the reasons why her mother and some of the kids at school are so cruel. She learns to confront them, help them to change, and even forgive them. And in doing so, she discovers the joy of living.

There are very few KIDS' ANIME, or indeed children's shows of any kind, that feature realistic disabled characters in major roles. This movie is an honorable exception. Weak hearts, cerebral palsy, and congenital conditions play a significant role in *Re-Birthday*, and are explicitly linked with bullying as children and adults home in on the visible difference of disability as an excuse for abuse. Writer and designer Shibuichi would direct the similarly themed MY SISTER MOMOKO at Magic Bus four years later. Director Dezaki, whose association with the studio goes back many years, was also executive producer on that title, so both clearly have a commitment to the themes of Kazuo Aoki's original story. The animation in this movie is no better than OK, but both the writing and story are absolutely inspiring. With so few shows presenting powerful, positive messages for children with disabilities, or those being bullied and doing the bullying, it is nothing short of a tragedy that this film hasn't been licensed and dubbed into English. See also HOUSE OF ACORNS and RUN.

REBORN *

2006. JPN: *Katekyo Hitman Reborn*. AKA: *Home Tutor Hitman Reborn*. TV series. DIR: Kenichi Imaizumi. SCR: Nobuaki Kishima, Hideki Mitsui, Kazuhisa Sakaguchi, Masashi Suzuki. DES: Masayoshi Tanaka, Masazumi Matsumiya. ANI: Masayoshi Tanaka, Masaki Hyuga. MUS: Toshihiko Sasaki. PRD: Artland, Reborn! Production Committee, d-rights, Dentsu, Marvelous Entertainment. 24 mins. x 203 eps. (TV), 26 mins. (online special), 3 mins. x 3 eps. (online special).

Tsunayoshi's parents are worried about his low test scores and rock-bottom self-esteem. He needs to study and to man up, so his mother hires a tutor, hoping to get a nice young man who will help and encourage the hapless teen. Instead she gets Reborn, a pint-sized childlike creature and a self-proclaimed Mafioso. Reborn tells Tsunayoshi that he's the next heir to the Vongola crime family and does all he can to help him become a true Godfather, including rounding up some minions for him. Reborn hopes to give him a stronger focus and greater willpower. Despite his determination not to be drawn into the world of crime, Tsunayoshi finds that he's becoming stronger, more confident and better at making friends.

Katekyo is a contraction of *katei kyoshi*, Japanese for "home tutor." "My Mom made me do extra study to become a Mafia crime lord" is a fascinating high concept, and Akira Amano's *Reborn!* manga exploits it to the full. The rationale for the childlike appearance of Reborn and his kind is plausibly presented and, unlike most anime, in which adult authority figures not engaged in teaching or the military have a worrying tendency to die or disappear, Tsunayoshi's family (and his Family) stick around, though naturally they never get in the way of the young protagonist and his friends and foes filling the screen with their squabbles, battles, and rites of passage. Despite a slow start—almost 20 episodes spent on scene-setting, character introduction, and comedy—it's endearing and silly, and the character designs, with their overtones of BLEACH and POLTERGEIST REPORT, are oddly appealing.

There are lacunae throughout the show, common in such long runs where slowdowns and flashbacks break up the impetus, trusting that fans are hooked and will keep coming back until the action picks up again. And of course there are the usual rehashes of anime tropes, from the girl who can't cook to collectible McGuffins like the infamous POKÉMON. Nevertheless, this uneven bit of fluff is a show you have to work at disliking. A stand-alone Internet episode, *Katekyo Hitman Reborn! Special*, was streamed on the *Shonen Jump* magazine website in 2010, taking the main characters on a tour of various holiday spots in Japan. There are also three three-minute DVD extras released in 2010 under the generic subtitle *Mr. Rebokku no Ciao Ciao Interview*.

REC *

2006. TV series. DIR: Ryutaro Nakamura. SCR: Reiko Yoshida. DES: Hideyuki Morioka. ANI: Hideyuki Morioka. MUS: Kei Haneoka. PRD: Shaft, TBS. 12 mins. x 10 eps.

Luckless 20-something Fumihiko Matsumaru has been stood up again by another date, and is just about to hurl his tickets into the trash when he meets Aka Onda, a pretty red-haired wannabe actress. Later that night, her apartment burns down and so she moves in "temporarily" with him, leading to yet another twist in the anime subgenre of not-quite-lovers becoming roommates. They must also work together without revealing their living arrangements, since Fumihiko works for a snack-food company, which hires Aka to voice the role of its mascot "cat-tree" in commercials. However, *REC*'s charm stems in part from its blatant appeal to an anime fan crowd, since while Aka may be obsessed with Audrey Hepburn, her personal vocation seems to lie in anime voice acting. If more proof were ever needed that anime has become its own self-referential fantasy world, this is it, with the "magical girlfriend" of anime cliché now transformed into a girl from the anime business itself, in an anime about people making anime. Based on the 2003 manga series by Q-taro Hanamizawa in the monthly *Sunday GX* magazine.

RECENTLY, MY SISTER IS UNUSUAL *

2014. JPN: *Saikin, Imoto no Yosu ga Chotto Okashiin da ga*. TV series, video. DIR: Hiroyuki Hata. SCR: Hideyuki Kurata. DES: Dai Suzuki. ANI: Dai Suzuki, Motohiro Taniguchi. MUS: Ryosuke Nakanishi. PRD: Project No.9,

Frontier Works, Bushiroad, Lantis, Media Factory, Showgate, Klockworx. 24 mins. x 12 eps. (TV), 24 mins. (v).

Mitsuya suffers a series of life-changing events, including her mother's remarriage, the injection into her family unit of elder stepbrother Yuya, and her parents' subsequent departure for foreign climes, leaving her stuck in the house with her new not-quite-sibling. Not-quite-incest soon ensues, but not in the usual way of anime **EROTICA AND PORNOGRAPHY**. Oh no, this time, Mitsuya is forced into compromising situations with Yuya in order to charge up the magic chastity belt that has been foisted on her by Hiyori, a ghost for whom the sexual attention of Yuya represents the final achievement required before opening a stairway to heaven. The story is sold as a romantic **COMEDY**, despite featuring a female lead compelled to seduce her own stepbrother. Meanwhile, Hiyori literally forces herself on Mitsuya, but sexual assault is apparently all right if they're both girls. To add injury to insult, the chastity belt only switches off for a limited period each hour, leading to a series of off-color gags about Mitsuya's bladder control. Based on the manga by Mari Matsuzawa in *Dragon Comics Age*. A "13th" episode was bundled with the DVD release, and there was apparently enough of a market in Japan for this nonsense for it also to be upgraded to a live-action film adaptation in 2014. The rating was "unsuitable for the under-15s," although the authors suggest it is "unsuitable for anyone." **◑**

RECORD OF LODOSS WAR *

1990. JPN: *Lodoss to Senki*. Video, TV series. DIR: Akinori Nagaoka. SCR: Mami Watanabe, Akinori Endo. DES: Yutaka Izubuchi, Nobuteru Yuki, Hidetoshi Kaneko. ANI: Eiko Yamauchi. MUS: Mitsuo Hagita. PRD: Madhouse. 30 mins. x 13 eps., 80 mins. (*Crystania Movie*), 40 mins. x 3 eps. (*Crystania*), 30 mins. (*Welcome to Lodoss*), 25 mins. x 27 eps. (*Heroic Knight*).

This video series based on the novels and gaming scenarios created by Ryo Mizuno and Hiroshi Yasuda presents role-playing games as they never were but should have been. In a world still reeling in the aftermath of a war between gods, a classic D&D party of warrior Parn, elf Deedlit, dwarf Ghim, magic-user Slayn, cleric Etoh, and thief Woodchuck set out to seek the aid of Wort the sage, a former adventurer whose early years were chronicled in the spin-off manga *Lady of Pharis*. The land of Lodoss is under threat from a revival of the power of darkness. A heroic king and his noble warlord have been turned to the dark side by an evil counselor, and the heroes of a former struggle are lending what support they can to the new young team as they travel to Wort's stronghold only to learn that he regards himself simply as an observer and is unwilling to use his great power to intervene. The dungeon party must travel on, trying to recruit allies for the fight against darkness among exotic kingdoms and dank forests, meeting evil Dark Elves, desert princes, and dragons guarding ancient treasures deep below the earth. At the end of the story, it seems that evil has been stopped in its tracks for the moment, and the young hero Parn has completed his journey from boyhood to manhood, his quest for himself.

The villains are dark and deadly enough to satisfy the keenest good-versus-evil aficionado, but they're neither motiveless nor entirely unsympathetic. One of the most tear-jerking scenes in the whole of anime occurs in episode 10, when tough-guy Ashram the Black Knight, noble servant of dark powers, affirms his eternal love for his elven mistress, Pirotessa, simply in the way he says her name as she dies in his arms. The "little people"—soldiers commanding outpost forts, thieves, and farmers—are shown in a sympathetic light, often more honorable and honest than the great kings and mages, and we learn that some of those who fought for the triumph of Light in days of yore are now on the side of Darkness. In his way the "good" sage Wort is more amoral than his dark counterpart, Karla the Gray Witch, who possesses men and topples empires to keep faith with her unshakable belief that good and evil must be kept in balance, and that when one has ruled for too long the balance must be made to shift.

Seductive music, especially the opening and ending themes, powerful faux-medieval and Art Nouveau design, and strong characters make for an attractive package. There's an effective opening sequence by veteran Rintaro, but the animation is generally undistinguished. The plotting circles and strays in places, and many elements of the dense backstory are hinted at though not explored, but the whole is involving enough to carry the viewer over such minor hiccups.

The first two videos also enjoyed a limited release in a "movie" edition in order to drum up support for the series. Ryutaro Nakamura's later movie and video sequel *Legend of Crystania* (1995 and 1996) proves less than satisfying. A promising concept is let down by low-rent designs, appalling animation, and editing that verges on the deranged in places—add to this a poor English dub and a different U.S. distributor with a nonexistent numbering policy. Set 300 years after the original and featuring characters who were supposed to be dead last time we looked, Ashram is possessed by the evil god Barbas, while Pirotessa assembles a new band of heroes to fight back. The already confusing plot of warring were-beasts is made even harder to unravel when the tape called "A New Beginning" turns out to be the last episode, coming after "Cave of the Sealed" and "Resurrection of the Gods' King."

The franchise returned briefly for Chiaki Koichi's theatrical short *Welcome to Lodoss Island* (1997), a squashed-down cartoon version rereleased on video with extra footage. In the post-**EVANGELION** boom, when producers desperately searched for anything to expand, the franchise was brought back once more, this time as Yoshihiro Takamoto's TV series *Record of Lodoss War: Chronicles of the Heroic Knight* (1998). A retelling of the second half of the original video series, *CotHK* adheres doggedly to the original books and hence rewrites some elements of anime continuity, with a number of former supporting characters in major roles, along with members of the original cast, who have hardly changed a bit, and some of whom seem to meet for the first time ... again. Young Spark fills the would-be paladin role occupied by Parn, now a bona fide hero, in the original video series. Barely competent mercenaries Shiris and Orson attack a free village and meet apprentice mage Cecil, a prissy, just-masculine version of elfin babe Deedlit from series one. Deedlit and Parn show up in time to stop a bloodbath when gentle giant Orson goes into berserker mode, and grown-up mage Slayn, also from series one, shows up with his wife and daughter in time to fill some of those expository gaps and get everyone organized into a dungeon party without too much bickering. Nothing much has changed in five years. There's another threat to the peace of the island and the supremacy of Light. Parn still idolizes the ultracool "mercenary king" Kashue and has no idea how to handle women. Deedlit still isn't sure of their relationship after five *years* of adventuring together. The world is still a reactionary place where Kashue can urge Parn, with complete sincerity, to become a king so that he can have the pleasure of treating him as an equal, and the lip service paid to serious issues with a brief refugee crisis doesn't hold up the real, important action of suborning priests and killing dragons. Despite a wonderful opening sequence, *CotHK* contains all of its predecessor's low-budget faults without any of its earnest, adventuring virtues. Yet the original, loaded with atmosphere and style, still has magic.

RECORDER AND RANDSELL *
2012. JPN: *Recorder to Randsell Do*. TV series. DIR: Hiroshi Kimura. SCR: Ryo Karasuma. DES: Naruyo Takahashi. ANI: Shiro Shibata, Toshiomi Izumi, Kata Suzuki, Kazumasa Takeuchi. MUS: Takaaki Anzai. PRD: Seven, Dream Creation, Takeshobo. 3 mins. x 13 eps. (TV1), 3 mins. x 13 eps. (TV2), 3 mins. x 13 eps. (TV3).
Two siblings have the same unusual problem: their looks. Atsushi is an elementary school kid who looks like a grown man; Atsumi is a 17-year-old high school girl who still looks like a child. Meme Higashiya's 2009 gag manga series is the source of this series of short gag cartoons, and its two follow-up series *R&R Re* in 2012 and *R&R Mi* in 2013.

RED BARON
1994. TV series. DIR: Akio Sakai. SCR: Junji Takegami, Kazuhiko Godo, et al. DES: Ryu Noguchi. ANI: Satoshi Hirayama. MUS: N/C. PRD: Tokyo Movie Shinsha, NTV. 25 mins. x 49 eps.
In the year 2020, the gladiatorial sport of Mecha Fighting (Metal Fighting in some sources) is the most popular spectator event. One hotheaded boy decides to become the champion pilot, operating

his Red Baron robot against all comers. A remake of a 1973 live-action series that featured men dressed up as giant robots—and they say there's no such thing as progress.

RED COLORED ELEGY
2007. JPN: *Sekishoku Elegy*. Video. DIR: Seiichi Hayashi. SCR: Seiichi Hayashi. DES: Seiichi Hayashi. ANI: Seiichi Hayashi. MUS: Keiichi Suzuki (Moon Riders). PRD: Toei Animation. 30 mins.
Ichiro and Sachiko are very much in love, but they can't communicate. He struggles to make a living from his comics, while her parents are eager to arrange a marriage for her. Struggling with poverty and melancholy, they drift through life side by side unable to say what they truly feel. This is part of Toei's *ga-nime* (ARGOT AND JARGON) series, adapted from director-writer Hayashi's manga of the same title, which was first published in *Garo* magazine in 1970. It summed up the spirit of counterculture, the movement for greater sexual and artistic freedom, and inspired Morio Agata's 1972 hit single, which is used as part of the soundtrack.

RED DATA GIRL *
2013. AKA: *RDG*. TV series. DIR: Toshiya Shinohara. SCR: Michiko Yokote. DES: Minako Shiba. ANI: Minako Shiba, Chisato Kawaguchi, Eriko Ito, Miyuki Nakamura. MUS: Masumi Ito, Myu. PRD: Kadokawa Shoten, Kids Station, Lantis, Klockworx, PA Works. 24 mins. x 12 eps.
Shrine maiden Izumiko Suzuhara has lived a sheltered life in the countryside, at least in part because her mother realizes that her strange abilities will cause her trouble in the modern world. If she takes off her special spectacles, she starts to see creatures from the spirit world, and if she touches an electrical device, it tends to malfunction. She is eventually revealed to be a medium capable of hosting Himegami (Divine Princess), a supernatural being with apocalyptic powers sufficient to wipe out the entire human race—which only makes the need to manage her abilities all the more pressing.
Ever since THE MELANCHOLY OF HARUHI SUZUMIYA there has been a subset within the anime-writing community that takes girls out of the gutter and elevates them

on pedestals in a new form of objectification—as hazards so dangerous that they need to be handled like nuclear waste. Izumiko is, on one level, another anime heroine struggling with superpowers (ELFEN LIED), but she is also, as the title obscurely teases, a "red data girl"—a species so rare as to be practically extinct. Like many an anime protagonist, there is the fearful possibility that her powers and good intentions might all too easily be exploited by evil forces. This series, based on a book by Noriko Ogawara, toys with the notion that Izumiko is a human "World Heritage Site," and hence unlikely to be allowed to make decisions about her own fate. Compare to similar jurisdictional issues over the female body to be found in GHOST IN THE SHELL and *The Bionic Woman*.

RED GARDEN *
2006. TV series, video. DIR: Ko Matsuo. SCR: Jukki Hanada, Tomohiro Yamashita, Mari Okada. DES: Kumi Ishii, Masatoshi Kai. ANI: Kumi Ishii. MUS: Akira Senju. PRD: Gonzo, Dentsu, GDH, Trinet Entertainment, TV Asahi. 24 mins. x 22 eps. (TV), 45 mins. (v).
Kate, Rachel, Claire, and Rose all wake feeling tired and dizzy, unable to recall anything that happened to them the night before. But this wasn't just well-to-do high school girls on a night out.... At school they learn that their classmate Lise is dead. She's just one of a spate of apparent suicides that has been spreading across New York, although their shock is soon compounded by the revelation that they, too, are all dead, killed by a monster in a mansion in the city.
The price of their resurrection is to fight for their lives night after night against humans turned into dog-like monsters. The girls take the deal: at least they'll still be New York teen princesses by day. And in between supernatural battles in the city's night-time streets, the new superpowers they seem to have acquired might just help them find out who got them into this fix.
It's GANTZ, but not as you know it. Replacing the video game machismo of the 2004 show with suspense and horror, *RG* reinvents its intense graphic violence as a game for girls. Taking anime right out of its Japanese high school comfort zone to New York creates some interesting, edgy

backgrounds and the overall look of the show is one of its principal charms. Its art style is striking, using elements of shojo manga and inventive design to create a look as visually distinctive as the Madhouse version of Ai Yazawa's divine **PARADISE KISS**. The narrative is unevenly structured and paced, but still delivers an interesting experience. The usual romantic-anime tensions around trust, friendship, and family become even more intense and painful as the girls learn more about the truth behind the suicides, and although the romantic twist isn't too hard to guess it's still poignant. The 2007 video *Red Garden: Dead Girls* is set after the TV series. Visually stunning and steeped in American TV culture, *Red Garden* handles the mix of Japanese origins and Western influences with aplomb. ◐

RED SHADOW

1987. JPN: *Kamen no Ninja Akakage*. AKA: *Masked Ninja Red Shadow*. TV series. DIR: Susumu Ishizaki, Kunihisa Sugishima, Tomoharu Katsumata, Kazuhisa Takenouchi. SCR: Yoshiyuki Suga, Toshiki Inoue, Mami Watanabe. DES: Akihiro Kanayama. ANI: Akihiro Kanayama, Michio Kondo. MUS: Shunsuke Kikuchi. PRD: Toei, Nippon TV. 25 mins. x 23 eps.

In medieval Japan, young temple boy Gennosuke disguises himself as the Red Shadow in order to fight the Cult of the Golden Eye, teaming up with color-coded allies that include the White and Blue Shadows. Another boy-ninja tale, this was one of the first "retro anime," since this nostalgic production was designed to remind parents of their own youth in 1967, when they could have read Mitsuteru Yokoyama's original manga and watched the live-action spin-off adventure TV series. The story was revived for Hiroyuki Nakano's live-action movie *Red Shadow* (2001).

RED-BLOODED ELEVEN

1970. JPN: *Akaki Chi no Eleven*. AKA: *Here Come The Superboys; Soccer Boy; Goal!* TV series. DIR: Takeshi Yamada, Yoshiyuki Tomino, Nobuhiro Okaseko. SCR: Tsunehisa Ito, Yoshi Suzuki. DES: Masahiro Ioka. ANI: Yoshiyuki Tomino, Masayuki Hayashi, Seiji Okada. MUS: N/C. PRD: NTV, DOGA Productions. 25 mins. x 52 eps.

At Shinsei high school, soccer is almost a combat sport and new team coach Teppei Matsuki is a fully paid up sadist who will push his team as hard as necessary to win. Headstrong school bad boy Shingo Tamai and his friend Ohira are determined not to be bullied into joining Matsuki's team; instead they set up a squad of their own, and at first play just for fun and struggle to keep up with Matsuki's team. As their skills progress, they play other teams and get stronger and craftier, until they face the crack Asakase high school squad and its star player Misugi Yan in the schools' final. In a tangle of subplots involving old rivalries and injuries, and a mixed-race player seeking his identity and his lost mother (who turns out to be in jail), Shingo develops his skills as a centerforward and looks forward to playing a visiting Brazilian squad. He is seriously injured in a game, but his talent, which even the legendary Brazilian Pele recognizes, is equaled by his determination. With the help of a friend of his old rival Matsuki, he recovers to help the team to victory. Definitely melodrama rather than a sports series proper, this is the first in the line of Japanese soccer soaps that stretches to **CAPTAIN TSUBASA** and beyond. Based on a manga by Ikki Kajiwara and Kosei Sonoda.

REDBREAST SUZUNOSUKE

1972. JPN: *Akado Suzunosuke*. AKA: *Red-Hips Suzunosuke*. TV series. DIR: Isao Takahata, Shigetsugu Yoshida, Tetsuo Imazawa, Minoru Okazaki. SCR: Haruya Yamazaki, Yoshitake Suzuki. ANI: Yoichi Kotabe, Shingo Araki, Hideo Kawauchi, Yoshinori Kanada, Tetsuo Imazawa, Yasuo Yamaguchi, Yoshifumi Kondo, Eiji Tamura, Hayao Miyazaki, Osamu Dezaki. MUS: Takeo Watanabe. PRD: Tokyo Movie Shinsha, Fuji TV. 25 mins. x 52 eps.

Suzunosuke Akado wishes to become a sword master, and begins to study with Shusaku Chiba, the leader of the Kitatatsu Single Sword School. Suzunosuke trains hard and also attracts the attention of his teacher's pretty daughter Sayuri. Meanwhile, the threat of civil war looms in Japan, with the mysterious Kimengumi group selecting opponents of their beliefs for attack. Suzunosuke stands up to them with his famous "swordless vacuum attack."

Based on a manga by animator Eiichi Fukui, and formerly the subject of a popular radio show, the reins in this anime production were handed to Tsunayoshi Takeuchi when Fukui died shortly after production commenced. Director Shigetsugu was nominally in charge, but temporarily obliged to hand things over to a young Isao Takahata when he was taken ill. Hayao Miyazaki and Osamu Dezaki also worked on this production as humble storyboarders, and the staff roster includes a number of Miyazaki's later collaborators, including Kanada and Kondo. The Suzunosuke story also became the subject of a live-action movie series directed by Bin Kado, Kimiyoshi Yasuda, and Kazuo Mori.

REDLINE *

2009. Movie. DIR: Takeshi Koike. SCR: Katsuhito Ishii, Yoji Enokido, Yoshiki Sakurai. DES: Katsuhito Ishii. ANI: Takeshi Koike, Hiroshi Hamasaki, Yoshiaki Kawajiri, Masanori Shino, Hiroyuki Aoyama. MUS: James Shimoji. PRD: Madhouse, Tohoku Shinsha. 102 mins.

It's all over for racer boy JP when his souped up Trans Am crashes at the finish of the illegal Yellowline contest on planet Dorothy. Meanwhile his double-crossing colleague Frisbee is merrily counting the cash from an evil interstellar syndicate that has rigged the race. The next race—the highly illegal, immensely prestigious Redline—is held only once every five years, and is scheduled to cross the face of Roboworld: a deeply private, heavily armed fascist dictatorship. Roboworld's Supreme Leader is determined to teach the racers a lesson by killing them all, preferably before the cameras of the galaxy's media outlets descend on Roboworld and take pictures of all his super-weapons, cyborg armies, and doomsday devices. The sheer risk is too much for several fellow racers, whose withdrawal from the competition puts JP back onto the starting grid, so long as he is prepared to cheat death in a race against killer opponents and enemy soldiers.

With a veritable bar-fight of contending characters and cameos from Katsuhito Ishii's earlier **HAL AND BONS**, **MOLE BROTHERS: FULL THROTTLE** and *Trava: Fist Planet* (**GRASSHOPPA**), *Redline* plays as if it is the finale of a massive series that unites multiple unrelated genres in the anime world: one participant is a fairy princess, another seems to have escaped from a beat-em-up arcade game, still another is a machine-man who is literally plugged into his vehicle. But our hero's nickname is "Sweet JP," a sneering epithet hurled at him by the others because he's too fair-minded to use landmines, rocket-propelled grenades, or tactical nukes just to win a race.

Redline is in love with the physicality of cars, replaying the love a young Ishii felt for MACHINE HAYABUSA. Even those racers who are not literally plugged in to their seats are twisted, bent, and broken by g-forces. The film's imagery is a 180-degree spinout from the naturalism of Isao Takahata or Satoshi Kon's careful re-creation of the real. Koike's filming frequently "crosses the line," switches directions, or bends the perspective of his characters as if they and their vehicles are symbiotic life forms. His anime feature is tricked out with vibrant primary colors and larger-than-life caricatures, hyper-real with the full toy-box of anime TROPES AND TRANSFORMATIONS. There is similar energy behind the microphones, with a voice cast of heavy-hitting stars, including Takuya Kimura of the boy-band SMAP (better known in anime circles as the lead in HOWL'S MOVING CASTLE) as JP, and silver-screen heart-throb Tadanobu Asano as Frisbee.

Redline is also, to Japanese eyes, a very "American" film, suffused with a love of muscle-cars and with a palette recalling a foreigner's arguably outmoded idea of what anime should be, much like KILL BILL: THE LEGEND OF O-REN. The film staked its international claims with an August 2009 premiere at Italy's Locarno International Film Festival, followed by showings in Australia, New Zealand, and the U.S.A. before its home premiere more than a year later. Its international credentials are embedded in the style and storyline. Ahead of being anime, ahead of being Japanese, ahead of being a major international feature, this is a movie by geeks, about geeks, for geeks: less *Top Gun*, more *Top Gear*.

REFRAIN BLUE

2000. Video. DIR: Norio Kashima. SCR: Takao Yoshioka. DES: Mayumi Watanabe. ANI: Mayumi Watanabe. MUS: N/C. PRD: Pink Pineapple. 30 mins. x 3 eps.
Nao is a girl in a state of some mental distress who walks into the sea and is rescued in the nick of time by Yoshihiro, a boy to whom she now latches on. He is returning to his hometown to fulfill a promise made seven years ago. It soon transpires that both are struggling to overcome the loss of a loved one, although their personal journey to healing is (a) being supervised by a mysterious spirit girl playing cupid, and (b) likely to result in nudity before the end of the show, this being from Pink Pineapple, and based on a game by elf. ◐

REI AND FUKO: SPECIAL DUTY AGENT

2006. JPN: *Tokumu Sosakan Rei to Fuko*. Video. DIR: Hideki Araki, Eisaku Wada. SCR: N/C, ZEQU. DES: Hideki Araki, Dairukabachi Q, Manabu Kodaira. ANI: Dairukabachi Q. MUS: Tomohiro Ushida. PRD: Pixy, Anime Antenna Iinkai. 30 mins. x 4 eps. (v1), 30 mins. x 2 eps. (v2).
Rei and Fuko are special agents fighting the war against drugs and crime in a future Tokyo devastated by earthquakes. However, things are worse than they envisaged—the forces of evil have supernatural tentacled backup. Expect sex, violence, gang rape, tentacle rape, and weird bodily fluids. Based on a porn game series by Black Lilith; a prequel entitled *Rei Zero* was released in 2010. ◐◑

REI REI *

1993. JPN: *Utsukushiki Sei no Dendoshi Rei Rei*. AKA: *Rei Rei the Sensual Evangelist*. Video. DIR: Yoshiki Yamamoto, Mihiro Yamaguchi. SCR: Michiru Mochizuki. DES: Kenichi Ishimaru. ANI: Oji Suzuki. MUS: Hiroyuki Ishizuka. PRD: KSS, AIC. 30 mins. x 2 eps.
Kaguya is a sexy spirit who wafts down from her home near the moon to solve sexual problems. Aided by cheeky goblin-cum-butler Pipi, she saves humanity from disaster by spreading the gospel of sexual freedom—as long as it's the freedom of *men* to have sex with whomever they choose, as long as they "really love" her. In the first story, schoolboy Mamoru lusts after arrogant Ikuko, who has no time for him since she has been corrupted by her lesbian teacher. Miss Manami, for her part, lusts after hunky local doctor Okabe, deciding to kill Ikuko so she can run off with him. Kaguya doesn't save the girl, but she does show Manami and Okabe the error of their ways and ensures that Ikuko, now properly ap-preciative of Mamoru, is restored to life before her cremation. A final scene cut from the Japanese version during production showed Manami and Oka-be getting their just desserts—each other.

Kaguya returns to help the nerdy Satoshi, a boy whose heart of gold is concealed under an obsession with as-tronomy that's boring his girlfriend Mika. No, Kaguya doesn't teach him social skills, just helps him "work through" his breast fixation, before turning him into bathwater so he can experience a girl up close. Everything works out in the end, but not before Satoshi is trapped inside a computer game, and Kaguya must en-dure the obligatory tentacle-rape to save him. Newly rejuvenated, Satoshi becomes a "real man" at last, ready to treat Mika in a fittingly dominant manner.

With an amusing pseudo-psycho-therapy subplot and some semblance of a story, *Rei Rei* compares very favorably to the lackluster erotica of the decade that followed it—thus making it even more of a surprise that this picaresque porno did not return for more than just these two episodes. Based on a manga by AIRBATS-creator Toshimitsu Shimizu, *Rei Rei* draws distantly on the *Taketori Monogatari*, one of the more famous JAPANESE FOLK TALES—the story of celestial Princess Kaguya whose search for an Earthbound husband proved fruitless. The same legend was pastiched very differently in QUEEN OF A THOUSAND YEARS and GU-GU GUNMO. After the American license lapsed, the show was rereleased in 2006 from a new distributor as *Rei Rei: Missionary of Love*. ◐

REIKO SHIRATORI I PRESUME

1990. JPN: *Shiratori Reiko de Gozaimasu*. AKA: *I'm Reiko Shiratori*. Video. DIR: Mitsuru Hongo. SCR: Ayako Okina. DES: Yumiko Suzuki. ANI: Keiko Hayashi, Takuya Saito. MUS: N/C. PRD: Ajia-do. 40 mins.
Nineteen-year-old Reiko Shiratori is a true material girl, devoted to style, snobbery, and snide put-downs. Thanks to her rich family, she feels superior to everyone she meets, but her high-class schooling has not prepared her for affairs of the heart. Refusing to admit her feelings for classmate Tetsuya Akimoto before it is too late, Reiko pursues him to Tokyo, where she enrolls at his university to try and win him back.

Based on a manga by Yumiko Suzuki, *RSIP* encapsulates the spirit of the money-mad 1980s, and was later adapted into a live-action TV series of the same name (*DE). Compare to the later HIS AND HER CIRCUMSTANCES, which also features a homecoming queen whose mask and halo slip.

RELIC ARMOR LEGACIAM

1987. Video. DIR: Hiroyuki Kitazume, Hideki Takayama. SCR: Akinori Endo. DES: Hiroyuki Kitazume, Hidetoshi Omori. ANI: Hiroyuki Kitazume. MUS: Tatsumi Yano. PRD: Atelier Giga. 50 mins.

The inhabitants of planet Libatia are under the mind control of the evil Daats. Professor Grace, escaping from this control, steals the giant robot Legacium and modifies it into a powerful weapon against them. When he is captured, his daughter Arushya manages to flee with the Legacium. Her friends Dorothy and Bric join her to fight Daats and liberate their homeworld.

RELIGION AND BELIEF

It is often said that the Japanese are "born Shinto, marry Christian, and die Buddhist," in recognition of their pragmatic attitude toward multiple beliefs. The same might be said of anime, in which the young are inculcated into rural traditions based on agrarian animism, dazzled in their teens with romance and marriage paraphernalia that is often drawn directly from Christian wedding iconography, and finally encouraged in old age to sacrifice their all for the greater good, be it as pestered parents or tormented mentors. One might interpose an additional stage, that anime children "grow up heathens," steeped as so many adventure anime are in the iconography of foreign myths.

Anime is a magpie medium, stealing flashy objects and solid building materials without discrimination; the exotic religions of the West offer rich pickings, especially as a source for icons and fetishes. As an ordinary teenage girl hearing voices, deemed to have magical powers, and defeating far stronger opponents to save her people, Joan of Arc is a prototype "magical girl": anime has used her story as inspiration for frothy shows like KAMIKAZE THIEF JEANNE and more serious works like TRAGEDY OF BELLADONNA. A shat-

tered, bleeding statue of the Virgin lends resonance to the climactic final battle between good and evil in WICKED CITY—set in a Christian church, where the heroine wields the combined powers of Death and the Madonna. Christ-like figures offer redemption in everything from FIST OF THE NORTH STAR to NAUSICAÄ OF THE VALLEY OF THE WIND. Of course, Europe and America also mine their own religious iconography for media purposes, which can lead to some confusion about which idols are being paid their due homage. The crucifix around the hero's neck in TOKYO BABYLON was inspired by pop icon Madonna, and not any Biblical character, while many of the Biblical analogies in SPRIGGAN and GHOST IN THE SHELL seem like so much set dressing.

It is sometimes difficult to make a distinction between religion, faith, and tradition. Faith, as in the individual response to the idea of the divine, is naturally less conspicuous than public practice, being also less open to examination and challenge. Tradition is where belief, religion, and history fade into the timeworn ritual backdrop of everyday life, particularly in the countryside, and hence often appears in anime for or about the very young. In their different ways both BOTTLE FAIRY and MY NEIGHBOR TOTORO allude to Japan's native Shinto religion, while JAPANESE FOLK TALES supply legendary inspirations for most anime, even if they are modernized or reimagined, as in the cases of USHIO AND TORA or SPIRITED AWAY. The anime KAMICHU goes even further and elevates a character to Shinto godhood. In PEACOCK KING the devotions of a young Buddhist monk are both set dressing and part of the storyline in a supernatural action-adventure. TENCHI MUYO!, USHIO AND TORA, ZENKI: THE DEMON PRINCE, and SHRINE OF THE MORNING MIST are all set in and around places of worship.

Like American comic creator Stan Lee before them, anime writers love mythology, with the gods of Greece, Rome, and Scandinavia cropping up in numerous guises, from the super-villains of SAINT SEIYA and ULYSSES 31 to the dysfunctional families of ARION or OH MY GODDESS! There's even an occasional nod to more exotic traditions, like the Polynesian tribal god NEORANGA, although once in Japan he quickly transmutes into a clunky yet

devoted family retainer—a cross between Lurch the butler from *The Addams Family* and an oversized, unstable rockery. While anime has yet to suffer a scandal like that which engulfed Lego's *Bionicles* in 2001, in which Maori representatives protested that their religion was demonstrably not a forgotten belief system, nor as open for abuse as the creators had thought, it has often stumbled into conflicts over what constitutes fair game in the inspirational stakes. Although many of Osamu Tezuka's works show a great respect for foreign religions and often used the crucifix as an icon of justice and transcendence, he was also the man who sanctioned the infamous "Christ's Eyeball" episode of ASTRO BOY—see CENSORSHIP AND LOCALIZATION. Cruciform imagery, much of it seemingly drawn from its appearance in misunderstood foreign movies rather than direct religious experience, often appears in anime. Examples include the Christ-metaphors of EVANGELION and an infamous episode of SAILOR MOON, heavily cut in the U.S. release, in which the supporting cast were all held captive on crystal crucifixes. Anime seems particularly enamored of Judaeo-Christian angels, either as figures of demure, cherubic innocence or gentle parental authority, in everything from the dramatic EARTHIAN to pornography like ANGEL CORE.

As in the West, many creators confuse witchcraft with Satanism, mixing their elements with impunity liable to shock some viewers. A similar confusion often substitutes the five-pointed pentagram of witchcraft (and/or demonology) with the six-pointed Jewish Star of David, witnessed as a symbol of sorcery in anime ranging from UROTSUKIDOJI to SILENT MÖBIUS. Notably, the artist Leiji Matsumoto refused to allow the use of a Star of David in this manner in an abortive remake of CAPTAIN HARLOCK, citing his unwillingness to cause religious offense. In the case of DEATH NOTE, it was the willingness of some viewers to embrace an anime's occult ideas, particularly in China where "superstition" runs counter to Communist doctrine, that led to its censure.

When anime uses religion as a story element, it is usually because of its ability to generate conflict. In HELLSING, the great schism of Christianity, which set Catholics against Protestants and devastated Europe for centuries, lives on despite a common enemy so powerful that both sides must fight it. In ANGEL SANCTUARY the conflict is the war of the fallen angels against the forces of Heaven, another concept born of Christian culture. Nuns and priests are authority figures or protectors of the weak, but more often their supposed disengagement from the world is subverted for dramatic effect, as with sexy priest Nicholas Wolfwood, heavily armed even by the standards of TRIGUN, or Sister Angela of ONE POUND GOSPEL. The sexual potential of nuns has been exploited in porn anime like HOLY VIRGINS and LEATHERMAN, but the concept of a woman vowed to gentleness and virtue, yet powerful and detached enough to deal in death, enhances the shock of violent retribution in such shows as SUIKODEN and CHRONO CRUSADE—a heavy weapon having more impact when wielded by a woman in a wimple.

In the late 1990s, *Animage* critic Maki Watanabe complained that too many anime followed Hollywood's lead in presenting Muslims as blood-crazed terrorists or ignorant peasants like those in LITTLE EL CID or GOSHOGUN, although it should also be noted that a significant number of postwar anime movies and TV specials drew on stories from A THOUSAND AND ONE NIGHTS. The scourge of history, religious fundamentalism, features in a few thoughtful modern anime like YUGO THE NEGOTIATOR and MASTER KEATON. Anime has also often embraced an educational role in the dissemination of religions. IN THE BEGINNING and SUPERBOOK both dramatized Bible stories, while Osamu Tezuka regularly used Buddhist and Shinto elements in his *Phoenix* stories (see SPACE FIREBIRD), and both Buddhism and humanism are strong influences on NIGHT ON THE GALACTIC RAILROAD. Anime's influence on the young and impressionable has also seen its use for preaching and recruitment, most conspicuously with the lavish movie productions of LAWS OF THE SUN and HERMES for the Institute for Research in Human Happiness (now renamed Happy Science), but also in lesser known works such as RAINBOW ACROSS THE PACIFIC or FAIRGROUND IN THE STARS, made as promotional vehicles for the Soka Gakkai Buddhist association. There was also a promotional anime

made for the AUM Shinrikyo organization before the 1995 Tokyo sarin gas attack, appearing to feature character designs by Shinji Aramaki, although the authors have not been able to obtain a credit list, and AUM representatives did not answer our requests for information. In the wake of the gas attack, the predilection of AUM's leader Shoko Asahara for apocalyptic science fiction, including but not limited to anime and manga, led some Japanese media to associate FANDOM's lunatic fringe with terrorism and religious cults. This later formed part of the inspiration for Kunihiko Ikuhara's PENGUINDRUM, the latter half of which is framed as a response, 16 years after the gas attack, to the likely effect it may have had on the children of the perpetrators.

Real religious figures and events appear in their historical context, as well as forming story elements in other shows, including the anime life of CONFUCIUS (although his belief system is still arguably not a religion) and the use of the martyrdom of Japanese Christians as a backdrop to NINJA RESURRECTION.

RENTAL MAGICA *
2007. TV series. DIR: Itsuro Kawasaki. SCR: Mamiko Ikeda, Makoto Sanda. DES: Minako Shiba, Masaru Ota. ANI: Minako Shiba. MUS: Jun Ichikawa, Takahito Eguchi. PRD: ZEXCS, Imagica, Kadokawa, NTT Docomo, Klockworx. 25 mins. x 24 eps.
When average Japanese teenager Itsuki Iba's father disappears, Itsuki is expected to take up the reins of the family business—a magical service agency renting out all kinds of spell-casters. But no amount of magic can help him deal with the horde of women demanding his attention. An absolutely stereotypical harem comedy (ROMANCE AND DRAMA) unredeemed by its earnest attempt to throw in all kinds of magic systems except the one that writes entertaining material; based on the 2004 light-novel series by Makoto Sanda with art by Pako.

RENTAMAN
1991. JPN: *Anime V Comic Rentaman*. Video. DIR: Takashi Watanabe, Osamu Tsuruyama, Masakazu Iijima, Eiko Toriumi. SCR: N/A. DES: N/A. ANI: N/A. MUS: N/A. PRD: Studio Pierrot. 74 mins. x 4 eps.

A short-lived, unrepeated experimental concept, *Rentaman* was a video magazine show serializing several short, episodic anime such as ABASHIRI FAMILY, AKAI HAYATE, the comedy *Hisashi Eguchi's Hisagoro Show*, and the thriller *Baku Yumemakura's Twilight Theater*. The serials were later compiled into stand-alone tapes, though the episodic nature of their origins goes some way toward explaining the cut-up storytelling of the two available in English.

RENZU *
2004. JPN: *Renzu—Futari no Kyori*. AKA: *The Distance Between the Two; Lens*. Video. DIR: Sanpo Edogawa. SCR: Isamu Hori. DES: Naomi Hayakawa. ANI: N/C. MUS: N/C. PRD: Five Ways, Wide Road. 30 mins.
Toru Shioda pushes his childhood friend Asuka Misaki out of the way of a speeding car—which saves her life, but causes him to have a leg injury that ruins his promising soccer career. He takes up photography instead, but his resentment and frustration lead him to try and rape Asuka, and the couple subsequently break up. His cram school teacher, a sexy and dominant woman, provides an outlet for these feelings, as does an attractive redhead he picks up while out girl-hunting with a friend, but his thoughts keep returning to Asuka, who still loves him despite his being so mixed up. A handful of explicit scenes gives the viewer what he bought this tape for, but there isn't time for much in the way of story or character development. Instead, this tale takes many of the childhood associations of romance anime like LOVE HINA and injects a note of bitterness and contempt—its message seemingly that sacrifice is all right, as long as it doesn't cost you anything. The title is a pun on both "lens" and *ren-zu*, "depictions of love." ⬤🅛🅝🅥

REPORTER BLUES
1990. TV series. DIR: Kenji Kodama. SCR: Ryuzo Nakanishi, Shuichi Miyashita. DES: Akio Sugino, Yukihiro Yokoyama. ANI: N/C. MUS: Pino Massara. PRD: TMS, Rever, RAI. 25 mins. x 52 eps.
Paris in the 1920s: Toni, a pretty young reporter for a daily newspaper, is crazy about the new jazz music that's sweeping Europe. In her spare time, she plays saxophone in a little jazz cellar. As she goes

about her daily work, she keeps running across the trail of one woman, Madame Lapin, who seems to be a very respectable lady, wealthy and influential and yet also involved in other, more dubious events. Toni's nose for a story could get her into serious trouble as she uncovers clues to a dangerous game.

One of the many Japanese-Italian coproductions masterminded by **SHERLOCK HOUND's** Marco Pagot, who cowrote the story with his brother Gi, this ran for two 26-episode series. The jazzy score and apealing designs from the designer of **COBRA** and **CAT'S EYE** make it attractive despite the somewhat run-of-the-mill detective stories. Broadcast on Japan's second satellite TV channel in 1991, the series ran on French TV early in the 1990s, but its biggest success has been in Italy.

REQUIEM FROM THE DARKNESS *

2004. JPN: *Kyogoku Natsuhiko Kosetsu Hyaku Monogatari*. AKA: *Kyogoku Natsuhiko KH Monogatari; Natsuhiko Kyogoku's Worldly Horror Stories*. TV series. DIR: Hideki Tonokatsu. SCR: Hiroshi Takahashi, Sadayuki Murai, Yoshinaka Fujioka, Yuu Kanbara. DES: Shigeyuki Miya. ANI: N/C. MUS: Kuniaki Haishima. PRD: Digiturbo, Nitroplus, Tokyo Movie Shinsha. 22 mins. x 13 eps.
The last years of the Tokugawa shogunate were a time of upheaval in Japan as the fast-changing 19th-century world invaded its ancient culture; yet the old tales of demons and goblins remained popular through the new era into the present. Author Momosuke Yamaoka, weary of writing for children, is on the road gathering material for a planned horror anthology book, which he intends to call *A Hundred Stories*. He meets three strange companions, shapeshifting birdcaller Nagamimi, puppeteer Ogin, and trickster monk Mataichi, who call themselves the Ongyo—see **YIN YANG MASTER**. They are "legend detectives," investigating the old tales to find the truth behind them and bring those responsible for wrongdoing to justice—compare to **MUSHI-SHI**. Each time he meets them, supernatural events and strange incidents follow, such as the capture of a *tanuki* rumored to be a shape-shifter (see **POM POKO**), or a criminal who keeps coming back from the dead.

Author Natsuhiko Kyogoku's original novel has echoes of **JUDGE** and *Zatoichi* (*DE), since Momosuke and his associates often act as agents of justice where no other justice can touch their victims, or classic tales of wanderers taking on jobs too dirty for the locals, such as **YOJIMBO**. His earlier horror works have won literary honors and found their way to the movie screen—*Kwaidan: Eternal Love (Warau Iemon)* and live-action TV, but this is the first anime based on his work. The color palette is limited and the worst of the gore implied rather than shown, which gives the show the spooky feel of late-night movies watched in a quiet, dark house. Many of the other staffers have backgrounds in both anime and live-action **HORROR AND MONSTERS**: Haishima composed the score for *Night Head* (*DE), for example, while **PERFECT BLUE** scenarist Murai also wrote episodes of *Wizard of Darkness* (*DE). **NV**

RESCUE KIDS

1991. JPN: *Kinkyu Hasshin Saver Kids*. AKA: *Saver Kids; Emergency Departure Rescue Kids*. TV series. DIR: Hajime Kamegaki, Keitaro Motonaga, Yasushi Nagaoka, Masanori Iijima. SCR: Shuichi Miyashita, Tadaaki Yamazaki. DES: Yasuo Otsuka, Osamu Nabeshima. ANI: Osamu Nabeshima. MUS: N/C. PRD: Studio OX, Tokyo Movie Shinsha, Sotsu Agency, TV Tokyo. 25 mins. x 50 eps.
Brothers Ken and Go and their sister Ran band together to defeat an evil genius in a Darth Vader-style helmet, plotting to take over the world with his "destroid" robot. They use all the resources of the family robot rental business to stop him in this domestic comedy. Any family-based science fiction series runs the risk of comparison with *Lost in Space*, especially if it throws in a villainous nemesis with delusions of grandeur. *RK* uses science fiction in the same way, as an exotic backdrop for the sibling bickering and minor domestic incidents that reflect its own society, rather than an exploration of alternative possibilities—although Japan has embraced the principle of the domestic robot more thoroughly than America. TMS marketed the show in Europe in the 1990s under the title *Rescue Kids*, and it was dubbed into Spanish and screened in South America. Based on an idea by **LUPIN III**—creator Monkey Punch.

RESCUE WINGS

2006. JPN: *Yomigaeru Sora*. AKA: *Revitalizing Sky*. TV series. DIR: Katsushi Sakurabi. SCR: Fumihiko Takayama, Seishi Minakami. DES: Tetsuya Takeuchi, Takashi Hashimoto, Toshiyuki Tokuda. ANI: Tetsuya Takeuchi, Takashi Hashimoto, Hiroshi Tomioka, Yutaka Karyu. MUS: Hayato Matsuo. PRD: JC Staff, Bandai Visual. 25 mins. x 13 eps.
Kazuhiro Uchida doesn't like his new job. He was training to be a fighter pilot with the Japan Air Self-Defense Force, but a lack of war (**SKY CRAWLERS**) means he has to carry out helicopter rescue missions instead. Resenting the discipline and routine, he gradually begins to realize the importance of the role—and the fact that there are no top guns in a rescue team. Action, adventure, realism, and not a streak of fantasy in sight make this an engaging show for those who've outgrown the superpowered-boy-ninja-of-the-month formula, although its complete lack of toy merchandising potential is a handicap in a market where most anime is **ADVERTISING AND SPONSORSHIP**. A 2009 live-action movie version was directed by Masaaki Tezuka, also known for *Godzilla vs MechaGodzilla* (2002) and *Samurai Commando Mission 1549* (2005.) Listen out for a musical homage to 1960s children's TV hit **MADCAP ISLAND**.

RESIDENT EVIL: DEGENERATION *

2008. JPN: *Biohazard: Degeneration*. Movie. DIR: Makoto Kamiya, Toyoshi Minamino. SCR: Shotaro Suga. DES: Naoyuki Onda, Takeshi Takakura, Shui Wen Tsai, Shiho Tamura, Fumi Sugawara, Decosuke, INEI. ANI: Atsushi Doi, Yukinobu Fujimatsu. MUS: Tetsuya Takahashi. PRD: Digital Frontier, CAPCOM, Sony Pictures Entertainment (Japan). 97 mins. (m1), 100 mins. (m2).
Seven years ago something very bad happened in Raccoon City after a pharmaceutical company had an accident with some of its experimental material. Now history threatens to repeat itself with the spread of a deadly virus. U.S. Agent Leon S. Kennedy and rescue worker Claire Reidfield race against time to try and prevent it in this CGI movie based on CAPCOM's hugely successful *Resident Evil* game series, known as *Biohazard* in Japan.

Video-game anime face constantly rising demands from fans, not just in terms of storyline but in terms of the animation itself (**Gaming and Digital Animation**). With so many games containing hours of animation, and so many aficionados holding decided views about their favorite characters, it's a struggle to create a satisfying scenario that looks as good as the game itself. Like *The Spirits Within* (**Final Fantasy**), this movie's CGI was state-of-the-art in 2009, but in a fast-developing medium that counts for little; we might as well be talking about *Do You Remember Love?* (**Macross**), and sadly, in story terms, *RE: Degeneration* is still far below the level of that glorious antique. CAPCOM and Sony virtually acknowledged this with an extremely limited theatrical release in Japan and the U.S.A.; it was never expected to pack movie theaters, but on DVD it sold respectably.

A second movie, *RE: Damnation* (*Biohazard Damnation*), appeared in September 2012, seemingly ahead of its scheduled release. This time Leon is in a fictional bit of the former Soviet Union: same mission, different babes, same huge crew required to make the pixels move. There are over 30 people credited on the animation team, twice that many on the CG team, almost 60 on the character team, 18 people working on cloth simulation, 23 on facial animation, and a team of 15 in Eastern Europe handling the models. With studios in Taiwan, China, and Thailand joining the party, and a team of Western motion-capture artists providing the movement for the lead characters, one might reasonably argue that this is just as much an international production as a Japanese one (**False Friends**). ⓥ

RESIDENTS OF THE ASHIARAI HOUSE
2010. JPN: *Ashiarai Yashiki no Junin-tachi*. Video. DIR: Yoshihide Ibata. SCR: N/C. DES: N/C. ANI: Yutaka Arai. MUS: Koichi Kikuchi. PRD: Studio NOA. 6 mins.
Based on Tokuichi Minagi's manga, this short anime tells the story of a hotpot dinner at the Ashiarai Yashiki apartment house, where Fukutaro Tamura lives with a motley crew of human, demon, and mythological neighbors. It was bundled with volume 10 of the limited edition collected comics, as a try-out for a possible animated series that didn't materialize. The voice actors who made the video also

voiced a three-part CD drama bundled with volume 11 of the same limited edition in 2011. A further CD drama with five separate stories was bundled with volume 12 in 2012, but no further animation has been announced—evidence that even a popular manga is still only one of many stories jostling for attention in the Japanese media market. A *yashiki* is an old-fashioned mansion, one of several archaic or foreign words for "house" commonly used in Japan to make an apartment block sound more interesting than it is (**Maison Ikkoku**).

REUNION
2011. Video. DIR: N/C. SCR: PON. DES: Hikaru Kinohara. ANI: Hikaru Kinohara. MUS: N/C. PRD: PoRO. 30 mins. x 2 eps.
Yuji is working through the summer, staying at his uncle's house. After an unsuccessful romance with local girl Saki and a completely accidental sexual encounter with a strange girl, he gets back to school only to find rookie teacher Rie and bad-girl Mao both after his body. How can a boy be expected to stay out of trouble? Based on an erotic game by Grand Cru. ⓞ

RG VEDA *
1991. JPN: *Seiden Rg Veda*. AKA: *Holy Scripture R(i)g Veda*. Video. DIR: Hiroyuki Ebata, Takamasa Ikegami. SCR: Nanase Okawa. DES: Mokona Apapa, Tetsuro Aoki, Kiichi Takaoka, Futoshi Fujikawa. ANI: Tetsuro Aoki. MUS: Nick Wood. PRD: Animate Film. 45 mins. x 2 eps.
Ashura the Lord of Heaven is betrayed by his wife and murdered by her lover, his chief general. The usurper rules for 300 years, until the day when the prophesied band of six warriors arrives to defeat him. But there are only five of them, so they wander around a bit looking for the missing slowpoke, while various people go on about "things that shall be" and "that which is written." By the time they find the latecomer, it's time for the credits to roll.

Based on a manga by the CLAMP artistic collective who gave us **CardCaptors**, *RV* is one of many of their works that has been poorly served in anime form. Like many anime designed as ads for much longer manga (e.g., **Compiler**), *RV* finishes before it's even begun, with the band of heroes heading off to do great deeds, frustrating

English-speaking fans who want to know how the story ends but cannot read the original.

The English dub uses genuinely British accents with mixed success; plummy goddesses ordering around minions sound rather good, but the iconoclastic gang of farting, bickering heroes seem like Enid Blyton's Famous Five on safari. Although George Roubicek's script is fine, *Rg Veda* suffers (like many anime) from being transliterated instead of translated. The fact that we're watching a Japanese fantasy retelling of Hindu myth is interesting, but the script keeps names in their Japanese form, so we never find out that Taishakuten is really Indra, Karura is Garuda (see **Karula Dances**), Kujaku is Mahamayuri Vidyarajni (see **Peacock King**), Kendappa is Gandharva, and Yasha is Yaksha. There are a few nice moments of fantasy, like the butterflies who are "messengers of darkness," and the mad Princess Aizen Myoo (Ragaraja, a red-skinned, three-eyed, six-armed *male* demon in the original), who imprisons Yasha in a castle of ice, but it's all been done better elsewhere—chiefly in the pious Indian coproduction **Ramayana**.

The production company pretentiously used Sanskrit orthography to write the title, not expecting the English distributors to mistake the opening two letters for initials—it's thus pronounced "Rig Veda" not "Ah Gee Veda."

RGB ADVENTURE
2006. TV series. DIR: Yuki Kinoshita, Yuichi Tachikawa. SCR: Naoyuki Sakai. DES: Yuki Kinoshita, Hidenori Nakahara. ANI: Masami Suda, Yuki Kinoshita, Takahiro Goto. MUS: Satoru Ida. PRD: ACC, Production, Yoyogi Animation Gakuin. 24 mins. x 6 eps.
An SF adventure based on the three primary colors of light—red, blue, and green—was made as an eight-minute CGI animation for a ride attraction in 1998, based on an idea by Monkey Punch. In 2005 producer Nobuyuki Sugenoya reworked the basic idea into entirely new characters and story and planned a 26-episode series. Two *Making of…* prequels were aired on TBS in November 2006, including staff interviews and English and Japanese versions of the 1998 CGI animation. However, only six complete episodes were broadcast, followed by an

"extra episode" made up of edited footage and an omnibus edition in January 2007. The reason given was "the circumstances of the production company." Five more episodes are rumored to be completed but never aired.

Although the remaining episodes were eventually released as a CD drama, rumors of censorship, sponsor withdrawal, and lawsuits surround the production, and at least one person credited as an animation director was removed from the official credits after stating on his own blog that he'd never even heard of the project. Another was the subject of a court case in Japan, alluding to unkept promises to animators. The crucial issue was a set of 23 character designs intended for one medium and exploited in another, much to the annoyance of an artist who didn't feel he'd been properly compensated in the first place. The Japanese judge's final ruling is freely available online, and makes for an intriguing window into conditions in the Japanese media in the early 1990s, as well as prevailing attitudes among certain managers, who seem to have hoped that "room and board" constituted reasonable part-payment for the creation of exploitable intellectual property. It is in order to avoid cases such as this that several companies assign copyright to house pseudonyms such as Hajime Yadate or Izumi Todo, rather than run the risk of facing angry designers who do not accept that their creations were work-for-hire created on company time. Compare to KIBA, which was similarly acrimonious and informative.

This mysterious oddity is entirely unrelated to the 2007 visual novel *RGB* illustrated by Hiro Suzuhira and its spin-off manga by Hina Shirogane.

RIDE BACK *
2009. JPN: *Rideback*. TV series. DIR: Atsushi Takahashi. SCR: Hideo Takayashiki. DES: Satoshi Tasaki, Kazuki Higashiji. ANI: Satoshi Tasaki. MUS: Takafumi Wada. PRD: Madhouse, Geneon, NEC Interchannel. 25 mins. x 12 eps.
The near future, in a world run by a monolithic group known as the Global Government Plan (GGP). Rin Ogata's dreams of following in her famous mother's footsteps with a ballet career were ended by injury, but the training proves unexpectedly useful when she goes back to college in an effort to rebuild her life. The balance and fine motor control that ballet gave her make her ideally suited to pilot a Rideback, a transforming motorcycle that draws her into the conflict between GGP and the resistance movement. Based on Tetsuro Kasahara's 2003 manga, this story of a girl rebuilding her life and seeking her true self is far more than a simple mecha adventure. It suffers from being too short, so the multiple story possibilities are simply sketched and not explored, but the engaging protagonist, beautiful animation, and subtle symbolism make it an intriguing package. ⓥ

RIDE OF THE VALKYRIE *
2004. JPN: *Ikusa Otome Valkyrie*. AKA: *I Dedicate Everything to You—The Valkyrie*. Video. DIR: Hiromi Yokoyama, Toshiharu Sato, Makoto Kanazawa, Tatsumi, Ken Raika. SCR: Makoto Kanazawa, Shinichiro Sawayama, Ryu Terano. DES: Hagio, Tatsumi, Makoto Tamaru, Mamoru Kobayashi, P-san Honda. ANI: Hagio, Tatsumi. MUS: N/C. PRD: Himajin Planning, Marigold (Cotton Doll), T-Rex. 30 mins. x 2 eps. (v1), 28 mins. x 2 eps. (v2, *Shinsho*), 30 mins. x 3 eps. (v3, *IOV2*), 30 mins. x 3 eps. (v3, *IOVG*).
Valkyries are the virgin warriors of the Norse god Odin (**RELIGION AND BELIEF**), but since this is a porn anime like **ARMY MAIDEN SUVIA** and not Norse mythology they have been stripped of their role as choosers of the slain for glory in Valhalla. Instead they protect humans from demon attacks. Duke, the half-human, half-Asgardian leader of the dark hordes, has been humiliated and ostracized for years because of his human blood, and is out for revenge. Now he's found a way through the Valkyries' defenses, thanks to the goddess Freya. Based on a porn game by Rune, this two-part video had several rereleases in Japan. A sequel followed in 2006, under the title *Ikusa Otome Valkyrie Shinsho*, and the second game was animated as *Ikusa Otome Valkyrie 2* in 2008. For *Ikusa Otome Valkyrie G,* based on the third game and made in 2012, Ryu Terano's script follows in the same track as its precursors, gleefully unbound by history or mythology; expect tentacles, large syringes, and perky girls with their hair in ribboned pigtails. ⓝⓥ

RIDING BEAN *
1989. Video. DIR: Yasuo Hasegawa. SCR: Kenichi Sonoda. DES: Kenichi Sonoda, Kinji Yoshimoto, Satoshi Urushibara, L. Lime, Yoshihisa Fujita. ANI: Masahiro Tanaka, Osamu Kamijo, Hiroya Ohira, Jun Okuda. MUS: David Garfield, Phil Perry. PRD: Artmic, AIC. 45 mins.
Bean Bandit is known as the Roadbuster; he's one of the best driver/couriers in the business. He makes a living on the outside edge of the law, but he's one of the good guys down deep, a true antihero with a heart of gold. He and his business partner, Rally Vincent, unwittingly get involved with psychotic kidnapper Semmerling, who sets them up to take the rap when her victim is killed, but they fight their way out in a hail of bullets and a screech of brakes. The story ends with nobody the winner and few survivors, but the kidnapper is "retired," permanently, and Bean and Rally live to keep on hustling.

This is one of the most interesting and watchable of anime actioners—made with a real love of Hollywood chase movies including *The Blues Brothers, Bullitt,* and *The French Connection.* Watch, too, for Japanese references to such anime as **LUPIN III**, especially in the cat-and-mouse relationship of cop and criminal. Some of the best car chases in anime are routed along the streets of Sonoda's beloved city of Chicago. Director Hasegawa also lets the darker side of Sonoda's manga show through the lighthearted take on an American genre; the violence and amorality of Semmerling's lifestyle are real and chilling, and her abusive, sadomasochistic relationship with an adoring child-slave is clearly spelled out without any need for sexual explicitness. Following the same studio disputes that truncated **BUBBLEGUM CRISIS**, ownership of the *Riding Bean* property became difficult to determine, and the franchise seemed finished. However, Sonoda recycled some of the characters and situations in his later **GUNSMITH CATS**—a radically different Rally becomes a bounty hunter, the child-sex subplot returns in the form of her partner Minnie May, and Bean himself has many cameo roles in the manga, though he does not appear in the anime. ⓛⓥ

RIN X SEN
2010. JPN: *Rin x Sen: Hakudaku Onna Kyoshi*

to Yarudomo. AKA: Rin x Sen: Steamy Woman Teacher and Her Violators. Video. DIR: Hiromi Yokoyama. SCR: Ren Soto. DES: Si Min Lee. ANI: Si Min Lee. MUS: N/C. PRD: Suzuki Mirano. 30 mins. x 2 eps.

Urara is looking forward to her wedding when her fiancé disappears. A debt collector comes to her house and says her fiancé owes money that she has to pay; she has no money so accepts his offer of a job at a boys' school to pay it off. The job involves gang rape and sexual slavery. Based on a porn game by Guilty+; a crossover with **RAN ® SEM**, entitled Rin x Sen + Ran® Sem Cross Mix was released in 2013. ❶❷❸

RIN: DAUGHTERS OF MNEMOSYNE ∗
2008. JPN: Mnemosyne—Mnemosyne no Musumetachi. TV series. DIR: Shigeru Ueda. SCR: Hiroshi Onogi. DES: Mitsuru Ishihara, Yumiko Kondo. ANI: Mitsuru Ishihara. MUS: Takayuki Negishi. PRD: Xebec, AT-X, GENCO, Showgate, VAP. 46 mins. x 6 eps.

Rin Asogi is not just an office lady. That's her cover for her private investigation agency work. With her cute little partner, Mimi, Rin explores the dark underbelly of modern society. But modern society doesn't mean much to her; Rin has far wider concerns, as the series soon reveals, spanning over 60 years of espionage by an unaging, undying protagonist. This series, which also has a book and manga adaptation published in the same year, was made as an anniversary project for AT-X, a channel with claims on the affections of those who like their anime sleazy and uncensored. **GUNSMITH CATS** it most emphatically isn't, though the older sister/jailbait/devoted comrades set-up of Rin and Mimi suggests that's what it would like to be; but if what you're after is sleazy entertainment masquerading as a sophisticated fantasy thriller, this is for you. ❶❷

RINGETSU ∗
2006. AKA: Bright Moon. Video. DIR: Yoshitaka Higuchi. SCR: Osamu Momoi. DES: Gaokun, Kiyotoshi Aoi, Hiromu Sato (Itaru Studio). ANI: Kenchi Hattori, Gaokun. MUS: N/C. PRD: Selen, Milky. 27 mins. x 3 eps. (v1), 28 mins. x 2 eps. (v2).

The Rindo family has been cursed for generations to bear only daughters. The sole way round the curse is to marry members of the Higetsu family and have a baby fast—by the next red moon. It seems to work, because Naoto Rindo was born. Now it's his turn to try curse-breaking with one of the four Higetsu sisters. Naturally there'll be some sampling to do, because this is based on a porn game by Selen. The sequel Shin (New) Ringetsu appeared in 2008 to promote the new game and involves Naoto's chosen sister Suzune falling into a coma and placing her soul in a toy ring. The only way to bring her out of the coma is for her younger sister Ayumi to wear the ring while having sex with Naoto and getting pregnant. ❶

RINGING BELL ∗
1978. JPN: Chirin no Suzu. AKA: Chirin's Bell. Movie. DIR: Masami Hata. SCR: Takashi Yanase. DES: Takashi Yanase. ANI: Shigeru Yamamoto, Sadao Miyamoto, Toshio Hirata. MUS: Taku Izumi. PRD: Sanrio. 46 mins.

Chirin the lamb is orphaned when the bad wolf Wor (the "Wolf King" in the U.S. dub) kills his mother. Chirin sets out for revenge but has a change of heart. Despairing of his weak nature, he begs the wolf to teach him how to be tough and learns how to be a predator from his parent's killer. Battered, bruised, and half drowned, the lamb is put through a heartless regime of torment until he is toughened into a vicious ram with a "reputation for ruthless killing." Two years later, Chirin is led by Wor in an attack on the farm where he was born. Seeing a ewe vainly fighting to protect her offspring, Chirin is reminded of his mother and turns on the wolf—killing his surrogate father. However, the rest of the flock is afraid of Chirin, and he remains an outcast, forced now to wander without any companionship at all. Chirin is "never seen again," though it is said that sometimes the sheep hear the distant tinkle of the bell around his neck.

A mind-bogglingly disturbing "children's film" that makes Bambi look like a comedy, **ANPANMAN**-creator Takashi Yanase's children's book is an unexpectedly nasty outing for the **HELLO KITTY** studio Sanrio, featuring sing-along lyrics such as "We will travel, wolf and ram, and we'll ravage all the land." Compare to **ON A STORMY NIGHT**. ❷

RINKAN CLUB
2011. AKA: Gang Rape Club. Video. DIR: Sadayamanawa. SCR: Konutan. DES: Sadayamanawa. ANI: N/C. MUS: N/C. PRD: Anime Lilith, Pixy. 27 mins. x 2 eps.

In feudal Japan a scorned woman set a terrible curse on those who mocked her. The Rinkan Club has sought to defuse the curse of Konohanasakuya-hime by selecting (or should that be kidnapping?) women who look like her at the new moon and full moon, and forcing them to submit to "public opinion." The public opinion is, of course, male, and the only resemblance required to the long-dead princess seems to be a set of knockers, because this is a porn anime based on a game by Lilith, with original character designs by Kohaku Sumeragi. ❶❷

RINTARO
1941–. Pseudonym for Masayuki Hayashi, often miscredited outside Japan as Taro Rin. Born in Tokyo, Rintaro graduated from Takada Middle School and began working in 1958 for Toei Animation. Subsequently, he has managed to turn up on the credits listings for most of the landmark anime of the latter half of the 20th century, beginning with **PANDA AND THE MAGIC SERPENT** (1958). He moved to Mushi Production in 1963 in time to work on both **ASTRO BOY** and **KIMBA THE WHITE LION** and became one of the early cheerleaders for Tezuka's move into limited animation as an artistic opportunity, and not merely a budgetary decision. After going freelance in the late 1960s, he worked on **CAPTAIN HARLOCK**, before gaining his feature direction debut with one of the **GALAXY EXPRESS 999** spin-offs in 1979. He was one of three directors of note deemed worthy of inclusion in the **NEO TOKYO** anthology (1987), and subsequent work has included further feature films and video work, such as **DAGGER OF KAMUI**, **FINAL FANTASY**, **DOOMED MEGALOPOLIS**, and **METROPOLIS**.

RIO: RAINBOW GATE ∗
2011. JPN: Rio RainbowGate [sic]. TV series. DIR: Takao Kato. SCR: Mayori Sekijima. DES: Hisashi Shimura, Ryoka Kinoshita. ANI: Hisashi Shimura. MUS: Atsushi Umebori. PRD: Xebec, avex entertainment, Pony Canyon. 24 mins. x 13 eps.

Rio Rollins is a casino dealer employed at the Howard Resort, an island casino. She's the daughter of another legendary dealer and is credited with bringing luck to gamblers just by walking past them, earning her the nickname "Goddess of Victory" (BLACK JACK). Her life changes when she befriends a little girl whose grandfather has come to play at the casino, and is drawn into a mysterious game called the Gate Battle. She's about to learn things about her family, friends, and boss that she never imagined, as the battle to be known as the world's greatest casino dealer unfolds. Based on KOEI Tecmo's *Rio* series of pachinko games, with original character design by Kotaro, but also recalling card-collection anime aimed at younger viewers, such as CARDCAPTORS and YU-GI-OH.

RISE AND FALL OF THE DINOSAUR KINGDOM, THE

1978. JPN: *Kyoryu Okoku no Kobo.* TV series. DIR: Eiichi Yamamoto. SCR: Eiichi Yamamoto. DES: Shigeo Itahashi. ANI: N/C. MUS: Hiroki Tamaki. PRD: Eizo Kiroku, Yomiuri TV, Nippon TV. 25 mins. x 6 eps.
After the first life-forms evolve on Earth, the world explodes into giant, terrifying action as the dinosaurs arrive. They are the strongest, largest creatures ever to walk on land; their achievements are chronicled in this brief documentary series that mixes diagrams, live-action photography (*not* of dinosaurs), and disappointingly cartoony dinosaur animation closer to *Barney* than *Jurassic Park*.

RISKY SAFETY *

1999. JPN: *Omishi Maho Gekijo: Risky/Sefty.* AKA: *Omishi Magical Theater Risky Safety.* TV series. DIR: Koji Masunari. SCR: Yosuke Kuroda. DES: Takuya Saito. ANI: Kazushi Nomura, Kenichi Hirano. MUS: Tamiya Terashima. PRD: APPP, Victor Entertainment, WOWOW. 8 mins. x 24 eps.
Tomboy apprentice Risky is trying to graduate as a fully-fledged agent of Death. She fixes on schoolgirl Moe Katsuragi as the victim who will prove she can handle the job. Unfortunately for her, she has been accidentally conjoined with apprentice angel Safety, a perky type who's always doing good and cheering things up. Whenever somebody says something nice, the good side of the duo takes over and Risky turns into Safety. Death-gods can only take someone's life when the person is feeling sad, and while Safety keeps Moe cheerful,

Risky has no chance of succeeding. Ray Omishi's manga combines the shifting changes of RANMA ½ and the "angel/demon on my shoulder" concept and wraps them in spun sugar, with the dark side as cute and lovable as the agent of light and Moe treating both like pets or toys, using them as confidantes and friends through mini-adventures based on Japanese folklore, festivals, and everyday life—compare to BOTTLE FAIRY. Shown as part of the *Anime Complex* slot on WOWOW with other shortform shows including NEORANGA and RIZELMINE.

RISTORANTE PARADISO *

2009. TV series. DIR: Mitsuko Kase. SCR: Shinichi Inotsume. DES: Itsuko Takeda. ANI: N/C. MUS: Ko-ko-ya. PRD: Flying Dog, Fuji Pacific MUS, Fuji TV, David Production. 23 mins. x 11 eps.
Nicoletta's mother Olga abandoned her when she was just a child, leaving her grandparents to raise her on a farm in the country. Now 21, Nicoletta heads to Rome and tracks down her mother, who has a new husband and a tiny restaurant. The restaurant has a unique style—its intimate space is staffed entirely by middle-aged waiters, all wearing spectacles. And they all have the manners of old-fashioned gentlemen—or, if you want to use the terminology of Japanese fangirls, butlers. Nicoletta's mother is horrified to see her daughter; her new husband married her not knowing she'd already been married and divorced. Desperate to keep their relationship secret, she puts her daughter to work in the restaurant kitchen where she's bullied by the cook in echoes of CINDERELLA and A LITTLE PRINCESS. Obviously their relationship needs a lot of work—but it's not the only love Nicoletta will learn about in Rome. This charmingly animated evocation of Rome, good food, and delightfully old-fashioned romance is based on Natsume Ono's 2005 manga, a tribute to a city, a cuisine, and a culture from a storyteller deeply in love with Italy.

RITA AND MACHIN

2010. JPN: *Rita to Nantoka.* AKA: *Rita et Machin.* TV series. DIR: Jun Takagi, Pon Kozutsumi. SCR: Yoichi Takahashi, Eriko Shinozaki, Yoshimi Narita, Gen Shiba. DES: Kazuhiro Hotchi, Kyoko Matsugae, Tomohiro

Maruyama. ANI: Saya Takamatsu. MUS: Yukie Mizugaki. PRD: Nippon Animation. 5 mins. x 26 eps.
Cheeky five-year-old Rita has the world's laziest dog. Their adventures and their day to day life with Mama and Papa, her teacher and friends, have made Jean-Philippe Arrou-Vignod and Olivier Tallec's picture books a hit all over the world, with translations into more than 15 languages. They could be compared to *Peanuts* except that the backgrounds are much more richly detailed and involve far more of the adult world than Charles Schulz's classic cartoon, where the characters have only the props absolutely necessary for the moment: Rita's world is a slightly updated version of "the Paris of our dreams" that made illustrator Raymond Peynet so popular in Japan.

RIZELMINE

2002. TV series. DIR: Yasuhiro Muramatsu, Hiroyuki Okuno. SCR: Naruhisa Arakawa. DES: Miwa Oshima. ANI: N/C. MUS: Toshihiko Sahashi. PRD: IMAGIN, m.o.e, Madhouse, WOWOW, Kid's Station. 15 mins. x 24 eps.
Fifteen-year-old Tomonori Iwaki comes home from school one day to find that the Japanese Government has married him to an insufferably perky 12-year-old girl. Rizel is the result of a government experiment in artificial humans, a prototype with the unfortunate design flaw of unleashing incredible destructive power by crying explosive tears when she feels sadness at being unloved. Merely adopting such replicants into a loving family with suitable role models doesn't seem to be an option, so they decide to make her happy by marrying her to a boy who doesn't want her—compare to FINAL APPROACH. The result is the search for love common to all *Pinocchio* clones from ASTRO BOY onward, combined with the pathological neediness of KEY THE METAL IDOL and the many, many "romantic" anime aimed at teenage couch-potato boys who think if they sit in their room long enough, FedEx will *deliver* them a girlfriend, and one who actively seems to enjoy being treated like a doormat. Based on a manga by DNANGEL creator Yukiru Sugisaki and part of the *Anime Complex Night* slot on WOWOW and Kid's Station, with 12 episodes shown between April and June and 12 between October

and December, alongside **HANAUKYO MAID TEAM** and the live-action *Steel Angel Kurumi Pure* (*DE). In the latter part of the run, Rizel gained the ability to transform into a well-endowed, older version of herself, in the style of **MARVELOUS MELMO**, thereby completing the box-ticking references to old magical-girl shows. **◎**

ROAD TO MUNICH

1972. JPN: *München e no Michi*. TV series, TV special. DIR: Masaaki Osumi. SCR: Soji Yoshikawa, Seiji Matsuoka. DES: Takeshi Osaka. ANI: Norio Yazawa. MUS: Takeo Watanabe. PRD: Nihon TV Doga, TBS. 25 mins. x 15 eps. (TV), 25 mins. (special).

After winning a bronze medal in the 1964 Tokyo Olympics and silver in Mexico in 1968, it seems like the Japanese men's volleyball team is in with a chance for gold. A harsh training regime begins in 1972 as the world prepares for the Munich Olympics, with the Japanese team under the firm management of Yasutaka Matsudaira.

Each episode introduces one of the players from the real-life team, often using real-world backgrounds, but using anime to depict the players themselves, since filming them for real would have been in contravention of Olympic rules on amateurs and sponsorship. Although the series ended before the final result, as with **YAWARA!** life imitated art, and the men's team won. A bonus "16th" episode, *Gold Medal of Tears* (*Namida no Kin Medal*), was made after the victory and broadcast in September 1972, in the timeslot that had been taken by *RtM*'s successor, **MON CHERIE COCO**. Considering the tragic implications of the title, it seems possible that the subject included not only the Japanese team's victory, but also some treatment of the effect on the competition of the infamous Munich Massacre, in which Palestinian terrorists kidnapped Israeli athletes and eventually gunned down their surviving hostages during an airport shootout with German police.

ROBBY AND KEROBBY

2011. JPN: *Robby to Kerobby*. TV series. DIR: Yu Ko. SCR: Yuji Kawahara. DES: Koji Watanabe, Etsuko Matsunaga. ANI: Fujio Suzuki. MUS: Kei Haneoka. PRD: A-1 Pictures, Aniplex, TV Osaka, We've, Inc., Yomiko Advertising. 52 eps x 25 mins.

A little robot and his little robot frog have slightly naughty adventures in the series for small children, created by Gen Kurosaki for Aniplex.

ROBIN AND HIS 100 FRIENDS

2010. JPN: *Robin-kun to Hyakunin no Otomodachi*. TV series. DIR: Max Weintraub. SCR: Hiroyuki Hashimoto. DES: N/C. ANI: N/C. MUS: Kentaro Kihara. PRD: PansonWorks, Sony Music Entertainment. 6 mins. x 13 eps.

Robin likes to work things out for himself and invent solutions alone. When his family moves from downtown to Green Village, he decides to make lots of friends. In simple pop-art pictures and vivid colors, this short show asks questions about true ecological awareness and real friendship. Panson Works specialize in creating character images that can be merchandised across a range of platforms, and Robin and his friends are already available as capsule toys, on socks and sandals, watches and t-shirts.

ROBIN HOOD *

1990. JPN: *Robin Hood no Daiboken*. AKA: *Great Adventures of Robin Hood; Robin Hood Junior*. TV series. DIR: Koichi Mashimo. SCR: Tsunehisa Ito, Katsuhiko Chiba, Hiroyuki Kawasaki. DES: Masamitsu Kudo, Tomohiro Hirata, Torao Arai. ANI: Masamitsu Kudo, Chuichi Iguchi. MUS: Fuminori Iwasaki. PRD: NEP, NHK, Tatsunoko. 25 mins. x 52 eps. (TV), 75 mins. (m).

In 12th-century England, the evil Baron Alwine and Abbot Hereford are in league with the devil in their quest for power. Alwine burns the entire Huntingdon family in their castle; only 14-year-old Robin and his three cousins Will, Winifred, and Barbara escape into the forest where they meet Friar Tuck, an old friend of Robin's father. He guides and protects the young orphans as best he can, and when they meet Little John and his band of teenage outlaws, they determine to fight for justice. The beautiful Marian Lancaster, daughter of a noble family, is kidnapped by the abbot, supposedly for marriage but really because he needs the crucifix she wears around her neck to unlock the magical secrets of Sherwood. Robin, Will, and Little John rescue Marian; then the refugees stay in the forest and fight the baron's agents, chiefly Gilbert, the Knight of the Black

Rose, who is Robin's rival for Marian's love. A character of contradictions, Gilbert is a good man bound to serve Alwine because the baron saved his sister's life.

Originally broadcast in a 39-episode run, extra episodes were made for the overseas market, particularly Italy and Germany, where the series was a great success. Though written by Tatsunoko producer Ippei Kuri, *RH* claimed to rely on the legend as retold by *Ivanhoe*-creator Walter Scott. It was the first of Tatsunoko's 1990s "fairy tale" series and was soon followed by the same studio's **SNOW WHITE**. Part of the story was also released as a feature-length movie edit. The series was released, at least partially, in English by Interfilm during the 1990s.

ROBIN JUNIOR

1989. JPN: *Wrestler Gundan Ginga-hen Seisenshi Robin Jr.* AKA: *Holy Warrior Robin Jr.* TV series. DIR: Masaharu Okuwaki. SCR: Hideki Sonoda, Satoru Nishizono. DES: Minoru Maeda, Satoshi Hirayama. ANI: Kazuyoshi Takeuchi. MUS: Hiroyuki Nanba. PRD: Tokyo Movie Shinsha, TV Tokyo. 25 mins. x 24 eps.

A set of superheroes modeled, as in the case of **BIKKURIMAN**, on the characters found on packets of candy. Their mission is to fight the attractively labeled Dark Power, a race of aliens intent on conquering the solar system.

ROBODZ *

2008. JPN: *Robodaizu—RoboDz—Kazagumo Hen*. AKA: *RoboDz Wind and Cloud Chapter*. TV series. DIR: Daisuke Nishio. SCR: Yoshimichi Hosoi. DES: Naoki Miyahara. ANI: Kazuhiro Nishikawa. MUS: DJ MITSU, nobodyknows+. PRD: Toei Animation, Walt Disney Television International Japan. 5 mins. x 26 eps.

An alien plans to conquer Earth as part of his plan for universal subjugation. This 3D short series has almost an aura of fate about it, not for what it is (forgettable) but for what it represents: the accomplishment of a long game plan to use anime as part of Japan's rehabilitation in the eyes of other nations after World War II. In 1958, with **PANDA AND THE MAGIC SERPENT**, Toei set out to become the Disney of Asia, producing a feature film based on Chinese legend to demonstrate their readiness to reach out to the rest of the world. Sixty years later, with Japan viewed by many teenagers in and beyond America as the coolest place on the planet, with anime and manga accepted as major world media, they partnered Disney's first official anime coproduction.

ROBOT CARNIVAL *

1987. Video. DIR: Katsuhiro Otomo, Atsuko Fukushima, Hiroyuki Kitazume, Mao Lamdo, Hideyuki Omori, Koji Morimoto, Yasuomi Umezu, Hiroyuki Kitakubo, Takashi Nakamura. SCR: Katsuhiro Otomo, Atsuko Fukushima, Hiroyuki Kitazume, Mao Lamdo, Hideyuki Omori, Koji Morimoto, Yasuomi Umezu, Hiroyuki Kitakubo, Takashi Nakamura. DES: Katsuhiro Otomo, Atsuko Fukushima, Hiroyuki Kitazume, Mao Lamdo, Hideyuki Omori, Koji Morimoto, Yasuomi Umezu, Hiroyuki Kitakubo, Takashi Nakamura. ANI: Katsuhiro Otomo, Atsuko Fukushima, Hiroyuki Kitazume, Mao Lamdo, Hideyuki Omori, Koji Morimoto, Yasuomi Umezu, Hiroyuki Kitakubo, Takashi Nakamura. MUS: Joe Hisaishi, Isaku Fujita, Masahisa Takeshi. PRD: APPP. 90 mins.

This anthology of robot stories is a sampler for some of the big names of anime and an excellent example of how one theme can be approached in a variety of different ways both in terms of script and design. It's also one of the easiest anime to show to foreign audiences because it has very little dialogue and lots of visual variety. The opening and closing sequences by Otomo and Fukushima take a wry look at what can happen when a seductive new diversion hits a tiny, poor community. A gigantic mechanical carnival rolls into town, a tinsel juggernaut crushing everything in its tracks, all bells and whistles and '30s-style dancing puppets, providing an opportunity for pure whiz-bang pyrotechnics on the part of the animators. The machine itself forms the title lettering, a neat conceit. At the end of the movie, this shimmering shrine to trash self-destructs taking the open-mouthed peasants with it. Kitazume's *Starlight Angel* is a boy-meets-girl-meets-giant-robot love story set in an amusement park and steeped in the style and atmosphere of the early 1980s; all the characters could have stepped straight out of the GUNDAM universe. Mao's *Cloud* is a more abstract piece whose narrative is buried in a series of beautiful, slow-moving images and hypnotic music, as a childlike robot walks slowly through a gathering storm into sunlight. Its purposely retro design and simple monotone pencil-sketch style look surprisingly contemporary in the 21st century. *Deprive* by Omori is another boy-girl-robot romance though with more of a heavy-metal edge. A young girl is torn from the arms of a handsome young man and kidnapped by an evil entity in KISS-type makeup. To rescue her, he must become his true self—a robot. Morimoto's *Franken's Gears* is a funny, quirky look at the limitations of science, in which an inventor overlooks the importance of tidiness and attention to detail and wrecks his own experiment. Kitakubo's *Tale of Two Robots* is a slapstick take on nationalism; a Japanese robot made of wood and operated by a band of kids must fight off the evil intentions of a mad white scientist and his brick-built alien war machine. *Nightmare* by Nakamura will make you very, very worried about being stranded in town after a drinking binge, as the detritus of urban life takes on ominous new shapes, and a drunk who misses his last train home is forced to watch their rampage and flee their strange leader. Umezu's *Presence* is the crown of a superb collection, a gem of a love story wrapped in a fable about the obsolescence of both people and technology and the responsibilities of the creator to his creation, enhanced by a seductive score whose main theme is unforgettable. The dialogue for this segment was dubbed into laughable "British" by Americans, which is unfortunate, but that's the only flaw in a superbly watchable film that is aging very gracefully, especially in comparison with some of the overhyped new material. Compare to the same year's NEO TOKYO and the later "showcase" anime MEMORIES.

ROBOT GIRLS Z *

2014. TV series. DIR: Hiroshi Ikehata. SCR: Kazuho Hyodo. DES: Tetsuya Kawakami. ANI: Tetsuya Kawakami. MUS: N/C. PRD: Toei Animation, Dynamic Planning, Studio Orphee. 10 mins. x 9 eps.

Robots from a number of classic Go Nagai shows, including DANGARD ACE, GRANDIZER, and MAZINGER Z are reimagined as pugnacious schoolgirls, who lurk around Nerima Ward in Tokyo, shilling for the miracle new energy source Photon Power. Occasionally they fight crime, in a spoof that cashes in on trends in cute, the Nerima location of several anime studios (NERIMA DAIKON BROTHERS), and aging fan-love for the shows of the 1970s.

ROBOT KING DAIOJA

1981. JPN: *Saikyo Robo Daioja*. AKA: *Strongest Robot Daioja*. TV series. DIR: Katsuyoshi Sasaki. SCR: Hiroyuki Hoshiyama, Yoshihisa Araki, Tsunehisa Ito, Akifumi Yoshida, Kosuke Yoshida, Sukehiro Tomita. DES: Nobuyoshi Sasakado, Kunio Okawara, Yutaka Izubuchi. ANI: Akihiro Kanayama. MUS: Michiaki Watanabe. PRD: Sunrise, TV Asahi. 25 mins. x 50 eps.

In the Edon protectorate of some 50 planets, the heir to the throne must make a grand tour of his realm at age 16, the better to serve his subjects. Traveling with Prince Edward Mito are Baron Kaikusu, Duke Skead, and female ninja Flora Shinobu. In their travels they run across many foul plots (the deadliest of which comes in the latter episodes, aimed at the heart of the monarchy itself!) that they unravel in the name of Mito's father, King Tokugar. At these times, Mito's, Kaikusu's, and Skead's small robots combine into one larger unit with the symbol of Edon on its chest—Robot King Daioja.

With a federation name that's a pun on Edo and a ruler's that's a pun on Tokugawa, *RKD* was inspired in part by the long-running samurai show *Mito Komon* (see MANGA MITO KOMON). *RKD* used many of the staff from UNCHALLENGEABLE TRIDER G7, but this show represents the end of the early Sunrise "combining robot" era that began with ZAMBOT 3. Sunrise wouldn't produce anything comparable until *Exkaiser* launched the BRAVE SAGA in 1990.

ROBOTAN *

1966. TV series. DIR: Hiroshi Ono. SCR: Tsuyoshi Danjo, Takuya Yamaguchi, Kasei Matsubara, Takashi Taka. DES: Moriyasu Taniguchi, et al. ANI: Moriyasu Taniguchi. MUS: Robotan Group. PRD: Ohiro, Fuji TV. 25 mins. x 104 eps. (TV1), 25 mins. x 33 eps. (TV2).

Based on a manga by Kenji Morita, the series revolves around alien household robot Robotan, who comes from planet

Roborobo and lives with an everyday Japanese family as a domestic servant and friend to the children. Like **DORAEMON**, his good intentions don't always work out, with comic consequences. The original series was made in Osaka by the short-lived Ohiro Planning. Production moved to Tokyo Movie Shinsha for the 20th-anniversary color remake *New Robotan* (1986) under director Masaharu Okuwaki.

ROBOTECH *
1985. TV series, video, movies. DIR: Robert Barron, Jim Wager. SCR: Gregory Snegoff, Robert Barron, Greg Finlay, Steve Kramer, Mike Reynolds, Steve Flood, Ardwight Chamberlain. DES: (see original shows). ANI: (see original shows). MUS: Ulpio Minucci. PRD: Tatsunoko Productions, Harmony Gold. 25 mins. x 85 eps. (TV), 80 mins. (m1), 90 mins.(m2), 90 mins. (m3).
In 1999, a giant alien battlecruiser crashes on Earth. The human race decides to stop fighting each other and unite in case the aliens ever come looking for their missing ship. Ten years on, the ship has been renamed the SDF-1 and reconstructed, but the global celebrations are interrupted by an alien attack. Earth's forces under Captain Gloval fight off the threat. As the SDF-1 attempts to save Earth, it uses its untested Spacefold drive and is transported deep into space, where it must fight a prolonged war with the invading Zentraedi fleet. Young pilot Rick Hunter finds himself in a complex triangular relationship with two very different women, ship's officer Lisa Hayes and singing star Lynn Minmay. After 36 episodes, known as the **MACROSS SAGA**, encounters with giant aliens, and big emotional tangles, the soap-in-space ended with the devastation of Earth and the deaths of several important characters. Fifteen years on, the story takes a new turn with the *Robotech Masters* saga. Rick Hunter has set off in SDF-3 to find the world of the Robo-tech Masters, but the Masters themselves are already heading the other way. Young cadet Dana Sterling, offspring of the first interspecies marriage, is thrown into the thick of the fighting when the Robotech Masters attack Earth in search of their lost "protoculture factory." She and her young comrades encounter a strange man who has spent years with the invaders and whose motives

are unclear, but who finally destroys his own culture to save them. In the interval between this Second Robotech War and the third season, *New Generation*, the Invid aliens arrive and conquer Earth. Terran defenders are too exhausted to resist, but a generation later, Scott Bernard and his reinforcements arrive to try and liberate their homeworld. Their task seems hopeless, but if they can somehow contact Admiral Rick Hunter and link up with his space fleet, Earth may have a chance.

The *Robotech* phenomenon is a curious hybrid of Japanese material and American ambition. Originally conceived as a U.S. video release, it was handed to Carl Macek to dub, and the first *Macross* tape, starring Japanese-American hero "Rick Yamada," was premiered at the 1984 World SF Convention. However, Harmony Gold made further deals to bring the show to TV and asked Macek to find a way of expanding it beyond 36 episodes, which is too small for TV syndication. He acquired **SOUTHERN CROSS** and **MOSPEADA** from the same studio, providing another 49 half-hour episodes of *similar* design and background. Macek renamed many of the characters, creating cross-generational links that were absent in the completely unlinked original series, and devised the concept of an ancient alien technology that could generate robots and weapons for space combat, rooted in a mysterious concept called "protoculture." The model-kit company Revell, owners of the *Macross* merchandise rights, already had a trademark line called *Robotech*, and a tie-in was born. The *Robotech* line, having been established before the series was conceived, included robots from shows not involved in Macek's rewrite, like **DOUGRAM** and **ORGUSS**, and did not include anything from *Southern Cross* or *Mospeada*.

The success of the concept led to the construction of *Robotech the Movie*, a dub for the U.S. market of the first part of **MEGAZONE 23**. Since this had absolutely nothing to do with the characters or story lines of any of the three original series, it was presented as a "side story" happening within the chronology of the Robotech Wars. Extra footage was animated for the film in Japan and included as a bonus on the Japanese *Megazone 23* release.

The story was to have continued in a

fourth segment focusing on the forgotten SDF-3. Though all 65 episodes were written for a Japanese-American coproduction, the project was never completed. The footage already shot (four partly completed episodes plus other material) was used to make up a single feature-length video, *Robotech II—The Sentinels*, the last animated installment of the saga.

Robotech gained such a hold on its American fans that it spun off into print with greater success. A series of novels by Jack McKinney (a pseudonym for James Luceno and Brian Daley) fills in many narrative gaps and explores many of the minor characters in greater depth, while *Robotech* comics have been produced by four different publishers over 14 years. Many of the comics and novels are based on the completed scripts for *Sentinels*, even though most were never filmed. The "close" of the *Robotech* saga is the final novel, *End of the Circle*. Similar recycling went on in Japan, where Tatsunoko placed some of the unused designs in the unrelated **ZILLION**.

Robotech attracts passionate response; fans either love or loathe it. Like **NAUSICAÄ**'s U.S. reedit, it is variously viewed as a welcome adaptation of unfamiliar material for a new, less adventurous audience, or a watered-down travesty of its origins. Its supporters cite a complex storyline with material rarely seen in U.S. animation— the unexpected deaths of much-loved characters, the fact that the good guys (humans) usually ended up losing, or even the introduction of a cross-dressing hero. Its detractors point out that all this was present in the original Japanese series and that the destruction of the internal logic and character relationships was unnecessary and excessive. The best way to describe it is probably not as anime but as an American reworking of the Japanese original, but, unlike most palimpsests, enough of the original text remains to entice viewers back to the source material.

Robotech: Shadow Chronicles (2005) is a 90-minute video sequel to the series, but is not technically anime as it was made by a predominantly American and Korean staff. It features the search for the missing Admiral Hunter and the introduction of a new adversary.

ROBOTICS;NOTES *

2012. TV series. DIR: Kazuya Nomura. SCR: Jukki Hanada, Naotaka Hayashi, Masahiro Yokotani, Toshizo Nemoto. DES: Chikashi Kubota. ANI: Satoshi Hagura, Seiko Asai, Hideki Takahashi. MUS: Asami Tachibana, Takeshi Abo, Yuki Hayashi. PRD: Aniplex, Fuji TV, Mages, Nitroplus, Production I.G, Sony Music Entertainment. 23 mins. x 22 eps.
Kaito Yashio and Akiho Senomiya are the only members of their school robotics club, which is threatened with disbandment unless they can cobble together a machine to impress the judges in a forthcoming robot competition. In hock to a number of benefactors for parts and materials, both start to realize that they are developing strange powers, and suspect that their new-found abilities are somehow connected to strange events in the world at large, and the annoying removal of their favorite anime show before the final episode reached the airwaves.

Starting wonderfully small, like an EVERYDAY ANIME about a bunch of losers working on a project that brings them a sense of community, and expanding into ever-greater circles of conspiracy and danger, *Robotics;Notes* is an admirable modern anime. It even makes great use of anime's growing trend for self-referentiality, as the conspiracy uncovered by the cast turns out to be linked obliquely to their favorite games and a much-loved TV show, taken off-air before its final episode, but with an influence no less powerful than that of *Gekiganger 3* in NADESICO. Unfortunately, it is a mixture of elements liable to please nobody, with the everyday soon becoming too surreal, and the surreal all too often weighed down by returns to the humdrum let's-build-a-robot subplot. It also suffers in comparison to its sister show STEINS;GATE (that semi-colon is supposed to be a clue), which similarly leapt ahead of itself in exponentially wild twists, but reached an arguably more satisfactory conclusion. Based on the visual novel (ARGOT AND JARGON) by 5pb, the story was also spun off into six different manga, reflecting the expectation that both younger and older teenagers would form the audience.

ROCKET GIRLS *

2007. TV series. DIR: Hiroshi Aoyama. SCR: Rika Nakase. DES: Kyuma Oshita, Atsushi Takeuchi, Takeshi Waki. ANI: N/C. MUS: Shinkichi Mitsumune. PRD: Mook Animation, Happinet Pictures. 25 mins. x 12 eps.
Yukari's father only hung around long enough to marry her pregnant mother, then disappeared. Now she's in high school and determined to track him down. Somehow or other she gets to the Solomon Islands where an unscrupulous private space contractor on the lookout for astronauts light enough to fly his mini-rockets decides that teenage girls are exactly what he needs. Before long, Yukari is one of a team of three girl astronauts— but is she any closer to finding her father? This pile of hokum and sugar actually turns out to be a pleasantly entertaining series, and the physics and financial aspects of commercial space travel are well presented without being too obvious. JAXA (the Japan Aerospace Exploration Agency) get a production cooperation credit, although in the three-dimensional world they have yet to employ high school girls as part-time astronauts.

ROCKET! BOKURA O TSUKI NI TSURETETTE SHIN GESSEKAI RYOKO

2008. AKA: *Rocket! Take Us to the Moon—The True "From The Earth to the Moon."* TV series. DIR: Kenichi Matsuzawa. SCR: Noriyuki Hori. DES: Takashi Narikawa, Shigeyuki Koresawa, Digital Noise, Toshikazu Ishiwata. ANI: Takashi Narikawa, Shigeyuki Koresawa, Digital Noise. MUS: Chikako Kobayashi (Suwara Production). PRD: Science Skills Promotion Organization, Shimizu Corporation, JAXA, Japan Jules Verne Study Group. 15 mins. x 5 eps.
London, 1882: airships promise a chance to explore new worlds, and a boy stows away on the airship taking the famous explorer Fogg (AROUND THE WORLD WITH WILLY FOGG) on his next adventure. A timeslip in a great storm takes them to the Japan of 2080. This adventure is aimed at introducing audiences to present-day and near-future Japanese technology through the characters of one of the nation's best-loved science fiction writers, Jules Verne. It was made with the collaboration of JAXA (the Japan Aerospace Exploration Agency) and shown on Japan's Science Channel. The show represents vocaloid idol Hatsune Miku's documentary debut and her first anime theme song. Noriko Namiki also contributes to the music with STUD-G providing for the opening theme *Radical Innovation*.

ROKUDENASHI BLUES

1992. JPN: *Rokudenashi Blues*. Movie. DIR: Takao Yoshizawa. SCR: Yoshiyuki Suga. DES: Masanori Morita. ANI: Yoshitaka Yashima. MUS: Fuminori Iwasaki. PRD: Toei. 25 mins.
A short "movie" based on Masanori Morita's 1988 manga in *Shonen Jump* magazine, in which Taison Maeda determines to be the toughest kid in his school, ruling over his fellow students with the power of his fists. Another distant homage to the U.S. boxer Mike Tyson was carefully buried in STREET FIGHTER II.

ROLLING RYOTA

1990. JPN: *Kogorashi Ryota*. Video. DIR: Masamune Ochiai. SCR: Yuki Kuroiwa. DES: Shinichi Nagasawa. ANI: Natsuki Aikawa, Shinichi Nagasawa. MUS: N/C. PRD: Knack. 45 mins. x 3 eps.
Former biker Takao Ryota becomes a bus driver, causing havoc in the streets by racing his bus against other vehicles. This anime was based on a manga by Hiroyuki Murata, who also created VOLLEY BOYS. Ryota, who sports a distinctive gangster punch-perm hairstyle, was originally voiced by Jutaro Kosugi, but he was replaced by Hiroya Ishimaru, the voice of Koji Kabuto in MAZINGER Z. **NV**

ROMAN *

2013. JPN: *Bakumatsu Gijinden Roman*. AKA: *Tale of a Righteous Man at the Fall of the Bakufu—the Wanderer*. TV series. DIR: Hirofumi Ogura. SCR: Tatsuto Higuchi, Yasuhiko Tamura, Atsuhiro Tomioka, Chinatsu Hojo. DES: Satoshi Hirayama. ANI: N/C. MUS: Hiroshi Takaki. PRD: TMS Entertainment, AT-X, Nippon Columbia, Sotsu Agency, Dax Production, TV Tokyo. 24 mins. x 12 eps.
Roman does not describe himself as a thief but a "getbacker" (GETBACKERS), who will steal back any goods that the owner feels have been wrongfully taken away. Since this includes things that have been stolen in the first place, this is an oddly intricate excuse, but Roman, like all anime thieves from CAT'S EYE onward, is in search of a justification for his actions. All? Not all, for LUPIN III was always honest about what he did for a living, and it should come as no

surprise to the viewer of this show that Roman's characters were originally designed by Lupin's creator Monkey Punch. In fact, the Lupin resemblances are so huge that you might be forgiven for thinking that you were watching a 19th-century respray of Monkey Punch's most famous creation. Roman, however, was born from a pachinko game, and the plotting reflects the kind of action one might expect to see on one of those mindless self-playing pinball devices—boxes to be ticked, wealth won in abundance only to be swiftly diminished once more, famine to feast in all fortunes, and surreal pay-offs.

ROMANCE AND DRAMA

The nature of anime favors spectacle—anime's mode of production often makes it better suited to special effects, science fiction, and fantasy. Human interest drama or romance can usually be made cheaply with live-action materials, and consequently appears in anime only rarely—HUMAN CROSSING is one of its best examples, although drama can also feature in crime shows such as DOMAIN OF MURDER and in psychological horror like PERFECT BLUE.

Regarded primarily as a children's medium, anime concentrated on comedic stories for its first decade. Its first demonstrably dramatic work was Noburo Ofuji's *Whale* (*Kujira*, 1927), in which a beautiful woman survives a shipwreck along with three male passengers who immediately begin fighting over her. They are distracted by the arrival of a whale, their hunting of which encourages its vengeful return, in a story that ends with the woman the sole survivor, riding on the whale's back. Early anime romances dealt with comedy and tragedy in equal parts, from the faithless husband's antics in THE WORLD OF POWER AND WOMEN (1932) to the heartbreak of MADAME BUTTERFLY (1940).

Some WARTIME ANIME remained humorous, although others put joking aside in order to warn audiences of the dangers lurking unseen, as in Sanae Yamamoto's *Defeat of the Spies* (*Spy Gekimetsu*, 1942). The postwar period brought increased access to Disney films such as *Bambi* (1942), encouraging Japanese animators to consider tragic scenes alongside the comedy of traditional children's entertainment. This maturing attitude to storytelling helped lift anime out of the single funny vignettes of cartoon shorts and into feature-length storytelling as found in THE LITTLEST WARRIOR (1961). However, the desire to appeal to a children's market continued to limit romantic plots or the seriousness of certain topics—WOOF WOOF 47 RONIN (1963) adapted a famous tragedy from the kabuki stage, tempered by the use of a cast of talking cartoon dogs which detracted from its dramatic weight.

As the cinema market slumped in the 1960s with the onslaught of television, Osamu Tezuka attempted to find a new niche with his erotic romances A THOUSAND AND ONE NIGHTS (1969) and CLEOPATRA: QUEEN OF SEX (1970). Anime, however, has never shied away from drama and tragedy, even in works intended for children, such as the harrowing RINGING BELL (1978) and KIMBA THE WHITE LION (1965).

The growth in the 1970s of the female manga market led to the adaptation of many more romance stories for animation. CANDY CANDY (1976) established many durable conventions of the girl's anime, including the orphan heroine victimized and persecuted like CINDERELLA, enjoying the attentions of a secret benefactor or admirer such as that found in DADDY LONG-LEGS, and enduring a series of torments while waiting for her Prince Charming, often in the company of a small furry animal. Such dramatic traditions even influenced the plots of anime supposedly based on historical fact, such as the breathless excitement of YOUNG PRINCESS DIANA (1986).

Homosexual longing and romance did not solely rely on the arrival of video, first appearing in the TV series PATALIRO (1982). However, video made it far easier for anime with more mature themes to go into production, such as the gay subtexts of SONG OF WIND AND TREES (1987). As the niche market expanded for amateur and professional comics featuring love between handsome young men, gay characters in anime gained wider acceptance. Science fiction and fantasy settings were also popular, as TIES OF LOVE and TOKYO BABYLON showed in 1992, but anime also made use of "real life" backdrops to tales of gay sexuality and its social consequences, like the family in OH FAMILY, football and music in ZETSUAI, and organized crime in KIZUNA. Girl-on-girl crushes are usually portrayed as innocent adoration, but sometimes with a lesbian subtext, as in UTENA.

The same period, however, also saw maturation of themes on TV, with extended romantic dramas such as TOUCH (1985) and MAISON IKKOKU (1986). Following the success of the alien spouse of URUSEI YATSURA (1981), romance in the 1990s often took on the characteristics of a dating simulation computer game, in which a male protagonist was obliged to work out which of several contenders would be the most appropriate choice for a happy ending. This has led to the "harem" tradition typified by TENCHI MUYO!, in which a single boy is surrounded by a cast of adoring females. The extremes to which this has been carried are exemplified by NEGIMA and HANAUKYO MAID TEAM, where the (underage) male protagonist is surrounded by literally dozens of women from whom to choose. Slacker mentality comes to the fore, with pretty girls that materialize by accident in lonely geeks' closets, or memoryless subplots that offer hope from forgotten childhood contacts. The archetypal lead for the harem show is often a solitary shut-in with borderline Asperger's Syndrome, alienated from friends and family and so inept and passive that his only hope of romance is either a past association occluded by amnesia (he was once loved, but has forgotten, as in LOVE HINA), or a future event about which he is told by time travelers, such as that in DNA^2 or KIRARA. There is no *now* for the harem show's point of identification; *now* is a miserable, dull, pointless time, although there may have been a dreamtime *then* when he was popular with girls, and might one day be a dreamtime *soon*, when he will be again, while the girls themselves are often "gamified" (see EROTICA AND PORNOGRAPHY), presented as puzzles to be solved or, as in CLANNAD, as prizes to be won by the resolution of box-ticking traumas. Many romantic interests also appear to be childhood friends, which is both a way of introducing labor-saving ready-made love objects and a form of nostalgia—modern urban Japanese yearning for the simpler associations of their rural pasts, when people genuinely could go to the same school as their parents, and everyone in a town would know each other from childhood, a concept known as *osana-najimi*. This trope is arguably best tackled in Makoto Shinkai's wonderful **FIVE CENTIMETERS PER SECOND**, which luxuriates in it without shying away from its pathological implications for arrested development. Recent years have also seen the rise of the "reverse harem" show, which, as the name implies, features a single female protagonist beset by an army of adoring boys, such as that to be found in **MARINA THE MANGA ARTIST GOES TO CAMELOT** (1990) and perpetuated in the male love-interests of **BOYS OVER FLOWERS** or **PARADISE KISS**.

The proliferation of quasi-incestuous titles (e.g., **SISTER PRINCESS** or **ONEGAI TEACHER**'s sequel *Onegai Twins*) may be another symptom of modern life—perhaps related to the shortage of real-world siblings noted in **BUBU CHACHA**. Living in close proximity to a sibling, humans in the real world are subject to the Westermarck Effect, a deadening of any mating impulses—in effect, the onset of a lack of sexual interest. Traditional China and Japan, however, both have many cases of "adopted" daughters, brought into a family as potential marriage candidates for the family's son, making the idea of romantic attraction to a stepsister less odd than it may at first appear in shows such as **MARMALADE BOY** (1995). However, it is worth noting that, to the modern, amoral, sedentary, couch-potato teenager, the logic of a love interest in one's own household may simply be that it does not involve having to walk so far.

ROMANCE IS IN THE FLASH OF THE SWORD II *

2001. JPN: *Romance wa Tsurugi no Kagayaki II*. Video. DIR: Yosei Morino. SCR: Yosei Morino. DES: Jun Sato, Takeshi Nakamura. ANI: Tomohiro Shibayama. MUS: N/C. PRD: Lemon Heart, Triple X. 30 mins. x 6 eps.
Keith (exotic name) is an adventurer and "honorable thief"—but don't expect **LUPIN III**. In a generic fantasy world, a series of repetitive scenarios with disposable characters have Keith rescuing and/or satisfying various women who either have plans for his body or have been molested by assorted unpleasant beings human and otherwise, usually with spectators—or both. Keith's "bodily fluids" are smeared

on a stone to release a powerful demon, whom he then defeats; a demonic monster molests priestesses for their sexual elixirs, but Keith sorts that out too; an evil duke hunts down and molests girls and men and plots against the crown until Keith arrives. He has sex in temples, in dungeons, on a swing, at a unicorn race, with a masseuse possessed by a ghost who's really a she-demon, and in a variety of other circumstances, while saving the world from various agents of darkness. Based on the 1999 erotic game, which was itself a sequel, hence the numerals "II" in the title—as with **STREET FIGHTER II**. ⬤Ⓝⓥ

ROMEO X JULIET *

2007. TV series. DIR: Fumitoshi Oizaki. SCR: Reiko Yoshida, Miharu Hirami, Kurasumi Sunayama, Natsuko Takahashi. DES: Daiki Hirada, Hiroki Harada, Masami Saito. ANI: Hiroki Harada. MUS: Hitoshi Sakimoto. PRD: Gonzo, CBC, G.D.H., SKY Perfect Well Think Co., Ltd. 25 mins. x 24 eps.
In Neo Verona, a floating city sustained by the great tree Escalus, the Montague family have ruled since taking power in a brutal coup 14 years ago. The former rulers from the Capulet family were wiped out, and their retainers can do nothing to defend the poor; that is left to a masked fighter for justice, the mysterious Red Whirlwind. But there is a direct heir to the Capulet line, the dead Prince's little daughter, Juliet, hidden and disguised as a boy for her own safety. She and the Red Whirlwind share a secret with Romeo, the heir of the House of Montague: that love takes no account of politics, logic, or good sense. With family loyalty, the weight of history, and a looming ecological disaster that could cripple Neo Verona, Juliet and her Romeo face drama, betrayal, loss, and tragedy for the sake of a love that could change their world, or destroy it.

William Shakespeare (a minor character in this sci-fi version of his own play) was never too proud to steal a good story, or too respectful to resist changing it for his audience. Gonzo's writing team, headed by Reiko Yoshida, have followed his lead, changing many details but keeping its beautiful outline and emotional denouement and borrowing embellishments where appropriate—**CASTLE IN THE SKY**'s mighty tree that holds the flying city

together, for example. The art and design team also borrow from many worlds and eras in putting together a magical city, entirely convincing from crumbling backstreets to lavishly decorated palace halls. Sakimoto's music is likewise note-perfect for the purpose. Despite a lapse in animation quality mid-run (unfortunately common to Gonzo productions), the visuals recover for the final episodes, so that nothing dilutes the impact of the ending. An exceptionally sensitive English dub script from a team headed by Taliesin Jaffe does justice to the language and inspiration of the story. Compare to **THREE MUSKETEERS**, which similarly took a familiar European story and ran it through the anime plot mangle. ⓥ

ROMEO'S BLUE SKY

1995. JPN: *Romeo no Aoi Sora*. AKA: *Romeo and the Black Brothers*. TV series. DIR: Kozo Kusuba, Shinpei Miyashita, Yasuo Iwamoto, Tomomitsu Matsukawa. SCR: Michiru Shimada. DES: Yoshiharu Sato. ANI: Yoshiharu Sato, Ei Inoue, Katsu Oshiro, Masaki Abe. MUS: Kei Wakakusa. PRD: Nippon Animation, Fuji TV. 25 mins. x 33 eps.
Romeo lives happily with his family in the Swiss Alps until a series of crop failures and his father's illness bring about tragic changes. To save his loved ones from ruin, he sells himself into slavery for 25 francs to Luini, called "God of Death," who travels poor country districts searching for child laborers to fuel the growing cities of Europe. He is taken to Milan and sold to a chimney sweep, and so becomes one of the "Black Brothers," the boys who keep the city's chimneys clear in great hardship. On the way he meets Alfredo, a boy with a mysterious past whose main aim in life is to find his beloved little sister, Bianca, and the two boys become close friends. In Milan he meets the fragile Angeletta, but her brother Anselmo is part of a local gang, the Wolf Pack, and despite Romeo's overtures of friendship, Anselmo begins a gang war. The Wolf Pack are not the only ones out for blood, as Alfredo is threatened by those who know his secret and will stop at nothing to prevent him claiming his rightful inheritance.

The story was based on the 1941 novel *The Black Brothers* (*Die Schwarzen Brüder*) by Lisa Tetzner, a German forced to flee the

Nazi regime to Switzerland because of her husband's Marxist leanings. She wrote her book to highlight the real-life scandal of child slavery in Europe—compare to **24 Eyes**, a similar protest. The anime adapted the story freely, though it retained the basic elements of the typical **World Masterpiece Theater** production—a classic tale of emotion and melodrama, set at a safe distance in time and space, with vulnerable but heroic young people enduring testing times in the struggle for survival. The lead character's name was changed from Giorgio, new characters were added, and the plot and conclusion altered, partly to fit a schedule originally planned for 39 episodes but finally forced to squeeze the story into 33.

RONIN WARRIORS *
1989. JPN: *Yoroiden Samurai Troopers*. AKA: *Armor Legend Samurai Troopers; Samurai Troopers*. TV series, video. DIR: Makoto Ikeda, Mamoru Hamazu. SCR: Junzo Toriumi, Yuki Onishi. DES: Norio Shioyama, Hideo Okamoto, Ariaki Okada. ANI: Norio Shioyama, Kisaraka Yamada. MUS: Osamu Tezuka. PRD: Sunrise, Nagoya TV. 25 mins. x 39 eps. (TV), 30 mins. x 3 eps. (v1), 30 mins. x 4 eps. (v2), 30 mins. x 5 eps. (v3).
Saint Seiya–style action, as the evil Lord Arago (Talpa in the U.S.) sends denizens of the Phantom World to invade Earth, and five teenage pretty-boys are given mystic suits of samurai armor that will enhance their own natural gifts, enabling them to fight back. Wildfire Ryo, Torrent Shin (Cye), Halo Seiji (Sage), Strata Toma (Rowen), and Hardrock Shu (Kento) can unite their suits to form Hariel's White Armor of Fervor. But Arago has already infiltrated the whole world. The boys' suits, plus all those worn by Arago's champions, are parts of a single incredibly powerful battle armor, broken up when Arago was defeated eons ago; now he wants to reunite them and make sure his conquest can't be overturned. The team members must overcome their own fears and weaknesses and face terrible dangers—their friends, too, are liable to be used by Arago as bait or bribes.

Looking suspiciously like an entire unbroadcast season cut into sections, the adventures continued on video with Mamoru Hamazu's *ST: Extra Story* (1989), in which our heroes go to the U.S. to investigate a mysterious news report that may point to new activity from Arago. One of them is captured and tortured by a demon who has teamed up with a human scientist to find the secrets of the Troopers' armor and use them to take over all five suits. A second series, *ST: Empire Legend* (1989), contains another tale of courage against supernatural evil, this time in Africa. In a kabuki-themed story arc redolent of **Gasaraki**, the final adventure of Makoto Ikeda's *ST: Message* (1991) has the boys returning to Japan to investigate mysterious forces at work in Shinjuku. While other members of the team face off against their female adversary Suzunagi, Seiji discovers evidence of an Edo-period play about "five boy warriors."

The series was screened as *Ronin Warriors* (1995) on American TV, with a title change occasioned by two other similarly named shows on the air at the time. Its Japanese origins remain clear, with onscreen Japanese text left in place and the lead character's name unchanged. It's very violent by U.S. standards even though there are few flesh-and-blood casualties, and the overall atmosphere of cruelty and menace is very powerful. **V**

ROOMMATE, THE *
2005. JPN: *Ki ni Naru Roommate*. AKA: *Horny Roommate*. Video. DIR: P Nakamura. SCR: P Nakamura. DES: Takafumi Hino. ANI: Takafumi Hino. MUS: N/C. PRD: Milky, Studio Ten, Image Works, GP Museum Pictures. 30 mins.
Failing his university entrance exam and dumped by his girlfriend, Yu rents a room and prepares for another try. But when he arrives at his new residence, he discovers that it is situated above a strip club, and performer Rei Asagiri is already living there. Before long, Yu is unable to cope with the distractions and decides to stop studying books and start studying girls. Based on the manga by Kaoru Yunagi, serialized in *Young Comic* monthly. **N**

ROOTS SEARCH *
1986. JPN: *Roots Search: Shokushin Buttai X*. AKA: *Roots Search: Life Devourer X*. Video. DIR: Hisashi Sugai. SCR: Michiru Shimada. DES: Sanae Kobayashi, Yasushi Moriki. ANI: Hiroshi Negishi. MUS: N/C. PRD: Production Wave. 44 mins.

The Tolmeckius Research Institute is impressed with its latest find, a psychic girl called Moira, who astounds them all when she starts experiencing terrible visions. When the orbital station is approached by a runaway ship, Moira's insight reveals that all is not as it seems. The ship has been occupied by a fearsome alien intelligence that mentally tortures its victims until they beg for the release of death. When the creature proves to be invincible, Moira resolves to make the ultimate sacrifice, although even death, it seems, cannot end the suffering.

There are shades of the more recent hit **Evangelion** in this SF tale that mixes Biblical elements with an *Alien* pastiche and a far more sinister interpretation of "God's" purpose. But that is where the resemblance ends for this creaky anime, unreleased in English until 1992, a time on the shelf that did not find it aging gracefully. **L**

ROSARIO + VAMPIRE *
2008. JPN: *Rozario to Vampire*. AKA: TP Sakura. TV series. DIR: Takayuki Inagaki. SCR: Hiroshi Yamaguchi, Ritsuko Hayasaka. DES: Mariko Fujita, Shigemi Ikeda. ANI: Satoru Kiyomaru. MUS: Kohei Tanaka, Shiro Hamaguchi. PRD: Gonzo, G.D.H., Happinet Pictures, Shueisha, Yomiko Advertising. 25 mins. x 13 eps. (TV1), 25 mins. x 13 eps. (TV2).
Tsukune wants to go to a private academy, but his high school grades are so awful that no will accept him, except one for *yokai*, traditional Japanese goblins, who attend disguised as humans (**Spooky Kitaro**). He's terrified that his fellow students will kill him, and determined to leave, until he falls for a beautiful vampire. Now he just has to hope nobody finds out that he's only human. Sticking faithfully to the harem formula (**Romance and Drama**), this series and its follow-up produce a show that sums up the genre. Action, humor, briskly executed and polished setpieces, crotch shots, and absurd situations are all delivered with slick ease. A second series *Rosario + Vampire Capu2* was made by the same crew and aired later in 2008, but to date Akihisa Ikeda's 2004 manga has inspired no more anime. **N**

ROSE OF VERSAILLES, THE *
1979. JPN: *Versailles no Bara*. AKA: *Lady Os-*

car. TV series. DIR: Tadao Nagahama, Osamu Dezaki, Yasuo Yamayoshi, Minoru Okazaki, Tetsuo Imazawa, Akinori Nagaoka. SCR: Yoshimi Shinozaki, Masahiro Yamada, Yukio Sugie, Hajime Hazama. DES: Shingo Araki, Michi Himeno, Akio Sugino, Ken Kawai, Tadao Kubota. ANI: Shingo Araki, Michi Himeno. MUS: Koji Makaino. PRD: Tokyo Movie Shinsha, Nippon TV. 25 mins. x 40 eps.

In 18th-century France, revolution is in the air, but for Oscar François de Jarjayes, the ties of tradition are all-powerful. Sole heir of an ancient family, she is given a man's name at birth and becomes the son her father wants. She succeeds so completely that she is soon one of the best fencers in France, promoted to Captain of the Guard of Marie Antoinette, Austrian child-wife of the Crown Prince. Both Oscar and Antoinette are women alone, forced into roles they did not choose and barred from love by duty. The Crown Princess of France loves a foreign nobleman, while the Captain of the Guard loves a childhood friend who is also a servant of her family. Both loves seem doomed, but both women must continue to live artificial public lives concealing real private agonies. A tangle of fascinating subplots and well-developed supporting characters, some historical and some invented, make this one of the most powerful and credible of anime TV series. As in Riyoko Ikeda's original 1972 manga, the sublime tale of love and loss ends with Antoinette going to the scaffold and Oscar leaving her life behind to share the struggle for freedom with her beloved André, dying in the assault on the Bastille.

Yet the two deaths are very different. Oscar's is a triumph of the human spirit, Antoinette's a failure. By stealing private happiness while supporting the feudal system that imprisons her as surely as the peasants, the proud, brave Antoinette has colluded in the lies and injustices that have made revolution inevitable. She dies because of her public role as a glittering cog in an increasingly useless machine, but in finally rejecting a system that separates people with artificial barriers of rank and property, Oscar asserts her own right to be fully human, regardless of gender or status. She dies, not because of, but rather *for* who and what she is. This cleverly subverts the familiar format of forbidden love between beautiful men (which would

give birth to the *shonen ai* manga genre) by making one of the pair a woman, but one so gifted in traditionally "masculine" skills that the idea of a truly equal relationship, with no element of dependency or weakness, can still be maintained.

The renowned Araki/Himeno team transformed Ikeda's black-and-white manga art into a colorful fantasy, and while the action is played strong, the romance is played with delicacy and pathos, keeping melodrama in check. Its roots are clearly in Tezuka's magical **PRINCESS KNIGHT**, and its influence is still strong in the 1990s TV hit **UTENA**. It is so popular in France that it is still screened occasionally on French TV and was also adapted as a live-action film, *Lady Oscar* (1979), directed by Jacques Demy. A live-action musical version is the jewel in the crown of Japan's Takarazuka theater troupe. *Rose of Versailles* deserves its classic rank. Despite its age and technical deficiencies, it still delivers powerful entertainment.

ROUGE

1997. JPN: *Ladies' Comic Video Rouge*. Movie. DIR: N/C. SCR: Haruko Kanzaki, Mizuki Iwase, Kei Misugi, Chika Taniguchi. DES: Haruko Kanzaki, Mizuki Iwase, Kei Misugi, Chika Taniguchi. ANI: N/C. MUS: N/C. PRD: Komine Communications. 40 mins. x 2 eps.

Bereaved strangers lose themselves in a sordid double life of prostitution but find love with each other. A loveless marriage blossoms through bondage. A trainee gets more than she bargained for when the head nurse takes the biology lesson to the limit. And a male beautician uses unorthodox methods to put color in a makeup artist's cheeks. Four erotically charged tales animated for a female audience, based on stories originally printed in the manga magazine *Rouge*. **N**

ROUJIN Z *

1991. AKA: *Old Man Z*. Movie. DIR: Hiroyuki Kitakubo. SCR: Katsuhiro Otomo. DES: Hisashi Eguchi. ANI: Satoshi Kon. MUS: Bun Itakura. PRD: APPP. 80 mins.

Old Mr. Takizawa, unable to care for himself, is selected as the guinea pig for an experimental robot bed designed to administer to his every need. Despite the protests of his nurse Haruko, the project gets underway, but the patient proves to

be more trouble than he's worth when he decides to take a trip to the seaside. The bed's true purpose becomes apparent; it's not for the care of the elderly at all, it's the prototype for a military model designed to revolutionize modern warfare. But with Mr. Takizawa at the controls, even the defanged civilian version manages to wreak considerable havoc, with the help of an ornery gang of geriatric hackers and despite the army's efforts to stop it. The ending, an **AKIRA** pastiche in which an ambulance is riddled with cybernetic tentacles, is followed by a surprise, which, on repeat viewing, you will see was planned all along.

There aren't many anime that begin with an old man wetting himself, but that's part of *Roujin Z's* originality. **AKIRA**-creator Otomo took a back seat for this satire on the developed world's aging population, limiting himself to script and design duties. Ridiculing the health service as **HUMMINGBIRDS** lampooned the privatization of the military, *Roujin Z* is entertaining and thought-provoking, with a witty script in the English-language version from George Roubicek. Arguably a superior story, it's fated to remain in *Akira*'s shadow owing to a drastically smaller animation budget. Watch for some clever touches, such as an underground battle lit in old-fashioned sepia tones and artificial scan lines on a TV screen, showing real attention to detail. Satoshi Kon worked on the backgrounds and later put this experience of designing lived-in environments to good use as the director of **PERFECT BLUE**.

ROURAN

2002. JPN: *Kiko Sen'nyo Rouran*. AKA: *Mysterious Steel Fairy Rouran*. TV series. DIR: Toshihiro Hirano. SCR: Sho Aikawa, Sho Egawa. DES: Naomi Miyata, Yutaka Izubuchi, Rei Nakahara, Masunori Osawa, Masakazu Okada, Katsuyuki Tamura. ANI: Kazuhiro Sasaki, Naomi Miyata. MUS: Yoshiro Kakimi. PRD: ZEXCS, Starchild Records, Kid's Station. 15 mins. x 28 eps.

A secret society is using monsters to invade Tokyo, and the peacekeeping force ASY opposes it with huge robots called Steel Hermits (Kosen), recruiting pilots wherever it can. Teenager Yamato Mikogami is sent out as a pilot of the Hermit Ginko when a huge monster attacks the city. After he lures the monster far out to sea and destroys it, a girl appears floating in the air, enveloped in a strange light. Named Rouran, she doesn't know who she is or where she comes from, but it seems she is fated to become the destroyer of worlds. Toshihiro Hirano is a hugely talented designer and director whose preferred scenarios involve cute girls in love with other cute teenagers (of either gender) being menaced by slime-dripping monsters or piloting heavy metal; he tends to favor gothic horror over straight tentacle porn. This show combines his great loves—cute girls, occult horror, and big robots—with the strongest emphasis on robots. Rouran bears an uncanny resemblance to director Hirano's earlier ICZER ONE, even to the extent of battling a rival counterpart in the manner of Iczers One and Two. See also SAIKANO.

ROZEN MAIDEN ★

2002. TV series. DIR: Mamoru Matsuo. SCR: Jukki Hanada, Mari Okada, Tsuyoshi Tamai. DES: Kumi Ishii. ANI: Kumi Ishii. MUS: Shinkichi Mitsumune. PRD: Memory Tech, Novic, Pony Canyon, TBS. 24 mins. x 12 eps. (TV1), 24 mins. x 12 eps. (TV2).
Spoiled teenager Jun Sakurada uses an incident at school as an excuse to shut himself in his room. Ordering everything he needs through his computer (and returning most of the packages just before payment is due), with a loving and supportive big sister to take care of everything else, he is stagnating in a comfortable cocoon. Then he receives a package he doesn't expect, containing an elaborate and beautiful antique doll—compare to STEEL ANGEL KURUMI and RIZELMINE. When he winds her mechanism, she springs into life and speaks to him. Her name is Shinku, and she's one of an elite "sisterhood" of dolls who take sibling rivalry to combative extremes. She has a rose-red gown, sweet face, and long blonde hair, but she also has a very powerful personality and Jun is forced to metamorphose out of his chrysalis of comfort and meet other doll owners as Shinku's "medium"—or her slave. A second series, *RM: Traumend*, followed in 2005 from the same crew. Based on a manga by "Peach Pit," the fanzine-turned-pro collective that also created DEARS, picking up neatly on the craze for

expensive customized dolls (like Volks' *Super Dollfie* line) which become as much part of their owners' lives as real people. Part of the relatively recent "Gothic Lolita" subgenre of anime, based on the fashion fad of the same name, and also found in PETITE COSSETTE and MOON PHASE.

RUBENKAISER

1977. JPN: *Gekiso! Rubenkaiser*. AKA: *Go Fast! Rubenkaiser; Rough Racer Rubenkaiser, Formula One*. TV series. DIR: Yasuo Hasegawa, Takashi Anno, Masahisa Ishida. SCR: Tatsuo Tamura, Atsuo Murayama. DES: Kazuyoshi Hoshino. ANI: Yuji Tanabe. MUS: Shunsuke Kikuchi. PRD: Wako, Green Box, Toei Animation, TV Asahi. 25 mins. x 17 eps.
Maverick racing driver Shunsuke Hayami is fired from the Arrow team when he disobeys a direct order from the pit. Before long, he is signed up by racing boss Ginjiro Arashi to drive the Rubenkaiser, a prototype Formula One vehicle designed by the late West German master racer George Kaiser, who also turns out to be Shunsuke's long-lost father, in a twist that will come as little surprise. Following their 1976 series MACHINE HAYABUSA, Toei made this further foray onto the tracks of Formula one racing. With an almost identical set-up—keen young drivers, a supportive pit and admin team, cute girl, cute kid, and fierce on-track rivalry—it did exactly the same job. However, forced to run opposite the new series of LUPIN III, *Rubenkaiser* suffered understandably low ratings and early cancellation. Manga versions were published in *Terebi Land* and *Terebi-kun* magazines.

RUIN EXPLORERS ★

1995. JPN: *Hikyo Tantei Fam and Ihrlie*. AKA: *Ruin Explorers Fam and Ihrlie*. Video. DIR: Takeshi Mori. SCR: Takeshi Mori. DES: Toshihisa Kaiya. ANI: Toshihisa Kaiya, Yoshiaki Yanagida, Takuya Saito. MUS: Masamichi Amano. PRD: Animate Film, Ajia-do. 30 mins. x 4 eps.
In a world filled with the relics of fallen civilizations, elf-catgirl Fam and her human companion Ihrlie search for a treasure known as the Ultimate Power. They meet Galuf, a traveler who claims to have a map revealing its location. Since Fam finds it hard to stay focused for more than a few seconds and Ihrie has a "horrible curse,"

it seems less than likely they will succeed, even if they weren't facing some stiff competition from the greatest evil wizard who ever lived. But they have a serious motive that says more about their friendship than their constant bickering. The Ultimate Power is the only thing that can free Ihrlie from her curse and enable her to fulfill her great magical potential. When she was a young apprentice, her carelessness so annoyed her teacher that he cast a spell to prevent her from using her powers. Every time she does so, she transforms out of human shape. She's been avoiding the problem by taking magical pills that enable her to transform back again, but they're almost all used up, so she can only use her magic in dire emergencies. They usually have to rely on Fam's less powerful magic instead.

Galuf, a sleazy merchant out for the treasure himself, is terrified of the various traps and defenses around the Ultimate Power, and he wants our heroines to go in there first. He also hires a crack pair of ruin explorers, sorceress Rasha and swordsman Migel, to make sure the Ultimate Power winds up in his hands. But the Ultimate Power alone won't actually do anything; it must be combined with a magic sword and mirror. Handsome Prince Lyle also wants the Ultimate Power, but for unselfish ends—to fight Rugodorull, a wise cleric corrupted by Dark Powers. Rugodorull has killed everyone else in Lyle's homeland and now wants to destroy all life on Earth. The six finally agree to work together to defeat Rugodorull. Their quest takes them across the seas to a magic island as they try to collect the items that will enable them to summon the Ultimate Power and save the world.

This D&D-style adventure was based on characters created by Kunihiko Tanaka for *Hobby Japan* magazine; compare its more successful contemporary, the lighthearted fantasy SLAYERS. The four episodes were released on two tapes by U.S. label ADV, which subtitled the first *Tales IN the Crypt* while the second is *Ruin Explorers 2: Profits and Prophecies*.

RUMBLING HEARTS ★

2002. JPN: *Kimi ga Nozomu Eien*. AKA: *Your Eternal Dream; Kiminozo; Eternity You Wish For; Rumble Hearts*. TV series, video. DIR:

Tetsuya Watanabe. scr: Katsuhiko Takayama, Kenichi Kanemaki. des: Yoko Kikuchi, Kanetake Ebikawa, Tomohiko Kawahara. ani: Yoko Kikuchi. mus: Abito Torai, Kenichi Sudo, Ryoji Minami. prd: Media Factory, Studio Fantasia, TV Kanagawa. 24 mins. x 14 eps. (TV), 25 mins. x 3 eps. (v).

After worshiping Takayuki Narumi from afar throughout her high school years, Haruka Suzumiya is finally pressured by her friend Mitsuki into confessing her feelings for him. The young couple overcome painful shyness and several teenage misunderstandings before each is sure of the other's love, but the future looks bright as they help each other to study for college entrance exams. Look away now if you are one of those people who complain *The Anime Encyclopedia* gives away all the plot twists, because after such an innocent and, seemingly, predictable start, Haruka is left in a coma by an accident. Takayuki falls into depression, shuts himself away, and does not even attend his own graduation ceremony. Mitsuki is so worried about him that she gives up a chance of a sports career in swimming, gets an ordinary office job, and even moves in with him. Gradually, she slips into depression herself as she thinks of what she has given up. He takes on part-time work at a restaurant, makes friends there, and is eventually settling into a comfortable rut when Haruka unexpectedly regains consciousness.

What follows is a cunning mainstream way of dealing with the yearnings across time of **Voices of a Distant Star**; compare to **24 Eyes**, which similarly finds a natural way to create "time travel." Haruka wakes up unaware that three whole years have passed until her younger sister Akane tells her. When Takayuki visits, Haruka wants to fill in the missing years, but mostly she wants to know if he's been dating anyone else, leaving him in the difficult position of explaining that he has shacked up with the girl who had brought them together. It was based on a dating sim game and manga by âge, which began as part of the adults-only erotica genre, although the anime, like later versions of the game, drops much of the nudity in favor of the romance. It does, however, occasionally cling to a misplaced desire to inject comedy into what is ultimately a rather dark and weepy storyline. Regardless, the result is an original variant

on the implicit promises and romantic tensions of **Love Hina** and its ilk, although live-action Japanese drama had been there before with *Since I Met You* (*DE), and American TV would take a similar approach in *Everwood* (2002). A three-part spin-off video, *Akane Maniax* (*Kiminozo Gaiden*, 2004), was a love story centered around Haruka's sister Akane, though the central characters from *Kiminozo* also appear. **Ⓝ**

RUN

1995. jpn: *5-to ni Naritai; Goto ni Naritai*. aka: *I Want 5th Place*; *Last But One*. Movie. dir: Mei Kato. scr: Yoko Yamamoto. des: Hotsubu Jizo. ani: Takashi Saijo, Izuru En, Kiyotaka Kanchiku. mus: Michiru Oshima. prd: Yoshifumi Ando, Amuse Video. 75 mins.

Ritsuko has one leg that doesn't work properly. Her mother is very protective of her, but when at last she gets the chance to go to school and make friends, some of the children tease her because of the odd way she walks. Nobody's perfect; some of her classmates have weird teeth or are overweight, her doctor can't see, and her mother can be so embarrassing. Ritsuko is determined to win through: somehow, with the support of her teacher, her doctor, and her embarrassing but loving mother, she's going to run in the relay team on sports day. Etsuko Kishikawa's original novel took a realistic look at real-world issues later addressed in **My Sister Momoko** and **Re-Birthday**: difference, disability, and bullying. The anime version was chosen as the Japan PTA's 35th summer vacation movie.

RUN, MELOS

1981. jpn: *Hashire Melos*. aka: *Run for Life*. TV special, movie, video. dir: Tomoharu Katsumata. scr: Keinosuke Uekusa. des: Toshio Mori. ani: Toshio Mori. mus: Katsuhiro Tsubono. prd: Toei, Visual 80, Fuji TV. 87 mins. (TVm), 107 mins. (m).

Melos is a simple Sicilian farmer traveling to see his sister's wedding when he is sentenced to death by Dionysius, the tyrant of Syracuse. He asks for a few days' grace to go to the wedding and promises to return immediately. The king agrees, but only if Melos can provide a hostage to guarantee his return—to be executed in his place if he fails. His old friend Seli-

nuntius volunteers, and Melos sets off for the wedding. Despite many misadventures and temptations along the way, Melos keeps his word and returns in the nick of time. Dionysius is so impressed by Melos' honesty and Selinuntius' trust in him that he frees them both.

Osamu Dazai's 1940 short story was based on Greek legend filtered through a poem by Schiller, but it has become a classic of *Japanese* literature. The simple story, hinging on the nature of friendship and the ability to keep faith, has a happy resolution that is bitterly ironic when one remembers that Dazai committed suicide.

Toei's TV special was followed in 1992 by a longer theatrical release directed and written by Masaaki Osumi. Despite the overall simplicity of the story, he manages to infuse the film with real tension and urgency, and he has excellent art direction and design to support his work, from the future directors of **Perfect Blue** and **Jin-Roh**, Satoshi Kon and Hiroyuki Okiura. Melos runs through ravishing backgrounds by Hiroshi Ono, whose talents also enhance such stellar titles as **Kiki's Delivery Service** and have recently been put to use by Hollywood on *The Tigger Movie*. This movie version was former pop idol Kazumasa Oda's first anime score and also a voice-acting debut for the singer Akina Nakamori, who played Melos' sister. The story was animated twice more for video—for the *Classic Children's Tales* series (1992), as a 30-minute stop motion short, and again for the *Famous Japanese Fables* series (1997), as a 10-minute short directed by Keisuke Morishita.

RUN=DIM *

2001. TV series. dir: Yasunori Kato. scr: Shingo Kuwana, Yasunori Kato. des: Yoshiaki Sato. ani: Sun Hwang Hyo. mus: Kuniaki Haishima. prd: Idea Factory, TV Tokyo. 25 mins. x 13 eps.

In the 21st century, much of Japan lies underwater after a rise in sea levels. The nation becomes more expansionist in its outlook as it loses more *lebensraum*, and JESAS, an arm of the military, is implicated in a corruption scandal. Green Frontier, an international ecology organization, discovers that JESAS has been earning foreign currency by taking nuclear disposal contracts but then illegally dumping the waste in space. After such promising sub-**PATLABOR** beginnings, the two sides then start fighting each other with giant robots piloted by 14-year-old children. It's 3-D CG, so the look changes for a new century, if not the plot.

RUNE SOLDIER *

2001. JPN: *Maho Senshi Riui*. AKA: *Magical Soldier Riui; Louie the Rune Soldier*. TV series. DIR: Yoshitaka Koyama. SCR: Katsuhiko Chiba, Nobuaki Kishima, Jiro Takayama. DES: Kazunori Iwakura. ANI: Takeshi Wada. MUS: Kenji Kawai. PRD: JC Staff, WOWOW. 25 mins. x 24 eps.

Louie is the adopted son of the headmaster of the prestigious Magician's Guild, and a beginning wizard. Unfortunately, he is also a hot-headed, muscle-bound lunk who prefers to use his fists to bash his way out of (and usually before that, into) trouble than to use magic. When a party of female adventurers—warrior Genie, thief Merrill, and priestess Melissa—discover that they need a magician to complete their planned raid on a dungeon, the only one they can find who is willing is Louie. Merrill and Genie, having already encountered him in less-than-ideal circumstances, reject his application. However, when he interrupts Melissa in the midst of a holy ritual to find the "hero" whom she is to serve (a man she imagines to be a stainless paladin), she discovers to her horror that her god has instead chosen Louie as her hero-designate. Mayhem ensues, in a combination of the role-playing-inspired adventure of **SLAYERS** with the boy-meets-babes set-up of **TENCHI MUYO!** Created by **RECORD OF LODOSS WAR**'s Ryo Mizuno, who wrote the manga (with art by Mamoru Yokota), which was serialized in *Dragon* magazine and *Dragon Jr* and supposedly set on an island north of Lodoss.

RUNNING BOY

1986. JPN: *Running Boy Star Soldier no Himitsu*. AKA: *Running Boy: Secrets of Star Soldier*. Movie. DIR: Tameo Ogawa. SCR: Junichi Ishihara, Kasumi Oka. DES: Oji Suzuki. ANI: Oji Suzuki, Hidemi Kamata. MUS: Yoichi Takahashi. PRD: Toho, Film Link International. 49 mins.

Genta Shinoyama is a kindhearted boy and video-game freak who helps drunken Nomoto in the street. Nomoto, a programmer for a major games company, befriends Genta but falls under suspicion when Genta's notes for a computer game are stolen. However, it is not Nomoto but Genta's friend Hideki who is the thief, a fact proven when Hideki sends the stolen idea to a magazine. Genta challenges Hideki to a duel, his chosen weapon—Nomoto's unfinished computer game *Bee's Hive*. The boys are trapped inside the game and must be guided out by Nomoto, who enlists the help of the famous Master Takahashi.

One of the first in the self-indulgent gaming tie-in subgenre (released the same day as **SUPER MARIO BROTHERS**), this anime was made by Hudson Soft, creators of the *Star Soldier* game, and it features a cameo by their popular designer Takahashi, who also sang the theme songs. It bombed at Japanese theaters, but game-based anime would dominate the 1990s, reaching their apotheosis with **POKÉMON**.

RURAL LEADER

1970. JPN: *Inakappe Taisho*. AKA: *Little Country Chief*. TV series. DIR: Hiroshi Sasakawa. SCR: Noboru Shiroyama, Naoko Miyake, Ryosuke Sakurai, Shigeru Yanagawa, Hisatoshi Hiraya, Tsunehisa Ito, Yoshiaki Yoshida. DES: Noboru Kawasaki. ANI: Tsuneo Ninomiya, Katsumi Endo. MUS: Katsuhiko Nakamura. PRD: Tatsunoko, Fuji TV. 25 mins. x 104 eps.

Creator Noboru Kawasaki allegedly based his story on the early career of a real Japanese judo champion, but turned it on its head for this comedy sports series. Northern boy Daizaemon Kaze is determined to become a great judo champion, with the help of his special trainer—Nyanko the cat. Comical high jinks ensue, in the first Tatsunoko series to be based on a preexisting manga, in this case from *Shonen Sunday*.

RURONI KENSHIN *

1996. JPN: *Ruroni Kenshin*. AKA: *Sword of Ruro; Vagabond Sword; Kenshin the Wanderer; Kenshin the Ronin; Samurai X*. TV series, movie, video. DIR: Kazuhiro Furuhashi, Hatsuki Tsuji. SCR: Michiru Shimada, Yoshiyuki Suga. DES: Hideyoshi Hamazu, Kuniyuki Ishii, Fumie Muroi, Hatsuki Tsuji. ANI: Masami Suda. MUS: Noriyuki Asakura. PRD: Studio Gallop, Studio Deen, Fuji TV. 25 mins. x 94 eps. (TV), 25 mins. x 1 ep. (v1), 90 mins. (m), 30 mins. x 4 eps. (v2), 125 mins. (m2), 40 mins. x 1 ep. (*Themes*), ca. 60 mins. x 2 eps. (v3, *Seiso Hen*), 45 mins. x 2 eps. (v4, *New Kyoto*).

It's 1878 in Japan, 11 years after the Meiji Restoration (see **OI! RYOMA**), and most of the revolutionaries have become just as corrupt as the government they once opposed. "Weakening" foreign influences have become ever stronger, and samurai have lost many of their past rights. Kenshin Himura is a former member of the revolutionary Isshin Shishi group—a reformed assassin who now uses a reverse-bladed sword to avoid ever killing again. He falls for the beautiful Kaoru Kamiya, the impoverished daughter of a swordsmaster whose school has fallen on hard times in the modern age. Kenshin stays at Kaoru's dojo, cooking and cleaning, while also finding the time to deal with some old enemies and scare off local ruffians and disaffected former students of Kaoru's school.

RnK began as a 1994 manga in *Shonen Jump* by Nobuhiro Watsuki, inspired in part by the true-life story of Gensai Kawakami, a 19th-century killer whose good looks often distracted his foes from his cold-blooded nature. Kawakami was useful to Japan's revolutionaries during the pre-Restoration period of civil unrest, but, a danger to the new order, he was imprisoned and executed on trumped-up charges in 1871. To add to the drama, Watsuki threw in a love interest and two more characters, the bratty kid Yahiko (supposedly based on the author's younger self, who was picked last for his school kendo team), and the supertough Sanosuke (based on the semihistorical Sanosuke Harada, hero of Ryotaro Shiba's novel *Burning Sword*). The TV series adapts two major story arcs, beginning with the "Tokyo" sequence mentioned above, followed by the "Kyoto" plotline in which another former revolutionary, Makoto, takes up Kenshin's old job, and with it a certain bitterness that the revolution hasn't gone the way he wanted it. Consequently, he plots to return Japan to chaos, but is thwarted by the actions of Kenshin and his associates.

The final sequence from the manga, "Revenge" was unfinished at the time that the anime reached that point in the story. Consequently, the "Revenge" arc was not adapted for the screen; instead, episodes 63 through 95 (the final episode being video-only) of the series went their own way, largely with "filler" episodes that had nothing to do with the manga. It is the loss in quality of these filler episodes that is credited with the serial's removal from the air, although such a criticism seems churlish when the filler episodes alone run for longer than many of *RnK*'s contemporaries.

Surprisingly popular in the U.S. in spite of featuring a hero who would have happily kicked Americans out of Japan, the *Ruro* TV series occasionally lapses into pointless comedy at the expense of its overall serious tone. The depiction of martial arts, however, while often not realistic, is respectful and detailed. Luckily this doesn't slow down the action; the battle sequences are well staged and directed. Attractive design and characterization, and the emotional and spiritual intensity of the main characters, make this an interesting and involving show. The *RnK* movie (1997, *Ishin Kokorozashi Samurai eno Chinkonka, Requiem for Ishin's Knight,* AKA *Samurai X: The Motion Picture*) takes the characters to Yokohama, where Kenshin once more faces a figure from his past. He saves the life of a man being attacked by bandits and finds that he and Shigure have a link—in his old, violent life, he killed Shigure's friend. Now, Shigure is planning a coup against the Meiji Government, which he believes to be as corrupt as its precursor, but his revolt has been infiltrated by elements in the government seeking to advance their own position. It fails, and Shigure is killed after he has surrendered by one of his treacherous supporters. Kenshin faces the betrayer of his former enemy and tests his vow never to kill again.

The 1999 video series, released in English as *Samurai X: Reflection* (*RnK: Tsuioku Hen*), is a flashback to Kenshin's youth, detailing the story of how he got the distinctive cross-shaped scar on his cheek. Free of the restrictions of TV broadcast, it is much darker than the TV version. The video series also exists in a 125-minute "movie" edit, with a fake widescreen appearance and cast/crew interviews. During the serial's long run, crucial moments of the plot were rerun in three clip-shows (billed as TV "specials"), while two more compilations of previous footage were rerun as "summer holiday specials." There was also an eight-part video release, *RnK: Popular Characters*, that purported to portray fan-favorite moments, though one is tempted to point out that a "fan" would buy the episodes anyway. A two-part sequel, released in English as *Samurai X: Trust & Betrayal* (2001, *RnK: Seiso Hen, RnK: Time Chapter*), features an appearance by Kenshin's son, while the substantially later sequel *RnK: New Kyoto Arc* (2011) retells the story from the point of view of the supporting character Misao Makimachi. A live-action film, titled simply *Rurouni Kenshin* (2012), was directed by Keishi Otomo. ●

RXXX: PRESCRIPTION FOR PAIN *

2002. JPN: *Ingoku Byoto*. AKA: *Obscene Prison Ward*. Video. DIR: Norihiko Nagahama. SCR: Rokurota Makabe. DES: MIE. ANI: MIE. MUS: Yoshi. PRD: YOUC, Digital Works (Vanilla Series). 30 mins.

Junichi is a young doctor, looking forward to the imminent retirement of his boss Tadahiko Mizuno, and the subsequent handover of the Mizuno hospital to him. Those familiar with the "nursing" subgenre of Japanese animation will know exactly what this is going to mean—see NIGHT SHIFT NURSES. Imagine, then, his irritation when Tadahiko's pert, sexy, competent daughter Serika arrives. Junichi now realizes that his sure-fire promotion is likely to go to the boss's daughter, unless he can stealthily take over the hospital through a dedicated campaign of bondage, degradation, and humiliation—yes, it's one of those anime. Accordingly, he begins molesting the nurses, some of whom enjoy it, and some of whom don't. Most are relatives of Serika and she, of course, is the grand prize, in an anime from the VANILLA SERIES, based, as usual, on an erotic computer game. For reasons we do not comprehend, the publicity for the American release calls the protagonist Junichi, whereas his name in the original Japanese version was Makoto. We don't think anyone's losing any sleep over it, though. ●N●V

RYOKO'S CASE FILES

2008. JPN: *Yakushiji Ryoko no Kaiki Jikenbo*. AKA: *The Strange Case Files of Ryoko Yakushiji*. TV series. DIR: Taro Iwasaki. SCR: Hiroyuki Kawasaki. DES: Junichiro Taniguchi, Atsuko Sasaki, Manabu Otsuzuki. ANI: Junichiro Taniguchi, Atsuko Sasaki. MUS: N/C. PRD: Dogakobo, GANSIS, Starchild Records. 23 mins. x 13 eps.

Ryoko is just 27 but she's already a superintendent in the Tokyo Metropolitan Police. A multilingual graduate from Tokyo University's prestigious Law Faculty, a crack shot, and a highly skilled martial artist, she's part of a very influential family, owners of one of Asia's top security companies, but she's chosen to work as a public servant. Still, she doesn't hesitate to use her family connections and assets if she needs help at work. Her number two is Assistant Inspector Junichiro Izumida, who is completely unaware that she adores him. Her loyal maids Lucienne and Marianne also form part of the team. Their beat is unusual: cases with apparent supernatural or paranormal connections.

This show is based on a series of books written by Yoshiki Tanaka and illustrated by Narumi Kakinouchi, which ran from 1998 to 2007 and spun off a manga by the pair in 2004 that ran to 2009. Tanaka is one of Japan's leading science fantasy novelists, best known as author of the epic novel series LEGEND OF GALACTIC HEROES, while Kakinouchi is the creator of VAMPIRE PRINCESS MIYU and an animation director and designer in her own right. With a pedigree like that, fans are entitled to expect polished, intelligent entertainment, and that's exactly what the show delivers. ●

RYU THE STONE AGE BOY

1971. JPN: *Genshi Shonen Ryu*. AKA: *Ryu the Early Man; Ryu the Cave Boy*. TV series. DIR: Masayuki Akehi. SCR: Tadashi Kondo, Kuniaki Oshikawa, Toyohiro Ando. DES: Kazuo Komatsubara. ANI: Mataharu Urata, Eiji Tanaka, Kazuo Hayashi, Hiroshi Wakabayashi. MUS: Takeo Watanabe. PRD: Toei Doga, TBS. 25 mins. x 22 eps.

Ryu is born with white skin in a primitive land where everyone else is dark-skinned. Left as a sacrifice to dinosaurs, he is found and reared by an ape, Kitty. When she is killed by a one-eyed Tyrannosaurus Rex, he sets out to avenge her and find his real mother. He makes friends with the beautiful Ran and her kid brother Don, but meets savagery and danger from men who fear his skin color and dinosaurs who just want to eat him, including a confrontation with the tyrannosaur which is scary despite the limitations of animation of the time. The animation style mixed both adult, dramatic images from Kazuo Komatsubara and more angular, primitive artwork for which Mataharu Urata used knives instead of brushes to apply the paint.

Based on Shotaro Ishinomori's manga *Ryu's Road* (*Ryu no Michi*), what first appears to be an anachronistic combination of *Tarzan* and *One Million Years B.C.* (1966) is later revealed as part of the plot. Ryu's mother is not a cavewoman at all, but an agent from the distant future, which helps explain not only Ryu's strange features, but eventually, the reasons that supposedly extinct dinosaurs are seen coexisting with cavemen. Ryu, Ran, and Don are also time travelers, and, in a lovely paradox, the enmity between Ryu and the tyrannosaur actually predates Ryu's own birth, since it was an adult Ryu that caused/will cause the dinosaur to lose an eye in the first place. Compare to **FLINT THE TIME DETECTIVE**, although the most obvious echoes are of Hanna-Barbera's *Dino Boy* (1965), in which a child of our own time falls out of a plane into a lost valley populated by dinosaurs.

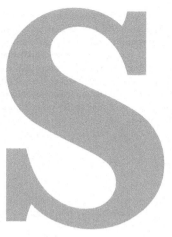

S.A. *

2008. JPN: *Special A*. TV series. DIR: Yoshika-zu Miyao. SCR: Jukki Hanada, Kenji Sugihara, Michiko Ito, Natsue Yoguchi, Yuko Kakihara. DES: Kiyotaka Nakahara, Ayumi Sugimoto. ANI: Kiyotaka Nakahara, Yuka Takemori, Kenji Fukazawa. MUS: Rie Mitsunaga, Shogo Kaida. PRD: AIC, GONZO, Dax Productions, Marvelous AQL, NAS, Pony Canyon, Showgate. 25 mins. x 24 eps.

Hikari's carpenter father loves to watch wrestling. So does his well-to-do buddy Takashima. What could be more natural than for two friends to introduce their six-year-old kids? If only they could have foreseen the consequences; Hikari vowed to beat Takeshima's boy Kei at wrestling and lost. Ever since then she's insisted on enrolling in the same schools as Kei, determined to beat him at something—anything. But it's never happened. She's always been one of the top two students in school, but Kei has always been number one. At the elite Hakusenkan academy, she's in the Special A class for top students and considers Kei her best friend and closest rival. Kei, meanwhile, is hopelessly in love with her.

School romances often center the action on a special group of students to enable the story to concentrate on just a few characters without seeming artificial. There are elements of **His and Her Circumstances** here too, with even older borrowings from **Ranma ½**. Maki Minami's 2003 manga doesn't concern itself with originality, nor does the anime version. Instead it takes a clutch of high-school wish-fulfillment stereotypes and surrounds them with imagery as cute and fluffy as an Internet picture of a basket of kittens. Nobody expects them to achieve world peace or a cure for the common cold; they're fine just as they are.

SABER MARIONETTES *

1995. Video, TV series. DIR: Masami Shimoda, Koji Masunari. SCR: Mayori Sekijima, Kenichi Kanemaki. DES: Tsukasa Kotobuki, Hidekazu Shimamura, Kazuo Nagai. ANI: Eiji Suganuma. MUS: Parome. PRD: Studio Juno, TV Tokyo. 30 mins. x 3 eps. (v, *R*), 25 mins. x 25 eps. (TV, *J*), 25 mins. x 6 eps. (v, *J Again*), 25 mins. x 25 eps. (TV, *J-X*), 25 mins. x 1 ep. (v, *J-X*).

In the late 22nd century, humanity spreads out from an overpopulated Earth. The colony ship Mesopotamia crashes on a distant world, and the six male survivors christen the planet Terra 2. Maintaining the species through cloning, the men establish six countries, each ruled by the pure clone of its founder: Japones, Sheien (probably China), New Texas, Peterburg (Russia), Geltland (Germany), and Romana (Italy).

Based on Satoru Akahori's comic novel in *Dragon* magazine, *SM* is a laughable simplification of the same body/soul concepts that informed the same year's **Ghost in the Shell**. It takes the **Adventures of Pinocchio** theme buried in so many robot anime and marries it to the ultimate variant on the magical-girlfriend and **Tenchi Muyo!** genres—a lone boy on a whole world of tailor-made women. It also features the most haphazard release schedule of any anime, jumping from video to TV, back to video, then back to TV, and finally finishing on video again! Two hundred years after mankind's arrival on Terra 2, clones of the originals live on, served by female-form "marionette" androids. Most are simply machines incapable of emotion or thought, but over time some have become more advanced. However the greatest leap—to androids with a "heart"—has yet to be made. An evil scientist and a psychotic villain are out to take over the state and double-cross each other, when the scientist is mowed down by a newly created android, Lime, made for Villey Junior, teenage son of a Romana dignitary. She and her fellow-marionettes Cherry and Bloodberry help Junior to save the day after fighting the bad guys and their powerful, vicious "sexadolls," depraved marionettes who get off on violence rather than sweet submission.

Resetting the plot to zero and recycling the same or similar characters in much the same way as *Tenchi Muyo!*, the series proper began the following year on TV with the prequel *Saber Marionette J*, set 200 years earlier. Japonese teenager Otaru discovers the marionette Lime in a hidden basement beneath a deserted museum (refer to the similar discovery of Ifrita in **El Hazard**). Otaru is considered odd because he prefers his relationship with his cute little puppet to the normal male-male relationships on his world. Lime is the first marionette to have a special "girly circuit," like a human heart, which gives her feelings. A little later, Otaru accidentally finds more such marionettes, Cherry and Bloodberry, with the same special circuit. The few marionettes with this circuit are "saber marionettes," and they have a secret purpose. They must achieve spiritual growth, seemingly by playing out the same corny fantasies as countless other anime babes, like getting into bed naked with their embarrassed man, fighting to be top bitch in his pack, participating in "talent" contests, cooking for him, and so on. Should this unlikely program of spiritual discipline enable them to transcend themselves, human females will "revive." The franchise itself revived on video with *SM J Again* (1997), which appeared to be six unbroadcast TV episodes of a tiresomely domestic nature, was released straight to video, and continued straight on from the series. The series bounced back onto TV as *SM J to X* (1998), with the predictable return of the previous series' bad-guy Faust, along with his team of pretty "Saber Dolls." The final episode was not broadcast on TV but is only available on video. **◐Ⓥ**

SABER RIDER AND THE STAR SHERIFFS *

1984. JPN: *Seijushi Bismarck*. AKA: *Star Gunner Bismarck*. TV series. DIR: Masami Anno, Tadamasa Takahashi, Hiroyuki Yokoyama, Norio Kashima, Akira Shigino, Hiroshi Yoshida, Rei Hidaka. SCR: Mitsuru Majima, Tsunehisa Ito, Kazusane Hisajima. DES: Shigeru Kato, Yasushi Moriki. ANI: Tadamasa Takahashi, Moriyasu Taniguchi. MUS: Osamu Totsuka. PRD: Studio Pierrot, Nippon TV. 25 mins. x 52 eps.

The New Frontier is an untamed region of space where the only law is the Star Sheriffs. From its space station, a team of brave young people—Saber Rider, Colt, Fireball, and April—ride out in their sheriff-shaped giant robot to defend the galaxy from bad guys like the Outriders. Before "versioning" for the U.S. market where, with its Wild West theme, it was inevitably headed, *SR&tSS* was set in the solar system, where the alien Deskula invaders had conquered Ganymede, and Earth was defended by the all-Japanese hero Shinji and his buddies, whose names were regarded (by the Japanese) as suitably Western—Bill, Richard, Marian, and Walter. When the series was altered for U.S. consumption, story editor Marc Handler (who went on to produce **VOLTRON**) had to make teen Texan Colt into the hero and sideline the original lead, Japanese kid Fireball, resulting in some hilarious scenes where other characters are looking at Fireball but supposedly listening to Colt. He also had problems with the amount of teenage drinking in the original, editing out all drunken behavior and moving many scenes from saloons to the "coffee shops" and "soda fountains" that were so much a part of the Old West.

SABU AND ICHI INVESTIGATE

1968. JPN: *Sabu to Ichi Torimono Hikae*. TV series. DIR: Rintaro, Mori Masaki, Shinichi Suzuki, Fumio Kurokawa, Eiji Kojima, Mami Murano, Kunihiko Okazaki, Masayuki Hayashi, Takeshi Tamiya, Tomoharu Katsumata, Noboru Ishiguro. SCR: Takao Suzuki, Keiichi Abe, Takashi Umebayashi, Yoji Nishikawa. DES: Shotaro Ishinomori. ANI: Akio Sugino, Mami Murano. MUS: Takeo Yamashita. PRD: Mushi, Studio Zero, Toei, NET. 25 mins. x 52 eps.

A detective story from Shotaro Ishinomori in which two Sherlock Holmes types solve a range of crimes in old Edo. Sabu, a young man in search of adventure, comes to the big city and becomes assistant to Saheiji, police chief of the Ryusenji quarter, who is almost crippled by rheumatism and spends much of his time bedridden. A local character, the masseur Ichi, turns out to be a very useful contact and helps Sabu in his efforts to keep Edo crime-free on behalf of his boss.

SACRED BLACKSMITH, THE *

2009. JPN: *Seiken no Katanakaji (Blacksmith)*. AKA: *Seiken no Blacksmith*. TV series. DIR: Masamitsu Hidaka. SCR: Masashi Suzuki, Rie Koshika. DES: Jun Nakai, Michie Watanabe. ANI: Jun Nakai, Yuko Matsui, Eiji Abiko, Naoaki Hojo. MUS: Tamiya Terashima. PRD: Manglobe, AT-X, Earth Star Entertainment, Media Factory, Nippon Cultural Broadcasting, Inc. 27 mins. x 12 eps. (TV).

Cecily Campbell is a feisty redhead determined to become a knight, like her father and grandfather before her, using the family's heirloom sword to defend their hometown from demonic attack. But she breaks it in a fight against a demon-crazed opponent. Luke, the taciturn young warrior who saves her, is a blacksmith, with the power to forge weapons that could save the world—assuming he has time in between saving Cecily from numerous threats. Still, her gift for making friends could turn out to be just as important in the battle for human survival. Based on Isao Miura's 2009 light-novel series, with art by Kotaro Yamada, this generic fantasy looks good, largely thanks to some lovely background work from Beijing Golden Pinasters and pleasant, if generic, character designs. The attitudes are also generic, with stock characters and tropes: Cicely's breasts a constant point of reference, a trick that was old when it was overused in **SLAYERS**. Overall this is pleasant enough, undemanding and useful if you want cuteness that doesn't involve *moe* schoolgirls and have a few hours you don't mind wasting. **Ⓥ**

SACRED SEVEN *

2011. TV series, movie, video. DIR: Yoshimitsu Ohashi, Yasuo Murai. SCR: Shin Yoshida, Kiyoko Yoshimura, Yuniko Ayana. DES: Mutsumi Inomata, Yuriko Chiba, Eiji Nakada, Jiro Kono. ANI: Eiji Nakada, Yuriko Chiba, Takuya Suzuki, Tatsuya Suzuki. MUS: Toshihiko Sahashi. PRD: Sunrise, Bandai Visual, Hakuhodo DY Media Partners, MBS. 24 mins. x 12 eps. (TV), 60 mins. (m), 12 mins. x 2 eps. (v).

Sixteen-year-old Alma Tandoji keeps to himself and likes it that way. He's unusually strong and once injured a number of his classmates. So when teen billionairess Ruri Aiba shows up at his place with her butlers and maids, he's unwilling to join in her schemes. Especially not when she spins a crazy yarn about her parents being killed by mystic Darkstones from outer space, her twin sister being turned into crystal, and Alma's dangerous rages not being his fault. It seems that 17 years previously, seven different types of alien crystals fell to earth, affecting a number of individuals and granting them strange powers. High school geology club suddenly gets much more interesting as monsters attack Japan, and Alma finds himself changing in unpredictable ways. Cue evil scientist, conflicted fighter for freedom, merchandisable mecha, sibling loyalty, and gemstone auctions.

Look out for homages to classic anime and live-action TV. Created by Sunrise house pseudonym Hajime Yadate, with designs by one of anime's bona fide legends—Inomata was one of the prime movers on **BIRTH**, regarded by many old school fans as the first video to show what the medium could do—this show looks and sounds good, but can't decide whether it's a boys' action adventure show, a knowing parody of classic anime, or a high school saga. The 2012 movie *Sacred Seven: Shirogane no Tsubasa* (*Sacred Seven: Wings of the Silver Moon*) has some new animation spliced into a recap of the show's best battles. Yasuo Muroi is credited as director, with Nakada and Chiba reprising their character design and animation director roles. Two 12-minutes "picture dramas" focusing on high school hijinks were spun off the movie as DVD specials. **V**

SACRILEGE *

2002. JPN: *Kaishun*. AKA: *Rejuvenation*. Video. DIR: Katsuma Kanazawa. SCR: Kazuhiro Oyama. DES: Hiroya Iijima. ANI: Shigenori Awai. MUS: N/C. PRD: Studio Kuma, Miami Soft. 30 mins. x 2 eps.
Lesbian cops Atsuko and Kei investigate a drug deal that has gone wrong, only to blunder into the activities of an evil cult. A sinister cabal of old men in search of immortality has found a drug that *almost* works. However, when tested on unsuspecting members of the public, it transforms them into crazed demonic rapists. Meanwhile, the shaven-headed female servants of the cabal realize that the cops are on their trail and do what they can to scare them off, which, with sad predictability, involves capture, bondage, torture, and sexualized violence. *Sacrilege* appears strangely old-fashioned, with rather ugly characters, a retro look and a rapacious plot that recalls 1990s tits-and-tentacles titles like **NIGHTMARE CAMPUS**. **CNV**

SADAMITSU THE DESTROYER *

2001. JPN: *Hakaima Sadamitsu*. AKA: *Destruction Devil Sadamitsu*. TV series. DIR: Shoichi Ohata, Yukihiro Matsushita. SCR: Masanao Akahoshi. DES: Akira Kikuchi, Tamotsu Shinohara. ANI: Masaaki Kannan, Koichi Ohata. MUS: N/C. PRD: Studio Deen, WOWOW. 25 mins. x 10 eps.
Sadamitsu Tsubaki is a self-proclaimed vigilante armed with a wooden sword. The Exiles are a group of interstellar criminals cast into space on a long and eternal orbit that unfortunately has Earth right in the middle of its trajectory. Earth is threatened by 20 million exiles, but Sadamitsu has an important ally—Junk, his sentient helmet,

made by the race who exiled the Exiles. However, Sadamitsu and Junk must also contend with Vulture, an intelligent spaceship sent to Earth to police Exile activity but which rejects Sadamitsu's help. **ULTRAMAN** meets **GUYVER**, based on a manga in *Ultra Jump* by Tadahiko Nakadaira.

SADAMOTO, YOSHIYUKI

1962–. Born in Yamaguchi Prefecture, Sadamoto sold his first manga work while still at university. He began working for the animation studio Telecom, before joining Gainax as a character designer on **WINGS OF HONNEAMISE**. He has subsequently been an animator on **THE SECRET OF BLUE WATER** and **GUNBUSTER** and was the character designer on **EVANGELION** and **.HACK**. He was also the author of the *Evangelion* manga, which achieved best-seller status before the series even aired, and is regarded as an alternate but valid continuity. As the designer of choice on Mamoru Hosoda's movies since **THE GIRL WHO LEAPT THROUGH TIME**, his personal style has become one of the most visible in modern feature anime outside the Ghibli axis.

SAIKANO *

2002. JPN: *Saishu Heiki Kanojo*. AKA: *She, The Ultimate Weapon*. TV series, video. DIR: Mitsuko Kase. SCR: Itaru Era. DES: Hisashi Kagawa, Hiroyuki Kanbe, Tomohiro Kawahara. ANI: Jeong Ho-Jang, Keuk Sun-Jeon, Seong Yong-An, Sun Hak-Jeon, Won Cheol-Seo, Yong Il-Park, Kazuhiro Tanaka, Ryo Sato. MUS: Takeo Miratsu. PRD: Shogakukan, Tohoku Shinsha, Toshiba EMI, Gonzo, CBC. 23 mins. x 13 eps. (TV), 30 mins. x 2 eps. (v).
Hokkaido teenager Shuji had a love affair with an older woman that has made him distant and mistrustful. Passive, shy fellow high school senior Chise has a crush on him, but she's the kind of girl who is constantly apologizing for needing to breathe. She finally steels herself to ask him out, and the pair are actually starting a real relationship, when a mass of bombers whose origin is unknown suddenly attacks Sapporo and flattens the city. It looks as if everyone will be killed, when a small point of red light streaks from the Sapporo television tower into the sky and destroys the bombers. Shuji is stunned to learn that the girl he's seeing is actually a

cyborg weapon in the Japan Self-Defense Force.
Saikano employs real-world Hokkaido settings, which were in vogue at the time thanks to the end of the long-running live-action TV show *From The North* (*DE, see also **DIAMOND DAYDREAMS**). It also shares that combination of teenage yearning and sci-fi combat that formed such a vital component of the same year's **VOICES OF A DISTANT STAR**. However, its clearest influences lie in the apparently doomed romance and fetishized girlfriendweapons of **MAHOROMATIC** and **LIMIT THE MIRACLE GIRL**. Where 20th-century anime might have allegorized pubescent or emotional turmoil with animal analogies or quasi-religious mysticism, the **CHOBITS** generation is more apt to understand human interactions in terms of hardware interfaces and software conflicts. So it is that Chise's ongoing "development" as a robot weapon causes her to overreact to an impending earthquake as if it is another attack. Meanwhile, Shuji develops a strange revulsion to his would-be girlfriend's declining humanity, and neither is able to cope with collateral damage caused by Chise's attempts to defend the Earth.
Some of anime's best drama springs from the marriage of teenage angst with physical events. The Japan of *Saikano* stands alone in a war against an unnamed foe (although in one scene a downed enemy pilot speaks English), beset by disasters both natural and military, with peripheral characters affording glimpses of the harsh life on the front line—shades here of **GUNPARADE MARCH** and **GUNBUSTER**. This could be read as an effective evocation of the modern world—as in **HOWL'S MOVING CASTLE**, civilization marches on regardless while contested in a savage war elsewhere—but is all the more striking for its relation to the traumas of the teen target audience. Later episodes allude to the closing scenes of Ridley Scott's *Blade Runner* (1982), as Chise and Shuji seek a life, of sorts, together. *Saikano* is also an anime with a brutally blunt and uncompromising antiwar message, rivaling **GRAVE OF THE FIREFLIES** in the accusatory way it approaches not the battles themselves, but their aftermath. Technology is regarded, even by the avuncular scientist who is Chise's "creator," as a curse that will drag

the entire human race on a course for destruction, toward a truly pessimistic denouement.

In the autumn of 2005, a two-part DVD from the same director gave another slant on the story. *Saikano: Another Love Song* tells the story of Chise's prototype, career officer Mizuki, who watches Chise's terrible potential unfolding while she must face the fact that she has reached the end of her own powers. Although billed as a "sidestory" to the original series, these two chapters are so integrated into the main story that they could have easily been inserted into its midpoint as two more episodes. The art style in both versions also manages to capture the delicate watercolor look of Shin Takahashi's original manga from *Big Comic Spirits* magazine. A live-action movie adaptation, *Saikano: The Last Love Song on this Little Planet*, was premiered at the Tokyo International Film Festival in 2005 and went on general release in Japan in 2006. **◊**

SAILOR MOON *

1992. JPN: *Bishojo Senshi Sailor Moon*. AKA: *Pretty Soldier Sailor Moon*. TV series, movie. DIR: Junichi Sato, Kazuhisa Takenouchi, Kunihiko Ikuhara, Yuji Endo, Hiroki Shibata, Masahiro Hosoda, Takuya Igarashi. SCR: Sukehiro Tomita, Yoji Enokido, Ryota Yamaguchi, Jun Maekawa, Kazuhiko Godo, Chitose Mizuno. DES: Kazuko Tadano, Ikuko Ito, Katsumi Tamegai. ANI: Kazuko Tadano, Ikuko Ito, Masahiro Ando, Hisashi Kagawa, Hideyuki Motohashi. MUS: Takanori Arisawa, Tetsuo Komuro, Kazuo Sano. PRD: Toei, Aoi, TV Asahi. 25 mins. x 200 eps., 60 mins. x 3 movies, 16 mins. (m, *Ami-chan*), 42 mins. (m, *Make Up*).

Usagi Tsukino (Serena in the U.S. version) is a cheerful but clumsy teenage crybaby. Nevertheless, she is fated to become Sailor Moon, leader of a team of brave girls: Ami (Amy/Mercury), Minako (Mina/Venus), Rei (Raye/Mars), and Makoto (Lita/Jupiter). Collectively, they are known as the Sailor Warriors (Sailor Senshi), or Sailor Scouts in the U.S. She meets a magical cat, Luna, and receives classic magical-girl items (including a wand and tiara) and superpowers to help her transform. In a past life, she was Moon Princess Serenity, beloved of Prince Endymion. That love will be reborn because Endymion has also been reincarnated as a human with the ability to magically transform into dashing hero (and occasional boy-damsel in distress) Tuxedo Kamen (Tuxedo Mask).

SM began as *Codename Sailor V* (1991, often confused with the unrelated **GRADUATION** spin-off *Sailor Victory*), a short-lived manga by Naoko Takeuchi in *Run-Run* magazine in which a teenage girl moonlights as a superhero wearing a distinctive sailor-style Japanese schoolgirl uniform. Reworked as a sequel which was published in *Nakayoshi* magazine as part of a cross-media promotion with the anime, the refashioned story now featured several color-coded heroines in the fashion of live-action team shows, as well as a supernatural spin—lunar reincarnations would also crop up in its contemporaries **PLEASE SAVE MY EARTH** and **BOUNTY DOG**. There are echoes of *Power Rangers* in the "monster-of-the-week" fight sequences in which our heroines take on ever more outrageously costumed baddies, but the show is saved from banality by the strength of its plotting, its earnest, honest romance, and its refusal to talk down to its audience. With reincarnation a given, the show is unafraid of death; the first season closes with a harrowing assault on the icy lair of the evil Queen Beryl, in which the entire cast is killed off (albeit temporarily). Needless to say, the sanitized U.S. release unconvincingly pretends they have merely been detained elsewhere.

It is unlikely that many of the girls who watched the first season were still glued to their TVs by the last episode in 1996, a ratings disaster the producers attempted to avoid by rebranding and refashioning the series to entice younger audiences. As *SM R[eturns]* in 1993, it introduced new foes from the Black Moon, who intend to destroy present-day Tokyo in order to prevent the founding of Crystal Tokyo in the future. It also introduced Chibi-Usa (Rini), Serena and Endymion's future daughter, who time-travels to stay with the girl who is/was/will be her mother. Rebranded again as Kunihiko Ikuhara's *SM S[uper]* in 1994, it introduced the controversially homoerotic Sailors Uranus and Neptune, who are in search of three mystic talismans. The talismans must be united to summon the Holy Grail, which is needed to locate the Messiah but must be kept out of the hands of Professor Tomoe and the Death Busters lest it summon the *Dark* Messiah. The new Sailors suspect (rightly) that Sailor Saturn is the Dark Messiah, splitting the group with in-fighting. By 1994's season *SM S[uper] S* (note the easy-to-confuse typography!), the focus of the show was gradually shifting away from Usagi and onto Chibi-Usa, thought to be more appealing to younger girls as the original target audience put childish things (i.e., merchandise) behind them. However, ratings hit an all-time low, partly because Chibi-Usa was unpopular, but also because Ikuhara's growing obsessions with fairy tales and subtexts (see his later **UTENA**) were lost on the target audience. Chibi-Usa befriends Pegasus, a flying horse, who enlists her help in keeping an important Golden Crystal from the evil Queen Nephrenia, leader of the Dead Moon Circus, who needs it to escape from her prison (inside a mirror) and conquer Earth. There was also a 48-minute *Super S* TV special, containing a trilogy of stories—a summary of the preceding seasons; a cruise-ship cutaway with Neptune and Uranus explaining why they are not appearing in this season; and a final part in which Chibi-Usa fights a monster inside a vampire castle.

For the final season, *SM Sailor Stars*, Chibi-Usa returns to the future, Mamoru leaves to study abroad, and the remaining Sailor Scouts must hold off Shadow Galactica, a group of evil Scouts led by Sailor Galaxia. They are aided in this by the Three Lights (AKA *Starlights*), a boy band who can transform into leather-clad girls in times of need.

There were also several theatrical outings—Ikuhara's *Sailor Moon R* (1993) takes place during the Nega Moon story in the TV series. An alien boy befriends the child who will grow up to be Tuxedo Mask, but, when they meet again as young adults, a misunderstanding leads to tragedy. The same year saw his *Make Up Sailor Senshi!* (AKA *Dreaming Moon*), a short film of animated character biographies and gossip. *Sailor Moon S The Movie* (1994) focuses on Luna, Sailor Moon's feline friend, who is rescued by and falls in love with a young astronomer caught up in the battle to save Earthwhen evil Princess Kaguya (see **REI REI**) plots to freeze it. Hiroki Shibata's *Sailor Moon SS* (1995) features Chibi-Usa's new friend, a modern-day Pied Piper, who leads all the local children toward a spaceship, and the Sailors must save them from being abducted. On the same bill was the short feature *Ami-chan's First Love* starring Sailor Mercury (always popular with the series' unexpectedly large audience of boys, because she did stuff with computers). The series was eventually brought to the U.S. with an indifferent dub, where it flopped, chiefly because it was shown at an insanely early time of the morning, edged into dead airtime by more powerful local interests. *SM*'s failure was an object lesson in how a multimedia sensation, heavily reliant on merchandising tie-ins, can crash without adequate support—Bandai would not make the same mistake with the later **POKÉMON**. Much imitated in modern anime such as **WEDDING PEACH**, *SM* has also been the subject of erotic parodies in **VENUS FIVE** and *Sailor and the Seven Balls*.

As the original *SM* viewers matured into a whole new demographic, a live-action TV series, with the official English title of *Pretty Guardian Sailor Moon* (2003) ran for 49 episodes and two DVD specials—somewhat longer than average in the world of Japanese TV, although its ratings were never quite as high as those of the anime. The release of the series coincided with a republication of the *SM* manga, with some sections rewritten or altered to make it conform closer to its latest "adaptation." The live version also introduced some new Sailors—Luna the cat occasionally transforming into the human-form Sailor Luna; a "Dark" version of Sailor Mercury after she is possessed by an antagonist; and a "Princess" form of Sailor Moon herself, when she is temporarily possessed by the spirit of her older self.

Although *Sailor Moon*'s late-era fortunes have been nowhere near as traumatic as those of **CANDY CANDY**, the franchise's creator has experienced some palpable ups and downs, including a tempestuous falling-out with her original publisher Kodansha, seemingly only smoothed over after several years of working for a rival. Much like J. K. Rowling in the West, Takeuchi enjoyed a level of success sufficient to give her substantially more clout

with publishers than many lesser creators (**POLAR BEAR CAFÉ**). This, combined with the temptations of married life (to **HUNTER x HUNTER** creator Yoshihiro Togashi) and motherhood, lured her away from the artistic treadmill for several years, in which her most notable manga creation was the semi-autobiographical *Princess Naoko Takeuchi's Return-to-Society Punch* (1998–2004). She did, however, bury the hatchet with Kodansha in time for the release of *Pretty Guardian Sailor Moon Crystal* (2014), a reboot of the anime series, billed as a celebration of its 20th anniversary.

SAILOR SUIT EXAMINATION FOR MARRIED WOMEN

2011. JPN: *Sailor-fuku Shinryo Tsumaka*. Video. DIR: Kiyoshiro Kato. SCR: Hideo Kobayashi. DES: Shintaro Nakata, Seihodo. ANI: Shintaro Nakata. MUS: N/C. PRD: YOUC, Digital Works. 30 mins. x 2 eps.

Student Nozomu is an amateur psychiatrist of some repute. Following in his late father's footsteps, he wants to work on the mental health of women. He believes that, through hypnosis, he can remove past mental trauma for teenage girls, who will then be able to experience a fulfilling school life. When his thesis is thrown out, he decides to prove his theories. So he gets his mother, her friends, and a school friend of his to dress up in sailor suits and play schoolgirls in his experiment. Porn anime based on the game by Rose Crown, part of the **VANILLA SERIES**. **N**

SAINT BEAST

2005. TV series. DIR: Harume Kosaka. SCR: Mayu Sugiura, Ryu Tamura. DES: Sakura Asagi. ANI: Toshiko Sasaki. MUS: N/C. PRD: Wonderfarm. 25 mins. x 6 eps. (v), 25 mins. x 13 eps. (TV, *Angel Chronicles*).

Two mighty angels angered the gods and were cast out of Heaven and sealed in prison. When they finally break free, Yuda the Kirin and Ruka the Phoenix decide to take revenge by conquering their former heavenly home. Soon the guardian spirits of Earth are disappearing. The Goddess calls upon the four Saint Beasts, angelic beings with the powers of their totem animals, to investigate. The four take human form and descend to Earth to live among humans and try to solve the mystery. The story is loosely based on Chinese legend,

with shades here of Sun Wukong's uproar in heaven from **JOURNEY TO THE WEST**, but also of the angelic angst of **SAINT SEIYA** and **EARTHIAN**, since it soon focuses on the relationships and pasts of the characters, whose chosen human forms are young, beautiful, and male. Yuda is a hunky, muscular redhead in his mid-20s, Ruka is a cute, spiky blond a year or so younger, and the Four Saint Beasts sent after them are 22-year-old Seiryu no Go, a dark-haired heroic hunk; 21-year-old Genbu no Shin, whose long green ponytail, spectacles, and interest in nature denote the brains of the party; purple-haired 20-year-old princeling Suzaku no Rei; and cute blond 19-year-old Byakko no Gai, the baby of the party, obsessed, like most teen gods, with TV, food, and shopping. Almost immediately, the Saint Beasts are diverted from their primary mission to find two missing brother Saints, half-human and half-angel, and settle into a country estate with them for some sub–**TENCHI MUYO!** domestic bickering. Ryusei no Kira is a bad boy in black leather who used to torment Go in childhood, and his kid brother Fuuga no Maaya immediately becomes Gai's soulmate and partner in goofing off. The primary plotline does reemerge as Yuda and Ruka wreak havoc among the lower ranks of the angels, and our heroes wrestle with the idea that their old friends could turn to the Dark Side. The character development and promising plot set-up isn't resolved in the short running time, leaving a sense of missed opportunity that detracts from the pretty art and design. Of course, what Western anime viewers lack is the vast backstory available in Japan in the manga and CD dramas. All the anime is intended to do is provide pretty moving pictures for the story's existing fans. Despite the boy-on-boy overtones, there's nothing sexually explicit here—go to the CD dramas for that. The music is undistinguished and the animation no more than acceptable, but boy-band fans will love it. Kei Arisugawa created *SB*, and **PHANTOM QUEST CORP**'s Juzo Mutsuki is credited on planning for the anime. The show is also packaged for promotion on mobile phone screens, at time of writing merely in terms of extras and character-based screen themes, although it would not surprise us at all if that is merely the beginning of a mobile broadcast effort like that of **LEGEND OF DUO**.

Nanako Shimazaki's *Saint Beast Angel Chronicles* (2007, *Saint Beast Koin Jojiji Tenshi Tan*) was a 13-episode prequel in which six angels are selected by the god Zeus to sort out troubles on Earth, only to reveal that the activities on the ground are distractions, aimed at keeping the gods' eyes away from far more dangerous plotting going on in heaven. See also **ANGEL TALES**, which is set in the same universe.

SAINT ELMO: APOSTLE OF LIGHT

1987. JPN: *Saint Elmo Hikari no Raihosha*. TV special. DIR: Tomoharu Katsumata. SCR: Hiroyasu Yamaura. DES: Katsumi Itahashi. ANI: Yasuhiro Yamaguchi. MUS: Michiru Oshima. PRD: Toei, Yomiuri TV. 84 mins.

A Jovian cloud-cruiser disappears in a strange accident, its pilot feared lost. The master "electrician" Issei Yuki is recalled to Osaka from his current proj-ect in Africa and dispatched to investigate. He discovers that there are problems on the giant orbital power station Saint Elmo that are creating electrical storms and threatening to plunge Earth into eternal darkness. In order to save his father's great project, and Mayu, the girl he loves, he tries to stop the Saint Elmo from falling into the sun. A very obscure TV anime, not broadcast in the Tokyo area, and therefore unknown to a large proportion of the *Japanese* audience. Despite a development credit from **CAPTAIN HARLOCK**–creator Leiji Matsumoto, *Saint Elmo* had its true genesis as a vanity project for the Kansai Electric Company, which wanted to do something to commemorate its 30th anniversary. Apparently, this hokey sci-fi show was it.

SAINT LUMINOUS MISSION HIGH SCHOOL

1998. JPN: *Sei Luminous Jogakuen*. AKA: *St. Luminous College*. TV series. DIR: Tetsuro Amino. SCR: Akira Oketani. DES: Hisashi Kagawa. ANI: Hisashi Kagawa, Tadashi Yoshida. MUS: Michiya Katakura. PRD: Pioneer, TV Tokyo. 25 mins. x 13 eps.

Two lucky guys become the first male pupils to attend the all-girl St. Luminous College, gaining a seemingly limitless supply of adoring classmates who can't wait to find out about the world of psychic investigation. A predictable rehash of

Pioneer's **TENCHI MUYO!** franchise with a cursory *X-Files* twist, this anime was based on an "original" idea by Kenji Terada.

SAINT OCTOBER

2007. AKA: *Seioku*. TV series. DIR: Masafumi Sato. SCR: Yuki Enatsu, Megumi Sasano, Yuka Yamada. DES: Shoji Hara, Kazuhiro Takahashi. ANI: Tomokazu Sugimura. MUS: Hiroshi Takaki. PRD: Studio Comet, Konami, Konami Digital Entertainmet. 25 mins. x 26 eps.

Three schoolgirls work for a detective agency in Arcana City. Kotono, the youngest member of the staff and the adopted daughter of the local Christian priest, meets a young boy who has lost his memory and saves him from a mysterious masked man who has been kidnapping young boys all over town. But it seems that the boy is more important than anyone imagined. He gives Kotono an extra magical power and in so doing regains his memory and his name—Juan. Can the girls track down the evil mastermind who set the kidnapper on Juan's trail? Can three Goth Loli girls save the world? Of course they can, because this amalgam of magical girl show, detective action, and *moe* fan service (**ARGOT AND JARGON**) is part of an assault on the market by game developer Konami. Our heroines get into and out of amazingly cute outfits and use a huge array of weapons, reflecting Konami's video-game heritage. The series was created for Konami by Shogo Kumasaka, also known for **FAIRY MUSKETEERS** and **SKY GIRLS**. A manga with art by Kiira ran in *Monthly Comic Blade* for a year from September 2006. There's also a clutch of soundtrack CDs and several artbooks. **Ⓝ**

SAINT SEIYA *

1986. JPN: *Seitoshi Seiya*. AKA: *Holy Fighters Seiya; Star Arrow; Zodiac Knights*. TV series, movie. DIR: Shigenori Yamauchi, Kozo Morishita, Kazuhito Kikuchi, Masayuki Akehi, et al. SCR: Takao Koyama, Yoshiyuki Suga, Tadaaki Yamazaki, et al. DES: Shingo Araki, Michi Himeno, Masahiro Naoi, Tadao Kubota, Fumihiro Uchikawa. ANI: Shingo Araki, Tetsuro Aoki. MUS: Seiji Yokoyama. PRD: Toei, TV Asahi. 25 mins. x 114 eps. (TV), 45 mins. (m1), 45 mins. (m2), 75 mins. (m3), 45 mins. (m4), 25 mins. x 13 eps. (*Hades*), 115 mins. (m5), 30 mins. x 6 eps. (v2).

Young martial artist Seiya and the Bronze Saints are sworn to protect Saori, the reincarnation of the Goddess Athena. Their magical armor is at the lower end of a divinely initiated pecking order that moves up through Silver and Gold Saints and even encompasses the sinister Black Saints, servants of a dark power who see Athena as the only barrier to their dominion. In the first series, Ikki and his Black Saints steal the legendary Gold armor. The battle to retrieve it seems hopeless, but the boys have their Cosmo, a kind of power in every living being that can be developed for good or evil. Combining their Cosmos with their individual skills and courage, they can beat seemingly invincible powers. Since evil can be reborn, their adversaries can reincarnate to fight them again. A complex plot builds through multiple story arcs in the TV series and the self-contained but linked movies, featuring mythologies from Greece, Scandinavia, China, and Christendom. The series ends with a multiepisode tale in which Poseidon captures Athena as part of a plot to create a new Great Flood; the Saints of Athena must defeat him and save the goddess, to save the world as we know it.

Based on the *Shonen Jump* manga by **BT'X**-creator Masami Kurumada, four movie outings followed: the first, Morishita and Kikuchi's *Saint Seiya* (1987, AKA *Legend of the Golden Apple*) pitted the boys against Eris, the goddess of Discord. The same year's *SS: Vicious Fight of the Gods* (*Kamigami no Nekki Tatakai*) was designed as the lead-in for the Norse-themed second season of the TV series, moving the action to the frozen wastes of Siberia (not quite Scandinavia, but easier for Japanese kids to find on a map) for a battle with the gods of Midgard over Odin's shield. The only full-length feature was *Legend of the Crimson Youth* (1988, *Makka no Shonen Densetsu*), in which Athena must fight Abel (the reincarnation of her elder brother, the sun god Apollo), and his cohorts Berenice and Jow, who wish to create a "new world of peace" by distinctly unpeaceful methods. Masayuki Akehi's *Armageddon Warriors* (45 mins., 1990) involves the awakening of Lucifer by the powers of the various evil deities Seiya and his companions have sent to Hades. It coincided with the ending of the TV series and proved to be the final outing for the Saints of Athena. The last incarnation of the series to date is the 13-part *Hades* chapter (*SS: Tenkai-hen*, 2002) which some sources file as a video series, as the makers intended, and others file as a television show, since it was made to resemble a TV series in 25-minute episodes and first appeared on pay-per-view television in Japan. A movie sequel to the Hades chapter was released in 2004 (*SS: Tenkai Hen Joso: Overture, SS: Heaven Chapter Defrost: Overture*), followed by a six-episode video spin-off *SS: Hades Chapter Inferno* (2005, *SS: Meio Hades Meikai-hen*).

Designers Araki and Himeno (**ROSE OF VERSAILLES**) work magic in both the series and movies, except for the last film, where Naoi's design is less successful. Yokoyama's music is suitably grand. Director Yamauchi stretches the series' tension like a bowstring for cliffhanger endings and midbattle episode breaks that kept audiences coming back for more. But despite its apparent teen appeal, a show that achieves much of its emotional impact through older boys and men fighting brave but naïve teenagers is disturbing, especially when strength and courage are rewarded with ever shinier weapons. *SS* and its close cousin **RONIN WARRIORS** should come with parental warning attached—though their influence, even into the girls' market, can be discerned throughout the **SAILOR MOON**–dominated 1990s. For those old enough to separate the complex strands of the story and keep its brutally seductive heroism in perspective, *SS* has many rewards.

The series was also adapted into a live stage musical in 1991, starring members of the boy-band SMAP. The anime itself was acquired for U.S. broadcast as *Knights of the Zodiac* by DIC Entertainment.

SAINT SLUT SCHOOL DATING DIARY THE ANIMATION

2013. JPN: *Sei Yariman Gakuen Enko Nikki the Animation*. Video. DIR: Takashi Nishikawa. SCR: Tan Uda. DES: Takashi Nishikawa, Shinji Katahara. ANI: Takashi Nishikawa. MUS: N/C. PRD: Pink Pineapple, Seven. 30 mins. x 2 eps.
Saiki is 45, an average salaryman with a nice wife, child, and suburban home. Then, after 20 years of marriage, his wife leaves with their child, and he has nothing left but drink and depression. One night he's drinking alone, as usual, when perky, curvaceous Miho approaches him. She's just one of the high school girls from Saint Marian Academy looking for no-strings sex. Based on a 2011 porn game from OrcSoft Team Goblin, back when they were a fan circle emerging into the professional world.

SAINT TAIL *

1995. JPN: *Kaito Saint Tail*. AKA: *Master Thief Saint Tail*. TV series. DIR: Osamu Nabeshima. SCR: Masaaki Sakurai, Masahiro Yokoyama. DES: Junko Abe, Shiro Kobayashi. ANI: Junko Abe. MUS: Seiji Suzuki. PRD: Tokyo Movie Shinsha, TV Asahi. 25 mins. x 43 eps.
Meimi is an ordinary Catholic schoolgirl who transforms at night into the daring thief Saint Tail. It's in the genes, as her mother was a notable burglar before marrying her stage-magician father, but she only steals from those who deserve it, or to help others. Her best friend, Seira, is a novice nun who somewhat heretically hears confessions from troubled parishioners and then blurts out the details to Meimi. Meimi then yells out, "It's showtime!" whereupon God Almighty transforms her into an angelic superthief in a costume based on a magician's female assistant: top hat, revealing bodysuit, and fishnet stockings. While Saint Tail restores valuable items to their true owners, the hapless police are unable to compete with her divinely assisted crime spree, though Meimi's classmate Asuka is the son of the beleaguered chief of police, determined to track down Saint Tail and hoping to capture Meimi's heart as well. A resurrection of two of the most successful themes of the 1980s—magical girls and TMS's own burglars-for-justice series **CAT'S EYE**—with a dash of Las Vegas showmanship and Catholic guilt. Meimi regrets the embarrassment she causes Asuka's father as she carries out God's work. Based on Megumi Tachikawa's manga.

SAKI: THE PLAYER *

2009. JPN: *Saki*. TV series. DIR: Manabu Ono, Kenji Seto. SCR: Tatsuhiko Urahata. DES: Masakatsu Sasaki, Hiroki Matsumoto. ANI: Masakatsu Sasaki. MUS: Takeshi Watanabe. PRD: Gonzo, Picture Magic, Lantis, Pony Canyon, Sotsu Agency, Square Enix, Klockworx, TV Tokyo. 24 mins. x 25 eps. (TV1), 25 mins. x 12 eps., 30 mins. x 4 eps. (TV2), 25 mins. x 13 eps. (TV3).
Saki's family is mahjong crazy, and whoever wins or loses, there's always trouble. So she has learned to play the game so precisely that she can guarantee a zero score every time, avoiding the risks of upsetting any of her difficult family and losing her allowance. When Saki starts high school, and is persuaded to join the mahjong club, her clubmates quickly realize that if she could use that astonishing ability to achieve high scores instead of low ones, the school would be in with a chance for the national high school mahjong championship. But can Saki learn to change her focus and deal with the new emotions and upheavals of high school life at the same time? Based on the 2006 manga by Ritz Kobayashi, *Saki* combines schoolgirl crushes and complex gameplay in an unlikely but entertaining story.

Mahjong has two major disadvantages as compared with, say, soccer or tennis in **SPORTS ANIME**: it is largely a game of luck, not skill, and it's played sitting down, so making it entertaining in a visual medium is hard. To make it work onscreen, Urahata and his animation crew employ a fascinating range of visual metaphors and techniques. Unfortunately the budget expended on this leads to severe cutbacks on animating the scenes of high school life that link the tournament sequences, leaving them lackluster. Gonzo left the series after episode 14, bequeathing Picture Magic with the task of stretching the budget over 11 more episodes. The uneven pacing of the story gave them no help. Seven eight-minute "picture dramas" by Gonzo were included as DVD extras and contain almost no animation, but give some background character material not featured in the TV version.

Nevertheless, the show was popular enough to get a spin-off. *Saki Achiga-hen episode of Side A* (*Saki: Achiga Chapter episode of side A*) was made by the same crew and production team with new Studio Gokumi, airing in 2012. There was a gap of six months between the airing of episode 12 and the four slightly longer "specials" screened between December 2013 and March 2013. A second season, *Saki*

Zenkoku-hen (*Saki: The Nationals*), followed in 2014. The same crew, bolstered by a new assistant director, are working with Studio Gokumi on a show that takes up Saki's story again.

SAKURA

1946. AKA: *Sakura: Haru no Genso.* AKA: *Cherry Blossom.* Movie. DIR: Sanae Yamamoto, Kenzo Masaoka. SCR: N/C. DES: Tatsumi Masae, Yosuke Kurosaki, Yasui Koyata. ANI: N/C. MUS: Carl Maria von Weber. PRD: Nippon Manga Eiga. ca. 5 mins.

Made in the aftermath of WWII by the surviving animators in Tokyo, *Sakura* depicts Kyoto in the springtime, concentrating on the traditional image of a trainee geisha, before moving on to shots of two puppies playing amid a shower of cherry blossoms, and butterflies who turn out to have human faces. Considering the style of a vignette set to classical music, the most obvious influence is likely to have been Disney's *Fantasia* (1940), although there is no record of the movie being screened in Japan during the war years—possibly the directors were inspired by the idea of *Fantasia*, rather than the actual sight of it, just as Osamu Tezuka's **METROPOLIS** was written without its creator having seen the film of the same name. *Sakura* was a bold effort at restarting Japan's collapsed animation industry, but was understandably substandard, considering the poor conditions in which it was made.

SAKURA DIARIES *

1997. JPN: *Sakura Tsushin.* AKA: *Sakura Communications.* Video. DIR: Kunitoshi Okajima. SCR: Kenji Terada. DES: Nobuyuki Takeuchi. ANI: Nobuyuki Takeuchi. MUS: Mitsuo Hagita. PRD: Kitty Films, Victor, Shaft. 25 mins. x 12 eps. (released on 6 tapes).

Toma Inaba is a dreamer, eager to get into university and begin adult life, but cursed to drift permanently around the outskirts. Arriving in Tokyo from the country to take his university entrance examinations, he fails after catching a bad cold. Said virus was contracted from his cousin and childhood friend, the pretty Urara Kasuga, who had visited him in his hotel room disguised as a prostitute as joke in an effort to boost his spirits, but whom he threw out after not recognizing her. Meanwhile, he has fallen in love with the beautiful but unattainable Mieko Yotsuba, who will only go out with a fellow student of the elite Keio University. He thus begins a life of boarding with Urara (who continues to chase him, and whose widower father is conveniently out of town) while attending a cram school to pass the next year's entrance exam and chasing Mieko (with whom he pretends to be a Keio student).

"When it comes to sex, she wrote the book on it," leers the hopeful box blurb, but the very fact that *SD* is released by ADV, rather than their erotic subsidiary brand Soft Cel, speaks volumes about its confused identity. While *SD* looks superficially like a faithful adaptation of the *Young Sunday* manga by U-Jin, the anime loses much of the original's appeal. Despite being U-Jin's most mature and entertaining work, *SD* was clearly optioned with the audience of **ANGEL** and **TALES OF …** in mind, vacillating between the sex farces of U-Jin's better-known works and the far more involving story of the original.

There are some clever moments that duplicate the spirit of the original. Each episode begins with a striking scene, as little-girl-lost Urara sits at her dresser and contemplates her reflection in the mirror, applying her warpaint and contemplating her next covert operation in this battle of the sexes. For the opening credits, Urara is filmed as if she is the only girl in the world, much the same as in the beginning of **VIDEO GIRL AI**. As with **OH MY GODDESS!**, the leads' association begins when they are children (a recurring trope in anime **ROMANCE AND DRAMA** for the next decade and beyond), but this is not a simple case of love at first sight—in the manga, it is the seven-year-old Touma who risks his life to protect Urara from her abusive father.

But like so many anime romances aimed at the onanistic male, *SD* paints a picture of a strange viewer, old enough to vote but somehow cursed with the emotional maturity of a child. Consequently, its female characters are dragged down to the level of the wanton Lolitas of **CREAM LEMON**, while its male lead becomes little more than a priapic **TENCHI MUYO!** Despite the more sophisticated story line of the original manga, the anime incarnation often slips into tawdriness, seemingly because the production team refused to believe that they could make an U-Jin anime without some eye candy. Released initially as a video series, and then broadcast the following year in a bowdlerized edition on television. **Ⓝ**

SAKURA TRICK *

2014. TV series. DIR: Kenichi Ishikura. SCR: Daishiro Tanimura, Kosuke Takeda, Kana Yamada, Kurone Shimiyasu. DES: Kyuta Sakai, Osamu Tayama. ANI: Hirofumi Morimoto, Kyuta Sakai, Yoichi Ishikawa. MUS: Ryosuke Nakanishi. PRD: Studio Deen, Hobunsha, Memory Tech, Pony Canyon, TBS. 24 mins. x 12 eps.

Based on a girls' love manga by Tachi, this is the story of Haruka and Yu, inseparable in junior high but now forced to sit on opposite sides of the classroom in senior high. As Yu begins to expand her social circle, Haruka feels jealous and decides that a lesbian affair is the way to make sure that she will be Yu's special best friend forever. And maybe this will finally prove to Yu that Haruka's breasts actually are D cups—Yu thinks they're C's.

We're not saying that lesbians can't be obsessed by breast size as much as straight guys, but that little clue bolsters our belief that this show (like most shows featuring hot high school girls with large breasts and few boundaries) is hoping to attract a wider audience. There's nudity right from the opening credits, and both the show and the episodes are labeled "trick" (a term used by American prostitutes of both genders). The talented crew could do better than reframing the high school crushes of **PROJECT A-KO** in a postmodern setting that regrettably leaves out the goofy fantasy. **Ⓝ**

SAKURA WARS *

1997. JPN: *Sakura Taisen.* Video, TV series. DIR: Takaaki Ishiyama, Ryutaro Nakamura. SCR: Hiroyuki Kawasaki, Satoru Akahori. DES: Hidenori Matsubara, Kosuke Fujishima. ANI: N/C. MUS: Kohei Tanaka. PRD: Bandai, TBS/MBS. 30 mins. x 4 eps. (v1), 30 mins. x 6 eps. (v2), 25 mins. x 25 eps. (TV), 85 mins. (m), 24 mins. x 1 ep. (v3, *Sumire*), 30 mins. x 3 eps. (v4, *École*), 30 mins. x 3 eps. (v5, *Nouveau*).

At the beginning of the 20th century, Earth fends off invading demons from another dimension. Suspecting that another attack is coming, a group of Japanese sci-entists perfect clunky war ma-chines in the early 1920s, discovering that they can only be effectively pi-loted by women with the right sort of virtuous energy. Assembling a team of anime archetypes (big-sisterly pla-toon leader Maria, tomboy Kanna, child Iris, maidenly Sumire, and alien Chinese girl Koh-ran/Hong-Lan), the scientists eventually find their perfect Girl Next Door, Sakura the swordswoman from Sen-dai. The Imperial Flower Combat Troop (since the platoons are chiefly named, Ta-karazuka theater style, after flowers) then prepares to resist the alien menace.

SW races through four years and a couple of flashbacks in order to set up the beginning of the Sega console game—hence occasional cutaways to the otherwise irrelevant life of Ichiro Ogami, the hapless naval officer who is the player's point of view in the game proper, as well as the introduction of Kanna, only to remove her, since she is absent at the beginning of the game. Designed to complement the game, it is nevertheless entertaining in its own right, with an appeal that crosses several anime subgenres—including robot combat, gaggles of girls à la **TENCHI MUYO!**, retro adventure in the style of **SUPER ATRAGON**, and hefty multimedia promotion. Fans were asked to buy into a complete "universe," including not just the novelization, but also a CD-ROM encyclopedia, two games, and the Taisho Romantic Society, a fan club of alternate historians with its own magazine. To top it all, the actresses appeared in several live-action musicals, drawing further paral-lels between the look of the show and the cross-dressing Takarazuka musical tradi-tion (particularly **ROSE OF VERSAILLES**) that inspired it.

Though *SW* does a masterful job of overcoming its computer-game origins, like **KISHIN CORPS** and creator Hiroi Oji's later **VIRGIN FLEET**, its innocuous revision-ism leaves a nasty taste in the historian's mouth—in the *real* 1920s, the only aliens the Japanese military were preparing to fight were the hapless inhabitants of Man-churia. Somewhat ironically, the period detail is quite exacting, with obsolete terms used for foreign countries, right-to-left writing in the prewar style, and even a character named Koh-ran, after a Japanese

actress who specialized in Chinese roles in prewar propaganda films.Each of the first four episodes focused on two of the members (including the two added for the second game, Orihime and Leni, both from the disbanded European Star Divi-sion), while the last two featured a two-part story about the entire troop. The franchise was upgraded to a TV series in 2000, which retold the story from the beginning, with the team forming a musical comedy troupe and setting off on a nationwide tour. For the game *SW3*, the action shifts to Paris in 1926, where Ichiro Ogami is put in charge of a new team of girls—big-sister-ly part-time thief Roberia, tomboy duchess Grecine, Vietnamese child Kokuriko, and girl-next-door Hanabi, a French-born Japanese girl. *Sakura Wars: The Movie* (*ST: Katsudo Shashin*, lit. *SW: The Motion Picture*), set in Tokyo after the events of *SW3* in Paris, appeared late in 2001. A new member, Lachette, formerly of the Star Division, joins the Imperial Flower Combat Troop to gain field experience in prepara-tion for the founding of the New York team. Meanwhile, an American industrial magnate, Brent Furlong, plots to replace the Troop with automated anti-demon robots, and then to conquer first Tokyo, next Japan, and eventually the world. The hackneyed plot is well presented, with lovingly detailed high-grade animation and art.

Three further video series duly fol-lowed, *SW: Sumire* (2002), *SW: École de Paris* (2003), and *SW: Le Nouveau Paris* (2004), the first a one-shot, and the latter two comprising three parts, each part 30 minutes long. *SW: Sumire* commemorates the retirement of both the character Sum-ire Kanzaki and her voice actress Michie Tomizawa. The multipart series both comprise three parts, each part 30 minutes long. Both related to the Paris-set third game, although by this time a fourth game was already out, set in 1927 and incorpo-rating 14 characters from the preceding installments of the franchise. A fifth game moves the action to New York with mainly new characters—if there is ever a new *SW* anime, this incarnation is a likely source.

SAKYO KOMATSU'S ANIME THEATER
1989. JPN: *Komatsu Sakyo Anime Gekijo*. TV series. DIR: Akira Nishimori. SCR: Sakyo Kom-

atsu. DES: Jun Ishikawa. ANI: Jun Ishikawa. MUS: N/C. PRD: Gainax, MBS. 3 mins. x 27 eps.

A series of adaptations of short stories, this anime's chief source of material is the *Punk Dragon* short-story collection by Sakyo Komatsu, best known for his novels *Japan Sinks* and *Resurrection Day* (the latter adapted into the live-action film *Virus*, 1980). In the anime world, Komatsu also worked with Tezuka on **SPACE FIREBIRD** and as a voice actor in **A THOUSAND AND ONE NIGHTS**.

SALAMANDER *
1988. Video. DIR: Hisayuki Toriumi. SCR: Kazuhito Hisajima. DES: Haruhiko Mikimoto, Yasuhiro Moriki. ANI: Toshiyasu Okada. MUS: Tatsushi Umegaki. PRD: Studio Pierrot. 60 mins., 50 mins., 60 mins.

In the year 2381, the aggressive galaxy-de-vouring parasites known as the Bacterians are heading for planet Gradius. In the first video, *Salamander Basic Saga: Meditating Paola*, ace pilot Stephanie and her team-mates, Eddie and Dan, find a beautiful girl in an abandoned spaceship. As she warns of the imminent Bacterian invasion, they wonder if she's an innocent victim or an agent of destruction. The lovely Paola reveals herself to be a Bacterian agent, and Stephanie's father makes the ultimate sacrifice to save Gradius from the invaders. For the second video, *Intermediate Saga*, Dan and Stephanie are called to planet Lo-tus, whose ruler, Lord British, needs their help. Despite courtly intrigues from rivals embittered at needing foreign aid, the Gradian pilots hold off another invasion. In *Advanced Saga: The Ambition of Gofar*, British comes to Gradius to sign a peace treaty and woo the reluctant Stephanie. She, however, is kidnapped by the Bacteri-ans and taken to their HQ on the artificial sun of Salamander, where they plan to rip out her brain and sew it into the skull of their agent Gofar. Stephanie's father, who has turned to the dark side, figures that her knowledge of the Gradian defenses will turn the battle in the invaders' favor. Needless to say, British and Dan save the day.

A brave stab at adapting the Konami arcade game *Gradius*, *Salamander* is ultimately defeated by the poverty of its source material. The love triangle between

Stephanie and the men is well-handled; she is tempted by riches, royalty, and marriage in the form of British as well as by career and camaraderie in the form of Dan. The ex-refugee Eddie is another intriguing character, drawn to the enemy agent Paola because she too does not really belong. A surprisingly cogent hard-science script and well-realized sequences that duplicate moments of gameplay for the fans are ruined by the worst subtitling in anime history, courtesy of Western Connection.

SALARYMAN KINTARO *

2001. TV series. DIR: Tomoharu Katsumata. SCR: Chikako Kobayashi, Sukehiro Tomita. DES: Masami Suda. ANI: N/C. MUS: N/C. PRD: 81 Produce, TBS. 25 mins. x 20 eps.

Kintaro Yajima was a biker gang leader with a ton of charisma and an attitude, until he fell in love and decided to settle down and have a family. Then tragedy struck when his young wife died in childbirth, leaving him alone to bring up their baby son. But Kintaro's biker past has given him a certain fearlessness that leads him to save the life of the CEO of Yamato Construction Company, immediately fast-tracking him into a management position for which his rough past often seems strangely suited.

Any similarities to **GTO** are purely intentional. Like its predecessor, *Salaryman Kintaro* is based on a manga, on this occasion by Hiroshi Motomiya in *Young Jump* magazine. Both titles enjoyed live-action incarnations (*DE) on primetime television, only converting to the anime format when interest (and budgets) had begun to die down. And, of course, both feature mavericks made good—handsome boys with hearts of gold, fighting to raise themselves out of an underclass youth into a respectable middle-class lifestyle.

The methods are often identical. Kintaro breaks up a fight on the day before he is due to start at Yamato Construction, leading to a chain of events that has him arriving for his first day at work in a police car—as with *GTO*, an old friend of his is now a cop. He must dodge the attentions of Yuki, a schoolgirl who makes it very clear that he can have anything he wants, and to whom he finds himself playing a surrogate father role—if, indeed, a surrogate father role includes breaking the jaw of her would-be boyfriend. Meanwhile, romance of sorts begins to unfurl in the style of SLOW STEP, as Kintaro gains the adoring attentions of Misuzu, a bar proprietess with a daughter of her own—this is a slight deviation from the plot of the live-action version, where Misuzu was the younger sister of Kintaro's late wife. Under the title *Kintaro*, the live-action series has also been broadcast with English subtitles on Hawaii's KIKU TV channel. There is also a 1999 live-action movie directed by Takashi Miike.

Salaryman Kintaro is a perfectly harmless anime, although its benign exterior hides tensions behind the scenes. This is an anime that really, really wants to be a live-action TV drama. Its set-ups and action all seem tailor-made for the real world, and there is little attempt to play to the strengths of the animated medium. As with **HUMAN CROSSING**, its action remains resolutely mundane, leaving the viewer with the nagging sensation that this ought to have stayed live, and its animated status is a reflection of the fact that its star was already on the wane—nobody, not even an anime viewer, likes to feel they are backing a losing horse. However, the possibility remains that the producers knew what they were doing all along, since *Salaryman Kintaro* enjoyed a new lease of life as one of the first TV shows to be made available for paid Internet download in Japan—the animated format makes for a better transfer and saving on memory for slower computers, while the live-action connection makes it more likely to appeal to viewers outside the limited anime "fan" bracket. In that regard, far from being a lame duck, this anime production may turn out to have been the kind of business decision that a corporate warrior like Kintaro would be proud of.

SAMURAI, THE

1987. Video. DIR: Kazuo Yamazaki. SCR: Takahiro Miki. DES: Takayuki Goto. ANI: Takayuki Goto. MUS: N/C. PRD: Studio Deen. 45 mins.

Takeshi Chimatsuri is a young martial artist whose rare sword is a gift from his father. He won it in a fair fight from the brilliant swordsman Kagemaru Akari, who was killed in the struggle. Now Akari's twin daughters, Toki and Kagedi, have come looking for Takeshi to avenge their father's death and retake the sword. Based on the manga serialized in *Young Jump* by Mitsuhiro Harunichi, this samurai soap opera fast devolves into a love comedy.

SAMURAI CHAMPLOO *

2004. TV series. DIR: Shinichiro Watanabe, Akira Yoshimura, Hiroyuki Imaishi, Kazuki Akane, Kazuyoshi Katayama, Tsukasa Sunaga. SCR: Dai Sato, Seiko Takagi, Shinji Obara. DES: Kazuto Nakazawa, Mahiro Maeda. ANI: Kazuto Nakazawa, Yumiko Ishii, Shinji Takeuchi. MUS: Fat Jon, Force of Nature, Nujabies, Tsutchie. PRD: Fuji TV, Manglobe. 25 mins. x 26 eps.

Two fighters in Edo-period Japan develop an instant dislike for one another, but keep crossing paths nonetheless. Mugen is a hick from the far south, while Jin is a self-styled noble—a literal odd couple with different class backgrounds, or at least, aspirations. All that unites them is their lack of interest in each other, and their indubitable fighting skills, leading Fuu, a waitress, to hire them to find a missing man—her father. The plot might sound like a thousand other samurai dramas, but *SC*'s play for originality comes in its unique style, in which the entire drama is framed with modern-day assumptions and music, as if a focus group of 14-year-old mallrats were obliged to recount a Kurosawa movie, and did so in their own distinctive argot.

As with his earlier **COWBOY BEBOP**, itself a deliberate mix of disparate musical and story genres, director Watanabe combines self-conscious cool with a tale of nobility fallen on hard times. His heroes are rake-thin free lances with hearts of gold, railing against institutions run by fat, pampered old men—the story not only of *SC*, but of conditions in the modern anime industry itself, and of its attitude toward its fellow samurai TV serials.

SC makes a fine virtue out of what could have been a terrible vice. It is, at heart, a crushingly old-fashioned show, with a studied punkishness dating back to the Vietnam-era *Monjiro* (*DE). Nor is its irreverent anime attitude anything new: **SAMURAI GOLD** was mixing up Edo period stories before *SC*'s target audience was even born. It dresses itself up with scratch editing and self-consciously anachronistic hip hop, perhaps less in the hope of attracting modern youth than in ensuring the censure of their elders—the ultimate test of *cool*, of course, is that your parents hate it. Sadly, its showy use of oh-so-20th-century music will cause it to age faster than it deserves; compare to similar faddery in **Bubblegum Crisis**.

However, *SC* also successfully reclaims the samurai drama for modern teens—a bold affirmation that stories about Japan's past do not have to be boring, staid Sunday night NHK epics for Dad. It boasts of its Internet generation's disrespect toward history, with onscreen cards that proclaim no interest in period accuracy, but while it may feign ignorance, it is made by people with a genuine and deep-seated appreciation of samurai lore. It steals ideas and set-ups from kabuki, TV, film, novels, and comics, uniting them all in an extended glorification of everything that ever made samurai worth pastiching in the first place. It mixes the thuggery of "Beat" Takeshi Kitano's 2003 postmodern *Zatoichi* with the sedate travelogue of **Manga Mito Komon** and all points in between, named after an Okinawan dish that is a mash-up of everything: *champloo*. Like Pink Floyd's *The Wall* (1979), it is a very smart, well-schooled product, which brags to an impressionable audience that it doesn't need an education. It is only in one episode, when a Japanese village takes on brutish American invaders in a symbolic baseball match, that the extent of the anachronisms and stereotypes are more likely to become obvious to a non-Japanese audience.

Its use of comedy is also sneakily subtle. Mugen and Jin might bicker like Tarantino hit men, but their odd-couple pairing is a timeless play-off between high and low culture, not dissimilar to other mismatched buddies like those in **Samurai Deeper Kyo**. Their humor is also often subtly directed at their underclass audience—Fuu is looking for a man who "smells of sunflowers," but Mugen, like most urban viewers, doesn't actually have a clue what a sunflower smells like.

The design work is heavily stylized, a cunning recognition of the fact that mismatched elements of period dramas and B-movies have established a wholly un-Japanese "samurai norm" in foreign countries, distracting us from the fact that the various episodes of this road movie don't really hang together. The show is

so stylish, so maniacally energetic, and so involved in its own mythology that it's easy to forgive its lack of substance, but it is an interesting experiment rather than a complete success. In years to come, it may be seen as a bridge that unites old traditions of Japanese TV and film with postmodern pastiches like **Afro Samurai**. **⊕Ⓥ**

SAMURAI DEEPER KYO *

2002. TV series. DIR: Junji Nishimura, Toshiya Shinohara, Masakazu Hashimoto. SCR: Hiroyuki Kawasaki, Masashi Sogo, Rika Nakase, Tetsuo Tanaka. DES: Manabu Fukuzawa, Michinori Chiba, Tamotsu Shinohara. ANI: Saburo Tanaka, Shinpei Tomo'oka, Noriko Kondo. MUS: N/C. PRD: Starchild Records, Studio Deen, TV Tokyo. 24 mins. x 26 eps.

At the great battle of Sekigahara in 1600, two great warriors fight a battle that ends in mystery. Kyoshiro Mibu and "Demon Eyes" Kyo both disappear when a meteor strikes the battleground. Four years later, in a land plagued by monsters, Kyoshiro is a traveling medicine salesman who has lost his memories of the past. He runs into female bounty hunter Yuya Shiina, on the road seeking her brother's killer, shortly before an attack by a powerful snake monster. Kyoshiro destroys it and Yuya uncovers his secret—Kyoshiro and Kyo now share one body in the style of **Ultraman** or **Bastard**, and Kyoshiro's mild-mannered persona is the host for Kyo's murderous one. Yuya decides to stick with him and turn him in for Kyo's bounty if she can; Kyo wants to find his own body and needs Kyoshiro until then—compare to the similar quest of a disembodied samurai in **Dororo**. As the "trio" travel through Japan, meeting more people from their pasts, they learn that the evil Nobunaga Oda was resurrected by the Mibu clan for their own ends and is responsible for the monsters plaguing Japan. The only hope for the country lies in the swordsmith Muramasa, Kyoshiro's former mentor, who has fashioned five magical weapons whose wielders stand the only chance of taking down Nobunaga. Kyoshiro finally manages to kill Nobunaga, only to see him resurrected again by his own clan, this time in Kyo's old body. The pair must work together to defeat him by forging the Muramasa swords into one, incredible dimension-warping weapon.

An additional Jekyll-and-Hyde twist is introduced when we discover that the two-in-one are also one-in-two—Kyo really *is* Kyoshiro, or rather his fighting self. When he fell in love with pacifist beauty Sakuya, Kyoshiro tried to divorce his warrior instincts from the rest of his personality and succeeded in creating another self to embody all the samurai battle instincts and fighting code. He has thus been at war with himself for the whole series. Adapted from Akimine Kamijyo's manga in *Shonen Jump*, the story includes references to many other historical and semi-historical characters like Sasuke Sarutobi (see **Magic Boy**) and, of course, Japan's arch-bogeyman Nobunaga himself. **⊕Ⓥ**

SAMURAI FLAMENCO *

2013. TV series. DIR: Takahiro Omori. SCR: Hideyuki Kurata. DES: Yoshimitsu Yamashita. ANI: Yoshimitsu Yamashita. MUS: agehasprings, Kenji Tamai. PRD: Manglobe, Aniplex, DeNa, Dentsu, Fuji TV, Hobibox, Movic, Kyoraku Industrial Holdings. 24 mins. x 22 eps.

Male model Masayoshi Hazama wants to be a superhero and is determined to achieve his dream, even though he lacks any of the abilities or contacts required. Still, if you build it, they will come, and his earnest wish soon attracts a number of oddball associates who fill the niches required for any self-respecting crime fighter. As his surrogate family of mentors and assistants slowly builds, Masayoshi begins to fight real crimes, and then *unreal* ones, as he encounters flamboyant super-villains as colorful as himself. *Samurai Flamenco* switches from one genre to another, beginning as a comedy before lurching into storylines that take its lead's hero-hood for granted, before suddenly sending him on the run and effectively turning him into an outlaw. While these abrupt changes of tone are initially jarring, they manage to keep the story fresh and intriguing, as if the entire show is being rebooted and remade with the same characters every few weeks. Compare to **Tiger and Bunny** for another postmodern take on superheroism, although much of the heart of *Samurai Flamenco* can be traced back somewhat further, to M. Night Shyamalan's *Unbreakable* (2000).

SAMURAI GIANTS

1973. AKA: *The Star Pitcher*. TV series. DIR: Tadao Nagahama, Satoshi Dezaki, Osamu Dezaki, Yoshiyuki Tomino. SCR: Seiji Matsuoka, Satoshi Dezaki, Haruya Yamazaki, Tomohiro Ando, Asako Tani. DES: Hideo Kawauchi. ANI: Yasuo Otsuka. MUS: Shunsuke Kikuchi. PRD: Eiken, TMS, Yomiuri TV (Nippon TV). 25 mins. x 46 eps.

The Giants baseball team is scouting for new talent and finds a high school player who can hit one massive home run after another. But the school star's great physical strength has a balancing weakness—he lacks control and can't pitch to save his life. Worried about this basic problem, he's not sure whether he should join the team or forget baseball and look for another, more conventional career. His girlfriend convinces him that he should join the Giants and work with the team on his weak point. With her encouragement, he's determined to become a star pitcher. Based on yet another baseball manga by STAR OF THE GIANTS–creator Ikki Kajiwara, working here with Ko Inoue.

SAMURAI GIRLS *

2010. JPN: *Hyakka Ryoran*. AKA: *A Hundred Flowers Blooming in Profusion*. TV series, video. DIR: KOBUN. SCR: Ryunosuke Kingetsu, Toshimitsu Takeuchi, Yuichi Kadota, Satoru Nishizono. DES: Tsutomu Miyazawa, Junichi Higashi. ANI: Tsutomu Miyazawa, Bum-Chul Chang, Masayuki Fujita, Rin-Sin. MUS: Tatsuya Kato. PRD: ARMS, GENCO, Gigno System Japan, Hobby Japan, Lantis, Media Factory, MOVIC, Showgate. 24 mins. x 12 eps. (TV1), 3 mins. x 6 eps. (v), 24 mins. x 12 eps. (TV2).

Japan in an alternate 21st century: the Tokugawa shogunate is still in power, but at some point they must have opened up to the West, because the current Americanized education system and the Western trend for exotic lingerie as street clothing is still in place. Samurai are now predominantly female, teenage, and improbably skilled at martial arts, but still need male trainers and handlers. High schools still have student councils, whose primary task is to oppress the student body. Teenage rebel Muneakira Yagyu bears the name of a renowned family of swordmasters (JUBEI-CHAN THE NINJA GIRL) and is sent to train new samurai. He discovers an innate ability for getting the best out of voluptuous girls named after legendary fighters of old, just by kissing them. He also acquires a sister who can transform into legendary warrior Jubei Yagyu, but in her own form is frequently without either functioning brain cells or clothes. There's an excuse for a plot, an upgrade system for the girls' skills, and some amazing action visuals, to compensate for the endless panty, boob, and butt shots.

Like MARIA†HOLIC and DOUJIN WORK, this is another title where a professional studio called on Tokyo Animator Gakuen for assistance, trading professional experience for cheap labor. They didn't return for the sequels. In 2010 KOBUN directed six three-minutes extras for the DVD release, entitled *Hyakka Ryoran Samurai Girls: Otome Ureshi Hazukashi Shoshi no Chigiri* (*Contract of the Blushing Warrior Maiden*). A new 12-episode TV series, released in English as *Samurai Bride*, aired in spring 2013 and was seemingly the result of a decision among the producers that there was not enough titillation, nudity, or objectification in the original series, and that what the girls really needed to do was open a maid café. The sole pleasure that the authors derive from this show is the similarity of the Japanese title to Chairman Mao's 1957 exhortation to "Let a Hundred Flowers Bloom," entirely coincidental, but liable to have old Communists spinning in their graves. **NV**

SAMURAI GOLD *

1988. JPN: *Toyamazakura Uchucho Yatsu no Na wa Gold*. AKA: *Cosmic Commander of the Toyama Cherry Trees; The Guy's Name Is Gold*. Video. DIR: Atsutoshi Umezawa. SCR: Akiyoshi Sakai. DES: Hiroyuki Kitazume. ANI: Hiroyuki Kitazume. MUS: Kentaro Haneda. PRD: Toei. 60 mins.

Late in the 21st century, Earth and its colonies are controlled by five Overseers working through EDO, a vast computer system. When Overseer Redklaad Mount is wounded by a would-be assassin, his estranged son, Gold, is dragged from a seedy downtown bar to investigate. On the space colony of Fedovar, Gold discovers that Redklaad is implicated in the death of the local ruler Duke Plenmatz, who died when the liner Ovconia crashed on its maiden voyage. After fighting with Plenmatz's vengeful son, Ion (his girlfriend Midi's brother), Gold goes missing, presumed dead. Posing as Gold, Ion returns to Earth, where he almost succeeds in sentencing Redklaad to death. Gold saves the day by baring his unique cherry-blossom tattoo, thus unmasking Ion's deception. Gold reveals that all the Overseers, not just his father, are guilty of orchestrating the crash of the Ovconia and murdering the shipbuilders who arranged it. Having challenged his rulers, Gold prepares to commit suicide but is stopped by EDO herself, who admits that she ordered the removal of Plenmatz without thinking of the consequences. EDO exonerates the Overseers, who were only following her orders, and sentences herself to deactivation. Gold becomes an Overseer, but still has time to return to his favorite bar, where Midi plays the piano, Ion serves the drinks, and Ion's former henchman, the Gay Blade, waits on tables.

A lighthearted sci-fi romp, distantly inspired by the life of Kinshiro Toyama, a figure who lived from 1793 to 1855. The character was popularized first in the kabuki play *Toyama no Kinsan* (1893), in which he is portrayed as a tattooed playboy who makes good when he becomes a magistrate, fighting corruption in Edo (old-time Tokyo) in the style of MANGA MITO KOMON. Dramatized by several novelists, including *SG*'s credited Tatsuro Jinde (who died in 1986) and Kyosuke Yuki, the character is best known in Japan through several live-action TV series (*DE). *SG*, however, is just an excuse for some laser swordplay and mild detective work, rounded off by an overlong courtroom finale. Very 1980s in both good and bad senses—Gold boasts a hideous mullet haircut, and the Gay Blade takes camp beyond the funny into the insulting, but Kitazume's stark pop-art colors and designs still retain a certain freshness. Similar samurai retellings occur in JUBEI-CHAN THE NINJA GIRL and CYBER CITY OEDO 808, while Toyama was parodied again in U-JIN BRAND. Another descendant of the original Toyama would turn up in DETECTIVE ACADEMY Q.

SAMURAI GUN *

2004. TV series. DIR: Kazuhiko Kikuchi. SCR: Hideki Sonoda. DES: Kenichi Onuki. ANI: N/C. MUS: Akifumi Tada. PRD: ADV Films, Avex, Inc.,

Studio Egg. 25 mins. x 12 eps., 25 mins. (v). A group of renegade samurai use forbidden firearms to fight an oppressive political system in the 1860s, masking up like ninja to take on the shogun and his corrupt supporters. But you don't stay shogun for long without a fair degree of low cunning, and the ruler creates his own force to take down the Samurai Guns by recruiting people with nothing to lose from the lowlife of the streets and taverns. Meanwhile, suspicions begin to arise about the true purpose of the Samurai Guns. The series focuses on one small Samurai Gun unit; half-blind half-breed Ichimatsu, Daimon, their liaison to their boss, and female performer Kurenai ("Scarlet"). Hard-drinking, low-living Ichimatsu's tragic past makes him hate violence, but his need to avenge his parents and sister explains why he's joined a group of assassins. He's also in love with a prostitute. All this goes to make up a suitably modern antihero—although readers might be forgiven for thinking this was a higher-tech variant on RURONI KENSHIN. A final episode was released as a "video exclusive."

As with so many other modern anime, from SAKURA WARS to PEACEMAKER KUROGANE, *SG* wants the best of both worlds—the freedom to do whatever it wants and the solid grounding that comes with historical references. The result, as ever, is a show that hopes its audience will know enough of its background to preempt its omissions, but still be ignorant enough to forgive its mistakes. Playing games with history is a difficult temptation, and simply piling in any interesting artifact makes a historical setting counterproductive. The gun was certainly known in Japan long before the 19th century, but other elements of *SG's mise en scene*, such as the submachine pistols on display, the zippers, and (although this is a churlish complaint considering other anime) even the Hollywood-implant breastsizes of female characters, come far later than the alleged time period in which this is set. The juxtaposition of Western and Eastern fight systems isn't as easy as *Kung Fu* and Terence Young's *Red Sun* made it look, and the fit here is sometimes awkward—as is the show's use of technology. The producers offer the spurious explanation that these are just "advances" on already existing technology that could theoretically have been carried this far by a secret organization with means and motivation. Based on a manga by Kazuhiko Kumagai in *Young Jump* magazine, and one of several productions in the early 21st century funded with a large injection of American money; ADV Films presumably hoping to find something that pleased audiences in both East and West. ⓛⓝⓥ

SAMURAI HAREM *

2009. JPN: *Asu no Yoichi*. AKA: *Yoichi's Tomorrows*. TV series. DIR: Rion Kujo. SCR: Hideyuki Kurata, Tatsuya Takahashi. DES: Noriko Morishima, Minoru Maeda. ANI: Yumiko Ishii, Hong Shen, Masami Nagata. MUS: Tomoki Kikuya. PRD: AIC, Akita Shoten, Geneon, Lantis, MOVIC, TBS. 24 mins. x 12 eps.
Yoichi's father took him up to the mountains when he was very young, to train him in the martial arts of the Divine Wind School. Now he's learned all his father can teach, so his devoted parent sends him to a much tougher school in a different wilderness—an urban martial arts school owned and operated by the four Ikaruga sisters. One could easily find echoes of RANMA ½, but that would flatter this show far beyond its merits. As the bluntly descriptive English title suggests, it's a harem comedy (ROMANCE AND DRAMA) that does nothing outstanding, made with the polished professionalism for which AIC is renowned.

SAMURAI PIZZA CATS *

1990. JPN: *Kyatto Ninden Teyande*. AKA: *Stealth Tales of the Kool Kat Gang*. TV series. DIR: Kunitoshi Okajima, Takeshi Serizawa, Shinji Sakai, Katsumi Kosuga. SCR: Satoru Akahori, Mayori Sekijima, Yumi Kageyama, Hiroyuki Kawasaki. DES: Noritaka Suzuki, Mayori Sekijima. ANI: Noritaka Suzuki, Yoshio Kabashima. MUS: Kenji Kawai (Shuki Levy, Haim Saban in Western version). PRD: Tatsunoko, TV Tokyo, Sotsu Agency. 25 mins. x 54 eps. (TV).
In the high-tech streets of Edolopolis (Little Tokyo), a fox (a rat in the English-language version) who has found his perfect role in life, cross-dressing politician Ko'on-no-Kami (Big Cheese), and his avian sidekicks, Kara-maru and Gennari-sai (Bad Bird and Jerry Atrick), plot against shogun Iei-Iei Tokugawa (Emperor Fred) and his ditzy, romance-obsessed rabbit daughter, Usa-hime (Princess Vi). To save the city from their evil plans, loyal dog retainer Wanko-no-kami (Big Al Dentei) calls for help from the Ninja Team Nyanki (Samurai Pizza Cats), who moonlight as superheroes while making and delivering the best pizza in town. Yattaro (Speedy Cerviche) is the leader of the team and fights with the unbeatable Magical Ginzu Sword. Sukoshii (Guido Anchovy), his smooth-talking comrade in arms and rival for the love of the beautiful Miss Omitsu (Lucille), fights with the Samurai Sunspot Umbrella. Pururun (Polly Esther), the hotheaded sex-kitten of the trio, uses the Cat's Paw Attraction technique, raising her paw like the "beckoning cat" statues in Japanese shops, while electromagnetic waves (represented by streams of fluttering hearts) pull her victims to her. She also throws heart-shaped *shuriken*. In a sly reference to the live-action show *Cyber Ninja*, for most of their missions, the Pizza Cats are launched from a giant revolver on the roof of the Pizza Parlor by their loyal (and frequently sarcastic) assistant, Otama (Francine). When they need extra clout they can use their own magnificent armored vehicle, Nyago-sphinx (Golden Sphinx); it can even transform into a giant robot, Nyago-king (The Great Catatonic).

With pizza-loving martial artists inspired by the *Teenage Mutant Ninja Turtles*, early writing credits for Satoru "Mr. Zany" Akahori, and even music from GHOST IN THE SHELL's Kenji Kawai in the original version, *SPC* is an anime classic. Many shows are ruined in translation, but *SPC* simply shrugged off the change of language and stayed insanely itself—in one memorable scene in the English version, the characters panic *because* they have been sent a note in Japanese. Brought to the West by Saban soon after its release, *SPC* was perhaps one of the last "translations" in the old 1970s *let's-just-make-it-up* style (see ROBOTECH). The improvised nature of the English-language version is, by definition, a very bad TRANSLATION, but, luckily, one that succeeds in retaining the madcap spirit of the original. Saban International, execrated in many quarters for its editing jobs on Asian material, brought together a team that not only understood what the show needed but actually seems to have enjoyed itself—an object lesson for the bored crews of many English anime dubs with grander pretensions. Edited episodes of the TV series were released on video in the U.S. as *SPC The Movie* (1991). The series made it into U.S. syndication in 1996; it had already been screened in Canada and Britain with some success and remains a fan favorite. Subsequent French, Spanish, and German editions were based on the English version, which means that a true translation of *SPC* has yet to be attempted in any Western language.

SAMURAI 7 *

2004. JPN: *Shichinin no Samurai*. AKA: *Seven Samurai; Akira Kurosawa's Samurai 7*. TV series. DIR: Toshifumi Takizawa, Hiroyuki Okuno. SCR: Atsuhiro Tomioka. DES: Hideki Hashimoto, Takuhito Kusanagi, Makoto Kobayashi. ANI: Hiroyuki Okuno, Katsuhisa Oono. MUS: Eitetsu Hayashi, Kaoru Wada. PRD: Gonzo, Sony Pictures Entertainment, Animax. 25 mins. x 26 eps.
Akira Kurosawa's classic 1954 movie gets the modern treatment with the question "What if *Seven Samurai* had been made in color as a science fantasy show with cooler, younger heroes?" This is, of course, a pointless query, and it's a tribute to the skills of the team rather than the money thrown at this version, allegedly made in "high definition" at double cost of a normal anime series, that the answer is not as awful as one might expect. We start with the basic Kurosawa story—seven penniless fighters are recruited by a group of yokels desperate to stop bandits from stealing their rice crop again. The pay is just their food, but they are all so far down on their luck (for a variety of reasons) that they accept. The story has been moved from the Edo period into a steampunk-pastiche future, in the aftermath of a great war in which the samurai lost their status and influence all over again.

Our heroes have been updated along with their world. The Toshiro Mifune character, Kikuchiyo, is now a tin man with an exhaust pipe on his head so he can let off steam, played for light relief rather than pathos. Seiji Miyaguchi's stoic samurai Kyuzo, who valued honor and sword skill above everything, has become an assassin for a crime boss. The leader of the gang, shaven-headed, dignified Kanbei, now has a mane of flowing hair.

The villains too have been updated—the Nobushi bandit gang are augmented humans with metal body modifications, living weapons capable of flight. In order to keep the link to the rice crop and the land as the essential story element, the remake postulates that these cyborg warriors can only be powered by eating rice, which is a fairly silly proposition in a starfaring society. The design is gorgeous, although it is sometimes betrayed by a poor interface between 2D and 3D animation—which, given the amount reputed to have been spent, and the number of shows that have handled this well, is inexcusable. So, too, is the noticeable drop in animation quality partway through; flashy openers that tail off into substandard animation are commonplace in modern anime, but most of the other offenders do not tempt fate by bragging about their high budgets.

As with **SAMURAI CHAMPLOO**, the show contains many references to other tales of Japan's past—there is even a nod to Goemon Ishikawa from **LUPIN III**, in a sequence where Kanbei leaps from a space cruiser and slices a destroyer in half in mid-air. But where Kurosawa's original depicted real people struggling with life-and-death problems at a time when the nation was in turmoil, *S7* is trying to be cool enough to catch the stunted attention spans of a generation for which poverty, danger, and personal responsibility are concepts more alien than tinplate warriors with exhaust pipes on their heads. **LNV**

SAMURAI SHODOWN: THE MOTION PICTURE *

1993. JPN: *Samurai Spirits*. TV special, video. DIR: Hiroshi Ishiodori, Kazuhiro Sasaki. SCR: Nobuaki Kishima, Masamuro Takimoto. DES: Kazunori Iwakura, Aoi Nanase. ANI: Kazunori Iwakura. MUS: Osamu Tezuka (mus). PRD: SNK, Ajia-do. 80 mins. (TVm), 30 mins. x 2 eps. (v).
One hundred years after their deaths at the hands of a former colleague, six legendary holy warriors are reborn to seek justice against the teammate who betrayed them into the hands of an evil god. Charlotte, Wan Fu, Nakoruru, Galford, and Tam Tam search the feudal province of Edo questing for their lost comrade, Haohmaru, and their sworn nemesis, Shiro Amakusa (see **NINJA RESURRECTION**). Will

the followers of the divine light triumph over the forces of the dark, or is the course of history destined to repeat itself? Yes to both, as our heroes fight and fight again. Based on a video game by SNK for the Neo Geo, this video series edited into a "movie" was widely considered a disappointment by game fans. Instead of blood, characters leak a milky white liquid, and the violence levels have been watered down to match. American fans suffered even worse—the androgynous lead villain was rewritten as a woman for the U.S. release.

In the video sequel *SS: Defeat of Ashura* (1999), spiky-haired Haohmaru is back with Rimururu, Nakoruru, and Galford and they're faced with a problem. Shiki, an old enemy of theirs, shows up badly hurt. Nakoruru wants to take her in, but Galford and Rimururu have other plans. They believe she should be destroyed because she's working for an agent of corruption that could destroy them all. Haomaru takes up his sword once again, to save Shiki's life and destroy the dark influence.

After the character of Nakoruru starred in a PC text adventure game, plans were announced to adapt it into a 13-part TV series. However, this project eventually transformed into a video "series," only the first chapter of which was ever released, as the 28-minute *Nakoruru* (2002).

SAMURAI: HUNT FOR THE SWORD *

1999. JPN: *Kaito Ranma the Animation*. AKA: *Swift-Blade Ranma ½*. Video. DIR: Masahiro Sekino. SCR: Mitsuhiro Yamada. DES: Hidekazu Shimamura. ANI: Hidekazu Shimamura. MUS: N/C. PRD: AIC, Animate Film. 30 mins. x 2 eps.
Edo-period swashbuckling with a touch of romance, based on a PC and PlayStation game. **V**

SAMURAI XXX *

2004. JPN: *Yoka no Ken*. AKA: *Blade of Fragrant Phantoms*. Video DIR: Naomi Hayakawa, Haruo Furuki. SCR: Rokurota Makabe. DES: Naomi Hayakawa. ANI: Fun Lee, Ganchan, Haru, Kero, MANE, Nagapon, Yasha. MUS: Yui Takase. PRD: Green Bunny, Kunoichi Partners, Hyper Space. 30 mins. x 2 eps.
Matagoro is a samurai who has no skills with any weapon except the one between his legs. So he's sent on a mission to find

a treasure map hidden on the backs of several female ninja. It will only show when they climax, which rather restricts the range of positions possible, though not as much as this kind of lame set-up restricts the story. A premise that was pretty weak in THOSE WHO HUNT ELVES has to support the usual grind of sex scenes strung around a disposable plot. Matagoro is also searching for his long-lost sister, who was (a) kidnapped by ninja as a child, and (b) isn't really his sister, thereby ensuring that not-quite-incest is in the cards before the show is over. Based on an "original story" by Naomi Hayakawa, who also brought us BEAST CITY. Not to be confused with *Samurai X*, for which see RURONI KENSHIN. ●▲◆

SAMURAIDER
1991. Video. DIR: Hideaki Oba. SCR: Masaru Yamamoto. DES: Moriyasu Taniguchi. ANI: Moriyasu Taniguchi. MUS: Mitsuo Takahama. PRD: Studio TV. 50 mins.
In a weak combination of samurai movie and BOMBER BIKERS OF SHONAN, Tokyo street-punk Masao buys a treasured FZR "katana" motorcycle and becomes a knight of the road, attacking criminals with a genuine *katana* sword. Based on the manga by Shinichi Sugimura in *Young Magazine*.

SANADA'S 10 BRAVE WARRIORS
2005. JPN: *Shinshaku Sengoku Eiyu Densetsu Sanada Ju Yushi The Animation*. AKA: *New Civil War Hero Legend of Sanada's Ten Samurai The Animation; Sanada's Samurai; Sanada 10, Brave Ten*. TV series, TV special. DIR: Keizo Shimizu. SCR: Shimao Kawanaka. DES: Keizo Shimizu. ANI: Satoshi Anakura. MUS: N/C. PRD: T.P.O., Group TAC, G&G Direction, Magic Bus, WOWOW. 25 mins. x 12 eps. (TV), 60 mins. (special).
Warlord Yukimura Sanada hires a band of brave fighters to help him in the struggle against Ieyasu Tokugawa (see YOUNG TOKUGAWA IEYASU). Their number includes the legendary Sasuke Sarutobi (see MAGIC BOY), the white-skinned foreigner Saizo Kirigakure, and deadly beauty Kiyomi Miyoshi. Although Sanada himself existed as a great warlord, his ten legendary warriors are just that—legendary, and best known to the Japanese TV audience through the 1975 puppet series *Ten Brave Warriors of Sanada* (*DE). As with the earlier HAKKENDEN, this anime remake capitalizes on

the crew's fond childhood memories of the puppet show, and hopes to recreate the historical fiction that brings them into conflict with Ieyasu Tokugawa and then allies them with the followers of defeated warlord Toyotomi for a display of heroism in defeat. The TV special was an hour-long prequel.

SANCTUARY *
1996. Video. DIR: Takashi Watanabe. SCR: Kenji Terada. DES: Hidemi Kubo, Hiroshi Kato. ANI: Hidemi Kubo. MUS: N/C. PRD: OB Planning, Toho. 70 mins.
Two Japanese survivors of the Khmer Rouge massacres in Cambodia vow to find a sanctuary even if they have to build it themselves. Returning to Japan, they take seemingly opposite paths—one becomes a politician, the other a gangster. As Asami and Hojo work their way through the linked worlds of politics and crime in modern Japan, they don't hesitate to do anything necessary to secure their own positions and stay true to their vow. Loyal to no one else, they find their friendship increasingly tested as they rise in their chosen fields. A prequel to the 1990 *Big Comic* manga by Sho Fumimura and CRYING FREEMAN–creator Ryoichi Ikegami, the style is glossy and international, the protagonists two sharp-suited young sharks navigating the murky seas of the 1990s without a scruple. It was also made as a live-action film. ●▲◆

SANDS OF DESTRUCTION *
2008. JPN: *World Destruction: Sekai Bokumetsu no Rokunin*. AKA: *World Destruction: Six People Who Will Destroy the World*. TV series. DIR: Shusuke Tada. SCR: Masahiro Yokotani. DES: Keita Matsumoto, Masanobu Nomura. ANI: Rui Kuroki. MUS: Yoshihiro Ike. PRD: Production I.G, Geneon, Sega. 24 mins. x 13 eps.
The story takes place in an alternate world in which humans are oppressed by a small but powerful elite of human-animal hybrids called beastmen. Morte is a fugitive, on the run from the beastmen who want the secret weapon she possesses—and means to use—to destroy the world. When she meets Kyrie in the beastman bar where he works, she decides to take him hostage, only to have his value disappear when the cat ears he's been wearing to

pass as a beastman fall off. The unlikely pair go on the run with a appealing little creature called Toppy, a teddy bear whose cute pirate headgear and eyepatch belie his talents.
There's a wealth of talent on this Nintendo-game-based story: Production I.G leading, 30-odd in-between studios including Studio Ghibli and Gonzo, a director whose credits include PRINCE OF TENNIS, and a writer with hits including NODAME CANTABILE on his resumé. But unless you're a fan of the games, it won't be long before you ask yourself what went wrong. It isn't just that the show is crashingly unoriginal, though ONE PIECE fans may feel pirate bear Toppy verges on the actionable. It isn't even that it's so uneven; the moments of superb animation are counterbalanced by sequences straight from the bargain bin, but Tada is clever enough to make a comic virtue out of cheap materials. It's the lack of any sense of a real story, where things happen for other reasons than to stack up enough bodies to get to the next level and characters develop in other ways than by acquiring magical gizmos. The main villain's comeuppance is as weak as that in TALES FROM EARTHSEA, largely thrown away for laughs, and the accumulation of destruction and backstory in the final episodes comes too late. ◆

SANKAREA: UNDYING LOVE *
2012. JPN: *Sankarea*. TV series, video. DIR: Mamoru Hatakeyama. SCR: Noboru Takagi. DES: Kyuta Sakai. ANI: Kyuta Sakai, Masaki Hyuga. MUS: Yukari Hashimoto. PRD: Studio Deen, Lantis, Kodansha, BS-TBS, Pony Canyon. 25 mins. x 12 eps. (TV), 25 mins. (v).
In the ultimate expression of "be careful what you wish for," zombie-obsessed teenager Chihiro embarks upon experiments to bring his dead cat back to life and ends up with a zombie girlfriend. Rea Sanka is the troubled daughter of a local family, subject to questionable treatment by her aging but inappropriate grandfather and now considerably freer in death than she ever was in life. Despite attempts by the narrative to keep things chaste and theoretical, there's no avoiding the fact that this story takes the idea of blank-slate, pre-abused girlfriends into the world of necrophilia, so thanks for that, anime. The more historically minded reader may

already notice, however, that in slowly decomposing before her boyfriend's very eyes, Rea is merely the latest in a string of disposable, temporary anime starter-women, dating back to LIMIT-CHAN THE MIRACLE GIRL and VIDEO GIRL AI. Based on the 2009 manga by Mitsuru Hattori, which ran in a spin-off title from *Shonen Magazine*.

SANPEI THE FISHERMAN

1980. JPN: *Tsurikichi Sanpei*. TV series. DIR: Eiji Okabe, Yoshimichi Nitta, Tameo Ogawa, Kiyoshi Harada, Yasuhiro Yamaguchi, Kazuyoshi Yokota, Fumio Kurokawa, Katsuhiko Yamazaki, Shigeo Koshi, Yasuhiro Imagawa. SCR: Mitsuru Majima, Tatsuo Tamura, Sukehiro Tomita. DES: Takao Yaguchi. ANI: Kazuyuki Okaseko, Takashi Saijo, Hidehito Kojima. MUS: Tatsuaki Sone, Hideyuki Yamamoto. PRD: Nippon Animation, Fuji TV. 25 mins. x 109 eps.

Having grown up in a distant mountain village in northeastern Japan, Sanpei Nihira is a gifted teenage fisherman, and this long-running series is the story of his struggle to catch as many fish as possible, all over Japan and even overseas. The bigger and meaner, the better he likes it, as he invents new techniques and exploits old ones learned from seasoned anglers to their limits in pursuit of more and more powerful fishy opponents. Based on Takao Yaguchi's 1973 manga that ran in both the weekly and monthly editions of *Shonen Magazine*—among the few attempts to present fishing as a combat sport (also see GRANDAR).

SANPEI THE KAPPA

1992. JPN: *Kappa no Sanpei*. Movie. DIR: Toshio Hirata. SCR: Shunichi Yukimuro. DES: Shigeru Mizuki. ANI: Tatsuo Kitahara. MUS: Kazuki Kuriyama. PRD: Nikkatsu. 90 mins. Japanese boy Sanpei befriends a *kappa* water-sprite and is soon accepted into a world of spiritual fun that lurks beneath the surface of modern Japan (see POM POKO). This movie was based on the 1962 manga by SPOOKY KITARO–creator Shigeru Mizuki and selected by the Japanese Ministry of Education as a worthy title.

SANSHIRO SUGATA

1981. JPN: *Sugata Sanshiro*. AKA: *Judo Story*. TV special. DIR: Yasumi Mikamoto. SCR: Fumio Konami, Kiyohide Ohara. DES: Monkey Punch. ANI: Kazuhide Yoshinaga. MUS: Talisman, Susumu Aketagawa. PRD: Tokyo Movie Shinsha, Fuji TV. 84 mins.

In the Tokyo of 1882, Sanshiro is a promising young martial artist who seeks a worthy teacher. He proves his ability by defeating 39 masters of jujitsu (who ridicule his choosing judo) and is taken in by their teacher, who continually tests him. He falls for local girl Sayo Murai and must fight her father at judo before defeating his greatest rival on the plain of Ukyogahara. Based on a novel by Tsuneo Tomita, best known in the West through its 1943 movie adaptation by a young Akira Kurosawa—though Kurosawa's version lacks the anime's comic-relief cat. The story, also included in ANIMATED CLASSICS OF JAPANESE LITERATURE, was an inspiration for the toy combat serial PLAWRES SANSHIRO, which supposedly starred the grandson of the original. Kurosawa's 1945 sequel was pastiched in later episodes of IRONFIST CHINMI, when Chinmi fights a foreign sailor. For more judo fun, see YAWARA!

SASAGAWA, HIROSHI

1936–. Sometimes read as Hiroshi Sasakawa. Born in Fukushima Prefecture he graduated from middle school and went to Tokyo, where he found work as an art assistant to Osamu Tezuka in 1956. His manga works included the original basis for GAZULA THE AMICABLE MONSTER, but in 1964 he left manga behind when he joined Tatsunoko Production, for which he animated SPACE ACE and parts of the TIME BOKAN series. He also wrote several science fiction novels.

SASUGA NO SARUTOBI

1982. AKA: *Idiot Ninja*. TV series. DIR: Koichi Sasaki, Masahisa Ishida. SCR: Takeshi Shudo, Masaki Tsuji, Tomoko Komparu, Shigeru Yanagawa. DES: Hiroshi Kanazawa, Jiro Kono. ANI: Hiroshi Kanazawa, Mutsumi Inomata, Masayuki, Shinichi Suzuki, Moriyasu Taniguchi. MUS: Joe Hisaishi. PRD: NAS, Tsuchida Pro, Fuji TV. 25 mins. x 69 eps. Sarutobi is the best pupil in his ninja school, but to look at him you'd never know it—he's as round as a butterball, and his superb fighting abilities are masked under a dozy demeanor. Both Mako, the prettiest girl in the school, and local bad-girl Mika see through his appearance to the hero underneath. Rivalry with the neighboring Spiner martial arts school is intense, but Sarutobi and his chums always come out on top. This cheerful comedy was based on Fujihiko Hosono's manga for Shogakukan, itself inspired by the earlier SASUKE and MAGIC BOY.

SASUKE

1968. JPN: *Sasuke*. TV series. DIR: Kiyoshi Onishi, Isao Kawachi. SCR: Junzo Tashiro. DES: Sanpei Shirato. ANI: Toyoo Ashida. MUS: Masashi Tanaka. PRD: TCJ, TBS. 25 mins. x 29 eps. (TV1), 25 mins. x 24 eps. (MSS). Sasuke's father sends him away to learn ninja techniques to defend the oppressed of feudal Japan from their overlords, the Tokugawa shogunate. Although just a little boy, he must fight the best warriors, armed to the teeth with swords, *shuriken*, nunchaku, and other deadly weapons. Based on the 1961 manga by Sanpei Shirato, which in its turn was inspired by a novel by Kazuo Den, the story of Sasuke was remade by Eiji Okabe for a much younger audience as *Manga Sarutobi Sasuke* (1979), a 24-episode series on Tokyo Channel 12, concentrating on Sasuke's feud with the rival ninja of the Iga clan. *Manga Sasuke Sarutobi* appears to have been released in an English compilation "movie" dub by Jim Terry Productions under the title NINJA THE WONDERBOY.

SATANIKA *

1997. Video. DIR: Takuji Endo. SCR: Glenn Danzig. DES: Yoshiaki Kawajiri. ANI: Junichi Hayama, Yoshihiko Umakoshi. MUS: Glenn Danzig. PRD: Datenshi, Madhouse. 3 mins. (25 mins.).

In a night-time urban-gothic setting redolent of WICKED CITY, demons leap between buildings and steal vehicles, causing mayhem. One such group is thwarted by the naked superheroine Satanika, a beautiful woman who transforms into a winged creature recalling DEVILMAN's Silene.

Screened at a couple of American conventions, this is an animated rock video sung by the wonderfully named Jenny Sexluv, featuring Glenn Danzig's Verotik comic character Satanika (MUSIC IN ANIME), with a color palette of reds and blues typical of the work of Yoshiaki Kawajiri. Although there is no dialogue, we have credited Danzig with the script, since he wrote the lyrics of the song, although arguably any sense of "script" might be better assigned to the storyboarder, Rintaro. The animation component is packaged inside a 25-minute showreel of live-action footage, comprising interviews with Danzig, Rintaro, director Endo, and producer Masao Murayama, all claiming to be planning a *Satanika* TV series, which never appeared. A decade and a half later, this rarity is more prized by anime encyclopedists for the time-capsule glimpse it affords inside Madhouse, an anime studio at work. Compare with similar foreigner-led enterprises, such as **KILL BILL: THE LEGEND OF O-REN**.

SATISFACTION, THE

1984. Video. DIR: N/C. SCR: N/C. DES: N/C. ANI: N/C. MUS: N/C. PRD: Zeros, Midnight 25, Sai Enterprise. 21 mins.

A campus beauty is admired by her fellow students, but her practiced air of coolness is actually a façade to hide her strong sex drive. She fantasizes about a series of sexual incidents, including a scene featuring a blue-furred demon seemingly inspired by **DEVILMAN**, who not only has a revolving phallus, but possibly the first appearance of tentacles in Japanese animated erotica. Subsequently, she is raped and degraded for real. **NV**

SATO, GEN

1960–. Born in Tokyo, he found part-time work at Toei Animation while still a student, but immediately after graduation he found work as a computer programmer outside the animation industry. He did not stay away from animation for long, and was lured back in by freelance work and then as a staffer at Ashi Production. After moving to Sunrise, he was assigned to work for Yoshikazu Yasuhiko. His design work and key animation have appeared in installments of the **GUNDAM** series, **TOMORROW'S NADJA**, and **CRUSHER JOE**, among others.

SATO, JUNICHI

1960–. Born in Aichi Prefecture, he studied film at the Fine Arts department of Nihon University, but dropped out to join Toei Animation in 1981. His animation debut was on the series **TENMARU THE LITTLE TENGU** (1983), but he is perhaps best known for his directorial work on

SAILOR MOON. Sometimes works under the pseudonyms Hajime Tendo or Kiichi Hadame. He is also the creator of more recent shows, such as **KALEIDO STAR** and **PRETEAR**.

SATO, YOSHIHARU

1958–. Born in Kanagawa Prefecture, he worked as a concept artist on **ANNE OF GREEN GABLES** and other children's anime, rising to key animator on **TREASURES OF THE SNOW** and **KATRI THE MILKMAID**. He was also a character designer on **POLLYANNA**.

SATO, YUZO

1960–. Born in Hiroshima Prefecture, he dropped out of Tokyo Design College to work for Sanrio on **SEA PRINCE AND THE FIRE CHILD**. Subsequently going freelance, his directorial debut was **BIO HUNTER**, and he has also worked as a concept artist on **CONFUCIUS**, among others.

SAVE ME, GUARDIAN SHAOLIN

1998. JPN: *Mamotte Shugogetten*. AKA: *Protect Me Shugogetten; Guardian Angel ShugoGetten*. TV series, video. DIR: Tatsuo Misawa, Satoshi Yamada, Keiji Hayakawa, Tetsuya Watanabe. SCR: Kenichi Yamada, Yasutoshi Yamada. DES: Ken Ueno. ANI: Masayuki Takagi, Hideyuki Motohashi. MUS: N/C. PRD: Toei, TV Asahi. 25 mins. x 22 eps. (TV), 30 mins. x 5 eps. (V).

Teenager Tasuke Shichiri is home alone while his parents travel in China. His father sends occasional presents; the first is a ring with a note—if someone of pure heart peers into it, a guardian from heaven will appear to protect them. No surprise that the heavenly body is a gorgeous teenage girl called Shaolin, whose sole destiny is to protect the "master" who releases her from 4,000 years of imprisonment. However, her naïveté about the modern world causes Tasuke more trouble (in the style of **DORAEMON**). Still, she has access to powerful spirits called Star Gods, who can use their special skills to help her. Father's second package contains a rod found in the same place as the ring, containing another spirit, also a gorgeous teenage girl whose sole destiny is to please her "master." Lu-An, confined for 1,652 years, can bring inanimate objects to life. By another strange coincidence, she and Shaolin are sworn rivals, often getting into fights

over Tasuke. To complicate matters even further, several of Tasuke's friends fall for the girls and do all in their power to entice the goddesses away, while a younger girl at Tasuke's school has a huge crush on him and is constantly trying to get rid of his supernaturally stacked slaves.

Based on the manga written by Sakurano Minene for *Shonen GanGan*, the similarity to **OH MY GODDESS!** reaches actionable proportions when a third goddess, Huang-Long, shows up to give Tasuke challenges (presumably to strengthen his character, which is normally the scriptwriter's job). Amazing—an average Japanese boy waits all through junior high school for a goddess to worship him, and then three show up at once! A video series, *New Legend: SMGS* (2000), further augmented by five CD dramas and a weekly radio show hosted by the characters, make up the grandly titled *Shugogetten Millennium Project*.

SAVE ME! LOLLIPOP *

2006. JPN: *Mamotte! Lollipop*. TV series. DIR: Noriyoshi Nakamura. SCR: Mitsutaka Hirota, Yoshimi Narita, Toshizo Nemoto, Yuka Yamada. DES: Rie Nishino, Akiko Ishida. ANI: Shinichiro Minami, Masaru Suda, Kei Takeuchi. MUS: N/C. PRD: Sunshine Corporation, Marvelous Entertainment. 25 mins. x 13 eps.

Twelve-year-old Nina Yamada loves sweets. So when she finds a hard white candy on her plate, she eats it. Unfortunately, it's a magical gem called the Crystal Pearl, and student sorcerers have to find it to pass their sorcery test. Luckily, the first of the students to find Nina are a couple of sweet, kindhearted guys called Zero and Ichi, who vow to band together to protect Nina from their rivals who mean to get the Pearl by any means necessary. She always dreamed of a hero to protect her from the world—now she has two! This is based on a 2002 girls' manga by Michiyo Kikuta, so the priceless opportunities for uncontrived toilet humor are completely ignored. Instead, the story is packed with tropes and clichés, moving from improbability to tedium and back by way of an outstandingly dull script and inexpensive animation. This won't worry the target audience, because little girls can enjoy almost anything wrapped in pastel colors, cute boys, and romance. But to reviewers who have seen it all before, and rather better done, this series is a disappointment.

SAY "I LOVE YOU" *

2012. JPN: Suki-tte Ii na yo. TV series. DIR: Toshimasa Kuroyanagi, Takuya Sato. SCR: Takuya Sato, Natsuko Takahashi, Michiko Yokote, Yuniko Ayana. DES: Junko Watanabe, Yoshiko Okuda. ANI: Junko Watanabe. MUS: Yuji Nomi. PRD: Gansis, Kodansha, Starchild Records, Zexcs. 24 mins. x 13 eps.
In this adaptation of Kanae Hazuki's manga from *Dessert* magazine (which features as a place of employment for one of the characters), awkward school wallflower Mei Tachibana accidentally kicks the handsome Yamato Kurosawa in the head. Yamato is immediately, and in Mei's opinion, inexplicably smitten with her, and pursues her as if she is the most beautiful girl in the world, in an artful, passionate entry in the anime ROMANCE AND DRAMA genre. Readers might scoff that the class hunk pursuing a dorky girl is no less ludicrous than a million harem anime premises for boys, but *Say "I Love You"* treats its heroine with heart and empathy, not the least in her recurring refusal to accept that Yamato's interest is anything more than some sort of blunt-force trauma. Viewers are assured that somewhere out there, everyone has that special someone, and that is surely the quintessence of romance, anime or otherwise.

SAYONARA ZETSUBO-SENSEI

2007. AKA: Farewell Mr. Despair. TV series, video. DIR: Akiyuki Shinbo. SCR: Kenichi Kanemaki, Fuyashi To, Yuichiro Oguro. DES: Hideyuki Morioka, Hiroshi Kato, Hirotsugu Kakoi. ANI: Hiroki Yamamura, Yoshiaki Ito, Hiroki Yamamura, Hideyuki Morioka, Mitsutoshi Kubota. MUS: Tomoki Hasegawa. PRD: SHAFT, Starchild Records. 25 mins. x 12 eps. (TV1), 25 mins. x 12 eps. (TV2), 24 mins. x 3 eps. (v1), 24 mins. x 13 eps. (TV3), 30 mins. x 2 eps. (v2).
Nozomu Itoshiki tends to expect the worst. In fact, he's probably the world's most determined pessimist. Since he's a high school teacher, you might feel some pessimism is understandable, even justified, but his is so extreme that one of his hobbies is planning his suicide. Even the three kanji of his name can be compressed into the two-kanji word *zetsubo*, or despair.

As the series opens he's trying to hang himself on a blossoming cherry tree, but is saved by a perky high school girl who tells him he can't possibly kill himself on such a beautiful day surrounded by such lovely trees. He flees to school to escape her overwhelming optimism, then finds that he's her new class teacher. What's more, everyone in the class has some weird trait or obsession. His abilities as a teacher, and his tendency to think everything through with brutal and unforgiving realism, will be tested to the full.

Koji Kometa's 2005 manga set out to satirize politics, media, and society in Japan, using literary, historical, and visual references to Japan's Taisho period, not the least Soseki Natsume's rural classroom drama BOTCHAN. It ran until 2012, and a dozen of the collected volumes are available in English at the time of writing. The anime follows the manga's lead in making frequent, often subtle references to pop culture, both in the number of parodies and homages to anime and manga, and in the apparently random thoughts and ideas written on the classroom chalkboard, behind credits and elsewhere onscreen. With Shinbo, director of PUELLA MAGI MADOKA MAGICA, in charge, arresting visuals and strong pacing are guaranteed. Stylish, reflective, and bleakly funny, the show references art from Aubrey Beardsley to Mike Mignola via *Peanuts*, anime from Sunrise to SHAFT via CASTLE OF CAGLIOSTRO, games, Internet forums, TV, movies, sport, and literature. (Watch for the blink-and-you'll-miss-it reference to the *Chronicles of Narnia*.) It even had its own mini-scandal when an opening animation showing Teacher and several girls in bondage or lesbian poses was changed after six uses for episode 10, with a note onscreen "The opening was not changed because of complaints."

Subsequent seasons displayed the punning humor of the show even in their titles, with prefixes that often had double meanings. A second TV series, *Vulgar/More Farewell Mr. Despair* (*Zoku Sayonara Zetsubo-Sensei*), aired in 2008, with a third, *Repent/Three Farewell Mr. Despair* (*Zan: Sayonara Zetsubo-Sensei*), in 2009. Three videos collectively entitled *Prison/Culmination Farewell Mr. Despair* (*Goku: Sayonara Zetsubo-Sensei*) appeared between October

2008 and February 2009, the first and third bundled with manga collections and the second as a stand-alone release. Confusingly, this is sometimes promoted as "series 2.5." Two more video episodes were released in 2009 and are sometimes called "series 3.5." Internet radio series and over 20 CD dramas have continued the story further.

SAZAE-SAN

1969. TV series. DIR: Kazuo Kobayashi, Satoshi Murayama, Takeshi Yamamoto, Yonehiko Watanabe. SCR: Masaki Tsuji, Noboru Shiroyama, Shunichi Yukimuro. DES: Toshihiro Osumi. ANI: N/C. MUS: Nobuyoshi Koshibe. PRD: Fuji TV. 7 mins. x 6500+ eps. (usually screened in batches of three).
Sazae Isono, her husband, Masato, their two children, and her mother live together in a small house in a quiet suburb of Tokyo. Each episode is simply a snippet of their daily life, running the gamut of putting up with noisy neighbors, sharing a public phone, or being polite to unwanted visitors.

Based on a manga serialized in the *Asahi Shinbun* newspaper from 1946 until 1974, *Sazae-san* was the most successful work by NASTY OLD LADY–creator Machiko Hasegawa. Its anime version adheres closely to her authorial style—no negative news items, no modern slang, no bad words, no electronic devices. Screenwriter Masaki Tsuji also reported that despite running for only seven minutes, the average *Sazae-san* script was so packed with incident and detail that it would often fill up 40 pages.

Still running 45 years later, the program has outlived both its manga incarnation and its creator, who died in 1992, but has garnered remarkably little attention outside Japan. This is, in part, because Hasegawa was vehemently opposed to merchandise spin-offs, severely limiting *Sazae-san*'s appearances not only in pencil cases, posters, and dolls, but also in video rereleases and foreign translations.

Appealing to a vast mainstream audience that does not otherwise watch animation, it remains the highest-rated anime on Japanese television, in 2014 maintaining an audience share around 25% (RATINGS AND BOX OFFICE). *Sazae-san* is thus the most popular anime in Japan and the longest-running cartoon in the world—a claim tardily acknowledged by Guinness World Records in 2013. Compare to the similar tone of **My Neighbors the Yamadas**.

The story also exists in a live-action version starring Chiemi Eri, which ran on TBS from 1965 to 1967 (*DE), while the creation of the story and the life of Hasegawa became the subject of an NHK series in 1979. A modern-day live-action reboot, *Sazae-san* (2010) ran for three short seasons, but already seemed curiously out of step—the story is so old that simple, physical issues such as the large size of the extended family are now anachronistic (**Bubu Chacha**). So, too, was the technology of the show's creation, with *Sazae-san* famously clinging on as the last Japanese cartoon to be made with cel animation. The studio only switched to full digital animation in 2013, presumably after the very last of the old-school animators had retired.

Modern-day episodes of *Sazae-san* end with the character appearing on screen and playing a *janken* (scissors-paper-stone) match with the viewer. This extra replaces the previous closing sequence, which ran from 1969 to 1991, in which *Sazae-san* would throw a peanut up in the air and catch it in her mouth. The peanut trick was taken off air in 1991 after a child choked to death while trying to imitate this feat.

SCARECROWMAN

2008. JPN: *Scarecrowman the Animation*. TV series. DIR: Yoshio Takeuchi. SCR: Megumi Hiyoshi. DES: Koichi Nishizuka, Takashi Miyano, Yuri Ishihara. ANI: Hisato Shioda. MUS: Koichiro Kameyama. PRD: Studio Hibari, TMS Entertainment, VAP. 25 mins. x 26 eps.
An old scarecrow has guarded a field for 20 years. One day, after being struck by lightning in a storm, he comes to life. He befriends the little daughter of a scarecrow shop owner and gradually finds his place in life in this CGI animation for small children.

SCARLET DEMON

1989. JPN: *Tokiiro Kaima*. Video. DIR: Wayu Suzumiya. SCR: Wayu Suzumiya. DES: Wayu Suzumiya, Atsushi Matoba. ANI: Atsushi Matoba. MUS: Kaoru Wada. PRD: Mushi. 20 mins. x 4 eps.
A "video comic" based on Wayu Suzumiya's manga about twin boys born to mixed human and dragon-god parentage. Passing their happy teens at a normal Japanese school, they are forced to defend their classmates from demonic attackers—a task made easier by their magical blood. Compare to **Legend of the Four Kings**.

SCARLET SANSHIRO

1969. JPN: *Kurenai Sanshiro*. AKA: *Judo Boy*. TV series. DIR: Jinzo Toriumi, Ippei Kuri, Hiroshi Sasagawa. SCR: Jinzo Toriumi. DES: Eiji Tanaka, Mitsuki Nakamura. ANI: Eiji Tanaka. MUS: Nobuyoshi Koshibe. PRD: Tatsunoko, Fuji TV. 25 mins. x 26 eps.
Saburo's father is a martial artist who dies in a fight with a mysterious one-eyed man outside the city gates. The boy sets out in search of his father's killer with only one clue: the killer left his glass eye at the scene of the crime. He meets, and fights, a lot of one-eyed people before he finally reaches the end of his quest, accompanied by his blood-red motorcycle, his mischievous junior pal Ken, and his faithful canine companion, Stupid. A run-of-the-mill adventure series of combat against mutants and mummies, characterized by some innovative filming techniques from Tatsunoko, including limited rotoscoping, strobe effects, and clever lighting.

SCHOOL

2011. Video. DIR: Shigeki Awai, Hisashi Tomii. SCR: Shin Ikari. DES: Keiji Ishihara. ANI: Keiji Ishihara. MUS: N/C. PRD: Hot Bear, Studio9MAiami. 30 mins. x 2 eps.
Kota goes to school in an old wooden schoolhouse in a small village. Three of his teenage girl classmates and his teacher all have the hots for him. This is based on one of Maya Miyazaki's porn manga so the outcome is predictable: sex on the beach, sex in the woods, sex in school, everything consensual and prettily rendered. **N**

SCHOOL DAYS *

2007. TV series, video. DIR: Keitaro Motonaga. SCR: Meizazu Numakichi, Makoto Uezu. DES: Junji Goto, Goichi Iwahata, Mitsuharu Miyamae Emi Suzuki, Jiro Kawano. ANI: Junji Goto. MUS: Kaoru Okubo. PRD: Animation Planet, Overflow, Stack, avex entertainment, Lantis, Marvelous Entertainment, Pony Canyon. 22 mins. (v1), 25 mins. x 12 eps. (TV), 24 mins. (v2), 19 mins. (v3).
Makoto falls in love with a beautiful girl who takes the same train to school every day. She's in his school, but not in his class. He enlists the help of his old friend Sekai to help him get to know Kotonoha, without realizing that Sekai is in love with him herself (compare to **Video Girl Ai**). The stage is set for another harem anime (**Romance and Drama**) based on a porn dating game, this time by Overflow.

It gained unexpected notoriety by a terrible coincidence. The final episode of the TV series contains extreme violence, and the day before it was to be aired, a 16-year-old Kyoto girl killed her father with an axe in somewhat similar circumstances. This led several TV stations to replace the episode with a soothing interlude of landscape film and classical music (**Censorship and Localization**).

A 22-minute Internet animation had been released in 2005, and two video spin-offs followed in 2008. *School Days OVA Special: Magical Heart Kokoro-chan* has all the characters from the game and anime playing roles in a fantasy good-vs-evil magical girl story. *School Days: Valentine Days* is the hot springs episode required by the laws of fan service (**Argot and Jargon**), ending with half a dozen girls fighting over who gets to give Valentine's Day chocolate to Makoto. **NV**

SCHOOL FOR THIEVES

1998. JPN: *Dorobo Gakko*. Video. DIR: Katsumi Hashimoto. SCR: Naoyuki Sakai. DES: Satoshi Kako. ANI: Katsu-mi Hashimoto, Kenzo Koizumi. MUS: Kenichi Kamio. PRD: Toei. 20 mins.
Based on a best-selling children's book by Satoshi Kako, this short features the self-explanatory goings-on at an educational institute with a difference. Also released as a double cassette with the same crew's 20-minute *Mr. Crow the Baker* (*Karasu no Panya-san*), another Kako story.

SCHOOL GIRL

2006. JPN: *Joseito*. AKA: *Female Student*. Video. DIR: Shutaru Oku. SCR: Tadashi Gozu. DES: Tadashi Gozu. ANI: N/C. MUS: Mako Kuwahara. PRD: Toei Animation, Gentosha. 24 mins.
Inspired by the writing of Osamu Dazai, this short video depicts a long-ago summer day in the life of a schoolgirl. Computer artist and painter Gozu's delicate images

and Kuwahara's music make perfect companions for this nostalgic trip. Director Oku has worked extensively on design in musical theater and ballet, contributing to a number of shows by the Takarazuka Revue. The very limited animation of Toei's *ga-nime* series (ARGOT AND JARGON) offers some interesting combinations of style and image.

SCHOOL GIRL: SPECIAL LESSON *

2000? JPN: *Heisei Jogakuen*. AKA: *Modern Girls School*. Video. DIR: N/C. SCR: N/C. DES: N/C. ANI: N/C. MUS: N/C. PRD: Obtain. 20 mins.

When Nakamura falls behind in class, she is summoned to school on a Sunday for some extra tutoring. It should come as no surprise to anyone who has seen DESPERATE CARNAL HOUSEWIVES that her teachers have only come in on the weekend because they have a secret plan to abuse and molest her in the name of education. A day of cruel "punishments" and lessons duly follows—or does it? A final twist questions whether Nakamura really didn't enjoy herself, and perhaps whether it happened at all. Possibly related to the *Heisei Jogakuin* series of live-action cheesecake DVDs—if it isn't, then the title is deliberately intended to imply that it is. ⬤⬤⬤

SCHOOL OF BONDAGE *

2004. JPN: *Inbaku Gakuen*. AKA: *School of Masochists*. Video DIR: Takefumi Goda. SCR: Miki Kano. DES: Yoshiten. ANI: Haraki. MUS: N/C. PRD: Studio Jam, Concept Films, Milky. 30 mins. x 3 eps. (v), 80 mins. (Best of).

Keisuke Shimizu has many problems at home, and as a result becomes a delinquent who treats women as sexual objects. But this is Japanese porn, so instead of youth custody or a sharp slap on the face from the nearest girl, he gets a visit from his class representative, the lovely Orie, who promises to be his sex slave for three months in an attempt to change his views about the power of true love. Stupidity of that order is fortunately rare in real life; the only possible category for this is fantasy. A "fourth" episode in the series is actually a "Best Of" compilation, the 80-minute movie edit released in America by a different company under the title *School of Masochists*. Based on a story in *Core* magazine by Nariaki Funabori. ⬤⬤

SCHOOL OF DARKNESS *

1995. JPN: *Inju Onna Kyoshi*. AKA: *Lust Beast Woman Teacher*. Video. DIR: N/C. SCR: N/C. DES: N/C. ANI: N/C. MUS: N/C. PRD: Pink Pineapple. 40 mins. x 3 eps.

When her boyfriend Taki becomes increasingly abusive toward her, school teacher Yoko is driven from him to seek lesbian comfort in the arms of her friend Ayano, who kindly offers to help her out by reading spells from a forbidden scroll shaped like a penis and supposedly made of demon skin. The mind boggles as to how anyone expects this to work out well—the scroll soon burrows inside her in the style of DEMON BEAST INVASION, turning her into a succubus intent on draining men of their life force. As in CAMBRIAN, BIBLE BLACK, and any number of other erotic anime you care to mention, an ancient evil has awoken, and now wishes to travel into our dimension to rape and abuse young girls. Considering how much of it goes on in other anime, the ancient evil will have to join the queue.

Episodes two and three take a slightly different tack and are only tenuously related, packing a number of schoolfriends off to the countryside with their teacher Miss Mizuno and her suspicious-looking fiancé. Countryside high jinks duly ensue, with the girls running into the woods for some furtive fumblings, before a storm disrupts the campsite and forces them to seek refuge in dark, forbidding woods.

With achingly predictable B-movie logic, the girls decide that the wisest move would be to split up. Instead of looking for help as agreed, two of them strip off at the first opportunity to go skinny-dipping. Meanwhile, their classmate Kyoko uses the separation of the group as a chance to seduce Miss Mizuno's fiancé, while men who have been overcome by the forces of lustful evil pursue other classmates around the woods. This is, as it turns out, because of the presence of a laughably Freudian giant vaginacreature, lurking underground and hoping to lure the cast into damnation. The authors only wish that there were a transcript of the pitch meeting for that one. Not to be confused with ANGEL OF DARKNESS, or any of the myriads of other tits-and-tentacles titles out there. ⬤⬤⬤

SCHOOL RUMBLE *

2004. TV series, video. DIR: Shinji Takamatsu. SCR: Tomoko Konparu, Miho Maruo, Natsuko Takahashi, Yuki Enatsu, Reiko Yoshida. DES: Hajime Watanabe. ANI: Katsuaki Kamata. MUS: Toshiyuki Omori, PRD: Marvelous Entertainment, Media Factory, Sotsu Agency, Starchild, Studio Comet, TV Tokyo. 23 mins. x 26 eps. (TV1), 23 mins. x 2 eps. (v1), 23 mins. x 26 eps. (TV2), 23 mins. x 2 eps. (v2).

Tenma Tsukamoto gets into the same class as the boy she's crazy about, only to hear that Oji Karasuma will transfer to another school next year. Desperate to get her man before the year is up, she tries everything to win his love, from shooting an arrow with a love letter attached straight at him to disguising herself as a nurse; she even ropes in her sister and her friends to help out. Meanwhile class troublemaker Kenji Harima has his eye on her, but she's no more interested in him that Oji is in her. Based on the manga in *Shonen Magazine* by Jin Kobayashi, and followed in 2005 by a two-part video sequel comprising a series of "outtakes" and bonus scenes that fill in gaps and add extra spin to situations already seen in the TV series. In the two-part video *School Rumble: Third Term* (2008), the previous 54 episodes are finally wrapped up; we find out why Karasuma has been so spaced-out and distant, see what makes Harima a good guy, and watch teenage girls get high on too much soda. And yes, people finally admit the feelings they've been discussing with everyone else in the school to the people who actually need to hear.

SCHOOL SPIRITS

1995. JPN: *Gakko no Yurei*. AKA: *Spirits/Ghosts of the School*. Movie. DIR: Norio Kashima. SCR: Masatoshi Kimura, Shigenori Kurii. DES: Shigenori Kurii. ANI: Shigenori Kurii. MUS: N/C. PRD: Toei. 45 mins. x 6 eps.

Another entry in the spooky-school genre typified by HERE COMES HANAKO, this anime is presented as short vignettes split roughly 50/50 between animation and live action. Based originally on chilling tales written for *My Birthday* magazine, it was disgracefully repackaged after the rental release as ten 15-minute tapes for retail. See also REAL SCHOOL GHOST STORIES.

SCI-FI HARRY

2000. TV series. DIR: Yasuhito Kikuchi, Katsuyuki Kodera. SCR: Kenichi Takashima, Mitsuhiro Yamada, Takeo Tsutsui. DES: Shinya Takahashi. ANI: Yuji Shigekuni, Keiji Tani. MUS: Jeanne D'Arc, Luca. PRD: APPP, TV Asahi. 25 mins. x 20 eps.

Harry McQueen is a shy 17-year-old who gets picked on by school bully Chris and his gang because they know he won't fight back. Harry's imagination is his escape route; fantasizing that he's the hero of one of his favorite TV shows, he retreats behind the screen into an imaginary world where he can kick Chris's butt. Then we begin to see another side to Harry. When his friend Kate, who has always stood up for him, is kidnapped by the bullies, Harry suddenly appears to save her, though he has no idea how or why. And then a bizarre series of murders occur. Based on the manga by *Night-Head*–creator Joji "George" Iida and Asami Tojo, set in the fantasyland of the U.S. (and loaded with American names, clearly aimed squarely at a foreign release from the get-go), this might at first sight seem an unlikely project for the studio that brought you JOJO'S BIZARRE ADVENTURES, but events soon take a turn for the surreal.

SCIENCE FICTION AND ROBOTS

The earliest science fictional works of Japanese animation date from the 1930s, with Shigeji Ogino's amateur film *Hyakunen-go Aru Hi* (1932, *One Day 100 Years Hence*) and Teizo Kato's ten-minute THE PLANE CABBY'S LUCKY DAY (1932). However, SF itself failed to catch on as an animated genre until the postwar period, particularly when Osamu Tezuka deliberately planned his ASTRO BOY (1963) as SF in reaction to the fantasies and fairy tales that dominated the medium. Tezuka's clean, spartan world also allowed for an extreme economy of animation, helping him to save money in the studio. Anime has favored science fiction ever since, not the least because more mundane genres can be less expensively reproduced with live action, whereas the ability to integrate special effects so readily makes anime a better choice for greater, cheaper spectacle.

The success of *Astro Boy* ushered in dozens of imitators, seemingly caught up in Japan's defeat "by aliens" and its subsequent reconstruction. Like *Superman*, the heroes of PRINCE PLANET (1965) and SPACE ACE (1965) are new arrivals on Earth, with quasi-magical powers or devices that can help their newfound allies. Like GIGANTOR (1963) and BIG X (1964), the Japanese emerge from World War II as the inheritors of a shameful history that may return to haunt them, but with great hope in industry and technology.

Whereas Astro Boy began as little more than a high-tech *Pinocchio* with superpowers, he was also the ultimate playmate for the average Japanese boy. Love of robots reflected a faith in the future that was not always justified, most famously in DORAEMON (1970), in which a time-traveling rescue mission goes periodically awry, courtesy of inadequate materials.

Go Nagai's MAZINGER Z (1972) presented robots not as radio-controlled toys or android companions, but as pilotable machines—hereafter, the term "robot" is strictly speaking an incorrect gloss, liable to be used freely by children but replaced with "mecha" by fans and academics who appreciate the distinction (ARGOT AND JARGON). Despite this, the term "robot" continued to be used, even by creators, even when the machines in question were demonstrably not robotic. Nagai's GETTER ROBO also featured a regular transformation sequence, in which separate modules would combine to form a super-robot—not only permitting the recycling of footage of the transformation sequence, but also encouraging the sales of not one, but three tie-in toys. The show was soon followed by a number of sequels, as well as anime based on Go Nagai's other manga in the same vein.

The broadcast of Gerry Anderson's *Thunderbirds* and *Captain Scarlet* in Japan ensured that by the 1970s, team shows fighting alien menaces were commonplace in live-action TV, combining the ensemble cast with the talents of miniature- and model-makers. In anime such as SKYERS 5 (1967), this led to color-coded teams of youths, often a cookie-cutter composition of leader, maverick, token girl, token child/comic relief, and "the other one." As with the live-action shows postdating *Goranger* (*DE; 1975) such shows were also likely to be unified around an arbitrary theme—cards, dinosaurs, or, in the case of BATTLE OF THE PLANETS, birds who were also ninja. The underlying themes of disparate entities combining into a transcendent whole was seen not only as a wonderful metaphor for teamwork, but also as an excellent excuse to sell multipart vehicle sets requiring all other elements to create one super-toy.

Star Trek (broadcast in Japan as *Great Battle in Space: Star Trek*) helped encourage a similar galactic quest in Japan, in the form of Leiji Matsumoto's (or, depending on which judge you obey, "Yoshinobu Nishizaki's") *Space Battleship Yamato* (1974), which made it to America as STAR BLAZERS. However, it would not do so until much later, in 1979, after the worldwide success of *Star Wars* (1977). Science fiction was the new fad, resulting in adaptations of classic American SF such as LENSMAN (1984) and CAPTAIN FUTURE (1978). Local competition came in the form of CAPTAIN HARLOCK (1984), but also most notably in GUNDAM (1979), a franchise still running to this day. Featuring angst-ridden combatants in giant robots, *Gundam* codified the concept of the "newtype." The baby boom generation, known as the "new breed" in Japan, was thus allegorized as a literal evolutionary leap, humans with psychic powers, radically different in abilities and expectations from the generation that preceded them. "Newtype" achieved a currency equivalent to that of *slan* in early American SF FANDOM, or *otaku* in modern anime—it remains the name of the world's best-selling anime magazine.

Gundam's only real rival was MACROSS (1982), which kept with the pilotable robots (although these could transform into space fighter-planes), and introduced the concept of defeating an enemy by singing at them. The concept offered considerable potential for new merchandise formats—spin-off albums. VOTOMS (1983) also offered an angle on "real robots," introducing the notion of a robot as merely a tool in a military arsenal, alongside more traditional technology. Hereafter, the "real robots" largely replaced the "super robots" of earlier genre shows like *Mazinger*.

Although *Gundam* and *Macross* presented some fresh angles on perennial themes, and NAUSICAÄ OF THE VALLEY OF THE WIND (1984) was a landmark in cinemas, anime SF only truly came into its own through video. It was the arrival of the video recorder that brought the potential for true science fiction, as opposed to the limited "sci-fi" of television. After the early experiment of **DALLOS** (1983), science fiction was established as a strong part of the anime world, with works including **MEGAZONE 23** (1985), **BUBBLEGUM CRISIS** (1987), and the first **APPLESEED** (1988). Video SF came into its own with **GUNBUSTER** (1988), conceived in loving homage to the sci-fi of the 1960s, and **PATLABOR** (1989), produced in an indignant reaction to the brutal apocalyptic world envisioned by *Mad Max 2: The Road Warrior* (1981) and **FIST OF THE NORTH STAR** (1984). SF also flourished in cinemas, in the form of two productions for which critical success came far in advance of actual profits—**WINGS OF HONNEAMISE** (1987) and **AKIRA** (1988). Notably, this period also saw the beginning of the long-running **LEGEND OF GALACTIC HEROES** (1988), a video series that survived primarily through subscriber orders, largely bypassing even video stores.

In the 1980s, Japan (and particularly Tokyo) became a motif in SF all its own, the future metropolis of William Gibson's novel *Neuromancer* (1984) and the Asian influences on the Los Angeles of Ridley Scott's *Blade Runner* (1982) helping to create further interest abroad in science fiction *from* Japan. In seeming inverse correlation to Japan's rising power on the world stage, the robots got smaller. The hulking, city-stomping behemoths of old reduced in size, evolving into the smaller personal vehicles of **MOSPEADA**, and the feminized "hard-suit" armor of **BUBBLEGUM CRISIS** (1987)—perhaps creators had less to prove, or, in the age of the Sony Walkman, saw that miniaturization was the new cool. Realizing that a primarily male audience would rather watch scantily clad girls, science fiction gained increasing numbers of female characters, until, after a decade of the likes of **DIRTY PAIR** (1985) and **SOL BIANCA** (1990), it was male characters that became the token castmembers. *Blade Runner* motifs returned in the android women of **AD POLICE** (1990), **ARMITAGE III** (1994), and **GHOST IN THE SHELL** (1995). Hideaki Anno's watershed **EVANGELION** (1995) was intended as the final word on the tropes and clichés of the giant robot genre, but instead ushered in another cycle of imitators such as **BRAIN POWERED** (1998) and

RAHXEPHON (2002). As the millennium approached, Japanese SF also began to look backward, both to the retro camp of shows like **GIANT ROBO** (1993) and **SUPER ATRAGON** (1995) and the martial fervor of **KISHIN CORPS** (1993) and **SAKURA WARS** (1997). **COWBOY BEBOP** (1998) stood out in the crowd simply for its sense of style—it began life as a Sunrise show deliberately written *without* giant robots, a refreshing change in a medium that seems to be overrun with them.

Modern science fiction anime occupy a gloriously wide selection of niches, from the intimate sensuality of **CHOBITS** (2002) to the dingy, dirty low-orbit world of **PLANETES** (2003) and the existential rebellion of **BLAME** (2003). The Wachowskis' *The Matrix* (1999) may have set many of the standards of modern-day media SF, but it did so in a manner that built on anime—its inspirations and homages can be clearly seen, both in the continuing hard-SF explorations of the *Ghost in the Shell* franchise, and in the large number of Japanese contributors to **THE ANIMATRIX** (2002).

SCIENTIFIC GUYS
2013. JPN: *Kagaku na Yatsura*. Video. DIR: Hiraku Kaneko. SCR: Katsuhiko Takeyama. DES: Masaya Nozaki. ANI: Masaya Nozaki. MUS: Shigeru Yoshida. PRD: Hoods Entertainment. 30 mins.
Nerdy teenager Haruki spends most of his time with two girls. But their happy threesome is ruined when love enters the equation, and both try to appeal to his affections by setting up rival Mechanical Science and Chemical Science clubs. Erotic hijinx ensue, although if someone set up a *Biological* Science club, they might like to point out that boobs don't naturally come in sizes that big. **Ⓝ**

SCOLD WITH DIRTY WORDS
2010. JPN: *Shikatte Ingo*. Video. DIR: Yoshinari Saito. SCR: N/C. DES: Yoshinari Saito. ANI: Yoshinari Saito. MUS: N/C. PRD: ChiChi No Ya. 20 mins.
This porn story is a novel take on workplace discipline and leadership styles—well, insofar as there is a story, and in 20 minutes you can't tell very much story if you have to leave most of the running time free for sex scenes. Rei Misaki is a junior education manager who has to motivate

a worker so demoralized he doesn't even like sex. She soon changes that. **Ⓝ**

SCOOPERS
1987. Video. DIR: Jun Hirabayashi, Hideo Watanabe. SCR: Monkey Punch. DES: Monkey Punch, Masakazu Abe. ANI: Hirohide Yashikijima. MUS: N/C. PRD: ACC, video Tech. 58 mins.
It's 2016, and Shambhala city reporter Yoko and her android boyfriend/bodyguard/cameraman Vito are hunting the enigmatic criminal Mr. X. Their search leads them to the Rainbow Tower, where Yoko is taken hostage and Vito must battle to save her by destroying the program of the Tower's central computer to prevent X's escape. Based on a manga by **LUPIN III**–creator Monkey Punch.

SCRAPPED PRINCESS *
2003. AKA: *Sutepri*. TV series DIR: Soichi Masui. SCR: Reiko Yoshida, Atsushi Yamatoya. DES: Takahiro Komori (aka Mogudan). ANI: Takahiro Komori. MUS: Hikaru Nanase. PRD: Kadokawa Shoten. 25 mins. x 24 eps.
Princess Pacifica Casull suffers from a bad case of fairy-tale curse, since her family was informed at the time of her birth that she was "the poison that will destroy the world"—a prophecy fated to come to pass on her 16th birthday, unless she dies first. Consequently, her parents the king and queen order their baby daughter's execution, although in a moment reminiscent of **SNOW WHITE**, the knight ordered to carry out the task cannot bring himself to do it. She is found and raised by a farmer's family, until she and her adopted siblings are forced to go on the run from followers of the evil god Mauser, and, despite brother Shannon's ability with the sword and sister Racquel's magical expertise, the attempts on her life get increasingly inventive. Meanwhile, the good knight Sir Leo has decided that Pacifica is his true love and insists on trying to protect her, although his efforts often cause more harm than good. As if that weren't enough, Pacifica's *real* twin brother back at the palace discovers that his sister is still alive and is forced to choose sides.

Often playing like **SLAYERS** with comedy teen angst, as Pacifica eternally frets that the world would be a happier place if she simply died, *Scrapped Princess* maintains a steady series of opponents and missions-of-the-week, while building up to Pacifica's final redemption and absolution. This fantasy series has attractive design and good character development and interaction to enliven the well-worn premise of a fantasy world growing out of a sci-fi global war. Based on an illustrated novel by Ichiro Sakaki and Yukinobu Asami, which was itself later adapted into a manga by Go Yabuki and serialized in the monthly *Comic Dragon*.

SCRYED

2001. TV series. DIR: Goro Taniguchi. SCR: Yosuke Kuroda. DES: Hisashi Hirai. ANI: N/C. MUS: N/C. PRD: Sunrise. 25 mins. x 26 eps.
In the near future, Kanagawa Prefecture becomes the "Lost Ground," an alternate reality where light and darkness duel for control of the locals' hearts. Sixteen-year-old Kazuma is an "Inner," a child who has never left the world of the Lost Ground, forced into conflict with powerful beings known as the Altered.

SEA CAT

1988. Movie DIR: Shunji Saida. SCR: N/C. DES: N/C. ANI: N/C. MUS: N/C. PRD: Oh Production, Anido. 20 mins.
Cats have nine lives. The central character of this experimental film needs them all. Lost at sea and adopted by a sea otter, he's abducted by a UFO as nuclear war breaks out and the oceans evaporate in the ensuing holocaust. Director Saida, a talented animator who worked on NAUSICAÄ OF THE VALLEY OF THE WIND and GRAVE OF THE FIREFLIES, pulled in a team of animators to contribute one shot each. The movie was never distributed but loaned out for small screenings, a method called "hall projection" in Japan.

SEA OF THE TICONDEROGA

1991. JPN: *Ticonderonga no iru Umi*. Movie. DIR: Yuji Himaki. SCR: Koji Kawakita. DES: Takao Kasai. ANI: Takao Kasai. MUS: N/C. PRD: Urban Project, Asmik, Kobushi Pro. 28 mins.
On December 5, 1965, a U.S. aircraft carrier is en route from Vietnam to Yokosuka, Japan. While conducting training exercises 80 miles off Okinawa, an A4 strike aircraft is loaded with a B43 hydrogen bomb, but it falls overboard and sinks in 16,000 feet of water. Based on the true story of the

USS Ticonderoga, which reached Japan two days later (on the anniversary of Pearl Harbor; nice touch). Neither side revealed the incident, nor that she was carrying atomic weapons in contravention of U.S. treaties with Japan. The plane, its pilot, and the bomb were never recovered, and the incident was only declassified in 1989, causing an outcry in Japan and resulting in this environmentally themed anime. The extra "n" in *Ticonderonga* may be a genuine error in transcription or an attempt to distance the story from real events, since the anime continues with Ashika, a boy from a Japanese fishing town, contacted by telepathic whales who bring him visions of fearful sea-monsters. Then again, if you were a whale given a choice between nuclear contamination and talking to Japanese fishermen, which would you choose? For more fun with the U.S. Navy, see SPACE FAMILY CARLVINSON.

SEA PRINCE AND THE FIRE CHILD *

1981. JPN: *Sirius no Densetsu*. AKA: *Legend of Sirius*. Movie. DIR: Masami Hata, Takuo Suzuki. SCR: Chiho Katsura. DES: Shigeru Yamamoto. ANI: Shigeru Yamamoto, Mikiharu Akabori. MUS: Koichi Sugiyama. PRD: Sanrio. 108 mins.
Prince Sirius comes from a family of water spirits and Princess Malta, daughter of Hyperia, from a family of fire spirits. The long and bitter war between the two makes the love of the two young protagonists impossible. When Sirius and Malta try to escape their parents' wrath, they are enveloped in a powerful storm conjured by the evil Algorac, Lord of the Winds. The Disneyesque animation style looks charming.

SEA STORY

2009. JPN: *Umi Monogatari: Anata ga Itte Kureta Koto*. AKA: *Sea Story: Things You Told Me*. TV series. DIR: Yu Ko, Junichi Sato. SCR: Yuka Yamada, Reiko Yoshida, Masahiro Yokotani. DES: Haruko Iizuka, Shichiro Kobayashi. ANI: Masato Kato, Haruko Iizuka, Akiko Matsuo, Kazuhiko Oriki. MUS: Ken Muramatsu. PRD: ZEXCS, CBC, Shochiku, T.O. Entertainment. 24 mins. x 13 eps.
Marin and Urin are two sisters who live in the sea, swimming with the fish, all the while longing to be on land. Sea dwellers are born from shells and don't have direct

family, but the two girls are inseparable. When they find a ring in the sea they decide to return it to its owner. After a long journey and many dangers they finally reach a remote Japanese island and meet a high school girl named Kanon. Kanon and Marin are drawn to each other because, unknown to them, they each wield the powers of their element, land and sea. Kanon tells the girls she threw the ring away because the boy who gave it to her is no longer her boyfriend, and flings it into the forest. The sisters go to look for it, and Urin accidentally breaks the seal of a forest shrine and unleashes a dark force. The powerful magician Senda was sealed away long ago; unless the powers of the sea and land can be combined, she will escape and wreak havoc on the world. This pretty anime is based on a pachinko game, claimed by its manufacturer, Sanyo Bussan, to be the most popular in Japan—a considerable boast in a place where pachinko parlors are so widespread. Two manga, one by Katsuragi following the anime storyline and one by Tonmi Narihara in a four-panel format, were launched in different magazines to help promote it. Compare to PONYO, which similarly refashions elements of THE LITTLE MERMAID, albeit in a far classier way.

SEA TURTLE AND THE BOY, THE

2008. JPN: *Umigame to Shonen*. TV movie. DIR: Tetsuo Yasumi, Ken Ushikusa. SCR: Nobuyuki Fujimoto. DES: Shuichi Seki, Minoru Nishida. ANI: Koichi Maruyama, Tadahiko Horiguchi. MUS: Motoi Sakuraba. PRD: Shin'ei Animation, TV Asahi. ca. 60 mins.
Wartime: Tetsuo and his mother and grandmother live in Naha on the island of Okinawa. Sea turtles have been nesting there from time immemorial. As Tetsuo and his friends see their families and lives shattered by events, the turtles too are affected by the horrors of war, and Tetsuo learns life and survival take many forms. A bleakly beautiful fable based on a story by Akiyuki Nosaka, author of GRAVE OF THE FIREFLIES, this TV special also inspired a new edition of the story, published by Studio Ghibli and illustrated by their legendary background artist Kazuo Oga.

SEA'S DARKNESS: MOON'S SHADOW

1988. JPN: *Umi no Yami, Tsuki no Kage*. AKA:

Darkness of the Sea, Shadow of the Moon. Video. DIR: Satoshi Dezaki. SCR: Hirokazu Mizude. DES: Setsuko Shibuichi. ANI: Akio Sugino, Yukari Kobayashi. MUS: N/C. PRD: Visual 80. 40 mins. x 3 eps.

These SF-horror adventures that were based on the 1987 manga in *Shojo Comic* by PURPLE EYES IN THE DARK–creator Chie Shinohara feature twin girls Ryusui and Ryufu, who discover they have unearthly powers that increase as the moon waxes. As a bonus, tape two contains a ten-minute anime based on Miyuki Kitagawa's *That Girl Is 1,000%* (*Ano Ko wa 1,000%*), a similar tale of haunting romance.

SECRET AKKO-CHAN *

1969. JPN: *Himitsu no Akko-chan.* AKA: *Akko-chan's Secret.* TV series. DIR: Hiroshi Ikeda, Keiji Hisaoka, Masayuki Akehi, Takeshi Tamiya, Yoshio Takami. SCR: Shunichi Yukimuro, Tomohiro Ando, Masaki Tsuji, Tadaaki Yamazaki. DES: Fujio Akatsuka. ANI: Shinya Takahashi. MUS: Asei Kobayashi. PRD: Toei, NET. 30 mins. x 94 eps. (TV1), 30 mins. x 61 eps. (TV2), 25 mins. (m6), 25 mins. (m7), 30 mins. x 44 eps. (TV3).

Helpful 10-year-old Akko usually takes good care of her belongings, especially her old mirror, brought back as a present from India by her father. She polishes it carefully every night before she goes to bed, but one night she accidentally breaks it. Very sad, she buries the pieces in the garden. That night, the spirit of the mirror wakes her and gives her another mirror to thank her for cherishing the old one. Her new present is a compact with the power to transform the owner into any person or animal she chooses if she says a magical word; but the fairy warns Akko that she must keep the spell, and the powers of the mirror, a secret. Akko uses her new powers to solve the problems of friends and neighbors in her quiet hometown, and, as her confidence grows, she transforms into animal shapes and even goes to other countries. Based on the 1962 manga series by Fujio Akatsuka, who also created OSOMATSU-KUN and GENIUS IDIOT BAKABON, *SA* was the next "magical girl" series after LITTLE WITCH SALLY and confirmed the appeal of the formula. The series was remade for Fuji TV in 1988 as *SA 2* (*Himitsu no Akko-chan 2*), with Hiroki Shibata as director and new character designs from

Yoshinori Kanemori, and was also made into two movies the following year, *SA* (*Himitsu no Akko-chan*) and *SA: It's the Sea! It's a Ghost!! Summer Festival* (*Himitsu no Akko-chan: Umi da! Obake da!! Natsu Matsuri*). Shibata returned for a *third* 28-episode TV season on TV Asahi in 1998, with character designs from Toshio Deguchi. A live-action film, *Eiga Himitsu no Akko-chan* (*Akko-chan the Movie*, 2012) was directed by Yasuhiro Kawamura.

SECRET ANIMA SERIES *

1997. AKA: (see below). Video. DIR: Kunimitsu Ikeda, Kaoru Tomioka, Hachi Saiga. SCR: Susumu Nanase, Doctor Emu. DES: Ran Hiryu, Protonsaurus, Mon-Mon, Yokihi, Yoshimasa Watanabe. ANI: Ruthie Tanaka, Jiro Makigata. MUS: N/C. PRD: Beam Entertainment. 30 mins. x 10 eps.

An umbrella series of adaptations of pornographic manga, which, unlike the similar COOL DEVICES, was broken up and released abroad as *separate* titles. *Mama* (#1–2, released in the U.S. as *Mama Mia*) was based on a manga by Ran Hiryu and features Yuichi, an orphaned boy who discovers that his frisky stepsister Mika has been seducing her own mother to prevent her getting her kicks from making any more porn videos. For the second part, a completely different boy (confusingly also called Yuichi) loses his adoptive father in the same traffic accident that leaves his adoptive mother in a wheelchair. Now the man of the house, Yuichi discovers that Dad used to play pervy games with Mom and Rika the maid, and Yuichi carries on the noble family tradition. *Chu²* (#3) consists of three far shorter tableaux from Protonsaurus, with a similar S/M theme to his work in *Cool Devices.* For U.S. release, it was combined with *Momone* (#4, AKA *The Naughty Professor*), another tale of bondage from Kazu Yoshinaga, under the title *Twisted Tales of Tokyo.* In *Dream Hazard* (#5), based on a manga from CREAM LEMON's Mon-Mon, timid schoolgirl Kaori buys a virtual-reality date in order to sublimate her desires for an upperclassman. Needless to say, things go horribly wrong, and she finds herself "virtually" subjected to the usual porn anime cavalcade of abuse, assault, rape, and torture. In *Four Play* (#6–7), based on the manga *2x1* by ETCHIIS-creator Yokihi, two boys are sent

to an absent classmate's home to deliver notes. However, the malingering Noriko instead seduces the sporty Junichi and eventually succumbs to the geekier charms of his quiet friend Satoshi. All three of them begin a series of sexual experiments, scandalizing their contemporaries in a Tokyo suburb. After several different scenes of naughtiness the foursome (Junichi's sister Miyuki turning up as an afterthought) agree that it's okay to do whatever they want, as long as nobody gets hurt. Junichi delivers an impassioned speech to that effect (at least, it might have been impassioned before the dubbers got hold of it) and the credits roll. In *Pianist* (#8), based on a manga by Yoshimasa Watanabe, concert pianist Seiji injures his wrist (sure he does) in a car accident, develops a crush on his robot nurse, and buys a slave-robot to remind him of her. When robot Yuna turns out to be a piano prodigy, he tries to secure her a record deal, only to discover that prejudice exists against nonhuman musicians. Finally, in Serina Kamuro's *Love²Police* (#9), three girls carry out secret missions in order to rescue boys from their virginity and any other frustrations. The final episode was JULIET (#10).

Unsurprisingly, these titles register a very low level of interest from all parties concerned—starting with the original creators, since only *Pianist* has a remotely interesting plot, and even that is riddled with holes. The sex is even less entertaining, let down by substandard animation. Most noticeable is the overuse of flashbacks, a relatively easy trick using digital animation, allowing, for example, multiple scenes of video playback as *Mama Mia*'s protagonist watches his stepmother's porno appearances on tape. The low budget also shows in traditional ways, such as very limited backgrounds in several episodes and heavy reliance on pans across single images. With such bad workmanship at the Japanese end, it comes as little surprise that the U.S. dubbing crews seem similarly disinterested in their material—both *Dream Hazard* and *Mama Mia* feature particularly bad performances from actors who clearly wish they were somewhere else. Producing porn will always be a thankless task, but *Secret Anima* is a particularly low-rent example of the genre, unlikely to satisfy fans of anime or erotica.

Mama Mia was later rereleased in the U.S. by Nu-Tech under the title *Ma Ma*. **🅛🅝🅥**

SECRET DESIRES *

2002. JPN: *Midara*. AKA: *Lewdness; Secret Desires: Passions of the Midara*. Video. DIR: N/C. SCR: N/C. DES: N/C. ANI: N/C. MUS: N/C. PRD: Museum Video, Milky. 30 mins. x 3 eps. College student Yuto Sawada picks up a video cassette that turns out to be magic—but all resemblance to **VIDEO GIRL AI** ends there. The tape shows the viewer his or her secret desires. Yuto sees himself winning an auction for the right to have sex with his stepsister. Anachronistic settings, bondage, and domination are a common theme of the fantasies on the tape; the idea of jerking off while watching *yourself* have sex is an uncomfortable one, especially when the sex you're having is nonconsensual. Based on a computer game by Mink. Compare to *Dream Hazard* in the **SECRET ANIMA SERIES**. **🅛🅝🅥**

SECRET FACE OF MY WIFE, THE

2010. JPN: *Watashi no Shiranai Mesu no Kao*. AKA: *The Unknown Face of My Wife*. Video. DIR: Shinichi Shimizu. SCR: Taifu Sekimachi. DES: Toshihide Masutate. ANI: Toshihide Masutate. MUS: N/C. PRD: Mary Jane, Studio Eromatik. 30 mins. Ichika and Masato are happily married until Masato gets an anonymous DVD of her having sex with someone else. This game-based porn anime tries to cover all bases—consensual bondage, consensual marital sex, voyeurism, rape, anal rape, watersports, and blackmail—but ends up as incoherent as it is unpleasant. **🅝🅥**

SECRET GARDEN, THE

1991. JPN: *Anime Himitsu no Hanazono*. AKA: *Anime Secret Garden*. TV series. DIR: Tameo Ogawa. SCR: Kaoru Umeno. DES: Hidemi Kubo, Aiko Katsumata. ANI: Hideki Kubo, Hiroshi Suzuki. MUS: Masaaki Matsumoto, Shiro Sagisu. PRD: Aubec, NHK. 25 mins. x 39 eps. Plain, awkward Mary is neglected by her pretty mother and military father. Orphaned in India, she is sent to live with her uncle in the north of England. She discovers that her cousin Colin is as lonely as she is—after his mother's death while giving birth to him, he is both indulged

and neglected by his heartbroken father and often kept locked away. But Mary's company and the fascinating project she has uncovered—finding and reviving his mother's secret garden—soon gets Colin back on his feet. When her uncle finally comes home, he finds a welcome he never imagined. Frances Hodgson Burnett's 1909 novel has been filmed many times in the West, and even made into a Broadway musical. The same author wrote **LITTLE LORD FAUNTLEROY** and **A LITTLE PRINCESS**.

SECRET HOT SPRING TOUR

2006. JPN: *Hito Meguri Rape 1: Waka Okami, Raichiru, Shokai Gentei Ban; Hito Meguri—Yokujo Jurin Onsen Ki*. AKA: *Hito Meguri the Animation*. Video. DIR: Banzo Tokita. SCR: Kaoru Takahashi. DES: Maro Akafuku. ANI: Noritomo Hattori. MUS: Akira Asano. PRD: Armor, Mary Jane, Kanto Doga. 30 mins. (v1), 20 mins. x 2 eps. (v2, *Kakure Yu*), 30 mins. (v3, *Shin*).
Chitose Yukino is in high school in her native resort town when her mother runs off with a man, leaving her to fend for herself and run the family inn. Before long she's raped by a guest from Tokyo and finds herself threatened by a gang who want to take the inn from her. Her childhood friend Mikio misinterprets the rape as consensual, so he calls in the yakuza because he wanted her for himself. In Porngameland, nothing says "I love you" to an abandoned teenage girl like judging her for her perceived sexual behavior and getting her gang-raped.

Based on a PC game from Riddle Soft, this did well enough that a sequel was released in 2010. Mikio, who wisely got out of town after the previous episode, comes back six months later to find Chitose more beautiful than ever, still running the inn and still getting it on with older men. We suspect that the "Pill Gates" credited for planning alongside Ponzu ("Poopy") Ittosai may be using a pseudonym, as may producer Katzen Hamburg. A release in 2013, *Hito Meguri Kakure Yu: Mao Hen*, is billed as a "sequel," with different main characters and Mikio back in a supporting role. There is also a new sequel to the original game, *Shin Hito Meguri*, by Potage, which also generated an anime adaptation in 2013. **🅝**

SECRET OF BLUE WATER, THE *

1990. JPN: *Fushigi na Umi no Nadia*. AKA: *Nadia of the Mysterious Seas; Nadia*. TV series, movie. DIR: Hideaki Anno, Shigeru Morikawa, Masayuki, Koji Masunari, Takeshi Mori. SCR: Toshio Okada, Hisao Okawa, Kaoru Umeno. DES: Yoshiyuki Sadamoto. ANI: Kazuto Nakazawa, Shunji Suzuki, Kazunori Matsubara, Yoshiaki Yanagida, Hideaki Anno. MUS: Shiro Sagisu. PRD: Gainax, Group Tac, NHK. 25 mins. x 39 eps. (TV), 90 mins. (m).
Paris is the scene of the 1889 International Exposition. Young inventor Jean meets circus acrobat Nadia. He rescues her from a strange gang of comical villains out to steal her necklace, and the pair set off on an amazing adventure that takes them far beneath the seas, and all around the world. They face racism in France and cold-blooded killing on a remote Pacific island, see a flying contest with Chitty-Chitty Bang-Bang as one of the entrants, and share a dream sequence in which they ride in something suspiciously like Thunderbird 2 (see **THUNDERBIRDS 2086**). They face the last remnants of Atlantis and join the fight to save the world from domination by a mad genius. Along the way they learn that their origins are less important than what they make of themselves, and that while love can conquer all, it doesn't guarantee a happy ending. The 1993 movie *Nadia of the Mysterious Seas the Movie: Fuzzy's Secret* takes up the story some years later, with Jean rescuing a mysterious girl and the impact this has on his stormy relationship with Nadia.

While working at Toho Studios in the 1970s, the young Hayao Miyazaki pitched a scenario to his bosses inspired by Jules Verne, creator of **ADRIFT IN THE PACIFIC**. Set in the late 19th century, *Around the World in 80 Days by Sea* would use two Vernean concepts—a trip around the world by two plucky characters on the run from bad guys, and the mighty submarine Nautilus, commanded by Captain Nemo, who has a secret past of his own. Toho didn't make the series but held onto the option. Miyazaki later used various elements of the idea in **FUTURE BOY CONAN** and **CASTLE IN THE SKY**, but it wasn't until the critical triumph of **WINGS OF HONNEAMISE** that Toho dusted off the outline and approached Gainax to turn it into a TV series.

SBW was conceived as a blatant pitch to the mass audience. Very rarely has this approach produced a show of such enduring charm and emotional validity. The combination of Vernean adventure, Dickensian richness of characterization (particularly in the comical semivillains Grandis, Sanson, and Hanson), nods and winks to more contemporary classics, and steampunk technology was irresistible, propelling the series to success and Nadia to an enduring place in the list of fans' favorite characters. In Nadia, the Gainax team created a heroine who was beautiful and independent yet alone and unsure of her place in the world, capable of anger and courage yet completely opposed to killing, a heroine of color and an animal rights advocate ahead of her time. Young hero Jean, a brilliant but naïve kid with total faith in technology and innocent of the world's deceits and cruelties, is an orphan as she is. The two are bonded by loss and alienation; despite the sunny color palette of the show and its upbeat pacing and music, the audience quickly realizes that a dark and terrible fate is always waiting just out of shot, threatening to engulf the young couple—the same team's later hit EVANGELION brought the lurking darkness into the foreground. The impact of several violent scenes—which are never gratuitous but likely to be shocking to a modern Western audience in a children's series—foiled an attempt in the mid-1990s to get the show onto U.K. television screens. *SoBW* was rereleased on DVD as *Nadia: SoBW* in the U.S. in 2001, just in time to invite insidious comparisons between it and the new Disney cartoon *Atlantis: The Lost Empire*. Though the filmmakers admitted to an interest in the works of Hayao Miyazaki, they denied any knowledge of *SoBW*—compare to the controversy surrounding KIMBA THE WHITE LION. ❤

SECRET OF CERULEAN SAND

2002. JPN: *Patapata Hikosen no Boken*. AKA: *Patapata Airship Adventure*. TV series. DIR: Yuichiro Yano, Kim Echoul, Go Yoonjae. SCR: Yuka Yamada, Koichi Masajima, Noriko Tanimura. DES: Kenji Yazaki, Kazuhide Tomonaga. ANI: Yuichi Takiguchi, Kazuhide Tomonaga. MUS: Daisuke Ikeda, Toshio Nakagawa. PRD: TAF, Tokyo Movie Shinsha, WOWOW, Koko Animation, Sega, ZET. 25

mins. x 26 eps.
Fifteen-year-old Jane Buxton hears that her eldest brother George has been executed for treason while off exploring distant lands. Meanwhile, her stepbrother William storms out of the family home as a result of an ongoing feud with Jane's father, who is soon on trial for embezzlement. Some time later, Jane receives a parcel in the mail containing a strange shard of blue stone (the "cerulean sand" of the English title). Realizing that this might be the mystical energy source for which George had been searching at the time of his reported death, Jane sets off to discover the truth and clear the family name.

The adventures of a plucky British teenager, in a world of deserts and airships in which the idea of honor is still important, may seem to echo the works of Hayao Miyazaki and Isao Takahata. However, any resemblance to CASTLE IN THE SKY stems from both stories drawing on the same source—the works of one of the most popular science fiction authors in Japan, the French writer Jules Verne (1828–1905). *SoCS* takes its inspiration from two of Verne's works, the first being *For the Flag* (1896, *Face au Drapeau*), in which an inventor discovers an incredibly powerful explosive and initially resolves to sell it to the highest bidder, regardless of his duty to his country. The second is *City in the Sahara* (1919, *L'Etonnante Aventure de la Mission Barsac*), Verne's last work, which was finished posthumously by his son. This anime version, a Japanese-Korean coproduction, changes the heroine's name from Joan to Jane, but otherwise clings to the broad strokes of the original, including its melodramatic face-off between the true-hearted Buxtons and the cruel intentions of their stepsiblings—shades here of an even more traditional family drama, stretching back to CINDERELLA. Both Verne's original stories dealt with scientists who must come to terms with their complicity in the use of their inventions for evil purposes—shades here for the Japanese audience of KIKAIDER and other antiheroes, but also of a genuine old-time fascination with technology and progress that was pastiched in STEAMBOY. The plot also revolves around Jane's discovery of a stone with a mysterious power—echoing the SECRET OF BLUE WATER, which was

itself inspired by the works of Verne. Such "coincidences" aside, the authors do not doubt for a moment that commercial concerns steered the producers' choice of material—Verne may have been conveniently out of copyright, but the chance to claim to be using his story while actually pastiching Miyazaki's must have been irresistible.

SECRET OF THE SEAL, THE *

1991. JPN: *Tottoi*. Movie. DIR: Noboru Ishiguro. SCR: Ryuzo Nakanishi. DES: Haruhiko Mikimoto, Masamichi Takano. ANI: Haruhiko Mikimoto. MUS: Koichi Sakata. PRD: Nippon Animation, Nikken Academy. 90 mins.
After the death of his mother, little Alexander moves with his father and sister to the Mediterranean island of Sardinia, where he is nicknamed Tottoi. In a grotto by the sea, he finds a baby seal and its mother. They've been thought extinct in the area for ten years, and he fears that if discovered they'll be shut up in an aquarium for scientific study or experimentation. But he is not sure he can even trust his friends among the islanders to help him keep the rare animals safe. Based on the novel by Gianni Padoan, the story has very strong similarities to FLY PEEK!, although the character style is more naturalistic.

SECRET SEX STORIES *

2003. JPN: *Sokan Rensa*. AKA: *Chain of Debauchery*. Video. DIR: Tomoyori Sasaki. SCR: Shigeaki Serida. DES: Aki Midori. ANI: Aki Midori. MUS: N/C. PRD: Animac. 30 mins.
Two short erotic vignettes appear in this anthology. The first features two hoodlums who break into a widow's house, hoping to steal her late husband's valuables. Instead, all they find are the widow and her daughter and proceed to hold them prisoner and subject them to sexual torment until the burglars get what they want.

The second story takes place in an art class, where the students' complaints about the unrealistic nature of mannequins has finally led the teacher to persuade a pretty young coed to pose for life drawing. The students gradually convince her to doff her clothes, in a striptease that ends with predictable results. In both cases, however, the female victims manage to some extent to turn the tables on their tormentors. Compare to the episode *Five*

Hour Venus in the CREAM LEMON SERIES.
🅛🅝🅥

SECRETS OF THE TELEPHONE CLUB

1991. JPN: *Terekura no Himitsu*. AKA: *Secret of the Teleclub*. Movie. DIR: Kan Fukumoto. SCR: Satoshi Yagi. DES: Akira Narita. ANI: Kan Fukumoto. MUS: N/C. PRD: Japan Home Video. 45 mins. x 2 eps.

A lonely man discovers the seedy world of the telephone club, where he can wait to receive calls from women desperate for sex. Soon he becomes a happy escort, taking the virginity of an appreciative client and helping an unhappy housewife find fulfillment. Sometimes they just want to talk, but this adaptation of Akira Narita's manga doesn't dwell for too long on those ones. Compare to CALL ME TONIGHT. 🅝

SEE IN AO *

2004. AKA: *See in Blue*. Video. DIR: Yoshikazu Yabe. SCR: Goro Mimyo. DES: Akira Kano. ANI: Sora Akino. MUS: N/C. PRD: Green Bunny. 30 mins. x 2 eps.

In a futuristic city on the sea, Kyoya teaches at an oceanography institute, where he has lived ever since he was rescued at sea by local girl Miyu. Miyu's twin sister Yui realizes that Miyu is attracted to Kyoya and plays matchmaker until the two are a happily copulating couple. It's only then that we are told Yui is not a human at all, but an android programmed to ensure that Miyu is always safe and happy. Yui has feelings for Kyoya herself, which conflict with her own programming and threaten to cause her entire system to crash—compare to other girlfriends with time limits, like VIDEO GIRL AI and MAHOROMATIC. After Miyu's unexpected death, Yui is on hand to help Kyoya mourn, which she does by taking her sister's place in Kyoya's bed.

With an erotic perspective on Isaac Asimov's "Laws of Robotics" (themselves adapted for Tezuka's ASTRO BOY), *See in Ao* has interesting potential, although it sorely lacks in execution with substandard digital animation and a ponderous pace. We also wonder how Kyoya can lose so much of his memory that he forgets who he is and how he got there, but not so much that he isn't able to function as a teacher. Based on a computer game from Alice Soft. In the U.S. release, the lead characters' names were pointlessly changed to Jim, Amy, and

Mizi, even though the show was subtitled and not dubbed—compare to HERITAGE FROM FATHER, which suffered similarly in its American release. 🅝

SEED OF THE MOUNTAIN PRINCESS

2007. JPN: *Akebi no Mi*. AKA: *Yamahime no Jitsu*. Video. DIR: Takato Shinno, Aoi Kira, Ken Harumachi, Ken Raika. SCR: Akira Sekai. DES: Takato Shinno, Hachinan Hara. ANI: Takato Shinno, Shigeki Awai, Hayate. MUS: N/C. PRD: Schoolzone, Studio Bluecat, MS Pictures (Milky). 26 mins. x 4 eps.

Episodes from Sanbun Kyoden's porn manga *Sankaku Apron*, in which a son finds that the Internet porn he's been eagerly devouring involves his mother. A typical housewife, but still so hot that her son Kazuya gets guilty thoughts about her, she's been blackmailed into video sex and bondage by a much older man. Soon other men and even one of Kazuya's fellow students get involved. Volume 2, *Akebi no Mi Dainikan—Masae* (*Seed of the Mountain Princess Vol. 2 - Masae*), appeared in 2009, followed in 2010 by *Akebi no Mi Daisankan—Kizuna* (*Seed of the Mountain Princess Vol. 3—Bonds*). Once again they tell the story of a son who lusts after his mother and finds she's having sex with other men. Also based on Kyoden's manga, in the same series, is *Akebi no Hana—Maho* (*Flower of the Mountain Princess*), a 2011 release that asks a different question: can a childhood friend become a lover (ROMANCE AND DRAMA), or will crossing the line destroy the relationship? Here the sex is teenage and no bondage is involved. 🅝🅥

SEIZE THE WIND

1988. JPN: *Kaze o Nuke*. Video. DIR: Kazunori Ikegami, Noboru Furuse. SCR: Sho Aikawa. DES: Noboru Furuse. ANI: Noboru Furuse. MUS: Masahiro Takami. PRD: Madhouse. 60 mins.

In a SPORTS ANIME that takes place in the world of motocross, 16-year-old Satoshi Ichimonji fights his way from the novice grade up to the Junior Cross championship. Motorcycle trickery abounds, alongside sporting hardships, and, of course, feckless foreign rival Jeff Anemoth. Based on the manga by SWORD OF MUSASHI–creator Motoka Murakami in *Shonen Sunday*.

SEKAI ICHI HATSUKOI *

2011. AKA: *World's Greatest First Love*.

Video, TV series. DIR: Chiaki Kon. SCR: Rika Nanase. DES: Yoko Kikuchi, Junko Shimizu, Yumiko Kondo. ANI: Yoko Kikuchi, Soon Yeon Kim, Takahiro Yasuda. MUS: Hijiri Anze. PRD: Studio DEEN, AT-X, Dax Production, Kadokawa, Klockworx. ?? mins. (v1), 24 mins. x 12 eps. (TV1), ?? mins. (v2), 24 mins. x 12 eps. (TV2).

Ritsu Onodera has always been independent-minded. He's got a good job as a literary editor at his parents' publishing company, but he quits and joins another publisher when jealous coworkers accuse him of trading on his family ties. At Marukawa Publishing he finds himself assigned to the girls' manga department, Emerald, though he has neither interest nor experience in the field. Worse, his editor-in-chief, Masamune Takano, is arrogant, presumptuous, and oddly familiar—in every sense of the word. Having been told he's useless, and kissed, by said editor-in-chief, Ritsu sets out to show how fast he can learn in this boys' love manga about high school crushes and what happens when they revive ten years later (ROMANCE AND DRAMA). Meanwhile other staff at the company, and the writers and artists they work with, have their own romantic issues to deal with.

If the inoffensive boys' love story doesn't grab you, the background of manga publishing might, as might the many English aphorisms ("One cannot love and be wise"; "Love and envy make a man pine") used for episode titles. It grabbed enough Japanese audience to justify a second series from the same crew. Based on a 2008 manga by Shungiku Nakamura, author of JUNJO ROMANTICA, both series were preceded a couple of weeks before airing by a video release under the same title. The first, in March 2011, was subtitled *Onodera Ritsu no Baai* (*Ritsu Onodera's Affair*) and the second, in September 2011, *Hatori Yoshiyuki no Baai*. The manga is ongoing, there are two series of books, and an animated feature film, *Gekijoban Sekai Ichi Hatsukoi: Yokozawa Takafumi no Baai*, along with a mini-movie, *Sekai Ichi Hatsukoi Valentine-hen*, in March 2014.

SEKI, SHUICHI

1946–. Born in Tokyo, he studied at a design college before finding work with TCJ (now Eiken). He worked as a concept artist on LEGEND OF KAMUI and eventually made his way up the ranks to character designer. Representative works include THE WIZARD OF OZ and TOM SAWYER.

SEKIREI *

2008. TV series. DIR: Keizo Kusakawa. SCR: Takao Yoshioka. DES: Shinpei Tomooka, Junichi Higashi, Akira Otsuka, Mie Kasai. ANI: Shinpei Tomooka. MUS: Hiroaki Sano. PRD: Seven Arcs, Aniplex, MOVIC. 25 mins. x 12 eps. (TV1), 25 mins. x 14 eps. (TV2).

Minato Sahashi is highly intelligent. He just looks like a loser because he can't cope under pressure. He's failed his college entrance exam twice and is in despair when he meets a mysterious girl and learns that he is actually an Ashikabi, a member of an elite group that has the right genes to be "masters" of the Sekirei, a group of 108 curvy women, cute girls, and hot young men with fighting powers to match their improbable physical endowments. They're engaged in a secret battle to save the world from evil, and the risks are immense: the Sekirei may not survive this contest and their masters risk losing them forever.

Yes, it's a harem (ROMANCE AND DRAMA) that tries to cover all bases, straight from the 2004 manga by Sakurako Gokurakuin, creator of SENSITIVE PORNOGRAPH. This show doesn't just contain fan service: it *is* fan service, completely unashamed. It's like POKÉMON, but with tits. It moves its predictable plot along at a brisk pace and gives characters what passes for development in a genre that is more about choosing your first puppy than anything else. A second series *Sekirei: Pure Engagement*, followed in 2010 from a crew largely unchanged except for the departure of art director Higashi. Ko Yoshinari came on board as animation director for the DVD special "Episode 0." Ⓝ

SEME CHICHI

2010. AKA: *Master Father*. Video. DIR: Manabu Nakasone. SCR: Hideo Kobayashi. DES: Manabu Nakasone, Seihodo. ANI: Manabu Nakasone. MUS: N/C. PRD: YOUC, Vanilla. 28 mins. x 2 eps.

Ex-prostitutes are persuaded to work as maids, with overtime as sex slaves to the family and friends of their "rescuer." Limited animation and clumsy psychological cruelty is hung onto a thin and tedious

plot in which a rich father and his artist son argue about his life choices. Based on the 2010 manga of the same title by Erect Sawaru, and part of the VANILLA SERIES. ⓃⓋ

SENBON MATSUBARA

1992. Movie. DIR: Satoshi Dezaki. SCR: Tetsuaki Imaizumi. DES: Setsuko Shibuichi. ANI: Keizo Shimizu. MUS: Masumi Hiyoshi. PRD: Magic Bus. 100 mins.

After suffering severe floods in 1753, the people of Senbon Matsubara in Shizuoka cooperate on flood prevention around the Kiso, Nagara, and Yuhi rivers. The people of Satsuma (Kumamoto Prefecture) endure great hardships after being forced to undertake the work by the central government, a subtle indication of the bad feeling that would foment into open rebellion the following century—see OI RYOMA!

SENGOKU BASARA: SAMURAI KINGS *

2009. AKA: *Devil Kings*. TV series, video, movie. DIR: Itsuro Kawasaki, Kazuya Nomura. SCR: Yasuyuki Muto. DES: Toru Okubo, Shunichiro Yoshihara, Iho Narita, Yoshito Takamine. ANI: Toru Okubo, Takaaki Chiba, Haruka Tanaka. MUS: Hiroyuki Sawano. PRD: Production I.G, Dentsu, Flying Dog, MBS, MOVIC, Shochiku, Central Japan Broadcasting, Pony Canyon. 24 mins. x 12 eps. (TV1), 24 mins. (v), 24 mins. x 12 eps. (TV2), ?? mins. (m).

The closing stages of Japan's civil war, at the dawn of the 17th century: an age of drama, romance, and extreme violence. At the heart of it all is the gifted warrior Nobunaga Oda, a man so powerful, so evil, and so strange that many believe him to be in league with demons (YOTODEN). Powerful samurai fight both for and against the Devil King, including young lords Masamune Date and Yukimura Sanada (SANADA'S TEN BRAVE WARRIORS). Some fight for the good of Japan, some for their own benefit, some for the pure joy of action in a world where the difference between good and evil is almost irrelevant, and only survival counts.

Nobunaga Oda has been the Demon King of Japanese folklore for much of anime's first hundred years, cropping up again and again in manga, pulp fiction, and animation as a man in league with, controlling, or tricked by dark forces. In Production I.G's absurdly grandiose yet

convincingly classy series, he's a force of pure evil, but there are plenty of other interesting characters around too. In the 2010 follow-up series *Sengoku Basara 2*, Hideyoshi Toyotomi is a flawed giant of immense strength, and the lesser samurai all have their own histories. These diverge, of course, from their real-life histories, in the interests of making the action and violence as vibrantly, chaotically over-the-top as possible. Reinterpreting Japanese history as a cross between *The Tudors*, FIST OF THE NORTH STAR, and DRAGON BALL, with costumes that are part glam rock and part history, and backgrounds that are often unexpectedly beautiful, *Sengoku Basara* celebrates the joys of excess.

This is no surprise, since the series is based on a string of video games of the same name by CAPCOM. Escalating levels of weaponry, skill, and power are built into the structure of the game, as are the ever-stronger bosses the player must defeat at each level. The final act of the drama, nominally set at the Battle of Sekigahara, is played out in the 2011 movie *Sengoku Basara—Samurai Kings: The Movie (Sengoku Basara: The Last Party)*. Both TV series also had an unscreened extra episode released on DVD. *Sengoku Basara II Katakura-kun* is a seven-part series of super-deformed short comedies released as DVD extras.

SENRAN KAGURA *

2013. AKA: *Dance of Flashing Chaos*. TV series. DIR: Takashi Watanabe. SCR: Takao Yoshioka. DES: Nan Yaegashi, Takashi Torii. ANI: Takashi Torii, Toshimitsu Kobayashi. MUS: Ruka Kawada. PRD: Artland, AT-X, GENCO, Lantis, Marvelous AQL, Media Factory, Showgate. 24 mins. x 12 eps.

Five Japanese schoolgirls are training in secret to be ninja at the Hanzo Academy, only to be confronted by five other Japanese schoolgirls, in training at the even more secret (and *evil*) Hiritsu Hebi academy. Everybody has big boobs. Based on a game by Marvelous AQL and Tamsoft.

SENSITIVE PORNOGRAPH *

2004. Video. DIR: Iroko Kagema, Hiroshi Kuruo. SCR: N/C. DES: Takebon. ANI: Takebon. MUS: N/C. PRD: Digital Works (Slash), Phoenix Entertainment. 30 mins.

Young manga artist Seiji is thrilled when he meets Sono, an older manga artist who has been an inspiration in his own career. He is surprised that Sono is equally thrilled to meet him, and the mutual admiration soon turns to mutual attraction. Meanwhile, in an apparently unrelated second chapter, a young male petsitter is given a "rabbit" to look after which turns out to be a man on a leash. Predictable couplings ensue; compare to **DARLING** and **MY SEXUAL HARRASSMENT**. Based on a manga by Ashika Sakura in *Magazine Magazine* [sic]. ◐

SENSUALIST, THE *

1990. JPN: *Ihara Saikaku: Koshoku Ichidai Otoko*. AKA: *Ihara Saikaku's Life of an Amorous Man*. Video. DIR: Yukio Abe. SCR: Eiichi Yamamoto. DES: Yukio Abe. ANI: Tomoko Ogawa, Masaharu Endo, Hiroyuki Kondo. MUS: Keiji Ishikawa. PRD: Groupier Productions. 53 mins.

The merchant Yonosuke decides to help his underling Juzo, a comical peasant who has made an unwise bet with a malicious acquaintance. The fool has bet his manhood that he will sleep with the famous courtesan Komurasaki on their first meeting, when any cultured person would know she would not dream of doing so for the richest and most intelligent man in the land, let alone this hayseed. Yonosuke has known her for a long time, and at his request, she agrees to help the poor fool out, not only giving him a night beyond his wildest dreams, but even writing a certificate of the event on his underwear in her most elegant calligraphy. Novelist Saikaku Ihara chronicled the follies and dramas of old-time Japan in his works. This film was based on just part of his *Life of an Amorous Man* (1682), retelling a few of the adventures of Yonosuke. The exquisite, jewel-like animation makes use of techniques that recall the traditional crafts of old Japan. Cels were not simply painted but embossed with the textures of leaves or fine fabrics. Genitals are not just pixilated or blacked out, they are transformed into symbolic representations from old woodcuts—a penis becomes the head of a tortoise, a vagina a splitting fruit or unfolding flower. Director Abe's pace is as slow and precisely calculated as a courtesan's every move, producing a hothouse atmosphere of elegant eroticism as far removed from the teenage crudities of

most porn anime as Edo is from modern Tokyo. A beautiful anime. ◐

SENTIMENTAL JOURNEY *

1998. TV series. DIR: Kazuyoshi Katayama, Keiichi Sato. SCR: Tsunehisa Arakawa. DES: Keiichi Sato, Madoka Hirayama. ANI: Madoka Hirayama. MUS: Toshiyuki Okada. PRD: Sunrise, TV Tokyo. 25 mins. x 12 eps.

Twelve friends are the heroines of this high school romance series, based on the game *Sentimental Graffiti*. Each episode focuses on one of them and her boyfriend problems—getting one, keeping one, making sure he's the right one. Aki is a violinist, Chie wants to be a folk guitarist, Chiho is the tough, sporty daughter of an *okonomiyaki* chef, Wakaba is an archer, Asako wants to be an artist, and Miyuki is fascinated with old-fashioned clothes. Players/viewers who insist on something out of the ordinary can plump for Emiru, who can see ghosts, or Honoka, who is afraid of *all* men. If that's not good enough for you, there are plenty of wounded souls to nurture—Yu pines for the man she last saw eight years ago, while Manami is consumptive, weak, and in need of a good cuddle. Asuka is a perky events manager whose bright exterior conceals a broken heart, while Rurika is bullied at school. A show about the everyday lives and little romantic problems of 12 teenage girls isn't exactly what we expect from the Sunrise studio, but since over a dozen **GUNDAM** kits have been sold for every inhabitant of Japan, doubtless there was an ulterior motive: selling new models and figurines to the chiefly male target audience. The same motivation inspires game-anime tie-ins like **TO HEART**.

SENYU *

2013. AKA: *War Hero*. TV series/TV special/Video/Movie. DIR: Yutaka Yamamoto. SCR: Michiko Yokote. DES: Ushio Tazawa. ANI: Ushio Tazawa. MUS: Daisuke Sakabe, Makoto Watanabe. PRD: Liden Films, Ordet, TV Tokyo, AT-X. 5 mins. x 13 eps. (TV1), 5 mins. x 13 eps. (TV2).

A thousand years after the evil Demon King was shut away to save the world, she escapes (the "king" is a girl, not unlike the antagonist of **ARCHENEMY AND HERO**). The ruler summons the 75 descendants of the hero who defeated evil all those years ago.

One of these hapless draftees is Alba, a confused soul who doesn't seem to stand much of a chance. But it is he who joins forces with the Demon King herself, in order to take down the *bad* demons who have smashed holes into his world. If that's confusing, it's probably supposed to be, in this animated adapation of Robinson Haruhara's screwball fantasy manga from *Jump Square*.

SEO, MITSUYO

1911–2010. Pseudonym for Norikazu Seo; sometimes also billed as Taro Seo. Born in Hyogo Prefecture, Seo went to Tokyo in the hopes of becoming an artist. After working briefly as one of Kenzo Masaoka's animators in Kyoto, he returned to Tokyo to make the talkie *Sankichi the Monkey* (1933, *Osaru Sankichi*; see **WARTIME ANIME**) and the *Norakuro* series. Inevitably drawn into the propaganda machine, Seo's *Momotaro's Sea Eagles* (1943, *Momotaro no Umiwashi*) was a success with both audiences and the Japanese Navy. Commissioned to make Japan's first full-length animated feature, **MOMOTARO'S DIVINE SEA WARRIORS** (1945), he completed the movie in time for an April 1945 release, although most children had been evacuated from Tokyo by that time. After the war, he made **THE KING'S TAIL** (1949, *Osama no Shippo*) before retiring from animation to illustrate children's books.

SEQUENCE

1992. Video. DIR: Naoto Takahashi. SCR: Tsunehisa Arakawa. DES: Ryunosuke Otonashi. ANI: N/C. MUS: Toshiyuki Watanabe. PRD: Studio Giants, Aoi Pro. 40 mins.

Suffering from a crippling memory loss ever since an accident at the age of six, Kara finds new hope, and a new mystery, when he is visited by a girl from his own future. Based on a manga in *Wings* magazine by Ken Mizuki.

SERAPHIM CALL *

1999. TV series. DIR: Tomomi Mochizuki. SCR: Go Sakamoto, Sadayuki Murai. DES: Aoi Nanase, Maki Fujii. ANI: Maki Fujii. MUS: Akifumi Oda. PRD: Media works, Sunrise, TV Tokyo. 25 mins. x 12 eps.

A sci-fi respray of **SENTIMENTAL JOURNEY**, in which 11 beautiful girls between the ages of 12 and 25—the Seraphim—live in the future city of Yokohama Neo Acropolis. Each of them has a different talent or hangup (in place of characterization), and each has a story devoted to her. Yukina is a high school science genius, but she's so afraid of men that she can't so much as pick up a pencil when one of them is looking at her. Tanpopo is 12, collects stuffed animals, and worries about growing up. Chinami is 16 and wants to open her own bakery and bring her divorced parents back together. Hatsumi is a sporty tomboy who's never been seen in a skirt in all her 18 years, but she's suddenly asked to model for an artist. Sakura and Shion are 16-year-old twins worried that romance may drive them apart. Their classmate Kurumi is a wannabe cartoonist in a slump, while Urara, also 16, is the daughter of the man who designed Neo Acropolis, and she loves him so much that she can't love a boy just yet. Ayaka is a spoiled rich kid whose father decides she needs to learn the value of money by getting a job at the age of 14. Saeno is the oldest at 25, an English teacher whose true passion is mathematics, but who runs into an equation she can't solve unless she uses her heart. The 11th girl is a legend: 18-year-old Kasumi, the goddess of Acropolis whom no one has ever seen. But on Christmas Eve all the Seraphim gather at the Acropolis Tower, hoping for their personal miracles to happen…. This collection of adolescent fantasies, some with an SF twist like Yukina's *Turn-A* GUNDAM parody robot, is designed to promote a game and sell related merchandise. Players can pick their favorite Seraph and get the idol card, *gachapon* toy (see VILLGUST), action figure, and so on. However, the only "game" that these characters were ever associated with was a by-mail interactive sequence in which readers of *Dengeki PC Engine* magazine (later renamed *Dengeki G's*) would fill in a storyline multiple choice or ideas for dating locations. These virtual girlfriends spanned a surprisingly long period in Media Works publications, first appearing in *Megami Tengoku* in 1996 and not waving a final farewell until 2000.

SERENDIPITY THE PINK DRAGON *

1983. JPN: *Serendipity Monogatari yori, Pure-to no Nakamatachi.* AKA: *The Story of Serendipity: Friends of Pure Island.* TV series, movie. DIR: Nobuo Onuki, Masayoshi Osaki, Mitsuo Kusakabe, Susumu Ishizaki, Keiji Hayakawa, Shigeru Omachi, Hiroyuki Yokoyama, Satoshi Inoue. SCR: Takeshi Matsuki, Tsunehisa Ito, Himiko Nakao. DES: Kazuo Tomizawa, Yoichi Kotabe, Yoshikuni Nishi. ANI: Kazuo Tomizawa, Yutaka Oka. MUS: Takeo Watanabe. PRD: Hokuto, Zuiyo Enterprises, Nippon TV. 25 mins. x 26 eps. (TV), 90 mins.

Based on an illustrated book by Steven Cosgrove and Robin James, this children's series tells the story of Corna, a little boy separated from his parents after an accident at sea washed him ashore on a remote South Pacific island with a large pink egg. The egg hatches and a cute little pink creature is born that soon grows into a large dragon. It's Serendipity, who is really a sea spirit, and who becomes the lost boy's friend. Corna's new home is governed by a queen who allows him to stay. A pretty little mermaid called Laura and many strange creatures live there. When the island is threatened by a pirate band come to steal its fabled treasure, the Mermaid's Tears, Corna and his comical friends fight to protect their home. Several episodes were also compiled into a 90-minute "movie" in 1989.

The theatrical release and TV series production were started by a subsidiary of Mizutaka Enterprises, but work was abandoned with 10 episodes in the can. Only after the completion of a further 16 episodes were the series and movie released. Both have been screened in Europe, and the movie is available on video in the U.S.

SERGEANT FROG

2004. JPN: *Keroro Gunso.* TV series. DIR: Yusuke Yamamoto, Junichi Sato. SCR: Satoru Nishizono, Mamiko Ikeda. DES: Fumitoshi Oizaki, Kunio Okawara. ANI: Asako Nishida, Fumitoshi Oizaki. MUS: N/C. PRD: Sunrise, NAS, Bandai Visual, TV Tokyo. 24 mins. x 357 eps.

Keroro is leading the advance guard of a frog-like alien army to planet Pokopen, which the locals call Earth. But he is captured by the natives and abandoned by his invasion fleet. Siblings Natsumi and Fuyuki Hinata take him home, where he has to do housework in return for a room in a haunted basement. He gradually settles in, comes to like his new home, and loses all interest in military glory when he discovers the delights of making plastic model kits. The other members of his platoon also find homes on Earth and comic mayhem ensues.

The theme of the alien observer of human foibles has been used in TV comedy from *My Favorite Martian* to *Third Rock from the Sun.* But Keroro follows a Japanese tradition dating back to EMPEROR OF THE PLUM PLANET, and also brings the army-issue kero ball, a device akin to Batman's utility belt, functioning as weapon, communicator, and general situation-saving MacGuffin—compare to DORAEMON. Supposedly based on Mine Yoshizaki's manga, but with an "original creator" credit for Yoshiyuki Tomino and Sunrise house pseudonym Hajime Yadate, the show is packed with references to Japanese science fiction like *Space Giants* (*DE, the live-action version of AMBASSADOR MAGMA) but the PlayStation 2 game packs in even more homages to all kinds of anime weapons, from GUNDAM's beam rifles to EVANGELION's Lance of Longinus. A movie followed in 2006.

SERIAL EXPERIMENTS LAIN *

1998. TV series. DIR: Ryutaro Nakamura, Shigeru Ueda, Akihiko Nishiyama, Masahiko Murata, Johei Matsuura. SCR: Chiaki Konaka. DES: Takahiro Kishida, Yoshitoshi Abe, Hiroshi Kato. ANI: Yuichi Tanaka, Masahiro Sekiguchi, Yoshihiro Sugai. MUS: Reichi Nakaido, Bôa. PRD: Pioneer, Triangle Staff, TV Tokyo. 25 mins. x 13 eps.

Shy 14-year-old Rein Iwakura meets a school friend on the Wired, a super-Internet that allows almost total immersion in cyberspace—but Chisa died by her own hand days ago. Now she says God is in the Wired. Understandably shaken, Rein is further baffled by a strange encounter in a club, where a junkie is so scared by her sudden, chilling response to his pestering that he kills himself. Rein learns more about the Wired, drawing her further into another existence, one where Lain, her second self, lives an independent life in the electronic impulses. In an identity crisis redolent of PERFECT BLUE, Lain starts putting in appearances in the real world, causing her double to wonder which of them is real. Uncertain of her true origins or existence, or of reality itself, Rein/Lain crosses paths with the godlike entity Deus (creator of the Wired, now dwelling inside it) in a surreal struggle. The listless analogue world of the late 20th century and the digital dream of the Wired combine to present a vision of the dominance of technology so nihilistic that at times it makes EVANGELION look almost sunny.

Real originality is rare in any field, but *SEL* skillfully perverts the two-as-one magical-girl tradition in an interesting Internet-inspired direction, fused with a paranoid Luddite technophobia. Much of the credit goes to ARMITAGE III–veteran Konaka and newcomer Abe, who has since created NIEA_7. Director Nakamura deliberately plays up the low-budget animation, making a virtue of 1990s cost-cutting by contrasting Rein's flat, unnatural daily life with the luxuriant, swirling CG images of the Wired itself. Much of the "action" takes place in cyberspace or inside Rein/Lain's skull, and the blurring of links and walls between objective and subjective reality is chillingly effective. Unlike in KEY THE METAL IDOL, Rein finds ordinary life messy and banal; weighing the so-called advantages of humanity, she is prepared to trade up, a sentiment guaranteed to appeal to troubled teens.

The concept would be refined in more magical terms in HAIBANE RENMEI, a later anime based on an earlier manga by Abe.

SERIKAWA, YUGO

1931–. Born in Tokyo, he studied German literature at Waseda University, before joining Toho as an assistant director after graduation. Inspired by the Japanese release of earlier Disney movies, he transferred to Toei Animation in 1959, soon rising to the rank of director. His works as director include NOBODY'S BOY REMI and CYBORG 009.

SERVANT PRINCESS *

2004. JPN: *Elufina: Servant Princess*. Video. DIR: Yoshitaka Fujimoto, Hiromi Yokoyama. SCR: Taifu Sekimachi, Osamu Momoi. DES: Toshide Masudate. ANI: N/C. MUS: N/C. PRD: Pink Pineapple. 30 mins. x 3 eps.
Princess Elfina (or sometimes Elufina) of Fiel is all set to marry Prince Kwan when the wicked Prince Viceard and his Valdland Army attack. Kwan is seriously injured, the castle is taken, and all the women of Fiel, Elfina included, are forced into sexual slavery—compare to EROTIC

TORTURE CHAMBER. The girls are humiliated and raped in the palace and made to urinate whenever and wherever they find the need. Prince Viceard's stepmother arrives and reveals that she was the prince's first love before her marriage to his father. Viceard, however, keeps himself busy by forcing Elfina's maid Ann to have sexual intercourse with Prince Kwan, Elfina's former betrothed, now comatose in a cell in what used to be his own dungeon. Clever typography means the Japanese title looked (*unintentionally*, of course) like LOVE HINA, but fans picking it up on that basis would feel shortchanged. It's a different type of fantasy with less romantic yearning and more sex, but the characterizations and motivations are just as improbable. ⬤🅝🅥

SERVANT X SERVICE *

2013. TV series. DIR: Yasutaka Yamamoto. SCR: Kento Shimoyama. DES: Terumi Nishii. ANI: Terumi Nishii, Marie Ino, Nia Tsuchida. MUS: monaca. PRD: Aniplex, ABC. 24 mins. x 13 eps.
A group of raw new recruits arrive to take up their posts as junior civil servants in the fictional Hokkaido town of Mitsuba—the clumsy Lucy Yamagami, the born listener Saya, and the slacker Yutaka. Office romance, troublesome locals, and bureaucratic tedium beset them in this adaptation of Karino Takatsu's manga series in *Big Gangan* magazine, which a cynical encyclopedist might suggest valorizes having an actual profession as some sort of fantasy realm for the magazine's implied readership of students and slackers. The characters certainly seem to be caught in a liminal world, unsure of whether to define themselves by the profession that occupies their waking hours or by the hobbies that they cram into their limited time off-duty.

Long-term anime viewers might discern in this EVERYDAY ANIME the gentle investigations of office life to be found in the likes of KAMEARI PARK PRECINCT or even PATLABOR, but without any LAW AND DISORDER to police, the cast of *SxS* are soon forced to turn to each other for much of their antics and action. The one surprise with this series is that it was animated at all—workplace dramas, even based on manga, are a dime a dozen in the live-action world (*DE), and it is a mystery why this one

wasn't similarly picked up by an enterprising TV channel for a primetime slot with real people.

SETON'S ANIMAL TALES

1989. JPN: *Seton Dobutsuki*. TV series. DIR: Takeshi Shirato, Eiji Okabe, Keiji Kawanami, Hiromitsu Morita, Masao Ito. Yoshikata Nitta. SCR: Yu Mizuki, Haruya Yamazaki, Sukehiro Tomita, Haruya Yamazaki, Tsunehisa Ito. DES: N/C. ANI: Kazutoshi Kobayashi, Hirohide Yashikijima. MUS: N/C. PRD: Nippon Animation, Eiken, TV Asahi. 25 mins. x 45 eps.
A series of stories taken from the work of Ernest "Black Wolf" Thompson Seton, the creator of BANNERTAIL THE SQUIRREL and MONARCH, THE BIG BEAR OF TALLACH. Born in England but a Canadian emigrant, Seton was the leader of the North American Boy Scout movement from 1910 to 1915, until he left over disagreements about the "military" aspects promoted by Lord Baden-Powell and James West. Setting up the "Woodcraft League," he promoted the healthy outdoor life with his 60 books and over 400 short stories and articles. A fraction of these were adapted for this anime series, including *Monarch* (again), *Wari the Fox*, *Bingo the Famous Dog*, *Link the Puppy*, *The Beaver of the Poplar Tree*, *Fox of Springfield*, *Snap the Heroic Puppy*, *Wolf of the Badlands*, and *Silver Fox of Yellowstone*, among others.

SEVEN CITIES

1994. JPN: *Nanatoshi Monogatari: Hokkyokukai Sensen*. AKA: *Story of Seven Cities: Arctic Sea Frontline*. Video. DIR: Akinori Nagaoka. SCR: Tomomi Nobe. DES: Katsumi Matsuda. ANI: Kasumi Matsuda. MUS: Hiroshi Sato. PRD: Sony Music Entertainment. 30 mins. x 2 eps.
In 2099, Earth has shifted off its axis and begins to rotate at an angle of 90% to the 20th-century equator. Three years of natural disasters follow, and when things settle down, Earth's ten billion population has died and only two million moon colonists remain. Some return to begin the repopulation of the world in seven new cities. The remaining colonists on the moon fear that their former neighbors might pose a threat and construct a ring of defense satellites to trap them on the newly repopulated homeworld—the Olym-

pus system destroys anything that travels more than 500 meters above the surface. Then the lunar colonists are wiped out by plague. Trapped beneath a defensive ring that will operate automatically for the next 200 years, the seven newly founded cities begin to fight one another. Moorbridge Jr., the son of the exiled ruler of Aquionia, becomes the ruler of New Camelot and leads a force to recapture his homeland. His superior tactician, Kenneth Guildford, leads an attack on an Aquionian supply base, but his victorious troops are subject to a counter-attack by the Aquionian hero Almaric Ashvail—compare to the similar well-matched foes of LEGEND OF GALACTIC HEROES, based on another novel by *SoSC* creator Yoshiki Tanaka.

SEVEN OF NANA *

2002. JPN: *Shichinin no Nana*. AKA: *Seven of Seven; NaNa 7 of 7*. TV series. DIR: Yasuhiro Imagawa. SCR: Mamiko Ikeda, Michiko Yokote, Yasuhiro Imagawa, Yasuko Kobayashi. DES: Asako Nishida, Mine Yoshizaki. ANI: N/C. MUS: Yoshihisa Hirano. PRD: AT-X, GENCO. 22 mins. x 25 eps.

Schoolgirl Nana Suzuki's dotty grandfather is using a crystal to separate light from the rainbow into its component seven colors. Unfortunately, he is using the family microwave as part of the experiment, and when Nana opens the door, the crystal explodes and splits her into six clones, each demonstrating just one aspect of the original. On one hand, there's the downbeat depressed Nana, the cheerful chirpy Nana, the clever Nana, the not-so-bright Nana, the nasty Nana, and the hypersensitive Nana. On the other hand, they've all acquired mystic powers, like the ability to fly. The original must now attempt to live with six wacky incarnations of herself—although the authors would like to point out that grandfather's "accident" presents an ideal solution to the problem Japan faces in RIZELMINE.

One of the constant gripes about team shows is that the team members are usually cardboard cutouts displaying one simplistic stereotype who have to work together to succeed. *7oN* could have made this a virtue by actually showing the process of an undeveloped young girl, looking at each aspect of her behavior and working out how to balance them into a rounded

personality. Instead it crashes SAILOR MOON into TENCHI MUYO!, as the seven Nanas converge on the original's school crush. Based on a story by director Imagawa.

SEVEN-COLORED DROPS

2007. JPN: *Nanatsu-iro Drops*. AKA: *Rainbow Drops*. TV series. DIR: Takashi Yamamoto. SCR: Michiru Shimada, Hiroko Naka, Yoshimi Narita. DES: Yukiko Ibe, Naoko Kosakabe. ANI: Yukiko Ibe, Takuji Yoshimoto, Kenichiro Ogata, Takafumi Hino et al. MUS: Etsuko Yamakawa. PRD: Studio Barcelona, AC Create, ASCII Media Works, Geneon Entertainment, Showgate, Yomiko Advertising. 25 mins. x 12 eps.

Quiet student Tsuwabaki is forced by one of his teachers to join the school gardening club, which has just two other members, both girls. Then a freakish mishap turns him into a stuffed dog. Only one chosen girl can capture the seven stardrops that will enable him to turn back. Luckily, there are a number of magically adept girls from another world hanging around the school, and so, as well as discovering the gentle innocence of first love, Tsuwabaki is sure to regain his own form. A prettily colored, innocent, and completely clichéd sugar overload of a show, surprisingly based on an erotic dating game by UNiSONSHIFT, released in 2006 for Windows PCs and ported onto other systems.

SEVERING CRIME EDGE, THE

2005. TV series. DIR: Yuji Yamaguchi. SCR: Tatsuhiko Urahata, Kurasumi Sunayama, Tomoyasu Okubo, Yu Mori. DES: Katsuzo Hirata. ANI: Katsuzo Hirata. MUS: Yasuharu Takanashi. PRD: AT-X, Media Factory, Pony Canyon, Studio Gokumi, Klockworx. 24 mins. x 13 eps.

Hairdresser Kiri Haimura discovers that his prized scissors are actually one of numerous "Killing Goods"—magical artifacts designed for use in a modern-day hunting game. They are also the only scissors in the world that can cut the cursed hair of the beautiful Iwai Mushanokoji, which grows back every night. Kiri is able to snip her into presentability on a daily basis, so that she can go to school like a normal girl, but he also becomes her protector when he realizes that the owners of all the other Killing Goods are converging on their town in

order to hunt the prize—Iwai herself.

This adaptation of Tatsuhiko Hikagi's manga in *Monthly Comic Alive* soon devolves into a surreal series of challengers-of-the-week, as new owners of Killing Goods—a sledgehammer, a syringe, knives, etc.—hunt Iwai, only to be defeated by Kiri in the fashion of the American anti-hero *Dexter*. Since Kiri and these killers (or "Authors" in the parlance of the story) each derive their powers from the obsessions of their murderous ancestors, the stage is set for a series of encounters deriving at least part of their bite from fetishization, perversion, and just plain weirdness. ❶

SEX CRAFT *

2003. JPN: *Gakuen Nanafushigi*. AKA: *High School Seven Mystery*. Video. DIR: Mamoru Yagoshi. SCR: Kazuharu Sato. DES: Yoshiten, Kazuhiro Ito. ANI: Yuki Mine. MUS: N/C. PRD: Studio JAM, Image House, Image Works, GP Museum Soft, Milky. 30 mins. x 2 eps.

Kumi and her chums play around with a ouija board and are soon possessed by spirits compelling them to steal sexual energy by seeking sex with men. An otherworldly rapist is on the loose, and exorcist Mia finds herself in grave danger when Kumi asks for her help. Despite Tadaaki Funabori's claim to producing the original work, there is an implied relationship to the 1991 TV series *High School Mystery: School of Seven Wonders (High School Mystery Gakuen Nanafushigi)*, produced by Studio Comet, which ran for 41 episodes on Fuji TV. Directed by Shin Misawa from a manga by psychic researcher Jiro Tsunoda, it was the story of a school plagued by dangerous psychic phenomena, but with more substantial 1980s-style costumes and less demonic fan service. ❶❶

SEX DEMON QUEEN *

2000. JPN: *Yarima Queen*. Video. DIR: Takeshi Aoki. SCR: Michiru Yari. DES: Mamoru Yasuhiko. ANI: Naoyuki Owada. MUS: N/C. PRD: AIC, Green Bunny. 30 mins.

Blue-haired sorceress Kuri/Cooley and her red-haired assistant Rima travel to a fantasyland with every intention of righting wrongs. When they rescue the green-haired girl Sour from a gang rape, she insists on paying back her saviors by taking them to an inn and having sex with them. Conveniently, Sour is a virgin reared in a secluded convent where the only form of education was a prolonged course in bestowing sexual pleasure. However, the Sex Demon Queen has other plans and dispatches her doglike demons to attack the girls—this is something to do with some missing magic rings, although they would be strange rings indeed if they were kept where the dogs end up looking.

After the many, many incidences in anime of not-quite-incest, *SDQ* tries something new with not-quite-bestiality—the demons only *look* like dogs, you see. The result is an anime with all the insane campery of VENUS FIVE, coupled with the forbidden acts hinted at in the backstory of the more mainstream HAKKENDEN. ❶❷❸

SEX PISTOLS
2010. Video. DIR: Koichi Yagami. SCR: N/C. DES: Fuku Hinata, Kazue Yoshizawa. ANI: Fuku Hinata. MUS: Hiroshi Takahashi. PRD: Tasogare Town. 30 mins. x 2 eps.
Norio thinks he's a pretty average guy, but he's suddenly attracting romantic attention he didn't expect. Turns out he's not just a normal high school boy—his DNA marks him out as one of a very special group of humans who didn't descend from primates but from reptiles, felines, ursines, and other exotic species. It doesn't make any of them look or behave differently from standard humans on the surface, but it makes Norio very attractive to some very attractive men. Based on Tarako Kotobuki's 2007 manga (retitled *Love Pistols* in English to avoid giving offense, which seems a bit silly given that the punk band has been around for far longer than the manga) and available in Japan in a "normal" and a "limited" edition. The main difference appears to be that the ¥3,500 price hike gets you a CD and other extra items. ❶

SEX TAXI *
2002. JPN: *Kojin Taxi*. AKA: *Private (Owned) Taxi*. Video. DIR: Ahiru Koike. SCR: Doji Sozoro. DES: Makoto Amamiya. ANI: Makoto Amamiya. MUS: N/C. PRD: Studio Jam, Milky. 30 mins. x 5 eps.
A nameless taxi driver arrives in a new town, using his peripatetic profession as a way to dig up dirt on local beauties. As in Martin Scorsese's *Taxi Driver* (1976), to which this erotic anime otherwise bears

no resemblance, passengers tend to forget their manners and their reticence in his presence and often inadvertently spill useful details about their private lives. He has a particular fetish for upper-class girls, especially in school uniforms, and strikes it lucky with a pair of pretty twins who have suppressed lesbian feelings for each other. This being one of *those* anime, they aren't suppressed for long, and our hero is soon dragging the girls back to his abandoned school lair for the usual rounds of domination and abuse. They are followed shortly afterward by more victims, as he compiles further blackmail evidence of the sort that would frighten only sheltered anime schoolgirls. A "Best Of" compilation is filed in some sources as a phantom sixth episode. ❶❷❸

SEX WARD *
2001. JPN: *Heisa Byoto*. Video. DIR: 1862 Kuboyama. SCR: Rokurota Makabe. DES: Joki Satsumaya. ANI: Mamoru Sakisaka. MUS: Yoshi. PRD: Digital Works (Vanilla Series). 30 mins. x 2 eps.
Satsuki Aoyanagi is the new recruit among the nurses, unaware that her long-time rival Naho has also signed up for the same ward. Before long, Satsuki is trying and failing to dodge the petty humiliations of Naho, as well as the lecherous attentions of the hospital chief Yutaka Ishikawa. Not to be confused with the similarly titled *Heisa Byoin*, filed in this book as NAUGHTY NURSES. Both titles, however, are entries in the erotic VANILLA SERIES. *Sex Ward* is filed as a "completed" title on its manufacturer's web page, despite an ending that was clearly intended to leave things open for a sequel. ❶❷❸

SEX WARRIOR PUDDING *
2004. JPN: *Famiresu Senshi Purin*. AKA: *Fami[ly] Res[taurant] Warrior Purin*. Video. DIR: Katsuma Kanazawa. SCR: Katsuma Kanazawa. DES: Isshi Hinoki. ANI: N/C. MUS: N/C. PRD: Milky. 30 mins. x 3 eps.
Shuta is an idle slacker devoted to pornographic computer games in the manner of the protagonist of AKIBA GIRLS. Imagine, then, his surprise (and our lack of it) when he inherits a restaurant from his father. The À La Mode diner is also the workplace for Shuta's would-be girlfriend Purin "Pudding" Nishimura and sex with the

staff soon ensues. One would hope that was enough for any erotic anime, but no, the restaurant is not merely packed with sexy waitresses in the style of VARIABLE GEO, but also with *operatives* in a Global Defense Agency, fighting against incursions from the heretofore unknown underground kingdom of Lividoll. Before long, the hordes of Lividoll have decided that the best way to conquer the world is to open a rival restaurant across the street, and then seduce all the customers away from the À La Mode. As plans go, it's hardly Operation Desert Storm, but it's a start. In one of the strange moves of the adult anime industry, the rights to the third and final episode were snapped up by a different company in America. ❶

SEXFRIEND *
2002. Video DIR: Kurige Katsura. SCR: Kurige Katsura. DES: Tadashi Shida. ANI: Tadashi Shida, Jiro Yamada. MUS: Toru Yukawa. PRD: Anime House, Green Bunny, Shinkukan. 30 mins. x 2 eps.
The sex-mad schoolgirl is a popular trope in porn; the male can abrogate all responsibility because she "made" him do it. The girl in this story is Mina Hayase and her target is classmate Tomohiro Takabe. Mina tells Tomohiro she doesn't want a boyfriend; she wants a "sexfriend," just for physical diversion with no strings attached. Aided and abetted by the school nurse, the pair spend most of their days in the nurse's office studying anatomy. At least it's consensual and, as is often the case with Green Bunny productions, well executed. "Sex Friend," or its contraction "SF," was a documented term in Japanese slang as early as 1992, making the only mystery with this title the length of time it took to appear. Based on a video game by Codepink/Stone Heads. ❶❷

SEXORCIST *
1996. JPN: *Ningyo Tsukai*. AKA: *Puppet Masters*. Video. DIR: Shigeru Yazaki. SCR: Kazuhiko Godo. DES: Kenji Teraoka, Kenichi Harada. ANI: Masao Tsutsumi. MUS: Kazuhiko Izu. PRD: Sente Studio. 45 mins.
The Silhouette robots of 2114 are virtual-reality "puppets" whose sensations of pleasure and pain can be passed on to their human operators. Enter Rika, a beautiful Silhouette manipulator thrown into a cor-

porate underworld where Silhouette-gladiators fight in death matches, and women are forced to endure assaults through the machines to which they are wired.

Despite being another smut session of screaming girls and leering perverts, *Sexorcist* has a lot to teach other game adaptations. The SF/erotica combination gives two extra angles to the dreary combat of TEKKEN or TOSHINDEN. Avoiding the halfhearted hackery of most porn, it really makes use of the SF setting—particularly in the separation of body and mind. In one chilling moment, Rika sees herself through the eyes of the Silhouette she is operating and notices that an assailant is sneaking up behind her.

In legal terms, the Silhouettes are not human, so they can perform more explicit acts than normally allowed by the Japanese censor. They also speak without moving their lips, allowing the animators to concentrate their budget on the fights and naked flesh. But while it may be an outstanding example of the genre, the genre is porn, and this offering also features bondage, tentacles, hypnotism, drugs, electric whips, and ceremonial rape. The PC game sequel to the original, featuring Rika's granddaughter, was released in the U.K. as *Bishojo Fighter*. ⓃⓋ

SEXTRA CREDIT *
2003. JPN: *Mejoku*. AKA: *Female Torture*. Video. DIR: Taifu Suginami. SCR: American Pie. DES: Taifu Suginami. ANI: Taifu Suginami. MUS: Yoshi. PRD: YOUC, Digital Works (Vanilla Series). 30 mins. x 2 eps.
Jotaro is a lonely teacher, frustrated by the utter lack of interest shown in him by the five sexy lady teachers at his school. He gains a new mission in life when he keeps a rebellious pupil behind after school and learns that the pair of them make a great team at hunting down female victims. Rape and abuse duly follow in another entry in the VANILLA SERIES, based on a computer game by LiLiM. ⒸⓃⓋ

SEXY MAGICAL GIRL *
2003. JPN: *Maho Shojo Ai*. AKA: *Magical Girl Ai*. Video. DIR: Hirohide Shikishima, Hiro Asano. SCR: Tsunekazu Murakami. DES: Mizuki. ANI: Mizuki. MUS: N/C. PRD: Milky (Red), GP Museum Pictures. 30 mins. x 5 eps. (v1) 30 mins. x 3 eps. (v2)

Akitoshi is an average boy in an average Tokyo suburb who suddenly starts noticing the very pretty Ai—although acquaintances inform him that she has always been in the neighborhood, merely escaping his notice in the past. While walking down a back alley, he disturbs a creature in the process of raping local girl Mikage and *almost* intervenes. Before he can truly behave in an active or heroic way, Ai herself steps in to fight the monster, which is an old-fashioned tentacled alien menace. After two episodes of saving Earth through tentacle sex, Ai suddenly disappears, leaving Akitoshi in a strange position akin to the one he had earlier—whereas previously he seemed to be the only person who hadn't noticed Ai, now he is the only one who seems to remember her. As with DEMON BEAST INVASION, this strange reset to zero is in fact a means of restarting a franchise that had already reached its natural end, with a substandard "second half" that plays more like an afterthought sequel. Ai duly returns and saves the day, again, after more tentacle rapist monsters, again. Based on a computer game by Colors.

The second series, *Magical Girl Love Trio* (2009, *Maho Shojo Ai San*), credited to Milky Pictures rather than the former cluster of companies, features three magic warriors, the original Ai with her colleagues Rin and Meg who battle the Yuragi demon rapists, although not all that successfully. ⒸⓃⓋ

SEXY SAILOR SOLDIERS *
2003. JPN: *Nami SOS!* Video. DIR: Masaharu Tomoda. SCR: Yamataro. DES: Shinichi Shigematsu. ANI: Shinichi Shigematsu. MUS: Riverside Music. PRD: Moonrock, APPP. 27 mins.
Nami Koishikawa is a waitress newly employed at a restaurant and is notable for her clumsiness and (as with all of the female characters in this one-shot) her overly generous bust. While putting out the trash at the end of her shift, she is accosted by a woman in a shredded costume, who hands her an amulet, saying that she can't do it anymore. Nami is puzzled, but heads home on the subway, only to be molested by a groper, whereupon she transforms into a magical girl à la SAILOR MOON—except that this only attracts the entire male population of the rail car to

join in until she makes her accidental escape by levitating through the roof of the train. Things grow worse when her boss shows up at her apartment, asking her to try on a new, much smaller uniform. He turns out to be a Sex Demon, and tells her that since she accepted the "Eye of Lust" amulet, she is now a Hunter ("Inma Hunter"—"Lust-Beast Hunter" in the original Japanese) whose pheromones are enhanced so that she may attract and destroy Sex Demons. She is eventually rescued by a team of four other Hunters, but not before much tentacle sex ensues. Without a sequel video, *SSS* is essentially a teaser for the manga by Chataro; a not-unworthy entry in the pornographic magical girl subgenre, which also includes VENUS FIVE, SEX WARRIOR PUDDING, and ANGEL BLADE. ⒸⓋ

SHADOW SKILL *
1995. JPN: *Kagewaza/Shadow Skill*. Video, TV series. DIR: Hiroshi Negishi, Hiroyuki Kuroda, Tsukasa Sunaga. SCR: Mayori Sekijima, Masashi Sogo. DES: Toshinari Yamashita, Fumitoshi Kizaki. ANI: Yoshio Murata, Fumitoshi Kizaki. MUS: Osamu Tezuka (mus), Tsutomu Ohira. PRD: Zero-G Room, Shadow Skill Project, Studio Deen, TV Tokyo. 45 mins. (v1), 30 mins. x 3 eps. (v2), 25 mins. x 26 eps. (TV).
In the kingdom of Kuldar (Karuta in the dub), there is only one way out of servitude—by becoming a gladiator in the arena (a thinly disguised Colosseum). Gladiators can become shavals (sevilles), the chosen knights of the kingdom. Ele Rag is the youngest of the 59 shavals, a mistress of the secret fighting art known as the Shadow Skill. She cares for Gau Ban of the Black Howling, a traumatized young orphan she found four years earlier. But Gau lives in a secret internal turmoil of honor and duty, watching Ele Rag's every move so that he may learn the Shadow Skill and become the brother she deserves.

SS was based on the 1992 *Comic Gamma* manga by Megumu Okada, praised in Japan for its meticulous internal logic. Okada has some great ideas, such as the Shadow Skill itself (a psychic martial art for slaves whose hands are bound) and magic in which each spell must be engaged in conversation before being unleashed. Okada's clan terminology creates "families" of people who aren't really related, defending the memories of "fathers" who weren't necessarily their biological parents. Like sumo wrestlers, clan adoption brings a new name, and like the samurai codes of old, the ignoble death of one's master forces a period of exile while the outcast seeks revenge. It also forbids the exile to use his or her former name, so *SS* contains a lot of people with very long and cumbersome handles. The man known as Screep Lohengrin of the White Running in the original manga is just plain "Louie" here, for example. Similar compressions devalue the rest of the production: mere moments after we're told that Gau is mute, he breaks his vow of silence to chat with the first stranger he meets. The anime *SS* is reduced to a simple kung-fu revenge tragedy, as a party that consists of two warriors (Ele and Gau), a magic-user (Fowari), and a ranger/cleric (Kiao Yu) square off against people who killed their fathers, and now must prepare to die (etc.). We're occasionally reminded of the original's evil Sorphan Empire, with tales of the King of the Moon or shots of a young Gau hunting a centaur, but the invaders are greatly underused.

The one-shot video *SS* soon made it to the U.K. through Manga Entertainment. It performed way beyond expectations in Japan and was followed in 1996 by an additional three-part series, also released in English, though cut into the feature-length *SS the Movie*. The dub was done in Wales, a land known for its own arcane language, though that's no excuse for the clunky dialogue or the outrageous moment when Kiao yells away soundlessly, presumably because nobody was paying attention to the visuals. The 1998 TV series, produced after the manga had switched publication to *Comic Dragon Junior*, was screened in a late-night slot and restored much of the manga's backstory. **LNV**

SHADOW STAFF, THE

A group of a dozen **EARLY ANIME** artists and technicians, also sometimes known as the Special Film Unit, officially known as the Toho Aviation Education Materials Production Office (Toho Koku Kyoiku Shiryo Seisaku-sho), which produced 21 **WARTIME ANIME** for military instructional use during the years 1939–44. Early work for the Ministry of Munitions included several installments in an *Industrial Science* series, explaining the uses of sheet metal, soldering, and several tools. With the absence of live-action documentary materials, the Shadow Staff also prepared four secret films for the Ministry of the Navy under the umbrella title *Principles of Bombardment*, used to train the pilots who attacked Pearl Harbor. Other works of note by the Shadow Staff include animated guides for identifying different classes of ships from the air, as well as guides to torpedo maintenance and dive-bombing. The group's longest work was *Principles of the Wireless: Triodes* (*Musen Riron: Sankyoku Shinkukan*, undated), thought to have been feature-length at eight reels and likely to have been completed *before* anime's "first" full-length movie, **MOMOTARO'S DIVINE SEA WARRIORS**. In straitened times with resources scarce, the Shadow Staff notoriously had access to better materials than those animators such as Tadahito Mochinaga, who were working on lower-priority propaganda. According to Soji Ushio's memoirs, posthumously published in 2007, producers on the Shadow Staff deliberately over-estimated their resource requirements by a factor of 300%, allowing the Toho studio to acquire vital extra film stock that was then handed over to more needy live-action productions, such as Akira Kurosawa's debut, *Sugata Sanshiro* (1943).

The films of the Shadow Staff have been largely absent from the historical record, in part because they were never shown in public, but also because they were "only 80% animated," and hence do not count as pure cartoons. However, the greatest enemy of their heritage was the fact that they were all destroyed in 1945 by animators who were understandably reluctant to discuss them in the postwar period. From asides in surviving testimonials, it is possible to guess whom the Shadow Staff comprised: Ikuo Oishi, Tomio Sagisu (AKA Soji Ushio), Shoji Ichino, Toshiro Wakabayashi, Mitsuyo Seo, and Eiji Tsuburaya are the main figures, although other names that can be assembled from partial credits include Masao Tamai, Saburo Fukuda, Eiichi Nagamura, Takeshi Mori, Yoshihito Matsuzaka, and Otori Watanabe. Several surviving members of the Shadow Staff would join forces with Nichido in the 1950s to form the basis for the company now known as Toei Animation.

SHADOW STAR NARUTARU *

2003. JPN: *Narutaru: Mukuro Naru Hoshi—Tama Taru Ko*. AKA: *Shadow Star Narutaru*. TV series. DIR: Toshiaki Iino. SCR: Chiaki Konaka. DES: Masahiko Ota, Keiji Hashimoto. ANI: Yuji Ushijima, Masayuki Fujita, Shiro Shibata, Hideaki Matsuoka. MUS: Susumu Ueda. PRD: Kid's Station. 23 mins. x 13 eps.
Cheerful schoolgirl Shiina Tamai lives alone with her jetpilot father. Swimming during a summer vacation with her grandparents, she almost dies when she is swept out to sea. Her life is saved by a strange star-shaped creature. She names him Hoshimaru—the Round Star—and they become friends. He can fly, transform into different shapes, and absorb objects into his body, and even though he doesn't talk, he and Shiina can understand each other. When she returns to school for the new year, Hoshimaru disguises himself as her backpack; but they learn that other children have also met strange creatures, some with their masters—and they're not all friendly. The creatures are called "dragons" and some of their young friends are easily manipulated through their own weaknesses—like arrogant Satomi who thinks she should be one of the elite running the world, or knife-crazy Akinori. A tale of alien invasion that starts out cute and perky and gets darker, based on the 1998 manga in *Comic Afternoon* by Mohiro Kito.

SHAKOTAN BOOGIE

1991. Video. DIR: Hiromitsu Sato, Junichi Shoji. SCR: Yukiyoshi Ohashi. DES: Hiroyuki Horiuchi. ANI: Hiroyuki Horiuchi, Hirotaka Kinoshita. MUS: Noriyuki Asakura. PRD: Studio Pierrot. 55 mins. x 4 eps.
It's girls, gangs, and cars in this adaptation of the 1985 manga in *Young Magazine*, by **LULLABY FOR WEDNESDAY'S CINDERELLA**–creator Michiharu Kusunoki. Local tough guys steal cars, switch the plates, and sell them, but not without racing them for a while against rival gangs. The anime continues the story where the 1987 live-action movie starring Kazuya Kimura left off. Compare to **INITIAL D**.

SHAKUGAN NO SHANA *

2005. AKA: *Shana of the Burning Eyes; Shana*. TV series. DIR: Takashi Watanabe. SCR: Yasuko Kobayashi. DES: Mai Otsuka. ANI: Shingo Fukuyo. MUS: Ko Otani. PRD: JC Staff, Animax, Chiba TV. 25 mins. x 24 eps.

Everyday Japanese student Yuji Sakai is attacked by a strange creature and saved by a girl with red hair and red eyes. Shana, for it is she, is a Flame Haze agent, whose job it is to hunt down Crimson Denizens, creatures from the Crimson Realm who are attempting to break into our world. Shana's mission is to protect Yuji, since there is supposedly something special about him that only gorgeous, nubile alien amazons can detect. Although initially presented as a tough, uncaring fighter, Shana inevitably warms to Yuji, particularly after they are forced to set up home in an URUSEI YATSU-RA–inspired cohabitation. Learning about the world through the highly inadvisable route of watching TV, Shana is soon asking Yuji to explain more about this "love" of which the soap operas continually speak. The authors are tempted to point out that a more realistic approach would have had her flicking through channel after channel and finding nothing but TENCHI MUYO! clones, questioning her existence, and debating the point of it all. Nevertheless, Shana and her associates are soon battling to save Yuji and his planet from Alastor, the ruler of the Crimson Realm, using a variety of fire-themed magic. Based on a series of books by Yashichiro Takahashi, illustrated by Noizi Ito. As with SLAYERS, calling them "novels" is a little presumptuous, as they are low on wordcount and high on illustrations, more like novelettes.

SHAMAN KING *

2001. TV series, specials. DIR: Seiji Mizushima. SCR: Katsuhiko Koide. DES: Akio Takami, Shinichi Yamaoka. ANI: Akio Takami. MUS: Toshiyuki Omori. PRD: NAS, TV Tokyo, Animax, Xebec. 23 mins. x 64 eps., 30 mins. x 3 eps. (special).

Shamans are people who can communicate with the supernatural and join with the spirits of the dead to use their skill and power. Teenager Yoh Asakura is a shaman, engaged to the ambitious Anna. She wants to marry the greatest shaman of all, the Shaman King. Once every 500 years a great contest, the Shaman Fight, gives the winner the chance to become Shaman King and wield great power by controlling the strongest spirits. The winner also gets to meet God. Yoh goes to Tokyo for the contest, along with his three faithful friends—Manta Oyamada, an undersized junior-high student who is scared of spirits but is able to see them, and whom Yoh has taken on as a de-facto apprentice; his spirit partner, a samurai named Amidamaru; and Anna, who is also a medium and is acting as his trainer. Along the way they meet strong opposition, misfit ghosts and would-be magicians, in a series whose high concept could be summed up as PHANTOM QUEST CORP meets DRAGON BALL. Based on a manga by Hiroyuki Takei, serialized in *Shonen Jump*. ●Ⓝ♥

SHAMANIC PRINCESS *

1996. Video. DIR: Mitsuru Hongo, Hiroyuki Nishimura. SCR: Asami Watanabe. DES: Atsuko Ishida. ANI: Atsuko Ishida, Masahiko Ogura, Hiroyuki Nishimura. MUS: Yoshikazu Suo. PRD: Bandai, Movic, Animate Film. 30 mins. x 6 eps.

Accompanied by Japolo, her ermine-like familiar (or "Partner"), Princess Tiara is sent from the Guardian World into our own dimension to prevent an imbalance in the cosmos. As a Magic User, this is her royal duty, since the Guardians must police the actions of indestructible, unpredictable Shadows. Disguised as a schoolgirl, Tiara must find Kagetsu, a being loyal to Yord, the godlike entity that is the Guardian World's source of power. Not only has Kagetsu stolen the Throne of Yord (a direct link to unfathomable powers), but he is also her ex-beloved, and the brother of her missing best friend, Sarah.

SP refers on occasion to the story of Daphne, who in Greek mythology was turned into a laurel tree to avoid the advances of Apollo—Sarah is actually trapped inside the Throne, which looks like a painting of laurel trees. But such literary pretensions are a red herring in themselves, since the six-strong committee that provided *SP*'s "story concept" are more interested in providing good-looking images. With painstakingly animated CG rose petals in the opening credits and ribbon-like adornments worthy of OH MY GODDESS!, they are not unsuccessful; girls duel with swords made of shadows and Tiara's luscious red hair transforms into unearthly wings beneath the light of the moon (a "moon-tree" in Japanese is a laurel). There are faint echoes of KIKI'S DELIVERY SERVICE in the European setting and mundane witchery, but *SP* is very much a designer's film, with sharp characters from RAYEARTH's Ishida and lush green backgrounds from SPRIGGAN's Hajime Matsuoka. It also has magical powers entrapped in sigils on the sorcerers' own skins, a peculiar fad from the mid-1990s also found in TATTOON MASTER. The switch in directors for the final two episodes also brings a switch in plotting—parts five and six are a prequel to the first four, creating an intriguing circular structure that plays with ideas of memory, dream, and reality.

SHAME ON MISS MACHIKO

1981. JPN: *Maitchingu Machiko Sensei*. TV series. DIR: Masami Anno, Keiichiro Mochizuki. SCR: Seiko Taguchi, Chiho Shioda, Kenji Terada, Yasuko Hoshikawa. DES: Ichiya Uenashi, Keiko Aono. ANI: Ichiya Uenashi, Norio Hirayama. MUS: Hiroki Inui. PRD: Studio Pierrot, Studio Gallop, TV Tokyo. 25 mins. x 95 eps.

Machiko is a young elementary-school teacher who does her utmost to solve the everyday problems faced by her little pupils. Unfortunately the situations and traps created by the little moppets always seem to involve Teacher losing some or all of her clothes, much to the delight of her class, and the utter disapproval of the Japanese PTA, which fulminated against lechery in a "children's" show (albeit one broadcast at 7:30 p.m.). The later CRAYON SHIN-CHAN would bring similar criticisms.

The story was remade as the live-action movie *Machiko Begins* (2005) starring Sayaka Isoyama and appears to have inspired the substantially more pornographic pastiche PANTY-FLASH TEACHER. ⓝ

SHAMELESS SCHOOL

1996. JPN: *Heisei Harenchi Gakuen*. AKA: *Modern-Era Shameless School*. Video. DIR: Koichi Kobayashi. SCR: N/C. DES: Go Nagai. ANI: Kimiyo Ono, Taseiko Hamazu. MUS: N/C. PRD: Pink Pineapple, KSS. 47 mins., 45 mins.

Yamanegi is determined to enjoy his school days—a desire made easier by attending a place of learning where the teachers are more interested in looking at girls' underwear and the classes are a non-stop party. This one-shot anime revived Go Nagai's controversial 1968 manga, originally run in *Shonen Jump*, much to the annoyance of PTA organizations all over Japan. Compare to Nagai's equally silly **KEKKO KAMEN**. **N**

SHANGRI-LA *

2009. TV series. DIR: Makoto Bessho. SCR: Hiroshi Onogi, Yutaka Izubuchi, Toshizo Nemoto, Yoichi Kato. DES: Range Murata. ANI: Daisuke Kamei, Miyuki Nakamura, Takeshi Kusaka, Yuichi Yoshida. MUS: Hitomi Kuroishi. PRD: Gonzo, Kadokawa Shoten, NTT Docomo, Sony PCL, Klockworx. 24 mins. x 24 eps.

Half a century after the Second Great Kanto Earthquake, global warming and the spread of a poisonous forest has fragmented Tokyo into isolated villages. In the wider world, carbon emissions credits are the only currency worth trading, and mighty corporations rule. Atlas Corp. is building a huge tower to house the Japanese in a more congenial environment, but progress is slow and places are allocated by lottery, leaving the majority of the population to scrape by living on the poisonous outside. Three teenage girls and a young soldier come together by strange paths: computer genius Karin, one of a gang raiding the world carbon markets for profit; the mysteriously powerful, apparently fragile Mikuni; and teen delinquent Kuniko, just out of two years' detention. Is she a terrorist or a freedom fighter? Probably both. Does this restrict the potential for fan service (**ARGOT AND JARGON**)? Not a bit. Makoto Bessho is still an inexperienced director here, but he knows the importance of panty shots and gratituous violence. This beautifully designed, sloppily plotted series promises so much and delivers rather less. The Range Murata character designs are a guilty pleasure; never have 18-year-olds looked so 12. **NV**

SHATTERED ANGELS *

2007. JPN: *Kyoshiro to Towa no Sora*. AKA: *Kyoshiro and the Eternal Sky*. TV series. DIR: Tetsuya Yanagisawa. SCR: Sumio Uetake. DES: Maki Fuji, Hisaharu Iijima. ANI: Maki Fuji. MUS: Mina Kubota. PRD: TNK, AT-X, Geneon Entertainment (USA), Studio Maus, Klockworx, Toshiba Entertainment. 24 mins. x 12 eps.

In the school-city of Academia, Ku Shiratori daydreams of meeting a handsome prince. A new transfer student arrives, looking just like the boy of her dreams, but things go wrong when he doesn't behave as she always imagined he would. But then she gets caught up in a fight between magical and mechanical creatures of a kind she's never seen before, and he rescues her. But will his odd friend Setsuna, with her habit of sucking the life out of others with a kiss, hamper their developing romance?

A whole city devoted to nothing but schools—not as far-fetched as it seems. To most schoolchildren, the school, home, and the places they hang out *are* the city; the rest might as well not exist. Creative duo Kaishaku, whose manga usually move quickly to anime, understand what junior high school readers want. *Shattered Angels* (which first appeared in manga form in 2006) is a crossover tale referencing earlier works such as **MAGICAL MEOW MEOW TARUTO**, **STEEL ANGEL KURUMI**, and *Destiny of the Shrine Maiden*. The result is a series that imports clichés not only from its genre—magical high school romance—but also from its sister stories and ends up too overwrought and tedious to be saved by the beautiful art and the skill lavished on it by the crew. It wants to reach the same level as **UTENA** or **SAILOR MOON**, but doesn't.

SHERLOCK HOUND *

1984. JPN: *Meitantei Holmes*. AKA: *Famous Detective Holmes*. TV series, movie. DIR: Hayao Miyazaki, Keiji Hayakawa, Seiji Okuda. SCR: Toshiyuki Yamazaki, Yoshihisa Araki, Hayao Miyazaki, Tsunehisa Ito. DES: Yoshifumi Kondo. ANI: Tsukasa Tannai, Seiji Kitahara. MUS: Kentaro Haneda. PRD: Tokyo Movie Shinsha, RAI, TV Asahi. 25 mins. x 26 eps. (TV), 45 mins. x 2 (m).

The great detective Sherlock Holmes and his faithful friend Dr. John Watson are in constant demand in Edwardian London to foil the evil schemes of Professor Moriarty, who is constantly out to steal some exotic treasure or cause havoc with his minions, Todd and Smiley. In this charming adventure series for children, they are transformed into anthropomorphic dogs (see also **DOGTANIAN AND THE THREE MUSKEHOUNDS**). Their adventures are full of charm, wit, and energy as they search for a missing train, track three mysterious lobsters, and defeat a "monster" in the Thames that is more than it seems. Adapted by **MONTANA JONES**–creator Marco Pagot from the original novels by Arthur Conan Doyle, this was Pagot's first work with Ghibli's giants. The series was very popular on TV in the U.K. and is still available on video in the U.S. The episodes *Blue Carbuncle* (#5) and *Sunken Treasure* (#9) were combined to make a 1984 theatrical release shown on a double bill with Miyazaki's **NAUSICAÄ**. A further two, *The Kidnapping of Mrs. Hudson* (#4) and *Air War Over the Cliffs of Dover* (#10), were combined to create a 1986 "movie" shown on a double bill with **CASTLE IN THE SKY**. A more realistic Sherlock Holmes would get on the trail of a French master thief: see **LUPIN THE MASTERTHIEF AND THE ENIGMA OF 813**. The first episode also exists in an alternate dub made by TMS for promotional purposes, which showcases more realistic British accents and renames Todd and Smiley as Nigel and Bruce.

SHE'S NO ANGEL

1994. JPN: *Tenshi Nanka ja nai*. AKA: *Somewhat Unangelic*. Video. DIR: Hiroko Tokita. SCR: Tomoko Konparu. DES: Yasuomi Umezu. ANI: Chuji Nakajima. MUS: Fujio Takano. PRD: Group Tac. 30 mins.

Based on the manga in *Ribon* magazine by **NEIGHBORHOOD STORY**–creator Ai Yazawa, this anime features the drama and romance centering on one girl's attempt to transfer schools.

SHIBA THE DOG'S PEACEFUL HEART

2006. JPN: *Shibawanko no Wa no Kokoro*. TV series. DIR: Keizo Kira. SCR: Minori Ikeno. DES: N/C. ANI: N/C. MUS: N/C. PRD: 3D, Moebius Town, NHK Enterprises, Hakusensha. 2 mins. x 80 eps.

Shiba-wanko, a dog, and Miike-nyanko, a calico cat, live together in a traditional Japanese house. Shiba is a gentle, loving creature who does all the housework and cooking, while Miike is a diva who does little apart from looking pretty. Together the pair learn the traditional Japanese way of peace and harmony, exploring the festivals, changing seasons, and rituals. Based on Yoshie Kawaura's 1998 picture books, this show took enormous care of the details—the Japanese credits include etiquette supervisors, Buddhist ritual advisors, incense advisors, and consultants on kabuki theater and traditional sweets. It's an enchantingly old-fashioned confection intended to teach children how to behave, and thus very useful to foreigners who want to learn the manners of polite Japanese society.

SHIBAI TAROKA

1993. JPN: *Shibai Taroka*. AKA: *Puttin' It On*. Video. DIR: Teruo Kogure. SCR: Shunsuke Amemura. DES: Shigeru Koshiba. ANI: Teruo Kogure. MUS: Toshio Okazawa. PRD: Toei, Knack. 30 mins. x 2 eps.
Hard-faced tough-guy Kusuta transfers to the Osaka area, where everyone is a hard-faced tough guy (see COMPILER). But appearances can be deceptive: he likes flowers and fairy stories. The girls love him, the guys hate him. There's trouble. Based on the 1993 manga in *Young Champion* by Shigeru Koshiba.

SHIBAYAMA, TSUTOMU

1941–. Born in Tokyo, he studied drama at Meiji University, joining Toei Animation after graduation and working on shows including KEN THE WOLF BOY and HUSTLE PUNCH. He moved to A Production (now Shin'ei Doga), and continued to work as a key animator and director, although his feature debut did not come until GO FOR IT, TABUCHI (1978).

SHIBUYA HONKY TONK

1988. Video. DIR: Masamune Ochiai. SCR: Masaru Yamamoto. DES: N/C. ANI: Tadashi Abiko. MUS: BORO. PRD: Tokuma Japan, Knack. 35 mins. x 4 eps.
Set in 1945, this is the story of teenager Naoya Abe, who comes from a good family but is fixated by the seeming glamour of organized crime. He manages to talk his way into working for the Todogumi, the clan that controls Tokyo's fashionable Shibuya area, but it's a lot tougher and less glamorous than he hoped. When his girlfriend is threatened and he kills a rival clan member, he decides to escape to London. Volume 2 sees him working in London as an assistant to photographer Aoki, but he manages to get himself involved in the theft of military secrets. When his criminal past comes to light, he's sent back to Japan to face the music, but

he survives and rises through the ranks of the Todogumi. Based on the semiautobiographical novel by Joji Abe, who also appears in a live-action section.

SHIDARA, HIROSHI

1936–. Born in Yamagata, he studied drama at Nihon University, and joined Toei's Kyoto office after graduation. He moved to Toei Animation in 1962, and his credits begin appearing on SPACE PATROL HOPPA by 1965. He was a supervising director on CANDY CANDY.

SHIGOFUMI: LETTERS FROM THE DEPARTED *

2008. JPN: *Shigofumi*. TV series, video. DIR: Tatsuo Sato. SCR: Ichiro Okochi. DES: Tetsuya Kawakami, Makoto Shiraishi, Nobuto Sakamoto. ANI: Tetsuya Kawakami, Fusako Nomura, Mayumi Okamoto, Satoshi Iwataki. MUS: Hikaru Nanase. PRD: JC Staff, Bandai Visual, GENCO. 24 mins. x 12 eps. (TV), 24 mins. (v).
Fumika and her talking staff Kanaka are postal workers. They deliver letters from the dead to the living. These letters—*shigofumi*—can only tell the truth; but when the living read them, the reaction isn't always positive. Fumika is dead, and does her job stoically, but when she encounters someone who knew her in life, her personal tragedy threatens to resurface from the world she has left behind.

This is a dark, disturbing series whose open-ended premise allows for the exploration of multiple stories. It embraces child abuse, teenage suicide, exploitation, mental illness, parental indifference, and cruelty, all the while weaving strands of Fumika's own story into the whole and leading us toward the conclusion sketched in the credits of the last TV episode and expanded on DVD in the unaired 13th episode. Despite a few logical flaws, an annoying sidekick in Kanaka, and a tendency to dehumanize all those involved in bullying, this strikingly original series serves up its violence and sexual content with considerable sensitivity. Seven *Shigofumi Picture Dramas* on the DVD contain some spoilers and so may be best watched after the series. Ryo Amamiya is credited as original creator, but the 2006–8 light-novel series with designs by Poko and art by Kohaku Kuroboshi was written by Tomoro

Yuzawa. Compare to A LETTER TO MOMO and COLORFUL: THE MOTION PICTURE. **NV**

SHIGURUI: DEATH FRENZY *

2007. JPN: *Shigurui*. TV series. DIR: Hiroshi Hamasaki. SCR: Kei Tsunematsu, Seishi Minakami. DES: Masanori Shino, Hidetoshi Kaneko. ANI: Masanori Shino. MUS: Kiyoshi Yoshida. PRD: Madhouse, Akita Shoten, Geneon Universal Entertainment, WOWOW. 25 mins. x 12 eps.
After long years of war, Japan has been united and pacified under a strong shogun. The seat of government has moved from the Imperial Palace at Kyoto to Edo. But after years of blood and death, it's hard to adapt to peace. When a great lord announces a fighting tournament, he decides it will be held with live steel, not wooden swords as in the past. The two best disciples of Japan's greatest swordsman will fight to determine who is the worthy heir to his school. One-armed Gennosuke Fujiki and blind Seigen Irako square off, only for the show to dive back in time to their earlier, friendlier days before they were wounded physically and mentally.

Adapted from Norio Nanjo's novel by way of Takayuki Yamaguchi's 2003 manga, this is one of the most grotesquely violent anime ever made. It's also one of the most insistent on its cultural context, not only within Japanese history but also within the traditions of Japanese film. And it's beautiful, in the way that Goya's horrific "black paintings" or a medieval *memento mori* tomb sculpture is beautiful: elegantly crafted, precisely balanced, finely honed to achieve a specific impact. If Akira Kurosawa had made an anime movie in his early years, it might look and sound like this. It wouldn't feel like this, though. Kurosawa's characters always retain their humanity, even when abandoning all pretence of morality, and, with it, hope.

Action horror with an artsy edge has always been home turf for Madhouse, and here the studio works to its highest standards of craftsmanship. They're also used to making stories that reduce all female characters to the level of trade goods, but even in a Madhouse movie there's usually one good girl saved or bad girl redeemed; here they're all used, then broken. Raising the bleak and chilling realism of feudal life to the level of fetish, Hamasaki directs this show like an arthouse movie made in a lunatic asylum where the guards have all been eaten by the inmates. Few other anime are as compellingly well-made, and even fewer focus so minutely on the vicious effects of a perfectly developed talent serving a narrow, formalistic worldview. Prepare to be amazed, but don't expect to be delighted. **NV**

SHIHO-CHAN

1996. JPN: *Maho no Shiho-chan*. AKA: *Magical Shiho-chan*. Video. DIR: Takashi Abe. SCR: N/C. DES: Minato Koimoro. ANI: Yasuhito Kikuchi. MUS: N/C. PRD: Pink Pineapple, KSS. 30 mins. x 2 eps.
Released from an icy tomb in the Antarctic, Vaj the talking penguin goes in search of a girl to protect Earth from danger by transforming into a more "adult" version of herself. This porno based on a *Young Magazine* manga by Minato Koimoro contains oblique references to **EVANGELION** that serve no purpose whatsoever. **N**

SHIKI *

2010. JPN: *Dead Demon*. AKA: *Corpse Demon*. TV series. DIR: Tetsuro Amino. SCR: Kenji Sugihara, Sawako Hirayabashi, Asami Ishikawa, Junichi Shintaku, Noboru Takagi. DES: Shinji Ochi, Ichiro Tatsuta. ANI: Shinji Ochi, Natsuki Watanabe, Akatsuki Koshiishi. MUS: Yasuharu Takanashi. PRD: Daume, Aniplex, Dax Productions, Dentsu, Fuji TV, Shueisha. 23 mins. x 22 eps.
Sotobamura is one of Japan's most isolated villages. It isn't even connected to a highway, and its residents—around 1,300 of them—live lives governed by old customs and rituals. Newcomers are rare, but the Kirishiki family have just moved in to the old mansion on the hill. And then people start falling ill with unexpected suddenness and dying just a few days after the first symptoms appear. Doctor Ozaki is looking for a scientific explanation, but the local priest thinks this may not be a scientific problem. It seems the village's newly dead, not content with resting peacefully in their graves like generations of their ancestors, may be coming back for more than just a last visit to their homes.
This is a classic vampire tale, told slowly, but with skill and care. The dead, undead, and not-yet-dead are treated as real people, each with something to say,

and these multiple voices and plotlines help the story stay compelling and engaging despite its slow pace. The visuals are as rich and detailed as the plot, and the action sequences are well done. Beautifully executed classic horror without gags or gimmicks is rare. *Shiki* may remind you of what you love about the genre, and why. Based on Ryu Fujisaki's 2007 manga adaptation of Fuyumi Ono's novel series. **V**

SHIMOKAWA, OTEN

1892–1973. Pseudonym of Sadanori Shimokawa, sometimes Hekoten Shimokawa. Born in Okinawa, Shimokawa moved to Tokyo at the age of seven after the death of his father, a school principal. He worked for the cartoonist Rakuten Kitazawa both before and after a stint in the Army General Staff as a trainee engineer. By 1912, he was a cartoonist for the satirical magazine *Tokyo Puck* and was commissioned in 1916 to make short animated cartoons for the Tenkatsu Studio. None of his animation work survives, but his *Mukuzo Imokawa the Doorman*, made in 1916 and released in January 1917, is widely regarded as the "first anime"—see **EARLY ANIME**. His work appears to have been made using the "chalkboard" method, in which a single image on a blackboard is photographed and rephotographed with minor alterations. Shimokawa's fifth film, *An Animation about Fishing* (1917, *Chamebozu, Uotsuri no Maki*), was also his last. Although he never worked in animation again, he enjoyed success in the 1930s writing manga for the *Sunday Yomiuri*, and post–World War II as an artist for *Nippon Manga Shinbun*. Controversially, none of Shimokawa's pioneering films survive, and the sole source for much of his animation achievement is an article he wrote himself in the 1930s that denied all knowledge of any fellow animators. As a result, some critics have approached his claims with a degree of suspicion, although recent years have unearthed enough evidence from his cameraman and contemporary articles to suggest that he was largely telling the truth.

SHIN HAKKENDEN

1999. JPN: *God Hakkenden*. TV series. DIR: Katsuyoshi Yatabe, Toshiaki Suzuki, Kenji Yoshida. SCR: Yasushi Hirano. DES: Atsuko

Ishida, Masahiko Okura. ANI: Moriyasu Taniguchi, Shinichiro Minami. MUS: N/C. PRD: Beam Entertainment, TV Tokyo. 25 mins. x 26 eps.
The year is 2588 in the system of Godworld and its eight satellites. Humanity came here in the distant past, after a long journey across the stars from Earth. Now the system is ruled by a loose coalition of powerful families: House Owari, House Meed, and House Iigy. The story begins when Kai, the heir to House Owari, attacks an icy planet. Living in a humble village on the surface is Ko, a young boy who is perpetually arguing with his father. When Kai's navy arrives, Ko takes his father's mighty Murasame sword to fight back, and his adventures begin. A sci-fi remake of **HAKKENDEN**. (Not to be confused with Pioneer's continuation of the original *Hakkenden* series, *Shin [New] Hakkenden*).

SHIN'EI DOGA

Literally "New Image Animation," or "New A Animation." Originally formed as A Productions (A Pro) in late 1965, its releases include the early Hayao Miyazaki work **PANDA GO PANDA**. The company was reorganized into its new form in 1976 by Daikichiro Kusube, a former employee of Tokyo Movie Shinsha. Its first notable work in its new incarnation was on **DORAEMON**. Prominent staffers have included Toshihide Yamada, Eiichi Nakamura, Susumu Watanabe, Keiichi Hara, and Toshihiko Ando. The company is still active today on productions such as **CRAYON SHIN-CHAN**.

SHINA DARK

2008. JPN: *Kuroki Tsuki no O to Soheki no Tsuki no Himegimi*. AKA: *Shina Dark: King of Dark Moon and Princess of Blue Moon*. Video. DIR: Akiyuki Shinbo. SCR: N/A. DES: N/C. ANI: Naoyuki Konno, Shinpei Tomooka. MUS: N/C. PRD: SHAFT, Lantis, GENCO. 8 mins.
Exoda, AKA Satan, is the Demon Lord of the magical island of Shina Dark. It has been sunk beneath the sea for years, but its Lord is said to be a legendary lust machine who will devastate the world if he is not constantly supplied with sacrificial maidens. These legends are far from the truth; Exoda, while definitely powerful, is a pleasant young man who just wants a quiet life, peace with his neighbors, and time to go fishing. But since reality can't

be allowed to get in the way of a good legend, the nations of the world send over a thousand girls to the island when it rises from the waves again. Now Exoda has over a thousand mouths to feed, and over a thousand girls who can't go back to their homes and families because they are regarded as tainted demon concubines. What's a guy to do? Well, in Bunjuro Nakayama and Yuraki Higa's manga he sets up an independent nation ruled by two of the girls to give them a new homeland. In the anime, he can't do much because it only runs for eight minutes. An anime that sums up the offensive logic of the harem genre (ROMANCE AND DRAMA) in just eight minutes is an achievement in itself, but this short compilation of four music videos has solid ground to build on. The manga ran from January 2006 to March 2009, and the music videos were compiled in DVD and bundled with a limited-edition manga volume in January 2008. ◑

SHINESMAN *

1995. JPN: Tokumu Sentai Shinesman. AKA: Special Duty Battle Team Shinesman. Video. DIR: Shinya Sadamitsu. SCR: Hideki Sonoda. DES: Kiyoharu Ishii, Atsuo Tobe. ANI: Kiyoharu Ishii. MUS: N/C. PRD: Sony, Animate Film. 30 mins. x 2 eps.

Hiroya Matsumoto is a bright young salesman working for Right Trading Company, devoted to his job and to his younger brother, Yota. But after work he swaps his business suit for red combat armor and puts in overtime as leader of the company's Special Duty Combat Unit division. He and his four colleagues Ryoichi Hayami (green), Shojo Yamadera (gray), Shotaro Ono (sepia), and Riko Hidaka (pink) are the Shinesman team. They're under the command of Kyoko Sakakibara of Human Resources and helped by support staff Hitomi Kasahara and Tsukasa Nakamura, and their sworn mission is to defend the Right Trading Company and the world from the invaders from Planet Voice, who are bent on conquering Earth. Sasaki, the prince of Voice, and his strategist sidekick, Seki, are already on Earth implementing the devious plan—through their company Science Electronics, they plan to take over the world through building a great business empire. They've started out with theme parks and a TV show that's wowing

kids everywhere; Yota is one of its biggest fans. This is a bizarre combination of Power Rangers and Wall Street, based on Minamu Tachibana's manga in Comic Bokke. Bad acting, recycled footage, silly dialogue, and insane plotting are presented as a satire—though since one gets plenty of that in anime anyway, it's tempting to suggest this is the same old same old, just presented "ironically." Another allegory of corporate competition, this time about video formats, can be discerned beneath the surface of ARMITAGE III.

SHINGU: SECRET OF THE STELLAR WARS *

2001. JPN: Gakuen Senki Muryo. AKA: College Chronicle Muryo. TV series. DIR: Tatsuo Sato. SCR: Tatsuo Sato. DES: Takahiro Yoshimatsu. ANI: Takahiro Yoshimatsu. MUS: Yuji Ono. PRD: Madhouse. 25 mins. x 26 eps.

In the year 2070, the Japanese government finally admits the existence of aliens after an "unidentified" flying object in Tokyo identifies itself as "the Seeker." A few days later, new student Subaru Muryo transfers to a school in Tenmo, a new town in Kanagawa Prefecture. He dresses and behaves oddly, inspiring fellow student Hajime Murata to investigate further—no prizes for guessing that Subaru is not of this Earth.

SHINING TEARS X WIND

2007. TV series. DIR: Hiroshi Watanabe. SCR: Hiro Masaki. DES: Yukiko Ban, Mariko Emori, Michiyo Miki. ANI: Yukiko Ban. MUS: Kei Haneoka. PRD: Studio DEEN, d-rights, Sega. 24 mins. x 13 eps.

Kiriya's home, Tatsumi Town, is plagued by mysterious disappearances, including his fellow student council members Soma and Kureha. Kiriya is beset by a vision of a mysterious girl with cat ears. There's a book with legends of an alternative world, and people are moving between the worlds and getting stuck. Dark forces are at play, magical weapons and powers abound, and there are many trials to overcome. Loosely based on Shining Tears, a 2004 Sega game by Tsuyoshi Sawada, with characters designed by master of cute girl art Tony, this is part of the Shining Force video-game series. The anime is simply a marketing tool for the 2007 game sequel, Shining Wind, in which all the main characters from Shining

Tears reappear. Airing a month before the game, the show helped to propel it to the top of the bestseller charts in its week of release.

SHINKAI, MAKOTO

1973–. Pseudonym for Makoto Niitsu, a writer and animator who arrived in the industry via GAMING AND DIGITAL ANIMATION and whose VOICES OF A DISTANT STAR is one of the landmark works of modern anime. Made practically solo, with off-the-shelf software in his own home, it turned Shinkai into the poster-boy of DIY animators and offered a tantalizing glimpse of new opportunities to bypass traditional channels of production and distribution in a wired world. Shinkai's work is distinguished by a concentration on ROMANCE AND DRAMA, even within science fictional framing devices, such as VoaDS, which uses relativity and space travel to symbolize the emotional distance between individuals. He would return to similar themes, largely stripped of SF trappings (EVERYDAY ANIME), in his later FIVE CENTIMETERS PER SECOND and THE GARDEN OF WORDS. Although he was swiftly co-opted into the professional anime world, handed the directorial reins for the feature-length THE PLACE PROMISED IN OUR EARLY DAYS and CHILDREN WHO CHASE LOST VOICES FROM DEEP BELOW, his best work remains in the niche that serves adult FANDOM—shorter works, released straight-to-video or shown only in limited screenings, without any restrictions imposed by wider appeals to the mainstream.

Shinkai maintains his contacts in the gaming world, with credits for animation segments in franchises such as DOUBLE WISH and WIND: A BREATH OF HEART. His work continues to reflect the yearnings and passion often implied in the audience of dating sims, but also the new angles and approaches associated with animators who have grown up with little experience of the cel tradition. In particular, he demonstrates a canny ability to play to his own strengths and limit his weaknesses, such as utilizing live reference materials for his backgrounds and environments. He remains an iconic figure for an entire generation of new animators all around the world, including China, where in 2009 the local series Xinling zhi Chuang (Spirit's Window) was caught lifting some of his work—recycling backgrounds, grabbing shots, and in one moment of quaintly demure piracy, putting longer skirts on some of his schoolgirls.

SHINSENGUMI FARCE

1989. JPN: *Shogeki Shinsengumi*. Video. DIR: Hiromi Noda, Takenori Kawata. SCR: Hiromi Noda. DES: Hiromi Noda. ANI: Michio Sato. MUS: N/C. PRD: ACC, Tanihara Studio, Random. 30 mins.

A comical depiction of the unrest caused by the arrival of Commodore Perry's black ships in 1853, as nationalists and *ultra*-nationalists fight over who should rule Japan in the name of the emperor (see OI RYOMA!). As the rival domains of Satsuma and Choshu jostle for power, the Shinsengumi organization becomes the emperor's "protectors" in Kyoto. Hyped on release as "the Shinsengumi as you've never seen them before," somewhat ironically since anime *never* seems to have portrayed the Shinsengumi as the vigilante extremists they actually were. Similarly sanitized versions would appear in ZEGUY, GINTAMA, and in Nagisa Oshima's live-action *Gohatto* (2000), which romanticized them as sexually confused pretty-boys.

SHIODOME CABLE TV

2011. TV series. DIR: FROGMAN. SCR: FROGMAN. DES: FROGMAN. ANI: Akihiro Saito, Mitsuo Sato. MUS: manzo, ti.o.pi. PRD: FROGMAN Co., DLE, NTV. 3 mins. x 22 eps.

Part of NTV's YURUANI? gag anthology show created by DLE, this was originated by FROGMAN for NTV, rather than based on a manga like the other six segments featured. It's a heavily fictionalized parody of life and work at *News Zero*, a news show running on cable TV for 15 years. The company president is a luridly suited statue of the Buddha and the bureau chief is a snake in a top hat. The closing credits are a perky masterpiece, with backing music that appears to have been scored on a Stylophone. Pure genius.

SHION

2008. Video. DIR: Shigenori Awai. SCR: Koichi Murakami. DES: Hiroya Iijima, Hifumi. ANI: Michitaka Yamamoto. MUS: N/C. PRD: Studio I.C., Studio Bambino, Studio Gadget, Pixy. 30 mins. x 4 eps.

Geist, an evil aggressor from another dimension, is being tracked by two voluptuous female warriors, Lidia and Sion. When the trio wind up in Hiroki's high school all hell breaks loose, and his friends, classmates, and teachers are drawn into the mayhem. Average schoolboys, over-endowed females, evil scientists, bondage, tentacle rape, blood, violence—yes, it's another porn fantasy anime based on a game by Black-Lilith. You get a three-minute bonus video with an alternate happy ending on the Japanese DVD. There's a Japanese online game of the same name by JSK that allows you to undress a purple-haired girl using only your mouse, but it doesn't look nearly as expensive as this. **NV**

SHION'S KING

2007. JPN: *Shion no O*. TV series. DIR: Toshifumi Kawase. SCR: Takashi Yamada. DES: Seiya Numata, Yutaka Mukumoto. ANI: Seiya Numata, Sunao Chikaoka. MUS: Kosuke Yamashita. PRD: Studio DEEN, Fuji TV, Pony Canyon, Yomiko Advertising. 23 mins x 22 eps.

Shion was only five when her parents were murdered in front of her in their home; the trauma took away her voice and her memory. Adopted by family friends, she began to play the Japanese chess game *shogi* and by the time she reaches the age of 11 she's a noted player. As her fame grows, she starts getting death threats and realizes that becoming a professional *shogi* player could lead her to her parents' killer; the only clue to her murder was a *shogi* board and one game piece, the King. But Shion knows the killer: he challenged her to her first ever game of *shogi* and terrified her into forgetting. This murder mystery based on Masaru Katori and Jiro Ando's 2004 manga is clever, well-paced, and entertaining. Compare with the very different approach to making anime about static table-top games entertaining in SAKI: THE PLAYER and HIKARU'S GO.

SHIOYAMA, NORIO

1940–. After his debut with HARRIS'S WIND, he joined forces with Ryosuke Takahashi to become one of the prime movers of the great era of robot anime. His first work as a character designer was on DAITARN 3, although he is probably best remembered today for RONIN WARRIORS.

SHIRAKAWA, DAISAKU

1935–. Pseudonym for Kenichi Takahashi. After early training in economics, he joined Toei Animation and worked on MAGIC BOY before working directly with Osamu Tezuka on JOURNEY TO THE WEST (1960). He subsequently worked as an animator on LITTLE NORSE PRINCE, MADCAP ISLAND, and many others, before leaving hands-on animation in 1968 to work as a producer for radio and television. He became a section leader at Media Center, a production planning house, in 1974.

SHIRATO, TAKESHI

1944–. After a debut as a key animator on TIGER MASK in 1969, he played a similar role in the productions of works including STAR BLAZERS and IKKYU. He has also been a concept artist and character designer and was the director of BENEATH THE BLACK RAIN.

SHIROW, MASAMUNE

1961–. Pseudonym for Masanori Ota. Born in Kobe, Shirow graduated from Osaka University of Arts. He achieved early fame as a manga creator, leading to an ill-starred role as director on his own BLACK MAGIC M-66, from which he eventually stepped down in favor of Hiroyuki Kitakubo mid-production. Subsequent adaptations of Shirow's manga work, such as GHOST IN THE SHELL, have traded on his name, but have been made without his direct involvement. Others, such as LANDLOCK and GUNDRESS, have utilized the bare minimum of Shirow's contribution (a single character design, for example) and trumpeted it as if he has made every frame.

SHINZO *

2000. JPN: *Mashurambo*. TV series. DIR: Tetsuo Imazawa. SCR: Mayori Sekijima. DES: Yoko Kamimura. ANI: Yoko Kamimura. Ken Ueno. MUS: N/C. PRD: Toei, TV Asahi. 25 mins. x 32 eps.

In the far future, the human race has lost a bitter war with the alien Matrixer life forms. Three hundred years after the Matrixer victory, a human boy and girl wake up from cryogenic suspension to discover that the Matrixers have overrun the surface of Earth and they are probably the last humans alive.

SHOCKING PINK

2011. AKA: *Pink Shock*. Video. DIR: Yoshitaka Fujimoto. SCR: Taifu Sekimachi. DES: Takayuki Noguchi. ANI: Yoshitaka Fujimoto. MUS: N/C. PRD: Studio Eromatick, Mary Jane. 17 mins. x 2 eps.

Three sisters claiming to be reincarnations of characters from ancient Chinese history corner average schoolboy Takaaki, claiming he's a reincarnation of their strategist. They're all in high school so this is just a grandiose excuse for a harem fantasy (ROMANCE AND DRAMA). Riosuke Yasui's 2008 porn manga is yet another reversioning of part of the story of GREAT CONQUEST: ROMANCE OF THE THREE KINGDOMS, and not an especially convincing one: reincarnations of ancient warrior princes usually want to make war, not love. Despite the alternate manga title, there's no relationship to 1986 video COSMOS PINK SHOCK. **N**

SHOCKING PINK GIRL MOMOKO

1990. Video. DIR: Masakatsu Tonokawa. SCR: Tetsuya Aikawa. DES: Tetsuya Aikawa. ANI: Hiroyoshi Sugawara. MUS: N/C. PRD: Apollon, Mook, Central AV. ca. 40 mins. x 2 eps.

The misadventures of a large-chested bimbo, based on Tetsuya Aikawa's manga in *Manga Sunday* magazine. She wants to be a star like Marilyn Monroe, but it's a tough route to the top, and it unsurprisingly involves taking off her clothes. **N**

SHOGUN WARRIORS

1977.

This is not an anime show, but it was the first major impact of anime robots on U.S. consciousness since ASTRO BOY. It's a brand name created by Mattel for a range of unrelated anime robot toys imported from Japan. Monogram also produced plastic kits of the toys, and in 1979 Marvel acquired permission to produce a comic book featuring the first three robots licensed, although the story lines and characters bear no relationship to the original Japanese series. The comic ran for 20 issues. By 1980, the line was at an end, but it was massively influential at the time; when FORCE FIVE was advertised in 1981, Jim Terry Productions' flier for the show labeled it "for the kids who have already bought $75 million worth of these Super Robot toys marketed by Mattel under the name of *The Shogun Warriors*." See also GODAIKIN. The names

used in the U.S. included (in order of U.S. release) Raydeen (*Brave Reideen*, see BRAVE RAIDEEN), Combatra (COMBATTLER V), Dangard Ace (DANGARD ACE), Mazinga and Great Mazinga (see MAZINGER Z), Daimos (see STARBIRDS), Dragun, Raider, and Poseidon (see GETTER ROBO G), GRANDIZER, and Voltus V (VOLTUS).

SHOJO SECT: INNOCENT LOVERS *

2008. Video. DIR: Ryuki Midoriki. SCR: Mayumi Ishida. DES: Hijirizuki, Minoru Maeda. ANI: Hijirizuki. MUS: Pinkman. PRD: Amarcord, MS Pictures (Milky). 27 mins. x 3 eps.

Shinobu was only a child when she met Momoko, but she fell in love with her then and there and her feelings have never changed. Momoko has forgotten about the past, but now that they're both in high school Shinobu hopes that their childhood promise of love can be revived. They're very different people—she's a promiscuous delinquent, Momoko is very straight-laced—but true love conquers in this girls' love harem. If you're offended by the idea of teachers seducing pupils, or by schoolgirl sexuality, give this anime adapted from Kenn Kurogane's 2005 manga a miss. **N**

SHOJO X SHOJO X SHOJO THE ANIMATION

2012. Video. DIR: Hideki Araki. SCR: Shinichiro Sawayama. DES: Hideki Araki. ANI: Hideki Araki. MUS: Koichi RX Kobe. PRD: T.I. Net, Pink Pineapple. 30 mins. x 2 eps.

Kengo's father was a cruel, sex-crazed tyrant, and Kengo fled his home as soon as he could. Seven years later, he receives a desperate plea for help from the five innocent young daughters of his father's concubines. Based on the 2011 porn manga by Myuto Akatsuki. **N**

SHOJYO KOAKUMA KEI *

2002. JPN: *Shojo Koakuma Kei*. AKA: *Girl Prostitution Kei; The Writhing Women*. Video. DIR: Noboru Yumejima. SCR: Sarasa. DES: Maruta. ANI: Makoto Motoguchi. MUS: N/C. PRD: IKIK Room, Five Ways (Wide Road). 30 mins.

Kyoichi is an ambitious young businessman who hopes to be the best in his field—it's just that his field happens to be prostitution. We first meet him setting up a client who likes young girls with Ayaka, who looks, sounds, and acts young but is

no helpless schoolgirl. The real female lead, though, is Yuri, who has a crush on Kyoichi and believes he helped her out of a bad situation. To repay him, she comes to work as a maid in his business and ends up servicing clients, unaware that Kyoichi actually set up her misfortune to put her in his debt. But there's more to Yuri than meets the eye, and Kyoichi's joke that his girls are "little devils" may not be a mere casual remark. The sex is adult and consensual, though tasteless, so this isn't one of the worst porn anime you'll ever see—but please be aware that this is no recommendation. **ON**

SHOKOJO THE ANIMATION

2011. AKA: *Girls Together*. Video. DIR: Tatsumi, Takaaki Kamihara. SCR: Shinichiro Sawayama. DES: Tatsumi. ANI: Kariya. MUS: : Koichi RX Kobe. PRD: Office Takeout, Pink Pineapple, T-Rex. 30 mins. x 2 eps.

After deflowering his little sister, our hero leaves home for a few years. On his return, little sister is now in middle school and they pick up where they left off. He's also screwing her cute, vulnerable best friend. The protagonist is faceless so that the viewer can more easily project onto him (no pun intended) in this underage incest/sex tale based on a porn game by Tanuki Soft. If you believe sex with people whose ages are barely into double figures can ever be consensual (LOLITA ANIME), you're the one this anime was made for. **N**

SHONEN ONMYOJI *

2006. AKA: *Teenage Sorcerer; Young Spirit Master*. TV series. DIR: Kunihiro Mori. SCR: Miya Asakawa, Kiyoko Yoshimura. DES: Shinobu Tagashira, Toshihisa Koyama. ANI: Kumiko Horikoshi. MUS: Ko Nagakawa. PRD: Studio DEEN, Frontier Works, Kadokawa. 24 mins. x 26 eps.

Masahiro is the grandson of the renowned sorceror-aesthete Abe no Seimei (YIN-YANG MASTER). To protect him from being sucked into the family business until he was older, his grandfather sealed away the sixth sense essential for a successful *onmyoji*—the ability to detect monsters. Then, when he turns 13, he meets a powerful spirit who turns out to be the companion and guide that he needs to unlock his inborn gifts and use them for good. But can he protect an imperial princess and help to neutralize a plot against his grandfather? A clichéd but charming historical mystery that succeeds through the strength of its character interactions and a multilayered story with some surprises amid the stereotypes. Based on a novel by Mitsuru Yuki, illustrated by Sakura Asagi.

SHOOT!

1994. JPN: *Aoki Densetsu Shoot*. AKA: *Blues Legend Shoot*. TV series, movie. DIR: Daisuke Nishio, Akinori Yabe, Takenori Kawata, Masahiro Hosoda, Tatsuo Misawa, Hiroyuki Kadono. SCR: Junji Takegami, Kazuhiko Godo. DES: Shingo Araki. ANI: Shingo Araki, Masami Abe, Toshio Takahashi. MUS: Yusuke Honma. PRD: Toei, Fuji TV. 25 mins. x 58 eps. (TV), 25 mins. (m).

Toshi joins his high school soccer team and is enjoying the training and social life to the full. Then, in the middle of the series, Kubo, the popular captain of the team, has a cardiac arrest on the field and dies. The rest of the series is the story of how Toshi and his teammates cope with this shattering loss (see TOUCH for a baseball drama along the same lines). The short film of the same title, also released in 1994, brings back many memories for the team members of their match against a squad from Germany, including an old friend of Kubo's. Based on the 1990 *Shonen Sunday* manga by Tsukasa Oshima.

SHOOTFIGHTER TEKKEN *

2003. JPN: *Koko Tekken-den Tough*. AKA: *High School Exciting Story: Tough*. Video. DIR: Yukio Nishimoto. SCR: Jin Munesue. DES: Fumitomo Kizaki. ANI: Yasuo Hasegawa. MUS: N/C. PRD: AIC, Spike. 45 mins. x 3 eps.

Iron Kiba, champion of the World Pro Wrestling circuit, is tough. Miyazawa is just as tough, if not tougher, and the pair have a long history in the dark and criminal underbelly of the pro wrestling scene. Miyazawa's boy Kiichi looks harmless, but with Dad's training and support from other fighters he becomes a master of the Nanshin Shadow style. Eventually Kiichi and Kiba will face each other in the ring, but not before you've watched three episodes of piledriver punches, bodyslams to the concrete, crushed bones, and buckets of gore. Yet another tournament series, but with no dragonballs, cute critters, or underwear jokes—instead it's a return to

Japanese professional wrestling, which has been an obsession with TV audiences ever since the earliest days of TV, when programmers fell in love with the sport because it only required one camera above the ring. The series also attempts to inject comedy, with stumbling results. Based on a manga by Tetsuya Saruwatari, who gave us even more ludicrous fighting in STORY OF RIKI. Inadvertently or otherwise, the English-language release title implies a nonexistent link with TEKKEN. **●**V

SHOTARO ISHINOMORI'S HISTORICAL ADVENTURES

1991. JPN: *Ishinomori Shotaro no Rekishi Adventure*. Video. DIR: Fuyu Kanno, Wara Sato. SCR: Masayuki Oiwa DES: Shotaro Ishinomori. ANI: N/C. MUS: N/C. PRD: Media Design. 50 mins. x 2 eps.

A two-part video series in which Dr. Teng (a researcher at the Time Institute) and his faithul *kappa* (water sprite) assistant Pasuke travel through time, first to the Battle of Sekigahara (1600) and then to the fourth Battle of Kawanakajima (1561). In the second installment, they then look in on the last stand of the Japanese underdog hero Yoshitsune in Hiraizumi (1189) and then, after spending so much time on the Genpei War, suddenly leap several centuries into the future, to cover the first time Nobunaga Oda used firearms in battle, at Nagashino (1575, see also YOTODEN). A mixture of live action and anime, described by Japanese sources as a "documentary with a touch of story," and presumably related in some way to Shotaro Ishinomori's multivolume manga history of Japan.

SHOWA STORY

2010. JPN: *Showa Monogatari*. TV series. DIR: Mitsuhiro Togo (eps. 1–4), Hiroshi Kugimiya (eps. 5–13). SCR: Yasushi Hirano, Miho Maruo, Naruhisa Arakawa, Sukehiro Tomita. DES: Tatsuo Yanagino, Takeshi Waki. ANI: Tatsuo Yanagino. MUS: Gido Hayashi. PRD: WAO! World, THINK Corporation. 25 mins. x 13 eps. (TV), 100 mins. (m).

It is 1964: the year of the Tokyo Olympics. The Yamazakis are an ordinary family living in the capital, where father Yuzo owns a small machine shop making parts for various industries with one employee. Oldest son Yoshi is at college, teenage daugh-

ter Kanoko is boy-crazy, and youngest son Kohei, the show's narrator, is a boisterous but kind-hearted kid. Mother stays at home and looks after the house, helped by Grandmother, who lives with them. Through Kohei's eyes we see the family's financial scrimping and saving, the everyday domestic details, and what family life was like in a year that brought huge excitement to Tokyo, but not much change to the business of getting by. A nicely detailed slice of Showa-period nostalgia, put into context by showing video clips and photos of the modern-day locations, timeshifting back to photos of the same places shot in 1964, and then animating them. Some sources list this as a 2011 series, since the first episode was broadcast only two days before the end of 2010. A movie version in 2011, *Showa Monogatari: Gekijo-ban*, carried the action up to the Tokyo Olympics themselves in October 1964. Compare to FROM UP ON POPPY HILL, which draws on a similar historical setting, and quite possibly for the same reason—the then-recent Japanese box office success of the three live-action nostalgia movies that began with *Always: Sunset on Third Street* (2005).

SHOYONOID MAKOTO-CHAN

1998. Video. DIR: Sai Imazaki. SCR: Sassai Ima. DES: Sassai Ima. ANI: Sai Imazaki. MUS: N/C. PRD: JVD. 30 mins. x 2 eps.

A deceased superheroine is brought back from the dead when her inventor father combines her with the body of an underage-seeming android. Then she takes her clothes off. An early entry in the notorious VANILLA SERIES. **Ⓝ**

SHRINE OF THE MORNING MIST *

2002. JPN: *Asagiri no Miko*. AKA: *Priestess of the Morning Mist; Maidens of the Morning Mist*. TV series. DIR: Yuji Moriyama. SCR: Ryoe Tsukimura. DES: Shoko Nakamoto. ANI: Yuji Moriyama. MUS: Tsuneyoshi Saito. PRD: Chaos Project. 12 mins. x 26 eps.

Teenager Tadahiro Amatsu has different colored eyes—one brown, one light hazel. One conceals a dark secret, which sets masked sorcerer Michimune Ayatachi and his band of demonic aides chasing after Tadahiro. The eye is linked to the spirit world, and what it sees there is able to cross into the human world. Michimune wants to use Tadahiro to bring the

Monster God into the world of men; meanwhile he'll settle for unleashing lesser monsters on mankind. But just when you need a spiritual defender, a whole harem of them turn up. Tadahiro's cousin, klutzy-but-kind trainee priestess Yuzu Hieda recruits four school friends to a shrine maiden defense force, and makes her older sister Kurako their trainer. Now the town has a fighting team to make them safe from demonic attack, and Tadahiro has a cousin who has had a crush on him since they were children, plus four of her friends, clogging up his life and our screen. The short run-time and monster-of-the-week format leaves little room for character development or plot innovation, but it's cute and repetitive enough to sell to both lovers of TENCHI MUYO! clones and those who go misty-eyed at the sight of traditionally dressed shrine maidens. Based on Hiroki Ukawa's manga, serialized in *Young King Ours*, the show was "conceived" by Ryoe Tsukimura, whose previous ideas have included the far superior EL HAZARD.

SHUFFLE!
2005. TV series. DIR: Naoto Hosoda. SCR: Katsuhiko Takayama, Katsumi Hasegawa, Masashi Suzuki. DES: Eiji Hirayama, Aoi Nishimata, Hiro Suzuhira. ANI: Eiji Hirayama. MUS: Kazuhiko Sawaguchi, Minoru Maruo. PRD: Shuffle! Media Partners. 24 mins. x 24 eps.
The gateways to the kingdoms of gods and demons are opened and can't be closed. In an ordinary suburb, the King of the Gods and his family move in on one side of the Tsuchimi family home, the King of the Demons and his family on the other. The teenage daughters of these two households set their sights on the human boy next door. Apparently they both fell in love with him years ago and have always wanted the chance to be near him, so the sudden availability of real estate in the human world is heaven-sent. But Rin already has a girl living with him—a childhood friend who is also in love with him. The three love rivals and their object all go to the same high school and … well, you can fill in the rest for

yourself. We have to admit we never expected a high concept that melds UROTSUKIDOJI with URUSEI YATSURA, but sadly that's *Shuffle*'s only claim to originality.

Shuffle! is a 2005 TV series based on a pornographic visual novel (ARGOT AND JARGON) by Navel, about a world in which gods, humans, and demons coexist. A familiar harem set-up (ROMANCE AND DRAMA), trope-heavy and predictable—could there be any way to squeeze more airtime and sponsorship money out of it? Taking a leaf from the EVANGELION primer on how to craft new money from used goods, the *Shuffle!* Media Partners got director Hosoda and his crew to recut the 24-episode series into a 12-episode recap with just one new episode thrown in at the end to lure fans on. Focusing on the story of each of the five individual girl characters, the "new" show aired in 2007.

SHUGO CHARA! *
2007. TV series. DIR: Kenji Yasuda. SCR: Michiru Shimada, Kazuhiko Inukai, Makoto Nakamura, Ryunosuke Kingetsu, Tomoko Koyama, Kenji Yasuda. DES: Fumihide Sai, Toshiyuki Sakae. ANI: Noritomo Hattori, Hiromi Masuda, Yukie Suzuki, Kazuhisa Kosuge. MUS: Di'LL. PRD: Satelight, Pony Canyon, TV Tokyo, TV Tokyo, Media Net. 24 mins. x 52 eps. (TV1), 24 mins. x 52 eps. (TV2), 24 mins. x 25 eps. (TV3).
Every child carries in its heart an egg containing the self he or she dreams of being. Resentment and failure can cause those eggs to become x-eggs, bringers of trouble and chaos. Amu is a shy girl who becomes a Guardian, dedicated to capturing x-eggs and restoring them to their original positive form. She does this with help from her own dream selves, alter egos (or Shugo Charas) called Dia, Ran, Miki, and Su. But Amu is only a sixth-grader, and ranged against her is the mighty Easter Corporation, whose one aim seems to be ensuring the spread of x-eggs, destroying childrens' self-belief and self-confidence, and making them dependent on commercial goods and superficial relationships.

The show's ambition goes beyond its budget; the plot and pacing are uneven, the design generic, the animation all over the scale from superb to almost unwatchable. But the concept and characters, based on Peach-Pit's 2006 manga, were strong enough to earn it another two TV seasons. *Shugo Chara! Doki!* aired in 2006 from the same crew and was followed in 2009 by *Shugo Chara! Party!*, which mixed short animated stories with appearances by the voice actresses who made up the *Shugo Chara Egg!* idol singer group. Carrying on the theme of secret dreams, the show also included an open audition for an unsigned elementary or junior high school-aged singer to join the group. The animated shorts were a series entitled *Shugo Chara! Dokki Doki!*, described as a "power-up" of *Shugo Chara! Doki!*, and a super-deformed comedy series called *Shugo Chara Pucchi Puchi!*

SHURA NO TOKI *
2004. JPN: *Mutsu Enmei-ryu Gaiden Shura no Toki*. AKA: *Untold Tales of the Mutsu Enmei School: Agent of Chaos*. TV series. DIR: Shin Misawa. SCR: Junji Takegami. DES: Takehiro Hamatsu. ANI: Takehiro Hamatsu. MUS: Yutaka Minobe (Wave Master). PRD: Studio Comet, Marvelous Music Publishing, Media Factory, Sotsueizo, TV Tokyo. 25 mins. x 26 eps.
The Mutsu clan practices an ancient unarmed martial art in Edo in the early 1600s. Big brother Yakumo crosses the path of swordmasters Musashi Miyamoto and Jubei Yagyu, and of young nobleman Kisshoumaru. Kisshoumaru is really a girl, Shiori, imitating a boy to protect the family inheritance, in the style of YOTODEN and KAI DOH MARU. An evil uncle wants "him" out of the way, and when Yakumo becomes "his" bodyguard the situation threatens to become even more complicated. Later episodes continue with later generations of the Mutsu clan, in the same family-saga style as JOJO'S BIZARRE ADVENTURES. Consequently, after episode 8 it focuses more on Iori, Musashi's young pupil, and his sometime rival Takato (a Mutsu clan member), thereby allowing the action to move 20 years further on, and

engineer a number of new conflicts with a number of new swordsmen from history and legend.

The action leaps ahead again, this time to the Meiji Restoration of the 19th century for the final tale, which features yet another descendant of the Mutsu clan, Izumi, who is caught up with the conflicts of the Shinsengumi in Kyoto—compare to **PEACEMAKER KUROGANE**. We are thus able to see a number of other famous figures, including Ryoma Sakamoto, in the final struggle over the supremacy of the samurai, which would eventually lead to the fall of the shogunate and the establishment of modern Japan.

Based on a manga by Masatoshi Kawahara in *Shonen Magazine*, it's easy to see *SnT*'s appeal—its dynasty of stubbly faced, good-hearted heroes sits astride samurai history like the Yagyu clan (see **NINJA SCROLL**), benefiting from action-packed careers with a vague nod toward educational storylines.

SHURATO

1989. JPN: *Tenku Senki Shurato*. AKA: *Heavenly Chronicle Shurato*. TV series, video. DIR: Mizuho Nishikubo, Takao Koyama, Ippei Kuri, Kazuhiro Mori, Shinji Takahashi, Satoshi Okada, Kiyoshi Murayama, Koji Masunari. SCR: Mayori Sekijima, Takao Koyama, Akinori Endo, Go Mihara. DES: Matsuri Okada, Masaki Nakao, Ammonite, Torao Arai. ANI: Masaki Nakao, Nobuyoshi Habara, Kenichi Okazaki. MUS: Hiroya Watanabe. PRD: Tatsunoko, TV Tokyo. 25 mins. x 36 eps. (TV), 30 mins. x 6 eps. (v).

Close friends Shurato and Gai are fighting in a martial arts tournament in modern-day Tokyo when they are hauled into another dimension and find that they have new powers bestowed by Asian gods and by *shakti*, animal totems with strange powers of their own. Shurato is one of the Eight Warriors of Vishnu, whose celestial kingdom is under threat of invasion from Asura. Gai is also one of these mystic warriors, but when Vishnu's treacherous general, Indra, turns the goddess into a statue and blames Shurato, Gai sides with Indra. The two close friends are now mortal enemies. Branded a traitor, can Shurato save Vishnu, her kingdom, and his friend? Can the two get back to their own lives? The series ended tragically, but six further

episodes were released on video in 1991 and 1992, extending the story.

Though possessing a Hindu-mythos setting redolent of **RG VEDA**, this is a series aimed squarely at the teenage boy market; a decade on, transforming the shakti into flying skateboards looks like a mistake. With the guiding hand of Tatsunoko's legendary producer Ippei Kuri on the tiller, *Shurato* delivers the goods. It was the number-one series in Japan in its year of release.

SHUSAKU *

1999. JPN: *Shusaku*. AKA: *Shameful*. Video. DIR: Jun Fukuda. SCR: Sakura Momoi. DES: Toshihide Masudate. ANI: Toshihide Masudate. MUS: N/C. PRD: Pink Pineapple, KSS. 30 mins. x 3 eps.

Secret lusts abound in a music school, where the teacher instructs his students in more than just carrying a tune. Based on a computer game by "Elf," and shamefully similar to **WAKE UP ARIA**. **N**

SHUTENDOJI *

1989. AKA: *Star Hand Kid; Star Demon; Shuten Doji*. Video. DIR: Junji Nishimura, Masaaki Sudo, Jun Kawagoe. SCR: Masashi Sogo. DES: Satoshi Hirayama. ANI: Hideyuki Motohashi. MUS: Fumitaka Anzai. PRD: Dynamic Planning, Studio Signal. 50 mins. x 4 eps.

Ryuichi Shiba is visiting the temple of his father's friend with his fiancée Kyoko in order to announce to his ancestors his intention to marry when two giant ogres crash through the space-time continuum. One of them is carrying a baby in his mouth, leaving it with them and promising to return in 15 years. Jiro Shutendo ("sent from heaven"), as they call the child, grows up to be a fine young man (albeit one who casts a giant, horned shadow) and is reluctant to return to his real parents when the allotted time expires.

Based on Go Nagai's 1977 manga for *Shonen Magazine*, *Shutendoji* replays the creator's earlier **DEVILMAN** but with solely Japanese mythical references. Drawing on one of the **JAPANESE FOLK TALES** in which Minamoto no Yorimitsu and several other warriors defeated an ogre who abducted a local maid, *Shutendoji* begins with two monsters fighting across time, crashing from medieval Kyoto, past the mystified

crew of a spaceship, before ending up in modern Japan. The first two episodes are concerned with Jiro's attempts to come to terms with his heritage and fight off his supernatural relatives. His teacher, possessed by evil, kidnaps Jiro's girlfriend, Miyuki, intending to use her as a sacrifice to open the interdimensional barrier that holds back the demons. He must also kill off the evil monk Jawanbo, whose son swears vengeance. By this point, however, Jiro has been thrown forward to the year 2100. He arrives in time to save the Iron Kaiser, a war cyborg sent on a suicide mission to protect its ship, the Alfard. Captain Persis Mahmoud (a **CUTEY HONEY** look-alike) promises to help return Jiro to his own time, a plan delayed by the revelation that Iron Kaiser is Jawanbo's son, whose life has been prolonged for decades with cybernetic implants, as he waits for the chance to avenge his father's death. For the finale, Jiro and his band must fight their way out of hell, while his adoptive human mother goes slowly insane, decorating the walls of her cell with pictures of hell, until Jiro's adoptive father destroys the pictures and saves Jiro's life. One of the better adaptations of Nagai's work, with a clever script, chilling visuals, and inspired plot twists that bridge time and space.

The original Shutendoji is a figure from medieval Japanese mythology: an ogre bested in combat by a famous samurai, who died at the foot of Mount Oe, and is still celebrated in a local festival each October. The name can be translated as "An Unearthly Child." See also **KAI DOH MARU** and **OTOGI ZOSHI**, which approach the same tale from a very different direction. **LNV**

SIAMESE CAT

2001. JPN: *Siam Cat*. AKA: *Siam Neko; Siam Neko: First Mission*. Movie. DIR: Masahiro Hosoda. SCR: Hiroshi Onogi. DES: Shingo Araki, Michi Himeno. ANI: Masuo Nakayama. MUS: Fujimaru Yoshino. PRD: Buyu. 90 mins.

Jun and Naomi are two pretty disc-jockeys who comprise "Siamese Cat," a secret government antiterrorist rapid-response team. Jun handles guns and martial arts, Naomi does communications and demolitions, while Mr. Kuritagachi, vice-president of the Cabinet Research Room, is their government contact. When the terrorist

Shunsuke Kaido (AKA Asian Tiger), kidnaps the Japanese prime minister, Siamese Cat goes into action, competing against a rival government's special force, Major Isurugi's Mighty Dog. *Charlie's Angels,* Japanese style, courtesy of **LUPIN III**–creator Monkey Punch.

SIBLING SECRET *
2002. JPN: *Unbalance.* Video. DIR: Juhachi Minamisawa. SCR: Miki Naruse. DES: Haruo Okawara. ANI: Haruo Okawara. MUS: Hiroaki Sano, Takeshi Nishizawa. PRD: Discovery. 30 mins. x 3 eps.
Mika has always had a crush on Jun, ever since he became her elder sister's boyfriend. Imagine, then, her guilty delight when her sister dies, leaving her free to chase Jun herself, and all in the name of mutual condolences. In this entry in the **DISCOVERY SERIES**, Jun initially tries to resist her charms, but eventually succumbs, although it is only then that he reveals that he and Mika's sister used to indulge in prolonged games of bondage and domination, to which he now subjects the shocked Mika. The third episode introduces a new character, Ritsuko, whose father is hoping to use her as leverage in order to take over the restaurant where Mika works. Coincidentally, another *Unbalance* (*DE) was the name of a coffee shop where psychic investigators would meet in early drafts of the script for the famous live-action TV series *Ultra Q.* The mind boggles at what they would have made of this. ●Ⓝ🅥

SIBLING STORIES
2009. JPN: *Gokyodai Monogatari.* TV series. DIR: Tetsuo Yasumi. SCR: Tetsuo Yasumi, Higashi Shimizu, Megumi Shimizu, Yuji Kawahara. DES: Shuichi Seki, Mayumi Okabe. ANI: Masae Otake. MUS: Masae Sagara. PRD: Shin-Ei, MSC. 19 mins. x 32 eps.
The Jinushi twins are elementary school kids who live in one of Tokyo's lower-class districts. Their interactions with the colorful characters of their neighborhood give a humorous picture of everyday life in a modern city. Based on Tetsu Adachi's award-winning 999 manga *Baka-Kyodai* (*Stupid Siblings.*)

SIGN OF THE OTAKU
1994. JPN: *Otaku no Seiza.* AKA: *Fanboy Constellation; An Adventure in the Otaku Galaxy.* Video. DIR: Atsuo Isamu. SCR: Masashi Sogo. DES: Hisashi Eguchi, Noboru Furuse, Hiroshi Motomiya. ANI: Tatsuo Okano. MUS: Aurora 5. PRD: KSS. 30 mins. x 2 eps.
A new idol group, the Aurora Girls, are the greatest threat to humankind ever known. They plan to wipe out civilization by spreading the otaku disease, a deadly virus that transforms ordinary people into hard-core anime fans. Packed with anime parodies, including affectionate homages to **OTAKU NO VIDEO**, this was based on an NES game that featured designs from Hisashi Eguchi and Hiroshi Motomiya, better known for **ROUJIN Z** and **MY SKY**.

SILENT MÖBIUS *
1991. Movie, TV series. DIR: Kazuo Tomizawa, Michitaka Kikuchi, Hideki Tonokatsu, Kunitoshi Okajima. SCR: Michitaka Kikuchi, Kei Shigema, Hiroyuki Kawasaki, Kenichi Kanemaki, Nami Narita, Katsuhiko Takayama. DES: Kia Asamiya (pseudonym for Michitaka Kikuchi), Michitaka Kikuchi, Yasuhiro Moriki, Yutaka Izubuchi, Masaki Tanaka. ANI: Michitaka Kikuchi, Masahide Yanasawa, Kunihiro Abe, Tetsuro Aoki, Nobuyuki Kitajima, Moriyasu Taniguchi. MUS: Kaoru Wada. PRD: AIC, Radix, TV Tokyo. 54 mins., 60 mins. (m), 25 mins. x 26 eps. (TV).
In the year 2028, Tokyo is overcrowded, polluted, and (unlike present-day Tokyo) occasionally attacked by demonic entities known as the Lucifer Hawks, who are using Japan's luckless capital as an interdimensional portal. Hence the formation of the Attacked Mystification Police Department, a unit designed to prevent the Lucifer Hawks from causing havoc. In a set-up not dissimilar to **BUBBLEGUM CRISIS**, the tough half-human leader Rally Cheyenne heads a group of uniformed beauties—cybernetic medium Lebia Maverick, Australian cyborg Kiddy Phenil, old-school Japanese mystic Nami Yamigumo, psychic dispatcher Yuki Saiko, and newest recruit Katsumi Liqueur, daughter of the arch-mage Gigelf and wielder of his sword Grospoliner. In mixing a cyberpunk look with occult imagery, *SM: The Motion Picture* is a visual feast. This is a dark, brooding anime aimed at an audience familiar with Kia Asamiya's original 1988 manga in *Comic Comp,* an assumption that may leave the uninitiated viewer feeling confused.

Matters are not helped by the extensive use of flashbacks—as with the manga, the narrative pattern is one of introducing "present-day" action in order to bracket a story from a character's past. Thus, for part of the action, Katsumi Liqueur is a hardened Lucifer-Hawk hunter and a member of the team, though several scenes also depict her as a fresh-faced arrival in 2024, unaware of the secrets that will be imparted to her by her dying mother. Though the first film ends in 2028, *SM 2* (1992), released on a triple bill with **WEATHERING CONTINENT** and the second part of **HEROIC LEGEND OF ARSLAN**, continues in 2025, with Katsumi's permission to leave Tokyo revoked, and her reluctant recruitment into the AMPD. Both movies share the same dark, brooding elegance; the ambience is definitely that of *Blade Runner,* with "spinner" vehicles flying through an almost permanently rain-swept Tokyo hiding terrors under its shiny carapace. They are triumphs of mood and atmosphere, with little in the way of narrative variety but lashings of cyber-noir style. There was also a 54-minute *Making of SM* video in the same year—*SM* was *very* popular in the Japanese fan community, which lapped up not only the manga and movies, but several novels, including a series of spin-offs set in the 19th century (during the last invasion of the Lucifer Hawks), a computer game from Gainax, and a series of CD dramas.

As studios scrambled for TV product in the wake of the success of **EVANGELION**, many old favorites were snapped up. *SM* was one of them, but the opportunity to reset to zero and remake the series was somewhat defeated by the low budgets of 1990s TV. Though 13 hours of running time allow for better fleshing-out of character backgrounds, the TV version disappointingly dumps much of the movies' style without adding much substance. Its animation and scripting are trite and undistinguished, limited time and budget watering down the impressive look of manga and movies; even the terrifying Lucifer Hawks now look more **ULTRAMAN** than Asamiya.

SILENT SERVICE, THE *
1995. JPN: *Chinmoku no Kantai.* TV special, video. DIR: Ryosuke Takahashi, Masamitsu

Hidaka, Koji Koshigoe. scr: Soji Yoshikawa, Akira Nishimori, Takeshi Ashizawa. des: Shigeru Kato, Hisashi Hirai, Kimitoshi Yamane. ani: Shigeru Kato, Keizo Shimizu, Hisashi Hirai. mus: Akira Senju. prd: Sunrise, video Champ, TBS. 100 mins. (TVm), 57 mins., 60 mins. (v).

As part of the surrender terms set at the end of WWII, Japan does not have an army so much as a "Defense Force." However, various interests have been developing the Seabat—a secret nuclear submarine created by both U.S. and Japanese ingenuity. It's on the cutting edge of military technology, armed with 50 of the most powerful nuclear weapons ever developed, manned by a crew believed to be dead, and led by Shiro Kaieda, an officer so devoted to the principle of peace that he will go to any lengths to uphold it. His ideas, however, differ somewhat from his superiors', as he steals the Seabat, renames it Yamato (see **Star Blazers**), and declares it to be an independent nation. Now former Japanese comrades and U.S. allies alike are equally determined to capture or destroy them. Kaieda is playing for the ultimate prize, by the rules he learned from America, with the most powerful weapon in the world to back him up.

Based on Kaiji Kawaguchi's controversial 1988 manga in *Comic Morning, SS* asked pertinent questions about Japan's role in the modern world, when, during the bubble economy of the 1980s, it was a major player on the world stage but hamstrung and embarrassed by its reliance on the unpredictable U.S. for defense (see **Sea of the Ticonderoga** and **Papa Mama Bye-Bye**). The anime version, however, was made after a succession of events that diluted the stirring message of the original, commencing with the collapse of the Soviet Union. After the Gulf War, from which the resource-hungry Japan benefited at the expense of other nations' soldiers, Japan was "invited" to join policing actions in Cambodia, negating much of the impact of the postwar restrictions on sending troops abroad. The war in the Balkans (a heavy influence on **Gasaraki**), with its succession of broken truces and pyrrhic victories, made foreign military involvement look distinctly unappealing. Accordingly, the pacifist movement in Japan now had two factions, those who

opposed war itself on moral grounds (see **Barefoot Gen**) and a growing number who simply couldn't see the point in wasting any money on it when the U.S. was doing such a fine job on its own. In other words, by the time *SS* got its premier as a TV movie on TBS, it had already been overtaken by history—though still a chilling controversy redolent of **Wartime Anime**, it was less of an anti-American manifesto than a modern-day **Deep Blue Fleet**—the opportunity to set up war-gaming scenarios between nominally friendly nations. Two further installments went straight to video but were not released abroad. Two other Kawaguchi manga, **Nine Love Stories** and **Hard and Loose**, were also adapted for anime. The flagship of the U.S. 7th Fleet, the Carl Vinson, would appear again in **Space Family Carlvinson**.

SILVER FANG

1986. jpn: *Ginga: Nagareboshi Gin*. aka: *Silver Tooth: Shooting Star Silver*. TV series. dir: Tomoharu Katsumata, Yugo Serikawa, Kazumasa Horikawa, Nobutaka Nishizawa, Masayuki Akehi, Tatsuo Higashino. scr: Mitsuru Majima, Kenji Terada. des: Joji Yanagise. ani: Koji Yanagise, Masaharu Endo, Tetsuro Aoki. mus: Goro Omi. prd: Toei, TV Asahi. 25 mins. x 21 eps., 25 mins. x 26? eps. (Weed). Gin, a beautiful dog with a silver-white coat, is third in a line of attack dogs trained by their master Gobei to fight with Aka Kabuto, the fearsome bear of the mountain. While hunting with Gobei, Gin meets his father, Riki, now the amnesiac leader of a pack of wild dogs determined to kill Aka Kabuto. The wild Riki and the domesticated Gin join forces and go in search of other brave dogs. Yoshihiro Takahashi's manga from *Shonen Jump* ran for several years, but the anime didn't do as well as other shaggy-dog tales like **Call of the Wild**.

Legend of the Silver Fang: Weed (2005) draws inspiration from **Kimba the White Lion**. Fourteen years after Gin's heroic battle with the great bear, another beast invades the peaceful valley where the dogs have been living. Gin's pregnant mate escapes, guarded by the fierce GB, a former hench-dog of Gin's who reveals a cruel streak in exile. Gin's son Weed endures torment at the paws of GB, until one fateful day when he stands up for himself

and exhibits some of the heroic spirit that made his father famous.

SILVER MAN

1991. jpn: *Gin no Otoko*. Video. dir: Koichi Ishiguro. scr: Keiji Michiyoshi. des: Hidetoshi Omori. ani: Hidetoshi Omori. mus: N/C. prd: JC Staff. 50 mins.

Nineteen-year-old university student Yuji decides to become a "host" at a city bar where lonely women will pay a cover charge for the pleasure of his company. He soon becomes a full-fledged male prostitute, claiming all the while that this is all an experiment in order to "better understand the hearts of women." Based on a minor manga in *Comic Morning* by **Climbing on a Cloud**-creator Hiroshi Motomiya, this predated the similar **Gigolo** by two years. **Ⓝ**

SILVER SPOON *

2013. jpn: *Gin no Saji*. TV series. dir: Tomohiko Ito, Kotomi Deai. scr: Taku Kishimoto. des: Jun Nakai. ani: Masako Matsumoto, Tomoko Suda, Atsushi Yamamoto, Shinichi Suzuki. mus: Shusei Murai. prd: A-1 Pictures. 24 mins. x 11 eps. (TV1), 24 mins. x 11 eps. (TV2).

Flunking the exams for his first-choice high school, Yugo decides to quit his native Sapporo and go for what first appears to be an easy option, taking a place out in the sticks at Yezo Agricultural High School. However, he is soon jolted out of his urban complacency by the discovery that his cosseted city-boy existence still relies on a panoply of rustic expertise—despite seeing himself on arrival as the cool kid in a class of yokels, he is soon overawed by the aspirations of would-be veterinarians, horse-breeders, and agronomists.

An unlikely follow-up to her **Fullmetal Alchemist**, Hiromu Arakawa's *Silver Spoon* rode on its bestselling predecessor's coattails, and draws deeply on the author's early life on a Hokkaido dairy farm. Arakawa enjoyed double luck—not only as the sure thing whose previous manga had topped the charts, but as the creator of a new title that began running mere weeks after the disastrous Great East Japan Earthquake in 2011. With northern Honshu a no-go area, the Japanese domestic travel industry swiftly began pushing Hokkaido as a safe and inviting tourist destination (see also

Francesca), sweeping the *Silver Spoon* manga up in the zeitgeist and propelling it swiftly to sales above a million.

Arakawa's original allegorizes the slacker mentality so popular with modern Japanese youth, matching it with a traditional and good-hearted assertion that kindness to others and a circle of friends is enough to get anyone through life with a smile on their face. In particular, we might note the use of the term Yezo for Yugo's school, invoking the samurai-era name of the island and old-world notions of Hokkaido as Japan's great cowboy frontier. The sharp-eyed viewer might also note a certain fresh-faced, apple-cheeked glorification of simple hard work and country living, denying much of the materialism of metropolitan Japan, as well as an arch willingness to confront mallrats with the visceral origins of the burgers on their plates. Although this is easily filed with the **Everyday Anime**, rural Hokkaido is exotic enough to function as a form of escapism all of its own, particularly for teenage viewers trapped in the pressure cooker of cram schools and mock examinations. A live-action movie followed in 2014.

SIMOUN *
2006. JPN: *Shimun*. TV series. DIR: Junji Nishimura. SCR: Akatsuki Yamatoya, Fukyoshi Oyamada, Junji Nishimura, Mari Okada. DES: Asako Nishida, Jin Seon Song, Shichiro Kobayashi. ANI: Asako Nishida. MUS: Toshihiko Sahashi. PRD: Studio DEEN, Bandai Visual, Sotsu Agency. 25 mins. x 26 eps.
Imagine a world in which everyone is born female and chooses a gender at the age of 17. The peaceful theocracy of Kyukoku is guarded by two-pilot flying machines known as Simoun. They can only be piloted by pairs of young girls who haven't yet chosen their sex, who are collectively known as Sibyllae. Despite their innocence, these girls can combine to activate a terrifying power that can destroy a huge number of enemies at once. When a powerful neighbor, industrialized Shokoku, attacks, the Sibyllae are granted exemption from gender-choosing for as long as they keep flying—or survive. But this leads to conflict in the ranks as Sibyllae lose beloved partners, have to choose new ones, and delay settling into their chosen adult roles. A newish excuse for lots of girl-

girl kissing (which is apparently essential to combat bonding—tell *that* to the Marines!) makes for a pretty girls'-love series with some interesting action sequences, like **Virgin Fleet** but with all the sexual conflicts within the ranks.

SIN IN THE RAIN
2006. Video. DIR: Hitoshi Haga. SCR: Yoshitaka Yano. DES: Kyuma Oshita, Noriko Oya. ANI: Koichi Hashimoto. MUS: N/C. PRD: Mook Animation, ES Entertainment. 22 mins.
Yui is terrified. She wanders the streets of the city, shocked and confused, until a stranger steps in. He tells her he's a private investigator. She tells him a strange tale of how she woke up and found herself alone with the body of her closest friend and confidante, her psychiatrist. It brought back memories of the tragedy of her childhood, when her parents were killed, and made her afraid that the police would make her the prime suspect in this new killing. A promising beginning is cut off short in a single episode; apparently more were planned but the sponsors pulled the plug. Based on a radio drama series by producer, director, and writer Yoshitaka Yano. **LV**

SIN SORORITY *
2002. JPN: *Utsukushii Emonotachi no Gakuen*. AKA: *School of Beautiful Games; Bigaku*. DIR: Yuji Uchida. SCR: Hideo Ura. DES: Shigenori Kurii. ANI: Haruto Fuyurai. MUS: Kenichi Kunishima. PRD: Mink, Milky, Museum Pictures. 30 mins. x 2 eps.
Shygirl Asuna has transferred to a select private school and is desperate to be accepted into its exclusive sorority. Student president Yurika, who prefers to be addressed as "Mistress," will only let her join if she agrees to a perverted sexual initiation ritual. Asuna doesn't like being raped at first but then finds she does, in an erotic anime based on the game by Mink. The title is sometimes contracted as Bigaku—which uses the characters for "Beautiful" and "School," but uses their alternate pronunciations. **LNV**

SIN: THE MOVIE *
2001. Video. DIR: Yasunori Urata. SCR: Carl Macek. DES: Dan Kongoji, Makoto Kobayashi. ANI: Dan Kongoji. MUS: Masamichi Amano. PRD: ADV Films, Phoenix Entertainment. 60 mins.

Late in the 21st century, Freeport is plagued by crime and corruption. Crack paramilitary unit HARDCORPS is there to sort it out. Hardman Colonel John Blade comes up against an enemy worthy of his steel in his latest case. Ruthless mogul Elixis Sinclaire, founder of multimillion-dollar biotechnology corporation SinTEK, has recently been developing something really big; at the same time, a wave of kidnappings in the city is baffling the regular law enforcement service. A U.S.-Japanese coproduction with two different subtitle scripts giving two story lines, this is an interesting experiment that's at least an effort to do something new with DVD's many possibilities. The original *Sin* computer game was bundled onto the same DVD.

SINDBAD THE SAILOR *
1962. JPN: *Arabian Night Sindbad no Boken*. AKA: *Arabian Night Sindbad Adventure*. Movie. DIR: Taiji Yabushita, Yoshio Kuroda. SCR: Osamu Tezuka, Morio Kita. DES: Yasuo Otsuka. ANI: Sanae Yamamoto. MUS: Isao Tomita, Masao Yoneyama. PRD: Toei. 81 mins.
Sindbad and his friend Ali meet an old man on the seashore who gives them the map to an island of treasure. They sail off in search of it but are imprisoned in one of the countries they visit. Released through the efforts of the beautiful Princess Samir, they head off once more but are pursued by the evil Grand Vizier, who wants the treasure for himself.

This Toei movie featured some innovative action behind the scenes, as animators pepped up the action sequences with rotoscoping. A human actor was filmed doing numerous martial arts moves, which were then traced by the animators for a fluidity of motion to rival those usually found in Disney films. This is unremarkable today, although worth mentioning solely because of the identity of the actor, a young martial artist called Shinichi "Sonny" Chiba, who would go on to find action-movie stardom (**Golgo 13**). After this popular, big-name feature inspired by **A Thousand and One Nights**, Sindbad would return for the unrelated *Arabian Nights: Sindbad's Adventure* (1975, *Sindbad no Boken*), a 52-episode Nippon Animation series on Fuji TV, directed by Fumio Kurokawa. Though aimed at a younger audience, the series crammed in more of the original, including the stories of Ali Baba (see **ALIBABA'S REVENGE**) and **ALADDIN AND THE WONDERFUL LAMP**.

SINS OF THE SISTERS *

1990. JPN: *Sei Michaela no Gakuen Hyoryuki*. AKA: *Tales of Saint Michaela's Academy*. Video. DIR: Hiroshi Fukutomi, Yorifusa Yamaguchi. SCR: Ryo Motohira, Masaru Yamamoto. DES: Michitaka Kikuchi. ANI: Tetsuro Aoki, Mitsuru Takanashi. MUS: N/C. PRD: Visual SD, Production Eureka, OL Production. 40 mins. x 2 eps., 45 mins. x 2 eps.

During the ill-fated Children's Crusade of A.D. 1212, Pope Innocent III double-crosses the loyal Christian soldiers and sells them to African slavers. Distraught at his betrayal by the very church he is sworn to serve, the children's leader, Hans, throws himself into the sea. Centuries later, he is reincarnated as a hermaphrodite in a convent school, where he seduces the girls and leads them in a bloody revolt against the oppressive nuns. Seizing control of the nuns' time tunnel, Hans (now called Aiko) and his/her chums travel back to Japan's Amakusa Rebellion (see **NINJA RESURRECTION**), where they fight the evil Christians. Eventually, all religions are wiped out in a worldwide atheist jihad, and the battle-hardened schoolgirls decide to go back in time again to save the original Hans from the slavers. Meanwhile, Hans/Aiko's lesbian lover, Rika, is brought back to life by Aron/Yuki, an evil nun out to retrieve her kamikaze pilot boyfriend from hell.

An everyday story of multiverse revenge, bare-breasted zombies, mass murder, and kung-fu schoolgirls—prime candidate for the most mind-boggling plot in anime, further mangled on U.S. release when only the final two episodes were released. Thus, the opening half of Hide Takatori's original novel is only discernible through flashbacks and occasional asides, while the complex (and paradoxical) rewrite of both European and Japanese history is buried amid a flurry of leaden dialogue and lesbian titillation. One of the funniest anime since **DRAGON HALF**, albeit unintentionally, with immortal lines like, "I must avert Yuki's evil plot, or else I will evaporate!" **Ⓝ**

SISTER 2: THE ANIMATION

2007. JPN: *Kateikyoshi no Oneesan the Animation: H no Hensachi Agechaimasu*.

AKA: *Home Teacher Miss the Animation: Increasing Deviations of Sex*. Video. DIR: Hideki Araki. SCR: Shinichiro Sawayama. DES: Hideki Araki. ANI: Hideki Araki. MUS: Koichi RX Kobe. PRD: Pink Pineapple. 40 mins. x 2 eps. (v1), 28 mins. x 2 eps. (v2).

Don't you just hate it when you come home for summer vacation after a tough year in school and find that your folks have hired live-in tutors to keep you busy all summer? Except that Toya's tutors are four hot older women and the kind of teaching they plan on doing won't come from textbooks. A sequel, *Kateikyoshi no Onee-san 2 the Animation: H no Hensachi Agechaimasu*, was released in 2010. Based on a game by the Berkshire Yorkshire label of Atelier Kaguya. **Ⓝ**

SISTER PARADISE

2011. JPN: *Imoto Paradise*. AKA: *Little Sister Paradise*. Video. DIR: Yamayana Wasada. SCR: Higashi Sonoman. DES: Masaaki Sakurai. ANI: N/C. MUS: N/C. PRD: Anime Antenna Iinkai, Labi Target, Mary Jane. 27 mins. x 2 eps. (v1), 20 mins. x 2 eps. (v2).

An otaku brother and his horny little sisters have the hots for each other. The girls appeal to his inner geek by dressing up as his favorite anime and porn game characters. MOONSTONE, which created the porn game on which this is based, obviously hit a winning formula because the two-part *Imoto Paradise 2* followed in 2012. **Ⓝ**

SISTER PRINCESS *

2001. TV series. DIR: Kiyoshi Ohata, Kazuo Nogami. SCR: Masaharu Amiya, Koichi Taki. DES: Yasunari Nitta. ANI: Osamu Kobayashi, Yasuo Okawara. MUS: Takayuki Hattori. PRD: Sunrise, TV Tokyo. 25 mins. x 26 eps. (TV1), 25 mins. x 13 eps. (TV2).

Disgraced when he fails his high school entrance exam, Wataru Minakami is sent by his father to a remote island school, where he is the sole boy in a population of 12 pretty girls. A bizarre mixture of **TENCHI MUYO!** and *The Prisoner* ensues.

Ultimately, Wataru's island idyll is disrupted by Akio, a confident, brash individual much like Wataru once was, who arrives with official notification that Wataru has finally gained a place in the educational institution of his choice—in fact, it transpires that Wataru never failed

the examination in the first place. He is consequently faced with a difficult decision: to remain in the solipsistic, anodyne world of his sisterly companions, or to take a chance on improving his lot in life by accepting his place at college. A second TV series, *SP Re Pure* (2002), offered even more of the same.

SISTERS

2008. JPN: *Aneimo*. Video. DIR: P. SCR: Taifu Sekimachi. DES: Tetsuro Aoki. ANI: Shinichi Shigematsu. MUS: N/C. PRD: Flavors Soft, MS Pictures (Milky). 30 mins. x 2 eps.

Takumi already has two childhood friends living next door, sisters who are devoted to each other and to him. Then his father remarries and two new stepsisters move into his house. Based on the porn game *Aneimo 2: Second Stage* by bootUP!, this is entitled *Aneimo Dai 1 Kan* (i.e., *Chapter 1: Square Sisters* in Japan), with the second episode being *Aneimo Dai 2 Kan: Triangle Lovers*. **Ⓝ**

SISTERS OF WELLBER

2007. JPN: *Wellber no Monogatari: Sisters of Wellber*. AKA: *Wellber Story: Sisters of Wellber*. TV series. DIR: Takayuki Hamana. SCR: Atsushi Maekawa. DES: Haruko Iizuka, Nariyuki Takahashi, Yoshinori Iwanaga, Seiko Akashi. ANI: Kenji Isobe, Haruko Iizuka, Nariyuki Takahashi. MUS: Akio Dobashi. PRD: Trans Arts Co., avex entertainment, Production I.G, WELZ Studio. 25 mins. x 13 eps. (TV1), 25 mins. x 13 eps. (TV2).

Princess Rita of Wellber is on the run. She stabbed her bridegroom-to-be, Prince Gernia of Sangatras, and his father wants her head on a platter as the price for not invading her country. Her father thinks the nearby kingdom of Greedom might help them prevent a war and gives Rita a petition to take to the King of Greedom. Accompanied by Tina, a feisty cat burglar on her own mission of revenge, and a machine with a human mind and spirit embedded in its metal casing, Rita sets out on her journey. But when this is accomplished, and she helps Tina look for her parents' killer, Rita learns some unpleasant truths about those she loves.

A second series, airing in 2008, is credited to Boyakasha, who wrote the spin-off manga *Muzzle Loader—Wellber no Monogatari*, but otherwise the senior crew is unchanged. A very slow start, and an uneven plot with enough cheesy twists to keep a buffet going all evening, are somewhat redeemed by decent production values and good action sequences. If you can get over your understandable annoyance at a show that emphasizes the need for its heroine to go "undercover," but then has her travel with a cyber-tank and a gun-toting babe in a bikini top, this is acceptably entertaining. **OV**

6 ANGELS
2002. Movie. DIR: Makoto Kobayashi. SCR: Yasushi Hirano. DES: Hiromi Kato, Makoto Kobayashi. ANI: Shoichi Masuo. MUS: Masamichi Amano. PRD: Eighty One Entertainment, Jpec System Co. Ltd. 100 mins.

In a post-apocalyptic world, the death penalty has been revoked. A nuclear test site in America has been converted into "Neo Purgatory," a prison for the worst criminals. The inmates are revolting, even before the Canyon family takes control of the prison to gain access to radioactive material and use it to wipe the world's slate clean. As the USA and Soviet Union face off, and mankind stands on the brink of extinction, a team of nubile young women in ludicrous outfits get an unexpected chance to save them. Doris, Marilyn, Naomi, and Maki are the "Rose Guard," a special police unit out to protect women from male brutality. Katherine is a stowaway on their patrol helicopter when it is shot down by Don Canyon and crashes into the test site. The Angels must now take down Don and his three psycho sons to save the world, with only their cute little rabbit-shaped pet high-grade war machine to help out. You may be surprised to learn that one of the rewards of success is to take over the Oval Office.

Created by Yasushi Akimoto, this movie lines up an experienced staff that knows its stuff. Given all that experience and talent, an end result like *Six Angels* is both baffling and disappointing—apart from some good CGI, there is very little onscreen to hold one's attention. Of course, the days when shows using scantily clad girl teams as weapons of mass entertainment were the hottest ticket in town are long past, but given the right slant the concept can still fly. Here, it doesn't. A preview/pilot, featuring a larger cast and somewhat different character designs, was prepared

roughly a year before the release of the film, leading to differing release dates in some sources. **ONV**

SKET DANCE *
2011. TV series. DIR: Keiichiro Kawaguchi. SCR: Shinichi Inotsume, Kazuyuki Fudeyasu, Junki Takegami. DES: Manabu Nakatake, Yutaka Mukumoto, Takashi Hiruma. ANI: Manabu Nakatake. MUS: Shuhei Naruse. PRD: Tatsunoko Pro, Dentsu, TV Tokyo. 25 mins. x 27 eps.

One of the easiest ways to meet people, make friends, and fit into high school is to join a school club. Even those who don't fit in anywhere can thrive in the right one (**K-ON**, etc.). Kaimei High's Living Assistance Club, affectionately known as SKET-dan, aims to help students with any of life's problems, big or small. SKET stands for "Support, Kindness, Encouragement, Troubleshoot," and when new student Teppei transfers in he soon finds he needs their help. They're an odd bunch: Bossun is super-bright but only when he's wearing his cap and goggles; Switch talks through a voice synthesizer in his laptop; and Himeko is extremely scary with a hockey stick—and they always seem to create chaos in the course of helping others. An episodic show packed with anime and pop-culture parodies, this is easy to dip in and out of and has plenty of charm.

SKETCHBOOK—FULL COLOR'S
2007. TV series. DIR: Yoshimasa Hiraike. SCR: Mari Okada. DES: Isao Sugimoto, Kenichi Tajiri. ANI: Satoru Fujimoto, Koichiro Ueda, Takashi Shiokawa. MUS: Ken Muramatsu. PRD: Hal Film Maker, AT-X, Mag Garden, Media Factory, Shochiku, TYO. 25 mins. x 13 eps.

Sora Kajiwara is a quiet, shy girl who loves to draw and adores cats. She lives in Fukuoka on the island of Kyushu. She's very easily frightened, often hiding from people or things she finds scary, and alongside this has a highly active imagination that can feed her fears. Even her younger brother, who loves her dearly, finds her childlike persona annoying at times. Although it takes her a long while to make friends and get to know people, joining the Art Club at school helps Sora come out of her shell. Based on Totan Kobako's 2002 manga, this slow, gentle slice of life manga is similar in pace and tone to **ARIA**,

from the same studio, though it lacks any science fiction elements. Six seven-minute "picture dramas" were made as extras for the DVD release.

SKIP BEAT *
2008. TV series. DIR: Kiyoko Sayama. SCR: Mayori Sekijima. DES: Tetsuya Kumagai, Riko Shinohara, Yusuke Takeda, Tomonori Kato. ANI: Mamoru Minakawa, Anna Yamaguchi, Masanori Kato, Beom Seok Hong. MUS: Akifumi Tada. PRD: Hal Film Maker, TV Tokyo. 25 mins. x 25 eps.

Kyoko has been in love with Shotaro since they were children (**ROMANCE AND DRAMA**). When he heads for Tokyo to follow his dream of being an idol singer, she goes with him. She keeps house and works three jobs to support him until his career takes off. Then she hears him talking about her to his manager and discovers that he doesn't care for her at all—she's just useful to have around as a maid and housekeeper. The worm turns with a vengeance: leaving Sho to do his own cooking and laundry, Kyoko changes her hair, her wardrobe, and her whole attitude. She decides to get revenge by becoming a star in her own right. But her journey to success—and revenge—is hampered by Sho's destruction of her ability to feel. Can she regain it and become the performer she was meant to be?

Based on Yoshiki Nakamura's 2002 manga, this series is a worthy successor to shows such as **YAWARA!**, in which a girl struggles to make a life for herself as well as serving her talent. Packed with comedy (including some inspired super-deformed sequences), drama, tension, and deep emotion, it also tells some truths about acting and the actor's life and does justice to all its characters, even charismatic, narcissistic Sho. Fast, funny, insightful, and nonstop entertaining in spite of its merely average animation, this is a series that shows the carbon-steel edge of determination under the sugar-sweet showbiz trappings and leaves you wanting more.

SKULL MAN, THE *
2007. TV series. DIR: Takeshi Mori. SCR: Yutaka Izubuchi, Hiroshi Onogi, Seishi Minakami, Shingo Takeba. DES: Jun Shibata, Yoshinori Sayama (mecha), Yutaka Izubuchi, Shingo Takeba. ANI: Jun Shibata, Toshiyuki Fujisawa,

Fumiaki Kota. MUS: Shiro Sagisu. PRD: BONES, Geneon Entertainment, Ishimori Entertainment, Toyokasei. 25 mins. x 13 eps.

In an alternate Japan, in the era of the Cold War, journalist Hayato Minagami comes back to his hometown to investigate a series of strange murders, allegedly committed by a man in a skull mask. The victims seem to be linked by a new religious cult, a local pharmaceutical company, and creatures that appear less than entirely human. Helped by ambitious young photographer Kiriko, he finds that the cult has links to both their pasts and the Skull Man may not be as he seems.

Shotaro Ishinomori's 1970 manga is the original inspiration for this series, but the image of the skull-masked protagonist was already embedded in Japanese popular culture thanks to the GOLDEN BAT novels of Ichiro Suzuki, illustrated by Takeo Nagamatsu, featuring an Atlantean put into suspended animation in an Egyptian sarcophagus to fight future evil. Ishinomori's character is more ambiguous, and the darkness and complexity of the story make this a truly adult anime, requiring and deserving thought and engagement from the viewer. With several plot threads left open, a follow-up is possible but has sadly not materialized.

SKY COLOR, WATER COLOR

2006. JPN: *Sora no Iro, Mizu no Iro.* AKA: *Color of the Sky, Color of the Water; SoraMizu.* Video. DIR: Banzo Tokita. SCR: Kaoru Takahashi. DES: Kazuya Kuroda, Tony. ANI: Megumi Ishihara, Kazuya Kuroda. MUS: Hiroki Kikuta. PRD: Taki Corp., Himajin Planning. 30 mins. x 2 eps.

Student photographer Hajime persuades transfer student Asa to pose for him and one thing leads to another. His old friend Natsume joins in and the two girls agree to share him, then end up sharing each other. The affair goes on all summer, then the three separate, to meet again at a railway station a year later. Based on a 2004 porn game by Ciel, with characters designed by Tony. ◐

SKY CRAWLERS *

2008. AKA: *The Sky Crawlers.* Movie. DIR: Mamoru Oshii. SCR: Chihiro Ito. DES: Tetsuya Nishio, Atsushi Takeuchi. ANI: Tetsuya Nishio. MUS: Kenji Kawai. PRD: Production I.G, Polygon Pictures. 122 mins.

In a world at peace, humanity's belligerent instincts find an outlet in a televised aerial war managed by competing private corporations. The pilots in the conflict are "Kildren," human clones who can be swiftly replaced with facsimiles in the event of their deaths. One such clone is Kannami, a new arrival at a European airbase, encountering the vestiges of his previous incarnation: former wingmen who accept him without a word, and an ex-lover resentful over the actions of an individual who both was and was not Kannami himself. Meanwhile in the skies overhead, the unseen enemy air ace "The Teacher" defeats all opponents.

Fully aware that they are disposable, the pilots develop odd quirks and self-destructive tendencies, confused by the simultaneous futility and immortality of their condition. It was this allegory of teenage apathy that first drew director Mamoru Oshii to the material of Hiroshi Mori's original 2001 novel, along with the resonances of industrial despondency within the anime business itself. The Kildren give their all in their enterprise, working with bad materials for the superficial praise of uncomprehending foreign dilettantes, at the expense of lives not lived and greater achievements unattempted (compare to similar undertones in BLOOD: THE LAST VAMPIRE). The release of *Sky Crawlers* came accompanied by Oshii's claim that atrophy of talent in the field had left him with no choice but to shoot the aerial combat sequences with computer graphics instead of more traditional animation. To be sure, the aerial combat is gloriously naturalistic, while the flat, affectless depictions of life on the ground, in which limp-haired teenagers mumble existential angst, is both a comment upon and product of the current state of Japanese animation. Mori and Oshii were also involved as consultants in the game *Sky Crawlers: Innocent Aces* for the Nintendo Wii console, while the early-21st-century implications of a life resting on the success of distant conflict can also be perceived in HOWL'S MOVING CASTLE and SUMMER WARS.

Sky Crawlers returns Oshii to his roots as a student watching European cineastes like Chris Marker and Ingmar Bergman, craftsmen who carefully controlled every cut and minutely observed every image. Oshii's movies are sometimes described as minimalist, and *Sky Crawlers* fits that bill. Its extravagance is all in the imagery, that maps multiple layers of meaning onto the characters and settings through focused, intense scripting, sound, and music. There are two ways to enjoy this film: treat it as a detective story requiring the closest possible attention to pick up every tiny clue; or just sit back and let the imagery of those astonishing flight sequences carry you away. ◐

SKY GIRLS

2006. video, TV series. DIR: Yoshiaki Iwasaki. SCR: Takao Yoshioka. DES: Kazunori Iwakura, Shigeki Kimoto, Mika Akitaka, Junya Ishigaki, Haruko Iizuka, Akira Suzuki. ANI: N/C. MUS: Shinkichi Mitsumune. PRD: JC Staff, Konami. 30 mins. (v), 25 mins. x 26 eps. (TV), 4 mins. x 9 eps. (TV2).

In the late 21st century alien artifacts like clusters of mechanical cells appeared. They had the ability to mimic other life forms by clustering together, and they have become formidable fighting monsters, mostly mimicking sea creatures. Humans named them WORMs, or Weapon of Raid Machines (presumably they weren't English-speaking humans), and within two years they had destroyed a third of the population of Earth. The war against the invaders cost humanity half its land mass, remade its geography, and killed most of the male population of military-service age. The majority of the military command are still older men, but the majority of pilots and combat troops are female. Girls and young women are selected for their innate skills and trained to pilot exoskeletons that combine the functions of glider, fighter plane, and mobile armor. A group of girls come together to train as pilots, but alongside their new military duties they have families, hopes, fears, loves, and secrets.

Konami is a content developer and publisher; the company is interested in ideas and images that can be applied to any or all of its products—from slot machines and arcade games to trading cards and health clubs. It's come a long way from its humble beginnings in 1969 as an Osaka jukebox repair and rental store. It wants franchises, and it has built or bought a whole stable from *Castlevania* and YU-GI-OH! to BOMBERMAN and FAR EAST OF EDEN. The Sky Girls concept, created for Konami by Shogo Kumasaka with designs by Humikane Shimada, is nothing new. The forming of an elite team to face high odds with new technology in unpromising circumstances has been the foundation stone of anime from GUNDAM through PATLABOR to VIRGIN FLEET. Cute pre-pubescent or just-pubescent girls form the cornerstone of the team, with some older types thrown in for variety. The fan service (ARGOT AND JARGON), while brief and relatively minimal, is a clear indicator of where this show sees its audience, and for them it works very well.

The *Sky Girls* video introduced the concept and the first three girl pilots in August 2006. It was almost a year before the TV series took off, adding more girls to the mix, followed swiftly by Eishi Ozeki's manga version in young mens' mag *Magazine Z*. The nine *Sky Girls TV DVD Specials* aired on Chiba TV between November 2007 and June 2008 to promote the DVD releases: they combine cute girls and fishing to supposedly comedic effect.

SKY OF THE TOWN TO BE

2010. JPN: *Yosuga no Sora*. AKA: *In Solitude Where We Are Least Alone*. TV series. DIR: Takeo Takahashi. SCR: Naruhisa Arakawa, Hiro Akitsuki, Masaharu Amiya. DES: Kanetoshi Kamimoto, Toshihiro Kohama. ANI: Kanetoshi Kamimoto, Go Suzuki, Kuniaki Masuda, Ryozo Sugiyama, Motoaki Sato. MUS: Bruno Wen-Li, Manabu Miwa. PRD: feel., GANSIS. 25 mins. x 12 eps.
Haruka's sister Sora is his twin, but appears much younger and behaves in a more childish way, partly because her health is fragile and partly because she's lazy and withdrawn. She adores her brother, and when their parents are killed in an accident the two are drawn even closer together. They decide to leave the city and move in with their grandparents in a small rural town where they used to visit for the summer. Old friends and old memories return and Haruka attracts the attention of other girls, but he and Sora find themselves more and more drawn to each other. Their world begins to crumble when their incest is discovered, and they find they may have to live apart. Both the

series and Takashi Mikaze's 2010 manga are based on an adult visual novel (ARGOT AND JARGON) by CUFFS, released for the Windows PC in December 2008. **Ⓝ**

SKYERS 5

1967. TV series. DIR: Seiji Sasaki, Takeshi Yamamoto, Takeshi Kawauchi, Satoshi Murayama. SCR: Norimasa Mayumi, Kenji Nakano. DES: Noboru Kawasaki. ANI: Shuichi Seki. MUS: Ichiro Tsukasa, Sanpei Akasaka. PRD: TCJ, Eiken, TBS. 25 mins. x 12 eps. (TV1), 25 mins. x 26 eps. (TV2).
When he receives a microfilm from a dying man, Shotaro becomes the target of the international arms syndicate Ghost, which kills his mother and sister. He is enlisted in Japanese International Secret Police, along with the agents Captain, Polka, Yuri, and Sampson. With Shotaro as their fifth team member, they form the "Skyers," a group of secret agents with high-tech gadgets, ready for the (almost) impossible mission of defeating Ghost's plans for world domination. Perhaps the earliest anime to introduce a five-strong team of Hero, Rogue, Big Guy, Comic Relief, and Token Girl (see BATTLE OF THE PLANETS). In 1971, the series was remade in color.

SLAM DUNK

1994. TV series, movie, TV specials. DIR: Yoshifumi Hatano, Nobuaki Nishizawa, Hiroyuki Kakudo, Masayuki Akehi, Kazuhisa Takenouchi, Satoshi Nakamura. SCR: Yoshiyuki Suga, Nobuaki Kishima. DES: Masaki Sato, Hidemi Kubo. ANI: Masaki Sato, Yoichi Onishi, Takahiro Kagami. MUS: Takanobu Masuda, BMF. PRD: Toei, TV Asahi. 25 mins. x 130 eps. (TV), 30 mins., 48 mins., 45 mins., 40 mins. (m), 50 mins. x 3 (TVm).
Hanamichi Sakuragi joins Shohoku High School as a senior and falls in love with gorgeous Haruko Akagi. But his romantic record in junior high was terrible—he's been dumped by 50 girls. This could have something to do with the fact that he's tall and skinny, with red hair, an attitude with very little respect for others, and tremendous fighting abilities; but whatever it is, he's determined to overcome his problem and win Haruko. She has a crush on someone else, Kaede Rukawa, who's only crazy about hoops, and when Hanamichi learns that her beloved older brother, Takenori, is captain of the Shohoku

basketball team, he decides to take up the sport. He gradually learns that there's a lot more to basketball than he ever imagined, and as he gets more and more involved with his teammates, he starts to use his strength for something other than fistfights.

Like Takehiko Inoue's original 1990 manga in *Shonen Jump*, SD depicts basketball games with loving realism, but with character development and plotting good enough to interest nonaddicts. More of the same would follow in the movie editions, *Slam Dunk* (1994), *SD: National Championships, Hanamichi Sakuragi* (1994, *SD: Zenkoku Seiha Da! Sakuragi Hanamichi*), *Shohoku's Biggest Crisis: Enter the Hanamichi* (1995, *Shohoku Saida no Kiki: Moero Sakuragi Hanamich*), and *Roaring Basketman Soul! Hanamichi and Ryukawa's Hot Summer* (1995, *Hoero Basketman Damashi: Hanamichi to Ryukawa no Nekki Natsumi*). There were also three "TV specials"—*SD:Decisions at Shohoku Basketball Club* (1994, *Ketsui no Shohoku Basuke-bu*); reedited versions of episodes 40 and 41, *SD: King of the Rebound* (1995, *Rebound-O*); and episodes 62 and 63, *SD Special* (1995).

SLAP UP PARTY

2009. JPN: *Slap Up Party: Arad Senki*. AKA: *Dungeon and Fighter: The Animation*. TV series. DIR: Lee Jin-Hyung, Takahiro Ikezoe. SCR: An Anm-Gyu, Jung Hun-Il, Kazuki Yamanobe, Kim Yun-Jong. DES: Tomokatsu Nagasaku, Hitoshi Tashiro, Satoshi Matsuhira. ANI: Kong Ji-Won, Choi Young-Hee, Hye-Ran Park, Jae Hyung Kim. MUS: Takeshi Nakatsuka. PRD: GK Entertainment, Gonzo. 24 mins. x 26 eps.
Swordsman Baron Abel wanders the world of Arad trying to find a cure for his demon-possessed right arm. This has earned him the title of Demon Swordsman and made him feared and shunned by almost everone he meets. His buxom companion Roxy, invisible to everyone but him, has the same problem and offers to help him find a way round it. She's a former Demon Swordsman whose spirit now resides in a sword. As they travel they meet other fighters and soon accumulate a merry band they call "Party." But destiny has more in mind for Baron than simply adventuring around with a goofy gang of pals. While the scenario undoubtedly echoes many quest/road trip anime from days gone

by—SORCERER HUNTERS, DRAGON BALL, even JOURNEY TO THE WEST—this incarnation originated in Korea, as a popular multi-player fight RPG called *Dungeon & Fighter*. Like all game-based anime, it balances on a thin line between boring dedicated players who'd rather be online choosing their own adventure and confusing new viewers who might go along with the show but have to assimilate a new world with lots of jargon and lots of fighting. This usually results, as here, in a rather meandering, unfocused plot, but the stereotype-packed action and gags keep things moving at a reasonable pace.

SLAVE DOLL: MAID TO ORDER *

2000. JPN: *Kowaremono Fragile Hearts*. Video. DIR: Kaoru Tomioka. SCR: N/C. DES: Noriyasu Takeuchi. ANI: Jiro Makigata. MUS: N/C. PRD: Green Bunny, Beam Entertainment. 25 mins. x 3 eps. (v1, *Fragile Hearts*), 25 mins. x 2 eps. (v2, *Kowaremono II*).
Aki is an expensive android, whose programming obliges her to do anything and everything her master demands. After subjecting her to a series of public humiliations, her owner sends her off to buy new parts, only to have her kidnapped and forced into a brief career as an erotic gladiator in the style of SEXORCIST. She is then (in the following year's *Kowaremono II*) put to work for a mad scientist who gives her the ability to transform into a superheroine, in a series of very loosely linked vignettes, based on an erotic computer game. ❶❶Ⓥ

SLAVE MARKET *

2002. JPN: *Dorei Ichiba*. Video. DIR: Michiru Takizawa. SCR: Naoki Tsuruoka. DES: Michiru Takizawa. ANI: Shoji Yanagisawa. MUS: Hiroaki Sano. PRD: Discovery. 30 mins. x 3 eps.
As the clouds of war beckon in the 17th century, Cassius arrives in Constantinople as an assistant to the European ambassador—yes, we know that Constantinople (Istanbul) is *in* Europe, but this is an erotic anime, not a geography lesson. His old friend Falco immediately takes him to the city's slave market where Bianca, a silver-haired slave girl who addresses him as "brother," soon catches his eye. However, even as Cassius takes his new acquisition home so he can begin manfully resisting the urge to molest her, Bianca's

own stalker begins to stalk her new owner.
Later episodes continue the pattern, as Cassius and his associates drift halfheartedly toward a plot involved with the beginning of the Thirty Years War, which is somehow reflected in whichever slave Cassius happens to pick up at the market. In episode 2, the slave-of-the-month is Cecilia, a girl who once believed she was betrothed to a prince, but somehow ends up sold at auction, already pregnant with her betrayer's child. Cassius's third purchase is Miya, an "African" slave whose vocal chords have been cut—"African" meaning that she has a slight tan. Cassius busily molests and degrades her, as is his wont, but becomes so obsessed with her that he refuses to hand her over to the mercenaries who come looking for her. Another entry in the DISCOVERY SERIES, complete with whips, chains, scatology, and water sports, like John Norman's *Gor* series without the feminist charm—yes, we are kidding. ❶❶Ⓥ

SLAVE NURSES *

2003. JPN: *Dorei Kaigo*. Video. DIR: Katsuma Kanazawa. SCR: Yoshio Takaoka. DES: Jiro Iwata. ANI: Jiro Iwata. MUS: Satoshi Shura. PRD: CherryLips, ARMS, Super Seven. 25 mins. x 3 eps.
All the "nurses" in the "hospital" have been seized by raging lusts. Every night sees them satisfying their urges with doctors, patients, and anyone else who passes by. Newly-hired male caregiver Yosuke has his own theories about what's behind this sudden surge of libido—but he doesn't want to uncover the truth too quickly because he's having too much fun joining in. It soon transpires that the music piped into the wards has additional, hypnotic side effects—it would be a rare anime medical institution that *wasn't* also a front for an unsanctioned experiment that had strange effects on the inhabitants! As the division of the female characters into standard wish-fulfillment archetypes (older woman, tomboy, the one with glasses…) suggests, this is based on a 2001 erotic computer game, on this occasion from Silkies. We would like to point out, for those that care about this sort of thing, that there are no actual nurses in this anime—the leading ladies are all unskilled teenage caregivers in a nursing home. De-

spite what is, considering the title, a rather important omission, this remains notable for its high production values—a welcome relief from run-of-the-mill CG animated dreck. ❶❶Ⓥ

SLAVE SISTERS *

1999. JPN: *Shimai Ijiri*. AKA: *Sisters Enslaved/ Tormented*. Video DIR: Mitsuhiro Yoneda. SCR: Nikukyu. DES: Meka Morishige. ANI: Y.O.U.C. MUS: Yoshi. PRD: YOUC, Digital Works (Vanilla Series). 30 mins. x 2 eps.
Yukari Isshiki and her younger sister Miku lose their parents and inherit their massive debts to a crime syndicate. They are given a choice—become sex slaves or die. Shunji Iwashiro is given the task of training them to please their new masters. Part of the VANILLA SERIES—compare to LOVE LESSONS, and based on a game by the company Nikukyu. ❶❶Ⓥ

SLAVES TO PASSION *

2001. JPN: *Hana Dorei*. AKA: *Glorious Slaves*. Video. DIR: Kanzaburo Oda. SCR: Rokurota Makabe, DES: Naomi Hayakawa, Hayato Teshima. ANI: Hayato Teshima. MUS: Yoshi. PRD: YOUC, Digital Works (Vanilla Series). 30 mins. x 2 eps.
Painter's apprentice Kaoru fantasizes about his master's beautiful wife Reiko, watching Master Aoki bind and dominate her, and then use the results as inspiration for his art. This continues until the fateful day that Aoki dies, leaving Reiko a griefless widow. Kaoru duly steps in to "console" her by taking up where his master left off, and adds her sister Karen to the group. However, Master Aoki's death is not the heart attack it was pronounced, and trouble ensues. Another entry in the VANILLA SERIES, based on a manga by Naomi Hayakawa, creator of BEAST CITY. ❶❶Ⓥ

SLAYERS *

1995. TV series, movie, video. DIR: Takashi Watanabe, Susumu Ishizaki, Kazuo Yamazaki, Masahito Sato, Yoshiaki Iwasaki, Moto Kawaguchi, Seiji Mizushima, Eiji Sato. SCR: Takao Koyama, Katsuhiko Chiba, Jiro Takayama, Tetsuko Watanabe, Yasushi Yamada, Katsumi Hasegawa. DES: Naomi Miyata, Kenji Teraoka, Toshihasa Higashi. ANI: Naomi Miyata, Kazuhiro Sasaki, Seiji Kikuchi, Mitsuru Abunai. MUS: Osamu Tezuka (mus), Vink. PRD: IG Film, SoftX, TV Tokyo.

25 mins. x 78 eps., (TV), 65 mins. (m1), 85 mins. (m2), 80 mins. (m3), 64 mins. (m4), 40 mins. (m5), 30 mins. x 3 eps. (v1), 30 mins. x 3 eps. (v2).

Hoping to obtain the Sword of Light, a powerful artifact wielded by the slow-witted Gourry Gabriev, flat-chested teen sorceress Lina Inverse decides to accompany him on his travels. The pair wander a sub–D&D world in search of fortune, helped and hindered by a changing stock company of sidekicks and adversaries, which include Amelia, a self-proclaimed Champion of Justice, the cursed swordsman Zelgadis, and the priestly prankster Xelloss. One of the most popular anime franchises of the 1990s, along with TENCHI MUYO!, *Slayers* remained a popular choice throughout the teens of its original 12-year-old target audience, leaping from Hajime Kanzaka's original 1989 short stories in *Dragon* magazine, illustrated by Rui Araizumi, to a long-running set of novels and the inevitable manga and anime spin-offs, eventually sliding from TV to video. Set in a complicated fantasyland supposedly in a neighboring plane of existence to the same creator's LOST UNIVERSE, it is the antidote to the deadly serious RECORD OF LODOSS WAR, with a cynical cast modeled on argumentative role-players. *Slayers* makes light of its own lumpen predictability, with the characters constantly bickering about food, being double-crossed by feckless clients, and lamenting the formulaic set-ups they face. Ridiculing its own shortcomings, *Slayers* has successfully kept a strong following that watches for what some might call biting satire, and others bad workmen blaming their tools.

The three 26-episode TV seasons (branded *Slayers, S Next,* and *S Try*) also came accompanied by a set of theatrical releases, beginning with *Slayers: The Movie* (1995). In order not to disturb the continuity of the ongoing TV series, writer/director Kazuo Yamazaki opted for a story from a spin-off continuity, the *S Special* tales set two years before Lina's first meeting with Gourry. While the TV show contained many running "gags" about breasts and the effect of menstruation on magic powers, it remained essentially asexual. However, with the absence of TV restrictions, the first and subsequent movies retain Naga from the stories, a

large-breasted, cackling sorceress and self-appointed traveling companion for the young Lina, her one-time enemy and sometime sidekick. Four further films followed: *S Return* (1996), *S Great* (1997), *S Gorgeous* (1998), and *S Premium* (2001). Meanwhile, the prequels also made it straight to video with *S Special* (1996, released in the U.S. as *S Dragon Slave* and *S Explosion Array,* AKA *S Book of Spells* on DVD) and *S Excellent* (1998). Naga and her breasts have become three very popular characters in the series, and long-term fans of the series wait eagerly to see how the writers can explain not only her disappearance between the end of *S Special* and the beginning of the original series, but also why she is never even mentioned after the events of the videos. Other spin-offs include the *Slayers* game for the SNES and *S Royal* for the Sega Saturn, the CD *S Etcetera,* and the CD-ROM *S Hyper.* In a final irony, the *Slayers* universe was sold as an add-on to the *Magius* role-playing game, bringing it full circle to the format that originally inspired it.

SLIGHT FEVER SYNDROME *

1996. JPN: *Binetsu Shokogun.* Video. DIR: Taiichi Kitagawa, Kozo Shirakawa. SCR: Rumi Miyamoto. DES: Kazunami Ota. ANI: Kazunami Ota. MUS: Hideyuki Tanaka. PRD: Yang Corporation, Caress Communications, Knack. 45 mins. x 2 eps.

Nubile, easily stimulated Mizuki combines the roles of nurse and health education teacher at a private high school (or "college" in the U.S. version). In other words, a feeble framing device for a succession of pornographic scenes in which students and teachers alike confess their experiences or seek her "help" with sexual problems. Mizuki tends to use a very hands-on approach with her students, especially when demonstrating all the various functions of the female anatomy. Then she starts to fall for Kirishima, one of her very attractive male students. In the second video, Mizuki catches him peeping at her sex session with a female colleague. She invites him to her apartment, finally starting to bring her work home with her. Based on the erotic manga by Rumi Miyamoto in *Penguin Club.* Ⓝ

SLIPPY DANDY

1987. TV series. DIR: Tameo Ogawa. SCR: N/C. DES: N/C. ANI: Hisatoshi Motoki. MUS: N/C. PRD: Meruhen, Fuji TV. 5 mins. x 4 eps.

Farcical thievery in the style of CAT'S EYE, as the pretty blonde photographer Audrey pursues the burglar Slippy Dandy, unaware that he is really Steve, the young college boy who worships her from afar. This series of shorts was shown as part of the variety show *Midnight Treasure Chamber* and made in a deliberately "American" style (meaning brashly bright colors and redundant sound effects plastered over the action in the style of the 1960s TV *Batman*).

SLOW STEP *

1991. Video. DIR: Kunihiko Yuyama. SCR: Toshimichi Saeki, Kenji Terada. DES: Tokuhiro Matsubara. ANI: Tokuhiro Matsubara. MUS: Hiroya Watanabe. PRD: Pastel, Youmex, OB. 45 mins. x 5 eps.

Minatsu is a lively, popular teenager and star of the girls' softball team. Her chief admirers are her childhood sweetheart, Akiba, and her perverse softball coach, Yamazakura. But while Minatsu falls for Kadomatsu, the boxing champ from a rival school, he is not interested in her. In fact, he is only interested in "Maria," a pretty girl with glasses, though he is unaware that "Maria" is really a disguise Minatsu uses to avoid a gang of thugs that's intent on getting back at her for reporting them in a hit-and-run incident. Kadomatsu and Akiba soon come to blows over their love for the same girl, and Coach Yamazakura, a former high school boxer himself, agrees to teach Akiba how to defend himself. Meanwhile, Coach's orphaned niece, Chika, is determined to find a wife for him so she can have a new mommy *and* daddy. Throw into this mix Somei, the newest teacher at the school, who's a gorgeous hunk but is scared of *all* women ... except Sawamura, the school bad-girl who wants Yamazakura for herself.

An addictive blend of softball, boxing, and nostalgic school-day intrigues that adapts the entirety of the short 1987 manga by Mitsuru Adachi in *Ciao* magazine. Not as well known as the same creator's TOUCH, H2, NINE, or MIYUKI, *SS* remains unavailable in the U.S. and has achieved the questionable distinction of being the

U.K.'s worst-selling anime from 1995 to 2000, a record broken only by the release of the KIMAGURE ORANGE ROAD videos. This is a great shame because it retains Adachi's masterful qualities of character interaction and observational comedy. The early episodes of quick-change farce are soon discarded for a complex mating dance, as Minatsu deftly deals with her suitors and tries to decide which (if any) to choose. Needless to say, after much comedy business divided, like the original manga, into seasonal chapters, the show ends happily with a spring wedding attended by several couples formed from the supporting cast.

SS is fascinating both for its portrayal of everyday Japan and for the "everyday" aspects that seem so alien to the Western viewer. These include the Japanese attitude toward smoking and sexual harassment, teen rebellion expressed through littering or (the horror!) buying alcohol from a vending machine, as well as the Japanese concept of what makes a man marriage material, and what aspirations a 17-year-old schoolgirl should have. A charmingly conservative story, with beautiful backgrounds and some wonderful humor, including the boys' vehement complaints about the service at a holiday resort, chiefly because they are unable to peek at the girls bathing. Parts three and four were run together as a single feature-length episode in the British version in a feeble attempt to avoid having to pay the classification board for two separate titles.

SLUTTY PRINCESS DIARIES *

2004. JPN: *Kijoku*. AKA: *Princesses Tortured*. Video. DIR: N/C. SCR: N/C. DES: N/C. ANI: N/C. MUS: N/C. PRD: Animac. 30 mins. x 3 eps.
Distol is a disinherited prince of Astaria, a small kingdom that has been bullied and invaded by its ruthless neighbor Bastarauge. Forced to live at the Bastarauge court with his stepmother as royal hostages, Distol is obliged to endure his incarceration alone when the former queen dies only a few days after arriving. He devotes the next eight years to learning the way of the sword, in the hope that one day he will be able to avenge his kingdom and stepmother, and perhaps also protect his stepsister Princess Qoona, who might be forced to take the late queen's place at the mercies of Bastarauge. Distol also

discovers that his stepmother was raped by the king of Bastarauge (so now he *really* wants to avenge her), and that Qoona is fated to be sacrificed in order to enact a sacred ceremony to keep a demon king imprisoned in an alternate dimension.

One way of helping Qoona is to ensure that Elena, a princess of Bastarauge, is corrupted, abused, and raped—this is something to do with magical spells and destinies, apparently. Consequently, Distol breaks into Elena's chambers and carries her off at the very beginning of this complex erotic fantasy anime, before pausing to recount the incidents described above in a long flashback that uses up much of the first episode.

The final episode finds Distol successfully breaking the "seal" that lies inside the body of Elena. It is only then that he realizes that he has been double-crossed, and that by doing so he has allowed the demon back *into* the world—his adviser in this was a witch who now turns out to be a servant of the demon lord Distol was hoping to keep away. Compare to EROTIC TORTURE CHAMBER, which similarly devoted massive amounts of time to setting up a story, leaving comparatively little time for the sex which is, we suggest, the reason that most people would be buying an anime with a title like that. ●🅝🅥

SMART-SAN

1978. JPN: *Haikara-san ga Toru*. AKA: *Miss "High Collar"; Fashionable Girl Passing By*. TV series. DIR: Yoshihiko Umakoshi, Kazuyoshi Yokota. SCR: Fumi Takahashi. DES: Tsutomu Shibayama. ANI: Tatsuhiro Nagaki, Eiji Tanaka, Takashi Saijo. MUS: Masuhiro Yamaguchi. PRD: Nippon Animation, TV Asahi. 25 mins. x 44 eps.
Early in the 20th century, pretty teenage tomboy Benio Hanamura is the spoiled only child of a major in the army. She studies martial arts and is much more direct than is considered proper for a young lady, even if it is the modern fashion. Benio is caught up in Japan's conflict between progress and tradition when her father decides to arrange her marriage to rich boy Shinobu, much against her will. According to custom, she is sent to her future husband's family home, but he is called up for war service and sent to the Russian front. Soon his family hears that he is missing,

believed dead. Benio eventually becomes a journalist and is astounded to meet Shinobu again some years later; he has lost his memory and believes he is Mikhailov, the husband of a Russian noblewoman. Benio becomes engaged to another man, but on their wedding day, Shinobu arrives at the ceremony, memory restored, to reclaim his bride just as a terrible earthquake hits the capital (see DOOMED MEGALOPOLIS).

Waki Yamato's original 1975 manga in *Shojo Friend* was hugely successful, but the anime didn't do as well; Nippon Animation cut it short earlier than planned. *Haikara* ("high collar") is a mild term of ridicule in 1920s Japanese slang—a fashion victim who slavishly adopts Western trends and fads.

SNOW NIGHT STORIES *

2004. JPN: *Setsuya Ichiya Monogatari*. Video. DIR: N/C. SCR: N/C. DES: N/C. ANI: N/C. MUS: N/C. PRD: schoolzone. 14 mins. x 3 eps.
Three short porn stories set in earlier times, with a Japanese title designed to recall the 1001 NIGHTS of Middle Eastern literature. "Thief" tells the story of a young wife left at home by her much older husband while he goes off to market. A thief arrives and steals more than he'd bargained for. "Female Pervert Warrior" is set in a time of feudal conflict, with a Princess and her loyal vassal on the run and meeting misfortune. "Disgraced Bride" focuses on a clan lord who just can't get enough of his beautiful royal bride, although she is rather less excited by the marriage and the sex. Feudal porn addicts might also like to check out OED48. ●🅥

SNOW QUEEN, THE

2005. JPN: *Yuki no Jo-O*. TV series. DIR: Osamu Dezaki, Kenji Hachizaki. SCR: Masashi Togawa, Makoto Nakamura, Michiru Shimada, Sukehiro Tomita, Tomoko Konparu. DES: Akio Sugino. ANI: Izumi Shimura, Miyuki Goto. MUS: Akira Senju. PRD: Tokyo Movie Shinsha, NHK. 25 mins. x 39 eps.
Kay and Gerda are childhood friends, separated when the evil actions of the legendary Snow Queen cause a shard of a mirror to become embedded in Kay's heart. He tearfully forces Gerda to leave him alone and heads off to the realm of the Snow Queen. Despite the admonitions of adults that Kay is lost to the world, Gerda insists

on looking for him. An adaptation of one of the **Tales of Hans Christian Andersen**, in apparent imitation of the earlier **World Masterpiece Theater** series, featuring the long-standing team of Dezaki and Sugino. As with **Cinderella**, there are a few alterations in the anime version, most notably the queen's quest to retrieve the many scattered shards of the "troll-mirror"—as in **Pokémon**, she's gotta catch 'em all.

SNOW WHITE

1994. JPN: *Shirayuki-hime no Densetsu*. AKA: *Story of Princess Snow White*. TV series. DIR: Kunitoshi Okajima. SCR: Tsunehisa Arakawa. DES: Yoshio Kabashima. ANI: N/C. MUS: N/C. PRD: Tatsunoko, NHK2. 25 mins. x 52 eps.
The evil Lady Crystal is affronted to hear that she is not "the fairest of them all" and orders the hunter Sampson to take her stepdaughter Snow White out into the forest and kill her. But Snow White escapes into the forest and hides with seven dwarves, hoping that some day her Prince Richard will come to save her and restore justice in the kingdom. This retelling of one of the most famous of **Grimms' Fairy Tales**, like the same studio's later **Cinderella**, expands the original to fill out an extended running time. In this case, Tatsunoko ensures that Snow White meets her Prince Charming early on in the events so that her intrigues, letters, and clandestine meetings with him allow for plenty of extra action. The finale returns to the original, poisoned apple and all. See also **Video Picture Book** and **Hello Kitty**.

Sailor Moon–director Junichi Sato would also create the "new *SW* story" **Pretear**, first as a manga drawn by Kaori Naruse for *Asuka* magazine, then as a TV anime. Refracting the legend through the prism of **Utena**, it features Himeno Awayuki, a Japanese teenager who discovers she is the "Snow Princess," fated to save the world from evil, assisted by seven bold "knights," who are, of course, fearsomely pretty boys.

SO, I CAN'T PLAY H *

2012. JPN: *Dakara Boku wa, H ga Dekinai*. TV series. DIR: Takeo Takahashi. SCR: Naruhisa Arakawa. DES: Kanetoshi Kamimoto. ANI: Kuniaki Masuda, Masakazu Yamazaki. MUS: Cher Watanabe. PRD: feel, AT-X, Dax, Fujimi Shobo, Geneon, Lantis, Sotsu, Klockworx.

24 mins. x ? eps.
Perverted teenager Ryosuke unwittingly becomes the energy source for the vampiric Grim Reaper Lisara, who feeds off his own lustful thoughts. He is therefore compelled, yes, *compelled* to pursue as many girls as possible, in as many perverted situations as possible, in order to preserve his energy levels and stay alive. Shades of **Ultraman** and **Urusei Yatsura**, repurposed for yet another festival of boobs. **Ⓝ**

SOAR HIGH! ISAMI *

1995. JPN: *Tobe Isami*. AKA: *Fly Isami*. TV series. DIR: Gisaburo Sugii, Tatsuo Sato. SCR: Hideo Takayashiki, Tomoko Konparu. DES: Kazuaki Mori. ANI: Kazuaki Mori, Yoshiko Sakurai. MUS: Hiroaki Serizawa. PRD: Tac, NHK. 25 mins. x 50 eps.
Isami, a 12-year-old girl with a newscaster mother and research-scientist father, fights against a secret organization, the "Black Tengu," that is trying to take control of the world. Eventually, the Black Tengu joins forces with the Serizawa industrial conglomerate, and Isami must recruit her friends and her father's inventions to fight back.

SOCCER FEVER

1994. TV series. DIR: Hitoshi Oda. SCR: Marco Pagot. DES: N/C. ANI: Kazuyoshi Takeuchi. MUS: N/C. PRD: RAI, Tokyo Movie Shinsha, NHK2. 26 mins. x 52 eps.
In the year of the World Cup tournament in the U.S., this series features British journalist Brian Thompson recounting anecdotes from various earlier World Cup games in other countries. Created by Marco Pagot (**Sherlock Hound**, **Reporter Blues**), the animation of this Japanese-Italian coproduction has much in common with European styles and shows characters considerably older than the usual school or college-age heroes like **Captain Tsubasa**. Korean animators followed the same lead with a special called *Spin Kicker* (1997) to cash in on the run-up to the 2002 World Cup.

SOFTENNI

2011. TV series. DIR: Ryoki Kamitsubo. SCR: Noboru Kimura, Takamitsu Kono, Takeyuki Ishida, Yosuke Kuroda. DES: Yuichi Oka, Yasuyuki Yuzawa. ANI: Taeko Hori, Yuichi Oka. MUS: Nijine. PRD: Xebec, AT-X, Geneon Univer-

sal Entertainment, Lantis, Studio Mausu, Klockworx. 24 mins. x 12 eps.
Asuna lives on a farm but she's crazy about tennis—specifically soft tennis, the version of the game played with a softer, lighter ball. A keen member of the Soft Tennis Club at school, she's keen to encourage her friends to win the next big tournament, but this wacky bunch may find it a challenge even with extra practice (**Sports Anime**). A slice of school life in short skirts and bright pastel colors, based on Ryo Azuchi's 2009 manga; most of the original's mild nudity was censored out for TV but the slightly perverted humor and lesbian fan service remain. Six two-minute "specials" were added for the DVD release. **Ⓝ**

SOL BIANCA *

1990. Video. DIR: Katsuhito Akiyama, Hiroki Hayashi, Hiroyuki Ochi. SCR: Mayori Sekijima, Hideki Mitsui. DES: Naoyuki Onda, Atsushi Takeuchi, Koji Watanabe, Kenji Teraoka, Satoshi Shimura. ANI: Kazuhiro Konishi, Naoyuki Onda, Koichi Arai, Takashi Takeuchi. MUS: Toru Hirano, Kosei Kenjo, Seiko Nagaoka. PRD: AIC, Pioneer. 60 mins. x 2 eps., 30 mins. x 6 eps.
Rim Delapaz wants to rescue his mother from the evil dictator Battros. He disobeys his father, stows away on a cruiser, and hopes that the rest of a plan will come to him before he arrives. But the cruiser is hijacked by pirates, the crew of the Sol Bianca, who are ready to throw Rim out of the airlock before he tempts them with the treasure that lies in Battros's vaults. The pirates decide to help Rim in his mission, but their landing team is ambushed by Battros's minions. As their fellow buccaneers mount a rescue mission, Rim's father decides it's time to mount a revolution, in which the crew of the Sol Bianca are caught.

Take a bunch of girls and a spaceship and you have a very wide range of possibilities. Luckily not all of them are pornographic (though see **Spaceship Agga Ruter**). Strangely redolent of *Blake's 7*'s Liberator, Sol Bianca is an alien ship faster than any other vehicle in space, while its pirate crew, in the eye-candy tradition of **Bubblegum Crisis**, are all female: laid-back, wine-drinking captain Feb; butch Janny, good with weapons but inclined to fly off the handle; complex, tough-but-fair April; intelligent but reserved June, whose empathic link with the ship and its guidance computer, G, has mysterious origins; and the very young May, with a penchant for frilly clothes but an ace engineer in the bargain. After the promising beginning, the second *SB* video slid into anime hackery, with the girls chased around by a rival pirate whose gun can disintegrate their clothes, and the ship overrun by clunky "viruses" that look like cybernetic worms. Though it ends on a cliffhanger with the suggestion that the Sol Bianca's original builders want her back, a third chapter of *Sol Bianca* never arrived—this is despite a popular reception in the English-speaking world, where it's available in two translations, of which Kiseki's, in the U.K., is the better. In the U.S., AD Vision published a short-lived spin-off comic called *SB: Treasure of the Lost Sun*, which featured the girls on an *Indiana Jones*–style treasure hunt, with no mention of their video antics.

Pioneer remade the series from scratch with *SB: The Legacy* (1999), featuring all-new character designs from Onda, a new script from Hideki Mitsui, and contributions from two stalwarts of the company's 1990s success: **ARMITAGE III**–director Ochi and **EL HAZARD**–composer Nagaoka. The revamped version takes the concept from the earlier series that Earth is semilegendary to the people of the far future, and then postulates a group of religious fanatics, the "Earthians," determined to preserve artifacts from the homeworld. This turns the crew of the SolBianca, somewhat pointlessly, from devil-may-care pirates into iconoclastic art thieves. *SB: The Legacy* also "updates" the characters, mostly ignoring the precedents of the first series. April is now captain, having found the Sol Bianca and put together a crew. Janny is still the muscle. June is still the brains, with a powerful symbiotic relationship with the ship and its computer. The biggest changes are in Feb, who still drinks but doesn't really seem to have a role in the crew, and May (now Meiyo), who supplants Rim as a stowaway and ship's mascot, though she too can link with the computer as June does. The computer can also take the form of a huge, shadowy woman, sometimes resembling the Christian Madonna and sometimes the goddess

Diana. As with most TV anime of the late 1990s, digital animation gives the show an overly "clean" look, though it adds considerable charm to the spaceships. Released almost simultaneously in Japan and the U.S., *SB: The Legacy* was derided in Japan for "smelling of butter;" in other words, it was a little too Americanized for Japanese tastes—though art connoisseurs will find a treasure trove of cultural references, from Dante's *Inferno* to Alphonse Mucha paintings.

SOLA *

2007. JPN: *Sora*. TV series, video. DIR: Tomoki Kobayashi. SCR: Jukki Hanada, Naoki Hisaya, Makoto Uezu, Kenji Sugihara. DES: Makoto Koga, Yoshinori Hirose. ANI: Makoto Koga. MUS: Hitoshi Fujima (Element Garden). PRD: Nomad, Bandai Visual, Iantis, Hakuhodo DY Media Partners. 25 mins. x 13 eps. (TV), 25 mins. x 2 eps. (v).
Fifteen-year-old Yorito loves to take photographs of the sky, especially at sunrise and sunset. While out taking pictures, he meets a mysterious girl, Matsuri, and finds out she is being chased by someone who wants to kill her. He invites her to stay at his house, even though she's not human. His older sister Aono is in the hospital, and he visits her every day with their friend Mana, Yorito's classmate. But neither Yorito nor Aono is what they seem, and the man who's trying to kill Matsuri is displaying great kindness and concern for a young girl who sleeps rough around the city. Matsuri is the catalyst who can restore the balance of things, but only through tragedy.

Designed by creator Naoki Hisaya (**KANON**) and artist Naru Nanao (**DA CAPO**) as a multimedia franchise, *Sola* made its debut in Hisaya's 2006 manga with art by Chako Abeno, with a drama CD before the TV show and videos in 2007, and a second drama CD in 2008. Two extra episodes were included in the DVD release, with episode 14 intended to occur between episodes 4 and 5 and episode 15 taking place the day before episode 1; in effect, the DVD release with its additional unscreened material, forms a "director's cut."

SOLTY REI *

2005. TV series. DIR: Yoshimasa Hiraike, Masashi Abe, Ryuichi Kimura, Yoshihiko Iwata.

SCR: Noboru Kimura. DES: Shujiro Hamakawa. ANI: Shujiro Hamakawa, Sawako Yamamoto, Shuichi Hara, Toshiharu Murata. MUS: Toshiyuki Omori. PRD: AIC, Gonzo, TV Asahi. 25 mins. x 24 eps. (+ 2 bonus eps.).
An amnesiac android girl is adopted by a bounty hunter as his own daughter, despite being on the run from an interstellar security bureau. In an act of stunning originality, the pursuing agents are named after cars. Oh no, wait a moment, see **RAYEARTH** and **VIPER GTS**. A manga spin-off later appeared in monthly *Comic Rex*, written by scenarist Kimura and drawn by Kazutaka Takimiya.

SOMEDAY'S DREAMERS *

2003. JPN: *Maho Tsukai ni Taisetsu na Koto; What Is Important for Magic Users*. AKA: *Important Things for Magic Users*. TV series DIR: Masami Shimoda. SCR: Norie Yamada. DES: Michinori Chiba, Nobue Yoshinaga. ANI: Keiko Kawashima. MUS: Takefumi Haketa. PRD: Daiei, JC Staff, Pioneer LDC, Rondo Robe, Viewworks, TV Asahi. 25 mins. x 12 eps. (TV1), 24 mins. x 12 eps. (TV2).
Country girl Yume Kikuchi has magical powers. That's not so unusual—in a nod to the *Harry Potter* fad, she lives in a land exactly like modern Japan, except for the presence of wizards as capable members of society, using their magic to do all kinds of jobs—in hospitals, schools, the police force, just about anywhere. When Yume's skills develop, she too will use them to help others under the guidance of the Ministry that controls magical activity. First, though, she has to pass her apprenticeship to the handsome mage Masami Oyamada, get used to life in the big city, and work out what's most important to her. If you thought **KIKI'S DELIVERY SERVICE** was a low-key story, wait until you see this. Despite ravishing art direction, the story is so slow and the characters so quiet, you could be back in **YOKOHAMA SHOPPING LOG**. Based on the manga in *Comic Dragon* by Kumichi Yoshizuki and Norie Yamada, this show is so laid back it's as if it never came off the page—pretty, sweet, and soporific; and often inverting the conventions of guy-gets-girls harem shows (**ROMANCE AND DRAMA**). In this story, we have a single hapless girl who ends up living amid a group of guys—the gullible Yume having inadvertently applied to live with Masami

on the assumption that she would be living with a girl.

The second season, *Someday's Dreamers II: Sora* (2008), directed by Osamu Kobayashi, repeats many of the same elements with different names. Now the heroine is Sora Suzuki, a country girl who promises her father that she will study magic in Tokyo. As she settles into her new life and studies, she becomes drawn to Gota, the cold-seeming, diffident boy who is not very good at magic. While the plot might be mundane in the extreme, Tokyo's own magic is beautifully depicted in the backgrounds, which make heavy use of photographs overlaid with animation to ground Sora's world in our own reality.

SONG OF RAIYANTSUURI

1993. JPN: *Raiyantsuuri no Uta*. AKA: *Song of Liang Chu Li* [?]. Movie. DIR: Seiji Arihara. SCR: Seiji Arihara, Toshiaki Imaizumi. DES: N/C. ANI: Takaya Ono. MUS: N/C. PRD: Mushi, Ringoro. 90 mins.

An indentured Chinese laborer, brought to Japan to work in a coal mine during WWII, manages to escape his captors. He hides out in the Japanese countryside, so far from human habitation that he does not realize when the war ends, with ultimately tragic results. Based on a story by Yoichi Takashi.

SONG OF THE BASEBALL ENTHUSIAST

1977. JPN: *Yakyukyo no Uta*. TV special, TV series, movie. DIR: Tameo Ogawa, Eiji Okabe, Hiroshi Fukutomi. SCR: Eiji Okabe, Haruya Yamazaki, Ryuzo Nakanishi, Shunichi Yukimuro. DES: Shinji Mizushima. ANI: Hidenori Kondo. MUS: Michiaki Watanabe. PRD: Nippon Animation, Fuji TV. 50 mins. (TVm), 25 mins. x 24 eps. (TV), 90 mins. (m).

Yuki Mizuhara is a teenage southpaw pitcher with outstanding ability, spotted by a talent scout for the Tokyo Mets. Brought into the team, "Yuki" is forced to reveal that he is really a she, but *Yuko* Mizuhara soon wins the affections of the scandalized players when she helps them in their ongoing feud against their rivals, the Hanshin Tigers. Based on the 1977 manga by MAN'S AN IDIOT–creator Shinji Mizushima, *SotBE* began as a double-length pilot episode released as a TV special just before Christmas, with the series proper starting in May

of the following year. Episodes 3–6 were also screened as full-length "specials" before being retailored as standard 25-minute chapters. Later episodes tried to move away from the Mizuhara story line (which was only one part of the original), but tales about other players on the team did not attract the same ratings—25 years on, it's the Mizuhara episodes that are still available on video. A movie, shown on a double bill with FUTURE BOY CONAN in 1979, focused on two players, the Northern Wolf and the Southern Tiger, whose rivalry gathers extra drama when it is revealed that they are twins separated at birth.

SONG OF THE CHIMNEY GHOSTS

1993. JPN: *Obake Entotsu no Uta*. Movie. DIR: Yutaka Ozawa. SCR: Yoko Yamamoto. DES: Takao Kasai. ANI: Takao Kasai. MUS: N/C. PRD: Asmik. 42 mins.

One day in 1945, children in Tokyo mistake the distant factory smoke of Shitamachi for ghosts in the sky, though their happy playtime is soon destroyed by the arrival of American bombers. Yet another childhood-innocence-obliterated-by-heartless-Allied-cruelty movie, this one based on a story by Katsumoto Saotome. Compare to the worthy BAREFOOT GEN or GRAVEYARD OF THE FIREFLIES, and their many inferior successors.

SONG OF THE LADYBUGS

1974. JPN: *Tento Mushi no Uta*. TV series. DIR: Masami Annai, Yukihiro Takahashi. SCR: Akiyoshi Sakai. DES: Noboru Kawasaki. ANI: N/C. MUS: Shunsuke Kikuchi. PRD: Tatsunoko, Fuji TV. 25 mins. x 104 eps.

Seven orphaned children decide to stay together and earn their own living. Even though their grandfather is very wealthy, he does nothing to help them, so they struggle to survive in difficult conditions. Based on the 1974 manga by STAR OF THE GIANTS–creator Noboru Kawasaki, another of whose works, *Inakappe Taisho*, was animated by Tatsunoko in 1970. No relation to the Candies pop trio's 1970s nuptial ditty "Ladybug Samba," sung in karaoke form at a wedding scene in EVANGELION.

SONG OF THE SHEEP

2003. JPN: *Hitsuji no Uta*. AKA: *Lament of the Lamb*. Video. DIR: Gisaburo Sugii. SCR: Gisaburo Sugii. DES: Yasuhiro Seo. ANI: Madhouse.

MUS: N/C. PRD: Madhouse. 30 mins. x 4 eps.

Kazuna's family has a gene that dare not speak its name—every now and then they have a child with a strange thirst for blood, but never call it vampirism and keep it quiet. Kazuna is afflicted as a child, and sent to live with the Eda family after his mother dies when he is only three years old. He has a normal, quiet family life and his foster mother wants to adopt him. Kazuna is unaware of his condition until he is a teenager and suffers several devastating attacks triggered by the sight of blood. His sister Chisana, a fellow sufferer, comes back into his life, and Kazuna learns the family secret and has to cope with the knowledge that his life is not going to be anything he expected. How does a young vampire live a normal life in the human world—presumably in a different way than the VAMPAIYAN KIDS? The original manga is by Kei Toume, author of WOLF'S RAIN. There is also a live-action theatrical version. Ⓥ

SONG OF WIND AND TREES

1987. JPN: *Kaze to Ki no Uta: Sei ni Naru ka na*. AKA: *Song of Wind and Trees: Sanctus—Can This Be Holy?* Video. DIR: Yoshikazu Yasuhiko, Tatsuya Hiramatsu. SCR: Keiko Takemiya. DES: Keiko Takemiya, Yoshikazu Yasuhiko. ANI: Yoko Kamimura. MUS: Nobuyuki Nakamura. PRD: Studio Gallop, Konami Kogyo, Herald. 60 mins.

At the end of the 19th century, a new academic year starts in a European boarding school for boys. Serious, devoutly religious Serge finds himself sharing a room with beautiful blond Gilbert Cocteau, an incorrigible flirt whom Serge correctly suspects of being homosexual. Gilbert's sweet nature and considerable physical charms gradually win over his suspicious and hostile roommate, and the pair become friends and lovers. But their relationship is under pressure from Serge's religious convictions and Gilbert's naturally flirtatious personality, which attracts plenty of offers from other boys, staff, and visitors. This tender, starry-eyed romantic melodrama was based on the 1976 manga by TOWARD THE TERRA–creator Keiko Takemiya.

SONIC SOLDIER BORGMAN *

1988. JPN: *Cho-on Senshi Borgman*. AKA: *Borgman; Supersonic Soldier Borgman*. TV series, movie, video. DIR: Hiroshi Negishi, Hiroshi Yoshida, Kiyoshi Murayama. SCR: Hideki Sonoda, Nobuaki Kishima, Sho Aikawa, Kiyoshi Murayama. DES: Michitaka Kikuchi, Koichi Ohata, Torao Arai, Takehiro Yamada. ANI: Masamitsu Kudo, Hideyuki Motohashi. MUS: Hiromoto Tobisawa. PRD: Ashi Pro, Nippon TV. 25 mins. x 35 eps. (TV), 25 mins. (m), 60 mins., 30 mins. x 3 eps. (v).

In the late 1990s, Tokyo is destroyed by four meteorites. In 2030, Megalo City in Tokyo Bay is infiltrated by a secret organization. Check: natural disaster, rebuilding, sinister organization—now all we need is a group of armored vigilantes. Our heroes Anice, Chuck, and Ryo are actually cyborgs (hence Borgman) created for a peaceful international deep-space probe, but the project head, Memory Geen, is the first to have been infiltrated by the alien Yoma, who plan to inherit the Earth since their own world is dying. The five battle-suited female cops of the World Criminal Police at first distrust and oppose the Borgman team, since fighting the Yoma is what they've been specially created and trained to do. Sound familiar? Post-**BUBBLEGUM CRISIS** but curiously more old-fashioned, *Borgman* is a stylistic bridge between earlier team shows and the dystopian heroes ushered in by *Alien, Blade Runner,* and *Terminator,* though none of them used a teaching career as cover for their hard-suited heroes. If you can ignore the presence of the annoying infants that this tactic welds into the story line and the somewhat simplistic characterization, this is a pleasant enough adventure for teens. Originator Kikuchi's design skills, helped by Ohata's monsters, propelled the show to success in Japan and a video revival four years later. The first video, *Midnight Gigs,* is a music compilation from the series, with some cast and crew information. The video release *The Borgman: The Last Battle* (1989), Murayama's movie *Lover's Rain* (1990), and the three-part video series *Borgman 2: New Century 2058* (1993, *B2: Shinseiki 2058*) carry the story forward to 2058 and a new Yoma attack. The survivors of the previous conflict unite with new allies to fight the old battles. Compare to the similarly themed **VIRUS**.

SONIC THE HEDGEHOG *
1996. Video. DIR: Kazunori Ikegami. SCR:

Mayori Sekijima. DES: Tsuneo Ninomiya, Haruo Miyakawa. ANI: Tsuneo Ninomiya. MUS: Mitsuhiro Oda. PRD: Sega, Taki Corporation. 25 mins. x 2 eps., 25 mins. x 78 eps. (*Sonic X*).

Sonic the Hedgehog's archnemesis, Dr. Robotnik, has been banished from the Land of Darkness by an evil Metal Robotnik. He tells Sonic that the Robot Generator has been sabotaged and will blow Planet Freedom to kingdom come. Sonic is reluctant to get involved until the president's daughter Sara turns on the charm, but as he sets off on his mission, he must defeat the Hyper Metal Sonic, a robot hedgehog (and *Terminator 2* homage) who's after his girl and his life.

Based on the video game series of the same name, the anime was released in English as *Sonic the Movie* to imply a budget and quality that simply weren't there. *StH* retains many favorites from the original, though Sonic's original hedgehog girlfriend, Amy, is replaced with the more human Sara. Hajime Kamegaki's later TV series *Sonic X* (2003) has Sonic and pals getting blown through the dimensions to Earth, where they team up with a 12-year-old boy to stop evil Dr. Eggman from collecting all seven Chaos Emeralds, which will give him absolute power. The first season ran a full year and was followed by a 26-episode second season.

SONODA, KENICHI
1962–. Born in Kumamoto, he worked for the Artmic studio as a designer of machinery and characters on shows such as **GALL FORCE** and **RIDING BEAN**. He retrieved elements of the latter story from the collapse of Artmic by writing them into a new manga story, **GUNSMITH CATS**, which was subsequently adapted into anime. His design work also appears in shows including Gainax's **WINGS OF HONNEAMISE** and **OTAKU NO VIDEO**.

SORA NO MANI MANI
2009. AKA: *At the Mercy of the Sky.* TV series. DIR: Shinji Takamatsu. SCR: Shinji Takamatsu. DES: Hajime Watanabe, Kuniaki Nemoto. ANI: Hajime Watanabe. MUS: Cooie Kaoru Okubo. PRD: Studio Comet, AT-X, Lantis, Marvelous Entertainment, Pony Canyon, Sony Pictures Entertainment (Japan). 24 mins. x 12 eps.

Bookworm Saku is moving back to his hometown after seven years traveling around Japan with his parents, thanks to his father's job. His last day in town was etched in his memory—he broke his arm trying to catch his friend Mihoshi as she fell out of a tree, and she didn't even come to wave him off. Now he has learned she was in the hospital as a result of the fall, and when they meet again in high school they rekindle their old friendship (**ROMANCE AND DRAMA**). Mihoshi persuades him to join the under-supported Astronomy Club with her, even though he'd prefer the literature club where the student council president, Fumie, is a member and has quite a crush on him. Other girls, too, have noticed the new boy, but for once this isn't a cue for a chorus of harem tropes. Instead a story of everyday school life extends gently as Saku and his friends, male and female, learn about life, love, and astronomy together. Adapting Mami Kashiwabara's manga from 2005, this is a sweet story of school life.

SORAN THE SPACE BOY
1965. JPN: *Uchu Shonen Soran.* TV series, movie. DIR: Tatsuo Ono. SCR: Kazuya Fujimoto, Ryu Mitsuse, Morimasa Matsumoto, Shota Fujimura, Masaki Tsuji. DES: N/C. ANI: Shizuko Sumeoka, Norio Yazawa. MUS: Kazuo Iba, Taku Izumi. PRD: TCJ, Eiken, TBS. 25 mins. x 96 eps. (TV) 25 mins. (m)

Professor Tachibana invents the Antisolar Bomb. Fearing it might be "put to the wrong uses" (it's a bomb!), he flees from Earth with his wife and child, but an accident befalls their capsule, and their son is the sole survivor. Raised by aliens on the planet Soran, the boy returns to Earth 15 times stronger than humans. Accompanied by his sidekick, Chappy the space squirrel, Soran rights wrongs on Earth, searching all the while for his long-lost sister. A muddled mixture of *Superman* and the James Bond movies. *Hyakuman doru Dokuro* (1965, *Million Dollar Skull*) was an episode-length "movie" shown as part of a summer vacation roadshow.

SORCERER HUNTERS *
1995. JPN: *Bakuretsu Hunter.* AKA: *Explosion Hunter.* TV series, video. DIR: Koichi Mashimo, Nobuyoshi Habara. SCR: Satoru Akahori, Hiroyuki Kawasaki, Masaharu

Amiya. DES: Keiji Goto, Toshihisa Kogawa. ANI: N/C. MUS: Kenji Kawai. PRD: Xebec. 25 mins. x 26 eps. (TV), 30 mins. x 3 eps. (v).

The place is the Spooner Continent. The benevolent Big Mama's last lot of defenders of peace and justice, the Haz Knights, failed to rid the land of evil sorcerers. Instead, she finds some unlikely replacements and names them the Sorcerer Hunters. Two are brothers, goofy lecher Carrot Glace, who's always hungry, and Marron Glace, who's quiet and refined. Despite their constant backbiting, they're devoted to each other. Then there's a big blond hunk named Gateau Mocha, who may be gay and secretly lusting after pretty-boy Marron. The other two are sisters, Tira Misu and Chocolate Misu, who dress in S/M style clothing when they go to work, complete with spike-heeled shoes and whips. They're both fixated on Carrot but don't fight over him because they're devoted to each other. They're all theoretically named after desserts, though to Western palates it's stretching things to call glazed carrots and chestnuts—literally carrot and marron *glacé*—a dessert.

The plot is riddled with internal contradictions. Many of the people our heroes are called on to help are stupid, superstition-ridden chumps not much better than the sorcerers who plague them. The supreme being, despite having a reassuringly maternal name and a sidekick whose name sounds like Daughter, has not been entirely honest with them. She's actually using each mission she gives them to train them for a bigger mission, one that will save the whole world from destruction, and she hasn't told them that Carrot is the ultimate weapon. Carrot (like innocent Rushe Lenlen in **BASTARD**) has the ultimate evil locked inside him. He can transform into a monster of enormous power, but he is completely unaware of this power and unable to control it. It only emerges when he is struck by magic, which happens rather a lot. The bad guy, Sacher Torte, is actually an ex-good guy, one of the Haz Knights who was driven to the dark side by despair over their failure to save the world from evil last time around. He knows about Carrot's power and wants to use it to destroy everything and start again with a clean slate. The survival of a planet depends on a hormonally challenged kid

and his love for his brother and friends. No wonder Big Mama is keeping it to herself. The three-episode video series is somewhat saucier than the TV anime, with more flesh on show and more gags. The first episode is a hot-springs story in which an unnaturally advanced child chases Tira and Chocolate while Carrot goes after his unnaturally youthful mother; amid all the fan service the producers allow the child to break the fourth wall repeatedly, getting into heated debate with the narrator. Episode two brings in the leader of the Haz Knights, androgynous swordsman Millefeuille, and once again shows the difference between TV and video; the restrained androgyne of the series is a gleeful, girl-fondling pervert. Carrot's multiple manga transformations, ignored in the TV series, are also showcased in the climactic final fight. The final episode flashes back to the characters' early lives but also provides comic relief, including Big Mama's karaoke turn.

Based on a manga in *Dengeki Comic Gao* by Satoru Akahori and Rei Omishi, *SH* is actually a rather enjoyable series, with more on offer than its slapstick wrappings indicate, including fun characters and wild designs. Though individual episodes may often stray into the banal territory that Akahori has done his utmost to claim, there are some interesting premises and plot twists like Sacher's origins, the Gateau-Marron relationship, and the genuine devotion between the two sisters competing for Carrot's affections. The second season of the TV series, which features Sacher's attempts to waken the destructive god slumbering inside Carrot, was renamed *Spell Wars: Sorcerer Hunters' Revenge* in the U.S.

SORCERER ON THE ROCKS *
1999. JPN: *Chivas 123*. Video. DIR: Kazuhiro Ozawa. SCR: Hiroyuki Kawasaki. DES: Yuki Mirai. ANI: Hisashi Abe. MUS: Nobuo Ito. PRD: Toho Video. 30 mins. x 2 eps.

Chivas Scotch is a loud, self-centered Chasemancer (magical bounty hunter) determined to tame the god Loki for a big reward, accompanied by his shapeshifting servant Kiss and nurse-out-of-water (and occasional bunny girl) Gin Phase. Beginning life in *Comic Gao* as yet another off-the-peg creation from **BEAST WARRIORS'**

Satoru Akahori and pseudonymous collaborator Yuki Mirai, it nevertheless stayed on video. In the cutthroat conditions of the early 21st century, it would take something more than 60 minutes of hackneyed magic to win a lucrative TV contract … we hope. Bought by ADV Films, though the name had to be changed in the U.S., where Chivas is a trademark.

SORI, FUMIHIKO
1964–. A prominent figure in the early-21st-century Japanese animation business, Sori is arguably an outsider, almost accidentally becoming a poster boy for motion-captured filmmaking as a spin-off from his live-action work. After studying at the University of Southern California, where he worked for James Cameron's Digital Domain on *Titanic*, he returned to Japan, where he spent several years at TBS producing computer graphics for effects, as well as the title sequences of notable live-action TV shows, such as *Beautiful Life*, *Stand Up*, and *Unsolved Cases* (*DE). In 2002, he demonstrated a masterful grasp of effects work in his live-action movie debut, *Ping Pong*, a tale of table tennis aficionados, for which Sori added digital ping-pong balls in order to make his actors look like world champions.

It was only after almost a decade using digital animation as a mere effect that Sori turned his hand to animation itself, first as the producer of the 2004 **APPLESEED** and then as the director of the acclaimed **VEXILLE**. Both films were less "animated" than they were movies with 100% special effects, using motion-capture in much the same way as Disney once used rotoscoping, as a means of using live actors to create the foundation for peerless animation. Although Sori has subsequently made *To* (**2001 NIGHTS**) and **DRAGON AGE: DAWN OF THE SEEKER**, it is possible that he is only a vistor in the anime world, liable to be tempted more permanently back to the greater risks but richer pickings of live action.

SOUL EATER *
2008. TV series. DIR: Takuya Igarashi. SCR: Akatsuki Yamatoya, Megumi Shimizu, Yoneki Tsumura. DES: Yoshiyuki Ito, Norifumi Nakamura. ANI: Yoshiyuki Ito, Koji Murai, Yoshiyuki Kodaira, Atsushi Hasebe, Hiroyuki Negishi.

MUS: Taku Iwasaki. PRD: BONES, Dentsu Inc., Media Factory, TV Tokyo. 25 mins. x 51 eps.

The Death Weapon Meister Academy teaches potential weapon meisters and their human weapons the techniques they need to go out and reap souls. To upgrade their powers to the highest level and elevate their weapon to a Death Scythe, the pairs must harvest the souls of 99 evil humans and one witch (likely to be a distant reference to the sword-collecting fetish to be found in the old story of **BENKEI VS USHIWAKA**). They also have to defend their hometown, Death City, from attacking monsters and magicians. Cue all-out action, goofy humor, dark, twisted family relationships, rivalries, and loyalties that go on beyond death. Atsushi Okubo's 2004 manga had a simple premise: magical technicians are able to wield the abilities of specially gifted, shapeshifting human partners as weapons. The idea of a talent residing in one party but useless without the control and guidance of a second party is well established in anime and is usually a hit with the teenage male audience. Guest appearances by Jack the Ripper, the Fisher King, the Flying Dutchman, Sherlock Holmes, and Al Capone do nothing to hurt the show's nonstop, slam-bang action. It won't stand up to detailed analysis but it's a lot of mindless fun. **Ⓥ**

SOUL HUNTER *
1999. JPN: *Sendai den Hoshin Engi*. AKA: *Immortal Tales of Hoshin Engi; Fengshen Yanyi; Hoshin Engi*. TV series. DIR: Junji Nishimura. SCR: Koji Ueda, Atsuhiro Tomioka, Masashi Sogo. DES: Masashi Kojima. ANI: N/C. MUS: Ryo Sakai. PRD: Studio Deen. 25 mins. x 26 eps.

In the 11th century B.C., the world is divided into two realms that coexist without any problem: Earth for humans and Heaven (actually Mount Kunlun, the Chinese Olympus), for immortals. Heaven has conferred on the young Immortal, Taikoubou, the mission of delivering Earth from the threat of the demon Immortal, Dakki, by capturing the 365 demons who are rampaging all over China. She and her aides have taken Emperor Zhou and in his name are bringing misfortune, famine, and slavery to the land. Taikoubou sets out to find warriors to support him in his mission and is joined by "Raishinshi" and

Nataku, while at the Imperial Palace Lord Chancellor Bunchu and Duke Kou Hiko seek to protect the imperial princes.

Based on Ryu Fujisaki's 1996 manga for *Shonen Jump*, which adapted a Chinese ghost story for a modern Japanese audience, it was noteworthy for the originality of his characters and his remarkable graphic treatment of drapery and costume. Although set in a specific time, everything seems deliberately incoherent, notably the presence of a hi-fi set-up during festivals (also seen in the *Monkey* live-action series). Occasional laziness in the animation is obscured behind flashy computer graphics.

SOUL LINK
2006. TV series. DIR: Toshikatsu Tokoro. SCR: Isao Shizuya, Katsumi Hasegawa. DES: Yoshihiro Watanabe, Mitsuharu Miyamae. ANI: N/C. MUS: Hiroyuki Sawano. PRD: Picture Magic. 24 mins. x 12 eps.

A space station is attacked by terrorists while a group of cadets are aboard on a training exercise. Now Ryota and his classmates are stranded in space, trying to survive and get back to Earth. But there is a mystery connecting the course instructor, Cellaria Markelight, and Ryota's older brother: it had to do with a strange virus. A "recap special" was issued in June 2006, presenting the story from two different girls' viewpoints. There are also three four-minute picture dramas made as DVD extras, with characters reminiscing about their pasts. **ⒸⓋ**

SOUL TAKER, THE
2001. TV series. DIR: Akinori Arafusa. SCR: Mayori Sekijima. DES: Akio Watanabe, Noriaki Tetsura. ANI: Haruo Sotozaki, Toshiaki Aida. MUS: N/C. PRD: Tatsunoko, WOWOW. 25 mins. x 13 eps.

Kyosuke Date comes home on a visit from his college dormitory to a devastating scene. His mother, Mio, has been assaulted and is dying in a sea of blood, a knife gripped in her shaking hand. Beautiful Maya Misaki is somehow or other on hand to help. The bewildered Kyosuke learns things he never knew about his family. He has a twin sister, Runa, who has a group of "other selves," beings called Flickers. She's on the run from both the mysterious organization known as the Hospital, men in

white with seemingly magical powers, and from robots sent by Kirihara Kontzern, a giant corporation. Kyosuke has to find his sister so that he can find out why their mother died, and why so much mystery surrounds his family. See also the *Soul Taker* spin-off, **NURSE WITCH KOMUGI**.

SOUND OF MUSIC, THE
1991. JPN: *Trapp Ikka Monogatari*. AKA: *Story of the Trapp Family; The Trapp Family Story*. TV series. DIR: Kozo Kusuba, Jiro Saito, Fujino Sadohara, Nobuaki Nakanishi. SCR: Ayo Shiroya. DES: Shuichi Seki. ANI: Katsu Oshiro, Hiromi Kato, Nobuhiro Hosoi, Koji Ito, et al. MUS: Shinsuke Kazato. PRD: Nippon Animation, Fuji TV. 25 mins. x 40 eps.

In pre-WWII Austria lives the von Trapp family—widowed Baron Georg and his seven children—who find their lives transformed by their new nanny, who reinforces their love of music, and eventually helps them escape the Nazis. This anime was based on Maria Augusta Kutschera von Trapp's account of her family's struggles that was published as *The Story of the Trapp Family Singers* (1949) and made world famous by the 1959 Rodgers and Hammerstein musical and the subsequent 1965 film starring Julie Andrews, which fictionalized the events considerably. Part of the **WORLD MASTERPIECE THEATER** series, this anime also takes many liberties with the story, chiefly to make it palatable to a younger audience. The series was also cut down into an 85-minute feature-length TV movie that covered roughly the same pacing and ground as the live-action movie. Compare to **NETTI'S MARVELOUS STORY**.

SOUND OF THE SKY *
2010. JPN: *Sora no Oto*. TV series. DIR: Mamoru Kanbe. SCR: Hiroyuki Yoshino. DES: Toshifumi Akai, Junya Ishigaki, Masatoshi Kai. ANI: Mamoru Kanbe, Takayuki Tanaka, Toshinori Fukushima, Toshifumi Akai. MUS: Michiru Oshima. PRD: A-1 Pictures, Aniplex. 24 mins. x 14 eps.

Fifteen-year-old Kanata is a serving soldier, reassigned during a ceasefire in a long war. Sent to a fort in the pretty, apparently quiet little town of Sieze, she finds herself part of an all-girl unit with three main tasks: to maintain the fortress, to uphold local tradition that a population of young maidens control a local demon, and prepare for the very unlikely event of an attack. All the girls have come from different backgrounds but all have their own secrets. The old melody "Amazing Grace" has a deep significance for Kanata—and, it turns out, for others.

Post-apocalypse, pre-1940s: an alternate world with charmingly quaint technology, oddly futuristic tanks and oddly familiar customs. Or they're familiar if you've watched enough anime where grabbing each other's breasts in any situation is normal behavior for girls. The maidens protecting the local population by keeping a demon in check recalls folklore as well as anime, and their doing dual duty as soldiers takes us back to **VIRGIN FLEET**. The mishmash of European cultures mixed in to Japan to make up their world isn't quite as engaging as in **KIKI'S DELIVERY SERVICE**, but the backgrounds and designs are charming enough. The characters, pure dating-game stereotypes, are also intended to charm but we've been around this block a few too many times for them to do anything else.

SOUTHERN CROSS *

1984. JPN: *Chojiku Kitai Southern Cross*. AKA: *Superdimensional Cavalry Southern Cross*. TV series. DIR: Yasuo Hasegawa, Tsukasa Sunaga, Masakazu Yasumura, Katsuhisa Yamada, Hiroshi Yoshida. SCR: Jinzo Toriumi, Hisato Kaganai, Tomoko Kawasaki, Kenji Terada. DES: Miya Sonoda, Hiroshi Ogawa, Hiroyuki Kitazume. ANI: Yutaka Arai. MUS: Tsutomu Sato. PRD: Tatsunoko, TBS. 25 mins. x 23 eps.

The human colony world of Grolier is attacked by the savage alien Zor. Jeanne Francaix, hotheaded commander of the 15th Squadron of the Southern Cross army, is on the front line. Her close friend Bowie Emerson, a passionate music lover, is one of her troop, and when he is taken prisoner by the Zor, he falls in love with alien singer Musika. Believing that most of the Zor don't want war but are being forced into it by their commanders, he escapes, promising Musika that he will come back for her. Meanwhile Jeanne has fallen in love with Seifrietti Weisse, an enemy pilot who has been captured in battle and lost his memory. She convinces him that he should join the human side and enlists him in her squadron despite

the protests of her commander, who is not convinced by his courage and success in battle. The lovers find new hope in a hidden outcrop of beautiful, thriving flowers uncontaminated by the devastation that both races have wrought. They also learn that the leaders of Zor are planning the total extinction of humanity. Seifrietti's memory returns, and he decides to return to the Zor base alone and eliminate the leaders in the hope that his people can live in peace with humans and that their world can survive.

SC was only one of a rich crop of robot series from this period, and not the most successful, but it achieved fame in the West when it became part of **ROBOTECH**, with changes to character names and relationships made to support the new continuity. Jeanne became Dana, half-breed daughter of Max and Miriya Sterling from the *Macross Saga* segment. It would be more than a decade before Max and Miriya's "real" daughter, Mylene Jenius, took to the screen in **MACROSS** 7. The rewrite also brought a different kind of ecological emphasis. Carl Macek's *SC* removed one of Grolier's moons in order to claim the story was set on a polluted Earth: as in **GUNBUSTER**, it is humans, not aliens who now present the greatest threat to the environment. Humanity is presented as a race of shortsighted idiots whose fight for survival obscures the fact that they have wrecked their own planet, forcing other species into extinction just as the Zor leaders seek to wipe them out.

SOUTHERN RAINBOW

1982. JPN: *Minami no Niji no Lucy*. AKA: *Lucy of the Southern Rainbow*. TV series. DIR: Hiroshi Saito, Shigeo Koshi, Kozo Kusuba, Takayoshi Suzuki. SCR: Akira Miyazaki. DES: Shuichi Seki. ANI: Eimi Maeda, Koichi Murata, Fumiko Morimoto, Noboru Takano. MUS: Koichi Sakata. PRD: Nippon Animation, Fuji TV. 25 mins. x 50 eps.

Lucy May is the youngest daughter of the Popple family. In 1836, she sets out with her mother, father, brothers Ben and Tob, and sisters Clara and Kate on the long voyage from England to Australia, which was then a mysterious and hazardous continent where colonists faced hardship but had the opportunity to become rich in their new homeland. The series

covers four years during which, after many struggles, the family sets up a successful business in the new city of Adelaide. Part of the **WORLD MASTERPIECE THEATER** series, this anime was based on a novel by Phyllis Piddington serialized in the Japanese magazine *Living Book*.

SPA OF LOVE *

2005. JPN: *Ryojoku Hitozuma Onsen*. AKA: *Rape Wife Onsen*. Video. DIR: P Nakamura. SCR: Shima Iizaki. DES: Kenji Hattori. ANI: Takahiro Toyomasu. MUS: N/C. PRD: Waki Pro, GP Museum Soft, Image House, Milky. 30 mins. x 2 eps.

Yuji arrives at a traditional Japanese inn with impeccable references, but soon things start to go wrong. He rapes the young hostess and the maids, and also targets three innocent housewives who are saying at the inn. More domination and abuse, in a traditional setting similar to that of **SWALLOWTAIL INN**—the Japanese publicity specifies sex in the bath and lactating breasts as two of the "delights" awaiting within. Based on a computer game by Strikes. **ⒷⓃⓋ**

SPACE ACE *

1965. JPN: *Uchu Ace*. AKA: *Ring-O*. TV series. DIR: Hiroshi Sasagawa, Toshio Kinoshita, Ippei Kuri, Tatsuo Yoshida, Seiji Okuda. SCR: Jinzo Toriumi. DES: Tatsuo Yoshida. ANI: Akiyuki Kuma, Tatsuo Yoshida, Seiji Okuda. MUS: Taku Izumi. PRD: Tatsunoko, Fuji TV. 25 mins. x 52 eps. (b/w).

The survivors of an alien race set out in search of an uninhabited planet where their civilization can be rebuilt. During the voyage, a single ship piloted by one little alien leaves the convoy and lands on Earth. Professor Tatsunoko of the Tatsunoko Institute discovers what he thinks is a giant shell on the sea bed and opens it to find the childlike pilot. A creature from planet Parum, "Ace" can use "space fuse" energy to perform amazing feats of strength and can fly through the air on a silver ring. With the professor's daughter Asari (Ginger), cub reporter Yadokari (Flash Scoop), and Ebo (Ibo) the robot dog, Space Ace fights off alien monsters and invaders by using a high-energy food supply maintained by Asari and stored in Ebo's flip-top nose. The Tatsunoko Studio's first production, planned as an answer to Osamu Tezuka's **ASTRO BOY**. *SA* featured Rei Osumi as a "science fiction adviser"—the author took the studio's money in return for such suggestions as shooting one's way out of trouble with a "platina ray." Broadcast on Australian TV; the first episode was remade in color in an unsuccessful attempt to gain a U.S. sale. Not to be confused with the American animation by Don Bluth for the wholly unconnected *Space Ace* game.

SPACE ADVENTURE COBRA *

1982. JPN: *Space Cobra* (TV); *Space Adventure Cobra* (m). TV series, movie. DIR: Osamu Dezaki, Toshio Takeuchi, Shunji Oga, Masaharu Okuwaki. SCR: Kenji Terada, Haruya Yamazaki, Kosuke Miki. DES: Akio Sugino, Shinji Otsuka. ANI: Akio Sugino, Koji Morimoto, Ryutaro Nakamura, Atsuko Fukushima, Chuji Nakajima, Jun Kawagoe, Hideo Nanba, Takuya Wada. MUS: Kentaro Haneda (TV), Osamu Shoji (m). PRD: Tokyo Movie Shinsha, Fuji TV. 103 mins. (m), 25 mins. x 31 eps. (TV).

Bored 24th-century salaryman Mr. Johnson buys a virtual vacation at the Trip Movie Corporation only to discover that his chosen holiday (the life of a space pirate) triggers real memories that he has suppressed. He discovers that he really *is* Cobra, a rogue with a price on his head who has a false arm hiding the mentally powered "psychogun." Fleeing the Galactic Guild, he encounters beautiful bounty hunter Jane Royale (Jane Flower), who has part of a treasure map tattooed on her shapely back. Her sisters Dominique and Catherine have the other pieces that reveal the location of the Supreme Weapon. Cobra springs Catherine from prison before tracking down Dominique, a police officer who has infiltrated the all-female Snow Guerrillas gang. Though Cobra claims to want the Supreme Weapon (and, like any Buichi Terasawa hero worth his salt, to see the girls naked), he is also intent on protecting the ladies from Crystal Boy, his golden cyborg rival, who lacks Cobra's qualms about skinning them alive to make the map more portable.

Keeping relatively close to Buichi Terasawa's 1978 manga in *Shonen Jump* magazine, the first season's quest for the MacGuffin Supreme Weapon ends with Cobra recruited by Dominique for

undercover work. Investigating Guild drug-smuggling on planet Laloux, he joins the Red Saxons, a sports team that plays the rugby/baseball hybrid *rugball*. Amid violent matches reminiscent of *Rollerball* (1975), he rises through the ranks to crack the case and win the championship. The series ends with a third arc, as Cobra locates Salamander, the entity behind the guild that's revealed to be an energy field controlled by the spirit of Adolf Hitler.

Predating *Total Recall* with its original premise, *SAC* is typical Terasawa, crammed full of leggy, disposable beauties who turn up, wiggle their assets, snog the hero, and then get shot. It's got plenty of ray-gun action, as well as the artist's other trademark—madly futurist designs based on contemporary technologies like motorcycles, cars, and planes.

The TV series was preceded by a feature, with a script written by Terasawa himself and Haruya Yamazaki—Miyazaki's amanuensis on **CASTLE OF CAGLIOSTRO**. The movie script shuffles the characters into a slightly different setting—in this version Jane Flower and her sisters Catherine and Dominique form the three aspects of the Empress of the Universe, ruler of the planet Myras, who will manifest when all fall in love with the same man (guess who?). Crystal Boy (AKA Necron) is now the personification of Death itself, tracking Cobra as he springs Catherine from jail and encounters Dominique on the Planet of the Snow Guerrillas. Clearly a dry run for the later series, changes made between the two include a new composer and the replacement of the original Cobra voice actor Shigeru Matsuzaki with Nachi Nozawa. *SAC* also steals from many SF movies, including *Barbarella* (1967), *Flash Gordon* (1980), the Genesis project from *Star Trek: Wrath of Khan* (1982), and the carbonite-freezing episode from *The Empire Strikes Back* (1980). The movie is often claimed as a sequel set two years *after* the TV events, though it requires remarkable suspension of disbelief to accept that Cobra would meet two trios of virtually identical girls with the same names, occupations, and troubles. Similarly, the movie version does not allude to Mr. Johnson's induction at the Trip Movie Corporation; Japanese audiences familiar with the manga could disregard any of the film's more far-fetched

or hallucinatory episodes as yet more evidence that this is all "really a dream"—not an option available to most English-speaking viewers. When dubbed for the U.K. market, Manga Entertainment replaced the Japanese soundtrack with all-new material from the group Yello. The decision gained *SAC* extra press coverage and papered over the cracks to make this antique film seem up-to-date, while the 1995 copyright date for the new score helped imply it was newer than it really was.

The series is popular to this day and has an ardent fan following in Japan and Europe. Scenes from the feature were also recycled for Matthew Sweet's pop promo "Girlfriend." However, its influence was strongest in Korea, where Cobra's relationship with Jane was shoddily rehashed with Hyesong and Marie Kim in Lee Hyun-se's *Armageddon* (1996). Other Terasawa works adapted as anime include **GOKU: MIDNIGHT EYE** and **KABUTO**.

SPACE DANDY *

2014. TV series. DIR: Shinichiro Watanabe, Shingo Natsume. SCR: Dai Sato, Kimiko Ueno, Keiko Nobumoto, Toh Enjoe, Shinichiro Watanabe. DES: Yoshiyuki Ito. ANI: Yoshiyuki Ito. MUS: Various. PRD: Studio Bones, TV Tokyo. 25 mins. x 13 eps. (TV1), 25 mins. x 13 eps. (TV2).

Handsome but clueless alien-hunter Dandy is a quiffy-haired spaceman, accompanied by an outmoded cleaning robot and a dim-witted cat-like Betelgeusian. He is supposed to chase after and register new alien species, but is much more interested in visiting every branch of Boobies, a mammary-minded "breastaurant" chain in space.

Your mileage may vary. *Space Dandy* has acquired an enthusiastic following among anime **FANDOM**, with any nay-sayers swiftly dismissed as sulking **COWBOY BEBOP** aficionados, annoyed that Shinichiro Watanabe's latest show is not a carbon copy of his most famous success. As comedy, it is certainly made with an appreciation that clichés are best rewarmed by confounding expectations, usually accomplished with throwaway sight-gags—reptilian alien boobs to taunt horny fanboys, for example, or a tragic lost lover who turns out to have been killed by her boyfriend's fiery breath rather than anything more malicious. That's not to say that the show doesn't have some clever ideas buried beneath its devil-may-care surface, much as SAMURAI CHAMPLOO bragged of its irreverence, while actually taking its inspirations very seriously. An episode that turns all the cast into zombies, for example, offers some intriguing riffs on pulp tradition, such as the consideration that being undead would allow one to leech off one's own life insurance.

But *Space Dandy*'s reduction to the absurd of the TROPES AND TRADITIONS of anime may have gone too far in its wilful removal of any jeopardy. With an opening episode in which the entire cast is killed, only to be resurrected for episode 2, it taunts its audience with a permanently available reset button. We've seen such things before, of course, in the likes of *South Park* and *Tom and Jerry*, but in *Space Dandy* they come across like the apotheosis of anime's cavalier attitude toward plot and story. After two decades of remakes and reboots that trample on previous continuities, *Space Dandy* presents the complete absence of continuity as a fait accompli. Certain anime have often served as little more than hooks to hang some characters in as they bumble around, mug to the camera, and sell themselves in merchandise form. *Space Dandy* takes that to its logical extreme—a fun joke, perhaps, but surely a joke that can only work once before people tire of it. **NV**

SPACE DEFENSE OFFICER TAA-BO

1991. JPN: *Uchu Boeitai Taa-bo*. AKA: *Space Self Defense Force Taa-Bo*. Movie, video. DIR: Masami Hata. SCR: Joji Iida, Anzu Nemuru. DES: Koichi Kadowaki. ANI: Toshiharu Akahori. MUS: Toyomi Kojima. PRD: Sanrio. 34 mins., 30 mins.
Interstellar crime-fighter Taa-bo fights the evil Scorpion Brothers in a short-lived attempt to introduce a more traditional hero to the Sanrio lineup. After his movie debut *Taa-Bo on the Planet of the Dragon Pavilion* (1991, *Taa-bo no Ryumiyasei Daitanken*), the character devolved to video, where he disappeared from view after *Taa-Bo on the Planet Where Time Stopped* (1993, *Taa-bo no Toki no Tomatta Sei*). The "movie" was also bundled onto a Sanrio anthology tape with mini-features of more popular stars HELLO KITTY and KEROPPI.

SPACE DEMON DAIKENGO

1978. JPN: *Uchu Majin Daikengo*. AKA: *Space Machine Daikengo; Space Devil/ God Daikengo*. TV series. DIR: Asahi Yahiro, Noriyasu Furukawa, Hiroshi Yamanouchi, Hideyoshi Ojika. SCR: Akiyoshi Sakai, Jinzo Toriumi, Satoshi Toyama, Ichiro Yamamura, Michio Fukushima, Hajime Mori. DES: Kunio Okawara, Mitsuki Nakamura, Motohiro Takahashi, Tadakazu Iguchi. ANI: Tadanori Tanabe, Kenzo Koizumi, Tadakazu Iguchi, Tsuneo Ninomiya. MUS: Hiroshi Tsutsui. PRD: Tori Pro, Studio Nue, Toei Animation, TV Asahi. 25 mins. x 26 eps.
There's intrigue afoot on planet Emperius. Prince Zamuson is murdered, but urges his younger brother Rygar to escape before dying at the hands of alien invaders. Believing the attackers were aided by local traitors, Rygar flees to avoid imprisonment. He has his sympathizers—beautiful Cleo, daughter of the corrupt Prime Minister, and two helpful robots, Anike and Otoke. Rygar revives the legendary giant spacerobot Daikengo, and he and his supporters fight the invading soldiers of the Magellan Empire, commanded by the evil Lady Baracross and her protege Roboleon, until peace is restored to Emperius and the galaxy. This is supposedly the first giant robot anime not to be focused on Earth (BATTLE OF THE PLANETS only acquired its deep-space focus in non-Japanese versions), and Daikengo is certainly the first robot to be able to open his mouth, show pointed fangs, and spit fire. The show was made by "Tori Pro," a group of defectors from the Tatsunoko studio, with whose productions this has many similarities.

SPACE FAMILY CARLVINSON

1988. JPN: *Uchu Kazoku Carlbinson*. Video. DIR: Kimio Yabuki, Tatsuo Suzuki. SCR: Michiru Shimada. DES: Yoshito Asari. ANI: Masahiro Kanno. MUS: Hiroya Watanabe. PRD: Toei. 45 mins.
A traveling-show troupe of aliens are playing cards when a vessel comes out of warp space and nearly crashes into their ship before crashing on planet Anika. The only survivor is a baby human girl, Corona. They decide to look after her, at least until somebody shows up to claim her. In order to equip themselves to play the part of the "normal" human family and friends the baby will need, they research information from the crashed ship's data banks and embark on one of the longest-running shows of their entire career. But they identify more and more with their roles, and when a ship comes for Corona five years later, they have *become* her family and friends.

Yoshito Asari's 1985 manga in *Shonen Captain* was a revamp of the popular SWISS FAMILY ROBINSON castaway theme that also inspired the U.S. comic *Space Family Robinson*, later known as *Lost in Space*. Mysteriously, the Nimitz-class U.S. aircraft carrier Carl Vinson visited Japan in the 1980s, though it seems likely that the use of its name is either coincidence or one of those meaningless puns that the Japanese find so entertaining (see SORCERER HUNTERS). As Chairman of the House Naval Affairs Committee from 1931 to 1947, the original Carl Vinson could be said to be personally responsible for the support and maintenance of the U.S. Navy during WWII, which hardly seems likely to have endeared him to the Japanese.

SPACE FIREBIRD *

1980. JPN: *Hi no Tori 2772: Ai no Cosmozone*. AKA: *Firebird 2772: Love's Cosmozone; Phoenix 2772*. Movie. DIR: Taku Sugiyama. SCR: Osamu Tezuka, Taku Sugiyama. DES: Shinji Ito, Tsuyoshi Matsumoto, Noboru Ishiguro. ANI: Kazuko Nakamura, Noboru Ishiguro. MUS: Yasuo Higuchi. PRD: Kadokawa, Tohoku Shinsha. 122 mins. (m), 60 mins. (v1, *Karma*), 48 mins. (v2, *Yamato*), 48 mins. (v3, *Space*), 25 mins. x 13 eps. (TV).
In the 22nd century, humans are bred to order, raised in laboratories, and selected for their roles from birth by a tyrannical government exploiting the planet to the verge of ecological collapse. Godot is lucky enough to be raised by the robot Olga, a warm, gentle mother-figure who looks like a fetishist's dream girl in her shiny red outfit and can transform into a whole range of fabulous toys and vehicles. He grows up to be a sensitive and intelligent young man who rebels against the harshness and cruelty of his society. While training to be a space pilot, he learns that he has a brother, Rock, who is one of the ruling class, selected for his intelligence and ruthlessness. He also falls in love with Lena,

an upper-class girl, and, because this is a crime against the State (and against Rock, her fiancé!), he is sent to a harsh prison planet. He is offered his freedom if he will capture the Space Firebird, a mystical creature whose blood can bestow immortality and everlasting power. The faithful Olga, who has followed him through all his troubles, joins him on his mission; she has always loved him and is determined to help him use the powers of the Firebird to revive the dying Earth.

Based on Osamu Tezuka's long-running series of 12 interlinked tales first begun in 1967 in the manga magazine *Com*, this magical love story contains many elements common in his work—the recycling of characters (**BLACK JACK** is the prison planet commandant), the use of comic characters and musical numbers straight out of Disney, the contrast between inner beauty and outer sham, supportive and exploitative relationships, and the visual inventiveness that makes every frame a pleasure. There are unexpected roles for Frederik L. Schodt and his fellow translator Jared Cook, credited along with SF writer Sakyo Komatsu as "planning brains."

The phoenix in *Space Firebird* is an eternal being who visits all parts of space and time in the course of the long-running *Phoenix* manga, which only finished in 1988, shortly before Tezuka's death in February 1989. The earliest chapters, created at the height of Tezuka's powers when he was also writing **ASTRO BOY**, are said to be the best. The third, fourth, and fifth chapters of the original were also animated for video by the Madhouse studio. The one-shots were supervised by Rintaro and seem to be a short-lived attempt to follow *SF* with the ten remaining chapters, though only these three were made. Rintaro's *Phoenix: Karma* (1986, *Hi no Tori: Hoo Hen*), also shown in cinemas on a double bill with **TIME STRANGER**, features the firebird's manifestation in ancient India, where it witnesses a conflict between a pirate king and a sculptor, who is, of course, making a statue of a phoenix. Toshio Hirata's *Phoenix: Yamato* (1987, *Hi no Tori: Yamato Hen*) moves to Japan for a retelling of the story of **YAMATO TAKERU**. The last episode, Yoshiaki Kawajiri's *Phoenix: Space* (1987, *Hi No Tori: Uchu Hen*), features the Earthbound starship ZFX-302

finding an icy planet whose occupants prefer death to life.

A 13-episode *Phoenix* TV series (*Hi no Tori*, 2004) was directed by Ryosuke Takahashi, and spanned the various incarnations of the story from Dawn to Future. It was coproduced by New York's WNET/13 PBS station.

SPACE PATROL HOPPER
1965. JPN: *Uchu Patrol Hopper*. AKA: (see below). TV series. DIR: Taiji Yabushita, Yoshio Ishihara, Yoshio Kuroda, Hiroshi Shidara, Masayuki Akehi. SCR: Taiji Yabushita, Susumu Ginga, Fumi Takahashi. DES: N/C. ANI: Masao Kumogawa. MUS: Shunsuke Kikuchi. PRD: Toei, NET. 25 mins. x 44 eps.
After being severely injured in a space accident, Earth boy Jun is saved by the Hopper Aliens, who give him a new cyborg body. With superhuman powers, Jun signs up for the space patrol along with fellow operatives Donkey, Pooh, Dar, Hook, and Professor Doc. After episode 27, the title was changed to *Patrol Team: Space Boy Jun* (*Patrol Tai: Uchukko Jun*). One of many 1960s also-rans in the wake of **ASTRO BOY**, including **PRINCE PLANET**, **SORAN THE SPACE BOY**, and **SPACE ACE**.

SPACE PIRATE MITO *
1999. JPN: *Uchu Kaizoku Mito no Daiboken*. AKA: *Stellarbusters; Great Adventures of Space Pirate Mito*. TV series. DIR: Takashi Watanabe, Koji Yasuda, Yoshio Nitta, Masahiko Murata, Shigeru Ueda, Kunitoshi Okajima. SCR: Hidefumi Kimura, Junko Okazaki. DES: Reibanji Ishigami. ANI: Masahiro Sekiguchi, Hiroshi Kanazawa. MUS: Hikaru Nanase. PRD: Sunrise, TV Tokyo. 25 mins. x 13 eps. (TV1), 25 mins. x 13 eps. (TV2), 4 mins. (v1, *Peaceful Days*), ? mins. (v2, *Mito Wars*).
Fifteen-year-old Aoi discovers that his mother is not a model working abroad at all. He discovers this when she is attacked in the cemetery by members of the space patrol, where she reveals that her adult body harbors Mito, a childlike female space pirate. Mito is his real mother, but, because she is an alien, she does not appear old enough to be. She reveals that Aoi is actually the heir to the throne of the Great Kingdom of the Milky Way, and they are chased by Lanban, the corrupt leader of the space patrol, who wants an artifact

that can make *him* king of the galaxy instead. A sci-fi take on the stories of Mitsukuni Tokugawa (see **MANGA MITO KOMON**), with a space pirate straight out of **TENCHI MUYO!**, this series only got more bizarre for its second season. In the second series, *Aoi and Mutsuki: A Pair of Queens* (JPN: *Uchu Kaizoku Mito no Daiboken: Futari no Joosama*), Aoi has fallen in love with Mutsuki, one of the space patrol officers sent after Mito, and suddenly turned into a girl. The newly female Aoi becomes Queen of the Milky Way but also continues to attend Japanese high school in disguise. The former Queen, Hikari, returns as a ghost and demands her throne back, setting the stage for more space piracy (in the name of the established order) and motherly interference from Mito (who seems to have been passed over in the succession). When released on video, the series also included bonus shorts—*The Peaceful Days of the People of Mito*, which is an immediate prequel to the first series and briefly introduces the cast in their "native environs," and *Mito Wars*, a music video of the second series' opening theme, which was an early experiment in full digital animation.

SPACE PIRATE SARA
2008. JPN: *Uchu Kaizoku Sara*. Video. DIR: Yanaha Sadayama. SCR: Shinichiro Sawayama. DES: Satoru Seura, Shinji Katahira. ANI: Yanaha Sadayama. MUS: N/C. PRD: Pixy. 26 mins. x 4 eps.
Sara Scorpion is out to find a treasure that will make her heir to the Imperial Throne: the Sword of Bernstein. She's distracted by weapons of a different kind when she runs into a little trouble en route. Based on a porn game by Lilith's Black Lilith, so expect gang rape, tentacles, and bestiality as well as space piracy. **🅝🅥**

SPACE RUNAWAY IDEON
1980. JPN: *Densetsu Kyoshin Ideon*. AKA: *Legendary God-Giant Ideon*. TV series, movie. DIR: Yoshiyuki Tomino, Masanori Miura, Toshifumi Takizawa. SCR: Sukehiro Tomita, Yuji Watanabe, Arata Koga. DES: Tomonori Kogawa, Submarine. ANI: Tomonori Kogawa. MUS: Koichi Sugiyama. PRD: Sunrise, TV Tokyo. 25 mins. x 39 eps. (TV), 185 mins. (m1), 99 mins. (m2).
In 2400, the human race and the Buff Clan are at war, but one young pilot be-

lieves that peace can be made between the two enemies. Meanwhile humankind has one last line of defense: advanced war machines retrieved from the destroyed colony world Solo, which can be combined into the super-robot Ideon—piloted by Cosmo Yuki, Casha Imhof, Tekuno, and Bento. Devised by Yoshiyuki Tomino in large part as a reworking of his popular GUNDAM, SRI had an even more outrageous main robot. It was formed from three giant trucks (Sol-Amber, Sol-Vainer, and Sol-Conver), each of which could become an independent war machine (Ideo-Delta, Ideo-Nova, or Ideo-Buster) and was armed with massive quantities of weaponry, including a small black-hole cannon. Any fan would call that serious play value, but the merchandising of SRI never took off as Gundam's did. Two films followed in 1982, shown on the same double bill. The first was a digest of episodes 1–32, the second of the finale, with bonus footage from the canceled episodes 40–43. Within five years, the coming of video would make such "movies" much rarer, and less popular with audiences—witness the outrage at the discovery that much of the EVANGELION: Death and Rebirth double bill was recycled TV footage.

SPACE SAGITTARIUS

1986. JPN: Uchusen Sagittarius. AKA: Spaceship Sagittarius. TV series. DIR: Kazuyoshi Yokota, Jiro Saito, Keiji Hayakawa. SCR: Nobuyuki Isshiki, Nobuyuki Fujimoto. DES: Sadahiko Sakamaki, Shuichi Seki, Noboru Takano. ANI: Hiroyoshi Sugawara. MUS: Haruki Mino. PRD: Nippon Animation, TV Asahi. 25 mins. x 77 eps.
Mr. Giraffe, a scientist, commissions Toppie and Lana, a mouse and frog with their own space haulage company, to take him in search of his teacher Anne, who disappeared while trying to prove her scientific theories on the dangerous planet Vega III. The pilots are dragged away from their loved ones (in Toppie's case, his pregnant wife, while Lana simply kisses his lasagna goodbye), and they are soon in trouble when facing a death sentence on the first planet they reach. Saved by the minstrel Sibip, they continue their journey. Based on the Italian comic Altri Mondi by Andrea Romoli, this charming little fantasy series brings together three animal astronauts who cruise the galaxy in the good ship

Sagittarius, with anthropomorphic adventures in the style of SHERLOCK HOUND and MONTANA JONES.

SPACE TRAVELERS: THE ANIMATION *

2000. Video. DIR: Takashi Ui. SCR: Katsuhiko Koide. DES: Takashi Okazaki. ANI: Noboru Takahashi. MUS: Toshiyuki Watanabe. PRD: Amuse Video, Fuji TV, Robot. 60 mins.
Plucky hero Hayabusa Jetter, his ingenue sidekick Irene Bear, muscle-mountain Crush Bomber, slimy Chinese trader Hoi, slinky femme fatale Gold Papillon, boomerang-throwing kid Black Cat, unstoppable space samurai Dragon Attack, mechanic Electric Sunny, and funky cyber-hipster Karl Hendrix fight to restore the honor of planet Earth after an apocalyptic interstellar incident. A parody of the giant-robot space operas of the 1980s, with homages to Star Wars and Star Trek thrown in, ST is cheap and derivative, though the producers would argue that this was at least part of the plan.
It began as a throwaway gag in Katsuyuki Motohiro's popular live-action movie Space Travelers (2000) in which a Tokyo bank robbery goes disastrously wrong. As the police surround the building, the staff and hostages volunteer to help the robbers bluff their way out; each is given a code name based on a character from the robbers' favorite cartoon, a nonexistent show called Space Travelers—hence the ridiculously large cast of anime archetypes. Scraps of animation were made as inserts for the original movie and are reused here—hence the strange pacing of the overlong opening credits that were not originally intended to be shown in this manner. The plot is a tired succession of fight scenes, a ludicrous transformation sequence, and an in-joke as the crew flies past the ruins of the Fuji TV building. An afterthought following the movie's success, ST was reputedly inspired by Motohiro's love of STAR BLAZERS, GUNDAM, and EVANGELION, though in execution it is a pale imitation of the 1970s hacksploitation of COWBOY BEBOP and all too obviously a product of the terminally low budgets of many 1990s anime. Ironically, it was Motohiro's previous film Bayside Shakedown (1999) that was said to have sounded the death knell for anime—not understanding its appeal to the teen audience, certain

producers backed away from making shows for that age group, only to discover that the producers' follow-up was just that. Motohiro himself would achieve significantly greater anime success with his later PSYCHO-PASS.

SPACE WARRIORS *

1980. JPN: Uchu Senshi Baldios. AKA: Space Warrior Baldios; Baldios. TV series, movie. DIR: Kazuyuki Hirokawa, Takao Yotsuji, Kunihiko Yuyama, Kazuya Yamazaki, Seiji Yamamuro, Junji Nishimura, Osamu Sekita. SCR: Akiyoshi Sakai, Jinzo Toriumi, Tomomi Tsutsui, Takeshi Shudo. DES: Osamu Kamijo, Hajime Kamegaki. ANI: Takeshi Tanaka, Toyoo Ashida. MUS: Kentaro Haneda. PRD: Ashi Productions, Tokyo 12 Channel. 25 mins. x 31 eps. (TV), 117 mins. (m).
Marin Reagan, a native of planet S1, flees a radioactive atmosphere and the persecutions of dictator Gattler, making his way to Earth. Gattler and the S-1 armies are on their way to take over the planet as a replacement for their hopelessly polluted homeworld, and Marin joins the team working to defend Earth from alien attack as the pilot of super-robot Baldios. Earth and S-1 are fated to come into final conflict, and the love-hate relationship between Marin and Aphrodia, commander of the S-1 forces, will finally be resolved. The show went off the air with another eight episodes to go, leading to protests from Japanese fans. The partly completed finale was assembled with some new footage from Toyoo Ashida to make a movie release, Space Warrior Baldios (1981, AKA Revenge of the Space Warriors, AKA SW: Battle for Earth Station S-1), showing the last battle between Gattler's spaceship Aldebaran and the Earth satellite base Blue Fixer under Commander Tsukikage. Gattler offers Aphrodia the chance to avenge her dead brother by killing Marin, but she can't do it and commits suicide. The ensuing battle destroys both armies and their weapons, and Marin, the sole survivor, is left to return to a devastated Earth with the body of the woman he truly loved. A 98-minute version of the movie was screened in Japan and is also available on video in the U.S.

SPACEKETEERS *

1978. JPN: SF Saiyuki Starzinger. AKA: SF Journey to the West Starzinger. TV series.

DIR: Yugo Serikawa, Kozo Morishita, Kazumi Fukushima. SCR: Tatsuo Tamura, Mitsuru Majima, Sukehiro Tomita. DES: Masami Suda. ANI: Masami Suda, Satoshi Kamimiya. MUS: Shunsuke Kikuchi. PRD: Toei, Fuji TV. 25 mins. x 73 eps.

As the Queen of the Great Planet at the center of the universe grows old, the harmony of the universe becomes unbalanced. Minerals and planets transform into evil starmen and attack other planets. In order to restore peace, the old queen must be replaced with a young, strong ruler who can keep her subjects in order. Princess Aurora is saved by scientist Dr. Kitty when the starmen attack the moon. He knows that she has the power to restore the harmony of the universe as the new ruler of the Great Planet, so she sets out in the spaceship Cosmos Queen with three companions charged to keep her safe: Sir Jogo (Arimos) from the planet of water, Don Hakka (Porkos) from the planet of fire, and rebel cyborg Jan Kugo (Jesse Dart), who wears a control circlet around his head. The starmen and other monsters try to stop them, but Aurora won't allow any creatures who were originally peaceful to be killed. She knows that if she fulfills her destiny, they will be restored to their former shapes and will once again live in harmony with their fellow beings.

Based on the *Terebi* magazine manga by CAPTAIN HARLOCK–creatorLeiji Matsumoto, this SF retelling of JOURNEY TO THE WEST was rebranded as *SFSS "II"* for its final nine episodes, in which the four have replenished the galactic energy provided by the old queen and go to the solar system of Girara, which is still unbalanced and needs Princess Aurora to restore it to normalcy. This time, the farewell to their princess is a final one, and her three companions must take their leave of her, but all of them (especially Kogo) leave their hearts in her keeping. Edited down to 26 episodes for U.S. release as part of the FORCE FIVE series, Jim Terry's new title and character names now misleadingly implied a space-going THREE MUSKETEERS. For the U.S. version, the characters are on a mission to the Dekos Star System, whose evil power source has caused the once-peaceful creatures of the universe to change into evil mutants.

SPACESHIP AGGA RUTER *
1998. JPN: *Space Opera Agga Ruter*. Video. DIR: Shigeru Yazaki. SCR: Masaki Kajishima, Hideyuki Kurata. DES: Masaki Kajishima, Kenji Teraoka. ANI: Katsuhisa Ito. MUS: T.K. Crow. PRD: AIC, Beam Entertainment. 30 mins. x 4 eps.

The evil Shiunk kills Taiyo's parents and leaves him to die in space. Rescued by the kindly android Kei, Taiyo is raised without human companionship for 15 years aboard her ship the Agga Ruter. Kei tells Taiyo to call her "Mother" and instructs him in the arts of love in a succession of Oedipally suspect scenes. When captured by the shrill space pirate Janis (who has been hired by Shiunk to steal the Agga Ruter), the pair prove to be perkily cooperative hostages, volunteering to cook and clean, rummaging in her underwear drawer, and reading out the funny bits from her diary. Janis is a descendant of Re-Formed Humans, ancient members of the Fighter civilization who recombined their DNA to survive on hostile worlds. Though she appears human, she turns into a were-tiger when reminded of abuse at the hands of her circus-ringmaster stepfather. Endowed with superhuman strength *and* bedroom prowess, Taiyo is the only man who can satisfy her, and the sexually sated Janis agrees to switch sides. The Agga Ruter, itself a Fighter relic (see the similar SOL BIANCA), lacks a vital component, which has been mistaken for a precious gem and put on display on the Millennium Mulecruise liner. The gang sneak in to steal it, but Shiunk (now disguised as the Joker with a bad blond wig) has followed them and arranged for their capture by a vicious green-eyed blonde, who is luckily not immune to Taiyo's charms.

A sci-fi porno made by the thinly disguised cast and crew of the TENCHI MUYO! series, whose audience was probably old enough by this point to appreciate the "joke." Even the humor is familiar, with Kei setting up a mock Japanese living room on the bridge of Janis's warship in order to teach her how to be a good wife (sexually available and a great cook). Taiyo is a dead ringer for the older but still passive hero of *Tenchi in Tokyo*, the Agga Ruter is a ship with all the weird properties of Jurai vessels, and the females are cookie-cutter *Tenchi* girlies. Compare to MASQUERADE,

which also appears to be reheated leftovers from the franchise. ◐

SPARKLING PHANTOM
1990. JPN: *Runohara Meikyu: Sparkling Phantom*. AKA: *Runohara Labyrinth: SP*. Video. DIR: Narumi Kakinouchi. SCR: Narumi Kakinouchi. DES: Kana Hoshino. ANI: N/C. MUS: N/C. PRD: Victor Entertainment. 45 mins.

This SF fantasy about a Japanese girl who is transported to an alternate world populated by fairies was based on the manga in *Hana to Yume* magazine by Kana Hoshino.

SPARROW'S HOTEL *
2013. TV series, video. DIR: Tetsuji Nakamura. SCR: N/C. DES: Daisuke Kusakari. ANI: N/C. MUS: N/C. PRD: Hotline, AT-X, Dream Creation, Takeshobo. 3 mins. x 12 eps. (TV) 3 mins. (v)

Short slice-of-life comedy based on the four-panel gag strip by Yuka Santo, in which the impossibly pretty Sayuri, who lists her best qualities as "large breasts and assassination," works in the titular hotel, occasionally putting her ninja-like skills to good use. Much of the comedy relies on the premise that an EVERYDAY ANIME is taken as seriously and dramatically as a thriller, with deadly stakes over whether or not the management snoop will uncover incompetence among the chamber maids, and whether or not anyone needs to kill the difficult customer in room #103. As if the cast of NINJA SCROLL were left to run Fawlty Towers. An unbroadcast "13th" episode was added to the DVD release.

SPECTRAL FORCE
1998. JPN: *Spectral Force*. Video. DIR: Yoshiaki Sato. SCR: Yoshiaki Sato. DES: Shinnosuke Hino, Tatsunori Nakamura. ANI: Katsuaki Tsubata. MUS: Toru Kobayashi. PRD: Idea Factory, Toon Works. 30 mins. x 2 eps.

This heroic fantasy has fighters duelling for supremacy in the world of Neverland (no relation to PETER PAN AND WENDY). Featuring copious computer graphics, it was based on the *Spectral Force* video game—note that the Japanese katakana title is more logically read as "Spectral Phase," but the English letters on the box insist otherwise.

SPECTRE
1991. JPN: *Boso Sengoku Shi Spectre/ Requiem*. AKA: *Racing Civil War Chronicle Spectre/Requiem*. Video. DIR: Yoichiro Shimatani. SCR: Yoichirio Shimatani, Ranko Ono. DES: Fumihide Sai, Hiroshi Kiyomizudera. ANI: Fumihide Sai. MUS: Takahiko Kanamaru. PRD: Apples, Miyuki Pro. 45 mins. x 2 eps.
Modern-day bikers make and break alliances with neighboring gangs, fight over the right to use a local petrol station, and are eventually united under a powerful leader. It's a replay of the events of Japan's 16th-century civil war, but with bikes instead of horses and knives instead of swords. Based on the manga by Jiro Ueno in *Weekly Playboy*. ❂

SPEED GRAPHER *
2005. TV series. DIR: Kunihisa Sugishima, Masashi Ishihama. SCR: Shin Yoshida, Yasuyuki Suzuki. DES: Yusuke Kozaki, Masashi Ishihama. ANI: Masashi Ishihama, Toyoaki Fukushima. MUS: Shinkichi Mitsumune. PRD: Gonzo, TAP, TV Asahi. 25 mins. x 24 eps.
Cameraman Tatsumi Saiga used to have a real job as a war photographer, but a strange chain of circumstances led him into the unprincipled end of the market among the paparazzi. Hanging around Tokyo scrabbling for salable shots, his perfectionism works against him. When he's hired to snap the exclusive Roppongi Club, he can't afford to say no, despite the difficulties. The club's location is secret, it's open only to the A-list, and rumor says that members get access to extraordinary powers through secret ceremonies and forbidden fantasies. When Saiga sneaks in and photographs one of these strange ceremonies, he's caught out by a goddess who, far from being angry, enables him to change into Speed Grapher, a superhuman entity with the power to make anything or anyone he photographs explode—an update of the old superstition that taking someone's photograph will steal his soul. Gorgeous 15-year-old Kagura wants to get away from the club before she becomes a bit player in someone else's twisted fantasy. They get out, but now face retribution from the cult.

SPEED RACER *
1967. JPN: *Mach Go Go Go*. AKA: *Mach 5, Go Go!* TV series. DIR: Tatsuo Yoshida, Ippei Kuri,

Hiroshi Sasagawa, Seitaro Hara, Hiroyuki Fukushima. SCR: Jinzo Toriumi, Tadashi Hirose, Takashi Hayakawa, Masaaki Sakurai, Masashi Kubota. DES: Ippei Kuri, Hiroshi Sasagawa. ANI: Masami Suda, Takashi Saijo. MUS: Nobuyoshi Koshibe, Michiru Oshima. PRD: Tatsunoko, Fuji TV, TV Tokyo. 25 mins. x 52 eps. (TV1), 25 mins. x 34 eps. (TV2), 3 mins. x 26 eps. (*Mach Girl*).
Go Mifune (Speed) is a young racing driver for his father Daisuke's (Pops Racer) Mifune Motors team (nameless in the U.S. version). His mother Aya (Mom Racer), irritating kid brother Kuo (Spritle), and pet monkey Senpei (Chim Chim) all work on the team along with Go's girlfriend, Michi (Trixie), and mechanic Sabu (Sparks). Go's success and the superb engineering of his racing car the Mach Five lead other jealous racers to try and put a spanner in the works, but they are foiled by the mysterious Masked Racer (Racer X), who also fends off master criminals and foreign spies. He's really Go's older brother Kenichi (Rex), a government agent who, for a variety of top-secret reasons, is compelled to work anonymously and cut himself off from his family. The series contained a surprising amount of violence and tension, and it had all the technical limitations of 1960s TV animation, but since distributors K. Fujita had successfully sold **MARINE BOY** to U.S. company Trans-Lux, it had a ready market for this new product.
Accepted by many of its fans as an American product from the first American TV screening in 1967, *Speed Racer* amended the Japanese original considerably. Actor/writer Peter Fernandez was entrusted with the task of toning down the Japanese version for U.S. consumption, and he ensured that no *Speed Racer* villain was ever killed by amending the scripts and inserting shots of stunned bad guys with cartoon planets and stars circling their heads.
A revival on MTV led to the making of a new 13-episode series, *The New Adventures of Speed Racer* (1993) by Fred Wolf Films in 1993; this really *was* an American cartoon. A proposed live-action feature film didn't get beyond concept stage, but 1994 brought us *Speed Racer the Movie*—a compilation of two series episodes with an episode of *Colonel Bleep* interspersed

with classic animated TV commercials of the 1960s to bulk out the running time to 80 minutes. Speed would also appear in a commercial for Volkswagen and a music video for Ghost-Face Killah. He returned to Japan, this time to TV Tokyo, in a 34-episode "30th anniversary" remake in 1997, with Pops renamed Daisuke Hibiki and new character Mai Kazami (photographer/love interest) along with her brother, Wataru (brat). The final season neglected the racing plot in favor of time travel. After hitting 555 kph while trying to outrun a tornado, Speed is catapulted through time to the year 2555, when the world is ruled by the evil dictator Handler. With his car newly converted to a fully operational time machine, Speed and the gang set off in search of the Ezekiel Wheel, an energy source that can change the future.
Seemingly produced in order to cash in on the Wachowski siblings' disappointing Hollywood movie adaptation the same year, Takashi Yamada's *Mach Girl* (2008) is a 26-part series of spin-off shorts, each three minutes long, in which sexy motorcycle ace Lip enters races on her amazing pink three-wheel bike, Mach Three. The look is astonishingly reminiscent of Hanna-Barbera's *Wacky Races* with our heroine as the Harajuku take on Southern belle Penelope Pitstop. The character style is fascinating, with many similarities to advertising illustrations of the 1960s, showing influences from artists such as Margaret Keane and Rune Naito.

SPELUNKER SENSEI
2011. Video. DIR: Minoru Ashina. SCR: N/C. DES: Shinpei Ogasawara, Yasutomo Ishii. ANI: Minoru Takehara. MUS: Mickey Miki. PRD: Studio Puyukai, Medicrie, indeprox, Kentaro Hattori. 30 mins.
Spelunker is a new physical education teacher with some very odd habits, chief among which is that he wears a hard hat with a light on the front all the time because his hobby is exploring caves. Oh, and he dies. Repeatedly. This nihilistic black comedy Flash animation is based on an online comic strip by Irem Software Engineering, a long-running cult favorite in Japan. It in turn was inspired by Tim Martin's 1983 Atari video game *Spelunker*, a notoriously difficult game with an absurdly

weak central character (**GAMING AND DIGITAL ANIMATION**).

Spelunkers have been using the name since the 1940s; like *otaku*, it's a term taken from more elevated language (its roots are in Latin and Greek), given a new usage as a self-claimed badge of honor, and often regarded as a form of ridicule by non-aficionados: serious cavers consider spelunkers deluded and dangerous amateurs. Aside from interesting etymological coincidence, this show illustrates how a niche product can be exploited long after its original release thanks to new technology. Build a loyal following, no matter how small, and providing you keep your costs low, you can monetize it for years, even generations. Compare to **EXCEL SAGA**, another **COMEDY** with a leading character who periodically drops dead and resurrects.

SPICE AND WOLF *
2008. JPN: *Okami to Koshinryo*. AKA: *Wolf and Spices*. TV series, video. DIR: Takeo Takahashi. SCR: Naruhisa Arakawa. DES: Kazuya Kuroda, Toshimitsu Kobayashi, Toshihiro Kohama, Yoshinori Shiozawa. ANI: Kazuya Kuroda, Si Min Lee, Back Min Kyoung, Yoshio Kosakai, Midori Otsuka, Toshimitsu Kobayashi. MUS: Yuji Yoshino. PRD: IMAGIN, Media Works, Pony Canyon, Kadokawa Pictures, MOVIC, Victor Entertainment, Brains Base, Marvy Jack, Flying Dog. 24 mins. x 12 eps. (TV1), 24 mins. (v1), 24 mins. x 12 eps. (TV2), 24 mins. (v2).
In one of those nonspecific fantasy worlds that's a bit like Europe in the Middle Ages but with some modern attitudes and manners, 25-year-old Kraft Lawrence is a peddler who makes his living traveling from town to town, buying and selling portable goods. Outside the town of Pasroe he finds a naked girl sleeping in his cart. She looks and behaves like a 15-year-old with pointy ears, a fluffy tail, and a penchant for nudity but is really a centuries-old pagan wolf goddess named Holo. For unexplained reasons the villagers worship this predatory being as the goddess of harvest, and, despite the complete disconnect between wolves and agriculture, Holo has kept the town supplied with good wheat harvests for years. But now she feels the townspeople have lost belief in her, and she wants to go back to her Northern homeland. Although as a wolf goddess she

ought in theory to be able to walk back into the wild when it suits her, she chose to wait for some human to come along and provide transport and company. As she and Lawrence set off on the road together, her ancient wisdom helps him to cope with currency fluctuations and major economic problems (compare to **ARCHENEMY AND HERO**). But despite living as a local goddess for many years, now she's on the move there could be serious trouble with the church.

The above synopsis of *S&W* should convince you that this show requires suspension of disbelief on multiple levels. Seasoned anime viewers are accustomed to the moral flexibility that accepts an underage girl as merely the current form of a mature woman capable of adult choices. They also know how very, very often nudity is an absolutely essential character tool rather than mere fan service, despite its being overwhelmingly more commonly required of female characters than male ones. Here, though, the mythological, metaphysical, religious, and economic intricacies and flexibilities are considerable, too. The plotlines are well crafted and the relationship between the two main characters is convincingly developed, despite heading toward sex with the inevitability of all relationships between a 15-year-old girl and 25-year-old man traveling together through a socially accommodating universe. Action scenes are well-handled and art is adequately cute.

The story of the first series takes in the first two *S&W* novels by writer Isuna Hasekura and artist Ju Ayakura, which appeared in 2006. The two stories are linked on the DVD release by *Wolf and a Tail of Happiness* (*Okami to Kofuku no Shippo*), a filler episode never aired in Japan, but inserted as episode 7 of the DVD series. A further unaired episode, *Wolf and the Amber-Colored Melancholy* (*Okami to Kohaku-iro no Yuutsu*), was added to the DVD release of second TV series *S&W II* (*Okami to Koshinryo II*) as Episode 0 The second TV series derives from books three and five of the original novels. **NV**

SPIDER RIDERS *
2006. JPN: *Spider Riders Oracle no Yushatachi*. AKA: *Spider Riders: The Heroes of Oracle*. TV series. DIR: Koichi Mashimo,

Takaaki Ishiyama. SCR: Hideki Shirane, Noboru Kimura, Yosuke Kuroda. DES: Yuko Iwaoka, Tomoaki Kado, Kenji Teraoka, Yoshihisa Koyama, Yuichi Mari. ANI: Yuko Iwaoka, Tomoaki Kado, Kosuke Kawazura, Tatsuya Oka. MUS: Fumitaka Anzai, Nobuhiko Nakayama, Tatsuya Kato, Tomomasa Yoneda. PRD: Bee Train, P.A.Works, Cookie Jar Entertainment, Yomiko Advertising. 24 mins. x 52 eps. (TV1), 24 mins. x 26 eps. (TV2).
Eleven-year-old Hunter Steele is on a hiking trip with friends when he is pulled into the fantastic underground world of Arachnia, where insects have grown to giant size and become the dominant species. He finds a welcome from an elite warrior team, the Spider Riders and decides to help them fight the evil Invectid, who threaten all of Arachnia. On his huge Battle Spider he takes part in jousting matches and fights to save the Oracle of Arachnia, the key to peace. But will he ever find his way home to the surface world?

Spider Riders is based on a trilogy by Canadian authors Tedd Anasti, Patsy Cameron-Anasti, and Stephen D. Sullivan. It first appeared as a 90-minute special on Canadian TV in March 2006 before airing in Japan in April of that year. The Canadian series premiere was in May and Kids WB screened it in the U.S.A. in June. The second series, *Spider Riders: Resurrected Sun* (*Spider Riders Yomigaeru Taiyo*), aired in Japan a year later in April 2007.

SPIRAL *
2002. JPN: *Spiral: Suiri no Kizuna*. AKA: *Spiral: Bonds of Reasoning; Lines of Reasoning*. TV series. DIR: Shingo Kaneko. SCR: Chinatsu Hojo, Katsuhiko Koide, Mitsuyasu Sakai, Tetsuo Tanaka. DES: Yumi Nakayama. ANI: Yumi Nakayama. MUS: Akira Mitake. PRD: SME VisualWorks, Sotsu Agency, TV Tokyo. 25 mins. x 25 eps.
Teenager Ayumu Narumi's older brother Kiyotaka, a renowned detective and pianist, disappeared two years ago. Now, Ayumu is accused of murder. School journalist Hiyono Yuizaki is determined to prove his innocence, and the pair team up to investigate both mysteries. A strange group calling themselves the Blade Children, who seem to know Kiyotaka, is at the center of a series of deaths and mysteries. Kiyotaka's wife Madoka, a police inspector,

is investigating them with her partner, but is ordered by her boss to back off. It seems there is more to the Blade Children than meets the eye, for they're also being killed off one by one by the ominous "Hunters." From the manga by Kyo Shirodaira with art by Eita Mizuno, serialized in *Shonen Gangan* and wholly unconnected to Junji Ito's manga *Spiral* (*Uzumaki*). A conspiracy story with real suspense is rare in any medium, and this is a good one, well served by a good script and nicely paced direction. **O**

SPIRIT OF WONDER *

1992. JPN: *Spirit of Wonder China-san no Yuutsu*. AKA: *SoW: Miss China's Melancholy; SoW: Miss China's Ring*. Video. DIR: Mitsuru Hongo, Takashi Anno. SCR: Michiru Shimada. DES: Yoshiaki Yanagida. ANI: Yoshiaki Yanagida. MUS: Kohei Tanaka. PRD: EMI, Ajia-do. 45 mins. (v1), 45 mins. x 2 eps. (v2).

Miss China runs a bar and boarding house in a small town. Her long-term residents are mad scientist Professor Breckenridge and his assistant, Jim Floyd (named for Heywood Floyd in *2001: A Space Odyssey*), whom she secretly loves. But she thinks Jim is smitten with local florist Lily and that her love is hopeless, until, for her birthday, he flies her to the moon and gives her a real moonstone ring.

Based on Kenji Tsuruta's delicately beautiful manga short stories serialized in *Afternoon* from 1986 onward, *SoW* harks back to a bygone age of Jules Verne, H.G. Wells, and similar Victorian-era science fiction. Tsuruta's output is fearfully slow, so it was little surprise that the anime incarnation was similarly tardy. A second *SoW* release, the *Scientific Boys' Club* (2001, *SoW: Shonen Kagaku Kurabu*), chiefly features Wendy Lindberg, a leading interplanetary ether theorist, who believes that light oscillates in "ether" just as sound oscillates in air and that one can therefore travel in space by airship using "ether convection." Her father, Gordon, and his eccentric old buddies from the Scientific Boys' Club plan to celebrate the club's 50th anniversary by flying to Mars using this method, a crackpot idea, which, like other insanely romantic schemes in Tsuruta's universe, pays off eventually. The two 35-minute *SBC* episodes each came with a 10-minute short to tie them in with the original 1992

video titled *China-san's Reduction* (*C-san no Shukusho*). Yanagida, who turned Tsuruta's fragile art into animation with such skill, returns on character design and art direction, and Anno directs.

SPIRITED AWAY *

2001. JPN: *Sen to Chihiro no Kamikakushi*. AKA: *Sen and Chihiro's Spirited Away*. Movie. DIR: Hayao Miyazaki. SCR: Hayao Miyazaki. DES: Hayao Miyazaki. ANI: Masashi Ando. MUS: Joe Hisaishi. PRD: Studio Ghibli. a. 125 mins.

After taking a wrong turn on the way to their new house, Chihiro's family end up in what appears to be the ruins of a theme park. As night falls, it transforms into a literal "ghost town." Chihiro's parents are changed into pigs, and she is forced to work in an unearthly bathhouse. Like many Miyazaki heroines before her, she is kind to those in need, and the new friends she meets come to her aid when her fellow indentured servant Haku is placed in grave danger.

Like a maverick diamondcutter, Miyazaki has made some innovative choices in the facets he carves. Like Mamoru Oshii's **PATLABOR** films, the leads in *SA* often seem like clueless bystanders in someone else's story. Its chills are sometimes lost on an audience that cannot read Japanese, such as the creepy moment when Chihiro walks through a harmless-seeming village, although the signs over the cafés in the background offer "Flesh," "Fresh Eyeballs," and "Dog." The most obvious "hidden" plotline is a romance between a human child and a river god, one of many forbidden loves in Japanese mythology, seen before in **USHIO AND TORA**. Another is a tale of warring sisters who live close by and continue to feud incessantly. The witch Yubaba's bathhouse is a meeting place for innumerable folktales old and new, some of which only have a single scene to charm us. We see the end, but not the beginning, of the tale of a river god polluted by litter-dumping (Miyazaki's obligatory environmental moment), the last part of the tale of a dragon-thief, and curious scenes from the life of No Face, a lonely, violent god desperate to be loved.

Miyazaki's eye for the fantastic does not disappoint, with desolate vistas of a world knee-deep in water, a train to nowhere (perhaps it shares a terminus

with **MY NEIGHBOR TOTORO**'s Catbus?), and a truly Grimm sense of the horrors that lie beneath the surface of the most innocent story. One critic controversially suggested that *SA* was a subtle allegory of life in a brothel, and like all the best fairy tales, the film is innocent, child-friendly, and psychologically disturbing all at once.

It shares the impenetrable ethnocentric references of Isao Takahata's **POM POKO** and a Japanese obsession with bathing and the smell of outsiders, but it seems to lack the humanity of **KIKI'S DELIVERY SERVICE**. Considering this is a story about a girl in a very inhuman world, that's probably part of the point, but the result could so easily have been the same as with **PRINCESS MONONOKE**—Nebraska mallrats prefer to watch the latest Jerry Bruckheimer, another Miyazaki film tanks in the U.S., and the fans blame Disney, who would really very much prefer it if Miyazaki remade **MY NEIGHBOR TOTORO** anyway and stopped doing animated pastiches of Tarkovsky and comedy allegories of union demarcation disputes involving a collective of soot-creatures. However, *Spirited Away* defied many expectations by winning an Academy Award for Best Animated Feature, gaining the film a new lease on life, and pushing Miyazaki to the forefront of anime's expansion abroad, despite the fact that much of his work is made in reaction to mainstream Japanese animation and is not really representative of it. His next directorial outing was **HOWL'S MOVING CASTLE**.

SPOOKY KITARO

1968. JPN: *Gegege no Kitaro*. AKA: *Spooky Ooky Kitaro*. TV series, movie. DIR: Yoshio Kuroda, Masao Murayama, Yasuo Yamaguchi, Yoshio Takami, Masayuki Akehi, Hiroshi Shidara, Keiji Hisaoka, Fusahito Nagaki, Hideo Furusawa, Masamune Ochiai, Hiroshi Wagatsuma, Tomoharu Katsumata, Isao Takahata, Takeshi Tamiya. SCR: Susumu Takaku, Masaki Tsuji, Shunichi Yukimuro, Tomohiro Ando. DES: Shigeru Mizuki, Yoshinori Kanemori. ANI: Mitsuo Hosoda, Masamune Ochiai, Hiroshi Wagatsuma, Shinya Takahashi. MUS: Taku Izumi. PRD: Toei, Fuji TV. 25 mins. x 65 eps. (TV1, b/w), 25 mins. x 45 eps. (TV2, color), 25 mins. x 108 eps. (TV3), 25 mins. x 7 eps. (TV4), 24 mins. (m1), 40 mins. (m2), 49 mins. (m3), 48 mins. (m4), 25 mins. x 92 eps. (TV5), 50 mins. (m5), 30 mins. (m6), 24 mins. (m7).

Kitaro is a little boy who lives with a gang of phantoms and figures from **JAPANESE FOLK TALES**, including his friends Rat Man, Cat Girl, and Piece-of-Paper. The spirit of his father possesses one of his eyeballs, which has grown tiny arms and legs and can climb about from its perch in his hair. His life may be strange in some of its details, but Kitaro is actually just a nice, ordinary Japanese boy who uses various magical artifacts, like his traditional coat and wooden shoes, to assist him in helping his human and nonhuman friends to resolve the problems that arise in their lives. Despite (or perhaps because of) reprising basic magical-girl and school-story concepts (the great thing about ghosts, of course, is that they *don't* have to go to school, as the theme song gleefully informs us), the series is charming and funny, with Kitaro's supernatural surrogate family presented as regular folks whose ditherings, weaknesses, and prosaic good-heartedness wouldn't be *too* out of place in **SAZAE-SAN**. **LITTLE DEVIL**–creator Shigeru Mizuki's 1965 manga in *Shonen Magazine* led to the first TV series, which then returned in color in 1971. The fashion for ghoulies and ghosties at the time was influenced by American TV and inspired other anime like **VAMPIRE**, **LITTLE GOBLIN**, and **MONSTER MAN BEM**. After a long hiatus, *SK* returned for a third series in 1985, now overseen by Osamu Kasai and Hiroki Shibata–in many ways a complete remake of the preceding two versions but with a few nods to the modern audience, such as the introduction of super-deformed "SD" scenes of a squashed-down Kitaro at humorous moments. Some later stories were all-new ideas based on viewer suggestions. During the same period, Toei also took the franchise into movie theaters, commencing with *SOK* (1985), which drew less on the original manga than on Mizuki's picaresque *Ghoulish Travels in Kitaro's World* (*Kitaro no Sekai Obake Ryoko*), then running in *Shonen King* magazine. Three more short movies followed in 1986: *Great Ghost War* (*Yokai Daisakusen*), featuring cameos from **DRACULA**, **FRANKENSTEIN**, and the Wolf-man, *Great Ghost Army—Destructive Monsters Arrive in Japan* (*Saikyo Yokai Guntai! Nippon Joriku*), and *The Big Revolt of Monsters from Another Dimension* (*Kyojigen Yokai no Dai*

Hanran). The short-lived TV series *SOK: Hell Chapter* (1988, *Jigoku Hen*) retold the story of Kitaro's origins, prompted by the opportunity to meet his parents' ghosts in the underworld. After that, the franchise lay dormant again until revived in 1996 by director Daisuke Nishio. This most recent incarnation, confusingly termed the "fourth" TV series, though technically being the fifth, also spun off into three more movies, Tomoharu Katsumata's *Giant Sea Monster* (1996, *Dai Kaiju*), Junichi Sato's *Ghost Knighter* (1997, *Obake Knighter*), and Takao Yoshizawa's *Monster Express! Ghost Train* (1997, *Yokai Tokkyu! Maboroshi no Kisha*). There was also a brief live-action series featuring Mizuki in a cameo role.

In interviews, Mizuki has been heard to suggest that traditional Japanese spirits are driven out of the modern world by the prevalence of electric light—that they need the shadows cast by candles and starlight to survive. This elegiac quality, alluding both to the advance of modernity and the transient nature of youth, can also be seen in modern fairy tales such as **POM POKO** and **SPIRITED AWAY**.

SPORTS ANIME

Sports anime have formed a vital part of the medium since its earliest days—the sublimated conflict of a sporting event, allowing both dramatic tension and a finishing line for which the opponents can strive, is readily appreciable by a younger audience. One of **AESOP'S FABLES** was adapted by Sanae Yamamoto in his single-reel *Tortoise and the Hare* (1924), but the first identifiable "sports anime" was Yasuji Murata's *Animal Olympics* (1928), in which a duck successfully wins the 800-meter gold, besting a bulldog, hippo, and camel. Inspired by the Amsterdam Olympics of the same year but played largely for laughs, the short film also includes a polar bear attempting to polevault, and a cheating pig, whose attempt to win the hurdles with the aid of a balloon is brought crashing back down to earth through the intercession of an elephant's well-thrown javelin. As war loomed in the 1930s, sports anime ironically clung to an American import, with animals competing again in Yasuji Murata's *Our Baseball* (1930) and Seiichi Harada's *Baseball in the Forest* (*Mori no Yakyu-dan*, 1934).

Firmly supported as a wholesome pursuit by the postwar Occupation forces, the game returned in Sanae Yamamoto's *Animal Great Baseball Battle* (*Dobutsu Dai-yakyu Sen*, 1949). The same year saw Hideo Furusawa's *Sports Tanuki* (*Sports Kotanuki*, 1949), in which a Japanese raccoon dog competes as a jockey in a horse race.

Real-world sporting events, particularly ones such as baseball, pro wrestling, or sumo, which could be covered by a single, unmoving camera, were early ratings draws for live-action TV, which had the effect of discouraging animators from attempting to replicate them. Early TV producers followed the lead of Osamu Tezuka in **ASTRO BOY**, who saw that anime's true potential lay in showing audiences sci-fi and fantasy—things they would not get so easily from live action. However, experiments in anime sports inevitably followed the national hysteria surrounding the 1964 Tokyo Olympics, in which the Japanese women's volleyball team took an unexpected gold medal. This success would generate a vast wave of sporting *manga*, which, once proving their popularity in print, would tempt producers to buy the rights for anime adaptation.

Although the protagonist of **HARRIS'S WIND** (1966) dabbled in many different disciplines, the first true TV sports anime did not arise until **STAR OF THE GIANTS** (1968)—tellingly, a show about the real-life Yomiuri Giants baseball team, part-owned by the same conglomerate that also owned the broadcaster, NTV. *SotG* pioneered techniques that have become mandatory in modern anime—framing a sporting contest with the zooms and freeze-frames of martial arts combat. Before long, many sports were represented in anime, including volleyball in **ATTACK NUMBER ONE** (1969), wrestling in **ANIMAL 1** and **TIGER MASK** (both 1969), boxing in **TOMORROW'S JOE** (1970), soccer in **RED-BLOODED ELEVEN** (1970), kick-boxing in **KICK FIEND** (1970), tennis in **AIM FOR THE ACE** (1973), and the self-evident **A KARATE-CRAZY LIFE** (1973) and **IN PRAISE OF JUDO** (1974). Almost all gravitated toward the common sports story—plucky outsiders winning against overwhelming odds, often in the face of personal bereavement, with family members and coaches seeming to have the life expectancy of the average rock drummer. Later seasons would replay the same story, but at a regional, national, or international level. In an interesting curio, ROAD TO MUNICH (1972) used animation in order to bypass Olympic competition restrictions concerning the use of players' images for "professional" purposes.

As merchandising began to play a bigger part in anime production, sports anime began to favor activities that offered better toy potential, most notably vehicular stories such as SPEED RACER (1967), MACHINE HAYABUSA (1976), and ARROW EMBLEM (1977). Baseball shows made a brief return in the late 1970s, only to be drowned in the merchandise-oriented sci-fi and fantasy of the 1980s. With most sports now relegated to one-shots or videos like PROGOLFER SARU (1982), baseball hung on by introducing romance, particularly in series based on the works of manga creator Mitsuru Adachi, such as MIYUKI (1983), NINE (1983), and TOUCH (1985). Other producers embraced commercial pressures with original cunning, making shows with improved foreign sales potential, such as the soccer favorite CAPTAIN TSUBASA (1983), which had guaranteed export audiences around the world, despite comparably little domestic interest. The more merchandise-oriented used sport as their excuse rather than their reason, with Olympic mascot shows like EAGLE SAM (1983) and MISHA THE BEAR CUB (1979), or completely unrelated releases that sought to exploit newfound awareness of event locations—it is no coincidence that TWELVE MONTHS went into production in the year of the Moscow Olympics, nor that YAWARA! enjoyed a revival in time for Atlanta. Arguably the most successful use of sports anime clichés in the late 1980s was not a sports anime at all but the sci-fi pastiche GUNBUSTER (1987), which even modeled its heroines' uniforms on those of the 1964 Japanese gymnastics team.

Since the early 1990s, sports anime have featured periodic revivals of baseball, soccer, and volleyball, among a scattering of ever stranger attempts to push the envelope with more obscure pursuits, such as the fishing of GRANDAR (1998) or the speedboat racing of MONKEY TURN (2004). Producers have also shied away from real-world games, preferring fantastical concoctions such as BATTLE ATHLETES (1997) and

EYESHIELD21 (2005). Modern children nowadays are less likely to play catch than they are to engage in more sedentary activities, such as the board gaming of HIKARU'S GO (2001) or the pachinko of the same year's PACHISLO KIZOKU GIN, though PRINCE OF TENNIS (also 2001) bucked the trend. The act of playing with a computer has itself become the subject of anime inquiry, from RUNNING BOY (1986) to BPS (2003). The greatest change, however, has been in a marked increase in martial arts tales, thanks to their relation to computer gaming—the ubiquitous STREET FIGHTER II (1994) and its clones. It could also be argued that "collecting" is the new sport, be it of digitized monsters in POKÉMON (1997), or of cards in DUEL MASTERS (2002). Sports even made its way into erotica, in the form of the volleyball-themed ANGELS IN THE COURT (2001) and the rhythmic gymnastics of PRINCESS 69 (2002). In the postmodern 21st century, sports anime often seem incorporated within the compass of EVERYDAY ANIME, in which the "real" world of physical sports and human contacts are valorized and approached with an almost anthropological fascination like the activities of some primitive lost tribe. We might consider anime such as BAMBOO BLADE (2007) in this context, not so much reflecting the real world as pleading with viewers to go out and find it.

SPOTLIGHT *

2002. Video. DIR: 1862 Kuboyama. SCR: Rokurota Makabe. DES: Hayato Nankodo. ANI: Hayoto Nankodo. MUS: Yoshi. PRD: Digital Works (Vanilla Series), Blue Gale. 30 mins. x 2 eps.

Pretty, pert Saori would love to be a pop idol, which is fortunate, because her mother Emiko has just inherited a music management company from her newly deceased second husband. However, she has also inherited a stepson, Masaki, who has an unhealthy obsession with his stepsister. In an updated and erotic inversion of the CINDERELLA motif, Saori gets the chance to front the Teinkle pop trio, much to the annoyance of the other two girls, Yuna and Erica, who begin bullying her for being such a privileged upstart. Masaki soon teaches them the error of their ways by tying them up and molesting

them, in typical VANILLA SERIES style—for this is one of *those*, based on a story by Blue Gale. Meanwhile, Masaki plots to make a move on Saori, while also enjoying the attentions of his stepmother, who sees in him something of his father, and offers to bed him for mutual companionship and general stress release. In the tradition of certain erotic computer games, some scenes neglect to put much effort into the male characters, drawing them instead as virtual silhouettes so that the "spotlight" is literally on the female victim. Compare to PARADE PARADE and PERFECT BLUE. ●🄽🅅

SPRIGGAN *

1998. AKA: *Striker*. Movie. DIR: Hirotsugu Kawasaki. SCR: Katsuhiro Otomo, Hirotsugu Kawasaki, Yasutaka Ito. DES: Hisashi Eguchi. ANI: Hisashi Eguchi. MUS: Kuniaki Haishima. PRD: TBS, Toho, Bandai, Studio 4°C. ca. 90 mins.

Explorers in Turkey find "Noah's Ark," a spaceship frozen in layers of ice. The clandestine ARCAM research organization, dedicated to recovering the artifacts of a lost prehistoric civilization, sends in its researchers but comes under attack from American agents who want the Ark's secrets for themselves. Yu Ominae, a Japanese schoolboy who is really one of ARCAM's elite "Spriggan" agents, heads for Turkey for a battle of wits against the Pentagon's high-powered Machiners Platoon led by the supersoldiers Fatman and Little Boy. They, however, report to the evil McDougal, a child prodigy whose powers are dangerously out of control. McDougal has realized that the Ark is a weather control device, and he intends to start a new Ice Age.

Inspired by the final shot of *Raiders of the Lost Ark* (itself an homage to *Citizen Kane*), Hiroshi Takashige and PROJECT ARMS–creator Ryoji Minagawa's 1989 manga in *Shonen Sunday* posited a secret society fighting to claim all the world's paranormal artifacts for good, with agents named after Celtic fairies that "protect important treasures in ancient ruins."

From the English lettering to the Chinese theme song, this is an anime made with the foreign audience in mind—the script was translated before the film was made in an attempt to secure foreign backing. The manga was originally translated into English as *Striker*, in a version that hid its strong anti-Americanism, though the film was made and released in the U.S. amid a post–*X-Files* willingness to cast the Pentagon as the bad guy. The anime project began life as a video of *Spriggan*'s "Berserker" chapters but was changed to the Ark plotline and upgraded to a theatrical release—close up it still looks like a video production inflated with extra capital. In a succession of bloody battles punctuated with Biblical apocalypse and government conspiracy, director Kawasaki recalls the whip-like cuts of **GHOST IN THE SHELL**, tearing from shot to shot to distract us from the sparse animation—*Spriggan* has less than a third of **AKIRA**'s cel count, which it hides with a breakneck pace worthy of Tsui Hark. "Supervisor" Katsuhiro Otomo's influence is clearest in the design of the Ark and the portrayal of the evil McDougal. Like the mutant children of *Akira*, he has a bluish pallor, a vocabulary that belies his age, and a voice provided by a genuine child actor.

A sequence from Kuniaki Haishima's score was lifted and reused in the Korean movie *Joint Security Area* (2001) and also in a British TV commercial for the Carphone Warehouse.

SPRING AND CHAOS *
1996. JPN: *Ihatov no Kenso: Kenji no Haru*. AKA: *Iwate Fantasy: Kenji's Spring*. TV special. DIR: Shoji Kawamori. SCR: Shoji Kawamori. DES: Takahiro Kishida. ANI: Takahiro Kishida. MUS: Shang-Shang Typhoon. PRD: Group Tac, Magic Bus, Animal, Triangle Staff, NTV. 53 mins.
A brief survey of the life and works of Kenji Miyazawa, animated for theatrical screenings in his hometown of Iwate during the centenary of his birth but only combined in this form for a December TV special. As in the adaptation of the same author's earlier **NIGHT ON THE GALACTIC RAILROAD**, the main roles are taken by cats, and all visible signs are written in Esperanto in honor of the author's devotion to the artificial language—hence Ihatov and not Iwate. Young Kenji, a pacifist, is at odds with Japan's increasingly militaristic society in the days before WWII. He is also determined to pursue a career as an author and poet, much to the chagrin of his levelheaded father. The story of

Miyazawa's brief life (he died in his 30s) is punctuated by brief interludes from his stories, in a style similar to the **DIARY OF ANNE FRANK**. Director Kawamori is better known today for **ESCAFLOWNE** and **MACROSS**.

SPRING LOVE MAIDENS
2008. JPN: *Harukoi Otome*. Video. DIR: Katsuma Kanazawa. SCR: Ryoga Ikari. DES: Akira Kano. ANI: Mamura Kubosaki. MUS: Tatsuhito Nakagawa. PRD: Studio9MAiami, D3, MediaBank. 28 mins. x 2 eps.
Saint Francesca Academy used to be an all-girls' school and still has a high percentage of female students. Akihito Hayasaka is in his second year there and is the only boy in his class. His fellow students include a novice nun, an athletic girl, a girl with a heart condition, a lesbian, and a girl *kendo* champion who's also the token rich girl and student council president. Akihito's clever, innocent younger sister Umi and his childhood sweetheart Yuika also go to Saint Francesca's. Can you hear the harem bells ringing? This is based on the visual novel (**ARGOT AND JARGON**) *Springtime Romance Maidens: Greetings from the Maidens' Garden* (*Harukoi Otome: Otome no Sono de Gokigen'yo*). It was developed by BaseSon and released in 2006. A character from their preceding game franchise **KOIHIME MUSO** also attends the school, building links between the products to cross-sell to fans. **Ⓝ**

SPRITE: BETWEEN TWO WORLDS *
1996. JPN: *Manami to Nami Sprite*. AKA: *Manami and Nami Sprite*. Video. DIR: Takeshi Yamaguchi. SCR: Tsutomu Senogai. DES: Shinobu Arimura. ANI: Takashi Wada. MUS: Plectrum. PRD: Toei. 40 mins. x 2 eps.
When his mother is taken ill, the irritating Toru is packed off to stay with "relatives" in Tokyo, where he meets the shapely Manami. Immediately smitten, he discovers that this demure girl next door has a hidden side, a second bad-girl personality called Nami who's ready to put out at the drop of a hat.

Ever since the early days of **CREAM LEMON**, the tawdry genre of anime Lolita porn has suggested that inside every underage girl there's a sexually mature adult bursting to get out, if only the right boy comes along with the magic password. You couldn't get much better than Toru—so

pathologically shy he can only search for sexual partners among his own family. And he's not the only one—this adaptation of Shinobu Arimura's manga alludes to a victim of childhood abuse, returning to the scene of the crime to face her demons. Blink and you'll miss it: a moment when Manami compares the size of Toru's member to her father's.

Where animation is limited, as it is here, voices have to carry a lot of the emotional weight, but the dubbing crew simply can't be bothered. The end result contains many silent hiatuses as the cast seemingly waits for canned laughter that never comes, and though **DEEP BLUE FLEET**–director Takeshi Yamaguchi tries to inject some arty moments (schoolgirls fighting with martial-arts moves based on common sports, waving grasses as lovers talk by a river), this is, like so many others of its ilk, a morally dubious attempt to package human pain as entertainment. **ⒸⓃ**

SPT LAYZNER
1985. JPN: *Aoki Ryusei SPT Layzner*. AKA: *Blue Meteor SPT Layzner*. TV series, video. DIR: Ryosuke Takahashi, Tetsuro Amino, Takashi Imanishi, Toshifumi Takizawa, Yoshitaka Fujimoto. SCR: Hiroyuki Hoshiyama, Fuyunori Gobu, Yasushi Hirano, Tsunehisa Ito, Ryosuke Takahashi. DES: Moriyasu Taniguchi, Kunio Okawara. ANI: Moriyasu Taniguchi. MUS: Hiroki Inui. PRD: Sunrise, Nippon TV. 25 mins. x 38 eps. (TV), 55 mins. x 3 eps. (v).
In 1996, Mars has been colonized by humans, with Russia and the U.S. both having established settlements on the planet. A group of Russian students, including Anna, David, Simone, and Arthur, is welcomed to an American base as part of a student exchange program. Eiji Asuka, child of a human father and a mother from planet Glados, is caught up in the beginnings of hostilities between the Americans and Russians and manages to save most of the students, but when Glados attacks Earth, he comes under suspicion purely because of his mixed blood. He and his giant robot, the "Blue Meteor" SPT (Super Powered Tracer) Layzner, are fated to play a key role in the conflict between planets. He is imprisoned by the Americans, considered a traitor by Glados, and has to fight his own sister Julia

in a war that results in the occupation of Earth under Glados leader Le Kain. The second part of the TV series begins on Earth in 1999, when three years of oppression have all but crushed human culture; the books, art, and learning of humankind are destroyed wherever they are found. Eiji and his young friends are living a hand-to-mouth existence as part of the resistance, while Julia has become the leader of a cult and a target for the aliens. As Eiji and Kain face each other for the last battle, Julia prepares to use her mystic powers to save Earth. The series is laden with emotional tension, with a dark emphasis on the cruelty of war and the corrupting effects of power. The early deaths of innocent civilians—including one of the original school party—set the tone; these are battles where nobody really wins and the good don't always survive. The series was taken off the air after episode 38, resulting in a confusing ending with Eiji simply left floating in space and a complex transfer to video. Initially, the series was released as three tapes: *Eiji 1996* and *Lu Kain 1999* (digests of episodes 1–24 and 26–37 respectively), incorporating extra, previously unseen footage, and *Act III: Seal 2000*, which contained the unbroadcast episodes 39 and 40. Set after the end of the war, Kain is still spoiling for a fight and prepares to reopen hostilities, but he is killed by his son Lu who takes control of Glados. Lu faces off against Eiji, but Julia manages to stop the fighting by warping Earth to a different part of the universe. *SPTL* was also released as another video series, the first two tapes comprising episodes 1–4, while the third contained episodes 15 and 28, supposedly because they were fan favorites. The entire 38-episode broadcast run was not released on video until 1997.

SPY OF DARKNESS *
1996. JPN: *Inju vs. Onna Spy.* AKA: *Lust-Beast vs. Female Spy.* Video. DIR: Hisashi Tomii, Tai Fujimoto. SCR: N/C. DES: N/C. ANI: Hideki Araki. MUS: N/C. PRD: Pink Pineapple, KSS. 45 mins.
When the government develops a high-tech cyborg as a secret military weapon, a failure in gene manipulation causes the experimental creature to become a sex beast, fueled only by its insatiable lust for women and utter destruction. The crea-

ture escapes and starts to abduct women, so the government assigns Anne, a sexy spy, to solve the crimes. When Anne finds the hideout where the creature is keeping the abducted women, she is caught in "an erotic battle of the sexes!" Another one for the pile. ⬤🅝🅥

SQUARE OF THE MOON *
2002. JPN: *Yoru ga Kuru.* AKA: *Night Is Coming.* Video. DIR: Yoshiyuki Okano. SCR: N/C. DES: Sachiko Yamamoto. ANI: Sachiko Yamamoto. MUS: N/C. PRD: Green Bunny, Alice Soft. 30 mins. x 4 eps.
College student Izumi and her fellow members of the Astronomy Club are in fact warriors from the Blue Moon, who have come to Earth to protect humanity from the evil Light Hunters. These evil creatures suck the life force out of their victims, by enveloping them with their tentacles and using psionic powers to make them believe that their sexual fantasies are being fulfilled. So, yes, it's **SAILOR MOON** and/or **VENUS FIVE** meets **DEMON BEAST INVASION**, based on the game from Alice Soft. ⬤🅝🅥

SQUID GIRL *
2010. JPN: *Shiryaku Ika Musume.* TV series, video. DIR: Tsutomu Mizushima. SCR: Michio Yokote, Mariko Kunisawa, Tsutomu Mizushima, Susumu Mitsunaka. DES: Masakazu Ishikawa, Kenichi Tatefuji. ANI: Masakazu Ishikawa. MUS: Tomoki Kikuya. PRD: Diomedea, Lantis, Pony Canyon, Klockworx, TV Tokyo. 24 mins. x 12 eps. (TV1), 24 mins. x 12 eps. (TV2), 24 mins. x 3 eps. (v1), 24 mins. x 3 eps. (v2).
Squid Girl is an unlikely avenger: a little girl with big ambitions and absolutely no abilities beyond extreme cuteness. The way the surface people abuse her undersea home drives her crazy, so she heads for the surface to invade the land and wreak retribution. Unfortunately her first victims, the Aizawa sisters, are no pushovers; they put her to work to pay for the damage she's caused to their restaurant, as a waitress and source of squid ink. As she makes friends in the human world, the conviction behind her big talk of revenge begins to waver.

Like **SERGEANT FROG** before it, *Squid Girl* is about winning hearts and minds more than conquest. It's sunny, silly, and rather

charming. Each episode is made up of three short segments, revealing its origins in Masahiro Anbe's episodic comedy manga from 2007.

SRUNGLE *
1983. JPN: *Aku Dai Sakusen Srungle.* AKA: *Great Subspace War Srungle; Gorilla Force.* TV series. DIR: Kazuya Miyazaki, Kenzo Koizumi, Tatsuya Kasahara. SCR: Masaru Yamamoto, Juzo Tsubota. DES: Yoshitaka Amano, MIC Group. ANI: Asao Takahashi, Satoshi Yamaguchi, Tsukasa Dokite. MUS: Masayuki Yamamoto. PRD: Kokusai Eiga, TV Asahi. 25 mins. x 53 eps.
Garrick Space Town, built in the habitable zone between the twin planets Baxas, is under threat from a criminal organization, calling itself, rather pathetically, Crime. Led by an android known as Fork-Razor, the police are powerless against its daring exploits. To help the forces of law to contain this android crime wave, Doctor Mandi (Captain Chance) forms the Gorilla team of brave space cops Jet, Sexy, Superstar, Magician, and Baby's-Face, equipped with powerful robotic weapons like the mighty Srungle. In this golden age of robot shows, there was plenty of dross around; with a TV run starting the week before Tomino's magical **DUNBINE**, this pedestrian cop show was never likely to fly. It isn't one of the more frequently highlighted entries on Amano's resume. However, it was picked up by Saban, crashed into another show, dressed up with a Top 40 soundtrack, and syndicated on American TV in 1985 as *Macron One* (see **GOSHOGUN**).

STAFFROOM AFTER SCHOOL
1994. JPN: *Hokago no Shokuinshitsu.* AKA: *Staffroom after Class.* Video. DIR: Kazuko Hirose. SCR: Mieko Koide. DES: Masayoshi Sudo. ANI: Masayoshi Sudo. MUS: N/C. PRD: Daiei, Tokuma. 30 mins. x 2 eps.
Despite his normal appearance, school-teacher Mitsuo is a whirlwind of homosexual lusts, and he can contain his desires no longer when, on his birthday, he blurts out his feelings to fellow art teacher Toshiaki. A secret romance develops, but, a year later, Mitsuo's parents try to fix him up with a nice girl. Based on the pretty-boy manga by Mieko Koide, who also wrote the script. 🅝

STAINLESS NIGHT *

1995. Video. DIR: Ryunosuke Otonashi. SCR: Akira Takano. DES: Ryunosuke Otonashi, Yuriko Chiba ANI: Ryunosuke Otonashi. MUS: N/C. PRD: Pink Pineapple, KSS. 30 mins. x 2 eps.

In the year 2020, hiking teenagers Mirei and Sayaka find a broken android in the mountains. It is the beautiful Linnear, who, once repaired, repays their kindness by having lesbian sex with them. Based on the manga by Kei Amaki, whose erotic works also appear in the CREAM LEMON collection. ⓝ

STAIRS *

2001. Video. DIR: Masashi Minamite. SCR: N/C. DES: N/C. ANI: Haraki. MUS: N/C. PRD: Milky, Museum Pictures. 30 mins.

Childhood friends Makoto and Une are attending cram school together. Makoto secretly lusts after Une and is crushed to discover that she now has a boyfriend. However, he soon discovers solace in the arms of new arrival Nonoka. Based on the erotic manga by Mikan R. ⓛⓝⓥ

STAR BLAZERS *

1974. JPN: Uchu Senkan Yamato. AKA: Space Cruiser Yamato; Space Battleship Yamato. TV series, movie, video. DIR: Noboru Ishiguro, Leiji Matsumoto, Eiichi Yamamoto, Yoshinobu Nishizaki, Takeshi Shirato, Toyoo Ashida. SCR: Keisuke Fujikawa, Maru Tamura, Eiichi Yamamoto, Yasushi Hirano. DES: Leiji Matsumoto, Studio Nue, Nobuhiro Okaseko, Toshiyuki Kubooka, Hiroyuki Kitazume, Aki Tsunaki, Nobuaki Nagano, Makoto Kobayashi, Atsushi Takeuchi, Keiji Hashimoto, Syd Mead. ANI: Toyoo Ashida, Yoshikazu Yasuhiko, Takeshi Shirato. MUS: Hiroshi Miyagawa, Kentaro Haneda. PRD: Westcape, Studio Take Off, Yomiuri TV (Nippon TV). 25 mins. x 26 eps. (TV1), 25 mins. x 26 eps. (TV2), 25 mins. x 25 eps. (TV3), 130 mins. (m1), 151 mins. (m2), 93 mins. (TVm/m3), 93 mins., 145 mins. (m4), 163 mins. (m5), 30 mins. x 3 eps. (v).

In 2199, the evil emperor Desslar (Desslock) orders the destruction of Earth. Radiation bombs from his planet Gamilas (Gamilon) have devastated the planet's surface and will make it uninhabitable within a year. Enemy cruisers have Earth under heavy surveillance so there's no chance to build a starship to fight back or escape. But the radiation that has dried up the oceans has exposed many old hulks, including the 250-year-old wreck of the WWII battleship Yamato (Argo). Tunneling under the surface, the authorities have secretly built a starship within the old hull. When Queen Starsha from the distant world of Iscandar offers Earth a device that can rid them of the deadly radiation if they'll just send a ship to fetch it, Captain Okita (Avatar) and a handpicked crew set out on the hazardous journey in the reborn Yamato. Young pilot Susumu Kodai (Derek Wildstar) has a grudge against the captain, who survived the battle that claimed Kodai's beloved older brother, Mamoru (Alex), but as time goes on, Kodai and the whole crew come to see the captain as a heroic father-figure whose responsibility to do everything in his power to save Earth is a heavy burden.

Despite looking faintly ridiculous to modern eyes, *Space Battleship Yamato* is one of the watersheds in anime history. A Japanese respray of *Star Trek*, it replaces pioneer exploration (or gunboat diplomacy) with oblique references to WWII—a desperate suicide mission, hounded by enemy vessels in red, white, and blue. The titular ship itself is the most obvious—at the time the greatest battleship ever built, it was sunk during a one-way mission to hold off the U.S. attack on Okinawa in 1945. Naval and aerial battle sequences are clumsily transposed to a space setting: ships "list" when holed in the hull and fighters are shot "down," although in space there isn't supposed to be a "down." Beyond the risible pseudophysics, however, *SBY* contained a supremely strong story line. *SBY* changed the way TV programmers thought about SF; previously it had been supposed that only very young audiences watched TV anime, and so there was no point in screening anything but giant-robot and *sentai* shows. The influence of the original series on a whole generation of Japanese animators is incredible, and it resulted in homages and cameos for the ship in many anime works. The green-skinned aliens seem to have inspired the design of the Zentraedi in MACROSS, while the teacher-pupil relationship of Okita and Kodai, born out of the captain's guilt over the loss of the pilot's close relation, never had a better reprise than in GUNBUSTER, where Coach Ota played the captain role to the full, even to the extent of dying before the end.

The show was the brainchild of writer Eiichi Yamamoto and THUNDERSUB-producer Yoshinobu Nishizaki, who poached many staff from his former employers Mushi Pro. It also features heavy involvement from CAPTAIN HARLOCK–creator Matsumoto, who drew many of the initial designs and also the spin-off manga. The show lived out a lukewarm and unremarkable initial run of 26 episodes, but in 1977 the advent of *Star Wars* rejuvenated network interest in sci-fi. The first movie, *SBY* (1977), is a compilation of the first TV series that gained a new lease on life abroad as *Space Cruiser*, with the Gamilas hordes renamed the Gorgons. Back in Japan, Tomoharu Katsumata's movie *Farewell to SBY: In the Name of Love* (*Saraba Uchusenkan Yamato: Ai no Senshitachi*, AKA *SBY: Warriors of Love*, 1978) seemed intended as the last word on the series, which ended with the Yamato destroyed, along with most of the main characters. Plainly, this would not be very useful for prolonging the franchise, leading to the same year's *SBY 2* TV series, which retold the events of the movie, but with a more open-ended finish that didn't kill everyone off. Earth's new age of peace is disrupted in 2201 by Emperor Zorder's Comet Empire. This was soon followed by Takeshi Shirato's *SBY: The New Voyage* (1979, *USY: Aratanaru Tabitachi*), a 95-minute TV special broadcast on Fuji TV, in which the Yamato has the chance to come to the aid of Earth's savior Queen Starsha when she suffers attacks by the Black Star Cluster Empire. *The New Voyage* was shown in 1981 in theaters on a double bill with the next genuine movie edition, Katsumata's *Be Forever Yamato* (1980, *Yamato yo Towa ni*), featuring Kodai and a crew that includes Starsha and Mamoru's daughter, Sasha, defeating the invading forces of commander Kazan of the Dark Empire.

However, *SBY*'s reissue as *Space Cruiser* was by no means the last of its English-language incarnations. The series made it to American TV screens as *Star Blazers* (1979). Claster Studios had acquired the first two series with its sights on marketing tie-ins for its toy division, Hasbro. Some changes were made for the U.S. market, notably to character names. Comic relief robot Analyzer and cyborg mechanic Sandor had been created well in advance of George Lucas's knockabout robot duo in *Star Wars*, but Analyzer was named IQ-9 in imitation of C-3PO. Some changes were made to cushion U.S. sensibilities; violence was toned down, and Dr. Sado's copious drinking became nonalcoholic. Despite an early lukewarm reception, American anime fans, as passionately loyal as their Japanese counterparts to the show they loved, began to screen episodes in convention video rooms. Its classic status on both sides of the Pacific was secured by fan interest and activity, to the extent where the full series and all five movies are still selling on video in the U.S. and Japan.

In 1980, a third Japanese TV series (also brought to the U.S.) moved the action further forward again to the year 2205, when new danger appeared in the Bolar Wars. During a battle between Galman Gamilas and the Bolar Commonwealth, a stray missile flies into the sun and renders it unstable. With only a year before the sun explodes, Kodai must restaff the Yamato with a crew fresh out of the academy and find a new Earth for the human race. In fact, by the end, the sun's stability is restored, leaving the grande finale of the Yamato's adventures to Takeshi Shirato's movie release *Final Yamato* (1983, *USY: Kanketsu*). For this conclusion, Okita (returned from the dead as an admiral) takes command of the ship in 2203 to defend Earth from Lugaral, priest-king of Dengil, a planet destroyed by a near-miss with the rogue planet Aquarius. The Aquarians are descendants of an advanced race that fled Earth during Noah's flood, and now they want to come home. The Yamato saves the galaxy once again, then sinks into the watery grave from which it was raised at the very beginning of the saga, there to remain until *Blade Runner*–futurist Syd Mead resurrected it in his much-trumpeted designs for the video series *Yamato 2520* (1995). Top-heavy with directors (Shirato, Nishizaki, and Shigenori Kageyama) and adding a stellar design team to rework Matsumoto and Kitazume's originals, this relaunch of the old ship failed to fly. It looks pretty, but the repetition of the teens-save-Earth concept lacks the passion and conviction of the old series. Some-

times the latest fashion just can't compete with the classics.

In recent years, the story has remained in the headlines largely through the acrimonious court battle that has raged between the two men claiming to be its creators. This seems to stem from their conflicting ideas of who was responsible for what in the original, with producer Yoshinobu Nishizaki claiming that the series was his idea, and artist Leiji Matsumoto counter-claiming that while the extant TV versions may belong to Nishizaki, it is he who has the right to make his own new versions. The court battle faded from view, particularly after Nishizaki's incarceration for several years on a cocktail of guns and weapons charges and parole violations. Ultimately, Nishizaki's death appears to have laid matters to rest, after an epic battle longer than the Argo's original mission. In a moment of historical irony, he died falling from his own boat, the Yamato— a "cruiser" that was the source of his insistence through many a romanization (although frustratingly not all) that the *senkan* (lit.: "battleship") of the Japanese title should be translated as the technically inaccurate "cruiser."

STAR CAT FULLHOUSE

1989. JPN: *Hoshineko Full House*. Video. DIR: Noboru Ishiguro. SCR: Noboru Ishiguro. DES: Noboru Sugimitsu, Haruhiko Mikimoto. ANI: Masahito Kitagawa. MUS: Kaoru Wada. PRD: Artland. 30 mins. x 4 eps.
This slapstick comedy is about three pretty girls struggling to earn a living as pilots of the Iron Goblin delivery vessel. The computer answers back, the space pirates are on their tail, and romantic entanglements with their clients cause friction in the trio. The final episode throws the alien Eterna race into the mix, but it's hardly **GUNBUSTER**.

STAR CHILD PORON

1974. JPN: *Hoshi no Ko Poron*. AKA: *Polon, Girl from the Stars; Poron the Star Child*. TV series. SCR: Tetsuyoshi Onuma, Setsuko Murayama. DES: N/C. ANI: Fumio Sakai. MUS: N/C. PRD: Nippon Animation, Jiho Eigasha. 5 mins. x 260 eps.
Poron is an alien child who comes in a flying saucer from the distant reaches of space to Earth. There, he soon encounters

the native life-forms, although as a new arrival, he is unaware that he has ignored humans, and instead befriends a rabbit, a bear, and a fox. This little-known science fantasy is not to be confused with **CHOBIN THE STARCHILD**, which started its TV run a month earlier.

STAR DRIVER *

2010. JPN: *Star Driver: Kagayaki no Takuto*. AKA: *Takuto's Radiance; Shining Takuto*. TV series, movie. DIR: Takayuki Igarashi. SCR: Yoji Enokido. DES: Yoshiyuki Ito, Shigeto Koyama, Takahiro Shikama, Yasuyuki Kai, Shinji Aramaki, Takeshi Waki, Hiroka Mizuya, Misa Mizuya, Kazuo Nagai, Tomoaki Okada. ANI: Yoshiyuki Ito, Shingo Abe. MUS: Satoru Kosaki, monaca. PRD: BONES, Aniplex, Dentsu, Bandai Namco Games, Square Enix, MBS. 25 mins. x 25 eps. (TV), 150 mins. (m).
On the remote Southern Cross Island, a secret society named The Glittering Crux is seeking giant transdimensional mobile suits, or cybodies, which have been hidden under the school for eons. Only certain specially gifted individuals, known as star drivers, can pilot these mighty weapons. Four shrine maidens living on the island are the magical seals that hold the cybodies immobile. Enter Takuto Tsunashi, a high school boy who has recently moved to the island. One of the shrine maidens, Wako, saved his life, and he feels he owes her a debt of honor. Along with Wako and her reluctant fiancé, Takuto is fated to be part of the mighty battle to protect the cybodies, and the world, from those who would use them for evil. He is the legendary Galactic Pretty Boy, the chosen pilot of the cybody Tauburn—the only one specially created for Earthlings.

There's a generous sprinkling of Go Nagai's **MAZINGER Z** here, a sprinkle of the doomed heroism of Leiji Matsumoto's *Starzinger* (**JOURNEY TO THE WEST**), a dash of **ZEORYMER**, even a twist of **DAITARN 3** in the love triangle. Yet Enokido manages to make the character archetypes of mecha anime (**SCIENCE FICTION AND ROBOTS**) come up fresh and shiny, and the art and design teams make the settings and robots look good. The battles are occasionally shaky in animation terms, but by the time that becomes an issue, you're likely to care about the characters enough not to mind. The pacing is not always consistent, but there's enough going on to carry viewers over the sticky patches. A show that could have been an unsuccessful rip-off of a great tradition ends up as an affectionate homage that can meet its noble ancestors without shame. **NV**

STAR DUST

1992. Video. DIR: Ichiro Itano. SCR: N/C. DES: Kazutoshi Kobayashi. ANI: Kazutoshi Kobayashi. MUS: Junichi Kanezaki. PRD: Yoyogi Animation Gakuin. 30 mins.

A misguided sci-fi tale of ecological police keeping *space* free from pollution in 2061. The quality of this anime is at least partly forgivable, though, for being an apprentice film made by students at the Yoyogi Animation academy. Only a few years later, budgets would become so tight in the anime business that members of the same college would become cheap labor on the far longer-running but equally amateurish GANDHARA.

STAR JEWEL

2011. Movie. DIR: Yoshiten. SCR: Katsuhiko Takayama. DES: Yoshiten. ANI: Yoshiten. MUS: N/C. PRD: Sugarboy, zyc, M No Violet. 42 mins., 45 mins.

Alien goddesses of darkness are exiled to Earth. To escape, they need to gather the light from the lives of human women by taking their jewelry—or rather, the jewelry of their souls, their "personality crystals." This leaves the victims as lifeless husks. The crystals will power their Sun Ship, allowing them to return to their home planet. The goddesses of light are sworn to prevent their return and bring them and their retractable penises to justice.

Yes, you read that correctly. We've seen a lot of dull, repetitive pornography in the course of researching this book (the things we do for you, dear reader …) but this was raised slightly above its shelfmates by the hooker-chic costumes, better than average fluidity of animation, the silliness of the concept, and the obvious passion of its creators. **N**

STAR OCEAN EX *

2001. TV series. DIR: Hiroshi Watanabe. SCR: Mayori Sekijima, Kenichi Kanemaki. DES: Ayako Kuroda. ANI: Ryoko Hata, Akira Matsushima. MUS: Motoi Sakuraba. PRD: Studio Deen, TV Tokyo. 25 mins. x 26 eps.

Claude is transported to Exvel, a world beyond time, where the fantasy adventures are what one might expect of an anime adaptation of a novel adap-tation of a PlayStation game. This anime was based on *Star Ocean Second Story* serialized in *Shonen Gan Gan* magazine, itself based on a computer game.

STAR OF DAVIDE

1989. JPN: *Davide no Hoshi*. Video. DIR: Yoichiro Shimatani. SCR: Akio Sato, Yoichiro Shimatani, Ranko Ono. DES: Masaaki Sato. ANI: Tatsuya Sotomaru. MUS: Takahiko Kanemaru. PRD: Apples, Miyuki Pro. 45 mins. x 5 eps.

Lustful creatures from another dimension are invading Earth, starting with the women, for a change. Based on the manga by Masaaki Sato, the fifth episode of this video series was rebranded *New SoD* (1991) and moved the sex and violence to the English countryside. A less fantastic (but equally distasteful) version of the story was also turned into *Star of David: Beauty Hunter* (1979), a live-action film directed by Norifumi Suzuki. **NV**

STAR OF THE GIANTS

1968. JPN: *Kyojin no Hoshi*. TV series, movie. DIR: Tadao Nagahama, Yoshio Kabashima (TV1); Tetsuro Imazawa, Satoshi Dezaki, Minoru Okazaki, Akinori Nagaoka (TV2). SCR: Tadaaki Yamazaki, Mamoru Sasaki, Masaki Tsuji, Ryohei Suzuki, Sumiko Hayashi, Tsunehisa Ito, Toru Sawaki, Yoshiaki Yoshida, Seiji Matsuoka (TV1); Toshiaki Imaizumi, Noboru Shiroyama, Yoshihisa Araki (TV2). DES: Noboru Kawasaki. ANI: Daikichiro Kusube, Hideo Kawauchi, Yasuo Otsuka, Yoshifumi Kondo, Tetsuo Imazawa, Toshiyuki Honda, Tetsuro Wakabayashi, Noboru Ishiguro, Soji Yoshikawa, Masaru Inoue, Shingo Araki, Takao Kasai. MUS: Takeo Watanabe. PRD: Tokyo Movie, Magic Bus, Yomiuri TV (Nippon TV). 25 mins. x 182 eps. (TV1), 90 mins. (m1), 70 mins. (m2), 70 mins. (m3), 60 mins. (m4), 30 mins. (special), 25 mins. x 52 eps. (TV2, *New*), 25 mins. x 23 eps. (TV3, *New 2*), 25 mins. x 13 eps. (TV4, *Hanagata*).

Hyuma Hoshi is a promising young baseball player who dreams of becoming a top star like his father before him. When he joins the famous Giants team, his father and friends all do their utmost to make sure he achieves his full potential

of becoming the star of the Giants. Based on the 1966 *Shonen Magazine* manga by Noboru Kawasaki and Ikki Kajiwara, *SotG* was the first SPORTS ANIME, the direct ancestor of the rest of the genre, including Kawasaki's later ANIMAL 1, as well as the girls' variants AIM FOR THE ACE, ATTACK NUMBER ONE, and their many imitators (STEREOTYPES AND ARCHETYPES). In bringing a sports plot to a medium previously dominated by juvenile adventure and sci-fi, it paved the way for other aspects of manga's diversity to cross over into animation. Some critics, including Hayao Miyazaki, have suggested that the Japanese people over-identified with the storyline in the aftermath of the Tokyo Olympics, seeing in the protagonist's rags-to-riches struggles and sacrifices a metaphor for the experience of all Japanese in the postwar period.

It also featured a number of stylistic innovations behind the scenes that would transform the nature of Japanese animation, commencing with the widespread use of xerography to transfer artists' linework directly to cels without an intermediate tracing stage (TECHNOLOGY AND FORMATS). This, in turn, allowed for considerable artistic experimentation, which became increasingly necessary as the long-running anime threatened to catch up with the ongoing manga series on which it was based. Although this condition is common today, and usually held off through the use of "filler" episodes to tread narrative water, *Star of the Giants* was the first time a TV anime company had faced the problem. Producer Keishi Yamazaki exhorted his writers to find a way of stretching the pages of the manga further and further, in a scheme that reached its apotheosis with a legendary "one-ball episode" written by Haruya Yamazaki. This exercise in hyperreality stretched the passage of a single ball, from pitcher, to batter, to outfield, to home plate, into 25 minutes, by darting from participant to participant, zooming in on their physical states and their internal monologues, freeze-framing moments of stellar action, and digressing into flashbacks and impressionistic representations of their state of mind.

Hence, *Star of the Giants* is remembered within the anime industry as being the harbinger of a whole series of hyper-real TROPES AND TRANSFORMATIONS used in the medium's storytelling thereafter, although there is some disagreement among its makers as to who should take the credit. While the scripts certainly set the tone, they were written in reaction to concerns at the production level, and much of the heavy artistic lifting was accomplished by the animators themselves. It has been suggested that part of the credit at least should go to the storyboarders, including Yoshiyuki Tomino (GUNDAM), for being able to make this arrested narrative work, or to the animators, led by Tadao Nagahama, for being able to put their tools to appropriate use. One might even suggest that the problem might not have arisen in the first place were it not for *Star of the Giants*'s unexpected appeal beyond the usual children's market, which was itself encouraged not only by a sporting tale sure to attract other groups, but a vitamin-drink sponsor, Oranamin C, with an adult market and, consequently, an interest in fostering adult audiences.

During the course of the original TV run, several reedits were screened in theaters as part of vacation anime festivals. The first, *SotG* (1969), was billed as the only chance for many viewers to see their favorite show in *color*—black-and-white TV sets being more common at the time. Other movie edits included *SotG: Big League* (1970, *Dai League Ball*), and the final game against the Yakult Swallows, *SotG: Confrontation at Shinjuku* (1970, *Shinjuku no Taiketsu*). Though *SotG* was popular in Japan, the mundane nature of its struggles, albeit leavened with some far-fetched training techniques lifted from martial arts, left it unlikely to be exported to the West. Hyuma's only appearance in the English-language version was in the 30-minute TV special *Star of the Giants vs. the Mighty Atom* (1969), a friendly match between the Giants and the characters from ASTRO BOY, which reached the U.S. as part of the latter series—renamed *Astro Boy vs. the Giants*. The series was followed by SAMURAI GIANTS, adapted from another Kawasaki manga, and by a later, much less successful sequel. *New [Shin] SotG* (1977) is set five years after the original and was broadcast at a time when the Yomiuri Giants were facing anime competition from the Tokyo Mets (see SONG OF THE BASEBALL ENTHUSIAST) and the Seibu Lions (see GO

FOR IT, TABUCHI). The final 23 episodes, rebranded as *New SotG II* (1979), deviated most from the original manga, introducing new regular characters, dumping Hyuma's girlfriend, and even killing off his father in the final episode, much to the original creators' annoyance.

The story was rereleased as a 13-episode series in October 2002, which used both footage from the original and newly animated scenes in order to retell the story from the point of view of supporting character Mitsuru Hanagata. In what may be an interesting precedent for a whole new subset of "post-anime" licensed adaptations, the original story was also repackaged and reanimated in India as *Suraj the Rising Star* (2012), with the baseball foundations entirely discarded in favor of a story about a promising cricketer, thickly populated with product placement from its Japanese backers.

STAR OF THE SEINE

1975. JPN: *La Seine no Hoshi*. AKA: *Star of La Seine; The Black Tulip*. TV series. DIR: Masaaki Osumi, Yoshiyuki Tomino, Satoshi Dezaki. SCR: Soji Yoshikawa, Mitsuru Majima. DES: Akio Sugino. ANI: Kazuo Yamazaki, Toshio Takagi. MUS: Shunsuke Kikuchi. PRD: Unimax, Fuji TV. 25 mins. x 39 eps.
Simone, illegitimate daughter of the King of Austria and an opera singer, is taken from court as a baby into the care of a Parisian florist and grows up as just another working-class girl in the French capital at the end of the 1700s. When the king's old friend the Comte de Voudrel recognizes her, he adopts her, and she discovers the secret of her birth. She learns to fence and teams up with the comte's son Robert, who secretly helps out the poor and needy using his secret identity as the Black Tulip. Thus is born the Star of La Seine, heroine of the Revolution. But despite her support of the people in their struggle to overthrow the nobility, Simone also has sympathy for her half-sister, Queen Marie Antoinette, and when the Revolution finally overthrows the monarchy, she and Robert rescue the queen's children and adopt them as their own. A popular adventure series that leaves the nods to historical accuracy to ROSE OF VERSAILLES (the heroine of the Revolution dresses in hotpants and boots more suited to 1970s

disco than 1780s swordfights), *SotS* did well in Europe, though Italy made Robert rather than Simone the titular hero. The *Black Tulip* title seems to have been engineered to imply an association with an unrelated 1850 novel of the same name by THREE MUSKETEERS–creator Alexandre Dumas.

STARBIRDS *

1978. JPN: *Tosho Daimos*. AKA: *Fighter/Champion Daimos; Fighting General Daimos*. TV series. DIR: Tadao Nagahama, Yoshikazu Yasuhiko, Kazuo Terada, Yoshihiro Takahashi. SCR: Masaki Tsuji, Fuyunori Gobu, Masaaki Sakurai. DES: Akihiro Kanayama, Studio Nue, Yutaka Izubuchi. ANI: Akehiro Kaneyama. MUS: Shunsuke Kikuchi. PRD: Sunrise, Toei, TV Asahi. 25 mins. x 44 eps. (TV).
Winged aliens from the dying planet Baam decide to conquer Earth and make it their new home. Heading up the resistance is Kazuya Ryusaku in the giant robot Daimos. During an enemy attack, Kazuya saves a girl called Erika. She's lost her memory, so both are completely unaware that she's the princess of the invading aliens, and they fall in love. When the truth emerges, she returns to her people to try and stop the war, while Kazuya is considered a traitor by his own people because he supports her wish for peace. The evil Emperor Olbam compels Erika to shoot her human lover; he survives and, not knowing that she is being forced to act against her will, decides to destroy the alien base in revenge. *Romeo and Juliet* with giant robots, the series didn't achieve the stellar popularity of Go Nagai's robot epics like GRANDIZER, its one claim to fame being the debut of PATLABOR's Yutaka Izubuchi as a guest robot designer on one episode. A 1980 "movie" was simply a theatrical showing of episode 24. In the U.S., the show was also edited into a 90-minute feature by New Hope Productions (see VOLTUS), broadcast on the Showtime cable network under the title *Starbirds*, with the robot renamed Dynamo and a new soundtrack deliberately redolent of *Star Wars*. See also SHOGUN WARRIORS.

STARCHILD RECORDS

Subsidiary of King Records, itself a subsidiary of the publishing house Kodansha, the Starchild label appears on many anime thanks to the dabbling of its chairman

Toshimichi Otsuki in anime production, such as **FLCL** and **MAGICAL SHOPPING ARCADE ABENOBASHI**.

STARLIGHT NOCTURNE

1989. JPN: *Kasei Yakyoku*. Video. DIR: Osamu Dezaki. SCR: Toshiaki Imaizumi. DES: Akio Sugino. ANI: Akio Sugino. MUS: Akira Mitake. PRD: Magic Bus. 30 mins. x 4 eps.
Complicated romance in early 20th-century Japan, as a baron's only daughter switches places with the maid who shares her birthday, causing confusion when each is more attracted to a man from the other's social background. The 1923 Tokyo earthquake (see **DOOMED MEGALOPOLIS**) brings matters to a close. Based on the manga by Masako Hirata.

STARRY SKY

2010. AKA: *Suta Suka*. TV series. DIR: Nobuhiro Takamoto. SCR: Makoto Nakamura. DES: Maki Fujii, Nariyuki Ogi. ANI: N/C. MUS: Tomoki Kikuya. PRD: Studio DEEN, Frontier Works, Sotsu Agency. 11 mins. x 26 eps.
Tsukiko has just enrolled in a new school—a formers boys-only establishment that has just turned co-ed. However, because it's in a rural area and has a rather specialized curriculum, she is the only female to enroll so far. Tsukiko encounters 13 handsome young men, each with a personality relating to the Houses of the Zodiac, including the mysterious 13th House, the House of the Serpent-Bearer, Ophiuchus.

As the show's short running time indicates, it was originally aired online before being shown on TV in 13 segments, two episodes at a time. It's based on a series of four 2009 visual novels (**ARGOT AND JARGON**) by Honeybee, aimed at female gameplayers. It spun off drama CDs, manga anthologies, and merchandise as well as this anime series. One of the manga, by Hal Minagawa, has been released in English. Unfortunately, as with many short manga-based anime, there isn't time to condense a long storyline with multiple characters into such a short compass, and the animation and design don't offer much by way of compensation. Not unattractive, but not especially memorable.

STARSHIP OPERATORS *

2005. TV series. DIR: Takashi Watanabe. SCR: Yoshihiko Tomizawa. DES: Fumio Matsumoto, Kimitoshi Yamane. ANI: N/C. MUS: Kenji Kawai. PRD: JC staff, Geneon, TV Tokyo. 25 mins. x 13 eps.
In a mix-up of **NADESICO** and **GUNDAM**, a group of cadets on a starship decide to take matters into their own hands when their homeworld Kibi is attacked by invaders. The crew of the Amaterasu declare war on the invaders, hoping to fund their unilateral defense effort by selling the TV rights to a galactic network—a sort of reality show, where instead of getting voted off, weekly losers are killed in the line of fire. The military plotline is leavened with plenty of girls in uniform and budding romance. Compare to **STELLVIA**.

STARSHIP TROOPERS

1988. JPN: *Uchu no Senshi*. AKA: *Space Warriors*. Video. DIR: Tetsuro Amino. SCR: Tsunehisa Ito, Sho Aikawa. DES: Hiroyuki Kitakubo, Yutaka Izubuchi, Kazumasa Miyabe, Studio Nue. ANI: Yoshinobu Inano. MUS: Hiroyuki Nanba. PRD: Sunrise, Bandai. 25 mins. x 6 eps.
Johnnie Rico loves the beautiful, willful Carmen, his high school sweetheart. When she signs up for the war against Earth's alien assailants, he follows suit in the hope of impressing her, but they get different assignments—she as a trainee pilot, he as an infantry grunt. From the studio that brought you **GUNDAM**, cited by its creator Tomino as one of his inspirations, this is an animated version of the Hugo-award winning 1959 novel by Robert Heinlein. Amino's version retains the scenes of training and combat but also focuses on time off the battlefield. His soldiers get into barroom brawls with disgruntled civvies, bury one of their comrades, and are then forced to attend his girlfriend's wedding to a new lover. The romance between Johnnie and Carmen becomes more central, ending with their tearful reunion in the hospital, to which they have both been evacuated with injuries. Carmen, absent for the bulk of the novel, has regular appearances in the anime to remind viewers what Johnnie is fighting for. In addition, each episode closes with Carmen bouncing along a beach in a bikini.

Johnnie's mother, Maria, also has a larger part to play. In the anime, she opposes Johnnie's enlistment, slapping his face as he prepares to leave. Her death is also made far more immediate; Amino's version keeps the trainees closer to Earth so that we see Johnnie and his platoon fighting fires at the Fall of Buenos Aires, unaware that his mother is breathing her last nearby. The only Japanese character in the original book, Private Shujumi, is not present in the anime, perhaps because a Japanese audience would not warm to a stereotypical martial artist. He is replaced by the jug-eared, happy-go-lucky Private Azuma, who has "dead meat" written all over him from day one.

Directing the adaptation amid the post–*Top Gun* glut of gung ho Hollywood movies, Amino tried to defang Heinlein's militarist text with some home truths about the evils of war, but he still ran into criticism at home for "over-Americanizing" the anime. Maybe he shouldn't have turned his Filipino hero into an all-American blond, but Paul Verhoeven's live-action *Starship Troopers* (1997) later followed the same route with Caspar van Dien looking about as Filipino as Bugs Bunny. One of Heinlein's references to real-world history managed to survive untouched in the anime; Johnnie's ship, the Rodger Young, is named after a real-life Ohio private who was posthumously decorated for singlehandedly destroying a Japanese gun emplacement in 1943.

STARZAN S

1984. JPN: *Okawari Boy Starzan S*. AKA: *Transforming Boy Starzan S*. TV series. DIR: Hidehito Ueda, Hiroyuki Tanaka, Masakazu Higuchi, Shinya Sadamitsu, Masayuki Kojima, Takaaki Ishiyama. SCR: Takao Koyama, Mayori Sekijima, Yoshiyuki Suga, Miho Maruo. DES: Yoshitaka Amano, Ammonite. ANI: Masayuki Hayashi. MUS: Kazunori Ishida. PRD: Tatsunoko, Fuji TV. 25 mins. x 32 eps.
The beautiful Jun Yagami sets out in search of her father, Mamoru, who was last seen searching for the world of Paratopia, where nobody ever grows old. Caught in a space storm with a group of feckless bounty hunters, she lands on the unexplored world of Kirakira. The world is riven by a war between the Zenobi tribe and a group of evil robots led by the metallic Darth Bellow. The bounty hunters join forces with Darth Bellow, while Jun supports the Zenobi and their "forest god," the human boy Starzan, who possesses a transforming

vehicle known as the Tobida Star. Conceived as a rather obvious mixture of *Star Wars* and *Tarzan*, this anime had robot toy tie-in potential ahead of the TRANSFORMERS sensation the following year.

STEALTH! KARATE CLUB

1990. JPN: *Osu! Karate-bu*. Video. DIR: Osamu Sekita. SCR: Hideo Nanbu. DES: Koichi Endo. ANI: Koichi Endo. MUS: Akira Yamazaki. PRD: JC Staff, Nippon Eizo. 50 mins. x 4 eps. Supertough high school kids duke it out in the Osaka area (see COMPILER), which, naturally, means that they're all in league with gangsters. Based on the 1985 manga by Koji Takahashi in *Young Jump* magazine. **V**

STEAM DETECTIVES *

1998. JPN: *Kaiketsu Shoki Tanteidan*. AKA: *Handsome Steam Detectives*. TV series. DIR: Kiyoshi Murayama. SCR: Tsunehisa Arakawa, Kenichi Araki. DES: Akio Takami, Satoshi Hashimoto. ANI: Akio Takami. MUS: N/C. PRD: Xebec, TV Tokyo. 25 mins. x 26 eps. Ten-year-old smartass Narutaki fights crime in the steampunk environs of Steam City. He is assisted by his loyal butler (shades of *Batman*) who has looked after him since his parents were killed by the malevolent Phantom Menace, and also by curvy 16-year-old nurse Ling Ling, daughter of a dead scientist, who not only shops, cooks, and wears a cute uniform, but also has her own magnificently clunky giant robot, Goriki. This intriguing mix of the diminutive CONAN THE BOY DETECTIVE with the nostalgic technology of GIANT ROBO is frittered away with low-quality animation and poorly conceived plots. Based on the 1995 manga by SILENT MÖBIUS–creator Kia Asamiya serialized in *Ultra Jump*.

STEAMBOY *

2004. Movie. DIR: Katsuhiro Otomo. SCR: Katsuhiro Otomo, Sadayuki Murai. DES: Katsuhiro Otomo. ANI: Shinji Takagi, Tatsuya Tomaru, Atsushi Irie, Katsumi Matsuda, Tsutomu Awada, Yasuyuki Shimizu, Hisashi Eguchi, Hirotsugu Kawasaki. MUS: Steve Jablonsky. PRD: Studio 4°C, Sunrise, Mash Room. 126 mins. (original version), 104 mins. (international version). In Manchester, England, in 1866, young James "Ray" Steam hopes to be an inventor like his father and grandfather. Receiving a parcel in the mail from his grandfather Lloyd, Ray becomes the new owner of the "steam ball," a prototype energy source that utilizes a supercompressed liquid—a similar catalyst to that in THE SECRET OF CERULEAN SAND. Ray's father Eddie is working with Scarlett O'Hara, the owner of the American O'Hara Foundation, whose impressive Steam Tower will be a feature of the Great Exhibition in London— compare to THE SECRET OF BLUE WATER which uses the later Paris Exhibition as a conduit to adventure. However, Lloyd and Eddie have fallen out over the tower's uses. Ray joins forces with inventor Robert Stephenson in order to thwart the O'Hara organization's plan to sell advanced steam-powered weapons at London's Great Exhibition, a trade fair that will attract the great and the good from all over the world.

As with many other anime hyped for their technical achievement (MACROSS *Plus* comes to mind, as does METROPOLIS, for which Otomo wrote the screenplay), *Steamboy* seems obsessed with the matter of its own creation. Eddie boasts to his son that the Steam Tower merely needs to exist and be seen to achieve its end. Some might argue the same for *Steamboy* itself, trumpeted as a flagship for anime abroad, ten years and $20.2 million in the making, constantly tweaked and remodeled to keep up with its notoriously perfectionist director's desire to remain at the cutting edge. However, this long-awaited follow-up, Otomo's first full-length anime feature as director since AKIRA, replays its predecessor's military-industrial conspiracy, dressed up in period costume and the exotic, inscrutable setting of England. As in Otomo's most famous work, the characters are plunged into a race over the mastery of an earth-shattering energy source, culminating in a long battle that levels buildings citywide with the cavalier attitude of a Godzilla. Like ASTRO BOY, *Steamboy*'s protagonist is torn between positive and negative father figures, but much of it comprises an overlong chase sequence, even in the "international version" that discards 20 minutes of footage from the original Japanese release—much of the jettisoned material coming from the early Manchester scenes.

Steamboy was commissioned in the mid-1990s, amid the same retro mood that saw other steampunk stylings such as SAKURA WARS or SUPER ATRAGON, with arch references to *Gone With the Wind* (1939) in its choice of leading lady. Its imagery recalls that of Otomo's "Cannon Fodder" segment in MEMORIES, while its love of steam power suggests the clunky contraptions of Hayao Miyazaki's CASTLE IN THE SKY and SHERLOCK HOUND. In its final moments, however, it also resembles the reconciliation and truce of HOWL'S MOVING CASTLE, with weapons of mass destruction temporarily thwarted and family values asserting themselves, however briefly, in the race to save London from the Steam family's FRANKENSTEIN technology. There is a certain irony that Otomo should employ so many devices from the 21st century in order to recreate a fantasy ideal of the 19th, particularly when if anything lets *Steamboy* down, it is the humble, low-tech want of an editor to take a red pencil to an overblown and strangely paced script. The movie enjoyed a new lease on life on DVD and was one of the first releases in the new Blu-ray format, in 2006. **V**

STEEL ANGEL KURUMI *

1999. JPN: *Kotetsu Tenshi Kurumi*. TV series. DIR: Naohito Takahashi, Kazuya Murata, Norihiko Sudo. SCR: Tsunehisa Arakawa. DES: Yuriko Chiba, Takeshi Ito, Toshihiko Sato. ANI: Yuriko Chiba. MUS: N/C. PRD: Kadokawa, Pony Canyon, WOWOW. 15 mins. x 24 eps. (TV1), 15 mins. x 4 eps. (v), 15 mins. x 12 eps. (TV2). In a 1920s Japan not unlike that of SAKURA WARS, a mad scientist (we know he's mad because he's called Professor Demon) has devoted the full power of his weird science to producing a robot whose deadly weapons are pink hair, a cute voice, and a French maid outfit. When a teenage boy sneaks into the basement for a peek, Kurumi decides *he's* her master. The 15-minute running time restricts what can be done to move the story along, but the audience's short attention span might work in favor of a concept that was hackneyed about three TENCHI MUYO! clones back. Realizing that a respray was all the audience's low expectations required, the producers returned in 2001 with a new series, which was just like the old one but set in the present day, with everyone's name now bearing the suffix

"Mark Two." That was worth it. A live-action version of the series was also made, under the title *Steel Angel Kurumi—Pure* (2002, *DE).

STEEL DEVIL
1987. JPN: *Daimaju Gekito Hagane no Oni*. AKA: *Violent Encounter Demon of Steel*. Video. DIR: Toshihiro Hirano. SCR: Sho Aikawa. DES: Naoyuki Onda, Koichi Ohata. ANI: Koichi Ohata. MUS: Masahiro Kawasaki. PRD: AIC, Tokuma Japan Communications. 60 mins. An experimental laser brings down a UFO on a remote island, and scientists Haruka and Takuya risk their lives to investigate. Accidentally opening a door to another dimension, Haruka is transformed into a giant mechanical warrior. In this derivative apocalyptic anime from ICZER-ONE-creator Hirano, ancient entities rise from their slumber of ages and fight in the sky above Shinjuku to herald the end of the rule of humanity. See also CYGUARD and GENOCYBER.

STEEL JEEG
1975. JPN: *Kotetsu Jeeg*. TV series. DIR: Masayuki Akehi, Yoshio Nitta, Kazuya Miyazaki, Masayuki Akehi, Yugo Serikawa, Masamune Ochiai, Nobutaka Nishizawa, Yasuo Yamayoshi. SCR: Hiroyasu Yamaura, Keisuke Fujikawa, Tomohiro Ando. DES: Kazuo Nakamura, Geki Katsumata. ANI: Kazuo Nakamura, Seiji Kikuchi, Koji Uemura, Sadao Tominaga. MUS: Michiaki Watanabe. PRD: Toei, NET. 25 mins. x 46 eps.
Hiroshi Shima is mortally injured in a racing accident but restored to life as a cyborg by his scientist father. Professor Shima is also investigating the relics of the ancient Jamatai kingdom, and he is murdered by the henchmen of their Queen Himika when he discovers a tiny bronze bell with supposed sorcerous powers. The modern inhabitants of Japan are attacked by the bell's ancient makers, but Hiroshi holds them off by interfacing with the head of a giant robot, Steel Robot Jeeg, also created by his father (a multitalented physiologist-cum-archeologist-cum-robot designer, it would seem). To complete its body and launch into space, he needs parts released by the space jet Big Shooter, piloted by his father's lovely assistant, Miwa Satsuki. The enemy has huge *haniwa* robots, called "clay phantoms," buried under

the soil of Japan, and only Jeeg can destroy them and save the world; but can cyborg Hiroshi suppress his human feelings for Miwa? After episode 29, the Jamatai invaders were replaced by a new enemy, the Ryoma Empire. Based on an idea by Tatsuya Yasuda and Go Nagai, creator of GRANDIZER, GETTER ROBO, and MAZINGER Z, *SJ* also ran as a manga in several children's publications. *Haniwa* in Japanese archeology are literally "circles of clay"—barrel-shaped terracotta cylinders topped by sculptures, used to mark the borders of burial grounds in ancient Japan. They date from the period when Queen *Himiko* ruled the state of *Yamatai* in the 3rd century A.D. (see DARK MYTH). Compare to similar ghosts of the past in PSYCHIC WARS and BLUE SEED.

STEEL THREE KINGDOMS *
2007. JPN: *Kotetsu Sangokushi*. TV series, video. DIR: Tetsuya Endo, Satoshi Saga. SCR: Natsuko Takahashi, Daisuke Watanabe, Kenichi Yamashita, Miharu Hirami, Shinichi Inotsume. DES: Chiyomi Tsukamoto, Yukio Okano, Koichi Hashimoto, Shigeru Morimoto, Hiroyuki Taiga, Takashi Ono. ANI: Koichi Hashimoto. MUS: Yuji Toriyama. PRD: Picture Magic, Konami Digital Entertainment, NAS. 25 mins. x 25 eps. (TV), 25 mins. (v).
The Imperial Seal is a mystical artifact that confers great powers on the warriors it chooses to defend it. Rikuson's family have been guardians of the Seal for generations until it was stolen by the charismatic but bloodthirsty Sonsaku. At the request of his foster father Komei, Rikuson offers to serve Sonsaku, even though Sonsaku killed his father—with the aim of finding out what the will of the Seal might be. Then Sonsaku is assassinated and the Seal is lost. As a much larger kingdom threatens two smaller ones, both ruled by mere boys, Rikuson sets out to recover the Seal.
GREAT CONQUEST: ROMANCE OF THE THREE KINGDOMS has inspired many anime and manga apart from this. It's a boys'-love story with nothing explicit in it, not even a chaste kiss; there is, however, plenty of drama, death, and tears. The heroes use a special armor known as "flame burst armor," which was intended to create heroic combat sequences. The character designs are fittingly beautiful, but the animation is scarcely worthy of the name, and the

pacing is woefully uneven. A manga, novelization, year-long radio show, drama CD, and stage opera all followed, and a 26th episode was aired in 2008 as a "special."

STEINS;GATE *
2011. TV series, video, movie. DIR: Hiroshi Hamasaki, Takuya Sato, Tomoki Kobayashi, Kanji Wakabayashi. SCR: Jukki Hanada, Masahiro Yokotani, Toshizo Nemoto. DES: Kyuta Sakai, Koji Eto. ANI: Kyuta Sakai. MUS: Jun Murakami, Takeshi Abo. PRD: WHITE FOX, AT-X, Frontier Works, Future Gadget Lab, Kadokawa, Media Factory, MOVIC, Nitroplus, Mages, Cinema Sunshine. 25 mins. x 24 eps. (TV), 25 mins. (v), ?? mins. (m).
Rintaro Okabe is a mad scientist—he says so himself. He thinks that the international scientific establishment, in the shape of international organization SERN (*sic*), is out to remake the world in line with its own desires, but then he and his friend Itaru accidentally invent something with far worse consequences. They create a transmitter to the past, and the messages they send in the course of their experiments change the present. Okabe realizes he's the only one who is aware of what's happening. How can he bring time back into line?
Taking one of science fiction's favorite paradoxes and turning it into a must-see TV series, *Steins;Gate* is one of the cleverest shows of its year, quite possibly of its decade. It cloaks its true nature under layers of geek-friendly psychobabble and fluff for long enough to draw you in to the world of this infuriating yet endearing pair of man-children and their acquaintances, including the haughty girl science genius Kurisu. The sly, subtle way that the protagonist turns out to be the very thing he most despises—the kind of scientist who'll reshape the world to his will without a thought for the consequences—sets us up for a thrill-ride denouement as he tries to undo the damage. Piling up the genre references into an Aladdin's cave of dreams and wishes and setting the whole thing in otaku dreamland Akihabara are master strokes, but they only set the scene for the twists and turns to come.
In a way, it's a good thing for the rest of anime that the style doesn't match the plotting. That would have made it unbeatable. As it is, the design and animation

do the job, but no more. **BLACK ROCK SHOOTER**'s game creator huke did the original character designs, strongly reminiscent of his work there. There's nothing much wrong with the design and animation, apart from a tendency to overuse talking-head shots and still frames—but what makes this show memorable is the plot and pace.

An extra TV-length episode by a new director was tagged on to the DVD and Blu-ray release of the series in Japan. A movie, *Steins;Gate Fuka Ryoiki no Déjà vu*, followed in 2013, bringing in new director Wakabayashi and picking up on an earlier romantic subplot. It was created by Mages, AKA Chiyomaru Shikura, composer and lyricist for several of the songs from the TV series.

It's unusual for such intelligent and focused science fiction to start out as a visual novel (**ARGOT AND JARGON**), but that's where Nitroplus launched *Steins;Gate* in 2009. Following on from **CHAOS;HEAD** and followed by **ROBOTICS;NOTES**, it was part of a series devoted to "hypothetical science," denoted by that tell-tale semi-colon in each title. Since then, there have been two more *Steins;Gate* games as well as five manga running in six magazines.

STELLA WOMEN'S ACADEMY *

2013. JPN: *Stella Jo-Gakuin Koto-ka C3-bu*. AKA: *High School Division Class C3*. TV series. DIR: Masayoshi Kawajiri. SCR: Katsuhiko Takayama, Mie Kaga, Takeshi Sakamoto, Yukihito Nonaka. DES: Manami Umeshita. ANI: Satoru Kiyomaru. MUS: Kotaro Nakagawa. PRD: Gainax, McRay, Movic, Pony Canyon, TBS. 24 mins. x 13 eps.

Yura Yamato is a new arrival at the titular women's academy, expecting a frilly fantasy of afternoon tea and lessons in deportment. Instead, she discovers that she is in a class of gun-nuts, co-opted into the C3 club ("command, control, and communications"), and thrown into a number of catch-the-flag wargames using airsoft guns.

Just when you thought anime had pushed as far as it could go, somewhere a brainstorming meeting throws out "**K-ON** with guns," and we're off again. Adapted from a 2010 manga by Ikoma and Getsumin, running in *Famitsu Comic Clear*, this is also a Gainax production, and embraces many of the ideas that makes Gainax such a winner with **FANDOM**. As with **GUNBUSTER**, early frivolous episodes give way to harder-hitting drama, while Yura's over-active imagination makes her *feel* (and envision for the viewer) each wargame as if it involves far more deadly firearms. Deep down, there is a tongue-in-cheek retelling of many of the tropes of **SPORTS ANIME**, but also many of the club-based school dramas that revolve around raising the money, and perky *let's-do-the-show-right-here* enthusiasm. Needless to say, there is a nerdy level of detail on the weapons themselves, even if they only shoot little plastic pellets. Compare to **GIRLS UND PANZER**, which does something similar … just with tanks.

STELLVIA *

2003. JPN: *Uchu no Stellvia*. AKA: *Stellvia of Space*. TV series. DIR: Tatsuo Sato. SCR: Ichiro Okochi, Katsuhiko Chiba, Katsuhiko Koide, Miho Sakai, Tatsuo Sato, DES: Makoto Uno, Naohiro Washio. ANI: Shigeru Ueda. MUS: Seiko Nagaoka. PRD: Foundation II, Xebec. 25 mins. x 26 eps.

A distant supernova triggered a huge electromagnetic pulse that brought mankind to the verge of extinction 189 years ago. With 99% of Earth's population destroyed, humanity has built huge space stations called "foundations" to try and prevent another such catastrophe. In 2356, 15-year-old Shima Katase passes the entrance exams for the Space Academy and sets out for the foundation Stellvia, hoping that she'll be ready to help out with the Great Mission, a plan to stop the aftershock from the first disaster causing more damage. First, though, she has to make friends, enemies, and rivals, and overcome her own fears and grow up. Yes, it's a high school story set in space. We've been on similar territory before, with the sublime **GUNBUSTER** exploring the insecurities of growing up enhanced by the time dilation effect, and a whole host of lesser stories starring an overly large cast of cute, slightly klutzy girls who are not the star student but try so hard that they eventually save the day. Parallels grow even stronger when the crew of the Stellvia find themselves having to deal with an alien attack. Writer-director Sato doesn't bring anything new to the table for *Stellvia*, despite its pretty design and animation—compare to **BATTLE ATHLETES**.

STEP-UP LOVE STORY, A *

2002. JPN: *Futari H.* AKA: *Futari Etchi*; *Futari Ecchi*; *H Together*. Video. DIR: Yuji Moriyama. SCR: Chiaki Konaka. DES: Yasuyuki Noda. ANI: N/C. MUS: Jun Watanabe. PRD: Geneon, Hakusensha. 30 mins. x 2 eps. (v1), 30 mins. x 2 eps. (v2).

Makoto is a 25-year-old man determined to save himself for his wedding night with the virginal Yura. But he's spent so long abstaining, he's not sure what to do next, and the only person prepared to teach him is his sexy sister-in-law, though she is soon joined by assorted other relatives, friends, and helpful strangers. The lessons begin with simple concepts and proceed through petting into bedroom role-play. Based on a manga by Katsu Aki in *Young Animal* magazine—not to be confused with **H TOGETHER**, which has a similar title in Japanese. **Ⓝ**

STEPMOTHER'S SIN *

2001. JPN: *Gibo*. AKA: *Stepmother*. Video. DIR: Takayoshi Mizuno. SCR: Rokurota Makabe. DES: Matsuri Ohana. ANI: Matsuri Ohana. MUS: Yoshi. PRD: Digital Works (Vanilla Series). 30 mins. x 2 eps.

Ever since witnessing a primal scene of his mother being unfaithful, Yusuke has developed a hatred of women that he directs in particular at members of his own family. Now divorced, his father is posted to a distant office, leaving Yusuke to live with his new stepmother-to-be Misako and Shiina, her daughter from a previous marriage. Meanwhile, Yusuke is conducting a secret affair with his cousin Mio, but also resolves to humiliate his new stepfamily. Shiina fantasizes about her stepbrother, but is then raped by him in front of her mother, who is so aroused by the incident that she then begs to be taken herself. Traumatized by the experience, Shiina allows herself to fall in with a street gang who end up raping her, too. Somewhat belatedly, Yusuke realizes the errors of his ways and that he actually loves Misako. He seeks her forgiveness, but she tells him that she has learned to love the sadistic sex he has taught him. This revelation causes Yusuke to lose control of his senses (as if he hadn't already!), and he is arrested after attacking a loving couple in the park. The police drag him back to Misako's house, where she is found in the middle of an orgy. She begs Yusuke to give her what she needs, but, in a surprise twist, the anime ends with the death of one of the leading characters. Precisely who is left to the viewer's imagination. ❶❷❸

STEPSISTER *

2002. JPN: *Gibomai*. Video. DIR: Toshihito Yura. SCR: Kentaro Mizuno. DES: Selen. ANI: Hitoshi Haga. MUS: Hiroaki Sano, Takeshi Nishizawa. PRD: Discovery. 30 mins. x 2 eps. Kyosuke has never really liked his stepmother Megumi, holding her personally responsible for the separation of his parents and his mother's untimely death soon after. But he rallies around when his famous painter father dies, and soon discovers that Megumi wants to hang onto a number of valuable paintings. As the negotiations over Kyosuke's father's estate continue, Megumi offers her daughter Yuna for Kyosuke's sexual diversion. Kyosuke begins a sadistic relationship with his stepsister, in an entry in the DISCOVERY SERIES, based on an erotic computer game by Selen. ❶❷❸

STEREOTYPES AND ARCHETYPES

Although we do not wish to draw too many links between Japan's traditional past and its modern-day entertainment, it is worth noting that much of the shorthand employed in story meetings and brainstorming sessions can break down into the *yakugara* character clichés established in the Japanese theater. In kabuki, for example, roles are broadly divided into protagonists and antagonists, with heroes divided into the gruff, "hot-headed" *aragoto*, and the more refined, elegant, even effeminate *wagoto* role—see SAMURAI CHAMPLOO, which copies these divisions to the letter. Other kabuki character clichés include the *jitsugoto*, who oppose evil with divine strength, although they are often broken and destroyed by their efforts. Female characters in kabuki were more simply divided into *wakaonnagata* (youthful princesses, courtesans, and other damsels in likely distress), *kashagata* (samurai wives, often good with a sword or a frying pan), and *akuba* (archetypal bad-girls, with street smarts, tattoos, and sass). These basic classes of character are further multiplied by three age groups—young, middle-aged, and old—to create most main characters

of the Japanese stage, although we have left out several subclasses, such as clowns, due to space limitations. Similarly, kabuki has six basic types of villain—evil princes (AKA "nation demolishers"), evil samurai, evil retainers, dishonest clerks, henchmen (often used for comic relief), and apprentices. Multiplied by the three age groups, they form 18 basic templates for villainy, from beautiful boy-villains who threaten the hero's would-be girlfriend, to scheming old uncles who are secretly in league with an enemy clan.

Anime in the early days of TV, particularly but not exclusively those with a sporting basis, would often use similar character archetypes. The viewer's point of identification is usually the character closest in age to the target audience, and often a supposed "natural" at the anime's central sport/activity, with a rough, unhoned talent that requires hard work and perseverance (GUNBUSTER's oft-repeated "*doryoku to konjo*") to turn into true ability. The catalyst that drives them into action in many instances is the loss of an elder family member—a father or sibling—although the lost relation may eventually reappear working for the enemy. The mentor figure is an associate of the one who is lost, attempting to assuage his/her own guilt or bereavement by pushing the lead character into ever better achievements. The mentor figure will also be likely to have a tragic fate, possibly due to some disease or affliction that s/he has kept from the protagonist, or otherwise a moment of supreme sacrifice. Note also that these archetypes are far from unique, as they delineate a mythic "hero's journey" that can also be found in Western media, most obviously *Star Wars* (1977), itself famously using Joseph Campbell's *Hero with a Thousand Faces* to define its archetypes. There will also be a childish sidekick, often for comic relief, and probably a dark mysterious stranger, who may turn out to be the long-lost relative. These dynamics, plus a few sports matches or battles, can normally carry a story healthily for 26 episodes. By the time the audience might notice they have seen it all before, they are probably already into a different year at school or following a different show—that, at least, is how the more cynical producers might excuse the use of such formulae.

The rise of merchandising led many manga and anime creators to follow larger cast templates, chiefly inspired by foreign imports. It was Gerry Anderson's *Thunderbirds* that introduced the Japanese to the toy-selling, audience-pleasing potential of an entire family of protagonists, most noticeable in SKYERS 5 (1967) and *Goranger* (*DE; 1975), which introduced the character roster of Hero, Rogue, Big Guy, Comic Relief, and Token Girl, often working for an avuncular scientist, and perhaps most recognizable in BATTLE OF THE PLANETS (1972).

Five lead characters allows for a healthy group dynamic and helps justify the sale of five toys instead of one. This format was further refined in girls' anime to remove men from the equation, creating groups of five heroines—or more precisely, a single point of identification, with four supporting cast members. HUMMINGBIRDS and early seasons of SAILOR MOON offer the best examples, with our klutzy, ugly-duckling Girl Next Door heroine, a hapless, self-doubting center, surrounded by a brusque Tomboy, a demure Maiden, a sophisticated Older Girl, and a Child (occasionally a feral one). Other female characters might include Foreign Girls, often depicted as blonde, loud, large-breasted, and stupid. It should be noted, however, that blonde hair, or indeed any other hair color, including green and purple, is not a racial signifier in anime, which often gives its characters ludicrous hair colors in order to aid identification. Similar concerns often lead to heavy accessorizing in female characters' hair.

Foreignness also plays an important part in the subject of gay erotica—many relationships in such anime being describable as a meek, submissive, dark-haired character, who is acted upon, dominated, or seduced by a more experienced, often elder, blonder character—even if the seducer is not demonstrably foreign, their actions will often be the least stereotypically Japanese.

The arrival of the dating simulation genre has also utilized the basic female archetypes of the team show, often turning gameplay into a form of personality test in which the computer tries to work out what kind of mate the player would most prefer—a bratty pop idol Child, perhaps, or a librarian Maiden, both likely candidates for *moe*, the modern fan obsession with unthreatening, childlike girls like something out of the LOLITA ANIME. Many dating sims introduce more than the basic character set (which, incidentally, the authors first divined by comparing the programming flowcharts on erotic dating sims), but additional girls are often variations on the basic themes. Such themes are readily translated into erotic anime, many of which are based directly on the games where the archetypes are most clearly used. Where romance is part of the story, even in mundane anime not related to dating sims, it is often assumed that the Girl Next Door character among a hero's love objects will be the eventual lucky lady—time-slip chapters of both the URUSEI YATSURA and DORAEMON stories imply that their heroes settle for their hometown girl, and not any exotic alien princesses or demon queens.

Japanese critics are often reluctant to admit that so many characters can be so easily delineated. Takashi Kondo's *Guide of Fantastic Beauties* (*Kusou Bishojo Tokuhon*, 1997), for example, prefers to plot female anime characteristics on six axes—Town vs.Country, Warlike vs. Peaceful, Adult vs. Child, Real vs. Ethereal, Fresh vs. Bitter, and the rather vague Sun vs. Moon. Furthermore, attempts by press liaisons to make something sound palatable to journalists can reduce any anime plot to predictable and unappealing stereotypes. Consequently, the phrase "Hot-headed and/or shy boy gets robot and/or several would-be girlfriends, and/or a childhood sweetheart who is a mysterious girl" is applicable to a depressingly large number of anime. Where a title first appeared in comic form, it has also become a hoary cliché to say "based on the popular manga," regardless of whether the manga was popular or not.

STINGIEST MAN IN TOWN, THE *

1978. JPN: *Machi Ichiban no Kechinbo*. TV special. DIR: Katsuhisa Yamada. SCR: Romeo Muller. DES: Paul Coker Jr. ANI: Kazuyuki Komori. MUS: Fred Spielman. PRD: Top Craft, Rankin/Bass, TV Asahi. 55 mins.
On a cold Christmas Eve in 1880s London, notorious miser Ebenezer Scrooge is visited in his sleep by three ghostly apparitions who teach him the errors of his ways and the meaning of Christmas. This U.S.-Japan coproduction based on Charles Dickens's 1843 novel *A Christmas Carol* was designed as a musical for the American market and made to order by the Japanese from a prerecorded voice and music track. Character designer Coker seems to have worked almost solely on festive cartoons back in the U.S., including *Frosty's Winter Wonderland* and *The Year without a Santa Claus*—he is better known as one of the artists on *Mad* magazine and an old hand at designing greetings cards for Hallmark. For the subsequent Japanese version, a new script was synchronized to the existing pictures: a rare case of an anime that genuinely has been *dubbed* in Japanese. The Japanese edition was broadcast on Christmas Eve 1978, a mere 24 hours after the U.S. premiere. Director Yamada would go on to make a variety of more obviously Japanese cartoons, including the high-spirited JUNK BOY and the spirit-slaying DEVIL HUNTER YOHKO. Dickens's OLD CURIOSITY SHOP was animated the following year by an unconnected crew.

STITCH!

2008. TV series. DIR: Masami Hata, Tetsuo Yasumi (TV3). SCR: Shoji Yonemura, Toko Machida, Satoru Nishizono, Yuko Kakihara, Ayako Kato, Higashi Shimizu, Kimiko Ueno. DES: Kenichi Shimizu, Yoshinori Kanemori, Hisashi Ikeda, Kaoru Ida, Yukio Abe, Nao Ikeda, Sachiko Ohashi, Toru Koga. ANI: Han Kwang Il, Shinchi Yoshikawa, Minoru Yamazawa, Minefumi Harada, Aya Nakanishi, Katsuya Yamamoto. MUS: Yoshihisa Suzuki. PRD: Madhouse Studios, Shin-Ei Animation, Walt Disney Television International Japan. 25 mins. x 26 eps. (TV1), 25 mins. x 30 eps. (TV2), 25 mins. x 30 eps. (TV3).
Alien experiment Stitch arrives on an island off the coast of Okinawa. He befriends a local girl, ten-year-old tomboy Yuna, and discovers a mystical power on the island that can grant his wish of being the strongest creature in the universe—providing he does enough good deeds. DRAGON BALL and a dozen other wish-quest adventures may spring to mind. Armed with a Good Deed Counter provided by his creator, scientist Jumba, he sets out to accumulate the 43 good deeds he requires. But his mischievous nature and tendency to get distracted sometimes mean he loses good deeds from his tally, rather than accumulating more.

This is an anime version of one of Disney's finest modern movies, specifically designed as an anime-influenced sequel to the movie for Japanese audiences aged 4–14. It has since been shown in other countries, including Finland, the Netherlands, and the U.K., although the U.S. screening was pulled from the schedules after only four episodes. A second series, *Stitch! The Mysterious Alien's Great Adventure* (*Stitch! Itazura Alien no Daiboken*), followed in 2009, with a third, *Stitch! Best Friends Forever* (*Stitch! Zutto Saiko no Tomodachi*), in 2010. Yasumi replaced Hata in the director's chair for series three.

STOP HIBARI-KUN

1983. JPN: *Stop Hibari-kun*. TV series. DIR: Satoshi Hisaoka, Tetsuo Imazawa, Yoshiaki Kawajiri, Hiroshi Sasagawa. SCR: Shigeru Yanagawa, Hiromi Asano, Tokio Tsuchiya, Hiroshi Koda, Tomomi Tsutsui, Takeshi Shudo. DES: Yoshinori Kanemori. ANI: Makoto Ito, Kazuo Tomizawa, Kiyoshi Matsumoto, Takao Kasai, Yasuomi Umezu. MUS: Koji Nishimura. PRD: Toei, Fuji TV. 25 mins. x 35 eps.
Yusaku Sakamoto is sent to live with a friend of the family after his mother's death—or should that be, a friend of the Family. Now he's living with Ibari Ozora, head of the Ozora crime syndicate, and Ozora's pretty daughters Tsugumi, Tsubame, Suzume, and Ko-chan. The prettiest "girl" of all, however, is Hibari, Ozora's eldest son, who has decided he likes life better if he dresses as a girl. This bizarre forerunner of TENCHI MUYO! combined with a cross-dressing *Godfather* was based on the 1982 manga in *Shonen Jump* by EIJI-creator Hisashi Eguchi.

STORY OF DONBE

1981. JPN: *Donbe Monogatari*. TV special. DIR: Fusahito Nagaki. SCR: Yota Tatsumachi, Keisuke Fujikawa. DES: Setsuo Monai, Akira Fukuda. ANI: Akira Fukuda. MUS: Hiroshi Takada, Kiyoshi Suzuki. PRD: Eiken, NTV. 84 mins.
Researcher Mutsugoro takes his family to a remote and uninhabited island near Hokkaido, to study the local population of wild bears. Nearby poachers make his life difficult, and he "inherits" an orphaned

bear cub, whom the family call Donbe and raise as one of their own. A dramatization of one Tadashi Hata's essays from his book *The Hokkaido Animal Kingdom*, the author himself provided authentic bear impersonations for the voice track, and is hence credited as Donbe's "voice actor."

STORY OF LITTLE LOVE

1984. JPN: *Chiisana Koi no Monogatari*. TV special. DIR: Toshio Hirata, Satoshi Dezaki. SCR: Shunichi Yukimuro. DES: Yoshiyuki Momose. ANI: Yoshishige Kosako. MUS: Shinsuke Kazato. PRD: Visual 80, MK, TBS. 84 mins.
Tiny schoolgirl Chiiko develops a crush on older boy Saly and believes herself to be his girlfriend, although Saly is already involved in a love triangle with Tonko, the girl he met on his summer vacation in the mountains. Based on a 1962 manga by Chikako Mitsuhashi.

STORY OF LITTLE MONICA, THE *

2002. JPN: *Little Monica Monogatari*. Movie. DIR: Joki Satsumaya. SCR: Rokurota Makabe. DES: Joki Satsumaya. ANI: Mamoru Yasaki. MUS: Yoshi. PRD: YOUC, Digital Works (Vanilla Series). 30 mins. x 2 eps.
Little Monica is a place, not a person, the idyllic seaside town to which protagonist (and accomplished ladies' man) Will returns after a long absence. However, the town is a shadow of its former self, having fallen under the sway of the evil ruler Kajo. Will finds out how much things have changed when he travels to the local theater, which has been turned into a stripjoint where Meow, a girl he has just met on the boat over, takes off her clothes before selecting a lucky audience member to have intercourse with her onstage—on this occasion, it is Will who is selected. Will has actually come back to Little Monica in order to be reunited with his childhood friend Celia, whose younger sisters Tina and Mei are intensely curious about boys and encourage Will to teach them the facts of life. He eventually does so, while helping out around the trio's restaurant (their mother having gone missing years before) and planning to make an honest woman out of Celia, while still fantasizing about Meow. He might also do something about the previously unmentioned prophecy as well, which predicts that someone will overthrow Kajo and restore the city's

goodness—though presumably that would mean no more stripper freebies for our hero. The series is notable for its high-gloss character designs and skilled use of CG animation—unlike many of its brethren in the VANILLA SERIES, the staff seems to know how bodies actually move. **LNV**

STORY OF RIKI

1989. JPN: *Riki-O*. AKA: *Power King; King Riki*. Video. DIR: Satoshi Dezaki. SCR: Kazumi Koide. DES: Akio Sugino. ANI: Yasuhiro Seo. MUS: Yoshimasa Nakajima. PRD: Magic Bus. 45 mins. x 2 eps.
In the near future, supertough guy Riki is sent to a private prison for a crime he didn't commit. He thrives, however, in the ultraviolent prison environment, fighting his way to the top of the pack and then out to freedom. Based on a manga by Masahiko Takakumi in *Business Jump*, this story was also made into Nam Nai Choi's live-action Hong Kong film *Story of Riki* (1992). Compare to the much later DEADMAN WONDERLAND.**V**

STORY OF SAIUNKOKU, THE *

2006. JPN: *Saiunkoku Monogatari*. AKA: *Color Cloud Palace*. TV series. DIR: Jun Shishido. SCR: Reiko Yoshida, Ayuna Fujisaki, Kurasumi Sunayama, Miho Maruo. DES: Miwa Oshima, Chikara Nishikura. ANI: Tatsuyuki Maeda, Nam Yul Park, Tomoko Shimizu. MUS: Kunihiko Ryo. PRD: Madhouse, NHK. 25 mins. x 39 eps. (TV1), 25 mins. x 39 eps. (TV2).
Saiunkoku is a world controlled by eight great houses, each named for a different color. The current emperor is a playboy with no interest in his job—he'd allegedly rather chase cute men. Shurei, impoverished daughter of an ancient family, agrees to become his concubine, hoping to make him a better ruler and herself a little more secure. But despite having agreed to be his concubine, she has no intention of succumbing to his advances. Aided by Seiran, a young man adopted by her father who has become the emperor's bodyguard, she sets out to become a court official. Much is against her—her poverty, her gender, and the number of men trying to entrap her into a relationship. But with her sharp mind, honesty, and determination, Shurei is determined to succeed, and she finds an unlikely ally in the emperor himself. This could so easily have been just

another lushly decorated reverse harem show (ROMANCE AND DRAMA). Instead, it's a delightfully affirmative romance in the old-fashioned sense of the word—an adventure where the heroine's travels through exotic places result in the discovery of herself. Based on Sai Yukino's novel illustrated by Kairi Yura, it was also turned into a manga in 2006. A second TV series followed in 2007, with the crew unchanged except for the writers. Compare to LIKE A CLOUD, LIKE A BREEZE.

STORY OF SUPERCONDUCTORS

1988. JPN: *Chodendo Monogatari*. TV special. DIR: Masayuki Oseki, Kenji Naito. SCR: Takashi Yamada, Hiroshi Aoki. DES: Isao Oji. ANI: Isao Oji. MUS: N/C. PRD: Studio Twinkle, Tokai TV. 60 mins.
The science department of the *Tosai Shinbun* newspaper investigates a story on superconductors, learning all about the mysterious world of subzero electrical conductivity, the Meissner Effect, Brian Josephson's work on "tunneling" (flow across an insulating layer without application of voltage), and implications for super-*computer* technology in the 21st century. Meanwhile, attractive reporter Miss Ohashi begins to find bespectacled scientist Dr. Arai rather attractive.

STORY OF THE SOYA

1984. JPN: *Soya Monogatari*. TV series. DIR: N/C. SCR: Masaru Yamamoto. DES: Shiro Murata, Hiroki Hayashi. ANI: Shiro Murata. MUS: Toshi Fukui. PRD: Kokusai Eiga, TV Tokyo. 25 mins. x 21 eps.
In 1978, the Antarctic survey vessel Soya calls in at Yamaguchi Prefecture's Moji port on her final voyage. Watching are Susumu Kozaki, a shipbuilder's son who was born on the day the Soya was launched, and his own son, Hiroshi. Susumu tells Hiroshi the story of the Soya, how it was commissioned by the Russians, and how the contract was canceled soon after launch. Renamed the Jishin Maru, the Soya bears witness to the events of the 1930s, as the dark clouds of war gather. The Soya might seem like an obscure vessel in world history, but it was also the survey ship that played a small part in the 1958 Second Cross-Winter Expedition, itself the subject of the live-action movie *Antarctica* (1983)—see RATINGS AND BOX

OFFICE. Hence, this drama series is able to cash in on the success of a film from the previous year—compare to CHOCCHAN'S STORY, which similarly finds an inexpensive angle to retell a better-known story.

STR.A.IN: STRATEGIC ARMORED INFANTRY *

2006. JPN: Soko no Strain. Video. DIR: Tetsuya Watanabe. SCR: Masanao Akahoshi. DES: Mariko Fujita, Kanetake Ebikawa, Tomohiro Kawahara. ANI: Riku Sato. MUS: Ryo Sakai. PRD: Studio Fantasia, Happinet Pictures, WOWOW. 25 mins. x 13 eps.

Sara has it all. A member of a top military family, whose older brother is a hero, she's outgoing and popular at her military academy. She's training to fly one of the Strain mecha (SCIENCE FICTION AND ROBOTS), complete with artificial brain interface. All this ends overnight when her beloved brother Ralph switches sides and leads a devastating attack on her training school. In one night, he destroys her position, her friendships, her expensive hardware, software, and her reputation. Changing her name, Sara sets out to work her way up from the bottom. One day, she plans to face Ralph in battle and redeem her family's honor. We were fascinated to learn that this show is a loose science fictional adaptation of A LITTLE PRINCESS. Sadly—and surprisingly, since everyone involved can do better—the leading character is far less likable and inspiring than Frances Hodgson Burnett's young heroine, and the pacing and lack of character development give a leaden overall feel. **V**

STRAIGHT AHEAD

2003. JPN: Massugu ni Iko. AKA: Let's Go Straight. TV series. DIR: Kiyotaka Isako. SCR: Aki Itami, Atsushi Yamatoya, Yoichi Kato. DES: Aki Tsunaki, Nanae Morita. ANI: Aki Tsunaki. MUS: Michiru Oshima. PRD: Yumeta, Yomiuri TV. 20 mins. x 4 eps. (TV1), 25 mins. x 5 eps. (TV2).

In the tradition of I AM A CAT and THE CALL OF THE WILD, a story is told from the point of view of an animal, in this case Mametaro the mongrel dog, who offers comment and insight into the personal life of his owner, Iku, a Japanese high school girl. Based on the 1993 manga from Bessatsu Margaret and Chorus magazines by "Kira." A second TV series followed in

2005, premiering on the Internet but later broadcast on Yomiuri TV.

STRAIT JACKET *

2007. Video. DIR: Shinji Ushiro. SCR: Ichiro Sakaki. DES: Yoshinori Yumoto, Hideki Fukushima, Rei Nakahara, Hiroki Matsumoto. ANI: N/C. MUS: Takeshi Yanagawa. PRD: feel. Manga Entertainment, T.O. Entertainment. 26 mins. x 3 eps.

If you use magic, you run grave risks. Magic can turn humans into monsters. That's even riskier in a world where humans can use advanced scientific techniques that monsters could seize and use to their own ends. Magicians wear special armor to guard against the transformation to demonic mode, but if this fails there's always the "Strait Jackets"—an elite class of Government-employed magic-users who can take down demons. When demon attacks begin to multiply out of control, resources are strained. The Government has to call in a rogue Strait Jacket and his mysterious, childlike sidekick, but their last hope is fighting inner demons of his own. This show would like to be Blade Runner with magic. It isn't. It's not very original (even the "Strait Jacket" containment principle is a feature of CASSHAN: ROBOT HUNTER), not very well animated, and not very interesting. **OV**

STRANGE DAWN *

2000. TV series. DIR: Shogo Kawamoto, Junichi Sato. SCR: Michiko Yokote. DES: Akihiko Yamashita. ANI: Miho Shimokasa. MUS: Kaoru Wada. PRD: HAL Filmmakers, WOWOW. 25 mins. x 13 eps.

Eri and Yuko are high school girls summoned into another world by Queen Aria. Her kingdom, Guriania, is at war with neighboring Barujitan, and she believes the two girls are witches who can use their mighty powers to end the conflict. But they don't have any powers, don't like each other, and don't want to work together—except that it seems like it's the only way they can get back to their own world. Predictably cute character designs, including a couple of childlike fantasy creatures that at least make a change from the usual magical animal sidekicks. But what sets Strange Dawn apart is the uses to which it puts its designs—the childish-seeming characters belie a plotline that is

unafraid to jump feet-first into war, bloodshed, and death. This is, unfortunately, exactly the sort of thing that TV companies don't want in their cutesy cartoons, leading to a patchy history of broadcast, suspension, and burial that has left Strange Dawn one of anime's forgotten shows, at least abroad. As with EL HAZARD, Junichi Sato's story concentrates on the mundane annoyances that might beset human beings in a fantasy world—regardless of the world that needs saving, the girls are more worried about finding a working toilet and how far they can stretch their limited laundry resources. Cunningly, the series also refuses point-blank to deal with the sort of questions that another series, such as ESCAFLOWNE, would have answered in the very first episode. We don't find out why the girls are so antagonistic toward each other, nor anything about their life in our own world—the lack of an introduction scene misleading the viewers and keeping them guessing throughout, and all for the better.

STRANGE LOVE *

1996. JPN: Hen. AKA: Strange. Video. DIR: Oji Suzuki. SCR: Mayori Sekijima. DES: Yasuomi Umezu. ANI: Chuji Nakajima. MUS: Goji Tsuno. PRD: Group Tac. 40 mins. x 2 eps.

Nerdy teacher (sorry, college professor) Sushiaki develops an obsession with one of his pupils, the impossibly proportioned Chizuru Yoshida. Torn with conflicting feelings in the hypocritical manner of HOMEROOM AFFAIRS, he discovers that she has been secretly appearing in commercials, in contravention of a school (sorry, college) rule that specifies no part-time jobs. Hoping to use this to his advantage, he realizes too late that he has become the plaything of a masterful tease. The "virginal" Chizuru is already sleeping with a rock star, but both men are left in the lurch when Chizuru falls for a female transfer student, Azumi Yamida. Despite several notable names in the crew, this is a creatively barren and often incoherent jailbait fantasy in the spirit of CREAM LEMON, complete with a few halfhearted homages to other anime such as PROJECT A-KO. Based on just part of the 1991 manga in Young Jump by Hiroya Oku, which sold more than five million copies, the story (and viewers) deserved better than this. Though the U.S.

Manga Corps release labels this as only *possibly* unsuitable for minors, it's probably unsuitable for anyone. **Ⓝ**

STRANGE+ *
2014 TV series, video. DIR: Takashi Nishikawa, Hiroyuki Furukawa. SCR: Takashi Nishikawa. DES: Hiroyuki Furukawa. ANI: Takashi Nishikawa, Itsuki Imazaki, Mihoko Ogawa, Yoichi Shimizu, Masato Okado, Tadashi Yoshida. MUS: N/C. PRD: Seven, Dax Production, Dream Creation. 5 mins. x 12 eps. (TV1), 5 mins. x 12 eps. (TV2), 5 mins. (v).
Kou's older brother Takumi left home for the big city and never wrote. So Kou sets off to find him and discovers he's working for an unusual detective agency whose oddball clients and weird cases are no stranger than their working methods, which include blowing up buildings with exploding rubber butts. And he's indulging his love for cross-dressing to the full. Yet despite the fact that his big brother looks like a teenage girl and is mad as a box of frogs, Kou doesn't want to lose him again. Since Takumi won't come home, Kou joins the agency's staff.

Short-form anime has been around from the beginning—when the expense of production and technical limitations made all films short-form—but it's reclaimed its old territory since the advent of broadband streaming. Where it costs a lot of money to acquire a VHS tape or DVD, viewers want a solid chunk of content; when animation costs nothing to download they are willing to be charmed by a few minutes' distraction. *Strange+* fits the bill, and delivers solid diversionary value, loading its run time with sight gags and references to classic mystery and detective shows like CAT'S EYE.

Star voice actor Jun Fukuyama, one of a glittering cast that knows exactly how to sell a goofy line, plays Takumi and sings the theme song. The second series *Shin Strange+* (pointlessly romanized as *Sin Strange+*, seemingly at the creators' insistence) nods ironically to this when Takumi reveals he wants to be Jun Fukuyama when he grows up. Manga creator Verno Mikawa's love of physical comedy is also carried over—you may see the bodies of the Three Stooges and the Marx Brothers amid the debris left by the frequent demolition of the fourth wall. *S+* also

packs in plenty of self-referential humor. An "unaired episode" was added to the Blu-ray/DVD release.

For those who think making something this short, nonsequential, and silly is easy, look at the crew list. Seven episode directors support Nishikawa, most also doubling up among the seven animation directors, and ten artists, including manga creator Verno Mikawa, are credited for the end card illustrations. Although both series were released in 2014, Mikawa's manga began its run in 2003, so it's had plenty of time to build up a cult audience and give the anime a flying start. **ⒸⓃ**

STRATOS 4 *
2003. TV series, video. DIR: Takeshi Mori. SCR: Katsuhiko Takayama. DES: Noriyasu Yamauchi, Tomohiro Kawahara. ANI: Noriyasu Yamauchi. MUS: Masamichi Amano. PRD: Bandai Visual, Columbia Music Entertainment, Studio Fantasia, TV Saitama. 23 mins. x 13 eps. (TV), 30 mins. x 2 eps. (v1), 30 mins. x 6 eps. (v2), 30 mins. x 6 eps. (v3).
In an Earth suffering a cometary bombardment (shades here of STAR BLAZERS), two new defensive programs keep the world safe. The front line is held by the Comet Blasters, top gun pilots based in space stations beyond Earth, armed with nuclear warheads to destroy meteors before they can penetrate the atmosphere. The second line is the Meteor Sweepers, ground-based pilots in supersonic planes who deal with any debris resulting from the space blasts. Heroine Mikaze is a teenager Meteor Sweeper trainee (in Okinawa, of course—see GUNBUSTER) who longs to become one of the elite Comet Blaster pilots. Like all teenage anime heroines, but most notably like her predecessor pilot in HUMMINGBIRDS, she has to struggle with her own shortcomings first, as she and her teammates learn the ropes.

Although the most obvious inspirations for *Stratos Four* are *Deep Impact* (1998) and *Armageddon* (1998), it often plays more like Gerry Anderson's *UFO* (1970), seen from the viewpoint of the Interceptor pilots and then filtered through teenage insecurity and powerlessness. Mikaze is a classic anime archetype: the daughter of renowned pilots, she flutters between an innate belief in her destiny to follow in the "family business" and teenage fretting

that she should be choosing her own path, and not merely aping her parents. Later episodes inject a note of seriousness—there may be on-base high jinks like any school anime, and sops to the anime audience like a comic-relief cat, not to mention the outrageous suspension of disbelief required to watch a bunch of inept schoolgirls flying jet fighters, and yet *Stratos Four* does not shy away from moments of danger and tension. Later episodes include subplots about how the loneliness of a space station posting can turn a girl's mind to same-sex relationships and the obligatory alien menace, although the former eventually turns out to have been created as a viral infection by the latter. For this, we largely have Studio Fantasia to thank—while the people who gave us AGENT AIKA have toned down their legendary obsessions a little, there is still much ogling of technical hardware and ample provision of female pulchritude for the male viewer. This may also explain the wholly unnecessary subplot that finds part-time work for some of the pilots in a Chinese restaurant, thereby permitting the animators to put them into slinky *cheongsam* dresses on occasion.

The TV series was followed by two video sequels: *Stratos Four: Return to Base,* in which the girls have to deal with a space station threatening to fall out of the sky, and *Stratos Four: Advance,* the first episode of which was broadcast on TV before its Japanese release. In *Advance,* the two male Meteor Sweepers are seconded off-island as test pilots for a new interceptor, while three new female trainees arrive, and the cast has to deal with the fallout—personal and political—of the first series. With a shortage of pilots, an escaped prisoner and the mysteries behind the crisis beginning to show themselves, the friends must make one more effort to ensure their beloved planet has a tomorrow. Director Mori gets a coscripting credit on the two-part video and is the sole writer on the six-parter, but otherwise the principal crew is unchanged. After the DVD release of *Stratos Four: Advance,* later episodes were also broadcast on TV, leading some sources to file it as a TV anime. The titular *Battle-Fairy Mave-chan* (2005), in a spin-off of the plane-oriented YUKIKAZE series, was an avowed *Stratos Four* fan.

STRAWBERRY EGGS *

2001. JPN: Ai! Mai! Mi! Strawberry Egg. AKA: I! My! Me! Strawberry Eggs. TV series. DIR: Yuji Yamaguchi. SCR: Yasuko Kobayashi. DES: Maki Fujii. ANI: Tetsuya Yanasawa. MUS: Keiichi Nozaki. PRD: TNK, WOWOW. 25 mins. x 13 eps.

Twenty-three-year-old hothead Hibiki Amawa is a boy from the far north of the Japanese mainland who wants to be a schoolteacher. With funds running low, he accepts the first job he can find, teaching (in drag!) at a school whose man-hating principal only hires female staff. Hibiki must then earn his students' respect, while keeping his true identity secret and battling the principal to keep the school from becoming girls-only—and to keep from falling in love, in a comedy from the studio that brought you HAND MAID MAY.

STRAWBERRY MARSHMALLOW

2005. JPN: Ichigo Mashimaro. TV series. DIR: Takuya Sato, Kazuhiro Ozawa, Mamoru Kanbe. SCR: Takuya Sato, Michiko Yokote, Jukki Hanada. DES: Kyuta Sakai. ANI: Kyuta Sakai, Tatsuya Abe. MUS: Tsuyoshi Watanabe. PRD: Domu, TBS, Geneon USA. 25 mins. x 13 eps.

Nobue Ito is a chain-smoking 20-something who is forced to endure the company of her little sister Chika and Chika's friends, who are supposedly cute, thereby marrying the comedy set-ups of AZUMANGA DAIOH with the world-weary surrogate mother of EVANGELION's Misato. Based on a manga by "Barasui" ("Rose Water") in Dengeki Daioh.

STRAWBERRY 100%

2005. JPN: Ichigo 100%. Video, TV series. DIR: Osamu Sekita. SCR: Tatsuhiko Urahata. DES: Kiyotaka Nakahara. ANI: N/C. MUS: Takayuki Negishi. PRD: Madhouse. 25 mins. x 4 eps. (v), 25 mins. x 24 eps. (TV).

Junpei Manaka heads up to the school roof for a view of his hometown, but instead gets a view of the distinctive strawberry pattern panties being worn by a girl who falls on him. Deciding that the scene would be interesting if recreated for an amateur film (it certainly wasn't in this supposedly professional one!), he seeks out the owner of the panties, only to discover that many of the girls in his school have similar underwear. 100%S is

based on the 2002–5 Shonen Jump manga by Mizuki Kawashita and manages the remarkable feat of recreating the sensation of watching a dull dating sim, despite no relation to any actual game. In an equally impressive anti-achievement, the manga's three-year run in Shonen Jump actually ended shortly after the broadcast of the show; one would expect TV to create renewed interest in a franchise, but apparently not in this case.

The TV version was preceded by the video "special" with the self-explanatory title 100% Strawberries: Love Begins!? Photography Training Camp, Indecisive Heart Going East to West (2004), in which Junpei manages to get a girl alone in a deserted mountain hut during a storm.

STRAWBERRY PANIC *

2006. TV series. DIR: Masayuki Sakoi. SCR: Tatsuhiko Urahata, Hideo Takayashiki, Kazuyuki Fudeyasu. DES: Kyuta Sakai, Yuka Okamoto. ANI: Si Min Lee, Naoko Nakamoto, Masayuki Tanaka, Seiya Numata, Takayuki Uchida. MUS: Yoshihisa Hirano. PRD: Madhouse Studios, Dwango, Ichigo-sha, Lantis, MOVIC, Marvelous Entertainment, Optrum, Yomiko Advertising. 25 mins. x 26 eps.

Aoi Nagisa's parents are working abroad, leaving her to start a new high school and live in the Astraea Dormitory with other pupils from three Catholic girls' schools. There she meets the class president of presidents, leading figure of all three schools, known as the Etoile. Shizuma is at the very top of the school social hierarchy, yet she finds herself drawn to this new girl. But Aoi is also attracting attention from other girls. Based on Sakurako Kimino's 2006 manga, this is a series loaded with schoolgirl melodrama and lesbian supertext but never quite attains the heart-wrenching emotional impact it's aiming for, largely due to a focus on the time-honored tropes and decorative details of girls' school romance rather than developing credible relationships between the characters. ◐

STRAY CATS OVERRUN

2010. JPN: Mayoi Neko Overrun. TV series. DIR: Shin Itagaki, Kenichi Yatani, Yoshimasa Hiraike, Akitaro Daichi, Michio Fukuda, Takashi Ikehata, Rion Kujo, Manabu Ono, Tomohiro Hirata, Takuya Sato, Keizo Kusa-

kawa, Junichi Sato. SCR: Noboru Kimura, Shin Itagaki, Yoshimasa Hiraike, Takashi Ikehata, Takuya Sato. DES: Naoko Nakamoto. ANI: Takahiro Sasaki, Yumiko Hara, Masakazu Ishikawa, Ikumoto Kimishima, Tomoko Iwasa, Tomoko Ishida, Yasuyuki Ebara, Toshimitsu Takechi, Yosuke Kabeshima, Hirokazu Hisayuki, Haruo Ogawara, Satonobu Kikuchi, Takahiro Sasaki, Kyoko Kotani. MUS: N/C. PRD: AIC, Frontier Works, Geneon Universal Entertainment, Shueisha, Klockworx. 25 mins. x 13 eps.

Takumi Tsuzuki is an orphan who lives with his unrelated "older sister" Otome and spends his days going to school and hanging out with his friends. Otome runs a café and patisserie called Stray Cats, and Takumi looks after the shop when she's out—which is often, because she's so good-hearted she travels far and wide helping others, even when it means she and Takumi have very little for themselves. One day, Otome brings a strange girl home to live with them. Nozomi is highly intelligent but totally lacking in social skills and has no understanding of personal boundaries, leading to highly personal remarks and inappropriate nudity. Her mysterious past is gradually uncovered and all the friends start to follow Otome's example of looking out for others. Based on a series of books by Tomohiro Matsu, illustrated by Peco, this is a warm-hearted but conventional and unoriginal harem story (ROMANCE AND DRAMA). The 13th episode is a compilation summarizing the series, an important aid when you consider that all 12 episodes were directed, storyboarded, and animated by different people. The lack of consistency generated by this approach is frequently confusing. Six three-minute specials were added to the DVD releases. ◐

STREET CORNER FAIRY TALES

1984. JPN: Machikado no Meruhen. Video. DIR: Mizuho Nishikubo. SCR: Takeshi Shudo. DES: Yoshitaka Amano. ANI: Heihachi Tanaka. MUS: Virgin VS. PRD: Kitty Films. 52 mins.

Hiroshi, a student in a Shinjuku high school, dreams of one day writing a children's book and is working hard to save enough money so that he can do it. He falls in love with a girl he meets by chance on the subway, and Hiroko becomes very important to the eventual realization of his dreams. Set to 17 pop tunes in the style of

CIPHER, this is not to be confused with Tezuka's **TALES OF THE STREET CORNER**, though the producers rather hoped it would be.

STREET FIGHTER II *

1994. JPN: *Street Fighter II; Street Fighter II Victory; SF Zero*. AKA: *Street Fighter II: The Movie; SF II TV; SF Alpha*. Movie, TV series, video. DIR: Gisaburo Sugii (m/TV); Eiichi Sato, Takuya Sato, Yukio Takahashi, Kuniaki Komura, Hideaki Shimada, Shigeru Yamazaki, Yutaka Arai (TV); Shigeyasu Yamauchi (v). SCR: Kenichi Imai, Gisaburo Sugii (m); Reiko Yoshida, Naoyuki Sakai (TV). DES: Shuko Murase, Minoru Maeda (m); Akira Kano, Junichiro Nishikawa, Yasuhiro Oshima, Satoshi Matsuoka (TV); Yoshihiko Umakoshi (v). ANI: Minoru Maeda (m); Yoshihiko Umakoshi (v). MUS: Tetsuya Komuro (m/TV); Chage and Aska, Hayato Matsuo, Masahiro Shimada (TV). PRD: Group Tac. 104 mins. (m), 25 mins. x 29 eps. (TV), 45 mins. x 2 eps. (v).

Evil Vega (M. Bison) is one of the leaders of the Shadowlaw organization intent on world domination. He is brainwashing martial artists in order to use them as secret agents and has kidnapped Ken Masters, a prominent street fighter. Ken's former sparring partner, Ryu, teams up with Interpol to track him down.

A film based on the sequel to CAPCOM's original computer *game*, *SFII*'s thin premise is a weak hook on which to hang a succession of fight scenes. However, Sugii's theatrical release sets the standard for the entire game-adaptation subgenre and has been much imitated by titles including **TOSHINDEN**, **ART OF FIGHTING**, **FATAL FURY**, and **SEXORCIST**. Though not the first game-based anime (see **SUPER MARIO BROTHERS**), *SFII* was arguably the most successful until **POKÉMON**. Many anime "movies" such as **TEKKEN** aren't "motion pictures" at all but straight-to-video nonsense given a pretentious title for foreign release. *SFII*, however, is a genuine theatrical feature, with computer graphics, lifelike fight animation, and a big budget. Unlike the live-action version released the same year starring Kylie Minogue and Jean-Claude Van Damme, the anime didn't have to try for a younger audience by cutting out the fights, nor was it limited by some cast members without any martial arts experience—the fights in *SFII* were coordinated by real-life fight choreographer Shinichi Shoji, and, since this is animated, every one's superb.

The derivative plot is a cunning conceit to gain as much of the feel of the game as possible without wasting too much time. Stealing from *Enter the Dragon* (1973), *SFII* maneuvers its characters into a set of standoffs engineered through a fighting contest and the idea that several of them are working as secret agents or in law enforcement. It also adds two elements that would become staples of fighting-game adaptations—a mind-control subplot to orchestrate fights between supposed allies, and a shower scene to showcase a female character in the nude.

Characters' billing comes partly determined by their popularity among fans and partly from their seniority. The American Ken and Japanese Ryu are two characters from the first game (1987), and the two gave the filmmakers the chance to have a male American in distress getting rescued by a hunky Japanese guy. Chun-Li and Guile (Interpol agents in the anime) were popular characters from the *SFII* game (1991), while Cammy's cameo role (as a brainwashed assassin) was largely determined by her standing with fans. Though a relative latecomer in *Super SFII* (1993), she gets to climb further up the billing by virtue of being a girl. The other characters get a chance to show their special moves in various bouts, but most of the film belongs to this central cast. Each featured character gets an obligatory rumble, but Sugii creates moments of genuine drama, most notably in a marvelously choreographed fight between Chun Li and Balrog (Vega), enhancing the tension with most of the violence offscreen or in partial shot. As in the game, the bad guys' names have been confusingly shuffled for legal reasons—M(ike) Bison, originally the name of the big African-American boxer character, was assigned to the supreme baddie in the Western release, while M. Bison's name is changed to Balrog, and Balrog's to Vega. The anime feature was resurrected for a *game* called *Street Fighter II Movie* (1996), which combined a normal *SFII*-style game with a semi-interactive version of the film, utilizing footage from the anime. This variant also included a few scenes of bridging animation not found in the bona fide

anime release. Almost two decades later in 2013, the film was rereleased in English on Blu-ray, with a dub track that mysteriously redacted much of Manga Entertainment's 1990s swearing. This presented purists with an odd dilemma—a bowdlerized edit that was actually more faithful to the original Japanese, but tinkered with the tone of the "original" dub.

The TV series *Street Fighter II V* (1995) serves as a prequel to the game, in which teen versions of Ryu and Ken are trounced by a young Guile and set off on an around-the-world trip to learn from "the best of the best." Though there is a heroic effort to introduce deeper backstories for the kung-fu clotheshorses of the game (Chun Li is a young Hong Kong tour guide, Fei Long is an action-film star, etc.), the TV series is undistinguished, and even Sugii's direction rarely rises above the barely necessary. Matters are not helped by an English dub that persistently mispronounces "Ryu" throughout—an achievement roughly equivalent to dubbing *Star Wars* with Han *Sulu*. However, amid the relatively undemanding audience of fighting-game fans, the TV series could be considered a success—it certainly outlasted many of its more "popular" contemporaries.

A final incarnation of the franchise was the two-part video series *SF Zero* (1999, renamed *SF Alpha* in the West, like its game incarnation). With a new director and scenarist better known for **BOYS OVER FLOWERS**, *Zero* keeps the "early years" aspect of the TV series, focusing on an even younger audience by introducing the game's popular schoolgirl fighter Sakura, as well as Ryu's previously unmentioned brother, Shun, who arrives from Brazil. Somewhat cynically dumping the previous continuity (Chun Li and Ryu meet for the first time, *again*, as if the producers do not expect any of the original audience to still be watching), *Zero* runs through a predictable set of clichés, as Ryu discovers his father's evil secret, is tempted by the dark side, and avenges the death of his teacher. *Zero* was partly funded by U.S. distributor Manga Entertainment, which edited it into a single feature-length edition in the expectation it would do as well as its predecessor. But while it often matches the kinetic action of its illustrious ancestor, complete with some good backgrounds, after half a decade of inferior copies of the original *SFII* movie, *Zero* simply looks like just another one. *Street Fighter II Ryu vs. Yomigaeru Fujiwara Kyo* (2004) was a manga boxed set featuring a complete run of Masaomi Kanzaki's manga and a 23-minute anime exclusive in which Ryu, Ken, Chun Li, and E. Honda are transported back in time. *Street Fighter Alpha Generations* (*Street Fighter Zero 2*, 2005) is a 50-minute video in which Ryu returns to the site of his education to pay homage to the spirit of his dead mentor, only to be tormented by the memory of his master's death and his desire to wreak revenge on his arch-rival, Goki.**🅥**

STRIKE WITCHES *
2007. TV series. DIR: Kazuhiro Takamura. SCR: Tsuyoshi Tamai, Takaaki Suzuki. DES: Kazuhiro Takamura, Hiromasa Ogura. ANI: Keiji Goto, Hironori Tanaka, Masami Goto, Shin Wakabayashi, Tomokazu Sugimura. MUS: Seiko Nagaoka. PRD: Gonzo, Kadokawa, NTT Docomo, Klockworx. 25 mins. x 12 eps.
In 1939 the Neuroi appeared. This mysterious new enemy attacked towns and cities, driving out all the survivors. Only magic, it appeared, could fight them. A new weapon called the Striker Unit amplified the powers of young female magic-users, and a new elite task force was born—the 501st Joint Fighter Wing, or the Strike Witches.

Strike Witches is based on the work of toy and action figure designer Humikane Shimada. Its origins indicate its approach: it's all about fan service (**ARGOT AND JARGON**). Most of the characters don't wear pants, nudity is *de rigeur,* and girl-on-girl sexual behavior occurs regardless of the fact that only one character is shown or implied to be lesbian. The standard tropes of fan service apply, with most major body and personality fetishes catered to, and another one added in for good measure. Anyone in love with the glamour and romance of World War II fighter aces and their marvelous machines will geek out over this show—once they get used to the idea that their heroes are represented by cute underdressed exhibitionist teenage girls.

The Battle of Britain is reenacted in this alternate universe, with Japan fighting on the same side as the Allies—and

reenacted magnificently, with director Takamura staging some superb battles and nail-biting setpieces. Nagaoka's music soars and roars in appropriately military fashion. Gonzo plunders anime history as well as world history, with stock characters and plot elements referring back to the real world with a knowing wink. Making no attempt whatsoever at originality, this show sets out to provide a certain type of fun for a certain type of fanboy, and does it very well. **🅝🅥**

STUDENT COUNCIL'S DISCRETION, A *
2006. JPN: *Seitokai no Ichizon: Hekiyo Gakuen Seitokai Gijiroku.* AKA: *Records of the Hekiyo Academy Student Council's Activities.* TV series. DIR: Takuya Sato, Kenichi Imaizumi. SCR: Jukki Hanada, Reiko Yoshida. DES: Kumi Horii, Masahito Onoda, Yuko Sugiyama. ANI: Kumi Horii, Masahiko Yoda, Masahito Onoda. MUS: Shuhei Kamimura, Tomohiro Anzai. PRD: Studio DEEN, AIC, AMG Entertainment, D. N. Dream Partners, Kadokawa, Klockworx. 24 mins. x 12 eps. (TV1), 24 mins. x 10 eps. (TV2).
The student council at Ken Sugisaki's private high school is chosen by popular vote. Unsurprisingly, the majority are extremely pretty girls. Ken, the secretary, is the only guy. He got elected by becoming the top-scoring student on all tests, but the cramming was worth it because now he gets to take the minutes of meetings surrounded by the cutest girls in school. These council meetings tend to devolve into chitchat about the latest school gossip in this **EVERYDAY ANIME** that would be a harem show (**ROMANCE AND DRAMA**) if it could be bothered to be anything but a frame for cute girl ciphers, originally created by Kira Inugami for Sekina Aoi's 2008 books and 2009 manga. The manga and novels combine *moe* (**ARGOT AND JARGON**), otaku and parody elements, and as befits a show aimed at a geek audience the anime started life online before making the leap to TV. Despite its almost total lack of substance it was popular enough to get a second season: *Student Council's Discretion Level 2* (*Seitokai no Ichizon Lv.2*) aired in 2012, again after streaming online. It was made at a different studio with an entirely different crew, and two of the voice actors from the original series were replaced. Not

to be confused with the previous year's **BEST STUDENT COUNCIL**.

STUDENT PRESIDENT HIKARU
2010. JPN: *Seito Kaicho Hikaru.* Video. DIR: Ryu Maiami. SCR: Shinichiro Sawayama. DES: Riku Kugahara. ANI: Riku Kugahara. MUS: N/C. PRD: Mary Jane, Studio Eromatick. 30 mins.
Three members of the student council— nun with a gun Seira, warrior girl Hikaru, and shrine maiden Yuki—are trying to cleanse their high school of perversion. It's a school devoted to training monster hunters and they finally defeat a terrible monster called Varmus. But he's revived by perverted magic and takes over their head teacher. Tentacle porn ensues as Varmus tries to breed monster babies from our heroines, and any other female who comes near. Based on a 2009 porn game by catwalkNERO. **🅝**

STUDIO DEEN
Formed in 1975 by a group of colorists from Sunrise, the studio took its name from **BRAVE RAIDEEN**, the first of the Sunrise shows on which it worked. It gained an Osaka regional subsidiary in 1991 and a Chinese subsidiary in 1994, thereby allowing it to cut costs on animation during the impecunious mid-1990s. The studio continues to enjoy a close relationship with the company that supposedly spawned it and can often be found on the credit listings of Sunrise anime. Notable works as a leading animation partner include **DIAMOND DAYDREAMS**, **FRUITS BASKET**, and the **PATLABOR** videos.

STUDIO FANTASIA
Formed in 1983 by former staffers from Tsuchida Production, Studio Fantasia appears to have been intended as a liability shield for what turned out to be the lucrative new world of straight-to-video animation. Its early works included stints on **CREAM LEMON** and later installments of **PROJECT A-KO**, establishing a reputation for "fan service"—wholly gratuitous nudity or quasi-nudity—that has made it a popular studio to this day, and led to the ludicrously unsubtle **AGENT AIKA** and **NAJICA**.

STUDIO 4°C
Sometimes Studio Yondo Shii. Formed by

a group that includes former Studio Ghibli and Nippon Animation employee Kyoko Tanaka and animator Koji Morimoto. Particularly prominent in anime that integrate digital animation, notably SPRIGGAN and STEAMBOY, but also found in such fluff as TWEENY WITCHES. The studio primarily focuses on producing experimental and postmodern animation shorts including its *Sweat Punch* shorts, segments of THE ANIMATRIX segments, NOISEMAN, and music videos for Glay, Ayumi Hamasaki, and Hikaru Utada.

STUDIO GHIBLI

Formed in 1985 by Tokuma Shoten for Hayao Miyazaki and Isao Takahata, and initially mostly staffed by former employees of Topcraft (q.v.), Ghibli's first notable work was on Miyazaki's CASTLE IN THE SKY. It has subsequently produced many of the most popular and acclaimed anime of the last 20 years, including MY NEIGHBOR TOTORO, GRAVE OF THE FIREFLIES, and KIKI'S DELIVERY SERVICE. Notable members include Hayao Miyazaki and Isao Takahata, and producer Toshio Suzuki, a former editor of Tokuma's *Animage* magazine, whose contacts ensure that the publication continues to get Ghibli-related exclusives. Ghibli became nominally independent of its parent company in 1992, but merged with Tokuma in 1997, after a deal struck the previous year with Disney to distribute Ghibli titles outside Japan—technically, it is now known as the Studio Ghibli Company. The most conspicuous effect was the higher profile distribution of PRINCESS MONONOKE in the United States. Miyazaki's next film, SPIRITED AWAY, was the first (and so far only) anime to win a Best Feature Animation Oscar. The studio became fully independent from Tokuma once more in 2005. The issue of how best to serve Ghibli's legacy has become paramount within the studio. Many in the anime world would agree that Ghibli essentially *is* the triumvirate of Miyazaki, Takahata, and Suzuki, and that with their inevitable retirement, it will be simply impossible for the studio to maintain its artistic heritage. The handover of Suzuki's power to Koji Hoshino, the former president of Walt Disney Japan, highlighted one potential path, of diversifying, Disney-style, into other market sectors peripheral to film-

making. There is now a Ghibli clothes label and a Ghibli Museum, and in a controversial decision, the studio's TALES FROM EARTHSEA and FROM UP ON POPPY HILL were directed by Hayao Miyazaki's son Goro, in what appears to have been an attempt to establish the word "Miyazaki" itself as a brand independent of the man who made it famous. However, Miyazaki's parting gift is arguably his reading list of 50 recommended children's books, which appears to have formed the basis for the studio's continued operation as a worthy successor to WORLD MASTERPIECE THEATER. The list includes *The Borrowers* and *Ronia the Robber's Daughter*, both of which have been released as part of the studio's post-Miyazaki strategy.

STUDIO LIVE

Founded by Toyoo Ashida in 1976, it became a public limited company in 1994. Notable staffers besides the founder include Kenichi Takeshita, Noriyasu Yamauchi, and Satoshi Nishimura. Production credits range from BAREFOOT GEN to GUYVER.

STUDIO PIERROT

Founded in 1979 by former employees of Tatsunoko, Pierrot soon acquired a reputation as the creator of the softer side of anime, particularly "magical girl" PASTEL YUMI, CREAMY MAMI, or FANCY LALA, many of which featured character designs by Akemi Takada and Koji Motoyama. Its roster of productions, however, is just as wide as any other company's—reputation aside, it also worked on HYPER POLICE and GTO. Usually billed today as just plain Pierrot, its modern successes include EMMA and SUGAR SUGAR RUNE.

STUDIO Z-5

The fifth incarnation of a company that initially went by the name of Studio Z, Z-5 was founded in 1980. Its high profile staffers have included Hajime Kamegaki and Hideyuki Motohashi, and works include LOVE HINA and FIREFIGHTER! DAIGO OF FIRE COMPANY M.

STUDY-A-BROAD *

2007. JPN: *Seisen Gakuin, Eisai Kyoiku*. AKA: *Holy Sleazy School; Crazy Gate*. Video. DIR: Anri Kirishima, Kenji Taru. SCR: Kusakai

Kokubunji, N/C. DES: Ryunosuke Karasawa, Atsushi Kawai, Osamu Ota. ANI: Shigenori Taniguchi, Aihane, Kyoichi Ohira. MUS: N/C. PRD: MS Pictures (JAM). 19 mins. x 2 eps.

One of the axioms of pornography is that you don't actually get very much for your money. Anime pornography tends to be short, if not always nasty and brutish, which presents a problem for foreign distributors. Their audiences are not necessarily habituated to paying the same sort of price for 20 minutes of animation as for a feature film or several TV episodes simply on the promise that it's transgressive. To have a salable product, studios sometimes find themselves compelled, as here, to bundle two unrelated episodes into a single release. Please bear in mind that, like two for one offers in supermarkets, this is not always a bargain.

The theme of both shows is sexual domination of schoolgirls. The first, *Crazy Gate* (*Eisai Kyoiku*), is based on a 2003 porn game by Amalgame that allowed players to sexually humiliate schoolgirls at an elite academy. In the anime, a male teacher is threatened by a female colleague with exposure about his former extracurricular activities with his pupils, so he rapes her and her schoolgirl sister and continues to expand his pupils' education. The second, *Holy Sleazy School* (*Seisen Gakuin*), features an unpopular teacher walking in on a girl masturbating with a glowing phallus-shaped artifact that turns girls into raging lust-crazed creatures. He is "chosen" by the object to acquire magical sex power and becomes irresistible.**NV**

SUBMARINE 707

1996. JPN: *Shinkai no Kantai Submarine 707F*. AKA: *Undersea Fleet Submarine 707F*. Video. DIR: Teruo Kogure, Jiro. SCR: Satoru Ozawa. DES: Masaaki Sudo. ANI: Masaaki Sudo, Teruo Kogure. MUS: N/C. PRD: Knack. 45 mins. x 2 eps.

Investigating a "Bermuda triangle" effect in the Pacific, the damaged submarine 707 is led to a vast undersea cavern by a white whale. 707 rests on the seabed for repairs but sinks beneath it to find the lost undersea empire of Mu (see SUPER ATRAGON). Queen Chiaka, ruler of Mu, has been thrown into a conflict with the surface world by bad-guy Red Silver's illegal drilling operations near her kingdom, and the crew of 707 must end the crisis before it destroys the world. An old-fashioned yarn based on Satoru Ozawa's 1963 submarine manga in *Shonen Sunday*, it was revived for the 1990s thanks to the dual influence of the nostalgic "retro" fashion ushered in by GIANT ROBO and the new-found popularity of submarine dramas post–SILENT SERVICE. A year later, Ozawa's BLUE SUBMARINE NO. SIX was also adapted into an anime, with far greater success.

SUBMARINE 707R *

2003. AKA: *Submarine 707 Revolution*. Video. DIR: Shoichi Masuo; Yuichi Wada, Kobun Shizuno. SCR: Hiroshi Onogi. DES: Jun Takagi, Minoru Murao, Kazutaka Miyatake. ANI: Minoru Murao, Nobuaki Nagano. MUS: Hideaki Kobayashi, Tatsuya Kozaki, Wave Master, Yutaka Minobe. PRD: Aniplex, Group TAC, Sony Music Entertainment. 48 mins. x 2 eps.

Under threat from an international terrorist organization, 11 nations form the Peace-Keeping Navy (PKN), only for the evil Admiral Red to crash his submarine into the PKN fleet and almost destroy it at the opening ceremony. Only commander Hayami of the Japanese sub 707R stands between him and victory, leading to a cat-and-mouse game on the high seas.

The submarine genre is understandably limited in its potential, leading elements of *Submarine 707R* to play like innumerable other underwater thrillers, most notably SILENT SERVICE and *The Hunt for Red October* (1990). Its clearest parallels, however, are with the criminal mastermind and plucky Japanese supersub of BLUE SUBMARINE NO. SIX, whose creator, Satoru Ozawa, also wrote the original 1963 manga of *707R*. *707R* really plays up its retro origins, often looking more like ASTRO BOY or GIGANTOR, both in its cartoonish design and the deliberate juxtaposition of it with more serious themes—it is worth remarking that where *707R* has an Admiral Red, there is a *Duke* Red in Tezuka's METROPOLIS.

Ozawa's work has been cited by many animators of the modern generation as a prime influence on their obsession with technology and sci-fi. Notable among them is EVANGELION-director Hideaki Anno, who is acknowledged here as the director of the opening credit sequence, leading some sources (and unscrupulous foreign distributors) to credit him with direction of the entire series.

SUBMARINE SUPER 99

2003. TV series. DIR: Hiromichi Matano. SCR: Keisuke Fujikawa. DES: Leiji Matsumoto, Katsumi Itabashi, Kichiro Harada. ANI: N/C. MUS: Shinichiro Mizobuchi. PRD: Vega Entertainment, AT-X, Tsuburaya. 25 mins. x 13 eps.

When the genius submarine designer Doctor Oki and his grandson Goro go missing, his other grandson Susumu immediately suspects the worst—that he has been kidnapped by the evil Helmet Party organization before he can spill their secrets to the world. Told that both his grandfather and elder brother are dead in an accident, Susumu sets off in Oki's prototype submarine, number 99. Susumu knows the 99 like the back of his hand, and is soon proving to be a useful addition to the crew. Before long, the crew of the 99 are at odds with the ruling clique of the undersea Ocean Empire, but even their supposed enemies have honorable men among them—faking the destruction of the 99 in order to allow it to escape.

It will come as no surprise to the reader that Dr. Oki and Goro are still alive and are being held prisoner by the ruler of the Ocean Empire, whose name is Hell Deathbird.

Deathbird wants Oki's latest super-invention, a powerful engine, in order to outfit a fleet of supersubs to seize control of the surface world. As in SUPER ATRAGON, the menacing "aliens" are actually from within the Earth, in this case a deep trench that leads to an "Underground Sea"—an "Undersea Sea," if you want to split hairs. Their world is under threat from the ever-growing spread of radiation poisoning, leading Susumu, once reunited with his family, to realize that the inhabitants of the Ocean Empire are not evil but simply misguided and misled by their leaders.

It is with a weary sigh that we note Leiji Matsumoto dusting off his old character designs yet again and reprising the basic plot of STAR BLAZERS underwater. The rationale, as ever, is that if something is not broken it should not be fixed, and that children's television is repetitive because it regularly finds itself addressing a completely new audience. That is all very well, but the hype for Matsumoto's work often clings defensively to his past glories, as if expecting more of the audience to be adults revisiting golden childhood memories than children who have never experienced them before. Consequently, this straight swap of new money for old rope is somewhat halfheartedly hyped as being in the "retro style," although even the most forgiving of modernday viewers surely must concede that the end result often seems less like a celebration of a popular creator's work than yet another tired, cynical rehash of it. Compare to THUNDERSUB, an earlier title for which Matsumoto plundered his own work, years before many of the target audience for *Submarine Super 99* were even born.

SUBMISSION CENTRAL *

2002. JPN: *Dokusen*. AKA: *Monopoly*. Video. DIR: Mitsuhiro Yoneda. SCR: Rokurota Makabe. DES: Meka Morishige. ANI: Meka Morishige. MUS: Yoshi. PRD: YOUC, Digital Works (Vanilla Series). 30 mins. x 2 eps.

Two boys make an Internet pact to take turns abusing and "training" a pair of kidnapped girls on camera, to be screened for an Internet audience that will later vote on who deserves to keep them. One of their victims, the hapless Tsumugi, does not initially realize that one of her captors is her own boyfriend Kyoshiro. Based on a computer game from "ruf"; another entry in the VANILLA SERIES. ●⓵Ⓥ

SUE CAT

1980. TV series. DIR: Takao Yotsuji. SCR: Tsunehisa Ito. DES: Front Publicity. ANI: Shinnosuke Mina. MUS: Akira Ito. PRD: Knack, Tokyo 12 Channel. 15 mins. x 40 eps.

Sue is a suburban Tokyo cat who enjoys climbing up on the roof to scat sing, beating out the rhythm with her tail, hoping that one day she'll become a star singer just like the human vocalists on TV. She talks her way onto the set of the NTV talent show *Who's the Star?* and becomes an overnight celebrity, soon forgetting all about her past life. As her life becomes a whirl of music hits, recording contracts, and product endorsements, she begins to wonder if she has sacrificed her personal life for stardom. As she reminisces about her happy kittenhood, she is found by her sisters, Lan and Miki, who convince her to return home to obscurity.

NTV and Crown Records, both real-life companies, have manufactured starlets before, so it's no surprise that they should do the same with a cat. This silly anthropomorphic "star is born" series was broadcast in double chunks in the Kansai region, and hence is listed as "30 mins. x 20 eps." in some sources. Later, very different satires of the idol-singer's life include **PERFECT BLUE** and **HUMMINGBIRDS**, while *Mis Print* (1997) was a much shorter-lived anime series about feline pop stars.

SUEZEN

Pseudonym for Shiro Iida, animator, born in Tokyo and often associated with Tatsunoko Production as a key animator and designer. His name appears on **WINGS OF HONNEAMISE** and **YADAMON**, and, so claim Japanese sources, the artist has also worked in secret for foreign studios including Disney and 20th Century Fox, although in what capacity nobody seems willing to say.

SUGAR *

2001. JPN: *Chicchana Yukitsukai Sugar*. AKA: *Cute Snowmancer Sugar; A Little Snow Fairy Sugar*. TV series. DIR: Shinichiro Kimura. SCR: Akiko Horii, Seishi Minakami, Tomoyasu Okubo, Yasunori Yamada. DES: Keiko Kawashima. ANI: Yumi Nakayama, Haruo Okawara, Makoto Yoshida, Yumiko Ishii. MUS: Shinkichi Mitsumune. PRD: TBS, Broccoli, JC STAFF, Kadokawa, Pioneer, BS-i. 25 mins. x 24 eps. (TV1), 24 mins. x 2 eps. (special).

Sugar is a trainee snow fairy who, with her friends Salt and Pepper, aspires to become a season fairy and help to create and control the weather on Earth using special musical instruments. In the town of Muhlenberg (based, after an extensive production crew "research trip," on one of three real-world Rothenburgs in Germany), they enlist the help of human schoolgirl Saga. As a mid-European girl who helps out in her grandmother's coffee shop, Saga has elements of the lead in **KIKI'S DELIVERY SERVICE** about her, but also happens to be one of the very few humans who can see fairies and who can help them in their quest to find the mythic "Twinkles" that makes flowers grow—compare to **BOTTLE FAIRY**. The search for Twinkles soon takes second place to other adventures, as the fairies report in to their elderly fairy boss and even, on one occasion, turn to the (cute) dark side when they fall in with a crowd of bad fairies. Later episodes suggest, as subtly and cutely as possible, that Saga is less helping the fairies than they are helping her, as the orphan girl tries to regain ownership of her late mother's piano—an allegory of grief and growing up like the many other imaginary friends found in other anime. Their adventures spun off a two-part TV summer special in 2003, in which Saga reminisces about the good old days. Based on a manga by Haruka Aoi and **PITA TEN**'s Koge Donbo. Relentlessly, criminally cute, but after day upon day of sex and samurai-related anime, a welcome change to anime encyclopedists.

SUGAR BUNNIES

2007. TV series. DIR: Hiroshi Kugimiya. SCR: Yoshio Urasawa, Chinatsu Hojo, Yumi Kageyama, Akiko Horii, Miho Mauro. DES: N/C. ANI: N/C. MUS: Go Takahashi. PRD: Asahi Production, Sanrio, TV Tokyo. 10 mins. x 27 eps. (TV1), 10 mins. x 26 eps. (TV2), 10 mins. x 26 eps. (TV3).

Sophia Cherbourg lives with her mama and papa above the family bookshop. She and her friend Francoise dream of becoming great pastry chefs when they grow up—after all, this is France, with a proud tradition of wonderful cooking. But there's an extra bit of magic in the air. Twin bunny brothers Shirousa and Kurousa have been sent to the human world by the Two Queens of Bunniesfield. Together with 12 of their twin bunny friends, they have a special task to fulfill. Disguised as dolls, they are soon discovered by Sophia and her friends in this sweet little **KIDS' ANIME** based on characters created by Sanrio. It premiered as a segment on Sanrio's TV show *Kitty Paradise Plus*. A second series, *Sugar Bunnies Chocolat!*, followed in 2008 with *Sugar Bunnies Fleur* in 2009.

SUGAR SUGAR RUNE

2005. JPN: *Sugar² Rune*. TV series. DIR: Yukihiro Matsushita, Hiroyuki Tomita, Kunitoshi Okajima, Masayuki Matsumoto. SCR: Reiko Yoshida, Mamiko Ikeda, Tomoko Konparu, Masahiro Okubo. DES: Noriko Otake. ANI: Noriko Otake, Park Sang-jin, Sawako Yamamoto. MUS: Shinkichi Mitsumune. PRD: Studio Pierrot, TV Tokyo. 25 mins. x 29 eps.

Chocola Meilleur and Vanilla "Ice" Mieux (no, really) are two sorceresses from the Magical Realm, each charged with the mission of collecting as much love as possible from the humans they meet, in the form of crystallized hearts that symbolize warm feelings. At stake is the throne of the Magical Realm itself, with the sweet-natured, mild-mannered Vanilla seemingly gaining much more human attention than the plucky redhead Chocola. In other words, another magical girl show revisiting the well-trodden ground of **LITTLE WITCH SALLY**, although this one appears to have been fast-tracked into production thanks to its familial connections—the "original" manga serialized in *Nakayoshi* magazine was created by Moyoko Anno, the wife of **EVANGELION**-director Hideaki Anno, who guests as an animation director on the opening sequence here. Chocola seems to have gained her name from the Japanese spelling of the French movie *Chocolat* (2000), which has a silent "t," and is hence no relation to Chocula in **DON DRACULA**. Compare to **BEWITCHED AGNÈS**, one of many magical-girl shows with which *Sugar Sugar Rune* shared the airwaves in its year of broadcast.

SUGII, GISABURO

1940–. Born in Shizuoka Prefecture, he left school at 16 and had many jobs, eventually joining Toei Animation in 1958. By 1961, he was working at Mushi Production, where he became a key animator and then director on **ASTRO BOY**, despite his initial protests that Osamu Tezuka's plans to cut costs on production meant that *Astro Boy* barely counted as "animated" at all. He left Mushi in 1967 to found Art Fresh with the Dezaki brothers, in which capacity he contributed as a key animator to shows including **JOURNEY TO THE WEST** and **DORORO**, on which he was a supervising director. The mini-studio arguably hired away much of the highest-level talent from Mushi and was infamously accused by Noboru Ishiguro of playing mah jong and drinking all week, before producing all their allotted anime cels in an overnight push on the day before each deadline.

In 1969, Sugii was one of the founding members of Group Tac, although he subsequently went fully freelance in 1985. Although his directorial work incorporates everything from THE TALE OF GENJI to TOUCH, arguably his most long-standing influence on the medium is his work on the first STREET FIGHTER II movie, which established a series of TROPES AND TRADITIONS for game adaptations that remain much imitated to this day.

SUGIYAMA, TAKU

1937–. Sometimes miscredited as Suguru Sugiyama. Born in Tokyo, he worked as an animator on PANDA AND THE MAGIC SERPENT, JOURNEY TO THE WEST, and THE LITTLEST WARRIOR, while still attending night school. He left anime to complete his education, graduating in Western-style art from Musashino College of Fine Arts (now Musashino Art University) in 1962. He returned to anime after graduation, working as an art director and assistant director for Iwanami Films, including a stint on the *Dolphin Prince* (see MARINE BOY), which was intended to become Japan's first color TV anime. He became a writer and director at Nippon Animation on shows including DOGTANIAN AND THE THREE MUSKEHOUNDS, DORORO, and ALICE IN WONDERLAND. He is also the author of several books on animation, including *The Anime Handbook, Young Anime Graffiti*, and *A Compendium of TV Anime.*

SUIKODEN *

1993. JPN: *Yokai Seki Suikoden*. AKA: *Demon Century Water Margin; Suikoden: Demon Century*. Video. DIR: Hiroshi Negishi. SCR: Mayori Sekijima. DES: Noboyuki Tsuru. ANI: Nobuyuki Tsuru. MUS: N/C. PRD: JC Staff. 46 mins.

Hotheaded country boy Nobuteru Sugo goes to town when his sister is abducted by an evil gang boss who is trying to buy up land in Shinjuku by blackmail and intimidation. Sugo meets other heroes who help him in his quest: one is a crossdressing martial artist who can disable a man without breaking a fingernail; another a Christian priest who believes in muscular, not to say aggressive, evangelism; and yet another a psychotic nun who is gentle as a lamb with orphan children but freaks out if anyone catches a glimpse of her tattoo.

Based on a story by IRRESPONSIBLE CAPTAIN TYLOR–creator Hitoshi Yoshioka that retold Shi Nai-an and Luo Guanzhong's 14th-century Chinese novel *Water Margin*

in a sci-fi setting, the final scene reveals that the characters are the reincarnations of the novel's Lin Chung, Hu San-Niang, and company, but this allusion is left unclear in an English dub that appears ignorant of the distant literary origins. Mitsuteru Yokoyama's unrelated 1969 *Water Margin* manga in *Kibo Life* was much more faithful to the original. It was never animated, but several of the characters were lifted wholesale for the later GIANT ROBO. For another rehash of the *Water Margin*, see HAKKENDEN. ◑◐

SUKEBAN DEKA *

1991. JPN: *Sukeban Deka*. AKA: *Bad Girl Cop*. Video. DIR: Takeshi Hirota. SCR: Takeshi Hirota. DES: Nobuteru Yuki. ANI: Masahiro Kase. MUS: Takashi Takao. PRD: JH Project, SIDO. 50 mins. x 2 eps.

Former high school tearaway Saki Asamiya soon ends up on the wrong side of the law and is stuck in the slammer just like her wayward mother. She is offered the chance to redeem herself by returning to school as an undercover agent to spy on the Mizuchi sisters' crime ring. It's an offer she can't refuse since it's the only way to gain her mother a reprieve from Death Row. Armed only with a police-issue yo-yo and a very bad attitude, Saki goes back to school and finds herself facing the Mizuchis and their father, a criminal hiding behind a cloak of respectability. As allies she has only a boy so fixated on her that he shaves his head to get her attention and Junko, an innocent young artist whose talents make her a target for one of the sisters.

Played in a deadly serious, deadpan manner that only accentuates its essential silliness, *SD* is an entertaining one-joke knockabout. Based on a 1976 manga by Shinji Wada in *Hana to Yume* magazine, it was soon co-opted for the male gaze in Hideo Tanaka's live-action TV series the same year. The anime version was released partway through a later series of live-action movie adaptations that also showcased cute young actresses in school uniforms. Ultimately, however, like its female lead, it's too bad to be good, and too good to be bad. After a DVD rerelease of the live-action *Sukeban Deka* series sold a surprising 130,000 copies in 2005, Toei announced that a new live-action movie was in the offing for 2006.

SUKISHO *

2003. JPN: *Suki na Mono wa Suki Dakara Shoganai!!* AKA: *If I Like Something Then There's Nothing You Can Do; Sukisyo*. TV series. DIR: Haruka Ninomiya. SCR: Mamiko Ikeda. DES: Mami Yamaguchi, Yuzu Tsutae. ANI: Zexcs. MUS: N/C. PRD: Zexcs, Chiba TV. 24 mins. x 13 eps.

Blue-haired, impulsive Sora Hashiba is good-looking but goofy. He falls out of a third storey window, goes into the hospital, and emerges with gaps in his memory. He has a new dorm-mate: pink-haired, enigmatic Sunao Fujimori claims to be a childhood friend but Sora can't remember him. As he begins to suspect his accident was no such thing and goes in search of the truth, he also starts to feel dangerously attracted to Sunao. Meanwhile, Sora and Sunao both begin to exhibit darker, hidden personalities, respectively called Yoru and Ran.

This originated as a computer game from Platinum Label, aimed at fans of "boys' love" stories, which spun off into a dozen novels. The anime version supposedly boasts an all-female staff, at least at the top echelons, presumably to assure the fangirls that all the right buttons will be pushed—though since the game seems to have managed this despite the presence of nasty unwelcome men, it seems like unnecessary hype.

_SUMMER

2006. JPN: *_Summer*. AKA: *Underbar Summer*. Video. DIR: Takahiro Okao. SCR: N/C. DES: Akio Uchino, Eiji Iwase. ANI: Megumi Noda. MUS: Takao Matsuura. PRD: Rikuentai, Soft Garage, HOOK. 25 mins x 2 eps.

Older readers will be reminded of the multiple-choice fantasy gamebooks of the 1980s in this adaptation of a "virtual novel" (ARGOT AND JARGON) originally released in 2005. Despite a profoundly unoriginal plot—average high school boy can't make up his mind which of his six female friends he likes enough to want to go out with—creators HOOK managed to spin off four light novels by Joji Kamio, four drama CDs, and these two short DVDs in 2006 and 2007. It's not easy to find a new angle on the harem genre (ROMANCE AND DRAMA), and based on the evidence of such releases we must assume its audience doesn't really want one. Most of those involved have more interesting things on their CVs. Character designer Uchino and animation director Noda worked with director Okao on a different kind of harem anime, *Antique Bakery*. Sound director Hajime Takakuwa and sound effects creator Yasuyuki Konno have anime credits going back over 15 years. Rikuentai assisted with the animation on *Hellsing Ultimate* in the same year, with _*Summer*'s director of photography Hiroyuki Chiba credited for photography assistance.

SUMMER DAYS WITH COO *

2007. JPN: *Kappa no Coo to Natsu Yasumi.* AKA: *Summer with Coo the Kappa.* Movie. DIR: Keiichi Hara. SCR: Keiichi Hara. DES: Yuichiro Sueyoshi, Takashi Nakamura. ANI: Yuichiro Sueyoshi. MUS: Kei Wakakusa. PRD: Shin-Ei Animation. 138 mins.

A single *kappa* water-spirit survives the changing world and environmental upheaval until he is found in modern Tokyo by schoolboy Koichi. Welcomed by Koichi's family, especially their dog Ossan with whom he can communicate by telepathy, Coo still longs for his own people. He and Koichi set out on a summer trip to the town of Tono, long associated with *kappa*, where others of his kind might have survived. But when he is faced with the attention of the world, and encounters a descendant of his father's murderer, Coo must decide whether there is any way for an ancient species to coexist with modern humans (compare to **POM POKO**).

Despite being adapted from a series of children's books by Masao Kogure, the opening sequence of the movie, 200 years in the past in ancient Edo, is more violent than we expect of a **KIDS' ANIME**. A samurai slaughters Coo's father, who had approached him seeking peace between their races, and an earthquake swallows Coo. Modern violence follows, when Koichi falls over while being bullied and breaks open a stone to see what he thinks is a fossilized turtle. *Kappa*, being water creatures, dry out and rehydrate quickly, and Koichi learns his mistake when he tries to wash his "fossil" clean.

What follows is a Japanese take on *E.T. The Extra-Terrestrial* (1982) from the director of TV episodes and no less than 13 movies in the **CRAYON SHIN-CHAN** series, on his way to even more serious work in

COLORFUL: THE MOTION PICTURE. Using a more naturalistic style than for *Shin-Chan*, but still grounding his characters in everyday events and emotions, Hara depicts both the gains and losses of growing up and the gradual loss of the natural world with realism and a certain amount of hope. Both Coo and Koichi are venturing into unknown territory with the certainties of past innocence left behind them. The friendship that sustains and nurtures both in their first steps into adulthood may not survive the changing world around them, let alone the changes both will go through as they grow up. They are literally worlds apart; yet they can reach across that space and be friends. A charming movie with a message of acceptance and hope that far outweighs its brief moments of violence. **V**

SUMMER STORM

2009. JPN: *Natsu no Arashi.* TV series. DIR: Shin Onuma, Akiyuki Shinbo. SCR: Katsuhiko Takayama, Deko Akao. DES: Kazuhiro Ota, Koji Azuma. ANI: Kazuhiro Ota, Yoshiaki Ito. MUS: Ken Sato. PRD: SHAFT. 24 mins. x 13 eps. (TV1), 24 mins. x 13 eps. (TV2).

Thirteen-year-old Hajime is staying with his grandfather in the country when he meets a strangely fascinating girl, Sayako Arashiyama, called Arashi for short. It turns out she's a ghost from World War II, and because the two of them can form a special connection they can travel back in time. Arashi recruits Hajime to help her in her mission to save others from the kind of untimely death she suffered. But there are other time-traveling ghosts around, not all as well-intentioned as Arashi, and some of the humans in town are very strange. With the constant threat of temporal paradox, a disaster to be avoided at all costs, Hajime and Arashi have their work cut out for them in this intriguing series based on Jin Kobayashi's 2006 manga. A second series, *Summer Storm: Open for Business (Natsu no Arashi! Akinai-chu),* followed in 2009 from the same crew. Historically minded readers may be aware of a similar subplot to the 1970s TV live-action series of **THE GIRL WHO LEAPT THROUGH TIME** (*DE), removed for the anime version.

SUMMER WARS *

2009. Movie. DIR: Mamoru Hosoda. SCR: Satoko Okudera. DES: Masaru Hamada,

Mina Okazaki, Takashi Okazaki, Yoshiyuki Sadamoto, Yoji Takeshige. ANI: Ryo Horibe, Hiroyuki Aoyama, Kazutaka Ozaki, Kunihiko Hamada, Shigeru Fujita. MUS: Akihiko Matsumoto. PRD: Madhouse Studios, D.N. Dream Partners, Kadokawa, NTV, VAP, Warner Bros., Yomiuri TV. 114 mins.

Teenage math geek Kenji agrees to help the school beauty Natsuki ("Summer Hope") on an unspecified task, only to discover that he must pose as her boyfriend at a family gathering in order to satisfy the conditions of a vow to her imposing great-grandmother Sakae. Out of place in Natsuki's country mansion, and overwhelmed by her extended family, Kenji inadvertently helps the rogue artificial intelligence Love Machine hack into the worldwide computer network OZ. With OZ compromised, modern society threatens to fall apart. Meanwhile, Natsuki's exiled uncle Wabisuke is back in town for Sakae's 90th birthday. But Wabisuke is also the creator of Love Machine, and needs the help of all the family to shut it down.

In the wake of the success of **THE GIRL WHO LEAPT THROUGH TIME**, Mamoru Hosoda and his team were obliged to come up with an original story—a high-pressure demand when much of the appeal of their previous film lay in the widespread popularity of its source material. Faced with such a a task, he appears to have cannibalized much of his own life, not only the basic premise behind his **DIGIMON** feature *Bokura no Wars* (release in the U.S. as part of the *Digimon Movie*), but also his personal confrontation with the teeming chaos of his fiancée's vast family.

Summer Wars is **GHOST IN THE SHELL** for the Facebook generation, with a self-aware artificial intelligence escaping from a sea of data and somehow attempting to influence the real world. Conceived as a ready-made summer classic for all the family, it carefully tips its hat to the values of any generation likely to be alive today, and turns its focus with naturalist grace upon the disappearing traditions of Japanese rural life when children are much more likely to be the solitary individuals of **BUBU CHACHA**. Himself an only child, Mamoru Hosoda frames *Summer Wars* not merely as a film for all the family, but a film for those without such a family at all. Kenji has a mother who is "busy at work" and a father working abroad. With no siblings, he is entirely alone, and swamped with the vivacious, noisy camaraderie of Natsuki's relatives.

Facing modern anime's stand-off between hand-drawn and computer-generated art, Hosoda embraces both, contrasting warm, organic depictions of rural life with a vibrant, super-abundant cyberspace. The juxtaposition of a wholly artificial world with the power to destroy the reality that created it and the peace and beauty of the countryside where Natsuki's family have lived for generations gives the film a visual tension to match its emotional impact.

This is no mere artistic conceit. In a narrative duplication of these contrasts, great grandma Sakae may not even own a modern phone, but she sits amid a network that proves easily to be the match of the World Wide Web—the endless rounds of gifts, kindnesses, and obligations that have held East Asian culture together for centuries. When the young adults fail to achieve anything with orders and chains of command, it's Sakae who pulls everything together by calling in a lifetime of favors. Meanwhile, the OZ virtual environment allegorizes the way in which Japan is connected to a wider world. The apparently harmless gaggle of online avatars, initially presented as little more than glorified **POKÉMON**, are soon shown to have the ability to exert damaging effects on everyday life, disrupting traffic, shutting down vital amenities, and threatening to end the world as the characters know it. In much the same fashion as **HOWL'S MOVING CASTLE** and **SKY CRAWLERS**, *Summer Wars* confronts the insular Japanese viewer with the sound and fury of distant battles, as modern life rests on a foundation of faraway conflicts.

At its heart, *Summer Wars* is also a secular holiday movie of the same stripe as **TOKYO GODFATHERS**, repackaging the sense of a seasonal special for a time when the Japanese are most likely to be with their families. *Summer Wars* is riddled with evocations of family gatherings—the awkward division of labor between newcomers in a stranger's kitchen and someone else's shed, sullen modern teenagers desperate to return to the online existence that defines them, or infants pushed into traditions and pastimes on which the older generation place a baffling value.

There are shadows, too, of the various backers, including baseball-crazy Yomiuri TV (**STAR OF THE GIANTS**), clearly hoping that the film will be a summer staple for years to come, and Nintendo, now a computer console giant, but originally the printer for the card-game Hanafuda that plays a critical role in the film's final act. Despite such corporate concerns, this feel-good summer movie is, ironically, one of the few that approaches the genius of Studio Ghibli's masterpiece **MY NEIGHBOR TOTORO**. Assured and effortlessly elegant, its story, script, plot, pacing, design, technique, and character combine to create the feeling that maybe, back in 2002, Studio Ghibli fired the natural successor to Hayao Miyazaki.

SUMMONING MR. AZAZEL *

2010. JPN: *Yondemasu yo Azazel-san*. AKA: *You're Being Summoned, Mr. Azazel*. Video, TV series. DIR: Tsutomo Mizushima. SCR: Daishiro Tanimura, Midori Goto, Susumu Mitsunaka. DES: Junichiro Taniguchi, Hiromasa Ogura, Akane Iwaguma. ANI: Junichiro Taniguchi, Seiji Kishimoto. MUS: Ryuji Takagi. PRD: Production I.G, Kodansha, Memory Tech, Starchild Records, Klockworx. 12 mins. x 3 eps. (v), 12 mins. x 13 eps. (TV1), 12 mins. x 12 eps. (TV2).

Azazel is a dog-shaped demon of lewdness, a pervert who specializes in sexual harassment and sexual embarrassment for others. His nemesis is human detective Akutabe, a cruel and sadistic master of the occult who uses his powers to make demons fear and serve him. He is also the employer and mentor of Rinko Sakuma, Azazel's current human partner. Their friends and colleagues, human and demon, form the backdrop to this gross comedy full of visual and verbal gags with something to offend almost everyone. Based on Yasuhisa Kubo's 2007 manga, the video series spun off a 2011 TV series under the same title. A further TV series, *Yondemasu Azazel-san Z*, followed in 2013.

SUMOMOMO MOMOMO *

2007. JPN: *Sumomomo Momomo—Chijo Saikyo no Yome*. AKA: *The Strongest Bride on Earth*. TV series, video. DIR: Nobuaki Nakanishi. SCR: Toshiki Inoue, Daisuke Ishibashi. DES: Ryoko Amisaki, Satoshi Matsudaira. ANI: Ryoko Amisaki, Aya Kano, Yuji Shigenuki.

MUS: 4EVER. PRD: Studio Hibari, Bandai Visual, Lantis, MOVIC, TV Asahi. 25 mins. x 22 eps. (TV), 25 mins. x 2 eps. (v).

Momoko is a teenage martial artist with a chauvinist father. He tells her no girl can master the family's ultimate fighting technique and the best he can hope for is to marry her off to a strong fighter and hope she produces a strong son. Unfortunately, he promised her before her birth to the unborn son of his best friend and fiercest rival in martial arts. Koushi has grown into a devout coward, who plans a career in law and freezes in terror whenever he sees violence. Despite this, Momoko falls madly in love with him, moves into his family home, and trains with his father to become the strongest fiancée ever. This show adapted from Shinobu Ohtaka's 2005 manga, also licensed in English, borrows its clothes from a host of earlier and better-dressed anime, including **URUSEI YATSURA** and **RANMA ½**, but never manages to achieve a style of its own. Two extra episodes, the predictable hot-spring battle episode and one where Koushi is kidnapped, were added to the DVD release.

SUNDAY WITHOUT GOD *

2013. JPN: *Kami-sama no Inai Nichiyobi*. TV series. DIR: Yuji Kumazawa. SCR: Tomoko Konparu. DES: Shinichi Miyamae. ANI: Shinichi Miyamae. MUS: Hiromi Mizutani. PRD: Madhouse, AT-X, Docomo Anime Store, memory Tech, Starchild, Klockworx. 24 mins. x 12 eps.

It has been 15 years since God officially gave up and turned his back on both heaven and the world (**RELIGION AND BELIEF**). As a result, the Earth is in a stage of advanced apocalypse, with the dead unable to leave, and wandering in a state of limbo despite their awful injuries. Trauma to the brain stem will immobilize one of these zombies, but only sanctioned burial by a qualified Gravedigger will permanently end their suffering. Ai Astin is 12 years old, born in the aftermath of the end of the world, and carrying on her lost father's mission as a Gravedigger. In the process, she wanders through a series of environments and polders against the end of days: some terrifying, some hopeful.

In much the same vein as **HUMANITY HAS DECLINED**, but with a decidedly less comedic touch, *Sunday Without God* taps into the

21st-century teenagers' sense of playing with all the cards stacked against them—the world is already in crisis, the food chain is facing imminent collapse, the climate is in freefall, Tohoku is a wasteland, and the political and economic solutions of previous generations turned out not to be the cure-alls they were promised to be. No wonder, then, that the second decade of this century has seen some impressive experiments in apocalypse and zombie fiction, from **ATTACK ON TITAN** to **TOKYO GHOUL** and **SANKAREA: UNDYING LOVE**. All have very different approaches to the same material, but all have the same underlying sense that the future is less a matter of evolution and more a matter of crisis management. Let's all hope they are wrong.

SUNNY BOARDINGHOUSE

1987. JPN: *Hiatari Ryoko.* AKA: *Ray of Sunshine; Staring into the Sun.* TV series, movie. DIR: Hiroko Tokita, Gisaburo Sugii, Satoshi Inoue, Hayato Ikeda, Mitsuru Hongo. SCR: Satoshi Yagi, Michiru Shimada, Tomoko Konparu, Higashi Shimizu, Hiroko Naka. DES: Minoru Maeda. ANI: Yoshihiro Kawamura, Kazuya Takeda. MUS: Hiroaki Serizawa (TV), Kohei Tanaka (m). PRD: Group Tac, Fuji TV. 25 mins. x 48 eps. (TV), 70 mins. (m).
Kasumi lives in a student hostel run by her aunt while studying and enjoying her other passion, running. Her fiancé, Kazuhiko, is at college in America. As she makes friends in the hostel, one boy, Yusaku, becomes especially close to her. Their friendship develops through comic moments, misunderstandings, and day-to-day events, with Kasumi's betrothal hanging over them like the Sword of Damocles. Based on a 1979 manga by Fumi Yamazaki and Mitsuru Adachi (creator of **TOUCH**), this is another of Adachi's specialty soap operas with sympathetic female characters, often with a sporting connection and a relationship dilemma. The movie finale *You Were in My Dreams Kasumi* (1988, *Kasumi Yume no Naka Kimi ga Ita*), shown on what must have been a weepy double bill with the **KIMAGURE ORANGE ROAD** feature, has the tanned Kazuhiko returning from the U.S. to become a motorcycle racer and demanding to marry Kasumi right away. Yusaku tries to keep a low profile, but at the last moment—literally, on the steps of the altar in church—he finally tells her he loves her, and she realizes that she really loves him. Luckily Kazuhiko is a good sport and encourages them to be together. Though credited to Sugii, the bulk of the movie was actually a directorial debut for Kimiharu Ono, Sugii's assistant on **TALE OF GENJI**.

SUNRISE

Formed as Sotsueisha in 1972 by refugees from the collapse of Mushi Production, rebranded as Nippon Sunrise in 1977 and as Sunrise in 1987. A part of the Bandai group since 1994, when many of its founding staff retired, shortly after selling a majority share to the studio's largest client in the toy industry and thereby securing its employees' futures. Its most famous work remains **GUNDAM**, but it has also worked on numerous other giant-robot shows, as well as **DIRTY PAIR**, **CITY HUNTER**, **OUTLAW STAR**, and **MAI-HIME**. It continues to refashion and update the "real robot" tradition, with more recent shows such as **GASARAKI**. See also **BANDAI NAMCO**. The company's most famous "employee" is the nonexistent Hajime Yatate/Yadate, a house pseudonym credited as a creator on various works to ensure that the company owns the intellectual property it generates.

SUNSET GUARDSMAN

1968. JPN: *Yuyake Bancho.* TV series. DIR: Renzo Kinoshita, Yoshiyuki Tomino. SCR: Yoshiaki Yoshida, Shunichi Yukimuro. DES: Renzo Kinoshita. ANI: Renzo Kinoshita, Nobuhiro Okaseko. MUS: Kenjiro Hirose. PRD: Tokyo TV Doga, Nippon TV. 10 mins. x 156 eps.
Tadaharu Akagi is a small but tough boy, transferred to Kiso Junior High, which is infamous for its badly behaved children. He is literally from the wrong side of the tracks—orphaned, he lives with his grandfather in a ramshackle house near the railway. One day at school, two of his classmates ask for his help in dealing with bullies. Though he is a strong fighter, he refuses, until the bullying becomes intolerable and he loses his temper. Samurai ethics at a modern school, as a bold hero resists violence and gets dewy-eyed whenever he sees a sunset.

SUPER ADDICTIVE

1994. JPN: *Cho Kuse ni Nariso.* AKA: *Heart Mark.* TV series. DIR: Tetsuya Endo, Mitsuo Kusakabe, Yasuhiro Matsuyama, Yoshiaki Iwasaki. SCR: Yorimichi Nakano, Takeshi Shudo, Tsutomu Nagai. DES: Toshiko Sasaki. ANI: Kazuhiro Sasaki, Seiji Kikuchi. MUS: Hiroshi Sakamoto. PRD: Studio Sensen, video Champ, NHK2. 25 mins. x 39 eps.
Idol singer Nagisa Shiratori disguises herself as a boy to attend school, hoping to prove her prowess at fighting and gain applicants for her father's undersubscribed martial arts school. Based on a manga in *Nakayoshi* magazine by Anzu Yoshimura and Yayoi Takano.

SUPER ATRAGON *

1995. JPN: *Shin Kaitei Gunkan.* AKA: *New Undersea Battleship.* Video. DIR: Kazuyoshi Katayama, Michio Fukuda. SCR: Nobuaki Kishima. DES: Yoshikazu Yasuhiko, Makoto Kobayashi, Masami Kosone. ANI: N/C. MUS: Masamichi Amano. PRD: Toho. 50 mins. x 2 eps.
In the troubled 1930s, the alien inhabitants of the sunken Pacific kingdom of Mu test the people of Earth by giving them a huge power source and waiting to see if they use it for good or evil. This classic case of bad timing leads to the U.S. and Japan each building a supersubmarine. Consumed with grief over his brother's death at Hiroshima (see **BAREFOOT GEN**), a gunner on the prototype battlesub Ra disobeys his captain's orders and opens fire on the American sub Liberty. The Ra and the Liberty ram each other and sink, and the Mu experiment is called off for 50 years.

Fast forward to the present, where Mu attack craft are spotted at the north and south poles. The United Nations prepare for battle, unaware that they have no chance of defeating the Mu battleships. Only the Raitself, lovingly restored in secret by the surviving first mate and his patriotic colleagues, can save the day, captained by the son of the original captain. Go, whose father went missing when he was a small child, is on a UN vessel sent to investigate the Mu weapons and is rescued by the Ra. Needless to say, he is troubled by the thought that the remote, forbidding "captain" may be his missing father, as the Ra takes on its enemy in naval action that recalls both **SILENT SERVICE** and **STAR BLAZERS**.

Shunro Oshikawa's original novel *Kaitei Gunkan* (1900) was a militaristic scientific romance, as if Jules Verne's Captain Nemo had decided to wage war on the Western powers in the Pacific. Combined with *Undersea Kingdom* (*Kaitei Okoku*), an unrelated "lost civilization" story by Shigeru Komatsuzaki (see **PROJECT BLUE EARTH SOS**), it was adapted into Ishiro Honda's live-action *Atragon* (1963, *Kaitei Gunkan*, AKA *Atoragan the Flying Supersub*), which featured special effects by Eiji Tsuburaya (see **ULTRAMAN**) and designs by Komatsuzaki, who was also one of Toho's senior illustrators.

Made in the middle of the retro boom ushered in by **GIANT ROBO**, the 1995 anime version keeps WWII, but now has to include three generations of the hero's family in the story in order to establish a link with Japan's martial past. As well as supremely Vernean technology like gravity lenses, *SA* injects an ambiguous note of 1990s conspiracy, suggesting that the battle between Terrans and Mu-ites is an accident in communication. Annette, exiled from Mu since the 1940s and prepared to help the Terrans, suggests that the entire conflict is a misunderstanding engendered by Avatar, the unbalanced Earth envoy of the Mu Empire. Sadly, however, none of these questions are answered, since *SA* is left open-ended, with the crew of the Rapreparing to dive beneath the sea and go in search of the Mu Empire itself. This was not in either of the previous versions of the story, and, although a journey to the center of the Earth seems quite fitting, *SA* never made it beyond episode 2. Mu (or Lemuria) is a "lost continent" in the Pacific that was originally suggested as an explanation for the distribution of Polynesians before Thor Heyerdahl's 1947 Kon-Tiki expedition demonstrated that they had probably scattered across the ocean on boats. As Asia's Atlantis, the place appears in many anime, including **WHITE WHALE OF MU**, **SUBMARINE 707**, **BRAVE RAIDEEN**, **MARINE EXPRESS**, and **FIGHT! OSPA**.

SUPER BABY
1994. JPN: *Osawaga Super Baby*. Movie. DIR: Junichi Sato. SCR: Junichi Sato. DES: Akira Inagami. ANI: Akira Inagami. MUS: N/C. PRD: Toei. 30 mins.
Kazuyoshi the bratty baby causes trouble for his long-suffering mother and elder sister, though he is often placated by his grandfather's creations—toy animals that can come to life. Then, when that plot idea seems to run out of steam, he transforms into Super Baby to fight crime. One of the few theatrical outings so forgettable as to never get a release on video.

SUPER GALS *
2001. JPN: *Super Gals Kotobuki Ran*. TV series. DIR: Tsuneo Kobayashi. SCR: Masashi Kubota. DES: Yoshiko Kuzumoto, Hiroto Tanaka. ANI: Keiichi Ishiguro, Takahiro Kitano. MUS: N/C. PRD: Studio Pierrot, TV Tokyo. 25 mins. x 26 eps. (TV1), 25 mins. x 26 eps. (TV2). Ran Kotobuki is the girliest girl in the fashion-conscious, shopping-crazy Tokyo district of Shibuya, but her parents and elder brother desperately want her to be a police officer like themselves. Based on the manga in *Ribon* magazine by Miho Fujii.

SUPER JETTER
1965. JPN: *Super Jetter Mirai kara Kita Shonen*. AKA: *Super Jetter, the Boy from the Future*. TV series. DIR: N/C. SCR: Ichiro Kanai, Takao Tsutsui, Masao Yamamura, Masaki Tsuji. DES: N/C. ANI: Kiyoshi Onishi. MUS: Takeo Yamashita. PRD: TCJ, Eiken, TBS. 25 mins. x 52 eps.
Time patrolman Jetter comes back from the 30th century in pursuit of the evil criminal Jagger, enlisting the help of pretty contemporary photographer Kaori Mizushima and her friend Professor Nishigoro. He fights crime in our time with three of the professor's inventions—a paralyzer ray, an antigravity belt, and a device that can stop time for 30 seconds.

SUPER KUMA-SAN
2003. AKA: *Super Bear*. TV special. DIR: Yukio Kaizawa. SCR: Hiromasa Tani. DES: Daisuke Yoshida. ANI: Daisuke Yoshida, Ayako Kurata, Haruki Miura, Nobuyoshi Hoshikawa. MUS: N/C. PRD: Toei Animation, Animax. 25 mins.
A large blue bear turns into a superhero to thwart bank robbers, in a one-shot anime based on the script that won the first Animax screenplay contest in 2002. Compare to **AZUSA WILL HELP**, which won the following year.

SUPER MARIO BROTHERS
1986. JPN: *SMB Peach Hime Kyushutsu Dai Sakusen*. AKA: *SMB: Struggle to Rescue Princess Peach*. Movie, video. DIR: Masami Hata. SCR: Hideo Takayashiki. DES: Nintendo, Shigeru Miyamoto, Takashi Tezuka. ANI: Maya Matsuyama. MUS: Toshiyuki Kimori. PRD: Nintendo. 60 mins. (m) ?? mins. x 3 eps. (v)
Italian plumber Mario is playing a computer game when Princess Peach calls out to him from the screen, begging him for help. He dives in to help save her from the evil Turtle tribe, aided by his loyal brother, Luigi. He must head for the game's Mushroom land, there to seek advice from the Mushroom sage. Released on the same day as **RUNNING BOY**, hence tied in the race to become the first anime based on a video game, *SMB* features the lovable character who first appeared in Nintendo's hit game *Donkey Kong*. A slightly different plot, involving the characters' efforts to save Princess *Daisy* from *dinosaurs*, would form the basis for Rocky Morton's live-action *SMB* (1993), starring Bob Hoskins. The franchise also returned as a short-lived three-part video anime in 1989, pointlessly retelling the fairy tales of **MOMOTARO**, **SNOW WHITE**, and *Rumplestiltskin*, but with the cast of the game *Super Mario Brothers 3*. The online Japanese Movie Database also contains a cryptic reference to a 21-minute film called *Super Mario Brothers 2* (1986), written by and starring one Jimmy Kobayashi. However, we have been unable to determine what it is.

SUPER MILK-CHAN *
1998. JPN: *Oh! Super Milk-chan*. TV series. DIR: Hideyuki Tanaka, Yoshio Nitta. SCR: Kiki Shiina. DES: Hideyuki Tanaka. ANI: Atsuko Nakajima. MUS: N/C. PRD: Pioneer, Fuji TV. 5 mins. x 14 eps. (TV1), 25 mins. x 25 eps. (TV2).
This spoof on 1970s spy thrillers and Bond movies has the cute and childlike Milk, a greedy, immoral brat with a passion for sushi, battling invading aliens, toxic monsters, and enemy snipers. After starting life as a short segment in the late-night *Flyer TV* show, Milk's adventures moved up to full half-hour status on satellite, with the same gang of regulars augmented by new characters like ghastly genius Professor Eyepatch. As the new series opens, Milk is holed up in her apartment with her two sidekicks, bottle-shaped and somewhat paranoid robot Tetsuko and little green

blob Hanage ("nose hair"), who resembles a particularly cute booger, complete with round eyes, bright pink nose, and stringy black mustache. Milk is beset by creditors and can't pay the rent. After her inept attempt at extortion from the local ant family fails, she is saved by a job offer from the president himself. He wants her to catch a counterfeiter with a Belgian waffle fixation. Visiting Eyepatch, who may have been Tetsuko's creator but now has a new toy, Robodog, a sniffer hound that can detect fakes, our little band sets up a roadside waffle stand to lure the villain into their net.

SUPER PIG *

1994. JPN: *Ai to Yuki no Pig-Girl Tonde Burin*. AKA: *Pig Girl of Love and Justice—Fly Burin*; *Tonde Burin*. TV series. DIR: Takayoshi Suzuki, Tatsuya Hirakawa, Masahiro Hosoda, Masahito Kitagawa, Kunihisa Sugishima, Teppei Matsuura. SCR: Minori Ikeno, Tomoko Ishizuka. DES: Hiromi Kato, Masamichi Takano. ANI: Kazuyoshi Sekiyuki, Takao Yamazaki, Kenichi Imaizumi. MUS: Goro Omi. PRD: Nippon Animation, Mainichi Broadcasting (MBS). 25 mins. x 51 eps.

Young Karin receives magical powers from a pig. Of all the magical girls, she gets the roughest deal, since instead of transforming her into a curvy, long-legged singing idol or magician, she gets to be the Pig of Justice. Not too happy at first, she buckles down and makes the best of her new powers. Everyone in town loves their cute little pink hero, and every time she does a good deed, she gets a magic pearl. When she's collected enough, she'll be allowed to choose her own transformation. But her father, a reporter, has sworn to find Pig's true identity. Based on a manga in *Ciao* magazine from Taeko Ikeda and Mari Mori, it's a somewhat original take on the magical-girl genre of LITTLE WITCH SALLY.

SUPER ROBOT GALATT

1984. JPN: *Choriki Robo Galatt*. AKA: *Change Robo Galatt*. TV series. DIR: Takeyuki Kanda, Osamu Sekita, Tetsuro Amino, Mamoru Hamazu, Hiroshi Negishi, Hideki Tonokatsu, Susumu Ishizaki, Shinya Sadamitsu. SCR: Hiroyuki Hoshiyama, Tsunehisa Ito, Yasushi Hirano, Takao Koyama. DES: Toyoo Ashida, Kunio Okawara, Koichi Ohata. ANI: Toyoo Ashida, Hiroshi Watanabe, Megumu Ishig-

uro. MUS: Masanori Sasaroku. PRD: Sunrise, Fuji TV. 25 mins. x 25 eps.

Ceaselessly inventing for 30 years in spite of recriminations and complaints from his neighbors, mad scientist Dr. Kiwi finally cooks up an "expanding super alloy" (see GODAIKIN) by combining scrap iron, sugar, Japanese radish, and boogers. He builds Jamboo, a superchange roboid, to ferry young Michael Marsh to and from school. Michael's associates Patty Pumpkin and Camille Cashmere have their own robots, too. But Jamboo changes into the powerful robot Galatt to fight the minions of the Space Real Estate Company, which plans to parcel Earth up and sell it on the open market. Not one of Sunrise's longer-running robot shows, *SRG* treats giant-robot combat primarily as a topic for gag and parody—compare to PREFECTURAL EARTH DEFENSE FORCE.

SUPER ROBOT WARS

2005. JPN: *Super Robot Wars Origin Generation: The Animation*. Video. DIR: Jun Kawagoe. SCR: Satoru Nishizono. DES: Ryo Tanaka, Yasuhiro Saiki. ANI: N/C. MUS: JAM Project. PRD: Brains Base. 30 mins. x 3 eps.

A series of robots built as an alien defense project cause more trouble than they are worth when they go rogue. Lesser, human-interfaced models go into combat against them—whichever way you want to dress it up, this means robots fighting, again, but this time the reason for the cliché is that this is a spin-off of a series of games, specifically *Super Robot Wars Original Generation*, that were made in a pastiche of the robot shows of the past and featured cameo appearances by many famous anime machines and pilots. So it is not derivative and disposable nonsense, then. However, this story takes place after the second release in the game series and restricts itself to robots and characters specifically created for the game, doubtless for copyright and licensing reasons.

SUPER ROBOT WARS ORIGINAL GENERATION: THE ANIMATION *

2005. JPN: *Super Robot Taisen Original Generation: The Animation*. Video, TV series. DIR: Jun Kawagoe, Hiroyuki Kakudo, Masami Obari. SCR: Satoru Nishizono, Takanobu Terada, Yuichiro Takeda, Tatsunosuke Yatsufusa. DES: Ryo Tanaka, Yasuhiro Saiki,

Hajime Katoki, Kunio Okawara. Masami Obari, Kazutaka Miyatake, Kenji Kato, Kenichi Hamazaki, Masahiro Yamane, Risa Ebata, Yukihito Ogomori, Shinya Mito. ANI: Masahito Yamashita, Yosuke Kabashima, Koji Iwaki. MUS: Naofumi Tsuruyama, Takuya Hanaoka, Yoshihisa Hirano. PRD: Bandai Visual, Brains Base, Oriental Light and Magic. Asahi Pro, Sotsu Agency. 27 mins. x 3 eps. (v), 25 mins. x 25 eps. (TV1), 25 mins. x 25 eps. (TV2).

A military demonstration goes badly wrong when the latest mass-produced giant robot models, the Bartoll, run amok and attack the assembled bigwigs. An evil mastermind is controlling them, and as his remote operating system uses human bodies for parts, he has no incentive to keep the carnage down. The pilots of the Earth Federation Army have to stop him before he and his metal army become unbeatable.

This slice of mind candy for giant robot fanatics presents every trope and trick of the super robot genre (SCIENCE FICTION AND ROBOTS) in a classy-looking, nicely animated slamfest that keeps the pedal to the metal in a series of spectacular set pieces. For those less invested in huge robots there's not much to hold the attention, and to the critical eye the designs are more generic than iconic, but if big shiny toys fighting other big shiny toys is your thing, this show delivers exactly what it says on the cover.

The show remakes a successful series of role-playing video games from Banpresto, which first appeared in 1991. Since expanded to cover a wide range of devices including mobile phones, the games are still being released and the franchise has extended into manga, radio and music, including live concerts, as well as anime and merchandise. The original concept brought together giant robots from many hit series to fight each other and mecha originated for the game; subsequently anime creators have paid homage to the games in works including LUCKY STAR, HAYATE THE COMBAT BUTLER, and Go Nagai's MAZINGER Z. The game *Super Robot Wars F Final* introduced Mazinkaiser, inspired by Nagai's creation and later absorbed into it when Nagai adopted it in his manga as the prototype of all the Mazinger robots.

The 2005 video series was successful enough that a TV series followed in 2006 with another in 2010. *Super Robot Wars OG: Divine Wars* has less robot action and more attempt at plot and character, cobbling together bits of plot from more famous robot series and ignoring the fact that this should be a robot show for people who don't like the politics in **GUNDAM**. It's rare for Bandai to miss the point of its own creations in such a lumpen manner, and it was four years before they returned to the series in 2010's *Super Robot Wars OG: The Inspector*, where a stunning opening battle sets a standard the rest of the series struggles to match. With seven designers, including director Obari, and a separate action director credit for Fujio Suzuki on the crew list, the team obviously understands the point of this show, but they never quite scale the heights of that first fight. One for mecha-heads only.

SUPER SONICO THE ANIMATION *

2014. JPN: *Soni Ani: Super Sonico the Animation*. TV series. DIR: Kenichi Kawamura. SCR: Yosuke Kuroda. DES: Masafumi Tamura, Yoshito Takamine. ANI: Masafumi Tamura. MUS: Go Sakabe. PRD: WHITE FOX, AT-X, Docomo Anime Store, GNCO, Good Smile Company, MOVIC, Nitroplus, Pony Canyon, Showgate, Klockworx. 24 mins. x 12 eps.
Life is nonstop for college students today, having to work and make a living while studying. Sonico models for pinups, plays in a band and helps out at her grandmother's restaurant. She needs to keep the jobs going, so when her bandmates are late for a gig, she has to start playing alone. And as a result, her life begins to change.

Super Sonico started life as a mascot character created by Santa Tsuji for the "Nitro Super Sonic" events held by game company Nitroplus. The backstory created for her has stayed the same for the show—she's an 18-year-old college student who is also a model and vocalist/guitarist for the three-girl band Fastest Speed in Space. She already had her own line of games and figures before the TV series launched, and has guested in other games.

The anime is brightly colored, packed with peekaboo moments and soft J-pop but almost totally lacking in plot or character development. You could read this as the story of a teenager's maturing into her own person. You could read it as a spoof on **K-ON**. Or you could read it as a T&A

collection for a **FANDOM** which has built to such a level that it can get a TV show greenlit—no mean achievement in cash-strapped times. Completists should note that the *Maho Shojo Sonico★Magica* animation was simply an April Fool's prank from Nitroplus, which released a one-minute "opening animation" on a "TV series" website in 2011. **◎★**

SUPER ZUGAN

1992. JPN: *Midnight Gamble Anime Super Zugan*. TV series. DIR: Junji Nishimura. SCR: N/C. DES: N/C. ANI: N/C. MUS: Haruo Mitsunami. PRD: Kitty Films, Fuji TV. 12 mins. x 42 eps.
This late-night mahjong anime using many of the staff from **RANMA ½** dredges through the clichés of sporting anime but adds more girls in states of undress. Based on a manga by Sayuki Katayama.

SUPERBOOK: VIDEO BIBLE *

1981. JPN: *Anime Oyako Gekijo*. AKA: *Anime Mother and Child Theater*. TV series. DIR: Masakazu Higuchi, Kenjiro Yoshida, Osamu Sekita, Susumu Ishizaki, Norio Yazawa. SCR: Akiyoshi Sakai, Kiichi Takayama, Tomomi Tsutsui, Kazuo Sato. DES: Akiko Shimomoto, Hajime Fukuoka. ANI: Kenjiro Yoshida, Osamu Sekita. MUS: Masashi Maruyama, Hiro Takada. PRD: Tatsunoko, Production Roots, TV Tokyo. 25 mins. x 26 eps. (TV1), 25 mins. x 52 eps. (TV2), 25 mins. x 26 eps. (TV3).
Professor's son Sho (Christopher) and his girlfriend, Azusa (Joy), are cleaning the attic when they discover an old Bible among the scattered books. A magical "Time Bible," it transports them to the Old Testament era, where they watch the greatest story ever told as it happens around them.

A different take on biblical studies from Tezuka's **IN THE BEGINNING**, this series was seemingly made to cash in on the Bible's status as a worthy international best-seller rather than through any overt religious impetus. The writers introduced Zenmaijikake (Gizmo), a wind-up crusader toy that is brought to life by the Time Bible, and attempted to involve the children in the stories, though events are predestined, so all they can do is *try* to change them—for example, Eve bites into the apple because Zenmaijikake's clockwork winds down before he can stop her, and, though he

shoots up a flare to warn Sho, the children cannot get there in time to stop Adam from taking a bite himself.

Bought for the U.S. market and reedited for the Christian Broadcast Network under the title *Superbook*, by the time the series reached video, its Japanese origins were almost completely occluded, though the voice actors in the English version included many from the cast of **SPEED RACER**. It was discredited in Christian circles for the introduction of modern characters—instead of making the original more accessible, it was more likely to confuse its young audience who were disappointed not to find robots and time-travelers in the *real* Bible.

A sequel the following year, *Adventures at Tondera [Flying] House*, kept the same **TIME BOKAN**–inspired kids-and-robot lineup for another 52 episodes; this time young Gen and female foil Kanna are caught in the rain and find shelter in a Western-style house in the forest. The guardian robot Kandenchin is building a time machine that, when struck by lightning, catapults the group into the past, where they witness further biblical events up to and including the story of Christ (though the Nativity and Resurrection had already been included in the former series). The sequel, *PC Travel Detectives* (1983, AKA *Trouble Shooters*), was set five years after their original adventures with the Time Bible, with an older Chris and Joy, accompanied by Chris's younger brother, Hisashi, thrown into the past by a magic computer.

SUPERCAR GATTIGER *

1977. JPN: *Cho Supercar Gattaiger*. TV series. DIR: Yukihiro Takahashi, Tadashi Hosono, Tsutomu Murai. SCR: Mitsuru Majima, Sukehiro Tomita, Haruya Yamazaki, Hideharu Iuchi, Hisashi Chiaki. DES: Shiro Yamaguchi (pseudonym for Shiro Murata), Mechaman. ANI: Shiro Yamaguchi (pseudonym for Shiro Murata). MUS: Hiroya Ishikawa. PRD: Eiwa, Tokyo 12 Channel. 25 mins. x 26 eps.
Racing driver Jo Kabuki is abandoned by his mother soon after his birth, and his scientist father dies in strange circumstances when a bomb explodes under his car. Now Jo is a member of the five-man Tiger Team—Hiroki, Ken, Katsumi, and, as in **SPEED RACER**, a token girl who is the professor's daughter, in this case Sachiyo

Tabuchi, daughter of the inventor of the 300-mph Solar Energy engines. When not racing all around the world, the team's supervehicles combine to form Gattiger, a mighty weapon that fights those of evil intent. Many of their races bring them up against the Demon Empire, whose leader, Emperor Black Demon, is not only Jo's grandfather, but also his father's murderer. Jo's mother, Queen Demon, was compelled to leave her loved ones out of loyalty to her own father. She works to support the Empire's semi-evil schemes (Black Demon only wants to conquer the world to put an end to war, though his assistant, Erich Bergen, has his own sadistic motives), but at moments of extreme danger, she shows up masked and disguised to save her son. Even though she always obeys her father (as a good daughter should), she still protects her child (as a good mother should)—for instance, when ordered to shoot Jo through the heart while Black Demon watches, she uses a tranquilizer instead of a bullet. Much loved by early American **FANDOM** for its hilariously over-the-top melodrama, it was based on an original idea by Hitoshi Chiaki and given a limited U.S. broadcast on some local TV stations for the Japanese community. Compare to **CYBERFORMULA GPX**.

SUPER-DEFORMED DOUBLE FEATURE *

1988. JPN: *Scramble Wars Tsuppashire! Genom Trophy Rally*. AKA: *Scramble Wars Get Going! Race for the Genom Trophy Rally; Scramble Wars; Ten Little Gall Force*. Video. DIR: Kenichi Yatagai, Hiroyuki Fukushima. SCR: N/C. DES: Kenichi Sonoda, Kimitoshi Yamane, Hiroyuki Kitazume. ANI: Toshiko Sasaki. MUS: Takehito Nakazawa. PRD: Artmic, Movic. 67 mins.
GENOM, the malevolent corporation of **BUBBLEGUM CRISIS**, is sponsoring a road race through the desert to the town of Bangor. "Super-deformed" (i.e., cute and squashed-down) versions of characters from *BGC*, **GALL FORCE**, **GENESIS SURVIVOR GAIARTH**, and **AD POLICE** are all taking part, and they all mean to win. The ensuing mayhem is straight out of *Wacky Races*, parodying the original shows with insane humor. The *GF* gals return in *Ten Little Gall Force*, a 1992 parody in which more super-deformed characters return to the studio

to make a documentary about the making of their movie and interact with animated versions of the crew.
The Western release combines the two completely separate Japanese videos of just over half an hour each, linked by their super-deformed art style of characters with heads out of all proportion to their squat, comical bodies. It's pure coincidence that the British release company also had its headquarters in a town called Bangor, though Wales has no deserts at present.

SUPERDIMENSION ROMANESQUE SAMY

1986. JPN: *Chojiku Romanesque Samy Missing 99*. Video. DIR: Seiji Okuda, Hidemi Kama. SCR: Seiji Okuda. DES: Moriyasu Taniguchi, Toru Yoshida. ANI: Yutaka Arai, Moriyasu Taniguchi. MUS: Hideo Goto. PRD: Aubec, Anime R. 59 mins.
The universe created by God is not eternal but can collapse if Satan has his way. Luckily, the forces of good are lined up to save the cosmos. This is all news to average Japanese teenager Samy, who is chased by supernatural pursuers and escapes from them into a place "beyond time." Samy and her friends Tokyo, Silver, and Dews must oppose the might of the evil Noa, with the aid of swords, sorcery, and cybernetic battle-suits. A mixture of **ALICE IN WONDERLAND** and **PLANET BUSTERS**.

SUPERNATURAL *

2011. JPN: *Supernatural the Animation*. TV series. DIR: Atsuko Ishizuka, Shigeyuki Miya. SCR: Naoya Takayama, Tatsuro Inamoto et al. DES: Shigeyuki Miya, Takahiro Yoshimatsu, Kenichi Tatefuji. ANI: Takahiro Yoshimatsu. MUS: Mark Ishikawa, Shusei Murai. PRD: Madhouse Studios. 23 mins. x 22 eps.
Sam and Dean Winchester are demon hunters. They inherited the job from their father, and now they travel across America killing supernatural creatures. Based on the American live-action TV hit, the anime condenses the first two live-action seasons and also features prologues from the boys' childhoods, extra story space for minor characters, and anime-only episodes incorporating Japanese folklore.
The Madhouse studio has had plenty of practice animating American hits, not always successfully. Here, they do their usual excellent job with the look of the show, but

the run time means that characters and situations have less space to develop, exposition feels rushed, and characterization is more exaggerated. The classic rock score of the American series has been largely replaced with new music. There's plenty for *Supernatural* geeks to nitpick over, but nothing really offensive or destructive of the original; the main question raised by the whole project is why bother? **①**

SURFSIDE HIGH SCHOOL

1999. TV series. DIR: Nobuyoshi Yoshida, Kenichi Maejima. SCR: N/C. DES: Tsutomu Ishigaki. ANI: N/C. MUS: N/C. PRD: Shogakukan, PolyGram, TBS. 7 mins. x 16 eps.
Late-night lineup of high school surfer dudes who dress like gangsters for TBS's after-midnight series of shorts. Drawn in a hard-edged caricature style, this series of shorts was based on a 1996 *Young Sunday* manga by Ken Sawai and screened as part of the *Wonderful* program.

SURVIVAL IN THE OFFICE

1990. JPN: *OL Kaizo Koza*. AKA: *O(ffice) L(adies) Remodeling Lecture*. Video. DIR: Hajime Ishigaki. SCR: Megumi Hikichi, Hiroshi Hashimoto. DES: Shinobu Arima. ANI: Yasushi Nagaoka. MUS: Michiru Oshima. PRD: TMS. 91 mins.
An Office Lady forgets to make a single photocopy, threatening the very fabric of existence in a Japanese company—or not. She muses on the ways to get through the week, including helpful advice on Goofing Off on Different Weekdays and The Right Thing to Say to Your Boss. Inspired by the column *Drop Dead! Stupid Office Ladies* in *Monthly Gendai* magazine. Released straight to video shortly after the same studio's **OLD MAN'S SURVIVAL GUIDE**, this is not to be confused with Risu Akizuki's manga *Survival in the Office* (*OL Shinka Ron*), which was released in English.

SURVIVAL: NO MAN'S PLANET

2003. JPN: *Mujin Wakusei Survive*. AKA: *Deserted Planet Survive; Uninhabited Planet Survive*. TV series. DIR: Yuichiro Yano. SCR: Shoji Yonemura. DES: Sadaichi Takiguchi, Hisashi Eguchi. ANI: Noriko Hara, Shuji Takahara. MUS: Takefumi Haketa. PRD: Madhouse, Telecom, NHK. 25 mins. x 52 eps.
In the 22nd century, a series of natural disasters on Earth has caused humanity

to move away into space and onto colony worlds. Fourteen-year-old Luna has been reared on colony Rocca A2 by her pet/nanny Chako, a pink cat-like robot, until she transfers to a new school, Soria Academy. However, her cosseted life is thrown into upheaval during a school trip to Jupiter's moon Io, where their craft is pulled into a giant gravitational storm. Only seven of the pupils make it into the escape pod with Chako and land on a blue planet, complete with monsters, ominously giant footprints, ancient ruins, mysterious voices, and a dwindling water supply. Meanwhile, their rescue ship is hijacked by three escaped prisoners who have no intention of using it to get them home.

Playing like a reversioning of *Lost In Space* (1965) or, if you prefer, a foreshadowing of *Lost* (2004) in space, this series even has its own man you love to hate in the form of the clever but selfish school dreamboat Howard, who tries to buy a passage off-planet with the convicts in exchange for spare parts. When he fails, the best hope for the party comes from a mysterious amnesiac boy named Adam, whose people may have left a space vessel somewhere on the planet. Compare also to **ADRIFT IN THE PACIFIC** and its sci-fi reprise **VIFAM**, both of which also marooned school children, although leaving plucky youngsters to find self-reliance is a staple of most anime aimed at a teenage audience—see **GUNDAM**. Some may also detect a few parallels with *They Were Eleven* (*DE).

This adventure series should not be confused with *Survival 2.7D*, a five-minute music video for Japanese pop group Glay, directed and designed by Koji Morimoto and animated and produced by Studio 4°C in 2004.

SUSIE AND MARVIE

1999. JPN: *Susie-chan to Marvie*. TV series. DIR: Shinya Sadamitsu, Scott Frazier. SCR: Noma Sabear. DES: Sonomi Makino. ANI: Nobuyoshi Habara. MUS: N/C. PRD: ShoPro, Xebec, NHK. 4 mins. x 104 eps.

Ten-year-old Susie is a daydreamer, while her one-year-old brother, Marvie, is a mischievous scatterbrain. They like to play with their neighbor Aunt Nana, and her lovable golden retriever, Hana. They also like to play with Professor Peabney, a dachshund inventor with a remarkable

resemblance to *Rocky and Bullwinkle*'s Professor Peabody. In the style of **DORAEMON**, the professor's inventions never quite go according to plan. These happy-go-lucky playtime adventures in a 1950s style were based on the 1994 manga by Noma Sabear serialized in *Sunshine* magazine.

SUZUKI, TOSHIMITSU

ca. 1950–. Anime producer who left Tatsunoko to found the Artmic studio, whose credits only show up on a limited number of video anime produced in a brief period between the mid-1980s and early 1990s. Since this straddled the post-**AKIRA** period where many in Western **FANDOM** discovered anime, Suzuki's works gained great attention—particularly **BUBBLEGUM CRISIS**, **RIDING BEAN**, and **GALL FORCE**. However, Artmic soon faced financial difficulties, leading to an exodus of creators and licenses that still has repercussions today. Some titles were abandoned mid-story, others picked up later under slightly different names and continuities. This confusion has even affected rights deals—the authors recall several occasions when rival companies have both believed themselves to be the sole sales agent for former Artmic products. Artmic licenses now largely reside with former coproduction partners Youmex and AIC—hence the remake *Bubblegum Crisis 2040*, on which Suzuki has a credit for being the "original creator," not for direct involvement with the actual production.

SUZUKI, TOSHIO

1948–. Born in Nagoya, Suzuki found employment at the publisher Tokuma Shoten shortly after graduating in literature from Keio University—where, at age 18, he read Akiyuki Nosaka's novella of **GRAVE OF THE FIREFLIES** and resolved one day to make a movie of it. After initial work on the magazine *Asahi Geino* ("Asahi Arts"), he became the editor of *Animage* magazine in 1978, in which capacity he commissioned Hayao Miyazaki's manga version of what was then a failed movie pitch—**NAUSICAÄ OF THE VALLEY OF THE WIND**. After assuring Miyazaki that he would not turn it into an anime, Suzuki subsequently talked his friend around. Suzuki is also credited with gaining a decent distribution deal for **MY NEIGHBOR TOTORO** by ensuring that it was

on a double bill with *Grave of the Fireflies*, and could thereby piggy-back on educational screenings for schools. Formally joining Studio Ghibli in 1991, Suzuki produced many movies for the company, as well as **GHOST IN THE SHELL**: *Innocence* for Mamoru Oshii, joining it in mid-production, at the same time as he was producing **HOWL'S MOVING CASTLE**.

Suzuki is also believed to be the author of the stern noninterference policy that prevented Buena Vista from bowdlerizing Ghibli movies for an American audience, famously sending a sword to his fellow producer Harvey Weinstein with the message attached: "No Cuts." A shrewd manipulator of the media, Suzuki often presented himself, with some degree of truth, as the no-nonsense manager who reined in the flightier ideas of the other creatives in the studio but also as the sharp thinker who would cut through the thorny problems of pride and preconception at Ghibli—the decision to hire Goro Miyazaki, the famous director's son, to helm **TALES FROM EARTHSEA** can largely be laid at Suzuki's feet.

In terms of the studio's peak era around **SPIRITED AWAY** and its managed decline in the subsequent decade, Suzuki should be regarded as just as important a figure as Miyazaki and Isao Takahata themselves. He announced his official retirement from producing in 2013, although he immediately moved into a new role as the studio's general manager, reflecting the increasing importance to Ghibli's bottom line of legacy and "events" above the creation of new films post-Miyazaki. In doing so, he arguably recognized that his recurring project over the preceding decade to nurture a successor to Miyazaki had failed, but not for want of trying.

SUZY'S ZOO

2011. JPN: *Suzy's Zoo Daisuki! Witzy*. AKA: *Witzy*. TV series. DIR: Hidekazu Ohara. SCR: Kaori Kita. DES: Suzy Spafford, Tetsuro Kodama. ANI: Noriyuki Omi. MUS: Wataru Maeguchi. PRD: Digital Media Lab, TBS. 2 mins. x 25 eps.

Witzy is a sweet little duck with an overactive imagination. She and her friends Boof, Lulla, Patches, and Elli Funt have brief, brightly colored CGI adventures in this **KIDS' ANIME**. It's based on the work of American artist and illustrator Suzy

Spafford, who founded Suzy's Zoo as a greeting card company in 1968. Compare with the greeting-card and gift genesis of **Hello Kitty**.

SWALLOWTAIL INN *

2003. JPN: *Ryokan Shirasagi*. AKA: *White Heron Inn*. Video. DIR: Juhachi Minamizawa. SCR: Joichi Michigami. DES: Dodoitsu, Tatsuya. ANI: Hanya. MUS: Hiroaki Sano, Takeshi Nishizawa, Sentaro. PRD: Discovery, AT-2 Project. 30 mins. x 2 eps.

When the owner of a traditional Japanese inn dies, the only way his widow Yuriko Shiratori can keep the inn going is by offering sexual services to selected guests, though even this scheme seems to fail due to her lack of skill. When a vagrant with memory loss is found wandering in the woods, kindhearted Yuriko takes him in, names him Kenji, and employs him to help out with odd jobs. Evidently his memory hasn't completely disappeared, as he is a good chef and has other hidden talents. He soon picks up on the specialty of the house, and offers Yuriko some tuition in unusual techniques to increase their income by improving the services they offer to their customers. Yuriko's husband's energetic younger sister Fuyuka soon arrives, and after mistaking Kenji for one of the special customers, pitches in to help with the guest parties. Her performance is disappointing and she also receives Kenji's special tutoring as they work toward the inn's profitability. Pretty visuals are unfortunately often marred by off-model characters, as well as a varying level of detail, but a resemblance to the female lead in **Ai Yori Aoshi** may interest connoisseurs of the genre. For us, it's sadly refreshing to find a porn anime where most of the sex is between consenting adults. Another entry in the **Discovery Series**, based on a game by Speed. 🅛🅝

SWAN LAKE *

1981. JPN: *Hakucho no Mizuumi*. Movie. DIR: Kimio Yabuki. SCR: Hirokazu Fuse. DES: N/C. ANI: Takuo Noda, Hiroshi Wagatsuma, Shunji Saita, Takashi Abe. MUS: Peter Tchaikovsky. PRD: Toei. 75 mins.

Princess Odette is bewitched by the wicked magician Rothbart; by day she is a swan, by night a girl. Prince Siegfried sees her transformation and falls in love with her.

He vows to break the spell and save the princess, but the spell may only be broken by the man who proclaims his undying love for her. At a ball, Siegfried dances with several girls, eventually finding the one whom he assumes to be Odette. Proclaiming his love, he discovers too late that it is Odile, Rothbart's daughter, breaking Odette's heart. Toei's animated version of Tchaikovsky's 1877 ballet won an award at the 1981 Moscow Film Festival. In a backhanded compliment to its artistic merits, 2,500 cels were stolen during production.

SWEET BLUE FLOWERS *

2009. JPN: *Aoi Hana*. TV series. DIR: Kenichi Kasai. SCR: Fumihiko Takiyama, Seishi Minakami, Yuniko Ayana. DES: Masayuki Onchi, Shichiro Kobayashi. ANI: Masayuki Onchi, Kazunori Iwakura. MUS: Takefumi Haketa. PRD: JC Staff, Fuji TV, Hakuhodo DY Media Partners, media Factory, Yomiko Advertising. 23 mins. x 11 eps.

Fumi thought her heart was broken when her beloved cousin, her first love, got married without even telling her. She retreated into books for the last year of middle school. Starting high school, she meets Akira, her best friend from ten years ago (**Romance and Drama**). The two girls rediscover their friendship and help each other cope with their romantic problems. And Fumi needs help when she starts dating a charismatic older girl who has problems of her own. This is a sensitive, low-key drama about young lesbians, not overly romanticized and with well-developed characters and situations. Takako Shimura's 2004 manga ran until 2013, but the anime didn't do well enough on DVD to get a second season.

SWEET HOME

2011. JPN: *Sweet Home: H-na Onee-san wa Suki Desu ka*. AKA: *Sweet Home: Don't You Just Love Pervy Big Sisters?* Video. DIR: Ryu Tamanomi. SCR: N/C. DES: N/C. ANI: N/C. MUS: N/C. PRD: MS Pictures (Celeb). 25 mins. x 3 eps.

Ryuichi lives alone until he is made homeless after a fire in his apartment building. He moves in with his stepmother and finds himself rooming with not one but five sexy women, all mad for him. Based on the 2007 porn game by STONEHEADS and CODEPINK. 🅝

SWEET MINT

1990. JPN: *Maho no Angel Sweet Mint*. AKA: *Magical Angel Sweet Mint*. TV series. DIR: Toshitaro Oba, Norio Takase, Kazuhiro Ozawa. SCR: Takao Koyama, Aya Matsui, Yoshimasa Takahashi, Masaharu Amiya. DES: Toshiyuki Tsuru. ANI: Himiko Ito, Hiroaki Sakurai, Yoshitaka Fujimoto. MUS: Osamu Morizuka. PRD: Ashi Pro, TV Tokyo. 25 mins. x 47 eps.

Another magical-girl series whose sweet heroine has a cute little bluebird as her magical friend and uses a magic compact (harking back to **Secret Akko-chan**) that transforms into anything she needs. The compact is a gift from Grandmother Herbe; when 12-year-old Mint opens the lid, the design of a crossbow engraved there actually turns into a bow whose arrow is tipped with a crystal heart. When she fires the arrow, the streaks of light from its facets transform her into a Magical Angel. From the studio that brought you **Gigi**, Mint has a similar origin—she is really a princess from the land of magic, sent to Earth to bring happiness to humans, taking up residence in the "Happy Shop" in the little town of Toal so she can carry out her mission.

SWEET SPOT

1991. Video. DIR: Gisaburo Sugii. SCR: N/C. DES: Kiyosuke Eguchi. ANI: Kiyosuke Eguchi. MUS: N/C. PRD: Tomason, Group Tac. 45 mins.

These "amusing" adventures of a golf-crazy Office Lady were based on a manga from *Weekly Spa!* magazine by Yutsuko Chudoji.

SWEET VALERIAN

2004. AKA: *Sweet Valerian*. TV series. DIR: Hiroaki Sakurai. SCR: Sayuri Oba. DES: Yoshiki Yamakawa. ANI: N/C. MUS: Double Oats. PRD: Madhouse, MBS, TBS. 4 mins. x 26 eps.

Stress is a killer in Japan, the country which has a specific word for working oneself to death—*karoshi*. In CLAMP's fictional Ajaran City, a group known as the Stress Team floats over the city spotting those whose stress levels are heading for meltdown and transforming them into monsters. To fight this menace, the "living enigma" Ear Hermit (a huge-eared purple head on legs) is on the lookout for a special team, and he finds it when Kanoko, Kate, and Pop go to take the test for a moped license. The Hermit ensures that instead they receive a "Valerian License" which enables them to transform into Sweet Valerian, defenders of justice in the form of prettily costumed fluffy bunnies—thereby obviating the need for them to have cute mascot sidekicks, since they are *their own* mascot animals. CLAMP's ability to run endless riffs on cute is truly staggering, especially as it is mixed with visual inventiveness, strong character and story skills, and a sense of fun. The style of this short series is flat, bright, and colorful, with a happy 1960s vibe, and the addition of elements like a whole UFO full of cute aliens and a talking mobile phone with a bad attitude only confirms our long held view that whatever CLAMP are on, we'd like some. In the real world, the herb valerian is supposedly a stress retriever. Note that some of the episodes were not initially broadcast on television, although it is unlikely that this minor snub would have been something that CLAMP got stressed about.

SWIMMY

1991. JPN: *Ganbare Swimmy*. AKA: *Go for It, Swimmy!* Movie. DIR: Hidetoshi Omori. SCR: Hideharu Iguchi. DES: Hidetoshi Omori. ANI: Hidetoshi Omori. MUS: Hideo Sato. PRD: OH Productions. 26 mins.
Swimmy, a black fish born into a shoal of red fish, tries to fit in amid adventures as he is chased by tuna and must evade the Great Octopus. Originally based on a children's picture book by Leo Lionni.

SWING OUT SISTERS

2011. AKA: SOS. Video. DIR: Toshihiro Watase. SCR: Toshihiro Watase. DES: N/C. ANI: Toshihiro Watase. MUS: Hito Yamato. PRD: SOS Production Committee. 30 mins.
Yuta's older sisters—sweet, feminine, big-breasted Chiyoko and tomboyish, strong-willed Chinatsu—fancy the pants off their little brother. It starts off with double entendres that Yuta is a bit too shy to pick up on, moves through sibling rivalry, and ends in yet more sex. Satomi Hino's color design is fresh and pretty but there's little else to recommend this silly story adapted from Taro Shinonome's 2005 porn manga. **Ⓝ**

SWISS FAMILY ROBINSON *

1981. JPN: *Kazoku Robinson Hyoryuki:*

Fushigi na Shima no Flowne. AKA: *Swiss Family Robinson: Mysterious Island of Flowne*. TV series. DIR: Yoshio Kuroda, Seiji Okuda, Michiyo Sakurai, Shigeo Koshi, Fumio Kurokawa, Hideo Fukuzawa, Fumio Ikeno, Takayoshi Suzuki, Taku Sugiyama. SCR: Shozo Matsuda. DES: Shuichi Seki. ANI: Michiyo Sakurai, Koichi Murata. MUS: Koichi Sakata. PRD: Nippon Animation, Fuji TV. 25 mins. x 50 eps.
The Robinsons leave Switzerland for Australia, but shipwreck strands them alone on a Pacific island. Gradually they build a home and a life there, but then find they are not alone—an old sailor and a young aborigine are also on the island. Helped by their new friends, they build a raft to try and reach Australia. One of Nippon Animation's **WORLD MASTERPIECE THEATER** series, this retelling of Johann David Wyss's 19th-century shipwreck tale has been adapted for TV and film many times before, but rarely with such charm. A series with moments of real beauty, owing much to Masahiro Ioka's backgrounds. See also **SPACE FAMILY CARLVINSON**. Dubbed by Saban and broadcast on the Family Channel (later known as Fox Family Channel).

SWITCH

2008. Video. DIR: Naoki Ohira. SCR: Natsuko Takahashi, Nobuaki Yamaguchi. DES: Takeshi Ito, Takeshi Takakura, Makoto Shiraishi. ANI: Takeshi Ito, Yasuyuki Ebara. MUS: Osamu Kubota. PRD: Actas, Frontier Works, Geneon Entertainment. 30 mins. x 2 eps.
Two newly appointed cops at Japan's Narcotics Control Department are childhood friends, unshakeably loyal to one another despite their very different personalities. Kai is a gentle, kindhearted soul—until he is threatened, when he switches personalities and becomes a killing machine. Hal is a brilliant, ruthless investigator who will use his charm on men and women alike to get his way. The pair and their young boss are determined to bring down a Chinese drug smuggling ring, but there's a connection with Kai's past that could threaten everything the team is working for. Based on the manga by Oto Saki and Tomomi Nakamura, AKA Naked Ape, this short series packs a lot of action and some character development into its runtime. The overall design, art style, and color palette are strongly influenced by **DEATH NOTE**,

along with the music and the darkness of the plot, but the show's cleanly executed plot twists and interesting central relationship make it more than just a copycat. **Ⓥ**

SWORD ART ONLINE *

2012. TV series/special. DIR: Tomohiko Ito. SCR: Munemasa Nakamoto, Naoki Shoji, Shuji Iriyama, Yoshikazu Mukai, Yukie Sugawara, Yukito Kizawa, Reki Kawahara. DES: Shingo Adachi, Takayuki Nagashima, Tetsuya Kawakami, Yuho Taniuchi, Kazuo Nakajima. ANI: Shingo Adachi, Tetsuya Kawakami, Ryuta Yanagi, Takahiro Shikama. MUS: Yuki Kajiura. PRD: A-1 Pictures, Aniplex, ASCII Media Works, GENCO, Bandai Namco. 23 mins. x 25 eps. (TV1), 100 mins. (special), 23 mins. x ?? eps. (TV2).
In 2022, a popular online game enables players to control avatars in a virtual world, a giant floating castle, and a wilderness, in which they have to progress to higher and higher floors fighting medieval villains. But *Sword Art Online* has a sinister twist. Players find themselves unable to log out, held captive by the game's creator unless they can defeat progressively more powerful bosses on 100 levels. And if they die in the game, they die in real life. The game's creator wants the usual real-world stuff: power, money, and getting the girl, all to be achieved by messing with teenagers' heads until, like hero Kirito, they question if they are truly themselves or simply artificial constructs.

Heavy on very pretty art and battle sequences and tediously light on story and character development, the show is based on Reki Kawahara's 2002 web novel series with art by abec, running in *Dengeki Bunko* magazine since 2009. A manga version with art by Neko Nekobyo commenced in June 2013 to support the launch of the TV series in July. Although the story is nothing new (**BTOOOM!**) and the concept has been used to better effect (**SUMMER WARS**) it caused considerable interest through its emphasis on the psychology of virtual reality and its understanding of how people completely uninterested in real-world society and economics can be deeply engaged in the same thing dressed up as a game. Further story arcs take in a floating world and winged fairy avatars, a gun-focused game with a currency exchangeable in the real world, and a world where time can be accelerated and slowed (see Kawahara's later novel and earlier anime ACCEL WORLD). Unfortunately, they also play host to the swift downgrading of the female lead, Asuna, from a formidable warrior and independent character to little more than a distressed damsel in the latter half.

A "special" compilation of the series was released online on New Year's Eve 2013 as *Sword Art Online Extra Edition*. As well as a segment in which the government sends a minister to get Kirito's opinion, new material focused on a fan service-laden "additional quest" in swimwear, along with the airing of a second series for TV broadcast in 2014. *SAOII* animates the Phantom Bullet story arc from the original novels, set in the gun-focused game "Gun Gale Online." **NV**

SWORD FOR TRUTH *

1990. JPN: *Shuranosuke Zanmaken: Shika-mamon no Otoko*. AKA: *Demon-slaying Sword of Shuranosuke: The Man with the Death-Sickle Crest*. Video. DIR: Osamu Dezaki. SCR: Jo Toriumi. DES: Akio Sugino. ANI: Akio Sugino. MUS: Toshiyuki Watanabe. PRD: Toei. 50 mins.
Lone samurai Shuranosuke strolls into 1636 Edo (the capital of Ieyasu, first Tokugawa shogun) and with one swipe of his legendary blade Onimaru, nonchalantly dispatches the giant white tiger that has been terrorizing the citizenry. The tiger is only the first wave of an assault by evil forces using demonic powers to kidnap Princess Mio then swap her for a magical dagger. Shuranosuke agrees to make the exchange but must then get the princess safely past a series of magical traps to return her to her no less treacherous household. But while the enemy has magic on its side, he has his own superb skills and the love of beautiful ninja-thief Orin.

Based on a novel by YOTODEN-creator Jo Toriumi, *SfT* oozes style and mystery, with gorgeous art direction by Yukio Abe. However, the limited animation that characterizes Dezaki's direction (e.g., BLACK JACK) lets it down—though optioned by Manga Entertainment in the hope it would be another NINJA SCROLL, it is nowhere near as good. To add insult to injury, the anime was infamously advertised with the fiendishly inaccurate line, "Ancient feudal Japan was ruled by clans of shoguns." A live-action version, *Legend of the Devil*

(1998), directed by Masaru Tsushima and starring the incandescently gorgeous Masaki Kyomoto as Shuranosuke, contains more of our hero's story than *SfT*, and retains plenty of the sex scenes, but has less convincing supernatural perils. **NV**

SWORD OF MUSASHI

1985. JPN: *Musashi no Ken*. AKA: *Sword of Musashi*. TV series. DIR: Toshio Kadota, Katsumi Minoguchi, Masamune Ochiai, Yuji Asada, Akinori Yabe, Hideki Tonokatsu, Kazutoshi Kobayashi, Kenjiro Yoshida. SCR: Masaru Yamamoto, Haruya Yamazaki. DES: Motoka Murakami. ANI: Makoto Kuniyoshi. MUS: Hidemi Sakashita. PRD: Eiken, TV Tokyo. 25 mins. x 72 eps. (TV1), 25 mins. x 72 eps. (TV2).
Born on the same day as Japan's legendary "Sword Saint" and named after him, too, the young Musashi Natsuki hopes one day to become as good with a sword as his famous namesake. Training hard at kendo at his home in Iwate, he is devastated by his father's death and transfers to a new dojo. There, however, he encounters not only new challenges, but also the bitter enmity of a new rival. Based on a manga by SEIZE THE WIND–creator Motoka Murakami in *Shonen Sunday*, *SoM* was rebranded after episode 49 as *SoM: The Teen Years* (1986, *Seishun-hen*), featuring Musashi's ongoing feuds with rival "samurai" from neighboring high schools. All set in the present day, this mixture of the clichés of SPORTS ANIME and samurai period drama drew its inspiration from the life of Musashi Miyamoto (see YOUNG MIYAMOTO MUSASHI).

SWORD OF THE DESTROYER

1992. JPN: *Hayo no Ken: Shikkoku no Masho*. AKA: *Sword of the Destructive Phantom: Jet-black Devilry*. Video. DIR: Setsuko Shibuichi, Shinichiro Kimura. SCR: Kazumi Koide. DES: Yukari Kobayashi. ANI: Yukari Kobayashi. MUS: Makihiko Araki. PRD: Magic Bus. 30 mins. x 2 eps.
Heroic fantasy in the ancient kingdom of Gandia, as the Fairy and Human realms choose their Princess of the Red Lotus, the only one who may wield the Sword of the Destroyer. Lots of Talking With Capital Letters, as battle-maid Raethril takes on the minions of the Prince of Darkness, rather unfortunately named Redial. Based on a best-selling novel by Shuko Maeda. **V**

SWORD OF THE STRANGER *

2007. JPN: *Stranger: Muko Hadan*. Movie. DIR: Masahiro Ando. SCR: Fumihiko Takayama. DES: Tsunenori Saito, Atsushi Morikawa. ANI: Tsunenori Saito, Yoshiyuki Ito. MUS: Naoki Sato. PRD: BONES. 102 mins.
Nanashi (No-Name) is a swordmaster on the run from a bloodstained past. He intends to leave his former life behind him and fight no more. Then he runs into little Kotaro, alone in the world except for his faithful dog Tobimaru. Boy and dog have fled from a monastery to escape soldiers from China's Ming dynasty as well as those of a local warlord. It appears the boy holds the key to a priceless secret, but he has no idea what it is. Among the pursuing Ming warriors is a Caucasian, Raro, whose only aim in life is to improve his sword skills. Among the defenders are ambitious men whose loyalty is negotiable. Neither Kotaro nor Nanashi is exactly what he seems. In fact, most of the characters are strangers in a strange land of bloodshed and greed.

Its Chinese travelers, a nod perhaps to the Seven Immortals of Chinese tradition, are perpetually young, but at a price. Like vampires, they have an immortality that must be recharged, junkies of an awful, killing addiction that leaves them craving human blood. And in a cruel twist, only the blood of a certain child will suffice. Where CONFUCIUS once said that a Great Sage would arise once every few generations, this old Chinese saw is perverted and sullied, turned into a quest not for a leader, or a savior, or a wise king, but for a simple fix for the old, twisted order.

Sword of the Stranger is set at a watershed moment in both Chinese and Japanese history, when both orders were set to topple. The visitors from "Ming" are the last representatives ever sent to Japan by a Chinese emperor. With the fall of the Ming dynasty in 1644, China would pass into the hands of a foreign power, the Manchus—the notorious "last" emperor, who abdicated in 1912, was still regarded by many of his subjects as a foreign usurper. The film depicts the occupants of a Japan exhausted after a century of civil war, reduced to mere peasants scraping out a subsistence existence, thieves with little to steal, and lone swordsmen, before the rise of the Tokugawa shoguns who would rule until their decline in the 19th century.

Classic *chambara* (Japanese swordplay) movies were made by men steeped in samurai tradition and legend. For this contemporary anime *chambara*, rookie director Ando also draws from the modern Hollywood tradition of a clear narrative arc and polished presentation. He takes a man with no name, a bratty kid on the run, and a dog and merges them into a reluctant team to take on a feudal lord and the Chinese army.

SotS says nothing new to existing fans of Japanese or Hollywood action flicks, and its characters and relationships were long established when Osamu Tezuka used them in **DORORO**. Where this debut movie scores is in presenting everything with style and panache, and punctuating the running time with magnificently animated action scenes, so superbly staged that all but the most critical audiences will be dazzled. There's no holding back as arteries spurt, limbs fly, and the body count rises. At 100 minutes, this could have grown tedious, and it's a tribute to Ando and his team that they manage to hold audience interest by balancing character and exposition with the passionate intensity of the combat scenes.

SotS shines on the big screen, showing off epic action sequences to advantage, and it's no surprise that it has won praise at festivals across Europe and got an award in Brazil for its technical qualities. We suggest you just enjoy it for what it is—a gorefest pure and simple, a swordplay epic sans wire-work that revels in the absolute simplicity of all-out action. **◑**

SWORD TALK

2010. JPN: *Katanagatari*. TV series. DIR: Keitaro Motonaga. SCR: Makoto Uezu, Seiko Nagatsu, Toko Machida. DES: Tsuyoshi Kawada, Tadashi Kudo. ANI: Tsuyoshi Kawada. MUS: Taku Iwasaki. PRD: WHITE FOX, Aniplex, Fuji TV, Kodansha, Lantis, MOVIC. 50 mins. x 12 eps.

Kiki Shikizaki was a legendary swordsmith who created 12 perfect weapons, *katana* of such beauty and power that many influential and dangerous people seek to own them. Female samurai Togame is employed by the government in Edo to make sure the swords fall into the proper hands. She enlists Shichika Yasuri, heir of

an ancient martial art tradition, to defeat swordfighters without using a sword. After spending years training on a isolated island with his sister, Shichika is ready to use his skills, but is a boy from the sticks with no social graces ready for an epic journey through the wild terrain of feudal Japan, all the while fighting off great warriors, ninja, rogues, and vagabonds?

This magnificent effort to transfer NisiOisin's book series and Dan Yoshii's original designs to the small screen has preserved both the best and worst of the original. The double-length episodes accommodate one novel's plot each, giving a satisfyingly complete narrative flow. The art style is distinctive and intriguing, and the animation is carefully composed to highlight each key moment, movement, and scene, creating an unusual and satisfying aesthetic experience. It's made for TV, but the quality of the art and the stylishness of the approach merits comparison with movies such as **THE SENSUALIST**. Very few shows create such impact on the small screen.

On the negative side, the weekly schedule highlights the extremely formulaic nature of the plots. Togame and Shichika always face fierce opposition but they always win the sword of the week. Tension and narrative surprise can come from character, and there's some of this in the developing romance between our hero and his employer and the way that romance forces both to confront their pasts; but all the other characters are as elegantly stylized as the art, as formulaic as the gorgeous figures in a Byzantine mosaic, or the paragons of **THE HAKKEN-DEN**. This creates an emotional distance that weakens the impact of the clever final twist. The series' other problem is its talkiness. NisiOisin's style is dialogue-heavy, and in this regard the show's fidelity to its creator is a drawback.

Don't allow that to put you off. This is an excellent series. The score is superb and the style is unique. But it's lacking in heart, and that, in the end, is what makes it a beautiful loser. **◑**

SYMPHOGEAR *

2012. JPN: *Senki Zessho Symphogear*. AKA: *Superb Song of the Valkryies: Symphogear*. TV series. DIR: Tatsufumi Ito. SCR:

Akifumi Kaneko. DES: Satoshi Koike, Takashi Nishimura, Thomas Romain. ANI: Satoru Fujimoto, Satoshi Koike. MUS: Noriyasu Agematsu, Elements Garden, Junpei Fujita, Hitoshi Fujima. PRD: Encourage Films, Satelight, Starchild Records, Aniplex, Bushiroad, Dwango, Good Smile Company, Kinyosha, Memory Tech. 24 mins. x 13 eps. (TV1), 24 mins. x 13 eps. (TV2).

Close friends Tsubasa Kazanari and Kanade Amo are a singing duo known as ZweiWing. They are drawn into a battle against alien invaders known as the Noise, who kill humans by turning them into carbon dust on contact. Piloting huge mecha (**SCIENCE FICTION AND ROBOTS**) and using **MUSIC** to activate weaponry known as Relics, they are an effective fighting team, until Kanade is killed saving the life of a younger girl from their school, Hibiki Tachibana. Tsubasa now views her music purely as a weapon. Two years later, Hibiki too joins in the fight against the Noise, using Kanade's old armor. Can she help to save the world while persuading Tsubasa to sing for joy again?

Based on the manga by Agematsu, Kaneko, and Elements Garden, this series tries to paint over its basic irrationality—everyone knows music attracts the Noise but all the fighters attend a music high school in a major city resulting in massive casualties—with industrial-strength coatings of schoolgirl angst and schoolgirl cuteness, and lots of high-sounding Germanic names for machines, weapons, and concepts. Mawkishness, fan service, mythological references, and hints of lesbian love set to music are not enough to save the show, but it was popular enough to get a second series. We regretfully assume that comparisons with **MACROSS** or **PUELLA MAGI MADOKA MAGICA** will remain unflattering. **◐**

SYMPHONY DREAM STORY

1985. JPN: *Symphony Yume Monogatari*. Video. DIR: Dojiro, Satoshi Harada, Yutaka Kuramoto. SCR: Gokiburi, Yuka Kurokawa. DES: N/C. ANI: N/C. MUS: N/C. PRD: Nippon Soft System. 75 mins.

Four short pornographic tales in the tradition of **CREAM LEMON**: *Naked after Class*, in which two school girls find something else to do beyond helping each other with their homework; *Telepathist Love Q315* (a complex pun also readable as *Telepathist*

IQ Saiko/Psycho), in which Earth can only be saved from alien invaders by the nubile bodies of young telepaths; *Punky Funky Baby*, which seems to be an erotic pastiche of the **DIRTY PAIR**; and *Shining May*, in which an idol singer takes to the spotlight in more ways than one. Supposedly "humorous" and also sold under the umbrella title "Little Mermaid Series." **Ⓝ**

SYMPHONY IN AUGUST

2009. JPN: *Hachigatsu no Symphony: Shibuya 2002–2003*. AKA: *8-gatsu no Symphony*. Movie. DIR: Akio Nishizawa, Hiroyuki Shimatsu, Satoshi Shimizu. SCR: Akio Nishizawa. DES: Tatsuo Yanagino, Tadashi Kudo. ANI: Shuichi Fujinaka, Tadashi Murakami, Hiroyuki Shimatsu, Tatsuo Yanagino. MUS: Makoto Kuriya, Tsubasa Shioya. PRD: WAO World. 112 mins.

Sixteen-year-old Ai wants to share her songs with the world. Supported and encouraged by her mother, she has always dreamed of succeeding in **MUSIC**. Now that her mother has passed away, she decides to set herself a goal: to perform for the public on the streets of Shibuya in Tokyo one thousand times. This true story is based on the autobiography of singer/songwriter Ai Kawashima, who also wrote and performed the theme song. Chief director Nishizawa founded animation company WAO World in 2000 with the goal of producing films that would be enjoyed by both parents and children while carrying messages to enrich the mind. The real-world Kawashima would eventually contribute songs to the soundtracks of anime including **ONE PIECE** and **THE PLACE PROMISED IN OUR EARLY DAYS**.

SYNAPI *

2001. Movie. DIR: Bak Ikeda. SCR: Bak Ikeda. DES: Bak Ikeda. ANI: N/C. MUS: N/C. PRD: Genome Entertainment Inc., Imagica Entertainment Inc. 5 mins.

This CG short about "the essence of communication" features a faceless female character who is desperately trying to communicate with the unseen hordes rushing around her. Shown at the Yubari International Fantastic Film Festival and New York's FantAsia film festival in 2001, it went on the festival circuit to worldwide acclaim. See also Ikeda's similar **PINMEN**. Not to be confused with *Schnappi the Little Crocodile*, a German cartoon character whose name romanizes in the same way when moved into Japanese characters.

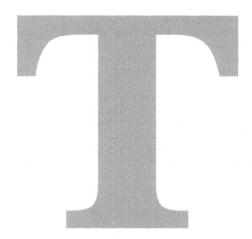

T&A TEACHER *

2004. JPN: *Shinkan*. AKA: *Sinkan*. Video. DIR: Hideki Araki. SCR: Hikaru Takeuchi. DES: Hideki Araki. ANI: Hideki Araki. MUS: Green Devil. PRD: Japan Home Video (Jewel), Shinkukan, Anime Antena [*sic*] Group. 26 mins.

Ayaka Yuki is a high school teacher, as well as the coach of the karate club and the daughter of the school's chairman. Beautiful and a provocative dresser, she is also quite willing to use her expert martial skills to keep order in her classroom—something that a delinquent student, Togawa, provokes her into when he is late to class, refuses to apologize, and then gropes her. Her father later chastises her for the incident, but her fellow teacher, Mr. Kitano, intervenes on her behalf (though his motives seem to not be entirely pure). The situation begins to deteriorate when Ayaka later finds herself in the grip of a mysterious, uncontrollable lust, and seeks privacy in the showers to relieve the "tension," only to have Togawa walk in and take advantage of her. His temerity lands him in the hospital when Ayaka eventually wakes up, but this only makes things worse for her.... A one-shot pornographic video with somewhat uneven production values (the art, though often good, often drops off in quality), this "series" is saved from going down the road trod before by DESPERATE CARNAL HOUSEWIVES, FAMILY OF DEBAUCHERY, and many others only by the lack of a second episode, though there is certainly room for it. Based on an erotic manga by Izumi Kyota, creator of KAREN. ○○

TA-CHAN KING OF THE JUNGLE

1994. JPN: *Jungle no Osama Ta-chan*. TV series. DIR: Hitoshi Nanba, Akitaro Daichi, Shigeru Ueda, Teppei Matsuura, Takaaki Ishiyama. SCR: Jinzo Toriumi, Akihiro Arashima, Satoshi Fujimoto, Toshiyuki Otaki, Takeshi Ito. DES: Yuka Kudo. ANI: Shigeru Kato, Chuji Nakajima, Kiyoshi Matsumoto, Masahiko Murata. MUS: Masatake Yamada. PRD: Amuse, TV Tokyo. 25 mins. x 50 eps.

A muscle-bound man in a loincloth fights evil kung-fu masters and vampires in darkest Africa. Though distantly inspired by Edgar Rice Burroughs's *Tarzan of the Apes* (1912), this series was filtered through a popular *Shonen Jump* manga by Masaya Tokuhiro.

TABOO CHARMING MOTHER *

2003. JPN: *Enbo*. AKA: *Captivating/Charming Mother; Erotic Heart Mother*. Video. DIR: Kan Fukumoto. SCR: Chiho Hananoki. DES: Tsuzuru Miyabi. ANI: Yuji Uchida, Kan Fukumoto, Shigenori Imoto. MUS: N/C. PRD: Big Wing, Milky, Museum Pictures. 30 mins. x 6 eps.

Only a year after marrying a significantly older man, Misako already feels that she is in a rut. Her stepson Kazuhiko treats her with distant disdain, and she hasn't had sex with husband Yosuke for two whole months. Initially, she is insulted and appalled by nuisance phone calls, although as time goes by, her frustrations in her private life cause her almost to welcome them. Over the course of several calls, her stalker talks her into using a sex toy he has left by her front gate in exchange for stopping the calls. Despite his telephonic absence, she begins using it obsessively—and even acquires another—unable to control her lust. When he inevitably telephones again, he persuades her to confess her fantasies. As time passes, it almost seems as if her life is improved by her illicit interludes of semi-forced onanism and phone sex—even her stepson seems to warm to her and addresses her at one point as "Mom." The identity of her caller is initially unclear, although considering the *Scooby Doo* size of the list of potential suspects, it shouldn't take anyone long to work out who it is. Later episodes introduce Misako's sister, Emiko, who is drawn into the maelstrom. Within the limited demands of anime porn, *TCM* is an intriguing title, much longer than the norm, and consequently able to stretch its suspense and sex scenes over several episodes. This is probably due at least in part to the size of the adult manga by Tsuzuru Miyabi that inspired it; compare to U-jin's SAKURA DIARIES. ○○

TACHUMARU THEATER

2010. JPN: *Tachumaru Gekijo*. TV series. DIR: OKN. SCR: Masaya Honda. DES: Makiko Watanabe. ANI: N/C. MUS: N/C. PRD: Tatsunoko Production. 25 mins. x 26 eps.

Tachu-mals are small, cute, super-deformed animals that have special fighting moves. You may think they're reminiscent of POKÉMON but they're even more redolent of characters created by Tatsunoko Studios, the "home of heroes." Look out for cute fur-folk mutated from BATTLE OF THE PLANETS, CASSHAAN: ROBOT HUNTER, and more in comical adventures.

TACTICAL ROAR

2006. TV series. DIR: Yoshitaka Fujimoto. SCR: Kazuho Hyodo. DES: Takeshi Ito. ANI: Takeshi Ito. MUS: Hikaru Nanase. PRD: Actas, TV Kanagawa, Bandai Visual, Lantis. 25 mins. x 13 eps.

Climate change has caused a supercyclone in the Western Pacific: the Grand Roar that shook the earth and flooded many nations. Shipping is vital to the new world economy and piracy is even more a curse than before, so companies spring up to provide escort ships for cargo and passenger liners. Young systems engineer Hyosuke Nagimiya is assigned to an escort ship with an all-girl crew, desperate to prove themselves competent officers. ◐

TACTICS *

2004. TV series DIR: Hiroshi Watanabe, Kazuhiko Inoue, Chiaki Kon, Shigeru Ueda. SCR: Kenichi Kanemaki, Hiroyuki Kawasaki, Katsuhiko Takayama, Masashi Kubota. DES: Tomomi Kimura. ANI: Yukiko Ban. MUS: Kei Haneoka. PRD: Medianet, MAG Garden, Studio Deen, TV Tokyo. 24 mins. x 25 eps.

Scholar Kantaro Ichinomiya researches folklore by day and goes ghostbusting by night in the manner of MUSHI-SHI. Hunting for an ogre-eating goblin, he releases a different kind of man-eater—hunky goblin Haruka, sealed inside a shrine and now out to form a very unusual monster-busting partnership with Kantaro. Kantaro's cute fox-spirit housekeeper Yoko doesn't approve of Haruka and Kantaro's partnership at first; nor does green blob Mu-chan, married to white goblin Sugino but carrying a torch for Kantaro. Based on the manga in *Comic Blade* by Sakura Kinoshita and Kazuko Higashiyama, this anime adaption adds a new character created specifically for TV—schoolgirl Suzu Edogawa falls for Haruka on sight. An old-time harem of spirits is a twist on the familiar theme geek-gets-girls, and this has more charm than the usual.

TAI CHI CHASERS

2007. JPN: *Tai Chi Senjimon*. AKA: *Tai Chi Thousand Character Text*. TV series. DIR: Hiroki Shibata. SCR: Hiromu Sato, Kazuhisa Okamoto, Kenichi Yamada. DES: Hisashi Kagawa, Takashi Kurahashi. ANI: N/C. MUS: N/C. PRD: KBS, Toei, Dongseo Univ., Iconix, JM Anime. 25 mins. x 39 eps.

Orphan Rai is astonished to find he's descended from an ancient race. In a parallel universe, his people the Tigeroids are locked in a centuries-long struggle with the Dragonoids to recover 500 lost tai chi symbols. Whoever recovers them will have the ultimate power to rule and defeat their enemies. Rai must develop his inborn talent for tai chi card battles to find the lost symbols as a champion Tai Chi Chaser. We're back in the world of KID'S ANIME, where kids emulate their heroes by buying and trading cards and other game paraphernalia to recreate their favorite battles on the playground. This Korean-Japanese coproduction uses Korean *hanja* symbols to represent the tai chi powers. It was licensed in the U.S.A. on 4Kids, but only 26 of the 39 episodes were actually shown prior to 4Kids filing for Chapter 11 bankruptcy in 2011.

TAIL OF TWO SISTERS *

1999. JPN: *Sister's Rondo: Charm Point 1*. Video. DIR: Yoshimaro Otsubo. SCR: Tedokoro Imaike. DES: Maron Kurase. ANI: N/C. MUS: N/C. PRD: Beam Entertainment, Akatonbo. 30 mins.

In this typical tale of anime abuse replaying the vengeful student/teacher set-up from ADVENTURE KID, new teacher Serina Kawano strikes up a very strange relationship with her pupil Masaya, submitting to his sadistic demands. Meanwhile, Serina's little sister, Yumi, is having boyfriend "troubles" of her own and doesn't understand how to keep her man. Needless to say, Serina has some advice for her. Not to be confused with the Korean horror movie, *Tale* [sic] *of Two Sisters* (2003). ◐

TAILENDERS

2009. Movie. DIR: Hisashi Sasaki, mebae, Makoto Ota, Masaru Kawahara. SCR: Hisashi Sasaki, mebae, Makoto Ota, Masaru Kawahara. DES: mebae. ANI: mebae. MUS: N/C. PRD: Picograph, Anime Innovation Tokyo. 27 mins.

Planet Terulus is plagued with mutated animals and giant earthquakes. Its cities are mobile, moving themselves around on wheels to avoid the worst excesses of nature, and its inhabitants amuse themselves with racing games. Top racer Shiro is horribly injured in an earthquake, and the only way to save him is to replace his heart

with part of his vehicle engine. Under race regulations this makes him a mere mechanical component, unqualified to compete with humans, so when a mysterious woman offers him the chance to regain his pride and his income—racing on a faraway world—he doesn't hesitate. This project was originally shopped around as the pilot episode of a series that never materialized, before being released as a movie: unfortunately this was in the same year as fan favorite REDLINE, which cornered the market in racing anime.

TAIMAN BLUES

1987. Video. DIR: Satoshi Dezaki. SCR: Machiko Kondo. DES: Yukari Kobayashi. ANI: Yukari Kobayashi. MUS: N/C. PRD: Magic Bus. 30 mins. x 5 eps.

A series grouping together two different stories linked by the biker theme. The three-part *Naoto Shimizu Chapter* is a tale of rivalry between two gangs, MND and Laku, and the personal vendetta between MND's Naoto and Laku's Yota, which lands Naoto in prison in the second (1988) episode. The third part of his story, his life after prison, was released in 1989. *Lady's Chapter* (1990) is devoted to a different set of characters, this time focusing on biker girls. Fifteen-year-old Mayumi has to move to the rough end of Osaka when her parents split and remarry. She meets Noriko, who helps her settle into her new life, and eventually moves in with her. Through Noriko's job at a petrol station, they get to know regular customer Big Bear and his biker gang, and eventually get into their own gang of girl racers. Based on a manga by Yu Furusawa.

TAISHO BASEBALL GIRLS *

2009. JPN: *Taisho Yakyu Musume*. TV series. DIR: Takashi Ikehata. SCR: Takashi Ikehata, Nobuhiko Amagawa, Masahiko Shiraishi. DES: Kanetoshi Kamimoto, Shichiro Kobayashi. ANI: Kanetoshi Kamimoto. MUS: Takayuki Hattori. PRD: JC Staff, Lantis, MOVIC, Pony Canyon, TBS, Tokuma Shoten. 24 mins. x 12 eps.

In 1925, Japan's Taisho period (SAKURA WARS) is in full swing and the nation, at least the urban and well-to-do part of it, is modernizing. Feisty 14-year-old high school girl Akiko is told by the man her parents have arranged for her to marry, a keen baseball player, that education is wasted on women and they should learn to run a household instead of going to school. She ropes in her friend Koume to form a girls' baseball team to prove him wrong. While their parents might not be quite so hidebound, they still see sports as a little too vulgar for women, so the girls have to start the team in secret. Actually learning the sport turns out to be even more of a challenge, but Akiko is determined to beat her fiancé's school team.

Atsushi Kagurasaka's book series, on which this SPORTS ANIME is based, is not especially strong on historical accuracy (*you* try to find a 1920s photograph showing Japanese schoolgirls with skirts above the knee) or even on baseball technique, but it has oodles of nostalgic charm. The anime follows the same route, director Ikehata using the innocence of the girls, and the contrast of modernity and old ways that marked out the era they inhabit, to create a sweet, light, gently humorous show that probably had grandmothers and their granddaughters watching all over Japan. Two five-minute "specials" from the same crew were included on the DVD release.

TAITO ROAD
1996. JPN: *Shinken Densetsu Taito Road*. AKA: *True Fighting Legend Taito Road*. TV series. DIR: Tatsuo Misawa. SCR: Kenichi Kanemaki, Kazuhiko Godo, Yoshihiko Tomizawa. DES: Michio Fukuda. ANI: Masahiro Masai. MUS: Koji Tsunoda. PRD: Toei, TV Tokyo. 25 mins. x 13 eps.
In a lackluster picaresque that tries to cash in on the successful STREET FIGHTER II franchise, a young man sets out to fight lots of people. ●

TAKADA, AKEMI
1955–. Born in Tokyo, Takada graduated from Tama Art University, and in the same year gained employment at Tatsunoko, where she worked for four years as a character designer on shows such as URUSEI YATSURA, before going freelance. An accomplished illustrator, her anime work includes a soft touch on KIMAGURE ORANGE ROAD and CREAMY MAMI, although she is perhaps best known for her membership in the Headgear collective and the key role

she played with former husband Kazunori Ito in the creation of PATLABOR.

TAKAHASHI, KATSUO
1932–. Born in Nagasaki, Takahashi grew up in Korea, which was a Japanese colony at the time. He was repatriated in 1945, and studied drama, film, and puppetry for four years before founding Chuo Productions (now Tokyo Chuo Productions) in 1958, specializing in children's entertainment and puppetry. He also wrote *Children's Education in the Age of Television*, an influential book in early Japanese broadcast media.

TAKAHASHI, RUMIKO
1957–. Born in Niigata Prefecture, Takahashi graduated from the history department of Japan Women's University. She had already been attending a manga workshop and found work as an assistant to Kazuo Umezu. She won a Shogakukan new writers prize in 1977 and went on to create the original manga for URUSEI YATSURA, MAISON IKKOKU, and RANMA ½, three of the defining manga works of the 1980s. She also appears as a "guest" designer on the credits for a few anime, as a design assistant on ADRIFT IN THE PACIFIC, and as the designer of a single character in CRUSHER JOE. Subsequently, her role in anime has been limited to that of the author of the manga on which many shows are based, notably the long-running INU YASHA, but also ONE-POUND GOSPEL and MERMAID'S FOREST. Her design credit on MOEYO KEN is for work on the original game on which the anime is based.

TAKAHASHI, RYOSUKE
1943–. Born in Tokyo, Takahashi dropped out of the literature department at Meiji University in order to begin full-time employment at Mushi Production, where he had already been working part-time. He went freelance in 1969, and became supervising director on ZERO TESTER. As a writer and director on VOTOMS, he was a key figure in the move toward the depiction of "realistic robots" (see Okawara, Kunio). He was also a supervising director on the 1979 remake of CYBORG 009, MAMA IS A FOURTH GRADER, and the *Knight of the Iron Dragon* segment in THE COCKPIT.

TAKAHATA, ISAO
1935–. Sometimes credited with the pseudonym Tetsu Takemoto. Born in Mie Prefecture, Takahata graduated from the French literature department of Tokyo University in 1959. Inspired by viewing Paul Grimault's cartoons in his student days, he joined Toei Animation in 1961 and worked on THE LITTLEST WARRIOR and THE LITTLE PRINCE AND THE EIGHT-HEADED DRAGON. His directorial debut came with LITTLE NORSE PRINCE, a financial flop despite critical acclaim, which led to his temporary retreat into television animation. Directorial posts followed at A Production (now Shin'ei Doga) and Zuiyo (now Nippon Animation), where he worked with his protégé and long-time collaborator Hayao Miyazaki on the landmark HEIDI and ANNE OF GREEN GABLES. Moving on to Tokyo Movie Shinsha and then freelance, he entered independent production with Miyazaki on NAUSICAÄ OF THE VALLEY OF THE WIND and had a pivotal role in Studio Ghibli, not only directing his own movies, such as the groundbreaking GRAVE OF THE FIREFLIES and POM POKO, but serving as producer on many of "Miyazaki's" masterpieces. In any other country, Takahata would be regarded as a national treasure—in an anime industry fixated on the successes of Miyazaki, the quiet achievements of this master filmmaker are often overlooked, despite a career rivaled in length and achievement only by that of Rintaro (q.v.).

TAKAMARU
1991. JPN: *Cho-Bakumatsu Shonen Seiki Takamaru*. AKA: *Super 19th-Century Boy Takamaru*. Video. DIR: Toyoo Ashida, Satoshi Nishimura. SCR: Toyoo Ashida, "Mindanao," Yuichiro Takeda. DES: Toyoo Ashida. ANI: Takahiro Yoshimatsu. MUS: Kohei Tanaka. PRD: JC Staff, Studio Live. ?? mins. x 2 eps. (v1), 25 mins. x 6 eps. (v2)
Set in the world of the Champion Kingdom, an imaginary island whose inhabitants follow a traditional samurai lifestyle, this is a tale of friendship and courage aimed at preteens. Based on director Ashida's manga in *Animedia* magazine. A second series, "New" Takamaru, followed in 1992–93. Compare to SHINSENGUMI FARCE.

TAKANE'S BICYCLE

2008. JPN: *Takane no Jitensha*. TV special.
DIR: Masashi Ikeda. SCR: Hayato Takagama.
DES: Sachiko Kamimura, Tadashi Kudo.
ANI: Sachiko Kamimura. MUS: N/C. PRD: A-1
Pictures, Animax. 27 mins.

Takane is promised a new bike if he places in the top 100 in an important exam. He comes in 112th, but tells his mother he's come in 92nd. His sister Tamaki is supposed to inherit his old bike, but when he accidentally breaks it she gets annoyed and accuses him of lying. One night he's out late, looking for his missing dog, when a strange young man offers him an exam answer sheet marked "92nd"—the proof of his story. He'll return it to the true owner unless Takane gives him something he doesn't need. So Takane offers his annoying little sister.

This story of selfishness and irresponsibility redeemed in the nick of time has echoes of CATNAPPED! It was the prizewinning script in the 6th Animax Awards—the prize being professional production of a young hopeful's script. CALLIGRAPHER was the next winner.

TAKAYASHIKI, HIDEO

1947–. Born in Iwate Prefecture, Takayashiki dropped out of Toyo University to pursue a career in scriptwriting, including work on LUPIN III, TOMORROW'S JOE, and the screenplay for the URUSEI YATSURA movie *Always My Darling*. He has also written many novelizations, including ones for the anime of DRAGON QUEST and SUKEBAN DEKA.

TAKE THE X TRAIN

1987. JPN: *X Densha de Iko*. AKA: *Let's Take the X Train*. Video. DIR: Rintaro, Tatsuhiko Urahata. SCR: Rintaro, Yoshio Urasawa. DES: Yoshinori Kanemori. ANI: Yoshinori Kanemori. MUS: Yosuke Yamashita. PRD: Madhouse. 50 mins.

Public-relations man Toru Nishihara is waiting on an underground station platform when he sees a phantom train. Ghosts are about to invade the human world, and Toru is co-opted by a secret military unit that has gathered the world's psychics to hold them off. Toru is threatened and cajoled into taking part, though the phantom train lays waste to the armed forces in a cataclysmic battle. The jazz number "Take the A-Train," whose

title inspired Koichi Yamano's original short story, appears at several points in this elegant little chiller and is sung over the closing credits by Akiko Yano.

TAKEGAMI *

1990. JPN: *Ankoku Shinden Takegami*. AKA: *Takegami: Guardian of Darkness*. Video. DIR: Osamu Yamasaki. SCR: Osamu Yamasaki. DES: Masami Obari. ANI: Masanori Nishii. MUS: Seiko Nagaoka. PRD: JC Staff. 45 mins. x 3 eps.

The lonely, homely Terumi has a crush on Koichi and sells her soul for beauty, agreeing to be possessed by an ancient dragon lord, who in return will make her more popular at school. Now everywhere she goes she is greeted by hissing cats and wilting flowers. And next time the school bullies come calling, she tears their souls apart. But Koichi has also been possessed, by a "kindly" spirit called Susano, although he (and anyone else who knows their JAPANESE FOLK TALES) has his doubts about who the good guys are, as the powerful beings fight an age-old war in modern Tokyo.

Despite a U.S. dub that adds to the suspense by not scrimping on the demonic voice effects, *Takegami* is a derivative tale of violent transformations that sits somewhere between GUYVER and SHUTENDOJI, with a dose of misogyny and lackluster fight scenes. Compare to LEGEND OF THE FOUR KINGS and DARK MYTH, which similarly retell ancient myth in a modern setting, but not as an excuse for getting into fights with girls. Reboxed in later years in the U.S. as just plain *Guardian of Darkness*. **NV**

TAKIZAWA, TOSHIFUMI

1953–. Born in Nagano Prefecture, Takizawa joined Tokyo Animation Film as an animator, soon moving on to Shin'ei Doga. He worked on CYBORG 009 and had his directorial debut working for Yoshiyuki Tomino on SPACE RUNAWAY IDEON. He subsequently went freelance.

TALE OF GENJI, THE *

1987. JPN: *Murasaki Shikibu Genji Monogatari*. AKA: *Murasaki Shikibu's Tale of Genji*. Movie. DIR: Gisaburo Sugii, Kimiharu Ono, Naoto Hashimoto. SCR: Tomomi Tsutsui. DES: Yasuhiro Nakura. ANI: Yasuo Maeda, Masahiko Murata, Masayuki, Yoshiyuki

Sadamoto, Minoru Maeda, Mahiro Maeda. MUS: Haruomi Hosono. PRD: Tac, Herald. 110 mins.

Hikaru Genji, son of Japan's Kiritsubo Emperor, is a brilliant and gifted young man stifled by the conventions of Heian court life, which offers no real outlet for his talent and energy except the arts and illicit love affairs. He is also haunted by memories of his mother, Lady Kiritsubo, who died when he was very young. He falls in love with his father's consort, Fujitsubo, but his own wife, Lady Aoi, and another lover, Lady Rokujo, will not give him up. The battle for sole possession of his heart is at the core of this film; despite being fought with courtly grace, it's a vicious and ultimately fatal contest, observed by the child Murasaki Shikibu, an orphan in Genji's care who will later become one of his loves.

Facetiously advertised as a "faithful adaptation" of Murasaki Shikibu's 11th-century novel, *ToG* was commissioned to mark the centenary of the *Asahi Shinbun* newspaper and the minor anniversaries for some of its affiliates. It unsurprisingly ditches most of the 1,000-page original, concentrating on a love triangle that formed just chapters 4–10 out of a total of 54. Though highly compromised by a recognizably modern script featuring several anachronisms of manner and etiquette, it is nevertheless a brave representation of the *spirit* of the original, and it is as stylistically rich as THE SENSUALIST. Sometimes, however, its attempt to be faithful can backfire—most notably in the confusingly "real" predominance of black hair, demonstrating all too well why so many anime prefer to differentiate characters with brighter colors and styles. Director Sugii takes enormous risks with pacing, composition, and narrative flow; he utilizes early computer graphics and live-action footage of flames and cherry blossoms. Many scenes are composed of static shots, and the exquisite delicacy of the imagery is given plenty of time to sink in—this film is *slow*. Heavy with the beauty and mood of a vanished age, the hothouse emotions of the court reflect Genji's own emotional turmoil, somewhat ill-served by a TRANSLATION and U.S. release that plays up the original's classical credentials but shies from offering any notes on the surviving poetic allusions. However, the true value of *ToG* does not lie in its relation to the original book at all but in its position as one of the small number of available anime that demonstrate the true diversity of the medium. Composer Hosono was one-third of the Yellow Magic Orchestra with Ryuichi Sakamoto and Yukihiro Takahashi. An erotic pastiche, "Bareskin Gen-chan," appeared as one of the stories in the historical porn series *Classical Sex-Zone* (1988). An unrelated 11-episode TV adaptation, *Genji Monogatari Sennenki* (2009, *Millennial Anniversary Tale of Genji*), was directed by Osamu Dezaki and was able to cram in marginally more of the incidents from the novel.

TALE OF HIKARI

1986. JPN: *Hikari no Densetsu*. TV series. DIR: Tomomi Mochizuki, Shinya Sadamitsu, Toriyasu Furusawa, Tetsuya Komori, Hirotsugu Hamazaki. SCR: Hideki Sonoda, Mayori Sekijima, Mami Watanabe, Yasushi Hirano. DES: Toyoko Hashimoto, Ammonite. ANI: Chuichi Iguchi. MUS: Koji Kawamura. PRD: Tatsunoko, TV Asahi. 30 mins. x 19 eps.
Teenage gymnast Hikari struggles to succeed in bitter rivalry with school supergymnast Diana Groichiva. A typical SPORTS ANIME in the tradition of AIM FOR THE ACE, the series was taken off the air before finishing the standard 26-episode run despite injecting a contrived romance with a young rock star. Based on the 1985 manga in *Comic Margaret* by Izumi Aso.

TALE OF THE NINJA RYUKEN

1991. JPN: *Ninja Ryuken Den*. AKA: *Ninja Ryu: the Dragon Sword Story*. Video. DIR: Mamoru Kanbe, Minoru Okazaki. SCR: Katsuhiko Nobe. DES: Satoshi Horiuchi. ANI: Satoshi Horiuchi. MUS: Toshiya Okuda. PRD: Studio Juno. 50 mins.
The scene is New York, where bioresearcher Ned Freidman announces a cure for cancer, although there are rumors of strange goings-on—screams are heard from his house, and large crates are transported from there to his laboratory. Modern-day ninja Ryu, along with CIA operative Robert and his team, go to investigate. But Ryu is really the avatar of ancient dragon gods, and this is only another stage in the eternal battle between good and evil.

Based on the video game known in the U.S. as *Ninja Gaiden*, *TNR*'s action is its biggest selling point. The beginning of the story, a running midnight brawl, is fluid and well depicted, with no dialogue, just the sound of footsteps and blade on blade. The characterization can be strange—if presenting feisty game character Irene as quiet and shy seems a contradiction in terms, making her a CIA operative scared to fire a gun is downright silly. There's an underdeveloped romantic subplot, and Robert gets more emphasis than game stars Ryu and Irene, as well as the video's best line, "Men love three things. We love fighting, we love alcohol, and we love women." **Ⓥ**

TALE OF THE PRINCESS KAGUYA, THE *

2013. JPN: *Kaguya-hime no Monogatari*. Movie. DIR: Isao Takahata. SCR: Isao Takahata, Riko Sakaguchi. DES: Kazuo Oga. ANI: Osamu Tanabe, Maiko Ueno. MUS: Joe Hisaishi. PRD: Studio Ghibli. 137 mins.
Okina, an elderly bamboo-cutter, discovers a tiny child in a bamboo stalk. He takes her home to his childless wife and names her Princess. If the nature of her discovery were not clue enough of magical origins, she soon grows with supernatural speed to become a beautiful young woman. Okina discovers gold dust and lavish clothing in the bamboo grove, and decides that they are his adoptive daughter's heavenly dowry.

Determined to live the good life, Okina moves his family to the city, where they are soon besieged by suitors, including the emperor himself. Princess, however, yearns for the simplicity of the country life that her parents have all-too-readily left behind.

Isao Takahata's first film in 14 years, loaded with references to his long career and his musings about the onset of old age, *The Tale of the Princess Kaguya* was swamped at the box office by the publicity and attention for his colleague Hayao Miyazaki's own grand finale, THE WIND RISES. The authors suspect that either production delays or its bloated running time ruined producer Toshio Suzuki's last great plan, to release both films on the same bill, closing the circle that began with GRAVE OF THE FIREFLIES and MY NEIGHBOR

TOTORO and guaranteeing the high-brow Takahata a share of Miyazaki's departing ticket sales. Instead, *TotPK* limped out four months later than its stablemate, to a lackluster reception, despite the assertion of many critics that it would ultimately be regarded as the better film. The cynical critic might suggest that Ghibli did everything it could to prove to itself and the public that it didn't need a Miyazaki (any Miyazaki) to produce a blockbuster, even to the extent of replacing the original intended composer with long-time Miyazaki collaborator Joe Hisaishi. But with Japanese box office takings of just $22 million against *The Wind Rises*' $135 million, the winner was clear.

Drawing on *Taketori Monogatari* (JAPANESE FOLK TALES), but also on the town-and-country divide central to his landmark HEIDI, Takahata's film eschews naturalism in favor of impressionistic line-work—this is animation that luxuriates in its animated status, ready to smudge backgrounds and shut out the real world in symbolic representations of its heroine's inner thoughts.

TALES FOR SLEEPLESS NIGHTS

1992. JPN: *Hara Yuko Nemurenu Yoru no Chiisana Ohanashi*. AKA: *Yuko Hara's Small Stories for Sleepless Nights*. Video. DIR: Kimiharu Ono. SCR: Eto Mori. DES: Shinji Nomura. ANI: Shinji Nomura. MUS: Yuko Hara. PRD: Group Tac, Victor Music Production. 33 mins. x 3 eps.
Three videos about cats—*Cat's Best Friend*, *Cat's Adventure*, and *Cat's Christmas*—each containing three smaller stories of feline fun. Based on a 1989 column in *Monthly Kadokawa* magazine by Yuko Hara, better known as the keyboard player/vocalist with the Southern All-Stars. In 1995, the videos were reedited for a cinema release, distinguished in records only by the addition of a star in between the creator's name and the rest of the title.

TALES FROM EARTHSEA *

2006. JPN: *Gedo Senki*. AKA: *Ged's Chronicle; Wizard of Earthsea*. Movie. DIR: Goro Miyazaki. SCR: Goro Miyazaki, Keiko Niwa. DES: Akihiko Yamashita. ANI: Takeshi Inamura. MUS: Tamiya Terashima. PRD: Studio Ghibli. 116 mins.
In a world where a mystical "balance" is apparently awry, Prince Arren kills his kingly father and goes on the run.

Captured by slavers, he is rescued by the wizard Sparrowhawk, who is investigating a series of portents that threaten the fabric of the universe and alter human behavior. Recuperating on a farm owned by Sparrowhawk's friend Tenar and her adopted daughter Therru, Arren confesses his crime and leaves, pursued by a doppelgänger. The slave-master Hare abducts Tenar and takes her to the fortress of Lord Cob, a sorcerer who is attempting to gain immortality, at the cost of the physical integrity of the known world. Cob tricks Arren into revealing his true name, thereby putting him under his power and inciting him to fight against Sparrowhawk. Therru, however, learns Arren's true name from his doppelgänger, and uses it to restore control over him. Cob attempts to kill Therru, but she transforms back into her true form, a dragon, and destroys him.

An adaptation of Ursula K. LeGuin's acclaimed *Earthsea* books, in particular the third volume, *The Farthest Shore*, *Tales from Earthsea* was controversially directed by a man whose former qualifications in the anime world had extended to being the director of the Studio Ghibli museum and, perhaps more handily, being the son of Hayao Miyazaki. Beginning with a patricide, and propelled by an underlying, vague eschatology suggesting that if motivations and actions don't make sense, that's *because* the world is falling apart, *Tales from Earthsea* forms another iteration in the tense handover of power between the founders of Studio Ghibli and a younger generation that eternally fails to live up to their legacy. The power behind the throne on *Tales from Earthsea* is the producer, Toshio Suzuki, seemingly acting on the findings of a survey that rated the surname Miyazaki as a more powerful brand than the name Studio Ghibli itself (**RATINGS AND BOX OFFICE**). His decision to put a Miyazaki, *any* Miyazaki, in charge of the film was hence greeted with some controversy, which Suzuki milked by leaking apocryphal gossip about a father/son falling-out. The younger Miyazaki certainly has a few bones to pick with his father, who was not only supposedly absent during his childhood making cartoons for everybody's else's kids like **PANDA GO PANDA**, but who also collaborated with his mother on a child-rearing book that documented

Goro's childhood for public scrutiny. The elder Miyazaki also set impossibly high standards that nobody else in Japan has managed to meet, making an unfavorable comparison a foregone conclusion, and dooming his son to pick up the Worst Director and Worst Film prizes at the Japanese equivalent of the Raspberry Awards, doled out by a public that justifiably felt it was being "handled." Matters were not helped by a hurt and negative review by LeGuin herself, who complained that she had sold the film rights to the studio that made **MY NEIGHBOR TOTORO**, only to discover that the project had been handed over to a man who had trained as a landscape gardener. This, too, is somewhat unfair, since the elder Miyazaki had tried to get the rights to *Earthsea* 20 years earlier, only to be rebuffed by LeGuin who had never heard of him; had she done her homework, he might have made this film himself instead of **KIKI'S DELIVERY SERVICE**.

Unsurprisingly, *Tales from Earthsea* is a minor Ghibli work, displaying little of the elder Miyazaki's magic, although only a fool would have expected anything more. If anything, it is somewhat more cartoony than earlier Ghibli works, with a character's "awful disfigurement" that seems more tasteful and carefully placed than some starlets' tattoos, and an over-saturated color scheme that sits uneasily with the naturalism of traditional Ghibli skies and backgrounds. It would have passed without notice in the anime canon were it not for the pedigree of its origins and its director, and the incitement of its own marketers to make that, rather than the film itself, the story. Suzuki's gambit to keep the brand alive worked to some extent and was extended in Goro Miyazaki's next film, **FROM UP ON POPPY HILL**, which was cowritten by his father.

TALES OF … *

1990. JPN: *Konai Shasei*. AKA: *Pictures from High School, The Tales Trilogy*. Video. DIR: Toshiyuki Sakurai, Takamasa Ikegami. SCR: Toshiyuki Sakurai. DES: Yuji Moriyama, Kinji Yoshimoto, Satoshi Urushihara. ANI: Yuji Moriyama, Kinji Yoshimoto, Satoshi Urushihara, Satoshi Hirayama. Masamune Ochiai. MUS: Takeshi Yasuda. PRD: Studio Fantasia. 40 mins. x 3 eps.
Barefaced and bawdy anime porn based

on short manga from **SAKURA DIARIES**– creator U-Jin. Broken into several short tableaux, it includes the infamous spoof **ULTRAMAN** episode where a giant businessman humps skyscrapers until a giant schoolgirl helps him out. It's the one with the naughty nurse looking for a soft spot in a bodybuilder, the college girls who will do absolutely *anything* for a free pizza, and the little match-girl who turns out to be the Ghost of Christmas Porn. Humor is the order of the day, with pastiches of **AIM FOR THE ACE** and **ASTRO BOY**—U-Jin is not afraid to laugh at himself, and at other dirty old men. His male characters are pathetic, hormonal losers in thrall to capricious little minxes. Everybody is desperate for sex, although, in a refreshing change from the rape fantasies that characterize so much anime porn, almost everybody has a good time. Strangely, the U.S. distributor has switched the running order, so that the second Japanese release is actually the first in the translated version. This means that the salaryman we see growing into a giant monster and being destroyed in "Sailor Warrior Akko" is inexplicably brought back from the dead for his cameo role on the train in "Lusty Long-Distance Commute." But since this anime is still on sale in Japan 11 years after its original release, whereas lesser erotica are swiftly deleted, such minor continuity bloopers are unlikely to put off the U.S. audience. Released in America as *Tales of Misbehavior, Tales of Titillation,* and *Tales of Sintillation.* The unrelated *Tales of Seduction* was a 2004 retitling of the anime filed in this book as **U-JIN BRAND**. Salacious punning fans may like to observe that the Japanese title, *konai shasei*, can also be read as "oral ejaculation." **Ⓝ**

TALES OF ETERNIA *

2001. TV series. DIR: Shigeru Ueda, Takeshi Nagasawa, Satoshi Sato. SCR: Hiroyuki Kawasaki, Satoru Nishizono, Katshuiko Takayama. DES: Akihisa Maeda, Mutsumi Inomata. ANI: Akihisa Maeda, Miko Nakajima. MUS: N/C. PRD: Xebec, Production I.G, WOWOW. 25 mins. x 13 eps.
Inferia and Celestia are in the midst of a religious war, which the locals (with the arrogance of religious fanatics everywhere) call the Extreme Light War. As diplomacy breaks down and things get

nasty, a young girl meets three teenagers near the borders of Inferia. She is Meldy, a Celestian, and according to her, both countries face a disaster called Grand Fall if they don't stop fighting. Eighteen-year-old Lid Harshel and his 17-year-old friends, Keal Zaibel and Fara Elstead, agree to help her, and together they set off for Belcarnu, legendary isle of everlasting summer, in search of a solution. Based on the PlayStation RPG of the same name, a follow-up to *Tales of Fantasia* and *Tales of Destiny*, the series credits Toshinori Otsuki as "Exclusive Production Director." No, we don't know what that means, either.

TALES OF HANS CHRISTIAN ANDERSEN *

1968. JPN: *Andersen Monogatari*. AKA: *Andersen Tales; The World of Hans Christian Andersen*. Movie, TV series. DIR: Kimio Yabuki (m), Masami Hata, Ichiro Fujita, Taku Sugiyama, Noboru Ishiguro, Makura Saki (pseudonym for Osamu Dezaki), Satoshi Dezaki (TV). SCR: Hisashi Inoue, Morihisa Yamamoto (m), Yoshiaki Yoshida, Shunichi Yukimuro, Eiichi Tachi, Koji Ito, Haruya Yamazaki, Seiji Matsuoka, Takeyuki Kanda, Keisuke Fujikawa. DES: Reiji Koyama (m), Toshihide Takeuchi, Shuichi Seki, Keiichi Makino (TV). ANI: Akira Daikuhara (m), Masami Hata. Shuichi Seki (TV). MUS: Seiichiro Uno (both). PRD: Toei (m), Zuiyo (Nippon Animation), Fuji TV. 80 mins. (m), 25 mins. x 52 eps. (TV).

Toei's 1968 movie interweaves the most famous of Andersen's stories into a Disneyesque musical around the tale of young Hans trying to get a ticket for the opera and gradually discovering his talent for telling stories. It focuses particularly on *The Red Shoes* and *The Little Match Girl*. A 73-minute version was dubbed for U.S. release as *The World of Hans Christian Andersen* (1971). Toei would mine Andersen's works for two further movies, LITTLE MERMAID and a version of THUMBELINA in 1978.

The 1971 TV series, also entitled *Andersen Monogatari*, retold many of the best-loved fairy tales collected by the Danish author, some in a single episode and some as an extended tale over several episodes. It employs the framing device of Candy, a girl who wishes to enter the Magic University and must collect 100 cards to do so by performing 100 good deeds—one shudders to think at the uses to which such a concept would be put post-POKÉMON. The large number of different staff members were encouraged to vary their styles (see JAPANESE HISTORY). This led to a wide range of looks and moods (some episodes are lighthearted, some darker) and some interesting stylistic experimentation. Compare to GRIMMS' FAIRY TALES.

TALES OF PHANTASIA *

2005. JPN: *Tales of Phantasia: The Animation*. Video. DIR: Takuo Tominaga, Shinjiro Shigeki. SCR: Ryunosuke Kingetsu. DES: Kosuke Fujishima. ANI: Noriyuki Matsutake. MUS: N/C. PRD: Namco, Geneon, Actus, Frontier Works. 30 mins. x 4 eps.

Warrior Cless Alvein is sent back in time to confront Dhaos, an evil sorcerer imprisoned by his parents. He is accompanied by Mint Adnade, a girl who has mastered the arts of healing, and a number of other companions forming an archetypal (dare we suggest, stereotypical) party of adventurers. As the character roster suggests, this is based on a role-playing game, in this case the long-running *Tales* ... series that began in 1995 with the Super Famicom (SNES) game of the same name. TALES OF ETERNIA is based on a later game in the same series.

TALES OF SYMPHONIA

2007. JPN: *Tales of Symphonia THE ANIMATION Sylvarant-hen*. AKA: *Tales of Symphonia The Animation: Sylvarant Chapter*. Video. DIR: Haruo Sotozaki. SCR: Ryunosuke Kingetsu. DES: Akira Matsushima, Hiromichi Ito. ANI: Akira Matsushima. MUS: Zizz Studio, Jin Aketagawa. PRD: ufotable, Frontier Works, Geneon. 33 mins. x 4 eps. (v1), 4 mins. (v2 special), 40 mins. x 4 eps. (v2), 6 mins. x 4 eps. (v2 special), 36 mins. x 3 eps. (v3), 6 mins. x 3 eps. (v3 special).

On the world of Sylvarant, a Chosen One is sent on a quest to reawaken the world's spirit and become its angel. Colette Brunel, the Chosen of Sylvarant, sets out on her journey with two good friends. Along the way she learns more strange and disquieting truths about the World Regeneration she is trying to achieve. Two worlds exist in balance: for Sylvarant to flourish, the other must perish. Do they have the right to endanger Tethe'alla, even to save their own world?

The *Tales of Symphonia (ToS)* anime franchise is part of a much larger one, based on the successful fantasy role-playing computer game by Namco (now Bandai Namco). This too is only a subfranchise of the *Tales of ...* series of computer games, which includes TALES OF PHANTASIA, *Eternity, Destiny, Rebirth* and VESPERIA, to name but a few. Unless they share a title, the games and anime are unrelated in story terms, each title presenting a different world but with a similar approach to storytelling and gameplay.

The *ToS* game was designed by Takashi Hasegawa with characters by Kosuke Fujishima (OH MY GODDESS!) and music by prolific game, anime, TV, and prog-rock composer Motoi Sakuraba. The anime forms a self-contained story arc based on the 2005 spin-off manga by Hitoshi Ichimura. The game included movie cut scenes animated by Gainax, and although ufotable's work on the anime isn't quite up to that standard, it is fluid, smooth, and convincing. The backgrounds are attractive, representing the world of the game well, which is, after all, the main function of this anime. The battles are rather disappointing: short and lacking in intensity and action. Character development can't really deliver many surprises, since the characters have to stay largely within their game confines.

In 2010 another four-part DVD series *ToS: Telle'atha Episode* (*Telle'atha-hen*) continues the story of Collette and her friends as they try to save both worlds. The DVD also featured four six-minute specials in which the characters chat about enhancing their roles in the show. This followed on from *ToS: Professor Kratos' Private Lesson* (*Kratos-sensei no Private Lesson*), the four-minute special added to the special DVD editions of *Sylvarant Chapter*, in which characters gave a short history of the world of *ToS*. The three-part *United Worlds Episode* (*Sekai Togohen*) wrapped up this story arc in 2011, with three more six-minute specials as DVD extras. **◑**

TALES OF THE ABYSS *

2008. TV series. DIR: Kenji Kodama. SCR: Akemi Omode. DES: Yoshihito Hishinuma, Junya Ishigaki, Shigemi Ikeda. ANI: Kazuchika Kise. MUS: Motoi Sakuraba. PRD: Sunrise, Bandai Visual, MBS, Namco. 25 mins. x 26 eps.

Luke is the spoiled and overprotected son of a noble house. His family's attitude is understandable: he was kidnapped seven years before the story starts and returned with absolutely no memory of anything before, even having to learn to walk all over again. Occasionally, a strange voice in his head calls to him, and as he grows up he yearns for a taste of freedom and adventure. When a woman breaks into his home to assassinate him, he gets his wish in a most unexpected way. Luke is about to find out more about himself, his family, and the world beyond his ancestral home …

The Namco role-playing computer game *Tales of the Abyss* (*TotA*) was released in 2005 to celebrate the tenth anniversary of the *Tales of …* gaming franchise, which includes TALES OF SYMPHONIA. Eighth in the series, with character designs by Kosuke Fujishima and music by Motoi Sakuraba, Shinji Tamura, and Moto Fujiwara, it included an abundance of comical skits as well as cut-scenes during gameplay. A manga version of *TotA* with art by Rei followed the game in 2006, with two more manga launched in 2009 as the TV series was coming to an end.

In visual terms, the series is an interesting change of pace from *Tales of Symphonia*. The characters, based on Fujishima's designs but reworked for animation, are broadly similar in style but the world is more baroque, with some interesting mecha concepts and art (SCIENCE FICTION AND ROBOTS). Unfortunately the plot focuses too closely on replaying scenes from the game, regardless of pace or clarity, and there are a number of unexplained and unresolved threads that may make perfect sense if you've played *TotA* but exclude the rest of us. **NV**

TALES OF THE STREET CORNER *

1962. JPN: *Aru Machikado no Monogatari*. Movie. DIR: Eiichi Yamamoto. SCR: Osamu Tezuka. DES: Osamu Tezuka. ANI: Shigeyuki Hayashi (Rintaro), Masaharu Mitsuyama, Tetsuro Amino, Gisaburo Sugii. MUS: Tatsuo Takai. PRD: Mushi Pro. 38 mins.

Posters on a street corner each tell their own story—a circus poster and several advertisements briefly come to life, and a pianist and a violinist from separate pictures fall in love. Meanwhile, a little

girl in a nearby garret apartment loses her doll, which finds a new friend in the mouse, playing in the gutter, who saves it from being swept away in a rainstorm. Military posters are slapped over the peacetime images, and the buildings are destroyed by enemy bombs. However, in the aftermath, the girl, the mouse, and her doll are all safe, and the military posters have blown away, revealing the originals underneath. There is no dialogue; the film tells its stories visually and notably in a limited animation form (TECHNOLOGY AND FORMATS), debunking the apocryphal story that Tezuka's first limited-animation production was the later ASTRO BOY. *Tales of the Street Corner* also relies to some extent on the limitations of *exhibition* at the time it was made, in that it was seemingly designed, like PIGGYBACK GHOST, to impress audiences at a single screening and then to do its job promoting its studio through attractive stills in brochures. Certainly, it does not hold up to prolonged scrutiny in the cold, repeatable light of the video age, but it was never intended to. Released in the U.S. on DVD as part of *The Astonishing Work of Tezuka Osamu* (2009). See also STREET CORNER FAIRYTALES.

TALES OF THICK-NECKED GEN AND I *

2010. JPN: *Ago Nashi Gen to Ore Monogatari*. TV series. DIR: N/C. SCR: N/C. DES: N/C. ANI: N/C. MUS: N/C. PRD: Bee Train. 8 mins. x 24 eps.

Gen is a hairy, thick-necked 30-something guy who runs a small shipping company and lives in an ordinary apartment house. He has absolutely nothing special about him, but he keeps trying to succeed in life, and with his pretty neighbor Haruko, even though he's doomed to fail.

This slice-of-life gag manga for ordinary working guys has been transferred to the screen as an EVERYDAY ANIME with the absolute minimum of animation—pans across frames, cut-out figures, occasional colored backgrounds, minimal sound effects, and lines from the manga read by actors. But since it was intended for an extremely small screen—the mobile phone—and for a non-geek audience, its technical shortcomings are irrelevant. Akira Hiramoto's 1998 manga was still running when it was adapted for mobile phone streaming channel BeeTV a decade on. It's not his only

work to attract attention: a live-action version of his erotic gag manga about young women, *Tales of the Over-the-Top Companion and I (Yarisugi Companion to Atashi Monogatari*—or if you prefer British vernacular—*Me and My Mad Mate)*, was made in 2011, and *Me and the Devil Blues*—the heavily fictionalized life of Delta bluesman Robert Leroy Johnson—was published in America in 2005. He's another of the galaxy of successful creators most Western fans have never heard of.

TALES OF VESPERIA: THE FIRST STRIKE *

2009. Movie. DIR: Kanta Kamei. SCR: Reiko Yoshida. DES: Tokuyuki Matsutake, Hiroshi Ono. ANI: Kazuchika Kise, Takuya Saito, Toshihisa Kaya. MUS: Akira Senju. PRD: Production I.G, Bandai Visual, Bandai Namco. 110 mins.

Ten years after a great war, the people of the planet Terca Lumireis use a powerful and mysterious substance called *aer* to help them fight off monsters and maintain human life. Yuri and Flynn, childhood acquaintances who have just joined up as knights, are taken under the wing of their corps leader Niren. Under his guidance their rookie enthusiasm is tempered and their friendship matures.

The *Tales of Vesperia* (*ToV*) game, tenth in the Namco *Tales of …* series, was released in Japan and the U.S.A. in 2008. The movie is a prequel to the game story. The plot is basic enough that any experienced gamer or fantasy reader will be able to predict it, but engaging and energetic enough to keep most entertained. Those who have played the *Tales of Vesperia* game will meet a number of new characters in the anime, though most, it must be said, are not extensively developed.

Production I.G has done its usual excellent job. The excellence would be almost monotonous if the results were not so utterly bewitching every time. The images are crisp, fluid, and gorgeous. The character and background designs carry echoes of Studio Ghibli, enhanced by the European feel of many of the buildings and settings, although here the influence is Spanish, rather than the North European cities loved by Hayao Miyazaki. The pacing, too, carries echoes of some Ghibli movies—it's leisurely, letting its scenarios evolve. Action sequences are well handled, but the overall feeling is one of evolving the storyline rather than rushing from one set piece fight to another. Fans of the game will find plenty to enjoy, but so will those who aren't.

TALES OF YAJIKITA COLLEGE
1991. JPN: *Yajikita Gakuen Dochuki*. Video. DIR: Osamu Yamasaki, Yoshihisa Matsumoto. SCR: Ayumu Watanabe. DES: Minoru Yamazawa. ANI: Minoru Yamazawa. MUS: Nobuhiko Kajiwara. PRD: JC Staff. 40 mins. x 2 eps. Forbidden love triangles at Mura'ame College, as Junko and Reiko become involved with boys they shouldn't, then discover that they are the last inheritors of the secrets of the ninja. Your average, everyday mix of romance and assassins, based on the 1982 girls' manga in *Bonita* magazine by Ryoko Shito.

TAMA AND FRIENDS *
1994. JPN: SAN-CHOME NO TAMA: *Uchi no Tama Shirimasen ka*. AKA: TAMA OF THIRD STREET: *Have You Seen/Do You Know My Tama?* TV series, movie. DIR: Hiroshi Takefuji, Kiyoko Sayama (TV), Hitoshi Nanba (m). SCR: Masumi Hirayanagi, Shige Sotoyama. DES: N/C. ANI: N/C. MUS: Michiko Yamakawa. PRD: Sony, TBS. 12 mins. x 36 eps. (TV), 40 mins. (m). Puppies and kittens hang out together in an infants' playground, where they get involved in numerous saccharine adventures. Tama, Doozle, Tiggle, and Momo then "share in fun-filled adventures that impart important social values." The anime was aimed at the very young and marketed in Japan as a kind of "Where's Waldo?"—its posters demanding "Have You Seen My Tama?" That it was optioned and "re-imagined" for broadcast in the U.S. by 4Kids almost makes one wish for the days of tentacle porn once more.

TAMA PRODUCTION
An animation house set up by Eiji Tanaka, a former employee of Mushi Production, Tama Pro became a limited company in 1970. It subsequently relocated much of its animation work to studios in China, particularly Shanghai in 1996. The studio also did minor work on foreign productions, such as the straight-to-video *American Tail: Mystery of the Night Monster* (1999). By 2008 the company was inactive, although

its debts carried on without it; it was declared bankrupt in 2011 by an act of the Tokyo court.

TAMAGOTCHI VIDEO ADVENTURES *
1997. JPN: *Eiga Tamagotchi Honto no Hanashi*. AKA: *True Tamagotchi Tales*. TV series. DIR: Masami Hata, Mitsuo Hashimoto. SCR: Hideki Mitsui. DES: Kenji Watanabe, Hideki Inoue. ANI: Kenji Watanabe. MUS: N/C. PRD: Bandai, Fuji TV. 9 mins. x 2 mins. 88 mins. (m1), 89 mins. (m2), 3 mins. x 12 eps. (TV, *Let's Go*), 15 mins. x 85 eps. (TV, *Tamagotchi!*), 25 mins. x 49 eps. (TV, *Yume Kira Dream*).
The Tamagotchi Museum doesn't have a display from Earth, so a group of Tamagotchi friends decide to go and collect appliances and artifacts from our world to make a display before the Great Gotchi realizes there isn't one. A blatant cash-in broadcast on Japanese TV in the wake of the Tamagotchi "virtual pet" boom, which combined the get-a-life-factor of pet rocks with the sonic irritation of other people's mobile phones. They were a brief fad in the mid-1990s, soon superseded by their "third generation" fighting versions, the DIGIMON. Both, however, were trounced in the marketplace by the multimedia phenomenon of Nintendo's POKÉMON.

Regardless, the franchise limps on in support of later editions of the toys, now numbering some 80 million, with iterations including two *Tamagotchi* movies in 2007 and 2008, and the TV serials *Let's Go Tamagotchi* (2009), just plain *Tamagotchi!* (also 2009), and *Tamagotchi: Yume Kira Dream* (2012).

TAMAKO MARKET *
2013. TV series. DIR: Naoko Yamada. SCR: Reiko Yoshida, Michiko Yokote, Jukki Hanada. DES: Yukiko Horiguchi. ANI: Yukiko Horiguchi, Nobuaki Maruki, Futoshi Nishiya, Kazumi Ikeda. MUS: Tomoko Kataoka. PRD: Kyoto Animation. 24 mins. x 12 eps. (TV), 83 mins. (m).
Tamako Kitashirakawa is the daughter of a traditional *mochi* (rice cake) maker. She is visited by Dera, a talking bird from a South Sea island, sent to Japan to find a bride for a local potentate. Dera, however, elects to stay, swiftly growing fat on rice cakes, and observing the idiosyncratic lives and

struggles of Tamako's Usagiyama shopping district.

Based on a manga by **K-ON** creator Kakifly, *Tamako Market* reunites his work with many of the same team who adapted *K-On*, albeit without much of *K-On*'s sense of purpose. Despite being crowded with pretty girls in a sop to the *moe* audience (ARGOT AND JARGON), the overarching narrative of the show is focused more on girls' choices over boys, as Dera comes to realize Tamako's secret love for the son of a rival *mochi*-making family, and his royal master inevitably comes to Japan in search of his putative bride. Like many EVERYDAY ANIME, the magical elements often seem like mere window-dressing for a wholly different subject—the sense of community to be found in local shopping districts, fast disappearing, in Japan as everywhere else, before a rising tide of homogenous shopping malls. A feature-length theatrical release, *Tamako Love Story* (2014), followed from the same team.

TAMALA 2010 *
2003. AKA: *A Punk Cat in Space*. Movie. DIR: Tol ("Tree of Life"). SCR: Tol. DES: Kentaro Nemoto, Tol. ANI: Kentaro Nomoto (2D), Michiro Tsutsumoto (3D CG). MUS: Homei Tanabe. PRD: Tol. 92 mins.
Orphan kitty Tamala heads off to Orion, much to the annoyance of her snake-charming human foster parent. En route, she finds herself in the city of Hate on Planet Q, where she befriends a cat called Michelangelo. Michelangelo later believes that Tamala has been murdered by Kentauros, an evil stalker who we also see sexually tormenting his pet mouse Penelope. Tamala, however, has a secret of her own, which is eventually revealed to Michelangelo by a maggot-infested zombie.

Loaded with ambient music, aimless vignettes, super-retro animation in a 1960s style, and highbrow bricolage, *Tamala 2010* has very little to do with punks, and much more to do with the art-house notion that audiences will be too afraid to say that something makes no sense. A well-known Japanese shipping company, whose logo is a cute little cat, once reputedly complained about the exploitation of their brand identity in KIKI'S DELIVERY SERVICE. Back then, their grievances were supposedly curtailed by making them coproducers.

But the same company is liable to be less than happy with *Tamala 2010*, which dares to suggest that a feline-themed postal service is really the modern-day front for an ancient cult of human sacrifice, which now lays waste in a different way, by encouraging the pointless consumption of worthless trash goods.

But *Tamala 2010* isn't quite as smart as it thinks it is. Like **HELLO KITTY** scripted by Samuel Beckett, with all the futile pretension that implies, it bolts together a series of random scenes, united only by grasping attempts to gain gravity by association. Visual and textual allusions abound, to everything from *Querelle* to **METROPOLIS**, **THE HAPPY PRINCE** to *2001: A Space Odyssey*, but beneath its knowing surfaces, *Tamala 2010* has little to say. Ultimately, it's a brilliant five-minute feline conspiracy thriller, ludicrously and counterproductively stretched to feature-length.

Shot primarily in a faux-monochrome that recalls *Felix the Cat*, its black and white frames are cunningly augmented with subtle spots of earthtones—browns, blues, and greens that give the film a surreal edge. There are also moments of computer graphics, color animation, and even a prolonged sequence of a real-life highway. *Tamala 2010* plays like the combined graduation shorts of a fine arts college, stuck in a blender and randomly reassembled. But if you want to put on a beret, stroke your goatee, sip espresso and tell the freshman semiotics class that it's all incredibly meaningful, then you'll help perpetuate the latest outing for the Emperor's new clothes.

One gets the impression that *Tamala 2010*'s makers realized this themselves, as much of what passes for "plot" is delivered in a rambling voice-over at the end of the movie, as if their tutor had told them they weren't going to get a grade at all unless they talked some sense. Until then, it comprises little more than self-conscious wackiness and an irritating feline ingenue, wandering through cheap animation that polite reviewers would call a triumph of irony. Since *Tamala 2010* soon gained its own merchandising line in the style of *Hello Kitty*, it is tempting to add that whatever worthy point its creators thought they were making has been well and truly blunted.

TAMAYURA

2010. Video, TV series. DIR: Junichi Sato. SCR: Junichi Sato, Reiko Yoshida, Yuka Yamada, Mamiko Ikeda, Tatsuhiko Urahata, Sayaka Harada. DES: Haruko Iizuka, Kenichi Tajiri. ANI: Masayuki Onchi, Hajime Watanabe, Kazunori Hashimoto. MUS: Nobuyuki Nakajima. PRD: Hal Film Maker, AT-X, BIGLOBE, McRAY, Shochiku, TYO Animations, Flying Dog. 20 mins. x 4 eps. (v), 25 mins. x 12 eps. (TV1), 24 mins. (v2), 24 mins. x 12 eps. (TV3). Fu Sawatari's father died five years ago, and she and her mother moved away from his old hometown. Now, entering her first year of high school, she moves back to Takehara, near Hiroshima, on Japan's Inland Sea (compare to **A LETTER TO MOMO**). She treasures her father's classic film camera, a Rollei 35S, and uses it to record her new life and the friends she makes as she settles back into the peaceful little town. Despite her shyness and clumsiness, she soon feels at home.

Sato, who also directed **ARIA**, brings the same sense of calm simplicity to this gentle **EVERYDAY ANIME** about the healing quality of mundane life. Nothing much happens. The characters don't change or develop much in the course of the first short series, but its charm and sweetness make a refreshing break from the hectic aggressiveness of much popular anime, like a weekend in a quiet seaside resort. It was popular enough to make the transition to TV in 2011 as *Tamayura—Hitotose*. TYO Animation took over animation duties from Hal Film Maker but the join is almost seamless. A second TV series, *Tamayura: More Aggressive*, followed in 2013.

TANSA 5

1979. JPN: *Kagaku Boken Tai Tansa 5*. AKA: *Science Adventure Command Tansa 5*. TV series. DIR: Shigeru Suzuki, Tameo Ogawa, Iku Suzuki, Kunihiko Okazaki, Osamu Sekita, Toshifumi Takizawa. SCR: Yoshihisa Araki, Sukehiro Tomita, Hiroyuki Hoshiyama, Tsunehisa Ito, Kenichi Matsuzaki, Takao Yotsuji, Yuji Watanabe. DES: Michiru Suzuki, DM Design. ANI: Michiru Suzuki. MUS: Goro Omi. PRD: Sunrise, TV Tokyo. 25 mins. x 33 eps. Tansa 5 is a five-member patrol team comprising Ryu, Daichi, Rui, Yumeto, and Hajime, whose Land, Aqua, and Sky Tansa vehicles can combine to form the predictably giant robot, Big Tansa. They also have the Time Tansa, a vehicle that allows them to travel an hour into the past, though they must return within their time limit or risk creating a paradox and leaving them lost forever. Their opponents are relics of the past—the forgotten civilization of Lemuria (see **SUPER ATRAGON**), found to be responsible for the statues on Easter Island—a handy ad for sister-company Bandai, which use the statues as the logo for its Emotion video range. In the tradition of team shows dating back to **BATTLE OF THE PLANETS**, one of the team members was doomed, in this case Yumeto, who was replaced halfway through the run by new team member Johnny.

TANSUWARASHI

2011. AKA: *Drawer Hobs*; *Drawer Kids*. Movie. DIR: Kazuchika Kise. SCR: Daishiro Tanimura. DES: Kazuchika Kise, Hiromasa Ogura. ANI: Toshihisa Kaya. MUS: Yasuo Sugibayashi. PRD: Production I.G. 23 mins. A *tansu* is an old-fashioned Japanese clothes chest or dresser, from the days when everyone's kimono could be folded flat and cedar or paulownia wood was a sensible choice to keep out moths. Not many city dwellers choose *tansu* nowadays: they're too big for many apartments. When office lady Noeru Hiragi receives an old dresser from her mother she gets an extra heirloom—the six goblin children who live in the chest, dedicated to the service of each generation of Higari women. They feel it is their hereditary duty to correct Noei's free-living ways and teach her to become a responsible adult and a fitting heir to her family tradition—compare to **A LETTER TO MOMO**. This charmingly simple movie is part of the 2010 Young Animators' Training Project, also known as *Anime Mirai*, an initiative funded by the Japanese Animation Creators' Association to give new talent a chance to work with top animators at a major studio.

TAOTAO THE PANDA

1981. JPN: *Shunmao (Xiong Mao) Monogatari Taotao*. AKA: *Panda Story Taotao*. Movie, TV series. DIR: Tatsuo Shimamura (m), Shuichi Nakahara, Kazuhiko Ikegami, Taku Sugiyama. SCR: Takeshi Takahashi (m), Keiji Kubota, Takeshi Shudo, Nobuko Morita, Osamu Kagami. DES: Shuichi Nakahara. ANI: Yusaku Sakamoto (m), Masao Kumagawa

(TV). MUS: Masaru Sato (m), Yasuo Tsuchida (TV). PRD: Shunmao, TV Osaka. 90 mins. (m), 25 mins. x 50 eps. (TV).

Chinese panda Taotao and his mate, Ang, are forced to flee when humans encroach on their natural habitat in Sichuan. Trapped and taken to a zoo in Europe, he becomes popular with the visitors, though animal psychologist Marie realizes that he is pining for his homeland. The first ever Sino-Japanese coproduction, this harks back to the panda boom of the 1970s (see **PANDA GO PANDA**) and was shown on a double bill with the live-action film *Tora-san's Promise* (see **TORA-SAN: THE ANIME**). Many of the same team went on to make the German coproduction *Taotao's Library—World Animal Stories* (1983, *Taotao Ehonkan Sekai Dobutsu Banashi*), in which a baby panda, coincidentally called Taotao, hears a number of stories at his mother's knee.

TAREPANDA

2000. AKA: *Lazy Panda; Papa Panda.* Video, TV series DIR: Takashi (aka Takashi Ui). SCR: N/C. DES: Hikaru Suemasa. ANI: Keitaro Mochizuki. MUS: N/C. PRD: Bandai Visual, San-X, Green Camel. 30 mins. (v), ca. 3 mins. x ca. 5 eps. (TV).

Tarepanda is a flat, lifeless panda, who excels at doing almost nothing. The slothful bear appears here in his own one-shot video, in which he is seen rescuing a Rapunzel bear, playing panda sumo, and racing in a very slow grand prix. The joke wears thin, however, when you realize you've just paid to watch a panda roll with tortuous slowness for several minutes, and that the "animation" ends all too soon to be replaced with an interview with the creature's creator and a live-action "Making Of" that shamelessly recycles much of the animation you've just seen. An obvious attempt by Bandai to seize some of the merchandising-led **HELLO KITTY** market— compare to the same company's **AFRO KEN**.

Designed in 1995 by Hikaru Suemasa for a range of character goods, Tarepanda was voted most popular toy in Japan in a 1999 magazine poll, and competitions to see how tall a stack could be built from his soft fabric body resulted in a record of 9.5 metres. In other words, to the delight of copyright owners San-X, a huge number of floppy little stuffed pandas were sold, and

this animated video was made, with a later TV series shown on Sony's Animax channel—although we believe that TV series to have comprised much of the footage already contained here, in short bursts.

TARI TARI *

2012. TV series. DIR: Masakazu Hashimoto. SCR: Masakazu Hashimoto, Michiko Yokote, Rika Sato. DES: Kanami Sekiguchi. ANI: Kanami Sekiguchi. MUS: Shiro Hamaguchi. PRD: PA Works, Dentsu, Good Smile Company, Infinite, Lantis, Bandai Visual, Shogate, Pony Canyon, Sotsu. 24 mins. x 13 eps.

Three mismatched schoolgirls form a Choir Club, in the hope that they can overcome their various identikit problems— childhood trauma, shyness, whatever. They are joined by two boys—one a shy badminton player, the other a recently returned transfer student, whose time in Austria has left him unfamiliar with Japanese customs. They battle all the usual obstacles of quirky teen clubs, including obstructive bureaucracy, disapproving teachers, and parental pressures. **K-ON** with choirs—they couldn't be bothered to think of anything new, so neither could we.

TARO MAEGAMI

1979. JPN: *Maegami Taro.* TV special. DIR: Hiroshi Saito. SCR: Akira Miyazaki. DES: Yoshiyuki Momose. ANI: Yoshiyuki Momose. MUS: Shinichi Tanabe. PRD: Nippon Animation, Fuji TV. 70 mins.

An elderly couple, childless through many years of love and sacrifice, is finally rewarded by the birth of a son whom they name Taro. Determined to help his impoverished home village, young Taro travels the world in search of the Water of Life, which legend says brings both peace and wealth. However, the water is guarded by an evil serpent which uses its powers as a weapon.

Based on the book by Miyoko Matsutani considered a children's masterpiece, this story was also adapted into another anime—**TARO THE DRAGON BOY**.

TARO THE DRAGON BOY *

1979. JPN: *Tatsu no Ko Taro.* AKA: *Taro the Dragon's Son.* Movie. DIR: Kirio Urayama. SCR: Kirio Urayama, Takashi Mitsui. DES: Yoichi Kotabe, Reiko Okuyama. ANI: Yoichi Kotabe, Yuji Endo, Osamu Kasai. MUS: Riichiro Ma-

nabe. PRD: Toei. 75 mins.

A young mountain boy named Taro searches for his mother who has been changed into a dragon. During his dangerous quest, he risks his own life to save others and fulfill his mission. Finally, Taro engages in a ferocious battle with the enchanted dragon. A beautifully animated film featuring animation from Kotabe, who also worked on the Miyazaki/Takahata **HEIDI**. Released on video in the U.S. in 1985, it was based on the same Miyoko Matsutani book adapted into **TARO MAEGAMI**, a TV special screened the following month. For another suspicious case of "simultaneous creation," see **THE WIZARD OF OZ**.

TATAMI GALAXY, THE *

2010. JPN: *Yojo Han Shinwa Taikei.* AKA: *4.5 Tatami Mythological Chronicles.* TV series. DIR: Masaaki Yuasa. SCR: Makoto Ueda, Masaaki Yuasa. DES: Nobutake Ito, Shinichi Uehara, Naruyo Kiriyama. ANI: Nobutake Ito. MUS: Michiru Oshima. PRD: Madhouse, Asmik Ace, Dentsu, Fuji TV, Kadokawa Hoten, SME, Toho. 25 mins. x 11 eps.

An unnamed third-year student at Kyoto University looks back on two years of college life, with not-always-helpful guidance from "god of matchmaking" Higuchi (compare to **SAKURA DIARIES**). Despite the number of possibilities opening up before him for the perfect campus life he dreamed of in high school, things always turn out unsatisfying in some way. With misdirection from his mischievous friend Ozu, and yearning to impress pretty but cold engineering student Akashi, he wanders down different paths to the same place. So what's a seeker of the perfect experience to do when time is running out and no experience turns out as he hopes?

Tomihiko Morimi's 2004 novel, set on the campus of Kyoto University, took an original approach to first-person reminiscence, lifting an idea from the replayable plotlines of computer games to show how different decisions might alter his hero's fate. A triumph of *what-if* speculation in the manner of **AMNESIA** or the "Endless Eight" time loop of **THE MELANCHOLY OF HARUHI SUZUMIYA**, each of the chapters of the novel takes place in a parallel universe in which the protagonist is enrolled in a different university society. The series echoes this adventurous approach to a degree unusual in TV anime. It was the first TV program to win the Japan Media Arts Festival Grand Prize for animation, the jury calling it a "richly expressive work that turns the limitations of TV on its head" with "unique scene layouts, characters' actions, and color scheme." The scope and daring of the design is certainly hard to match in other anime, and the cool, clever plot shows it off to perfection.

This is a seriously grown-up show that provides whizzing visual hamster wheels to distract and seduce, but encourages the viewer to look behind its glossy surfaces to the ideas they obscure. Its title refers to the size of the pokey "four-and-a-half mat" room in which the protagonist is doomed to spend his entire university life unless he goes out and does *something*, even if any decision comes accompanied by regrets about what might have been. If you want style over substance, you can choose it here; but *Tatami Galaxy* lets you have both. It may be Yuasa's best work, matching his tricksy artsy games with a scenario better than anything he's created so far. **L🐙**

TATSUNOKO PRODUCTION

Founded in 1964 by manga artist Tatsuo Yoshida with his brothers Kenji and Toyoharu (who used the pseudonym Ippei Kuri), Tatsunoko Pro soon established a reputation in influential television shows, including **Speed Racer** and **Battle of the Planets**. The company was famous for experimenting with new **Technology and Formats** and embraced xerography (machine-tracing), air-brush painting to aid with explosions, and transmitted light effects for the passage of bullets in its landmark **Animentary**. All these technical processes had more long-lasting applications in the realm of SF, where they were used to impart realistic robot action, the glows of rocket engines, and other soon-to-be-common tropes in **Science Fiction and Robots**. The studio has also established many sister companies and spin-off subsidiaries, including IG Tatsunoko, now better known as Production I.G. Notable staffers include Hiroshi Sasagawa, Hidehito Ueda, and Tetsuya Kobayashi. Many famous creators had their first break working for Tatsunoko, including illustrators such as Yoshitaka Amano and Akemi

Takada. The studio celebrated its 40th anniversary with the Madhouse-influenced **Karas**. The company's products are easily identified by its seahorse logo, a *tatsunoko* in Japanese being a "dragon's child," the word for a seahorse/seadragon, but also a reflection that the founding father of the company was "Tatsuo" Yoshida. Tatsunoko was bought in 2005 by the toy company Takara, but in 2014 was 54% owned by the channel NTV. Lesser board members include Production I.G, the talent agency Horipro, and Takara. See also Bee Train and Xebec.

TATTOON MASTER *

1996. Video. DIR: Kazuyuki Hirokawa. SCR: Yosuke Kuroda. DES: Hiroyoshi Iida. ANI: Hideki Araki. MUS: Harukichi Yamamoto. PRD: AIC, KSS. 30 mins. x 2 eps.

While his anthropologist mother is off studying the remote Tattoon tribe, Hibio (Eric) sulkily does the housework for his inept father, a pornographic filmmaker. He believes his mother to be dead, and she very nearly was, since she angered the Tattoons, who were ready to kill her. Unbeknownst to Hibio, his mother has bought her life by offering his hand in marriage to the Tattoon chieftainess Nima (Bala), who arrives in Tokyo weapons in hand, magical powers at the ready, and all set to marry him. This is not a welcome thought to the misogynist Hibio, whose sole experience of women has been his father's models, his feckless mother, and his militant feminist class president Fujimatsu (Lisa), a keen archer who carries her bow everywhere, and, for reasons utterly incomprehensible, wants Hibio for herself. Yet another alien-girl-adores-geek scenario, it traces a long line back to **Urusei Yatsura** but is sadly lacking any of its predecessor's virtues—a failed attempt to take the well-worn clichés in a new direction resulting in a uniformly unlikable cast. Based on a manga in *Ultra Jump* by Masahisa Tadanari.

TAYUTAMA: KISS ON MY DEITY *

2009. JPN: *Tayutama*. TV series. DIR: Keitaro Motonaga. SCR: Makoto Uezu, Hiro Akitsuki et al. DES: Haruo Ogawara, Kazuto Shimoyama. ANI: Haruo Ogawara. MUS: Shigenobu Okawa, Yutaka Minobe. PRD: SILVER LINK, 5pb., Marvelous Entertainment, Media Factory, Russell. 24 mins. x 12 eps.

Yuri Mito is an ordinary Japanese high school boy whose family are hereditary keepers of an ancient shrine. When he finds an ancient relic in the woods, a beautiful goddess appears and tells him to leave it alone, but despite his good intentions a magical seal is broken and a number of dangerous entities, called *tayuti*, are now loose in the world. Not only does Yuri have to resolve the war between these beings and get them back under control before anyone gets hurt, but he's suddenly acquired a divine fiancée and a harem (**Romance and Drama**) of other beauties. If you hear echoes of **Tenchi Muyo!** they're dim and distant ones. Kiss my deity, indeed: this anime adapted from the visual novel (**Argot and Jargon**) by Lump of Sugar is the mental equivalent of eating cotton candy until you're sick. It's not offensive, except to the intelligence of all women and most men, and it's not harmful in small quantities, but if you watch too many shows like this your brain will get fat and toothless. **🐙**

TBS, OR TOKYO BROADCASTING SYSTEM

TV channel originally established as "KRT" in 1955, and the original home of the *Adventures of Superman*, a foreign import that may have inspired rival channel Fuji TV to commission **Astro Boy** in competition. In more recent times it continues to fight Fuji TV for market share, often scheduling its own anime in direct opposition to its competitor. TBS screens anime in all three major blocks, early morning for the kids, prime time for an older audience, and in the graveyard shift for fans. The Mainichi Broadcasting System (MBS) is an affiliate of TBS, as is the *Mainichi Shinbun* newspaper.

TEACH ME PLEASE

2007. JPN: *Oshiete Re: Maid*. AKA: *Teach Me Please! Maid Re-education*. Video. DIR: ;p. SCR: Taifu Sekimachi. DES: Jun Hi. ANI: Noritomo Hattori. MUS: N/C. PRD: MS Pictures, Oshiete Re: Maid Production Committee. 30 mins. x 2 eps.

Four girls who have failed to fulfill their dream of graduating from maid academy and developing a close relationship with a master of their very own are given one last chance. Millionaire schoolboy Akito accepts a contract to have them live in his mansion for special training. If they can win his approval, they can all graduate. Never mind the pornography, the whole concept of this show is offensive on so many levels that it ought to win some kind of award. Based on a porn game by UNiSONSHIFT Accent. ◐

TEACHER TANK ENGINE
1996. JPN: *Kikansha Sensei*. Movie. DIR: Kozo Kusuba. SCR: Takuro Fukuda. DES: Shuichi Seki. ANI: Toshitsugu Saita. MUS: Kei Wakakusa. PRD: Nippon Animation. 100 mins.
A modern spin on BOTCHAN, as a clueless city boy becomes a supply teacher on a remote Japanese island, slowly gaining the trust of the canny locals. Based on a novel by Shizu Ijuin, the anime features live-action stars as many of the voices, including Yumi Adachi, Kin Sugai, and Shigeru Muroi, as well as the author himself.

TEACHER'S PET *
2000. JPN: *Natural*. Video. DIR: Kan Fukumoto. SCR: Fairy Tale. DES: Mizuki Sakisaka. ANI: Tadaji Tamori. MUS: N/C. PRD: Beam Entertainment, Green Bunny. 30 mins. x 2 eps. (v1), 30 mins. x 2 eps. (v2, *Another*), 30 mins. x 4 eps. (v3, *Duo*).
New teacher Haruhiko Shimotsuki comes home to find pretty student Chitose Misawa in his apartment, offering herself and her undying love to him. Naturally he takes her up on her proposal, though matters are complicated by the fact that she is the younger sister of his ex-girlfriend Mariko, by the covert nature of their relationship, and his insistence on training her as his sex slave in time-honored S/M fashion.

In *Natural Another*, the direct sequel (issued in America with *Natural* under the title *Teacher's Pet*), Haruhiko further complicates matters by sleeping with another student and by accepting his colleague "Professor" Takagi's (this taking place per the English TRANSLATION at a "college") advances, only to abuse her in the same fashion as Chitose, all in the name of breaking their wills to comply with his. Still, this is one of the better instances of the "training" genre of erotic anime, if only because the participants are (mostly) willing, the training mostly refrains from physical violence (emotional violence is

another matter) and bodily fluids, and the production values are relatively high (as is to be expected from Green Bunny). These episodes were followed by *Natural2 Duo* and were based on the games by F&C. Not to be confused with Izumi Aso's 1989 romantic manga of the same name. ◐

TEARS TO TIARA *
2009. TV series. DIR: Tomoki Kobayashi. SCR: Ryo Tamura. DES: Masahiko Nakata, Izumi Hoki. ANI: Masahiko Nakata. MUS: Takayuki Hattori. PRD: Oriental Light and Magic, WHITE FOX, Bushiroad, Dwango, Good Smile Company, Hakuhodo DY Media Partners, Lantis, MOVIC, Pony Canyon, Showgate, T3WORKS. 24 mins. x 26 eps.
The Ancient Kingdom's rule of the island of Erin is under threat from the rise of the Divine Empire. The Goidelic tribe are about to sacrifice the beautiful virgin priestess Riannon to revive demon king Arawn so that he can lead the resistance against the Empire. Riannon survives thanks to Arawn, and he joins her and her brother Arthur to lead the struggle.

This is almost a sibling show to UTAWARERUMONO, made by Oriental Light and Magic and based on an Aquaplus game. In fact, it's based on an Aquaplus game that was *itself* based on an Aquaplus game—it derives from the non-porn version of a porn game. We admit, the use of all those Dark Age British names (albeit wonkily spelled), and the references to Arthurian legend and the Roman Empire, had us intrigued. The scenario also has echoes of BASTARD!!, with the awakened demon warrior the only one who can save those who imprisoned him, and of *Lord of the Rings* in Arawn's and Riannon's chosen band of Elf and human followers.

It's a very good-looking show, but those who want Dark Age accuracy will be disappointed: there are still strong fan service elements (ARGOT AND JARGON) though the original game's erotic approach has been muted for TV. But the characters are clichéd and the pacing is uneven, leading to some tedious passages: it takes half the series to completely set things up, and then the final battle sequences drag through four episodes. For a much more interesting take on Dark Age Britain and Ireland, we refer you to Yuho Ashibe's remarkable manga *Crystal Dragon*.

TECHNOLOGY AND FORMATS
We cover several anime "firsts" in our section on EARLY ANIME, and reiterate here that the development of anime remains directly tied to new developments and applications of media technology—film from 1917, television from the late 1950s, video from the late 1970s, and digitization from the early 1980s. When the only resource available was a film camera, anime remained beholden to the film medium, with Oten Shimokawa drawing his *Mukuzo Imokawa the Doorman* (*Imokawa Mukuzo Genkanban no Maki*, 1917) in chalk on a blackboard.

Animators all over the world soon realized that while foreground figures would need to move on a frame-by-frame basis, background images could often remain unchanged from shot to shot. Paper-cut animators began to experiment with translucent paper in order to create multiple layers of action on a screen. The animation "cel," a clear piece of celluloid (nitro-cellulose), presented the ideal solution, allowing animators to draw partial images on uniformly shaped, identically sized squares of transparent film. These could be layered one on top of the other on a rostrum and then photographed by an overhead camera in order to create a multilayered image. A "multiplane" set-up, enabling the separate levels to be manipulated at different degrees of parallax, hence creating a better sense of depth, first reached Japan in 1941, when Tadahito Mochinaga built one for Mitsuyo Seo's *Ant Boy* (*Ari-chan*, 1941).

Cels and rostrum cameras became the basic tools of the anime world for the next 50 years. Images could be kept in exact "registration" from shot to shot by the use of sprocket holes at their edges ("perforations and pegs"). These are not seen in the finished film, since they occur beyond "TV Safety"—that is, beyond the area of the image that will actually be photographed. Jimmy T. Murakami reported his frustration at Toei in the late 1950s, where animators still insisted on holding cels together by the less exacting means of paperclips. Peter Chung has observed that the pegs in Japanese drawing boards are fixed in place, whereas those in America can be rotated on hinges. This, he suggests, allows American artists a better opportunity to test and retest their work in progress, but forces Japanese animators to trust in their first draft, or to embrace a more impressionistic, less "naturalistic" form of animation.

The ability to reuse elements also led to certain choices in filmmaking, such Osamu Tezuka's decision to have a spartan, barely furnished future in ASTRO BOY, and a robot protagonist whose limb positions, once drawn on cels, could be reused from episode to episode. Although cels are transparent, too many of them stacked one on top of another can cause lower levels to appear murky, generally limiting the number of cels in use to three—a foreground, a background, and some kind of change onscreen, be it a hand gesture or a moving mouth. Five levels of cel are usually considered to be the maximum, although the need to pour in extra light can cause a leeched, bleached quality reducing the vivacity of any colors. This, however, was exploited by Mamoru Oshii, who adopted a "bled" color scheme for his PATLABOR movies. The need for light in order to ensure good photography also made it time-consuming to realistically depict night sequences in cel animation, as it requires animators to use murkier, grayer grades of standard colors. Katsuhiro Otomo's AKIRA, which contains many night sequences, is a particularly good example of the painstaking efforts required. This issue was resolved with the adoption of digital animation in the late 1990s, which effectively allowed day-for-night shooting at the flick of a switch and ushered in a whole slew of vampire and werewolf stories as a result.

The opportunity to reuse backgrounds also led to an understandable craftsmanship—anime can have wonderful skies, sunsets, and lush backgrounds, since the painters can afford to concentrate their efforts on an image that will be used for more than a single 24th of a second. Animators can also treat the image through the use of camera filters or effects placed on the rostrum camera itself, often using improvised methods, such as those employed in some episodes of FIST OF THE NORTH STAR. Not all cels are the regulation screen shape. Long panning shots, for example, might be drawn onto elongated cels, in order to keep a single unbroken

image onscreen. Horizontal movement is thereby achieved by moving the *cel*. Vertical movement, such as zooms, can be achieved by moving the *camera*, which is attached to a fixed rail.

Anime were initially shot on 16mm and then transferred to video for broadcast using a standard telecine process. However, some anime were shot on other forms of film—MAGIC BOY (1959) was the first anime to be shot using the Cinescope process, a deliberate attempt to match the same methods used on Disney's *Lady and the Tramp* (1955). Disney's *Sleeping Beauty* (1959) was the first feature cartoon to be shot on 70mm film, although this achievement largely passed the Japanese by, since prints of the film in Japan were in 35mm. Consequently, Japanese sources in search of the opportunity to discuss Japan's "first" 70mm film tend to fall back on METAMORPHOSES/WINDS OF CHANGE (1978), which was an American-Japanese coproduction, but did contain a 70mm sequence directed by Sadao Miyamoto. Other technological breakthroughs in anime include 3D, first used for the final episode of NOBODY'S BOY REMI (1977) and occasionally wheeled out for children's movies, and stereo sound, first used in the BATTLE OF THE PLANETS movie (1978).

With 24 frames per second of traditional film, it is theoretically possibly to change the onscreen image 24 times per second—animating "on ones." However, this was rarely done, even by Disney in the cel age, where globally animators seemed to settle that animating on "twos," i.e., 12 times per second, was more than enough to deliver fluid motion on all but the most complex of shots. As a result, the industrial definition of "full" animation is not, as one might expect, animating on ones, but on twos. Japanese television animation tends to follow Osamu Tezuka's decision to animate on threes, i.e., at eight images per second, which can make for a jerky, staccato movement onscreen but allows studios to bring in work on budget and on time in the treadmill of television. There is nothing physically preventing the Japanese from doing "full" animation—nothing, that is, except the financial restrictions born of the relatively low returns that the Japanese animation industry usually expects—see RATINGS AND BOX OFFICE.

A major change behind the scenes in anime came during the late 1960s, when studios began to use a Xerox camera to transfer pencil drawing directly onto cels. This "xerography," or in Japanese "machine tracing," not only made an entire echelon of tracers redundant, but it also allowed much more of the key artists' work to make it to the final image. Anime came to favor scrappier, sketchier stylings and more daring artistic experimentations such as deformation and compression, by key animators sure that less of their creation would be sanded down in the tracing process. Most notable in these experiments was STAR OF THE GIANTS, in which a number of them were used to conceal the fact that the anime version was swiftly catching up with the original manga and the animators were flailing in search of means to slow the action down. This, in turn, created a new trend of hyper-reality in the animated image, accentuating freeze-frame, cutaways, flashbacks, and dramatizations of human emotion, many of which became commonplace in the anime tradition (TROPES AND TRANSFORMATIONS).

The arrival of video recorders in the late 1970s caused a radical change in the nature of viewers' access to animation. Suddenly, it was possible to re-watch and re-view, and even to send and swap tapes with fellow aficionados. It was hence possible to create an anime FANDOM, both inside Japan and beyond its borders, and it was not long before producers realized that the presence of a small but dedicated audience of adult viewers offered the potential of a new direct-sales market bypassing theaters and television channels. The first video anime, DALLOS (1983), changed anime's method of distribution, not the technology that actually made it. The lower overheads required to put video cassettes and laserdiscs, then DVDs, into stores allowed producers to try more experimental works. Video also allowed for private viewing, and hence the return of EROTICA AND PORNOGRAPHY.

In addition, video permitted the ready export of anime abroad, where original formats were sometimes confused. AI CITY, made as a movie for screening in cinemas, went straight to video outside Japan, whereas the original APPLESEED, released straight-to-video in Japan, was released in cinemas in some territories, blowing up artwork originally intended for the small screen to the work's arguable detriment. The mixture of original formats often led to false expectations among rights-buyers and audiences abroad. Anime's initial boom in the English-speaking world was spearheaded by *movies*—**AKIRA**, **UROT-SUKIDOJI**, and **CASTLE OF CAGLIOSTRO**—but largely comprised *videos*, with a predictable drop in quality. Nor were many of the videos stand-alone titles, leading to increased confusion, particularly in cases such as **RG VEDA**, where a Japanese release was left open-ended, with the expectation that audiences would follow the rest of the story in a manga version simply unavailable to the American mainstream at the time.

In the mid-1990s, the expansion of television networks and the reduction in video budgets led to a new form of distribution. Instead of releasing niche programming onto video, some producers sold it at a cheap rate to television networks, who would then broadcast it during the late-night "graveyard shift." What once might have been released in the 1980s as a video series of six one-hour episodes would now be broken into 12 or 13 half-hour episodes, with the concomitant budgetary savings of more recyclable opening and ending credit sequences. Essentially, the idea was to have a video release in which the fan was expected to bring his own tape—Japanese magazines even published guides on how to get the best from home taping. The rise of the late-night anime led to a different type of content, with the late-night anime largely unsuitable for primetime. Although not a problem in Japan, this has led to more confused expectations abroad, as anime distributors buy "TV serials" that they find to be almost impossible to sell for broadcast without **CENSORSHIP AND LOCALIZATION**.

The ability to store and manipulate images digitally is the most crucial innovation in the anime business since the adoption of the cel, and its repercussions are still playing out. During the recession of 1974, producers at Toei first began exploring the possibilities of using computers to streamline the animation process. Primitive computers were used at first to control "tablework" (increments for zooms and pans on the rostrum camera), but eventually integrated into a company-wide system, Computer-Aided Toei Animation System (CATAS) set up by Fujitsu in the 1980s. In the years after an episode of **THE YEARLING** (1983) was digitally composited, much anime still appeared to be 2D; it was largely made inside a computer. As the price of computer power dropped, Toei installed a high-speed data cable between its Tokyo base and its Phillipines subsidiary, and in 1991 was the first company to use the Revolutionary Engineering Total Animation System (RETAS), a software suite from Celsys corporation that swiftly became the Japanese industry standard for 2D animation.

The cel animation industry has now been replaced by new methods of production, which we cover in greater detail in our entry on **GAMING AND DIGITAL ANIMATION**. But the new technology has also exerted a strong influence on the type of anime that gets made. Just as anime once favored TV serials or videos, it now favors increasingly smaller episodes, easier to stream online, download, and view on personal devices such as a PSP or iPod. This also allows many anime producers to invent a new excuse for what they have always done—cutting their budgets.

TECHNOPOLICE 21C *

1982. JPN: *Technopolis 21C*. AKA: *Techno Police*. Movie. DIR: Masashi Matsumoto, Shoji Kawamori. SCR: Mamoru Sasaki, Kenichi Matsuzaki, Masaru Yamamoto, Hiroyuki Hoshiyama. DES: Yoshitaka Amano, Kazumasa Miyabe. ANI: Norio Hirayama, Kogi Okawa. MUS: Joe Hisaishi. PRD: Studio Nue, Artmic, Toho, Dragon Production. 79 mins. In the year 2001 (which still seemed quite a long way off in 1982), the police force uses robots to minimize risk to human personnel in fighting crime. The Technopolice is the special squad of cops and robots set up to use the new technology to its best effect. But a crime wave is sweeping Centinel City, and the police have almost lost control. When a powerful experimental tank is hijacked, hotheaded rookie cop Kyosuke (Ken) is thrown in at the deep end. In a high-tech Road Ranger car (a step up from his own beloved Lotus Seven, which he proudly describes as a "collector's item"), he sets out on a death-defying chase through the streets. Luckily he's got the best Techroid (Technoid) backup on the force, three superb robots: his own Blader (Blade), who throws a pair of cuffs to catch villains as they flee; pretty Scanny, the computer hacker partner of token girl Eleanor; and Vigoras (Vigorish), a big, strong robot to partner his big, strong sidekick Kosuga. With their help, he may just manage to stay alive long enough to capture the crooks, disarm the tank, and save Eleanor; but not even his instinct for outguessing the criminals can help him outwit the political machinations behind the hijack and bring the culprits to justice. Based on an idea by Toshimitsu Suzuki, who would return in **BUBBLEGUM CRISIS** with hard-suits bearing a certain resemblance to the Techroids. Also note the cameo appearance of two cute girl traffic cops in a small car, distantly foreshadowing **YOU'RE UNDER ARREST!**

TEEKYU

2005. TV series. DIR: Shin Itagaki. SCR: Shin Itagaki. DES: Shin Itagaki. ANI: Shin Itagaki. MUS: N/C. PRD: Mappa, Dax Production, Snowdrop. 2 mins. x 12 eps. (TV1), 2 mins. x 12 eps. (TV2), 2 mins. x 12 eps. (TV3). Four girls, only one of whom can actually play tennis, join the school tennis club and then spend all their time hanging out, talking about nothing, and only occasionally getting on the court, seemingly mainly as an excuse to wear miniskirts for a bit. Written by Roots, drawn by Piyo, *Teekyu* favors a cartoonish grasp of reality at all times, with characters often depicted as goddesses, devils, multi-armed balls of anger, and sex objects—*everything* in this **SPORTS ANIME** is presented as a squashed-down, super-deformed version of reality, because the cast take nothing seriously, certainly not tennis, and probably not life itself. **K-ON**, but with tennis.

TEKKAMAN *

1975. JPN: *Uchu Kishi Tekkaman*. AKA: *Tekkaman the Space Knight; Space Knight Tekkaman*. TV series, video. DIR: Hiroshi Sasagawa, Hideo Nishimaki, Eiko Toriumi, Seitaro Hara (TV1), Hiroshi Negishi, Akihiko Nishiyama, Kazuya Yamazaki, Hideki Tonokatsu (TV2), Hideki Tonokatsu (v). SCR: Jinzo Toriumi, Akiyoshi Sakai, Hiroshi Sakamoto (TV1), Mayori Sekijima, Hiroyuki Kawasaki, Satoru Akahori, Tetsuko Watanabe, Katsuhiko Chiba (TV2), Hiroyuki Kawasaki (v). DES: Yoshitaka Amano, Kunio Okawara (TV1), Yoshinori Sayama, Hirotoshi Sano, TO III O [sic] (TV2), Hirotoshi Sano, Yoshinori Sayama, Rei Nakahara (v). ANI: Masami Suda, Tsuneo Ninomiya (TV1), Shigeru Kato (TV2), Akira Kano (v). MUS: Bob Sakuma (TV1), Kaoru Wada (TV2), Shigeki Kuwara (v). PRD: Tatsunoko, NET (now TV Asahi) (TV1), Tatsunoko, TV Tokyo (TV2). 25 mins. x 26 eps. (TV1), 25 mins. x 49 eps. (TV2), 30 mins. x 6 eps. (v).

A space-borne version of **BATTLE OF THE PLANETS**, as the invading Waldstar aliens (Waldarians in the U.S. dub) are opposed by Joji Minami (Barry Gallagher), a young man who can wear the powerful Tekkaman battle armor designed by Professor Amachi (Dr. Edward Richardson). The professor's daughter, Hiromi (Patricia), the teleporting alien Andro Umeda, and space furball Mutan support him in his fight on the starship Terra Azzura. Not unlike Vega in **HARMAGEDON**, Andro is a survivor from another world ravaged by the enemy, helping humans avert a similar disaster on their own world. In the Japanese version, the situation was considerably more desperate, since Earth is on the verge of ecological collapse, and the human race will perish without a new home. Conversely, in the U.S. version, the human ships that first encounter the Waldarians are simply looking for new worlds to colonize. Created by Jinzo Toriumi and Akira Toyama from an idea by Ippei Kuri, the original TV series ends with Earth saved, but at the price of the hero's life—though it is highly likely that his "death" was only a cliffhanger that would have been revealed as a red herring in episode 27, had the unpopular series not been pulled off the air only halfway through its original planned run of 52 episodes.

The concept was revived for a new series, *SK Tekkaman Blade* (1992), screened in the U.S. as *Teknoman*. This time, the alien Radamu kidnap humans to use them as living weapons, almost invincible once they conjure up the alien Tekkaman armor. One such human, known only as D-Boy, escapes from their control and makes his way to Earth, whose defenders, undecided as to how far to trust him, still need his armor and its power to have a chance of saving the planet. The classic team-show jealousies, misunderstandings, and romantic love tangles back up a plot with plenty of fighting action, and D-Boy's past tragedy is gradually revealed. In the video series *SK Tekkaman Blade* 2 (1994), ten years have elapsed since the events of the second TV series, and D-Boy returns to save Earth again. The marketing-led emphasis on starlets in the 1990s means that this time the Tekkaman Support Team consists of several beautiful young girls, each of whose voice actresses made a tie-in single. **V**

TEKKEN *

1998. AKA: *Iron Fist*. Video. DIR: Kunihisa Sugishima. SCR: Ryota Yamaguchi. DES: Masaaki Kawabata. ANI: Masaaki Kawabata. MUS: Kazuhiko Sotoyama. PRD: Foursome. 30 mins. x 2 eps. (v), 58 mins. (m).

Sometime in the near future, cloning has been outlawed by the Darwin Treaty, but an international crime-fighting organization suspects that super-rich weapons magnate Heihachi Mishima is planning something nasty. Meanwhile Kazuya, Mishima's son, is out to kill him. Mishima thought the best way to train his gentle, good-hearted son was by throwing him into a ravine. The boy survived only thanks to his raging thirst for revenge and has now become a superb martial artist in his own right. A prestigious martial arts tournament on Mishima's private island off Hong Kong, attended by the best fighters from all over the world, offers Kazuya the chance to achieve his aims. His childhood friend Jun wants to bring him back from his chosen path of hatred, but his father aims to Turn Him To The Dark Side.

This game-based anime incorporates characters from all three *Tekken* versions then available. *Tekken* pays lip service to the police thriller angle exploited in the past by **STREET FIGHTER II**, casting Jun Kazama as a lady investigator with an international crime-busting syndicate. Both in anticipation of the large Chinese market and in recognition of the ideal way to engineer as many fight scenes as possible, it also pastiches Bruce Lee movies—hence the martial arts tournament on a millionaire's private island, the promised fight through the floors of a central tower, and the Hong Kong setting. Though the plot meanders toward a massive fight at Mishima's lair, which would, of course, be the tournament featured in the game itself, the events of the game only take place off-screen for a few fleeting seconds. The script takes the macho posturing of games to mind-boggling extremes, and as a rundown of all the available clichés, *Tekken* has the lot, including a childhood flashback, bad dreams, sibling rivalry, a shower scene, an evil corporation, a female assassin, a psychic girl agent, graphic breaking bones, a gentle giant, a girl in a sailor suit, a broken punching bag, incompetent minions, Russian androids, a self-destruct sequence, and a baddie who lives to fight another day. As a small bonus, it also includes stealth dinosaurs and a boxing kangaroo. As well as adding the pretentious subtitle "the motion picture," the English-language release replaced the original soundtrack with music from popular beat combos, including Offspring and Corrosion of Conformity.

Set between the fifth and sixth iterations of the game (in an "alternate storyline," so not actually between them at all), the digitally animated film *Tekken: Blood Vengeance* (2011) features several characters going undercover at a Japanese school, where the Mishima corporation turns out to be conducting genetic experiments on the students, in the search for Shin Kazama, a mutant who carries an immortality gene. Directed by Yoichi Mori, the film owes much of its appeal to a script by Dai Sato that earnestly takes the posturings and pomposities of the concept and invests them with a hilariously portentous seriousness. Almost as if the characters are unaware they are in a comedy, it is suffused with double-entendres and camp homoeroticism, turning out to be immensely entertaining, although not necessarily in the manner that its producers may have originally intended. A post-apocalyptic live-action film, *Tekken* (2010) was directed by Dwight H. Little but universally panned in Japan, where Katsuhiro Harada, director of the game series, publicly called it a poor effort made without Namco's participation, owing to a "cruel contract." **V**

TEKKONKINKREET *

2006. AKA: *Black and White*. Movie. DIR:

Michael Arias, Hiroaki Ando. scr: Anthony Weintraub. des: Shojiro Nishimi. ani: Chie Uratani, Masahiko Kubo. mus: Plaid. prd: Studio 4 Degrees C. 111 mins.

Orphans Kuro (Black) and Shiro (White) consider themselves to be the uncrowned kings of the slum known as Treasure Town, meting out rough justice in the streets, and determined to resist the efforts of a corporation that wishes to tear down their home in order to build an amusement park. Based on the manga by Taiyo Matsumoto, published in English as *Black and White*, this film marked the feature debut of Michael Arias, one of a tiny handful of non-Japanese to get anywhere at all in the Japanese animation business, with a career that has scored many behind-the-scenes triumphs in digital TECHNOLOGY AND FORMATS, and oft-overlooked contributions to others' successes, such as ANIMATRIX and PATEMA INVERTED. His feature directorial debut, however, seems more designed to showcase the cutting edge of modern animation than the heart and humanity of Matsumoto's original, not helped by a cliché-ridden script. In Japan, where the local TRANSLATION allegedly sanded down much of Anthony Weintraub's dialogue, the film gained substantially better accolades, although its release at the peak of anime's production, and its unfortunate flaws, have conspired to keep it relatively obscure among international fans. Compare to the same studio's MIND GAME, to which the film makes several references. **V**

TELEPATHY GIRL RAN, THE
2008. jpn: *Telepathy Shojo Ran.* TV series. dir: Makoto Nakamura. scr: Makoto Nakamura. des: Ushio Tazawa, Minoru Yasuhara. ani: Shinichi Suzuki. mus: Yoshihiro Ike. prd: TMS Entertainment, NHK. 25 mins x 26 eps.
Ran is a teenager and a telepath. Midori, another telepath, starts out as her rival and becomes her friend. With Ran's childhood friend and crush Rui, and Ran's older brother Rin, the girls learn how to deal with their abilities, accept the concept of being "different," and enjoy resolving the various mysteries that crop up around them. This is a pleasant series for preteens and young teenagers that presents important ideas—accepting yourself, accepting others, doing your best, helping out when you can, and taking a positive approach

to life—in an enjoyable, undemanding format; entertaining and not preachy. Based on the series of nine books, written by Atsuko Asano between 1999 and 2008.

TEMPLE THE BALLOONIST
1977. jpn: *Fusen Shojo Temple-chan.* aka: *Hot Air Balloon Girl Temple; Tiffany's Traveling Band; Sabrina's Journey.* TV series dir: Seitaro Hara. scr: Jinzo Toriumi, Shigeru Yanagawa. des: Akiko Shimamoto. ani: Kazuhiko Udagawa. mus: Nobuyoshi Koshibe. prd: Tatsunoko, Fuji TV. 25 mins. x 26 eps.
Deep in the Alps lies the tiny village of Green Grass, the home of Temple, a pretty, curly haired girl who wears a drum majorette's outfit and dreams of becoming a musician. On a stormy night, she meets Puffy the cloud, who whisks her away to a magical hot-air balloon. Riding in the balloon, Temple and Puffy see several musicians fleeing from robbers. Rescuing them in the nick of time, they discover that their new traveling companions are animal musicians—Tommy the cat, who plays his whiskers like a mouth harp, Quincy the horn-playing duck, Nicky the flutist mouse, along with Scrapper the orphan drummer boy. Picaresque adventures ensue, with a halfhearted aim of eventually returning Temple to her home—compare to THE WIZARD OF OZ—in a Tatsuo Yoshida creation whose little leading lady's bright attitude and golden curls seem designed to recall the Shirley Temple whose name she appears to share. There were several attempts to sell the story to the American TV market in the 1980s, hence the multiple alternate titles employed in advertising flyers by Harmony Gold. However, we have no record of the show's TRANSLATION or broadcast in English.

TEN LITTLE FROGS
1998. jpn: *10-piki (Juppiki) no Kaeru.* Video. dir: Masahiro Hosoda. scr: Miyako Ando. des: Hirokazu Ishiyuki. ani: Hirokazu Ishiyuki. mus: Kenichi Kamio. prd: Toei, Trans Arts. 20 mins. x 2 eps.
Ten frogs set out in search of adventure in their swamp, sailing in a boat made from a running shoe. Based on the children's book by Hisako Madokoro and Michiko Nakagawa, the story of the frogs returned in a second episode, in which they went to a summer festival.

TEN TOKYO WARRIORS *
1999. jpn: *Tokyo Jushoden.* aka: *Ten Captains of Tokyo.* Video. dir: Hikaru Takanashi, Noboru Ishiguro. scr: Tetsuya Oishi. des: Sawako Yamamoto. ani: Sawako Yamamoto. mus: N/C. prd: Five Ace, Beam Entertainment. 27 mins. x 6 eps.
Long ago, ten brave warriors defeated the Demon King and his legion of "Kyoma" warriors. But in present day Tokyo, Shindigan, a servant of the Kyoma, is determined to resurrect her master and restore his rule on Earth. You will not be surprised to hear that the warriors are reborn in the manner of IKKI TOUSEN, since schoolboy Jutto Segu discovers that he is the reincarnation of one of the original heroes, and that the time has come for him to fight again. A rehash of DOOMED MEGALOPOLIS, doomed by a repetitive monster-of-the-moment format with formulaic plots and characters, based on a novel by Taku Atsushi that was also adapted into a manga by Satoru Kiga, whose illustrations were used as the basis for the characters in this anime version. A CD drama was also produced in Japan. **OV**

TEN TOP TIPS FOR PRO BASEBALL
1983. jpn: *Proyakyu o 10-bai Tanoshiku Miru Hoho.* aka: *How to Make Pro Baseball Ten Times More Exciting.* Movie. dir: Kiyoshi Suzuki. scr: Junichi Ishihara, Toshiharu Iwaida. des: Hisaichi Ishii. ani: Tsutomu Shibayama, Osamu Kobayashi, Satoshi Dezaki, Tsukasa Sunaga. mus: Kazuo Otani. prd: Tokyo Movie Shinsha for Film Link (1), Magic Bus for Film Link (2). 95 mins. (m1), 106 mins. (m2).
Based on the two books of career reminiscences by real-life Hanshin Tigers baseball star Takenori Emoto. Mixing live action and animation to tell humorous anecdotes from professional baseball (nine short tales in nine "innings"), the film was followed by a sequel in 1984, largely because it made a billion yen at the Japanese box office. The fact that an adult audience had gone to see an "animated" film would become part of the argument in favor of video releases aimed specifically at adults, and help feed the otaku video boom of the 1980s.

TENAMONYA VOYAGERS *
1999. Video. dir: Katsuhito Akiyama, Akiyuki Shinbo. scr: Ryoei Tsukimura. des: Masashi

Ishihama, Noriaki Tetsura, Naoyuki Konno. ANI: Takashi Azuhara. MUS: Masamichi Amano. PRD: Studio Pierrot. 30 mins. x 4 eps. Rookie schoolteacher Ayako Hanabishi volunteers for a posting in the middle of nowhere only to find that the school has closed down before she arrives. Far from home with no money, she meets Wakana Nanamiya, a Japanese girl on a sports scholarship, who is also stranded. The brash, tough girl Paraila has never seen the girls' homeland, and she inspires the others to pool their resources and head for home. However, their train is attacked en route, and the girls realize too late that Paraila is wanted by the police and using them as cover. So begins a road-movie set-up that would make a perfect live-action film of the week, somewhat redundantly transformed into an anime space opera. Compare to **AWOL**, which similarly augmented a real-world drama with pointless sci-fi trappings. An inferior Japanese fish-out-of-water comedy to Tsukimura's earlier **EL HAZARD**, *TV* mixes obvious quick fixes (a space-going *bullet*-train after **GALAXY EXPRESS 999**) with halfhearted visual gags (spaceships like battering rams that deposit a 20th-century police car inside a criminal's ship). There are regular breaks for cheesy shots of Tatsue Yokoyama, the dogged police officer who never quite catches them—the filmmakers would have you believe that this is an "homage" to pulp detective shows of the 1970s, though it looks suspiciously like a poverty of ideas masquerading as irony. There are some genuinely funny moments born of the onscreen ensemble, and occasionally some tongue-in-cheek observations in the style of a poor man's **GUNBUSTER**, but like so many 1990s anime comedies, *TV* thinks it's a lot funnier than it really is (see also **JUBEI-CHAN THE NINJA GIRL**), and it stops abruptly with a cynical narration that unhelpfully adds, "And for some reason, this is the end." It will, however, remain forever in the anime history books as the first to be released in the U.S. straight to DVD without ever gracing the old-fashioned VHS format.

TENCHI MUYO! *

1992. JPN: *Tenchi Muyo! Ryo Oh Ki.* AKA: *This Way Up!; No-Good Tenchi; No Need for Tenchi; Heaven and Earth Prince.* Video, TV series, movie. DIR: Hiroki Hayashi, Kenichi Yatagai, Kazuhiro Ozawa, Yoshiaki Iwasaki, Shinichi Kimura, Koji Masunari, Satoshi Kimura. SCR: Naoko Hasegawa, Masaki Kajishima, Hiroki Hayashi, Ryoei Tsukimura, Yosuke Kuroda, Satoru Nishizono. DES: Masaki Kajishima, Atsushi Takeuchi, Takeshi Waki. ANI: Takehiro Nakayama, Wataru Abe. MUS: Seiko Nagaoka, Christopher Franke, Ko Otani, Tsuneyoshi Saito. PRD: AIC, Pioneer, TV Tokyo. 30 mins. x 6 eps. (v, *Ryo-ohki 1*), 45 mins. (v sp., *Carnival*), 30 mins. x 6 eps. (v, *Ryo-ohki 2*), 27 mins. (v sp., *Mihoshi*), 25 mins. x 26 eps. (TV1, *Universe*), 40 mins. 48 mins. 40 mins. (v, *Sammy*), 95 mins. (m1, *In Love*), 25 mins. x 26 eps. (TV2, *Sammy*), 25 mins. x 26 eps. (TV3, *Tokyo*), 60 mins. (m2, *Daughter*), 95 mins. (m3, *Forever*), 25 mins. x 26 eps. (TV4, *GXP*), 30 mins. x 6 eps. (v, *Ryo-ohki 3*), 30 mins. (v, *Ryo-ohki* finale), 25 mins. x 26 eps. (TV5, *Sasami*).

Tenchi Masaki is a quiet, average teenager who lives in the family shrine with his father and grandfather, goes to school, and does nothing much—until the day he accidentally releases a malevolent creature from the family shrine (compare to **USHIO AND TORA**). It transforms into a hot babe, space pirate Ryoko, and her hots are aimed at Tenchi. Then another alien babe, Jurai Princess Ayeka, arrives with her sweet little sister, Sasami. She too fancies Tenchi, but she's got another reason for hating Ryoko—a past tragedy that robbed her of her intended husband. When ditzy Space Officer Mihoshi falls out of the skies onto the Masaki household and pink-haired alien professor Wasshu shows up, the scene is set for a romantic farce in which the girls fight for Tenchi's affections while he fights off various galactic threats and gradually uncovers the truth about his family. There's also a mascot "cabbit" (cat/rabbit), the titular Ryo-Oh-Ki, which likes carrots and will one day grow into a spaceship.

The "unwelcome guest" genre, in which a hapless boy is saddled with a magical babe, is a popular high concept in anime. It's a genre rich in mind-boggling situation comedies: girlfriend-as-alien (**URUSEI YATSURA**), girlfriend-as-elfin-nymphomaniac (**ADVENTURE KID**), girlfriend-as-the-Norse-embodiment-of-the-concept-of-Being (**OH MY GODDESS!**), girlfriend-as-time-traveling-ghost-of-future-dead-wife (**KIRARA**). *Tenchi*

is its 1990s apotheosis; a show about a boy stuck with more girls than he can shake a stick at, every one of them feverishly competing for a chaste peck on the cheek. Originally conceived as a spoof vacation episode of **BUBBLEGUM CRISIS**, *Tenchi* reached screens in this heavily rewritten form—however, along with the girl-heavy cast, the idea that it was okay to just goof off for an episode or two became ingrained. Sasami's regular plea that things can always stay the same "forever and ever" is perhaps the most bowel-emptyingly fearsome line in televisual history, striking greater dread into the audience than any horror movie. Though the first video series of *Tenchi* was witty, funny, and charming, the premise was repeated *ad nauseam* by a creative team happy to simply coast along. Later incarnations of the series reorder a few plot elements into what some might call alternate universes, and others lazy continuity. In hindsight, *Tenchi* has become regarded as one of the harbingers of the *moe* subgenre of anime, in which plot, continuity, and pretty much anything else take second place to doltish enthusing over the female characters (**EROTICA AND PORNOGRAPHY**).

The Pioneer corporation, searching for an easily repeatable franchise to rival Sunrise's **BRAVE SAGA** or Tatsunoko's **TIME BOKAN**, hyped *Tenchi* to insane extremes, and the series clambered onto TV screens with the new-look *Tenchi Universe* (Ryoko *crashes* on Earth while being *pursued* by Mihoshi; see the subtle difference?), which moves the action into space for its second season. A further TV series, *Tenchi in Tokyo*, packed our boy off to college—but a dimensional portal let his harem pop up for "unexpected" visits. At the time of its U.S. release, Pioneer's blurb proclaimed it was the "same old Tenchi," which was at least honest.

The series proper "ended" with three expensive movies, beginning with *Tenchi Muyo in Love* (1996), which paid out for music from *Babylon 5*–composer Christopher Franke. Shamelessly ripping off *Back to the Future*, Tenchi must travel back in time to unite his courting parents. Despite high production values and an involving plot, the movie is let down by the serial's vastly overpopulated cast—the number of characters demanding a scene to steal often makes it resemble crowded game-based anime like STREET FIGHTER II. In typical *Tenchi* style, the movie *Daughter of Darkness* (1997, AKA *Midsummer's Eve*) half-heartedly inverts the previous plot, featuring the cast visited by a character from the *future*, claiming to be Tenchi's daughter. The final movie, *Tenchi Forever* (1999), features Tenchi kidnapped by yet another obsessive female and spirited into a parallel world where his adoring harem have to find him. *Tenchi Muyo GXP* (2002) is yet another retelling, a 26-episode TV series supposedly rooted more in the continuity of the video serials, moving the focus away from Tenchi, who joins the galactic police, and onto his young classmate Seina Yamada, a shy, retiring child who believes that he, like Ataru in URUSEI YATSURA, has the worst luck in the world. Amid a main plot about a pirate guild's plan to seize control of the galaxy, the usual geek-gets-girls "comedy" ensues.

A third video series ran for six episodes, and a bonus finale (the "21st" episode in the cumulative video continuity), ran from 2003 to 2005.

With the dogged staying power of a mutant cockroach, the franchise might not necessarily have pleased the crowds (ratings were unremarkable), but it certainly pleased studio executives, in a time of refocused expectations that favored a small audience of fan consumers over a large audience of television viewers. *Tenchi* was a fertile breeding ground for other shows during the 1990s—most notably the superior EL HAZARD, which was made by bored staffers Hayashi and Tsukimura, and the pornographic pastiches SPACESHIP AGGA RUTER and MASQUERADE. Two video "specials" also introduced a superheroine, who returned in her own video series *Magical Princess Pretty Sammy*, which followed the classic magical-girl-show pattern (see LITTLE WITCH SALLY), and, predictably, ran a string of subplots about the grown-up girls competing for first place in Tenchi's affections. Little Sasami, however, was safely remodeled as his sister, allowing an 8-year-old girl to adore a 17-year-old guy without a hint of impropriety and simultaneously securing her claim to be big bro's Number One. The series has some enjoyable moments—one episode is a wholly unsubtle dig at Bill Gates's Mi-

crosoft empire—but ultimately it's a show about cute little girls for much older boys who really should know better. The video series was itself rehashed for Japanese TV as the jaw-droppingly camp 26-episode *Magical Girl Pretty Sammy* (*Magical Project S*). The relationships and premises are completely reworked, but this time, apart from the odd cameo appearance, Tenchi and friends are sidelined. Sammy has a mother and father and a whole bunch of elementary school friends and is more interested in talking to her best friend Misao (who is also her unwitting adversary Pixie Misa) than mooning over boys. Marketed in Japan for the little-girl audience, the series received inexplicably high ratings in Nagoya but has proved unpopular with Western *Tenchi* fans, perhaps because it abandons most of the series' established tropes in favor of those of standard magical-girl shows.

Pretty Sammy returned in the TV series *Sasami's Magical Girl Club* (2006), which ran for 26 episodes, split into two "seasons." **Ⓝ**

TENGRI THE BOY OF THE STEPPES
1977. JPN: *Sogen no Ko Tengri*. Movie. DIR: Yasuo Otsuka. SCR: Osamu Tezuka. DES: Yasuo Otsuka. ANI: Yasuo Otsuka, Hayao Miyazaki. MUS: Michio Mamiya. PRD: Snow Brand Milk Products, Sakura Eiga-sha, Shin-Ei Animation. 22 mins.

Tengri, a hunter boy on the steppes of Central Asia, develops a cross-species friendship with Tartar, a young calf. During a bitterly cold winter, Tengri is ordered to kill Tartar for food, but cannot bring himself to slaughter the beast and instead "loses" it in a blizzard. Years later, with the help of a grateful Tartar, Tengri saves the village by discovering the secret of cheese, thereby allowing milk products to be preserved far past the day on which they are extracted.

This trite and rather silly promotional cartoon for a dairy company occupies a prime place in the history of anime as the only film directed to completion by Yasuo Otsuka, lead animator on CASTLE OF CAGLIOSTRO and a revered mentor at Studio Ghibli. It was, supposedly, the cause of his decision never to go near the director's chair again, from the plot dashed off by Osamu Tezuka in mere

minutes, to the gripes of the labor union that underestimated the time required to draw great vistas and then demanded overtime to meet the requirements, to the lackluster premiere, where everyone sat glumly through the film and shrugged that it was fit for the purpose. *Tengri* languished in obscurity thereafter, only screened at the Snow Brand dairy to a generation of baffled schoolchildren, before Otsuka mentioned the film in his autobiography and casually recalled that his layout assistant had been a young artist called Hayao Miyazaki. When the news got back to the dairy, the film was rereleased in a deluxe DVD that somehow stretched the running time to over an hour, presumably with a Making Of, or perhaps some recipes for cheese.

TENJHO TENGE *
2004. JPN: *Tenjo Tenge*. AKA: *Everything Above Heaven; Everything Under Heaven*. TV series, video, TV special. DIR: Toshifumi Kawase. SCR: Toshiki Inoue. DES: Takahiro Umehara. ANI: Takahiro Umehara, Studio Madhouse. MUS: Yasunori Iwasaki. PRD: DR Movie, Madhouse, Nagoya Broadcasting Network, TV Asahi. 23 mins. x 24 eps. (TV), 24 mins. x 2 eps. (v), 92 mins. (special).

Young punks Soichiro Nagi and his best friend, Afro-Japanese Bob Makihara, join Todo Academy, a high school with a high delinquent population and a number of martial arts clubs that fight for supremacy under the iron regulation of the student council. They meet up with the stunningly beautiful Natsume twins, Maya and Aya, and are drawn into a closed world of highly advanced skills and unruly emotions. Both sisters see something special in Soichiro; Aya falls for him, and Maya, whose ex-boyfriend allegedly killed his best friend, their brother, sees him as a fighter with huge but as yet untapped potential. The pair find themselves in the twins' exclusive Juken club, opposed to the student council and its powerful, mysterious leader Mitsuomi, who also happens to be Maya's ex. The combination of teenagers simultaneously flouting authority and regulating their own anarchy through hierarchies as arcane and restrictive as anything in the adult world is familiar—just compare to BOYS OVER FLOWERS or UTENA. But don't come here for philosophy because you'll get eye candy instead; *TT* is all about defying the laws of physics and gravity with slam-bang fighting action and enormous breasts. Based on the manga by "Oh! Great," the TV series led to a two-part video spin-off from the same director, entitled *TT: Ultimate Fight*, and a prequel "special," *TT: Past Chapter* (2005). **L N V**

TENMARU THE LITTLE TENGU

1983. JPN: *Bemubemu Hunter Kotengu Tenmaru*. TV series. DIR: Hiroshi Shidara, Yuji Endo, Atsutoshi Umezawa, Takeshi Shirato, Junichi Sato. SCR: Tadaaki Yamazaki, Akiyoshi Sakai, Katsuhiko Taguchi. DES: Kiichiro Suzuki. ANI: Masami Abe, Takeshi Shirato. MUS: Hiroshi Tsutsui. PRD: Toei, Fuji TV. 25 mins. x 19 eps.

Prince Tenmaru leaves the land of the tengu (crow-spirits) in pursuit of 108 evil creatures who have invaded the human realm. He hides out at the apartment of pretty Earth girl Yoko. A mixture of the gentle humor of **DORAEMON** with the ghostbusting of **DORORON ENMA**, *Tenmaru* was the anime debut of future **SAILOR MOON**–director Junichi Sato.

TENTACLE AND WITCHES

2011. Video. DIR: Tsukasa Kaido. SCR: Kometan. DES: Mayu Furuse, Hiroaki Kawabe. ANI: Mayu Furuse. MUS: N/C. PRD: OZ Inc., Pixy. 30 mins. x 4 eps.

Teenage peeping tom Ichiro spies on his curvaceous teacher Ms. Yuko and learns she's a witch! Apprentice witch Lily sets up a spell to punish him, but it goes wrong and he's turned into a tentacle monster. Now, as everyone knows, tentacle monsters have to absorb energy from witches by having sex with them. Otherwise they go berserk and attack other girls. Luckily two witches are willing to help out. Based on the porn game *Tentacle and Witches* by Lilith Mist—yes, we know there is more than one tentacle, but the Japanese licensors insist that it refers to the single monster, not the number of his appendages. **N**

TEPPEN

1995. AKA: *Summit*. Video. DIR: Yota Minagawa, Fumi Shirakawa. SCR: Tomohiro Ando, Masashi Reishi. DES: Masashi Yusono. ANI: Hidemizu Kita. MUS: N/C. PRD: Toei. 50 mins. x 2 eps.

In an adaptation of Takanori Onari's manga from *Young Jump* magazine, teenage tough-guy Satoshi gets into fights at school and has run-ins with the police. **V**

TERROR IN RESONANCE *

2014. JPN: *Zankyo no Terror*. TV series. DIR: Shinichiro Watanabe. SCR: Shoten Yano, Hiroshi Seko, Jun Kumagai, Senta Ihara. DES: Kazuto Nakazawa, Shinobu Tsunkei, Hidetoshi Kaneko. ANI: Kazuto Nakazawa, manabu Akita, Tomohiro Kishi. MUS: Yoko Kanno. PRD: Mappa, Aniplex, Fuji TV, Kyoraku Industrial Holdings. 23 mins. x 11+ eps.

High summer: Tokyo reels under a terrorist attack. The perpetrators are two teenagers, self-named Nine and Twelve, collectively known as Sphinx. Their grievances are at first unknown, though we learn they stem from their shared past at a mysterious institute. As the government and the police scramble to identify and contain them, Nine and Twelve play a game of cat and mouse, befriending the policeman who untangles their complex puzzles and leading the police on a dance of destruction. Then a girl called Five shows up, part of their past, out to stop their present endeavors.

Far removed from Watanabe's much-lauded **SPACE DANDY**, *TiR* looks back at the great conspiracy shows of the 1980s, from **MEGAZONE 23** to **AKIRA**—shows that have a special and terrible resonance in these days of disaffected youth prosecuting jihad under the radar of the authorities they see as oppressors.

The show is rooted in the present, with America's influence on Japan called into question. YouTube and social media are shown as vital tools of both terror and the war against it, information roaming free and out of government control, inviting the young to make up their own minds and build their own allegiances. There's a carefully built and paced undercurrent of acknowledgment that nothing is simple and no one is entirely good or evil. Like **DEATH NOTE**, the show invites some sympathy for its self-consciously brilliant anti-heroes, and reinforces this by indicating that they have been horrifically abused. It nods to *Akira* again, and to *The Uncanny X-Men*, in its hints of government experiments on those with special abilities.

A show with Watanabe and the divine Yoko Kanno on board will always be worth seeing and hearing. This one oozes style, intelligence, and lean, cool elegance, and the music is pitch-perfect: episode 8 opens with an English-language pop track packed with the sunny, bright-eyed perfection of the Beach Boys at the top of their harmonious and positive game, building for the sucker punch that follows. **L V**

TEXHNOLYZE *

2003. TV series DIR: Hirotsugu Hamazaki, Kojiro Tsuruoka, Sayo Yamamoto, Takayuki Hirao. SCR: Chiaki Konaka, Noboru Takagi, Shin Yoshida, Takeshi Konuta. DES: Shigeo Akahori, Morifumi Naka, Toshihiro Nakajima. ANI: Shigeo Akahori. MUS: Hajime Mizoguchi, Keishi Urata. PRD: Fuji TV, Madhouse, Pioneer, Rondo Robe. 24 mins. x 22 eps.

Centuries after mankind first burrowed underground to live in "experimental" cities, the descendants of the original colonists are fighting for control of the near-derelict city of Lux. Orphan Ichise is a prizefighter who gets involved with a corrupt promoter and literally loses an arm and a leg. He becomes the guinea pig of a female scientist working on the Texhnolyze project, and receives new limbs and enhanced fighting powers. This in turn makes him the favored protégé of Onishi, leader of an organization with a mysterious power over Lux. Girl prophet Ran offers him the chance to find out who he really is and what his destiny holds. Created by Yoshitoshi Abe, whose fascination for labyrinths and processes of evolution led to the modern anime classics **SERIAL EXPERIMENTS LAIN** and **HAIBANE RENMEI**, this is a beautifully designed dystopia, although built on foundations set by many others—see *Robocop*, **MEGAZONE 23**, **AD POLICE**, and even the previous year's **TOKYO UNDERGROUND**. **L V**

TEZUKA, OSAMU

1928–89. Born in Osaka Prefecture, Tezuka graduated in medicine from Osaka University, although he was already writing manga in his teens, and never practiced as a doctor—his pursuit of a medical education may have been a form of conscientious objection in wartime Japan. He is often termed the "God of Manga" or "Father of Manga." He is one of the giants of postwar Japanese comics, and the author of over 500 volumes of comics, although his manga output need not concern us here, save in his youthful associations with other artists, dramatized in WE'RE MANGA ARTISTS: TOKIWA VILLA. He was able to be so prolific, at least in part, through his adoption of a "production line" system that institutionalized the practices already present in the comics industry of farming out different work to multiple assistants. Tezuka's ability to delegate not only set paradigms for other comics artists, but also encouraged him to diversify into animation with his company Mushi Production. Seeing TV as an opportunity to advertise his comics, and vice versa, Tezuka helped create anime as we know it with his groundbreaking ASTRO BOY, KIMBA THE WHITE LION, and PRINCESS KNIGHT. His decision to undercharge for animation production, a failed attempt to head off competition by undercutting their prices, forever doomed the anime business to have a product that required external investment—this has been termed "Tezuka's curse" by some critics and has left anime eternally beholden to ADVERTISING AND SPONSORSHIP. His early successes stumbled in the late 1960s, as Mushi Production lost money, causing Tezuka to embark on more "adult" fare such as A THOUSAND AND ONE NIGHTS and questionable deals which found creations such as his TRITON OF THE SEA ending up in the hands of others. Tezuka left Mushi Pro in 1971 as the company spiraled into chaos, and returned with Tezuka Productions, a new company that continued to make meaningful contributions to the anime world, particularly in the often-overlooked world of TV specials such as PRIME ROSE. For details of the lifelong work by which Tezuka would probably have preferred to be remembered, see SPACE FIREBIRD. Tezuka is one of the founding fathers of Japanese animation, since it was he, along with Shotaro Ishinomori and Mitsuteru Yokoyama, who first created many of the manga tropes and traditions that are replayed every season in modern anime. He grossly overspent on his early TV anime titles, but thereby ensured that his studio rounded up the most talented graduates of Toei's animation education program and that his art style dominated the early days of the medium. He was also active in selling anime to America, visiting the U.S. and encouraging its fledgling fanbase. He

was the president of the Japan Animation Association until his death, and was succeeded by Kihachiro Kawamoto. See also MUSHI PRODUCTION; TEZUKA PRODUCTIONS. Some older sources repeat Tezuka's claim that he was born in 1926, a deception that he maintained in his youth in order to convince his editors that he was an adult manga creator and not a teenage prodigy.

TEZUKA PRODUCTIONS

Also Tezuka Pro. Founded by Osamu Tezuka in 1968 as a company to produce *comics*, Tezuka Pro was a separate entity, and therefore shielded from any liability when the anime company Mushi Production collapsed in the early 1970s. It was able to continue operating and diversified into animation production; its first anime, MARVELOUS MELMO, was released before Mushi even officially closed. Tezuka Pro is hence the company responsible for most of Tezuka's anime output in the last two decades of his life, such as TV specials like BANDAR BOOK. Since his death, the company has maintained a strong presence in the industry, with an unofficial mission statement to ensure that everything Tezuka ever wrote will eventually be animated. Recent applications of this policy have seen anime of METROPOLIS, BLACK JACK, and an ASTRO BOY remake, all designed to keep Osamu Tezuka's legacy alive.

THAT'LL DO NICELY

1991. JPN: *Nyuin Bokki Monogatari: O Daiji ni*. AKA: *Hospitalization Surprise Story: That'll Do Nicely*. Video. DIR: Yoshitaka Koyama, Naoko Kuzumi. SCR: Yoshitaka Koyama. DES: Koichi Arai. ANI: Yoshio Mizumura. MUS: Michiya Katakura. PRD: Tokyo Kids. 45 mins. x 2 eps.
Ayumu Nerima is hospitalized after a motorcycle accident, but he soon perks up when he discovers that everyone on the ward is desperate for sex, from the nurses to the unwed-teenager mother next door. A predictable farce based on a manga by Maki Otsubo in *Manga Action* magazine—compare to O-GENKI CLINIC. **N**

THERE GOES SHURA

1994. JPN: *Shura ga Yuku*. Video. DIR: Masamune Ochiai. SCR: Yu Kawanabe. DES: Aiko Kamada. ANI: Teruo Kogure. MUS: Hideyuki Tanaka. PRD: Knack. 50 mins. x 2 eps.

The assassination of a Shinjuku gang boss starts a trail of blood-soaked revenge, ending with a nasty shoot-out between yakuza in Kyushu. Based on the original manga in *Comic Goraku* by Yu Kawanabe (who also wrote EMPEROR OF THE SOUTH SIDE) and Masato Yamaguchi. **V**

THERE GOES TOMOE

1991. JPN: *Tomoe ga Yuku*. Video. DIR: Takaaki Ishiyama. SCR: Asami Watanabe. DES: Matsuri Okuda. ANI: Masayuki Goto. MUS: Katsuhiro Kunimoto. PRD: Beam Entertainment. 45 mins. x 2 eps.
In this adaptation of Yumi Tamura's manga from *Bessatsu Shojo Comic*, Tomoe Oshima is a bad-girl biker who cherishes a hidden love for stuntman Tokoro. Since the heroine takes her name from Tomoe Gozen, the famous 12th-century womanwarrior, it might be prudent to file this story with SPECTRE, another adaptation of Japanese history into a modern setting.

THERMAE ROMAE *

2012. TV series, video. DIR: Azuma Tani. SCR: Azuma Tani, Mamoru Nakano. DES: Toshimitsu Takechi. ANI: Toshimitsu Takechi. MUS: N/C. PRD: Dentsu, DLE, Fuji TV, Sony Music Entertainment, Toho. 110 mins.
In A.D. 128, Roman bathhouse architect Lucius Modestus is fired for his inability to embrace new developments in technology. Luckily for him, he discovers that the trauma of almost drowning can propel him through time to the land of modern Japan, where he swiftly learns about and then steals innovations from Japanese bath-houses, including fruit-flavored milk, bidets, and boiled eggs. Back in his own era, he swiftly becomes the toast of Rome, only to attract the unwelcome attention of Emperor Hadrian himself.
Mari Yamazaki's original 2008 manga series in *Comic Beam* was followed in January 2012 by this cheapo Flash-animation comedy series, seemingly designed to drum up interest in the live-action movie of the same name, starring Hiroshi Abe in the leading role and released in Japanese cinemas that April. The U.S. release collates the three original TV episodes, as well as two bitty video releases and a single further episode that was released on the Internet in the month of the film's premiere—their individual lengths

were roughly 15 minutes each, although the rate of their release was somewhat haphazard, with the first two TV episodes containing two chapters each, and the second video release inexplicably containing three.

THEY ARE MY NOBLE MASTERS *

2008. JPN: *Kimi ga Aruji de Shitsuji ga Ore de*. AKA: *You Are the Master I Am the Servant*; *KimiAru*. TV series. DIR: Susumu Kodo. SCR: Jun, Takahiro. DES: Fumio Matsumoto, Masatoshi Muto. ANI: Fumio Matsumoto, Yuichi Yoshida. MUS: Hitoshi Fujima, Noriyasu Agematsu. PRD: A.C.G.T. 25 mins. x 13 eps. Ren Uesugi and his sister Mihato leave home after family troubles. They move to the city, but with no money, they have to find work. So they become servants to the three rich Kuonji sisters, and join their harem of maids and manservants. Based on an erotic visual novel (**ARGOT AND JARGON**) by Minato Soft, but quite mild in terms of pornographic content, focusing more on clichéd softcore fan service and comedic parody incidents than plot or character. **N**

THEY WERE ELEVEN *

1986. JPN: *Juichi-nin Iru*. Movie. DIR: Satoshi Dezaki, Tsuneo Tominaga. SCR: Toshikai Imaizumi, Katsumi Koide. DES: Akio Sugino, Keizo Shimizu. ANI: Keizo Shimizu, Yukari Kobayashi, Kenichi Maejima. MUS: Hirohiko Fukuda. PRD: Kitty Films. 91 mins. An interplanetary group of 10 military academy cadets set out on their end-of-course test. They have to take an elderly spaceship out into space and survive 53 days without outside help. Any one of them can give up, but if so, they all fail. Then they find there are 11 people on board. One of them is an imposter, and they can't contact the academy to find out who it is or whether it's all part of the test. A series of incidents and accidents, trivial at first, grow increasingly threatening, and their personal strengths and weaknesses, as well as the social and political agendas of their different races, have a wider impact than on the outcome of this test alone. The anime version of Moto Hagio's suspenseful 1975 manga is delicate but powerful, a miniature gem.

THIRD: THE GIRL WITH THE BLUE EYE, THE *

2006. JPN: *The Third: Aoi Hitomi no Shojo*. TV series. DIR: Jun Kamiya. SCR: Shinsuke Onishi. DES: Shinichi Yamaoka, Naohiro Washio, Hachidai Takayama, Yoshimi Umino. ANI: Eri Yuzuki, Junki Honma. MUS: Megumi Ohashi. PRD: Xebec, Kadokawa Shoten, T.O. Entertainment, Klockworx, WOWOW. 24 mins. x 24 eps.
Honoka is a misfit. Born into a post-apocalyptic future where Earth is controlled by powerful beings known as The Third, she shares their characteristic third eye (compare to **3 x 3 EYES**). This serves as a port for data access and communication, as well as a caste mark, but Honoka's third eye is blue, not red, so her peers declared her a mutant and left her with the humans. She travels from town to town in her intelligent tank Bogie, across desolate deserts teeming with huge mutated insects, trying to make a living without killing. When she must use her *katana*, she does it so gracefully that people call her the Sword Dancer. She has to avoid The Third's cyborg enforcer Blue Breaker, whose duty it is to kill any human using or owning high-level technology, and Joganki, a high-ranking Third who has a particular interest in her. Then she picks up a beautiful, mysterious guy who turns out to have healing powers.

Ryo Hoshino's book series, illustrated by Nao Goto, began its run in 1999, with a manga version from the same team commencing serialization in 2005. The reason for its ongoing success is twofold: meticulous world-building and a thoughtful, philosophical background that shapes both the story and the characters. The animated version absorbs influences from Studio Ghibli, Jamie Hewlett's *Tank Girl*, and other anime as diverse as **GUNSMITH CATS**, **DESERT PUNK**, and **KINO'S JOURNEY**, to make a show that's something out of the ordinary. Although the animation can be uneven in places, it's mostly good and occasionally impressive—overall this is one of Xebec's best-ever productions. The characters and their beautifully realized world more than make up for the occasional technical lapses.

30,000 MILES UNDER THE SEA

1970. JPN: *Kaitei Sanman Mile*. Movie. DIR:

Takeshi Tamiya. SCR: Katsumi Okamoto. DES: Makoto Yamazaki. ANI: Reiko Okayama, Sadao Kikuchi, Michihiro Kanayama. MUS: Takeo Watanabe. PRD: Toei. 60 mins. Returning home from an ocean trip, young Isamu meets the beautiful sea-dweller Angel on a volcanic island. Attacked by a fiery dragon, Isamu and Angel escape on the observation boat See Through (a punning reference to the Sea View in Irwin Allen's 1961 *Voyage to the Bottom of the Sea*), and Angel invites Isamu to see her undersea kingdom of Atlas. As Isamu is preparing to return to dry land, Atlas is attacked by the evil king, Magma VII, who reveals that he is planning to use the dragon to seize control of the surface world. The fate of Earth and Ocean is placed in the hands of Isamu and Angel for the final battle against the invading king.

This was the fourth Toei adaptation of a Shotaro Ishinomori story (the previous one was **FLYING GHOST SHIP**), but this popular manga artist's work continue to appear in a variety of different anime for many decades to come, from the SF of **CYBORG 009** to the economics education of **JAPAN INC**. Director Tamiya would go on to direct another kids-save-the-world

THIRTY-YEAR-OLD'S HEALTH AND PHYSICAL EDUCATION, A

2011. JPN: *Sanjussai no Hoken Taiiku*. AKA: *30-sai no Hoken Taiiku*. TV series. DIR: Mankyu. SCR: Ryo Akiyama. DES: Sao Tamado. ANI: N/C. MUS: N/C. PRD: Gathering. 12 mins. x 12 eps.
Hayao and Natsu are both 30-year-old virgins until the gods decide to bring them together. Daigoro and his little brother Macaron are Gods of Sexual Love, sent from heaven to make sure office worker Hayao gets over his nervousness and gets it on, even if that means practicing on the gods themselves until he can get up enough nerve to try a girl. Timid librarian Natsu gets a visit from twin goth-Loli goddesses Pi-chan and Ku-chan to do the same for her. In the cause of helping their charges achieve sexual freedom, both sets of deities will do anything, however crude, tasteless, or offensive.

No giggling at the back of class, please: this isn't porn, it's educational. Or at least, that's the intention. Japan's falling birthrate is caused by the reportedly low levels of sexual activity among its citizens. This anime is based on a guidebook by Mitsuba, published in 2008, designed to educate older virgins about how to find potential sex partners and what to do with them. A manga version by Rikako Inomoto followed in 2010, after a national survey claimed that activity in Japan's bedrooms was disappointingly infrequent for most. Director Mankyu has previous experience with short, humorous anime—see **WITH THE LORDS** and **UTSURUN DESU**—but the educational purpose of the series is hampered by the levels of censorship required for TV broadcast. It may improve when seen uncensored, but we can't offer any guarantees.

THIS BOY CAN FIGHT ALIENS *
2011. JPN: *Kono Danshi, Uchujin to Tatakaemasu*. Video. DIR: Sobi Yamamoto. SCR: Sobi Yamamoto. DES: Sobi Yamamoto. ANI: Sobi Yamamoto. MUS: N/C. PRD: CoMix Wave. 28 mins.

A series of alien invaders are sent to conquer Earth, although for reasons not initially clear, they are expected to first fight Kakashi, a troubled, amnesiac Japanese boy who must defeat them on a patch of pre-determined ground. Sobi Yamamoto's home-made anime, inspired very much by the success of **VOICES OF A DISTANT STAR** and released by the same production company, takes a winningly female stance on the posturings and declarations of sci-fi anime made for boys. Like the fan artists and appropriations of the *yaoi* movement (**ARGOT AND JARGON**), she posits a reluctant warrior, unsure of why he needs to go through the ridiculous performance of beating up aliens-of-the-week, doubting the honor of the organization and society that desires him to do so, and struggling with his homoerotic feelings for his handsome handler. The U.S. release includes three shorter works by Yamamoto, on similar themes.

Yamamoto's *This Boy Caught a Merman* (2012, *Kono Danshi Ningyo o Hiroimashita*), also released in English, also takes a well-used cliché of boys' anime and filters it through a *yaoi* lens—a teen who jumps into the sea and is saved by a hunky merman, with all the interspecies issues that is sure to create.

THIS UGLY YET BEAUTIFUL WORLD *
2004. JPN: *Kono Minikuku mo Utsukushii Sekai*. AKA: *Konomini; The Ugly & Beautiful World*. TV series. DIR: Shoji Saeki. SCR: Tomoyasu Okubo, Sumio Uetake, Shin Itagaki, Shoji Saeki, DES: Kazuhiro Takamura, Yo Yoshinari. ANI: Kazuhiro Takamura. MUS: Tsuyoshi Watanabe. PRD: Gainax, SHAFT, Geneon, Rondo Robe, MOVIC, TBS. 24 mins. x 12 eps.

Bored part-time motorcycle courier Takeru Takemoto has a close encounter of the third kind when he finds an alien girl in the glow of a strange light in the woods. Later, one of his friends encounters a second, similar girl. Based on an original concept by Hiroyuki Yamaga and Shoji Saeki, this science-fiction tale introduces alien entities that are not "living" organisms by our definition, but can mimic human beings. Their function is to help humans experience the beauty of emotion, such as joy or surprise—they often seem to achieve this by jiggling, the true hallmark of a Gainax anime. This is the 20th-anniversary work from the renowned studio, which previously collaborated with the SHAFT production house on **MAHOROMATIC**. **N**

THOSE WHO HUNT ELVES *
1996. JPN: *Elf o Karu Monotachi*. AKA: *Elf Hunters*. TV series. DIR: Kazuyoshi Katayama, Tatsuo Okazaki, Hiroshi Fukutomi. SCR: Masaharu Amiya, Masashi Kubota. DES: Keiji Goto, Akira Furuya. ANI: Keiji Goto. MUS: Susumu Aketagawa. PRD: Group Tac, TV Tokyo. 25 mins. x 24 eps.

A trio of adventurers is transported (with their T-74 tank) to a world inhabited by elves. Elven leader Celcia accidentally destroys the spell to send them back. Luckily fragments were copied onto the skin of five elves (and you can bet they aren't fat, old male elves, either) so fighter Junpei, actress Airi, and schoolgirl tank pilot Ritsuko must find them to get home. Crashing quest into skin-flick, with the emphasis on stripping the elves rather than skinning them, there are a few plot twists designed to amuse *Beavis and Butthead* viewers (firebrand Celcia transforms herself into an ugly dog and gets stuck, ho ho) and some with wider appeal (all the spell fragments our heroes find are easily visible without removing a stitch of clothing from their hosts.) There are nods to **DOMINION**

in Ritsuko's devotion to her tank, and **EL HAZARD** in Junpei's obsession with finding decent curry in this alien world. Based on an "original" manga by Yutaka Yagami in *Dengeki Comic Gao*. **LN**

THOUSAND AND ONE NIGHTS, A *
1969. JPN: *Senya Ichiya Monogatari*. AKA: *A Thousand and One Nights*. Movie. DIR: Eiichi Yamamoto, Osamu Tezuka. SCR: Kazuo Fukuzawa. DES: Osamu Tezuka, Eiichi Yamamoto. ANI: Kazuko Nakamura, Sadao Miyamoto. MUS: Isao Tomita. PRD: Mushi Pro. 128 mins.

Aldin the water-seller (modeled upon French star Jean-Paul Belmondo) carries the beautiful Miriam away from a Baghdad slave market where she is just about to be sold to Havahslakum, the spoiled son of the chief of police. They spend a night of passion in a house they believe to be deserted but is actually a hideaway for the pervert Suleiman, who has been watching them. The police arrest Aldin on suspicion of Suleiman's murder, and a heartbroken Miriam dies shortly after giving birth to his child. In fact, the murder was committed by Havahslakum's father's assistant, Badli, who not only covets the chief's job but has also been arranging secret trysts between Kamhakim, leader of the 40 thieves, and the chief of police's wanton wife. Badli plays all sides against each other, allowing the thieves to escape to make his boss look incompetent but also raping Kamhakim's tomboyish daughter, Mahdya, to break her spirit. He has even had sex with a crocodile, believing an ancient prophecy that promises a kingdom to anyone who can manage it. Aldin escapes from jail, steals some treasure from the 40 thieves, and escapes with Mahdya, who soon deserts him when he succumbs to temptation on an island of nymphomaniacs. Discovering they are really snake-women, Aldin flees and eventually finds a great treasure after many more adventures.

Many years later, two interfering jinn cause Aldin and Miriam's daughter, Yahliz (now Badli's stepdaughter), to fall in love with Aslan the shepherd boy. In search of her lover while disguised as a man, Yahliz is forced to marry a king's daughter, a lesbian who is extremely pleased to discover her new "husband's" secret. The princess helps Yahliz find Aslan, and they return to Baghdad in time for the arrival of

"Sindbad," who is really Aldin in disguise. After a feud with the king (engineered by Badli, of course), Aldin becomes ruler and Badli his vizier. Badli fakes Aslan's death and persuades Yahliz to join Aldin's harem. Aslan is saved by the two jinn, one of whom turns into a lioness to pleasure the lions who are supposed to devour him, and returns in time to prevent Aldin from committing incest with his own daughter. Mahdya kills Badli in belated revenge for her father's death, and Aslan and Yahliz become the new rulers, leaving Aldin penniless but happy once more.

During a mini-boom of Japanese interest in the *Arabian Nights* (which would turn thoroughly sour with the Oil Shocks and subsquent recession of the early 1970s), Astro Boy–creator Tezuka published his own manga adaptations and subsequently adapted them into this sumptuous film, faithfully including erotic elements often dropped from modern versions. As well as stirring orientalist music from composer Isao Tomita (who scored several Tezuka anime), it included early contributions from future big names Akio Sugino, Gisaburo Sugii, and Osamu Dezaki as lowly animators. For reasons known only to himself, Tezuka also invited several famous novelists to contribute to the production as voice actors in minor roles. Unsung talents included *Silence*-author Shusaku Endo and the science fiction writers Yasutaka Tsutsui and Sakyo Komatsu. Komatsu would return to help Tezuka in a more sensible capacity on Space Firebird. There have been several Japanese versions of the same classic cycle of stories, including Alibaba's Revenge, A Thousand and One Nights, Aladdin and the Wonderful Lamp, and Sindbad the Sailor. An English-dubbed version, running at approximately 100 minutes, was released in America at the turn of the 1970s, but sank without a trace and may even be lost. There is, however, an extant English-subtitled print, screened at festivals under the title *A Thousand and One Nights*, with a song on the soundtrack that clearly identifies the hero as "Aldin," and not the Aladdin one might expect. Tezuka went on to make a far less successful erotic movie, Cleopatra: Queen of Sex. See also Video Picture Book. **◐**

THREE MUSKETEERS, THE

1987. JPN: *Anime Sanjushi*. TV series, TV special, movie. DIR: Kunihiko Yuyama, Tetsuro Amino, Takashi Watanabe, Keiji Hayakawa, et al. SCR: Yasuo Tanami, Jack Production. DES: Mitsuki Nakamura, Shingo Ozaki, Hatsuki Tsuji. ANI: Hatsuki Tsuji, Shojuro Yamauchi. MUS: Kohei Tanaka. PRD: Studio Gallop, Gakken, Toei, NHK. 25 mins. (TVm), 25 mins. x 52 eps. (TV), 45 mins. (m).

In 17th-century France, young D'Artagnan leaves his home village to travel to Paris and find fame and fortune, serving his King as a Musketeer like his father before him. So far, so close to the 1844 novel by Alexandre Dumas *père*. In Paris, he defeats the plots of evil Cardinal Richelieu and Milady against Louis XIII, aided by his fellow Musketeers and mentors Athos, Porthos, and Aramis, and by the queen's beautiful maid, Constance. The familiar Dumas tale was popularized in Japan by *D'Artagnan's Story*, an 11-volume series of novels by Yoshihiro Suzuki, with accompanying artwork by Lupin III–creator Monkey Punch. The *3M* anime adapts the first volume of this version, with two major additions to the Dumas original—D'Artagnan's orphan boy assistant Jean, and the fact that Aramis is actually a *woman*, in a cross-dressing homage to Rose of Versailles. The series, which began in October, was piloted the previous May with a 25-minute TV special *Chase the Iron Mask* (*Tekkamen o Oe*). For the latter half of the series, the animators would draw on the same events, from Dumas' *Man in the Iron Mask* through the tenth book in Suzuki's series. The series was recut again into the movie *Aramis' Adventure* (1989, *Aramis no Boken*), which rearranged flashbacks with new footage set a year after the final episode. Lune is a 16-year-old girl from the Swiss Alps, who falls in love with François, a young man she meets in the forest. Believing him to have been murdered, she adopts a man's disguise and changes her name to Aramis, hoping to track down the man who ordered his death. Naturally, this turns out to have been his twin brother, Louis XIII, in a surprise that dovetails beautifully with the original source material. For very different animated versions, see Dogtanian and the Three Muskehounds, Keroppi, and Puss in Boots.

3×3 EYES *

1991. JPN: *Sazan Eyes*. Video. DIR: Daisuke Nishio, Kazuhisa Takenouchi. SCR: Akinori Endo, Yuzo Takada. DES: Koichi Arai, Tetsuya Kumagai, Hiroshi Kato. ANI: Koichi Arai, Tetsuya Kumagai. MUS: Kaoru Wada. PRD: Tabac, Toei. 30 mins. x 4 eps. (v1), 49 mins., 45 mins., 50 mins. (v2).

Yakumo Fuji loses his father in an accident in Tibet but gains a new responsibility. He must help a 300-year-old immortal, the last of the race that once ruled Earth, who lives in a symbiotic relationship with a 16-year-old girl called Pai. Yakumo is killed rescuing Pai but is brought back to life as her zombie protector. Now both of them begin a quest to become human.

Creator Yuzo Takada began as an assistant to Judge's Fujihiko Hosono, and here combines the "walking dead" hero of Ultraman with the ancient immortals of Tezuka's Three-Eyed Prince. Takada's *3x3 Eyes* manga suggests that all myths are the vestigial race-memory of a great conflict between extradimensional entities. Mixing the treasure-hunting elements of *Indiana Jones* with a mythopoeic buddy-movie, Pai and Yakumo search the world for artifacts that might help them. The mawkish romance between the two (made frankly irritating in an English dub that gives Pai a grating screech in place of a voice) is nicely contrasted with their magical personae—shy-boy Yakumo is an indestructible zombie, and puppy-fat ingenue Pai disappears completely when her third eye opens, revealing a powerful being with a demonic disregard for human life. In this way, *3x3 Eyes* is perhaps the most dramatically interesting spin-off from Cream Lemon's schizophrenic "Lolita" concept and is mercifully asexual.

A second series, *3x3 Eyes: Legend of the Divine Demon* (1995, *Sazan Eyes: Seima Densetsu*), followed after Takada's successful Blue Seed, with Pai losing her memory in Hong Kong and living as a schoolgirl in Japan. The new story, featuring input from Takada himself, takes the pair to Mount Kunlun, China's version of Olympus, where they join forces with some priests and a man with a really bad Australian accent to find the "key" to Pai's dimension. Covering only the first five volumes of the ongoing original, *3x3 Eyes* remains one of those truncated anime series consistently beset with rumors of its imminent return to the screen.

THREE-EYED PRINCE

1985. JPN: *Mitsume ga Toru; Akumajima no Prince Mitsume ga Toru*. AKA: *The Three-eyed Prince on Devil's Island*. TV special, TV series. DIR: Yugo Serikawa (TVm), Hidehito Ueda, Yusaku Saotome, Keiichiro Mochizuki, Shinichi Matsumi (TV). SCR: Haruya Yamazaki (TVm), Mayori Sekijima, Reiko Naka, Tsunehisa Arakawa. DES: Osamu Tezuka (TVm), Kazuhiko Udagawa (TV). ANI: Shigetaka Kiyoyama, Hiroshi Wagatsuma, Masami Abe (TVm), Kazuhiko Udagawa, Yoshiaki Matsuhira (TV). MUS: Kazuo Otani (TVm), Toshiyuki Watanabe (TV). PRD: Toei, Tezuka Pro, Nippon TV, Tezuka Pro, TV Tokyo. 85 mins. (TVm), 25 mins. x 47 eps. (TV). Sharaku is a high school student but his naïve manner, youthful face, and bald head make him look like a kindergarten kid, and he usually has some kind of bandage or dressing on his forehead. If he didn't, the world would be in trouble, for he is the last descendant of a three-eyed race who once ruled the world with advanced technology and vast intelligence. His mother left him to be raised at Dr. Inumochi's home shortly before she was killed by a mysterious lightning blast. Sharaku's friend is the local priest's daughter, Wato, a tomboy and aikido expert who knows his secret. She loves his "true" self, an arrogant but lonely superbeing, and looks after and protects his childlike human persona. She's also the one who usually has to take off his third-eye covering so he can save the situation when they get into some kind of trouble with magical phenomena, and she puts it back on again to prevent him taking over the world once the danger is past. Based on a manga by Osamu Tezuka, in which he hoped to combine the look of Elmer Fudd with the adventures of Sherlock Holmes—note an investigative character "Sha-rak," whose faithful assistant is addressed as "Wat-san." A heavy influence on the later **3x3 EYES**.

THRILLER RESTAURANT

2009. JPN: *Kaidan Restaurant*. AKA: *Ghost Story Restaurant*. TV series, movie. DIR: Yoko Ikeda, Masayuki Ochiai. SCR: Shoji Yonemura, Higashi Shimizu, Miho Maruo. DES: Akira Takahashi, Yoshito Watanabe. ANI: Akira Takahashi. MUS: Hiroshi Takaki. PRD: Toei Animation, TV Asahi. 24 mins. x 23 eps. In the old Tokyo suburb of Yamazakura, development has come to a standstill: modern buildings and old apartment blocks stand side by side. Ako Ozora is an elementary school student and her life is quiet until Sho Komoto transfers to her class from a school in London. He's handsome, outgoing, and widely traveled. He's got a fund of scary stories from all over the world. When he hears that strange phenomena are happening in Yamazakura, he asks Ako to take him to an old restaurant that has been abandoned for years on the outskirts of town. What will be on the menu for Ako and her friends?

Based on Miyoko Matsutani's long and successful series of children's books, with art by Kumiko Kato and Yoshikazu Takai, this show promises **HORROR AND MONSTERS** with no magic involved. Each episode has the ghostly waiter at the restaurant introducing Ako, Sho, and their friends to three short scary stories for those of a nervous disposition.

Toei's studio in the Philippines provided much of the in-between animation and digital painting with some of the key animation outsourced to Korea and Shanghai. The result was a show that frequently rated in the top ten anime of the week throughout its run. In summer 2010 a hybrid live-action/anime movie *Theater Version: Thriller Restaurant (Gekijoban Thriller Restaurant)* paired teenage screen star Ayano Kudo with other popular TV and movie actors and the animated ghosties. Compare with **SPOOKY KITARO**, another chiller with a live-action movie version, and with the original *Kwaidan*—ghostly tales by Yakumo Koizumi, better known as the 19th-century European immigrant Lafcadio Hearn.

THUMBELINA

1978. JPN: *Andersen Dowa: Oyayubi-hime*. AKA: *Andersen's Tale: Thumbelina; Princess Thumb*. Movie, TV series. DIR: Yugo Serikawa (m), Hiromitsu Morita, et al. (TV2). SCR: Ikuko Oyabu (m), Akiyoshi Sakai, Shigeru Yanagawa, Yu Mizuki (TV1). DES: Osamu Tezuka, Satoshi Fukumoto (m), Usagi Morino (TV). ANI: Tatsuji Kino (m), Usagi Morino (TV). MUS: Shunsuke Kikuchi (m), N/C (TV). PRD: Toei, Tezuka Pro (m), Enoki Film, TV Tokyo (TV). 64 mins. (m), 25 mins. x 26 eps. (TV). The movie made by Tezuka's studio for Toei is a straightforward adaptation of the classic fairy tale. A tiny girl, only as long as a man's thumb, is born to a childless woman, abducted by frogs who want her to marry their son, but escaping instead (with the help of a kindly bumblebee, a Tezuka addition) to find a real prince without having to kiss the frog first. It's utterly charming. One of the ever-popular **TALES OF HANS CHRISTIAN ANDERSEN**, the story was adapted again by Megumi Nagata (see **PRISM SEASON**), and again as a TV series, *The Story of Princess Thumbelina* (1994, *Oyayubi-hime Monogatari*). A feature-length edit of this series was apparently released on home video in the U.S. as *Thumbelina*. The series was also shown in Spanish on Puerto Rican TV.

THUNDERBIRDS 2086 *

1982. JPN: *Kagaku Kyujotai Technovoyager*. AKA: *Scientific Rescue Team Technovoyager*. TV series. DIR: Noboru Ishiguro, Yasuo Hasegawa, Katsuhito Akiyama, Hiromichi Matano, Shigeo Koshi. SCR: Hideki Sonoda, Noboru Ishiguro, Kazuo Yoshioka, Takayuki Kase, Shiro Ishimori, Keiji Kubota. DES: Kenzo Koizumi, Kunio Aoi, Kazuto Ishikawa. ANI: Katsu Amamizu, Mitsuru Ishii, Yasushi Nakamura. MUS: Kentaro Haneda, Koji Makaino. PRD: Jin, Green Box, AIC, Tohoku Shinsha, Fuji TV. 25 mins. x 24 eps. In 2066, the World Federation Supreme Council appoints former astronaut Dr. Gerard Simpson (pointlessly renamed Warren Simpson in the U.S. dub) to run the International Rescue Organization. Based on a remote Pacific island, he leads a group of kids who pilot the "Techno Voyager" vehicles to save people in danger—Captains Raiji Hidaka (Dylan Beyda) in One, Sammy Edkins Jr. (Johnathan Jordan Jr.) and Eric Jones (Jesse Rigel) in Two, Gran Hanson (Gran Hansen) in Three, Catherine Heywood (Kallan James) in Four, and token brat Paul Simpson ("Skipper" Simpson) getting under everyone's feet.

The concept of the five-strong team had already been popularized in anime by **BATTLE OF THE PLANETS**, but the other similarities between *Technovoyager* and the British cult puppet show *Thunderbirds* (1966) might be considered actionably obvious. Luckily for him, producer Banjiro Uemura was head of Tohoku Shinsha and also of ITC Japan, part of the international corporation that owned the Thunderbirds copyright—*if* he found the resemblance too close for comfort, he would have had to sue *himself*. Uemura had already made ZERO TESTER, which by his own cautious admission "learned from" *Thunderbirds*. In 1977, he had held extensive talks with *Thunderbirds*-creator Gerry Anderson about a new animated series to be called first *Thunderhawks*, then *Terrahawks: Order to Recapture Earth*. During the outlining process, much of Anderson's original idea was discarded in favor of new plot elements from Sukehiro Tomita and designs from Yoshikazu Yasuhiko. Set in the year 2085, it was to be the story of second-generation immigrants from the rest of the solar system, returning to reconquer their homeworld, which has been overrun by aliens led by the evil "Queen Mother." The show stalled in the early stages, because the Japanese network MBS claimed there was no call for sci-fi. *Star Wars* opened in Japan just a few months later, by which time the project was already canceled.

However, several parties reused elements of the proposal in later shows—writer Tomita with MOSPEADA, Anderson with his puppet show *Terrahawks* (1983), and Uemura with *Technovoyager*.

Technovoyager flopped in Japan (only 18 episodes were screened on its initial run), but in his capacity as head of ITC Japan, Uemura was able to sell it to ITC's American arm, and, in 1983, the full run was broadcast in America as "*Thunderbirds 2086*, an ITC Entertainment Production"—transformed into a *bona fide* ITC production after the fact. The new title recognized the show's debt to *Thunderbirds*, but where the British only allowed for a handful of rescue craft, the Japanese team could call on no less than 17, enabling them to investigate crime and save lives on land, under the sea, in the air, and in space. The coincidental and remarkably convenient confusion of the letters B and V in Japanese allowed for the "Techno Voyager" vehicles to have the letters "TB" on their sides. The extensive vehicle lineup and stock hero team characters were close to the Japanese *Terrahawks* outline, while the *Terrahawks* puppet series released in

Britain reputedly had many elements of the British outline—with the Queen Mother renamed Zelda. In another moment of chance cross-cultural pollination, both *Terrahawks*' Zeroids and GUNDAM's Haro were spherical robots.

The confusion continued when the six unbroadcast episodes of *Technovoyager* were exported back to Japan as part of *Thunderbirds 2086*, two 90-minute videos with the U.S. dub (by SPEED RACER's Peter Fernandez) left intact for added exoticism. Meanwhile, in a final irony, an "anime" version of *Terrahawks* did eventually reach Japanese screens; when the puppet show was broadcast in Japan, its opening sequence was replaced with new Japanese-made animated footage, directed by Satoshi Dezaki. Hideaki Anno, a big enough fan of the original *TB* to produce the Japanese-made documentary *The Complete Thunderbirds*, would acknowledge his own debt to Gerry Anderson with numerous homages in EVANGELION.

THUNDERBOYS

1996. JPN: *Itsuka no Main:* Kaminari Shonen Tenta Sanjo. AKA: *Forever Main*. Video. DIR: Hiromichi Matano. SCR: Isao Shizudani. DES: Shushi Mizuho. ANI: Mitsuharu Otani. MUS: Teppei Sato. PRD: Toei. 45 mins.
Tokyo bikers race and fight, and race, and fight. Based on the manga in *Young Jump* by Shushi Mizuho. 🅛🅥

THUNDERCATS *

2011. TV series. DIR: Sean Song, Yoshiharu Ashino. SCR: Todd Casey, Tab Murphy. DES: Takahiro Tanaka, Koji Watanabe, Toru Hishiyama, Yusuke Yanagisawa. ANI: Masayuki Kato, Sadahiko Sakamaki, Takuo Tominaga. MUS: Kevin Kliesch. PRD: Studio 4°C, Warner Brothers Animation. 25 mins. x 26 eps.
Thundera is under attack by the lizard people. Lion-O and the Thundercats set out on a quest for the Book of Omens to restore peace, but their old enemies Mumm-Ra and Slythe will do anything to foil them. This remake of the 1980s U.S. Rankin/Bass TV series (FALSE FRIENDS) is a Japanese-American coproduction that aims to combine elements of anime with Western animation, made primarily for airing in the West—unlike the original which was a work-for-hire project created in America by Tobin "Ted" Wolf and animated in Ja-

pan for the Western market. Jules Bass and Arthur Rankin, Jr. (both now retired) are credited as executive producers with Eiko Tanaka as animation producer. Only one of the original voice actors has returned— Larry Kenney, the original Lion-O, now plays the hero's father in the 2011 version. The character of talking cat Snarf has been changed, presumably as a mark of respect for the late Bob McFadden, who created the character, and Jim Meskiman, the character designer on the 1985 series, provides voices for supporting characters in several episodes. *Thundercats* is listed in line with our principle of considering all animation made with a primarily Japanese crew as anime, but it should be noted that the writing and approach is entirely American. Like the Marvel Comics adaptations from Madhouse, the body may be made in Japan but the soul comes from somewhere else entirely. This is not a criticism, simply an observation: America makes some fine stories, but they're not Japanese, however they're dressed.

THUNDERSUB *

1979. JPN: *Uchu Kubo Blue Noah*. AKA: *Space Carrier Blue Noah*. TV series. DIR: Kazunori Takahashi, Tomoharu Katsumata, Masahiro Sasaki, Kunihiko Okazaki, Shiro Murata, Teppei Matsuura. SCR: Hideaki Yamamoto, Kiyoshi Matsuoka, Takashi Yamada. DES: Yukiyoshi Hane. ANI: Kenzo Koizumi. MUS: Masaaki Hirao. PRD: Westcape Corporation, Yomiuri TV (Nippon TV). 25 mins. x 27 eps.
In the year 2050, Earth is invaded by the alien Godom race, known rather more grandly in the Western version as the Force of Death. Ninety percent of humanity is wiped out, but their last hope lies in the secret Point N1 Base on Minamidori Island. There, the great aircraft carrier Blue Noah is nearing completion. With a young crew led by the inventor's son Makoto Kusaka (Earth commander's son Colin Collins in the U.S. version), it launches fighters to save the world, but the project isn't yet complete, and the ship must get to other secret Points to complete its construction, powered by a pendant passed on to the hero by his dying father.

As if taking a WWII battleship and sending it on a star trek wasn't ludicrous enough, this Earthbound follow-up to STAR BLAZERS somehow failed to recapture the magic of its predecessor. It wasn't until episode 21 that the ship justified its "Space Carrier" title, picking up a star drive at Point N9 that finally allowed it to get out of the water. Though 27 episodes were made, the first 4 were not shown in their original form but cut together into a feature-length "TV special" to open the series. Unlike the Yamato, however, the Blue Noah did not return for a sequel. See also **ODIN**, another attempt by producer Yoshinobu Nishizaki to make money out of ships sailing in space.

TIBETAN DOG, THE *

2012. JPN: *Tibet Inu Monogatari: Kin'iro no Dorje*. Movie. DIR: Masayuki Kojima. SCR: Naoto Inoue. DES: Shigeru Fujita. ANI: Ken Baba, Yutaka Minowa, Kunihiko Hamada, Kunihiko Sakurai, Masaru Kitao, Tsutomu Awada. MUS: Shusei Murai. PRD: Madhouse, China Film Group, Ciwen Pictures. 90 mins.
After the death of his mother, young Tenzing (Tianjing in Mandarin) is sent away from his home town of Xi'an, and out to the prairie lands beneath the Tibetan mountains, where his father Lageba is a small-town physician. Tenzing is initially a reluctant transplant to the countryside, particularly when he is obliged to help out by becoming a shepherd, although he makes a newfound friend in the form of Dorje, a golden-furred Tibetan mastiff that he nurses back to health after a fight with another dog (compare to **WHITE FANG** and **CALL OF THE WILD**).

With China and Japan eternally at odds over obscure southern islands and cultural controversies like **DEATH NOTE**, more business-minded souls seem to have prevailed in this international coproduction, with a feel-good story about a politically sensitive subject, using Japanese talent but with presumably enough Chinese money and labor to get around the People's Republic's hefty quota on foreign film imports. For this reason, the film's "original" state is officially in Chinese; the Japanese **TRANSLATION** is presumably a dub made after the initial release, synchronized to pictures that were originally voiced in Mandarin, although this does not explain why the credited screenwriter is Japanese.

Yang Zhijun's best-selling source novel *Zang Ao* (2005, *Tibetan Mastiff*) was set in China's troubled 1950s and played to the Chinese sense of Tibet as an untamed wilderness requiring the sacrifice and patronage of good-hearted workers, although neither Lageba nor his son appear to be ethnic *Han* Chinese, but rather local Tibetans. In that regard, Tenzing is less participating in the colonization of Tibet than he is returning to his own roots, not that this made much difference in either Japan or China, where the film put an end to high-level feature collaboration for a while by ignominiously flopping. In a moment of historical irony, it was suggested that part of its poor performance was down to the assumption by audiences that it was a Chinese cartoon (**FALSE FRIENDS**), and not one of those better-made Japanese ones we keep hearing about.

TICO OF THE SEVEN SEAS

1994. JPN: *Nanatsu no Umi no Tico*. AKA: *Tico and Nanami*. TV series. DIR: Jun Takagi, Jiro Fujimoto, Shinpei Miyashita, Kozo Kusuba, et al. SCR: Hideki Mitsui, Aya Matsui, Noriyuki Aoyama, Asako Ikeda, Toru Noborito. DES: Satoko Morikawa, Shigeru Morimoto, Kazue Ito. ANI: Yoshiharu Sato, Masaru Oshiro, Koichiro Saotome, Ei Inoue, Azumayami Sugiyama. MUS: Hibiki Mikazu. PRD: Nippon Animation, Fuji TV. 25 mins. x 39 eps.
Little Nanami travels the world's oceans with her father, Scott Simpson, an oceanographer, in search of adventure and on the track of a legendary luminous whale said to have played a vital role in the evolution of life on Earth. Their captain is Alphonso, a brave fishermen and the owner of the good ship Peperonchino. Rich, beautiful Cheryl Melville talks her way on board in search of adventure, with her butler, and refuses to leave. Nanami's special friend, the orca Tico, swims alongside their boat as they search for the whale through the seven seas. When an unscrupulous team of scientists gets to the whale first, Nanami and Tico rescue it in the hope of learning its secrets and sharing them with the rest of the world. This is one of Nippon Animation's rare series *not* based on a classic novel; the story was created for the company by Akira Hiroo. Beautiful designs and a plot combining adventure with ecological correctness make a charming children's series. Episode 31 was not broadcast but included on the laserdisc release.

TIDE-LINE BLUE *

2005. TV series. DIR: Umanosuke Iida, Dan Odawara, Keiko Oyamada. SCR: Yuka Yamada, Megumi Sasano. DES: Sadakazu Takiguchi, Kimitoshi Yamane, Akihiko Yamashita. ANI: Kazuhide Tomonaga, Mineko Ueda. MUS: Tsuneyoshi Saito. PRD: Telecom, TV Asahi. 25 mins. x 13 eps.
It has been 14 years since the terrifying Hammer of Eden disaster, in which a meteorite strike on the Earth wiped out six billion lives and caused a massive rise in the sea levels. Aoi, the secretary-general of what's left of the United Nations, hopes to persuade the remnants of the globe to pull together, while Gould, a maverick submarine captain, stands up to the New United Nations by declaring war on them in the Ulysses, a rogue nuclear submarine. So, **EVANGELION** meets **SILENT SERVICE**, with the unsurprising presence of Satoru Ozawa, creator of **BLUE SUBMARINE NO. SIX**, among the committee members who came up with the plot. Compare also to **SUBMARINE SUPER 99**, which similarly featured two brothers separated by conflict—in this case, a boy called Keel is our teenage point-of-view character in the town of Yabitsu, attacked by Gould, while Keel's brother Tean is one of the men onboard Gould's sub.

TIES OF LOVE

1992. JPN: *Ai no Kusabi*. AKA: *Ties of Affection; Bonds of Love*. Video. DIR: Akira Nishimori, Kazuhito Akiyama. SCR: Naoko Hasegawa, Rieko Yoshihara. DES: Katsumi Michihara, Naoyuki Onda. ANI: Koichi Arai, Takeyoshi Nakayama. MUS: Toshio Yabuki. PRD: AIC. 60 mins. x 2 eps.
The future city of Tanagra is governed by a computer entity known as Jupiter but administered by the Parthia syndicate, whose members are drawn from the aristocratic group known as Blondys. Social tensions bubble under its serene, ordered surface; disaffected political groups are plotting to kill the most important syndicate member, Jason Mink. But there's an even more pressing destabilizing factor in Jason's life: he has fallen deeply and embarrassingly in love with his "pet" Riki, a boy from the wrong side of the tracks who, like many young men and women with no other options, has voluntarily become a sex slave. Neither Jason nor Riki can admit the

ties that hold them, even to themselves; leaving aside their pride, both would be outcasts. Jason gives Riki a vacation, a chance to go back to the slums and find his old friends again, but a meeting with his former lover leads to tragedy.

Based on the novel by Rieko Yoshihara, which was illustrated by JOKER's Katsumi Michihara, *ToL's* society is reminiscent of ancient Greece; not only are the institutions of power restricted to a certain class, but women are completely excluded from significant roles. All the key power relationships we see, including sexual ones, are between men. Ironically, the Jupiter computer manifests as feminine: like Kusanagi in GHOST IN THE SHELL, she's a man-made idea of the female in a world run by masculine elites. There is sexually explicit material but the violence is mostly emotional. Like most anime about homosexual love, this was originally made for a *female* audience. **NV**

TIGER AND BUNNY *

2011. JPN: *Tiger to Bunny*. TV series, movie. DIR: Keiichi Sato, Yoshitomo Yonetani (m1). SCR: Masafumi Nishida, Tomohiro Suzuki, Yuya Takahashi. DES: Masakazu Katsura, Kenji Hayama, Masaki Yamada, Kenji Ando, Kinichi Okubo. ANI: Kenji Hayama, Toshimitsu Kobayashi, Yoshikazu Kon. MUS: Yoshihiro Ike. PRD: Sunrise, Bandai Visual, MBS, Asatsu DK, Shochiku, T-Joy. 25 mins. x 25 eps. (TV), 93 mins. (m1), 100 mins. (m2). In an alternate world, those with special superpowers, known as "Next," make a living by protecting the people like old-style superheroes. They get ranked through "hero points" and have corporate backers requiring them to wear logos on their costumes (ADVERTISING AND SPONSORSHIP). There's even a reality show, *Hero TV*, with the winner of the year's rankings being crowned "King of Heroes." Veteran hero Wild Tiger—AKA Kotetsu T. Kaburagi—has been slipping in the rankings, and his old-school preference for saving lives regardless of the cost has bankrupted his sponsors (DIRTY PAIR). The ruthless corporation that buys up his contract decides to monetize the investment by pairing him up to create *Hero TV's* first superhero duo. They choose cute young rookie Barnaby "Bunny" Brooks as the other half of the team. Blond, babyfaced Brooks definitely

appeals to the younger demographic that simply doesn't get Wild Tiger—but appealing to his new partner is an entirely different matter.

Brad Bird's remarkable 2004 movie *The Incredibles* put superheroes into a postmodern world where they were not wanted. Zack Snyder's *Watchmen* (2009) had them mired and sullied in a past where nationalism and patriotism fought a rearguard action against individual control: the superhero gone off track, flawed, and compromised, but still master of his fate and captain of his soul. *Tiger and Bunny (T&B)* brings them right into the 21st century, in our world of increasing globalization and corporate control—a world more akin to Norman Jewison's *Rollerball* (1975) in which not even a superhero can be free and the only way to survive is by selling out to the suits or standing together for no gain but friendship and commonwealth: the superhero as the reckless idealist he was born to be.

Despite breaking no molds with regard to the way the superhero genre treats women, *T&B* is a lovable show as well as a clever one. Its structure weaves one-shot tales into an overarching web of background threads, its central characters face convincing personal conflicts and problems apart from their relationship, and its writers really understand the way celebrity, personality, and control interweave inside and outside the glitzy media world. A sure sign of its intelligence is that the second half of the show builds an even stronger story on the foundation of the first. It looks slick and stunning, with as much awareness of visual trends as social ones. Its art is as flashy and as well-founded as its story. The music zips along, meshing with the story and art to create a strong audience-grabbing net.

In the spirit of monetization, the logos of real as well as fictional companies feature on the heroes' costumes. There have also been spin-offs galore: games, toys, a stage play, and (of course) comics. Katsura and Mizuki Sakakibara illustrated the manga written by Masafumi Nishida, published in 2012; two more manga have followed. The year 2012 also saw the release of the movie *T&B: The Beginning (Gekijoban TIGER & BUNNY: The Beginning)*, which interleaved elements of

the first two episodes with new footage. A second film, *T&B: The Rising* (2014), featured all-new animation and a new plot in which an industrial bigwig takes over Apollon Media, fires Tiger, and briefly forces Bunny to pair up with a lackluster new hero, Golden Ryan.

TIGER MASK

1969. TV series, movie. DIR: Takeshi Tamiya, Kimio Yabuki, Tomoharu Katsumata, Fusahito Nagaki, Hiroshi Shidara, Yoshio Kuroda, Yasuo Yamaguchi (TV1), Kozo Morishita, Shigenori Yamauchi, Hideki Takayama, Tomoharu Katsumata, Masayuki Akehi, Kazuo Yamazaki, Osamu Sekita (TV2). SCR: Masaki Tsuji, Tadashi Kondo, Tomohiro Ando (TV1), Haruya Yamazaki (TV2). DES: Naoki Tsuji. ANI: Keijiro Kimura, Koichi Murata (TV1), Tsukasa Abe (TV2). MUS: Shunsuke Kikuchi (both). PRD: Toei, Yomiuri TV (Nippon TV) (TV1), Toei, TV Asahi (TV2). 25 mins. x 105 eps. (TV1), 47 mins., 53 mins., 25 mins. (m), 25 mins. x 33 eps. (TV2). Naoto Date has a secret identity as masked wrestler Tiger Mask, part of a crude school of fighting that is more violence than art. Overcome by guilt when an opponent's death puts his little son in an orphanage, the hard man devotes himself to the well-being of the orphans and works to improve their lives in the only way he knows how—by fighting. He also aims to raise the standards of the ring and ensure that fighting is recognized as an honorable art, not mere violence.

Based on a 1968 manga in *Bokura* magazine by KARATE-CRAZY LIFE's Ikki Kajiwara and ZERO SEN HAYATO–creator Naoki Tsuji, *TM* soon made it to theaters, as episodes were edited into seasonal "movies"—*TM* (1970, #9), *TM: War Against the League of Masked Wrestlers* (1970, #23, 25 and 26), and *TM: The Black Demon* (1971, #56).

A 1981 follow-up series is set after Naoto's death—he was killed saving the life of a child. A new opponent, Outer Space Mask, not endorsed by any of the national wrestling federations, bullies his way into the ring and injures a young wrestler. Tatsuo, a great fan of Tiger Mask who once lived in the orphanage he supported, intervenes wearing his hero's old mask and is accepted into the fraternity of masked wrestlers, where he becomes a major star. Champion of the oppressed and weak, he hides his secret wrestling identity under the everyday clothes of a sports journalist, echoing that other champion of the weak, *Superman.* The character remains an iconic figure in Japanese popular culture; a live-action movie remade the story for a new generation in 2014. **ⓥ**

TIME BOKAN
1975. AKA: *Time Fighters; Time Ma-chine.* TV series. DIR: Hiroshi Sasagawa, Takao Koyama, Katsuhisa Yamada, Hideo Nishimaki (TV1), Seitaro Hara (TV2), Takao Yotsuji (TV4). SCR: Jinzo Toriumi, Haruya Yamazaki, Keiji Kubota, Tsunehisa Ito, Shigeru Yanagawa (TV1), Akiyoshi Sakai (TV2), Masaru Yamamoto (TV4), Satoru Akahori. DES: Tatsuo Yoshida, Yoshitaka Amano, Kunio Okawara. ANI: Eiji Tanaka, Hidemi Kubo, Hitoshi Sakaguchi. MUS: Masayuki Yamamoto, Masaaki Jinbo. PRD: Tatsunoko, Fuji TV. 25 mins. x 61 eps. (TV1), 25 mins. x 108 eps. (TV2), 25 mins. x 53 eps. (TV3), 25 mins. x 52 eps. (TV4), 25 mins. x 52 eps. (TV5), 25 mins. x 58 eps. (TV6), 25 mins. x 20 eps. (TV7), 30 mins. x 2 eps. (v), 25 mins. x 26 eps. (TV8).

Junko and Tanpei are the grandchildren of a mad inventor who produced a time machine, went off into history, and simply vanished. They're determined to find him, but they're not the only ones. The scandalously dressed villain Madame Margot, with her hapless sidekicks, Birba and Sgrinfia, are also on his trail, and on the trail of a massive diamond lost somewhere in time. The ending could be viewed as an anticlimax—the professor returns to the present under his own steam—but in this case the journey, with its slapstick perils, crazy creatures, and interventions by wicked but inept villains, is more than the destination.

Time Bokan was only the first chapter in an epic saga of insanity on every level: design, characterization, and plot. With often-cited similarities to *Wacky Races,* and machines and performances that went further and further over the top, Ippei Kuri produced the first series based for Tatsunoko Production and remained in charge throughout its increasingly silly but lovable progress to classic status.

Like Sunrise's **BRAVE SAGA**, both the crew and central concept of the series remained through successive sequels, with only superficial changes. Only the characters' looks and the wonderful machines, de-

signed to spin off into toy merchandising, displayed any variation—the robots and vehicles became so lucrative that a new one was introduced every episode.

Its successor, *TB Series Yattaman* (1977), came only a week later. Ganchan, descendant of a line of inventors, has made his own robot car, Yatta One, and takes his girlfriend and mechanic for a celebratory meal. Unfortunately they go to a restaurant run by sexy Miss Doronjo and her comic sidekicks, Tonzura and Boyakei. They are members of a gang under orders to find a powerful artifact, the Dokurostone (Skullstone), which can locate hidden treasure and is really the head of a mighty extraterrestrial called Dokurobei, who is just using the crooks to retrieve it. Ganchan and his friends must stop the crooks, but the quest takes them all over the world and through time. Though the plot is an obvious respray, art directors Toyo'o Ashida, Kazuhiko Itada, and Takashi Nakamura brought *visual* freshness and invention.

Once again, as one series ended another began, the following year's *TBS Zendaman* (1978). This time young Tetsu and his girlfriend Sakura race through time in their robots, Zendalion and Zendagorilla, to fight the trio of villains headed by sexy Miss Mujo. A short *Zendaman* movie premiered in spring 1980, but the new series *TBS Time Patrol Tai [Team] Otasukeman* was already on the air. In an achingly familiar set-up, Miss Atasha, Dovalski, and Sekovitch are seeking an artifact that will enable the shadowy Tonmanomanto to dominate the world. Hikaru and Nana spring to the rescue in their increasingly incredible machines, chasing or chased by the villains through time and space. An *Otasukeman* movie was screened in spring 1981 as once again the new series *TBS Yattodetaman* had just begun on TV. Princess Domenica's rule is challenged by the theft of the Cosmopavone, a magical bird whose powers (like Tezuka's **SPACE FIREBIRD**) can bring peace and healing. She calls on two of her ancestors, a boy and a girl from the 1980s, for help against hot-tempered Princess Mirenjo and her henchmen.

The sixth series, *TBS Gyakuten Ippatsuman* (1982, AKA *Ippatsuman Returns*), revolved around Homuran and Harubo, owners of the time delivery company

Timelease, who set off to make a delivery to another era and find themselves pursued by Munmun, Kosuinen, and Kyokanchin, representatives of rival firm Sharecowbellies, who are now calling themselves the Clean Aku Trio. Then Ippatsukiman shows up to help Timelease, and they realize that there's more to this job than they thought. The final series, *TBS Itadakiman* (1983), moves the starting point for the journey to Oshaka Academy, where the headmaster orders three students, Hoshi, Sagosen, and Hatsuo, to find the pieces of an artifact called the Oshakapuzzle, now scattered throughout the world. Meanwhile three "ronin" (students waiting to retake entrance exams) called Yanyan, Dasainen, and Tonmentan are also looking for the puzzle, which will give the finder strange powers. As before, the titular hero comes to the aid of the good guys.

Falling ratings brought the show to an end after reasonably long innings, though it returned to video once its young audience was old enough to rent. Members of the original crew reunited one last time for the *Wacky Races* homage *Time Bokan Royal Revival* (1993), which pits all seven trios of villains from the original series in a race against each other. The prize is supposedly the leading role in the next episode.

However, there was no next episode until *Thieving Kiramekiman* (2000, *Kaito Kiramekiman*), an eighth series that reordered the archetypes to make goodnatured criminals the protagonists. The handsome Puff is sent back 500 years to our time to rescue his ancestor, Professor Rikkid. Everybody needs the treasure known as the Gold Eye, and Puff teams up with the pretty teenager Lips to form the Kiramekiman cat-burglar team. They are pursued by a trio of bumbling French cops, while Lips' own father is the chief of police—a combination of elements of **CAT'S EYE** and **LUPIN III**. This most recent incarnation in the franchise was shown on TV Tokyo. There was also an unrelated Fuji TV series *Time Travel Tondekeman* (1989), directed by Kunihiko Yuyama.

TIME OF EVE *
2008. JPN: *Eve no Jikan.* Video, movie. DIR: Yasuhiro Yoshiura. SCR: Yasuhiro Yoshiura.

DES: Ryusuke Chayama, Kazuhiro Hotchi, KODAMA. ANI: Ryusuke Chayama. MUS: Toru Okada. PRD: Studio Rikka, DIRECTIONS. 15 mins. x 6 eps. (v), 106 mins. (m)

Androids are taken for granted in human society. Most people treat them like household appliances, though some have more empathy—after all, the only practical difference between androids and humans, apart from better behavior, is a digital ring floating over their heads. But fraternizing with androids is frowned on. Riko has always toed the acceptable social line, but then his household android Sammy, made to appear female, goes missing. He and his friend Masaki trace its footsteps and find an unusual café—a café where all are welcome, but discrimination between androids and humans is not permitted. Here he will rediscover an important part of himself.

Packed with references to sci-fi favorites, this is anime made by and for fans. Isaac Asimov's Three Laws of Robotics are specifically invoked, and Osamu Tezuka's discourse on the status and treatment of robots underlies the show's framework. The title is a reference to a line from the end credits of **YOKOHAMA SHOPPING LOG**, which has very similar themes, and there are references to *R.U.R., Blade Runner,* and *THX1138.* Yoshiura's **PALE COCOON** is also referenced. The same team, along with similar inspirations from Asimov and Tezuka, would be reunited in **PATEMA INVERTED**.

The series was successful online, attracting considerable attention. Its website hinted at a second series, which has yet to materialize, but a movie was edited from the episodes, with a new theme song by Yuji Kajiura performed by J-Pop divas Kalafina. This was screened at festivals worldwide, but was only available outside Japan through the U.S. iTunes store as a download. In 2013 Pied Piper, Inc., DIRECTIONS Inc., and Studio Rikka launched a Kickstarter to raise $18,000 for an international Blu-ray release of the movie edit.

TIME PALADIN SAKURA

2011. JPN: *TP Sakura—Time Paladin Sakura—Jiku Boeisen.* AKA: *TP Sakura—Time Paladin Sakura—Space-Time Self-Defense Match.* Video. DIR: Takehiro Nakayama. SCR:

Naoki Tozuka. DES: Makoto Koga, Masatoshi Muto. ANI: Makoto Koga. MUS: Tatsuya Kato. PRD: Nomad, Bandai Visual, Bushiroad, Lantis. 25 mins. x 2 eps.

Sakura Yoshino is a lively third-grader who has inherited secret magical powers from her grandmother. He and her cousin Junichi Asakura gain power from a magical cherry tree. With their classmate Suginami and android schoolgirl Miharu, they have various lighthearted adventures in this alternate-world spin-off from the **DA CAPO** series.

TIME STRANGER

1986. JPN: *Toki no Tabibito Time Stranger.* AKA: *Time Traveler Time Stranger.* Video. DIR: Mori Masaki. SCR: Atsushi Yamatoya, Mori Masaki, Toshio Takeuchi. DES: Moto Hagio, Koji Morimoto. ANI: Takuo Noda, Hiroshi Fukutomi, Toshio Hirata, Yoshiaki Kawajiri, Kunihiko Sakurai, Yasuomi Umezu. MUS: Ryoichi Kuniyoshi. PRD: Project Team Argos, Madhouse. 91 mins.

A minibusload of modern-day teenagers is hijacked by Jiro Agino, a time-traveler from the future, who drags them back to WWII Tokyo, and then to feudal Japan. They arrive at Azuchi Castle in 1582, just before the surprise attack that will/did/could result in the death of Nobunaga Oda. Jiro has determined that this is a critical moment in history, and that, had Nobunaga survived, Japan would have been spared the seclusion and stagnation of the Tokugawa period—forecasting that when Western powers arrived in the 19th century they would not have been able to treat Japan as a second-class nation. This in turn would have created a better political climate in the Pacific, and averted Japan's involvement in WWII! The gang is faced with a dilemma—to change history by warning Nobunaga (portrayed with a sympathy rare in his other anime appearances such as **YOTODEN**), or to keep quiet and risk dying in the coming "surprise" attack. Meanwhile, far-future assassin Toshito Kutajima arrives to terminate Jiro's meddling, while schoolgirl Tetsuko "Teko" Hayasaka unhelpfully falls in love with Nobunaga's page-boy Ranmaru. Considering the famous names all over the crew (note **THEY WERE ELEVEN**'s Hagio designing alongside future **MEMORIES**-director Morimoto), it's a real mystery why this was never

picked up for U.S. release. Based on a young adult SF novel by Taku Mayumura. In 2003, the unrelated anime **GOSHOGUN** *Étranger* was released in the U.S. under the confusing title of *Time Stranger,* in what we can only assume was a deliberate attempt to annoy the authors of the *Anime Encyclopedia.*

TIME STRANGER KYOKO

2001. JPN: *Jiku Ihojin Kyoko Chokora ni Omakase.* AKA: *Time Stranger Kyoko: Leave It to Chocola.* Video. DIR: Masatsugu Arakawa. SCR: Fumihiko Shimo. DES: Hiroyoshi Iida. ANI: Hiroyoshi Iida. MUS: Koshu Inaba. PRD: Production I.G, Transarts. 11 mins.

A number of girls stand watch as guardians for the future of the world, their sub–**SAILOR MOON** ranks including Sakataki the Crystal Stranger, Hizuki the Ice Stranger, and of course, Kyoko Suomi, the Time Stranger. None of that's important right now, however, because the king's robot assistant is trying to organize a birthday party for him, in a spin-off tale that only tenuously relates to the 2000 manga in *Ribon* magazine by **FULL MOON**–creator Arina Tanemura. Although made for video, this short was shown in a few venues as part of a *Ribon* promotional tour, hence its being filed as a "movie" in some sources. **LNV**

TIME TRIO

1988. JPN: *Zukkoke Sanningumi Zukkoke Jiku Boken.* AKA: *Bumbling Trio's Time Travel Adventure.* Video. DIR: Hidehito Umeda. SCR: Takao Koyama. DES: Kazuo Maekawa. ANI: Takashi Saijo. MUS: Masayuki Yamamoto. PRD: Tama. 57 mins.

Hachibe, Mochan, and Hakase are three young newshounds for their elementary-school newspaper. While trying to spy on their pretty teacher, Yukiko, they are flung back into the Edo period where they meet another beautiful authority figure, this time a princess struggling to control her domains. Based on a best-selling children's book by Masayoshi Nasu. Compare to **ZEGUY**. They were back in 1995 as the leads in a one-shot TV special, and again in 2004 in a 26-episode series.

TIMID VENUS

1986. JPN: *Okubyo-na Venus.* Video. DIR: Hiroyuki Kadono. SCR: Koichi Arai. DES: Hiroyuki Kitakubo, Shingo Araki, Michi Himeno. ANI:

Michi Himeno. mus: Ami Osaki. prd: Victor. 20 mins.
Young singer Hiromi is packed off to New York shortly after the release of her debut single and told to train hard for her first concert. A short anime made with a semi-documentary feel.

TO HEART *
2000. TV series. dir: Naohito Takahashi. scr: Hiroshi Yamaguchi. des: Yuriko Chiba. ani: Shichiro Kobayashi. mus: Kaoru Wada. prd: KSS, Sun TV, Oriental Light and Magic (OLM). 25 mins. x 13 eps. (TV1), 4 mins. x 6 eps. (v extras), 25 mins. x 13 eps. (TV2), 25 mins. x 13 eps. (TV3, To Heart 2), 30 mins. x 3 eps. (v1), 30 mins. x 2 eps. (v2), 20 mins. x 2 eps. (v3), 30 mins. x 2 eps. (v4).
Akari and her childhood friend Hiroyuki walk to high school together every day. After school Akari, Hiroyuki, and their friends Shiho and Masashi attend school sports clubs and hang out at restaurants and karaoke spots. Their classmates include a rich girl who belongs to the school's Black Magic Club and a robot maid sent to school to collect data on Japanese student behavior. So it's just another typical Japanese high school, and Hiroyuki is just another typical Japanese high school boy who, despite being a lazy, sarcastic guy, finds himself solving various people's problems and thus surrounded by pretty girls who would do anything for him. But the trouble is, they don't seem to have much idea of anything *to* do. Episode one depicts the first day of the fall school term, and revolves around choosing new seating assignments for Hiroyuki, Masashi, and Akari's class—which involves much arguing until Hiroyuki steps in—and then a trip to a karaoke spot. Episode two shows the angst generated when Masashi and Shiho each obtain two tickets to a popular band's concert without the other's knowledge, and Hiroyuki and Shiho (who never seem to rub each other the right way) are tasked with telling their friends of the opposite gender that only two of the quartet can attend. Subsequent episodes either introduce further characters (and their problems) or depict similar minor crises.
Created by a group of artists calling itself AQUAPLUS, this is another anime based on a 1997 "love simulation game" for the PlayStation and designed to sell

merchandise depicting the cute characters. The anime shifts the original's focus from Hiroyuki to Akari, presumably to lure in a female audience who wouldn't take kindly to being regarded as the "prize" in a game. It's not overtly sexual; rather it creates the fantasy life most lonely Japanese teenagers would apparently like to have, which, on the evidence of this show, is a quiet one. A series of often comic shorts was included as part of the television series' video release.
The *third* TV series was based on another game story, hence the confusing name of *To Heart 2* (2005). A series of later video releases revisited the characters in a series of new combinations, with each episode focusing on one particular girl from the ever increasing ensemble.

TO LOVE-RU *
2008. jpn: To LOVEru—Trouble. aka: Trouble, To Love You. TV, video. dir: Takao Kato, Atsushi Otsuki. scr: Akatsuki Yamatoya, Katsuhiko Chiba, Saki Hasemi, Takao Kato, Yasutomo Yamada, Naoko Marukawa, Takeyuki Ishida, Yukari Matsumura. des: Yuichi Oka, Keito Watanabe, Mika Nakamura, Yoshimi Umino, Naritsuki Ogi. ani: Tsuyoshi Nakano, Natsumi Doi, Yuichi Oka, Akio Takami, Kazumi Ono, Kaiji Tani, Maria Ichino. mus: Takeshi Watanabe. prd: Xebec, TBS, Triple A, Geneon, avex entertainment, Shueisha. 24 mins. x 26 eps. (TV1), 25 mins. x 6 eps. (v1), 24 mins. x 12 eps. (TV2), 24 mins. x 12 eps. (TV3), 25 mins. x 2 eps. (v2), 25 mins. x 2 eps. (v3).
Rito Yuki is smitten with his high school idol Haruna, but can't bring himself to tell her. Instead he comes home night after night and sulks in the bathtub, where he is eventually visited by Lala, princess of planet Deviluke, who has sought his unlikely protection in order to avoid marriage to one of the unsuitable suitors pressed upon her by her royal father. This fan-service-packed love comedy has been done better (and funnier) on TV as URUSEI YATSURA then as a porn video in VISIONARY. On this occasion, the "original" story is based on the manga by Saki Hasemi with art by Kentaro Yabuki, which has spun off further manga, TV, and video releases since its debut in 2006. A video of the same title followed in 2009, with six stories based on Lala's penchant for inventing comically

unreliable devices like those DORAEMON pulls out of his tummy. The 2010 TV series *More To Love-Ru (Motto To LOVERu)* brings in another harem trope (ROMANCE AND DRAMA), this time from granddaddy of harem anime TENCHI MUYO! as Lala and Rito are joined by her little sisters and friends. Another TV series, 2012's *To Love-Ru Darkness (To LOVERu—Trouble—Darkness),* introduces a golden-haired assassin hired by one of Lala's suitors to kill Rito, and she naturally ends up as part of the harem. This was preceded the same year by a video of the same title, animating further chapters of the manga as asides to the TV continuity. ◐

TO-Y
1987. Video. dir: Mamoru Hamazu. scr: Izo Hashimoto. des: Naoyuki Onda. ani: Naoyuki Onda. mus: Masayuki Matsuura. prd: Studio Gallop. 60 mins.
To-Y, leader of the up-and-coming band Gasp, has an intense rivalry with another young musician, Yoji. An ambitious manager, Miss Kato, tries to use this to persuade him to dump his band and let her manage his solo career. She plays him and Yoji off against each other and threatens to stop Gasp playing a big open-air concert that is vital to their career. In the end To-Y decides that playing his own kind of music with his own kind of people is more important than manufactured pop success, and this commitment pays off when he and Gasp set up their own gig near the open-air concert and draw a good crowd. An enjoyable pop soap opera based on Atsushi Kamijo's 1985 manga from *Shonen Sunday Comics Wide*, it had added cred thanks to music director Matsuura, a member of hit band PSY-S, who also have a single on the soundtrack, along with Zelda, Barbee Boys, Street Sliders, Kujira, and more.

TOBIDASE! BATCHIRI
1966. aka: *Jump to It, Batchiri*. TV series. dir: Kumi Yamamoto. scr: Hitoshi Narihashi. des: Mitsuteru Okamoto. ani: Batchiri Group. mus: Kunio Miyauchi. prd: Nippon TV. 10 mins. x 132 eps.
The adventures of jug-eared schoolboy detective Batchiri, who can solve cases that baffle the police, thanks to his brilliantly ingenious mind. An early precursor of CONAN THE BOY DETECTIVE.

TODAY IN CLASS 5-2

2006. JPN: *Kyo no Go no Ni*. TV series, video. DIR: Makoto Sokuza, Tsuyoshi Nagasawa. SCR: N/C. DES: Tadashi Kojima, Mitsuo Miyamoto, Sunao Chikaoka, Yuka Hirama. ANI: Tadashi Kojima, Sunao Chikaoka. MUS: Toru Yukawa, Kei Haneoka. PRD: Shinkuukan, Xebec, Starchild Records. 29 mins. x 4 eps. (v), 23 mins. x 13 eps. (TV).

Ryota is a bright, energetic fifth grader in elementary school who always manages to get into perverted situations with his classmates. If you are disturbed by sexual innuendo relating to children—adult jokes told in cute, childlike voices, very young characters with little or no idea that what they're doing is inappropriate—then Coharu Sakuraba's manga and the show it inspired really isn't for you. Each episode is divided into five periods of the school day, and is a slice-of-life story with a sexual twist, framing jokes and curiosity about the opposite sex and bodily functions as part of normal childhood development—as, indeed, they are for the age group depicted in the show, although to judge from online fan feedback that doesn't appear to be the age group watching it. A TV series followed in 2008: the TV team also made a video bundled as an extra with the special edition of the collected manga in 2009. It was entitled *Today in Class 5-2: Treasure Chest (Kyo no Go no Ni Takarabako)*. ❶❷

TODAY WE START OUR LOVE

2010. JPN: *Kyo, Koi o Hajimemasu*. Video. DIR: Shigeyasu Yamauchi. SCR: N/C. DES: Junichi Hayama, Yusuke Takeda. ANI: Junichi Hayama. MUS: Masaru Sugimoto. PRD: JC Staff, Shogakukan, Shogakukan-Shueisha Productions. 20 mins. x 2 eps.

Hibino Tsubaki starts high school in the same class as a rude boy with the same surname as her. Kyota behaves as though she owes him when he cuts her hair, makes crude demands, steals her first kiss, and says he'll make her his woman. But it turns out that he's got some painful secrets in his past. Can he help Hibino overcome her low self-esteem and deal with her selfish kid sister if she helps him deal with his issues? Based on Kanan Minami's 2007 manga.

TODAY'S ASKA SHOW

2012. JPN: *Kyo no Asuka Show*. TV series. DIR: Masato Jinbo. SCR: Taishi Mori. DES: Masashi Kudo. ANI: Masashi Kudo. MUS: Tomoki Kikuya. PRD: Silver Link. 3 mins. x 20 eps. In this short series based on the manga of Taishi Mori, clueless blonde teenage ingénue Asuka (or Aska in the company's English press releases) embarks upon a series of everyday activities, only to find herself in a series of embarrassing clothing emergencies that display her underwear (at very least) to shocked passers-by. Jailbaity "entertainment," and nowhere near as amusing as it thinks it is, this online series was designed for distribution to cellphones, and came accompanied by an *Aska* app, which took the form of the animated heroine leaving messages on the viewer's phone. ❶

TODO, IZUMI

A house pseudonym used by workers at Toei Animation in the creation of some anime serials, including **PRECURE** and **TOMORROW'S NADJA**. Compare to Hajime Yatate, the nonexistent man who invents stories for Sunrise, or Saburo Yade, who has supposedly dreamed up many of the teamshows made by Tsuburaya.

TOEI ANIMATION

Founded in 1956 as the animation arm of the film studio Toei, the company's first and most important acquisition was Nippon Doga (AKA Nichido), the small studio formed in 1947 by Sanae Yamamoto and Kenzo Masaoka. The company was known as Toei Doga until 1998, when the *doga* part of its name was translated into English as Toei Animation. For simplicity's sake, we have referred to the company as Toei Animation throughout this book. As the inheritor of Japan's prewar **EARLY ANIME** tradition, and as the instigator of Japan's postwar feature anime with **PANDA AND THE MAGIC SERPENT**, Toei can be seen as the cradle of the modern Japanese animation business, not only in the establishment of a long tradition of cinema animation, but in training much of the talent that was then poached by rivals at the start of the TV era—this latter leading to its nickname as "Toei University." Its movie releases included early classics of Japanese feature animation, including **LITTLE NORSE PRINCE** and **PUSS IN BOOTS**, whose leading feline Perrault remains the studio's mascot character—"a cat," commented one producer only partly in jest, "to devour the [Disney] Mouse." Despite its successes, it was unable to compete at a local level with the higher-budget releases of Disney, and enjoyed longer term success in television—some of its early work including **KEN THE WOLF BOY**, **LITTLE WITCH SALLY**, and **TIGER MASK**. As a feature of the move into TV and the same general slump in finances that killed off Mushi Production, Toei put many staff on temporary or freelance contracts in the early 1970s. A number of them responded by forming their own limited companies as suppliers to Toei, leading to the foundation of many of the small studios of today. As one of the largest production studios, Toei's home in north Tokyo's Nerima Ward attracted other anime specialty companies, both spin-offs and originals (the situation is analogous to Hewlett-Packard and California's Silicon Valley). Today, Nerima is the site of dozens of other production houses, as well as several of the best-known manga creators. More recent successes for the studio have included **NARUTO** and **ONE PIECE**, which have taken the studio's work to a wide international audience. The creator Izumi Todo, responsible for the studio's long-running **PRECURE** franchise among others, is a house pseudonym, deriving from "TOei DOga, oIZUMI studio."

TOFU BOY

2011. JPN: *Tofu Kozo*. Movie. DIR: Gisaburo Sugii, Masaaki Kawahara. SCR: Gisaburo Sugii, Kiyomi Fujii, Mao Aoki. DES: Shigeru Fujita, Nobuhito Sakamoto. ANI: Kazuaki Kawakita. MUS: S.E.N.S. PRD: Lapiz, EXACT 3D, Avant, BROSTA TV, CYBIRD, Dentsu, Epic Records Japan, Fuji TV, Kadokawa Shoten, Warner Bros. Pictures Japan, TIS. 86 mins. A little *yokai* (goblin) from the Edo period is a big disappointment to his family, especially his father, the leader of all *yokai*. He can't scare anyone and is compelled to hang on to a plate of tofu to avoid vanishing into thin air. According to Japanese folklore the tofu should be deadly, but he's too sweet to harm anyone. At last, tired of being scolded and shouted at, he sets out to find his mother, with only a Daruma doll for companion. He ends up in the human world, where he finds new friends and new courage.

This was trumpeted by Warner as Japan's first fully 3D anime, overlooking the claims of a bunch of others. It has, however, sufficient claims on attention in its own right. Sugii has always been unafraid to let the story dictate both style and pace; his assured direction plus the insanely energetic *yokai* give this film based on Natsuhiko Kyogoku's original novel its own charm.

TOHO

Founded in 1932 as the Tokyo-Takarazuka Theater company (the characters for which contract to "To-Ho" in Japanese, and conveniently also mean "Eastern Treasure"), Toho's international reputation is largely founded on its production of the movies of Akira Kurosawa and the famous *Godzilla* series. However, it has also produced or distributed many anime productions, including **LUPIN III**, **TOUCH**, and the movies of Studio Ghibli. In 2012, clearly annoyed with only taking part of the money from distributing films made by others, Toho entered the field of anime production, directly investing in several new titles in order to benefit as both distributor and producer. Its foray into such dangerous waters began with **MAJESTIC PRINCE**.

TOKA GETTAN

2007. TV series. DIR: Yuji Yamaguchi. SCR: Tomomi Mochizuki, Ai Shimizu, Mamiko Noto. DES: Asako Nishida, Toshihisa Koyama. ANI: Asako Nishida. MUS: Akifumi Tada. PRD: Studio DEEN, avex entertainment. 25 mins. x 26 eps.
Kamitsumihara, ancestral home of the Kamiazuma clan, is a place where magic and legend can still be glimpsed. Toka Kamiazuma meets a young girl named Momoka and their meeting brings an ancient legend to life. This series looks absolutely glorious, with beautiful art and dreamlike, delicate color. Unfortunately it wraps its themes of violence, abuse, survival, and predestination in a chronology so convoluted that following it is just too much effort, especially given the plot holes and contrived occurrences. Even watching the series back to front doesn't help, though much of the story is told in reverse. A spin-off of **MOONLIGHT LADY**, which in turn is based on a porn game by CARNELIAN. **ⒸⓃⓋ**

TOKAIDO GHOST STORIES

1981. JPN: *Tokaido Yotsuya Kaidan*. AKA: *Ghost Stories of Tokaido/Yotsuya*. TV special. DIR: Hajime Suzuki. SCR: Sadatoshi Yasunaga. DES: N/C. ANI: N/C. MUS: N/C. PRD: TMS, Telecom, Fuji TV. 54 mins.
Set in 1636, this is the story of Iemon, who plans to kill his wife, Oiwa, hoping to inherit her wealth and marry his new, rich ladylove. Though his slow poisoning scheme pays off, he escapes justice in this world but not in the next, as Oiwa's ghost returns to haunt him at every turn. A TV special based on Japanese ghost stories, for which one segment consisted of an animated tale.

TOKIMEKI MEMORIAL

1999. AKA: *Heartbeat Memorial*. Video. DIR: Hajime Kamegaki, Akira Nishizawa. SCR: Yosuke Kuroda. DES: Hideyuki Motohashi. ANI: Hideyuki Motohashi, Yasunori Tokiya. MUS: N/C. PRD: Studio Pierrot. 40 mins. x 2 eps. (v), 25 mins. x 25 eps. (TV).
Kirameki High School has a beautiful romantic legend. If on graduation day a girl confesses her love to a boy under the old tree in the school grounds, the two will have a long and happy life together. Twelve girls are in their last five months before graduation: Shiori Fujisaki, the principal character; her best friend Megumi Mikuhara; the beautiful but vain Mira Kagami; and the others consisting of Saki Nijino, Ayako Katagiri, Nozomi Kiyokawa, Yuko Asahina, Yuina Himoo, Yukari Koshikii, Yumi Saotome, and Miharu Tatebayashi. The first episode is essentially an introduction to all the characters, but in the second, as Rei Ijuin's Christmas party approaches, Shiori must decide whether to let her beloved know her true feelings.
Based on a 1994 dating game by Konami, which required the player to win one of the girls' hearts over a game span that was supposed to occupy three years of high school and end at graduation, this video spin-off matches the game story closely and uses the same voice actresses, though the character designs are slightly different. Launched for the PC Engine, the original game spun off ten further titles in PlayStation, Sega Saturn, Game Boy, PC, Mac, and arcade incarnations, plus a radio chat show, radio dramas, and a long list of merchandise. Nobuhiro Takamoto's TV

series *Tokimeki Memorial: Only Love* (2006) introduces a new protagonist with links to the original game, only later revealed.

TOKIMEKI TONIGHT

1982. AKA: *Heartbeat Tonight*. TV series. DIR: Hiroshi Sasagawa, Akinori Nagaoka, Tsutomu Shibayama, Teruo Kogure, Hideo Yoshisawa, Noboru Ishiguro, Tomomi Mochizuki. SCR: Toshio Okabe, Takao Koyama, Tomomi Tsutsui, Fuyunori Gobu, Akiyoshi Sakai. DES: Koi Ikeno. ANI: Keiichi Takahashi, Keiko Yoshimoto, Gisaburo Sugii. MUS: Kazuo Otani. PRD: Group Tac, Nippon TV. 25 mins. x 34 eps.
Ranze looks like any other teenage girl, but she's the daughter of a vampire and a female werewolf. You can imagine how that would cramp your style bringing friends home after school, so she leaves her family to try and live a normal life. But then, just as she's enjoying falling in love with school hunk Shinpeki, she begins to manifest powers of her own. Strict laws forbid creatures of the night from marrying humans, and it seems that everything's going to go wrong for her—but in the end, luckily, Shinpeki turns out to be the long-lost son of Satan. Based on the 1982 manga by **NURSE ANGEL LILIKA SOS**–creator Koi Ikeno.

TOKIO PRIVATE POLICE *

1997. JPN: *Tokio Kido Police*. AKA: *Tokio Mobile Police*. Video. DIR: Moriichi Higashi. SCR: Yu Yamato. DES: Harunaga Kazuki, Satoshi Teraoka. ANI: Harunaga Kazuki. MUS: An Fu. PRD: Beam Entertainment. 30 mins. x 2 eps.
In 2034 Tokyo is beset by a giant-robot crime wave. With personnel numbers slashed on the police force, the government is forced to subcontract to private companies—compare to similar privatizations in **HUMMINGBIRDS**. Hence the Tokio (*sic*) Private Police, although the subject of this anime is less concerned with fighting future crime and more with erotic diversions. A cast roster that is a thinly disguised reference to **PATLABOR** duly assembles, with section chief Shibata trying to keep his affair with a captain under wraps, and new recruit Noriko arriving at the run-down Ginza branch, and getting laid on her first day.
Episode two features some robot action as well, although that's not the kind of

action that viewers of this short-lived series are likely to be looking for. The authors are not entirely sure why the world needs an erotic parody of *Patlabor*, but here it is. **◐**

TOKKO *
2006. TV series. DIR: Masashi Abe. SCR: Mitsuhiro Yamada. DES: Koji Watanabe, Maho Takahashi. ANI: Kazuo Takigawa, Koji Watanabe. MUS: Takamasa Aoki, Koji Sekiguchi. PRD: AIC Spirits, Group TAC, Shochiku, Three Light, WOWOW. 24 mins. x 13 eps.
Ranmaru Shindo and his little sister Saya survived a murder spree that left most of those who lived in their apartment complex, including their parents, dead. Now he has bad dreams, in which a topless woman with a sword pops in to finish off the nightmare creatures. Nevertheless, he's grown up and qualified to join the police department. He soon finds the topless lady is no dream, and the real nightmares are worse than he imagined. Add medieval alchemists, demons, and souped-up superfast zombies, and life is about to get even more dangerous as he joins the special unit known as Tokko, dedicated to keeping Japan safe from the kind of terror that claimed his parents.

Before filing for bankruptcy in 2010, Group TAC were *old*-old-school, founded in 1968, predating Madhouse, Ghibli, and a dozen more fan-favorite studios. But that's not why this show feels so old-fashioned. It's packed with interesting ideas but the execution lets it down—ironic, for a show that derives so much of its watchability from excessive execution, with body parts flying around the screen like confetti at a wedding on a windy day. Beyond the amount of gore, the action scenes are not well animated, with many corners cut and shortcuts taken. The two leads are badly underwritten, with little character and limited opportunity for the audience to care about them. The pacing is very uneven, and key facts and characters are dropped like dei ex machina in the final episodes. **◐◑Ⓥ**

TOKYO BABYLON *
1992. Video. DIR: Koichi Chiaki, Kumiko Takahashi. SCR: Tatsuhiko Urahata, Hiroaki Jinno. DES: Kumiko Takahashi. ANI: Kumiko Takahashi. MUS: Toshiyuki Honda. PRD: Animate Film. 50 mins., 55 mins.
Subaru Sumeragi lives in Tokyo with his twin sister, Hokuto. A fey, gentle young man, he's a psychic by heritage and by trade, often called on by the police to assist on investigations that stump all normal crime-fighting methods. Each of the two videos (the second appeared in 1994) focuses on one case: the first a murder for power and money that is complicated when a bereaved young woman, out for revenge, unleashes psychic forces she can't control; and the other a genuinely chilling look into the world of a psychopathic serial killer. The stories contrast Subaru's unworldly gentleness with the cynical and self-seeking city dwellers around him. The religious symbols are leftover 1980s fashion statements rather than deep philosophical references—a superficial quality only emphasized by a truly awful English-language musical interlude. The real importance of *TB* is its part in the movement of elements from girls' manga into the commercial mainstream—though the U.K. distributors did hype it by falsely claiming that the tape contained scenes of phone sex! Both videos are enjoyable in their own right but are only fragmentary glimpses of CLAMP's much larger manga universe, missing many of its facets. Subaru has a part in the earth-shaking events of **X: THE MOVIE**, in which the genial vet who has been his friend, suitor, and mentor, reveals his darker side, and the ancestral links between their two families are finally resolved.

TOKYO GHOUL *
2014. TV series. DIR: Shuhei Morita. SCR: Chuji Mikasano. DES: Kazuhiro Miwa. ANI: N/C. MUS: Yutaka Yamada. PRD: Pierrot, Tokyo MX TV. 24 mins. x 12 eps.
Hapless college boy Ken Kaneki is attacked by his would-be girlfriend Rize and seemingly saved when his assailant is crushed mid-assault by a falling girder. Rize is a *ghoul*—a vampiric predator that must eat fresh human meat to survive—but Ken is inadvertently co-opted into her species when overly helpful medics at the hospital save his life by transplanting her organs into him. He is now a hybrid, suffering the same overwhelming addiction to human flesh as other ghouls, but also disgusted by his condition. Prevented from committing suicide by the quasi-immortality that comes as a side effect of ghoulhood, Ken is plunged into the shadowy society of his new tribe, while desperately trying to keep his condition secret.

Sui Ishida's original 2011 manga in *Weekly Shonen Jump* was one of the best-sellers of its era, neatly catching a zeitgeist of self-doubt brought about by ecological paranoia, terrorist threats, and nationwide austerity measures. Ken's condition is a perfect allegory for the unwitting guilt of modern Japanese youth—saddled with an environmental and political situation not of their own making and facing the karmic debt of living in a late capitalist society, supported by predatory conflicts and unseen hardships elsewhere in the world. It is thus not only a fine contribution to modern anime in the vein of **SUMMER WARS**, but also a worthy iteration of the deep-set subtexts to be found in many a zombie and vampire story, confronting modern society with the visceral torments that lie beneath the surface—easily worthy of comparison with *True Blood* and *The Walking Dead*. With particularly nasty means of killing and consuming their prey, the ghouls take the gore quotient to such extremes that much of it was blanked out in the original simulcast and only restored on home video (**CENSORSHIP AND LOCALIZATION**). Such atrocities of **HORROR AND MONSTERS** jar rather unexpectedly with the show's only real failing—a recurring motif of out-of-place coffee shop comedy, as if the Taliban ran a teahouse. **Ⓥ**

TOKYO GODFATHERS *
2004. Movie. DIR: Satoshi Kon, Shogo Furuya. SCR: Keiko Nobumoto, Satoshi Kon. DES: Kenichi Konishi, Satoshi Kon. ANI: Kenichi Konishi. MUS: Keiichi Suzuki. PRD: Madhouse. 92 mins.
Three tramps—alcoholic Gin, transvestite Hana, and teen runaway Miyuki—find an abandoned baby while searching through the trash on Christmas Eve, a set-up familiar to cowboy movie fans as a sly reference to John Ford's *Three Godfathers* (1948), itself a refashioning of Harry Carey's early silent movie *The Three Godfathers* (1916). They decide to return the infant to its mother, only to plunge into a whirl of scandal, kidnapping, and attempted murder, all on the one day when Tokyo is supposed to be quiet.

Like Satoshi Kon's earlier **PERFECT BLUE**, *TG* initially seems like a strange choice for animation. With so many real-world locations, why not film it with real people? But nobody in the metropolitan government was going to approve a live-action film depicting a shanty town in the shadow of Tokyo's distinctive twin-tower metropolitan government offices, nor were many of today's TV idols likely to sign up for a tale of grunge and poverty, however happy the ending. The clincher would have been the snow. It is popularly believed that it only falls in Tokyo once every ten years—the presence of snow being the first of this movie's many Christmas miracles, and far cheaper to achieve with animation.

Satoshi Kon's choice of subject matter is an act of faith in itself—framing the relentless hope and happiness of a Christmas comedy in the stark, realist tones of his other work. The baby's arrival sends the tramps scurrying to buy water instead of booze at their local convenience store, much to the shop assistant's surprise. Hana jokes in the soup line that he is "eating for two," only to shock the charity worker the following day when he does indeed turn up with a babe in arms. In its comedy and sentimentality, *TG* is the closest thing we'll see to an anime pantomime, an end-of-year revel that turns everything on its head—even down to the Japanese voice actors, who are often cast against type, and with some amusing cameos. The opening sequence cunningly inserts production credits into the storefronts and graffiti surrounding the action; the ending is a souped up version of Beethoven's *Ode to Joy*—to the Japanese, the ultimate Christmas song.

TG also finds divine inspiration and beauty in everyday events, such as a wounded tramp seeing an angel, who turns out to be a bargirl in fancy dress. It may have three wise men (one and a half of whom are actually female), but its nativity story is not limited to Christian lore. A cemetery becomes a treasure trove as the tramps search for votive offerings of *sake*, and the film's stand-in for Santa Claus, white beard and all, can only perform his task properly if he dies doing it. The movie also alludes to Akira Kurosawa's *Rashomon*, which similarly features old men bickering over a foundling child in a storm, but at its

heart is a search for kindness and warmth in materialist Japan.

TG shows a side of Tokyo that tourists rarely see, a side that many anime fans will find less believable than the heroic ninja, giant monsters, and transforming robots produced by audiencechasers whose talent only extends to riffs on the latest fashion. It is also, like **AKIRA**, a love letter to the city. Kon renders its back alleys, shabby corners, and blue-collar areas with the same devotion that Otomo gave to the neon overload of its glittering uptown districts. Kon's leading characters are mostly confused and hapless but with an inner core of humanity that redeems their weakness. Ultimately, all are attempting to reunite themselves with "families" they have abandoned, believing their crimes to be unpardonable, whereas all their loved ones want for Christmas is for them to walk back in through the door. The story is compassionate but unsentimental—a work of honest emotion on the level of **MY NEIGHBOR TOTORO** or Frank Capra's Christmas masterpiece *It's a Wonderful Life*—and we can't, sadly, say that about very many anime. **LV**

TOKYO KIDS

Studio formed in 1990 by former employees of Studio Gallop and Tokyo Movie Shinsha, and particularly strong in digital compositing. Representative works include **HIKARIAN** and **SUSIE AND MARVIE**.

TOKYO MAGNITUDE 8.0 *

2009. TV series. DIR: Masaki Tachibana. SCR: Natsuko Takahashi, Yoichi Kato, Hiroko Kazui. DES: Atsuko Nozaki, Mika Nakajima. ANI: Atsuko Nozaki, Yukie Akitani, Atsushi Hasebe, Eiji Inomoto. MUS: Ko Otani. PRD: BONES, Kinema Citrus, Asmik Ace, Dentsu, Fuji TV, SME, Toho. 23 mins. x 11 eps. Right at the start of summer vacation in 2012: first year middle schooler Mirai takes her kid brother Yuki to a robot exhibition on Odaiba, the artificial island in Tokyo Bay. A huge undersea tremor starts a quake that topples Tokyo Tower and the Rainbow Bridge, ruining the city in seconds. Helped by motorbike delivery woman Mari Kusakabe, Mirai and Yuki try to get back home to Setagaya, on the west side of town, not knowing what they'll find there.

It's hard to believe, writing in the aftermath of Japan's devastating 2011 earthquake, that anyone in Japan would need reminding of the terrifying impact of these events; but when this anime aired, the last major quake (in Kobe) was 14 years in the past (**THE DAY THE EARTH SHOOK**), and children the age of heroine Mirai had no memory of such disaster. Mirai is a typical preteen girl, bored by everything and taking her family and home for granted. The events of the quake and the realization of how helpless she and her brother would be without a friendly adult to look out for them is an object lesson unlikely to have been lost on the young audience. Wishing you could lose your little brother is one thing; actually losing him as the city falls apart around you is quite another. Their struggle to deal with events even with adult help is believable, making up for the slightly incongruous depiction of a disaster in a major city with minimal panic, mass good behavior, and absolutely no looting.

Blood and bodies are kept to a minimum and there's nothing gratuitous, but the dirt and desperation are realistically shown. There's considerable effort to get the science of earthquakes and disaster management right, from the exposed anchor bolts of Tokyo Tower being scrutinized by engineers to the shocking sequence where a bridge collapse creates a huge wave that adds even more horror to the disaster. Much of this show is uncomfortable to watch, especially for those of us lucky enough to live in regions where earthquakes are few and small. It was also, of course, inadvertently prophetic of events in northeastern Japan in 2011, which themselves exerted an adverse influence on anime then in production—in the real year 2012, many anime were affected by power cuts and shortages, or censored owing to a sudden outbreak of taste (**KAIJI; BECAUSE I DON'T LIKE MY BIG BROTHER AT ALL**). See also **GYO: TOKYO FISH ATTACK**, which seemed to allegorize the experience in a different way.

TOKYO MAJIN *

2007. JPN: *Tokyo Majin Gakuen Kenpuchu To*. AKA: *Tokyo Demon Campus Sword Style Scroll*. TV series. DIR: Shinji Ishihara. SCR: Toshizo Nemoto, Shinji Ishihara, Atsuko Terasaki. DES: Jun Nakai, Koki Nagayoshi,

Masahiro Sato, Yoshihiro Nakamura. ANI: Jun Nakai. MUS: Takayuki Negishi. PRD: AIC Spirits, BeSTACK, Asmik Ace, Animax, Marvelous AQL, Showgate. 25 mins. x 14 eps. (TV1), 25 mins. x 12 eps. (TV2).

Tokyo's dragon stream has been disrupted. Demons and zombies prowl the night; a demonic rock god directs hordes of attack-crows; revolution and murder are in the air. A few ordinary teenagers are endowed with superior abilities. But can they learn to join forces and control their powers in order to save the city and their loved ones?

This series is based on a 2002 PlaySta-tion game created by Shuho Imai. It's as sprawling and messy as a game-based show can get, pulling in every element of the game world and letting it rip in an orgy of narrative chaos, with characters swirling and switching and goofy moments punctuating the extreme darkness. But what it does well, remarkably well considering its paper-thin plotting and hyperactively inept editing, is deliver action, gore, and magical battles. Like DOOMED MEGALOPOLIS before it, it realizes that kicking spirit ass makes up for many other shortcomings as far as the young male audience is concerned. This is undoubtedly what secured a second series in the same year, made by the same crew. *Tokyo Majin Part 2* (*Tokyo Majin Gakuen Kenpuchi To Dainimaku*) gives our heroes a new enemy in the form of a mysterious group of assassins, but otherwise sticks to what worked the first time around. **LV**

TOKYO MARBLE CHOCOLATE

2007. Video. DIR: Naoyoshi Shiotani. SCR: Masaya Ozaki. DES: Fumiko Tanikawa, Kyoji Asano, Shichiro Kobayashi. ANI: Kyoji Asano. MUS: Takeshi Yanagawa. PRD: Production I.G, BMG Japan, Frontier Works. 27 mins. x 2 eps.

A love story told from two viewpoints: Yudai can't express his feelings, while his girlfriend Chizuru has problems keeping a relationship going. This should be their first Christmas together but Yudai's gift goes disastrously wrong. As the pair chase off in different directions, can this help them find the answers that will bring them back together again? Made to celebrate the 20th anniversary of BMG Japan, inspired by songs from BMG artists SEAMO and Sukima Switch, it gave the performers

voice cameos, and Shiotani his directorial debut.

TOKYO MOVIE SHINSHA

Also known as TMS. Founded in 1964 by former puppeteer Yutaka Fujioka as a company to work on BIG X, the company originally operated as plain "Tokyo Movie" until 1976, when a refinancing deal led to the appendation of the phrase "New Company," or *Shinsha*, to its name. It has also traded variously as Kyoiku Tokyo Shisha (Education Tokyo Office) and Thomas Entertainment. The company has worked on many anime serials and movies, including AKIRA, GOLGO 13, ROSE OF VERSAILLES, MONSTER RANCHER, and LUPIN III. In 2005, the games corporation Sega announced that it had acquired a 50.2% stake in TMS, linking the animation studio to Sega's products in much the same way as the relationship of Bandai Namco to its own component companies such as Sunrise. The TMS company is now 100% owned by Sega-Sammy Holdings. Just as Toei's Nerima location has attracted related industries to settle nearby, TMS shares its neighborhood in Tokyo's north-western Suginami district with many other animation companies, including Sunrise and Madhouse. TMS itself wholly owns the subsidiary Telecom Animation Film, founded in 1978.

TOKYO PIG *

1988. AKA: *Fairweather Pig; Clear Day with Occasional Pig*. Movie, TV series. DIR: Toshio Hirata. SCR: Toshio Takeuchi, Hideo Takayashiki. DES: Kazuo Komatsubara. ANI: Kazuo Komatsubara. MUS: N/C. PRD: OH! Productions, TV Tokyo. 45 mins. (m), 25 mins. x 61 eps. (TV).

Eight-year-old Noriyasu writes and draws in his diary, discovering later that *everything* he writes in it comes true, even if it involves talking pigs and strange adventures. This adaptation of the children's picture book by Shiro Yadakara was revived for a TV series in 1997, directed by Shinichi Watanabe and written by Yoshio Urasawa, with Harebuta's ("Sunny Pig"'s) ability to "smell" people's true intentions getting him into many scrapes.

TOKYO REQUIEM *

2005. JPN: *Tokyo Chinkonka*. Video. DIR:

Kazuyuki Honda. SCR: Kazuyuki Honda. DES: Akira Kano. ANI: Kazuyuki Honda. MUS: N/C. PRD: Milky, Studio Jam. 30 mins. x 2 eps.

A secret society in Tokyo is intent on kidnapping four "priestesses," each the mistress of a particular element of Fire, Water, Earth, or Wind. Their use in a clandestine, and no doubt unpleasant, ceremony is prophesied to herald the return of an evil god—as one might expect, if one has seen DOOMED MEGALOPOLIS. Having already captured and ritually ravished the Priestess of Earth, their second target is Homura Kamishiro, an attractive red-haired schoolgirl and part-time prostitute, who is soon infected with a magical feather that causes her to be constantly aroused and in need of satisfaction. Hiroto "The Avenger" Nambu steps in—he is an agent of another society, dedicated to opposing the previous one, and now functioning as the girl's protector and occasional sexual partner. Based on a manga by Nishiki Nakamura published in 2002, this is supposedly a multipart complete adaptation, although so far only two episodes have appeared. **LNV**

TOKYO REVELATION *

1995. JPN: *Shin Megami Tensei: Tokyo Moku-jiroku*. AKA: *True Goddess Reborn: Tokyo Revelation*. Video. DIR: Osamu Yamasaki. SCR: Mamiya Fujimura. DES: Kenichi Onuki. ANI: Minoru Yamazawa. MUS: Yoshihiro Ike. PRD: JC Staff. 29 mins. x 2 eps. (v), 25 mins. x 50 eps. (TV), 25 mins. x 52 eps. (TV2).

Pale loner Akito Kobayashi sells his soul to Satan, and swears to assemble large quantities of the element Magnetite in order to open a gateway to hell. He transfers to a new school, where he swiftly turns all the local girls into vessels of demonic possession and sets his sights on class beauty Saki, whose pliant young body contains massive amounts of Magnetite. Ranged against him are a motley crew of schoolkids, including two ninja in disguise, a teen witch, and handsome occult hobbyist Kojiro. This junior version of UROTSUKIDOJI has sorcerous computer geeks summoning devils through the Internet, necromantic heavy petting, a harpy who's an obvious rip-off of DEVIL-MAN's Silene, a clueless cast who don't know their Hecate from their athame, and some of the cheesiest dialogue known to man, including, "It's not every day I meet ninjas who are demon slayers…. I wouldn't be surprised if you were the reincarnation of some great goddess." Kojiro is the reincarnation of Tokyo's guardian deity Masakado (see DOOMED MEGALOPOLIS), his golden retriever has been possessed by the Hound of Hell (see CARD CAPTORS), and, if the plot wasn't trashy enough for you, it's actually a remake—this is a slightly more faithful adaptation of the novel and computer game already available in anime form as DIGITAL DEVIL STORY. Before you can say "Buffy," Satan is stalking Tokyo, teen witch Kyoko's been excommunicated for performing sex magic, and there's a faint whiff of homoeroticism redolent of the later X: THE MOVIE, as Akito confesses his love for Kojiro, albeit in a doomed, unrequited sort of way. The whole thing is tied up in a fiendishly rushed ending, with the characters yelling plot details at each other while the credits roll over them.

In 2000, the franchise was revived to promote a new version of the game on the Nintendo Gameboy. In *Goddess Reborn Devichil* (*Shin Megami Tensei Devichil*), 11-year-old soccer-loving schoolboy Setsuna flees indoors when rocks begin to rain from the sky. He meets token female Mirai Kaname and her scientist father, Kokai, who explains that the raining rocks are a sign that Magical King Lucifer has returned to terrorize the planet and is trying to break out of the parallel "magic" Earth to subdue the everyday world. Mirai, however, is one of the "Devil Children," a carrier of the "Devil Genome" that will allow her to fight Lucifer in the style of Go Nagai's *Devilman*. As demonstrated by the younger age group, the early morning broadcast, and the availability of the game in "Black" and "Red" editions, the new generation of the franchise has more in common with POKÉMON than with the story that originally inspired it. *Tokyo Revelation 2* (2002), a new version of the game, featured CG animation as part of its gameplay, and the game series eventually evolved into PERSONA. ⬤Ⓝⓥ

TOKYO TRIBE 2

2006. TV series. DIR: Tatsuo Sato. SCR: Tatsuo Sato. DES: Masahiro Emoto, Koji Eto, Junichi Higashi. ANI: Cindy Yamauchi. MUS: MURO. PRD: Madhouse, SANTASTIC! Entertainment, WOWOW. 24 mins. x 13 eps.

In the urban jungle where gangs of young men fight for territory, you're only as strong as your last fight and the tribe you run with. Gang war, decapitations, baseball bats, *katana*, cars, hos, and bitches and the constant drive and grind of a hip-hop score pack out a show where humor is grim and romance is nonexistent. Based on Santa Inoue's manga *Tokyo Tribe 2*—released in English as *Tokyo Tribes* [sic] and retaining its "2" in this anime incarnation in order to demonstrate to fans that it is based on the 1997 sequel, not the earlier 1993 "1" manga that featured several of the same characters. The art style picks up on Inoue's distinctively different character designs and opens a window on a side of Japan that's a million miles from shrine maidens and *moe* idols. The first three or four episodes are mostly devoted to setting up characters and relationships—a bold move, since it expects the fighting-mad audience to invest without seeing the goods—but then an old-school plot kicks in, part yakuza flick, part World War II drama, and all testosterone, and we're in familiar ground. This is FIST OF THE NORTH STAR for guys who are too self-consciously hip to buy *Fist of the North Star*. ⬤Ⓝⓥ

TOKYO UNDERGROUND *

2002. TV DIR: Hayato Date. SCR: Satoru Nishizono. DES: Yuji Moriyama. ANI: Shim Hyunok. MUS: Akifumi Tada. PRD: Studio Pierrot, TV Tokyo, Dentsu. 24 mins. x 26 eps.
Based on the manga in *Shonen Gangan* magazine by Akinobu Uraku, this is the story of a world under the streets and subway tunnels of Tokyo, where a group of powerful children with the ability to control the elements live a secret life. Rumina Asagi meets them after his first day at high school, when he comes home to a big hole in his back yard and two strange girls, fragile Ruri and feisty Chelsea, in his house. When Ruri is dragged back to the netherworld below Tokyo, Rumina joins forces with Chelsea and his schoolfriend Ginnosuke to get her back from the adults who hold her prisoner—he feels obliged to do this, because he has already died once rescuing her, and has now been brought back from the dead with new elemental powers into the bargain—compare to POLTERGEIST REPORT.

Director Hayato Date was a member of

the team that made NARUTO, a fan favorite of the early 21st century that similarly made light of more serious questing issues. He also made BUBU CHACHA, a kid's show for the very young that subtly revealed the strains of modern life, featuring a protagonist in need of rescue and companionship. *TU*'s Ruri is not merely a damsel in distress, she is a girl reared in a hermetically sealed world, cut off, as characters observe, from the sun and sky. Japanese comics and animation have seen many such exiles, both in times gone past, and in a recent resurgence since 9/11 and the invasion of Iraq. Like Japan itself, the fantasy realms of anime are often isolated from the rest of the globe. In the hidden worlds of *TU*, we see a similar distant conflict to that in HOWL'S MOVING CASTLE, and a nationunder-siege like that of HEAT GUY J. *Tokyo Underground* also reflects the iPod generation's general lack of affect. In a reversal of the twists of *The Matrix*, our intrepid heroes face a completely new environment, unlike anything they have ever encountered. Their first thought, however, is how much it reminds them of a film set—similar designer apathy for slightly older kids appears in *TU*'s contemporary, GANTZ.

TOKYO UNIVERSITY STORY

2005. JPN: *Tokyo Daigaku Monogatari: Kamen Ronin Ban*. AKA: *Tokyo University Story: Episode of the Masked Ronin*. Video. DIR: Jiro Fujimoto. SCR: Tatsuya Egawa. DES: Tadashi Shida. ANI: N/C. MUS: N/C. PRD: Sega, HMP, Shogakukan. 30 mins. x 2 eps.
Handsome, promising student Naoki finds his academic prospects crumbling around him when he is distracted by the pretty Haruka. Despite apparent similarities to SAKURA DIARIES, this video series is based on a much older manga in *Big Comic Spirits* from GOLDEN BOY–creator Tatsuya Egawa, which celebrated the tenth anniversary of its first publication in 2003. The story was also adapted into a 1994 live-action TV series (*DE), and a 2006 live-action movie, directed by Egawa himself. The anime features bonus commentary tracks from the Japanese voice actors—which are relatively rare in Japanese anime releases, although such extras have long been a staple of the English-language anime community.

TOKYO VICE *

1988. Video. AKA: *The Tokyo Project*. DIR: Osamu Yamasaki. SCR: Minami Machi Bugyosho. DES: Kenichi Onuki. ANI: Osamu Tsuruyama. MUS: Karioka. PRD: Minami Machi Bugyosho. 60 mins.

Teenagers Junpei, Akira, and Keiko get involved in corruption on a grand scale when one of them is slipped a computer disk in a Shinjuku club by someone whose life is just about to be terminated. The bad guys are prepared to do anything to recover the disk, including tracking Junpei with a military satellite, kidnapping his sister Kumiko, chasing him in a helicopter gunship, and suppressing all media coverage of the cataclysmic aftermath. As usual, the police (in the form of Inspector Sakamoto and his team) are some way behind the young heroes in getting to the root of the problem, which leads to an explosive showdown with the corrupt corporation's secret weapon, a heavily armed robot. Like its U.S. inspiration *Miami Vice*, *TV* flirts with low life but is basically clean-cut, cute, and earnest. The action (the main point of an action show) is rather patchy; apart from the admittedly good final fight, there's a motorcycle/helicopter chase and a shootout with some suits, and that's your lot. We know that real investigators spend most of their time playing with computers and questioning suspects, but we don't necessarily want to watch the whole process.

Later rereleased in the U.S. by Media Blasters as *Tokyo Project*.

TOM OF T.H.U.M.B. *

1967. JPN: *001/7 Oyayubi Tom*. AKA: *Tom Thumb, 001/7*. TV series. DIR: Yasuji Mori. SCR: Toshio Shino (translator). DES: N/C. ANI: Yasuji Mori, Takao Kasai. MUS: Asei Kobayashi. PRD: Toei, Videocraft, NET. 6 mins. x 26 eps.

Secret agent Tom and his faithful assistant, Swinging Jack, are accidentally zapped by a Miniaturization Ray, and are now small enough to fit into pockets. This actually makes them more, not less, effective as secret agents, and they become employees of the Tiny Humans Underground Military Bureau. From their new secret hideaway inside a desk, they pop out in a tiny sportscar, ready to battle against MAD, an organization hellbent on world conquest.

A diminutive variant on James Bond, with the U.S. title a reference to *The Man From U.N.C.L.E.*, *ToT* was a coproduction between Toei Animation and the U.S. company Videocraft, made as a companion piece to **THE KING KONG SHOW**. The same companies also produced several other cartoons, including *The Mouse on the Mayflower* and *The Smokey Bear Show*. Among the many other "American" shows that technically qualify as anime are **MIGHTY ORBOTS**, the **ROBOTECH** sequel *Sentinels*, and **THE STINGIEST MAN IN TOWN**.

TOM SAWYER *

1980. JPN: *Tom Sawyer no Boken*. AKA: *Adventures of Tom Sawyer; Tom and Huck*. Movie, video, TV series. DIR: Hiroshi Saito, Shigeo Koshi, Takayoshi Suzuki. SCR: Akira Miyazaki, Mei Kato, Yoshiaki Tomita, Tadahiko Isogai, Takeshi Kiyose, Seijiro Kamiyama. DES: Shuichi Seki. ANI: Yoshishige Kosako, Yoshitaka Gokami, Noboru Takano, Michiyo Sakurai, Akio Sugino. MUS: Katsuhisa Hattori. PRD: Nippon Animation, Fuji TV. 25 mins. x 49 eps., 105 mins. (m).

Tom is a boy who lives in a small town on the banks of the Mississippi River in 19th-century America. He and his best friend, orphan Huck, hang out together and make mischief in and out of school. Their shenanigans include a balloon ride, a river trip, and a rescue of an innocent person from the false accusations of Indian Joe. Based on Mark Twain's 1876 novel, this **WORLD MASTERPIECE THEATER** series was edited into a feature-length movie entitled *Tom and Huck* for U.S. video release. An English dub of the series by Saban was shown as part of HBO's Family Showcase, alternating in the 7:30 a.m. timeslot with **LITTLE WOMEN**. Twain's follow-up, **HUCKLEBERRY FINN**, was also turned into an anime.

TOMATO-MAN

1992. JPN: *Sarada Ju Yushi Tomato Man*. AKA: *Tomato-man and the Knights of the Salad Table*. TV series. DIR: Hiroshi Sasagawa, Teppei Matsuura, Shinichi Watanabe, Hiromichi Matano. SCR: Masaaki Sakurai, Yukiyoshi Ohashi. DES: Futago Kamikita, Yoshiko Hashimoto. ANI: Michio Shindo, Hiroshi Kagawa. MUS: N/C. PRD: Animation 21, TV Tokyo. 25 mins. x 50 eps.

The Kingdom of Salad is a beautiful dreamland where vegetables, fruits, and insects try, often unsuccessfully, to live together in peace and harmony. When the wicked Bug-Bug gang casts an evil sleep spell on beautiful Princess Peach, King Boo-Melon sends for "the Withered Plum," an old hermit believed to have magical powers, to awaken the princess from her eternal sleep. To help protect the king, Plum uses his magical powers to create a group of mighty warriors from ordinary food, the Knights of the Salad Table. Tomato-man, the last of the knights created by Plum, is the hero of the show. One of the few TV shows to attribute disruptive political intent to fruit and vegetables.

TOMINO, YOSHIYUKI

1941–. Born in Kanagawa Prefecture, he graduated in film from the Fine Arts department of Nihon University. He joined Mushi Production in 1964, where he soon became a writer and director on **ASTRO BOY**. He went freelance after three years and taught at Tokyo Designer Gakuin College, before being tempted back into the anime business as a director on **TRITON OF THE SEAS**, **BRAVE RAIDEEN**, and **STAR OF THE SEINE**. His greatest contribution to the anime world came with his involvement in giant-robot shows, adding notes of pathos and tragedy to **DAITARN 3**, **ZAMBOT 3** and his most famous creation, **GUNDAM**. For this and the realization that in his anime no major character was safe, he later gained the nickname "Kill 'em All Tomino." As a proponent of real robots (**SCIENCE FICTION AND ROBOTS**) and a prominent director at the turn of the 1980s when the existence of adult fans was first recognized, Tomino became something of a champion for anime with mature themes. In February 1981, at the launch event for the first *Gundam* movie, he issued a "proclamation of a new century" (*shinseiki sengen*, see also **EVANGELION**), decreeing that the **ASTRO BOY** generation had come of age, and that the time was right for anime to also grow up. He has since occupied a slippery, liminal position among fans, as both a proponent of the otaku revolution and as a symbol of the very mass-produced dole against which the otaku revolution, at least initially, contended.

He also wrote the lyrics to many of the songs associated with his shows, using the pseudonym Iogi Rin, and is credited with several novels, including the trilogy released in English as *Mobile Suit Gundam: Awakening, Escalation, Confrontation.* Tomino has occasionally struck out at the success of *Gundam*, protesting that it is all he is known for in FANDOM, despite a varied resumé that stretches all the way back to the earliest days of Japanese television animation. Among his oft-overlooked achievements is his grasp of storyboarding, in which capacity he was arguably a major influence on the groundbreaking style of STAR OF THE GIANTS and for which he is the author of the standard Japanese industry textbook for all aspiring animators. Never afraid to speak his mind, Tomino frequently plays up his role as the cantankerous old man of the anime business and rants about the shortcomings of the business and its fans in a magazine column that is often debatably tongue-in-cheek.

TOMITA, KUNI

?–. A former storyboard artist for Madhouse on productions such as CYBER CITY OEDO 808 and WICKED CITY, Tomita relocated to America in 1990. She subsequently brought a Japanese touch to local shows such as *Invasion America* (1998) and *X-Men: Evolution* (2000).

TOMITA, SUKEHIRO

1948–. Sometimes miscredited as Yukihiro Tomita; a pseudonym for Hiroshi Tomita. Born in Saitama Prefecture, Tomita worked briefly in the business world before becoming a screenwriter on SPACEKETEERS. Subsequent work has included SPACE RUNAWAY IDEON, MACROSS, and GALL FORCE, for which he wrote a novel spin-off. He also works as a manga scriptwriter, and hence is often associated with the manga adaptations or precursors of his anime work.

TOMORROW'S ELEVEN

1979. JPN: *Ashita no Yusha Tachi*; Ashita no Eleven-tachi AKA: *Heroes of Tomorrow*. TV special. DIR: Kozo Morishita. SCR: Seiji Matsuoka. DES: Hiroshi Motomiya. ANI: Susumu Shiraume. MUS: N/C. PRD: Toho, Nippon TV. 85 mins.
In 1978, as the World Under-21 Soccer Championships draw near, amateur Jiro Ipponji is still living on a Hokkaido ranch with his sister Yuki, caring for his beloved horse, Golden Leg, and romancing his girlfriend, Yoko. The withdrawn loner is approached by Shin Mizuki and coach Matsumoto to play for Japan's national team. He agrees, becoming a formidable attacker. I think they make him leave his horse at home, though. Made as part of the hype for the 1979 championships, which were held in Japan. Compare to CAPTAIN TSUBASA.

TOMORROW'S JOE *

1970. JPN: *Ashita no Joe*. AKA: *Rocky Joe*. TV series, movie. DIR: Osamu Dezaki, Hideo Makino, Seiji Okuda, Yuki Kobayashi, Toshio Hirata. SCR: Shunichi Yukimuro, Tadaaki Yamazaki, Seiji Matsuoka, Haruya Yamazaki, Hiroshi Saito, Tsunehisa Ito. DES: Akio Sugino, Akihiro Kanayama, Shingo Araki. ANI: Akio Sugino, Akihiro Kanayama, Shingo Araki. MUS: Tadao Yagi (TV1); Ichiro Araki (TV2). PRD: Mushi, Fuji TV; TMS, Nippon TV. 25 mins. x 79 eps. (TV1), 153 mins. (m1), 25 mins. x 47 eps., 120 mins. (m2).
One of SPORTS ANIME's great legends, this is the story of Joe Yabuki, a 15-year-old from the wrong side of the tracks, living by his wits in Tokyo, who meets Danbei, a once-great boxing coach now seeking refuge from his past in drink. Both see something they need in the other—Joe a source of free meals, Danbei a potentially great fighter and a reason to live. Under the cloak of training with Danbei, Joe carries on a life of petty crime, eventually getting caught and sent to prison. Over a year inside, he finally realizes that Danbei was offering him both friendship and a future, and he carries on with the training regime the two had set up. On his release, he begins a successful boxing career. As he rises through the ranks, his main rival is Toru Rikiishi, a prison acquaintance, who dies tragically in a bout with Joe at the end of the series, leaving the champion devastated.

TJ is the most famous creation of Tetsuya Chiba, also known for WEATHER PERMITTING, I'M TEPPEI, and NOTARI MATSUTARO. His 1968 *Shonen Magazine* manga was drawn from a script by KARATE-CRAZY LIFE's Ikki Kajiwara, who used the pseudonym Asao Takamori since he was also writing STAR OF THE GIANTS for a rival magazine at the time. The story was also adapted as a 1970 live-action film. It continued to attract readers after the series it inspired had ended, and in 1980, with a second series in production for Nippon TV, the first series was edited to feature length for theatrical release, providing background for new fans and a reminder of the story for older ones. Though many of the old crew returned to work on the sequel, *TJ2* also featured new directors, including Mizuho Nishikubo and Toshio Takeuchi. It opens as Joe, having given up boxing after Riki's death, is brought back to the ring through the encouragement of his friends. This time, as in the manga, the tragic death at the end of the series is Joe's own, and fans were inconsolable. The second anime movie, premiered in 1981 was an edit of this series, released by Taiseng Video as *Champion Joe*, and so far the only incarnation of this series to be translated into English. The title *Rocky Joe* was adopted for Western sale in an attempt to cash in on the popularity of Sylvester Stallone's live-action film series, obscuring the fact that Joe was there first. ❶

TOMORROW'S NADJA

2003. JPN: *Asu no Nadja*. AKA: *Nadja of Tomorrow*. TV series. DIR: Takuya Igarashi. SCR: K. Y. Green, Tomoko Konparu, Yoshimi Narita, Yumi Kageyama. DES: Kazuto Nakazawa. ANI: Akira Inagami, Mitsuru Aoyama. MUS: Keiichi Oku. PRD: Toei Animation, TV Asahi. 25 mins. x 50 eps.
Over a century ago, pretty blonde 13-year-old Nadja lives in an orphanage in an unspecified part of Europe, until the arrival of a mysterious package makes her think her mother may still be alive. She joins a traveling circus in an effort to find her origins. Two mysterious men attempt to steal her heart-shaped brooch, but she is rescued by handsome, aristocratic Francis Harcourt. When you learn that the strangers keep chasing after her to try and get her heirloom jewel, you may detect a certain similarity to SECRET OF BLUE WATER; this will quite probably be enhanced by the arrival of a perky boy Nadja's age, a cute red-headed preschool moppet and not one, but two, friendly young lions. Based on the manga in *Nakayoshi* magazine, written by Izumi Todo and drawn by Yui Ayumi, this mines the long tradition of children in search of their loved ones, like NOBODY'S BOY REMI and NOBODY'S GIRL. A

game spin-off duly followed.

TONA-GURA!

2006. TV series. DIR: Tatsuya Abe. SCR: N/C.
DES: Shinji Ochi, Michie Watanabe. ANI: Shinji
Ochi, Hironori Tanaka. MUS: Tomoki Kikuya.
PRD: Daume, Hatsukoi no Veranda Aikokai.
25 mins. x 13 eps.
Kazuki can't wait for her childhood friend
(**ROMANCE AND DRAMA**) Yuji to move back
next door. She had a huge crush on him
when he came over to her house to play,
and their older sisters were friends. Now
Yuji wants to play much rougher games
and Kazuki is appalled at the pervert he's
become. What on earth happened to their
innocent childish promises? With the "fan
service" elements of Hidetaka Kakei's
manga toned down for TV viewing, what's
left is a broad, pervy slice-of-life comedy
with a minimal plot jerry-built from clichés, and very average art. **V**

TONARI NO SEKI-KUN *

2014. AKA: The Boy at the Next Desk; The
Master of Killing Time. TV series. DIR: Yuji
Muto. SCR: Takuma Morishige. DES: Masae
Otake. ANI: Masae Otake. MUS: Akifumi
Tada. PRD: Shin-Ei Animation, Media Factory, Shogakukan-Shueisha Productions,
Starchild Records. 8 mins. x 21 eps.
Master slacker Seki-kun turns prissy model
schoolgirl Rumi's life upside down as he
pulls off prank after time-wasting prank,
right under the eyes of their teacher, who
never notices a thing. In fact, when she
tries to put a stop to his antics, Rumi gets
into trouble. Something of a one-trick
pony, and rather longer than most of its
jokes, this show has a difficult balancing
act to perform—ensuring the main gag
doesn't get too old—and limited resources
of plot, character and art style to build
beyond it. Made by long-established studio
Shin-Ei, home of **DORAEMON**.

TONDE MON PE

1982. JPN: Tonde Mon Pe. AKA: Mon-Pe.
TV series. DIR: Shigetsugu Yoshida, Junzo
Aoki, Hideharu Iuchi, Saburo Kawashima,
Masaharu Okuwaki. SCR: Chifude Asakura,
Yoshiaki Yoshida, Masaaki Sakurai, Kenji
Terada. DES: Kazu Mitsui. ANI: Takao Kasai.
MUS: Yuikihide Takekawa. PRD: Tokyo Movie
Shinsha, TV Asahi. 25 mins. x 42 eps.
Fifteen-year-old country girl Mon-Mon

dreams of being a fashion designer and
gets a job as an au pair to a rising star
designer, Mrs. Kano, her baby girl PePe,
and her silly writer husband. But PePe can
make toys and animals do very odd things.
Mon's employers don't seem to notice anything odd is going on, and she finds her
dream job turning into a chaotically cute
trial of wits she has no chance of winning.
She's a sweet girl, hardworking and kind,
but very unsophisticated and simply not
used to walking teddy bears and talking
stuffed animals. She eventually decides to
leave her job and go home, but psychic
baby PePe, who has come to love her, finds
a way to make sure she stays.

TONY'S HEROINE SERIES

2009. JPN: Tony's Heroine Series: Kanojo
wa Hanayome Kohosei? Cinderella Series.
Video. DIR: Shinichi Shimizu. SCR: Kai Kimu-
hakei. DES: Kujira Akishima. ANI: Kujira Akishima. MUS: N/C. PRD: Melissa, MS Pictures.
27 mins. x 2 eps.
A young man is told that he is heir to a
fortune. To claim his birthright he must
find a girl with a cherry blossom birthmark
on her neck. However, this only shows up
when she's having an orgasm. To train the
inexperienced young man and help in his
quest, he is sent a beautiful ninja/maid
named Zero. With her help he embarks on
an odyssey, checking out a shrine maiden,
policewoman, nurse—the standard fantasy
figures. Meanwhile, his shy girlfriend
has her own issues. There's sex, but no
violence, in this porn anime based on the
illustrations of Tony, a man who has made
a career out of drawing just what he
likes—cute underdressed girls. **N**

TOP SECRET, THE

2008. JPN: Himitsu: The Revelation. TV
series. DIR: Hiroshi Aoyama. SCR: Satoshi Suzuki, Sumino Kawashima, Sotaro Hayashi,
Takafumi Tsuzuki. DES: Kyuma Oshita,
Tomoyuki Shimizu. ANI: Kyuma Oshita. MUS:
Yoshihisa Hirano. PRD: Madhouse Studios,
D.N. Dream Partners, NTV, VAP. 25 mins. x
26 eps.
Memory Reproduction Imaging (MRI) has
advanced to the stage where government
detectives are able to retrieve up to five
years of memories from the corpses they
find at crime scenes. The story concentrates on the forensic pathologists at the

9th Institute of Police Science, who can
arrive at the scene of any criminal tragedy,
and with a little scientific jiggery-pokery,
delve into the memories of the dead body
(thereby finding a scientific rationale for
the otherwise magical pursuits of **GHOST
TALKER'S DAYDREAM**).
Adapted from Reiko Shimizu's manga
Himitsu—The Top Secret, this interesting
premise is well executed, with a necessarily episodic case-by-case plot linked by
mature, well-developed characters and
involving ideas about ethics, morality, and
intrusion into private life. But it is worth
noting that Shimizu's original manga
ran in Melody, a girls' manga magazine,
and was hence a world removed from
the science fictional trappings one might
expect if the same sort of story were told
for boys (**GHOST IN THE SHELL**). Shimizu
does not seem to be all that interested
in the usual implications of setting a
Crime Scene Investigation comic 50 years
in the future. Her characters meet in
anonymous offices, or are depicted in
extreme close-up with little space for the
backgrounds. The incidental details of life
in the future, which would be sufficient
to occupy Masamune Shirow for entire
volumes of vistas and splash pages, are
entirely inconsequential to Shimizu, who
instead wears the future setting like a
minor plot point, sufficient to give her
characters what really interests her—the
chance to poke around in the emotional
lives of dead strangers. In that regard,
with its concentration on the priorities
and fixations of the recently dead—what
really matters to people when they realize
that their life is over—the storyline shares
many concerns with the liminal, Buddhist-
influenced philosophizing of **COLORFUL:
THE MOTION PICTURE**.
Whereas SF for boys often delivers
vacant, 2D characters in vivid worlds,
Shimizu does the opposite for her female
fans. Her A.D. 2060 looks exactly like
the present day, but she cares about the
people who live in it, and the foggy, dying
ghosts of their memories, depicted in
a heavily pointillist style as if broadcast
through a dot-matrix printer. Some might
see this as a failure when translated to
anime form—certainly, the lack of an
English-language release of this anime
implies that foreign distributors see it

as somehow flawed for the traditional market of SCIENCE FICTION AND ROBOTS. The authors prefer to see it as a fascinating example of how manga (and the anime that draw upon them) can approach the same material from such interesting and varied angles. **OV**

TOPCRAFT

Animation company formed in 1972 by several former employees of Toei, including Toru Hara, a former producer on LITTLE NORSE PRINCE, whose work in the late 1960s revolved around managing Toei's work-for-hire for foreign clients. Although the studio's first work was on MAZINGER Z for its "parent" company Toei, it was soon lured away by the American Rankin/Bass company to work on foreign animation. Its first job was on episodes of the series *Kid Power* (1972). Amid the local chaos caused by the collapse of Mushi Production, Topcraft employees worked on TV specials for Rankin/Bass, including *20,000 Leagues Under the Sea* and TOM SAW-YER. Later years saw the company working on anime only when times were lean; while Topcraft may have done occasional work on bona fide anime such as TIME BOKAN, LUPIN III, and LITTLE KOALA, the company's efforts were aimed at chasing dollars from Rankin/Bass specials such as *The First Easter Rabbit* (1976). Topcraft thereby managed to appear on the credits of many supposedly foreign cartoons, including *Barbapapa* (1973), *Doctor Snuggles* (1979), and *The Hobbit* (1977). Topcraft had no connection with Ralph Bakshi's animated *Lord of the Rings*, but when Bakshi's work ended partway, Topcraft and Rankin/Bass cunningly fashioned their own *Return of the King* (1980) as a sequel of sorts to *The Hobbit*! However, most of Topcraft's work in this period was unknown in Japan, with only THE STINGIEST MAN IN TOWN being broadcast in Topcraft's home country. The high points of Topcraft's work for the U.S. include *The Last Unicorn* (1982) and *The Flight of Dragons* (1982). Subsequently, Topcraft was commissioned to work on Hayao Miyazaki's NAUSICAÄ OF THE VALLEY OF THE WIND. Those remaining members of Topcraft's staff who had not left during the high-pressure creation of *Nausicaä* stayed on and formed the core of the new Studio Ghibli. Their first work as Ghibli

was CASTLE IN THE SKY. Some members of Topcraft split to form Pacific Animation Corporation (PAC), under which auspices they continued to work for Rankin/Bass on such productions as *Thundercats* (1985).

TOPO GIGIO

1988. TV series. DIR: Shigeo Koshi, Noboru Ishiguro, Masahito Kitagawa, Shigeru Omachi. SCR: Noboru Ishiguro, Tomoo Tadaoki. DES: Susumu Shiraume. ANI: Tadaichi Iguchi, Hirokazu Ishino. MUS: Nobuyoshi Koshibe. PRD: Nippon Animation, TV Asahi. 25 mins. x 34 eps.

By the 25th century, mice have evolved into a sentient species, gaining bigger heads, shorter tails, and the power of speech. Topo Gigio is a mouse space pilot sent on an exploration mission who accidentally returns to the 20th century, before the establishment of peaceful diplomatic relations between humans and mice. Landing in Santa Catalina City, he finds that humans still think of mice as either pets or pests, cats are still the enemy, and mouse society is still underground, but a nine-year-old girl, Jean, learns his secret and helps him.

Created by the Italian author Maria Perego, the famous mouse was introduced to Japanese children in a series of adventures getting his friends into and out of trouble (compare to future cat DORAE-MON). These included rescuing mouse rebel Kurt and his fat friend Per from numerous scrapes, foiling the plots of head cat Megalo, helping mouse inventor Doc with his devices, and even meeting with Dracula. After episode 21, the series was rebranded as *Dreaming Topo Gigio (Yume Miru Topo Gigio)*.

TOPPUKU VIOLENT RACERS

1996. JPN: *Toppuku Kyoso Kyoku*. AKA: *Symphony of Violent Racers in Battle-dress*. Video. DIR: Yoshimasa Yamazaki. SCR: Narihiko Tatsumiya. DES: Kenzo Koizumi. ANI: Kenzo Koizumi. MUS: N/C. PRD: Taki. 42 mins. x 2 eps.

The Sea Monkey biker gang fights over its turf. Yet another bikers-beat-each-other-up anime, this one based on a manga by Yu Furuzawa. Compare to BOMBER BIKERS OF SHONAN. **OV**

TOPSTRIKER

1991. JPN: *Moero Topstriker!* AKA: *Burn Topstriker; Enter the Topstriker*. TV series. DIR: Ryo Yasumura, Akira Shimizu, Shigeru Yamazaki, Masahito Kitagawa. SCR: Yoshiyuki Suga, Yoshimasa Takahashi. DES: Nobuhiro Okaseko. ANI: Nobuhiro Okaseko. MUS: N/C. PRD: Nippon Animation, TV Tokyo. 25 mins. x 49 eps.

Hikari Yoshikawa arrives in Italy to develop his soccer skills with the Columbus team under top trainer Bertini and Dr. Robson, who used to be a top-level English player— he is, as anyone acquainted with the current state of the English game would realize, rather old. Hikari has some problems with rival player Cesare but eventually leads the team to the final, losing with honor, and is selected by Robson for a new international team, the Jupiter Wings. This consists of talented players from all over the world who haven't been selected for their national teams. The aim is to compete with the best at the international level, but with so many strong personalities involved, it will take time and effort to get them to work together. The story has a similar premise to 1992's FREE KICK FOR TOMORROW, but without the focus on the family relationships of the hero; the presentation of the game itself was more realistic than in many earlier series. It was screened in France as *School for Champions*, with Hikari renamed Benjamin, Cesare called Mark, and almost every Japanese name removed from the credits—a yellow card for local boy Thibault Chatel for crediting himself as director.

TORA-SAN: THE ANIME

1998. JPN: *Otoko wa Tsurai yo: Torajiro no Wasurenagusa*. AKA: *It's Tough to Be a Man: Torajiro's Forget-Me-Not*. TV special. DIR: Setsuko Shibuichi, Satoshi Dezaki. SCR: Tadao Hayashi. DES: Kenichiro Takai. ANI: Kenichiro Takai. MUS: Naoki Yamamoto. PRD: Eiken, TBS. 95 mins.

Torajiro Kuruma is an itinerant peddler, eternally unlucky in relationships but forever prepared to help others in need. In this case it is the singer Lily, who asks for his aid in Hokkaido but rejects his offer of love. A tragicomedy spun off from Yoji Yamada's long-running "Tora-san" series, which produced 48 movies, starting with *It's Tough to Be a Man* (1969, *Otoko wa Tsurai yo*). The franchise, arguably the most successful movie series on the planet, was thrown into chaos by the death of its leading man Kiyoshi Atsumi late in 1996. The character had a brief cameo, played by a double, in Yamada's live-action *The Man Who Caught the Rainbow* (1997), but this anime version can be seen as an attempt to move into a medium where the absence of the star would be less noticeable. The original was pastiched in the anthropomorphic anime **DORATARO**, and its 28th installment was shown on a double bill with **TAO-TAO THE PANDA**.

TORADORA! *

2008. AKA: *Tiger x Dragon*. TV series. DIR: Tatsuyuki Nagai. SCR: Mari Okada, Matsuto Higuchi, Junko Okazaki, Masahiro Yokotani. DES: Masayoshi Tanaka, Chikako Shibata. ANI: Masayoshi Tanaka, Tomoyuki Shitaya. MUS: Yukari Hashimoto. PRD: JC Staff, GENCO, Starchild Records, Yomiuri Advertising. 24 mins. x 25 eps.

Ryuji is a really nice guy but for some reason people find his looks very intimidating—they say he has "delinquent eyes." For the second year of high school he's in the same class as his best friend Yusaku and his secret crush Minori Kushieda, along with her diminutive best friend Aisaka Taiga, who's secretly crazy about Yusaku. The teeny tiger (*tora* in Japanese) and the gentle dragon (*doragon*) team up to snag their dream dates in this sweet romantic comedy that's not your usual lame high school story. Mari Okada (**BLACK BUTLER**) leads a writing team that understands how to make the target audience feel good, while director Nagai has prior experience on sweet stories with **TWIN ANGEL**. Not to be confused with **TIGER AND BUNNY**.

TORIKO *

2011. TV series. DIR: Akifumi Zako, Hiroaki Miyamoto. SCR: Isao Murayama, Tomoko Taguchi, Yoichi Takahashi. DES: Hisashi Kagawa, Masahiro Shimanuki, Masanobu Nomura, Shinichi Imano. ANI: Hisashi Kagawa, Kazuya Hisada. MUS: Hiromi Mizutani. PRD: Toei Animation, Fuji TV, Shueisha, Yomiuri Advertising. 25 mins. x 139 eps.

In a world where the gourmet experience has become the height of cultural aspiration, the *bishokuya*—luxury food hunters or "Gourmet Hunters"—are sought-after specialists. Toriko is one such, hired by restaurants and multimillionaires to track down and provide the finest, rarest foods in the world and arrange the ultimate dinner. His huge strength and deep insight into the animal kingdom enable him to capture the fiercest and most stealthy of rare animals and deliver them to the top table. Traveling with him is Komatsu, a feeble, timid Japanese chef who'll endure all the terror and discomfort to extend his skills. But an evil organization is sending out its super-robots to hinder their quest.

This is not some insane dream. This show really is **FIST OF THE NORTH STAR** crashed into *Man v. Food*. Cranking the dial up higher than *Spinal Tap*, Toriko finds ever bigger, ever deadlier plants and animals, then slices, dices, and fricassees them with the help of his tiny chum. The show's world is evoked on a scale reminiscent of the grandest space operas. It's sadly limited by the endless repetition built into its high concept, but its cast of fabulously campy characters in zingy colors is so rich and imaginative that fun is hard to avoid. This madcap tale, based on the manga by Mitsutoshi Shimabukuro, depicts a world of pure play and oral gratification built on the deeply buried and not-so-absurd notion that we're eating the world to extinction. A movie, *Theater Version Toriko Gourmet Spirit Supermeal Treasure Special Menu (Gekijoban Toriko Bishoku Shin no Choshoku Takara (Special Menu)*, followed in summer 2013, preceded by a crossover TV special (episode 99) with characters from **ONE PIECE** and **DRAGON BALL** entitled *Dream 9 Toriko & One Piece & Dragon Ball Z Cho Collaboration Special*.

The oddest thing about *Toriko* is that it feels so out of its time. "Gourmet" manga, anime, films, and television serials were a feature of Japan's booming 1980s economy, most famously with Juzo Itami's live-action movie *Tampopo* (1985). Shimabukuro's *Toriko* manga arrived in 2008 in *Shonen Jump* magazine, seemingly a generation late to the party, but also carnivalizing and lampooning the whole genre as a ridiculous, excessive pursuit of consumption for consumption's sake—a foodie show combined with the gotta-catch-em-all mentality of **POKÉMON**. For many Japanese teens, this is how their parents' yuppie youth must look.

TORIUMI, HISAYUKI

1941–. Sometimes miscredited as Eiko Toriyumi. Born in Kanagawa Prefecture, he graduated in law and politics from Chuo University in 1966. He found work as a writer and director at Tatsunoko on **BATTLE OF THE PLANETS** and subsequently wrote many other anime, including **SALAMANDER**, **TEKKAMAN**, and **THE MYSTERIOUS CITIES OF GOLD**. He was a founding member of Studio Pierrot, but is now a freelance novelist.

TOSHINDEN *

1996. JPN: *Toshinden; Battle Arena Toshinden*. Video. DIR: Masami Obari. SCR: Masaharu Amiya, Jiro Takayama. DES: Tsukasa Kotobuki, Kazuto Nakazawa, Masahiro Yamane. ANI: Hiroshi Kato. MUS: Kensuke Shiina. PRD: Animate Film. 30 mins. x 2 eps.

Uranus, leader of a powerful secret organization cleverly called "The Organization," wants to build an army of indestructible, invincible warriors. To foil the plan, the world's indestructible, invincible warriors reunite. Eiji, Sophia, and tooth-rottingly cute little Ellis are among the chosen ones, but Uranus' minions are gradually picking off the opposition and time is running out. Yet another game-based clone in the **STREET FIGHTER II** mode—a large cast of two-dimensional video game "characters" brought to the screen in a cynical promotion, each given barely enough screentime to have a fight and use their little combat catchphrases or moves. Meanwhile, the big-haired Eiji embarks on a halfhearted quest for his missing brother, with risible attempts at depth resulting in immortal dialogue like, "We both know your brother killed my dad."

Obari's direction starts off well, with a line of soldiers aiming guns upstaged by a journalist aiming a camera. He pastiches the **AKIRA** manga as the robotic Sho takes on a U.S. aircraft carrier, then shifts the scene to a Chinatown set-up redolent of his later **VIRUS**. But this remains an anime-by-numbers that ticks every perfunctory box of a game adaptation—including a female character in a shower scene (Sofia actually manages to put her clothes back on while jumping through a window), fights between allies engineered through "mind-control," and a big fight at a secret hideout (in this case, two nicely inconspicuous skyscrapers). **Ⓥ**

TOUCH

1985. TV series, movie, TV special. DIR: Gisaburo Sugii, Hiroko Tokita, Naoto Hashimoto, Akinori Nagaoka. SCR: Yumiko Takahoshi, Shigeru Yanagawa, Tomoko Konparu. DES: Minoru Maeda, Shichiro Kobayashi. ANI: Yasuo Maeda, Masako Goto, Hajime Watanabe. MUS: Hiroaki Serizawa. PRD: Toho, Group TAC, Fuji TV. 25 mins. x 101 eps. (TV), 93 mins., 80 mins., 85 mins. (m), 60 mins. x 2 (TVm).

When his popular twin brother is killed in an accident, Tatsuya tries to fill his shoes, both on their high school baseball team and romantically with Minami, the team's manager. A moving and involving story based on the 1981 manga in *Shonen Sunday* by SLOW STEP–creator Mitsuru Adachi. *Touch* the anime was a huge hit, both in Japan, where its rating topped 30%, and in Europe. The series transferred into theaters for three movie editions—*T: Ace without a Backstop* (1986, *Sebango no Nai Ace*), *T2: Goodbye Gift* (1986, *Sayonara Okurimono*), and *T3: You Are Too Right* (1987, *Kimi wa Torisugi Daa to ni*)—ending with the team about to play the national championship finals and Tatsuya asking himself if he has succeeded either on the field or in love. The closing credits of the series rolled without showing fans the outcome of the big game, or giving answers to either of Tatsuya's questions. Over a decade later, released in a period that also saw the long-delayed ending of KIMAGURE ORANGE ROAD, the TV special *Miss Lonely Yesterday—Are kara, Kimi wa … (1998, MLY: Since Then, You've …)* takes place three years after that fateful match and shows us how Tatsuya and Minami have dealt with life and their own relationships outside the protective routines of school days. Series director Sugii and original designer Maeda returned for this follow-up. After it gained outstanding 23.3% ratings, it was only a matter of time before a further follow-up was announced: *Crossroads: Whereabouts of the Wind* (2001, *Crossroads: Kaze no Yukue*). In this latest installment, Tatsuya joins the minor U.S. team the Emeralds, and he soon finds himself courted by the team owner's young daughter, Alice Vormont. Meanwhile, Minami becomes a sports photographer's assistant, and the two nonlovers' paths are fated to cross

once again. Adachi's baseball manga also reached anime in H2, MIYUKI, and NINE.

TOURNAMENT OF THE GODS *

1997. JPN: *Toshin Toshi II*. AKA: *Battle City II*. Video. DIR: Takehiro Nakayama. SCR: Takehiro Nakayama. DES: Takehiro Nakayama. ANI: Takehiro Nakayama. MUS: N/C. PRD: Pink Pineapple, KSS. 30 mins. x 3 eps.

At the Battle Tournament, fighters struggle to become proclaimed the supreme "Battle God." The victor of each gladiatorial bout gets the possessions of the vanquished, including their female partner. Sid, a mere fourth-level fighter, enters the tournament not because he wants to find his way through the maze and become an "angel eater" (use your imagination), but rather because he wants to win the hand of his beloved Azuki. Even though Sid wins the day with his pure heart, he is infected with a bizarre drug by the evil Aquross and becomes subject to incredible sexual urges that must be satisfied by copulation with angels. Though the superior SEXORCIST got there first, this erotic anime is based on a computer game that came even closer to the original inspiration—even the Japanese title is designed to look almost, but not quite, exactly like TOSHINDEN. ⚫NⓋ

TOWANOQUON *

2011. AKA: *Towa no Quon*. Movie. DIR: Umanosuke Iida. SCR: Toshizo Nemoto. DES: Toshihiro Kawamoto, Kuniaki Nemoto. ANI: Toshihiro Kawamoto, Yeong Beom Kim, Shigeru Fujita, Takeshi Yoshioka. MUS: Kenji Kawai. PRD: BONES, Bandai Visual, Hakuhodo DY Media Partners, Lantis, MOVIC, Showgate, Sony PCL. 50 mins. x 6 eps.

Tokyo, the future: in a world controlled by The Order, children who look normal are suddenly acquiring special powers and abilities. The Order considers them dangerous deviants to be hunted down and exterminated by its cyborg secret police, Custos. Quon is one of a group of Attracters, as these mutants describe themselves, trying to save as many of these children as he can. From their hideout under an abandoned amusement park, they brave danger and risk death to save others and uncover the secret behind their powers.

In Japan, where there is a steady cinema audience for animation, it's possible to release a short theatrical feature or a

multipart theatrical series, sometimes on a shared bill with other titles to make up a full program. Some studios put together bills of their hit anime series to generate extra holiday revenue and publicity. So BONES was able to release *Towa no Quon* as a series of six short movies under six subtitles: *The Ephemeral Petal (Utakata no Kaben), Dancing Chaos Orchid (Konton no Ranbu), Complicity of Dreams (Mugen no Renza), Roaring Anxiety (Guren no Shoshin), Return of the Invincible (Sozetsu no Raifuku),* and *Eternal Quon (Towa no Quon).*

BONES set a high bar in the first movie with a thrillingly kinetic opening sequence strongly reminiscent of SWORD OF THE STRANGER, and managed to maintain the quality of the animation through most of the succeeding episodes. Director Iida, in what would be his last production before his death, manages to maintain interest in a story strongly reminiscent of American mutant superhero comics, but better executed and more involving than Madhouse's Marvel Comics collaborations such as BLADE and IRON MAN. Kenji Kawai provides a powerful orchestral score, matched for sheer bombast by the hard-rock closing theme "Reckless" by Lazy, which truly goes up to 11.

TOWARD THE TERRA *

1980. JPN: *Terra e*. Movie. DIR: Hideo Onchi. SCR: Hideo Onchi, Chiho Shioda. DES: Masami Suda. ANI: Masami Suda. MUS: Masaru Sato. PRD: Toei. 119 mins.

Earth is a distant memory. Five hundred years after a revolution replaced human government with computer-aided totalitarianism, machines control every aspect of human life. Artificially created children are examined on reaching adulthood—telepaths are weeded out and destroyed. These "Mu" rejects marshal their strength in a desperate attempt to escape this hostile environment. They need a dynamic leader who can take them to a world of their own, where they can live without fear of persecution. Meanwhile the computers declare that a fugitive Mu is at large, and Keith, one of the elite caste who work for the computers, realizes that his servant Jonah is more than he seems to be.

Keiko Takemiya, author of SONG OF WIND AND TREES, wrote this science-fiction epic for *Manga Shonen* in 1977, and the anime remains close to the original style—boys' manga from a girls' artist. Despite the old-fashioned character designs, the film has held up well. The story handles familiar science-fiction concepts with assurance: Orwellian social and political oppression, computers that dictate human-kind's every move, mutant monsters shunned and hunted by humans, and pilgrims braving danger for a freer world. The film does not shy away from death, and, though violence and gore are kept low-key, some scenes are disturbing.

Osamu Yamasaki's 24-episode TV remake, *Toward the Terra* (2007) uses its longer running time to present a more faithful and in-depth adaptation of the original manga, commencing with a six-episode arc about a boy called Jomy as he embraces his status as a Mu, before suddenly lurching off to an entirely different story about Keith, a scholar prodigy on a space station. Subtle clues dropped during the telling of Keith's story reveal it as a narrative that is entwined with that of Jomy's, before both become involved in the titular search for Earth, facing the temptation along the way of settling for a different world that might even turn out to be a nicer place to live. **Ⓝ**

TOWER OF DRUAGA, THE *

2008. TV series. DIR: Koichi Chigira. SCR: Shoji Gatoh. DES: Akiko Asaki, Takuhito Kusanagi. ANI: Akira Amemiya, Hye Jin Lee, Yeong Beom Kim. MUS: Hitoshi Sakimoto. PRD: Gonzo, Dentsu. 24 mins. x 12 eps. (TV1, *Aegis of Uruk*), 24 mins. x 12 eps. (TV2, *Sword of Uruk*).

After years of struggle, the armies of Uruk have fought back the demons in the immense tower of Druaga and built a fortress on the first floor. Young explorer Jil decides to seek the fabled Blue Crystal Rod, a powerful magical treasure rumored to be on the top floor of the Tower, guarded by the legendary (and supposedly long-dead) Druaga himself. But he and his small party of adventurers are not the only ones planning to scale the upper levels. Every five years there's a summer lull in demon activity, and other interested parties—including Jil's older brother—plan to make the most of the opportunity. The scene is set for an anime that parodies the role-playing tropes it's based on and presents some fascinating stylistic diversions

wrapped around astonishingly kinetic action sequences.

Based on the 1984 Namco arcade game *The Tower of Druaga*, the events of the anime are set 60 years after the events of the game, with an all-new cast—though two of the game characters make brief appearances, and one sequence features the cast in a gaming arcade, playing the original. The changes wrought in the story and cast were minor compared to those in the media world since its appearance: there's no need to go to an arcade when games can be played anywhere on your cellphone. The series streamed over the Internet worldwide on the same day as its Japanese TV broadcast, alongside **BLASS-REITER**—the first ever global simultaneous streaming of multiple series from a major studio. Gonzo's parent company GDH stated that they wanted to showcase "a legal alternative to illegal file-sharing and downloading." They highlight a major shift in audience habits. The teenage market at which the show is aimed wants its media mobile, personal, and on-demand. With illegal streaming cutting their income to shreds, studios catering to this market had to adapt or die, and this enjoyably lightweight series thus became a bellwether for the future of mass visual media (**TECHNOLOGY AND FORMATS**).

TOWER OF ETRURIA

2003. Video. DIR: Motoaki Ishu. SCR: Yuji Suzuki. DES: Ryosuke Morimura. ANI: Ryosuke Morimura. MUS: N/C. PRD: Milky, Museum Pictures. 30 mins. x 2 eps.

In an erotic variant on the fairy tales of Rapunzel and Sleeping Beauty, an evil witch kidnaps the beautiful princess Cecilia, imprisoning her in a supposedly impregnable tower. While the princess is abused and tortured, her royal parents decree that they will offer her hand in marriage to the brave knight who rescues her. The warrior Albion duly volunteers, although this is an anime that concentrates more on the princess's misery than the quest to end it—compare to **BLOOD ROYALE**. Based on a manga by Hiyo Hiyo in *Core* magazine. **ⓛⓃⓋ**

TOWN WHERE YOU LIVE, A

2012. JPN: *Kimi no Iru Machi: Tasogare Kosaten*. AKA: *A Town where You Live—Twi-*

light Crossing. Video, TV series. DIR: Yasuhiro Yoshiura, Hiroshi Kobayashi, Shigeyasu Yamauchi. SCR: Momoko Murakami, Reiko Yoshida. DES: Ryusuke Chayama. ANI: Akira Takata. MUS: Keiichi Oku. PRD: Tatsunoko, Gonzo, Kodansha. 24 mins. x 2 eps. (v), 20 mins. x 12 eps. (TV).

Haruto Kirishima's father allows his friend's daughter Eba to live with with his family so that she can attend Haruto's high school for a while. She and Haruto were friends as toddlers (**ROMANCE AND DRAMA**) but now things have changed; Haruto has a crush on classmate Nanami. The stage is set for a high school romantic comedy based on Koji Seo's manga: when Eba goes back to Tokyo, Haruto hopes to hook up with her on a school trip, but Nanami gets in the way. The two-part video contains some spoilers for the manga storyline.

TP TIME PATROL BON

1989. TV series. DIR: Kunihiko Yuyama. SCR: Shunichi Yukimuro. DES: Tsukasa Fusanai. ANI: Tsukasa Fusanai. MUS: Hiroshi Tsutsui. PRD: Studio Gallop. 25 mins. x 26 eps.

A lackluster **TIME BOKAN** rip-off from **DORAEMON**-creators Fujiko-Fujio, in which Japanese schoolboy Heibon is enlisted in the efforts of the time patrol to keep the past out of trouble. Compare to **FLINT THE TIME DETECTIVE**.

TRAGEDY OF BELLADONNA *

1973. JPN: *Kanashimi no Belladonna*. Movie. DIR: Eiichi Yamamoto. SCR: Eiichi Yamamoto, Yoshiyuki Fukuda. DES: Kuni Fukai. ANI: Gisaburo Sugii, Shinichi Tsuji, Yasuo Maeda. MUS: Nobuhiko Sato. PRD: Mushi Pro. 89 mins.

In medieval France, country-boy Jean falls in love with country-girl Jeanne. As part of a strange ritual, the local landlord forces himself on Jeanne, and then allows his soldiers to gang rape her. Jean's hand is cut off when he fails to raise enough funds for the war coffers. Losing faith in God, Jeanne starts to have conversations with the Devil. Both Jean and the villagers throw her out, believing her to be possessed, and the disillusioned girl devotes herself to the Devil. Based on the 1862 novel *La Sorcière* by Jules Michelet, it adapts the story of Joan of Arc for an adult art-house audience, using a combination of still frames and animation deliberately aimed at breaking free of the full-animation mold and extending anime's "artistic" potential. That, at least, is the official story. *Belladonna* was the last of three films made for an adult audience by Mushi, though before production began Osamu Tezuka had already lost control of the company. Of those who did work on it, many were so aghast at the low budget that they used pseudonyms, including Reiko Okuyama, billed as Reiko Kitagawa. Director Eiichi Yamamoto's memoirs deride it as a "patchwork film" and "inanimate animation," better described as a series of panning shots across still images. The film was made to fulfil contractual demands, but had a drastically cut budget in order to amortize the shortfall on CLEOPATRA: QUEEN OF SEX, the budget of which had in turn been cut in an attempt to pay for cost overruns on A THOUSAND AND ONE NIGHTS, and thereby representing the final, inevitable consequence of the kiting of cheques and budgets by Osamu Tezuka since ASTRO BOY in 1963. The first English-language version of this film was prepared for the reception at a foreign film festival (probably Berlin in 1973), where *Belladonna* was supposedly greeted with enthusiastic applause. Producers had vainly hoped that foreign receipts for *Belladonna* would drag it into the black, but it was not to be. ◐

TRAGIC SILENCE *

2005. JPN: *Shojo Yugi*. AKA: *Girl Game*. Video. DIR: Tsuyoshi Kano. SCR: Miki Kano. DES: Wataru Yamaguchi. ANI: N/C. MUS: N/C. PRD: Onion Studio, Five Ways. 30 mins. x 2 eps. Luticia is a girl from a clan of vampires, who finds herself falling into forbidden love with Sho, her human childhood friend. Luticia's vampire relatives are very strict about avoiding human relationships—normal people are to be regarded as a food source, not potential bedmates, although this does not seem to have prevented Luticia's clan-mate Rick sleeping with Elana, a woman in a nearby town. This sets up an obvious tension between the humans of the village and the vampires that they now realize are dwelling in their midst. Although many vampires and humans appear to be in forbidden relationships, it's the one between Luticia and Sho that forms the focus of this short erotic anime—dumping the angst of *Romeo and Juliet* into a setting more akin to

DRACULA: SOVEREIGN OF THE DAMNED. Based on an original story by Hashiba Hayase. ◐◐◐

TRAINING WITH HINAKO

2009. JPN: *Isshoni Training: TRAINING WITH HINAKO*. AKA: *Training Together: Training with Hinako*. Video. DIR: Iku Suzuki, Shinichiro Kimura. SCR: Muneshige Nakagawa. DES: Ryoko Amisaki, Katsuhiro Hashi, Toshiya Nakamura. ANI: Ryoko Amisaki, Isao Sugimoto. MUS: Raito. PRD: Studio Hibari, Primastea. 24 mins. (v1), 40 mins. (v2), 35 mins. (v3). Hinako was once a human being, but turned into an anime character in her second year in middle school. She's a very well-developed girl in great shape, and a supporting actress in a magical girl anime. But her true mission in anime life is to encourage otaku to exercise, and that's exactly what she does in this exercise video with inevitable fan service (ARGOT AND JARGON). Its popularity led to a second video in 2010, *Isshoni Training SLEEPING WITH HINAKO*, about the joys of the sleepover and the exercises you can do then. This was followed the same year by *Isshoni Training 026: Ofuro* (or *The Bath*, subtitled *Bathtime with Hinako and Hiyoko*). Our heroine and her cute little friend show exercises you can do in, before, and after the bath. This episode came with a micro SD card to enable you to take Hinako's exercise tips with you—presumably into the bathroom. The "026" does not appear to relate to the *Hinako* series so hunting the missing 23 episodes would be a pointless exercise. ◐

TRAINSPOTTER'S JOURNEY

2007. JPN: *Tetsuko no Tabi*. TV series. DIR: Akinori Nagaoka. SCR: Kazuhiko Soma. DES: Yuka Kudo, Shinji Kawai. ANI: N/C. MUS: Cheru Watanabe, SUPER BELL Z. PRD: Group TAC, Attic Arcade, Shogakukan, Toei Video, Tohoku Shinsha. 20 mins. x 13 eps. Naoe Kikuchi is a manga artist in desperate need of a job when a travel writer asks her to join him on an epic journey. He's Japan's biggest train geek, Hirohiko Yokomi. He's already visited all 4,636 Japan Rail stations. Now his mission is to visit the remaining 5,207 private stations, and he wants her along to record the epic journey. Since Naoe's editor is a huge train freak too, her fate is sealed: she and Yokomi set off to travel the iron roads of Japan and

turn the experience into a manga.

This anime is based on their true-life experience and the manga that came out of it. A note at the front of the manga apologizes for the lack of drama: they get on trains, look out of the window, buy snacks, get off, wait on platforms, and that's about it. Yet very, very few anime and manga record the real life of Japan as carefully and effectively as this one (EVERYDAY ANIME), and believe it or not, this has substantially more incident and drama than the massive subgenre of travel videos in Japan that literally do nothing more than point a camera out of the window of a moving train, along the entirety of a given line. If you've ever traveled on Japan's railway network you may find yourself nodding in recognition; if you haven't—well, this is the next best thing. The characters vary, too—a number of people included in the later episodes caught the train with Naoe and Yokomi because they read about their trip in a previous episode of the manga. Only reality could feel quite so surreal; compare to RAIL WARS.

TRANSFORMERS *

1985. JPN: *Tatakae Cho Robot Seimeitai Transformers*. AKA: *Fight Super Living Robots Transformers*. TV series, movie. DIR: (Japan) Takayuki Nakano, Shoji Tajima (TV1–2), Katsutoshi Sasaki, Takao Yoshizawa (TV3–5), Mika Iwanami (BW), Osamu Sekita (Car-Robot). SCR: (Japan) Katsushige Hirata (translator, TV1–2), Keisuke Fujikawa (TV3–5), Tomohiro Ando (v), Mika Iwanami (BW). DES: (Japan) (TV1–2), Ban Magami (TV3–5, v). ANI: N/C. MUS: Shiro Sagisu (TV1–2), Kazunori Ishida (TV3–5, v). PRD: Toei, Nippon Animation, Toei; TV Asahi; TV Tokyo. 25 mins. x 64 eps. (TV1), 25 mins. x 30 eps. (TV2), 25 mins. x 35 eps. (TV3), 25 mins. x 35 eps. (TV4), 25 mins. x 35 eps. (TV5), 25 mins. x 36 eps. (TV1, *Beast Wars*), 25 mins. x 36 eps. (TV2, *BW*), 25 mins. x 36 eps. (TV3, *BW*), 25 mins. x 39 eps. (*Car-Robot*), 25 mins. x 39 eps. (*Car Robot*), 25 mins. x 52 eps. (*Armada*), 25 mins. x 52 eps. (*Energon*), 25 mins. x 52 eps. (*Galaxy Force*).
Far out in the galaxy is a planet where life has evolved in mechanical, rather than organic, form: Cybertron, a world of intelligent transforming robots. Two forces struggle for control of the planet—the

evil Destrons (Decepticons in the U.S. version) led by Megatron (later upgraded to Galvatron), and the heroic Cybertrons (Autobots), led by Convoy (Optimus Prime). The energy that sustains the planet is running out and the good guys build a huge starship, the Ark, to look for new energy sources. The Destron too have their own starship, and after their plotting leads to both ships being flung far back in time to Earth, good and bad robots are buried under the crust of our planet until, in the 20th century, they are awakened by the eruption of a volcano. Remodeling themselves to allow transformation into automobiles, jets, and other indigenous technology in order to conceal their presence from the local population, they plan to carry on their war on Earth. The Cybertrons team up with a few humans who stumble across their base, but the Destrons see humankind as inferiors to be enslaved or removed.

A U.S.-Japanese coproduction and the **POKÉMON** of its day, *Transformers* was originally made to order by Toei from scripts and designs prepared in the U.S. It was based on a toy line by Takara that was not originally known as *Transformers* until it was licensed to Hasbro for Western markets. Though nothing particularly new (**MACROSS** was way ahead of the game with transforming robots) or believable (a consistent sense of scale disappearing for good), the concept of two-toys-in-one wormed its way into boys' hearts, and there it stayed.

Transformers: The Movie (1986) was notable for a voice cast including Orson Welles, Eric Idle, and Leonard Nimoy. It moved the action back to the robots' homeworld in 2005. Supposedly designed to bridge the gap between the first and second series, it was not shown in Japan, creating the first wobbles of confusion that would eventually split the franchise into four distinct and contradictory continuities. Optimus Prime dies, handing on leadership of the Cybertrons to Ultra Magnus, who in turn passes on the leadership to Rodimus Prime. On the dark side, Megatron is remodeled by the mighty Unicron, an even nastier Force of Evil that goes around the galaxy eating planets, into a new leader named Galvatron—possibly after his Japanese

self, who appeared in a new TV series the same year.

Transformers 2010 (1986) continued the story without reference to the movie continuity, ending with another heroic self-sacrifice for Convoy and featuring a whole range of new transforming toys. The format of "new transformations to fight new battles" was set, and from here on the complications multiplied, with U.S. and British comics from Marvel taking the story in separate directions, while the animated version continued in Japan. Originated completely in Japan, the third series, *Transformers Headmasters* (1987), has the goodies led by Fortress Maximus and Galvatron still leading the Destrons, as the search for new energy sources goes on across the galaxy.

The fourth series, *Transformers Chojin Master Force* (1988), introduces a new breed of robots, known as Pretenders, that can mix with human beings. The Destron have been driven off Earth, but under their leader Metalhawk, the few remaining Cybertron Pretenders are fighting to defend humans from a demonic force. The transformations that sold toys were still paramount, with the robot characters changing into other forms such as starfighters. The fifth season, *Transformers: Victory* (1989), focuses around Star Saber, the Galaxy's greatest swordsman, who leads the Cybertron to protect Earth from the menace of Deathsaurus.

Transformers Z[one] (1990), in which a supernatural evil has resurrected the Destron, was canceled, and instead it was released straight to video as a 25-minute special. The series returned with a vengeance as *Beast Wars* (1998) on TV Tokyo, which reduplicated its checkered origins for a whole new generation. Though now using computer animation (from *ReBoot* creators Mainframe) the franchise began once more as a U.S.-Japan coproduction, which was then continued in Japan as *Beast Wars Second* (1998), *Beast Wars Neo* (1999), and *Beast Wars Metals* (1999). Just to confuse things, there was an additional non-anime Beast Wars sequel, *Beast Machines* (2000), animated in Canada by Mainframe, and only later exported back to Japan as *Beast Wars Returns*. A twist was borrowed from *Jurassic Park* as the two opposing robot ships crashed on planet

Gaea and the good guys merged with local animals, while the bad guys linked up with fossil dinosaur DNA, enabling the protagonists to transform into cyber-versions of the local fauna both alive and extinct. The Destron (Predacon in the English version) under souped-up T-Rex Galvatron (Megatron) want the planet's mysterious energy source, and the Cybertron (Maximals) under Live-Convoy (giant gorilla Optimus Primal) mean to stop them.

Transformers: Car-Robot (2000, released in America as *Transformers: Robots in Disguise*) returned to cel animation and the basic vehicle-to-robot transformation on which the series originally made its name. At the beginning of 2001, it was rebranded as *Transformers: Powerful Cars*. The next series was a true international coproduction between America and Japan, the 52-episode *Transformers: Armada* (2002, subsequently released in Japan as *Transformers: Micron Legend*), focusing on a group of special, smaller Transformers known as Mini-cons in America (Microns in Japan), who flee to Earth being pursued by the larger, bullying versions. The difference between the American and Japanese versions is not limited to the language track—the American version was rushed into production and onto the airwaves, resulting in numerous bloopers and substandard animation that were cleaned up for the localized version in Japan, which had more time to work on the materials.

Despite such embarrassments, the coproduction method clearly made things a little easier for both sides, and the cross-Pacific collaboration continued in *Transformers: Energon* (2004, released in Japan as *Transformers: Super Link*), set ten years after the events of the previous series and featuring two new twists. The Transformers themselves are locked in a struggle to seize the powerful element known as Energon, but the series also introduces the other great robot gimmick—the *Energon* continuity robots can not only transform, but they can also *combine*.

The emphasis on quests and collection was continued in the next international coproduction, *Transformers: Cybertron* (2005, released in Japan as *Transformers: Galaxy Force*), in which a black hole threatens to destroy the galaxy, and both Autobots and Decepticons rush to acquire the MacGuffins of the season—the Planet Forces (Cyber Planet Keys in Japan) that will allow them to control the energies involved and save the universe, or conquer it, or something.

With the concept still selling toys to a new generation of six-year-old fans, and "vintage" 1980s items acquiring collectible status, it seems the *Transformers* concept will run and run. Edits of various series were also rebroadcast as seven "TV specials" throughout the period and were also shown as *Beast Wars* "movies" in 1998 and 1999. There have also been two computer-animated *Robotmaster* DVDs released as special deals with toy packets, which feature characters from several of the continuities. *Transformers Takara* is a special DVD release of episodes from the original series previously unseen outside Japan. The American *Transformers* "live-action" film (the term seems strange considering how much CG animation was used instead) in 2007, and its sequels, initiated a new movie franchise for Hasbro, arguably representing the apotheosis of Hollywood's interest in Japanese products that began with **PRINCESS MONONOKE** and **POKÉMON**.

TRANSLATION

Translation is the rendering of any text into another language, replicating the original author's intent and tone. A difficult enough task in simple conversation, it is even more difficult when languages are as different in structure as Japanese and English. Since an anime is not the work of a single creative, translating Japanese animation requires a series of decisions concerning the intent, not only of the original author, but also of some of the actors. Translation in the anime world is often a labor of love—it is no coincidence that many translators are surprisingly young, idealistic, and ready to take intern-level salaries for complex work that in other sectors would usually require at least one, if not two university degrees and a decade of linguistic experience.

The basic form of translating anime is the subtitle—a text-based translation superimposed on the film. When movies are screened at film festivals, distributors sometimes supply a print with white subtitles. When viewed at a high resolution on a cinema screen, such subtitles are clear and

easily read; however, the same subtitles can often fade into the image when viewed on a television screen. This is a handy means of discouraging piracy, although some distributors have not realized the qualitative loss inherent in using such "white on white" subtitles for home video releases, where they tend to bleed and disappear into white backgrounds.

"Hard subtitles" are part of the finished image; "soft subtitles" are digital in origin, and can be turned on or off depending on the language needs of the viewer. Preferred subtitles in anime are usually yellow or white outlined in black (a type style called drop shadow), although some companies use multiple colors to denote different speakers or even onscreen titles to translate signs or background details not part of the main dialogue.

True translation requires a rare set of skills—a mastery of the Source Language (in this case, Japanese) and the ability to write fluently and professionally in the Target Language (English). In order to facilitate sales abroad, some Japanese companies provide a "spotting list"—a very basic translation, often prepared by someone in the Japanese office who is not an English native-speaker. Some Western distributors, particularly before the 1990s, liked to believe that spotting lists were close enough to the original dialogue to completely remove the need for a translator. However, many spotting lists, summarizing rather than translating dialogue, missing jokes, puns, and exact meanings, often neglecting songs or onscreen credits altogether, are next to useless in preparing a professional quality translation.

Translators usually require a copy of the source program with a burned-in timecode (BITC)—an onscreen counter that allows each line's location to be identified to the precise fraction of a second. It is also usual to request a copy of the Japanese script. Anime scripts were often hand-written until the mid-1990s, but today are largely word-processed, and divide neatly into descriptions of onscreen action (at the top of the page), and dialogue (on the lower half of the page). In this regard, they bear a closer resemblance to scripts used in English-language commercials, rather than the playbook format used for English-language screenplays and theater scripts.

Subtitle scripts must be fitted within a limited space on screen, forcing subtitlers to limit their language, often condensing or summarizing meaning. As with all translation, one must walk a delicate line between the communicative (what people say) and the referential (what they mean). This is particularly difficult translating Japanese into English, since word order, honorifics, and cultural differences can often ruin punchlines or moments of drama and need to be carefully considered. A perennial problem is translating simple forms of address, since Japanese are often apt to call one another by titles rather than names, creating a dissonant sense in a viewer who hears the word: "Senpai!" but reads the translation "Motoko!"

The fees offered for translation vary widely. The lowest payment we have seen for an anime script was barely 0.03% of the highest, reflecting the variation in both skills and expectations in the industry. The ideal translators are fluent speakers of both source and target languages, with an appropriate level of skill in the target language to have sold books or scripts of their own, but the prices for such individuals often prove prohibitive. Company accountants argue that it makes far better economic sense to hire a translator to do a "basic" translation into English and a rewriter who will then polish the script. This can lead to generational loss, also known as semantic drift, where the meanings of certain phrases will mutate from the original author's intent, since the rewriter rarely understands enough of the original to check. It also leads to a form of job-title inflation—merely having a "translation" is no longer enough; instead we must now talk of "English-language adaptations," or "trans-creations."

Subtitled releases appeal to roughly 10% of the anime-buying market. Outside the fan community, in some mainstream sectors and particularly on television, it is more normal to see "dubbed" anime—that is, anime whose Japanese language track has been replaced by an English-language track. As a rule of thumb, a dubbed release costs ten times as much to produce, but can sell ten times as many copies and is more easily sold to television. The expense is incurred through the need to hire voice actors and a recording studio. Early dub releases, made for the children's market and often subject to drastic CENSORSHIP AND LOCALIZATION, often had dub scripts with names, plots, and even locations differing entirely from the original—the location of BATTLE OF THE PLANETS was moved into space, that of MOSPEADA back to Earth. Since the 1990s, when the Japanese origin of anime became a selling point in itself, even dub translations have aspired to a more faithful reproduction of the original. There are, however, still some exceptions, such as the brief vogue for "fifteening," in which anime were refitted for an older audience by the addition of superfluous bad language, and the occasional improvisational throwback such as GHOST STORIES. Some English-language rewriters even go so far as to credit themselves as the "authors" of a script, regardless of the person who actually wrote it or the often uncredited figure who translated the script into English.

The voice track in an anime is usually separate from the Music and Effects track (or M&E). This allows for a far easier process, although there have been cases in the anime world where the M&E track has been lost or damaged—such as the original GUNBUSTER, which has never been dubbed into English owing to the prohibitive costs of reconstructing the audio from the ground up. Recording is usually done using an Automated Dialogue Replacement process (ADR, known as post-synching in Britain), in which single lines or scenes can be dropped in and manipulated digitally, one at a time. Digital editing processes allow for lines to be moved fractionally ahead or behind, speeded up or slowed down in order to achieve synchronized lip movements (lip sync), although the limited nature of Japanese animation sometimes means that lips do not necessarily sync completely, even in the Japanese original. The movement of characters' mouths is sometimes known as "lip flaps" in America, and the process of synching known as "fitting the flaps"—a term which did not survive in Britain, where it sounds laughably obscene.

Dialogue recording for actors is commonly done one voice at a time, in order to allow for audio manipulation, and to avoid paying a performer by the hour to largely sit and watch other actors work.

Some anime dubs are recorded with ensemble casts, although the immediacy and interactivity of such performances is often outweighed by the extra studio time spent doing retakes. Actors are sometimes brought in to the studio in twos and threes to record all the sequences in which they share screen time. There is thus no single method employed in recording dialogue, but often a mix of all three, even over the course of dubbing a single title. "Making Of" documentaries often imply a prevalence of ensemble casts, purely because they are usually shot for technical reasons on the "crowd-scene" day when most of the cast will be available for interviews.

A subtitle script is subject to further rewrites for performance, both for ease of delivery and fitting the flaps. The worst cases of semantic drift can often occur on the spot, as actors misread, mispronounce, or misinterpret lines. For this reason, the best choice for ADR directors is usually whoever wrote the ADR script—there are several in the modern anime industry who started as voice actors or translators and progressed through ADR rewriting to directing.

Translators are also obliged to make a judgment call on "ad libs" in the original script, where the Japanese screenwriter calls for the cast to improvise. Whether to faithfully reproduce whatever the Japanese actors said on the day of their recording (which may then have been matched by the animators in onscreen business) or to interpret the "author's intent" as being one of letting the English-language actors similarly improvise is one of the no-win situations of anime translation. Incidences of semantic drift are more common in dubbing, and the subject of increased indignation among fans at the liberties they believe to have been taken with the original script. Matters are often confused further by the use of "Engrish," English words adorning box art or press materials in Japan, frequently misspelled, which then establish themselves within FANDOM as the "approved" terms.

Translators on dubs are often obliged to make another judgment call, particularly with humor, as to whether they should reproduce the exact meaning of a line, or instead substitute it with a different line that will induce the same effect in

the viewer—be it a belly laugh, shocked surprise, or a groan. It appears traditional in anime fandom for the translator to take the blame for anything a fan doesn't like, particularly if the fan has learned a little Japanese and can use the occasion to boast of his own supposed skill. The best example of this is the controversy over Kosuke Fujishima's *Aa Megamisama*, which was initially (and excellently) translated as OH MY GODDESS!, only to incur the wrath of fans who knew enough Japanese to read the letters "*aa*" but not enough to know that it could be a contraction of "*anna ni.*" A later incarnation of the series was subsequently released as *Ah My Goddess*, an inferior translation that nevertheless matched the Engrish title already seen on Japanese materials, and hence greeted as somehow more "correct." Similarly, Streamline Pictures felt obliged to release the LUPIN III movie *Secret of Mameux* under the title *Secret of Mamo*, since the latter title was already popular in fandom, and the producers had given up fighting.

Some humor can be unintentional, leaving translators with a further problem—whether to faithfully translate an author's text if doing so would make it seem laughable to foreign audiences. Even the great Osamu Tezuka was unable to resist making a few English puns with his character's names, which often makes them difficult to translate, while spelling and names in GUNDAM and CAPTAIN HARLOCK have been a source of constant argument between self-appointed interpreters of the original creators' will.

Fans, however, are not the worst enemy of translators, and can often lend diligent and impressive support. Fandom has potentially limitless time to debate and correct its understanding of any anime it chooses, whereas translators are unable to predict what project will be the next to land in their laps. Time itself can be the most crushing limitation on a translator's performance. In one case, the translator was driven to an airport freight terminal at two in the morning to meet the tape directly from the plane, with eight hours to translate the script, for a producer who wanted a master ready for one o'clock in the afternoon, ready for review copies to be made and biked over to magazines by two. He made the deadline, although

SAMURAI GOLD hasn't won any awards.

Another controversy in the anime world concerns "dubtitling," in which a distributor uses a dubbing script as the source for subtitling, often repeating alterations for lip-sync and actors' ad libs rather than a scriptwriter's original prose. This often creates subtitles that do not appear to translate the onscreen Japanese dialogue at all, and is greatly frowned upon in fandom. However, fandom's censure sometimes extends too far, deriding perfectly reasonable translation decisions as dubtitling, simply because they do not match the critic's preferred translation to the precise letter.

Semantic drifts can sometimes range further than the original target language, in cases where a "second generation" translation is prepared from the English text. Although most European distributors claim to translate direct from Japanese, there are cases of companies using some or all of an English-language translation in the preparation of the version in their own language. In the eyes of anime companies, this is usually a victimless crime, although it can be galling for English-language translators to see others taking the credit for their work and hard-won skills. This practice was common in the early 1990s, but now seems to have faded away, largely because many European anime translators are now better paid and better trained than their English-language counterparts.

TRAP

2011. JPN: *Wana: Hakudaku Mamire no Ho-kago*. AKA: *Trap: Stained After School*. Video. DIR: Hiromi Yokoyama. SCR: Tsuyako Shinomiya. DES: Si Min Lee. ANI: gonbee, Kiriko Satsuma. MUS: N/C. PRD: Suzuki Mirano. 30 mins. x 2 eps.

Raika's brother commits suicide under mysteriously motiveless circumstances. She decides to infiltrate his all-male school to find out the truth behind his death. But her identity is discovered and she finds herself facing gang rape with other girls caught in the same trap. Based on the computer game by Guilty. **⊙Ⓥ**

TRAP AROUND THE TOWN: STEAMY BODIES

2010. JPN: *Machi-gurumi no Wana: Haku-daku ni Mamireta Shitai*. Video. DIR: N/C. SCR:

minamikaze. DES: Hikaru Kinohara. ANI: N/C. MUS: N/C. PRD: PoRO. 28 mins. x 2 eps.

Atsuko, a newly qualified teacher, comes to work at the school where her younger sister is a pupil and her father is a clerk. The headmaster's son, a troubled young man, is also a student and manages to blackmail Atsuko into sex under threat of getting her whole family kicked out of school. Then his father and others join in. Soon men from the neighborhood are involved, and Atsuko's kid sister is drawn into their net. Based on an erotic game by Syrup whose basic premise is that young women aren't safe anywhere. **⊙Ⓥ**

TRAVELER IN DARKNESS WITH HAT AND BOOKS

2004. JPN: *Yami to Boshi to Hon no Tabibito*. AKA: *Yamibo*. TV series. DIR: Yuji Yamaguchi. SCR: Hideki Shirane, Rika Nakase, Tomomi Mochizuki, Toshifumi Kawase. DES: Asako Nishida. ANI: Kyuta Sakai. MUS: Akifumi Tada. PRD: Studio Deen, MBS. 25 mins. x 13 eps.

Eve is one of the overseers at the Great Library, an interdimensional institution where multiple realities from the entire universe are contained within books—at least, that is how it appears in our dimension. Eve, however, has lived many lives in these other worlds and has had many names, all while searching for a particular girl, in a multiverse drama recalling the works of Neil Gaiman and Roger Zelazny. Compare to READ OR DIE. Based on an erotic game by Root, with designs by Carnelian.

TREASURE CASTLE IN THE DESERT

2008. JPN: *Sabaku no Takara no Shiro*. Video. DIR: Tomoharu Katsumata. SCR: Chikako Kobayashi. DES: Katsumi Aoshima. ANI: Katsumi Aoshima. MUS: Seiji Yokoyama. PRD: Shinano Planning. 31 mins.

Yuta turns up at school on his birthday, and is given a sketch of himself by one of the other children. He curtly dismisses this heartfelt, handmade gift with the comment that he was hoping for something else—he has already been prattling incessantly about computer games, and so we may presume that he would have preferred one of those. In geography class, where the children are allowed to pick a place on the world map to learn about, Yuta inadvertently picks Dunhuang,

the Buddhist sacred site in the western Chinese desert (RELIGION AND BELIEF). Yuta daydreams about its legendary "treasures"—which he imagines as crowns, swords, and jewels—and later that day, falls asleep in his room.

He dreams that he is dragged into a photograph of the desert, where a pair of talking camels, Kinpo and Gingaku, offer to take him to the treasures. After a foreshadowing encounter with a mirage in the desert, Yuta reaches Dunhuang, a temple complex carved into a cliffside, perpetually threatened by a rain of sand from the encroaching dunes above. There, he meets an old Chinese man, who has the Sisyphean task of sweeping away the sand, "to protect the treasures of Dunhuang," and a young Chinese girl, Youlan, who values her hand-made doll more than any treasure Yuta has heard of—he witlessly talks, once again, of soccer balls and model aeroplanes.

Of course, the real treasure in question is Buddhist scripture and self-knowledge, which the thick-headed Yuta takes the rest of this short film to comprehend, in another anime parable based on a children's book by Daisaku Ikeda, leader of the Sokagakkai International organization. *Treasure Castle in the Desert* retains some of the cloying bonhomie of Ikeda's earlier RAINBOW ACROSS THE PACIFIC, along with the oddly subversive implication also found in his FAIRGROUND IN THE STARS, that only rude, selfish, and otherwise naughty children will get the chance to have any fun. However, it also pushes its anti-materialist message with a degree of subtlety, as Yuta stares in wonder at the ancient Buddhist paintings on some of the cave walls. Predictably, the paintings come to life to illustrate a few choice pieces of Buddhist philosophy, leaving the newly awoken Yuta with an interest in TV documentaries about Central Asia, and, we hope, less of a childish self-regard. The word "Sabaku" in the title is written in hiragana, occluding the precise intention of the homophone terms for "desert" and "judgment"—the title hence puns on the material treasure house of the sands and a metaphorical choice over what a house of treasure really is.

TREASURE ISLAND *

1965. JPN: *Shin Takarajima; Dobutsu Takarajima*. AKA: *New Treasure Island; Animal Treasure Island*. TV special. DIR: Osamu Tezuka (TVm), Hiroshi Ikeda (m1), Osamu Dezaki, Toshio Takeuchi, Hideo Takayashiki (TV1). SCR: Osamu Tezuka (TVm), Satoshi Iijima, Hiroshi Ikeda (m1), Haruya Yamazaki, Hajime Shinozaki (TV1). DES: Osamu Tezuka (TVm), Yasuji Mori (m1), Akio Sugino (TV1). ANI: Gisaburo Sugii (TVm), Yasuji Mori (m1), Akio Sugino (TV1). MUS: Isao Tomita (TVm), Naoki Yamamoto (m1), Kentaro Haneda (TV1). PRD: Mushi, Fuji TV (TVm), Toei (m1); Tokyo Movie Shinsha, Nippon TV (TV1). 52 mins. (TVm), 78 mins. (m1), 25 mins. x 26 eps. (TV1), 90 mins. (m2).

Jack the wolf sea-pirate is killed in a harbor inn. The innkeeper's rabbit son, Jim, finds a treasure map on the old sea-wolf and sets out to find the booty, berthing on a ship crewed by other animals, chartered by the deer Dr. Livesay and financed by the pig Squire Trelawney. He befriends Silver, another wolf, who is revealed as the leader of the local pirates when they seize control of the ship. Eventually, the pirates find the island on the map and go in search of buried treasure. The anime then deviates from Robert Louis Stevenson's original 1881 story, in a style that not only contains elements of creator Osamu Tezuka's occasional heavy-handed moralizing, but also his genius. As the animals near the treasure, they lose their anthropomorphic characteristics, devolving back to a feral state and running off into the jungle. Eventually, only Silver and Jack are left, and Silver struggles between the two states. Reasoning that no treas-ure is worth losing one's "humanity" to animal greed, Silver and Jack leave the treasure behind. This anthropomorphic adaptation should not be confused with Shichima Sakai and Osamu Tezuka's 1947 manga *Shin Takarajima*, which shares the title but not the concept. Some sources list this as the first-ever anime "TV special," a somewhat pointless distinction since it was not the first one-shot anime to be broadcast—see **INSTANT HISTORY**. The U.S. release was colorized for Fred Ladd by animators in Seoul, who ensured that it was the South Korean flag, not the Japanese one, that the animals accidentally raise in a throwaway visual gag.

Hiroshi Ikeda's *Animal Treasure Island* (1971, *Dobutsu Takarajima*) deviated further from the original. The human Jim Hawkins and his mouse companion Lex set sail in a toy boat, pursued by a porcine Long John Silver (perhaps thanks to animator Hayao Miyazaki, who worked on the production). Jim also joins forces with a third party in search of the map, Captain Flint's granddaughter Cathy. At the climax, the treasure is found to be at the bottom of a drained lake, a conceit later reused in Miyazaki's **CASTLE OF CAGLIOSTRO** and ripped off in other anime, including **LADIUS** and **BEAST WARRIORS**. It was released in the U.S. as just plain *Treasure Island*, coincidentally featuring many of the same voice actors from the U.S. dub of the earlier version.

A more faithful version came in the form of the TV series *Treasure Island* (1978), director Dezaki's follow-up to his **NOBODY'S BOY REMI** for TMS. This version restored the human characters from the original but did insist on giving Jim Hawkins a leopard cub for a pet. As well as directing, Dezaki provided storyboards under his pseudonym of Makura Saki, and this version was also reedited into a "movie" release, with Takeuchi credited as director and Dezaki as assistant. The series has been screened in Europe and run in Spanish on Puerto Rican TV.

TREASURES OF THE SNOW

1983. JPN: *Alps Monogatari: Watashi no Annette*. AKA: *My Annette: Story of the Alps*. TV series. DIR: Kozo Kusuba. SCR: Kenji Yoshida. DES: Issei Takematsu. ANI: Issei Takematsu, Eimi Maeda, Yoshiharu Saito. MUS: Ryohei Hirose. PRD: Nippon Animation, Fuji TV. 25 mins. x 48 eps.

In the remote Swiss village of Rossiniere, local bully Lucien causes Annette's younger brother Dani to fall into a valley and break his leg. The 13-year-old Annette vows revenge on Lucien, determined to damage his life in any way she can, although she eventually realizes that a truly good person should forgive others, even if they do wrong to them. Based on the 1950 children's book with a heavy Christian subtext by Patricia M. St. John, the anime version added many sequences not found in the original story, taking several episodes, for example, to cover the

years leading up to the fateful leg-breaking incident. Compare to another **WORLD MASTERPIECE THEATER** Alpine story, Johanna Spyri's **HEIDI**.

TREE IN THE SUN, A *

2000. JPN: *Hidamari no Ki*. TV series. DIR: Gisaburo Sugii, Rei Mizuno. SCR: Tatsuhiko Urahata. DES: Marisuke Eguchi. ANI: Noriyuki Fukuda, Masahiro Kitazaki. MUS: Reiko Matsui. PRD: Madhouse, Nippon TV. 25 mins. x 25 eps.

At the end of the Tokugawa period, as Americans enter feudal Japan, two young men come of age. Manjiro Ibutani is a samurai through and through, beholden to his lord and obliged to lay down his life before his honor. But Manjiro's code is put to the test by a succession of humiliations, such as guarding the U.S. consul and commanding a unit composed of lowly farmers. Eventually, Manjiro becomes one of the fundamentalists who refuse to modernize (see **OI RYOMA!**); he is unable to survive in the brave new world of the late 19th century. But Ryoan, the doctor who tends his wounds, is very different. Ryoan has studied Western-style medicine and appreciates all the good that can be learned from the foreign powers. Both love their country and want to help their people, but in very different ways—compare to **SANCTUARY**, which similarly observes life from two very different perspectives. Based on the 1981 manga by Osamu Tezuka and partly inspired by the life of his own great-grandfather, Ryoan Tezuka, a 19th-century doctor. Broadcast with English subtitles in the U.S. on Asahi Homecast.

TREE OF PALME, A *

2001. JPN: *Parumu no Ki*. AKA: *Palm Tree; Wooden Palm*. Movie. DIR: Takashi Nakamura. SCR: Takashi Nakamura. DES: Toshiyuki Inoue. ANI: Mamoru Sasaki. MUS: Takashi Harada. PRD: Palm Studio, GENCO, Kadokawa, Toho. 136 mins.

On planet Arcana, a mystic tree is said to absorb the memories of the civilization where it takes root. A sentient android boy, Palme, is made from this wood to care for his maker's sick wife. When she dies, he is paralyzed with grief and loses all sense of purpose. Then blue-skinned Koram, a woman warrior of the Sol tribe, arrives at their home fleeing a group of armed pursuers, and he mistakes her for his dead mistress. She asks Palme and his maker to take a mysterious egg to the sacred region of Tama. When his maker is killed by Koram's attackers, Palme takes over and journeys through Arcana, encountering danger and friendship and learning what it is to be human. This Japanese take on *Pinocchio* is beautifully rendered, with backgrounds by Mutsuo Koseki, whose work is better known from NAUSICAÄ OF THE VALLEY OF THE WIND and CASTLE IN THE SKY. Attractive and interesting designs show stylistic echoes of CATNAPPED; but it's poorly paced and the character of Palme himself is not sympathetic. ●

TRIANGLE *
1998. JPN: *Terra Story*. Video. DIR: Yukihiro Makino. SCR: Yutaka Hidaka. DES: Hiro Asano. ANI: Hiro Asano. MUS: N/C. PRD: Daiei. 30 mins. x 2 eps.
Nineteen-year-old Keisuke gets a whirlwind education in the art of love from several enthusiastic ladies. Will they help him win the woman of his dreams? And will she mind some extra company? Based on a computer game, so the answers are probably yes and no. ●

TRIANGLE HEART—SWEET SONGS FOREVER
2000. Video DIR: Akiyuki Shinbo. SCR: Maki Tsuzuki. DES: Satoshi Ishino. ANI: Satoshi Ishino. MUS: Hiroaki Sano. PRD: Starchild. 30 mins. x 4 eps.
Fiasse Christella, headmistress of a renowned music school, is a former singer who still does a charity World Tour every year. Her mother left her very wealthy, and mysterious evildoers covet both her and her inheritance. Her old friends Ellis McGaren and brother/sister swordmasters Kyoya and Miyu Takamachi are drafted to protect her. The World Tour is coming up and Fiasse is determined that the show must go on. The story is based on a computer game by Ivory. It took two and a half years to release the four episodes on video, but Tsuzuki spun a creator credit for the immensely more successful LYRICAL NANOHA TV series off them in 2004 and 2005.

TRIANGLE STAFF
Company formed in 1987 by defectors from numerous anime companies, the first

work for which was animation on the video remake of DEVILMAN. Notable staffers have included Ryotaro Nakamura, Noriyuki Suga, and Takashi Hirokawa.

TRIGUN *
1998. JPN: *Trigun*. TV series. DIR: Satoshi Nishimura. SCR: Yosuke Kuroda. DES: Takahiro Yoshimatsu. ANI: Yoshimitsu Ohashi. MUS: Tsuneo Imahori. PRD: Madhouse, TV Tokyo. 25 mins. x 26 eps. (TV), 90 mins. (m).
A space Western in the style of EAT-MAN, set in one of those star systems that look exactly like the fantasy American West, if you ignore the two suns and the presence of a pair of female insurance investigators. Derringer Meryl and Stungun Millie, both as cute as pie, are there to keep an eye on a one-man destruction machine named Vash the Stampede, to try and minimize the collateral damage and expense of his shootouts. But Vash, a fabled gunman chased by every bounty hunter in the area, is not just another bad guy. He avoids killing at any cost and only fires off one of his mighty weapons to prevent injury to others. When you get right down to it, he's just a skinny geek with spiky hair and a good nature, whose main passions in life are food and girls. With hot lead flying from just about every other direction, Vash doesn't fire a single shot until episode 5. He also raises issues such as exploitation of natural resources and the ethics of murder. And in Nicholas Wolfwood, a sexy young Christian priest whose weapons (wielded only in a good cause) include a portable confessional and a huge cross packed with weaponry, he's created an unusual antagonist. Ranged against him are his real enemies, the Gung-Ho Guns, whose secret agenda is to blacken his reputation by provoking him into murder. Based on Yasuhiro Nightow's original manga in *Young King Ours*, *Trigun* enjoyed surprising success in the overseas market, sufficient to justify another installment, although this only became apparent midway through the first decade of the 21st century when royalty figures became available. The movie follow-up *Trigun: Badlands Rumble* (2010) hence went into production a decade after the original series had finished and was steered primarily by interest in the English- and Spanish-speaking territories. ●

TRINITY BLOOD *
2005. TV series. DIR: Tomohiro Hirata, Daisuke Chiba. SCR: Atsuhiro Tomioka, Yuji Hosono, Masahiro Sekino, Masayuki Kojima. DES: Atsuko Nakajima, Thores Shibamoto. ANI: Atsuko Nakajima, Yasuomi Umezu. MUS: Takahito Eguchi. PRD: AIC, Madhouse, Hanjin, FAI, Angle, Anime Aru, Gonzo. 24 mins. x 24 eps.
In a post-apocalyptic scenario not dissimilar from that in VAMPIRE HUNTER D, a race of vampires faces up to a new threat, long-lived humans who have modified their bodies with cybernetic implants and nanotechnology. Peter Abel Nightroad is an agent for the Vatican but is also a secret operative in Ax, a special tactical unit run by the maverick Cardinal Catherina—compare to HELLSING and CHRONO CRUSADE. Based on a novel by the late Sunao Yoshida, although it is likely that the anime made it into production more through the artwork that accompanied the text, since artist Kiyo Kujo later adapted it into a manga for *Asuka* magazine. ●●●

TRIP TREK
2003. TV series. DIR: Shoji Nishimoto. SCR: N/C. DES: N/C. ANI: Kenji Hagita, Shoji Nishimoto. MUS: n3o. PRD: Estrella, Manglobe, bb-anime, Contents Japan, Sunrise. 6 mins. x 4 eps. (v1), 8 mins. x 8 eps. (v2).
Half-girl, half-demon, Zocco is a cute and zanily disturbing little redhead with a spooky toy rabbit, Mimime, created for her by her missing mother. The pair go hunting for Mama in this short fantasy series, narrated by a fly called Catherine who claims to be her missing mother. Their simply drawn world is populated with horror show and fairy tale tropes, spooky toys, and strange animals, rather as if THE GREGORY HORROR SHOW were to be remade as KIDS' ANIME. Mimime has a zippered pouch in its stomach from which Zokko produces a book of spells and various artifacts, in a nod to DORAEMON. Originally aired online, it was produced in a fascinating array of English accents with Japanese subtitles. Eight more episodes were later made in Japanese. These seem to have been released from 2007 online, although several Japanese sources give the official release date for the 12-episode series as 2010—possibly the DVD release date. Digital distribution does not, it turns out, make

it any easier for encyclopedists to check their facts. The score is rather cool.

TRISTIA OF THE DEEP-BLUE SEA *

2004. JPN: *Aoi Umi no Tristia*. AKA: *Tristia; Blue Ocean of Tristia*. Video. DIR: Hitoyuki Matsui. SCR: Kazuharu Sato. DES: Eiji Komatsu. ANI: ufotable zippers. MUS: Norihiko Tsuru, Yuriko Nakamura. PRD: Kogado Studio, Inc., Kumasan Team, Inc., The Klockworx. 30 mins. x 2 eps.

It's been ten years since the ocean city of Tristia was ravaged by dragon attacks, and Nanoca, granddaughter of the great inventor Prospero Flanka, still dreams of carrying on his work and restoring the city to its former glory. That's enough plot for a Miyazaki movie, but not for an anime based on a computer game like this one. Accordingly, Nanoca's rival Panavia Tornado challenges her to enter the upcoming Golem Building Contest, in which inventors compete to create a useful household magical robot. Many of the characters are named after aircraft, which, we're sure you'll agree, more than makes up for any other elements that may seem derivative or futile. Cute girls and Roman centurion-inspired robot designs hint that this may not be rocket science, although a leading lady who aspires to be a great engineer is at least a welcome change from the usual anime roster of wannabe pop idols and doormats. ⓁⓃⓋ

TRITON OF THE SEA

1972. JPN: *Umi no Triton*. TV series, movie. DIR: Yoshiyuki Tomino. SCR: Seiji Matsuoka, Masaki Tsuji, Yuki Miyata, Chikara Matsumoto, Minoru Onotani. DES: Osamu Tezuka. ANI: Yukiyoshi Hane. MUS: Yoshimasa Suzuki. PRD: Animation Staff Room, Westcape; Office Academy. 25 mins. x 27 eps. (TV), 74 mins. (m).

Poseidon rules the depths of the sea cruelly, imposing his will through armies of vicious creatures. Little Triton's parents died resisting him, and now the boy carries on their struggle, helped by the intelligent and gentle female dolphin Lukar and by little mermaid Pipi. *Triton* began life as a 1969 manga in the *Sankei Shinbun* and was first animated as the unreleased eight-minute pilot *Blue Triton* (1971, *Aoi Triton*). Taken from Osamu Tezuka by skullduggery behind-the-scenes, both *Triton* and

WANSA-KUN may have been birthed by the ASTRO BOY creator, but they were reared by other hands.

TRI-ZENON

2000. JPN: *Muteki Trizenon*. AKA: *Invincible Trizenon*. TV series. DIR: Takashi Watabe, Matsuo Asami, Hiroshi Kimura. SCR: Katsumi Hasegawa, Takao Yoshioka. DES: Naomi Miyata, Rei Nakahara. ANI: Naomi Miyata, Naoko Yamamoto. MUS: Kenji Kawai. PRD: Ganges, Kadokawa, TBS. 25 mins. x 22 eps.

"Hot-blooded and straightforward" Akira Kamui lives with his father and kid brother, Ai. His mother is mysteriously missing, and Japan is under threat from alien invaders. To fight the enemy, Akira has help from his childhood friend Kana, with whom he constantly squabbles, his dog Gon, the enigmatic but cute Shizuku, and sisters Uma and Riku (complete opposites), as well as Rama, a girl from an old Japanese family, and Umu, the standoffish singer of a local amateur band. Akira's rival Jin, who is strong, handsome, cool, and really nice, and Jin's sister Ena make up the rest of the team. Conceived as a multimedia project by Rui Araizumi, its publicity claims that *Tri-Zenon* will simultaneously encompass manga, anime, and novels, with each freestanding enough to be enjoyed independently, but together forming a complex interweaving story. A man's reach should exceed his grasp, but this may be rather too ambitious for the creator and team that gave us SLAYERS.

TROPES AND TRANSFORMATIONS

Anime's most common stylistic device is the appearance of the characters themselves. Many, but not all, creators take their lead from Osamu Tezuka (himself working in imitation of the Fleischers' Betty Boop and Disney's Mickey Mouse) in using visual "pedomorphism"—many anime characters have skulls more like those of babies than adults, with large, widely spaced eyes and a drastically reduced lower jawline, often creating a pointed chin and small mouth. Much imitated by foreign artists who claim to draw in a "manga style," this tradition is more related to the concerns of anime, with large eyes to help convey expression and emotion, and a reduced mouth size to lessen the time spent animating lip movements. According to Isao Takahata,

Japanese animators get away with limited mouth movements because speaking Japanese only requires three mouth positions in reality, whereas English requires eight. Perfected with Tezuka's ASTRO BOY, this drawing style is now commonplace in anime, in manga based on anime designs, and consequently in much graphic art from Japan. It is merely one of many art styles used in Japanese comics, but the one most likely to appear in the kinds of works that are usually adapted for animation.

Unreal proportions do not merely apply to the faces of anime characters. In anime for the young, the baby motif is often continued for the whole body, with an outsized head and, occasionally, feet and short legs. In anime for older viewers, torso and leg dimensions are elongated to create tall, elfin body shapes, although, as in Western comics, the boys are sometimes given carved, muscular physiques, and many girls get large breasts. Regardless of the proportions of characters in a show, they may sometimes devolve into squasheddown, "super-deformed" (SD) cartoon versions of themselves in moments of intense agitation, or sometimes in entire SD spin-offs in which the cast remains permanently in a cartoon parody state.

Anime hairstyles have their own traditions. Period pieces like THE TALE OF GENJI will sometimes use natural shades for all characters, but the combination of black Asian hair and limited animation can make it difficult to tell them apart. In general, anime characters are differentiated by blatantly unreal coloring—it is not unusual in a cast of all-Japanese characters to find black hair alongside foreign variants like red, blond, and brown, and artificial shades like pink, blue, and green. Similarly, many characters have instantly recognizable hairstyles. Anime boys have quiffs and spikes in their hair that remain in constant position for ease of animation (but may occasionally droop into their line of sight), while girls have complex accessorizing. Drawing plaits or braids is unnecessarily fiddly for artists on a short deadline, but bows or ponytails with distinctive scrunchies are much quicker to draw and often present another excuse for brightly colored adornment. Such hairstyles can make anime girls seem younger than their age, but help make a hero's five love-objects at least a little different.

Anime clothing is similarly differentiated, with a cast line up of girls likely to be dressed in mini-skirts, trousers, shorts, and long dresses, usually in direct reflection of their characters. Some anime, such as HUMMINGBIRDS, even feature the rather desperate inclusion of a pair of pants with one long leg and one short—an apparent attempt to do something offbeat. The only place where clothing is not set apart in this way is in female underwear, for reasons based on animation concerns and erotic subtexts. Animators at Studio Fantasia, long-time purveyors of soft-core titillation like AGENT AIKA, reported that overly lacy or frilly underwear was simply too time-consuming to animate. Distinguishing underwear with straightforward colors often backfired, since a pair of red or blue panties could look too much like gym-wear or a swimsuit, and hence lost much of its erotic edge. Instead, the default setting for anime underwear became plain white panties (Studio Fantasia taking this to an extreme, where they had their own identifiable style of panty, worn by both protagonists and antagonists), which are not only easier to draw, but can also carry an erotic charge based on Japanese censorship—a blank space in the image as a substitute for what is hidden beneath it.

The slapstick and externalized emotions common to cartoons around the world also play a major part in anime comedy. Lechery can be signaled by drool or nosebleeds (a sign of high blood pressure caused by sexual arousal), or an elongated philtrum that accentuates pursed lips; anger by enlarged and throbbing veins, red face, or steam coming out of the ears; panic or relief by an exaggerated sweat drop on the brow or hair; romance by the sudden eruption in the frame of hearts and flowers. Sight gags can work even when the visual grammar of the medium is a little unfamiliar. One does not have to know much about Japan to enjoy many of the visual gags in PROJECT A-KO, whose very title is a spoof on a Jackie Chan movie, or to get the joke when LUPIN III, eyes bugging out and body suddenly rigid as an arrow, spots yet another cute girl.

Another visual trope in anime is the exaggerated freeze-frame. The use of a single still image for a prolonged period represents an obvious saving in animation costs (taken to ludicrous extremes in later episodes of EVANGELION), but also accentuates moments of high drama. A samurai holding still, waiting for his opponent's head to fall off, or a freeze-frame of kung-fu action, inadvertently resembles the *mie*—a held-pose used to similar effect in kabuki drama. It has since been much copied in live-action science fiction, most notably the "bullet time" sequences of *The Matrix* (1999), which ironically spent large amounts of money imitating an anime trope originally designed to save on a budget. Sometimes, a heroic pose is accompanied by a gleam of highlighting on a character's sword or armor with a chiming sound effect. This can also be parodied by a self-confident (male) character producing the same effect from his white teeth, or even his glasses. Unconfirmed popular myth asserts that this is the origin of the Jamaican slang term *bling*, for jewelry or other conspicuous accessories.

Anime excels at adapting visual devices from manga and inserting them into action. This hyper-reality first came to the fore in STAR OF THE GIANTS, when writers and animators collaborated on a series of ruses to extend and dramatize sequences of baseball games, soon adapted to many other SPORTS ANIME. Sudden crash-zooms into character's eyes, often accompanied by a *bling* sound effect and the narrowing of the screen, can denote steely resolve or intense rivalry between two characters. Watery, starry eyes and a sudden outbreak of hearts, flowers, or soft-focus is used to show a girlish crush or adoration. Silence itself can be illustrated by a sound effect, with an uncomfortable pause, perhaps in the wake of an unfunny joke, marked only by the calling of distant crows. A clonking sound of hollow bamboo is a reference to the *shishi odoshi* ("deer-scarer"), a pivoted bamboo tube used as part of a Japanese water landscape that fills up with water until it tips, hitting against a stone, and denotes the passage of time. Sometimes anime will even steal sound effects directly from manga and write them onscreen. There is even a manga "sound effect" for total silence—the word *shiin*, which can sometimes be seen onscreen as an additional visual gag.

Until the advent of video, anime's audience was primarily juvenile, and anime fictions often deal with the politics of exclusion and inclusion, filial duties, and family obligations—such as ASTRO BOY's *Pinocchio*-inspired yearning to become a real child and, when that fails, his *Superman*-inspired quest to do good for the human race. Juvenile and teenage anime viewers are in an a permanent liminal state, facing the pressures of puberty and adolescence, and wishing both to grow up fast and never to grow up at all. Anime deals with these concepts by injecting story lines of transformation, allowing its characters to experiment with becoming something different—the superhero duality of Clark Kent and Superman, later remodeled with the symbiotic existence of ULTRAMAN, but also that of the "magical girls" like MARVELOUS MELMO (1971), able to transform into an older, more sophisticated version of herself. The magical girls form a crucial and often overlooked sector of anime's output, ignored by critics and journalists who tend to favor the "male" genres of sci-fi and sports. But they are just as likely to spin off into merchandise and other media, have just as dedicated a fan base, and just as intricate a pathway into postmodern maturity, with intriguing commentaries provided in modern remakes such as PENGUINDRUM and PUELLA MAGI MADOKA MAGICA, although such shows may arguably seem more "mature" because they have incorporated elements designed to appeal to male fans.

Anime for girls had often drawn directly on the cross-dressing traditions of the Takarazuka musical theater, particularly Osamu Tezuka's PRINCESS KNIGHT (1967) and Riyoko Ikeda's ROSE OF VERSAILLES (1979), creating a subgenre running all the way to UTENA (1997), in which heroines become their *own* knights in shining armor. The notion of girls assuming men's clothing is given the weight of history in YOTODEN (1987) and OTOGI ZOSHI (2004), where the heroines assume the roles of dead or sick brothers. Despite the inclusion in MOSPEADA (1983) of a hunky hero who likes women and also dresses up as one, men's cross-dressing efforts often get less respectful presentation—such as a gentle comic sideswipe at school cross-dressing in HERE IS GREENWOOD (1991). In the same year, OKAMA REPORT and 3x3

Eyes presented more sympathetic cross-dressers, but in 1992 Go Nagai lowered the tone of the whole girls' school genre with **Delinquent in Drag**. The right and wrong way for a samurai to cross-dress is graphically illustrated in **Peacemaker Kurogane** (2003). Note that transvestism is distinct from transsexuality, a topic most famously treated in **Ranma ½** (1989), whose hero regularly transformed into a heroine and back again, forcing him to deal with both sides of the battle of the sexes.

One of the most important innovators in the anime of transformation is Go Nagai, who gave male viewers the sight of a superheroine whose clothes regularly disintegrated in **Cutey Honey**, and another whose "costume" left her almost completely naked in **Kekko Kamen**. These, however, were mere diversions compared to his true achievements in the boys' market, notably the pilotable robot **Mazinger Z**, which could combine with other robots to form a super-robot. This simple device not only generated a powerful pester factor among children who would demand all the toys in order to reenact their favorite moments from the show, it also allowed for a prolonged transformation sequence, and hence the weekly reuse of preexisting anime footage.

Such transformations have been a common feature of anime ever since, reaching their apotheosis with **Macross** and the **Transformers**, created during a general reduction in the size of toys during the 1980s. Smaller toys were easier to store and transport, not just for children but for toy companies, and the reduction in size was compensated for by increased variation and functionality—more intricate moving parts that allowed each model to be "two toys in one."

Anime is currently engaged in one of its biggest transformations, its format and scheduling shifting from a communal experience delivered at set times in theaters and on TV to infinitely mutable packets of data accessed on a handheld device. This reflects a change in society, camouflaging the big idea in a colorful wrapper. New tropes and transformations will doubtless emerge as a result.

TROUBLE CHOCOLATE *

1999. TV series. DIR: Tsuneo Tominaga. SCR:

Hideki Sonoda. DES: Chizuko Kusakabe. ANI: Robot, Junichi Takaoka. MUS: N/C. PRD: AIC, TV Asahi. 25? mins. x 20 eps.

Timid teenager Cacao, a student at the Microgrand Academy, spends more time lusting after gorgeous green-haired Hinano next door than studying, even though the classes on offer include magic. His magic professor, Professor Garner, reveals that, since he's over 120 years old, it's time for him to stop goofing around and move on to the next stage of his magical education. As Cacao slowly starts to regain his memory, he recalls that not only has he already achieved his ends with Hinano, but she also isn't quite as human as she seems. Most males forget how old they are at some point, but very few forget who they've slept with, so Cacao isn't the brightest apple in the barrel, and his continuing progress may be problematic.

TROUBLE EVOCATION

1997.Video. DIR: Masakazu Amiya. SCR: Ryoga Ryuen. DES: Ryoga Ryuen. ANI: Inatsugi Shimizu. MUS: N/C. PRD: Pink Pineapple, KSS. 30 mins. x 2 eps.

Hideya is visited every night by the cute sex-kitten Leah, who falls in love with him. One day she is ordered back to Hell by Satina, but Hideya begs her to stay. In this erotic variant on **Oh My Goddess!** based on **Zankan**-creator Ryoga Ryuen's manga originally serialized in *Kitty Time*, Leah is so shocked by the strength of his feelings that she starts to take off her clothes. **⊗**

TROUBLED TIMES

1991. JPN: *Michite Kuru Toki no Muko ni*. AKA: *Toward a Time of Trouble*. TV special. DIR: Eiko Toriumi. SCR: Eiko Toriumi. DES: Takayuki Goto. ANI: Hisatoshi Motoki. MUS: Teruhiko Sato. PRD: Studio Pierrot, Nippon TV. 80 mins.

It's a fantasy adventure as tribal boy Bokudo, his red-deer guardian spirit, and the chieftain's pretty daughter Faya go hunting in the Gobi Desert. A one-shot adaptation of Koji Suzuki's novel *Paradise*, which won the 1991 Japan Fantasy Novel Award.

TRUE BLUE

2005. Video. DIR: Sakura Momoi, Kuro Kawasaki, Yota Nobitome. SCR: Sakura Momoi, Juliet Hanata, PON, Kuro Kawasaki. DES:

Yoshiyuki Kodaira, Hideki Arai, Hikaru Kinohara, Kenchi Hattori. ANI: Noritomo Hattori, Kimiko Mitsui, Si min Lee, Kenchi Hattori. MUS: N/C. PRD: Himajin Planning, PoRO. 28 mins. x 2 eps. (v1), 30 mins. (v2, *Gaiden*), 30 mins. x 2 eps. (v3, *Triangle Blue*), 30 mins. x 2 eps. (v4, *Dark Blue*), 25 mins. x 2 eps. (v5, *Innocent Blue*).

High school idol Aoi is in love with her childhood friend and next door neighbor Akito. He rescued her once when they were much younger and they've been devoted to each other ever since (**Romance and Drama**). But then Aoi is raped and abused by her physical education teacher Mr. Shudo. When Akito finds out he's devastated, but powerless to stop it, because Aoi is learning to enjoy it. This nasty little anime, based on a rape game by LiLiM Darkness, had a sequel, *True Blue Gaiden* (*TV Side Story*), in the same year. Akito tries to forget about Aoi with a new love, Kaya, who is also blackmailed into having sex with someone else as part of Shudo's plan to draw her into his perverted web. *Triangle Blue* (2009) has no character link to the earlier story, and has older protagonists, but again follows the theme of a girl and guy parted when the girl is abused by a sexual predator and starts to like it. It was animated by PoRO.

In the same year PoRO released *Dark Blue*, another high school rape tale in which Yukito's sister is blackmailed by a teacher, raped, and begins to enjoy it, while Yukito sees the girl he loves having sex with his best friend. In 2011 Himajin Planning picked up the LiLiM Darkness franchise again for *Innocent Blue*, the story of a married nurse, her younger cousin, who she considers almost as a little brother, and a predatory older doctor. It appears that, as the fanbase for the original game grew out of high school, the creators continued to provide them with age-appropriate **Erotica and Pornography**: in 2012 LiLiM Darkness released a new game, *Wedding Blue*, starring a young couple and the superintendant of their apartment building. **⊗Ⓥ**

TRUE LOVE STORY

2003. AKA: *True Love Story: Summer Days, and yet...* Video. DIR: Hidehito Ueda. SCR: Masashi Takimoto, Naotaka Hayashi. DES: Tatsuya Oka. ANI: N/C. MUS: Ryo Sakai. PRD:

KSS. 30 mins. x 3 eps.
Another story set in a high school where a bevy of cute girls covering all the teenage wish-fulfillment stereotypes surround one ordinary teenage boy.

TRUE TEARS *
2008. TV series. DIR: Junji Nishmura. SCR: Mari Okada, Junji Nishura, Mayumi Morita. DES: Kanami Sekiguchi, Yusuke Takeda, Satoko Shinohara. ANI: Kanami Sekiguchi, Jae Seon Heo, Yuko Yoshida. MUS: Hajime Kikuchi. PRD: P.A. Works, Bandai Visual. 24 mins. x 13 eps.
When Hiromi's father dies, leaving her an orphan, she moves in with the Nagakami family. A year on, she seems to be coping with her grief, but her classmate Shin-ichiro Nagakami is convinced that she must be holding back the tears because, while she's outgoing and cheerful at school, she is quiet and withdrawn at home. He's also having problems at school with a strange girl named Noe, who's oddly fixated on the school's pet chickens, and being pressured into learning to a traditional Japanese dance. At least he can still hang out with his old friends Aiko and Miyokichi at Aiko's family store. Set in Toyama Prefecture, where anime studio P.A. Works is based, *True Tears* features authentic Toyama landscapes that can be visited by fans (similar vistas form the backdrop for Mamoru Hosoda's SUMMER WARS and WOLF CHILDREN). The beautiful settings are the most interesting thing about this sentimentality-by-numbers high school romance. A visual novel (ARGOT AND JARGON) of the same name appeared in 2006, but the story and characters were entirely different, and the creative team is unconnected with the anime.

TRUSTY GINJIRO
1991. JPN: *Koha Ginjiro*. Video. DIR: Koichi Ishiguro. SCR: Hirokazu Mizude. DES: Kazuya Takeda. ANI: Kazuya Takeda. MUS: N/C. PRD: Animate Film, Visual 80. 45 mins. x 3 eps.
After the death of his elder brother, Ginjiro Yamazaki appoints himself his parents' protector. Transferred to a new school, he gets into a lot of fights, as one might expect in an anime from MY SKY–creator Hiroshi Motomiya, this one based on a 1975 manga originally serialized in *Shonen Jump*. ◗

TSUBASA CHRONICLE *
2005. TV series, movie. DIR: Koichi Mashimo. SCR: Hiroyuki Kawasaki. DES: Minako Shiba. ANI: Minako Shiba, Yukiko Ban, Takao Takegami. MUS: Yuki Kajiura. PRD: Bee Train, Production I.G, NHK. 25 mins. x 26 eps. (TV), 60 mins. (m), 29 mins. x 3 eps. (*Tokyo Revelations*), 29 mins. x 2 eps. (*Spring Thunder*).
Wannabe archeologist Syaoran is dragged in an unexpected career direction when his childhood friend, Sakura the Clow Princess, loses her memory. Syaoran is advised by a witch that he must recover the scattered pieces of Sakura's memory from a number of points in space and time—a quest tinged with tragedy, since if he succeeds, she will still not know who he is. Memory loss might be an apt subject to bring up for the CLAMP collective of creators as well, who, in imitation of the eternal self-referential recycling of Leiji Matsumoto (see SUBMARINE SUPER 99), have simply dumped characters from some of their earlier works into a vaguely defined quest narrative. So it is that we have two characters from CARDCAPTORS joining forces with a number of elements and creatures from RAYEARTH to chase after a new MacGuffin. As in the case of the "original" manga, also created by CLAMP, there are also frequent crossovers with xxxHOLIC—most notably in the case of the *Tsubasa Chronicles* movie spin-off, *TC: Chronicles of the Princess of Birdcage-land* (2005, *Tsubasa Chronicle: Torikago no Kuni no Himegimi*), which was shown in a double bill with the xxxHOLIC movie *A Midsummer Night's Dream*.
The quest continues in much the same vein in the three-part *Tsubasa Tokyo Revelations* (2007), as Syaoran and his beloved Princess Sakura continue to wander various worlds with friends and foes from the rest of the CLAMP universe. It looks very pretty but has little else to interest anyone not already heavily invested in the creators' self-referential world, lacking much in the way of character development or story variation from previous outings. A sequel of sorts, or at least a further adventure with the same characters, appeared in 2009. In the two-part *Tsubasa: Spring Thunder* (*Tsubasa Shunraiki*) our heroes escape a world trying to keep them in, but leave Sakura trapped in a dream world.

Syaoran goes to save her, but his clone also shows up, and pretty magical battles follow without resolving anything much. Makes X: THE MOVIE look like a model of narrative drive and clarity.

TSURITAMA *
2012. TV series. DIR: Kenji Nakamura. SCR: Toshiya Ono, Toko Machida, Shinsuke Onishi. DES: Atsuya Uki. ANI: Ayako Matsumoto, Tomoko Sudo. MUS: Kuricorder Quartet. PRD: A-1 Pictures, Aniplex, Dentsu, Fuji TV. 24 mins. x 12 eps.
Bad-tempered new kid Yuki befriends a group of Enoshima guys who are similarly ostracized, for various reasons. Paramount among them is Haru, an alien trying to stay undercover in small-town Japan, and Akira, an Indian agent of Defense Universal Confidential Keepers (or DUCK for short), who has transferred to Enoshima's local school to observe Haru's behavior. Local loner Natsuki doesn't seem like friends-material but is soon teaching the other three how to fish, an activity that exposes them to ongoing concerns about strange phenomena just off-shore.
Haphazardly mixing science fiction with COMEDY, Tsuritama sometimes reeks of desperation, as if a production committee decided to tick every available box in their original pitch. There have been shows about fishing; there have been shows about aliens … we're not sure if the world really needed a show about aliens learning how to fish, but that's what pushing the envelope gets you.
Connected by a causeway to the mainland, Enoshima is an island in central coastal Japan that offers some of the closest beach space to Tokyo. It therefore offers something of a vacation feel to Tokyo audiences.

TSURU-HIME
1990. JPN: *Tsuru Hime Jaaaa!* AKA: *Princess Tsuru; Crane Princess*. TV series. DIR: Tameo Ogawa, Yoshihiro Yamaguchi, Yoshiko Sasaki, Shigeru Ueda, Koichi Sasaki. SCR: Hirokazu Mizude, Tadashi Hayakawa, Tameo Ogawa. DES: Yoshiko Tsuchida. ANI: Hiromi Muranaka. MUS: N/C. PRD: Aubec, Nippon TV. 17 mins. x 67 eps.
The ugly Princess Tsuru makes life hell for everyone in the samurai-era Hagemasu Castle. This gag anime was based on the

manga in *Margaret* magazine by Yoshiko Tsuchida.

TSURUPIKA HAGEMARU-KUN
1988. AKA: *Little Baldy Hagemaru*. TV series. DIR: Hiroshi Sasagawa, Tetsuo Yasumi, Tsukasa Sunaga, Hiroyuki Sasaki, Teruo Kogure, Koichi Sasaki, Junji Nishimura. SCR: Masaaki Sakurai. DES: Munekatsu Fujita. ANI: Akira Kawajima, Katsuhiko Yamazaki. MUS: Kuni Kawauchi. PRD: Shinei Doga. 25 mins. x 58 eps.
In this adaptation of the four-panel gag strip by Shinbo Nomura, ten-year-old brat Hagemaru Hageda causes mischief all over his small Japanese suburb.

TSUYOKISS COOL X SWEET
2006. AKA: *Tsuyo-kiss*. TV series. DIR: Shinichiro Kimura. SCR: Yasutomo Yamada. DES: Yoshimi Agata, Kuniaki Nemoto. ANI: N/C. MUS: I've, Little Non, Yuichi Nonaka. PRD: Studio Hibari, Trinet, Candy Soft. 25 mins. x 12 eps.
Sunao starts a new school and finds there's no theater club. She decides to start one, but for some reason the class president is blocking her efforts. And then her childhood friend Leo turns up and romance starts to blossom (ROMANCE AND DRAMA). This pervy slice-of-life school comedy packed with fan service (ARGOT AND JARGON) is not especially distinguished in any way. It's based on a game by Candy Soft.

TV ASAHI
Often abbreviated in Japanese broadcast listings as "EX," this channel began life in 1957 as NET—Nippon Educational Television. Subsequently renamed Asahi National Broadcasting (ANB—Zenkoku Asahi Hoso) in 1962. Asahi has a large number of children's titles and often appears to stick to long-running family franchises instead of short bursts of riskier entertainment like TV Tokyo. It is the home of both DORAEMON and CRAYON SHIN-CHAN. The newspaper the *Asahi Shinbun* is a related company.

TV TOKYO
Established as Television Tokyo Channel 12 in 1964 by the Foundation for Science and Technology, TV Tokyo, or "TX," is a subsidiary of the *Nihon Keizai Shinbun* newspaper. A smaller channel with a far greater interest in niche programming, TV Tokyo is the home of many of the anime series recognizable to Western teenagers, particularly the short-run shows lasting for 13 episodes. The channel's biggest anime successes are arguably POKÉMON and NARUTO, although it was also the home of many modern favorites, including EVANGELION and COWBOY BEBOP (see also WOWOW). TV Tokyo also runs the dedicated anime satellite channel Anime Theater X (AT-X).

TWD EXPRESS: ROLLING TAKEOFF
1987. Video. DIR: Kunihiko Yuyama. SCR: Izo Hashimoto. DES: Kazuyuki Kobayashi. ANI: Kazuyuki Kobayashi. MUS: Minoru Yamazaki. PRD: Gakken, Shochiku. 55 mins.
Space cargo workers Ken Kato, Duke Stern, and Ivan Sernikov run the Tiger Wolf Dragon Express service, but they land themselves in big trouble when they rescue the beautiful android Rina. She is being pursued by the evil Baron Gohdam, who wants her so he can seize control of the superpowerful Hydra. Based on a manga in *Comic Nora* by Yuki Hijiri, it was also shown in some theaters on a double bill with the MAPS movie.

TWEENY WITCHES *
2004. JPN: *Maho Shojo Tai Arusu*. AKA: *Magical Girl Squad Alice*. TV series. DIR: Yoshiharu Ashino, Yasuhiro Aoki, Toru Yoshida. SCR: Shinji Obara. DES: Daisuke Nakayama. ANI: Studio 4°C. MUS: Tamiya Terashima. PRD: Tohoku-shinsha, Dentsu, Beyond C, NHK. 9 mins. x 40 eps. (TV), 23 mins. x 6 eps. (v).
Fifth-grade schoolgirl Alice dreams of having magical powers. One day she's pretending to study in class, but the book on her desk is a magical one that transports her to a forest. She meets and befriends witches-in-training Eva and Sheila, and it seems her dreams are about to come true. This is not, perhaps, what one would immediately expect from a creation of IRIA's Keita Amemiya, whose remarkable live-action fantasies (*Hakaider, Moon over Tao*) have a grittier edge. However, that darkness soon emerges. Alice, who has always imagined that magic powers are there to be used for good, finds her wonderland can be as harsh and unjust as her own world—senior witches are enslaving other magic beings. She and her new witch sisters free an elf from captivity, but like many Amemiya characters, they find the price of doing good is high. In the magic world releasing a captured elf is a criminal act, and they are punished by a curse that will prevent them from growing up until the elf is recaptured—shades here of THOSE WHO HUNT ELVES, without the kinky undertones. The later video series, *Tweeny Witches: The Adventure* (2007), seems to have been initially planned as a second season on TV, but downgraded before its broadcast.

TWELVE KINGDOMS, THE *
2002. JPN: *Juni Koku-ki; Juni Kokki*. AKA: *Chronicle of Twelve Kingdoms; Record of Twelve Countries*. TV series. DIR: Tsuneo Kobayashi. SCR: Sho Aikawa. DES: Hiroto Tanaka, Yuko Kusumoto. ANI: Hiroto Tanaka. MUS: Kunihiko Ryo. PRD: Studio Pierrot, NHK, Sogovision. 25 mins. x 45 eps.
Unhappy teenager Yoko Nakajima is suddenly confronted by a strange man who says she is his queen and he is her sworn subject. He fights off a group of beastdemons before taking her and two of her classmates into another world, where people from Earth are hunted fugitives. The friends and their protectors wander the lands, trying to survive and find out why they are there and how to get home.

Based on a series of novels begun in 1991 by Fuyumi Ono, the first story arc in *The Twelve Kingdoms* often plays like a new version of ESCAFLOWNE or FUSHIGI YUGI. We have, of course, a Japanese girl transported to an otherworldy kingdom—the early episodes coincidentally based on the book SEA'S DARKNESS: MOON'S SHADOW, although they have no relation to the Chie Shinohara story of the same name. Yoko's "difference" is telegraphed from the earliest moments by her naturally red hair. Whereas anime hair colors are often wholly random and unrealistic, the script soon calls attention to Yoko's, when her parents urge her to dye it black in order to fit in. A brown-red deviation from the normal black is what happens when you try to bleach Japanese hair and is often used in fiction to suggest a girl is something of a wild-child. This has led, ironically, to Japanese girls who genuinely do not have standard-issue black hair being forced to dye their hair black in the manner to which Yoko's parents are alluding. Yoko, it is alleged, is one of the latter, a straight-A student who has been voted class president, but who is being led away from her previous childish things by the allegorical temptations of the 12 kingdoms.

By the sixth episode, however, the story has taken a radical departure, dumping Yoko into the company of a number of beast-like creatures in a more surreal setting. Yoko's adventures start to take on elements of THE WIZARD OF OZ, or, more properly, *The Lion, The Witch and the Wardrobe*, as Yoko discovers that she really is fated to be queen of one of the lands and that only her successful ascension to the thrown can restore the sundered and ruined kingdoms. In another parallel with both Oz and Narnia, the focus of the story leaves its original protagonist for long periods of time, concentrating on some of her associates. In the next story arc, based on the Ono novel *Sea's Wind: Maze's Shore*, there are also elements of the lost children of HAIBANE RENMEI, in a series of fairytales that unite the stories of mundane, urban tragedy in our own world with the incarnation of fantastic creatures in the 12 kingdoms.

Later chapters, based on the novel *Ten Thousand-League Wind: Dawn's Sky*, see Yoko becoming ruler of one of the kingdoms and forced to deal with the aftermath of her lessthanillustrious predecessor, alongside politicking by some of her rival queens and long tangents that discuss some of their own backstories. A few final stories prepare the ground for a last battle, as Yoko rides off to save her newfound home.

The original novels presented a sprawling saga, distantly inspired, in the fashion of LIKE A CLOUD, LIKE A BREEZE, by Chinese history and mythology. However, it is worth noting that the stories have been shuffled and rearranged for this anime version. Two of them, "Correspondence" and "Ally of the Moon," were originally short stories, and are dealt with in just two episodes, while others stretch over many chapters. The final story arc, five episodes that draw on the novel *Eastern Sea God, Western Ocean*, almost exhausts the original source material featuring Yoko, although other books about other cast members still remain unadapted. As with IRONFIST CHINMI, the exhaustion of the original

material left the producers with the difficult choice of pressing on regardless and diverging from the original even further, or calling a hiatus with the vague hope of restarting if the material became available. Hence, although originally planned as a 68-episode series, *The Twelve Kingdoms* currently grinds to a halt at episode 45 with some plot elements left unresolved; an unfortunate fate for an anime that has gained a large and appreciative following for its literally novelistic density and complex relationships. Two PlayStation 2 spin-offs also followed.

TWELVE MONTHS *

1980. JPN: *Mori wa Ikiteiru.* AKA: *The Forest Is Alive.* Movie. DIR: Kimio Yabuki, Tetsuo Imazawa. SCR: Tomoe Ryu, Kimio Yabuki. DES: Yasuhiro Yamaguchi. ANI: Takashi Abe, Takao Kasai, Shinya Takahashi. MUS: Vladimir Grifutsov. PRD: Toei. 65 mins.

Sent out to collect spring flowers in midwinter by the wicked queen, Anya believes her life is lost, but she is saved by the spirit of her mother, who chases the snow from the forest. Anya is helped by the 12 spirits of the months of the year, each one a handsome prince, and within an hour, the once-barren winter wood is awash with the colors of spring. A Cinderella-like fairy tale based on a story by Soviet poet Samuel Marshack and featuring powerful orchestrations from the Leningrad Symphony Orchestra.

24 EYES

1980. JPN: *Nijushi no Hitomi.* TV special. DIR: Akio Jissoji, Shigetsugu Yoshida. SCR: Sumie Tanaka. DES: Kazuyuki Honma. ANI: Junsaburo Takahata, Hiromi Yokoyama, Kanetsugu Kodama. MUS: Takeo Watanabe. PRD: TMS, Fuji TV. 84 mins.

Young Miss Oishi is the new school teacher on the island of Shodoshima in 1928. When she injures her leg, her 12 students visit her at home and discover that she cycles nine miles every day to teach them. Miss Oishi transfers to a new school in time to see her students five years later (1933). In 1941, the boys go off to war, preferring a glorious military career to a humdrum home life. Four years later, a widowed Miss Oishi comes out of retirement to teach once again—her new students including a sister and a daughter

of the original class. The surviving class of 1928 arrange a reunion and buy her a new bicycle.

Based on the book by Sakae Tsuboi, *24 Eyes* draws lightly on Tsuboi's years at the periphery of Japanese anarchist counterculture and her disgust that "pacifist" Japan was rearming during the Korean war. The book was also adapted into a live-action film by former propagandist Keisuke Kinoshita in 1954. Made after the previous year's DIARY OF ANNE FRANK made WWII an acceptable subject for TV, this anime remake mixes animation with live-action (old Tsuburaya studio hand Jissoji handling the former, HELLO SPANK–director Yoshida the latter) to depict different times of Miss Oishi's life. The story was remade again as the fully live-action *Children on the Island* (1987). Many other anime would copy *24 Eyes'* concentration on children, recognizing that a cast too young to have started WWII need not be held accountable for those who actually did. Hideaki Anno would pay homage to *24 Eyes* in GUNBUSTER with a scene in which a teacher bids farewell to a class including the daughter of her former classmate.

21 EMON WELCOME TO SPACE

1981. JPN: *21 Emon: Uchu e Irasshai.* Movie. DIR: Tsutomu Shibayama. SCR: Masaki Tsuji. DES: Yuko Yamamoto. ANI: Michishiro Yamada. MUS: Shunsuke Kikuchi. PRD: Fujiko F, Shogakukan, Shinei. 93 mins.

In the 21st century, would-be space pilot Emon discovers that he is the sole heir to the dilapidated Tsuzureya Inn in Tokyo. But the inn hasn't changed since the 19th century, and customers no longer find it quaint. Realizing that Emon can be "persuaded," the owners of the Galaxy Hotel chain invite him on a space holiday to get him away from his inheritance. Emon is accompanied on the trip by his wacky potato-digging robot, Gonsuke, and the all-powerful alien, Monga.

The Fujiko-Fujio team behind ESPER MAMI and MOJACKO were heavily involved in this adaptation of their series from *Corocoro Comic*, even to the extent of singing the theme song themselves. The film was shown on a double bill with another Fujiko-Fujio production, the DORAEMON short *What Am I for Momotaro?*, and reuses the footage for one scene in which Doraemon and Emon briefly share each other's movie.

TWILIGHT OF THE COCKROACHES *

1987. JPN: *Gokiburi no Tasogare*. AKA: *Cockroach*. Movie. DIR: Hiroaki Yoshida. SCR: Hiroaki Yoshida. DES: Yoshinori Kanemori. ANI: Toshio Hirata. MUS: Morgan Fisher. PRD: TYO, Kitty Films. 105 mins.

Naomi, an attractive young cockroach, enjoys the easy life with her boyfriend, Ichiro, and other roaches in Mr. Saito's apartment. This is because the lazy Saito lets the roaches eat the scraps from his table and never tries to hurt them. Hans, a hard-bitten fighter-roach from the other side of the yard, is a rival for Naomi's affections, but he eventually returns to his own people. Naomi embarks on the long quest across the yard (50 human feet, an incredible distance) to find him. There, she discovers that Hans did not lie, and that other humans are engaged in an all-out war to exterminate the roaches; Hans and his people are fighting a suicidal battle they cannot win. The unthinkable happens when Momoko, the woman across the yard, moves in with Saito—a newly house-proud Saito kills off the roaches. Soon, only Ichiro and the pregnant Naomi are left, then he too is killed. Naomi escapes to give birth to a new litter, and a new generation of cockroaches, just that little bit more resistant to human poisons, is ready for a rematch.

A very *Japanese* insect movie that mixes a neighborly human romance with the anthropomorphized characters of *Hoppity Goes to Town* and the apocalyptic armageddon of WWII—*A Bug's Death*, if you will. Beginning with Naomi's first encounter with the human female, the film is chiefly told in flashback, lending it the weight of inevitable tragedy that also characterizes GRAVE OF THE FIREFLIES. Shot in a mixture of live action (the humans) and animation (the roaches) that is all the more impressive in these days of digital easy-fixes, it mixes the comic spectacle of humans battling their only serious rivals for planetary domination, with the heroic defensive actions of a tiny community facing impossible odds. The director reportedly thought of his cockroaches as a metaphor for the way the Japanese appear to the rest of the world—he meant as selfish, parasiti-

cal trading partners, though many foreign critics saw other parallels, particularly in *TotC*'s glorification of fanatical suicide missions and its insect cast's self-assured belief that they will, eventually, become the masters of Earth. A fascinating and unexpectedly entertaining experiment, comparable in some regards with the U.S. movie *Joe's Apartment* (1996), which also featured a single guy who shared his apartment with roaches. **V**

TWILIGHT OF THE DARK MASTER *

1997. JPN: *Shihaisha no Tasogare*. AKA: *Twilight of the Master*. Video. DIR: Akiyuki Shinbo. SCR: Duanne Dell'Amico, Tatsuhiko Urahata. DES: Hisashi Abe. ANI: Hisashi Abe. MUS: Keiji Urata. PRD: Madhouse. 46 mins.

In the beginning, the Great Mother created a Demon Master, an adversary designed to test the mettle of human beings. However, the Demon Master exceeded its design specifications, and the Great Mother had to create a Guardian to protect humankind. Eons later, in the year 2089, a strange force transforms the Japanese Eiji—he turns on his lover Shizuka, mutilates her, and escapes into the city. Determined to give her mutated fiancé the release of death, Shizuka pursues him, accompanied by a police detective and Shijo, an androgynous man who is the current Guardian. As in DOOMED MEGALOPOLIS, the monster terrorizing the city is simply a pawn of the true evil, in this case the Demon Master himself, who is asserting his powers through a new illegal muscle-enhancement drug. This predictable sci-fi gorefest was based on the manga by Saki Okuse and originally serialized in *Wings* magazine. **LNV**

TWILIGHT Q

1987. JPN: *Twilight Q Toki no Musubime—Reflection; Twilight Q 2—Meikyu Bukken File 538*. AKA: *TQ: A Knot in Time; TQ2 Labyrinth Article File 538*. Video. DIR: Tomomi Mochizuki, Mamoru Oshii. SCR: Kazunori Ito. DES: Akemi Takada, Katsuya Kondo. ANI: Shinji Otsuka. MUS: Kenji Kawai. PRD: Studio Deen. 30 mins. x 2 eps.

Mayumi is on holiday when she finds an old camera while swimming. Out of curiosity she has the film developed—only one frame can be saved. The picture shows her with a young man she has never met. Re-

turning to her holiday base to investigate, she learns from the camera manufacturer that this model hasn't even been made yet. She finds herself caught up in weird events that take her back in time to WWII and forward to her own graveside. This unsettling paradoxical tale is seemingly without meaning, a bizarre entry in the girls' anime catalogue. The second story takes matters even further into fantasy, opening with the transformation of an airship into a giant carp and focusing on a small girl, seemingly the reincarnation of a powerful deity, and a mysterious detective in shades. He's a Tokyo detective who wants to find out why every aircraft over his town has suddenly vanished without a trace. The magic of the transformation sequence is unforgettable, but there's little that could be described as action.

The surreal goings-on in this short-lived "twilight zone" were made by the crew of PATLABOR but owe a heavy debt to the 1960s live-action show *Ultra Q[uestion]* (a forerunner of ULTRAMAN). Whereas its predecessor threatened to "apart your soul and going into the mystery zone [*sic*]," this modern update preferred to "take over your reality and disable the stop button."

TWIN

1989. JPN: *Bakuso Circuit Roman Twin*. AKA: *Racing Circuit Romance Twin*. Video. DIR: Noboru Ishiguro, Osamu Sekita. SCR: Takashi Yamada. DES: Tsuneo Ninomiya. ANI: Tsuneo Ninomiya, Koichi Endo. MUS: N/C. PRD: Japan Home Video. 80 mins.

Hyo Hibino grows up a confused orphan after his mother dies giving birth to him—alternately blaming himself for her death and believing himself to be invulnerable. He gets the perfect opportunity to prove it when he becomes a motorcycle racer. An anime based on the 1986 *Young Sunday* manga by **F** and DASH KAPPEI–creator Noboru Rokuda.

TWIN ANGEL *

2008. JPN: *Kaito Tenchi Twin Angel*. AKA: *Heaven and Earth Thief Twin Angel*. Video, TV series. DIR: Tatsuyuki Nagai, Yoshiaki Iwasaki. SCR: Hideyuki Kurata, Michiko Ito, Hideki Shirane, Shogo Yasukawa. DES: Makoto Koga, Yoshinori Hirose, Ryoichi Oki, Takahiro Yoneda. ANI: Makoto Koga, Ryoichi

Oki. MUS: Kenichiro Oishi. PRD: Nomad, Sammy, JC Staff, Kadokawa. 30 mins. x 2 eps. (v), 25 mins. x 12 eps. (TV).

Haruka and Aoi are best friends in school. After school, they thwart evil plots as the Twin Angels, Red Angel and Blue Angel. This anime, based on the pachinko game of the same name, is completely unrelated to the porn anime entitled *Twin Angels* (**TWIN DOLLS**). In 2011 it became a TV series from an entirely new crew. *Twin Angel Twinkle Paradise* (*Kaito Tenshi Twin Angel: Kyun Kyun Tokimeki Paradise!!*) is a sweet and otherwise undistinguished magical girl show that has been streamed online in Europe and the U.S.A. with subtitles.

TWIN BEE PARADISE

1999. Video. DIR: Kazuhiro Takamoto. SCR: Yasunori Ide. DES: Akihiro Asanuma. ANI: Akihiro Asanuma. MUS: N/C. PRD: Public & Basic, Beam Entertainment. 30 mins. x 3 eps.

Fresh from the video game that spawned them, the Twin Bee team is carted off for an intergalactic adventure, complete with big hair, babies, and UFOs. The series was preceded by a 1994 "episode zero," which must have made for one of the slowest anime productions in history.

TWIN DOLLS *

1994. JPN: *Seijuden Twin Dolls; Inju Seisen Twin Angels*. AKA: *Holy Beast Story Twin Dolls; Lust Beast Crusade Twin Angels*. Video. DIR: Kan Fukumoto. SCR: Oji Miyako. DES: Rin Shin. ANI: Akira Ojo. MUS: Teruo Takahama. PRD: Dandelion. 45 mins. x 2 eps. (*Dolls*), 30 mins. x 4 eps. (*Angels*).

The one thing you can be pretty sure of in anime is that people who look like ordinary high school girls rarely are. Mai and Ai are professional demon hunters, descended from an immortal being, dedicated to defending mankind (and, in particular, high school grrrl-kind) from the demons of the Pleasure Underworld. They are appointed guardians of the infant Messiah who will save the world. For once tentacles aren't used as penis substitutes—instead the crew animates optimistic renditions of the real thing. This openness doesn't last long as the story introduces one of the most meretricious of all plot devices, the "orb of orgasm"; pop it in a woman's mouth and she'll *enjoy* being raped. Historical and mythical figures are

used as set dressing in the background of an unpleasant exercise in taking money for old rope.

For reasons we've never been quite able to fathom, the franchise not only changed its Japanese title to *Twin Angels*, but also gained itself a new U.S. distributor, moving from Softcel to Anime 18 for the distribution of the 1995 sequel. In *Angels*, the sorcerer-nuns must defend their charge, Lord Onimaro (who is 21, allegedly), from another demon assault, when Kama and Sutra, the King and Queen of Seduction, drag him off to a ritual orgy. Onimaro's guardian Dekinobu worries that if he succumbs to his demonic heritage, he will become the Demon King and his legion of sex-crazed monsters will subdue the world. He makes a predictable choice and has the twins stripped and tortured for his pleasure, planning to have them sacrificed. But Dekinobu is determined to rescue Onimaro from his destiny, even if it costs him his life.

Angels adds staggering naïveté to its other offenses—what hormonally normal male, offered the career choice of ordinary human or Demon King with ultimate power, is going to be persuaded into the paths of righteousness by two "19-year-old" bimbos who can't even find sensible underwear? It is difficult, however, to completely write off any show that has immortal dialogue like, "Commence creation of an evil sex barrier!" and a scene featuring two miniskirted girls on a stormy school roof trying to hang onto a magic staff while lightning transforms it into a giant penis. **LNV**

TWIN ELF PRINCESSES

2009. JPN: *Elf no Futago Hime: Willan to Arsula*. AKA: *Elf Twin Princesses: Willan and Arsula*. Video. DIR: Ken Raika (as P-San Honda). SCR: Shinichiro Sawayama. DES: Mamoru Kobayashi. ANI: Mamoru Kobayashi. MUS: N/C. PRD: T-Rex, Marigold (Cotton Doll). 30 mins.

Humans and elves live side by side, but elves rule the world because of their intelligence and maturity. Then humans rebel, and a marriage of convenience is proposed to stop the war. Arsula is selected as the bride, but she and her twin sister Willan, who is also her guard, are kidnapped by monsters under the control

of half-human, half-elf Darsh. Based on a porn game by Lune, so fill in the rest yourself. **N**

TWIN LOVE

2004. JPN: *FUTAKOI/Futakoi Alternative*. TV series. DIR: Nobuo Tomizawa, Takayuki Hirao, Masashi Abe. SCR: Tomoko Konparu, Miho Maruo, Masahiro Yokotani, Katsumi Terato, Kazuharu Sato, Ryunosuke Kingetsu. DES: Mineko Ueda, Toshimitsu Kobayashi. ANI: Toshimitsu Kobayashi. MUS: Hajime Kikuchi, Shunsuke Suzuki, Tatsuya Murayama, Toshimichi Isoe. PRD: Feel, Flag, UFO Table, Media Works. 25 mins. x 13 eps. (TV1), 25 mins. x 13 eps. (TV2).

Ninth-grader Nozomu Futami moves back to his childhood hometown to live alone, boarding and helping out in a temple so he can go to school while his father works overseas. He welcomes the chance to get reacquainted with his childhood friends, twins Sumireko and Kaoruko Ichijo, and hopes to get closer to them both; but his school is overrun with girl twins, plus a few pairs of siblings for variety. There's a local legend about twin girls falling in love with the same boy, and he is set to become the beneficiary. However, as with the **D3 SERIES** tales *Lustful Mother* and *Lustful Sister*, this twinstory has a literal twinstory—a second tale runs in parallel, in which redheads Sara and Souju Shirogane work as assistants in a private detective agency that has recently been taken over by the son of the original owner. The trio run into trouble with local gangsters, and high jinks ensue. This series was also adapted as a manga in *Comic Dengeki Daioh* with art by Kanao Araki. Yes, it's yet another geek-gets-girls show, this time based originally on a magazine story and illustrations by Hina Futaba and Mutsumi Sasaki.

TWIN PRINCESSES FROM THE MYSTERIOUS STAR

2005. JPN: *Fushigi-boshi no Futago Hime*. TV series. DIR: Junichi Sato, Shogo Kawamoto. SCR: Rika Nanase, Kiyoko Yoshimura. DES: Akemi Kobayashi, Hiroko Kazui, Junichi Azuma, Yuka Ohashi. ANI: Akemi Kobayashi, Terumi Nishii, Yasutoshi Niwa. MUS: Kotaro Nakagawa. PRD: Hal Film Maker, NAS, TV Tokyo. 25 mins. x 51 eps. (TV1), 25 mins. x 52 eps. (TV2).

The Mysterious Star is a hollow body

with the life-giving Kingdom of the Sun at its center. Around the core sun, seven kingdoms coexist. When the sun begins to fail, Fine and Rain, the twin princesses of the Sun Kingdom, decide to use their magic to save all seven realms. However, the evil Chancellor of the Moon Kingdom is out to seize power and will stop at nothing to achieve his aims. Prince Bright is possessed by the Chancellor's evil. Helped by the spirit of Princess Grace, a princess who died saving the seven kingdoms from darkness, Fine and Rain set out to collect the Grace Stones and save the world.

This candy-striped take on the magical girl concept is a rainbow-colored journey through the various kingdoms, packed with adventures in baking, jewelry-making, décor, festivals, fashion, and romance, as the girls make friends and allies, learn to work with and consider others, and try to become better princesses. Along the way they meet with setbacks and failures, but there's nothing in *Twin Princesses* to distress even the smallest of girls.

Originally conceived by Birthday, the show had its roots, not in manga or a game, but in a concept webpage put up by the group in 2003 to showcase the characters and their world in the hope of marketing the idea. TV Tokyo and NAS came onboard a year later and the concept was developed into an anime series, with manga, merchandise, and software following. The second TV series *Twin Princesses of the Mysterious Star—Gyu!* (*Fushigiboshi no Futago Hime Gyu!*) appeared in 2006 from the same team. That year it came in at number 65 in a poll to find the 100 favorite anime on Japanese TV. The show was popular overseas as well as at home, screened in Spain, Italy, Portugal, and the Philippines as well as in Taiwan.

TWIN SIGNAL *
1995. Video. DIR: Takashi Sogabe. SCR: N/C. DES: Toshiko Sasaki. ANI: Toshiko Sasaki. MUS: Takeshi Suzuki. PRD: Tokyo Kids. 28 mins. x 3 eps.
A-S Signal is the newest, most sophisticated Human Formed Robot (HFR) in the Atrandom series, created by Professor Shinnosuke Otoi, a brilliant engineer. Signal looks like a cute 16-year-old boy, programmed to be "big brother" to the professor's grandson, Nobuhiko. Made

of the revolutionary material MIRA by a secret process, Signal is the constant target of kidnap attempts and other efforts to steal the Professor's secrets. But there's one small problem with the process— whenever Nobuhiko sneezes, Signal transforms from a normal teenage boy into a sweet three-year-old super-deformed dwarf. Chibi Signal, as he's known in this state, is phenomenally cute and obsessed with eating chocolate, but his powers as a bodyguard are severely compromised.

Luckily, lots of pretty-boy robots pop up to help Signal out. They are earlier models in the Atrandom series. Signal's older brother and prototype, Pulse, also lives with the Otoi family as does Code, a robot bird also made by the same secret techniques. Based on the early chapters of the *Shonen GanGan* manga by Sachi Oshimizu, which has also spun off novels and drama CDs.

TWINKLE HEART
1986. JPN: *Twinkle Heart: Gingakei made Todokanai*. JPN: *Twinkle Heart: No Stop Til The Milky Way*. Video. DIR: Seiji Okuda. SCR: Kenji Terada. DES: Sachiko Yamamoto. ANI: Moriyasu Taniguchi. MUS: N/C. PRD: Project Team Argos. 45 mins.
On a distant planet, the treasure of Love is being sought by planetary ruler Ogod. Three insufferably cute aliens—Cherry, Lemon, and Berry—join in the search and finally reach Earth. In order to look for information about the treasure, they decide that the best course would be to turn their spaceship into a hamburger bar, so as to blend in with the natives and listen for any intelligence. A comedy, in case you were wondering.

TWINS AT ST. CLARE'S
1991. JPN: *Ochame na Futago Clare Gakuen Monogatari*. AKA: *Story of Mischievous Twins at Clare College*. TV series. DIR: Masaharu Okuwaki, et al. SCR: Haruya Yamazaki, Michiru Shimada. DES: Shuichi Seki. ANI: Keiko Sasaki, Satoshi Hirayama, Toshiharu Mizutani. MUS: Masahiro Kawasaki. PRD: Tokyo Movie Shinsha, Nippon TV. 25 mins. x 26 eps.
Patricia and Isabel are identical twins whose rich parents decide that their girls should learn the true values of life. They don't feel their expensive, luxurious

school is making a very good job of this, so instead they send them to St. Clare's, a much simpler school. At first the girls resent this, seeing it as a step down the social ladder. Their privileged background doesn't help them adjust to life as members of a community unimpressed by wealth. They are determined to win respect, but because they're completely unused to communal life, they rebel against the rules, going on strike, stealing, and causing all sorts of trouble. Instead of the school's best students they become its biggest troublemakers, but they eventually settle down, make friends, and learn to value and respect others while having lots of fun. There are midnight feasts, adventures, and all the things people do at boarding school in novels like the 1941 book by Enid Blyton that inspired this series. Unfortunately real English boarding schools were never so exciting, but Japanese audiences didn't care; nor did those across Europe. TMS followed with another twin story, ME AND I: THE TWO LOTTES.

TWO DOWN, FULL BASE
1982. AKA: *Two Out, Bases Loaded*. TV special. DIR: Tsutomu Shibayama. SCR: Seiichi Yashiro. DES: Michishiro Yamada, Hideo Kawauchi. ANI: Tsutomu Shibayama, Kenichi Onuki. MUS: Yusuke Hoguchi, Joe Hisaishi. PRD: Group Tac, Ajia-do, Toho, Fuji TV. 85 mins.
Musuke "Shorty" Sato is a shortstop for the local junior baseball team, the Eggs, who is asked by his mother to look after some money for her. He foolishly lends it to Tower and Dump, the school bad-boys, and must enlist the help of the pitcher's pretty little sister.

TWO FACIALS OF EVE, THE *
2004. JPN: *Masho no Kao*. AKA: *Fiendish Face*. Video. DIR: Kirin Morishiba. SCR: Joichi Michigami. DES: Sawa Oo. ANI: Sawa Oo. MUS: Hiroaki Sano. PRD: AT-2 Project, Discovery. 30 mins.
High schooler Keiichi Hayama fantasizes about having sex with his childhood friend Tomo Aihara at the school's pool, only to have his fantasy invaded by a stranger—a young woman who materializes in Tomo's place, and proceeds to take Keiichi. Keiichi arrives home after school that day to find the woman from his fantasy

masturbating in his bedroom. His foster mother surprises him while he is peeping, only to have the woman emerge from the room at the far end of the hall, to be introduced as his foster mother's niece Reika, whose parents died in a traffic accident and who will be living with them. Reika, who seems to be possessed of mysterious powers, continues her attempts to seduce Keiichi at every turn, eventually getting her way by blackmailing Keiichi into submitting. Meanwhile, Keiichi's foster sister Akane also harbors a secret crush for him, in yet another instance of pseudo-incest in anime. *The Two Facials of Eve* is also an instance of an anime porn title without a conclusion—no explanation is given of Reika's abilities, nor are any of the other plot threads tied up. Based on a 1997 game from Mink, the anime's release apparently inspired a 2005 remake, appropriately titled *Nymphomania*, and part of the DISCOVERY SERIES. **N**

TWO ON THE ROAD

1992. JPN: *Two on the Road: Itsumo Futari de*. AKA: *Always the Two of Us*. Video. DIR: Hirotoshi Hayasaka, Seizo Watase. SCR: Seizo Watase. DES: Seizo Watase. ANI: N/C. MUS: BEGIN. PRD: Cure. 37 mins., 30 mins.
Two anthologies of short stories, 13 in all, based on originals by CHALK-COLORED PEOPLE–creator Seizo Watase. As with other adaptations of Watase's work, they are set to music—stories here include *Ashes of Love, White Fish/Blue Fish, Dance on the Sands, Glider, Handbag Mirror, Blue Snow*, and *Living in the World*. Though several early ones were broadcast on the WOWOW satellite channel, this qualifies more as a video production.

TWO TAKAS, THE

1984. JPN: *Futari Taka*. TV series. DIR: Takao Yotsuji, Hiroko Tokita, Junichi Sakata, Hiroshi Negishi. SCR: Sukehiro Tomita, Hideo Takayashiki, Yuji Watanabe, Yasushi Hirano. DES: Shiro Murata, Akira Nakanishi. ANI: Shiro Murata, Yasuhiro Moriguchi. MUS: Joe Hisaishi. PRD: Movie International, Fuji TV. 25 mins. x 32 eps.
Two boys both named Taka ("Hawk") are both passionate motorcyclists and both determined to be champions. The similarity ends there; one's a rich kid from a good family, one's from the wrong side of the

tracks, constantly fighting with his mother. Then they learn that, following a fire in the maternity unit where they were born, two babies were accidentally swapped over.
Based on Kaoru "AREA 88" Shintani's 1981 manga in *Shonen Sunday*, this was the last Movie International production. The studio closed down before it could be completed, so only by reading the manga could fans find out how the story ended; but the series gave them Hisaishi's music by way of compensation.

2001 NIGHTS *

1987. JPN: *Space Fantasia 2001 Nights*. Video. DIR: Toshio Takeuchi. SCR: Chiho Katsura. DES: Akio Sugino, Takashi Watanabe. ANI: Hisatoshi Motoki, Noboru Tatsuike. MUS: Satoshi Kadokura. PRD: TMS. 57 mins.
In 2085, a sleeper ship carrying the embryos of the "Robinson Family" launches for planet Ozma. A community begins to thrive onboard the ship, and when it reaches Ozma 375 years later, the terraformed planet is settled peacefully. Then, a second ship arrives, captained by yet another Robinson, who urges the colonists to help spread the human race even further into space. Owing much more to *2001: A Space Odyssey* than SWISS FAMILY ROBINSON, this majestic video was shot in "Super Perspective Technique" (whatever that is) to capture the photo-real quality of Yukinobu Hoshino's original 1984 *Action Comics* manga. Note also the homages to THE WIZARD OF OZ.
Hoshino's original presented such rich material for anime adaptation that it was no surprise it was approached a second time. Fumihiko Sori, director of VEXILLE, adapted two other stories for the straight-to-video *To* (2009). The title is a reference in Japanese to an insurmountable distance (something like "To Infinity … "), but in English it is a common preposition, obscuring the work from many search engines and making it hard to find; in some territories, it was released as *To: 2001 Nights* in an attempt to tag it better with potential audiences. Highlighting Sori's trademark digital animation, the video release sadly scrimps on the script, despite some neat high concepts in *Elliptical Orbit*, in which a husband and wife are obliged to come to terms with the relativity effects of trips beyond the solar system, keeping her

young while he ages, and *Symbiotic Planet*, in which two lovers from rival colonies are confronted by a hostile environment that out-dangers their Earthbound prejudices. Only the Sori version was released in English.

TWO'S COMPANY

1998. JPN: *Futari Kurashi*. AKA: *Two People Living Together*. TV series. DIR: Futa Morita. SCR: Fumihiko Shimo. DES: Masayuki Hirooka. ANI: Masayuki Hirooka. MUS: Katsuo Ono. PRD: TBS. 5 mins. x 36 eps.
The romantic misadventures of an out-of-work manga artist, based on a manga by working manga artist Kenjiro Kakimoto. These shorts were broadcast as part of the late night *Wonderful* program. **N**

TYPHOON IN ISE BAY

1989. JPN: *Ise-wan Taifu Monogatari*. AKA: *Story of the Typhoon in Ise Bay*. Movie. DIR: Seijiro Kamiyama, Yasuo Iwamoto. SCR: Seijiro Kamiyama. DES: Masahiro Kitazaki. ANI: Masahiro Kitazaki. MUS: Masao Haryu. PRD: Mushi. 90 mins.
This self-explanatory true story of a 1959 storm that decimated Western Japan was directed by Kamiyama, who also wrote the original book.

TYRANT FALLS IN LOVE, THE

2010. JPN: *Koi Suru Bo-kun*. Video. DIR: Keiji Kawakubo. SCR: Yukino Hiro. DES: Tomoko Hirota. ANI: N/C. MUS: N/C. PRD: Prime Time. 30 mins. x 2 eps.
Tetsuhiro is crazy about his hot friend Soichi. Unfortunately Soichi is straight, homophobic, and a bossy, arrogant person. But Tetsuhiro's determined to bring out his good side, in this anime based on the first five episodes of Hinako Takanaga's boys' love manga. In fact he's so determined that even if Soichi keeps saying no, he'll find a way to get him. Lovely art and two lead characters who are as strong and stubborn as each other make up for the rather cramped plot. Avoid if you don't like rape fantasies. **NV**

TYTANIA *

2008. AKA: *TP Sakura*. TV Video Movie. DIR: Noboru Ishiguro. SCR: N/C. DES: Noboru Sugimitsu, Kazutaka Miyatake, Koji Ito, Yasutoshi Kawai. ANI: Yuya Iwashita. MUS: Hiroshi Takaki. PRD: Artland, Columbia ME, EEJ,

Happinet, MICO, ogo Visio, Sony PCL, Three Light, Wrightstaff. 30 mins. x 26 eps.

The star empire of Valdana is under the control of the powerful Tytania clan. The clan's four leading noblemen are jockeying for position as successor to the head of the family when an unexpected defeat by a minor general of a small city-state attracts their attention. Meanwhile, a determined, naïve, and beautiful princess sets out from home as a hostage to the Tytania court. Will the Tytanian Dukes retain their power? Will they squabble and destroy their powerbase? Will the resistance forces destroy them? As the game plays itself out over a huge canvas of star systems, even the most minor pieces can make a difference.

This epic space opera is based on an as-yet-unfinished series of novels by Yoshiki Tanaka, creator of the sublime LEGEND OF GALACTIC HEROES, as well as HEROIC LEGEND OF ARSLAN and LEGEND OF THE FOUR KINGS. Artland, the studio that has animated the whole of the epic *LoGH* story, picks up the torch again for this new and strikingly similar tale, with Noboru Ishiguro in the director's chair. Haruhiko Mikimoto and Katsumi Michihara originally designed the characters, and Ishiguro's team doesn't mess with success, leaving this show looking as stunning as its precursor. Sadly, the space battle scenes are as slow and complex as the *LoGH* ones, without the combination of engagement with the characters and plot complexity that made them so compelling. The polish and beauty of the design and animation can't make up for the missing sense of dash and daring.

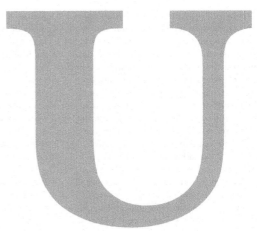

U-JIN BRAND *

1991. Video. DIR: Osamu Sekita. SCR: Satoru Akahori. DES: Yumi Nakayama. ANI: Yumi Nakayama. MUS: Nobuo Ito. PRD: JC Staff, Animate. 45 mins.

Three short stories based on U-Jin's erotic manga, similar in style to ANGEL and TALES OF ... In the first story, a songwriter can produce hits for teenage idol singers—but only after he gets to know the girl *really* well. Despite his constant calendar of seductions, he secretly loves innocent Akiyo, with whom he must one day work and try on his irresistible charm. The other two chapters are linked tales of Toyama no Benbei, a righter of wrongs in the tradition of Toyama no Kinsan (see SAMURAI GOLD). In the first, he is called in to avenge a girl wronged by a serial seducer, who claims he will still respect her if they do the deed, then dumps her because she is no longer a virgin. In the second, he is brought in to solve the problem of a young man who doesn't want to dump his career prospects along with his unwelcome engagement to the boss's daughter. In 2004 the title was rereleased in the U.S. as *Tales of Seduction*. ⓝ

UCHUREI

2009. TV series. DIR: Ryoko Yabuki (ROBOT). SCR: Kentaro Ushio. DES: Takuya Inaba. ANI: Chota Akatsuki, Kazunori Hirai, Reiji Erada, Takayuki Sekiguchi. MUS: Tatsuhiko Iino. PRD: drop, ROBOT, TV Tokyo. 3 mins. x 12 eps.

Takashi is a normal high school boy who gets involved in a strange accident one summer, and winds up living with the ghost of a space alien. He names it Uchurei (a contraction of the Japanese for "alien's ghost," *uchujin no yurei*) and intends to keep it as a pet, then finds himself possessed. Comedic fun ensues; compare to ULTRAMAN, which might be similarly parsed as a tale of alien possession.

UDAGAWA, TOKI

?–. Born in Kanagawa, Udagawa went to Tokyo to study drama at Waseda University, but soon found part-time work as a puppeteer and performed on the original puppet version of MADCAP ISLAND. Dropping out of Waseda, he became a full-time performer in the Hitomi-za puppetry troupe. In 1983, he moved into anime by becoming the producer of KAKKUN CAFÉ.

UFO ROBOT DAI APOLLON *

1976. JPN: *UFO Senshi Dai Apollon*. AKA: *UFO Warrior Dai Apollon, Shadow World*. TV series. DIR: Tatsuo Ono. SCR: Takao Koyama, Okihara Matsumoto, Noboru Shiroyama, Soji Yoshikawa, Seiji Matsuoka. DES: Toyoo Ashida. ANI: Keijiro Kimura, Takashi Kakuta, Yoshiyuki Tomino, Toyoo Ashida, Satoshi Dezaki, Seiji Okuda. MUS: Masahisa Takeichi. PRD: Eiken, TBS. 25 mins. x 39 eps.

Sixteen-year-old Takeshi forms a football team at the Blue Sky Orphanage. One day after a game, he's alone on the field when a warrior of light on a mighty steed appears and points his sword at Takeshi's chest. Takeshi loses consciousness, waking later to find a mark in the shape of a sun over his heart. He is really the son of the king of planet Apollon, spirited away to Earth by his father's faithful retainer, Rabi, in order to avoid the prince's death at the hands of the usurper General Dazaan. His heart contains the "Key Energy" of his planet, which allows him to control the space ship Rabi cunningly hid on the ocean floor—it contains several flying saucers, a dart-shaped flyer with detachable motorcycle, and the three component vehicles Edda (Head), Trangu (Trunk), and Legga (Leg) that combine to form the giant robot Dai Apollon. Using his Key Energy, Takeshi can painfully synchronize with the robot, allowing him to operate it as an extension of his own body. The separate vehicles are piloted by his teammates Miki, Choko, and Goro, whose clothes magically change into their football jerseys whenever they shout "U! F! O!" Using the robot, Takeshi hopes to set his planet free and release his mother from imprisonment. Based on the 1974 *Shonen King* manga by OISHINBO-creator Tetsu Kariya and Shigeru Tsuchiyama, though since the original featured a 15-year-old orphan called Akira defeating demons with the powers of 108 heroes (see SUIKODEN), and no giant robot anywhere to be seen, it's a wonder the producers bothered to pay for the rights at all.

UFO SUMMER

2005. JPN: *Iriya no Sora, UFO no Natsu*. AKA: *Iriya's Sky, UFO Summer*. Video. DIR: Naoyuki Ito. SCR: Michiko Yokote. DES: Eiji Komatsu, Yoshinori Sayama, Takeyasu Kurashima. ANI: N/C. MUS: Hiroshi Takagi. PRD: Toei Animation, Happinet. 30 mins. x 6 eps.

Naoyuki Asaba is a withdrawn boy who likes watching the sky and daydreaming about UFOs. One summer night, he sneaks into his school's swimming pool and encounters a distant-seeming girl who claims her name is Iriya Kana. The two shyly become friends as Naoyuki teaches her to swim, but she is soon whisked away by stern-faced minders. Naoyuki begins to suspect, as does anyone who has seen MAHOROMATIC or SAIKANO, that Iria is part of a clandestine military project, fighting a "secret" war in parts unknown, but he must also contend with the predictable arrival of Iria at his school at the beginning of the new semester. But while this might appear to have all the hallmarks of innumerable other anime, its closest influence is not the above-mentioned tales, but the elegiac longing and tragedy of VOICES OF A DISTANT STAR. Based on a novel by Mitsuhito Akiyama.

UFO ULTRAMAIDEN VALKYRIE *
2002. JPN: Enban Ojo Walküre. AKA: UFO Princess Valkyrie; UFO Battlemaiden Valkyrie; UFO Princess Valkyrie. TV series, video. DIR: Shigeru Ueda, Nobuhiro Takagi. SCR: Ryoe Tsukimura. DES: Maki Fujii. ANI: Tetsuya Yanagisawa, Hiroshi Kubo. MUS: Kenji Kawai. PRD: Toshiba EMI, Kid's Station, Media Factory, UHF Group, TNK. 24 mins. x 12 eps. (TV1), 24 mins. x 12 eps. (TV2), 30 mins. x 6 eps. (v).
Princess Valkyrie crash-lands on Earth, right on top of bathhouse owner Kazuto. She can only save him from death by giving him part of her soul. Naturally, she gives him the teenage half and reverts to her child persona. Kazuto and his friends have to try and get her back to normal and explain away the space ship stuck in the roof, although this becomes less of a talking point as more crashes occur. Alien girls crashing into the human world and developing crushes on an ordinary boy with an old-fashioned occupation may sound familiar, but nonetheless Ryoe Tsukimura, creator and screenwriter of EL HAZARD, is credited with the series concept. The pseudonymous Kaishaku, creator of KANNAZUKI NO MIKO, "originated" the idea in the manga of the same name, although similarities to TENCHI MUYO! and BIRDY THE MIGHTY are obvious. The second series, December Nocturne (Junigatsu no Yasokyoku), followed in October 2003 with the arrival of the mysterious Valkyrie Ghost, another alien girl whose main agenda is getting

Kazuto for herself but who also reveals more of the mysterious past of Valkyrie's home planet of Valhalla. A third series, subtitled Deluxe, was announced for 2004 but instead our happy band of Tenchi clones got a video series, Bride of the Star Spirit Season (Seiretsu no Hanayome). The show's Japanese title reflects the German pronunciation of the word valkyrie, presumably better known to the Japanese than the Anglo-Saxon variant thanks to the Richard Wagner opera Die Walküre (1862).

ULTIMATE GIRLS
2005. JPN: U.G.: Ultimate Girl [sic]. TV series. DIR: Yuji Moto. SCR: Satoru Nishizono. DES: Hideyuki Morioka. ANI: Seiji Matsuda. MUS: Moka. PRD: m.o.e., Studio Matrix. 13 mins. x 12 eps.
In a retread of the premise for ULTRAMAN, three young girls decide that they want to get a closer look at one of the giant monsters that has been periodically attacking their city. They get what they wanted, only to be crushed to death by UFO-man, the giant superhero who has been protecting humanity from danger by battling the creatures. However, UFO-man is a kindly and public-spirited individual, who brings the girls back from the dead on the condition that they agree to take over the task of saving the world. A sequel was originally hinted later the same year, although this had transformed into a mere audio-drama bonus extra on the DVD release of the TV series. However, lowbudget transformations form part of the appeal of this series, which cheekily makes a comedy virtue out of everdecreasing funding for animation. Whereas old-school anime often used transformation sequences to recycle footage, Ultimate Girls does not even go that far, instead showing a picture of the city from a distance, an arrow pointing to the street where one of the girls is transforming and a thermometer-style horizontal menu, as if a file is downloading, with the message "Please Wait." Meanwhile, it even finds a new excuse for cheesecake, since the girls' embarrassment at losing their clothes is what powers the release of their destructive energies. At least, that is how things are supposed to work, except teammember Tsugumi is such an exhibitionist that she rarely gets embarrassed enough to generate any monster-destroying energy

of her own. A manga version also ran in Dengeki Gao magazine.

ULTIMATE SUPERMAN R
1991. JPN: Kyukyoko Chojin R. Video. DIR: Ayumi Shibuki. SCR: Toshiko Uehara. DES: Toyomi Sugiyama. ANI: Toyomi Sugiyama. MUS: Masayuki Yamamoto. PRD: Studio Core. 75 mins.
Average Japanese teenager Ichiro Tanaka is really an android, programmed to take over the world by mad scientist Hiroshi Narihara. He enlists the help of the school photography club, which is probably a bad idea. Based on the comedy manga by PATLABOR-creator Masami Yuki, this anime was also spun off into several audio dramas.

ULTIMATE TEACHER, THE *
1988. JPN: Kyofun no Bio-Ningen: Saishu Kyoshi. AKA: Fearsome Bio-Human: The Last Teacher. Video. DIR: Toyoo Ashida. SCR: Monta Ibu. DES: Atsuji Yamamoto, Mandrill Club. ANI: Noriyasu Yamauchi. MUS: Miyuki Otani. PRD: Studio Live, SME. 60 mins.
Ganpachi Chabane, half-man, half-cockroach, is the result of a genetic experiment. This makes him a natural teacher in the eyes of many teenagers, so when he escapes from the lab where he was created, he heads straight for Emperor High School and installs himself on the staff. His idea of education agrees with that of the pupils—both see it as a battleground where only the strong survive. The school is overrun by student gangs; Chabane has to defeat the leader of the strongest gang, pretty martial artist Hinako Shiratori, if he's to keep his class in line. Luckily Hinako has a weakness; if she isn't wearing her lucky blue bloomers emblazoned with a cute white cat, she has no confidence at all in her fighting skills and changes from powerhouse to pushover. The U.S. TRANSLATION calls these "lucky gym shorts," but the U.K. version's "velvet pussy panties" is much more in line with the crude tone of the whole package. Mystifyingly released in theaters on a double bill with the LEGEND OF GALACTIC HEROES movie, it features a theme song by famous Japanese pop band the Kome-Kome Club. Atsuji Yamamoto also wrote a manga version for Animage Comics. The video was released as just plain Ultimate Teacher, without its "the"

in the U.K., although probably only anime encyclopedists and their proofreaders are liable to know or care. ◉

ULTRA B

1987. TV series, movie. DIR: Hiroshi Sasagawa, Tetsuo Yasumi, Teruo Kogure, Kazuhiro Mori, Fusahito Nagaki. SCR: Masaaki Sakurai, Masaru Yamamoto, Nobuaki Kishima, Hirokazu Mizude. DES: Fujiko-Fujio "A." ANI: Keisuke Mori. MUS: Shunsuke Kikuchi. PRD: Shinei Doga, TV Asahi. 20 mins. (m), 25 mins. x 51 eps. (TV).

One night, Michio chases a UFO to see where it lands. He is taken inside it and encounters a mysterious baby, Ultra B (AKA UB). Though at first the only strange thing about him is his pathological obsession with drinking milk, UB soon reveals that he has superpowers when he moves in with Michio's family—a fact that causes humorous misunderstandings in the style of DORAEMON. The 1988 "movie" outing *UB: Dictator B.B. from the Black Hole* featured the arrival of the evil, pterodactyl-riding "Black Baby," whom UB defeats with the aid of his cohorts Super Baby Robot and Muscle Bird. Another work from PROGOLFER SARU–creator Motoo Abiko, formerly half of the Fujiko-Fujio duo, for *Fujiko-Fujio Land* magazine, its appearance in a glorified vanity publication perhaps explains the tiredness of the idea.

ULTRA GRAN

1982. JPN: *Hitotsuboshi-ke no Ultra Baa-san*. AKA: *Ultra Granny of the Hitotsuboshi Family; Super Grandma*. TV series. DIR: Kenji Hirata, Satoshi Inoue. SCR: Yoshiyuki Suga, Shigeru Mizuno, Hiroko Naka. DES: Toshio Kitahara. ANI: Takumi Manabe, Takao Yamazaki. MUS: Masayuki Yamamoto. PRD: Knack, Yomiuri TV (Nippon TV). 25 mins. x 13 eps.

Seventy-year-old Granny Hitotsuboshi acts like a teenager and cares nothing about the effect her quick tongue and accident-prone nature have on those around her. Her crazy schemes create chaos for her family, which includes hard-pressed salaryman Eitaro, exam-obsessed mother Kinuko, consumptive grandson Kenichi, toddler Todome, and Antonio the local tramp. Based on a gag manga by Meme Akutagawa—compare to SAZAE-SAN and MY NEIGHBORS THE YAMADAS.

ULTRA MANIAC *

2003. TV series, video. DIR: Shinichi Masaki, Nanako Shimazaki. SCR: Hisayoshi Kato, Miho Maruo, Shiki Masuda, Yasuko Oe. DES: Miho Shimogasa. ANI: Maki Fujii. MUS: Toru Yugawa. PRD: Animax, Ashi Pro, Studio Aqua, Studio Jack, Studio Ox. 30 mins. (v), 23 mins. x 26 eps. (TV).

Nina is in line for the title of Princess of the Magic Kingdom. To qualify for consideration, she and her transforming talking cat Rio have to travel to Earth to improve her magic skills, in the sorcerously self-improving manner of LITTLE WITCH SALLY and KIKI'S DELIVERY SERVICE. But she is involved in an accident on her flying scooter, and as a result she meets and befriends Ayu Tateishi, a sporty, kindhearted, and popular girl in her second year at middle school. She tries to use her magic to help her friend's romantic endeavors, with comic results; but she also has to decide if she will follow her destiny or stay on Earth. From the age of its protagonists and the trappings (cute magic creature sidekick, magic equipment, and transformation sequences) this appears to be a magical-girl show, but it deviates from the classic canon by making the magical girl second lead in the style of E-CHAN THE NINJA. There are also a few nods to a more modern magic—Nina doesn't have a wand or bracelet, but a sentient PDA that she plugs into a treasure casket to work her spells. Her aim in the TV series is to retrieve five magical stones, although once she achieves this she realizes, like BEWITCHED AGNÈS, that she rather likes the human world and would prefer to stay. The original manga in *Ribon* magazine is by MARMALADE BOY–creator Wataru Yoshizumi, but designed to appeal to a younger audience. A one-shot video, which we presume to be related to *Ribon*-reader screenings like that of FULL MOON, featured Nina helping Ayu win a tennis match.

ULTRAMAN *

1979. JPN: *The Ultraman*. Movie, TV series. DIR: Eiko Toriumi, Masahisa Ishida, Takashi Anno, Katsuyuki Tsuji, Takeshi Shirato, et al. (TV1), Masayoshi Ozaki (TV2), Mitsuo Kusakabe (USA, Company), Hiroshi Sasagawa (v), Tetsuro Amino (*Tsuifun*), Mitsuo Kusakabe (Company), Hiroko Tokita (*Love and Peace*). SCR: Keiichi Abe, Soji Yoshikawa,

Hiroyuki Hoshiyama, Yasushi Hirano (TV1), Hiroko Naka, Keiji Kubota (TV2), John Eric Seward (USA), Hiroshi Hashimoto (v). DES: Tsuneo Ninomiya, Kunio Okawara, Shoji Kawamori (TV1), Yoshihiko Shinozaki (TV2), Kazuo Iimura (USA), Tsuneo Ninomiya (v), N/C (*Love and Peace*). ANI: Tsuneo Ninomiya (TV1), Osamu Kamijo (TV2), Kazuo Iimura (USA), Tsuneo Ninomiya, Hiroko Minamimoto (v), Yutaka Miya (*Tsuifun*), Noriko Nishimiya (Company), Haruo Takahashi (*Love and Peace*). MUS: Kunio Miyauchi (TV1, TV2), Shinsuke Kazato (USA), N/C. PRD: Sunrise, Tsuburaya, TBS, Tsuburaya, NHK2, Tsuburaya, Hanna-Barbera, Tsuburaya, Triangle Staff. 30 mins. x 50 eps. (TV1), 25 mins. (m, *Kids*), 10 mins. x 26 eps. (TV2, *Kids*), 10 mins. x 26 eps. (TV3, *Mother*), 80 mins. (USA), 30 x 6 eps. (v), 30 mins. (*Tsuifun*), 60 mins. (Company), 80 mins. (*Love and Peace*).

After an apprenticeship in special effects on films ranging from *The War at Sea from Hawaii to Malaya* (see WARTIME ANIME) through the original *Godzilla* to Kurosawa's *Throne of Blood* (for which he made the forest move), Eiji Tsuburaya started the famed "monster studio" that bears his name. The live-action *Ultraman*, one of the enduring icons of Japanese TV, evolved from *Ultra Q* (1966), an SF drama series in the *X-Files* mode featuring the investigation of mysterious beings and events. As *Ultraman* (also 1966), it was taken over by the monsters and became a battle between the heroic Ultrans, citizens of Nebula M78, and their human allies, against often absurd but compelling monster opponents. It is still one of the most popular toy lines in Japan, with legions of new plastic monsters released every year.

The Ultraman (1979), broadcast during the period that reruns of the live-action series prepared the audience for *Ultraman 80*, commences with glowing symbols appearing over major cities like Tokyo, Paris, and New York. A new tactical team, the Space Garrison, is set up by the Earth Defense Force and discovers they are signs of a higher civilization from another dimension, the Ultrans, who came to Earth in ancient times. To fight evil in our dimension, they need human help. Young pilot Hikari flies out into space to investigate and is transported by a beam of light into another dimension, where he meets an Ultran and agrees to the merging of their life forces (a symbiotic rebirth often pastiched in later anime, from **BIRDY THE MIGHTY** on up). Hikari can now use the star-shaped "Beam Flasher" on his forehead to transform into Ultraman Joneas (AKA Joe). He can fight the monsters and aliens that menace Earth, and thanks to the lower cost of animation, he has a much wider range of power-rays than any of his live-action brothers. Episodes from this series were edited into a feature-length video, *The Adventures of Ultraman* (1982), for the U.S. market only. It focuses on Hikari's journey and meeting with the Ultran, and the space warfare elements. A few translated episodes were also released in the U.S. video market on one tape as *Ultraman II*.

Ultraman Kids (1984) was more humorous, a short movie of cute kiddie versions of the Ultraman family and their monster rivals. In April 1986 they got their own series, *Ultraman Kids Proverb Stories* (*Kotowaza Monogatari*), in which Ultraman Zoffy and friends reenact wise maxims for little ones. The two final episodes were not broadcast. A second kids' series moved from Ultraman's home on TBS to the NHK2 satellite channel—the **FROM THE APENNINES TO THE ANDES** pastiche *30 Million Light Years in Search of Mother* (1991, *Haha o Tazunete 3,000 Man Konen*).

The serious movie *Ultraman: The Adventure Begins* (1987; retitled just plain *Ultraman USA* in Japan) was a Japanese-American coproduction between Tsubaraya and Hanna-Barbera and based on a story by Noboru Tsubaraya. Three stunt pilots survive a fatal crash thanks to three aliens from M78, who have linked life forces with the pilots and made them part of the Ultra-Force. The aliens' mission is to destroy four evil Sorkin Monsters hatched from asteroids that have crashed onto New Orleans, San Francisco, Denver, and New York. Ultra-Scott, Ultra-Chuck, and token woman Ultra-Beth now have a secret base inside Mount Rushmore and another under a golf course, plus three robots to help them out.

The video series *Ultraman Graffiti* (1990) featured more cartoony adventures for mini-versions of the Ultra brothers—a style that continues to dominate the franchise, at least in its animated incarnation. It was

followed by Tetsuro Amino's video release *Ultra-Violent Battle—Comet War-God Tsuifun* (1996, *Chotoshi Gekiden—Suisei Senshin Tsuifun*). In the late 1990s, the live-action *Ultraman* was influenced by the postmodern angst of **EVANGELION**, resulting in the more serious *Ultraman Gaia* TV series, written in part by **SERIAL EXPERIMENTS LAIN**'s Chiaki Konaka. The Sturm und Drang of the *Gaia* movies was balanced in theaters by new cartoon Ultrakids features, Mitsuo Kusakabe's *Ultraman Company* (1996) and Hiroko Tokita's *Ultraman: Love and Peace* (1999), featuring animation by Triangle Staff. This is the most recent animated incarnation of the series to date, though the original is often referenced in shows including **PROJECT A-KO**, **URUSEI YATSURA**, **PATLABOR**, **DOCTOR SLUMP**, and the feline parody *Ultranyan* (1997).

ULTRAVIOLET: CODE 044 *

2008. TV series. DIR: Osamu Dezaki. SCR: NC. DES: Akio Sugino. ANI: Akio Sugino, Moriyasu Taniguchi. MUS: Shusei Murai. PRD: Madhouse Studios, Sony Pictures Entertainment (Japan). 25 mins. x 12 eps.

044 is a phenomenally strong soldier whose combat abilities have been boosted by viral gene manipulation. The downside is that her lifespan is shortened, but that doesn't worry her government bosses. When sent in to destroy the Phage troops and their leader, she finds herself unable to kill an injured Phage soldier. Even though this makes her a traitor, targeted by her own side as well as the enemy, she goes on the run with him. And even when she learns that he could destroy her, she still can't bring herself to kill him.

This is an anime version of the 2006 sci-fi movie *Ultraviolet*; some sources also quote a comic book origin, misled by the movie's title sequence featuring covers from the nonexistent series, specially created as background for the credits. Romi Park, the Korean-Japanese actress who was the original voice of Edward Elric in **FULLMETAL ALCHEMIST**, plays the title role with aplomb. Director Dezaki (who died in 2011) and Sugino are old-school anime aristocracy. They were both still in their teens when **ASTRO BOY** hit Japan's small screens, part of the young cohort working for Osamu Tezuka at his new studio and making up the rules of TV anime as they

went along. Tezuka Productions, the studio they joined more than half a century ago, is still active and gets an animation assistance credit. The mix of Dezaki, Sugino, and Madhouse produces a curious hybrid, old-fashioned in the positive sense of the term. The series is redolent of the '80s, when the world was heading for a cyberpunk future and shows like **BUBBLEGUM CRISIS**, all hot chicks with sexy armor, ruled the airwaves. It doesn't offer anything new, but it's solidly entertaining. **◐**

ULYSSES 31 *

1981. JPN: *Uchu Densetsu Ulysses 31*. AKA: *Space Legend Ulysses 31*. TV series. DIR: Bernard Deyries, Tadao Nagahama, Kazuo Terada, Seiji Okuda. SCR: Ryohei Suzuki, Jean Chalopin, Nina Wolmark. DES: Shingo Araki, Michi Himeno, Studio Nue, Manchu, Noboru Tatsuike, Shinji Ito, Yuki Motonori. ANI: Shingo Araki, Toyoo Ashida. MUS: Kei Wakakusa (Denny Crokett, Ike Egan, Haim Saban, Shuki Levy for Western version). PRD: DIC, Tokyo Movie Shinsha, TV Nagoya (TV Asahi). 25 mins. x 26 eps. (only 12 shown in Japanese broadcast, 1988).

Preparing for a routine journey back to his home on 31st-century Earth, starship captain Ulysses runs into trouble on planet Troy when his son, Telemachus, is captured by the disciples of the Cyclops. Killing the Cyclops to save Telemachus, Ulysses brings down the wrath of the god Zeus, who puts his crew into suspended animation and wipes the navigation systems of his ship, the Odyssey. Accompanied only by Telemachus, Numinor, and Yumi, the alien siblings from planet Zotra, and the intensely annoying robot No-no, Ulysses must wander the stars in search of the Kingdom of Hades to awaken his crew and find the way back home.

A ridiculously contrived sci-fi reworking of Homer's *Odyssey*, accomplished in such an endearing and exciting fashion as to become one of the best-loved anime in Europe, *Ulysses 31* was the first French-Japanese coproduction. It was also the last for **ROSE OF VERSAILLES**' Tadao Nagahama, who died during production. Producer Jean Chalopin would return with the equally memorable **MYSTERIOUS CITIES OF GOLD**, before his output sank into the financially lucrative but creatively impoverished doldrums of the toy tie-ins *Rainbow Brite* (also made with Japanese staff) and *Care Bears*. He next surfaced in the anime world when his Studio DIC provided the English dub of SAILOR MOON.

The basis of the story (the gods, their human servants, and the obstacles they place in Ulysses' way) has hardly changed, except that Telemachus accompanies our hero rather than staying at home to fight off his mother Penelope's suitors as he did in the original. The addition of new characters doesn't jar; there are so many fantastic beings in the story already that a sweet alien telepath and an annoying robot with an appetite for metal fit right in. The design team makes the best of what it has, with classy machines from Manchu (AKA French designer Phillippe Bouchet), reworked by Studio Nue and SAINT SEIYA–designer Araki. His version of Ulysses had to be toned down by Deyries at final approval stage; the director wanted a pacifist hero, so most of the Japanese-originated futuristic sidearm designs were discarded. The show remains deservedly popular, despite the annoying robot—most notable among its many achievements, a Homeric episode in which the SF Ulysses travels back in time to meet the Greek original and the faithful Penelope. For this episode alone, *Ulysses 31* is an anime classic.

UMISHO
2007. JPN: *Kenko Zenrakei Suieibu Umisho*. AKA: *Kenko Nude Swimming Club Umisho*. TV series. DIR: Koichiro Sotome. SCR: Mamiko Ikeda, Masahiro Yokotani. DES: Rie Nishino. ANI: Rie Nishino. MUS: Yasumasa Sato. PRD: Artland, Geneon, Pony Canyon, Marvelous Entertainment. 25 mins. x 13 eps.
Average high school boy Kaname lives on an island, but can't swim. So he joins his school swimming club to learn. It's full of weirdos and freaks and he's getting nowhere with his swimming when a transfer student from Okinawa joins the club. Amuro is a perky, happy-go-lucky girl who swims nude, but that isn't the only reason Kaname is drawn to her—she reminds him of a mermaid he saw once in his early childhood. A story and characters constructed from the High School Hentai Cliché Kit, spiced with nudity and fan service and leavened with goofy humor, make this a predictable brainless offering, but if you're in the mood for something

mildly funny and completely undemanding, you could do much worse. It's based on Mitsuru Hattori's 2006 manga. ◐

UN-GO *
2011. AKA: *Un-Go Defeated Detective Yuki Shinjuro*. TV, movie. DIR: Seiji Mizushima. SCR: Sho Aikawa. DES: pako, Yun Kouga, Takeshi Waki, Takashi Miyamoto. ANI: Hiroko Yaguchi, Kazumi Inadome, Yuko Yazaki. MUS: NARASAKI. PRD: BONES, Dentsu, Fuji TV, Sony Music Entertainment, Toho. 24 mins. x 11 eps. (TV), 48 mins. (m), 30 secs. x 10 eps. (web).
Japan, the near future, in the aftermath of war: Shinjuro Yuki stalks the mean streets seeking out crime and corruption, a master detective aided by his mysterious assistant Inga. So why is he generally known as the "defeated detective?" Because, despite his brilliant work, credit for solving the crime goes to "super detective" Ronroku Kaisho. Kaisho just happens to be the guy in control of Tokyo's communications infrastructure. While Sherlock Holmes acquired his public reputation from the pulp fiction of his flatmate Dr. Watson, Kaisho is able to ensure that credit for Yuki's discoveries is as deeply buried as the discoveries themselves. Uncovering the truth sometimes requires supernatural help, but it's only half the battle: getting the truth out into public view can be next to impossible.

Un-Go is an entertaining show with plenty of intriguing ideas—Inga's take on vampirism and the nature of her/its deal with Shinjuro are prime examples—but it falls frustratingly short of its promise. The crimes themselves are spectacularly well conceived, original, and often with powerful emotional impact, but they are generally underdeveloped. The relationship between the two detectives—almost that of Holmes and the hapless Inspector Lestrade, from Lestrade's point of view—is also frustratingly underused. Nevertheless, there's enough interest to keep all but the pickiest mystery fan involved, and the supernatural get-out-of-jail card isn't overused.

BONES animates the show superbly, with slick cinematic values that keep the show moving like a beautifully staged ballet. Every frame has something of interest, repaying repeated watching. The elegant

designs and backgrounds and Shihoko Nakayama's well-chosen color palette create a creepily credible world, with old-school touches like the masked villains reminding us that this may be the future, but it's strongly rooted in the past.

The story is based on the work of Japanese novelist and essayist Ango Sakaguchi, who died in 1955. Japan was still recovering from the devastation of the Second World War, and the Allied Occupation had ended, so daily life was much like the world of *Un-Go*. A manga adaptation by J-ta Yamada began serialization in *Newtype Ace* a month before the TV show aired. An "alternative version" written by Sho Aikawa with art by Yun Kouga (EARTHIAN) and "pako" started running in *Newtype* on the same day. Ten Flash animation shorts by BONES were streamed on the Internet, starting a few days before the first episode aired on TV and ending on the same day as the final episode, under the title *Un-Go: Inga's Diary (Un-Go Inga Nikki)*. A movie prequel, *Un-Go Episode 0 Inga-ron (Un-Go Episode 0: Karma Theory)*, premiered in November 2011 while the TV show was running and was made by the same team.

UNCHALLENGEABLE TRIDER G7
1980. JPN: *Muteki Robo Trider G7*. AKA: *Invincible Robo (T) Rider G7*. TV series. DIR: Katsutoshi Sasaki, Seiji Kikuchi, Iku Suzuki, Takao Yoshikawa. SCR: Hiroyuki Hoshiyama, Tsunehisa Ito, Kenichi Matsuzaki, Katsutoshi Sasaki, Sukehiro Tomita, Fuyunori Gobu. DES: Nobuyoshi Sasakado, Kunio Okawara, Yutaka Izubuchi. ANI: Nobuyoshi Sasakado, Akihiro Kanayama, Keijiro Kimura, Norio Shioyama. MUS: Kurando Kaya. PRD: Sotsu Agency (Sunrise), TV Nagoya (TV Asahi). 25 mins. x 50 eps.
When his father dies in 1985, young Watta Takeo inherits the family space transport firm. Despite the fact that the president is just a schoolkid, the company has to fight for survival in a competitive world with rivals and space pirates at every turn. Watta manages to succeed and keep the company going thanks to Professor Navarone's giant robot, Trider G7. Looking forward to the workhorse robots of PATLABOR and back to the boy-and-his-bot sagas of Go Nagai, the series mixes school and home scenarios with space battles—compare to John Stanley's American comic *O.G. Whiz*,

which similarly featured a boy "dragged" away from school and forced to play with expensive supertoys.

UNDERSEA ENCOUNTER *

1981. JPN: *Kaitei Daisenso Ai no Niman Mile*. AKA: *War Beneath the Sea: 20,000 Miles for Love*. TV special. DIR: Ippei Kuri. SCR: Mamoru Sasaki. DES: Akemi Takada, Kunio Okawara. ANI: Takashi Saijo. MUS: Hiroaki Suzuki. PRD: Tatsunoko, Nippon TV. 72 mins.

All the nations of Earth are crumbling before the might of Darius, ruler of the Gabia Empire. Meanwhile, childhood friends Ben and Ricky are sailing on the oceans in search of the lost city of Atlantis. When their ship is sunk, they are rescued by Captain Nemo in his submarine Nautilus. The captain reveals that he knows the location of Atlantis and offers to take them there.

Dubbed in the early 1980s by Harmony Gold and broadcast as afternoon filler in several U.S. cities, this obscure TV movie was two years in the making, shot on 35mm film, and the first lead design job for **PATLABOR**'s Akemi Takada. Directorial assistant Koichi Mashimo would later be given charge of another ship's commander, the less heroic **IRRESPONSIBLE CAPTAIN TYLOR**. The character of Nemo would reappear in **SECRET OF BLUE WATER**, an even freer adaptation of Jules Verne's original story.

UNICO *

1981. Video, movie. DIR: Toshio Hirata, Mami Murano. SCR: Masaki Tsuji. DES: Osamu Tezuka. ANI: Shigeru Yamamoto, Akio Sugino, Yoshiaki Kawajiri, Kazuo Tomizawa. MUS: Yukihide Takakawa, Micky Yoshino, Godiego, Ryo Kitayama, Iruka. PRD: Madhouse, Sanrio Eiga, Tezuka Pro. 25 mins. (v), 90 mins. x 2 (m).

Exiled from Paradise by a malevolent goddess, Unico the baby unicorn is blown on the West Wind, finding troubled souls and helping them before he moves on again. Originally appearing as a color Osamu Tezuka manga in *Lyrica* magazine, Unico first showed up on TV in the pilot *U:Black Cloud, White Feather* (1979, *Kuroi Kumo Shiroi Hane*), eventually released straight to video. In this version, he arrives in a heavily polluted city, where he is befriended by a rat. While sharing a meager meal with

the rat, Unico finds out that the sick girl upstairs can only be cured by the destruction of the local factories and chemical plants. As soon as Unico has brought sunlight back to the town, the West Wind returns to carry him away, before depositing him in yet another desolate place, alone and with no memory of the past.

The TV series wasn't picked up, but the movie *Fantastic Adventures of Unico* (1981) presents the backstory, showing the gods jealous of baby Unico's happiness. They command the West Wind to take him away from his mother and abandon him on the Hill of Oblivion, but the West Wind hasn't the heart to do it, instead leaving Unico in the Land of Mists. When the gods learn of the deception, they send the evil Night Wind to finish the job, and the West Wind saves Unico's life by racing to the Land of Mists and snatching Unico away from the friends he has made there. A second movie, *U in the Land of Magic* (1983, *Maho no Shima e*), again opens with the amnesiac Unico in a strange place, once more making friends thanks to his open, happy nature and willingness to help those in trouble. This time a puppet, maltreated by humans, has been brought to life and given magical powers by the mysterious energy of sunlight. Kuruku has vowed to revenge himself on all humanity by turning humans and animals into puppets and imprisoning them on his magical island. Helped by a little girl and boy, Unico tries to save Kuruku but cannot convince him there is more to life than hate. As Unico's new friends are reunited with their families, he is once again torn away by the West Wind, who tells him the gods will soon find him because of the happiness he has created. Given such a bleak scenario, it's perhaps not surprising that the TV series was not picked up, but the movies—whose art style is not the same as the pilot episode—have acquired their own overseas following thanks to a U.S. video release. Compare to similar Sanrio-sponsored misery in **RINGING BELL**.

UNIVERSITY GIRLS *

2005. JPN: *Joshidai H Sodanshitsu*. AKA: *Female Student Perverse Consultation Room*. Video. DIR: N/C. SCR: N/C. DES: N/C. ANI: N/C. MUS: N/C. PRD: Obtain. 30 mins.

Schoolgirl, sorry, college student Madoka

goes to see her counselor for advice on her studies, only to find herself submitting to a series of sexual advances. Compare to **DESPERATE CARNAL HOUSEWIVES**, which has the same basic premise. **Ⓝ**

UNKNOWN GIRLFRIEND, THE *

2008. JPN: *Kemeko-DX*. AKA: *Kemeko Deluxe*. TV series. DIR: Tsutomu Mizushima. SCR: Yoshimi Narita. DES: Isao Sugimoto, Yoji Yoshikawa. ANI: Goro Sessha, Yuhei Mitsui. MUS: Ryuji Takagi. PRD: Hal Film Maker, AC Create, Askey Media Works, Geneon, Klockworx, Yomiuri Advertising, YTV. 24 mins. x 12 eps.

A teenage boy is reminiscing about his first love, a pink-haired girl he met when they were just children (**ROMANCE AND DRAMA**). Suddenly a strange cute-style robot bursts into his room and announces that she is his wife. The pilot emerges, a pink-haired girl who looks like a grown-up version of the girl our hero Sanpeita fell in love with all those years ago. And this is just the beginning of an avalanche of clichés, more than enough to engulf a better show than this one. Shows like **HARE + GUU** can handle clichés and make them part of the humor; that doesn't happen here. Based on the 2006 manga by Masakazu Iwasaki, the show is just as packed with nods and winks to the older fanboy audience as it is with clichés: costumes from **EVANGELION** and **LA BLUE GIRL**, references to **FLCL** and **STREET FIGHTER II**, lines from **SOUL EATER**, plus a parody of classic Hollywood movies and a few frames of footage from another anime. That might keep you awake. **Ⓝ**

UNKO-SAN JUNJOHA

2010. AKA: *Shit Naïve School*. TV series. DIR: Hasama Iya. SCR: Fue Tsuna, Yorimitsu Sakamoto. DES: MAD BARBARIANS. ANI: Misae Honma, Kokoro Tsutsumi. MUS: The Singing Heroes. PRD: Iyasakado Film. 3 mins. x 13 eps.

On a legendary island shaped like an unusually regular turd, a population of turd-people and insanely aggressive animals go about their hilarity-packed day to day lives. Central character Yoshiko Un is known as Unko-san, but you're unlikely to meet her—the island appears only to the fortunate few, to whom they give good luck. Created by Katsuya Saito and Masumi Ito of MAD BARBARIANS, a group they founded in 2000 to create characters for marketing and merchandising purposes around the key concepts of MAD, POP, ROCK, CUTE. They had an exhibition in Los Angeles in 2008 as part of their plan for world domination—or so claims their website. These little turds were widely merchandised as part of a trend for jokey "good luck" mascots. **◑**

UNTIL THE MOONRISE

1991. JPN: *Takeda Tetsuya no Tsuki ga Noboru made ni* AKA: *Tetsuya Takeda, Until the Moonrise; Tsuki ga Noboru made ni*. Video. DIR: Eiichi Yamamoto. SCR: Eiichi Yamamoto. DES: Kazuo Tomozawa. ANI: Kazuo Tomozawa, Sai Imazaki, Neri Mimana. MUS: N/C. PRD: Grouper Productions. 40 mins.

A father and daughter in Japan climb to the top of a ridge to watch the moonrise. As they wait, an old man tells them his story. An adaptation of Tetsuya Takeda's story about the relationship between a Japanese child and an American soldier.

UNTIL THE UNDERSEA CITY

1969. JPN: *Kaitei Toshi no Dekiru made (31 Nen go no Nihon)*. AKA: *Until the Undersea City: Japan in 31 Years*. TV special. DIR: Eiichi Yamamoto, Yusaku Sakamoto. SCR: Tadaaki Yamazaki. DES: Shuji Kimura. ANI: Jiro Fujimoto. MUS: N/C. PRD: Mushi, Nippon TV. 45 mins.

Taro Yamamoto has devoted his life to designing an undersea city. In 1972, he joins Tokyo Electronics, where he meets and eventually marries the pretty submariner Kazuko. He moves out to Tama New Town (see POM POKO) and is present at the launch of the submarine Mambo in 1983. In 1986, construction finally begins on the undersea city of Oceanacopia. It is completed in 1997, and three years later, in the futuristic-sounding year of 2000, Taro finally gets to gaze on his creation.

URAHATA, TATSUHIKO

1963–. Born in Wakayama Prefecture, he joined Madhouse in 1983 as a writer. His subsequent scripts have included RAIL OF THE STAR and HIT HARD, DREAMERS!

URBAN SQUARE

1985. JPN: *Urban Square Kohaku no Tsuigeki*. AKA: *Urban Square: Chasing Amber*. Video. DIR: Akira Nishimori. SCR: Kazunori Ito. DES: Akemi Takada, Chiharu Sato. ANI:

Hideyuki Motohashi. MUS: Chicken Chuck. PRD: Network. 55 mins.

Ryu Matsumoto is a screenwriter who sees a murder in Kobe, but his testimony is ignored by police because the body has vanished without a trace. Eager to prove he's not crazy and worried that he may have attracted the attention of the murderers, Ryu hires private detective Mochizuki to protect him and investigate. Similarities with cult live-action movie *Blow-Up* (1966) are unlikely to be coincidental. **◐**

URDA: THE THIRD REICH *

2003. AKA: *Urda*. Online series. DIR: Romanov (Kazuhiro) Higa. SCR: Romanov Higa. DES: Romanov Higa, Tetsuya Watanabe. ANI: Romanov Higa. MUS: Junki Shimizu. PRD: Romanov Films. 5 mins. x 5 eps.

In the summer of 1943, Nazis in Europe uncover a crashed spaceship that allows them to manipulate time and change the course of the war—a hackneyed concept in science fiction, but one that achieved new prominence in Asia with the release of the Korean-Japanese alternate history movie *2009: Lost Memories* (2002). Hitler sets up the URDA project to exploit the technology, and the Allies send in spy Erna Kurtz. Ex-commando Erna uncovers the plot and finds that she is already closely linked to it through her relationship to project commander Glimhild Kurtz. She tries to rescue the young girl who is the subject of the URDA tests—and claims to be from the future. This one-man show with an almost entirely unknown cast is a prime example of how the Internet is changing the way we get our entertainment. Made in CGI but intended to look like full cel animation, its only link with the anime establishment is the presence of designer, producer, and director Watanabe, who also has a background in CGI, but is here credited with the design of the vehicles. The short format works well for streaming and new platforms like mobile phones, but it takes a very skillful director to do anything other than make eye candy in such a restricted timeslot. A generation with its attention span attuned to MTV is unlikely to worry about such details as depth of character and plot development, but those who love anime for the freedom it gives the writer have legitimate cause for concern and may be reassured by this

confident debut, which packs a lot into its tiny parcels. The *URDA* series was also cut together and shown as a "movie" at the Tokyo International Film Festival in 2005. Compare to VOICES OF A DISTANT STAR and LEGEND OF DUO, both of which also showcase potential new directions for the anime world in the early 21st century. **◐◑**

URIQPEN: ANIMAL RESCUE LEAGUE *

1974. JPN: *Uriqpen Kyudotai*. TV series. DIR: Hiroshi Sasagawa, Seitaro Hara. SCR: Jinzo Toriumi. DES: Akio Sugino. ANI: Jun Tanaka. MUS: Shunsuke Kikuchi. PRD: Tatsunoko, Fuji TV. 5 mins. x 156 eps. (also broadcast as 26 different 30-min. strips).

Four young animals, rabbit Seitaro Usagi, squirrel Risu, bear Kuma, and penguin Penguin (U-Ri-Ku-Pen), are part of a team of brave young animals that rescues others in peril—a sort of animal THUNDERBIRDS 2086. Other team members included a dog, a boar, a deer, a koala, a mouse, a seagull, and a lion, but the title would have become too unwieldy even for such a long-running show if they'd all been included in the acronym, although it would have been fun listening to announcers say, "And now, it's time for *Uriqpen-inu-bu-shi-ko-nezu-kamome-shi*." The animals would win a prize for completing a mission, as would the viewers, who were encouraged to write in and guess which of the creatures would save the world by each Friday (a single mission stretched over a week of TV). Created by Mitsuru Kaneko, this show was given a limited broadcast on some American local TV stations for the Japanese community.

UROTSUKIDOJI *

1987. JPN: *Chojin Densetsu Urotsukidoji*. AKA: *Legend of the Overfiend: Wandering Child; Wandering Kid*. Video, movie. DIR: Hideki Takayama. SCR: Sho Aikawa, Goro Sanyo, et al. DES: Rikizo Sekimae, Shiro Kasami, Keiichi Sato, Keiji Goto, Tetsuya Yanasawa. ANI: Tetsuya Yanasawa. MUS: Masamichi Amano. PRD: JAVN, Angel. 45 mins., 55 mins., 55 mins. (v1, *U1*), 55 mins., 50 mins. (v1 part 2), 108 mins. (m1, *U1*), 88 mins. (*U2*), 60 mins., 50 mins., 50 mins. (v3, aka *U3*), ca. 80 mins. (m3, aka *U3*), 40 mins. x 3 eps. (v4, aka *U4*), ca. 40 mins. (v5, aka *U5*), 45 mins. x 3 eps. (v6, aka *The Urotsuki*).

Every three thousand years, a superbeing is born who will unite the three separate dimensions of humans, demons, and Jujin "man-beasts," bringing about a new world. Man-beast Amanojaku is determined to track down this "Chojin," and after 300 years of wandering, locates demonic forces at work in 1993 Japan. Teenager Nagumo impregnates schoolgirl Akemi, rupturing the fabric of the universe and ushering in the apocalypse. Akemi goes into hibernation for a century to await the birth of her child (the Chojin), and Earth is ravaged by a nuclear war. Decades later, in a Japan ruled by former industrialist Caesar, the Chojin is born early because of the arrival in Tokyo of his diametrical opposite, the Kyo-O (translated variously as Mad King, or Lord of Chaos). Buju, a man-beast hybrid, elopes with Caesar's daughter, Alecto, and finds the Kyo-O in a temple shortly before he is killed. Buju is brought back to life by the Kyo-O (a young girl called Himi whose growth is rapidly accelerated) and overthrows Caesar. He vows to take Himi to Osaka to confront the Chojin. Despite the efforts of the Chojin to stop him, he eventually succeeds— Chojin drinks a drop of the blood from Himi's first menstruation, and the world is restored to normality.

Based on the violent and pornographic 1985 manga by Toshio Maeda for *Wani* magazine, **Urotsukidoji** is the best-known of the anime "nasties" released in English in the 1990s. A fiercely complex cycle of rape and redemption, it even seems to have confused its Japanese crew—the first three episodes take place in Osaka, the next two are set *before* the third episode, with the same characters inexplicably moved to Tokyo. This leap backward seems designed to incorporate the Kyo-O subplot, vital to the rest of the series, but unnecessary if the series were to end early; though considering that the series has an eschatologically cyclical plot (like its contemporary **Gall Force**), it is conceivable that one is set several eons after the other! Perplexity continued in the English-language market, where the series was dubbed by three different companies using different actors and contradictory translations. The first five-part video series was edited into the two "movies," *Legend of the Overfiend* and *Legend of the Demon Womb*. Note that *Demon Womb* was numbered in Roman numerals as "Urotsukidoji II,"

thereby causing the *second* series, *Return of the Overfiend*, to gain the misleading numeral of *Urotsukidoji III*. In the U.S. all five video episodes appeared, numbered 1 to 5 in order of release, to add to the confusion. The massive and (to the Japanese originators) completely unexpected success of the series in English led to the making of two sequels. The four-part *Return of the Overfiend* (1993) featured the postholocaust chapters, followed by *Inferno Road* (1995), which concludes the saga in three parts. However, though the series is complete in the U.S., *Inferno Road* was delayed by the British censor for three years. Eventually, the final chapter alone was permitted a release in 2001—the British DVD sheepishly includes the scripts of the banned episodes to compensate. *Urotsukidoji V: The Final Chapter* (1996) is a mysterious curio in the history of the saga, intended as the first installment of yet another series. Despite being abandoned partway through production, with some of the animation still jerky and incomplete, it was nonetheless released in Japan and Germany and claims to introduce the real Chojin at last, dropping many of the newer characters and returning to a continuity that seems to owe more to the earlier episodes of the series. This, however, could have made no difference—as with some installments of **Gall Force**, the ending of *Urotsukidoji IV* implied that some characters had been shoved back through a time or dimensional loop, and hence would be reexperiencing certain elements of the saga again, albeit with some changes.

The story was remade again as *Urotsukidoji: New Saga* (aka *The Urotsuki*, 2002), a three-part video series made as part of the erotic **Vanilla Series**. In a return to the subject matter and characters of the original series, Amanojaku evades prison and hides out at a Japanese high school; along with the usual sex and violence, there is an increased concentration, in the style of *Inferno Road*, on the childhoods of the protagonists, designed to show how they might grow up into the kind of beastly people they ultimately turn out to be. In this version, the Chojin is renamed the Ultra God.

Urotsukidoji amply achieves Maeda's overriding narrative aim—to demonstrate that the only way to win in this world

is to die young before your dreams are shattered. The question for his critics, in both the pro- and anticensorship lobbies, is whether the poetry of the end justifies the gross extremity of the means. Since *Urotsukidoji*, many other Maeda works have been adapted, including **Demon Beast Invasion**, **Adventure Kid**, **La Blue Girl**, **Nightmare Campus**, and **Demon Warrior Koji**. Though the *Urotsukidoji* saga is now complete in manga form, recent spin-offs have included stories of the Chojin's earlier manifestations in human history, leaving a rich vein of material for potential further anime installments. Scenes from *Urotsukidoji*, **MD Geist**, and **Perfect Blue** were shown onstage as part of Madonna's *Drowned World* tour in 2001. **LNV**

URUSEI YATSURA *

1981. AKA: *Those Obnoxious Aliens; Weird Folk from Planet Uru; Noisy People.* TV series, movie, video. DIR: Mamoru Oshii, Keiji Hayakawa, Tameo Ogawa, Kazuo Yamazaki, Satoshi Dezaki, Katsuhisa Yamada, Setsuko Shibuichi. SCR: Hiroyuki Hoshiyama, Masaru Yamamoto, Shunsuke Kaneko, Ichiro Itabashi, Takao Koyama, Kazunori Ito, Michiru Shimada, Tomoko Konparu, Hideo Takayashiki. DES: Akemi Takada, Torao Arai, Setsuko Shibuichi, Kumiko Takahashi. ANI: Katsumi Aoshima, Yuichi Endo, Tsukasa Dokite, Yukari Kobayashi, Kumiko Takahashi. MUS: Shinsuke Kazato, Izumi Kobayashi, Fumitaka Anzai, Masamichi Amano, Toshiyuki Omori, Mitsuru Kotaki. PRD: Studio Pierrot, Kitty Films, Fuji TV. 25 mins. x 218 eps. (TV), 101 mins., 98 mins., 90 mins., 95 mins., 85 mins., 77 mins. (m), 45 mins. x 2 eps., 57 mins., 30 mins. x 2 eps., 25 mins. x 6 eps. (v).

The alien Oni race decide to invade Earth but offer to leave if Earth's champion can defeat theirs at a game of tag. But the randomly selected Earth champion is Ataru Moroboshi, a hapless Japanese teenage lecher. Racing the beautiful Princess Lum, Ataru tricks her by stealing her bikini top and wins the game. Earth is saved, but he has gained an alien fiancée living in his closet. She may be sexy, but she has the power to electrocute him if he goes near another girl and is fiercely jealous of his many love interests, including his Earth-girl paramour, Shinobu.

One of Western **Fandom**'s favorites,

based on the 1978 *Shonen Sunday* manga by Rumiko Takahashi, this romantic comedy mixes sci-fi with JAPANESE FOLK TALES and suburban life. Takahashi has a dark side, but she keeps it for her horror stories like MERMAID'S FOREST; in most of her work, creatures of all planets share the same failings and desires, and there is more of a gulf between male and female than there can ever be between human and alien.

The TV series (sadly showing its age in terms of animation quality) introduces us to Lum, her unlikely beloved Ataru, the unluckiest, laziest, and most lecherous boy on Earth, and their associates, including his helplessly uncomprehending parents, her dreamboat ex-boyfriend, Rei, her bratty cousin, Ten-chan, and her many pretty friends. The original series is loaded with topical domestic humor in the manner of a Japanese *Simpsons*, but though little of this survives TRANSLATION, the fresh, funny slapstick and situations do, along with an educational quantity unforeseen by the original filmmakers. *UY*'s depiction of mundane *Japanese* life is a window onto a culture alien to many Western fans, a fact cleverly exploited in the studiously annotated subtitled releases from AnimEigo. The TV series is a delight from beginning to end and absolutely deserves its fan-favorite status; its stablemate RANMA ½, originally made for an audience too young to remember the early *UY*, has attained a similar status simply by copying it.

The movies and videos are all variations on the same theme—love, and the crazy deceptions we play in its name. The first two movies are directed by GHOST IN THE SHELL's Mamoru Oshii and designed by Kazuo Yamazaki. *Only You* (1983) introduces another alien fiancée for Ataru, and shows Lum's desperate attempts to save him from walking to the altar with Elle, a girl who rules a planet with décor straight out of a rose-strewn Harlequin fantasy. In the surreal *Beautiful Dreamer* (1984), the characters are caught up in Ataru's recurring dream, enabling Oshii to play with perceptions of reality within the conventional format of a romantic comedy. Yamazaki moved up to direct *Remember My Love* (1985) with character designs by Takada. This tale of transdimensional travel, obsessive love, and the line between childhood and adulthood remains, for all its lunatic

wrappings (such as Ataru transformed into a pink hippo and a Bradburyesque nightmare circus that later showed up in NEO-TOKYO and SAILOR MOON), the purest SF story ever achieved by the *UY* team. *Lum the Forever* (1986) was again directed by Yamazaki and designed by Takeda, with DIRTY PAIR's Dokite directing the animation. The gang is making a film, with Lum as the star, but all the surrounding activity, including the cutting down of an ancient cherry tree, has awakened a curse that may change their lives forever and lead to the loss of the things they value most. *UY The Final Chapter* (1988, *Kanketsuhen*) puts the romantic boot on the other foot; instead of Ataru running after some cute girl, Lum is carried off by an alien hunk named Lupa, to whom, it appears, her grandfather promised her in marriage when she was still a baby. Neither Ataru nor Carla (Lupa's girlfriend) is pleased, and the chaos culminates in yet another game of tag to decide the fate of Earth. Dezaki directed Konparu's screenplay with designs by Shibuichi. Typically, the "final chapter" wasn't—the last *UY* movie was actually *Always (Itsudatte) My Darling* (1991), made when *UY* had been supplanted on TV by *Ranma*, reversing the previous plot for a kidnap tale in which Ataru is carried off by an alien princess named Lupica, and Lum sets out to get him back with a little help from biker goddess Benten and snow princess Oyuki. It was made by a new team, with Yamada in the director's chair, Takayashiki joining Konparu on screenplay, another Takahashi (Kumiko) designing and directing the animation, and music from Koteki.

The ever-increasing cost of movie-making coincided with the rise of the video format that started with DALLOS in 1983, leading to changes in release formats. In 1986, the Japanese *UY* fan club began screening "exclusive" mini-movies at public events, soon revealed to be advance copies of the straight-to-video *UY* releases *Ryoko's September Tea Party* and *Memorial Album*. Both stories used flashback footage from the series with about 15 minutes of new framing animation to recount the past history of the characters and episodes from the story line—a useful way of hooking new video buyers to boost TV series sales on video. A new story, *Inaba The Dream*

Maker (1987), featured a transdimensional white rabbit and answered the question of what happens when you unlock doors in time and space without knowing where they lead. Next up was the insanely funny *Raging Sherbet* (1988), in which flying alien ice-cream cones carry out kamikaze revenge attacks on Lum's greedy girlfriend Ran. Ghost love story *Nagisa's Fiancé* appeared the same year. Then 1989 brought four new romantic comedy stories. *I Howl at the Moon* has Ataru gobbling Lum's cooking and turning into a wolf. *Catch the Heart* has hard-nosed Ran involved in chaos when a spirit gives her a candy that makes capturing the heart of the one you love a breeze. *Goat and Cheese* shows the problems of ancient and incomprehensible family curses when Mendo's father breaks one by taking a picture in front of the statue of great-grandfather's goat, and *The Electric Household Guard* gives Mendo a new servant with eyes only for his sister, Kyoko. In 1991 the series was rounded off with *Terror of Girly-eye Measles*, in which Ataru's womanizing ways spread an alien virus all over town, and *Date with a Spirit*, in which he tries to date a pretty ghost haunting sorceress Sakura's fiancé. An improvisational dub of two episodes by minor British celebrities was screened as *Lum the Invader Girl* (2000) as part of a "Japan Night" on a U.K. digital channel, BBC Choice (now BBC Three).

URUSHIHARA, SATOSHI

1966–. Sometimes credited as Satoshi Urushibara. Although briefly employed by Toei Animation, Urushibara soon went freelance, peddling his distinctive illustration work as a character designer for games and anime, and was founder of the manga studio Ars Work (*sic*). ANOTHER LADY INNOCENT is representative of his style—a master with flesh tones and the female form, which has often led him to erotica such as TALES OF…, where his talents seem best employed. Attempts have also been made to put him to work in more mainstream areas, such as LEGEND OF LEMNEAR or PLASTIC LITTLE, but his best-known successes are probably as a designer on the *Langrisser* and *Glowlancer* computer games.

USAVICH

2006. TV series. DIR: Satoshi Tomioka.
SCR: Satoshi Tomioka. DES: Aguri Miyazaki,
Satoshi Tomioka. ANI: Satoshi Tomioka. MUS:
Hironori Ueno. PRD: Kanaban Graphics, MTV
Japan, Viacom. 90 secs. x 13 eps. (TV1),
90 secs. x 13 eps. (TV2), 90 secs. x 13 eps.
(TV3), 90 secs. x 13 eps. (TV4), 90 secs. x
13 eps. (TV5).

Prison Break crashed into *Tom and Jerry* and
set in 1962, in a Soviet Union populated
by rabbits: that's *Usavich,* and it's utterly,
mind-blowingly, insanely brilliant. Hapless
Putin and laid-back Kirenenko are two
prisoners of the State. We don't know their
crime but we do know they're as crazy as
the system that imprisons them—well,
almost. We follow them through their
escape with a gender-dysmorphic chick
and a frog, their life on the run, and their
increasingly demented adventures. Maybe
Prison Break is a less helpful comparison
than the surreal, politically motivated
1960s British series *The Prisoner*, the focus
on action emerging from character is just
as intense.

Satoshi Tomioka is known for his
astonishing CGI animation. He graduated
from Tokyo University of Agriculture and
Technology and joined CGI animation
studio Dream Pictures in 2002, setting up
his own company, Kanaban Graphics, the
same year. He worked with Katsuhiko Ishii
on HAL AND BONS, and made prizewinning
short films alongside his day job making
commercials. In 2006 MTV commissioned
the first series of *Usavich*, cocreated with
Agura Miyazaki. Further series from the
same team followed in 2007, 2008, 2011,
and 2012, perfectly formed bite-size packages of intelligent fun that every animator
could learn from and every animation fan
can enjoy.

USELESS ANIMALS

2005. JPN: *Damekko Dobutsu*. TV series. DIR:
Setsuko Shibuichi. SCR: Mitsuyo Suenaga.
DES: Yukari Kobayashi. ANI: Yukari Kobayashi.
MUS: Tsunta Kobayashi. PRD: Magic Bus, Kid's
Station. 5 mins. x 26 eps.

When he is not found to be suitably
savage or lupine in demeanor, Uruno
is declared to be a useless wolf and cast
out. He wanders the world until he finds
the Useless Forest, populated solely by
animals that have similarly failed to live up
to their stereotypes. This, however, is not
all good—a near-sighted owl may be no
threat, but Uruno is threatened and ha-
rangued by a bad-tempered rabbit whose
"useless" quality is to be violent, not cute at
all, and rather dangerous. However, he is
tempted to stay in the forest when he falls
for the cute cheetah Chiiko, in an anime
that mixes the out-of-character anthro-
pomorphics of ON A STORMY NIGHT with a
cast that often resembles children dressed
up as animals for a kindergarten play.
Nor are the animals "realistic" in our own
sense, since there is space in the Useless
Forest for fantasy creatures like an alcoholic unicorn and a timid winged horse.
Beneath the cutesy subtext is a staple of
many Japanese movies and live-action TV
serials—a group of comical no-hopers
somehow finding their way in life through
their friendship.

USHIO AND TORA *

1992. JPN: *Ushio to Tora*. Video. DIR: Kunihiko
Yuyama. SCR: Kenji Terada, Kunihiko Yuyama.
DES: Tokuhiro Matsubara. ANI: Tokuhiro Matsubara. MUS: Shiro Sagisu. PRD: Pastel, Toho.
30 mins. x 11 eps.

Ushio Aotsuki is the grandson of a priest
and guardian of an ancient temple,
where (so he is told) the malevolent spirit
Nagatobimaru (Lord Long-Flyer) has been
imprisoned for centuries, impaled on the
magical Spear of Beast. He discovers the
old legends are true when he inadvertently
releases the spirit. Invisible to others, Tora
(as Ushio calls Nagatobimaru) claims he
would dearly love to eat Ushio but cannot
get close to him while Ushio hangs onto
the spear. The second-sight provided by
the spear allows Ushio to see a whole
world of spirits living amid our own, and,
in an unlikely team with Tora, he sets out
busting ghosts in the neighborhood. These
include a stone centipede in a school
storeroom, sickle-carrying weasels, a group
of flying heads, and floating clouds of bad
vibes.

Combining a reluctant-buddies/un-
welcome-guest plot with modern rewrites
of JAPANESE FOLK TALES, *U&T* began as a
1990 *Shonen Sunday* manga by Kazuhiro
Fujita, only parts of which are adapted
here. Despite the obvious potential for a
long-running TV series (the manga tops
30 volumes), *U&T* stayed on video and
fizzled out in the mid-1990s, while its inferior contemporary TENCHI MUYO! ripped
off its premise and, presumably, found a
more enduring audience by swapping the
ghostbusting for interminable flirting. The
show comes laden with arch observations
on modern Japan in the style of POM
POKO—the samurai-era Tora cannot eat today's people because they daub themselves
with sickly perfumes; the sickle-weasels
must disguise themselves as humans to survive; and a sea monster made of drowned
souls is rendered invulnerable by modern
pollution. As in DEVIL HUNTER YOHKO, new
construction disturbs the ancient dead,
while modern children are their inheritors
and saviors—Ushio is the descendant of a
warrior-mage, and his friend Mayuko the
reincarnation of an exorcist. This anime
also features some unexpected changes
of tone—despite their antagonism, Ushio
and Tora complement each other like
signs of the Chinese zodiac (*ushi*/ox and
tora/tiger), and it is Ushio who leaps to
Tora's defense when he is pursued by
talisman master Piao, a Cantonese exorcist
who mistakenly believes Tora killed
his family. Similarly, while Ushio spars
constantly with local tomboy Asako, he is
prepared to fight for her against Tsubura,
the spirit of a water wheel who wishes to
carry her away (this episode is the only
one not taken directly from the manga).
The series ends with a spoof episode, the
C[omical] D[eforme] Theater, in which cartoon versions of the characters fight, sing
songs, and eventually appear in their own
zany silent movie. There was also an audio
spin-off on the *U&T Original Album*, which
featured music "inspired by" the series
from Seikima-II guitarist Ace Shimizu (see
HUMANE SOCIETY).

A welcome antidote to the teen wish-
fulfillment pap that dominated much of
the anime market throughout the 1990s,
U&T is by turns funny, exciting, and
reflective, distinguished by two separate
translations, of which the U.S. version by
ADV is the superior. **LV**

UTA NO PRINCE-SAMA: MAJI LOVE
1000% *

2011. AKA: *Prince's Song: Maji Love 1000%*;
UtaPuri. TV series. DIR: Yu Ko. SCR: Tomoko
Konparu, Michiru Shimada, Makoto Naka-
mura. DES: Mitsue Mori, Saho Yamane. ANI:

Mitsue Mori. mus: Elements Garden. prd: A-1 Pictures, Broccoli, Dwango, MOVIC, Showgate, Starchild Records. 25 mins. x 13 eps. (TV1), 25 mins. x 12 eps. (TV2).

Haruka wants to be a songwriter, because a song helped her at a difficult time in her life. She's delighted to win a place at a top performing arts academy with a guaranteed agency placement if she graduates. The headmaster was a famous singer, her homeroom teacher is a current idol, and the place is packed with young, beautiful talent. Normally, every aspiring writer is paired with a potential idol—but Haruka finds herself with six gorgeous "princes of song" as her partners. The only snag is that she's not allowed to date any of them. You heard the harem alert ringing: but before you make for the emergency exit, you might want to check out a show that revels in its stereotype. The clichés of palatial school, cookie-cutter harem boys, vivid colors, and relentlessly perky J-pop are executed with determined precision. OURAN HIGH SCHOOL HOST CLUB or MASK OF GLASS it's not, but if you know any preteen girls (or if you remember being a fan of The Osmonds), *Prince's Song* may appeal. The show was based on a 2010 manga created by Kanon Kunozuki with art and story by Utako Yukihiro. It had enough charm for the local audience to get a second series, *Prince's Song: Maji Love 2000%*, in 2013.

UTA—KATA *

2004. aka: *One Song/Poem Piece*. dir: Keiji Goto. scr: Hidefumi Kimura. des: Megumi Kadonosono. ani: Akiko Nagashima, Koichiro Ueda. mus: Harumi Ono. prd: TV Kanagawa, Bandai Visual, gimik, HAL Filmmaker. 24 mins. x 12 eps. (TV), 30 mins. (v).

In a reprise of the premise of E-CHAN THE NINJA, Japanese schoolgirl Ichika stares into a mirror to discover another girl staring back at her. Her new companion is Manatsu (lit.:: "Midsummer"), who grants her magical powers that will only last for the summer, in an allegory of the end of childhood and one last vacation before the responsibilities of the grown-up world start to impinge—compare to MAHOROMATIC. However, all is not sweetness and light, as there are hints that this has happened before and that Ichika is the target of a mysterious plot conceived by the woman next door. A number of well-known manga

illustrators, including Ken Akamatsu and Koshi Rikudo, provide "guest" designs for the costumes into which Ichika changes in each episode.

A one-shot video sequel followed, *Twin Summers of the First Winter* (2005, *Shoto no Futanatsu*) in which Satsuki, believing herself to be alone once more, encounters an apparent doppelgänger of Manatsu during the winter. The new girl claims to be Mafuyu (or "Midwinter"), in a rather pointless rehash that to some minds betrays the elegiac quality of the original series—if everything can be reset and reprised à la TENCHI MUYO!, where's the drama?

UTAWARERUMONO *

2006. aka: *The Song of Dreams*; *The One Being Sung*. TV, video. dir: Tomoki Kobayashi, Kenichiro Katsura. scr: Makoto Uezu, Takamitsu Kono. des: Masahiko Nakata, Kenji Kato, Kenichiro Katsura, Toshiki Nishi. ani: Tomohiro Koyama, Masahiko Nakata, Shinichi Yoshino, Yumenosuke Tokuda, Kenichiro Katsura, Yasuyuki Noda. mus: Hijiri Anze, Miyu Nakamura. prd: Oriental Light and Magic, AQUAPLUS, Chaos Project, Frontier Works. 23 mins. x 26 eps. (TV), 30 mins. x 3 eps. (v).

A mysterious masked man is found in the forest, injured and with no memory of who he is and how he came to be there. His bony mask cannot be removed, but a family of healers takes him in, and their small village welcomes him. A wicked emperor is oppressing the land and forces of magic and nature are awake. Hakuoro, as his rescuers name him, sets out to defend those who have become his family and soon finds himself leading the nation against evil.

This is a formulaic fantasy show whose main selling point is the impressively realized world that unfolds with the story. Unfortunately the characters and plot lack similar depth, making *Utawarerumono* forgettable unless you're a fan of AQUAPLUS, creators of this erotic game/visual novel franchise (ARGOT AND JARGON). The anime is based on a 2005 manga spun off the game by Aro Shimakusa. A three-part video telling stories not included in the TV series appeared in 2009 under the same title.

The show was involved in a copyright controversy in 2010. Nippon Kanko Sho-

kai, a company providing art and promotional materials for the tourism industry, withdrew artwork allegedly traced from a number of franchises including *Utawarerumono*, K-ON, and THE MELANCHOLY OF HARUHI SUZUMIYA.

UTENA *

1997. jpn: *Shojo Kakumei Utena*. aka: *Revolutionary Girl Utena*; *La Fillette Revolutionnaire Utena*; *Ursula's Kiss*. TV series, movie. dir: Kunihiko Ikuhara, Shingo Kaneko, Toru Takahashi, Tatsuo Okazaki, Akihiko Nishiyama, Katsushi Sakurabi, Takafumi Hoshikawa, Shigeo Koshi, Hiroaki Sakurai. scr: Yoji Enokido, Noboru Higa, Kazuhiro Uemura, Ryoei Tsukimura. des: Chiho Saito, Shinya Hasegawa. ani: Shinya Hasegawa, Tomoko Kawasaki, Yuji Matsukura. mus: Shinkichi Mitsumune, J.A. Seazar. prd: Be-Papas, JC Staff, TV Tokyo. 25 mins. x 39 eps. (TV), 85 mins. (m).

Pink-haired tomboy Utena Tenjo (a surname infuriatingly mispronounced throughout the U.S. dub) is an eighth grader at Otori Academy. She clings to the memory of her childhood encounter with a mysterious "prince" as she wept by the grave of her parents. Though she cannot remember his face (refer to CANDY CANDY), she treasures the rose signet ring he gave her and, for reasons not totally clear, resolves to dress and behave as a boy until she finds him again.

Otori is a teen fantasy, where teachers live in fear of the student council and sputter impotently at pupils' "witty" comebacks, the boys and girls are all beautiful, and dueling is the number-one occupation. Fencers regularly meet for ritual combat within a gargantuan hall (part of the school, yet also a separate dimension), where they fight for the right to the hand of Anthy, the "Rose Bride" whose body is a living sheath for a sword. Victorious in battle, Utena becomes Anthy's betrothed, though the student council do what they can to topple her because they are searching for the ultimate duelist who will summon forth the divine power known as "Dios."

Portentous and pretentious in equal amounts, *Utena* quite literally invests teenage crushes and schoolgirl intrigues with world-shattering significance. Created by director Ikuhara, with several other staffers from his earlier SAILOR MOONS, and Chiho Saito, who drew the *Utena* manga for *Ciao* magazine, it artfully perverts mundane school life into a quest of fantastic proportions. It also features swordplay and cross-dressing in the swashbuckling tradition of PRINCESS KNIGHT and ROSE OF VERSAILLES, to which it owes a heavy aesthetic debt. Director Ikuhara acknowledges a strong influence from TRAGEDY OF BELLADONNA, the film that inspired him to work in anime. Like the tarot-themed episodes of ESCAFLOWNE, *Utena* presents its heroine with a series of subtext-laden duels to test her mettle, forging her into a suitable messiah. Highly sensual though rarely explicit, its premise is ironically close to that of an UROTSUKIDOJI that replaces sex and violence with pure, infinite yearning. On Japanese TV, *Utena* thrived in the vacuum left by the conclusion of EVANGELION, though it was not without controversy—in a ludicrous outbreak of racism, the TV Tokyo switchboard received complaints that love interest Anthy was "black."

Many better-known fairy tales are mixed and matched with situation comedy: one character proudly displays a "designer pendant" that is nothing more than a cowbell, then slowly transforms into a cow before the others' eyes. In another, tomboy Utena and twee Anthy swap personalities after a particularly hot curry. Amid all the school high jinks, the central story continues, as girls pine for their princes, boys for their princesses, and a plot with the vague aims of "bringing revolution and attaining eternity" advances ever onward. Ikuhara brings sensibilities and themes from his own *Sailor Moon S* episodes to this unlikely confection of swords and roses, mirroring the rollercoaster of teenage emotions in a whirl of seductive imagery. Unlike SLAY-

ERS, which mixes "real" elements into its fantasy world for comic effect, *Utena* coats the real world in fantasy but lets the sharp edges show through. Beautiful clothes and skill with a sword can't ward off the pain of inadequacy and loss—though they certainly *look* good. The series too places increasing emphasis on style over substance as it progresses, becoming ever more surreal, with additional digital effects in the last season.

The movie *Adolescence of Utena* (1999) offers a retelling of the story in a fantasy that summarizes its main themes in a succession of vignettes rather than providing a logical conclusion. It's therefore incomprehensible to anyone who has not seen the preceding series; a hallucinogenic whirl of tortured relationships, floating roses, flying cars, flashing blades, and gorgeous costumes.

UTSUNOMIKO

1989. AKA: *Celestial Prince*. Movie, video. DIR: Fumio Kurokawa (m), Tetsuo Imazawa (v). SCR: Kenji Terada, Sukehiro Tomita (m), Junji Takegami, Sukehiro Tomita (v). DES: Mutsumi Inomata (m), Teruyoshi Yamazaki (v). ANI: Chuichi Iguchi, Kazuya Kise. MUS: Kunihiro Kawano (m), Masahiro Kawasaki (v). PRD: Nippon Animation, Toei Animation. 83 mins. (m1), 30 mins. x 13 eps., 75 mins. (m2). Based on Keisuke Fujikawa's novel of mythical 7th-century Japan, the first movie, subtitled *Earth Chapter*, introduces the divine child Utsunomiko, born with a tiny horn on his head but otherwise a normal mystic hero. Trained with a group of friends by the mysterious priest Ojino, he is a fine fighter but will only ever use a bamboo staff. When the group is forced to fight a cruel overlord and his diabolical allies, they must prove their courage and strength to save their friends. In the

video series, subtitled *Heaven Chapter*, Imazawa used Inomata's designs but completely changed the staff. Yamazaki redesigned the characters, and new music was provided by Kawasaki. Ojino gives the friends a magic Phoenix ship that takes them to heaven, but Utsunomiko finds the gods can be just as cruel as humans, and he fights them for the rights of the people, eventually changing into his god-form as the only way to win and finally meet his father, the supreme lord of heaven. The clash between the "new" Buddhist practices and native Shinto spirits, as well as the civil disorders of the time, form the backdrop to a series of richly designed adventures, and the video animation is (unusually) better than that of the 1988 film, allowing for better appreciation of the subtlety of Inomata's work. The 1990 film *U: Heaven Chapter* was a short reworking of the video series.

UTSURUN DESU

2009. Video. DIR: Mankyu. SCR: N/C. DES: N/C. ANI: N/C. MUS: N/C. PRD: Utsurun Desu Production Committee, Toho. 30 mins. x 3 eps. An adaptation of Sensha Yoshida's four-panel nonsense gag manga, which ran from 1989 to 1994, this anime follows the same pattern, telling surreal jokes through a series of strange characters led by an otter with a man's face (or a man in an otter suit), a human-faced fly, a mushroom in a red muffler, and many more. Norio Wakamoto of GUNBUSTER fame is among the voice cast; director Mankyu also made gag manga spin-off WITH THE LORDS. This was made for streaming to mobile phones by NicoNico Douga before appearing on DVD. A 1992 live-action video written by Yoshida and directed by Keizo Kira and Norikazu Tanaka also featured an 11-minute animated segment.

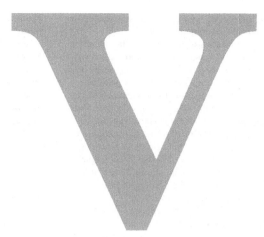

VALKYRIA CHRONICLES

2009. JPN: *Senjo no Valkyria GALLIAN CHRONICLES*. TV series, video. DIR: Yasutaka Yamamoto, Nobuhiro Kondo. SCR: Michiko Yokote, Akatsuki Yamatoya, Kento Shimo-yama, Hiroshi Onogi. DES: Atsuko Watanabe, Yoshio Tanioka, Kazuko Tadano. ANI: Atsuko Watanabe, Keiko Nakaji, Yu Yonezawa. MUS: Hitoshi Sakamoto. PRD: A-1 Pictures, Aniplex, Sega, Animax. 23 mins. x 26 eps. (TV1), 23 mins. x 2 eps. (v1), 23 mins. x 2 eps. (v2). Imperial forces attack a border town in Gallia. Three of the defenders—Welkin Gunther, his adopted sister Isara, and the captain of the Town Watch, Alicia Melchiott—escape and join the militia defending their country. While fighting to repel the invaders, they begin to learn the true purpose of the invasion itself.

The world of *Valkyria Chronicles*, loosely based on Europe in the 1930s, comes from the computer game of the same name released by Sega in 2008. The game was considered groundbreaking thanks to its innovative tactical gameplay, and quickly built a following in Japan and the U.S.A. The anime, like many of its ilk, takes popular characters and a senario from the game; minor variations are not enough to worry fans of the original. Considering it's set in wartime, the depiction of violence is quite restrained, though there are a few graphic scenes. The writing, weak and somewhat confusing in the first half, improves as the series progresses, although the characters fail to shake the imrpint of the cookie-cutter. Design and animation are satisfactory, though not especially striking or impressive. Overall the show

is enjoyable enough, but missable unless you're a diehard fan of the franchise.

Two manga, with art by Kito En and Kyusei Tokita respectively, followed the game launch in 2008, with an anthology manga a year later, after the anime had ended its first TV run. Two drama CDs appeared alongside the TV series. The first video episodes were released as extras on the TV series DVD, and are generic anime extras, taking the characters to the beach and a local festival, where all popular anime characters must eventually go whether relevant to their context or not. The second video, *Valkyria Chronicles 3: Unrecorded Stories (Senjo no Valkyria 3 Ta ga Tame no Juso)* appeared in 2011. It's a separate story: a renegade squadron known as "The Nameless" sets out to protect civilians from both sides, and is consequently considered an enemy by both. **Ⓥ**

VALKYRIE TRAINING

2009. JPN: *Valkyrie Chokyo Semen Tank no Ikusa Otome 10-nin Shimai*. AKA: *Valkyrie Training: Seed Tank Competition—10 Virgin Sisters*. Video. DIR: Hiromi Yokoyama. SCR: PON. DES: Hikaru Kinohara. ANI: N/C. MUS: N/C. PRD: Jinnan Studio, PoRO. 29 mins. x 2 eps.
The Valkyries are the peacekeepers between the three realms: the land of the gods, the human world, and the world of the dead. Now the peace has begun to break down, and one of the Valkyries has been possessed by a vengeful force. Before long they're discarding bits of their lingerie-armor and losing their all to a variety of warriors in this anime based on

a porn game by MBS TRUTH. There are indeed ten sister Valkyries in this story, which means things soon get repetitive. Scholars of Norse myth (**RELIGION AND BELIEF**) should definitely avoid this; it will only upset them. Some of the Valkyries wear horned helmets (which the Vikings never did) and one, the redheaded Grimgerde, actually cuts the end off the horns so she can thread her ponytails through, combining battle armor and hair accessory in a fashion as far from historical accuracy as one can imagine. **ⓁⓃⓋ**

VALVRAVE THE LIBERATOR *

2013. JPN: *Kakumeiki Valvrave*. TV series. DIR: Ko Matsuo. SCR: Ichiro Okochi, Jun Kumagai. DES: Tatsuya Suzuki. ANI: Tatsuya Suzuki. MUS: Akira Senju. PRD: Sunrise, Aniplex, Bandai, Dentsu, MBS, Movic, Starchild Records. 24 mins. x 13 eps. (TV1), 24 mins. x 13 eps. (TV2).
Seventy-one years after the proclamation of a new era, much of humanity is scattered throughout the solar system or living on the inner surface of a Dyson Sphere, built around an artificial sun. Old, rather outdated Cold War enmities have followed humanity into space, with the two superpowers ARUS and Dorssia squabbling over resources and territory. Haruto Tokishima is a teenage citizen of the neutral nation of JIOR, thrust into the conflict when Dorssian raiders attack his school in search of the military prototype under construction beneath it. Like dozens of anime heroes before him (**GUNDAM**), Haruto is *left with no choice* but to clamber aboard the Valvrave machine (for such it is), and fight them

off, becoming in the process a new soldier in the ongoing conflict.

Overblown, over-the-top, but deadly serious, *Valvrave* replays many concerns of the Sunrise studio and its ongoing efforts to sell as many robot toys as possible. As the human-shield implications of Haruto's school suggest from the very first episode, children in Haruto's world are being fed a series of lies and exploitative commands by their elders and supposed betters, plunging Haruto into conspiracies and espionage alongside the more traditional mecha conflict of power-ups and tactics.

Later episodes introduce more Valvrave units, more conspiracies, and a controversial, apparently nonconsensual sex scene, even more controversially shrugged off by its victim as nothing to get worked up about. But even then, "serious" is the watchword, with no attempts by the crew to titillate—at least not here. As with so many other Sunrise shows, *Valvrave* is all about the SCIENCE FICTION AND ROBOTS, and the usual teen mistrust of adult authority figures.

VAMPIRE

1968. TV series. DIR: Tsutomu Yamada, Tei Mafune. SCR: Yasuhiro Yamaura, Masaki Tsuji, Toshiro Fujinami, Tomohiro Ando, Shunichi Yukimuro, Yoshiyuki Fukuda. DES: Osamu Tezuka. ANI: Renzo Kinoshita. MUS: Hikaru Hayashi. PRD: Mushi Pro, Fuji TV. 25 mins. x 26 eps.

Toppei Tachibana is an everyday worker at the Mushi Pro company, who is secretly one of the Clan of Night's Weeping, a were-creature. Mr. Morimura, a reporter from the *Daily Times* researching vampires, discovers that Toppei transforms into a wolf whenever he sees a full moon and starts to chronicle both his activities and his secret feud with other clan members. A self-referential series from Tezuka, disastrously mixing animated supernatural creatures with live-action footage, shot in and around his own studios—the ASTRO BOY–creator would later do his best to edge *Vampire* out of his biography. Tezuka, Toppei's boss in real life and onscreen, plays himself in the series, while behind the scenes are several staff borrowed from ULTRAMAN's Tsuburaya studios and respected art-house animator Renzo

Kinoshita (see WARTIME ANIME). Compare to the later BORN FREE.

VAMPIRE HUNTER D *

1985. JPN: *Vampire Hunter D*. Movie. DIR: Toyoo Ashida. SCR: Yasushi Hirano. DES: Yoshitaka Amano, Noriyasu Yamaura. ANI: Hiromi Matsushita. MUS: Tetsuya Komuro. PRD: Ashi Pro. 80 mins., 102 mins.

Ten thousand years in the future, humanity lives in a quasi-medieval society overrun by the vampires who keep them in a state of feudal subjugation and terror. When Count Lee claims Doris as his next bride, a mysterious cloaked stranger in a big hat, known only as "D," rides into town on a huge horse and saves her. The townspeople want to give her up to pacify the count, but Doris has fallen in love with her vampire-hunter savior. "D" has to clean out the nest of vampires, but he's not without problems of his own. His hand has an independent life and nags him mercilessly, and his own background as a half-vampire is the cause of much inner conflict.

The film is based on a long series of novels by Hideyuki Kikuchi, who also created WIND OF AMNESIA, WICKED CITY, and DARKSIDE BLUES. Despite the Hammer-horror trappings, at heart *VHD* is more like a vampire Western. The character designs, based on Amano's illustrations for the novels, may entice lovers of his smoky, elegant watercolors and baroque game characters, but they were radically simplified to cut animation costs, with only traces of the artist's hand remaining, mostly in still frames.

Based on Kikuchi's third novel, *D: Demon Deathchase*, and first shown unfinished and unedited as a "work in progress" at the Fantasia 2000 festival; a second film, *VHD Bloodlust*, was directed and scripted by NINJA SCROLL's Yoshiaki Kawajiri. D, revealed as a half-vampire or "dhampir," is one of several hunters hired to rescue Charlotte, the daughter of a wealthy family, who has been kidnapped by a vampire; but she has fallen in love with her captor. Does he kill them both, or allow her to escape the misery of human life and flee to another planet with her lover? Characters are designed by Yutaka Minowa, monsters by Yasushi Nirasawa, and animation is by Madhouse. ❸❹

VAMPIRE KNIGHT *

2008. TV series, TV special. DIR: Kiyoko Sayama. SCR: Mari Okada. DES: Asako Nishida, Kazuhiro Ito. ANI: Asako Nishida, Atsuko Watanabe, Eiji Suganuma. MUS: Takefumi Haketa. PRD: Studio DEEN, Aniplex, NAS, Softbank Creative Corp., TV Tokyo. 24 mins. x 13 eps. (TV1), 24 mins. x 13 eps. (TV2), 3 mins. (special).

Yuki Cross is the adopted daughter of the headmaster of Cross Academy. She remembers nothing of her life before a winter night ten years ago, when one vampire attacked her and another saved her. Now she's sworn to protect the vampire race. Her father's school runs both day and night classes: in the daytime the ordinary students attend, and at night the "elite"— including Yuki's savior, Kaname—come to class. Yuki and her childhood friend Zero are the prefects who ensure that neither class impinges on the other. Zero hates and fears vampires, and is guarding a dark and terrible secret. He isn't the only one …

Matsuri Hino's 2004 manga pre-empted Stephenie Meyer's *Twilight*, which also sent vampires to high school. This absurd concept appears designed to make red-hot sexy undead people more acceptable to the average teenager. Unfortunately, at least in the hands of Sayama and Okada, it also renders them … *fluffy*. Most of the vampires in this show are cute pets. But then, most of the characters are dull and featureless, and the heroine is one of the weakest on record. The only thing *Vampire Knight* has in common with HELLSING is that the cute girl was saved from a vampire by a vampire. In the case of *Vampire Knight*, however, the vampire then turned into a typical high school hero and the cute girl became a wet blanket. In story terms this cannot be considered an unmixed blessing. The art is extremely pretty, although not even Aubrey Beardsley at his graphic best could save this show, as unfortunately the animation is too weak to give the art a decent chance. Some vampires induce terror: this lot induce boredom.

Nevertheless, a second season made by the same team, *Vampire Knight Guilty*, continued the story from the first season in the same year. This time the noble Kaname intervenes to save Zero from the consequences of his own bigotry. A three-minute special was added to the 2008 DVD release.

VAMPIRE PRINCESS MIYU *

1988. JPN: *Kyuketsuki Miyu*. AKA: *Vampire Miyu*. Video, TV series. DIR: Toshihiro Hirano. SCR: Sho Aikawa, Yuji Hayami. DES: Narumi Kakinouchi, Yasuhiro Moriki (v), Megumi Kadonosono, Kenji Teraoka (TV). ANI: Narumi Kakinouchi, Masahiro Nishii. MUS: Kenji Kawai. PRD: AIC, Pony Canyon. 30 mins. x 4 eps. (v), 25 mins. x 26 eps. (TV).
Himiko is a cynical, charlatan "medium" faced with a real-life case of demonic possession in Japan's former capital of Kyoto. There, amid sleepy, leafy lanes, she witnesses a battle between the Shinma, evil "demon-god" creatures from another dimension, and Earth's only protector, a vampire princess called Miyu.

Like Claudia in Anne Rice's *Interview with the Vampire*, Miyu is a former human who bears a vampire curse, trapped forever in a world of teenage angst. Motivated sometimes less by a sense of justice than by her own raging hormones, she pushes a succubus away from a man she secretly wants herself, parades Lolita-fashion around her devoted servant (and former enemy) Larva, and slowly worms her way into Himiko's life. Like PET SHOP OF HORRORS, *VPM* features the ghostbusting odd-couple of a mundane person from our world and a flashy spellcaster from the next. The olde-worlde charm of Kyoto makes a nice change from the sprawling city of Tokyo, particularly when the animation has aged so well. But amid the long, long silences and dark, meaningful glances, *VPM* is a mass of contradictions. As Himiko points out in a rare moment of lucidity, Miyu walks around in daylight, licks up holy water, and can crush a crucifix in her bare hands—so for the peculiarly picky audience of vampire folklorists, *VPM* is little more convincing than the execrable BEAST CITY. Furthermore, since she often seems only to be protecting people so she can chow down on their jugular veins, what exactly makes her any better than the creatures she is supposed to be fighting? Don't expect any answers, because Miyu (and, it would seem, her creator Narumi Kakinouchi) would rather smile condescendingly and tell you that you could never understand rather than

admit they don't know either.

Sometimes this approach pays off, especially when the story reverses the roles of the sexes. It makes a change to see a predatory succubus chasing after a young *male* virgin, or indeed to see a vain pretty-*boy* selling his soul to the devil to keep his looks forever. There are some great ideas, such as the girl who loses her mind because she is kept alive by blood transfusions from her dying parents, or alien parasites that feed off people's dreams. But such moments are few, making for an elegantly chilling and curiously watchable anime that constantly promises more than it delivers.

The video series is based on Kakinouchi's 1988 manga and directed by her husband, one of Japan's masters of horror and creator of ICZER-ONE. In 1997, it was snapped up for TV adaptation amid the post-EVANGELION boom when so many old video shows were reborn as cheap but at least *partly* market-tested TV. The TV series, conceived by Kakinouchi, Hirano, and Yuji Hayanami, introduced new characters such as Miyu's little bat-winged rabbit Shina, and another servant, Reiha, a snow demon who detests Miyu and also has the power to send Shinma back to the shadows. Reiha confides in her doll while chirpy human schoolgirl Chisato balances Miyu's coldness and further enhances the disturbing links between magic and childhood. Megumi Kadonosono reworks the character designs without obvious disharmony, and Kenji Kawai's music is just as evocative and elegant. Hirano (by this point using his real first name of Toshiki) disliked some of the changes required by Japanese TV censorship, including the removal of much of the projected second episode story line, and restored the deletions for the video release in 1998. Another Kakinouchi project, *Vampire Princess Yui*, the story of a girl whose mother was bitten by Miyu while pregnant, was published in manga form but not animated. **V**

VAMPIRE WARS *

1990. Video. DIR: Kazuhisa Takenouchi. SCR: Hiroyuki Hoshiyama. DES: Hideki Hamazu, Hiroyuki Kitazume. ANI: Hideki Hamazu. MUS: Kazz Toyama. PRD: Toei. 50 mins.
Japanese agent Kosaburo Kuki (sort of) hides out in Paris in the company of

dialogue-challenged whores and meets Lamia Vindaw, a girl who's sort of chummy with "vampires," who are really a galaxy-spanning alien race that have achieved immortality by storing life-giving energy in their bodies. Human blood provides a weak source of this energy, but Lamia's altered body chemistry has a uniquely powerful version. It's just what the aliens need to revive their king, trapped in a deep sleep in Transylvania ever since the visitors arrived five thousand years ago. Meanwhile, Monsieur Lassar of the French Secret Service thinks there is a connection between a terrorist attack on a NASA base in Arizona and the murder of a CIA man in Paris, and he hires Kuki to find out. Naturally, it's Lamia who is the key, though the more interesting elements of the backstory are only revealed in the final moments of this awful anime, which is little more than a commercial for the opening chapters of the best-selling Kiyoshi Kasai novel on which it is based. Most but not all anime novel adaptations suffer in the transition, mainly from being cut down to fit a 50-minute running time—barely enough to contain the average short story. However, such bastard children of the industry are often sold off at a bargain price to foreign companies (for obvious reasons), though any who pay for them discover at their cost that there is negligible pressure to rush out the next part—thus the interminable wait over the next episodes of HEROIC LEGEND OF ARSLAN.

The original Lamia of vampire legend was Queen of Libya and one of Zeus's many lovers. She was transformed into a child-eating monster, giving her name to a race of ghoulish female demons with a craving for blood. This tired story does no credit to its ancient antecedents. **BNV**

VAMPIYAN KIDS

2001. JPN: *Nanchatte Vampiyan*. AKA: *Vampire Vegetarians*. TV series. DIR: Masaaki Yuasa (pilot), Masatsugu Arakawa. SCR: N/C. DES: Suzuka Yoshida (pilot), Kayoko Nabeta (pilot), Miyako Yazu. ANI: Hiroyuki Nishimura, Kanami Sekiguchi, Kayoko Nabeta, Masahiro Sato, Takayuki Hamana, Taketomo Ishikawa, Tsuyoshi Ichiki, Yuichiro Sueyoshi. MUS: Ko Otani (pilot), Toshihiko Sahashi. PRD: Fuji TV, Production I.G, IKIF +, Ogura Workshop. 25 mins. x 26 eps.

A vampire family that survives on orange juice instead of blood can't call itself "vampire"—hence the name *vampiyan*. The father can't even scare humans and is sent into exile in the human world to scare 1,000 people before he is permitted to return home. But his daughter Sue falls in love with human boy Ko and doesn't want to go back. The whole show appears to have undergone a transfusion between the pilot (screened at the 2004 Future Film Festival in Italy) and release—the main crew and cast members, except for Ko and Mama, were all replaced. Notably, the voice of "Papa" in the pilot was provided by Kenji Utsumi, who has voiced vampires on other occasions, such as the similarly comedic **DON DRACULA** and the more traditional **DRACULA: SOVEREIGN OF THE DAMNED**.

VANDREAD *

2001. TV series. DIR: Takeshi Mori, Hitoyuki Matsui. SCR: Atsuhiro Tomioka, Natsuko Takahashi. DES: Mahiro Maeda, Kazuya Kuroda, Tomohiro Kawahara. ANI: Takahiro Fujii, Satoshi Kawano. MUS: N/C. PRD: Gonzo, Media Factory, WOWOW. 23 mins. x 12 eps. (TV1), 23 mins. x 12 eps. (TV2), 75 mins. (Integral), 75 mins. (Turbulence).
War has been raging for generations between the all-male planet Talac and the all-female planet Majel. Suspend disbelief as to how they keep this up, then imagine that they are invaded by a common enemy and forced to settle their differences for a united counter-attack. The first meeting of 16-year-old Talac engineer Hibiki Tokai and Majel babe Dirda is unplanned; he gets tired of his mundane job assembling robots and plots to steal one of his own. He stows away on a Talac immigration ship, but then the ship is attacked by a Majel pirate. But, despite their races' history of separate development, Hibiki and Dirda will eventually work things out.

The script cleverly exploits the mutual attraction/repulsion of teenagers of opposite sexes, though the visuals resort to standard fan-service ogling of female charms. *Vandread Integral* (AKA *Vandread: Taidohen*, 2001) was a feature-length edit of the first series broadcast as a TV movie to set the scene for part two. *Vandread: Turbulence* (AKA *Vandread: Gekitohen*, 2003) was a similar recapitulation of the second

season. Both included a minor amount of new footage.

VANILLA SERIES *

1997. Video. DIR: Rion Kujo, Norihiko Nagahama, Teruaki Murakami, Mitsuhiro Yoneda, Rokurota Makabe, Sotsuki Mitsumura, Kanzaburo Oda, Takayoshi Mizuno, Naomi Hayakawa, Hiroyuki Yanase. SCR: Nikukyu, Rokurota Makabe, Naruhito Sunaga. DES: Raihiken (aka Ken Raika), Matsuri Ohana, Ryosuke Morimura. ANI: Raihiken, Tetsuya Ono, Meka Morishige, Takeshi Okamura, Shinichi Omata. MUS: Yoshi. PRD: YOUC, Digital Works. 30 mins. x 4 eps. (Love Doll), 2 eps. (Shoyonoid Makoto-chan), 1 ep. (Co-Ed Affairs), 3 eps. (A Heat for All Seasons), 4 eps. (Mei King), 2 eps. (Slave Sisters), 1 ep. (Office Affairs), 1 ep. (Sins of the Flesh), 2 eps. (Bondage Mansion), 1 ep. (Endless Serenade), 2 eps. (Girl Next Door), 2 eps. (Dark), 4 eps. (Nightmare Campus), 2 eps. (Campus), 2 eps. (Holy Virgins), 2 eps. (Private Sessions), 2 eps. (Punishment), 2 eps. (Sex Ward), 2 eps. (Slaves to Passion), 2 eps. (Stepmother's Sin), 2 eps. (Hooligan), 2 eps. (I Love You), 2 eps. (Classroom of Atonement), 2 eps. (Spotlight), 2 eps. (Submission Central), 2 eps. (Story of Little Monica), 3 eps. (The Urotsuki/New Saga), 2 eps. (Debts of Desire), 2 eps. (Rxxx: Prescription for Pain), 2 eps. (Maid Service), 1 eps. (Ingoku Byouto), 2 eps. (Hardcore Hospital), 2 eps. (Voyeur's Digest), 2 eps. (Perverse Investigations), 2 eps. (Xpress Train), 2 eps. (Wicked Lessons), 2 eps. (Private Sessions 2), 2 eps. (Hot For Teacher), 2 eps. (Chains of Lust), 2 eps. (Naughty Nurses), 2 eps. (Bondage 101), 2 eps. (Milk Money), 3 eps. (Angel Blade), 2 eps. (Anyone You Can Do), 2 eps. (Internal Medicine), 2 eps. (My Brother's Wife), 2 eps. (Sextra Credit), 2 eps. (Duchess of Busty Mounds), 2 eps. (Invasion of the Booby Snatchers), 2 eps. (Gold Throbber), 2 eps. (Elfen Laid), 2 eps. (Mother Knows Breast), 2 eps. (Virgin Auction), 2 eps. (Invisible Man), 2 eps. (Sex Exchange), 2 eps. (Horny Ladies), 2 eps. (Milf Mansion), 2 eps. (Booby Life), 2 eps. (Sinners Paradise), 2 eps. (Cosplay Sex Machine), 2 eps. (Classmate's Mother), 2 eps. (Enspelled), 2 eps. (Bijukubo), 2 eps. (Gropesville).
The Vanilla Series is the Digital Works company's umbrella title for numerous unrelated pornographic anime in the style

of **COOL DEVICES** or the **DISCOVERY SERIES**, largely based on lecherous computer games. With many unrelated one-shot or two-part titles, the Vanilla Series has been greatly overrepresented in the American market, since its titles have been separated, renamed, and sold as several dozen anime releases—many have their own entries in this book, but we have assembled this chronological umbrella entry in an attempt to make some sense of it. Most of the original games are erotic variants of the "dating simulation" engine, in which a protagonist's choices in a role-playing environment lead him not to treasure or freedom, but to the perfect girl of his dreams. Consequently, plotlines often revolve around a roster of half a dozen female stereotypes, differentiated through hair color and nonthreatening personality traits.

The first release from the production team was **LOVE DOLL** in 1997, although its role as the inaugural title for the franchise was only really assigned retroactively. Similar membership to a Vanilla "line" would be assigned to the 1998 releases **SHOYONOID MAKOTO-CHAN** and **CO-ED AFFAIRS**.

The Sega Saturn-originated *Heat for All Seasons* (*Kiss Yori*, 1999) features Masato, an aspiring novelist who moves to a seaside town for a working vacation while looking for candidates for a summertime fling. Masato's friend Oka finds his dream girl working at a restaurant, but Masato rekindles his love with his old highschool sweetheart, Chisato, before juggling her with a succession of other girls in the style of an erotic **TENCHI MUYO!**Released originally in three seasonally themed chapters, the English-language version initially featured a title change to *Summer Heat, Autumn Heat,* and *Winter Heat,* before being repackaged as *Heat for All Seasons*.

Mei King (1999) is another outbreak of the **CREAM LEMON** virus, as a man called Cane falls in love with the spirit of a woman trapped inside the body of a young girl called Charlotte. In *Sins of the Flesh* (*Ikenie*, AKA *Holy Sacrifice*, 1999), talented artist Adolfo wants to enter the Church and live out his days painting angels, though temptations of the flesh present themselves in the form of the country girl Michaela, with predictable results. **SLAVE SISTERS** and **OFFICE AFFAIRS** followed the same year, demonstrating Vanilla's ongoing obsessions with both young girls and scenarios of bondage, coercion, and domination.

Bondage Mansion (*Kinbaku no Yakata*, 2000) featured extensive scenes of the same in a secluded forest hideaway, perpetrated by a father upon his daughters. A different variant on the incest theme was presented in the same year's ENDLESS SERENADE, while GIRL NEXT DOOR presented a vaguely consensual variant on the dating sim theme, whereas *Dark* (*Daraku*, AKA *Degeneration*, 2000), featuring more coerced sex, didn't.

In 2001, the Vanilla Series almost doubled its output, jumping on the erotic horror bandwagon with an adaptation of Toshio Maeda's NIGHTMARE CAMPUS, classroom bondage in PRIVATE SESSIONS, CLASSROOM OF ATONEMENT, *Campus*, and *Punishment* (*Korashime*). The "gentler" side of pornography continued with I LOVE YOU, while bondage and wife-coveting continued in SLAVES TO PASSION and STEPMOTHER'S SIN. The year also saw a further concentration on fantasy in the literal sense, with ANGEL BLADE and *Hooligan: The Quest for the Seven Holy Dildos* (released in Japan as just plain *Hooligan*), in which a botched "science experiment" transports a Japanese boy to another time and place where he must obtain a series of magical artifacts from the usual roster of stereotyped females—a more quest-oriented variant on the erotic dating sim. The same year saw the nursing craze in Japanese erotica reaching its peak—a line the authors suspect can be traced from the mainstream TV show *Leave It to the Nurses* (*DE), through to erotic rip-offs in the computer games world in 1999, and the subsequent success of NIGHT SHIFT NURSES, the flagship title of the rival Discovery Series. Not to be outdone, the Vanilla Series retaliated with SEX WARD, and by mixing nurses *and* nuns in HOLY VIRGINS.

The nursing themes continued into 2002, with the release of Vanilla's INGOKU BYOUTO, and HARDCORE HOSPITAL. Erotic horror continued with the release of *The Urotsuki*, the newest incarnation of the UROTSUKIDOJI franchise (released in America as *Urotsukidoji: New Saga*), while less violent fantasies appeared in THE STORY OF LITTLE MONICA. Coercion and domination returned in SUBMISSION CEN-

TRAL and DEBTS OF DESIRE, while SPOTLIGHT mixed the not-quite-incest genre with a tale of a female singer seeking the bigtime. *Maid Service* (*Maid no Yakata: Zetsubo-hen*, AKA *Maid Mansion: Chapter of Despair*, 2002) featured an orphan, Momoko, who must perform menial services for the rich youth Takaaki if she is to earn enough to pay for her college tuition.

By 2003, Vanilla appeared to be establishing an annual roster of subgenres in those areas of anime erotica proven to work in the market. In *Wicked Lessons* (*Gakuen no Shuryosha*, AKA *Hunter of the Campus*, 2002), an abusive youth forces his raped and orphaned stepsister to help him chase girls at a college, all "to get back at his father." Meanwhile, school (or "college") abuse and sex continued in HOT FOR TEACHER, P.I.: PERVERSE INVESTIGATIONS, and *Private Sessions 2*. Hospitals continued to perform beyond the call of duty in NAUGHTY NURSES, while *Chains of Lust* (*Ryojoku no Rensa*, 2003) featured two workers at an erotic video store who decide to make a porn movie without acquiring the consent of their female performers—the authors wonder if this is an erotic variant on the contemporary self-referential genre in the mainstream that also gave us ANIME SHOP-KEEPER.

A similar spread of titles covered all of the Vanilla Series' main bases in 2004, with school bondage in SEXTRA CREDIT and BONDAGE 101, and hospital abuses in RXXX: PRESCRIPTION FOR PAIN. However, the year also saw a marked increase in the number of incest and not-quite-incest tales, particularly involving a fetish for lactating women. This is nothing new in erotic anime, and dates at least as far back as PROFESSOR PAIN in 1998, but 2004 alone saw the Vanilla Series releasing MILK MONEY, ANYONE YOU CAN DO... I CAN DO BETTER, and *My Brother's Wife* (*Aniyome*, 2004).

The new direction, with its concentration on older, fuller-figured women (at least compared to the jailbait of earlier incarnations), continued with *Duchess of Busty Mounds* (*Mama Haha*, 2005), INVASION OF THE BOOBY SNATCHERS, and *Mother Knows Breast* (*Chibo*, 2005, lit. *Perverse Mother*). The franchise also released *Group Groper Train* (*Shudan Chikan Densha*, 2005, released in the U.S. as *Gold Throbber*), ELFEN LAID, and VIRGIN AUCTION.

The year 2006 was presumably some cause for celebration for the Vanilla Series, having reached its 100th title. The vagaries of release schedules make it unclear exactly which DVD represented Vanilla's attainment of three-figure smut, but by our unreliable calculations, it was probably *Invisible Man* (*Tomei Ningen*, 2006). Male characters in some erotic anime games have often been rendered invisible or translucent in the past, and some anime have found ways to remove the image of male participants from the action in order to show more female flesh (be it through tentacles at a distance in erotic horror, or transforming a character into a girl's bathwater as in REI REI). *Invisible Man* takes the concept literally, often allowing for the anime to incorporate the genre of live-action pornography known as "POV" (point-of-view), in which the girls address and interact with the camera as if it is the male viewer himself. *Invisible Man* features an old man who takes supreme advantage after ingesting a drug that makes him disappear. A similar concept can be seen in the Japanese box art to *Stepsister* (2006, the characters say *Gimai* but the *furigana* alongside demands it be read as "Imoto," or "Younger Sister"; released in English as *Sex Exchange*)—not to be confused with the Discovery Series title of the same name—which features a semi-naked girl about to perform a sexual act on her knees, smiling up at the viewer/buyer. However, the onscreen action itself is more traditional, both in terms of the way it is filmed and in the plotting the title suggests, which is old-school Vanilla Series not-quite-incest.

Subsequent releases have included *Horny Ladies and the News* (2007, *Joku Ana*), *My Classmate's Mother* (2007, *Classmate no Okaasan*), *Milf Mansion*, and *Enspelled* (2007, *Okusama wa Mahotsukai*), the latter deliberately playing on the "my wife is a witch" concept of *Bewitched*. Many of the titles remain bluntly descriptive in Japanese and bawdily evocative in English TRANSLATION, leading to such concoctions as *Last Train to Gropesville* (2008, *Hissatsu Chikan Nin*, a pun on "Last Train to Clarksville," by the Monkees), *Sinners Paradise* (2008, *Shitsurakuen*), *Booby Life* (2008, *Oppai Life*), *Like a Mother* (2009, *Mama Puri*), *Cosplay Sex Machine* (2009, *Jinko Shojo: Henshin Sex Android*), *The Cougar Trap* (2009, *Musuko no Tomodachi ni Okasarete), Bijukubo* (2010, currently untranslated but literally *Hot Mother*), and *My Lover Is a Celebrity* (2012, *Cele Kano*). **N**

VARIABLE GEO *

1996. Video. DIR: Toru Yoshida. SCR: Yosuke Kuroda. DES: Takahiro Kimura. ANI: Takahiro Kimura. MUS: Harukichi Yamamoto. PRD: KSS. 30 mins. x 3 eps.
This ridiculously puerile anime was based on a video game that must have seemed like a really good idea at the time. Waitresses from rival restaurants meet in public fighting bouts in which they pound each other into submission (see STREET FIGHTER II). The ultimate winner gets $10 million and some prime real estate in the city of her choice. The loser must strip off her clothes and humiliate herself in front of the audience (see SEXORCIST). Meanwhile, a shadowy secret organization (see TOSHINDEN) is planning to use the ultimate winner's DNA to breed the ultimate warrior (see TEKKEN). Plucky heroine Yuka Takeuchi punches and kicks her way through a series of opponents from the game (see all of the above), in a succession of ludicrous set pieces that show off fighting catchphrases and special moves (ditto). Working conditions in the fighting-evil trade have obviously gone downhill—this never happened to the Knight Sabers. It lasts 90 minutes. Life's too short, really. Trust us. **NV**

VASSALORD

2013. Video. DIR: Kazuto Nakazawa. SCR: N/C. DES: Nariyuki Takahashi, Chieko Miyagawa, Yuji Kaneko. ANI: Kazuto Nakazawa, Hidekazu Kaneko, Hiroki Fujiwara, Akira Tabata. MUS: Sumire Kokushoku. PRD: Production I.G, MAG Garden. 28 mins.
The Vatican likes to keep its hands clean, so it employs some unlikely angels. Cyborg vampire Charley Chrishunds is one of them: the slave of vampire playboy Johhny Rayflo, forced to serve him because he refuses to drink human blood and so can only feed from a vampire. The pair fight rogue vampires, and each other, when not having sex. Then they start to investigate a mysterious branch of the Unitarian Church. Nanae Chrono's 2006 manga has such an irresistibly daft high concept that it's hard to imagine why it took so long

to animate. Sadly, too many characters and too much story make this a very over-egged pudding. The plot is fugitive and the pace never lets up, adding to the impression of complete incoherence. The quality of Production I.G's art and animation is strikingly good, creating the distinct impression that this is really a visual pitch for a TV series. **V**

VEGETABLE FAIRIES

2007. JPN: *Yasai no Yosei N.Y. Salad.* TV series, movie. DIR: Hiroaki Matsu, Keisuke Toshimna. SCR: Hiroaku Matsu. DES: Tetsuo Kodama, Ayuko Matsumura, Kiyotaka Kawata. ANI: Noriyuki Omi. MUS: Koichi Fujino. PRD: Digital Media Lab, NHK. 5 mins. x 26 eps. (TV1), 5 mins. x 26 eps. (TV2), 35 mins. (m1).
In a New York kitchen after dark, when everyone is asleep, the salad fairies wake and begin their day. Seemingly ordinary vegetables open into enchanting little creatures with their own quirks and personalities.
    Sometimes people surprise you. Artist/ illustrator Yoshitaka Amano, designer of VAMPIRE HUNTER D, creator of tales of love and despair such as BIRD SONG, wrote and illustrated *N.Y. Salad,* the book on which this sweet kiddies' series is based. Using a combination of CG animation and delicate drawings, the secret life of the salad fairies of New York—where Amano now lives—is revealed in art strongly reminiscent of 1930s children's illustration in its whimsical beauty. A second TV series followed in 2008, and a theatrical feature, narrated like the series by actress Tomoyo Harada, in 2010. A further movie, *Vegetable Fairies N.Y Salad Quiz Theater (Quiz Gekijo),* was promised in summer 2013, although at the time we went to press, we saw no sign of it.

VENUS FILES, THE *

2003. JPN: *Megami Tantei FILE 01.* AKA: *Goddess Detective File 01; Vinus Files.* Video. DIR: Shinichi Shimizu. SCR: Aoi Ichinoe. DES: Noboru Jitsuhara. ANI: Mikio Fujiwara. MUS: N/C. PRD: Five Ways, JHV (Video2). 30 mins. (v1), 30 mins. x 2 eps. (v2).
Beautiful detectives Karen and Rio of the Goddess Detective Agency take on a case involving drugs and rape, which arouses painful memories for Rio—her sister was murdered by a gang of sex-starved drug

dealers. Can she control her emotions and bring the case to a successful conclusion? And can Karen avoid being turned on by the lurid details of the case? This porn anime is based on the manga by Jamming, whose manga KAMYLA was also adapted by Five Ways. In 2004 Karen and Rio were back with a two-part version of the same story, *The Venus Files Video 2* (*Shin Ban Megami Tantei VINUS FILE—Zenpen/Kohen* or *True Edition Goddess Detective VINUS FILE First Part/Sequel*). **NV**

VENUS FIVE *

1994. JPN: *Sailor Senshi Venus Five.* AKA: *Sailor Warriors Venus Five.* Video. DIR: Satoshi Inoue, Kan Fukumoto. SCR: Wataru Amano. DES: Rin Shin. ANI: N/C. MUS: N/C. PRD: Daiei. 45 mins. x 2 eps.
Five beautiful teenage girls are destined to battle the evil Inma Empire led by the perverted Necros. The empire aims to revive the god Apollo from his ten-thousand-year slumber in order to gain his near-infinite power. And the only thing that will revive a god is … yes, you've guessed it, the sexual secretions of certain beautiful high school girls. Unfortunately for the bad guys, our heroines have been recruited by the Goddess of Love to ensure that the power of evil doesn't triumph, and Aphrodite has even sent them a talking cat to help them. A shameless SAILOR MOON parody based on a manga by Jin Ara, *V5* is aimed straight at the fans who dream of seeing more than just a flash of thigh in those transformation sequences. The girls mimic the Sailor Scouts every way they can—fighting poses, speeches, costumes, all are so close to the original that they could be twins. There, however, all similarity ends, as the cat talks dirty, the tentacles multiply, and the smut takes over. This is for all those out there who snicker at a bad guy called Count Uranus, as well as connoisseurs of Immortal Dialogue like, "Let me entice you to the very summit of lust." **NV**

VENUS TO MAMORU *

2006. JPN: *Mamoru-kun ni Megami no Shukufuku o!* AKA: *Mamoru Was Blassed By A Goddess!* TV series. DIR: Itsuro Kawasaki. SCR: Mari Okada. DES: Yuka Takashina, Shinobu Tsuneki (mecha), Mitsuo Miyamoto. ANI: Hironori Tanaka. MUS: Noriyasu Agematsu. PRD: ZEXCS, WOWOW. 25 mins. x 24 eps.

A mysterious magical power known as "Beatrice" is wielded by a few specially gifted people. Only one school in the world specializes in training those with this power, and Mamoru is accepted there because of his high intelligence. He becomes aide to the student council president, Ayako, a girl from a high-ranking political family who is one of the most powerful Beatrice users in the world. She's adored by a number of guys in the school for her power and her beauty. Mamoru is short and very childish-looking, but he's a good-hearted boy who turns out to have quite a lot of magical power himself. So the hero of NEGIMA is catapulted into the world of URUSEI YATSURA, disguised with a few harem trappings but really just the setting for a sweet but unmemorable high school romantic comedy, based on the 2006 light-novel series by Hiroki Iwata, illustrated by Toshiyuki Sato.

VENUS VERSUS VIRUS *

2007. TV series. DIR: Shinichiro Kimura. SCR: Yasutomo Yamada. DES: Yoshimi Agata, Katsuhiro Hashi, Kazushige Kanehira. ANI: Kim Sang Yoeb. MUS: Hikaru Nanase. PRD: Studio Hibari, Lantis, MOVIC, Pony Canyon, Sony PCL. 24 mins. x 12 eps.
Sumire has always been able to see ghosts, and nobody has ever believed her. When a mysterious girl saves her from a monster, she becomes part of a group called Venus Vanguard. The group, operating from an antique store that forms their cover, exists to exterminate evil spirits, or "viruses," that prey on human souls. Lucia, her rescuer, is a powerful fighter, but Sumire turns out to have astonishing ability against viruses. Yet all she wants is to live a normal life and have a boyfriend. Old-school fans may see echoes of BUBBLEGUM CRISIS in this set-up, but they shouldn't get too excited. This show based on Atsushi Suzumi's 2005 manga tries desperately hard to be cool, stylish, and exciting and fails on all counts. A weak first episode and unmemorable characters are not even lightened by fan service; despite the show being misdescribed in some sources as *yuri* (lesbian) it has no sexual content. ❶

VENUS WARS *

1989. JPN: *Venus Senki*. AKA: *Venus War Chronicle*. Movie. DIR: Yoshikazu Yasuhiko.

SCR: Yuichi Sasamoto, Yoshikazu Yasuhiko. DES: Hiroyoshi Yokoyama, Yoshikazu Yasuhiko, Sachiko Kamimura, Hirotoshi Sano, Makoto Kobayashi, Shichiro Kobayashi. ANI: Yoko Kamimura. MUS: Joe Hisaishi. PRD: Triangle Staff, Kugatsu-sha. 104 mins.
Young journalist Susan Sommers arrives on Venus to cover the war between its two nation-states just before the troops of Ishtar take the capital and overcome the armies of Aphrodia. She meets a group of young motorcycle punks, the Killer Commandos, led by Hiro. Previously engaged in racing other gangs around a makeshift circuit in scenes reminiscent of *Rollerball*, Hiro and some of his team fight a guerrilla action against the occupying forces of Ishtar, and Susan soon loses her journalistic objectivity as she is drawn into the struggle. Based on one of Yasuhiko's own manga, and with music by the man who has given both Hayao Miyazaki and Beat Takeshi some unforgettable themes, this glossily produced and well-designed film ought to be a classic, but it just misses the mark. Sasamoto contributes an intelligent script in which our young hotheads learn that not all adults are brain-dead, not all organization is tyranny, and not all action is sensible. There's plenty to interest the genre fan, including some good action sequences and fine mecha designs, yet the film lacks the emotional edge and perverse power of Yasuhiko's earlier ARION. A similar Venusian Cold War standoff would appear in BLACK MAGIC.

VERY PRIVATE LESSON *

1998. JPN: *Kyokasho ni Nai!* AKA: *Not in the Textbook!* Video. DIR: Hideaki Oba. SCR: Hideaki Oba. DES: Masahiko Yamada. ANI: Etsuro Tokuda, Masahiko Yamada. MUS: Ryuichi Katsumata. PRD: AIC. 30 mins. x 2 eps.
High school teacher Oraku and his colleague Satsuki hope to marry one day. Meanwhile, one of his students has fallen in love with him. Aya is a beautiful and spoiled delinquent; her father, a very wealthy man, only wants his princess to be happy, so much so that she insists she moves in with the man she loves. So what's the problem with having a beautiful teenager move in, with Daddy's blessing? Aya is a Mob princess in the style of THE GOKUSEN; her father's money comes from

organized crime, and while he's happy for her to do whatever she wants, if she doesn't stay a virgin he'll kill whoever is responsible. So Oraku has to become Aya's chaperone. Meanwhile, if anyone finds out he is living with one of his students, his career and his future marriage to Satsuki will both go down the drain. You may recall HOMEROOM AFFAIRS, MY WIFE IS A HIGH SCHOOL STUDENT, or HAPPY LESSON at this point. Based on a long-running manga by Kazuto Okada. ❶❻

VEXILLE *

2007. JPN: *Vexille 2077 Nippon Sakoku*. AKA: *Vexille: 2077 Isolation of Japan*. Movie. DIR: Fumihiko Sori. SCR: Fumihiko Sori, Haruka Handa. DES: Atsushi Yasuoka, Daisuke Nakayama, Kazuya Nomura, Atsushi Takeuchi, Toru Hishiyama. ANI: N/C. MUS: Paul Oakenfold, M.I.A., Basement Jaxx, Asian Dub Foundation. PRD: Oxybot, avex entertainment, CCRE CO, Shockiku, Shogakukan, TBS. 110 mins.
By the mid-21st century, Japan had perfected biotechnology and robotics, extending human lifespans. Daiwa Heavy Industries was a world leader in the field. However, the United Nations decided that this research was a threat, and imposed a ban on future development of robotics in 2067. Japan cut itself off from the rest of the world in protest: trade continues, but people and information cannot pass in or out. Ten years later, a U.S. special forces unit codenamed SWORD, led by machine-hating commander Vexille Serra, is sent to infiltrate and gather intelligence. What Vexille finds shocks her, and will shake the world.

This fascinating premise not only echoes Japan's *sakoku* isolation period from the 17th to the late 19th century, but also the censure of Japan in 1933 by the League of Nations, and sets the scene for a cyberpunk movie from many of the production crew of the earlier CGI APPLESEED. Some suspiciously minded encyclopedists might even suggest that the entire project could have started life as a sequel, but has had Masamune Shirow's serial numbers filed off it to save money, leaving only a heroine who is a dead ringer for Deunan Knute and a story that could very easily be slotted back into the franchise that might have birthed it. The movie opens strongly, with some interesting CGI and elegantly simplified characters moving over minutely detailed backgrounds, providing eye candy aplenty. However, the plot and characters fail to deliver on the early promise: things begin to flag in the first half hour, and the rapidly opening plot holes swallow all chance of recovery.

Sori's animation begins in a glistening chrome future but must incorporate a far grungier, grittier setting when the scene switches to Japan. He accomplishes this with much the same aplomb as the animators of **METROPOLIS**, using digital technology to capture sequences invested with analogue realism. The soundtrack and animation are good, and if this were a music video anthology that would be enough; setting it up as a movie only raises expectations Sori and his crew largely fail to fulfill. However, one might argue that in chosing a blockbuster model to emulate, Sori dooms himself to a predictable, explosive, attack-focused finale in which the dust blows away to reveal people punching each other bare-handed in the ruins.

That's not to say that it doesn't contain some remarkable feats of performance capture and effects, and some wonderful touches. The facial animation is so detailed that it is literally possible (indeed *necessary* in one crucial, silent moment) to read the characters' lips. Moreover, subtle changes in lighting at the end suggest that Vexille has been changed for the better by her experience, retaining the coloration and warmer glow of the Japan she has left behind.

VICE PRINCIPAL

2009. JPN: *Kurutta Kyoto Danzai no Gakuen.* AKA: *Maddened Vice Principal: Convict Academy.* Video. DIR: Ahiru Koike. SCR: Ken Kida. DES: Hiroya Iijima. ANI: N/C. MUS: N/C. PRD: Studio9MAiami, Jya no Michi wa Hebi Soft. 28 mins.
When the principal of a Tokyo school is fired for having sex with a student, the vice-principal, hitherto a model of respectability, takes over. And since all the teaching staff are sex maniacs, he decides it's best to uphold the old school traditions. Unusual uses for a cane and improper dress on the sports field are the order of the day; unorthodox use is made of gymastic sashes and even the school rabbit hutch isn't safe in this anime based on a porn game by Jya no Michi wa Hebi Soft. But if you want school perversions to be *fun,* we suggest you try **KEKKO KAMEN.** 🅛🅝

VICIOUS *

2001. Video DIR: Sakura Harukawa. SCR: N/C. DES: N/C. ANI: N/C. MUS: N/C. PRD: Five Ways. 30 mins. x 2 eps.
In what appears to be Victorian or Edwardian Britain at the turn of the 20th century, a household is still struggling to come to terms with the death of its much-loved mother in a fall down the stairs six months earlier. Daughter Angela feels that her father is cold-hearted and distant and despises him for seeking solace in the arms of the maid, Bridget. Perhaps out of spite, perhaps in an attempt to assuage her own loneliness, Angela decides that she will lose her virginity to John the butler. Although John fears reprisals from his boss, he eventually succumbs to Angela's charms. However, Angela's mood changes when she learns that John and Bridget plan to leave her father's employment, turning the latter half of this erotic anime into a tale of murder and revenge. 🅛🅝🅥

VICKY THE VIKING *

1974. JPN: *Chiisana Viking Vickie.* AKA: *Vickie the Little Viking.* TV series. DIR: Hiroshi Saito, Noboru Ishiguro, Kiyoshi Harada. SCR: Yuji Fusano, Hiroshi Kaneko, Akira Saiga, Takeshi Hidaka, Chikao Katsui. DES: Shuichi Seki. ANI: Shinichi Tsuji. MUS: Seiichiro Uno. PRD: Zuiyo, Taurus Film, Fuji TV. 25 mins. x 77 eps.
Vicky is the son of Halvar, chief of a little Viking village. He'd rather play than learn to fight, but he is compelled to go on one of the village's raiding expeditions where he manages to foil the plans of the enemy, Sven the Terrible, through his quick wits and courage. Adapted from a series of stories by Runer Jonsson, this German-Japanese coproduction holds the seeds of a great tradition—Zuiyo later became Nippon Animation, whose **WORLD MASTERPIECE THEATER** series was dedicated to bringing classic stories from the West to Japanese TV.

VICTORY PITCHER

1987. JPN: *Shori Tosha.* Video. DIR: Hiroki Shibata. SCR: Akane Nishiura. DES: Noriko Umeda. ANI: Katsumi Aodori. MUS: Akihiko Matsumoto. PRD: Toei. 72 mins.
Baseball coach Hoshiyama offers a chance to turn professional to Katsumi Kunimasa, a star member of the student squad that won the summer tournament. The young girl becomes a star pitcher for the Chunichi Dragons (conveniently, the team her father owns), and, after a year of triumphs, she leads them to victory in the national championships at legendary Koshien Stadium. Based on the manga by No-riko Umeda, this anime may be compared to the other girl-playing-baseball story **SONG OF THE BASEBALL ENTHUSIAST.** The Dragons team members are all based on the real-life team, though their opponents are fictional. At the time, the real-life Hoshiyama was a commentator, but fact was eventually true to fiction, and he became the manager for the real-life Dragons.

VIDEO GIRL AI *

1992. JPN: *Denno Shojo Ai.* AKA: *Cyber Girl Ai; Electric Girl Ai.* Video. DIR: Mizuho Nishikubo. SCR: Satoru Akahori. DES: Takayuki Goto. ANI: Takayuki Goto. MUS: Nobuyuki Shimizu. PRD: Production I.G, Tatsunoko. 30 mins. x 6 eps.
Average-guy Yota loves girl-next-door Moemi. But Moemi has a crush on local hero Takashi, and to make it worse, Takashi is a nice guy and Yota's best friend. Enter Ai, a disposable alien girl who escapes from a dating video and resolves to get Yota together with his true love. But before you can say "Cyrano de Bergerac," Ai secretly longs for Yota, too. Ai is a "video girl," designed to distract and amuse, programmed, like all video, with a definite time limit. When her relationship with Yota moves from being a disposable, casual entertainment into more dangerous territory, the "copyright authorities" step in. Yota, Moemi, Ai, and their friends move through the tortuous dance of teenage emotion and sexual longing, beautifully conveying the agonies of alienation and embarrassment inherent in growing up, and also learning that time will not always be on their side.

An unwelcome guest/magical girlfriend tale in the tradition of **URUSEI YATSURA** and **OH MY GODDESS!,** playing straight to the gallery with fan-service asides and a loving appreciation of the loser male psyche. Satoru Akahori's script masterfully recreates a world of teenage desperation, far from the madcap comedies for which he is normally known. From the opening shot in which Ai addresses the audience directly, through the regular stuck-record repetition of Moemi's declaration of love for the wrong man, Akahori demonstrates that there's more to him than the slapstick of SORCERER HUNTERS. But occasional moments of unnecessary physical comedy intrude on what could have been a great emotional farce, and sporadic outbreaks of Katsura's trademark panty shots further undermine a show that, at heart, is all heart. After shoving the couple together, Ai immediately breaks them up—a schizophrenic characterization that is one of Ai's biggest flaws. She fluctuates unevenly between bitchy best friend, infuriating tease, and doormat mother-substitute, while Moemi is part drippy little girl, part sassy schemer. Yota himself is half lovable dork, half *annoying* dork, his own wavering interest in his love objects often reduced to comparisons of breast size or cooking ability.

Director Nishikubo's clever camerawork fades the entire world into the background so that only the self-obsessed leads get any screen time, replicating overexposed shots of school life to turn every dingy corridor into a pathway of dreamy bright nostalgia. He puts similar thought into the opening credits, which feature a fully rendered Ai skipping through a world that's often only half-formed, as if the camera itself has eyes only for her. Nishikubo's pauses emphasize the secret language of women, lingering for long moments as Ai and Moemi alternate between friendship and rivalry. The series considerately ends before outstaying its welcome (see TENCHI MUYO!), and an excellent dub completes the package. A live-action movie, video *Girl Ai* (1991), was directed by Ryu Kaneda from a script credited to both creator Katsura and scenarist Masahiro Yoshimoto.

VIDEO PICTURE BOOK

1988. JPN: *Video Anime E-Hon*. Video. DIR: Noriaki Kairo. SCR: Noriaki Kairo, Shin Yukuba. DES: N/C. ANI: Shunji Saita. MUS: Masahito Maekawa. PRD: Mushi Pro. 12 mins. x 50 eps.
A vast library of classic tales animated in bite-sized chunks, including a number

from AESOP'S FABLES, GRIMMS' FAIRY TALES, TALES OF HANS CHRISTIAN ANDERSEN, and A THOUSAND AND ONE NIGHTS. Some of the titles include JOURNEY TO THE WEST, *Jack and the Beanstalk*, CINDERELLA, ALICE IN WONDERLAND, SNOW WHITE, A LITTLE PRINCESS, THE WIZARD OF OZ, LITTLE WOMEN, *Little Red Riding Hood*, *Hansel and Gretel*, LITTLE MERMAID, *The Ugly Duckling*, HEIDI, TREASURE ISLAND, PETER PAN AND WENDY, *The Little Match Girl*, *Gulliver's Travels*, DADDY LONG-LEGS, ROBIN HOOD, LITTLE LORD FAUNTLEROY, SECRET GARDEN, *Frog Prince*, THREE MUSKETEERS, NOBODY'S BOY REMI, NOBODY'S GIRL, and ADRIFT IN THE PACIFIC. A similar concept was on sale at the same time in Aubec's 26-volume *Video Anime Picture Book Theater: World Masterpiece Children's Stories*.

VIE DURANT

2003. AKA: *Lasting Life*. TV series. DIR: Hiroshi Negishi. SCR: Takamitsu Otorino. DES: Yukari Watanabe. ANI: N/C. MUS: Hiroyuki Kozu. PRD: Marin Entertainment, RADIX, Durant Project. 8 mins. x 8 eps.
The melting Antarctic has submerged much of the world in water. With humans almost extinct, cloning becomes the preferred method of reproduction. But there is another way for some to survive: the way of the vampire. Seven young men cling to life and seek the salvation of the mysterious "Mother." Originally streamed over the Animate TV broadband site, this short series is directed by Hiroshi Negishi and also generated a CD drama. Negishi always comes up with something watchable, and Watanabe's character designs are very attractive, making this little-known show a good bet for light entertainment.

VIEWTIFUL JOE *

2004. TV series. DIR: Takaaki Ishiyama. SCR: GGB. DES: Yukiko Ohashi, Nobuaki Nagano. ANI: Masaki Kubomura. MUS: N/C. PRD: Capcom, Group Tac, TV Tokyo. 25 mins. x 51 eps.
Everyday slacker Joe has only two interests in life, and arguably, the screen hero Captain Blue takes precedence over Silvia, Joe's oftenneglected girlfriend. But when villains from the Movieworld snatch Silvia from a cinema and drag her into an alternate dimension, Joe chases after her into the screen. He gets to be Viewtiful Joe, a superhero in training who tries to rescue

his beloved, while learning tips on the superhero lifestyle from the aging, portly Captain Blue. Incorporating heavy doses of the underrated Arnold Schwarzenegger vehicle *The Last Action Hero* (1993), *Viewtiful Joe* dutifully recreates the look of the Capcom game that premiered the year before. It contains loving sideswipes at Japanese-style superheroes like ULTRAMAN, but also a terrifying English dub, with slacker slang and wanna-be streetwise hip hop argot that already sounds self-conscious and dated—compare to SAMURAI CHAMPLOO.

VIFAM

1983. JPN: *Ginga Hyoryu Vifam*. AKA: *Galactic Tales of Vifam; Galactic Wanderer Vifam; Round Vernian Vifam*. TV series. DIR: Takeyuki Kanda, Susumu Ishizaki, Tetsuro Amino, Osamu Sekita, Seiji Okuda, Junji Nishimura, Kazuo Yamazaki. SCR: Hiroyuki Hoshiyama, Yasushi Hirano, Tsunehisa Ito. DES: Toyoo Ashida, Kunio Okawara, Shoji Sato. ANI: Toyoo Ashida, Hiroshi Watanabe, Hideyuki Motohashi, Yasushi Nagaoka, Makoto Ito. MUS: Toshiyuki Watanabe. PRD: Sunrise, TBS. 25 mins. x 46 eps. (TV), 50 mins. x 4 eps. (v), 25 mins. x 12 eps. (TV2).

The Terran colony of Kreado is attacked by alien Kuktonian invaders, and when the adult crew of its orbiting space station are all killed, it is up to their 13 surviving children to fight back. Eventually, they reactivate the old starship Janus from dry dock and prepare to head for their homeworld—a trip fraught with perils both on the planets they pass and within the labyrinthine corridors of the Janus itself. It's a sci-fi remake of ADRIFT IN THE PACIFIC, and *Vifam*'s ludicrously overpopulated cast returned in 1984 for video adventures *V: News from Catcher* (*Catcher kara no Tayori*), *V: Gathering of the Thirteen* (*Atsumatta Jusannin*), *V: The 12 Fade Away* (*Kieta Juninin*, also shown in theaters), and *V: Kate's Reflections* (*Kate no Kioku*). The fact that the 4 video episodes follow on from the TV series, break down into eight 25-minute acts, and would have taken the series to a full year's 52 episodes makes it likely that they were the final unbroadcast episodes of the series.

The series was remade by Toshifumi Kawase as *Vifam 13* (1998), reuniting many of the old crew for a production that used previously unfilmed scripts as its basis. For the *V13* story arc, the crew rescue baby Kukto twins from a derelict ship and are forced to juggle child-care with their continuing mission.

VILLGUST

1992. JPN: *Kyoryu Densetsu Villgust*. AKA: *Armored Dragon Legend Villgust*. Video. DIR: Katsuhiko Nishijima. SCR: Satoru Akahori. DES: Katsuhiko Nishijima. ANI: Katsuhiko Nishijima. MUS: Kohei Tanaka. PRD: Animate Film. 30 mins. x 2 eps.

Two separate groups of adventurers meet up in a faux-medieval European village in the alternate universe of Villgust. Wannabe paladins Kui, Yuta, and cute girls Kris and Fanna are full of high ambitions to protect the land and rid it from evil, while catgirl Ryugia, Marobo the dog-man, Bostof the elf, and cute little girl Lemi are more interested in finding something to eat. They've actually been sent by the presiding goddess of the land to rid Villgust of a dark, evil force that looks suspiciously like Jabba the Hutt. Gabadi is a wicked oppressor with a large band of thoroughly nasty disposable minions, but he's devoted only to his pet frog, Antoinette. Gabadi succeeds in tricking Kui and company into fighting Ryugia (who has a penchant for bikini-style armor, an infantile food fetish, and a set of claws borrowed from X-Man Wolverine) and her friends—the very people intended by Heaven to be their allies! He wants them to destroy each other so that there is no opposition to his evil plans. More through luck than judgment, our heroes eventually start fighting his minions instead of each other, and they battle their way through a tornado, flying slabs of rock, snake-headed monsters, and tentacles to rid the land of his evil and bring peace back to Villgust.

Bandai originated the *gachapon* concept—small plastic toys enclosed in egg-shaped cases and sold for small change in street-corner vending machines. The name is said to be the sound of the egg-shaped cases falling from the machine. These sweet little creatures influenced video games, card games, and manga—Nintendo created the *Villgust* role-playing game based on them, and from that came this video series. So if anyone asks you which came first, it was definitely the egg.

VIOLENCE JACK *

1986. JPN: *Violence Jack Harlem Bomber; Violence Jack Jigokugai; Violence Jack Hell's Wind*. AKA: *VJ Slum-king; VJ Hell Town [Evil Town]; VJ Hell's Wind*. Video. DIR: Seiji Okuda, Ichiro Itano. SCR: Sho Aikawa, Takuya Wada, Makio Matsushita. DES: Takuya Wada, Moriyasu Taniguchi. ANI: Takuya Wada, Moriyasu Taniguchi. MUS: Hiroshi Ogasawara. PRD: Ashi Pro, Studio 88, Dynamic Planning. 40 mins. (*Harlem/Slumking*), 59 mins. (*Hell Town*), 60 mins. (*Hell's Wind*).

A comet strikes Earth and causes a chain reaction of other cataclysms. In Japan, the fault line gives way in the mother of all earthquakes, while the long-dormant volcano Mount Fuji erupts in a spectacular cloud of ash and lava. Survivors trapped in the Tokyo subway system turn into savage tunnel tribes. Gangs of motorcycle bandits roam the land in search of resources. And through the midst of it all walks Violence Jack, a mountain of a man with superhuman strength, inhuman fangs, and absolutely no scruples. Jack is an elemental force, wandering the desolate land like hell's own lawman, coming to the rescue of the assaulted, raped, and injured survivors, but not before the camera has permitted us a long, lingering look at their torments. These include stabbings, shootings, eviscerations, chainsaw decapitation, and someone eating his dead lover.

Often thought to be an inferior remake of FIST OF THE NORTH STAR, *VJ* actually predates it, starting as a 1973 manga in *Goraku* magazine, as the sequel to Go Nagai's DEVILMAN. The video necessarily condensed much of the epic original (Nagai's longest) into a broader, more basic, and much less shocking package, though it remains extremely violent and nasty even when censored—the U.K. running time is considerably shorter than the original. The lead character, with "the strength of a gorilla and teeth of a wolf, blood boiling with the fire of prehistory," is named for the huge jackknife he carries, and the anime focuses on his volcanic nature rather than the tangle of subplots and reincarnations of the manga. The basic post-apocalyptic plots of the video version (with knowing winks to *Mad Max*) were originally intended to have some internal coherence but were released in the wrong order outside Japan. The first episode,

showing the comet hitting Earth and explaining that Jack is the personification of the Grim Reaper, born from a mound of skulls, is actually *Slumking*, which was inexplicably the *last* episode to be released in the English version. To be fair, the muddled running order hardly makes any difference. The then boss of U.K.'s Manga Entertainment, Mike Preece, coined the term "beer-and-curry movie" for those anime destined to be watched by a group of inebriated teenage boys in search of sex and violence, and *VJ* is exactly what he meant. Those with higher hopes for the anime industry find the show embarrassingly infantile, including the English-language voice cast, who all appear to be using pseudonyms. ●⚫Ⓥ

VIOLIN OF THE STARRY SKY

1995. JPN: *Hoshizora no Violin*. Movie. DIR: Setsuo Nakayama. SCR: Toshiaki Imaizumi. DES: Mitsuharu Miyamae. ANI: Kazunori Tanahashi. MUS: Kazuki Kuriyama. PRD: Takahashi Studio. 90 mins.

Based on Noboru Wada's true story of the life of the Shinshu violinmaker Kikuji Ozawa (1916–98), who pursued his dream to make and play violins even as the clouds gathered for World War II. Violin music is provided by soloist Mio Umezu.

VIOLINIST OF HAMELIN, THE

1996. JPN: *Hamelun no Violin*. AKA: *Violin of Hamelin*. Movie, TV series. DIR: Takashi Imanishi, Junji Nishimura, Hiroshi Morioka, Akira Shimizu. SCR: Takashi Imanishi, Yasuhiro Imagawa. ANI: Toshimi Kato. ANI: Toshimi Kato. MUS: Kohei Tanaka. PRD: Nippon Animation, Studio Deen, TV Tokyo. 50 mins. (m), 25 mins. x 25 eps. (TV).

Fifteen years ago, Queen Horn of Sforzando tried to shut evil out of the world of Staccato with a powerful spell, but not even the strongest spell lasts forever, and now Horn's strength is failing. Evil Hell King Bass is trying to break through the barrier and release the "supreme leader" Great Chestra (in Japanese "Oh-kestra"), a dark being of unparalleled power who is trapped somewhere in Staccato. Horn's estranged daughter, Flute, is the only person who can save Sforzando from the inrush of darkness. She's been in hiding for 15 years, but now she is called by her mother to return to Sforzando. She sets out for the capital with her childhood friend and guardian, Hamel, but on the way they have many strange adventures and meet old and new friends. Hamel learns more about the mystery of his past and the strange horn on his head.

Based on a 1991 manga in *Shonen GanGan* by Michiaki Watanabe, *VoH* mixes tragedy and suspense with humor. On the way to becoming a moving picture the story developed a split personality. In 1996, it became a funny movie and was followed soon after by a much darker and more serious TV series—insofar as anything can be dark and serious when the protagonists' main weapons, as well as their names, are musical instruments. The animation in the TV series is noticeably low-budget, too, which caused controversy when the director himself publicly complained about the limited materials he had to work with.

VIPER GTS *

2002. Video. DIR: Masami Obari. SCR: P. Warrior, Kunitoshi Watanabe. DES: Kenichi Hamazaki. ANI: Kenichi Hamazaki, Kazuhiro Yamada. MUS: Takehiro Kawabe. PRD: Frontline, Moonrock, Studio G-1 Neo. 30 mins. x 3 eps.

Girl-demon Carrera and her partner Rati and self-appointed rival Mercedes form part of a demonic sales force, like Avon ladies but with spells. Their mission is to attract the attention of humans in need of magical aid, which they then grant in exchange for their victims' immortal souls. Teenage wimp Ogawa summons Carrera looking for vengeance on everyone who's ever picked on him. When she turns up to grant his wish, he takes one look at her oiled and wobbling endowments and decides to wish for something else instead. In a surprising plot twist, she discovers that he is massively well endowed and develops a crush on him. However, her contract fulfilled, she returns to whence she came, much to Ogawa's disappointment. She is duly punished for overstaying her time, and Ogawa begins summoning other demons in an attempt to regain her company, resulting in Mercedes' appearance, after which she also conceives a longing for him. But they aren't his only fans—the angels also muscle in. It's their duty to save Ogawa and the demonic duo, so they kidnap Carrera and Rati to Heaven, and

despite being cute females, they sprout penises and anoint the sinners liberally with "holy water from God's Tool." Ogawa and Mercedes thereafter mount a rescue mission, to assault Heaven and save the victims from the fate of salvation-by-rape. Nobody can say Masami Obari lacks a sense of the ridiculous—although divine sperm has been done before in **MASQUERADE**—nor the ability to produce high quality animated pornography. *Viper GTS*, despite its simple plot, shines above the great majority of anime porn for its excellence in character design, art, and animation. Combining two geeky wet dreams in one (the characters are named after top-marque cars, Rati being *Mase*rati, and the series is named for the $90K Dodge dream machine), he must be laughing himself silly all the way to the bank. Based on a computer game by Sogna, which was little more than an erotic, satanic take on **OH MY GODDESS!**—if you accept naming elements after automobiles as originality, then Sogna's claim to have created an "original story" won't annoy you. ⬤Ⓝ

VIPER'S CREED *

2009. TV series. DIR: Shinji Aramaki, Hiroyuki Kanbe. SCR: Masanao Akahoshi. DES: Ai Ota, Akira Tanisaki, Keiichi Hasegawa. ANI: Kazuyuki Kitahara. MUS: N/C. PRD: AIC Spirits, Digital Frontier, Sony Pictures Entertainment. 24 mins. x 12 eps.

Global warming has flooded much of the world's surface and the unrest led to a third world war. In the aftermath, cities hire private military corporations to protect them from the lawlessness and terrorism bred by the new conditions. Relations between the mercenaries and regular military and police aren't good, adding to the tensions. This show comes with excellent cyberpunk credentials; it was created by the **APPLESEED** remake director Shinji Aramaki, but despite interesting ideas and attractive-looking armor and mecha the story flags and the characters are not involving. It was pulled from American TV channel G4 after only four episodes, later to be released on DVD.

VIRAGO IN DUNGEON

1991. JPN: *Ozanari Dungeon: Kaze no To.* AKA: *Perfunctory Dungeon: Tower of the Wind.* Video. DIR: Hiroshi Aoyama. SCR: Hideki

Sonoda. DES: Minoru Maeda. ANI: Yoshikazu Takiguchi, Yasuo Otsuka. MUS: Kazz Toyama and Secret Plans. PRD: Tokyo Movie Shinsha. 30 mins. x 3 eps.

Three adventurers are hired by King Gazelle to steal the Dragon Head relic from the Shrine of Fire. Mocha (sexy elf-babe warrior), Blueman (funny animal cat-thief), and Kilieman (dog-wizard) are startled out of their larcenous intentions when the relic introduces itself to them as Morrow and asks to be taken, not to Gazelle's Tower of Fire, but to the Tower of Wind. Morrow is an organic program that can transform the Tower of Wind into an ultimate weapon called the Space Dragon. Gazelle, he says, is just a frontman for the real enemy, a mysterious being out to control the Space Dragon and destroy the world. Based on the 1987 *Comic Nora* manga by Motoo Koyama, who named the characters after the brands of coffee he was drinking while drawing the series— Mocha, Blue Mountain, and Kilimanjaro.

VIRGIN AUCTION *

2005. JPN: *Shojo Auction.* Video. DIR: Aim. SCR: Akaroh Kamagui. DES: Mie. ANI: Mie. MUS: Yoshi. PRD: Digital Works/Vanilla, YOUC. 30 mins. x 2 eps.

Another in the "slave auction" sub-sub-genre of the *chokyo* (training) subgenre, this series is unusual in that virtually none of the training is shown—it concerns itself primarily with the characters' relationships and interactions—and it is a production original to Digital Works (producers of the **VANILLA SERIES**, of which this is one), instead of being based on another company's game or manga. Shirohebi ("White snake"—see **PANDA AND THE MAGIC SERPENT**) Sukamu and Rongai Shijima are charged by their unseen bosses with training virgins for one night stands with the highest bidder. As in **LOVE LESSONS**, the virgins are volunteers—in this group of three, "Umi" (all of the girls are known only by *noms d'amour*) is attempting to earn enough money to pay off her fiancé's father's debts, foreigner "Gin" is seeking to finance her revenge against her Japanese con-man father, who abandoned her and her mother, while "Yukina" keeps her motives a secret. Gin is eventually sold to the head of a cult, and finds that her father is the power behind its throne, much to her satisfaction. Umi's services are bought by a shy, bullied geek from old money (who hopes that losing his virginity will make him "cool"); he takes Shirohebi's advice, and makes a new start. Yukina "escapes," in a plot cooked up so that Shirohebi may buy her; in exchange for her services, Rongai takes revenge on Yukina's rapist

The production values are better than have been the norm in recent *Vanilla Series* outings—the red tint that haunted such series as **HOOLIGAN** is gone, and overuse of digital animation loops is absent, as are obvious frame-to-frame continuity errors. While lacking much of a plot, this is a relatively inoffensive piece of porn; compare to the much nastier **SLAVE SISTERS** and *Fallen Idol Rina* in the **COOL DEVICES** series. A DVD player game was spun off from the series. **ⓁⓃⓋ**

VIRGIN FLEET *

1991. JPN: *Seishojo Kantai Virgin Fleet*. AKA: *Holy Maiden Fleet Virgin Fleet*. Video. DIR: Masahiro Hosoda. SCR: Yasuhiro Imagawa. DES: Hiroyuki Kitazume. ANI: Hiroyuki Kitazume. MUS: Masanobu Ito. PRD: Beam Entertainment. 30 mins. x 3 eps.
In the 1930s, a group of teenage girls in a Japanese military academy train with a mysterious psychic energy that includes, among other things, weather control and telekinesis and can only be controlled by a few young female virgins. Years before in WWI, a similar team called the 36 minstrels somehow succeeded in controlling this force and was able to put an end to the fighting. With the political situation growing ever more tense, the Soviet Union spying on its neighbors and trying to steal military secrets, and internal squabbling between the leaders of Japan, the nation desperately needs that power once more. A survivor of the Minstrel force is now highly placed in the military command and her daughter heads the academy—but she hasn't inherited her mother's power, which causes some friction between them. And out of the squabbling, shallow band of young ladies in her care, the one who emerges as able to release virgin energy is Shiokaze, who is engaged and whose boyfriend is pressuring her to leave the academy and marry him right away. Sadly, he's not the only man in the story who takes sexism to comic levels—the local military

leaders trot out all the clichés about a woman's place in war without any sense of irony, though in the U.S. dub the director and actors substitute a level of overacting that approaches talent in itself.

VF is part of the subgenre that includes creator Hiroi Oji's earlier **SAKURA WARS**, in which 20th-century military history isn't quite the way the West remembers it. In Oji's cute, squeaky-clean universe, Japan only wants to unleash the massive destructive force of virgin energy to *prevent* more killing—compare to similarly far-fetched avoidances of history in **KISHIN CORPS** and **SUPER ATRAGON**. However, this anime remains curiously endearing, full, like **GUNBUSTER**, of the martial enthusiasm of an undefeated Japan (see **WARTIME ANIME**), with well-animated backgrounds, sepia-toned flashbacks, and intriguing *neverwhen* aircraft designs. The story has some interesting moments and makes a few pointed observations on the real thoughts and feelings of teenagers about jealousy, love, and sex, but like many video anime, it starts a whole raft of subplots that don't go anywhere.

VIRGIN TOUCH *

2002. JPN: *Flutter of Birds: Toritachi no Habataki*. Video. DIR: Yoshitaka Fujimoto. SCR: Sumishi Aran, Rei Tachibana. DES: Masaki Takei, Tatsuhito Kurashiki. ANI: Tatsuhito Kurashiki. MUS: N/C. PRD: Pink Pineapple. 30 mins. x 2 eps. (v1), 30 mins. x 2 eps. (v2).
After eight years away in the big city, Yusaku is invited to come back to his remote hometown and work for a while in his uncle's clinic. He arrives back home to find that much has changed. Although he left as just another teenager, he returns as a respected authority figure, and his childhood friend Ibuki has grown into a pretty doctor herself. Yusaku is a heartthrob for the impressionable local nurses and some of the patients at the clinic. Not all the afflictions seem to be serious—some appear to be curable through the handy expedient of sexual intercourse, but it's not as if viewers of this mildly erotic anime wouldn't have been expecting that. Based on a computer game released the previous year by Silkies. **Ⓝ**

VIRTUACALL *

1997. JPN: *Virtuacall 2*. Video. DIR: Kaoru

Tomioka. SCR: Tetsuya Oseki. DES: N/C. ANI: Mitsuru Fujii. MUS: N/C. PRD: Fairy Dust. 45 mins. x 2 eps.
Virtuacall is the latest development in phone-sex clubs—a virtual meeting service that lets you see, hear, and even touch the man or woman of your dreams. Emily decides to use the service to help Hasegawa, a friend from her apartment building. She desires him, but he seems reluctant to make a move. She plans to assist in building his confidence and improving his chances of scoring by introducing him to Virtuacall for some online practice sessions. The anime is based on a Sega Saturn game; compare to similar cybersex in **SECRET ANIMA**'s *Dream Hazard*. **Ⓝ**

VIRTUA FIGHTER *

1995. TV series. DIR: Hideki Tonokatsu. SCR: Tsutomu Kamishiro, Kuniaki Kasai, Natsuko Senju. DES: Ryo Tanaka, Hiroshi Ono. ANI: Ryo Tanaka. MUS: Kaori Ohori. PRD: Tokyo Movie Shinsha, TV Tokyo. 25 mins. x 35 eps.
Based on Sega's successful video game, the story hinges around young martial artist Akira Yuki and his travels in search of his inner self. This involves lots of fighting. Luckily he meets lots of other people who also want to find themselves through fighting. He teams up with Pai Chan, a Chinese girl who is fighting to find her fiancé, and Jacky, who is fighting to find his sister Sara, and they fight lots of people "for honor, love, and revenge." The almost concurrent appearance of the **STREET FIGHTER II** TV series obviously had nothing to do with it, and an artist like Ono, who did the ravishing backgrounds for **DOG OF FLANDERS**, is wasted here. **Ⓥ**

VIRUS

1997. JPN: *Virus Buster Serge*. TV series. DIR: Masami Obari. SCR: Masami Obari, Jiro Kaneko, et al. DES: Masami Obari, Natsuki Mamiya. ANI: Masami Obari, Kazuto Nakazawa. MUS: Toshiyuki Omori. PRD: JC Staff, Plum, TV Tokyo. 30 mins. x 12 eps.
In 2097 Hong Kong, virtuality is preferable to the real world. The Internet has a mind of its own. Cloning is outlawed. Vast supercomputers run on biological software, but the combination of genetics and cybernetics places human beings at the mercy of digital viruses, some of which are accidents, some of which are the work

of the infamous "Incubator." The STAND is an elite task force that terminates viruses with extreme prejudice. Serge is a brainwashed assassin, plotting the death of STAND captain Raven. But when Serge is "cured" of his desire for vengeance, he joins the team. Impossibly proportioned token female Erika is just dying to get to know him better. But Serge is less popular with the two gunslinging officers, Macus and Joichiro, who don't want an ex-assassin for backup. The team must learn to work together and to exorcise the demons from their own past—the viruses feed on skeletons in the mental closet.

With its possessed human hosts, *Virus* shares themes with **GHOST IN THE SHELL** and glossy horror moods out of **SILENT MÖBIUS**. It combines the angst of **EVANGELION** and the superheroes of **SONIC SOLDIER BORGMAN**, artfully concealing a tiny budget and breakneck schedule with great splashes of special effects, clever uses of shadow, and superfast cuts. Its appeal to audiences is nicely, if perhaps cynically, manufactured; the makers assume that a male SF audience is already guaranteed, so they concentrate on the brooding, pouting, pretty-boys to drag in female fans. Fight scenes are carefully interwoven with character development; the end-of-episode cliffhanger is just as likely to be a terrifying revelation from the past as a physical threat. However, like the equally beautiful **DARKSIDE BLUES**, *Virus* has a frustrating tangle of subplots and relationships running into dead ends with no time to resolve them. For those who really can't wait to get more of the high-tensile battle action and the darkly erotic aura of the male cast, the Sega Saturn game and later PlayStation spin-off *Virus: The Battle Field* use the original cast voices and design. The hip-hop group Dragon Ash had its big break with the anime's opening theme, going on to record music for **DT EIGHTRON** and Kinji Fukasaku's live-action *Battle Royale* (2001). **V**

VISIONARY *

1995. AKA: *Vixens*. Video. DIR: Teruo Kogure, Taichi Kitagawa. SCR: Ryo Saga. DES: Tomohiro Ando. ANI: Tomohiro Ando. MUS: Masahiko Kikuchi. PRD: Knack, Beam Entertainment. 40 mins., 45 mins., 30 mins.

Ujita is a geeky high school boy who has no luck whatever with women and gets grief from the local bullies, until one day his computer malfunctions. Out pops sexy Doreimon, from another dimension (or back from the future—the script can't decide which) to solve all of his problems, in a cheeky parody of **DORAEMON**. Just like the hapless cat, she can grant all of Ujita's wishes (in exchange for room and board), but things don't always work out as she plans or he hopes, either in his attempt to date (and bed) the school's beauty, Reika, or to seduce a university co-ed. Later episodes continue the short pornographic comedies in the style of creator U-Jin's similar **TALES OF …**, with "Skydiving in Love," about the romantic and naïve rich boy Tadashi ("Koban") Okamura, his pragmatic ladies'-man friend Toru ("Sameo") Yabe, and his earthy love interest Shiori Hanamura; "New Century Queen," which looks into the backroom and bedroom deals between a Tokyo television channel's production executives, the schoolgirls who aspire to stardom, and their arrangement of affairs to their mutual satisfaction; and the last episode, "The Vampire Tradition," in which female "university" students confront the source of their friends' disappearances. *Visionary* brings a sense of fun that is too often missing from most anime porn, and many of its female characters are notable for their spunk and self-determination, rather than being the usual doormats. The series was later repackaged under the title *Vixens*. **OV**

VISITOR

1998. TV series. DIR: Atsushi Tokuda. SCR: Kazunori Ito. DES: Akemi Takada. ANI: N/C. MUS: Keiichi Matsuzaki. PRD: COM NT, WOWOW. 50 mins. x 3 eps.

In the year 2099, one of NASA's Apollo rocket capsules is found in the Mongolian desert, where it appears to have been for 65 million years. Meanwhile on Mars, a strange black artifact of unknown origins is eating one of the planet's moons. Earth ship Davide is sent to investigate and is sucked into the vortex. Lila Mochizuki and her companions are suddenly a long, long way from home. Entirely computer-generated animation faintly reminiscent of Supermarionation is one of the earliest in a style of animation likely to dominate the medium in the 21st century—motion-capture against CG backgrounds fast becoming the only viable means of making anime in an age of atrophied artistic skills and cheap computer power. This anime was intended for video but premiered on the satellite channel WOWOW. Later repackaged as a feature-length movie edit. Compare to **A.LI.CE** and **AURORA**.

VITAMINX ADDICTION

2011. Video. DIR: Keiichiro Kawaguchi. SCR: StoryWorks. DES: Satonobu Kikuchi. ANI: N/C. MUS: N/C. PRD: Nomad, Lantis. 25 mins. x 3 eps.

Yuri Minami is starting her second year of teaching at the elite Seitei Gakuen, an exclusive private school that teaches all ages from kindergarten to college. She's assigned to a class of seniors who have seen off all their previous teachers with ulcers or neuroses. Can she tame the bad boys of the upper crust and get them into college? Of course she can, because this is based on the dating simulation game *VitaminX* by D3.

VIVIDRED OPERATION *

2013. TV series. DIR: Kazuhiro Takamura. SCR: Hiroyuki Yoshino, Shigeru Morita, Tensai Okamura. DES: Kazuhiro Takamura. ANI: Yuki Ito. MUS: Hideyuki Fukasawa. PRD: A-1 Pictures, ANiplex, Dentsu, MBS, Movic. 24 mins. x 12 eps.

In a future mercifully free of the usual dystopian apocalypse, Ayane Isshiki grows up in a seaside town close to the Manifestation Engine, a miracle power source that has solved the energy crisis and ended pollution all at once. Unfortunately, this cure-all is soon under attack by alien forces called the Alone, leading Ayane and her companions to be recruited into a defense force utilizing fantastic inventions with powers barely distinguishable from magic. They also do so in skimpy outfits, just because. But it's the "indistinguishable from magic" part that really sets this show out, as a sci-fi invasion is held off by a bunch of ladies who use the combining powers and artifacts of Power Rangers, but in the style of many a magical girl.

VOICE ACTING

Voice acting in the earliest of the **EARLY ANIME** was not part of the finished work, since Japanese animation was in existence for at least a decade before the introduction of audio. Instead, anime would be screened to a musical accompaniment, although many would also employ a live *benshi* (narrator) to fill in dialogue and story elements in the style of similar performances in the Japanese puppet theater or magic lantern shows—as in the world of live-action film, there was never any such thing as a "silent" movie.

Voice work in early anime was often of secondary concern, with "actors" pulled in from available staff. When casting the two combatants in **BENKEI VS. USHIWAKA** (1939) animator Kenzo Masaoka chose Mrs. Masaoka to play the diminutive hero, and himself as the hulking brute Benkei. Dialogue from several American films was stolen to add exotic foreign language scenes to **WARTIME ANIME**, including snatches from Popeye's enemy Bluto, who appears as an Allied soldier in *Momotaro's Sea Eagles* (1943). Sometimes the effect can be unintentionally surreal—in the middle of the battle sequence in **MOMOTARO'S DIVINE SEA WARRIORS** (1945), an American voice can be heard hailing a taxi. The first genuine English-language voice actor in anime appears in the closing moments of the same film, as the tremulous and cowardly British soldier who attempts to renegotiate the terms of his surrender. The uncredited actor is clearly a native speaker, but with a strange delivery that seems either to be a calculated attempt to make his dialogue unusable, or perhaps, more chillingly, the sign of a man in genuine fear for his life.

In the 1950s, as Toei and Mushi began to make animated features in imitation of Disney, famous Japanese personalities were often chosen to appear in anime, although not always on account of their acting skills. Osamu Tezuka's **A THOUSAND AND ONE NIGHTS** (1969) and **CLEOPATRA: QUEEN OF SEX** (1970) bizarrely include vocal performances from a number of famous Japanese authors, including Shusaku Endo, Yasutaka Tsutsui, and Sakyo Komatsu.

The rise of television saw an exponential rise in the number of vocal performers in Japan, creating an entire voice acting industry in order to dub foreign television productions into Japanese. Anime voice acting often exploited this fact with casting decisions whose relevance is all but lost on a non-Japanese audience, hiring the Japa-

nese "voices" of famous American screen stars to portray anime characters with similar profiles. Yasuo Yamada, who was until his death the voice of **LUPIN III**, was also renowned for playing Clint Eastwood, while Lupin's sidekick Jigen was played by Kiyoshi Komori, the Japanese voice of Lee Marvin. Similar casting "coincidences" continue to the present day, with numerous bigname anime voice actors also playing big names from Hollywood, although it is less common for a Hollywood star to have one single Japanese actor play all their roles.

The popular anime voice actors of today include Akio Otsuka, best known as Batou in **GHOST IN THE SHELL**, who is also the voice of Jonathan Frakes (Commander William Riker) in *Star Trek: The Next Generation*. Yasunori Matsumoto played both V-daan in **BEAST WARRIORS** and Brad Pitt in *Se7en*; Kappei Yamaguchi is the voice of **INU YASHA** and Bugs Bunny; and the versatile Koichi Yamadera has voiced not only **COWBOY BEBOP**'s Spike Spiegel, but also Jim Carrey, Eddie Murphy, Robin Williams, and Tom Hanks. Many famous voice actors end up typecast—consistently given the same kind of role, be it as a juvenile lead, a maverick rebel, or a slow lunk. This can limit the audience's perception of their abilities, but can also prove to be beneficial on fast schedules—an actor who has played three hot-headed heroes in the past week probably knows what he's doing when given a fourth. Sometimes anime can exploit these associations in reverse—**EVANGELION** famously cast several prominent voice actors against type, in a decision that generated superb performances. Anime voice actors are also liable to enjoy spin-off careers in radio and music, and many have their own radio shows or albums. Modern anime exploits this by using voice actors in radio dramas or games as an experiment to test the market for a later anime version.

Voice acting in Japan is usually recorded a substantial way into the production process, often while the actors watch the animatics (in Japanese, the "Leica reel")—a precisely timed video of storyboards that allows them a sense of how the finished product will look. Types of voice-acting, however, fall into four distinct categories: *afureco* ("after-recording") after anima-

tion has been made; *atereco* ("substitution recording") to replace a foreign dialogue track in dubbing; the rare *prereco* ("presentation recording") in the Disney model, recording the voice track before the animation is made; and the rarest *mitereco* ("observation recording") in which the actors are filmed in order to allow animators to imitate their expressions.

Many voice recording facilities in Japan run around the clock in order to get the best returns from their investment in expensive machinery. This, along with union rules, has made child actors rare in anime voice work:they tend only to appear in movie productions, which require less studio time than a long-running series, and can also afford the higher prices of daytime booking. In the cheaper, longer-running worlds of video and TV, child parts are often played by adult women, notably Masako Nozawa, who is the Japanese voice of both talking pig *Babe* (1995) and **DRAGON BALL Z**'s Goku, and Megumi Ogata, who has voiced male anime protagonists from **EVANGELION** to **YU-GI-OH**. Most Japanese voice actors are professionally trained as such, and hence know to monitor and preserve the talent that earns their living. In one notable choice, Akira Kamiya, the voice of Ken in **FIST OF THE NORTH STAR**, decided upon his trademark high-pitched attacks because falsetto yells would be easier to repeat and maintain over a long series than gruff growls. Such considerations can often elude less experienced actors abroad, some of whom have temporarily damaged their vocal chords, lost their voices, or been forced to drop out of long-running productions.

The concept of a voice acting **FANDOM** first arrived in Japan in the early 1980s, with newly founded magazines such as *Newtype* and *Animage* in search of fresh subjects for articles, and the rise in voiceacting spin-offs occasioned by Mari Iijima's role as the singer Lin Minmei in **MACROSS**. For the video-based anime industry, with a primarily male fan-base, a heavy concentration on voice *actresses* was inevitable, with some of the most popular stars including Megumi Hayashibara (the female **RANMA ½**, but also Audrey Tautou in *Amélie*), Kotono Mitsuishi (the lead in **SAILOR MOON**, but also sometimes heard as Cameron Diaz and Natalie Portman),

Aya Hisakawa (Sailor Mercury *and* Natalie Portman, again), and Chisa Yokoyama (Pretty Sammy in **TENCHI MUYO!**, but also Winona Ryder and Alicia Silverstone). Anime voice actors are also popular choices as columnists in magazines, and not merely those associated directly with the anime world. Fumi Hirano, who was once the voice of Lum in **URUSEI YATSURA**, still writes a column on the world of fish for *Big Comic*. This is not quite as bizarre as it may first seem, since she left the acting business to marry a wealthy fish market entrepreneur. Although, on second thought, it is still pretty weird.

Voice acting in the Western world has developed similar personality cults, beginning with the realization that many American voice actors were often locally available, easy on the eye and good with crowds—all excellent reasons to invite them to conventions. Many American voice actors have become fixtures on the convention circuit, including stars from anime of yesteryear such as Corinne Orr (**SPEED RACER**) and Amy Howard Wilson (**STAR BLAZERS**). Voice actor attendance at conventions has grown exponentially during the 1990s and beyond, particularly since Japanese guests can be expensive to invite and usually do not speak English. It is not uncommon for American anime conventions to have many more American voice actors than Japanese guests.

Whereas video anime tend to use relative unknowns, often rendered all the more unknowable by the use of pseudonyms to preserve union status, anime movie releases in America regularly use "stunt-casting"—the use of actors famous elsewhere. Incidences date back to the use of Frankie Avalon in *Alakazam the Great* (1960, see **JOURNEY TO THE WEST**), and have included cameo anime performances from Orson Welles and Leonard Nimoy (in the **TRANSFORMERS** movie). This has even happened in Japan, where the producers of the **ARMITAGE III** movie *Polymatrix* decided to make it extra exotic by hiring foreign actors and releasing the movie in English in Japan, with the voices of Kiefer Sutherland and Elizabeth Berkley.

American stunt-casting roles have become even more noticeable in recent years with the release of Studio Ghibli films in America, utilizing such talents as Lauren Bacall and Jean Simmons (**HOWL'S MOVING CASTLE**), or Kirsten Dunst and Debbie Reynolds (**KIKI'S DELIVERY SERVICE**). Similar casting decisions have been made with regard to the voices in some modern porn anime, in which erotic stars such as Asia Carrera, Kobe Tai, and Alexa Rae have been used to dub anime, in the presumed hope that fans of their live-action work will also pick up their porn voice-overs for the sake of completeness. This was also tried with some erotic anime in Japanese, such as the casting of adult video starlets in the original Japanese language track of **ADVENTURE KID**. Players of the actor game "Six Degrees of Kevin Bacon" will be disappointed to hear that although he voiced the eponymous *Balto* (1995), he has not appeared in an anime. However, he did costar with Kiefer Sutherland in *Flatliners* (1990), which should help anyone playing a version that links to the anime world.

VOICES AT WORK

2010. JPN: *Koe de Oshigoto! The Animation*. Video. DIR: Naoto Hosoda. SCR: Masashi Suzuki. DES: Satoru Kiyomaru, Hiroki Matsumoto. ANI: Satoru Kiyomaru. MUS: N/C. PRD: Studio Gokumi, Pony Canyon. 30 mins. x 2 eps.

Kanna's older sister Yayoi has always been a true friend to her, in spite of their 12-year gap in ages. She's done so many things for Kanna, and she's a great role model—hardworking, loving, and straighttalking. On Kanna's 16th birthday Yayoi invites her to visit her workplace, an erotic video-game company, for the first time. They're developing a new game and need a young voice actress. After all her sister has done for her, how can Kanna refuse? She finds she can actually have an orgasm just using her imagination, but that isn't always necessary. Azure Konno's 2008 manga forms the basis for a series in which a sister grooms her younger sibling to work in the sex trade. In an unexpected display of restraint, Pony Canyon delayed the release of the second episode by a month after the 2011 earthquake. ⬤⬤

VOICES OF A DISTANT STAR *

2002. JPN: *Hoshi no Koe*. AKA: *Voice of the Stars*. Video. DIR: Makoto Shinkai. SCR: Makoto Shinkai. DES: Makoto Shinkai. ANI: Makoto Shinkai. MUS: Tenmon. PRD: CoMix Wave International, Mangazoo. 25 mins.

Noboru and Mikako are ordinary Japanese teenagers in love: they walk each other home from high school, hang out at the convenience store, and dream of a future together. When mysterious aliens attack a human colony on Mars, Mikako is accepted for a United Nations military program. She becomes a Tracer, piloting a giant robotic combat suit on a series of training missions, before circumstances force her mothership to take successively greater warp jumps away from home. Her wouldbe boyfriend waits back in Japan, hoping for his mobile phone to ring with a text message from his 15-year-old girlfriend. Every now and then, it does… but Mikako's texts can only travel at the speed of light. Her *now* becomes his *then*, separated by days, then weeks, then months….

Such tales of robots and romance initially seem little removed from a hundred other anime since the groundbreaking **ZAMBOT 3**, but *Voices* remains a touchstone of 21st-century anime not for its story, but for the means of its execution. This is a work so saturated with its creator's sensibility and personality that watching it is like reading a private diary—its strongest literary influences are the phantom girlfriends in the works of novelist Haruki Murakami, separated from a narrator by obstacles both physical and metaphysical. Its brevity is a great virtue, forcing Shinkai to enhance the emotional charge. This is useful, too, since unforgiving critics might otherwise focus on its minor flaws, such as the "future" technology that simply slaps spaceships and robots onto the present day (the phones already look dated), or a closing song that often sounds like a cat in pain. However, *Voices* is truly one of the most beautiful and powerful anime of recent years and its creator has become a posterboy for the new generation of have-a-go amateur animators. Shinkai assembled much of it solo, using software packages liberated from his dayjob at a computer games company, and originally played the lead himself while conscripting his fiancée to play Mikako. In pushing for the fan-friendly audience, in his designs and plotting, in incidents, in scenes, and even in some shots, Shinkai's debt to **GUNBUSTER** is so great that it verges on the actionable. But Shinkai's constant reference to the 1988 classic is only one of several homages—look out, too, for passing train cars destined for the "U.N. Spacy" of the **Macross** saga.

As multimedia corporations fight over increasingly smaller TV ratingsshares and pump out endless dross based on bad computer games, *Voices* shows what one man can achieve in his living room. Of course, Shinkai had a little help from the Mangazoo corporation, which eventually provided financial and logistic support (including revoicing the audio for the mass-market release), but *Voices* is essentially put together with a high-end personal computer and commercially available software. In that regard, it brings the medium fullcircle, to the homemade concoctions of **Early Anime**.

The DVD release includes both Japanese voice tracks, as well as Shinkai's earlier short film *She and Her Cat*. Compare also to the same year's **Saikano**, with which it shares several story elements and attitudes. *Voices* also enjoyed an extensive run at a small western Tokyo cinema, so is filed in some sources as a "movie." Shinkai followed *Voices* with the feature-length **The Place Promised in Our Early Days**, which revisits many of the same themes.

VOLLEY BOYS

1997. JPN: *Kogyo Aika Volley Boys*. AKA: *Industrial Lament Volley Boys*. Video. DIR: Kunihiko Yuyama. SCR: Hiroshi Koda. DES: Hiroyuki Murata. ANI: N/C. MUS: N/C. PRD: Toho. 50 mins. x 2 eps.
Sex-starved teenage boys at Kudo High School sign up for the *girls'* volleyball team—hoping that if they build it, the girls will come, to a year that has no girls in it at all. This spin-off from Hiroyuki Murata's 1988 manga in *Young Magazine* mixes *Field of Dreams* with **Ping Pong Club**.

VOLTAGE FIGHTER GOWCAISER *

1996. JPN: *Chojin Gakuen Gowcaiser*. AKA: *Superhuman Academy Gowcaiser*. Video. DIR: Masami Obari. SCR: Kengo Asai. DES: Masami Obari. ANI: Masahiro Yamane. MUS: Airs. PRD: JC Staff, GaGa. 45 mins. x 3 eps.
Isato Kaiza's (Isato Goka's) athletic skills have won him a place at the Belnar Institute, a school for those with some outstanding gift, and this being an Obari anime, all the female students have at least

two. But the institute's mysterious founder has a hidden agenda—he is using the arcane powers of his Caizer Stones to control his students by giving them superhuman fighting skills, while he is controlled by a beautiful, seemingly female but definitely inhuman entity. Isato's friend Kash has given him a Caizer Stone and with it the power to transform into armored hero Gowcaizer; he learns that just about everyone else he knows has similar powers of transformation. Alas, the script doesn't. It starts with some interesting ideas, but many never develop. A subplot about incest between a brother and sister at school is well developed, largely because it provides an excuse for more sex and fighting; another, about a teacher's involvement in the government's attempts to keep an eye on things at the institute, is more or less ignored because it doesn't. The interesting relationship between the founder and his control remains unexplained. Perhaps the plan was to take all these ideas further if the video had spun off into a TV series, but it never happened. Based on a computer game (though it only uses some of the characters), with plenty of action and plenty of Obari's trademark fan service, *Gowcaizer* remains just another beat-'em-up with fantasy tropes thrown in. The videos were also edited into a feature-length *Gowcaiser* "movie." **Ⓝ Ⓥ**

VOLTRON *

1981. JPN: *Hyakujuo Go-Lion, Kiko Kantai Dairugger XV*. AKA: *Beast Centurion Go-Lion, Machine Platoon Dairugger XV; Lion Force Voltron*. TV series. DIR: Katsuhiko Taguchi, Kazuyuki Okaseko, Kazushi Nomura, Hiroshi Sasagawa. SCR: Susumu Takaku, Ryo Nakahara, Masaaki Sakurai. DES: Kazuo Nakamura. ANI: Kazuo Nakamura, Moriyasu Taniguchi, Akira Saijo. MUS: Masahisa Takeshi. PRD: Toei, Tokyo 12 Channel. 25 mins. x 125 eps.
Reptile Emperor Dai Bazal of planet Garla (AKA Zarkon of planet Doom in the American version) has built a galaxy-conquering army by transforming kidnapped enemies into fighting monsters. On a mission to Earth his forces kidnap some of its people, including our unsuspecting heroes Akira, Takashi, Tsuyoshi, Isamu, and Hiroshi. They are carried off to a conquered world for transformation. Stealing an enemy

ship, they escape and manage to reach the palace of Princess Fara, where they learn that five ancient robot lions can combine to form one mighty robot. Impressed by their courage, the dead emperor (in hologram form) gives them the power to operate the machines, form the robot, and free the galaxy from the forces of evil in just 52 episodes.

In the U.S. version, Earth was the headquarters of the peace-loving planetary federation known as the Galaxy Alliance, and Sven, Keith, Lance, Pidge, and Hunk were Space Explorers sent on a mission to planet Arus, recently devastated by Zarkon. Their objective was the Lion Force, Arus's five greatest weapons, which could merge to form the super-robot Voltron. They find that Princess Allura has survived the devastation of her world and is struggling to overthrow Zarkon's evil rule, and they join her as the pilots of the five robot lions that combine to make up Voltron. In the original story Akira is killed in battle (Sven is merely wounded, since American heroes can't die) and Fara/Allura takes his place on the team.

The *Golion* series was bought for U.S. syndication as *Voltron: Defender of the Universe!*, with scripts "written" by Jameson Brewer and Howard Albrecht. Presaging the later treatment of **Robotech**, it was combined with an unrelated show to bulk out the running time. *Dairugger XV* (1982) was a 56-episode show, also from Toei, renamed *Vehicle Team Voltron* in the U.S. In the original Japanese version, Earth is enjoying a period of unparalleled prosperity thanks to its alliances with the people of the planets Mila and Sara. The president of the Terran League initiates a mission to explore space beyond our galaxy, and the starship Rugger-Guard sets out on its mission. Attacked by a ship of the Galveston Empire, Rugger-Guard sends out its best line of defense—Dairugger XV, a giant robot made up of 15 different mecha, each with its own pilot. As with **Gold Lightan** and other shows of the period, there is a far-fetched origin—15 players on a team in rugby, a sport whose only other anime appearance is in **Wartime Anime**.

In the U.S. version, Voltron technology was brought back to Earth after the struggle with Zarkon in the earlier *Lion Force Voltron* segment of the series. The

Galaxy Alliance used it to build their own, even larger Voltron made up of 15 smaller robots and sent it out of our galaxy on the spaceship Explorer to find habitable new planets. The Drule dictatorship, whose homeworld was dying of pollution, sent ships to tag along behind the Explorer and try to steal any habitable worlds for themselves. The 15 pilots of the Explorer had to do battle both with natural forces like volcanoes on the worlds they discovered and with the Drule. Eventually the Drule population revolted, the planet exploded, and the "good" Drule were rescued by Voltron and relocated to new homes.

The producers intended to refashion LIGHTSPEED ELECTROID ARBEGAS as the third part of the series, but the show was canceled. However, merchandising by U.S. toy distributors Matchbox further confused matters by including the "stackable" robot hero from *Arbegas* as "Voltron II." The toy boxes show stills from all three anime, with Dairugger as "Voltron I" and GoLion as "Voltron III," claiming that the Arbegas robot is part of the Voltron story line, though he never appears in the TV show. Riding on the momentum created by *Star Wars* and sales of space battle toys, *Voltron* was successfully rerun on U.S. cable TV in the early 1990s. World Events Productions ran a 90-minute special in 1983 then syndicated the series as a half-hour daily show, tied into the merchandising of toy weaponry. *Lion Force* did better than *Vehicle Team Voltron* with its new audience, to the extent that new episodes were commissioned from Japan especially for the American market—creating a total run for the combined *Voltron* series of 125 episodes. In one of these, the "recovered" Sven rejoined the team just in time to help defeat Zarkon. The sequel *Voltron: The Third Dimension* (1998, AKA *Voltron 3D*) was an all-American 3-D CG motion-capture version made by *Babylon 5*'s effects company Netter Digital. In this version, the team is joined by Zarkon himself, who has seen the error of his ways, and fights to defeat Zarkon's evil son Lotor—you can tell he's evil because he has a *scar*.

VOLTUS *

1977. JPN: *Cho Denji Machine Voltes V*. AKA: *Super Electromagnetic Machine Voltes 5*. TV series. DIR: Tadao Nagahama, Yoshiyuki

Tomino, Yukihiro Takahashi. SCR: Koichi Taguchi, Masaki Tsuji, Fuyunori Gobu. DES: Akihiro Kanayama, Nobuyoshi Sasakado. ANI: Akihiro Kanayama. MUS: Hiroshi Tsutsui. PRD: Sunrise, Toei, TV Asahi. 25 mins. x 40 eps.

The three Go brothers, Kenichi, Daijiro, and Hiyoshi, and their friends Ippei Mine and Megumi Oka pilot the giant robot Voltes V in the battle against the people of planet Bozan, who are trying to add Earth to their galactic empire. But the prince of Bozan, Hainel, claims to be the Go boys' half-brother; he says their father was an alien, sent to Earth many years before. How can they fight their own flesh and blood, can Earth trust them, and might this point to a way forward for both peoples?

After Sunrise made COMBATTLER V for Toei, it followed up with this repeat performance—the undisputed star of which is Hainel, the first baddie to be a real hit with the female audience, many of whom wrote in demanding that he survive. Originally dubbed in Japan by William Ross for a U.S. theatrical release, the relatively faithful version was scrapped by new owners "New Hope Productions," which replaced it with a soundtrack more like *Star Wars* and eventually sold it to the Christian Broadcast Network. The company similarly tried to capitalize on George Lucas' success by refashioning STARBIRDS.

VOLUPTUOUS CRAVING

2007. JPN: *En-yoku*. Video. DIR: Motoyagi Yamamoto. SCR: Kusakai Kokubunji. DES: Motoyagi Yamamoto, Hachiman Hara. ANI: Motoyagi Yamamoto, Eisaku Wada. MUS: FUJIMOTO. PRD: MS Pictures (BOOTLEG), Tsukasa Shobo. 30 mins.

So how exactly does an English teacher wind up chained on the couch in the school nurse's office? The voluptuous Mizuho seduces one of her students, Naria, but has a rival for his affections: Yukiha, a girl his own age who also goes to their school. You can predict the outcome, but any woman who wears a black bra under a white shirt obviously has no regard for the consequences of her actions. Based on the 1997 porn manga *En-yoku* by Tsuzuru Miyabi and storyboarded by Heisaku Wada. ●●

VOOGIE'S ANGEL *

1997. JPN: *Denno Sentai Voogie's Angel*. AKA: *Cyber Battle Team Voogie's Angel*. Video. DIR: Mamoru Takeuchi. SCR: Mamoru Takeuchi. DES: Masami Obari. ANI: Masami Obari. MUS: Satoshi Yuyama. PRD: JC Staff, Beam Entertainment. 30 mins. x 3 eps.

A hundred years after Earth is invaded by aliens, the last remnants of the human race dwell in underwater "Aqua Bases." A team of five cybernetically enhanced women is trained for the purpose of carrying out guerrilla attacks against the occupying forces. Earth's last best hope for salvation is Voogie's Angel. Playing like a warped version of *Stingray*, *VA* delivers some interesting moments. The cutesy-conventional girl cyborg team (good sort, tough girl, kid sister, nice Japanese girl) and their scientist father-figure go from the aliens-invade-earth scenario, via space battles and embarrassing "comic" scenes, to the extremely violent fight in the second episode in which our heroes are smashed almost to a pulp. Then there's the black-and-white GUNBUSTER homage in episode 3, which shows how each of the cyborgs died tragically and was then rebuilt in enhanced form. The fight for human freedom shows the cyborgs what it means to be truly human but doesn't explain why cyber-enhanced women usually have gravity-defying breasts or why swimwear is the battle dress of preference in Obari-designed shows. A radio and CD drama in 1996 preceded the video release. Spin-offs include a manga in *Comic Gamma* and a "side story" *Onward! Super Angels* that features the characters in super-deformed mode (see SUPER-DEFORMED DOUBLE FEATURE). The series was also released on DVD in the 70-minute feature-length "director's cut" *VA: Forever and Ever* (1998), containing extra footage. ●

VOTOMS *

1983. JPN: *Sokokihei Votoms*. AKA: *Armored Trooper Votoms; ScopeDog*. TV series, video. DIR: Ryosuke Takahashi, Haruka Miyako, Tatsuya Matsuno, Toshifumi Takizawa, Hiroshi Yoshida, Yukihiro Takahashi, Masakazu Yasumura. SCR: Fuyunori Gobu, Soji Yoshikawa, Jinzo Toriumi, Ryosuke Takahashi, Takashi Imanishi. DES: Norio Shioyama, Ryosuke Takahashi, Kunio Okawara (TV, v), Yutaka Izubuchi (v94). ANI: Norio Shioyama. MUS:

Hiroki Inui. PRD: Sunrise, TV Tokyo. 25 mins. x 52 eps. (TV), 60 mins. x 3 eps. (v), 30 mins. x 4 (v94), 22 mins. x 12 eps. (v09), 50 mins. x 6 eps. (v10a), 50 mins. (v10b), 50 mins. (v10c), 50 mins. (v11).

On a distant world, the Perfect Soldier is finally created after genetic manipulation and a breeding program lasting centuries, but by the time this happens, the war has almost ended. The politicians and scientists who bred him either want him dead or want to use him in other, more sinister ways. But Chirico Cuve isn't a machine—he's a human being, and he's determined to find out who is responsible for all this. As the war ends he is separated from his unit, thrown into a series of desperate situations, enslaved, used as a gladiator in robot combat, enlisted as a mercenary, and meets the love of his life, only to discover that she too is a Perfect Soldier.

The first video, *The Last Red Shoulder* (1985), is a continuation of the story after the end of the TV series. Chirico leaves Udo City in search of his beloved Fiana. In *Big Battle* (1986), he finds her being held hostage by Bararant in an experimental facility near Koba City, and he and his comrades have to fight their way in to save her. 1987's *Red Shoulder Document: The Roots of Treachery* is a prequel to the TV series and shows Chirico's origins as part of a genetic experiment and recruitment into the Red Shoulder group. In 1994 Takahashi brought the same team together for a four-part video adventure set 32 years after the end of the TV series. Chirico and Fiana have been in cryo-sleep together for all that time, but now a new threat has arisen, and it's time for them to fight again. An extra item on the first tape, *Votoms Briefing*, filled in the backstory for those who missed the series 11 years earlier.

The "real robot" concept was born out of a conviction that the weapons of the future would not be made of shiny metal in clean, bright primary colors. Instead, creator Takahashi posited an environment where fighting machines were grim, functional workhorses, many past their prime and headed for the scrapheap. Designer Okawara wanted to create suits that looked as if they could be made in a 20th-century factory, designed so that the toys that would inevitably be spun off the series could be posed and moved exactly like

their animated inspirations (unlike many of the suits he'd designed for **GUNDAM**) and smaller in scale than his designs for **DOUGRAM**. In just one of the serial's many inspired touches, many Votoms machines have "roller-skates" to permit speedy movement; while it sounds incongruous, it functions as a challenge to the *Gundam* machines, which Takahashi regarded as unrealistically mobile on the ground.

Robots, which started out in anime primarily as cool toys to even up the odds for the little guy (children, the human race, or the Japanese) against a big, hostile world (adults, alien invaders, or foreign competition), had been seen right from the first as having as much potential for destruction as for good. **GIGANTOR** could be used by evil men just as easily as by perky little Jimmy Sparks—the power lay in the hands of whoever held the remote control. Takahashi and his fellow writers and directors extended this idea into the whole range of future military technology (VOTOMs is an acronym for Vertical One-man Tank for Offensive Maneuvers), showing robots and scientifically enhanced superbeings as just another weapon in the arsenal of the politicians, and war as a vicious, dehumanizing process in which honor and courage came from the individual, rather than any religion or value system, and could be crushed as easily as an insect (see **GREY: DIGITAL TARGET**). It also didn't hurt that *Votoms'* hero resembled Steve McQueen (lead character in the Western *Junior Bonner*, an early inspiration for the anime), whose laconic combination of little-boy charm and man's-man toughness was hugely popular with Japanese audiences.

The concept and the appealingly gritty realism of Takahashi's future war vision spun off another video series set in the same universe, as the title signals. Written by Takahashi but directed by Takeyuki Kanda, *Armored Trooper Votoms: Armor Hunter Merowlink* (1988, *Kiko Ryohei Merowlink*) is the story of a young rookie who is the sole survivor of a platoon cut down by bungling and treachery higher up the ranks. Framed for desertion and the deaths of his colleagues, he vows to avenge them; each of the 12 25-minute episodes shows one act of vengeance on an individual betrayer. A brilliantly paced

series richly meriting a Western release, it combines good character development and edge-of-the-seat tension. There are points when *Merowlink* doesn't simply suspend disbelief but knocks it out cold, especially in the final episode with an escape sequence as silly on calm reflection as it is absolutely convincing while you watch. Sequences of extreme violence and deliberate cruelty are carefully calculated to enhance the effect of this stunning rite-of-passage tale. The series was a major inspiration for the *Heavy Gear* role-playing war- and video-game franchise, which now has its own CGI cartoon series. Note that *Votoms* has many recap episodes and fix-ups of preexisting videos, which are sometimes mistaken for original episodes. These recapitulations are *ATV: Highlights, Stories of the ATV 2, Woodo, Kammen, Sansa,* and *Quant*.

Fifteen years after the last of the video spin-offs, a number of new iterations extended the franchise and filled several narrative gaps, beginning with the 12-part video series *Armored Trooper Votoms: The Pailsen Files* (2009, also in a movie edit), followed by the six-part video series *Phantom Chapter* (2010) and the one-shots *Case Irvine* (2010), *Finder* (2010), and *Alone Again* (2011). These twilight releases seemed to reflect an understanding on the part of the producers that *Votoms* was one of the blue-chip titles that had gathered a "silver otaku" following of middle-aged men with an enduring interest in the models and the franchise. However, as creator Takahashi once joked at a Scottish film festival: "*Votoms* and golf have a lot in common. They both take a long time, and they are both quite boring to watch!" **LV**

VOYAGE OF THE TSUSHIMA

1982. JPN: *Tsushima-maru: Sayonara Okinawa*. AKA: *The Tsushima: Farewell Okinawa*. Movie. DIR: Osamu Kobayashi. SCR: Shoichiro Okubo, Koji Senno. DES: Osamu Kobayashi. ANI: Tsutomu Shibayama, Hideo Kawauchi. MUS: Haruya Sugita. PRD: Ajia-do. 70 mins. On August 22, 1944, the Japanese freighter Tsushima Maru flees Okinawa for the mainland with a cargo consisting primarily of evacuees, the crew divided over whether to steer a zigzag course or simply to steam at full speed for safety. Her luck runs out off Akuseki Island, Kagoshima, when she is struck three times by torpedoes from an American submarine. The ship sinks with the loss of 1,484 lives, including 738 children. Based on a true story dramatized by Tatsuhiro Oshiro in book form in 1961, this movie ends with a roll call of those who did not survive. The wreck of the Tsushima Maru itself was not located until 1997.

VOYEUR'S DIGEST ★

2002. JPN: *Bad End*. Video. DIR: Kanzaburo Oda. SCR: Rokurota Makabe; DES: Mario Yaguchi. ANI: Mario Yaguchi. MUS: Yoshi. PRD: YOUC, Digital Works (Vanilla Series). 30 mins. x 2 eps.

Student Toshiki Mikimoto is the secret proprietor of an underground newspaper, which exposes trouble and corruption in his school. At least, that's how he rationalizes it to himself; in fact, his newsletter is more of a scandalous gossip column, making slanderous accusations about certain coeds, in the hope that Toshiki's fellow students will take it upon themselves to "punish" the alleged transgressors. When a group of students duly take the bait and rape one of their number, Toshiki is on hand to record everything for prosperity. In the second episode, he similarly stalks another voluptuous coed, in an erotic anime in the VANILLA SERIES, based on a computer game. The original title was presumably changed in the American release in order to prevent people like us making snide and unjustified remarks about the beginning and middle not being all that good either. Compare to CLASSROOM OF ATONEMENT, which shares many plot elements. ⬤🅝🅥

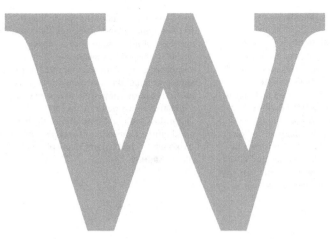

WA WA WA WAPPI-CHAN
2006. TV series. DIR: N/C. SCR: N/C. DES: Rucola Nicola. ANI: Rucola Nicola. MUS: N/C. PRD: WOWOW. 30 mins. x 26 eps. (TV1), 30 mins. x 26 eps. (TV2).

In a world where past and future connect, cute little catgirl Wappi-chan learns the meaning of phrases and words rooted in Japanese culture by interacting with the strange beings and spirits who inhabit Watt Warp Town. Narrated by Gingabanjo, with Azusa Yamamoto providing the voice of Wappi-chan alongside Junichi Kawamoto and Satoshi Inoue as her companions Wabi and Sabi, and turning her repeated question *nananosa*—what is it?—into a catch phrase. A second 26-episode series followed the first in 2007; some Japanese sources list them as four 13-episode seasons. Rucola Nicola is a partnership between Rucola Hamada and Etsuhiro Hamada, founder of FAT'S Co., to create and develop characters for use in anime, manga, and illustration.

WAGNARIA!! *
2010. JPN: *Working!!* TV series. DIR: Yoshimasa Hiraike, Atsushi Otsuki. SCR: Yoshimasa Hiraike, Kazuho Hyodo, Noboru Kimura, Rika Sogo, Takao Yoshioka, Michiko Ito, Shogo Mukai, Michiko Yokote. DES: Shingo Adachi, Kenichi Tajiri, Ryoka Kinoshita (TV2). ANI: Shingo Adachi. MUS: monaca. PRD: A-1 Pictures, Aniplex, Yomiuri TV. 25 mins. x 13 eps. (TV1), 25 mins. x 13 eps. (TV2)., 25 mins. x 13 eps. (TV3).

In a small town on Japan's northern island of Hokkaido, there's a family restaurant called Wagnaria. Sota Takanashi gets a job there to help his widowed office lady mother to support his four abusive and unstable sisters. He soon finds that none of his coworkers could exactly be described as normal, either. The slow-paced stories present snippets from their lives, relying largely on the characters for humor. Therein lies its problem: if you don't find the concept of an elementary school dominatrix and jokes about mentally challenged people with big boobs funny, and you aren't fixated on cute girls regardless of content, you may struggle to see the point of *Wagnaria!!* Neverthless, enough people did get the joke to lead to a second 13-episode series in 2011 and a third announced for 2015. It's based on the 2005 manga *Working!!* by Karino Takatsu. **V**

WAITING IN THE SUMMER *
2012. JPN: *Ano Natsu de Matteru.* TV series. DIR: Tatsuyuki Nagai. SCR: Yosuke Kuroda. DES: Taraku Uon, Masayoshi Tanaka. ANI: Masayoshi Tanaka, Yukie Hiyamizu. MUS: I've, Maiko Iuchi. PRD: JC Staff, AT-X, Bushiroad, Geneon Universal, Showgate, GENCO. 24 mins x 12 eps.

Amateur teenage filmmaker Kaito Kirishima seems to suffer from selective amnesia after filming a strange phenomenon one night. He returns to school none the wiser and with nothing particularly different about his life, apart from the sudden presence of a beautiful red-haired transfer student, Ichika Takatsuki. Ichika takes a great interest in the well-being of Kaito, much to the annoyance of his childhood friend (**ROMANCE AND DRAMA**) Kanna, who can usually be found trying to attract his attention with revealing and figure-hugging outfits—just one of a series of love polygons that arise.

Reuniting the core crew of **PLEASE TEACHER**, *Waiting in the Summer* might appear on the surface to be the preamble to yet another harem show. It is, however, very much an old-fashioned romance, a refreshing change in a genre that gaming has largely transformed into box-ticking character Sudoku, shuffling a bunch of female **STEREOTYPES AND ARCHETYPES** until the viewer gets what he thinks he wants. But *WitS* connections to old-school anime extend even further—it is soon revealed, in case you hadn't guessed already, that Ichika is an alien, introducing a science fictional undertone that, as in **KIMAGURE ORANGE ROAD**, can often be disregarded for episodes at a time. Meanwhile, Ichika's reason for her initial interest in Kaito is eventually revealed as guilt, in a plot device lifted ultimately from **ULTRAMAN** (and also used in **BIRDY THE MIGHTY**) with the unwitting Kaito killed by her crashing spaceship and restored to life using nanotechnology. In a typical anime touch, Kaito's miracle cure can only be maintained through the exchange of saliva, so it's lucky that Ichika is enthusiastic about kissing him. In another traditionalist touch, perhaps inspired by the look of nostalgic anime like **WHEN THEY CRY**, or more likely J. J. Abrams' *Super 8* (2011), Kaito eschews the easy fixes of digital or video technology and pursues his filmmaking hobby using an antiquated celluloid camera inherited from his grandfather. Beyond the central romance, much of the serial's greatest joy is to be found in its depiction of a bunch of friends making a film together, although as with many other modern anime (see COLORFUL: THE MOTION PICTURE) the authors wonder whether the narrative is highlighting and celebrating the activity itself, or rather the presence of actual, real-life friends.

WAKE UP ARIA *

1998. JPN: Wake Up, Aria: Majokko Virgin Kiki Ippatsu. AKA: Wake Up, Aria: Magical Girl Virgin in Danger. Video. DIR: Komari Yukino. SCR: Komari Yukino. DES: Hideo Ura. ANI: Hideo Ura. MUS: Rika Hanasaki. PRD: Cosmos Plan (Uchuu Kikaku), Zuwaigani, Friends, Media Station. 30 mins.

Pretty young musician Aria goes to Golden Breast Island in search of an education and finds herself in the company of several other pretty, musically minded girls, including the Chinese Yang Hiren, and the Indian twins Luna and Monica. However, the Royal Elegance Music School is just a front for the lusts of its principal and vice-principal, Mr. Karma and Ms. Shinbi. Every student they see ends up brainwashed into performing sexual acts for and with the perverse pair. Aria must escape the island alive, but not before she gets a good "education" in this predictable porno. ⓛⓝⓥ

WAKE UP, GIRLS! *

2014. TV series/movie. DIR: Yutaka Yamamoto. SCR: Toko Machida. DES: Sunao Chikaoka, Takanori Tanaka. ANI: Sunao Chikaoka, Keisuke Goto. MUS: monaca, Satoru Kosaki. PRD: Ordet, Tatsunoko Pro, AT-X, avex ent., Gakken, Good Smile Company, Sega, Sotsu Co., Ltd., Tatsunoko Pro, TOHO, TV Tokyo, Ultra Super Pictures, Wake Up, Girls! Partners. 60 mins. (m), 24 mins. x 12 eps.

A talent agency in the boondocks loses its last client. The jaded, chain-smoking manager and her assistant hatch a plan to put together an idol singer group and make easy money. The girls they find are mostly raw, unpolished, and eager, except for one who was badly burned by a previous idol experience.

WUG! is a concept that's been around the block, but here it's executed with charm, flashes of originality and a huge amount of skill. It started with a movie, WUG! Shichinin no Idol (WUG! Seven Idols),

screened the day the series commenced. It goes on to flesh out its cookie-cutter idols and allows them to use their own natural voices instead of the usual helium register of the J-pop idol. All this is, of course, part of a minutely planned campaign to launch the career of the "real" Wake Up Girls. These plans included a visit to an American anime convention in the summer of 2014, for which two of the group showed up late because they had to take high school exams on the Friday, then leave early to get back to school on Monday.

Around these sweet young wannabes revolves a huge crew carefully picked by their watchful management team, for the anime as for the live shows. An idol's time in the sun is usually brief, but a concept that's set up and marketed right from the start can have a long and very lucrative life. CDs, concerts, merchandise, and endorsements can all have returns dwarfing the advertising and rights revenues from the anime itself.

WUG! isn't a great show and the girls' music isn't great music; but it's pleasant, optimistic, and buoyant, its story of struggling to overcome given resonance by an episode where the girls visit the city of Kesennuma, hometown of one of their number and one of the cities devastated by the tsunami that followed 2011's Great East Japan Earthquake. And it's a textbook example of the creation and management of an idol group in both the real and fictional universe.

WALKURE ROMANZE *

2013. TV series. DIR: Yusuke Yamamoto. SCR: Kazuyuki Fudeyasu, Masaya Honda. DES: Kenichiro Katsura. ANI: Kenichiro Katsura, Akihiro Takata. MUS: N/C. PRD: 8 Bit, Frontier Works, AT-X, Lantis, Pony Canyon, Klockworx. 24 mins. x 12 eps.

Four perky female heroines jostle for the attention of a single boy, Takahiro, who has the unlikely skill of being a good jousting coach in a school that inexplicably relies on jousting to settle scores. Based on an erotic game … with jousting. We don't know why, either.

WALLFLOWER, THE *

2006. JPN: Yamato Nadeshiko Shichi Henge. AKA: Japanese Maiden Seven Transmutations; YamaNade. TV series. DIR: Shinichi

Watanabe. SCR: Haruka. DES: Yasuko Sakuma, Yumi Kudo. ANI: Yasuko Sakuma. MUS: Hiromi Mizutani, Yasuharu Takanashi. PRD: Nippon Animation, Pony Canyon, TV Tokyo. 25 mins. x 25 eps.

Based on Tomoko Hayakawa's manga from 2000, this is the story of four stunningly handsome but otherwise flawed young men who share the perfect city home: they rent rooms in a huge mansion, and their landlord is so sweet and friendly that they all call her Auntie. Then Auntie asks them a favor: her teenage niece Sunako is coming to live with her, and she wants the boys to turn her into a "proper young lady." To sweeten the deal she agrees to waive their rent if they succeed—but if they fail, it will triple. The boys accept the challenge, only to find that Sunako is a strange, antisocial young woman who would rather be a hermit than have anything to do with them.

Taking on the ugly-duckling concept that inspired George Bernard Shaw's Pygmalion, director Watanabe throws cookie-cutter characters and extreme situations into the pot with wild abandon and comes up with something charmingly original and often hilarious. Keeping faith with Hayakawa's original concept, he shows Sunako in distorted form, as an impressionistically modified character, for most of the story. She doesn't believe in her own beauty, seeing herself as ridiculous at best and hideous at worst; allowing her outward appearance to mirror her self-image gives weight to the times when she appears as her true self. Other characters are modified in the same way as required. The art and animation are good, with interesting visual ideas, making this one of the most entertaining male harem shows around (ROMANCE AND DRAMA).

WALT DISNEY ANIMATION JAPAN

Animation company using the staff and resources of the Pacific Animation Corporation (q.v.), acquired by Disney in 1988. The company continued to work in its previous incarnation's capacity of below-the-line on American cartoons, particularly Disney straight-to-video sequels such as Pocahontas II. Industry legend holds that the Japanese studio was largely tasked with animating action sequences, whereas comedy was handled by an Australian sister-studio.

Motoyoshi Tokunaga, the company chairman, ensured that WDAJ had an alternate revenue stream by setting up a subsidiary company, Spectrum, at the same address and utilizing many of the same staff, in order to take on non-Disney work without using the Disney brand or finances. As Spectrum, his animators worked on cartoons including *Batman: The Animated Series*, before shutting down in 1998. Many of the staff then migrated either in-house to the parent company, or across to Production I.G.

The studio was closed in 2004 shortly after the completion of *Pooh's Heffalump Movie*, initially with the promise that 30 of the hundred staff would be transferred to America. However, few could speak English and most dispersed elsewhere in the Japanese animation business. A core of some 70 staff continued under Tokunaga as The Answer Studio, in which capacity they worked on Japanese titles such as **THE GARDEN OF WORDS** and foreign contracts such as Marvel's *Next Avengers* (2007). Staffers from Walt Disney Animation Japan also set up Tama Production, largely to subcontract work for the parent company. Tama closed in 2008, although several of its members went on to form Drop, best known for animating a promo video for the rock group Radiohead.

WANDABA STYLE *

2003. JPN: *Moso Kagaku Series Wandaba Style*. AKA: *Delusion Science Series Wandaba Style; Fantasy Chemistry Series Wandaba Style*. TV series. DIR: Nobuhiro Takamoto. SCR: Juzo Mutsuki. DES: Shoji Hara, Gaku Miyao, Koji Nakakita. ANI: TNK. MUS: Try Force. PRD: Wonderfarm, TNK, Kid's Station, Chiba TV. 25 mins. x 12 eps.

Top manager Michael Hanagata cobbles together girl band Mix Juice from four has-been singers whose careers are going nowhere. Ayame Akimo is a folk singer whose brain is away with the fairies most of the time. Himawari Natsuwa sings Japanese classics with so little success that she also has to work on a construction site. Former child star Sakura Haruno is getting by selling her panties over the Internet. Yuri Fuyude plays such hard-edged rock that she can't get a gig anywhere. Michael's plan is to make a fortune by getting the girls to play the first ever concert on

the moon. That suits boygenius billionaire Susumu Tsukumo (aged 13) who wants to find an eco-friendly means of space travel and thinks the girls will make excellent test subjects to supplement his cute personal android Kiku 8. Homages to anime like **EXCEL SAGA** and **PUNI PUNI POEMI** as well as Gerry Anderson's *Thunderbirds* and the *Super Mario* games make this a lightweight cavalcade of sight gags. Creator Juzo Mutsuki also edited and wrote the lyrics for the theme song.

The slang term *wandaba* originates in the martial music by Toru Fuyuki that once accompanied scenes of military preparation or launch in the old live-action *Ultraman Returns* (*DE, 1971)—parodied in **FANDOM** as a tune that went "wandabad-abadabadaba." It has come to signify any launch sequence or scene of steely, belligerent resolve, and was also appropriated for the name of the male protagonist, Wan Dabada, in **BEAST WARRIORS**.

WANDERING BAWDY LUNATICS

2009. JPN: *Samayou Midara na Lunatics*. Video. DIR: Yukihiro Makino. SCR: Yukihiro Makino, Mamoru Abiko. DES: Yuji Ushijima, Hifumi. ANI: Kazuya Shirogane. MUS: N/C. PRD: Pixy, Lilith. 27 mins. x 2 eps.

Beautiful princess Eifa and her brother Alois are crazy about each other, but can't express their love because of their status. Then Eifa, who is set to be queen, is cursed by an ambitious witch who wants the role for herself. First she is given a potion that renders her unable to control her passions, so that the siblings' incestuous love is exposed and they are banished. Then she and Alois are put under a spell that makes them occupy one body, female at night and male by day, in a thin echo of *Ladyhawke* (1985). Alois seeks help from another witch. But how can he repay her? If you never knew that incest is forbidden to the upper classes purely for reasons of status, or that they wore fishnet stockings in medieval times, you may learn something from this anime based on a porn game by Lilith's Lilith Mist label, with original characters by Sasayuki; but beware, it carries a tentacle rape warning. **NL**

WANDERING SON *

2011. JPN: *Horo Musuko*. TV series. DIR: Ei

Aoki. SCR: Mari Okada. DES: Ryuichi Makino, Akira Ito. ANI: Ryuichi Makino. MUS: Keiichi Okabe, Satoru Kusaka. PRD: AIC, Aniplex, Dentsu, Enterbrain, Fuji TV. 23 mins. x 11 eps.

Shuichi Nitori is a quiet, sensitive boy. Sometimes, when he's sure he won't be caught out, he dresses as the girl he really wants to be. Then he transfers to a new school. Amid the bewildering array of new people he meets, one stands out: Yoshino Takatsuki, who sits next to him, a tomboy who doesn't want to be a girl. As both approach their teenage years, they know their bodies will soon mature and lock them into roles they don't want. They also know that many people—including their loved ones—don't understand their dilemma. They scarcely understand it themselves, and as time passes Nitori wonders what his true feelings are.

Tackling a complex issue with empathy and sensitivity, Mari Okada's script shines, giving all the characters a credible weight and enabling us to see even the unpleasant and unsympathetic as real people. The ignorance and injustice of many areas of society are highlighted without making viewers feel they're being preached at. Meanwhile, director Aoki and the crew provide pretty, delicately colored backgrounds and designs, through which the characters move at a gentle pace. The way the color is allowed to fade near the edges of a scene, as if we're looking at an unframed watercolor, is beautiful and adds a distancing effect to a story that is, at times, almost unbearably poignant.

Despite the lack of event and action, Aoki adds tension where it's needed—a sequence where footsteps outside a closed door herald the approach of a bully is especially powerful. Awkward silences, uncomfortable glances, lowered eyes, all telegraph emotion quietly yet powerfully. The music is simple and beautiful. This is a magical series, one of very few to address the issues facing transgender or gender-conflicted children with the respect and love they deserve, but so rarely find.

WANDERING SUN

1971. JPN: *Sasurai no Taiyo*. TV series. DIR: Chikao Katsui, Yoshiyuki Tomino, Masayuki Hayashi, Ryosuke Takahashi. SCR: Hiroyuki Hoshiyama, Shunichi Yukimuro, Michio Su-

zuki, Tadaaki Yamazaki, Haruya Yamazaki, Tsunehisa Ito, Isao Okishima. DES: Yoshikazu Yasuhiko. ANI: Hayao Nobe. MUS: Taku Izumi. PRD: Mushi, Fuji TV. 25 mins. x 26 eps.
Miki and Nozomi are two would-be singers. Miki's rich parents will go to any lengths to give their little princess her heart's desire, but the more talented Nozomi comes from a deprived background. The daughter of a deceased noodle seller, Nozomi must struggle to support her blind mother and make sacrifices on the way to achieving the success that her natural guitar-strumming ability deserves. Based on a manga in *Shojo Comic* by Keisuke Fujiwara and Mayumi Suzuki.

WANGAN MIDNIGHT

2007. AKA: *Bayside Midnight*. TV series. DIR: Tsuneo Tominaga. SCR: Nobuaki Kishima. DES: Hisashi Kagawa, Hideaki Yokoi, Michiko Morokuma. ANI: Kanemori Yasuda (3D). MUS: Atsushi Umebori. PRD: A.C.G.T., OB Planning. 25 mins. x 26 eps.
Tokyo's Shuto Expressway has the longest, straightest stretch of road in the whole of Japan. It's known as the *wangan*, or bayside, and car junkies and speed freaks gather there for street racing. The traffic is heavy and wrecks and accidents are common. It doesn't deter high school boy Akio Asakura, who has just lost a race to Tatsuya Shima's legendary Porsche 911 Turbo, known as the Blackbird. Akio is looking for a car that can beat the Blackbird. The car he finds in a junkyard comes with a dark history: it's known as the Devil Z and its last owner died in it, racing the Blackbird. He had the same name as Akio. But Akio's willing to take a chance on the Devil Z because its modifications might just give him the edge over Shima.
Lovers of *The Fast & The Furious* movies will be right at home with this street-racing anime. So will James Dean fans, picking up on the visual references in Akio's clothing and the nods to the allegedly cursed Porsche in which the young star died. But the point of this SPORTS ANIME is not really the cars but the relationships of characters to their vehicles, to each other, and to the unofficial, unregulated sport that makes them willing to throw away time, money, and even their lives for the thrill of the race. It's not just a clone of director Tominaga's other street racing show, INITIAL D,

any more than is Michiharu Kusunoki's original 1992 manga, serialized in *Big Comics Spirits* and *Young* magazine. The racing style is strikingly different, a straight speed rush down the expressway as against the other show's hairpin bends, up to four cars competing instead of two, and a different, slightly grittier cast of characters. It also starts off slowly, as Akio builds his relationship with Devil Z and Tominaga builds ours with him and his friends and foes. The mechanical details are perfect—the show has been described as a tutorial in how to build an engine. But this isn't just a car manual; when the action starts, it's pedal to the metal, as fast and furious as the most rabid speed freak could wish. Compare to REDLINE, for a radically different feel of racing from the inside, and SKY CRAWLERS, which oddly mirrors the sense of returning to the scene of the crime.

WANNA-BE'S *

1986. Video. DIR: Yasuo Hasegawa. SCR: Toshimitsu Suzuki. DES: Kenichi Sonoda, Yoshiharu Shimizu, Shinji Araki, Kimitoshi Yamane, Hideki Kakinuma. ANI: Yoshiharu Shimizu. MUS: Hiroshi Arakawa, Seikima-II. PRD: Artmic, Animate Film, AIC. 45 mins.
Eri Fuma and Miki Morita are young female pro-wrestlers who fight under the professional name Wanna-Be's. They struggle to rise through the ranks and challenge the champions, not realizing that they are embroiled in a plot to test a secret muscle-enhancing drug. Will it be enough to help them defeat mutated monsters, though? A hilarious look at the sport that's so popular in Japan, with some thinly disguised "guest appearances" by real girl wrestling stars—compare to the similar wrestling in-jokery of CRUSHER JOE and METAL FIGHTERS MIKU.

WANSA-KUN

1973. AKA: *Little Wansa*. TV series. DIR: Eiichi Yamamoto, Minoru Tanaka, Masami Hata, Noboru Ishiguro, Norio Yazawa, Minami Asa. SCR: Keisuke Fujikawa, Maru Tamura, Fumio Ikeno, Eiichi Yamamoto, Hitoshi Hidaka. DES: Shinji Nagashima. ANI: Hiromitsu Morita, Toyoo Ashida. MUS: Yasushi Miyakawa. PRD: Tomi Pro, Anime Room, Mushi, Fuji TV. 25 mins. x 26 eps.
Wansa the little white dog comes to town and befriends neighborhood boy Kota. His

"people," however, are the neighborhood dogs, who introduce him to a hidden life of triumph and tragedy as the local canines fight a vicious turf war with their cat enemies. Wansa falls in love with local puppy Midori and pines for his mother, *presumed* dead in typical anime fashion. Based on the 1971 manga written by Tezuka for *Tezuka Magazine Leo* and starring the mascot character of the Sanwa Bank, this musical comedy, faintly redolent of *Lady and the Tramp*, was the last TV series made by the beleaguered Mushi studio. It, along with TRITON OF THE SEA, was effectively lost to its creator through copyright foul-ups and is not a "true" Tezuka work.

WARTIME ANIME

With the Japanese invasion of China in the 1930s, the fairy tales and fables of EARLY ANIME were gradually co-opted into the military machine, the anime creators tempted by offers of funding and, for the first time, wide distribution. Early emphasis was on austerity and unity in the face of potential threats. Yasuji Murata's *Masamune and the Monkeys* (*Saru Masamune*, 1930) dwells on the virtues of righteous intervention, depicting an incident in which the swordsmith Masamune comes to the aid of a monkey, and is consequently bestowed with the blade that will one day save his own life. Like many other anime from the period, such as the early SF anime THE PLANE CABBY'S LUCKY DAY, it tacitly advanced Japan's demands for an East Asian "co-prosperity sphere," and her right to interfere in the affairs of other countries in order to overthrow Western imperialism. Murata's *Aerial Momotaro* (*Sora no Momotaro*, 1931) featured a war between penguins and albatrosses on a remote island near the South Pole, broken up by the timely arrival of the Japanese hero Momotaro. Yoshitaro Kataoka's *Bandanemon the Monster Exterminator* (*Bandanemon: Bakemono Taiji no Maki*, 1935) focused on a tough Japanese hero who comes to the aid of oppressed villagers, volunteering to clear an infestation of *tanuki* from a nearby castle. The shape-changing creatures have disguised themselves as beautiful women (with shades of Betty Boop) in order to distract him from his mission. Yasuji Murata revisited the plot of DREAMY URASHIMA with his *One Night at a*

Bar (*Izakaya no Ichiya*, 1936), the Dragon King's Palace of legend presented as a drunken hallucination by a man who, like the Japanese nation itself, has yet to wake up to reality—in this case, the inevitability of conflict.

In the wake of the League of Nations' condemnation of Japan's expansion into Manchuria, attacks on foreign powers became more blatant. In Takao Nakano's *Black Cat Banzai* (*Kuroneko Banzai*, 1933), a peaceful parade of toys is disrupted by a fleet of flying bat-bombers, each ridden by a clone of Mickey Mouse. Snake-marines with machinegun mouths land on the beach, and the invaders kidnap a doll. The islanders beg for help from a book of JAPANESE FOLK TALES, which obligingly disgorges Momotaro, Kintaro, and several other Japanese folk icons. The story ends with a celebration, as all the dead trees sprout cherry blossoms.

Shiho Tagawa's popular manga character NORAKURO joined up in Yasuji Murata's *Corporal Norakuro* (*Norakuro Gocho*, 1934). This comprised another warning about drunkenness, in which the titular stray dozed off and dreamed he was attacked by monkeys. The emphasis on humor continued with the uncredited *Sky Over the Shanghai Battle-Line* (*Sora no Shanhai Sensen*, 1938), in which two comical Japanese pilots observed the Chinese war theater in a biplane. Similarly, Noboru Ofuji's *Aerial Ace* (*Sora no Arawashi*, 1938) featured another pilot fighting giant clouds in the shape of Popeye and Stalin—FOREIGN INFLUENCES were no longer welcome.

In 1939, the increasingly oppressive Japanese government passed a Film Law bringing the media under greater central control and also creating new openings for local animators by banning foreign imports. In the same year, a group of a dozen animators, including Tadahito Mochinaga and Ikuo Oishi, were drafted into the Toho Aviation Materials Production Office, also known as the "Shadow Staff," to make instructional films for military use, including the *Principles of Bombardment* series (1940–41) claimed by the animator Soji Ushio to have been used for training the pilots who attacked Pearl Harbor. The onset of war with America in 1941 brought greater funding, but also greater pressures on filmmakers. Kajiro Yamamoto com-

pleted his live-action *The War at Sea from Hawaii to Malaya* (*Hawaii-Marei Okikaisen*, 1942) in just six months, recreating Pearl Harbor with special-effects footage from Eiji Tsuburaya, creator of *Ultraman* (*DE). Its success prompted the Japanese Navy to attempt similar triumphs with animation, ordering Mitsuyo Seo to make *Momotaro's Sea Eagles* (*Momotaro no Umiwashi*, 1943). Retelling the Momotaro folktale with enemy caricatures, the film pushed the boundaries of animation in Japan with an unprecedented running time of 37 minutes, although several privately screened works of the Shadow Staff reached similar lengths during the same period, and some, such as *Principles of the Wireless: Triodes* (*Musen Riron: Sankyoku Shinkukan*) may have even approached feature length. With animation cels in short supply (nitro-cellulose was a crucial ingredient in gunpowder), Seo's animators were forced to wash their materials in acid and reuse them for this tale of the bombing of Pearl Harbor in fairy-tale form, destroying the original artwork even as they shot each frame of animation. In order to get the right voice for a caricature of *Popeye*'s Bluto, seen on the deck of a sinking ship, they also sampled the original straight from a reel of the American print—copyright law hardly being an issue at the time. The film was immensely popular with children on release, and was even screened in the palace for Prince Akihito (the future Heisei Emperor). The Navy authorized Seo to make an even longer sequel, and the result was Japan's first full-length animated feature, MOMOTARO'S DIVINE SEA WARRIORS.

Other anime of the 1940s show signs of increasing desperation, as Japanese defeats become harder to ignore. Sanae Yamamoto's *Defeat of the Spies* (*Spy Gekimetsu*, 1942) depicts Roosevelt and Churchill sending three agents onto Japanese soil, although they are swiftly unmasked. In Ryotaro Kuwata's *Human Rugby Bullets* (*Tokkyu Nikudan Sen*, 1943), a sports match between Japanese dogs and foreign monkeys attempts to make light of Japan's use of the *taiatari* ramming attack—a chilling precursor to the following year's *kamikaze* attacks. Animation was also a major component of the ten-minute short *Nippon Banzai* (1943), best described as Japan's *Why We Fight*. In it, evil British

soldiers are shown oppressing the natives of Asia beneath a hot sun, which segues into the rising sun of Japan's flag. Cartoon fish dance in and out of the wreck of the HMS *Prince of Wales*, while Chiang Kai-Shek is first portrayed as a marionette (with his wife, operated by Allied "advisers"), then as a gleeful child with a toy plane (a snide reference to the Flying Tigers). The anime sequence ends with Roosevelt impeached and Churchill's trademark cigar falling from his mouth in shock, before returning to live-action footage exhorting young men to join up.

In the aftermath of the war, the works of the Shadow Staff and many propaganda movies were destroyed by both sides in an attempt to suppress the past. The surviving animators in Tokyo worked on SAKURA, although it was hobbled by both limited materials and the unfortunate undertones of its poetic imagery, with cherry blossoms now indelibly associated with the war era. Anime struggled for some time amid conditions of deprivation in which many had understandably more pressing problems, and early postwar anime are largely feel-good FANTASY AND FAIRY TALES such as *The Magic Pen*. Sanae Yamamoto would help re-create anime with the establishment of his studio Nippon Doga (Nichido) in 1947. Bought by Toei in 1956, the company would form the foundations of Toei Animation, and with it, the beginnings of the anime industry as we know it today.

The war, however, remained a taboo subject for a decade, with the anomalous exception of ZERO SEN HAYATO and occasional references as origin stories in shows such as GIGANTOR and BIG X. As the babyboomers reached maturity, several anime began alluding to the war through future allegories such as STAR BLAZERS, and the devastation wrought by the giant aliens of MACROSS.

After the success of the anime DIARY OF ANNE FRANK, producers realized the value of children as protagonists—caught up in a conflict not of their own making, the brutalized innocents of BAREFOOT GEN, GRAVE OF THE FIREFLIES, and their many imitators allowed history without discussion of responsibility. The Hiroshima Peace Festival film prize became dominated by Renzo Kinoshita, whose short anime included *Pica-Don* (1978, the nickname of the bomb that destroyed Hiroshima), **THE FLYING FISH IS TAKEN ILL**, *LastAir Raid Kumagaya* (1990), and the unfinished project *Okinawa*. Outside the art-house theaters however, popular representations of the war became increasingly fantastic, as a nostalgic craze for "retro" anime transformed into an obsession with rewriting history—**KISHIN CORPS** and **SAKURA WARS** would have met with joyous approval from the government censor in 1941.

WAT PO AND US

1988. JPN: *Wat Po to Bokura no Ohanashi*. AKA: *The Story of Us and Wat Po; Watt Poe*. Video. DIR: Shigenori Kageyama. SCR: Shozo Uehara. DES: Mutsumi Inomata, Shohei Kohara, Takahiro Tomoyasu, Torao Arai. ANI: Mutsumi Inomata. MUS: Satoshi Kadokura. PRD: Diva, Konami. 55 mins.

The life of a tiny fishing village is disrupted when Wat Po, a horned white whale who is the village's guardian spirit, vanishes. The creature used to attract fish for the people to catch. Local boy Jam, hearing strange music wafting down from the mountains, sets out with three friends and his dog in search of the sound. Attacks by monsters scare his friends away, but he finds a mountain lake where a lovely young girl called Selene is playing music to Wat Po. At first she's afraid and tries to flee in winged armor. Her people, the Birdoes, are technologically far in advance of the village folk, but they hid inside the mountain generations ago after a terrible war devastated and polluted the land. They used their power of flight to bring Wat Po from the sea to the landlocked lake. Selene and Jam decide to rescue Wat Po and try to bring their peoples back together, but Jam's disappearance is arousing old hatreds and may even rekindle the long-ago war.

An eco-saga with a strong antiwar message in the vein of **FUTURE BOY CONAN** and **GREEN LEGEND RAN**, it fails to match up to the same team's work on **WINDARIA** and **LEDA: THE FANTASTIC ADVENTURE OF YOHKO**.

WATAMOTE *

2013. JPN: *Watashi ga Motenai no wa, Do Kangaetemo Omaera ga Warui!* AKA: *No Matter How I Look at It, It's You Guys' Fault That I'm Not Popular*. TV series. DIR: Shin Onuma. SCR: Takao Yoshioka. DES: Hideki Furukawa.

ANI: Hideki Furukawa, Michio Hasegawa. MUS: Sadesper Record. PRD: Silver Link. 24 mins. x 12 eps. (TV), 30 mins. (v).

Withdrawn, antisocial teenager Tomoko Kuroki has inadvisably attempted to learn all about the world by playing dozens of dating sim games. Witlessly believing that her middle school angst will transform, like a butterfly, into high school popularity, she experiences a crushing series of disappointments when high school turns out to comprise yet more of the same humiliations and ostracisms (compare to **LOVE, CHUNIBYO, AND OTHER DELUSIONS**). Almost friendless, and completely out of touch when it comes to human interactions, she embarks upon a series of projects to gain the attention and admiration of her fellow students, only to fail miserably.

Based on a manga by Nico Tanigawa in *Gangan Online*, *Watamote* ably and humorously charts the obsessions and concerns of self-absorbed teenagers, not the least Tomoko's constant refrain that all the problems she creates for herself are actually everybody else's fault. The series functions well as a satire of many clichés found in anime set in schools, and also as a cringe-inducing study of almost everyone's teen years (and dare we suggest, anime **FANDOM**), fraught with disasters in personal hygiene, awkward human interactions, and counter-productive reinventions. Those fans who don't watch through their fingers in terrified recognition might also notice many in-jokes referencing contemporary anime, including **THE MELANCHOLY OF HARUHI SUZUMIYA**, **K-ON**, **ANOTHER**, and **PUELLA MAGI MADOKA MAGICA**.

WATANABE, KAZUHIKO

1932–97. Born in Tokyo and a graduate of Tokyo University of Fine Arts, Watanabe's first anime work was a paper-cut animation version of **AESOP'S FABLES**. His subsequent animations have included the prize-winning *Princess Kaguya* and *The Little Match Girl*—much of his work comprises fairy tales and parables drawn from **JAPANESE FOLK TALES** and the **TALES OF HANS CHRISTIAN ANDERSEN**.

WATANABE, SHINICHI

1964–. AKA Nabeshin. Often appearing as a cameo character in his own work (look out for someone with an afro

hairdo, particularly in **EXCEL SAGA** and its spin-offs), Watanabe is a modern director with a strong track record in comedy and parody, although his stature often seems artificially inflated through the coincidental resemblance of his own name to that of Shinichiro Watanabe (q.v.).

WATANABE, SHINICHIRO

1965–. After early work on **MACROSS** *Plus*, Watanabe soon established a reputation as a modern, "groovy" director, overseeing both **COWBOY BEBOP** and **SAMURAI CHAMPLOO**. He also featured as one of the directors on **THE ANIMATRIX**, setting him apart as one of Japan's top anime creatives, despite a very limited cinema output so far. Not to be confused with Shinichi Watanabe (q.v.).

WATARU

1988. JPN: *Majin Eiyuden Wataru*. AKA: *Legend of Devilish Heroism Wataru*. TV series, video. DIR: Hideharu Iuchi, Michio Fukuda, Masamitsu Hidaka, Nobuhiro Kondo, Katsuoshi Yatabe, Yutaka Kagawa. SCR: Yoshiaki Takahashi, Ryosuke Takahashi, Hiroyuki Kawasaki, Takao Koyama, Hiroko Naka. DES: Toyoo Ashida, Kazunori Nakazawa. ANI: Toyoo Ashida. MUS: Junichi Kanezaki, Satoshi Kadokura. PRD: Sunrise, Nippon TV. 25 mins. x 45 eps. (TV1), 25 mins. x 28 eps. (TV2), 30 mins. x 4 eps. (v).

After school, ten-year-old Wataru doesn't go straight home—instead he slips into an alternate world where he is the pilot of a huge super-deformed comical robot and fights to deliver the world from the oppression of an evil magician with the help of the cute but overexciteable Tora-chan. Luckily these adventures only last a few seconds in our world, or his mother would wonder why he was late for dinner. A huge success in Japan, the first series spun off a remake series with the prefix *Cho* [*Super*] and the four-part video series *W: Tales of Endless Time* (*W: Owarinaki Toki no Monogatari*).

WATCH WITH MOTHER

1988. JPN: *Mama Ohanashi Kikasete*. TV series. DIR: Keiji Hayakawa. SCR: Shunichi Yukimuro. DES: Yuzo Sato. ANI: N/C. MUS: N/C. PRD: Staff 21, Nippon TV. 8 mins. x 15 eps. Short animated films of well-known **JAPANESE FOLK TALES**, including the stories of **TARO MAEGAMI**, *The Riceball Family*, *The*

Master of Catching Stars, Thunder Is the Bridegroom, and *The Elephant's Sneeze.* Shown as part of the children's variety program, *Tondeke Gutchonpa.*

WATER SPIDER MONMON
2006. JPN: *Mizugumo Monmon.* Movie. DIR: Hayao Miyazaki. SCR: Hayao Miyazaki. DES: Yoichi Watanabe. ANI: Atsuko Tanaka, Hiromasa Yonebayashi. MUS: Rio Yamase. PRD: Studio Ghibli. 15 mins.
Monmon is a diving bell spider who catches a glimpse of a water strider and falls in love. She's naturally wary of her strange suitor, and he lives his entire life underwater while she lives hers on the surface. Can their love blossom? This enchanting short film was made by Hayao Miyazaki for screening at the Studio Ghibli Museum. The art and animation is of Ghibli's usual stellar standard and the simple, quirky story is a charming look at the idiocy and the courage of a love that ignores all barriers. Thematically, its mismatched lovers prefigure those in Miyazaki's later PONYO.

WAVE OF RAGE
1998. JPN: *Soliton no Akuma.* AKA: *Sea of Angels—Waves of Devils; Devil of the Solitons.* Movie. DIR: Toshio Takeuchi, Jun Kawagoe. SCR: Masashi Sogo. DES: Hisatoshi Motoki. ANI: Hisatoshi Motoki. MUS: N/C. PRD: Locomotion, Japan Cinema Associates. 90 mins.
Deep below the sea off the coast of Okinawa, the Ocean Technopolis is at the forefront of humankind's efforts to adapt to catastrophically rising sea levels, but it's caught in the middle of escalating tensions between Japan and Taiwan. Taiwan is already blaming Japan for the disappearance of its submarine Shui Long, though the vessel was actually destroyed by an underwater monster enraged by the testing of a new Japanese holophonic sonar device. Fleeing the creature, the Japanese submarine Hatsushio inadvertently leads its pursuer to Technopolis. The serpentine creature attacks the underwater city, trapping several tourists on the sea floor. Atsushi Kurase, head of the nearby Helios Oil underwater drilling rig, is trying to organize a rescue operation—his estranged wife and daughter, Qiu Hua and Mei Ling, are trapped on a stricken tourist submarine. He sees the Hatsushio and calls on

it for aid. The sub cannot publicly refuse, but its commander is given orders that if Atsushi or any rescuees should realize the top-secret nature of its mission, they are to have a "fatal accident." Though the tourists are saved, the cast is now trapped on the damaged Sea Turtle 200, Helios Oil's underwater platform. They are contacted by the Solitons, underwater creatures made from pure energy, who reveal that a rogue one of their race is responsible for the attacks and that only a human mutated into Soliton form can stop it. To save his daughter, Kurase volunteers, destroying the menace with the aid of the Hatsu-shio. This derivative combination of *The Abyss* and *The Hunt for Red October* was redeemed in Japanese eyes by its well-conceived setting—a 21st-century Asia riven by international tension, with Japan, Taiwan, and China provocatively cast as superpowers in a new Cold War. Based on the 1995 novel by Katsufumi Umehara. For more underwater action, see BLUE SUBMARINE NO. SIX and SILENT SERVICE. **V**

WE WERE THERE
2006. JPN: *Bokura ga Ita.* TV series. DIR: Koichiro Sotome, Akitaro Daichi. SCR: Mamiko Ikeda, Mizuki Ogawa, Yuka Yamada. DES: Nobuaki Shirai, Chikako Shibata. ANI: Akemi Hayashi, Akiko Nakano, Hideyuki Arao. MUS: Jun Abe, Seiji Muto. PRD: Artland, Marvelous Entertainment, Pony Canyon, Shogakukan. 26 mins. x 26 eps.
A 15-year-old in a new high school decides that her ambition is to make as many friends as she can. At first school is a hard grind, but she gradually makes friends with others in her class. Then she meets someone she thinks is the rudest boy in school—yet he's very popular. There must be another side to him. Can she find it?
    Director Sotome and his crew create a pretty, delicately animated world, in a watercolor style reminisicent of HONEY AND CLOVER (though with slightly stronger inking), imitating a girl's-eye view of teen romance. The script also reflects the tendency to obsess over tiny details common to new loves: although the drama and angst is low-key and on a real-life scale, rather than the epic excesses of, say, CODE GEASS, there's plenty of it. This sweet, sometimes funny, and sometimes thought-provoking show about love, loss,

and leaving the past behind, is based on Yuki Obata's 2002 manga. **N**

WE WITHOUT WINGS: UNDER THE INNOCENT SKY *
2011. JPN: *Oretachi ni Tsubasa wa Nai.* AKA: *OreTsuba; We Without Wings.* TV series, video. DIR: Shinji Ushiro. SCR: Takamitsu Kono, Kojiro Nakamura, Takashi Aoshima, Jackson O. DES: Kumi Ishii, Chikara Nishikura. ANI: Kumi Ishii, Eri Baba, Masatsugu Yamamoto, Takao Takegami. MUS: Acchorike. PRD: Nomad, Lantis, Marvelous AQL. 25 mins. x 12 eps. (TV), 24 mins. (v).
Three young men live apparently unconnected lives in the city of Yanagihara. As we follow their interactions with their families and the girls they meet through a cold winter, it slowly becomes apparent that the threads linking their lives are potentially very dark indeed.
    Despite the confusion of the first three episodes, which throw seemingly random cast members onscreen without much in the way of introduction or explanation, this show is more interesting than most anime adapted from porn games—it is an adaptation of a "visual novel" (ARGOT AND JARGON) by Navel, which has also inspired three manga. Underlying the fan service and adult comments obscenely placed in the mouth of a child, there's an examination of obsession and mental illness that makes this one of anime's great rarities—a harem show worth watching. A video with "nakedness plus" from the same team was bundled with a release of the PC game. **NL**

WE'RE MANGA ARTISTS: TOKIWA VILLA
1981. JPN: *Bokura Mangaka: Tokiwa So Monogatari.* AKA: *WMA: Tokiwa Villa Story.* TV special. DIR: Shinichi Suzuki, Kazumi Fukushima, Atsutoshi Umezawa. SCR: Masaki Tsuji, Kazuo Koike. DES: Shotaro Ishinomori. ANI: Takao Kasai. MUS: Nozomu Aoki. PRD: Toei, Aoi, TBS. 84 mins.
Possibly the single most influential address in the postwar history of Japanese comics, Tokiwa was the apartment complex where a group of stellar artists lived in 1953. Hiro Terada, Motoo Abiko and Hiroshi Fujimoto (the pair who worked as Fujio-Fujiko), Shotaro Ishinomori (then plain Ishimori), and Fujio Akatsuka shared the

trials and tribulations of being struggling young artists and writers with no money and no luck with editors or girls, with a spirit of insane youthful enthusiasm that enabled them to survive the lean years and emerge as stars of the manga firmament. The Tokiwa building was demolished in 1981, prompting both this anime and NHK's rival live-action documentary *Tokiwa Villa of My Youth*. In allowing the manga characters to come to life for some sequences, the anime version was the greater success. The story was revived for Jun Ichikawa's live-action movie *Tokiwa: The Manga Apartment* (1996). The idea that a dormitory might form a last-ditch community for inhabitants who have otherwise been let down by more traditional social ties has since become common in manga and anime, such as **MAISON IKKOKU** and **PET GIRL OF SAKURASOU**.

WEATHER PERMITTING

1984. JPN: *Ashita Tenki ni Naare*. AKA: *Tomorrow If the Weather Holds*. TV series. DIR: Hisaya Takabayashi, Hiroyoshi Mitsunobu, Kenjiro Yoshida. SCR: Noboru Shiroyama. DES: Tetsuya Chiba. ANI: Hiroshi Kanazawa, Kazuo Tomizawa, Akira Kasahara. MUS: Masakazu Togo. PRD: Fuji TV, NAS. 25 mins. x 47 eps.
Taro is a short, fat food-addict who is obsessed with golf—the one sport that doesn't object if its players amble around the field slowly. He astounds observers with his golfing skill but eventually becomes so devoted to the game that he excludes everything else from his life. Based on a 1980 manga by **TOMORROW'S JOE**–creator Tetsuya Chiba.

WEATHER REPORT GIRL *

1994. JPN: *Otenki Oneesan*. AKA: *Weather Woman*. Video. DIR: Kunihiko Yuyama, Takashi Watanabe. SCR: Kunihiko Yuyama. DES: Naomi Miyata. ANI: Shinji Sato. MUS: Fumihiko Kurihara. PRD: OB Planning, Toho. 45 mins. x 2 eps.
A determined young woman gets her big break in TV when the regular weather girl goes on vacation. Regardless of the barometer, Keiko sets temperatures and ratings soaring as she uses her clothing, or lack of it, to illustrate the trends and turns the serious stuff of the weather report into a song and dance routine. When the original weather girl gets back

from her holiday and finds her replacement so popular, the fur begins to fly! Not everyone at the TV station (named ATV, but clearly intended to be a pastiche of the real-world national broadcaster NHK) likes the new-style weather report, though, and rivals in the boardroom and on the screen are out to end Keiko's career. Based on the 1992 manga in *Young Magazine* by Tetsu Adachi, *WRG* also spawned the live-action film *Weather Woman*, directed by Tomoaki Hosoyama, starring Kei Mizutani as the exhibitionist heroine. **○**

WEATHERING CONTINENT, THE

1992. JPN: *Kaze no Tairiku*. AKA: *Continent of Wind*. Movie. DIR: Koichi Mashimo. SCR: Koichi Mashimo. DES: Mutsumi Inomata, Nobuteru Yuki. ANI: Kazuchika Kise. MUS: Michiru Oshima. PRD: IG, Kadokawa. 60 mins.
The long history of the continent of Atlantis is coming to an end; its once-great cities are crumbling to dust, and it is almost completely deserted after a series of natural disasters. Its few surviving people are under constant threat from scavengers and bandits. Water is increasingly scarce; the winds that scour the land carry no rainclouds, and most of the rivers and springs have long dried up. Across this desolate landscape walk three travelers: Tieh, an androgynous young mystic devoted to the Moon Goddess, Boyce, a mercenary warrior, and Lakshi, a feisty young person who is really the princess Lakshi Arun Ard. Through a series of strange events, they find themselves in a long-dead city where they face the anger of departed souls disturbed by a group of pirates plundering their comfortable afterlife. Tieh and Lakshi must confront their own demons, and all three of the companions must fight to escape the grip of Death and return to a world that, while dying, still has something to offer them.
Originally released on a triple bill with **SILENT MÖBIUS** 2 and **HEROIC LEGEND OF ARSLAN** 2, this hypnotically slow tale was based on a novel by Sei Takekawa with illustrations by Mutsumi Inomata, on which Yuki's character designs are based. A manga by Masaeda Hashimoto followed in *Dragon* magazine.

WEB DIVER

2001. JPN: *Denno Boken-ki Webdiver*. AKA:

Cyber Adventure Web Diver. TV series. DIR: Hiroshi Negishi, Kunitoshi Okajima. SCR: Mayori Sekijima. DES: Shigetsugu Takahashi. ANI: N/C. MUS: N/C. PRD: NAS, Radix, TV Tokyo. 25 mins. x N/D eps.
In the year 2100, children are able to transform themselves into data, allowing them to interact in a "magical" cyberworld. When the cyberworld is attacked by the evil Wills Program Deletron, Japanese kids Kenta and Aoi hold them off with the aid of the Web Knight Gradion, which looks uncannily like a giant robot.

WEB GHOST PIPOPA *

2008. JPN: *NetGhost PiPoPa*. TV series. DIR: Shinichiro Kimura. SCR: Yasutomo Yamada. DES: Marcow Himawari, Naomi Iwata. ANI: Toshiaki Sato, Daisuke Tsumagari. MUS: Motoyoshi Iwasaki. PRD: Studio Hibari, AT-X, TV Tokyo. 25 mins. x 51 eps.
Elementary schoolboy Yuta hates most modern technology but loves his cellphone. That's unfortunate because he lives in a city entirely run by computers. He gets a mysterous email on his phone and when he opens it he's sucked into "net space." There he meets three feisty little creatures named Pit, Pot, and Pat—PiPoPa for short, an allusion to the Japanese onomatopoeia for the beeps of a touchpad. They take him on adventures between the human world and netspace, helping him to make new friends and become more comfortable with technology. Director Kimura has made stories based on new uses for familiar technology before: in **CHARGER GIRL JUDEN-CHAN** the heroines are mobile charging stations for the depressed, like battery chargers, while **OH! EDO ROCKET** uses a firework for space travel. Creator Naomi Iwata's previous work includes material for both adults and children, including the quirky, unsettling **GREGORY HORROR SHOW**.

WEDDING PEACH

1995. JPN: *Ai Tenshi Densetsu Wedding Peach*. AKA: *Legend of Love Angel WP*. TV series, video. DIR: Kunihiko Yuyama, Norihiko Sudo, Yuji Asano, Toshiaki Suzuki, Yoshitaka Fujimoto. SCR: Sukehiro Tomita, Kenji Terada, Hideki Sonoda, Yukiyoshi Ohashi. DES: Kazuko Tadano. ANI: Yuri Isseki, Mariko Fujita, Moriyasu Taniguchi. MUS: Toshiki Hasegawa. PRD: NAS, KSS, TV Tokyo. 25 mins. x 51 eps.,

30 mins. x 4 eps. (v).
Three adolescent girls—one good, one bad, one silly—band together to fight evil as the Love Angel and her, er, bridesmaids. Yes, where SAILOR MOON fought evil with the power of love and makeup, *WP* uses bridal finery. Naturally, the ditzy one (Momoko, AKA Wedding Peach) is the bride and lead fighter of evil, with the intellectual and the bad girl (Yuri and Hinagiku, AKA Angel Lily and Angel Daisy, respectively) as her sidekicks. All this has its roots in an ancient battle between the devils, led by Reine Devilla, who wants to banish all love from Earth, and the angels, led by Queen Aphrodite, who wants to preserve it. So the queen picked three ordinary high school girls and gave them magical items to enable them to transform into their wedding-day alter egos. Unlike most magical girls, they transform in three stages—from school uniform to wedding dress or bridesmaid's outfit to sexy lightly armored battlesuits. (Why wedding dress, you ask? To build up the power of Love, *obviously!*) The series ended with the world made safe for Love, but in 1997 our heroes returned in the four-part video series *WP DX*; they're enjoying a quiet vacation when a monster attacks Earth, and Aphrodite gives them back their powers to fight once more for love and truth. Tomita, who wrote the manga of *WP* for *Ciao* magazine, was also a writer on SAILOR MOON, and Tadano worked as a designer on the first two *SM* TV series.

WEE WENDY *

1984. JPN: *Tongari Boshi Memoru*. JPN: *Memoru and Her Pointed Hat; Little Memole*. TV series. DIR: Osamu Kasai, Yukio Misawa, Junichi Sato, Hiroshi Shidara. SCR: Shunichi Yukimuro, Chifude Asakura, Ryoko Takagi. DES: Ginichiro Suzuki. ANI: Ginichiro Suzuki, Takashi Saijo. MUS: Nozomu Aoki. PRD: Toei, TV Asahi. 25 mins. x 50 eps. (TV), 15 mins. (m).
Space travelers from the planet Rilulu crash-land on Earth, where, like the characters in DAGON, they discover that they are tiny compared to the giant local inhabitants. Sneaking away from her parents, Memoru and her friends hitch a ride on the back of an owl and befriend the bedridden child Marielle. Eventually, a Rilulu rescue craft arrives to take them home,

but as she prepares to leave, Memoru realizes that her departure will break Marielle's heart, and she decides to stay. The series was followed by a 15-minute "movie" outing, which combined elements of episodes 1, 2, 7, 24, and the reunion of Memoru and Marielle in episode 25. Cut and released as *Wee Wendy* on U.S. VHS under the Just For Kids label in 1989, with a running time of 100 minutes.

WEEKLY SHIMAKO

2011. JPN: *Shukan Shimako*. TV series. DIR: FROGMAN. SCR: FROGMAN. DES: N/C. ANI: Akihiro Saito, Mitsuo Sato. MUS: manzo, ti.o.bi. PRD: DLE Inc, happyproject.Inc, NTV. 3 mins. x 22 eps.
A short gag anime based on Kenji Hirokane's business manga character, Kosaku Shima, part of the YURUANI? anthology show. The segment, or the character, must appeal to the director since he also voiced the leading role. The original manga character first appeared in 1983 as *Section Chief Kosaku Shima* in *Morning* magazine, and his career has entertained adult Japanese readers ever since, through multiple promotions, migrations, a prequel charting his early days, up to the present day's *President Kosaku Shima*. He has hence served as a witness and icon to Japan's economic rise, fall, and recovery—famous enough to poke fun at himself in this humorous outing but also invested with enough gravity to narrate another series, *Kosaku Shima's Asia Success Story* (*Shima Kosaku Asia Risshiden*, 2013), in which cartoon characters and animated graphics presumably explained why the Chinese now own everything.

WEISS KREUZ *

1998. AKA: *White Cross; Night Hunters*. TV series, video. DIR: Kiyoshi Egami, Masami Obari. SCR: Isao Shizuya, Shigeru Yanagawa, Sukehiro Tomita. DES: Tetsuya Yanasawa. ANI: Tetsuya Yanasawa. MUS: Weiss. PRD: Animate Film, TV Tokyo. 25 mins. x 25 eps. (TV), 25 mins. x 2 eps. (v), 25 mins. x 13 eps. (TV2).
Why *shouldn't* four pretty teenage male florists fight evil when the shop closes for the night? Our heroes hate the crime and murder stalking the big city and harming the innocent, so they roam the streets offing as many of the bad guys as they can; they may be florists, but they're no shrink-

ing violets when it comes to pest control. Unlike the Knight Sabers (but like *Charlie's Angels*), they have an external authority—a mystery man known only as Persia. As the series progresses they find that more of the drug rings and terrorist factions they take out are connected to one hugely powerful family, pointing to a coldly planned conspiracy.

With a concept straight from BUBBLEGUM CRISIS and a cast out of SAINT SEIYA via GUNDAM W, *WK* was made to promote Weiss, a band manufactured from four young voice actors, purportedly based on an idea by their lead singer, Takehito Koyasu, and first serialized as a novel in *Animage*. A number of interesting *Doomwatch*-style SF concepts lurk in the plotlines (like the attempt to infest the water supply with flesh-eating bacteria), but relentless cuteness always wins out, and every episode has a downbeat ending designed to pluck at the heartstrings of the intended junior-high-school-girl audience. Giving one of the boys a Wolverine-style steel claw and making him a biker jock isn't enough to give the show real teeth; it loses out in the crime-fighter stakes to *BGC* and can't compete with ZETSUAI for angst. For sheer prettiness, though, the characters take some beating, and the series is fabulous eye candy. Released in the U.S. under the title *Knight Hunters*.

Weiss Kreuz Glühen (AKA *Knight Hunters Eternity*, 2002) was a second TV series, in which the boys find themselves at a mysterious academy, troubled by student suicides and violence in a similar set-up seemingly inspired by *Challenge From the Future* (*DE). The series introduced two new pretty boys, Sena and Kyo, and radically different character designs by Toshimitsu Kobayashi, as an indirect result of an ongoing dispute with the original character designer Kyoko Tsuchiya. Three of the original *WK* voice actors also appeared together in GET BACKERS, leading to a boost among fans for the latter series among *WK* aficionados.

WELCOME TO IRABU'S OFFICE *

2009. JPN: *Kuchu Buranko*. AKA: *Flying Trapeze*. TV series. DIR: Kenji Nakamura. SCR: Manabu Ishikawa, Isao Murayama, Tomoko Taguchi. DES: Takashi Hashimoto, Shoji Tokiwa. ANI: Takashi Hashimoto. MUS:

Hideharu Mori. PRD: Toei Animation, Asmik Ace, Bunshun, Dentsu, Fuji TV, Sony Music Entertainment. 25 mins. x 11 eps.

Over nine days, 11 patients come to see psychiatrist Dr. Irabu and his sulky, sexy nurse Mayumi. They find an arrogant, self-centered man-child with little or no empathy for their troubles. He rarely prescribes anything stronger than a vitamin shot, forcing them to confront their issues and either resolve them or learn to live with them. They see him differently depending on their condition, or perhaps depending on how he perceives their need. For those unclear about the mental health issues involved, a live doctor pops up onscreen to explain.

Hideo Okuda's 2004 short story collection *Trapeze* also inspired a TV drama and a stage show. The anime version collected several awards in Japan for film technology as well as style and substance. It looks good—vivid, edgy, and unsettling, but compulsively watchable and sometimes reminiscent of Terry Gilliam at his best. The story structure is simple and repetitive, but as the episodes unfold we begin to see the connections between the characters, forming an overall theme: that empathy and acceptance can impart a degree of dignity and control to those often denied it by a terrifying world. Delivering its insights with style, humor, and an inventive, appropriate soundtrack packed with pings, whirrs, Japanese Christmas songs, and effortless irony, this is one of the most interesting shows of its year. ◐

WELCOME TO THE NHK *

2006. JPN: *NHK ni Yokoso!* TV series. DIR: Yusuke Yamamoto. SCR: Satoru Nishizono. DES: Masashi Ishihama, Takahiko Yoshida, Hiroshi Igaki. ANI: Takahiko Yoshida. MUS: Pearl Brothers. PRD: Gonzo, NHK ni Yokso! Production Team. 24 mins. x 24 eps.

Tatsuhiro Sato is 22 and NEET—not in employment, education, or training. He's also a *hikikomori*, or shut-in. For the past four years he's stayed indoors most of the time, living on an allowance from his parents, watching trashy TV and Internet porn in his garbage-filled apartment. He firmly believes that he is being persecuted by the Japanese Shut-in Society, the *Nihon Hikikomori Kyokai*, or NHK, an evil organization whose intention is to produce a

world filled with people like him (no relation, of course, to NHK, the Japanese public broadcaster). His next-door neighbor plays appalling anime music at ear-shattering volume. He knows he can't go on like this but has no idea how to change. Then a girl comes into his life asking him to sign up for her big project: to save *hikikomori* from their self-imposed prison.

The tragicomic chaos of the inner self is this show's territory (compare to **WATAMOTE**), and it uses satire, comedy, and melodrama to illuminate the dark corners of a terrifying dissociative disorder. Although its drug references and nudity are considerably toned down from the manga inspired by Tatsuhiko Takimoto's original novel, it loses none of their psychological depth and power. The music reflects this confusion, with exquisitely timed switches between grunge rock, acoustic blues, J-pop, and eerie minimalism. The art, especially Studio Easter's backgrounds, serves the story similarly well, with fantastic and realistic environments created in equally convincing depth and detail. While the animation isn't Gonzo's finest, it works well enough, especially during character closeups that reveal inner turmoil and change.

Sato, pushed on by his would-be savior Misaki, revisits people and events from his past to try and unlock the door to a better future. As in **WE WITHOUT WINGS**, there is more to his fears than meets the eye. The slow, initially perplexing way the story unfolds reflects his feelings and fears and the way rejection and scorn add to Sato's own confusion and reluctance to face the world. His efforts to create a porn game might seem a stupid way to try and impress a girl, but seen in context any bridge out of his terrifying fantasy world, however shaky, looks good. Asking big, scary questions and acknowledging that most of our answers are very shaky, *Welcome to the NHK* is that rare thing—an anime series that's entertaining, disturbing, and seriously worthwhile in equal parts.

WELCOME TO THE SPACE SHOW *

2010. JPN: *Uchu Show e Yokoso*. Movie. DIR: Koji Masunari. SCR: Hideyuki Kurata. DES: Masashi Ishihama, Kazuo Ogura. ANI: Masashi Ishihama. MUS: Yoshihiro Ike. PRD: A-1 Pictures, Aniplex, Dentsu. 136 mins.

Five children come to a tiny village deep in the woods for a summer camp. Their rural idyll is disrupted when they find what looks like a small dog, injured and in need of help. But "Pochi" is really an alien, attacked by poachers while seeking a mysterious substance coveted throughout the universe. In gratitude for their rescue he takes them into space, but the adventure turns sour when reports of the attack that injured him cause the authorities to ban travel between Earth and the Moon. Stranded in space, the children have to earn enough money to persuade someone to take them home before their parents find out they aren't at camp any more.

Although the standard of the animation is a little uneven at times, the movie is aimed squarely at the primary school age-bracket of the young protagonists, and they are unlikely to be as hypercritical as the largely adult Western audience. Its sense of adventure and fun carries viewers over the occasional preachy passages in Kurata's script, which is helped by his wide-ranging influences and inspirations. The narrative potpurri is a match for the bright and varied visuals. Like **POKÉMON** the film allows its young stars to visit exciting alien worlds that are reassuringly like home, from social structures to fast food. Like **MY NEIGHBOR TOTORO** it allows them to befriend strange and powerful forest creatures. Like **SPIRITED AWAY** it requires them to take on adult responsibilities and save themselves when the situation turns nasty. Fans of children's fiction will also spot nods to classics such as **THE PSAMMEAD** and the *Chronicles of Narnia*.

This could have resulted in a visual and narrative mess but under Masunari's hand it turns into a midnight feast, leaving the viewer sugar-rushed and replete with candy and pop. The adventure is upbeat and entertaining, and while the show is low on serious issues and the "mysterious substance" is anticlimactic, it's still a treat. Based on an idea by "Besame Mucho," a pen name for the same creative team of Masunari, Kurata, and producer Tomonori Ochikoshi that previously collaborated on **KAMICHU!**

WET SUMMER DAYS *

2003. JPN: *Suika*. AKA: *Melon*. Video. DIR: Yasuhito Kikuchi. SCR: Mitsuhiro Yamada,

Kazuhiro Ota. DES: Kazuhiro Ota. ANI: Shigeru Ikehata. MUS: Kamin. PRD: Studio A.P.P.P., Moon Rock, Circus. 30 mins. x 3 eps.

Tokiwa is a quiet seaside hamlet far from the city and the hometown of Sayaka Shirakawa, an artist's daughter going steady with a local boy. It's based on a dating sim game, hence the swift divergence of the story into tales of five girls who are so "different" that it takes different hats and hairstyles to remind you which is which. The storyline, however, takes on an element of doom and gloom—such as the rumor in the village that Sayaka's father paints corpses—in accordance with the Japanese tradition that holds that summertime is the best occasion for ghost stories, in order to keep the blood cold. Later episodes veer away from Sayaka to incorporate Akira, a student returning to the town for the summer vacation who discovers that his childhood friend Itsuki appears to have become a shrine maiden. A third man, Hiroshi, also encounters a local girl in the third episode, and once more what appears to be a simple tale of young love drifts into unexpected revelations and implications of tragedy. As with ONE: TRUE STORIES and several other anime of recent years, this title appears to exist in two incarnations back in Japan, both with and without the more explicit scenes. **N**

WHAT'S MICHAEL?

1985. Video, TV series. DIR: Yuichi Higuchi, Katsumi Kosuga, Norio Yazawa, Kunitoshi Okajima, Hideki Hirojima, Satoshi Okada, Seiji Okuda. SCR: Masaaki Sakurai, Yoshio Urasawa, Koji Tanaka, Osamu Nakamura, Nobuaki Kishima, Mayumi Shimazaki, Tomoko Konparu, Megumi Sugiwara. DES: Norio Kashima, Katsuyoshi Kanemura. ANI: Norio Kashima. MUS: Makoto Kobayashi, Koji Makaino. PRD: Kitty Films, TV Tokyo. 56 mins. (v1), 60 mins. (v2), 25 mins. x 45 eps. (TV).

Michael is a fat orange cat who lives with a pair of well-meaning but very stupid humans who fondly imagine he is their pet. But Michael's own daily life is rich in all kinds of little incidents and upheavals—avoiding local bad cat Nyazilla, a monster against whom Michael knows he'll always come out worse, scrounging food from local stores, meeting up with his animal friends, and keeping the humans amused as best he can. And Michael also

has a fantasy life even his fellow feline Garfield would envy, with cat corporations, cat nightclubs, and his own imitation of a dancing American megastar also called Michael. His adventures continued in 1988 with another video and a TV series. Based on the 1984 manga in *Comic Morning* by Makoto Kobayashi, itself the happy musings of an indulgent pet-owner rather than the more biting satire of I AM A CAT. *WM* was the first show to begin on video and then transfer to TV, and it is a must for cat-lovers and fans of observational humor.

WHAT'S UP MECHADOC?

1984. JPN: *Yoroshiku Mechadoc*. TV series. DIR: Hidehito Ueda, Takaaki Ishiyama, Hiroyuki Tanaka, Masayuki Kojima, Shinya Sadamitsu. SCR: Kenji Terada, Hirohisa Soda, Takao Koyama, Mayori Sekijima. DES: Tatsunoko Anime Office, Ammonite. ANI: Hideyuki Motohashi, Chuichi Iguchi. MUS: Hirokazu Takahashi. PRD: Tatsunoko, Fuji TV. 25 mins. x 30 eps.

Jun Kazama is crazy about cars and loves to tune his engines to top performance; he can make even a standard manufacturer's model run above spec. With Kazumichi Nakamura and Kiyoshi Noro, he sets up a tuning shop called Mechadoc in Yokohama, helped by Kanzaki, the owner of the nearby Paddock teashop. Competing with a rival store owned by the scheming Wataru Hochi, they tune up biker gangs and befriend female car-nut Reiko Ono. Eventually Jun is so drawn into the world of custom cars that he races against rival mechanics' masterpieces—compare to the much later INITIAL D. Based on the 1982 *Shonen Jump* manga by Ryuji Tsugihara.

WHEN MARNIE WAS THERE *

2014. JPN: *Omoide no Marnie*. AKA: *Marnie of my Memories*. Movie. DIR: Hiromasa Yonebayashi. SCR: Hiromasa Yonebayashi, Keiko Niwa, Masashi Ando. DES: Masashi Ando. ANI: Masashi Ando. MUS: Takatsugu Muramatsu. PRD: Studio Ghibli, Toho, Buena Vista Home Entertainment, Hakuhodo, KDDI, Mitsubishi, NTV. 103 mins.

The asthmatic, withdrawn 12-year-old Anna is sent away from Sapporo to northern Hokkaido to stay for the summer with relatives. She befriends Marnie, the mysterious, ethereal blonde girl who lives in a nearby house that is said to be haunted.

Often feeling, like many late Ghibli works, as if a committee is imitating the glory days, this adaptation of Joan G. Robinson's 1967 novel replays many familiar Ghibli themes, including absent or departed parental figures, elegies to country living, and plucky heroines. Comments about the blue tinge in Anna's eyes and the fact that the family who once lived in the deserted villa were "foreigners" are enough to telegraph many of the supposed twists miles ahead, turning much of the narrative into an unspooling description of the *how*, rather than the *what*. A heavy shroud of melancholy also evokes similar contemporary features, most notably COLORFUL: THE MOTION PICTURE and A LETTER TO MOMO, but *Marnie* marks both an ending and a beginning. It was released in July 2014, shortly before the announcement that Studio Ghibli would be putting its feature production department on hiatus, seemingly in recognition that the heart had gone out of its output with the departure of Hayao Miyazaki (THE WIND RISES) and the failure of Isao Takahata's THE TALE OF THE PRINCESS KAGUYA to set the box office alight. This seems rather an unfair commentary on ARRIETTY director Hiromasa Yonebayashi, who does a perfectly workmanlike job on this feature. Meanwhile, the Hokkaido setting plays into the continued promotion of Japan's northern island for domestic tourism (FRANCESCA; SILVER SPOON), born out of a fear that nobody dares take the narrow road to the deep north now that it traverses the cursed wastelands of the 2011 Great East Japan earthquake and tsunami.

WHEN THEY CRY *

2007. JPN: *Higurashi no Naku Koro ni; Higurashi no Naku Koro ni: Kai*. AKA: *The Season When Cicadas Cry; When They Cry II: Solutions*. TV series, video. DIR: Chiaki Kon, Toshifumi Kawase, Hideki Tachibana. SCR: Toshifumi Kawase, Rika Nakase, Fumihiko Shimo. DES: Kyuta Sakai, Kazuya Kuroda, Chikako Shibata. ANI: Seiya Numata, Kyuta Sakai, Tomoyuki Abe, Hiromitsu Hagiwara, Hiroshi Tomioka. MUS: Kenji Kawai. PRD: Studio DEEN, Frontier Works, Geneon Universal Entertainment, Sotsu Agency. 26 mins. x 24 eps. (TV1), 24 mins. x 24 eps. (TV2), 23 mins. (v1), 30 mins. x 5 eps. (v2), 30 mins. x 4 eps. (v3).

During the long, hot summer of 1983, Keiichi Maebara transfers to the mountain village school of Hinamizawa. It's so small that all the grades are taught together in one classroom. He soon makes friends with four girls, Rina, Rika, Mion, and Satoko, and joins their club, playing all kinds of card and board games. But there's a mystery around the annual festival for the local god. Every year for the past four years, someone has been murdered on the day of the festival and someone else has gone missing. As strange and horrifying events unfold, Keiichi's ordinary life becomes terrifyingly extraordinary.

Created by gaming circle 07th Expansion as a visual novel (ARGOT AND JARGON), the first anime series *Higurashi no Naku Koro ni* also spun off six manga following the different scenarios of the game and one adapting an unperformed stage play by 07th Expansion member Ryukishi07 that formed the original basis of the game. There were also two live-action movies in 2008 and 2009. The structure of the plot follows that of the game—and, incidentally, that of Akira Kurosawa's *Rashomon*—unfolding in a series of scenarios that look at events from different perspectives. Only by taking all the perspectives into account can the viewer begin to piece together what has happened and why. It's a puzzle box, intricate and beautifully crafted, all the drawers and compartments overflowing with blood and horror (HORROR AND MONSTERS). Story arcs, either posing questions or offering answers, start off innocently but lead down dark and violent paths that may be blind alleys, offering an array of possible endings in which nobody's survival is guaranteed. Meanwhile, the 1980s setting adds a new chill for modern viewers, depriving the Facebook generation of the security blankets of mobile phones, search engines, and GPS technology, all of which have compromised the locked-room limits of many modern thrillers (compare to ANOTHER). It makes a big difference to the experience, and prevents the audience shouting "JUST GOOGLE IT!" every few minutes.

The unique selling point of this franchise is its mixture of gore, psychological horror, and cute, wide-eyed moppets of a type more normally seen in much lighter, sweeter shows. To see a Lolita-type girl in school uniform is one thing: to see her standing behind the hero with a cleaver in her tiny hand, about to dye them both red with blood, is quite another. Characters you have come to like, even love, cannot be trusted. Their cute little catch phrases suddenly sound sinister, and you dread what might lie behind those bland expressions.

The mystery still leaves unanswered questions, which were only partly resolved in the second TV series *When They Cry II: Solutions* (2007). The emphasis shifts from Keiichi to his friend Rina, who is determined to break the cycle of hatred that has led to so much death. The same crew is in charge, maintaining the suspense and tension from the first series. The characters are still stereotypes, but the weight of expectation around these tropes served them well in the first series and still does. The DVD release for this series has 24 COMEDY snippets of one minute or less as an extra. This series had three manga adaptations, and as with the first series each manga focuses on events from a different viewpoint.

A 23-minute video, *Higurashi no Naku Koro ni Gaiden: Nekogoroshi-hen* (*When They Cry Extra Chapter: Cat Killing Story*), also appeared in 2007. Taking Keiichi and the girls to an abandoned village, it presents a self-contained mystery set in a haunted quarry. A five-part video series in 2009, *Higurashi no Naku Koro ni: Rei* (*When They Cry: Gratitude*), forms the true sequel to the second TV series. It gives Rika a leading role, opening and closing with an episode of light relief. In the middle three episodes the whole world is changed by Rika's guardian goddess. Rika has to choose between a version of her life in which the sin and tragedy of the past never happened and Hinamizawa is an Eden, but without some of the people she loves, or one where the hot blood flows but friends missing from Eden are still present. Compare to ANOTHER.

The four-part video series *Higurashi no Naku Koro ni: Kira* (*When They Cry: Glitter*, 2011) is a parallel-world tale turning Rika and Satoko into magical girls and completely abandoning the mystery and horror for fan service and fun to celebrate the tenth anniversary of the franchise. A new video series, *Higurashi no Naku Koro ni: Kaku: Outbreak* (*When They Cry: Outbreak, 2013*), resets the story to zero and brings Keiichi and Rena together to deal with a mysterious virus that seals off the village in 1983. 🅥🅛

WHISPER OF THE HEART *

1995. JPN: *Mimi o Sumaseba*. AKA: *Prick Up Your Ears; If You Listen Closely/Carefully*. Movie. DIR: Yoshifumi Kondo. SCR: Hayao Miyazaki. DES: Yoshifumi Kondo, Satoshi Kuroda. ANI: Kitaro Kosaka. MUS: Yuji Nomi. PRD: Studio Ghibli. 111 mins.

Imaginative, intelligent 14-year-old Shizuku Tsukishima secretly longs to be a writer, reading anything she lays her hands on. Observing that the same name continually crops up on the borrower's lists of books she takes from both the school library and from the public library where her father works, she wonders who this Seiji Amasawa, who shares her taste in reading, might be. When they do finally meet, Seiji upsets her by criticizing her work, and she storms off. Idly following a cat she sees getting off her train, she finds herself in a chic residential area. Wandering into an antique store, she befriends the shopkeeper (eventually revealed as Seiji's grandfather) and becomes intrigued by Baron, an elegantly dressed German cat-doll. Shizuku and Seiji learn that they share a love of music, and with his violin playing and her singing, they soon become closer.

Baron himself appears in Shizuku's dream and shows her a magical fantasy world, which Shizuku begins to turn into a story. Grandfather encourages her to continue writing, while reminiscing about his prewar youth in Germany, where he loved and lost the owner of Baron's lady-doll companion. But Seiji's future plans threaten their growing friendship—he is taking two months off school to have special violin tutoring. If he shows promise, his father has agreed to let him go to Italy and study to become a professional musician. Meanwhile, their friendship and her writing project are distracting Shizuku from her schoolwork and may even mean she fails her exams.

A gentle, beautifully executed movie based on a manga by Aoi Hiiragi, which, like KIKI'S DELIVERY SERVICE, juxtaposes flights of fantasy (Shizuku's daydreams of journeys with Baron) with commonplace realities (Shizuku's "failure" in the eyes of her teachers). It revolves around the stresses of love and ambition, the need to lay the groundwork of both careers and relationships, and the difficulty of balancing it all when your head and heart are awhirl. It marries the lush production values common to Studio Ghibli productions with a new directorial vision that, sadly, developed no further. Director Kondo died, just into his 40s, soon after the film was released. A sequel, *Happy Times* (*Shiawase na Jikan*), exists in manga form, while the real-world location, Tama Hills, also got the Ghibli treatment in POM POKO. It is implied that one of the stories that Shizuku ends up writing is the basis for another anime, THE CAT RETURNS, while the fantasy world shown to her by Baron is revisited in IBLARD TIME.

WHISPERED WORDS *

2009. JPN: *Sasameki Koto*. TV series. DIR: Eiji Suganuma. SCR: Hideyuki Kurata. DES: Masami Inomata, Yukihiro Shibutani. ANI: Masami Inomata. MUS: Shigeomi Hasumi. PRD: AIC, Flying Dog, Fuji TV, Media Factory, T.O. Entertainment. 24 mins. x 13 eps. Sumika is in love with her classmate and friend Ushio. Ushio is openly lesbian, but Sumika isn't her type—she likes cute little girls, whereas her tall, sarcastic, overachieving friend is anything but cute. Ushio even finds a cross-dressed boy cuter than her, and she doesn't intend to lose a great friendship by declaring her feelings when there's no chance.

This endearingly funny and often heart-wrenching romance is based on a manga by Takashi Ikeda, and will carry you back to the days when waiting for The One to phone you was an occasion of almost unbearable tension, and a single look or gesture created high drama. Realistic characters, all capable of pettiness and stupidity, all convincing, will warm your heart, while the simplicity of the design and animation support a story that is generally well told, although later episodes never quite match the precise and polished perfection of the first. The lesbian focus is well and respectfully handled, but this isn't a series about gender choices: it's about the agony of young love. Everyone, of every orientation—even the most macho fanboy—can empathize with that.

WHISTLE!

2002. TV series. DIR: Hiroshi Fukutomi, Shin Misawa. SCR: Shunichi Yukimuro, Takashi Yamada, Nobuaki Kishima. DES: Tadami Komura. ANI: Tadami Komura, Masateru Kudo. MUS: Toshihiko Sahashi. PRD: Marvelous Entertainment, Animax. 24 mins. x 39 eps. Sho Kazamatsuri wants to be a pro soccer player. He's not very talented, but that's a perfect qualification for the role of hero in a TV anime series about developing your own skills through effort and determination while learning to work as part of a team. Leaving a prestigious high school because he's unable to rise very far in its renowned soccer team, he enrolls at Sakura Junior High and finds that at last he can get to play, albeit for the underdogs. Based on the *Shonen Jump* manga by Daisuke Higuchi, this is a standard boys' sports series, the bread and butter of anime.

WHITE ALBUM *

2009. AKA: *W.A.* TV series. DIR: Akira Yoshimura, Taizo Yoshida. SCR: Hiroaki Sato. DES: Ko Yoshinari, Shinji Katahira. ANI: Osamu Sakata. MUS: Hitoshi Fujima, Junpei Fujita. PRD: Seven Arcs, Starchild Records. 25 mins. x 26 eps. (TV1), 25 mins. x 12 eps. (TV2). It's 1986. Cassette tapes rule music, cell phones are newfangled gadgets the size of bricks, and as far as everyone except the military is concerned, the Internet doesn't exist (WHEN THEY CRY). Toya Fujii's life has been turned upside-down. His girlfriend Yuki has become a famous idol singer, and her management company wants her to cool their relationship. Her fans want him to stay faithful and loyal to support her. Other girls want him to forget her and turn to them. Her fame has rubbed off on him and brings some old acquaintances back into his circle. And his life isn't just about her: his father is ill, and he's trying to keep up with his university studies. His relationships and feelings matter as much as hers—at least, they do to him.

The 1980s, with their exaggerated styles and disco beats, are the new nostalgic focus for those too young to remember the '60s when the Beatles' groundbreaking *White Album* appeared. Authentic 1980s shows like TO-Y can look too dated to an audience reared on modern CGI: *White Album* steps neatly into the gap. Loaded with insert songs and styled to look like the present's idea of a groovy past, it looks and sounds perfect for its target market. Toya's reaction to his situation is disappointingly typical, but his indecision and turmoil, and the shallowness of his world, ring uncomfortably true to life.

Adapting the first series from an erotic game by Leaf for Aquaplus, writer Sato takes the unusual step of stripping out the sex apart from one scene in a car—and even there, the activity doesn't go much beyond kissing and the steam is generated by the writing and animation. Another surprise comes in the animation from Seven Arcs. Not always distinguished for the quality and fluency of their work, the team turns in a solid, workmanlike job, segueing seamlessly from caricature to more realistic animation and handling delicate expressions and pastel colors well. The second season added Seiya Numata as director, Fumiaki Maruto as writer, and Satelight as the animation studio.

WHITE FANG

1982. JPN: *Shiroi Kiba White Fang Monogatari*. AKA: *White Fang Story*. TV special. DIR: Soji Yoshikawa, Takeyuki Yokoyama. SCR: Shiro Hagiwara. DES: Yoshikazu Yasuhiko. ANI: Yoshikazu Yasuhiko, Tsuneo Ninomiya. MUS: Hitoshi Komuro. PRD: Sunrise, TBS. 85 mins. A hunter living in the forests of North America rears and trains a superb white wolf to become his faithful companion. Based on the classic novel by Jack London, author of CALL OF THE WILD, this was the first non-SF show from GUNDAM studio Sunrise.

WHITE WHALE OF MU, THE

1980. JPN: *Mu no Hakugei*. AKA: *Moby Dick 5*. TV series. DIR: Tetsuo Imazawa, Yasuo Yamayoshi, Akinori Nagaoka, Minoru Okazaki, Satoshi Dezaki. SCR: Hiroyuki Hoshiyama, Kenichi Matsuzaki, Masaaki Sakurai, Hideo Takayashiki. DES: Shunzo Aoki. ANI: Takao Kasai. MUS: Kentaro Haneda. PRD: Tokyo Movie Shinsha, Yomiuri TV (Nippon TV). 25 mins. x 26 eps. The people of Atlantis are defeated by the people of Mu (see SUPER ATRAGON) and send their planet through a time slip to escape. Thirty thousand years later, at the end of the 20th century, the White Whale, last remnant of the forgotten civilization of Mu, awakes from her slumber, causing massive natural disasters all over Earth. The escaped Atlanteans have emerged from their time tunnel, and the flying cybernetic White Whale assembles a group of young children on Easter Island to protect the Earth. Ken (the leader), Mamoru (the cocky one), Rei (the token girl), Shin (the fat one), and Manabu (the bratty brain) serve Princess Madora, daughter of King La-Mu. This far-fetched mixture of **Battle of the Planets** and **Blue Submarine No. Six** was based on an original story by Motoo Fukuo and is infamous in early U.S. **Fandom** for its naked winged cherub, who was quite obviously male. A transforming whale would also appear in **Ladius**.

WICKED CITY *
1987. JPN: *Yoju Toshi*. AKA: *Demon Beast City; Supernatural Beast City; Monster City*. Video. DIR: Yoshiaki Kawajiri. SCR: Kisei Cho. DES: Yoshiaki Kawajiri, Masao Maruyama, Kazuo Oga. ANI: Kenichi Ishikawa. MUS: Takeshi Nakazawa, Hironobu Kagoshima. PRD: Madhouse. 80 mins.
A state of stalemate exists between our world and the next dimension, and while "Black Guard" agents from both sides play a game of espionage, representatives from the two worlds prepare to sign a treaty. Renzaburo Taki is an undercover human, forced to partner up with the sexy, deadly Makie. Charged with guarding the uncooperative and lecherous old ambassador Giuseppe Maiyart, the pair become attracted to each other, though relationships between a human and a denizen of the Dark Realm are most inadvisable. In the climactic final battle between good and evil they learn that they are vital to the future of both worlds, and the love they have developed is more than just coincidence.
Made for the theaters with a relatively large budget, *WC* is vastly superior to the later straight-to-video **Demon City Shinjuku**, with which it is often confused, and indeed shares a writer, director, and studio. However, it still comes lumbered with risible *"Oh Taki!"/ "Oh, Makie!"* dialogue, perfunctory sex scenes, and a misogynistic obsession with Bad Girls From The Dark World. The final showdown in a church also throws in a contrived twist to wrap up the story, tearing vast holes in the preceding plot as it does so.
Darkside Blues–creator Hideyuki

Kikuchi's original novel cleverly exploited the fantasies of bored businessmen. Taking the viewer from bar to office to airport to hotel, it walks through the scenery of a company rep's humdrum life, enlivening each familiar place with dangerous sex and vicarious violence. *WC* was the first film to show the distinctive style of **Ninja Scroll**'s Kawajiri, whose trademark blue-red lighting is leavened here with artful fog effects and moody shadows. The first set piece says it all: a fight to the death beneath the wheels of a taxiing jumbo jet, with superfast fists making a virtue of the low animation cel count, an imitation shaky-cam effect right out of a Sam Raimi film, and superfast cutting to hide the joins, borrowed from Hong Kong action master Tsui Hark. Tsui would repay the compliment in 1993 when he produced a live-action version of *WC* in Hong Kong, featuring Leon Lai as Taki and Michele Reis as Makie.
Amid the dark palette and piano-wire tension, Kawajiri demonstrates a marvelously gothic sense of the unbreakable link between sex and death. The predatory nature of most sexual relationships, set out in Taki's opening encounter with a spider-woman whose vagina is lined with teeth, is contrasted in true Hammer-horror fashion with the purity of his relationship with Makie, whose inner self is affected but not changed by the sexual horrors she endures. For Makie, transformation and transcendence come when the deadly power of her fighting skill is lifted to another level by motherhood; Death and the Madonna become one. **ⒸⓃⓋ**

WIDOW *
2004. JPN: *Mibojin: Numeriau Niku-yoku yo Midara ni Nureru Mitsuko*. AKA: *Widow: Slimy Lust and a Dirty Wet Honey Pot*. Video. DIR: Ahiru Koike. SCR: Sosuke Kokubunji. DES: KAZU. ANI: Ahiru Koike. MUS: N/C. PRD: Milky, Studio Jam. 30 mins. x 2 eps.
Some time after the death of his brother, Kaoru returns to Japan to help settle the estate. This requires him meeting his brother's widow Taeko for the first time. Kaoru soon discovers that his old flame Miyuki is now the tutor to Taeko's younger sister Chiyoko and that all the residents of the house have a history of sex games in a secret underground basement.

As might be expected in an erotic anime such as this, it is not all that long before Kaoru is offering sexual condolences to his widowed sister-in-law, thereby exercising erotic anime's perennial obsessions with not-quite-incest and the use of bereavement as a means of sexual entrapment. **ⒸⓃⓋ**

WIFE EATER *
2003. JPN: *Tsumamigui*. Video. DIR: Hiromi Yokoyama. SCR: Himajin Planning, Taifu Sekimachi. DES: Toshide Matsudate. ANI: N/C. MUS: N/C. PRD: Pink Pineapple, SOFTGARE. 30 mins. x 2 eps.
The work of Rumiko Takahashi has inspired many imitations, some of which do their inspiration little credit. **Maison Ikkoku**'s young widow in a rooming house has become something of a porno paradigm, here crashed into the "unexpected alien visitor" genre, with a dash of **Slow Step** in its little girl latching on to every passing adult to try and find a new family. To vary things a bit and avoid any unjustified claims of copyright infringement, it's an apartment complex, not a boarding house, and the landlord runs a sex shop from his room. The widow is shy Chiho, and the guy with a crush on her is Satoru. He has no idea how to win her heart, but sex with new tenant Kanae, an experienced married woman who knows what women want, will surely help him to his goal, in an erotic anime that spends much longer than usual setting up its prescribed sex scenes. An "episode 0" was released, with a preview of the first episode and some additional bonus footage. The title plays with puns and slang terms for transitory affairs and eating with one's fingers. Based on a computer game from Alice Soft. **ⒸⓄ**

WIFE IN MOURNING
2010. JPN: *Mofuku Tsuma: Yurushite Anata? Watashi Yowai Mobijin desu*. AKA: *Wife in Mourning: Pardon me? I'm a Fragile Widow*. Video. DIR: Hidekai Oba. SCR: Akira Nintai. DES: Hayate. ANI: Akira Kano. MUS: N/C. PRD: schoolzone, Marigold (Girls Talk). 30 mins.
Honami dreamed of a happy family life with her new husband Satoshi and his relatives, but he was older than her and died on their honeymoon. Satoshi's sister Sayako blames Honami for his death. She

raised his son Manabu and wants him to help her take revenge. This is based on a porn game by Lune so they're all soon having sex. **ⓝⓥ**

WIFE IS MICAEL?, THE
2012. JPN: *Oku-sama wa Micael?* Video. DIR: Yoshiten. SCR: Yoshiten. DES: Yoshiten. ANI: Yoshiten. MUS: N/C. PRD: Chichi No Ya, Studio Parrot. 30 mins. x 2 eps.
Newlyweds Shinichi and Mika have their lives turned upside-down by the arrival of Furu, an alien creature that can transform into articles of clothing. Shinichi works at a hospital, so before long, nurses are involved, while Mika gets enmeshed in a series of bickering arguments with her talking underwear. We just write this stuff down. Although its own press releases already seem to be translating this as *The Wife Is Micael?*, we would be remiss in our encyclopedic duties if we did not point out that the "Oku-sama wa…" construction is usually used in the Japanese mainstream to allude to a number of TV shows with the title *My Wife Is a …* (see also *DE), as in MY WIFE IS A HIGHSCHOOL STUDENT. **ⓝ**

WIFE PIGEON
2011. JPN: *Hato no Oyome-san.* AKA: *HatoYome.* TV series. DIR: Kiminori Tagami. SCR: N/C. DES: N/C. ANI: Akina Watanabe. MUS: N/C. PRD: DLE Inc, happyproject.Inc, NTV. 3? mins. x 22 eps.
Based on a 1999 gag manga by Haguki, this simply animated story is all about a girl who marries into the Hato (pigeon) family, where she encounters many strange animals and comical situations. It was animated as part of NTV's comedic anthology show YURUANI?

WIFE SQUEEZING
2008. JPN: *Tsuma Shibori.* Video. DIR: Ken Raika. SCR: N/C. DES: N/C. ANI: N/C. MUS: N/C. PRD: MS Pictures (Milky). 30 mins. x 2 eps.
Kosuke's father has arranged a marriage for him without consulting him, and moves his wife-to-be Madoka in with him. Madoka's widowed sister Sakura also moves in to chaperone them, so naturally he ends up having sex with both of them. Then he pours out his heart to his childhood friend, bar owner Himeka, with predictable results. Based on a porn game by Alice Soft. **ⓝ**

WIFE WITH WIFE *
2005. JPN: *Tsuma Tsuma.* AKA: *Tsuma X Tsuma.* Video. DIR: Ao Tengen. SCR: Kazunari Kume. DES: Naoki. ANI: Naoki, Ao Tengen. MUS: N/C. PRD: Animac. 30 mins. x 2 eps.
In a set-up seemingly ripped from the derivative world of Japanese TV, Kotaro inherits Sakura Market from his late father, only to discover that his small, independent grocery business is under assault from the grasping Kaneyu Corporation, which is run by his long-lost brother. Since this is an erotic anime, the plot soon veers off the competitive track into the growing feelings between Kotaro and his stepmother, an older woman who was still significantly younger than her first husband. Meanwhile, Kotaro also finds out that service with a smile can lead to a different kind of servicing, when he offers to carry groceries home for lonely housewife Toko, and she repays him with sexual favors.

The second story is unrelated to the first, and features newlyweds Yosuke and Akira (Akira being a girl's name here), whose sex life gets off to a bumpy start thanks to the tiring process of moving house so soon after their wedding. But their union comes under even stronger pressure when Yosuke begins his new job as an assistant director and is almost immediately seduced by red-haired actress Atsuko. The first episode is based on the game *Tsuma X Tsuma 3,* while the second is based on the game *Tsuma X Tsuma 1.5*—note that as with GUN X SWORD and HUNTER X HUNTER, the "X" in the Japanese title is silent. The the art and animation of the series are above the usual par for CGI anime porn, and although these episodes are currently all there are, with two other *TXT* games still unadapted, other installments may follow. Not even the two episodes here have fully conclusive endings—in the first, the takeover attempt is unresolved and two characters remain untouched (with one's backstory untold as well); in the second, Atsuko remains determined to get Yosuke. **ⓛⓝⓥ**

WIFE-LOVE DIARY
2010. JPN: *Aisai Nikki.* Video. DIR: Dosan Saito. SCR: Kosaku Shima. DES: Jisakikeusu. ANI: Jisakikeusu. MUS: N/C. PRD: Gramme, Pink Pineapple. 30 mins.
Beautiful, gentle Sanae has been married

for four years, and her husband Keisuke finds he can no longer have sex with her. Because this is porn, he doesn't discuss it with her to work things out. Instead, he asks a subordinate at work, who's a bit of a stud, to come and seduce her. Naturally he watches them and records their sessions, and finds himself getting horny again. This was originally an erotic game by ORCSOFT, so unfortunately there is no chance that Sanae will get so furious that she kicks both of them where it hurts, divorce Keisuke, and marry a clergyman or anime encyclopedist. **ⓝ**

WIFE'S MOTHER SAYURI
2011. JPN: *Tsuma no Haha Sayuri.* Video. DIR: Mitsuhiro Yoneda. SCR: N/C. DES: N/C. ANI: Ichiro Yamadari. MUS: N/C. PRD: YOUC, MS Pictures, Digital Works/Vanilla. 27 mins. x 2 eps.
When Akihiro's wife cheats on him, his mother-in-law Sayuri comes around to apologize. She says this is all her fault. When she was bringing up her daughter alone, she worked as a call girl and the blood of prostitutes runs in their veins, or something. Comforting his distraught mother-in-law, he notices how hot she is, and works out a way she can make it up to him. She's eager to replace her daughter, and their friends Fuji and Shizue soon get involved, in this anime based on a porn game by CATTLEYA. Part of the VANILLA SERIES. **ⓝ**

WIFE-SWAP DIARIES
2009. JPN: *Hitozuma Kokan Nikki.* Video. DIR: Manabu Nakasone. SCR: Hideo Kobayashi. DES: Manabu Nakasone, Hodo Sei, Kuro Neko. ANI: Manabu Nakasone. MUS: Shikemoku. PRD: YOUC, Digital Works/Vanilla. 30 mins. x 2 eps.
Koichi and his wife's sex life has evaporated, like that of many married couples with kids, but they get along. One day his neighbor Kimihiko suggests they swap wives, video each other's activities, and watch them. They know this will include rape because one of the women won't be willing, but they decide to go ahead anyway. Twosomes, threesomes, and not very well animated sex ensue, in this porn based on a game by ANIM with characters by MUMU. Part of the VANILLA SERIES. **ⓝⓥ**

WILD ARMS *

1999. TV series. DIR: Toshiaki Kawasaki. SCR: Aya Matsui, Hideki Mitsui. DES: Kanami Sekiguchi, Yasuo Miyazawa. ANI: Minoru Yamazawa, Kanami Sekiguchi. MUS: Miyuki Otani. PRD: B-Train, WOWOW. 25 mins. x 22 eps.

On the planet Far Gaia, Loretta, a dark and deadly Crest Sorceress who wields a powerful magic based on tarot cards (flavor of the month since ESCAFLOWNE and CARDCAPTORS) leads a team of strange talents. Shaian looks like a little boy, but he's really a 25-year-old scientist and a sharpshooter of no mean skill. His main aim is to get his grown-up body back. But he's not the only one around who conceals his age—team genius Jerusha is a cute pink bunnykin who won't see 5,000 again. Even cute little turquoise-haired Mirabelle is really a Noble Red Vampire under that sweet exterior. A spaghetti Western that mixes cute fantasy and frontier adventure based on the PlayStation RPG, this doesn't have the same protagonists as the game; producer Sony decided to throw in a few little kids.

WILD CARDZ *

1997. JPN: The Crown Knights: Jaja Uma Quartet. AKA: Crown Knights: Wild Horse Quartet. Video. DIR: Yasushi Nagaoka. SCR: Hideki Sonoda, Hiromitsu Amano. DES: Noritaka Suzuki. ANI: Keisuke Watanabe. MUS: N/C. PRD: Animate Film. 25 mins. x 2 eps.

The story follows four defenders of the Card Kingdom as they try to defend it from a series of game-themed aggressors such as battle mecha shaped like giant chessmen and oversize mahjong tiles. As usual, the four defenders are girls of high school age and uniform cuteness who possess supernatural powers. The two episodes released form one long battle sequence, giving the impression that they come from the middle of a much longer story that might as a whole possess some substance. Or it might not—the whole thing was conceived as a "reader-input media mix" strategy in two magazines, which eventually grew into this short-lived video and a couple of audio dramas.

WILD 7 *

1994. Video. DIR: Kiyoshi Egami. SCR: Ginzo Choshiya. DES: Hisashi Hirai, Akira Takeuchi.

ANI: Hisashi Hirai. MUS: Kazushi Umezu. PRD: Animate Film. 50 mins. x 2 eps.

A team of seven killers from Death Row, led by a reform school escapee, is equipped with motorcycles and a license to terminate with extreme prejudice, Police Captain Kusanami showing touching but wholly unjustified faith in their ability to discriminate between bad guys and innocent bystanders. Their first assignment, bringing in a gang of bank robbers, turns into a running firefight through downtown Tokyo that piles taxpayers' bodies on the sidewalks. W7: Biker Knights followed in 1995. A shady politician and his crime-lord buddy decide to discredit our heroes even more by forming their own look-alike gang which will race through Tokyo and—here's the twist—kill innocent bystanders *deliberately*. Based on a 1969 manga by Mikiya Mochizuki, inspired by the *Dirty Dozen* (1967), and predating CYBER CITY OEDO 808, the anime version does its utmost to outgross MAD BULL 34, with which it also shares the same standard of writing and English dubbing—so bad it's almost good. *Wild 7 Another* (2002) was a TV version of the franchise, directed by Sumio Watanabe. The series also existed in a live-action variant, broadcast in 1972 (*DE). ◑

WILD STRIKER

2002. JPN: Hungry Heart Wild Striker. TV series. DIR: Satoshi Saga. SCR: Yoshiyuki Suga. DES: Kenichi Imaizumi. ANI: Tetsuro Aoki. MUS: Nobuyuki Nakamura. PRD: Animax, Fuji TV, Nippon Animation. 24 mins. x 52 eps.

Sixteen-year-old Kyosuke Kano is in the first year of high school. He quit soccer in junior high, but when he is inveigled into managing the female soccer team at his new high school, his love for the game rekindles and he starts to play again, eventually becoming one of the world's best strikers. Yoichi Takahashi, who wrote and drew the original manga *Hungry Heart*, also wrote and drew the manga that became Japan's most famous soccer anime, CAPTAIN TSUBASA, and was formerly married to Akari Hibino, voice of the young Tsubasa. Broadcast in Latin America, Portugal, and the Philippines but as yet unshown in English, despite sponsorship from sports shoe maker Puma.

WILD SWANS, THE

1977. JPN: Sekai Meisaku Dowa: Hakucho no Oji. AKA: Swan Princes. Movie. DIR: Nobutaka Nishizawa, Yuji Endo. SCR: Tomoe Ryu. DES: Takashi Abe, Hideo Chiba. ANI: Takashi Abe. MUS: Akihiro Komori. PRD: Toei Animation. 62 mins.

A widowed king remarries, but his frequent visits to his six sons and daughter annoy his new bride. Since she's the daughter of a witch, she is in a position to solve the problem in an interesting way; her spell transforms the six brothers into swans. Only their sister, Elisa, escapes, and she must follow her brothers and find a way to break the spell and bring them home. Based on a dark story found in both the TALES OF HANS CHRISTIAN ANDERSEN and GRIMMS' FAIRY TALES. The Japanese title, rather sneakily, throws in the term "World Masterpiece Fairytales," implying a nonexistent relationship to the World Masterpiece Theater series from rival studio Nippon Animation.

WILLFUL IDOL

1990. JPN: Kimama ni Idol. Video. DIR: Junichi Sato. SCR: Koichi Yomogi. DES: Kenichi Koya. ANI: Seiji Kikuchi. MUS: Toshitaro. PRD: Tabac. 50 mins.

Three pretty girls want to make it big as pop stars, but it's tough on their way to the top. Based on a manga in *Comic Burger* by Kenichi Koya, *WI* was distinguished by a marketing gimmick that had the three lead voice actresses taking to the stage for real in an early attempt at multimedia promotion. Compare to the earlier GLORIOUS ANGELS, which didn't try to manufacture its own hype, or the later PERFECT BLUE, which documented what can happen when you do.

WILLOW TOWN

1993. JPN: Tanoshii Willow Town. AKA: Happy Willow Town; Wind in the Willows. TV series. DIR: Tameo Ogawa, Masahito Sato, Yasuo Yamayoshi, Shigeru Omachi, Yutaka Kagawa. SCR: Takao Koyama, Hideki Mitsui, Yoshimasa Takahashi, Yumi Kageyama, Toshiyuki Machida, Kenichi Yamada. DES: Toshiyasu Okada. ANI: N/C. MUS: N/C. PRD: Enoki Films, TV Tokyo. 25 mins. x 25 eps.

Kenneth Grahame's enchanting novel *The Wind in the Willows* (1908) is the basis for a series about the happy little world of the animals who live along the riverbank. Toad's boastful nature and the evil ferrets and weasels who live in the Wild Wood threaten everyone's quiet lives until the brave Ratty, Mole, Badger, and Toad band together to ensure that they can all live happily ever after. The series ends with them all saying their farewells before hibernating for the winter.

WIND: A BREATH OF HEART

2004. Video, TV series. DIR: Tsuneo Tominaga (v), Mitsuhiro Togo (TV). SCR: Mami Watanabe (v), Akiko Horii, Takamitsu Kono (TV). DES: Koji Watanabe (v), Shinichi Yoshino (TV). ANI: Koji Watanabe (v), N/C (TV). MUS: N/C (v), Tatsuya Murayama (TV). PRD: venet, KSS (v), Radix, AT-X (TV). 30 mins. x 3 eps. (v), 12 mins. x 13 eps. (TV).

Makoto Okano and his sister Hinata return to their hometown, a mysterious, remote place where everyone except him seems to have a magical power. They settle in for lessons with their smooth-tongued classmate Tsutomu and Makoto's child-hood friend Kasumi, until the day that the sound of a harmonica draws Makoto to the roof of the school. There, he finds Minamo, his childhood sweetheart, in a romantic anime seemingly designed to marry the teen troubles of LOVE HINA to the muggle-headed adventures of ALICE ACADEMY and CROMARTIE HIGH, which similarly featured "mundane" attendees in a place where everyone else was gifted. In such a glorification of the merely average, we can see elements of Japanese media's perennial obsession with klutzy ugly ducklings such as SAILOR MOON. This anime exists in two versions, which inexplicably appear to have entered production simultaneously. Since both are based on a gaming franchise created by "minori," the authors assume that different incarnations of the game were licensed separately—compare to similar simultaneous creation problems that have led to confusion with NIGHT SHIFT NURSES. The differing versions take their origins from different branches of the game's potential endings. One rendition, given away free with one of the games, presents the story from the point of view of one character. The video version condenses the entire plot, while the longest incarnation, the TV version, concentrates on just two endings available from

the story. The original game featured a sequence of animation by Makoto Shinkai, creator of VOICES OF A DISTANT STAR.

WIND NAMED AMNESIA, A *

1990. JPN: *Kaze no Na wa Amnesia*. AKA: *The Wind's Name Was Amnesia; Wind of Amnesia*. Movie. DIR: Kazuo Yamazaki. SCR: Kazuo Yamazaki, Yoshiaki Kawajiri. DES: Satoru Nakamura, Morifumi Naka. ANI: Satoru Nakamura. MUS: Kazz Toyama, Hidenobu Takemoto. PRD: Madhouse. 80 mins.

In 1997, a mysterious wind wipes the minds of most of the human race. In a Montana research facility, crippled cyborg Johnny retains human memories; when he is saved from an attack by a bestial human, he names his rescuer Wataru ("drifter") and starts teaching him to talk. When Johnny dies, Wataru sets off to search for other survivors. In San Francisco he meets Sophia, who listens to his story and pointedly refuses to tell him hers. They wander across America until Sophia feels like telling Wataru the story behind the wind, 20 minutes before the end. Then there's a showdown with a law-enforcement robot that's been stalking Wataru since San Francisco, a perfunctory sex scene, and a finale that implies there's hope, even when the rest of the film has demonstrated that there isn't.

A Wind of Amnesia has a fascinating "high concept," based on a novel by DARKSIDE BLUES–creator Hideyuki Kikuchi, but after the bold, broad strokes of the original idea (coincidentally similar to Thomas Calvert McClary's 1934 story *Rebirth*), it swiftly devolves into mundane cliché little better than FIST OF THE NORTH STAR. Transforming into an aimless road movie, it shifts gear into a quest to rescue a damsel in distress whose people still have the intelligence of chimps but have nonetheless managed to set up a society based around ritual human sacrifice. Wataru then teaches a former policeman how to be human again (by showing him how to use a shotgun), before making a brief stop at the obligatory "false paradise." In other words, despite being made for the movies as a stand-alone production, it still has the picaresque feel of a cut-up TV series, amateurishly crashing George R. Stewart's *Earth Abides* (1949) into Harlan Ellison's *A Boy and His Dog* (1969). The script suggests

early on that the "wind" could be a psionic experiment gone wrong, or perhaps even rather stupid aliens who prefer to wipe humanity's mind as part of a preemptive strike, but there's no mystery here. Despite having the answers to everything, Sophia refuses to tell Wataru (or us) for a full 60 minutes, preferring instead to play devil's advocate with mind-boggling inconsistency, railing against the civilized charade of a computer-controlled city in the Nevada desert but vigorously defending the rights of savages who want to sacrifice virgins. Quite possibly, she is simply too embarrassed to tell the truth about an alien intervention plot device whose incoherence would not be matched until GREEN LEGEND RAN. The rest of the script is similarly shoddy—no thought is given as to why people wear clothes, considering that they have forgotten what they were for, and an "Eternal City" is supposedly built "at the beginning of the 21st century" when we've already been told that the film is set in 1999. There is a brief treatment of the idea that humanity might be better off this way, but it was done far more convincingly in GREY: DIGITAL TARGET. Artistically, this is a departure for the Madhouse studio, full of airy, wide-open spaces that are a far cry from the dark urban sprawls of WICKED CITY. **⦿⦿**

WIND OF EBENBOURG *

2003. JPN: *Ebenbourg no Kaze*. Video. DIR: Yosei Morino. SCR: Yosei Morino. DES: N/C. ANI: N/C. MUS: Satoshi Shura. PRD: Amumo, Studio Ego. 30 mins. x 2 eps.

Ronsard is a small town in the Grand Duchy of Ebenbourg in exotic 19th-century Europe. Its new lord is Claude MacDonald, who was a poor student in even more exotic England until the former lord, Eric, was exiled. Claude finds out about his inheritance when the counselor for Ronsard, beautiful bespectacled Sophie, seeks him out. They are both virgins, and to seal the pact of his new inheritance they have to have sex. That done and an assassination attempt foiled, Claude learns that as well as inheriting Eric's title and mansion, he also inherits his maid. Mylene is quite willing to serve the new master exactly as she served the old one, but carries on seeing Eric off duty. The pair plot to kill the Grand Duke and implicate Claude so

Eric can take power over all Ebenbourg. Meanwhile Claude starts to remember his past, when he made a childhood promise to another maid, Charlotte. *The Prisoner of Zenda* crashes into Japan's French maid fetish with predictably pretty and vacuous results. **ⒸⓃⓋ**

WIND RISES, THE *

2013. JPN: *Kaze Tachinu*. AKA: *The Wind Is Rising*. Movie. DIR: Hayao Miyazaki. SCR: Hayao Miyazaki. DES: Kitaro Kosaka. ANI: Kitaro Kosaka. MUS: Joe Hisaishi. PRD: Studio Ghibli. 126 mins.

Japanese boy Jiro Horikoshi is plagued by magic-realist dreams of flight and aeroplanes, in which the figure of the Italian aircraft designer Giovanni Caproni challenges him to create a thing of beauty. He becomes an engineering student and experiences a number of setbacks, including industrial intrigues and the Great Kanto Earthquake of 1923, during which he first encounters Naoko, the woman who will become his wife. He dedicates himself to the development of his dream project, the Mitsubishi A5M, even as Naoko succumbs to tuberculosis.

With his much-postponed retirement finally looming for real, Hayao Miyazaki was seemingly given *carte blanche* by Studio Ghibli to do anything he liked, so long as it was one last feature film to rake in the cash. He chose this loose adaptation of Tatsuo Hori's short story "The Wind Has Risen" (1936–37), tying up a number of recurring themes in his own life and work. His love of flight and aerial perspective, a major feature of many of his films since NAUSICAÄ, comes to the fore, along with a young aircraft designer in the idealistic mold of Tombo from KIKI'S DELIVERY SERVICE. Whereas Ghibli's TALES FROM EARTHSEA was haunted by the idea of Hayao Miyazaki the father, reluctantly passing on his mantle, *The Wind Rises* is about Hayao Miyazaki the son, fondly remembering the life and attitudes of his own father Katsuji, whose Miyazaki Airplane factory made rudders for Mitsubishi planes during World War II. Arguably, the director-writer's bulletproof guarantee of no studio interference might have also shielded him from the otherwise welcome contributions of an editor's red pencil—the repetitive nature of some of the character interactions could be said to inflate the running time some 20 minutes past its welcome. The interwar development, design, and discarded concepts of aircraft, such as those to be seen in the European setting of PORCO ROSSO, is hence also an intensely personal story for Miyazaki, who seems here to be puckishly defying a studio establishment that would really much prefer him to make something nice and safe, like a sequel to MY NEIGHBOR TOTORO. Inevitably, in writing a fictionalized biography of the man who would go on to design the notorious Mitsubishi Zero fighter plane, Miyazaki was drawn into ongoing controversies about Japan's wartime role (WARTIME ANIME). Although his protagonist experiences hand-wringing doubt about the uses to which his work is put by the military, this was not good enough for many critics and audiences abroad, particularly in South Korea, where the film was derided ahead of its release for its "moral repugnance." Lines assigned to Caproni ask Jiro if the world is better with or without pyramids, seen by many to dismiss and diminish the slave laborers who were required for both the pyramids and the Japanese military-industrial complex. Moreover, Jiro's concerns remain devotedly, purely aesthetic, annoyed at the corruption and misuse of things of beauty, rather than the real-world deaths that would ultimately result from his work. Miyazaki's last movie is hence a thorny argument, critically acclaimed and panned in equal measure, annoying both the left and right wings in its native Japan. But this is surely what he intended all along; if this was to be his last testament, it is also a beautiful and uncompromising statement of everything that Hayao Miyazaki is, born as an innocent into the world created by the father-figures of 1930s Japan, imbued with a love of art and design, repurposed for unexpected uses (HEIDI), praised as the poster-boy of an industry that he has often railed against, even as it destroys much of what he personally holds dear (PRINCESS MONONOKE), and ultimately expected to speak and act as an ambassador for Cool Japan, despite his personal misgivings. In this regard, *The Wind Rises* might also be considered alongside the figure of SPIRITED AWAY's Kamaji, toiling away in the boiler room, as an allegory of its creator's own life in the anime industry.

We might also view this final movie as a companion piece to both HOWL'S MOVING CASTLE and PONYO in its further reflections on Miyazaki's marriage to the young animator Akemi Ota, who wed him while they both worked at Toei and retired to bring up their sons. *HMC* was a fantasy reading of the perils and penalties of marriage to a charismatic, gifted, and obsessive creator. *Ponyo* is usually considered a reflection on Miyazaki's relationship with his son Goro, but it has just as much to say about unreliable absentee husbands and the women who love them. It roots the fantasy of *HMC*'s odd yet idealized nuclear family in the everyday world of long spousal absences spent wrangling recalcitrant domestic systems, children, and the kind of work that fits around them.

The Wind Rises reframes this love story as a melodrama, in which the beautiful, consumptive heroine runs out into the snow to die alone rather than distract the loving but wholly work-focused genius from the truly important things in his life. In all these reversionings, the genius remains devoted to his self-chosen task and the loyal and supportive female remains equally devoted to facilitating his worldview. However often he reinvents the story, Miyazaki arrives at the same conclusion: men must work and women, even the feistiest of them, must fill their lonely hours by doing everything else.

WINDARIA *

1986. JPN: *Windaria Senki Densetsu*. AKA: *Legend of Windaria Chronicle; Once Upon a Time*. Movie. DIR: Kunihiko Yuyama. SCR: Keisuke Fujikawa. DES: Mutsumi Inomata, Shigenori Kageyama, Shohei Kohara, Shigeru Katsumata, Toshihiko Sato. ANI: Mutsumi Inomata. MUS: Satoshi Kadokura. PRD: Kaname Pro. 101 mins.

After centuries of peace, the Kingdom of Paro (the Shadowlands) is under the reign of an arrogant king, Draco, who sees himself as a mighty conqueror. The neighboring Kingdom of Isa (Lunaria), realizing that it would be the first target for any expansionist plans, tries to keep Paro peacefully under control by rationing the fresh water flowing through Isa's system of locks and canals. As war looms, their heirs Prince Jil (Roland) and Princess Aanasu (Veronica) love one another, but family loyalty makes their union impossible; she chooses death for both in a twist on *Romeo and Juliet*. A happily married farming couple, Izu (Alan) and Malin (Marie), are drawn into the conflict when the agents of both countries try to buy Izu's services. Seeing a chance for adventure and wealth working for Paro, he tries to sneak out of his home in the middle of the night, but Malin wakes and makes him promise to return to her even as she promises to wait for him, no matter what happens. His betrayal of his country and his marriage buys him the sophisticated toys he covets—elegant clothes, a fast bike, an upper-class girl who would never look at a mere farmer—but costs him dearly. His new masters try to have him killed; when he runs for home he finds it destroyed, his village devastated, most of his old friends dead. Only the ghost of his beautiful wife lingers to say a final farewell. Painfully, he learns that he can't buy his way back into the past he has betrayed. Presiding over the conflict between tradition and modernity, a huge "tree of life" symbolizes the enduring power of nature.

Based on Keisuke Fujikawa's novel, written at a time when Japan was beginning to realize how much it had already thrown away in its rush to modernize, this Asian romance has wider meaning for a world whose small economies and ecosystems are increasingly under threat. Katsumata's backgrounds are pure delight, and although the robots of Windaria are rarely mentioned among its many pleasures, this is partly because Kohara does such a good job of integrating them carefully into their faux-feudal societies. This genuinely thoughtful fantasy has a good mix of action and reflection and a score whose sweeping grandeur reflects the beauty of the visuals.

WINDY TALES

2004. JPN: *Fujin Monogatari*. TV series. DIR: Junji Nishimura. SCR: Hiroaki Jinno. DES: Masatsugu Arakawa. ANI: Nobutoshi Ogura. MUS: Kenji Kawai. PRD: Production I.G, Sky PerfecTV. 25 mins. x 13 eps.

After her new schoolteacher Taiki uses a miraculous control over the wind to save her life, schoolgirl Nao Ueshima resolves to travel to his home village to find out more. She discovers that Taiki's powers are nothing strange in his birthplace, since everyone in the remote mountain village is also a "wind handler" or *kazetsukai*. The anime is distinguished by a strangely angular art style reminiscent of **RYU THE STONE AGE BOY**. The anime was adapted from a screenplay that won the Best Anime Plan Grand Prix in 2002.

WINGMAN

1984. JPN: *Yume Senshi Wingman*. AKA: *Dream Warrior Wingman*. TV series. DIR: Tomoharu Katsumata, Yugo Serikawa, Masayuki Akehi, Hideo Watanabe, Hiroyuki Kadono, Shigeo Koshi. SCR: Akiyoshi Sakai, Sukehiro Tomita, Shigeru Yanagawa. DES: Yoshinori Kanemori. ANI: Masamune Ochiai. MUS: Keiichi Oku. PRD: Toei, TV Asahi. 25 mins. x 47 eps.

Some of the greatest battles take place not in the waking world, but in dreams. Warriors capable of transforming into powerful armored beings can intervene in our world to save those in danger. When superhero-obsessed teenager Kenta sees a girl literally fall out of the sky, he has no idea what's about to happen. Aoi has a "dream note," a kind of promissory paper: whatever you write on it will come true. Kenta writes that he wants to be the superhero Wingman, protecting everyone from the evil Rimel, ruler of the fourth-dimensional land of Powdream. And it happens—he's a superhero! But Rimel sends his minions into the real world in disguise to steal the dream note and so prevent Wingman from foiling his plans. He also wants to break up the growing friendship between Kenta and Aoi. Based on the 1983 *Shonen Jump* manga by Masakazu Katsura, creator of **VIDEO GIRL AI** and **DNA²**.

WINGS OF HONNEAMISE *

1987. JPN: *Oneamisu no Tsubasa*. AKA: *Royal Space Force; Royal Space Force: A Wing of Honnêamise*. Movie. DIR: Hiroyuki Yamaga. SCR: Hiroyuki Yamaga, Hiroshi Onogi. DES: Yoshiyuki Sadamoto. ANI: Hideaki Anno, Yuji Moriyama, Fumio Iida, Yoshiyuki Sadamoto. MUS: Ryuichi Sakamoto, Yuji Nomi, Koji Ueno. PRD: Bandai, Gainax. 120 mins.

Shiro Lhadatt is a dropout, a wannabe pilot who wasn't good enough to get into the navy air corps. Instead, he joins the only organization that will have him, a ragtag group of misfits called the Royal Space Force. Underfunded, undermotivated, and under extreme pressure, they race to get a man in space, but nobody believes it's possible. Nobody, that is, except for Shiro and his would-be girlfriend, a religious zealot called Lequinni. Space is waiting for humanity as a whole, but the project to reach it is the result of two nations' political and military agendas. Our hero joins up for all the wrong reasons but eventually realizes that he can turn the "fake dream" of his government's PR campaign into a real dream, and he becomes the first man in space. Despite the political skullduggery that follows, he refuses to let go of the hope that the reality just might redeem all the failure and sacrifice of history and give us another chance to soar.

One of anime's greatest successes despite a "poor" box office performance relative to its inflated budget, *WoH* is a peculiarly Japanese take on the U.S.-Soviet space race—an outsider's view of the gung ho ideals of *The Right Stuff*, moved to an alien world to emphasize the viewer's own alienation. Made by the young, fiendishly talented Gainax collective during the heyday of anime's (and Japan's) bubble era, modest plans for an inexpensive video one-shot mushroomed into a lavish cinema feature with many interfering patrons, which would take years to earn back its immense budget. As an example of many attempts to "fix" it at the distribution stage when it was already complete, it was misleadingly advertised in Japan as a film in the style of **NAUSICAÄ OF THE VALLEY OF THE WIND**, with a name-change similarly designed to imply resonances with the Miyazaki classic—"The Something of Something." "Honneamise" is never mentioned in the film proper, but is supposedly a reference to the country where the action takes place. The word "Wings" was suggested by an earnest airline company sponsor who wanted something aerial in the title. Despite such metatextual fudges, this is one of the shining examples of how cerebral and intelligent anime can be, far removed from the sex and violence that stuffs Western anime catalogues, and rewards repeat viewings if only for the meticulous design of every aspect of its world. The language, the names, the maps, and even the telegraph poles all scream to be recognized as triumphs of world-building almost unequalled elsewhere in science-fiction film. Even the minutiae of everyday life are knocked ever-so-slightly out of kilter, with little touches like triangular spoons, unidentifiable foods, and sunrise in the north.

Gainax, which later made **GUNBUSTER** and **EVANGELION**, is made up of *true* science-fiction fans. Space is their religion; they fervently believe that it's human-kind's destiny to leave the cradle of Earth and spread out among the stars. The film's closing moments are their manifesto: a march of progress from the earliest times until the climactic moment, a final leap into space as war rages around the launch-pad. *WoH* is a marvelous film, improved all the more by music from *Merry Christmas, Mr. Lawrence*'s Ryuichi Sakamoto and a fluent adaptation (though allegedly far removed from the original) from LA Hero, which was bought out during production and rebranded as the American arm of Manga Entertainment. A sequel, *Blue Uru*, has been promised for over a decade but thus far has only materialized in the form of a Gainax video game. *WoH* also exists in an ill-fated 1987 dub version from Go East, under the title *Star Quest—* which rearranged some scenes, changed some names, and was reputedly so bad that it was hidden from sight after its poorly received L.A. premiere. Compare to the similarly unfortunate treatment suffered by *Nausicaä* as *Warriors of the Wind.* ●

WINTER SONATA

2009. JPN: *Fuyu no Sonata*. AKA: *Winter Love Story*. TV series. DIR: Daisuke Nakayama. SCR: Kim Hyeong-Wan. DES: Daisuke Nakayama, Hiroshi Ono. ANI: Mayu Ito, Daisuke Nakayama, Masae Nakayama. MUS: N/C. PRD: G&G Entertainment, JM Animation, Studio Comet. 25 mins. x 26 eps.
Yu-Jin loses her high school sweetheart Jun-Sang when they uncover a tragic truth about their parents from an old photograph. After ten years, she decides it's time to move on and agrees to marry a childhood friend, Sang-Hyuk. Just as they are about to announce their engagement, she meets a newcomer to Seoul who looks exactly like her lost love. Is it possible that two people could resemble each other so exactly? As the winter passes the drama

that tore Yu-Jin and Jun-Sang apart becomes the backdrop to a new story.

Based on a 2002 live-action drama from Korean TV that was a huge hit in Japan, this is a fascinating study in the migration of culture. The anime version, largely designed and animated in Japan, not only depicts the faces of the original Korean cast but employed 23 of them to provide the voice track in Korean. This was aired in Japan with subtitles. Production company G&G has a respectable history in anime, contributing to productions such as **YUGO THE NEGOTIATOR** and **KALEIDO STAR**, but this is probably their most revolutionary piece of work for reasons unconnected with the animation. Studio Fuga contributed the delicately beautiful backgrounds.

WISH UPON THE PLEIADES *

2011. JPN: *Hokago no Pleiades*. AKA: *Afterschool Pleiades*. Video. DIR: Shoji Saeki. SCR: Daisuke Kikuchi, Shoji Saeki. DES: Daisuke Kikuchi, Hiroshi Kato. ANI: Mai Otsuka. MUS: N/C. PRD: Gainax, Fuji Heavy Industries Ltd. 6 mins. x 3 eps., 7 mins.
Teenager Subaru is sitting outside with her telescope, watching the night sky, when she sees a strange meteor divide. She's soon drawn into a weird world where her schoolfriend Aoi turns out not to be an exhibitionist cosplayer, but part of a magical group hunting bits of an alien engine so that a little creature from the Pleiades star system can use it to go home. They're opposed by Minato, a boy who looks like the younger brother of Howl from **HOWL'S MOVING CASTLE** and whose allegiance to evil is signaled by a hot uniform and two little horns of red hair. The story of magical miniskirted high school witches fighting a cute bad boy in space to help an annoying but endearing little creature is cunningly peppered with visual references to CLAMP, Ghibli, and other preteen and family favorites, with end credits packed with highly merchandisable art. Made by Gainax, this pretty piece of nonsense was created for online streaming in conjunction with car manufacturer Subaru (the Japanese name for the Pleiades star cluster): car promotion that doesn't mention cars, seemingly aimed at people who are at least a decade away from buying one in a bizarre application of the arts of **ADVERTISING AND SPONSORSHIP**. The characters, in

squashed-down form as seen in the end credits, have also appeared in a "manners movie" in Japanese cinemas, reminding filmgoers to turn off their phone and avoid annoying other patrons.

WITCH CRAFT WORKS *

2014. TV series. DIR: Tsutomu Mizushima. SCR: Michiko Yokote, Reiko Yoshida, Tsutomu Mizushima. DES: Yukie Hiyamizu, Tomonori Kuroda. ANI: Shinji Itadaki. MUS: Technoboys Pulcraft Green Fund. PRD: JC Staff, Bandai Visual, Hakuhodo DY Media Partners, Kodansha, MOVIC, Sony PCL. 24 mins. x 12 eps.
Honoka is an ordinary guy in high school. Ayaka is the school "princess"—rich, clever, tall, busty, and pretty. So why does she call him "master" and start taking such an interest in him? She even walks to school with him (when surely a girl with her background should be dropped at the gates by her chauffeur). And what about those legions of robot rabbits, and the transfer students who turn out to be enemy witches? All this should tell you that you're watching a high school harem anime (**ROMANCE AND DRAMA**) with a few small twists. The ending theme makes gleeful and tasteless super-deformed fun of the torture meted out to witches down the ages by most cultures. Otherwise, there's nothing new in this anime based on Ryu Mizunagi's 2010 manga. ●●

WITCH HUNTER ROBIN *

2002. TV series. DIR: Shuko Murase, Yohei Miyahara, Kumiko Takahashi. SCR: Aya Yoshinaga, Shuko Murase, Toru Nozaki. DES: Kumiko Takahashi, Hajime Sato, Michiaki Sato, Yoshinori Sayama, Shinji Aramaki, Toshihiro Nakashima. ANI: Hiromitsu Morishita, Iwao Teraoka, Toshihiro Nakashima. MUS: Taku Iwasaki. PRD: Bandai Visual, Sunrise. 24 mins. x 26 eps.
In present-day Japan, use of magic—called CRAFT—is an everyday occurrence. It's more about extrasensory perception and enhanced mental powers than the spells-and-potions variety of magic. Anyone using CRAFT for evil is branded a witch, likely to be hunted down by an official body, the STN (*Solomon Tokatsu Nin'idantai*—or Solomon Secret Action Group). But it goes even further; STN mastermind Solomon, based in Europe, tracks down individuals with witch genes

in their ancestry and takes action against anyone with emerging latent abilities, visiting the sins of their forebearers on later generations. Six skilled witch hunters form the operational arm of STN-Japan, out to protect the population from misuse of magic. The team's father figure, Takuma Zaizen, combines the roles of M and Q from the James Bond mythos, as the man who gets the hottest weapons for the team and the controller of their field activities. When one of the team is lost in action and a new member joins them, the team's equilibrium is upset. Gentle, reserved Robin Sena, Japanese but raised in an Italian convent, is just 15 and has an uncanny ability to control fire, but her relationships with her new teammates prove more difficult to manage, and the political undercurrents of their work create more conflict. A moody, gray-black color palette and restrained design create an atmosphere of repressed emotion—later episodes play up the literal witch hunts in a new form of cold war, marrying the paranoia of Arthur Miller's *The Crucible* (1953) to the paranoid conspiracies and switches in allegiance of *Alias* (2001). Compare to **HELLSING** and **CHRONO CRUSADE**, which similarly allegorized modern conflicts with myth and magic. The original concept is credited to Sunrise's house pseudonym Hajime Yadate and director Murase. A live-action version was supposedly planned by the American Sci-Fi channel, but dropped in 2005.

WITCHBLADE *

2006. TV series. DIR: Yoshimitsu Ohashi. SCR: Yasuko Kobayashi. DES: Kazuyuki Matsubara, Makoto Uno. ANI: N/C. MUS: Kazunori Miyake. PRD: Gonzo, CBC, TBS. 25 mins. x 26 eps. Police officer Masane Amo suffers from amnesia in 22nd-century Japan, initially unaware that she is the latest in a long line of blade wielders—fierce warrior women who deploy the legendary "witchblade" in the service of justice. Based on the American comic created by Marc Silvestri, which was set in the 1990s, this science-fiction spin-off uses the hereditary nature of the witchblade to establish a continuity sufficiently far from the original to allow a different story.

WITCHES

1992. JPN: *Nozomi Witches*. Video. DIR: Gisa-

buro Sugii. SCR: Gisaburo Sugii. DES: Kosuke Eguchi. ANI: Kosuke Eguchi. MUS: Hiroaki Serizawa. PRD: Tac. 50 mins. x 3 eps. Ryutaro is an average high school student until the beautiful Nozomi takes an interest in him. Clever, a superb athlete, and fancied by every boy in class, she decides that Ryutaro has real potential, and her belief in him soon pushes him all the way to the Olympic boxing trials. But does she see him as anything but a sporting project? Based on the *Young Jump* manga by Toshio Nobe. **Ⓥ**

WITH THE LORDS *

2010. JPN: *Tono to Issho*. Video, TV. DIR: Mankyu. SCR: Mankyu. DES: Aki Watanabe, Masaya Yokoyama. ANI: Minoru Takehara, Mari Takada. MUS: Keiichi Sugiyama. PRD: Gathering, Frontier Works, Yomiuri TV. 30 mins. (v1), 1 min. x 12 eps. (TV), 4 mins. (v2), 3 mins. x 12 eps. (TV2). Oh, those wacky warlords! Antics of the great men of Japan's civil war era –Masamune Date, Nobunaga Oda, Mitsuhide Akechi, and Kenshin Uesugi—are presented with a nudge, a wink, and very little regard for propriety. Based on Oba-Kai's hit samurai comedy manga, running since 2007, and preceded by two drama CDs in 2009, the first video had J-Pop superstar Gackt providing the voice of warlord Kenshin Uesugi, a role he had already played in a New Year's Eve TV special. It was followed the same year by *With the Lords: One Minute Theater* (*Tono to Issho Ippunkan Gekijo*) and by *Tono to Issho 1.5*, a 4-minute video. The second TV series, *With the Lords: Eyepatch of Ambition* (*Gantai no Yabo*), followed in 2011, length extended to 3 minutes. As all these times run a little short for DVD, the crew made a further 20-minute film about how director Mankyu persuaded Gackt to take the voice role. So if you want to see animation of Gackt in the bath, order the DVDs from any good Japanese retailer.

WIZARD BARRISTERS *

2014. JPN: *Wizard Barristers Benmashi Cecil*. TV series. DIR: Yasuomi Umetsu. SCR: Michiko Ito. DES: Yasuomi Umetsu, Kazuo Ogura. ANI: Yasuomi Umetsu, Tatsuya Tomaru, Katsumi Masuda. MUS: Kayo Konishi, Yukio Kondo. PRD: ARMS, GENCO, Pony Canyon, Showgate. 24 mins. x 12 eps.

Tokyo, 2018: humans and wizards live together, mostly peacefully. When problems arise, the police and ordinary courts deal with the humans, while wizards are tried in a separate court system with barristers who are also magic users—and wizard-catchers on the side. At the almost actionably young age of 17, Cecil (no, not Cecile, that would make too much sense) has just qualified as a Wizard Barrister. With her lecherous frog familiar she sets out to navigate the wizardly legal world—which is just as ready to make inappropriate assumptions about a hot young chick whose taste in dress is a little extroverted as, say, the ordinary legal world.

So far, so *Legally Blonde*, crashed winningly into *Harry Potter*, but *WB* has a trick up its sleeve in the form of its creator, director, art, and animation director Yasuomi Umetsu. This shows in the superbly polished, beautifully paced first episode— everything done so well it seems effortless until you compare it with the legion of lesser series of this type. Long-term Japanwatchers might also appreciate the cutesy and matter-of-fact way that the show crams in notions of immigration and extraterritoriality, linking it in an unexpected and misleadingly humorous way with some of the darker themes of shows like **SAKURA WARS**, **GINTAMA**, and **DANCE ON THE VAMPIRE BUND**. It wouldn't be as much fun if it was called *Sharia Barristers.…*

Umetsu has been doing what's now called *moe* for over three decades. He has serious chops for violence and fan service too—he made **KITE**—and both are present here, though to a lesser extent than some of his earlier work. He knows what his audience expects and delivers it in a polished, action-packed package. Nothing surprising here, just solid skill deployed in a popular format. **ⒸⓋ**

WIZARD GIRL AMBITIOUS

2011. Video. DIR: N/C. SCR: PON. DES: Megumi Ishihara, Do Ichimotsu. ANI: N/C. MUS: N/C. PRD: PoRO. 30 mins. Meet Asuka: cute, vain, ambitious, and a wizard. Her outfit of choice—like those of all the other magical girls we meet— threatens wardrobe malfunctions on an epic scale with every jiggle. This poses no barrier to non-wizardly activity with fantasy guys, in this anime based on a porn game from Sugar Pot. The art is pretty but the excuse for a plot is as flimsy as the clothes. It never ceases to amaze us that cultures capable of making hold-up stockings hold up on skinny little legs under any orc or tentacle assault can't make a bra that stays in place around boobs the size of basketballs.

WIZARD OF OZ, THE *
1984. JPN: *Oz no Maho Tsukai*. Movie, TV series. DIR: Masaru Tonogochi, Masaharu Endo, Hiromitsu Morita. SCR: Akira Miyazaki, Takafumi Nagamine, Hiroshi Saito. DES: Shuichi Seki (TV), N/C (m). ANI: Shinya Takahashi, Minoru Kobata, Akio Sakai, Joji Yanase, Toshio Kaneko. MUS: K. S. Yoshimura (TV), Joe Hisaishi (m). PRD: Itoman, Panmedia, TV Tokyo. 25 mins. x 52 eps. (TV), 60 mins. (m, 78 mins. in the U.S.).
Brunette Kansas girl Dorothy Gale and her dog, Toto, are whisked away to the magical land of Oz, where she joins forces with a Tin Woodman, a Scarecrow, and a Cowardly Lion, following the Yellow Brick Road to the Emerald City, from whence she hopes to return home. Based on *The Wonderful Wizard of Oz* (1900), *The Marvelous Land of Oz* (1904), *Ozma of Oz* (1907), and *The Emerald City of Oz* (1910) from L. Frank Baum's 14-volume series, *WoO* was first broadcast abroad in 1984 but not shown in Japan until 1986. It was dropped by NHK and eventually screened on TV Tokyo, though the final two episodes were crammed into an hour-long special. On video, the separate story arcs were condensed into 90 minutes each and released across four two-tape sets—thereby existing in feature-length chunks, often leading to their confusion with the Fumihiko Takayama anime movie version. The Takayama *Wizard of Oz* (1982, though not released in Japan until 1986) is a 60-minute movie (78 in the U.S.) with a blonde Dorothy. It keeps closer to the plot of the first book only, just like the famous live-action 1939 Judy Garland adaptation. Curiously, Akira Miyazaki is credited as a screenwriter in both blonde and brunette versions, which, despite the contradictory international release dates, must have begun production almost simultaneously! Both were seen in the U.S. before being shown in Japan.

A video of a Japanese Oz puppet show, *WoO: Dorothy's Adventure* (1991, *Dorothy* *no Daiboken*), is also filed in some anime sources. See also the sci-fi remake **GALAXY ADVENTURES OF SPACE OZ**, the distantly related **OZ**, and **VIDEO PICTURE BOOK**.

WIZARDRY
1991. Video. DIR: Shunsuke Shinohara. SCR: Masaru Terajima. DES: Satoshi Hirayama, Yasushi Hirayama. ANI: Yasushi Nagaoka. MUS: Soji Kawamura. PRD: TMS. 50 mins.
Evil wizard Werdna has stolen a powerful amulet from crazy King Trebor and constructed a ten-level dungeon right under the king's own castle, where he and the amulet are hiding. The king offers a reward for the recovery of his property, so hero Shin Garland takes up the challenge and joins a band of adventurers to descend into the wizard's lair. Based on the computer game of the same name designed by AnimEigo founder Robert Woodhead and Roe R. Adams III.

WOLF CHILDREN *
2012. JPN: *Okami Kodomo Ame to Yuki*. AKA: *Wolf Children Ame and Yuki*. Movie. DIR: Mamoru Hosoda. SCR: Mamoru Hosoda, Satoko Okudera. DES: Yoshiyuki Sadamoto. ANI: Takaaki Yamashita. MUS: Masakatsu Takagi. PRD: Studio Chizu, Madhouse. 117 mins.
Nineteen-year-old college student Hana falls for a classmate, only to discover that her man is a lycanthrope. Unphased by this revelation, she eventually becomes the mother to his two children. Struggling, after his death, as the single parent not merely of typically boisterous kids, but of shape-shifting were-children, Hana moves to rural Toyama in order to give her unorthodox family more space.

The third movie production from the team who made **THE GIRL WHO LEAPT THROUGH TIME**, *Wolf Children* is another film that draws indirectly on Mamoru Hosoda's personal life. It repeats the countryside vistas of his home prefecture from **SUMMER WARS**, but progresses from the earlier film's in-law encounters to young parenthood and life choices. Ame (Rain) and Yuki (Snow) are superb anime creations, able to literally sprout fur and fangs like many **TROPES AND TRANSFORMATIONS**, but also allegorical of the branching paths that face us all as we age. Their names are deliberately evocative—both Rain and Snow are formed from water, but turn out radically different, just as one wolf child is inspired to embrace human society, while the other is increasingly drawn to the animal realm.

Perhaps more than any previous film by Hosoda, *Wolf Children* affords us a glimpse of the sort of work he might have turned in had he stayed at Studio Ghibli. There is much of **MY NEIGHBOR TOTORO** in the way the characters dwell within a numinous and natural world, at odds with modernity, and of **PRINCESS MONONOKE** in the atavistic allure of the wild. But *Wolf Children* is also a triumph, in a way, of **EVERYDAY ANIME**, not shying away from the mundane disasters and triumphs of child-rearing, as well as the bittersweet inevitability of growing up and letting go.

WOLF GUY
1992. Video. DIR: Naoyuki Yoshinaga. SCR: Toshikazu Fujii. DES: Osamu Tsuruyama. ANI: Atsushi Aono. MUS: Kenji Kawai. PRD: JC Staff. 30 mins. x 6 eps.
Akira Inugami is infected with a terrible poison. The only known antidote has an unfortunate side effect—it turns him into a werewolf. He opts for survival but then has to cope with his new desires and with the attention of the military, which is interested in using his affliction for its own purposes. Based on the series of novels by Kazumasa Hirai, who also wrote **HARMAGEDON** and episodes of **8TH MAN**.

WOLF'S RAIN *
2003. TV series, video. DIR: Tensai Okamura. SCR: Keiko Nobumoto, Aya Yoshinaga, Dai Sato, Doko Machida, Miya Asakawa, Tensai Okamura. DES: Toshihiro Kawamoto, Shinji Aramaki, Shingo Takeba, Tomoaki Okada. ANI: Ayumi Karashima, Hiroki Kanno, Keiichi Sato, Kenji Mizuhata, Koichi Horikawa, Koji Osaka, Masahiro Koyama, Naoyuki Onda, Ryuji Tomioka, Satoshi Osawa, Shigeki Kuhara, Takahiro Omori, Tomoaki Kato, Toshihiro Kawamoto, Toshihiro Nakajima. MUS: Yoko Kanno. PRD: Bandai Visual, BONES, Fuji TV. 25 mins. x 26 eps. (TV), 30 mins. x 4 eps. (v).
In a post-apocalyptic future, humans think wolves have been hunted to extinction; but some survive, and have learned to pass for human in a new twist on the werewolf legend (or indeed on **POM POKO**). Lone wolf Kiba is on a quest to find the legend-

ary Lunar Flowers, whose scent can lead the wolves to a paradise where they can live freely and without fear. Tsume is a renegade wolf who betrayed his pack and now lives as a human-form scavenger. Full of self-loathing, he first opposes Kiba but then joins him. Hige and Toboe are hardly more than cubs, but once they learn about Kiba's quest they join him. The pack meets Cheza, a girl engineered from plants, who can open the way to the paradise of the Lunar Flowers; but others are seeking the key for their own ends. Only after tragedy and suffering will the four young wolves attain paradise—which, in a typical anime twist, soon turns out to be more than originally expected, with the science-fictional future of the original setting also alluding to a secret past that links humans, wolves, and another, even more sinister foe. This, however, can stretch the viewer's patience a little—despite a relatively low running time, the series suffered from production delays and scheduling conflicts that led to its broadcast in several different slots, with hiatuses that led to four recap episodes. If the makers had spent less time recounting the story so far, they might have had more than enough space to finish the entire run within the requisite 26 episodes. Instead, the story wasn't finished on TV, but on video, numbered as if to comprise TV episodes 27–30. Yoko Kanno's musical team and the Warsaw Philharmonic do a beautiful job of supporting the atmosphere and character development. The art and design are moody, dark, and understated, making for a technically unadventurous but attractive series. Original creator Keiko Nobumoto, who similarly documented a loner's quest in the future world of **COWBOY BEBOP**, delegated story and art duties on the manga adaptation to Toshitsugu Iida. On a historical note, wolves were worshiped by northern Japan's indigenous Ainu race, but were wiped out by 1905—the extinction of wolves regarded as a sign of the march of progress and the dismissal of the old gods, in the style of **PRINCESS MONONOKE**.

WOLVERINE *

2011. TV series. DIR: Rintaro, Hiroshi Aoyama. SCR: Kengo Kaji. DES: Hisashi Abe, Katsushi Aoki. ANI: Yoshio Kosakai, Fumiaki Usui, Hisashi Abe. MUS: Tetsuya Takahashi.

PRD: Madhouse, Sony Pictures Entertainment (Japan). 23 mins. x 12 eps. Wolverine is a mutant with hyper-enhanced senses, animal-like reflexes, psychic ability, retracting claws on each hand, and accelerated healing genes. He's fallen in love with Mariko Yashida, and she's vanished. He learns that her crime-boss father has taken her back to Japan, so he goes to rescue her.

Like **IRON MAN** before it, this is an anime version of a well-loved Marvel comic, and a complete mess. Madhouse's artistry and the dedication of its animators cannot make a short, stocky, middle-aged American hero with an excess of body hair into a lean, high-cheekboned, almost hairless 20-something anime guy without losing almost everything of the character in the process. Yes, it's conceivable he could be younger in this story, but taller? Putting voice actor Milo Ventimiglia from American TV hit *Heroes* on the English dub is similarly ill-judged, as Marvel's renownedly gruff blue-collar chap now sounds like a surfer dude. Cheaply animated action scenes full of jump-cuts and motion blur combine with a script fully of silly concepts and worse lines. The main benefit of this show is that it makes you realize *Iron Man* could have been worse.

WOMAN SPY TORTURE

1999. JPN: *Onna Spy Goumon: Teki no Kichi wa Nyotai Goumon Tokoro*. AKA: *Woman Spy Torture: The Enemy Base as a Place of Female Torture*. Video. DIR: Kazuo Matsushita. SCR: N/C. DES: N/C. ANI: N/C. MUS: N/C. PRD: Applause Media Entertainment, Matsushita Okoku. 65 mins.

Three pretty female agents (described as sisters in the PR blurb) are caught infiltrating an enemy embassy and tortured with escalating levels of pain. This particular anime, however, is notable for its prolonged scenes of *tickling*. This eventually progresses to "forced" orgasms and slut-shaming, since apparently being naked before one's enemies is worse than being tickled. A 1980s styling seemingly recalls the mainstream sister-burglars of **CAT'S EYE**, possibly inadvertently. Made by a company better known for its live-action material, which went bust shortly after the release, making this one of the most frightfully obscure anime we could think of. The

producers will be tickled pink that we even know about it. **NV**

WOMEN AT WORK *

2005. Video. JPN: *The Guts*. DIR: Hideki Araki. SCR: Koichi Murakami. DES: Hideki Araki. ANI: Hideki Araki. MUS: Meeon. PRD: Animac. 30 mins. x 2 eps. Slacker university student Akiyoshi Nakajima is rebuffed by the object of his affections, who tells him he is unreliable and weedy. He decides to kill two birds with one stone by applying for a job on a construction site. Soon after arriving, he is forced to take an "entrance exam" which involves having sex with Hiroko Miike, the pretty 30-something site manager. Impressed with his performance, she puts him on the work detail, where he is soon offered sex galore by the desperate women he encounters. A rare anime foray into the world of construction worker porn, in which for some reason not only the women but also some of the men appear to have large breasts. Based on one of a series of erotic games by Complet's (*sic*). **N**

WONDER BEAT SCRAMBLE

1986. JPN: *Wonderbeat S*. TV series. DIR: Satoshi Dezaki, Seiji Arihara. SCR: Toshiaki Imaizumi, Kazumi Koide, Noboru Shiroyama, Hideo Takayashiki, Toshiyuki Tanabe, Yoshihisa Araki. DES: Setsuko Shibuichi, Keizo Shimizu, Yuichi Higuchi. ANI: Toshio Nitta. MUS: Ryo Yonemitsu. PRD: Mushi, Magic Bus, TBS. 25 mins. x 24 eps. In the year 2121, Professor Sugida disappears during an experiment in medical miniaturization, for which he has been inserted within a patient's body. His son, Susumu, is allowed to join the White Pegasus team sent to rescue him and is miniaturized to board the mini-vessel Wonderbeat. The seven-man crew discovers that the professor, far from being dead, has been kidnapped by the alien creature Hieu as the first step in its quest for world domination. It's anime's homage to *Fantastic Voyage* (1966), or, if you'd rather, *Invasion of the Body Snatchers* (1956), seen from the inside out. Each episode finishes with a live-action mini medical lecture, from **ASTRO BOY**'s Osamu Tezuka, who was also the executive producer. Compare to the similar **MICROID S**.

WONDERFARM
Production company established in 1996, whose works include **COSPLAY COMPLEX**, **HAND MAID MAY**, and **SAINT BEAST**.

WONDERFUL GENIE FAMILY *
1969. JPN: *Hakushon Daimao*. AKA: *Bad King Haxion/Atchoo*. TV series. DIR: Hiroshi Sasakawa, Tsuneo Ninomiya. SCR: Junzo Toriumi. DES: Tatsuo Yoshida. ANI: Shigeru Yamamoto, Yukihiro Takahashi, Takashi Saijo. MUS: Shosuke Ishikawa. PRD: Tatsunoko, Fuji TV. 25 mins. x 52 eps.
In this modern-day parody of **ALADDIN AND THE WONDERFUL LAMP**, a jinni and his family can be summoned from their imprisoning bottle by a Sneeze (Dad), a Sniff (Mom), and a Yawn (the eternally tired daughter). Created by producer Tatsuo Yoshida, the series bears a strong resemblance to the original **COMET-SAN**, sharing with it an original inspiration in *I Dream of Jeannie* and *Bewitched* (see **BEWITCHED AGNÈS**) and a remake in the early years of the 21st century. Original director Hiroshi Sasakawa returned for *Akubi-chan* (*Yobarete Tobidete Akubi-Chan/ Call Her Up and Out She Flies: Akubi-chan*), a 26-part TV series on Kid's Station that was successful enough to generate a 13-part TV sequel in 2002. However, at the time of writing, only the original 1969 series has been broadcast in the U.S.

WOOF WOOF 47 RONIN
1963. JPN: *Wan Wan Chushingura*. AKA: *Woof Woof Chushingura; Doggie March*. Movie. DIR: Daisaku Shirakawa, Hiroshi Ikeda. SCR: Satoshi Iijima, Daisaku Shirakawa. DES: Seiichi Toriizuka. ANI: Akira Daikuhara, Hayao Miyazaki. MUS: Urahito Watanabe. PRD: Toei. 81 mins.
Lock the puppy lives happily in the peaceful forest until outlaws Kira the tiger and Akamimi the fox murder his mother. Lock enlists Goro, an aging stray dog, to help him in his quest for revenge, and they assemble a band of dogs to bring justice against the killers where the law has failed. Based an idea by executive producer Osamu Tezuka, itself inspired by the kabuki play *Chushingura* (which exists in many forms, the earliest known dating from 1706), also known as *Treasury of Loyal Retainers* or *The 47 Ronin*. The original story dates from 1701, when Lord Asano of Ako Castle was provoked into drawing his sword and wounding his guest, the high-ranking samurai Kira. Asano was forced to commit suicide, but the castle steward Oishi assembled 46 loyal retainers, who murdered Kira, and then committed ritual suicide in 1703. The anime version is far simpler, dumping matters of etiquette and loyalty in favor of an archetypal quest for revenge, with only Oishi (Lock) and Kira surviving in any recognizable form. Its title seems deliberately intended to recall the Japanese name of Disney's *Lady and the Tramp* (1955), which was released in Japan in 1956 as *Woof Woof Story* (*Wan Wan Monogatari*). The final showdown in the snow, also present in the original, made the film ideal for its release just before Christmas. Compare to the similarly canine **DOGTANIAN AND THE THREE MUSKEHOUNDS**. A young Hayao Miyazaki was one of the animators.

WORDS WORTH *
1999. Video. DIR: Kan Fukumoto. SCR: N/C. DES: Rin Shin. ANI: Rin Shin. MUS: N/C. PRD: Beam Entertainment, Green Bunny. 30 mins. x 5 eps., 5 mins. (bonus), 30 mins. x 2 eps. (*WW: Gaiden*).
The forces of light and darkness fight to obtain the scattered pieces of the Words Worth, a stone monolith with magical powers. Our hero, Astral, illegally acquires a sword license and dives into the conflict between the rival realms, only to be blasted 20 years into the future by a sorcerer. Suffering from amnesia, he is eventually reunited with his old companions and the daughter of a previous liaison and confronted with the revelation that he is the son of a great swordsman and the father of the figure who will reunite the sundered realms. This sensual fantasy epic was based on the pornographic computer game from Elf, although as ever, this was more like a "visual novel" that practically played itself and only rarely sought the "player's" input in decisions (**ARGOT AND JARGON**). As per usual, there is a prophecy about a legendary swordsman, ladies in diaphanous veils, and lots of shagging, along with a complex family dynamic redolent of the messianic ending to **UROTSUKIDOJI**. A five-minute bonus sequence of "comedy" scenes was included in the Japanese box set. Hisashi Tomii's *WW: Gaiden* (*Outer Story*) introduces the warrior-women Persia and Sabrina, and their prison tribulations, seemingly in a flashback to the war between light and shadow.

The original game also had a spin-off, set during the 20-year hiatus in the anime plot, in which **NONOMURA HOSPITAL** and *Words Worth* swapped a couple of characters for just long enough for them to get naked. The anime series has the dubious honor of being banned in Canada, where the Border Services Agency deemed it obscene in 2007. ◐

WORLD CONQUEST ZVEZDA PLOT *
2014. JPN: *Sekai Seifuku: Boryaku no Zvezda*. AKA: *World Conquest: Star Strategy*. TV series. DIR: Tensai Okamura. SCR: Tensai Okamura, Meteo Hoshizora, OKSG, Shotaro Suga. DES: Kohaku Kuruboshi, Keigo Sasaki, Shigemi Ikeda, Yukiko Maruyama. ANI: Sanae Shimada, Masahiro Sekiguchi, Hatsue Koizumi, Hiroyuki Kaido, Satoshi Sakai. MUS: Tatsuya Kato. PRD: A-1 Pictures, Aniplex, Dentsu Inc, Ichinjinsha, MBS, MOVIC, Notes (Type-Moon). 24 mins. x 13 eps.
Asuta Jimon is cast out of the family home with no money and nowhere to go after an argument with his father. But he's as kindhearted as he is foolish: he shares the only food he has with a little girl he meets on the street and gets a big surprise. Kate Hoshimiya is a little girl with big dreams. She has her own secret organization devoted to world conquest, a master plan, and the technology to back it up. But the Japanese government is onto her—they have appointed a three-girl fighting force called White Light to put an end to the Zvezda threat. And by a not entirely odd twist of fate for an anime plot, the father who kicked Jimon out into the cold is Governor of Tokyo, with his own secret ambitions of conquest.

Bizarre comic battles, wisecracks, and a whole Scooby gang of sidekicks and heavies, all competently executed, bring the story to life. In a determined assault on the market, three manga adaptations started at the same time as the TV series. Sharp-eyed readers might wonder if the use of a Russian name for the Zvezda organization points to real-world political confrontations over Japan's northern territories (**GIOVANNI'S ISLAND**), but to the best of our knowledge the dispute is not a war against forces under the command of a barely dressed baby Lolita, and the Governor of Tokyo is not trying to annex the whole of Japan. Not yet. **NV**

WORLD GOD ONLY KNOWS, THE *

2010. JPN: *Kami Nomizo Shiru Sekai*. TV series, video. DIR: Shigehito Takayanagi. SCR: Hideyuki Kurata, Tatsuya Takahashi, Tamiki Wakaki. DES: Akio Watanabe. ANI: Toshie Kawamura, Yoshikazu Samura. MUS: Hayato Matsuo. PRD: Manglobe, Geneon Universal, TV Tokyo. 24 mins. x 12 eps. (TV1), 24 mins. x 12 eps. (TV2), 24 mins. (v1), 24 mins. (v2), 24 mins. (v3).

High-schooler Keima Katsuragi has absolutely nothing to do with girls. In fact, he has as little as possible to do with any non-virtual scenario. All of Keima's attention is occupied by the dreamgirls of the dating sim games he plays online—and there, he never fails to score. In fact, he's known as "the God of Conquest" because no virtual female has ever been able to resist him. But then Keima finds himself trapped in a life-or-death deal to help Elsie, a cute, incompetent, and absurdly named demon, to dispel demonic possessors of local girls, by making them fall in love with him.

Based on a manga by Tamiki Wakaki, which ran in *Shonen Sunday*, TWGOK cleverly has its cake and eats it—replaying the conquest-of-the-week of many a bawdy anime, but with a new, noble cause. Success in each exorcism for Keima also means that his patient loses all memory of him, thereby resetting his quest back to zero. It lampoons the ridiculous nature of dating sims while finding an excuse for their gameplay to work in the real world. The women Keima must seduce are "gamified" puzzles to be solved like the STEREO-TYPES AND ARCHETYPES of many a sim-based anime (EROTICA AND PORNOGRAPHY); but they are that way *because* they have been possessed by dim-witted demons.

A riff on Akira Kurosawa's mighty *Rashomon* shows one episode from four viewpoints, and there are sly visual nods to hit anime including THE MELANCHOLY OF HARUHI SUZUMIYA, DRAGON BALL, and DORAEMON (all stories about damaged superbeings) as well as nods to Osamu Tezuka's classic outsider BLACK JACK and the misfit-packed GUNDAM canon. Game fans will have fun spotting other homages. Alongside these knowing nudges to the geek community, there's plenty of light comedy and a second season revealing that Keima retains an emotional link to the girls he has "freed."

WORLD MASTERPIECE THEATER

After the success of Isao Takahata and Hayao Miyazaki's HEIDI, Nippon Animation began a long-term project to adapt numerous Western children's favorites into anime. Originally sponsored by the soft drink company Calpis, the *WMT* (*Sekai Meisaku Gekijo*) series began in 1975 with DOG OF FLANDERS. The Calpis sponsorship continued in the following years with FROM THE APENNINES TO THE ANDES, RASCAL RACCOON, and NOBODY'S GIRL. Without Calpis, but firmly established as Nippon Animation's yearly cash cow by 1979 (compare to Tatsunoko's TIME BOKAN, Sunrise's BRAVE SAGA and GUNDAM, or Tokyo Movie Shinsha's LUPIN III), the *WMT* series continued with ANNE OF GREEN GABLES, TOM SAWYER, SWISS FAMILY ROBINSON, SOUTHERN RAINBOW, TREASURES OF THE SNOW, KATRI THE MILKMAID, A LITTLE PRINCESS, POLLYANNA, LITTLE WOMEN, LITTLE LORD FAUNTLEROY, PETER PAN AND WENDY, DADDY LONG-LEGS, THE SOUND OF MUSIC, THE BUSHBABY, LITTLE MEN, TICO OF THE SEVEN SEAS, and ROMEO'S BLUE SKY. By 1996, however, the franchise was showing signs of increasing strain—LASSIE was taken off the air and replaced with *Remi: A Child without a Home*, a remake of NOBODY'S BOY REMI that deviated so far from the original as to betray the entire raison d'etre of the franchise. The *WMT* never recovered and was laid to rest after 21 years, though the earlier shows were soon given a new lease on life through video. Though the English-language market has been dominated in successive waves by the likes of ROBOTECH, AKIRA, UROTSUKIDOJI, and POKÉMON, anime in Europe is far more likely to be known through the high-quality children's entertainment for which the *WMT* became justly famous. In his memoirs, the producer Toshio Okada reported his feeling that many animators regarded *WMT* as the only work really worth doing, and that contracts on fan-friendly productions were something that many studios only took on as a distant second place. By the early 21st century, most if not all of the *WMT* anime had also been released in 90-minute movie edits on DVD.

In 2007, the series was briefly revived with a new sponsor, House Foods, under which it made a new version of LES MISÉRABLES (2007), an adaptation of THE ORPHANS OF SIMITRA (2008), and a prequel to ANNE OF GREEN GABLES (2009). Its legacy, once again obliquely related to the efforts of Hayao Miyazaki, can be seen in Studio Ghibli's 21st-century move into adaptations of classic children's stories; the retiring Miyazaki left a list of 50 children's books worthy of adaptation, through which his successors appear to be working with releases such as ARRIETTY.

WORLD OF AIKA-CHAN, THE

1993. JPN: *Aika-chan no Chikyu*. Video. DIR: So Sugiyama. SCR: So Sugiyama. DES: Shunji Saita. ANI: Shunji Saita. MUS: N/C. PRD: Tech. 33 mins.

The author of the manga *Secrets of the World* was only 12 years old, and she died days after completing it. Aika Tsubota's parents published her environmentally themed story in her memory, and this one-shot anime was the eventual result, sponsored in part by a charity opposing the pollution of the oceans. In 1995, *Secrets of the World* itself was animated as a two-part video series under the auspices of the Japanese Department of the Environment.

WORLD OF NARUE, THE *

2003. JPN: *Narue no Sekai*. TV series. DIR: Toyoo Ashida, Hiromitsu Morita. SCR: Yu Sugitani. DES: Takaaki Hirayama. ANI: Mika Takahashi, Takaaki Hirayama. MUS: Takayuki Negishi. PRD: BeSTACK, Imagica, Media Factory, Pony Canyon, Toshiba Digital Frontier. 25 mins. x 12 eps.

Kazuto Iizuka is an ordinary Japanese 14-year-old until his new classmate Narue Nanase bludgeons a puppy with a bat, claiming that it is an alien invader about to eat him. In fact, Narue is not lying. Although she has been raised on Earth, she is the daughter of a man who works for the Galactic Federation. Kazuto thereby gains the alien girlfriend common to so many anime since URUSEI YATSURA, who is not merely a love interest, but also a defender of the Earth—see SAIKANO, MAHOROMATIC, and ... well, most of the anime on the shelves of your local anime store. Later episodes tick further boxes of the modern harem show, since cute cyborg girls are soon also hanging around with Kazuto, while time-dilation effects à la **Gunbuster** ensure that Narue's older sister is actually younger than her, and also comes to stay. There are several superficial references in the story to classic science-fiction novels, particularly Robert Heinlein's *Door into Summer* (1957) and A.E. van Vogt's *World of Null-A* (1948) to which the title is a punning reference.

WORLD OF POWER AND WOMEN, THE
1932. JPN: *Chikara to Onna no Yo no Naka*. AKA: *In a World of Power and Women*. Movie. DIR: Kenzo Masaoka. SCR: Tadao Ikeda. DES: Tadao Ikeda. ANI: Mitsuyo Seo, Seiichi Harada, Saburo Yamamoto. MUS: Masanori Imasawa. PRD: Shochiku, Masaoka Eiga. ca. 10 mins.
A nameless husband and father of four lives in fear of his wife, a statuesque beauty who towers above him. One night, she hears him talking in his sleep, either dreaming or reminiscing about an affair with a typist at his place of work. The angry wife turns up at the company on the pretext of delivering lunch for her husband and loses her temper when she sees him flirting with the typist. The husband helpfully suggests that the women settle their differences with a boxing match. The typist overcomes her opponent with tickling, but the victory goes to the wife, in anime's first "talkie." Despite a 1932 production date, the movie did not receive its premiere until April the following year. Reputedly one of the first Japanese cartoons to use cel animation (**Technology and Formats**), this film's production methods would soon become the norm—with the opening of a Japanese factory producing cels in 1934, almost all Japanese animation would soon adopt the new methods for the next six decades.

WORLD WAR BLUE *
2012. JPN: *Aoi Sekai no Chushin de*. AKA: *At the Center of a Blue World*. TV series. DIR: Tetsuya Yanagisawa. SCR: Crimson, Takao Fuso. DES: Maki Fujii, Takeshi Kanda. ANI: Maki Fujii. MUS: Tomohiko Kishimoto. PRD: 5th Avenue, S-Wood, Team Crimson. 24 mins. x 3 eps.
Gear is a young man from the Segua Kingdom who has lost both his father and his best friend to an ongoing war with the nearby Ninteldo Empire. He joins up in the ongoing fight for the territory of Consume, putting his special attribute of incredible speed to use in the conflict. Based on a manga by Anatasia Shestakova and Crimson, this title is one of the most baffling in the anime world. Not for its central conceit, which openly allegorizes the console wars between a thinly disguised Sega and Nintendo (**Gaming and Digital Animation**), nor for its characters, which comprise reversionings of many popular gaming characters, beginning with the blue-haired Gear, who is a remake of **Sonic the Hedgehog**. No, what stumps us is that the notoriously litigious, picky, and obstructive Japanese licensing business, particularly as represented by two major corporations, has somehow been content and let this continue. When certain Japanese companies even try to throw their weight around regarding the content in an *Anime Encyclopedia*, the authors are agog with admiration that someone managed not only to get such a satire off the ground in manga form, but into an anime version as well.

WOUNDED MAN
1986. JPN: *Kizuoibito*. Video. DIR: Satoshi Dezaki, Takao Takeuchi. SCR: Tetsuaki Imaizumi, Kazuo Koike. DES: Keizo Shimizu. ANI: Keizo Shimizu. MUS: Noriaki Yamanaka. PRD: Toei, Magic Bus. 30 mins. x 5 eps.
TV reporter Yuko Soka visits gold-rush Brazil in order to interview Keisuke Ibaragi, AKA Rio Baraki, the quarterback of the football team. After predictably becoming lovers, the pair go in search of an Amazon treasure in the company of Peggy, a shipbuilder. The girls eventually meet with death for the crime of being eye candy in a macho anime—this one based on a manga by the same team of Kazuo Koike and Ryoichi Ikegami that produced **Crying Freeman** and **Sanctuary**. Keisuke discovers that his mother, Natsuko, Yuko, and Peggy were killed by the mysterious secret group GPX. Boiling with revenge, he finally confronts the two men responsible in a showdown on a sinking aircraft carrier. **LNV**

WOW! MR. MASARU!
1998. JPN: *Sexy Commando Gaiden! Sugoi yo!, Masaru-san*. AKA: *Sexy Commando Side Story!, Wow! Mr. Masaru*. TV series. DIR: Akitaro Daichi. SCR: Kyosuke Usuta. DES: Toshihide Masudate. ANI: Toshihide Masudate. MUS: Harukichi Yamamoto. PRD: M-BAS, TBS. 10 mins. x 48 eps.
Teenager Masaru is the top fighter at his school in a number of martial arts—karate, judo, boxing, and more. But he wants to get even better. He goes off into the mountains for three months and returns as the "Sexy Commando." His new special technique is to stun opponents with weird fighting poses, then attack before they can gather their wits. Based on the 1995 *Shonen Jump* manga by Kyosuke Usuta, these shorts were serialized as part of the *Wonderful* variety program. **V**

WOWOW
Sometimes rendered as "World Wide Watching." A subscription satellite broadcaster formed in competition with NHK's satellite services in 1991, WOWOW soon became the home of many foreign movies and import television, including *The Simpsons* and *South Park*. The channel was also host to some of the more controversial anime of the 1990s—**Cowboy Bebop** may have been shown on TV Tokyo, but its missing episodes were only restored on WOWOW. Other representative works for the channel include **Paranoia Agent** and **Ergo Proxy**.

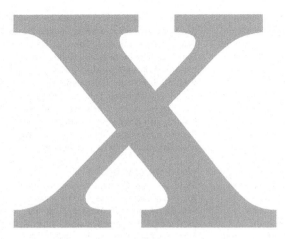

X-MEN *

2011. TV series. DIR: Fuminori Kizaki. SCR: Mitsutaka Hirota, Hideo Takayashiki. DES: Ai Yokoyama, Takashi Okazaki. Shigemi Ikeda. ANI: Michinori Chiba, Hisashi Abe, Ai Yokoyama. MUS: Tetsuya Takahashi. PRD: Madhouse Studios, Sony Pictures Entertainment. 24 mins. x 12 eps.

Professor Charles Xavier and his X-Men head for Japan, where a mutant girl has disappeared in mysterious circumstances. Still reeling from the death of one of their colleagues, the team face a challenge from an anti-mutant group calling itself the U-Men. Will the beautiful Japanese protege of their former adversary Emma Frost, the White Queen of the Hellfire Club, help them? Or will Mastermind—better known as Jason Wyngarde—and his cohorts triumph? Fans of British TV of the 1970s will smile at Marvel's nod to actor Peter Wyngarde, his best-known character *Jason King*, and his role in the Hellfire Club episode of the British TV show *The Avengers*—nothing to do with the American comicbook/movie team of the same name. There's something to smile about for other viewers, many of whom were disappointed by the Madhouse take on IRON MAN, in that the story and characters here are fairly close to the established *X-Men* canon. However, this third series of Marvel's classic comic/anime collaborations with Madhouse has its problems. The animation is good and the action scenes are densely, even chaotically, animated. On the other hand Japan itself seems very sparsely populated, both in mutant and human terms. There are a number of plot

holes and those who have already seen WOLVERINE will spot a major plot element being recycled. As in other Marvel-Madhouse collaborations of the period, the story is credited to Britain's Warren Ellis. Disappointingly, several big-name evil mutants, including the Professor's arch-rival Magneto, show up only in the end credits.

X-TREME TEAM

1998. JPN: *Totsugeki! Pappara-tai*. AKA: *Attack! Sprinkle Squad*. TV series. DIR: Kenichi Maejima. SCR: Natsuki Matsuzawa. DES: Yukari Kobayashi. ANI: N/C. MUS: N/C. PRD: Media Works, TV Tokyo. 25 mins. x 26 eps.

This spoof of anime's teens-save-Earth genre starts with rumors of an imminent alien invasion. The world mobilizes to establish the United Earth Defense Forces, the most powerful of whom are, of course, in Japan. When the promised alien invasion doesn't arrive, however, the SWAT teams resort to mercenary activities, fighting crime, chasing terrorists, and even delivering valuables as security guards. They also organize "friendly" competitions with rival defense teams. A tongue-in-cheek comedy about what might have happened if, say, the cast of EVANGELION was all ready for the Angels, but the Angels forgot to come. We derive our translated title here from that used in broadcasts in the Philippines.

X: THE MOVIE *

1996. AKA: *X: 1999*. Movie, video, TV series. DIR: Rintaro. SCR: Nanase Okawa, Mami Watanabe. DES: Nobuteru Yuki. ANI: Nobuteru Yuki. MUS: Yasuaki Shimizu, X-Japan. PRD:

Madhouse. 98 mins. (m), 25 mins. (v), 25 mins. x 24 eps. (TV).

Two groups of psychic warriors, known as the Seven Seals of the Earth Dragon and the Seven Harbingers of the Heaven Dragon, fight to save the world or destroy it. The battle is fought in modern Tokyo but draws on landmarks of the city's historic and spiritual past as both shields for Earth and levers to trigger its destruction. Subaru and Seishiro (characters from CLAMP's earlier TOKYO BABYLON) fight on opposing sides and end up destroying each other without resolving the struggle. Kamui, a psychic of enormous power, witnesses the fight and is so devastated that he flees Tokyo. But running can't save him; it is his destiny to join one side or the other and decide the fate of Earth. He finally returns to Tokyo to avenge the death of his mother, but to protect his friends Fuma and Kotori (whom he has loved since childhood), he refuses to take sides in the decisive battle. But Fate has decided otherwise. Fuma is Kamui's opposite number, the balance to his powers in the scales of destiny. When Fuma is seduced by the Earth Dragon's powers and kills his own sister, Kotori, Kamui finally joins the other side. The two friends must fight each other to decide if the world survives or ends.

Based on the manga in *Asuka* magazine from the CLAMP collective, *X* was preceded by lots of hype and a 25-minute music video made with the rock group X-Japan, suitably titled *X2*. But the amount that has to be cut from a huge, unfinished saga to make it into a coherent feature-length script can destroy the subtlety of a story and alienate fans of the original. Faced with compressing the massive melodrama without upsetting its fans, director Rintaro opted for style and emotion over clarity and substance. The look and mood of the original are there, just don't expect it to make much sense in terms of plot. The "1999" was dropped from the title for its English-language release since it didn't reach video until 2000. Yoshiaki Kawajiri's *X* TV series followed in 2001, preceded by an "episode zero" released on video, which included teasers of the show to come, but also footage that was not reused in the TV series proper. Put into production when the direction of the manga storyline was clearer, and taking advantage of the longer running time afforded by TV, the series revisits the story of the movie, but with greater opportunities for character development.

XABUNGLE

1982. JPN: *Sento Mecha Xabungle*. AKA: *Battle Mecha Xabungle; The Bungler*. TV series, movie. DIR: Yoshiyuki Tomino, Toshifumi Takizawa, Osamu Sekita, Iku Suzuki, Yasuhiro Imagawa. SCR: Tsunehisa Ito, Soji Yoshikawa. DES: Kunio Okawara, Yutaka Izubuchi. ANI: Tomonori Kogawa, Akihiro Kanayama. MUS: Koji Makaino. PRD: Sunrise, TV Asahi. 25 mins. x 50 eps. (TV), 86 mins. (m).

On planet Zola, the purebred Innocents live inside a sealed dome, unable to survive in the inhospitable environment. The Civilian underclass, who live out in the wilderness, regard the Innocents' rocket launches as "ascensions of light" and do not question their assigned roles as rockmen (bluestone miners), freighters (traders), and sand-rats (desert-dwellers). Civilian Jiron Amos believes his rockman father was murdered and steals the new Walker Machine Xabungle, quarrelling all the way with the pretty land-ship captain Elche. He sets out on the land-ship Iron Gear to learn the truth about his father's death, but the whole planet has another truth to learn. For generations all Zolans have believed that they were descended from colonists from the planet Earth, but they never left the homeworld—Zola *is* the Earth, devastated by centuries of exploitation.

A more jocular robot show than its

contemporaries, *Xabungle* (i.e., "The Bungler") featured an inept hero and giant robot battles often played for laughs, set against a background that mixes parts of **GREY** and **NAUSICAÄ** with Westerns—homages extend as far as having a Clint Eastwood clone among the characters, along with a look-alike of Sunrise's all-time great antihero Char Aznable. A deliberate attempt to break the serious mold of Sunrise robot shows (by Tomino, the man whose name remains synonymous with **GUNDAM**), it also predates **PATLABOR** in its depiction of robots as everyday working tools. The story reappeared in 1983 in a feature-length edit, *Xabungle Graffiti*, screened alongside the two **DOUGRAM** short movies. Wild West imagery would return years later in **TRIGUN** and **EAT-MAN**.

XAM'D: LOST MEMORIES *

2008. JPN: *Bonen no Xamd*. AKA: *Xamd—Lost Memory*. TV series. DIR: Masayuki Miyaji. SCR: Masayuki Miyaji, Megumi Shimizu, Yuichi Nomura, Hiroshi Onogi. DES: Ayumi Kurashima, Takashi Aoi. ANI: Ayumi Kurashima, Seiichi Hashimoto. MUS: Michiru Oshima. PRD: BONES, Aniplex, Sony Computer Entertainment. 25 mins. x 26 eps.

What if you were one of the lucky ones, living in a place of peace and plenty while nearby areas were caught up in the hell of war? And what if one day, for no obvious reason, you were flung into the battle? Teenage protagonist Akiyuki is unlucky enough to be caught in a terrorist attack that changes him into a fusion of man and mecha (shades of **GUYVER**). As his home is ground under martial law, he becomes the weapon everybody wants and has to go on the run.

This hugely inventive series is full of character threads that lead nowhere, with more plot holes and loose ends than a bad piece of knitting, but it's also one of the most joyous, energetic, and enjoyable anime of its year. Crammed with enough ideas for a two-year story arc, its messy plot is rescued by its magnificently drawn characters, whose key moments of triumph and tragedy resonate as if they were real. The design shows cultural difference and technological variance with a loving subtlety not seen in many anime since **WINGS OF HONNEAMISE**. Hiroko Umezaki's color design is as powerful as Oshima's

score, both of them emphasizing and angling the ambience of each scene with subtle skill. BONES has created a series that's far from flawless, but almost better than flawless: clever, humane, and packed with character and invention, and with the same 21st-century taste as **SUMMER WARS**—that peaceful Japan is an island of tranquility in an unstable world. Although it was constructed and eventually broadcast as a television series, it had its premier several months earlier on the Sony PlayStation Network download service, leading some sources to file it as a "Net" animation.

XANADU: LEGEND OF DRAGONSLAYER

1988. JPN: *Xanadu Dragonslayer Densetsu*. Video. DIR: Atsutoshi Umezawa. SCR: Haruya Yamazaki. DES: Koichi Arai. ANI: Koichi Arai. MUS: Seiji Yokoyama. PRD: Nippon Falcom, Toei. 50 mins.

The evil magician Reichswar has killed the King to gain possession of a magic crystal; now he means to use its power to rule the whole of Xanadu. Then the widowed Queen Rieru is kidnapped. One brave young warrior, wielding the magic blade Dragonslayer, goes to her rescue. It's all based on the role-playing game *Xanadu*, as if you couldn't guess.

XEBEC

Formed in 1995 by former employees of Tatsunoko, Xebec functions as a subsidiary of its parent company, contributing animation to shows including **ZOIDS**, **PILOT CANDIDATE**, and **LOVE HINA**. Prominent staffers include Takashi Sudo, Nobuyoshi Habara, Akio Takami, and Makoto Uno. The company takes its name from a three-masted Mediterranean pirate ship.

XENOSAGA: THE ANIMATION

2005. TV series. DIR: Shigeyasu Yamauchi. SCR: Yuichiro Takeda. DES: Nobuteru Yuki, Hiroyuki Okawa. ANI: Masayuki Sato. MUS: Kosuke Yamashita. PRD: Happinet, Toei, TV Asahi. 25 mins. x 12 eps.

Four thousand years after humanity abandoned the Earth, a human vessel carrying a KOS-MOS battle android is attacked by alien enemies. In an inversion of the perils of **BLACK MAGIC M-66**, KOS-MOS turns out to be a model that resembles a pretty girl, which self-activates in order to save the life of its creator Shion. The ship destroyed, Shion and her creation are thrust into the middle of the ongoing war between humanity and the Gnosis aliens in an anime based on the PlayStation game of the same name—in fact, it is *so* based on the game that the cast often seem to assume that the viewer only requires summaries of plot details from the PlayStation version, often making it impenetrable to viewers who do not already know what is going to happen.

XI AVANT

2011. JPN: *Xi AVANT*. AKA: *Cross i Avant*. Movie. DIR: Kenji Kamiyama. SCR: Kenji Kamiyama. DES: Satoko Morikawa, Atsuko Sakaki, Yusuke Takeda. ANI: Satoru Nakamura. MUS: Kenji Kawai. PRD: Production I.G. 3.5 mins.
The near future. Cellphones have continued to develop and social networking is more powerful than ever. Government employee Kaoru is ordered to locate a missing man. His phone guides him every step of the way as he travels from Japan to Barcelona, where a clue picked up at Gaudi's famous cathedral takes him on a chase across town. Kenji Kamiyama's film, is still just four minutes of footage shown in Japanese cinemas in April 2011 with the *Stand Alone Complex: Solid State Society* movie (**GHOST IN THE SHELL**). It was also streamed on the NTT DoCoMo Xi website, since their new mobile phone service forms a key part of the story. It looks classy and well-animated, but with no release date or further update on the horizon, it may turn out to be just a very fancy commercial for a new phone service.

XPRESS TRAIN *

2003. JPN: *Chikan Densha*. AKA: *Groper Train; Lovely Train*. Video. DIR: Taifu Suginami. SCR: Yuta Takahashi. DES: Takashi Itani. ANI: Yuji Kamizaki. MUS: Yoshi. PRD: YOUC, Digital Works (Vanilla Series). 28 mins. x 2 eps.
Salaryman Kazuo loses his job after he is wrongfully accused of groping a woman on the subway. The actual culprit is an old lecher who calls himself the "God of Groping," who takes the down-at-heels Kazuo on as his 500th apprentice. Soon Kazuo is learning the way of successful groping—and picking up handy tips like avoiding women in groups, women on mobile phones, or women who look like they might put up a fight—all targets which the talented Kazuo goes after with relish. However, both gropers are in for a surprise when they run into Reiko, a woman who actually enjoys being felt up by strangers. Making a comedy out of one of Japan's most prevalent commuting annoyances, this entry in the **VANILLA SERIES** even manages to turn tragedy into porn, as the dying old groper persuades one of his victims to administer hand relief to the only part of his body that still has any blood in it. ●N

XTRA CREDIT *

2002. JPN: *Reiju Gakuen*. AKA: *Domination Academy*. Video. DIR: Shigeru Kohama. SCR: Rokurota Makabe. DES: Yoshihito Kato. ANI: Motokazu Murakami. MUS: Hiroaki Sano, Takeshi Nishizawa. PRD: Discovery. 30 mins. x 2 eps.
Keiko is a young, attractive school teacher, sorry, professor at an elite academy, who secretly enjoys being the pin-up of all the boys. Feeling under threat by the arrival of the equally attractive new teacher Miyuki, Keiko arranges for her rival to be "taught" her true place in the order of things, which involves molestation, rape, and assault, as per usual. An entry in the **DISCOVERY SERIES**, not to be confused with the similarly titled **SEXTRA CREDIT**. ●NV

XXXHOLIC *

2005. Movie, TV series. DIR: Tsutomu Mizushima. SCR: Ageha Okawa, Michiko Yokote. DES: Kazuchika Kise. ANI: N/C. MUS: N/C. PRD: Production I.G, TBS. 60 mins. (m), 25 mins. x 24 eps. (TV).
In anime's answer to *The Sixth Sense* (1999), Kimihiro Watanuki has the ability to see and interact with ghosts. He is approached by a woman called Yuko, who offers to cure him of his affliction, but only if he agrees to work for her. Based on the manga by CLAMP, which began running in *Young* magazine in 2003. After the movie *xxxHOLIC: A Midsummer Night's Dream* (*Manatsu no Yoru no Yume*), which shared a double bill and several plot elements with CLAMP's **TSUBASA CHRONICLE**, a TV series followed in 2006. In one of anime's many counter-intuitive readings, the "xxx" in the title is silent.

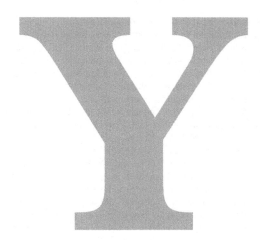

YABUKI, KIMIO
1934–. Born in Fukushima Prefecture, Yabuki graduated from Tokyo National University of Fine Arts and Music in 1958 and found work with Toei's Kyoto studios as an assistant director in live action. Transferring to Toei Animation in 1962, his anime directorial debut was on KEN THE WOLF BOY, and his breakthrough work was on PUSS IN BOOTS. He moved to Toei's advertising division in 1970, officially leaving anime behind, although he subsequently went freelance in 1973, returning to the anime world to work on such titles as CALIMERO.

YABUSHITA, TAIJI
1903–86. Born in Osaka, Yabushita graduated from the photography department of Tokyo School of Arts (now Tokyo National University of Fine Arts and Music) in 1925. He worked briefly for Shochiku before leaving to make films for the Ministry of Education. Joining Nippon Doga (Nichido), he made *A Baby Rabbit's Tale* (1952, *Ko-usagi Monogatari*) and *Kappa Kawataro* (1955). With Nippon Doga's sale to Toei, Yabushita became the director of production for Toei Animation, in which capacity he was sent to the U.S. to learn how Disney had industrialized the animation process. He should hence be considered a major player in Toei's quest to become "the Disney of the East." After the 13-minute *Lost Kitten* (1957, *Koneko no Rakugaki*), he oversaw the flowering of Toei's animated features, including PANDA AND THE MAGIC SERPENT (1958), MAGIC BOY (1959), and JOURNEY TO THE WEST (1960).

He subsequently moved into teaching, and although he wrote textbooks on animation, tragically he does not seem to have committed his own memoirs to paper, despite witnessing the meteoric rise of Japanese animation in the 1960s.

YADAMON
1992. TV series. DIR: Kiyoshi Harada, Takaya Mizutani, Yoshiko Sasaki, Koichi Takada. SCR: Minami Okii. DES: SUEZEN. ANI: Masahiko Murata, Hideaki Sakamoto, Kenichi Shimizu. MUS: Koji Makaino. PRD: Group Tac, NHK. 8 mins. x 170 eps.
Yadamon is a little witch who lives with Jan and his parents in the near future. Maria, Jan's mother, is a biologist and spends her time performing experiments. Yadamon is an inquisitive girl, and, like most magical friends (see DORAEMON), she frequently gets Jan into trouble. Like all good magical girls, she has a cute little magical pet, Taimon, who can not only talk but also stop time for a short while.

The series aired every weekday; the 21-week first run accounted for 110 episodes. Starting out on NHK, the second series aired on NHK's Educational Channel in 1993. For the linguistically curious, *iya-damon* is a cute way for little girls to say "no," which might be useful for the heroine of YOIKO.

YADATE, HAJIME
Also sometimes Hajime Yatate. A house pseudonym employed by Sunrise in order to assign some or all of the intellectual property in a new concept to the studio itself. Yadate's name appears on most of

the company's giant robot shows.

YAGAMI'S FAMILY TROUBLES
1990. JPN: *Yagami-kun no Katei no Jijo*. AKA: *Yagami's Family Circumstances; Affairs at the House of Yagami*. Video. DIR: Shinya Sadamitsu. SCR: N/C. DES: Kei Kusunoki, Kazuchika Kise. ANI: Kazuchika Kise. MUS: Ichiro Nitta. PRD: IG Tatsunoko, Kitty Films. 30 mins. x 3 eps., 55 mins.
Yagami's mother looks as if she's just 16 and is as cute as anything; despite finding this embarrassing, he can't help lusting after her in a combination of Oedipus *and* Lolita complexes! All his classmates, and his teacher, and the local delinquent, are in love with his mother; as well as fighting each other over who loves her most, they get together to plot ways of getting rid of their common enemy, Yagami's father. Dad has problems of his own as the love object of a secretary in his office, but once his coworker discovers he has such a pretty "young" wife, she turns her affections instead to Yagami. No wonder the poor boy's confused. Things could hardly get worse when a new student who looks almost exactly like Yagami's mother joins his class—and it's a boy. The 1986 *Shonen Sunday* manga by OGRE SLAYER–creator Kei Kusunoki pushed the envelope of family values, but the spin-off video is a low-budget effort aimed at exploiting the manga fan base. The series was repackaged into an edited one-shot *Decisions* (*Yorinuki*) the same year.

YAIBA
1993. JPN: *Kenyu Densetsu Yaiba*. AKA: *Leg-*

end of Brave Swordsman Yaiba. TV series. DIR: Kunihiko Yuyama, Norihiko Sudo, Sadao Suzuki, Hiroshi Yoshida, Osamu Sekita, Akitaro Daichi, Kazuya Murata, Yasuhiro Matsumura, Eiichi Sato. SCR: Kenji Terada, Yukiyoshi Ohashi, Isao Shizuya. DES: Norihiro Matsubara, Katsuyoshi Kanemura. ANI: Norihiro Matsubara, Tadashi Hirota, Kazuto Nakazawa. MUS: Kohei Tanaka. PRD: Pastel, TV Tokyo. 25 mins. x 52 eps.

Leaving the distant isle where he and his father studied samurai skills, Yaiba Kurogane comes home with his animal friends—a tiger and a vulture. He stays with his father's old adversary, Raizo, and Raizo's cute daughter, Sayaka, enrolling in her high school. Here he has to face school kendo champion Takeshi Onimaru, possessor of a demonic sword. Yaiba goes into the mountains to learn from ancient sword master Musashi (see **YOUNG MIYAMOTO MUSASHI**) and gets not just new skills but also a magic sword of his own, the legendary Sword of the Thunder God. All he has to do is stay true to the samurai spirit within him and collect seven magic spheres to enhance his sword's power, and then he can vanquish all evil. But he and Takeshi aren't the only people with conquest in mind. Princess Moon, the Thunder God's old adversary, is out to conquer Earth, and Yaiba and Takeshi must forget their quarrel and unite to save the world. Adapted from the first successful manga by **CONAN THE BOY DETECTIVE**–creator Gosho Aoyama, *Yaiba* has many similarities with its smarter younger brother, mixing action, drama, and humor.

YAMADA'S FIRST TIME *

2010. JPN: *B-gata H-kei*. AKA: *B-Stream, H-Group*. TV series. DIR: Yusuke Yamamoto. SCR: Satoru Nishizono, Kazuyuki Fudeyasu, Natsue Yoguchi. DES: Yuko Yahiro, Michiyo Miki. ANI: Yuko Yahiro. MUS: Hitoshi Fujima, Junpei Fujita. PRD: HAL Film Maker, AT-X, Dax Pro, Dentsu, Happinet Pictures, Mages, McRAY, NEC, Shueisha, TYO Animations. 25 mins. x 12 eps.

Yamada (her first name is never revealed) is a beautiful high school student who wants to have casual sex with 100 partners before she graduates. There are two problems: she's a virgin, and she thinks her vulva looks weird. So she decides to find a fellow virgin for her first partner,

reasoning that he won't have any grounds for comparison. She picks a boy at random in a bookstore because he looks inexperienced—but given her own lack of experience, how will Yamada seduce him? This show is a great rarity—an erotic comedy that allows a girl to be outgoing and openly, even aggressively, interested in sex, without making her into a slut or punishing her for her normality. Based on a four-panel comic strip by Yoko Sanri that ran in *Weekly Young Jump* from 2004 to 2011, its characters and situations have the ring of authenticity and considerable charm. **Ⓝ**

YAMAGA, HIROYUKI

1962–. Born in Niigata Prefecture, Yamaga was an obsessive fan whose love of film found new directions at Osaka University of Arts. After making a live-action wine commercial (and hence being not quite the inexperienced fan-made-good of industry legend), he directed the inaugural movie for the 1981 Daicon III SF convention with fellow students Hideaki Anno and Takami Akai. Yamaga was only 24 years old when work began on **WINGS OF HONNEAMISE** (1987), which he was to direct, before becoming the president of the Gainax animation company. Despite acclaimed directorial work on **GUNBUSTER** (1988), Yamaga soon disappeared behind the scenes as Gainax involved itself in computer games. He was technically "president-at-large" for 14 years, only returning actively to direction with **MAHOROMATIC** (2001).

YAMAMOTO, EIICHI

1940–. Born in Kyoto Prefecture, he attended several schools in different parts of Japan before leaving high school to work at a pharmaceutical company. He quit in 1958 to pursue an animation career, firstly with Ryuichi Yokoyama's Otogi Pro, joining Mushi Production in 1961, and soon gaining directorial credits on **ASTRO BOY** and **KIMBA THE WHITE LION**. He also directed **TRAGEDY OF BELLADONNA** (1973) before leaving the troubled Mushi to work on **STAR BLAZERS**. Yamamoto left anime entirely in the late 1970s to work on the NTV series *Wonderful World Travel*, in the course of which he spent much time filming abroad. He returned to anime with **OSHIN**

(1984) and a number of video works, including **THE SENSUALIST**, which he scripted. He also worked in an advisory capacity on **UROTSUKIDOJI**, and published a semi-fictionalized account of his days at Mushi, *The Rise and Fall of Mushi Pro* (*Mushi Pro no Koboki*, 1989), which remains a major source of behind-the-scenes information on anime in the 1960s.

YAMAMOTO, SANAE

1898–1981. Pseudonym of Zenjiro Yamamoto. Born in Chiba Prefecture, he began working part-time for Seitaro Kitayama's animation company Kitayama Eiga, while still a student of Japanese art. After the Great Kanto Earthquake and Kitayama's subsequent relocation to Osaka, Yamamoto stayed in Tokyo to found Yamamoto Manga Productions. His *Mountain Where Old Women Are Abandoned* (1923, *Obasuteyama*) was the earliest anime extant until the rediscovery of Junichi Kouchi's *Sword of Hanawa Hekonai*, AKA *The Blunt Katana* (1917)—the Natsuki Matsumoto discovery of 2005 has yet to be satisfactorily dated (**EARLY ANIME**). He labored for some time on *Jar* (not dated, *Tsubo*), an instructional film for the Ministry of Education, and moved into political advertisements and propaganda in the 1930s. His most notable propaganda work was *Defeat of the Spies* (1942, *Spy Gekimetsu*). Post–World War II, he assembled surviving animators in the Tokyo area to form Nippon Doga, a company eventually merged into Toei to form Toei Animation, where he was a major mentor to many of the following generation. Yamamoto played an executive role in Japan's early features **PANDA AND THE MAGIC SERPENT**, **MAGIC BOY**, and *Alakazam the Great* (see **JOURNEY TO THE WEST**).

YAMAMOTO YOHKO *

1995. JPN: *Sore Yuke! Uchu Senkan Yamamoto Yoko*. AKA: *Go! Space Battleship Yoko Yamamoto; Starship Girl Yamamoto Yohko*. Video. DIR: Akiyuki Shinbo. SCR: Yuji Kawahara, Mayori Sekijima, Masashi Kubota. DES: Kashiro Akaishi, Kazuto Nakazawa (v), Akio Watanabe (TV). ANI: Hiroyuki Morinobu. MUS: N/C. PRD: JC Staff, Tee-Up, TV Osaka. 30 mins. x 7 eps. (v), 25 mins. x 26 eps. (TV). In A.D. 2990, the human race has been split into two spacefaring empires, Terra and Ness. With Terra on a losing streak in the ritualized "war games," scientist Rosen creates a time machine, sending emissaries back to 20th-century Earth to recruit new warriors by testing them with familiar-looking arcade games. He finds schoolgirl Yoko and convinces her to time-travel after school to the battlefront, where she and several other girls from her school must adapt their arcade game skills to real combat. This is yet another spin on *The Last Starfighter* (see also **BATTLE ATHLETES**), with video-game style duels in advanced machines that look like a cross between a Formula One racing car and a goldfish. The alleged "girl power" is presented, in the tradition of **GUNBUSTER**, for the titillation of a male audience, but there are a few fun visual tricks, like cockpits that disappear in battle, leaving the pilot apparently floating in space. Based on a novel by Taku Atsushi, also adapted as an audio drama. Episode four is renumbered "episode zero," and reintroduces the characters for the second "season." This episode "zero" was never released in the U.S. *YY* returned as a TV series in 1999.

YAMAMURA, KOJI

1964–. Born in Aichi Prefecture, he began a career making corporate videos after graduating from Tokyo Zokei University in 1987. He had already made several short cartoons in his student days and moonlighted on several anime productions, including a stint as a character designer on the NHK educational program *Playing in English* (*Eigo de Asobo*). He also worked as an illustrator on a very simple show designed to teach Japan's *kana* syllabary to very young viewers. He made his name, however, with several 8mm short films, one of which, **MOUNT HEAD**, was nominated for a Best Short Animation Oscar. Yamamura's accolade would have made him one of the most famous figures in the anime world, were it not for **SPIRITED AWAY**'s Oscar win for Best Feature Animation the same year, news of which largely swamped his own quiet achievement.

YAMASAKI, OSAMU

1962–. Born in Kumamoto Prefecture, Yamasaki began his animation career at Kaname Productions in 1981, before going freelance in 1985, just in time to cash in on the boom in production caused by the arrival of video. After a directorial debut on **YOTODEN** (1987), he also worked as director on **TAKEGAMI** (1990) and **TOKYO REVELATION** (1995).

YAMATO TAKERU

1994. JPN: *Yamato Takeru.* TV series. DIR: Hideharu Iuchi, Shinichi Masaki, Nobuhiro Kondo, Jiro Saito, Takeshi Yoshimoto. SCR: Masaharu Amiya, Kenichi Araki. DES: Koichi Ohata. ANI: Takahiro Kishida, Moriyasu Taniguchi, Akira Kasahara. MUS: Takahiro Kishida. PRD: Nippon Animation, TBS. 25 mins. x 37 eps. (TV), 25 mins. x 2 eps. (v).
On planet Yamato, a twin birth is a bad omen for the throne, so when two brothers are born to the queen, one of them must be killed. But Takeru is saved through the intervention of the gods and survives to return and claim the throne (and the beautiful princess) as fate has decreed. For this sci-fi clash of robotic armor indistinguishable from "magic," creator Masami Yuki took his inspiration from one of Japan's oldest stories. The original Yamato Takeru's epic expedition was recorded in two of Japan's oldest historical texts, the *Kojiki* (A.D. 712) and *Nihon Shoki* (A.D. 720), and he and Princess Ototachibana are jointly credited as founders of many real shrines. Ancient sources sometimes embroider the bare cloth of supposed history—Takeru is alleged to have defeated Kumaso warriors by disguising himself as a woman and getting them drunk, and he was to have saved the plains from Ainu arsonists by cutting away the burning brush with his sword. The weapon, known thenceforth as *Kusanagi* ("Grass-Cutter"), became one of the Imperial Treasures of Japan, lending its name to several anime protagonists, most notably Motoko Kusanagi in **GHOST IN THE SHELL**.
The final two episodes were not broadcast but were released on video in 1997 under the title *Yamato Takeru: After War.* The beginning of a fourth season that never materialized, they are set three years after the original, with Takeru now 16 years old, having to defend his homeworld from samurai-style robot invaders from planet Izumo in a "flying magic fortress." See also **LITTLE PRINCE AND THE EIGHT-HEADED DRAGON** and the live-action version of the legend released in the West as *Orochi the Eight-Headed Dragon.*

YAMAZAKI, KAZUO

1949–. Born in Tokyo, Yamazaki dropped out of high school to work in anime, gaining credits on shows for Madhouse, Sunrise, and Studio Deen, among others. His directorial debut came with an episode of the live/animation hybrid show **BORN FREE** in 1976. Later works have included the remake of **TIGER MASK**, **URUSEI YATSURA**, and **MAISON IKKOKU**. More recent years have seen him move away from directing into storyboarding on shows such as **ARGENTO SOMA**.

YAMAZAKI KING OF SCHOOL

1997. JPN: *Gakko O Yamazaki.* AKA: *School King Yamazaki.* TV series. DIR: Tsuneo Tominaga. SCR: Kazumi Koide, Taku Ichikawa. DES: Hiroshi Ikeda. ANI: Shinichi Suzuki. MUS: N/C. PRD: Bandai, TV Tokyo. 25 mins. x 33 eps.
A bratty six-year-old declares himself the "King of School." In a rip-off of the earlier **CRAYON SHIN-CHAN**, this adaptation of Manabu Kashimoto's manga from *Corocoro Comic* features kleptomania, disobedience, and fighting.

YANBO, NINBO AND TONBO

1995. JPN: *Yanbo Ninbo Tonbo.* TV series. DIR: Seitaro Hara, Tatsuo Okazaki, Shigeo Koshi, Mamoru Kanbe. SCR: Satoshi Nakamura. DES: Takumi Izawa. ANI: Katsumi Hashimoto, Hiroshi Kagawa, Kazuhiko Udagawa. MUS: N/C. PRD: Image K, NHK2. 25 mins. x 39 eps.
An old 1950s NHK radio drama featuring the three titular monkey brothers, this anime updates the story for the '90s audience of the original broadcasters' new satellite channel. The brothers try some crow soup, start a fire on the mountain, and race the king of the Pig People—like kids do.

YANKI: RIDE LIKE THE WIND

1989. JPN: *Yanki Reppu-tai.* AKA: *Yanki Wind Gang.* Video. DIR: Tetsuro Imazawa. SCR: Ryunosuke Ono, Yasushi Ishikura. DES: Masahide Hashimoto. ANI: Hideki Kakinuma. MUS: Tetsuro Kashibuchi. PRD: Toei. 50 mins. x 6 eps.
Impossibly tough and hairsprayed biker boys and girls fight turf wars in the streets, with much revving of motors and "you killed my buddy, prepare to die" dialogue. This lackluster latecomer to the genre

typified by **BOMBER BIKERS OF SHONAN** was based on the *Sho-nen Magazine* manga by Masahide Hashimoto, whose hero was *so* tough that he transferred schools 20 times. Only a Japanese tough guy would continue to go at all! **L V**

YASUHIKO, YOSHIKAZU

1947–. Born in Hokkaido, he dropped out of Hirosaki University midway through a degree in Western history in order to go to Tokyo and become an animator at Mushi Production. His early anime work included stints on **WANDERING SUN** and the second series of **MOOMINS**. With the demise of Mushi Pro, he was one of the early defectors to what would become Sunrise, ideally placing him to work as a director and character designer on that studio's output, most notably as a defining character designer in the **GUNDAM** and **DIRTY PAIR** series. His other works in anime include **CRUSHER JOE** and **GIANT GORG**, and he has also contributed to anime adaptations of his manga work, including **ARION** and **VENUS WARS**. Also known as "YAS," the name with which he signs his artwork.

YASUJI'S PORNORAMA

1971. JPN: *Yasuji no Pornorama Yatchimae!* AKA: *Yasuji's Pornorama: How About That!* Movie. DIR: Takamitsu Mitsunori. SCR: Yoshiaki Yoshida. DES: Yasuji Tanioka. ANI: Michiru Suzuki. MUS: Kiyoshi Hashiba. PRD: TV Tokyo. 101 mins.
Three incidents in the life of Busuo ("Fatso"), the lecherous hero of Yasuji Tanioka's anarchic 1970 manga *Yasuji's Course on Being an Utter Brat* (*Yasuji no Metameta Gaki Michi Koza*). Though produced by TV Tokyo, these cartoon erotica were "too hot for television" and screened instead in theaters. With the failure of **CLEOPATRA: QUEEN OF SEX** the previous year, anime pornography would disappear for a generation after this, until straight-to-video releases made **LOLITA ANIME** possible. **N**

YAT BUDGET! SPACE TOURS

1996. JPN: *YAT Anshin! Uchu Ryoko*. TV series. DIR: Hitoshi Nanba, Takuya Sato, Tsuneo Kobayashi, Kazuhiro Sasaki. SCR: Keiko Hagiwara, Ryo Motohira, Mineo Hayashi, Yutaka Hirata. DES: Yuka Kudo. ANI: Yuka Kudo. MUS: Kenji Kawai. PRD: Tac, NHKEP. 25 mins. x 75 eps.

The Yamamoto Anshin Travel Company's latest luxury space tour hits an unexpected setback when the ship warps into an unknown part of space, ruled by a race of fishlike humanoids called the Gannon, who don't like their visitors. "Luxury" is a misnomer; the ship is a pile of junk, the captain is fat and grumpy, and, with the exception of the stewardess—his daughter Katsura—and the boy who's crazy about her, most of the crew are robots or aliens, and all of them are weird. Beset by pretty shark-boys out for their blood, with restless passengers, and the normally quiet Katsura ready to bash someone with her monkey wrench, how will our gang of misfits get their passengers home? To make matters worse, they've got a stowaway—squirrel-girl Marron, who can turn herself into a little pink ball but doesn't seem to have many other useful survival skills. This cute, colorful slapstick SF show, created by Shinji Nishikawa, was a departure for NHK's educational division. Something the anime industry *itself* should have learned from was a stroboscopic sequence in the final episode, which produced fainting and convulsions in some viewers in March 1997. Nine months later, a similar sequence in **POKÉMON** would make international headlines.

YATTOKAME TANTEIDAN

2007. AKA: *Great Detective Team Yattokame*. TV series. DIR: Takuo Suzuki. SCR: Yuji Kawahara, Tetsuo Yasumi. DES: Junichi Seki, Minoru Yasuhara. ANI: Saburo Takada, Junichi Seki. MUS: N/C. PRD: TV Aichi. 20 mins. x 14 eps.
A 74-year-old lady who runs a candy store in downtown Nagoya is the center of a group of senior citizens and neighborhood children who investigate local mysteries and crimes. Based on the novels by Yoshinori Shimizu, this charming cross-generational concept with a strong regional focus seems like ideal family viewing. Two live-action specials were screened on Tokai TV, a TV drama was shown on CBC TV, and there were also stage performances. However, only 14 of the planned 26 episodes were completed and broadcast, with Shimizu announcing in a TV interview that the anime had been censored. Backgrounds, incidentally, were provided by the Beijing Golden Pinasters

Animation Company, which now has work on over 30 Japanese titles to its credit.

YAWARA! *

1989. JPN: *Yawara! The Gentle Judo Girl*. AKA: *A Fashionable Judo Girl*. TV series, movie, TV special. DIR: Hiroko Tokita, Katsuhisa Yamada, Akio Sakai, Junichi Sakata. SCR: Toshiki Inoue, Yoshiyuki Suga. DES: Yoshinori Kanemori. ANI: Kunihiko Sakurai, Hirotsugu Yamazaki. MUS: Eiji Mori. PRD: Kitty Films, Yomiuri TV. 25 mins. x 124 eps. (TV), 60 mins. (m), 90 mins. (TVm).
Teenage judo genius Yawara Inokuma (who shares the surname of the gold medalist from the 1960 Tokyo Olympics) wants to get to the Barcelona Olympics and fulfill her grandfather Jigoro's dream of making her a judo champion under his coaching. But she also wants a life of her own outside of training schedules and competitions—her best friend, the plain Fujiko, also strives hard to be a top-class sportswoman. Yawara attracts two suitors, playboy Kasamatsuri and young sports reporter Matsuda. With them come rivals to create anime love polygons—Matsuda is also desired by the buxom photographer Kuniko, while rich-bitch judoist Sayaka sees herself as the perfect companion to Kazamatsuri. To make matters even more complicated, Sayaka's trainer is Yawara's own estranged father, Kojiro—determined that his daughter is toughened by a truly worthy opponent.
Based on the 1986 manga in *Big Comics Spirits* by **MASTER KEATON**–creator Naoki Urasawa, *Yawara!* is one of the better successors to **AIM FOR THE ACE**, always ready to lay sports aside for more human-interest drama. Her love for her crusty old grandfather is equal to her determination to go to school, have fun with her friends, and maybe even fall in love; this is the main cause of conflict in both manga and anime. The first season ends, in true sports-anime style, with Yawara's defeat of her Soviet rival, Tereshkova, as *glasnost* takes hold. The series was a hit with more than just the female audience. Life imitated art as it drew to a close with Tokita's movie *Wiggle Your Hips* (1992, *Soreyuke Koshinuke Kids*), shown on a double bill with the **RANMA ½** feature *Nihao My Concubine*. As the anime Yawara went off to the Barcelona Olympics in 1992, 16-year-old real-life judoist Ryoko

Tamura won a silver medal at the actual Barcelona games and was immediately christened "Yawara-chan" by the Japanese media. Four years later, the series was revived for a feature-length TV special, Morio Asaka's *Yawara!: Only You* (*Y: Zutto Kimi no Koto ga …*), in which Yawara defeats Sayaka in Atlanta and faces another of her father's protégés in the finals, the French Marceau. The real-life Tamura dutifully obliged by winning another silver at the real-life Atlanta Olympics. Four more years later, Tamura finally won gold in Sydney. For other judo-related struggles, see SANSHIRO SUGATA.

YAWARAKAME

2009. AKA: *A Bit on the Soft Side*. TV series. DIR: N/C. SCR: N/C. DES: N/C. ANI: N/C. MUS: N/C. PRD: ufotable, Bee TV. 2 mins. x 26 eps.
Made for mobile phones and broadcast on Bee TV, this children's comedy show is remarkable for the dedication of voice actor Miyuki Sawashiro, who plays every character, male, female, human, and non-human. It's a joint project between Yu Yagami, creator of THOSE WHO HUNT ELVES and DOKKOIDA?!, and anime studio ufotable.

YEARLING, THE *

1983. JPN: *Kojika Monogatari*. AKA: *Little Deer Story*. TV series. DIR: Masaaki Osumi. SCR: Shunichi Yukimuro, Eiichi Tachi, Mitsuru Majima, Soji Yoshikawa. DES: Shuichi Seki. ANI: Shuichi Seki. MUS: Koichi Sugiyama. PRD: MK Production, NHK. 25 mins. x 52 eps.
Based on the book by Marjorie Kinnan Rawlings about an orphaned fawn and the 12-year-old boy who finds it and rears it. Jody lives in grinding poverty on an isolated homestead in the Florida swamps in 1807. As he grows toward manhood and the fawn grows into an adult deer, Jody struggles with the difficulties of keeping a relationship going with a wild thing while still respecting its own nature. *The Yearling* was Osumi's last anime directing job—he left to work in the theater. Released in several European languages during the 1990s, we believe that a drastic edit of this show may have surfaced in America on a single VHS under the title *Country Hearts*. However, the series occupies a notable but largely unnoticed place in the history of GAMING AND DIGITAL ANIMATION, since its

second episode was entirely composited inside a computer, despite appearing on the surface to be standard 2D cel work. It was hence an experiment and harbinger of the way that almost all anime would be made a decade later.

YIN-YANG MASTER

2003. JPN: *Onmyoji: Yoen Emaki*. AKA: *Yin-Yang Master: Scroll of Passionate Phantoms; Yin-Yang Mistress*. Video. DIR: Kazuhiko Yagami. SCR: Rokurota Makabe. DES: N/C. ANI: N/C. MUS: Salad. PRD: Milky, T-Rex, Museum Pictures. 30 mins. x 2 eps.
In the Taisho period of the early 20th century (see ARISA), Japan is drifting inexorably toward war, and dark evils stalk the streets of Tokyo. Baffled detective Hiromasa Miyamoto decides to seek supernatural help by visiting the Master of Yin and Yang (or should that be Mistress?), Abe no Seimei, a voluptuous sorceress who has the power to command and control the nymphlike goddesses who rule the four directions of the compass. Then everybody's clothes come off and they have sex. Not to be confused with the medieval supernatural TV series *The Yin-Yang Master* (*DE), the movie adaptations of which would have been in Japanese video stores at the same time as this erotic anime was released. Based on a computer game. The original, male, Abe no Seimei appears in numerous other anime, including OTOGI ZOSHI and DOOMED MEGALOPOLIS, while his fictional grandson is the star of SHONEN ONMYOJI. ●🄻🄽🅅

YIN-YANG MISTRESS

2009. JPN: *Onmyoji Ayakashi no Megami: Inran Jubaku*. AKA: *Goddess of Yin-Yang Magic: Lascivious Curse*. Video. DIR: N/C. SCR: N/C. DES: N/C. ANI: N/C. MUS: N/C. PRD: T-Rex, MS Pictures. 28 mins. x 2 eps.
An evil goddess is absorbing the life force of a young human male as a means to absolute power. Four lesser goddesses try to stop her, but two of them also fall under her evil control. Can the others save the day? Can they awaken the spirit of the great yin-yang magician Abe no Seimei (YIN-YANG MASTER), or will tentacle porn take over the world? Sometimes we think it already has. 🄽🅅

YIN-YANG WAR

2004. JPN: *Onmyo Taisenki*. TV series. DIR: Masakazu Hishida. SCR: Junko Okazaki. DES: Michio Fukuda. ANI: Ayako Kurata. MUS: Yoko Fukushima. PRD: NAS, Sunrise, TV Tokyo. 25 mins. x 52 eps.
Riku Tachibana is raised by his grandfather, a strange old man who teaches him innumerable hand positions and signals in an impenetrable code. It gets so that this form of sign language comes as second nature to Riku, much to his classmates' amusement, until the day that he discovers they have a purpose. Grandfather is a sorcerer, who has secretly taught Riku the movements necessary to summon magical powers. Now all Riku needs to do is work out which sign creates which sorcery—and of course, save the world, while combating a number of other kids who use devices and signals to summon their own monsters, in the manner of DIGIMON.

YO SHOMEI MUSEUM LINE

2006. JPN: *Yo Shomei Bijutsukan LINE*. Video. DIR: Yu Nakai. SCR: N/C. DES: N/C. ANI: N/C. MUS: N/C. PRD: Toei Animation, Gentosha. 24 mins.
A beautiful presentation of the paintings of renowned Japanese artist Yo, set to natural sounds of wind, water and thunder. Beautiful wallpaper, excellent for relaxation, and a very pleasant addition to Toei's wide-ranging *ga-nime* line (ARGOT AND JARGON) in which artists and musicians are invited to interpret imagery, with or without stories, through limited animation. Director Nakai often works in music video with artists including JackKnife, The MODS, and Bonnie Pink.

YOIKO

1998. AKA: *Pretty Girl, Pretty Child*. TV series. DIR: Takahiro Omori, Jun Matsumoto, Kiyotaka Matsumoto, Kenichi Takeshita. SCR: Sukehiro Tomita, Yukiyoshi Ohashi, Shigeru Yanagawa. DES: Yugo Ishikawa. ANI: N/C. MUS: Shigeru Chiba. PRD: Studio Pierrot, TBS. 25 mins. x 20 eps.
The agenda of this late-night series is hinted at by the title's wordplay. Fuka Esumi is just a little girl at elementary school, but her body is almost that of a grown woman. This gets her into all kinds of problematic situations that a little girl her age isn't equipped to handle. Same

old same old (see **Cream Lemon**) gets new names, faces, and clothes. Based on Yugo Ishikawa's *Big Spirits* manga, this anime incongruously mixes childish school-room gags with prurient nudity. **N**

YO-KAI WATCH *

2014. JPN: *Yokai Watch.* TV series. DIR: Shinji Ushiro. SCR: Yoichi Kato. DES: Masami Suda, Miho Tanaka. ANI: N/C. MUS: Kenichiro Saigo. PRD: OLM. 24 mins. x 34+ eps.

Eleven-year-old Keita Amano frees a *yokai*—a Japanese spirit—from 190 years of imprisonment. Twin-tailed cat spirit Whisper is duly grateful and promises to protect Keita from supernatural dangers that he previously didn't know existed. He gives Keita a watch that allows him to see other *yokai*, and together they become *yokai* troubleshooters.

The concept for this simple but well-executed sub-**Pokémon** show was created by Level-5 and first appeared as a Nintendo 3DS game in July 2013. A second game followed in July 2014. The games offer the option of a boy or girl protagonist, and the promotional machine logically developed this into two manga. One written and drawn by Chikako Mori, starring Fumika Kodama, began serialization in girls' magazine *Ciao* in December 2013. A boys' version starring Keita, by Noriyuki Konishi for *CoroCoro Comic,* won the Best Children's Manga category at the Kodansha Annual Manga Awards in May 2014. Nobody on Earth has even bothered to hyphenate the word *yokai* before, but our title here reflects the insistence of the Japanese creators.

YOKOHAMA SHOPPING LOG

1998. JPN: *Yokohama Kaidashi Kiko.* AKA: *Going Shopping in Yokohama.* Video. DIR: Takashi Anno. SCR: Takashi Anno. DES: Atsushi Yamagata. ANI: Atsushi Yamagata. MUS: Gontiti. PRD: Ajia-do. 29 mins. x 2 eps.

This is either a sweet tale of a young girl's everyday life in a quiet suburb or a mold-breaking SF adventure in which an android searches for meaning in a world plagued by global warming. Alpha Hasseno is a humanoid robot girl who lives in the countryside of a future Japan, near what used to be Yokohama. Though Yokohama today is a big coastal city partly built on reclaimed marshland, in this fu-

ture much of Japan's urban infrastructure has been destroyed as global warming has put much of the world underwater. Her area is safe for the moment, but storms and floods are a constant threat. She runs a coffee shop, Café Alpha, in the absence of her owner, but she doesn't know where he is or when he will return. She's happy to wait, meanwhile serving coffee to the local characters. But in the course of her daily life and her shopping trip into Yokohama city—a trip that shows us how her world differs from ours—she meets other people, even another robot, and starts to wonder about her own life and purpose. The arrival of a parcel containing her creator's diary adds to the mystery. Based on the manga by Hitoshi Ashinano in *Comic Afternoon* magazine from 1994 onward.

YOKOHAMA THUGS

1993. JPN: *Yokohama Bakkure-tai.* Video. DIR: Mineo Goto, Masamune Ochiai. SCR: Shunsuke Amemura. DES: Satoshi Kuzumoto. ANI: N/C. MUS: N/C. PRD: Toei. 50 mins. x 4 eps.

It's all gags and fighting as gangster Tsunematsu Narita (the "biggest idiot in Yokohama") causes havoc in the neighborhood with his two henchmen. Based on the *Shonen Champion* manga by Satoshi Kuzumoto. **V**

YOKOHAMA'S FAMOUS KATAYAMA

1992. JPN: *Yokohama Meibutsu: Otoko Katayama-gumi.* AKA: *Yokohama's Famous Male Katayama Gang.* Video. DIR: Yoshinori Nakamura, Osamu Sekita. SCR: Hideo Nanba. DES: Masafumi Yamamoto. ANI: Masafumi Yamamoto. MUS: Quarter Moon. PRD: JC Staff, Nippon Eizo. 50 mins. x 2 eps.

Motorcycle gangsters with "a comical touch," as Hiromi Katayama, leader of the Yokohama biker gang Crazy Babies, tries to proclaim a one-month moratorium on violence while he trains new recruits, though his Tokyo rival, the Mad Emperor, has other ideas. Based on the manga in *Shonen Magazine* by Akira Yazawa. Compare to **Bomber Bikers of Shonan**.

YOKORENBO: IMMORAL MOTHER

2009. Video. DIR: N/C. SCR: N/C. DES: N/C. ANI: N/C. MUS: N/C. PRD: Suzuki Mirano. 29 mins. x 2 eps.

Based on a video game by Guilty+, this is the story of a sexually unsatisfied, preda-

tory mother who has sex with her son while she thinks he's asleep. Being a devoted son, and not a very heavy sleeper, he decides to make mother happy by "raping" her—although one might wonder, given the scenario, why rape is required. Then his sister gets involved, too. **NV**

YOKOYAMA, MITSUTERU

1934–2004. Born in Kobe, he left high school and worked for four months in a bank before quitting to become a manga artist. He is one of the most influential manga artists of the postwar era, fully deserving of consideration alongside Osamu Tezuka and Shotaro Ishinomori, although his role specifically in anime is largely limited to that of the creator of a couple of important titles. With **Gigantor**, he defined many of the tropes and traditions that would lead to Japan's giant robot anime; with **Little Witch Sally**, he established much of what is now taken for granted in the "magical girl" tradition. His other works include **Babel II**, and a manga adaptation of *The Water Margin*, which was used as the basis for the TV series of the same name (*DE).

YOMA: CURSE OF THE UNDEAD *

1988. JPN: *Yoma.* AKA: *Blood Reign; Curse of the Undead.* Video. DIR: Takashi Anno. SCR: Sho Aikawa. DES: Matsuri Okuda. ANI: Matsuri Okuda. MUS: Hiroya Watanabe. PRD: Animate Film, JC Staff. 40 mins. x 2 eps.

In medieval Japan, the constant battles between rival warlords have left the land ravaged and prey to evil; the spirit world is ever-present. When the great warlord Shingen Takeda dies, one of his ninja, Maro, tries to escape from the clan, and his best friend, Hikage, is sent to hunt him down. He comes to a village where people seem to have no memory of their earlier lives, and he falls in love with Aya, a woman he meets there; but he learns that it's really just a fattening ground for people who don't want to live because of past sadness. They are kept in a state of happy forgetfulness while being held as sacrificial food for a demonic giant spider that has drawn Maro into its coils. When he destroys the god and breaks the spell, his beloved Aya remembers her past sorrows and kills herself. The second part of the story, *Maro's Evil Fang*, released in 1989, reveals that the spider god was only part of a huge conspiracy to allow the Demon Kings of the Land and Sea to unite as one and unleash all the devils in the world on mankind. Through a ninja girl named Aya, who looks exactly like his dead love, and the ghost of Maro's beloved Kotone, Hikage learns that only by killing his friend can he prevent this evil, but Maro offers him the chance to become a Lord of Hell. After a final bloody battle, it seems that evil has been defeated; but on the road, Aya and Hikage take a baby from the arms of a dead woman and see that it looks exactly like Maro. Is evil simply reborn again and again? Based on an original story by Kei Kusunoki, creator of **Ogre Slayer** and **Yagami's Family Troubles**, this is an elegant and chilling story, much subtler than the blockbuster **Urotsukidoji**, with which it shares the rebirth-of-evil theory. **ⓥ**

YONA YONA PENGUIN *

2009. Movie. DIR: Rintaro. SCR: Tomoko Konparu. DES: Katsuya Terada, Cedric Babouche. ANI: Loïc Miermont, Stephane Brillon. MUS: Toshiyuki Honda. PRD: Madhouse, Shochiku, Denis Friedman Productions, Storm Lion. 85 mins.

Six-year-old Coco missses her daddy. Since he died, she's been going out late at night in the penguin suit he gave her, playing alone in the streets and trying to make sense of her loss. What can a flightless bird do when someone she loves flies far, far away? Coco needs a miracle: not the trashy tinsel kind you can buy in a toyshop, but the kind you make for yourself from the dreams and memories in your heart, with just a little help from others who need you.

Yona Yona Penguin uses similar materials to **My Neighbor Totoro**: a very small girl protagonist, secret worlds of childhood where myth and fantasy can walk the same path as the mundane, flight as metaphor and motif, inventive visuals, a wonderful score and an exquisite sense of pace and framing. It is first and foremost a delightful film for children, but in the hands of an intelligent filmmaker, a delightful film for children can speak to many others.

Adults will note many similarities to the work of director Rintaro's mentor Osamu Tezuka, especially in the use of vertical space and movement, the sense of enclosure and shadow as threat and prison, and the theme of the old and greedy perverting the boundless, unfocused energy of youth for their own ends. The transitions between the film's many levels are beautifully handled, both visually and in story terms. One early transition sequence is a stunning metaphor for modern childhood, a mad mix of commercialism and tradition, safety and danger, abundance and trashy excess.

The art direction and writing play with references across the spectrum of Asian and Caucasian culture, from the seven gods of good fortune to the hierarchy of the Heavenly Host, from *Dante's Inferno* to the subtleties of Dali and Escher, to baby-images in the style of Mabel Lucie Atwell or Anne Geddes. The Christian heaven is coolly surreal, like the foyer of some deranged yet tasteful megalomaniac corporation more interested in preserving its brand image than getting its hands dirty in the realms below. Disney references and a nod to singing duo The Peanuts jostle among many playful echoes and inventions in the film's other worlds. The heroine's hometown, seen in darkness like the one in Gisaburo Sugii's **Night on the Galactic Railroad** or Rintaro's night circus in **Neo-Tokyo**, is packed with fantastical architecture and the potential for danger.

The film has been screened at a number of festivals and cinemas, including the Barbican Cinema in London and in several U.S. cities, and released in France, Portugal, and Brazil. It's a coproduction with French company Denis Friedman Productions, previously known at home for work on *Asterix*.

Yona Yona Penguin is beautifully crafted, warmly humane, and generous to all its characters. It has the courage to see the world at a child's eye-level and move at a child's pace. It explicitly recognizes the real villain of every piece, the one all the guys in black hats stand in for, the gunman no-one can outdraw. Rintaro's film, made from a child's perspective, tells us that acceptance is the secret of joy—not a passive acceptance, but an open, dynamic response to the potential for good in every person, the possibilities in every situation, the magic at the heart of the world.

YONNA IN THE SOLITARY FORTRESS

2006. JPN: *Hanare Toride no Yonna*. Movie. DIR: Kengo Takeuchi. SCR: Kengo Takeuchi. DES: Kengo Takeuchi. ANI: Kengo Takeuchi. MUS: Toshio Okazawa. PRD: CoMix Wave Inc. 34 mins.

Yonna and her brother Stan were cast out of their village and now live in an abandoned castle, pursued by the authorities because of their special powers. The siblings rebuff all advances, even though the Government apparently wants to use their power to benefit others—so an agent infiltrates the castle while another makes an open approach. Kengo Takeuchi's solo project is obviously a labor of love and skill, a full CGI animation that shows his roots in Squaresoft and on *The Spirits Within* (**Final Fantasy**). But, beautiful as it looks and luscious as the backgrounds are, the story is slow and the character development minimal.

YOSHI

A pseudonym credited with almost all of the musical accompaniments to the erotic **Vanilla Series**, thereby inadvertently becoming one of the most prolific composers in anime.

YOSHIDA, TATSUO

1932–77. Born in Kyoto, Yoshida grew up in the war years, and found work in 1945 as an illustrator for newspapers including the *Kyoto Shinbun*. He subsequently moved into manga creation, and was one of the early innovators who realized the cross-promotional possibilities of television, founding the Tatsunoko studio in 1962 with his brothers Kenji and Toyohiro (AKA Ippei Kuri). His output included **Space Ace**, **Hutch the Honeybee**, and the **Time Bokan** series, although Tatsunoko is probably best known in the west for **Battle of the Planets** and **Speed Racer**.

YOSHIMOTO, KINJI

1966–. Animator and illustrator whose work has included character design on **La Blue Girl**, mechanical design on **Riding Bean**, and several collaborations with Satoshi Urushihara, most notably **Legend of Lemnear** and **Plastic Little**.

YOSHIMUNE

2006. TV series. DIR: Hiroaki Sato. SCR:

Hiroaki Sato, Junko Okazaki. DES: Hiroyuki Horiuchi, Shigemi Ikeda. ANI: Haruo Ogawara. MUS: Akifumi Tada. PRD: Gonzo, Atelier Musa, Chiba TV, TV Tokyo MX, TV Kanagawa, TV Aichi. 24 mins. x 24 eps.

Based on a pachinko slot machine game by Daito Giken, named after the eighth Tokugawa shogun, one of Japan's greatest rulers, this alternate-world comedy takes a "super-deformed," cartoonish slant on the Edo period. Samurai culture, historical dress and homes, and candlelit rooms co-exist with modern items like motorbikes, cell phones, microwave ovens, computers, and nightclubs—history, but with more conveniences. There's subplot in the style of **1001 NIGHTS**, with ruler Yoshimune sneaking out of his castle disguised as his alter ego Yoshi to go among his people and try to solve their problems. Charmingly silly.

YOTODEN *

1987. JPN: *Sengoku Kitan Yotoden*. AKA: *Civil War Chronicle of the Magic Blades*; *Wrath of the Ninja*. Video. DIR: Osamu Yamasaki. SCR: Sho Aikawa. DES: Kenichi Onuki, Junichi Watanabe. ANI: Kenichi Onuki. MUS: Seiji Hano. PRD: MTV, JC Staff. 40 mins. x 3 eps.

In 1582, demons possess the warlord Nobunaga Oda, acting through his adviser Ranmaru Mori. The only weapons that can fight the demons are three magical weapons—a sword, a pike, and a dagger—each in the possession of a different ninja clan. The Kasami clan holds the dagger, and when the demons wipe out the rest of her family, teenage Ayame assumes the masculine name Ayanosuke and sets out to avenge her clan. Sakon of the Hyuga clan has the sword, and Ryoma of the Hakagure clan the pike. As the demons try to prevent them from using the magic weapons, their loved ones are killed and their homes destroyed. They think they have foiled the plot by killing Nobunaga and Ranmaru, but the dead were only impersonators. Ranmaru has a master plan, centuries in the making, to build a bridge between hell and Earth and give the world over to the rule of the Demon God. The three blades reunite in a titanic battle at Azuchi Castle, where victory is won at a terrible cost (compare to **TIME STRANGER**, which approaches the same events from a science-fictional viewpoint).

As with most ninja stories, **SWORD FOR TRUTH**–creator Jo Toriumi's original *Yotoden* novel owes more to 20th-century fiction than 16th-century fact. Treading the same ground as **NINJA SCROLL**, it assumes that the real-life events of Japan's civil war went hand-in-hand with black magic, and that Nobunaga united Japan, not with the foreign guns of the history books, but with demon armies. Ninja with '80s haircuts duck and dive their way in and out of real historical events like superpowered Forrest Gumps with throwing-stars, led by an ice-cool heroine whose gorgeous voice is from the refreshingly unsqueaky Keiko Toda. The story ends with a demonic battle that carries visceral, ultraviolent overtones of the contemporary **UROTSUKIDOJI** series, also written by scenarist Aikawa. **OV**

YOU AND ME *

2011. JPN: *Kimi to Boku*. TV series. DIR: Mamoru Kanbe. SCR: Reiko Yoshida. DES: Masayuki Onchi, Masatoshi Kai, Tomoyuki Aoki, Yukie Inose. ANI: N/C. MUS: Elements Garden, Masato Nakayama. PRD: J.C.Staff, Aniplex, MOVIC, NAS, Square Enix, TV Tokyo. 24 mins. x 13 eps. (TV1), 24 mins. x 13 eps. (TV2).

Four boys, friends since kindergarten, still hang out together in high school. Then a half-Japanese, half-German, all-disruptive guy joins their class, and relationships with their girl classmates start to get complicated. Friendship, though, makes everyday life in high school survivable in this sweet story based on Kiichi Hotta's 2005 manga. It's not a harem anime, or a boys'-love anime. It's not especially well animated. It's just a lovely, emotionally honest story, feel-good anime without a guilty pleasure in sight. Although it couldn't be accused of hyper-realism—few teenage boys are this sensitive and sweet to each other—its fantasies of an idealized childhood will resonate with many an adult who wishes their high school years had been more like this. The same team worked on the second series *You and Me. Season 2 (Kimi to Boku. 2)* in 2012, except for music where Elements Garden's Masato Nakayama worked solo (as on **MY LITTLE MONSTER**).

YOU LOOK DELICIOUS

2010. JPN: *Miyanishi Tatsuya Gekijo: Omae Umaso da na*. AKA: *Tatsuya Miyanishi*

Theater: You Look Delicious. TV series, movie. DIR: Masaya Fujimori. SCR: Hiroaki Jinno, Osamu Murakami. DES: Yoshiaki Yanagida, Takashi Nakamura, Masayuki Sekine. ANI: Yoshiaki Yanagida. MUS: Tamiya Terashima. PRD: Ajia-Do, TV Tokyo. 5 mins. x 20 eps. (TV), 90 mins. (m).

Once upon a long, long time ago, there was a big, hungry tyrannosaur who found a lost baby ankylosaur. His first thought was "You look delicious!" But somehow, instead of eating it, he ended up adopting it. Tatsuya Miyanishi's delightful picture book is adapted in this **KIDS' ANIME**, which was first screened every weekday for a month, starting a week before the premiere of the movie *You Look Delicious* (*Omae Umaso da na*). This was made by the same core team as the series, somewhat extended to meet the demands of feature-length animation—chief animation director Yanagida headed up a team of ten animation directors for the movie. The movie story starts as a prequel to the series: a maiasaura hatches a lost egg and raises the infant tyrannosaur with her own baby, even though her terrified herd rejects the family. When the young tyrannosaur realizes his true nature, he leaves his adopted mother and sibling for their own good. Then he finds an ankylosaur hatchling ...

Comparable to the heartrending premise of **RINGING BELL**, the happy ending required for tinies makes this comforting viewing for adults. The big surprise of the movie is the total change in animation and design style. The series uses Miyanishi's quirky picture-book art and very limited animation; the movie is in the more rounded, semi-realistic style often used for kiddy anime features, with a much brighter, softer color palette.

YOU'RE UNDER ARREST! *

1994. JPN: *Taiho Shichauzo*. Video, TV series, movie. DIR: Hiroshi Watanabe, Kazuhiro Furuhashi, Junji Nishimura, Takeshi Mori. SCR: Michiru Shimada, Michiko Yokote, Kazuhisa Sakaguchi (TV), Masashi Sogo (m). DES: Atsuko Nakajima, Toshihiro Murata, Hiroshi Kato. ANI: Yasuhiro Aoki (TV), MUS: Ko Otani (TV), Kenji Kawai (m). PRD: Studio Deen, Toei, TBS. 30 mins. x 4 eps. (v), 25 mins. x 47 eps. (TV), 24 mins. x 1 ep. and 6 mins. x 20 eps. (special), 25 mins. x 26 eps. (TV2), 88 mins. (m), 26 mins. (v2).

Miyuki is a gentle, reserved young woman, but for all that she's an ace driver in her working life as one of Tokyo's police officers. Natsumi is hot-headed, impulsive, and disorganized. She too is a Tokyo police officer, in the motorcycle division, and, when the two are teamed up, she doesn't think she and Miyuki will ever hit it off. But from their first important case, a pursuit of a reckless driver with a deadly agenda, they come to rely on each other and value each other's good qualities.

This pretty, innocuous, and astoundingly sanitized cop show takes the mismatched-partners cliché, removes almost all jeopardy, and hopes to muddle through on infantile foolery, female flesh, and an anal attention to audio effects—particularly engine noises. Based on the manga by **OH MY GODDESS!**–creator Kosuke Fujishima, *YuA* flips incessantly between car chases and mawkish flirting at the station house, creating a peculiar combination of *CHiPs* and a school disco. The 1996 TV series that followed the four videos—quite literally, with the first episode numbered as episode 5—is pure soap opera, following day-to-day life at the station and expanding the roles of their colleagues, in particular Officer Ken Nakajima, whose romance with Miyuki forms an ongoing subplot. The episodes pack in much fan service and even a little violence, like Miyuki trying to electrocute a pervert, but there's nothing to merit real concern on these counts. A new series, *YuA: Special* (1999), comprised much shorter episodes, screened as part of the *Wonderful* program. The 1999 movie, directed by Nishimura, did much the same thing with a bigger budget for its story of an abandoned car full of weaponry and the danger that arises from its discovery. The series also spun off into audio dramas, wittily written by former **PATLABOR**-scenarist Michiko Yokote, including *Police Stories* and *Only One*. The latter CD features the girls getting jobs as the pop group "Tokyo Policewoman Duo," in which guise they record the worst song ever made, the "We Are Policewomen" rap. In taking the genre that gave us "Cop Killer" and using it to extol the virtues of driving safely, the song is the perfect summary of the series as a whole. It returned for a 26-episode TV season in spring 2001. In 2002, the show was also adapted into a

live-action TV series (*DE), and returned to anime form with *YUA: No Mercy* (AKA *YUA in America*), in which the girls are transferred to the LAPD, and end up chasing a former Japanese detective who has stolen Miyuki's car—not quite *The Shield*.

YOUMEX
Anime company established in 1985 by Junji Fujita, a former employee of the music company King Records. Youmex was a coproducer in several of the video anime of the 1980s and early 1990s, including **SLOW STEP**, **AD POLICE**, and **HUMMINGBIRDS**, although Youmex's achievements were marred by the financial difficulties it inherited from its collapsed **BUBBLEGUM CRISIS**–partner Artmic. The company was subsequently bought out by Toshiba EMI (AKA TOEMI), for whom Fujita went to work in 1998.

YOUNG ASHIBE
1991. JPN: *Shonen Ashibe*. TV series, video. DIR: Noboru Ishiguro. SCR: Daiki Ike, Toshiaki Sasae, Katsuhide Motoki. DES: Hiromi Morishita. ANI: Kiyotoshi Aoi. MUS: Toshiyuki Arakawa. PRD: Nippon Eizo, TBS. 8 mins. x 111 eps. (TV1), 8 mins. x 75 eps. (TV2). The story of a cute little boy and his pet white sea lion was a successful *Young Jump* 4-panel strip by Hiromi Morishita, selling five million copies of its six collected volumes by the end of 1992. The first TV series starring Chika Sakamoto in the leading role spun off 25 more episodes of *YA2* in 1992, with Minami Takayama taking over the role.

YOUNG FUJIMARU THE WIND NINJA
1964. JPN: *Shonen Ninja Kaze no Fujimaru*. AKA: *Young Fujimaru the Wind Ninja*. TV series. DIR: Daisaku Shirakawa, Kimio Yabuki, Takeshi Shirato, Hiromi Uchida, Michiru Takeda. SCR: Satoshi Iijima, Jiro Yoshino, Daisaku Shirakawa, Minoru Tanaka. DES: N/C. ANI: Daikichi Kusube, Akira Daikuhara. MUS: Koichi Hattori. PRD: Toei, NET. 25 mins. x 65 eps.
The first animated version of one of Sanpei Shirato's popular ninja manga about a young boy who is carried away by an eagle and brought up by ninja, who instruct him in secret combat techniques and almost magical fighting arts. The warlords of Japan are fighting over the mystical Book

of Dragon Smoke, a scroll detailing how to make special weapons (presumably gunpowder). Fujimaru becomes involved in the conflict with his pacifist love-interest, Midori, and fights against his rival, Jupposai of the Fuma clan, as well as the Iga ninja and the evil southern barbarians.

Shirato was determined to show Japanese life in the Tokugawa shogunate as faithfully as possible, with attention to historical detail, but, although the style of the TV series is quite realistic, it was aimed at a relatively young audience. Shirato's **SASUKE** follows the same pattern, though he would get to appeal to a more adult audience with **LEGEND OF KAMUI**. The original manga in *Bokura* magazine was originally known as *Ninja Clan* but had a name change for the anime to associate it closer with the show's sponsor—Fujisawa Pharmaceuticals.

YOUNG HANADA
2002. JPN: *Hanada Shonen Shi*. AKA: *History of Young Hanada*. TV series. DIR: Masayuki Ojima. DES: Yoshinori Kanemori. ANI: Satoshi Yoshimoto. MUS: Yoshihisa Hirano. PRD: Madhouse, NTV. 25 mins. x 25 eps. Elementary schoolboy Ichiro Hanada is the kind of kid who gets into constant trouble. He receives nine stitches on his head after he is hit by a truck, only to discover that his accident has given him the new ability to see ghosts. What's worse, they all want him to help them out with their unfinished business around his home village, in this lighthearted comedy from the manga in *Uppers* magazine by Makoto Isshiki. Although rather obscure in its home country, *Young Hanada* enjoyed a new lease on life in Asia, particularly in Taiwan, where it rode a trend born in equal parts of *The Sixth Sense* (1999) and a local Chinese cartoon, Wang Shaudi's *Grandma and Her Ghosts* (1998). Its sunny, simple rural backgrounds are deceptive—it won the Best Animation prize at the 2003 Asian Television Technical and Creative Awards. The theme songs were provided by the Backstreet Boys.

YOUNG KINDAICHI FILES
1996. JPN: *Kindaichi Shonen no Jiken Bo*. AKA: *Young Kindaichi's Casebook*. Movie, TV series. DIR: Daisuke Nishio. SCR: Takeya Nishioka, Michiru Shimada, Hiroshi Motohashi,

Akinori Endo, Toshiki Inoue. DES: Shingo Araki; Hidemi Kubo. ANI: Shingo Araki. MUS: Kaoru Wada. PRD: Toei Animation, Nippon TV. 90 mins. (m), 25 mins. x 148 eps. (TV), 90 mins. (m).

Hajime Kindaichi, grandson of a famous detective, swears on the name of his grandfather to solve every murder case he finds. He's 17, a bit of a delinquent with a bad record of attendance at his high school, but he's got a mind like a steel trap, a gift for sleight-of-hand, and a lot of help from childhood friend Miyuki Nanase.

Based on the 1992 manga in *Shonen Magazine* by Yozaburo Kanari and Fumiya Sato, *YKF* features the descendant of a famous sleuth—the Kosuke Kindaichi created by crime novelist Seishi Yokomizo in 1946, whose most famous cases include *The Man with Three Fingers* and the live-action movie *The House of Inugami* (1976). As with LUPIN III, there were legal wrangles with the indignant executors of the original, though these were resolved with an out-of-court settlement as the series' popularity steadily increased. The manga spun off into a 1995 live-action TV series, and the first volume was adapted into Nishio's anime movie *YKF: Murder at the Hotel Opera* (1996). *YKF* rode a post-*X-Files* wave of interest in detective stories, making it and rival CONAN THE BOY DETECTIVE two of the greatest anime hits of the 1990s. Rather than limiting the mysteries to the 25-minute sessions of single episodes, writers favored two- and three-part dramas, increasing the suspense and readily lending themselves to feature-length video releases. Just some of Kindaichi's TV cases include *The Waxworks Murders, Death by the Devil's Symphony*, and *The Killer on the Haunted Train*. Araki's designs for the 1997 TV series were revamped by Hidemi Kubo for the 1999 movie *Deep Blue Slaughter*, in which Kindaichi hunts a murderer stalking a newly built Okinawa beach-resort.

YOUNG MIYAMOTO MUSASHI

1982. JPN: *Shonen Miyamoto Musashi: Wanpaku Nitoryu*. AKA: *Young Miyamoto Musashi: Naughty Way of Two Swords*. TV special. DIR: Yugo Serikawa, Hideo Watanabe. SCR: Shizuo Nonami. DES: Kazumi Hattori, Hiroshi Wagatsuma. ANI: Hiroshi Wagatsuma, Moriyasu Yamaguchi, Satoshi Hirayama. MUS: N/C. PRD: Toei, Fuji TV. 84 mins.

Four-year-old Bennosuke sees his father, a great swordmaster, killed by an even better man, Hirata. Since he knows he isn't old enough or skilled enough to take revenge, he becomes Hirata's disciple. When he's mastered the secrets of the sword and invented the technique of fighting with two at once, he kills Hirata and assumes the name Musashi. Based on the life of Musashi Miyamoto (Miyamoto Musashi, 1584–1645), often said to be the greatest swordsman in Japanese history, author of *The Book of Five Rings*, and subject of Eiji Yoshikawa's famous series of novels. In this incarnation, however, his life bears an uncanny similarity to the plot of RINGING BELL. This anime version of Musashi's life was based on Renzaburo Shibata's novel *The Duellist*, with character designs lifted from Kazumi Hattori's later manga adaptation. See SWORD OF MUSASHI.

YOUNG PRINCESS DIANA

1986. JPN: *Niji no Kanata e: Shojo Diana-hi Monogatari*. AKA: *End of the Rainbow: Young Princess Diana Story*. TV special. DIR: Hidemi Kubo. SCR: Seiji Matsuoka. DES: Yutaka Arai. ANI: Oji Suzuki, Animation 501. MUS: N/C. PRD: Tachyon, Aubec, NTV, TV Asahi. 114 mins. Born in 1961, Diana Spencer is a child of the British aristocracy. Her parents divorce when she is six years old, and she goes to live with her father and grandmother. Sent away to boarding school, Diana is shy and withdrawn, but a sweet-natured girl who helps the maid with the washing-up and excels at pet care—winning the best-guinea-pig contest. Isolated when her father remarries, Diana throws herself into swimming and ballet, hoping that one day her prince will come. Then she meets Charles, the heir to the throne, never imagining that one day she will become his wife.

Screened a few days before the arrival of the real-life Charles and Diana on a royal visit to Japan, this could well be described as the highlight of scenarist Matsuoka's career—his later KAMA SUTRA hardly compares! The early life of the late Princess Diana is plundered with, in anime terms, only minor alterations; voiced by NAUSICAÄ-actress Sumi Shimamoto. The mind boggles at how this might have been "improved" with a few giant robots and invading aliens, but sadly it was not to be. The appeal is obvious to a Japanese audience reared on CINDERELLA and denied intrusive media access to their own royals—though the upbeat ending is particularly ironic considering the protagonist's later fate.

YOUNG TOKUGAWA IEYASU

1975. JPN: *Shonen Tokugawa Ieyasu*. DIR: Takeshi Tamiya, Kimio Yabuki. SCR: Hisao Okawa. DES: Shingo Araki, Takeshi Shirato. ANI: Shingo Araki, Shoji Iga. MUS: Takeo Watanabe. PRD: Toei Animation, NET (TV Asahi). 25 mins. x 20 eps.

At the age of six, young Takechiyo Matsudaira (the future Ieyasu Tokugawa) is involved in a hostage exchange between his beleaguered samurai family and the powerful Oda clan. At 14, he officially reaches manhood, and is given the name Motoyasu Matsudaira. He begins his military career by opposing the Oda clan before deciding to ally himself with its new leader, Nobunaga.

Historical series on TV are a safe bet—parents think they're educational and advertisers like to be associated with worthy cultural products. Tokugawa was the third of the three great warlords who ended Japan's Civil War period, Nobunaga Oda being the first. The series glamorizes his boyhood with demons and ninja, poking a finger at parents who thought it was all going to be highschool curriculum stuff. Manga spin-offs ran in *Terebiland* magazine, among others.

YOUNGER SISTER JUICE

2003. JPN: *Imotojiru*. Video. DIR: Ken Raika. SCR: Shinichiro Sawayama. DES: Mamito Tayama. ANI: Mamito Tayama. MUS: N/C. PRD: T-Rex, MS Pictures (Milky), Pink Pineapple, Office Take Off. 30 mins. x 2 eps. (v1), 40 mins. x 2 eps. (v2), 28 mins. x 2 eps. (v3). Akira has a new stepmother and three stepsisters. While Dad is on an archeological dig, Akira somehow winds up in bed with his stepmother and finds himself in the power of the Sumerian goddess Inanna. Inanna demands that he collect the love juices of his three sisters in cursed jars before the next full moon, or face a horrible fate.

For those with specific fetishes, an alternative version, *Older Sister Juice: Leave It to the Three Shirakawa Sisters* (*Anejiru: Shirakawa Sanshimai ni Omakase*), was made in

2006 by Pink Pineapple. This time the boy has been brought up by his grandmother but goes to live with his newly remarried mother, archeologist stepfather, and three hot older stepsisters. Same cursed jars, same supernatural treat. Unsurprisingly based on an erotic video game of the same title by Atelier Kaguya's Berkshire Yorkshire label, this led to a second two-part adventure in 2010: *Anejiru 2 The Animation: Shirakawa's Three Sisters Set Menu* (*Anejiru 2 THE ANIMATION: Shirakawa Sanshimai ni Omakase*). A substantial amount of footage from the 2006 video is reused in flashback, and the story continues with more older-sister sex after the curse is lifted. **DEVILMAN** also starts with a kid named Akira whose archeologist parents uncover ancient evil, but it's a lot more interesting than this. Go Nagai was in the business of creating new formulae, not merely exploiting old ones. **Ⓝ**

YOUTH LITERATURE

2009. JPN: *Aoi Bungaku*. AKA: *Blue Literature*. TV series. DIR: Morio Asaka, Tetsuro Araki, Shigeyuki Miya, Ryosuke Nakamura, Atsuko Ishizuka. SCR: Satoshi Suzuki, Ken Iizuka, Mika Abe, Sumino Kawashima, Atsuko Ishizuka, Yuji Kobayashi. DES: Takeshi Obata, Tite Kubo, Takeshi Konomi, Tomoyuki Shimizu, Mio Isshiki, Shinichi Uehara, Hidetoshi Kaneko. ANI: N/C. MUS: Hideki Tanuchi, Shusei Murai. PRD: Madhouse, Hakuhodo DY Media Partners, Happinet, McRay, MOVIC, MTI, Three Light, Visionaire. 24 mins. x 12 eps.

An animated adaptation of six classics of Japanese literature, including *No Longer Human* (*Ningen Shikkaku*) and **RUN MELOS** by Osamu Dazai, *Kokoro* by Soseki Natsume, *Hell Screen* (*Jigoku Hen*) and *The Spider's Thread* (*Kumo no Ito*) by Ryunosuke Akutagawa, and *In the Forest, Under Cherries in Full Bloom* (*Sakura no Mori no Mankai no Shita*) by Ango Sakaguchi. Although the overall quality of scripting is uneven, this is a valiant attempt to use anime to attract young people to classic literature. Compare to **ANIMATED CLASSICS OF JAPANESE LITERATURE**.

YOZAKURA QUARTET

2008. JPN: *Yozakura Shijuso*. AKA: *Quartet of Evening Cherry Blossom; Quartet of Cherry Blossoms in the Night*. TV series, video. DIR: Ko Matsuo. SCR: Jukki Hanada. DES: Satonobu Kikuchi. ANI: Satonobu Kikuchi. MUS: Akio Dobashi. PRD: Nomad, TBS. 24 mins. x 12 eps.

Three superpowered girls and one ordinary boy form a quartet of teen heroes defending the suburb of Sakurashin, a crossing point between the human and demon worlds. Suzuhito Yasuda's manga was first published in 2006 and is still running. The anime was less successful, but there was a three-part video series, *Yozakura Quarter—Sea of Stars* (*Hoshi no Umi*) in 2010.

YS *

1989. Video. DIR: Jun Kamiya, Takashi Watanabe. SCR: Tadashi Hayakawa, Katsuhiko Chiba. DES: Tetsuya Ishikawa, Hideaki Matsuoka, Hiroyuki Nishimura. ANI: Tetsuya Ishikawa, Hiroyuki Nishimura. MUS: Michio Fujisawa. PRD: Urban Project; Tokyo Kids. 30 mins. x 7 eps. (v1), 30 mins. x 4 eps. (v2).

Adol, a young swordsman in the magical kingdom of Esteria, must save the world from demonic destruction by gathering six sacred books and bringing them to the Goddesses on Precious Mountain. Based on the NES game by Nippon Falcom that has also spun off a manga by Sho Hagoromo, a series of novels, and other merchandise. *Ys: Palace of the Celestial Gods* (1992, *Tenku no Shinden*) was a second video series based on the events of the second game. Set on the flying island of Ys, it featured Adol in another quest. There was also a 60-minute animated music video, *Ys Special Collection: All About Falcom*.

YU-GI-OH *

1998. JPN: *Yugi-O*. AKA: *King of Games*. TV series, movie. DIR: Hiroyuki Kadono, Yoko Ikeda, Satoshi Nakamura, Keiji Hayakawa, Kunihisa Sugishima. SCR: Junji Takegami, Toshiki Inoue, Yasuko Kobayashi, Kenichi Kanemaki, Katsuhiko Chiba. DES: Shingo Araki, Michi Himeno. ANI: Masayuki Takagi. MUS: BMF. PRD: Studio Gallop, Nippon Animation, TV Asahi. 25 mins. x 27 eps. (TV1), 25 mins. x 224 eps. (TV2), 25 mins. (m1), 25 mins. x 180 eps. (TV3), 25 mins. x 154 eps. (TV4), 101 mins. (m2; 90 mins. in U.S.), 61 mins. (m3).

Game-mad Japanese boy Yugi is victimized by the school bullies and obsessed with an ancient Egyptian Millennium Puzzle. The successful player acquires a second thoroughly evil and nasty persona. Yugi can now transform into a vengeful, powerful figure; he can bring game monsters to life and deal out retribution to local evildoers, as well as to those who used to bully him, by forcing them to play a "dark game" on his terms. When he accidentally awakens the Guardian of Darkness, he and his friends are dragged into an adventure that features his own father reincarnated as a Pegasus and a showdown at a real-world gaming convention against his archenemy, who in our dimension is the president of the Industrial Illusion Company. Armed with another Egyptian artifact, the Millennium Eye, Yugi becomes the strongest duelist, in an anime/manga/collectible card game tie-in commissioned in the wake of **POKÉMON**. Based on the manga by Kazuki Takahashi serialized in *Shonen Jump*, it was followed by several more seasons, including *YO: Duel Monsters* (which ran until 2004), *YO: GX* (2004–8), and *YO: 5D's* (2008–11). This is a kids-get-even fantasy so some sequences are quite violent—like the one where our hero pours petrol down the trousers of an armed robber and keeps him at bay with a cigarette lighter. A 30-minute movie formed part of 1999's Toei Anime Fair bill, and the franchise achieved its arguable peak with the release of a full-length feature, *YO: The Movie—Pyramid of Light* (2004). The later film, *YO: Bonds Beyond Time* (2010), was also shown in cinemas despite barely scraping feature length, and 11 minutes of that constituted the story so far. Such excesses, however, were deemed necessary for an installment that used a complex time-travel plot to unite the original Yugi with his successors Jaden Yuki and Yusei Fudo, the heroes of the later series, in order to defeat a common enemy. Regardless, this was memorably panned by one British film magazine as nothing more than "a shouty advert for more stuff you don't want." **Ⓥ**

YUGO THE NEGOTIATOR *

2004. DIR: Seiji Kishi, Shinya Hanai. SCR: Kazuharu Sato, Kenichi Kanemaki. DES: Takahiko Matsumoto, Kenichi Imaizumi. ANI: N/C. MUS: N/C. PRD: G&G Direction, Artland, Kid's Station. 25 mins. x 13 eps.

Based on the manga by Shinji Makari and Shu Akana, this is the story of Yugo Beppu, a negotiator who works to free hostages, resolve standoffs, and save lives in tense situations all around the world. Yugo is a young man of high intelligence who speaks many languages fluently; he is physically and mentally strong enough to withstand any form of torture; however, the qualities that make him stand out above others in his field are his humanity, compassion, and his superb instinct for when and how far to trust others. His missions in this series take him first to Pakistan, where he agrees to negotiate for the lost-cause handover of a girl's father, and then Siberia, where he is tasked with locating a rich man's lost granddaughter, whose wing of the family was separated from her relatives by the upheavals of the Russian revolution.

Yugo has little of the menace-of-the-week set-ups so common to anime. Instead, it divides into two broad story arcs, more like two three-hour movies than a 13-episode TV series, and each animated by a different production team. It also flies in the face of many anime conventions, without recourse to the robots or science-fictional distractions of many other shows. In its reliance on tension and psychological profiling, its portrayal of a man of peace in a brutal world, Yugo is one of the more interesting anime of modern times, mixing up the intelligent protagonist of **MASTER KEATON** with real-world issues far removed from much of modern anime's content.

YUKI

1981. Movie. DIR: Tadashi Imai. SCR: Akira Miyazaki. DES: Tetsuya Chiba. ANI: Shinichi Tsuji. MUS: Chito Kawachi. PRD: Mushi, Nikkatsu. 89 mins.

Demons threaten the peaceful existence of a group of peasants who live in Japan's far north during the Muromachi period (1338–1573). However, the villagers have the aid of Yuki, a snow fairy who dwells among them in human form, and her beloved horse, Fubuki (Snowstorm). Though based on the story by Takasuke Saito, itself drawing on **JAPANESE FOLK TALES**, elements of this anime seem to coincidentally foreshadow the far more famous **PRINCESS MONONOKE**.

YUKI TERAI—SECRETS *

2000. JPN: *Yuki Terai Secret Films*. TV series. DIR: Kenichi Kutsugi. SCR: N/C. DES: N/C. ANI:

N/C. MUS: N/C. PRD: Fuji TV, Frog Entertainment. 79 mins.

The virtual idol Yuki Terai is a lively 17-year-old who supposedly lives just outside Tokyo. She stars in this entirely computer-generated animation made up of six short segments, mostly SF and fantasy, but including a sequence where she is a singer in a French café-bar and another where she must shut down a critical machine at the other end of a space ship—yes, this involves running down a very long corridor while klaxons blare and lights flash. There is also a trailer for an unmade World War II epic. These disparate shorts are little more than showreels for computer animators, made at that point in the early 21st century when developments in computer animation could still surprise on a monthly basis. The production credits imply that they were first seen as part of a larger show on Fuji TV, hence our classification of them as "television," and neither the "video" nor "movie" that some foreign distributors have attempted to imply. In the wake of *Final Fantasy: The Spirits Within* (2001), of course, computer animation has gone underground again, and prides itself on *not* being noticed, making Yuki Terai one of the creations of the brief flurry of CG-hype that also gave us **VISITOR, AURORA, MALICE DOLL,** and **BLUE REMAINS**. The rights for *Yuki Terai* were picked up by Escapi and released in the U.K. and northern Europe, alongside DVDs of similar showreels, *Virtual Stars* (1999) and *Cybervenus Feifei* (2001). The discs are sometimes sold under the umbrella label for the whole series: *Virtually Real.*

YUKIKAZE *

2002. JPN: *Sento Yosei Yukikaze*. AKA: *Battle Fairy Yukikaze*. Video. DIR: Masahiko Okura. SCR: Hiroshi Yamaguchi, Yumi Tada, Masahiko Okura, Masashi Sogo, Ikuto Yamashita, Seiji Kio. DES: Yumi Tada, Masahiro Aizawa, Koichi Hashimoto, Ikuto Yamashita, Seiji Kio, Atsushi Takeuchi, Kanetake Ebikawa, Masahiko Sekino, Masaru Kato. ANI: Koichi Hashimoto, Masahiro Sekino. MUS: Satoshi Mishiba, Dogen Shiono (The KANI), Clara. PRD: Bandai Visual, Victor Entertainment, Gonzo. 25 mins. x 5 eps. (v1), 30 mins. (v2). Thirty-three years after opening an interdimensional gate above the Ross Ice Shelf in Antarctica, and attacking a supply plane

to McMurdo Station, the alien JAM have been beaten back to the other side of the portal, the green-skyed, twin-sunned world of Fairy. The Fairy Air Force, an organ of the United Nations, continues the fight, which has been all but forgotten by the rest of Earth-bound humanity. One of its pilots is Lt. Rei Fukai, whose charge is a fighter plane so advanced it has developed sentience—the titular Yukikaze. Fukai is a member of the FAF's Special Air Force, a small unit devoted to observing and gathering data on the aerial battles between the JAM and the FAF, but ordered to never interfere, lest doing so jeopardize the collected information. However, Fukai and Yukikaze are increasingly drawn into battle with the JAM, an enemy humanity has never seen clearly and about which it knows very little. In an ideological twist reminiscent of **GUNBUSTER**, the JAM are a machine-based race who regarded humans as mere adjuncts to the machines they created but who have realized their mistake and have begun to change and adapt their strategy and tactics, much to the detriment of humans. As the story progresses, Fukai and Yukikaze, with their unique rapport, assume a pivotal role in the war against the JAM.

Just as Shoji Kawamori did for **MACROSS** *Plus*, the team based its fighter technology on study visits to the Komatsu air force base, so the mecha designs are state-of-the-art and the whole show is imbued with a passion for *Top Gun* antics—perhaps explaining why Tom Cruise himself would eventually option the original novel in 2013 for a putative *Yukikaze* movie project. The Gonzo team pulls out all the visual stops, with the work of color coordinator Eriko Murata looking particularly strong and providing a wonderful sense of atmosphere—compare to **BLUE SUBMARINE NO. SIX** and **AREA 88**.

The series began as a collection of linked short stories published in 1984 by Chohei Kanbayashi, in which the JAM have their portal at the *north* pole, and which revealed that Yukikaze ("Blizzard") took its name from the most famous destroyer in the Japanese navy in World War II. Publicity at the time of *Yukikaze's* American release mystifyingly boasted that it had recently won the "Japanese Nebula" Seiun award, although the winner was a 20th-anniversary revised edition—its original publication date being a much surer indicator of its cutting-edge originality, since many foreign audiences may have otherwise assumed it to be a rip-off of the movie *Stealth* (2005). Anniversaries seem to have played an important part in the commissioning process, since *Yukikaze*'s anime incarnation went into production to mark the 20th anniversary of Bandai's Emotion video label. Much was made at the time of its amazingly realistic animation of planes; the show does seem to spend an inordinate amount of time presenting fetishized views of aerial battles, which may have been entertaining then but may seem to the more jaded to look like so many modern-day combat flight simulators.

Yukikaze also generated an odd spin-off in the form of *Yukikaze Mave-chan* (2005), a one-shot video based on some doodles drawn by designer Ikuto Yamashita when his hard drive was temporarily down. Elfin Mave is one of a group of girls fighting the alien Jam in another world. When she runs into a strange boy, she naturally leaps into the attack with her knives. Her companion Super Sylph rescues the boy, who turns out to be a human called Rei; he has no idea how he was sucked into the girls' world, because he was just minding his own business at an anime convention. It turns out that the world was created by the desires of anime fans, and the girls represent the archetypes fans like best—at least it's honest!

Mave is a happy person, fun to be around, but her two big knives warn anyone not to mess with her. Super Sylph is a gentle, quiet girl, tall and curvy. Sly and slinky chatterbox Sylph bickers constantly, and childlike Fand is strange and silent. But the worst danger is not from aliens but from the fans' minds shifting on to home and dinner—as the convention draws to an end, the world created from its collective dream starts to collapse. An intriguing adaptation of the guilt trip attitude of **KEY OF THE METAL IDOL**, itself an emotional approach to the brutal realities of the entertainment industry.

YUKIMURO, SHUNICHI
1941–. Born in Kanagawa Prefecture, he enrolled in the Eighth Scenario Writing Workshop for television drama, "graduating" in 1961. His early work was for Nikkatsu, although subsequently his name has somehow found its way onto over 3,000 scripts for television, including many anime such as **SAZAE-SAN**, **KIMBA THE WHITE LION**, **MOOMINS**, and **SPOOKY KITARO**.

YUME-IRO PATISSIÈRE *
2009. AKA: *Dream-Colored Pastry Chef; Rainbow-Colored Pastry Chef*. TV series. DIR: Iku Suzuki. SCR: Takashi Yamada, Yoshimi Narita. DES: Yukiko Akiyama, Eiko Tsunoda, Yoshimi Narita, Kuniaki Nemoto. ANI: Yukiko Akiyama, Hideaki Isa, Kenji Matsuoka, Koji Yamagata. MUS: Megumi Ohashi. PRD: Studio Pierrot. 20 mins. x 50 eps. (TV1), 20 mins. x 13 eps. (TV2).

Fourteen-year-old Ichigo wants to be a top pastry chef like her grandmother. When she gets the opportunity to enroll in the elite Saint Marie Academy, a specialist patisserie school, she can't believe her luck. Here she enters a magical world—not simply through the new friends she makes and the wonderful teachers, but thanks to the Sweets Spirits, magical beings who choose human partners to make their dreams come true.

Based on Natsumi Matsumoto's manga of 2008, this is a sweet, pretty series for girls and was successful enough to get a second series, *Yumeiro Patissière SP (Special) Professional*, in 2010. Here Ichigo and friends graduate from the junior classes into high school, to hone their cooking skills further and deal with the challenges of teenage life—romance, dreams, and difficulties. The production team is largely unchanged—there's a new art director, **GUN X SWORD**'s Nemoto, and chief animation director Akiyama hands his chair to Yamagata and helms the opening and ending sequences. Compare to **ANTIQUE BAKERY**, which similarly explores the magical world of cake.

YUMERIA *
2004. TV series. DIR: Keitaro Motonaga. SCR: Makoto Uezu, Yosuke Kuroda. DES: Shinobu Nishioka, Yasuhiro Moriki. ANI: N/C. MUS: N/C. PRD: Studio Deen, BS-i. 24 mins. x 12 eps.

Tomokazu Mikuri discovers that in his dreams he can visit the alternate world of Yumeria, populated by pretty girls, where he is welcomed as a hero who can save the oppressed kingdom from destruction at the hands of the Faydoom invaders. Sub–**TENCHI MUYO!** "comedy" soon ensues, as Tomokazu and a number of real-world associates get to travel to the alternate world and, well, hang out. Not an erotic anime, although it is loaded with puerile excuses to ogle girls, many of who either appear underage, act like they might as well be, or are Tomokazu's relatives. Based on a video game—*yume* is Japanese for dream.

YU-NO *
1998. Video. DIR: Katsuma Kanazawa. SCR: Osamu Kudo. DES: Tetsuro Aoki. ANI: Takeo Takahashi, Yasushi Nagaoka. MUS: N/C. PRD: Pink Pineapple, KSS. 30 mins. x 4 eps.

Takuya falls for the woman his father marries after his mother's death. Yes, it's yet another almost-but-not-quite incest story; compare to **CREAM LEMON** and **COOL DEVICES**. Ⓝ

YUN-YUN PARADISE
1995. JPN: *YunYun Paradise*. Video. DIR: Hiroshi Yamakawa. SCR: N/C. DES: N/C. ANI: Inatsugu Shimizu. MUS: N/C. PRD: Pink Pineapple, AIC. 30 mins.

This "love comedy" features Yun-Yun, a suspiciously young-looking Chinese girl, falling in love with a Japanese boy. Based on a novel from the same Napoleon imprint that gave us **EROTIC TORTURE CHAMBER**. Ⓝ

YURUANI?
2011. TV series. DIR: Various. SCR: Various. DES: Various. ANI: Various. MUS: Various. PRD: FROGMAN Co., DLE, NTV. 30 mins. x 22 eps.

An anthology show created by DLE, collecting half a dozen flash-animated short gag manga including Kenshi Hirokane's **WEEKLY SHIMAKO** based on his successful business manga, Haguki's **WIFE PIGEON**, **FLOP-CAT** by Masayuki Kitamichi, Hidekichi Matsumoto's *Really! Mr Reibai*, Yukari Taninami's **OK!! EKODA** about a single woman in Tokyo drifting through the clubs and bars using feigned silliness to prey on men, and a short version of school gag cartoon **DOUBLE J** by Eiji Nonaka (episodes 12–22 only). *Shiodome Cable TV*, an original creation by NTV, was also included.

YURUMATES
2009. TV series, video. DIR: Tomohiro Tsukimisato, Tomohiro Yamanishi, Hamu Arai,

Yoshihide Yuzumi. scr: Yoshihide Yuzumi, Shinsuke Takahashi. des: saxyun, Takeshi Oda, Akiko Ishida. ani: Hamu Arai, Yoriko Yamazaki, Aya Tabuchi, Takeshi Oda. mus: Shuji Katayama. prd: Triple A, indeprox, indigo line, Yokohama Studio, C2C, Takeshobo. 3 mins. x 12 eps., 3 mins. special (v1), 34 mins. (v2), 3 mins. x 13 eps. (TV1), 3 mins. x 13 eps. (TV2).

Country girl Yurume moves to Tokyo to study at a cram school for the entrance exams for Tokyo University. She rents a small room in Maison du Wish, an old house where three other students—two girls and a guy—live the slacker lifestyle. The four become friends and share the experiences of student life, from coping with the extremes of Tokyo weather to cooking and fending for themselves. Based on a four-panel gag strip by saxyun, each episode is a tiny slice of student life (EVERYDAY ANIME). This means that, unlike the similarly themed MAISON IKKOKU, there is no time to develop the characters, let alone romances between them, but the simply animated series presents everyday tropes of Japanese life charmingly. The series was bundled onto a DVD with a special bonus episode and followed in 2011 by the six-episode DVD *Yurumates Ha?* In 2012 Yurume, having flunked her extrance exam, gets to try again on TV in *Yurumates 3D* and follow-up series *Yurumates 3D Plus*.

YURUYURI *

2011. aka: *Easygoing; Slow Yuri*. TV series. dir: Masahiko Ota. scr: Takashi Aoshima, Hideaki Koyasu, Itsumi Kono, Kenji Sugihara, Takamitsu Kono. des: Chiaki Nakajima, Shunsuke Suzuki, Studio Fuga. ani: Chiaki Nakajima, Junichiro Taniguchi, Tsubasa Ito, Shinji Ochi, Shinya Ojiri. mus: Yasuhiro Misawa. prd: Dogakobo, Nanamori, Cospa, Dax Production, Pony Canyon, Showgate, TV Tokyo. 24 mins. x 12 eps. (TV1), 24 mins. x 12 eps. (TV2).

Akari Azaka and three friends are the only members of the Amusement Club at this middle school. Unlike most Japanese school clubs, the Amusement Club has no stated aim or interest—its members just amuse themselves in whatever way they please. There are lesbian/bisexual overtones but no explicit depictions of sexual activity.

How do you reproduce a titan of *moe*,

a mega-hit cash cow like **K-ON** or **THE MELANCHOLY OF HARUHI SUZUMIYA**? That's a question that has kept many an anime studio burning the midnight oil. The answer, obviously, is to find something new that several cute girls can do together. *Yuruyuri* takes a unique approach in that it shows very cute girls doing absolutely nothing (except ponder their potential sexual orientations) in humorous ways. Based on Namori's ongoing 2008 manga, this is a pretty and harmless way to waste half an hour—chicken soup for the *yuri*-addicted soul (ARGOT AND JARGON), though those who like some story and character development with their anime will find it unsatisying. A second series, *Yuruyuri ♪♪*, was made by the same core team and aired in 2012, and a spin-off manga *Omuroke* appeared in the same year.

YUTAKA OZAKI FROM THIS RULE ... GRADUATION

2004. jpn: *Kono Shihai kara no Sotsugyo—Ozaki Yukata*. Video. dir: Junichi Hayama. scr: N/C. des: N/C. ani: Junichi Hayama. mus: Yukata Ozaki. prd: Karinto Factory, Isotope, Toei Animation. 43 mins.

Age and youth were important factors in the music of Yutaka Ozaki. He captivated the hearts of an entire generation of Japanese teenagers, but his obsession with teenage years as the *only* worthwhile time hid a great insecurity within himself. Ozaki sung of the empty victory of graduation, but never finished school himself; he wrote of adults waiting to seize children's minds, but took their money himself as part of the adult music machine. Ozaki was that saddest of popular heroes, a teen hero who preached nonconformity, who could only watch in terror as he slowly outgrew his audience.

This musical tribute-biography of the legendary Japanese singer/guitarist is narrated by his long-time producer Akira Sudo over five tracks by Ozaki. His most famous is "Graduation" itself, which begins as a valedictory song, self-congratulatory anthem: "At last we're free from fighting the adults in disbelief, we have the freedom we so desperately wanted." But "Graduation" turns nasty very fast, as the happy, proud student suddenly starts asking difficult questions: "What happened to our dreams? Where do we put our anger

now?" The threshold of adulthood is not regarded with hope or eagerness, but with a bitter elegy for, literally, the best years of the singer's life.

This TV special covers the era from before Ozaki's debut up to his Tokyo Dome appearance in 1988. In 1992 he was found drunk and unconscious in a Tokyo alleyway, admitted to and then discharged from hospital, and died a few hours later. He was just 26. Toei's *ga-nime* (ARGOT AND JARGON) series website gives the length as 43 minutes, but several sales sites have 35 minutes.

YUYAMA, KUNIHIKO

1952–. Born in Tokyo and developing an interest in animation while still at high school, Yuyama worked as an inbetweener on episodes of **STAR BLAZERS** and **BRAVE RAIDEEN**. He was a concept artist and storyboarder on the foreign coproduction *Barbapapa* (1973) and joined Aoi Productions in 1978. The same year, he had his directorial debut while working for Aoi on **GALAXY EXPRESS 999**, and soon struck up a successful working partnership with the screenwriter Takeshi Sudo on **GOSHOGUN**. By 1982, he had been promoted to "chief director," an overseeing role on **GIGI AND THE FOUNTAIN OF YOUTH**. While remaining in TV during the 1980s, he also played a leading role in anime's exodus into video. His work showed a mastery of elements for a female audience, most obvious in his **THREE MUSKETEERS** spin-off, *Aramis' Adventure*. After his underrated **USHIO AND TORA**, he gained true fame through his involvement with two later works—**SLAYERS** and **POKÉMON**.

YUYUSHIKI *

2013. aka: *Yuyu Style*. TV series. dir: Kaori. scr: Natsuko Takahashi, Pierre Sugiura, Sayaka Harada. des: Hisayuki Tabata. ani: Majiro, Reiko Nozaki, Keisuke Kojima, Akiko Matsuo, Atsushi Hasebe. mus: Asuka Sakai. prd: Kinema Citrus, Tezuka Pro, Tokyo MX TV, Tsuyoshi Kusano Design, Art Box, Husio Studio. 25 mins. x 13 eps.

Three schoolgirls hang out and talk about life, in an occasionally funny gag anime that often centers on their life in the school Data Processing Club. Based on a manga by Komata Mikami, serialized in *Manga Time Kirara* magazine.

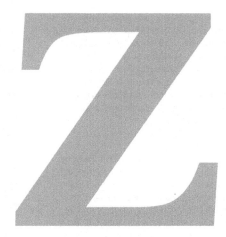

Z-MIND *

1999. JPN: *Shishunki Shojo Gattai Robo Zee-Mine*. AKA: *Adolescent Pretty-Girl Synchro Robot Z-Mine*. Video. DIR: Yasuhiro Matsumura. SCR: Fuyunori Gobu. DES: Kamo Namimaru, Kenta Aoki. ANI: N/C. MUS: Toshiki Inoue. PRD: Sunrise. 25 mins. x 6 eps.

Ayame, on her way home from viewing the cherry blossoms, is attacked by strange men and dragged, along with three other girls, into a new role as a transforming-robot pilot. It was made in a deliberate 1970s style (compare to the '60s retro of **GATE KEEPERS**), even down to a mysterious male who pops up to give advice (shades of *Charlie's Angels*). Displaying all the hallmarks of an **EVANGELION** clone that arrived too late, only to discover that the TV boom had slumped, it sidled out sheepishly onto video.

Z/X IGNITION *

2014. JPN: *Z/X*. AKA: *Zillions of Enemy X*. TV series. DIR: Yuji Yamaguchi. SCR: Kurasumi Sunayama. DES: Junko Watanabe, Yasuhiro Yamako. ANI: Junko Watanabe. MUS: Yasuharu Takanashi. PRD: Telecom Animation Film. 24 mins. x 12 eps.

Five dimensional portals open and monsters from man's darkest fantasies surge out to devastate the world. After three years of research mankind comes up with a new weapon—a card that can control the monsters they call Z/X and make them fight for humans. Although these card devices are supposed to be available only to the forces of law and order, kids and teens get hold of them and use them to stage fights. Meanwhile a motley band of inter-dimensional heroes fights to save the world, or at least the Japanese bit of it.

Yes, it's **POKÉMON**, but nastier, and with less narrative clarity. Based on a collectible card game, this apology for a coherently plotted show pitches elves, angels, magical beasts, dinosaurs, high school kids, and Alexander the Great into the city of Kobe to fight it out with lots of flashy lights and sharp objects. There's a character from another world who is still described as half-Japanese and half-German. The game which inspired this, by Nippon Ichi Software and Broccoli, was given away for free at card shops and game events in Japan and made available to print online. Judging from the anime, we think this is still too expensive, but there's also a manga. We understand the title should be pronounced *ZEX*, though we can think of a few other short snappy terms to describe it. **V**

ZAION: I WISH YOU WERE HERE *

2001. AKA: *I Wish You Were Here*. TV series. DIR: Seiji Mizushima. SCR: Natsuko Takahashi. DES: Yasuhiro Oshima. ANI: Yasuhiro Oshima, Yasufumi Soejima. MUS: N/C. PRD: Gonzo. 25 mins. x 4 eps.

In May 2002, a terrorist group sets off a gas explosion in Atlanta, Georgia. It is the first of many incidents across the U.S., though the perpetrators' motives are a mystery. Only unclear photographs of (surprise, surprise) a "mysterious girl" provide any clue. They seem to be linked in some way to Project I, a top secret operation by an international collective of scientists, who are rumored to be working on a "Multi-purpose Operative Being" experiment in sentient cybernetics. A mixture of conspiracies and espionage from Gonzo, combining CG elements of the studio's earlier **BLUE SUBMARINE NO. SIX** with the identity crisis of **SERIAL EXPERIMENTS LAIN**.

ZAKURO *

2010. JPN: *Otome Yokai Zakuro*. AKA: *Maiden Spirit Zakuro*. TV series. DIR: Chiaki Kon. SCR: Mari Okada, Mayumi Morita. DES: Shinya Hasegawa, Hiroshi Kato, Izumi Yasuki. ANI: Shinya Hasegawa, Junko Yamanaka, Yuko Matsushita. MUS: Masaru Sugimoto. PRD: JC Staff, Aniplex, Lantis, NAS, TV Tokyo. 24 mins. x 13 eps.

In an alternate 19-century Japan, humans and *yokai* magical beings live side-by-side, and sometimes even interbreed. Three young soldiers are assigned to special duty with the Ministry of Spirit Affairs. They will partner three half-*yokai*, half-human girls (included the eponymous fox-eared heroine) to investigate and resolve issues arising between the two cultures, in the interests of justice and social harmony.

Lily Hoshino's original 2006 manga from *Comic Birz* magazine raises issues still current in Japan, about the cost of integration with alien cultures, the problems of racism, and the fear of obliteration by greater powers. It also has undercurrents of the gap between the very different worlds of modernist "human" boys and traditional "spirit" girls (an allegory explored elsewhere in the likes of **SAKURA WARS** and **VIRGIN FLEET**), and a bawdier, rural culture whose natural joy and openness is being destroyed by the pretensions and prejudices of the modern world—an idea familiar everywhere in anime from **Pom Poko** to **Ushio and Tora**. Elegantly designed, skillfully directed by Kon (who is already in danger of getting a reputation for offbeat, saucy comedy with **Arakawa Under the Bridge** and **Junjo Romantica**), and with lovable characters, this is a very appealing show.

ZAMBOT 3

1977. JPN: *Muteki Chojin Robot Zambot 3*. AKA: *Invincible Superman Zambot 3*. TV series. DIR: Yoshiyuki Tomino, Minoru Onodani, Susumu Yukita, Takao Yotsuji, Shinya Sadamitsu, Kazuyuki Hirokawa, Kazuya Yamazaki. SCR: Fuyunori Gobu, Yoshihisa Araki, Soji Yoshikawa. DES: Yoshikazu Yasuhiko, Ryoji Hirayama, Studio Nue. ANI: Tadaichi Iuchi, Green Box, Kazuo Tomozawa. MUS: Takeo Watanabe, Hiroshi Matsuyama. PRD: Sunrise, Nagoya TV (TV Asahi). 25 mins. x 23 eps.

The last descendants of an extraterrestrial race take refuge on 19th-century Earth when their homeworld of Bial is destroyed by the treacherous Gaizoku. Several generations later, a Gaizoku advance force led by "Killer the Butcher" attacks Earth, and the local population accuses the descendants of the original refugees of bringing down trouble on the planet. They decide to use the ships their fathers arrived in to fight the mechanical monsters. These ships include the giant robot Zambot 3, made up by combining three different machines. Young Kappei, the robot's pilot, is assisted by Uchita and Keiko. The enemy has a very nasty way of killing; they implant explosive devices in their prisoners' bodies and can set them off at any time, even after the prisoners have returned to their homes and families. The tragic climax has Uchita and Keiko killed in a valiant effort to fight off the enemy, presaging the angst to come in Tomino's **Gundam**, for which this can reasonably be regarded as a test run. Notable for beginning as a lighthearted parody of earlier robot shows, before descending into tragedy—compare with **Gunbuster** and **Evangelion**. **Ⓥ**

ZANKAN

1996. JPN: *Mato Kidan Zankan*. AKA: *Killer Mischief*. Video. DIR: Motoaki Isshu. SCR: N/C. DES: N/C. ANI: Sugiko Enkai. MUS: N/C. PRD:

Pink Pineapple, KSS. 30 mins. x 2 eps. At the turn of the 21st century, Earth is conquered by demons, and only the two sexy "Riot" girls can save the universe, by having lots of sex. That's a surprise. Based on a manga by **Trouble Evocation**–creator Ryoga Ryuen. **Ⓝ**

ZATCH BELL *

2003. JPN: *Kinshoku no Zatch; Konjiki no Zatch Bell*. AKA: *Gash Bell; Golden Zatch Bell*. TV Series, movie. DIR: Tetsuji Nakamura, Atsuji Shimizu. SCR: Atsushi Yamatoya, Hiro Masaki, KOHEIMUSHI, Takashi Yamada, Yoshimi Narita, Yuji Hashimoto. DES: Ken Otsuka. ANI: Ken Otsuka, Hideki Hashimoto. MUS: Ko Otani. PRD: Fuji TV, Toei Animation, Yomiko Advertising Inc. 25 mins. x 140 eps. (TV), 85 mins. (m1), 83 mins. (m2).

There can be only one, and that doesn't just apply in *Highlander*. The *mamono*, a race of tiny demons, is trying to find a new ruler. Candidates are sent into the human world to pick a human master and then fight other demon contenders, using spells from their differentcolored magic books, until only one is left alive. Perky little blond demon Zatch started out wanting to win so he could be a benevolent demon king and stop them fighting each other, but then lost all memory of his past life: clues to the past are hidden in his magical red book. He pairs up with lonely, apathetic schoolboy Kiyomaro Takamine, who is isolated at school because his classmates are jealous of his intelligence. The scene is thereby set for another tale of a child with a strange playmate, combining the otherworldly mentor of **Hikaru's Go** with the seemingly endless quest for material acquisition of **Pokémon**. It's perhaps no coincidence that Zatch's voice actress is Ikue Otani, the voice of Pikachu. The series also spawned two movies, *Konjiki no ZB: Unlisted Demon 101* (*KnoZB: 101 Banme no Mamono*, 2004), in which Zatch and Kiyomaro stumble into another world and risk being stuck there forever unless they can solve a crime, and *KnoZB: Attack of the Mechavulcan* (*KnoZB: Mechavulcan no Raishu*, 2005), in which Zatch's friend Vulcan 300 is transformed into a giant menacing robot. Based on the manga by Makoto Raiku in *Shonen Jump*.

ZEGAPAIN *

2006. TV series. DIR: Masami Shimoda. SCR: Mayori Sekijima, Ken Oketani, Sadayuki Murai, Masashi Kubota, Katsuhiko Takayama. DES: Akihiko Yamashita, Rei Nakahara, Noriyuki Jinguji, Takayuki Yanase. ANI: Takao Maki. MUS: Ayako Otsuka. PRD: Dentsu, Sunrise, TV Tokyo. 24 mins x 26 eps. Keen swimmer Kyo wants to keep his highschool swimming club going. Then he sees a beautiful girl on the diving board—a girl all his friends tell him doesn't exist. But Kyo sees her again and is drawn into a strange game where he pilots a mecha to fight off alien invaders. Although he believes himself to be playing an immersive virtual-reality game, glitches in his daily life lead him to develop a sense of paranoia about which of his two realities is genuine.

Zegapain is an interesting concept, exploring once more the modern disconnection between the daily life of the average teen and his evenings spent immersed in other worlds at a computer or game console. It has a well-told, multi-layered story and an elegant, bittersweet finish. Unusually for TV, the cheap, repetitive early animation improves as it progresses, although the mecha action isn't its strongest point. This probably explains why such an intelligent, likable show didn't go further as an anime, although in its day it did flourish into several gaming spin-offs and two novels. Takehiko Ito is credited as cocreator with Hajime Yadate, the Sunrise house name that secures the company's rights in a property.

ZEGUY *

1992. JPN: *Unkai no Meikyu Zeguy*. AKA: *Labyrinth of the Sea Clouds: Zeguy*. Video. DIR: Shigenori Kageyama. SCR: Shigenori Kageyama. DES: Aki Tsunaki. ANI: Akinobu Takahashi. MUS: Soichiro Harada. PRD: KSS. 40 mins. x 2 eps. Time-traveling troubleshooters Toshizo and Gennai (from the ultranationalist Shinsengumi organization of 19th-century Japan) must prevent the evil Himiko (Japan's ancient ruler, see **Dark Myth**) from opening a gateway to our world. They have two sailor-suited schoolgirls to help them but are lined up against a squad of smart enemies, including Leonardo da Vinci. Sadly, however, da Vinci is one of the only historical references that have survived in the dub version of this comedy romp— many of the clever references of the original script are sanded away by a distributor uneasy with "ethnocentric" allusions. Fun despite the dumbing-down, it's notable for a rare moment in a Manga Entertainment release when a character is chastised for using a rude word. Re-released in 2004 in the U.S. as *Mask of Zeguy*.

ZENKI: THE DEMON PRINCE *

1995. JPN: *Kishin Doji Zenki*. AKA: *Demon-God Boy Zenki*. TV series. DIR: Junji Nishimura. SCR: Ryota Yamaguchi, Masashi Sogo, Hitoshi Tokimura. DES: Hideyuki Motohashi, Torao Arai. ANI: Hideyuki Motohashi. MUS: Goji Tsuno. PRD: Studio Deen, Kitty Films, TV Tokyo. 25 mins. x 51 eps.

A thousand years ago, a sorcerer sealed the demon Zenki in stone to protect the world. Chiaki, a direct descendant, lives in modern Tokyo, where her grandmother has taught her the forbidden spell that breaks Zenki's bonds. To save her own world, she must use the spell, set Zenki free, and try to harness his power to fight off the spirits that are attacking modern Japan. The problem is, this involves his living with her in the family temple, and when he isn't casting spells as a superb hunk of menacing magical manhood, he takes the form of an annoying little brat who's every girl's worst nightmare of a kid brother. The director of **RANMA ½** must know something about milking a franchise for its last drop of humor, but he doesn't have much to work with here—just an average kids' TV series and not a patch on **USHIO AND TORA**. Based on the manga in *Shonen Jump* by Hide Tanikiku and Yoshihiro Kuroiwa.

ZENMAI ZAMURAI

2006. AKA: *Turnkey Samurai*. TV series. DIR: Tetsuo Yasumi, Kazumi Nonaka. SCR: Tetsuo Yasumi, Ryota Yamaguchi, Hiroshi Onogi. DES: Momoko Maruyama, Ryotaro Kuwamoto. ANI: N/C. MUS: Jun Miyake. PRD: A-1 Pictures, Noside, NHK Education. 5 mins. x 175 eps.

Two hundred years ago, a somewhat incompetent thief fell down a well and died during one of his crimes. Resurrected by the God of Bounty, he is fitted with a clockwork key in his head that will wind

down and kill him once more unless he continually performs good deeds. His chief tool in this enterprise is Dumpling Sword that can shoot food into the mouths of wrongdoers, if used often enough for them to see the error of their ways. His traveling companion is Mamemaru, an incontinent ninja in training.

Running for four years on NHK Education, this children's series offered an off-the-wall interpretation of the proverb "Ichinichi Ichizen" ("A Good Deed Every Day"), using a character originally designed for the same creators' **DEKO BOKO FRIENDS** but kept aside. Much of the design work involved a clockwork version of Edo-period Tokyo—starting with Zenmai's key, which is positioned to resemble a samurai topknot. If Zenmai performs enough good deeds, he will be released from his cycle of torment, although the series seems to have simply disappeared from the airwaves into reruns without a definite denouement.

ZENO: LOVE WITHOUT LIMITS

1999. JPN: *Zeno: Kagirinaki Ai ni*. Movie. DIR: Takashi Ui. SCR: Takashi Ui, Shigeki Chiba. DES: N/C. ANI: Satoshi Mutsukura. MUS: N/C. PRD: Robot, Media Vision. 90 mins.

Father Zeno is a Polish priest who lived in Japan during the 1930s and fell in love with the land and its people. In the aftermath of World War II, he comes back with a mission to help the children of Japan who have been orphaned by war, fire, flood, or earthquake.

ZEORYMER HADES PROJECT *

1988. JPN: *Meio Kikaku Zeorymer*. AKA: *Hades Project Zeorymer*. Video. DIR: Toshihiro Hirano. SCR: Sho Aikawa. DES: Michitaka Kikuchi, Yasuhiro Moriki. ANI: Michitaka Kikuchi. MUS: Eiji Kawamura. PRD: AIC, Artmic. 30 mins. x 4 eps.

Scientist Masaki Kihara rebels against his employers, the Haudragon crime syndicate. He destroys seven of the huge Hakkeshu robots he created for their top-secret Hades Project and hides the eighth and most powerful, the Zeorymer. Fifteen years later, the Haudragon have almost rebuilt the Hakkeshu, but the government has the Zeorymer and means to use it to thwart the criminals' plans. It needs the right pilot—a clone of its creator. Luckily, the government has one it had made

earlier. Fifteen-year-old Masato is about to find out that his whole life so far has been a lie, and that he was created in a test tube for the sole purpose of going into battle as the pilot of the greatest war machine the world has ever seen. Unless he can destroy the Hakkeshu and thwart Haudragon's plans, the world will plunge into an abyss of nuclear destruction.

Hirano gives this dark, tense scenario all the menace and nastiness that he brought to **ICZER-ONE** a year earlier, while the atmosphere and design work fore-shadow Kikuchi's later **SILENT MÖBIUS**. But there are no nasty alien in-vaders here—all the evil and suffering, as well as all the near-magical technology that created the magnificently spiky robots, is the work of humans; like **GUNDAM**, this reminds us that science fiction doesn't need aliens. Masato's emotional struggle and the near-disintegration of his personality are portrayed with melodramatic emphasis. This is a minor work by the standards of its stellar team but still has much of interest to offer. **LV**

ZERO G ROOM

Studio founded in 1991 by director Hiroshi Negishi, along with fellow animators Takuya Saito and Toshinari Yamashita, eventually merged into the planning company Radix. Works include **SAKURA WARS** and the **TENCHI MUYO!** movies.

ZERO NO MONO *

2001. AKA: *Nothing; Worthless*. Video. DIR: Ryuichi Kimura. SCR: Saki Hosen. DES: Akira Kano. ANI: Haruo Okuwara. MUS: N/C. PRD: Studio March, Milky, Museum Pictures. 30 mins.

A nameless slacker protagonist fantasizes about abusing and humiliating the girls in his dull college class. After he is snubbed by snooty coed Riko, he stalks her and attempts to torment her with a thrown jar of semen. She instead reacts with interest, much to his surprise, and he follows her to her destination—a house where her "Master" is busily abusing another girl. Riko actually enjoys the pain, and soon it is she who is in charge, in yet another bondage anime. Our language warning is stronger than usual on this title, since the dub by Nu-Tech inserts outrageous quantities of swear words. Not that anyone buying this sort of thing is likely to be shocked by anything so mild as bad language. Based on an anonymous story by the artist "Zero no Mono," from the series *Women at the Crossroads* (*Onna no Ko no Tsuji*), in the publication *Waning Moon* (*Tsuki ga Kakeru*). **ⓁⓃⓋ**

07-GHOST *

2009. JPN: *Seven Ghost*. TV series. DIR: Nobuhiro Takamoto. SCR: Natsuko Takahashi, Yoichi Kato. DES: Maki Fujii, Yutaka Miya, Hirotsugu Kakoi. ANI: Yukiko Ban. MUS: Kotaro Nakagawa. PRD: Studio DEEN, avex entertainment, Hakuhodo, Ichijinsha, YTC. 25 mins. x 25 eps.
An orphaned amnesiac prince fights his way out of slavery into an elite Imperial military academy thanks to his magical combat powers, but is imprisoned, escaping only with the protection of the Church. He sets out on a quest to find the truth about those who overthrew his homeland, killed his father, and enslaved him. His best friend dies and he faces fierce opposition from within the very Church that protects him. He must decide who his true friends are and how he will use his powers, assuming he survives.

The original manga by Yuki Amemiya and Yukino Ichihara has been running since 2005 and has been collected into 14 volumes, so the anime covers only a tiny portion of the complex plot. Nevertheless, it gives a fair summary of the charms of the story—its pretty-boy heroes and villains, its arcane hierarchy wrapped in mystical terms from an invented system of magic, and its appropriation of such exotic European concepts as the Catholic priesthood and the German language. But since anime is made in color with sound, it can—and does—pump up the emotional volume faster and harder than the slow burn of a long-running manga.

A successful manga seduces its readers into an ongoing relationship with the characters using minimal means—ink, paper, and storytelling skills. Unless you can transfer that loyal audience to the small screen, your anime doesn't last for long. But the needs of the TV audience are very different; they're easily distracted and it's difficult to keep them focused on one story. Just dressing it up in bright colors doesn't work. For every hugely successful

TV anime, every **MACROSS** or **FULLMETAL ALCHEMIST**, there are dozens like *07-Ghost*: competent, attractive, and forgettable.

Borrowing the artistic sensibility of CLAMP, dressing it up with gewgaws borrowed from **JOJO'S BIZARRE ADVENTURE** and **UTENA**, art director Kakoi and the design team make vivid if overdecorated frames. Director Takamoto does a good job, but the battles go on for too long and the constant voiceovers and flashbacks destroy anything resembling pace. Seen one luridly lit significant moment emphasized by choral music and drumrolls, seen them all.

It's Gothic, it's pretty, and you can get it with English subtitles online, but—in common with many recent anime—it hasn't had a physical English-language release, at the time of writing. That, in itself, is evidence of how far the industry has changed since we last updated this book.

ZERO SUM GAME *

2001. JPN: *Sex Crime: Zero Sum Game*. Video. DIR: Kaoru Toyooka, Hotaru Arisugawa. SCR: Guts Maro. DES: N/C. ANI: Shigeru Sasaki. MUS: Yasuaki Fujita. PRD: Blue Eyes, Picol Aibu. 30 mins.
A romantic future seems to beckon for Yuka and her boyfriend Yazaki, until a fateful night when he takes her to see the band Zero Sum in concert. Lead singer Keith knows Yazaki from their student days and also carries a torch for Yuka. At the backstage party, he ensures that Yazaki gets drunk and volunteers to escort him home, leaving Yuka at the mercy of a gang rape by the other band members. In the aftermath, Yuka decides to tell Yazaki what has happened, but Keith, who wants her for himself, convinces her instead to work through her trauma—unsurprisingly, this involves repeatedly having sexual intercourse with him. The result is yet another erotic anime that requires its female victims to be "broken in" through rape and domination. Based on a manga by Naizo Kudara. **ⓁⓃⓋ**

ZERO TESTER

1973. TV series. DIR: Ryosuke Takahashi, Yoshiyuki Tomino, Seiji Okuda. SCR: Fuyunori Gobu, Haruya Yamazaki, Kazushi Inoue, Soji Yoshikawa. DES: John Dettault, Crystal Art Studio. ANI: Kazuo Nakamura, Kazuhiko Udagawa, Yoshikazu Yasuhiko. MUS: Naoki

Yamamoto. PRD: Tohoku Shinsha, Soei, Kansai TV (Fuji TV). 25 mins. x 66 eps.
A series of space accidents turn out to be the work of the Armanoid aliens, who plan to conquer Earth. Professor Tachibana gathers a team around him at the Future Science Invention Center and prepares five state-of-the-art vehicles for Shin, Go, Lisa, and Captain Kenmotsu. Three of the Tester vehicles combine to make the giant Zero Tester robot, which successfully sees off the Armanoid invasion in 39 episodes. The rest of the series, retitled *ZT: Save the Earth!* (*Chikyu o Mamotte!*), was aimed at a younger age group and featured an attack by the new Gallos aliens.

An early gathering of many of anime's future greats, particularly for the **GUNDAM** series, this Gerry Anderson "homage" escaped complaint from the Japanese division of ITC because *Thunderbirds* (1965) was distributed in Japan by Tohoku Shinsha, who also produced *ZT*! Tohoku producer Banjiro Uemura would eventually work with Gerry Anderson himself on the abortive *Terrahawks* anime, and he would go it alone with the blatant **THUNDERBIRDS 2086**. Crystal Art was eventually renamed Studio Nue.

ZERO-SEN HAYATO

1964. TV series. DIR: Kazuo Hoshino, Tomio Sagisu. SCR: Satoru Kuramoto, Tomio Sagisu. DES: Tomio Sagisu. ANI: Saburo Sakamoto, Fujio Watanabe. MUS: Takeo Watanabe. PRD: P Productions, Oricomi, Fuji TV. 25 mins. x 41 eps.
Hayato Azuma, grandson of one of the Iga ninja clan, becomes a Zero-sen fighter pilot in the South Seas. Launching from Atsugi Island, he and his 34 ace pilot associates (including other descendants of ninja) fight as the Bakufu Team, under their commander Miyamoto, against a large number of opponents from nations whose insignia and nationality remain coyly unidentified. The only postwar anime for a generation after **WARTIME ANIME** to refer to WWII itself, this was based on the manga by **TIGER MASK**–creator Naoki Tsuji and features much repurposing of wartime experiences by Tomio Sagisu (Soji Ushio), who had been a member of the military instruction animation team known as the "Shadow Staff." In one memorable scene, the animators used footage from the

live-action *War at Sea from Hawaii to Malaya* (see **Ultraman**) as a background.

009-1 *

2005. JPN: *Zero Zero Nine One*. TV series. DIR: Naoyuki Konno. SCR: Shinsuke Onishi. DES: Fujio Suzuki, Naoyuki Konno, Yusuke Takeda. ANI: Naoyuki Konno. MUS: Taku Iwasaki. PRD: Ishimori Entertainment Inc., Ishimori Productions, TBS, Aniplex. 25 mins. x 12 eps. (TV) 25 mins. (v).

One hundred forty years in our future, the world is divided into Eastern and Western blocs, and the arms race is as fierce as ever. Alongside nuclear weapons, cyborgs have been developed into sophisticated and deadly agents for their respective powers. Mylene Hoffman, AKA 009-1, is one of the best weapons in the Western Block's arsenal. She's also one of a team of terrifyingly skilled women working for her handler, the mysterious Zero.

Shotaro Ishinomori created the *009-1* manga in 1967, as a spicier version of his 1964 hit **Cyborg 009**—the digits in the title deliberately recall the term *kunoichi* (a homonym for "nine of one"), then a buzzword for a female ninja. This anime version, made eight years after his death and updated for an audience with a different definition of sophistication, emphasizes the fan-service elements yet retains some of the period vibe of the original. Imagine *Charlie's Angels* set in the world of early James Bond films, but with elements of fantasy that might have been borrowed from the British TV series *The Avengers*—mutants, cyborgs, evil masterminds, well-meaning but inept boffins, and excursions into high camp. It's not classy—there's some less-than-sophisticated weaponry, like shoes that spit needles and guns embedded in women's breasts—but the action rattles along at a good pace. Although character development and strong story points are neglected in favor of hot babes and an episodic structure that makes *The Man From U.N.C.L.E.* look masterfully plotted, there's still enough going on to keep spy fans and peeping toms entertained.

Director Konno was a key animator back in the '90s, with credits including the **Tenchi Muyo!** franchise and **Armitage III**. His passion for the craft of animation still burns, judging from the number of credits here: chief animation director, animation

director, key animation, opening and ending animation, storyboard. He also shares character design credit with Suzuki, who got his start as an in-betweener on Madhouse's **Wicked City** in 1987. Composer Iwasaki is probably better known to anime fans for his work on the **Ruroni Kenshin** shorts, **Black Butler**, and **JoJo's Bizarre Adventures** on TV. Here he provides music to spy by with true retro flair. It's not his fault that his sultry sax riffs, invariably tied to sex scenes, become a Pavlovian trigger, a subliminal signal to get ready for some mild onscreen titillation or go and make a cup of tea, depending on your preference.

ZETSUAI *

1992. JPN: *Zetsuai 1989*. AKA: *Desperate Love 1989; Everlasting Love 1989*. Video. DIR: Takuji Endo, Kazuo Yamazaki. SCR: Tatsuhiko Urahata. DES: Tetsuro Aoki, Kazuchika Kise. ANI: Tetsuro Aoki. MUS: Kenji Kawai, Yasunori Honda. PRD: Madhouse. 45 mins., 33 mins., 45 mins.

Takuto Izumi, a high school soccer star, has a dark family secret—his mother's obsessive love for his father led to murder. Superstar idol singer Koji Nanjo has a terrible family background, with long-standing animosity between him and his eldest brother, and his middle sibling clinging to the elder. With their problems, the two should never even contemplate a relationship, but Koji has fancied Izumi since he first saw him; even when he finds out Izumi isn't, as he thought, a girl, he can't get him out of his mind. His obsessive love is the last thing Izumi needs, but as Koji pursues the relationship and Koji's friend Katsumi Shibuya becomes a friend to Izumi, too, love grows between the desperately needy pair despite Izumi's reluctance to accept it. It's tested by the hostility of Koji's family, which doesn't hesitate to threaten Izumi's chance of an international soccer career.

Bronze Cathexis (1994), a 33-minute "image" video concentrating on Koji, features five pop promos set to animation (as with **Cipher**) directed by some of the star directors of the Madhouse studio: Katsuyuki Kodera, Yoshiaki Kawajiri (who storyboarded *Zetsuai*), Koichi Chiaki, Toshio Hirata, and Rintaro.

A further video, *Bronze: Zetsuai since 1989* (1996), directed by Yamazaki and

designed by Kise, shows Izumi leaving for a soccer tour. When Koji doesn't show up to see him off, he gets worried and starts to wonder why. In fact, Koji has had a minor car accident, but as a result Izumi starts pondering over their whole relationship.

Based on the ongoing 1990 manga in *Margaret* by Minami Ozaki, *Zetsuai* is one of the greatest icons of *shonen ai*—gay erotica for a female audience. The video versions show only a tiny segment of the angst-ridden multicharacter story, and though there's not much explicit sex, there is a lot of blood—accidents and self-inflicted wounds abound. Koji and Izumi have become *shonen ai*'s Romeo and Juliet, and a similarly tragic ending probably awaits. "Everlasting Love" is Ozaki's preferred English title, either through deliberate irony or simply poor **Translation**. **(NV)**

ZETTAI SHONEN

2005. AKA: *Absolute Boy*. TV series. DIR: Tomomi Mochizuki, Hiroshi Negishi, Kenichi Imaizumi. SCR: Kazunori Ito, Miwa Kawasaki, Tatsuya Hamazaki. DES: Masayuki Sekine. ANI: Hiroshi Kawaguchi, Hiroyuki Horiuchi, Kenichi Imaizumi, Koji Watanabe, Yuko Yamamoto, Nobuyuki Hata. MUS: Hikaru Nanase. PRD: Studio One Pack, Ajia-do, Studio Fuga, Trilogy Future, Anime Aru, NHK. 25 mins. x 26 eps.

Ayumu Aizawa is sent by his mother to stay with his father—a posting he initially regards with some reluctance, although his consent is bought with the bribe of a mountain bike. But on his rides around the remote village of Tana, he encounters a series of strange phenomena that lead him to believe that something weird is going on in the woods—glowing lights through the trees, a local girl who knows more than she lets on, and a small child eerily attired in the clothes that Ayumu himself wore when he was younger. It's all due to fairies, apparently, in a surreal take on *The X Files*.

ZILLION *

1987. JPN: *Akai Kodan Zillion*. AKA: *Red Tracer Zillion; Red Photon Zillion*. TV series, video. DIR: Hiroshi Hamazaki, Tetsuya Kobayashi. SCR: Tsunehisa Ito, Mayori Sekijima. DES: Mizuho Nishikubo, Kunio Aoi, Ammonite. ANI: Takayuki Sato. MUS: Jun Irie. PRD: Tatsunoko, Nippon TV. 25 mins. x 31 eps., 45 mins. (v).

In the year 2387, a group of human colonists live on the planet Maris, hailed as a "second Earth." However, the colonists are attacked by the Noza aliens—Maris' only hope is a captured alien weapon system known as the "Zillion Gun." Three of these fall into the hands of the defenders, and a team of brave young freedom fighters calling themselves the White Nauts/ Nuts (White Knights in the U.S. release) fight for their people's survival. The 1988 video release *Burning Night* was a one-shot written and directed by Nishikubo, set in the peacetime after the aliens have been seen off. Former comrades Champ, Dave, JJ, and cute girl Apple form a rock band (see **DANCOUGAR**) but have to call on their old combat skills again when Apple is kidnapped by a criminal gang. Made just after **ROBOTECH** *Sentinels* was canceled, *Zillion* incorporated some of the design work undertaken for the aborted project by Tatsunoko. The whole series was based on a toy—a photoelectric gun used for Lazer Tag—and only 5 of the 31 episodes, plus *Burning Night* (released as *Zillon Special: BN*) appeared on video in the U.S.

ZIPANG

2004. TV series. DIR: Kazuhiro Furuhashi, Daisuke Tsukushi, Hideki Okamoto, Hiromichi Matano, Takashi Yamana, Yukihiro Matsushita. SCR: Kazuhiro Furuhashi, Yuichiro Takeda. DES: Yoshihiko Umakoshi, Sanpei Ohara, Yasuhiro Nishinaka. ANI: Akira Kasahara, Hirofumi Morimoto, Masashi Matsumoto. MUS: Toshihiko Sahashi. PRD: Studio Deen, TBS. 25 mins. x 26 eps.

The modern-day Japanese Kongo-class AEGIS destroyer Mirai ("Future") is transported back in time to the eve of the Battle of Midway and faced with the difficult decision to intervene in World War II or to sit back and watch its countrymen die in the battle. The commander initially adopts a strictly defensive position (itself an ironic pastiche of Japan's own postwar constitutional stance), only to find trouble coming his way when the crew inadvertently rescue Major Kusaka, an officer who was, historically, supposed to have died at Midway. After much bickering, the ship heads for Singapore, where executive officer Kadomatsu discovers that the presence of the Mirai has already altered the timeline too far for history to play out as they

remember it. Consequently, after seven episodes of hand-wringing indecision, they decide to weigh in on the Japanese side, and set course for Guadalcanal. Ultimately, the Mirai is destined for a showdown involving the quintessential WWII vessel, the Yamato—see **STAR BLAZERS** for its better-known appearance in an earlier anime. Based on the 2001 manga by **SILENT SERVICE**–creator Kaiji Kawaguchi, serialized in *Comic Morning* magazine, this series also owes obvious debts of inspiration to Don Taylor's *Final Countdown* (1980), in which an American aircraft carrier falls through time to witness Pearl Harbor, and the Sonny Chiba vehicle *Time Slip* (1981), in which modern Japanese soldiers stumble across time into Japan's civil war. Compare to **DEEP BLUE FLEET**.

ZOIDS *

1999. TV series. DIR: Yoshio Kado, Nobuyoshi Habara, Shingo Kobayashi. SCR: Katsuyuki Sumisawa, Kazuhiko Koide. DES: Tadashi Sakazaki. ANI: Taro Ikegami. MUS: Akira Takahashi. PRD: Xebec, Sho-Pro, MRS, JRK, TBS. 25 mins. x 67 eps. (TV1), 25 mins. x 26 eps. (TV2), 25 mins. x 26 eps. (TV3; 13 eps. in U.S.), 25 mins. x 50 eps. (TV4).

Van is just an ordinary kid, but his life changes forever when a capsule crashes outside his village and he defends it from bandits. The occupants are a sleek metallic dinosaur and a beautiful girl. The girl, Phina, says that her companion, Jeek, is a zoid. Van sets off with them on an adventure he could never have imagined, a battle against Deathsaura.

Promoting toys is what kids' robot shows are all about; Bandai's **GUNDAM** franchise is just one example. Here, though, is a show that starts out with a range of toys that have been on sale since 1982, a motor-driven range of construction kit toys by Tomy, with a name made from an Engrish combination of *ju* ("beast") and "android," making *ju-oids*. The artwork has a split personality, using CG on the Zoids (under the supervision of Nobuyoshi Habara) but aiming for a cel-animated look overall. At the beginning of 2001, the series was rebranded as *New Century Zoid Slash Zero* (*Zoid Shinseki/0*) with episode 68, moving away from the martial theme of the earlier episodes and concentrating instead on gladiatorial zoid combat. A manga spin-off

was serialized in *Corocoro Comic*. A third series, *Zoids: Fuzors* (2003) was made in Japan but first broadcast in the U.S.—unusually, the Japanese broadcast is marginally improved on the American, which was canceled after 13 episodes. In Japan, it ran for 26 and featured several tweaks to the animation. The post-apocalyptic fourth series *Zoids: Genesis* (2006–7) is set in a world so markedly different from its predecessors that fans remain in disagreement as to whether it can be the same place, even though it features many of the machines from the preceding series, which might be supposed to have taken place in its distant past.

ZOMBIE-LOAN

2007. TV series, special. DIR: Akira Nishimori. SCR: Atsuhiro Tomioka, Yuka Yamada. DES: Chiharu Sato, Norifumi Nakamura. ANI: Makoto Furuta, Yuriko Nagaya. MUS: Hiroyuki Sawano. PRD: XEBEC M2, E-Net Frontier, NAS, Super Vision, TV Asahi. 24 mins. x 13 eps. (TV), 23 mins. x 2 eps. (special).

Schoolgirl Michiru Kita has *shinigami* eyes—she can see a dark ring round a person's neck and watch as it quickly darkens and they die. Now, two boys in her class have dark rings round their necks. It turns out that Chika and Shito should have been killed in an accident, but instead they made a deal with a secret supernatural loan office, called the Zombie-Loan. It loans them extra life as long as they hunt zombies in return. At first they plan to kill Michiru, but they soon decide to draw her into their zombie-hunting work, which only creates even more trouble. Compare with **D.GRAY-MAN** and **GHOST HUNT**, very different stylistically but with similar themes. The series was originally planned to run for more than 20 episodes but had to be cut short due to what PR calls "unknown circumstances." There was enough footage unscreened for two 23-minute specials released on the seventh DVD volume. Based on a manga in *G-Fantasy* magazine by the Peach-Pit duo, creators of **ROZEN MAIDEN**.

ZONE OF THE ENDERS *

2001. JPN: *Zone of Enders*. Video, TV series. DIR: Tetsuya Watanabe. SCR: Shin Yoshida. DES: Madoka Hirayama, Tsutomu Suzuki, Tsutomu Miyazawa. ANI: Kumi Horii. MUS:

Hikaru Nanase. PRD: Sunrise, TV Tokyo. 55 mins. (v), 25 mins. x 26 eps.

In A.D. 2167, humankind has established colonies in space. Jupiter colony Antilla is the farthest human settlement from Earth, so its residents are called Enders. Leo Stenbuck, an introverted Ender, goes along with his friends (who bully him most of the time) to a U.N. Space Force facility to steal from their junkyard, but he gets caught. At the same time, fanatical Martian military ruling party Z.O.E. hijacks the Antilla colony. His home turned into a battlefield, Leo witnesses the deaths of his friends. Scared and weighed down with guilt, he runs from the scene determined to find the reasons behind the attack. In April 2001, the video *ZoE 2167* and the *ZoE Dolores* TV series were both released alongside the PlayStation game, which itself has a solid crew including GUNDAM and *Metal Gear Solid* veteran Nobuyoshi Nishimura. The anime version is set five years before the events of the game.

ZOO WITHOUT AN ELEPHANT

1982. JPN: *Zo no Inai Dobutsuen*. Movie. DIR: Yasuo Maeda. SCR: Hikaru Saito. DES: Junji Nagashima. ANI: Minoru Aoki. MUS: Kuni Kawauchi. PRD: Tac, Herald. 80 mins.

After the war, concerned brother Hide promises his critically ill sister Miyoko that he will arrange for her to see a real elephant. But when he goes to the zoo to find one, an old man tells him of the tragic day when the zoo animals were slaughtered. Compare to GOODBYE LITTLE HIPPO, a similar tale of wartime deprivation.

ZORRO THE MAGNIFICENT *

1996. JPN: *Kaiketsu Zorro*. AKA: *Magnificent Zorro; Z for Zorro*. TV series. DIR: Katsumi Minoguchi, Kenichi Hirano, Yasuhiro Matsumura, Masakazu Amiya, Takeshi Yamaguchi, Akiyuki Shinbo. SCR: Sukehiro Tomita, Yasushi Hirano, Takashi Yamada, Hideki Sonoda, Isao Shizuya. DES: Hisashi Kagawa. ANI: Hirotoshi Takaya, Masaaki Endo. MUS: N/C. PRD: Tohoku, Ashi productions, NHK2. 25 mins. x 52 eps. (TV), 106 mins. (m). Based on the stories by Johnston Mc-Culley, which first appeared in *All-Story Weekly* in 1919, this Italian coproduction, only 46 episodes of which aired in Japan, chronicles the adventures of a heroic freedom fighter (El Zorro, "The Fox") struggling to defend the independence of the people of 19th-century California from their Spanish rulers. Like the Hollywood feature film *Mask of Zorro* (1999), *ZtM* is set a generation later, with Zorro's son taking up the mantle and rapier. The series was

reportedly dubbed into English, although the authors have not seen any evidence of this beyond an entertainingly awful 106-minute movie edit, credited to Village Productions of Dagenham, U.K., which misspells the director's name as Mino Guti (*sic*) and often gives only surnames for the Japanese staff.

With McCulley conveniently out of copyright, *Zorro* is a popular franchise in animation—Hayao Miyazaki planned a *Kaiketsu Zorro* series in 1982 but it never appeared. Other animated adventures of Zorro include the 1981 Filmation series and a 2000 Warner Bros. remake. *Zorori the Magnificent* (1993, *Kaiketsu Zorori*) is an unrelated 30-minute feature directed by Toshio Takeuchi that featured two popular episodes from a Zorro-pastiche children's book by Miho Mizushima and Yutaka Hara, with animals in all the main roles. Zorro, of course, is played by a fox. This Zorori returned as the hero of a 52-episode series on Nagoya TV in 2004, directed by Hiroshi Nishikiori. Zorori, accompanied by his twin boar assistants, and with a self-proclaimed desire to become the Prince of Mischief, came back once more in his own 53-minute anime movie *Kaiketsu Zorori: The Race for the Mysterious Treasure* (*Nazo no Otakara Daisakusen*, 2006).

Selected Bibliography

Film Index

Name & Subject Index

SELECTED
BIBLIOGRAPHY

BOOKS

Acuff, Daniel with Robert Reiher. *What Kids Buy and Why: The Psychology of Marketing to Kids*. New York: Free Press, 1999.

AJA [Association of Japanese Animations (*sic*) and Tokyo Bureau of Industrial and Labor Affairs]. *Anime no Text; Anime Gyokai o Mezasu Hito no Tame ni [Anime Text: For Those Aiming for the Japanese Animation Industry]*. 3 vols. + DVD. Tokyo: AJA, 2008.

Akita, Takahiro. "Manga Eiga no Warai to Eiyu: Momotaro to Senso" ["Laughter and Heroes in Cartoon Films: Momotaro and the War"]. In Kenji Iwamoto, ed., *Eiga to Dai To-A Kyoeiken [Film and the Greater East Asia Co-Prosperity Sphere]*, pp. 255–68. Tokyo: Shinwasha, 2004.

Animage. *The Art of Japanese Animation I: 25 Years of Television Cartoons*. Tokyo: Tokuma Shoten, 1988.

_____. *The Art of Japanese Animation II: 70 Years of Theatrical Films*. Tokyo: Tokuma Shoten, 1989.

_____. *Best of Animage: 20th Anniversary*. Tokyo: Tokuma Shoten, 1998.

Aosaka, Tomoyuki, et al. *Contents Business in China: Hendo suru Shijo, Taito suru Sangyo [Contents Business in China: Fluctuating Markets, Emerging Industry]*. Tokyo: Shoeisha, 2007.

Ban, Toshio, and Tezuka Productions. *Tezuka Osamu Monogatari: Manga no Yume, Anime no Yume 1960–1989 [The Tezuka Osamu Story: Dreams of Manga, Dreams of Anime 1960–1989]*. Tokyo: Asahi Shinbunsha, 1992.

Baricordi, Andrea, et al. *Cartoonia Anime: guida al cinema d"animazione giapponese*. Bologna: Granata Press, 1991.

Baskett, Michael. *The Attractive Empire: Transnational Film Culture in Imperial Japan*. Honolulu: University of Hawai'i Press, 2008.

Beier, Carl. "Film Briefing of Air Crews." In *Hollywood Quarterly* 1:2, January 1946, pp. 236–37.

Bernardi, Joanne. *Writing in Light: The Silent Scenario and the Japanese Pure Film Movement*. Detroit: Wayne State University Press, 2001.

Chun, Jayson. *"A Nation of a Hundred Million Idiots"? A Social History of Japanese Television 1953–1973*. New York: Routledge, 2007.

Clements, Jonathan. "The Mechanics of the US Anime and Manga Industry." In *Foundation: The Review of Science Fiction*, no. 64, Summer 1995, pp. 32–44.

_____. *Schoolgirl Milky Crisis: Adventures in the Anime and Manga Trade*. London: Titan Books, 2009.

_____, and Barry Ip. "The Shadow Staff: Japanese Animators in the Toho Aviation Education Materials Production Office 1939–1945." In *Animation: An Interdisciplinary Journal* 7(2), July 2012, pp. 189–204.

_____, and Motoko Tamamuro. *The Dorama Encyclopedia: A Guide to Japanese TV Drama Since 1953*. Berkeley: Stone Bridge Press, 2003.

Condry, Ian. "Anime Creativity: Characters and Premises in the Quest for Cool Japan." In *Theory, Culture & Society*, 2009, no. 26, pp. 139–163.

_____. *The Soul of Anime: Collaborative Creativity and Japan's Media Success Story*. Durham, NC: Duke University Press, 2013.

Denison, Rayna. "Anime tourism: discursive construction and reception of the Studio Ghibli Art Museum." In *Japan Forum* 22 (3–4), 2010. pp. 545–63.

Endo, Homare. *Chugoku Doman Shinjinrui: Nihon no Anime to Manga ga Chugoku o Udokasu [The New Breed of Chinese "Dongman": Japanese Cartoons and Comics Animate China]*. Tokyo:

Nikkei BP, 2008.

Funamoto, Susumu, ed. *Anime no Mirai o Shiru: Post-Japanimation Keyword wa Sekaishi + Digital [Understanding the Future of Anime: Post Japanimation the Keywords are Global + Digital]*. Tokyo, Ten Books, 1998.

Gan Sheuo Hui. "To Be or Not To Be: The Controversy in Japan over the 'Anime' Label." In *Animation Studies*, vol. 4 (2009), pp. 35–44.

Gill, Tom. "Transformational Magic: Some Japanese Superheroes and Monsters." In D. P. Martinez, ed., *The Worlds of Japanese Popular Culture: Gender, Shifting Boundaries and Global Cultures*. Cambridge: Cambridge University Press, 1998. pp. 33–55.

Goldschmidt, Rick. *The Enchanted World of Rankin/Bass: A Portfolio*. Issaquah, WA: Tiger Mountain Press, 1997.

Haraguchi, Masahiro, ed. *Animage Pocket Data Notes*. Annual. Tokyo: Tokuma Shoten, 1989–2000.

Hase, Masato. *Eiga to Iu Technology Keiken [Cinema and Technological Experience]*. Tokyo: Seikyusha, 2010.

Hatakeyama, Kenji, and Masakazu Kubo. *Pokémon Story*. Tokyo: Nikkei BP, 2000.

High, Peter. *The Imperial Screen: Japanese Film Culture in the Fifteen Years' War 1931–1945*. Madison: University of Wisconsin, 2003.

Hikawa, Ryusuke. "Anime Tokushu Giho no Hensen" [Alterations of Anime Special Techniques]. In Makoto Misono, ed., *Zusetsu Terebi Anime Zensho [Complete Book of TV Animation: Illustrated]*, pp. 181–214. Tokyo: Hara Shobo, 1999.

Hiramatsu, Keiichiro, ed. *Terebi 50-nen in TV Guide: The TV History of 50 Years*. Tokyo: Tokyo News Tsushinsha, 2000.

Horibuchi, Seiji, and Manami Iiboshi. *Moeru America: Beikokujin wa Ikanishite Manga o Yomuyo ni natta ka [Turning America On: Was It Possible for Americans to Somehow Become Manga Readers?]*. Tokyo: Nikkei Business Publishing, 2006.

Hoshiyama, Hiroyuki. *Hoshiyama Hiroyuki no Anime Scenario Kyoshitsu [Hoshiyama Hiroyuki's Anime Screenplay Classroom]*. Tokyo: Raichosha, 2007.

Hotta, Junji. *Gainax Interviews*. Tokyo: Kodansha, 2005.

Hu, Tze-yue. "The Animated Resurrection of the Legend of the White Snake in Japan." In *Animation*, vol. 2 (March 2007), pp. 44–61.

_____. "Dare no Mukete no Animation ka: Shusen Chokugo no Animation Eiga" [Animating for Whom in the Aftermath of a World War]. In Kenji Iwamoto, ed., *Senryoka no Eiga: Kaiho to Kenetsu [Film Under the Occupation: Emancipation and Censorship]*, pp. 243–67. Tokyo: Shinwasha, 2009.

_____. *Frames of Anime: Culture and Image-Building*. Hong Kong: Hong Kong University Press, 2010.

Ikeda, Koichi. *Char e no Chinkonka: Waga Seishun no Akai Suisei [A Requiem for Char Aznable: My Youth as the Red Comet]*. Tokyo: Wani Books, 2007.

Ikeda, Noriaki, and Hideaki Ito. *Renzoku Ningyogeki no Subete [All About NHK Puppet Serials]*. Tokyo: Enterbrain, 2003.

Inoue, Akito. *Gamification: Game ga Business o Kaeru [Gamification: How Games are Changing Business]*. Tokyo: NHK Shuppan, 2012.

Inoue, Shinichiro, ed. *Anime DVD Kanzen [Complete] Catalogue*. Tokyo: Kadokawa Shoten, 2000

Inoue, Takeo. *Niju Seiki Anime Daizen [Encyclopaedia of 20th Century Animation]*. Tokyo: Futabasha, 2000.

Inui, Naoaki. *That's TV Graffiti: Gaikoku Terebi Eiga Sanjugonen no Subete [All About 35 Years of Foreign TV and Films]*. Tokyo: Film Art-sha, 1988.

Ishiguro, Noboru, and Noriko Ohara. *Terebi Anime Saizensen: Shisetsu Anime 17 Nenshi [The Frontline of Television Animation: A Personal History of 17 Years in Animation]*. Tokyo: Yamato Shobo, 1980.

Ishikawa, Mitsuhisa. *Animation Gyokai, Itanji Producer no Genjoriki Kakumei [The Animation Industry and a Non-conformist Producer's On-the-Spot Revolution]*. Tokyo: KK Bestsellers, 2009.

Ito, Go. *Tezuka Is Dead: Hirakareta Manga Hyogenron e [Tezuka is Dead: Postmodernist and Modernist Approaches to Japanese Manga]*. Tokyo: NTT Shuppan, 2005. Wording of title translation is that in the Japanese edition.

Iwabuchi, Koichi. *Recentering Globalization: Popular Culture and Japanese Transnationalism*. Durham, NC: Duke University Press, 2002.

_____. *Feeling Asian Modernities: Transnational Consumption of Japanese TV Dramas*. Hong Kong: Hong Kong University Press, 2003.

_____. "How "Japanese" is *Pokémon?*" In Joseph Tobin, ed., *Pikachu's Global Adventure: The Rise and Fall of Pokémon*, pp. 53–79. Durham, NC: Duke University Press, 2004.

Iwamoto, Kenji, ed. *Nippon Eiga no Tanjo [The Birth of Japanese Film]*. Tokyo: Shinwasha, 2011.

Iwasaki, Yoshikazu, et al., eds. *Osamu Tezuka*. Tokyo: National Museum of Modern Art, 1990.

Kadokawa, Haruki. *Waga Toso: Furyo Seinen wa Sekai o Mezasu [My Struggle: A Delinquent Youth Aims for the World]*. Tokyo: East Press, 2005.

Kajiyama, Sumiko. *Suzuki Toshio no*

Ghibli Book. Tokyo: Nikkei Business Bunko, 2009.

Kano, Seiji. *Nippon no Animation o Kizuita Hitobito [The People Who Built Japanese Animation].* Tokyo: Wakakusa Shobo, 2004.

Kataoka, Yoshiro. "Nippon no Anime Shijo" [The Japanese Animation Marketplace]. In Mitsuteru Takahashi and Nobuyuki Tsugata, eds., *Anime-gaku [Anime Studies],* pp. 152–83. Tokyo: NTT Shuppan, 2011.

Kato, Akiko. *Nihon no Ningyogeki 1867–2007 [Japanese Puppet Theater 1867–2007].* Tokyo: Hosei Daigaku, 2007.

Kato, Mikiro. *Animation no Eiga-gaku.* Kyoto: Rinsen Shoten, 2009

Katsuno, Hirofumi, and Jeffrey Maret. "Localizing the Pokémon TV series for the American Market." In Joseph Tobin, ed., *Pikachu's Global Adventure: The Rise and Fall of Pokémon,* pp. 80–107. Durham, NC: Duke University Press, 2004.

Kawai, Ryu. "Saigo no Shonintachi" [The Last Witnesses]. In Tatsuo Shibayama and Shuji Kobayashi, et al., *Mushi Pro Tenamonya: Dare mo Shiranai Tezuka Osamu [Mushi Pro Maverick: The Tezuka Osamu That Nobody Knows],* pp. 12–13. Tokyo: Kuraki-sha Bijutsu, 2009.

Kimura, Makoto. "Anime Business no Kihon Model" [A Basic Model of the Anime Business], in Mitsuteru Takahashi and Nobuyuki Tsugata, eds., *Anime-gaku [Anime Studies],* pp. 115–51. Tokyo: NTT Shuppan, 2011.

Kinema Junpo Eiga Soko Kenkyusho [Kinema Junpo Film Integration Research Office]. *"Nichijokei Anime" Hit no Hosoku [The Rules for Making a Hit "Mundane Anime"].* Tokyo: Kinema Junpo-sha, 2011a.

_____. *Anime Producer no Shigoto-ron [On The Profession of the Anime Producer].* Tokyo: Kinema Junpo-sha, 2011b.

Kitamura, Hiroshi. *Screening Enlightenment: Hollywood and the Cultural Reconstruction of Defeated Japan.* Ithaca: Cornell University Press, 2010.

Kitano, Taiitsu. *Nippon Anime Shigaku Kenkyu Josetsu [An Introduction to the Historical Study of Japanese Animation].* Tokyo: Hachiman Shoten, 1998.

Komaki, Masanobu. *Animec no Goro [My Time at Animec].* Tokyo, NTT Shuppan, 2009.

Komatsuzawa, Hajime. "Momotaro's Sea Eagle." In Mark Nornes and Yukio Fukushima, eds., *The Japan/America Film Wars: World War II Propaganda and Its Cultural Contexts,* pp. 191–95. Langhorne, PA: Harwood Academic Publishers, 1994.

_____. "Princess Iron Fan (Saiyuki)." In Mark Nornes and Yukio Fukushima, eds., *The Japan/America Film Wars: World War II Propaganda and Its Cultural Contexts,,* pp. 225–29. Langhorne, PA: Harwood Academic Publishers, 1994.

Komori, Ikuya, and Shinichi Suzuki. *Zero no Shozo: Tokiwa-so kara Umareta Anime Kaisha no Monogatari [Portrait of the Zero: The Story of the Anime Company Born from Tokiwa-so].* Tokyo: Kodansha, 2012.

Kon, Satoshi. *Kon's Tone: Sennen Joyu e no Michi [Kon's Tone: The Road to Millennium Actress].* Tokyo: Shobunsha, 2002.

Kondo, Takashi. *Kuso Bishojo Yomihon [The Guide of Fantastic Beauties].* Tokyo: Bessatsu Takarajima-sha, 1997.

Koyama-Richard, Brigitte. *Japanese Animation: From Painted Scrolls to Pokémon.* Paris: Flammarion, 2010.

Kurosawa, Akira. *Something Like an Autobiography.* New York: Vintage Books, 1983.

Kurosawa, Kiyoshi; Inuhiko Yohota; et al. *Anime wa Ekkyo suru [Anime in Transition].* Tokyo: Iwanami Shoten, 2010.

Kuwahara, Keisuke. "Animation ni Okeru Oto to Ugoki no Hyogen: Tetsuwan Atomu no Chushin ni" [The Appearance of Sound and Movement in Animation: Astro Boy]. In *Japanese Journal of Animation Studies,* vol. 9 (2008), no.1A, pp. 25–32.

Kushida, Makoto. *Ani Kuri 15 DVD x Materials.* Tokyo: Ichijinsha, 2009.

Ladd, Fred, with Harvey Deneroff. *Astro Boy and Anime Come to the Americas: An Insider's View of the Birth of a Pop Culture Phenomenon.* Jefferson, NC: McFarland, 2009.

Lamarre, Thomas. *The Anime Machine: A Media Theory of Animation.* Minneapolis: University of Minnesota Press, 2009.

Ledoux, Trish, ed. *Anime Interviews: The First Five Years of Animerica Anime and Manga Monthly.* San Francisco: Cadence Books, 1997.

Lent, John, ed. *Animation in Asia and the Pacific.* Eastleigh, Hampshire: John Libbey, 2001.

Linsenmaier, Timo. "Why Animation Historiography?" In *Animation Studies,* vol. 3, 2008. pp. 51–59

Litten, Frederick. "Starving the Elephants: The Slaughter of Animals in Wartime Tokyo's Ueno Zoo." In *The Asia-Pacific Journal,* vol. 38-3-09 (September 21, 2009).

_____. "On the Earliest (Foreign) Animation Films Shown in Japanese Cinemas." http://litten.de/fulltext/nipper.pdf [accessed January 11, 2013].

_____. "Some remarks on the first Japanese animation films in 1917." http://litten.de/fulltext/ani1917.pdf [accessed June 1, 2013].

_____. "Japanese color animation from ca.1907 to 1945." http://litten.de/fulltext/color.pdf [accessed 17th June 2014].

Lurçat, Liliane. *A cinq ans, seul avec Goldorak: le jeune enfant et la télévision.* Paris: Éditions Syros, 1981.

MacWilliams, Mark, ed. *Japanese Visual Culture: Explorations in the World of Manga and Anime.* Armonk, New York: M.E. Sharpe, 2008.

Masuda, Hiromichi. *Anime Business ga Wakaru [Understanding the Animation Business].* Tokyo: NTT Shuppan, 2007.

_____. *Motto Wakaru Anime Business [Understanding the Anime Business More].* Tokyo: NTT Shuppan, 2011.

Matsumoto, Natsuki. "Eiga Torai Zengo no Katei-yo Eizo Kiki: Gento, Animation, Gangu Eiga" [Domestic Imaging Appliances During the Advent of Film: Magic Lanterns, Animation, and Toy Films]. In Kenji Iwamoto, ed., *Nippon Eiga no Tanjo [The Birth of Japanese Film],* pp. 95–128. Tokyo: Shinwasha, 2011a.

Matsumoto, Satoru. "Digital Jidai no Anime Ryutsu" [Anime Distribution for the Digital Age]. In Mitsuteru Takahashi and Nobuyuki Tsugata, eds., *Anime-gaku [Anime Studies],* pp. 184–98. Tokyo: NTT Shuppan, 2011b.

McCarthy, Helen. *Hayao Miyazaki: Master of Japanese Animation.* Berkeley: Stone Bridge Press, 1999.

_____. "The Development of the Japanese Animation Audience in the United Kingdom and France." In John A. Lent, ed., *Animation in Asia and the Pacific,* pp. 73–84. Eastleigh, Hampshire: John Libbey, 2001.

_____. *The Art of Osamu Tezuka: God of Manga.* Lewes: Ilex Press, 2009.

_____, and Jonathan Clements. *The Erotic Anime Movie Guide.* London: Titan Books, 1998.

McGray, Douglas, moderator. "Otaku Unmasked: The Life, Death and Rebirth of Japan's Pop Culture." November 30, 2005. http://www.japansociety.org/otaku_unmasked [accessed June 23, 2014].

Mikami, Koji. "Anime Seisaku Shuho to Gijutsu" [Anime Production Methods and Techniques], in Mitsuteru Takahashi and Nobuyuki Tsugata, eds., *Anime-gaku [Anime Studies],* pp. 70–112. Tokyo: NTT Shuppan, 2011.

Minakawa, Yuka. *Nippon Doga no Koboshi: Shosetsu Tezuka Gakko. [The Rise and Fall of Japanese Animation: The Story of the Tezuka School].* 2 vols. Tokyo: Kodansha, 2009.

Misono, Makoto, ed. *Zusetsu Terebi Anime Zensho [Complete Book of TV Animation: Illustrated].* Tokyo: Hara Shobo, 1999.

Miyao, Daisuke. "Before Anime: Animation and the Pure Film Movement in Pre-War Japan." In *Japan Forum* 14 (2), 2002, pp. 191–209.

Miyazaki, Hayao. *Starting Point: 1979–1996.* San Francisco: Viz Media, 2009.

_____. *Turning Point: 1997–2008.* San Francisco: Viz Media, 2014.

Mochinaga, Tadahito. *Animation Nitchu Koryuki [A Chronicle of Sino-Japanese Animation Interchange].* Tokyo: Toho Shoten, 2006.

Mori, Yasuji. *Mogura no Uta: Animator no Jiden [The Mole's Song: An Animator's Autobiography].* Tokyo: Animage Bunko V, 1984.

Nagayama, Yasuo. *Sengo SF Jiken Shi: Nihonteki Sozoryoku no 70-nen [An Event History of Postwar SF: 70 Years of Japanese Imaginative Power].* Tokyo: Kawade Books, 2012.

Napier, Susan. *Anime from Akira to Howl's Moving Castle: Experiencing Contemporary Japanese Animation.* New York: Palgrave Macmillan, 2006.

Nash, Eric. *Manga Kamishibai: The Art of Japanese Paper Theater.* New York: Abrams, 2009.

NHK Hoso Bunka Kenkyusho. *Terebi Shicho 50-nen [50 Years of Television Ratings].* Tokyo: NHK Shuppan, 2003.

Nichigai Associates. *Mangaka Anime Sakka Jinmei Jiten [Writers of Comics in Japan: A Biographical Dictionary].* Tokyo: Nichigai Associates, 1997.

Nippon Animation. *25 Shunen Kinen Nippon Animation Zensakuhinshu [25th Anniversary Memorial: Nippon Animation Complete Works Compendium].* Tokyo: Planet Publishing, 2001.

Nishizaki, Yoshinobu. "My Anime Life: Yamato ni Itaru made, Yamato ni Ketsubetsu suru made" [My Anime Life: Until Yamato Arrives, Until Yamato Departs]. In *My Anime* #1, 1981, pp. 100–104.

Nomura Research Institute. *Otaku Shijo no Kenkyu [Research in the Otaku Marketplace].* Tokyo: Toyo Keizai, 2005.

Nornes, Abe Mark (Markus), and Fukushima Yukio, eds. *The Japan/America Film Wars: World War II Propaganda and Its Cultural Contexts.* Langhorne, PA: Harwood Academic Publishers, 1994.

Ogata Emiko. *Animation no Senkakusha Ofuji Noburo: Koko no Tensai [Animation Pioneer Ofuji Noburo: Isolated Genius].* Tokyo: Kinokuniya, 2010. Sleeve notes to the DVD of the same name.

Oguro, Yuichiro. *Anime Professional no Shigoto: Kono Hito no Hanashi o Kikitai 1998–2001 [Anime Professionals' Occupation: I Want to Listen to This Person's Story]*. Tokyo: Asuka Shinsha Animestyle Archive, 2006.

_____, et al. *Plus Madhouse 02: Kawajiri Yoshiaki*. Tokyo: Kinema Junposha, 2008.

_____, et al. *Plus Madhouse 04: Rintaro*. Tokyo: Kinema Junposha, 2009.

_____. *Anime Creator Interviews: Kono Hito no Hanashi o Kikitai 2001–2002 [Anime Creator Interviews: I Want to Listen to This Person's Story]*. Tokyo: Kodansha, 2011.

Okada Toshio. *Otakugaku Nyumon [An Introduction to Otakuology]*. Tokyo: Ota Shuppan, 1996.

_____. *Yuigon [Testament]*. Tokyo: Chikuma Shobo, 2010.

Okamoto Rei. "Portrayal of the War and Enemy in Japanese Wartime Cartoons." In *Journal of Asian Pacific Communication*, vol. 7, nos. 1 and 2, 1996, pp. 5–17.

Okawa, Hiroshi. *Kono Ichiban no Jinsei [This Number One Life]*. Tokyo: Jitsugyo no Nipponsha, 1963.

Okubo, Ryo. "Utsushi-e kara Eiga e: Eizo to Katari no Keifu" [From Reflected Pictures to Film: A Genealogy of Image and Speech]. In Kenji Iwamoto, ed. *Nippon Eiga no Tanjo [The Birth of Japanese Film]*, pp. 64–94. Tokyo: Shinwasha, 2011.

Ono, Kosei. "Tadahito Mochinaga: The Animator Who Lived in Two Worlds." In *Animation World Magazine*, 4.9 (December 1999). www.awn.com.

Oshii, Mamoru. *Tariki Hongan Shigoto de Makenai Nanatsu no Chikara [Salvation Through Outside Help: Seven Powers for Work That Does Not Fail]*. Tokyo: Gentosha, 2008.

Osmond, Andrew. *Satoshi Kon: The Illusionist*. Berkeley: Stone Bridge Press, 2009.

Otomo, Katsuhiro. *Kaba: Otomo Katsuhiro Artwork*. Tokyo: Kodansha, 1989.

Otsuka, Eiji, and Osawa Nobuaki. *Japanimation wa Naze Yabureru ka [Why Does Japanimation Fail?]*. Tokyo: Kadokawa, 2005.

Otsuka, Yasuo. *Sakuga Asemamire [Sweating over Animation]*. Revised and Expanded Edition. Tokyo: Tokuma Shoten, 2001.

_____. *Little Nemo no Yabo [The Prospect of Little Nemo]*. Tokyo: Studio Ghibli, 2004.

_____, and Yuki Mori. *Otsuka Yasuo Interview: Animation Juo Mujin [Otsuka Yasuo Interview: Animation Rush of Business]*. Tokyo: Jitsugyo no Nipponsha, 2006.

Oyama, Kumao, and Hayashi Nobuyuki, eds. *Animation Kantoku Dezaki Osamu no Sekai [The World of Animation Director Dezaki Osamu]*. Tokyo: Kawade Shobo Shinsha, 2012.

Pang Laikwan. "The Transgression of Sharing and Copying: Pirating Japanese Animation in China." In Chris Berry, Nicola Lascutin, and Jonathan D. Mackintosh, eds., *Cultural Studies and Cultural Industries in Northeast Asia: What a Difference a Region Makes*. Hong Kong: Hong Kong University Press, 2009. pp. 119–134.

Patten, Fred. *Watching Anime, Reading Manga: 25 Years of Essays and Reviews*. Berkeley: Stone Bridge Press, 2004.

Pelliteri, Marco. *The Dragon and the Dazzle: Models, Strategies and Identities of Japanese Imagination, A European Perspective*. Latina: Tunué, 2010.

Power, Natsu. *God of Comics: Osamu Tezuka and the Creation of Post-World War II Manga*. Jackson: University of Mississippi Press, 2009.

Royal, Ségolène. *Le ras-le-bol des bébés zappeurs*. Paris: Éditions Robert Laffont, 1989.

Ruh, Brian. *Stray Dog of Anime: The Films of Mamoru Oshii*. New York: Palgrave Macmillan, 2004.

Saito, Takao. *Kajiwara Ikki Den [Biography of Kajiwara Ikki]*. Tokyo: Shinchosha, 1995.

_____. *Kajiwara Ikki: Yuyake o Miteita Otoko [Kajiwara Ikki: The Man Watching the Sunset]*. Tokyo: Bungei Bunko, 2005.

Sakurai, Takamasa. *Anime Bunka Gaiko [Anime Cultural Diplomacy]*. Tokyo: Chikuma Shinsho, 2009.

_____. *Nippon wa Anime de Saiko suru: Kuruma to Kaden ga Gaika o Kasegu Jidai wa Owatta [Japan Renewed by Anime: The Age of Earning Foreign Exchange from Cars and Electronics Has Ended]*. Tokyo: Ascii Shinsho, 2010.

Schodt, Frederik L. *Inside the Robot Kingdom: Japan, Mechatronics and the Coming Robotopia*. Tokyo: Kodansha International, 1988.

_____. *The Astro Boy Essays: Osamu Tezuka, Mighty Atom, and the Manga/Anime Revolution*. Berkeley: Stone Bridge Press, 2007.

Seto, Tatsuya, et al. *Nippon no Anime: All About Japan Anime*. Tokyo: Takarajima-sha (*Bessatsu Takarajima*, no. 638), 2002.

Sharp, Jasper. "Between Dimensions: 3D Computer Generated Animation in Anime." In Menzel, Martha-Christine, et al., eds., *Ga Netchu: The Manga Anime Syndrome*, pp. 120–133. Frankfurt am Main:

Deutsche Filmmuseum, 2008.

_____. *Historical Dictionary of Japanese Cinema*. Lanham, MD: Scarecrow Press, 2011.

Shimokawa, Oten. "Nihon Saisho no Manga Eiga Seisaku no Omoide" [Recollections of the First Cartoon Film Production in Japan] in *Eiga Hyoron*, no. 3, 1974. p. 39.

Standish, Isolde. *A New History of Japanese Cinema: A Century of Narrative Film*. London: Continuum, 2006.

Steinberg, Marc. "Immobile Sections and Trans-Series Movement: Astroboy and the Emergence of Anime." In *Animation*, vol. 1 (November 2006), pp. 190–206.

_____. "Anytime, Anywhere: Tetsuwan Atomu Stickers and the Emergence of Character Merchandizing." In *Theory, Culture & Society*, 2009, no. 26, pp. 113–38.

_____. *Anime's Media Mix: Franchising Toys and Characters in Japan*. Minneapolis: University of Minnesota Press, 2012.

Stevenson, Richard. *Degrees of Freedom: The influence of Fansubbing on Mainstream Subtitling Practices*. MSc dissertation, University of Edinburgh, 2010.

Stingray and Nichigai Associates, eds. *Anime Sakuhin Jiten [Dictionary of Animation Works]*. Tokyo: Nichigai Associates, 2010.

Sugiyama, Taku. "Terebi Anime no Zenshi: Toei Chohen Anime no Jidai" [The Prehistory of TV Anime: The Era of Toei Long-form Animation]. In Misono Makoto, ed., *Zusetsu Terebi Anime Zensho [Complete Book of TV Animation: Illustrated]*, pp. 91–120. Tokyo: Hara Shobo, 1999.

Sunrise. *Sunrise Anime Super Data File*. Tokyo: Tatsumi Shuppan, 1997.

Suzuki, Shinichi. *Anime ga Sekai o Tsunagu [Anime Connects the World]*. Tokyo: Iwanami Junior Shinsho, 2008 [Suzuki 2008a in citations].

Suzuki, Toshio. *Eiga Doraku [Film Hobby]*. Tokyo: Pia, 2005.

_____. *Shigoto Doraku: Studio Ghibli no Genba [Work Hobby: On the Spot at Studio Ghibli]*. Tokyo: Iwanami Shinsho, 2008 [Suzuki 2008b in citations].

Tada, Makoto. *Kore ga Anime Business da [This Is the Anime Business]*. Tokyo, Kosaido, 2002.

Tajima, Osamu. *Sekai no Kodomotachi ni Yume o: Tatsunoko Pro no Soshisha Tensai—Yoshida Tatsuo no Kiseki [A Dream for the Children of the World: The Essence of Tatsunoko Pro's Founding Genius Yoshida Tatsuo]*. Tokyo: Mediax, 2013.

Takahashi, Mitsuteru, and Nobuyuki Tsugata, eds. *Anime-gaku [Anime Studies]*. Tokyo: NTT Shuppan, 2011.

_____. "Animation ni Okeru Jinzai Ikusei" [The Training of Capable Personnel for Animation"]. In Mitsuteru Takahashi and Nobuyuki Tsugata, eds., *Anime-gaku [Anime Studies]*, pp. 253–84. Tokyo: NTT Shuppan, 2011.

_____, and Yuji Nunokawa. "Nihon Anime no Genjo to Mirai" [The Current and Future Condition of Japanese Animation]. In Mitsuteru Takahashi and Nobuyuki Tsugata, eds., *Anime-gaku [Anime Studies]*, pp. 307–17. Tokyo: NTT Shuppan, 2011.

Takahashi, Ryosuke. "Tokichiro o Kidotte" [Sensing Tokichiro]. In Tatsuo Shibayama and Shuji Kobayashi, et al., *Mushi Pro Tenamonya: Dare mo Shiranai Tezuka Osamu [Mushi Pro Maverick: The Tezuka Osamu that Nobody Knows]*, pp. 60–63. Tokyo: Kuraki-sha Bijutsu, 2009.

_____. "Anime Enshutsu-ron: Anime ni Okeru Enshutsu, mata Kantoku to wa" [On Anime Production: Concerning Anime Production and Direction]. In Mitsuteru Takahashi and Nobuyuki Tsugata, eds., *Anime-gaku [Anime Studies]*, pp. 47–69. Tokyo: NTT Shuppan, 2011a.

Takahashi, Takeo, and Yasuo Tsukahara, "Pocket Monster Incident and Low Luminance Visual Stimuli." In *Pediatrics International* 40 (6), 1998. pp. 631–37.

Takahashi, Toshie. *Audience Studies: A Japanese Perspective*. London: Routledge, 2010.

Takahata, Isao. *Eiga o Tsukuri-nagara Kangaeta Koto [Thoughts While Making Movies]*. Tokyo: Tokuma Shoten, 1991.

_____. *1991–1999 Eiga o Tsukuri-nagara Kangaeta Koto II [Thoughts While Making Movies II]*. Tokyo: Tokuma Shoten, 1999.

Takamoto, Iwao, with Michael Mallory. *Iwao Takamoto: My Life with a Thousand Characters*. Jackson: University Press of Mississippi, 2009.

Takeda, Yasuhiro. *The Notenki Memoirs: Studio Gainax and the Men Who Created Evangelion*. Houston: AD Vision, 2005.

Takefuji, Tetsuro. *Animesoft Kanzen Catalog*. Tokyo: Kadokawa Shoten, 1993.

Takemura, Mana. *Majokko Days [Magical Girl Days]*. Tokyo: Bug News Network, 2009.

Takeuchi, Osamu, et al. *Gendai Manga Bijutsukan [The Encyclopaedia of Contemporary Manga 1945–2005]*. Tokyo: Shogakukan, 2006.

Tanaka, Tatsuo. "Net-jo Chosakuken Hogo Choka wa Hitsuyo ka—Anime Doga Haishin o Jirei Toshite [Is It Necessary to

Strengthen Intellectual Property Rights on the Net?—With Reference to Precedents in Animation Distribution]. Tokyo: Research Institute of Economy Trade and Industry. RIETI Discussion Paper Series 11-J-010, 2011.

Tanizaki, Akira. "Anime Mechanic Hensen Shi" [The Historical Transformation of Anime Mechanics]. In Misono Makoto, ed., *Zusetsu Terebi Anime Zensho [Complete Book of TV Animation: Illustrated]*, pp. 155–82. Tokyo: Hara Shobo, 1999.

Tatsunoko. *Tatsunoko Pro Anime Super Data File*. Tokyo: Tatsumi Shuppan, 1999.

Tezuka, Osamu. *Boku no Manga Jinsei [My Manga Life]*. Tokyo: Iwanami Shinsho, 1997.

———. *Boku wa Mangaka [I Am a Comic Artist]*. Tokyo: Nihon Tosho Centre, 1999.

Tezuka Productions. *Tezuka Osamu Gekijo [The Animation Filmography of Osamu Tezuka]*. Tokyo: Tezuka Productions, 1991.

Tobin, Joseph, ed. *Pikachu's Global Adventure: The Rise and Fall of Pokémon*. Durham, NC: Duke University Press, 2004.

Tokugi, Yoshiharu. "OVA no Jugonen" [Fifteen Years of Original Video Animation]. In Makoto Misono, ed., *Zusetsu Terebi Anime Zensho [Complete Book of TV Animation: Illustrated]*, pp. 305–30. Tokyo: Hara Shobo, 1999.

Tokyo Movie Shinsha. *TMS Anime Super Data File*. Tokyo: Tatsumi Shuppan, 1999.

Tomino, Yoshiyuki. *Dakara Boku wa … Gundam e no Michi [And So I … The Road to Gundam]*. Tokyo: Kadokawa Sneaker Bunko, 2002. Reprint of Tokuma Shoten edition, 1981, with new Afterword.

———. *Tomino ni Kike! [Ask Tomino!]*. Tokyo: Animage Bunko, 2010.

Toriumi, Jinzo. *Anime Scenario Nyumon [An Introduction to Anime Screenwriting]*. Tokyo: Eijinsha, 1987.

Tsugata, Nobuyuki. "Research on the Achievements of Japan's First Three Animators." In *Asian Cinema*, vol. 14.1, 2003, pp. 13–27.

———. *Nihon Animation no Chikara: Hachijugo-nen no Rekishi o Tsuranuku Futatsu no Jiku [The Power of Japanese Animation: Two Axes Running Through Its 85-Year History]*. Tokyo: NTT Shuppan, 2004.

———. *Animation-gaku Nyumon [An Introduction to Animation Studies]*. Tokyo: Heibonsha, 2005.

———. *Nihon Hatsu no Animation Sakka Kitayama Seitaro [Japan's First Animation Creator: Kitayama Seitaro]*. Kyoto: Rinsen Shoten, 2007a.

———. *Anime Sakka toshite no Tezuka Osamu: Sono Kiseki to Honshitsu [Tezuka Osamu as an Anime Auteur: His Locus and Substance]*. Tokyo: NTT Shuppan, 2007b.

———. "Ofuji Noburo Sakuhin List" [Filmography of Ofuji Noburo] in *Animation no Senkakusha Ofuji Noburo: Koko no Tensai [Animation Pioneer Ofuji Noburo: Isolated Genius]*. Tokyo: Kinokuniya, 2010. Sleeve notes to the DVD of the same name.

———. "Nihon no Shoki Animation no Shoso to Hattatsu" [Aspects and Development of Early Animation in Japan]. In Kiyoshi Kurosawa, Inuhiko Yohota, et al., *Anime wa Ekkyo suru [Anime in Transition]*, pp. 9–30.Tokyo: Iwanami Shoten, 2010.

———. "Anime to wa Nani ka" [What is Anime?]. In Mitsuteru Takahashi and Nobuyuki Tsugata, eds., *Anime-gaku [Anime Studies]*, pp. 3–23. Tokyo: NTT Shuppan, 2011.

———. "Anime no Rekishi" [The History of Anime]. In Mitsuteru Takahashi and Nobuyuki Tsugata, eds., *Anime-gaku [Anime Studies]*, p. 24–44. Tokyo: NTT Shuppan, 2011.

———. *Terebi Anime Yoake Mae: Shirarezaru Kansai-ken Animation Koboshi [Before the Dawn of TV Anime: A History of the Rise and Fall of Forgotten Kansai-area Animation]*. Tokyo: Nakanishiya, 2012.

Tsuji, Masaki. *TV Anime no Seishunki [The Early Days of TV Anime]*. Tokyo: Jitsugyo no Nipponsha, 1996.

———. *Bokutachi no Anime Shi [Our Anime History]*. Tokyo: Iwanami Junior Shinsho, 2008.

Tsukada, Hiro'o, ed. *Nippon Onseisaku Sakusha Meikan [Directory of Japanese Audio Production]*. Tokyo: Shogakukan, 2004.

Ubukata, Tow. *Ubukata-shiki Anime & Manga Sosaku-juku* [The Ubukata-method Anime & Manga Story Cram School]. Tokyo: Takarajimasha, 2009.

Uchiyama, Takashi. "Nihon to Kaigai no Anime Seisaku [Animation Policy in Japan and Overseas]. In Mitsuteru Takahashi and Nobuyuki Tsugata, eds., *Anime-gaku [Anime Studies]*, pp. 230–50. Tokyo: NTT Shuppan, 2011.

Ushiki, Riichi. "Anime to Chiteki Zaisan Ho" [Anime and Intellectual Property Law]. In Mitsuteru Takahashi and Nobuyuki Tsugata, eds., *Anime-gaku [Anime Studies]*, pp. 201–29. Tokyo: NTT Shuppan, 2011.

Ushio, Soji. *Yume wa Ozora o Kakemeguru: Onshi Tsuburaya Eiji Den [Dreams Fly Around in a Big Sky: The Life of My Mentor Tsuburaya Eiji]*. Tokyo: Kadokawa Shoten, 2001.

———. *Tezuka Osamu to Boku [Tezuka Osamu and I]*. Tokyo: Soshisha, 2007.

Vogel, Harold. *Entertainment Industry Economics: A Guide for Financial Analysis.* 7th edition. Cambridge: Cambridge University Press, 2007.

Wada-Marciano, Mitsuyo. *Japanese Cinema in the Digital Age.* Honolulu: University of Hawai'i Press, 2012.

Yamaguchi, Katsumi, and Yasushi Watanabe. *Nihon Animation Eiga Shi [A History of Japanese Animation].* Osaka: Yubunsha, 1977.

Yamaguchi, Yasuo, ed. *Nihon no Anime Zenshi [Complete History of Japanese Animation].* Tokyo: Ten Books, 2004.

Yamamoto, Eiichi. *Mushi Pro no Koboki: Ani Meita no Seishun [The Rise and Fall of Mushi Production: The Youth of "A. Nimator"].* Tokyo: Shinchosha, 1989.

Yamamoto, Y., and Mikiro Kato. "Selective Animation to iu Gainen Giho" [Conceptual Techniques in Selective Animation] in Mikiro Kato, *Animation no Eiga-gaku [Animation Film Studies].* Kyoto: Rinsen Shoten, 2009.

Yamamura, Koji. *Animation no Sekai e Yokoso [Welcome to the World of Animation].* Tokyo: Iwanami Shoten, 2006.

Yamazaki, Keishi. *Terebi Anime Damashii [Spirit of TV Anime].* Tokyo: Kodansha Gendai Shinsha, 2005.

Yokoyama, Ryuichi. *Yokoyama Ryuichi: Waga Yugiteki Jinsei [Yokoyama Ryuichi: My Playful Life].* Tokyo: Nippon Tosho Center, 1997.

MAGAZINES

Animage (Japan). 1978–.

AnimeUK/AnimeFX (U.K.). 1991–96.

Animeland (France) 1991–.

Animerica (U.S.). 1993–2005.

AX (Japan). 1998–2001.

Manga Mania/Manga Max (U.K.). 1993–2000.

Newtype (Japan). 1984–.

Newtype USA. 2002—2008.

Protoculture Addicts (Canada). 1988–2008.

ONLINE SOURCES (JAPANESE)

tvgroove.com

www.fujitv.co.jp

www.geocities.co.jp/Playtown/3064/

www.ja.wikipedia.org

www.jmdb.ne.jp

www.ktv.co.jp

www.ntv.co.jp

www.tbs.co.jp

www.tv-asahi.co.jp

www.ytv.co.jp

www3.justnet.ne.jp/~a_matsu/Ashi.htm

ONLINE SOURCES (ENGLISH)

www.akadot.com

www.allanime.org

www.animeacademy.com

www.animenewsnetwork.com

www.animeondvd.com

www.animeresearch.com

www.anipike.com

www.google.co.jp

www.hentaineko.com

www.imdb.com

www.wikipedia.org

TITLE INDEX

Use this index to find all films and publications mentioned in the text. Included here are official titles plus many of their variants and alternates in English and Japanese. Films whose formal titles begin with numbers are listed both at the top of the index and throughout the alphabetical listings, as if their numerals were written out. Alphabeticization follows the "index by word," system, which can sometimes produce nonintuitive results. If you do not find an entry where you expect it to be, look up and down the adjoining listings.

NAME & SUBJECT INDEX

Use this index to find names of people and studios as well as references to thematic entries throughout the text. Studios may appear under more than one name or variant spelling. Alphabeticization follows the "index by word," system, which can sometimes produce nonintuitive results. If you do not find an entry where you expect it to be, look up and down the adjoining listings.

Endo, Shigeo, 231, 633, 678

Murakami, Koichi, 187, 748, 930
Murakami, Kotaro, 11
Murakami, Maki, 320, 456
Murakami, Momoko, 858
Murakami, Motoka, 353, 734, 812
Murakami, Motokazu, 242, 936
Murakami, Naoki, 160, 242
Murakami, Osamu, 944
Murakami, Ryuchi, 533
Murakami, Takashi, 345, 369, 378
Murakami, Teruaki, 84, 175, 185, 231, 303, 305, 650, 655, 892
Murakami, Tsunekazu, 270, 351, 741
Murakami, Tsutomu, 149
Muraki, Kazuma, 25
Muraki, Kazumasa, 481
Muraki, Shintaro, 152
Muraki, Yasushi, 216
Murakoshi, Shigeru, 441
Muramatsu, Hisao, 135
Muramatsu, Jiro, 388
Muramatsu, Ken, 447, 730, 757
Muramatsu, Takatsugu, 469, 918
Muramatsu, Yasuhiro, 694
Muramatsu, Yujiro, 71
Muramoto, Katsuhiko, 375, 409
Muramtasu, Jiro, 175
Muranaka, Hiromi, 869
Murano, Mami, 78, 252, 709, 882
Murano, Moribi, 61, 169, 548, 568
Murao, Minoru, 375, 452, 799
Murasaka, Yoko, 481
Murasaki, Shikibu, 818
Murase, Shuko, 37, 174, 232, 287, 327, 340, 578, 796, 927
Murata, Akira, 3, 875
Murata, Drill, 93, 112
Murata, Eiken, 601
Murata, Eriko, 949
Murata, Goro, 416
Murata, Hajime, 318, 747
Murata, Hiroyuki, 698, 904
Murata, Jiro, 608
Murata, Kazuya, 55, 204, 236, 287, 787, 938
Murata, Koichi, 155, 485, 545, 633, 769, 811, 842
Murata, Masahiko, 50, 76, 152, 240, 300, 382, 401, 737, 772, 815, 818, 937
Murata, Osamu, 174
Murata, Range, 92, 452, 744
Murata, Satoshi, 36, 222, 225
Murata, Shiro, 566, 792, 807, 840, 875
Murata, Shunji, 240, 461, 607
Murata, Toshiharu, 64, 92, 292, 325, 356, 551, 662, 764
Murata, Toshihiro, 945
Murata, Yasuji, 221, 454, 553, 588, 778, 911, 912
Murata, Yasuji, 553
Murata, Yasushi, 222, 553
Murata, Yoshihito, 140
Murata, Yoshio, 741
Murayama, Atsuo, 703

Murayama, Isao, 856, 916
Murayama, Kazumitsu, 659
Murayama, Kimisuke, 578
Murayama, Kiyoshi, 11, 92, 147, 373, 407, 437, 492, 752, 766, 787
Murayama, Ko, 357
Murayama, Kosuke, 611
Murayama, Masao, 93, 277, 305, 495, 724, 777
Murayama, Osamu, 207
Murayama, Satoshi, 407, 459, 567, 588, 725, 759
Murayama, Setsuko, 783
Murayama, Tatsuya, 152, 873, 924
Murayama, Toru, 7
Murayama, Yoshimitsu, 22
MURO, 851
Muroi, Fumie, 128, 152, 331, 500, 535, 705
Muroi, Shigeru, 827
Muroi, Yasuo, 710
Murota, Yuhei, 482
Murotani, Tsunezo, 252
Muroyama, Mayumi, 537
Murphy, Eddie, 902
Murphy, Marty, 633
Murphy, Tab, 840
Musa, Atelier, 944
Musashi Project, 567
MUSE, 24, 260, 276, 314, 347, 420, 529, 621
Museum Soft, 10, 22, 81, 94, 177, 187, 471, 510, 552, 628, 652, 739, 769
Mushi Pro(ductions), 21, 27, 35, 40, 46, 64, 92, 140, 141, 153, 191, 203, 206, 227, 233, 238, 252, 262, 272, 320, 345, 347, 365, 368, 369, 416, 420, 421, 433, 437, 449, 460, 495, 496, 507, 514, 524, 548, 555, 565, 568, 573, 582, 588, 600, 633, 635, 675, 693, 709, 726, 765, 782, 800, 804, 817, 822, 823, 835, 837, 846, 852, 853, 855, 858, 859, 864, 875, 883, 890, 897, 902, 911, 930, 938, 940, 948
MUSIC HEROES, 360
Music in Anime, 16, 70, 188, 238, 316, 348, 412, 428, 443, 483, 511, 522, 536, 555, 556, 585, 643, 649, 723
Music, Charlotte Russe, 586
Mussorgsky, Modest, 633
Mutaguchi, Hiroki, 156, 320, 491
Muto, Ayato, 185
Muto, Gion, 158
Muto, Kazuhiro, 22, 127
Muto, Kei, 587
Muto, Masatoshi, 399, 836, 844
Muto, Mirin, 652
Muto, Seiji, 276, 324, 462, 535, 914
Muto, Yasuyuki, 63, 76, 113, 129, 138, 180, 363, 394, 510, 628, 629, 682, 735
Muto, Yoshiaki, 272
Muto, Yuji, 152, 204, 321, 349, 632, 854
Mutsu, Toshiyuki, 62
Mutsuki, Juzo, 26, 163, 182, 189, 342, 631, 712, 910
Mutsukura, Satoshi, 953

Muzushima, Tase, 489
MW Films, 7
My Video, 198, 375, 382, 526, 596, 732
Mybic, 276
Myu, 528, 641, 660, 685
Myung-jin, Lee, 672

n3o, 865
Na-Ga, 24, 413, 414, 472, 726, 761, 912
Nabe, 4, 162
Nabeshima, Osamu, 138, 144, 149, 166, 169, 204, 225, 484, 606, 670, 690, 714
Nabeta, Kayoko, 468, 891
NAC, 378, 658
Nagae, Tom, 76
Nagae, Toshikazu, 225
Nagahama, Hiroshi, 188, 261, 463, 555
Nagahama, Norihiko, 532, 629, 706, 892
Nagahama, Tadao, 145, 247, 332, 379, 394, 552, 565, 627, 668, 702, 719, 784, 785, 880, 905
Nagahama, Tadao, 565
Nagai, Go, 4, 83, 125, 162, 174, 183, 185, 186, 190, 206, 214, 259, 293, 309, 318, 323, 341, 392, 414, 420, 423, 470, 500, 518, 528, 549, 565, 578, 612, 613, 617, 618, 661, 665, 673, 674, 696, 728, 743, 744, 752, 783, 785, 788, 806, 851, 868, 881, 898, 947
Nagai, Go, 565
Nagai, Kazuo, 368, 708, 783
Nagai, Keisuke, 399
Nagai, Noriaki, 426
Nagai, Shinpei, 175, 489, 633, 654
Nagai, Takeshi, 426
Nagai, Tatsuyaki, 127
Nagai, Tatsuyuki, 30, 367, 382, 555, 561, 856, 872, 908
Nagai, Tomoyoshi, 608
Nagai, Tsutomu, 804
Nagai, Yuji, 626
Nagaishi, Takao, 678
Nagakawa, Ko, 608, 749
Nagakawa, Kotaro, 159
Nagakawa, Takashi, 419
Nagaki, Funahito, 219
Nagaki, Fusahito, 15, 47, 62, 110, 112, 205, 206, 476, 514, 518, 777, 791, 842, 879
Nagaki, Tatsuhiro, 261, 262, 444, 762
Nagakubo, Masakazu, 419
Nagamachi, Hideki, 388
Nagamatsu, Kiyoshi, 292
Nagamatsu, Takeo, 758
Nagamatsu, Tatsuo, 311
Nagamine, Takafumi, 929
Nagamine, Tatsuya, 72, 389, 647
Nagamori, Keiyo, 288
Nagamori, Masato, 534
Nagamori, Yoshihiro, 58, 346, 438
Nagamura, Eiichi, 742
Nagano, Akane, 302
Nagano, Atsuko, 584
Nagano, Mamoru, 101, 183, 258, 259, 268,

Topcraft, 265, 344, 612, 613, 616, 798, 855

ABOUT THE AUTHORS

JONATHAN CLEMENTS (1971–) has worked as a translator, voice actor, or dubbing director on over 70 anime, including **GREY: DIGITAL TARGET, SOL BIANCA**, and **MUSASHI: DREAM OF THE LAST SAMURAI**. He was formerly the editor of *Manga Max* magazine, a contributing editor of *Newtype USA*, and is now a contributing editor to *The Encyclopedia of Science Fiction*, with special responsibility for China and Japan. He is currently a Visiting Professor at Xi'an Jiaotong University, China. Among his many published works is *Anime: A History* (British Film Institute, 2013), which received a 2014 *CHOICE* Award as one of the year's outstanding academic titles.

HELEN MCCARTHY (1951–) was the founding editor of *Anime UK magazine*, editor of *Manga Mania* magazine, and the author of *Anime! A Beginner's Guide*, the first book in the English language on the medium. She has appeared in several anime as a voice actress and produced the U.K. release of **BEAST WARRIORS**. Her subsequent publications include *Hayao Miyazaki: Master of Japanese Animation, 500 Essential Anime You Must Own*, and *The Art of Osamu Tezuka: God of Manga*, which won the Harvey Award, and *A Brief History of Manga* (Ilex, 2014).

CPSIA information can be obtained
at www.ICGtesting.com
Printed in the USA
LVOW03*0839240117
521977LV00003B/7/P